KU-180-197

READINGS IN

# knowledge acquisition and learning

## AUTOMATING THE CONSTRUCTION AND IMPROVEMENT OF EXPERT SYSTEMS

*Edited by Bruce G. Buchanan & David C. Wilkins*

MORGAN KAUFMANN PUBLISHERS

SAN MATEO, CALIFORNIA

Sponsoring Editor: *Michael B. Morgan*
Production Manager: *Yonie Overton*
Production Editor: *Carol Leyba*
Editorial Coordinator: *Douglas Sery*
Cover Designer: *Ross Carron Design*
Additional Composition: *SuperScript Typography*
Pasteup: *Jeanne Sakai-Chan, JC Graphics*
Proofreaders: *Fran Taylor and Gary Morris*
Additional Production Services: *Judy Weiss*
Printer: *Edwards Brothers, Inc.*


Morgan Kaufmann Publishers, Inc.
Editorial Office:
2929 Campus Drive, Suite 260
San Mateo, CA 94403

© 1993 by Morgan Kaufmann Publishers, Inc.
All rights reserved
Printed in the United States of America

No part of this publication may be reproduced, stored in a retrieval system, or transmitted in any form or by any means—electronic, mechanical, photocopying, recording, or otherwise—without the prior written permission of the publisher.

96  95  94  93      4  3  2  1


**Library of Congress Cataloging-in-Publication Data**

Readings in knowledge acquisition and learning : automating the construction and
   improvement of expert systems / edited by Bruce G. Buchanan & David C. Wilkins.
      p.    cm.
   Includes bibliographical references (p.  ) and indexes.
   ISBN 1-55860-163-5
   1. Knowledge acquisition (Expert systems)  2. Machine learning.  I. Buchanan,
Bruce G.   II. Wilkins, David C.
QA76.76.E95R42   1993
006.3'3—dc20                                                    92-38384
                                                                    CIP

# Contents

# Preface

The relevance of knowledge-based systems to most fields of science, engineering and the professions is now widely recognized. And since the creation of MYCIN, the first expert system, two decades ago, many techniques have been developed to automate partially or fully the creation of knowledge-based expert systems.

The first goal of this book is to provide a primary source of papers for those who wish to harness the accumulated store of semi-automatic and automatic knowledge acquisition techniques, and for those who wish to extend the state of the art. Many of the advances in techniques have been recent; indeed, 70% of the papers in this book were published within the last five years. Advances have been made in acquiring knowledge for a range of expert systems and a diversity of knowledge structures.

The second goal of this book is to increase the cross-fertilization between the subfields of knowledge acquisition and machine learning. Historically, almost all of the best work in automatic learning (e.g., Michalski's AQ15 rule learning, Mitchell's Version Spaces, Quinlan's ID3 decision tree learning) was closely tied to a challenging real-world application domain. More recently, a dichotomy has emerged, so that now knowledge acquisition work focuses on interactive tools for complex real-world application domains, and machine learning focuses on automatic methods for simple domains or simple knowledge-based system architectures. We hope this book will contribute to greater interaction between the fields of knowledge acquisition and machine learning, each of which has so much to learn from the other.

The third goal of this book is to provide a source of articles for AI researchers *outside* of knowledge-based systems who wish to take a more knowledge-intensive approach to problem solving and to automate the acquisition of this knowledge. All areas of artificial intelligence – automatic programming, commonsense reasoning, expert systems, natural language processing, robotics, vision – are moving toward more knowledge-intensive methods of problem solving and hence they all face the tedious process of acquiring and maintaining the relevant knowledge.

This volume includes overview articles as well as papers about particular knowledge acquisition methods. The overview articles are included to introduce major topics and to help structure one's reading and understanding of issues surrounding knowledge acquisition. Clarity of presentation was a primary criterion for selection of the overviews. For articles about particular methods, selection criteria include clarity as well as the development of a new method or technique, demonstration that the method has been implemented and tested, and solid evidence that the technique has an impact on the creation of knowledge-based systems. Several of the method articles are "classic" papers that are frequently cited and that motivated much subsequent work.

The breadth of coverage of this book has prevented the inclusion of many excellent papers. Because so many of the included articles are recent and have extensive bibliographies themselves, the reader will be able to pursue topics of interest through the entry points provided here. We also strongly recommend *Readings in Machine Learning*, edited by Jude Shavlik and Thomas Dietterich, to the interested reader. Of the nearly 100 articles contained in both books, only 12 overlap.

Early versions of this book have been successfully used over the last four years as a textbook for mixed graduate and undergraduate courses. Selection of subsets of papers from the book allows specialized courses to be tailored to focus on machine learning, knowledge acquisition, or advanced topics in knowledge-based systems. Suggestions for using this book as a text in different courses are described in Appendix A.

## Acknowledgments

The authors gratefully acknowledge the suggestions and reviews provided by John Boose, Tom Dietterich, Brian Gaines, Tom Gruber, Pat Langley, Doug Lenat, John McDermott and Tom Mitchell. We are greatly indebted to Marianne Winslett for carefully reading the final version of this book and suggesting many useful revisions.

The selection of papers for the volume was strongly influenced by our experience teaching the course and by feedback from the students. Particularly helpful critiques of papers were produced by Michael Barbehenn, Carl Kadie, Donald Lee, Dan Oblinger, Vance Morrison, Ziad Najem and Dale Russell.

An appointment as a Fellow in the Center for Advanced Study at Illinois provided release time from teaching to work on this book. Support was also provided by ONR grant N00014-88K0124. We gratefully express our appreciation for the excellent secretarial assistance provided by Sharon Collins and Lucille Jarzynka. We thank Mike Lake, Vance Morrison, Ray Olsen and Dershung Yang for assistance that allowed us to meet the publication deadline. And we appreciate the conscientious effort of Mona Q. Dabbah and Ziad Najem in helping to create a detailed index with many cross-references that bridge the fields of machine learning and knowledge acquisition.

In the years spent working on this book, Michael Morgan was a constant source of help and encouragement, and we are very grateful for his support. We also express our thanks to Carol Leyba, Douglas Sery, and William Baxter for the care they gave to the creation of this book.

Bruce G. Buchanan
Pittsburgh, Pennsylvania

David C. Wilkins
Urbana, Illinois

September, 1992

# Acknowledgements

The editors are pleased to thank the following authors and publishers for permission to include copyrighted material in this volume.

Anderson, J. R. (1990). Development of expertise. From COGNITIVE PSYCHOLOGY AND ITS IMPLICATIONS, 3rd edition, chapter 9, pages 256–288, by John R. Anderson. Copyright © by W. H. Freeman and Company. Reprinted by permission of the author and publisher.

Barstow, D. R. (1985). Domain-specific automatic programming. *IEEE Transactions on Software Engineering*, 11(11):1321–1336. Reprinted with permission of the author and publisher.

Booker, L. B., Goldberg, D. E., and Holland, J. H. (1989). Classifier systems and genetic algorithms. *Artificial Intelligence*, 40(1-3):235–282. Reprinted with permission of the authors and publisher.

Boose, J. H. (1989). A survey of knowledge acquisition techniques and tools. *Knowledge Acquisition*, 1(1):3–37. Reprinted with permission of the author and publisher.

Boose, J. H. and Bradshaw, J. M. (1987). Expertise transfer and complex problems: using AQUINAS as a knowledge-acquisition workbench for knowledge-based systems. *International Journal of Man-Machine Studies*, 26(1):3–28. Reprinted with permission of the authors and publisher.

Bratko, I. (1989). Qualitative modelling and learning in KARDIO. In *Proceedings of the Fifth Australian Conference on Applications of Expert Systems*, pages 1–22, Sydney. Reprinted with permission of the author.

Buchanan, B. G. and Smith, R. G. *The Handbook of Artificial Intelligence*, edited by A. Barr, P. Cohen, E. A. Feigenbaum, ©1989 by Addison-Wesley Publishing Company, Inc. Addison Wesley. Reprinted with permission of the authors and publisher.

Carbonell, J. G. (1986). Derivational analogy: A theory of reconstructive problem solving and expertise acquisition. In Michalski, R. S., Carbonell, J. G., and Mitchell, T. M., (eds.), *Machine Learning: An Artificial Intelligence Approach*, volume 2, chapter 14, pages 371–392. Morgan Kaufmann Publishers. Reprinted with permission of the author and publisher.

Chandrasekaran, B. (1986). Generic tasks in knowledge-based reasoning: High-level building blocks for expert system design. *IEEE Expert*, 1(3):23–29. Reprinted with permission of the author and publisher.

Cheeseman, P., Kelly, J., Self, M., Stutz, J., Taylor, W., and Freeman, D. (1988). Autoclass:

A Bayesian classification system. In *Proceedings of the Fifth International Conference on Machine Learning*, pages 54–64, Ann Arbor, Michigan. Reprinted with permission of the authors and publisher.

Clancey, W. J. (1988). Acquiring, representing, and evaluating a competence model of diagnostic strategy. In Chi, M., Glaser, R., and Farr, M., (eds.), *The Nature of Expertise*, chapter 12, pages 343–418. Lawrence Erlbaum Press. Reprinted with permission of the author and publisher.

Davis, R. (1979). Interactive transfer of expertise: Acquisition of new inference rules. *Artificial Intelligence*, 12(2):409–427. Reprinted with permission of the author and publisher.

Dietterich, T. G. (1989). Limitations on inductive learning. In *Proceedings of the Sixth International Workshop on Machine Learning*, pages 124–129. Reprinted with permission of the author and publisher.

Eshelman, L., Ehret, D., McDermott, J., and Tan, M. (1987). MOLE: a tenacious knowledge-acquisition tool. *International Journal of Man-Machine Studies*, 26(1):41–54. Reprinted with permission of the authors and publisher.

Falkenhainer, B., Forbus, K., and Gentner, D. (1989). The structure-mapping engine: Algorithm and examples. *Artificial Intelligence*, 41(1):1–63. Reprinted with permission of the authors and publisher.

Fikes, R. E., Hart, P. E., and Nilsson, N. J. (1972). Learning and executing generalized robot plans. *Artificial Intelligence*, 4(3):189–208. Reprinted with permission of the authors and publisher.

Forsythe, D. E. and Buchanan, B. G. (1989). Knowledge acquisition for expert systems: Some pitfalls and suggestions. *IEEE Transactions on Systems, Man, and Cybernetics*, 19(3):435–442. Reprinted with permission of the authors and publisher.

Gaines, B. R. (1989). The quantification of knowledge: Formal foundations for knowledge acquisition methodologies. In Raz, Z., (ed.), *Methodologies for Intelligent Systems*, volume 4, pages 137–149. North-Holland. Reprinted with permission of the author and publisher.

Gennari, J. H., Langley, P., and Fisher, D. (1989). Models of incremental concept formation. *Artificial Intelligence*, 40(1-3):11–63. Reprinted with permission of the authors and publisher.

Gentner, D. (1989). The mechanisms of analogical learning. In Vosniadou, S. and Ortony, A., (eds.), *Similarity and Analogical Reasoning*. Cambridge University Press, London. Reprinted with permission of the author and publisher.

Ginsberg, A., Weiss, S. M., and Politakis, P. (1988). Automatic knowledge base refinement for classification systems. *Artificial Intelligence*, 35(2):197–226. Reprinted with permission of the authors and publisher.

Golding, A. R. and Rosenbloom, P. S. (1991). Improving rule-based systems through case-based reasoning. In *Proceedings of the 1991 National Conference on Artificial Intelligence*, pages 22–27, Anaheim. Reprinted with permission of the authors and The MIT Press, Inc.

Gruber, T. G. (1989). Automated knowledge acquisition for strategic knowledge. *Machine Learning*, 4(3-4):293–336. Reprinted with permission of the author and publisher.

Guha, R. V. and Lenat, D. B. (1990). CYC: A midterm report. *AI Magazine*, Fall, pages 32–59, copyright ©1990, American Association for Artificial Intelligence. Reprinted with permission of the authors and publisher.

Hammond, K. J. (1990). Explaining and repairing plans that fail. *Artificial Intelligence*, 45(1-2):173–228. Reprinted with permission of the author and publisher.

Hinton, G. E. (1989). Connectionist learning procedures. *Artificial Intelligence*, 40(1-3):185–234. Reprinted with permission of the author and publisher.

Kodratoff, Y. and Tecuci, G. (1987). Techniques of design and DISCIPLE learning apprentice. *International Journal of Expert Systems*, 1(1):39–66, JAI Press, Inc. Reprinted with permission of the authors and publisher.

Laird, J. E., Rosenbloom, P. S., and Newell, A. (1986). Chunking in SOAR: The anatomy of a general learning mechanism. *Machine Learning*, 1:11–46. Reprinted with permission of the authors and publisher.

Lenat, D. B. (1978). The ubiquity of discovery. *Artificial Intelligence*, 9(3):257–285. Reprinted with permission of the author and publisher.

Marcus, S. and McDermott, J. (1989). SALT: A knowledge acquisition language for propose-and-revise systems. *Artificial Intelligence*, 39(1):1–37. Reprinted with permission of the authors and publisher.

McDermott, J. (1988). Preliminary steps toward a taxonomy of problem-solving methods. In Marcus, S., (ed.), *Automating Knowledge Acquisition for Knowledge Based Systems*, chapter 8, pages 120–146. Kluwer Academic Publishers. Reprinted with permission of the author and publisher.

Michalski, R. S. (1983). A theory and methodology of inductive learning. *Artificial Intelligence*, 20(2):111–161. Reprinted with permission of the author and publisher.

Michalski, R. S. (1990). Toward a unified theory of learning: Multistrategy task-adaptive learning. Technical Report MLI90-1, George Mason University. Expanded version of Toward a unified theory of learning: An outline of basic ideas. *Proceedings of the First World Conference on the Fundamentals of Artificial Intelligence*, Paris, July 1-7, 1991. Reprinted with permission of the author.

Mitchell, T. M., Utgoff, P. E., and Banerji, R. (1983). Learning by experimentation: Acquiring and refining problem-solving heuristics. In Michalski, R. S., Carbonell, J. G., and Mitchell, T. M., (eds.), *Machine Learning: An Artificial Intelligence Approach*, pages 163–190. Morgan Kaufmann Publishers. Reprinted with permission of the authors and publisher.

Mitchell, T. M., Keller, R. M., and Kedar-Cabelli, S. T. (1986). Explanation-based generalization: A unifying view. *Machine Learning*, 1(1):47–80. Reprinted with permission of the authors and publisher.

Mitchell, T. M., Mahadevan, S., and Steinberg, L. I. (1990). LEAP: A learning apprentice for VLSI design. In Kodratoff, Y. and Michalski, R. S., (eds.), *Machine Learning: An Artificial Intelligence Approach*, volume III, pages 271–301. Morgan Kaufmann Publish-

ers. Reprinted with permission of the authors and publisher.

Mooney, R. J. (1992). Explanation generalization in EGGS. In DeJong, G., (ed.), *Investigating Explanation-Based Learning*, chapter 2, pages 20–59. Kluwer Academic Publishers. Reprinted with permission of the author and publisher.

Musen, M. A. (1989). Automated support for building and extending expert models. *Machine Learning*, 4(3-4):347–376. Reprinted with permission of the author and publisher.

Porter, B. W., Bareiss, R., and Holte, R. C. (1990). Concept learning and heuristic classification in weak-theory domains. *Artificial Intelligence*, 45(3):229–263. Reprinted with permission of the authors and publisher.

Quinlan, J. R. (1986). Induction of decision trees. *Machine Learning*, 1(1):81–106. Reprinted with permission of the author and publisher.

Shavlik, J. W., Mooney, R., and Towell, G. G. (1991). Symbolic and neural learning algorithms: An experimental comparison. *Machine Learning*, 6(1):111–143. Reprinted with permission of the authors and publisher.

Shaw, M. L. G. and Woodward, J. B. (1990). Modeling expert knowledge. *Knowledge Acquisition*, 2(2):179–206. Reprinted with permission of the authors and publisher.

Swartout, W. R. (1983). XPLAIN: A system for creating and explaining expert consulting programs. *Artificial Intelligence*, 21(3):285–325. Reprinted with permission of the author and publisher.

Wielinga, B. J., A. T. Schreiber, and J. A. Breuker (1992). KADS: A modelling approach to knowledge engineering. *Knowledge Acquisition*, 4(1):5–53. Special issue on 'The KADS approach to knowledge engineering'. Reprinted with permission of the author and publisher.

Wilkins, D. C. (1990). Knowledge base refinement as improving an incomplete and incorrect domain theory. In Kodratoff, Y. and Michalski, R. S., (eds.), *Machine Learning: An Artificial Intelligence Approach*, volume III, pages 493–514. Morgan Kaufmann Publishers. Reprinted with permission of the author and publisher.

# Chapter 1

# Overview of Knowledge Acquisition and Learning

## 1 Introduction

The primary goal of a knowledge-based system is to make expertise available to problem solvers (e.g., decision makers, designers, troubleshooters, and planners) who need reliable answers quickly. Since the commercial appearance of expert systems around 1980, thousands of knowledge-based systems have been put into service around the world (Feigenbaum et al., 1988; Waterman, 1988). They represent and use heuristic knowledge of the same kinds that specialists use, frequently obtained from the specialists themselves. Until the advent of expert systems, no computer applications – in industry, government, health, defense, or anywhere else – represented and used the same kinds and quantities of knowledge that are now commonly used in expert systems.

The technology for building knowledge-based applications of artificial intelligence, i.e., "expert systems," has evolved rapidly as knowledge-based systems have become ubiquitous. Although many principles underlying the design and construction of useful knowledge-based systems have by now been well characterized and disseminated, knowledge-based systems are still difficult and time-consuming to construct. The

difficulty stems partly from their emphasis on qualitative formulations of knowledge, on knowledge that is "second nature" to experts but has never been well-codified, and on imprecise knowledge that guides human problem solvers through a complex, messy, and imprecise problem.

The fundamental axiom of designers of knowledge-based systems is that a system's performance is tied directly to the quality and quantity of its encoded knowledge. This has been called the "knowledge principle" (Feigenbaum, 1977; Lenat and Feigenbaum, 1987), frequently shortened to "Knowledge is power." Unfortunately, the very specialized, informal knowledge obtained from experts that makes symbolic reasoning systems useful also is difficult to obtain, as opposed to the formalized, general knowledge found in textbooks (Forsythe et al., 1992). Also, expertise is frequently so well integrated into problem-solving practice that it is "tacit knowledge" (Polanyi, 1964) and no longer readily accessible for explanation. These characteristics underlie the often-mentioned problem of the "knowledge acquisition bottleneck" (Hayes-Roth et al., 1983).

This volume surveys many of the techniques, and surrounding issues, that have been advanced to facilitate the construction of high performance reasoning systems. The history of interest in learning within artificial intelligence is as old as the field itself. Learning, after all, is an important – some would say essential – component of intelligent behavior. In the early years of artificial intelligence, Minsky (Minsky, 1961b) included learning and induction among the problems that had to be addressed in artificial intelligence and surveyed the early literature (Minsky, 1961a). At the same time, McCarthy called attention to the critical role that knowledge representation plays in building computer programs that learn from experience (McCarthy, 1958). In his famous paper describing the "Advice Taker," he argues that a prerequisite for machine learning is the ability to represent knowledge in structures that can be modified when a person tells the program new things.

A major division in the work represented in this volume is between techniques that exploit the fundamental "knowledge principle" through knowledge obtained from experts and represented explicitly, and techniques that build knowledge into programs in other ways or that represent it implicitly. This division is reflected in the design of the performance programs themselves. Knowledge-based systems, of course, explicitly encode knowledge symbolically and require techniques for acquiring that knowledge. Adaptive controllers, perceptrons, statistical pattern recognition systems, genetic algorithms, and neural networks, on the other hand, can provide high performance solutions to problems without using heuristic knowledge encoded symbolically. They make essential use of knowledge, but their knowledge is built into their structure, methods, or assumptions. Their knowledge is amenable to modification only through limited channels, such as bit strings or coefficients in polynomials.

Another major division of the techniques represented in this volume lies in the extent to which people are or are not involved in the construction of the performance program. For example, a software engineer or systems analyst (acting as a knowledge engineer) may interview a person who is expert in solving the problem that the target software is supposed to address. Or, an expert may interact with editing programs to describe the strategies and tactics that the target software should follow. Or, an automated machine learning program might infer from a large database the principles that past experience indicates will solve similar problems in the future.

The tools for knowledge acquisition described in this book are shown in Figure 1, along with some well-known and well-documented AI performance programs. The vertical axis in Figure 1 represents the complexity of the knowledge structures that are accessible to modification and addition through knowledge acquisition. Knowledge structures in a program can be arbitrarily complex and thus are at the top; coefficients in polynomials are syntactically simple and thus are near the origin. In any case, as McCarthy points out, only knowledge that is represented explicitly and modularly is amenable to examination and change by another program. The reason for assigning control rules as having greater complexity than domain rules is because the order in which they are stored in the knowledge base more often implicitly encodes additional knowledge.

The horizontal axis in Figure 1 represents the degree to which human interactions can be facilitated or reduced through automation. Hand coding, with nothing but a text editor to change knowledge structures, is the least automated approach, as all considerations of syntactic correctness, semantic consistency, completeness and the like are the programmer's responsibility. At the other end of the scale, researchers are seeking ways to make programs learn from experience with little or no human intervention. Even with full automation, machine learning programs still require considerable effort when they are applied to data from a new domain with new features and new constraints. Note that a program's position in the chart implies nothing about the quality of its performance: some of today's most reliable, most complex systems (e.g., automatic landing systems for commercial aircraft) are constructed manually.

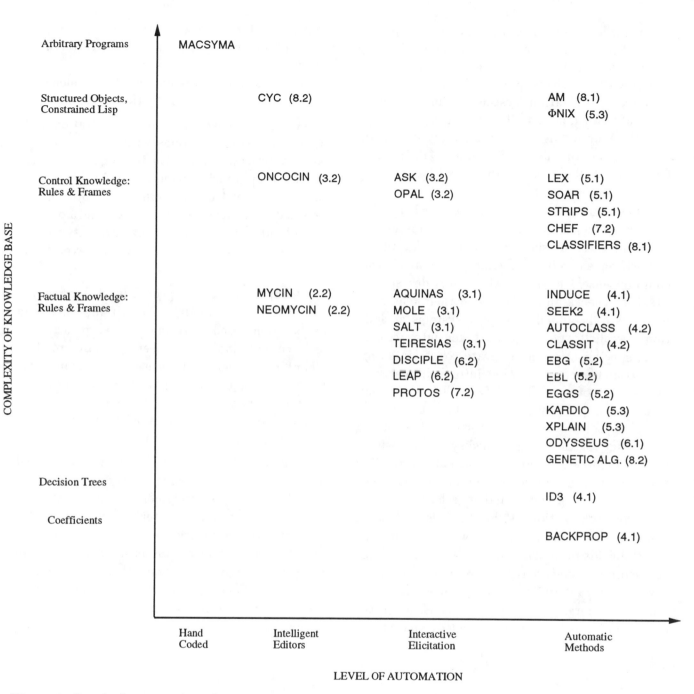

Figure 1: Level of automation of program construction vs. complexity of the knowledge structures that are added explicitly by knowledge acquisition.

A number of the acquisition tools shown in Figure 1 can fit into several columns, and so the placement is largely a matter of degree. For example, PROTOS has an initial automatic phase for early knowledge acquisition and then uses interactive elicitation during knowledge base refinement. Another example would be LEAP, which has an initial elicitation phase wherein the expert types in the knowledge missing from the knowledge base. But this is followed by an automatic phase in which the knowledge is validated and then checked to see if it can be generalized.

Knowledge engineering is not shown in Figure 1 because it involves more than changing knowledge structures. Knowledge engineering involves working with experts in project definition, resource identification, system testing, and many other activities, as described in Hayes-Roth et al. (1983). A knowledge engineer mainly does manual elicitation of knowledge and uses editing tools built into shell systems; substantial hand coding may be required as well.

There are still many types of knowledge that knowledge-based systems do not represent and use well; these present challenges for knowledge acquisition as well. For example, nontechnical, commonsense knowledge often provides specialists with checks and balances in their reasoning, but it is only added to expert systems as additional explicit "facts" to be taken into account. Also, specialists often integrate constraints from the geometry of a situation into their reasoning in a variety of ways that defy explicit statement. Thus the papers in this book do not present a complete solution to the problem of acquiring knowledge for knowledge-based systems. Instead, they provide important and useful information about what can be done today and about the issues in extending the available techniques.

The organization of this book is as follows. Chapter 1 contains two overview papers that survey the fields of machine learning and knowledge acquisition, respectively. The remaining chapters cover important tools and techniques, both current and emerging, plus important issues in the design and construction of knowledge-based systems. Chapter 2 focuses on the nature and acquisition of human expertise and the architecture of second-generation expert systems. These topics are essential for understanding the problems addressed by knowledge acquisition systems.

Chapter 3 covers interactive elicitation techniques; for expert systems with complex knowledge structures, interactive techniques are often the only approach currently applicable to the task. Chapter 4 covers inductive approaches to knowledge acquisition. These are the most successful automatic approaches at present, and are of primary relevance to classification expert systems.

Chapter 5 covers primarily deductive approaches to knowledge acquisition, including explanation-based learning, speedup learning, and compilation from deep domain models. Chapter 6 covers apprenticeship learning systems. An apprenticeship is the most powerful method human experts use to refine their expertise, and apprentice systems offer similar promise for refining knowledge-based systems.

Chapter 7 covers analogical and case-based approaches; these provide a way of using past experience that is fundamentally different from induction. Finally, Chapter 8 covers discovery and commonsense learning. To be effective, analogy, discovery, and commonsense learning require much larger knowledge bases than are currently available. Nevertheless, these techniques hold promise for some important parts of the knowledge acquisition problem.

# Section 1.1

# Overviews

The articles in this section provide broad overviews of the two distinct but closely related fields of machine learning and knowledge acquisition.

The research communities of these two fields are largely separate, each with its own areas of emphasis, journals and conferences. Traditionally, machine learning researchers have emphasized concept learning with approaches that are completely automatic; an example is inductive concept learning from a library of preclassified training examples. In contrast, knowledge acquisition researchers emphasize a broad range of expert tasks with semi-automatic approaches that have a human expert in the acquisition loop; an example is an interactive tool to elicit design knowledge from a human expert.

The first article, by Michalski, provides an excellent introduction and orientation to the field of machine learning. It addresses such fundamental issues as defining learning, describing the different types of learning, relating the different types of learning to each other, and describing how they can be combined.

The second article, by Boose, provides a comprehensive survey of the field of knowledge acquisition. The article communicates very well the range of knowledge-based application problems that have been explored, and the range of problem-solving methods used by expert systems to solve these problems. Emphasis on problems and methods provides an excellent framework for categorizing the knowledge acquisition tools that have been developed to date.

Additional broad or specific overviews can be found by consulting Appendix B, which provides an annotated guide of the literature. Approximately ninety books are listed in this selected guide. The organization of Appendix B reflects the chapter and section organization of this book. Additionally, it lists the most useful journals in the area of knowledge acquisition and learning.

# TOWARD A UNIFIED THEORY OF LEARNING:
## Multistrategy Task-adaptive Learning

### Ryszard S. Michalski

### Abstract

Any learning process can be viewed as a self-modification of the learner's current knowledge through an interaction with some information source. Such knowledge modification is guided by the learner's desire to achieve a certain outcome, and can engage any kind of inference. The type of inference involved depends on the input information, the current (background) knowledge and the learner's task at hand. Based on such a view of learning, several fundamental concepts are analized and clarified, in particular, analytic and synthetic learning, derivational and hypothetical explanation, constructive induction, abduction, abstraction and deductive generalization. It is shown that inductive generalization and abduction can be viewed as two basic forms of general induction, and that abstraction and deductive generalization are two related forms of constructive deduction. Using this conceptual framework, a methodology for *multistrategy task-adaptive learning* (MTL) is outlined, in which learning strategies are combined dynamically, depending on the current learning situation. Specifically, an MTL learner analizes a "triad" relationship among the input information, the background knowledge and the learning task, and on that basis determines which strategy, or a combination thereof, is most appropriate at a given learning step. To implement the MTL methodology, a new knowledge representation is proposed, based on the *parametric association rules* (PARs). Basic ideas of MTL are illustrated by means of the well-known "cup" example, through which is shown how an MTL learner can employ, depending the above triad relationship, emprical learning, constructive inductive generalization, abduction, explanation-based learning and abstraction.

## 1. INTRODUCTION

The last few years have seen an extraordinary growth and diversification of research in machine learning, and one can expect a continuation of this trend in the predictable future. While previously established areas, such as empirical symbolic learning, discovery systems and explanation-based learning have continued to be quite active (e.g., Laird, 1988; Segre, 1989; Porter and Mooney, 1990), some new areas have been very rapidly expanding, such as neural net learning (e.g., Barto and Anderson, 1985; Touretzky, Hinton and Sejnowski, 1988; and Fisher et al., 1989), genetic algorithm based learning (Holland, 1986, 1987; Davis, 1987; Goldberg, 1988; and Schafer, 1989), and computational learning theory (e.g., Haussler and Pitt, 1988; Ehrenfeucht, 1988; COLT 1990, 1991).

While past machine learning has been primarily oriented toward single-strategy systems, more recent research has been increasingly concerned with building systems that integrate two or more learning strategies. Single strategies are inherently limited as each of them applies only to a range of problems. To extend the capability of machine learning programs it is necessary to build systems that integrate various stategies. Among most known such systems are Unimem

An earlier and shorter version of this paper was presented at the ONR Workshop on Knowledge Acquisition Arlington, VA , November 6-7, 1989, and subsequently published in *Reports of Machine Learning and Inference Laboratory* . MLI-90-1, AIC, GMU, 1991.

(Lebowitz, 1986), Odysseus (Wilkins, Clancey, and Buchanan, 1986), Prodigy (Minton et al., 1987), DISCIPLE-1 (Kodratoff and Tecuci, 1987), GEMINI (Danyluk, 1987 and 1989), OCCAM (Pazzani, 1988), IOE (Dietterich and Flann, 1988) and ENIGMA (Bergadano et al., 1990). For some other examples see (Segre, 1989, Porter and Mooney, 1990). With few exceptions, most existing multistrategy systems are concerned with integrating some relatively simple empirical method, an analytic method, and possibly also an analogy, and the integration is done in a rather predefined way.

An open and ever challenging problem for machine learning research is to develop a system that would integrate a whole spectrum of learning strategies, and would be able to decide by itself which strategy(ies) is most suitable in any given learning situation. Humans are clearly able to apply a great variety of learning strategies depending on the problem at hand, and machine learning systems should try to ultimately match this ability.

In the context of the above mentioned proliferation of various learning methods and directions, and the interest in multistrategy systems, there is a need for a theoretical framework that would clarify the relationship among the diverse research strategies and methods, and provide a conceptual foundation for integrating them into effective multistrategy systems.

This paper represents our initial results toward such goals. Viewing learning as essentially a goal-guided multiple inference process (though not always explicit), it clarifies several fundamental concepts in learning, such as analytic and synthetic learning, derivational and hypothetical explanation, constructive induction, abduction, abstraction and deductive generalization. Based on the described conceptual framework, it then introduces a concept of *multistrategy task-adaptive learning* (MTL), in which multiple learning strategies are combined dynamically, according to the task at hand.

The objective of research on MTL is to develop a methodology, which for any learning task can recognize what learning strategy, or combination thereof, is likely to be the most effective for solving it (hence, the term "task-adaptive"). The key idea is that any learning process can be viewed as a derivation of desired knowledge from the input information according to the principle of computational economy. What is "desired" knowledge depends on the task the learner wants to perform. How the learner proceeds to obtain this knowledge (learning strategy) depends on what is the most effective way to utilize the available information and the learner's prior knowledge. Recent experiments in cognitive science show that when people have to reason in order to answer a question, they utilize knowledge that is most easily available to them. For example, when they have a choice of the knowledge source, they typically rely on their personal knowledge rather than on the knowledge supplied to them externally (Michalski, Boehm-Davis and Dontas, 1989).

The underlying aims of this work are to explain the relationships among basic learning strategies and research directions in a simple conceptual sense, rather than in a formal sense, so to clearly expose the main issue of the paper, that of viewing learning as a unified process in which diverse inference types are synergistically employed toward always the same goal, that of improvement of the learner's knowledge/skill through an interaction with some information source. In this spirit, the proposed MTL methodology is also presented through a conceptual explanation and illustration of the main ideas and the reasons behind them, rather than by giving specific algorithmic solutions and implementational details. These and related issues would take up much more space, and will be the subject of a separate publication.

The presented work is an extension and an elaboration of the ideas presented earlier in (Michalski and Ko, 1988; Michalski and Watanabe, 1988; Michalski, 1989 & 1990, Ko and Michalski, 1990). It also draws upon many ideas developed by others in the field of machine learning and cognitive science. We start with an outline of the inference-based learning theory and a discussion of basic learning strategies.

## 2. INFERENCE-BASED THEORY OF LEARNING

A key idea in symbolic learning is that the learner acquires desired knowledge through some form of reasoning - inductive, analogical, or deductive. In special cases, learning involves only copying the information provided by a source ("rote learning"), or syntactically transforming it and/or selecting from it some parts ("learning by instruction'). These cases, however, are not central to understanding the learning behavior, and will not be discussed here.

A learning process is activated by the input information, obtained from a teacher or from a learner's environment (external or internal). Such a process involves the learner's prior knowledge ("background knowledge"), and is motivated by the learner's desire to achieve some goal (to solve a problem, to understand given facts or observations, to perform a task, etc.). The learning goal defines the criteria for determining the relevant parts of prior knowledge, choosing the learning strategy, evaluating acquired knowledge, selecting the most preferred hypothesis among the candidate ones, etc. The goal also plays a major role in determining the amount of effort the learner should extend in pursuing any specific strategy.

Thus, learning can be viewed as a process of transforming input information into the desired knowledge by the use of inference and under the guidance of the learner's goal. Because a learning act may involve any type of inference, a complete theory of learning must therefore include also a theory of all types of inference. These ideas provide a framework for what we call the *inference-based theory of learning* (Figure 1).

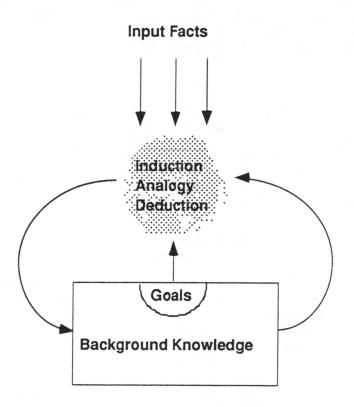

*Figure 1*. An Illustration of the inference-based theory of learning

The input information ("input") can be facts, observations, concept instances, previously formed generalizations, or any other knowledge. The input activates segments of the learner's background knowledge (BK) that are most relevant to it from the viewpoint of the current learning task. This is done by making matches between the input and hierarchically organized knowledge segments (see knowledge representation in section 5).

A major tenet of this theory is that the primary inference type performed in any learning act is determined by a "triad" relationship that involves the input, background knowledge and the current learning task. This primary inference defines the "learning strategy." The strategy is inductive, if the input consists of one or more facts, and/or previously generated descriptions existing in the learner's BK, and the task is to generalize the facts and/or improve the descriptions so that the resulting knowledge is useful for solving some new problems. It is analogical, if the input is "similar" to what the learner already knows, and the task is to make a decision about the input that would take advantage of the similar past experience. It is deductive, if the input is principally entailed by what the learner already knows (i.e., BK), but the relevant parts of BK are not efficient or directly useful for the learner, and the learning task is to transform these parts into a better form.

The results of inference are assimilated into BK, so that the next act of learning will involve the modified BK. To achieve such a step-wise knowledge improvement, any knowledge acquired by the learner in some learning act must be expressed in the form compatible with other knowledge stored in BK. A learning process with such an ability is called *closed-loop learning*.

In summary, the inference-based theory states that in order to learn, an agent needs to be able to perform transformations of knowledge, i.e., to perform *inference*, and to have *memory* which supplies the learner with the background knowledge needed for performing the inference, and records the results of the inference in the form useful for future use. Without either of the two abilities, no learning can be accomplished (except for "rote" learning," which involes essentially no inference). Thus, one can concisely say that:

*Learning = Inferencing + Memorizing*

While these ideas seem to clearly apply to symbolic learning, it may appear that they do not apply to neural net learning, reinfocement learning or genetic algorithm based learning. In fact, they do apply, because these approaches also perform a generalization, specialization or similization operations on input information, except that they do them implicitly rather than explicitly, as in symbolic systems. They also have the ability to memorize results of their learning for future use, although, again, they do it in a distributed way, rather than localized way. An explicit representation of inference operations performed by a neural net or genetic algorithm is described in (Wnek et al. (1990),who employ the so-called *diagrammatic visualization* of learning processes.

Another question may be what is the main purpose of this theory, in particular, whether it is intended to be a cognitive theory, which explains information processes in human (or animal) learning. The answer is that our intention is to develop a theory that is sufficiently general that unessential biological and implementational aspects can be ignored, but sufficiently specific that it accounts for major information processes occuring in diverse forms of learning, whether they exist in nature or not. The success of the theory can be measured by its ability to characterize and explain conceptual relationships among methods and paradigms studied in machine learning, or in human learning. We deliberately avoid being too formal, so that we can primarily stress the ideas and intuitions behind different concepts, learning strategies and their interrelationships.

Many proposed ideas have been inspired by observing how people or animals learn, but no claims are made that this is a cognitive theory. It is hoped, however, that the presented outline of the theory will be helpful for fostering our understanding of learning processes in general, and for implementing more advanced learning systems.

## 3. THE ROLE OF EXPLANATION IN LEARNING

It is a well-known fact that it is difficult to learn anything without understanding it. At the early stage of development humans, of course, acquire a lot of information by rote, but among mature individuals rote learning plays a minor role. Understanding, in turn, is a result of self-creating or receiving a satisfactory explanation. The notion of explanation, however, needs clarification.

In explanation-based learning (Mitchell, Keller and Kedar-Cabelli, 1986; DeJong and Monney, 1986; DeJong, 1986 and 1988; ), an explanation is the process of deductively applying the learner's prior knowledge (domain knowledge and an abstract definition of the goal concept) to demonstrate that a given example is an instance of the goal concept. The obtained proof is then used to restructure the learner's concept definition, to make it more efficient or useful ("operational").

In inductive learning, producing some form of an "explanation" of the observed facts is the main purpose of learning. Through induction, a scientist builds a theory explaining an observed phenomenon, or a medical researcher develops a general description of a disease (Michalski, 1983). Such a description, especially if it is stated in terms of causal relations, serves as an "explanation" of the disease, and of the patient's symptoms.

In the field of machine learning, inductive learning has been implemented in several forms. Its simplest form, empirical inductive learning, generates "explanations" in the form of simple general descriptions (rules, decision trees, equations, etc.) of the given examples. In empirical inductive learning these descriptions are typically expressed in terms of the attributes selected from those used in describing individual examples. Though such empirical generalizations hardly deserve to be called explanations, they satisfy the primary condition for an explanation, as they entail the input examples. For example, the rule "if there is smoke, there is fire" may be a generalization of some observations, but it does not give a "real" explanation of the phenomenon. Only in knowledge-based induction, i.e., constructive induction or abduction (see sec. 4), can the result of learning be a "true" explanation. This is because such induction is capable of creating descriptions in terms of high level concepts and/or causal relationships (e.g., Hoff, Michalski and Stepp, 1983; Mehler, Bentrup and Riedesel, 1986; O'Rorke, Morris and Schulenburg, 1989).

The above shows that the word "explanation" can be used in more than one sense, and it is not easy to capture its meaning formally. The Webster's Third International Dictionary states that "an explanation is an act or process of explaining," and that it "consists in successfully comparing a new phenomenon with an older and more familiar one." While such an "explanation" of explanation sounds intuitively correct, in order to make it computational, one needs to better specify the meaning of "comparing" in this definition.

It appears that one can adequately capture the meaning of "comparing" by assuming that it means a demonstration that the new phenomenon is a logical consequence of the old familiar one. Thus, the process of explanation involves proving such a logical consequence, i.e., it involves deduction.

We postulate that creating an explanation of some observation involves, in general, constructing two components (Michalski and Ko, 1988):

- an *explanatory hypothesis*, which, together with a reasoner's background knowledge, entails the observation ("strongly" or "weakly"), and

- an *explanatory structure*, which demonstrates this entailment.

where a "strong" entailment means a logical entailment, and a "weak" entailment means a plausible or probabilistic entailment.

To illustrate these components, let us use an example concerning the U.S. space shuttle Challenger disaster on January 28, 1986, and Richard Feynman's experiment to explain the reason for this disaster. During a launch of a shuttle there are always vibrations that cause the rocket joints to move a little. Inside the joints are the so-called O-rings, which are supposed to expand to make a seal. However, if the O-rings do not expand, hot gas can escape through the joints, which can start a fire. Thus, if the O-rings lose their resiliency just for a second or two, this could cause an accident.

In a televised meeting of the presidential commission investigating the accident, Richard Feynman made the famous O-ring and ice-water demonstration. He put a sample of the rubber from the O-rings in a clamp, and submerged it for a while in a glass of ice-water. Then he took the rubber out, and showed that when the clamp was undone, the rubber did not spring back.

Thus, the experiment showed that the rubber of the O-rings loses resiliency at low temperatures. This information is what we characterized above as explanatory hypothesis. To explain the accident one also needs background knowledge, that if the rings lose resiliency, hot gas can escape through the O-rings, which, in turn, can cause the observed fire, and the rocket explosion. One also needs to know that on the morning of the launch, the temperature was 29 oF, which is low. The line of reasoning (a sequence of steps) from the explanatory hypothesis combined with background knowledge to the phenomenon being explained is what we call the explanatory structure.

## Defining Explanation

We call an observation, a process, or anything that is supposed to be explained, the *explanatory target* (ET). To explain an ET to an agent (or to oneself) one needs to show that the *explanatory hypothesis* (EH), plus the agent's *background knowledge* (BK) entails the ET. As we stated before, the sequence of steps demonstrating this entailment is the explanatory structure (ES). In brief, ES demonstrates that EH and BK strongly or weakly entails ET, which we write as:

$$\text{EH \& BK} \mathrel{|\!\!>} \text{ET} \tag{1}$$

In some situations, the explanatory hypothesis does not need to be constructed, because the background knowledge itself entails ET. In the example about the Challenger accident, if it were well known that the rubber used in O-rings loses resiliency at low temperatures, there would have been no need for Feynman's demonstration. In such situations, the explanatory structure simply demonstrates that:

$$\text{BK} \mathrel{|\!\!>} \text{ET} \tag{2}$$

In the most general case, the background knowledge may be incorrect or inconsistent with respect to an observation, and the total explanatory hypothesis may also involve modifications of the background knowledge. In such a case, instead of BK, we would have a modified BK*:

$$\text{EH \& BK*} \mathrel{|\!\!>} \text{ET} \tag{3}$$

For example, suppose that in the Challenger example the background knowledge includes an erroneous belief that nothing could be wrong with the O-rings. In this case, the explanatory hypothesis would include not only the knowledge that the rubber O-rings are not resilient at low temperatures, but also a correction of the erroneous belief.

The explanatory hypothesis (in the Challenger example, "the rubber of O-rings loses resiliency at low temperatures") may be obtained in several ways. It may be obtained through an experiment, and a generalization of the results. In our example, the observation "the rubber loses resiliency in a glass of ice-water" can be generalized to "the rubber loses resiliency at low temperatures" (thus, it will lose resiliency when exposed to the cold air). Such a process of making generalized statements solely on the basis of experimental observations is *empirical induction*.

To come up with the idea to make such an experiment, however, one needs to perform knowledge-based induction, i.e., constructive induction (see section 4). The background knowledge might involve rules, such as:

"If there is a leak, the gas escapes through. If the gas is very hot, and gets in contact with flammable material, then it might cause a fire."

A fire has been observed. By reasoning backward (from consequences to premises), one could hypothesize that there might have been a leak. What could cause a leak? Many things could cause a leak. For example, if rubber of the O-rings would shrink due to vibrations, and did not spring back, this would cause a leak. Since properties of materials change with temperature, let us then see how the rubber of O-rings behaves in the kind of temperature observed on the day of the flight. Conducting such reasoning leads one to the idea of making an experiment, like the one made by Feynman.

Alternatively, one may generate the explanatory hypothesis by drawing an analogy. Feynman might have known, for example, that some specific rubber material, similar to the one used in the O-rings, looses resiliency in low tempretures. Through analogy he could then generate the explanatory hypothesis involving O-rings. Another way to get the explanatory hypothesis is to deduce it from a general theory. In our example, it would be a theory about the behavior of different rubber materials at different temperatures.

Finally, the explanatory hypothesis can be received directly from a source of information. For example, Feynman, instead of making a demonstration, might have referred to a technical document stating the properties of this specific rubber material. This is a form of learning by instruction. (Of course, the information in the document could have been a result of prior experiments).

The above methods of creating an explanation of observations correspond to fundamental learning strategies - learning by empirical induction, by constructive induction, by analogy, by deduction, and by instruction, respectively.

## Types of Explanation

We distinguish between two basic types of explanation, one in which the explanatory hypothesis is not needed because background knowledge is sufficient to explain the ET, and the second in which explanatory hypothesis has to be created through some form of plausible inference (empirical induction, constructive induction or analogy). Accordingly to these two cases we have two types of explanation:

- *derivational* (or *deductive*) explanation, which consists only of an explanatory structure demonstrating through deductive reasoning that the knowledge already possessed (knowledge supplied by some source plus the agent's prior knowledge) implies the explanatory target , and

- *hypothetical* (or *inductive*) explanation, which consists of an explanatory hypothesis and an explanatory structure demonstrating that this hypothesis together with the learner's background knowledge implies the explanatory target. The explanatory hypothesis is created by inductive reasoning or analogy (which can be viewed as induction and deduction combined).

Learning processes that involve making primarily derivational explanations are called *analytic*. Their main result or purpose is restructuring prior knowledge into a form that is better in some sense (e.g., more efficient, easier to understand, or operational), or strengthening the belief in the prior knowledge. This form of learning has also been called "learning at the symbol level" (Dietterich, 1986).

Learning processes that involve making primarily inductive explanations are called *synthetic*. Their main result or purpose is to hypothesize new knowledge, i.e., knowledge not contained in the deductive closure of the learner's background knowledge. This form of learning has also been called "learning at the knowledge level" (Dietterich, 1986). Synthetic learning methods can, in turn, be classified into *empirical induction* (in which the role of prior knowledge is limited), and *constructive induction* (in which prior knowledge plays a significant role).

One may ask how these ideas relate to skill acquisition through practice, as such processes seem to involve little reasoning. This question is related to the previously mentioned issue about learning in connectionist or neural nets and genetic algorithms. In skill acquisition, there is no explicit execution of symbolic rules of inference. However, by comparing the input information (e.g., training examples or practice exercises) with the observed behavior on new cases, one can say that, from the conceptual viewpoint, the above processes do implicitly perform operations logically equivalent to those of generalization, analogy or specialization. For example, the famous Pavlov's experiments have shown that dogs perform instinctively certain limited generalizations of sound, smell or other sensory signals, without any explicit reasoning. As we pointed out before, neural nets, as well as genetic algorithms are able to perform generalization, specialization or analogy, but not in an explicit form.

The next section discusses a classification on learning processes from the viewpoint of basic types of knowledge representation used, and then analizes in a greater detail the synthetic and analytic learning paradigms.

## 4. BASIC TYPES OF LEARNING

### 4.1 Fundamental learning strategies

Inference-based learning theory treats learning as an inference process that involves input facts and the learner's prior knowledge. If the results of this inference are evaluated as important, they are stored for future use, and this completes a single learning process. The major type of inference involved in a learning process defines the learning strategy. The lowest level strategy is when there is no inference done by the learner, and the inputs are stored as they are received (*direct knowledge implantation* or *rote learning*). The next level strategy is when there is only a selection of information from and/or syntactic transformation of the source information (*learning by instruction*). This type of strategy is central to current methods of knowledge acquisition for expert systems.

The above two strategies involve little knowledge transformation (inference) on the part of the learner, and are not considered central for the field of machine learning. The next level strategies are classified generally to analytic and syntetic. The goal of an analytic strategy is to improve in some sense the knowledge already possesed by reformulating it to a better form. The primary inference type used is deduction. The goal of a syntetic strategy is to create new knowledge that goes beyond the input facts. The primary inference types are induction and analogy.

### 4.2 A classification based on the type of input and output knowledge

Both analytic and syntetic strategies can be classified on the basis of the comparison of the type of knowledge that a learner starts with and the type of knowledge acquired. From this viewpoint, learning methods can be classified into four basic types:

DD   (Declarative to Declarative) - The initial knowledge is in a declarative form, and the derived knowledge is also in a declarative form. For example, in explanation-based generalization (Mitchell, Keller and Kedar-Cabelli, 1986), the initial knowledge is an example (a declarative description of some fact or observation with an associated class) plus the learner's background knowledge (domain knowledge, goal concept plus some domain-independent knowledge, i.e., relevant inference rules). The deductively derived output is "operational" knowledge (knowledge in the form useful for a given application). Another example is empirical induction from examples, where the input is typically a collection of observations stated in a declarative form, and the output is a generalization, also stated in such a form. Knowledge compression (reformulation) is also an example of DD learning.

DP   (Declarative to Procedural) - The initial knowledge is in a declarative form, and the derived knowledge is in a procedural form. For example, advice taking or automatic programming are forms of the DP analytic method, because the input is some advice or a program specification typically in declarative form, and the output is a procedure for actually accomplishing the desired task (e.g., Bierman, Guiho and Kodratoff, 1984, Amarel, 1986; Mostow, 1986). Acquiring new skill can also be viewed as a DP learning task in which the initial knowledge includes a mental representation of what one should be able to do and observed results of trying, and the output knowledge is the improved control mechanism.

PD  (Procedural to Declarative) - The initial knowledge is in a procedural form, e.g., an algorithm or a process developing in time, and the output is in a declarative form, e.g., a declarative description of this algorithm or process. If the input is a complete process, and the produced description just builds a "true" declarative description of it, then we have PD analytic learning. On the other hand, if a learner generalizes a description beyond the observable process, then we have a synthetic PD learning. Program SPARC that discovers rules for predicting sequences of objects is an example of synthetic PD learning (e.g., Dietterich and Michalski, 1986; Michalski, Ko and Chen, 1987).

PP  (Procedural to Procedural) - The starting knowledge is procedural, as is the derived knowledge. Skill improvement with practice, automatic program optimization and the analogy-based program transformation are examples of PP learning.

As mentioned in the previous section, a major distinction between analytic and synthetic methods is in the type of explantion they generate, derivational and hypothetical. The next section will explore these two strategies in a greater detail, and define various subclasses of these two classes of methods.

## 4.3 Analytic Learning

As mentioned earlier, analytic learning involves an analysis of the input information in terms of the learner's relevant prior knowledge (domain-dependent and domain-independent), and then creation of desirable knowledge on the basis of this analysis. The primary type of inference engaged in this process is deductive, although in more recent versions of explanation-based learning, there can be some inductive inference involved also. A "pure" analytic learning method performs only a truth-preserving knowledge transformation, and thus the validity of the derived knowledge depends entirely on the validity of the input information and the background knowledge. If the initial knowledge is valid, so is the derived knowledge. Such pure analytic learning creates no "new" knowledge, but a more useful reformulation or specialization of the initial knowledge (i.e., the learner's prior knowledge, plus input information, such as a concept example supplied by a teacher).

### Explanation-based learning

The most well-known form of analytical learning is explanation-based learning (Mitchell, Keller and Kedar-Cabelli, 1986; DeJong and Mooney, 1986). Other forms include "operationalization" (Mostow, 1983) and automatic program synthesis (e.g., Bierman, Guiho and Kodratoff, 1984).

Let us analyze explanation-based learning (EBL) in terms of the ideas presented above. In EBL, given an instance of a concept, the learner first determines an explanatory structure (proof) showing that the instance is indeed an example of the concept. An abstract concept definition ('goal concept"), relevant domain knowledge and domain-independent knowledge (inference rules) are assumed to be known to the learner a priori. All these components constitute what we call learner's background knowledge. The produced explanatory structure is then used to create a reformulation of the concept definition, so that it is more useful ("operational") for classifying future instances. This operational concept description is a generalization of the original instance and a specialization of the abstract concept definition. The underlying assumption is that future concept instances to be classified will be in the same form as the initial (training) instance.

Thus, (pure) EBL assumes that the learner's background knowledge (BK) is adequate to establish an explanatory structure explaining a given instance (i.e., the explanatory target ET), and there is no need for an explanatory hypothesis. The learner only seeks the explanatory structure that demonstrates that

$$BK \models ET \tag{4}$$

holds, where $\models$ denotes logical (strong) entailment. The explanatory structure can be in the form of a proof tree generated by a theorem prover showing that the abstract concept definition (goal concept) is satisfied by a given example. The explanatory structure is then used to develop more effective knowledge. For example, in the ARMS system (Segre, 1987), given an initial plan for joining two assembly components, an example provided by a teacher and BK describing simpler goals, the system determines a more effective plan for joining components.

In short, in EBL, the learner relies primarily on BK, and the example serves as a focus of attention for learning. Once an explanatory structure is established, it is used to generalize the input example to the extent that the created operational knowledge BK* still subsumes ET, i.e., $BK^* \models ET$.

If BK is inadequate (inconsistent, incomplete or intractable), an explanatory structure cannot be established without postulating change in the background knowledge or hypothesizing some new knowledge. Thus, the applicabiltiy of this approach and the validity of its results depend on whether the background knowledge is complete and valid.

## Constructive deduction

While studing properties of constructive induction (see next section) it occured to us that one could formulate a symmetric form of learning, which we call *constructive deduction*. This form uses background knowledge to deductively transfrom input information to a more abstract description, more general description or both. Creating a more abstract description is called *abstraction*; while creating a more general description by deduction is called *deductive generalization*. In both cases, learning involves applying truth-preserving rules of inference (domain-dependent or domain-independent) to the input information. Abstraction transfers a description of an entity from a more specific language to a less specific, in which certain details are ignored. Generalization extends the set of entities that are referred to in a description. These two processes often co-occur, and this is probably the reason why these two terms are sometimes confused.

For example, transforming a statement "My workstation has a Motorolla 25-MHz 68030 processor" to "My workstation is quite fast" is an abstraction. To make such a transformation, one needs (domain-dependent) background knowledge that a processor with the 25-MHz clock speed is quite fast, and therefore the computer can be viewed as quite fast. On the other hand, transforming a statement "John lives in Fairfax, Virginia" to "John lives in the United States" is a deductive generalization, because the set of locations where John lives is extended. This is a deductive generalization, because the resulting statement is a logical consequence of the initial input description and background knowledge. To make such a transformation one needs domain-dependent background knowledge that Virginia is a part of the United States, and that if somebody lives in some subarea, which is a part of a greater area, then the person also lives in the greater area. The last piece of knowledge is a special case of the transitivity of set membership, which is domain independent knowledge. For a more discussion of deductive generalization, see (Michalski and Zemankowa, 1989). Finally, consider a transformation of a statement "John has two cats, Kicia and Vicia, in his appartment" into "John has pets in his residence." This trasformation involves both abstraction and deductive generalization.

To simply characterize the difference between an abstraction and a generalization, consider an expresssion

$$d(A) = p \tag{5}$$

which states that a descriptor (an attribute or predicate) takes value p for the set of entities A. Changing (5) to a statement in which d and/or p is substituted by a more abstract/general descriptor is an abstraction. Changing (5) to a statement in which A is replaced by a larger set is a generalization (can be deductive or inductive, depending on the meaning of d).

Inference rules used in constructive deduction may change the terms used in a description from low level observable concepts to highly abstract and/or general concepts. This way, constructive deduction is a vehicle for creating abstract descriptions. Notice, that constructive deduction generates knowledge that is a logical consequence of given premises (input information and the background knowledge), and therefore its pure form does not introduce elements of uncertainty. It can introduce uncertainty, if the rules of inference are plausible rather than crisp. Because constructive deduction uses deduction as the primary form of inference, it is classified as a form of analytic learning.

## 4.4 Synthetic Learning

In synthetic learning, the system strives to create desired knowledge by hypothesizing it through some form of inductive inference. Although the primary inference type involved is inductive, a synthetic learning process always involves also some deductive inference (e.g., to test whether a generated hypothesis accounts for an observation).

Unlike deduction, induction has been a subject of a long-standing debate, and different authors have defined it in different ways. One view is that it is merely empirical reasoning from particulars to universals without using prior knowledge. Another view is that induction includes every inference process under uncertainty, i.e., any inference that is not strictly deductive (e.g., Holland et al, 1986). These two views seem to be extreme points of a spectrum. The first one is too narrow, as it does not reflect the basic scientific thought on this subject going back to Aristotle, which characterizes induction as the fundamental inference underlying any process of creating new knowledge (see the reference under Aristotle). The second view seems to be overly general, as it includes processes such as approximate deduction. Our view is that induction is simply a process opposite of deduction. While deduction is a derivation of consequents from given premises, induction is a process of hypothesizing premises that entail given consequents. Strict deduction is truth-preserving, and strict induction is falsity-preserving. The intersection of these two types is tautological inference, which is both truth-preserving and falsity-preserving (i.e., equivalence preserving).

Empirical reasoning from particulars to universals, which we call *empirical inductive generalization*, is a simple, knowledge-poor, form of reasoning from effects to premises. As we show below, it can be viewed as a reasoning that traces backward certain *domain-independent* rules of inference ("generalization rules"; Michalski, 1983).

A more general form is *constructive induction*, which may trace backward both *domain-dependent* rules, as well as domain-independent background knowledge rules. In this formulation, constructive induction includes *constructive inductive generalization*, which uses BK rules to create higher level generalizations, *constructive inductive specialization*, which uses BK to hypothesize specializations (Michalski and Zemankowa, 1990; see an example below), and *abduction*, a form of reasoning introduced by Peirce in his classic and very influential treatise on Elements of Logic (see the reference under Peirce).

Abduction, as defined by Peirce, also called by him *retroduction*, is "the operation of adopting an explanatory hypothesis ...that would account for the facts (or some of them)." Here is an exerpt from his treatise (chp. II, sec.1):

> *The surprising fact, C, is observed;*
> *But if A were true, C would be a matter of course*
> *Hence, there is reason to suspect that A is true.*

Thus, abduction is creating a hypothesis that would entail the observation ("..if A were true, C would be a matter of course"). It is interesting to observe that this definition is equivalent to the definition of induction, if one interprets the undefined concept of "explanatory hypothesis" more broadly, namely that it can be in the form of a generalization. In this sense, this definition includes, as a special case (probably unintentionally), empirical inductive generalization. Clearly, a generalization of an observed fact must account for the fact. For example, suppose one observes that a particular painting of Polacci was sold very high, and hypothesizes that perhaps all paintings of Polacci are very expensive. If such a generalization is adopted as true, then the statement that the particular Pollaci's painting is expensive would be  "a matter of course."

As we show below, in Peirce's abduction a hypothesis is created by "tracing backward" certain *domain-dependent rules*. Because constructive induction places no constraints on what type of background knowledge rules are employed, it can create causal explanations or other explanatory hypotheses, as well as inductive generalizations.

The initial formulation of constructive induction (Michalski, 1983) emphasized using domain knowledge to develop new concepts or attributes, beyond those supplied in the input. Depending on the type of domain knowledge involved, the new concepts so created can serve as explanatory hypotheses. Therefore, in general, the idea of constructive induction includes a knowledge-based creation of explanations, and this has led us to the use of the term "constructive induction" in the current form.  Both, empirical inductive generalization and constructive induction can be viewed as forms of "reverse" reasoning, as opposed to deduction that can be viewed as "forward" reasoning. Therefore, we find it conceptually more attractive to consider them as two forms of inductive inference, rather than to view them as totally distinct forms of inference.

There is another issue related to abduction. Peirce was not very concerned with the issue of a preference criterion for choosing an explanatory hypothesis. This issue, however, is important when there is more than one hypothesis that explains the given facts. Thus, in general,  a preference criterion has to be included as an important component of processes of creating hypotheses.

In view of the above, our general formulation of inductive inference is that, given an observation statement (OS) and background knowledge (BK), the reasoner searches for a hypothesis (H), consistent with BK, such that H & BK strongly or weakly entails OS, which we write as:

$$\text{H \& BK } |> \text{ OS} \tag{6}$$

and that the hypothesis satisfies a *preference criterion*. The preference criterion expresses the desirable properties of the hypothesis from the viewpoint of the reasoner's goals. For example, the reasoner may have a preference (or a bias) for a simpler hypothesis, and/or more plausible one according to the BK,  and/or a hypothesis that uses concepts easy to test, etc.  A preference criterion may also allow to generate an inconsistent and/or incomplete hypothesis, if such a hypothesis is more effective for its expected use.  For example, we usually prefer to use the Newton's laws of motion, although they are, in general,  less consistent with the facts than Einstein's theory.

By identifying H with explanatory hypothesis EH and OS with explanatory target ET, equation  (6) becomes identical to (1), which characterizes the concept of explanation. Thus, the above shows that induction can be viewed as a process of creating explanations that satisfy some preference criterion. We  distinguish between two basic types of induction:

- *Empirical induction*, in which the system creates an inductive hypothesis primarily on the basis of the given facts, that is without much use (or need) of domain-dependent background knowledge BK.  Empirical induction involves primarily domain-independent generalization rules. Domain-dependent knowledge plays only a supportive role, for example,  that of providing the constraints on the set of possible attribute values, specifying relations that hold among these attribute values and influencing the preference criterion.

- *Constructive induction (knowledge-based induction)*, in which the process of creating a hypothesis depends strongly on the domain-dependent background knowledge, as well as domain-independent .

In the literature, the terms empirical induction and inductive generalization are often viewed as equivalent. This view is not correct, because inductive generalization can not only be empirical, but also constructive, that is, it may involve a significant amount of domain knowledge. For example, creating a general scientific theory describing a class of entities (e.g., creating a physical law) is a form of inductive generalization, but may not be what we would call an empirical induction, because it may involve concepts far beyond the observables. Another example is a generalization of the statement "I saw John in his office on Monday, Wednesday and Sunday evenings" to "John is an unusually hard working employee." The second statement is a constructive inductive generalization, but strictly speaking is not an empirical induction. This is because to generate such a hypothesis one also needs to know about the work of other employees and to know that being in one's office in the evenings means working beyond normal expectations.

Finally, one should note that induction and generalization are two different processes. As indicated earlier, just as induction does not always produce a generalization, generalization is not always inductive (Michalski and Zemankova, 1989).

Let us now consider in greater detail empirical and constructive inductive learning.

### Empirical inductive learning

In empirical inductive learning, BK is small and inadequate for constructing an explanatory structure for a given observation(s). The learner generalizes examples observed to create a consistent and complete description of them in terms of concepts used in describing observations (or closely related ones). Such a description implies the observed facts and, thus, can be viewed formally as an explanatory hypothesis, EH (an " empirical " generalization or explanation).

In machine learning, programs constructing empirical generalizations typically use only descriptive concepts that are selected from among those used in describing original observations. Such "surface" induction is called *selective induction* .

In learning from examples, P denotes a description that characterizes all positive examples and none of the negative examples (assuming that they are distinct). There can be many Ps which consistently and completely characterize a given finite set of examples, and therefore empirical learning needs some preference criterion for judging such admissible hypotheses. The essence of practical implementations of empirical learning is determining the simplest or most efficient expression for P.

The above describes a *crisp* empirical induction, which creates generalizations that strongly (or strictly) imply the observations. For example, after observing that John has come to various meetings punctually, one might hypothesize that he always comes to meetings punctually. The crisp empirical induction is falsity-preserving (if the input includes a false statement, the generalization is necessarily false). Another form is *soft* empirical induction that produces generalizations that weakly imply the observations. The latter form of empirical induction is not necessarily falsity-preserving. For example, observing someone coming late to a meeting several times, one might generalize that this person *usually* comes late to meetings.

Statements produced by empirical induction are usually not causal explanations, because they do not typically involve any causal relationships, but only correlations. They tend to be used, however, as explanations in everyday reasoning. For example, a person may ask, "Why is this tennis table green?" and someone may answer, "All tennis tables are green." This is not a "real" explanation, but people give such answers as "explanations."

Empirical induction has been the most active research area in machine learning, and there are many successful implementations of empirical learning programs. Most of them either generate rules [e.g., the AQ-based family of programs (Michalski, 1973)], or decision trees [the ID3-based family of programs (Quinlan, 1979)].

### Constructive induction

In constructive induction (Michalski, 1983), the learner uses *domain-dependent* as well as domain independent background knowledge to hypothesize concepts and/or relations that characterize input information. The hypothesized concepts can be generalizations of the input facts, can be causal explanations of the facts, or they can be specializations of the input knowledge. If the engaged background knowledge involves causal dependencies that are "traced back," then the created hypothesis provides a causal explanation of the observation(s). If the input is general knowledge rather than specific facts, constructive induction involves using background knowledge to hypothesize lower level or more specific knowledge (which implies the more general one). To illustrate the latter, suppose that input information is that azalias grow in Virginia. From that general knowledge, one my hypothesize that azalias may also grow in Fairfax, a city in Virginia. This type of reasoning is called *inductive specialization* (Michalski and Zemankowa, 1989).

As we mentioned earlier, we view inductive inference as a general form of inference that includes empirical generalization and constructive induction. Such a view is consistent with a long tradition of science - starting with views of Aristotle, as expressed in his fundamental treatise *Posterior Analytics* (see reference under Aristotle). Such a view is also quite satisfying intellectually, because it treats both empirical induction and constructive induction as different forms of reverse reasoning, namely as a reasoning from effects to premises that imply them. Such premises can be generalizations or causal descriptions. A simple form of constructive induction can be characterized as follows.

*Given:*

• Background knowledge consiting of domain-dependent rules

$$(\text{For all } p \in \textbf{P}, \ Q(e, p) \ ==> \ (\text{For all } t \in \ T, \ S(e, t)) \tag{7}$$

where $Q(e, p)$ and $S(e, t)$ are certain predicates,

and domain-independent rules used in empirical induction, such dropping a condition, climbing generalization tree, etc. (Michalski, 1983).

• Input $S(e, t_1)$, $S(e, t_2)$, $S(e, t_3)$,..., where $t_1, t_2, t_3, ... \in T$.

*Hypothesize:*

$$\text{For all } p \in \textbf{P}, \ Q(e, p) \tag{8}$$

For example, suppose one believes that being well-organized, i.e., consistently well-organized over time, implies the ability to come to meetings punctually. If one observes John coming to several meetings punctually, then one might *constructively* hypothesize that John is well-organized.

As another example, suppose that one believes that being hardworking implies working after hours. If one sees several students from the AI Center working after hours a few times, then one might hypothesize that all students of the AI Center are hardworking. In these examples one can see how constructive induction may involve both empirical generalization (over the students), and an abduction of an abstract concept ("hardworking"). To show that the above form includes abduction, consider a classic example of abductive inference presented by Peirce (see reference under Peirce):

*Given*

BK:         Location(bean, BAG)   ==>   Color(bean, white)

            ("Beans in this BAG are white")

Input:      Color (Bean1, white)

            ("Color of Bean1 is white")

*Determine*

Hypothesis:   Location(Bean1, BAG), i.e., "Bean1 is from the BAG".

As one can see, the above inference can be interpreted as "tracing backward" a domain-dependent rule. For another illustration of abduction consider, for example, the problem of recovery from failed proofs (Cox and Pietrzykowski, 1986; Duval and Kodratoff, 1990). In these works, the system abductively creates the minimal hypothesis needed for completing a proof by "tracing backward" certain domain knowledge rules.

In general, constructive induction is reasoning that may trace backward and/or forward certain domain-independent rules (e.g., rules of generalization), and/or domain-dependent rules (expressing domain knowledge), so that the result is a hypothesis that together with BK entails the initial input. Thus, constructive induction can be viewed as the most general form of induction, and abduction as a special type of such constructive induction.

A major limitation of inductive learning (empirical or constructive) is that it produces hypotheses that may be incorrect, because induction is not, in general, a truth-preserving inference. Even if the input facts are all correct, the produced generalization may not be correct. On the other hand, analytic learning, if it is based on strict deduction, guarantees that the improved knowledge is correct.

It may be interesting to point out a certain symmetry between synthetic (inductive) and analytic (deductive) methods. Analytic learning produces correct knowledge only to the extent to which the learner's initial knowledge (handcrafted into the system, or induced from cases) is *correct and complete*. If the initial knowledge is incorrect or incomplete, the results may be incorrect also. On the other hand, empirical inductive learning may also produce provably correct results. This is the case when the set of input facts (examples) is *correct and complete*, in the sense that it spans all representative examples (this does not necessarily mean the whole space of examples). Such a situation is described, for example, in (Michalski and Negri, 1977), where an inductive learning program produced provably correct rules for distinguishing between a win and draw positions in a chess endgame. Analytic and synthetic methods are not mutually exclusive, but are overlapping; methods that perform an equivalence-preserving knowledge transformation are both analytic and synthetic.

The uncertainty of inductive inference is a property inherently connected with any process of knowledge creation, including all scientific activities, and cannot be avoided in principle. The certainty of deduction is based on the certainty of the premises, but the premises have originally been created by induction.

## 5. A MULTICRITERION CLASSIFICATION OF LEARNING PROCESSES

Learning processes can be classified according to many criteria. Among particularily relevant criteria are the type of learning strategy used, the research orientation, the type of knowledge representation employed, the application area, etc. Classifications based on such single criteria have been discussed in (Carbonell, Michalski and Mitchell, 1983) and (Michalski, 1986).

This section proposes a classification of learning processes that is based on several interrelated criteria (Figure 2). In one general stucture, the classification shows basic characteristics of all major machine learning approaches and paradigms. Its primary purpose is to help the reader to get a general view of the whole field of machine learning.

As any classification, the classification can be judged by the degree to which it illustrates important distinctions and relations among various categories. The categories presented are not to be viewed as having precisely delineated borderlines, but rather as labels of central tendencies that can transmute from one to another by differently emphasizing various principal components. This interpretation reflects our view of multistrategy learning as an integration of basic inference processes, which are combined in different ways appropriately for the task. The classification criteria include the primary purpose of the learning method, the type of input information, the type of primary inference employed, and finally, the role of the learner's prior knowledge in the learning process.

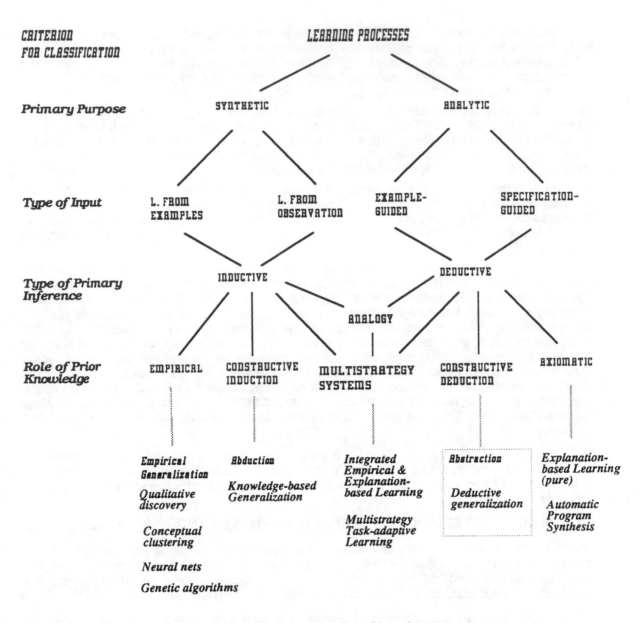

*Figure 2.* A multicriterion classification of learning processes.

As discussed above, from the viewpoint of the primary purpose, learning methods can be classified into synthetic and analytic. The primary purpose of synthetic methods is to create new or better knowledge. The primary purpose of the analytic methods is to transform the prior knowledge into a better form, so that is can better serve some goal. The knowledge so transformed does not allow the learner to solve more problems, but to solve them more effectively.

If the input to a synthetic learning method are examples classified by an independent source of knowledge, for example, a teacher, an expert, or an "oracle," then we have *learning from examples*. When the input are facts that need to be described or organized into a knowledge structure by the learner itself, then we have *learning from observation*. The latter is exemplified by learning by discovery, conceptual clustering and theory formation.

The primary type of inference used in synthetic learning is induction. As described in section 4.1, inductive learning can be empirical (BK-poor) or constructive (BK-intensive). Most work in empirical induction has been concerned with empirical generalization of concept examples using attributes selected from among those present in the descriptions of the examples (hence, such induction is sometimes called "selective" ; Michalski, 1983). Another form of empirical learning includes quantitative discovery, in which learner constructs a set of equations characterizing given data. Learning methods employed in neural nets or genetic algorithms are also viewed as forms of empirical inductive learning. They typically rely on relatively small amounts of BK, and their primary inference type is inductive. This inference, however, is not executed in an explicit way, like in typical symbolic methods, but in an implicit way.

In contrast to empirical induction, constructive induction is knowledge-intensive, as it uses BK to create high-level characterizations of the input information. This input information can be in the form of low level specific facts or already generalized descriptions. As described above, abduction can be viewed as a form of constructive induction, which "traces backward" certain domain-dependent knowledge rules.

For completness, let us mention that there are two other classifications of inductive methods, not shown in this classification. One is based on the way facts or examples are presented to the learner. If examples are presented and processed all at once, then we have one-step or non-incremental inductive learning. If they are processed one by one, or in portions, and the system may have to modify the hypothesis after each input, we have an incremental inductive learning.

The second classification is based on the method of interpreting or matching instances with concept descriptions. Mathing an instance with a concept description can be done in a direct way, or can employ a substantial amount of background knowledge and inference. For example, case-based or exemplar-based methods employ matching procedures that allow the system to recognize new examples that do not directly match any past example (e.g., Bareiss, Porter and Wier, 1990). Such a process can be characterized as a "dynamic" induction that is performed during the matching process (or the recognition process). Learning methods based on the two-tiered concept representation (Bergadano et al., 1990) also use a sophisticated matching procedure. In general, they can employ any type of inference in matching an instance with a concept representation (Michalski, 1990).

Analytic methods can be divided to those that are guided by an example in the process of knowledge reformulation (example-guided) and those that start with a specification (specification-guided). The former category includes explanation-based learning (e.g., DeJong et al. 1986), explanation-based-generalization (Mitchell et al., 1986), and explanation-based specialization (Minton, 1986; Minton et al., 1987). The primary inference method in analytic learning is deduction. If deduction is based on axioms ("domain theory"), then it is called axiomatic. Explanation-based generalization can be viewed as an example of an axiomatic method, because it is based on a pure deductive process that utilizes complete and consistent background knowledge. This knowledge playes the role analogous to the axioms in formal theories.

Analytic methods that involve deductive transformations of description spaces and/or imperfect background knowledge and/or plausible rules of deductive inference are classified as methods of "constructive deduction." This class also includes abstraction, as it utilizes background knowledge to create descriptions at a lower level of detail, while basically preserving the truth of the description. Results of abstraction are typically statements expressed in a higher level language.

Another form of constructive deduction is deductive generalization that creates more general statements, in the sense that they include more entities. Such statements are logically implied by the source statements, in contrast to statements generated by inductive generalization, which imply the source statements. These two processes are put into a dotted rectangle, to indicate they do not seem to correspond to any major current research areas. They are simply suggested as potential research areas, as a result of making the above classification. This can be viewed as a kind of the "Mendeleiev periodic table effect."

In general, constructive deduction is a knowledge-based process of transforming descriptions from one representation space or language to another, which preserves information important for an assumed goal. Abstraction is classified as a constructive deduction, which transforms a description at a high level of detail to a description at a low level of detail, while preserving the truth of the relations and/or properties relevant to the assumed goal. In other words, while reducing the total information content of the original description, abstraction preserves the information important to performing an implicitly or explicity defined goal. Depending on the goal, a given description can be abstracted in many different ways. Each such process is essentially deductive, as it is not supposed to introduce or hypothesize any information that is not contained in the initial description or information source, or which cannot be deductively inferred from it using the learner's BK. The difference between constructive deduction and what we call axiomatic deduction is that the former emphasizes a change in the representation space or language, and may use a variety of knowledge transformations, rather then strictly logic-based formal methods. A "pure" constructive deduction is truth-preserving; however, in general, it can involve rules of plausible reasoning, and in this case ceases to be truth-preserving.

As mentioned before, abstraction is sometimes confused with generalization. Note that generalization transforms descriptions along the set-superset dimension and may be falsity-preserving, as in the case of inductive generalization, or truth-preserving, as in the case of deductive generalization (Michalski and Zemankowa, 1990; see also below). In contrast, abstraction transforms descriptions along the level-of-detail dimension, and is truth-preserving with regard to the characteristics of the entity(ies) important for the assumed goal. While generalization often uses the same description space (or language), abstraction typically involves a change in the representation space (or language). The reason why generalization and abstraction are frequently confused may be attributed to the fact that many processes include both of them.

Deductive generalization is concerned with making generalizations that are logical deductions from the base knowledge. It differs from abstraction as it moves from considering a set to considering a superset, and typically uses the same representation formalism. For example, transforming a statement " George Mason University is in Fairfax" to "George Mason University is in Virginia" is a deductive generalization. In contrast, changing a high resolution digitized satellite image of Fairfax into a low resolution image is a simple form of abstraction. A more sophisticated abstraction would be to use the high resolution image and appropriate BK to create a map of Fairfax, which emphasizes important (according to the goal) aspects of the area. Research on problem representation, transformation of problem representation spaces, determination of a representative set of attributes, deductive transformation of a knowledge base, and related topics can be classified under the rubric of constructive deduction.

In parallel to multistrategy systems, that combine several strategies, one can also distinguish multirepresentation learning systems (not shown in the classification). Such systems would employ various forms of constructive deduction or induction to create and use representations at different levels of abstraction, and/or apply different description languages in the process of learning. The use of these descriptions and languages would depend on the task at hand, and on the application domain. Such systems thus are capable of changing the representation of the original problem statements. The importance of this area has been acknowledged very early by pattern recognition researchers (Bongard, 1970), as well as by AI researchers (Newell, 1969; Amarel, 1970). Nevertheless, it received relatively little attention during recent years. Among notable exceptions are (Amarel, 1986; Mozetic, 1989)

Summarizing, one can distinguish three pairs of reasoning/learning mechanisms. Each pair contains two opposite processes, and is concerned with different aspects of knowledge transformation. Two of these pairs have been relatively well-explored in machine learning: deduction/induction and generalization/specialization. The third pair, which has been relatively less studied, consists of abstraction and its reverse, which may be called *concretion* (Webster's dictionary defines it as being a process of concretizing something). These three types of mechanisms can be combined in different ways, giving some classical, well-known reasoning mechanisms, and some less known. The classical ones include inductive generalization and deductive specialization. Less investigated are inductive specialization, abstraction, deductive generalization, inductive concretion and other.

The above "grand" classification appears to be the first attempt to characterize and relate to each other all major methods and subareas of machine learning within one general scheme. As such, this attempt may suffer from various weaknesses and imprecision, and can be criticized on various grounds. Its primary purpose is to try to help the reader, especially a novice in this field, to view different learning mechanisms and paradigms as parts of a one general structure, rather than as a collection of unclearly related components and research efforts. By analyzing this classification, the reader may be stimulated to improve it or to develop a new, more adequate one.

# 6. MULTISTRATEGY TASK-ADAPTIVE LEARNING

The ideas presented above have shown the relationships among different forms of explanation and different types of learning. They have shown, in particular, the relationship between the two most active and complementary methodologies for building learning programs: empirical learning, which primarily exploits data, and analytical learning, which primarily exploits prior knowledge. While both these methodologies are useful for some domains of application, most practical learning problems seem to fit neither the empirical nor the analytic paradigm. This is because most practical problems involve to a significant extent both prior knowledge and new facts, and the prior knowledge is often incomplete and/or not totally correct.

This section discusses a general approach to learning that attempts to unify several learning approaches and to build a learning system of much greater capability than those using only one type of approach. The proposed *multistrategy task-adaptive learning* integrates empirical learning, constructive induction, learning by instruction, explanation-based learning and conceptual clustering. Ultimately, it is intended to integrate also learning by analogy and case-based reasoning (which can be viewed as a form of analogical reasoning).

Given a fact or an observation, one can distinguish five types of relationship between the fact and the learner's prior knowledge. First, the fact may be new or partially new to the learner, neither confirming nor disconfirming the learner's prior knowledge, or, if it is not economical to test for this property, one assumes that the fact is new. Second, the fact may contradict some segment (a rule or a rule set) of the learner's prior knowledge. Third, the fact may be implied (or may imply) some segment of the learner's prior knowledge. Fourth, the fact may be similar in certain respects (in terms of abstract relations, rather than low level attributes) to some segment of the learner's knowledge. Fifth and finally, the fact may be already known to the learner (i.e., strictly match some knowledge segment).

Current empirical and constructive induction systems are concerned primarily with handling the first and the second cases. "Pure" explanation-based learning is concerned with handling the third case. The more recent methods of explanation-based learning attempt to address situations in which the learner's knowledge is insufficient (first case), or inconsistent with the prior knowledge (second case), or the prior knowledge is intractable (first case). Learning by analogy and case-based reasoning are concerned with handling the fourth case. Very few symbolic learning systems handle the fifth case other than by ignoring such inputs (Slimmer and Granger, 1986). In neural networks and genetic algorithms a repetition of the input is not ignored, but those systems do not have the ability to recognize that the input is repeated.

Our work on the MTL learning methodology is intended ultimately to handle all five cases in an integrated fashion. Thus, to explain how this methodology works, one needs to explain how it would handle all these cases. Before we move to this topic, however, we first need to introduce the knowledge representation to be used in the proposed methodology.

## Knowledge representation

A multistrategy task-adaptive learning system (briefly, an *MTL learner*) has to be able to represent and use knowledge created by different learning strategies. This means, in particular, that it has to be able to employ knowledge created by one learning process as an input to another learning process. The other learning process may be using the same learning strategy or a different strategy. As mentioned earlier, learning with such a property is called the closed-loop learning.

Another property of a constructive learner concerns its reaction to repetitive information. Traditional symbolic learning methods typically use a knowledge representation (e.g., rules or semantic networks) that does not change if a new instance repetitively satisfies the given concept description. A constructive learner needs a representation that could change even if an instance is shown to satisfy a concept description. The reason is that such cases should be used for increasing a degree of confirmation of the concept description. An MTL learner should also be able to decrease such a degree in some situations.

To satisfy the above requirements, we assume that the basic component of the learner's background knowledge (BK) is a *parameterized association rule* (PAR), whose general form is:

$$\text{CTX:}\quad \text{AS:}\quad \text{L-PREMISE} \longleftrightarrow \text{R-PREMISE: } \textit{M-Parameters} \tag{9}$$

where

L-PREMISE and R-PREMISE denote the left and right sides of a PAR, respectively. They are expressed as conjunctive statements or terms. The statements may include *internal disjunction* and terms may be *compound* (Michalski, 1983).

<---> denotes a bi-directional *association*, which is instantiated into a more specific relationship according to AS.

AS stands for the *association specification*, which defines the type and properties of the association. An association can be instantiated to many specific types and defined with different degree of precision. For example, AS may state that the association is an implication between statements or a mutual dependency between terms. A term dependency is, e.g., that "smoking is related to lung cancer." When more knowledge about this dependency is obtained, the association may become a functional dependency, e.g., that "smoking two or more packs a day shortens the life span by 10 years on the average." In general, the association may be a strong (logical) or weak (plausible or probabilistic) implication or equivalence, mutual dependency between terms, equality, correlation, causal relationship, decision assignment, precedence relation, and other. AS may include a quantification expressed in the from of an ordinary quantifier or a *numerical quantifier* (Michalski, 1983). A numerical quantifier may state, e.g., that there are two or more objects in a set S to which the PAR applies or that there are specifically three objects in S to which the PAR applies. When AS is not specified, the association takes a default meaning. The default meaning may be that if the premises are statements, then the association is implication; and if the premises are terms, it is *mutual dependency* (Collins and Michalski, 1989).

CTX denotes a *context* for the association, that is a characterization of the conditions under which the PAR applies. When the CTX is not specified, a default context is assumed.

*M-Parameters* (*merit* parameters) represent numerical or qualitative properties of the association, which characterize its strength in both directions, the number of times the association has been satisfied or not satisfied by input events, and other parameters, such as those introduced in the theory of plausible reasoning (Collins and Michalski, 1989). Each time a PAR is evoked and either satisfied or not satisfied, the appropriate parameters are updated.

An input fact may match the whole or part of either premise, or both premises of a PAR. For example, a description of an object may match the left premise, and its classification by a teacher may match the right premise. PARs are organized into *segments*. A segment is collection (a "parset") of rules that are related in some way. For example, a segment may describe a single concept or a few closely related ones. Segments may be (statically or dynamically) organized to larger units, called *schemas*.

This form of knowledge representation is based on ideas stated in the theory of human plausible reasoning proposed by Collins and Michalski (1989), and in the *annotated predicate calculus* (Michalski, 1983). In particular, the PAR is a generalization of the rules for mutual implication and term dependency. The concepts used in PARs (attributes, relations, etc.) are organized into *dynamic hierarchies*, such as described in that theory.

Although PARs are significantly more general than productions used in genetic algorithms (e.g., Holland, 1986 and 1987), they share with them the property of having some numerical score(s) attached to them. PARs permit one to represent a large class of descriptions and relationships. For example, a single PAR may represent a condition-action rule, such as "if the second valve is broken, call a mechanic"; a term dependency, such as "pressure and volume are inversely proportional "; a causal relationship, such as "if the pressure goes beyond 3 atmospheres, this indicator will move up"; a quantified implication, such as " 60% of objects observed have property P", as well as ordinary implications or equivalences.

## Outline of the method

We will now outline our preliminary ideas about how an MTL learner might learn in different situations, in particular, how it could react to the above described different types of relationship between an input, background knowledge (BK) and a learning goal. We assume that the input consists of information (e.g., a fact, a concept example or a rule) supplied by an external source, or information resulting from an impass in processing of an input according to some strategy. In the latter case, processing of the input may involve activating another learning strategy. For example, in the process of determining if a fact is implied by BK (i.e., in attempting to explain the fact), the learner finds that some parts of it are explainable by BK, and some other parts may represent new information. The parts that are explainable are processed by an analytical learning strategy, and the parts that are new may activate a synthetic learning process.

We assume that the general learning goal (a default goal) is to derive any "useful" information from the input, make sense of it and assimilate it into the knowledge base. More specific learning goals, such as to generalize facts to generate a rule, to create a conceptual classification of facts, to reformulate a part of BK into a more efficient knowledge, to determine new knowledge on the basis of an analogy between the input and some past knowledge, etc. are supplied from a supervisory control system.

Presented ideas are concerned only with aspects of building or updating a knowledge base, and not with issues of using the knowledge for problem solving. Given input information, the learner determines which of the five cases above ("processing methods") is involved. The rules and segments in BK are indexed in various ways to facilitate this process. The learner performs a "deductive" matching of the information with BK to determine if it satisfies (or is satisfed by) some rule, or at least is consistent with the rules. Such a matching is called "deductive" because it may involve several steps of deduction.

A limited amount of resources is available for this process, and if they are exceeded, a failure is communicated. In such a case, the information is assumed to be (pragmatically) new to the system. Rule generalization or specialization is done by applying various inference rules, such as those described in (Michalski, 1983). Any input is first evaluated for "relevance" to the learner's goal(s).

Such an evaluation is based on a quick classification of the input to some category, and the category is related to the goal(s). If the input passes such a "relevance test," a learning process is activated.

### 1. The input represents pragmatically new information

Generally, this case handles situations that require some form of synthetic learning (empirical learning or constructive induction), or learning by instruction. Given an input, the learner searches for a part of BK that is "hierarchically related" to it. For example, it may be a part describing the concept being exemplified by the input, but neither entailing it, nor contradicting it. If this effort succeeds, the relevant part is generalized, so that it accounts for this input and possibly other information stored previously. The resulting generalizations and the input facts are evaluated for "importance," and those that pass an *importance criterion*, are stored (a process that involves storing representative past facts is called *learning with partial memory of the past*). If there is no knowledge "hierarchically related" to the input, the input is stored, and the control is passed to case 4.

### 2. The input is implied by, or implies a part of BK

This case represents a situation when it is determined that there is a part of BK that accounts for the input, or is a special case of it. The learner creates a derivational explanatory structure that links the input with the involved BK part. Depending on the learning task, this structure can be used to create a new ("operational") knowledge that is more adequate for future handling of such cases. If the new knowledge passes an "importance criterion," it is stored for future use. This mechanism is related to the ideas on the utility of explanation based-learning (Minton, 1988). If the input represents a "useful" result of a problem solving activity, e.g.," for given state x, it was found that a useful action is y", then storing such a fact as a rule is similar to chunking in SOAR (Laird, Rosenbloom, and Newell, 1986). If the input information (e.g., a rule supplied by a teacher) implies some part of BK, then an "importance criterion" is applied to it. If the input passes this criterion, it is stored, and an appropriate link is made to the part of BK that is implied by it. In general, this case handles situations requiring some form of analytic learning.

### 3. The input contradicts some part of the learner's BK

The system identifies the part of BK that is contradicted by the input information, and then attempts to specialize this part. If the specialization involves too much restructuring, and/or the confidence in the input is low, no change to this part of BK is made, but the input is stored. When some part of BK has been restructured to accommodate the input, the input is also stored, but only if it passes an "importance criterion." If contradicted knowledge is a specific fact, this is noted, and any knowledge that was generated on the basis of the contradicted fact may have to be revised. In general, this case handles situations requiring a correction of BK through some form of synthetic learning and, generally, managing inconsistency.

### 4. The input evokes an analogy to a part of BK

This case represents a situation when the input does not match any background fact or rule exactly, nor is "hierarchically" related to any part of BK, but there is a similarity between the fact and some part of BK at a higher abstraction level. That is, unlike in case 1, in which the system tries to directly match the fact with a knowledge segment, in this case, matching is done at a higher level of abstraction, using generalized attributes or relations. If the fact is "sufficiently important" it is stored with an indication of an similarity (analogy) to a background knowledge segment, and with the specification of the aspects (abstract attributes or relations) defining the analogy. For example, an input describing a lamp may evoke an analogy to the part of BK describing the sun, because both lamp and sun match in terms of an abstract attribute "produces light."

*5. The input is already known to the learner*

This case occurs when the input matches exactly some part of BK (a stored fact, a rule or a segment). In such a situation, a measure of confidence associated with this part is updated.

Summarizing, in multistrategy task-adaptive learning, any act of receiving information that passes a *relevance test* (that checks if the input information is suffficiently relevant to the goals of the leraner) activates learning process. The learner employs deductive inference when an input fact is consistent with, implies, or is implied by the background knowledge; analogical inference when it is similar to some part of past knowledge; and inductive inference when there is a need to hypothesize a new and/or more general knowledge. It also learns when input facts confirm its knowledge, by reinforcing current beliefs.

## 7. SIMPLE EXAMPLE: Learning the Concept of a Cup

To illustrate briefly some of the ideas described above, let us use a well-known example of learning the concept of "cup" (Mitchell, Keller and Kedar-Cabelli, 1986). The example is deliberatly oversimplified, so that major ideas can be presented in a very simply way (Figure 3).

The top part of the figure presents an abstract concept definition (abstract CD) for the concept "cup," the domain rules, a description of an example of a cup (specific object description or specific OD), an abstract object description (abstract OD), and an operational concept description (operational CD). An abstract concept definition describes the concept of "cup" in abstract/general terms, while an abstract object definition describes the specific object in such terms.

The bottom part of the figure summarizes information that is assumed to be given and to be learned using different learning approaches: constructive deduction (abstraction), explanation-based learning, empirical induction, constructive induction (in cases of generalization and abduction), and the proposed multistrategy task-adaptive learning. For simplicity, some details are omitted, and the example does not illustrate the mechanism of updating the strength of the rules, nor analogical reasoning. Figures 4, 5 and 6 give more details about some of the learning processes, specifically, about abstraction, constructive generalization and abduction.

A more practical, but less general example is described in (Ko and Michalski, 1989). It shows how a system learns a general schema for creating a plan for putting together simple assemblies, for example, a bell. The schema is developed by an incremental improvement and testing of intermediate schemas.

## 8. CONCLUSION

The aims of this work are to create a theoretical framework for characterizing and unifying basic learning strategies, and to develop an experimental integrated learning system based on it. The proposed MTL methodology stems from the inference-based theory of learning that considers learning as an inference process, whose useful results are stored for future use. This process involves input information, the learner's prior knowledge, and the goal of learning. It may employ any kind of inference - deductive, analogical or inductive.

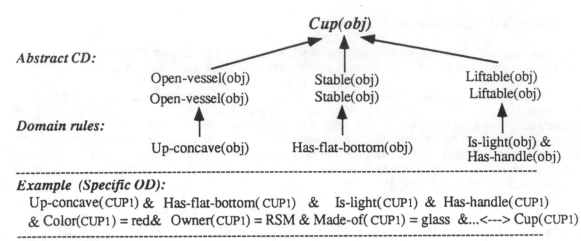

*Example (Specific OD):*
   Up-concave( CUP1) &  Has-flat-bottom( CUP1)  &   Is-light( CUP1) & Has-handle( CUP1)
   & Color(CUP1) = red&  Owner(CUP1) = RSM & Made-of( CUP1) = glass &...<---> Cup(CUP1)

------------------------------------------------------------------------------------

*Abstract OD:*
   Open-vessel( CUP1) & Stable( CUP1) & Liftable( CUP1)  &   ... <---> Cup(CUP1)

------------------------------------------------------------------------------------

*Operational CD:*
   Up-concave(obj) & Has-flat-bottom(obj) & Is-light(obj) & Has-handle(obj) <---> Cup(obj)

------------------------------------------------------------------------------------

|  | *Given:* |  | *To be learned:* |
|---|---|---|---|
| **Constructive Deduction** *(Abstraction)* | Example<br>Domain rules | ▷ | Abstract  OD |
| **Explanation-based Learning** | Abstract CD<br>Domain rules<br>Example | ▷ | Operational CD |
| **Empirical  Induction** | Examples<br>Partial BK' | ⊀ | Operational CD |
| **Constructive  Induction** *(Generalization)* | Domain rules<br>Example(s) | ⊀ | Abstract CD |
| **Constructive Induction** *(Abduction)* | Example(s)<br>Abstract CD | ⊀ | Domain rules |
| **Multistrategy Cooperative Learning** | Any of the above and other combinations, depending on what is the input, what the learner knows already and what is to be learned | | |

OD and CD denote object and concept descritpion, respectively. CUP1 stands for a specific cup;  obj denotes a variable.  BK' denotes  some partial background knowledge, e.g.,  a specification of the value sets of the attributes and the type of the attributes. Operators ▷ and ⊀  denote deduction and induction, respectively.

*Figure 3.* Learning various aspects of the concept of "cup"  using different strategies.

## Learning Process:    EX&DR --> OD

*Constructive Deduction*  Example
*(Abstraction)*  Domain rules  ⊬  Abstract OD

---

## *Given:*

### 1. INPUT
*New Example:*

Up-concave(CUP1) & Is-light(CUP1) & Has-handle(CUP1) & Owner(CUP1)=RSM &
Color(CUP1)=red & Made-of(CUP1)=glass & Has-flat-bottom(CUP1) <----> Cup(CUP1)

### 2. BACKGROUND KNOWLEDGE

**Domain rules**    Open-vessel(obj)        Stable(obj)        Liftable(obj)

↑        ↑        ↑

Up-concave(obj)        Has-flat-bottom(obj)        Is-light(obj) &
Has-handle(ob

### Other Relevant Knowledge

Container(obj) <---- Open-vessel(obj) & Stable(obj)

....

### 3. GOAL
To derive an abstract description of this example.

---

### STEPS:
1. Determine relevant domain rules
2. Apply the rules to the given example and create an abstract OD

## *Learned:*

An abstract OD:

**Cup(CUP1) <---> Open-vessel(CUP1) & Stable(CUP1) & Liftable(CUP1) &...**

After applying other relevant knowledge, even more abstract OD can be created:

**Cup(CUP1)    <--->    Container(CUP1) & Liftable(CUP1) &...**

*Figure 4.* An illustration of abstraction.

**Learning Process:**                    **EX&DR --> AC**

*Constructive Generalization*        Example(s)    ⊬    Abstract CD
                                      Domain rules

---

## *Given:*

### 1. INPUT

*Examples::*
Up-concave(CUP1) & Is-light(CUP1) & Has-handle(CUP1) & Owner(CUP1)=RSM &
Color(CUP1)=red & Made-of(CUP1)=glass & Has-flat-bottom(CUP1) <----> **Cup(CUP1)**

Up-concave(OBJ2) & Is-heavy(OBJ2) & Has-handle(OBJ2) & Owner(OBJ2)=RSM &
Color(OBJ2)=grey & Made-of(OBJ2)=wood & Has-flat-bottom(OBJ2) <----> **Jar(OBJ2)**

Up-concave(OBJ3) & Is-light(OBJ3) & Made-of(OBJ3)=glass & Has-flat-bottom(OBJ3)
No-handle(obj) <----> **Jar(OBJ3)**

### 2. BACKGROUND KNOWLEDGE

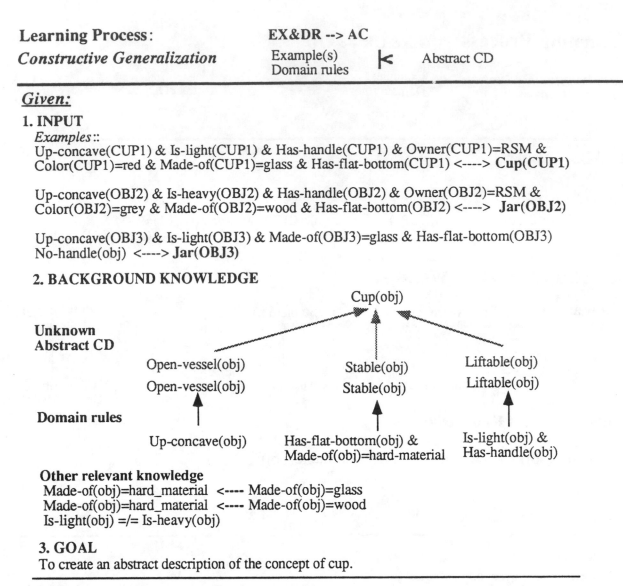

**Other relevant knowledge**
Made-of(obj)=hard_material <---- Made-of(obj)=glass
Made-of(obj)=hard_material <---- Made-of(obj)=wood
Is-light(obj) =/= Is-heavy(obj)

### 3. GOAL
To create an abstract description of the concept of cup.

---

### STEPS:
**1.** Analyze the relationship between the input and the BK in the context of GOAL
**2.** If the current abstract description of the cup BK is incomplete, hypothesize additional rule(s),
   to make it complete

## *Learned:*
An abstract concept description:
                **Cup(obj) <---- Open-vessel(obj) & Stable(obj) & Liftable(obj)**

*Figure 5.* An illustration of constructive generalization

**Learning Process:**      **EX&AC --> DR**

*Abduction*      Example(s)
               Abstract CD   ⊬   Domain rules

---

## *Given:*

### 1. INPUT

*An example:*
Up-concave(CUP1) & Is-light(CUP1) & Has-handle(CUP1) & Owner(CUP1)=RSM &
Color(CUP1)=red & Made-of(CUP1)=glass & Has-flat-bottom(CUP1) <----> Cup(CUP1)

### 2. BACKGROUND KNOWLEDGE

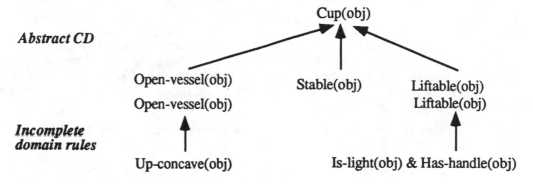

*Abstract CD*

*Incomplete domain rules*

*Other relevant knowledge*

Stable(obj) <~~/~~~> Owner(obj) & Color(obj)   (no mutual dependency)
Stable(obj) <~~~~> Type-of-bottom(obj)   (mutual dependency)
Type-of-bottom(obj) = {uneven, flat, leg-supported,...}
Type-of-bottom(obj) = <value>   ==>   Has-<value>-bottom(obj)

### 3. GOAL
To determine domain knowledge that justifies the abstract concept definition.

---

**STEPS:**
1. Analyze the relationship between the input and the BK in the context of GOAL
2. If the BK is insufficient, hypothesize additional domain rule(s), that are
    consistent with example and BK.

## *What is learned :*

A new domain rule:
            **Stable(obj) <== Has-flat-bottom(obj)**

*Figure 6.* An illustration of abduction.

Among important assumptions for this work are that a learning system should be capable of acquiring knowledge from any input and be able to use knowledge gained in one learning task in any new learning task (i.e., be capable of the "closed-loop" learning).

The MTL methodology is intended ultimately to include capabilities for empirical learning, chunking, constructive induction, learning by instruction, reinforcement learning, explanation-based learning, conceptual clustering, learning by analogy and case-based reasoning. An important component of the MTL methodology is the cognitive theory of plausible reasoning (Collins and Michalski, 1989), which provides a formal structure for implementing various forms of such reasoning. In the complete implementation of the MTL, plausible reasoning is supposed to play a double-level function. The first-level function is to generate lines of reasoning that relate the input information to the learner's background knowledge and goals, and determine the most plausible conclusions. These conclusions are to be stored as results of learning, and integrated with the rest of the learner's knowledge. The second-level function is to generate, on request, explanations of the results of learning in terms of high-level human-oriented concepts and structures. It is our strong believe that an advanced learning system should not only be able to learn, but also to explain to human counterparts what knowledge it acquired or modified during any learning process. When a learning system is a part of a knowledge system (e.g., an expert system), the explanatory capabilites for learning should be integrated with explanatory capabilities for the system's performance. It may be worth mentioning, that while a significant amount of research has been done on the development of explanatory capabilities for performance of knowledge-based systems (e.g., Tanner, 1990), relatively little has been done so far on the development of explanatory capabilites for learning systems.

To demonstrate some aspects of MTL learning, a prototype system, called NOMAD, has been implemented (Ko, 1989). NOMAD is a planning system that learns from planning experiences, and has been developed in connection with the Intelligent Explorer (IEX) project at the GMU Center for Artificial Intelligence. In the future work we plan to explore the utility of the INDUCE 4 program for incremental structural learning (Mehler, Bentrup, and Riedesel, 1986), and the DISCIPLE integrated learning system (e.g., Tecuci and Kodratoff, 1990) for implementing an MTL system.

The presented ideas are at an early state of development, and many issues have not been resolved. For example, future resaerch should address the question of the development of a flexible control of the execution of different learning strategies, handling input information whose different components need to be processed separately, but in a globally coordinated way, the access and manipulation of a large collection of parameterized association rules (PARs), or the methods for updating and using various parameters associated with PARs. Future research may also explore the utility of genetic algorithms in the MTL methodology. A genetic algorithm might be used, e.g., for evolutionary optimization of many parameters involved in MTL.

In closing, our goals in developing the MTL methodology are to explore research issues involved in the integration of different learning strategies, and to understand how various strategies can best be utilized in different learning situations. This understanding may give insights into learning processes in general, and help to build more powerful and efficient multistrategy learning systems.

Such systems are needed for many practical tasks in which a learning system starts with inadequate knowledge, and needs to use facts or experience to extend or improve it in some sense. There are two general areas where such systems may be particularily useful: extraction of knowledge from large databases and knowledge acquisition for expert and advisory systems. In both these areas, to derive useful knowledge in different situations no single learning strategy is usually sufficient, and knowledge learned must be understandable by a human user. Among specific application tasks one can list all kinds of diagnostic problems, decision making, planning systems, system design, economical prediction, resource management, robot navigation, automated assembly, and high level sensory signal interpretation.

## Acknowledgements

The author expresses his gratitude to Hugo De Garis, Ken De Jong, Kejitan Dontas, Bob Giansiracusa, Heedong Ko, Yves Kodratoff, David Littman, Elizabeth Marchut, Pawel Stefanski, Gheorge Tecuci, Janusz Wnek and Jianping Zhang for many insightful comments and suggestions that significantly helped to improve earlier versions of the paper. Thanks also go to Gara Barham and Janet Holmes for stylistic suggestions and proofreading.

This research was supported in part by the Defense Advanced Research Projects Agency under the grant administered by the Office of Naval Research No. N00014-K-85-0878, and in part by the Office of Naval Research under grants No. N00014-88-K-0397 and No. N00014-88-K-0226.

## References

Adler, M. J., Gorman (Eds.) The Great Ideas: A Synoptic of Great Books of the Western World, Vol. 1, Ch. 39, *Encyclopedia Britannica*, 1987.

Aristotle, Posterior Analytics, in *Great Books of the Western World*, vol.8, R.M. Hutchins (ed.), Encyclopedia Britannica, Inc. 1987.

Amarel, S., "Program Synthesis as a Theory Formation Task: Problem Representations and Solution Methods," in *Machine Learning: An Artificial Intelligence Approach Vol.II,* Morgan Kaufmann, Los Altos, CA, R. S. Michalski, J. G. Carbonell and T. M. Mitchell (Eds.), 1986.

Aristotle, *Posterior Analytics*, in *The Works of Aristotle Volume 1*, R. M. Hutchins (Ed.), Encyclopedia Britannica, Inc., 1987.

Bareiss, E. R., Porter, B. and Wier, C.C., PROTOS, An Exemplar-based Learning Apprentice, in *Machine Learning: AN Artificial Intelligence Approach vol. III*, MOrgan Kaufmann, 1990.

Barto, A.G., and Anderson, C.W., "Structural Learning in Connectionist Systems," *Proceedings of the 7th Conference of the Cognitive Science Society*, pp. 43-53, 1985.

Bergadano, F., Matwin, S., Michalski, R.S. and Zhang, J., Learning Two-tiered Descriptions of Flexible Concepts: The POSEIDON System, *Machine Learning and Inference Raports, No. MLI-3*, Center for Aritificial Intelligence, George Mason University, 1990.

Bierman, A. W., Guiho, G., and Kodratoff, Y. (Eds.), *Automatic Program Synthsis Techniques*, Macmillan Publishing Company, New York, pp. 517-552, 1984.

Carbonell, J. G., Michalski R.S. and Mitchell, T.M., An Overview of Machine Learning, in *Machine Learning: AN Artificial Intelligence Approach*, Michalski, R.S., Carbonell, J.G., and Mitchell , T. M. (Eds.), Morgan Kaufmann Publishers, 1983.

Collins, A., and Michalski, R.S., "The Logic of Plausible Reasoning: A Core Theory," *Cognitive Science*, Vol. 13, No. 1, pp.1-49, 1989.

Cox, P.T., Pietrzykowski, T., "Causes for Events: Their Computation and Applications" *Proceedings of the Eighth International Conference on Automated Deduction*, Oxford, 1986.

Danyluk, A.P., "The Use of Explanations for Similarity-Based Learning," *Proceedings of IJCAI-87*, pp. 274-276, Milan, Italy, 1987.

Danyluk. A. P., "Recent Results in the Use of Context for Learning New Rules," Technical Report TR-98-066, Philips Laboratories, 1989.

Davis, D., *Genetic Algorithms and Simulated Annealing*, Pitman Press, Cambridge, MA, 1987.

DeJong, G. and Mooney, R., "Explanation-Based Learning: An Alternative View," *Machine Learning Journal*, vol 2, 1986.

DeJong, G.F., "An Approach to Learning from Observation," in *Machine Learning: An Artificial Intelligence Approach, Vol. II*, Morgan Kaufmann, Los Altos, CA, R. S. Michalski, J. G. Carbonell and T. M. Mitchell (Eds.), pp. 571-590, 1986.

DeJong, G. F. (Ed.), *Proceedings of the 1988 Symposium on Explanation-Based Learning*, Stanford University, March, 1988.

DeJong, K.A., and Spears, W., "Using Genetic Algorithms to Solve NP-Complete Problems," *Proceedings of the 3rd International Conference on Genetic Algorithms and their Applications*, Fairfax, VA, 1989.

de Kleer, J., "An Assumption-Based Truth Maintenance System," *Artificial Intelligence*, vol. 28, No. 1, 1986.

Dietterich, T.G., "Learning at the Knowledge Level," Machine Learning, Vol. 1, No. 3, pp. 287-316, 1986.

Dietterich, T.G., and Flann, N.S., "An Inductive Approach to Solving the Imperfect Theory Problem," *Proceedings of 1988 Symposium on Explanation-Based Learning,* pp. 42-46, Stanford University, 1988.

Dietterich, T.G., and Michalski, R.S., Learning to Predict Sequences, in *Machine Learning: An Artificial Intelligence Approach Vol. II*, Morgan Kaufmann, Los Altos, CA, R.S. Michalski, J.G. Carbonell and T.M. Mitchell (Eds.), pp. 63-106, 1986.

Duval B., and Kodratoff Y. "A Tool for the Management of Incomplete Theories: Reasoning about Explanations" in *Machine Learning, Meta-Reasoning and Logics,* P. Brazdil and K. Konolige (Eds.), Kluwer Academic Press, pp. 135-158, 1990.

Ehrenfeucht, A., Haussler, D., Kearns, M., and Valiant, L., "A General Lower Bound on the Number of Examples Needed for Learning," *Proceedings of the 1988 Workshop on Computational Learning Theory COLT'88,* pp. 139-154, MIT, 1988.

Fisher, D.H., McKusick, K., Mooney, R., Shavlik, J.W., and Towell, G., "Processing Issues in Comparisons of Symbolic and Connectionism Learning Systems," *Proceedings of the 6th International Workshop on Machine Learning*, pp. 169-173, Ithaca, NY, 1989.

Goldberg, D.E., *Genetic Algorithms in Search, Optimization, and Machine Learning*, Addison-Wesley, 1989.

Haussler D. and Pitt, L. (Eds.), *Proceedings of the 1988 Workshop on the Computational Learning Theory* (COLT 88), Morgan Kaufmann Publishers, San Mateo, CA, 1988.

Hoff, B., Michalski, R.S. and Stepp, R., INDUCE 2 - a program for learning structural descriptions from examples, Intelligent Systems Group Reports, No.83-1, Department of Computer Science, University of Illinois at Champaign-Urbana, 1983.

Holland, J.H., "Escaping Brittleness: The Possibilities of General-Purpose Learning Algorithms Applied to Parallel Rule-based Systems," in *Machine Learning: An Artificial Intelligence Approach, Vol. II*, Morgan Kaufmann, Los Altos, CA, R. S. Michalski, J. G. Carbonell and T. M. Mitchell (Eds.), pp. 499-570, 1986.

Holland, J.H., "Genetic Algorithms and Classifier Systems: Foundations and Future Directions," *Proceedings of the 2nd International Conference on Genetic Algorithms*, pp. 82-89, Cambridge, MA, 1987.

Holland J. H. Holyoak K. J., Nisbett R. E. and Thagard, P R., Induction: Processes of Inference, Learning and Discovery, The MIT Press, Cambridge, MA 1986.

Ko, H., "Assembly Planning Through Constructive Learning Approach," to appear in *Machine Learning and Inference Reports*, Center for AI, George Mason University, 1989.

Ko, H. and Michalski, R.S., "Types of Explanation and Their Role in Constructive Learning," to appear in *Machine Learning and Inference Reports*, Center for AI, George Mason University, 1989.

Kodratoff, Y., and Tecuci, G., "DISCIPLE-1: Interactive Apprentice System in Weak Theory Fields," *Proceedings of IJCAI-87*, pp. 271-273, Milan, Italy, 1987.

Laird, J.E., (Ed.), *Proceedings of the Fifth International Conference on Machine Learning*, University of Michigan, Ann Arbor, June 12-14, 1988.

Laird, J.E., Rosenbloom, P.S., and Newell A., "Chunking in SOAR: the Anatomy of a General Learning Mechanism," *Machine Learning*, Vol. 1, No. 1, pp. 11-46, 1986.

Lebowitz, M., "Integrated Learning: Controlling Explanation," Cognitive Science, Vol. 10, No. 2, pp. 219-240, 1986.

Mehler, G., Bentrup, J., and Riedesel, J., "INDUCE.4: A Program for Incrementally Learning Structural Descriptions from Examples," *Reports of Intelligent Systems Group*, Dept. of Computer Science, University of Illinois at Urbana-Champaign, 1986.

Michalski, R.S., "Discovering Classification Rules using Variable-valued Logic System $VL_1$," *Proceedings of the Third International Joint Conference on Artificial Intelligence*, Stanford, 1973.

Michalski, R. S., "Theory and Methodology of Inductive Learning," *Machine Learning: An Artificial Intelligence Approach*, R. S. Michalski, J. G. Carbonell, T. M. Mitchell (Eds.), Tioga Publishing Co., 1983.

Michalski, R.S., Understanding the Nature of Learning: Issues and Research Directions, in *Machine Learning: AN Artificial Intelligence Approach Vol. II*, Michalski, R.S., Carbonell, J.G., and Mitchell , T. M. (Eds.), Morgan Kaufmann Publishers, 1986.

Michalski, R. S., "Concept Learning," *Encyclopedia of Artificial Intelligence*, E. Shapiro (Ed.), John Wiley & Sons, January, 1987.

Michalski, R.S., LEARNING FLEXIBLE CONCEPTS: Fundamental Ideas and a Method Based on Two-tiered Representation, in *Machine Learning: AN Artificial Intelligence Approach vol. III*, MOrgan Kaufmann, 1990.

Michalski, R. S., Ko, H. and Chen, K., "Qualitative Prediction: The SPARC/G Methodology for Describing and Predicting Discrete Processes," in *Expert Systems*, P. Dufour and A. Van Lamsweerde (Eds.), Academic Press Incorporated, pp. 125-158, 1987.

Michalski, R.S.and Ko, H., "On the Nature of Explanation or Why Did the Wine Bottle Shatter," *Proceedings of the AAAI Workshop on Explanation-based Learning*, Stanford University, March 1988.

Michalski, R.S. and Negri, P., "An Experiment on Inductive Learning in Chess End Games," *Machine Representation of Knowledge, Machine Intelligence 8*, E. W. Elcock and D. Michie (Eds.), Ellis Horwood Ltd., New York, pp. 175-192, 1977.

Michalski, R. S. and Watanabe, L., "Constructive Closed-loop Learning: Fundamental Ideas and Examples," *Reports of Machine Learning and Inference Laboratory*, 1988.

Michalski, R.S., D. Boehm-Davis, D. and Dontas, K.,"Plausible Reasoning: An Outline of Theory and Experiments," *Proceedings of the Fourth International Symposium on Methodologies for Intelligent Systems*, Charlotte, NC, North Holland, October 12-14, 1989.

Michalski, R. S. and Zemankova, M., "What is Generalization: An Inquiry into the Concept of Generalization and its Types," to appear in *Reports of Machine Learning and Inference Laboratory*, MLI 90-6, Center for Artificial Intelligence, George Mason University, 1990.

Minton, S., "Quantitative Results Concerning the Utility of Explanation-Based Learning," *Proceedings of AAAI-88*, pp. 564-569, Saint Paul, MN, 1988.

Minton, S., Carbonell, J.G., Etzioni, O., et al., "Acquiring Effective Search Control Rules: Explanation-Based Learning in the PRODIGY System," *Proceedings of the 4th International Machine Learning Workshop*, pp. 122-133, University of California, Irvine, 1987.

Mitchell, T. M., Keller, T., and Kedar-Cabelli, S., "Explanation-Based Generalization: A Unifying View," *Machine Learning Journal*, Vol. 1, January 1986.

Mostow, J., "Machine Transformation of Advice into a Heuristic Search Procedure," in *Machine Learning: An Artificial Intelligence Approach, Vol. I*, pp. 367-403, R. S. Michalski, J. G. Carbonell and T. M. Mitchell (Eds.), Morgan Kaufmann, Los Altos, CA, 1986.

O'Rorke, P.V., Morris, S., and Schulenburg, D., "Theory Formation by Abduction: Initial Results of a Case Study Based on the Chemical Revolution," *Proceedings of the 6th International Workshop on Machine Learning*, pp. 266-271, Ithaca, NY, 1989.

Pazzani, M.J., "Integrating Explanation-Based and Empirical Learning Methods in OCCAM," *Proceedings of EWSL-88*, pp. 147-166, Glasgow, Scottland, 1988.

Peirce, C.S., *Elements of Logic* in Collected papers of Charles Sanders Peirce (1839-1914), Ch. Hartshorne and P.Weiss (Eds.), The Belknap Press Harvard University Press, Cambridge, MA, 1965.

Quinlan, J. R., "Discovering Rules from Large Collections of Examples: A Case Study", *Expert Systems in the Microelectronic Age*, D. Michie (Ed.), Edinburgh Univ. Press, Edinburgh, 1979.

Schafer, D. (Ed.), *Proceedings of the 3rd International Conference on Genetic Algorithms*, George Mason University, June 4-7, 1989.

Segre, A. M., "Explanation-Based Learning of Generalized Robot Assembly Plans," PhD thesis, *UILU-ENG-87-2208*, Coordinated Science Laboratory, University of Illinois, January 1987.

Segre, A. M. (Ed.), *Proceedings of the Sixth International Workshop on Machine Learning*, Cornell University, Ithaca, New York, June 26-27, 1989.

Slimmer, J.C. and Granger, R.H., Jr., "Incremental Learning from Noisy Data," *Machine Learning*, 1, pp.317-354, 1986.

Smolensky, P., "Connectionist AI, Symbolic AI, and the Brain," *Artificial Intelligence Review 1*, pp. 95-109, 1987.

Tanner, M.C., Explaining Kowledge Systems:Justifying Diagnostic Conclusions, PhD thesis, Department of Computer Science and Information Science, Ohio State University, 1990.

Tecuci G. and Kodratoff Y., "Apprenticeship Learning in Imperfect Domain Theories," in *Machine Learning: An Artificial Intelligence Approach, Vol. III*, Y. Kodratoff and R. S. Michalski (Eds.), Morgan Kaufmann, Los Altos, CA, 1990.

Touretzky D., Hinton, G., and Sejnowski, T. (Eds.), *Proceedings of the 1988 Connectionist Models*, Summer School, Carnegie Mellon University, June 17-26, 1988.

Wilkins, D.C., Clancey, W.J., and Buchanan, B.G., *An Overview of the Odysseus Learning Apprentice*, Kluwer Academic Press, New York, NY, 1986.

Wnek, J., Sarma, J., Wahab, A.A. and R. S. Michalski, R.S., COMPARING LEARNING PARADIGMS VIA DIAGRAMMATIC VISUALIZATION: A Case Study in Concept Learning Using Symbolic, Neural Net and Genetic Algorithm Methods, Proceedings of the 5th International Symposium on Methodologies for Intelligent Systems, University of Tennessee, Knoxville, TN, North-Holland, October 1990.

# A survey of knowledge acquisition techniques and tools

JOHN H. BOOSE

*Knowledge Systems Laboratory, Advanced Technology Center, Boeing Computer Services, P.O. Box 24346, Seattle, WA 98124, USA*

*(Based on a paper presented at the AAAI Knowledge Acquisition for Knowledge-Based Systems Workshop, Banff, November, 1988)*

Knowledge acquisition tools can be associated with knowledge-based application problems and problem-solving methods. This descriptive approach provides a framework for analysing and comparing tools and techniques, and focuses the task of building knowledge-based systems on the knowledge acquisition process. Knowledge acquisition research strategies discussed at recent Knowledge Acquisition Workshops are shown, distinguishing dimensions of knowledge acquisition tools are listed, and short descriptions of current techniques and tools are given.

## 1. Application problems and problem-solving methods

In this section a framework for describing problems and problem-solving methods is presented. Knowledge acquisition tools will then be mapped on to this framework.

Several incompatible taxonomies exist for categorizing knowledge-based application problems. One common scheme, illustrated below, divides them into *analysis* (interpretation) problems and *synthesis* (construction) problems (Clancey, 1986). Generally, analysis problems involve identifying sets of objects based on their features. One characteristic of analysis problems is that a complete set of solutions can be enumerated and included in the system. Synthesis (generative, or constructive) problems require that a solution be built up from component pieces or subproblem solutions. In synthesis problems there are too many potential solutions to enumerate and include explicitly in the system.

Analysis and synthesis problems can be broken down into sub-problem areas. We will use the following classification in the remainder of the discussion, although the same knowledge acquisition tool mapping idea can be applied to other problem taxonomies.

### Analysis problems

Classification—categorizing based on observables.
Debugging—prescribing remedies for malfunctions.
Diagnosis—inferring system malfunctions from observables.
Interpretation—inferring situation descriptions from sensor data.

This document will be periodically updated and re-published. If you have additional information or revisions concerning knowledge acquisition tools and techniques, please contact the author.

1042-8143/89/010003 + 35$03.00/0

© 1989 Academic Press Limited

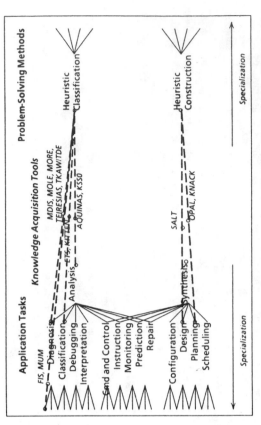

FIG. 1. Knowledge acquisition tools may be associated with relationships between application problems and problem-solving methods.

*Synthesis problems*

Configuration—configuring collections of objects under constraints in relatively small search spaces.
Design—configuring collections of objects under constraints in relatively large search spaces.
Planning—designing actions.
Scheduling—planning with strong time and/or space constraints.

*Problems combining analysis and synthesis*

Command and control—ordering and governing overall system control.
Instruction—diagnosing, debugging, and repairing student behavior.
Monitoring—comparing observations to expected outcomes.
Prediction—inferring likely consequenes of given situations.
Repair—executing plans to administer prescribed remedies.

Relationships exist between problems and problem-solving methods. For instance, the *heuristic classification* problem-solving method has been used for many knowledge-based systems that solve analysis problems (Clancey, 1986), and is employed in a variety of knowledge-based system development tools, or "shells" (S.1, M.1, EMYCIN, TI-PC and so on). In heuristic classification, data is abstracted up through a problem hierarchy, problem abstractions are mapped onto solution abstractions, and solution abstractions are refined down through the solution hierarchy into specific solutions.

General methods for solving synthesis problems are sparse; Clancey classified these methods under *heuristic construction*. Usually, a specific method is developed to solve a particular problem (such as SALT's propose-and-revise method or OPAL's skeletal-plan-refinement method), but it may be difficult to generalize the method. Some form of directed backtracking or cyclic constraint exploration is often used to explore the problem space.

Many problems require a combination of analysis and synthesis problem-solving methods. For instance, Clancey outlines a maintenance cycle requiring monitoring, prediction, diagnosis, and modification; this would combine aspects of heuristic classification and heuristic construction.

## 2. Knowledge acquisition research strategies

Musen proposed that knowledge acquisition tools could be associated with specific problems or specific problem-solving methods (Musen, Fagan, Combs & Shortliffe, 1987). In a related manner, we propose to classify tools with problems *and* problem-solving methods, since most problems are strongly linked to certain types of problem-solving methods. Consequently, certain types of domain knowledge and possibly control knowledge should be acquired to build the corresponding knowledge-based system. This idea was discussed at the First AAAI-Sponsored Knowledge Acquisition for Knowledge-Based Systems Workshop held in Banff, Canada, in November, 1986 (Gaines & Boose, 1988). Builders of interactive knowledge acquisition tools were asked to try and classify their research and the

research of others in terms of these relationships. Figure 1 shows a possible mapping of such relationships at a high level in Clancey's problem classification hierarchy and a problem-solving method classification hierarchy. Lower levels in the problem hierarchy would be sub-problems (i.e. trouble shooting and symptom analysis would be found under diagnosis) and the leaves of the problem hierarchy would be specific application problems to be solved.

Knowledge acquisition tool research fell into several categories. Descriptions and references for the tools mentioned here are given later.

### Research strategy 1

*Find and clarify knowledge acquisition techniques for a problem-to-method relationship (usually a domain specific problem employing a highly specialized method using much domain knowledge, or a general problem employing a general method with little domain knowledge).*

Examples for specific problem domains ("bottom up") include OPAL, STUDENT, FIS, and MUM.
Examples for general analysis problems ("top down") include ETS, KITTEN, KRITON, AQUINAS, and KSS0.

### Research strategy 2

*Pick a problem, find and develop knowledge acquisition techniques for an applicable method, and then see if the method and strategies will generalize to another related problem.*

Examples ("middle out") include TEIRESIAS, MDIS, MOLE, MORE, INFORM, KNACK, SALT, and TKAW.

### Research strategy 3

*Develop languages for defining and describing problems and methods.*
Examples include the work of Bylander & Mittal (1986), Bylander & Chandrasekaran (1987) and Gruber & Cohen (1987).

### Research strategy 4

*Build intelligent editors to help AI programmers construct large knowledge bases.*
Examples include CYC and KREME.

Research strategy 4 was controversial. Opponents argued that knowledge should be tested for specific purposes as it is acquired rather than being constructed in a "use-vacuum". This usually means that the tool has a link to or contains an embedded performance system. Proponents of the strategy stated that future expert systems will require large knowledge bases to avoid problems of brittleness and narrowness of scope and to be able to perform analogy and discovery, and that tools to build and manage large knowledge bases should be developed now.

## 3. Knowledge acquisition tools: dimensions, techniques, and descriptions

Six Knowledge Acquisition for Knowledge-Based Systems workshops have been held since 1986 (see the bibliography for proceedings information):

First AAAI-Sponsored Knowledge Acquisition for Knowledge-Based Systems Workshop, Banff, Canada, November, 1986;
First European Acquisition for Knowledge-Based Systems Workshop, Reading, England, September, 1987;
Second AAAI-Sponsored Knowledge Acquisition for Knowledge-Based Systems Workshop, Banff, Canada, October, 1987;
Second European Knowledge Acquisition for Knowledge-Based Systems Workshop, Bonn, Germany, June, 1988;
Integration of Knowledge Acquisition and Performance Systems Workshop, AAAI-88, St. Paul, August, 1988;
Third AAAI-Sponsored Knowledge Acquisition for Knowledge-Based Systems Workshop, Banff, Canada, November, 1988.

Future workshops include:

Third European Knowledge Acquisition for Knowledge-Based Systems Workshop, Paris, France, July, 1989;
Fourth AAAI-Sponsored Knowledge Acquisition for Knowledge-Based Systems Workshop, Banff, Canada, October, 1989.

Representative knowledge acquisition techniques and tools presented at these workshops are described and analysed below. First, an analysis of tools and tool dimensions is shown. Then, knowledge acquisition techniques and methods are listed and briefly described, along with computer-based tools, if any, that employ them. Finally, representative tools are listed, described, and referenced.

### Knowledge acquisition tool dimensions

AQUINAS, a knowledge acquisition tool in use at The Boeing Company, was used prior to one of the Knowledge Acquisition Workshops to classify the tools and develop tool dimensions (references for AQUINAS appear below).

Knowledge in AQUINAS is represented, in part, in repertory grids. Objects appear along one axis of the grid and dimensions or traits appear along the other axis. AQUINAS helps the expert develop, analyse, refine, and test knowledge. A preliminary grid developed for the knowledge acquisition tools is shown in Fig. 2. An expanded version of this grid is shown in the Appendix. This grid reflects the author's view of state of the tools as of June, 1988. Eventually, AQUINAS elicited the following set of knowledge acquisition tool dimensions:

### Application task dimensions

—*Level of generality* (domain dependence)—how domain-dependent is the tool?
—*Analysis/synthesis*—What broad categories of application tasks can the tool address?
—*Specific task*—Has the tool been built for a specific task? If so, what is the task?
—*Application statistics* (number and size of applications)—How many applications have been built with the tool? How diverse are they? How large are they? How much of the finished system did the tool help build?

### Knowledge acquisition techniques and methods (these are listed separately below)

### Modeling dimensions

—*Deep modeling/shallow modeling*—Are "deep" models or "causal" models elicited?
—*Multiple/single methods for handling uncertainty*—What techniques, if any, are used to model uncertainty?

### Representations

—*Expertise representation method* (cognitive maps, concepts, correlations, decision tables, frames, goal structures, hierarchies, operators, probability distributions, relations, repertory grids, rules, scripts, tables).
—*Knowledge types* (causal knowledge, classes conceptual structures, constraints, control, covering, example cases, explanations, facts, goals, judgments, justifications, preferences, procedures, relations, spatial, strategic, temporal, terminology, uncertainties).

—*Multiple knowledge view/few knowledge views*—How many ways are there to look at elicited knowledge? What, if any, knowledge transformation techniques are employed?

## System use

—*Automated tool/semi-automated tool/manual technique*—How much of the technique is implemented as a computer program? How "smart" is the tool? Is effective tool use dependent on the user, or does the tool offer semi-automated or automated assistance?

—*Efficiency of use; speed of use*—How hard is the tool to use? How efficient is knowledge elicitation and modeling? How well are the techniques implemented?

—*Implementation stage* (planned, in progress, implemented, tested, in use, past use).

—*Life cycle support* (one-shot use to complete cycle support)—How much of the knowledge engineering and system delivery life cycle does the tool support?

—*System in use/system not in use*—Is the tool currently in use? Was the tool previously in use? Will the tool be in use in the future?

—*Training needed*—How much training is needed to use the tool? Can experts use the tool directly?

—*Users* (end-users of expert system, decision makers, experts, knowledge engineers, AI programmers needed)—Who are the targeted users of the tool?

AQUINAS performed several analyses of the knowledge. For example, an implication analysis produced by AQUINAS showed logical entailments between different dimensions (Fig. 3). A similarity analysis among dimensions showed, for example, that EFFICIENT.AND.FAST.TO.USE was closely coupled to LITTLE.TRAINING.NEEDED. A similarity analysis among tools showed, for example, high similarity between ETS, KITTEN, and PLANET, and low similarity between FIS and KSS0 (similarity scores were produced for each pair of dimensions and each pair of tools).

AQUINAS also produced several "scatter tables" showing clusters of tools plotted on successive pairs of dimensions. Figure 4 (domain independence *vs* task class) shows strong concentrations of knowledge acquisition tools for diagnostic tasks, but few knowledge acquisition tools for synthesis problems. Figure 5 shows that, generally, it is easier to automate tools that are more domain-dependent. Figure 6

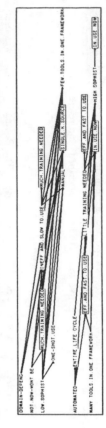

FIG. 3. AQUINAS was used to produce implications showing logical entailment between tool dimensions.

FIG. 2. A preliminary repertory grid developed using AQUINAS to help analyse knowledge acquisition tools. Nominal as well as ordinal dimensions are represented. *Distributions* of values exist when values in the grid are preceded by "***"; the highest value in the distribution is shown. Full distributions for the grid are shown in tables in the Appendix.

```
INTERACTIVE.TRAIT
 1. (5) APPL.DOMAIN: (CLASSIFICATION C-AND-C CONFIGURATION DIAGNOSIS DESIGN MANAGEMENT MONITORING PLANNING REI
 2. (5) AUTOMATION-GUIDANCE: MANUAL(1)/AUTOMATED(5) [ORDINAL,1]
 3. (5) DOMAIN-INDEPENDENCE: DOMAIN-INDEPENDENT(1)/DOMAIN-DEPENDENT(5) [ORDINAL,1]
 4. (5) EFFICIENCY: EFF.AND.FAST.TO.USE(1)/INEFF.AND.SLOW.TO.USE(5) [ORDINAL,1]
 5. (5) IMPL.STAGE: (PLANNED IN-PROGRESS IMPLEMENTED TESTED IN-USE) [NOMINAL,]
 6. (5) IN-USE: IN-USE.NOW(1)/NOT.IN-USE(5) [ORDINAL,1]
 7. (4) K-REP: (COGNITIVE-MAPS CONCEPTS CORRELATIONS DECISION-TABLES FRAMES GOAL-STRUCTURES HIERARCHI
 8. (4) K-TYPE: (CONSTRAINTS CONTROL LOWERING EXPLANATIONS FACTS JUDGMENTS JUSTIFICATIONS PREFERENC
 9. (5) LEARNING COMPONENT: (AUTOMATIC INTERACTIVE NONE) [NOMINAL,]
10. (5) LIFE.CYCLE: ONE-SHOT.USE(1)/ENTIRE.LIFE.CYCLE(5) [ORDINAL,1]
11. (5) LEVEL.OF.SOPHIST.: LOW.SOPHIST(1)/HIGH.SOPHIST(5) [ORDINAL,1]
12. (5) METHODS-TECHNIQUES: (ANALOGY APPR-LEARNING INTERVIEWING CONSISTENCY-V-ANALYSIS DEC-TREE-II
13. (4) K-SOURCES: SINGLE.K.SOURCE(1)/MULTI.K.SOURCE(5) [ORDINAL,1]
14. (4) TRAINING: LITTLE.TRAINING.NEEDED(1)/MUCH.TRAINING.NEEDED(5) [ORDINAL,1]
15. (4) UNCERTAINTY-REP: (CF PROBABILITIES SYMBOLIC OTHER NONE) [NOMINAL,]
16. (5) USERS: (ES-USERS DEC-MAKERS EXPERTS KE AI-PROGRAMMERS) [NOMINAL,]
17. (5) WORKBENCH: MANY.TOOLS.IN.ONE.FRAMEWORK(1)/FEW.TOOLS.IN.ONE.FRAMEWORK(5) [ORDINAL,1]
```

## Features

—*High-level techniques/low-level techniques*—How sophisticated are the techniques used?

—*Learning component* (automatic, interactive, none)—If there is a learning component in the tool, how powerful is it? Is it automatic or interactive?

—*Multiple features/few features*—How many techniques are integrated in a single framework? How well do multiple techniques support each other?

—*Multiple knowledge sources support*—Is there specific support for eliciting, analysing, or delivering knowledge from multiple experts or other sources?

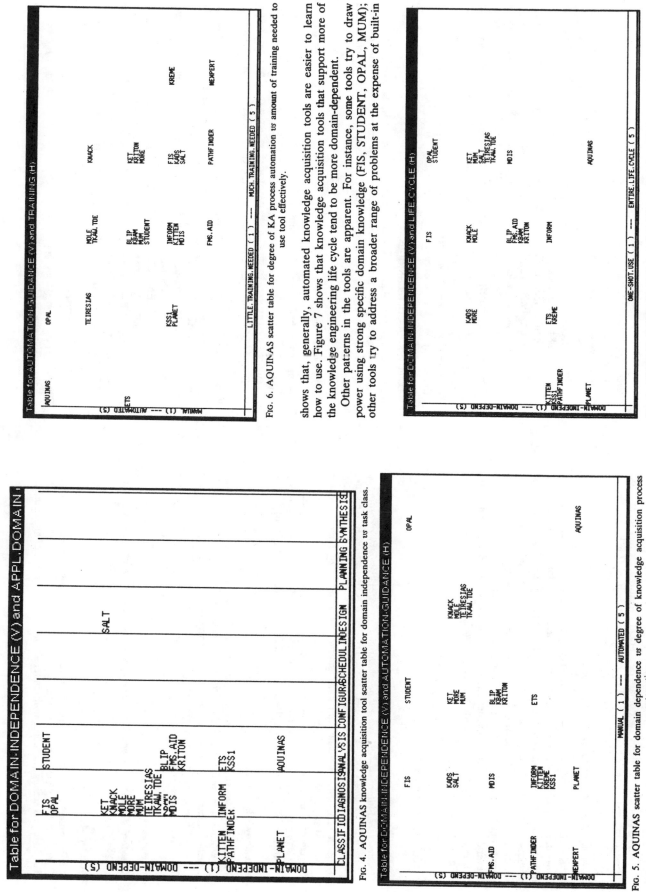

Fig. 4. AQUINAS knowledge acquisition tool scatter table for domain independence vs task class.

Fig. 5. AQUINAS scatter table for domain dependence vs degree of knowledge acquisition process automation.

Fig. 6. AQUINAS scatter table for degree of KA process automation vs amount of training needed to use tool effectively.

Fig. 7. AQUINAS scatter table for domain independence vs knowledge engineering life cycle support.

shows that, generally, automated knowledge acquisition tools are easier to learn how to use. Figure 7 shows that knowledge acquisition tools that support more of the knowledge engineering life cycle tend to be more domain-dependent.

Other patterns in the tools are apparent. For instance, some tools try to draw power using strong specific domain knowledge (FIS, STUDENT, OPAL, MUM); other tools try to address a broader range of problems at the expense of built-in domain-specific problem-solving power (ETS, KITTEN, AQUINAS). The few tools that address synthesis problems are domain dependent. Most researchers seem to be interested in applying their tools to more domain independent and/or harder tasks.

**Knowledge acquisition techniques and methods**

In this section, knowledge acquisition methods and techniques presented at various Knowledge Acquisition Workshops are listed and briefly described. Techniques are divided into *manual* techniques and *computer-based* techniques. Computer-based techniques and tools are further divided into *interactive* and *learning-based* techniques and tools. This section is meant to serve as a reference for those interested in obtaining more information about these techniques and tools.

Several papers also discussed issues such as the future of knowledge acquisition systems and the evolving nature of the knowledge engineering process (Gaines, 1987a, b, 1988a, b).

3.1. MANUAL TECHNIQUES

**Interviewing**

**Unstructured interview**—*ask general questions and hope for the best, recording as much as possible* (Kidd & Cooper, 1985; Trimble & Cooper, 1987; Welbank, 1987a)

**Focused interview**—*interview with open questions and a list of topics to cover* (Bradshaw, 1989; Welbank, 1987b)

**Structured interview**—*interview with strict agenda and list of specific questions relating to features of system* (Bradshaw, J. M., 1989; Freiling, Alexander, Messick, Rehfuss & Shulman, 1985; Slocombe, Moore & Zelouf, 1986)

**Active knowledge engineer roles**

**Participant observation**—*knowledge engineer becomes an apprentice or otherwise participates in the expert's problem-solving process* (Welbank, 1987b)

**Teachback interview**—*knowledge engineer demonstrates understanding of expertise by paraphrasing or solving a problem* (Johnson & Johnson, 1987)

**Tutorial interview**—*expert delivers a lecture* (Welbank, 1987b)

**Brainstorming**

**Crawford slip method**—*rapidly generate a large number of ideas* (Rusk & Krone, 1984)

**Psychology-based**

**Card sorting**—*sort objects on cards to help structure knowledge* (Gammack & Young, 1984; Welbank, 1987b)

**Psychological scaling** (including multidimensional scaling)—*use scaling techniques* to help structure knowledge (Burton, Shadbolt, Hedgecock & Rugg, 1987; Saaty, 1981; Young & Gammack, 1987)

**Overcoming bias**—*recognize and correct bias from knowledge sources* (Cleaves, 1987; Moray, 1985; Stephanou, 1987)

**Protocol analysis** (case walk-through/eidetic reduction/observation/process-tracing)—*record and analyse transcripts from experts thinking aloud during tasks* (Belkin, Brooks & Daniles, 1987; Breuker & Wielinga, 1987b; Ericcson & Simon, 1984; Gammack & Young, 1984; Welbank, 1987b; Glover, 1983; Johnson, Zaulkernan & Garber, 1987; Killin & Hickman, 1986; Littman, 1987; Waldron, 1985; Wetter & Schmalhofer, 1988)

**Uncertain information elicitation**—*expert encodes uncertainty about the problem* (Beyth-Marom & Dekel, 1985; Hink & Woods, 1987; Kahneman, Slovic & Tversky, 1982; Pearl, 1986; Shafer & Tversky, 1985; Spetzler & Stael von Holstein, 1983; Stael von Holstein & Matheson, 1978; Tversky, Sattah & Slovic, 1987; Wallsten & Budescu, 1983).

**Wizard of Oz technique**—*an expert simulates the behavior of a future system* (Sandberg, Winkels & Breuker, 1988)

3.2. COMPUTER-BASED TECHNIQUES

When specific computer-based tools implement these methods, the name of the tool is listed. Computer-based tools are described and referenced below. Work describing methods not implemented as computer-based tools are listed and referenced as a "Method".

**Interactive techniques**

**Psychology-based and interviewing methods**

Automated/mixed-initiative interviewing—*the tool interviews the expert*
AQUINAS, ASK, CAP, ETS, KITTEN, KNACK, KRIMB, KRITON, KSS0, MDIS, MOLE, MORE, ODYSSEUS, PLANE, PROTOS, ROGET, SALT, TEIRESIAS, TKAW

Protocol analysis (Case walk-through/Eidetic reduction/Observation/Process-tracing)—*record and analyse transcripts from experts thinking aloud during tasks*
KRITON, LAPS, MEDKAT

Psychological scaling (including multidimensional scaling)—*use scaling techniques to help structure knowledge*
AQUINAS, KITTEN, KSS0, PATHFINDER, PLANET

Methods—(Butler & Corter, 1986; Gaines & Shaw, 1981; Kelly, 1955)

Repertory grids/PCP—*use personal construct psychology and related methods to elicit and analyse knowledge*
AQUINAS, ETS, FMS-AID, KITTEN, KRITON, KSS0, PLANET

**Task/method/performance exploitation**

Domain exploitation (single application)—*rely heavily on the domain for knowl-edge acquisition guidance*

FIS, LAS, LEAP, OPAL, PROTOGE, STUDENT

Problem-solving method exploitation—*use information about the problem-solving method to guide knowledge acquisition*
AQUINAS, CLASSIKA, FMS-AID, KNACK, MDIS, MOLE, MORE, SALT, TEIRESIAS, TKAW

Performance system (*direct link or embedded*)—*generate knowledge that may be directly tested*
AQUINAS, ASK, BLIP, ETS, KAE, KNACK, KRITON, LAPS, LEAP, MDIS, MOLE, MORE, MUM, ODYSSEUS, OPAL, PROTOGÉ, ROGET, TEIRESIAS, TKAW, SALT

## Modeling

Decision analysis—*perform probabilistic inference and planning using influence diagrams*
INFORM
Methods—(Bradshaw & Boose, 1989; von Winterfeldt & Edwards, 1986)

Modeling (*deep models, causal models, cognitive models, conceptual models, mediating representations, task-level models*)—*use or generate models of the domain, possibly independent of a tool or a specific application*
ASTEK, BLIP, CLASSIKA, FIS, KADS, KRIMB, MACAO, NEXPERT, ONTOS, OPAL, PROTOGÉ
Methods—(Addis & Bull, 1988; Alexander, Freiling, Shulman, Rehfuss & Messick, 1987; Hayward, Wielinga & Breuker, 1987; Johnson, 1987; Johnson, 1988; Linster, 1987; Morik, 1987b; Regoczei & Plantinga, 1986; Schreiber, Breuker, Bredeweg & Wielinga, 1988; Twine, 1988; Woods & Hollnagel, 1987; Young & Gammack, 1987)

Consistency analysis—*analyse knowledge for consistency*
BLIP, FIS, KNAC, MUM, TEIRESIAS

Physical model simulation—*use basic laws to drive physical models through simulation*
SIMULA

## Multiple experts

Delphi—*gather information from people independently*
MEDKAT

Multiple source—*elicit and analyse knowledge from multiple sources separately and combine for use*
AQUINAS, ETS, MEDKAT, KITTEN, KSS0
Methods—(Gaines, 1987a, b; Mittal & Dym, 1985)

## Other sources of knowledge

Textual analysis/natural language analysis—*generate knowledge directly by analysing text*
KRITON, KSS0, KBAM, PROPOS/EPISTOS, WASTL

## Learning-based techniques

Analogy—*apply knowledge from old situations in similar new situations*
CYC, TEIRESIAS

Apprenticeship learning—*learn by watching experts solve problems*
DICIPLE, ISG, LEAP, LEDA, ODYSSEUS, PROTOS, OPAL, STUDENT

Decision tree induction/analysis; question scheduling—*generate, analyse decision trees*
CART, ID3
Methods—(Bramer, 1987; Cox, 1988; Goodman & Smyth, 1988; Pettit & Pettit, 1987)

Example selection—*select an appropriate set of examples for various learning techniques*
Methods—(Blythe, Corsi & Needham, 1987; Rissland, 1987)

Explanation-based learning—*deduce a general rule from a single example by relating it to an existing theory*
ACES, INDE, LAS, LEAP, OCCAM, ODYSSEUS, SRAR
Method—(Kodratoff & Manago, 1987; Kodratoff, 1987)

Genetic algorithm—*genetic operators (crossing-over, mutation, inversion) are used to adapt a system's behavior*
Method—(Pettit & Pettit, 1987)

Induction of models from experience
AM, ATOM

Mimicking expert behavior
INDUCE

Performance feedback—*performance feedback is used to reinforce behavior*
AQUINAS, MOLE, PERCEPTRON, PROTOS, STELLA

Rule/knowledge induction—*generate rules from other forms of knowledge*
AQ, AQUINAS, BLIP, ETS, KSS0, INSTIL
Methods—(Buntine, 1987; Cleary, 1987; Delgrande, 1987; Goodman & Smyth, 1989; Rissland, 1987; Sebag & Schoenauer, 1988; Witten & MacDonald, 1988)

Similarity-based learning—*learn similarities from sets of positive examples and differences from sets of negative examples*
BLIP, GINESYS, ID3, ILROD, INC2, INDE, INSTIL
Method—(Schroder, Niemann & Sagerer, 1988)

Systemic principles derivation—*use general principles to derive specific laws*
OBJ

## Computer-based knowledge acquisition tools descriptions and references

Knowledge acquisition tools presented and discussed above are briefly described and referenced here. Interactive tools in current use are described in terms of the problem-method framework, intended user, uses, and features.

ACES—*learn heuristics for fault diagnosis from device descriptions using explanation-based learning* (Pazzani, 1987)
Problem: fault diagnosis
Method: explanation-based learning.

Uses, systems built:
Features: supports incremental knowledge base construction focussing on different problem-solving aspects, enables knowledge formalization by using special tables, forms, and hierarchies; uses MED2 shell.

CYC—*acquire and use knowledge through the use of analogy and a large existing knowledge base* (Lenat, Prakash & Shepard, 1986)
Problem and method: undefined.
Intended user: AI programmer.
Uses, systems built: store "common sense" knowledge needed to understand encyclopedia articles.
Features: classification of common sense of knowledge primitives.

DICIPLE—*integrate various machine learning techniques to adopt to available theories* (Kodratoff & Tecuci, 1988)

ETS—*interview experts using repertory grid-based methods and test the knowledge* (Boose, 1984, 1985, 1986a, b)
Problem: classification.
Method: heuristic classification.
Intended user: domain expert.
Uses, systems built: wide range of small analytic system prototypes for knowledge engineering project start-up and feasibility analyses.
Features: based on personal construct psychology (repertory or rating grid methods); embedded analysis, refinement, testing, and knowledge base shell generation.

FIS—*tie knowledge acquisition closely to the fault diagnosis domain* (De Jong, 1986)
Problem: mechanism diagnosis.
Method: heuristic classification.
Intended user: AI programmer.
Uses, systems built: fault isolation systems—radar units.
Features: causal models built with replaceable components, tests, attached rules; consistency check; rule induction.

FMS-AID—*combine repertory grid methods and Newell and Simon's problem space concept to manufacturing problems* (Garg-Janardan & Salvendy, 1987)

GINESYS—*use confirmation rules, a form of redundant knowledge, to learn in noisy domains* (Gams, 1988)

ID3—*learn similarities and differences from training sets by optimizing global parameters* (Quinlan, 1983, 1987)

ILROID—*perform logic-based induction on Horn clauses to learn knowledge of relevance* (Dutta, 1988)

INC2—*perform learning by observation using hill-climbing through a space of hierarchical classification schemes* (Hadzikadic, 1988)

INDE—*generate rules on the basis of counterexamples combining explanation-based learning and similarity-based learning* (Terpstra & van Someren, 1988)

INDUCE—*mimic an expert's behavior* (Michalski & Chilausky, 1980)

INFORM—*elicit knowledge using decision analysis techniques* (Moore & Agogino, 1987)
Problem: mechanical diagnosis.
Method: heuristic classification.

Intended user: AI programmer.
Uses, systems built: attitude control.
Features: heuristics examine atypical features and hypothesize potential faults; device models confirm or deny hypothesized faults.

AM—*induce models from experience* (Davis & Lenat, 1982)

AQ—*induce rules from sets of positive and negative training examples* (Michalski, 1983)

AQUINAS—*elicit and model information using a knowledge acquisition workbench including hierarchically-structured repertory grid-based interviewing and testing and other methods* (Boose & Bradshaw, 1987a, b; Kitto & Boose, 1987, 1988; Boose, 1988; Bradshaw & Boose, 1989; Shema & Boose, 1988; Boose, Bradshaw & Shema, 1988)
Problem: analysis.
Method: heuristic classification.
Intended user: domain expert.
Uses, systems built: wide range of analytic tasks (decision aid for one-shot decisions, knowledge-based system development and delivery, group decision aid, shell front-end, situation insight and analysis).
Features: workbench of tool kits: personal construct psychology methods; hierarchical structuring aids; induction; multiple expert analysis and reasoning; support for elicit, analysis, test, expand cycles.

ASK—*acquire strategic knowledge from experts using a justification language* (Gruber, 1988)
Problem: problems where problem-solving strategy is important.
Method: analysis.
Intended user: expert, AI programmer.
Features: addresses encoding examples, biasing generalization, new term problem.

ASTEK—*combine multiple paradigms for knowledge editing in a natural language discourse framework* (Jacobson & Freiling, 1988)

ATOM—*induce models from experience* (Gaines, 1977)

BLIP—*construct organized domain models automatically by learning from sloppy models* (Morik, 1987a; Wrobel, 1988; Kietz, 1988)
Problem and method: used to acquire problem-solving independent knowledge.
Intended user: expert.
Features: "Sloppy modeling" of intermediate knowledge.

CART—*employ cross-validation to produce appropriately-sized decision trees* (Crawford, 1989)
Problem: classification.
Uses, systems built: display fault classification, flower classification.
Features: partitions measurement space into decision tree using concept induction.

CLASSIKA—*use expert-directed techniques to capture aspects of classification problem-solving* (Gappa, 1988)
Problem: classification.
Method: heuristic classification.
Intended user: expert.

Intended user: domain expert.

Uses, systems built: model-based diagnosis of electro-mechanical systems.

Features: decision analysis techniques—influence diagrams as knowledge representation.

INSTIL—*acquire knowledge using similarity-based learning combining aspects of both numeric and symbolic approaches* (Kodratoff & Manago, 1987a)

ISG—*link evidence to situations by synthesizing rules from interesting situations using an apprenticeship learning approach* (Wisniewski, Winston, Smith & Kleyn, 1986)

Problem: classification.

Intended user: AI programmer, expert.

Uses, systems built: geological formation analysis.

Features: synthesize rules from situation-manifestation pairs by exploiting error propagation information.

KADS—*elicit and model knowledge decoupled from the design and implementation of the system* (Breuker & Wielinga, 1987a; Anjewierden, 1987; Tong & Karbach, 1988; Schreiber et al., 1988)

KAE—*capture scene analysis expertise* (Tranowski, 1988)

KBAM—*use natural language explanations to construct a domain-specific knowledge base* (Silvestro, 1988)

Problem: concept classification.

Method: explanation-based learning.

Intended user: expert.

Uses, systems built: course descriptions.

Features: natural language explanation analysis.

KET—*provide a graphical interface and analyse relationships to help experts write rules* (Esfahani & Teskey, 1987, 1988)

Problem: analysis.

Method: heuristic classification.

Intended user: expert, AI programmer.

Features: elicitation of rules for the shell RBFS.

KITTEN—*interview experts using repertory grid-based methods* (Shaw & Gaines, 1987; Shaw & Woodward, 1988)

Problem: classification.

Method: heuristic classification (uses NEXPERT shell)

Intended user: domain expert.

Uses, systems built: range of small analytic system prototypes.

Features: based on personal construct psychology (rating grid methods); text analysis to feed rating grids; linked to multi-user participant system.

KNAC—*use acquired assimilation knowledge to help enter new knowledge in a knowledge base* (Lefkowitz & Lesser, 1988)

Problem: analysis.

Method: heuristic classification.

Intended user: expert.

Features: help integrate new knowledge into an existing POISE system knowledge base.

KNACK—*elicit and use knowledge about evaluation report generation* (Klinker, Bentolila, Genetet, Grimes & McDermott, 1987; Klinker, Genetet & McDermott, 1988)

Problem: design evaluation and reporting.

Method: heuristic classification.

Intended user: domain expert.

Uses, systems built: electro-mechanical system design evaluation and reporting for nuclear hardening.

Features: gathers report outlines, phrases, and run-time procedures for filling in reports; generates shells that evaluate designs and produce reports.

KREME—*include multiple-representations in a knowledge editing environment* (Abrett & Burstein, 1987)

Problem: analysis.

Method: heuristic classification.

Intended user: AI programmer.

Uses, systems built: examine steam plant operations (STEAMER).

Features: knowledge base editor; multiple views of knowledge.

KRIMB—*interview experts and build diagnostic domain models* (Cox & Blumenthal, 1987)

Problem: diagnosis.

Intended user: expert.

Features: intelligent questioning, reliability analysis of domain models.

KRITON—*combine repertory grid interviewing and protocol analysis to build knowledge at an intermediate level* (Diederich, Ruhmann & May, 1987; Diederich, Linster, Ruhmann & Uthmann, 1987; Linster, 1988)

Problem: analysis.

Method heuristic classification.

Intended user: domain expert, AI programmers.

Uses, systems built: configuration of office equipment (in progress).

Features: combines repertory grids, protocol analysis, content analysis; knowledge editor.

KSS0—*elicit knowledge with a repertory grid-based interviewing tool including text analysis, behavior induction, and psychological scaling techniques* (Gaines, 1987a, t, 1988; Gaines & Sharp, 1987; Shaw & Gaines, 1987; Shaw, 1988)

Problem: analysis.

Method: heuristic classification (uses NEXPERT shell).

Intended user: expert.

Features: workbench of tool kits: personal construct psychology methods; multiple expert analysis; text analysis, behavior induction, and psychological scaling.

LAPS—*interweave protocol analysis and completeness querying* (di Piazza, 1988)

Problem: diagnosis.

Method: heuristic classification.

Intended user: knowledge engineer and expert.

Features: protocols are analysed and aggregated; tables are formed for M.1.

LAS—*use apprenticeship learning to learn by watching experts solve problems* (Smith, Winston, Mitchell & Buchanan, 1985)

LEAP—*use apprenticeship learning to learn steps in VLSI design by watching experts solve problems* (Mitchell, Mahadevan & Steinberg, 1985)

LEDA—*acquire knowledge for chip architecture design by interactively generalizing design plans* (Franztke & Herrmann, 1988)

MACAO—*model expert knowledge based on empirical and conceptual schemes* (Aussenac, Frontin & Soubie, 1988)
Intended user: knowledge engineer, expert.
Uses, systems built: overseeing bus lines.
Features: represent schemes from experts as graphs containing procedural and declarative knowledge.

MDIS—*experts are interviewed to describe mechanisms in a top-down structured manner for diagnostic problems* (Antonelli, 1983)
Problem: mechanical diagnosis.
Method: heuristic classification.
Intended user: domain expert.
Uses, systems built: mechanical systems—jet engines.
Features: top-down structured model elicitation, causal reasoning, simulation, multiple diagnostic strategies.

MEDKAT—*automate the Delphi technique to gather information from multiple experts* (Jagannathan & Elmaghraby, 1985).

MOLE—*exploit information about how problems are solved to elicit scarce diagnostic knowledge and use feedback to fine tune the knowledge* (Eshelman, Ehret, McDermott & Tan, 1987; Eshelman, 1988)
Problem: mechanical diagnosis.
Method: heuristic classification.
Intended user: domain expert.
Uses, systems built: diagnosis—steel rolling mill, coal-burning power plant.
Features: distinguishing among and reasoning about covering differentiating, and combining knowledge; understanding how to infer causal direction and support values.

MORE—*exploit information about how problems are solved to elicit extensive diagnostic knowledge* (Kahn, Nowlan & McDermott, 1985a, b)
Problem: mechanical diagnosis.
Method: heuristic classification.
Intended user: domain expert.
Uses, systems built: diagnostic tasks.
Features: nets built around hypotheses, symptoms, and tests.

MUM—*evidential combination knowledge and control knowledge are elicited for medical problems* (Gruber & Cohen, 1987)
Problem: medical diagnosis.
Method: heuristic classification.
Intended user: AI programmer.
Uses, systems built: medical diagnosis; used with MU system.
Features: use of task-level primitives to capture domain knowledge at expert's level of abstraction.

NEXPERT—*include multiple-representations in a knowledge editing environment with a performance component* (Rappaport, 1987, 1988)
Problem: analysis.
Method: heuristic classification.
Intended user: AI programmer.
Uses, systems built: commercial shell.
Features: knowledge base editor, multiple knowledge views.

OBJ—*use general principles to derive specific laws* (Goguen & Meseguer, 1983)

OCCAM—*learn to predict outcomes of economic sanction episodes using explanation-based learning* (Pazzani, 1987)
Problem: prediction.
Method: explanation-based learning.
Intended user: AI programmer.
Uses, systems built: economic sanction episodes.
Features: generalize from the outcome of previous incidents.

ODYSSEUS—*refine and debug knowledge using apprenticeship learning techniques* (Wilkens, Clancey & Buchanan, 1987)

ONTOS—*build domain models using cognitive and linguistic factors* (Monarch & Nirenburg, 1987)

OPAL—*tie knowledge acquisition closely to the cancer treatment domain* (Musen et al., 1987)
Problem: administration of cancer therapy.
Method: skeletal plan refinement.
Intended user: domain expert.
Uses, systems built: cancer therapy management (in ONCOCIN).
Features: use semantics of application domain (vs knowledge structure or problem-solving method) to manage knowledge acquisition.

PATHFINDER—*use psychological scaling techniques to help structure knowledge hierarchically* (Cooke & McDonald, 1987)

PLANET—*use repertory grids for psychological interviewing and analysis* (Shaw, 1984; Gaines & Shaw, 1986)
Problem: classification.
Uses, systems built: used by psychologists and others for computer-based repertory grid elicitation.
Features: repertory grid elicitation and analysis.

PROPOS/EPISTOS—*transform text into a meaning representation and then perform epistemological analysis using pragmatic fields* (Moller, 1988)

PROTOGÉ—*edit the conceptual model of another knowledge acquisition tool* (OPAL) for skeletal plan refinement tasks (Musen, 1988)

PROTOS—*use exemplar-based learning in an apprenticeship learning system* (Bareiss, Porter & Wier, 1988)
Problem: analysis.
Method: heuristic classification.
Intended user: expert.
Uses, systems built: clinical audiology.
Features: use inductive and deductive techniques to retain, index, and match exemplars.

ROGET—*interview experts and produce conceptual structures of the domain* (Bennet, 1985)
Problem: medical diagnosis.
Method: heuristic classification.
Intended user: expert.
Uses, systems built: used to generate knowledge bases for EMYCIN.
Features: elicits conceptual model from the expert by asking for concepts and support relationships.

SALT—*elicit and deliver knowledge for constructive constraint satisfaction tasks* (Marcus, McDermott & Wang, 1985; Marcus, 1987; Stout, Caplain, Marcus & McDermott, 1988)
Problem: configuration, scheduling.
Method: propose-and-revise (directed backtracking).
Intended user: domain expert.
Uses, systems built: physical system configuration (elevator configuration); simulation lab resource scheduling.
Features: expert knowledge consists of parts or modules, constraints, and what to do when constraints are violated.

SIMULA—*use basic laws to derive physical models through simulation* (Nygaard & Dahl, 1981)

SRAR—*use explanation-based learning techniques to develop intelligent tutoring systems* (Boy & Nuss, 1988).
Intended user: AI programmer.
Uses, systems built: flight management training.
Features: combine explanation-based learning with an authoring language (PLATO) and an observer model (built in NEXPERT Object).

STELLA—*performance feedback is used to reinforce behavior* (Gaines & Andreae, 1966)

STUDENT—*tie knowledge acquisition closely to the statistical consulting domain* (Gale, 1987)
Problem: statistical analysis classification.
Method: heuristic classification.
Intended user: domain expert.
Uses, systems built: statistical consulting.
Features: domain primitives (frames) that specify what information is relevant to data analysis.

TEIRESIAS—*model existing knowledge to monitor refinements and help debug consultations* (Davis & Lenat, 1982)
Problem: medical diagnosis.
Method: heuristic classification.
Intended user: domain expert.
Uses, systems built: MYCIN, systems built with EMYCIN.
Features: rule-based repair through errors of commission and omission; suggestion of new rules based on statistical models.

TKAW/TDE—*exploit information about how problems are solved to elicit trouble-shooting knowledge* (Kahn, Breaux, Joeseph & DeKlerk, 1987)
Problem: mechanical diagnosis.

Method: heuristic classification.
Intended user: domain expert, AI programmer.
Uses, systems built: trouble-shooting electro-mechanical systems.
Features: mixed-initiative environment, concentrates on search control in trouble-shooting tasks.

WASTL—*acquire knowledge for a natural language understanding system based on KADS methodology* (Jansen-Winkeln, 1988)

## 4. Discussion

The first part of this paper presented a framework for associating knowledge acquisition tools with knowledge-based application problems and problem-solving methods. Specific tools and tool classes were associated with specific application problems and methods (i.e. AQUINAS is associated with analysis problems and the heuristic problem-solving method; SALT is associated with configuration and design applications and a specialized form of heuristic construction).

These associations help define the depth and breadth of current knowledge acquisition research. Our research using AQUINAS has lead us to try and build a broad link (multiple integrated tool sets) between a general application problem class (analysis problems) and a powerful problem-solving method (heuristic classification). Other successful work has led researchers to tightly couple knowledge acquisition tools to a domain problem (for example, FIS, STUDENT, OPAL).

Current research strategies were mentioned. Associations in the problem-method framework where no tools exist can point out promising areas for new research. For example, can special types of knowledge acquisition tools be associated with debugging problems and heuristic classification, or with planning and new specializations of heuristic construction?

This descriptive approach provides a framework for studying and comparing tools. It also emphasizes the need for a more refined application problem hierarchy, and the need to recognize and generalize new problem-solving methods.

The rest of the paper analysed dimensions and relationships among the tools and techniques, and classified and briefly described current knowledge acquisition tools and methods. It is hoped that this reference work will be useful both as an introduction and to those who pursue this field of research.

Thanks to Roger Beeman, Miroslav Benda, Jeffrey Bradshaw, William Clancey, Brian Gaines, Catherine Kitto, Ted Kitzmiller, Sandra Marcus, Mark Musen, Art Nagai, Doug Schuler, Mildred Shaw, David Shema, Lisle Tinglof-Boose, and Bruce Wilson for their contributions and support. Aquinas and ETS were developed at the Knowledge Systems Laboratory, Advanced Technology Center, Boeing Computer Services in Seattle, Washington.

## References

ABRETT, G. & BURSTEIN, M. H. (1987). The KREME knowledge editing environment, special issue on the 1st Knowledge Acquisition for Knowledge-Based Systems Workshop, 1986, Part 4. *International Journal of Man–Machine Studies*, **27**, 103–126; also in J. H. BOOSE & B. R. GAINES, Eds (1988). *Knowledge-Based Systems: Knowledge Acquisition Tools for Expert Systems*, vol. 2, pp. 1–24. New York: Academic Press.

ADDIS, T. R. & BULL, S. P. (1988). A concept language for knowledge elicitation. *Proceedings of the 2nd European Knowledge Acquisition Workshop (EKAW-88)*, Bonn, June, pp. A1.1–16.

ALEXANDER, J. H., FREILING, M. J., SHULMAN, S. J., REHFUSS, S. & MESSICK, S. L. (1987). Ontological analysis: an ongoing experiment, special issue on the 1st Knowledge Acquisition for Knowledge-Based Systems Workshop, 1986, Part 3. *International Journal of Man–Machine Studies*, **26**, 473–484; also in J. H. Boose & B. R. Gaines, Eds (1988). *Knowledge Acquisition Tools for Expert Systems*, vol. 2, pp. 25–38. New York: Academic Press.

ANJEWIERDEN, A. (1987). The KADS system. *Proceedings of the 1st European Workshop on Knowledge Acquisition for Knowledge-Based Systems*, Reading University, September, pp. E2.1–12.

ANTONELLI, D. (1983). The application of artificial intelligence to a maintenance and diagnostic information system (MDIS). In *Proceedings of the Joint Services Workshop on Artificial Intelligence in Maintenance*, Boulder, CO.

AUSSENAC, N., FRONTIN, J. & SOUBIE, J.-L. (1988). Macao: a knowledge acquisition tool for expertise transfer. *Proceedings of the 2nd European Knowledge Acquisition Workshop (EKWA-88)*, Bonn, June, pp. 8.1–12.

BAREISS, E. R., PORTER, B. W. & WEIR, C. C. (1988). Protos: an exemplar-based learning apprentice, special issue on the 2nd Knowledge Acquisition for Knowledge-Based Systems Workshop, 1987. *International Journal of Man–Machine Studies*, **29**, 549–562.

BELKIN, N. J., BROOKS, H. M. & DANIELS, P. J. (1987). Knowledge elicitation using discourse analysis, special issue on the 1st Knowledge Acquisition for Knowledge-Based Systems Workshop, 1986, Part 4. *International Journal of Man–Machine Studies*, **27**, 127–144; also in B. R. Gaines & J. H. Boose, Eds (1988). *Knowledge-Based Systems: Knowledge Acquisition for Knowledge-Based Systems*, vol. 1, pp. 107–124. New York: Academic Press.

BENNET, J. S. (1985). A knowledge-based system for acquiring the conceptual structure of a diagnostic expert system. *Journal of Automated Reasoning*, **1**, 49–74.

BEYTH-MAROM, R. & DEKEL, S. (1985). *An Elementary Approach to Thinking Under Uncertainty*, translated and adapted by S. Lichtenstein, B. Marom & R. Beyth-Marom. Hillsdale, N.J.: Lawrence Erlbaum.

BLYTHE, J., CORSI, P. & NEEDHAM, D. (1987). An experimental protocol for the acquisition of examples for learning. *Proceedings of the 1st European Workshop on Knowledge Acquisition for Knowledge-Based Systems*, Reading University, September, pp. F1.1–13.

BOOSE, J. H. (1984). Personal construct theory and the transfer of human expertise. In *Proceedings of the National Conference on Artificial Intelligence (AAAI-84)*, Austin, Texas, pp. 27–33.

BOOSE, J. H. (1985). A knowledge acquisition program for expert systems based on personal construct psychology. *International Journal of Man–Machine Studies*, **23**, 495–525.

BOOSE, J. H. (1986a). *Expertise Transfer for Expert System Design*. New York: Elsevier.

BOOSE, J. H. (1986b). Rapid acquisition and combination of knowledge from multiple experts in the same domain. *Future Computing Systems Journal*, **1**, 191–216.

BOOSE, J. H. (1988). Uses of repertory grid-centred knowledge acquisition tools for knowledge-based systems, special issue on the 2nd Knowledge Acquisition for Knowledge-Based Systems Workshop, 1987. *International Journal of Man–Machine Studies*, **29**, 287–310.

BOOSE, J. H. & BRADSHAW, J. M. (1987a). Expertise transfer and complex problems: using Aquinas as a knowledge acquisition workbench for expert systems, special issue of the 1st Knowledge Acquisition for Knowledge-Based Systems Workshop, 1986, Part 1. *International Journal of Man–Machine Studies*, **26**, 3–28; also in J. H. Boose, & B. R. Gaines, Eds (1988). *Knowledge-Based Systems: Knowledge Acquisition Tools for Expert Systems*, vol. 2, pp. 39–64. New York: Academic Press.

BOOSE, J. H. & BRADSHAW, J. M. (1987b). AQUINAS: a knowledge acquisition workbench for building knowledge-based systems. *Proceedings of the 1st European Workshop on Knowledge Acquisition for Knowledge-Based Systems*, Reading University, September, pp. A6.1–6.

BOOSE, J. H., BRADSHAW, J. M. & SHEMA, D.B. (1988). Recent progress in Aquinas; a knowledge acquisition workbench. *Proceedings of the 2nd European Knowledge Acquisition Workshop (EKAW-88)*, Bonn, June, pp. 2.1–15.

BOY, G. & NUSS, N. (1988). Knowledge acquisition by observation: application to intelligent tutoring systems. *Proceedings of the 2nd European Knowledge Acquisition Workshop (EKAW-88)*, Bonn, June, pp. 11.1–1.4.

BRADSHAW, J. (1988). Shared causal knowledge as a basis for communication between expert and knowledge acquisition system. *Proceedings of the 2nd European Knowledge Acquisition Workshop (EKAW-88)*. Bonn, June, pp. 12.1–6.

BRADSHAW, J. M. (1989). Strategies for selecting and interviewing experts, Boeing Computer Services Technical Report, in preparation.

BRADSHAW, J. M. & BOOSE, J. H. (1989). Decision analytic techniques for knowledge acquisition: combining situation and preference models using Aquinas, special issue on the 2nd Knowledge Acquisition for Knowledge-Based Systems Workshop, 1987. *International Journal of Man–Machine Studies*, in press.

BRAMER, M. (1987). Automatic induction of rules from examples: a critical analysis of the ID3 family of rule induction systems. *Proceedings of the 1st European Workshop on Knowledge Acquisition for Knowledge-Based Systems*, Reading University, September, pp. F2.1–31.

BREUKER, J. & WIELINGA, B. (1987a). Knowledge acquisition as modeling expertise: the KADS methodology. *Proceedings of the 1st European Workshop on Knowledge Acquisition for Knowledge-Based Systems*, Reading University, September, pp. B1.1–8.

BREUKER, J. & WIELINGA, B. (1987b). Use of models in the interpretation of verbal data. In A. Kidd. *Knowledge Elicitation for Expert Systems: A Practical Handbook*, New York: Plenum Press.

BUNTINE, W. (1987). Induction of horn clauses: methods and the plausible generalisation algorithm, special issue on the 1st Knowledge Acquisition for Knowledge-Based Systems Workshop, 1986, Part 3. *International Journal of Man–Machine Studies*, **26**, 499–520; also in B. R. Gaines & J. H. Boose, Eds (1988). *Knowledge-Based Systems: Knowledge Acquisition for Knowledge-Based Systems*, vol. 1, pp. 275–298. New York: Academic Press.

BURTON, A. M., SHADBOLT, N. R., HEDGECOCK, A. P. & RUGG, G. (1987). A formal evaluation of knowledge elicitation techniques for expert systems: domain 1. *Proceedings of the 1st European Workshop on Knowledge Acquisition for Knowledge-Based Systems*, Reading University, September, pp. D3.1–21.

BUTLER, K. A. & CORTER, J. E. (1986). Use of psychometric tools for knowledge acquisition: a case study. In W. A. Gale. *Artificial Intelligence and Statistics*, pp. 295–320. Menlo Park: Addison-Wesley.

BYLANDER, T. & CHANDRASEKARAN, B. (1987). Generic tasks in knowledge-based reasoning: the 'right' level of abstraction for knowledge acquisition, special issue of the 1st Knowledge Acquisition for Knowledge-Based Systems Workshop, 1986, Part 2. *International Journal of Man–Machine Studies*, **26**, 231–244; also in B. R. Gaines & J. H. Boose, Eds (1988). *Knowledge-Based Systems: Knowledge Acquisition for Knowledge-Based Systems*, vol. 1, pp. 65–80. New York: Academic Press.

BYLANDER, T. & MITTAL, S. (1986). CSRL: a language for classificatory problem-solving and uncertainty handling. *AI Magazine*, August.

CLANCEY, W. (1986). Heuristic classification. In J. Kowalik, Ed. *Knowledge-Based Problem-Solving*. New York: Prentice-Hall.

CLEARY, J. G. (1987). Acquisition of uncertain rules in a probabilistic logic, special issue on the 1st Knowledge Acquisition for Knowledge-Based Systems Workshop, 1986, Part 4. *International Journal of Man–Machine Studies*, **27**, 145–154; also in B. R. Gaines & J.

H. Boose, Eds (1988). *Knowledge Acquisition for Knowledge-Based Systems: Knowledge Acquisition for Knowledge-Based Systems*, vol. 1, pp. 323–332. New York: Academic Press.

Cleaves, D. A. (1987). Cognitive biases and corrective techniques; proposals for improving elicitation procedures for knowledge-based systems, special issue on the 1st Knowledge Acquisition for Knowledge-Based Systems Workshop, 1986, Part 4. *International Journal of Man–Machine Studies*, **27**, 155–156; also in B. R. Gaines & J. H. Boose, Eds (1988). *Knowledge-Based Systems: Knowledge Acquisition for Knowledge-Based Systems*, vol. 1, pp. 23–34. New York: Academic Press.

Cooke, N. M. & McDonald, J. E. (1987). The application of psychological scaling techniques to knowledge elicitation for knowledge-based systems, special issue on the 1st Knowledge Acquisition for Knowledge-Based Systems Workshop, 1986, Part 3. *International Journal of Man–Machine Studies*, **26**, 533–549; also in J. H. Boose & B. R. Gaines, Eds (1988). *Knowledge-Based Systems: Knowledge Acquisition Tools for Expert Systems*, Vol. 2, pp. 65–82. New York: Academic Press.

Cox, L. A. & Blumenthal, R. (1987). KRIMB: an intelligent knowledge acquisition and representation program for interactive model building, *Proceedings of the 1st European Workshop on Knowledge Acquisition for Knowledge-Based Systems*, Reading University, September, pp. E3.1–17.

Cox, L. A. (1988). Designing interactive expert classification system that acquires knowledge 'optimally'. *Proceedings of the 2nd European Knowledge Acquisition Workshop (EKAW-88)*, Bonn, June, pp. 13.1–16.

Crawford, S. L. (1989). Extensions to the CART algorithm, special issue on the 2nd Knowledge Acquisition for Knowledge-Based Systems Workshop, 1987. *International Journal of Man–Machine Studies*, in press.

Davis, R. & Lenat, D. B. (1982). *Knowledge-Based Systems in Artificial Intelligence*. New York: McGraw-Hill.

De Jong, K. (1986). *Proceedings of the First Knowledge Acquisition for Knowledge Based Workshop*, Banff, November. pp. 20.0–20.8.

Delgrande, J. P. (1987). A formal approach to learning from examples, special issue on the 1st Knowledge Acquisition for Knowledge-Based Systems Workshop, 1986, Part 2. *International Journal of Man–Machine Studies*, **26**, 123–142; also in B. R. Gaines & J. H. Boose, Eds (1988). *Knowledge-Based Systems: Knowledge Acquisition for Knowledge-Based Systems*, vol. 1, pp. 163–182. New York: Academic Press.

Diederich, J., Ruhmann, I. & May, M. (1987). KRITON: a knowledge acquisition tool for expert systems, special issue on the 1st Knowledge Acquisition for Knowledge-Based Systems Workshop, 1986, Part 1. *International Journal of Man–Machine Studies*, **26**, 29–40; also in J. H. Boose & B. R. Gaines, Eds (1988). *Knowledge-Based Systems: Knowledge Acquisition Tools for Expert Systems*, vol. 2, pp. 83–94. New York: Academic Press.

Diederich, J., Linster, L., Ruhmann, I. & Uthmann, T. (1987). A methodology for integrating knowledge acquisition techniques. *Proceedings of the 1st European Workshop on Knowledge Acquisition for Knowledge-Based Systems*, University of Reading, September, pp. E4.1-11.

Dutta, S. (1988). Domain independent inductive learning of relevance. *Proceedings of the 2nd European Knowledge Acquisition Workshop (EKAW-88)*, Bonn, June, pp. 15.1–13.

Ericcson, K. A. & Simon, H. A. (1984). *Protocol Analysis: Verbal Reports as Data.* Cambridge, MA: The MIT Press.

Esfahani, L. & Teskey, F. N. (1987). KET, a knowledge encoding tool. *Proceedings of the 1st European Workshop on Knowledge Acquisition for Knowledge-Based Systems*, Reading University, September, pp. E5.1-11.

Esfahani, L. & Teskey, F. N. (1988). A self-modifying rule-eliciter. *Proceedings of the 2nd European Knowledge Acquisition Workshop (EKAW-88)*, Bonn, June, pp. 16.1–16.

Eshelman, L., Ehret, D., McDermott, J. & Tan, M. (1987). MOLE: a tenacious knowledge acquisition tool, special issue on the 1st AAAI Knowledge Acquisition for Knowledge-Based Systems Workshop, 1986, Part 1. *International Journal of Man–*

Machine Studies, **26**, 41–54; also in J. H. Boose & B. R. Gaines, Eds (1988). *Knowledge-Based Systems: Knowledge Acquisition Tools for Expert Systems*, vol. 2, pp. 95–108. New York: Academic Press.

Eshelman, L. (1988). MOLE: a knowledge acquisition tool that buries certainty factors, special issue on the 2nd Knowledge Acquisition for Knowledge-Based Systems Workshop, 1987, *International Journal of Man–Machine Studies*, **29**, 563–578.

Frantzke, J. & Herrmann, J. (1988). Requirements for computer-aided knowledge acquisition in an ill-structured domain: a case study. *Proceedings of the 2nd European Knowledge Acquisition Workshop (EKAW-88)*, Bonn, June, pp. 21.1–13.

Freeman, P. (1985). Knowledge elicitation—a commercial perspective. *Proceedings of the 1st International Expert System Conference*, London, October.

Freiling, M., Alexander, J., Messick, S., Rehfuss, S. & Shulman, S. (1985). Starting a knowledge engineering project: a step-by-step approach. *AI Magazine*, Fall, 150–164.

Gaines, B. R. (1977). System identification approximation and complexity. *International Journal of General Systems*, **3**, 145–174.

Gaines, B. R. (1987a). An overview of knowledge acquisition and transfer, special issue on the 1st Knowledge Acquisition for Knowledge-Based Systems Workshop, 1986, Part 3. *International Journal of Man–Machine Studies*, **26**, 453–472; also in B.R. Gaines & J. H. Boose, Eds (1988). *Knowledge-Based Systems: Knowledge Acquisition for Knowledge-Based Systems*, vol. 1, pp. 3–22. New York: Academic Press.

Gaines, B. R. (1987b). Knowledge acquisition for expert systems. *Proceedings of the 1st European Workshop on Knowledge Acquisition for Knowledge-Based Systems*, Reading University, September, pp. A3.1–4.

Gaines, B. R. (1987c). How do experts acquire expertise? *Proceedings of the 1st European Workshop on Knowledge Acquisition for Knowledge-Based Systems*, Reading, England, September 1987, pp. B2.1-11.

Gaines, B. R (1988a). Advanced expert system support environments, special issue on the 2nd Knowledge Acquisition for Knowledge-Based Systems Workshop, 1987. *International Journal of Man–Machine Studies*, in press.

Gaines, B. R. (1988b). Second generation knowledge acquisition systems. *Proceedings of the 2nd European Knowledge Acquisition Workshop (EKAW-88)*, Bonn, June, pp. 17.1–14.

Gaines, B. R. & Andrae, J. H. (1966). A learning machine in the context of the general control problem. *Proceedings of the 3rd Congress of the International Federation for Automatic Control*, London: Butterworths.

Gaines, B. F. & Boose, J. H. (1988). A summary of the AAAI-sponsored Knowledge Acquisition for Knowledge-Based System Workshops. *AI Magazine*, in press.

Gaines, B. R. & Sharp, M. (1987). A knowledge acquisition extension to notecards. *Proceedings of the 1st European Workshop on Knowledge Acquisition for Knowledge-Based Systems*, Reading University, September, pp. C1.1–7.

Gaines, B. F. & Shaw, M. L. G. (1981). New directions in the analysis and interactive elicitation of personal construct systems. In M. L. G. Shaw, Ed. *Recent Advances in Personal Construct Technology*. New York: Academic Press.

Gaines, B. R. & Shaw, M. L. G. (1986). Interactive elicitation of knowledge from experts. *Future Computing Systems*, **1**, 151–190.

Gale, W. A. (1987). Knowledge-based knowledge acquisition for a statistical consulting system, special issue on the 1st AAAI Knowledge Acquisition for Knowledge-Based Systems Workshop, 1986, Part 1. *International Journal of Man–Machine Studies*, **26**, 55–64; also in J. H. Boose & B. R. Gaines, Eds (1988). *Knowledge-Based Systems: Knowledge Acquisition Tools for Expert Systems*, vol. 2, pp. 109–118. New York: Academic Press.

Gammack, J. G. & Young, R. M. (1984). Psychological techniques for eliciting expert knowledge, in R & D in expert systems. *Proceedings of the 4th Expert System Conference*, Warwick, Max Bramer, Ed. Cambridge: Cambridge University Press.

Gams, M. (1988). A new breed of knowledge acquisition systems uses redundant knowledge. *Proceedings of the 2nd European Knowledge Acquisition Workshop (EKAW-88)*, Bonn, June, pp. 18.1–7.

JOHNSON, N. E. (1988). Knowledge elicitation for second generation expert systems. *Proceedings of the 2nd European Knowledge Acquisition Workshop (EKAW-88)*, Bonn, June, pp. 23.1–10.

JOHNSON, P. E., ZAULKERNAN, I. & GARBER, S. (1987). Specification of expertise: knowledge acquisition for expert systems, special issue on the 1st Knowledge Acquisition for Knowledge-Based Systems Workshop, 1986, Part 2. *International Journal of Man–Machine Studies*, **26**, 161–182; also in B. R. GAINES & J. H. BOOSE, Eds (1988). *Knowledge-Based Systems: Knowledge Acquisition for Knowledge-Based Systems*, vol. 1, pp. 125–146. New York: Academic Press.

KAHN, G., NOWLAN, S. & McDERMOTT, J. (1985a). Strategies for knowledge acquisition. *IEEE Transactions of Pattern Analysis and Machine Intelligence*, PAMI-7 (3), pp. 511–522.

KAHN, G., NOWLAN, S. & McDERMOTT, J. (1985b). MORE: an intelligent knowledge acquisition tool. *Proceedings of the 9th Joint Conference on Artificial Intelligence*, Los Angeles, CA, August, pp. 581–584.

KAHN, G. S., BREAUX, E. H., JOESEPH, R. L. & DEKLERK, P. (1987). An intelligence mixed-initiative workbench for knowledge acquisition, special issue on the 1st AAAI Knowledge Acquisition for Knowledge-Based Systems Workshop, 1986, Part 4. *International Journal of Man–Machine Studies*, **27**, 167–180; also in J. H. BOOSE & B. R. GAINES, Eds (1988). *Knowledge-Based Systems: Knowledge Acquisition Tools for Expert Systems*, vol. 2, pp. 161–174. New York: Academic Press.

KAHNEMAN, D., SLOVIC, P. & TVERSKY, A., Eds (1982) *Judgment Under Uncertainty: Heuristics and Biases*. Cambridge: Cambridge University Press.

KELLY, G. A. (1955). *The Psychology of Personal Constructs*. New York: Norton.

KIDD, A. L. & COOPER, M. B. (1985). Man–machine interface issues in the construction and use of an expert system. *International Journal of Man–Machine Studies*, **22**, 91–102.

KIETZ, J-U. (1988). Incremental and reversible acquisition of taxonomies. *Proceedings of the 2nd European Knowledge Acquisition Workshop (EKAW-88)*, Bonn, June, pp. 24.1–11.

KILLIN, J. L. & HICKMAN, F. R. (1986). The role of phenomenological techniques of knowledge elicitation in complex domains. *Expert Systems '86*, Brighton.

KITTO, C. M. & BOOSE, J. H. (1987). Heuristics for expertise transfer: the automatic management of complex knowledge acquisition dialogs, special issue on the 1st Knowledge Acquisition for Knowledge-Based Systems Workshop, 1986, Part 2. *International Journal of Man–Machine Studies*, **26**, 183–202; also in J. H. BOOSE & B. R. GAINES, Eds (1988). *Knowledge-Based Systems: Knowledge Acquisition Tools for Expert Systems*, vol. 2, pp. 175–194. New York: Academic Press.

KITTO, C. M. & BOOSE, J. H. (1989). Selecting knowledge acquisition tools and strategies based on application characteristics, special issue on the 2nd Knowledge Acquisition for Knowledge-Based Systems Workshop, 1987. *International Journal of Man–Machine Studies*, in press.

KLINKER, G., BENTOLILA, J., GENETET, S., GRIMES, M. & McDERMOTT, J. (1987). KNACK: report-driven knowledge acquisition, special issue on the 1st AAAI Knowledge Acquisition for Knowledge-Based Systems Workshop, 1986, Part 1. *International Journal of Man–Machine Studies*, **26**, 65–80; also in J. H. BOOSE & B. R. GAINES, Eds (1988). *Knowledge-Based Systems: Knowledge Acquisition Tools for Expert Systems*, vol. 2, pp. 195–210. New York: Academic Press.

KLINKER, G., GENETET, S. & McDERMOTT, J. (1988). Knowledge acquisition for evaluation systems, special issue on the 2nd Knowledge Acquisition for Knowledge-Based Systems Workshop, 1987. *International Journal of Man–Machine Studies*, **29**, 715–733.

KODRATOFF, Y. & MANAGO, M. (1987). Generalization in a noisy environment: the need to integrate symbolic and numeric techniques in learning, special issue on the 1st Knowledge Acquisition for Knowledge-Based Systems Workshop, 1986, Part 4. *International Journal of Man–Machine Studies*, **27**, 181–204; also in B. R. GAINES & J. H. BOOSE, Eds (1988). *Knowledge-Based Systems: Knowledge Acquisition for Knowledge-Based Systems*, vol. 1, pp. 299–322. New York: Academic Press.

KODRATOFF, Y. (1987). Machine learning and explanations. *Proceedings of the 1st European*

GAPPA, U. (1988). Classica: a knowledge acquisition system facilitating the formalization of advanced aspects in heuristic classification. *Proceedings of the 2nd European Knowledge Acquisition Workshop (EKAW-88)*, Bonn, June, pp. 19.1–16.

GARG-JANARDAN, C. & SALVENDY, G. (1987). A conceptual framework for knowledge elicitation, special issue on the 1st Knowledge Acquisition for Knowledge-Based Systems Workshop, 1986, Part 3. *International Journal of Man–Machine Studies*, **26**, 521–532; also in J. H. BOOSE & B. R. GAINES, Eds (1988). *Knowledge-Based Systems: Knowledge Acquisition Tools for Expert Systems*, vol. 2, pp. 119–130. New York: Academic Press.

GOGUEN, J. A. & MESEGUER, J. (1983). Programming with parametrized abstract objects in OBJ. *Theory and Practice of Programming Technology*. Amsterdam: North-Holland.

GOODMAN, R. M. F. and SMYTH, P. (1989). Learning from examples using information theory, special issue on the 2nd Knowledge Acquisition for Knowledge-Based Systems Workshop, 1987, *International Journal of Man–Machine Studies*, in press.

GROVER, M. D. (1983). A pragmatic knowledge acquisition methodology. *Proceedings of the 8th International Conference of Artificial Intelligence*, Karlsrue, West Germany, pp. 436–438.

GRUBER, T. R. (1988). Acquiring strategic knowledge from experts, special issue on the 2nd Knowledge Acquisition for Knowledge-Based Systems Workshop, 1987. *International Journal of Man–Machine Studies*, **29**, 579–598.

GRUBER, T. R. & COHEN, P. R. (1987). Design for acquisition: principles of knowledge system design to facilitate knowledge acquisition, special issue on the 1st Knowledge Acquisition for Knowledge-Based Systems Workshop, 1986, Part 2. *International Journal of Man–Machine Studies*, **26**, 143–160; also in J. H. BOOSE & B. R. GAINES, Eds (1988). *Knowledge-Based Systems: Knowledge Acquisition Tools for Expert Systems*, vol. 2, pp. 131–148. New York: Academic Press.

HADZIKADIC, M. (1988). Inc2: a prototype-based incremental conceptual clustering system. *Proceedings of the 2nd European Knowledge Acquisition Workshop (EKAW-88)*, Bonn, June, pp. 20.1–13.

HAYWARD, S. A., WIELINGA, B. J. & BREUKER, J. A. (1987). Structured analysis of knowledge, special issue on the 1st Knowledge Acquisition for Knowledge-Based Systems Workshop, 1986, Part 3. *International Journal of Man–Machine Studies*, **26**, 487–499; also in J. H. BOOSE & B. R. GAINES, Eds (1988). *Knowledge-Based Systems: Knowledge Acquisition Tools for Expert Systems*, vol. 2, pp. 149–160. New York: Academic Press.

HINK, R. F. & WOODS, D. L. (1987). How humans process uncertain knowledge: an introduction for knowledge engineers. *AI Magazine*, Fall, 41–53.

IVEY, A. E. & SIMEK-DOWNING, L. (1980). *Counseling and Psychotherapy: Skills, Theories, and Practice*. Englewood Cliffs, NJ: Prentice-Hall.

JACOBSON, C. & FREILING, M. J. (1988). ASTEK: a multi-paradigm knowledge acquisition tool for complex structured knowledge, special issue on the 2nd Knowledge Acquisition for Knowledge-Based Systems Workshop, 1987. *International Journal of Man–Machine Studies*, **29**, 311–328.

JAGANNATHAN, V. & ELMAGHRABY, A. S. (1985). MEDKAT: multiple expert delphi-based knowledge acquisition tool. *Proceedings of the ACM NE Regional Conference*, Boston, October, pp. 103–110.

JANSEN-WINKELN, R. M. (1988). An approach to knowledge acquisition in the natural language domain. *Proceedings of the 2nd European Knowledge Acquisition Workshop (EKAW-88)*, Bonn, June, pp. 22.1–15.

JOHNSON, L. & JOHNSON, N. E. (1987). Knowledge elicitation involving teachback interviewing. In A. KIDD, Ed. *Knowledge Elicitation for Expert Systems: A Practical Handbook*. New York: Plenum Press.

JOHNSON, N. E. (1987). Mediating representations in knowledge elicitation. *Proceedings of the 1st European Workshop on Knowledge Acquisition for Knowledge-Based Systems*, Reading University, September, pp. A2.1–10.

MORIK, K. (1987a). Acquiring domain models, special issue on the 1st Knowledge Acquisition for Knowledge-Based Systems Workshop, 1986, Part 1. *International Journal of Man–Machine Studies*, **26**, 93–104; also in J. H. BOOSE & B. R. GAINES, Eds (1988). *Knowledge-Based Systems: Knowledge Acquisition Tools for Expert Systems*, vol. 2, pp. 245–256. New York: Academic Press.

MORIK, K. (1987b). Knowledge acquisition and machine learning—the issue of modeling. *Proceedings of the 1st European Workshop on Knowledge Acquisition for Knowledge-Based Systems*, Reading University, September, pp. A4.1–4.

MUSEN, M. A., FAGAN, L. M., COMBS, D. M. & SHORTLIFFE, E. H. (1987). Use of a domain model to drive an interactive knowledge-editing tool, special issue on the 1st AAAI Knowledge Acquisition for Knowledge-Based Systems Workshop, 1986, Part 1. *International Journal of Man–Machine Studies*, **26**, 105–121; also in J. H. BOOSE & B. R. GAINES, Eds (1988). *Knowledge-Based Systems: Knowledge Acquisition Tools for Expert Systems*, vol. 2, pp. 257–274. New York: Academic Press.

MUSEN, M. (1988). Conceptual concepts of interactive knowledge acquisition tools. *Proceedings of the 2nd European Knowledge Acquisition Workshop (EKAW-88)*, Bonn, June, pp. 26.1–15.

NYGAARD, K. & DAHL, O. J. (1981). The development of the SIMULA languages. In R. L. WEXELBLAT, Ed. *History of Programming Languages*, pp. 439–480. New York: Academic Press.

PAZZANI, M. J. (1987). Explanation-based learning for knowledge-based systems, special issue on the 1st Knowledge Acquisition for Knowledge-Based Systems Workshop, 1986, Part 3. *International Journal of Man–Machine Studies*, **26**, 413–434; also in B. R. GAINES & J. H. BOOSE, Eds (1988) *Knowledge-Based Systems: Knowledge Acquisition for Knowledge-Based Systems*, vol. 1, pp. 215–238. New York: Academic Press.

PEARL, J. (1956). Fusion, propagation and structuring in belief networks. Technical report CSD-850022, R-42-VI-12, Cognitive Systems Laboratory, Computer Science Department, University of California, Los Angeles, April.

PETTIT, E. J. & PETTIT, M. J. (1987). Analysis of the performance of a genetic algorithm-based system for message classification in noisy environments, special issue on the 1st Knowledge Acquisition for Knowledge-Based Systems Workshop, 1986, Part 4. *International Journal of Man–Machine Studies*, **27**, 205–220; also in B. R. GAINES & J. H. BOOSE, Eds (1988). *Knowledge-Based Systems: Knowledge Acquisition for Knowledge-Based Systems*, vol. 1, pp. 333–350. New York: Academic Press.

DI PIAZZA, J. S. (1988). Laps: an assistant for debriefing experts. *Proceedings of the 2nd European Knowledge Acquisition Workshop (EKAW-88)*, Bonn, June, pp. 14.1–17.

QUINLAN, J. R. (1983). Learning efficient classification procedures and their application to chess end games. In R. S. MICHALSKI, J. G. CARBONELL & T. M. MITCHELL, Eds. *Machine Learning, An Artificial Intelligence Approach*. Tioga Publishing Company.

QUINLAN, J. R. (1987). Simplifying decision trees, special issue on the 1st Knowledge Acquisition for Knowledge-Based Systems Workshop, 1986, Part 5. *International Journal of Man–Machine Studies*, **27**, 221–234; also in B. R. GAINES & J. H. BOOSE, Eds (1988). *Knowledge-Based Systems: Knowledge Acquisition for Knowledge-Based Systems*, vol. 1, pp. 239–252. New York: Academic Press.

RAPPAPORT, A. (1987). Multiple problem spaces in the knowledge design process, special issue on the 1st Knowledge Acquisition for Knowledge-Based Systems Workshop, 1986, Part 3. *International Journal of Man–Machine Studies*, **26**, 435–452.

RAPPAPORT, A. (1988). Cognitive primitives, special issue on the 2nd Knowledge Acquisition for Knowledge-Based Systems Workshop, 1987. *International Journal of Man–Machine Studies*, **29**, 733–747.

REGOCZEI, S. & PLANTINGA, E. P. O. (1986). *Proceedings of the First Knowledge Acquisition for Knowledge Based Systems Workshop*, Banff, November. pp. 38.0–38.19.

RISSLAND, E. L. (1987). The problem of intelligent example selection, *Proceedings of the 2nd Knowledge Acquisition for Knowledge-Based Systems Workshop*, Banff, October. pp. 16.0–16.25.

*Workshop on Knowledge Acquisition for Knowledge-Based Systems*, Reading University, September, pp. A5.1–9.

KODRATOFF, Y. & TECUCI, G. (1988). Learning at different levels of knowledge. *Proceedings of the 2nd European Knowledge Acquisition Workshop (EKAW-88)*, Bonn, June, pp. 3.1–17.

LEFKOWITZ, L. S. & LESSER, V. R. (1988). Knowledge acquisition as knowledge assimilation, special issue on the 2nd Knowledge Acquisition for Knowledge-Based Systems Workshop, 1987. *International Journal of Man–Machine Studies*, **29**, 215–226.

LENAT, D., PRAKISH, M. & SHEPARD, M. (1986). CYC: using common sense knowledge to overcome brittleness and knowledge acquisition bottlenecks. *AI Magazine* **6**(4), 65–85.

LINSTER, M. (1987). On structuring knowledge for incremental knowledge acquisition. *Proceedings of the 1st European Workshop on Knowledge Acquisition for Knowledge-Based Systems*, Reading University, September, pp. D1.1–8.

LINSTER, M. (1988). Kriton: a knowledge elicitation tool for expert systems. *Proceedings of the 2nd European Knowledge Acquisition Workshop (EKAW-88)*, Bonn, June, pp. 4.1–9.

LITTMAN, D. C. (1987). Modeling human expertise in knowledge engineering: some preliminary observations, special issue on the 1st Knowledge Acquisition for Knowledge-Based Systems Workshop, 1986, Part 1. *International Journal of Man–Machine Studies*, **26**, 81–92; also in B. R. GAINES & J. H. BOOSE, Eds (1988). *Knowledge-Based Systems: Knowledge Acquisition for Knowledge-Based Systems*, vol. 1, pp. 93–106. New York: Academic Press.

MARCUS, S., MCDERMOTT, J. & WANG, T. (1985). Knowledge acquisition for constructive systems. In *Proceedings of the 9th Joint Conference on Artificial Intelligence*, Los Angeles, August, pp. 637–639.

MARCUS, S. (1987). Taking backtracking with a grain of SALT, special issue on the 1st Knowledge Acquisition for Knowledge-Based Systems Workshop, 1986, Part 3. *International Journal of Man–Machine Studies*, **26**, 383–398; also in J. H. BOOSE & B. R. GAINES, Eds (1988). *Knowledge-Based Systems: Knowledge Acquisition Tools for Expert Systems*, vol. 2, pp. 211–226. New York: Academic Press.

MICHALSKI, R. S. & CHILAUSKY, R. L. (1980). Knowledge acquisition by encoding expert rules versus computer induction from examples—a case study involving soybean pathology. *International Journal of Man–Machine Studies*, **12**, 63–87.

MICHALSKI, R. S. (1983). Theory and methodology of inductive learning. In R. S. MICHALSKI, J. G. CARBONELL & T. M. MITCHELL, Eds. *Machine Learning, An Artificial Intelligence Approach*. Tioga Publishing Company.

MITCHELL, T. M., MAHADEVAN, S. & STEINBERG, L. I. (1985). LEAP: a learning apprentice for VLSI design. *Proceedings of the International Conference on Artificial Intelligence*, 1985, Los Angeles.

MITTAL, S. & DYM, C. (1985). Knowledge acquisition from multiple experts. *AI Magazine*, Summer 32–36.

MOLLER, J. U. (1988). Knowledge acquisition from texts. *Proceedings of the 2nd European Knowledge Acquisition Workshop (EKAW-88)*, Bonn, June, pp. 25.1–16.

MONARCH, I. & NIRENBURG, S. (1987). The role of ontology in concept acquisition for knowledge-based systems. *Proceedings of the 1st European Workshop on Knowledge Acquisition for Knowledge-Based Systems*, Reading University, September, pp. E1.1–14.

MOORE, E. A. & AGOGINO, A. M. (1987). INFORM: an architecture for expert-directed knowledge acquisition, special issue on the 1st Knowledge Acquisition for Knowledge-Based Systems Workshop, 1986, Part 2. *International Journal of Man–Machine Studies*, **26**, 213–230; also in J. H. BOOSE & B. R. GAINES, Eds (1988). *Knowledge-Based Systems: Knowledge Acquisition Tools for Expert Systems*, vol. 2, pp. 227–244. New York: Academic Press.

MORAY, N. (1985). Sources of bias and fallibility in humans. *Workshop on Knowledge Engineering in Industry*, University of Toronto, May.

RUSK, R. A. & KRONE, R. M. (1984). The Crawford Slip Method (CSM) as a tool for extraction of expert knowledge. In G. SALVENDY, Ed. *Human-Computer Interaction*, pp. 279–282. New York: Elsevier.

SAATY, T. L. (1981). *The Analytic Hierarchy Process*. New York: McGraw-Hill.

SANDBERG, J., WINKELS, R. & BREUKER, J. (1988). Knowledge acquisition for intelligent tutoring system. *Proceedings of the 2nd European Knowledge Acquisition Workshop (EKAW-88)*, Bonn, June, pp. 27.1–12.

SCHREIBER, G., BREUKER, J., BREDEWEG, B. & WIELINGA, B. (1988). Modeling in KBS development. *Proceedings of the 2nd European Knowledge Acquisition Workshop (EKAW-88)*, Bonn, June, pp. 7.1–15.

SCHRODER, S., NIEMANN, H. & SAGERER, G. (1988). Knowledge acquisition for a knowledge based image analysis system. *Proceedings of the 2nd European Knowledge Acquisition Workshop (EKAW-88)*, Bonn, June, pp. 29.1–15.

SEBAG, M. & SCHOENAUER, M. (1988). Generation of rules with certainty and confidence factors from incomplete and incoherent learning bases. *Proceedings of the 2nd European Knowledge Acquisition Workshop (EKAW-88)*, Bonn, June, pp. 28.1–20.

SHAFER, G. & TVERSKY, A. (1985). Languages and designs for probability judgment. *Cognitive Science*, **9**, 309–339.

SHALIN, V. L., WISNIEWSKI, E. J., LEVI, K. R. & SCOTT, P. D. (1988). A formal analysis of machine learning systems for knowledge acquisition, special issue on the 2nd Knowledge Acquisition for Knowledge-Based Systems Workshop, 1987. *International Journal of Man–Machine Studies*, **29**, 429–446.

SHAW, M. L. G. (1984). Interaction knowledge elicitation. *Proceedings of the Canadian Information Processing Society Annual Conference*, Calgary, Canada.

SHAW, M. L. G. (1988). Problems of validation in a knowledge acquisition system using multiple experts. *Proceedings of the 2nd European Knowledge Acquisition Workshop (EKAW-88)*, Bonn, June, pp. 5.1–15.

SHAW, M. L. G. & GAINES, B. R. (1987). Techniques for knowledge acquisition and transfer, special issue on the 1st Knowledge Acquisition for Knowledge-Based Systems Workshop, 1986, Part 5. *International Journal of Man–Machine Studies*, **27**, 251–280.

SHAW, M. L. G. & WOODWARD, J. B. (1988). Validation in a knowledge support system: construing consistency with multiple experts, special issue on the 2nd Knowledge Acquisition for Knowledge-Based Systems Workshop, 1987. *International Journal of Man–Machine Studies*, **29**, 329–350.

SHEMA, D. B. & BOOSE, J. H. (1988). Refining problem-solving knowledge in repertory grids using a consultation mechanism, special issue on the 2nd Knowledge Acquisition for Knowledge-Based Systems Workshop, 1987. *International Journal of Man–Machine Studies*, **9**, 447–460.

SILVESTRO, K. (1988). Using explanations for knowledge base acquisition, special issue on the 2nd Knowledge Acquisition for Knowledge-Based Systems Workshop, 1987. *International Journal of Man–Machine Studies*, **29**, 159–170.

SLOCOMBE, S., MOORE, K. D. M. & ZELOUF, M. (1986). Engineering expert system applications. *Expert Systems-86*, December, Brighton.

SMITH, R. G., WINSTON, H. A., MITCHELL, T. M. & BUCHANAN, B. G. (1985). Representation and use of explicit justifications for knowledge base refinements. *Proceedings of the 9th International Joint Conference on Artificial Intelligence*, Los Angeles.

SPETZLER, C. & STAEL VON HOLSTEIN, C. (1983). Probability encoding in decision analysis. In R. HOWARD & J. MATHESON, Eds. *Readings on the Principles and Applications of Decision Analysis*, vol. 2, pp. 601–626. Palo Alto, CA: Strategic Decisions Group.

STAEL VON HOLSTEIN, C. & MATHESON, J. E. (1978). *A Manual for Encoding Probability Distributions*. Menlo Park, CA: SRI International.

STEPHANOU, H. (1987). Perspectives on imperfect information processing. *IEEE Transactions on Systems, Man, and Cybernetics*, **17**, 780–798.

STOUT, J., CAPLAN, G., MARCUS, S. & McDERMOTT, J. (1988). Toward automating recognition of differing problem-solving demands, special issue on the 2nd Knowledge Acquisition for Knowledge-Based Systems Workshop, 1987. *International Journal of Man–Machine Studies*, **29**, 599–611.

TERPTRA, P. P. & van SOMEREN, M. W. (1988). Inde: a system for knowledge refinement and machine learning. *Proceedings of the 2nd European Knowledge Acquisition Workshop (EKAW-88)*, Bonn, June, pp. 30.1–8.

TONG, X. & KARBACH, W. (1988). Filling in the knowledge acquisition gap: via Kads' models of expertise to Zdest-2's expert systems. *Proceedings of the 2nd European Knowledge Acquisition Workshop (EKAW-88)*, Bonn, June, pp. 31.1–17.

TRANOWSKI, D. (1988). A knowledge acquisition environment for scene analysis, special issue on the 2nd Knowledge Acquisition for Knowledge-Based Systems Workshop, 1987. *International Journal of Man–Machine Studies*, **29**, 197–214.

TRIMBLE, G. & COOPER, C. N. (1987). Experience of knowledge acquisition for expert systems in construction. *Proceedings of the 1st European Workshop on Knowledge Acquisition for Knowledge-Based Systems*, Reading University, September, pp. C5.1–14.

TVERSKY, A., SATTAH, S. & SLOVIC, P. (1987). *Contingent Weighing in Judgment and Choice*. Menlo Park, CA: Stanford University.

TWINE, S. (1988). From information analysis toward knowledge acquisition. *Proceedings of the 2nd European Knowledge Acquisition Workshop (EKAW-88)*, Bonn, June, pp. 6.1–15.

WALDRON, V. R. (1985). Process tracing as a method for initial knowledge acquisition. *Proceedings of the 2nd IEEE Conference on AI Applications*, Florida, December.

WALLSTEN, T. & BUDESCU, D. (1983). Encoding subject probabilities: a psychological and psychometric review. *Management Science*, **29**, 151–173.

WELBANK, M. (1987a). Knowledge acquisition: a survey and British Telecom experience. *Proceedings of the 1st European Workshop on Knowledge Acquisition for Knowledge-Based Systems*, Reading University, September, pp. C6.1–9.

WELBANK, M. (1987b). Knowledge Acquisition Update, Insight Study No. 5, Systems Designers, England.

WETTER, T. & SCHMALHOFER, F. (1988). Knowledge acquisition from text-based think-aloud protocols: situational specification for a legal expert system. *Proceedings of the 2nd European Knowledge Acquisition Workshop (EKAW-88)*, Bonn, June, pp. 33.1–15.

WILKENS, D. C., CLANCEY, W. J. & BUCHANAN, G. G. (1987). Knowledge base refinement by editing abstract control knowledge, special issue on the 1st Knowledge Acquisition for Knowledge-Based Systems Workshop, 1986, Part 5. *International Journal of Man–Machine Studies*, **27**, 281–294.

von WINTERFELDT, D. & EDWARDS, W. (1986). *Decision Analysis and Behavioral Research*. Cambridge: Cambridge University Press.

WISNIEWSKI, E., WINSTON, H., SMITH, R. & KLEYN, M. (1986). Case generation for rule synthesis, *Proceedings of the 1st Knowledge Acquisition for Knowledge-Based Systems Workshop*, Banff, November, pp. 41.0–41.19.

WITTEN, I. H. & MACDONALD, B. (1988). Using concept learning for knowledge acquisition, special issue on the 2nd Knowledge Acquisition for Knowledge-Based Systems Workshop, 1987. *International Journal of Man–Machine Studies*, **29**, 171–196.

WOODS, D. D. & HOLLNAGEL, E. (1987). Mapping cognitive demands and activities in complex problems solving worlds, special issue on the 1st Knowledge Acquisition for Knowledge-Based Systems Workshop, 1986, Part 2. *International Journal of Man–Machine Studies*, **26**, 257–275; also in B. R. GAINES & J. H. BOOSE, Eds (1988). *Knowledge-Based Systems: Knowledge Acquisition for Knowledge-Based Systems*, vol. 1, pp. 45–64. New York: Academic Press.

WROBEL, S. (1988). Design goals for sloppy modeling systems, special issue on the 2nd Knowledge Acquisition for Knowledge-Based Systems Workshop, 1987. *International Journal of Man–Machine Studies*, **29**, 461–477.

YOUNG, R. M. & GAMMACK, J. (1987). Role of psychological techniques and intermediate representations in knowledge elicitation. *Proceedings of the 1st European Workshop on Knowledge Acquisition for Knowledge-Based Systems*, Reading University, September, pp. D7.1–5.

# Appendix: detailed repertory grid tables for interactive knowledge acquisition tools

These tables were generated by Aquinas from the repertory grid in Fig. 2 (shown below). They show the grid ratings in more detail; in particular, distributed rating are shown. For example, in the first table, some tools have distributed ratings (more than one value) for the trait K.REP-EXPERTISE—the direct representation for expertise. These tables reflect the author's view of the state of the tools as of June, 1988.

INTERACTIVE.TRAIT
1. (5) APPL_DOMAIN: (CLASSIFICATION  C-AND-C CONFIGURATION DIAGNOSIS DESIGN MANAGEMENT MONITORING PLANNING REP)
2. (5) AUTOMATION-GUIDANCE: (MANUAL(1)/AUTOMATED(5)) [ORDINAL, 1]
3. (5) DOMAIN-INDEPENDENCE: (DOMAIN-INDEPEND(1)/DOMAIN-DEPEND(5)) [ORDINAL, 1]
4. (5) EFFICIENCY: EFF. AND FAST TO USE(1)/INEFF. AND SLOW TO USE(5) [ORDINAL, 1]
5. (5) IMPL_STAGE: (PLANNED IN-PROGRESS IMPLEMENTED TESTED IN-USE) [NOMINAL, 1]
6. (5) IN-USE: IN-USE. NOW(1)/NOT NOW-WONT BE(5) [ORDINAL, 1]
7. (4) K-REP-EXPERTISE: (COGNITIVE-MAPS CONCEPTS CORRELATIONS DECISION-TABLES FRAMES GOAL-STRUCTURES HIERARCHI
8. (4) K-TYPE: (CONSTRAINTS CONTROL COVERING EXPLANATIONS FACTS JUDGMENTS JUSTIFICATIONS PREFERENCES PREFER)
9. (5) LEARNING-COMPONENT: (AUTOMATIC INTERACTIVE NONE) [NOMINAL, 1]
10. (5) LIFE_CYCLE: ONE-SHOT-USE(1)/ENTIRE LIFE_CYCLE(5) [ORDINAL, 1]
11. (5) LEVEL_OF_SOPHIST: LOW SOPHIST(1)/HIGH_SOPHIST(5) [ORDINAL, 1]
12. (5) METHODS-TECHNIQUES: (ANALOGY APPR-LEARNING INTERVIEWING CONSISTENCY-ANALYSIS DEC-ANALYSIS DEC-TREE-I)
13. (4) K-SOURCES: SINGLE K-SOURCE(1)/MULTI K-SOURCES(5) [ORDINAL, 1]
14. (4) TRAINING: LITTLE TRAINING NEEDED(1)/MUCH TRAINING NEEDED(5) [ORDINAL, 1]
15. (4) UNCERTAINTY-REP: (CF PROBABILITIES SYMBOLIC OTHER NONE) [NOMINAL, 1]
16. (4) USERS: (ES-USERS DEC-MAKERS EXPERTS KE AI-PROGRAMMERS) [NOMINAL, 1]
17. (5) WORKBENCH: MANY TOOLS IN ONE FRAMEWORK(1)/FEW TOOLS IN ONE FRAMEWORK(5) [ORDINAL, 1]

1. APPL_DOMAIN
2. AUTOMATION-GUIDANCE
3. DOMAIN-INDEPENDENCE
4. EFFICIENCY
5. IMPL_STAGE
6. IN-USE
7. K-REP-EXPERTISE

1. AQUINAS
ANALYSIS
5
3
3
IN-USE
1
0.5 REP-GRIDS
0.25 PROB-DISTRIBU
0.25 HIERARCHIES

2. BLIP
ANALYSIS
3
3
IN-PROGRESS
0.8 RULES
0.2 HIERARCHIES

3. ETS
ANALYSIS
3
2
1
IN-USE
1
REP-GRIDS

4. FIS
DIAGNOSIS
2
5
IN-PROGRESS
0.7 RULES
0.3 HIERARCHIES

## Bibliography

### PROCEEDINGS FROM KNOWLEDGE ACQUISITION WORKSHOPS

The *Proceedings of the 1st AAAI-sponsored Workshop on Knowledge Acquisition for Knowledge-Based Systems*, Banff, Canada, November 2–6, 1986, were published in the *International Journal of Man–Machine Studies* in the January, February, April, August, and September issues in 1987. The proceedings are also available in an indexed two-volume set in the Knowledge-Based Systems Series: GAINES, B. R. & BOOSE, J. H., Eds (1988). *Knowledge Acquisition for Knowledge-Based Systems*, vol. 1. London: Academic Press. BOOSE, J. H. & GAINES, B. R., Eds (1988). *Knowledge Acquisition Tools for Expert Systems*, vol. 2. London: Academic Press.

The *Proceedings of the 1st European Workshop on Knowledge Acquisition*, Reading, U.K., September 1–3, 1987, will be published as an Academic Press book. Copies of the proceedings distributed at the workshop are available directly from Tom Addis, Department of Computer Science, Reading University, Whiteknights, PO Box 220, Reading RG6 2AX, U.K. for 39 pounds (Tom Addis@reading.ac.uk).

The *Proceedings of the 2nd AAAI-sponsored Workshop on Knowledge Acquisition for Knowledge-Based Systems*, Banff, Canada, October 19–23, 1987, will be published in the *International Journal of Man–Machine Studies* in 1988 (August, September, October, November, and others), and in Academic Press books in 1989.

The *Proceedings of the 2nd European Workshop on Knowledge Acquisition*, Bonn, June 19–22, 1988, copies of the proceedings distributed at the workshop are available directly from Marc Linster, Institut for Applied Information Technology, German Research Institut for Mathematics and Dataprocessing, Schloss Birlinghoven, Postfach 1240, D-5205 St. Augustin 1, West Germany (GMD will invoice you for DM68.00 plus postage).

The *Proceedings of the 3rd AAAI-sponsored Workshop on Knowledge Acquisition for Knowledge-Based Systems*, Banff, Canada, November 7–11, 1988, will probably be published in the *International Journal of Man–Machine Studies*, and in Academic Press books in 1990. Copies of the proceedings distributed at the workshop are available directly from SRDG Publications, Department of Computer Science, University of Calgary, Calgary, Alberta, Canada. T2N 1N4 (send order, draft, or check drawn on US or Canadian bank for US$65.00 or CDN$85.00).

---

**Legend (attribute codes used in the tables below):**

1. APPL.DOMAIN
2. AUTOMATION-GUIDANCE
3. DOMAIN-INDEPENDENCE
4. EFFICIENCY
5. IMPL.STAGE
6. IN-USE
7. K-REP-EXPERTISE
8. K-TYPE
9. LEARNING.COMPONENT
10. LIFE.CYCLE
11. LEVEL.OF.SOPHIST.
12. METHODS-TECHNIQUES
13. K-SOURCES
14. TRAINING
15. UNCERTAINTY-REP
16. USERS
17. WORKBENCH

**Tool data:**

```
17. MORE
  INTERACTIVE
  1
  3
  0.5 PCP.REP-GRIDS
  0.2 PERFORMANCE-SY
  0.2 INTERVIEWING
  4
  NONE
  AI-PROGRAMMERS
  0.6 EXPERTS
  0.4 KE

18. MUM
  INTERACTIVE
  1
  3
  0.4 PCP.REP-GRIDS
  0.3 INTERVIEWING
  0.15 MULTI-K-SOURC
  2
  OTHER
  0.6 EXPERTS
  0.4 KE
  DIAGNOSIS
  IN-PROGRESS
  0.6 RULES
  0.4 FRAMES
  0.33 COMBINING
  0.2 CONTROL
  0.6 JUDGMENTS
  NONE
  3
  0.8 PROB-SOLVING-M  UNIQUE-UNCERTAINTY
  0.2 INTERVIEWING
  1
  CF
  0.6 EXPERTS
  0.4 KE
  3

19. NEXPERT
  AUTOMATIC
  3
  3
  0.4 INTERVIEWING
  4
  CF .75 EXPERTS
  0.25 AI-PROGRAMMER
  3 AI-PROGRAMMER
  ANALYSIS
  1
  IN-USE
  3
  0.8 RULES
  0.2 FRAMES
  0.2 CONSTRAINTS
  0.2 FACTS
  NONE
  3
  5
  NONE
  AI-PROGRAMMERS
  4

20. OPAL
  INTERACTIVE
  3
  1
  0.6 PROB-SOLVING-M
  0.2 PERFORMANCE-SY
  0.2 INTERVIEWING
  1
  3
  NONE
  0.8 EXPERTS
  0.2 KE
  DIAGNOSIS
  5
  TESTED
  1
  0.8 SCRIPTS
  0.2 CONCEPTS
  0.6 PROCEDURAL
  0.2 STRATEGIC
  0.2 FACTS
  4
  0.5 MODELING
  0.34 DOMAIN-EXPLOI
  0.16 PERFORMANCE-S
  2
  NONE
  EXPERTS
  5

21. PATHFINDER
  CLASSIFICATION
  2
  1
  3
  IN-PROGRESS
  2
  3
  REP-GRIDS
  0.6 JUDGMENTS
  0.4 RELATIONSHIPS
  NONE
  1
  PSYCH-SCALING
  0.5 PCP.REP-GRIDS
  0.4 PSYCH-SCALING
  2
  NONE
  0.6 KE
  0.4 EXPERTS
  3

22. PLANET
  CLASSIFICATION
  2
  2
  IN-PROGRESS
  REP-GRIDS
  JUDGMENTS
  0.6 JUDGMENTS
  0.4 RELATIONSHIPS
  NONE
  3
  0.5 PCP.REP-GRIDS
  0.4 PSYCH-SCALING
  2
  NONE
  0.8 EXPERTS
  0.4 KE

23. SALT
  DESIGN
  0.6 CONFIGURATION
  0.4 CONFIGURATION
  3
  4
  IN-USE
  3
  0.8 FRAMES
  0.2 SCRIPTS
  0.2 CONCEPTS
  0.2 CONSTRAINTS
  NONE
  4
  0.4 PROB-SOLVING-M
  0.25 PERFORMANCE-S
  0.25 DOMAIN-EXPLOI
  1
  NONE
  0.6 EXPERTS
  0.4 AI-PROGRAMMERS
  5

24. STUDENT
  ANALYSIS
  3
  3
  3
  TESTED
  3
  0.6 FRAMES
  0.4 RULES
  0.7 FACTS
  0.3 CONSTRAINTS
  INTERACTIVE
  4
  DOMAIN-EXPLOITATIO
  1
  NONE
  0.6 EXPERTS
  0.4 EXPERTS
  4

25. TEIRESIAS
  DIAGNOSIS
  4
  4
  IN-USE
  2
  RULES
  0.9 JUDGMENTS
  INTERACTIVE
  0.4 INTERVIEWING
  0.3 PERFORMANCE-SY
  0.2 PROB-SOLVING-M
  1
  CF
  0.6 EXPERTS
  0.3 KE
  4

26. TKAW.TDE
  DIAGNOSIS
  4
  3
  IN-PROGRESS
  0.4 HIERARCHIES
  0.3 SCRIPTS
  0.3 RULES
  0.6 RELATIONSHIPS
  0.2 PROCEDURAL
  0.2 FACTS
  NONE
  3
  0.6 INTERVIEWING
  0.4 DOMAIN-EXPLOIT
  1
  NONE
  0.8 EXPERTS
  0.4 KE
  4
```

# Chapter 2

# Expertise and Expert Systems

Knowledge acquisition is the construction of knowledge structures for knowledge-based systems, through manual, semi-automated (interactive), or automated techniques. Much of the reason for slow progress in knowledge acquisition stems from the need to understand first the nature of expertise, then the need to understand how to design an expert system that captures the richness of this expertise. Only after settling the issues of expert system knowledge organization, representation and inference can one define the knowledge acquisition problem. Despite twenty years of experience since the advent of first-generation MYCIN-style expert systems, much current machine learning research assumes that the performance element to be improved is this type of primitive program. The purpose of this chapter is to introduce the reader to the nature and variety of human expertise, and to the organization of advanced expert system architectures that simulate this expertise.

Expert systems share many similarities with two other AI application domains that require large amounts of domain-specific knowledge: natural language processing and commonsense reasoning. Much of the challenge in all three of these domains is in determining which architecture of the problem-solving program should be improved, and this remains an open research problem. It is difficult to discover how to learn automatically the knowledge needed by a natural language program without an understanding of the design of such a program in the first place. Not only does the design and organization of the knowledge-based system define the learning problem, but this organization often is at the heart of the source of power of the learning method.

A significant aspect of expertise is an ability to use knowledge in the domain for multiple purposes. For example, a piece of knowledge in a natural language processing system is often of equal importance for language generation, language recognition, and language learning. Human experts can often use their knowledge for multiple purposes: expert problem solving, explanation, learning, teaching, critiquing, and the like.

Section 2.1 describes how human expertise and its acquisition are different from other forms of human reasoning. Section 2.2 describes expert systems, the ways they are different from other types of computer programs, and some of the implications of these differences for knowledge acquisition.

Note that the references for the Anderson and Buchanan et al. papers in this chapter are in Appendix C.

# Section 2.1

# Expertise and Its Acquisition

The three papers in this section provide an introduction to what we know about human expertise and describe some of the challenges involved in getting an expert to communicate this expertise in a way that allows an expert system to be constructed. Much of the work on the nature of expertise contrasts the problem-solving approaches of experts and novices.

The article by Anderson in Section 2.1.1 summarizes and integrates the experimental evidence from psychology regarding human expertise and its development. The evidence shows that expertise is a distinct dimension of human intelligence, different from, say, natural language or vision. Even though the fields of experts differ widely, there are many commonalities, such as the power law of practice, the stages of expertise acquisition, and how acquisition is affected by practice.

The article by Shaw and Woodward in Section 2.1.2 describes the types of mental models that human problem solvers have of their own expertise, and the extent to which their mental models are explicit and accessible via introspection. The paper covers the relationships between the mental models that people create and the type of conceptual models that can serve as the basis for an expert system. The paper describes the challenges that are faced when experts are asked to communicate and reason about mental models and conceptual models.

The article by Wielinga, Schreiber and Breuker in Section 2.1.3 describes a particular approach to the development of a conceptual model, called the KADS approach. KADS' aim is the development of a knowledge engineering methodology that will allow the construction of a knowledge-based system. The paper is based in part on the experience of using the KADS methodology to construct over 40 knowledge-based systems in Europe. The terminological complexities and vagaries of the KADS model reflect the inherent difficulty of creating a formalized methodology for the early stages of constructing a knowledge-based system.

The article by Forsythe and Buchanan in Section 2.1.4 identifies some of the pitfalls that the current knowledge engineering practices are susceptible to and provides suggestions on how they can be avoided.

# Development of Expertise

## J.R. Anderson

### *Summary*

1. Skill learning occurs in three steps: (1) a cognitive stage, in which a description of the procedure is learned; (2) an associative stage, in which a method for performing the skill is worked out; and (3) an autonomous stage, in which the skill becomes more and more rapid and automatic.

2. Time to perform a task is a power function of the amount of practice on the task. Such a function implies that continued practice is of continued but ever diminishing benefit to the task performance.

3. There are a number of factors modulating the effects of practice: spacing of practice increases learning; skills can be learned better if independent parts are taught separately; subjects learn more rapidly if they are given immediate feedback.

4. *Proceduralization* refers to the process by which people convert their declarative, factual knowledge of a domain into a more efficient procedural representation.

5. *Tactical learning* refers to the improvement that comes about because people learn familiar subsequences of problem-solving steps that appear in multiple problems.

6. *Strategic learning* refers to the improvement that comes about because people learn the optimal way to organize their problem solving for a particular domain.

7. Problem solving also improves in a domain because people learn how to represent problems in the domain in terms of abstract (not surface-level) features that facilitate the problem solving.

8. As people become expert in a domain their memory for problems improves both because they learn the patterns that appear in these problems and because they can commit to memory more patterns in a problem.

9. Training in a particular skill transfers to another skill to the extent that the second skill involves use of the same facts, productions, and patterns. It is difficult to find any transfer between totally different cognitive skills and it is difficult to find any negative transfer between any cognitive skills.

It may sometimes seem that at every turn we are being faced with a novel problem, but generally we are achieving goals in domains that are highly familiar—speaking a language, driving a car, solving column addition, and the like. Here our behavior is often so automatic that it is difficult to even recognize that we are solving a problem. However, if we look at novices—someone trying to communicate in an unfamiliar language, a person behind the wheel of a car for the first time, a child learning addition—we can see that these can be difficult and quite novel problem domains. Through practice, however, we have become relatively expert. The skills just mentioned are ones at which a large fraction of the population becomes expert. There are other skills at which only a small fraction becomes expert—playing chess, doing science, hitting major league pitching, and so on. Nevertheless, it appears that development of expertise in these specialized areas is really no different than in the more general areas.

The references for this paper can be found in Appendix C: Addendum to Chapter 2 (pp. 879 ff.).

encoding (see the distinction between declarative and procedural representations at the beginning of Chapter 8) of the skill; that is, they commit to memory a set of facts relevant to the skill. Learners typically rehearse these facts as they first perform the skill. For instance, when I was first learning to shift gears in a standard transmission car, I memorized the location of the gears (e.g., "up, left") and the correct sequence of engaging the clutch and moving the stick shift. I rehearsed this information as I performed the skill.

In this stage the learners are using domain-general problem-solving procedures (see the distinction between domain-general and domain-specific procedures in Chapter 8) to perform and are using the facts they have learned about the domain to guide their problem solving. Thus, they might have a general means–ends production, such as:

IF    the goal is to achieve a state $X$
      and $M$ is a method for achieving state $X$
THEN  set as a subgoal to apply $M$

Applied to driving, if the goal is to go in reverse and if the learner knows that moving the stick shift to the upper left will put the car into reverse, then this production would set the subgoal of moving the gear to the upper left. The knowledge acquired in the cognitive stage is quite inadequate for skilled performance. There follows what is called the *associative stage.* Two main things happen in this second stage. First, errors in the initial understanding are gradually detected and eliminated. So, I slowly learned to coordinate the release of the clutch in first gear with the application of gas in order not to kill the engine. Second, the connections among the various elements required for successful performance are strengthened. Thus, I no longer had to sit for a few seconds trying to remember how to get to second gear from first. Basically, the outcome of the associative stage is a successful procedure for performing the skill. In this stage, the declarative information is transformed into a procedural form. However, it is not always the case that the procedural representation of the knowledge replaces the declarative. Sometimes the two forms of knowledge can coexist side by side, as when we can speak a foreign language fluently and still remember many rules of grammar. However, it is the procedural, not the declarative, knowledge that governs the skilled performance.

The output of the associative state is a set of procedures specific to the domain. So, for instance, rather than using the general means–ends production above in driving, the learner may develop a special production for moving into reverse:

William G. Chase, late of Carnegie-Mellon University, was one of our local experts on expertise. He had two mottos that summarize much of the nature of expertise and its development:

No pain, no gain.

When the going gets tough, the tough get going.

The first motto reflects the fact that no one develops expertise without a great deal of hard work. Richard Hayes (1985), another CMU faculty member, has studied geniuses in fields varying from music to science to chess. He found that no one reached genius levels of performance without at least 10 years of practice.[1] Chase's second motto reflects the fact that the difference between relative novices and relative experts increases as we look at more difficult problems. For instance, there are many chess duffers who could play a credible, if losing, game against a master when they are given unlimited time to choose moves. However, they would lose embarrassingly if forced to play lightning chess, where they have only 5 s per move.

Chapter 8 reviewed some of the general principles governing problem solving, particularly in novel domains. This research has provided a framework for analyzing the development of expertise in problem solving. Research on expertise has been one of the major new developments in cognitive science. This is particularly exciting because it promises to have implications for education of technical or formal skill in areas such as mathematics, science, and engineering.

This chapter begins with a look at the general characteristics of the development of expertise in a skill. Then we will consider what factors might underlie the development of expertise. Finally, we will consider the vexing question of how skill might transfer from one domain of expertise to another.

## Stages of Skill Acquisition

It is typical to distinguish among three stages in the development of a skill (Anderson, 1983; Fitts & Posner, 1967). Fitts and Posner call the first stage the *cognitive stage.* In this stage subjects develop a declarative

[1]Frequently cited as an exception to this generalization is Mozart, who wrote his first symphony when he was 8. However, his early works are not of genius caliber and are largely of historical value only. Schonberg (1970) claims that Mozart's great works were produced after the twentieth year of his career.

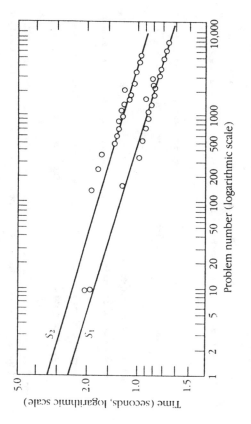

**Figure 9-1.** Improvement with practice in time taken to add two numbers. Data are given separately for two subjects. Both time and problem number are plotted on a logarithmic scale. (Plot by Crossman, 1959, of data from Blackburn, 1936.)

IF   the goal is to go in reverse
THEN  set as subgoals
  1. To disengage the clutch
  2. Then to move the gear to the upper left
  3. Then to engage the clutch
  4. Then to push down on the gas

The third stage in the standard analysis of skill acquisition is the *autonomous stage*. In this stage, the procedure becomes more and more automated and rapid. No sharp distinction exists between the autonomous and associative stage. The autonomous might be considered an extension of the associative stage. Because facility in the skill increases, verbal mediation in the performance of the task often disappears at this point. In fact, the ability to verbalize knowledge of the skill can be lost altogether. This autonomous stage appears to extend indefinitely. Throughout it, the skill gradually improves.

Two of the dimensions of improvement with practice are speed and accuracy. The procedures come to apply more rapidly and more appropriately. Anderson (1982) and Rumelhart and Norman (1978) refer to the increasing appropriateness of the procedures as *tuning*. For instance, consider our production for moving into reverse. It is only applicable to an ordinary three-speed gear. The process of tuning would result in a production that had additional tests for the appropriateness of this operation. Such a production might be:

IF   the goal is to go in reverse
  and there is a three-speed standard transmission
THEN  set as subgoals
  1. To disengage the clutch
  2. Then to move the gear to the upper left
  3. Then to engage the clutch
  4. Then to push down on the gas

## The Power Law of Practice

Figure 9-1 is a graph of some data from Blackburn (1936) showing the improvement in performance of mental addition as a function of practice. Blackburn had two subjects, $S_1$ and $S_2$, perform 10,000 addition problems! The data are plotted on a log–log scale. That is, the abscissa is the logarithm of practice (number of additions) and the ordinate is the logarithm of time per addition. On this log–log plot, the data for two subjects approximate a straight line. Similar straight-line functions relating practice to performance time have been found over a wide range of tasks. In fact, virtually every study of skill acquisition has found a straight-line function on a log–log plot. There is usually some limit to how much improvement can be achieved, determined by the capability of musculature involved, age, level of motivation, and so on. There do not appear to be any cognitive limits on the speed with which a skill can be performed. In fact, one famous study followed the improvement of a woman whose job was to roll cigars in a factory. Her speed of cigar making followed this log–log relationship over a period of 10 years. When she finally stopped improving, it was discovered that she had reached the physical limit of the machinery with which she was working!

The linear relationship between time ($T$) and log practice ($P$) can be expressed as:

$$\log(T) = A - b \log(P)$$

which can be transformed into

$$T = aP^{-b}$$

where $a = 10^A$. In Chapter 6 we discussed such power functions in memory (see Figure 6-5). Basically, these are functions where the de-

functions illustrate that the benefit of further practice rapidly diminishes, but that no matter how much practice we have had, further practice will help a little.

Kolers (1979) investigated the acquisition of reading skills using materials such as those illustrated in Figure 9-3. The first type of text (*N*) is normal, but the others have been transformed in various ways. In the *R* transformation, the whole line has been turned upside down; in the *I*

*Factors Affecting Practice*

N   *Expectations can also mislead us; the unexpected is always hard to
    perceive clearly. Sometimes we fail to recognize an object because we

R   [spatially transformed text]

I   [spatially transformed text]

M   [spatially transformed text]

rN  [spatially transformed text]

rR  [spatially transformed text]

rI  [spatially transformed text]

rM  [spatially transformed text]

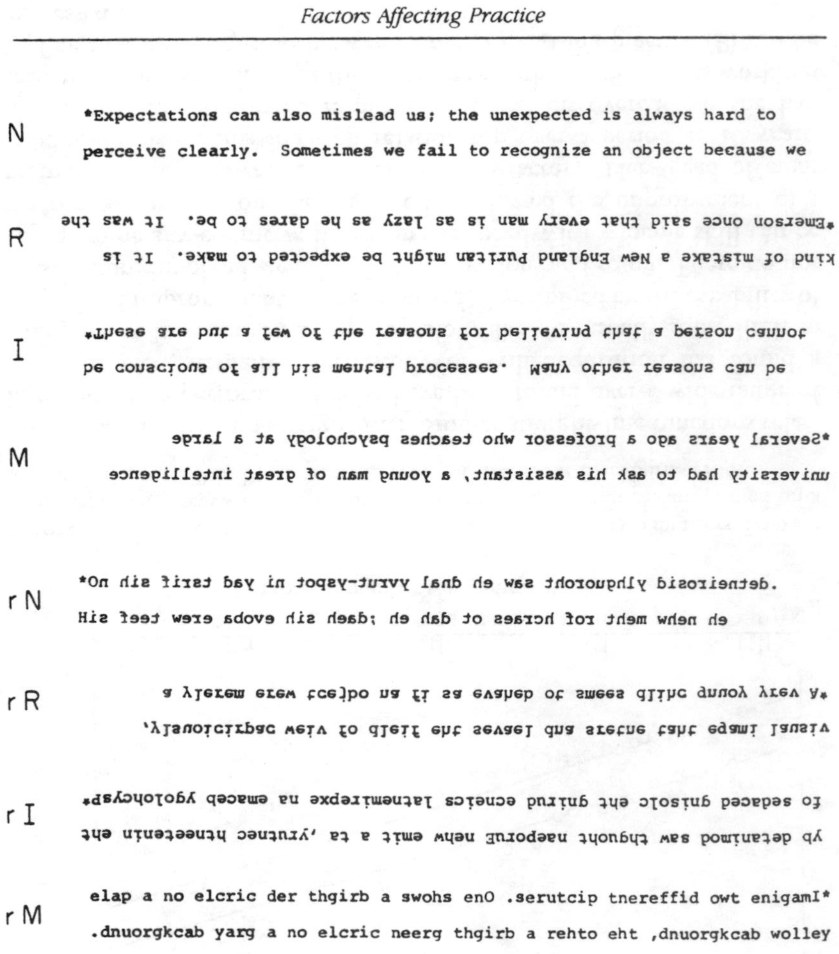

**Figure 9-3.** Some examples of the spatially transformed texts used in Kolers's studies of the acquisition of reading skills. The asterisks indicate the starting point for reading. (From Kolers & Perkins, 1975.)

crease in processing time with further practice becomes small very rapidly.

Effects of practice have also been studied in domains involving complex problem solving, such as giving justifications for geometrylike proofs (Neves & Anderson, 1981). Figure 9-2 shows a power function for that domain, in terms of both a normal scale and a log–log scale. Such

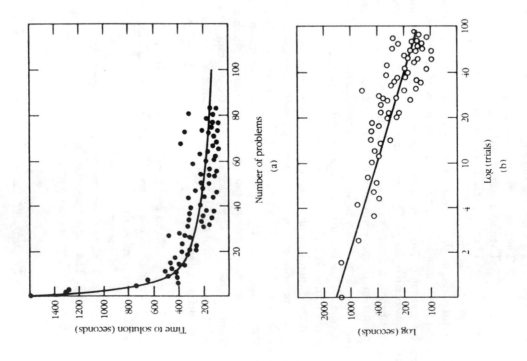

**Figure 9-2.** Time to generate proofs in a geometrylike proof system as a function of the number of proofs already done: (a) function on a normal scale, $RT = 1410P^{-55}$; (b) function on a log–log scale.

transformation, each letter has been inverted; in the M transformation, the sentence has been set as a mirror image of standard type. The rest are combinations of the several transformations. In one study, Kolers looked at the effect of massive practice on reading inverted (I) text. Subjects took more than 16 min to read their first page of inverted text as compared with 1.5 min for normal text. Following the initial test of reading speed, subjects practiced on 200 pages of inverted text. Figure 9-4 provides a log–log plot of reading time against amount of practice. In this figure, practice is measured in terms of number of pages read. The change in speed with practice is given by the curve labeled *Original training on inverted text*. Kolers interspersed a few tests on normal text; data for these are given by the curve labeled *Original tests on normal text*. We see the same kind of improvement for inverted text as in the Blackburn study (i.e., a straight-line function on a log–log plot). After reading 200 pages, Kolers's subjects were reading at the rate of 1.6 min per page, almost the same rate as subjects reading normal text.

Kolers brought his subjects back a year later and had them read inverted text again. These data are given by the curve in Figure 9-4 labeled *Retraining on inverted text*. This time for the first page of the inverted text, subjects took about 3 min. Compared with their performance of 16 min on their first page a year earlier, subjects were displaying an enormous savings, but it was now taking them almost twice as long to read the text as it did after their 200 pages of training a year earlier. They had clearly forgotten something. As the figure illustrates, subjects' improvement on the retraining trials showed a log–log relationship between practice and performance, as had their original training. Subjects took 100 pages to reach the same level of performance that they had initially reached after 200 pages of training.

## Factors Affecting Practice

Although practice is very important for the development of a skill, you should not think that this is all that is involved. The nature of the practice and the circumstances surrounding it can be very important. This is just the same as the effect of practice on the development of factual or declarative memories (Chapters 6 and 7). Practice was important there, too, but there were numerous modulating factors. In fact, it seems that some of the principles which apply to declarative memory also apply to memory for procedures. For instance, we discussed in Chapter 7 the powerful effects that spaced study can have on the learning of verbal materials. Spacing appears to have even more profound effects on skill learning. The inefficiency of massed practice was shown in one study involving intensive training in Morse code during World War II (reported in Bray, 1948). Students were found to learn as rapidly with 4 hours of practice as with 7 hours of practice. The 7-hour subjects were effectively wasting the 3 extra hours of practice crammed into the day. Similar advantages of spaced practice are found for the learning of more cognitive skills. For instance, Gay (1973) has shown that spaced practice of algebra rules results in better retention than massed practice.

## Part Versus Whole Learning

Students working to acquire a skill frequently ask whether it is better to try to learn and practice the whole skill or to learn and practice parts of the skill, putting them together later. In the area of motor skills, the answer to this question depends on whether the parts to be practiced are independent. If they are, it is better to practice the parts separately. For

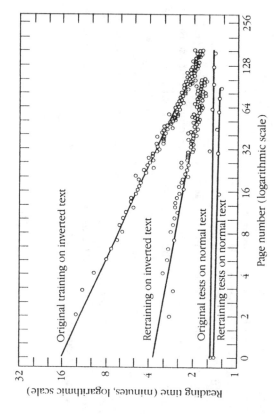

**Figure 9-4.** The results for readers in Kolers's reading-skills experiment (1976) on two tests more than a year apart. Subjects were trained with 200 pages of inverted text with occasional pages of normal text interspersed. A year later they were retrained with 100 pages of inverted text, again with normal text occasionally interspersed. The results show the effect of practice on the acquisition of the skill. Both reading time and number of pages practiced are plotted on a logarithmic scale. (From Kolers, 1976. Copyright by the American Psychological Association. Reprinted by permission.)

instance, Koch (1923) taught subjects a rather bizarre skill—to type finger exercises using two typewriters simultaneously, one hand per typewriter. There were two groups of subjects—those who practiced each hand first and those who tried immediately to use both hands. The group that started by practicing with separate hands was better when they switched to both hands than the group that started with both hands, and they maintained this superiority with further practice. In contrast, experiments on tasks that require careful integration show superiority for whole learning over part learning. For example, in playing the piano it is better to try to learn the whole sequence rather than to try to integrate subsections of a sequence.

Much of education seems designed to decompose a complex skill into independent subcomponents, and to teach each separately. Gagne (1973) has argued that many skills in education can be decomposed into subskills and these into subsubskills, and so on. The lower-level skills are prerequisites to the higher skills. For instance, calculus assumes algebra as a subcomponent, which assumes arithmetic as a subcomponent, which assumes basic counting skills as a subcomponent. Gagne argued that the key to successful educational plans was to identify the correct hierarchy of subskills. The educational curriculum should be designed to teach separately each of the subskills in the hierarchy.

## Knowledge of Results

Subjects learn a skill more rapidly if they receive feedback as to whether their skill attempts are correct and how they are in error (for a classic review of research on feedback see Bilodeau, 1969). The amount of time between the action and the feedback is important—an expected relationship, since for feedback to be useful, the action must be active in memory. After a delay, it may be hard to recall just what led to incorrect result.

Recently, Lewis and Anderson (1985) looked at this relationship in learning to play a maze game on the order of Dungeons and Dragons. In one condition, players received immediate feedback after making a wrong move. In a second condition, the consequences of a wrong move became apparent only after the next move, when players found themselves in a bad situation. As predicted, subjects learned to play the game better in the condition of immediate feedback.

On the other hand, there are a number of situations where immediate feedback or too much feedback can be harmful. Schmidt, Young, Swinnen, and Shapiro (1989) had subjects practice simple motor skills such as moving a shaft in a precise time. They contrasted giving subjects feedback about how much they were off the target time after every trial of practice or in a summary after 15 trials. Subjects appeared to learn more in the summary condition as measured by a final retention test. Schmidt et al. argue that subjects can become too dependent on feedback. It is also the case that processing the feedback can interfere with learning the task. Just how much feedback to present and when is a rather subtle issue. Private human tutors appear to be quite tuned to needs of students. Bloom (1984) compared the effectiveness of students learning with private tutors versus in a standard classroom. He found that the average student with a private tutor was doing better than 98 percent of the students in the standard classroom. Unfortunately, private tutors are very expensive and it is not possible to provide every student with a full-time private tutor.

One of the promises of computer-assisted instruction is that it would be an economical means of providing students with feedback that is tuned to their learning needs. Of course, it also requires a great deal of intelligence to provide such feedback. Endowing computers with sufficient intelligence has been a major stumbling block. However, there have been some successes (Anderson, Boyle, Farrell, & Reiser, 1984; Sleeman & Brown, 1982). These successes have relied heavily on cognitive psychology and artificial-intelligence research. We will be describing some of this research in the last chapter of this book.

## The Nature of Expertise

We have discussed so far in this chapter some of the phenomena associated with skill acquisition. An understanding of the mechanisms behind these phenomena has come from examining the nature of expertise in various fields of endeavors. In the last decade or so there has been a great deal of research looking at expertise in such domains as mathematics, chess, computer programming, and physics. This research compares people at various levels of development of their expertise. Sometimes this research is truly longitudinal and will follow students from their introduction to a field to their development of some expertise. More typically such research samples people at different levels of expertise. For instance, research on medical expertise might look at students just beginning medical school, residents, and doctors with many years of medical practice. This research has begun to identify some of the ways that problem solving becomes more effective with experience. Below we will review some of these dimensions of the development of expertise.

## Proceduralization

There are dramatic changes in the degree to which subjects rely on declarative versus procedural knowledge. This is illustrated in my own work on the development of expertise in geometry (Anderson, 1982). One student had just learned two postulates for proving triangles congruent—the side-side-side (SSS) postulate and the side-angle-side (SAS) postulate. The side-side-side postuate states that if three sides of one triangle are congruent to the corresponding sides of another triangle, the triangles are congruent. The side-angle-side postulate states that if two sides and the included angle of one triangle are congruent to the corresponding parts of another triangle, the triangles are congruent. Figure 9-5 illustrates the first problem the student had to solve. The first thing he did in trying to solve this problem was to decide which postulate to use. The following is a portion of his thinking-aloud protocol, during which he decided on the appropriate postulate:

"If you looked at the side-angle-side postulate (long pause) well $RK$ and $RJ$ could almost be (long pause) what the missing side. I think somehow the side-angle-side postulate works its way into here (long pause). Let's see what it says: 'Two sides and the included angle.' What would I have to have to have two sides. $JS$ and $KS$ are one of them. Then you could go back to $RS = RS$. So that would bring up the side-angle-side postulate (long pause). But where would Angle I and Angle 2 are right angles fit in (long pause) wait I see how they work (long pause) $JS$ is congruent

to $KS$ (long pause) and with Angle 1 and Angle 2 are right angles that's a little problem (long pause). OK, what does it say—check it one more time: 'If two sides and the included angle of one triangle are congruent to the corresponding parts.' So I have got to find the two sides and the included angle. With the included angle you get Angle 1 and Angle 2. I suppose (long pause) they are congruent to each other. My first side is $JS$ is to $KS$. And the next time one is $RS$ to $RS$. So these are the two sides. Yes, I think it is the side-angle-side postulate." (Anderson, 1982, pp. 381–382)

After reaching this point the student still went through a long process of actually writing out the proof, but this is the relevant portion in terms of assessing what goes into recognizing the relevance of the SAS postulate.

After a series of four more problems (two were solved by SAS and two by SSS), we came to the student's application of the SAS postulate for the problem illustrated in Figure 9-6. The method-recognition portion of the protocol follows:

"Right off the top of my head I am going to take a guess at what I am supposed to do: Angle $DCK$ is congruent to Angle $ABK$. There is only one of two and the side-angle-side postulate is what they are getting to." (Anderson, 1982, p. 382)

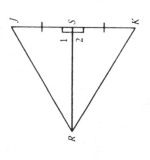

Given: $\angle 1$ and $\angle 2$ are right angles
$JS \cong KS$
Prove: $\triangle RSJ \cong \triangle RSK$

**Figure 9-5.** The first geometry proof problem encountered by a student after studying the side-side-side and side-angle-side postulates.

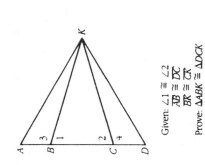

Given: $\angle 1 \cong \angle 2$
$AB \cong DC$
$BK \cong CK$
Prove: $\triangle ABK \cong \triangle DCK$

**Figure 9-6.** The sixth geometry proof problem encountered by a student after studying the side-side-side and side-angle-side postulates.

## Tactical Learning

As students practice problems they come to learn the sequences of moves required to solve the problem or portions of the problem. This is referred to as *tactical learning* in that a tactic refers to a method that accomplishes a particular goal. For instance, Greeno (1974) found that it took only about four repetitions of the hobbits and orcs problem (see discussion surrounding Figure 8-4 from the previous chapter) before subjects could solve the problem perfectly. Subjects were learning in this experiment the sequence of moves to get the creatures across the river. Once learned they could simply recall the sequence without further search.

In more complex domains problems do not repeat but components of problems do repeat and students remember the solutions to these components. For instance, consider the problem in Figure 9-7. As students gather expertise in geometry problem solving they learn to recognize that they should infer that the triangles *ACM* and *BDM* are congruent because they have two pairs of congruent sides and the included angles are in a vertical angle (or opposite angle) configuration. This is a repeating subpattern that appears in multiple geometry problems. In effect they have learned the following production rule:

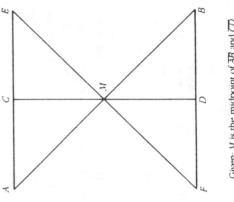

Given: *M* is the midpoint of $\overline{AB}$ and $\overline{CD}$
Prove: *M* is the midpoint of $\overline{EF}$

**Figure 9-7.** An advanced problem for high school geometry students.

A number of things seem striking about the contrast between these two protocols. One is that there has been a clear speedup in the application of the postulate. A second is that there is no verbal rehearsal of the statement of the postulate in the second case. The student is no longer calling a declarative representation of the postulate into working memory. Note also in the first protocol that there are a number of failures of working memory — points where the student had to recover information that he had forgotten. The third feature of difference is that in the first protocol there is a piecemeal application of the postulate by which the student is separately identifying every element of the postulate. This is absent in the second protocol. It appears that the postulate is being matched in a single step.

These transitions are like the ones that Fitts and Posner characterized as belonging to the associative stage of skill acquisition. The student is no longer relying on a verbal recall of the postulate, but has advanced to the point where he can simply recognize the application of the postulate as a pattern. We can represent this ability by the following production rule:

IF    the goal is to prove triangle 1 is congruent to triangle 2
      and triangle 1 has two sides and an included angle that
      appear congruent to two sides and an included angle of
      triangle 2

THEN  set as subgoals to prove the corresponding sides and angles
      congruent
      and then to use the side-angle-side postulate to prove
      triangle 1 congruent to triangle 2

Thus, the student has converted the verbal or declarative knowledge of the postulate into a procedural knowledge as embodied in the production rule above.

A similar result is reported by Sweller, Mawer, and Ward (1983). They studied the development of expertise in solving simple kinematics problems and looked at how often subjects wrote down basic formulas involving velocity, distance, and acceleration such as $v = at$, where $v$ is velocity, $a$ is acceleration, and $t$ is time. They found that initially subjects would write these formulas down to remind themselves of them but later on they would only write these equations with constants from the problem substituted for some of the variables — for example, $v = 2*10 = 20$. Thus, the formula was only implicit in their problem solving rather than being explicitly recalled.

**Table 9-1** *Typical Novice Solution to a Physics Problem*

To find the desired final speed $v$ requires a principal with $v$ in it, say

$$v = v_c + 2at.$$

But both $a$ and $t$ are unknown, so that seems hopeless. Try instead

$$v^2 - v_0^2 = 2ax.$$

In that equation $v_0$ is zero and $x$ is known, so it remains to find $a$. Therefore try

$$F = ma.$$

In that equation $m$ is given, and only $F$ is unknown, therefore use

$$F = \Sigma F\text{'s}.$$

which in this case means

$$F = F_g'' - f$$

where $F_g''$ and $f$ can be found from

$$F_g'' = mg \sin \Theta,$$
$$f = \mu N,$$
$$N = mg \cos \Theta.$$

With a variety of substitutions, a correct expression for speed,

$$v = \sqrt{2(g \sin \Theta - \mu g \cos \Theta)l},$$

can be found.

Adapted from Larkin, 1981.

---

IF    there are two triangles
      and they have two pairs of congruent sides
      and these sides combine to form a vertical-angle
      configuration
THEN  conclude the angles are congruent because of vertical angles and conclude the triangles are congruent because of the side-angle-side postulate

This rule will put in place one inference along the path to developing the full proof for this problem.

## Strategic Learning

The discussion above was concerned with how students learn tactics that are sequences of moves to solve subproblems. There are also changes at the strategic level, which is concerned with how students organize their solution to the overall problem. Learning how to organize one's problem solving is referred to as *strategic learning*. The clearest demonstrations of such strategic changes have been in the domain of physics problem solving. Larkin (1981) compared novice and expert solutions on problems like the one in Figure 9-8. A block is sliding down an inclined plane of length $l$ where $\theta$ is the angle between the plane and the horizontal. The coefficient of friction is $\mu$. The subject's task is to find the velocity of the block when it reaches the bottom of the plane. Table 9-1 gives a typical novice solution to the problem and Table 9-2 gives a typical expert solution.

The novice solution typifies the method of *working backward*. It starts with the unknown, which is the velocity $v$. Then the novice finds an equation to calculate $v$. However, to calculate $v$ by this equation it is necessary to calculate $a$, the acceleration. So an equation is found involving $a$; and so the novice chains backward until a set of equations is found that enable solution of the problem.

The expert, on the other hand, uses similar equations but in the completely opposite order. The expert starts with quantities that can be directly computed, such as gravitational force, and works toward the desired velocity.

Larkin has shown that on such problems, experts and novices typically apply physics principles in just the opposite order. She developed a computer model that is able to simulate the development from a novice to expert with practice. This was done within a production-system framework. Novices start out with productions for working backward and slowly develop productions that make forward inferences.

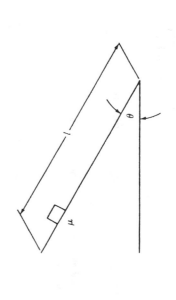

**Figure 9-8.**   A sketch of a sample physics problem. (From Larkin, 1981.)

calculated so $v$ can be calculated. This puts a severe strain on working memory and can lead to errors. Reasoning forward eliminates the need to keep track of subgoals. However, to successfully reason forward one must know which of the many possible forward inferences are relevant to the final solution. This is what the expert learns with experience. The expert learns to associate various inferences with various patterns of features in the problem.

It is not the case that all domains see this shift from backward to forward problem solving. A good counterexample is computer programming (Anderson, Farrell, & Sauers, 1984; Jeffries, Turner, Polson, & Atwood, 1981). Both novice and expert programmers develop programs in what is called a *top-down* manner. That is, they work from the statement of the problem to subproblems to sub-subproblems, and so on, until they solve the problem. For instance, Figure 9-9 illustrates part of the development of a plan for a program to calculate the difference in mean

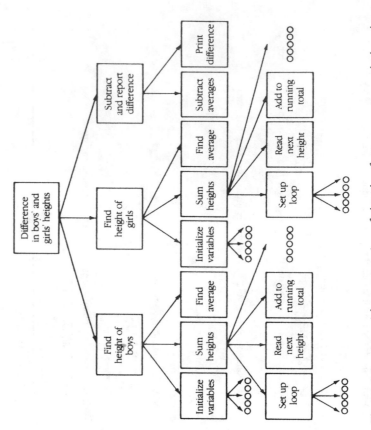

**Figure 9-9.** A partial representation of the plan for a program to calculate the difference in mean height between boys and girls in a classroom.

**Table 9-2** *Skilled Solution to a Physics Problem*

The motion of the block is accounted for by the gravitational force,

$$F_g'' = mg \sin \Theta$$

directed downward along the plane, and the frictional force,

$$f = \mu mg \cos \Theta$$

directed upward along the plane. The block's acceleration $a$ is then related to the (signed) sum of these forces by

$$F = ma$$

or

$$mg \sin \Theta - \mu mg \cos \Theta = ma.$$

Knowing the acceleration $a$, it is then possible to find the block's final speed $v$ from the relations

$$l = \tfrac{1}{2}at^2$$

and

$$v = at$$

Adapted from Larkin, 1981.

Novice students are simulated by means–ends productions such as:

> IF  the goal is to calculate quantity $x$
>      and there is a physics principle that involves $x$
> THEN  try to use that principle to calculate $x$

So, given the goal of calculating the acceleration, $a$, this production might invoke the use of the equation $v = v_0 + at$ (velocity equals initial velocity plus acceleration times time). With experience, however, her system developed productions that modeled expert students:

> IF  the quantities $v$, $v_0$, and $t$ are known
> THEN  assert that the acceleration $a$ is also known

A similar shift from backward reasoning to forward reasoning also occurs in geometry. There are real advantages to be had by forward reasoning in domains such as geometry and physics. Reasoning backward involves setting goals and subgoals and keeping track of them. For instance, the student must remember that he or she is calculating $F$ so $a$ can be

height between boys and girls in a classroom. First, the problem is developed into the subproblems of (1) calculating the mean height of the boys; (2) calculating the mean height of the girls; (3) subtracting the two. The problem of calculating the mean height of the boys is divided into the goals of adding up the heights and dividing by the number of boys. And so the program development continues until we get down to statements in the language such as:

$$\text{AVERAGE} = \text{TOTAL/NUMBER}$$

This top-down development is basically the same thing as what is called *working backward* in the context of geometry or physics. It is noteworthy that there is not a change to working forward as programmers become more expert. This is in sharp contrast to geometry and physics, where experts do change to working forward. This contrast can be understood by considering the differences in the problem domains. Physics and geometry problems have a rich set of givens that are more predictive of solutions than is the goal. In contrast, there is nothing in the typical statement of a programming problem that corresponds to the givens which would guide a working forward or bottom-up solution. The typical problem statement only describes the goal and often does so with information that will guide a top-down solution. Thus, we see that development of expertise does not follow the same course in all domains. Rather, experts adapt themselves to the characteristics of a particular domain.

Another difference has been noted between expert and novice development of computer programs (Anderson, 1983; Jeffries, Turner, Polson, & Atwood, 1981). Experts tend to develop problem solutions breadth first, whereas novices develop their solutions depth first. The differences are not striking with a simple problem like Figure 9-9, but can become quite dramatic with more complex programs that have more complex plans. The expert tends to expand a full level of the plan tree before going down to expand the next level, whereas the novice will expand the first problem down to its lowest levels. Thus, an expert will have decided on a basic plan of calculating both the boys' and the girls' heights in the figure before working out all the details of calculating the boys' heights, whereas the novice will completely work out the plan for the boys' heights before considering the plan for the girls' heights. The expert's approach is called breadth first because a whole layer of tree is created at a time. The novice's approach is called depth first because of the tendency to first complete the leftmost branch of the tree right to the bottom. There are good reasons for the expert's approach. Programming prob-

lems are typically nonindependent (see the discussion on p 238). Therefore, the solution of a later problem can often impact on the solution of an earlier problem. For instance, you might want to write a program to calculate the boys' heights in such a way that the same program could be used to calculate the girls' heights. Experts, because of breadth-first expansion, are likely to see these dependencies among subproblems.

In summary, it is not the case that the transition from novices to experts involves the same changes in strategy in all domains. Different problem domains have different structures that make different strategies optimal. What we see in the development of expertise in a domain is the discovery of those strategies which are optimal for that domain. Physics experts learn to reason forward while programming experts learn breadth-first expansion.

## Problem Representation

Another dimension of expertise is that problem solvers learn to represent problems in ways that enable more effective problem-solving procedures to apply. This can be nicely demonstrated in the domain of physics. Physics, being an intellectually deep subject, has principles that are only implicit in the surface features of a physics problem. Experts learn to see these implicit principles and represent problems in terms of them.

Chi, Feltovich, and Glaser (1981) asked subjects to classify a large set of problems into similar categories. Figure 9-10 shows sets of problems that their novices thought were similar and the novices' explanations for the similarity groupings. As can be seen, the novices chose surface features, such as rotations or inclined planes, as their bases for classification. Being a physics novice myself, I have to admit these seem very intuitive bases for similarity. Contrast these classifications with pairs of problems that the expert subjects saw as similar in Figure 9-11. Problems that are completely different on the surface were seen as similar because they both involved conservation of energy or they both used Newton's second law. Thus, experts have the ability to map surface features of a problem onto these deeper principles. This is very useful because the deeper principles are more predictive of the method of solution. This shift in classification from reliance on surface features to deeper features has been found in a number of domains, including mathematics (Silver, 1979; Schoenfeld & Herrmann, 1982), computer programming (Weiser & Shertz, 1983), and medical diagnosis (Lesgold, Rubinson, Feltovich, Glaser, Klopfer, & Wang, 1988).

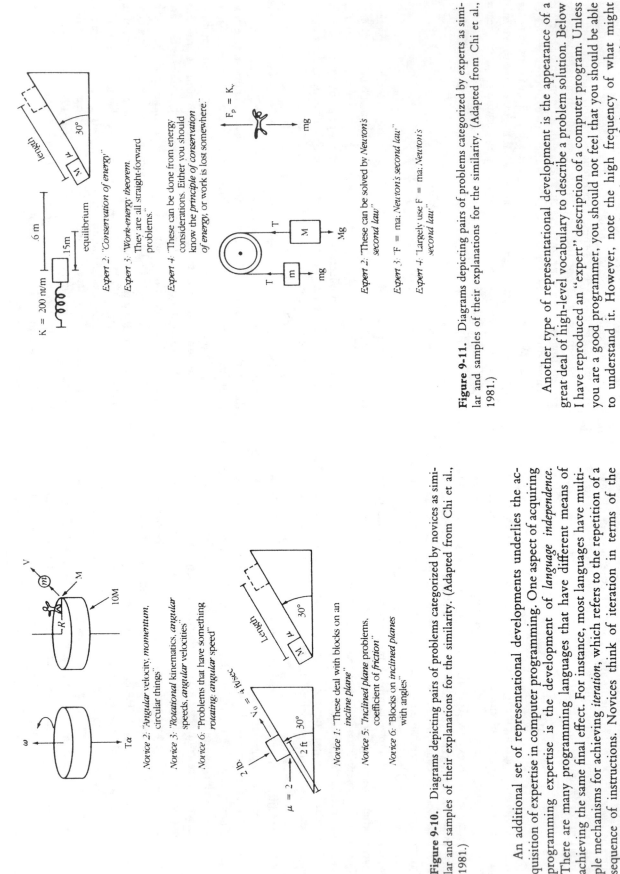

**Figure 9-10.** Diagrams depicting pairs of problems categorized by novices as similar and samples of their explanations for the similarity. (Adapted from Chi et al., 1981.)

**Figure 9-11.** Diagrams depicting pairs of problems categorized by experts as similar and samples of their explanations for the similarity. (Adapted from Chi et al., 1981.)

An additional set of representational developments underlies the acquisition of expertise in computer programming. One aspect of acquiring programming expertise is the development of *language independence.* There are many programming languages that have different means of achieving the same final effect. For instance, most languages have multiple mechanisms for achieving *iteration,* which refers to the repetition of a sequence of instructions. Novices think of iteration in terms of the mechanisms of a particular language. Experts think of iteration in the abstract, independent of any particular language. This is much like the development observed in physics, where experts perceive problems in terms of abstract principles.

Another type of representational development is the appearance of a great deal of high-level vocabulary to describe a problem solution. Below I have reproduced an "expert" description of a computer program. Unless you are a good programmer, you should not feel that you should be able to understand it. However, note the high frequency of what might appear to be jargon. (I have italicized some of the more striking instances.) Actually, each of these instances of jargon is attached to an important programming construct and enables the programmer to more economically represent and think about the plan for the program:

*BKT-DELETE* is implemented as the *standard list deletion plan*. Inputs are a *key* and a *list of entries*. The plan is a *search loop* using two *pointers*: a pointer to the *current entry* which is *initialized* to the *input list*, and a *trailing pointer* which is initialized to *NIL*. On each *iteration*, it *tests the key* of the *first element* of the current list. If it is equal to the input key, it *splices the current element* out of the list by *RPLACD'ing the previous pointer*.

Thus, one important dimension of growing expertise is the development of a set of new constructs for representing the key aspects of a problem.

## Problem Memory

One of the surprising discoveries about expertise is that experts seem to display a special enhanced memory for information about problems in their domain of expertise. This was first discovered in the research of de Groot (1965, 1966), who was attempting to determine what separated master chess players from weaker chess players. It turns out that chess masters are not particularly more intelligent in domains other than chess. de Groot found hardly any differences between expert players and weaker players—except, of course, that the expert players chose much better moves. For instance, chess masters consider about the same number of possible moves before selecting their move. In fact, if anything, masters consider fewer moves than chess duffers.

However, de Groot did find one intriguing difference between masters and weaker players. He presented chess masters with chess positions (i.e., chessboards with pieces in a configuration that occurred in a game) for just 5 seconds and then removed the chess positions. The chess masters were able to reconstruct the positions of more than 20 pieces after just 5 seconds of study. In contrast, the chess duffers could reconstruct only 4 or 5 pieces—an amount much more in line with the traditional capacity of working memory (see Chapter 6). It appears that chess masters build up patterns of 4 or 5 pieces that reflect common chessboard positions as a function of their massive amount of experience in games. Thus, they remember not individual pieces but these patterns. In line with this analysis, if the players are presented with random chessboard positions rather than ones that are actually encountered in games, no difference is demonstrated between masters and duffers. Both types of subjects can reconstruct only a few chess positions. The masters also complain about being very uncomfortable and disturbed by such chaotic board positions.

This basic phenomenon of superior expert memory for meaningful problems has now been demonstrated in a large number of domains, including the game of Go (Reitman, 1976), electronic circuit diagrams (Egan & Schwartz, 1979), bridge hands (Engle & Bukstel, 1978; Charness, 1979), and computer programming (McKeithen, Reitman, Rueter, & Hirtle, 1981; Schneiderman, 1976). One might think that the memory advantage shown by experts is just a working memory advantage, but research has shown that their advantage extends to long-term memory. Charness (1976) compared experts' memory for chess positions immediately after they had viewed the positions or after a 30-second delay filled with an interfering task (like the Peterson and Peterson task discussed in Chapter 6). Class A chess players show no loss in recall over the 30-second interval, unlike other subjects, who show a great deal of forgetting. Thus, expert chess players, unlike duffers, have an increased capacity to store information about the domain. Interestingly, these subjects show the same poor memory for three-letter trigrams as ordinary subjects. Thus, their increased long-term memory is *only* for the domain expertise.

Chase and Simon (1973) examined the nature of the *patterns* or *chunks* used by masters. They used a chessboard-reproduction task, as illustrated in Figure 9-12. The subjects' task was simply to reproduce the positions of pieces of a target chessboard on a test chessboard. In this task, subjects glanced at the target board, placed some pieces on the test board, glanced back to the target board, placed some more pieces on the test board, and so on. Chase and Simon defined as a chunk those pieces that subjects moved following one glance. They found that these chunks tended to

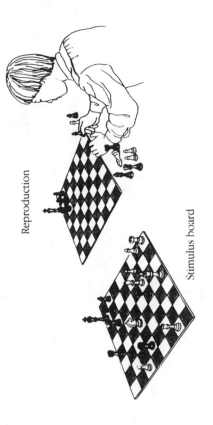

Reproduction

Stimulus board

**Figure 9-12.** The reproduction task in Chase and Simon (1973). Subjects were to reproduce the configuration of pieces on the reproduction board. (Adapted from Klatzky, 1979.)

Experts appear to be able to remember more patterns as well as larger patterns. Some of the evidence for this was in an experiment by Chase and Simon where they had subjects recall chess boards as did de Groot (in contrast to the reproduction task illustrated in Figure 9-12). They tried to identify the patterns that their subjects used to recall the chess boards. They found that subjects would tend to recall a pattern, pause, recall another pattern, pause, etc. They found that they could use a two-second pause to identify boundaries between patterns. With this objective definition of what a pattern is, they could then explore how many patterns were recalled. In comparing a master chess player with a beginner they found large differences in both measures. The pattern size of the master averaged 3.8 pieces while it was only 2.4 for the beginner. However, the master also recalled an average of 7.7 patterns per board while the beginner recalled only an average of 5.3. Thus, it seems that the experts' memory advantage is based not only on larger patterns but also on the ability to recall more of them.

The strongest evidence that expertise involves the ability to remember more patterns as well as larger patterns comes Chase and Ericsson (1982), who studied the development of a simple but remarkable skill. They watched a subject, SF, increase his digit span, which is the number of digits that he could repeat back after one presentation. As discussed in Chapter 6, the normal digit span is about 7 or 8 items, just enough to accommodate a telephone number. After about 200 hours of practice, on Saturday, December 15, 1979, SF was presented with 81 random digits at the rate of 1 digit per second. He proceeded to reel off the 81 digits perfectly. Figure 9-13 illustrates how his memory span grew over 264 training trials.

What was behind this feat of superhuman memory? In part, SF was learning to chunk the digits into meaningful patterns. He was a long-distance runner, and part of his technique was to convert digits into running times. So, he would take four digits, like 3492, and convert them into "Three minutes, 49.2 seconds – near world-record mile time." Using such a strategy he could convert a memory span for 7 digits into a memory span for 7 digit patterns of length 3 or 4. This would get him to a digit span in the 20s, far short of his eventual performance. Gradually, he developed what Chase and Ericsson called a *retrieval structure*, which enabled him to recall 22 such patterns. This retrieval structure was very specific; it would not generalize to retrieving letters rather than digits. Chase and Ericsson hypothesize that part of what underlies development of expertise in other domains such as chess is development of retrieval structures, which allows superior recall for past patterns.

define meaningful game relations among the pieces. For instance, more than half of the masters' chunks were pawn chains (configurations of pawns that occur frequently in chess).

Simon and Gilmartin (1973) estimate that masters have acquired on the order of 50,000 different chess patterns, that they can quickly recognize such patterns on a chessboard, and that this ability is what underlies their superior memory performance in chess. This 50,000 figure is not unreasonable when one considers the years of devoted study that becoming a chess master takes.

What might be the relationship between memory for so many chess patterns and superior performance in chess? Newell and Simon (1972) speculated that, in addition to learning many patterns, masters have also learned what to do in the presence of such patterns. Basically, they must have something on the order of 50,000 productions in which the condition (the IF part) of a production is a chess pattern and its action (the THEN part) is the appropriate response to that pattern. For instance, if the chunk pattern is symptomatic of a weak side, the response of the production might be to suggest an attack on the weak side. Thus, masters effectively "see" possibilities for moves; they do not have to think them out. This explains why chess masters do so well at lightning chess, in which they have only a few seconds to move.

So, to summarize, chess experts have stored the solutions to many problems that duffers must solve as novel problems. Duffers have to analyze different configurations, try to figure out their consequences, and act accordingly. Masters have all this information stored in memory, thereby claiming two advantages. First, they do not risk making errors in solving these problems, since they have stored the correct solution. Second, because they have stored the correct analysis of so many positions, they can focus their problem-solving efforts on more sophisticated aspects and strategies of chess.

Chess players become masters only after years of playing. They have to be able to store a great deal of information about chess to be experts. Native intelligence is no substitute for knowledge (there is more on this topic in Chapter 14).

It had been thought that better expert memory rested solely on possession of more and larger patterns with which to encode the problem. The advantage of the expert in chess was like the advantage of someone who knows English in remembering a sentence — in the latter case one can remember words and phrases and not individual letters. However, there is increasing reason to believe that the memory advantage goes beyond experts' ability to encode the problem in terms of familiar patterns.

manipulated successfully in the streets. For example, if a child had correctly calculated the total cost of five lemons at 35 cruzeiros a piece on the street, the child was given the following written problem:

$$5 \times 35 = ?$$

The results showed that, whereas children solved 98 percent of the problems presented in the situated context, they solved only 37 percent of the problems presented in the laboratory context. It needs to be stressed that these problems involved the exact same numbers and mathematical operations. Interestingly, if the problems were stated in the form of word problems in the laboratory, performance improved to 74 percent. This runs counter to the usual finding, which is that word problems are more difficult than equivalent "number" problems (Carpenter & Moser, 1982). Apparently, the additional context provided by the word problem allowed the children to make contact with their pragmatic strategies.

While the study of Carraher et al. showed a curious failure of expertise in real life to transfer to the classroom, the typical concern of educators is whether what is taught in one class will transfer to other classes and the real world. At the turn of the century educators were fairly optimistic on this issue. A number of educational psychologists subscribed to what has been called the Doctrine of Formal Discipline (Angell, 1908; Pillsbury, 1908; Woodrow, 1927), which held that studying such esoteric subjects as Latin and geometry was of significant value because it served to discipline the mind. Formal Discipline subscribed to the faculty view of mind, which extends back to Aristotle and was first formalized by Thomas Reid in the late eighteenth century (Boring, 1950). The faculty position held that the mind was composed of a collection of general faculties, such as observation, attention, discrimination, and reasoning, which were exercised in much the same way as a set of muscles. The content of the exercise made little difference; most important was the level of exertion (hence the fondness for Latin and geometry). Transfer in such a view is broad and takes place at a general level, sometimes spanning domains that share no content. For example, training in chess should transfer to computer programming since both skills involve the use of the general reasoning faculty.

At the beginning of this century Thorndike undertook a research program extending some 30 years to show that transfer was much narrower in scope than would be predicted by the Doctrine of Formal Discipline. According to Thorndike, the mind was not composed of general faculties but rather of specific habits and associations, which provided a person with a variety of narrow responses to very specific

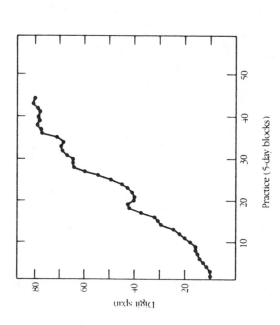

**Figure 9-13.** The growth in the memory span of the subject SF with practice. Notice how the number of digits he can recall increases gradually but continually with the number of practice sessions. (From Chase & Ericsson, 1982.)

## Transfer of Skill

As noted, Chase and Ericsson's subject SF was unable to transfer memory span skill from digits to letters. This is an almost ridiculous extreme of what is becoming a depressing pattern in the development of cognitive skills. This is that these skills can be quite narrow and fail to transfer to all other activities. Chess experts do not appear to be better thinkers for all their genius in chess. An amusing example of the narrowness of expertise is the study of Carraher, Carraher, and Schliemann (1985). They investigated the mathematical strategies used by Brazilian school children who also worked as street vendors. On the job, these children used quite sophisticated strategies for calculating the total cost of orders involving different numbers of different objects (e.g., the total cost of four coconuts and twelve lemons), and what's more, they could perform such calculations reliably in their heads. Carraher et al. actually went to the trouble of going to the streets and posing as customers for these children, making certain kinds of purchases and recording the percentage of correct calculations. The experimenters then asked the children to come with them to the laboratory, where they were given written mathematics tests that involved the same numbers and mathematical operations that had been

stimuli. In fact, the mind was regarded as just a convenient name for countless special operations or functions (Stratton, 1922). Thorndike's theory of transfer was the Theory of Identical Elements, which stated that training in one kind of activity would transfer to another only if the activities shared common situation-response elements:

One mental function or activity improves others in so far as and because they are in part identical with it, because it contains elements common to them. Addition improves multiplication because multiplication is largely addition; knowledge of Latin gives increased ability to learn French because many of the facts learned in the one case are needed in the other. (Thorndike, 1906, p. 243)

Thus, Thorndike was happy to accept transfer between diverse skills as long as it could be shown that the transfer was mediated by identical elements. Generally, however, he concluded that:

the mind is so specialized into a multitude of independent capacities that we alter human nature only in small spots, and any special school training has a much narrower influence upon the mind as a whole than has commonly been supposed. (p. 246)

In his first series of experiments (Thorndike & Woodworth, 1901), Thorndike subjected the strong version of the Doctrine of Formal Discipline to an empirical test. The strong version, as presented above, claims that transfer ranges across diverse tasks when those tasks involve the same general faculty. In one study, no correlation was found between memory for words and memory for numbers. In another, accuracy in spelling was not correlated with accuracy in arithmetic. Thorndike interpreted these results as evidence against the general faculties of memory and accuracy.

Thorndike formulated his Theory of Identical Elements in what proved to be an overly narrow manner. For instance, he argued that if you solved a geometry problem which involved one set of letters for points you would not be able to transfer to a geometry problem with a different set of letters. The research that we examined in the previous chapter indicated that this is not true. Transfer is not tied to identity of surface elements. There is in some cases very large positive transfer between two skills that have the same logical structure even if they have different surface elements (see Singley & Anderson, 1989, for a review). Thus, for instance, there is large positive transfer between different word processing systems, between different programming languages, and between using calculus to solve economic problems and using calculus to

solve problems in solid geometry. However, all the available evidence is that there are very definite bounds on how far skills will transfer and that becoming an expert in one domain will have little positive benefit in becoming an expert in a very different area. There will be positive transfer only to the extent that the two domains involve use of the same facts, productions, and patterns—i.e., the same knowledge.

There is a positive side to this specificity in transfer of skill. This is that there seldom seems to be negative transfer, in which learning one skill makes a person worse at learning another skill. Interference, such as occurs in memory for facts (see Chapter 7), is almost nonexistent in skill acquisition. Polson, Muncher, & Kieras (in press) provide a good demonstration of lack of negative transfer in the domain of text editing. They had subjects learn one text editor and then learn a second, which was designed to be maximally confusing. Whereas the command to go down a line of text might be $n$ and the command to delete a character might be $k$ in one text editor, $n$ would mean to delete a character in another text editor and $k$ would mean to go down a line. However, subjects experienced overwhelming positive transfer in going from one text editor to the other because the two text editors worked in the same way, even though the surface commands had been scrambled.

There is only one clearly documented kind of negative transfer in the case of cognitive skills. This is like the Einstellung effect discussed in the previous chapter. Students can learn a way of solving a problem in one skill, which is no longer optimal for performing another skill. So, for instance, someone may learn tricks in algebra to avoid having to perform difficult arithmetic computations. These tricks may no longer be necessary when one goes to an environment where there are calculators to perform these calculations. Still students show a tendency to continue to perform these unnecessary simplifications in their algebraic manipulations. This is really not a case of failure to transfer. This is a case of transferring knowledge that is no longer useful.

# Remarks and Suggested Readings

The work on the development of expertise in cognitive skills is a relatively recent phenomenon. The papers by Chase and Simon (1973) and Larkin, McDermott, Simon, and Simon (1980) are already considered classics. Lesgold (1984) reviews many of the concepts. The books edited by Anderson (1981) and Chi, Glazer, and Farr (1988) contain numerous recent papers on the topic. An issue of the 1985 *Canadian Journal of*

*Psychology*, edited by Charness, is devoted to the topic. Card, Moran, and Newell (1983) describe interaction with computer systems, especially text editors. Schneiderman (1976) reviews many aspects of computer programming. Soloway, Bonar, and Ehrlich (1983) have done some excellent research on programming in Pascal.

This chapter has focused mainly on the development of cognitive skills. However, considerable research has been done on the development of motor skills. Reviews can be found in Fitts and Posner (1967), Kelso (1982), Schmidt (1982), and Stelmach and Requin (1980). Rosenbloom and Newell (1983) have done a production-system analysis of practice and transfer in the domain of perceptual-motor skills. Singley and Anderson (1989) provide a review of research of transfer and a modern version of Thorndike's Theory of Identical Elements cast in terms of production systems.

# Modeling expert knowledge

MILDRED L. G. SHAW AND J. BRIAN WOODWARD

*Knowledge Science Institute, Department of Computer Science, University of Calgary, Calgary, Alberta, Canada T2N 1N4*

*(Received 23 August 1989 and accepted in revised form 10 January 1990)*

The main difficulties in knowledge acquisition from domain experts stem from the variety of forms of knowledge, the various representations of knowledge, and the problems in making these explicit and accessible. There is, at present, no systematic overall methodological framework for knowledge acquisition to guide the organization and arrangement of the appropriate application of the many manual and automated techniques and methods used for knowledge acquisition. In considering these problems it is appropriate to draw on studies in cognitive science and associated disciplines to examine the models of the expert and the demands and goals of the task. This paper develops the modeling processes involved from the perspective of the expert trying to communicate his view of a target system and transfer it into computer implementable form. It identifies the distinct processes of elicitation, analysis and implementation, the knowledge representations of the intermediate knowledge bases which can be used to help the expert review and refine his conceptual model, and the computer knowledge bases which may be unrecognizable by the expert as related to his developing models. Finally, several methods of knowledge aquisition are reviewed in the context of these models.

## Introduction

The field of knowledge acquisition requires a methodological framework which logically supports the process of knowledge acquisition, identifies the characteristics of the products of knowledge acquisition, and offers a set of ordered assumptions about the nature of knowledge and its characteristics. Making expert knowledge explicit in all its forms challenges the knowledge engineer. Beginning with the domain problem, the initial objectives of knowledge acquisition are to identify both the characteristics of the task situation and the method used by the problem solver to address the task. Without the determination of these two general areas of knowledge, the task of the knowledge engineer becomes an undirected search for whatever knowledge appears to fit the operational formalism chosen for the final computer knowledge base.

If the task demands can be identified and the problem-solving method of the expert ascertained, the types of knowledge required become identifiable. Procedures can then be developed to elicit these types of knowledge, either new procedures or, more likely, those borrowed and modified from other disciplines. These next four sections identify the problems of current approaches and the underlying philosophical, conceptual and methodological issues.

## The "patchwork" approach to knowledge acquisition

Current approaches to knowledge acquisition are based on a variety of methods and techniques, mostly imported from other disciplines and adapted for use in knowledge acquisition. Often a technique has been imported to address a specific issue or problem and then its use is generalized for other purposes. Psychology has offered entity-attribute grids (Shaw & Gaines, 1987; Boose & Bradshaw, 1987) protocol analysis (Ericsson & Simon, 1984) and some forms of interviewing (LaFrance, 1987). Linguistics has offered implicit knowledge structures for text analysis (Woodward, 1988) and forms of discourse analysis, ontological and conceptual analysis (Belkin, Brooks & Daniels, 1986; Hirst & Regoczei, 1989). Epistomology has offered knowledge hierarchies (Hayward, Wielinga & Breuker, 1986). The machine learning field has provided induction techniques (Forsyth & Rada, 1986). Artificial intelligence has provided a number of knowledge representation formalisms, inference procedures, and the development of generic structures (McDermott, 1988; Chandrasekaran, 1988), and more procedures are being brought from the area of systems analysis (McGraw & Harbison-Briggs, 1989).

As each method was incorporated into knowledge acquisition, it brought with it assumptions about the nature of knowledge and how knowledge was represented. The assumptions are often implicit, but usually begin to emerge in the knowledge representation language (e.g. entity-attribute grids assume that distinctions are critical primitives underlying knowledge), but also assumptions often remain implicit as in some forms of interviewing.

The assumptions made about knowledge are reflected in the procedures of the knowledge acquisition method or technique. Methods which emphasize the use of "task-like" situations (e.g. think-aloud protocols) which provide prompts and cues to draw out or elicit responses are assumed to provide the required knowledge. Methods which emphasize the labeling, selecting, coding or reordering of linguistic material (e.g. discourse analysis, KADS) are assumed to provide an *a priori* structure or schema. The assumptions about knowledge contained in the structure activity also require elucidation.

Borrowing methods from other disciplines has helped address the growing knowledge acquisition problem for knowledge based systems and has helped to provide a variety of useable techniques and methods. However, this approach has also resulted in the knowledge acquisition area resembling a patch-work quilt whereby methods and techniques are strung together in a pragmatic rather than systematic fashion. One may ask whether the elicitation, analysis and implementation processes make inconsistent, even conflicting, assumptions about knowledge.

Due to the lack of a systematic framework for knowledge acquisition it is extremely difficult to organize and arrange the proper and appropriate application of the techniques and methods for knowledge acquisition. When and why to apply a particular technique is often left up to the predilections of the knowledge engineer or the availability of a program for that method.

Some researchers have attempted to solve the problem by extending those methods imported from other areas or by developing a very precise, well-formalized and very powerful method. An example of the first solution is the KADS

© 1990 Academic Press Limited

development. Particular assumptions reflecting the epistomological underpinnings of knowledge representation were used to develop a complex system of knowledge analysis. Examples of the second solution are the knowledge acquisition methods developed by Chandrasekaran (1988) and McDermott (1988). These researchers developed specific methods for identifying repeatable activity during the solution of a problem as the certain types of problems. These repeatable procedures were then formalized to identify adequate knowledge to emulate the expert which acts as a basis for knowledge acquisition.

Twine (1989) offers a suggestion for another solution to the "patchwork" problem. He proposes that we begin by making a very clear distinction between "method" and "methodology". A methodology requires the development of a set of guidelines, assumptions and eventually principles which bring order to a field. In the case of knowledge acquisition, a clearly defined methodology would provide a set of criteria for identifying, ordering and comparing the variety of methods for knowledge acquisition. It would also provide a framework for identifying the "gaps" in knowledge acquisition techniques and methods. Once a gap was found, the methodology would aid in the principled development of new tools which meet methodological requirements. Finally, the methodology provides a framework for logically supporting the knowledge acquisition process, for identifying the characteristics of the products of knowledge acquisition and for making decisions about the nature of knowledge and its characteristics. In this paper we develop a general methodological framework for knowledge acquisition methods that clarifies their underlying assumptions and classifies their structures.

## Philosophical issues

The primary philosophical issue in knowledge acquisition may be seen as the contrast between the rational/objectivist approach to knowledge versus the constructivist approach (Woodward, 1989). A rational/objectivist approach defines a problem as the observable gap between a given goal or predefined standards of performance and the present state of affairs (Nystedt, 1983). Knowledge is presumed to be a body of information acquired by people, something that can be transferred, borrowed, stored, displayed, packaged and bought or sold like any other commodity. Within this framework, the "task" is an objectively defined set of situational demands which must be met or addressed in order to close the gap. Assumptions are that the gap can be objectified, that the problem-solving process addressing the task can be identified and agreed upon and that the problem can be decomposed into sub-problems. Diagnostic tasks in one domain should be the same as diagnostic tasks in other domains. This philosophical position ignores the presence of the problem-solver; or at the very least, reduces the problem-solver to a container for replicable problem-solving procedures.

In contrast, the constructivist approach defines a problem as an artifact of cognitive processes (Nystedt, 1983) and problem-solving is defined as problem-formulation combined with the steps taken to arrive at cognitive closure (e.g. satisfaction, reduction of dissonance). Problems may be sub-divided but more likely they are reformulated. This approach assumes that the goal may be shared with others but there may be numerous individual methods of reaching the goal.

Different experts in the same domain may use different problem-solving methods to solve the same problem. This philosophical position reflects a view which recognizes the problem-solver as central to problem-solving. The problem-solver constructs the knowledge needed for the problem to be solved. For knowledge acquisition, the focus is on identifying the features of the task which are salient to the problem-solver and making explicit the cognitive procedures which are used. Knowledge about the task is only used as it is seen through the eyes of the problem-solver (Compton & Jansen, 1989).

Both approaches assume that tasks and methods may be classified based on various qualities and characteristics. This is useful for knowledge acquisition. If knowledge engineers can recognize the *task characteristics* and the *problem-solving method* of the expert and match the two, then knowledge base development takes on a more methodical, less idiosyncratic flavor (Welbank, 1987). The salient types of knowledge can be identified and algorithms for the processing of this knowledge constructed or selected. However, there does not yet exist a taxonomy of either task characteristics of problem-solving methods which can assist knowledge engineers throughout the knowledge acquisition process (Woodward, 1989). Also there is no useful scheme for mapping specific task demands with problem-solving processes.

## Conceptual issues

The conceptual difficulties in knowledge acquisition stem from a lack of consensus on what framework can be used for representing the task demands and problem-solving method (Clancey, 1989). The concept of *mental models* has been developed by a number of researchers in cognitive science. Johnson-Laird (1983) operationalizes this concept as logical propositions represented by quasi-logical propositions. This approach recognizes mental models as the "micro" level whereas Graesser and Clarke (1985) identify "general knowledge structures" as unique and self-contained mental models. This same level of operationalization is demonstrated by other examples of general knowledge formats or packages such as frames (Minsky, 1975), scripts and/or plans (Schank & Abelson, 1977), productions (Anderson, 1983), memory organization packages (Schank, 1982), and thematic abstract units (Winston, 1984).

At the "macro" level, the mental models concept can be operationalized as styles of problem-solving. Styles refer to the general approach taken by the problem-solver in addressing a variety of tasks. An example of this level of definition is the formalizing of modes of inquiry. Churchman's (1971) book on inquiry identifies five major schools of western philosophy which provide the basis for different types of problem-solving systems. Each system is characterized by its definition of knowledge, how this form of knowledge is combined, what constitutes a solution and the differing strengths and weaknesses of the inquiry process. Lockian, Leibnitzian, Kantian, Hegelian and Singerian inquiring systems are outlined. This scheme has been translated into a practical tool which attempts to identify an individual problem-solver's mode or style of inquiry (Harrison & Bramson, 1982).

The conceptualization of mental models at the levels outlined offers useful representation schemes and operational definitions, but these lack an overall framework which would help to organize and arrange the various schemes or models

and behavior. The mental model affects the form and representation of the conceptual model and is, in turn, constrained by the language and behavioral representational system. It is this conceptual model that is available to others and the one which requires further translation and representation by other modeling activities. As the mental model is unavailable to an observer, the conceptual model is taken to represent the model used to address the task demands of the target system.

The conceptual model becomes the focus of further modeling efforts. Knowledge engineers, or automated knowledge acquisition systems, take these models and enforce an order through the underlying models implicit in their elicitation procedures from the introspection of the expert about his interaction with the target system. The conceptual model provides a set of primitives which are communicated to the analysis processes and recognized by the analytic methods used (which, in turn, are directed by models of their own). The *intermediate knowledge base* is produced from the conceptual model through the elicitation and informal analysis procedures which rely on the introspection and communication of it from the expert. There is no direct link between the mental and conceptual models, between the cognitive processes, or between the elicitation and analysis procedures, but the processes are iterated back and forth, the models providing new data for the procedures which in turn select parts of the essential features from the models until the intermediate knowledge base emerges.

The objective of this modeling activity is to select a set of primitives from the conceptual model which can be used for another model. This activity requires an ordered and systematic procedure of its own. Representing the primitives of the conceptual model necessitates another medium and another representation structure. What is generated is a series of models of the conceptual model of the target system, in various forms of refinement and representation. These models are usually designed to represent different primitives which are considered important to the task. Primitives, which represent facts of the domain, are included with the inferencing procedures. Also, forms of strategic processes which guide the use of domain knowledge primitives and the inferencing processes are included. The result of this activity is a new model of the conceptual model, which is the model of the conceptual model of the target system. This model represents the interrelationships between the task demands of the target system and the model for addressing the demands of the conceptual model. It represents the salient features of the task and its context.

Each successive model requires a representational schema, another medium of representation, and an ordered procedure for translating one representation to another. The model of the conceptual model of the target system should contain the necessary primitives to recreate the operation of the mental model (Norman, 1983). There may be many models of the conceptual model of the target system that can perform the same activity of simulating the mental model. The model of the conceptual model of the target system represents the final working or operational model. By formally analysing this, a computer knowledge base may be identified and coded in the representation language. As in earlier stages, this process may be iterated and refined by extracting knowledge structures produced until the computer

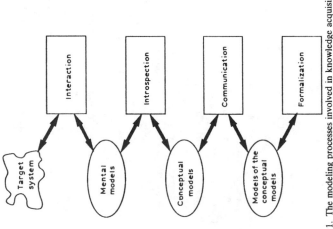

FIGURE 1. The modeling processes involved in knowledge acquisition.

of knowledge. Norman (1983) points out that the first requirement is to define the system that the expert is interacting with, "the system that the person is learning or using, by definition, the *target system*". Figure 1 shows the relationships between the target system, the mental models of the expert, the conceptual models of the expert and the processes of interaction with the target system, introspection about the interaction, communication of the introspection, and formalization of the communication. No intrinsic model exists in the target system, but rather an ordered or repetitive sequence of activities or events. A variety of potential models are possible for this target system which represents the "task".

Using Norman's terminology, the expert interacts with the target system and may produce many *mental models* of the target system. The perceptual system of the expert is capable of isolating and defining "primitives" by representing them in symbolic form. There is some debate in cognitive science about the nature of these representations and about the level at which the representations are confirmed. Empirical research suggests that it is possible for various models to exist at different levels in perceptual and cognitive processes (Paivio, 1977; Fodor, 1980; Pylyshyn, 1984.

The next modeling process results in a model of the model of the target system. Norman refers to this as the *conceptual model* of the target system because it is the model that is reflected in communicating the mental model to other entities. The conceptual model finds representation in the communication primitives of language

exist in the target system, only ordered or repetitive sequences of events. The *mental models* represent unexpressed, uncommunicated knowledge in the expert's mind—fragmentary, partial models generated to account for his or her purposeful interaction with the target system. At this stage primitives in the situation are isolated and defined. The *conceptual models* represent the models of the models of the target system. They represent knowledge expressed in a linguistic form which can be communicated to others. They are not formal and not necessarily consistent and usually require further refinement. They are the focus of further modeling. The *models of the conceptual models* of the target system are more formally expressed and available for communication, interpretation and discussion with others. They may encompass a variety of media and consist of a series of models which represent the interrelationships of task characteristics as modeled by the problem-solver.

## Methodological issues

Methodologically, the field of knowledge acquisition is characterized by a variety of systems, each useful for a selected type of knowledge. Confusion exists between elicitation methods and analysis methods. Norman's modeling framework also offers a way out of this methodological dilemma in knowledge acquisition. Any procedures which aid in the transition, or translation, from the mental model to the conceptual model, may be called *knowledge elicitation* methods. These procedures (interviewing, laddering, brain-storming, repertory grids, MOLE, SALT, etc.) are designed to draw out and represent forms of knowledge. In responding to the elicitation stimuli, the problem-solver arranges his or her knowledge in linguistic form (verbal and behavioral) according to the structure of the prompts. The elicitation methods are particular to specific types of knowledge and must be chosen appropriately. The conceptual model is, however, a rough model of the mental model of the target system and must be further refined into an operational form.

The translation step from the conceptual model to the model of the conceptual model of the target system can be seen as *knowledge analysis* because the end result is a knowledge model or qualitative model (Clancey, 1989) based on the linguistic primitives in the conceptual model. These methods, such as the analysis portion of KSS0 (Gaines & Shaw, 1987), induction programs (Dietterich & Michalski, 1981; Quinlan, 1987; Gaines, 1989), Cognosys (Woodward, 1988), protocol analysis (Ericsson & Simon, 1984), perform analyses on the elicited knowledge and result in another model of knowledge. These models may undergo numerous iterations. The result is a methodological distinction between elicitation and analysis procedures. This suggests the need for operationally connecting the elicitation and analysis procedures through the intermediate knowledge base which is done, for instance, in KSS0 resulting from the earlier work of Shaw (1980).

Integration of a flexible range of tools is of paramount importance (Gaines, 1987) especially with automated knowledge acquisition methods. With current systems, the knowledge engineer is allowed few degrees of freedom. If the current domain does not conform to the tool, the domain is sometimes "redefined" to fit the tool. Manual methods, on the other hand offer a flexibility and adaptability not found

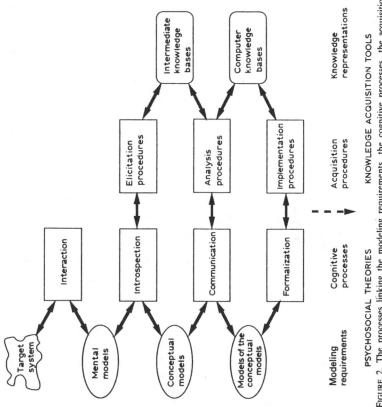

| Modeling requirements | Cognitive processes | Acquisition procedures | Knowledge representations |
|---|---|---|---|
| PSYCHOSOCIAL THEORIES | | KNOWLEDGE ACQUISITION TOOLS | |

FIGURE 2. The processes linking the modeling requirements, the cognitive processes, the acquisition procedures and the knowledge bases.

knowledge base is sufficiently well implemented to represent the model of the conceptual model of the target system as shown in Figure 2.

This method of development inherently links the task demands and the problem-solving method, and models of the conceptual model of the target system which are developed, must maintain these connections (Woodward, 1989).

The complete modeling process for the knowledge acquisition phase of development is shown in Figure 2. This shows the links from one part of the model to another and emphasizes the essentially iterative and refining nature of knowledge acquisition. The left side of the figure uses Norman's terminology applied to an expert involved a problem-solving task. It shows the social effect of communication of his problem-solving in a goal-directed situation, where the goal is to produce a computer implementation of his knowledge. The right side shows the computer-based knowledge acquisition and representation tools.

In summary, the *target system* is the focal point for the problem-solver, who has patterns of activity or knowledge inherent to the context or situation. No models

with automated tools but frequently offer help with only a part of the elicitation and analysis tasks required for knowledge acquisition.

## Properties of mental models

Assumptions made about the mental models are propagated to later models. A simple formulation of the components required for mental representational activity come from the description of verbal reports (Ericsson & Simon, 1984) which are considered as reflecting a subset of the information held in the short-term memory. Cognitive processes are postulated as a sequence of internal states successively transformed by a series of information process. Also, information is assumed to be stored in several different memories which reflect different capacities and display different capacities and accessing characteristics (p. 11).

The mental model, or the cognitive representations in the human knowledge source, represents that which knowledge engineers attempt to discover and model. These models represent two different processes. The first is the forming of models. Models are formed during information gathering when "some basic level concepts and relationships [are selected] on the basis of perceptual input and prior expectations" (Gilhooly, 1987, p. 23). New situations are initially categorized in terms of an existing model but if this one is insufficient then a new model is developed (Kelly, 1955) from basic concepts or by combining parts of existing models. The second use of models is in prediction and problem solving. The models suggest a set of hypotheses about the system under study. The hypotheses change as new information is perceived and incorporated (Kelly, 1955).

For knowledge acquisition, the nature of these models requires elucidation because elicitation techniques often assume (implicitly or explicitly) particular cognitive structures and processes. For example, the generic task approach (Chandrasekaran, 1988) assumes that problem-solving can be modeled as a series of "modular" processing activities using specific types or forms of knowledge. Elicitation of these processes and the knowledge forms required act as the basis for knowledge acquisition activity.

In order for elicitation procedures to be more useful, the underlying assumptions about knowledge and knowledge processes require elucidation and definition. The structures and descriptions of knowledge types, roles and functions require objectification and definition to be useful to the knowledge engineer. This is accomplished when a well developed theory underlies the elicitation (and hopefully the analysis method as well) and is used to make assumptions about the structure of knowledge. KSS0 (Gaines & Shaw, 1987) is based on Kelly's (1955) method of repertory grids within the framework of personal construct psychology. Cognosys (Woodward, 1988) uses the method of generic knowledge structures (Graesser & Clark, 1985) as a method within the framework of implicit knowledge structures. These methods make very definite assumptions about the nature of knowledge and the inference processes at play in the mental model. Other researchers (Craik, 1943; Johnson-Laird, 1983; Gentner & Gentner, 1983; Norman, 1983) use the concept of mental models to outline and define the components of knowledge. It has also been postulated that various mental models exist at various levels in the perceptual and cognitive faculties (Paivio, 1977; Fodor, 1980; Pylyshyn, 1984).

## Properties of introspection and elicitation procedures

Elicitation techniques for knowledge acquisition support introspection of the expert and act as classification grammars for linguistic elements and linguistic levels. After the task situation has been selected, instructions are normally given to the expert in order to generate verbal and/or behavioral events. These events are collected, then ordered or parsed into useful phrases which form the conceptual model. The specific instructions act as a constraint on the mental model material in that they structure the verbal material from the expert. The method of collection may result in fairly complete collection such as video recording or partial collection such as note-taking.

There appear to be few variations on the main types of elicitation procedures. Each type involves assumptions about the type of knowledge or information and where it resides. Ericsson and Simon (1984) note that information can be elicited retrospectively, inferentially, descriptively, or by direct questioning. In the first case, retrospective elicitation is assumed to tap information stored in the short-term memory if the time between the completion of the task and the elicitation procedure is not too long. It is assumed that the expert can describe the heeded information used for task completion.

When given instructions to report on the steps in solving the task, the expert will make inferences about what he or she "must" have thought. Inferentially generated material in elicitation procedures constrains the expert's responses by requiring information that is plausible. The information tapped in this case may or may not have anything to do with the heeded material or those salient knowledge cues used in completing the task. Rather, the communication context between the knowledge engineer, or knowledge acquisition tool, and the expert becomes more salient.

Descriptive types of elicitation take the form of thought descriptions at the time of completing the task. These types of elicitation instructions promote the verbalization of information which is currently in short-term memory. It is assumed that the verbalization processes do not interfere with the completion of the task or influence the processes required for task completion (Ericsson & Simon, 1984). The vocalizations are assumed to be a commentary on the problem-solving method used while the expert is completing the task.

Direct probing is assumed to elicit pieces of information directly from the short-term memory with no need for intervening accessing cues. If the information is not in short-term memory, then the direct probing can still be used to elicit information in long-term memory by way of accessing cues. LaFrance's (1987) grid is based on the assumptions that information is stored in many different memories and so can be accessed using a variety of probes.

The information resulting from the above elicitation types may reflect different qualities of verbal material. The simplest verbal material in the conceptual model results from direct verbal descriptions of the information heeded while completing the task. Very little effort is required by the expert for this activity because the information points within the awareness of the expert while completing the task are simply labeled.

More complex material comes into the conceptual model from elicitation when the expert begins to describe the thought content of the mental model in short-term memory. This information assumes an "observer" role such that the expert is able to describe the thought processes and knowledge roles which are salient and relevant to the task. It is assumed that these verbalizations are descriptions of the mental model in action or descriptions of the mental model in past action.

The most complex level of verbalization occurs when the expert begins to explain the thought processes, thoughts, ideas, hypotheses or motives required when completing the task. The act of explanation requires the linking of cues in short-term memory to earlier information and/or to information in long-term memory. This need to link information not currently in the short-term memory results in an increase in the amount of information and may even alter the salience and relevance of the information (Ericsson & Simon, 1984, p. 79).

Elicitation procedures implicitly assume characteristics about the form of knowledge they intend to elicit; they select and order some of the information available in the mental model. The elicitation procedure uses its "theory" to constrain the types of "entities" which the expert believes pertain to a certain purpose or task. These entities may be physical objects or procedures, design components, cases, etc. Then, the expert is asked to describe the distinctions between and among the objects. This form of retrospective elicitation uses its background theory to identify the required elements of the mental model and produces a severly constrained, but highly functional, conceptual model and intermediate knowledge base in the completed entity-attribute grid. The grid can then be used as the basis for a variety of analyses.

## Properties of conceptual models

For knowledge acquisition, this model is the final outcome of elicitation activity. The elicitation procedures structure the information from the expert and it is assumed that this information reflects some of the available knowledge characterizing the expert's mental representation of the particular task as it is interpreted and represented by the elicitation procedures. The conceptual model acts as the first available representation or model of the expert's thinking processes and knowledge concerning the task situation. It contains representations of communicable information about the mental model.

In most cases, the conceptual model is represented in the form of linguistic structures. Because of this representation formalization, a number of assumptions are made about the information available due to the use of linguistic structures. A basic assumption is that linguistic structures are an adequate, reliable and valid means of studying human thought process. This assumption has been the basis for much of the modern research on linguistics (e.g. Chomsky, 1975) but has not been explicitly stated in knowledge acquisition work. It is possible to extend this main assumption to make it more applicable to knowledge acquisition by outlining a number of assumptions about knowledge and cognitive processes which apply in knowledge acquisition work.

In linguistics it is postulated that the linguistic material produces a surface-structure representation of a base-grammar, that operations are performed on the base grammar to produce a communicable description of the underlying representation. The view of transformational grammarians (e.g. Chomsky, 1975; Gazdar, 1981; Bresnan, 1982) is that deep structure relations are transformed through a semantic analysis to produce surface, or linguistic, representations. Elicitation methods appear to affect the integration processes of the transformations, and depend upon this tranformational process in that such procedures constrain the types of surface-structure components and relations possible.

It is the nature of the linguistic material which allows the knowledge engineer the opportunity of making inferences about the material. Graesser and Clark (1985, p. 14) suggest that much of the meaning of the conceptual model is not exclusively in the text. Inferences can be drawn based on contextual cues, on the linguistic material itself, on the goals of the comprehender, on the degree of shared knowledge between the generater and reader of the conceptual model and, finally, about the knowledge structures in long-term memory. The richness of the conceptual model depends somewhat on the elicitation process, and the usefulness of the linguistic representation of the conceptual model lies in the knowledge engineer's ability to generate meaning based on properties of the linguistic structure.

It must also be assumed that the linguistic material somehow reflects abstract structures in the mind which make knowledge possible. The production of linguistic structures are assumed to reflect these mind-based structures and processes. That knowledge engineers and knowledge acquisition methods are able to aid in the linguistic description of internally represented structures and processes has not been proven experimentally but is assumed to be true. We believe that what we elicit is an approximate representation of knowledge; assumptions are made about the ability of linguistic material to capture the expert's intrinsic competence and internalized knowledge.

Ericsson and Simon (1984, p. 221) make specific assumptions about the cognitive mechanisms underlying verbal descriptions. They state that:

- Verbalizable cognitions can be described as states that correspond to the contents of short-term memory (i.e. to the information that is in the focus of attention);
- The information vocalized is a verbal encoding of the information in short-term memory;
- The verbalization processes are initiated as thought is heeded;
- The verbalization is a direct encoding of the heeded thought and reflects its structure;
- Units of articulation will correspond to integrated cognitive structures; and
- Pauses and hesitations will be good predictors of shifts in the processing of cognitive structures.

## Properties of intermediate knowledge bases

Most knowledge engineers, and knowledge acquisition systems, produce multiple and varied intermediate knowledge bases. Welbank (1987) interviewed a number of knowledge engineers and discovered that there is much variety in how knowledge engineers deal with linguistic material from the conceptual model. Idiosyncratic, *ad hoc*, methods were reflected in the use of a variety of diagramatic methods and representation procedures. There is more activity in the knowledge acquisition community which has focused on the production of procedures for generating intermediate representations of the conceptual model material (e.g. Johnson & Johnson, 1987).

Intermediate knowledge bases are best characterized in terms of their functions. One main function is as a representation for display to the expert so that validation and confirmation are possible. A diagram is useful to help confirm understanding of the expert's mental model. A second function is to act as a focal point for further elicitation; the initial elicitation acts as the foundation for acquiring more information. An example is the development of a domain dictionary composed of term definitions (McGraw & Harbison-Briggs, 1989) which constitutes domain vocabulary. Another example is the development of ontological categories based on the syntactic position of words. A noun suggests a static object; a verb suggests action and change; adverbs and adjectives suggests style and distinctions. Attributes or distinctions can be elicited and combined in groups.

Intermediate knowledge bases are characterized by structures and forms based on qualities already inherent in the natural language structure of the conceptual model rather than on a formalized analysis procedure. Because of their functional properties, intermediate knowledge bases are formally-produced, partially-ordered, linguistically-based, and inherently unstable structures.

## Properties of communication and analysis procedures

Informal analysis procedures support the expert's first attempts at communication and draw out meaning from the linguistic material of the conceptual model and the partial orderings and structures of the intermediate knowledge bases. Informal analysis procedures are used to identify underlying, implicit or assumed knowledge structures in the elicited material. These procedures are usually theory-laden in that they reflect assumptions made about the structure of knowledge and how the structures can be operationalized. These analysis procedures are possible only because of an underlying theoretical framework which justifies the labeling and ordering of the material. They are possible also because of their formality and consistency. They reflect a step-by-step, algorithmic nature and are capable of being applied consistently to elicited material.

Analysis procedures usually begin with some form of encoding of the linguistic material from the conceptual model or from the intermediate knowledge bases. Encoding of these materials impose an *a priori* framework over the conceptual model and intermediate knowledge base material. This framework identifies the "required" linguistic primitives and labels or categorizes them. For example, in the KADS method (Breuker & Wielinga, 1987), verbs or groups of verbs in the text are viewed as "knowledge sources" in the sense that verbs indicate action and that action is usually done to something to produce something else. Knowledge sources are considered as producers of structure or meaning. Nouns or groups of nouns are, in turn, considered as objects which function as either inputs to knowledge sources or as the products or outputs of knowledge sources.

Once material has been coded, more formal analysis techniques group the encoded material into various structural configurations which aid communication of the material to other people and processes. Groups of encoded material are distinguished which can then be ordered, compared, matched, or constructed to

produce more meaningful knowledge structures. In Cognosys (Woodward, 1988) "knowledge units", noun–verb–noun phrases, are labeled as events, states, goals or styles. These are then connected to other knowledge units on the basis of linking rules (Graesser & Clark, 1985). Only knowledge units of certain types can be linked to others. Once the linking is complete, the categories are used to develop a variety of sub-structures which appear evident in the task. For example, goal-oriented sub-structures identify the ultimate goal and sub-goals. Implication sub-structures identify implicit connections within the task.

## Properties of models of the conceptual models

The results of formal analysis procedures produce a well-defined, conceptually ordered, theoretically consistent model of the task and context under consideration. This model can be viewed as a completed theory of knowledge, based on consistent use of concepts and a methodical application of formal rules which is able to trace the origins of how and why the knowledge was constructed, and document its transformations. The model of the conceptual model stands as the formalized representation of the more expressive conceptual model.

The model viability is ensured by containing all the necessary elements which allow the implementation process. Addis (1989) has identified three necessary components of knowledge which may be applied to the models of the conceptual models: first, each model should contain the required declarative knowledge reflecting tacit and factual knowledge inherent in the problem-solving method and in the task demands; second, the inference knowledge which operates on the declarative forms is necessary to identify the transformation or processing steps used; third, heuristic knowledge is required which sometimes act as special constraints, sometimes as inferences and sometimes as strategic procedures.

This model of the conceptual model is also characterized by formal interrelationships between task demands, external to but perceived by the problem solver, and the problem-solving method used by the problem-solver (Woodward, 1988). Task cues and their meanings are represented in the model and these cues are directly linked to inference, heuristic and declarative structures.

## Properties of formalism and implementation procedures

Implementation processes draw upon the formalized structure of the model of the conceptual model. Based on well established principles of artifical intelligence and underlying assumptions about knowledge, these processes select, order, arrange and represent elements of the model in a form conducive to operation in a computer-based knowledge system. Inference, heuristic and declarative knowledge are all coded into formats which reflect their different natures and functions. A variety of declarative knowledge forms are used to build portions of the knowledge base. Inference knowledge is represented by the ways in which the declarative knowledge is processed and manipulated. Heuristic knowledge is represented as meta- or control knowledge.

Due to the number of possible formal methods of implementation, different aspects of the model of the conceptual model may be selected. Rule-format coding

TABLE 1
*Some major knowledge acquisition techniques classified according to the presupposed model assumed, and the procedures used for elicitation, analysis and implementation.*

| Method | Presupposed model | Elicitation procedures | Analysis procedures | Implementation |
|---|---|---|---|---|
| **Interviewing** (LaFrance, 1987) (Johnson & Johnson, 1987) | General but weak | Interview: unstructured semi-structured structured | Extraction and organization of domain concepts | Not supported |
| **Protocol analysis** (Ericsson & Simon, 1984) Johnson, Zualkernan & Garber, 1987) | Possibility of adequate introspection | Recall of introspection | Extraction and organization of domain concepts | Not supported |
| **Empirical induction** (Quinlan, 1987) (Diettrich & Michalsky, 1981) Gaines, 1989) | Domain structure already identified; large dataset of expert behavior available | Collect large data-set of expert protocols (evaluations and decisions) | Induction of decision rules | Backward chaining rule-based system |
| **Generic ontologies** (Breuker & Weilinga, 1987) | Applicable multi-level ontology for knowledge representation | Structured interview; protocol analysis | Fit ontological structure to problem | Logic-based interpretation of structure |
| **Problem-solving ontologies** (McDermott, 1988) Chandrasekaran, 1988) | Existence of applicable generic problem-solving methods | Elicit repetitive process of problem-solving in domain | Fit generic problem-solving methods to observed behaviours | Parameterize implementation of generic problem-solving methods |
| **Implicit knowledge structures** (Woodward, 1989) | Implicit knowledge structures | Recall expert problem-solving behavior in domain | Identification of noun-verb phrases | Use as a basis for semantic net, frame or rule-based coding formalizations |
| **Entity-attribute grids** (Gaines & Shaw, 1987) (Boose & Bradshaw, 1987) | Knowledge characterized by distinctions made | Elicit entities in domain and distinctions between them | Conceptual clustering to confirm domain structure; induction to determine constraints | Generate classes, properties, methods, objects and values |

differs from frame-based coding which differs from logic-based coding. The appropriate choice depends on whether the required knowledge structures are represented in an applicable form within the model of the conceptual model. An efficient model would allow many implementation methods.

## Properties of computer knowledge bases

This final result reflects the multiple methods used in this process. The computer knowledge base represents a theory of knowledge that was constructed through the elicitation, analysis and implementation processes and based the assumptions underlying the representations in each modeling phase. Declarative knowledge is usually represented separately from the inferential knowledge but once complete, the final knowledge base operates in algorithmic fashion.

The first part of the paper has identified the primary characteristics of knowledge acquisition processes to be the underlying models and presuppositions they make, and the elicitation, analysis and implementation procedures used. The next section analyses some widely used knowledge acquisition techniques in these terms. The table below summarizes the techniques surveyed, how they relate to the presupposed models and the procedures used in the elicitation, analysis and implementation techniques used in each case.

## Some major techniques for the acquisition of knowledge

### INTERVIEWING

Interviewing (McGraw & Harbison-Briggs, 1989) is used to identify tasks and major concepts, to structure and refine already-acquired information. Unstructured interviews are appropriate when the knowledge engineer wants to explore an issue or the goal is to establish rapport and to get a broad view. It facilitates the description of the domain in a way that is easy for the expert to understand. However, the data acquired is often unrelated and difficult to integrate due to its lack of structure. It may not allow gathering of specific knowledge and takes time and training to do well. Also, similar questions may be asked in future sessions and this may annoy the expert. Alternatively, structured interviews have the advantages of forcing organization on the interview and being very goal-directed. They attempt to remove distortion from experts subjectively and allow better integration of material after the interview. They force the expert to be systematic, and the knowledge engineer is able to identify gaps in the material which act as a basis for further questions. The purpose of the session is clear to the expert. However, they need more preparation by the knowledge engineer who must study the background material extensively.

During the interview, of any kind, the knowledge engineer must decide on a note taking approach, for example, video- or audio-taping, each of which has advantages and disadvantages. Both open and closed questions can be used. Open questions are broad and place few constraints on the responder. They are used for determining scope of understanding, response certainty, and the models used. These questions like *what*, *why*, *how* allow the expert to express information the knowledge engineer does not know about. He or she can obtain the expert's vocabulary, concepts, frames of reference, and can help with explanations and underlying theory. Closed questions

(LaFrance, 1987) to bring information and rules from long-term memory. This process is vulnerable to influence by the structures of the communication situation between expert and knowledge engineer.

This method assumes a neutral stance with respect to types of knowledge elicited, although the question content itself makes assumptions about what knowledge is important and required. The encoding procedures developed for the results of interviewing (e.g. discourse analysis) are left to provide some implication of the nature of the acquired knowledge.

The result of interviewing is a very rich, but extremely unstructured and perhaps somewhat invalid (Bainbridge, 1986) conceptual model. On the other hand, the conceptual model allows a great number of intermediate knowledge bases which may be developed, described, demonstrated, redefined, etc. These intermediate knowledge bases act as useful indicators of validity and as stimuli for further elicitation.

There exist few formal procedures for the analysis of unstructured material. Even though these other procedures are being adapted from other disciplines, they do not yet meet the requirements of producing a model of the conceptual model. The results of grounded theory and of the systemic grammar method actually result in a better conceptual model. Jumping from a conceptual model to coding processes without the aid of a model of the conceptual model may account for much of the difficulty and inaccuracy of the interviewing method of knowledge acquisition.

## PROTOCOL ANALYSIS

This includes both observations of expert behavior and expert verbalizations. Two examples which are widely used, are Verbal Reports as Data (Ericsson & Simon, 1984) and the Specification of Expertise (Johnson, Zaulkernan & Garber, 1987). Ericsson's method uses concurrent and retrospective verbalization for elicitation. "Concurrent report" reveals the sequence of heeded (attended to) information and "retrospective report" reveals the sequence of specific cognitive processes. A think-aloud transcript is then encoded into segments (assertions, propositions, reading, doing arithmetic, visual searching, long-term memory recall, generalizing combinations) and relations of code are derived from verbs, propositions and adjectives. "Arguments" are often nouns phrases representing information relevant to the task. The method is based on the facts that:

• heeded (attended to) information is identified by analysis of corresponding verbalization through inference and task analysis;
• the original encoding should reflect as closely as possible the verbalized information, preferably by automated or semi-automated means;
• encoding uses a problem space approach (behaviour is a search through a problem space involving the step-by-step accumulation of knowledge);
• the model distinguishes information directly stored in memory (facts, experiences, perceived events and behaviour in past situations) from information generated or produced by inference (reactions and behaviour in hypothetical situations);
• the criteria for inferring underlying cognitive processes from thinking aloud protocols are relevant to task analysis and consistency with preceding verbalizations;

such as *who, where, when, which* tend to set limits on the type, level and amount of information the expert provides since they often provide a choice of alternatives such as a bipolar or multiple choice response. These are used more for clarifying or probing questions or as feedback as they are less time consuming for specific information. Note-taking is much easier but sometimes one can get too little information as they may stop the expert from volunteering information. Closed questions require an excellent command of vocabulary and concepts from the knowledge engineer. On balance a combination of open and closed questions is preferable.

One example of semi-structured interviewing is the Knowledge Acquisition Grid (LaFrance, 1987). This is a matrix of knowledge types and forms where the forms of knowledge are *layouts, stories, scripts, metaphors* and *rules-of-thumb*; and the knowledge question types are *grand tour, cataloging categories, ascertaining attributes, determining inter-connections, seeking advice* and *cross-checking.*

Examples of a "grand tour" are distinguishing boundaries of the domain, perspective, goals organization, e.g. Please describe the kinds of things you do. Examples of "cataloging" may be an organized taxonomy of expert terms and concepts, e.g. How would you group and subgroup these things? Examples of "ascertaining attributes" are distinguishing features and ranges of values, e.g. Describe similarities and differences of concepts. Examples of "determining interconnections" are uncovering relationships and casual model(s), e.g. Why? Examples of "seeking advice" include revealing strategies, e.g. Which conditions warrant which actions? Finally, examples of "cross-checking" are validation concerns, e.g. knowledge engineer plays naive, devil's advocate, poses hypothetical situations and asks How sure are you? Are there exceptions?

The teachback technique of Johnson and Johnson (1987) is a semi-structured interviewing method based on Pask's (1975) teachback techniques and Systemic Grammar Networks from Linguistics. This method attempts to formalize a functional approach to grammar. It is an intermediate representation used to teach back to the expert the knowledge acquired in the interview. It results in a mediating representation which is a machine language independent formalism between verbal data and software development environments. It is used as a tool to help proceed on early elicitation and conceptualization for synthesizing knowledge from talk with experts. The expert is encouraged to use his or her own words to express facts, procedures and abstractions which are recorded. The transcript is segmented, paraphrased, indexed and annotated by the knowledge engineer and the results captured in a systemic grammar network and checked and amended with the expert. It is mainly used as a means to prepare explicit descriptions of knowledge for the use of the development team to construct an associative network, graphs composed of nodes joined by links. It is said to be a generative form which captures all relevant information but excludes absurdities.

Interviewing protocols whether structured or unstructured, specific or general, probing or expansive, usually require a retrospective approach by the expert. This method makes implicit assumptions about the processing of knowledge but little about the nature of knowledge. Interviewing assumes that knowledge expressed by the expert is based on the question prompts and is used by the expert during task completion. Further, this knowledge needs to come into short-term memory before the expert can answer and that the expert needed to use some set of accessing cues

Elicitation takes the form of a variety of "thinking-aloud" activities while completing the task of interest. As the expert thinks aloud, the entire linguistic material is recorded and usually transcribed. The transcription can then be parsed or ordered for later coding or encoding. The conceptual model is rich and contains generated material as opposed to retrospective material (e.g. interviewing) and can be used to develop domain dictionaries and parsings based on discourse analysis procedures (e.g. Belkin, Brooks & Daniels, 1986).

Analysis procedures vary for protocol analysis because this method was developed as a generic elicitation strategy. Johnson, Zaulkerman and Garber (1987) used a method of encoding and ordering of the protocol material. Categories such as cues, triggers, goals, activities, etc. were ordered in graphical form to give a well-defined, formally ordered model of the conceptual model. The KADS method also uses protocol analysis but uses a much different theoretical approach to analysing the conceptual model.

A variety of coding methods are available but the choice depends on the analysis procedures used and the nature of the model of the conceptual model.

## DOMAIN ONTOLOGIES

These include the KADS methodology or Knowledge Acquisition Design System (Breuker & Wielinga, 1987) which deals with the whole process from domain organization to developing a complete system. It breaks the domain organization into stages where the problem is decomposed into component parts and the analysis of knowledge is separated from its machine implementation. Data is then collected and tested to modify the framework. The three refinement cycles are applied: orientation which includes the acquisition of vocabulary, the assessment of characteristics, the selection of the model and a test for problem feasibility; problem identification in which structures of domain concepts are uncovered, the functional analysis of the prospective expert system and task analysis; and problem analysis where the analysis of the user and operational environment results in the basic architecture of the system. At this point knowledge primitives are identified such as objects, knowledge sources, structures, strategies and models. Interpretation models are produced using a top-down model-driven approach which may include notions of causality, time, space, change and task-dependent concepts.

Building interpretation models is done by knowledge identification and knowledge conceptualization where knowledge primitives are ordered using relationships such as is-a, part-of, causes, depends-on, consists-of, defines, and several types of analysis are performed. The system is then coded using guidelines laid down.

Underlying the KADS method of knowledge acquisition is a philosophically-based theory of knowledge. Epistemologically, knowledge is considered a multi-level phenomenon. Each level represents a different level of complexity and functionality (Hayward, Wielinga & Breuker, 1986). They integrate the four degrees of depth at which questions about knowledge can be asked, that is, questions at the *individual*, *conceptual*, *formalism* and *mechanism* levels suggested by Sloman (1980), with the five types of knowledge *implementational*, *logical*, *epistemological*, *conceptual* and *linguistic* suggested by Brachman (1979). They identify the five levels as being "knowledge identification", "knowledge conceptualisation", "epistemological

- information in focal attention is vocalized directly or is encoded, recovery implies decoding;
- segments are analysed using syntax, pauses and intonation;
- each segment is independent (the context is ignored for the reason cited above);
- encoding involves finding a category expressing the same information as the segments.

The advantages of this method are that it can provide a complete record using both concurrent and retrospective reports, then after definition of problem space and segmentation of the protocol the analysis can be automated or the task made much easier for the coder as it focuses the coder's attention on the segments. It requires consistency and explicitness of underlying assumptions, vocabulary and inference rules and the automated encoding lessens the risk of incorrect inference. A comparison of thinking aloud protocols shows a very high consistency for practised skills and successive protocols show stable task strategies and cognitive representations. On the other hand, retrospective reports may leave out important detail and include inferences and generated information (plausible explanations). It is often difficult to tell if the expert pays attention to the knowledge engineer's instructions. The expert cannot report cues allowing recognition of stimuli since these are in long term memory and his short term memory retains goals and intentions longer than heeded information. There are also incompleteness problems. For example, thought in a non-oral form is much faster; the knowledge engineer cannot instruct a juggler to slow down!

The Specification of Expertise (Johnson, Zaulkerman & Garber, 1987) is one way of using the material gained from protocol analysis. It is a psychology based manual technique in which the expert thinks aloud while working. It encompasses a syntactic and semantic analysis of the protocol using operations, episodes, and data cues. Expertise is characterized by semantic categories, actions abilities, goals, conditions, strategies and solutions. It is based on the facts that thinking is not directly observable, especially that of an expert with considerable compiled knowledge and practice and that expertise is characterized by generativity and is a kind of knowledge that is used to perform a task. Part of this knowledge is represented by a set of abilities for problem solving. The representation or specification of expertise consists of: possible solutions and components of solutions; relevant information or data needed; goals for solutions; permissible ways to move between intermediate solutions and the abilities needed to make a transition.

This psychologically-based method of knowledge acquisition makes assumptions about knowledge from an information processing point of view. The method assumes that an individual is able to describe the contents of his or her own short-term memory as if the individual had an internal observer watching information come and go from working memory. Ericsson and Simon (1984) demonstrate support for this method and its underlying assumptions about cognitive information processing but little is stated about the nature of knowledge, apart from stating that perceptual information about environmental cues and internal cognitive processes are within the awareness of the "observer".

analysis", "logical analysis" and "implementational analysis". Knowledge cannot be considered uni-dimensional. This assumption indicates knowledge is not complete without taking into account all levels and their relationships.

Elicitation methods in KADS are designed to develop linguistically rich protocols of expert behavior. Broader than just protocol analysis, the KADS method generates a variety of verbal protocols from specialized interviews, thinking-aloud instructions, introspection and user-dialogues. The resulting conceptual models are rich linguistic models which are parsed partially on the basis of syntactical position of the words to form domain vocabularies, diagrams, etc. and are sometimes used to identify the format of the final model of the conceptual model.

Analysis procedures (Breuker & Wielinga, 1987) follow closely the multi-level theory of knowledge. Objects, knowledge sources, tasks and strategies are all hierarchically ordered levels pulled out of the conceptual models and intermediate knowledge bases. The final model of the conceptual model is a rich and highly organized formal model called an interpretation model.

Coding procedures are represented by logic-based methods and structures. It is not yet clear how much of the richness of the model of the conceptual model survives the transformation into the computer knowledge base. Other coding methods may be possible with the rich model of the conceptual model but have not, as yet, been described.

PROBLEM-SOLVING ONTOLOGIES

These are exemplified by *role-limiting methods* (McDermott, 1988) and *generic tasks* (Chandrasekaran, 1988), and reflect a somewhat different nature than most other methods in that they are highly structured and highly specific elicitation procedures based on a great deal of effort prior to elicitation. Both are based on the assumption that there exist repetitive processes of problem-solving used by the expert to complete a task; these methods concentrate first on identifying the repetitive roles of knowledge or those processes of knowledge use. The types of knowledge required are defined by the requirements of the processes.

Role-limiting methods strongly guide knowledge collection and encoding having a broad scope of applicability and providing help in specifying what knowledge needs to be collected to perform a particular task. A role-limiting method typically consists of a simple loop over a sequence of five to ten steps. For example, MOLE is a knowledge acquisition tool for generating expert systems that do heuristic classification. The method has the following control knowledge: determine the events that explain the symptoms; differentiate among several candidates by ruling out explanatory connections or candidate explanatory events, or by providing sufficient support for a candidate or reason for preferring some explanatory connections; get this information and apply it; at this stage, if new symptoms are revealed, go back and perform the sequence again.

Chandrasekaran is aiming to raise the level of knowledge structures from rule type systems to generic tasks which are problem-solving procedures for specific tasks. Elicitation is highly structured and specific in that an algorithm is defined for a problem and an automated elicitation mechanism is developed to structure the expert's verbalizations. If the problem-solving method is, for example, heuristic

classification within a diagnostic task, then certain types of knowledge such as symptoms, hypotheses, and differentiation information are requested of the expert. The conceptual model and the model of the conceptual model are identical in this method. Implementation methods are very specific due to the nature of the model of the conceptual model, and the computer knowledge bases which result are automatically built from the elicitation, analysis and implementation procedures.

IMPLICIT KNOWLEDGE STRUCTURES

These are used in linguistics, and one method resulting from this approach is Cognosys (Woodward, 1988) which is mainly used in domain organization to structure the domain in order to isolate and organize key areas of content. The expert provides a description statement of the overall domain and a list of general objectives which must be met in order to solve problems or make decisions successfully within the domain. He must then produce short paragraphs which are descriptive of the task required to meet each objective. These may be articles provided by the expert, such as case studies, text books or operating manuals. The knowledge engineer takes these and analyses the tasks into categories. He also completes the concept description categories and clarifies and elaborates such things as temporal relationships, event and state sequences, goal specification, cause-effect relationships, inferences, hierarchical relationships. It is important at this stage to clarify the domain boundaries with the expert and discuss specific problems in the domain. He may identify other sources of domain knowledge before he identifies knowledge acquisition methodologies and tools, report formats and inference processes. A general knowledge structure is then produced by the knowledge engineer from which goal structures, cause-effect structures, implicational structures and taxonomic structures are identified and isolated.

This linguistic-based method of knowledge acquisition is based on the theory of implicit knowledge structures which underlie general knowledge structures (Woodward, 1988). This method assumes that knowledge structures consist of discrete units which are linked and stored together in memory. When a word is chosen (in linguistic form), it is assumed that there exist a number of semantic meanings attached to the word. The word represents the tip of a meaning iceberg. This representation is not completely static but contains variable links which are partially sensitive to context. When words are chosen for textual material to describe, explain, or label symbolic entities, they can be used to identify the underlying or implicit knowledge structures.

This conceptual model is rich and requires further ordering but it is partially constrained by the objective-task breakdown. A variety of intermediate knowledge bases are possible. Lists of structural concepts (nouns) and functional concepts (verbs) result from the parsing of the textual material. Attributes describing each of the concepts are listed and more may be elicited. Contextual information about each concept can be stored.

The analysis procedures require the application of rules by the knowledge engineer who identifies noun-verb-noun phrases, assigns them a type and then links the phrases with a restricted set of arcs based on the meanings in the paragraphs (Woodward, 1988). These procedures follow directly from the theory of implicit structures and identify generic structures which define set-relations, goal-sequences, implications, cause-effect relationships and temporal sub-structures.

The set of sub-structures for each task and objective represents the model of the conceptual model. This formalized model then acts as the basis for semantic net, frame, or rule-based coding formalisms to generate a computer knowledge base.

### ENTITY-ATTRIBUTE GRIDS

These are derived from the repertory grids of personal construct theory (Kelly, 1955) which is one example of a modeling system that externalizes human processes. The personal construct theory model views the individual as an anticipatory system anticipating the future as a hypothesized replication of the past; constructs about the world change as a result of feedback about the predictions or actions on it. This is a systemic theory of human cognition based on the single primitive of a construct, or dichotomous distinction. Constructs are:

> transparent templets which [a person] creates and then attempts to fit over the realities of which the world is composed. (Kelly, 1955)

He proposes that all human activity can be seen as a process of anticipating the future by construing the replication of events:

> Constructs are used for predictions of things to come, and the world keeps rolling on and revealing these predictions to be either correct or misleading. This fact provides a basis for the revision of constructs and, eventually, of whole construct systems. (Kelly, 1955)

Hence his psychological model of the person is strongly epistemological and concerned with the way in which the person models his or her experience and uses this model to anticipate the future. The anticipation may be passive, as in prediction, or active, as in action. Kelly developed his theory in the context of clinical psychology and hence was concerned to have techniques which used it to by-pass cognitive defences and elicit the construct systems underlying behavior. This is precisely the problem of knowledge engineering.

A repertory grid (Shaw, 1980) is a two-way classification of data in which events are interlaced with abstractions in such a way as to express part of a person's system of cross-references between his personal observations or experience of the world (elements or entities), and his personal constructs or classifications of that experience (attributes). It is a way of representing personal constructs as a set of distinctions made about entities relevant to the problem domain. In the development of expert systems the entities might be key elements in the problem domain such as oil-well sites or business transactions, and the attributes express what the particular expert sees as the crucial distinctions between the entities in the context of the problem.

This psychologically-based method of knowledge acquisition assumes that the mental model is partially characterized by distinctions made about the target system by the expert and used to help make predictions about the world. Mental categories are present in which objects act as instances of those categories. These distinctions can be represented by bi-polar relationships and objects in the world can be distinguished on the basis of the bi-polar relationships.

The entity-attribute grid elicitation procedures follow very directly from the

assumptions. Within a given situational or contextual system, objects are elicited which have something to do with the context. Distinctions are elicited by offering triads of objects and asking why two of the objects are the same but different from the third. The distinctions are defined by bipolar descriptions and the remaining objects are ranked upon the bi-polar dimensions depending on the extent to which they are characterized by the distinctions at one or the other end of the dimension. An assumption made by the procedure is that all necessary objects and distinctions are elicited in this manner.

The result of this activity is a very clean conceptual model but one which is limited in linguistic terms. The grid does not capture all that occurs or all the background knowledge that is used when completing the elicitation exercise. If one were to tape record a session while a grid was elicited while the expert worked under thinking aloud instructions, a fuller conceptual model would be obtained which could include explanations for why choices were made, the decision-making verbalizations and the descriptions of the new understanding acquired by the expert. An intermediate knowledge base becomes available from the elicitation. Any grid which results is part of the conceptual model and may act as one possible intermediate knowledge base in that it reflects a partial ordering of the material in the complete conceptual model.

A variety of analyses for conceptual clustering, and visualization of the domain can be completed using the distance-based ratings in the grid (Shaw, 1980; Shaw & Gaines, 1986). These will aid the expert in reviewing and defining the domain structure in his conceptual model. At a more formal stage of analysis, classes, objects etc. can be produced using empirical induction.

### EMPIRICAL INDUCTION

This is basically a method that can be applied to obtain a set of rules (or equivalent) from a set of cases (Forsyth & Rada, 1986). It is necessary to have a training set of critical (or other—see Gaines, 1989) cases which encompass crucial and complete information. The cases are distinguished by a set of attributes, in a similar way to the repertory grid attributes. The decision of the expert in each of the cases is also needed and an induction algorithm such as ID3 (Quinlan, 1987). ID3, or Interactive Dichotomizer 3, works the best if the data is not corrupted by "noise". A subset of a certain size (window) is selected from the training set and and algorithm applied to derive a rule for this window. All exceptions to this rule are noted and the algorithm re-applied with these exceptions until none are found. When the whole set of rules are found they are formed into a decision tree.

Induce (Dietterich & Michalsky, 1981) is another induction algorithm based on earlier experience with a system called AQ11. A search technique is used to explore the set of examples and generalize very specific rules formed from an initial subset of the training set. There are many other induction systems, notable are Prism (Cendrowska, 1987) and Induct (Gaines, 1989). In general, the quality of the induced results depends on the quality of the initial training set which must be drawn up by an expert. The resulting rules are usually tested on a quite separate set of examples than the training set, and the final set of rules discussed with the expert (Hart, 1987).

Gaines (1989) reports a study of the tradeoff between expertise transfer and the number of cases required for induction. The results indicate that a mixture of correct rules, adequate rules, a critical set of cases described in terms of a set of relevant (or including some irrelevant) attributes, and even some incorrect decisions can produce the same minimal set of correct decision rules. In other words, the lack of a first class expert who can abstract overt knowledge from his model, and represent it clearly in an intermediate knowledge base can be offset by the analysis process which produces the computer knowledge base. There is scope for further exploration of this insight into the relationship between empirical induction and expertise transfer.

## Conclusion

In this paper we have identified one of the major problems in knowledge acquisition as the lack of an overall methodological framework which logically supports the process of knowledge acquisition, identifies the characteristics of the products of knowledge acquisition, and offers a set of ordered assumptions about the nature of knowledge and its characteristics. We have shown the modeling processes involved from the perspective of the expert trying to communicate his view of the target system and transfer it into computer implementable form. We have identified the distinct processes of elicitation, analysis and implementation, but have not gone beyond this stage of development of a knowledge-based system. Finally, we have identified the separate knowledge representations of the intermediate knowledge bases which can be used to help the expert review and refine his conceptual model, and the computer knowledge bases which may be unrecognizable by the expert as related to his developing models.

Many manual and automatic elicitation methods exist. Some are well-founded in basic underlying theories from established disciplines, but the majority are based on *ad hoc* methods that seem to work. What has to be established by the advocates of these various methods is an underlying justification, not only from another discipline, but also from a well-established and tested discipline such as psychology, linguistics, philosophy or systems theory. Any less well-established theories need, in turn, to be grounded in a basic discipline.

Shaw and Gaines (1987) list requirements for a computer-based knowledge support system which will support the expert in his or her endeavours to externalize problem-solving behaviors:

• The knowledge support system should be domain independent;
• The knowledge support system should be directly applicable by experts without intermediaries;
• The knowledge support system should be able to access a diversity of knowledge sources including text, interviews with experts, and observations of expert behaviour;
• The knowledge support system should be able to encompass a diversity of perspectives including partial or contradictory input from different experts;
• The knowledge support system should be able to encompass a diversity of forms of knowledge and relationships between knowledge;

• The knowledge support system should be able to **present knowledge** from a diversity of sources with clarity as to its derivation, **consequences and structural relations**;
• Users of the knowledge support system should be able to apply the knowledge in a variety of familiar domains and freely experiment with its implications;
• The knowledge support system should make provision for validation studies;
• As much of the operation of the knowledge support system as possible should be founded on well-developed and explicit theories of knowledge acquisition, elicitation and representation;
• As the overall knowledge support system develops it should converge to an integrated system.

These requirements provide a first checklist for developers, users and supporters of existing systems and techniques. In addition, we would include support of the analysis phase of knowledge acquisition in such a way that the conceptual model of the expert is preserved as much as possible, and the analysis results in knowledge representation schemes that can be adequately applied in computerized knowledge bases. The above requirements are a start in aiding people to assess more completely the validity or otherwise of assumptions made about the types of knowledge which is being elicited by the various tools and techniques. Clearly, they must be designed to support the expert as much as possible and to help him or her in preserving an existing series of models that lead to effective interaction with the target system.

Financial assistance for this work has been made available by the Natural Sciences and Engineering Research Council of Canada. We are grateful to many colleagues for discussions which have highlighted many of the issue raised in this paper, and in particular to Brian Gaines for his critical comments and stimulating discussions.

## References

ADDIS, T. (1989). The science of knowledge: a research program for knowledge engineering. *Proceedings of the Third European Workshop on Knowledge Acquisition for Knowledge-Based Systems (EKAW'89), Paris, France (June)*.
ANDERSON, J. R. (1983). *The Architecture of Cognition*. Cambridge, MA: Harvard University Press.
BAINBRIDGE, L. (1986). Asking questions and accessing knowledge. *Future Computing Systems*, **1**, 143–149.
BELKIN, N. J., BROOKS, H. M. & DANIELS, P. J. (1986). **Knowledge elicitation using discourse analysis** In J. H. BOOSE, & B. R. GAINES, Eds., *Proceedings of the First AAAI Knowledge Acquisition for Knowledge-Based Systems Workshop. Banff (November)* pp. 3-0-3-16.
BOOSE, J. H. & BRADSHAW, J. M. (1987). Expertise transfer and complex problems: using AQUINAS as a knowledge acquisition workbench for knowledge-based systems. *International Journal of Man–Machine Studies*, **26**, 3–28.
BRACHMAN, R. J. (1979). On the epistemological status of semantic networks. In N. V. FINDLER, Ed., *Associative Networks.*, New York: Academic Press.
BRESNAN, J. Ed. (1982). *The Mental Representation of Grammatical Relations*. Cambridge, MA: MIT Press.
BREUKER, J. & WIELINGA, B. (1987). Use of models in the interpretation of verbal data. A. KIDD, Ed, *Knowledge Elicitation for Expert Systems: A Practical Handbook*. New York: Plenum Press.

CENDROWSKA, J. (1987). An algorithm for inducing modular rules. *International Journal of Man–Machine Studies*, **27**, 349–370.

CHANDRASEKARAN, B. (1988). Generic tasks as building blocks for knowledge-based systems: the diagnosis and routine design examples. *The Knowledge Engineering Review*, **3**, 183–211.

CHOMSKY, N. (1975). *Logical Structure of Linguistic Theory*. New York: Plenum Press.

CHURCHMAN, C. W. (1971). *Design of Inquiring Systems*. New York: Basic Books.

CLANCEY, W. (1989). Viewing knowledge bases as qualitative models. *IEEE Expert*, **4**, 9–23.

COMPTON, P. & JANSEN, R. (1989). A philosophical basis for knowledge acquisition. *Proceedings of the Third European Workshop on Knowledge Acquisition for Knowledge-Based Systems (EKAW'89) Paris, France (June)*.

CRAIK, K. J. W. (1943). *The Nature of Explanation*. Cambridge: Cambridge University Press.

DIETTERICH, T. & MICHALSKY, R. (1981) Inductive learning of structural descriptions. *Artifical Intelligence*, **16**(3), 257–294.

ERICSSON, K. A. & SIMON, H. A. (1984). *Protocol Analysis: Verbal Reports as Data*. Cambridge, MA: MIT Press.

FODOR, J. A. (1980). *Representations*. Cambridge, MA: MIT press.

FORSYTH, R. & RADA, R. (1986). *Machine Learning Applications in Expert Systems and Information Retrieval*. Chichester: Ellis Horwood.

GAINES, B. R. (1987). Advanced expert system support environments. In J. H. BOOSE & J. GAINES, Eds., *Proceedings of the Second AAAI Knowledge Acquisition for Knowledge-Based Systems Workshop. Banff (October)*. pp. 8-0-8-14.

GAINES, B. R. (1989). An ounce of knowledge is worth a ton of data: quantitative studies of the trade-off between expertise and data based on statistically well-founded imperical induction. *Proceedings of 6th International Workshop on Machine Learning, San Mateo. California*: Morgan Kaufmann (June).

GAINES, B. R. & SHAW, M. L. G. (1987). Knowledge support systems. *ACM MCC-University Research Symposium*, pp. 47–66. Austin, Texas: MCC.

GAZDAR, G. (1981). On syntactic categories. *Philosophical Transactions of the Royal Society of London. Series B*, **295**, 267–83.

GENTNER, D. & GENTNER, A. L. (1983) Flowing waters or teeming crowds: mental models of electricity. In D. GENTNER & A. STEVENS, Eds., *Mental Models*. Hillsdale, NJ: Erlbaum.

GILHOOLY, K. J. (1987). Mental modelling; a framework for the study of thinking. In. D. N. PERKINS, J. LOCHHEAD & J. C. BISHOP, Eds., *Thinking: the Second International Conference*. Hillsdale, NJ: Erlbaum.

GRAESSER, A. C. & CLARK, L. F. (1985). *Structures and Procedures of Implicit Knowledge*. New Jersey: Ablex.

HARRISON, A. & BRAMSON, (1982). R. M. *Styles of Thinking*. New York: Doubleday.

HART, A. (1987). Role of induction in knowledge elicitation. In A. L. KIDD, Ed., *Knowledge Acquisition for Expert Systems: A practical handbook*. New York: Plenum.

HAYWARD, S. A., WIELINGA, B. J. & BREUKER, J. A. (1986). Structured analysis of knowledge. In J. H BOOSE & B. R. GAINES, Eds., *Proceedings of the First AAAI Knowledge Acquisition for Knowledge-Based Systems Workshop. Banff*. pp. 18-0-18-6.

HIRST, G. & REGOCZEI, S. (1989). On "extracting knowledge from text": modelling the architecture of language users. *Proceedings of the Third European Workshop on Knowledge Acquisition for Knowledge-Based Systems (EKAW'89) Paris, France (June)*.

JOHNSON, L & JOHNSON, N. E. (1987). Knowledge elicitation involving teachback interviewing. A. KIDD, Ed., *Knowledge Elicitation for Expert Systems: A Practical Handbook*. New York; Plenum Press.

JOHNSON, P. E. (1986). Cognitive models of expertise. *Symposium on Expert Systems and Auditor Judgment*. University of Southern California.

JOHNSON, P. E., ZUALKERNAN & GARBER, S. (1987). Specification of expertise: *International Journal of Man-Machine Studies*, **27**, 161–181.

JOHNSON-LAIRD, P. N. (1983). *Mental Models: Towards a Cognitive Science of Language, Inference and Consciousness*. Cambridge: Cambridge University Press.

KELLY, G. A. (1955). *The Psychology of Personal Constructs*. Norton: New York.

LAFRANCE, M. (1987). The knowledge acquisition grid: a method for training knowledge engineers. *International Journal of Man–Machine Studies*, **27**, 245–255.

McDERMOTT, J. (1988). Preliminary steps towards a taxonomy of problem solving methods. In S. MARCUS, Ed., *Automating Knowledge Acquisition for Expert Systems*. Boston: Kluwer.

McGRAW, K. L. & HARBISON-BRIGGS, K. (1989). *Knowledge Acquisition Principles and Guidelines*. New Jersey: Prentice Hall.

MINSKY, M. (1975). A framework for representing knowledge. In P. H. WINSTON, Ed., *The Psychology of Computer Vision*. McGraw Hill: New York.

NORMAN, D. A. (1983). Some observations on mental models. In D. GENTNER & A. STEVENS, Eds., *Mental Models*. Hillsdale, NJ: Erlbaum.

NYSTEDT, L. (1983). The situation: a constructivist approach. J. A. ADAMS-WEBBER & J. C. MANCUSO Eds., *Applications of Personal Construct Theory*. New York: Academic Press.

PAIVIO, A. U. (1977). Images, propositions and knowledge. In J. M. NICHOLAS, Ed., *Images, Perception and Knowledge*. Amsterdam: Reidel.

PASK, G. (1975). *Conversation, Cognition and Learning*. Amsterdam: Elsevier.

PYLYSHYN, Z. W. (1984). *Computation and Cognition*. Cambridge, MA.: MIT Press.

QUINLAN, J. R. (1987). Simplifying decision trees. *International Journal of Man–Machine Studies*, **27**, 221–234.

SCHANK, R. C. & ABELSON, R. (1977). *Scripts, Plans, Goals, and Understanding*. Hillsdale, NJ: Erlbaum.

SCHANK, R. C. (1982). Reminding and memory organization: an introduction to MOPs. In W. G. LEHNERT & M. H. RINGLE, Eds., *Strategies of Natural Language Comprehension*. Hillsdale, NJ: Erlbaum.

SHAW, M. L. G. (1980). *On Becoming a Personal Scientist*. London: Academic Press.

SHAW, M. L. G. & GAINES, B. R. (1986). Interactive elicitation of knowledge from experts. *Future Computing Systems*, **1**, 151–190.

SHAW, M. L. G. & GAINES, B. R. (1987). KITTEN: Knowledge Initiation and Transfer Tools for Experts and Novices. *International Journal of Man–Machine Studies*, **27**, 251–280.

SLOMAN, A. (1980). *The Computer Revolution in Philosophy*. Hemel Hempstead UK: Harvester.

TWINE, S. (1989). A model for the knowledge analysis process. *Proceedings of the Third European Workshop on Knowledge Acquisition for Knowledge-Based Systems (EKWA'89) Paris, France (June)*.

WELBANK, M. (1987). Knowledge acquisition update: Insight study #5. *Systems Designers*. Camberley, Surrey, UK: Pembroke Broadway.

WINSTON, P. H. (1984). *Artificial Intelligence*. (second edition). Reading: Prentice-Hall.

WOODWARD, B. (1988). Knowledge engineering at the front-end: defining the domain. J. H. BOOSE & B. R. GAINES, Eds., *Proceedings of the Third AAAI Knowledge Acquisition for Knowledge-Based Systems Workshop. Banff (November)*. pp. 37-1-37-25.

WOODWARD, B. (1989). Integrating task demands and problem-solving methods to develop useful taxonomies for knowledge acquisition. *Proceedings of the Third European Workshop on Knowledge Acquisition for Knowledge-Based Systems (EKAW'89) Paris, France (June)*.

# KADS: a modelling approach to knowledge engineering

B. J. Wielinga, A. Th. Schreiber and J. A. Breuker

*Department of Social Science Informatics, University of Amsterdam, Roetersstraat 15, NL-1018 WB Amsterdam, The Netherlands*

This paper discusses the KADs approach to knowledge engineering. In KADS, the development of a knowledge-based system (KBS) is viewed as a modelling activity. A KBS is not a container filled with knowledge extracted from an expert, but an operational model that exhibits some desired behaviour that can be observed in terms of real-world phenomena. Five basic principles underlying the KADS approach are discussed, namely (i) the introduction of partial models as a means to cope with the complexity of the knowledge engineering process, (ii) the KADS four-layer framework for modelling the required expertise, (iii) the re-usability of generic model components as templates supporting top-down knowledge acquisition, (iv) the process of differentiating simple models into more complex ones and (v) the importance of structure—preserving transformation of models of expertise into design and implementation. The actual activities that a knowledge engineer has to undertake are briefly discussed. We compare the KADS approach to related approaches and discuss experiences and future developments. The approach is illustrated throughout the paper with examples in the domain of troubleshooting audio equipment.

## 1. Introduction

This paper discusses results of a European research project commonly known as the KADS project (ESPRIT-I P1098). This project aimed at the development of a comprehensive, commercially viable methodology for knowledge-based system (KBS) construction. When the KADS project was conceived, in 1983, little interest in methodological issues existed in the AI community. The prevailing paradigm for building knowledge-based systems was rapid prototyping using special-purpose hard- and software, such as LISP machines, expert system shells etc. Since then, many organizations have become aware of the fact that KBS development from an organizational point of view does not differ much from the development of other types of information systems. Aspects of KBS development such as information analysis, application selection, project management, user requirement capture, modular design, re-usability etc, are similar to those encountered in conventional system development. Problems that frequently occur in conventional information system development projects are amplified in the case of KBS development. The wider capabilities of KBS technology allow more complex applications, which have a stronger impact on organizational structure than most conventional systems and often require a more sophisticated user–system interaction than is the case with conventional systems. Additionally, KBS development poses a number of problems of its own.

1042-8143/92/010005 + 49$03.00/0

© 1992 Academic Press Limited

An often-cited problem in KBS construction is the *knowledge acquisition bottleneck*. It turns out to be very difficult to extract the knowledge that an expert has about how to perform a certain task efficiently in such a way that the knowledge can be formalized in a computer system. The actual realization of a KBS often poses problems as well. The reasoning methods that are used in KBSs are not always fully understood. Although the AI literature abounds in methods and techniques for modelling reasoning processes, their description is not uniform and unambiguous. So, the need for a sound methodology for KBS development has become recognized over the last few years.

In this paper we will discuss the principles that comprise the framework on which the KADS methodology is founded and describe its main ingredients.

## 2. Views on knowledge acquisition

During the knowledge acquisition process the knowledge that a KBS needs in order to perform a task, is defined in such a way that a computer program can represent and adequately use that knowledge. Knowledge acquisition involves, in our view, at least the following activities: *eliciting* the knowledge in an informal—usually verbal—form, *interpreting* the elicited data using some conceptual framework, and *formalizing* the conceptualizations in such way that the program can use the knowledge. In this paper we will mainly focus on the interpretation and formalization activities in knowledge acquisition. Elicitation techniques have been the subject of a number of recent papers and their role in the knowledge acquisition process is now reasonably well-understood (Breuker & Wielinga, 1987; Neale, 1988; Diaper, 1989; Meyer & Booker, 1991).

Traditionally the knowledge acquisition process was viewed as a process of extracting knowledge from a human expert and transferring the extracted knowledge into the KBS. In practice this often means that the expert is asked what rules are applicable in a certain problem situation and the knowledge engineer translates the natural language formulation of these rules into the appropriate format. Several authors (Hayward, Wielinga & Breuker, 1987; Morik, 1989) have pointed out that this transfer-view of knowledge acquisition is only applicable in very few cases. The expert, the knowledge engineer and the KBS should share a common view on the problem solving process and a common vocabulary in order to make knowledge transfer a viable way of knowledge acquisition. If the expert looks at the problem or the domain in a way different from the knowledge engineer, asking for rules or similar knowledge structures and translating them into the knowledge representation language of the system does not work.

A different view of knowledge acquisition is that of a modelling activity. A KBS is not a container filled with knowledge extracted from an expert, but an operational model that exhibits some desired behaviour observed or specified in terms of real-world phenomena. The use of the models is a means of coping with the complexity of the development process.

Constructing a KBS is seen as building a computational model of desired behaviour. This behaviour can coincide with behaviour exhibited by an expert. If one wants to construct a KBS that performs medical diagnosis, the behaviour of a physician in asking questions and explaining the problem of a patient may be a good

starting point for a description of the intended problem-solving behaviour of the KBS. However, a KBS is hardly ever the functional and behavioural equivalent of an expert. There are a number of reasons for this. Firstly, the introduction of information technology often involves new distributions of functions and roles of agents. The KBS may perform functions which are not part of the experts repertory. Secondly, the underlying reasoning process of the expert cannot often be explained fully. Knowledge, principles and methods may be documented in a domain, but these are aimed at a human interpreter and are not descriptions of how to solve problems in a mechanical way. Thirdly, there is an inherent difference between the capabilities of machines and humans. For example, in an experiment in a domain of configuring moulds (Barthélemy, Frot & Simonin, 1988) a decision was made to generate all possible solutions instead of the small set generated by experts. The decision was guided by the fact that, for a machine, it presents no problem to store a large number of hypotheses in short-term memory, whereas for humans this is impossible.

So, in the modelling view, knowledge acquisition is essentially a constructive process in which the knowledge engineer can use all sorts of data about the behaviour of the expert, but in which the ultimate modelling decisions have to be made by the knowledge engineer in a constructive way. In this sense knowledge engineering is similar to other design tasks: the real world only provides certain constraints on what the artefact should provide in terms of functionality, the designer will have to aggregate the bits and pieces into a coherent system.

In this paper we will adopt the modelling perspective of knowledge acquisition. We discuss the principles that underlie the KADS approach to building knowledge-based systems, namely:

- (i) The introduction of multiple models as a means to cope with the complexity of the knowledge engineering process (Section 3).
- (ii) The KADS four-layer framework for modelling the required expertise (Section 4).
- (iii) The re-usability of generic model components as templates supporting top-down knowledge acquisition (Section 5).
- (iv) The process of differentiating simple models into more complex ones (Section 6).
- (v) The importance of structure-preserving transformation of models of expertise into design and implementation (Section 7).

Although a description of the use of KADS in practical KBS projects is outside the scope of this article, we look briefly at the actual knowledge engineering process (Section 8). We also compare the KADS approach to other approaches (Sections 10 and 11). Finally we discuss experiences and future developments (Sections 10 and 11).

The approach is illustrated throughout the paper with examples, most of them in the domain of diagnosing and correcting malfunctions of an audio system.

## 3. Principle 1: multiple models

The construction of a knowledge-based system is a complex process. It can be viewed as a search through a large space of knowledge-engineering methods, techniques and tools. Numerous choices have to be made with regard to elicitation, conceptualization and formalization. Knowledge engineers are thus faced with a jungle of possibilities and find it difficult to navigate through this space.

The idea behind the first principle of KADs is that the knowledge-engineering space of choices and tools can to some extent be controlled by the introduction of a number of *models*. A model reflects, through abstraction of detail, selected characteristics of the empirical system in the real world that it stands for (DeMarco, 1982). Each model emphasizes certain aspects of the system to be built and abstracts from others. Models provide a decomposition of knowledge-engineering tasks: while building one model, the knowledge engineer can temporarily neglect certain other aspects. The complexity of the knowledge-engineering process is thus reduced through a divide-and-conquer strategy.

In this section we discuss a number of models, namely (i) the organizational model, (ii) the application model, (iii) the task model, (iv) the model of cooperation, (v) the model of expertise, (vi) the conceptual model and (vii) the design model.

We use the term *knowledge engineering* in a broad sense to refer to the overall process of KBS construction (i.e. the construction of all these models and the artefact) and the term *knowledge acquisition* in a more restricted sense to refer to those parts of this construction process that are concerned with the information about the actual problem solving process. The scope of the present article is limited to the knowledge acquisition aspects. Other knowledge engineering aspects are only briefly addressed.

3.1. ORGANIZATIONAL MODEL, APPLICATION MODEL AND TASK MODEL

In KADS we distinguish three separate steps in defining the goals of KBS construction, namely, (i) defining the *problem* that the KBS should solve in the organization, (ii) defining the *function* of the system (which can be either humans or possibly other systems) and (iii) defining the actual *tasks* that the KBS will have to perform.

In this section we discuss three models that address parts of this three-step process. The first two are discussed briefly as these are outside the scope of this article.

*Organizational model*

An organizational model provides an analysis of the socio-organizational environment in which the KBS will have to function. It includes a description of the functions, tasks and bottlenecks *in the organization*. In addition, it describes (predicts) how the introduction of a KBS will influence the organization and the people working in it. This last activity can be viewed as a type of *technology assessment* (de Hoog, Sommer & Vogler, 1990)). We have found (de Hoog, 1989; van der Molen & Kruizinga, 1990) that it is dangerous to ignore the impact of the interaction between the construction of a KBS and the resulting changes in the organization. Neglecting this aspect may lead to realize that the system that is not accepted by its prospective users. It is also important to realize that the process of KBS construction itself can, by its nature (for instance, through extensive interviewing), change the organization in such a way that it becomes a "moving target" (van der Molen &

Kruizinga, 1990). The result may be that the final system is aimed at solving a problem that does not exist any more in the organization. We are convinced that the organizational viewpoint is important throughout the KBS construction process.

*Application model*

An application model defines what problem the system should solve in the organization and what the function of the system will be in this organization. For example, the daily operation and fault handling of an audio system can pose serious problems for people who are not familiar with or just not interested in more than the superficial ins-and-outs of such a system. A potential solution to this problem could be the development of a knowledge-based system. The function of this system would be to ensure that the owner of the audio system is supported in the process of correcting operational malfunctions of the audio system.

In addition to the *function* of the KBS and the *problem* that it is supposed to solve, the application model specifies the *external constraints* that are relevant to the development of the application. Examples of such constraints are the required speed and/or efficiency of the KBS and the use of particular hardware or software.

*Task model*

A task model specifies how the function of the system (as specified in the application model) is achieved through a number of tasks that the system will perform. Establishing this relation between function and task is not always as straightforward as it may seem. For example, consider a problem such as the medical care of patients with acute infections of the bloodstream. One approach to solve this problem is to perform the following tasks: (i) determine the identity of the organism that causes the infection and (ii) select, on the basis of that diagnosis, the optimal combination of drugs to administer to the patient. In real life hospital practice however, the recovery of the patient is the primary concern. So, if identification of the organism proves difficult, e.g. because no laboratory data are available, a therapy will be selected on other grounds. In fact, some doctors show little interest in the precise identity of the organism causing an infection as long as the therapy works. Stated in more general terms: given a goal that a system should achieve, there may be several alternative ways in which that goal can be achieved. Which alternative is appropriate in a given application depends on the characteristics of that application, on availability of knowledge and data and on requirements imposed by the user or by external factors.

With respect to the content of the task model, we distinguish three facets: (i) task decomposition, (ii) task distribution and (iii) task environment.

*Task decomposition.* A task is identified that would achieve the required functionality. This task is decomposed into sub-tasks. A technique such as *rational task analysis* is often used to achieve such a decomposition. We call the composite top-task a "real-life task", as it often represents the actual task that an expert solves in the application domain. The sub-tasks are the starting point for further exploration, such as the modelling of expertise and cooperation. A simple decomposition of a real-life task in the audio domain is shown in Figure 1.

Each separate task is described through an input/output specification, where the output represents the goal that is achieved with the task and the input is the

### 3.2. MODEL OF COOPERATION

The task model consists of a decomposition of the real-life task into a number of primitive tasks and a distribution of tasks over agents. The model of cooperation contains a specification of the functionality of those sub-tasks in the task model that require a cooperative effort. These tasks can for instance be data acquisition tasks activated during problem solving or various types of explanation tasks. Such tasks are called *transfer* tasks, as they involve transferring a piece of information from the system to an external agent or vice versa.

There is thus a clear dependency between the model of cooperation and the model of expertise. Some of the sub-tasks will be achieved by the system, others may be realized by the user. For example, in a diagnostic task in the audio example, the system may suggest certain tests to be performed by the user, while the user will actually perform the tests and will report the observed results back to the system. Alternatively, the user may want to volunteer a solution to the diagnostic problem while the system will criticize that solution by comparing it with its own solutions.

The result is a model of cooperative problem solving in which the user and the system together achieve a goal in a way that satisfies the various constraints posed by the task environment, the user and the state-of-the-art of KBS technology. The modelling of cooperation is outside the scope of this paper, but is discussed in more detail in de Greef and Breuker (1992, this issue), de Greef, Breuker and de Jong (1988a) and de Greef and Breuker (1989).

### 3.3. MODEL OF EXPERTISE

Building a model of expertise is a central activity in the process of KBS construction It distinguishes KBS development from conventional system development. Its goal is to specify the problem solving expertise required to perform the problems solving tasks assigned to the system.

One can take two different perspectives on modelling the expertise required from a system. A first perspective—one that is often taken in AI—is to focus on the computational techniques and the representational structures (e.g. rules, frames) that will provide the basis of the implemented system. A second perspective focuses on the behaviour that the system should display and on the types of knowledge that are involved in generating such behaviour, abstracting from the details of how the reasoning is actually realized in the implementation. These two perspectives correspond to the distinction Newell (1982) makes between respectively the *symbol level* and the *knowledge level.*

We take the second perspective and view the model of expertise as being a knowledge-level model. The model of expertise specifies the desired problem solving behaviour for a target KBS through an extensive categorization of the knowledge required to generate this behaviour. The model thus fulfills the role of a *functional specification* of the problem solving part of the artefact. As stated previously, it is not a cognitive model of the human expert. Although the construction of the model of expertise is usually guided by an analysis of expert behaviour, it is biased to what the target system should and can do.

In modelling expertise we abstract from those sub-tasks that specify some form of cooperation with the user. For example, in the audio domain we could identify two tasks that require such interactions: *performing a test* and *carrying out a*

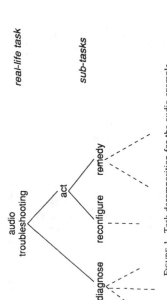

FIGURE 1. Task decomposition for the audio example.

information that is used in achieving this goal. What constitutes the goal of a task is not always self-evident. Even for a seemingly well-understood task such as diagnosis, it is not always clear what a diagnosis of a faulty system means. A diagnosis could be the identification of a subsystem (a component of an audio system) that malfunctions, or it could be a full causal model of how a malfunction came about. Similarly the result of a design task could be a detailed description of the structure of a system (e.g. a device for monitoring patients in an intensive care unit) or it could be a description of the functionality, structure and use of the device. *Task distribution.* The task distribution is the *assignment* of tasks to *agents.* Example agents are the KBS, the user or some other system. The last two agents are called *external* agents. Given the task decomposition the knowledge engineer has to decide what sub-tasks to assign to the system and what tasks to the user. These decisions constitute essentially cognitive engineering problems (Roth & Woods, 1989): they should be made on the basis of an analysis of the user requirements and expectations, the knowledge and skills that the user has and the potential capabilities and limitations of the system.

*Task environment.* The nature of the task-domain itself usually enforces a number of constraints on how the task can be performed. We call the constraints the *task environment.* For example, the task environment of a support system for handling malfunctions in an audio system could consist of the following constraints:

(i) The KBS is not a physical part of the audio system.
(ii) It has no sensors to make observations (and thus depends on the user to do this).
(iii) It has no robot arm to perform reconfigurations and/on repairs (and thus again depends on the user to do this).
(iv) The KBS users will be novices, who are not expected to be able to understand technical terms or to examine the interiors of the audio system.

The constraints posed by the task environment influence both the scope and the nature of the models of expertise and cooperation (see below).

The task model and its role in specifying system–user interaction is discussed in more detail in de Greef and Breuker (1992, this issue).

**Phenomena**                    **Models**

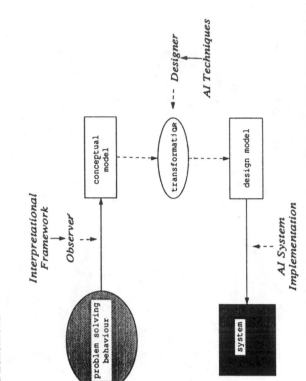

FIGURE 2. Role of the conceptual model and the design model in the knowledge acquisition process.

reconfiguration. In the model of expertise, such interaction or *transfer* tasks are specified more or less as a black box (see Section 4.3). The detailed study of the nature of these transfer tasks is the subject of the modelling of cooperation.

As the model of expertise plays a central role in KBS development, its details are discussed extensively in Section 4.

### 3.4. CONCEPTUAL MODEL = MODEL OF EXPERTISE + MODEL OF COOPERATION

Together, the model of expertise and the model of cooperation provide a specification of the behaviour of the artefact to be built. The model that results from merging these two models is similar to that is called a *conceptual model* in database development. Conceptual models are abstract descriptions of the objects and operations that a system should know about, formulated in such a way that they capture the intuitions that humans have of this behaviour. The language in which conceptual models are expressed is not the formal language of computational constructs and techniques, but is the language that relates real world phenomena to the cognitive framework of the observer. In this sense conceptual models are subjective, they are relative to the cognitive vocabulary and framework of the human observer. Within KADs we have adopted the term "conceptual model" to denote a combined, implementation-independent, model of both expertise and cooperation.

### 3.5. DESIGN MODEL

The description of the computational and representational techniques that the artefact should use to realize the specified behaviour is not part of the conceptual model. These techniques are specified as separate *design decisions* in a design model. In building a design model, the knowledge engineer takes external requirements such as speed, hardware and software into account. Although there are dependencies between conceptual model specifications on the one hand and design decisions on the other, in our experience building a conceptual model without having to worry about system requirements makes life easier for the knowledge engineer.

The separation between conceptual modelling on the one hand and a separate design step on the other has been identified as both the strength and the weakness of the KADS approach (Karbach, Linster & Voß, 1990).

The main advantage lies in the fact that the knowledge engineer is not biased during conceptual modelling by the restrictions of a computational framework. KADs provides a more-or-less universal framework for modelling expertise (see the next section) and although computational constraints play a role in the construction of such models (cf. Section 6) experience† has shown that this separation enables knowledge engineers to come up with more comprehensive specifications of the desired behaviour of the artefact. The disadvantage lies in the fact that the knowledge engineer, after having built a conceptual model, is still faced with the problem of how to implement this specification. In Section 7 we discuss some principles that can guide the knowledge engineer in this design process.

Figure 2 summarizes the different roles which the conceptual model and the design model play in the knowledge engineering process. An observer (knowledge

† See Section 10 for an overview of applications developed with the KADS approach.

engineer) constructs a conceptual, knowledge-level, model of the artefact by abstracting from the behaviour of experts. This abstraction process is aided by the use of an interpretational framework, such as generic models of classes of tasks or task-domains. The conceptual model is real-world oriented in the sense that, it is phrased in real-world terminology and can thus be used as a communication vehicle between knowledge engineer and expert. The conceptual model does not take detailed constraints, with regard to the artefact, into account. The desing model, on the other hand, is a model that is phrased in the terminology of the artefact: it describes how the conceptual model is realized with particular computational and representational techniques.

Figure 3 shows the dependencies between the models discussed in this section. Connections indicate that information from one model is used in the construction of another model. The actual activities in the construction process do not necessarily have to follow the direction from organization model to system. In fact, several life-cycle models have been developed, each defining various phases and activities in building these models. The first life-cycle model developed in KADS (Barthélemy, Edin, Toutain & Becker, 1987) was of the water-fall type. At the end of the KADS project, a new life-cycle was defined (Taylor *et al.*, 1989) based on the concept of a spiral model (Boehm, 1988).

The nature of knowledge engineering thus becomes a process that bridges the gap between required behaviour and a system that exhibits that behaviour through the

for modelling expertise is outlined. Slightly different versions of this KADS approach to modelling expertise (usually called the "four-layer model") have been presented in Wielinga and Breuker (1986), Hayward et al. (1987), Schreiber et al. (1988) and in Breuker and Wielinga (1989).

Two basic premises underly the ideas presented here. First, we assume that it is possible and useful to distinguish between several generic types of knowledge according to different *roles* that knowledge can play in reasoning processes. Second, we assume that these types of knowledge can be organized into several *layers*, which have only limited interaction. A first distinction that is often made is the distinction between *domain knowledge* and *control knowledge*. Here we will take such a separation of knowledge in two layers one step further, and will argue for a refined distinction of different types of control knowledge at three levels.

The categories in which the expertise knowledge can be analysed and described are based or epistemological distinctions: they contain different types of knowledge. We distinguish between, (i) static knowledge describing a declarative *theory* of the application domain (domain knowledge), (ii) knowledge of different *types of inferences* that can be made in this theory (first type of control knowledge), (iii) knowledge representing *elementary tasks* (second type of control knowledge) and (iv) *strategic knowledge* (third type of control knowledge).

Each of these categories of knowledge is described at a separate level. The separation reflects different ways in which the knowledge can be viewed and used. In the following sections each of the four categories of knowledge distinguished in KADS is discussed in more detail.

The distinction between different types of knowledge is not new. Several authors have reported ideas which pertain to the separation of domain and control knowledge, and have proposed ways to increase the flexibility of control in expert systems. The work of Davis (1980) introduced explicit control knowledge as a means of controlling inference processes in a flexible way. In the NEOMYCIN system (Clancey, 1985a) different functions of knowledge are explicated by separating domain knowledge and control knowledge and by introducing an explicit description of the strategies that the system uses. Pople (1982) has stressed the problem of the right task formulation. He considers it to be a fundamental challenge for AI research to model the control aspects of the reasoning process of expert diagnosticians which determines the optimal configuration of tasks to perform in order to solve a problem.

### 4.1. DOMAIN KNOWLEDGE

The domain knowledge embodies the *conceptualization* of a domain for a particular application in the form of a *domain theory*. The primitives that we use to describe a domain theory are based on the epistemological primitives proposed by Brachman and Schmolze (1985): concepts, properties, two types of relations and structures.

#### Concept

*Concepts* are the central objects in the domain knowledge. A concept is identified through its name (e.g. amplifier).

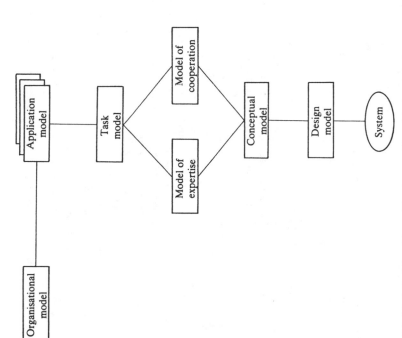

FIGURE 3. Principle 1: Partial models provide a decomposition of the knowledge-engineering task.

creation of a set of models. Summarizing, we can say that the KADS modelling view of knowledge engineering gives rise to a methodology that involves the construction of a variety of models in the course of the knowledge engineering process. Each model represents a particular view on the KBS. They allow the knowledge engineer to cope with the complexity of the knowledge engineering process through a "divide-and-conquer" strategy.

The remainder of this article focuses mainly on the model of expertise, as it plays such a central role in KBS development.

## 4. Principle 2: modelling expertise

The major challenge for any modelling approach to KBS construction is to find an adequate answer to the question of how to model expertise. It is this aspect of the system that distinguishes KBS development from the development of conventional systems. As discussed previously, we require, of the resulting model of expertise, that it is independent of a particular implementation. In this section a framework

TABLE 1

*A domain schema for diagnosing faults in an audio-system*

| Primitive | Name | Description |
|---|---|---|
| Concept | component | The elements of the audio system |
| Relation between concepts | component IS-A component | Sub-type hierarchy of components of the audio system |
| Relation between concepts | component SUB-COMPONENT-OF component | Part-of hierarchy of components of the audio system |
| Property | component:state-value | Components have properties describing the state that components are in at some moment in time. |
| Relation between expressions | component:state-value CAUSES component:state-value | Causal relations that specify how normal state-values of components are causally related to each other. |
| Concept | test | Test that can be performed to establish a state of an audio system. |
| Property | test:value | Possible outcomes of a test. |
| Relation between expressions | test:value INDICATES component:state-value | A relation describing which internal state is indicated by a particular test outcome. |

*Property/value*

Concepts can have *properties*. Properties are defined through their name and a description of the values that the property can take. For example, amplifier has a property power with as possible values on/off.

*Relation between concepts*

A first type of relation is the relation between concepts, for example amplifier is-a component. The most common relations of this type are the sub-class relation and the part-of relation. Several variants of these two relations exist, each with its own semantics.

*Relation between property expressions*

A second type of relation is the relation between expressions about property values. An expression is a statement about the value(s) of a property of a concept, e.g. amplifier:power=on.† Examples of this type of relation are causal relations and time relations. An example of a causal relation in the audio domain could be:

```
amplifier:power-button=pressed CAUSES amplifier:power=on
```

*Structure*

A structure is used to represent a complex object: an object consisting of a number of objects/concepts and relations. For example, the audio system as a whole can be viewed as a structure, consisting of several components and relations (part-of, wire connections) between these components.‡

The choice of this set of primitives is, in a sense, arbitrary and probably somewhat biased by the types of problems that have been tackled with KADS. The problem is to find a subset that provides the knowledge-engineer with sufficient expressive power. One could consider including additional special-purpose primitives such as mathematical formulae. There is clearly a link here with research in the field of semantic database modelling (see, for an overview, Hull & King, 1987).

The primitives are used to specify what we call a *domain schema* for a particular application. A domain schema is a description of the *structure* of the statements in the domain theory. It is roughly comparable to the notion of a signature in logic.§ For example, in a domain schema we could specify that the domain theory contains part-of relations between component concepts without worrying about the actual tuples of this relation. We prefer to use the term "schema" rather than "ontology" to stress the fact that the domain theory is the product of knowledge engineering and thus, does not necessarily describe an inherent structure in the domain (as the word "ontology" would suggest).

The domain schema specifies the main decisions that the knowledge engineer makes with respect to the *conceptualization* (Genesereth & Nilsson, 1987; Nilsson,

† We use the shorthand ⟨concept⟩:⟨property⟩ for "the ⟨property⟩ of ⟨concept⟩".

‡ The term "structure" as used here should not be confused with the "structural descriptions" in KL-ONE.

§ The relation between property expressions corresponds to an axiom schema; structures correspond to a sub-theory.

1991) of the domain. For example, when a domain schema for a diagnostic domain is constructed, a decision has to be made whether "correct" or "fault" models (or both) are part of the domain theory. Parts of a domain schema often re-appear in similar domains and could be re-used (see Section 5 for a more detailed discussion of re-usability). The domain schema also provides convenient handles for describing the way in which inference knowledge uses the domain theory. Issues related to the interaction between domain knowledge and inference knowledge are discussed in the next section.

An example domain schema of a simple domain theory for diagnosing faults in an audio system is shown in Table 1.† Two types of concepts appear in this theory: *components* and *tests*. Both components and tests can have properties: respectively a *state-value* and a *value*. Two relations are defined between concepts of type "component": *is-a* and *sub-component-of*. In addition, two relations between property expressions are defined: (i) a *causal* relation between state values of components, and (ii) an *indicates* relations between test values and state values. Figure 4 shows some domain knowledge in the audio domain. The domain

† The description of the domain schema given here is rather informal. For example, nothing is said about cardinality (e.g. can a property have one or more values at some point in time). Techniques exist for describing these schemata in a more precise and formal way, e.g. (Davis & Bonnel, 1990; Hull & King, 1987).

knowledge description follows the structure defined in the domain schema of Table 1.

Domain knowledge can be viewed as a declarative theory of the domain. In fact, adding a simple deductive capability would enable a system, in theory (but, given the limitations of theorem-proving techniques, not in practice), to solve all problems solvable by the system. The domain knowledge is considered to be relatively task-neutral, i.e. represented in a form that is independent of its use by particular problem solving actions. There is ample evidence (Wielinga & Bredeweg, 1988) showing that experts are able to use their domain knowledge in a variety of ways, e.g. for problem solving, explanation, teaching etc. Separating domain knowledge embodying the theory of the domain from its use in a problem solving process, is a first step towards flexible use and re-usability of domain knowledge.

### 4.2. INFERENCE KNOWLEDGE

At the first layer of control knowledge, we abstract from the domain theory and describe the inferences that we want to make in this theory. We call this layer the *inference layer*. An inference specified at the inference level is assumed to be *primitive* in the sense that it is fully defined through its name, an input/output specification and a reference to the domain knowledge that it uses. The actual way in which the inference is carried out is assumed to be irrelevant for the purposes of modelling expertise. From the viewpoint of the model of expertise no control can be exercised of the internal behaviour of the inference. One could look upon the inference as applying a simple theorem prover.

Note that the inference is only assumed to be primitive with respect to the model of expertise. It is very well possible that such a primitive inference is realized in the actual system through a complex computational technique.

In the KADS model of expertise we use the following terms to denote the various aspects of a primitive inference.

### Knowledge source

The entity that carries out an action in a primitive inference step is called a *knowledge source*.[†] A knowledge source performs an action that operates on some input data and has the capability of producing a new piece of information ("knowledge") as its output. During this process it uses domain knowledge. The name of the knowledge source is supposed to be indicative of the type of action that it carries out.

### Meta-class

A knowledge source operates on data elements and produces a new data element. We describe those elements as *meta-classes*. A *meta-class* description serves a dual purpose, (i) it acts as a *placeholder* for domain objects, describing the *role* that these objects play in the problem solving process, and (ii) it points to the *type(s)* of the domain objects that can play this role.

Domain objects can be linked to more than one meta-class. For example, a

[†] The term "knowledge source" was inspired by Clancey's (1983) use of this term as a process that generates an elementary piece of information. Its intended meaning corresponds only roughly to the meaning of the term in blackboard architectures.

| is-a | Properties of components: | | causes | deck:power = on and<br>deck:function = play and<br>cable-connection:deck amplifier = present<br>   causes<br>amplifier:input-signal = deck |
|---|---|---|---|---|
| component<br> <br>audio tape speaker left ....<br>system deck system speaker | deck:function   (stop, play, rew, ff, pause)<br>deck:power   (on, off)<br>amplifier:power   (on, off)<br>amplifier:input-signal   (deck, tuner, CD, ...)<br>.... | | | amplifier:input-signal = deck<br>amplifier:input-selection = deck<br>   causes<br>amplifier:output-signal = deck<br>...... |
| sub-component-of<br> <br>audio system<br> <br>speaker     tape<br>system amplifier deck<br> <br>left  / \<br>speaker ..... | Properties of tests:<br> <br>deck-power-switch:   (pressed, not pressed)<br>input-selector   (deck, tuner, CD, ...)<br>.... | | indicates | deck-power-switch = pressed<br>indicates<br>deck-power = on<br> <br>input-selector = X<br>   indicates<br>amplifier:input-selection = X<br>...... |

FIGURE 4. Domain knowledge of the audio system using the schema described in Table 1.

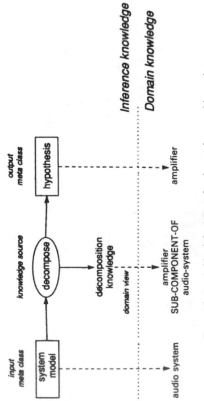

FIGURE 5. A primitive inference performing an decomposition action.

particular component of an audio system could play the role of a *hypothesis* at one point in time and the role of *solution* at some other instant. The name "meta-class" is inspired by the fact that it provides a "meta" description of objects in a domain "class".† An input data element of a knowledge source is referred to as an *input* meta-class; the output as an *output* metaclass. Each meta-class can be the input and/or output of more than one knowledge source.

*Domain view*

The *domain view* specifies how particular parts of the domain theory can be used as a "body of knowledge" by the knowledge source.

Figure 5 describes a primitive inference in the audio domain with example references to domain knowledge. At the inference level a *decomposition* inference is specified. The action that is performed in this inference is the decomposition of a composite model of the audio system into sub-models. *System model* and *hypothesis* are examples of meta-classes. They describe the role that domain objects like audio-system and amplifier can play in the problem solving process. The *decompose* knowledge source achieves its goal, the generation of a new hypothesis, through the application of decomposition knowledge. The domain view of this inference specifies that tuples of the SUB-COMPONENT-OF relation in the domain theory can be used as decomposition knowledge. Figure 5 shows one applicable tupel of this relation.

A somewhat more formal specification of the *decompose* inference is given below. The arrow specifies how inference knowledge maps on to domain knowledge.

**knowledge-source** *decompose*
**input-meta-class:**
    system-model → component
**output-meta-class:**
    hypothesis → component

**domain-view:**
```
decomposition(system-model, hypothesis) →
sub-component-of(component, component)
```

Note that this specification only refers to elements of the schema of the domain theory. Both *system model* and *hypothesis* are place holders of objects of type "component" and describe the role these objects play in the inference process. In this particular example the domain view refers to just one type of knowledge in the domain theory, namely the SUB-COMPONENT-OF relation. In principle, however, there could be several of these mappings.†

There are distinct advantages in separating the domain theory from the way it is viewed and used by the inferences:

(i) The separation allows multiple use of essentially the same domain knowledge. Imagine for example a knowledge source *aggregate*, that takes as input a set of components and aggregates them into one composite component. This knowledge source could use the same SUB-COMPONENT-OF relation, but *view* it differently, namely as aggregation knowledge. Such an inference could very well occur in a system that performs configurations of audio systems.

(ii) Domain knowledge that is used in more than one inference is specified only once. In this way, knowledge redundancy is prevented.

(iii) It provides a dual way to *name*‡ domain knowledge: both use-independent and use-specific. Knowledge engineers tend to give domain knowledge elements names that already reflect their intended use in inferencing and keep changing the names when their usage changes. We would argue that both types of names can be useful and should be known to the system—for example, for explanation purposes.

(iv) The scope of the domain theory is often broader than what is required for problem solving. For example, explanatory tasks (in KADS defined in the model of cooperation) often require deeper knowledge than is used during the reasoning process itself.

This is not to say that we claim that a domain theory can in general be defined completely independent of its use in the problem solving process. The scope and the structure of the domain knowledge has to meet the requirements posed by the total set of inferences. In many applications there are interactions between the process of conceptualizing a domain and specifying the problem solving process. We are convinced, however, that it is useful to *document* them at least separately.

As stated previously, the primitive inference steps form the building blocks for an application problem solver. They define the basic inference actions that the system can perform and the roles the domain objects can play. The combined set of primitive inferences specifies the basic inference capability of the target system. The set of inference steps can be represented graphically in an *inference structure*. The

---

† It should not be confused with the meaning of this term in object-oriented systems.

† We omit here the details of specifying the mapping between a domain view and a domain theory. See for a more detailed discussion, Schreiber *et al.* (1989b).

‡ We would argue that the whole activity of knowledge acquisition is in fact, for a large part, a matter of giving (meaningful) names.

(iv) A selection of an observable, for which a value is to be obtained (the *finding*).

(v) A comparison of the observed *finding* and the predicted *norm*.

The inference structure defines the vocabulary and dependencies for control,† but *not* the control itself. This latter type of knowledge is specified as task knowledge.

### 4.3. TASK KNOWLEDGE

The third category contains knowledge about how elementary inferences can be combined to achieve a certain goal. The prime knowledge type in this category is the *task*. Tasks can achieve a particular *goal*. The relations between tasks and goals are in principle many-to-many. Task knowledge is usually characterized by a vocabulary of control terms; for instance, indicating that a finding has been processed or a hypothesis has been verified.

Tasks represent fixed strategies for achieving problem solving goals. Several researchers (Clancey, 1985a; Gruber, 1989) have pointed out that task knowledge is an important element of expertise. The competence model of the diagnostic strategy of NEOMYCIN (Clancey, 1985a) is an example of what we call task knowledge. Clancey describes the sub-tasks of this strategy via meta-rules. The main difference between his approach and our approach is that he refers directly in these meta-rules to the domain knowledge. In KADS, tasks only refer to inferences and not explicitly to domain knowledge.

We use the following constructs to describe task knowledge:

*Task*

A task is a composite problem solving action. It implies a decomposition into sub-tasks. The application of the task to a particular (sub-)problem results in the achievement of a goal.

*Control terms*

The vocabulary used. A control term is nothing more than a convenient label for a set of meta-class elements. The label represents a term used in the control of problem solving, e.g. "differential" or "focus". Each control term is defined through the specification of a mapping of this term on to sets of meta-class elements (e.g. the differential is the set of all active hypotheses).

*Task structure*

A decomposition into sub-tasks and a specification of the control dependencies between these sub-tasks.‡ The decomposition can involve three types of sub-tasks: (i) composite problem solving tasks: inferences specified in the inference layer, (ii) primitive problem solving tasks: a task specified in the task layer. (In principle, this could be a recursive invocation of the same task.) and (iii) transfer tasks: tasks that require interaction with an external agent, usually the user.

† We use the term *control* here to refer to the process of controlling the execution of knowledge sources. We are not referring to more detailed, symbol-level forms of control such as search control in the application of a computational technique. See Schreiber, Akkermans & Wielinga (1991) for a more elaborate discussion on these different types of control.

‡ We agree with Steels (1990) that "control structure" is a more appropriate term for this type of structure. The term "task structure" is used here mainly for historical reasons.

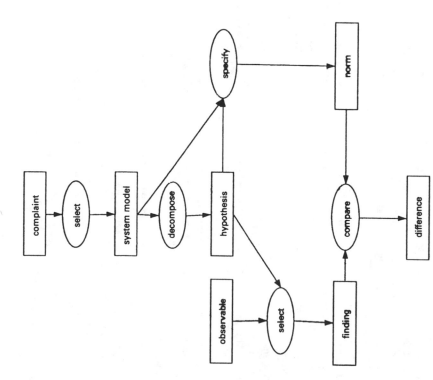

FIGURE 6. An inference structure for diagnosing faults in an audio system.

inference structure thus specifies the problem solving *competence* of the target system.

Figure 6 presents such an inference structure for the audio domain. The inferences specify a top-down and systematic approach to find a sub-model of the audio system that behaves inconsistently. The following inferences appear in the inference structure:

(i) A selection of a (sub-part) of the audio system (*system model*) on the basis of a *complaint*.

(ii) A decomposition of some part of the system into a number of sub-components that play the role of *hypothesis*.

(iii) A prediction of a *norm*-value for a hypothesis. The norm is a value of a test that is consistent with the normal state of the hypothesis.

The dependencies between the sub-tasks are described as a structured-English procedure such as used in conventional software engineering (DeMarco, 1978), with selection and iteration operators.

The conditions in these procedures always refer to control terms and/or meta-class elements, e.g. "**If** *the differential is not empty* **then**...".

There is interaction between the task knowledge in the model of expertise on the one hand and the model of cooperation on the other, with respect to the specification of the transfer tasks. Transfer tasks are more-or-less specified as a black box in the model of expertise (for more details, see de Greef & Breuker, 1992, this issue): (i) *obtain*: the system requests a piece of information from an external agent. (The system has the initiative.), (ii) *present*: the system presents a piece of information to an external agent. (The system has the initiative.), (iii) *receive*: the system gets a piece of information from external agent. (The external agent has the initiative.) and (iv) *provide*: the system provides an external agent with a piece of information. The external agent has the initiative.

An example task-knowledge specification for our audio domain is shown below. It consists of three tasks. The first task is *systematic-diagnosis*. The goal of this task is to find a sub-system with inconsistent behaviour at the lowest level of aggregation. The task works under the single-fault assumption. On the basis of a complaint, an applicable system model is selected. This selection task corresponds to the knowledge source *select* specified in the inference layer. Subsequently, hypotheses in the differential are generated through the *generate-hypotheses* sub-task. In the sub-task *test-hypotheses* these hypotheses are then tested to find an inconsistent sub-system. This hypothesis then becomes the focus for further exploration. The generate-and-test process is repeated, until no new hypotheses are generated (i.e. the differential is empty).

```
task systematic-diagnosis
goal
    find the smallest component with inconsistent behaviour,
    if one.
control-terms
    differential=set of currently active hypotheses
    inconsistent-sub-system=sub-part of the system with
        inconsistent behaviour
task-structure
systematic-diagnosis(complaint→inconsistent-sub-
    system)=
    select(complaint→system-model)
    generate-hypotheses(system-model→differential)
    REPEAT
        test-hypotheses(differential→inconsistent-sub-
            system)
        generate-hypotheses(inconsistent-sub-system→
            differential)
    UNTIL differential=∅
```

For readability purposes, the names of knowledge sources are italicized in the task structure. The arrows in the task structure describe the relation between input and output of the sub-task. Note that all arguments of tasks and conditions are either explicitly declared control terms (*differential*) or meta-class names.

The task *generate-hypotheses* is a very simple task. It just executes the *decompose* knowledge source.

```
task generate-hypotheses
goal
    generate new set of hypotheses through decomposition
control-terms-
task-structure
    generate(system-model→differential)=
    decompose(system-model→differential)
```

The task *test-hypotheses* tests the hypotheses in the differential sequentially until an inconsistency is found (*difference = true*). Testing is done through a kind of experimental validation: a norm value is predicted and this value is compared with what is actually observed. *Obtain(observable, finding)* is an example of a transfer task, that starts an iteration with the user to obtain a test value. How the transfer task is carried out, should be specified in the model of cooperation.

```
task test-hypotheses
goal
    test whether a hypothesis in the differential behaves
        inconsistently
control-terms-
task-structure
    test(differential→hypothesis)=
    DO FOR EACH hypothesis∈differential
        specify(hypothesis→norm)
        select(hypothesis→observable)
        obtain(observable→finding)
        compare(norm+finding→difference)
    UNTIL difference=true
```

If one abstracts from the control relations between sub-tasks and assumes a fixed task decomposition, the set of task structures can be represented graphically as a tree. The tree for systematic diagnosis is shown in Figure 7. Such a decomposition of a task assigned to the system is in fact a further refinement of the decomposition specified in the task model (see Section 3).

## 4.4. STRATEGIC KNOWLEDGE

The fourth category of knowledge is the *strategic knowledge*.† Strategic knowledge determines what goals are relevant to solve a particular problem. How each goal is achieved is determined by the task knowledge. Strategic knowledge will also have to deal with situations where the afore-mentioned knowledge categories fail to produce

† Gruber (1989) uses the term "strategic knowledge" in a different way. His strategic knowledge is, in many aspects, similar to the task knowledge in KADS.

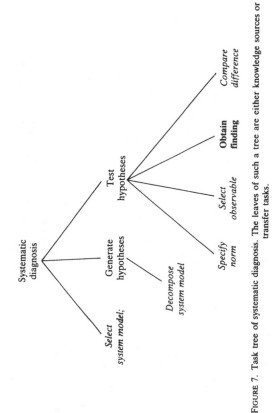

FIGURE 7. Task tree of systematic diagnosis. The leaves of such a tree are either knowledge sources or transfer tasks.

| knowledge category | | organisation | knowledge types |
|---|---|---|---|
| strategic | *controls* | strategies | plans / meta rules |
| task | *applies* | tasks | goals / control terms / task structures |
| inference | *uses* | inference structure | knowledge source / meta class / domain view |
| domain | | domain theory | concept / property / relations |

FIGURE 8. Synopsis of the KADS Four-Layer Model.

a partial solution. For example, the problem-solving process may reach an impasse because information is not available or because contradictory information arises. In such cases the strategic reasoning should suggest new lines of approach or attempt to introduce new information, e.g. through assumptions (cf. Jansweijer, 1988; Jansweijer, Elshout & Wielinga, 1989).

Strategic knowledge concerns, among other things, the dynamic planning of task execution. However, most systems developed with the KADS approach used only fixed task decompositions and had little or no strategic knowledge. In our opinion, this does not mean that strategic knowledge is unimportant or superfluous. When knowledge engineers have to construct more complex and flexible knowledge-based systems than presently is usually the case, we think a much more detailed exploration of strategic knowledge will be necessary. We have recently started to work on an ESPRIT project named REFLECT where the central topic is the exploration of strategic knowledge. Apart from dynamic planning, strategic knowledge can also enable a system to answer questions such as "Can I solve this problem?" (Voß et al., 1990). For the moment, however, the study of the nature of strategic knowledge remains mainly a research topic.

### 4.5. SYNOPSIS OF THE MODEL OF EXPERTISE

The four knowledge categories (domain, inference, task and strategic knowledge) can be viewed as four levels with meta-like relations in the sense that each successive level interprets the description at the lower level. In Figure 8 these four levels and their interrelations are summarized.

The four-layer framework is a structured but informal framework. This means that the specifications are sometimes not as precise as one might want them to be and thus may be interpreted in more than one way. This has led to research aimed at defining a formal framework for representing models of expertise (van Harmelen

& Balder, 1992, this issue; Wetter, 1990). The price paid for a greater amount of precision in formal specifications is, however, a reduction in conceptual clarity. In our view, there is a place for both informal and formal representations in the knowledge engineering process. The use of both informal and formal model representations is a major topic of research in the KADS-II project.

The four-layer framework for knowledge modelling has been successfully used as a basis for structured acquisition and description of knowledge at an intermediate level between the expertise data obtained from experts, test books etc. and the knowledge representation in an implemented system (de Greef & Breuker, 1985). From a knowledge-level viewpoint, the present four-layer model captures knowledge categories that are quite similar to those encountered in other models in the literature. However, differences in opinion exist about where to situate particular types of knowledge. This point will be discussed in more detail in Section 9.

## 5. Principle 3: re-usable model elements

There are several ways in which models of expertise can be used to support the knowledge acquisition process. A potentially powerful approach is to *re-use* (structures of) model elements. When one models a particular application, it is usually already intuitively clear that large parts of the model are not specific for this application, but re-occur in other domains and/or tasks. KADS (as do most other approaches to knowledge modelling) makes use of this observation by providing a knowledge engineer with predefined sets of model elements. These libraries can be of great help to the knowledge engineer. They provide the engineer with ready-made building blocks and prevent him/her from "re-inventing the wheel" each time a new system has to be built. In fact, we believe that these libraries are a *conditio sine qua non* for improving the state-of-the-art in knowledge engineering.

In this section, two ways of re-using elements of the model of expertise are discussed: (i) *typologies* of primitive inference actions (knowledge sources) and (ii) *interpretation models*. In principle, however, the re-usability principle holds for all models in the KBS construction process.

## 5.1. TYPOLOGIES OF KNOWLEDGE SOURCES

In Breuker *et al.* (1987) we have defined a tentative typology of primitive problem solving actions (knowledge sources) which has been the basis of a considerable amount of models. The typology is based on the possible operations one can perform on the epistemological primitives defined in KL-ONE (Brachman & Schmolze, 1985). This set of primitives consists of: concept, attribute (of concept), value (of attribute), instance (of concept), set (of concepts) and structure (of concepts).

In the typology of inferences we view these primitives not as data-structures but as epistemological categories. Their actual representation in a system may be quite different (e.g. in terms of logical predicates rather than KL-ONE like constructs).

Table 2 gives an overview of the typology of knowledge sources used in KADS. The inferences are grouped on the basis of the type of operation that is carried out by the knowledge source: *generate concept/instance, change concept, differentiate values/structures* and *manipulate structures*. A detailed description of the inferences mentioned in Table 2 is given in Breuker and Wielinga (1989).

Although this typology has been a useful aid in many analyses of expertise, it has a number of important limitations:

(i) The selected set in Table 2 is in a sense arbitrary. For example, we could have added other operations on sets such as *join, union* or *merge.*

(ii) The ontology on which the typology is based is of a very general nature and hence weak. The operations are defined more or less independent of tasks and/or domains. Often, it is difficult for the knowledge engineer to identify how an inference in a particular application task must be interpreted.

(iii) A more serious limitation is that some inferences cannot be adequately classified because they require another ontological framework. For example, operations on causal relations such as abduction and differentiation cannot be represented in a natural way.

We consider the study of more adequate taxonomies of inferences to be a major research issue. Potentially, taxonomies are very powerful aids for the knowledge engineer. In a new research project (KADS-II) we are exploring the possibility of describing taxonomies that are specific for classes of application domains such as technical diagnosis. These taxonomies will be based on a much more task-specific ontology.

It is interesting to see that, from a different angle, the "Firefighter" project (Klinker *et al.*, 1991) is aiming at similar results. An important goal of this project is to look at what they call *mechanisms* that are used in various applications, detect commonalities between these mechanisms and construct a library of mechanisms that can be re-used in other applications. These mechanisms appear to have the same grain size as the knowledge sources in KADS. The main difference is that mechanisms have a computational flavour.

## 5.2. INTERPRETATION MODELS

Typologies of elements of a model of expertise, such as a typology of knowledge sources, represent a first step into the direction of re-usability. A further step would be to supply *partial models* of expertise such as models without all the detailed domain knowledge filled in. Such partial models can be used by the knowledge engineer as a template for a new domain and thus support top-down knowledge acquisition. In KADS such models are called *interpretation models*, because they guide the interpretation of verbal data obtained from the expert.

The KADS interpretation models are models of expertise *with an empty domain layer*. Interpretation models describe typical *inference* knowledge and *task* knowledge for a particular task. As these descriptions are phrased in domain-independent terminology, they are prime candidates for re-use in other domains. For example, the inference and task description of the audio domain could very well be applied to another domain where some device is being diagnosed. In Breuker *et al.* (1987) interpretation models for a large number of tasks are presented. One of these is the model for systematic diagnosis as presented in this paper.

### Example interpretation model

Another model in this library is that of the *monitoring* task. This model has been used in applications ranging from process control (Schrijnen & Wagenaar, 1988) to software project management (de Jong, de Hoog & Schreiber, 1988). It is also interesting because it illustrates how different tasks can apply the same set of inferences in different ways.

TABLE 2

*A typology of knowledge sources*

| Operation type | Knowledge source | Arguments |
|---|---|---|
| Generate concept/instance | instantiate | concept → instance |
| | classify | instance → concept |
| | generalize | set of instances → concept |
| | abstract | concept → concept |
| | specify | concent → concept |
| | select | set → concept |
| Change concept | assign-value | attribute → attribute-value |
| | compute | structure → attribute-value |
| Differentiating values/structures | compare | value + value → value |
| | match | structure + structure → structure |
| Structure manipulation | assemble | set of instances → structure |
| | decompose | structure → set of instances |
| | transform | structure → structure |

```
task model-driven monitoring
    goal
        execute a monitoring cycle in which the system
            actively acquires new data
    control-terms
        active-parameters=set of parameter
    task-structure
        monitor(discrepancy)=
            select(system-model, active-parameter)
            DO FOR EACH parameter ∈ active-parameters
                specify(parameter→norm)
                select(parameter→observable)
                obtain(observable→finding)
                compare(norm+finding→difference)
                classify(difference+historical-data→discrepancy)
```

The second task, *data-driven monitoring*, is initiated through incoming data. It contains a *receive* statement representing a transfer task in which an external agent (a human user or another system) has the initiative (see Section 4.3). The values received are checked against expected values for the observables concerned. Resulting differences are subsequently classified in discrepancy classes.

```
task data-driven-monitoring
    goal
        execute a monitoring cycle when a new value of an
            observable is received by the system
    task-structure
        monitor(discrepancy)=
            receive(observable-set→finding)
            DO FOR EACH observable ∈ observable-set
                select(observable+system-model→parameter)
                specify(parameter→norm)
                compare(norm+finding→difference)
                classify(difference+historical-data→discrepancy)
```

*Selecting an interpretation model from the library*

The library of interpretation models consists of a number of models that can be used to describe the reasoning process in various applications.

The knowledge engineer is guided in deciding which interpretation model to choose for a particular application through a decision tree. Part of this tree is shown in Figure 10. The decision tree is based on a taxonomy of task types. This taxonomy is a modified and extended version of Clancey's (1985b) description of problem types which in turn was derived from Hayes-Roth, Waterman and Lenat (1983: p 14). The decision points in this tree concern features of the solution space, the problem space and the required domain knowledge types.

The first decision point concerns the availability of information about the structure of the system involved in a task. The term "system" refers here to the

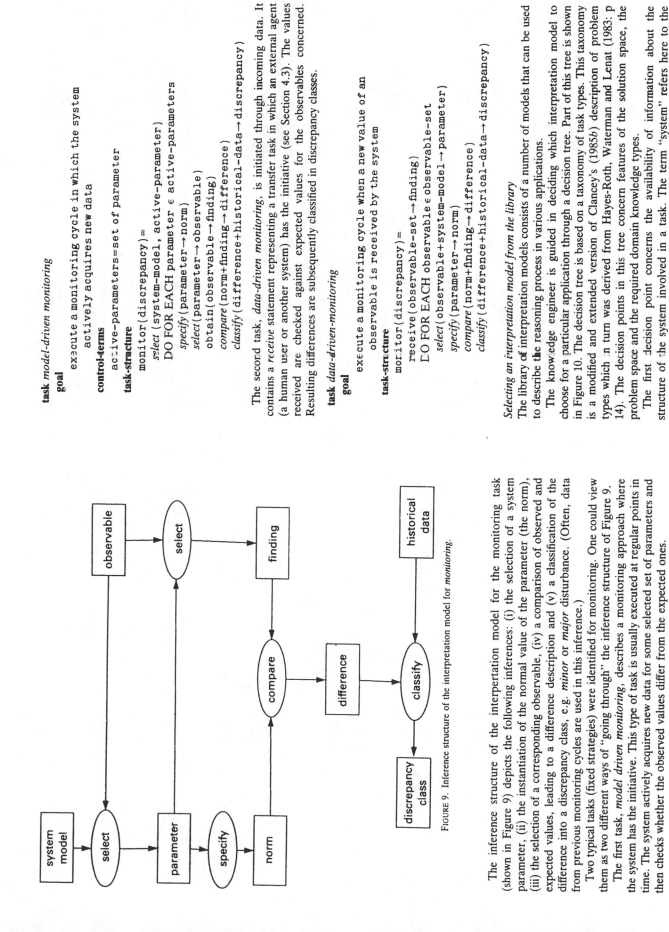

FIGURE 9. Inference structure of the interpretation model for *monitoring*.

The inference structure of the interpretation model for the monitoring task (shown in Figure 9) depicts the following inferences: (i) the selection of a system parameter, (ii) the instantiation of the normal value of the parameter (the norm), (iii) the selection of a corresponding observable, (iv) a comparison of observed and expected values, leading to a difference description and (v) a classification of the difference into a discrepancy class, e.g. *minor* or *major* disturbance. (Often, data from previous monitoring cycles are used in this inference.)

Two typical tasks (fixed strategies) were identified for monitoring. One could view them as two different ways of "going through" the inference structure of Figure 9.

The first task, *model driven monitoring*, describes a monitoring approach where the system has the initiative. This type of task is usually executed at regular points in time. The system actively acquires new data for some selected set of parameters and then checks whether the observed values differ from the expected ones.

audio domain, we focused only on the diagnostic sub-task. In actual practice the repair/remedy task also needs to be addressed. This may result in a combination of (parts of) two or more interpretation models. An example of this process of combining is described in Hayward (1987).

A number of researchers have developed knowledge acquisiton tools that are based on the notion of a generic model of the problem solving task. For example, ROGET (Bennet, 1985), MOLE (Eshelman *et al.*, 1988) and BURN (Klinker *et al.*, 1991) are all systems that drive the knowledge acquisition dialogue with an expert through a strong model of the problem solving process. This model prescribes what domain knowledge is needed to build an actual expert system. In OPAL (Musen *et al.*, 1988) this approach is taken one step further. The conceptual model is OPAL is not just a model of the problem solving process (i.e. the upper three layers in the KADS framework) but also contains templates of the domain knowledge needed. As a consequence OPAL can present the expert with detailed forms that he or she can fill in with the details of an application domain. Although this approach is very powerful indeed, it has limitations in scope and applicability.

## 6. Principle 4: knowledge differentiation

The use of template descriptions such as interpretation models provides a powerful tool for knowledge acquisition. However, applying such a template to a particular domain will often reveal that the model does not completely fit the data on human expertise. Most interpretation models embody only a minimal set of inferences necessary for solving a problem with this method. The model needs to be further refined. This process of refinement is called *knowledge differentiation*.

Knowledge differentiation is guided by several types of characteristics of the application domain: e.g. the nature of the knowledge in an application domain (e.g. "are causal models available?"), the constraints posed by the task environment (e.g. the required certainty of a solution) and computational constraints: it is possible to find computational techniques that realize the specified behaviour.

In the "Components of Expertise" framework (Steels, 1990) these characteristics are called "task features" and the three categories respectively *epistemic, pragmatic* and *computational* task features.†

### 6.1. TWO DIFFERENTIATIONS OF SYSTEMATIC DIAGNOSIS

The model of systematic diagnosis can be differentiated in various ways. We discuss two differentiations relevant to the audio domain.

The plain model of systematic diagnosis (of which the inference structure is shown in Figure 6) presupposes that the applicable system model is *selected* using knowledge about fixed decompositions of the system being diagnosed. However, the configuration of an audio system is usually not fixed. System elements such as a CD-player, a second tape-deck, head phones or additional speakers may or may not be present. This potential problem can be handled by replacing the simple *select* inference with a more complicated *assemble* inference (Figure 11).

† In the Components approach the task features are used for dynamic run-time task-decomposition in an actual system. In KADS, knowledge differentiation is primarily seen as a knowledge engineering activity, which could be (but does not need to be) reflected in the design of the KBS (in other words, it could result in fixed task decompositions).

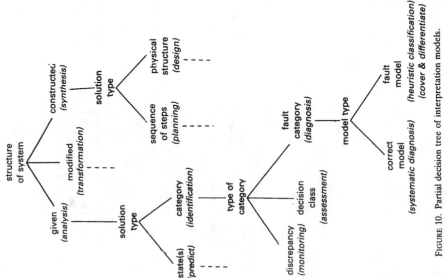

FIGURE 10. Partial decision tree of interpretation models.

central entity in the application domain, e.g. the audio system in the audio domain, the patient in a medical domain, the device in a technical domain etc. Other decision points concern, for example, the type of solution (state, category, types of categories etc.) and the nature of the domain knowledge (fault-model or correct-model of the system). The leaves of the decision tree are associated with one or more interpretation models that specify typical inference and task knowledge for modelling this task. For example, the interpretation model for *monitoring* task presented earlier, is associated with the *monitoring* task in Figure 10. This model is chosen if (i) the structure of the system is given, (ii) the solution is a category and (iii) this solution category is not a fault category nor a decision class, but a simple discrepancy between observed and expected behaviour.

It should be noted that in many real-life applications the task is a compound one: it consists of several basic tasks. For example, in the model of expertise for the

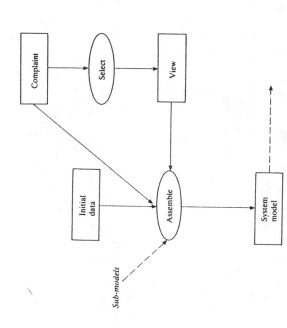

FIGURE 12. Differentiating the model of Systematic Diagnosis: introducing multiple system models representing different views.

### 6.2. MODEL CONSTRUCTION OPERATORS

Thus far, we have presented the process of constructing a model of expertise more-or-less as a two-step process: (i) the selection of an interpretation model from the library and (ii) the differentiation of the model on the basis of characteristics of the application domain.

More recently, we are considering a somewhat more dynamic view of the model construction process. This view has been influenced by the work of Patil (1988) on medical diagnosis. He shows how one can start with a simple model of diagnosis, such as generate-and-test, and start a gradual refinement process of this model on the basis of application characteristics, such as the ones discussed earlier. This approach would require a different organization of the library of template models, namely not as a flat set of models but as a set of *model construction operators*. These model construction operators can be applied to a model and result in a more complex model. The two differentiations of systematic diagnosis can be viewed as examples of such operators. Model construction operators can also be identified on a more general level. If one studies the inference structures of systematic diagnosis (Figure 6) and of monitoring (Figure 9), it becomes clear that they share a common set of related inferences, namely the process of checking the expected value of a parameter against the observed value. Figure 13 shows this set of inferences. One could view this set as a potential model construction operator.

Representing template models in the form of such model construction operators is attractive because it captures the way in which knowledge engineers actually build these models

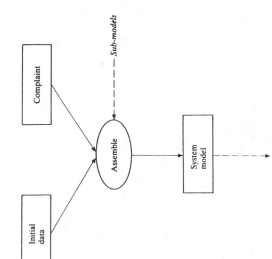

FIGURE 11. Differentiating the model of Systematic Diagnosis: *system model assembly* instead of selection.

In this assemble step additional data (*initial data* in Figure 11) about the audio system are used to construct an applicable system model. An epistemic requirement for this differentiation is that additional domain knowledge can be made available, namely: (i) a definition of potential system elements of an audio system, possible hierarchically organized (cf. the *sub-models* in Figure 11) and (ii) configuration rules for assembling an actual model from the possible system elements.

This modification of the plain inference structure of systematic diagnosis thus leads to a slightly more complex model with additional domain knowledge requirements. A second, more complicated, differentiation concerns the introduction of multiple system *views*. Often, there are various ways of decomposing a device. Each decomposition represents a different view on the system. Well-known views are functional and physical decompositions. In the audio domain, one can think of the system as, for example, an *electrical* system or as a *sound transformation* system. The faulty component can only be found if the right view is selected.

Allowing multiple views also introduces additional complexity in the model of expertise. It implies an additional decision in the inference process concerning view selection. Davis (1984) suggests that initial view selection is usually done on the basis of characteristics of the problem (the *complaint*) using domain heuristics. In Figure 12 shows the additional inferences necessary for handling multiple views. In this case the epistemic requirement on additional decomposition knowledge is even stronger: for each view sub-models and configuration rules should be present in the domain theory. In addition, heuristics about how to select a view need to be made available.

Introducing multiple views also involves additional task structure complexity. If one view fails to provide a solution, another view needs to be selected and the process is repeated. We omit here the specification of this extended task structure.

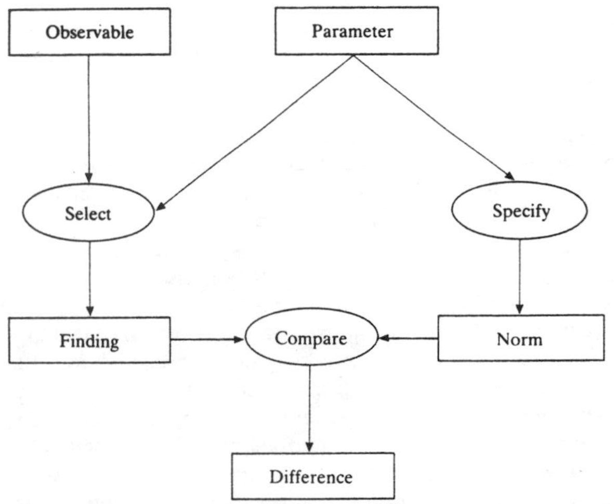

## 7.2. APPROACHES TO DESIGN

By definition, knowledge-level models such as the KADS conceptual models do not contain all information necessary for the implementation of a system. The design problem can be defined as the selection (or possibly development) of appropriate representations and computational techniques for the elements in the conceptual model. In principle, the designer is free to make any set of design decisions that results in meeting the specifications. In fact, a number of successful applications have been built that used standard design techniques (Readdie & Innes, 1987a; Benus & van der Spek, 1988). Often this was due to external requirements that forced the use of, for example, first-generation expert system shells that supply only a very limited set of AI techniques.

However, from a methodological point we strongly favour a *structure-preserving design*. With structure-preserving we mean that for the final system it should be possible to relate the elements of conceptual model to identifiable computational constructs. A structure-preserving design has a number of advantages:

*Explanation*

One important advantage is a wider possible scope for explanations that can be generated by the system. First-generation expert systems were only able to give explanations by paraphrasing their code (e.g. MYCIN). It is now commonly accepted that this is not sufficient to understand the reasoning process of the KBS. Preserving the structure of the conceptual model makes it possible to generate explanations at the level of the language of the conceptual model (Clancey & Letsinger, 1984).

Figure 14 shows part of the interface of a prototype shell that we developed for operationalizing models of systematic diagnosis. The shell was used to implement a KBS for the audio domain (Lemmers, 1991). The interface allows the user to trace the reasoning of the KBS in the vocabulary of the conceptual model at various levels through: (i) the task that is being executed and its structure, (ii) the inference structure in which an inference is highlighted when it is being executed, (iii) the bindings of control terms and meta-classes (i.e. the current state of "working memory") and (iv) the domain knowledge that is used by inferences that are executed.

The interface is a simple example of providing a user insight into the reasoning process of the KBS.

*Maintenance and debugging*

Another advantage has to do with the maintenance and the debugging of a KBS. The preservation of the structure of the conceptual model makes it possible to trace an omission or inconsistency in the implemented artefact back to a particular part of the conceptual model. Also, knowledge redundancy is prevented.†

† Similar goals with respect to explanation and maintenance are pursued in the Explainable Expert Systems (EES) approach (Neches, Swartout & Moore, 1985). In EES the structure-preserving property is guaranteed through an automatic transformation process.

FIGURE 13. Model construction operator: checking the expected value of a parameter against the observed value.

## 7. Principle 5: structure-preserving design

Unlike most other approaches to knowledge modelling, the KADS models of expertise have no direct computational interpretation: they are not executable. In this section we discuss various issues that are related to the process of operationalizing the model of expertise:

(i) The trade-off between conceptual modelling and design.
(ii) The structure-preserving approach to design and its advantages.
(iii) An overview of the detailed design decisions in a structure-preserving design process.
(iv) Support for a structure-preserving design process.
(v) Computational adequacy of systems built on the basis of a non-executable knowledge-level model.

### 7.1. TRADE-OFF BETWEEN CONCEPTUAL MODELLING AND DESIGN

It is important to realize that there is a trade-off between (i) extending the conceptual model and (ii) a more elaborate specification during design. The decision whether to do the former or the latter depends on whether one is interested from the conceptual-model point of view in exercising explicit control on the execution of a computational technique. The borderline between conceptual model and design is thus, in a sense, governed by the level of *granularity* that is required of the conceptual model. For example, in OFFICE-PLAN (a system for allocating offices to employees, see Karbach, Linster & Voß, 1989) the actual allocation inference is modelled as one knowledge source *assign* in the conceptual model and is realized in the actual system through a complex constraint satisfaction technique. If it would have been necessary to exercise control on this technique, then one would need to model constraint satisfaction "at the knowledge level".

## Inference knowledge

For each knowledge source a corresponding computational technique needs to be selected that can realize this inference. A technique consists of three types of elements: (i) an algorithm, (ii) input-output data structures and possibly additional temporary data structures, and (iii) a representation of domain knowledge.

The algorithm embodies the method for realizing the inference and specifies the local, symbol-level, control. The representation of the input-output data structures corresponds to the meta-classes and should be synchronized within the set of knowledge sources. The chosen domain knowledge representation (e.g. production rules) implies the requirement that the representation of the domain theory can be *viewed* in this way.

In AI research a number of (groups of) computational techniques have been developed such as production systems, state-space search, parsing, classification and matching. Detailed studies have been performed to unravel the criteria for choosing a technique within one group such as hierarchical classification (Goel, Soundarajan & Chandrasekaran, 1987) and logical representation and deduction (Reichgelt & van Harmelen, 1986). In Schreiber *et al.* (1989a) criteria for choosing a particular group of techniques are discussed. Often, knowledge engineers use, within one system, only one or two groups of techniques. In that case the chosen group of techniques takes the role of a design *paradigm*. For example, in NEOMYCIN (Clancey, 1985a) four (forward chaining) production system techniques are provided. Each inference applies one of these production system techniques. Applying only one type of technique, such as production systems, in one particular KBS minimizes the interaction problems with the design of other parts of the system (in particular, the domain theory, as it requires just a single representational formalization), but apart from that there is no compelling reason to adhere strictly to this approach.

## Domain knowledge

We view the domain knowledge as an elaborate database (with much more sophisticated representational primitives than conventional databases provide). Computational techniques require an access path into this database. A crucial design decision concerns the choice of the representation technique(s) for the domain theory. This representation has to meet the requirement posed by the set of "domain views". In other words, one should be able to view (or rewrite) the domain representation in such a way that it meets the demands of the computational techniques implementing knowledge sources. In addition, the representational technique should allow the specification of knowledge needed for other purposes, such as explanation. These requirements usually follow from the specification of the model of cooperation.

If the knowledge engineer works within a particular paradigm, such as production systems, the choice of the representational technique is usually obvious: the domain representation technique is the same as the representation used by the chosen type of computational technique.

In most existing systems no clear difference is made between use-specific and use-independent representations of elements of the domain-theory. In such cases the design is not fully structure-preserving. It also implies that the advantages of separating these the domain theory and the domain view (see Section 4.2) do not

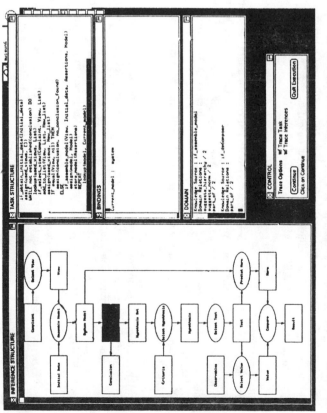

FIGURE 14. Prototype interface for tracing the execution of a system for systematic diagnosis in the vocabulary of the model of expertise. The inference structure is shown on the left and is a refined version of the one presented in this paper. The *decompose* knowledge source is currently being executed. The task structure, the bindings (e.g. the system model that is currently being decomposed) and the domain knowledge used by the decompose knowledge source (a part-of relation) are shown on the right. The window in the lower-right corner allows the user to trace the reasoning process at the task and/or inference level.

## Knowledge acquisition tools

A related advantage is that the conceptual model and its links to the artefact can be used to guide the use of knowledge acquisition tools and techniques. For example, techniques such as repertory grid and induction algorithms can be used to generate not *any* knowledge but a *particular type* of knowledge. This approach to knowledge acquisition support allows much more focused use of tools and therefore increases the interpretability and the quality of their results. This approach is currently being pursued in the ACKNOWLEDGE project (Shadbolt & Wielinga, 1990).

### 7.3. DETAILED DESIGN DECISIONS

In this sub-section we discuss typical design decisions. The scope of the section is limited to decisions with respect to elements of the model of expertise. A more detailed description of these decisions can be found in Schreiber *et al.* (1987) and Schreiber *et al.* (1989a). Decisions concerning the design of inference knowledge are discussed first, because these decisions influence other decisions, notably the design of the domain knowledge base.

hold for the final system. This can mean that problems arise, particularly in the area of maintenance. For example, it could lead to multiple presence in the domain theory of essentially the same knowledge (knowledge redundancy).

*Task knowledge*

Given the set of tasks specified in the conceptual model (consisting of both problem solving tasks and of transfer tasks) the designer has to make two—interrelated—decisions.

(i) The choice of a control technique for executing tasks. Examples of such control techniques are an agenda mechanism, a blackboard, a skeletal planning technique or a simple procedure hierarchy.

(ii) The choice of how to represent and update the run-time data. These data can be viewed as the "working memory" of the KBS. This working memory contains the data that are manipulated by the tasks and the inferences, e.g. the current state of the differential, the findings etc. The control terms and the meta-classes specified in the conceptual model form the basis for the representation of working memory: they often re-appear in the final system as labels for (sets of) working memory elements.

Most existing KBSs use a simple monotonic technique of updating working memory. We expect that in the next generation KBS's more complex techniques, such as truth-maintenance techniques, will be used more often. Note that the ue of such a technique can pose additional requirements on the output produced by computational techniques realizing primitive inferences. An example of such an additionally required output is the "justification" used in an ATMS (de Kleer, 1986).

*Strategic knowledge*

Most conceptual models that have been constructed do not contain a large amount of strategic knowledge. In many of these systems the strategic part has been "compiled out" into fixed task decompositions with possibly a few strategic decision points that can be influenced by the user (cf. de Greef, Schreiber & Wielemaker, 1987, Part II, Section 3.4).

If more elaborate strategic knowledge is present, the following techniques could be applicable:

(i) A production system containing a set of meta-rules with states of working memory as conditions and task activations and/or changes to working memory (e.g. assumptions) as actions.

(ii) An extended blackboard technique such as the "Blackboard Control Architecture" (Hayes-Roth, 1985), where the scheduling part represents the strategic knowledge.

(iii) One can also view the strategic knowledge as a separate meta-system, the PDP system is an example of this approach (Jansweijer, Elshout & Wielinga, 1986). This approach is also currently being pursued in the REFLECT project (Reinders et al., 1991).

## 7.4. SUPPORT FOR THE DESIGN PROCESS

The design decisions should lead to a mapping from the elements of the conceptual model on to elements of the implementation environment. In KADS we have developed a notation for supporting this structure-preserving design process through intermediate design descriptions (Schreiber et al., 1989b). It is also possible to support the knowledge engineer in this transformation process through the development of a dedicated computational framework that provides: (i) a number of predefined representational and computational techniques, and (ii) a programming environment that more-or-less predefines how elements of the conceptual model should be mapped on to constructs in this environment (for example, by providing constructs called "knowledge source" etc.).

In such a computational framework most of the design decisions discussed earlier are hard-wired. The use of a dedicated framework minimizes the number of design decisions that have to be made for implementing the system given a conceptual model, because most of the these decisions have already been taken by the designers of the environment. Model-K (Karbach et al., 1991) and ZDEST-2 (Tong, He & Yu, 1988; Karbach, Tong & Voß, 1988) are computational environments that (partially) allow such a mapping of KADS conceptual models on to an implementation. A potential problem with this type of approach is that the environment may not provide all the necessary techniques for a particular application. As any other design process, the design of a knowledge-based system is by its nature open-ended, i.e. the solution space is infinite.

## 7.5. COMPUTATIONAL ADEQUACY

One major objection to the use of knowledge-level models in the KBS development process is the potential computational inadequacy of such models. Since knowledge-level models do not specify the control regime in full detail they are apt to potential combinatorial explosion behaviour. Although it is true in principle that this problem may occur, the structure of the models proposed here provides important safeguards against the computational inadequacy. The knowledge that is specified in a KADS four-layer model cannot be used in arbitrary ways: it has to fulfill certain typing requirements and can only be applied within the constraints specified by the model. For instance, a piece of domain knowledge of a certain type can only be used for abstraction inferences, not for all types of inference steps. Our introduction of knowledge sources and task structures generally yields the possibility of selecting specific rules or theories needed to produce a certain inference. In this way the knowledge-level model provides a *role-limiting* (McDermott, 1989) constraint to knowledge. Role limitations translate to *access* limitations at the symbol level and hence reduce the combinatorial explosion (Schreiber et al., 1991).

## 8. The knowledge-acquisition process

The description of the various models can be seen as the *product* of KBS construction. With respect to the *process* of KBS construction, KADS provides two ways of support: (i) a description of phases, activities and techniques for knowledge engineering and (ii) computerized support tools. Both are briefly discussed in this section.

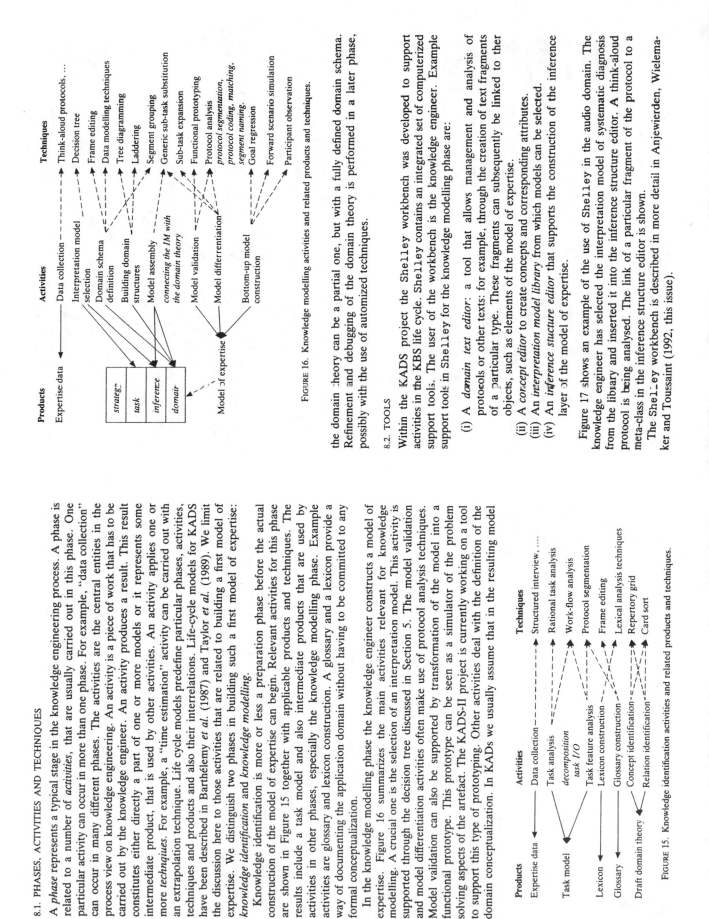

FIGURE 16. Knowledge modelling activities and related products and techniques.

FIGURE 15. Knowledge identification activities and related products and techniques.

the domain theory can be a partial one, but with a fully defined domain schema. Refinement and debugging of the domain theory is performed in a later phase, possibly with the use of automized techniques.

## 8.2. TOOLS

Within the KADS project the Shelley workbench was developed to support activities in the KBS life cycle. Shelley contains an integrated set of computerized support tools. The user of the workbench is the knowledge engineer. Example support tools in Shelley for the knowledge modelling phase are:

(i) A *domain text editor*: a tool that allows management and analysis of protocols or other texts: for example, through the creation of text fragments of a particular type. These fragments can subsequently be linked to ther objects, such as elements of the model of expertise.
(ii) A *concept editor* to create concepts and corresponding attributes.
(iii) An *interpretation model library* from which models can be selected.
(iv) An *inference stucture editor* that supports the construction of the inference layer of the model of expertise.

Figure 17 shows an example of the use of Shelley in the audio domain. The knowledge engineer has selected the interpretation model of systematic diagnosis from the library and inserted it into the inference structure editor. A think-aloud protocol is being analysed. The link of a particular fragment of the protocol to a meta-class in the inference structure editor is shown.

The Shelley workbench is described in more detail in Anjewierden, Wielemaker and Toussaint (1992, this issue).

## 8.1. PHASES, ACTIVITIES AND TECHNIQUES

A *phase* represents a typical stage in the knowledge engineering process. A phase is related to a number of *activities*, that are usually carried out in this phase. One particular activity can occur in more than one phase. The activities are the central entities in the process view on knowledge engineering. An activity is a piece of work that has to be carried out by the knowledge engineer. An activity produces a result. This result constitutes either directly a part of one or more models or it represents some intermediate product, that is used by other activities. An activity applies one or more *techniques*. For example, a "time estimation" activity can be carried out with an extrapolation technique. Life cycle models predefine particular phases, activities, techniques and products and also their interrelations. Life-cycle models for KADS have been described in Barthélemy et al. (1987) and Taylor et al. (1989). We limit the discussion here to those activities that are related to building a first model of expertise. We distinguish two phases in building such a first model of expertise: *knowledge identification* and *knowledge modelling*.

Knowledge identification is more or less a preparation phase before the actual construction of the model of expertise can begin. Relevant activities for this phase are shown in Figure 15 together with applicable products and techniques. The results include a task model and also intermediate products that are used by activities in other phases, especially the knowledge modelling phase. Example activities are glossary and lexicon construction. A glossary and a lexicon provide a way of documenting the application domain without having to be committed to any formal conceptualization.

In the knowledge modelling phase the knowledge engineer constructs a model of expertise. Figure 16 summarizes the main activities relevant for knowledge modelling. A crucial one is the selection of an interpretation model. This activity is supported through the decision tree discussed in Section 5. The model validation and model differentiation activities often make use of protocol analysis techniques. Model validation can also be supported by transformation of the model into a functional prototype. This prototype can be seen as a simulator of the problem solving aspects of the artefact. The KADS-II project is currently working on a tool to support this type of prototyping. Other activities deal with the definition of the domain conceptualization. In KADs we usually assume that in the resulting model

In the approach taken at Ohio State University (Bylander & Chandrasekaran, 1988; Chandrasekaran, 1988) the implementation environment consists of so called "generic tasks". A generic task (GT) is a combination of a problem (e.g. classification) and a problem-solving method (e.g. hierarchical classification) with particular knowledge and inference requirements. GTs can perform quite general information-processing tasks. The assumption is that by combining a relatively small set of GTs one can solve a large number of problems. The problem-solving methods in the GT approach have a somewhat smaller grain size than the interpretation models in KADS.

In the approach taken at DEC (McDermott, 1989; Marcus & McDermott, 1989; Eshelman et al., 1988) a number of systems were built that provide an operational-ization of a particular problem solving method, such as "propose & revise" and "cover & differentiate". The terminology used to describe these methods is such that during knowledge acquisiton the expert can be prompted for domain knowledge in a high-level, method-specific language, e.g. ''What are symptoms that the system should be able to explain?''. The problem solving methods have a similar grain size as the KADs interpretation models. More recently (Klinker et al., 1991), the emphasis in this approach has shifted to the construction of an integrated environment in which the knowledge engineer can configure such single-task knowledge acquisition systems from a set of predefined mechanisms. As remarked in Section 5.1, the research on a typology of mechanisms is very close to aims in KADS.

In the PROTEGE (Musen, 1989) approach the problem is addressed that experts find it difficult to enter knowledge in a method-specific format. In this approach two steps are distinguished in building ONCOCIN-like systems: the knowledge engineer uses PROTEGE to specify the required domain knowledge in method-specific terms; PROTEGE then generates a knowledge acquisition tool called p-OPAL that enables the expert to enter knowledge in domain-specific terms. This dual way of naming domain knowledge is similar to the approach advocated in KADS. The PROTEGE system presupposes a single-task model, based on the skeletal planning method of ONCOCIN (Shortliffe, et al., 1981).

All models used in these last three approaches are hard-wired to particular computational constructs. As stated earlier, compared to the KADS approach this is both an advantage and a disadvantage.

The "Components of Expertise" (CoE) approach (Steels, 1990) is in many aspects similar to KADS. The main differences with KADS are the dynamic view on task decomposition based on task features and the absence of an explicit description of inference knowledge such as meta-classes. A dedicated computational framework has been developed for CoE models (Vanwelkenhuysen & Rademakers, 1990). Research aiming at a synthesis of KADS and CoE is in progress within the KADS-II project.

The "Ontological Analysis" approach (Alexander et al., 1988) describes know-ledge in three categories: (i) the static ontology describing the primitive objects, properties and relations, (ii) the dynamic ontology describing the state space of the problem solver and the actions that can make transitions in this space, and (iii) the epistemic ontology describing methods that control the use of knowledge of the first two categories. These three categories resemble closely the domain, inference and

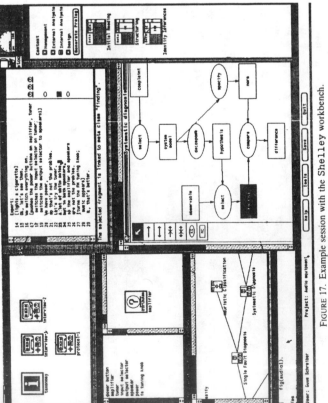

FIGURE 17. Example session with the Shelley workbench.

## 9. Relation to other approaches

We make no claim that all ideas underlying KADS are new. On the contrary, work of other researchers has heavily influenced the work on KADS. In this section we discuss a number of these approaches and relate them to the KADS approach.

Brachman (1979) proposed five levels for describing knowledge: the linguistic, the conceptual, the epistemological, the logical and the implementational level. Brachman and also Clancey (1983) showed that the epistemological level of Brachman is the "missing" level in the description of knowledge-based systems. We interpret Newell's knowledge level as a combined description of Brachman's conceptual and epistemological level. In the KADS model of expertise the domain knowledge roughly corresponds to the conceptual level and the three other categories to the epistemological level. The KADS design description (Newell's symbol level) corresponds to the logical level.

The work of Clancey has had a large impact on KADS. Clancey (1983, 1985b) introduced the notion of an inference structure in the description of the model of heuristic classification (HC). In the work on NEOMYCIN (Clancey, 1985a) a similar type of task decomposition is found as is used in the task layer in KADS. The main difference is that there is no explicit relation between the tasks in NEOMYCIN and the inferences in the HC model. These tasks refer directly to the domain knowledge, whereas the tasks in KADS reference the domain knowledge only indirectly via primitive inferences.

task knowledge in KADS. The formalizations used in Ontological Analysis are based on algebraic specification languages.

Although terminology is different, a common view appears to emerge based on the idea that different types of knowledge constitute the knowledge level and that these different types of knowledge play different roles in the reasoning process and have inherently different structuring principles. One salient characteristic is that all approaches distinguish between structural domain knowledge and control knowledge. In addition, various kinds of control knowledge are distinguished, like global control of how to go about the task as a whole, and local control knowledge specifying how and/or when to carry out certain individual actions.

There are also relations between KADS and conventional software engineering approaches. The introduction of multiple models was inspired by work of DeMarco (1982). As pointed out in Section 4.1, issues concerning modelling of domain knowledge are quite closely related to research in semantic database modelling. Software engineering techniques are used in KADS, e.g. a form of data-flow diagrams (for inference structures) and structured English (for task structures). Life-cycle models using a water-fall approach (Barthélemy et al., 1987) and a spiral model approach (Taylor et al., 1989) have been defined in KADS.

## 10. Experiences

The KADS approach has been (and is being) used in some 40–50 KBS projects. Not all these projects used "pure" KADS. The core activities of Bolesian Systems, a Dutch company, are teaching and applying an earlier version of KADS under the name SKE (Structured Knowledge Engineering). Other companies, such as Arthur Andersen Consulting and commercial partners in the KADS-I project, have incorporated KADS into their own methodology.

Within the KADS-1 project the approach has been tested in a number of experiments in domains such as commercial wine making (Wielinga & Breuker, 1984) statistical consultancy (de Greef & Breuker, 1985; de Greef, et al. 1988b), the integration qualitative reasoning approaches (Bredeweg & Wielinga, 1988), network management (Krickhahn et al., 1988: Readdie & Innes, 1987b), mould configuration (Barthélemy et al., 1988), mixer configuration (Wielemaker & Billault, 1988), technical diagnosis (Wright et al. 1988), insurance (Brunet & Toussaint, 1990) and credit card fraud detection (Land et al., 1990). Other applications include re-engineering of ONCOCIN (Linster & Musen, this issue), process control (Schrijnen & Wagenaar, 1988), chemical equipment (Schachter & Wermser, 1988), room planning (Karbach et al., 1989), social security (de Hoog, 1989), software project management (de Jong et al., 1988), diagnosis of movement disorders (Winkels & Achthoven, 1989), and paint selection (van der Spek, van der Wouden & Ysbrandy, 1990). The last two systems and the credit card system have been in operational use for some time.

A recent publication for the commercial AI community (Harmon, 1991) commented that "before KADS, most of the methodologies were vague prescriptions rather than systematic step-by-step models for large-scale systems development efforts". On the basis of the success of KADS-I, the CEC has decided to fund a second ESPRIT project (KADS-II) with the aim to arrive at a de facto European standard for KBS development.

This is not to say that we think that the approach described in this paper has no deficiencies: on the contrary. It is clear that a group of KADS users find certain aspects of KADS attractive, but it is also recognized that there are many weaknesses in current KADS. The first KADS user meeting (Überreiter & Voß, 1991) in which some 40, mainly German, KADS users participated, provided a good overview of the strong and weak points of KADS. Among the strong points are:

(i) The distinction between various models, especially the distinction between the model of expertise and the design.

(ii) The framework for modelling expertise. Especially the inference structures are mentioned by many people as an intuitively appealing way of describing the reasoning process and as a communication vehicle with domain experts.

(iii) The library of interpretation models. Although this library is far from complete, it has still provided useful starting points for many applications.

The list of weaknesses is considerably longer. A selection:

(i) The vocabulary in the four-layer framework for describing domain knowledge and task knowledge is not expressive enough.

(ii) The typology of knowledge sources is too general. The precise meaning of the knowledge sources is ambiguous.

(iii) The library of interpretation models is incomplete and needs serious revision. For example, coverage of synthetic tasks is marginal.

(iv) KADS does not provide enough support for operationalizing conceptual models.

(v) KADS gives you a vocabulary, but it provides little support for the modelling process.

In short, the experiences show that the KADS approach has some interesting and attractive features, but that it still needs a lot of work before it can really be considered a "comprehensive methodology". In addition, controlled validation studies are necessary to show that KADS actually provides advantages compared to other approaches. The work of Linster & Musen (1992, this issue) can be seen as a step in this direction.

## 11. Future developments and conclusions

In this paper we have taken the position that knowledge acquisition is to a large extent a constructive activity: models of several aspects of the task and domain have to be built before implementing a knowledge-based system.

Looking at the future of knowledge acquisition from this point of view raises the obvious question of how AI and knowledge-based systems themselves can support the various modelling processes. Recent developments in the area of knowledge-acquisition tools provide some directions in how this could be done.

Given the modelling approach to knowledge acquisition it is of vital importance that a knowledge engineer has some language in which the various models can be formulated. Such a language is not only important for the knowledge-acquisition process itself, but also for communicating models and comparing models for different tasks. A comparative analysis of the problem-solving methods embodied in KBSs will advance the knowledge-acquisition activity from an art to a proper engineering discipline. Although there is currently little consensus on what the ingredients and vocabulary of such a modelling language should be, the various ideas appear to converge. The result of the synthesis of the KADS and the CoE approach, which is currently being pursued and in which ideas from other approaches are also taken into account, may be a starting point for such a language. In our view, it is also worthwhile investigating the different types of knowledge and their relationships from a more formal point of view. Attempts are being made in this direction (see van Harmelen & Balder, 1992, this issue). Such a formal account of knowledge models clarifies at least some of the notions that have been used in a rather informal way so far.

If a common language for defining conceptual models of problem-solving processes became accepted, it would be of great interest to study the large collection of problem-solving models that currently exist. A consolidation and integration of the models in the KADS interpretation model library (Breuker et al., 1987), the generic probelm-solving models of Chandrasekaran and co-workers (Chandrasekaran, 1988), the models underlying the various model-driven knowledge acquisition tools (McDermott, 1989) and various other models in the literature, could provide the knowledge-engineering community with an invaluable tool for knowledge acquisition. Also, such a collection of generic models could be the basis of powerful knowledge-acquisition tools that communicate both with experts and with knowledge engineers.

Looking beyond the traditional knowledge-engineering paradigm where the knowledge engineer does most of the work, we envisage an important role for knowledge about models in knowledge-acquisition tools that integrate traditional knowledge-acquisition techniques and automated learning techniques. One of the major problems in this area is that of integrating knowledge of various sources. A system that has knowledge about the kinds of knowledge that it needs to acquire can exercise much more focused control on the acquisition process and hence solve at least part of the integration problems.

## Acknowledgements

We gratefully acknowledge the contributions to the work reported here from Anjo Anjewierden, Jean-Paul Billault, Bert Bredeweg, Massoud Davoodi, Paul de Greef, Simon Hayward, Robert de Hoog, Ton de Jong, Maarten van Someren, Peter Terpstra and Jan Wielemaker. Many other co-workers of ESPRIT Project 1098 participated in discussion, applications and validations of the ideas presented here.

Anjo Anjewierden, Frank van Harmelen, Marc Lister, Jacobijn Sandberg and three anonymous referees provided valuable comments on earlier versions of this paper.

This research was largely carried out in the course of the KADS-I project. This project was partially funded by the ESPRIT-I Programme of the Commission of the European Communities as project number 1098. The partners in this project were STC Technology Ltd., SD-Scicon plc., KBSC of TRMC (all UK), NTE NeuTech (Germany), Cap Sesa Innovation (France), and the University of Amsterdam (The Netherlands).

The production of this article was supported by the KADS-II project. This project is partially funded by the ESPRIT Progrmame of the Commission of the European Communities as project number 5248. The partners in the project are Cap Gemini Innovation (The Netherlands), Cap Gemini Logic (Sweden), Netherlands Energy Research Foundation ECN (The Netherlands), ENTEL SA (Spain), IBM France (France), Lloyd's Register (UK), Swedish Institute of Computer Science (Sweden), Siemens AG (Germany), Touche Ross MC (UK), University of Amsterdam (The Netherlands) and the Free University of Brussels (Belgium). This paper reflects the opinions of the authors and not necessarily those of the consortia.

## References

ALEXANDER, J., FREILING, M., SHULMAN, S., REHFUSS, S. & MESSICK, S. (1988). Ontological analysis: an ongoing expriment. In J. BOOSE & B. GAINES, Eds. Knowledge-Based Systems, Volume 2: Knowledge Acquisition Tools for Expert Systems, pp. 25–37. London: Academic Press.

ANJEWIERDEN, A., WIELEMAKER, J. & TOUSSAINT, C. (1992). Shelley—computer-aided knowledge engineering. Knowledge Acquisition, 4, 109–125.

BARTHÉLEMY, S., EDIN, G., TOUTAIN, E. & BECKER, S. (1987). Requirements analysis in KBS development. ESPRIT Project P1098 Deliverable D3 (task A2), Cap Sogeti Innovation.

BARTHÉLEMY, S., FROT, P. & SIMONIN, N. (1988). Analysis document experiment F4. ESPRIT Project P1098, Deliverable E4.1, Cap Sogeti Innovation.

BENNET, J. (1985). ROGET: A knowledge-based system for acquiring the conceptual structure of a diagnostic expert system. Journal of Automated Reasoning, 1, 49–74.

BENUS, B. & VAN DER SPEK, R. (1988). The Paint Expert: report on the development of a knowledge-based system for naive users. Master's thesis, University of Amsterdam, Faculty of Psychology.

BOEHM, B. (1988). A spiral model of software development and enhancement. IEEE Computer, 61–72.

BRACHMAN, R. (1979). On the epistemological status of semantic networks. In N. FINDLER, Ed. Associative Networks, New York: Academic Press.

BRACHMAN, R. & SCHMOLZE, J. (1985). An overview of the KL-ONE knowledge representation system. Cognitive Science, 9, 171–216.

BREDEWEG, B. & WIELINGA, B. (1988). Integrating qualitative reasoning approaches. In Proceedings of ECAI-88, Munich, pp. 195–201.

BREUKER, J. & WIELINGA, B. (1987). Use of models in the interpretation of verbal data. In A. KIDD, Ed. Knowledge Acquisition for Expert Systems, a Practical Handbook, New York: Plenum Press.

BREUKER, J., WIELINGA, B., VAN SOMEREN, M., DE HOOG, R., SCHREIBER, G., DE GREEF, P., BREDEWEG, B., WIELEMAKER, J., BILLAULT, J.-P., DAVOODI, M. & HAYWARD, S. (1987). Model Driven Knowledge Acquisition: interpretation models. ESPRIT Project P1098 Deliverable D1 (task A1), University of Amsterdam and STL Ltd.

BREUKER, J. A. & WIELINGA, B. J. (1989). Model Driven Knowledge Acquisition. In P. GUIDA & G. TASSO, Eds. Topics in the Design of Expert Systems, pp. 265–296. Amsterdam: North-Holland.

BRUNET, E. & TOUSSAINT, C. (1990). A KADS application in insurance. ESPRIT project P1098, Deliverable E9.1, Cap Sesa Innovation.

BYLANDER, T. & CHANDRASEKARAN, B. (1988). Generic tasks in knowledge-based reasoning: The 'right' level of abstraction for knowledge acquisition. In B. GAINES & J. BOOSE, Eds. Knowledge Acquisition for Knowledge Based Systems, Volume 1, pp. 65–77. London: Academic Press.

CHANDRASEKARAN, B. (1988). Generic tasks as building blocks for knowledge-based systems: the diagnosis and routine design examples. The Knowledge Engineering Review, 3(3), 183–210.

CLANCEY, W. (1983). The epistemology of a rule based system—a framework for explanation. Artificial Intelligence, 20, 215–251. Also, Stanford Heuristic Programming Project, Memo HPP-81-17, November 1981, also numbered STAN-CS-81-896.

CLANCEY, W. (1985a). Acquiring, representing and evaluating a competence model of diagnostic strategy. In CHI, GLASER, & FAR, Eds. Contributions to the Nature of Expertise.

CLANCEY, W. (1985b). Heuristic classification. Artificial Intelligence, 27, 289–350.

CLANCEY, W. & LETSINGER, R. (1984). NEOMYCIN: Reconfiguring a rulebased expert system for application to teaching. In W. CLANCEY & E. SHORTLIFFE, Eds. *Readings in Medical Artificial Intelligence: the First Decade*, pp. 361–381. Reading: Addison-Wesley.

DAVIS, J. & BONNEL, R. (1990). Producing visually-based knowledge specifications for acquiring organizational knowledge. In B. WIELINGA, J. BOOSE, B. GAINES, A. SCHREIBER & M. VAN SOMEREN, Eds. *Current Trends in Knowledge Acquisition*, pp. 105–122. Amsterdam: IOS Press.

DAVIS, R. (1980). Metarules: Reasoning about control. *Artificial Intelligence*, **15**, 179–222.

DAVIS, R. (1984). Diagnostic reasoning based on structure and behavior. *Artificial Intelligence*, **24**, 347–410.

DE GREEF, P. & BREUKER, J. (1985). A case study in structured knowledge acquisition. In *Proceedings of the 9th IJCAI*, p. 390–392, Los Angeles.

DE GREEF, P. & BREUKER, J. (1989). A methodology for analysing modalities of system/user cooperation for KBS. In J. BOOSE, B. GAINES & J GANASCIA, Eds. *Proceedings of the European Knowledge Acquisition Workshop, EKAW'89*, pp. 462–473, Paris, France.

DE GREEF, P. & BREUKER, J. (1992). Analysing system-user cooperation. *Knowledge Acquisition*, **4**, 89–108.

DE GREEF, P., BREUKER, J. & DE JONG, T. (1988*a*). *Modality: An analysis of functions, user control and communication in knowledge-based systems*. ESPRIT Project P1098, Deliverable D6 (task A4), University of Amsterdam.

DE GREEF, P., BREUKER, J., SCHREIBER, G. & WIELEMAKER, J. (1988*b*). StatCons: Knowledge acquisition in a complex domain. In *Proceedings ECAI'88*, Munich.

DE GREEF, P., SCHREIBER, G. & WIELEMAKER, J. (1987). *The StatCons case study*. ESPRIT Project P1098, Deliverable E2.3 (experiment F2), University of Amsterdam.

DE HOOG, R. (1989). Een expertsysteem, bijstand voor bijstand. *Informatie & Informatiebeleid*, **7**(1), 47–53. (In Dutch.)

DE HOOG, R., SOMMER, K. & VOGLER, M. (1990). *Designing knowledge-based systems; a study of organisational aspects*. Technical Report Report W17, ISBN 90 346 2400 5, Dutch Organisation for Technological Aspects for Technological Research NOTA. (In Dutch.)

DE JONG, T., DE HOOG, R., & SCHREIBER, G. (1988). Knowledge acquisition for an integrated project management system. *Information Processing and Management*, **24**(6), 681–691.

DE KLEER, J. (1986). An assumption-based TMS. *Artificial Intelligence*, **28**, 127–162.

DEMARCO, T. (1978). *Structured Analysis and System Specification*. New York, Yourdon Press.

DEMARCO, T. (1982). *Controlling Software Projects*. New York: Yourdon Press.

DIAPER, D., Ed. (1989). *Knowledge Elicitation: principles, techniques and applications*. Series in Expert Systems. Chichester: Ellis Horwood Ltd.

ESHELMAN, L., EHRET, D., MCDERMOTT, J. & TAN, M. (1988). MOLE: a tenacious knowledge acquisition tool. In J. BOOSE & B. GAINES, Eds. *Knowledge Based Systems, Volume 2: Knowledge Acquisition Tools for Expert Systems*, pp. 95–108. London: Academic Press.

GENESERETH, M. & NILSSON, N. (1987). *Logical Foundations of Artificial Intelligence*. Los Altos, California: Morgan Kaufmann.

GOEL, A., SOUNDARAJAN, N. & CHANDRASEKARAN, B. (1987). Complexity in classificatory reasoning. In *AAAI-87*, pp. 421–425.

GRUBER, T. (1989). The acquisition of strategic knowledge. In *Perspectives in Artificial Intelligence, Volume 4*. San Diego: Academic Press.

HARMON, P. (1991). A brief overview of software methodologies. *Intelligent Software Strategies*, **VII**(1), 1–19. Newsletter. Circulation office: 37 Broadway, Arlington. MA 02174 USA.

HAYES-ROTH, B. (1985). A blackboard architecture for control. *Artificial Intelligence*, **26**(3), 251–321.

HAYES-ROTH, F., WATERMAN, D. & LENAT, D. (1983). *Building Expert Systems*. New York: Addison-Wesley.

HAYWARD, S. (1987). How to build knowledge systems; techniques, tools, and case studies.

In *Proceedings of 4th annual ESPRIT conference*, pp. 665–680. Amsterdam: North-Holland.

HAYWARD, S. WIELINGA, B. & BREUKER, J. (1987). Structured analysis of knowledge. *International Journal of Man-Machine Studies*, **26**, 487–498.

HULL, R. & KING, R. (1987). Semantic database modelling: Survey, applications, and research issues. *ACM Computing Surveys*, **19**, 201–260.

JANSWEIJER, W. (1988). *PDP*. PhD thesis, University of Amsterdam.

JANSWEIJER, W., ELSHOUT, J. & WIELINGA, B. (1986). The expertise of novice problem solvers. In *Proceedings ECAI'86*, Brigthon.

JANSWEIJER, W., ELSHOUT, J. & WIELINGA, B. (1989). On the multiplicity of learning to solve problems. In H. MANDL, E. DE CORTE, N. BENNETT, & H. FRIEDRICH, Eds. *Learning and Instruction: European research in an international context*, pp. 127–145. Oxford, UK: Pergamon Press.

KARBACH, W., LINSTER, M. & VOß, A. (1989). OFFICE-PLAN: Tackling the synthesis frontier. In D. METZING, Ed. *GWAI-89: 13th German Workshop on Artificial Intelligence, Informatik Fachberichte* **216**, pp. 379–387. Berlin: Springer Verlag.

KARBACH, W., LINSTER, M. & VOß, A. (1990). Model-based approaches: One label—one idea? In B. WIELINGA, J. BOOSE, B. GAINES, G. SCHREIBER, & M. VAN SOMEREN, M. Eds. *Current Trends in Knowledge Acquisition*, pp. 173–189. Amsterdam: IOS Press.

KARBACH, W., TONG, X. & VOß, A. (1988). Filling in the knowledge acquisition gap: via KADS models of expertise to ZDEST-2 expert systems. In *Proceedings of EKAW '88*, Bonn.

KARBACH, W., VOß, A., SCHUKEY, R. & DROUWEN, U. (1991). Model-K: Prototyping at the knowledge level. In *Proceedings Expert Systems '91, Avignon, France*, pp. 501–512.

KLINKER, G., BHOLA, C., DALLEMAGNE, G., MARQUES, D. & MCDERMOTT, J. (1991). Usable and reusable programming constructs. *Knowledge Acquisition*, **3**, 117–136.

KRICKHAHN, R., NOBIS, R., MAHLMANN, A. & SCHACHTER, M. (1988). Applying the KADS methodology to develop a knowledge-based system. In *Proceedings ECAI'88, Munich*, pp. 11–17 London: Pitman.

LAND, L., TAYLOR, R., MULHALL, T., KILLIN, J. & BINGHAM, T. (1990). *Credit card fraud identification knowledge-based system*. ESPRIT Project P1098, deliverable F12.1, KADS-F12-d1-00-. KBSC of Touche Ross Management Consultants, London.

LEMMERS, M. (1991). *A shell for systematic diagnosis: structure-preserving design of a KBS*. Master's thesis, University of Amsterdam, Social Science Informatics.

LINSTER, M. & MUSEN, M. (1992). Use of KADS to create a conceptual model of the ONCOCIN task. *Knowledge Acquisition*. **4**, 55–87.

MARCUS, S. & MCDERMOTT, J. (1989). SALT: A knowledge acquisition language for propose-and-revise systems. *Artificial Intelligence*, **39**(1), 1–38.

MCDERMOTT, J. (1989). Preliminary steps towards a taxonomy of problem-solving methods. In S. MARCUS, Ed. *Automating Knowledge Acquisition for Expert Systems*, pp. 225–255. The Netherlands: Kluwer Academic Publishers.

MEYER, M. & BOOKER, J. (1991). *Eliciting and Analyzing Expert Judgement: A Practical Guide, Volume 5 of Knowledge-Based Systems*. London: Academic Press.

MORIK, K. (1989). Sloppy modeling. In K. MORIK, Ed. *Knowledge Representation and Organisation in Machine Learning*. Berlin: Springer Verlag.

MUSEN, M. (1989). *Automated Generation of Model-Based Knowledge-Acquisition Tools*. Research Notes in Artificial Intelligence. London: Pitman.

MUSEN, M., FAGAN, L., COMBS, D. & SHORTLIFFE, E. (1988). Use of a domain model to drive an interactive knowledge editing tool. In J. BOOSE & B. GAINES, Eds. *Knowledge-Based Systems, Volume 2: Knowledge Acquisition Tools for Expert Systems*, pp. 257–273. London. Academic Press.

NEALE, I. (1988). First generation expert systems: a review of knowledge acquisition methodologies. *The Knowledge Engineering Review*, **2**, 105–145.

NECHES, R., SWARTOUT, W. & MOORE, J. (1985). Enhanced maintenance and explanation of expert systems through explicit models of their development. *IEEE Transactions Software Engineering*, **11**, 337–1351.

NEWELL, A. (1982). The knowledge level. *Artificial Intelligence,* **1982,** 87–127.

NILSSON, N. (1991). Logic and artificial intelligence. *Artificial Intelligence,* **47,** 31–56.

PATIL, R. (1988). Artificial intelligence techniques for diagnostic reasoning in medicine. In H. Shobe, & AAAI, Eds., *Exploring Artificial Intelligence Survey Talks from the National Conferences on Artificial Intelligence,* pp. 347–379. San Mateo, California: Morgan Kaufmann.

POPLE, H. (1982). Heuristic methods for imposing structure on ill-structured problems: The structuring in medical diagnosis. In P. Szolovits, Ed., *Artificial Intelligence in Medicine,* pp. 119–190 Boulder CO: Westview Press.

READDIE, M. & INNES, N. (1987a). *Network management: KBS design document.* ESPRIT Project P1098, Deliverable E3.2a, SciCon Ltd. (UK).

READDIE, M. & INNES, N. (1987b). *Network management: Requirements analysis and feasibility analysis.* ESPRIT Project P1098, Deliverable E3.1a, SciCon Ltd. (UK).

REICHGELT, H. & van HARMELEN, F. (1986). Criteria for choosing representation languages and control regimes for expert systems. *Knowledge Engineering Review,* **1,** 2–17.

REINDERS, M., VINKHUYZEN, E., VOß, A., AKKERMANS, H., BALDER, J., BARTSCH-SPORL, B., BREDEWEG, B., DROUVEN, U., van HARMELEN, F., KARBACH, W., KARSSEN, Z., SCHREIBER, G. & WIELINGA, B. (1991). A conceptual modelling framework for knowledge-level reflection. *AI Communications,* **4.**

ROTH, E. M. & WOODS, D. (1989). Cognitive task analysis: An approach to knowledge acquisition for intelligent system design. In P. GUIDA & G. TASSO, Eds. *Topics in Expert System Design,* pp. 233–264, Amsterdam: North-Holland.

SCHACHTER, M. & WERMSER, D. (1988). A sales assistant for chemical measurement equipment. In *Proceedings ECAI'88, Munich,* pp. 191–193, London: Pitman.

SCHREIBER, G., AKKERMANS, H. & WIELINGA, B. (1991). On problems with the knowledge level perspective. In L. STEELS & B. SMITH, Eds. *AISB91: Artificial Intelligence and Simulation of Behaviour,* pp. 208–221, London: Springer Verlag. Also in J. BOOSE & B. GAINES, Eds. *Proceedings Ban, '90 Knowledge Acquisition Workshop,* pp. 30-1–30-14. University of Calgary: SRDG Publications.

SCHREIBER, G., BREDEWEG, B., DAVOODI, M. & WIELINGA, B. (1987). *Towards a design methodology for KBS.* ESPRIT Project P1098, Deliverable D8 (task B2), University of Amsterdam and STL Ltd.

SCHREIBER, G., BREDEWEG, B., de GREEF, P., TERPSTRA, P., WIELINGA, B., BRUMET, E., SIMONIN, N. & WALLYN, A. (1989a). *A KADS approach to KBS design.* ESPRIT Project 1098, Deliverable B6 UvA-B6-PR-010, University of Amsterdam & Cap Sogeti Innovation.

SCHREIBER, G., BREUKER, J., BREDEWEG, B. & WIELINGA, B. (1988). Modeling in KBS development. In *Proceedings of the 2nd European Knowledge Acquisition Workshop,* Bonn, GMD-Studien **143,** pp. 7.1–7.15. St. Augustin. GMD. Also in: *Proceedings of the 8th Expert Systems Workshop,* Avignon, 1988.

SCHREIBER, G., WIELINGA, B., HESKETH, P. & LEWIS, A. (1989b). *A KADS design description language.* ESPRIT Project 1098, Deliverable B7 UvA-B7-PR-007, University of Amsterdam & STC Technology Ltd.

SCHRIJNEN, L. & WAGENAAR, G. (1988). Autopes: the development of an expert system for process control. In M. van SOMEREN, & A. SCHREIBER, Eds. *Proceedings First Dutch AI Conference NAIC'88,* pp. 58–71, University of Amsterdam. Department of Social Science Informatics. (In Dutch.)

SHADBOLT, N. & WIELINGA, B. (1990). Knowledge based knowledge acquisition: the next generation of support tools. In B. WIELINGA, J. BOOSE, B. GAINES, G. SCHREIBER & M. van SOMEREN, Eds. *Current Trends in Knowledge Acquisition,* pp. 313–338, Amsterdam: IOS Press.

SHORTLIFFE, E., SCOTT, A., BISCHOFF, M., CAMBELL, A., van MELLE, W. & JACOBS, C. (1981). ONCOCIN: An expert system for oncology protocol management. In *IJCAI-81,* pp. 876–881.

STEELS, L. (1990). Components of expertise. *AI Magazine,* Summer issue. Also as: AI Memo 88–16, AI Lab, Free University of Brussels.

TAYLOR, R., PORTER, D., HICKMAN, F., STRENG, K.-H., TANSLEY, S. & DORBES, G. (1989). System evolution—principles and methods (the life-cycle model). ESPRIT Project P1098, Deliverable Task G9, Touche Ross.

TONG, X., HE, Z. & YU, R. (1988). A survey of the expert system tool ZDEST-2. In *Proceedings ECAI'88, Munich,* pp. 113–118, London: Pitman.

ÜBERREITER, B. & VOß, A., Eds. (1991). *Materials KADS User Meeting, Munich, February 14/15 1991.* Siemens AG ZFE IS INF 32, Munich Perlach. (In German).

van der MOLEN, R. & KRUIZINGA, E. (1990). *OKS GAK: a feasibility study.* Master's thesis, University of Amsterdam, Department of Social Science Informatics. (In Dutch).

van der SPEK, R., van der WOUDEN, H., & YSBRANDY, C. (1990). The paint advisor. *Expert Systems,* **7**(4), 190–198.

van HARMELEN, F. & BALDER, J. (1992). $(ML)^2$: A formal language for KADS models of expertise. *Knowledge Acquisition,* **4,** 127–161. Also as, Technical Report ESPRIT Project P5248 KADS-II/T1.2/TR/ECN/006/1.0, Netherlands Energy Research Centre ECN.

VANWELKENHUYSEN, J. & RADEMAKERS, P. (1990). Mapping knowledge-level analysis on to a computational framework. In L. AIELLO, Ed. *Proceedings ECAI'90, Stockholm,* pp. 681–686, London: Pitman.

VOß, A., KARBACH, W., DROUVEN, U. & LROEK, D. (1990). Competence assessment in configuration tasks. In L. Aiello, Ed. *Proceedings of the 9th European Conference on AI, ECAI'90,* pp. 676–681, London: Pitman.

WETTER, T. (1990). First-order logic foundation of the KADS conceptual model. In B. WIELINGA, J. BOOSE, B. GAINES, G. SCHREIBER & M. van SOMEREN, Eds. *Current Trends in Knowledge Acquisition,* pp. 356-375. Amsterdam: IOS Press.

WIELEMAKER, J. & BILLAULT, J. (1988). *A KADS analysis for configuration.* ESPRIT Project P1098, Deliverable E5.1, University of Amsterdam.

WIELINGA, B. & BREDEWEG, B. (1988). Knowledge and expertise in expert systems. In G. van der VEER & G. MULDER, Eds. *Human-Computer Interaction: Psychonomics Aspects,* pp. 290–297. Berlin: Springer-Verlag.

WIELINGA, B. & BREUKER, J. (1984). Interpretation of verbal data for knowledge acquisition. In T. O'SHEA, Ed. *Advances in Artificial Intelligence,* pp. 41–50, Amsterdam: ECAI, Elsevier Science publishers.

WIELINGA, B. & BREUKER, J. (1986). Models of expertise. In *Proceedings ECAI'81,* pp. 306–318.

WINKELS, R. & ACHTHOVEN, W. (1989). Methodology and modularity in ITS design. In *Artificial Intelligence and Education,* pp. 314–322, Amsterdam: IOS Press.

WRIGHT, I., HAYBALL, C., LAND., L. & MULHALL, T. (1988). *Analysis report experiment F6.* ESPRIT Project P1098, Deliverable E6.1, STC Technology Ltd. & Knowledge Based Systems Centre.

# Knowledge Acquisition for Expert Systems: Some Pitfalls and Suggestions

DIANA E. FORSYTHE AND BRUCE G. BUCHANAN

*Abstract* —Although data for building a knowledge base are often gathered during face-to-face interviews between experts and knowledge engineers, practical problems of communication between a knowledge engineer and an expert are rarely addressed in the expert systems literature. The paper presents some preliminary conclusions from an ongoing study in which ethnographic techniques are being applied to the problem of identifying and mitigating difficulties of communication between knowledge engineers and experts.

## I. INTRODUCTION

ALTHOUGH the technology of representing and using knowledge in expert systems has been a major focus of artificial intelligence (AI) research for three decades, the practical problems of building such systems have only recently become a topic of research. In this paper we address the problem of identifying and mitigating difficulties of communication in the process of eliciting information from one or more human experts for the purpose of building a knowledge base.[1]

Knowledge acquisition (KA) has come to be seen as a bottleneck in the process of building expert systems [1]. This task, sometimes called "extracting knowledge from human experts," can be slow, inefficient, and frustrating for expert and knowledge engineer alike. As Stefik and Conway [2] noted,

"...knowledge acquisition is sometimes considered a necessary burden, carried out under protest so that one can get on with the study of cognitive processes in problem solving."

Manuscript received March 3, 1988; revised August 10, 1988. This work was supported in part by US West, in part by the National Institute of Health (grant no. 5P41 RR-00785), and in part by Boeing (contract no. W271799).

D. E. Forsythe was with the Knowledge Systems Laboratory, the Department of Computer Science, Stanford University, Stanford, CA and is now with the Intelligent Systems Laboratory, the Department of Computer Science, Mineral Industries Building, Room 212, University of Pittsburgh, Pittsburgh, PA 15260.

B. G. Buchanan was with the Knowledge Systems Laboratory, Stanford University, Stanford, CA and is now with the Intelligent Systems Laboratory, the Department of Computer Science, Mineral Industries Building, Room 206, University of Pittsburgh, Pittsburgh, PA 15260.

[1]In this paper we distinguish between "knowledge acquisition" and "knowledge elicitation". Knowledge acquisition typically involves gathering information from one or more human experts and/or from documentary sources, ordering that information in some way, and then translating it into machine-readable form. Sometimes knowledge acquisition includes face-to-face interviewing of the expert(s) by the knowledge engineer(s). We refer to this interview process as "knowledge elicitation."

Several years later [3], the same problem persists:

"Collecting and encoding the knowledge needed to build an ITS [intelligent tutoring system] is still a long and difficult task and substantial project resources must still be allocated to this stage. Of course, the lack of good high-level tools for knowledge acquisition is a serious problem..."

There have been numerous attempts to solve the knowledge acquisition bottleneck. One approach has involved the development of automated or semi-automated methods of knowledge acquisition. These include intelligent editors, such as Teiresias [4], Roget [5], Mole [6], More [7], and ETS [8]. Another approach has been the creation of tools for aiding in the conceptualization of a knowledge base. Such tools include protocol analysis [9] and personal construct theory [10]. A third approach involves the development of heuristics for knowledge engineering [1], [11].

Characteristic of all such proposed solutions from within the AI community is a tendency to focus on higher-level issues such as classifying information collected from the expert or insuring that this information is complete, while glossing over detailed questions of how to gather the material in the first place. Although KA typically requires a lengthy interview process, it would be impossible to learn how to carry out an interview from the AI literature alone. When actual problems of face-to-face data collection are addressed, reference to such notions as "chemistry" and "rapport" implies a certain sense of helplessness among practitioners about how to approach the task [12]. While recent publications have come closer to addressing some of the practicalities of interviewing for KA [13]–[18], they still suffer from the general tendency to name methods without providing much information on how to apply them.[2] To date there is nothing in the AI literature that

[2]To illustrate this point, we take an example from one of the better recent books on the subject of KA methodology. On "The elicitation of data on domain knowledge," Breuker and Wielinga [46] provide the following advice: "Because written sources hardly ever contain information on how knowledge is used, other data have to be elicited from experts by interview techniques, and in particular by thinking-aloud procedures." They then name six "elicitation techniques" and list the types of data each is intended to elicit. Although this passage appears in a volume intended as a practical handbook, however, and Breuker and Wielinga are clearly aware that knowledge elicitation is not just a matter of common sense, they do not in fact provide practical information on how to carry out the procedures they name. Reading the passages mentioned here, for example, the reader is left with such questions as the following. What sort of "focused interview," "thinking-aloud procedures," and so forth do the authors have in mind here, and how should a knowledge engineer go about learning and applying them? What do

©1989 IEEE. Reprinted, with permission, from *IEEE Transactions on Systems, Man, and Cybernetics*; 19:3, pp. 435-442; May/June 1989.

could serve as a useful "how to" guide for the novice knowledge engineer.[3]

In short, we know a good deal about how to represent and manipulate knowledge in expert systems, but have very little systematic understanding of how best to gather that knowledge in the first place. Attention to this problem is a priority for speeding up and teaching knowledge acquisition. Recognition of this state of affairs prompted us to approach the knowledge acquisition problem from a new perspective. Reasoning that the design of heuristics for knowledge acquisition should begin with a detailed understanding of the knowledge elicitation process itself, we decided to undertake research on that topic.

This paper presents our initial report on this research. The first section introduces the interdisciplinary anthropoligical study of knowledge elicitation (ASKE) project. Next, we discuss the choice of anthropological methodology for the project, pointing out the relevance of anthropology to knowledge engineering in general. In the third section we give examples of pitfalls that we have observed in the knowledge elicitation process, including problems related to both interviewing technique and conceptual approach. And finally, we draw some preliminary conclusions based on our work to date.

## II. AN EMPIRICAL STUDY OF KNOWLEDGE ELICITATION

In 1986 we inaugurated a research initiative on knowledge acquisition. One of the projects begun under that initiative is the ASKE project, which uses anthropological methods to analyze knowledge elicitation as a process of face-to-face communication. ASKE is a qualitative empirical study: we are observing and analyzing the processes by which knowledge engineers acquire and order the domain knowledge to be encoded in their systems. The outcome of this research will be an improved understanding of the KA process itself—including some of its pitfalls—and the development of heuristics for coping with or (better yet) avoiding such difficulties.

We recognize that many factors determine the success or failure of a knowledge engineering effort. For example, knowledge engineers must be technically competent. Communication skills on the part of both knowledge engineers and experts are clearly important, as are many other social and technical factors involved in building a computer program for human use. In this study, we have chosen to focus primarily on the communication skills of the knowledge engineer as one important determinant of success.

ASKE is an interdisciplinary project primarily involving anthropology and AI. The central component of the pro-

ject is observation of face-to-face knowledge elicitation in a range of scientific and engineering projects, including both academic and commercial settings. These observational data are supplemented with material drawn from interviews with AI professionals and from extended participant observation in a Silicon Valley AI lab. In addition, we draw upon data taken from our own videotapes of novice knowledge engineers engaged in practice interviews with real experts.

Anthropology is involved in two ways. First, we are using anthropological field methods to gather information about communication during the knowledge acquisition process. Second, we believe that some of the same methods (in particular, participant observation and interviewing methods) are appropriate approaches to include in the repertoire of knowledge engineering.

This study has been underway for a year and a half, and is still in progress. To date Forsythe has completed eighteen months of participant observation in the AI lab, over 200 h of formal meeting observations involving 12 projects, and about 80 h of formal observation of KA sessions. Of the latter, ten hours were recorded on videotape.

## III. THE APPROPRIATENESS OF ANTHROPOLOGICAL METHODOLOGY

While artificial intelligence has drawn heavily on linguistics and psychology, it has paid much less attention to the neighboring disciplines of anthropology and qualitative sociology.[4] In the areas of both problem definition and methodology, however, there is a great deal of overlap between the concerns of AI and those of these other social science disciplines. With respect to the definition of problems for research, all three are concerned with investigating how human beings understand, organize, process and make use of symbolic information. With respect to methodology, anthropologists and qualitative sociologists rely on the same primary data-gathering methods as knowledge engineers—face-to-face interviewing of one or more specialist individuals, supplemented by the use of documentary evidence and observational data. From the standpoint of a social scientist this disciplinary overlap is striking,[5] a fact reflected in a growing literature in which the methods of anthropology and sociology have been applied to the analysis of AI-related problems [19]–[28].

There are also some noteworthy differences between these disciplines, two of which deserve mention here be-

---

"factual knowledge," "support knowledge," etc. mean, and how can a knowledge engineer recognize them?

[3]Several companies, including Digital Equipment Corporation, Texas Instruments, and Teknowledge, have created training courses in knowledge engineering methodology. However, since the written materials that accompany these courses are not in the public domain, we are unable to evaluate their contents.

[4]The lack of discussion about possible connections between sociology and AI has been noted by Woolgar, [47] who comments: "Although the associations between AI, on the one hand, and disciplines like psychology and philosophy, on the other, have been widely recognised and lengthily debated in terms of the implications of one for the other, the important possibility of an association between AI and *sociology* has hardly been noticed. On the few occasions it is alluded to, sociology is assigned the role of dealing with matters left over by other disciplines" [original emphasis].

[5]In fact, from a methodological standpoint knowledge engineering would seem to have more in common with the fieldwork orientation of anthropology and qualitative sociology than with the experimental orientation of many in the cognitive sciences.

cause of their potential utility for AI. First, whereas AI is a relatively new discipline with a newly-emerging body of theory, the social sciences have built up an extensive literature on the nature and functioning of human intelligence in a range of naturally occurring cultural, social and material contexts. This literature can offer AI some relevant theory and vocabulary. It can also serve as a useful counterbalance to the psychological data derived from contrived experimental settings on which many AI researchers rely for information about the nature of human thought. Second, while (as we have noted) the AI literature contains little discussion of data-gathering methodology for knowledge acquisition, the conduct of face-to-face research has been a major topic in anthropology and qualitative sociology, again resulting in a large body of literature.

Two sections of that literature are of particular interest for knowledge engineers. First, the discussion on qualitative methodology [29], especially interview methodology [30]–[32], offers numerous pointers for increasing the success of knowledge elicitation and analysis. Second, the literature on the ethnographic method of research used by anthropologists discusses ways of combining directive and nondirective interviewing with observation and the use of documentary material. Ethnographic methodology has been developed to facilitate data-gathering in the informal, unstructured, and sometimes unpredictable situations typically encountered by anthropologists in the course of field research [33]–[35]. It is particularly relevant to knowledge engineers for two reasons. First, knowledge elicitation involves data-gathering under conditions that are in many ways comparable to those in which anthropologists are accustomed to work. For example, the ethnographic approach explicitly recognizes the fact that in the early stages of research, knowledge engineers/fieldworkers not only do not know the answers they are seeking, they do not even know the right questions to ask. Becoming familiar with a particular domain implies learning to understand the types of questions and answers that have meaning in that domain. And second, the method promotes the collection of uncodified "common sense" knowledge as well as knowledge that is formally ordered. As AI researchers have noted, both kinds of knowledge may be necessary if expert systems are to function in anything but very narrowly specified domains [36], [37].

Recognition of the common ground between anthropology and artificial intelligence is just beginning to emerge in the AI community:

"Anthropologists, it could be argued, are also in the ontology and inventory business. They visit foreign cultures and as part of their field work, attempt to compile an explicit ontology. We believe that KA for systems development is fundamentally an anthropological activity." [38]

The ASKE project grew out of the insight that this overlap can be of considerable benefit to knowledge engineers. Not only do the theory and methodology of the social sciences constitute a valuable resource for AI, but the ethnographic method itself can be applied to contribute to the analysis and solution of the knowledge acquisition problem.

## IV. SOME PITFALLS OF KNOWLEDGE ELICITATION

There is a great deal more to understanding what an expert says and does than what one can obtain from interview material alone, or from interview material supplemented by textbooks. Such material is not self-evident: it must be interpreted [20], [39]. This job requires, for example, that one sift through the experts' reports about their own thoughts and actions, and add in information that was not reported but that is necessary for understanding the nature of their expertise. This may include tacit knowledge [40], contextual information, and unreported actions that experts may or may not be aware of, but which nevertheless constitute part of the process being modeled. For instance, in a project modeling the expertise of a scientist skilled at assessing the credibility of statistical studies, the expert produced a detailed list of formal statistical criteria that he used to judge methodological quality. After hours of watching him engaged in this task, however, we realized that he consistently paid attention to other information that he had not reported. This included social factors (e.g., the reputation of the statisticians involved in the studies, and whether or not he knew them personally).

To an anthropologist it appears obvious that the best approach to knowledge elicitation would be to apply ethnographic methodology. In this case, knowledge engineers would attach themselves to an expert or group of experts as participant observers for a period of weeks or months. This would enable them to learn as much as possible about a particular sort of expertise by observing, questioning, and attempting to apply the skills themselves, while simultaneously learning about the social and material context in which the expertise is normally constituted and practiced. Such participant observation would provide knowledge engineers with the opportunity to notice and collect informal, uncodified information, some of which may not be directly accessible to the experts themselves.

At the present time, however, few knowledge engineers have received any training in ethnographic methods and few seem open to trying this approach. On the contrary, under pressure of time and money, most appear to want to spend less rather than more time with their experts [23]. Recognizing this state of affairs, we focus here on proposing change of a more modest kind. Since knowledge elicitation generally involves face-to-face interviews with one or more experts, the discussion below aims at encouraging knowledge engineers to undertake these interviews in a more informed and self-conscious way.

Knowledge engineers—particularly novices—can encounter various difficulties in connection with the communication aspects of knowledge acquisition. In this section we list examples of two of the types of pitfalls that we have observed during interview sessions.[6] Errors of the first type

---

[6] These are only two out of several possible types of pitfalls. Our data also demonstrate that knowledge engineers encounter difficulties that relate to such factors as nonverbal communication and the spatial organization of the interview setting. In later publications we will present

reflect problems in interview technique, in which the knowledge engineer mis-applies or fails to apply appropriate interview strategies. Errors of the second type involve inappropriate assumptions that knowledge engineers may bring to the job of face-to-face data-gathering.

Maxims for knowledge engineering have been formulated before. They tend to be extremely general, not to be based upon systematic observation of knowledge acquisition, and not for the most part to concern themselves with problems of communication between knowledge engineer and expert. For example, of the 43 maxims offered by Buchanan *et al.* [1], only three relate to knowledge elicitation.[7] In contrast, the communicative processes of knowledge elicitation are our major concern. We are particularly interested in alerting knowledge engineers to the importance of communication on the nonverbal as well as the verbal level. Although few knowledge engineers seem to be aware of this fact, the way in which they ask questions of the expert may influence the success of their enterprise as much as the content of those questions.

### A. Interviewing Problems

Because interviewing takes place through the medium of conversation, and because the latter is an everyday activity, knowledge engineers sometimes assume that KA is just a matter of chatting with the expert. As Gorden [41] comments, "To the uninitiated, interviewing is 'just talking to people!'" The influence of this attitude among knowledge engineers can be seen in two examples from the literature. First, in an article on "methods for knowledge acquisition," Olson and Rueter [42] describe interviewing in the following terms:

> "Interviews are the most common method for eliciting knowledge from the expert. In conversation, the expert reveals the objects he/she thinks about, how they are related or organized, and the process he/she goes through in making a judgement, solving a problem, or designing a solution. There are simple guidelines that can be followed to make interviewing efficient."

Second, one of Gammack's "rules of thumb" is, "If interviewing comes naturally to both parties, then interview methods may be fruitful." [43]

These statements sound naive. Interviewing does not just happen: the knowledge engineer must make it happen. Far from coming naturally, interviewing is a difficult task that requires planning, stage-management, technique, and a lot of self-control. It also demands skills very different from—indeed, in some cases opposite to—those usually required of graduate students, corporate employees, or

programmers. Unfortunately, it is very easy to interview badly, with the result that one may learn little and/or alienate the expert. Below we outline some of the shoals that knowledge engineers must navigate during the interview process. No simple solutions are presented here; indeed, interviewing is such a particularistic process that no general solutions could be presented to many of these problems. Rather, our goal is to increase awareness of the problems themselves, since that is the first step toward finding appropriate solutions.

*1) Obtaining Data versus Relating to the Expert as a Person:* Experts are people with personalities and agendas of their own, and they frequently have the authority to refuse further interviews. Successful interviewing requires negotiating and maintaining a balance between obtaining data and acknowledging the expert as a person and a professional. To some extent, these two goals are in conflict: our data include examples of interviewers who were highly personable but didn't learn much about their topic, and others who were so topic-oriented that the expert felt irritated and even abused. Concerning a knowledge engineer in the first category, the expert commented, "He wasted my time." Concerning one in the second, the expert said, "He treated me like a dog!"

*2) Twin Dangers of Over- and Under-Directedness:* Interviewing also requires maintaining a balance between being directive and being responsive. This principle applies in several senses, including both decisions concerning the subject-matter of particular interviews and the degree of intrusiveness used by the interviewer in steering the expert. Knowledge engineers must find a middle ground between deciding upon an approach and a list of questions beforehand, and being completely open to changing approach on the basis of what the interviewee says and does. Similarly, they must consciously weigh the cost in time and efficiency of letting a loquacious expert carry on at will, versus the possible cost in good-will (and possibly data) of interrupting repeatedly to keep the expert on course. Again, our data include a range of examples. Some interviewers were so preplanned that they ignored the expert when he/she showed irritation or suggested that their approach was inappropriate. For example, some stuck stubbornly to a case-based approach when the interviewee was trying to tell them rules. On the other hand, some interviewers were so nondirective and so unplanned that they simply floundered without appearing to have any approach in mind. Surprisingly, perhaps, some interviewers managed during the same session to be both under- and overdirective, veering between the two extremes. Once again, the goal is balance: steering the interviewee gently while remaining open to the possibility of having to change course.

*3) Fear of Silence and Failing to Listen:* Some interviewers don't allow the expert sufficient time to speak. This may be the result of nervousness and/or a rapid interactional rhythm on the part of the interviewer. Novice knowledge engineers may confuse an interview with an examination, and waste time unnecessarily trying to demonstrate their own competence to the expert. Simple as

---

further material on pitfalls in knowledge elicitation. We will also take up related questions such as the problem of knowledge engineering configuration (e.g. the effects on knowledge elicitation of the size, structure, and composition of the knowledge engineering team and the expert team).

[7]Buchanan et al. urge the knowledge engineer to "record a detailed protocol of the expert solving at least one prototypical case" [1, p. 161], to "use the terms and methods that the experts use" [1, p. 164], and to "watch (the expert) doing examples" as well as talking with him/her [1, p. 164].

it sounds, it is imperative to learn to listen; for many interviewers this requires considerable self-control. Silence is an ally in this task. Knowledge engineers should not be afraid to sit silently for a while in case the expert has more to add, or in order to gather their own thoughts. We observed knowledge engineers who were so afraid to let the conversation lag that they fired questions at the expert without really listening to the responses. In such cases no one's goals were met: the experts were offended because they didn't feel they had been heard, while the knowledge engineers gathered information that was less accurate than it could have been.

*4) Difficulty Asking Questions:* Asking good questions well is an art. Knowledge engineers may encounter several problems in this area. First, for some knowledge engineers, questioning the expert at all is clearly difficult. The age, gender, status, and cultural background of both interviewer and expert are likely to affect this situation. After all, an interview is a social encounter as well as a professional one. It is impossible usefully to prescribe a particular strategy or style: our observations illustrate that the tactics appropriate in any particular situation depend on the individual knowledge engineer and expert involved. For example, of two female experts we have observed so far, one preferred to be treated deferentially; she responded best to female interviewers and to a young male knowledge engineer of Chinese background. In contrast, the other expert responded well to a less deferential approach, apparently pleased that a rather brash male interviewer found her approachable. Clearly, face-to-face knowledge acquisition demands considerable sensitivity and flexibility on the part of the knowledge engineer (and the expert) to be able to assess and adjust to the social constraints posed by the interview. Whatever the tone of the interaction, the interviewer must actively question the expert. The worst pitfall of all is to fail to ask for information.

Second, since the questions one asks influence the answers one gets, knowledge engineers need to pay attention to question formulation. Almost everyone finds it challenging to formulate carefully worded questions that are appropriate to a particular domain, interactional situation, and stage of research. This is especially difficult when the domain is unfamiliar. Payne [44] provides a useful discussion of some of the issues involved in question formulation. Our own observations suggest that novice knowledge engineers in particular should beware of the following.

- Asking long, complicated, repetitious questions. Ask one short, clear question at a time and then stop talking. Resist the temptation to repeat and elaborate questions.
- Using AI vocabulary not necessarily known to the respondent. Try to speak the expert's language.

Third, a lack of awareness of different types of questions makes it difficult to conduct an interview. Knowledge engineers must have at their command a repertoire of questions that perform such tasks as:

- probing for further information ("Tell me more about that") and checking for completeness ("Is there anything else?");
- asking for clarification ("I don't understand; could you explain?", "How does that relate to our topic?");
- following up points mentioned by the expert ("How/why/when do you do that?", "What do you do next?");
- prompting to keep the expert talking ("I see", "Um hmm"); and
- feeding back information to check on its accuracy ("Let me try to summarize—please correct me if I'm wrong").

*5) Interviewing Without a Record:* Interviewing is difficult in part because it requires the knowledge engineer to pay attention on many levels at once. In addition to asking questions and monitoring progress on the substantive level, knowledge engineers must maintain awareness of time, personality, interactional and sometimes political factors, as well as hardware and software requirements of the proposed expert system. Given these demands, it is inevitable that the interviewer will miss—or fail to grasp the significance of—some of what the expert says. Therefore, it is necessary that some sort of objective record of each interview be maintained. The easiest and least obtrusive recording device is a small tape recorder. Like many of our points in this section, this may appear obvious; but only a minority of the knowledge engineers we have observed have actually recorded their sessions on tape. Too often, knowledge engineers seem to trust their memories and their handwritten notes.

To sum up these comments on interview technique, no single approach or method will work all the time; rather, an interviewer must be able to draw upon a repertoire of approaches. It pays to prepare carefully ahead of time, planning what seems like a sensible way of focusing the interview, but remaining flexible in case this turns out not to be the best way of doing things. An interview is a social occasion during which social convention and personalities enter in significant ways. It is necessary to analyze the expert's personality, interactional style, and tolerances, and adapt oneself to them. This requires flexibility. Knowledge engineers also need to be aware of their own personality, interactional style, etc., and to try to keep them under control while interviewing.

### B. Conceptual Problems

A second category of pitfalls in knowledge acquisition is conceptual errors that have methodological implications. Three such assumptions will be mentioned here.

*1) Treating Interview Methodology as Unproblematic:* Some knowledge engineers seem to perceive the question of interview methodology as trivial or "just a matter of common sense" [23]. One AI professional we interviewed likened explicit discussion of how to interview to telling grown-ups how to tie their shoes. In response, we would like to point out that common sense is anything but common: as Minsky [45] notes, "what people vaguely call common sense is actually far more intricate than most of the technical expertise we admire." The KA bottleneck is a matter of clear concern to knowledge engineers themselves. We suggest that there is a connection between this bottleneck and the apparent reluctance to take seriously the question of interview methodology. This point has major implications for expert systems development, because interview technique may affect the quality of the data gathered as well as the time it takes to collect them. If the information that goes into a knowledge base is poorly understood or incomplete, the most sophisticated representation or inference schemes will not produce a good system. As Gorden [41, p. 4] points out:

> "It is clear that no amount of refinement in data analysis can counteract the effects of faulty data-collection methods that provide raw information which is false, distorted, or incomplete. Nevertheless, there is still a tendency for the advances in data-gathering methodology to lag behind those in data analysis."

Gorden [41, pp. 4–5] identifies several causes of this attitude, two of which are relevant here:

> "First, there is an unfortunate tendency to consider data gathering as a lower status activity than data analysis or theorizing about the data. ...Another barrier to the actual application of the best data-gathering methods is the fact that it often costs more in time or money to collect valid data than it does to collect invalid data. Of course, this is a false economy if any real decisions are to be based on the data."

*2) Blaming the Expert:* Knowledge engineers often blame the expert for difficulties encountered in the elicitation process. This attitude was expressed in interviews; for example, one experienced knowledge engineer asserted that "experts are a cantankerous lot." It is also reflected in the literature (e.g., [12]). However, where AI scientists resort to speculation about the psychological difficulties of experts in dealing with knowledge engineers or computers, the experienced ethnographic fieldworker suspects a lack of interviewing expertise on the part of the knowledge engineers involved and/or an inappropriate pairing between interviewer and expert.

*3) Reifying Knowledge:* Knowledge engineers appear to think of knowledge as a material entity, a thing that lends itself to extraction like a diseased tooth [23]. As Kidd also pointed out, the language used to talk about knowledge acquisition serves to obscure the nature of the process.

> "A popular view of KA has been to consider experts' heads as being filled with bits of knowledge and the problem of KA as being one of 'mining those jewels of knowledge out of their heads one by one' [Feigenbaum and McCorduck, 1983]. ...The analogy is misleading; there is no *truth* in that sense. Rather, it is the case that KA involves the following:
> 1) Employing a technique to elicit data (usually verbal) from the expert.
> 2) Interpreting these verbal data (more or less skillfully) in order to infer what might be the expert's underlying knowledge and reasoning process.

> 3) Using this interpretation to guide the construction of some model or language that describes (more or less accurately) the expert's knowledge and performance.
> ...Knowledge engineers need to recognize that this is the basic process in which they are engaging..." [48].[8]

Rather than conceptualizing knowledge as a material entity, we suggest that it is more useful to view it as shared understanding produced through the collaborative efforts of interviewers and respondents [49], [50]. Knowledge that may be needed by knowledge engineers is "stored" not only in the experts' conscious models but also in their unarticulated understanding of the world and the task at hand, and in the social and physical milieux that form the normal context of the experts' work [20], [22], [28].

## V. THE NONTECHNICAL NATURE OF THESE PITFALLS

Accustomed to thinking in terms of technical problems with technical solutions, knowledge engineers may be unimpressed by the fact that the KA pitfalls identified here are nontechnical in nature. However, we believe that this is one reason they are pitfalls for knowledge engineers, since the training and biases of the latter may lead them to overlook such difficulties. Since the ASKE project began, we have been asked about "the latest knowledge acquisition techniques" by colleagues who clearly did not want to hear about other disciplines or about ideas that could be categorized as "just common sense." However, many important insights seem obvious once they have been articulated; the trick is to notice and articulate them. Furthermore, people do not always do what is obvious. Therefore, we repeat that every factor just discussed has been observed repeatedly to interfere with the knowledge acquisition process.

## VI. CONCLUSION

In this paper, we have pointed out that discussion of knowledge acquisition methodology in the AI literature has neglected consideration of the methodology involved in gathering data in a face-to-face context. Both this fact and the spontaneous comments of knowledge engineers suggest that this topic is widely viewed in the field as trivial and/or self-evident. However, observations of actual knowledge acquisition sessions reveal that knowledge engineers not infrequently commit errors in interview technique that are severe enough to alienate the expert and/or to jeopardize the amount or quality of data gathered during the interview. To an anthropologist this is not surprising, since social scientists do not view interview technique as self-evident. On the contrary, anthropological common sense suggests that there is a link between the knowledge acquisition problem, and the naive approach apparently taken by many knowledge engineers to both the

[8]Kidd's reference is to E. Feigenbaum and P. McCorduck *The Fifth Generation*. New York: Addison-Wesley, 1983.

theory and the practice of acquiring knowledge from experts through the medium of face-to-face interaction.

The job of the present-day knowledge engineer is not exclusively technical; it requires communication skills in several areas, one of which is knowledge elicitation. It follows that the education of knowledge engineers should not be exclusively technical either. At best, it should include formal training in the social sciences. At the least, it should include training in interview methodology (which is aided by the use of videotaped practice interviews to give specific feedback on interview style and content), in interview theory (covering such topics as question formulation, interactional rhythm, and nonverbal communication), and in the sociology of knowledge.

## REFERENCES

[1] B. G. Buchanan, D. Barstow, R. Bechtel, J. Bennet, W. Clancey, C. Kulikowski, T. Mitchell, and D. A. Waterman, "Constructing an expert system," in *Building Expert Systems*, F. Hayes-Roth, D. A. Waterman, and D. B. Lenat, Eds. Reading, MA: Addison-Wesley, 1983.

[2] M. Stefik and L. Conway, "Toward the principled engineering of knowledge," *AI Magazine*, Summer 1982, p. 4.

[3] J. R. Miller, "Human computer interaction and intelligent tutoring systems," MCC Tech. Rep. No. HI-294-86, *Handbook of Intelligent Tutoring Systems* in M. C. Polson and J. J. Richardson, Eds. Hillsdale, NJ: Lawrence Erlbaum Associates, 1987, p. 27.

[4] R. Davis, *Applications of Meta Level Knowledge to the Construction, Maintenance and Use of Large Knowledge Bases*. Stanford, CA: Computer Science Dept., Stanford Univ., 1976.

[5] J. S. Bennett, "ROGET: A knowledge-based system for acquiring the conceptual structure of a diagnostic expert system," *J. Automated Reasoning*, vol. 1, no. 1, 1985.

[6] L. Eshelman and J. McDermott, "MOLE: A knowledge acquisition tool that uses its head," in *Proc. Fifth Nat. Conf. Artific. Intell.*, Philadelphia, PA, 1986.

[7] G. Kahn, S. Nowlan, and J. McDermott, "MORE: An intelligent knowledge acquisition tool," in *Proc. Ninth Int. Joint Conf. Artificial Intell.*, Los Angeles, CA, 1985.

[8] J. H. Boose, *Expertise Transfer for Expert System Design*. New York: Elsevier, 1986.

[9] D. A. Waterman and A. Newell, "Protocol analysis as a task for artificial intelligence," *Artificial Intell.*, vol. 2, no. 3–4, 1971.

[10] J. H. Boose, *Expertise Transfer for Expert System Design*. New York: Elsevier, 1986, pp. 33–50.

[11] W. J. Clancey, "The knowledge engineer as student: Metacognitive bases for asking good questions," *Learning Issues for Intelligent Tutoring Systems*, H. Mandl and A. Lesgold, Eds. New York: Springer Verlag, 1988.

[12] R. H. Hill, Automating knowledge acquisition from experts. MCC Tech. Rep. Number AI-082-86, Microelectronics and Computer Technology Corp., Austin, TX, 1986.

[13] A. Hart, *Knowledge Acquisition for Expert Systems*. New York: McGraw-Hill, 1986.

[14] R. R. Hoffman, "The problem of extracting the knowledge of experts from the perspective of experimental psychology," *AI Magazine*, Summer 1987.

[15] A. L. Kidd, Ed., *Knowledge Acquisition for Expert Systems — A Practical Handbook*. New York: Plenum, 1987.

[16] M. LaFrance, "The knowledge acquisition grid: A method for training knowledge engineers," in *Proc. Knowledge Acquisition for Knowledge-Based Systems Workshop*. Banff, AB, Canada, 1986.

[17] J. R. Olson and H. H. Rueter, "Extracting expertise from experts: Methods for knowledge acquisition," *Expert Systems*, vol. 4, no. 3, 1987.

[18] D. S. Prerau, "Knowledge acquisition in the development of a large expert system," in *AI Magazine*, Summer 1987.

[19] J. Blomberg, "Social interaction and office communications: Effects on user evaluation of new technologies," *Technology and the Transformation of White Collar Work*, R. Kraut, Ed. Hillsdale,

[20] NJ: Erlbaum Press, 1986.

[20] H. M. Collins, "Expert systems and the science of knowledge," *The Social Construction of Technological Systems: New Directions in the Sociology and History of Technology*, W. E. Bijker, T. P. Hughes, and T. J. Pinch, Eds. Cambridge, MA: MIT Press, 1987.

[21] ___, "Expert systems, artificial intelligence, and the behavioural co-ordinates of skill," *The Question of Artificial Intelligence: Philosophical and Sociological Perspectives*, B. Bloomfield, Ed. London: Croom Helm Ltd., 1987.

[22] H. M. Collins, R. H. Green, and R. C. Draper, "Where's the expertise? Expert systems as a medium of knowledge transfer," *Expert Systems 85*, M. Merry, Ed. Cambridge: Cambridge Univ. Press, 1985.

[23] D. E. Forsythe, "Engineering knowledge: An anthropological study of an artificial intelligence laboratory," presented to meeting of the Society for Social Studies of Science, Worcester, MA, Nov. 19–22, 1987.

[24] L. Gasser, "The integration of computing and routine work," *ACM Trans. Office Inform. Syst.*, vol. 4, no. 3, 1986.

[25] ___, *The Social Dynamics of Routine Computer Use in Complex Organizations*. Los Angeles, CA: Computer Science Dept., Univ. of Southern California, 1984.

[26] J. E. Orr, "Narratives at work: Story telling as cooperative diagnostic activity," *Field Service Manager: The Journal of the Association of Field Service Managers International*, vol. 11, no. 6, 1987.

[27] ___, "Talking about machines: Social aspects of expertise." In The ARI Project: Section III: Research in Modeling, Reasoning, and Expertise: Four Papers from Research into the Semantics of Procedures, a final report to the Army Research Institute, Contract MDA 903-83-C-0189, Xerox Palo Alto Research Center, Palo Alto, CA, July 1987.

[28] L. Suchman, *Plans and Situated Actions: The Problem of Human-Machine Communication*. New York: Cambridge Univ. Press, 1987.

[29] A. L. Strauss, *Qualitative Analysis for Social Scientists*. New York: Cambridge Univ. Press, 1987.

[30] R. L. Gorden, *Interviewing — Strategy, Techniques, and Tactics*, 4th ed. Chicago, IL: The Dorsey Press, 1987.

[31] R. L. Kahn and C. F. Cannell, *The Dynamics of Interviewing — Theory, Technique, and Cases*. London: Wiley, 1961.

[32] E. G. Mischler, *Research Interviewing*. Cambridge, MA: Harvard Univ. Press, 1986.

[33] R. F. Ellen, Ed., *Ethnographic Research*. London: Academic Press, 1984.

[34] O. Werner and G. M. Schoepfle, *Systematic Fieldwork*. Newbury Park, CA: Sage Publications, 1987.

[35] R. H. Wax, *Doing Fieldwork: Warnings and Advice*. Chicago, IL: Univ. Chicago Press, 1971.

[36] D. B. Lenat and E. A. Feigenbaum, "On the thresholds of knowledge," in *Proc. Tenth Int. Joint Conf. Artific. Intell.*, Milan, Aug. 23–28, 1987.

[37] D. Lenat, M. Prakash, and M. Shepherd, "CYC: Using common sense knowledge to overcome brittleness and knowledge acquisition bottlenecks," *AI Magazine*, vol. 6, no. 4, 1986.

[38] S. Regoczei and E. P. O. Plantinga, "Ontology and inventory: A foundation for a knowledge acquisition methodology," in *Proc. Knowledge Acquisition for Knowledge-Based Syst. Workshop*, Banff, AB, Canada, 1986, p. 8.

[39] J. Breuker and B. Wielinga, "Use of models in the interpretation of verbal data," *Knowledge Acquisition for Expert Systems — A Practical Handbook*, A. L. Kidd, Ed. New York: Plenum Press, 1987, p. 19.

[40] M. Polanyi, *The Tacit Dimension*. New York: Doubleday, 1965.

[41] R. L. Gorden, *Interviewing — Strategy, Techniques, and Tactics*. Homewood, IL: The Dorsey Press, 1975, p. 32.

[42] J. R. Olson and H. H. Rueter, "Extracting expertise from experts: Methods for knowledge acquisition," *Expert Systems*, vol. 4, no. 3, p. 153, 1987.

[43] J. G. Gammack, "Different techniques and different aspects on declarative knowledge," *Knowledge Acquisition for Expert Systems — A Practical Handbook*, A. L. Kidd, Ed. New York: Plenum Press, 1987, p. 160.

[44] S. L. Payne, *The Art of Asking Questions*. Princeton: Princeton Univ. Press, 1963.

[45] M. Minsky, *The Society of Mind*. New York: Simon and Schuster, 1988, p. 72.

[46]    J. Breuker and B. Wielinga, "Use of models in the interpretation of verbal data," *Knowledge Acquisition for Expert Systems — A Practical Handbook*, A. L. Kidd, Ed. New York: Plenum Press, 1987, pp. 21–22.

[47]    S. Woolgar, "Why not a sociology of machines? The case of sociology and artificial intelligence," *Sociology*, vol. 19, no. 4, 1985, p. 558.

[48]    A. L. Kidd, "Knowledge acquisition; An introductory framework," in *Knowledge Acquisition for Expert Systems — A Practical Handbook*. New York: Plenum, 1987, pp. 2–3.

[49]    C. L. Briggs, *Learning How to Ask: A Sociolinguistic Appraisal of the Role of the Interview in Social Science Research*. Cambridge: Cambridge University Press, 1986.

[50]    E. G. Mischler, *Research Interviewing*. Cambridge, MA: Harvard University Press, 1986.

edge Systems Laboratory, Stanford University, Stanford, CA. She is now a Research Scientist at the Intelligent Systems Laboratory, the Department of Computer Science, University of Pittsburgh, Pittsburgh, PA. Her main research interest is in applying anthropological perspectives and methods to artificial intelligence, both descriptively (conducting an ethnographic study of an artificial intelligence laboratory) and prescriptively (in ongoing research on the problems of knowledge elicitation and explanation).

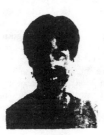

**Diana E. Forsythe** received the B.A. degree in anthropology from Swarthmore College, Swarthmore, PA, in 1969, and the M.A. and the Ph.D. degrees in anthropology and social demography from Cornell University, Ithaca, NY, in 1973 and 1974, respectively.

She has held teaching and research positions at universities in the United States, Great Britain, and the Federal Republic of Germany. In 1986 she began to focus on problems of artificial intelligence, and spent two years at the Knowl-

**Bruce G. Buchanan** received the B.A. degree in mathematics from Ohio Wesleyan University, Delaware, OH, in 1961 and the M.S. and Ph.D. degrees in philosophy from Michigan State University, East Lansing, MI, in 1966.

He was Professor of Computer Science Research and Co-Director of the Knowledge Systems Laboratory at Stanford University, Stanford, CA.

He is now Professor of Computer Science, Medicine, and Philosophy at the University of Pittsburgh, Pittsburgh, PA. He is also Adjunct Professor of Computer Science at Carnegie-Mellon University, Pittsburgh, PA and a Senior Fellow in the Center for Philosophy of Science at Pittsburgh. His main research interest is artificial intelligence, in particular, knowledge acquisition and machine learning, scientific hypothesis formation, and environments for building expert systems. He was one of the principals in the design and development of Dendral, Meta-Dendral, Mycin, E-Mycin, and Protean systems.

Dr. Buchanan is Secretary-Treasurer of AAAI and an editor of Artificial Intelligence and Machine Learning.

# Section 2.2

# Expert Systems and Generic Problem Classes

In the foreward to the MYCIN book (Buchanan and Shortliffe, 1984), Allen Newell referred to expert systems as generating a "need to redraw the intellectual map of artificial intelligence." The purpose of this section is to introduce the reader to this important class of AI program.

The paper in Section 2.2.1, by Buchanan and Smith, provides a broad overview of expert systems. It describes the aspects of expert systems that make them distinct from conventional programs, and the range of tasks for which expert systems have been successfully constructed. The article concludes with a description of the limitations of expert systems, and the directions for future research that these limitations suggest.

The most extensive exploration of the important idea of generic problem classes has been undertaken by John McDermott's research group. The article by McDermott in Section 2.2.2 summarizes the lessons learned from implementing approximately a dozen role-limiting methods for actual real-world domains.

Chandrasekaran's article in Section 2.2.3 also provides insight into the nature of generic classes; his paper describes a taxonomy of problem-solving methods. His article argues for the importance of encoding the knowledge relevant to a generic task at the correct level of abstraction.

The article in Section 2.2.4, by Clancey, provides a very nice description of NEOMYCIN, a second-generation expert system. The article describes how NEOMYCIN explicitly represents strategy knowledge at a meta-level rather than embedding it procedurally in base-level domain rules as was done in MYCIN. The explicit representation of strategy knowledge facilitates use of a knowledge base and shell code for multiple purposes, such as learning, critiquing, and tutoring.

For additional information about expert systems, we refer the reader to *Building Expert Systems* (Hayes-Roth et al., 1983). This book, the first ever written about expert systems, is still worth reading for its introduction and clarification of many issues ranging from conceptualization to evaluation of systems.

# Chapter XVIII

# Fundamentals of Expert Systems

Bruce G. Buchanan—University of Pittsburgh
Reid G. Smith—Schlumberger Laboratory for Computer Science, Austin

## CHAPTER XVIII:  FUNDAMENTALS OF EXPERT SYSTEMS

The references for this paper can be found in Appendix C: Addendum to Chapter 2 (pp. 879 ff.).

## A. OVERVIEW

EXPERT SYSTEMS are among the most exciting computer applications to emerge in the last decade. They allow a computer program to use expertise to assist in a variety of problems such as diagnosing failures in complex systems and designing new equipment. Using artificial intelligence (AI) work on problem solving, they have become a commercially successful demonstration of the power of AI techniques. Correspondingly, by testing current AI methods in applied contexts, expert systems provide important feedback about the strengths and limitations of those methods. In this review we present the fundamental considerations in designing and constructing expert systems, assess the state of the art, and indicate directions for future research. Our discussion focuses on the computer science issues, as opposed to issues of management or applications.

*Characterization and Desiderata*

Expert systems are distinguished from conventional programs in several important respects. Although none of the characteristics in the following list are missing entirely from other well-designed software, all of them together describe a distinct class of programs. Note that few expert systems exhibit all of the following five desiderata to the same degree. An expert system is a computer program that:

a. *Reasons with domain-specific knowledge that is symbolic* as well as numerical (this is what we mean by calling an expert system a knowledge-based system).

b. *Uses domain-specific methods that are heuristic (plausible)* as well as following procedures that are algorithmic (certain).

c. *Performs well* in its problem area.

d. *Explains* or makes understandable both what it knows and the reasons for its answers.

e. *Retains flexibility.*

One expert system that meets these conditions is the Dipmeter Advisor System (Smith and Young, 1984; and Smith, 1984). Its task is to help petroleum engineers determine the "map" of geological strata through which an oil well is being drilled, e.g., the depth and the dip, or "tilt" of individual layers of sandstone, shale, and other rocks. It meets our desiderata in the following respects:

1. The knowledge used is partly mathematical (e.g., trigonometry) but largely nonnumeric geological knowledge (e.g., how sand is deposited around river beds).

2. Its reasoning is based on heuristics that well-logging experts use to interpret data from boreholes.

3. It aids specialists, providing interpretations better than those of novices.

4. It uses a variety of graphical and textual displays to make its knowledge understandable and to justify its interpretations.

5. It is flexible enough to be modified and extended frequently, without rewriting the programs that interpret the knowledge.

Figure A–1 shows an example of what the Dipmeter Advisor System's computer screen looks like, as an illustration of what the user of an expert system might see. This figure shows the input data and a partial explanation for a conclusion drawn by the system. The left-hand column shows natural gamma radiation against depth (which increases from the top of the screen to the bottom). To its right is shown dip against depth. Individual dip estimates (called "tadpoles") show the magnitude of the dip as horizontal position, depth as vertical position, and azimuth as a small direction line. Dip patterns, detected by the system, are explained in the text to the right.

Desiderata (a) and (b)—symbolic reasoning and heuristic methods—define expert systems as artificial intelligence programs. Desideratum (c) separates high-performance programs from others. By specifying human specialists as a standard of comparison, this condition also suggests using the knowledge of specialists to achieve high performance. Predefining the scope of problem solving to a narrow "slice" through a domain (still smaller than the slice mastered by most human specialists) has become a pragmatic principle of design. As covered in the following discussion, bounding the scope of the problem in advance avoids many of the challenges of building a generally intelligent robot that would behave appropriately in a wide range of situations.

Desiderata (d) and (e)—understandability and flexibility—are less frequently cited and less frequently achieved than (a) through (c). They may be seen as a means of achieving high performance, but they are included here to highlight their importance in designing and implementing any expert system. Understandability and flexibility are important both while expert systems are being designed and when they are used. During design and implementation, not all the requisite knowledge is in hand because not even specialists can say precisely what a program needs to know. As a result, expert systems are constructed incrementally. Important to understandability is the use of the same terminology that specialists and practitioners use. Understanding the static knowledge base allows us to decide what knowledge needs to be added to improve performance. Understanding the dynamics of the reasoning is also important in deciding what to change. Flexibility is thus needed to allow the changes to be made easily. Explanations help designers, as well as end users, understand the reasons for a program's conclusions. This capability is especially important when end users accept legal, moral, or financial responsibility for actions taken on a program's recommendations.

## Examples

Many expert systems are in routine use (see AAAI, 1989; Rauch-Hindin, 1986; Buchanan, 1986; Walker and Miller, 1986; Harmon and King, 1985, for lists of examples). Some of the best known, such as XCON and the Dipmeter Advisor System (produced by Digital Equipment Corporation and Schlumberger, respectively) have been used commercially for many years. The programs shown in Table A–1 were chosen because they illustrate a variety of problem types and contexts of use. Roughly two classes of problems are addressed in these several systems:

1. Problems of interpreting data to analyze a situation.

2. Problems of constructing a solution within specified constraints.

Within each category are listed several different examples under general task names that are descriptive but not necessarily distinct.

We should note several points about these two lists of problems. First, there is no clear, unambiguous taxonomy of problem types that is independent of the methods used to solve problems. Perhaps the best characterization of the types of problems is with respect to the *methods* used to solve them. For example, heuristic classification problems (Clancey, 1985, and Chandrasekaran, 1986) are those that are solved by a method of the same name. This method assumes a predefined, enumerated list of possible solutions—such as MYCIN's list of antimicrobial drugs (Buchanan and Shortliffe, 1984)—and a set of heuristics for selecting among them efficiently—such as MYCIN's rules.

Second, for some problems we can specify a narrow enough scope so that the list of possible solutions is short enough for programs to deal with (dozens or hundreds, but not millions). For other problems we must

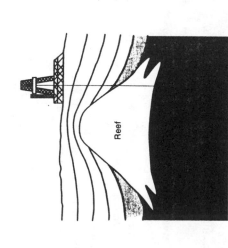

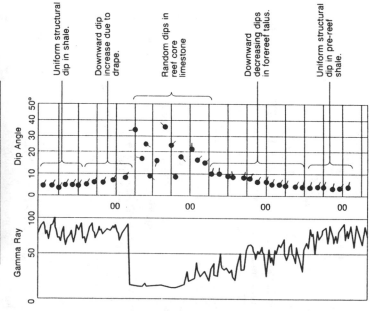

Figure A–1.    Screen from Dipmeter Advisor System.

## TABLE A-1

Several Examples of Expert Systems Working in Various Problem Areas.

### CLASS I: PROBLEMS OF INTERPRETATION

*Data Interpretation*

Schlumberger (Dipmeter Advisor)—interpret down-hole data from oil well boreholes to assist in prospecting (Smith and Young, 1984).

St. Vincents Hospital (Sydney)—aid in interpreting diagnostic tests on thyroid function (Horn et al., 1985).

NL Baroid (MUDMAN)—determine causes of problems in drilling oil wells and recommend additives to the drilling fluid that will correct them (Kahn and McDermott, 1986).

*Equipment Diagnosis*

General Motors (VIBRATION)—determine causes of vibration noises and recommend repairs (Teknowledge, 1987).

Kodak (BLOW MOLDING INJECTION ADVISOR)—diagnose faults and suggest repairs for plastic injection molding machines (Teknowledge, 1987).

AT&T (ACE)—provide troubleshooting and diagnostic reports on telephone cable problems (Miller et al., 1985).

General Electric (CATS)—diagnose problems in diesel-electric locomotives (Sweet, 1985).

*Troubleshooting Process*

Hewlett-Packard—diagnose causes of problems in photolithography steps of wafer fabrication (Cline et al., 1985).

Elf Aquitaine Oil Company (DRILLING ADVISOR)—demonstrate reasoning used to find the cause of drill bit sticking in oil wells and to correct the problems (used for training) (Rauch-Hindin, 1986).

*Monitoring*

IBM (YES/MVS)—monitor and adjust operation of MVS operating system (Rauch-Hindin, 1986).

National Aeronautics and Space Administration (LOX)—monitor data during liquid oxygen tanking process (Kolcum, 1986).

*Preventive Maintenance*

NCR (ESPm)—monitor computers in the field, analyze error logs, and suggest preventive maintenance procedures before a computer fails (Teknowledge, 1987).

## TABLE A-1 Continued

*Screening*

U.S. Environmental Protection Agency (EDDAS)—determine which requests for information fall under the exceptions to the Freedom of Information Act (Feinstein and Siems, 1985).

*Credit Authorization*

American Express (AA)—assist in authorizing charges from card members or in determining that a request is suspect or fraudulent (Klahr et al., 1987).

*Financial Auditing*

Arthur Young (ASQ)—assist auditors with planning and developing approaches to field audits (Hernandez, 1987).

*Software Consulting*

AT&T (REX)—advise persons on which package to use for their problems and how to use them (Rauch-Hindin, 1986).

*Equipment Tuning*

Lawrence Livermore National Laboratory (TQMSTUNE)—specify parameter settings to bring a sensitive instrument into alignment (Rauch-Hindin, 1986).

*Inventory Control*

Federal Express (INVENTORY SETUP ADVISOR)—help decide whether or not to stock spares in inventory of 40,000 parts (Teknowledge, 1987).

### CLASS II: PROBLEMS OF CONSTRUCTION

*Configuration*

Digital Equipment Corporation (XCON)—translate customers' orders for computer systems into shipping orders (Rauch-Hindin, 1986).

*Design*

Xerox (PRIDE)—design paper-handling systems inside copiers and duplicators (Mittal et al., 1985).

GM Delco Products (MOTOR EXPERT)—generate information necessary to make production drawings for low-voltage DC motor brushes by interacting with designers (Rauch-Hindin, 1986).

*Loading*

U.S. Army (AALPS)—design loading plan of cargo and equipment into aircraft of different types (AALPS, 1985).

(continued)

readily achieved by giving a program substantial subject-specific knowledge than by giving it the general axioms of the subject area plus a powerful, but general, deductive apparatus. The DENDRAL program represented many specific facts about organic chemistry in a variety of ways and used those facts in rather simple inferences (see Article VII.C2, Vol. II). For example, it represented the masses and valences of atoms as values of attributes; it represented classes of unstable chemical compounds as partial graph structures in a table; and it represented certain major patterns of molecular fragmentation in a mass spectrometer as predictive rules. From this work emerged the first principle of expert system building, as enunciated by Feigenbaum (Feigenbaum et al., 1971): "In the knowledge lies the power." The concept of a knowledge base has consequently become central in expert system.

In contrast, most other AI work of the day concerned reasoning by such general methods as theorem proving. Researchers sought to give programs power by means of general planning heuristics, exhibited, for example, in problem areas where knowledge about the objects of the domain was almost irrelevant. A favorite problem area was the so-called "Blocks World" of children's blocks on a table. General knowledge about stability and support, plus general knowledge about planning and constraint satisfaction, allowed programs to reason, say, about the sequence of operations needed to stack blocks in a specified order (see Section XV.A, Vol. III).

From the beginning (1950s–1960s), work in AI focused on two main themes: psychological modeling and search techniques (see Chapters II and XI). Expert systems build on much of that work, but they shift the focus to representing and using knowledge of specific task areas. Early work used game playing and reasoning about children's blocks as simple task domains in which to test methods of reasoning. Work on expert systems emphasizes problems of commercial or scientific importance, as defined by persons outside of AI. Newell calls MYCIN "the original expert system" (Foreword to Buchanan and Shortliffe, 1984) because it crystallized the design considerations and emphasized the application (see Article VIII.B1, Vol. II). In the 1970s, work on expert systems developed the use of production systems (see Article III.C4, Vol. I), based on the early work in psychological modeling. In the 1980s, fundamental work on knowledge representation evolved into useful object-oriented substrates (Stefik and Bobrow, 1986). Expert systems continue to build on—and contribute to—AI research by testing the strengths of existing methods and helping define their limitations (Buchanan, 1988).

Hardware developments in the last decade have made a significant difference in the commercialization of expert systems and in the rate of their development. Standalone workstations provide special hardware for AI programming languages, high-resolution interactive graphics, and

---

TABLE A-1 *Continued*

*Planning*

Hazeltine (OPGEN)—plan and prepare "operations sheets" of assembly instructions for printed circuit boards (Rauch-Hindin, 1986).

Hughes Aircraft (HI-CLASS)—set up sequence of hand-assembly steps for printed circuit boards (Hi-Class, 1985).

*Scheduling*

Westinghouse (ISIS)—plan manufacturing steps in Turbine Component Plant to avoid bottlenecks and delays (Fox and Smith, 1984).

Babcock & Wilcox—automate generation of weld schedule information (e.g., weld procedure, pre-heat, post-heat, and nondestructive examination requirements) (Rauch-Hindin, 1986).

*Therapy Management*

Stanford Medical Center (ONCOCIN)—assist in managing multistep chemotherapy for cancer patients (Hickam et al., 1985).

---

define a generator of alternatives, which can only be exercised with strong guidance.

Third, some problems reason with a "snapshot" of a situation and provide a static assessment; others require monitoring a data stream.

Fourth, some problems are solved routinely by people who have little specialized training; others are problems that highly skilled persons solve with considerable effort.

Fifth, the scope of competence of most of these programs is narrow and well defined. To the extent that a problem is open-ended (or "open-textured," i.e., requires reasoning about unbounded lists, such as the intended meanings of a sentence), it is *not* a good candidate for an expert system.

Sixth, criteria of the success of most of these programs are well defined; e.g., either a suggested repair fixes a problem or it does not.

*Historical Note*

Expert systems emerged as an identifiable part of AI in the late 1960s and early 1970s with the realization that application of AI to science, engineering, and medicine could both assist those disciplines and challenge AI. The DENDRAL (Lindsay et al., 1980) and MACSYMA (Moses, 1971) programs suggested that high performance in a subject area such as organic chemistry or algebraic simplification was more

## B.  FUNDAMENTAL PRINCIPLES

ALL AI PROGRAMS, including expert systems, represent and use knowledge. The conceptual paradigm of problem solving that underlies all of AI is search (i.e., a program, or person, can solve a problem by searching among alternative solutions). Although immediately clear and simple, this formulation does not tell us how to search a solution space efficiently and accurately. The number of possible solutions may be astronomical, so exhaustive consideration of alternatives is out of the question. Therefore, most expert systems use heuristics to avoid exhaustive search, much as experts do. For example, the Dipmeter Advisor System is expected to delineate significant strata through which an oil well borehole penetrates. There are many hundreds of these in a one- or two-mile borehole. Then it is expected to classify the strata in any of several dozen geological categories. These interpretations are not totally independent: the endpoints of significant intervals are partly determined by the types of rock formations, and the identification of a type is partly determined by the identity of formations immediately above or below. Considerable knowledge of geology keeps the program from exhaustively searching this large, combinatorial space.

For problem areas in which experts are acknowledged to be more efficient and accurate than nonspecialists, it is reasonable to assume that what the experts know can be codified for use by a program. This is one of the fundamental assumptions of knowledge engineering, the art of building expert systems by eliciting knowledge from experts (Hayes-Roth, et al., 1983).

The term "expert system" suggests a computer program that performs at the pinnacle of human expertise, or one that models a human expert's thought processes. However, designers of expert systems subscribe to neither of these implications. Although high performance is a goal, a system need not equal the best performance of the best individuals to be useful: well-timed advice from a "good" system can help novices avoid trouble. On the other hand, programs can sometimes outperform the specialists by being more systematic in their reasoning. A commitment to achieving high performance, though, is not a commitment to achieving consistently unexcelled performance.

Similarly, designers of expert systems build into their programs much of the knowledge that human specialists have about problem solving. But they do not commit to building psychological models of how the

large address spaces in small boxes at affordable prices (Wah, 1987). These have simplified development since it is no longer necessary to depend on large, time-shared central mainframes for development and debugging. They also provide an acceptable answer to questions of portability for field personnel. Development of expert systems—and the languages and environments (called "shells") for building them—in standard languages such as CommonLISP and C have essentially eliminated the last barriers to portability.

To a certain extent, a knowledge base is a database. The essential differences between knowledge bases and databases are flexibility and complexity of the relations. Current research on AI and databases, which are sometimes called expert database systems (Kerschberg, 1986) is reducing these differences. A knowledge base requires an organizational paradigm plus data structures for implementation. Together these two parts constitute the representation of knowledge in an AI program. Elements of a knowledge base may also be interpreted directly as pieces of the program, which is partly what we mean by the complexity of the relations expressed.

The contents of a knowledge base include domain-specific facts and relations. But many expert systems explicitly state generic facts and relations as well. For example, types and properties of various mathematical relations, or general knowledge of English grammar, may be included in a knowledge base. Also, many knowledge bases include declarative descriptions of the problem-solving strategy in meta-level statements (about how to use the domain-specific knowledge).

Elements of knowledge needed for problem solving may be organized globally around either the primary objects (or concepts) of a problem area or around the actions (including inferential relations) among those objects. For example, in medicine we may think primarily about the evidential links among manifestations and diseases, and the links among diseases and therapeutic actions, and secondarily about the concepts so linked. In this paradigm, we concentrate on the knowledge that allows inferences to be drawn and actions to be taken—the "how to" knowledge. Alternatively, we might organize medical knowledge primarily around the taxonomy of diseases and the taxonomy of their manifestations and secondarily around the inference rules that relate manifestations to diseases and problems to treatments. In this second paradigm, we concentrate on what might be called the "what is" knowledge. These two conceptual views are known as *action-centered* or *object-centered* paradigms for representing knowledge. They have counterparts at the implementation level in program organization.

For each type of representation, we may identify the primitive unit and the primitive action. The primitive unit, in the case of action-centered representations, is the fact (e.g., the freezing temperature of water is 0 degrees C). Primitive facts are linked in conditional sentences by rules ("If . . . then . . ." statements). Note that these links may reflect causal associations based on theory, or empirical associations based on experience. An example from the Dipmeter Advisor System, which is an abbreviated causal description as found in geology texts, is shown in Figure B–1. It is one of a set used to perform sedimentary environment analysis. This rule is attempted only after the system has determined that the overall sedimentary environment is a deltaic plain.

expert thinks. The expert may describe how he or she would like others to solve problems of a type, as well as how he or she actually solves those problems. The expert system is a model of something, but it is more a model of the expert's model of the domain than of the expert.

One of the fundamental principles in the design of expert systems is the separation of knowledge about the domain (say, geology or medicine) from the programs that reason with that knowledge. This is sometimes briefly stated as separation of the knowledge base and the inference engine (Davis, 1982). The architecture of an expert system is a commitment to both the representation of knowledge and the form of reasoning.

In this section we attempt to elucidate principles that underlie architectural choices made to facilitate the design, implementation, fielding, and evolution of expert systems. We focus on the following important aspects: representation of knowledge, reasoning methods, knowledge base development, explanation (of both the contents of the knowledge base and of the reasoning process), tools used to facilitate system construction, and validation of performance. In the discussion, we relate each of the classes of choices to desiderata (a)–(e) for expert systems as enumerated in Section A. Finally, we conclude with a brief summary of factors that indicate when an expert systems approach is appropriate.

## B1.   Representation of Knowledge

A HALLMARK OF an expert system is the use of specific knowledge of its domain of application (say, geology or medicine), applied by a relatively simple reasoning program. In this simple characterization, the term "knowledge base" is taken to mean the collection of knowledge of the domain, and the term "inference engine" refers to the programs that reason with that knowledge.

The phrase "knowledge programming" has been used to emphasize this aspect of building an expert system. The single most important representational principle is that of declarative knowledge enunciated by McCarthy in the formative years of AI (McCarthy, 1958). (See also Winograd's discussion of this principle in Winograd, 1975.) Simply put, this principle states that knowledge about facts and relations in the world must be encoded in an intelligent program explicitly, in a manner that allows other programs to reason about it, as opposed to relying on programs and subroutines to compute new facts. Arbitrary FORTRAN or LISP procedures, for example, cannot be explained or edited by other programs (although they can be compiled and executed), whereas stylized attribute-value pairs, record structures, or other, more complex data structures can be.

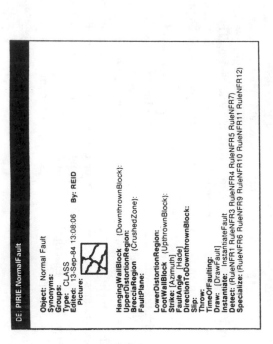

**Figure B–2.  Dipmeter Advisor System object.**

ual attribute (slot) names are shown in boldface (e.g., **Hanging-Wall-Block**). Where used, synonyms for attribute names are enclosed in braces (e.g., {Downthrown-Block}). The "type" of each attribute value is shown in square brackets (e.g., the value of the **Strike** slot is expected to be a datum of type [Azimuth]).

Smalltalk (Goldberg and Robson, 1983) was one of the early languages that showed both the power of objects as programming constructs and the power of an integrated graphical programming environment. Many commercial expert-system shells now contain an object-oriented component (Stefik and Bobrow, 1986).

The primitive action in action-centered representations is often referred to as *firing a rule*: If the premise conditions of a conditional rule are true in a situation, take the actions specified in the consequent part of the rule. For example, in a medical system, conclude that an organism may be streptococcus if its gram stain is positive. This style of programming began as production systems, made popular by Newell's work in the 1960s (see Chapter 2 of Buchanan and Shortliffe, 1984).

Given that rule-oriented programming often involves making deductions, it has been argued that various forms of logic are well suited for use in expert systems. Simple systems have used propositional logic; more complex systems have used first-order predicate logic; and there is ongoing research in the use of higher order logics to express relations among beliefs, temporal relations, necessity, and uncertain information

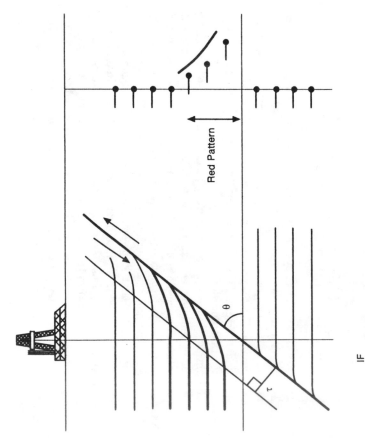

IF    *there exists a normal fault pattern (p), and*
      *there exists a red pattern (p1),*
          *such that the length of p1 <50 ft., and*
          *such that p1 is above the fault plane pattern of p,*

THEN  *specialize p to be a late fault pattern*

**Figure B–1.  Dipmeter Advisor System rule.**

Conversely, the primitive unit of an object-centered representation is the object with a number of attributes (called *slots*) and values (e.g., a spur gear with number-of-teeth = 24, material = cast-steel, and diameter = 5 cm). Objects typically also encapsulate procedures (called *methods*). In addition, they may contain defaults, uncertainty, relations to other objects (e.g., generalizations and parts), and a variety of other information. An object can be viewed as a structured collection of facts. Minsky (Minsky, 1975) popularized the use of objects (then called *frames*) for AI (see Article III.C7, Vol. I). An example of an object definition from the Dipmeter Advisor System is shown in Figure B–2. This model encapsulates information about normal or tensional geological faults. Individ-

(both the uncertainty with which data must be regarded in many real systems and the uncertainty about the strength of heuristic rules, which reflects a lack of detailed understanding of a domain) (Allen, 1984; Allen and Koomen, 1983; Szolovitz and Pauker, 1978; Pearl, 1986; Pearl, 1989; Shafer et al., 1989).

In object-centered representations, the primitive action is called *sending a message*: If an action needs to be taken (e.g., a value of an attribute is needed), send a request to the object that can take the action (e.g, compute, or conclude, the value). For example, in a geology system, send the *Analyze-Sedimentary-Environment* message to an instance of the Borehole-Interval object. The effect is to perform an arbitrary action, which could include drawing inferences. In our example, the action performed is to draw conclusions about the geological "story" of sedimentation at a specific depth interval penetrated by the oil rig's drill. This style of object-oriented programming was defined by Hewitt (1977).

In terms of data structures, objects are much like record structures. Each object has a number of fixed fields. Unlike record structures, however, new fields can be added to objects during a computation. Objects are typically divided into two types: instances and classes. Instances represent individuals in a domain (e.g., a specific depth interval from 1200 to 1225 feet in a specific borehole). Classes represent sets of individuals (e.g., any depth interval). They define the common characteristics of the individuals that are their instances. Classes are usually organized into hierarchies according to different relations. The most common relations are the specialization, subclass, or "is-a" relation (e.g., a reverse geological fault is a kind of geological fault) and the "part-of" relations (e.g., a fault plane is part of a geological fault). Object-oriented systems allow arbitrary relations to be encoded, but they often provide efficient support for one or two specific relations.

To support the characteristics of expert systems listed in Section A, representation mechanisms must have sufficient expressive power to state, clearly and succinctly, both "what is" knowledge and "how to" knowledge. (This distinction and an important early discussion of representing facts about the world—the "what is" knowledge—are in McCarthy and Hayes (1969). Expressive power has both design-time and run-time implications. One of the key problems for designers of expert systems is the management of complexity. Impoverished representation mechanisms force designers to encode information in obscure ways, which eventually leads to difficulty in extending and explaining the behavior of expert systems. Representation mechanisms that permit efficient compilation and structuring of knowledge reduce run-time requirements of both time and memory.

As an example, an object-oriented language allows some information to be stated once, in an abstract class, and accessed (by inheritance) in

a large number of subclasses. A representational mechanism that does not allow this forces designers to confront the complexity of stating essentially the same information many times. This may lead to inconsistency and difficulty in updating the information. It also has an obvious memory cost. At run time, each of the separate encodings of the information may have to be considered individually, resulting in an obvious performance penalty. An example of a taxonomic hierarchy is shown in Figure B-3.

To facilitate the incremental development of expert systems, representation schemes must also be extensible. Since there is rarely a complete specification of either the problem or the knowledge required to solve it, incremental development is required. When new concepts, attributes, and relations are added incrementally, a designer must not be forced to recode substantial portions of the knowledge already encoded.

Experience has shown that declarative, modular representations are useful for expert systems. Some information is more difficult to encode

**Figure B–3.** Dipmeter Advisor System tectonic feature hierarchy.

in the action-centered paradigm, whereas other information is more difficult in the object-centered paradigm. For example, sequencing of actions is difficult to encode in an action-centered paradigm. The same is true of information that is essentially static such as causal or structural descriptions. On the other hand, object-centered representations have no built-in inference mechanism beyond inheritance (although they support them, and many commercial shells have an integrated rule-oriented component). In addition, in some domains, subclasses are "soft," and it may be inappropriate to wire in hard distinctions between classes. For example, in geology, classification of rocks according to lithology (sandstone, shale, and carbonate) is not firm because the end members are mixed to varying degrees. Consequently, there is no single answer to the question, "Which representation method is best?" Action-centered and object-centered paradigms are in fact two ends of a spectrum of representational possibilities. The two emphasize different aspects of modeling. Contemporary expert systems often use heterogeneous representational paradigms, but they attempt to integrate them into a uniform framework. As systems become more complex, it will be more and more difficult to maintain a uniform view.

The problem of representation spans from deciding globally what to represent through deciding locally how to use the data structures of a specific programming language. At the global level, designers (sometimes called *knowledge engineers*) must determine an overall organizational paradigm within which an expert system can reason effectively. Since the knowledge engineer and the expert are discussing at this point the objects and relations that are important enough to name, this phase is sometimes called determining the ontology. As an organizing principle, it is important that the ontology of the expert system closely reflect the ontology of the experts. Otherwise, the experts will not be able to understand and debug the system's reasoning.

## B2.  Reasoning Methods

INFERENCE METHODS are required to make appropriate and efficient use of the items in a knowledge base to achieve some purpose such as diagnosing a disease. Logically speaking, the two rules of inference most used in problem solving are *modus ponens* ("If A implies B and you know A, then infer B") and *modus tollens* ("If A implies B and you know not-B, then infer not-A") (see Section XII.B, Vol. III). Linking several applications of modus ponens together is sometimes called the "chain rule" because inferences are chained together in a sequence:

$$
\begin{array}{l}
A \\
A \rightarrow B \\
B \rightarrow C \\
C \rightarrow D \\
\hline
\text{Therefore, } D
\end{array}
$$

In addition to these two simple rules, rules of quantification are sometimes used. For example, "If all As are Bs and x is an A, then x is a B." With a few simple rules of inference such as these driving the problem solving, a knowledge base full of many special facts and relations about the problem area can provide the expertise on which high performance is based.

Some expert systems (e.g., those written in PROLOG) use a theorem prover to determine the truth or falsity of propositions and to bind variables so as to make propositions true. Others use their own interpreters in order to incorporate more than a theorem prover provides—most importantly, capabilities for controlling the order of inferences, strategic reasoning, and reasoning under uncertainty. Most fielded rule-based expert systems have used specialized rule interpreters that are not based directly on logic. To some extent this reflects timing—efficient PROLOG interpreters and compilers that can be integrated with other systems have only recently become available. However, it also reflects a need for more flexible styles of inference (in addition to a theorem prover's depth-first backtracking) and control over the strategies guiding the order of inferences.

### Controlling the Order of Inferences and Questions

From a logical point of view, the order in which new facts are derived is irrelevant, if all logical consequences of the initial facts are to be considered. However, for pragmatic reasons, expert systems often need to be selective about which facts to consider and which consequences to pursue. Space and time are often limited, for example, and it may also be important to develop a line of reasoning, and an order in the inferences, that a user can follow.

Matching the premise clauses of all rules—or the templates of all objects—in a knowledge base against each new situation can be prohibitively expensive where there are many rules or objects, and many new situations created in the course of problem solving. Rules and object definitions often contain variables that can be bound in many different ways, thus creating additional ways that they can match a situation. Rule interpreters commonly provide mechanisms for compilation of rules and rule-matching procedures (Brownston et al., 1985). In addition, all but the simplest rule-based systems organize and index rules in groups

wired into forward- and backward-chaining systems. Two successful prototypes based on this paradigm are the HEARSAY-II and HASP systems. In both cases, acoustic data are received and need to be interpreted (as a spoken English sentence in HEARSAY-II or as a description of types and locations of ships in the ocean in HASP). Opportunistic processing, blackboard architecture, and specific systems, including HEARSAY-II and HASP, are described in Chapter XVI of this volume. As data are received over time, hypotheses are revised. With each revision, new ambiguities arise, which can be resolved by reprocessing old data or looking for new signals.

Object-centered expert systems generally make inferences with rules, and thus include one or more of the rule-based reasoning paradigms. They also include built-in mechanisms for inheritance of features of one object from another. For example, individual persons will inherit defining characteristics of the classes they belong to so that the default characteristic diet of Joe Jones is inferred to be omnivorous, provided that the object representing Joe has been defined to be an instance of the class object of omnivores.

## Using Explicit Strategies

Any simple reasoning paradigm may need refinement and coordination in order to reflect a complex decision strategy such as medical diagnosis. There are many high-level strategies for solving problems that have been discussed in the AI literature such as means-ends analysis, stepwise refinement, or plan-generate-and-test.

Many environments—or *shells*—for building expert systems provide a built-in problem-solving paradigm at a conceptual level. EMYCIN and its commercial derivatives, for example, work under the strategy of evidence gathering, in which data are collected for and against hypotheses (individually or in classes). Then the data, and the facts inferred from them, are weighed (using a built-in weighting function) in order to decide which hypothesis is best supported by the data. This is a description at the conceptual level; at the implementation level this is all accomplished using backward and forward chaining. (This paradigm is sometimes called *heuristic classification* (Clancey, 1985) because data and heuristics are used to classify a situation into one of a fixed number of categories.)

Representing strategic knowledge explicitly is an important trend in expert systems. It is especially important whenever there is no clear choice as to the best strategy and some experimentation with prototype systems may be required—under different strategies—to determine good

in order to control the expense of matching and invocation. Rule groups (called *rule sets, tasks,* or *control blocks*) are also used to control the expert system's focus of attention in order to make interactions with users more comprehensible.

Rule-based expert systems are often organized around one (or a combination) of three different reasoning paradigms: forward, backward, and opportunistic reasoning.

Forward reasoning from data to conclusions is used when the cost or inconvenience of gathering and filtering low-level processing data is low and there are relatively few hypotheses to explore. A forward-chaining system starts with a collection of facts and draws allowable conclusions, adding those to the collection and cycling through the rules. The stopping conditions vary from stopping with the first plausible hypothesis to stopping only when no more new conclusions can be drawn. The XCON computer configuration system is a classic example of a forward-chaining system.

Backward reasoning is goal-directed and does not require all relevant data to be available at the time the inferences are begun. It is also more appropriate when a user supplies many of the data, and when the user cares about the order in which data are requested. MYCIN is a classic example (see Article VIII.B1, Vol. II). A backward-chaining system starts with a hypothesis (goal) to establish and asks, in effect, "What facts (premise clauses of rules) would need to be true in order to know that the hypothesis is true?" Some of these facts may be known because they were given as initial data, others may be known after asking the user about them, and still others may be known only after starting with them as new subgoals and then chaining backward. The stopping conditions vary from stopping with the first hypothesis found true (or "true enough") to stopping only after all possibly relevant hypotheses have been explored.

Opportunistic reasoning combines some elements of both data-directed (forward) and goal-directed (backward) reasoning. It is useful when the number of possible inferences is very large, no single line of reasoning is likely to succeed, and the reasoning system must be responsive to new data becoming known. As new data are observed, or become known, new inferences can be drawn; and as new conclusions are drawn, new questions about specific data become relevant. An opportunistic reasoning system can thus set up expectations that help discriminate a few data elements from among an otherwise confusing mass.

The key element of such a system is an agenda of actions with an associated scheduler that enables explicit decisions to be made about which actions are to be taken (e.g., which rules to apply, whether to apply them in a forward- or backward-chaining manner, and which object is to be the focus of attention). Such decisions, by contrast, are hard-

ities with some variation of Bayes's Theorem (Gorry, 1970). This method is based on a solid formalism, but it requires either frequency data or subjective estimates for many combinations of events.

3. Fuzzy Logic—Represent the uncertainty of propositions such as "John is tall" with a distribution of values; then reason about combinations of distributions (Zadeh, 1979). This is intuitively appealing because it is based on ordinary linguistic concepts. It is computationally more complex than other mechanisms, however, because it propagates uncertainty through distributions of values.

4. Criterion Tables—Assign categories or weights to clauses in rules based on their relative importance in drawing conclusions (e.g., major and minor findings associated with a disease); then allow a conclusion to be drawn if sufficient numbers of clauses in each category are true (Kulikowski and Weiss, 1982). This simple mechanism is computationally very fast. It fails to capture gradations between categories, however, and thus lacks the expressive power to reason in some complex problem areas.

5. Certainty Factors (CFs)—Assign single numbers to propositions, and to associations among propositions, representing increases in belief—either probabilities or a combination of probabilities and utilities; then use MYCIN's formulas to determine the CFs for inferred beliefs (Buchanan and Shortliffe, 1984). This calculus has been frequently used and has been shown to have a formal interpretation in probability theory (Heckerman, 1986).

A general problem with methods 2 through 5 is arriving at a coherent set of numbers. Typically these are obtained from experts over several iterations, with empirical testing, because valid, objective numbers are not available. Another problem is that one person's subjective estimates are not always applicable in novel situations, nor are they always easy for others to change.

## Summary

There is no single answer to the question, "Which inference method is best?" Each expert system, or system-building shell, provides a nearly unique set of choices for controlling inferences, using strategies, and reasoning under uncertainty. Some also contain methods for backtracking (recovering from local failures), critiquing (making no recommendations unless the user needs them), reasoning about shapes or positions, and reasoning about temporal dependencies. Most present-day systems allow no modification of the inference methods they use. This is a shortcoming that has not received widespread attention, but that sometimes causes system builders to make inappropriate or unhappy choices

and bad choices. It is also important because users may be puzzled about the line of reasoning of an expert system when the expert's strategy for attacking a problem (and thus the expert system's approach) differs from that of the user. With an explicit representation of the strategic rules or procedures, an expert system can explain those just as it explains its domain-level knowledge.

MYCIN's metarules, a solution to this problem in the late 1970s, represent knowledge of reasoning strategy as rules (Buchanan and Shortliffe, 1984). They differ from the other "domain knowledge" rules in the system in that they refer to those rules in some of their premise or conclusion clauses:

IF <medical context> AND there are rules that mention fact A and rules that mention fact B,

THEN reason with the rules mentioning A before the others.

Strategies can also be represented as an organization of steps to perform, in a stylized definition of a procedure (Clancey, 1986; Hickam et al., 1985; Laird et al., 1987; Newell and Simon, 1976; Gruber, 1987; Marcus, 1987; Hayes-Roth, 1985).

### Reasoning Under Uncertainty

Reasoning under uncertainty is essential in problem areas outside of logic and mathematics, in which information is incomplete or erroneous. In every empirical discipline from physics to biology and engineering to medicine there is rarely complete certainty about having *all* the data or about the accuracy of the data. Data are never complete enough; tests that would confirm or disconfirm a hypothesis are often too expensive or too risky to perform. Measurement errors are known to occur. Thus expert systems must address these problems if they are to be useful in the real world.

Several methods are used in expert systems to deal with uncertainty arising from either uncertain and incomplete data, or uncertain associations between data and conclusions. The major methods for addressing these issues are listed below.

1. Abstraction—Assume that the uncertainty is small and can safely be ignored, thus treating all knowledge as categorically true (Szolovits and Pauker, 1978). The method is extremely simple and efficient to use. It often works. However, many problems require more precision in estimating uncertainty.

2. Bayes's Theorem—Use prior and posterior probabilities to represent less than certain data and associations; then compute new probabil-

because they must work with an inference procedure within a shell in which someone else made those choices.

## B3.   Knowledge Base Development

FOR THE LAST decade, everyone involved has referred to the process of putting knowledge into a knowledge base as a "bottleneck" in building expert systems (Hayes-Roth et al., 1983). Usually this process involves two persons (or teams): an expert whose knowledge is to be partially mirrored in the knowledge base, and a knowledge engineer who interviews the expert to map his or her knowledge into the program's data structures holding the knowledge base. The process is time consuming and difficult, yet the performance of the resulting expert system depends on its being done well. This is exacerbated by the fact that knowledge base design often involves integrating knowledge of several experts because relying on a single expert may cause implicit assumptions to be overlooked. A survey conducted by SRI International indicates that the average cost of developing an application (knowledge engineering plus end-user interface alone) is about $260,000. For small systems, these costs are about $5,000; for large systems, more than $1.5 million (Fried, 1987). Note that these estimates do not include the cost of constructing an expert system shell.

Much of the process of knowledge engineering is engineering. Yet there are several difficult issues of a fundamental nature wrapped up in the steps of the process.

1. During the first step, problem assessment, the knowledge engineer must match the characteristics of the proposed problem against the characteristics of known solution methods. Unfortunately there are no expert systems that match a description of a problem to a best method for solving it.

2. The second major step is exploratory programming, in which a few experimental prototypes are constructed quickly—first as a proof-of-concept, and then with successively larger fractions of an expert's knowledge—showing that a part of the problem can be (partially) solved with that knowledge encoded in a specific environment. Two substantial issues here are

   a. Formulating an accurate conceptual framework, including terminology, to allow knowledge to be added incrementally.

   b. Iterating with—not just passively listening to—the expert efficiently to elicit what he or she knows about the problem that is relevant for the expert system.

3. Developing the knowledge base to increase both the breadth and depth of the system's competence is the third major step. This step takes the most time (several person-years), but it is relatively straightforward if steps 1 and 2 have been done well. One difficult issue here is anticipating characteristics of end users and their context of use. Another is deciding which new facts and relations are and which are not relevant for the system's performance and understandability in context. The competing paradigms for making this decision—and for knowledge engineering generally—may be called *model-directed* and *case-directed* knowledge base development. In the former, the knowledge base is largely developed along the lines of a model, or theory, of the problem area. In the latter, it is largely developed in response to errors exhibited in solving test cases. Neither is entirely adequate by itself; knowledge engineers must use both. Whatever combination of development paradigms is used, there is no clear stopping criterion for development. This presents problems in providing for continual additions and modifications to a knowledge base—the extensibility mentioned earlier.

4. The last step of the process is software engineering, that is, ensuring that the system fits into the end users' environment, is responsive to their needs, and so on. The difficult issues at this step are not unique to expert systems. It is included as a reminder that a successful application requires more than developing a knowledge base.

## B4.   Explanation

ONE OF THE defining criteria of expert systems is their ability to "explain" their operation. Early forms of explanation focused on showing the line of reasoning, typically a sequence of rule firings, that led to a particular conclusion This was normally done in stylized natural language (Part Six of Buchanan and Shortliffe, 1984). The user could ask the system questions of the form, "How did you conclude . . . ?" In a sense it is an extension to the kind of dialog that was originally shown in the SHRDLU system (Winograd, 1972; Article IV.F1, Vol. I). That system answered questions by actually looking in its environment and on its own goal stack (i.e, agenda of goals and subgoals).

Although natural language interfaces were used almost exclusively in early expert systems, powerful, low-cost graphics workstations have fueled a trend toward graphic interfaces, for example, the STEAMER system, used to train naval personnel to operate steam power plants onboard ships (Hollan et al., 1984). Contemporary systems often provide mixed natural language and graphical interfaces, for example, the Drilling Advisor (Rauch-Hindin, 1986).

Lines of reasoning, for example, the Guidon-Watch System (Richer et al., 1985) may be shown as graphs that permit user interaction to explore alternative possible lines of reasoning. Perhaps this makes clear the fact that current explanation facilities are much like sophisticated program debugging systems, they permit the programmer/user to examine system operation in high-level terms, rather than in terms of the low-level machine instructions actually executed. There is a trend today toward recording justifications that underlie the items in the knowledge base (Smith et al., 1985). These can be used to augment explanations. Research is ongoing to enable expert systems themselves to use this information.

The term "explanation" can also be used to cover examination of the static knowledge base. Object-oriented representations and sophisticated graphics facilities enhance the ability of a domain specialist to understand what has been encoded (Smith et al., 1987). As found in the GUIDON system (Clancey, 1986) (see Article IX.C6, Vol. II), however, such facilities do not in and of themselves constitute a tutoring system.

We could argue that the user of a conventional FORTRAN program can also examine the "knowledge base" of the program. Depending on how the program is written, this is true to a certain extent. It would typically be done with a text editor. One thing that sets expert systems apart, however, is their ability to be queried in the run-time context. Whereas a conventional program can be examined only statically, an expert system can be examined dynamically. It is true that a programmer can examine the stack of a conventional program with a debugger, but such programs do not maintain an explicit goal stack or line of reasoning. This is not a statement about implementation language but rather about system design style.

## B5.    System-Building Tools/Shells

When the first commercial expert systems were being developed, the developers faced two major problems:

1. Eliciting and encoding the domain knowledge to solve the problem at hand.
2. Building programming systems with which to encode/apply the knowledge.

There were almost no generally applicable rule interpreters or object-oriented programming languages. Most of the early "shells" had been

constructed in universities as parts of specific applications. They typically made too many assumptions about either the domain of application or the problem-solving methods to be used. Furthermore, they typically could only be used by highly trained specialists. Finally, their run-time, space, and implementation language requirements precluded their use in a wide variety of environments. Nevertheless, these shells represented generalizations, in code, of principles learned from experience with prior expert systems.

One of the most practical effects of the recent commercial application of expert systems has been the development of many dozens of robust shells and tool sets (Bundy, 1986; Gevarter, 1987; Harmon, 1987; and Richer, 1986). These shells range in capability from those that can support little more than experimentation with rule-based techniques to those that can support efficient development and operation of substantial systems. A few of the more powerful shells are used to support current research in expert systems. The shells are implemented in a number of programming languages (e.g., LISP, C, and PROLOG) and run on a variety of hardware, including inexpensive PCs, workstations, and mainframe computers.

Today, users can expect a high-end shell to offer support for a number of programming paradigms. The two most common are rule-oriented programming and object-oriented programming. Both forward and backward chaining are standard, as is support for structuring rules into collections (or rule sets) according to task. Typically rules are efficiently compiled into code in the underlying implementation language. Not all rule languages are extensible. The OPS5 rule language, for example, allows new action functions to be defined but does not allow new matching predicates (Brownston et al., 1985).

When support for object-oriented programming is provided, it includes multiple inheritance, message-passing, and active values. A common way to combine rules and objects is to construct a method that responds to a message by applying a set of rules, with either forward or backward chaining. Such a method may also be invoked in response to a change in an active value. The REACTORS system, for example, uses active values to respond to changes in the operating conditions of a nuclear power plant to invoke rules that suggest new responses (Rauch-Hindin, 1986).

Some shells provide support for uncertainty in rules and in facts. The certainty factor calculus originally developed for the MYCIN system is widely used. Complete integration of inexact reasoning and objects has not yet been achieved. It is currently limited to support of uncertainty for slot values. Support for uncertainty in interobject relations is less common.

In the early years of commercial systems, expert systems were designed as standalone tools. As a result, they were not well integrated with database management systems, large numerical packages, or other existing software and systems. Today's commercial systems are considerably better integrated with other uses of computers. It is now common to see support for mixed language environments (e.g., with some code in LISP and some in C).

Over the past few years increasing attention has been focused on tools to support interaction between humans and expert systems. There are two major reasons for this:

1. In many fielded systems, the end-user interface accounts for a substantial portion of the overall system and success depends heavily on the quality of user interaction (Smith, 1984).

2. The knowledge acquisition process is simplified and enhanced when the expert can readily examine the evolving knowledge base and directly interact with the system to refine its understanding of the domain (Davis and Lenat, 1982).

It has also been found that the tools used to represent domain knowledge and strategy knowledge (e.g., objects and rules) can be applied to structuring user interfaces. Extensible systems and tools have been developed to support interaction requirements for knowledge engineers, experts, and end users (Smith et al., 1987).

## B6.  Validation

THERE ARE many dimensions along with which we might wish to judge an expert system. The three most important of these are computational, psychological "look and feel," and performance. Computational issues include speed, memory required, extensibility, portability, and ease of integration with other systems. Psychological issues include ease of use, understandability and "naturalness," and online help and explanation. Performance issues—the sine qua non—include the scope of competence, percentage of false positive and negative solutions (false alarms and misses), and time or money saved. Some involve evaluations of the static knowledge base (e.g., its scope), whereas others involve looking at the program in use (e.g., its ease of use or statistics on correctness). (See Cohen and Howe, 1989 and 1988 for specific recommendations.)

Formal validations of expert systems are rarely published, if done at all. The formal validation of MYCIN's performance (Part 10 of Buchanan and Shortliffe, 1984) stands out as an exception. In that study, outside evaluators reviewed the therapy recommendations for several randomly selected patients as made by MYCIN and nine persons whose expertise

ranged from acknowledged specialist to medical student. The evaluators (in a blinded study) judged MYCIN's recommendations to be indistinguishable from those of the specialists. In practice, expert systems are validated in the same way as conventional software. Developers mostly demonstrate that a new system solves a variety of difficult problems before it is turned over to end users (O'Keefe et al., 1987). A few of the end users then try the new system in context on a large number of cases, often in parallel with the old method for solving these problems. Any errors that are detected are fixed. When the end users and their managers are convinced of the program's effectiveness, the program is put into routine use, often at a single site first.

With small conventional programs, we often test each branch of each subroutine with boundary values of variables to assure ourselves that the program's parts behave as specified. With large systems, complete testing is not possible, and software engineering practices prescribe testing boundary conditions, exercising new code under as many variations as possible, and empirical testing with a variety of cases—with no guarantees of complete testing. As a consequence, programmers (as well as managers) hesitate to make any changes at all in code that has worked in the past for fear that unforeseen errors will be introduced.

In an expert system, each element of the knowledge base can be examined in the same fashion as a single, small subroutine. As with subroutines, the places where unforeseen errors occur are in the interactions among the elements. These have to be uncovered by empirical tests—running the program on a large random sample of problems (within the specified scope) and determining which cases are solved correctly and which are not. In the absence of a complete logical analysis that proves the correctness of both the knowledge base and the inference engine, we must analyze performance empirically. The criteria for "acceptable" levels of errors of any type, however, must be determined by weighing costs of errors of each type against the benefits of correct solutions.

## B7.  Reasons for Using the Methods of Expert Systems

IN GENERAL, the main issues in building expert systems can be classed as issues of complexity, interpretability, and explicit, modular forms of knowledge. In this section we summarize some of the factors that suggest using expert systems instead of conventional software. Note that many of the points are true of the programming technology that underlies AI programs in general—not simply expert systems.

can do this kind of detailed introspection, examining their procedures as well as their data.

In order for this capability to be used effectively, it is important that the knowledge be represented explicitly (declaratively) and uniformly, and that it be applied in a relatively uniform manner. Although it may be possible in principle to reason about pure LISP code, in practice it is extremely difficult—for humans as well as programs. Thus a simpler syntax, like objects or rules, is usually defined as the fundamental representation, and an interpreter is written for that syntax.

*Knowledge*

Specialized knowledge of a problem area is the key to high performance. And the key insight from AI has been that representing a program's knowledge declaratively provides considerable advantages over hard-wiring what a program knows in coded subroutines. There is a continuum, of course, from parameterized procedures to completely stylized, understandable, high-level procedure descriptions. For different purposes, designers of expert systems use different ways of representing knowledge explicitly, but they all focus on the knowledge—representing it, reasoning with it, acquiring it, and explaining it. Today's expert systems demonstrate the adequacy of current AI methods in these four areas, for some well-chosen problems. Shells, or system-building environments, codify many of the present methods.

*Complexity: Problems, Project Management, Systems*

Often when we begin designing an expert system, neither the problem nor the knowledge required to solve it is precisely specified. Initial descriptions of the problem are oversimplified, so the complexity becomes known only as early versions of the system solve simple versions of the problem. Expert systems are said to approach competence incrementally. A declarative, modular representation of knowledge, applied in a uniform manner, is the key to managing this kind of complexity. Time after time, commercial developers of expert systems report that one major benefit of building a system has been that they, and others in the organization, better understand the problem and the information requirements for a solution.

The traditional life-cycle model of software construction and maintenance presumes that problems are well specified. An alternative model, used in constructing expert systems, is exploratory programming, in which problem definition and problem solution are mutually reinforcing. A key element in exploratory programming is a powerful, integrated development environment (Sheil, 1984).

Conventional software can in principle be written by good programmers to solve any problem that an expert system solves. Frequently a system that is initially constructed in a shell system is rewritten in FORTRAN, PL/I, C, or some other well-known language. Constructing the system in the first place, however, requires considerably more ability than most, or unless the shell system (itself in C or some other language) provides an interpreter for elements in its knowledge base.

*Interpretation*

One of the facilities commonly used to advantage in expert systems is evaluation—*EVAL* to the LISP programmer. This facility allows the user (or the system itself) to specify a query or arbitrary computation to the running system and evaluate it in the run-time context. It lays open to examination the entire state of the system and its environment, including the knowledge base, the line of reasoning, agenda, and so on. This is the sense in which programs written in interpretive languages like LISP are said to themselves constitute data. It is one of the most important facilities on which an expert system depends. It allows a system to reason not only about incoming data but also about past inferences and even about how it makes inferences. To a certain extent, operating systems also perform this kind of introspection. However, these systems can usually only be tuned in a number of predefined ways, according to a fixed set of parameters; operating systems typically cannot look at their own procedures. By contrast, expert systems in principle

II) contains about 2,600 rules, with another 50,000 links among roughly 600 diseases (objects), and 80 manifestations (slots) per disease (chosen from approximately 4,500 manifestations in all). Numbers like these are difficult to compare for many reasons: there may be substantial differences in the level of conceptual detail covered in a rule in different shells (e.g., EMYCIN vs OPS5); there is more in a knowledge base than rules and object names; complex procedures contain considerable knowledge, even though not represented declaratively; and a single concept, or a single clause in a rule, may stand for something very complex (e.g., "state of the patient") or for something quite straightforward (e.g., "patient's age").

An approximate characterization of the complexity of present-day knowledge bases is shown in Table C–1. Assuming that the facts are represented as object-attribute-value triples (e.g., "the identity of Organism-2 is *E. coli*"), it makes some sense to ask how many there are. The numbers in Table C–1 represent empirical, not theoretical, upper bounds on several key parameters. With problems much smaller than those in Table C–1, along these dimensions, the flexibility of expert systems may not be required. With much larger problems, resource limitations (especially time for construction) may be exceeded. There are complications,

TABLE C–1.

Approximate Measures of Complexity of Expert Systems Built Routinely in the Late 1980's.

| *Vocabulary* | |
| --- | --- |
| # Objects | 1,000s of objects or classes of objects |
| # Attributes | 10–250 named attributes per object |
| # Legal values | 3–100 discrete values per attribute, or arbitrarily many discrete ranges of values of continuous attributes |
| *Inferential Relations* | |
| # Rules or Taxonomic Links | 100s to 1,000s |
| Depth of Longest Reasoning Chains | 2–10 steps from primary data to final conclusion |
| Breadth of Reasoning | 2–10 ways of inferring values of any single attribute |
| Degrees of Uncertainty | Facts and relations may be expressed with degrees of uncertainty beyond "true or false" (or "true, false, or unknown") |

# C.  STATE OF THE ART

SEVERAL recent books and publications provide extensive overviews and details about the state of the art. See, for example, Feigenbaum et al. (1989), Waterman (1986), Rauch-Hindin (1986), Mishkoff (1985), and Scown (1985), plus numerous current journals and newsletters such as *Expert Systems, IEEE Expert, AI Magazine, Expert System Strategies,* and *The Applied Artificial Intelligence Reporter.* In this section we encapsulate our own understanding of what can be done easily with standard tools, and distinguish that from work that requires ingenuity or new research because present methods are inadequate.

## C1.  Size of System

THE NUMBERS of expert systems and persons working on them have grown to the point where building expert systems has become routine. This is especially true for small, rule-based systems, and many companies are choosing to develop many small systems instead of concentrating on one or two "big wins" (Feigenbaum et al., 1989). A few expert system shells have small upper limits on the size of the knowledge bases that can be accommodated, mostly for reasons of memory size of the underlying personal computer. Even systems that today are counted as modestly large or complex mention only a few thousand objects (or classes of objects) or a few thousand rules. These limits may be due more to experts' and knowledge engineers' limitations in keeping track of larger numbers of items (and their interactions)—and to managers' unwillingness to spend more than 12–24 months in developing a system—than to hardware or software limits. New technology will be required for managing knowledge efficiently, however, when we try to build knowledge bases that contain millions of items. (See Lenat et al., 1986, for work in progress on methods for defining and managing truly encyclopedic knowledge bases.)

Although it is difficult to characterize the size of a system, either numerically or symbolically, there are some rather crude ways of describing how large present systems are. For example, MYCIN contained about 1,000 rules and 20 class names, and XCON contains about 6,000 rules and 100 class names. The INTERNIST system (see Article VIII.B3, Vol.

however, because classes may be defined for arbitrarily many instances; and attributes may take on continuous values (e.g., any real number). So, instead of showing only the number of rules, Table C–1 indicates the depth and breadth of the chains of inferences. It also suggests that knowledge bases are more complex when they must deal with uncertain facts and relations.

As developers attempt to encode more information in objects (attempting to make fewer assumptions about how the knowledge will be used), the number of rules tends to be reduced. This occurs because the rules are written to be applied to members of hierarchically organized classes of objects and not just to single individuals. An important strategy in scaling up from a small system to a large one is to find nearly independent subproblems and build subsystems that address them, with other subsystems addressing the (few) interactions. When followed, this simple idea keeps the complexity of the composite system from growing exponentially with the number of objects or facts being related.

The amount of detail required in a knowledge base is determined by the degree of precision required in the solution to a problem. If a diagnostic system, for example, is useful in locating errors within large, replaceable components (such as an aircraft's radar system), it need not reason about all the individual parts within the component. This would be reflected especially in the size of the vocabulary and the depth of the reasoning. Often this consideration is called the *grain size* or *granularity* of the description.

The time it takes to build a system varies greatly depending on the scope of the problem and the expectations about the end product. A prototype that is expected to demonstrate feasibility on a small troubleshooting problem, for example, may be built by a single person in one to ten weeks. A fully developed system ready for field use on a complex problem, on the other hand, may take a team of several persons one to three years or more. One measure of our increased understanding of knowledge programming is that students are now routinely assigned one-term class projects that would have been two-year doctoral research projects a decade ago.

## C2.  Type of System

SEVERAL TYPES of problems for which systems can be built were listed earlier in the categories: interpretation and construction. We lack a robust taxonomy of problem types (among the most complete so far is the one proposed in Chandrasekaran, 1986), so the individual examples still provide a better characterization of the types of problem than general descriptions. Most expert systems described in the open literature address problems of data interpretation, mostly for purposes of trouble-shooting or equipment diagnosis. They are mainly organized around the method of evidence gathering, in which evidence is gathered for and against a fixed set of hypotheses (or solutions), and the answer(s) with the best evidence is selected (Buchanan and Shortliffe, 1984). This is also known as *catalog selection* or *heuristic classification* (Clancey, 1985). Most commercial shells address problems of this type. However, more and more systems are being built for problems of the second category, construction, and shell systems are emerging to handle the myriad constraints that shape a design, assembly, configuration, schedule, or plan.

## C3.  Some Observed Limitations

EXPERT SYSTEMS are designed to solve specific problems in well-circumscribed task domains in which specialists can articulate the knowledge needed for high performance. Current methods for designing and building them have limitations, naturally, so that attempts to implement and use an expert system may not always be successful. Working within known limitations is more likely to lead to success, however, than working without regard for them.

The observations about the limitations of today's tools highlight opportunities for further research. Taken together with current research, the limitations also point to extensions of our methods that can be expected in the future. In the following subsections we mention several pieces of current research on some of these topics, and additional ones that are likely to advance the state of the art over the next several years. This is not a complete list by any means, but it points to several areas of active work in which improvements are likely. It is also not a list that does justice to any of the topics or any piece of work mentioned.

Traditionally, research in artificial intelligence generally has focused on problems of *knowledge representation* and knowledge use, or *reasoning*. Advances in these fundamental areas will certainly advance the state of the art of expert systems. There are additional demands that expert systems make on programmers, however, because of the desired high performance, flexibility, and understandability. The corresponding areas of research in expert systems work are known as problems of *robustness* and *validation*, *knowledge acquisition* and *maintenance* of knowledge bases, and *explanation*.

In addition, several problems crop up repeatedly in work on expert systems that are broader issues of software engineering or computer science generally. Pragmatic problems of putting expert systems into actual routine use involve research on the *integration* of expert systems with existing applications software, the *security* of knowledge and data in expert systems, design *specification* and *testing*, and the costs and logistics of *hardware* for AI applications. There is also considerable work on *interfaces* and *human factors* whose advances will make a difference in future expert systems.

**Expertise.** Expert systems work within narrow areas of expertise (Davis, 1982 and 1989). Technical domains, in which terms are well defined and in which subproblems can be solved separately, are more amenable to the introduction of expert systems than more open-ended domains. Engineering and business are thus better problem domains than political science and sociology. When the limitations are well understood, there is little problem in using an expert system reliably for substantial gains in productivity, and many of the notable successes are of just this sort (Feigenbaum, 1989).

Difficulties arise, however, when a user of a system expects that the system can solve a problem for which the knowledge or reasoning principles are totally inadequate. Often, regrettably, this is the fault of the designers; sometimes it is the result of overselling on the part of the user; and sometimes the result of misunderstanding on the part of the user; and sometimes the result of blind spots or errors in the program.

Applications over the last several years have become larger and more complex. In the past we had to choose between building a 3,000-rule (or 5,000-object) system that is either narrow and deep, or shallow and broad. Mostly it has been easier to demonstrate proficiency and utility with the former. With advances in our methods for dealing with very large problems, we will be able to have both breadth and depth. Several of the techniques from AI that help us manage large, combinatorial problems will also apply to large expert systems. These include problem decomposition, omitting (nearly) irrelevant details, reasoning at successively finer levels of detail, and reasoning at a strategic level before (and during) problem solving.

**First Principles.** The domain models used by expert systems are not generally the theoretical first principles of textbooks, but are a looser collection of facts and associations (Davis, 1987). Expert systems rely more on special-case formulations of relations than on "first principles." Although a set of general principles such as Maxwell's equations governs the behavior of a large class of devices, designers of expert systems prefer to codify special cases, exceptions, and empirical associations, as well as some causal associations, in order to put the general principles in forms that can be applied more quickly and more precisely. As a result, they are unable to fall back on a better theory in some situations. There is substantial research in AI on using first principles in reasoning, much of it in the area of electronics troubleshooting (Davis, 1987). As this matures, it will allow us to build expert systems that blend the theoretical soundness of the first principles with the precision of special-case exception clauses that map the theory into the world of practical applications.

**Limits of Knowledge.** Expert systems tend to perform well on the classes of cases that have been explicitly considered but may fail precipitously on new cases at the boundaries of their competence (Davis, 1987; Lenat, 1936). In part this is due to lack of knowledge of first principles. The performance of humans is more robust. As we reach the extent of what we know about a problem area, we often can give appropriate answers that are approximately correct, although not very precise—and we know that we have reached the limits of our knowledge. For expert systems, the standard solution today is to codify rules that screen out cases that are outside the intended scope in order to further ensure that the system is being used in an appropriate way. Current research on reasoning from a sound theoretical basis mentioned earlier will help overcome this problem. The general approach is to back up (or perhaps replace) the specialized rules that are now encoded by expressions of a sound theory. Thus, when a system finds few or no specialized items in its knowledge base covering a situation, it can resort to reasoning from first principles. It can also use the theory to check the plausibility of conclusions reached by using the specialized knowledge.

**Self-knowledge.** Expert systems have little or no self-knowledge, and thus do not have a sense of what they do not know (Lenat et al., 1983). Although expert systems can often give explanations of what they know, they do not have a general "awareness" of what the scope and limitations of their own knowledge are. Meta-level knowledge, such as rules of strategy, can offset this shortcoming in special situations but does not constitute a general capability.

**Commonsense Knowledge.** Expert systems can only represent commonsense knowledge explicitly and do not use commonsense modes of reasoning such as analogical reasoning or reasoning from the most similar recent case (McCarthy, 1983). Designers of current expert systems resolve this by assuming that users can exercise some common sense, and by specifying common facts explicitly when needed. The INTERNIST system, for example, contains about 100,000 commonsense medical facts such as "males do not get pregnant" and "aspirin obscures the results of thyroid tests" (personal communication from R. Miller). The challenge is to construct a "commonsense reasoning component" that is general enough to avoid errors that "any fool" would avoid and specific enough to reason reliably and efficiently. Current research on case-based reasoning attends to some of these difficulties (See, for example, the 1989 Proceedings of the Case-based Reasoning Workshop, published by Morgan-Kaufman, San Mateo, CA).

hoc." In this regard, though, expert systems are not in a much different state than other software in which complex reasoning with heuristics defies proofs of correctness. There is considerable research on formalizing the reasoning methods of AI programs and combining those with a predicate calculus representation of knowledge.

**Knowledge Context.**  Expert systems may fail if the user's conceptual framework is not the same as that of the expert and others on the design team (Winograd and Flores, 1986). Knowledge engineers work under the assumption that the experts they work with know the context of intended use and the intended users' terminology and point of view. This may result in misuse of a system when a user attaches different meaning to terms than did the expert who designed the knowledge base. There are no safeguards built into today's systems to test this assumption. Thus the challenge is to provide enough ways of explaining what is in a knowledge base to make its contents clear to all users. But a simple, more pragmatic remedy is to make members of the intended user community on the design team.

A related problem is that the conceptual view of the design team—even if only a single expert—may change over time, and thus maintaining a knowledge base over time becomes difficult.

**Explicit Knowledge.**  The knowledge of expert systems must be made explicit; they have no intuition (Dreyfus and Dreyfus, 1986). So far, the problems that have been most successfully solved with expert systems have been those in which inferential knowledge is easily formulated as rules and the organization of objects and concepts is easily formulated as taxonomic (class-subclass-instance) hierarchies and partwhole hierarchies. Reasoning by analogy or by intuition is still too unpredictable (and ill-understood) to use in high-performance systems. Because expert systems depend on knowledge formulated explicitly, it is important to develop better methods for facilitating the process through which experts articulate what they know. Any task for which knowledge cannot be articulated for any reason is not a good candidate for an expert system.

**Reusable Knowledge.**  Knowledge bases are not reusable (Lenat, 1986). Since the cost of building a knowledge base is substantial, it is desirable to amortize it over several related expert systems, with unique extensions to cover unique circumstances. For example, many medical systems use facts about anatomy and physiology, yet often each encodes those facts specifically for use in a unique way. The challenge is to develop knowledge representations that can be used efficiently, independent of the specific context of use. By contrast, considerable progress has been made in building lower level components of expert systems that are reusable—this has led to the widespread use of expert system shells. Representing knowledge in structured objects improves the chances of reusability, and substantial current research is exploring this and other means of improving reusability of knowledge bases (see, for example, Lenat, 1986).

**Learning.**  Expert systems do not learn from experience (Schank, 1983). Research on machine learning is maturing to the point where expert systems will be able to learn from their mistakes and successes. Learning by induction from a large library of solved cases is already well enough understood to allow induction systems to learn classification rules that an expert system then uses (Michie et al., 1984; Michalski et al., 1986). Prototype systems have been built that emphasize learning in context, sometimes called explanation-based learning or apprentice learning, which appears to hold promise for expert systems (Mitchell et al., 1986). The challenge is to design learning mechanisms that are as accurate as knowledge engineering but are more cost effective.

**Reasoning Methods.**  It is generally not possible to prove theorems about the scope and limits of an expert system because the reasoning is not formal (Nilsson, 1982). Although some systems are implemented in a logic programming language such as PROLOG, or otherwise use predicate calculus as a representation language, many systems are more "ad

# D. DESIGN PRINCIPLES AND SUMMARY

## D1. Design Principles

OUT OF THE experimental work with expert systems over the last five to ten years, several "architectural principles" of expert systems have emerged. In 1982, Davis (1982) articulated an early set of principles based on experience with a few rule-based systems. (See also McDermott, 1983, for another set of generalizations and Chapter 5 of Hayes-Roth et al., 1983, and practical advice for knowledge engineers.) Given additional experience, we can augment and refine these principles. Note that many of these "principles" in fact represent design tradeoffs. Where appropriate, we identify the relative advantages of each side of tradeoffs.

*Modular, Declarative Expressions of Knowledge Are Necessary*

1. *Represent all knowledge explicitly.* This simplifies the explanation of system behavior as well as refinement, both by human designers and by the system itself. The main feature of an expert system is the suite of specific knowledge it has about its domain of application. For reasons of extensibility and flexibility, it is important to separate the abstract concepts and relations of the target domain from inferences that can be made in the domain, i.e., "what is known" from "how to use it."

2. *Keep elements of the knowledge base as independent and modular as possible.* When updating rules or links among objects, the fewer the interactions with other parts of the knowledge base the easier the isolation and repair of problems. Although complete independence of rules or objects is impossible (without complex, lengthy descriptions of the context of relevance), partitioning the knowledge base into small, nearly independent modules facilitates maintenance. Common partitionings include:

   a. Domain-specific knowledge (e.g., a model of structural geology, which could be used in a variety of applications).
   b. Task-specific knowledge (e.g., the knowledge of how to use the model of structural geology, together with a model of the data sensed by a dipmeter tool, to interpret the data in terms of geological structures).
   c. Knowledgeable interaction with developers and users.
   d. Problem-solving knowledge (e.g., strategies like top-down refinement and least-commitment constraint propagation).
   e. Other domain-independent knowledge (e.g., commonsense facts and mathematics).

3. *Separate the knowledge base from the programs that interpret it.* Historically this has been phrased as "separate the knowledge base and the inference engine" (Davis, 1982).

4. *Consider interaction with users as an integrated component.* It is important to avoid dealing with user interaction issues in an "add on" manner, after the expert system has been designed. High-quality user interaction frameworks are often essential to end-user utility. They are also important to widen the knowledge acquisition bottleneck.

5. *Avoid assumptions about context of use.* Extending a knowledge base is made difficult when assumptions about how the individual packets of knowledge will be used are implicitly encoded. For example, important premise conditions of a rule may be omitted because the system developer knows the context in which that rule will be applied (as noted earlier with the sample rule from the Dipmeter Advisor system). This is also important if domain-specific knowledge bases are to be reused for a variety of applications.

*Uniformity, Simplicity, Efficiency, and Expressive Power Are Interdependent*

1. *Use as uniform a representation as possible,* although specialized representations are often worth the cost of translating among representations because they may improve run-time performance and simplify knowledge acquisition.

2. *Keep the inference engine simple.* A program's ability to reason about its actions depends on its ability to reason about the way it makes inferences, and complex inference procedures make this task more difficult. However, this must be balanced against problems that simplicity may cause in expressing knowledge in "appropriate" ways and in run-time efficiency.

3. *An object-centered paradigm offers the most flexibility,* and thus the most expressive power, even though there is a logical equivalence among representational choices.

4. *Be sure the reasoning is based on sound, conceptually simple strategic knowledge.* A knowledge base is more than a bag of facts and relations; it is used for a purpose, with a reasoning strategy in mind. The clearer that strategy is, the more coherent the knowledge base

will be. Again, however, this must be balanced against possible deterioration in run-time performance.

### Redundancy Is Desirable

*Exploit redundancy.* One advantage of a modular representation of the domain knowledge is that it allows the system to explore multiple lines of reasoning. By contrast, a conventional program typically has a single procedure with a fixed sequence of steps for achieving a goal. Reasoning with uncertain or missing data, or with knowledge that is uncertain or incomplete, requires building redundancy into the reasoning to allow correct conclusions to be drawn in spite of these deficiencies.

## D2.  Summary

EXPERT SYSTEMS use AI methods for representing and using experts' knowledge about specific problem areas. They have been successfully used in many decision-making contexts in which:

1. Experts can articulate much of what they know (e.g., in training manuals).

2. Experts can reason qualitatively (e.g., based on what they have learned from experience) to augment the formulas in textbooks.

3. The amount of knowledge required to solve problems is circumscribed and relatively small.

Although many interesting and important research problems remain open, expert systems—and the shell systems that make them easy to build—encapsulate solutions to many problems associated with the representation, use, acquisition, and explanation of knowledge. The engineering solutions used in today's expert systems are not without limits, but they are well enough understood and robust enough to support commercial applications of importance. Many applications are in routine use, with annual savings of millions of dollars each (AAAI, 1989; Feigenbaum et al., 1989), and all of them were built with the tools and methods developed in the last decade or so. Future research will extend the scope of the commercial successes, but there is no limit to the number of systems that can succeed using tools available today.

### Acknowledgments

Eric Schoen and David Hammock assisted in generating the Dipmeter Advisor System figures. The ideas in this chapter synthesize articles by and discussed with many friends and colleagues, no one of whom will agree with every statement (including this one). We are grateful to them all. An earlier version of this paper appeared in the *Annual Review of Computer Science* 1988, Vol. 3: 23–58.

# 8. Preliminary Steps Toward a Taxonomy of Problem-Solving Methods

*John McDermott*

## Abstract

Although efforts, some successful, to develop expert systems (application systems that can perform knowledge-intensive tasks) have been going on now for almost 20 years, we are not yet very good at describing the variations in problem-solving methods that these systems use, nor do we have much of an understanding of how to characterize the methods in terms of features of the types of tasks for which they are appropriate. This chapter takes a few steps toward creating a taxonomy of methods -- a taxonomy that identifies some of the discriminating characteristics of the methods expert systems use and that suggests how methods can be mapped onto tasks.

## 8.1. Introduction

The various research efforts described in this book are experiments in automating the programming process by building tools, each of which knows what sort of knowledge is required to solve some class of tasks. The research is interesting to the extent that the scope of at least some of the tools is fairly broad; that is, the kinds of knowledge that a tool knows how to collect and represent are useful for solving a significant number of real tasks in a variety of domains.

This chapter presents problem solving as the identification, selection, and implementation of a sequence of actions that accomplish some task within a specific domain. A problem-solving method provides a means of identifying, at each step, candidate actions. It provides one or more mechanisms for selecting among candidate actions. Finally, it ensures that the selected action is implemented and often provides a mechanism that allows the actual effect of the action to be compared with the expected or desired effect. To a first approximation, a method's control knowledge comprises (1) an algorithm specifying when to use what knowledge to identify, select, and implement actions, together with (2) whatever knowledge the method has for selecting among candidate actions. The knowledge it uses to identify candidate actions and to implement the action selected is not control knowledge. In traditional expert systems terminology, a problem-solving method is called an inference engine. The inference engine comes with all of the control knowledge needed to solve some class of tasks; none of the knowledge in its knowledge base is (supposed to be) control knowledge.

Control knowledge can vary from being extremely unspecific to the actual task at hand to being tightly wrapped around task details. This chapter is an attempt to describe a way of classifying inference engines and the knowledge they use for action selection in terms of the specificity of the control structures to task features. This focus leads to the identification of inference engines that are somewhat limited in scope, but that provide substantial assistance in automating the task types they cover. There are task families for which control knowledge that strongly abstracts from task details is adequate for selecting the next action. The point of this chapter is that to the extent that such task families can be identified, there is a real opportunity for radically simplifying the programming enterprise. In this chapter, I will refer to the knowledge that is specific to a particular task instance as task-specific knowledge. Almost all of the knowledge that a method uses to identify and implement actions is task-specific knowledge. Knowledge used to select among candidate actions that depends on details of particular task instances is also task-specific knowledge. This chapter makes three claims:

- There are families of tasks that can be adequately performed by methods whose control knowledge strongly abstracts from the peculiarities of any of the family members.

- A method whose control knowledge is not very task-specific will use task-specific knowledge for identification and implementation that is highly regular; each piece of task-specific knowledge will play one of a small number of roles; thus the method will provide strong guidance with respect to what knowledge is required to perform a particular task and how that knowledge should be encoded.

- The clarity of these knowledge roles, and thus the strength of the guidance provided by a method, diminishes with the increasing diversity of the information required to identify candidate actions and to define the conditions that must obtain in order for an action to be implemented.

In this chapter, methods that strongly guide knowledge collection and encoding will be called **role-limiting methods**.

During the 1960's, a significant piece of the AI community's attention was devoted to identifying and analyzing what Newell has called the **weak methods** [Laird 83]. The weak methods are called weak because their usefulness is only weakly constrained by task features; each is potentially applicable to a broad set of task types. They typically achieve this generality with simple control structures that require additional control knowledge to be supplied before the method can be applied. The Hill Climbing method, for example, requires control knowledge in the form of a task-specific evaluation function that determines whether a candidate action will move the system closer to or farther from a solution. Since one can imagine a weak method whose control knowledge contains only a small amount of task-specific knowledge (a Hill Climbing method, for example, whose evaluation function consists of comparing the value of just one feature of one class of objects), weak methods would seem to be likely instances of role-limiting methods. But a weak method is more open with respect to control than a role-limiting method can be; a weak method does not put any limits on the nature or complexity of the task-specific control knowledge it can use. A role-limiting method can be viewed as a specialization of a weak method that predefines the task-related control knowledge the method can use.

The MYCIN experiments [Buchanan 84], which ran through most of the 1970's, introduced a role-limiting method. The MYCIN inference engine is an example of a method, heuristic classification [Clancey 84], that is similar to the weak methods in that it is a very simple control structure. However, it differs from weak methods in that the task-related control knowledge the method uses is included in the definition of the method. One of the most important insights of the MYCIN project was that, given that no control knowledge needs to be added to the method before it is applied, it should be possible to fully understand the interdependencies between the control knowledge and whatever other knowledge the method will need. This in turn, can substantially simplify the task of the method user who has to formulate the task-specific knowledge for identification and implementation of actions in a way that allows the control knowledge to operate on it effectively.

The thesis of this book is that role-limiting methods are an important class of methods because they both have a quite broad scope of applicability and also provide substantial help in specifying what knowledge needs to be collected to perform a particular task and how that knowledge can be appropriately encoded. Methods that allow task-specific control knowledge to be added as a knowledge base is built up cannot provide as much help in determining what knowledge needs to be collected or how it should be encoded; this is because the requirements for task-specific knowledge cannot be known until the additional control knowledge is defined, and that is not known at method definition time. We have created support for this thesis by developing automatic knowledge-acquisition tools for collecting and encoding the knowledge required by five different role-limiting methods.

There has not been much attention given to identifying role-limiting methods. Clancey's description of heuristic classification is surely the most complete, but he doesn't attempt to identify others. Chandrasekaran has identified a number of methods for generic tasks [Chandrasekaran 83, Chandrasekaran 86]; however he has not discussed the interdependencies between his methods and the task-specific knowledge they operate on.

The underlying idea here is that if we take seriously the knowledge-base/inference-engine distinction that expert system developers have made so much of, it should be possible to devise a set of role-limiting methods, where each method defines the roles that the task-specific knowledge it requires must play and the forms in which that knowledge can be represented. A review of a number of role-limiting methods in the next section will show the sense in which their task-specific knowledge is highly regular and will show the implications of each piece of knowledge participating in one of a few roles. The methods provide strong guidance. This is what we would expect given that each of the methods is a simple control structure, since the simplicity of the control structure will not allow a knowledge base with little regularity to be effectively exploited. The situation is different with the weak methods. For weak methods, the task-specific evaluation function can be arbitrarily complex, and thus the method can be shaped to exploit knowledge that is highly irregular. A role-limiting method typically consists of a simple loop over a sequence of 5 or 10 steps.

Some of the steps operate on significant bodies of task-specific knowledge, and within a step there is no control; that is, it makes no difference in what order the actions that can be performed are performed.

It is the regularity of the task-specific knowledge that a role-limiting method requires that makes automating the building of expert systems a tractable task. A couple of examples may make this more concrete. Two of the knowledge-acquisition tools discussed in this book are MOLE and SALT. Each program that MOLE creates uses the cover-and-differentiate problem-solving method -- a method suitable for certain types of diagnostic tasks. A MOLE-built program searches a space of possible explanations. The explanation space can be represented by one or more graphs where each node is an event and the unidirectional links represent possible explanatory relationships. The values of some nodes must be provided externally; the values of other nodes can then be inferred. The cover-and-differentiate method assumes that the intial state is a set of one or more symptoms. The method has the following control knowledge:

1. Determine the events that potentially explain (that is, cover) the symptoms.

2. If there is more than one candidate explanation for any event, then identify information that will differentiate the candidates by

   - ruling out one or more of the explanatory connections,

   - ruling out one or more of the candidate explanatory events,

   - providing sufficient support for one of the candidate explanatory events,

   - providing a reason for preferring some of the explanatory connections over others.

3. Get this information (in any order) and apply it (in any order).

4. If step 3 uncovers new symptoms, go to step 1.

This control knowledge is sufficient for performing diagnostic tasks in a wide variety of domains. Most of the task-specific knowledge for action identification and implementation comes into play in steps 1 and 2. In step 1, each symptom that needs to be explained generates the set of events, any of which might explain that symptom. Each piece of task-specific knowledge relevant to this step associates a symptom with an event. The form of each piece of knowledge must be such that touching a symptom returns the set of associated events. In step 2, four kinds of task-specific knowledge are potentially relevant; each of these four kinds of knowledge provide hypothesis differentiation of one of the four types identified above. The form of each piece of knowledge must be such that touching a candidate explanatory event returns a description of the information that will help confirm or disconfirm that event.

Each program that SALT creates uses the propose-and-revise problem-solving method -- a method suitable for certain types of constructive tasks. The design space can be represented by a graph where each node is a partial design and the unidirectional links represent possible design extensions. The propose-and-revise method assumes that the initial state is a set of specifications. The method has the following control knowledge:

1. Extend a design and identify constraints on the extension just formed.

2. Identify constraint violations; if none, go to step 1.

3. Suggest potential fixes for a constraint violation.

4. Select the least costly fix not yet attempted.

5. Tentatively modify the design and identify constraints on the modification just formed.

6. Identify constraint violations due to the revision; if any, go to 4.

7. Remove relationships incompatible with the revision.

8. If the design is incomplete, go to 1.

Most of the task-specific knowledge that the method uses comes into play in steps 1, 3, and 5. The knowledge in those three steps play three roles: Each piece of knowledge describes a possible plan extension, defines a constraint, or describes a possible fix for a constraint violation. In step 1, a partial design is extended or a constraint is identified. Either of the first two kinds of task-specific knowledge may be relevant. The first describes a possible

```
If two of the candidate actions are
    to configure an RA60 drive
    to configure another type of drive
        that uses the same cabinet type,
Then prefer configuring the RA60 next.


If two of the candidate actions are
    to configure a rack-mountable device
    to configure a free standing tape
        drive or a tape drive that is to be
        bolted to the CPU cabinet,
Then prefer configuring the non-rack-mountable
    device next.


If two of the candidate actions are
    to configure a rack-mountable device
        whose subtype is not RV20A or RV20B
    to configure a different rack-
        mountable device whose subtype is
        not RV20A or RV20B,
and no cabinet has been selected,
and the second device is not bundled with
    an available cabinet,
and there is an available cabinet or tape
    drive in which the devices can be
    placed,
and it is desirable to place the first
    device in the cabinet before the
    second device,
Then prefer configuring the first device.
```

design extension; the form of pieces of this kind of knowledge must be such that a partial design can extend itself in some manner. The second kind of task-specific knowledge relevant in this step defines a constraint; the form of pieces of this kind of knowledge must be such that the extension of a partial design identifies that constraint on the partial design. In step 3, a violated constraint associated with a partial design identifies a potential fix. Each piece of task-specific knowledge associates a set of fixes with a constraint and indicates the cost of using each of those fixes to solve the problem; the form of each piece of knowledge must be such that the existence of the constraint violation returns the set of associated fixes. The task-specific knowledge required in step 5 is the same as that required in step 1.

Hopefully these two examples illustrate the nature of the control knowledge that one finds in role-limiting methods. The control knowledge is useful for deciding what to do next only within the context of a particular task type. But the two tasks illustrated here, and the other three illustrated in the next section, are tasks that are performed in a wide variety of domains. Thus the role-limiting methods have a quite broad scope of potential applicability. It is likely to turn out that there are hundreds of role-limiting methods; it is also likely that there will be an even larger number of task types in which the control knowledge required to perform the task adequately can only be acquired as the other task-specific knowledge needed for the task is acquired. Chapter 7, on RIME, addressed the issue of how to provide assistance in defining methods and in imposing structure on task-specific knowledge in situations where role-limiting methods are not applicable.

To lend support to the claim that there are tasks that are difficult to cast in role-limiting methods, we will look briefly at a small piece of XCON (or R1) [McDermott 82]. The version of XCON that has recently been reimplemented using the RIME methodology is organized as problem spaces. One of the problem spaces, Select-Device, has as its overall purpose to determine the next device to configure. The problem space has 46 pieces of task-specific knowledge, 15 of which are pieces of control knowledge; each piece of control knowledge prefers a candidate action over another candidate. Four examples should give some sense of the level of detail in which the control knowledge is immersed:

```
If two of the candidate actions are
      to configure a box-mountable device
      to configure a different box-mountable
      device,
  and the first device is bundled with the
      system,
  and there is a selected cabinet or box
      in which the devices can be placed,
  and it is desirable to place each of the
      devices in the selected cabinet or
      box,
Then prefer configuring the first device.
```

Because selection of the action to perform next is so intimately tied to the details of the type of system being configured, and because the nature of the considerations that lead to preferring one action over another change as new products are developed, it is not possible to predefine what control knowledge will be required to perform XCON's task. Thus, the task cannot be done with a role-limiting method. XCON's task also exemplifies a task in which the information required to identify candidate actions and to define the conditions under which an action may be implemented is highly diverse. Thus, even if a role-limiting method could be used for the task, within each of the roles that the method would impose there would be substantial diversity, and thus the method would provide less assistance with the collection and encoding of task-specific knowledge than for any of the other tasks discussed in this chapter.

In section 8.2, six knowledge-acquisition tools are described. The first five of these tools each presuppose a particular role-limiting method; each tool elicits information that its method demands and constructs a knowledge base that the method can use. The sixth tool, SEAR, assists the user in defining problem-solving methods and in using the method definition to determine what task-specific knowledge, including control knowledge, needs to be collected and how it should be encoded.

## 8.2. A Few Data Points

Four of the six knowledge-acquisition tools described in this section (MOLE, SALT, KNACK, and SIZZLE) are treated in detail in chapters 3 through 6. The other two tools (YAKA and SEAR) do not have chapters devoted to them because they are not yet sufficiently well-developed to warrant it. YAKA is included in this section because it is, in many respects, quite similar to MOLE, and thus can give us some insight into the relative power and scope of closely related methods. SEAR is included because, although it is still in the early stages of development, it is closely related to the RIME methodology introduced in chapter 7.

In order to make it easy to compare the tools presented in this section, the form of each of the following subsections is identical.

The first part of each subsection begins with a list of what characteristics a task must have in order for the method presupposed by the tool to be suitable; this list is followed by another indicating what additional task characteristics make the method particularly suitable. Then there is a brief description of the problem-solving behavior of the systems built using the knowledge-acquisition tool, and this is followed by a few examples of how these systems perform representative tasks. The first example in each subsection provides illustrations of each of the necessary and desirable task characteristics.

The second part of each subsection begins with an identification of the intended users of the tool. This is followed by a brief description of how the knowledge-acquisition tool (as opposed to the systems it builds) works and examples of the kinds of knowledge the tool collects.

### 8.2.1. MOLE

**Possible Tasks.**

MOLE is a tool for building diagnostic expert systems whose role-limiting method is *cover-and-differentiate* (a form of heuristic classification). A task must have the following characteristics in order for cover-and-differentiate to be an appropriate method: (1) There is an identifiable set of problem states or events (for example, symptoms, complaints, abnormalities) each of which must be explained or accounted for (that is, covered). (2) An exhaustive set of candidate explanations (that is, hypotheses, explanatory events) that cover these events can be statically pre-enumerated. The method is most appropriate for tasks that, in addition, have the following characteristics: (3) There is information that will help differentiate the candidate explanations for each abnormal event. (4) Usually only one candidate explanation is applicable at any given time per event (the single fault assumption).

MOLE includes a performance system ($MOLE_P$) that interprets the knowledge base generated by the knowledge-acquisition tool ($MOLE_{KA}$). $MOLE_P$'s task-specific control knowledge guides it iteratively through the following steps: It asks the user for the complaints that are present. It next activates the candidate hypotheses that will explain these complaints. It then queries the user about the presence or absence of states or events that will help it differentiate these hypotheses.

Examples of MOLE-built systems:

**Diagnosing car engine problems.** $MOLE_P$ asks the user if certain noticeable malfunctions of a car engine are present (for example, the engine is not running smoothly). If it is told that the engine is not running smoothly, MOLE activates the hypotheses that might explain this abnormality (for example, the engine is overheating, there is incomplete combustion, the valves are bad). MOLE next queries the user about events or states that will differentiate these explanations (for example, incomplete combustion is indicated by black deposits on the spark plugs). If incomplete combustion is the most likely explanation of the engine not running smoothly, its possible causes are activated (for example, a maladjusted carburator or maladjusted rockers are potential causes of incomplete combustion). MOLE then queries the user about events or states that will differentiate these explanations.

Cover-and-differentiate is an appropriate method for this task because the task has the following characteristics: (1) It is possible to identify a set of complaints that motivate car users to seek help (for example, the car won't start, the engine makes a loud noise when idling). (2) Once a complaint is identified, possible explanations can be statically pre-enumerated (for example, the battery is dead, a fuel line is blocked). (3) The problem-solving process can be naturally represented as a process of differentiating possible explanations of the complaints (for example, knowing that the engine won't crank differentiates in favor of the battery being dead rather than a blocked fuel line as an explanation for why the car won't start). (4) Usually only one actual explanation is necessary per complaint (for example, if it is discovered that the car won't start because the battery is dead, then other explanations are probably irrelevant).

**Diagnosing problems in a steel-rolling mill.** A steel-rolling mill processes steel by rolling bars of steel into thin sheets. MOLE asks the user if there are any defects in the product (for example, the steel is too narrow or too thin). If it is told that the steel is too narrow, MOLE activates the hypotheses that will explain this abnormality (for example, the steel was too narrow coming out of the preprocessor, the rolls are worn out, or there is too much tension between stands). MOLE next queries the user about events or states that will differentiate these explanations (for example, if there is no oscillation of the roll, then it is probably not worn out). Since MOLE assumes that every abnormal event has a cause, if MOLE can rule out all but one of the explanations of an event, it will accept the remaining explanation. For example, if MOLE can rule out both that the steel is too narrow coming out of the preprocessor and that the roll is worn out, then it will accept as the explanation of the steel being too narrow that there is excessive tension between stands. Acceptance of this hypothesis will in turn activate hypotheses that explain the excessive tension between stands (for example, there is an overload or a looper malfunction).

**Diagnosing inefficiencies in a coal-burning power plant.** The boiler is the central unit in a coal-burning power plan. Problems rarely prevent the boiler from functioning, but they are major sources of inefficiency that can waste millions of dollars of fuel as well as dump tons of pollutants into the atmosphere. MOLE asks the user if there are any events or states indicating that the plant is working inefficiently (for example, the ash is dark). MOLE activates the hypotheses that will explain this state (for example, there is high excess air, low excess air, or large fuel particles). MOLE queries the user about events or states that will differentiate these explanations (for example, the oxygen reading differentiates the high and low excess air hypotheses from the large particles hypothesis). These hypothesized events in turn can be explained by other events (for example, possible explanations for large fuel particles are a pulverizer malfunction and a wrong setting of the pulverizer).

## Using MOLE to Develop Application Systems.

Section 8.2.1 described the kinds of tasks that the MOLE performance programs perform and gave an indication of the types of information those performance programs ask their users for. In this section, we look at the knowledge that the performance programs need in order to perform such tasks and indicate how the MOLE knowledge-acquisition tool elicits that knowledge from domain experts. MOLE$_{KA}$ is intended to be used by domain experts who need not know anything about programming. The expert must provide the following types of task-specific knowledge:

- Complaints or abnormalities.
- Explanations (that is, possible causes) for these complaints.
- Differentiation knowledge (that is, information that will help differentiate these possible complaints).

MOLE$_{KA}$ begins by asking the expert to list the complaints or abnormalities that would motivate someone to seek diagnostic help. It next asks for possible explanations for each of these complaints. MOLE then asks whether these explaining events or states in turn have relevant explanations, and so on. Finally, MOLE seeks information that will enable it to differentiate these candidate explanations. This is done both statically and dynamically. Static differentiation looks at the knowledge base and makes sure that each hypothesis can in principle be differentiated from its competitors. Dynamic differentiation compares the diagnosis of the performance system for some case with an expert's diagnosis, and if they differ, elicits information that will help differentiate hypotheses in this situation.

Examples of task-specific knowledge that domain experts provided for the three diagnostic tasks described earlier:

**Diagnosing car engine problems:**

*Complaints:* car won't start, engine not running smoothly.

*Explanations:* the engine not running smoothly is explained by incomplete combustion, engine overheating, or problems with valves, crankshaft, pistons, or cylinders.

*Differentiation:* carbon deposits on the spark plugs point to incomplete combustion as the problem.

**Diagnosing steel-rolling mill problems:**

*Complaints:* steel too thin, too thick, too wide, too narrow.

*Explanations:* the steel too narrow is explained by the steel entering the rolls being too narrow, a worn out roll, or by too much tension between stands.

*Differentiation:* an oscillation of the looper roll indicates a worn out roll; a major imbalance between rolls indicates the problem must be either a worn out roll or a tension problem, but the problem is not that the steel is too narrow upon entry.

**Diagnosing inefficiencies in a coal-burning power plant:**

*Complaints:* dark ash, high fly ash flow, high bottom ash flow, loss in gas.

*Explanations:* dark ash is explained by high excess air, low excess air, and large particles; high fly ash flow is explained by high excess air and small particles.

*Differentiation:* a high or low oxygen reading identifies high or low excess air; the absence of high fly ash flow rules out high excess air.

## 8.2.2. YAKA

### Possible Tasks.

YAKA is a tool for building diagnostic expert systems whose role-limiting method is a combination of *qualitative reasoning* and *cover-and-differentiate*. A task must have the following characteristics in order for this method to be appropriate: (1) There is an identifiable set of problem states or events (for example, symptoms, complaints, abnormalities) each of which must be explained or accounted for (that is, covered). (2) A model of the normal functioning of the system can be provided, and this model can be characterized in terms of qualitative equations between state variables describing components and conduits. The method is most appropriate for tasks that, in addition, have the following characteristics: (3) Candidate explanations that are external to the functional model (faults) can be expressed as disturbances affecting the functioning of a conduit or component, hence changing its equation(s). (4) There is information that will help differentiate candidate faults for each abnormal event. (5) Usually only one fault is applicable at any given time per event.

YAKA includes a performance system ($YAKA_P$) that interprets the knowledge base generated by the knowledge-acquisition tool ($YAKA_{KA}$). $YAKA_P$'s task-specific control knowledge guides it iteratively through the following steps: Given a variable whose value is abnormal at time t, $YAKA_P$ traces back through the equations upon which the variable is dependent until equations are found whose independent variables are all measured. If this set of equations is inconsistent, then YAKA identifies (by a process of substitution) all faults (represented by equations) that potentially account for the inconsistency. On the other hand, if the set of equations is consistent, YAKA treats the measured variables whose values explain the problem as abnormal values and repeats the process. Once a set of candidate faults has been identified, YAKA makes use of heuristic knowledge that will enable it to differentiate them.

An example of a YAKA-built system:

**Diagnosing problems in a refinery process.** An oil refinery is quite complex but it can be described in terms of a relatively small number of component and conduit types (for example, pipes, tanks, valves, pumps). The task is to track down where a problem is occuring. Given a symptom at time t such as a low value for the state variable "tank-level", $YAKA_P$ evaluates the equation upon which the value of the tank-level is dependent, $dL/dt = Fin - Fout$, at time $t1 = t$ - time-delay of the equation. If this equation holds, the symptom is caused by an abnormal value in one of the variables it is dependent upon (Fin or Fout), so YAKA repeats the process with this variable. If the equation is violated, the problem is caused by a disturbance preventing the tank from performing its function correctly (for

example, a leak in the tank). YAKA generates the fault hypotheses that can affect the tank and tests the equations relevant to these faults (for example, for the leak in the tank, $dL/dt < Fin - Fout$). The fault hypotheses corresponding to equations that hold are marked as possible; the others are rejected. If there is no hypothesis, YAKA points out that there is a problem "around the tank". In this manner, YAKA generates a set of hypotheses that are plausible explanations for the observed symptom (for example, leak in the tank, leak in the inlet pipe) and then uses a MOLE-like approach to differentiate them.

The method is appropriate for this task because the task has the following characteristics: (1) It is possible to identify a set of complaints that motivate refinery operators to seek help (for example, tank-level too low). (2) It is possible to describe the system in terms of components (for example, tanks) and conduits (for example, pipes), and it is possible to derive from this and a library of generic qualitative equations, a functional model, in terms of qualitative equations ($dL/dt = Fin - Fout$). (3) Faults can be expressed as disturbances affecting the functioning of a component or conduit; that is, disturbances of its characterizing equation(s) (for example, the leak in the tank is characterized by the new equation: $dL/dt < Fin - Fout$). (4) There is knowledge available to differentiate the faults (for example, evidence of a leak, liquid on the floor, near the tank). (5) Usually only one fault is applicable (for example, if there is a leak in the tank, then it is unlikely that there is also a leak in the inlet pipe).

## Using YAKA to Develop Application Systems.

$YAKA_{KA}$ is intended to be used by domain experts. Two levels of expertise are required; neither requires any knowledge of programming. The first level requires an understanding of qualitative physics as well as a theoretical understanding of the domain in order to build a library of generic qualitative equations and faults. This level of expertise is needed only initially for a given domain. The second level requires no understanding of qualitative physics but requires instead familiarity with the physical structure and functioning of specific applications. The experts must provide the following types of task-specific knowledge:

- A *library* of generic equations and faults (provided by experts with first-level expertise).

- A *structural model* of the system.
- *Refinements* of the functional model generated by YAKA, including cardinal time-delays of the equations, and refinements of the general equations proposed by YAKA.
- Descriptions of possible *faults* in terms of the changes they can induce in the equations.
- *Differentiation* knowledge (that is, information that will help differentiate possible faults having the same direct effect).

YAKA$_{KA}$ uses the structural model plus the library of generic equations to derive a functional model -- a set of equations characterizing the functioning of each component. The expert may need to complete, refine and confirm this set of equations. YAKA provides a step-by-step qualitative simulation algorithm, to help the expert in this process, which includes the acquisition of the cardinal time-delays for the equations. YAKA classifies faults as conduit faults and component faults. It is able to generate the conduit faults and some of the component faults from a library. YAKA asks the expert about the others, and then updates its library. The faults are characterized as disturbances that will affect or replace equations of the normal functioning of components, and thus are represented locally with respect to a component and its connections. Finally, YAKA groups the faults that have the same direct effect and asks the expert for differentiating knowledge.

Examples of task-specific knowledge that domain experts provided:

**Diagnosing problems in a refinery process:**

*Library*: dL/dt = Fin - Fout.

*Structural model*: There is a tank connected to two pipes (conduits) -- one for inlet flow and the other for outlet flow.

*Refinement*: In the functional model generated by YAKA, the conduits are characterized by variables such as flow-rate and pressure, and the tank by its level, and also by the following qualitative equation:

$$dL/dt = Fin - Fout$$

As a refinement, the expert adds that for this particular tank, this equation has a time-delay of t1.

*Faults*: a leak in the tank (a component fault), characterized by the following equation:

$$dL/dt < Fin - Fout,$$

a leak in a pipe between the tank and the flow-rate sensor of the inlet pipe (a conduit fault), affecting the value of Fin in the above equation.

*Differentiation*: liquid around the bottom of the tank.

### 8.2.3. SALT

**Possible Tasks.**

SALT is a tool for building constructive expert systems whose role-limiting method is *propose-and-revise*. A task must have the following characteristics in order for propose-and-revise to be an appropriate method: (1) Procedures can be specified to determine a starting point or most preferred, likely value for each piece of the design. (2) For each design constraint, remedies (indicating what to do if the constraint is violated) can be specified in the form of modifications to the design. The method is most appropriate for tasks that, in addition, have the following characteristic: (3) There is not a high level of potential conflict in preferences for alternative design extensions.

A SALT-built system's task-specific control knowledge guides it iteratively through the following steps: It first accepts a set of specifications (which may include a partial design) and proposes additions to the design while checking for constraint violations. If a constraint is violated, the system finds the least costly fix or combination of fixes that will eliminate the violation, and applies them. This propose-and-revise process continues until no more additions can be made to the design and no constraints are violated.

Examples of SALT-built systems:

**Configuring an elevator system.** Elevator configuration involves designing an elevator system from an initial set of specifications, which include architectural specifications and customer preferences. VT, a SALT-generated system, first verifies the consistency of the input specifications (for example, that the number of front openings plus the number of rear openings equals the total number of openings). It then proposes design extensions (for example, selecting the smallest motor that can supply the required horsepower) until a constraint is violated. It eliminates a violation by implementing the least costly fix or fixes (which are expressed in terms of nonoptimal modifications to previous design extensions).

Propose-and-revise is an appropriate method for this task because the task has the following characteristics: (1) Procedures can be specified for determining an initial value for each piece of the elevator design (for example, use the least expensive piece of equipment that has a chance of being acceptable). (2) Each constraint that may be violated has at least one remedy (for example, equipment can be moved and/or more expensive equipment can be used). (3) The amount of potential conflict in preferences for alternative design extensions is low. Alternatives for individual design parameters can be selected using a single property (for example, minimizing weight) and while preference for alternative remedies to constraint violations involves multiple considerations (for example, minimizing cost and maximizing customer satisfaction) alternatives can be categorized into 12 ordered preference classes.

**Task scheduling in an engineering department.** Task scheduling involves adding a new job to an existing schedule. The job is specified in terms of its attributes and any constraints on the its schedule (for example, deadlines promised to the customer). The schedule comprises the dates each job will enter and leave each subdepartment and details about how it will be handled in each one. The purpose of Scheduler, a SALT-generated system, is to schedule each job as it comes in with a minimum of disruption to the existing schedule. Scheduler first schedules the job without regard for possible constraint violations (for example, overloads in departments and promised delivery dates not met are ignored). It then examines all the constraint violations, picks the most important one (for example, a promised delivery date not met), implements the least costly fix for that constraint (for example, hurry the job through a particular department), and rebuilds the schedule as before.

**Using SALT to Develop Application Systems.**
SALT is intended to be used by domain experts who need not know anything about programming, but who do have a formalized grasp of their domain. The expert must provide the following types of task-specific knowledge:

- *Procedures* for obtaining initial values *for pieces of the design.*
- *Procedures for* obtaining any *constraints* on these values.
- Local *remedies* for violated constraints (that is, remedies that do not have to address the possibility that they may cause other constraints to be violated).

SALT begins by asking the user to specify any of the three types of knowledge listed above, in any convenient order. When the user is done, SALT checks that all pieces of the design mentioned by the user have associated procedures (or are inputs), that all constraints that might be violated have remedies, that pieces with multiple procedures have disjoint preconditions, and so forth. SALT also analyzes the knowledge base to ensure that there are no loops among procedures, and if there are, it will ask the user to specify a new procedure for initially estimating one of the pieces and convert its original procedure into a constraint, which then requires remedies.

Examples of task-specific knowledge that domain experts provided:

**Configuring an elevator system:**

*Procedures for pieces of the design:* select the smallest motor that can produce horsepower greater than the maximum required horsepower, place the car platform 1.25 inches from the door sill at the front of the shaft.

*Procedures for constraints:* a model 38 machine can be used only with a 25, 30, or 35 hp motor (for mechanical reasons); if there is no counterweight guard, there must be a minimum of 1 inch between the car platform and the counterweight (due to safety regulations).

*Remedies:* upgrade to the next larger motor (a more expensive, less optimal choice); select a smaller car platform (which would be a change to the customer's specifications).

Task scheduling in an engineering department:

*Procedures for pieces of the design:* an order spends two weeks in the Contract Coordination Department; the Contract Coordination Department's load for each week is a weighted sum of all the jobs in that department for that week.

*Procedures for constraints:* the Contract Coordination Department's maximum load for each week is a weighted sum of each of the people in the department who will be working that week.

*Remedies:* delay the job's entry into the department until it can handle it, rush the job through a previous department in order to get the job into Contract Coordination before the overload.

### 8.2.4. KNACK

Possible Tasks.

KNACK is a tool for building expert systems, called WRINGERs, whose role-limiting method is acquire-and-present. A task must have the following characteristics in order for acquire-and-present to be an appropriate method: (1) A report is a suitable means of documenting the task (that is, it is possible to document the task with a report). (2) A relatively small set of concepts cover the substance of what is contained in all of the reports for any particular task. The method is most appropriate for tasks that, in addition, have the following characteristic: (3) A report is an essential means of documenting the task (that is, it is necessary to document the task with a report).

A WRINGER's task-specific control knowledge guides it iteratively through the following steps: It first identifies all relevant pieces of information that are appropriate to acquire next and determines what procedures can be used to gather that information. It then selects one piece of information to acquire next and a strategy for acquiring it. A WRINGER applies the selected strategy and integrates the gathered information with whatever information it already has. This acquisition process goes on until the WRINGER has tried to gather all of the information it thinks it needs. WRINGER then produces a report, which documents the task.

Examples of KNACK-built systems:

**Reporting on designs of electromechanical systems that may be suboptimal from a hardening perspective.** Nuclear hardening involves the use of specific engineering design practices to increase the resistance of an electromechanical system to the environmental effects of a nuclear event. Designers of electromechanical systems usually have little or no knowledge about the specialized analytical methods and engineering practices of the hardening domain. The purpose of this WRINGER is to assist a designer in presenting given designs of electromechanical systems such that hardening experts have readily available the information they need to evaluate the system from a hardening perspective. The WRINGER first gathers information about the ElectroMagnetic Pulse (EMP) environment (for example, rise time, electrical field). It then asks for the geometry and a description of the major components of the system (for example, cables, equipment, protections). Values for system and environment properties are determined through various analytical methods, depending on the level of description of the system -- the poorer the description is, the more conservative are the underlying assumptions (for example, normal operating environment, screen analysis, resistor analysis). This analysis can continue down to the level of individual semiconductors (for example, bulk resistance of a diode, transfer impedance of a cable). The WRINGER's output is a report about the design of the system.

Acquire-and-present is an appropriate method for this task because the task has the following characteristics: (1) A report is a suitable means of documenting the design of an electromechanical system (for example, a Program Plan is the primary top-level report covering all phases of the design process, a Design Parameters Report presents a detailed system description). (2) The reports are all quite similar and quite focused (for example, 43 concepts cover the substance of what is contained in a Program Plan; 92 concepts cover the substance of what is contained in a Design Parameters report). (3) A report is an essential means of presenting the design of an electromechanical system (for example, government requirements prescribe that the design of an electromechanical system be presented in the form of both a Program Plan and a Design Parameters Report).

**Assisting with the creation of a project proposal.** A first step in starting a new project is typically the creation of a project proposal. The proposal must be concise and contain all the information management needs to accept or reject the project. The purpose of this WRINGER is to assist a project leader in creating a project proposal such that management has readily available the information needed to make a decision. The WRINGER asks for information about the planned project (for example, objectives, functionality, motivation, research or engineering issues, related issues, methodology, resources, schedule, and tasks). It then produces a proposal.

**Assisting with the definition of requirements for software systems.** Defining requirements for new software is a complex process. It involves functionally decomposing the software into basic modules, defining the data requirements, and integrating the new software with the existing software environment. The purpose of this WRINGER is to assist a systems analyst in functionally decomposing a high-level description of a planned software system into basic modules and in defining the data requirements for each of the modules. The WRINGER first gathers information about high-level functions (for example, major groups involved, main activities of the groups). It then assists the systems analyst in functionally decomposing that description into basic modules (for example, Determine Drawing Identification, Get Drawing Standards). In a next step the WRINGER assists in defining the data requirements for the modules (for example, input for Get Drawing Standards is model-type; output of Get Drawing Standards is a list of drawing standards). The WRINGER produces a technical document describing the requirements for the software system. This includes an executive summary that presents the information management needs to evaluate whether the planned software will be a valuable enhancement to the existing software environment.

**Using KNACK to Develop Application Systems.**

KNACK is intended to be used by domain experts who need not know anything about programming. The expert must provide the following types of task-specific knowledge:

- A *domain model*.
- A *sample report*.
- *Sample strategies* for acquiring specific information.

In an initial interaction, KNACK acquires a preliminary model of a domain. The domain model describes the concepts and the vocabulary that experts use in performing their task. KNACK also requires a sample report as an initial input. The sample report is a document that exemplifies the output a WRINGER is expected to produce. Once the sample report is provided and an initial domain model is defined, KNACK interacts with a domain expert to integrate the sample report with the domain model. The integration process generalizes the sample report, making it applicable to different applications. KNACK then instantiates the generalized examples with known concept representatives taken from the domain model and displays several differently instantiated examples for each generalization. The expert edits any examples that make implausible statements. KNACK uses those corrections as additional knowledge to refine its generalizations and the domain model. Once the expert is content with KNACK's understanding of the sample report, KNACK elicits knowledge about how to customize the generalized sample report for a particular application. The expert defines sample strategies that a KNACK-generated expert system, a WRINGER, will use to acquire values instantiating the concepts in the generalized fragments. KNACK displays sample instantiations for review and correction by the expert.

Examples of task-specific knowledge that domain experts provided:

**Reporting on designs of electromechanical systems that may be suboptimal from a hardening perspective:**

*Domain model:* cable, enclosure, threat, aperture (concepts); type, resistive component of pin voltage, length of shield, transfer resistance of shield, current on shield (concept characteristics for cable); power cable, signal cable (concept representatives for cable).

*Sample report fragment:* The power cable penetrates the S-280C enclosure and induces 0.4 volts on the window of this enclosure.

*Sample strategy:* (Formula) Resistive Component of Pin Voltage = Length of Shield * Transfer Resistance of Shield * Current on Shield

### 8.2.5. SIZZLE

**Possible Tasks.**

SIZZLE is a tool for building expert systems whose role-limiting method is *extrapolate-from-a-similar-case*. Characteristics that a task must have in order for extrapolate-from-a-similar-case to be an appropriate method are: (1) A large collection of validated cases is available. (2) Experts have a notion of the overall degree of similarity between different cases. (3) Knowledge exists of how to adjust a case solution as a function of changes to the case problem. The method is most appropriate for tasks that, in addition, have the following characteristics: (4) The problem is to determine needed quantities of various resources for some process when the precise nature of the process is not very well understood. (5) The set of factors that need to be considered is very large. (6) The quality of a solution can be characterized as incrementally better or worse, rather than as categorically acceptable or not acceptable, when compared to some other solution.

A SIZZLE-built system's task-specific control knowledge guides it iteratively through the following steps: It asks for enough information about a particular sizing problem to identify other, similar, already-solved problems in a knowledge base of cases. It then uses those differences between the solved and unsolved cases to determine how to extrapolate from the known solution to the new solution.

An example of a SIZZLE-built system:

**Sizing the requirements for a computer system.** Computer-system sizing involves creating a generic description of a computer system that will provide adequate computational resources for some set of intended uses. Sizer, a SIZZLE-generated system, asks the user to identify how many of various kinds of workers will be using the computer system. Sizer then looks in its knowledge base of cases for the two cases that are most similar to the case at hand. It uses simple techniques to extrapolate from each known solution to create a solutions for the new case. If the two solutions for the new case are very similar, it proposes one of them to the user; if not, it suggests to the user that its knowledge base needs to be more dense in the area of the new case.

---

**Assisting with the creation of a project proposal:**

*Domain model:* project, objective, task, software (concepts); name, description (concept characteristics for software); KNACK, WRINGER (concept representatives for software).

*Sample report fragment:* The objective of the NAC WRINGER project is to refine KNACK, a knowledge-acquisition tool currently being developed at CMU, so that it can be used to build expert systems that assist with the design of computer networks.

*Sample strategy:* (Question) What are the objectives of the NAC WRINGER project?

**Assisting with the definition of requirements for software systems:**

*Domain model:* external function, function requirements (concepts); name, processing steps (concept characteristics for external function); define bundle geometry, produce system schematics manual (concept representatives for external functions).

*Sample report fragment:* Projected impact of requirements for the external function, Define Bundle Geometry: an interface must be built between the electronic/electrical workstation and the software ASGR.

*Sample strategy:* (Inference) Because Define Bundle Geometry is an external function for the software Electronic/Electrical Workstation, and Define Bundle Geometry must get data from the Electronic/Electrical Workstation, and Define Bundle Geometry is a function of the software ASGR, and there is no interface between ASGR and the Electronic/Electrical Workstation, the impact of Define Bundle Geometry is: an interface must be built between the software Electronic/Electrical Workstation and ASGR.

Extrapolate-from-a-similar-case is an appropriate method for this task because the task has the following characteristics: (1) Thousands of validated cases are available. (2) Experts have a notion of the overall degree of similarity between different cases (for example, experts can indicate how close two cases are on the basis of how many of various kinds of users will be using the system). (3) Knowledge exists of how to adjust a case solution as a function of changes to the case problem (for example, for a particular class of cases, each additional analyst will require 5 megabytes of disk). (4) The problem is to determine needed quantities of various computing resources, but there is no good model of how the computer is going to be used. (5) The set of factors that would need to be considered to determine how much computing resource each worker in the organization requires is very large. (6) An incremental change to a computing system sizing solution of a given quality results in a solution that is incrementally more or less good, rather than a solution that is categorically acceptable or unacceptable.

**Using SIZZLE to Develop Application Systems.**

SIZZLE is intended to be used by domain experts who need not know anything about programming. The expert must provide three types of task-specific knowledge:

- A population of *sized cases*.
- Case *indexing knowledge*.
- *Extrapolation knowledge* that will allow a sizer to extrapolate from the solved case to the unsolved case.

SIZZLE permits the expert to build a sizer by specifying sizing cases and user models and indexing into them by means of a discrimination tree of case features. This capability is provided primarily by a rule generator, which translates a source file of case features, cases, and user resource-demand models into rules. Integrated with every such sizer is a mechanism that permits the user to interactively define new sizing cases and to test their effect upon the performance of the system as a whole.

Examples of task-specific knowledge that domain experts provided:

**Sizing the requirements for a computer system:**

*Sized cases*: a case includes a description of the types and quantities of users of the system, paired with a characterization of the required computing resources along such dimensions as user disk space, number of disk spindles, and number of mips.

*Indexing knowledge*: a discrimination tree that classifies cases on the basis of industry and organizational function.

*Extrapolation knowledge*: computer user demand models that define solution features (for example, total user disk space required) with respect to the number of given types of user (for example, accountants) in the region of the case space in which a sizing case lies.

### 8.2.6. SEAR

This subsection will differ in format somewhat from the previous five. SEAR, the tool described here, does not presuppose a particular role-limiting method, but instead provides a capability for allowing developers to define a set of methods, some of which might have substantial amounts of task-specific control knowledge and which collectively will be particularly appropriate for some class of tasks. SEAR is intended to be a guide to and an enforcer of the RIME methodology described in chapter 7. SEAR currently provides only very modest assistance to the user of the RIME methodology; however a description of SEAR is included here because of the potentially strong complementarity between SEAR and the other tools described in this chapter.

**Possible Tasks.**

SEAR is a set of tools for developing higher-level knowledge-acquisition tools as well as applications systems. A task must have the following characteristics in order for SEAR to be an appropriate tool: (1) There is no known role-limiting method suitable for the task that is to be automated. (2) A set of methods for performing the task can be defined. The method is most appropriate for tasks that, in addition, have the following

There are two reasons why MOLE is being developed using RIME: (1) As with XCON, there is no known role-limiting method suitable for the task of acquiring knowledge for a heuristic classifier. (2) It seems quite likely that some, if not many, of the systems that MOLE might be used to build will not be able to do the task the real world imposes on them using the particular heuristic classification method MOLE presupposes. Therefore, MOLE is being implemented in RIME to allow the MOLE developer to more easily create method variants.

**Using SEAR to Develop Higher-Level Tools and Application Systems.** SEAR is intended to be used by fairly knowledgeable system designers, with strong programming backgrounds, who wish to build an application system or a knowledge-acquisition tool. These users will need to be able to define new methods and specify how knowledge is to be structured for particular domains. The SEAR method-definer tool will allow designers to define and combine problem-solving methods to create a knowledge-impoverished skeleton. Then, people with more modest programming skills can go to work with the rule-definer to add the knowledge necessary for a viable application. Other planned extensions to SEAR include a debugging assistant and a testing assistant.

Currently, the only tool available for use is a method-knowledgeable rule analyzer. This tool checks that an application system's knowledge is represented in a fashion appropriate for the particular problem-solving methods the system uses. Senior developers define the problem-solving methods and define rule types for each method. The SEAR rule analyzer ensures that the rules in these systems follow the requirements specified for the rule types.

## 8.3. Conclusions

Five role-limiting methods have been identified and briefly described. The scope of applicability of a role-limiting method, because it is a method for performing a particular type of task, is less broad than that of a weak method. But role-limiting methods, unlike weak methods, have little, if any, task-specific control knowledge. This characteristic makes role-limiting methods good foundations on which to build knowledge-acquisition tools, since knowing in advance all of the control knowledge that a method will

characteristic: (3) A lot of what makes the task challenging is deciding what to do next based on a variety of task details.

A SEAR-built system uses whatever collection of problem-solving methods its developers have defined.

Examples of systems whose developers SEAR assisted:

**Configuring a computer system.** Computer-system configuration involves two interdependent activities: (1) the customer's order must be determined to be complete; if it is not, whatever components are missing must be added to the order; and (2) the spatial relationships among the components (including those added) must be determined. XCON starts with a set of unrelated components and incrementally builds up the set of relationships among the components, adding components where necessary, until a functional system has been defined. A great deal of XCON's attention is devoted to deciding which extension to make next; because it spends significant energy deciding what to do next, it seldom needs to backtrack.

SEAR is an appropriate knowledge-acquisition tool for this task because the task has the following characteristics: (1) There is no known role-limiting method suitable for the task. The most likely candidate, SALT's propose-and-revise method, appears unsuitable because there is a high level of potential conflict among preferences for alternative design extensions in XCON's task. (2) Six methods have been defined for XCON; the number of steps in each method range from 4 to 10. (3) XCON's most frequently used method, *propose-apply*, is designed for tasks in which substantial amounts of task-specific control knowledge must be brought to bear in order for it to decide what action should be performed next.

**Acquiring knowledge for a heuristic classifier.** $MOLE_{KA}$ has also been reimplemented using the RIME methodology. As was mentioned above, MOLE begins its knowledge-acquisition efforts by asking the expert to list the typical complaints or abnormalities that would motivate someone to seek diagnostic help. MOLE next asks for possible explanations for each of these complaints. MOLE then asks whether these explaining events or states in turn have relevant explanations, and so on. Finally, MOLE seeks information that will enable it to differentiate, both statically and dynamically, these candidate explanations.

## Acknowledgements

Tom Cooper, Larry Eshelman, Serge Genetet, Keith Jensen, Georg Klinker, Herve Lambert, Sandy Marcus, Dan Offutt, and Jeff Stout provided substantial assistance in formulating the tool descriptions in this chapter. Judy Bachant, Rex Flynn, John Laird, David Marques, Tom Mitchell, Allen Newell, Elliot Soloway, and Bill Swartout provided extremely helpful comments on earlier drafts.

use gives substantial insight into what kinds of task-specific knowledge will be required and into how that knowledge can be appropriately encoded.

Although several expert systems have been developed using the knowledge-acquisition tools described in this book, we do not yet have even a good guess as to what percentage of tasks can be adequately performed by systems that have no task-specific control knowledge. The RIME methodology was created to deal with building systems whose tasks cannot be performed adequately without task-specific control knowledge. It provides two kinds of assistance: (1) It can help guide the definition of previously undefined role-limiting methods. (2) It can assist with the collection of task-specific control knowledge for tasks that can only be solved effectively (for example, efficiently enough) if a great deal of control knowledge is brought to bear. The rewrite of XCON exemplifies both. Previous reports on XCON [Bachant 84, McDermott 82] have characterized the system as strongly data-driven; the data drove the system in two ways: (1) to apply appropriate task-specific knowledge, and (2) to select among competing pieces of task-specific knowledge. The initial version of XCON did not distinguish between the knowledge required for these two kinds of activities. The RIME methodology forces the developer to clearly distinguish between knowledge to be used to select among candidate actions and knowledge to be used to identify and implement actions.

We have gotten a little ways toward a taxonomy of problem-solving methods -- or at least toward a way of thinking about what a taxonomy might look like. It is possible that as we spend more energy analyzing methods, we will discover that all tasks can be performed adequately with only modest amounts of task-specific control knowledge. I doubt it, however. Systems like XCON and MOLE$_{KA}$ have control knowledge that appears to be very closely tied to the peculiarities of their tasks. It is more likely that a fairly large number of role-limiting methods will be identified, each of which can solve a range of similar problems. These methods will serve as the jumping-off point for a large number of methods that use substantial amounts of task-specific control knowledge whose only common denominator is the underlying role-limiting method. Thus, in addition to the strong assistance role-limiting methods give to automating the collecting and encoding of task-specific knowledge, they also give us the means of developing a helpful taxonomy.

# References

[Abrett 87]      Abrett, G., and M. Burstein.
The KREME knowledge editing environment.
*International Journal of Man-Machine Studies*
27(2):103-126, 1987.

[Bachant 84]     Bachant, J., and J. McDermott.
R1 revisted: Four years in the trenches.
*AI Magazine* 5(3):21-32, 1984.

[Boose 84]       Boose, J.
Personal construct theory and the transfer of human
expertise.
In *Proceedings of the Fourth National Conference on
Artificial Intelligence*. Austin, Texas, 1984.

[Boose 87]       Boose, J., and J. Bradshaw.
Expertise transfer and complex problems: Using
AQUINAS as a knowledge acquisition workbench for
expert systems.
*International Journal of Man-Machine Studies*
26(1):3-28, 1987.

[Brown 87]       Brown, D.
Failure handling in a design expert system.
*Computer-Aided Design* 17(9):436-441, 1987.

[Buchanan 84]    Buchanan, B., and E. Shortliffe.
*Rule-Based Systems: The Mycin Experiments of the
Stanford Heuristic Programming Project.*
Addison-Wesley, Reading, Massachusetts, 1984.

[Carbonell 85]   Carbonell, J.
*Derivational Analogy: A Theory of Reconstructive
Problem Solving and Expertise Acquisition.*
Technical Report, Carnegie Mellon University,
Department of Computer Science, 1985.

[Chandrasekaran 83]
Chandrasekaran, B.
Towards a taxonomy of problem solving types.
*AI Magazine* 4(1):9-17, 1983.

[Chandrasekaran 86]
Chandrasekaran, B.
Generic tasks in knowledge-based reasoning: High-level
building blocks for expert system design.
*IEEE Expert* 1(3):23-29, 1986.

[Charniak 83]    Charniak, E.
The Bayesian basis of common sense medical diagnosis.
In *Proceedings of the Third National Conference on
Artificial Intelligence*. Washington, D.C., 1983.

[Clancey 83]     Clancey, W.
The advantages of abstract control knowledge in expert
system design.
In *Proceedings of the Third National Conference on
Artificial Intelligence*. Washington, D.C., 1983.

[Clancey 84]     Clancey, W.
Classification problem solving.
In *Proceedings of the Fourth National Conference on
Artificial Intelligence*. Austin, Texas, 1984.

[Clancey 85]     Clancey, W.
Heuristic classification.
*Artificial Intelligence* 27(3):289-350, 1985.

[Clancey 86]     Clancey, W.
From Guidon to Neomycin and Heracles in twenty short
lessons.
*AI Magazine* 7(3):40-77, 1986.

[Cohen 83]       Cohen, P., and M. Grinberg.
A theory of heuristic reasoning about uncertainty.
*AI Magazine* 4(2):17-24, 1983.

[Davis 79]       Davis, R.
Interactive transfer of expertise: Acquisition of new
inference rules.
*Artificial Intelligence* 12(2):121-157, 1979.

[Davis 82]       Davis, R., and D. Lenat.
*Knowledge-Based Systems in Artificial Intelligence.*
McGraw-Hill, New York, New York, 1982.

[Dechter 85]     Dechter, R., and J. Pearl.
The anatomy of easy problems: A constraint-satisfaction
formulation.
In *Proceedings of the Ninth International Joint
Conference on Artificial Intelligence.* Los Angeles,
California, 1985.

[Dechter 87]     Dechter, R., and J. Pearl.
The cycle-cutset method for improving search
performance in AI applications.
In *Proceedings of the Third Conference on Artificial
Intelligence Applications.* Orlando, Florida, 1987.

[Diederich 87]     Diederich, J., I. Ruhmann, and M. May.
KRITON: A knowledge acquisition tool for expert
systems.
*International Journal of Man-Machine Studies*
26(1):29-40, 1987.

[Dietterich 82]     Dietterich, T.
Learning and inductive inference.
In P. Cohen and E. Feigenbaum (editors), *The Handbook
of Artificial Intelligence.* Morgan Kaufmann, Los
Altos, California, 1982.

[Doyle 79]     Doyle, J.
A truth maintenance system.
*Artificial Intelligence* 12(3):231-272, 1979.

[Doyle 85]     Doyle, J.
Reasoned assumptions and pareto optimality.
In *Proceedings of the Eighth International Joint
Conference on Artificial Intelligence.* Los Angles,
California, 1985.

[Eshelman 86]     Eshelman, L., and J. McDermott.
MOLE: A knowledge acquisition tool that uses its head.
In *Proceedings of the Fifth National Conference on
Artificial Intelligence.* Philadelphia, Pennsylvania,
1986.

[Eshelman 87a]     Eshelman, L., D. Ehret, J. McDermott, and M. Tan.
MOLE: A tenacious knowledge acquisition tool.
*International Journal of Man-Machine Studies*
26(1):41-54, 1987.

[Eshelman 87b]     Eshelman, L.
MOLE: A knowledge acquisition tool that buries
certainty factors.
In *Proceedings of the Second Knowledge Acquisition for
Knowledge-based Systems Workshop.* Banff, Canada,
1987.

[Forgy 81]     Forgy, C.
*The OPS5 Users Manual.*
Technical Report, Carnegie Mellon University,
Department of Computer Science, 1981.

[Fox 83]     Fox, M., S. Lowenfield, and P. Kleinosky.
Techniques for sensor-based diagnosis.
In *Proceedings of the Eighth International Joint
Conference on Artificial Intelligence.* Karlsruhe,
West Germany, 1983.

[Freuder 82]     Freuder, E.
A sufficient condition for backtrack-free search.
*Journal of the Association for Computing Machinery*
29(11):24-32, 1982.

[Gale 87]     Gale, W.
Knowledge-based knowledge acquisition for a statistical
consulting system.
*International Journal of Man-Machine Studies*
26(1):55-64, 1987.

[Gruber 87a]     Gruber, T., and P. Cohen.
Design for acquisition: Principles of knowledge-system
design to facilitate knowledge acquisition.
*International Journal of Man-Machine Studies*
26(2):143-159, 1987.

[Gruber 87b]     Gruber, T.
Acquiring strategic knowledge from experts.
In *Proceedings of the Second Knowledge Acquisition for
Knowledge-based Systems Workshop.* Banff, Canada,
1987.

[Harman 86]     Harman, G.
*Change in View: Principles of Reasoning.*
The MIT Press, Cambridge, Massachusetts, 1986.

[Herman 86]    Herman, D., J. Josephson, and R. Hartung.
               *Use of DSPL for the Design of a Mission Planning*
               *Assistant.*
               Technical Report, Ohio State University, Department of
               Computer and Information Science, 1986.

[IntelliCorp 87]    IntelliCorp.
                    *KEE 3.0 Training Manual.*
                    IntelliCorp, Mountain View, California, 1987.

[Kahn 84]      Kahn, G., and J. McDermott.
               The MUD system.
               In *Proceedings of the First IEEE Conference on Artificial*
               *Intelligence Applications.* Denver, Colorado, 1984.

[Kahn 85a]     Kahn, G., S. Nowlan, and J. McDermott.
               Strategies for knowledge acquisition.
               *IEEE Transactions on Pattern Analysis and Machine*
               *Intelligence* 7(5):511-522, 1985.

[Kahn 85b]     Kahn, G., S. Nowlan, and J. McDermott.
               MORE: An intelligent knowledge acquisition tool.
               In *Proceedings of Ninth International Conference on*
               *Artificial Intelligence.* Los Angeles, California, 1985.

[Kahn 87a]     Kahn, G.
               TEST: A model-driven application shell.
               In *Proceedings of the Sixth National Conference on*
               *Artificial Intelligence.* Seattle, Washington, 1987.

[Kahn 87b]     Kahn, G., E. Breaux, P. DeKlerk, and R. Joseph.
               A mixed-initiative workbench for knowledge acquisition.
               *International Journal of Man-Machine Studies*
               27(2):167-179, 1987.

[Kahn 87c]     Kahn, G.
               From application shell to knowledge acquisition System.
               In *Proceedings of Tenth International Joint Conference*
               *on Artificial Intelligence.* Milan, Italy, 1987.

[Kahn 87d]     Kahn, G., E. Breaux, R. Joseph, and P. DeKlerk.
               An intelligent mixed-initiative workbench for knowledge
               acquisition.
               *International Journal of Man-Machine Studies*
               27(2):167-179, 1987.

[Klinker 87a]  Klinker, G., J. Bentolila, S. Genetet, M. Grimes, and
               J. McDermott.
               KNACK -- Report-driven knowledge acquisition.
               *International Journal of Man-Machine Studies*
               26(1):65-79, 1987.

[Klinker 87b]  Klinker, G., C. Boyd, S. Genetet, and J. McDermott.
               A KNACK for knowledge acquisition.
               In *Proceedings of Sixth National Conference on Artificial*
               *Intelligence.* Seattle, Washington, 1987.

[Klinker 87c]  Klinker, G., S. Genetet, and J. McDermott.
               Knowledge acquisition for evaluation systems.
               In *Proceedings of the Second Knowledge Acquisition for*
               *Knowledge-based Systems Workshop.* Banff, Canada,
               1987.

[Laird 83]     Laird, J., and A. Newell.
               *A Universal Weak Method.*
               Technical Report, Carnegie Mellon University,
               Department of Computer Science, 1983.

[Laird 87]     Laird, J., A. Newell, and P. Rosenbloom.
               SOAR: An architecture for general intelligence.
               *Artificial Intelligence* 33(1):1-64, 1987.

[Lenat 86]     Lenat, D., M. Prakash, and M. Shepherd.
               CYC: Using common sense knowledge to overcome
               brittleness and knowledge acquisition bottlenecks.
               *AI Magazine* 6(4):65-85, 1986.

[Marcus 85]    Marcus, S., J. McDermott, and T. Wang.
               Knowledge acquisition for constructive systems.
               In *Proceedings of Ninth International Conference on*
               *Artificial Intelligence.* Los Angeles, California, 1985.

[Marcus 87]    Marcus, S.
               Taking backtracking with a grain of SALT.
               *International Journal of Man-Machine Studies*
               26(4):383-398, 1987.

[Marcus 83a]   Marcus, S., J. Stout, and J. McDermott.
               VT: An expert elevator configurer that uses knowledge-
               based backtracking.
               *AI Magazine* 9(1):95-112, 1988.

[Marcus 88b]     Marcus, S.
A knowledge representation scheme for acquiring design knowledge.
In C. Tong and D. Sriram (editors), *Artificial Intelligence Approaches to Engineering Design.* Addison-Wesley, Reading, Massachusetts, forthcoming, 1988.

[McDermott 82]     McDermott, J.
R1: A rule-based configurer of computer systems.
*Artificial Intelligence* 19(1):39-88, 1982.

[McDermott 86]     McDermott, J.
Making expert systems explicit.
In *Proceedings of Tenth Congress of the International Federation of Information Processing Societies.* Dublin, Ireland, 1986.

[Miller 82]     Miller, R., H. Pople, and J. Myers.
INTERNIST-1, an experimental computer-based diagnostic consultant for general internal medicine.
*New England Journal of Medicine* 307(8):468-476, 1982.

[Mitchell 85]     Mitchell, T., S. Mahadevan, and L. Steinberg.
LEAP: A learning apprentice for VLSI design.
In *Proceedings of the Ninth International Joint Conference on Artificial Intelligence.* Los Angeles, California, 1985.

[Mittal 86]     Mittal, S., and A. Araya.
A knowledge-based framework for design.
In *Proceedings of the Fifth National Conference on Artificial Intelligence.* Philadelphia, Pennsylvania, 1986.

[Musen 87]     Musen, M., L. Fagan, D. Combs, and E. Shortliffe.
Using a domain model to drive an interactive knowledge-editing tool.
*International Journal of Man-Machine Studies* 26(1):105-121, 1987.

[Neches 84]     Neches, R., W. Swartout, and J. Moore.
Enhanced maintenance and explanation of expert systems through explicit models of their development.
In *Proceedings of IEEE Workshop on Principles of Knowledge-Based Systems.* Denver, Colorado, 1984.

[Newell 81]     Newell, A.
The knowledge level.
*AI Magazine* 2(2):1-20, 1981.

[Omohundro 87]     Omohundro, S.
Efficient algorithms with neural network behavior.
*Complex Systems* 26(1):273-347, 1987.

[Pearl 86]     Pearl, J.
Fusion, propagation and structuring in belief networks.
*Artificial Intelligence* 29(3):241-288, 1986.

[Pople 82]     Pople, H.
Heuristic methods for imposing structure on ill-structured problems.
In P. Szolovits (editor), *Artificial Intelligence in Medicine.* Westview Press, Boulder, Colorado, 1982.

[Schank 82]     Schank, R.
*Dynamic Memory: A Theory of Reminding and Learning in Computers and People.*
Cambridge University Press, Cambridge, England, 1982.

[Schank 86]     Schank, R.
*Explanation Patterns: Understanding Mechanically and Creatively.*
Lawrence-Erlbaum Associates, Hillsdale, New Jersey, 1986.

[Shafer 76]     Shafer, G.
*A Mathematical Theory of Evidence.*
Princeton University Press, Princeton, New Jersey, 1976.

[Shortliffe 76]     Shortliffe, E.
*Computer-Based Medical Consultation: Mycin.*
Elsevier, 1976.

[Smith 85]     Smith, R., H. Winston, T. Mitchell, and B. Buchanan.
Representation and use of explicit justifications for knowledge base refinement.
In *Proceedings of the Ninth International Joint Conference on Artificial Intelligence.* Los Angeles, California, 1985.

[van de Brug 85]  van de Brug, A., J. Bachant, and J. McDermott.
Doing R1 with style.
In *Proceedings of the Second IEEE Conference on Artificial Intelligence Applications*. Miami, Florida, 1985.

[van de Brug 86]  van de Brug, A., J. Bachant, and J. McDermott.
The taming of R1.
*IEEE Expert* 1(3):33-38, 1986.

[vanMelle 81]  van Melle, W., A. Scott, J. Bennet, and M. Peairs.
*The EMYCIN manual*.
Technical Report, Stanford University, Heuristic Programming Project, 1981.

[Waterman 85]  Waterman, D.
*A Guide to Expert Systems*.
Addison-Wesley, Reading, Massachusetts, 1985.

[Weiss 78]  Weiss, S., C. Kulikowski, S. Amarel, and A. Safir.
A model-based method for computer-aided medical decision-making.
*Artificial Intelligence* 11(1, 2):145-172, 1978.

[Smith 86]  Smith, S., M. Fox, and P. Ow.
Constructing and maintaining detailed production plans: Investigations into the development of knowledge-based factory scheduling systems.
*AI Magazine* 7(4):45-60, 1986.

[Soloway 87]  Soloway, E., J. Bachant, and K. Jensen.
Assessing the maintainability of XCON-in-RIME: Coping with the problems of a VERY large rule-based system.
In *Proceedings of the Sixth National Conference on Artificial Intelligence*. Seattle, Washington, 1987.

[Stallman 77]  Stallman, R., and G. Sussman.
Forward reasoning and dependency-directed backtracking in a system for computer-aided circuit analysis.
*Artificial Intelligence* 9(2):135-196, 1977.

[Stefik 81a]  Stefik, M.
Planning with constraints (MOLGEN: Part 1).
*Artificial Intelligence* 16(2):111-140, 1981.

[Stefik 81b]  Stefik, M.
Planning and meta-planning (MOLGEN: Part 2).
*Artificial Intelligence* 16(2):141-170, 1981.

[Stout 88]  Stout, J., G. Caplain, S. Marcus, and J. McDermott.
Toward automating recognition of differing problem-solving demands.
*International Journal of Man-Machine Studies*, forthcoming, 1988.

[Sussman 80]  Sussman, G., and G. Steele, Jr.
CONSTRAINTS -- A language for expressing almost-hierarchical descriptions.
*Artificial Intelligence* 14(1):1-39, 1980.

[Swartout 83]  Swartout, W.
XPLAIN: A system for creating and explaining expert consulting systems.
*Artificial Intelligence* 21(3):285-325, 1983.

[Szolovits 78]  Szolovits, P., and Pauker, S.
Categorical and probabilistic reasoning in medical diagnosis.
*Artificial Intelligence* 11(1, 2):115-144, 1978.

# Generic Tasks in Knowledge-Based Reasoning: High-Level Building Blocks for Expert System Design

B. Chandrasekaran

Ohio State University

In the view of our research group at the Laboratory for Artificial Intelligence Research, the field of expert systems is stuck in a level of abstraction that obscures the essential nature of the information processing tasks that current systems perform. The available paradigms often force us to fit the problem to the tools rather than fashion the tools to reflect the structure of the problem. This situation is caused by a failure to distinguish between what we might call the information processing level (or the knowledge level, in Allen Newell's words) and the implementation language level. Most available languages, be they rule-, frame-, or logic-based, are more like the assembly languages of the field than programming languages with constructs essential for capturing the essence of the information processing phenomena.

We wish to provide a critique of the abstraction level of the currently dominant approaches and propose an alternative level of abstraction. The proposed alternative not only clarifies the issues but also makes possible tools and approaches that help in system design, knowledge acquisition, and explanation.

## Information processing tasks in knowledge-based reasoning

It seems intuitively clear that there are types of knowledge and control regimes that are common to diagnostic reasoning in different domains, and we similarly expect to find common structures and regimes for, say, design as an activity. In addition, we will also anticipate that the structures and control regimes for diagnostic reasoning and design problem solving will, generally speaking, be different. However, looking at the formalisms (or equivalently, the languages) commonly used in expert system design, we see that the knowledge representation and control regimes do not typically capture these distinctions. For example, in diagnostic reasoning we might wish to speak generically in terms of malfunction hierarchies, rule-out strategies, setting up a differential, etc.; while for design, the generic terms might be device/component hierarchies, design plans, ordering of subtasks, etc.

Ideally we would like to represent diagnostic knowledge in a domain by using the vocabulary appropriate for the task. But typically the languages in which the expert systems have been implemented have sought uniformity across tasks and have thus sacrificed clarity of representation at the task level. The computational universality of representation languages such as Emycin or OPS5—any computer program can be written more or less naturally in these languages— often confuses the issue, since after the system is finally built it may not be clear which portions represent domain expertise and which are programming devices. In addition, the control regimes that these languages come with (in rule-based systems they are typically variants of hypothesize-and-match, such as forward or backward chaining) do not explicitly indicate the real control structure of the system at the task level. For example, the fact that R1[1] performs a linear sequence of subtasks—a very special and atypically simple version of design problem solving—is not explicitly

©1986 IEEE. Reprinted, with permission, from *IEEE Expert*; 1:3, pp. 23-29; June 1986.

encoded: The system designer so to speak "encrypted" this control in the pattern-matching control of OPS5.

These comments need not be restricted to the rule-based framework. It is possible to represent knowledge as sentences in a logical calculus and use logical inference mechanisms to solve problems. Knowledge could also be represented as a frame hierarchy with procedural attachments in the slots. It is relatively straightforward to rewrite Mycin,[2] for example, in this manner (see Szolovits and Pauker[3]). In the logic-based approach the control issues would deal with choice of predicates and clauses, and in the second approach they would be at the level of, for example, which links to pursue for inheritance. None of these choices have any direct connection with the control issues natural to the task.

There is an opposite aspect to control. Because of the abstraction level relative to the information processing task, some control issues are artifacts of the representation. In our opinion these are often misinterpreted as issues at the knowledge level. For example, rule-based approaches often concern themselves with syntactic conflict resolution strategies. When the knowledge is viewed at the appropriate level, we can often see the existence of organizations of knowledge that bring up only a small, highly relevant body of knowledge without any need for conflict resolution at all. Of course, these organizational constructs could be "programmed" in the rule language (metarules are meant to do this in rule-based systems), but because of the status assigned to the rules and their control as knowledge-level phenomena (as opposed to the implementation-level phenomena, which they often are), knowledge acquisition is often directed toward strategies for conflict resolution, whereas they ought to be directed to issues of knowledge organization.

This is not to argue that rule representations and backward- or forward-chaining controls are not natural for some situations. If all a problem solver has in the form of knowledge in a domain is a large collection of unorganized associative patterns, then data-directed or goal-directed associations may be the best the agent can do. But that is precisely the occasion for weak methods such as hypothesize -and-match (of which the above associations are variants), and, typically, successful solutions cannot be expected in complex problems without combinatorial searches. Typically, however, expertise consists of much better organized collections of knowledge, with control behavior indexed by the kinds of organization and forms of knowledge they contain.

We have found six generic tasks that are very useful as building blocks for the construction (and understanding) of knowledge-based systems. These tasks cover a wide range of existing expert systems. Because of their role as building blocks, we call them elementary generic tasks. While we have been adding to our repertoire of elementary generic tasks for quite some time, the basic elements of the framework have been in place for a number of years. In particular, our work on MDX[4,5] identified hierarchical classification, hypothesis matching, and knowledge-directed information passing as

three generic tasks and showed how certain classes of diagnostic problems can be implemented as an integration of these generic tasks. (In the past we have also referred to them as problem-solving types.) Over the years we have identified several others: object synthesis by plan selection and refinement,[6] state abstraction,[7] and abductive assembly of hypotheses.[8] This list is not exhaustive; in fact, our ongoing research objective is to identify other useful generic tasks and understand their knowledge representation and control of problem solving.

## Examining some generic tasks

Each of the generic tasks will be described in somewhat greater detail. Abstractly, the generic tasks can be characterized by providing information about (1) a task specification in the form of generic types of input and output information; (2) specific forms in which the basic pieces of domain knowledge are needed for the task, and specific organizations of this knowledge particular to the task; and (3) a family of control regimes appropriate for the task. The explanations will be both concrete and abstract, employing historical examples.

The first three generic tasks are best described by means of the MDX example. In the late 1970's, at about the time Mycin and rule-based systems had captured the imagination of many researchers and drawn attention to knowledge-rich problem solving, we began a project on medical diagnosis. The MDX system that resulted was the product of collaboration between four researchers: myself; Jack Smith, a member of the medical faculty at Ohio State University; and Fernando Gomez and Sanjay Mittal, graduate students in our group. The MDX system embodies many of the ideas that eventually resulted in the theory of generic tasks.

**Hierarchical classification.** Gomez recognized that the core process of diagnosis can be thought of as a classificatory problem-solving process, that is, one of identifying a patient case description as a node in a disease hierarchy. This led him to consider the nature and organization of knowledge and the control processes required for hierarchical classification. The following briefly summarizes the more detailed account given elsewhere[9] of classificatory problem solving for diagnosis.

Let us imagine that corresponding to each node of the classification hierarchy alluded to earlier we identify a diagnostic hypothesis. The total diagnostic knowledge is then distributed through the conceptual nodes of the hierarchy in a specific manner to be discussed shortly. The problem solving for this task will be performed top down, that is, the topmost concept will first get control of the case, then control will pass to an appropriate successor concept, and so on. In the medical example, a fragment of such a hierarchy might resemble Figure 1. More general classificatory concepts are higher in the structure; more particular ones are lower in the

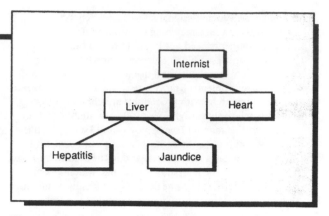

**Figure 1.** A diagnostic hierarchy.

hierarchy. It is as if Internist first establishes that there is in fact a disease, then Liver establishes that the case at hand is a liver disease, while, say, Heart, etc., reject the case for not being in their domain. After this level, Jaundice may establish itself, and so on.

Each of the concepts in the classification hierarchy contains "how-to" knowledge to enable it to decide how well the concept matches the data (see the next section on hypothesis matching) and whether the concept can be established to some degree or rejected. When a concept rules itself irrelevant to a case, all its successors also get ruled out; thus, large portions of the diagnostic knowledge structure never get exercised. On the other hand, when a concept is properly invoked, a small, highly relevant body of knowledge comes into play. We note in passing that because of their role, the concepts are also called "specialists." (Thus the entire conceptual hierarchy is a community of specialists.)

The problem solving that goes on in MDX is distributed. The problem-solving regime implicit in the structure can be characterized as an *establish-refine* type. That is, each concept first tries to establish or reject itself. If it succeeds in establishing itself, it keeps track of which observations it can "cover" (account for), and the refinement process is invoked. This consists of seeing which of its successors can establish itself. Typically, this process goes on until enough tip nodes (specific diseases or, more generally, classificatory hypotheses) are established to cover all the observations.

This discussion of the problem solving in MDX is oversimplified and incomplete; nevertheless, it should be noted that certain kinds of multiple diseases can be handled, including diseases that are secondary to other diseases. Further discussion of these aspects of MDX is available in the literature.[5] MDX uses a simple version of classificatory control. We have recently investigated some of the more complex issues in control for hierarchical classification.[10] But the important point is that the control issues for classification are not merely subsumed in the control issues, such as forward or backward chaining, for rule languages, but have a separate conceptual existence. Furthermore, classification has a homogeneous family of control, a distinct hierarchical organization, and specific types of knowledge associated with it. This point can be repeated for each of the generic tasks.

**Hypothesis matching, or assessment.** While MDX as a whole is engaged in classification, what about the problem solving of each of the specialists, namely, the classificatory concepts, which, when called upon, attempt to establish themselves? Generally, the data and the knowledge needed for establishment both have a good deal of uncertainty associated with them—the sort of uncertainty that Mycin attempted to handle with its "uncertainty factors." Basically, the information processing task for establishing a concept is to match a concept against relevant data and determine a degree of fit. But this matching process itself is independent of its application for classification and has a generic

character of its own. It could be used just as readily by a planner to select from among alternative plans; the features of the problem will be the data, and the plan's degree of appropriateness will be the result of the matching process. In the case of classification, the matching can be interpreted as degree of likelihood, but in the case of plan selection, the interpretation is "appropriateness," or "applicability."

Consistent with the idea that this form of matching is a generic activity, our work in MDX revealed that the matcher —we call the task "hypothesis matching"—required distinctly separate forms of knowledge, organization, and control. The task involves hierarchical symbolic abstraction. An abstraction of the data is computed in the form of a degree of fit; it is symbolic because the abstraction is presented as one of a small number of discrete qualitative measures of fit ("definite," "very likely,"..."definitely not") and hierarchical because the final abstraction is computed from intermediate conceptual abstractions, which can in turn be computed from other intermediate ones, or from raw data.

For example, assume that the evidence for a disease D can be of three kinds, chemical, physical, and historical, and that values of several laboratory tests together determine the strength of chemical evidence, while a number of specific observations during a physical examination are used to determine the strength of physical evidence, and so on. Further assume that each of the raw observations can be converted into one of a small set of appropriate symbolic values, for example, "abnormally high," "high," "normal," etc. For MDX, human experts were consulted to determine the combinations of values that would result in a specific degree of strength for an abstraction. For example, to a question such as "Given an abnormally high value for test 1, a moderately high value for test 2, and a normal value for test 3, what, in your judgment, is the strength of chemical evidence?" the expert might reply "very high." Given that the number of possible symbolic values for each level is kept low, and that a number of combinations will be judged not possible by experts, the tables that incorporate such judgments are typically sparse and computationally very manageable. This process is repeated until the top-level abstractions can be readily computed. The theory of uncertainty handling implicit in this approach is discussed elsewhere.[5,11,12] The relevant point here is that this problem of matching hypotheses against data is a general subtype of reasoning useful in a number of different contexts.

**Knowledge-directed information passing.** Now consider the following situation in classificatory problem solving. Suppose a piece of knowledge in the liver specialist states, "If history of anesthetic exposure, consider hepatitis." But what if there is no mention of anesthetics in the patient record even though his history indicates recent major surgery? We would expect a competent physician to infer possible exposure to anesthetics in this case and therefore consider hepatitis. Mittal[13] noted that the reasoning involved to make this inference is not classificatory but involves a form of generic task that we call *knowledge-directed information passing*. In our work on MDX, we were led to the creation of a separate subsystem called PATREC for performing this inference. The literature will provide interested readers with details on PATREC.[5,14]

The knowledge about each data concept—not the values for a particular patient, but general domain knowledge such as default values for attributes, strategies for inferring them if they are not available, etc.—is stored in a frame, and these concepts are typically organized in a frame hierarchy. (These frames also have pointers to the actual data values for particular instances, but that is largely a matter of implementation and need not be discussed further.)

Briefly, this form of reasoning involves accessing a frame that stores either the desired datum or information about how the value of the datum might be obtained, including possible default values. For instance, in the above example the frame corresponding to "anesthetics" will examine its portion of the database and find nothing in it, but it will find knowledge of the following kinds: (1) check if particular types of anesthetics were administered; (2) check if any major surgery was performed, and if so answer "yes"; (3) if answer is "no" by any of the above inferences, default answer is "no." In this particular case it will find no record of various specific anesthetics and will check the "surgery" frame, which will have its own knowledge in the form "Check various kinds of surgeries," and eventually it will infer that major surgery was performed. The anesthetics concept can then infer that the patient had been exposed to anesthetics. Mittal[13] has worked out a complex theory of organization of such databases, including issues of temporal reasoning of certain types.

**Abductive assembly.** MDX viewed diagnosis as largely classificatory, but we have since been building a more comprehensive framework for diagnostic reasoning in which diagnosis is viewed as building a hypothesis that best explains the data. The underlying information processing task can be conveniently thought of as having two components: In one, hypotheses are generated, each with some attached degree of plausibility and a list of observations it can account for (typically the number of hypotheses would be a small subset of the hypothesis space in general); in the other, a subset of these hypotheses is assembled into a composite hypothesis so as to satisfy various criteria of "best coverage."

In the RED system for antibody identification,[8] we propose an architecture for this problem. Our plan calls for an MDX-style system, working with a classifier, matcher, and a data abstractor, to produce a small number of highly plausible classificatory hypotheses, and an assembler uses them to build a best explanatory composite. The assembly process itself is again quite generic; given a set of hypotheses and an account of what they can explain, the abductive assembly problem solving is useful to produce a composite that best explains the data. Dendral[15] and Internist[16] can both be thought of as systems with components that perform this type of reasoning.

Josephson[8] has analyzed the problem-solving process needed for this form of reasoning. The knowledge that the assembler needs is in the form of causal or other relations (such as incompatibility, suggestiveness, special case of) between the hypotheses and relative significance of data items. A simplified version of the control regime for problem solving can be given as follows: Assembly and criticism alternate. In assembly, a means-ends regime, driven by the goal of explaining all the significant findings, is in control. At each stage, the best hypothesis that offers to explain the most significant datum is added to the composite hypothesis so far assembled. After each assembly, the critic removes explanatorily superfluous parts. This loops until all the data are explained or until no hypotheses are left.

## Other generic tasks

The generic tasks described so far were motivated by our investigation of diagnostic reasoning, though they can all be used as building blocks for other types of problem solvers. In the early 1980's, we began to investigate design problem solving and identified *routine design,* a form of problem solving wherein the way to decompose a design problem is already known, and compiled "design plans" are available for each major stage in design. We distinguished this form of design problem solving (class 3 design, as we called it) from situations in which even the components of the object being designed are unknown (class 1), or situations in which the components are known but design plans are not available in a compiled form (class 2). These three classifications are not meant to be a rigorous account of the design process but to give a feeling for the spectrum of difficulty of the design task, with class 3 being the most routine. We are talking about design as an abstract activity; it can be applied to concrete things such as mechanical devices or abstract objects such as plans or programs. In fact, we have applied the following ideas to the construction of a mission-planning assistant in the domain of military logistics. A number of planning systems, such as the Molgen system,[17] can be brought under this framework.

**Hierarchical design by plan selection and refinement.** In our group, Brown[18] investigated the forms of knowledge and

> **We speak of design
> as an abstract activity,
> but it can be applied to both
> abstract and concrete things.**

control for class 3 design. The Aircyl system, which captures the mechanical design expertise in the domain of air-cylinder design, is a result of this study.

Typically, knowledge for this type of design activity comes in two forms:

(1) The object structure is known at some level of abstraction; that is, typical components of a device under design and their configuration are known. For example, in the Aircyl domain the general structure of the air cylinder under design is known—the air cylinder is not being invented—but the actual dimensions and choice of material are to be made case-specific.

(2) Design plans are available for each part in the structure. These plans have knowledge to help make some design choices for that component, and they also invoke subcomponent designs for refining the design at that level of abstraction. This knowledge is organized as a hierarchy of design specialists, mirroring the device-component hierarchy of the object structure. Each specialist has design plans which, as mentioned, can be used to make commitments for some dimensions of the component.

The control regime for routine design is top-down in general. The following is done recursively until a complete design is worked out: A specialist corresponding to a component of the object is called; it chooses a plan based on some specification, instantiates and executes some part of the plan, which in turn suggests further specialists to call to set other details of the design. Plan failures are passed up until appropriate changes are made by higher level specialists, so that specialists who failed may succeed on a retry.

Design is generally a complex activity. However, the realization of a design by invoking a design plan, which makes some commitments and also calls other plans for refinement, is an elementary building block for design and has a great deal of generality.

**State abstraction.** Now let's look at a generic task for predicting consequences of actions. Often when actions are contemplated on a complex system, we would like to be able to predict their consequences to the system's functionality. (For example, "What will happen if valve A is closed in this process plant?") The reasoning necessary for this task requires some type of qualitative simulation. One such type occurs when expertise in the domain is available in a highly compiled form, that is, when the reasoner has knowledge about the structure of the device or system (the components and how they are connected), the functionality of the components and how they relate to the functionality of the system as a whole, and when he has compiled knowledge about how state changes to components affect their functionality. Typically, experts in a domain would need to have knowledge of this form in order to evaluate proposed actions very quickly. In this reasoning, the proposed action is interpreted as a state change in the component, and the change in the functionality of the component is inferred. This change in functionality is in turn interpreted as a state change of the

higher level subsystem of which the component is a part, and the change in that subsystem's functionality is then inferred, and so on. In the example above, the closing of the valve will be used to infer the loss of function "cooling water output" of the component "cooling water inlet." Assuming that this is a component of the cooling system, the change in functionality of the component can be interpreted as a change of state in the cooling system. This chain of reasoning can be recursively carried on until the effect on the functionality of the whole system can be inferred.

Abstractly, then, the following characterization of this task can be given.

*Task specification:* Given a change in some state of a system, provide an account of the changes that can be expected in the functions of the system.

*Form of knowledge:* < change in state of subsystem > → < change in functionality of subsystem = change in state of the immediately larger system >.

*Organization of knowledge:* Knowledge of the above form is distributed in conceptual specialists corresponding to system/subsystems. The way these conceptual specialists are connected mirrors the way the system/subsystem is put together.

*Control regime:* The control regime is basically bottom-up and follows the architecture of the system/subsystem relationship. The changes in states are followed through, interpreted as changes in functionalities of subsystems, until the changes in the functionalities at the level of abstraction desired are obtained.

The literature offers a concrete example of this task.[7]

## Viewing existing expert systems in this framework

Let's look at some of the better known expert systems from the perspective of the framework developed so far in this article.

Mycin's task is to classify a number of observations describing a patient's infection as resulting from one or another organism, and, once this is done, to instantiate a plan with parameters appropriate to the particular patient situation. We have shown elsewhere[19] how the diagnostic portion of Mycin can be recast as a classification problem solver with a more direct encoding of domain knowledge and a control structure directly appropriate to this form of problem solving.

Prospector[20] classifies a geological description as one of a previously enumerated set of formations.

Internist[16] generates candidate hypotheses by a form of enumeration (plausibility scoring and keeping only the top few) and uses a form of abductive assembly. These two types of problem solving alternate.

Dendral[15] generates candidate hypotheses by a form of hypothesis matching and uses a form of abductive assembly that puts together the best molecular hypothesis from the fragments produced by the matching process.

Note that in the above analysis we have not mentioned rules (Mycin), networks (Prospector), graphs (Dendral), etc., which are the means of encoding and carrying out the tasks. This separation is one reason we are tempted to refer to this level of analysis as the "right" level of abstraction.

## Complex generic tasks

Earlier we contrasted diagnosis and design as examples of distinctively different but generic problem-solving activities. Note, however, that diagnosis was not included as one of the generic tasks discussed, and only a type of design was included. There are, in fact, other levels at which generic phenomena are reported. Some expert system researchers point to the existence of generic problem areas such as process control problems, and there are attempts to provide AI programming environments with constructs that can specify generic process-control structures for particular instances. What is the relation between these generic phenomena and the ones we have been discussing?

Further distinctions will aid understanding. Typically, many tasks that we intuitively think of as generic are really complex generic tasks. That is, they are further decomposable into components that are more elementary in the sense that each of them has a homogeneous control regime and knowledge structure. For example, what we call the diagnostic task—generic in the sense that it may be quite similar across domains—is not a unitary task structure. Diagnosis may involve classificatory reasoning at a certain point, reasoning from one datum to another at some other point, and abductive assembly of multiple diagnostic hypotheses at yet another point. Classification, as we have seen, has a form of knowledge and control behavior that is different from those for data-to-data reasoning, which in turn are dissimilar in these dimensions to assembling hypotheses. Similar arguments apply with even greater force to generic problem areas such as process control. Thus diagnosis, design, process control, etc., are "compound" processes, while the phenomena we have been discussing are more "atomic." Hence the term "building blocks" in the title.

Let's assume we have a complex, real-world, knowledge-based reasoning task and a set of generic tasks for each of which we have a representation language and a control regime to perform the task. If we can perform an epistemic analysis of the domain such that (1) the complex task can be decomposed in terms of the generic tasks, (2) paths and conditions for information transfer from the agents that per-

form these generic tasks to the others which need the information can be established, and (3) knowledge of the domain is available to encode into the knowledge structures for the generic tasks, then the complex task can be "knowledge-engineered" clearly and successfully. Notice that an ability to decompose complex tasks in this way brings with it the ability to characterize them in a useful way. We can see, for example, that the reason we are not yet able to handle difficult design problem solving is that we are often unable to find an architecture of generic tasks in terms of which the complex task can be constructed.

Clancey's work on classification problem solving[21] can be contrasted with our generic task on hierarchical classification. For Clancey, classification problem solving is an identifiable phenomenon that occurs within a number of expert systems. However, it is not a unitary building block structure in his analysis. For example, he includes as part of classification a component called data abstraction, which roughly corresponds to the functionality of our knowledge-directed data inference component. The latter functionality, however, is not uniquely needed for classification; it could be used by a planner just as well, since a stage of data abstraction can also be involved in planning. Thus, what Clancey has called heuristic classification is in reality a compound task in our analysis and can be broken down into more elementary problem-solving tasks for greater clarity. Furthermore, identifying classification problem solving as separate from data abstraction enables us to associate a form of knowledge, an organization, and a control regime with each of the tasks, thus truly giving them the status of building blocks. This has advantages for knowledge encoding and system building, as we will see.

## Building blocks for knowledge-based systems

Discussions of knowledge representation normally assume that one uses some language to represent knowledge about a domain and then uses various procedures to operate on the knowledge to make inferences to produce solutions to problems. Whatever the preferred knowledge representation used—OPS5, Emycin, predicate calculus, semantic nets, frames, etc.—this point of view permeates the field. We have argued that this separation of knowledge from its use leads to a number of difficulties. However, our generic-task approach suggests an alternative point of view: that the representation of knowledge should closely follow its use, since the form of knowledge is tied to its use, and that there are different organizations of knowledge for different types of problem solving.

Ideally, we need knowledge representation languages that will enable us to directly encode knowledge at the appropriate level by using primitives that naturally describe the domain knowledge for a given generic task. The problem-solving behavior for the task can then be automatically controlled by regimes appropriate for the task. If done correctly, this would simultaneously facilitate knowledge representation, problem solving, and explanation.

For each generic task, the form and organization of the knowledge directly suggest the appropriate representation for encoding the domain knowledge. Since there is a control regime associated with each task, the problem solver can be implicit in the representation language. That is, as soon as knowledge is represented in the shell corresponding to a given generic task, a problem solver that uses the control regime on the knowledge representation created for the domain can be created by the interpreter. This is similar to what representation systems such as Emycin do, but note that we are deliberately trading generality at a lower level for specificity, clarity, richness of ontology, and control at a higher level.

We have designed and implemented representation languages for a number of these generic tasks, and other languages are on the way. Languages for classification (CSRL)[12,22] and object synthesis by selection and refinement (DSPL)[6] have been reported in the literature. The current version of CSRL includes facilities for hypothesis matching, but a language called HYPER for hypothesis matching and assessment will soon be available separately. A simple version of the state abstraction task language is available now. A database language called IDABLE and an abductive assembly language called PEIRCE will soon be available from our laboratory and will complete the current list of high-level building-block tools.

All these languages will make it possible to encode the knowledge directly at the level of abstraction appropriate for the task. But these are not mere knowledge representation languages; they are really shells, and once the knowledge is represented, they and their associated control regimes together become a problem-solving agent. It is in this sense that these languages are building blocks.

Building an expert system for a complex task using these languages involves matching portions of problem solving with various generic tasks. To the extent that such a mapping is possible—the really difficult task in expert system construction turns out to be this kind of epistemic analysis—this compound task is realizable by using our approach. As indicated earlier, a number of existing expert systems can in fact be analyzed and reencoded in this manner.

One aspect of this approach has not been discussed because of space limitations but is at least worth noting. Since the problem solving is decomposed into distinct problem-solving activities by a number of different structures, there is a need to integrate the activities by making it possible for these various structures to communicate with each other. As it turns out, all our implementations use a message-passing communities-of-specialists paradigm, and thus such communication and integration can be handled naturally in our framework.

> *While there are candidates, is there a holy grail in AI— a uniform mechanism to explain and produce intelligence?*

There has been an ongoing search in artificial intelligence for the "holy grail" of a uniform mechanism that will explain and produce intelligence. This desire has resulted in a number of candidate mechanisms—from perceptrons of the 1960's through first-order predicate calculus to rules and frames— to satisfy this need. Another school, often called the "scruffies," has proposed AI theories with a multitude of knowledge entities and mechanisms. While these programs have been more or less successful at their tasks, they have nevertheless been subject to the charge of *ad hoc*-ness from the proponents of simpler and more uniform mechanisms. This article takes the middle ground. A multitude of mechanisms do exist, but they constitute an armory of generic information-processing strategies available to intelligent agents. That they are generic is what rescues them from the charge of *ad hoc*-ness, while their multiplicity yields an ability to match the information-processing strategy to the problem faced by the problem solver and the type of knowledge he has available.

This position is not an argument for or against any of the mechanisms that have been repeatedly proposed. Even if some intelligent agent can be built out of perceptrons of appropriate types, or implemented entirely in a rule language or within a logic representation, it does not follow that the conceptual problems in the design of intelligent artifacts would vanish. There are problems to be solved at higher levels of abstraction before the artifact can be built. This article proposes an appropriate level of abstraction at which to discuss the issues in the design of knowledge-based problem solving.

Ease and clarity in system design and implementation, along with knowledge acquisition at a more conceptual level, are some of the main advantages of our approach. Of course, there are advantages in other dimensions as well. For example, elsewhere I have described how this approach directly helps in providing clearer explanations of problem solving in expert systems.[23] The approach has a number of other implications. For example, uncertainty handling in problem solving is best viewed as consisting of different types of each kind of problem solving rather than as a uniform general method. In the literature,[11,12,24] we have described a method of uncertainty handling that is especially appropriate for classification problem solving.

## Acknowledgments

This research was supported by Air Force Office of Scientific Research grant 82-0255, National Science Foundation grant MCS-8305032, and the Defense Advanced Research Projects Agency, RADC contract F30602-85-C-0010. I would like to thank John Roach for inviting me to write this article, and one of the reviewers, who made especially useful comments.

## References

1. J. McDermott, "R1: A Rule-Based Configurer of Computer Systems," *Artificial Intelligence,* Vol. 19, No. 1, 1982, pp. 39-88.

2. E. H. Shortliffe, *Computer-Based Medical Consultations: MYCIN,* Elsevier-North Holland, New York, 1976.

3. P. Szolovits and S. G. Pauker, "Categorical and Probabilistic Reasoning in Medical Diagnosis," *Artificial Intelligence,* Vol. 11, No. 1-2, 1978, pp. 115-144.

4. B. Chandrasekaran, S. Mittal, F. Gomez, and J. Smith, "An Approach to Medical Diagnosis Based on Conceptual Structures," *Proc. Sixth Int'l Joint Conf. Artificial Intelligence,* Aug. 1979, pp. 134-142.

5. B. Chandrasekaran and S. Mittal, "Conceptual Representation of Medical Knowledge for Diagnosis by Computer: MDX and Related Systems," in *Advances in Computers,* M. Yovits, ed., Academic Press, 1983, pp. 217-293.

6. D. C. Brown and B. Chandrasekaran, "Expert Systems for a Class of Mechanical Design Activity," *IFIP WG5.2 Working Conf.,* Sept. 1984.

7. B. Chandrasekaran, "Towards a Taxonomy of Problem-Solving Types," *AI Magazine,* Vol. 4, No. 1, winter/spring 1983, pp. 9-17.

8. John R. Josephson, B. Chandrasekaran, and J. W. Smith, "Assembling the Best Explanation," *Proc. IEEE Workshop Principles of Knowledge-Based Systems,* IEEE Computer Society, Los Alamitos, Calif., Dec. 1984. Revised version available from Laboratory for Artificial Intelligence Research, Ohio State University.

9. F. Gomez and B. Chandrasekaran, "Knowledge Organization and Distribution for Medical Diagnosis," *IEEE Trans. Systems, Man and Cybernetics,* Vol. 11, No. 1, Jan. 1981, pp. 34-42.

10. J. Sticklen, B. Chandrasekaran, and J. R. Josephson, "Control Issues in Classificatory Diagnosis," *Proc. Ninth Int'l Joint Conf. Artificial Intelligence,* Aug. 18-24, 1985.

11. B. Chandrasekaran, S. Mittal, and J. W.Smith, "Reasoning with Uncertain Knowledge: The MDX Approach," *Proc. First Ann. Joint Conf. American Medical Informatics Assoc.,* May 1982, pp. 335-339.

12. T. C. Bylander and Sanjay Mittal, "CSRL: A Language for Classificatory Problem Solving and Uncertainty Handling," *AI Magazine,* summer 1986, to appear.

13. S. Mittal, *Design of a Distributed Medical Diagnosis and Database System,* doctoral dissertation, Dept. of Computer and Information Science, Ohio State University, 1980.

14. Sanjay Mittal, B. Chandrasekaran, and Jon Sticklen, "Patrec: A Knowledge-Directed Database for a Diagnostic Expert System," *Computer,* Vol. 17, No. 9, Sept. 1984, pp. 51-58.

15. B. Buchanan, G. Sutherland, and E. A. Feigenbaum, "Heuristic DENDRAL: A Program for Generating Explanatory Hypotheses in Organic Chemistry," in *Machine Intelligence 4,* B. Meltzer and D. Michie, eds., American Elsevier, New York, 1969.

16. H. W. Pople, "Heuristic Methods for Imposing Structure on Ill-Structured Problems," in *Artificial Intelligence in Medicine,* P. Szolovits, ed., Westview Press, 1982, pp. 119-190.

17. Peter Friedland, *Knowledge-Based Experiment Design in Molecular Genetics,* PhD thesis, Computer Science Department, Stanford University, 1979.

18. D. C. Brown, *Expert Systems for Design Problem-Solving Using Design Refinement with Plan Selection and Redesign,* dissertation, Ohio State University, 1984.

19. Jon Sticklen, B. Chandrasekaran, J. W. Smith, and John Svirbely, "MDX-MYCIN: The MDX Paradigm Applied to the MYCIN Domain," *Int'l J. Computers and Mathematics with Applications,* Vol. 11, No. 5, 1985, pp. 527-539.

20. Richard O. Duda, John G. Gaschnig, and Peter E. Hart, "Model Design in the Prospector Consultant System for Mineral Exploration," in *Expert Systems in the Microelectronic Age,* D. Michie, ed., Edinburgh University Press, 1980, pp. 153-167.

21. William J. Clancey, "Classification Problem Solving," *Proc. Nat'l Conf. Artificial Intelligence,* Austin, Tex., 1984, pp. 49-55.

22. T. Bylander, S. Mittal, and B. Chandrasekaran, "CSRL: A Language for Expert Systems for Diagnosis," *Proc. Int'l Joint Conf. Artificial Intelligence,* Aug. 1983, pp. 218-221.

23. B. Chandrasekaran, "Generic Tasks in Expert System Design and Their Role in Explanation of Problem Solving," *Proc. Office of Naval Research Workshop on Distributed Problem Solving,* May 16-17, 1985, National Academy of Sciences, to appear.

24. B. Chandrasekaran and Michael C. Tanner, "Uncertainty Handling in Expert Systems: Uniform vs. Task-Specific Formalisms," in *Uncertainty in Artificial Intelligence,* Laveen N. Kanal and John Lemmer, eds., North Holland Publishing, 1986, in press.

**B. Chandrasekaran** has been at Ohio State University since 1969, where he directs the AI group. He is currently professor of computer and information science. From 1967 to 1969 he was a research scientist with the Philco-Ford Corporation in Blue Bell, Pennsylvania, working on speech- and character-recognition machines. His major research activities are currently in knowledge-based reasoning.

Chandrasekaran received his bachelor of engineering degree with honors from Madras University in 1963 and his PhD from the University of Pennsylvania in 1967. He is associate editor for AI of *IEEE Transactions on Systems, Man and Cybernetics* and chairs the society's Technical Committee on AI. He was elected a fellow of the IEEE in 1986.

The author's address is Laboratory for Artificial Intelligence Research, Department of Computer and Information Science, Ohio State University, Columbus, OH 43210.

# 12 Acquiring, Representing, and Evaluating a Competence Model of Diagnostic Strategy

William J. Clancey
Stanford Knowledge Systems Laboratory

## INTRODUCTION

Over the past decade, a number of Artificial Intelligence programs have been constructed for solving problems in science, mathematics, and medicine. These programs, termed "Expert Systems" (Duda & Shortliffe, 1983; Feigenbaum, 1977) are designed to capture what specialists know, the kind of non-numeric, qualitative reasoning that is often passed on through apprenticeship rather than being written down in books. However, these programs are not generally intended to be *models* of expert problem-solving, neither in their organization of knowledge nor their reasoning process. Consequently, difficulties have been encountered in attempting to use the knowledge formulated in these programs outside of a consultation setting, where getting the right answer is mostly what matters. Their application to explanation and teaching, in particular, (Brown, 1977a; Clancey, 1983a; Swartout, 1981) has necessitated closer adherence to human problem-solving methods and more explicit representation of knowledge. That is, building expert systems whose problem-solving must be comprehensible to people requires a close study of the nature of expertise in people.

NEOMYCIN (Clancey & Letsinger, 1984) is a consultation system whose knowledge base is intended to be used in a tutoring program. While MyCIN (Shortliffe, 1976) is the starting point, we have significantly altered the representation and reasoning procedure of the original program. Unlike MyCIN, NEOMYCIN's knowledge is richly organized in multiple hierarchies; distinction is made between findings and hypotheses; and the reasoning is data- and hypothesis-directed, not an exhaustive, top-down search of the problem

space. Most importantly, for purposes of explanation and teaching, the reasoning procedure is abstract, separate from knowledge of the medical domain. The knowledge base is also broadened to take in many disorders that might be confused with the problem of meningitis diagnosis, the central concern of the MYCIN program. Together, the knowledge base and reasoning procedure constitute a model of how human knowledge is organized and how it is used in diagnosis.

In practical terms, we are interested in determining what we can teach students about diagnosis and how this knowledge might be usefully structured in a computer program. In general terms, we want to know what design would enable an expert system to acquire knowledge interactively from human experts, to explain reasoning to people seeking advice, and to teach students. Figure 12.1 shows how a program like NEOMYCIN relates to these three perspectives, providing an idealized overview of our goals.

In teaching, GUIDON2 will use NEOMYCIN's knowledge to model a student's problem solving. A strong parallel occurs in the process of building NEOMYCIN: "Knowledge acquisition" is a process of modeling a human expert's problem-solving, in which the modeler is the learner and the expert is the teacher. Similarly, to provide explanations of advice, a "user model" of the client is required. In all three settings — teaching, knowledge acquisition, and consultation explanation — a model is constructed of the person

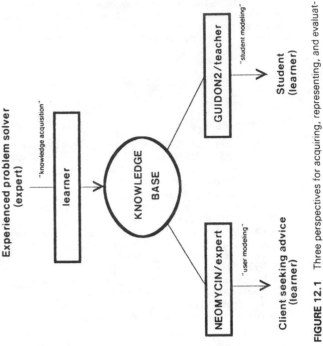

**FIGURE 12.1** Three perspectives for acquiring, representing, and evaluating expertise.

interacting with the program, and a common knowledge base (NEOMYCIN) is used. We give different names to the modeling process — student modeling, knowledge acquisition, and user modeling — but the principles are essentially the same. We must determine: What is this person telling me about what he knows? What does he want to know about my knowledge? The purpose of NEOMYCIN research is to determine what kind of knowledge representation facilitates interacting with people in these three settings — as teacher, learner, and expert problem-solver. Indeed, we take the strong stand that a program is not an "expert" system, and certainly not a model of reasoning, unless it is proficient in these multiple, complex settings (see Anderson & Bower, 1980, for a similar discussion).

We don't have such a central program today, and most knowledge acquisition is done between people. But we can still capitalize on the analogies to learn how people organize their knowledge, how they model other people's knowledge, and how they explain what they know in dialogues. For example, we can compare a physician's explanations in knowledge acquisition dialogues to what he tells his students in the classroom. What we learn from this study can be incorporated in a user modeling program. All along we refine our model of diagnostic reasoning.

There are many overlapping perspectives to such a study. For example, in modeling medical diagnosis, we must sort out modeling of disease processes, general search procedures, explanation techniques, pedagogical strategies for interrupting students, and so on. In this paper, we examine NEOMYCIN as it is currently constructed from the perspective of what we might call *the psychology of medicine*. We are interested in issues of model acquisition, representation, content, and evaluation. In particular, we will consider the following questions:

1. Why does NEOMYCIN work? How could a model derived from a problem-solver's explanations about his behavior actually solve problems? That is, what must be true about an *explanation* of reasoning for it to be part of a procedural model?

2. What aspects of the model are *empirical*, based on observations of an expert's behavior and his explanations? What aspects are *rational*, based on mathematical and logical assumptions about the nature of knowledge and the task domain?

3. What capabilities of human reasoning are assumed by the *procedural language* for representing diagnostic strategy? How are considerations of *cognitive economy* incorporated?

4. What constraints imposed by the problem space are implicit in the *content* of the diagnostic procedure? What *correctness and efficiency* considerations derive from these task constraints?

5. What must be true about the nature of expertise and task domains for a model of reasoning to be expressed as an *abstract procedure*, wholly separate from the domain knowledge it operates upon?

6. Given that expert knowledge is highly "compiled" into domain-specific form, and that novices do not always know the right procedures, whom does NEOMYCIN model? If NEOMYCIN's abstract procedure of diagnosis is a *grammar*, constituting a model of *competence*, what are the difficulties of extracting such a grammar from expert behavior?

7. What part do multiple settings for using expertise play in evaluating the *sufficiency* of the model? How can knowledge of the underlying cognitive and task constraints be used to evaluate the *plausibility* of the model?

In pursuing these questions, we adopt different perspectives for formalizing and studying the model. We view it as:

• an *opportunistic strategy for remembering "compiled knowledge" of disorders* — emphasizing that diagnosis is an indexing problem. The diagnostic procedure operates upon a network of stereotypic knowledge of disorders, that is, knowledge derived from the experience of diagnosing many cases, not a working model of the human body and how it car be faulted;

• a *set of operators for establishing the space of diagnoses* — emphasizing that diagnosis is at heart a search problem whose bounds must be established and explored systematically;

• a *procedure derived from cognitive, sociological, mathematical, and case-experience constraints* — emphasizing that the determinants of efficiency and correctness are implicit in the procedure, below the level of diagnostic behavior;

• a *grammar for parsing information-gathering behavior* — emphasizing the domain-independent character of the diagnostic procedure, how it selects from a well-structured "lexicon" of medical knowledge and specifies the "discourse structure" of the diagnostic interview.

Building a large, complex program is necessarily iterative, with early versions serving as sketches of the idealized model. Like artists, we start with an idea, represent it, study what we have done, and try again. The state of AI and computational modeling is such that — if it were an artist's body of work — an exhibit of his or her completed paintings would be very small. NEOMYCIN is not a completed program, but a sketch that this chapter studies and critiques. It is reasonable to address the previous questions now to lend some methodological clarity to the enterprise.

Four major sections follow. In the *acquisition* section we illustrate how we collect and parse diagnostic behavior. (A detailed protocol analysis appears in Appendix II.) In the *description* section, we present an overview of our perspective on the search problem of medical diagnosis. (The entire diagnostic procedure appears in Appendix IV.) The *representation* section describes NEOMYCIN's strategy and domain knowledge architecture in detail, along with a summary of constraints implicit in the procedure. Finally, the *evaluation* section considers tests for determining the sufficiency and plausibility of the model. We conclude by considering what NEOMYCIN reveals about the nature of expertise and its implications for teaching.

## ACQUIRING THE MODEL:
## KNOWLEDGE ENGINEERING AND PROTOCOL ANALYSIS

### Related Work and Scope of Effort

In conventional knowledge engineering (Hayes-Roth et al., 1983), an expert system is constructed by an interview process. A program is constructed and critiqued in an iterative manner. In this way, the resident "expert" frequently picks up the jargon and tools of artificial intelligence: He learns how to formalize his knowledge in some structured language, using editing programs and explanation systems to construct a "knowledge base" with the desired problem-solving ability.

NEOMYCIN was constructed in a different way. Our teaching goals required that we improve MYCIN's representation. We found that MYCIN's rule formalism made it necessary to proceduralize all knowledge, combining facts with how they were to be used (Clancey, 1982, Clancey, 1983a). With this experience in mind, we decided not to devise yet another formalism by which an accommodating physician might distort what he knew. Instead, we started (in 1980) by presenting problems to the physician to learn about his knowledge and methods from scratch. Our original objective was just to make explicit a taxonomy of diseases and subtype relations among findings; but the clarity of the approach used by our expert (and its difference from MYCIN's) ultimately encouraged us to construct the model that became NEOMYCIN's diagnostic procedure.

This investigation was influenced in many ways by previous work. For example, Pauker and Szolovits (1977) constructed a model of diagnostic reasoning, called PIP, concurrent with the development of MYCIN. Thus, we knew that a psychological approach, instead of a purely engineering approach, could be used for constructing an expert system without a loss in problem-solving performance. Other studies (such as Elstein, Shulman, & Sprafka, 1978; Kassirer & Gorry, 1978; Miller, 1975; Patil, Szolovits, & Schwartz, 1982; Rubin, 1975), as well as that of Benbassat and Schiff-

mann, 1976, strongly suggested that diagnostic strategy constitutes a separate, significant body of knowledge that might be interesting to formalize independent of medical facts themselves. Furthermore, previous research in teaching problem-solving strategies with instructional programs using AI techniques (e.g., Brown, Collins, & Haris, 1977; Papert, 1980; Wescourt & Hemphill, 1978), suggested that it would be useful to go beyond MYCIN's purely domain-specific rules and make explicit the underlying general search procedure.

In related psychological research, Feltovich, Johnson, Moller, and Swanson (1984) used fixed-order diagnostic problems to demonstrate the effect of knowledge organization on reasoning. Could we formalize an ideal organization of knowledge for MYCIN's meningitis domain? In AI, Davis (1980) designed a construct he called a "metarule" for controlling reasoning, but he had presented only two examples in MYCIN's domain. Could this representation be generalized for formalizing a complete diagnostic procedure? Concurrent studies at the Learning Research Development Center and CMU (Anderson, Greeno, Kline, & Neves, 1981; Chi, Feltovich, & Glaser, 1981; Feltovich, Johnson, Moller, & Swanson, 1984; Larkin, McDermott, Simon, & Simon, 1980) were concerned with modeling differences between experts and novices in geometry and physics problem-solving. Could we "decompile" MYCIN's knowledge into the components an expert had learned from experience and compiled into specific procedures and rules? Finally, in our previous research (Clancey, 1983a; Clancey, 1984), we had found a convenient epistemologic framework for characterizing the content of an explanation. Could this be used for directing and analyzing a knowledge acquisition dialogue?

In summary, the process of acquiring the NEOMYCIN model from expert interviews is disciplined by three greatly different perspectives:

- *Psychology:* The new program, unlike MYCIN, should embody a model of diagnosis that students can understand and use themselves. Moreover, a program that captures general principles of data- and hypothesis-directed reasoning can be used as the basis for a student model. (See page 385.)

- *Knowledge Engineering:* The new program, unlike MYCIN, should separate control knowledge from the facts it operates upon. The diagnostic procedure should be represented in a well-structured way, just like the medical knowledge, so that it will be accessible for explanation and interpretation in student modeling. See Clancey, 1983a for detailed discussion.

- *Epistemology:* The new program, unlike MYCIN, should distinguish among findings, hypotheses, evidence (finding/hypothesis links), justifications (why a finding/hypothesis link is true), structure (how findings and hypotheses are related), and strategy (why a finding request or hypothesis comes to mind). See Clancey, 1983a for detailed discussion, also see page 364.

Besides not filling in some predetermined representation, we have been wary of incorporating ad hoc features into the model just because the computer allows them. In particular, we are especially wary of all scoring mechanisms: We want every hypothesis and finding request either to be based on explicit principles or to be totally arbitrary. It is essential that NEOMYCIN avoid numeric calculations that cannot be expressed in terms of facts and procedures known and followed by people. We use MYCIN's evidence-weighing scheme (certainty factors) to signify strength of association; but focus decisions, such as selecting a hypothesis to test and a finding to request, primarily follow from relations among findings and hypotheses (such as "sibling," and "necessary cause").

Furthermore, in proceeding in this principled way, we have avoided making the mechanisms more complex than our empirical observations of physicians' reasoning or the cases to be solved warrant. For this reason, we have not included in the model diagnostic considerations that play an important part in several other programs (Chandrasekdelaran, Gomez, & Mittal, 1979; Pauker & Szolovits, 1977; Pople, 1982). These include: differentiation of the disease on the basis of organ system involvement; a problem-oriented approach (trying to explain the data); consideration of multiple causes; and use of probabilistic information. We have minimized these concerns by focusing on diagnosis of meningitis and diseases that might be confused with it. Of course, some of these considerations may be incorporated as we continue to develop the program.

Our research approach could be characterized as "making a push to the frontier." Some of our results might not stand up because the problems considered are not broad enough. But we will have demonstrated, as a first attempt, that certain epistemologic and knowledge-engineering distinctions are useful for constructing a program that can solve problems and explain what it knows.

As another perspective, we want to determine what good teachers know about their own knowledge and problem-solving methods that students would profit from being taught. In assembling a runnable computational model, we must fill in some details, such as strength of belief and activation of memory. We do this in a minimal way, devising just enough mechanism to get the behavior we want (on our small set of test cases). So, for example, we use the MYCIN certainty factor mechanism because it is convenient and simple enough. We have much to learn about what teachers *know* about their knowledge and problem solving, and much of what we do falls in the realm of the traditional computer science problem of design-

ing an appropriate programming language to encode these structures and procedures. Thus, our first interest is to replicate what people know about what they do; we are only secondarily interested in formalizing models of how the mind works (e.g., activation of knowledge), and not at all in mathematically deriving optimal models that might replace or augment what people do.

With our objective of constructing a tutoring program with useful capabilities, the purpose of NEOMYCIN research is not to make the best medical diagnostic program, but to demonstrate a representation methodology for separating kinds of knowledge and formalizing strategies in domain-independent form. The problem domain is sufficiently complex to be challenging, and we have formalized a sufficient subset of diagnostic strategies to provide an interim report on our approach. We have uncovered a number of cognitive problems of interest that have been little studied, particularly that of how focus of attention changes during diagnosis.

## The Hypothesize-and-Test Theory of Diagnosis

In studying diagnostic behavior, we used the epistemologic framework previously mentioned and evolved a set of terms for describing the process of diagnosis. Terms that appear frequently in subsequent sections, such as "task" and "differential," are defined in Appendix I.

In addition, we began with the traditional model of diagnosis, which says that each request for case information, or each finding, directly relates to some hypothesis (Figure 12.2). This model suggests several problems for investigation (points corresponding to numbers in the figure):

1. Where do the initial hypotheses come from?
2. How does the problem-solver choose a finding to confirm or test a hypothesis?
3. What causes attention shift to a new hypothesis?
4. How does the problem-solver know when he or she is done?

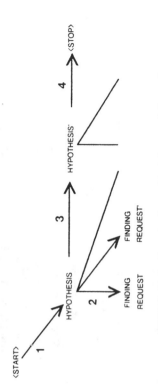

**FIGURE 12.2**  Hypothesize and test theory of diagnosis.

We define a *diagnostic strategy* to be the control structure that regulates these four decisions. This hypothesize-and-test theory drove our initial investigations, but the NEOMYCIN model eventually became much more complex.

**Knowledge Acquisition Technique**

With our interest in formalizing the reasoning process of diagnosis, it is particularly important to allow experts to request problem findings in whatever order they desire. Our main concern is to determine what task and domain knowledge leads to each finding request. Contrary to the protocol-collection procedure most often used today (Ericsson & Simon, 1980; Kuipers & Kassier, 1984; Newell & Simon, 1972) with a minimal number of interruptions, we frequently ask the expert specific questions. In retrospect, this is not always done in a consistent way, and is sometimes so late that the expert has clearly moved ahead (see Line 30 in Appendix II). However, the expert appears to be quite tolerant of interruptions, perhaps from his teaching experience, though of course he might not be typical in this respect.

The questioning techniques we use are listed here, in somewhat idealized form.[1]

- Epistemologic distinctions:
  - Be concerned about the specificity of a finding request: Is it a general maneuver or does he have a specific hypothesis in mind?
  - When asking why a finding came to mind, distinguish between strategic and causal explanations.
  - Distinguish between substances and processes; watch out for composed explanations that leave out intermediate processes or refer to substances as if they were processes.
  - Do not delve into explanations of causal mechanisms that go beyond the expert's level of reasoning.
  - Ask for definitions and try to detect synonyms, which might be misunderstood as representing different entities.
- Interactive considerations:
  - Immediately after a finding is requested, and before supplying the information, ask why the finding came to mind (otherwise new hypotheses might be used to rationalize the request).
  - When the expert indicates that he has formed some hypotheses, ask him to list his differential (this encourages completeness).
  - When a specific hypothesis is being tested, ask about ordering of data requests: Are these "routine" questions for the hypothesis, or has the expert been reminded of some particular correlation or causal process?
  - When the expert appears to be changing his task and/or focus without commenting, confirm this and find out why.
  - Watch for assumptions made by the expert: What is he inferring from the context of his dialogue with you and not explicitly confirming? Ask why certain questions were not asked.

---

[1]Typical of our attempt to apply expertise in multiple settings, we use such generalizations of our own behavior as expectations of what a student or client watching NEOMYCIN might want to know.

**Illustration of Level of Protocol Analysis**

We introduce our analysis of an expert's problem-solving and explanation protocol with an excerpt (Figure 12.3) from the end of the case we analyze in Appendix II. Phrases are broken to separate different kinds of statements; MD = the medical expert, KE = the knowledge engineer. (Again, we choose the term "knowledge engineer" to make clear that this is not presented as a formal psychological experiment.) Brief annotations illustrate our terminology. Annotations always *precede* the protocol section they pertain to.

The analysis shows how findings, hypotheses, and tasks are typically related. Lines L5 to L7 are most interesting in this aspect. Here we see plainly the interaction of task knowledge (stating a list of tested hypotheses), focus of attention (hematoma), and application of domain knowledge (what causes hematoma). The hypothesis in focus, hematoma, was tested by considering what could have caused it. (Interestingly, the physician is so caught up in his role as clinician that he addresses the KE as if he were the patient.)

It is also worth noting that the expert states in L2 that he is planning to go back to ask for more information. Again, in L9 he characterizes his own behavior in general terms. This is typical of the abstract statements this expert makes about diagnosis. His "explanations" of what he does abstractly characterize his problem-solving procedure: "Formulate a differential" and "ask more questions." An important aspect of these explanations is that they are not arbitrary "rationalizations," but are abstract descriptions of a procedure that could generate his finding-requests and hypotheses. They do not necessarily correspond to steps of a procedure that he consciously considers, but are rather the "syntax" of his behavior. The expert's statements constitute a set of tasks and goals that can be fleshed out as an executable procedure. This is obviously important if the model we construct from the expert's explanations is to solve problems successfully and to be useful in teaching. We know that our expert was an unusually good teacher, therefore we cannot expect that every expert's explanations would have this property.

Finally, this excerpt illustrates how during the process of reviewing the differential (a task) the expert realizes that a hypothesis should be tested or refined (broken into subtypes or causes). We do not view this as an error on his part. Father, as the expert says in L9, reviewing is a deliberate maneuver for being complete; it helps bring other diagnostic tasks to mind. NEOMYCIN does not behave in this way because it is a simplified model that does not precisely model how knowledge of diseases is stored or recalled. This level of modeling may very well be useful for understanding the basis of diagnostic strategies, as well as for considering the space of alternative strategies people are capable of and the causes of errors.[2]

## OVERVIEW OF THE DIAGNOSTIC MODEL

### Flow of Information

Figure 12.4 provides an overview of the flow of information during diagnosis. The loop begins with a "chief complaint," one or more findings that supposedly indicate that the device is malfunctioning. These findings are supplied by an *informant*, who has made or collected the observations that will be given to the problem solver. By forward reasoning, hypotheses are considered. They are focused upon by a general search procedure, leading to attempts to test hypotheses by requesting further findings.

Keep in mind that this diagram shows the flow of information, not the invocation structure of the tasks. TEST-HYPOTHESIS regains control after each invocation to FINDOUT and FORWARD-REASON. Similarly, the subtask within ESTABLISH-HYPOTHESIS-SPACE that invoked TEST-HYPOTHESIS will regain control after a hypothesis is tested. Tasks can also be prematurely aborted and the "stack popped" in the manner described on page 365.[3]

---

[2] As it becomes clear later, we might link NEOMYCIN's metarules to the domain memory model used by Kolodner in the CYRUS program (Kolodner, 1983). In this paper, we present prosaic summaries of the underlying memory constraints (Appendix IV and p. 371, many of which bear striking resemblance to Kolodner's results, such as the importance we give to disease process features for differentiating among diseases.

[3] An obvious alternative design is to place tasks, particularly PROCESS-FINDING and PURSUE-HYPOTHESIS, on an agenda, so findings to explain and hypotheses to test can be more opportunistically ordered (e.g., see Hayes-Roth & Hayes-Roth, 1979). It is possible that the procedural decomposition of reasoning in NEOMYCIN, which suitably models an expert's deliberate approach on relatively easy cases, will prove to be too awkward for describing a student's reasoning, which might jump back and forth between hypotheses and mix data- and hypothesis-directed reasoning in some complex way.

*A task has been completed . . .*

L1 MD: I've gotten a pretty good data base,

*A new task is planned . . .*

L2 so I am going to go back and just ask a couple more questions.

*There is a differential . . .*

L3 I have formulated in my own mind what I think some of the possibilities are.

L4 KE: Can you tell me what you think are some of the possibilities?

*The differential is stated . . .*

L5 MD: I think that there is a very definite possibility that this patient does not have an infectious disease. She could have brain tumor, or a collection of blood (hematoma) in her brain from previous head trauma.

In reviewing, the expert notices that the task

"PURSUE-HYPOTHESIS (focus = mass lesion)"

was not completed; all of the causes have not been considered. So the problem-solving process shifts task and focus:

task: TEST-HYPOTHESIS (hematoma)
evidence rule: head-trauma -> hematoma
task: FINDOUT (head-trauma)

L6 (That is a question I should have asked, by the way . . . )

L7 Have you had any recent head trauma?

L8 KE: Head trauma, no.

L9 MD: You'll find that this happens to physicians. As they formulate their differential diagnosis and then they go back and ask more questions.

L11 KE: What comes after . . . ?

L10 MD: Then I would say a chronic meningitis.

**FIGURE 12.3** Example of protocol analysis.

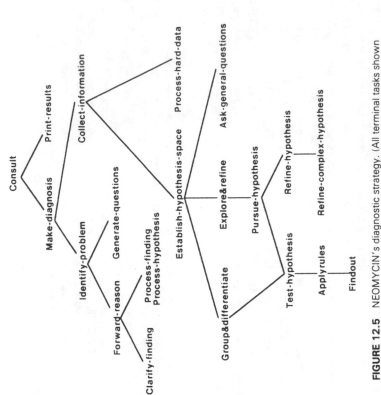

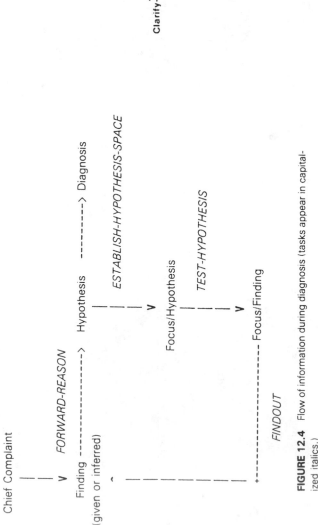

**FIGURE 12.4**    Flow of information during diagnosis (tasks appear in capitalized italics.)

**FIGURE 12.5**    NEOMYCIN's diagnostic strategy. (All terminal tasks shown here except PRINT-RESULTS invoke FINDOUT directly or through APPLYRULES.)

## Tasks for Structuring Working Memory

Figure 12.5 shows the general calling structure of tasks in the diagnostic procedure. An important perspective behind the design of this procedure is that the diagnosis can be described abstractly as a process in which *the problem solver poses tasks for himself in order to have some structuring effect on working memory.* Metarules for doing a task bring appropriate sources of knowledge to mind. Thus, it is very important that the procedure is structured so that the tasks make sense as things that people try to do.

Diagnosis involves repetitively deciding what data to collect next, generally by focusing on some hypothesis in the differential. If we examine the kind of explanations a physician gives for why he is requesting a finding, we find that most refer to a hypothesis he is trying to confirm; this is the conventional view of diagnosis. But we find that a number of requests are *not directed at specific hypotheses or relate to a group of hypotheses.* The problem solver describes a more *general effect that knowledge about the finding will have on his thinking.* For example, information about pregnancy would "broaden the spectrum of disorders" that he is considering. He considers fever and trauma, very general findings, in order to "consider the things at the top." Thus, besides being focused on particular hypotheses, finding requests are intended to affect the differential in some way—for

example, to restrict it categorically or to rule out unusual causes. We call the overall task of collecting circumstantial evidence (through a patient's history and physical examination) "establishing the hypothesis space" because it is oriented toward circumscribing the space of diseases that must be considered.

Structurally, we relate this heuristic search to multiple hierarchical organizations of disorders. Figure 12.6 illustrates our model in general terms. The problem solver receives initial information that "places him in the middle" of some hierarchical organization of known diseases. We show here an etiological hierarchy (defined later). In the protocol we analyze in Section II "chronic-meningitis" was first considered, not "infection," something at the top of the hierarchy, or "tb-meningitis" something at the bottom. The process of diagnosis then involves massaging this set of initial guesses by first "looking up" for general evidence that establishes the class, and then "looking down" to be as specific as possible. To establish a diagnosis, the physician must not only attempt to collect direct evidence for it but must establish paths upward through the multiple hierarchies in which the diagnosis is contained.

Put another way, the physician tries to form a set of possibilities that includes the "right answer" and then narrows down the possibilities to a small, treatable number. This is why a premium is placed on questions that would "broaden the spectrum of possibilities that must be considered" or, alternatively, lend confidence that the typical, a priori, most likely diseases under consideration are appropriate.

To repeat the main point, *we explain finding requests in terms of the effect they are intended to have on the differential.* And moreover, at each point, as findings are requested that could have a certain effect, we say that the *task* of the problem solver is to bring about this effect on his thinking, to change what he is considering or to in some respect give him confidence. Each effect provides structure to the problem in some way: characterizing, refining, or confirming the causes that must be considered. Figure 12.7 shows graphically how each of the operators affect the space of hypoth-

eses.[4] This analysis is of course strongly inspired by Simon's study of the role of the problem space and how it pertains to ill-structured problems (Newell & Simon 1972; Simon & Lea, 1979). Pople, in work concurrent to ours, has developed this point very well and appears to adopt the same "task-oriented" terminology for the proposed CADUCEUS follow-on to INTERNIST (Pople, 1982). (Patil, Szolovits, & Schwartz 1981) has defined operators for constructing alternative causal models to explain findings on multiple levels of detail. Returning to Elstein's study of medical problem-solving (Elstein, Shulman, & Sprafka, 1978), we find similar experiments and analyses of how a physician reasons about alternative formulations of the problem he or she is trying to solve. Finally, the idea of an *information-gathering strategy* for classifying objects or phenomena was pioneered by Bruner (Bruner, Goodnow, & Austin, 1956), in experiments that allowed the problem solver to order data requests, so the different strategic motivations could be studied.

### Problem Formulation and Other Approaches to Diagnosis

It is worth noting that this model of diagnosis differs from a Bayesian model

---

[4]The objective is to put the "right answer" into the box labeled "differential." Possible answers, hypotheses, are focused on, confirmed, grouped, differentiated, and refined. The box is broadened to include other hypotheses by asking general questions. Determining a finding may involve requesting it or determining another finding. Findings must be explained (accounted for causally) with respect to the differential.

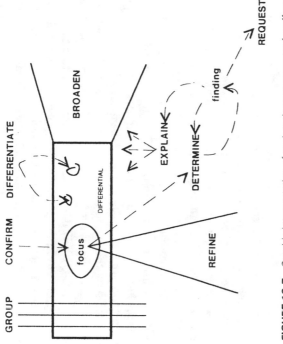

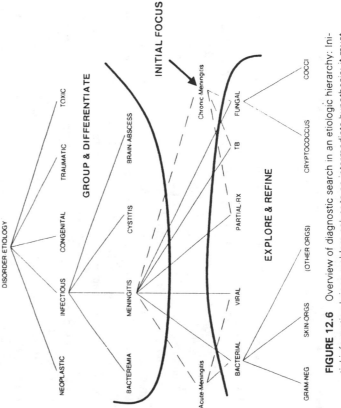

**FIGURE 12.7** Graphic interpretation of each task as an operator for affecting working memory. (See text for elaboration.)

**FIGURE 12.6** Overview of diagnostic search in an etiologic hierarchy: Initial information brings problem-solver to an intermediate hypothesis; it must be confirmed by considering classes containing it, and then it must be refined by considering more specific disorders.

in its emphasis on a structured search. The problem solver is not just working with lists of diseases. There are general maneuvers for contrasting, exploring, and seeking evidence in terms of *relations* among diseases. Nor is this model what medical students are taught in textbooks. Students are commonly given an outline of all data that they might collect, organized by "social history," "previous illness," and so on, suggesting that medical diagnosis is a process of collecting data in a fixed order. The result is that students sometimes collect information by rote, without thinking about hypotheses at all!

The aspect of problem solving that involves forming a set of initially unrelated hypotheses and then finding ways to group, contrast, and refine them is often called "initial problem formulation." The capabilities of NEOMYCIN and systems like PIP (Szolovits & Pauker, 1978) and CADUCEUS (Pople, 1982) should be contrasted with the exhaustive top-down analysis used by programs like MYCIN and CENTAUR (Aikens, 1981). In a sense, the process of "looking up" into categories serves as a "big switch" as conceived in the General Problem Solver (Newell & Simon, 1972). It is the operation of viewing the overall problem in dramatically different ways: Did the patient fall and hit his head? Does he have an emotional problem? Is there a congenital weakness in the vascular system? Is there a tumor? Has the patient been infected by a virus? Did the patient consume something toxic? Diagnosing each of these dramatically different processes requires bringing specialized knowledge into play. So we might imagine constructing specialized subsystems of knowledge to deal with infectious disease diagnosis, psychological analysis, and toxic drug disorders, and integrating them by the GROUP-AND-DIFFERENTIATE procedure of comparing and contrasting likely categories of disease.

## A Causal Model of What Happened to the Patient

So far we have described diagnosis in terms of heuristics for carrying on an efficient search of a combinatorially large space. However, it must be remembered that a diagnosis is not just a label, but constitutes *a model of the patient*. This model is a causal story of what has happened to bring the patient to his current state of illness. The general questions of diagnosis regarding travel, job history, medications, and so forth (the categories emphasized to a student) seek to circumscribe the external agents, environments, or internal changes (due to age, pregnancy, or diseases) that may have affected the patient's body. Thus, "establishing the hypothesis space" is more precisely characterized as "establishing the space of causes."

The following protocol excerpt provides a typical causal story, showing how a finding request is intended to establish the space of causes that must be considered:

KE: What about pregnancies? Why is that important?

MD: When I asked about compromised host, that includes a wide spectrum of problems. The pregnant woman is probably the most common compromised host, in that during the pregnancy period women are more susceptible to dissemination of certain types of infections, and cocci is a classic of that. Whereas most of us would localize cocci to the lungs, pregnant women disseminate cocci to the meninges more commonly. The same thing happens with TB.

KE: Would it be fair to say that the question about pregnancy is not necessarily specific to the possibility of a cocci infection, but is of more general interest?

MD: Yes, I think it is of more general interest. It is pertinent to cocci, but would also be considered perhaps in other areas, because it would change your thinking a bit, the pregnant woman having a little different spectrum of infection than a regular, normal person.

Here the expert supplies a causal explanation for how pregnancy affects the body, mentioning the very important concept of "dissemination" – spread of an infectious agent in the body. In trying to establish a causal story of an infectious disease, the physician looks for general evidence of exposure, dissemination, and impaired immunoresponse— all of which are necessary for an infection to take place, regardless of the specific agent. Importantly, diseases can be ruled in or out on the basis of general evidence for these *phases* in the causal process, so the physician needn't directly try to rule in or out all of the specific diseases. Thus, the process of establishing the space of causes reduces to considering broad categories of evidence (e.g., "compromised host" implies impaired immunoresponse), rather than focusing narrowly on every specific causal mechanism and agent that might be involved. Moreover, this might be generalized even further by characterizing some causal stories as "unusual" and others as "typical." Thus, establishing the space of possibilities reduces to determining whether the patient is "typical," or whether "unusual processes" might be occurring. In this style of diagnosis, characteristic of our domain, diagnosis is categorical, with essentially no concern for low-level causal arguments.

In his analysis of the patient, the physician's "process-oriented approach" is manifested in several ways. The most obvious are the general questions (ASK-GENERAL-QUESTIONS) for determining whether the patient has had related problems in the past. This is a key maneuver for circumscribing the problem space. For example, by asking if the patient has been hospitalized, one learns about all serious illnesses the patient has had. This is an excellent starting point for determining what causal processes might be implicated in the current disease. Learning that there have been no previous hospitalizations, illnesses, medications prescribed, and so on, the problem solver can be reasonably sure that he has an accurate database for making decisions: He knows what has affected this patient and can infer that everything else is "typical" or "what one might expect." Thus, the use of general questioning is perhaps the most heuristically powerful technique in medical diagnosis. The anatomically oriented "review of systems" is similar, particularly as a spatial reminder of possible diseases, but it is not used by NEOMYCIN.

Constructing a model of the patient is often described informally as forming a "picture of the patient." The physician establishes the sequence in which findings were manifested and factors this with information about prior problems and therapies, using their time relations to match possible causal connections. For example, a fever might be a precursor to an illness that later manifests itself by abdominal pains. Thus, the physician is not just matching a set of symptoms to a disease; he is matching the order in which the symptoms appeared and how they changed over time to his knowledge of disease processes—a much richer organization than a mere list of symptoms. The physician remembers the sequence, knowing what symptoms to expect or to ask about, based upon his knowledge of the underlying causal process that relates the symptoms to one another.

Another way to understand the importance of process knowledge is to logically consider the importance of differentiating between hypotheses. In a pure sense, this does not mean to confirm them independently, but to gain information that will favor one and disfavor another. This is the sense in which diagnosis is a process of modeling the patient. When the interpretation is ambiguous, it is necessary to gain more information. Discrimination in this way presupposes that there is some *dimension* for comparison. That is, we must have some common way for viewing the competing diseases. In NEOMYCIN, we call this the *disease process frame*. Its *slots* are the features of any disease—where it occurs, when it began, its first symptom, how the symptoms change over time, whether it is a local or "systemic," and so on. This frame applies to more than disease processes, of course. For example, it can be used in the "oil spill problem" (Hayes-Roth et al., 1983) to diagnose the causes of oil spills by their frequency, amount, change over time, periodicity, and location in the network of drainage ditches.

The following excerpt from a class discussion with our expert illustrates how this kind of process orientation is critical to causal reasoning:

TEACHER: Think of the common anemias that a young person might get, and think of anemia in general. There are two ways to look at it. You start out with an adequate number of red cells and you reach the point of being anemic; there are two ways you can do it. You're losing blood excessively, or you're not making enough to replace your normal losses. These divide anemia into two major categories: production deficits or loss of blood. So you can talk about reasons that a young person might lose blood.

Basically, to lose enough blood to become anemic either you are losing it in your stool, GI bleeding, . . . what's a good question about GI bleeds, or the most common reason for blood loss in the United States is what? What physiologic function causes people to lose blood?

STUDENT: Menstruation. She said that it was normal.

TEACHER: Normal. Normal menstrual periods, okay. So now the question is if you don't get a good history for excessive blood loss then you question, are people producing blood adequately? You can have some serious derangement in production such as sickle cell anemia, or they may not have the basic substrates.

Even here, causal reasoning is categorical, with general consideration of production deficiency, loss of product, or substrate (input) limitation.

## Structure of Knowledge

The hypothesis space is structured in many different ways, with different purposes. For example, an etiological taxonomy, based on the *ultimate origins* of disorders, can be contrasted with an "organ system taxonomy," also used in medicine, which is a strict hierarchy by location of the disorder. Siblings of the etiologic taxonomy are alternative causes for a given disease process, which is why the etiological taxonomy is favored over the organ system taxonomy for focusing search during diagnosis.

The task of establishing the hypothesis space blends the good human ability to detect familiar patterns (by data-directed associations) with a critical analysis that considers alternatives and unusual possibilities, with different indexing schemes used for these purposes. Studies indicate that medical experts differ from novices precisely by their ability to call to mind useful categories of disease (Feltovich, et al., 1984). For example, in diagnosis of congenital heart disease, the expert learns the list of causes associated with abnormal noises on the left side of the heart. Feltovich calls this the *logical competitor set*. Significantly, this grouping is often orthogonal to the traditional hierarchies given in textbooks. Similarly, a subset of hypotheses can be remembered by labeling them, as in meningitis we refer to "the unusual causes of bacterial meningitis." Thus, over time the expert evolves a complex organization of hypotheses that is more finely indexed than a simple hierarchy (Feltovich, 1980). The expert efficiently circumscribes the possible causes by relating a familiar interpretation with unlikely but important causes that might be confused with it.

### Activation of Knowledge

Modeling human reasoning requires some model of the activation of knowledge. The idea is basic in medical diagnosis: Any given fact about the patient might have many real-world implications, but only those relevant to diagnostic hypotheses should come to mind. As a simple example, consider a physician who is told that the patient has pets. The expert, diagnosing a possible infectious disease, might ask, "Does the patient have turtles?" Some sort of intersection match has occurred that activated salmonella as a diagnosis (because it is a bacterial infectious disease). If the leading hypothesis had been cancer, it is less likely that the salmonella association with turtles would have come to mind when pets were mentioned. If so, we would say that a shift in focus of attention occurred. A model of data- and hypothesis-directed reasoning, such as NEOMYCIN, must specify how data is used and how focus of attention changes.

Most programs use a form of "spreading activation" (Anderson & Bower, 1980; Rumelhart & Norman, 1983; Szolovits & Pauker, 1978) by which knowledge structures are brought into consideration based on their proximity. NEOMYCIN's model incorporates these dimensions:

- *Context*: In simple terms, this concerns when relations between findings and hypotheses are realized. The value of known findings is realized when a new hypothesis is triggered (see PROCESS-HYPOTHESIS). Support for previously considered hypotheses (ancestors and immediate descendants of the differential) is realized when a new finding is received (see PROCESS-FINDING). These are called *focused forward-inferences*.

- *Strength of association*: "Antecedent rules" are applied immediately (discussed on page 371).

- *Level of effort*: Intermediate subgoals are only pursued when applying "trigger rules," interpreting "hard findings," or deliberately attempting to confirm a hypothesis.

### Summary of NEOMYCIN'S Reasons for Gathering Information

One measure of complexity of NEOMYCIN's model of diagnosis is the number of reasons for requesting a finding. In MYCIN the only reason for asking a question was to apply a rule that concluded about some "goal." This is analogous to the hypothesis and test, "single-operator" view presented

in Figure 12.1 NEOMYCIN's tasks in essence give more structure and meaning to the data-gathering process. Besides testing a hypothesis, the program has the following direct motivations for gathering information (with related tasks in parentheses):

- *follow-up questions that specify previous information* (Given that the patient has a fever, the program will ask what the temperature is.) (CLARIFY-FINDING)

- *process-oriented follow-up questions* (When did a headache begin, how severe is it, where is it located?) (CLARIFY-FINDING)

- *process-oriented discrimination questions* (To discriminate between meningitis and brain-abscess, determine if the disorder is spread throughout the central nervous system or is localized.) (GROUP-AND-DIFFERENTIATE)

- *triggered questions* (Given that the patient has a stiff neck, we might immediately ask whether he has a headache or other neurological symptoms, because of the possibility that this might be meningitis.) (FORWARD-REASON)

- *general questions to determine the availability or presence of findings and tests* (To determine whether the CSF is cloudy, a lumbar puncture must be taken.) (FINDOUT)

- *general questions to establish that the relevant history is complete* (Has the patient been hospitalized recently? Is he taking any medications?) (ASK-GENERAL-QUESTIONS)

The expert-teacher's directives to students are the primary source for formulating the tasks of NEOMYCIN's diagnostic procedure (Appendix III).

## REPRESENTING THE MODEL: STRATEGY AND DOMAIN KNOWLEDGE

NEOMYCIN's abstract and explicit diagnostic procedure distinguishes it from other AI programs. The procedure is *abstract* because it is separated from the domain knowledge—a feature common to frame-oriented systems. The procedure is *explicit* because it is represented in a well-structured way, not arbitrary code—a feature common to rule-based systems.[5] (Rumelhart & Norman, 1983, provides a good, up-to-date discussion of the declarative/procedural distinction.) Here we discuss these two knowledge representations.

---

[5]That is, the procedure is expressed in a language for which we can write an interpreter that can reason about how tasks are invoked, as well as their input and output: The notation is *declarative*.

**Representing Strategy: Tasks, Metarules, and End Conditions**

As already described, the strategy part of the model is represented as subprocedures we call tasks. Each task has an *ordered* list of rules, sometimes called a "rule set," associated with it.[6] We call them *metarules* because they reason about which domain rules (more generally, "domain relations") should be applied to the problem. The metarules determine which causal, subtype, definition, or disease process relations will be exploited for purposes of adding hypotheses to the differential—contrasting hypotheses, focussing on a hypothesis, refining a hypothesis, confirming a hypothesis, or determining whether a finding is present.

For example, the FORWARD-REASON metarule that says, "If there is a red-flag finding, then do forward reasoning with it," is using the relation "red-flag finding" to index the knowledge base. More specifically, this metarule causes red-flag (or significant, abnormal) findings to be considered first. We say that the relation "red-flag finding" *partitions* set of findings. This is the typical way in which metarules use relations that organize domain knowledge to select findings, hypotheses, and relations to apply to the problem at hand. To the degree that a concept like "red-flag finding" can be given a consistent meaning in several problem domains, the diagnostic procedure is domain-independent. It is plausible that we might construct such a theory of knowledge organization because relations like "red-flag finding" are completely defined by how they are used by the diagnostic procedure.

A task has associated with it a description of how its metarules are to be applied. (To "apply a rule" means to determine whether the "if part" of the rule is satisfied [i.e., the rule "succeeds"]; and, if so, to carry out the action specified in the "then part" of the rule.) There are four possibilities:

1. *simple, try-all*: All of the metarules are applied once in sequence (a simple procedure of multiple steps).

2. *simple, don't-try-all*: The metarules are applied in sequence until one succeeds, then the task is complete (control returns to the calling task) (a "do one" selection).

3. *iterative, try-all*: the metarules are applied in order, repetitively, until no rule succeeds (a simple loop; NEOMYCIN currently has no tasks of this type, probably because "try-all" suggests constantly changing methods or following a breadth-first approach).

4. *iterative, don't-try-all*: The metarules are applied in order, with control returning to the head of the list each time a rule succeeds, until no rule succeeds (a "pure production system").

---

[6]Currently, there are 33 tasks and 80 metarules; thus the procedure is highly structured, with relatively few steps or methods for achieving any one task.

The "if part" of a metarule generally examines the working memory and domain knowledge. The "then part" invokes another task, applies a domain rule, or requests a finding of the informant.

A task generally has an argument, known as the *focus* of the task, or that part of the working memory it is operating upon (a finding, hypothesis, or domain rule). A task can have only one focus, but it might be a list, such as the entire differential.

A history is kept of which tasks have been done, recording the focus, if appropriate. Metarules reference this history, for example to determine if a particular hypothesis has been pursued. Other bookkeeping, such as resetting global registers that characterize the state of the differential, is handled by rules applied before or after the task metarules.

A task may have an *end-condition*, which is evaluated whenever a metarule succeeds. If it is satisfied, the task is aborted. Importantly, end-conditions can be inherited from tasks higher on the stack, and each task along the way will be aborted. End-conditions describe either *preconditions*, which must be true for it to make sense to be doing the task (see the end-condition of EXPLORE-AND-REFINE) or *what the task is trying to achieve* (when it can be halted — see GENERATE-QUESTIONS). NEOMYCIN's end-conditions all refer to the differential: the presence of strong evidence for a "competing" hypothesis; the presence of a hypothesis in a new, unexplored category; an "adequate" differential to begin a diagnosis. Some tasks are always allowed to go to completion (indicated by an end-condition of DONTABORT). We can think of the end-condition mechanism as a means for "backing out of a procedure" when it becomes inappropriate or its goal is no longer of highest priority.

In summary, the knowledge for applying tasks—knowledge for controlling metarules, focussing, bookkeeping, and interrupting—constitutes a knowledge base in its own right.

Figure 12.8 summarizes how the diagnostic procedure interacts with domain knowledge. Figure 12.9 shows a task definition and a metarule ex-

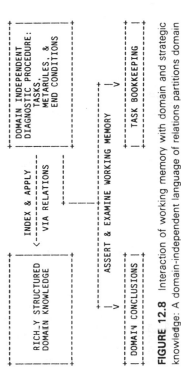

**FIGURE 12.8** Interaction of working memory with domain and strategic knowledge: A domain-independent language of relations partitions domain knowledge enabling a domain-independent procedure to index and selectively apply facts.

**States.**  There are two kinds of states: findings and hypotheses. *Findings* are observations describing the problem. There are two kinds of findings: soft (circumstantial or historical) and hard (laboratory or direct measurements). *Soft findings* tend to be categorical, weak, and easily determined. *Hard findings* are specific, strong, and often costly, dangerous, or time-consuming to determine. *Hypotheses* are partial descriptions of the disorder process causing the findings; that is, hypotheses explain the findings and constitute the problem-solver's diagnosis.[7]

**Causal and Subtype Relations**

Findings and hypotheses can be related by cause and subtype. Various larger structures are built out of these parts:

• *Etiological taxonomy:* a subtype hierarchy of hypotheses. These are the ultimate causes of disorders. For example, in medicine, these hypotheses include poisoning, an injury from falling down, infection by a virus, and psychological problems (refer to Figure 12.6). Associated with each hypothesis are findings or other hypotheses that it causes or that are caused by it. Hypotheses lower in the tree inherit properties of all hypotheses on the path to the root ("ANY-DISORDER"). Thus, bacterial meningitis has manifestations common to all infectious processes, such as fever and inflammation. The leaf-node hypotheses are the most specific causes, usually those that can be treated to alleviate the disorder.

The etiological taxonomy is actually a "tangled hierarchy" based on process relations. Proceeding below INFECTIOUS-PROCESS, the relations of each level are: "location," "chronicity," "class of causal agent," and "causal agent." For example, children of MENINGITIS are ACUTE-MENINGITIS and CHRONIC-MENINGITIS. Thus, each level of the taxonomy further characterizes *the kind of process* in some way. Under this interpretation, the top level of the etiological hierarchy pertains to events in the life process of the device: design, birth, ingestion, growth, injury, and so on. We have found this characterization of the etiological taxonomy to be useful in our initial attempts to apply it to computer software diagnosis.

There may be multiple etiologies requiring treatment. For example, a traumatic injury, such as falling and hitting one's head, can cause certain

[7]Technically, distinctions among states, such as "hypothesis," "soft finding" and "red-flag finding," are unary relations, which we express in metarules as (HYPOTHESIS $STATE), (SOFT-FINDING $STATE) and (RED-FLAG-FINDING $STATE). The states themselves are relations (e.g., (HEADACHE $PATIENT)), though as shorthand we write them as atomic propositions (e.g., HEADACHE). Thus, we write (HYPOTHESIS HEADACHE), rather than (HYPOTHESIS (HEADACHE $PATIENT)).

```
(TASK CONTROL KNOWLEDGE)
  (TASKTYPE PROCESS-FINDING SIMPLE)
  (TASK-TRY-ALL-RULES PROCESS-FINDING)
  (ENDCONDITION PROCESS-FINDING DONTABORT)
  (TASKFOCUS PROCESS-FINDING $FOCUS-FINDING)
  (LOCALVARS PROCESS-FINDING (RULELST SUPERFINDINGS FOCUSQS))
  (ACHIEVED-BY PROCESS-FINDING (METARULE069 . . .))
  (DO-AFTER PROCESS-FINDING (RULE381))

(TYPICAL METARULE)
  (IF (AND (SOFT-FINDING $FOCUS-FINDING)
           (ACTIVE-HYP $HYPOTHESIS)
           (EVIDENCE-FOR $FOCUS-FINDING $HYPOTHESIS $RULE $CF)
           (UNAPPLIED $RULE))
      (TASK APPLYRULE $RULE))

(AUXILIARY RULE)
  (IF (OR (DIFFERENTIAL $HYPOTHESIS)
          (AND (DIFFERENTIAL $H1)
               (CHILD $HYPOTHESIS $H1))
          (AND (DIFFERENTIAL $H2)
               (TAXONOMIC-ANCESTOR $HYPOTHESIS $H2)))
      (ACTIVE-HYP $HYPOTHESIS))
```

**FIGURE 12.9**  Internal form of the task PROCESS-FINDING and one of its metarules (''apply rules using the finding to conclude about a hypothesis in focus'').

pressed in internal form, using the MRS language, a form of predicate calculus (Genesereth, Greiner, & Smith, 1981). (In MRS notation, $X will match whatever term is in the database and once bound will maintain that value in the rest of the expression.) Note that intermediate relations, such as ''active hypothesis,'' are also defined by rules written in MRS. Further details about the advantages of the MRS notation and NEOMYCIN's procedural language for representing strategy appear in Clancy & Brock (in press).

New strategies are generally expressed by writing new metarules and tasks and defining appropriate new structural relations for indexing domain knowledge. In summary, the control language constructs include: tasks, controlled metarules, problem-solving history, end-conditions, primitive actions (ask, conclude, apply a rule), and a relational language for organizing domain knowledge (referenced by the conditional part of metarules). Domain knowledge and its organization is considered in the next section.

**Representing Domain Knowledge:**
**States, Relations, and Strengths**

Domain knowledge consists of states, unary and binary relations defined on states and other relations, and information about the strength of relations.

is usually true about the world. For example, males do not become pregnant; we can't determine directly if a 1-year-old has a headache; adults do not frequently suffer from ear infections. Because there tends to be a different underlying relation for each case we have encountered, this knowledge is currently proceduralized in NEOMYCIN in the form of "don't ask" rules. For example, "If the patient is under 2 years old, don't ask if he has a headache."

• *Definitional*: a finding can be defined in terms of other findings. For example, a neonate is a person under five months of age.

• *Process feature*: a finding or hypothesis can characterize in more detail the process partially described by another finding or hypothesis. For example, the patient's temperature characterizes the finding that he has a fever. A pain can be characterized by location and change in severity over time. Every hypothesis in the etiological taxonomy can be characterized by a set of similar process features. Thus, each process feature constitutes a relation upon which a generalization hierarchy can be based. For example, an organ-involvement hierarchy of hypotheses is based on an hierarchy of locations. (While our work has clarified these distinctions, in our limited domain and with our current knowledge base, we use such multiple hierarchies only in the most limited way.)

Figure 12.10 summarizes how findings and hypotheses can be related.

### Strength of a Relation

Associated with causal relations is a "certainty factor" (CF), as used in MYCIN. For convenience in associating a CF with a causal relation between states, and to signify that the association is a heuristic that omits de-

```
FINDING  subsumes
         is source of
         is further characterized by (process features are)
         defines
         is usually related to (don't ask when)

FINDING  is evidence for (causes or caused by)

         HYPOTHESIS  has process subtypes
                     is etiologic parent of
                     is caused-by

                     HYPOTHESIS
```

**FIGURE 12.10**  Summary of basic domain relations in NEOMYCIN.

forms of bacterial meningitis. Here the treatable cause is really two etiologies: the bacteria must be treated and, if the patient is elderly, some means must be found to prevent the patient from falling again. (In medicine, this relation is sometimes called a "complication" (Szolovits & Pauker, 1978).)

• *Causal network*: hypotheses that characterize general states, neither findings (directly observed) nor etiologic hypotheses (pertaining to specific processes), which are related by cause. To give them a name, we call these general characterizations of abnormal conditions in the device *state/categories*. An example in medicine is "unusual space-occupying substance in the brain," a nonobservable condition, which can have many etiologies. We have found it useful to distinguish between *substances* (or structural features) and *processes*. This does not lead to a complete causal model, but it does provide a useful discipline for our level of representation.[8]

• *Hypothesis subtype hierarchies*: hypotheses (either etiologic or state/category) related by subtype. For example, INTRACRANIAL-MASS has subtypes INTRACRANIAL-TUMOR, INTRACRANIAL-HEMATOMA, and INTRACRANIAL-MASS-OF-PUS. Substances are subtypes of substances; processes are subtypes of processes.

• *Finding subsumption hierarchies*: a presupposition hierarchy of findings. For example, HEADACHE subsumes HEADACHE-SEVERITY, HEADACHE-SEVERITY subsumes HEADACHE-DURATION, and so on, because consideration of headache severity presupposes that the patient has a headache. In NEOMYCIN, a subsumption hierarchy is just a concise way of expressing inference relations among findings. Subsumption can be further characterized by relations such as "component of" and "specialization of" – distinctions we have not yet found to be useful for performance, but that might be useful for teaching.

### Source, World-fact, Definitional and Process Relations

Other domain relations are:

• *Source*: a finding can be the source of a set of findings that are collected together. For example, the complete blood analysis is the source of the white cell count.

• *World-fact*: findings can be related by factual relations based on what

---

[8]One potential difficulty is that this representation is more principled than common medical knowledge. For example, in some cases we found that our expert made no distinction among a substance causing a lesion, the lesion itself, and its functional effects. Thus, a tumor is referred to as a type of lesion, a bit like saying that a pair of scissors is a kind of cut. Traversing a more articulated network may require different strategies than those used by the physician. Indeed, to turn the argument around, composition of relations through "compilation," or blurring of cause/subtype distinctions, as we observed in our expert, may be useful for efficient search. See Clancey (1985) for further discussion.

current problem description and partial solution ("working memory");

- the organization of domain knowledge ("long-term memory");
- the manner in which knowledge is retrieved ("activation criteria").
- *Computational or mathematical constraints:* properties of combinatorial, categorical, and probabilistic search.
- *Assumptions about the world:* disorder patterns, determined by the frequency of problems previously encountered, in turn determined by device weaknesses and external influences on devices. These assumptions or expectations can be used to constrain search.
- *Sociological economy:* to make the correct diagnosis, with the least expenditure of money and time, with due regard for the value placed on life and equipment, and efficiently communicating information needs and decisions.

In using a categorical search, asking general questions first, requesting hard data sparingly after consideration of soft data, maintaining focus until leads have been exhausted, and so on, etc., the problem solver is satisfying these constraints. We make an attempt in Appendix IV to indicate how the constraints are evidenced by individual metarules and their ordering. The main constraints of concern are correctness, efficiency (speed), and minimizing mental effort. Correctness is best evidenced by the systematic search of ESTABLISH-HYPOTHESIS- SPACE; efficiency, by the categorical reasoning of GROUP-AND-DIFFERENTIATE and the use of general questions by FINDOUT; and minimizing mental effort, by the nature of focus changes in PROCESS-FINDING and EXPLORE-AND-REFINE. The constraints can also be grouped in terms of the problem solver's goals (reflecting cognitive and sociological constraints) and constraints imposed by the task domain (mathematical and statistical).

Each task corresponds to some condition the problem solver is trying to make true; the metarules and task control knowledge constitute a procedure for making the condition true. We say that tasks *proceduralize* constraints (VanLehn & Brown, 1979), that is, they seek to *satisfy constraints by conditional actions*. For example, one of the correctness constraints relevant to EXPLORE-AND-REFINE is that all hypotheses placed on the differential must be pursued eventually. One of the ordered metarules for this task says, "If there is a sibling of the current focus that has not been pursued, then invoke PURSUE-HYPOTHESIS with the sibling as focus." Thus, subtasks with a given focus are invoked to satisfy constraints.

The structural properties of NEOMYCIN's domain knowledge reveal an interesting set of cognitive and task domain constraints. However, these properties are a strong reflection of the cases the model has been developed upon, so they are just a set of unrefuted or convenient (known to be false in general) assumptions:

tails, the relation is called a *rule* and given a name. For example, "double vision is caused by increased intracranial pressure," is a rule with CF 0.8. We call the "if part" of the rule the *premise* and the "then part" the *conclusion*.[9] A rule premise is stated as a conjunction and each part involving a finding or hypothesis is called a *conjunct*.

Certainty is dynamically propagated through the network of states by a fairly complicated scheme. Basically, the maximum positive certainty is propagated upward and the minimum negative certainty downward through the multiple hierarchies. Assuming a closed world, a parent will be negative if all of its children are negative. Assuming mutual exclusivity, a sole believed child will inherit all the belief of its believed parent. The "cumulative" CF used in reasoning combines the CF directly inferred from rules with the propagated certainty.

A rule whose strength is very strong might be labeled as being an antecedent or trigger rule. These are defined in terms of activation criteria:

- A causal relation that is *definite*, having a certainty of 1.0, is generally labeled as an *antecedent rule*, so named because the rule will be considered, as part of the program's forward reasoning, when the premise of the rule is known to be true. For example, the double-vision rule is so labeled, so the program will conclude that the patient is experiencing increased intracranial pressure just as soon it learns that the patient has double vision.

- If an antecedent rule is also labeled as a *trigger rule*, then the program will attempt to satisfy the premise of the rule (by gathering additional findings if necessary) as soon as some specified part of the premise (one or more conjuncts) is satisfied.

## Implicit Constraints of the Diagnostic Procedure

Metarules for tasks, as well as subtasks in the action of a metarule, are often ordered, and the criteria for this ordering is not explicit in the model. These ordering criteria are *constraints* which the problem solver is trying to satisfy or which are imposed by his or her reasoning ability. From our study of the metarules, we have identified several sources of constraints in diagnosis:

- *Cognitive Economy:* to incur the least costs in terms of mental effort, acting within the constraints of human memory and reasoning capability; specifically,
  - the size or organization constraints of memory for holding the

[9]Technically, we should call the "if part" the *antecedent* and the "then part" the *consequent*, but we reserve these terms for characterizing the indexing schemes for applying rules.

model's language and is always reliable (see FINDOUT). Interactional methods for talking to patients are certainly a key part of what students learn in the classroom diagnosis games. In the six classroom transcripts we have analyzed, one third of the teacher's interruptions (10 of 30) are directed at giving practical advice of this sort.

In summary, at this stage in NEOMYCIN's development we are developing a procedural language that enables the program to articulate its reasoning. By studying the procedures we write down in this language, we may become able to represent them at a more principled level, in terms of the constraints they seek to satisfy. See Clancey, in press, for a significant expansion of this point. Also see page 383 for a discussion of an expert's awareness of constraints on his behavior.

## EVALUATING THE MODE: SUFFICIENT PERFORMANCE AND PLAUSIBLE CONSTRAINTS

Having considered how NEOMYCIN's model is acquired and represented, we now turn to its evaluation: A general discussion of what the program really is, what it says about the nature of expertise, and what its limitations are. Evaluation is very difficult. At this time, we can only hope to explicate the issues and discuss how we're handling them, rather than describe formal, completed experiments.

In considering evaluation, we take NEOMYCIN as it exists today as an incomplete artifact, and we ask, "What is it?" What kind of program is it? What is its basis in fact? What does it tell us about human reasoning? About knowledge engineering? About computational modeling? This is an opportunity to take stock of the enterprise, criticize the program, and try to determine what has been accomplished.

Four perspectives are useful for evaluating the program, to be considered in this order:

1. *Performance:* Does the program run? Does its behavior (question asking and diagnosis) suitably match, on some domain of problems, the expert behavior we seek to model?

2. *Articulation:* Is the level of explicitness of the representation appropriate? Do the program's explanations of its behavior correspond to the statements made by an expert teacher explaining the tasks and rationale of diagnosis to students?

3. *Accuracy:* Does the program model human reasoning? Are the constraints of the tasks what experts seek to satisfy in their problem solving? Are the implicit assumptions about correctness, efficiency, and cognitive economy justified?

4. *Completeness:* Is the program a comprehensive model of diagnostic

• Every problem that will be encountered can be uniquely characterized in terms of some single disorder that has been diagnosed before (an assumption known to be false in general). These "etiologies" can be organized hierarchically in multiple ways, particularly according to process relations.

• Evidence for disorders is generally weak, requiring categorical reasoning and inheritance of belief.

• There are no "deep" causal models that explain the normal functioning of the device's behavior (an assumption known to be false in general). Therefore, reasoning does not benefit from complete structural (anatomical) information about the device.

• There are few "pathognomonic" findings; that is, findings that clearly identify the disorder.

• Nevertheless, groups of findings strongly "trigger" hypotheses because of the high frequency with which the disorder exhibits that pattern of findings, the disorder's relatively high a priori probability over other hypotheses that explain the findings, and/or the fact that it is a serious and treatable disorder.

• Patterns in finding/hypothesis relations make it possible to characterize findings as "nonspecific" versus "red-flag," "a good general question," "a good follow-up question."

The tasks and metarules are deliberately formalized at a level of detail that will be useful for providing explanations to a student in a tutoring system. However, it is becoming apparent that constraint information is essential for deciding what parts of the model should be emphasized during teaching and what parts might differ with individual abilities and preferences. For example, we might explain student errors by systematically relaxing the constraints of the procedure. We are currently extending the model to include annotations that indicate: what is arbitrary and not part of the model (e.g., order of GENERATE-QUESTIONS metarules); what may reasonably vary among individuals (order of PROCESS-FINDING metarules); what no person could logically expect to do differently (doing FORWARD-REASON before information is received); what individuals might do differently, but which would violate the principles of the idealized model (e.g., doing EXPLORE-AND-REFINE before GROUP-AND-DIFFERENTIATE).

Note that NEOMYCIN's procedure doesn't reflect some of the most important constraints useful for the "present illness interview," namely the constraints of human interaction that require the problem solver to paraphrase finding requests in multiple ways and to cross-check information ("interface constraints"). We assume that the informant speaks the

reasoning? Are the domain knowledge structures and search techniques complete for some domain of problems?

The first two perspectives are concerned with the *sufficiency* of the model for different settings requiring expertise (refer to Figure 12.1). The second two perspectives examine whether this is a *plausible* model of human competence and whether it captures the full range of human diagnostic behavior. We evaluate NEOMYCIN's acquisition and representation from these perspectives in the sections that follow.

## Performance of the Model: Problem Solving

Perhaps a nontrivial point, a prerequisite for claiming that NEOMYCIN is a model at all is that it runs: It "computes" behavior that we can match against the behavior of people. This is a property of the representation of the diagnostic procedure; it is structured into recursive subprocedures, with control information for stopping and printing results. Its activities are to gather information and construct a solution. Contrast this with the constraints (given on page 371) which the tasks implicitly satisfy. Such statements might capture what problem solvers try to accomplish and the background in which they work, but they do not specify the *process* by which consideration of specific domain knowledge and actions taken in the world interact. NEOMYCIN's metarules combine considerations of domain knowledge (via indexing relations) and working memory to conditionally invoke the right subtasks (with the right focus) to satisfy the task constraints.

NEOMYCIN solves problems at least as well as MYCIN. In particular, its conclusions are reasonably close to MYCIN's for the ten cases used in a double-blind evaluation of MYCIN (Yu et al., 1979). However, we demand much more of NEOMYCIN. Unlike MYCIN, it should:

• Reason in a focused, hypothesis-directed way. For example, if the infection is chronic, it should not explore acute subtypes of meningitis. In contrast, MYCIN's question-asking is undirected and exhaustive for all types of meningitis.

• Consider meningitis from initial information and decide what tests to request, such as a lumbar puncture. MYCIN is told that the patient has meningitis and that certain laboratory tests are available. NEOMYCIN must begin with more general, nonspecific findings such as "headache" and "malaise," consider meningitis, and decide when a lumbar puncture would be too dangerous to do.

• Consider competitors of meningitis and know when they are more likely. MYCIN has no knowledge of migraines, tension headaches, brain abscesses, etc. NEOMYCIN carries on a "differential diagnosis," know-

ing when to consider these competitors and how to contrast them.

• Reason more generally about findings; for example, determine what lab test to request, based on subtype and definitional information.

There are other differences in performance (e.g., as specified in the task FINDOUT and FORWARD-REASON), but these are the main ones. Our main technique for testing (and developing) the program is to run cases with different correct diagnoses, but having very similar initial findings. This tests the program's ability to elicit relevant additional information and to adopt different lines of reasoning appropriately. Trivially, the program should not always pursue meningitis. The same evaluation technique is essential for measuring completeness of the model as well. Evaluation of the order of questioning pertains most closely to matters of accuracy and is considered on page 379.

A not insignificant question is, "Why does NEOMYCIN work correctly at all?" There are two aspects to this. First, how can abstract explanations given by a physician (e.g., "look for associated symptoms"), coded as tasks and metarules, produce the right answer? Second, what is the nature of reasoning that allows us to completely separate the domain knowledge from the reasoning procedure? The issue of explanation is treated here; the more general characterization of reasoning is treated in the final section of this chapter.

It is plausible that the expert's explanations should constitute at least the outline of an effective procedure. Recall from the first section of this chapter that all behavior is explained in terms of the *effect* it will have on the expert's thinking. He says, "I'm trying to form and test my hypothesis set in some way." Indirectly, we take this to be his general *task* at that point — what he is trying to do — and write rules that will invoke that task and carry it out. A procedure written to have *the same effects on working memory* will generate the same questions as does the expert, with the same final diagnosis, and can be characterized abstractly by the same explanations supplied by the expert.

The question has a deeper side, however. Do NEOMYCIN's metarules really come from the expert? What do we supply from our knowledge of the constraints of diagnosis? All of the major tasks bear some relation to the expert's explanations, visible most clearly in the classroom discussions when he tells students what they should and should not be doing. (Recall the examples on page 364.) Most of the rules for FORWARD-REASON, FIND-OUT, and ESTABLISH-HYPOTHESIS-SPACE are *inferred* from conclusions the expert states and the questions he asks. But the nature of the inferences are different. For example, FORWARD-REASON and FIND-OUT consist of lists of metarules using straightforward domain relations such as SUBSUMES. That is, we inductively abstract patterns from expert behavior, based on our evolving knowledge of the relations among findings and hypotheses. The simple coappearance of findings in a problem solution is often sufficient to suggest metarules. (For example, the subsumption relation among findings suggests why "travel" would be mentioned at the same time as "lived in Mexico.")

However, ESTABLISH-HYPOTHESIS-SPACE is *a procedure involving search of a taxonomy.* We have to infer both the domain relations and subprocedures from patterns in the expert's questions. Explanations point the way at critical times, and the classroom discussions seem to confirm most of our analysis, as strategies we learn inductively are often stated explicitly in class (particularly the idea of looking up, then down the etiological taxonomy). But most of our confidence in the completeness of the procedure is based on *mathematical considerations of set manipulations,* concepts the expert never mentioned. The idea of getting the right answer into the differential, even at just the highest categorical level, and then winnowing down makes good mathematical sense. In this way, the metarules are designed to work: The constraints of set theory are adhered to at every turn.

In summary, NEOMYCIN's model is not supplied directly by the expert. It is *constructed* by relating his behavior to mathematically logical maneuvers within the data- and hypothesis-driven reasoning scheme. However, our views are strongly guided by the expert's emphasis on what he is trying to do — what he can accomplish, through new evidence, in terms of getting the right answer.

The relation of *empirical* and *rational* approaches for constructing a model has been a subject of much debate (e.g., see Anderson & Bower, 1980). Our methodology is summarized in Figure 12.11. Given the logical basis for much of the model, we might wonder whether

we could construct a proof that the program will always output the right diagnosis. One approach is to break the proof into parts:

1. Prove that the hypothesis that explains the findings or some more general hypothesis will be put into the differential.
2. Prove that it and its ancestors will be examined.
3. Prove that it will be refined to its subtypes and causes.

There are many subtle interactions to consider. For example, considering a hypothesis requires inferring evidence for it by some rule. A rule not applied immediately might be considered later. If a rule is not a trigger rule, it still might be invoked by the GENERATE-QUESTIONS task, but this task won't be invoked if the differential is already "adequate." Thus, a hypothesis might not be considered if belief in some alternative explanation is strong enough. Also, the problem is ultimately reduced to proving that the knowledge base's finding/hypothesis relations are complete and correct, a difficult assumption to start with and difficult to prove independently.

However, this analysis can be used to complement the usual test of running cases. Stepping through it, we discovered that NEOMYCIN did not examine ancestors of state/category hypotheses — a GROUP-AND-DIFFERENTIATE metarule was missing. We conclude that this approach is a worthwhile cross-check for developing the model.

### Performance of the Model: Articulating Reasoning

Evaluating the explanation capability of NEOMYCIN is perhaps best done in a tutorial setting. Does the program use appropriate terminology? Does the program explain its question-asking with appropriate generalizations? A prototype explanation system demonstrates during problem-solving that the program's level of representation is apparently close to the terminology used by the expert (Hasling, Clancey, & Rennels, 1984). As we begin to use NEOMYCIN for teaching, major explanation issues include: (a) the proper mix of abstract and concrete statements; (b) terminology (e.g., task names like ESTABLISH-HYPOTHESIS-SPACE have to be restated); and (c) use of a model to selectively present and summarize reasoning.

One very interesting test of the program's ability to articulate its reasoning involves use of a "student modeling" program. We have transcripts of the discussions of six cases in a classroom, in which one student interviews (and diagnoses) another student who is pretending to have a particular illness. Can we combine a program that uses NEOMYCIN's model with some (hopefully) simple pedagogical rules, to predict not only when the teacher will interrupt the student/physician but (because of model violation) predict

*EMPIRICAL*
Observed Diagnostic and Explanation Behavior of Expert   =====>

**Tasks/Metarules**
Abstracted patterns of knowledge and search and effect on working memory

*RATIONAL*
<=====   Mathematical and Logical Analysis

*Working Program*
(requires that theory be sufficient to solve problems and hence explain phenomena in the world)

**FIGURE 12.11**   Combined empirical and rational methodology (After Anderson & Bower, 1980).

3. The expert used the information tentatively, planning to try to disconfirm the hypothesis or the single finding upon which it was based, should this conclusion play a pivotal part in the final analysis (e.g., should it suggest that a dangerous, invasive test is necessary). That is, he is capable of retracting his conclusions and reconsidering his decisions.

Having listed these, we can now argue about whether other alternatives should be included, as well as which is most likely. Furthermore, given that most researchers would probably opt for the third ("allow retractions") alternative, and NEOMYCIN now uses the second ("assume reliability"), we can proceed to construct cases in which the program's behavior would fail to be an accurate model of how people reason, thus testing the hypothesis that NEOMYCIN is inaccurate in a particular way.[10]

## Difficulties of Extracting Principles from Compiled Knowledge

One effect of experience is that simple domain facts are proceduralized into specific rules for using them, and that rules for controlling reasoning are composed and generalized. This effect is called "knowledge compilation" (Neves & Anderson, 1981). In attempting to formulate a competence model, we want to carefully decompose these rules and state how knowledge is used, separately from the facts themselves. That is, we want to "decompile" expert knowledge, to the extent possible, to get at the primitive knowledge organization and control that lie behind it. Evaluation of accuracy of the model takes place at this lower level.

However, separation of domain facts and abstract control may be difficult if compilation occurs in a principled way. A result of compilation might be systematically mistaken for a new principle, a primitive step of the diagnostic strategy. For example, consider a case in which a finding counts against a hypothesis. Suppose further that the hypothesis has not been considered yet, but is a "child" of some hypothesis that is about to be refined. Now, would the negative evidence be *consciously* noticed by the problem solver at refinement time, when the "children" are logged as hypotheses to pursue (placing them in the differential); or would it not occur until the problem solver focuses on that hypothesis and tries to confirm it? (Similarly, if you are using an agenda, do you note the evidence while putting the

---

[10]Indeed, taking this example, the inability to change conclusions that have been used to form other conclusions is very basic. We should examine the entire model critically from this perspective. For example, we are probably missing FORWARD-REASON metarules that detect that a prior conclusion must be changed or task interruptions (end conditions) that trigger reconsideration of the patient model.

also what he will say? To do this, we either would need more case discussions in NEOMYCIN's domain, or would need to expand the program's domain of expertise.

### Accuracy of the Model

By reduction of the metarules to constraint assumptions, and the separating out of accuracy in the *implementation* of the constraints, arguments about accuracy are reduced to showing that the principles upon which the model is based are valid. NEOMYCIN's design, in which the reasoning procedure is stated in a special, well-structured language, completely separate from the domain knowledge, helps makes these principles clear. We start by writing down how knowledge, working memory, and task behavior interact; then we study what we have written down. With the components of the model factored out this way, each can be examined for plausibility: Could human knowledge be structured hierarchically with multiple indices? Could working memory include a list of hypotheses? Does NEOMYCIN allow its differential to get "too long"? Is the recursive, single-argument invocation structure of tasks plausible? Similarly, we might evaluate the end condition mechanism, means for restoring context, and so on. In fact, there are three considerations, though with some common constraints: the *task/metarule control language, the content of the metarules, and the representation of domain knowledge.*

### Competitive Argumentation

Our primary technique for constructing the model is a form of "competitive argumentation" described by VanLehn (1983; VanLehn, Brown, & Greeno, 1984). We enumerate alternative designs and choose among them in a principled way. For example, in the extended protocol (Appendix II, line 5), observe that the expert mentions evidence for increased intracranial pressure and goes on to use this information immediately. When NEOMYCIN was first given this case, it gathered additional information because "diplopia" did not make increased intracranial pressure certain. Why didn't the expert do this? We list some alternative "designs":

1. The expert *had* made a definite conclusion; NEOMYCIN's evidence rule is incorrect.

2. The expert knew of nothing that could disconfirm his current belief in increased intracranial pressure, and he believed that the current evidence was fully reliable and not susceptible to retraction. So there was no need to gather additional evidence; the current belief was high enough to be useful in any way.

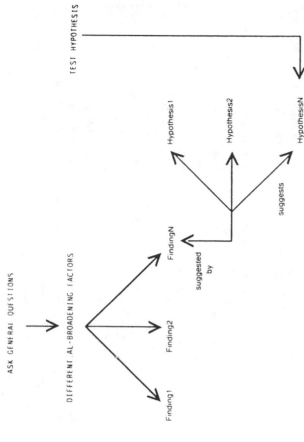

**FIGURE 12.12** Finding request interpreted as a "compiled" general question or a deliberate attempt to confirm a hypothesis.

task of pursuing the hypothesis on the agenda [and decide not to schedule it], *or* when you go to do the task?) It appears that there are no simple answers. It all depends on how long ago the finding was revealed, what the problem solver was thinking about at the time, how strongly he is swayed by other hypotheses, and so on.

A similar example suggests that we are dealing with a general problem about attention and focusing. Does the problem solver notice that a task such as testing a hypothesis is trivially done in some context, when he is looking for a new focus (e.g., in EXPLORE-AND-REFINE when examining hypotheses to pursue). Or is this noticed after the operation is scheduled and begun? Put another way, should the metarule predicate do look-up only and require the invoked task to observe and record completion?

In an expert, compilation of knowledge probably combines scheduling and task behavior. In a novice the separation might be more complete, so that although his behavior is methodical it is also clumsy, and inefficient by not being adapted to routine problems. This suggests that NEOMYCIN is a model of *competence*—what the expert is capable of doing (at the task level), rather than the actual operations (*performance*) he does for any given case. He is traveling on familiar roads and takes shortcuts that are compositions of primitive steps.

In building NEOMYCIN, it has been difficult to isolate unambiguous, principled paths by which the expert indexes knowledge. In some cases, more than one inference path is possible. Indeed, when information is useful for general questions I always ask" rather than "something I need to confirm a specific hypothesis" (see Figure 12.12). In general, it can be unclear whether the expert is *indexing via findings* (asking things he knows will usefully modify his differential) or *indexing via hypotheses* that he currently cares about. As expert reasoning tends to be more data-directed (Chi et al., 1981), subgoals are set up by "trigger rules" (see PROCESS-FINDING in Appendix IV), rather than arising from a hypothesis-directed line of questioning (TEST-HYPOTHESIS). Rubin's model (Rubin, 1975) and ours differ in this respect. In fact, trigger rules occupy an interesting midway point in our model: They are a form of "compiled" knowledge that beginners need to be taught immediately if they are not to be extremely inefficient. Follow-up questions (CLARIFY-FINDING) are another manifestation of compiled knowledge that must be distinguished from deliberate attempts to confirm a hypothesis.

A model of competence is an idealized, "interpreted" statement of expert reasoning—the conscious steps an expert follows when reasoning in a "careful" mode, rather than routinely solving problems. We claim that the expert's knowledge, full of shortcuts as it is, can be expanded into princi-

pled steps (or alternative principled procedures).[11] A principled procedure is an "interpretive simulation" in which the outward behavior of data requests and conclusions is matched, but many intermediate steps (e.g., decide to EXPLORE-AND-REFINE, choose a focus, REFINE-HYPOTHESIS, TEST-HYPOTHESIS, choose a finding) would only be consciously followed by a novice (knowing the right procedure) or an expert faced with a difficult problem.

---

[11]For example, we disallow a rule of the form, "Headache and fever triggers meningitis," because fever is evidence for an infection and meningitis is a kind of infection. The link between fever and meningitis should be made via propagation of belief from the "parent," infectious process. Otherwise, the evidence of a fever is considered redundantly. However, we allow a specialized rule stating "headache and high fever," or its more correct generalization, "headache and evidence for a fulminating infection," because the information about severity is not factored into the belief that the patient has an infection. In general, when we study a rule of the form "A implies B," we must always ask whether there is some hypothesis X in the knowledge base, where X implies B, meaning that the new rule should state that A implies X. In the example given here, we might also decide to have fever trigger infectious process, and write an ordinary evidence rule of high CF that headache implies meningitis. If the patient has a fever, infectious-process will be triggered; meningitis will then be "active" and noticed should it become known that the patient has a headache (see PROCESS-FINDING in Appendix IV and the metarule stated in Figure 12.9).

Furthermore, we must distinguish composition of procedure and medical knowledge with compilation of the medical knowledge base itself. As a set of schemas characterizing diseases, domain knowledge is knowledge of patterns in the world. The problem solver asks, "Of all the problems I have encountered in the world or am likely to encounter, what are the common causes, the serious findings, the general questions important to ask early on? What are the important causes, and useful follow-up questions?" These patterns all relate to importance in terms of *usefulness* (of a finding, based on the number of evidence links or its ability to discriminate) and *likelihood* (of a hypothesis). Thus, by case experience or general knowledge of the problem population, associations are specialized and abstracted, moving to the level of *heuristic knowledge* as opposed to simple facts about cause and subtype. By some form of structural analysis, it may become possible to derive a theory of when a finding would be a good general, trigger, or follow-up question in a given domain. (See Clancey in press for further discussion.)

In summary, in identifying primitive steps and knowledge relations in the diagnostic model, we need to be clear about:

- *Kinds of knowledge:* Figure 12.13 summarizes the basic elements of NEOMYCIN's diagnostic model. The model consists of domain knowledge relations (kinds of patterns); reasoning tasks for using this knowledge (a classification procedure concerning focus and activation of associations); and constraints that could be used to derive the procedure (the rationale for the procedure).

- *Kinds of "knowing":* We claim that a good teacher knows the domain relations and the general tasks for manipulating the differential. He can talk about this knowledge; it is not just reflected in his behavior. In class-

room explanations, the teacher also mentions many social constraints, as well as some logical constraints (regarding search of trees) and some case experience constraints (such as correlations among findings). This is the substance of what we want to teach students.

However, some of the parts of NEOMYCIN's procedure, particularly FORWARD-REASON, describe what experts do and what is essential to construct a complete, runnable model. We believe that these tasks, corresponding to the "cognitive constraints," are generally not consciously considered by experts and needn't be taught. These tasks are not known in the same sense that "serious causes of sore throat" are known; they are automatic, they are how the mind does diagnostic classification. Perhaps FORWARD-REASON and its metarules are more a description of how the hardware works, rather than of a particular software program or strategy. Does ESTABLISH-HYPOTHESIS-SPACE fall in between, so that grouping and refining categories is automatic, but profits from conscious direction (to be aware of and cope with knowledge gaps)? Thus, given that NEOMYCIN is a model of what experts *do*, we must distinguish between the processor and the program, and then overlay a secondary description of what experts *know about what they do.*

We might conclude that a good teacher knows much more about problem solving than the average practitioner. But it is interesting to conjecture that the mark of an expert is precisely this *metaknowledge* of how he reasons: He knows that there are procedures, that these procedures derive from constraints that problem solving must respect, and that there is a mode of reflective reasoning for checking his behavior for completeness and consistency, both for solving difficult problems and for justifying his conclusions (teaching).

- *Origin and development of knowledge:* As discussed in this section, associations can be learned directly by rote (e.g., trigger rules), composed from primitive associations (e.g., headache and fever suggesting meningitis), generalized from experience (e.g., patterns of serious causes of a disease), or instantiated from more general principles (e.g., testing a given hypothesis might be learned as a specific set of things to do, following the principles for testing any hypothesis in general). Complicating the analysis, what is compiled from experience by one problem solver might be taught by rote to another. Finally, in relating behavior to motivational principles or a plan, we must remember that even a sequence of behavior could be generated by more than one plan. It is even possible that automatic behavior is nondeterministic, in the sense that the problem solver's actions are explained by multiple plans (compiled paths of association) and that no single intention consciously produced his actions (J.S. Brown, personal communication, 1986).

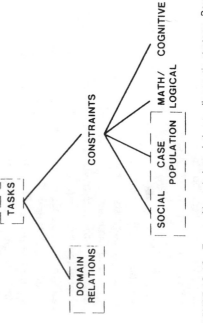

**FIGURE 12.13**  Types of knowledge relating to diagnostic strategy. Boxes indicate what a physician teacher can articulate.

W2: Have you had a lot of sore throats?

W1: No.

M1: So your throat is getting worse? Is that what you are saying?

W1: Well, it's really bothering me and it just keeps dragging on. And before when I've had a sore throat, I had if for a few . . . a couple days.

M1: I see.

W1: It would be gone, but it just keeps dragging on and I'm just feeling terrible.

M2: Does anything make the sore throat better? Have you tried gargling?

W1: Um, well I haven't really done too much about it. I just thought it would go away, but it hasn't and as they said I'm just . . . I'm feeling really tired and not feeling very good.

M1: Your sore throat is always as painful when you get up in the morning or is it getting worse during a certain time of the day?

W1: Well, I guess I haven't noticed too much difference.

M1: I see.

TEACHER: Let me ask you a question. When you ask these questions about whether gargling makes it better or worse, or whether it's better certain times of the day, are you thinking about how that's going to help you move down different differential diagnoses?

M1: Uh huh.

**FIGURE 12.14**  Classroom discussion illustrating a diagnostic error.

The decomposition of knowledge types in NEOMYCIN has allowed us to make substantial progress toward characterizing what physician teachers know and communicate with their students. However, we have barely begun to properly account for the origin and development of this knowledge.

### Using a Competence Model to Explain Variant Behavior

By assumption, the "careful mode" of reasoning is principled. A good way to extract these principles is to give experts difficult problems. In this way we characterize the nature of expertise and how experts and novices might differ. In particular, as already suggested, a principled analysis of mechanisms has real relevance for explaining errors that people make in diagnosis.

A good example of a principled error appears in the classroom excerpt of Figure 12.14. Several students are interviewing the student W1, who is pretending to be a patient. The students' questions about sore throats are not random. The students appear to be looping in the task of CLARIFY-FINDING, following the principle of characterizing a finding in terms of the process (see Figure 12.15, parse 1). The error or misconception is that not every process question you might ask will be useful. If the students know the strategy of characterizing a finding, they are applying it at the right time with the right focus, but their knowledge base is not right: What are the useful follow-up questions to ask about a sore throat? In fact, there might not be any in general; instead a causal analysis should be undertaken (form a hypothesis and test it).

Given that the "useful follow-up questions" are determined by case experience, this analysis suggests that some parts of "compiled knowledge" may normally be taught directly, rather than learned from experience. That is, *experiential knowledge—knowledge about how to efficiently solve problems, given a certain population of cases—may be learned by apprenticeship, rather than individual practice.* Trigger rules and useful general questions, two other forms of "compiled knowledge" in NEOMYCIN, are probably also taught directly to students.

An alternative analysis of the sore throat protocol is that the students might not know what causes a sore throat, so their differential is inadequate. They might be following the strategy of ELABORATE-DATUM, a subtask of GENERATE-QUESTIONS, attempting to elaborate known symptoms until some new clue triggers a hypothesis. This illustrates how we might explain student behavior in a principled way in terms of the expert's diagnostic procedure operating on different domain knowledge. Having stated the procedure separately from the medical knowledge, we have a basis for inferring what students are doing, the state of their working memory (e.g., an inadequate differential), and hence their knowledge of domain relations. Thus, even if we don't need to teach the diagnostic procedure, it is useful for motivating teaching of domain facts and for detecting deficiencies.

We can of course generate an infinity of interpretations if we relax the assumption that the student's procedures are correct. For example, perhaps stuck with an inadequate differential, the students don't know enough to do GENERATE-QUESTIONS, but are instead attempting to "repair" their procedure. They can't continue, so they are looping on the last successful operation. In addition, they might not know the useful follow-up questions to ask, but they know the principle that allows them to generate candidates. This kind of analysis could be pursued by competitive argumentation.

As another example of an incorrect procedure, consider the issue of when TEST-HYPOTHESIS can be interrupted. Suppose a finding becomes known that is relevant to some hypothesis that was previously considered, but that is not the current focus. Under what conditions does the problem solver notice the association and when will he actually shift attention to pursue the other hypothesis? Under one scheme, used by NEOMYCIN, "processing a finding" means deliberately widening attention to notice the relevance to any activated hypothesis. Under another scheme, the problem solver might only observe the relevance of findings to his current focus. The narrowly focused problem solver might never realize the significance of data to other hypotheses he cares about.

The very notion of a "task" as something that the problem solver does deliberately, a thinking problem he imposes upon himself, allows us to distinguish among problem solvers according to the tasks they bring upon themselves in various situations, such as when a new finding is revealed. When distinctions in the model have implications for correctness of the diagnosis, it will be important that the model be annotated at this level of detail, so the teaching program can know and point out the important tasks the students are failing to do.

## Completeness of the Model

Whereas "accuracy" is concerned with the correctness of the assumptions and constraints of the diagnostic procedure, "completeness" is concerned with coverage of the model: Does a wider population of problems require more problem-solving techniques? Given the association between metarules and constraints, this question approximates asking whether we have identified all of the relevant constraints that the task demands, and taken into account all of the relevant capabilities of human reasoning.[12] As already stated, NEOMYCIN's problem domain does not require all forms of diagnostic reasoning that have been studied elsewhere. Without attempting to examine the underlying issues, we simply list many of the limitations we know about:

• Reasoning about structure and function of the body (Davis, 1983; Genesereth, 1984).

[12]Naturally, testing the program for accuracy may suggest ways in which the program is incomplete (e.g., the possibility of retracting conclusions).

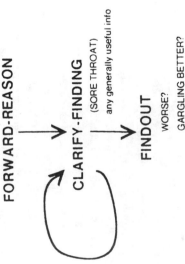

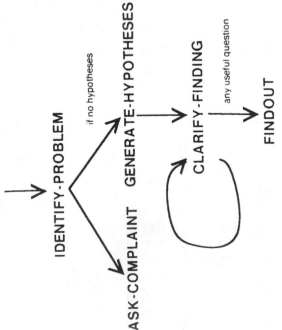

**FIGURE 12.15**   Alternative parses of student behavior shown in Figure 12.14.

work, which is the main product of this effort. Here the main considerations are both *psychological*, at the level of interrupting and restoring focus of attention and metalevel reasoning about an agenda of tasks; and *representational*, at the level of belief maintenance, the constructed model of the problem, and intersection-search procedures.

## Summary of Evaluation

We have argued that evaluation of the accuracy and completeness of the model should focus on the assumed constraints pertaining to knowledge structure, task requirements, human memory, and reasoning. Evaluation of performance and articulateness requires exercising the program in different, complex settings, including consultation, teaching, and learning. More specifically, we find ways in which the same knowledge must be used in multiple ways. We examine how a particular knowledge organization (e.g., subsumption) is used by different strategies and how a given strategy is applied in different contexts for a single case. Multiple cases enable us to vary the task, preventing us from tailoring strategies to particular cases, and revealing not only where the model falls short but what properties of the task domain made the model appear adequate in other cases. Applying the model to other domains, such as computer software failure diagnosis, further reveals unprincipled or inadequately specified parts of the model (e.g., what is an etiological taxonomy?), and brings out assumptions about the task domain that are implicit in the model (e.g., the nature of the informant).

- Analogical reasoning using "device models" (Gentner & Stevens, 1983).
- Interview techniques for getting reliable information from laymen (e.g., commonsense ways of detecting weight loss; finding out whether the patient has had rheumatic fever; knowing what the "white pill" is).
- Description of causality and disease processes on multiple levels of abstraction (Patil, et al., 1981).
- Distinguishing among different forms of "subsumption."
- Temporal reasoning: onset and progression of disease.
- Using probabilistic information about findings, such as frequency information, to bias and rule out hypotheses.
- Determining whether there is adequate evidence for a hypothesis should be contextual, taking into account other hypotheses and unexplained findings (Cohen & Grinberg, 1983).
- The problem solver must strive for coherency by explaining the "important" findings and explaining findings inconsistent with each other or which violate expectations formed by his hypotheses. The program's "differential" should be a "case specific model" (Patil, et al., 1982) that merges findings and hypotheses.
- A real-world expert must deal with multiple, interacting, concurrent problems. The problem solver must separate causes from complications (Pople, 1982; Rubin, 1975; Szolovits & Pauker, 1978).
- NEOMYCIN's causal network is too simplistic to determine the completeness of its strategies. For example, when the causal connections between data and the taxonomy are long and complex, it is not feasible to follow each path (possible cause), testing and confirming intermediate states along the way (Pople, 1982). However, as mentioned in the section "The Hypothesize-and-test theory of diagnosis," such an articulated model may even require different strategies than used by people, for it poses different search problems. We speculate that experts are searching a highly composed model of disorders, not based on clear subtype and causal distinctions, but allowing for highly efficient search.
- Urgency, cost, the ability to treat a disease, and human values in general must be factored into the model explicitly.

Demonstrating the difficulty of this problem, the exclusions are more complex than what the model includes. Of course, the aim of the work has been to develop a representation useful for teaching, not the most comprehensive model of diagnosis. It is premature to "flesh out" the model in all possible ways. However, gaps in the model require that we argue for its extensibility, particularly within the task/metarule/end-condition frame-

## CONCLUSIONS

The driving force in NEOMYCIN's development has been to design a knowledge representation that can be used to model human diagnostic reasoning and explanation capability. The essential (and novel) aspect of the design is representation of the diagnostic procedure as abstract tasks that capture what structural effect the problem solver is trying to have on his evolving model of the problem. These tasks are invoked in a rule-like way that strongly emphasizes the problem solver's use of relational knowledge about the domain in choosing his or her next move.

What is the nature of reasoning that enables such a model of expertise to work? First, there must be relatively more stereotypical situations (tasks and metarule conditions) than special case rules. It must be possible for problem solving to proceed step-by-step in a principled way (even if this would be unnecessary for the experienced problem solver), without the user encountering combinatorial problems. Second, knowledge about possible solutions and problem features must be richly structured. These relations

early on. The orientation toward "things to think about" is directly useful for teaching. Particularly, the idea of thinking in a hypothesis-directed way must be encouraged (but is this because students simply lack the automatic associations?). Perhaps the grammar or logic of diagnosis need not be conveyed explicitly, but certainly it is useful for a teacher of medicine to know it. How often have teachers criticized students, when the latter were just following the procedure used by experts for coping with limited knowledge?

The idea of teaching students strategies or "how to think" has received considerable attention from AI researchers. Papert's work with LOGO (Papert, 1980) is perhaps the most well-known experiment in applying computational ideas to help problem solving in general. Our work raises interesting questions in this regard. For example, could someone familiar with our description of EXPLORE-AND-REFINE in terms of "looking up and looking down," and viewing diagnosis as a set-construction activity, provide *better* explanations than those given by our expert-teacher? That is, having studied the constraints of the task more systematically than has the expert, can we give students a better idea of what they should be trying to do?

A teacher using NEOMYCIN's model could go a step beyond Polya (1957) and others (e.g., Schoenfeld, 1981) who have tried to teach reasoning strategy to students. To contrast this with other research in teaching general strategies, we emphasize the role of domain relations ("structural knowledge") in selecting among different operators that affect the hypothesis space. From our perspective, Polya's heuristics might seem vague and unworkable (Newell, 1983) because:

1. They are not presented as parts of a comprehensive task structure or metastrategy (as pointed out by Schoenfeld).
2. They lack a premise part that refers to working memory, the situation in which the problem solver will find them to be useful for something he is trying to do; that is, they are not stated as conditional operators.
3. The way in which they index particular mathematical solution methods is not clearly worked out; that is, the domain relation vocabulary is missing.

NEOMYCIN's relational vocabulary consists of causal, subtype, and process relations that classify and link findings and hypotheses. Some of the specific terms considered in this chapter are: finding, soft-finding, red-flag finding, substance, and process location. These terms are like parts of speech and syntactic units that classify and organize the problem solver's domain lexicon. This is *knowledge for organizing knowledge:* a means for expressing and using knowledge.

provide means for multiple, orthogonal hierarchical indexes that greatly facilitate search. Note that these constraints are general; they are what enable us to form *any* abstract model of strategy.

One purpose of NEOMYCIN has been to develop a language for representing abstract strategies. Follow-on work is concerned with using them in explanation (Hasling, et al., 1984) and constructing a student model (London & Clancey, 1982). There are many advantages that can be useful in building any expert system (Clancey, 1983b). In our continuing development we are slowly, but constantly, adding to the strategic model. We are still at the point where a carefully chosen case will reveal one or two important limitations in the model. In short, we are following an "enumeration methodology": Writing what we want to study in some language, and organizing the collection to find underlying themes, and further developing the language to express important distinctions.

How applicable is the diagnostic procedure to other domains? The limitations described in section "A Causal Model of What Happened to the Patient" suggest that the model is far from complete. For example, electronic diagnosis often requires low-level causal analysis, working backward from symptoms to component failures (Davis, 1983). However, at a higher and more functional level, particularly for an expert who has debugged a particular device such as a given television or automobile model many times, we can expect that stereotypical matching as in infectious disease diagnosis will occur. In this sense, NEOMYCIN's diagnostic procedure will carry over to other domains. It should be viewed as a subset of a complete procedure, rather than as a specialized or oversimplified model.

What is the relation of NEOMYCIN to what the expert does? The model can be used to explain his or her behavior in the sense that it can generate it; but above the level of finding requests and hypotheses, the procedure is an abstraction, not steps the expert always consciously considers. In this sense, the diagnostic procedure is a *grammar* for parsing a series of information-gathering questions. By analogy with the grammar of natural language, it may reflect the innate nature of human reasoning, specifically how knowledge is remembered. Given that the procedure we have formalized operates entirely upon stereotypic knowledge of disorders, it can be characterized as a *procedure for searching classification knowledge.* Or, since all knowledge may be in some sense compiled (e.g., encoded hierarchically as differences from patterns), the diagnostic procedure is analogous to Kolodner's "executive strategies" for remembering (Kolodner, 1983). However, the NEOMYCIN model pertains to the entire information-gathering procedure of diagnosis, not just a single probe of memory.

As a matter of practice, the diagnostic procedure has some of the same value to an expert that knowledge of grammar provides for a writer. As in grammar, some elements of diagnosis must be taught or at least enforced

plish a certain task, think about some finding (or hypothesis) that is related to your current hypotheses (or known findings) by the X relation. "To refine a hypothesis, consider common causes. What are the common causes of a sore throat?" As a self-directive, this is an example of metacognition. Strategies orient the problem solver toward constructing and refining an appropriate problem space. They constitute the *managerial knowledge* by which the problem solver directs his or her attention and so brings his or her expertise to bear on the problem. Having gone beyond MYCIN's single-layer, "quick association" model of thinking (as Schoenfeld has character-ized traditional expert systems), we are poised to experiment with teaching strategic reasoning.

Indeed, we have now entered a strange sort of loop in our research. We are teaching the diagnostic strategy to research assistants to make them better computer program debuggers. (The general question, "Has the patient un-dergone surgery?" becomes "Has this program been edited since it last worked?") This experience suggests ways to generalize the model, helps us to develop ways to teach it, and may enable us to implement the teaching program itself more efficiently. And so again we find ourselves amid the complex web of learning, teaching, and problem solving.

## APPENDIX I: BASIC TERMINOLOGY OF DIAGNOSIS

*Diagnostic Problem*: A situation in which a device exhibits behavior (find-ings) that suggest that it is malfunctioning. A diagnostic problem has a "cause" that, for our purposes, is one of a set of known processes (hypotheses). Example: A severe headache for a week and double vision in a patient is a diagnostic problem.

*Finding*: An observable problem feature, generally characterizing the problem in a very narrow, nonexplanatory way. In medicine, these are signs, symptoms and laboratory data. Example: A headache is a finding.

*Hypothesis*: An interpretation of findings in terms of underlying sub-stances and processes that produce them. A hypothesis can be said to "ex-plain" the findings. Example: "Space-occupying substance in the brain" is a hypothesis.

*Differential*: The most specific set of hypotheses that the problem solver is considering. By the "single-fault assumption" these hypotheses are mutu-ally exclusive and therefore competing. Example: A typical differential might be brain abscess and chronic meningitis.

*Domain Knowledge*: Findings, hypotheses, and relations among them that enable inferences to be drawn about their applicability. Example: Medi-cation "subsumes" antibiotics, analgesics, and steroids. Example: An "evi-dence relation" links a finding to a hypothesis that causes or might be caused by it, as viral meningitis is caused by exposure to the disease.

*Task*: What the problem-solver is trying to do with respect to findings, hypotheses, and his or her domain knowledge. A task is accomplished by a procedure of ordered conditional actions, called metarules. We say that the metarules "achieve" the task. For example, the metarules of the task PURSUE-HYPOTHESIS test and refine a given hypothesis. Primitive tasks are to request information about a finding and to make an inference about a finding or hypothesis.

*Focus*: The finding, hypothesis, or differential that is the argument to a task; for example, the hypothesis that the problem solver is trying to test.

*Metarule*: A conditional statement that partially accomplishes a task by invoking subtasks. For example, "If the task is to establish the space of hypotheses relevant to this problem and the differential has been reduced and refined, then ask general questions." Metarules are either conditional steps in a procedure or ordered alternative methods for accomplishing a task.

*Constraint*: Some condition that the problem solver must try to satisfy, such as to solve the diagnostic problem in the shortest amount of time; or some limitation or capability of his ability to reason that he must cope with, such as his ability to remember the extent of his knowledge or the differential.

## APPENDIX II: DETAILED ANALYSIS OF A PROTOCOL

In the protocol that follows, annotations indicate the NEOMYCIN tasks that would generate the finding requests and hypothesis assertions made by the expert.[13] Numbers in parentheses refer to numbered statements that sup-port the interpretation. Annotations precede the expert behavior they are intended to explain. This analysis illustrates the knowledge acquisition tech-nique, the nature of the diagnostic problem, and the model's representa-tion in terms of tasks, focus, and domain relations. Note that the metarules that cause the tasks to be invoked are not indicated here; they are listed in Appendix IV. Figure 12.16 shows a parse tree of the physician's five data requests, which appear *italicized* in the protocol. By comparison with Figure 12.5, this protocol can be seen to illustrate the central part of the diag-nostic procedure, but not most of the tasks.

[13] Although we have a prototype modeling program that can generate similar annotations, they are still not nearly as good as what we can do by hand. In the interest of making NEO-MYCIN's model as comprehensible as possible, it seems best to show here the best interpreta-tions we can supply.

ESTABLISH-HYPOTHESIS-SPACE
- GROUP AND DIFFERENTIATE
  - TEST-HYPOTHESIS (BRAIN-MASS-LESION)
  - FINDOUT (FOCALSIGNS)
    - WEAKNESS 10
    - FEVER 16
  - TEST-HYPOTHESIS (INFECTION)
    - TB EXPOSURE 24
    - TEST-HYPOTHESIS (TB-MENINGITIS)
      - TB PNEUMONIA 26
- EXPLORE-AND-REFINE
  - PURSUE-HYPOTHESIS (CHRONIC-MENINGITIS)
    - TEST-HYPOTHESIS (COCCIDIOMYCOSIS)
      - SJ VALLEY TRAVEL 29

**FIGURE 12.16**   Parse with respect to the diagnostic model of the five questions asked in the protocol.

1 KE:   What I wanted to do different in these cases is to pick cases where I thought you might have to request more information than what I gave originally so we can look at a little bit of that process. In these cases especially, you can be as complete as possible in telling me what you are thinking.

2 MD:   So you just want to give me skeleton data?

3 KE:   Yes, we'll see how it goes. I am going to try to follow the general principle we had established, which was to tell you why the person was in the hospital and how they got to the point where the lumbar puncture was done.

4   First example: A 15-year-old female. A two-week history of headache, nausea, vomiting; and diplopia one day prior to admission.
    task = IDENTIFY-PROBLEM
    task = FORWARD-REASON (headache, nausea, vomiting, diplopia, headache-duration, nausea-duration, vomiting-duration, diplopia-duration)
    structural knowledge: diplopia is a serious (red flag) CNS finding
    task = PROCESS-FINDING (diplopia)
    task = APPLY-ANTECEDENT-RULES (causes of diplopia
    evidence rule: diplopia caused-by increased-pressure-in-brain (6)

    task = PROCESS-FINDING (diplopia-duration)
    task = APPLY-ANTECEDENT-RULES (mentioning diplopia-duration)
    definition: max(duration of CNS findings) = CNS-problem-duration (5)

5 MD:   (I think this would be a very good case to illustrate whether you should do a lumbar puncture or not.) This is somebody who has evidence of perhaps a pressure buildup in the brain for a two-week period of time.
    [Causal explanation: how pressure buildup causes diplopia]

6   The diplopia comes because as the pressure builds up in the brain, you can't focus your eyes properly. It is a very sensitive indicator. One of the nerves that enervate the movement of the eyes together is the first one that is impaired as the pressure builds up,
    task = PROCESS-HYPOTHESIS (increased-pressure-in-brain) (7)

7   so that I would be concerned in this situation of increased pressure in the brain
    task = APPLY-ANTECEDENT-RULES (causes of increased-pressure-in-brain)
    evidence rule: increased-pressure-in-brain -> brain-mass-lesion)

    task = PROCESS-HYPOTHESIS (brain-mass-lesion) (8)
    add differential: brain-mass-lesion
    task = PURSUE-HYPOTHESIS (brain-mass-lesion)
    task = REFINE-HYPOTHESIS (brain-mass-lesion)
    structural knowledge: brain-mass-lesion subsumes brain-tumor, hematoma, and collection of pus.

8   and worry about tumor—a mass lesion of some type: a collection of blood, a collection of pus.
    task = PROCESS-FINDING (serious-CNS-finding)
    task = APPLY-ANTECEDENT-RULES (serious-CNS-finding)
    evidence rule: serious-CNS-finding -> meningitis (9)
    task = PROCESS-HYPOTHESIS (meningitis)
    add differential: meningitis
    task = APPLY-EVIDENCE-RULES (known findings activated by meningitis)
    evidence rule: CNS-problem-duration -> chronic-meningitis (9, 22)
    replace differential: meningitis -> chronic-meningitis

9   If it is a meningitis it is clearly a chronic one because we are talking about a two-week history.
    task: GROUP-AND-DIFFERENTIATE (brain-mass-lesion, chronic-meningitis)
    structural knowledge: brain-mass-lesion is a focal process; (12) chronic-meningitis is a systemic process.
    task: FINDOUT (focal-manifestations) (13)
    structural knowledge: focal-manifestations subsume diplopia (13)
    structural knowledge: focal-manifestations subsume weakness (14)
    task: FINDOUT (weakness)

10  The next historical question that I would want to know: *Does she have any weakness anywhere in her body? One side weaker than the other?*

11 KE: *Why do you ask that?*

12 MD: Since this picture is very suggestive of a focal lesion in the brain,

13  I am wondering if there are any focal manifestations other than double vision,
    [Causal explanation: that brain problem affects body extremity]
    [Structural knowledge: focal neurological findings subsume one-sided hand-weakness and leg-weakness]

14  e.g., "My hand right has been very weak" and I would wonder if there is something happening in the brain which enervates the right hand. Or, has she been having trouble walking, with one leg being weaker than the other, or is her balance off. Those are what are called focal neurological findings.

15 KE: Okay. Focal signs in general . . . unknown.
    task: GROUP-AND-DIFFERENTIATE (brain-mass-lesion, chronic-meningitis)
    structural knowledge: chronic-meningitis is an infection
    task: TEST-HYPOTHESIS (infection) (18)
    evidence rule: fever -> infection (21)
    task: FINDOUT (fever)

16 MD: *Has she had fevers?*

17 KE: Unknown.

18  I think that is an important question to help distinguish between an infectious cause versus a noninfectious cause.

19  [Structural knowledge: blood clot = hematoma and brain tumor are not infectious causes]

20 KE: A noninfectious cause being a blood clot or brain tumor.

21 MD: So the fact that if there weren't a fever, that would suggest . . . ?

22  Not having a fever does not necessarily rule out an infection. But if she had a fever, it would be more suggestive of it.
    The situation we are dealing with is a chronic process.
    task: TEST-HYPOTHESIS (chronic-infection)
    evidence rule: low grade fever -> chronic-infection (23)

23  Sometimes with chronic infections fever can be low or none at all.
    task: PURSUE-HYPOTHESIS (chronic-meningitis)
    task: REFINE-HYPOTHESIS (chronic-meningitis)
    structural knowledge: chronic-meningitis subsumes TB-meningitis, fungal-meningitis, and partially-rx-bacterial-meningitis (33)
    add differential: TB-meningitis, fungal-meningitis, and partially-rx-bacterial-meningitis
    task: EXPLORE-AND-REFINE (TB-meningitis, fungal-meningitis, and partially-rx-bacterial-meningitis)
    task: PURSUE-HYPOTHESIS (TB-meningitis)
    task: TEST-HYPOTHESIS (TB-meningitis)
    evidence rule: tuberculosis-exposure - > TB-meningitis
    task: FINDOUT (tuberculosis-exposure)

24  *Has she had any exposure to tuberculosis?*

25 KE: No. No TB risk.
    task: PROCESS-FINDING (negative TB-risk)
    task: FINDOUT (TB-risk)
    structural knowledge: TB-risk subsumes tuberculosis-pneumonia
    task: FINDOUT (tuberculosis-pneumonia)
    structural knowledge: pneumonia subsumes tuberculosis-pneumonia (26)
    task: FINDOUT (pneumonia)

26 MD: *No recent pneumonia that she knows of? Tuberculosis-pneumonia?*

27 KE: Let me see how complete "TB risks" is. According to MYCIN, they include one or more of the following: Positive intermediate trans-PPD; history of close contact with person with active TB; household member with past history of active TB;

atypical scarring on chest x-ray; history of granulomas on biopsy of liver, lymph nodes, or other organs.
task: FORWARD-REASON
(+PPD, contact-TB, family-TB, x-ray-TB, granulomas)
structural knowledge: TB-risk subsumes +PPD, contact-TB, family-TB, x-ray-TB, granulomas

28 MD: That's pretty solid evidence against a history of TB.
task: EXPLORE-AND-REFINE (fungal-meningitis and partially-rx-bacterial-meningitis)
task: PURSUE-HYPOTHESIS (fungal-meningitis)
task: REFINE-HYPOTHESIS (fungal-meningitis)
structural knowledge: likely fungal-meningitis causes are coccidiomycosis and histoplasmosis (33)
add differential: coccidiomycosis and histoplasmosis
task: PURSUE-HYPOTHESIS (Coccidiomycosis)
task: TEST-HYPOTHESIS (Coccidiomycosis)
evidence rule: San-Joaquin-Valley-travel -> Coccidiomycosis
task: FINDOUT (San-Joaquin-Valley-travel)
structural knowledge: travel subsumes San-Joaquin-Valley-travel (29)
task: FINDOUT (travel)

29     *Has she traveled anywhere? Has she been through the Central Valley of California?*

30 KE: You asked TB risks because?

31 MD: I asked TB risks because we are dealing here with an indolent (chronic) infection since we have a two-week history.

32     I am thinking, even before I have any laboratory data,

33     of infections, chronic infections are most likely. So I'll ask a few questions about TB, cocci, histo and other fungal infections.

34 KE: Histo is a fungal infection?
[structural knowledge: histo location is Midwest]
[structural knowledge: cocci location is Arizona and California]

35     Histoplasmosis is a fungus infection of the Midwest. Cocci is the infection of Arizona and California.

36 KE: So you are focussing now on chronic infections. Why would you look at the history now before doing anything else?

37 MD: I am trying to approach it as a clinician would. Which would be mostly to get a lot of the historical information and do a physical exam, then do a laboratory.

38     A lot of times, people think *from* the laboratory, whereas I think you should think *for* the laboratory. People are talking more about that now, especially because the cost of tests are an issue. You can get a lot from just talking with the patient. I could ask for the LP results, then go back and ask questions. But without knowing the LP results, which would bias me in the way I am going to ask the questions.

39 KE: This helps you. . . .

40 MD: This is the way you approach a patient.

## APPENDIX III:
## EXPERT-TEACHER STATEMENTS OF DIAGNOSTIC STRATEGY

We summarize here the general principles of the model, with excerpts from expert problem-solving and classroom protocols. The tasks of the model are a set of directives for changing focus, testing hypotheses, and gathering information. Note the expert-teacher's method of combining abstract and concrete explanations.

• ESTABLISH-HYPOTHESIS-SPACE — Establish the breadth of possibilities, then focus.

TEACHER:     . . . All the cases we have had have fit pretty nicely into trying to establish a breadth of possibilities and then focussing down on the differential within one of the categories.

• GROUP-AND-DIFFERENTIATE — Ask yourself, "What are the general processes that could be causing this?"

TEACHER:     Do you have in mind certain types of sore throats that . . . ? Because the types of questions that you ask early on, once you have a sense of the problem, would be to ask a couple of general questions maybe that could lead you into other areas to follow up on, rather than zeroing in.

STUDENT:     Ok.

TEACHER:     I was asking that because I think it's important to try to be as economical as possible with the questions so that each question helps you to decide one way or the other. At least with sore throat and my conception of sore throat, I have a hard time thinking of how different types of pain and different types of relief pattern are going to mean different etiologies to the sore throat. . . .

TEACHER (different case): What diseases can wind up in congestive heart failure? Congestive heart failure is not a diagnosis, it's kind of an end-stage physiology and there are lots of diseases that lead into congestive heart failure; lots of processes, one is hypertension. What's the other most common one? There are two that are common in this country. One is hypertension, what's the other most common one?

STUDENT: Atherosclerosis?

• TEST-HYPOTHESIS — Ask yourself, "How can I check this hypothesis?"

TEACHER: How can you check whether someone is anemic? What question might you ask?

• ASK-GENERAL-QUESTIONS — Ask general questions that might change your thinking.

TEACHER: Well, that's an important question I think. Sometimes you can ask it very generally, like, "Is there anything... have you had any major medical problems or are you on any medications?" Then people will come back and tell you. And that's an important issue to establish, whether somebody is a compromised host or a normal host because a normal host... Then you have a sense of what the epidemiology of diseases is in a normal host... When you talk about compromised host, you're talking about everything changing around, and you have to consider a much broader spectrum, different diagnoses. So, you might ask that question more specifically, you know, "Are you taking any medications or do you have any other medical problems, like asthma," or sometimes they're taking steroids. Those types of general questions are important to ask early on, because they really tell you how soon you can focus down.

STUDENT: Are you on any medication right now?

• GENERATE-QUESTIONS — Try to get some information that suggests hypotheses.

TEACHER: You're jumping around general questions and I think that's useful. I don't know where to go at this point. So this is the appropriate time for a kind of a "buckshot" approach ... every direction till we latch onto something that we can follow up, because right now we just have a very non-specific symptom.

TEACHER (later): Ok, so we think about infectious, but what other things might be running through your mind in terms of broadening out again? We've got a new set of findings now, besides fever and sore throat, we have...

• EXPLORE-AND-REFINE — Scan the possibilities and choose one to explore in more detail.

TEACHER: Anything else? Well there are probably a couple of other areas to think about, ... you know, like autoimmune diseases, inflammation of the throat... Why don't we get back to infections now, because we have a story of fever and sore throat, that is a common problem with infectious diseases. So we're talking about strep throat, we're talking about upper-respiratory, viral... Any other type of infectious problem...?

STUDENT: ... Pneumococcus would give you sore throat too, right?

TEACHER: Pretty rarely.

TEACHER (different case): Well, how about some questions about mononucleosis now. I'd have you zero in on that.

• FORWARD-REASON — Ask yourself, "What could cause that?" Look for associated symptoms.

TEACHER: Well, what's another possibility to think about in terms of weakness? What do a lot of older people think of when they just think of being weak, a common American complaint. Or a common American understanding of weakness. How about tired blood?

STUDENT: Iron deficiency.

TEACHER: I think of anemias.

TEACHER (different case): Most important is to develop a sense of being reasonably organized in approaching the information base and trying to keep a complete sense of not homing in too quickly. Look for things to grab onto, especially if you have a nonspecific symptom like headache, weakness. Ten million people in the country probably have a headache at this given point in time. What are the serious ones, and what are the benign ones? Look for associated symptoms. Some associated symptoms definitely point to something severe, while others might not.

• REFINE-HYPOTHESIS — Ask yourself, "What are the common causes and the serious, but treatable causes?"

TEACHER: What anemias do young people get?

## APPENDIX IV: THE DIAGNOSTIC PROCEDURE

This section describes in detail the content of NEOMYCIN's metarules. The tasks are listed in depth-first calling order, assuming that they are always applicable (refer to Figure 12.5). For each substantial task (FORWARD-REASON, FINDOUT, ESTABLISH-HYPOTHESIS-SPACE and its subtasks), we attempt to list exhaustively all of the implicit assumptions about task and cognitive constraints proceduralized by the metarules. These are an essential part of the model. The model is constantly changing; this is a snapshot as of July 1985. To give an idea of how the program is evolving, metarules now on paper are listed as " < <proposed> > ."

### CONSULT

This is the top-level task. A single metarule unconditionally invokes MAKE-DIAGNOSIS and then prints the results of the consultation. (We have disabled MYCIN's therapy routine because the antibiotic information was out of date; it would be invoked here.)

### MAKE-DIAGNOSIS

A single unconditional metarule invokes the following tasks: IDENTIFY-PROBLEM, REVIEW-DIFFERENTIAL, and COLLECT-INFORMATION. REVIEW-DIFFERENTIAL simply prints out the differential, modeling a physician's periodic restatement of the possibilities he or she is considering. (In a teaching system, this would be an opportunity to question the student.) Hypothesis-directed reasoning is done by COLLECT-INFORMATION.

### IDENTIFY-PROBLEM

The purpose of this task is to gather initial information about the case from the informant, particularly to come up with a set of initial hypotheses.

1. The first metarule unconditionally requests "identifying information" (in medicine, the name, age, and sex of the patient) and the "chief complaint" (what abnormal behavior suggests that there is an underlying problem requiring therapy). The task FORWARD-REASON is then invoked.

2. If no diagnoses have been triggered (the differential is empty), the task GENERATE-QUESTIONS is invoked.

### FORWARD-REASON

The metarules for FORWARD-REASON iterate over the list of new conclusions, first invoking CLARIFY-FINDING for each finding and then PROCESS-FINDING for each serious or "red-flag" finding. PROCESS-FINDING is then invoked for nonspecific findings and PROCESS-HYPOTHESIS for each hypothesis. These tasks perform all of the program's forward reasoning.

It is important to "clarify" findings, that is, to make sure that they are well specified, before doing any forward reasoning. Thus, before considering that the patient has a fever, we first ask what his temperature is. "Red-flag" in contrast with "nonspecific" findings often trigger hypotheses; they are serious, indicative of a real problem to be treated and not just a "functional" imperfection in the device;[14] nonspecific findings may very well be explained by the hypotheses that red-flag findings quickly suggest. These considerations are all matters of cognitive economy, means to avoid backtracking and to make a diagnosis with the least search.

### CLARIFY-FINDING

Using subsumption and process relations among findings, these metarules seek more specific information about a finding, asking two types of questions:

1. Specification questions (e.g., if the finding is "medications," program will ask what drugs the patient is receiving).

2. Process questions (e.g., if the finding is "headache," the program will ask when the headache began).

### PROCESS-FINDING

The metarules for this task apply the following kinds of domain rules and relations in a forward-directed way:

---

[14] In medicine, a headache usually indicates a functional, as opposed to an "organic," disorder. By analogy, a high load-average in a time-sharing computer often indicates a functional disorder, just a problem of ordinary "life" — though, like a headache, it may signify a serious underlying disorder.

1. Antecedent rules (causal and definitional rules that use the finding and can be applied now).

2. Generalization (subsumption) relations (e.g., if the finding is "neurosurgery," the program will conclude that "the patient has undergone surgery").

3. Trigger rules (rules that suggest hypotheses; the program will pursue subgoals if necessary to apply these rules). If a nonspecific finding is explained by hypotheses already in the differential, it does not trigger new hypotheses.

4. Ordinary consequent rules that use soft findings to conclude about activated hypotheses (those hypotheses on the differential, plus any ancestor or immediate descendent).[15]

5. Ordinary consequent rules that use hard findings, as above, but subgoaling is allowed.

6. (<<Proposed>> Rule out considered hypotheses that do not account for a new red-flag finding.)

7. (<<Proposed>> Refine current hypotheses that can be discriminated into subtypes on the basis of the new finding.[16]

These metarules (and their ordering) conform to the following implicit constraints:

- The associations that will be considered first are those requiring the least additional effort to realize them.

  Effort in forward reasoning, an aspect of what has also been called *cognitive economy*, can be characterized in terms of:

  - *immediacy* (the conclusion need only be stated *vs.* subgoals must be pursued or the problem solver must perform many intersections of the differential, related hypotheses, and known findings)

  - *relevance* (make conclusions focused with respect to current findings and hypotheses vs. take actions that might broaden the possibilities, require "unrelated" findings, and change the focus).

- The metarules are directed at efficiency by:

  - Drawing inferences in a data-directed way, rather than doing a search when the conclusions are needed. The primary assumption here is that the structure of the problem space makes forward reasoning more efficient.

  - Drawing all possible focused inferences (each metarule is tried once, but executes all inferences of its type) and refining findings to a useful level of detail by asking more questions (not hypothesis-directed).

In summary, the order of forward reasoning is based on cognitive issues, not correctness.

## PROCESS-HYPOTHESIS

These rules maintain the differential and do forward reasoning:

1. If the belief in the hypothesis is now less than .2, and it is in the differential, it is removed.

2. If the hypothesis is not in the differential and the belief is now greater than or equal to .2, it is added to the differential. The task APPLY-EVIDENCE-RULES is invoked. This task applies rules that support the hypothesis, using previously given findings (the hypothesis might not have been active when the data was processed). Only rules that succeed without setting up new subgoals are considered.

3. (<<Proposed>> If the belief is very high (greater than .8) and the program knows of no evidence that could lower its belief, then the hypothesis is marked as explored, equivalent to completing TEST-HYPOTHESIS.)

4. (<<Proposed>> Apply ordinary consequent rules that use soft findings to conclude about new activated hypotheses.)

5. If the hypothesis has been explored (either because of the previous rule or the task TEST-HYPOTHESIS is complete), then generalization (subsumption) relations and antecedent rules are applied.

Adding a hypothesis to the differential is bookkeeping performed by a

---

[15]Should the concept of a trigger rule be generalized to allow specification of any arbitrary context? In particular, is the idea of applying rules relevant to children of active hypotheses just a weak form of trigger rule? Perhaps the "strength" of an association corresponds to the *extent of the context* in which it will come to mind. Trigger rules are simply rules which apply to the entire domain of medical diagnosis. We might associate rules with intermediate contexts as well, for example, the context of "infectious disease diagnosis."

Resolving this issue may make moot the issue of whether trigger rules should be placed before ordinary consequent rules. Their relevance is more directly ascertained; applying consequent rules in a focussed, forward way requires intersection of the new finding with specific hypotheses on the differential and their descendents. Trigger rules also have the payoff of indicating new hypotheses. However, if applying a trigger rule requires gathering new findings and then changing the differential, some cost is incurred in returning to consider the ordinary consequent rules afterward.

[16]This would again promote refocussing, and thus the cost of losing the current context. An agenda model could explain the ability to realize these new associations and come back to them later.

6. If some more specific finding is known to be present, then this finding can be concluded to be present, too. (E.g., if the patient is receiving steroids, then the patient is receiving medications.)

7. If the finding is normally requested from the informant, but shouldn't be asked for this kind of problem, then try to infer the finding from other information.[18]

8. If the "finding" is really a disorder hypothesis (we are applying a rule that requires this information), then invoke TEST-HYPOTHESIS (rather than backward chaining through the domain rules in a blind way).

9. If the informant typically expects to be asked about this finding, then request the information, and then try to infer it, if necessary.

10. Otherwise, try to infer the finding, then request it.

The constraints that lie behind these rules are:

• Economy: use available information rather than drawing intermediate inference or gathering more information. Keep the number of inferences and requests for data to a minimum. Solve the problem as quickly as possible.

• First requesting more general information attempts to satisfy the economy constraint, but assumes that more than one specific finding in the class will eventually be considered and that the general finding is often negative. Otherwise, the general question would be unnecessary.

• It is assumed that the informant knows and consistently uses the subsumption relations used by the problem solver, so the problem solver is entitled to rule out specific findings on the basis of general categories. For example, knowing that the patient is pregnant, the informant will not say that she is not a compromised host. General questions help ensure completeness. When a more general question is asked, a different specific finding than the one originally of interest could be volunteered. Later forward reasoning could then bring about refocussing.

• Typical of the possible interactions of domain knowledge that must be considered, a finding with a source must not be subsumed by ruled-out findings; otherwise, considering the source would be unnecessary, and doing it first would lead to an extra question. Obviously, if there are too many interactions of this sort, the strategic "principles" will be very complex and slow to apply in interpreted form.

[18]"Inferring" means to use backward chaining. Given that source and subsumption relations have already been considered at this point, only definitional rules remain to be considered. That a finding should not be asked is determined by the "don't ask when" relation, requiring the task APPLYRULES to be invoked in the premise of this metarule.)

---

LISP function. While NEOMYCIN's differential is a list, it cannot really be separated conceptually from the hierarchical and causal structures that relate hypotheses. The hypothesis is not added if a descendent (causal or subtype) is already in the list. If an ancestor is in the list, it is deleted. If there is no previous ancestor or descendent, the program records that the differential is now "wider" — an event that will effect aborting and triggering of tasks. Thus, the differential is a memory-jogging "cut" through causal and subtype hierarchies.

The ordering of PROCESS-HYPOTHESIS metarules is cognitively based, as for PROCESS-FINDING, but follows a more logical procedural ordering: bookkeeping of the differential, recognition of more evidence, completion of consideration, and drawing more conclusions. The orderliness of this procedure again reflects the cognitive (and computational) efficiency of locally realizing and recording known information before drawing more conclusions (i.e., returning to the more general search problem).

## FINDOUT

This task models how the problem solver makes a conclusion about a finding that he wants to know about. (This is a greatly expanded and now explicit version of the original MYCIN routine by the same name (Shortliffe, 1976). The rules are applied in order until one succeeds:

1. If the finding concerns complex objects (such as cultures, organisms, or drugs) then a special Lisp routine is invoked to provide a convenient interface for gathering this information.

2. If the finding is a laboratory test whose source is not available or whose availability is unknown, then the finding is marked as unavailable. (E.g., if it is not known whether the patient had a chest x-ray, nothing can be concluded about what was seen on the chest x-ray.)

3. If the finding is subsumed by any more general finding that is ruled out for this case, then the finding is ruled out also. (E.g., if the patient has not received medications, then he has not received antibiotics.)

4. As a variant of the above rule, if any more general finding can be ruled out that has not been considered before, then the finding can be ruled out.[17]

5. If any more general finding is unknown, then this specific finding is marked as unavailable.

[17]That is, the premise of this metarule invokes FINDOUT recursively. To do this cleanly, we should allow tasks to return "success" or "fail."

Note that we could have added another metarule to rule out a general class if all of its more specific findings have been ruled out, but the "closed-world assumption" does not make sense with NEOMYCIN's small knowledge base.

## APPLYRULES

NEOMYCIN has "internal" tasks that control how domain rules are applied: "only if immediate" (antecedent), "with previewing" (looking for a conjunct known to be false), and "with subgoaling." An important aspect of NEOMYCIN as a cognitive model is that new findings, coming from rule invocation, are considered in a depth-first way. That is, the conclusions from new findings are considered before returning to information gathered earlier in the consultation. Implementing this requires "rebinding" the list of new findings (so a "stack" is associated with rule invocations) and marking new findings as "known" if no further reasoning could change what is known about them, thus adding them to the list of findings to be considered in forward reasoning. The basic assumptions are that the informant does not retract findings, that the problem solver does not retract conclusions, and that FORWARD-REASON is done for each new finding.

## GENERATE-QUESTIONS

This task models the problem solver's attempt to milk the informant for information that will suggest some hypotheses. The program generates one question at a time, stopping when the differential is "adequate" (the end condition of the task). The differential is adequate in the early stage of the consultation if it is not empty; otherwise the belief in some considered hypothesis must be "moderate" (defined as a cumulative CF of .3 or greater, the measure used consistently in domain rules to signify "reasonable evidence").

The metarules generate questions from several sources, invoking auxiliary tasks to pursue different lines of questioning:

3. Any rule using previous data that was not applied before because it required new subgoals to be pursued is now applied.
4. The informant is simply asked to supply more information, if possible.

This task illustrates the importance of record-keeping during the consultation. These metarules refer to which tasks have been previously completed, which findings have been fully specified and elaborated, and hypothesis relations that have been considered.

## ASK-GENERAL-QUESTIONS

These questions are the most general indications of abnormal behavior or previously diagnosed disorders, useful for determining whether the case is a "typical" one that is what it appears to be, or an "unusual" problem, as described at the beginning of this chapter. These are of course domain-specific questions. They generalize to: Has this problem ever occurred before? What previous diagnoses and treatments have been applied to this device? When was the device last working properly? Are there similar findings manifested in another part of the device? Are there associated findings (occurring at the same time)? These questions are asked in a fixed order, consistent with the case-independent, "something you do every time" nature of this task.

## COLLECT-INFORMATION

These rules carry out the main portion of data collection for diagnosis; they are applied iteratively, in sequence, until no rule succeeds:

1. If there are hypotheses appearing on the differential that the program has not yet considered actively, then the differential is reconsidered (ESTABLISH-HYPOTHESIS-SPACE) and reviewed (REVIEW-DIFFERENTIAL).[19] If the differential is not "adequate" (maximum

1. General questions (ASK-GENERAL-QUESTIONS).
2. Elaboration of previously received data (ELABORATE-DATUM). (The subtask ELABORATE-DATUM asks about subsumed data. For example, if it is known that the patient is immunosuppressed, the program will ask whether the patient is receiving cytotoxic drugs, is an alcoholic, and so on. The subtask also requests more "process information." For example, it will ask how a headache has changed over time, its severity, etc.)

[19]To avoid recomputation, the function for modifying the differential sets a flag when new hypotheses are added. It is reset each time the task ESTABLISH-HYPOTHESIS-SPACE completes. Generally, the goal of each task (e.g., GENERAL-QUESTIONS-ASKED) is used for history-keeping; but tasks like ESTABLISH-HYPOTHESIS-SPACE are invoked conditionally, multiple times during a consultation, as the program loops through the COLLECT-INFORMATION metarules. The use of flags brings up questions about the mind's "register" or "stack" capabilities, whether NEOMYCIN should use an agenda, and so on. In our breadth-first approach to constructing a model, we hold questions like this aside until they become relevant to our performance goals.

CF below .3), an attempt is made to generate more hypotheses (GENERATE-QUESTIONS).

2. If the hypotheses on the differential have all been actively explored (ESTABLISH-HYPOTHESIS-SPACE completed), then laboratory data is requested (PROCESS-HARD-DATA).

## ESTABLISH-HYPOTHESIS-SPACE

This task iterates among three ordered metarules:

1. If there are ancestors of hypotheses on the differential that haven't been *explored* by TEST-HYPOTHESIS, then these are considered (GROUP-AND-DIFFERENTIATE). (For computational efficiency, the records *parents-explored* and *descendents-explored* are maintained for each hypothesis.)

2. If there are hypotheses on the differential that haven't been *pursued* by PURSUE-HYPOTHESIS, then these are considered (EXPLORE-AND-REFINE).

3. If all general questions have not been asked, invoke ASK-GENERAL-QUESTIONS.

The constraints satisfied by this task are:

- All hypotheses that are placed on the differential are tested and refined (based on correctness).

- Causal and subtype ancestors are considered before more specific hypotheses (based on efficiency and assuming that the best model for explaining findings is a known stereotype disorder, and that these stereotypes can be taxonomically organized).

### Group-and-Differentiate

This task attempts to establish the disorder categories that should be explored:

1. If all hypotheses on the differential belong to a single top-level category of disease (appear in one subtree whose root is at the first level of the taxonomy), then this category is tested. Such a differential is called "compact"; the concept and strategy come from Rubin (1975).

2. If two hypotheses on the differential differ according to some process feature (location, time course, spread), then ask a question that dis-criminates on that basis. (This is the metarule that uses orthogonal indexing to group and then discriminate disorders.)

3. If there is some hypothesis whose top-level category has not been tested, then test that category. (E.g., consider infectious-process when there is evidence for chronic-meningitis.)

The first metarule is not strictly needed since its operation is covered by the third metarule. However, we observed that physicians remarked on the presence of an overlap and pursued the single category first, so we included this metarule in the model.

The second metarule uses process knowledge to compare diseases, as described early in this chapter.

To summarize the constraints behind the metarules:

- When examining hypotheses, intersection at the highest level is noticed first. The etiological taxonomy is assumed to be a strict tree.

- Use of process knowledge requires two levels of reasoning: mapping over all descriptors, and intersecting disorders based on each descriptor. This is more complicated than a subtype intersection, requiring more effort, so it is done after testing the differential for compactness. For this maneuver to be useful, disorders must share a set of process descriptors.

- Because a stereotype disorder inherits features of all etiological ancestors, these ancestors must be considered as part of the process of confirming the disorder (a matter of correctness). This assumes that knowledge of disorders has been generalized and "moved up" the tree (perhaps an inherent property of learning, the effect is beneficial for search efficiency). Furthermore, circumstantial evidence that specifically confirms a disorder can only be applied if ancestors are confirmed or not ruled out. That is, circumstantial associations are context-sensitive.

## TEST-HYPOTHESIS

This is the task for directly confirming a hypothesis. The following methods are applied in a pure-production system manner:

1. Preference is first given to findings that trigger the hypothesis.

2. Next, causal precursors to the disease are considered. (For infectious diseases, causal precursors include exposure to the disease and immunosuppression.)

3. Finally, all other evidence is considered.

Each metarule selects the domain rules that mention the selected finding in their premise, and conclude about the hypothesis being tested. The MYCIN domain rule interpreter is then invoked to apply these rules (in the task APPLYRULES). (So applying the rule will indirectly cause the program to request the datum.) After the rules are applied, forward reasoning using the findings and new hypothesis conclusions is performed (FORWARD-REASON).

<<Proposed>>: The task aborts if belief is high (CF greater than .8), and if no further questioning can make the belief negative. The task also aborts if there is no belief in the hypothesis, and if only weak evidence (CF less than .3) remains to be considered after several questions have been asked.
Relevant constraints are:

- Findings bearing a strong relation with the hypothesis are considered first because they will contribute the most weight (a matter of efficiency).

- Disconfirming a hypothesis involves discovering that required or highly probable findings—causal precursors or effects—are missing. NEOMYCIN's domain lacks this kind of certainty. Therefore, the program does not use a "rule-out" strategy.

- The end conditions attempt to minimize the number of questions and shift attention when belief is not likely to change (a matter of efficiency).

### EXPLORE-AND-REFINE

This is the central task for choosing a focus hypothesis from the differential. The following metarules are applied in the manner of a pure production system:

1. If the current focus (perhaps from GROUP-AND-DIFFERENTIATE) is now less likely than another hypothesis on the differential, then the program pursues the stronger candidate (PURSUE-HYPOTHESIS).
2. If there is a child of the current focus that has not been pursued, then it is pursued (this can only be true after the current focus has just been refined and removed from the differential).
3. If there is a sibling of the current focus that has not been pursued, then it is pursued.
4. If there is any other hypothesis on the differential that has not been pursued, then it is pursued.

This task is aborted if the differential becomes wider (see PROCESS-HYPOTHESIS), a precondition that requires doing the task GROUP-AND-DIFFERENTIATE.
Relevant constraints are:

- All selection of hypotheses is biased by the current belief (a matter of efficiency).

- Focus should change as soon as the focus is no longer the most strongly believed hypothesis (a matter of correctness; perhaps at odds with minimizing effort, due to the cost of returning to this focus).

- Siblings are preferred before other hypotheses (a matter of cognitive effort to remain focused within a class; also a matter of efficiency, insofar as siblings are mutually exclusive diagnoses).

### PURSUE-HYPOTHESIS

Pursuing a hypothesis has two components: testing it (TEST-HYPOTHESIS), followed by refining it (REFINE-HYPOTHESIS). After these two metarules are tried (in order, once), the hypothesis is marked as pursued.

Pursuing self followed by children brings about depth-first search. (Specifically, PURSUE-HYPOTHESIS puts the children in the differential and EXPLORE-AND-REFINE focuses on them.) This plan is based on the need to specialize a diagnosis (correctness), to remain focused (minimizing cognitive effort), and to consider more general disorders first (efficiency).

### REFINE-HYPOTHESIS

The effect of this task is to put taxonomic children or the causes of a state/category into the differential. If the hypothesis being refined has more than four descendents, a subset of possibilities is considered (REFINE-COMPLEXHYPOTHESIS). For each child considered, the task APPLY-EVIDENCE-RULES is invoked (see PROCESS-HYPOTHESIS).

In order to reach a diagnosis in the etiologic taxonomy, this task requires that there be causal or subtype links from state/category hypotheses into the taxonomy, allowing them to be "refined" as etiologic hypotheses.

### REFINE-COMPLEX-HYPOTHESIS

Two metarules are used to select the common and unusual causes of the hypothesis. Ordinary domain rules, marked accordingly, are used to define these sets. The assumption is that, if only a few specializations can be considered (for economy), one should consider the common as well as the serious, unusual causes (for correctness). The less important hypotheses will be covered by the strategies of asking general questions and focused forward reasoning.

## PROCESS-HARD-DATA

Briefly, special functions are used to assemble a set of "hard findings" that support hypotheses on the differential, reduce them to a set of "sources" (a lumbar puncture is the source for the CSF findings), and request the sources from the informant. Subsumption and definition relations are used to infer the sources. Contraindications (dangerous side effects) of gathering certain information is also considered. As described in PROCESS-FINDING, rules used by these findings are applied with subgoaling enabled. The program will return to GROUP-AND-DIFFERENTIATE and EXPLORE-AND-REFINE new hypotheses as necessary.

## ACKNOWLEDGMENTS

We are especially grateful to the late Timothy Beckett, M.D., for serving as the expert-teacher in this research. Reed Letsinger participated in early discussions and helped implement the program. Bob London, Diane Hasling, Curt Kapsner, M.D., David Wilkins, and Mark Richer have also contributed to the development of NEOMYCIN. I would like to thank Lewis Johnson for his careful reading and helpful suggestions. This chapter was prepared in September 1983, then revised in February 1984 and August 1985.

This research has been supported in part by joint funding from ONR and ARI, Contract N00014-79C-0302, and more recently by ONR Contract N00014-85K-0305 and a grant from the Josiah Macy, Jr. Foundation. Computational resources are provided by the SUMEX-AIM facility (NIH grant RR 00785). NEOMYCIN is implemented in INTERLISP-D.

## REFERENCES

Aikins, J. S. (1981). Representation of control knowledge in expert systems. In *Proceedings of the First AAAI* (pp. 121-123). Stanford, CA.

Anderson, J. R., & Bower, G. H. (1980). *Human associative memory: A brief edition.* Hillsdale, NJ: Lawrence Erlbaum Associates.

Anderson, J. R., Greeno, J. G., Kline, P. J., & Neves, D. M. (1981). Acquisition of problem-solving skill. In J. R. Anderson (Ed.), *Cognitive skills and their acquisition* (pp. 191-230). Hillsdale, NJ: Lawrence Erlbaum Associates.

Benbassat, J., & Schiffmann, A. (1976). An approach to teaching the introduction to clinical medicine. *Annals of Internal Medicine, 84,* 477-481.

Brown, J. S., Collins, A., & Harris, G. (1977). Artificial intelligence and learning strategies. In A. O'Neill (Ed.), *Learning Strategies.* New York: Academic Press.

Bruner, J. S., Goodnow, J. J., & Austin, A. A. (1956). *A study of thinking.* New York: Wiley.

Chandrasekaran, B., Gomez, F., Mittal, S. (1979). An approach to medical diagnosis based on conceptual schemes. *Proceedings of the Sixth International Joint Conference on Artificial Intelligence* (pp. 134-142), Tokyo.

Chi, M. T. H., Feltovich, P. J., & Glaser, R. (1981). Categorization and representation of physics problems by experts and novices. *Cognitive Science, 5,* 121-152.

Clancey, W. J. (1982). Applications-oriented AI research: Education. In A. Barr and E. Feigenbaum (Eds.), *The handbook of artificial intelligence.* Los Altos: Morgan Kaufmann.

Clancey, W. J. (1983a). The epistemology of a rule-based expert system: A framework for explanation. *Artificial Intelligence, 20,* 215-251.

Clancey, W. J. (1983b). The advantages of abstract control knowledge in expert system design. *Proceedings of the National Conference on AI* (pp. 74-78). Washington, DC.

Clancey, W. J. (1984). Methodology for building an intelligent tutoring system. In W. Kintsch, J. R. Miller, & P. G. Polson (Eds.), *Method and tactics in cognitive science* (pp. 51-83). Hillsdale, NJ: Lawrence Erlbaum Associates.

Clancey, W. J. (1985). Heuristic classification. *Artificial Intelligence, 27,* 289-350.

Clancey, W. J. (in press). Representing control knowledge as abstract tasks and metarules. In M. J. Coombs & L. Bolc (Eds.), *Computer expert systems.* New York: Springer-Verlag.

Clancey, W. J., & Letsinger, R. (1984). NEOMYCIN: Reconfiguring a rule-based expert system for application to teaching. In W. J. Clancey & E. H. Shortliffe (Eds.), *Readings in medical artificial intelligence: The first decade* (pp. 361-381). Reading: Addison-Wesley.

Cohen, P. R., & Grinberg, M. R. (1983). A framework for heuristic reasoning about uncertainty. *Proceedings of the Eighth International Joint Conference on Artificial Intelligence* (pp. 355-357). Karlsruhe, West Germany.

Davis, R. (1980). Meta-rules: Reasoning about control. *Artificial Intelligence, 15,* 179-222.

Davis, R. (1983). Diagnosis via causal reasoning: Paths of interaction and the locality principle. *Proceedings of the National Conference on AI* (pp. 88-94). Washington, DC.

Davis, R., & Lenat, D. (1982). *Knowledge-based systems in artificial intelligence.* New York: McGraw-Hill.

Duda, R. O., & Shortliffe, E. H. (1983). Expert systems research. *Science, 220,* 261-268.

Elstein, A. S., Shulman, L. S., & Sprafka, S. A. (1978). *Medical problem solving: An analysis of clinical reasoning.* Cambridge, MA: Harvard University Press.

Ericsson, K. A., & Simon, H. A. (1980). Verbal reports as data. *Psychological Review, 87,* 215-251.

Feigenbaum, E. A. (1977). The art of artificial intelligence: I. Themes and case studies of knowledge engineering. *Proceedings of the Fifth International Joint Conference on Artificial Intelligence* (pp. 1014-1029). MIT, Cambridge, MA.

Feltovich, P. J., Johnson, P. E., Moller, J. H. & Swanson, D. B. (1984). *The role and development of medical knowledge in diagnostic expertise.* Presented at the 1980 Annual meeting of the American Educational Research Association. In W. Clancey & E. H. Shortliffe (Eds.), *Readings in medical artificial intelligence: The first decade.* New York: Addison-Wesley.

Genesereth, M. R. (1984). The use of design descriptions in automated diagnosis. *Artificial Intelligence, 24,* 411-436.

Genesereth, M. R., Greiner, R., & Smith, D. E. (1981). *MRS Manual.* (Heuristic Programming Project Memo HPP-80-24). Stanford, CA: Stanford University.

Gentner, D., & Stevens, A. (Eds.). (1983). *Mental Models.* Hillsdale, NJ: Lawrence Erlbaum Associates.

Swartout, W. R. (1981). Explaining and justifying in expert consulting programs. *Proceedings of the Seventh International Joint Conference on Artificial Intelligence* (pp. 815–823). Vancouver, Canada.

Szolovits, P., & Pauker, S. G. (1978). Categorical and probabilistic reasoning in medical diagnosis. *Artificial Intelligence, 11*, 115–144.

VanLehn, K. (1983). Human procedural skill acquisition: Theory, model and psychological validation. *Proceedings of the National Conference on Artificial Intelligence* (pp. 420–423). Washington, DC.

VanLehn, K., Brown, J. S., & Greeno, J. (1984). Competitive argumentation in computational theories of cognition. In W. Kintsch, J. R. Miller, & P. G. Polson (Eds.), *Method and tactics in cognitive science* (pp. 235–262). Hillsdale, NJ: Lawrence Erlbaum Associates.

VanLehn, K., & Brown, J. S. (1980). Planning nets: A representation for formalizing analogies and semantic models of procedural skills. In R. E. Snow, P. A. Frederico, & W. E. Montague (Eds.), *Aptitude learning and instruction: Cognitive process and analysis*. Hillsdale, NJ: Lawrence Erlbaum Associates.

Wescourt, K. T., & Hemphill, L. (1978). *Representing and teaching knowledge for troubleshooting/debugging* (Tech. Rept. 292). Stanford: Stanford University, Institute for Mathematical Studies in the Social Sciences.

Yu, V. L., Fagan, L. M., Wraith, S. M., Clancey, W. J., Scott, A. C., Hannigan, J. F., Blum, R. L., Buchanan, B. G., & Cohen, S. N. (1979). Antimicrobial selection by a computer: A blinded evaluation by infectious disease experts. *Journal of the American Medical Association, 242*, 1279–1282.

Hasling, D. W., Clancey, W. J., Rennels, G. R. (1984). Strategic explanations for a diagnostic consultation system. *The International Journal of Man-Machine Studies, 20*, 3–19.

Hayes-Roth, B., & Hayes-Roth, F. (1979). A cognitive model of planning. *Cognitive Science, 3*, 275–310.

Hayes-Roth, F., Waterman, D., & Lenat, D. (Eds.). (1983). *Building expert systems*. New York: Wesley.

Kassirer, J. P., & Gorry, G. A. (1978). Clinical problem solving: A behavioral analysis. *Annals of Internal Medicine, 89*, 245–255.

Kolodner, J. (1983). Maintaining organization in a dynamic long-term memory. *Cognitive Science, 7*, 243–280.

Kuipers, B., & Kassirer, J. P. (1984). Causal reasoning in medicine: Analysis of a protocol. *Cognitive Science, 4*, 363–385.

Larkin, J. H., McDermott, J., Simon, D. P., & Simon, H. A. (1980). Models of competence in solving physics problems. *Cognitive Science, 4*, 317–348.

London, B., & Clancey, W. J. (1982). Plan recognition strategies in student modeling: Prediction and description. *Proceedings of the Second AAAI* (pp. 335–338). Pittsburgh, PA.

Miller, P. B. (1975). *Strategy selection in medical diagnosis*. (Tech. Rep. AI-TR-153). Cambridge, MA: MIT, Artificial Intelligence Laboratory.

Neves, D. M., & Anderson, J. Jr. (1981). Knowledge compilation: Mechanisms for the automatization of cognitive skills. In J. R. Anderson (Ed.), *Cognitive skills and their acquisition* (pp. 57–84). Hillsdale, NJ: Lawrence Erlbaum Associates.

Newell, A. (1983). The heuristic of George Polya and its relation to artificial intelligence. In R. Groner, M. Groner, & W. F. Bischof (Eds.), *Methods of heuristics*. Hillsdale, NJ: Lawrence Erlbaum Associates.

Newell, A., & Simon, H. A. (1972). *Human problem solving*. Englewood Cliffs: Prentice-Hall.

Papert, S. (1980). *Mindstorms: Children, computers, and powerful ideas*. New York: Basic Books.

Patil, R. S., Szolovits, P., & Schwartz, W. B. (1981). Causal understanding of patient illness in medical diagnosis. *Proceedings of the Seventh International Joint Conference on Artificial Intelligence* (pp. 893–899). Vancouver, Canada.

Patil, R. S., Szolovits, P., & Schwartz, W. B. (1982). Information acquisition in diagnosis. *Proceedings of the National Conference on AI* (pp. 893–899). Pittsburgh, PA.

Pauker, S. G., & Szolovits, P. (1977). Analyzing and simulating taking the history of the present illness: Context formation. In Schneider & Sagvall-Hein (Eds.), *Computational linguistics in medicine* (pp. 109–118). Amsterdam, North-Holland.

Pauker, S. G., Gorry, G. A., Kassirer, J. P., & Schwartz, W. B. (1976). Toward the simulation of clinical cognition: Taking a present illness by computer. *American Journal of Medicine, 60*, 981–995.

Polya, G. (1957). *How to solve it: An aspect of mathematical method*. Princeton, NJ: Princeton University Press.

Pople, H. (1982). Heuristic methods for imposing structure on ill-structured problems: The structuring of medical diagnostics. In P. Szolovits (Ed.), *Artificial Intelligence in Medicine* (pp. 119–190). Boulder, Westview Press.

Rubin, A. D. (1975). *Hypothesis formation and evaluation in medical diagnosis*. (Technical Rep. AI-TR-316). Cambridge, MA: MIT, Artificial Intelligence Laboratory.

Rumelhart, D. E., & Norman, D. A. (1983). *Representation in memory*. (Tech. Rep. CHIP-116). San Diego: University of California, Center for Human Information Processing.

Schoenfeld, A. H. (1981). *Episodes and executive decisions in mathematical problem solving*. (Tech. Rep. unnumbered). Presented at the 1981 AERA Annual meeting. Los Angeles: Hamilton College, Mathematics Department.

Shortliffe, E. H. (1976). *Computer-based medical consultations: MYCIN*. New York: Elsevier.

Simon, H. A., & Lea, G. (1979). Problem solving and rule induction. In H. A. Simon (Ed.), *Models of thought*. New Haven: Yale University Press.

# Chapter 3

# Interactive Elicitation Tools

Chapters 1 and 2 have presented frameworks and perspectives that show how the different techniques for acquiring knowledge for a knowledge-based system can be seen as sharing many of the same concerns. Foremost among the common concerns are the nature of the expertise to be acquired and its representation in programs that assist in solving problems in an application domain.

This chapter introduces a set of interactive tools for knowledge acquisition that have been developed to assist in the knowledge engineering process by organizing, representing, checking, and refining knowledge obtained from experts. These tools can be thought of as "smart editors" that know about the correct form of expressions in the knowledge base (i.e., their syntax) and know something of the intended use of those expressions by a reasoning program (i.e., their semantics). Some of these tools may be used directly by an expert without sophisticated programming skills; most of the tools require the assistance of a knowledge engineer as well as a domain expert.

The first knowledge engineering tools were simply syntactic checking added to a LISP editor. In DENDRAL, for example, a very crude interac-tive editor asked for the individual parts of rules (left-hand side, right-hand side, name, etc.), assembled them into a single rule with matching parentheses, and then inserted the new expression into the rule base. DENDRAL's approach was possible because of the ease with which LISP allows a program to manipulate fragments of programs such as rules.

INTERLISP became available at the time work began on MYCIN (Buchanan and Shortliffe, 1984), and INTERLISP's sophisticated set of editing tools made it considerably easier to implement editing tools for MYCIN's knowledge base. Davis saw the possibility of making MYCIN's rule editor, TEIRESIAS, an active and intelligent participant in knowledge acquisition, an insight that underlies all the work in Chapter 3.

Interactive elicitation still requires many assumptions, as will be seen from the readings in this chapter. Nevertheless, tools for interactive elicitation have made a large difference in the ease with which knowledge-based systems can be constructed and have made commercial applications of knowledge-based systems cost-effective.

For the interested reader, one of the best recent discussions of "classical" knowledge engineering techniques can be found in Scott et al. (1991). That book includes a short annotated bibliography, organized to serve as a structured entry into the literature on knowledge engineering. Another useful resource is found in Gaines and Boose (1988a) and Gaines and Boose (1988b), a collection of important papers on knowledge acquisition that were first presented at an annual Banff Knowledge Acquisition for Knowledge Based Systems Workshop.

# Section 3.1

# Eliciting Classification Knowledge

Since most commercial expert system shells are oriented toward heuristic classification tasks, most knowledge elicitation tools are too. Heuristic classification is now well understood, and that is all the more reason why intelligent knowledge elicitation assistants are focused on knowledge for classification tasks.

In Section 3.1.1, Davis presents the groundbreaking TEIRESIAS system. TEIRESIAS is oriented toward the syntax of rule-based systems and the task of heuristic classification, but its techniques are quite general.

Three important assumptions built into TEIRESIAS are addressed by other papers in this chapter. First, TEIRESIAS was developed to transfer expertise, based on the model that knowledge packets (e.g., rules or clauses) were obtained from an expert and given to a program. At the time the metaphor of "mining the heads of experts"\for "knowledge gems" seemed appropriate, but only because we failed to see that TEIRESIAS was actually helping an expert conceptualize and construct the rules. Later, experts working with knowledge engineers on commercial systems described some of the work as formulating new knowledge to deal with situations no one had thought of before.

Second, TEIRESIAS knew how to assist in constructing knowledge bases for a "MYCIN-style problem" but knowledge about the type of problem was largely built into the acquisition program. In the early days of EMYCIN, it was not clear that EMYCIN was set up to deal easily with structured selection, or heuristic classification, problems. (All of the work in Section 2.2, for example, post-dates TEIRESIAS.)

Third, Davis explicitly assumed that TEIRESIAS would be used to refine a knowledge base that was already mostly defined. Bennett has articulated three stages of knowledge acquisition, "beginning," "middle," and "end-game," corresponding to knowledge base conceptualization, implementation, and refinement. Bennett used terminology from chess because in knowledge acquisition, as well as in chess, different strategies are required in the different stages. TEIRESIAS addresses only the end-game stage.

The AQUINAS system of Boose and Bradshaw, presented in Section 3.1.2, is different from TEIRESIAS in that AQUINAS is based on techniques developed in psychology for structuring a conceptual space. The methods, originally developed by Kelly, are based on a representation called repertory grids. Using this representation in a systematic way gives a knowledge engineer a powerful tool for eliciting the names of the features that specialists use to classify and discriminate among objects in a domain.

The MOLE system of Eshelman et al., described in Section 3.1.3, is an important member of a class of tools developed by McDermott and colleagues that are based on role-limiting knowledge. These tools are based on the well-founded assumption that we need more than one kind of problem-solving system in order to solve commercially important problems. Therefore, MOLE and similar tools exploit the specialized knowledge about a task type in order to provide meaningful assistance to knowledge engineers and experts who are building performance systems that assist people who perform the task.

# Interactive Transfer of Expertise: Acquisition of New Inference Rules

**Randall Davis***

*Computer Science Department, Stanford University, Stanford, CA 94305, U.S.A.*

Recommended by Jacques Pitrat

ABSTRACT

*TEIRESIAS is a program designed to provide assistance on the task of building knowledge-based systems. It facilitates the interactive transfer of knowledge from a human expert to the system, in a high level dialog conducted in a restricted subset of natural language. This paper explores an example of TEIRESIAS in operation and demonstrates how it guides the acquisition of new inference rules. The concept of meta-level knowledge is described and illustrations given of its utility in knowledge acquisition and its contribution to the more general issues of creating an intelligent program.*

## 1. Introduction

Where much early work in artificial intelligence was devoted to the search for a single, powerful, domain-independent problem solving methodology (e.g., GPS [14]), more recent efforts have stressed the use of large stores of domain-specific knowledge as a basis for high performance. The knowledge base for this sort of program (e.g., DENDRAL [11], MACSYMA [13]) is traditionally assembled by hand, an ongoing task that typically involves numerous man-years of effort. A key element in constructing a knowledge base is the transfer of expertise from a human expert to the program. Since the domain expert often knows nothing about programming, the interaction between the expert and the performance program usually requires the mediation of a human programmer.

We have sought to create a program that could supply much the same sort of assistance as that provided by the programmer in this transfer of expertise task. The result is a system called TEIRESIAS[1] [5–8], a large INTERLISP [19] program

* Author's current address: 545 Technology Square, MIT, Cambridge, MA 02138, U.S.A.

This work was supported in part by the Advanced Research Projects Agency under ARPA Order 2494; by a Chaim Weizmann Postdoctoral Fellowship for Scientific Research, and by grant MCS 7–02712 from the National Science Foundation. It was carried out on the SUMEX Computer System, supported by the NIH Grant RR-00785.

[1] The program is named for the blind seer in *Oedipus the King*, since, as we will see, the program, like the prophet, has a form of "higher order" knowledge.

*Artificial Intelligence* **12** (1979), 121–157

Copyright © 1979 by North-Holland Publishing Company

This paper originally appeared in the journal, *Artificial Intelligence*, Vol. 12, No. 2, and is reprinted here with permission of the publisher, Elsevier, Amsterdam.

designed to offer assistance in the interactive transfer of knowledge from a human expert to the knowledge base of a high performance program (Fig. 1).

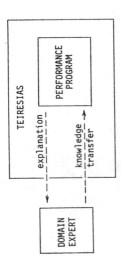

FIG. 1. Interaction between the expert and the performance program is facilitated by TEIRESIAS.

Information flow from right to left is labelled *explanation*. This is the process by which TEIRESIAS clarifies for the expert the source of the performance program's results and motivations for its actions. This is a prerequisite to knowledge acquisition, since the expert must first discover what the performance program already knows and how it used that knowledge. Information flow from left to right is labelled *knowledge transfer*. This is the process by which the expert adds to or modifies the store of domain-specific knowledge in the performance program.

Work on TEIRESIAS has had two general goals. We have attempted first to develop a set of tools and empirical methods for knowledge base construction and maintenance, and sought to abstract from them a methodology applicable to a range of systems. The second, more general goal has been the development of an intelligent assistant. This task involves confronting many of the traditional problems of AI and has resulted in the exploration of a number of solutions reviewed below.

This paper describes a number of the key ideas in the development of TEIRESIAS and discusses their implementation in the context a specific task (acquisition of new inference rules[2]) for a specific performance program (a rule-based computer consultant). While the discussion deals with one particular task, system and knowledge representation, several of the main ideas are applicable to more general issues concerning the creation of intelligent programs.

## 2. Meta-Level Knowledge

A central theme that runs through this and related papers [5–8] is the concept of *meta-level knowledge*. This takes several different forms as its use is explored, but can be summed up generally by saying that a program can "know what it knows". That is, a program can not only use its knowledge directly, but may also be able to examine it, abstract it, reason about it, and direct its application.

[2] Acquisition of new conceptual primitives from which rules are built is discussed in [7], while the design and implementation of the explanation capability suggested in Fig. 1 is discussed in [5].

To see in general terms how this might be accomplished, recall that one of the principal problems of AI is the question of representation and use of knowledge about the world, for which numerous techniques have been developed. One way to view what we have done is to imagine turning this in on itself, and using some of these same techniques to describe the program itself.

The resulting system contains both *object-level* representations describing the external world, and *meta-level* representations which describe the internal world of representations. As the discussion of "rule models" in Section 7 will make clear, such a system has a number of interesting capabilities.

## 3. Perspective on Knowledge Acquisition

We view the interaction between the domain expert and the performance program as *interactive transfer of expertise*. We see it in terms of a teacher who continually challenges a student with new problems to solve and carefully observes the student's performance. The teacher may interrupt to request a justification of some particular step the student has taken in solving the problem or may challenge the final result. This process may uncover a fault in the student's knowledge of the subject (the debugging phase) and result in the transfer of information to correct it (the knowledge acquisition phase).

Other approaches to knowledge acquisition can be compared to this by considering their relative positions along two dimensions: (i) the sophistication of their debugging facilities and (ii) the independence of their knowledge acquisition mechanism.

The simplest sort of debugging tool is characterized by a program like DDT, which is totally passive (in the sense that it operates only in response to user commands), is low ... l (since it operates at the level of machine or assembly language), and knows nothing about the application domain of the program.

Debuggers like BAIL [16] and INTERLISP's break package [19] are a step up from this since they function at the level of programming languages like SAIL and INTER-LISP.

The explanation capabilities in TEIRESIAS, in particular the "how" and "why" commands (see [5] and [9] for examples), represent another step, since they function at the level of the control structure of the application program. The guided debugging which TEIRESIAS can also provide (illustrated in Section 6) represents yet another step, since here the debugger is taking the initiative and has enough built-in knowledge about the control structure that it can track down the error. It does this by requesting from the expert an opinion on the validity of a few selected rules from among the many that were invoked.

Finally, at the most sophisticated level are knowledge-rich debuggers like the one found in [2]. Here the program is active, high-level, and informed about the application domain, and is capable of independently localizing and characterizing bugs.

By independence of the knowledge acquisition mechanism, we mean the degree of human cooperation necessary. Much work on knowledge acquisition has emphasized a highly autonomous mode of operation. There is, for example, a large body of work aimed at inducing the appropriate generalizations from a set of test data (see, e.g., [3] and [12]). In these efforts user interaction is limited to presenting the program with the data and perhaps providing a brief description of the domain in the form of values for a few key parameters; the program then functions independently.

Winston's work on concept formation [21] relied somewhat more heavily on user interaction. There the teacher was responsible for providing an appropriate sequence of examples (and non-examples) of a concept.

In describing our work, we have used the phrase "interactive transfer of expertise" to indicate that we view knowledge acquisition as information transfer from an expert to a program. TERESIAS does not attempt to derive knowledge on its own, but instead tries to "listen" as attentively as possible and comment appropriately, to help the expert augment the knowledge base. It thus requires the strongest degree of cooperation from the expert.

There is an important assumption involved in the attempt to establish this sort of communication: we are assuming that it is possible to distinguish between basic *problem-solving paradigm* and *degree of expertise*, or equivalently, that control structure and representation in the performance program can be considered separately from the content of its knowledge base. The basic control structure(s) and representations are assumed to be established and debugged, and the fundamental approach to the problem assumed acceptable. The question of *how* knowledge is to be encoded and used is settled by the selection of one or more of the available representations and control structures. The expert's task is to enlarge *what* it is the program knows.

There is a corollary assumption, too, in the belief that the control structures and knowledge representations can be made sufficiently comprehensible to the expert (at the conceptual level) that he can (a) understand the system's behavior in terms of them and (b) use them to codify his own knowledge. This insures that the expert understands system performance well enough to know what to correct and can then express the required knowledge, i.e., he can "think" in those terms. Thus part of the task of establishing the link shown in Fig. 1 involves insulating the expert from the details of implementation, by establishing a discourse at a level high enough that we do not end up effectively having to teach him how to program.

## 4. Design of the Performance Program

### 4.1. Program architecture

Fig. 2 shows a slightly more detailed picture of the sort of performance program that TERESIAS is designed to help construct. (The performance program described here is modelled after the MYCIN program [17, 9], which provided the context

within which TERESIAS was actually developed. (The essential elements of MYCIN's design.) The *knowledge base* is the program's store of task specific knowledge that makes possible high performance. The *inference engine* is an interpreter that uses the knowledge base to solve the problem at hand.

FIG. 2. Architecture of the performance program.

The main point of interest in this very simple design is the explicit division between these two parts of the program. This design is in keeping with the assumption noted above that the expert's task would be to augment the knowledge base of a program whose control structure (inference engine) was assumed both appropriate and debugged.

Two important advantages accrue from keeping this division as strict as possible. First, if all of the control structure information has been kept in the inference engine, then we can engage the domain expert in a discussion of the knowledge base and be assured that the discussion will have to deal only with issues of domain specific expertise (rather than with questions of programming and control structures) Second, if all of the task-specific knowledge has been kept in the knowledge base, then it should be possible to remove the current knowledge base, "plug in" another, and obtain a performance program for a new task.[3] The explicit division thus offers a degree of domain independence.

It does not mean, however, that the inference engine and knowledge base are totally independent: knowledge base content is strongly influenced by the control paradigm used in the inference engine. It is this unavoidable interaction which motivates the important assumption noted in Section 3 that the control structure and knowledge representation are comprehensible to the expert, at least at the conceptual level.

In this discussion we assume the knowledge base contains information about selecting an investment in the stock market; the performance program thus functions as an investment consultant. MYCIN, of course, deals with infectious disease diagnosis and therapy selection, and the rules and dialog shown later dealt with that subject initially. The topic has been changed to help keep the discussion phrased in terms familiar to a wide range of readers, and to emphasize that neither

[3] Two experiments of this sort have been performed with the MYCIN system, and suggest that this sort of "plug compatibility" of knowledge bases is a realistic possibility for a range of tasks.

the problems attacked nor the solutions suggested are restricted to a single domain of application or performance program design. The dialog is a real example of TEIRESIAS in action with a few words substituted in a medical example:

e.g., *E. coli* became *AT&T*, *infection* became *investment*, etc.

An example of the program in action is shown in Section 6. The program interviews the user, requesting various pieces of information that are relevant to selecting the most appropriate investment, then prints its recommendations. In the remainder of this paper the "user" will be an expert running the program in order to challenge it, offering it a difficult case, and observing and correcting its performance.

### 4.2. The knowledge base

The knowledge base of the performance program contains a collection of decision rules of the sort shown in Fig. 3. (The rule is stored internally in the INTERLISP form, the English version is generated from that with a simple template-directed mechanisms.) Each rule is a single "chunk" of domain specific information indicating an *action* (in this case a conclusion) which is justified if the conditions specified in the *premise* are fulfilled.

The rules are judgmental, i.e., they make inexact inferences. In the case of the rule in Fig. 3, for instance, the evidence cited in the premise is enough to assert the conclusion shown with only a weak degree of confidence (0.4 out of 1.0). These numbers are referred to as *certainty factors*, and embody a model of confirmation described in detail in [18]. The details of that model need not concern us here; we need only note that a rule typically embodies an inexact inference rather than an exact rule.

RULE 027

If    [1.1] the time scale of the investment is long-term,
       [1.2] the desired return on the investment is greater than 10%, and
       [1.3] the area of the investment is not known,
then AT&T is a likely (0.4) choice for the investment.

```
PREMISE ($AND (SAME OBJCT TIMESCALE LONG-TERM)
              (GREATER OBJCT RETURNRATE 10)
              (NOTKNOWN OBJCT INVESTMENT-AREA))

ACTION   (CONCLUDE OBJCT STOCK-NAME AT&T 0.4)
```
Fig. 3. Example of a rule.

Finally, a few points of terminology. The premise is a Boolean combination of one or more *clauses*, each of which is constructed from a *predicate function* with an *associative triple (attribute, object, value)* as its argument. For the first clause in Fig. 3, for example, the predicate function is SAME, and the triple is "*timescale of investment* is *long-term*". (The identifier OBJCT is used as a placeholder for the specific object to be referred to; the actual binding is established each time the rule is invoked.)

### 4.3. The inference engine

The rules are invoked in a simple backward-chaining fashion that produces an exhaustive depth-first search of an and/or goal tree (Fig. 4). Assume that the program is attempting to determine which stock would make a good investment. It retrieves (the precomputed list of) all rules which make a conclusion about that topic (i.e., they mention STOCK-NAME in their action), and invokes each one in turn, evaluating each premise to see if the conditions specified have been met. For the example shown in Fig. 4, this means first determining what the timescale of the investment ought to be. This is in turn set up as a subgoal, and the process recurs.

The search is thus depth-first (because each premise condition is thoroughly explored in turn); the tree that is sprouted is an and/or goal tree (because rules may have OR conditions in their premise); and the search is exhaustive (because the rules are inexact, so that even if one succeeds, it was deemed to be a wisely conservative strategy to continue to collect all evidence about the subgoal.)

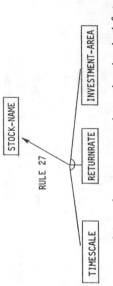

FIG. 4. Control structure of the performance program is an exhaustive, depth-first search of an and/or goal tree.

We have noted earlier that the expert must have at least a high-level understanding of the operation of the inference engine and the manner of knowledge representation to enable him to express new knowledge for the performance program. That level of understanding is well supplied by the information in Sections 4.2 and 4.3, together with an equally brief summary of the model of confirmation described in [18]. This should make plausible the assumption in Section 3 that the expert might indeed be able to understand these things sufficiently without having to deal with details of implementation. Note too that TEIRESIAS's basic design and the notion of interactive transfer of expertise does not depend on this particular control structure, only on the (non-trivial) assumption that an equally comprehensible explanation can be found for whatever control structure is actually used in the inference engine.

## 5. A Word about Natural Language

Natural language has not been a major focus of this work, and for the most part the simplest techniques have been used that would support the level of performance required. For instance, all questions and responses from TEIRESIAS are either performed, or manufactured by filling in templates with appropriate words (as evidenced the occasional appearance of phrases like "a area"). Where answers are free text (rather than multiple choice), the system relies primarily on the keyword- and template-oriented techniques described in Section 7.3.4. There is no parser in the system, in part to minimize processing time, and in part because users often give ungrammatical responses.

## 6. Example of TEIRESIAS in Operation

In the interaction shown below, the expert is challenging the investment advisory program with a particular case, observing the program's performance, and then making the necessary correction to the knowledge base. The bug encountered here was created by deleting an existing rule from the knowledge base and removing all references to it. The expert then repairs the bug by tracking down the source of the problem and teaching the system the "new" rule.

The deleted rule was chosen to make possible an acquisition example that displays a large number of TEIRESIAS's capabilities in a single example. It is special in no other sense, however, and offers a real trace of the system in action.

In the trace below, computer output is in mixed upper and lower case in this font, user responses follow a double asterisk and are in **BOLD CAPITALS**, and commentary appears as {*indented italics inside braces*}. The example is also divided into five phases for later reference.

**Investment Advisory Program**

User?
** RD

Hello, Randy.

{*The expert identifies himself to the program, and then, responding to the program's inquiries, describes a particular case as a test of performance.*}

(1) Investor's name?
**FRED SMITH

(2) Age?
**40

(3) Present taxable income?
**40,000

(4) Number of dependents?
**3

(5) Occupation?
**LAWYER

(6) Amount of previous investment experience? (slight = less than one year; moderate = 2 to 4 years; extensive = more than 4 years)
**MODERATE

(7) Does the investor subscribe to the Wall Street Journal, or any securities market newsletters?
**Y

{*Most of the consultation with the performance program has been edited out for brevity (see [5] for a complete example). The interaction continues with the program printing out its conclusions.*}

The following investments appear to be the most appropriate at this time:
Varian-Corporation
America 1-Telephone-and-Telegraph

{*At this point TEIRESIAS steps in, and since the interaction is with an expert (rather than an ordinary user), it requests an evaluation of the performance program's results.*

*From here on the dialog takes place between TEIRESIAS and the expert, with the performance program in the background being manipulated by TEIRESIAS.*}

{**Phase I: tracking down the bug**}

{*The expert indicates that the results are incorrect...*}

Are all these correct?
+ + **N

{*... and then specifies the problems.*}

Are there any missing?
+ + **Y
Which one(s)?
+ + ** **DIGITAL-EQUIPMENT DATA-GENERAL**
Are there any that shouldn't have appeared?
+ + ** Y
Which one(s)?
+ + ** **AT&T**

Do you want to
(1) track down the problem yourself, or
(2) allow me to guide the debugging, or
(3) ignore it for now and fix it another time?
Type 1, 2 or 3
+ + * * 2

{*The first option allows the expert to use the explanation facilities described in [5] to track down the problem. The facility indicated by the second option is based on a model of the control structure of the performance program that allows a simple algorithmic search for the error, and will be demonstrated here. The third is for human engineering purposes, and allows the expert to sidestep this whole process if desired.*}

We'll start with the AT&T first.

{*Heuristics derived from our experience in debugging rule-based systems are built into* TEIRESIAS. *One such heuristic suggests that the best approach is to (1) track down one problem at a time, and (2) start with a result that shouldn't have appeared (if there is one). Experience indicates that this class of bug is often a manifestation of a deeper bug causing several problems, so curing it will often solve several problems at once.*}

The following rules were used in deducing that the investment should be AT&T:

RULE 027
Since [1.1] the area of the investment is not known, and
[1.2] the desired return on the investment is greater than 10%, and
[1.3] the time scale of the investment is long-term,
then AT&T is a likely (0.4) choice for the investment.

Is this rule correct?
+ + * * Y
Should its premise have failed for this case?
+ + * * Y
Which clause of the premise should have been false? [give #]
+ + * * 1

{*The expert indicates that this rule should have failed, so the debugging continues by looking further back in the chain. Had he indicated that rule 27 had been invoked properly, then* TEIRESIAS *would have indicated that the problem was probably a missing rule which tended to* **rule out AT&T**.}

No conclusions were reached concerning the area of the investment.

Should it have been possible to conclude an area?
+ + * * Y
{*The error might have been a failure to rule out an investment area.*}

Which one?
+ + * * **HIGH TECHNOLOGY**

There were no rules successfully invoked in the attempt to deduce that the area of the investment should be high-technology.

The following (potentially applicable) rules were NOT executed because the starred [**] clause failed:

RULE 116
If (1) the desired return on the investment is greater than 10%,
(2) the time scale of the investment is long-term,
**(3) the number of dependents of the client is less than 3,**
(4) the age (in years) of the client is less than or equal to 35
then there is evidence (0.4) that the area of the investment should be high-technology.

RULE 050
If (1) the time scale of the investment is long-term,
(2) the desired return on the investment is greater than 10%,
**(3) the risk class of the investment is speculative**
then there is evidence (0.6) that the area of the investment should be high-technology.

Are all these rules correct?
+ + * * Y
Should any of them have been successfully invoked?
+ + * * N

{*This would have been the case if one of the starred premise clauses were false because it was "stepped on" by yet another rule further back in the chain.*}

Is there a rule missing?
+ + * * Y

Ok, then I need a rule that would allow me to deduce that the area of the investment should be high-technology.

Would you like to give me such a rule now?
+ + * * Y
Good...

{*To review briefly: the expert is tracking down the reason why the system incorrectly concluded that the stock to invest in was AT&T. Shown below is the sequence of rules which were involved:*}

RETURN
TIME SCALE
**DEPENDENTS**
AGE      —RULE 116→
                            →AREA
TIME SCALE—RULE 050→   RETURN   —RULE 027→AT&T
RETURN                 TIME SCALE
**RISK CLASS**

*AT&T appeared because the system executed Rule 27 successfully. This occurred in part because investment area was unknown. Investment area was unknown because all rules to conclude it (Rules 50 and 116) failed.*

*Since the expert believes all existing rules are correct, the knowledge base must be missing a rule that will conclude about investment area, in particular, that the area should be high-technology. Such a rule will cause area to be known, inhibiting Rule 27, fixing at least this first problem.*

*Note how sharply focussed the issue has become, for both the expert and* TEIRESIAS, *as a result of the large amount of contextual information available. The expert is not being asked to "discuss the stock market"; instead the system can at this point say*

*... I need a rule that would allow me to deduce that the area of the investment should be high technology.*

*and it must be a rule which is invokable in the current situation. Thus it is easier for the expert to specify a rule that may never before have been explicitly stated or recognized as such. This can be an important advantage in any domain where the knowledge is not yet fully formalized.*

*The contextual information is useful for* TEIRESIAS *as well. The information provides a number of expectations about the content of the rule which are used both in understanding what the expert types in, and in checking the new rule to make sure that it does indeed solve the problem at hand. Details of this process are explained below.*

*The trace continues with the expert typing in the rule...}*

{Phase II: interpreting the rule}
The new rule will be called RULE 383

If:  1. **THE CLIENT'S INCOME TAX BRACKET IS 50%**
and  2. **THE CLIENT IS FOLLOWING UP ON MARKET TRENDS CAREFULLY**
and  3.
Then: 1. **THERE IS EVIDENCE (0.8) THAT THE INVESTMENT AREA SHOULD BE HIGH TECHNOLOGY**
and  2.

This may take a few moments...

*{Generally on the order of 10 to 30 seconds of cpu time.}*

This is my understanding of your rule:

RULE 383

If   (1)  The client's income-tax bracket is 50%, and
     (2)  The market has followed an upward trend recently, and
     (3)  The client manages his assets carefully,
then there is evidence (0.8) that the area of the investment should be high-technology

*{*TEIRESIAS's *initial interpretation is not entirely correct (and the example was chosen in part for this reason). The first line of text and the conclusion have been interpreted correctly, but the second line has been turned into two clauses (numbers 2 and 3) in the system's initial attempt at understanding. (The expert occasionally types what should be two separate clauses as one line of text. The system is capable of handling this, but this same capability at times produces spurious clauses like No. 3).*

*This level of performance results primarily from the system's simple word-by-word approach to meaning. While the result is in part incorrect, it will become clear below that the interpretations are both "reasonable" and "consistent" in light of the techniques used.}*

**{Phase III: modifying the interpretation}**

Okay? (Yes or No)
+ + ∗∗ **N**

*{The expert indicates there is a problem with the interpretation, and uses* TEIRESIAS's *rule editor to specify the changes needed.}*

Change premise?
+ + ∗∗ **Y**

What clause should be changed in premise? (type HELP for list of commands)
+ + ∗∗ **CHANGE 2**

Suppose (2) were changed to read:
(2) The client follows the market carefully
Would that be ok?
+ + ∗∗ **Y**

*{Several simple heuristics are invoked to select the next most likely interpretation, based on the English source of this clause and the set of interpretations already rejected. In this case the second choice is correct.}*

Then you'll probably want to delete:
(3) The client manages his assets carefully
Correct?
+ + ** Y

*{TEIRESIAS enforces certain consistency constraints on its interpretation of the English text. One of these constraints indicates that if the new interpretation of clause No. 2 is correct, then clause No. 3 must have arisen spuriously (since, among other things, it requires a different interpretation for the word carefully).}*

Anything else?
+ + ** ?
(1) the client's income-tax bracket is 50%
and (2) the client follows the market carefully
and (3) ⟨deleted⟩

Anything else?
+ + ** N

Change action?
+ + ** N

This is my understanding of your rule:

RULE 383

If: (1) the client's income-tax bracket is 50%, and
(2) the client follows the market carefully,
then there is evidence (0.8) that the area of the investment should be high-technology.

Okay? (Yes or No)
+ + ** Y

*{This is the standard test of comprehension: the original English text has been turned into a rule coded in LISP, and is then retranslated back into English for approval. Compare the results with the expert's original input. Now that the expert is satisfied that TEIRESIAS understands the rule that he entered, TEIRESIAS checks several things about the rule to see if it is satisfied with the rule content.}*

*{Phase IV: "second guessing"}*

I hate to criticize, Randy, but did you know that most rules about what the area of an investment might be, that mention:
the income-tax bracket of the client, and
how closely the client follows the market
ALSO mention:

[A] The amount of investment experience of the client
Shall I try to write a clause to account for [A]?
+ + ** Y

*{The mechanism that makes possible this sort of "second guessing" by the system is explained in detail below. Briefly, the system maintains a model of its own knowledge. In checking to see how this new piece of information "fits in" to that model, it discovers that its expectations have been only partially met. It indicates to the expert what expectations were left unfulfilled, and asks if it should attempt to fill in the missing parts.}*

How about:
[A] The amount of investment experience of the client is moderate
Ok?
+ + ** Y

*{The expert agreed to the inclusion of the new clause and TEIRESIAS is able to construct a plausible guess as to its content. Note that it must be possible to invoke the new rule in the current situation, in order to fix the known bug. TEIRESIAS uses this fact to guide its construction of the new clause. Details of this process are explained below.}*

Also, most rules about what the area of an investment might be ALSO conclude about:
[A] The desired risk classification of the investment
Shall I try to write a clause to account for [A]?
+ + ** N

*{The system noticed another unfulfilled expectation concerning the action part of the rule, but the expert always has the option of overriding the system's suggestions, and does so.}*

*{Phase V: final checkout, bookkeeping, rerunning the consultation}*

The rule now reads:

RULE 383

If (1) the income-tax bracket of the client is 50%, and
(2) the client follows the market carefully, and
(3) the amount of investment experience of the client is moderate,
then there is evidence (0.8) that the area of the investment should be high-technology.

Please describe briefly why you added (or changed) this rule.
Type an empty line when done.

+ +**THE SYSTEM FAILED TO REALIZE IT COULD CONCLUDE
+ +**INVESTMENT AREA, AND THIS ALLOWED RULE 027 TO BE
+ +**INVOKED INAPPROPRIATELY
+ +**

{Experience suggests that in building any large knowledge base it is very useful to keep fairly detailed records about the source of various contributions. The new rule is automatically tagged with a range of such information (including author, date, and a record of the consultation which prompted its creation), along with any comments which the expert may care to make for his own future reference.}

RULE 383 has now been added to the knowledge base.

I will now rerun the consultation to check the effectiveness of your new rule. Get comfortable, since this may take a bit.
Also, new questions may be asked as a result of this new rule. If a question is printed, please answer it with reference to this current client.

.

{The consultation is then rerun, but all the previous answers are saved, so the expert can in most cases just watch it proceed. This has been edited out here for brevity.}

The following investments appear to be the most appropriate at this time:

Varian-Corporation
Data-General
Digital-Equipment

Well, it appears that things are straightened out.

{The new conclusions are the ones the expert indicated earlier as the correct answers. This does not go unnoticed.}

Are all these values correct now?
+ +**Y

{As always, however, the expert gets the last word, and TEIRESIAS waits for approval before proceeding.}

Good, then the problem's been fixed.

{How is it that three errors disappeared with the addition of one rule? This is explained schematically below:}

*RULE 116*
*RULE 050*
RULE 383→AREA—→RULE 027*→AT&T
— RULE 084 →DATA-GENERAL
DIGITAL-EQUIPMENT

*As before, Rules 116 and 50 failed (hence the **'s), but now the new rule, 383, has succeeded, supplying a value for investment area. This in turn means that Rule 27 now fails, as hoped.*
*However, Rule 84, which requires a value of area, failed last time because the system was unable to deduce one. Now that Rule 383 supplies one, Rule 84 can fire, and it turns out to yield the missing answers.}*

## 7. How it all Works

### 7.1. Overview of the main ideas
Before reviewing the trace in more detail, we describe the ideas which make possible the capabilities displayed. The list below serves primarily to name and briefly sketch each in turn; the details are supplied in reviewing the example.

#### 7.1.1. Knowledge acquisition in context
Performance programs of the sort TEIRESIAS helps create will typically find their greatest utility in domains where there are no unifying laws on which to base algorithmic methods. In such domains there is instead a collection of informal knowledge based on accumulated experience. This means an expert specifying a new rule may be codifying a piece of knowledge that has never previously been isolated and expressed as such. Since this is difficult, anything which can be done to ease the task will prove very useful.

In response, we have emphasized knowledge acquisition in the context of a shortcoming in the knowledge base. To illustrate its utility, consider the difference between asking the expert

    *What should I know about the stock market?*

and saying to him

    *Here is an example in which you say the performance program made a mistake. Here is all the knowledge the program used, here are all the facts of the case, and here is how it reached its conclusions. Now,* **what is it that you know and the system doesn't** *that allows you to avoid making that same mistake?*

Note how much more focussed the second question is, and how much easier it to answer.

#### 7.1.2. Building expectations
The focussing provided by the context is also an important aid to TEIRESIAS. In particular, it permits the system to build up a set of expectations concerning the

knowledge to be acquired, facilitating knowledge transfer and making possible several useful features illustrated in the trace and described below.

### 7.1.3. *Model-based understanding*

Model-based understanding suggests that some aspects of understanding can be viewed as a process of matching: the entity to be understood is matched against a collection of prototypes, or models, and the most appropriate model selected. This sets the framework in which further interpretation takes place, as that model can then be used as a guide to further processing.

While this view is not new, TEIRESIAS employs a novel application of it, since the system has a model of the knowledge it is likely to be acquiring from the expert.

### 7.1.4. *Giving a program a model of its own knowledge*

We will see that the combination of TEIRESIAS and the performance program amounts to a system which has a picture of its own knowledge. That is, it not only knows something about a particular domain, but in a primitive sense it knows what it knows, and employs that model of its knowledge in several ways.

### 7.1.5. *Learning as a process of comparison*

We do not view learning as simply the addition of information to an existing base of knowledge, but instead take it to include various forms of comparison of the new information with the old. This of course has its corollary in human behavior: A student will quickly point out discrepancies between newly taught material and his current stock of information. TEIRESIAS has a similar, though very primitive, capability: It compares new information supplied by the expert with the existing knowledge base, points out inconsistencies, and suggests possible remedies.

### 7.1.6. *Learning by experience*

One of the long-recognized potential weaknesses of any model-based system is dependence on a fixed set of models, since the scope of the program's "understanding" of the world is constrained by the number and type of models it has. As will become clear, the models TEIRESIAS employs are not hand-crafted and static, but are instead formed and continually revised as a by-product of its experience in interacting with the expert.

### 7.2. Phase I: tracking down the bug

To provide the debugging facility shown, TEIRESIAS maintains a detailed record of the actions of the performance program during the consultation, and then interprets this record on the basis of an exhaustive analysis of the performance program's control structure (see [5] for details). This presents the expert with a comprehensible task because (a) the backward-chaining technique used by the performance program is sufficiently straightforward and intuitive, even to a non-programmer; and (b) the rules are designed to encode knowledge at a reasonably high conceptual level. As a result, even though TEIRESIAS is running through an exhaustive case-by-case analysis of the preceding consultation, the expert is presented with a task of debugging *reasoning* rather than *code*.

The availability of an algorithmic debugging process is also an important factor in encouraging the expert to be as precise as possible in his responses. Note that at each point in tracking down the error the expert must either approve of the rules invoked and conclusions made, or indicate which one was in error and supply the correction. This is extremely useful in domains where knowledge has not yet been formalized, and the traditional reductionist approach of dissecting reasoning down to observational primitives is not yet well established.[4]

TEIRESIAS further encourages precise comments by keeping the debugging process sharply focussed. For instance, when it became clear that there was a problem with the inability to deduce investment area, the system first asks which area it should have been. It then displays only those rules appropriate to that answer, rather than all of the rules on that topic which were tried.

Finally, consider the extensive amount of contextual information that is now available. The expert has been presented with a detailed example of the performance program in action, he has available all of the facts of the case, and has seen how the relevant knowledge has been applied. This makes it much easier for him to specify the particular chunk of knowledge which may be missing. This contextual information will prove very useful for TEIRESIAS as well. It is clear, for instance, what the *effect* of invocation of the new rule must be (as TEIRESIAS indicates, it must be a rule that will "deduce that the area of the investment should be high-technology"), and it is also clear what the *circumstances* of its invocation must be (the rule must be invokable for the case under consideration, or it won't repair the bug). Both of these will be seen to be quite useful (see Sections 7.3.3 and 7.6).

### 7.3. Phase II: interpreting the rule

As is traditional, "understanding" the expert's natural language version of the rule is viewed in terms of converting it to an internal representation, and then re-translating that into English for the expert's approval. In this case the internal representation is the INTERLISP form of the rule, so the process is also a simple type of code generation.

There were a number of reasons for rejecting a standard natural language understanding approach to this problem. First, as noted, understanding natural language is well known to be a difficult problem, and was not a central focus of this research. Second, our experience suggested that experts frequently sacrifice

[4] The debugging process does allow the expert to indicate that while the performance program's results are incorrect, he cannot find an error in the reasoning. This choice is offered only as a last resort and is intended to deal with situations where there may be a bug in the underlying control structure of the performance program (contrary to our assumption in Section 3).

precise grammar in favor of the compactness available in the technical language of the domain. As a result, approaches that were strongly grammar-based might not fare well. Finally, technical language often contains a fairly high percentage of unambiguous words, so a simpler approach that includes reliance on keyword analysis has a good chance of performing adequately.

As will become clear, our approach to analyzing the expert's new rule is based on both simple keyword spotting and predictions TEIRESIAS is able to make about the likely content of the rule. Code generation is accomplished via a form of template completion that is similar in some respects to template completion processes that have been used in generating natural language. Details of all these processes are given below.

### 7.3.1. Models and model-based understanding

To set the stage for reviewing the details of the interpretation process, we digress for a moment to consider the idea of models and model-based understanding, then explore their application in TEIRESIAS.

In the most general terms, a model can be seen as a *compact, high-level description of structure, organization, or content* that may be used both to *provide a framework for lower-level processing*, and *to express expectations about the world*. One particularly graphic example of this idea can be found in the work on computer vision by Falk [10] in 1970. The task there was the standard one of understanding blocks-world scenes: the goal was to determine the identity, location, and orientation of each block in a scene containing one or more blocks selected from a known set of possibilities.

The key element of his work of interest here is the use of a set of *prototypes* for the blocks, prototypes that resembled wire frame models. While it oversimplifies slightly, part of the operation of his system can be described in terms of two phases. The system first performed a preliminary pass to detect possible edge points in the scene and attempted to fit a block model to each collection of edges. The model chosen was then used in the second phase as a guide to further processing. If, for instance, the model accounted for all but one of the lines in a region, this suggested that the extra line might be spurious. If the model fit well except for some line missing from the scene, that was a good hint that a line had been overlooked and indicated as well where to go looking for it.

While it was not a part of Falk's system, we can imagine one further refinement in the interpretation process and explain it in these same terms. Imagine that the system had available some *a priori* hints about what blocks might be found in the next scene. One way to express those hints would be to bias the matching process. That is, in the attempt to match a model against the data, the system might (depending on the strength of the hint) try the indicated models first, make a greater attempt to effect a match with one of them, or even restrict the set of possibilities to just those contained in the hint.

Note that in this system, (i) the models supply a compact, high-level description of structure (the structure of each block), (ii) the description is used to guide lower level processing (processing of the array of digitized intensity values), (iii) expectations can be expressed by a biasing or restriction on the set of models used, and (iv) "understanding" is viewed in terms of a matching and selection process (matching models against the data and selecting one that fits).

### 7.3.2. Rule models

Now recall our original task of interpreting the expert's natural language version of the rule, and view it in the terms described above. As in the vision example, there is a signal to be processed (the text), it is noisy (words can be ambiguous), and there is context available (from the debugging process) that can supply some hints about the likely content of the signal. To complete the analogy, we need a model, one that could (a) capture the structure, organization, or content of the expert's reasoning, (b) be used to guide the interpretation process, and (c) be used to express expectations about the likely content of the new rule.

Where might we get such a thing? There are interesting regularities in the knowledge base that might supply what we need. Not surprisingly, rules about a single topic tend to have characteristics in common — there are "ways" of reasoning about a given topic. From these regularities we have constructed *rule models*. These are abstract descriptions of subsets of rules, built from empirical generalizations about those rules, and are used to characterize a "typical" member of the subset.

Rule models are composed of four parts (Fig. 5). They contain, first, a list of EXAMPLES, the subset of rules from which this model was constructed.

EXAMPLES    the subset of rules which this model describes

DESCRIPTION    characterization of a "typical" member of this subset
      characterization of the premise
      characterization of the action
        which attributes "typically" appear
        correlations of attributes

MORE GENERAL    pointers to models describing more general

MORE SPECIFIC    and more specific subsets of rules

FIG. 5. Rule model structure.

Next, a DESCRIPTION characterizes a typical member of the subset. Since we are dealing in this case with rules composed of premise-action pairs, the DESCRIPTION currently implemented contains individual characterizations of a typical premise and a typical action. Then, since the current representation scheme used in those rules is based on associative triples, we have chosen to implement those characterizations by indicating (a) which attributes "typically" appear in the premise (action) of a rule in this subset, and (b) correlations of attributes appearing in the premise (action).[5]

Note that the central idea is the concept of *characterizing a typical member of the subset*. Naturally, that characterization would look different for subsets of rules, procedures, theorems, or any other representation. But the main idea of characterization is widely applicable and not restricted to any particular representational formalism.

The two remaining parts of the rule model are pointers to models describing more general and more specific subsets of rules. The set of models is organized into a number of tree structures, each of the general form shown in Fig. 6. At the root of each tree is the model made from all the rules which conclude about ⟨attribute⟩ (e.g., the INVESTMENT-AREA model), below this are two models dealing with all affirmative and all negative rules (e.g., the INVESTMENT-AREA-IS model), and below this are models dealing with rules which affirm or deny specific values of the attribute.

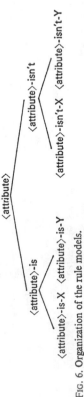

FIG. 6. Organization of the rule models.

These models are not hand-tooled by the expert. They are instead assembled by TEIRESIAS on the basis of the current contents of the knowledge base, in what amounts to a very simple (i.e., statistical) form of concept formation. The combination of TEIRESIAS and the performance program thus presents a system which has a model of its own knowledge, one which it forms itself.

The rule models are the primary example of meta-level knowledge in this paper (for discussion of other forms, see [5] and [8]). This form of knowledge and its generation by the system itself have several interesting implications illustrated in later sections.

Fig. 7 shows a rule model; this is the one used by TEIRESIAS in the interaction shown earlier. (Since not all of the details of implementation are relevant here, this discussion will omit some. See [5] for a full explanation.) As indicated above, there is a list of the rules from which this model was constructed, descriptions characterizing the premise and the action, and pointers to more specific and more general models. Each characterization in the description is shown split into its two parts, one concerning the presence of individual attributes and the other describing correlations. The first item in the premise description, for instance, indicates that "most" rules about what the area of an investment should be mention

[5] Both (a) and (b) are constructed via simple thresholding operations.

the attribute *rate of return* in their premise; when they do mention it they "typically" use the predicate functions SAME and NOTSAME; and the "strength", or reliability, of this piece of advice is 3.8 (see [5] for precise definition of the quoted terms).

The fourth item in the premise description indicates that when the attribute *rate of return* appears in the premise of a rule in this subset, the attribute *timescale of the investment* "typically" appears as well. As before the predicate functions are those typically associated with the attributes, and the number is an indication of reliability.

```
INVESTMENT-AREA-IS

EXAMPLES    (RULE116 0.3)
            (RULE050 0.7)
            (RULE037 0.8)
            (RULE095 0.9)
            (RULE152 1.0)
            (RULE140 1.0))

DESCRIPTION
PREMISE    ((RETURNRATE SAME NOTSAME 3.8)
            (TIMESCALE SAME NOTSAME 3.8)
            (TREND SAME 2.8)

            ((RETURNRATE SAME) (TIMESCALE SAME) 3.8)
            ((TIMESCALE SAME) (RETURNRATE SAME) 3.8)
            ((BRACKET SAME) (FOLLOWS NOTSAME SAME)
                            (EXPERIENCE SAME) 1.5))

ACTION     ((INVESTMENT-AREA CONCLUDE 4.7)
            (RISK CONCLUDE 4.0)

            ((INVESTMENT-AREA CONCLUDE) (RISK CONCLUDE) 4.7))

MORE-GENL  (INVESTMENT-AREA)
MORE-SPEC  (INVESTMENT-AREA-IS-UTILITIES)
```

FIG. 7. Example of a rule model.

### 7.3.3. Choosing a model

It was noted earlier that tracking down the bug in the knowledge base provides useful context, and, among other things, serve to set up TEIRESIAS's expectations about the sort of rule it is about to receive. As suggested, these expectations are expressed by restricting the set of models which will be considered for use in guiding the interpretation. At this point TEIRESIAS chooses a model which expresses what it knows thus far about the kind of rule to expect, and in the current example it expects a rule that will "deduce that the area of the investment should be high-technology."

Since there is not necessarily a rule model for every characterization, the system chooses the closest one. This is done by starting at the top of the tree of models, and descending until either reaching a model of the desired type, or encountering a leaf of the tree. In this case, the process descends to the second level (the INVESTMENT-AREA-IS model), notices that there is no model for INVESTMENT-AREA-IS-HIGH-TECHNOLOGY at the next level, and settles for the former.[6]

7.3.4. *Using the rule model: guiding the natural language interpretation*

TEIRESIAS uses the rule models in two different ways in the acquisition process. The first is as a guide in understanding the text typed by the expert, and is described here. The second is as a means of allowing TEIRESIAS to see whether the new rule "fits in" to its current model of the knowledge base, and is described in Section 7.5.

To see how the rule models are used to guide the interpretation of the text of the new rule, consider the second line of text typed by the expert. Each word is first reduced to a canonical form by a process that can recognize plural endings and that has access to a dictionary of synonyms. We then consider the possible connotations that each word may have (Fig. 8a). Here connotation means the word might be referring to one or more of the conceptual primitives from which rules are built (i.e., it might refer to a predicate function, attribute, object, or value). One set of connotations is shown.[7]

Code generation is accomplished via a "fill-in-the-blank" mechanism. Associated with each predicate function is a *template*, a list structure that resembles a simplified procedure declaration, and gives the order and generic type of each argument to a call of that function (Fig. 8b). Associated with each of the primitives that make up a template (e.g., ATTRIBUTE, VALUE, etc.) is a procedure capable of scanning the list of connotations to find an item of the appropriate type to fill in that blank.

The whole process is begun by checking the list of connotations for the predicate function implicated most strongly (in this case, SAME; see [5] for details), retrieving the template for that function, and allowing it to scan the connotations and "fill itself in" using the procedures associated with the primitives. The set of connotations in Fig. 8a produces the LISP code in Fig. 8c. The ATTRIBUTE routine finds the attribute TREND, the VALUE routine finds an appropriate value (UPWARD), and the OBJect routine finds the corresponding object type (MARKET) (but following the convention noted earlier, returns the variable name OBJCT to be used in the actual code).

```
THE CLIENT  IS  FOLLOWING  UP   ON  MARKET  TRENDS  CAREFULLY
                   ↓                  ↓         ↓          ↓
           PREDICATE FUNCTION       VALUE      OBJ     ATTRIBUTE
```

FIG. 8a. Connotations.

```
FUNCTION     TEMPLATE
SAME         (OBJ ATTRIBUTE VALUE)
```

FIG. 8b. Template for the predicate function SAME.

```
(SAME OBJCT TREND UPWARD)
The general trend of the market is upward
```

FIG. 8c. The resulting code.

There are several points to note here. First, the interpretation in Fig. 8c is incorrect (the system has been misled by the idiom "following up"); we'll see in a moment how it is corrected. Second, there are typically several plausible (syntactically valid) interpretations available from each line of text, and TEIRESIAS generates all of them. Each is assigned a score (the "text score") indicating how likely it is, based on how strongly it was implicated by the text (details in [5]). Finally, we have not yet used the rule models, and it is at this point that they are employed.

We can view the DESCRIPTION part of the rule model selected earlier as a set of predictions about the likely content of the new rule. In these terms the next step is to see how well each interpretation fulfills those predictions. Note, for example, that the third line of the premise description in Fig. 7 "predicts" that a rule about investment area will contain the attribute *market trend*, and the clause generated from the connotations in Fig. 8a fulfills this prediction. Each interpretation is scored (employing the "strength of advice" number in the rule model) according to how many predictions it fulfills, yielding the "prediction satisfaction score".

This score is then combined with the text score to indicate the most likely interpretation. Because more weight is given to the prediction score, the system tends to "hear what it expects to hear" (and that leads it astray in this case).

7.3.5. *Rule interpretation: sources of performance*

While our approach to natural language is very simple, the overall performance of the interpretation process is adequate. The problem is made easier, of course, by the fact that we are dealing with a small amount of text in a restricted context, written in a semi-formal technical language, rather than with large amounts of text in unrestricted dialog written in unconstrained English. Even so, the problem

[6] This technique is used in several places throughout the knowledge transfer process, and in general supplies the model which best matches the current requirements, by accommodating varying levels of specificity in the stated expectations. If, for instance, the system had known only that it expected a rule which concluded about investment area, it would have selected the first node in the model tree without further search.

TEIRESIAS also has techniques for checking that the appropriate model has been chosen and can advise the expert if a discrepancy appears. See [5] for an example.

[7] The connotations of a word are determined by a number of pointers associated with it, which are in turn derived from the English phrases associated with each of the primitives. For instance, one of the primitives—the attribute TREND—has associated with it the phrase *the general trend*. Hence when the English word *trends* is found in the text of the rule, it is first changed to *trend* by the canonicalization process, then the connotation pointers are checked, yielding the attribute TREND.

It is possible to have sets of interpretations other than the one shown and TEIRESIAS considers them all. The number of possibilities is kept constrained by enforcing several types of consistency This and other details are omitted here for the sake of brevity; see [5] for a complete description.

of interpretation is substantial. TEIRESIAS's performance is based on both the application of the ideas noted in Section 7.1 (notably the ideas of building expectations and model-based understanding) and the use of two additional techniques: the intersection of data-driven and model-driven processing, and the use of multiple sources of knowledge.

First, the interpretation process proceeds in what has been called the "recognition" mode: it is the intersection of a bottom-up (data-directed) process (the interpretations suggested by the connotations of the text) with a top-down (goal-directed) process (the expectations set up by the choice of a rule model). Each process contributes to the end result, but it is the combination of them that is effective.

This intersection of two processing modes is important where the interpretation techniques are as simple as those employed here, but the idea is more generally applicable as well. Even with more powerful interpretation techniques, neither direction of processing is in general capable of eliminating all ambiguity and finding the correct answer. By moving both top-down and bottom-up, we make use of all available sources of information, resulting in a far more focussed search for the answer. This technique is applicable across a range of different interpretation problems, including text, vision, and speech.

Second, in either direction of processing, TEIRESIAS uses a number of different sources of knowledge. In the bottom-up direction, for example, distinct information about the appropriate interpretation of the text comes from (a) the connotations of individual words (interpretation of each piece of data), (b) the function template (structure for the whole interpretation), and (c) internal consistency constraints (interactions between data points), as well as several other sources (see [5] for the full list). Any one of these knowledge sources alone will not perform very well, but acting in concert they are much more effective (a principle developed extensively in [15]).

The notion of program-generated expectations is also an important source of power, since the selection of a particular rule model supplies the focus for the top-down part of the processing. Finally, the idea of model-based understanding offers an effective way of using the information in the rule model to effect the top-down processing.

Thus our relatively simple techniques supply adequate power because of the synergistic effect of multiple, independent sources of knowledge, because of the focussing and guiding effect of intersecting data-directed and goal-directed processing, and because of the effective mechanism for interpretation supplied by the idea of model-based understanding.

### 7.4. Phase III: modifying the interpretation

TEIRESIAS has a simple rule editor that allows the expert to modify existing rules or (as in this example) indicate changes to the system's attempts to understand a new

rule. The editor has a number of simple heuristics built into it to make the rule modification process as effective as possible. In dealing with requests to change a particular clause of a new rule, for instance, the system re-evaluates the alternative interpretations, taking into account the rejected interpretation (trying to learn from its mistakes), and making the smallest change possible (using the heuristic that the original clause was probably close to correct). In this case this succeeds in choosing the correct clause next (Fig. 8d shows the correct connotations and resulting code).

```
THE CLIENT IS FOLLOWING  UP ON MARKET TRENDS  CAREFULLY
       →   →   →                              →
      OBJ SAME ATTRIBUTE                     VALUE

          (SAME OBJCT FOLLOWS CAREFULLY)
          The client follows the market carefully
```

FIG. 8d. The correct interpretation.

There are also various forms of consistency checking available. One obvious but effective constraint is to ensure that each word of the text is interpreted in only one way. In the trace shown earlier, for instance, accepting the new interpretation of clause 2 means clause 3 must be spurious, since it attempts to use the word *carefully* in a different sense.

### 7.5. Phase IV: "second guessing", another use of the rule models

After the expert indicates that TEIRESIAS has correctly understood what he said, the system checks to see if *it* is satisfied with the content of the rule. The idea is to use the rule model to see how well this new rule "fits in" to the system's model of its knowledge—i.e., does it "look like" a typical rule of the sort expected?

In the current implementation, an incomplete match between the new rule and the rule model triggers a response from TEIRESIAS. Recall the last line of the premise description in the rule model of Fig. 7:

```
((BRACKET SAME) (FOLLOWS NOTSAME SAME)
                (EXPERIENCE SAME) 1.5)
```

This indicates that when the tax BRACKET of the client appears in the premise of a rule of this sort, then how closely he FOLLOWS the market, and how much investment EXPERIENCE he has typically appear as well. Note that the new rule has the first two of these, but is missing the last, and the system points this out.

If the expert agrees to the inclusion of a new clause, TEIRESIAS attempts to create it. Since in this case the agreed upon topic for the clause was the amount of investment EXPERIENCE of the client, this must be the attribute to use. The rule model suggests which predicate function to use (SAME, since that is the one paired with EXPERIENCE in the relevant line of the rule model), and the template for this function is retrieved. It is filled out in the usual way, except that TEIRESIAS checks the record of the consultation when seeking items to fill in the template blanks. In this case only a VALUE is still missing. Note that, as the answer to question 6 of the consultation, the expert indicated that the amount of experience was MODERATE, so TEIRESIAS uses this as the value. The result is a plausible guess, since it ensures that the rule will in fact work for the current case (note the further use of the "debugging in context" idea). It is not necessarily correct, of course, since the desired clause may be more general, but it is at least a plausible attempt.

It should be noted that there is nothing in this concept of "second guessing" which is specific to the rule models as they are currently designed, or indeed to associative triples or rules as a knowledge representation. The fundamental point was that mentioned above of testing to see how the new knowledge "fits in" to the system's current model of its knowledge. At this point the system might perform any kind of check, for violations of any established prejudices about what the new chunk of knowledge should look like. Additional kinds of checks for rules might concern the strength of the inference, number of clauses in the premise, etc. Checks used with, say, a procedural encoding might involve the number and type of arguments passed to the procedure, use of global variables, presence of side effects, etc. In that case, for example, we can imagine adding a new procedure to a system which then responds by remarking that "... *most procedures that do hash-table insertion also have the side effect of incrementing the variable* NUMBRELE-MENTS. *Shall I add the code to do this?*" In general, this "second guessing" process can involve any characteristic which the system may have "noticed" about the particular knowledge representation in use.

Note also that this second use of the rule model is quite different than the first. Where earlier we were concerned about interpreting text and determining what the expert actually said, here the task is to see what he plausibly *should have* said. Since, in assembling the rule models, TEIRESIAS may have noticed regularities in the reasoning about the domain that may not yet have occurred to the expert himself, the system's suggestions may conceivably be substantive and useful.

Finally, all this is in turn an instance of the more general notion of using meta-level knowledge in the process of knowledge acquisition: TEIRESIAS does not simply accept the new rule and add it to the knowledge base, but instead uses the rule model to evaluate the new knowledge in light of its current knowledge base. In a very simple way, learning is effected as a process of examining the relationships between what is already known and the new information being taught.

### 7.6. Phase V: final checkout, bookkeeping, rerunning the consultation

Now that both the expert and TEIRESIAS are satisfied, there is one final sequence of tests to be performed, reflecting once again the benefit of knowledge acquisition in context.

At this point, TEIRESIAS examines several things about the rule, attempting to make sure that it will in fact fix the problem uncovered. In this case, for instance, the action of the new rule should be a conclusion about investment area, the area mentioned should be high technology, and the conclusion should be affirmative. The premise should not contain any clauses which are sure to fail in the context in which the rule will be invoked. All these are potential sources of error which would make it obvious that the rule will not fix the bug.

The rule in the current example passes all the tests, but note what would have happened if the user had (perhaps accidentally) typed *the client's income tax bracket is 20%*.

The rule now reads:

RULE 383

If (1) the client's income tax bracket is 20%, and
(2) the client follows the market carefully, and
(3) the amount of investment experience is moderate,
then there is evidence (0.8) that the area of the investment should be high-technology.

Sorry, but this won't work. For Fred Smith, clause No. 1 ("the client's income tax bracket is 20%") is sure to fail. Would you like to change the rule?
+ + * *

(Since the answer to question 3 of the consultation indicated that the client had a taxable income of $40,000, TEIRESIAS is able to determine [by referring to the appropriate tables] that his tax bracket would not be 20%, hence the rule can't succeed). The expert then has the option of either editing the current rule or writing a new one (since the one he wrote may be correct, only inapplicable to the current problem). If he edits it, the tests are run again, until TEIRESIAS is satisfied that there is nothing obviously wrong with the rule.

There are also a number of straightforward bookkeeping tasks to be performed, including hooking the new rule into the knowledge base so that it is retrieved and invoked appropriately (e.g., in this case it gets added to the list of rules that conclude about INVESTMENT-AREA),[8] and tagging it with information which will make it easier to maintain the large and constantly changing body of rules (e.g., the name of the rule author, date of creation, author's justification for adding the rule, a pointer to the consultation which prompted its creation, etc.).

At this point, the system also performs any necessary recomputation of rule models. The operation is very fast, since it is clear from the action part of the rule

[8] Note that these tests require the ability to dissect and partially evaluate the rule. The same function template which is used as a pattern for constructing rules is also used as a guide in this dissection and partial evaluation process. See [5] for details.

which models may need to be recomputed, and the EXAMPLES part of the model then supplies the names of the other relevant rules. TEIRESIAS then reruns the performance program as a sub-process, and checks the results to see if all the problems have been repaired.

## 8. Other Uses for the Rule Models

Two other uses have been developed for the rule models, which demonstrate capabilities made possible by meta-level knowledge.

### 8.1. "Knowing what you know"

The MYCIN system has the ability to answer simple natural language questions about the knowledge base. In response to a question like "*How do you determine the identity of an organism causing an infection?*", that system will print the relevant rules. But a rule model, as a generalization of an entire class of rules, answers the question, too. Fig. 9 shows one example, taken from the stock market example we have been using.

---

\*\*HOW DO YOU DECIDE THAT THE UTILITIES GROUP IS AN APPROPRIATE AREA FOR INVESTMENT?

Rules which conclude that an appropriate area for investment is the utilities group generally use one or more of the following pieces of information:

the desired rate of return of the investment
the income-tax bracket of the client
the time-scale of the investment

Furthermore, the following relationships hold:
If a rule mentions the income-tax bracket of the client, it also typically mentions the time scale of the investment as well.

RULE 247, RULE 45, RULE 123, and RULE 206 conclude that an appropriate area for investment is the utilities group. Which of these (if any) would you like to see?
\*\*

---

Fig. 9. "Knowing what you know."

By simply "reading" the rule model to the user, TEIRESIAS can supply an overview of the knowledge in the relevant rules. This suggests the structure of global trends in the knowledge of the expert who assembled the knowledge base, and thus helps to make clear the overall approach of the system to a given topic.

### 8.2. "Knowing what you don't know"

Another use of the models demonstrates that, in a primitive fashion, they give TEIRESIAS a model of what it *doesn't* know. There are models in the current system made from between 2 (the defined minimum) and 35 rules. We have defined a metric to measure the "strength" of a model, and base it on both the total number of rules from which the model was constructed and the strength of the inference of each of those rules. The entire model set is kept ordered from weakest to strongest, giving the system some indication of its likely competence on a range of subjects. In a very primitive way, it thus gains a knowledge of where it is ignorant.

This makes possible a new option for the expert. Instead of adding a rule to fix a bug, he can ask the system what it would like to learn.

---

— — \*\* WHAT WOULD YOU LIKE TO KNOW?
Answer
 –Y for yes
 –N for no, or
 –Q to quit this.
There are only 2 rules for concluding that the name of the stock to invest in would be Homestake-Mining.
Would you like to give me a rule for that? [Y, N, Q]
+ + \*\* N
There are only 2 rules for concluding that the risk class of an investment should be speculative.
Would you like to offer a rule for that? [Y, N, Q] + + \*\* Y
The new rule will be called RULE 384
  If (1)

---

Fig. 10. "Knowing what you don't know."

The system cycles through the rule models in order, indicating the weakest topics first. This is, of course, a first order solution to the problem of giving the system an indication of its areas of ignorance. A better solution would supply an indication of how much the system knows about a subject, compared with how much there is to know. There surely are subjects for which three or four rules exhaust the available knowledge, while for others a hundred or more rules may not suffice. The issue is related to work described in [4] on closed vs. open sets. That paper offers some interesting strategies for allowing a program to decide when it is ignorant and how it might reason in the face of the inability to store every fact about a given topic.

There appear to be no easy ways to deduce the incompleteness of the knowledge base using only the information stored in it. It is not valid to say, for instance, that there ought to be even a single rule for every attribute (how could an investor's name be deduced?). Nor is there a well-defined set of attributes for which no rules are likely to exist. Nor is it clear what sort of information would allow the incompleteness to be deduced.

The issue is a significant one, since a good solution to the problem would not only give TEIRESIAS a better grasp of where the performance program was weak, but would also provide several important capabilities to the performance program itself. It would, for example, permit the use of the "if it were true I would know" heuristic in [4]. Roughly restated, this says that "if I know a great deal about subject S, and fact F concerns an important aspect of S, then if I don't already know that F is true, it's probably false." Thus, in certain circumstances a lack of knowledge about the truth of a statement can plausibly be used as evidence suggesting that the statement is false.[9]

## 9. Assumptions and Limitations

The work reported here can be evaluated with respect to both the utility of its approach to knowledge acquisition and its success in implementing that approach.

### 9.1. The interactive transfer of expertise approach
As noted, our approach involves knowledge transfer that is interactive, that is set in the context of a shortcoming in the knowledge base, and that transfers a single rule at a time. Each of these has implications about TEIRESIAS's range of applicability.

Interactive knowledge transfer seems best suited to task domains involving problem solving that is entirely or primarily a high level cognitive task, based on a number of distinct, specifiable principles. Consultations in medicine or investments seem to be appropriate domains, but the approach would not seem well suited to those parts of, say, speech understanding or scene recognition in which low level process play a significant role.

The transfer of expertise approach presents a useful technique for task domains that do not permit the use of programs (like those noted in Section 3) which autonomously induce new knowledge from test data. The autonomous mode may most commonly be inapplicable because the data for a domain simply don't exist yet. In quantitative domains (like mass spectrum analysis [3]) or synthesized ("toy") domains (like the line drawings in [12]), a large body of data points is easily assembled. This is not currently true for many domains, consequently induction techniques cannot be used. In such cases interactive transfer of expertise offers a useful alternative.[10]

[9] This is another useful form of meta-level knowledge.
[10] Where the autonomous induction technique can be used, it offers the interesting advantage that the knowledge we expect the system to acquire need not be specified ahead of time, nor indeed even known. Induction programs are in theory capable of inducing "new" information (i.e., information unknown to their author) from their set of examples. Clearly the interactive transfer of expertise approach requires that the expert know and be able to specify precisely what it is the program is to learn.

Knowledge acquisition in context appears to offer useful guidance wherever knowledge of the domain is as yet ill-specified, but the context need not be a short-coming in the knowledge base uncovered during a consultation, as is done here. Our recent experience suggests that an effective context is also provided by examining certain subsets of rules in the knowledge base and using them as a framework for specifying additional rules. The overall concept is limited, however, to systems that already have at least some minimal amount of information in their knowledge base. Earlier than this, there may be insufficient information to provide any context for the acquisition process.

Finally the rule-at-a-time approach is a limiting factor. The example given earlier works well, of course, because the bug was manufactured by removing a single rule. In general, acquiring a single rule at a time seems well suited to the later stages of knowledge base construction, in which bugs may indeed be caused by the absence of one or a few rules. We need not be as lucky as the present example, in which one rule repairs three bugs; the approach will also work if three independent bugs arise in a consultation. But early in knowledge base construction, where large sub-areas of a domain are not yet specified, it appears more useful to deal with groups of rules, or, more generally, with larger segments of the basic task (as in [20]).

In general then, the interactive transfer of expertise approach seems well suited to the later stages of knowledge base construction for systems performing high-level tasks, and offers a useful technique for domains where extensive sets of data points are not available.

### 9.2. TEIRESIAS as a program
Several difficult problems remain unsolved in the current implementation of the program. There is, for instance, the issue of the technique used to generate the rule models. This process could be made more effective even without using a different approach to concept formation. While an early design criterion suggested keeping the models transparent to the expert, making the process interactive would allow the expert to evaluate new patterns as they were discovered by TEIRESIAS. This might make it possible to distinguish accidental correlations from valid inter-relations, and increase the utility and sophistication of TEIRESIAS's second guessing ability. Alternatively, more sophisticated concept formation techniques might be borrowed from existing work.

There is also a potential problem in the way the models are used. Their effectiveness in both guiding the parsing of the new rule and in "second guessing" its content is dependent on the assumption that the present knowledge base is both correct and a good basis for predicting the content of future rules. Either of these can at times be false and the system may then tend to continue stubbornly down the wrong path.

The weakness of the natural language understanding technique presents a substantial barrier to better performance. Once again there are several improvements that could be made to the existing approach (see [5]), but more sophisticated techniques should also be considered (this work is currently underway; see [1]).

There is also the difficult problem of determining the impact of any new or changed rule on the rest of the knowledge base, which we have considered only briefly (see [5]). The difficulty lies in establishing a formal definition of inconsistency for inexact logics, since, except for obvious cases (e.g., two identical rules with different strengths), it is not clear what constitutes an inconsistency. Once the definition is established, we would also require routines capable of uncovering them in a large knowledge base. This can be attacked by using an incremental approach (i.e., by checking every rule as it is added, the knowledge base is kept consistent and each consistency check is a smaller task), but the problem is still substantial.

## 10. Conclusions

The ideas reviewed above each offer some contribution toward achieving the two goals set out at the beginning of this paper: the development of a methodology of knowledge base construction via transfer of expertise, and the creation of an intelligent assistant.

In the near-term they provide a set of tools and ideas to aid in the construction of knowledge-based programs and represent a few empirical techniques of knowledge engineering. Their contribution here may arise from their potential utility as case studies in the development of a methodology for this discipline.

*Knowledge acquisition in the context of a shortcoming in the knowledge base*, for instance, has proved to be a useful technique for achieving transfer of expertise, offering advantages to both the expert and TEIRESIAS. It offers the expert a framework for the explication of a new chunk of domain knowledge. By providing him with a specific example of the performance program's operation, and forcing him to be specific in his criticism, it encourages the formalization of previously implicit knowledge. It also enables TEIRESIAS to form a number of expectations about the knowledge it is going to acquire, and makes possible several checks on the content of that knowledge to insure that it will in fact fix the bug.

In addition, because the system has a *model of its own knowledge*, it is able to determine whether a newly added piece of knowledge "fit into" its existing knowledge base.

A second contribution of the ideas reviewed above lies in their ability to support a number of intelligent actions on the part of the assistant. While those actions have been demonstrated for a single task and system, it should be clear that none of the underlying ideas are limited to this particular task, or to associative triples or rules as a knowledge representation. The foundation for many of these ideas is the concept of meta-level knowledge, which has made possible a program with a limited form of introspection.

The idea of *model-based understanding*, for instance, found a novel application in the fact that TEIRESIAS has a model of the knowledge base and uses this to guide acquisition by interpreting it as predictions about the information it expects to receive.

The idea of *biasing the set of models* to be considered offers a specific mechanism for the general notion of *program-generated expectations*, and makes possible an assistant whose understanding of the dialog was more effective.

TEIRESIAS is able to "second guess" the expert with respect to the content of the new knowledge by using its models to *see how well the new piece of knowledge* "*fits in*" *to what it already knows*. An incomplete match between the new knowledge and the system's model of its knowledge prompts it to make a suggestion to the expert. With this approach, learning becomes more than simply adding the new information to the knowledge base; TEIRESIAS examines as well the relationship between new and existing knowledge.

The concept of meta-level knowledge makes possible *multiple uses of the knowledge in the system*: information in the knowledge base is not only used directly (during the consultation), but is also examined and abstracted to form the rule models (see [8] for additional examples).

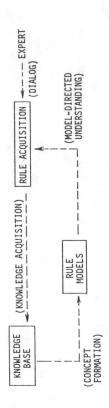

FIG. 11. Model-directed understanding and learning by experience combine to produce a useful feedback loop.

TEIRESIAS also represents a synthesis of the ideas of model-based understanding and learning by experience. While both of these have been developed independently in previous AI research, their combination produces a novel sort of feedback loop (Fig. 11). Rule acquisition relies on the set of rule models to effect the model-based understanding process. This results in the addition of a new rule to the knowledge base, which in turn prompts the recomputation of the relevant rule model(s).[11]

This loop has a number of interesting implications. First, performance on the acquisition of the next rule may be better, because the system's "picture" of its knowledge base has improved — the rule models are now computed from a larger set of instances, and their generalizations are more likely to be valid.

[11] The models are recomputed when any change is made to the knowledge base, including rule deletion or modification, as well as addition.

Second, since the relevant rule models are recomputed each time a change is made to the knowledge base, the picture they supply is kept constantly up to date, and they will at all times be an accurate reflection of the shifting patterns in the knowledge base. This is true as well for the trees into which the rule models are organized: they too grow (and shrink) to reflect the changes in the knowledge base.

Finally, and perhaps most interesting, the models are not hand-tooled by the system architect, or specified by the expert. They are instead formed by the system itself, and formed as a result of its experience in acquiring rules from the expert. Thus despite its reliance on a set of models as a basis for understanding, TEIRESIAS's abilities are not restricted by the existing set of models. As its store of knowledge grows, old models can become more accurate, new models will be formed, and the system's stock of knowledge about its knowledge will continue to expand. This appears to be a novel capability for a model-based system.

## ACKNOWLEDGMENTS

The work described here was performed as part of a doctoral thesis supervised by Bruce Buchanan, whose assistance and encouragement were important contributions.

## REFERENCES

1. Bonnett, A., BAOBAB, a parser for a rule-based system using a semantic grammar, Stanford University HPP Memo 78-10, Stanford CA, U.S.A. (1978).
2. Brown, J. S. and Burton, R. R., Diagnostic models for procedural bugs in mathematical skills, *Cognitive Science 2* (April–June 1978), pp. 155–192.
3. Buchanan, B. G. and Mitchell, T., Model-directed learning of production rules, in: Waterman and Hayes-Roth (Eds.), *Pattern-Directed Inference Systems* (Academic Press, New York, 1978), pp. 297–312.
4. Carbonell, J. R. and Collins, A. M., Natural semantics in artificial intelligence, Proc. Third International Joint Conference on AI, Stanford, CA (August 1973), pp. 344–351.
5. Davis, R., Applications of meta-level knowledge to the construction, maintenance, and use of large knowledge bases, Stanford University HPP Memo 76-7 (July 1976).
6. Davis, R., Generalized procedure calling and content-directed invocation, Proc. of the Symposium on Artificial Intelligence and Programming Languages, *SIGART/SIGPLAN* (combined issue, August 1977), pp. 45–54.
7. Davis, R. Knowledge acquisition in rule based systems—knowledge about representations as a basis for system construction and maintenance, in: D. Waterman and F. Hayes-Roth (Eds.), *Pattern-Directed Inference Systems* (Academic Press, New York, 1978), pp. 99–134.
8. Davis, R. and Buchanan, B. G., Meta-level knowledge: overview and applications, Proc. Fifth International Joint Conference on AI, Cambridge, MA (August 1977), pp. 920–927.
9. Davis, R., Buchanan, B. and Shortliffe, E. H., Production rules as a representation for a knowledge-based consultation system, *Artificial Intelligence 8* (February 1977), pp. 15–45.
10. Falk, G., Computer interpretation of imperfect line data, Stanford University AI Memo 132 (August 1970).
11. Feigenbaum, E. A., et al. On generality and problem solving, *Machine Intelligence 6* (1971), pp. 165–190.
12. Hayes-Roth, F. and McDermott, J., Knowledge acquisition from structural descriptions Proc. Fifth International Joint Conference on AI, Cambridge, MA (1977), pp. 356–362.
13. Mathlab Group, The MACSYMA Reference Manual, MIT Lab. for Computer Science (September 1974).
14. Newell, A. and Simon, H., *Human Problem Solving* (Prentice-Hall, Englewood Cliffs, NJ, 1972).
15. Reddy, D. R., et al. The HEARSAY speech-understanding system: an example of the recognition process, Proc. 3rd IJCAI, Stanford, CA (1973), pp. 185–193.
16. Reiser, J. F., BAIL—A debugger for SAIL, AI Memo 270, Stanford University, AI Lab. (October 1975).
17. Shortliffe, E. H., MYCIN: *Computer-based Consultations in Medical Therapeutics* (American Elsevier, New York, 1976).
18. Shortliffe, E. H. and Buchanan, B. G., A model of inexact reasoning in medicine, *Mathematical Biosciences 23* (1975), pp. 351–379.
19. Teitelman, W., *The INTERLISP Reference Manual*, Xerox Corp. (1975).
20. Waterman, D., Exemplary programming, in: D. Waterman and F. Hayes-Roth (Eds.), *Pattern-Directed Inference Systems* (Academic Press, New York 1978), pp. 261–280.
21. Winston, P. H., Learning structural descriptions from examples, Project MAC TR-76, MIT, Cambridge, MA (September 1970).

*Received 8 December 1978*

# Expertise transfer and complex problems: using AQUINAS as a knowledge-acquisition workbench for knowledge-based systems

JOHN H. BOOSE AND JEFFREY M. BRADSHAW

*Knowledge Systems Laboratory, Boeing Advanced Technology Center 77–64, Boeing Computer Services, P.O. Box 24346, Seattle, WA 98124, U.S.A.*

Acquiring knowledge from a human expert is a major problem when building a knowledge-based system. Aquinas, an expanded version of the Expertise Transfer System (ETS), is a knowledge-acquisition workbench that combines ideas from psychology and knowledge-based systems research to support knowledge-acquisition tasks. These tasks include eliciting distinctions, decomposing problems, combining uncertain information, incremental testing, integration of data types, automatic expansion and refinement of the knowledge base, use of multiple sources of knowledge and providing process guidance. Aquinas interviews experts and helps them analyse, test, and refine the knowledge base. Expertise from multiple experts or other knowledge sources can be represented and used separately or combined. Results from user consultations are derived from information propagated through hierarchies. Aquinas delivers knowledge by creating knowledge bases for several different expert-system shells. Help is given to the expert by a dialog manager that embodies knowledge-acquisition heuristics.

Aquinas contains many techniques and tools for knowledge acquisition; the techniques combine to make it a powerful testbed for rapidly prototyping portions of many kinds of complex knowledge-based systems.

## Obtaining and modeling expertise

### EXPERTISE TRANSFER SYSTEM

The Expertise Transfer System (ETS) has been in use in Boeing for more than 3 years. Hundreds of prototypical knowledge-based systems have been generated by ETS. The system interviews experts to uncover key aspects of their problem-solving knowledge. It helps build very rapid prototypes (typically in less than 2 h), assists the expert in analysing the adequacy of the knowledge for solving the problem, and creates knowledge bases for several expert system shells (S.1, M.1, OPS5, KEE, and so on) from its own internal representation (Boose, 1984, 1985, 1986).

The tools in ETS are now part of Aquinas, a much larger system. Aquinas was developed to overcome ETS's limitations in knowledge representation and reasoning (Fig. 1). Due to these limitations, ETS was usually abandoned sometime during the knowledge-acquisition process. Typically project approaches were explored or feasibility was assessed for several days or a week, and then development continued in some other expert system shell. While the use of the tool in this way saved substantial time (typically 1 or 2 calendar months from a 12–24-month project), it was desirable to explore new approaches for making the system more powerful.

---

### Features of AQUINAS

Improved process efficiency:
Rapid feasibility analysis;
Multiple alternative testing with little resource expenditure;
Expert enthusiasm;
Easier to learn expert-system and knowledge engineering concepts;
Group knowledge elicitation and decision making.
Faster knowledge-base generation:
Very rapid prototyping;
Vocabulary identification;
Solution elicitation;
Trait elicitation through triads and other methods;
Hierarchies;
Problem decomposition;
Reasoning at varied levels of abstraction.
Improved knowledge-base quality:
Embedded testing and feedback during the knowledge elicitation process;
Multiple knowledge representations;
Multiple methods for handling uncertainty based on needed precision, convenience;
Tools for comparing knowledge from different experts to show similarities and differences;
Consultation systems giving consensus and dissenting opinions from multiple sources of knowledge;
Analytic tools.
Better knowledge-base maintenance and comprehensibility:
Case-based knowledge source-based elicitation, structure, analysis;
Knowledge at higher levels of abstraction;
Single central source generation of expert-system shell knowledge bases;
Knowledge libraries.
Extensions to personal construct theory methods:
Manipulation of rating grids in hierarchies;
Multiple variable scale types;
Many analytic tools in a single framework;
Interactive testing and debugging of rating grid knowledge.

FIG. 1. Aquinas is a knowledge-acquisition workbench that provides a variety of capabilities.

---

### AQUINAS TASKS AND TOOL SETS

Aquinas is a collection of integrated tool sets. They share a common user interface (the dialog manager) and underlying knowledge representation and data base (Fig. 2). Each set of tools addresses a general knowledge-acquisition task and embodies sets of strategies that support the task. Many of these strategies will be illustrated later.

### TASK: ELICIT DISTINCTIONS

Gaines (in press) has characterized knowledge acquisition as: "the modeling of events enabling adequate prediction and action". In this view, a *distinction* is the primitive concept underlying the representation of knowledge and the formal theory of modeling. Systems that acquire problem-solving knowledge seek to establish qualitative and quantitative distinctions that lead to effective prediction and action, while weeding out distinctions that are redundant or inconsequential.

*Eliciting distinctions with Aquinas*

*Personal construct psychology.* George Kelly's personal construct theory (Kelly, 1955) provides a rich framework for modeling the qualitative and quantitative

0020-7373/87/010003 + 26$03.00/0

© 1987 Academic Press Inc. (London) Limited

analysis and display tools. Aquinas can analyse a rating grid in many ways to help the expert refine useful distinctions and eliminate those that are inconsequential or redundant. Distinctions captured in grids can be converted to other representations such as production rules, fuzzy sets, or networks of frames.

## TASK: DECOMPOSE PROBLEMS

Experts building large knowledge bases face the task of decomposing their problem in ways that enhance efficiency and clarity. In our previous work using ETS, the difficulty of representing complex problems in a single rating grid became clear. First, a single rating grid can represent only "flat" relations between single solutions and traits. No deep knowledge, causal knowledge, or relationship chains can be shown. A second limitation was that only solutions or traits at the same level of abstraction could be used comfortably in a single grid. Finally, large single grids were often difficult to manipulate and comprehend.

### Problem decomposition strategies in Aquinas

*Hierarchies.* Hierarchical tools in Aquinas help the expert build, edit, and analyse knowledge in hierarchies and lattices. These hierarchies allow the expert to break up complex problems into pieces of convenient size and similar levels of abstraction. Hierarchies in Aquinas are organized around *solutions, traits,* knowledge sources (i.e. *experts*), and *cases.*

Nodes in the four hierarchies combine to form rating grids. In the most simple case, the children of a node in a solution hierarchy supply the solutions along the top of a grid; the children of a node in a trait hierarchy supply the traits down the side of a grid. Rating values within the grid provide information about the solutions with respect to each trait (Fig. 3).

In eliciting knowledge for complex problems it is sometimes difficult for the expert to identify conclusion sets whose members are at similar, useful levels of granularity. For instance, in an engine diagnostic system, the expert may include the repair solutions "engine", "battery", "ignition coil" and "electrical system". "Engine" and "electrical system" are at more general levels of structural and functional abstraction than "battery" and "ignition coil". Mixing more general and more specific solutions in the same rating grid causes problems during trait elicitation, since traits useful in differentiating "engine" from "electrical system" problems are not necessarily those useful in discriminating "ignition coil" from "battery" problems.

*Solution hierarchies.* Solutions are grouped in specialization hierarchies within Aquinas. This structure aids experts in organizing large numbers of solutions that may exist at different levels of abstraction. For example, a solution class named "vehicle" is a superclass (parent or prototype) to "car" and "truck" subclasses. The "car" class can serve in turn as a parent to a class of specific car models or to a particular instance of a car.

*Trait hierarchies.* Characteristics of a particular level in the solution hierarchy can be structured in trait hierarchies. For instance, in a knowledge base for a Transportation Advisor, the solutions exist in hierarchies of vehicles. Each level in the solution hierarchy has a trait hierarchy that contains information needed to select solutions at that level. A trait hierarchy attached to the "vehicle" abstraction level of a solution hierarchy, for instance, may contain information about general

distinctions inherent in an expert's problem solving knowledge. Expertise Transfer System (ETS) is a set of tools used by the expert to elicit, analyse, and refine knowledge as rating grids. In a rating grid, problem solutions—*elements*—are elicited and placed across the grid as column labels, and traits of these solutions—*constructs*—are listed alongside the rows of the grid (Fig. 3, taken from the Programming Language Advisor). Traits are first elicited by presenting groups of solutions and asking the expert to discriminate among them. Following this, the expert gives each solution a rating showing where it falls on the trait scale.

Many of the strategies used in building a rating grid are extensions of ideas in the work of Kelly and in the PLANET system (Gaines & Shaw, 1981; Shaw & Gaines, in press *a, b*). These strategies include triadic elicitation, corner filling, and multiple

| Dialog manager | | | | | | |
|---|---|---|---|---|---|---|
| ETS Repertory grid tools | Hierarchical structure tools | Uncertainty tools | Internal reasoning engine | Multiple scale type tools | Induction tools | Multiple expert tools |
| Object-oriented DBMS | | | | | | |
| CommonLoops/CommonLisp | | | | | | |

FIG. 2. The Aquinas workbench is a collection of integrated tool sets that support various knowledge-acquisition tasks.

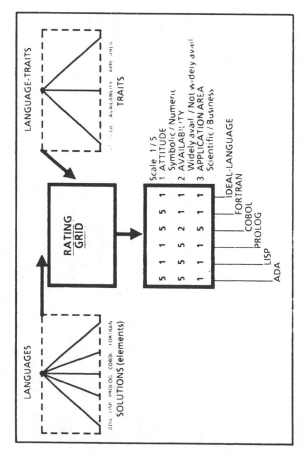

FIG. 3. Rating values in different hierarchies combine to form *rating grids*. The children of a node in a *solution hierarchy* supply the solutions along the top of the grid; the children of a node in a *trait hierarchy* supply the traits down the side of a grid.

use type, relative speed, cost, and so forth for the types of vehicles in the hierarchy. The "car" subclass is attached to a car trait hierarchy that contains information useful in selecting a particular car.

Two other hierarchies are formed in Aquinas (Fig. 4).

*Expert hierarchies.* Expert hierarchies represent multiple knowledge sources as structured groups. Each node in the expert hierarchy may represent an individual, an aspect of an individual, a group, or an independent knowledge source. Information from multiple experts may be independently elicited and analysed, then weighted and combined to derive joint solutions to problems. Analyses can be performed that show similarities and differences among experts. Experts each have their own solution and trait hierarchies, which may or may not overlap those of others. Each expert's unique problem-solving strategies and information are preserved.

*Case hierarchies.* Case hierarchies define subsets of the knowledge base appropriate to solving a particular class of problems. For example, in a knowledge base of information about vehicles, a user may want to include different knowledge for selecting a vehicle for going over land than for going over water. A land case and a water case may be created, each drawing on a subset of the expert pool knowledgeable in those areas. Additional levels may be created for short or long land trips, cost considerations, and so on. A hierarchy of cases allows the knowledge base to be developed, modified, and maintained based on specific classes of situations. Eventually the lower leaves in case hierarchies become specific consultation instances when the knowledge is tested and used to solve a specific problem.

*From hierarchies to rating grids.* A rating grid is built by combining values associated with nodes in each of the four basic hierarchies. Relationships between nodes do not have to be strictly hierarchical; lattices may be formed when more than

one parent points to the same child. The expert defines the current rating grid by selecting appropriate nodes in the hierarchies.

Figure 5 shows selected map nodes (case: K-ACQUISITION; expert: WEC; solution: WEC.ELEMENT; trait: WEC.ELEMENT.TRAIT) that define the rating grid of Fig. 3. Each different collection of nodes (at least one from each hierarchy) describes a rating grid. A rating grid could be a single column or row, or even a single cell. Inversely, each cell in a rating grid is uniquely described by its location in the four hierarchies.

In a sense, each rating grid is four-dimensional. Any two of these dimensions are shown at once as rows and columns in a given grid. Usually solutions and traits are shown, but sometimes it is useful to show other combinations. For instance, a grid could display the ratings of several experts across the top with particular solutions down the side. The associated trait and case nodes would be shown to the side of the grid. Often the ratings displayed summarize or generalize information from different nodes in the hierarchies; this issue is discussed later.

*Techniques for defining and exploring hierarchies.* Strategies for helping the expert build and refine hierarchies in Aquinas include laddering, cluster analysis, and trait value examination. Some of these strategies will be demonstrated in the section describing the Programming Language Advisor.

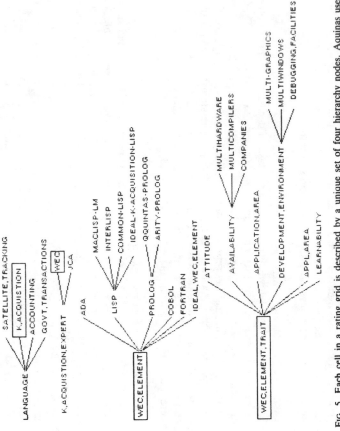

FIG. 5. Each cell in a rating grid is described by a unique set of four hierarchy nodes. Aquinas users specify rating grids by selecting sets of nodes (either the nodes themselves or their children).

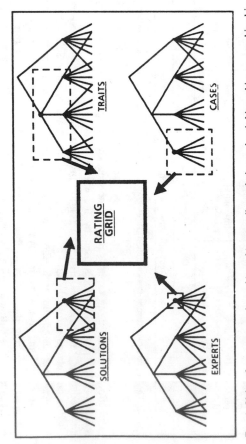

FIG. 4. Values from *expert* and *case hierarchies* as well as solution and trait hierarchies are combined in many ways to form rating grids. Relationships between nodes do not have to be strictly hierarchical; lattices may be formed when more than one parent points to the same child.

TASK: SPECIFY METHODS FOR COMBINING UNCERTAIN INFORMATION

A major limitation of most current knowledge engineering tools is that they do not allow experts to specify how specific pieces of information should be combined (Gruber & Cohen, in press). Most tools either tend to use fixed, global numeric functions to compute values or restrict the expert to purely symbolic representations of uncertainty. Ideally, flexibility and comprehensibility could be achieved by allowing experts to specify how information should be combined locally either by selecting from a set of commonly accepted combining functions (e.g. as done by Reboh & Risch, 1986; Reboh, Risch, Hart & Duda, 1986) or by defining their own method.

## Combining uncertain information in Aquinas

In Aquinas, uncertain knowledge, preferences, and constraints may be elicited, represented, and locally applied using combinations of several different methods. These methods may be classified into three main types: absolute, relativistic, and probabilistic.

*Absolute reasoning.* Absolute (categorical) reasoning involves judgments made with no significant reservations. It "typically depends on relatively few facts, its appropriateness is easy to judge, and its result is unambiguous" (Szolovitz & Pauker, 1978). For example, in selecting a programming language, users may be able to say with certainty that they would be interested only in languages that run on an Apple Macintosh or that they will not consider a language that costs more than $400, regardless of other desirable characteristics. Experts can also build these types of absolute constraints into the knowledge associated with an Aquinas rating grid.

*Relativistic reasoning.* Unfortunately, not all judgments can be absolute. Many involve significant trade-offs, where information and preferences from several sources must be weighed. Even if criteria for the ideal decision can be agreed on, sometimes it can be only approximated by the available alternatives. In these cases, Aquinas incorporates a variety of models and approaches to relativistic reasoning, including MYCIN-like certainty factor calculus (Adams, 1985), fuzzy logic (Gaines & Shaw, 1985), and the Analytic Hierarchy Process (AHP, Saaty, 1980).

*Probabilistic and user-defined reasoning.* In the current version of Aquinas, some limited propagation of probabilistic information is made possible by allowing discrete distributions on rating values. Future versions of Aquinas will have more complete models for the elicitation (Alpert & Raiffa, 1982; Spetzler & Stal von Holstein, 1984; Wallsten & Budescu, 1983) and analysis of probabilistic information including Bayesian (Howard and Matheson, 1984; Cheeseman, 1985; Henrion, 1986; Pearl 1986; Spiegelhalter, 1986), Dempster–Shafer (Shafer, 1976; Gordon & Shortliffe, 1985), and other approaches (Shastri & Feldman, 1985). Users may also define their own methods for combining and propagating information.

The availability of different inference methods within a single workbench allows users and experts flexibility in adapting Aquinas to the problem at hand. Methods are currently selected based on the cost of elicitation, the precision of the knowledge needed, convenience, and the expert's preference. Future research will suggest heuristics for helping experts select appropriate methods and designs for particular types of questions (e.g. Shafer & Tversky, 1985). These heuristics will be incorporated into the Aquinas dialog manager.

## TASK: TEST THE KNOWLEDGE

McDermott (1986) has emphasized the inseparability of acquired knowledge from the role it plays in problem solving. Within a given knowledge-acquisition tool, the problem method must be available to the expert as the knowledge base is being constructed so that incremental testing and refinement can take place.

## Testing knowledge in Aquinas

A mixed-initiative reasoning engine within Aquinas supports consultations. The model of problem solving currently used in Aquinas is that of multiple knowledge sources (experts) that work together in a common problem-solving context (case) by selecting the best alternatives for each of a sequential set of decisions (solutions). Alternatives at each step are selected by combining relevant information about preferences (relativistic reasoning), constraints (absolute reasoning) and evidence (probabilistic reasoning).

For many structured selection problems, a more specialized version of this model seems adequate. After analysing several expert systems for classification, Clancey (1986) suggested that many problems are solved by abstracting data, heuristically mapping higher-level problem descriptions onto solution models, and then refining these models until specific solutions are found (Fig. 6). This is also similar to the establish-refine cycle used in CSRL (Bylander & Mittal, 1986; Chandrasekaran, 1986; Bylander & Chandrasekaran, in press). In the version of Aquinas described in this paper, data abstraction is carried out within hierarchies of traits, and solutions are refined as information is propagated through solution hierarchies.

While the current version of Aquinas works best on those problems whose solutions can be comfortably enumerated (such as those amenable to the method of heuristic classification), we are interested in generalizing Aquinas to incorporate synthetic (constructive) problem-solving methods such as those in SALT (Marcus, in press).

## TASK: INTEGRATE DIVERSE DATA TYPES

Problem solving in knowledge-based systems often involves combining symbolic and numeric information. Qualitative and quantitative aspects are complimentary rather

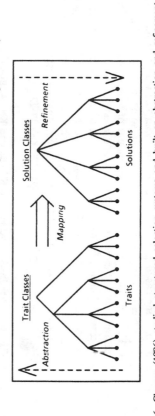

FIG. 6. Clancey (1986) studied structured selection systems and built an abstraction and refinement model. Inference in Aquinas typically occurs in a bottom-up fashion through the trait hierarchies and in top-down fashion through the solution hierarchies.

than opposing considerations, so knowledge-acquisition tools need to represent such information flexibly and conveniently. In our work with ETS, we found that it was inconvenient to represent certain types of problem-solving information solely using Kelly's constructs. Unordered variables, such as a set of computer types, had to be represented as a series of bipolar traits (VAX/NOT-VAX, IBM/NOT-IBM, and so on) when it would have been easier to combine them into a single nominal trait (a COMPUTER trait whose values are VAX, IBM, and so on).

Experts also apply different levels of precision at different points in the knowledge-acquisition process. For example, in some instances it might be sufficient to know that an object is hot or cold. At a later point, it may be important to know the exact temperature of the object. Levels of precision must also be appropriately flexible. ETS only dealt with ordinal ratings on a scale from 1 to 5, not probabilities or exact numeric values.

*Integrating data types within Aquinas*
In Aquinas, various trait (attribute) scale types can be elicited, analysed, and used by the reasoning engine. Traits are currently described according to the level of measurement of their rating scales, which is determined by the expert. The level of measurement depends on the presence or absence of four characteristics: *distinctiveness, ordering in magnitude, equal intervals,* and *absolute zero* (Coombs, Dawes & Tversky, 1970). These four characteristics describe the four major levels of measurement, or types of traits: nominal (unordered symbols), ordinal, interval, and ratio (Fig. 7). The additional information about trait types gives increased power to analytical tools within Aquinas and allows experts to represent information at the level of precision they desire.
Ratings may be generated through several methods:

(1) *Direct.* An expert directly assigns a rating value for a trait and an element. If an exact value is unknown, Aquinas helps the expert derive an estimate (Beyth-Marom & Dekel, 1985). If fine judgments are needed, Aquinas can derive a set of ratio scaled ratings from a series of *pairwise comparisons* (Saaty, 1980). Aquinas also contains tools for encoding of probability distributions on specific values. The value with the highest probability is displayed in the grid, but all appropriate values are used in reasoning and may be edited with graphic distribution aids.
(2) *Derived.* Incomplete grids can be automatically filled through propagation of

rating values from another grid through the hierarchies (e.g. from lower-to higher-level grids, different experts, or different cases).

*Precision and cost.* Increased precision and specificity in knowledge acquisition allow increased problem-solving power but usually at some cost (Michalski & Winston, 1985). This cost is reflected in both the amount of work needed to elicit the additional information and increased complexity and greater number of steps in the reasoning process. Aquinas tries to minimize this cost by eliciting more precise information only when it is needed to solve critical portions of the problem. If, for example, Aquinas finds that it cannot sufficiently discriminate between solutions from simple rating values between 1 and 5, it may suggest that the user perform a series of pairwise comparisons to increase the sensitivity of judgments.

TASK: AUTOMATIC EXPANSION AND REFINEMENT OF THE KNOWLEDGE BASE
Knowledge-acquisition tools can increase their leverage by suggesting appropriate expansions and refinements of the knowledge based on partial information already provided by the expert. Michalski (1986) has discussed the advantages of incorporating learning strategies within conventional knowledge-acquisition tools.

*Expanding and refining knowledge with Aquinas*
Several types of tools make inductive generalizations about existing knowledge. Generalizations can be examined by the expert and used to refine the knowledge, and are used by the reasoning engine. Sometimes, Aquinas may suggest that traits be deleted after analysing the knowledge through a process that is similar to the simplification of decision tables (Hurley, 1983, Michalski, 1978) and decision trees (Quinlan, 1983).

Learning strategies in Aquinas include simple learning from examples (e.g. selective induction on lower level grids to derive values for higher level grids), deduction (e.g. inheritance of values from parents), analogy (e.g. derivation of values based on functional similarity of traits), and observation (e.g. constructive induction based on cluster analysis). The dialog manager (described below) also contains various learning mechanisms.

TASK: USE MULTIPLE SOURCES OF KNOWLEDGE
Future knowledge-acquisition systems can neither assume a single source of expertise nor a closed world. In ETS, we began experimenting with strategies for manually combining ETS knowledge from several domain experts (Boose, in press). Others in our laboratory have been involved in developing methods for cooperative problem-solving (Benda, Jagannathan & Dodhiawala, 1986).

*Using multiple sources of knowledge in Aquinas*
Knowledge from multiple experts (or other knowledge sources) can be analysed to find similarities and differences in knowledge, and the degree of subsumption of one expert's knowledge over another (Gaines & Shaw, 1981). Information from analyses can be used to guide negotiation among experts. The reasoning engine uses knowledge from user-specified and weighted sources and gives consensus and dissenting opinions.

| RATING SCALE | DESCRIPTION | EXAMPLES |
| --- | --- | --- |
| Nominal | Unordered set | LANGUAGE: {ADA COBOL LISP} |
| Ordinal | Ordered set | COLD/HOT: {1 2 3 4 5} |
| | | SIZE: {SMALL MEDIUM LARGE} |
| Interval | Ordered set with measurable intervals | SMALL-INTEGERS: {1 2 3 4 5 6 7} |
| | | F-TEMP: {32..112} |
| Ratio | Ordered set with measurable intervals and an absolute origin | HEIGHT: {0.01 0.0' ..} |

FIG. 7. Aquinas expands the knowledge representation capability of rating grids from personal construct theory by allowing the use of several types of rating scale values. Scale types are selected for convenience, precision, or efficiency of value entry.

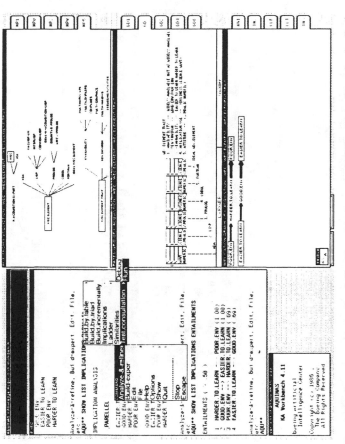

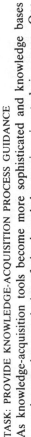

FIG. 8. Aquinas screen showing developing hierarchies for expert WEC, a rating grid, and an implication analysis graph of the grid.

## TASK: PROVIDE KNOWLEDGE-ACQUISITION PROCESS GUIDANCE

As knowledge-acquisition tools become more sophisticated and knowledge bases grow larger, the complexity of the knowledge engineering task increases. One approach to managing this complexity is to implement some form of apprenticeship learning program that is available to the expert (e.g. Wilkins, in press).

### Providing process guidance in Aquinas

A subsystem called the dialog manager contains pragmatic heuristics to guide the expert through knowledge acquisition using Aquinas. Its help is important in the use of Aquinas, given the complexity of the Aquinas environment and the many elicitation and analysis methods available to the expert. The dialog manager makes decisions about general classes of actions and then recommends one or more specific actions providing comments and explanation if desired. This knowledge is contained in rules within the dialog manager in Aquinas. A session history is recorded so that temporal reasoning and learning may be performed (Kitto & Boose, in press).

## Using Aquinas: building a programming language advisor

Aquinas is written in Interslip and runs on the Xerox family of Lisp machines. Subsets of Aquinas also run in an Interslip version on the DEC Vax and a "C/UNIX"-based portable version. The Aquinas screen is divided into a typescript window, map windows showing hierarchies, rating grid windows, and analysis windows (Fig. 8). Experts interact with Aquinas by text entry or by mouse through pop-up menus.

Following are the steps in a Aquinas session in which an expert is building a Programming Language Advisor. Novice software engineers and project managers would use such a system to help select programming languages for application projects. Aquinas guides the expert in putting knowledge into Aquinas's knowledge base, and continues through the making of a knowledge base for the S.1 expert-system shell. These steps are:

(1) ELICIT CASES AND THE INITIAL GRID (SOLUTIONS, TRAITS AND RATINGS)
The expert is first asked to specify the behavior of Aquinas's dialog manager. Then the expert enters several problem test cases and selects one for analysis. The *knowledge-acquisition language* case is selected (satellite tracking, accounting and government transaction cases are also entered). The cases are added to the case hierarchy and appear in the *map window* (Figure 8; upper right corner). Eventually experts may be able to select and modify grids and cases from a library; we expect that in several years this library will contain hundreds of hierarchies of grids.

The expert chooses to think about a language for developing a knowledge acquisition testbed, and enters potential candidates (Fig. 9). After five languages are entered, Aquinas adds an *ideal language* for this problem. This would be an ideal solution for the knowledge-acquisition case. The languages are added to the solution hierarchy as children. Then Aquinas asks the expert to enter traits based on differences and similarities between languages. This is the heart of Kelly's interviewing methodology. Aquinas uses it in several different ways as knowledge is expanded through elicitation and analysis.

Aquinas initially assumes that traits will be bipolar with ordinal ratings between 1 and 5. The expert is asked to rate each solution with regard to each trait, but the expert may specify different rating scales (unordered, interval, or ratio). Aquinas later assists in recognizing and changing types of rating scales.

Aquinas also elicits information about the importance of each trait. This knowledge is used later in the decision-making process.

(2) ANALYSE AND EXPAND THE INITIAL, SINGLE GRID
Once a grid is complete, an analysis is performed to show *implications* between various values of traits (see the lower right-hand window in Fig. 8). Implications are read from left to right, and the thickness of the arc shows the strength of the implication (HARDER TO LEARN implies POOR DEVELOPMENT ENVIRONMENT). A method similar to ENTAIL (Gaines & Shaw, 1985; Shaw & Gaines, in press) derives implications. Rating grid entries are used as a sample set and fuzzy-set logic is applied to discover inductive implications between the values. This method uncovers higher-order relationships among traits and later helps build trait hierarchies. The expert can also use an interactive process (implication review) to analyse and debug this information; the expert may agree or disagree with each implication. If the expert disagrees, the knowledge that led to the implication is

associated with an instance of the case under consideration. These values may be appended with a certainty factor and/or the tag ABSOLUTE to show an absolute constraint. Consultation questions are ordered according to a computed benefit/cost ratio that depends on both the generated system (e.g. entropy of a given trait, Quinlan, 1983) and the specified expert (e.g. cost of obtaining information) parameters. The questions may also be ordered according to an arbitrary specification given by the expert. Performance is measured by comparison of experts' expectations with Aquinas consultation results.

Two methods are available in Aquinas for turning rating values in grids into solution recommendations. One approach for turning rating values in grids into solution recommendations involves mapping this information onto certainty factor scales. Each rating in the grid is assigned a certainty factor weight based on its *relative strength* (a 5 is stronger than a 4), the *relative weight* the expert has assigned to the trait, and any *absolute constraints* that the expert has specified for the trait. In the test consultation, EMYCIN's certainty factor combination method (Adams, 1985) is used to combine the certainty factors. The result is a rank-ordered list of solutions with certainty-factor assignments. These certainty factors are also used when rules are generated for expert-system shells.

Another approach available employs Saaty's Analytic Hierarchy Process to order a set of possible solutions. Grid information obtained through pairwise comparisons or through regular rating grid methods is mapped onto *judgment matrices*. The *principal eigenvector* is computed for each matrix; the eigenvectors are normalized and combined to yield a final ranking of the solutions. Each solution has a score between $0{\cdot}0$ and $1{\cdot}0$. In a knowledge base consisting of multiple grids, these values are propagated through the hierarchies.

(4) BUILD HIERARCHIES (STRUCTURED AS SOLUTIONS AND TRAITS IN MULTIPLE GRIDS) FROM THE FIRST GRID

Next, the dialog manager recommends that the expert expand the trait and solution hierarchies by performing a *cluster analysis* (Fig. 10). Aquinas uses a method of single-link hierarchical cluster analysis based on FOCUS (Shaw & Gaines, in press *a*) to group sets of related solutions or traits. The junctions in the clusters can be seen as conjectures about possible new classes of solutions or traits. These more general trait or solution classes may be named and added to the hierarchies. *Laddering* is also used to find traits at varying levels of abstraction (Boose, 1986). "Why?" questions are used to find more general traits;

What is a new trait that says why you think GOOD-DEVELOPMENT-ENVIRONMENT should be true of a LANGUAGE for K-ACQUISITION?
AQU** FASTER SYSTEM DEVELOPMENT.

"How?" questions help find more specific traits:

How could a language for K-ACQUISITION be characterized by WIDELY-AVAILABLE?
AQU** RUNS ON MULTIPLE HARDWARE
AQU** MANY COMPILERS AVAILABLE.
AQU** MANY COMPANIES OFFER.

---

```
--- ELICITING ELEMENTS ---
Please enter a list of LANGUAGE elements for K-ACQUISITION, one to a line. When you're
done, enter a RETURN. Try to include at least one LANGUAGE that would NOT be good for K-
ACQUISITION (a counter example)
AQU** ADA
AQU** LISP
AQU** PROLOG
AQU** COBOL
AQU** FORTRAN
AQU** (CR)
Can you imagine a new ideal LANGUAGE for K-ACQUISITION?
AQU** YES
For now, it will be called IDEAL-K-ACQUISITION-LANGUAGE

--- BUILDING TRAITS BY TRIADS ---
When answering the following questions, remember to keep the K-ACQUISITION case in
mind

Think of an important attribute that two of ADA, LISP, and PROLOG share, but that the other
one does not. What is that attribute?
AQU** SYMBOLIC
What is that attribute's opposite as it applies in this case?
AQU** NUMERIC
What is the name of a scale or concept that describes
SYMBOLIC/NUMERIC?
AQU** ATTITUDE

Think of an important trait that two of LISP, PROLOG, and COBOL share, but that the other
one does not. What is that trait?
AQU** WIDELY AVAILABLE
What is that trait's opposite as it applies in this case?
AQU** NOT AS WIDELY AVAILABLE
What is the name of a scale or concept that describes WIDELY-AVAILABLE/NOT-AS-WIDELY-
AVAILABLE?
AQU** AVAILABILITY

--- FILLING IN RATINGS ---
Please rate these things on a scale of 5 to 1, where 5 means more like SYMBOLIC and 1 means
more like NUMERIC. If neither one seems to apply, enter N(either). If both seem to apply, enter a
B(oth). If you would like to change the range or type of scale, enter C(hange scale)
SYMBOLIC(5) NUMERIC(1)
ADA ** 5
LISP ** 1
PROLOG ** 1
COBOL ** 5
FORTRAN ** 5
IDEAL-K-ACQUISITION-LANGUAGE ** 1
```

FIG. 9. Aquinas asks the expert for an initial set of potential solutions to the first problem case. Then, the solutions are presented in groups of three, and the expert gives discriminating traits. Ratings are entered for each solution for each trait.

reviewed, and the expert can change the knowledge or add exceptions that disprove the implication (Boose, 1986). Certain types of *implication patterns* are also uncovered. Discovery of *ambiguous* patterns, for example, may mean that traits are being used inconsistently (Hinkle, 1965; Boose, 1986).

After the initial grid is complete, the dialog manager suggests a method to help the expert expand the grid. The method depends on the size of the grid, analysis of information in the grid, session history, and so on. The dialog manager inserts the appropriate command on the screen. The expert may change this recommendation or accept it by entering RETURN.

(3) TEST THE KNOWLEDGE IN THE SINGLE GRID
The dialog manager next recommends that the grid knowledge be tested by running a consultation. The expert is asked to provide desirable values for the traits

--- TEST CONSULTATION --

Would you like to run an EXISTING or NEW consultation?

AQU** **EXISTING**

What is the name of this existing consultation?

AQU** **LISP-PROLOG-ADA-ONLY**

This test consultation is named K-ACQUISITION LISP-PROLOG-ADA-ONLY.

Which K-ACQUISITION alternatives you would like to consider in this consultation (LISP-PROLOG-ADA-ONLY). Enter them one to a line If you wish all solutions to be considered, type ALL When done, press RETURN

AQU** **MAC-LISP-LM**

AQU** **INTERLISP**

AQU** **COMMON-LISP**

AQU** **QUINTUS-PROLOG**

AQU** **ADA-1**

AQU** **(CR)**

The following experts know about MACLISP-LM, INTERLISP, COMMON-LISP, QUINTUS-PROLOG, and ADA-1: WEC JCA. Would you like to exclude or weight any of these experts?

AQU** **NO**

Please indicate the desired trait selection values for LISP-PROLOG-ADA-ONLY solutions. Press RETURN to indicate agreement with the default values, or type in a new value Values may be appended with a certainty factor in the form ' 8' and/or the word ABSOLUTE to indicate that the value is an absolute constraint when selecting a type of LANGUAGE for K-ACQUISITION

(WIDELY-AVAILABLE(5), 1 0)** **(CR)**

(GOOD-DEVELOPMENT-ENVIRONMENT(5), 1.0)** **(CR)**

(LOW-COST(<45000 DOLLARS-US), 1 0, ABSOLUTE)(NOTE: THIS INCLUDES HARDWARE FOR A WORKSTATION)** **<30000 DOLLARS-US 1.0 ABSOLUTE**

:

FIG. 11. The expert tests the knowledge by running a consultation. The expertise of two experts is used and consensus and dissenting solutions are given (see Fig. 12).

in selecting a particular version of Lisp, Prolog, or ADA for a knowledge acquisition project. Because of the many potential solutions, the user is given the opportunity to specify a subset for consideration. The solutions in this subset are called *solution candidates*.

Aquinas then asks for a set of absolute and preferred trait values for this consultation. The user enters an absolute constraint that only languages with a delivery cost of less than $30 000 will be considered. Patterns of constraints may be entered by using key words such as AND and OR. The user may accept default values entered in a previous consultation by pressing the RETURN key. If a default value has not been previously specified and the user types RETURN, the trait will be ignored in the inference process for this consultation. The user's preference for

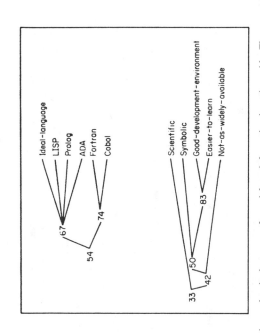

FIG. 10. Solution and trait clusters are formed from information in rating grids. The expert is asked to label nodes and expand clusters where possible; new traits are used to expand the hierarchies.

Experts stop expanding the trait hierarchies when they are able to provide direct grid ratings at these more specific trait levels. Ratings need not be explicitly given at each level of the trait and solution hierarchies, but can often be inferred from other grids in the knowledge base (e.g. induction from more specific examples or inheritance from more general ones) (Lieberman, 1986).

(5) USE SEVERAL RATING VALUE TYPES (TRANSFORM ORDINAL RATINGS TO NOMINAL AND INTERVAL RATINGS) TO REPRESENT KNOWLEDGE

Aquinas helps the expert convert a trait with ordinal values (DELIVERY-COST: HIGH-COST(5)/LOW-COST(1)) into a trait with ratio scaled rating values (DELIVERY-COST: (1500–60 000) DOLLARS-US). The expert re-rates the solutions in terms of the new values and these values appear on the grid Aquinas provides several forms of estimation help. Four estimation procedures are provided: START-&-MODIFY, EXTREME-VALUES, DECOMPOSITION, and RECOMPOSITION (Beyth-Marom & Dekel, 1985). In this instance, the EXTREME-VALUES procedure first asks for the least and greatest DELIVERY-COST one could imagine for the type of Lisp being considered. Through a series of questions, Aquinas helps shrink this range until a satisfactory estimate is given.

Aquinas also helps the expert change trait scale types by checking values associated with particular kinds of traits. For instance, bipolar traits that receive only extreme ratings (e.g. RUNS ON VAX/RUNS ON IBM) may be better represented with an unordered trait (e.g. COMPUTER TYPE).

(6) TEST KNOWLEDGE IN HIERARCHIES; TEST KNOWLEDGE FROM MULTIPLE EXPERTS

Another expert adds knowledge about programming language selection to the knowledge base and tests it. In the first consultation (Fig. 11), the user is interested

HARDWARE type is partitioned among three manufacturers by pairwise comparison (Fig. 12), which generates a ratio scaled set of preferences (Saaty, 1980).

The results of the consultation are presented to the user. For each solution, the *consensus* recommendation of the experts consulted is presented, followed by the weight of each expert that contributed to the recommendation. With multiple experts, it may sometimes be useful to examine a set of recommendations from a *dissenting* expert or group of experts. Since WEC's recommendations differed most from the consensus, these are listed as a dissenting opinion.

A general model illustrating the inference propagation path was shown in Fig. 6. For each expert consulted and for each level in that expert's solution hierarchy, a partial problem model is constructed, evaluated, and abstracted in a bottom–up fashion through the trait hierarchy of that solution level. Through this process the solution is refined as the children of the best solutions are chosen for continued evaluation. Bottom–up abstraction takes place again in the trait hierarchy at the new solution level, and the cycle continues until all remaining solution candidates have been evaluated. Then an ordered list of solution candidates is obtained and combined with the results from other experts. This information from a single case may then be combined, if desired, with information from other cases to derive a final ranking of solution candidates. Users may override this general model of inference propagation by specifying explicit inference paths and parameters.

(7) EDIT, ANALYSE AND REFINE THE KNOWLEDGE BASE, BUILDING NEW CASES
Once the experts have entered information about one case, they describe additional cases. They could start from scratch by entering a list of relevant solutions and traits, but that would be inefficient if there were significant overlap in those required by a previously entered case and a new one (Mittal, Bobrow & Kahn, 1986). Aquinas allows an expert to copy pieces of hierarchies (and, optionally, their associated values) between cases. Information copied in this way can be modified to fit the new context. This facility may also be used to copy pieces of hierarchies between experts.

(8) FURTHER EXPAND AND REFINE THE KNOWLEDGE BASE
Hierarchies and rating grids continue to be used during the session to expand and refine the knowledge base. Work in progress is shown in Fig. 8. Aquinas contains a variety of other tools to help analyse and expand the knowledge base.

*Comparison of experts (sources)*
The MINUS tool (Shaw & Gaines, 1986) compares grids from different experts on the same subject and points our differences and similarities. This information has been used to manage structured negotiation between experts (Boose, 1986). SOCIOGRIDS features (Shaw & Gaines, in press *a*) will be available in the future to display *networks* of expertise. Nodes and relations in these networks show the degree of subsumption of one expert's grid over grids from other experts.

*Incremental interviewing*
Aquinas can use an incremental dialog to elicit new traits and solutions, one at a time, from the expert (Boose, 1986). This is useful when the expert does not have a list of solutions to start a grid and in other situations during knowledge refinement.

*Trait value examination*
New solutions can be identified by asking the expert to "fill in holes" in the values of trait ranges. For instance, no solution may exist with a rating of 2 on some ordinal trait scale; the expert is asked if one can be identified:

What is a new LANGUAGE that would receive a value of 2 on the scale SCIENTIFIC(5)/BUSINESS(1)?

New traits can also be identified by forming triads based on ratings: if LISP and

```
:
(COMPANIES(VAX 33, IBM 33, ATT 33), 1 0)** PAIRWISE
Please compare these values of HARDWARE with regard to their importance in contributing to an
overall high score for a particular type of LANGUAGE for K-ACQUISITION in the context of LISP-
PROLOG-ADA-ONLY.

Please compare VAX and IBM. Enter:
VAX = IBM if VAX and IBM are equally important
VAX>IBM or VAX<IBM if one of the pair is weakly more important
VAX>>IBM or VAX<<IBM if one is demonstrably or very strongly more important
VAX>>>IBM or VAX<<<IBM if one is absolutely more important
AQU** VAX<IBM

Please compare VAX and ATT. Enter:
VAX = ATT if VAX and ATT are equally important
VAX>ATT or VAX<ATT if one of the pair is weakly more important
VAX>>ATT or VAX<<ATT if one is strongly more important
VAX>>>ATT or VAX<<<ATT if one is demonstrably or very strongly more important
VAX>>>ATT or VAX<<<ATT if one is absolutely more important
AQU** VAX>>>ATT
:

Results for test consultation K-ACQUISITION LISP-PROLOG-ADA-ONLY:
1: INTERLISP   (47 (WEC 5, JCA 5))
2: QUINTUS- PROLOG  (40. (WEC 1 0))

Would you like to see the dissenting opinion for this consultation?
AQU** YES

The following dissenting opinion was given by WFC
Overall agreement with consensus  79
1: QUINTUS PROLOG (.40)
2: INTERLISP (.39)
```

FIG. 12. Test consultation (continued). The expert specifies "run-time" values for traits, entering an absolute cost constraint, and performing a pairwise comparison task to derive relative values for hardware. Consensus and dissenting opinions are given along with the weighted contributions of each expert.

PROLOG are rated 5 on SCIENTIFIC(5)/BUSINESS(1), and ADA is rated 4, the expert is asked:

What is a new trait having to do with SCIENTIFIC/BUSINESS that makes LISP and PROLOG similar yet different from ADA?

*Trait range boundary examination*
Important traits can frequently be identified by exploring the boundaries of trait ranges:

You said that the range of DELIVERY-COST for LISP for the K-ACQUISITION case was 1500 to 60000 DOLLARS-US. Can you think of any conditions in the future that might make DELIVERY-COST LESS THAN 1500?
AQU** YES
Enter conditions in terms of traits, one to a line; enter a RETURN when done.
AQU** HARDWARE BREAKTHROUGH-LISP ON A CHIP
AQU** (CR)

Can you think of any conditions in the future that might make DELIVERY-COST GREATER THAN 60000?
AQU** YES
Enter conditions in terms of traits, one to a line, enter a RETURN when done.
AQU** VERY POWERFUL HARDWARE
AQU** PARALLEL ARCHITECTURES AVAILABLE
AQU** (CR)

*Completeness checking*
A single grid can be used as a table of examples. If the table is incomplete, the expert is asked to fill in other examples (Boose, 1986).

*Combine similar traits*
Sometimes different labels are used for the same underlying concept. This can be discovered when a similarity analysis is performed (functionally equivalent traits with different labels may be uncovered). If the expert cannot think of a new solution to separate identical traits, then the traits may be combined into a single trait.

(9) GENERATE RULES FOR EXPERT-SYSTEM SHELLS
The expert is the judge of when the point of diminishing returns has been reached within Aquinas. When such a point is reached, a knowledge base is generated for an expert-system shell, and development continues directly in that shell. Similarity and implication analyses allow experts to determine whether traits or solutions can be adequately and appropriately discriminated from one another. The system provides correlational methods for comparing the order of Aquinas recommendations with an expert's rankings.

Aquinas can generate knowledge bases for several expert-system shells (KEE, KS-300/EMYCIN, LOOPS, M.1, OPS5, S.1, and others). The knowledge contained in grids and hierarchies is converted within Aquinas into rules, and the rules are formatted for a particular expert-system shell. Appropriate control knowledge is also generated when necessary. Rules are generated with screening clauses that partition the rules into subsets. An *expert clause* is used when expertise from multiple experts is weighted and combined together. A *case clause* controls the focus of the system during reasoning.

Four types of rules are generated:

(1) *Implication rules* are generated from arcs in the implication graph and conclude about particular traits. The conclusion's certainty factor is proportional to the strength of the implication. The use of implication rules restricts search and lessens the number of questions asked of users during consultations;

(2) *Solution rules* conclude about a particular solution class. The conclusion's certainty factor is derived from a combination of the *grid rating strength* and the *trait weight*;

(3) *Absolute rules* are generated when the expert places an absolute constraint on the value of a trait. Sometimes information about absolute constraints is included elsewhere when knowledge bases for expert system shells are generated;

(4) *Specialization/generalization rules* are derived from information in the hierarchies and are used to propagate hierarchical information.

## Discussion

### GENERAL ADVANTAGES AND DISADVANTAGES OF AQUINAS

*Improved process efficiency and faster knowledge-base generation*
Aquinas inherits the advantages of ETS: rapid prototyping and feasibility analysis, vocabulary, solution and trait elicitation, interactive testing and refinement during knowledge acquisition, implication discovery, conflict point identification, expert-system shell production, and generation of expert enthusiasm (Boose, 1986). It is much easier for users to learn knowledge-based system concepts through using Aquinas than through reading books or attending classes (i.e. rules are automatically generated and used dynamically in consultations; new vocabulary is incrementally introduced).

ETS, still in use at Boeing, has been employed to build hundreds of single-grid prototype systems. Single grids as large as 42 × 38 (1596 ratings) have been built. Alternative approaches may be tested with little expenditure of resources. Knowledge bases have been generated for expert-system shells that contain over 2000 rules. Typically, something on the order of a 15 × 10 grid is built that generates several hundred rules.

Over 30 prototype systems have been built during the development of Aquinas (an AI book consultant, and AI tool advisor, a course evaluation system, a customer needs advisor, a database management system consultant, an investment advisor, a management motivation analyser, a personal computer advisor, a personality disorder advisor, a product design and impact advisor, a robotic tool selector, a Seattle travel agent, and a wine advisor, among others). Some of these systems contain thousands of ratings arranged in hierarchical grids. The Programming Language Advisor session took less than 2 h with each of the two experts.

*Improved knowledge-base quality*

Aquinas offers a rich knowledge representation and reasoning environment. We believe that Aquinas can be used to acquire knowledge for significant portions of the most structured selection expert-system problems. Hierarchies help the expert break down problems into component parts and allow reasoning at different levels of abstraction. Varying levels of precision are specified, with multiple types of rating scales when needed. Multiple methods for handling combining uncertain information are available based on needed precision and convenience. Knowledge from multiple experts may be combined using Aquinas. Users may receive dissenting as well as consensus opinions from groups of experts, thus getting a full *range* of possible solutions. Disagreement between the consensus and the dissenting opinion can be measured to derive a *degree of conflict* for a particular consultation. The system can be used for cost-effective group data gathering (Boose, in press).

Analytic tools help uncover inconsistencies and circularities in the growing knowledge base.

*Better knowledge-base maintenance and comprehensibility*

Elicitation, structuring, analysis, and testing of knowledge is based on specific cases. When knowledge in Aquinas is updated, it is done so with respect to a specific case. Addition of new knowledge in this way can be strictly controlled by the expert; the tendency for local changes to degrade other cases is thus curbed.

The expert builds and refines knowledge in rating grids and hierarchies—not directly in production rules. As a result, knowledge at this higher level of abstraction is more compact, comprehensible, and easier to maintain.

The growing collection of rating grids and case knowledge represents an important resource for building a variety of knowledge-based systems. Knowledge is stored explicitly with associated problem cases, making knowledge bases easier to update and maintain.

Currently, a user may copy and change any portion of the Aquinas knowledge base during a consultation. In the future, each expert will be able to protect areas of knowledge. The expert may believe protection is necessary because some knowledge should not be changed or because the knowledge has commercial value.

*Extensions to personal construct theory methods*

Aquinas significantly extends existing personal construct theory methods. Rating grid knowledge can be tested and used interactively to make decisions; rating grid information may be arranged and coupled in hierarchies; multiple rating scale types are available (not just bipolar ordinal scales); many grid analysis tools are available in a single workbench.

*Process complexity*

Aquinas is not as easy to use as was ETS using single grids. There are many elicitation and analysis tools for a novice to understand; the decision-making process and inference engine can be set up to work in several different ways. We expect that continuing improvements in the dialog manager will help make the system more comprehensible and decrease the learning time for new users.

THEORETICAL ISSUES—KNOWLEDGE ELICITATION

Personal construct psychology methods provide no guarantee that a *sufficient* set of knowledge will be found to solve a given problem. Aquinas attempts to expand the initial subset of solutions and traits based on problem-solving knowledge for specific cases. The goal is to solve enough cases to that the knowledge is sufficient to solve *new* cases. This is the methodology of knowledge engineering in general; Aquinas helps make the process explicit and manageable.

Hierarchical decomposition can be used to build intuitive, comprehensible models that seem to behave in reasonable ways. One disadvantage is that some problems do not easily fit the hierarchical model. It also may be true that a particular problem would best be represented by a *collection of conflicting hierarchies* (hierarchies for mechanical problems tend to model structure *or* function, not both, and both may be necessary).

The use of multiple rating value types provides more flexibility, convenience, and precision in representing knowledge. However, deciding a particular type of variable to use can be a complex task. The dialog manager offers some assistance, but the expert usually must learn appropriate usage of rating types through experience.

Experts develop Aquinas knowledge bases serially. In the future, we would like to build a participant system in which many experts could dynamically share rating grids and hierarchies (Chang, 1985).

ANALYSIS AND INFERENCE

Multiple analysis tools and elicitation methods in Aquinas help the expert think about the problem in new ways and tend to point conflicts and inconsistencies over time. Lenat (1983*a, b*) argues that knowledge representations should shift as different needs arise. This should lead to a better problem and solution descriptions, and, in turn, to better problem solving.

Inference in Aquinas is efficient because the problem space is partitioned. Information in the trait hierarchies is attached to particular levels of solutions. Although no formal studies have been conducted, consultation results using the methods described above seem reasonable.

Rule generation for expert-system shells is straightforward. Development of the knowledge base can continue in an expert system shell that may offer advantages of speed, specialized development and debugging facilities, and inexpensive hardware.

FUTURE DIRECTIONS

We intend to build a knowledge-acquisition environment that includes specific domain knowledge for specialized application areas and can acquire knowledge for synthetic problems, combining features from other knowledge acquisition tools such as MDIS (Antonelli, 1983), DSPL (Brown, 1984), MORE (Kahn, Nowlan & McDermott, 1985), MOLE (Eshelman, Ehert, McDermott & Tan, in press), and TKAW (Kahn, Breaux, Joeseph & De Klerk, in press).

Presently Aquinas works best on those problems whose solutions can be comfortably enumerated (*analytic* or *structured selection* problems such as classification or diagnosis) as opposed to problems whose solutions are built up from components (*synthetic* or *constructive* problems such as configuration or planning).

Simple classification can be thought of as a single-decision problem (handled by ETS). Complex structured selection problems may require a set of linked data abstraction/solution refinement decisions (Aquinas). The next step may be to generalize this process to acquire and represent knowledge for planning, configuration, and design problems where the order of linked decisions in solution hierarchies may represent precedence of events or goals rather than just solution refinement. In these problems hierarchies may be assembled at consultation time rather than constructed totally in advance as they are currently. Grid cells might sometimes contain an arbitrary computation rather than a rating. These would include results of functions (such as found in spreadsheets) or data base retrievals. Deeper models of the structure and function of physical systems could be modeled.

An important step in expanding the knowledge-acquisition workbench concept is the linking together of other specialized tools. At the Boeing Knowledge Systems Laboratory we are investigating ways of integrating diverse knowledge representations from different laboratory projects so that this may be more easily accomplished. In the domain of knowledge acquisition, we feel that the approach used in SALT (Marcus, McDermott & Wang, 1985; Marcus & McDermott, in press; Marcus, in press) is particularly promising. SALT is a system that interviews experts to build knowledge bases for certain types of constructive problems (its first use was to configure elevators). We are also interested in generating knowledge sources for BBB, a blackboard system that has been successfully applied to a variety of problems (Benda, Baum, Dodhiawala & Jagannathan, 1986).

Development of the Aquinas workbench will continue in an incremental fashion. Techniques will be continuously integrated and refined to build an increasingly more effective knowledge-acquisition environment.

Thanks to Roger Beeman, Miroslav Benda, Kathleen Bradshaw, William Clancey, Brian Gaines, Cathy Kitto, Ted Kitzmiller, Art Nagai, Doug Schuler, Mildred Shaw, David Shema, Lisle Tinglof-Boose, and Bruce Wilson for their contributions and support. Aquinas was developed at the Knowledge Systems Laboratory, Advanced Technology Center, Boeing Computer Services in Seattle, Washington.

## References

ADAMS, J. (1985). Probabilistic reasoning and certainty factors. In BUCHANAN, B. & SHORTLIFFE, E., Eds, *Rule-Based Expert Systems. the MYCIN Experiments of the Stanford Heuristic Programming Project.* Reading. Massachusetts: Addison-Wesley.

ALPERT, M. & RAIFFA, H. (1982). A progress report on the training of probability assessors. In KAHNEMAN, D., SLOVIC, P. & TVERSKY, A. Eds, *Judgment under Uncertainty: Heuristics and Biases,* New York: Cambridge University Press.

ANTONELLI, D. (1983). The application of artificial intelligence to a maintenance and diagnostic information system (MDIS). *Proceedings of the Joint Services Workshop on Artificial Intelligence in Maintenance,* Boulder, Colorado.

BENDA, M., BAUM, L. S., DODHIAWALA, R. T. & JAGANNATHAN, V. (1986). Boeing blackboard system. *Proceedings of the High-Level Tools Workshop,* Ohio State University, October 1986.

BENDA, M., JAGANNATHAN, V. & DODHIAWALA, R., On optimal cooperation of knowledge sources. *Workshop on Distributed Artificial Intelligence,* Gloucester, Massachusetts.

BEYTH-MAROM, R. & DEKEL, S. (1985). *An Elementary Approach to Thinking under Uncertainty.* London: Lawrence Erlbaum Associates.

BOOSE, J. H. (1984). Personal construct theory and the transfer of human expertise. *Proceedings of the National Conference on Artificial Intelligence,* Austin, Texas.

BOOSE, J. H. (1935). A knowledge acquisition program for expert systems based on personal construct psychology. *International Journal of Man-Machine Studies,* 23, 495-525.

BOOSE, J. H. (1936). *Expertise Transfer for Expert System Design.* New York: Elsevier.

BOOSE, J. H. (1937). Rapid acquisition and combination of knowledge from multiple experts in the same domain. *Future Computing Systems Journal* In press.

BROWN, D. E. (1984). Expert systems for design problem-solving using design refinement with plan selection and redesign. Ph.D. Thesis, Ohio State University, CIS Department, Columbus, Ohio.

BYLANDER, T. & CHANDRASEKARAN, B. (1987). Generic tasks in knowledge-based reasoning: the "Right," level of abstraction for knowledge acquisition. *International Journal of Man-Machine Studies.* In press.

BYLANDER, T. & MITTAL, S. (1986). CSRL: a language for classificatory problem solving and uncertainty handling. *AI Magazine,* August.

CHANDRASEKARAN, B. (1986). Generic tasks in knowledge-based reasoning: high-level building blocks for expert system design. *IEEE Expert,* Fall.

CHEESEMAN, P. (1985). In defense of probability. *Proceedings of the Ninth International Joint Conference on Artificial Intelligence,* Los Angeles, California.

CLANCEY, W. (1986). Heuristic classification In KOWALIK, J. Ed., *Knowledge-Based Problem-Solving.* New York: Prentice-Hall.

COOMBS, C. H., DAWES, R. M. & TVERSKY, A. (1970). *Mathematical Psychology.* Englewood Cliffs, New Jersey: Prentice-Hall.

ESHELMAN, L., EHRET, D., McDERMOTT, J. & TAN, M. (1987). MOLE: a tenacious knowledge-acquisition tool *International Journal of Man-Machine Studies.* In press.

GAINES, B. R. (1987). An overview of knowledge acquisition and transfer. *International Journal of Man-Machine Studies.* In press.

GAINES, B. R. & SHAW, M. L. G. (1987). New directions in the analysis and interactive elicitation of personal construct systems. In SHAW, M. L. G. Ed, *Recent Advances in Personal Construct Technology.* New York: Academic Press.

GAINES, B. R. & SHAW, M. L. G. (1985). Induction of inference rules for expert systems. *Fuzzy Sets and Systems.*

GORDON, J. & SHORTLIFFE, E. (1985). The Dempster-Shafer theory of evidence. In BUCHANAN, B. & SHORTLIFFE, E. Eds, *Rule-Based Expert Systems: the MYCIN Experiments of the Stanford Heuristic Programming Project.* Reading, Massachusetts: Addison-Wesley.

GRUBER, T. & COHEN, P. (1987). Design for acquisition principles of knowledge system design to facilitate knowledge acquisition. *International Journal of Man-Machine Studies.* In press.

HENRION, M. (1986). Propagating uncertainty by logic sampling in Bayes' networks. *Proceedings of the Second Workshop on Uncertainty in Artificial Intelligence,* Philadelphia, Pennsylvania.

HINKLE, D. N. (1965). The change of personal constructs from the viewpoint of a theory of implications. *Ph. D. Thesis,* Ohio State University, Ohio.

HOWARD, R. A. & MATHESON, J. E. (1984). Influence diagrams. In HOWARD, R. A. & MATHESON, J. E. Eds, *Readings on the Principles and Applications of Decision Analysis,* Menlo Park, California: Strategic Decisions Group.

HURLEY, R. (1983). *Decisions Tables in Software Engineering,* New York: Van Nostrand Reinhold.

KAHN, G., NOWLAN, S. & McDERMOTT, J. (1985). MORE: an intelligent knowledge acquisition tool. *Proceedings of the Ninth Joint Conference on Artificial Intelligence,* Los Angeles, California.

KAHN, G. S., BREAUX, E. H., JOESEPH, R. L. & DEKLERK, P. (1987). An intelligent mixed-initiative workbench for knowledge acquisition. *International Journal of Man-Machine Studies.* In press.

KELLY, G. A. (1955). *The Psychology of Personal Constructs,* New York: Norton.

SPETZLER, C. & STAL VON HOLSTEIN, C. (1983). Probability encoding in decision analysis. In HOWARD, R. & MATHESON, J. Eds, *Readings on the Principles and Applications of Decision Analysis*, Vol. 2. Palo Alto, California: Strategic Decisions Group.

SPIEGELHALTER, D. J. (1986). Probabilistic reasoning in predictive expert systems. In KANAL, L. N. & LEMMER, J. Eds, *Uncertainty in Artificial Intelligence*. Amsterdam: North-Holland.

SZOLOVITZ, P. & PAUKER, S. (1978). Categorical and probabilistic reasoning in medical diagnosis. *Artificial Intelligence*, **11**.

WALLSTEN, T. & BUDESCU, D. (1983). Encoding subject probabilities: a psychological and psychometric review. *Management Science*, **29**.

WILKINS, D. C. (1987) Knowledge base debugging using apprenticeship learning techniques. *International Journal of Man–Machine Studies*. In press.

KITTO, C. & BOOSE, J. H. (1987). Heuristics for expertise transfer: the automatic management of complex knowledge-acquisition dialogs. *International Journal of Man–Machine Studies*. in press.

LENAT, D. (1983a). The nature of heuristics. *Artificial Intelligence*, **19**,

LENAT, D. (1983b). The nature of heuristics. *Artificial Intelligence*, **21**.

LENAT, D., PRAKASH, M. & SHEPARD, M. (1986). CYC: using common sense knowledge to overcome brittleness and knowledge acquisition bottlenecks. *AI Magazine*, **6**.

LIEBERMAN, H. (1986). Using prototypical objects to implement shared behavior in object-oriented systems. *Proceedings of the Object-Oriented Programming Systems, Languages, and Applications Workshop*, Portland, Oregon

MARCUS, S., McDERMOTT, J. & WANG, T. (1985). Knowledge acquisition for constructive systems. *Proceedings of the Ninth Joint Conference on Artificial Intelligence*, Los Angeles, California.

MARCUS, S. & McDERMOTT, J. (1987). SALT: a knowledge acquisition tool for propose-and-revise systems. *Carnegie–Mellon University Department of Computer Science technical report*. In press.

MARCUS, S. (1987). Taking backtracking with a grain of SALT. *International Journal of Man–Machine Studies*. In press.

McDERMOTT, J. (1986). Making expert systems explicit. *Proceedings of the IFIP Congress*, Dublin, Ireland.

MITCHALSKI, R. S. (1978). *Designing Extended Entry Decision Tables and Optimal Decision Trees Using Decision Diagrams*. Urbana, Illinois: Intelligent Systems Group, University of Illinois.

MICHALSKI, R. S. & WINSTON, P. (1985). Variable precision logic. *MIT AI Memo*, Artificial Intelligence Laboratory, Massachusetts Institute of Technology, 857.

MICHALSKI, R. S., *Machine Learning*. Plenary talk at the *AAAI Knowledge Acquisition for Knowledge-Based Systems Workshop*, Banff, Canada, November, 1986.

MITTAL, S., BOBROW, D. & KAHN, K. (1986): Virtual copies: at the boundary between classes and instances. *Proceedings of the Object-Oriented Programming Systems, Languages, and Applications Workshop*, Portland, Oregon.

PEARL, J. (1986). Fusion, propagation and structuring in belief networks. *Technical report CSD-850022, R-42-VI-12*, Cognitive systems Laboratory, Computer Science Department, University of California, Los Angeles, California.

QUINLAN, J. R. (1983). Learning efficient classification procedures and their application to chess end games. In MICHALSKI, R. S., CARBONELL, J. G. & MITCHELL, T. M. Eds, *Machine Learning—An Artificial Intelligence Approach*, Vol. 1. Tioga: Palo Alto, California.

REBOH, R. & RISCH, T. (1986). SYNTEL: knowledge programming using functional representations. *Proceedings of National Conference on Artificial Intelligence (AAAI-86)*, Philadelphia, Pennsylvania.

REBOH, R., RISCH, T., HART, P. E. & DUDA, R. O. (1986). Task-specific knowledge representation: a case study. *Proceedings of the High-Level Tools Workshop*, Ohio State University.

SAATY, T. L. (1980). *The Analytic Hierarchy Process*. New York: McGraw–Hill.

SHAFER, G. (1976). *A Mathematical Theory of Evidence*. Princeton: University Press.

SHAFER, G. & TVERSKY, A. (1985). Languages and designs for probability judgment. *Cognitive Science*, **9**, 309–339.

SHASTRI, L. & FELDMAN, J. (1985). Evidential reasoning in semantic networks: a formal theory. *Proceedings of the Ninth International Joint Conference on Artificial Intelligence*, Los Angeles, California.

SHAW, M. L. G. & GAINES, B. R. (1987a). PLANET: a computer-based system for personal learning, analysis, negotiation and elicitation techniques. In MANCUSO, J. C. & SHAW, M. L. G. Eds, *Cognition and Personal Structure: computer Access and Analysis*. Praeger Press. In press.

SHAW, M. L. G. & GAINES, B. R. (1987b). Techniques for knowledge acquisition and transfer. *International Journal of Man–Machine Studies*. In press.

# MOLE: a tenacious knowledge-acquisition tool

LARRY ESHELMAN, DAMIEN EHRET, JOHN McDERMOTT & MING TAN

*Department of Compuer Science, Carnegie Mellon University, Pittsburgh, Pennsylvania 15213, U.S.A.*

MOLE can help domain experts build a heuristic problem-solver by working with them to generate an initial knowledge base and then detect and remedy deficiencies in it. The problem-solving method presupposed by MOLE makes several heuristic assumptions about the world, which MOLE is able to exploit when acquiring knowledge. In particular, by distinguishing between covering and differentiating knowledge and by allowing covering knowledge to drive the knowledge-acquisition process, MOLE is able to disambiguate an under-specified knowledge base and to interactively refine an incomplete knowledge base.

## 1. Introduction

MOLE (Eshelman & McDermott, 1986) is an expert-system shell that can be used in building systems that do heuristic classification. It is both a performance system which interprets a domain-dependent knowledge base and a knowledge-acquisition tool for building and refining this knowledge base. MOLE the performance system presupposes that the task can be represented as a classification problem: some object is selected from a set of pre-enumerable candidates (e.g. faults, diseases, components) on the basis of weighted evidential considerations (e.g. symptoms, cues, requirements) (Clancey, 1984, 1985; Buchanan & Shortliffe, 1984). MOLE the knowledge-acquisition tool builds a knowledge base by eliciting knowledge from the domain expert guided by its understanding of how to represent the knowledge required by its problem-solving method, and discovers missing knowledge and refines the knowledge base guided by its understanding of how to diagnose what knowledge the problem-solving method might be missing.

MOLE belongs to a family of knowledge-acquisition tools which get their power by paying close attention to the problem-solving method used by their performance systems (McDermott, 1986, Gruber & Cohen, in press). Examples of such systems are TEIRESIAS (Davis & Lenat, 1982), ETS (Boose, 1984), MORE (Kahn, Nowlan & McDermott, 1985a,b), KNACK (Klinker, Bentolila, Genetet, Grimes & McDermott, in press), SALT (Marcus, McDermott & Wang, 1985), and SEAR (van de Brug, Bachant & McDermott, 1985). MOLE resembles the first three systems in that its method can be described as a variant of heuristic classification. It differs from them in that its problem-solving method incorporates certain explicit assumptions about the world which, along with several assumptions about how experts express themselves, are exploited during the knowledge-acquisition process.

Our goal has been to make MOLE smart—i.e. to enable it to build a reasonable knowledge base with a minimal amount of information elicited from the expert. Our research strategy has been to overly restrict (or so it seems at first) the information that MOLE can elicit from the expert and then to search for heuristics that will enable it to build from this limited information a knowledge base that can perform the given task reasonably well. In this paper we shall describe the results of this strategy. In section 2 we describe the method presupposed by MOLE and the set of knowledge roles imposed by the problem-solving method. In section 3 we describe how MOLE's knowledge of its performance system's method is exploited in knowledge acquisition.

## 2. MOLE's method

MOLE the knowledge-acquisition tool gets its power from its knowledge of the problem-solving method of MOLE the performance system. In this section we shall describe the method used by MOLE the performance system. MOLE's problem-solving method is a variant of heuristic classification. MOLE selects or classifies candidate hypotheses on the basis of "rules" associating the candidates with various evidential considerations. However, unlike some heuristic classification systems such as MYCIN, these rules are not just arbitrary implications among arbitrary facts about the world (Szolovits & Pauker, 1978). By making certain assumptions about the world and interpreting the rules or associations in light of these assumptions, MOLE is able to obtain considerable leverage for its knowledge acquisition. MOLE's problem-solving method consists of the following steps:

(1) ask what symptoms need to be explained;
(2) determine what hypotheses will explain or cover these symptoms (Covering Knowledge);
(3) determine what information will differentiate among the hypotheses covering any symptom (Differentiating Knowledge);
(4) ask for that information;
(5) if any differentiating knowledge needs to be explained, go to 2;
(6) pick the best combination of viable hypotheses that will explain all of the symptoms (Combining Knowledge)
(7) if there is information that will affect the viability of some combination of hypotheses, ask for that information, and go to 2;
(8) display the results.

Central to MOLE's method is the distinction between evidence that needs to be explained or covered by some hypothesis and evidence that helps differentiate among hypotheses. The former, Covering Knowledge, reflects two basic assumptions that MOLE makes about the world:

(1) exhaustivity: every abnormal finding has an explanation—i.e. some candidate hypothesis will account for it;
(2) exclusivity: explanations should not be multiplied beyond necessity—i.e. do not accept two hypotheses if one will do.

The exhaustivity assumption enables MOLE to interpret the hypothesis-symptom associations in its domain model causally. Every symptom is assumed to have a cause. If a symptom is not explained by one hypothesis, it must be explained by another. The exclusivity assumption is a version of Occam's razor: all other things

0020-7373/87/010041 + 14$03.00/0

© 1987 Academic Press Inc. (London) Limited

being equal, parsimonious explanations should be favored. As a general rule of thumb, the types of events represented by hypotheses are fairly rare, so it is unlikely that several occur simultaneously. (Of course, two such events might be interrelated, but then this should be represented by combining knowledge).

An important corollary follows from the exhaustivity and exclusivity assumptions: accept the best candidate relative to its competitors—i.e. a candidate may "win" by ruling out competing candidates. Because symptoms must be explained by some hypothesis (exhaustivity), one of the hypotheses must be true. And because only one hypothesis is likely to be true (exclusivity), we can drive up the support of one hypothesis by driving down the support of its competitors or vice versa. This provides the basis for MOLE's second kind of knowledge role, Differentiating Knowledge.

Differentiating Knowledge enables MOLE to evaluate the relative likelihood of hypotheses explaining the same symptom. MOLE understands four types of differentiating knowledge:

Anticipatory Knowledge;
Circumstantial Knowledge;
Refining Knowledge;
Qualifying Knowledge.

In all four cases, the knowledge helps differentiate which hypothesis is the most likely explanation of a symptom. Anticipatory Knowledge is closely tied to Covering Knowledge. Given the Covering Knowledge that event $E_1$ explains event $E_2$, Anticipatory Knowledge is the additional information that the presence of $E_1$ is likely to lead to $E_2$, or alternatively, that the absence of $E_2$ tends to rule out $E_1$. Circumstantial Knowledge, like Covering Knowledge, associates evidence with hypotheses. But unlike Covering Knowledge, the evidence does not have to be explained or covered. Circumstantial Knowledge is merely correlated—positively or negatively—with the hypothesis. Such evidence indicates that the hypothesis is more or less likely to be true, but there is no presumption that one of the hypotheses with which it is associated must be true. Refining Knowledge points to distinguishing features of a symptom which indicate that a proper subset of the hypotheses covering it are more likely to contain the correct explanation. By refining the symptom, MOLE is able to differentiate among the hypotheses that might explain the unrefined symptom. Qualifying Knowledge is any background condition which qualifies the strength of an association. A qualifying condition may either strengthen an association or weaken (or completely mask) an association.

MOLE the performance system seeks to explain all the symptoms which are present. Covering Knowledge and Differentiating Knowledge are used to determine local explanations. Combining Knowledge, on the other hand, is instrumental in integrating the local explanations into a global explanation. Once the hypotheses which best cover or explain each symptom that needs to be covered have been discovered, Combining Knowledge is used to select the best combination of hypotheses that will explain all the symptoms that are present. More specifically, Combining Knowledge overrides MOLE's default method for combining hypotheses. MOLE classifies active hypotheses in one of three categories: accept, reject, or indeterminate. Hypotheses that are clearly better than any of their competitors at

explaining some symptom are tentatively accepted. Hypotheses which are not accepted and are not needed to explain any symptoms because these symptoms are explained by some accepted hypothesis are rejected. All other active hypotheses are classified as indeterminate. Among the indeterminate hypotheses MOLE tries to find the smallest viable set that will explain all the unexplained symptoms. Combining Knowledge overrides MOLE's default procedure and recommends a less parsimonious combination of hypotheses.

We have mainly used MOLE to build knowledge bases for diagnostic tasks. However, we have described MOLE's method so that no particular type of domain is presupposed, for we suspect that there is a much wider range of tasks for which MOLE would be useful. For example, MOLE might be used in a domain whose task is component selection. Covering Knowledge would link the components (hypotheses) with requirements that must be met (symptoms). Differentiating Knowledge would be information indicating what tradeoffs can be made between various components. Combining Knowledge would be heuristics suggesting how to select a combination of components if no single component met a set of overlapping requirements.

Since most of our research has involved diagnostic problems, we will illustrate MOLE's method and the knowledge roles presupposed by its method with an example of a system which diagnoses problems in a coal-burning power plant. The knowledge base built by MOLE the knowledge-acquisition tool enables MOLE the performance system to diagnose problems connected with the boiler, the central unit in a power plant. The problems rarely prevent the boiler from functioning, but they are a major source of inefficiency. A boiler that is functioning inefficiently can waste millions of dollars of fuel as well as dump tons of pollutants into the atmosphere.

Suppose, for example, the operator notices that there is a loss in gas and that the ash leaving the boiler is dark. These are two symptoms that need to be covered or explained. The loss in gas has two potential explanations: (1) a high gas temperature; (2) high excess air. The other symptom, dark ash, has three potential explanations; (1) high excess air; (2) low excess air; (3) large fuel particles. For each symptom present, MOLE tries to differentiate among the potential causes. For example, when there is high excess air, there is a strong expectation (anticipatory knowledge) that there will be a high fly ash flow. If this expectation is not met, support for the high excess air hypothesis is driven down. Consequently, support for the competing explanation, high gas temperature, is driven up and becomes the likely explanation for the loss in gas. Since high excess air is also a potential explanation for the dark ash, support for its competitors, low excess air and large fuel particles, is also driven up. MOLE tries to differentiate further between these two hypotheses. For instance, if the flame temperature is not low, contrary to what one would expect if there is low excess air, then support for the low excess air hypothesis is also driven down, leaving large fuel particles as the most likely explanation for the dark ash. Once MOLE has finished locally differentiating the hypotheses covering each symptom that is present, MOLE looks at what combination of hypotheses will best explain all the symptoms. In this case MOLE will accept two hypotheses, high gas temperature and large fuel particles, since the only hypothesis which will explain all the relevant symptoms has been ruled out by the absence of a high fly ash flow. Having accepted these two hypotheses, MOLE next sees whether they, in turn, can be treated as symptoms that are explained by higher-level hypotheses. In this case, they both have higher-level explanations. For example, the large fuel particles can be explained by either the setting of the pulverizer or by a malfunction of the pulverizer. Knowing that the grinder had recently been maintained would provide circumstantial evidence that a malfunction is unlikely and thus drive up the likelihood that the setting of the pulverizer is the explanation for the large fuel particles. MOLE continues until it has attempted to explain every event that can be explained.

In the next section we will draw from our experiences with the power-plant diagnosis task to illustrate how MOLE uses its knowledge of its method to guide the knowledge-acquisition process both when generating the initial knowledge base and when refining it.

## 3. Knowledge acquisition

Usually it is not a very hard to elicit knowledge from an expert. The hard problem is eliciting the right sort of knowledge. Knowledge needs to be in such a form that it will be applied to the problem in the right way at the right time. The first step in satisfying this need is to identify explicitly the appropriate problem-solving method for the task and the types of knowledge roles relevant for this method. Once this is done, it is fairly easy to build a knowledge collector. However, if the ultimate goal is to replace the knowledge engineer with an automated system, rather than providing the knowledge engineer with a programming tool, then two troublesome features of the knowledge-acquisition process must be addressed:

(1) indeterminateness: when specifying associations between events, the expert is likely to be fairly vague about the nature of these associations and events;
(2) incompleteness: the expert will probably forget to specify certain pieces of knowledge.

The indeterminateness problem reflects the fact that experts are not accustomed to talking about the associations between events in a way that precisely fits the problem-solving method's pre-defined knowledge roles. Since our ultimate goal is to develop a knowledge-acquisition tool that replaces the knowledge engineer, the burden is upon the knowledge-acquisition system to make sense of whatever information the domain expert is willing to provide. Although the expert can be encouraged to be as specific as possible, a smart knowledge acquisition tool must be able to tolerate ambiguity and indeterminateness.

The incompleteness problem is the problem of how to identify missing or incorrect knowledge. The expert, no matter how qualified and thorough he may be, is going to forget to mention certain special circumstances. And sometimes the expert will make mistakes. Thus, a smart knowledge-acquisition tool needs to be able to incrementally add knowledge to the knowledge base, refine existing knowledge, and sometimes correct existing knowledge.

The indeterminateness problem and the incompleteness problem dominate the two phases of knowledge acquisition: (1) the gathering of information for constructing the initial knowledge base; and (2) the iterative refinement of this knowledge base. During the first phase, MOLE mainly relies upon static techniques of analysis.

MOLE examines specific associations and events in light of the context provided by the surrounding structures. MOLE concentrates on disambiguating the information provided by the expert, although MOLE also tries to recognize areas where the knowledge is obviously incomplete. During the second, dynamic phase, MOLE and the expert interact in order to refine the knowledge base. The expert gives MOLE a test case and tells MOLE the correct diagnosis. If MOLE the performance program comes to an incorrect conclusion, MOLE the knowledge-acquisition tool tries to determine the source of the error and recommends possible remedies. Typically, this means adding knowledge or qualifying existing knowledge, but sometimes the interpretation provided in the previous phase needs to be revised.

In the following two subsections, we shall discuss the techniques MOLE uses during both the construction and refinement phases of knowledge acquisition.

### 3.1. CONSTRUCTING THE INITIAL KNOWLEDGE BASE

MOLE initiates the knowledge acquisition process by asking the expert to list the events—i.e. hypotheses and evidence—that are commonly relevant to the expert's domain and to draw associations between pairs of events. This information is easy to elicit from the expert, although the expert will often overlook certain associations or events. However, in order for MOLE to be able to fashion this network of events and associations into a knowledge base suitable for diagnosis, four additional pieces of information are needed:

(1) the type of event (i.e. whether observed or inferred);
(2) the type of evidence an association provides (e.g. covering evidence, anticipatory evidence);
(3) the direction of an association (e.g. does $E_1$ explain $E_2$ or vice versa);
(4) the numeric support value attached to an association.

MOLE understands that experts are not very good at providing such information and so does not require that the expert provide a fully specified network of associations. Instead, MOLE relies on its expectations about the world and how experts enter data in order to mold an under-specified network of associations into a consistent and unambiguous knowledge base.

The most critical piece of information is the association type. Both the direction and support value of an association are dependent upon its type. The problem with directly asking the expert for the association type is that it is hard to convey to the expert what these types mean. The distinction between covering and circumstantial evidence, for example, is part of MOLE's jargon, not the expert's. But the problem is not simply a matter of finding a translation from MOLE's jargon into terminology that the expert can understand. The indeterminacy is deeper than this. Not only does the expert have difficulty distinguishing among types of evidence, often he cannot decide whether an event should be classified as evidence rather than a hypothesis. He may not even be sure whether he should say it is observed or inferred. Perhaps it can be observed, but only with difficulty. For example, one of the causes of a misbalance of convection is the presence of fouling. Whether the operator can see signs of fouling depends upon what part of the boiler it is occurring. On those occasions when he cannot observe fouling, he still may be able to infer fouling. Furthermore, even if an event is observed, it can function as a

However, if the expert indicates that he is not sure about the temporal direction, MOLE will try to elicit more information in order to clarify the nature of the association. It could be that the association is circumstantial, or, more likely, that one event is really a direct indication of the other event. For instance, a small, red flame is a direct indication of a low flame temperature. Although MOLE interprets the flame temperature as explaining the flame size and color, the expert may be reluctant to put a temporal direction on this relationship.

The final type of information that MOLE needs in order to fashion the initial network of associations into a knowledge base is each association's support value. However, experts do not like providing numeric support values and are not very good at it. In our experience, when experts are asked to indicate the degree of support of some piece of evidence for a hypothesis by selecting a number within a fixed range, they will think about the question for a while and then almost inevitably choose some number near the middle of the range. Fortunately, it turns out that the support values do not have to be very accurate, and that on the basis of a few simple assumptions MOLE can assign default support values that are just as good, if not better, than those assigned by the expert. (They subsequently can be adjusted by MOLE during dynamic analysis).

MOLE's method for assigning support values for covering evidence follows directly from MOLE's exhaustivity and exclusivity assumptions. The assumption that every symptom can be explained by some hypothesis plus the assumption that only one of the covering hypotheses is likely to be the explanation suggests that the positive support provided by the presence of a symptom should be distributed among the hypotheses and should sum to 1·0. Since MOLE initially has no information how this support should be distributed, it makes the default assumption that the support values for any symptom should be equally divided among the hypotheses which explain it.

The method for assigning support values for anticipatory evidence has a weaker rationale. MOLE assumes that if an expert spontaneously mentions a piece of anticipatory knowledge, then it is the sort of information that is likely to have a significant impact; thus, a relatively high support value is assigned. The problem, then, is to determine when an expert is spontaneously entering anticipatory evidence. As was explained earlier, covering evidence and anticipatory evidence are closely linked. They enable MOLE to reason in both directions between two events.

If $E_1$ explains $E_2$, then the occurrence of $E_2$ provides some evidence for $E_1$. If in addition there is a strong anticipatory connection between the events, then the occurrence of $E_1$ increases the likelihood of $E_2$. MOLE pays attention to the direction of this supporting relationship. If the expert indicates that $E_1$ supports $E_2$ and that $E_1$ is temporally prior, then MOLE will infer that the expert is spontaneously entering an anticipatory association. MOLE will also assume that there is a covering association between the two events. On the other hand, if the temporal and supporting directions are different—e.g. if $E_1$ supports $E_2$, and $E_2$ is prior to $E_1$—MOLE assumes that the expert is entering a covering association, and assumes, until evidence to the contrary, that there is no strong anticipatory association.

MOLE has one other opportunity to identify anticipatory associations in the initial phase of knowledge acquisition. MOLE monitors the static knowledge base

hypothesis. Suppose that fouling can be observed and that a low heat transfer needs to be explained. A misbalance of convection competes with a misbalance of radiation as explanations of a low heat transfer. If fouling is discovered before the radiation explanation of a low heat transfer has been resolved, then fouling serves as evidence for a misbalance of radiation. On the other hand, if it has already been ascertained that there is a misbalance of radiation, then the fouling provides the explanation.

After several unsuccessful attempts to find ways of unambiguously eliciting the association types from the expert, we discovered that we are looking for the solution in the wrong place. In the three domains that we have explored most extensively, the only associations that the experts have ever spontaneously entered are covering and anticipatory associations. Instead of having to worry about identifying half a dozen knowledge roles, we only have to worry about two. In a sense there is no identification problem at all, since every anticipatory association can be interpreted as a covering association and vice versa. However, the anticipatory strengths of some covering associations are so weak that they can be ignored in practice. So the problem is to identify which covering associations provide significant anticipatory evidence. We shall return to this question when we discuss how MOLE determines the support values of associations.

On reflection, it is not very surprising that the initial knowledge-acquisition process generates just these two types. The starting point in diagnosis is a set of events that need to be explained. MOLE asks for the names of these events and their potential explanations, and then for explanations of these explanations. The knowledge-acquisition process is driven by covering knowledge and to a lesser extent anticipatory knowledge. Other types of knowledge are secondary and tend to be overlooked by the expert. For example, given that low excess air needs to be explained, the most common explanations will occur to the expert—e.g. the fan power has been exceeded or there is a leak in the duct. While he is thinking about fan power it may occur to him that if he knows that a valve is malfunctioning, he will anticipate that the fan power has been exceeded. On the other hand, it is unlikely to occur to him that the installation date of the duct is a relevant circumstance for determining the likelihood of a leak. When providing covering knowledge, the expert is biased toward thinking of events causing other events. He tends to overlook circumstances or states that are correlated with an event except in the context of some actual test case.

Given the expert's bias toward providing only covering associations, finding out the direction of these covering associations would seem to be a straightforward matter. All we need to do is ask the expert whether $E_1$ explains $E_2$ or vice versa. Unfortunately, about 20% of the time experts reverse the direction. When the expert says that $E_1$ explains $E_2$ what he may mean is that $E_1$ explains why he would accept $E_2$, not that $E_1$ is the physical explanation of $E_2$. The same confusion occurs with cause and effect language. Sometimes the expert will say that $E_1$ causes $E_2$ and mean that the occurrence of $E_1$ "caused" him to think of $E_2$ as the explanation of $E_1$. We have found that the most reliable directional information that can easily be elicited from the expert is an association's temporal direction—i.e. which event occurs first. MOLE assumes, all things being equal, that the temporal direction is a reliable indicator of the explanatory direction. If, for example, the expert says that $E_2$ supports $E_1$ and that $E_1$ precedes $E_2$, MOLE assumes that $E_1$ explains $E_2$.

and notes any symptoms which have hypotheses that cannot be differentiated. MOLE assumes that if the expert provides several explanations for some event, then he probably can provide knowledge that will differentiate among them. For example, suppose that MOLE learns during the initial construction of the knowledge base that low excess air can be explained by either the fan power being exceeded or by a leak in the duct, but is not told about any evidence that would help differentiate between these hypotheses. MOLE will ask the expert how he can tell which hypothesis is the cause of low excess air. The expert may indicate that if there is no loud noise coming from the wind box, then MOLE can rule out that there is a leak. This will enable MOLE, at least in principle, to differentiate the two hypotheses.

Before discussing the second phase of knowledge acquisition, something should be said about the absence of any stress on qualifying knowledge during the first phase. Based on the descriptions of other diagnostic systems, one might expect that for a system to perform adequately most associations would need a large number of qualifications. If MOLE did not distinguish between covering and differential knowledge and simply tried to build rules associating evidence with hypotheses, then, no doubt, its initial network of associations would require many qualifications. However, because of the emphasis that MOLE puts on covering knowledge, MOLE tends to build multi-layered networks with sparse connections rather than flat networks where several layers of information need to be compiled into one rule. By asking for the explanations of a symptom rather than the conditions for accepting a hypothesis, MOLE naturally discovers intermediate events which mediate between the bottom-level symptoms and the top-level hypotheses. The knowledge base for diagnosing boiler problems, for example, consists of eight levels of explanation and has as much depth as it has breadth.

However, there is a price to pay for the heavy reliance on intermediate events. There is the danger that redundant pathways are drawn between events. MOLE needs to check for duplicate pathways. For example, in one session MOLE was told that the two explanations for a misbalance of convection are fouling and low excess air. However, in a later session MOLE learned that low excess air can be explained by the fan power being exceeded which, in turn, can be explained by fouling. Thus, there is a direct path from fouling to misbalance of convection and an indirect path through fan power being exceeded and low excess air. The question is whether the direct path is an actual causal path or whether it represents a compiled version of the longer path. MOLE has no way of knowing the answer, but it is important that MOLE notice such occurrences and ask the expert about them.

## 3.2. REFINING THE KNOWLEDGE BASE

In the previous section, we mentioned that MOLE checks to make sure that hypotheses can in principle be differentiated. If they cannot, MOLE tries to elicit knowledge from the expert that will enable it to differentiate among them. However, such static techniques of refinement are quite limited. The expert typically needs a richer context to remind him of missing knowledge, and MOLE needs a richer context in order to be able to distinguish a wider range of association types. The needed context is provided by feedback from the expert during dynamic analysis. The expert gives MOLE a test case and tells MOLE the correct diagnosis.

If MOLE the performance system has come to an incorrect diagnosis, MOLE the knowledge-acquisition tool tries to determine the source of the errors and recommends possible remedies.

In the remainder of this section we will discuss MOLE's techniques for doing dynamic analysis. These techniques reflect the three types of knowledge roles understood by MOLE: Covering Knowledge, Differentiating Knowledge, and Combining Knowledge.

### 3.2.1. Differentiating knowledge

If MOLE's diagnosis does not match that supplied by the expert, MOLE first determines whether or not the diagnosis would have been reachable if the hypotheses had been differentiated differently. If it is so reachable, then MOLE looks for missing differentiating knowledge which will shift the support among the hypotheses. An important consideration, when looking for differentiating knowledge, is whether the needed shifts can be accomplished globally or locally. A global solution may be possible if the raising or lowering of some hypothesis's likelihood will affect the explanations of several symptoms in the right direction and so have a global effect. If a global solution is not possible, then the shifts must be made locally by shifting support among hypotheses which explain the same symptom. (Sometimes what looks like a global problem is actually a collection of several local problems).

*Anticipatory Knowledge.* If a global solution appears possible, MOLE will first focus on identifying anticipatory knowledge. As was explained in our discussion of static analysis, if the expert spontaneously enters a covering association, MOLE cannot tell whether the two events are also linked by an anticipatory association, so it only generates a covering association. MOLE now examines whether there are any inactive covering associations which would have the desired effect if they were also interpreted as anticipatory assumptions.

For example, knowing that a loss in gas is explained by either a high gas temperature or high excess air, and that a high fly ash flow is explained by either very small fuel particles or high excess air, and not having any information to differentiate between these pairs of hypotheses, MOLE will accept high excess air as the explanation for both symptoms and reject the other two hypotheses. MOLE's reasoning is that since it does not have any reason to favor the other two hypotheses over high excess air, high excess air is the best choice because it alone can explain both symptoms. However, when given this case, the expert told MOLE that it was wrong—it should have rejected high excess air and accepted high gas temperature and very small fuel particles. MOLE recognized that if there was some evidence that could drive down the likelihood of high excess air, then the likelihood of the other two hypotheses would be driven up. Noting the absence of an event which provides covering evidence (a high oxygen reading) which would have been explained by high excess air, MOLE reasoned that if these two events were also linked by anticipatory knowledge, then the absence of a high oxygen reading would tend to rule out the high excess air hypothesis. MOLE asked the expert whether the absence of a high oxygen reading ruled out high excess air. The expert confirmed that it did.

*Circumstantial Knowledge.* If a global solution appears possible, and no anticipatory knowledge is discovered, MOLE focuses on circumstantial knowledge. One reason that circumstantial knowledge is given less priority than anticipatory knowledge is that we have found that anticipatory knowledge is more common. But a more important reason is that anticipatory knowledge is tied to covering knowledge and so the existing covering knowledge provides the richer context which MOLE tries to exploit first. Even when MOLE interprets a piece of knowledge as circumstantial, it does so tentatively, keeping in mind that in another example it may learn that it should be interpreted as anticipatory knowledge.

In our previous example, if MOLE had not known anything about the relevance of a high oxygen reading and the expert had entered it for the first time, then MOLE would have interpreted it as circumstantial evidence. If MOLE later learned that a high oxygen reading needs to be explained by high excess air, then it would add a covering association and reinterpret the circumstantial association as an anticipatory association.

*Refining Knowledge.* If the problem is local to a symptom (i.e. the hypotheses which need to be differentiated explain a common symptom), MOLE will ask the expert whether there are many features of the symptom which narrow the set of the hypotheses that are the likely causes.

So far in the power-plant domain we have not found any occasion for refining a symptom. However, in other domains refinement has been useful. For example, in a system that diagnoses automobile problems the symptom that the car would not start was refined to include the feature of whether or not the engine cranked. This feature is used to distinguish the hypothesis that the battery is dead from alternative explanations for the car not starting such as being our of gas, faulty spark plugs, and carburetor problems.

*Qualifying Knowledge.* Qualifying knowledge can adjust existing anticipatory, circumstantial, and refining knowledge. If such knowledge exists but its support is in the wrong direction, or in the right direction but is too weak, MOLE asks if there is any background condition which would strengthen or weaken the existing association in the right direction. In addition qualifying knowledge can be added in conjunction with an anticipatory association. This, in effect, adds a condition which strengthens a potential anticipatory association into one that has a significant impact.

For example, when trying to acquire knowledge that would lead it to accept that the fan power is being exceeded as the explanation for low excess air, and so reject a leak in an air duct as the explanation, MOLE looked for potential anticipatory knowledge. It knew that there was evidence of fouling and that this could cause the fan power to be exceeded, but discovered that the link was too weak to have the needed effect. This suggested to MOLE that it should ask the expert whether there was any condition which would make it very likely that the fan power would be exceeded when there was fouling. The expert confirmed that fouling almost always leads to the fan power being exceeded when there is a heavy load.

*Adjusting Support Values.* If the expert fails to provide any special knowledge which will differentiate among the hypotheses in the needed fashion, then there are three possibilities: (1) there is a need for combining knowledge; (2) the numeric support values are wrong and need to be adjusted; (3) a combination of locally differentiating evidence is needed, instead of a single globally differentiating piece of knowledge. MOLE's choice of what to explore first will depend on the "maturity" of the network and the reliability of feedback from the expert. It is easier for the expert to understand and respond to questions about locally differentiating evidence, so this option is usually tried first, provided the network is mature.

However, early in the refinement phase the most likely possibility is that the support values are wrong. After all, the support values are simply MOLE's guesses based on the structure of the network. The most common change is a shift of a symptom's support from some of its hypotheses to others. For example, there are only two hypotheses explaining the fan power being exceeded—fouling and a malfunction of a valve—so MOLE initially set the support value of each association to 0·5. However, fouling is much more likely than a valve malfunction, unless the fan has not been maintained for a long time. In a test case where the fan power had been exceeded and there was no further evidence for favoring fouling over a malfunction of a valve, MOLE could not decide between the two hypotheses. The expert indicated, however, that MOLE should have picked fouling. After failing to elicit any knowledge from the expert that would help it differentiate between these two causes, MOLE decided that its apportionment of support between the two hypotheses must be mistaken and shifted support from the malfunction of a valve hypothesis to the fouling hypothesis.

### 3.2.2. Covering knowledge

So far we have examined the case where MOLE would have reached the correct diagnosis if it has differentiated among the hypotheses differently. If differentiation is not the problem, then MOLE looks for missing covering knowledge. There are two possible cases: (1) a hypothesis should be rejected but cannot be because it is needed to explain some otherwise unexplained symptom; (2) a hypotheses should be accepted, but it was rejected because it is not needed to explain any symptom.

If a hypothesis fails to be rejected because it is needed to explain some symptom, then MOLE asks the expert for an alternative explanation of the symptom. For example, MOLE discovered that low excess air was a possible explanation of dark ash after being told in a test case that both of the hypotheses that it considered possible explanations for the dark ash should be rejected. MOLE reasoned that dark ash must have an explanation that it did not know about, and asked the expert for this explanation.

Suppose the expert had told MOLE that there is no alternative explanation; yet, the two explanations that it knows about are incorrect. MOLE considers two possibilities: (1) the symptom report is mistaken; (2) the evidence is not really a symptom—i.e. it has misinterpreted the event as covering evidence. MOLE would first inquire whether it is possible that the reported observation that there is dark ash could be mistaken. If it can be, MOLE would lower the default certainty for the report of this event. Then if it is again faced with a situation where there is evidence against both the explanations for this symptom, it will reject them both and suggest that a mistaken report (or mistaken observation) is the most likely explanation for the reported symptom. On the other hand, if the expert is quite certain about this reported symptom, then MOLE would examine how it can most coherently reinterpret the association—e.g. interpret the association as a circumstantial association instead of a covering association.

If a hypothesis is mistakenly rejected because it is not needed to explain anything, then MOLE asks the expert if there is some symptom that is present which can be explained by this hypothesis. For example, MOLE learned about the high stack gas temperature reading in a test case where it wrongly rejected high gas temperature as an explanation for loss in gas. MOLE the performance system had reasoned that since high excess air was needed to explain high fly ash and could also explain loss in gas, the high gas temperature was not needed. However, upon being informed that it should not have rejected high gas temperature, MOLE the knowledge-acquisition tool reasoned that there must be some piece of evidence that high gas temperature explained which was not explained by any other hypothesis. MOLE asked the expert for this information, and was told that the missing piece of evidence was the fact that the stack gas temperature reading was high.

### 3.2.3. Combining knowledge

But what if the expert indicates that there is no missing evidence that needs to be explained by the rejected hypothesis? MOLE reasons that it is probably missing some combining knowledge. If its hypotheses are properly differentiated locally and there is no missing piece of evidence for the hypothesis to explain, then this must be a case where the best explanation for some symptom is the combination of several hypotheses. It should be stressed that MOLE's default strategy will accept several explanations for a set of symptoms, provided each hypothesis is the best explanation of at least one symptom. What distinguishes the case where combining knowledge is needed is that several hypotheses are needed to explain one symptom. MOLE, with the guidance of the expert, acquires a rule for handling this special case.

For example, a misbalance of radiation and a misbalance of convection are alternative explanations for low heat transfer. Furthermore, the misbalance of convection hypothesis is only needed to explain the low heat transfer. When MOLE has reason to accept a misbalance of radiation as the explanation of low heat transfer, its default combining strategy will dictate that it reject the misbalance of convection hypothesis as unneeded. When told that this diagnosis was wrong, MOLE first looked for some symptom which a misbalance of convection explains but a misbalance of radiation does not. Upon learning that there are was no such symptom, MOLE reasoned that it must be missing a special combining rule, and asked the expert for the circumstances that lead him to accept both misbalance of radiation and misbalance of convection. In this case, it is the presence of low excess air.

As MOLE has evolved, dynamic analysis has increasingly taken on a more important role. By not insisting that the expert identify an event's type or an association's direction during the construction phase if he is uncertain about its value, the knowledge base used in the refinement phase is less determinate than it would otherwise be. These indeterminate associations provide MOLE with variable pieces of information when doing dynamic analysis. Whenever MOLE learns that it has made an incorrect diagnosis and has located the portions of the network where there is likely to be missing knowledge, indeterminate associations in these parts of the network are prime candidates for the missing knowledge. And since MOLE knows something about these associations—e.g. what events they connect—it can be quite certain how they should be interpreted even if the expert is not.

## 4. Conclusion

MOLE illustrates how much power a knowledge-acquisition tool can obtain from a set of domain independent heuristics about the knowledge-acquisition process and the nature of the world as it relates to diagnosis. MOLE plays the role of an experienced knowledge engineer who is able to work in conjunction with a domain expert and build a diagnostic system, even though the knowledge engineer has little or no knowledge of the domain. Like such a hypothetical knowledge engineer MOLE begins with no knowledge of the target domain nor any understanding of the domain's vocabulary. By interpreting its assumptions about the world in terms of explicit knowledge roles that guide heuristic classification and by exploiting a few heuristics about how domain experts are likely to express themselves, MOLE is able to extract intelligently from the expert information relevant for building a reasonable knowledge base for performing the given diagnostic task.

We want to thank Gary Kahn and Sandra Marcus for helpful suggestions in the development of MOLE. We also would like to thank Holger Sommer for serving as MOLE's expert in the power plant domain and for the useful feedback that he provided in the development of MOLE.

## References

Boose, J. (1984). Personal construct theory and the transfer of human expertise. In *Proceedings of the National Conference on Artificial Intelligence*. Austin, Texas, 1984.

Buchanan, B. & Shortliffe, E. (1984). *Rule-based Systems: the Mycin experiments of the Stanford Heuristic Programming Project*. Reading, Massachusetts: Addison–Wesley.

Clancey, W. (1984). Classification problem solving. *Proceedings of the National Conference on Artificial Intelligence*, Austin, Texas, 1984.

Clancey, W. (1985) Heuristic classification. *Artificial Intelligence*, **27**, 289–350.

Davis, R. & Lenat, D. (1982). *Knowledge-Based Systems in Artificial Intelligence*. McGraw-Hill.

Eshelman, L. & McDermott, J. (1986). MOLE: a knowledge acquisition tool that uses its head. *Proceedings of the National Conference on Artificial Intelligence*, Philadelphia, Pennsylvania, 1986.

Gruber, T. & Cohen, P. (1987). Design for acquisition: designing knowledge systems to facilitate knowledge acquisition. *International Journal of Man–Machine Studies*. In press.

Kahn, G., Nowlan, S. & McDermott, J. (1985a). Strategies for knowledge acquisition. *IEEE Transactions on Pattern Analysis and Machine Intelligence*, **7**, 511–522.

Kahn, G., Nowlan, S. & McDermott, J. (1985B). MORE: an intelligent knowledge acquisition tool. *Proceedings of Ninth International Conference on Artificial Intelligence*, Los Angelos, California, 1985.

Klinker, G., Bentolila, J., Genetet, S., Grimes M. & McDermott, J. KNACK—report-driven knowledge acquisition. *International Journal of Man–Machine Studies*. In press.

Marcus, S., McDermott, J. & Wang, T. (1985). Knowledge acquisition for constructuve systems. *Proceedings of Ninth International Conference on Artificial Intelligence*, Los Angelos, California, 1985.

McDermott, J. (1986). Making expert systems explicit. *Proceedings of 10th Congress of the International Federation of Information Processing Societies*, Dublin, Ireland, 1986.

Szolovits, P. & Pauker, S. (1978). Categorical and probabilistic reasoning in medical diagnosis. *Artificial Intelligence*, **11**, 115–144.

van de Brug, A., Bachant, J. & McDermott, J. (1985). Doing R1 with Style. *Proceedings of the Second IEEE Conference on Artificial Intelligence Applications*, Miami, Florida, 1985.

# Section 3.2

# Eliciting Design Knowledge

Tasks that involve constructing a solution are generally called design problems, in contrast to data interpretation or analysis problems. Design problem solvers usually apply constraints to refine a partial solution, in order to find acceptable designs that satisfy all or most of the constraints. Design problems include:

- one-dimensional design of schedules and plans, where items are laid out on a time line in a way that satisfies global or local constraints;

- two-dimensional design of layouts and configurations of parts onto a planar spatial representation, where relative or absolute positions of objects may be specified in the geometrical constraints;

- three-dimensional design of artifacts, such as engines and airplanes, where the geometrical constraints become more complex.

Marcus' SALT system described in Section 3.2.1 is a tool for acquiring knowledge about design systems that may be solved by a method called propose-and-refine. SALT illustrates, once again, the leverage that a knowledge acquisition tool can gain from having its own knowledge of the specialized task for which the performance program is being constructed.

Musen's work on OPAL and PROTEGE, presented in Section 3.2.2, focuses on the acquisition of procedural knowledge, namely plans and procedures for managing the therapy of cancer patients. OPAL uses knowledge of therapy planning to help in acquiring the specialized knowledge of oncology therapy that was used in the ONCOCIN system. PROTEGE is a further abstraction, namely, a tool that could be used by knowledge engineers to construct OPAL and similar systems.

The ASK system of Gruber, presented in Section 3.2.3, explicitly recognizes the importance of strategy knowledge in constructing a high-performance program. A strategy can be thought of as an abstract plan for solving a problem; thus strategic knowledge is a kind of design knowledge. ASK provides a knowledge engineer with the ability to monitor a problem-solving session and to refine the strategic knowledge when the system selects a suboptimal action to perform next.

# SALT: A Knowledge Acquisition Language* for Propose-and-Revise Systems

**Sandra Marcus**

*Advanced Technology Center, Boeing Computer Services, P.O. Box 24346, M/S 7L-64, Seattle, WA 98124, U.S.A.*

**John McDermott**\*\*

*Department of Computer Science, Carnegie-Mellon University, Pittsburgh, PA 15213, U.S.A.*

Recommended by Sanjay Mittal

ABSTRACT

*SALT is a knowledge acquisition tool for generating expert systems that can use a propose-and-revise problem-solving strategy. The SALT-assumed method incrementally constructs an initial design by proposing values for design parameters, identifying constraints on design parameters as the design develops and revising decisions in response to detection of constraint violations in the proposal. This problem-solving strategy provides the basis for SALT's knowledge representation. SALT uses its knowledge of the intended problem-solving strategy in identifying relevant domain knowledge, in detecting weaknesses in the knowledge base in order to guide its interrogation of the domain expert, in generating an expert system that can perform the task and explain its line of reasoning, and in analyzing test case coverage. The strong commitment to problem-solving strategy which gives SALT its power also defines its scope.*

## 1. Introduction

Many successful tools for automating knowledge acquisition for expert systems have taken the approach of focusing on one particular problem-solving method to be used by the systems they generate [1, 7, 11, 15, 18, 34]. The narrow focus simplifies the task of making clear the roles that knowledge plays

*NaCl.

\*\*Current address: Digital Equipment Corporation, DLB5-3/E2, 290 Donald Lynch Blvd., Marlboro, MA 01752, U.S.A.

0004-3702/89/$3.50 © 1989, Elsevier Science Publishers B.V. (North-Holland)

*Artificial Intelligence* **39** (1989) 1–37

This paper originally appeared in the journal, *Artificial Intelligence*, Vol. 39, No. 1, and is reprinted here with permission of the publisher, Elsevier, Amsterdam.

SALT is a program that acquires knowledge from an expert and generates a domain-specific knowledge base compiled into rules. SALT then combines this compiled knowledge base with a problem-solving shell to create an expert system. SALT maintains a permanent, declarative store of the knowledge base which is updated during interviews with the domain expert and which is the input to the compiler/rule-generator. It is this intermediate language which represents knowledge by function.

SALT makes use of its understanding of the roles knowledge will play in the problem-solving strategy it assumes. It is one of few knowledge acquisition tools for systems that construct, rather than select, a solution. (See [22, 34] for descriptions of two others.) SALT is intended for use by domain experts to create and maintain systems that perform constraint-satisfaction tasks such as designing an artifact or constructing a schedule. A SALT-generated system uses a propose-and-revise method. The expert system constructs an approximate plan or design by proposing a value for one parameter of the design at a time and checks to see whether each parameter satisfies all constraints on it. Whenever constraint violations are detected, the system will revise past decisions, for example, by changing a parameter value in some way that is dependent on the constraint violated. This problem-solving strategy defines multiple roles that knowledge can play in the system. For this method, there is much interaction among pieces of knowledge in different roles. The high degree of interaction means that it is sometimes difficult for someone adding knowledge to the system to understand how each new piece of knowledge added will fit with what is already in the knowledge base. SALT uses its assessment of the completeness, consistency and adequacy of the knowledge base to guide its interrogation of the user.

The next section describes how knowledge roles define the relevant pieces of knowledge that must be acquired by SALT. Section 3 describes the knowledge base built up from these pieces during an interview and the analyses used to identify and respond to gaps and inadequacies in the knowledge base. Section 4 describes SALT's compilation procedure to create an expert system. The SALT-generated explanation capability is discussed in Section 5. Section 6 looks at a SALT-generated explanation facility for assessing the coverage of test problem sets. Section 7 briefly describes our explorations in understanding SALT's applicability.

## 2. Acquiring Relevant Knowledge Pieces

A functional knowledge representation helps identify what knowledge is relevant to acquire; that is, it identifies what domain knowledge is required by the problem-solver in order to solve the problem. A SALT-generated problem-solver creates a design by proposing values for design parameters, checking constraints on those parameters, and revising values if constraints on proposed parameters are violated. There are three roles that knowledge can play in such

in finding a solution. Role definition provides several advantages [3–6, 21, 25, 33]:

(1) A knowledge acquisition tool needs a clear notion of the function of the knowledge required by the system it is building so that it knows what information to ask for. Questions to domain experts like "How do you perform your job?" are too undirected to produce useful material for constructing an expert system. Knowledge of the ways domain knowledge can be used provides focus for interrogating domain experts.

(2) A functionally represented knowledge base can be examined to judge the expert system's adequacy to perform the task for which it is intended. For example, a knowledge acquisition tool that understands how knowledge will be used can have strategies for identifying places where knowledge is missing and for eliciting remedial knowledge.

(3) Understanding the roles knowledge plays allows the knowledge acquisition tool to generate a problem-solving system that knows how to apply the gathered knowledge when appropriate. This is because the knowledge gathered is identified by role and the problem-solving strategy itself specifies when during problem-solving each role is applicable. This also leaves open the possibility of using the same knowledge base representation with distinct variations in problem-solving strategy that use the same knowledge roles but differ in when they apply the knowledge in those roles.

(4) In order for an expert system to describe to a user how it makes its decisions, an explanation facility must have an understanding of the function of the knowledge the system uses. The common demands on knowledge representation from both explanation and knowledge elicitation are not surprising since in the former, the expert system must "transfer" knowledge to its user while in the latter, the human domain expert must have the means to transfer knowledge to the knowledge acquisition tool. One advantage of this relationship is that a function-based knowledge representation scheme used by a knowledge acquisition tool can be incorporated into the expert system it generates to serve that system's explanation facility.

(5) For most expert systems, it is impractical to enumerate all of the potential problems a system will need to solve. But a well-chosen set of sample problems can be used to help assess the validity of the system. Selection criteria for the sample set which take into account how knowledge will be used can help ensure that relevant characteristics of the knowledge base will be tested.

(6) An understanding of the roles knowledge plays during problem-solving is crucial in mapping a domain expert's problem description onto a problem-solving strategy. The more the AI community understands about how to do this for specific problems and problem-solving strategies, the better position we will be in to develop methods to match problem-solvers and tools to problems in general.

a problem-solving strategy:

(1) PROPOSE-A-DESIGN-EXTENSION,
(2) IDENTIFY-A-CONSTRAINT on a part of the design,
(3) PROPOSE-A-FIX for a constraint violation.

These are the relevant kinds of knowledge that SALT needs to acquire in order to serve the problem-solver.

In acquiring this knowledge, SALT follows a piecemeal, bottom-up strategy of elicitation, where the grain size and identification of the pieces is determined by these knowledge roles. Our experience with human designers and schedulers is that they are fairly good at describing individual considerations for constructing a solution for their domain. They can extemporaneously list many of the constraints that the solution needs to satisfy. They can consult manuals of formulas and tables for producing values for individual design parameters. But they are less clear on how the individual steps should fit together, how to organize them into a system. In addition, domain experts need help in organizing pieces into a system when later pieces are added as a system evolves over time or when a system must represent expertise from multiple experts, each expert in a different part of the problem. SALT aids users by allowing them to enter knowledge piecemeal starting at any point. SALT then cues for appropriate links, keeps track of how the pieces are fitting together and warns the user of places where pieces might be missing or creating inconsistencies.

In order to illustrate what it looks like to supply pieces of knowledge through SALT, we will use examples based on knowledge acquired in building VT. VT [19] is a SALT-generated expert system currently in use at Westinghouse Elevator Company that custom designs elevator systems. VT takes as input customer requirements, such as how fast the elevator should travel and what its carrying capacity should be, as well as architectural details about the building it will service, such as floor heights and wall-to-wall dimensions in the elevator shaft. VT must produce a list of quantities, ordering codes and other parameters for all equipment required, including some routine modifications of standard equipment, and an equipment layout customized to the elevator shaft.

When a SALT interview is initiated, the user is shown a menu like the one below for indicating the type of knowledge to be entered or viewed. These knowledge types correspond to the knowledge roles identified above. PROCEDURE is used to describe a procedure for determining the value for a proposed design extension. CONSTRAINT is used to identify a constraint and supply a procedure for determining its value. FIX is used for specifying potential remedies for specific constraint violations. The user may begin the interview by electing to enter any of these types of knowledge.

1 PROCEDURE   Enter a procedure for a value
2 CONSTRAINT  Enter constraints on a value
3 FIX         Enter remedies for a constraint violation
4 EXIT        Exit interviewer

Enter your command [EXIT]:

The knowledge role identifications assumed by SALT force domains experts to carve their knowledge into these pieces in return for the guidance SALT provides in putting the pieces together. SALT users are given the following guidelines to help them fit their knowledge into the SALT schema: A PROCEDURE must be given for every design parameter needed to describe the completed design.[1] The PROCEDURE should, as far as possible, take into account all of the considerations, or constraints, that affect the specification of a value. When this is not possible, as, for example, in the case of under-constrained parameters, the user should use PROCEDURE to specify a preferred choice given the considerations available. CONSTRAINT is used to identify limits on the value of a design parameter that are not captured in the specification of the PROCEDURE but should be explicitly checked before a solution can be reached by the generated expert system. FIX must be used to suggest revisions to decisions in response to a violation of tests expressed by CONSTRAINT knowledge. Revisions may change the values of inputs, design parameters or constraints. Users get the maximum benefit of SALT's analytic capabilities if they do not enter FIXes until the other pieces are in place.

Each piece of knowledge entered must be associated with a value name. For PROCEDURE, it is the name of the value that will be determined by the procedure. For CONSTRAINT, it is the name of the value which is constrained. For FIX, it is the name of the violated constraint. These value names are relevant in tying the pieces of knowledge together as described below in Section 5. Once a user selects a knowledge type and supplies the desired value name, SALT displays a schema of prompts for information associated with the knowledge role selected. The identification of what responses to the prompts are allowed, or interpretable by SALT, is somewhat application dependent (see Section 7). A default schema for supplying a procedure for determining the value of CAR-JAMB-RETURN is shown below:

1 Name:         CAR-JAMB-RETURN
2 Precondition: NONE
3 Procedure:    CALCULATION

[1] PROCEDUREs may also be entered for determining intermediate values that are used to determine design parameters. The user may mention such intermediate values the first time by directly entering a PROCEDURE for them or by using them in a PROCEDURE for some other value. In the latter case, SALT will prompt for PROCEDUREs for them if they are not otherwise supplied.

4 Formula:
5 Justification:

Enter your command [EXIT]:

SALT's prompts for information are given on the left. Users fill in the schema by indicating the number of the prompt and then typing the knowledge requested by the prompt. A completed schema is shown below:

| | | |
|---|---|---|
| 1 | Name: | CAR-JAMB-RETURN |
| 2 | Precondition: | DOOR-OPENING = CENTER |
| 3 | Procedure: | CALCULATION |
| 4 | Formula: | [PLATFORM-WIDTH – OPENING-WIDTH]/2 |
| 5 | Justification: | CENTER-OPENING DOORS LOOK BEST WHEN CENTERED ON THE PLATFORM. |

The precondition specifies that this procedure should only be used on cases in which the value assigned to DOOR-OPENING is CENTER. The type of procedure is a calculation using the formula given on line 4. (Information on how DOOR-OPENING, PLATFORM-WIDTH and OPENING-WIDTH receive values must be supplied by the user through separate PROCEDUREs.) In this case the value of CAR-JAMB-RETURN is under-constrained by the limits placed on it; this procedure supplies a preferred value. The justification states why this value is preferred.

A second example will illustrate a PROCEDURE screen that uses a method other than CALCULATION. Below is a completed screen for a PROCEDURE for MACHINE-MODEL:

| | | |
|---|---|---|
| 1 | Name: | MACHINE-MODEL |
| 2 | Precondition: | NONE |
| 3 | Procedure: | DATABASE-LOOKUP |
| 4 | Table name: | MACHINE |
| 5 | Column with needed value: | MODEL |
| 6 | Parameter test: | MAX-LOAD >= SUSPENDED-LOAD |
| 7 | Parameter test: | DONE |
| 8 | Ordering column: | HEIGHT |
| 9 | Optimal: | SMALLEST |
| 10 | Justification: | THIS PROCEDURE IS TAKEN FROM STANDARDS MANUAL IIIA, P. 139. |

When the procedure DATABASE-LOOKUP is selected, the user is presented with a set of subprompts asking for details for locating the value to be retrieved. In the display above, the name of the table and column from which the value is retrieved are SALT-generated defaults. Each parameter test lists a test to be performed on entries (rows) of the table to decide which are viable candidates for retrieval. In this case the entry must have a listing under the column MAX-LOAD which is greater than or equal to the SUSPENDED-LOAD, a separately generated value. Finally, if more than one entry under MODEL meets this test, ORDERING-COLUMN and OPTIMAL are used to determine a preferred candidate. Here the user indicates that the entry with the SMALLEST HEIGHT is the most desirable.

The crucial information needed to use a constraint is an indication of what value it constrains[2] and an indication of the nature of the limit it places on that value. This information is conveyed in response to the first two prompts in the examples below. In addition the user must give a procedure for specifying a value for the constraint, and prompts for this information are identical to those on the PROCEDURE screen. Two examples are given below:

| | | |
|---|---|---|
| 1 | Constrained value: | CAR-JAMB-RETURN |
| 2 | Constraint type: | MAXIMUM |
| 3 | Constraint name: | MAXIMUM-CAR-JAMB-RETURN |
| 4 | Precondition: | DOOR-OPENING = SIDE |
| 5 | Procedure: | CALCULATION |
| 6 | Formula: | PANEL-WIDTH*STRINGER-QUANTITY |
| 7 | Justification: | THIS PROCEDURE IS TAKEN FROM INSTALLATION MANUAL I, P. 12b. |

| | | |
|---|---|---|
| 1 | Constrained value: | MOTOR-MODEL |
| 2 | Constraint type: | CHOICE-SET |
| 3 | Constraint name: | CHOICE-SET-MOTOR-MODEL |
| 4 | Precondition: | NONE |
| 5 | Procedure: | DATABASE-LOOKUP |
| 6 | Table name: | MACHINE |
| 7 | Column with needed value: | COMPATIBLE-MOTORS |
| 8 | Parameter test: | MODEL = MACHINE-MODEL |
| 9 | Parameter test: | DONE |
| 10 | Ordering column: | NONE |
| 11 | Justification: | THIS PROCEDURE IS TAKEN FROM STANDARDS MANUAL IIIA, P. 154. |

[2] This schema requests the user to supply a single name of a value that is constrained. This imposes some conventions on how constraint knowledge is expressed when a constraint affects more than one value. If $x$ and $y$ are parts of the solution whose sum is constrained to be less than $z$, the SALT user must define an intermediate value, for example $sumxy$, that is constrained by $z$. And if $z$ is a maximum for $x$ and a maximum for $y$, the user can enter two different names for $z$, such as $maximum$-$x$ and $maximum$-$y$, with the same value.

In the generated system, whenever a constraint violation is detected, the problem-solver will consider ways that it can revise decisions it has made in order to make the design fit the constraint. The crucial domain information the problem-solver needs is an identification of the value to change, how to change it and some idea of the expert's preference for this revision relative to others that might be tried.

| | |
|---|---|
| 1 Violated constraint: | CHOICE-SET-MOTOR-MODEL |
| 2 Value to change: | MOTOR-MODEL |
| 3 Change type: | UPGRADE |
| 4 Preference rating: | 8 |
| 5 Reason for preference: | Changes major equipment sizing |

This suggested fix for a violation of CHOICE-SET-MOTOR-MODEL would upgrade the value of MOTOR-MODEL, that is, would select a model using the criteria of the table lookup for MOTOR-MODEL, but choose the next less preferred (or more costly) model. The user may suggest more than one potential fix for the same constraint violation. For example, an upgrade of MACHINE-MODEL might also fix a violation of CHOICE-SET-MOTOR-MODEL. The rating of preference is used to compare the current fix to other proposed fixes that have been or might be entered. Specifying what revisions should be made in response to a constraint violation is one of the most difficult tasks of a domain expert supplying knowledge. We will describe how SALT aids the user in filling in such a knowledge piece in the next section.

## 3. Analyzing How the Pieces Fit Together

In representing the knowledge pieces, SALT must make clear how these pieces interact during problem-solving. An understanding of decision interaction is needed particularly for analyzing the completeness of the knowledge base, its compilability and its adequacy in converging on a solution. For this purpose, connections represented in the knowledge base express how decisions based on one piece of knowledge affect decisions based on others, where the observable effect of a decision on the solution is the assignment of a value to an input, design parameter or constraint.

SALT's representational scheme is built around the framework of a dependency network. For SALT, each node in the network is the name of a value the expert system must acquire or generate; this can be the name of an input, a design parameter or the name of a constraint. There are three kinds of directed links that represent relations between nodes:

(1) "Contributes-to" will link $A$ to $B$ if the value of $A$ is used in a procedure to specify a value for $B$.

(2) "Constrains" will link $A$ to $B$ if $A$ is the name of a constraint and $B$ is the name of a design parameter and the value of $A$ places some restriction on the value of $B$.

(3) "Suggests-revision-of" will link $A$ to $B$ if $A$ is the name of a constraint and a violation of $A$ suggests a change to the currently proposed value of $B$.

Each of these links is derived from a knowledge piece. One of the anchors of the link is the value name asked for when the SALT user enters a piece of knowledge, and the other is extracted from the knowledge supplied. (SALT users can enter synonym lists for each value name. These synonyms are used to help the user establish appropriate connections and browse the knowledge base.) Each knowledge piece supports the links derived from it with more refined knowledge describing the nature of the link:

(1) "Contributes-to" links are supported by PROCEDUREs and the procedure parts of CONSTRAINTs that tell how contributors are combined to specify the value of the node pointed to.

(2) "Constrains" links are supported by a specification of the nature of the restriction taken from CONSTRAINT knowledge pieces.

(3) "Suggests-revision-of" links are supported by a declaration of the nature of the proposed revision (e.g., direction and amount of change) and its relative preference specified in FIX knowledge pieces.

An example of the connections that would be generated from the pieces given in Section 2 is shown in Fig. 1. "Contributes-to" links are shown as solid-line arrows, "constrains" by dotted-links, and "suggests-revision-of" by broken-line.

Once the user enters some knowledge, SALT guides further knowledge elicitation by using its understanding of how the problem-solver will use the knowledge. Some interrogation is driven by a rather broad notion of completeness checking. Other interactions amount to delivering a kind of compile error warning combined with guidance on how to correct the error by re-defining knowledge roles or adding knowledge. Finally some guidance is aimed at making sure that the knowledge given will be adequate to converge on a solution.

### 3.1. General completeness

When a piece of knowledge is added to the knowledge base store, it may create new nodes in the network. When a new node is added, SALT checks for the existence of other links that may point to or from that node. SALT expects

determine the same node. For example, an overlap in preconditions would exist if there were one formula for CAR-JAMB-RETURN when DOOR-OPENING = CENTER and one when [DOOR-OPENING = CENTER AND DOOR-SPEED = SINGLE]. Similarly, there would be no unique path to MOTOR-TORQUE for a speed of 250 if one procedure was applicable for speeds less than 300 and another for speeds greater than 200. The user is warned of such overlaps in preconditions. In addition, SALT checks to see whether preconditions on procedures allow at least one path to be followed for the values checked in the preconditions. If a user requested precondition checking on the knowledge base shown in Fig. 1, the following warning messages would be issued:

SIDE was mentioned as a legal value for DOOR-OPENING but the case: [DOOR-OPENING = SIDE] is not considered in preconditions for CAR-JAMB-RETURN.

CENTER was entered as a legal value for DOOR-OPENING but the case: [DOOR-OPENING = CENTER] is not considered in preconditions for MAXIMUM-CAR-JAMB-RETURN.

It is not necessary for a user to address all precondition warnings. The cause of the warnings is sometimes intentional. The warnings are given to remind the user in case knowledge was inadvertently left out. Failure to address a problem with uniqueness will result in the problem-solver's random selection between alternative paths. Failure to address a warning of a missing link will mean that no value will be assigned at that node on the identified cases.

### 3.2.2. Acyclicity in dependency

If each step in the path in assigning values that the problem-solver follows includes all relevant considerations, the resulting expert system will be a least commitment system in the sense that, like MOLGEN [29, 30], it will not make a decision until all necessary information is available. In supplying procedures to propose design extensions, SALT users are asked to include all relevant considerations needed to determine a value. The most basic compilation strategy, the one SALT uses, tries to create a least commitment system by compiling each procedure with data-driven control. A procedure to determine a value will be eligible for use when all values that contribute to it have been specified. If, however, there is a cycle in the dependency network, this eligibility requirement will never be met for the procedures on the loop. SALT detects loops in the dependency network and will guide the expert in setting up the knowledge base for propose-and-revise to get values for all nodes on the loop.

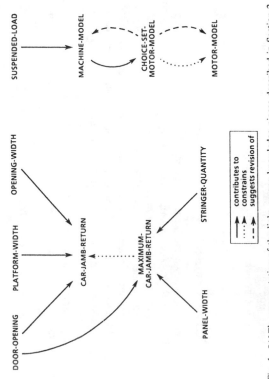

Fig. 1. SALT's representation of the links among knowledge pieces described in Section 2.

"contributes-to" links to every node in the network unless the node represents a "ground," that is, an input or a constant. It therefore checks to make sure that all nodes have procedures associated with them that will either supply "contributes-to" links or identify the node as an input or constant. If a procedure is not stored for a node, SALT will ask the user for one. SALT also considers potential "constrains" and "suggests-revision-of" links that might emanate from a node. SALT requests the user to supply constraints for any nonconstraint value and fixes for a violation of any constraint identified in the course of the interview.

### 3.2. Compilability

The task of the problem-solver is essentially to find a path through the network, assigning values at each node, that leads to quiescence, a state in which all constraints have been checked and satisfied. The compiler essentially proceduralizes these paths. Most of the compilability issues enter into checking whether for a given set of inputs a unique and complete path can be found through the dependency network.

### 3.2.1. Uniqueness and connectedness

SALT checks for the uniqueness and connectedness of paths by analyzing the coverage of sets of preconditions on multiple procedures that might be used to

Figure 2 shows a section of the knowledge base after the following procedures have been added:

```
HOIST-CABLE-QUANTITY = SUSPENDED-LOAD/HOIST-CABLE-STRENGTH
HOIST-CABLE-WEIGHT   = HOIST-CABLE-UNIT-WEIGHT
                       *HOIST-CABLE-QUANTITY
                       *HOIST-CABLE-LENGTH
CABLE-WEIGHT         = HOIST-CABLE-WEIGHT + COMP-CABLE-WEIGHT
SUSPENDED-LOAD       = CABLE-WEIGHT + CAR-WEIGHT
```

It is clear from this representation that the procedures cannot be applied in a strict forward-chain. When the problem-solver reaches the loop, it will become stuck since it cannot have all the information needed to apply any procedure without having the results of applying the procedure itself. When SALT detects such a loop, it delivers the following message:[3]

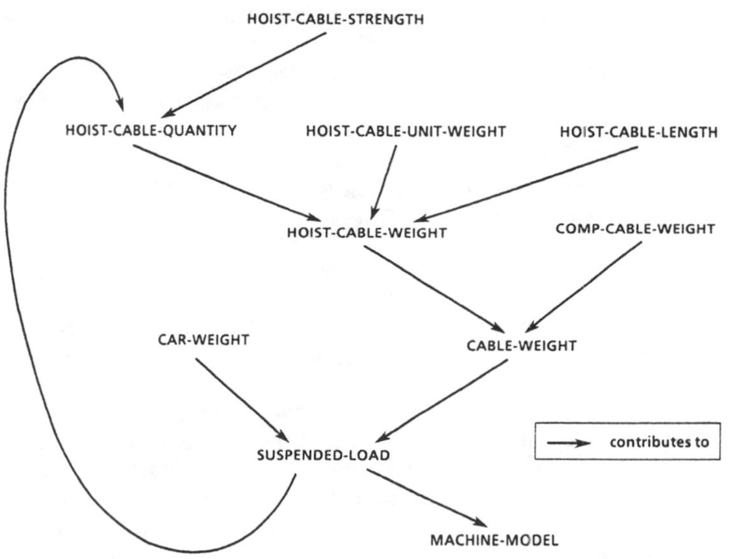

In the procedures I have been given, there is a loop. The list below shows the values on the loop; each value uses the one below it and the last uses the first:

1 HOIST-CABLE-QUANTITY
2 SUSPENDED-LOAD
3 CABLE-WEIGHT
4 HOIST-CABLE-WEIGHT

In order to use any procedure, I need some way of getting a first estimate for one of the names on the list. Which one do you wish to estimate?

In supplying a new procedure for proposing a value for one of the nodes on the loop, SALT users are coached to provide a way of determining the most preferred value given what the problem-solver could know at that point. This means that users can use any information that predicts the quality and success of the choice as long as the new procedure does not create additional cyclicities in the dependency network. In this example, the user elected to estimate HOIST-CABLE-QUANTITY. The procedure uses CAR-WEIGHT to rule out values of HOIST-CABLE-QUANTITY the expert knows cannot be used and then selects the smallest HOIST-CABLE-QUANTITY that might be used since this incurs the smallest possible dollar cost.

```
1  Name:                     HOIST-CABLE-QUANTITY
2  Precondition:             NONE
3  Procedure:                DATABASE-LOOKUP
4  Table name:               HOIST-CABLE
5  Column with needed value: QUANTITY
6  Parameter test:           MAX-LOAD > CAR-WEIGHT
7  Parameter test:           DONE
8  Ordering column:          QUANTITY
9  Optimal:                  SMALLEST
10 Justification:            THIS ESTIMATE IS THE SMALLEST
                             HOIST CABLE QUANTITY THAT CAN
                             BE USED ON ANY JOB.
```

Enter your command [EXIT]:

SALT does not need to be told that this procedure to propose a design extension does not contain all of the information that should go into making the decision; that information was contained in the original procedure. Therefore, SALT proposes to change the role of the original procedure for HOIST-CABLE-QUANTITY as identifying a constraint that must be explicitly checked after the value for HOIST-CABLE-QUANTITY is proposed. SALT tells the user this and asks for the additional information required by that role, namely a

Fig. 2. Knowledge base showing cyclicity in dependency.

[3] Sometimes loops are detected at this level of analysis that would never occur at runtime because of preconditions. For example, one set of procedures may say "If DOOR-OPENING=SIDE, $A = 3$ and $B = A + C$" and another "If DOOR-OPENING=SIDE, $B = 3$ and $A = B + C$". Based on potential dependency, $A$ contributes to $B$ and $B$ contributes to $A$, but both of these contributions will not be active on a given run. If such a case were detected, SALT would ask the user if this in fact is the case; i.e., if it's true that DOOR-OPENING will not be CENTER and SIDE at the same time. If that is the case, the loop is ignored.

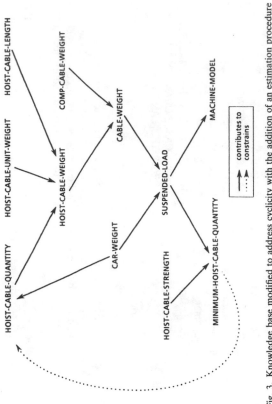
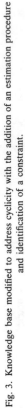

Fig. 3. Knowledge base modified to address cyclicity with the addition of an estimation procedure and identification of a constraint.

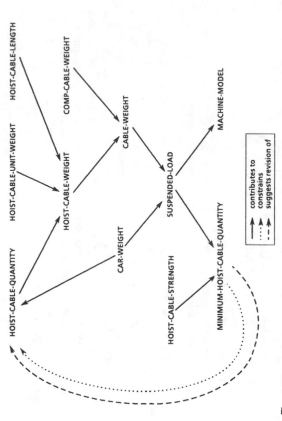
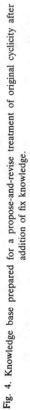

Fig. 4. Knowledge base prepared for a propose-and-revise treatment of original cyclicity after addition of fix knowledge.

specification of what kind of constraint the value is:

The procedure you originally gave for HOIST-CABLE-QUANTITY will be used as a check of the estimate. How does the value arrived at by that procedure limit the estimate? [MINIMUM]: ⟨cr⟩

MINIMUM contained in brackets is SALT's suggested default, which in this example the user accepts by typing a carriage return (⟨cr⟩). The knowledge base, shown in Fig. 3, now contains a knowledge piece for a new constraint, MINIMUM-HOIST-CABLE-QUANTITY.

Now that SALT has knowledge of a new constraint, checks for general completeness will require the user to supply a suggested fix the problem-solver can use if the constraint is violated. If the user now exits from the interview, SALT will issue the following request:

I have no knowledge of fixes for MINIMUM-HOIST-CABLE-QUANTITY. Do you wish to specify any now? [SAVE]:

The completed proposed fix is shown below:

1  Violated constraint:       MINIMUM-HOIST-CABLE-QUANTITY
2  Value to change:           HOIST-CABLE-QUANTITY
3  Change type:               INCREASE
4  Step type:                 SAME
5  Rating of undesirability:  4
6  Reason for undesirability: Changes minor equipment sizing

The problem-solver should consider increasing HOIST-CABLE-QUANTITY by the same amount that it fell below the minimum. Figure 4 shows the knowledge base after the addition of this piece of fix knowledge.

One final piece of SALT advice is the prompt for a ceiling on the increase of HOIST-CABLE-QUANTITY:

I have no knowledge of a procedure for MAXIMUM-HOIST-CABLE-QUAN-TITY which could bound the increase of HOIST-CABLE-QUANTITY called for by a fix for MINIMUM-HOIST-CABLE-QUANTITY. Would you like to specify one now? [SAVE]:

The knowledge base now calls for the problem-solver to start with the smallest quantity of hoist cables possible and to use that estimate to make other equipment selection and sizing decisions. It will then use the results of those decisions to calculate the smallest quantity of hoist cables that would be required using that estimate. If the estimate is equal to or greater than this calculated minimum, the current design is fine. If it is less, hoist cable quantity will be increased by the amount that it fell below the minimum, and the process is repeated using this new estimate for hoist cable quantity. If the calculated minimum ever exceeds the specified maximum, the problem-solver will stop increasing hoist cable quantity and reach a dead end; it will then declare that no solution is possible for this over-constrained job.

Filling in a knowledge piece for a fix for MINIMUM-HOIST-CABLE-QUANTITY creates a propose-and-revise treatment for the original cycle in the dependency network. Revision itself will explicitly introduce a cycle into the problem-solver's path through the network. Spotting how a cycle like increasing HOIST-CABLE-QUANTITY in the small knowledge base shown in Fig. 4 could go awry is fairly simple. The next section deals with problems with convergence caused by interactions among revisions for different constraints.

### 3.3. Convergence

In order for a propose-and-revise problem-solver to move toward a solution, it needs control knowledge identifying what revision is appropriate to make when a proposed design does not meet a constraint. In addition to trying to converge on a solution if one is possible, the problem-solver must also attempt to optimize the solution. In general, there is not enough knowledge contained in procedures to extend a design and identify constraints to figure out how to achieve this second goal. Domain knowledge is required to specify what revisions are feasible and which are preferable.

SALT starts acquiring a knowledge piece for a fix by asking the user to consider one constraint violation at a time. As with SALT's elicitation of procedures to propose a design extension, every local consideration that relates to the decision. Then SALT uses analyses of the knowledge base to figure out if this is a sound approach for the problem-solver to take; i.e., does the knowledge base have enough knowledge for the problem-solver to converge on a solution? The basic pieces of fix knowledge—what to change, how to change it and its relative preference—can be used to predict convergence and could be used to help the user understand what additional knowledge might help guide the search. This section describes how the basic fix knowledge piece is acquired and the analyses that use the knowledge.

In many cases, deciding what parts of the proposed design to revise in order to remedy an individual constraint violation can be nontrivial. In principle, any value which contributes to the constraint or its constrained value might serve as potentially helpful revisions. If the dependency network is very dense, the user may have difficulty recalling all contributors. SALT helps by reading out the relevant part of the network on request. The message SALT produces is shown below:

```
Contributors to HOIST-CABLE-QUANTITY:
1  CAR-WEIGHT
Contributors to MINIMUM-HOIST-CABLE-QUANTITY
2  HOIST-CABLE-STRENGTH
3  SUSPENDED-LOAD
     CAR-WEIGHT
4    CABLE-WEIGHT
5      HOIST-CABLE-WEIGHT
6      HOIST-CABLE-UNIT-WEIGHT
7      HOIST-CABLE-QUANTITY
         CAR-WEIGHT
8      HOIST-CABLE-LENGTH
9      COMP-CABLE-WEIGHT

Give the number of the one you want to work on (0 for new) [0]: 7
```

The level of contribution is represented by indentation. The leftmost values contribute directly to MINIMUM-HOIST-CABLE-QUANTITY. The values indented one level below SUSPENDED-LOAD contribute directly to it and so on. In this case, the user suggests a revision of HOIST-CABLE-QUANTITY as a potential remedy for a violation of MINIMUM-HOIST-CABLE-QUANTITY. The user might suggest a change to some other value as well, for example, to CAR-WEIGHT.

Given that procedures used in proposing a value for a design extension are the ones the expert would prefer in an under-constrained case, potential fixes must be less preferred than the originally preferred value. What the problem-solver needs from the expert is some indication of the relative preference of a change to one design parameter, for example, to HOIST-CABLE-QUANTITY, compared to some other change it might make, for example, to CAR-WEIGHT. SALT allows the domain expert to supply a list of reasons why revisions could be less preferred than the originally proposed value. (This list is modifiable by the domain expert.) The list used for VT is shown below:

```
 1  Causes no problem
 2  Increases maintenance requirements
 3  Makes installation difficult
 4  Changes minor equipment sizing
 5  Violates minor equipment constraint
 6  Changes minor contract specifications
 7  Requires special part design
 8  Changes major equipment sizing
 9  Changes the building dimensions
 0  Changes major contract specifications
-1  Increases maintenance costs
-2  Compromises system performance
```

These effects are ordered from most to least preferred. The reasons mainly reflect concerns for safety and customer satisfaction as well as dollar cost to the elevator company. Because of the dissimilarity in the nature of the negative effects, relative position on this scale is significant but absolute position is not. For example, an increase of HOIST-CABLE-QUANTITY changes minor equipment sizing. This cost can be measured directly in dollars. It is preferred to a decrease in CAR-WEIGHT, which changes major contract specifications. This is associated with a cost measured in less concrete terms of additional effort required for contract negotiations with a probable loss in customer satisfaction.

The information provided in a fix piece gives the problem-solver what it needs to start a revision. As a default strategy, the problem-solver might begin revision as soon as a single constraint violation is detected and start by trying the most preferred fix associated with that constraint, then the next less preferred fix and so on until the constraint no longer registers as violated. If fixes for one constraint violation have no effect on other constraint violations, this strategy guarantees that the first solution found will be the most preferred. However, it is possible that remedies selected for one constraint violation may aggravate constraint violations that occur elsewhere in the network.

For example, Fig. 5 shows a section of a knowledge base containing antagonistic constraints. These two constraints are connected to the values they constrain by dotted-line arrows at the bottom. Above these is the portion of

the dependency network that links the constraint-constrained pairs to their potential fix values. In order to make the figure more readable, not all contributors are shown. In addition, "suggests-revision-of" links have been omitted. Instead, suggested revisions in response to a violation of MAXIMUM-MACHINE-GROOVE-PRESSURE are surrounded by rectangles while suggested revisions for violations of MAXIMUM-TRACTION-RATIO are enclosed in ovals.

Based on the knowledge in this part of the knowledge base, SALT can detect the possibility of a problem-solving scenario involving thrashing such as this one: The problem-solver derives values for MACHINE-GROOVE-PRESSURE and finds that MACHINE-GROOVE-PRESSURE is greater than the maximum. The problem-solver responds by decreasing CAR-SUPPLEMENT-WEIGHT. This decreases CAR-WEIGHT which in turn decreases SUSPENDED-LOAD. This decreases MACHINE-GROOVE-PRESSURE, the desired effect, but also increases TRACTION-RATIO. An increase in TRACTION-RATIO makes it more likely for it to exceed its maximum. A violation of MAXIMUM-TRACTION-RATIO calls for an increase of COMP-CABLE-UNIT-WEIGHT which in turn increases COMP-CABLE-WEIGHT, CABLE-WEIGHT and SUSPENDED-LOAD. Increasing SUSPENDED-LOAD increases MACHINE-GROOVE-PRESSURE making it more likely to violate MAXIMUM-MACHINE-GROOVE-PRESSURE. At this point, the scenario could repeat itself.

In order to alert the user to the possibility of thrashing caused by interacting fixes, SALT produces a listing of chains of interacting fixes such as the one shown below. Each chain originates from a constraint whose fixes make other constraints more likely to be violated. Fixes are shown in parentheses under the constraint they address and give the value to change and the direction of change. Embedded beneath each fix is a list of constraints that they might aggravate. If fixes for any of the constraints in this second tier make other constraints more likely to be violated, these are added to the chain and so on. Loops are flagged when a constraint recurs in the chain.

The message shown in Fig. 6 represents SALT's report on the fix interaction in this part of the knowledge base. This display indicates to the SALT user that three suggested fixes for a violation of MAXIMUM-TRACTION-RATIO make a violation of MAXIMUM-MACHINE-GROOVE-PRESSURE more likely while three proposed fixes for a violation of MAXIMUM-MACHINE-GROOVE-PRESSURE also make a violation of MAXIMUM-TRACTION-RATIO more likely. Lack of embedding under the fix CWT-TO-PLATFORM-DISTANCE and lack of embedding or looping from the fix HOIST-CABLE-QUANTITY indicate that the proposed changes to these values do not hinder ability to satisfy constraints elsewhere in the network.

On the basis of SALT's identification of potential constraint violations, the SALT user can specify that these constraints should be treated as antagonistic. SALT stores knowledge about constraint antagonism with the knowledge to identify a constraint. The problem-solver

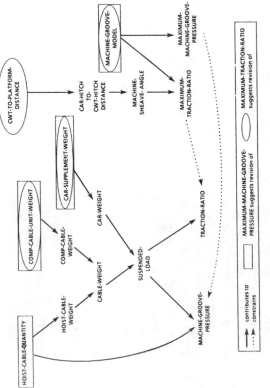

Fig. 5. Knowledge base illustrating antagonistic constraints.

combined with a problem-solving control shell, also written in OPS5. In providing SALT with this rule-generation capability, our goal was to demonstrate the feasibility of this approach. We wanted to show that a compiler could be written that could go from the declarative representation of the knowledge base which supports effective knowledge elicitation strategies to a functional expert system.

An outline of the activities of the problem-solver during a run will make it easier to understand the SALT rule-generation procedure. The problem-solving control shell shifts control between the phases of problem-solving and uses domain-specific knowledge to decide what other domain-specific knowledge to apply next. The flow of control of the problem-solving strategy as it makes use of the pieces of knowledge is as follows: The expert system starts with a forward-chaining phase in which procedures to propose design extensions and identify constraints are eligible to apply. The control in this constructive phase is data-driven; any step can be taken as soon as the information called for by the procedure associated with the step is available. As it extends the design, the expert system also builds a dependency network which, for each fact, records which other facts were used to derive it.

Demons are used to check for constraint violations; whenever a constraint and the value it constrains are known, they are compared. Whenever the system detects a constraint violation, it selects alternatives in order of decreasing preference from a pre-enumerated set of possible fixes. Combinations of changes may also be tried, where fixes are selected to be combined in order of preference.

The problem-solver then investigates the success of the revision. The expert system first verifies that no constraints on the revised value itself are violated by the change. It then makes the proposed change and works through the implications according to its knowledge for proposing design extensions and identifying constraints. If the constraint is not identified as antagonistic to others, the problem-solver explores revision implications until it has enough knowledge to evaluate the originally violated constraint. If a proposed change violates the constraints, it is rejected and another selection is made. This lookahead is limited because it only considers constraints on the revised value and the originally violated constraint. If the constraint is identified as belonging to an antagonistic set, lookahead is extended to include evaluation of the other constraints in the set. If others in the set are violated, the problem-solver will keep track of combinations of revisions for the set it has tried and not repeat any. The purpose of this lookahead is to limit the work done in exploring the implications of a proposed guess until the system has reason to believe it is a good guess.

Once a good guess has been identified, the system applies a truth maintenance system; i.e., it uses the dependency network constructed during the forward-chaining phase to identify and remove any values that might be

```
*
MAXIMUM-TRACTION-RATIO
*
(CWT-TO-PLATFORM-DISTANCE, Down)

(COMP-CABLE-UNIT-WEIGHT, Up)
MAXIMUM-MACHINE-GROOVE-PRESSURE
  (MACHINE-GROOVE-MODEL, Down) —— **LOOP**
  (HOIST-CABLE-QUANTITY, Up)
  (COMP-CABLE-UNIT-WEIGHT, Down) —— **LOOP**
  (CAR-SUPPLEMENT-WEIGHT, Down) —— **LOOP**

(CAR-SUPPLEMENT-WEIGHT, Up)
MAXIMUM-MACHINE-GROOVE-PRESSURE
  (MACHINE-GROOVE-MODEL, Down) —— **LOOP**
  (HOIST-CABLE-QUANTITY, Up)
  (COMP-CABLE-UNIT-WEIGHT, Down) —— **LOOP**
  (CAR-SUPPLEMENT-WEIGHT, Down) —— **LOOP**

(MACHINE-GROOVE-MODEL, Up)
MAXIMUM-MACHINE-GROOVE-PRESSURE
  (MACHINE-GROOVE-MODEL, Down) —— **LOOP**
  (HOIST-CABLE-QUANTITY, Up)
  (COMP-CABLE-UNIT-WEIGHT, Down) —— **LOOP**
  (CAR-SUPPLEMENT-WEIGHT, Down) —— **LOOP**
```

Fig. 6. SALT's report on the fix interaction.

then knows to deal with these constraints as a set in order to keep track of what combinations of revisions for this set it has tried. The additional information that SALT then asks for is very sparse. For every set of antagonistic constraints, SALT asks the user to order the constraints according to how important they are to fix. Then if the problem-solver can't fix all constraint violations, it at least knows the best place to stop. This is a somewhat brute force approach to prevent thrashing. How to more effectively elicit domain knowledge about what tradeoffs should be made and how to compile the information to efficiently achieve tradeoffs is still an open research issue not addressed by this study.

## 4. Compiling the Knowledge Base

A functional knowledge base representation provides the key to how and when the knowledge should be used during problem-solving. SALT proceduralizes the domain-specific knowledge base into rules written in OPS5 [12] and these are

inconsistent with the changed value. This includes removing the effects of previous fixes if the current change will cause a re-evaluation of the constraint which they remedied. The expert system then re-enters the data-driven constructive phase for extending the design with the new data.

To describe the generation of the domain-specific rules used in a problem-solving episode, we will detail how knowledge in each of the three main knowledge roles is proceduralized by SALT. We will describe the six main rule types in roughly the order in which the rule type first appears during a run; the exact order of firing is defined by the control described in each rule.

For PROPOSE-A-DESIGN-EXTENSION, the knowledge the user provides consists of a description of a procedure. A completed screen of knowledge is shown below:

Knowledge Piece 1:

1 Name:          CAR-JAMB-RETURN
2 Precondition:  DOOR-OPENING = CENTER
3 Procedure:     CALCULATION
4 Formula:       [PLATFORM-WIDTH − OPENING-WIDTH]/2
5 Justification: CENTER-OPENING DOORS LOOK BEST
                 WHEN CENTERED ON THE PLATFORM.

An example of an English translation of an OPS5 rule for a "constructive" PROPOSE-A-DESIGN-EXTENSION is shown below:

Rule 1:

IF    values are available for DOOR-OPENING, PLATFORM-WIDTH and OPENING-WIDTH, and

      the value of DOOR-OPENING is CENTER, and

      there is no value for CAR-JAMB-RETURN,

THEN  Calculate the result of the formula [PLATFORM-WIDTH − OPENING-WIDTH]/2

      Assign the result of this calculation as the value of CAR-JAMB-RETURN.

      Leave a trace that DOOR-OPENING, PLATFORM-WIDTH and OPENING-WIDTH contributed to CAR-JAMB-RETURN.

      Leave a declarative representation of the details of the precondition and calculation and its justification.

Leaving a trace of contributions builds up the dependency network used by the truth maintenance system and explanation. A declarative representation of the knowledge base is used by the explanation facility.

At the same time as the problem-solver is building a description of the proposed design, it is specifying constraints that apply to parts of that design. A completed screen from an interview is shown below:

Knowledge Piece 2:

1 Constrained value: CAR-JAMB-RETURN
2 Constraint type:   MAXIMUM
3 Constraint name:   MAXIMUM-CAR-JAMB-RETURN
4 Precondition:      DOOR-OPENING = SIDE
5 Procedure:         CALCULATION
6 Formula:           PANEL-WIDTH * STRINGER-QUANTITY
7 Justification:     THIS PROCEDURE IS TAKEN FROM
                     INSTALLATION MANUAL I, p. 12b.

For every piece of IDENTIFY-A-CONSTRAINT knowledge, a rule is generated that both supplies a procedure for specifying a value for the constraint and provides the crucial identifying information to the problem-solver:

Rule 2:

IF    values are available for DOOR-OPENING, PANEL-WIDTH, and STRINGER-QUANTITY, and

      the value of DOOR-OPENING is SIDE, and

      there is no value for MAXIMUM-CAR-JAMB-RETURN,

THEN  Calculate the result of the formula PANEL-WIDTH * STRINGER-QUANTITY.

      Assign the result of this calculation as the value of MAXIMUM-CAR-JAMB-RETURN.

      Identify this value as a constraint of type MAXIMUM on CAR-JAMB-RETURN.

      Leave a trace that DOOR-OPENING, PANEL-WIDTH and STRINGER-QUANTITY contributed to MAXIMUM-CAR-JAMB RETURN.

      Leave a declarative representation of the details of the precondition and calculation and its justification.

The next rule type generated uses knowledge in the PROPOSE-A-FIX role. This rule uses a collection of pieces of fix knowledge like the one below:

Knowledge Piece 3:

| | | |
|---|---|---|
| 1 | Violated constraint: | MAXIMUM-CAR-JAMB-RETURN |
| 2 | Value to change: | STRINGER-QUANTITY |
| 3 | Change type: | INCREASE |
| 4 | Step type: | BY-STEP |
| 5 | Step size: | 1 |
| 6 | Preference rating: | 4 |
| 7 | Reason for preference: | Changes minor equipment sizing |

For every constraint that can be violated, a rule is generated that suggests all of the potential fixes to the problem-solver:

Rule 3:

IF    there has been a violation of MAXIMUM-CAR-JAMB-RETURN,

THEN  Try an INCREASE of STRINGER-QUANTITY BY-STEPs of 1. This costs 4 because it CHANGES MINOR EQUIPMENT SIZING.

Try a SUBSTITUTION of SIDE for DOOR-OPENING. This costs 8 because it CHANGES MAJOR EQUIPMENT SIZING.

Try a DECREASE of PLATFORM-WIDTH BY-STEPs of 2 in. This costs 10 because it CHANGES MAJOR CONTRACT SPECIFICATIONS.

The final three rule types are used to explore the success of a proposed fix or fix combination in a lookahead context before extending the proposed design on the basis of the proposed revision. In order to do this, the problem-solver uses PROPOSE-A-DESIGN-EXTENSION knowledge to draw out the implications of the change suggested by the fix and IDENTIFY-A-CONSTRAINT knowledge to reevaluate the value of the constraint under the change. In operation, the lookahead contexts function in a way that is similar to possible worlds in KEE [16]. What is significant here is that a SALT analysis of the knowledge base is used to compile instructions that set up the entry conditions of the possible world and limit exploration within it.

The fourth rule type directs the problem-solver to propagate the change to just those values that contribute to either the violated constraint or its constrained value. SALT conducts a search through the dependency network in order to generate the actions in these rules. The list of values to "FIND" essentially limits the lookahead by the generated expert system to the immediate constraint violation under repair.

Rule 4:

IF    MAXIMUM-CAR-JAMB-RETURN has been violated, and

the problem-solver has decided on which changes to try,

THEN  FIND-CAR-JAMB-RETURN and

FIND-MAXIMUM-CAR-JAMB-RETURN.

This rule directs control to a set of lookahead rules which take the proposed fix changes and propagate the values through the relevant PROPOSE-A-DESIGN-EXTENSION and IDENTIFY-A-CONSTRAINT procedures. Rules used for propagating lookahead differ from the first two constructive groups with respect to the circumstances under which they fire. No additional kinds of knowledge need be collected from the user beyond the ones described so far. SALT will generate Rule 5 using Knowledge Piece 1 and Rule 6 using Knowledge Piece 2.

Rule 5:

IF    the active command is to FIND-CAR-JAMB-RETURN, and

any of DOOR-OPENING, PLATFORM-WIDTH or OPENING-WIDTH has been revised, and

the most recently derived value (mrdv) of DOOR-OPENING is CENTER, and

there is no revised value for CAR-JAMB-RETURN,

THEN  Calculate the formula [mrdv of PLATFORM-WIDTH − mrdv of OPENING-WIDTH]/2.

Assign the result of this calculation as the value of CAR-JAMB-RETURN.

Mark this value as revised.

Rule 6:

IF    the active command is to FIND-MAXIMUM-CAR-JAMB-RETURN, and

any of DOOR-OPENING, PANEL-WIDTH or STRINGER-QUANTITY has been revised, and

the mrdv of DOOR-OPENING is SIDE, and

there is no revised value for MAXIMUM-CAR-JAMB-RETURN,

THEN    Calculate the result of the formula mrdv of PANEL-WIDTH * mrdv of STRINGER-QUANTITY.

Assign the result of this calculation as the value of MAXIMUM-CAR-JAMB-RETURN.

Identify this value as a constraint of type MAXIMUM on CAR-JAMB-RETURN.

Mark this value as revised.

When asked to compile the knowledge base, SALT proceduralizes the knowledge pieces into these six rule types. Roughly, for every piece of PROPOSE-A-DESIGN-EXTENSION knowledge and every piece of IDENTIFY-A-CONSTRAINT knowledge, SALT generates one constructive rule and one lookahead rule. For each constraint, a rule for directing the lookahead is also generated if its fixes propose direct changes to values other than the constraint or its constrained value (i.e., the change needs to be propagated through intermediate values in order to re-evaluate compliance with the constraint) or if the constraint is a member of an antagonistic set.

It is probably clear from this description of SALT's generation capability that the compiler allows the problem-solver to use the knowledge base in a form fairly directly reflecting the form in which it was acquired from the domain expert. This has advantages in explaining the expert system's line of reasoning and supporting interactive problem-solving with the user of the expert system. SALT-generated systems are similar in architecture to EL [28], an expert system that performs analysis of electrical circuits, and CONSTRAINTS [32], a related shell, which show similar advantages. There are some important differences. CONSTRAINTS allows the user to direct backtracking in a way similar to SALT-generated systems when run in interactive mode or performing what-if explanation (see Section 5). CONSTRAINTS, however, does not use domain knowledge of fix preferences to automatically revise decisions. EL's decision of where to backtrack to is based solely on the dependency network's record of what guesses contributed to the conflicting constraints. Furthermore, EL is committed to a search which will try all possible combinations of all guesses, although it prevents thrashing by keeping track of combinations already tried and never repeating a combination.

Even though there is fairly close correspondence between acquired knowledge and compiled knowledge, the SALT compiler does process the knowledge to improve the efficiency of the problem-solver. For example, SALT identifies the relevant sphere of influence of a revision in addressing a particular constraint violation and contains the problem-solver in that sphere until quiescence is reached. SALT also identifies in advance where thrashing could take place and narrows its try-all-possible-combinations approach to just those

areas where thrashing is likely to occur. Substantial work has been done to develop domain-independent algorithms for efficiently ordering value assignments in a class of constraint-satisfaction problems [8, 9, 13]. In these problems, generation of any solution which satisfies all constraints constitutes success. In general, this is not true in domains for which SALT is intended. In domains like VT's, domain-specific considerations such as cost and customer satisfaction affect preference for solutions. These domain-specific considerations directly affect the decision ordering compiled by SALT; SALT-generated systems will try for plausible, preferred solutions first. However, the control derived from domain-specific constraints and preferences is sometimes underdetermined; multiple decision orderings may be possible. Other shells and problem-solving systems that perform tasks similar to the ones SALT is intended to acquire employ efficiency strategies in ordering decisions to propose design extensions. These strategies are hand-coded by the system designers of systems such as MPA [14] written in DSPL [2], OPIS [27] and PRIDE [23]. There is a potential for SALT either to generate similar goal structures in compiling the knowledge base or to support a user in describing top-level strategies by supplying useful proposals and analyses [20].

## 5. Explaining Problem-Solving Decisions

A SALT-generated expert system explains its decisions using records of the problem-solver's use of the domain knowledge pieces. The dependency network built up for the truth maintenance system can provide the foundation for a very useful explanation facility [10, 32]. The network is augmented by the details of the contribution relation; e.g., a description of an algebraic formula or the relation between values required by a precondition. In addition, the problem-solver records constraint violations encountered in developing a design and adjustments to the proposed design that it makes. Explanation pieces these individual actions together to describe the problem-solver's line of reasoning.

The explanation facility offers the user a choice of a small number of query types. The *how* query mainly supplies a kind of trace facility and can be thought of as asking the question *How did you determine the value of x?* Explanation looks for the appropriate node in the dependency network that recorded the decision of the problem-solver's assignment of a value to x. The dependency network provides pointers to the actual values that were used in determining the value in question.

If the user were to ask the expert system how the machine groove pressure was determined, it would respond with a message such as:

The MACHINE-GROOVE-PRESSURE (90.0307) = SUSPENDED-LOAD (6752.3042)/([MACHINE-SHEAVE-DIAMETER (30) * 0.5] * HOIST-CABLE-QUANTITY (5))

The machine groove pressure was determined by a calculation, which is displayed both in terms of the names of the system values and the values assigned to them.

A *why* query would produce the justification for the procedure:

THIS PROCEDURE IS TAKEN FROM STANDARDS MANUAL II, p. 13.

The *how* query also finds possible reasons why a design parameter or constraint in the system might have a value which the expert believes to be unexpected. A value changed by a revision in response to a constraint violation can look unusual to a user, particularly if the value changed is an input or if a low-preference fix was required. An example is shown below:

Explain: *how hoist cable quantity*

The HOIST-CABLE-QUANTITY (4) was determined by a fix:

The MAXIMUM-MACHINE-GROOVE-PRESSURE constraint was violated.
The MACHINE-GROOVE-PRESSURE was 149.5444, but had to be <=119. The gap of 30.544 was eliminated by the following action(s):
    Increasing HOIST-CABLE-QUANTITY from 3 to 4

Of course, it is a simplification of the process of extending a design to say that a value is determined by its direct contributors or "unusual" decisions that directly change its value. Everything upstream in the dependency network contributes to the proposed value. Explanation allows the user to step back through the network by repeated questioning and provides default queries after each answer to aid in this. Explanation also searches the upstream network on its own and in answering any *how* query also reports any unusual decisions made about upstream contributors. In searching for reasons why *x* may be unusual, explanation will examine all of the items which directly contributed to *x*, as well as the items used in evaluating any preconditions on *x*'s method. This examination is recursive in that each of these contributors is also examined similarly, and so on until explanation "grounds out" on either inputs or constants.

The following is an example of an unusual explanation:

Explain: *how supported load*

The SUPPORTED-LOAD (1796.574) =
MAX[SUPPORTED-LOAD-CAR-TOP-FULL (1759.741)
    SUPPORTED-LOAD-CAR-BOTTOM-FULL (1796.574)
    SUPPORTED-LOAD-CAR-TOP-EMPTY (1742.178)
    SUPPORTED-LOAD-CAR-BOTTOM-EMPTY (1696.701)]

The value for SUPPORTED-LOAD may be unusual because:
The MACHINE-MODEL was changed due to a CHOICE-SET constraint on the HOIST-CABLE-DIAMETER. (Depth = 3)

The "depth" mentioned indicates how far upstream the contributor is.

The explanation facility does more than just examine past decisions; it also performs some hypothetical reasoning to demonstrate the effect of alternative decisions the user suggests. The generated system offers two hypothetical queries: The user may ask why the value of a variable was not the one the user expected (*why not*). The user may also ask what would happen if the value of a variable were changed to something else (*what if*). For *why not* explanations, the system will report any changes to contributors to the variable that would have to be made in order to have the value come out to be the one expected. For *what if* explanations, the system displays how output values would differ from those for the original run.

Hypothetical explanations are relatively simple to generate given SALT's knowledge representation scheme. What the system must do in order to answer hypothetical queries is very closely related to how it resolves constraint violations. The expected or desired value becomes a kind of dynamic constraint and the system applies "fixes" that would allow the currently proposed value to be the one the user proposes. SALT collects this explain-fix knowledge with a format very similar to that used for regular problem-solving fixes. SALT then generates domain-specific rules very similar to the two types of fix rules above and the explanation facility uses many of the domain-independent fix control and truth maintenance rules used for problem-solving.

Two examples of *why not* responses to the query "why not safety model B4" are shown below:

The SAFETY-MODEL (currently B1) could be B4, but that is less desirable because it has a larger HEIGHT. A SAFETY-MODEL of B1 was selected because it met the following constraints:

Its MAX-SPEED (500) was at least as much as the SPEED (250).
Its MAX-PLATFORM-WIDTH (93) was not less than the PLATFORM-WIDTH (70).
Its MIN-PLATFORM-WIDTH (54) was not more than the PLATFORM-WIDTH (70).

In this case the user's expectation is possible, but not preferred. Here explanation locates all constraints in the system which constrained the safety-model (including implicit constraints in database calls) and reports them.

The following is the opposite case; the suggested value would be preferred, but is not possible, except perhaps by changing values upstream (e.g., introducing non-preferred values elsewhere).

If the user does not wish to implement the fix, the system will accept suggestions from the user to use other fixes that it knows about or to use new fixes. These suggestions are accepted in the same structured language that SALT uses to acquire pieces of fix knowledge. The problem-solver will then attempt the fix and report the results for user acceptance before continuing.

SALT-generated expert systems automatically log records of user-overrides. The system maintainers can then read the log file and decide whether the knowledge base should be changed to reflect new priorities on old fixes or to add new fix knowledge. If the knowledge base should be changed, they can enter the appropriate knowledge through SALT. This provides SALT-generated systems with a kind of debug/apprentice function with a human "programmer" in the loop. As with true learning apprentice systems, such as LEAP [22] and LAS [26], the system's ability to provide this communication link is based on an explicit model of how domain knowledge is used by the problem-solver.

## 6. Evaluating Test Case Coverage

For tasks which require constructive problem-solving methods, it is not practical to enumerate all of the possible solutions. It is also not possible to collect a suite of test cases that will produce all possible solutions. However, testing is required to help judge the validity of an expert system. Understanding the ways in which knowledge could be used by the problem-solver can help analyze a set of test cases to see whether important features of the system's problem-solving behavior are being exercised in that set.

For any expert system, the most important behavior to test is the behavior that is hardest to predict based on the building blocks from which the system was created. It is the interaction of individual pieces that is hardest to understand. In SALT-generated systems, the most derivative behavior, the behavior that is furthest from the step-by-step procedures given by the expert, is what the system does when a constraint violation is detected. For this reason, any validity test should observe a violation of each constraint that the system knows about and should observe the implementation of every suggested kind of revision for each constraint violation. Since individual pieces of fix knowledge are collected with a local focus on a single constraint violation, an even bigger concern is seeing how revisions for different constraint violations interact. Therefore, a validity test should also observe every potential fix interaction.

SALT sifts through the knowledge base to generate a list of all constraints and a list of all suggested fixes for these constraints. SALT also uses the analysis described in Section 3.3 on Convergence to generate a list of sets of potentially interacting fixes. These generated lists are used by a module of the domain-independent control shell to screen a set of test cases. As test cases are run, the

---

A SAFETY-MODEL of B4 would have been used (instead of B6) if:
The PLATFORM-WIDTH were 82 instead of 84.

*What if* can be thought of as asking the question *What would happen if I changed x to be a particular value?* In response to this query, the user is shown the impact that change would make on the design parameters.

Explain: *what if safety model B4*

The SAFETY-MODEL is currently B1.
If it were B4, the following changes would occur:

| NAME: | ACTUAL: | PROPOSED: |
|---|---|---|
| MACHINE-GROOVE-PRESSURE | 114.118 | 155.563 |
| TRACTION-RATIO | 1.80679 | 1.76682 |
| CWT-OVERTRAVEL | 49.835 | 52.835 |
| CAR-BUFFER-REACTION | 26709.4 | 27652.4 |
| CWT-STACK-PERCENT | 84.1122 | 88.148 |
| CWT-BUFFER-REACTION | 19684 | 20627.0 |
| CWT-PLATE-QUANTITY | 90 | 94.3184 |
| CWT-WEIGHT | 4921.0 | 5156.76 |
| CAR-BUFFER-LOAD | 6677.35 | 6913.11 |
| CAR-WEIGHT | 3677.35 | 3913.11 |
| DEFLECTOR-SHEAVE-DIAMETER | 25 | 20 |
| CAR-BUFFER-BLOCKING-HEIGHT | 18 | 17.125 |
| HOIST-CABLE-MODEL | (4) – 0.5 | (3) – 0.5 |
| CAR-RUNBY | 6.125 | 6 |
| SAFETY-MODEL | B1 | B4 |

Would you like to implement this [NO]:

As indicated in the last line of this example, *what if* explanation allows the user to change decisions that the system made after a run is completed. The generated system also allows users to affect decisions during a run when set in interactive mode. Whenever a revision is made, the system will pause after lookahead and provide the explanation below.

The MAXIMUM-TRACTION-RATIO constraint has been violated.
The TRACTION-RATIO is 1.806591, but must be <= 1.783873.
The gap of 0.272000E – 01 can be eliminated by the following action(s):
  Decreasing CWT-TO-PLATFORM-FRONT from 4.75 to 2.25
  Upgrading COMP-CABLE-UNIT-WEIGHT from 0 to 0.5

Should this be implemented [YES]:

module uses these lists to check off what has been tested. This module aims to make sure that within the test case set, each constraint is violated and each fix for each constraint violation is tried in at least one of the test cases. In addition, for each chain of interacting fixes, the test-case checker notes whether within some single test case, all of the constraints on the chain are violated. The test coverage evaluator can be used to identify test cases that don't check additional features off the list and can be used to describe particular features not covered by the test suite.

## 7. Understanding SALT's Scope

Understanding the roles that knowledge can play in problem-solving helps map a task's problem-solving demands onto a problem-solving system. Creating knowledge acquisition tools that are explicit about how knowledge is used in the systems they generate and testing their applicability to different problem-solving domains is a way to begin to understand how to make this mapping. To date, we have only two data points for SALT: custom designing elevator systems and flow-shop scheduling. SALT was developed in the context of building VT, the expert elevator designer whose task was described briefly in Section 2. All of the examples described so far have been based on the generation, maintenance and running of VT. SALT's second use was its extension to develop a prototype for a flow-shop scheduler [31]. The scheduler's task is to route an order for an escalator or elevator system through departments for engineering, manufacturing and delivering it.

The keystone to the SALT approach is the knowledge role definition that SALT assumes in order to create its internal representation of the knowledge base. Based on our interviews with the domain expert, the scheduling domain knowledge does fit these roles. The initial schedule for an order is determined by PROPOSE-A-DESIGN-EXTENSION procedures that set up preferred (i.e., routine) handling of an order. Knowledge that can IDENTIFY-A-CONSTRAINT includes such considerations as the limited order-handling capacity of each department and promised complete dates for various events for particular orders. In response to a constraint violation, such as a schedule's exceeding a department's capacity, the expert has PROPOSE-A-FIX knowledge that may recommend revising schedules of particular orders in ways that will repair the constraint violated.

The ability to identify a correspondence between SALT-assumed knowledge roles and the domain knowledge for the scheduler meant that the knowledge could be represented using SALT's primitives: nodes representing value assignments connected by relations of contribution, constraint and revision. This representation is used by a number of functions described above. In order to provide some of these functions for the scheduling domain, SALT had to be extended. Analyses of how the knowledge pieces fit together, explanation, and evaluation of test case coverage remained pretty much intact. Areas where the original, VT version of SALT became cumbersome and/or inappropriate were in the details of the language used to acquire the knowledge pieces and the operation of the compiled system.

### 7.1. Acquiring relevant knowledge pieces

Although the knowledge roles used to identify relevant pieces are appropriate for the scheduler, a user interface based on these pieces for a scheduling application can be rather cumbersome. Some of the awkwardness has to do with how legal responses are defined for some of the prompts associated with each knowledge piece. For example, for VT all preconditions were easily expressed in terms of comparisons of values using $>$, $>=$, $<$, $<=$, $=$, $<>$ (greater than, greater than or equal to, less than, less than or equal to, equal to, and not equal to). Giving SALT an understanding of ways of describing time relations would have made the system easier to use for scheduling. In order to state that a PROCEDURE should be used only if event $A$ occurred before event $B$, the user would have to say something like "the value of the date at event $A$ must be $<$ the value of the date at event $B$". We made a brief exploration into providing a kind of editor to allow the user to define domain terms like "before" and "after" that could be used as shorthand for the longer expression. Even this doesn't go quite far enough. For example, it would have been even better if the expert could convey knowledge about the routine schedule by laying out a critical path diagram with associated durations which SALT could then translate into PROCEDUREs to extend a proposed design. An interface such as this would have been more in the spirit of OPAL [24] or KNACK [17]. Creation of such customized interfaces is not necessary but would definitely improve SALT's ease of use for the scheduling domain.

Aside from the awkwardness, there was a critical lack in the means for expressing preference in a piece of fix knowledge. For VT, the expert could supply a ranked list of negative effects that revisions could have on a proposed design that applied to virtually any design VT was likely to encounter. For the scheduler, the expert could identify in advance of any run some properties of the value that might be revised. However, the identification of the exact value could only be made at run time on the basis of what orders were input and their effect on the overall schedule. For example, suppose a constraint on the capacity of the electrical engineering department was exceeded by assignment of an order to that department in week 29. A potential revision would be to reschedule one of the orders currently in EE in week 29 to be processed there in week 30 instead. Selection of which order to reschedule should be based on priority associated with the job and any contract deadlines it has to meet. SALT was extended to allow the expert to supply evaluation functions as part of a piece of fix knowledge. These functions would then be evaluated during run time to select the order to reschedule with minimal job priority and maximal slack time till deadline.

### 7.2. Compiling the knowledge base

Just as the knowledge that the problem-solver should use in handling revisions differed between the two domains, how the problem-solver performed revisions also differed somewhat. There were two major changes in going from VT to the scheduler—both affect the pre-compiled control shell and one required changes in the routines for compiling the knowledge base.

In order to make use of evaluation functions like the one described in Section 7.1, the problem-solver should wait until it completes a proposed schedule for all orders before it responds to constraint violations. Completing a rough schedule gives it the information it needs to evaluate where best to reschedule. This contrasts with VT which responds to constraint violations as soon as they are detected, i.e., as soon as a constraint is identified and the constrained value proposed. This immediate attention helps prevent costly elaboration based on what might be a bad guess.

For the same reason, VT performs a limited lookahead. This helps identify a locally good guess before elaborating on it. The scheduler completes a reschedule after every revision. This is because if the reschedule fails, information gained in completing the reschedule will be used in the evaluation to select another revision.

The added expressive capability that allows users to supply evaluation functions for indicating what value to revise created a version of SALT that is useful for both VT and the scheduler. Where there are mutually exclusive variations in SALT's assumed problem-solving shell and compiler, such as when to do constraint checking, we are currently maintaining a unified SALT by offering a user-operated switch. What we hope to do is develop SALT's knowledge of when to apply or recommend such switches.

### 8. Conclusion

SALT has proved quite useful in generating and maintaining VT. VT's first SALT-acquired knowledge base was entered by an elevator engineer with moderate exposure to AI. VT was handed over to the organization that now uses it in April, 1985, with 1300 SALT-generated rules. Since then SALT has been used regularly by elevator engineering personnel to debug, refine and add to the knowledge base. By summer of 1986, VT had 3062 total rules; 2130 of these were generated by SALT. SALT essentially rides herd on the system development. This makes the approach we took in developing SALT a very useful methodology for large knowledge-based systems.

SALT makes a strong commitment to the problem-solving strategy that will be used for the task it will acquire. This allows SALT to represent domain-

specific knowledge according to the role it will play in finding a solution for any task that can use this basic strategy. This commitment gives it considerable power in identifying relevant domain knowledge, in detecting weaknesses in the knowledge base in order to guide its interrogation of the domain expert, in generating an expert system that can perform the task and explain its line of reasoning, and in analyzing test case coverage. An exploration into understanding SALT's applicability highlighted a number of areas in which SALT could be strengthened.

SALT is weak in its ability to elicit knowledge to handle tradeoffs among alternatives both for selecting an original value to extend a proposed design and for selecting a revision to the proposal. Currently a user can enter such knowledge. For example, some design tasks may require selection of parts involving tradeoffs among attributes of the parts. A user of the current SALT could enter a procedure for proposing candidates, a procedure for calculating a function for evaluating how well each fits the design requirements, and yet another procedure for using the evaluation function to make the selection. However, entering this knowledge requires quite a bit of AI sophistication. We need to improve SALT's ability to acquire tradeoff knowledge.

For any SALT-stored knowledge base, represented appropriately for propose-and-revise, there are some options in how to use the knowledge. Although SALT has created a useful expert system, SALT might better exploit the representation to improve the efficiency of the systems it creates. For example, efficiency can become a factor in deciding what part of the dependency network the problem-solver should work on first or when it should do constraint-checking. In using SALT in different domains, we hope to understand how to automate compilation strategies that can respond to such efficiency issues using its analysis of this knowledge representation framework.

ACKNOWLEDGMENT

We would like to thank Gilbert Caplain, Michael Gillanov, Charles Pepe, Emile Servan-Schreiber, Paul Sitruk, Junpu Wang, and Tianran Wang who contributed to the coding of SALT. We would also like to thank Jeff Stout for his work on the problem-solving strategy and control shell assumed by SALT and for his participation in the scheduling project. We are indebted to Robert Roche, first domain expert for VT and first user of SALT, for feedback and suggestions that were incorporated into the SALT design. Many of the ideas contained in this paper were presented in a discussion group attended by Larry Eshelman, Gary Kahn, Tom Mitchell, and Allen Newell, and we are very grateful for their input. We are also indebted to B. Chandrasekaran, Georg Klinker, Steve Smoliar and Bill Swartout for their very useful comments on an earlier draft of this paper.

REFERENCES

1. Boose, J., Personal construct theory and the transfer of human expertise, in: *Proceedings AAAI-84*, Austin, TX (1984).
2. Brown, D., Failure handling in a design expert system, *Comput.-Aided Des.* **17** (1985) 436–441.

3. Chandrasekaran, B., Towards a taxonomy of problem solving types, *AI Mag.* **4** (1983) 9–17.

4. Chandrasekaran, B., Generic tasks in expert system design and their role in explanation of problem solving, Tech. Rept., Ohio State University, Department of Computer and Information Science, Columbus, OH (1986).

5. Clancey, W., The advantages of abstract control knowledge in expert system design, in: *Proceedings AAAI-83*, Washington, DC (1983).

6. Clancey, W., Heuristic classification, *Artificial Intelligence* **27** (1985) 289–350.

7. Davis, R., Buchanan, B.G. and Shortliffe, E., Production rules as a representation for a knowledge-based consultation program, *Artificial Intelligence* **8** (1977) 15–45.

8. Dechter, R. and Pearl, J., The anatomy of easy problems: A constraint-satisfaction formulation, in: *Proceedings IJCAI-85*, Los Angeles, CA (1985).

9. Dechter, R. and Pearl, J., The cycle-cutset method for improving search performance in AI applications, in: *Proceedings IEEE Conference on Artificial Intelligence Applications*, Orlando, FL (1987).

10. Doyle, J., A truth maintenance system, *Artificial Intelligence* **12** (1979) 231–272.

11. Eshelman, L. and McDermott, J., MOLE: A knowledge acquisition tool that uses its head, in: *Proceedings AAAI-86*, Philadelphia, PA (1986).

12. Forgy, C., OPS5 user's manual, Tech. Rept., Carnegie-Mellon University, Department of Computer Science, Pittsburgh, PA (1981).

13. Freuder, E., A sufficient condition for backtrack-free search, *J. ACM* **29** (1982) 24–32.

14. Herman, D., Josephson. J. and Hartung, R., Use of DSPL for the design of a mission planning assistant, Tech. Rept., Ohio State University, Department of Computer and Information Science, Columbus, OH (1986).

15. Kahn, G., Nowlan S., and McDermott, J., MORE: An intelligent knowledge acquisition tool, in: *Proceedings IJCAI-85*. Los Angeles, CA (1985).

16. KEE 3.0 training manual. IntelliCorp. Mountain View, CA (1987).

17. Klinker, G., Boyd, C., Genetet, S. and McDermott, J., A KNACK for knowledge acquisition, in: *Proceedings AAAI-87*. Seattle, WA (1987).

18. Marcus, S., McDermott. J. and Wang, T., Knowledge acquisition for constructive systems, in: *Proceedings IJCAI-85*, Los Angeles. CA (1985).

19. Marcus, S., Stout, J. and McDermott, J., VT: An expert elevator designer that uses knowledge-based backtracking, Tech. Rept., Carnegie-Mellon University, Department of Computer Science, Pittsburgh, PA (1986); also: *AI Mag.* **8** (1987) 41–58.

20. Marcus, S., Understanding decision ordering from a piecemeal collection of knowledge, in: *Proceedings AAAI Workshop on Knowledge Acquisition for Knowledge-Based Systems*, Banff, Alta. (1988).

21. McDermott, J., Making expert systems explicit, in: *Proceedings IFIP Congress*, Dublin, Ireland (1986).

22. Mitchell. T., Mahadevan. S. and Steinberg, L., LEAP: A learning apprentice for VLSI design. in: *Proceedings IJCAI-85*, Los Angeles, CA (1985) 573–580.

23. Mittal. S. and Araya. A... A knowledge-based framework for design, in: *Proceedings AAAI-86*, Philadelphia, PA (1986) 856–865.

24. Musen, M., Fagan, L., Combs, D. and Shortliffe, E., Use of a domain model to drive an interactive knowledge-editing tool, *Int. J. Man-Mach. Stud.* **26** (1987) 105–121.

25. Neches, R., Swartout, W. and Moore. J., Explainable (and maintainable) expert systems, in: *Proceedings IJCAI-85*, Los Angeles, CA (1985).

26. Smith, R.G., Winston, H.A., Mitchell, T.M. and Buchanan, B.G., Representation and use of explicit justifications for knowledge base refinement, in: *Proceedings IJCAI-85*, Los Angeles, CA (1985).

27. Smith, S., Fox, M. and Ow, P., Constructing and maintaining detailed production plans: Investigations into the development of knowledge-based factory scheduling systems, *AI Mag.* **7** (1986) 45–60.

28. Stallman, R.M. and Sussman, G.J., Forward reasoning and dependency-directed backtracking in a system for computer-aided circuit analysis, *Artificial Intelligence* **9** (1977) 135–196.

29. Stefik, M., Planning with constraints (MOLGEN: Part 1), *Artificial Intelligence* **16** (1981) 111–139.

30. Stefik, M. Planning and meta-planning (MOLGEN: Part 2), *Artificial Intelligence* **16** (1981) 141–169.

31. Stout, J., Caplain, G., Marcus, S. and McDermott, J., Toward automating recognition of differing problem-solving demands, *Int. J. Man-Mach. Stud.* **29** (1988) 591–611.

32. Sussman, G.J. and Steele, G.L., Jr, CONSTRAINTS: A language for expressing almost-hierarchical descriptions, *Artificial Intelligence* **14** (1980) 1–39.

33. Swartout, W., XPLAIN: A system for creating and explaining expert consulting systems, *Artificial Intelligence* **21** (1983) 285–325.

34. van de Brug, A., Bachant, J. and McDermott, J., The taming of R1, *IEEE Expert* **1** (1986) 33–42.

*Received November 1986; revised version received January 1988*

Machine Learning, 4, 347-375 (1989)
© 1989 Kluwer Academic Publishers, Boston. Manufactured in The Netherlands.

# Automated Support for Building and Extending Expert Models

MARK A. MUSEN                MUSEN@SUMEX-AIM.STANFORD.EDU
*Medical Computer Science Group, Knowledge Systems Laboratory, Stanford University, Stanford, California 94305-5479*

**Abstract.** Building a knowledge-based system is like developing a scientific theory. Although a knowledge base does not constitute a theory of some natural phenomenon, it does represent a theory of how a class of professionals approaches an application task. As when scientists develop a natural theory, builders of expert systems first must formulate a model of the behavior that they wish to understand and then must corroborate and extend that model with the aid of specific examples. Thus there are two interrelated phases of knowledge-base construction: (1) model building and (2) model extension. Computer-based tools can assist developers with both phases of the knowledge-acquisition process. Workers in the area of knowledge acquisition have developed computer-based tools that emphasize either the building of new models or the extension of existing models. The PROTEGE knowledge-acquisition system addresses these two activities individually and facilitates the construction of expert systems when the same general model can be applied to a variety of application tasks.

**Key Words.** knowledge acquisition, knowledge engineering, human-computer interaction, visual languages, domain modeling

## 1. Introduction

*Knowledge acquisition* is the process of eliciting the expertise of authorities in an application area and of formalizing that knowledge within a computer program. From the time of McCarthy's [1968] early proposal for the "Advice Taker" (a theoretical program that could act on the statements about the world that its users typed into it in predicate logic), workers in artificial intelligence (AI) have described tools that could facilitate the knowledge-acquisition process. Knowledge acquisition often is depicted as the cumbersome activity whereby expertise is transferred from the minds of application specialists to those of the computer scientists who build expert systems (knowledge engineers), and thence to the knowledge bases of expert systems. Most builders of knowledge-acquisition tools consequently perceive knowledge acquisition as a problem in *knowledge flow*.

The depiction of knowledge acquisition as the transfer of expertise has caused many researchers to view knowledge engineers as middlemen, whose naiveté in the application area impedes communication and clogs the pipeline during knowledge extraction. Davis' [1976] landmark knowledge-acquisition program, TEIRESIAS, was predicated on the proposition that, if domain experts could enter their knowledge directly into expert systems, the need for knowledge engineers during the refinement of new knowledge bases would be eliminated. Although Davis' suggestion was influential, TEIRESIAS never actually was used by the expert physicians for whom it was intended. During the more than one dozen years that have ensued since the development of TEIRESIAS, a score of computer-based knowledge-acquisition tools have been constructed, most designed to eliminate the need for knowledge engineers [Boose 1989]. Despite this nearly universal goal, not one of these tools has supplanted the humans needed to assist application specialists in the construction and maintenance of production-quality expert systems [Kitto 1989]. Although current knowledge-acquisition tools may greatly facilitate the process, development of most expert systems still requires intermediaries and still is often bottlenecked.

The emphasis on knowledge transfer and the view of the knowledge engineer as an intermediary, however, have hindered the recognition that knowledge acquisition is a creative and inventive activity. When knowledge engineers interview application specialists to develop expert systems, they begin to form mental models of how the experts solve problems; the experts, of course, have mental models of their own that attempt to capture their professional problem-solving behavior. In the course of building the expert system, both the knowledge engineers and the experts continually revise their respective mental models. Although the knowledge engineers and the application specialists may have very different mental models at the outset of their collaboration, the models eventually converge. This convergence is possible (1) because the knowledge-acquisition process forces all parties to commit their mental models to a fixed, publicly examinable form—typically, the emerging knowledge base; and (2) because the frequent consideration of examples and test cases forces the system builders to assess, corroborate, and revise their models. The often-cited difficulties of knowledge acquisition can be ascribed, in general, to creating and agreeing on a shared model of problem solving [Winograd and Flores 1986; Regoczei and Plantinga 1987].

The creation of a knowledge base is much like the creation of a scientific theory. Unlike traditional scientists, however, builders of expert systems are not concerned with the elaboration of theories of natural phenomena; these knowledge engineers instead seek to develop theories of expert behavior. In constructing a knowledge base, system builders first define a general model (or theory) of the application task to be performed. In the case of the MYCIN system [Buchanan and Shortliffe 1984], for example, that general task model was one of diagnosing and treating infectious diseases. Given the initial model, MYCIN's developers validated and revised that model as necessary, attempting to fit the model to specific clinical problems. Once the essential model was worked out, it was then extended to include knowledge of particular kinds of bacteremia and, later, of meningitis. For example, after the basic system had been designed, the developers of MYCIN augmented the program's knowledge base to permit diagnosis and treatment of bacterial, fungal, viral, and tuberculous meningitis by making four separate extensions to the original MYCIN model.

Thus knowledge acquisition can be viewed as comprising two interrelated phases: (1) building a general task model—that is, creating an *intention* of the proposed system's behavior; followed by (2) filling in the specific content knowledge in the domain that is consistent with the general model—that is, creating *extensions* [Addis 1987]. In this paper, I shall discuss the special nature of these two stages of knowledge acquisition, with an emphasis on the kinds of computer-based tools that can facilitate the two phases. Knowledge-acquisition systems such as ROGET [Bennett 1985] are *model-building* tools that are particularly well suited to help knowledge engineers and application specialists to develop theories of expert problem solving. Other systems, such as OPAL [Musen, et al. 1987], are *model-extending* tools that are best used by domain experts working along to define specific applications. Recent work on the PROTÉGÉ knowledge-acquisition system [Musen 1989a, b] demonstrates

how a model-building tool can help knowledge engineers to fashion a general task model, such that that model then can be used by a second model-extending tool to permit experts to define specific applications. In particular, PROTÉGÉ allows system builders to create general models of application tasks that can be solved with the method of skeletal-plan refinement [Friedland and Iwasaki 1985]; PROTÉGÉ then generates automatically knowledge-acquisition tools like OPAL that domain experts can use to enter the content knowledge for individual applications.

## 2. The Problem of Creating Models

Computer-based knowledge-acquisition tools, unlike traditional machine-learning programs, assume that knowledge will be formalized as the consequence of an interaction with a human expert. This interaction, which undeniably constitutes the greatest strength of the knowledge-engineering approach, also is the source of substantial liability. Application specialists cannot simply transfer their expertise to a computer, and knowledge-acquisition programs often cannot accept an expert's entries at face value. Understanding why a direct transfer of expertise is impossible points both to a major distinction between current research in knowledge acquisition and work in machine learning, and motivates important design decisions made in the construction of PROTÉGÉ.

Like the construction of other large pieces of software, the engineering of knowledge-based systems requires significant creativity on the part of system builders. Creativity is essential because the application specialists whose professional acumen is to be encoded as a knowledge base often cannot verbalize how they actually go about solving problems. Experts may not be merely inarticulate in explaining their behavior; they frequently are tongue-tied for reasons stemming from the very nature of human intelligence.

### 2.1. The Paradox of Expertise

Human cognitive skills appear to be acquired in at least three generally distinct stages of learning [Fitts 1964; LaBerge and Samuels 1974; Johnson 1983]. Although different authors have used different terms to describe the three phases, there is concordance regarding the qualitative changes that occur in the way that people seem to retrieve information during problem solving. Initially, there is the *cognitive* stage, during which an individual identifies the actions that are appropriate in particular circumstances, either as a result of direct instruction or from observation of other people. In this stage, the learner often verbally rehearses information needed for execution of the skill. Next comes the *associative* phase of learning, in which the relationships noted during the cognitive stage are practiced and verbal mediation begins to disappear. With repetition and feedback, the person begins to apply the actions accurately in a fluent and efficient manner. Then, in the final *autonomous* stage, the learner *compiles* the relationships from repeated practice to the point where he can perform them without conscious awareness. Suddenly, the person performs the actions appropriately, proficiently, and effortlessly—without thinking. The knowledge has become *tacit* [Fodor 1968].

There is substantial evidence that, as humans become experienced in an application area and repeatedly apply their know-how to specific tasks, their knowledge becomes compiled

that they do not always work. Slovic and Lichtenstein [1971], for example, asked stock brokers to weight the importance of various factors that influenced these brokers' investment decisions. A regression analysis of *actual* decisions made by the stock brokers revealed computed weights for these factors that were poorly correlated with the brokers' subjective ratings. More important, there was a *negative* correlation between the accuracy of introspection and the stock brokers' years of experience. More recently, Michalski and Chilausky [1980] found that decision rules elicited from plant pathologists for the diagnosis of soybean diseases performed less accurately than did a rule set that was automatically induced by application of the AQ11 algorithm to a library of test cases. (The experts' actual diagnoses were used as the gold standard against which the two sets of rules were judged.)

Many workers in knowledge acquisition have consequently argued for the elicitation of *authentic* (as opposed to reconstructed) methods of reasoning in hopes of improving expert-system performance [Johnson 1983; Cleaves 1987; Meyer, et al. 1989]. The goal is determination of the behaviors actually used by experts in performing relevant tasks. Acquisition of authentic knowledge, not surprisingly, requires more than just posing direct questions and asking application experts to introspect. Despite intense research to develop non-biasing interviewing techniques [for example, Ericsson and Simon 1984], psychometric methods [for example, Cooke and McDonald 1987], and ethnographic approaches [for example, Belkin et al., 1987], the elicitation of authentic problem-solving strategies remains cumbersome and often is impractical. The translation of authentic reasoning methods (when such methods can be elicited) into current knowledge-system architectures in a manner that avoids artifacts due to the knowledge-representation language itself also is an unsolved problem.

Knowledge engineers, therefore, must apprehend both the authentic and the reconstructed knowledge derived from application specialists and must assess that knowledge objectively. The engineers serve the important function of detecting gaps in the knowledge and of helping the application specialists to fill those gaps by defining plausible sequences of actions that can achieve the necessary goals. Knowledge engineers thus create theories of how the experts tacitly solve problems. The knowledge bases that embody those theories may not achieve the same level of performance as do the procedures actually used by domain experts, but the knowledge bases nevertheless can be observed, extended, and easily disseminated to other people in need of advice. It is incorrect to view a knowledge base as an embodiment of some human's problem-solving expertise. Knowledge bases instead represent only *models* of expert behavior—models that attempt to approximate, but that do not reproduce, the actual problem-solving steps used by humans [Clancey 1986].

When attempting to automate knowledge acquisition, we must identify the roles that knowledge engineers—and that computer-based tools—can play in either the creation or the extension of expert models. The PROTÉGÉ system has been developed under the premise that, at present, it is neither possible nor desirable to build tools to automate the entire knowledge-acquisition process. We can find data in support of that proposition by examining how knowledge engineers and experts have tried to use previous knowledge-acquisition tools to develop practical knowledge bases. Some automated tools help system developers to craft a model of the application task to be performed. Other tools assume that a model of the task area already exists. We now consider these two classes of knowledge-acquistion programs in detail.

and thus inaccessible to their consciousness. Experts lose awareness of what they know. The knowledge that experts acquired as novices may be retrievable in a *declarative* form, yet the skills that these professionals actually practice are *procedural* in nature [Anderson 1987]. Although there is no consensus on how such procedural knowledge is stored within the nervous system [Rumelhart and Norman 1983], the inability of experts to *verbalize* these compiled associations is well accepted [Nisbett and Wilson 1977; Lyons 1986]. The consequence is that the special knowledge that we would most like to incorporate into our expert systems often is that knowledge about which experts are least able to talk. Johnson [1983] has identified this phenomenon as *the paradox of expertise.*

The paradox is confirmed by experimental data, as well as by much acedotal experience. Johnson [1983], for example, reports that he once enrolled in classes at the University of Minnesota Medical School as part of his investigation of the process of medical diagnosis. At the same time, Johnson had the opportunity to study a medical colleague (one of his teachers) caring for patients on the hospital wards. Johnson compared the physician's observed clinical behavior with the diagnostic methods his colleague was teaching in the classroom. To Johnson's surprise, the medical-school professor's behavior in practice seemed to contradict what the teacher professed. When confronted with these observations, Johnson's subject responded:

Oh, I know that, but you see I don't know how I actually do diagnosis, and yet I need to teach things to students. I create what I think of as plausible means of doing tasks and hope students will be able to convert them into effective ones. [Johnson 1983, p. 81]

The clinician in this example recognized explicitly that he could not verbalize his compiled expertise in medical diagnosis. The problem for knowledge engineers and for builders of knowledge-acquisition tools, however, is that people rarely know the limits of their tacit knowledge. When asked to report on their compiled expertise, subjects often volunteer plausible answers that may well be incorrect. In experimental situations, subjects have been shown to be frequently (1) unaware of the existence of a stimulus or cue influencing a response, (2) unaware that a response has been affected by a stimulus, and (3) unaware that a cognitive response may have even occurred. Instead, subjects give verbal reports of their cognition based on prior causal theories from their nontacit memory [Nisbett and Wilson 1977]. Furthermore, because Western culture mistakenly teaches us that accurate introspection somehow should be possible [Lyons 1986], people freely explain and rationalize their compiled behaviors without recognizing that these explanations frequently are incorrect.

### 2.2. *Authentic and Reconstructed Strategies*

When asked questions about tacit processes, experts volunteer plausible answers that may not reflect their true behavior. These believable, although sometimes inaccurate, responses are known as *reconstructed* reasoning methods [Johnson 1983]. Reconstructed methods typically are acknowledged and endorsed by entire problem-solving communities. They form the basis of most major textbooks. The disadvantage of these methods, however, is

## 3. Tools for Creating Task Models

When building an expert system, developers must first perform a requirements analysis and must identify the *task* that the expert system will perform. Then, knowledge engineers and application specialists traditionally must work together to construct a model of the proposed system's behavior. This model generally corresponds to the developers' theory of how the expert actually solves problems. Much of the necessary modeling activity entails what Newell [1982] refers to as *knowledge-level analysis*—determining (1) the goals for an intelligent system, (2) the actions of which the system is capable, and (3) the knowledge that the system can use to select actions that can achieve the goals. The process of knowledge-level analysis makes no assumptions about the set of symbols with which the expert system ultimately will be encoded (that is, about the rules, frames, or other data structures within the knowledge-representation language). The concern at this stage is only the *behaviors* of which the system will be capable.

There is increasing agreement in the literature that system builders should model the behavior of a proposed system at the knowledge level before they begin to implement the system. One modeling approach centers on defining abstract, domain-independent strategies known as *problem-solving methods* that can form the basis of languages that system builders can use to describe specific application tasks [Clancey 1985; McDermott 1988]. For example, Clancey's [1985] model of the method of *heuristic classification* includes abstract notions such as (1) *conclusions* that the problem solver may select from a pre-enumerated set, (2) *solution-refinement hierarchies* that allow the problem solver to narrow down the set of conclusions that it makes, (3) *data-abstraction hierarchies* that allow the problem solver to generalize from specific input data, and (4) *heuristics* that link abstractions of the user's input data to potential solutions.

Clancey derived the heuristic-classification model from a retrospective analysis of the behavior of a number of expert systems. Knowledge engineers, however, can apply such models of problem solving *prospectively* when they create new knowledge bases, structuring and clarifying the models that they create. Given an application task, such as MYCIN's task of identifying potential causes of infectious disease, developers can use the domain-independent concepts in the heuristic-classification model to define the intended behavior of an evolving system without reference to individual data structures that might be required to implement that behavior within the computer. By relating task-specific knowledge (such as attributes of possible infectious deseases) to well-understood problem-solving methods (such as the method of heuristic classification), developers clarify the roles that the knowledge plays in the system's production of recommendations, facilitating both the encoding and the maintenance of that system [McDermott 1988].

Researchers in AI have identified a number of domain-independent problem-solving methods that can assist system builders in the creation of knowledge-level models [Clancey 1985; Chandrasekaran 1986; McDermott 1988]. Considerable work concentrates on the elucidation of still other models of problem solving, particularly methods that might be applied to tasks that cannot be performed using classification. Although there is increasing consensus on the importance of the modeling approach, the knowledge-acquisition literature is fragmented by the use of inconsistent terminology. For example, whereas many researchers use the term *problem-solving method* for these abstract strategies [Clancey 1985; McDermott 1988; Boose 1989; Musen 1989c], workers at Ohio State University advocate the term *generic task* [Chandrasekaran 1986]. Yet most authors use the word *task* (without the "generic" modifier) to refer to an application problem to be solved. Unfortunately, the distinction between a *task* and a *generic task* often confuses both readers and authors. The developers of the KADS system for knowledge acquisition [Breuker and Wielinga 1987] use the expression *interpretation model* to refer to the formalization of a problem-solving method. In this paper, I consistently use the expression *problem-solving method*—or simply *method*—when referring to an abstract solution mechanism. The term *task* denotes the statement of an application problem, without regard to how that problem might be solved.

A source of additional confusion may arise in this paper, however, because there often are two kinds of models under discussion. First, there are models of *methods*, which represent sets of both terms and relationships for describing abstract, domain-independent solution strategies. Second, there are models of *tasks*, which represent terms and relationships for defining application problems to be solved. Frequently, system builders use the terms and relationships of a model of a problem-solving method (for example, heuristic classification) to define the specific terms and relationships that are needed to model an application task (for example, organism identification in MYCIN). If the task can be solved using the method, then the model of the method can provide a structure for the model of the task. Indeed, task models often can be viewed as direct extensions (or instantiations) of models of problem-solving methods [Musen 1989c].

Recently, several workers have developed computer-based knowledge-acquisition tools that expand this notion of relating task-specific knowledge to a predefined model of a problem-solving method [for example, Bennett 1985; Eshelman 1988; Marcus 1988]. Each of these tools presupposes a model of a different problem-solving method. Knowledge engineers use the terms and relationships in these models of problem solving to create new models for the solution of application *tasks* (Figure 1). In this paper, I refer to these method-oriented programs as *model-building* tools, because these tools help their users to devise and refine task models. To create the task models, users *extend* a pre-existing model of some problem-solving method. Each extension defines how the domain-independent method can be used to solve a particular application task.

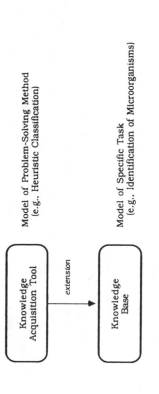

*Figure 1.* Creating a task model. Knowledge-acquisition tools such as ROGET contain models of domain-independent problem-solving methods. Users of such tools extend the problem-solving models to define specific application tasks.

ROGET [Bennett 1985], for example, was a knowledge-acquisition tool that contained a model of diagnosis that was a specialized form of heuristic classification. The program asked its user to identify the *problems* to be diagnosed, the *causes* of those problems, and the *data* that could be used to suggest, to confirm, or to rule out those causes and problems.

A user's dialog with ROGET created a knowledge-level specification of the application task, which was then translated into EMYCIN symbols that could form the basis of a working consultation program. The knowledge engineer, however, modeled the application task (for example, the organism-identification task in MYCIN) in terms of the abstract notions of "problems," "causes," and "data." The developer never had to think in terms of the production rules or other data structures that EMYCIN ultimately would require to generate the proper diagnostic behavior.

A number of analogous method-based tools have been described subsequently, including MORE [Kahn, Nowlan, and McDermott 1985], MOLE [Eshelman 1988], and SALT [Marcus 1988]. PROTÉGÉ (which I shall describe in Section 5) is also of this class. Each of these tools provides a language that allows its users to create models of how application tasks can be solved. In each case, that language is one of a particular problem-solving method. Like ROGET, both MORE and MOLE assume that a user's task can be solved using a specialized form of heuristic classification. PROTÉGÉ and SALT, on the other hand, adopt problem-solving methods in which the solution is constructed. The method assumed by PROTÉGÉ is a specialized form of skeletal-plan refinement [Friedland and Iwasaki 1985]. The method built into SALT is a constraint-satisfaction strategy known as *propose and revise*.

Tools such as MORE, MOLE, and SALT allow their users to do much more than to create models of application tasks. Users of these tools also *extend* the task models that they develop with the many domain-specific facts that are necessary to generate complete knowledge bases. Unlike PROTÉGÉ, these other tools do not sharply distinguish between the activities of building models and those of extending them. However, because the process of task-model extension is necessarily preceded by that of task-model creation, it is appropriate to view such method-based tools as knowledge-acquisition aids that assist users in building task models.

In principle, all these model-building tools can be used by domain experts working alone. Indeed, mechanical engineers used SALT to develop an expert system that configures elevators for new buildings [Marcus 1988]. Such method-based tools, however, are used most effectively by knowledge engineers [Musen 1989c]. The terms and relationships of the problem-solving models assumed by the tools (for example, terms in ROGET such as "problems" and "causes") have precise semantics—distinct from these terms' vernacular meanings—that may not be clear to untrained users. A naive user who recognizes such terms as familiar lexical entities, but who may not appreciate the subtleties of the problem-solving model that the terms denote, will be incapable of translating his mental model of a domain task into an effective knowledge base. More important, the tacit nature of human expertise often makes it difficult for application specialists independently to develop robust models of their own behavior. For example, Kitto [1989] reports that when domain experts attempted to use the KNACK knowledge-acquisition tool [Klinker 1988] without the aid of knowledge engineers, the experts' inability to create models of the tasks to be performed constituted

a major stumbling block. The entry of instantiating knowledge to extend task models that already had been developed with help from knowledge engineers, however, was much more straightforward for these experts.

## 4. Tools for Extending Task Models

Regardless of whether a computer-based tool is used to help developers to fashion the task model, after a knowledge engineer and domain expert have created a model of the intended behavior of the expert system, that model must be validated. An important form of validation is to ascertain how well the model applies to closely related application tasks. For example, given a task model that correctly identifies the presence of infections involving one class of micro-organism, system builders will want to confirm that the model can be extended to identify additional classes of potential pathogens. In this phase of knowledge acquisition, the developers test their model by establishing how that model applies to new situations. The system builders' original knowledge-level model is an *intention* of how problem solving occurs; each specific situation for which the model can be shown to apply is an *extension* of that model.[1]

Although creating a knowledge base may be difficult, extending an existing model is less cognitively taxing. Whereas experts may not be able to introspect and to articulate the *process knowledge* that allows them to solve problems [Johnson 1983; Winograd and Flores 1986], these experts certainly are adept at volunteering the *content knowledge* that may be either consistent or inconsistent with a given model. For example, a physician may not be able to provide a coherent description of how he actually diagnoses infectious diseases, but he may be able to describe readily the differences between bacterial and fungal meningitis. Thus, although knowledge engineers typically are needed to help to craft an initial task model, application experts may require little assistance either in extending an existing model or in identifying specific situations in which a given model fails. The frequently raised concern that the experts may not articulate authentic knowledge becomes moot when the specification of only content knowledge is at issue.

The automated knowledge-acquisition tools that are most suited for direct use by domain experts consequently are those that ask their users to extend existing models, rather than to create new ones [Musen 1989c]. Such tools both assume a predefined problem-solving method and incorporate a model of a *class* of application tasks; users extend the general task model to define specific applications (Figure 2). Unlike the detailed task models that knowledge engineers create and extend using tools such as MOLE and SALT, the task models that developers build into this latter set of model-extending knowledge-acquisition tools remain relatively abstract; the models are *intentions*. Rather than describing a particular task to be performed, these models define the characteristics of classes of application tasks that users might want to specify.

An example of such a tool is OPAL [Musen, et al. 1987], which was built by our laboratory to streamline knowledge acquisition for a medical expert system known as ONCOCIN [Tu, et al. 1989]. OPAL contains a model of the general task of administering cancer therapy and asks physicians to extend that model to specific cancer-therapy plans. OPAL's task model presupposes that patients will be treated with groups of drugs called *chemotherapies*. OPAL

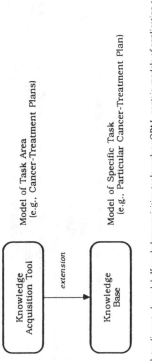

Model of Task Area
(e.g., Cancer-Treatment Plans)

*extension*

Model of Specific Task
(e.g., Particular Cancer-Treatment Plan)

*Figure 2.* Extending a task model. Knowledge acquisition tools such as OPAL contain models of application-task areas. Users of tools such as OPAL extend the general task models to define specific applications (for example, particular cancer-treatment plans).

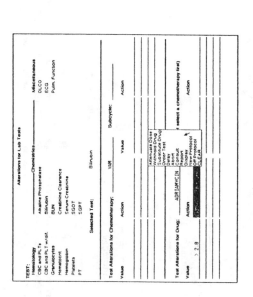

*Figure 3.* OPAL form for actions related to laboratory-test results. In this form, the physician is specifying how therapy should be modified if the level of bilirubin in a patient's blood is elevated to more than 2.0 mg/dl.

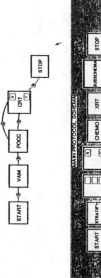

*Figure 4.* OPAL flowchart language. OPAL allows physicians to create visual programs corresponding to the procedural specification of chemotherapies (CHEMO) and X-ray therapies (XRT) in a given cancer-treatment plan. Below the region where the flowchart is entered is a palette of reference icons, used to add new nodes to the graph. The specification that has been entered in this figure calls for a single course of VAM chemotherapy to be given, followed by administration of POCC chemotherapy until the parameter CR (complete response) becomes *true*.

does not require its user to stipulate how chemotherapies are administered; such a model was developed by the knowledge engineers who built OPAL. Rather, the program asks its physician-user only to identify the sequence of chemotherapies in a particular treatment plan, to enter the doses of the relevant drugs, and to indicate how the administration of chemotherapy must be modified in response to changes in a patient's condition. Although the individual treatment plans are complex, the pre-existing task model reduces the process of defining new cancer treatments to simply filling in the blanks of graphical forms from menus (Figure 3), or to piecing together sequences of icons using a graphical flowchart language [Figure 4; Musen, et al. 1988]. OPAL thus solicits from the user an extension to its predefined task model that specifies a new treatment plan; the program then automatically generates from that extension a knowledge base that can be interpreted by the ONCOCIN system to carry out that plan.

The task model in OPAL makes assumptions regarding everything from the nature of chemotherapy to the kinds of conditions that can mandate modifications to a physician's treatment plan. Such assumptions define a *closed world*. There is no way to add new concepts to the model. OPAL allows physicians to create novel instantiations of existing concepts (for example, a user can readily define a previously unknown drug or chemotherapy), but the general classes of concepts in the model are predetermined. The task model tends to be sufficient, however, because of the highly stylized nature of cancer therapy. Because the terms in the model have precise, intuitive meanings that match the physicians' common usage of these terms, it is relatively simple for application specialists to fill in the blanks and to connect the flowchart icons in proper sequence to define new therapies. In 1986 alone, physicians used OPAL to enter 36 cancer-treatment plans. Each plan could be entered in a few hours or days. Previously, knowledge engineers and cancer specialists had typically required several weeks of work to encode each such plan using traditional, manual techniques.

System builders construct tools such as OPAL with the assumption that they will create multiple extensions to a given task model (for example, that they will create multiple chemotherapy knowledge bases). It would not be practical to incur the expense of programming such a tool if the system were not to be used repeatedly. There are a number of application areas where knowledge engineers have built tools to facilitate the construction of multiple,

related knowledge bases. For example, Freiling and Alexander [1984] developed INKA to aid knowledge acquisition for an expert system that troubleshoots electronic instruments; each knowledge base created with INKA specifies fault-detection strategies for diagnosing a particular device. Similarly, Gale [1987] built a program called Student to aid knowledge acquisition for an expert system that advises researchers on the use of data-analysis programs; each knowledge base produced with Student specifies the use of a different statistical routine. In diverse domains such as medical therapy, event scheduling, and process control, system builders would benefit from tools such as OPAL that allow application experts to work alone, extending pre-existing task models to specify the knowledge that defines new task instances.

Although model-extending tools such as OPAL can be powerful in allowing domain specialists to author large knowledge bases without the concurrent need for knowledge engineers, each such tool is necessarily tied to a specific task model. For example, if someone is not interested in constructing a knowledge base for cancer chemotherapy, OPAL is useless to him. Tools such as OPAL can play a significant role in the life cycle of expert systems when developers require multiple knowledge bases for sets of related domain tasks. The challenge for tool builders is to recognize appropriate application areas and to generate such domain-specific programs rapidly and efficiently.

Building the models that form the basis of systems such as OPAL and Student is itself a problem in knowledge acquisition. Constructing such task-specific tools thus constitutes another kind of bottleneck. OPAL, for example, required 3.5 person-years to develop before any knowledge bases could be encoded. Building OPAL was cumbersome because, whenever developers altered their model of cancer therapy, OPAL had to be reprogrammed. More important, because that task model was not represented explicitly within OPAL, refining the model required knowledge engineers to modify LISP expressions throughout the system's program code; there was no knowledge-level representation of the model. These obstacles to maintaining OPAL, and the desire to transfer the methodology to application areas other than cancer therapy, prompted the development of PROTÉGÉ.

## 5. Generation of Tools that Extend Task Models

A tool for *building* task models (such as ROGET), which presupposes a particular problem-solving method, is best used by knowledge engineers to create knowlede-level models of the tasks that expert systems will perform. On the other hand, a tool for *extending* task models (such as OPAL), which presupposes a particular set of application tasks, can be used by application experts independently to define specific task instances. The two classes of tools are each suited for distinct phases of the expert-system life cycle. Because model building is invariably followed by model extension—and because the process of model extension often uncovers deficiencies in the original model that need to be repaired—an important goal is to make the use of these two types of tools as integrated as possible. An example of the necessary integration has been achieved with the research system called PROTÉGÉ [Musen 1989a, b].

### 5.1. The PROTÉGÉ System

PROTÉGÉ is a knowledge-acquisition tool that, like ROGET, assumes a particular problem-solving method—namely, a variant of skeletal-plan refinement [Friedland and Iwasaki 1985]. In performing skeletal planning, a problem solver decomposes a problem's abstract (skeletal) solution into one or more constituent plans that are each worked out in more detail than is the abstract plan. These constituent plans, however, may themselves be skeletal in nature and may require further distillation into subcomponents that are more fleshed out. The refinement process continues until a concrete solution to the problem is achieved.

The expert systems that PROTÉGÉ ultimately constructs produce as their output fully instantiated plans for their users to follow. In the cancer-chemotherapy domain, for example, such plans provide the details of the treatment that physicians should prescribe for an individual patient at specific stages of therapy. The method of skeletal-plan refinement has been applied to practical tasks not only in the ONCOCIN system [Tu, et al. 1989], but also in Friedland's [1979] MOLGEN program and in various versions of the Digitalis Therapy Advisor [Silverman 1975; Swartout 1981]. The method is well suited for applications that require construction of solutions for which the problem solver's reasoning does not need to concentrate on the details of selecting and ordering individual plan operators. In tasks that can be solved by skeletal-plan refinement, the availability of substantial domain knowledge makes it possible for the nuances of operator selection and of constraint satisfaction to be precompiled into the skeletal plans themselves. The problem-solving method consequently avoids search in favor of the instantiation of predefined partial plans [Friedland and Iwasaki 1985].

PROTÉGÉ allows a system builder to create an explicit model of a set of application tasks that can be solved by skeletal-plan refinement. PROTÉGÉ then *generates automatically* a knowledge-acquisition tool like OPAL that is custom-tailored for the set of application tasks that was modeled (Figure 5). PROTÉGÉ recently has been used to construct *p-OPAL*, a knowledge-acquisition tool for the cancer-therapy domain that reproduces the functionality of OPAL. A second program created using PROTÉGÉ, called *HTN*, allows physicians to enter treatment plans for the management of patients with hypertension [Musen 1989a]. Unlike OPAL, which required many months to program by hand, both p-OPAL and HTN were generated with PROTÉGÉ after only a few days of work.

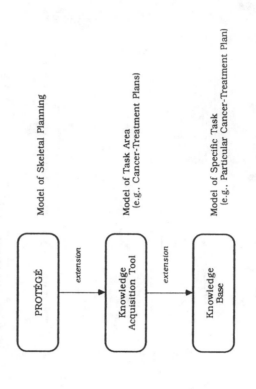

PROTÉGÉ — Model of Skeletal Planning

*extension*

Knowledge Acquisition Tool — Model of Task Area (e.g., Cancer-Treatment Plans)

*extension*

Knowledge Base — Model of Specific Task (e.g., Particular Cancer-Treatment Plan)

*Figure 5.* Creating and extending task models with PROTÉGÉ. Knowledge engineers extend the model of skeletal-plan refinement in PROTÉGÉ to create general task models; the application-specific tools that PROTÉGÉ generates then allow domain experts to extend those task models to define individual applications.

With PROTÉGÉ, a knowledge engineer defines a task model by filling out a series of graphical forms in a manner similar to the way in which oncologists fill out the forms in OPAL. As in OPAL, the PROTÉGÉ forms cluster together related information for presentation to the user and allow data to be examined and edited using direct-manipulation techniques. Although both PROTÉGÉ and OPAL acquire knowledge using hypermedia interfaces [Conklin 1987] and share common styles of human–computer interaction, the nature of the knowledge that users enter into the two systems is quite different. Whereas OPAL acquires knowledge of specific application tasks, PROTÉGÉ acquires knowledge of general task areas. Users enter into OPAL knowledge that is expressed in terms of that program's predefined model of cancer-therapy administration. The knowledge that users enter into PROTÉGÉ, on the other hand, is couched in terms of a predefined model of skeletal-plan refinement.

When PROTÉGÉ is first activated, the system's main menu appears on the workstation screen (Figure 6). This form allows access to other PROTÉGÉ forms that are available at the next organizational level. Via the main menu, the user can cause forms to be displayed that allow him to enter and edit the terms and relationships in a task model.

Task models created using PROTÉGÉ have the same three general components as does the cancer-therapy task model that was hand-coded into OPAL: (1) the *planning entities* in the domain from which the target expert system will refine its skeletal plans (for example, concepts such as the administration *chemotherapies and drugs* in oncology), (2) *actions* that can modify the application of one of the planning entities (for example, concepts such as *attenuating* the dose of a drug or *delaying* treatment), and (3) *input data* that will be entered by the user of the target expert system, the values of which may determine whether any of the *actions* should be applied (for example, concepts such as *laboratory-test results*).

The challenge for PROTÉGÉ users is to create a model of the task area under consideration that can be represented using the terms and relationships of the predefined skeletal-planning model. The knowledge engineer and domain specialist thus must examine the application area and discern the kinds of abstract plans that experts may construct. The developers then map the components of those plans into a hierarchy of PROTÉGÉ *planning entities* and establish the attributes of those plan components that are relevant during problem solving. The users also must determine how experts may modify the standard plans in the task area on the basis of external conditions, modeling such potential plan alterations as a set of PROTÉGÉ task *actions*. Finally, the knowledge engineer and application specialist must consider those external features that may bear on the system's recommendations. These features are modeled as *input data* in PROTÉGÉ's terminology. The PROTÉGÉ interface assists the developers by providing an explicit structure and a convenient notation for recording the components of the task model. Nevertheless, knowledge engineers and application specialists still must collaborate using traditional techniques to elucidate that model in the first place.

The mechanics of entering a task model in PROTÉGÉ are straightforward. For example, selecting PLANNING ENTITIES from the main menu in Figure 6 causes PROTÉGÉ to display the corresponding form for defining the components of skeletal plans in the relevant application domain. Figure 7 shows this planning-entities form filled out for the hypertension-therapy task, as was done to produce the HTN knowledge-editing tool. In the figure, the knowledge engineer has specified that the most general component of a plan is called a *protocol*, and that a problem solver may refine hypertension protocols into more detailed plans that entail the prescription of *tablets*, the ordering of *tests*, and the passage of *wait* periods. The specifications for these components say nothing about the particular kinds of tablets that might be prescribed or the precise tests that might be ordered during the administration of a particular treatment protocol for high blood pressure; the specifications form only an *intention* of the application tasks that are possible in the hypertension domain. Once PROTÉGÉ generates a knowledge-editing tool based on this task model, then application specialists can enter the *extensions* to the model that define individual treatment plans. The problems of building a task model and of extending that model are therefore separated.

In addition to the form for PLANNING ENTITIES in Figure 7, PROTÉGÉ contains eleven other forms that knowledge engineers fill in to describe various aspects of a task model [Musen 1989a]. Each form acquires information related to a particular topic (attributes of planning entities, properties of attributes of planning entities, actions, attributes of actions, and so on). All the forms contain blanks for making entries, as well as icons that allow transfer from one form to the next. When the user selects with the mouse pointing device a triangular-arrow icon in one of these forms, PROTÉGÉ displays a new form for entry

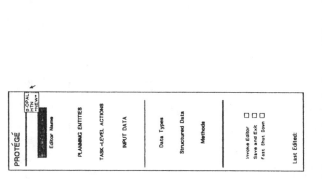

*Figure 6* PROTÉGÉ main-menu form. This form asks the user for the name of the knowledge-editing system for which specifications are to be entered or edited using PROTÉGÉ. Once the name has been entered via the pop-up menu, the user can access forms for various topics by selecting the blanks in the menu. The top three items (PLANNING ENTITIES, TASK-LEVEL ACTIONS, and INPUT DATA) correspond to the three principal components of PROTÉGÉ's model of skeletal planning.

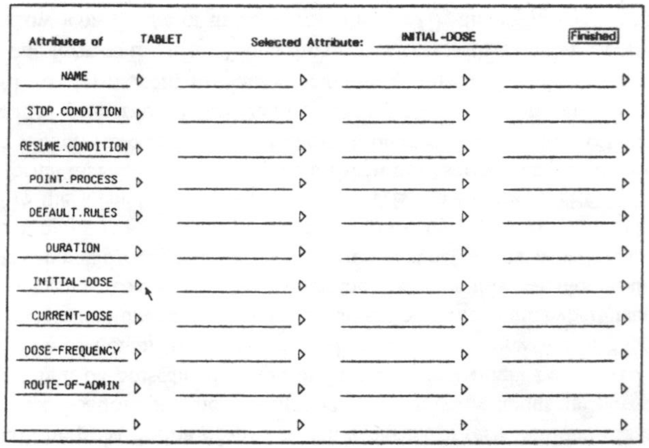

Figure 8. PROTÉGÉ form for attributes of planning entities. This form lists the attributes of the selected class of planning entity—in this case, tablet. PROTÉGÉ enters the first six attributes automatically, as these are common to all classes. The knowledge engineer types in the remainder of the attributes. Selecting one of the arrows causes PROTÉGÉ to display another form that describes the properties of the corresponding attribute.

knowledge engineer's entries are consistent with information that has been stipulated previously. The specifications that the user enters into PROTÉGÉ are stored as n-tuples in a relational database. When the user selects invoke editor from the PROTÉGÉ main menu (see Figure 6), the system queries the database and constructs a knowledge-acquisition tool based on those data that is tailored for the intended application area.

The semantics both of the knowledge engineer's entries into PROTÉGÉ and of the relational-database schema are grounded in the system's predefined model of skeletal-plan refinement. Thus, when a user indicates that hypertension protocols comprise the administration of tablets, tests, and wait periods (as in Figure 7), the intention of these compositional relationships is established by the meaning ascribed to relationships among plan components in the model of skeletal planning. In interacting with PROTÉGÉ, a knowledge engineer consequently uses his understanding of the terms and relationships in the skeletal-planning model to define task-specific concepts in a domain-independent manner.

For each attribute of each task-specific entity that the knowledge engineer describes for PROTÉGÉ (see Figure 8), the engineer must determine how the attribute is associated with a particular distinguishing value and what the data type of that value is. For each such attribute, the knowledge engineer must indicate whether the corresponding value is constant for all instances of that entity. If the value is indeed fixed, then the knowledge engineer simply enters that value into PROTÉGÉ. (For example, the ROUTE-OF-ADMINISTRATION attribute of all instances of antihypertensive tablets has the value oral.) If the value varies depending on circumstances that can be determined only at the time that the skeletal plan is refined, then the knowledge engineer indicates to PROTÉGÉ how the target expert system can ascertain that value at run time. (For example, the CURRENT-DOSE attribute of all tablets has an integer value that the target expert system computes via rules that are invoked

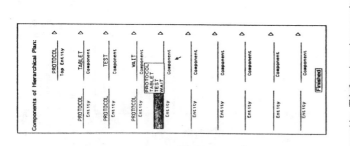

Figure 7. PROTÉGÉ form for planning entities. This form is used to enter the planning entities in an application area and to specify their compositional hierarchy. The knowledge engineer types in the names of the entities using the right column. Before the engineer can type in the name of a new entity, however, he must first identify the "parent" entity of which the new entity is a component. In the hypertension-therapy domain, PROTOCOLS comprise the administration of TABLETs, TESTs, and WAIT periods. Selecting the arrow next to the blank filled in with the word TABLET would open the PROTÉGÉ form in Figure 8.

of information at the next lower level of detail. For example, if the knowledge engineer selects the arrow next to the blank for the TABLET planning entity in Figure 7, PROTÉGÉ will open up a form for editing the attributes of TABLETs (Figure 8). PROTÉGÉ uses just one form to solicit the attributes of all planning entities that the knowledge engineer may define. Because different entities necessarily have different attributes, however, the way that the knowledge engineer fills out the form will depend on the particular entity that the attributes of which are to be entered. When the knowledge engineer selects an arrow next to one of the attributes listed in Figure 8, another PROTÉGÉ form appears for editing the properties of the indicated attribute. Thus, PROTÉGÉ uses a hierarchy of graphical forms that acquire knowledge at increasingly fine levels of granularity. All forms in the system permit the user to return to the more general form from which the current form was invoked by selecting an icon labeled finished.

Whenever possible, PROTÉGÉ allows the user to fill in the necessary blanks by making selections from pop-up menus that the system generates dynamically. This approach not only minimizes the amount of typing that is necessary, but also helps to ensure that the

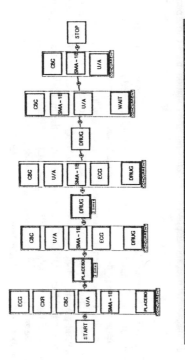

*Figure 9.* HTN flowchart environment. The HTN knowledge-editing tool includes a graphical language with which physicians draw out the sequence of steps in a protocol for antihypertensive drugs. All task-specific features of this language were derived from the explicit task model that knowledge engineers created previously using PROTÉGÉ. Compare this flowchart with the diagram constructed using OPAL in Figure 4.

at the time of each patient consultation.) Alternatively, the value of an attribute may be independent of consultation-related conditions, but contingent on the particular *instance* of the planning entity. (For example, the value of the INITIAL-DOSE attribute of antihypertensive drugs may vary from tablet to tablet, but still may be a constant for any individual tablet instance.) These instance-specific values represent elements of domain knowledge that can be precompiled into the skeletal plans that the target expert system ultimately will refine. The knowledge-acquisition tools that PROTÉGÉ generates allow users to define such instance-specific values for particular application tasks. In entering these values, users of the PROTÉGÉ-generated tools extend the general task model that the knowledge engineer created using PROTÉGÉ, describing individual applications within the task area.

### 5.2. Custom-Tailored Model-Extending Tools

The knowledge-acquisition tools that PROTÉGÉ creates produce as their output usable knowledge bases. These knowledge bases allow an expert-system shell extracted from the ONCOCIN program (called *e-ONCOCIN*) to solve application tasks via the method of skeletal planning. Users of the PROTÉGÉ-generated knowledge-acquisition tools, however, are not required to think in terms of either the structure of these knowledge bases or the skeletal-planning method. Instead, the users view their interactions in terms of the task model developed using PROTÉGÉ. Like OPAL, the tools generated by PROTÉGÉ help their users to create new knowledge bases by facilitating the extension of task models, and thus are intended for use directly by application specialists [Musen 1989c].

The hypertension-therapy model discussed previously has been used by PROTÉGÉ to create a knowledge editor, *HTN*, that allows physicians to construct knowledge bases for hypertension management [Musen 1989a]. The description of planning entities entered into the PROTÉGÉ form in Figure 7, for example, provides the basis for a graphical environment in HTN in which users depict the procedures for carrying out individual hypertension protocols (Figure 9). The model of skeletal-plan refinement built into PROTÉGÉ assumes that effecting any given plan component necessarily entails carrying out a sequence of operations involving instances of plan components at the next level of granularity. Because the task model entered into PROTÉGÉ states that hypertension protocols comprise the administration of tablets, tests, and wait periods (see Figure 7), the HTN user automatically is presented with a flowchart language for indicating how individual hypertension protocols are composed of a sequence of instances of precisely such elements. The domain-independent icons with which the user represents the flow of control (namely, START, STOP, RANDOM-IZE, and DECIDE) and the SUBSCHEMA icon with which he creates graphical subroutines are built into the graphical language; however, the domain-specific icons (namely, TABLET, TEST, and WAIT) are derived from the task model defined at the PROTÉGÉ level. The flowchart shown in Figure 9 describes a typical experimental protocol in which researchers first administer a placebo tablet for three visits, while monitoring the patients' baseline blood pressure. The physicians then prescribe an active antihypertensive drug for several visits, then withhold all medication and observe the patients for any withdrawal effects. Concurrent with this procedure, a number of laboratory investigations are performed at designated intervals.

When knowledge engineers use PROTÉGÉ to generate knowledge-editing tools for other application areas, similar flowcharting environments are created; the task-dependent aspects of those environments, of course, reflect the models created at the PROTÉGÉ level. Unlike the flowchart language in OPAL, the PROTÉGÉ-generated languages can be modified easily by the knowledge engineer. The developer needs only to edit the task model using PROTÉGÉ and then to regenerate the corresponding knowledge editor. The PROTÉGÉ-derived tools transparently convert the flowchart diagrams that users draw on the workstation screen into augmented transition networks (ATNs) that are incorporated within the knowledge bases of the target expert systems. The e-ONCOCIN inference engine uses these ATNs to determine how instances of skeletal-planning entities (for example, specific hypertension protocols) should be refined into their component skeletal plans from one consultation to the next. Thus, the ATN constructed from the flowchart in Figure 9 would specify that, on the first e-ONCOCIN consultation for a particular patient, the *protocol* should be refined to include the administration of an electrocardiogram (ECG), a chest X-ray study (CXR), a complete blood count (CBC), a urinalysis (U/A), and a blood-chemistry panel (SMA-18)—all of which are instances of *tests*—and that the administration of a placebo *tabler* also should occur. On the occasion of the subsequent consultation for the patient, the ATN would indicate that refinement of the *protocol* plan requires only the administration of *placebo*.

In addition to the flowcharting environments, the tools created by PROTÉGÉ incorporate a variety of graphical forms that are much like those in OPAL (see Figure 3). The domain-specific features of the forms in the PROTÉGÉ-generated system, however, are derived from the explicit task models that knowledge engineers create using PROTÉGÉ. Figure 10, for example, shows one of the graphical forms in HTN. This form allows hypertension

PROTÉGÉ-generated tool does not need to be concerned with the often-thorny issues of working out the semantics of such actions; the user merely selects the predefined actions from the menu. The user, however, still must understand and agree to the semantics established by the developers who created the relevant task model in the first place.

### 5.3. The Performance Element: e-ONCOCIN

The e-ONCOCIN shell has been derived from the ONCOCIN cancer-chemotherapy advice system [Tu, et al. 1989] in much the same way that EMYCIN was distilled from the MYCIN program [Buchanan and Shortliffe 1984]. The shell comprises (1) an inference mechanism that instantiates frame hierarchies using methods such as production rules, ATNs, attached procedures, and queries to the expert-system user, (2) a database for storing time-dependent information that was either entered by the end user or concluded by the system during previous consultations [Kahn, Ferguson, Shortliffe, and Fagan 1986], and (3) a graphical user interface that acquires data from the user and that displays the recommendations concluded by the system. The systems created by PROTÉGÉ therefore must deliver to e-ONCOCIN (1) a knowledge base, (2) a database schema, and (3) specifications for constructing the user interface. These three functional components are encoded as a set of objects in an object-oriented programming language [Lane 1986]. Representation of the simple hypertension protocol described in Section 5.2 (see Figures 9 and 10) required HTN to generate 177 objects.

Users interact with e-ONCOCIN much as they do with the original ONCOCIN system [Lane, et al. 1986]. Each time that a consultation is run on a particular case, the user enters data into a time-oriented spreadsheet (Figure 11). Because the complete spreadsheet is typically too large to be displayed on the workstation screen in its entirety, the interface is divided into sections, such that each section refers to a specific class of input data or to a different portion of e-ONCOCIN's recommendation. With the mouse, users select specific sections of the spreadsheet to examine and then enter current input data into the rightmost column of the indicated sections. (The interface makes it convenient for the users to examine data from previous consultations and to review the recommendations that e-ONCOCIN suggested during these past encounters, because the data are displayed chronologically by column.) After all the current data have been entered, e-ONCOCIN completes its refinement of the relevant skeletal plan and displays the system's recommendation in the corresponding portion of the spreadsheet. In Figure 11, the recommendation appears in the sections labeled *tablets* and *tests*.

The e-ONCOCIN system, like any expert-system shell, assumes a particular knowledge-representation syntax (namely, a hierarchy of frames with attached productions rules and ATNs). The semantics of e-ONCOCIN knowledge bases are determined operationally by the behavior that results when the inference engine is applied to those frames, production rules, and ATNs. At the same time, e-ONCOCIN's behavior can be described in terms of the skeletal-planning model that is built into PROTÉGÉ. When a PROTÉGÉ-generated tool is used to build an e-ONCOCIN knowledge base, the tool automatically constructs the frames and other symbols that will cause e-ONCOCIN's activity during a consultation to match the task model that the knowledge engineer first created with PROTÉGÉ and that the application specialist extended using the resultant tool.

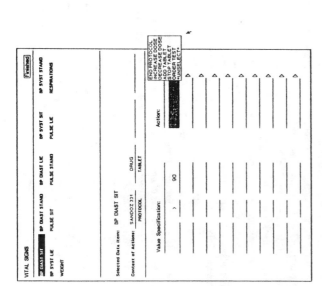

*Figure 10.* HTN form for vital-sign measurements. This form allows physician experts to enter actions to take within hypertension protocols in response to changes in a patient's vital signs. Here, the expert is about to specify actions for e-ONCOCIN to recommend whenever the treating physician notes that a patient's diastolic blood presure (when measured with the patient in the sitting position) is greater than 90 mm Hg. All task-specific features of this form were derived from the explicit task model created at the PROTÉGÉ level. Compare with the OPAL form in Figure 3. (SYST stands for *systolic*; DIAST stands for *diastolic*; STAND, SIT, and LIE indicate whether the patient is standing, sitting, or lying down when the corresponding measurement is taken.)

specialists to indicate how therapy should be modified in response to changes in a patient's vital signs. A list of possible vital-sign measurements that knowledge engineers previously entered into PROTÉGÉ appears at the top of this form. The HTN form in Figure 10 allows physician-experts to indicate actions that e-ONCOCIN should recommend if the end user notes that any of a patient's vital signs (blood pressure, pulse, weight, or respiratory rate) is elevated, depressed, or within a particular range. In the figure, the expert is about to enter the specification that, if a patient's diastolic blood pressure (measured with the patient in the sitting position) is greater than 90 mm Hg, then the dose of the drug that the patient is taking should be increased. (The expert indicates by how much to increase the dose using another form that HTN subsequently displays.) The menu of permitted actions shown in Figure 10 includes choices such as *end protocol*, *add tablet*, and *order test*. When knowledge engineers created the hypertension task model, the meanings of these actions were specified. Although the hypertension-related actions are relatively simple, in domains such as cancer chemotherapy, task actions can be quite complex and can affect a variety of plan components simultaneously [Musen 1989a]. An application specialist who enters knowledge into a

## 6. Discussion

For over 20 years, many workers in AI have viewed knowledge acquisition as a problem in the transfer of expertise. Concentrating on the issue of knowledge transfer, these researchers have tried to identify impediments to successful knowledge acquisition and have suggested that automated tools can help to improve knowledge flow. Historically, the knowledge engineer is perceived as an intermediary who must interview the expert and then transform the expert's rules of thumb into representations that can be interpreted by the computer. Because the knowledge engineer is inexperienced in the application area and because the expert is unable to envision how his knowledge might be captured within the knowledge base, failures in communication are inevitable. In the traditional view, the knowledge-acquisition bottleneck occurs because of these communication difficulties; if the application experts could somehow record their knowledge directly, without having to explain everything to the knowledge engineers, the development and maintenance of knowledge bases would be accelerated.

From the time of TEIRESIAS, the knowledge-acquisition community has struggled to build tools that might allow application specialists to work alone, bypassing the need for knowledge engineers. Although the knowledge-base-maintenance features of TEIRESIAS were never put into practical use, the program set a standard for how most researchers believed automated knowledge-acquisition tools should function. At conferences and in the literature, developers of new tools boast whenever application specialists have been successful in encoding portions of their knowledge without assistance from human intermediaries. Although such examples are laudable, what often is missing from these reports is careful evaluation of the results that have been achieved. It is often impossible to know how to assign credit for a tool's apparent success. What features of the tool, of the application specialist, or of the situations in which the tool was used were most relevant? More important, knowledge entered directly by application specialists themselves is unlikely to be *authentic* (see Section 2.2). Whenever domain experts use knowledge-acquisition tools without the mediating influence of a knowledge engineer, system builders must be willing to accept that the entered knowledge may not reflect the behavior that the experts actually exhibit in practice. Whether the discrepancy significantly degrades the performance of the target expert system almost never is assessed.

OPAL, for example, is a tool that cancer specialists often use alone without the aid of knowledge engineers. Like most knowledge-acquisition programs, there are many aspects of OPAL that never have been evaluated formally. Once the system was put into routine use, however, the obvious rapidity with which oncology protocols could be encoded using OPAL made knowledge engineers unenthusiastic, to say the least, about engaging in academic experiments that required manual knowledge-engineering techniques. At the same time, because the knowledge that users entered into OPAL was never tacit (but rather entailed content know edge about the doses of drugs and the sequencing of chemotherapies), system builders never saw the need to question the authenticity of the physicians' specifications. Indeed, knowledge bases created with OPAL have been shown to achieve expert-level performance [Shwe, et al. 1989].

The acquisition of authentic knowledge becomes an issue when system builders create new task models. It is during this early stage of knowledge acquisition that developers

|  |  | | | | | | | |
|---|---|---|---|---|---|---|---|---|
| **Vital Signs** | BP SYST LIE | | | | | | | |
| | BP SYST SIT | 150 | 156 | 155 | 154 | 140 | 138 | 125 |
| | BP SYST STAND | | | | | | | |
| | BP DIAST LIE | | | | | | | |
| | BP DIAST SIT | 100 | 105 | 103 | 103 | 95 | 92 | 85 |
| | BP DIAST STAND | | | | | | | |
| | PULSE LIE | | | | | | | |
| | PULSE SIT | | | | | | | |
| | PULSE STAND | | | | | | | |
| | RESPIRATIONS | | | | | | | |
| | WEIGHT | | | | | | | |
| **Tablets** | TABLET | PLACEBO | PLACEBO | PLACEBO | | | | |
| | DOSE TO GIVE | 1 | 1 | 1 | | | | |
| | DOSE FREQUENCY | BID | BID | BID | | | | |
| | TIME BETWEEN VISITS | 7 | 7 | 7 | | | | |
| | TABLET | | | DRUG | DRUG | DRUG | DRUG | DRUG |
| | DOSE TO GIVE | | | 1 | 2 | 3 | 3 | 3 |
| | DOSE FREQUENCY | | | BID | BID | BID | BID | BID |
| | TIME BETWEEN VISITS | | | 14 | 14 | 14 | 14 | 14 |
| **Tests** | TEST | ECG | | ECG | | | | ECG |
| | TEST | CXR | | | | | | |
| | TEST | CBC | | CBC | | | | CBC |
| | TEST | U/A | | U/A | | | | U/A |
| | TEST | SMA-18 | | SMA-18 | | | | SMA-18 |
| | Urinalysis | | | | | | | |
| | Hematology | | | | | | | |
| | Adverse Reaction | | | | | | | |
| | Chemistry | | | | | | | |
| **Time** | Day | 12 | 19 | 26 | 2 | 16 | 30 | 13 |
| | Month | Jul | Jul | Jul | Aug | Aug | Aug | Sep |
| | Year | 87 | 87 | 87 | 87 | 87 | 87 | 87 |

*Figure 11.* Interface for e-ONCOCIN expert systems. In addition to a knowledge base describing a particular hypertension protocol, HTN generates a user interface for e-ONCOCIN based both on the general task model entered into PROTÉGÉ and on the specific hypertension protocol entered into HTN. The interface consists of a spreadsheet, with each column representing the occurrence of a different e-ONCOCIN consultation regarding the same patient case. In the figure, the sequence of tablets and tests that have been administered corresponds with the HTN flowchart diagram in Figure 9.

The model of skeletal planning that knowledge engineers extend at the PROTÉGÉ level to create new task models ultimately is constrained by the limitations of the e-ONCOCIN shell. Thus, a plan described with PROTÉGÉ can be refined only in a top-down manner, because the current e-ONCOCIN architecture does not include a general mechanism for performing backtracking to satisfy constraints [Tu, et al. 1989]. Similarly, the input data described at the PROTÉGÉ level must be associated with only discrete time intervals that correspond with elements of past or current plans—a restriction that reflects the semantics of the e-ONCOCIN temporal data model [Kahn, Ferguson, et al. 1986]. Future work in our laboratory to enhance the capabilities of the e-ONCOCIN shell ultimately will allow application refinement of the problem-solving model built into PROTÉGÉ and will expand the applicability of the system. In the absence of a *meta*-metalevel editor to alter PROTÉGÉ's method-specific assumptions, such changes will require manual reprogramming.

forms help to break up a knowledge engineer's entries into manageable portions, and the relationships among the forms emphasize the relationships among the components of the user's specifications. The same advantages in knowledge presentation accrue in model-extending tools as well. Users of programs such as OPAL and those generated by PROTÉGÉ benefit from graphical presentation formats that accentuate the relationships among large numbers of entries and that organize those entries coherently.

PROTÉGÉ offers the additional advantage that users can extend a predefined model of problem solving in two discrete stages. Knowledge engineers first extend a model of skeletal-plan refinement to create a task model. Domain experts then extend that task model (itself an extension of the model of the method) to define individual applications. By viewing knowledge acquisition as the process of task-model formation followed by the process of task-model extension, system builders can think critically about these two phases of the expert-system lifecycle and can identify features of knowledge-acquisition tools best suited for each phase. Rather than concentrating on whether the need for knowledge engineers has been obviated by a particular tool—and implicitly assuming that eliminating the knowledge engineers is a necessary and sufficient metric of success—developers can consider the *roles* that knowledge engineers might play in helping application specialists to build models. The knowledge engineer should be regarded as a potential partner, rather than as an inherent marplot, allowing workers in AI to develop more effective strategies for acquiring and representing the tacit knowledge that separates experts from novices. At the same time, by recognizing the ease with which application specialists can enter the content knowledge that extends pre-existing models, developers can build tools such as OPAL that experts can indeed use independently.

The PROTÉGÉ system demonstrates a divide-and-conquer strategy that separates the model-building work that application specialists best perform with the aid of knowledge engineers from the model-extending work that application specialists easily can perform independently. At the PROTÉGÉ level, knowledge engineers work with domain experts to build models of tasks that can be solved using the method of skeletal-plan refinement. These models can then be used as the foundation for custom-tailored knowledge-editing tools. PROTÉGÉ is used to map out the structure of the task and, consequently, the *process* by which a problem solver might arrive at a recommendation. The tools that PROTÉGÉ generates, on the other hand, acquire knowledge about the *content* of specific plans. Although these two phases of knowledge acquisition sometimes may be strictly sequential in nature, attempts to enter content knowledge frequently point out deficiencies in the initial task model; PROTÉGÉ's division of labor allows knowledge engineers to alter the task model easily whenever application specialists encounter problems during their model-extension work. (With OPAL, changes to the task model always required cumbersome reprogramming of LISP code.)

The decision regarding the optimum way to separate task knowledge into a fixed, reusable portion and a variable, application-specific portion is an important judgment that all PROTÉGÉ users must face. The declaration of the classes of entities in the domain and the attributes of those entities is necessarily part of the task model entered into PROTÉGÉ. The values of those attributes, however, may either be predefined as part of the task model (or have predefined methods by which the attributes' values may be concluded) or be identified as content knowledge to be entered by the user of the tool that PROTÉGÉ generates.

formulate their initial theories of how experts solve problems. It is also during this early stage that knowledge engineers—and computer-based tools—can greatly facilitate the modeling process.

Many workers in AI have described expert-system knowledge bases as unstructured collections of rules that correspond with the problem-solving heuristics actually used by experts. In this traditional view, the rules are considered to be modular and independent; each rule thus lacks relationships with other rules in the knowledge base and is devoid of any preordained role in problem solving. Recently, however, the elucidation of heuristic classification [Clancey 1985] and of other problem-solving methods [Chandrasekaran 1986; McDermott 1988] has provided an alternative perspective that offers much more guidance to the programmers who develop and maintain complex knowledge bases. In this new light, expert-system behavior need not be caused by the seemingly random results of one "modular" rule triggering the invocation of another; rather, such behavior can result from the application of coherent, domain-independent strategies. Emphasizing these problem-solving methods allows sytem builders to clarify the roles that elicited knowledge plays in arriving at a task solution and provides a structure by which to direct further knowledge-elicitation work. The use of an explicit model of problem solving (such as that of heuristic classification) when creating the incipient task model in no way guarantees that knowledge engineers will obtain authentic knowledge from application specialists. The model's framework simply helps system builders to structure the elicited knowledge and to determine where there still may be gaps.

Models of problem-solving methods vary in the assumptions that they make about the tasks to which the method can be applied. Very general methods, such as heuristic classification, make few assumptions and, therefore, have tremendous applicability. A great many diagnostic tasks and plan-selection operations, for example, can be represented as extensions of the heuristic-classification model. The generality of the model, however, limits the structure that the heuristic-classification model can impose on the way that knowledge engineers represent domain tasks. There is a direct tradeoff between the applicability of a problem-solving model and the guidance that the model can provide for system builders. The more specialized, less widely applicable models incorporated within programs such as MOLE [Eshelman 1988] and SALT [Marcus 1988] have, in practice, been more helpful to developers attempting to structure domain tasks than have more abstract models such as heuristic classification. The advantage of the more specialized models is that they provide greater assistance in distinguishing the different ways in which a problem solver may use domain knowledge to arrive at a solution. To apply these more detailed models, however, system builders must be able to foresee whether a proposed method will be successful in addressing the task at hand, or whether that method will prove to be too restrictive.

Models of problem solving, when embodied within a computer-based tool, are much more useful to system developers than are models that are mapped out only on paper. The ability to translate a user's extensions of the model into machine-readable knowledge bases is an obvious advantage. A more subtle, but perhaps more important, benefit arises because automated tools can facilitate the presentation of complex systems. The graphical forms in PROTÉGÉ, for example, group together related data and emphasize the relationships entered by the user. Each transition from one form to another moves the user's view of the task model that he is creating to a different level within an abstraction hierarchy. The

Whether an attribute's value should be considered a constant element of the task model or part of the application-specific content knowledge is determined by the nature of the task domain and by the role that attribute plays in problem solving.

Although demonstrated within the context of the skeletal-planning method, the PROTÉGÉ approach also should apply to other methods of problem solving. For example, if the system were adapted for an inference engine that is well-suited for solving problems using heuristic classification (such as EMYCIN), knowledge engineers then would use PROTÉGÉ to create models of classification tasks, rather than models of planning tasks. A knowledge engineer, for instance, might use PROTÉGÉ to describe the set of classification problems that is encountered during geological mineral exploration, as was done in the Prospector system [Reboh 1981]. A knowledge-acquisition tool generated by PROTÉGÉ then could be used by expert geologists to enter specific ore-deposit models. The ore-deposit models could be converted to knowledge bases for expert systems that workers in the field would use to determine the most favorable drilling sites for particular minerals.

Where there are multiple, related tasks within an application area—and when there is thus the need to construct multiple knowledge bases—the PROTÉGÉ approach offers a considerable advantage. The difficult problem of creating a computational model of the domain task does not disappear; the need for knowledge engineers to help application specialists to build such a model does not disappear either. Nevertheless, the methodology allows system builders to confront only a single bottleneck. If knowledge engineers and domain experts first use tools such as PROTÉGÉ to build the required task models, those experts then can go to work on their own, extending those task models to define multiple knowledge bases. The models incorporated within the tools that PROTÉGÉ generates, however, may not always account for all the professional behaviors that system builders ultimately may observe in an application area. When the user of a PROTÉGÉ-generated tool is unable to extend the given task model to specify a required action (that is, if he must unexpectedly describe an entity that is not within the original model), the task model may have to be augmented at the PROTÉGÉ level.

Like natural theories that are proposed, tested, and revised, the models constructed by knowledge-acquisition tools display a distinct life cycle. Workers in AI have built a variety of tools, each addressing different aspects of this modeling process. Tools such as ROGET assist developers with the initial model-building phase when the task still may be ill defined. Tools such as OPAL aid in the final model-extending phase, when the task area is well understood and end users require multiple, related knowledge bases. The new challenge is to integrate these approaches, allowing model building to be followed by model extension, providing continuous assistance from the time that the application task is first identified to the time that the final knowledge base is disseminated to end users.

PROTÉGÉ is the first step toward that integration. Workers in AI, however, have not yet identified an optimal technology for acquiring knowledge for expert systems, and even less is known about acquiring domain knowledge for the purposes of building knowledge-acquisition tools. Consequently, there will be substantial opportunities for research as the PROTÉGÉ approach is broadened to other task areas, to other problem-solving methods, and to other knowledge-system architectures. In the process of expanding the techniques demonstrated by PROTÉGÉ, we shall be able to learn more about the structure and applicability of new problem-solving methods and about the modeling of domain tasks.

## Acknowledgments

Development of OPAL and PROTÉGÉ was supported in part by grants LM-07033 and LM-04420 from the National Library of Medicine. Computing facilities were provided by the SUMEX-AIM resource under NIH grant RR-00785. Lyn Dupré, Tom Gruber, and Sandra Marcus provided valuable comments on an earlier draft of this paper.

## Notes

1. We also could refer to each situation in which the model applies as an *instantiation*, although many authors reserve that word for descriptions of symbols within a knowledge-representation language. In this paper, therefore, I use the term *extension*.

## References

Addis, T.R. 1987. A framework for knowledge elicitation. In *Proceedings of the First European Workshop on Knowledge Acquisition for Knowledge-Based Systems*, Reading University, Reading, England.

Anderson, J.R 1987. Skill acquisition: Compilation of weak-method problem solutions. *Psychological Review*, 94: 192-210.

Belkin, N.J., Brooks, H.M., and Daniels, P.J. 1987. Knowledge elicitation using discourse analysis. *International Journal of Man-Machine Studies*, 27: 127-144.

Bennett, J.S. 1985. ROGET: A knowledge-based system for acquiring the conceptual structure of a diagnostic expert system. *Journal of Automated Reasoning*, 1: 49-74.

Boose 1989. A survey of knowledge acquisition techniques and tools. *Knowledge Acquisition*, 1: 3-37.

Breuker, J., and Wielinga, B. 1987. Use of models in the interpretation of verbal data. In A.L. Kidd (Ed.), *Knowledge acquisition for expert systems: A practical handbook*. London: Plenum.

Buchanan, B.G., and Shortliffe, E.H. 1984. *Rule-based expert systems: The MYCIN experiments of the Stanford heuristic programming project*. Reading, MA: Addison-Wesley.

Chandrasekaran, B. 1986. Generic tasks for knowledge-based reasoning: High-level building blocks for expert system design. *IEEE Expert, 1*: 23-30.

Clancey, W.J. 1985. Heuristic classification. *Artificial Intelligence, 27*: 289-350.

Clancey, W.J. 1986. Viewing knowledge bases as qualitative models. (Technical Report KSL-86-27). Stanford. CA: Knowledge Systems Laboratory, Stanford University.

Cleaves, D.A. 1987. Cognitive biases and corrective techniques: Proposals for improving elicitation procedures for knowledge-based systems. *International Journal of Man-Machine Studies, 27*: 155-166.

Conklin, J. 1987. Hypertext: An introduction and survey. *Computer. 20*: 17-41.

Cooke, N.M., and McDonald, J.E. 1987. The application of psychological scaling techniques to knowledge elicitation for knowledge-based systems. *International Journal of Man-Machine Studies, 26*: 533-550.

Davis, R. 1976. *Applications of Meta Level Knowledge to the Construction, Maintenance, and Use of Large Knowledge Eases*. Ph.D. thesis, Technical Report STAN-CS-76-564. Stanford University, Stanford, CA.

Ericsson, K.A. and Simon. H.A. 1984. *Protocol analysis: Verbal reports as data*. Cambridge, MA: MIT Press.

Eshelman. L. 1988. MOLE: A knowledge-acquisition system for cover-and-differentiate systems. In S. Marcus (Ed.), *Automating knowledge acquisition for expert systems*. Boston: Kluwer Academic Publishers.

Fitts, P.M. 1964. Perceptual-motor skill learning. In A. Melton (Ed.), *Categories of human learning*. New York: Academic Press.

Fodor, J.A. 1968. The appeal of tacit knowledge in psychological explanation. *Journal of Philosophy. 65*: 627-640.

Friedland, P.E 1979. *Knowledge-Based Experiment Design in Molecular Genetics*. Ph.D. thesis. Technical Report STAN-CS-79-771. Stanford University, Stanford, CA.

Silverman, H.A. 1975. *A digitalis therapy advisor.* (Technical Report MAC/TR-143). Cambridge, MA: Massachusetts Institute of Technology.

Slovic, P., and Lichtenstein, S. 1971. Comparison of Bayesian and regression approaches to the study of information processing in judgment. *Organizational Behavior and Human Performance, 6:* 649–744.

Shwe, M.A., Tu, S.W., and Fagan, L.M. 1989. Validating the knowledge base of a therapy-planning system. *Methods of Information in Medicine, 28:* 36–50.

Swartout, W.R. 1981. *Producing Explanations and Justifications of Expert Consulting Programs,* Ph.D. thesis. Technical Report MIT/LCS/TR-251, Massachusetts Institute of Technology.

Tu, S.W., Kahn, M.G., Musen, M.A., Ferguson, J.C., Shortliffe, E.H., and Fagan, L.M. 1989. Episodic monitoring of time-oriented data for heuristic skeletal-plan refinement. *Communications of the ACM,* in press.

Winograd, T., and Flores, F. 1986. *Understanding Computers and Cognition: A New Foundation for Design.* Norwood, NJ: Ablex.

Friedland, P.E., and Iwasaki, Y. 1985. The concept and implementation of skeletal plans. *Journal of Automated Reasoning, 1:* 161–208.

Freiling, M.J., and Alexander, J.H. 1984. Diagrams and grammars: Tools for mass producing expert systems. In *The First Conference on Artificial Intelligence Applications* (pp. 537–543). Denver, CO: IEEE Computer Society Press.

Gale, W.A. 1987. Knowledge-based knowledge acquisition for a statistical consulting system. *International Journal of Man-Machine Studies, 13:* 81–116.

Johnson, P.E. 1983. What kind of expert should a system be? *Journal of Medicine and Philosophy, 8:* 77–97.

Kahn, G., Nowlan, S., and McDermott, J. 1985. Strategies for knowledge acquisition. *IEEE Transactions on Pattern Analysis and Machine Intelligence. PAMI-7:* 511–522.

Kahn, M.G., Ferguson, J.C., Shortliffe, E.H., and Fagan, L.M. 1985. Representation and use of temporal information in ONCOCIN. In *Proceedings of the Ninth Annual Symposium on Computer Applications in Medical Care.* Baltimore, MD: IEEE Computer Society Press.

Kitto, C.M. 1989. Progress in automated knowledge acquisition tools: How close are we to replacing the knowledge engineer? *Knowledge Acquisition,* in press.

Klinker, G. 1988. KNACK: Sample-driven knowledge acquisition for reporting systems. In S. Marcus (Ed.), *Automating knowledge acquisition for expert systems.* Boston: Kluwer Academic Publishers.

LaBerge, D., and Samuels, S.J. 1974. Toward a theory of automatic information processing in reading. *Cognitive Psychology, 6:* 293–323.

Lane, C.D. 1986. *Ozone reference manual.* (Technical Report KSL-86-40). Stanford, CA: Knowledge Systems Laboratory, Stanford University.

Lane, C.D., Walton, J.D., and Shortliffe, E.H. 1986. Graphical access to medical expert systems: II. Design of an interface for physicians. *Methods of Information in Medicine, 25:* 143–150.

Lyons, W. 1986. *The disappearance of introspection.* Cambridge, MA: MIT Press.

Marcus, S. 1988. SALT: A knowledge acquisition tool for propose-and-revise systems. In S. Marcus (Ed.), *Automating knowledge acquisition for expert systems.* Boston: Kluwer Academic Publishers.

McCarthy, J. 1968. Programs with common sense. In M. Minsky (Ed.), *Semantic information processing,* Cambridge, MA: MIT Press.

McDermott, J. 1988. Preliminary steps toward a taxonomy of problem-solving methods. In S. Marcus (Ed.), *Automating knowledge acquisition for expert systems.* Boston: Kluwer Academic Publishers.

Meyer, M.A., Mniszewski, S.M., and Peaslee, A. 1989. Use of three minimally-biasing elicitation techniques for knowledge acquisition. *Knowledge Acquisition, 1:* 59–71.

Michalski, R.S., and Chilausky, R.L. 1980. Knowledge acquisition by encoding expert rules versus computer induction from examples: A case study involving soybean pathology. *International Journal of Man-Machine Studies, 12:* 63–87.

Musen, M.A., Fagan, L.M., Combs, D.M., and Shortliffe, E.H. 1987. Use of a domain model to drive an interactive knowledge-editing tool. *International Journal of Man-Machine Studies, 26:* 105–121.

Musen, M.A., Fagan, L.M., and Shortliffe, E.H. 1988. Graphical specification of procedural knowledge for an expert system. In J. Hendler (Ed.), *Expert systems: The user interface.* Norwood, NJ: Ablex.

Musen, M.A. 1989a. *Automated generation of model-based knowledge-acquisition tools.* London: Pitman.

Musen, M.A. 1989b. An editor for the conceptual models of interactive knowledge-acquisition tools. *International Journal of Man-Machine Studies,* in press.

Musen, M.A. 1989c. Conceptual models of interactive knowledge-acquisition tools. *Knowledge Acquisition, 1:* 73–88.

Newell, A. 1982. The knowledge level. *Artificial Intelligence, 18:* 87–127.

Nisbett, R.E., and Wilson, T.D. 1977. Telling more than we can know: Verbal reports on mental processes. *Psychological review, 84:* 231–259.

Reboh, R. 1981. *Knowledge engineering techniques and tools in the Prospector environment.* (Technical Report 243). Menlo Park, CA: SRI International.

Regoczei, S., and Plantinga, E.P.O. 1987. Creating the domain of discourse: Ontology and inventory. *International Journal of Man-Machine Studies, 27:* 235–250.

Rumelhart, D.E., and Norman, D.A. 1983. *Representation in memory.* (Technical Report CHIP 116). San Diego, La Jolla, CA: Center for Human Information Processing, University of California.

Machine Learning, 4, 293-336 (1989)
© 1989 Kluwer Academic Publishers. Boston. Manufactured in The Netherlands.

# Automated Knowledge Acquisition for Strategic Knowledge

THOMAS R. GRUBER GRUBER@SUMEX-AIM.STANFORD.EDU
*Knowledge Systems Laboratory, Computer Science Department, Stanford University, Stanford, CA 94305*

**Abstract.** *Strategic knowledge* is used by an agent to decide what action to perform next, where actions have consequences external to the agent. This article presents a computer-mediated method for acquiring strategic knowledge. The general knowledge acquisition problem and the special difficulties of acquiring strategic knowledge are analyzed in terms of *representation mismatch*: the difference between the form in which knowledge is available from the world and the form required for knowledge systems. ASK is an interactive knowledge acquisition tool that elicits strategic knowledge from people in the form of *justifications* for action choices and generates *strategy rules* that operationalize and generalize the expert's advice. The basic approach is demonstrated with a human-computer dialog in which ASK acquires strategic knowledge for medical diagnosis and treatment. The rationale for and consequences of specific design decisions in ASK are analyzed, and the scope of applicability and limitations of the approach are assessed. The paper concludes by discussing the contribution of knowledge representation to automated knowledge acquisition.

**Key Words.** knowledge acquisition, knowledge engineering, human-computer interaction, strategic knowledge, knowledge representation

## 1. Introduction

Knowledge acquisition is the transfer and transformation of knowledge from the forms in which it is available in the world into forms that can be used by a knowledge system (adapted from [Buchanan, et al. 1983]). In the context of this article, knowledge in the world comes from people and knowledge in the system is implemented with formal symbol structures—knowledge representations. Knowledge acquisition is a multifaceted problem that encompasses many of the technical problems of knowledge engineering, the enterprise of building knowledge systems. Deciding what knowledge can be used by a program, how to represent it, and then eliciting it from people and encoding it in a knowledge base are all aspects of the knowledge acquisition problem. The inherent difficulty of these tasks makes knowledge acquisition a fundamental obstacle to the widespread use of knowledge system technology.

The research reported here addresses the problem of acquiring strategic knowledge from people. In particular, the article presents an approach by which an interactive computer program assists with the knowledge acquisition process. The general term *automated knowledge acquisition* refers to computer-mediated elicitation and encoding of knowledge from people.

The first section of this article provides a theoretical analysis of the general knowledge acquisition problem and introduces the problem of acquiring strategic knowledge. Section 2 reviews the techniques of automated knowledge acquisition in terms of the theoretical framework developed in the first section and motivates the present work. Section 3 describes the automated knowledge acquisition tool called ASK. Section 4 demonstrates the program with a human-computer dialog. Sections 5, 6, and 7 provide an analysis of the scope of applicability, assumptions, and limitations of the system, and a discussion of key design decisions. A concluding section summarizes the contribution of the design of knowledge representations to the development of knowledge acquisition tools.

### 1.1. The Knowledge Acquisition Problem as Representation Mismatch

Most knowledge systems are built by knowledge engineers rather than by the domain experts who provide the knowledge. A long-standing goal of a course of knowledge acquisition research has been to replace the knowledge engineer with a program that assists in the direct "transfer of expertise" from experts to knowledge bases [Davis 1976]. Yet the problem has eluded a general solution; no existing knowledge acquisition program can build a knowledge system directly from experts' descriptions of what they do.

Why is knowledge acquisition difficult to automate? It seems that the "transfer" metaphor is misleading. Clearly, the form in which knowledge is available from people (e.g., descriptions in natural language) is different from the form in which knowledge is represented in knowledge systems. The difference between the two forms of knowledge, called *representation mismatch* [Buchanan, et al. 1983], is central to the problem of knowledge acquisition. Because of representation mismatch, one cannot merely transfer knowledge from human to machine. The knowledge acquisition tool must actively elicit knowledge in a form that can be obtained from domain experts and map elicited knowledge into the executable representations of the knowledge system. The mapping is difficult to automate because the requirements for building a working system (e.g., operationality, consistency) differ from the requirements for a human expert describing a procedure to another person. In order to automate knowledge acquisition, one must provide a method for overcoming representation mismatch.

The following discussion introduces three aspects of representation mismatch—modeling, operationalization, and generalization—as an explanatory framework with which to understand the problem of knowledge acquisition. The general issues and the specific problems of acquiring strategic knowledge are described within this framework.

*1.1.1. Dimensions of Representation Mismatch* The *modeling* or formalization problem is a fundamental kind of representation mismatch. A knowledge system can be thought of as a qualitative model of systems in the world, including systems of intelligent activity [Clancey 1989]. While the model embodied by a knowledge system is informed by the behavior of human experts, it is not designed as a model of the experts' knowledge or their cognitive processes [Winograd and Flores 1986]. From this point of view, knowledge acquisition is a creative rather than imitative activity, resulting in a computational model that makes distinctions and abstractions not present in the initial language of the expert. Because of the difference between descriptions of behavior and computational models of action, the task of knowledge acquisition requires a model-building effort beyond that of rendering the expert's utterances in formal notation. Morik [1988] illustrates the modeling problem with the example of building a natural language-understanding system. The builder of such a system does not interview experts in natural language understanding (native speakers) but experts in modeling the formal structure and mechanisms of language (linguists). Furthermore, the system-builder must adapt the expert's concepts (a theory of syntax) to the needs of a computational model (a parser) and sometimes invent new concepts (semantic networks).

The *operationalization* aspect of representation mismatch refers to the difference between descriptions of what the system should accomplish, given by domain experts, and the operational methods for achieving those objectives required by a computer program. Two senses of operationalization have been identified in the machine learning literature: making advice executable [Mostow 1983] or more useful [Keller 1988].[1] Knowledge acquisition involves both kinds of operationalization in the service of performance goals such as recommending an effective drug therapy or designing an efficient electric motor. To make a therapy recommendation executable, a knowledge engineer might build an interface that justifies a recommendation and requests the results. To make the advice "minimize cost, maximize speed" more useful, the engineer might decide to use a redesign algorithm and elicit more knowledge from the expert about ways to cut costs and fine tune performance by modifying existing designs. The methods in which expert-supplied specifications are operationalized may require concepts and terminology unfamiliar to the domain expert.

A third dimension of representation mismatch is *generalization*: the difference between a set of specific examples of desired input/output performance and a more concise representation that will enable a system to perform correctly on a larger class of input situations. It is frequently observed that it is much easier to elicit examples of expert problem solving than general rules or procedures that cover the examples. The available form of knowledge (classified examples) needs to be mapped into a more useful representation (general class descriptions).

Problems of modeling, operationalization, and generalization are ubiquitous in knowledge acquisition. We will now see how they are manifest in the case of a particular kind of knowledge, strategic knowledge.

*1.2. The Problem of Acquiring Strategic Knowledge*

*1.2.1. Strategic Knowledge.* *Strategic knowledge* is knowledge used by an agent to decide what action to perform next, where actions can have consequences external to the agent. The more general term *control knowledge* refers to knowledge used to decide what to do next. What constitutes an action and its consequences depends on how one characterizes what the agent can *do*. For knowledge systems that make recommendations to people (e.g., "increase dosage of drug D") or control physical systems (e.g., "close valve V"), actions have consequences that are observable in the world outside of the agent. For problem-solving programs based on state–space search, an action may be the firing of a rule or an operator. For such an agent, *search-control knowledge* is used to choose internal actions that increase the likelihood of reaching a solution state and improve the speed of computation. The research reported here distinguishes knowledge for deciding among actions with consequences in the external world because the goal is to acquire strategic knowledge from domain experts without reference to the symbol-level organization of the knowledge system.

For descriptive purposes, strategic knowledge is also distinguished from the *substantive knowledge* of a domain, knowledge about what is believed to be true in the world. Both substantive and strategic knowledge underlie expertise in many domains. For example, a robot uses substantive knowledge to recognize and interpret situations in the world (e.g., an obstacle in its path) and strategic knowledge to decide what to do (to go around or over it). A lawyer uses substantive knowledge to identify the relevant features of cases and strategic knowledge to decide which case to cite in defense of an argument. A diagnostician uses substantive knowledge to evaluate evidence pro and con hypotheses and uses strategic knowledge to decide among therapeutic actions. In general, substantive knowledge is used to identify relevant states of the world, and strategic knowledge is used to evaluate the utility of possible actions given a state.

*1.2.2. Representation Mismatch for Strategic Knowledge*    Although progress has been made in automating the acquisition of substantive knowledge used in classification [e.g., Bareiss 1989; Boose and Bradshaw 1987; Eshelman 1988], strategic knowledge is typically imparted to systems by knowledge engineers using implementation-level mechanisms. The difficulty of acquiring strategic knowledge directly from experts can be seen within the framework of the three aspects of representation mismatch introduced earlier.

First, strategic knowledge presents serious modeling problems. While substantive knowledge might be acquired in a perspicuous form, such as rules mapping evidence to hypotheses, strategic knowledge about choosing actions is often represented with programming constructs, such as procedures or agenda mechanisms. At least in principle, rules that encode substantive knowledge can be written in a process-independent context; experts can specify how to classify situations in the world without worrying about the mechanism by which the specifications are interpreted. However, specifying knowledge that affects the order and choice of actions involves building a computational model of a process.

Consider the problem of modeling the strategy of a medical *workup*: the process of gathering data, assessing the results, and planning treatment for an individual patient. Although medical diagnosis is often described as a static classification problem (i.e., to classify *given* data), in medical practice evidence for a diagnosis is gathered over time, and the actions that produce evidence are chosen strategically. In modeling the workup, requests for patient data, laboratory tests, diagnostic procedures, and options for trial therapy are treated as actions. Substantive knowledge is used for the classification task, identifying likely causes for a given set of findings. In addition, strategic knowledge is used to decide what action to take next when the data are not all in.

In the MYCIN system, much of the knowledge that determined question ordering and decisions about laboratory tests was represented with screening clauses, clause ordering, and "certainty factor engineering"—implementation-level manipulations of the rules to achieve the intended strategic behavior [Clancey 1983a]. This knowledge could not be acquired easily with the available rule editors and debugging support tools [Buchanan and Shortliffe 1984] because the strategy was implicit in the engineering tricks rather than the content of the rules. Since MYCIN, more explicit representations of strategic knowledge have been devised, such as the control blocks of S.1 [Erman, Scott, and London 1984] and the high-level control languages of BB1 [Hayes-Roth, et al. 1987]. Because these advances are general-purpose languages for control, rendering strategic knowledge in a computational model remains a programming task.

The acquisition of strategic knowledge also highlights the operationalization aspect of representation mismatch. At the *knowledge level* [Newell 1982], the strategic knowledge of an agent may be specified as a set of behavioral goals that the agent should attempt to achieve. While it is possible to elicit specifications of desired behavior at the knowledge level from experts, it is far more difficult for experts (and knowledge engineers) to specify *how* a knowledge system should achieve these goals.

For example, during conventional knowledge acquisition for a knowledge system called MUM [Cohen, et al. 1987], knowledge engineers interviewed a practicing physician for the purpose of modeling his diagnostic strategy for patients reporting chest and abdominal pain. MUM's task was to *generate* workups for chest pain patients, choosing one action at a time, waiting for the outcome of previous action. When asked to describe how to choose diagnostic tests, the expert would mention goals such as "do the cheap, quick tests first" and "protect the patient against a dangerous disease." This is nonoperational advice. To make it operational requires specifying how actions achieve goals (e.g., the diagnostic and therapeutic effect of actions), how to determine the currently relevant goals (e.g., when is a dangerous disease suspected), and how to balance competing objectives (e.g., cost, timeliness, diagnostic power, therapeutic value).

Third, the generalization aspect of representation mismatch is exhibited by the problem of acquiring strategic knowledge. By definition, experts are good at what they do; it does not follow that they are good at generalizing what they do. In particular, it is much easier to elicit *cases* of strategic decisions—choices among actions in specific situations—than to elicit general strategies.

For example, in the MUM domain of chest pain workups, the physician makes a series of decisions about actions. He typically starts with a set of questions about patient history, then performs a physical examination (in a knowledge system, steps in the examination are also implemented as requests for data), and then plans and executes a series of diagnostic tests and trial therapeutic actions, until sufficient evidence for a conclusive diagnosis or recommended therapy has been found. For MUM it was feasible to elicit example workups corresponding to actual patients. These workups can be viewed as very specific plans. Each step in the workup, each choice of what to ask to try next, is the result of a strategic decision. However, generalizations about classes of strategic decisions were not present in the original workup descriptions but developed by retrospective analysis of the cases and followup consultation with the expert. Within a single workup there may be several actions chosen for the same reasons (e.g., "do the cheap, quick tests first"), and there may be common reasons across workups (e.g., "gather enough evidence to recommend therapy").

Although cases of specific workups can be acquired in the form of directed graphs, they are not general enough for a knowledge system. First, they are specific to individual patients, and workups differ over individuals. Second, these plan-like procedures are extremely brittle; if any action cannot be taken (e.g., because the results of a test are not available), then the procedures fail. Third, because they only record the results of strategic decisions, workup graphs fail to capture the underlying reasons for selecting actions in the prescribed order. This third problem reveals a subtle form of representation mismatch: although it is possible to elicit reasons for past strategic decisions, these reasons alone do not constitute a *generative* strategy. A generative strategy plans new workups based on the strategic knowledge that gave rise to existing workups.

The work reported in this article is motivated by the problem of acquiring knowledge that underlies strategic decisions and putting it in operational, general form. The next section lays out some of the techniques for addressing the problem.

## 2. Techniques for Overcoming Representation Mismatch

Interactive tools can assist with knowledge acquisition by overcoming representation mismatch. This section reviews the techniques used by existing knowledge acquisition tools and motivates the approach taken in ASK. The techniques are presented in the context of the three aspects of representation mismatch.

### 2.1. Incorporating Models into Knowledge Acquisition Tools

Conventionally, the modeling problem for knowledge acquisition is handled by the knowledge engineer, who is responsible for building the knowledge system. The engineer analyzes the *performance task* (the problem to be solved by the knowledge system) and designs a program for applying knowledge to perform the task. A performance task is defined in terms of the input and output requirements of the system and the knowledge that is available. Tasks can be described at multiple levels of abstraction, from the functional specifications for a single application to input/output requirements for a general class of tasks. A *problem solving method* is the technique by which a knowledge system brings specific knowledge to bear on the task. When the computational requirements and methods for a *class* of tasks are well understood, a domain-independent problem-solving method can be designed, such as heuristic classification [Chandrasekaran 1983; Clancey 1985].

A *task-level architecture* consists of a knowledge representation language (a set of representational primitives) and a procedure implementing the problem-solving method designed to support knowledge systems for a class of performance tasks [Chandrasekaran 1986; Gruber and Cohen 1987]. The procedure, which in this article is called the *method* for short, is a mechanism by which knowledge stated in the architecture's knowledge representation is applied to perform one of the tasks in the abstract class of tasks for which the architecture is designed. The representation and the method of a task-level architecture are tightly coupled. Each method defines *roles* for knowledge: ways in which knowledge is applied by the method [McDermott 1988]. The algorithm that implements the method in a program operates on statements in the associated representation language. The primitive terms in the representation correspond to the roles of knowledge. For example, Chandrasekaran [1987] and his colleagues have built architectures for *generic tasks* such as hierarchical classification and routine design. Each generic task is described in terms of the function to be performed (an abstract description of the performance task), a knowledge representation language (the set of primitive terms), and a control strategy (the procedure that implements the method). Chandrasekaran uses the term *generic task problem solvers* to refer to task-level architectures. Task-level architectures can facilitate knowledge acquisition. Like a virtual machine, the architecture supports a set of method-specific representation primitives for building a knowledge system. Much of the model-building effort can be put into the design of the architecture, and the representational primitives can hide the implementation details. As a consequence, the architecture can reduce representation mismatch by presenting a task-level representation language comprehensible to the domain expert [Bylander and Chandrasekaran 1987; Gruber and Cohen 1987; Musen 1989].

Interactive knowledge acquisition tools can help overcome representation mismatch by employing special techniques for eliciting and analyzing knowledge in architecture-supported representations. Some tools help analyze the task requirements to choose among existing methods and instantiate an architecture with domain terminology. For example, ROGET [Bennett 1985] offers help in choosing among a small set of particular heuristic classification methods and elicits domain-specific instantiations of the input, output, and intermediate concepts for the selected method.

Other tools specialize in eliciting the knowledge for the roles required by the problem-solving method. For example MOLE [Eshelman 1988] uses an instantiation of the heuristic classification method called cover-and-differentiate. The knowledge acquisition tool specializes in the elicitation of knowledge for roles such as "covering knowledge" and "differentiating knowledge." Similarly, SALT [Marcus 1988] is based on the propose-and-revise method for constructive problem solving, and elicits knowledge for proposing design extensions, identifying constraints, and backtracking from violated constraints.

Tools of another category specialize in a particular formulation of knowledge, independent of how the knowledge will be applied to particular tasks. For example, repertory grid tools elicit knowledge in the form of a two-dimensional matrix of weighted associations between "elements" and "traits" [Boose and Bradshaw 1987; Shaw and Gaines 1987]. These tools use a task-independent elicitation technique to help the user identify traits and elements and the strengths of associations among them and provides detailed analyses of the information. The user interprets the feedback in terms of a particular task, such as a procurement decision or an evaluation of policy alternatives.

On the other end of the spectrum are elicitation tools that are customized to the problem-solving method and a specific task in a domain. An example is OPAL, which acquires protocols used in the domain of cancer therapy [Musen, Fagan, Combs, and Shortliffe 1987]. The problem-solving method is a kind of skeletal-plan refinement, and the performance task is to manage cancer-therapy protocols modeled as skeletal plans. OPAL elicits knowledge from experts entirely in domain-specific terms and in forms that correspond to paper and pencil representations familiar to the experts. Because the tool has almost completely eliminated the representation mismatch due to modeling, it has been used successfully by physicians with little experience with computation [Musen 1989].

The acquisition of strategic knowledge, as it has been defined, is not supported by conventional task-level architectures. In fact, all of the built-in methods of the architectures mentioned above are implemented with procedures that themselves encode a control strategy. To the extent that the strategy is implemented by the method, it cannot be acquired by tools that assume the method is fixed.

However, it is possible to design an architecture for a restricted class of tasks that require domain-specific strategic knowledge. The method for such an architecture should define roles for strategic knowledge, just as MOLE's method defines roles for substantive knowledge, such as knowledge for proposing explanations that cover an abnormal symptom. As will be described in Section 3, ASK was designed with an architecture that represents

strategic knowledge as rules that map situations to desired actions. In this architecture, strategic knowledge is limited to three roles for associating features in the agent's current model of the world with classes of appropriate actions. As will be discussed in Section 6, the restricted roles for strategic knowledge reduce the scope of what needs to be acquired and simplify how elicited knowledge is operationalized and generalized. They also limit the class of strategies that can be acquired.

## 2.2. Eliciting Knowledge in Operational Terms

Automated knowledge acquisition tools can address the operationalization aspect of representation mismatch by limiting what is elicited from the user to representations of knowledge that are already machine-executable—that is, to elicit knowledge in the form in which it will be used for performance or in some form that can be compiled into the runtime representation. An alternative approach is to provide a nonoperational "mediating representation" for eliciting the conceptual structure of a domain and then *manually* building a system that operationalizes the specifications [Johnson and Tomlinson 1988]. A rule editor is a simple example of a tool that elicits knowledge in a form that can be directly executed.

The technique of eliciting knowledge directly in executable form is reminiscent of the single representation trick [Dieterich, et al. 1982] in which the learning agent is given training data in the same representation as the language used for describing learned concepts. Using this technique in a knowledge acquisition tool replaces the problem of making the elicited input executable (operationalization) with the assumption that the elicitation language is representationally adequate. A language is representationally adequate if all of the relevant domain knowledge can be stated in the representation.

The success of tools employing this technique depends in part on whether the elicitation interface can make the operational semantics of the representation comprehensible to the user. For example, although TEIRESIAS paraphrases rules into English, the user needs to know more than English to understand them. TEIRESIAS depends on the assumption that the user can understand the backward-chaining model [Davis 1976].

Well-designed user interface techniques can help make the computational model of the architecture comprehensible to the user. For example, the OPAL tool facilitates the acquisition of cancer treatment protocols with a form-filling interface, emulating paper-and-pencil forms familiar to its users [Musen, et al. 1987]. Similarly, spreadsheet applications are made comprehensible by presenting a familiar metaphor. The interface design goal is to minimize the conceptual distance between the user's understanding of the system's mechanism and the system's presentation of the options afforded by the computational model [Hutchins, Hollan, and Norman 1986].

A tool that acquires knowledge in an executable representation can also offer intelligent assistance by analyzing the consequences of *applying* the knowledge. For example, SALT elicits fine-grained rules for repairing local constraint violations in a design task. One of the consequences of using backtracking from local constraint violations is that the user can unintentionally define cycles in the dependency network, in which repairing one constraint violation introduces another. SALT can analyze the elicited knowledge, identify cycles, and offer assistance to the user in specifying different routes for backtracking [Marcus 1987].

It is difficult to acquire strategic knowledge in executable form without forcing the expert to understand symbol-level mechanisms such as procedures and priority schemes. There is a tension between the requirement to provide the user with a language that is comprehensible and yet sufficiently powerful to implement the strategy. There are some techniques that help elicit specifications of control, such as visual programming interfaces for building transition networks [Musen, Fagan, and Shortliffe 1986] and graph-drawing tools for specifying decision trees [Hannan and Politakis 1986]. However, the strategic knowledge that can generate decisions among actions is *implicit* in transition networks and decision trees. ASK's representation of strategic knowledge was designed to correspond to the form in which experts can describe their strategic knowledge: justifications for specific actions in specific situations. As will be explained in Section 3, ASK elicits justifications for choices among actions in terms of features of strategic situations and actions. ASK's design ensures that the features mentioned in justifications are operational; the features are well-defined functions and relations that hold over objects in a knowledge base representing the current state of problem solving.

Like all tools that elicit knowledge in executable form, ASK is based on the assumption of representational adequacy discussed above. There are two ways this assumption can fail: the computational model is inadequate for describing the desired strategy, or the set of terms in the existing knowledge representation is incomplete. The former problem is a function of the architecture, as discussed above. The problem of incomplete terms can be handled in an interactive tool if the user is given the chance to define new terms with the representational primitives provided by the architecture.

Since defining terms for a knowledge system is an operationalization task, it is a challenge to provide automated assistance. A promising approach is exemplified by PROTÉGÉ, a tool that helps the knowledge engineer define domain-specific instantiations of architecture-level representational primitives [Musen 1989]. PROTÉGÉ generates OPAL-class elicitation tools meant for the domain expert in which the vocabulary is fixed. ASK provides a means for defining new features in the context of eliciting justifications, as demonstrated in Section 4.6. By design, ASK integrates the acquisition of new features and the acquisition of knowledge that uses the features.

### 2.3. Integrating Mechanical Generalization with Interactive Knowledge Elicitation

Machine learning techniques are an obvious answer to the generalization aspect of representation mismatch. There are many well-established techniques for generalization from examples [Dietterich and Michalski 1983]. Because inductive generalization is inherently underconstrained, these techniques all depend on some kind of *bias* to direct the learner toward useful or relevant generalizations [Mitchell 1982; Utgoff 1986]. Bias can be provided to a learner by supplying a highly constrained generalization space, defined by the language for representing learned concepts, such as LEX's pattern-matching language [Mitchell, Utgoff, and Banerji 1983]. Bias can also come from the choice of features in the training examples, as in the feature vectors used by decision tree algorithms [Quinlan 1986].

A knowledge acquisition tool can capitalize on existing techniques if they are augmented with the appropriate bias. One approach would be to build the necessary bias into the tool.

If the bias is itself important domain knowledge, however, this approach limits the usefulness of automating the knowledge acquisition process, since the tool would have to be modified for each domain. Instead, a knowledge acquisition tool can provide means for the *user* to contribute bias—to guide the generalization toward useful concepts. The user can contribute bias by carefully selecting training examples [Winston 1985], by identifying their relevant features, and by evaluating machine-generated generalizations. While the human provides pedagogical input and evaluation of results, the tool can apply syntactic generalization operators and check for consistency with a database of training cases. The resulting human-machine synergy is a more powerful acquisition technique than either manual knowledge engineering or traditional inductive learning.

Knowledge-based learning techniques such as explanation-based learning [DeJong and Mooney 1986; Mitchell, Keller, and Kedar-Cabelli 1986] are strongly biased by the domain theory provided by the system builder. Inserting a human in the learning loop can help overcome the dependence of the learning technique on the quality of the built-in knowledge. For example, in an experiment with SOAR in the domain of algebraic simplification, a human intercedes during problem solving to help the system learn search-control knowledge [Golding, Rosenbloom, and Laird 1987]. When the system needs to choose among algebraic simplification operators for a specific equation, the human recommends an operator to apply or provides a simpler equation to solve. The system uses a domain theory of algebraic simplification to find useful chunks that generalize the situation (the class of equations) in which the recommended operator should be applied. In the absence of a complete domain theory, one can imagine the human pointing out relevant parts of the equation to chunk.

To integrate generalization techniques into a knowledge acquisition tool, the knowledge to be acquired must be represented in such a way that syntactic generalizations of statements in the representation correspond to semantic generalizations in the knowledge [see Lenat and Brown 1984]. For strategic knowledge, this means formulating the selection of actions in terms of classification. For example, a common technique for programs that learn search-control knowledge is to formulate the knowledge for selecting actions as pattern-matching expressions that identify situations in which operators would be usefully applied [Benjamin 1987; Laird, Newell, and Rosenbloom 1987; Minton and Carbonell 1987; Mitchell, Utgoff, and Banerji 1983; Silver 1986]. Because of this formulation, syntactic generalizations of the expressions to which an operator had been applied during training correspond to classes of situations to which the operator might be useful in the future.

ASK's representation of strategic knowledge is designed to exploit syntactic generalization operators. Knowledge about what action to do next is formulated as predicates that describe situations in which equivalence classes of actions are useful. In the absence of a theory to infer the utility of actions, ASK acquires strategic knowledge from people.

### 3. The ASK Knowledge Acquisition Assistant

ASK is an interactive knowledge acquisition assistant. It acquires strategic knowledge from the user of a knowledge system, called the performance system. The strategic knowledge acquired by ASK is used by the performance system to decide what action to perform on each iteration of a control cycle. With additional strategic knowledge, the performance system should be able to make better decisions about what to do in various situations.

The basic approach is to elicit strategic knowledge from the user in the form of *justifications* for specific choices among actions, and then operationalize and generalize the justified choices in the form of *strategy rules* that associate situations with classes of appropriate actions.

This section presents an overview of the knowledge acquisition procedure, and then covers in more detail the strategy-rule representation and the knowledge system architecture that supports it. Section 4 demonstrates ASK with examples from a knowledge system for planning workups of chest pain.

### 3.1. *The Knowledge Acquisition Dialog*

ASK orchestrates a mixed-initiative dialog with the user. The basic steps in the knowledge acquisition dialog are shown in Figure 1.

ASK is invoked by the user of the performance system. At run time, the performance system executes a simple control loop. On each iteration the system selects a set of recommended actions, the user picks one, and then the system executes it. The results of the actions are recorded, and then the system continues by selecting the next set of recommended actions. If the user disagrees with the system's recommended actions on any iteration, she can interrupt the control loop and initiate a knowledge acquisition dialog.

The first step of the knowledge acquisition dialog is to elicit a critique from the user. A critique is a labeling of what the system did wrong in terms of choosing actions. The system recommends a set of actions at each iteration of the control cycle because they are all equally appropriate in the current situation, according to the existing strategic knowledge. The user

critiques the system's choices by selecting an action that the system should have chosen (the positive example) and one that the system should not have chosen (the negative example). The positive and negative examples do not have to be in the set of the system's initial choices (which may be empty). The user also characterizes the system's error in recommending actions, indicating, for instance, whether the positive example is merely preferred to the negative example or whether the negative example should not have been considered at all.

Next, ASK performs credit assignment analysis by examining how the current set of strategy rules matched the positive and negative examples. The output of this analysis is a learning objective that specifies what a new strategy rule would have to match and not match and what it should recommend in order to accommodate the user's critique and be consistent with existing strategy rules.

Then ASK elicits justifications from the user. From the user's perspective, justifications are explanations or reasons why an action should or should not be recommended, in terms of relevant features of the current situation. From ASK's perspective, justifications are facts about the state of knowledge base objects in the current working memory of the performance system; the set of justifications corresponds to the set of features that should be mentioned in matching strategy rules. ASK suggests an initial seed set of justifications, based on how existing strategy rules fired. The user adds justifications by clicking on features of objects displayed in windows on the screen. The justification interface allows the user to browse through the knowledge base for relevant objects. If the set of existing features is inadequate, the user can define new features within the justification interface.

When the user indicates that she is finished and has specified a set of justifications that are sufficient to distinguish the positive and negative examples, ASK generates a new strategy rule from the justifications. The new strategy rule is generalized by syntactic induction operators to apply to a range of situations and an equivalence class of actions. For example, where a specific action appears in a justification, ASK puts a variable in the corresponding clause of a strategy rule. Similarly, if a justification mentions a specific value for a feature, ASK may build a strategy-rule clause that matches a *range* of values for that feature.

Finally, the new rule is paraphrased and the operational effects of the new rule are presented to the user for approval. If the user agrees that the new rule improves the system's choices of actions, the rule is added to the strategic knowledge base of the performance system, and the control cycle is continued.

Details of the knowledge acquisition dialog are demonstrated with examples in Section 4. First some background on the performance system architecture and the representation for strategic knowledge is required.

### 3.2. *The MU Architecture*

ASK is integrated with an architecture for knowledge systems called MU [Cohen, Greenberg, and Delisio 1987; Gruber and Cohen 1987]. As depicted in Figure 2, a performance system built in MU consists of a substantive knowledge base, typically for heuristic classification, and a strategic knowledge base for controlling actions.[2] This division of knowledge is typical of architectures that support control knowledge, such as BB1 [Hayes-Roth 1985]. MU organizes the substantive knowledge as a symbolic inference network, where inferences are

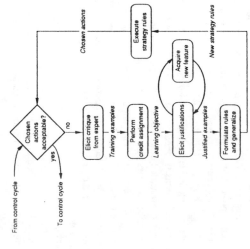

*Figure 1.* The ASK knowledge acquisition dialog.

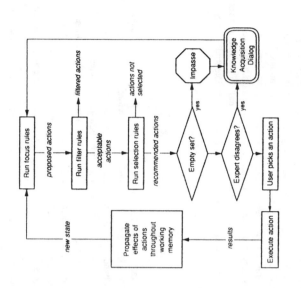

*Figure 3.* The strategy rule control cycle.

The strategy-rule control cycle corresponds to the method of task-level architectures described in Section 2.1. It specifies how strategic knowledge is brought to bear in the decision about what action to do next. The propose-filter-select algorithm defines three roles for strategic knowledge: specifying the conditions under which actions might be applicable, inappropriate, and preferable. Its design stipulates that actions are chosen iteratively, waiting for the effects of the execution of the previous action before making the current decision. The algorithm also assumes that the context of the decision, the *strategic situation*, is defined in terms of currently available features of the state of the performance system. Thus, strategy rules are *not* general-purpose control rules, useful for writing arbitrary programs. Rather, the strategy-rule control cycle supports a style of reasoning that has been called *reactive planning* [Agre and Chapman 1987; Chapman and Agre 1987; Firby 1987; Kaelbling 1987]. The form of strategic knowledge is restricted to facilitate automated knowledge acquisition. The consequences of this design are made explicit in later sections.

The left-hand side (If part) of a strategy rule is a conjunctive expression, with variables, that specifies a strategic situation and the set of recommended actions for that situation. The left-hard side expression matches against the values of control features that reflect the properties and dynamic state of objects in working memory, including objects that represent actions. The right-hand side (Then part) of a strategy rule indicates whether the matching actions should be proposed, filtered, or selected in the matching situation.

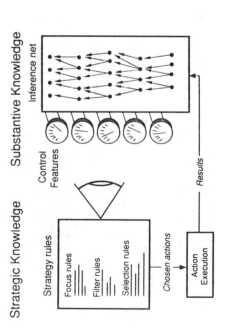

*Figure 2.* The MU architecture with strategy rules.

propagated from evidence to hypotheses by local combination functions. The inference network serves as the working memory of the system at runtime. The state of the network is abstracted by *control features*, which are functions, attributes, and relations over knowledge base objects.[2] The strategic knowledge is organized in a separate component, which examines the state of working memory via control features and selects actions to execute. MU was designed to support a variety of experiments in strategic reasoning, so the architecture does not include a built-in problem solving method or control strategy. The strategy-rule representation was developed for the study of knowledge acquisition in ASK.

### 3.3. *Strategy Rules*

Strategic knowledge acquired by ASK is represented in the form of *strategy rules*, inspired by the metarules that represent diagnostic strategy in NEOMYCIN and HERACLES [Clancey 1988; Clancey and Bock 1988]. Strategy rules map *strategic situations* to sets of recommended actions. Strategic situations are states of the working memory of a performance system. In the MU architecture, strategic situations are states of the inference network.

The strategy-rule control cycle, shown in Figure 3, specifies how strategy rules are applied in a performance system to decide among actions. At each iteration of the control cycle, strategy rules recommend the actions that are appropriate to perform next. There are three types of recommendations, corresponding to three categories of strategy rules. *Focus rules* propose a set of possible actions at each iteration. *Filter rules* prune actions that violate constraints. *Selection rules* pick out subsets of the proposed and unpruned actions that are most desirable in the current situation to form the final set of recommended actions. One of the actions in the recommended set is chosen by the user and executed. The effects of the action are then propagated through working memory.

### 3.4. Examples from the Chest Pain Domain

Here are some examples of strategy rules and control features from a system for planning workups for chest pain that will be used to demonstrate ASK in Section 4.

The following *focus rule* proposes actions that are general questions (e.g., age, sex, etc.) when the set of active hypotheses, called the differential, is empty.

```
Rule Ask-intake-questions   a focus rule
    ''Ask general questions when at a loss.''
    If: (IS (differential) :EMPTY)
        (IN ?ACTION (members-of general-questions))
    Then: (PROPOSE ?action history-and-exam)
```

The strategic situation in this rule is specified by the condition that the value of the differential object is empty. The set of recommended actions is generated by the relation members-of applied to the object general-questions, which is a class of actions. The right-hand side operator PROPOSE specifies that the values bound to the variable ?ACTION should be proposed under these conditions, and that the goal history-and-exam should be posted.

The expression (differential) refers to the set of hypotheses on the differential. It is a control feature defined in the MU inference network as:

```
VALUE of DIFFERENTIAL          a control feature
    ''The set of active hypotheses''
    SET-OF ?Hypothesis IN hypotheses SUCH-THAT
        trigger-level of ?Hypothesis IS triggered AND
        level-of-support OF ?Hypothesis IS-NOT disconfirmed
    OR
        level-of-support OF ?Hypothesis IS-AT-LEAST supported
```

Another focus rule, shown below, is complementary to Ask-intake-questions. It proposes actions that potentially provide diagnostic evidence when the differential is *not* empty, and labels this state with the goal gather-evidence-for-differential.

```
Propose-diagnostic-evidence          a focus rule
    ''Gather evidence for current hypotheses.''
    If: (IS (differential) :NONEMPTY)
        (IN ?ACTION (potential-evidence differential))
    Then: (PROPOSE ?ACTION gather-evidence-for-differential)
```

The expression (potential-evidence differential) refers to a control feature that returns the set of actions that are potentially diagnostic for hypotheses on the differential. This set is computed dynamically by a function that calls a MU service for analyzing the inference network [Cohen, Greenberg and Delisio 1987].

A very simple *filter rule* prevents actions from being recommended if they have already been executed. In some domains actions may be executed repeatedly. That is why the don't-repeat policy is encoded in the following rule instead of built in to the basic control loop.

```
Filter-executed-actions          a filter rule
    ''Do not repeat actions''
    If: (IS (executed? ?ACTION) yes)
    Then: (FILTER ?ACTION)
```

The following *selection rule* is enabled under the goal history-and-exam. It recommends those actions that are cheap to perform and that can potentially produce data that would trigger new hypotheses.

```
Select-cheap-triggering-data          a selection rule
    ''Prefer cheap actions that might trigger hypotheses.''
    If: (IN history-and-exam (current-goals))
        (IS (potentially-triggered-by ?ACTION) :NONEMPTY)
        (≤ (cost ?ACTION) cheap)
    Then: (SELECT ?ACTION)
    Shadows: Select-triggering-data, select-free-evidence.
             select-cheap-evidence
```

The terms current-goals, potentially-triggered-by, and cost refer to control features. The set of actions recommended by this rule are those with some hypotheses on their potentially-triggered-by feature and whose cost feature is not more than cheap. The feature potentially-triggered-by is computed from the definitions of triggering conditions for hypotheses, stated in a rule-like form. For example, the hypothesis classic-angina is triggered when "the chief-complaint is pain or pressure and pain-quality is vise-like and the chief-complaint-location is substernal." This rule will recommend the action of asking for the chief-complaint-location because it potentially triggers a hypothesis and it is cheap.

### 3.5. The Shadowing Relation Among Strategy Rules

Within each strategy-rule category (focus, filter, selection), rules are matched in an order specified by a precedence relation called *shadows*, which is a partial order based on the generality of left-hand sides. If a rule succeeds (matches some objects), then the more general rules that it shadows are pruned (prevented from being fired). Generality is defined in terms of the features mentioned in a rule and the range of values specified for each feature. For example, the selection rule shown above, Select-cheap-triggering-data, shadows (takes precedence over) more general rules mentioning the same features. It shadows the more general rule Select-cheap-evidence, which recommends any action that is cheap. In turn, Select-cheap-evidence shadows the rule Select-free-evidence because the former matches actions with costs of cheap or free. The global effect of a family of selection rules in which the more specific rules shadow the more general is to choose those actions judged to be acceptable by the most constraining criteria. The shadows relation is a symbolic alternative to a numeric function for combining the recommendations of each rule into a single measure of utility. Further details can be found in [Gruber 1989].

## 4. A Knowledge Acquisition Dialog with ASK

In this section, ASK will be demonstrated in the context of a performance system that generates diagnostic workups for patients reporting chest and abdominal pain. The performance system is a reimplementation of the MUM knowledge system [Cohen, et al. 1987]. MUM's task is called *prospective diagnosis*, which is to choose diagnostic actions as a physician would, asking questions in an intelligent order and balancing the potential costs of diagnostic tests and trial therapy with the evidential and therapeutic benefits.

### 4.1. What the Performance System Already Knows

In experiments with ASK, the performance system is given MUM's substantive knowledge about the diagnosis of chest pain, implemented in the MU architecture in an inference network. The inference network contains hypotheses, data-gathering actions, intermediate conclusions, and combination functions that represent inferential relations such as the evidential support for hypotheses given patient data. MUM's original strategy was written by knowledge engineers in Lisp. In the ASK experiments, the strategic knowledge is represented in strategy rules.

In the dialog shown here, the performance system starts with a small but incomplete set of strategy rules, and the user extends them to improve strategic performance. ASK can also be used without any existing strategy rules. In a separate experiment reported in [Gruber 1989], ASK was used to acquire a set of strategy rules that replicates the original MUM strategy. However, since ASK makes use of existing strategy rules and control features in acquiring new strategic knowledge, it can be more helpful in specializing an existing strategy than in building a strategy from scratch. Thus the dialog in this section will show ASK being used to extend an existing set of rules that represent a general strategy for prospective diagnosis.

### 4.2. Running the Performance System

A MU performance system runs the basic control loop that was introduced in Section 3.3. At each iteration, strategy rules recommend some set of actions as candidates. From the system's point of view, these recommended actions are equivalent. Given the current strategic knowledge, the system could select among them arbitrarily. The user of a MU system is given the choice to "break the tie" and pick one action to execute. In the chest pain application, executing an action typically causes a request for data (e.g., symptoms or test results). That data is entered into the inference network, where it may change the evidential support for active hypotheses and trigger new hypotheses.

We begin the knowledge acquisition dialog at a point at which the user has already run the performance system through the first several actions in a case (namely, the cheap and easy questions about the history and the physical examination data). At this point, the system has run out of cheap actions and the Propose-diagnostic-evidence rule (Section 3.4) recommends a set of diagnostic actions. The user has the option to pick one of the recommended actions for execution or to teach the system to refine its strategy.

The following menu shows the system offering a set of recommended actions during an iteration of the control cycle of the performance system. Instead of choosing an action, the user initiates the dialog with ASK to "teach the system to improve its choices." (An item with a box drawn around it signifies that the user has selected it with the mouse.) The user sets up this diagnostic situation because it demonstrates a weakness in the system's strategy. The system needs to be more selective in choosing among diagnostic tests and trial therapeutic actions such as the seven offered in the menu.

### 4.3. Eliciting the User's Critique

ASK elicits a critique from the user by presenting the list of the system's chosen actions and asking what should have been done differently. It first asks for the general category of error, to help determine whether the problem is with focus, filter, or selection rules:

Then it asks for a positive example, an action that should have been recommended, and a negative example, an action that should not have been recommended. It is assumed that the user will choose a positive example that is representative of a class of actions that should be recommended in this situation, and a negative example that represents a class of actions to distinguish in this situation. In the interaction shown below, the user indicates that the action EKG should have been distinguished from the action Upper-GI-series, which is a reasonable alternative (i.e., a near miss).

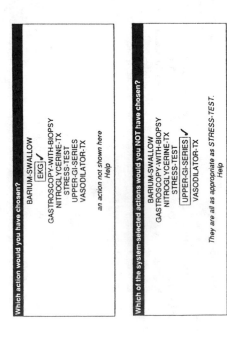

**Which action would you have chosen?**

BARIUM-SWALLOW
EKG ✓
GASTROSCOPY-WITH-BIOPSY
NITROGLYCERINE-TX
STRESS-TEST
UPPER-GI-SERIES
VASODILATOR-TX

*an action not shown here*
*Help*

**Which of the system-selected actions would you NOT have chosen?**

BARIUM-SWALLOW
GASTROSCOPY-WITH-BIOPSY
NITROGLYCERINE-TX
STRESS-TEST
UPPER-GI-SERIES ✓
VASODILATOR-TX

*They are all as appropriate as STRESS-TEST.*
*Help*

### 4.4. Credit Assignment Analysis

Using the information provided by the user, ASK performs a credit assignment analysis. The credit assignment algorithm examines how existing strategy rules matched in this situation and determines the requirements for a new rule that would account for the critique. The algorithm makes strong use of the distinction between focus, filter, and selection rules and the way they are applied in the strategy-rule control cycle. For example, if the positive example was not proposed by any focus rules, the algorithm prescribes learning a focus rule that proposes it. Alternatively, if both the positive and negative examples are recommended by selection rules, then the algorithm prescribes learning a selection rule that matches the positive example, fails to match the negative example, and shadows the selection rules that recommended the negative example. In the sample session, ASK determines that it needs to acquire a selection rule, specializing the Propose-diagnostic-evidence rule, such that the new rule matches EKG and does not match Upper-GI-series. The complete credit assignment algorithm can be found in [Gruber 1989].

### 4.5. Eliciting Justifications

In the next stage of the dialog, the user provides justifications for choosing the positive example over the negative example. Justifications are specified as features of the current strategic situation and features of actions. In the example session, the strategic situation is

characterized by the state of hypotheses on the differential. A feature shared by the actions recommended by the system (including the positive and negative examples) is that they potentially provide evidence for hypotheses on the differential. In the current example, the user must provide additional justifications that distinguish the positive example EKG from the negative example Upper-GI-series.

The user interface for asserting justifications consists of two windows containing mouse-sensitive text. The "relevant objects window" displays the values of features of a set of objects from the knowledge base. The "justifications window" contains a list of justifications in the form of natural language sentences. Each justification is a description of the value of a feature of some relevant object.

ASK initializes the relevant objects window with a set of knowledge base objects that might be relevant to the current control decision. An object is considered relevant if it is one of the positive or negative examples (actions), a current goal, an instance of a class representing some aspect of the global state of the inference network, or if it is mentioned in a strategy rule matching the positive or negative examples. The user is provided with tools for browsing the knowledge base to find additional relevant objects.

ASK also initializes the list of statements in the justification window with *seed justifications* which represent the system's reasons for selecting the current actions. Seed justifications are derived from the clauses of strategy rules matching the positive and negative examples. In the windows shown below, objects and justifications have been seeded by ASK.

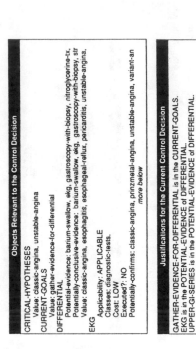

**Objects Relevant to the Control Decision**

CRITICAL-HYPOTHESES
    Value: classic-angina, unstable-angina
CURRENT-GOALS
    Value: gather-evidence-for-differential
DIFFERENTIAL
    Potential-evidence: barium-swallow, ekg, gastroscopy-with-biopsy, nitroglycerine-tx,
    Potentially-conclusive-evidence: barium-swallow, ekg, gastroscopy-with-biopsy, str
    Value: classic-angina, esophagitis, esophageal-reflux, pericarditis, unstable-angina.
EKG
    Applicability: APPLICABLE
    Classes: diagnostic-tests.
    Cost: LOW
    Executed?: NO
    Potentially-confirms: classic-angina, prinzmetal-angina, unstable-angina, variant-an
                        *more below*

**Justifications for the Current Control Decision**

GATHER-EVIDENCE-FOR-DIFFERENTIAL is in the CURRENT-GOALS.
EKG is in the POTENTIAL-EVIDENCE of DIFFERENTIAL.
UPPER-GI-SERIES is in the POTENTIAL-EVIDENCE of DIFFERENTIAL.

The user asserts a justification by selecting a feature of one of the objects presented in the relevant objects window. When a justification is selected, ASK paraphrases the fact in the justifications window. In the following interaction, the user indicates that EKG should have been chosen because it has low cost. Using the mouse, the user selects the statement "Cost: low" from the relevant objects window, and the statement "The COST of EKG is low" shows up in the justification window, as depicted below.

knowledge engineers (e.g., dynamic relations written in Lisp). ASK knows about how features are implemented in MU and makes it possible to acquire some of the more simple features, such as static attributes, interactively. To help make architecture-dependent terms such as "inferential value" concrete to the user, ASK offers instances of features types from the current knowledge base as exemplars. In the menu below, the user indicates that the time-required feature is an attribute of actions, analogous to the cost feature.

**What kind of feature is TIME-REQUIRED?**
an attribute of actions (like COST) ✓
a class of actions (like DIAGNOSTIC-TESTS)
an object (like DIFFERENTIAL)
an inferential value computed by rules (like LEVEL-OF-SUPPORT)
a dynamic relation (like POTENTIALLY-CONFIRMS)
*more below*
*Help*

To complete the definition of a static attribute, ASK elicits information about the domain, data type, possible values, order, cardinality, and default value for the feature, and constrains the user's choices whenever possible.

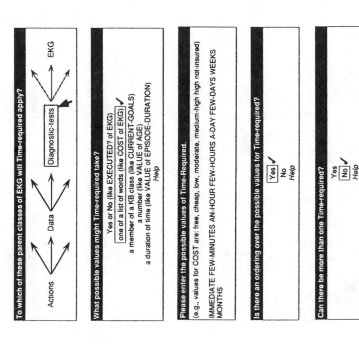

**To which of these parent classes of EKG will Time-required apply?**
Actions    Data    Diagnostic-tests    EKG

**What possible values might Time-required take?**
Yes or No (like EXECUTED? of EKG)
one of a list of words (like COST of EKG) ✓
a member of a KB class (like CURRENT-GOALS)
a number (like VALUE of AGE)
a duration of time (like VALUE of EPISODE-DURATION)
*Help*

**Please enter the possible values of Time-Required.**
(e.g., values for COST are: free, cheap, low, moderate, medium-high high not-insured)
IMMEDIATE FEW-MINUTES AN-HOUR FEW-HOURS A-DAY FEW-DAYS WEEKS MONTHS

**Is there an ordering over the possible values for Time-required?**
Yes ✓
No
*Help*

**Can there be more than one Time-required?**
Yes
No ✓
*Help*

At this point the user could tell ASK that she was finished. If the set of justifications satisfied the learning objective, ASK would then turn the justifications into a new strategy rule. In this session, however, the user wishes to add more justifications. In particular, the user wants to say that EKG is appropriate in this situation not only because it has low cost, but also because it takes little time to perform. To be able to say this in the language of justifications, the user needs to define a new feature.

### 4.6. Acquiring a New Feature

To define a new feature is to implement an attribute, function, or relation over some set of objects in the knowledge base. ASK can help the user define a new feature. Playing the role of a knowledge engineer, ASK elicits the information needed to implement the feature in the MU architecture. The interaction below shows the user defining a new feature called "time required." The user starts by clicking on the EKG object in the relevant objects window, bringing up the following menu:

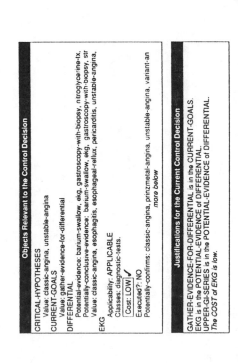

**Objects Relevant to the Control Decision**
CRITICAL-HYPOTHESES
  Value: classic-angina, unstable-angina
CURRENT-GOALS
  Value: gather-evidence-for-differential
DIFFERENTIAL
  Potential-evidence: barium-swallow, ekg, gastroscopy-with-biopsy, nitroglycerine-rx,
  Potentially-conclusive-evidence: barium-swallow, ekg, gastroscopy-with-biopsy, str
  Value: classic-angina, esophagitis, esophageal-reflux, pericarditis, unstable-angina,
EKG
  Applicability: APPLICABLE
  Classes: diagnostic-tests.
  Cost: LOW ✓
  Executed?: NO
  Potentially-confirms: classic-angina, prinzmetal-angina, unstable-angina, variant-an
  *more below*

**Justifications for the Current Control Decision**
GATHER-EVIDENCE-FOR-DIFFERENTIAL is in the CURRENT-GOALS.
EKG is in the POTENTIAL-EVIDENCE of DIFFERENTIAL.
UPPER-GI-SERIES is in the POTENTIAL-EVIDENCE of DIFFERENTIAL.
*The COST of EKG is low.*

**EKG**
Display unit
Remove Object
Apply an existing feature
Define a new feature ✓

**What shall we call the new feature of EKG?**
TIME-REQUIRED

After obtaining a name for the feature, ASK needs to determine its general type. The type of a feature is a symbol-level property, dependent on the knowledge-base architecture. MU supports several varieties of control features, many of which are best implemented by

Once the intentional properties of the feature are acquired, the values of the feature applied to the elements of its domain are elicited. For static attributes, ASK presents a table of the objects to which it applies, and the user specifies the value of the feature for each object. In the current example, the user enters the value of the time-required feature for all diagnostic tests, including the training examples EKG and Upper-GI-series. The table below shows the value of time-required for EKG, after it was entered by the user.

**Please choose a default value for Time-required.**

    immediate
    few-minutes
    an-hour
    few-hours
    a-day
    few-days
    weeks
    months
    No default is applicable ✓
                        Help

**Time-required of Diagnostic-tests**

| | |
|---|---|
| Angiogram | unknown |
| Barium-swallow | unknown |
| Cardiac-enzyme | unknown |
| Chest-xray | few-hours |
| Cholesterol-level | unknown |
| Echo-cardiogram | unknown |
| EKG | few-minutes ✓ |
| Flat-plate-of-the-abdomen | unknown |
| Gall-bladder-series | unknown |
| | *More below* |

### 4.7. Using the New Feature in Justifications

When the expert has finished defining time-required, the system can use it as any other feature and ASK can offer it as a possible justification. The dialog now returns to the justification interface, where the user selects the time-required as a justification for choosing EKG over Upper-GI-series:

**Objects Relevant to the Control Decision**

CRITICAL-HYPOTHESES
  Value: classic-angina, unstable-angina
CURRENT-GOALS
  Value: gather-evidence-for-differential
DIFFERENTIAL
  Potential-evidence: barium-swallow, ekg, gastroscopy-with-biopsy, nitroglycerine-rx,
  Potentially-conclusive-evidence: barium-swallow, ekg, gastroscopy-with-biopsy, str
  Value: classic-angina, esophagitis, esophageal-reflux, pericarditis, unstable-angina,
EKG
  Applicability: APPLICABLE
  Classes: diagnostic-tests.
  Cost: LOW
  Executed?: NO
  Potentially-confirms: classic-angina, pinzmetal-angina, unstable-angina, variant-an
  Potentially-triggered: None.
  Time-required: FEW-MINUTES ✓
  Value: unknown
                        *more below*

**Justifications for the Current Control Decision**

GATHER-EVIDENCE-FOR-DIFFERENTIAL is in the CURRENT-GOALS.
EKG is in the POTENTIAL-EVIDENCE of DIFFERENTIAL.
UPPER-GI-SERIES is in the POTENTIAL-EVIDENCE of DIFFERENTIAL.
*The COST of EKG is low.*
*The TIME-REQUIRED of EKG is few-minutes.*
*The TIME-REQUIRED of UPPER-GI-SERIES is a-day.*

At this point in the dialog, the user has indicated that the cost and time required of actions are factors to consider when choosing actions. The first three justifications represent the factors that the system would consider and were suggested by ASK. The user could have removed some of these seed justifications but did not in this case. From the combined set of justifications, ASK can generate a new strategy rule.

### 4.8 Generating and Generalizing a Strategy Rule

Given the user's justifications, ASK formulates a new strategy rule that accounts for the expert's critique of the system's performance. The new rule causes the expert's preferred action to be selected on the next iteration.

The left-hand side of the new rule is constructed by transforming the list of justifications into left-hand-side clauses. The transformation from justifications to rule clauses is fairly straightforward. The internal representation of justifications is very similar to the clause form of strategy rules. The right-hand-side recommendation (in this case, SELECT) was decided by the credit assignment analysis. In the current example, ASK forms the following rule:

```
IF   (IN gather-evidence-for-differential (current-goals))
     (IN ?ACTION (potential-evidence differential))
     (≤ (cost ?ACTION) low)
     (= (time-required ?ACTION) few-minutes)
     THEN (SELECT ?ACTION)
```

In the process of forming rule clauses from justifications, ASK applies generalization operators. One operator is called *turning constants into variables*. In the strategy rule above, references to EKG have been replaced with the free variable *?ACTION*, which is bound at runtime by the strategy-rule interpreter to each action that has been proposed and has not been filtered. The result is that the rule recommends the class of actions sharing the features of EKG in the justifications: the cost and time required.

Another generalization operator is *extending the reference* of a feature from a test of equality to a test over some range or set of permissible values. In the example strategy rule, the ≤ operator specifies that the third clause will succeed when the action has any value of cost equal to or less than low. ASK used a heuristic for applying this generalization; it found another selection rule that used ≤ for the cost feature.

In this example, however, ASK has no a priori information to help in extending the reference of the new feature, time-required. It asks the user for guidance by posing hypothetical variants on the current case to obtain boundary conditions on the acceptable range for the time-required clause in this rule. Since ASK lacks common sense, it has to ask whether the user would still accept the EKG if it takes no time at all:

**What if the Time-required of EKG were IMMEDIATE? Would you still choose it?**
Yes
No
Help

Then ASK offers near-miss cases:

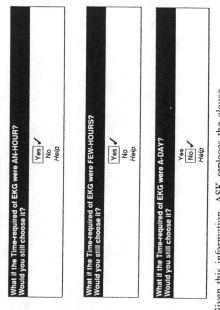

**What if the Time-required of EKG were AN-HOUR? Would you still choose it?**
Yes
No
Help

**What if the Time-required of EKG were FEW-HOURS? Would you still choose it?**
Yes
No
Help

**What if the Time-required of EKG were A-DAY? Would you still choose it?**
Yes
No
Help

Given this information, ASK replaces the clause

    (= (time-required ?ACTION) few-minutes)

with the clause

    (≤ (time-required ?ACTION) few-hours).

### 4.9 Verifying a Rule

To evaluate the face validity of the generated rule, ASK presents a paraphrased translation to the user for verification. It also shows the operational consequences of the rule.

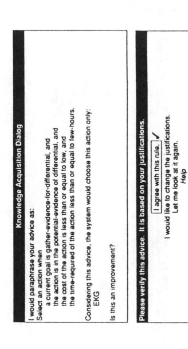

**Knowledge Acquisition Dialog**

I would paraphrase your advice as:
Select an action when
  a current goal is gather-evidence-for-differential, and
  the action is in the potential-evidence of differential, and
  the cost of the action is less than or equal to low, and
  the time-required of the action less than or equal to few-hours.

Considering this advice, the system would choose this action only:
  EKG

Is this an improvement?

**Please verify this advice. It is based on your justifications.**
I agree with this rule. ✓
I would like to change the justifications.
Let me look at it again.
Help

This completes one session of the knowledge acquisition dialog. With the new strategy rule, the performance system now recommends only the positive example, EKG, when the goal is to gather evidence and the actions are potentially diagnostic. The new selection rule fails to match the negative example and the other proposed actions, and it shadows the more general rule that formerly matched all seven actions.

The next subsection demonstrates how ASK can be used to acquire tradeoffs in a utility space. It is not essential to understanding the basic approach.

### 4.10. Acquiring Tradeoffs

The strategy rule just acquired is one of a family of rules that together constitute a strategy for selecting diagnostic actions. Selection rules can be viewed as tradeoffs among features, and a family of selection rules represents a set of acceptable tradeoffs. The new rule specifies that a moderate amount of time is acceptable if the cost is low and the diagnosticity is moderate.

In terms of utility theory, the new rule occupies a region in a space with dimensions defined by the features measuring diagnosticity, cost, and timeliness. Points in this space can be interpreted as the values of a multiattribute utility function [Keeney and Raiffa 1976]. The dimensions are attributes and the regions represent values of equivalent utility. The shadows relation among rules corresponds to a partial order over values of utility; some regions have higher utility than others in the same attribute space. For example, because of the shadows relation, the new rule takes precedence over selection rules that mention only cost or time-required. The region corresponding to the new rule can be interpreted as having higher utility. In other words, actions selected by the new rule are preferred over actions that would have been selected by shadowed rules.

To illustrate how ASK can be used to acquire other tradeoffs in the same space, this subsection sketches a second session where the user finds an exception to an existing rule. In this second scenario, the user runs the performance system on a case where initial data provides evidence that the patient could have a very serious condition which requires immediate diagnosis. In this situation, the system suggests a set of actions that are potential evidence for hypotheses on the differential and have low cost. However, the user indicates that the system should ignore cost and concentrate on evidence that is potentially *conclusive* for hypotheses that are *critical*. The relevant objects and justification windows appear as follows:

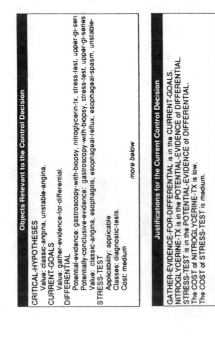

**Objects Relevant to the Control Decision**

CRITICAL-HYPOTHESES
  Value: classic-angina, unstable-angina.
CURRENT-GOALS
  Value: gather-evidence-for-differential.
DIFFERENTIAL
  Potential-evidence: gastroscopy-with-biopsy, nitroglycerin-tx, stress-test, upper-gi-seri
  Potentially-conclusive-evidence: gastroscopy-with-biopsy, stress-test, upper-gi-series
  Value: classic-angina, esophagitis, esophageal-reflux, esophageal-spasm, unstable-
STRESS-TEST
  Applicability: applicable
  Classes: diagnostic-tests.
  Cost: medium          *more below*

**Justifications for the Current Control Decision**

GATHER-EVIDENCE-FOR-DIFFERENTIAL is in the CURRENT-GOALS.
NITROGLYCERINE-TX is in the POTENTIAL-EVIDENCE of DIFFERENTIAL.
STRESS-TEST is in the POTENTIAL-EVIDENCE of DIFFERENTIAL.
The COST of NITROGLYCERINE-TX is low.
The COST of STRESS-TEST is medium.

The positive example is Stress-test, which was not selected by the system because its cost was more than low. The negative example is Nitroglycerine-tx, which was selected by the system. The justifications in the window shown above were seeded by ASK; they correspond to the clauses of the strategy rules that picked Nitroglycerine-tx and not Stress-test.

In the justification session, the user tells ASK to consider *conclusive* evidence for *critical* hypotheses. The set of critical hypotheses is already represented by a knowledge-base object. Critical-hypotheses is defined as a set of hypotheses that are active (and therefore on the differential) and time-critical (a feature of hypotheses). The relationship between conclusive evidence and critical hypotheses *is not* currently represented by a feature. The relationship *is* currently defined for the set of hypotheses on the differential. Since the set of critical hypotheses and the differential share the same domain, the feature implementing the potentially-conclusive-evidence relationship can be applied to the critical-hypotheses object. The user accomplishes this by clicking on the critical-hypotheses object and performing the operations shown in the following windows.

**CRITICAL HYPOTHESES**

Display unit
Remove Object
Apply an existing feature ✓
Define a new feature

**Members of the class FEATURES**

ACTIVE-P
APPLICABILITY
CLASSES
COST
CRITICALITY
DIAGNOSTIC-DATA
EXECUTED?
EXPECTED-COST
GENERALITY
LEVEL-OF-SUPPORT
NETWORK-DEPENDENTS
POTENTIAL-EVIDENCE
POTENTIALLY-CONCLUSIVE-EVIDENCE ✓
POTENTIALLY-RULES-OUT
POTENTIALLY-TRIGGERED
TIME-CRITICALITY
TRIGGER-LEVEL
VALUE

The feature potentially-conclusive-evidence was conveniently defined to work for any set of hypotheses, and critical-hypotheses is a set of hypotheses. As a result, when the user applies the feature to critical-hypotheses, the set of potentially conclusive evidence for critical hypotheses is immediately computed. The newly-applied feature is displayed in the relevant objects window and becomes available as a justification. The updated relevant objects window shows the value of the feature as the singleton set containing the action Stress-test. In the window shown below the user selects this fact as a justification for choosing the stress test.

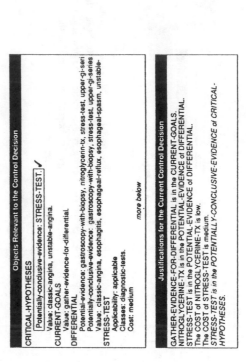

**Objects Relevant to the Control Decision**

CRITICAL-HYPOTHESES
  Potentially-conclusive-evidence: STRESS-TEST. ✓
  Value: classic-angina, unstable-angina.
CURRENT-GOALS
  Value: gather-evidence-for-differential.
DIFFERENTIAL
  Potential-evidence: gastroscopy-with-biopsy, nitroglycerin-tx, stress-test, upper-gi-seri
  Potentially-conclusive-evidence: gastroscopy-with-biopsy, stress-test, upper-gi-series
  Value: classic-angina, esophagitis, esophageal-reflux, esophageal-spasm, unstable-
STRESS-TEST
  Applicability: applicable
  Classes: diagnostic-tests.
  Cost: medium          *more below*

**Justifications for the Current Control Decision**

GATHER-EVIDENCE-FOR-DIFFERENTIAL is in the CURRENT-GOALS.
NITROGLYCERINE-TX is in the POTENTIAL-EVIDENCE of DIFFERENTIAL.
STRESS-TEST is in the POTENTIAL-EVIDENCE of DIFFERENTIAL.
The COST of NITROGLYCERINE-TX is low.
The COST of STRESS-TEST is medium.
*STRESS-TEST is in the POTENTIALLY-CONCLUSIVE-EVIDENCE of CRITICAL-HYPOTHESES.*

With this set of justifications, ASK generates the rule paraphrased to the user as follows:

Some representational limitations of the strategy-rule approach to control were revealed in another experiment in which ASK was used to reimplement NEOMYCIN's diagnostic strategy. One difference between ASK's strategy rules and NEOMYCIN's tasks and metarules [Clancey 1988; Clancey and Bock 1988] is the way in which the problem-solving state is represented. In NEOMYCIN, metarules are invoked by tasks, and tasks are invoked like subroutines with arguments. Some of the problem-solving state is represented by the calling stack for task invocation. In addition, metarules access and set global variables. These computational properties make certain kinds of strategic knowledge easier to represent. The task structure serves as a natural representation for goal-directed control, and the global variables and task arguments encourage a strategy with a persistent focus on the "current hypothesis" and "current finding." In contrast, ASK's strategy rules have no hierarchical calling structure and cannot set global variables. As a consequence, it is difficult to implement a goal-directed (top-down) strategy or to manipulate the differential as a data structure. ASK's representation and the corresponding elicitation metaphor is more suited to acquiring an opportunistic strategy.

In principle, one can completely reproduce the observable behavior of the NEOMYCIN strategy using ASK, because the strategy-rule language together with MU's control features are Turing complete. In practice, knowledge engineering skills were required to coerce the desired behavior from strategy rules, mainly by defining control features. For example, the engineer using ASK had to define special control features to correspond to NEOMYCIN's "current hypothesis" and "pursued hypothesis" which were stated more naturally with metarules and variables in the NEOMYCIN language. The engineering effort went into defining sophisticated features. ASK is more helpful for building up associations between existing features and actions in strategic decisions.

## 6. Analysis: Scope of Applicability, Assumptions, and Limitations

Although the approach taken with ASK is independent of any domain, it necessarily sacrifices generality for power. The ASK approach commits to a method of applying strategic knowledge that iteratively chooses among individual actions, employs strategy rules for the representation, and bases new knowledge on justifications of choices of actions. As a consequence, ASK has limited scope and requires some strong assumptions. This section will characterize the scope of applicability of ASK in terms of properties of a class of performances tasks and will explicate the critical assumptions and limitations that are inherent in the approach.

### 6.1. Characteristics of Tasks to Which ASK Applies

The problems to which ASK can be applied are those for which expert strategy is essential to the performance task and for which the strategy-rule knowledge representation and MU architecture are adequate. This is not a circular definition; it states that the applicability of the acquisition tool depends largely on the adequacy of the performance representation. Representational adequacy is judged with respect to the class of performance tasks and

---

```
Select an action when
  a current goal is gather-evidence-for-differential, and
  the action is in the potential-evidence of differential, and
  the action is in the potentially-confirming-evidence of critical-hypotheses, and
  the cost of the action is ignored.
```

The final clause of the rule is a positive form of the *dropping conditions* generalization operator. It specifies explicitly that the cost criterion, which was mentioned in the system's existing rule, should be overridden by this new rule. The ignore clauses are used in determining the shadowing relationship among strategy rules (Section 3.5). This new rule will shadow the existing rule. The operational effect is that the actions that are potentially conclusive for critical hypotheses will be selected regardless of cost, if there are any such actions and hypotheses; otherwise, actions that provide evidence for any active hypotheses and have low cost will be selected.

## 5. Experience Using ASK

This section reports briefly on some test sessions performed to evaluate ASK. More detailed analysis of these experiments and the positive and negative results may be found in [Gruber 1989].

ASK has been tested for the *prospective diagnosis* task [Cohen, Greenberg, and Delisio 1987] in the domain of chest pain, which is the problem addressed by the MUM system and used as an example performance system in this article. The original MUM strategy, the strategic phase planner described in [Cohen, et al. 1987], was written by a knowledge engineer as a set of knowledge sources implemented in Lisp. ASK was used by its designer to (re)acquire MUM's strategic knowledge from scratch in the form of strategy rules.

ASK was also tested with the physician who served as the domain expert for MUM. He was able to add domain-specific strategic knowledge to an existing general strategy in dialogs like those demonstrated in Section 4. In one session, the original domain expert taught a colleague how to use ASK. In general, this experience suggested that the following conditions are important for success at helping the domain expert teach a diagnostic strategy to ASK:

• The relevant control features are defined in advance (e.g., potentially-conclusive-evidence relation of Section 4.10) or are analogous to existing features (e.g., the definition of time-required, which is analogous to cost, can be elicited by example as shown in Section 4.6). When new features have no analog, then it may require knowledge engineering skills to define them. The problem of defining features is discussed in Section 6.3.

• The user understands the opportunistic control model that underlies the strategy-rule representation. If the user does not understand how the strategic knowledge is used, he or she may not give ASK useful information upon which to build strategy rules. For example, when the second physician used ASK for the first time, he tried to get it to follow a procedure-like plan: e.g., ask *all* the history and examination questions before proposing *any* diagnostic tests. This caused ASK to construct an overly general strategy rule, as described in Section 6.3.

In general, the opportunistic style of control afforded by ASK's representation *generates* plans based on underlying reasons for taking plan steps (actions), when they are available. A memory-based planner unfolds and *instantiates* stored plans, in which individual actions need no independent justification. Applications requiring domain-specific strategic knowledge often do both styles of reasoning about action. *Within* an ONCOCIN protocol, for example, actions may be modified or dropped for reasons relating to the dynamic situation (e.g., the condition of the patient). Strategic knowledge for modifying steps within a plan could be formulated in strategy rules and acquired with ASK if the position of an action in a plan were abstracted as a control feature. In ONCOCIN this knowledge is, in fact, represented with rules that are indexed by protocols.[3]

*Local action-selection criteria can avoid global pitfalls.* Computer players of adversarial games often are based on static evaluation of position. Their strategy for selecting a next move is to choose the action that scores best on the evaluation function. If the evaluation function can be structured as a conjunctive expression over features, ASK could be used to acquire it. For example, ASK can acquire the kind of strategy learned by Waterman's poker player: mappings from descriptions of the board and the opponent to betting actions [Waterman 1970]. A game-playing strategy based on mappings from features of game situations to classes of moves will succeed if the features are usefully predictive—if what looks good locally does not lead to global pitfalls.

A borderline negative example is chess, where strategy is often played out over several moves, and evaluation functions are prone to horizon effects. If the right features can be found, strategy rules can map them to actions and ASK can acquire them. If the features invented by the user lead to pitfalls, then acquiring rules that use these features will not produce a globally optimal strategy.

In general, strategy rules support the reactive style of reasoning, where features are immediately available. In contrast, search-based planning can explore the outcomes of actions into the simulated future and back up the evaluation of the utility of the results. Therefore, ASK can be useful for tasks in which the effects of actions cannot be accurately predicted. The features acquired by ASK combine predictions of effects and the expected utility of effects.

*An optimal decision among actions is not required or possible for every choice of actions.* The chest pain application is both a positive and negative example. Most of the evidence-gathering questions, tests, and therapies are chosen with relatively simple measures of utility, such as qualitative measures of diagnosticity, efficacy, and cost. In practice, the data and necessity to elicit probabilities and numeric estimates of utility for every possible combination of actions is not present. However, a negative example in the same domain is the *last* strategic decision that is typically made (or avoided): deciding whether to perform angiography and consequently open heart surgery. This decision has been successfully modeled using the techniques of decision analysis [Pauker and Kassirer 1981].

There is no reason in principle why ASK's model of selecting actions cannot be described in terms of expected utility, nor is there any fundamental reason why a Bayesian utility function could not be used as a feature in strategy rules. The practical difference is in how a utility model is constructed. A set of strategy rules form a qualitative model of the utility

the problem-solving method for which a representation is designed (see Section 2.1). So, ASK's applicability will be characterized in terms of tasks for which the strategy-rule representation and the strategy-rule control cycle are appropriate.

The major characteristics of tasks to which ASK would apply are as follows:

*Actions can be selected one at a time (as opposed to sequences of action).* A task for which this characteristic often holds is reactive planning for robots, where uncertainty about the world and real-time constraints necessitate acting without projection. Robots controlled by reactive planners select actions on the basis of immediate features of the environment, without projecting the consequences of several possible sequences of actions and picking the best sequence.

A task for which selecting actions one at a time is *not* appropriate is planning a set of drugs to cover an infection. MYCIN's therapy algorithm, for example, selects a collection of drugs to cover a set of infectious organisms using an algorithm written in Lisp [Clancey 1984]. This task necessitates reasoning about the *collective* properties of groups of drugs and organisms. Since the utility of individual actions depends strongly on the other actions to be selected at the same time, the strategy-rule representation could not capture the desired drug-selection expertise. (If every possible collection of drugs was represented as a "superaction," then strategy rules could represent drug-selection criteria. However, this is not feasible for large numbers of drugs, and it reduces all strategic reasoning to a single decision.)

*Actions can be related directly to the situations in which they should be chosen.* A positive example of a task with this property is selecting legal cases for argument, where cases are treated as actions. The merits of each case can be represented with features that describe its individual properties and its relationships to other cases and the current fact situation (e.g., Ashley's [1989] *dimensions*). A case-selection strategy might be modeled by relating the relevant features of legal situations to the features of cases that may be cited in the specified situations. For instance, in a trade secrets situation one might cite cases that make a claim about whether and how secrets were disclosed.

A negative example is the management of cancer treatment plans, the domain of the performance system ONCOCIN [Tu, et al. 1989]. The strategy for cancer treatment in ONCOCIN is represented with *protocols*: skeletal plans that are instantiated with therapeutic actions for particular patients. In attempting to model the individual treatment steps as actions in ASK, we found that the justifications for choosing the next action in cancer protocols were often statements of the form "because drug V is a member of the drug combination VAM, which is the next chemotherapy to be administered to this patient according to protocol 20-83-1" rather than "VAM is useful for small cell lung cancer because this combination can help prevent the tumor becoming resistant." The justifications also did not include a description of the context in which drugs V, A, and M are competing with other possible drugs. The knowledge underlying the recommendation of the VAM drug combination is compiled into the skeletal plan for a protocol. In this domain it is unrealistic to expect the experts to justify treatment plans with underlying reasons for their use, because by their very nature protocols are experiments designed to *test* the effectiveness of treatment strategies.

of actions, where the union of actions recommended by rules are treated as equivalent. A multiattribute decision model [Keeney and Raiffa 1976] makes finer-grained, numeric estimates of the relative utility of each attribute, and combines them to rank the recommended actions.

## 6.2. Critical Assumptions

ASK makes progress in automating the acquisition of strategic knowledge, but many aspects of this difficult problem are not solved. What is left for further work is revealed by the key assumptions that the ASK approach makes about the available knowledge and the people that can provide it. Some key assumptions are discussed here, and a more complete list is supplied in [Gruber 1989].

*Requirements on the substantive knowledge.* The ASK approach assumes that substantive knowledge of the performance system: 1) is already acquired or can be acquired; 2) is correct; and 3) is sufficient for making the distinctions necessary for the strategic knowledge.

The control features used by ASK depend on existing substantive knowledge in the inference network of a MU performance system. For example, in diagnostic tasks, much of the important substantive knowledge is found in combination functions which specify how evidential support values and other inferential values are propagated through the inference network. In the MU environment, combination functions are acquired with a symbol-level interface—editors that present and elicit knowledge in the same form as it is used (i.e., rules, slot values, etc.). ASK assumes that the MU interface is adequate for acquiring substantive knowledge.

A more serious problem is the assumption that the substantive knowledge is correct. ASK's credit assignment algorithm determines what type of rule to acquire and which objects the rule must match and not match. The algorithm is based on the assumption that the features mentioned in existing strategy rules are correct. To account for the discrepancy between system and user actions, a new rule must match different features or different values of features than the existing strategy rules. If the features return incorrect values for some actions, this algorithm cannot correctly attribute the blame.

Finally, ASK assumes that the features that are already defined or are easily defined within the existing knowledge base are sufficient for representing the desired strategy. The experiment in reimplementing NEOMYCIN described in Section 5 was an opportunity to test this assumption. NEOMYCIN's strategy makes heavy use of the subsumption relation among hypotheses. For example, one metarule specifies that, "If the hypothesis being focused upon has a child that has not been pursued, then pursue that child." The CHILD metarelation assumed by this rule is a subsumption relation among hypotheses that was not present in the MUM knowledge base used in our experiment. It was simply not possible to acquire this strategic knowledge without reorganizing the substantive knowledge base (i.e., identifying abstract categories of diseases and relating them in a hierarchy to the existing diseases).

In general, the overall effectiveness of ASK in acquiring strategic knowledge is bounded by the difficulty of representing the relevant control features for the domain.

*Validity of experts' justifications for acquiring strategy.* It was argued in Section 1 that the acquisition of strategic knowledge is difficult because domain experts do not normally express their strategy in a form that is generative, operational, and general (i.e., because of representation mismatch). However, it is observed that experts *can* give justifications for specific strategic decisions. The approach taken in ASK requires a strong assumption: that experts' justifications form a valid basis for acquiring the strategic knowledge of systems. There are several ways that this assumption might be wrong.

One way is the problem of tacit knowledge—that the knowledge we wish to acquire from experts is not explicitly present in what they tell us. An influential theory in cognitive science argues that the knowledge underlying expertise is often tacit due to the process of *knowledge compilation* [Anderson 1986]. As experts learn problem-solving strategies from experience in a domain, they internalize the useful associations between situations and actions and become unaware of the inferential steps that they may have made as novices. For example, physicians in an educational setting may teach diagnostic strategy one way and practice it another way. In experimental settings, when people are asked to account for their decisions retrospectively they often refer to causal theories or judgments of plausibility rather than the pertinent stimuli and their responses [Nisbett and Wilson 1977]. And some writers argue that the difference between being able to act and being able to talk about action is fundamental—that computer models of action are essentially incapable of capturing the real basis for action [Winograd and Flores 1986].

If experts cannot account for their strategic decisions, ASK cannot acquire the strategic expertise in a program. There is a difference, however, between assuming that experts can describe their own cognitive processes and assuming that they can justify their behavior. ASK only depends on the latter assumption. The assumptions that experts can provide valid justifications may be reformulated as the requirement that experts be good teachers. Remember that ASK is designed to acquire knowledge for choosing actions that are observable and, therefore, objectively justifiable. The fact that medical school professors may not practice what they preach does not mean that the justifications are invalid. On the contrary, good teachers can account for behavior in a principled way and in objective terms, even though their compiled expertise may not follow from their explanations.

A second problem with the reliance on expert-supplied justifications is the assumption that domain experts can invent useful abstractions of the domain—the right control features. In the same way that an autonomous machine-learning program is limited by the description language provided by the program author, a knowledge acquisition system such as ASK is dependent on the abstraction skills of the user.[4] ASK relies on the user to invent features that not only are sufficient to distinguish actions in specific cases, but also lay out a space of relevant generalizations. This assumption would be unfounded if the expert defined a unique feature for every training case: the resulting strategy—a lookup table of special cases—would be brittle. It is also possible that an expert can describe useful features in natural language but cannot implement them.

The validity of an assumption about the skill level of users is an empirical question, and the answers will depend on the subjects and the tasks. ASK helps frame the research question by distinguishing between the ability to *invent* the necessary features, which is structured by the elicitation of justifications, and the *implementation* of features, which is partially supported by a symbol-level interface for defining features. If an ASK user cannot implement a feature but knows what it should represent, she calls the knowledge engineer. The acquisition of features (new terms) is an interesting area for further study.

*6.3. Major Limitations*

Two of the fundamental limitations to the approach taken in ASK are discussed in this section. A more complete analysis is given in [Gruber 1989].

**6.3.1. Reliance on Knowledge Engineering Skills** It should be clear from the preceding discussion that ASK depends on the ability of the user to define and implement control features. The fact that many features are not easy to implement means that ASK is still limited by the operationalization aspect of representation mismatch. The problem of operationalizing terms is relevant to any learning system whose description language can be extended by the user. Although ASK provides a helpful interface for defining new features, some new features require programming to implement. The problem is not a matter of learning the notation; one needs to know a lot more than the syntax of Lisp to be able to implement control features that capture sophisticated assessments of the state of problem solving. To implement a feature such as the potentially conclusive-evidence relation, one needs to understand the workings of the MU architecture at the symbol level. That is the expertise of knowledge engineers, not domain experts.

There is a way in which ASK's elicitation technique can actually aggravate the problem of representation mismatch. ASK is designed to present the "user illusion" [Kay 1984] of an interface that accepts *explanations* for strategic decisions. In contrast, a symbol-level acquisition tool such as TEIRESIAS [Davis 1976] supports a straightforward interface to rules without disguising them as anything else. The problem with a system such as ASK that presents a knowledge-level interface to the user but internally makes symbol-level distinctions is that the user's model of how the system works can differ significantly from how the system actually functions. If the user's model is inaccurate, she cannot predict what the system will do with what is elicited. The result is a breakdown in communication and a failure in the knowledge acquisition process.

One of the experiments in which ASK was used by physicians illustrates a case in which the user's ignorance of the operational semantics of strategy rules resulted in an unintended strategy. The expert wanted to teach the system to ask all applicable questions of one class before asking any applicable questions of another. He answered ASK's prompts in such a way that the credit assignment algorithm determined that it needed to acquire a filter rule, when in fact a selection rule was needed. When the expert explained (with justifications) that questions of one type should *not* be selected, ASK generated a filter rule that prohibited questions of that type from *ever* being selected, which is a gross overgeneralization. The error was not apparent until all the actions from the first class were exhausted and the system could not suggest any more actions to perform. To have avoided this problem, the user would have had to understand the operational difference between filter and selection rules and the correspondence between his answers to ASK's prompts and the type of rule being acquired.

**6.3.2. Overgeneralization Due to the Lack of a Training Set** Although ASK uses generalization operators, it differs from most inductive learning techniques in that it does not learn from a large training set of examples. The user is responsible for choosing training examples that will produce useful generalizations. Unfortunately, the lack of a large training set limits the extent to which ASK can help with the generalization problem.

It is easy to generate strategy rules with ASK that are overly general, because of the elicitation technique. Adding justifications specializes the resulting strategy rule; doing nothing leaves it general. Consider two strategic situations in the medical workup. In the early phase, actions are selected for their low cost and minimal diagnosticity. In later phases, actions that offer a potentially significant diagnostic or therapeutic value are selected at higher cost, even if lower-cost actions are available. If the selection rules for the first phase were acquired without any clauses identifying the strategic situation (i.e., features of the early phase), then the rules acquired for the early phase would also match when the later phase arose. There is no knowledge-free way for ASK to anticipate the missing clauses that specify the context in which a rule should apply.

In practice, overgeneralizations of this type are discouraged by starting with an initial set of strategy rules that specify the basic strategic situations to distinguish. These rules serve as the basis for seed justifications (Section 4.5) upon which the user builds a set of justifications for a specific case. The knowledge engineer can provide a set of very general strategy rules, anticipating some of the situations in which domain-specific tradeoffs will arise. Then the major role of the user is to *specialize* the general strategy with application-specific strategic knowledge. Overgeneralizations are still likely, however, when the user fails to elaborate the features of a novel context in which a selection is made among specific actions.

If ASK kept a library of training cases, it might be able to check newly formed rules for inconsistency with past training and prevent excessive overgeneralization. Each case in a library would need the values of all relevant features of the positive and negative examples and the features specifying the strategic situation. When a new rule is proposed, it could be tested against the stored case. If the new rule recommended a different outcome than the stored case, and did not shadow the rule associated with the case, then the two rules would be inconsistent. Unfortunately, keeping a library of cases is not trivial because the space of features can grow with experience. If a new rule mentions a new feature, it is incomparable with previous cases that did not mention the feature, unless the feature is static (i.e., its value does not change during the execution of the performance system). A general solution is to store a snapshot of the entire working memory with each case, so that all possible relevant features could be derived. This solution could be expensive. The whole issue of how to store experience for future learning is an intriguing avenue for research. Some promising approaches have been developed for case-based learning systems [e.g., Bareiss 1989; Hammond 1989].

**7. Discussion: Key Design Decisions**

Design decisions are often hidden sources of power in AI systems. This section discusses a few characteristics of ASK's design as they relate to its function as an automated knowledge acquisition tool.

The strategy-rule representation supported by ASK is neither a novel way of formulating strategy nor an ad hoc design. For the purpose of *implementing* strategic knowledge, a procedural representation such as a Lisp function or an augmented transition network would have been more flexible. The goals in designing a representation for ASK are to be able to capture strategic knowledge in an executable form *and* to be able to elicit it from experts.

Strategy rules were designed to represent mappings between states of the inference network, work and equivalence classes of actions, for each of three operations: propose, filter, and select. The declarative clausal form of strategy rules allows for execution by conventional unification-style matching and corresponds to the structure of justifications. Limiting the operational effects of rules to propose, filter, and select operations simplifies credit assignment and conflict resolution. The result is a representation in which strategic knowledge can be acquired.

Two of the design decisions that led to this representation are critical to ASK's techniques for automated knowledge acquisition. First, strategic knowledge has been formulated as classification knowledge. Second, a global strategy is represented as a family of strategy rules with fine-grained effects. The rationale for each decision is given below.

### 7.1. Formulating Strategic Knowledge as Classification Knowledge

Strategy rules structure knowledge about what to do next as knowledge for classification: associations between strategic situations and classes of actions. The following capabilities follow from this design.

***The ability to use conventional machine learning techniques.*** ASK can use simple syntactic induction operators for generalization (turning constants into variables, dropping conditions, and extending reference). Whereas the problem of learning sequences and procedures with internal states is very hard [Dietterich and Michalski 1986], the problem of learning classification rules is well understood [Dietterich and Michalski 1983]. If mappings from states to actions define the classes of state descriptions in which actions are appropriate, a learner can generalize control knowledge by generalizing class descriptions.

***The ability to elicit machine-understandable information at the knowledge level.*** ASK can elicit applicability conditions for control decisions in machine-understandable terms, because the justifications from the user's point of view correspond to clauses in the rule representation. The list of justifications can be elicited in any order, since they are used as conjuncts in the class descriptions.

***The ability to use simple explanations for input and output.*** ASK can use simple template-based natural language generation to provide explanations. ASK's explanations are just lists of facts relevant to the current control decision paraphrased in English; they are essentially the same as justifications. ASK can get away with this simple explanation technique because every control decision is a flat match of situations and associated actions. Because there is no implicit state, such as there is in an evolving control plan, the context of the decision to choose an action is fully explained by the clauses of matching strategy rules. The English explanation—paraphrases of instantiated clauses—corresponds to what is happening at the symbol level.[5]

The use of explicit, abstract control knowledge for explanation was developed in the work of Swartout, et al. [Swartout 1983; Neches, Swartout, and Moore 1985] and Clancey [Clancey 1983a, 1983b]. ASK follows the principle arising from their work that an explanation of surface behavior should correspond to the structure of the system's strategy. However, in contrast to serious attempts at knowledge-system explanation, ASK's explanations do not describe the goal structure and focusing behavior of the system because the performance architecture does not support the corresponding control mechanisms (e.g., goal stacks, tasks, etc.).

***The inability to acquire goal-directed plans.*** As a consequence of formulating strategy as simple classification, it is awkward to acquire goal-directed strategy with ASK. To capture the knowledge for reasoning about action at different abstraction levels, the strategy-rule representation would have to be extended to support hierarchical planning in the sense of ABSTRIPS [Sacerdoti 1974]. Currently, all strategy rules within each category (propose, filter, select) are matched in parallel at each iteration. In one extension proposed in [Gruber 1989], the rules would be partitioned into abstraction levels; at each level, rules would choose the subgoals for the lower abstraction level until the subgoals at the lowest level are grounded in individual actions. It is not clear whether the added structure would compromise the comprehensibility of the elicitation technique; this is a question for future research.

### 7.2. Formulating Strategy as Fine-Grained Reactions

Recall the third aspect of representation mismatch: domain experts have more difficulty devising a general procedure that accounts for their strategic expertise than describing what they actually do in specific cases. ASK shows that strategic knowledge can be acquired from experts if it is elicited in the context of specific choices among actions and then generalized. This is possible because strategy rules model local decisions about actions that can be generalized to classes of situations and actions. In theory, what appears to be a global strategy can emerge from a series of local strategic decisions. For example, Chapman and Agre [1986] propose that complex, coherent behavior arises from the continued activation of situation-action structures without top-down control.

There is empirical support for the notion that globally coherent plans can be acquired by eliciting the knowledge for local decisions. For example, SALT succeeds at acquiring knowledge about how to construct globally satisfactory solutions to a class of design problems [Marcus 1987, 1988]. SALT elicits from designers knowledge about constraints among individual parts—information that is relatively easy to specify—and offers help for putting the pieces together. SALT's results are relevant to ASK because constructing a solution requires managing the *process* by which parts are assembled under constraints; this is similar to managing the selection of actions. SALT can acquire the requisite knowledge from experts because it decomposes the larger task of assembling a solution into small decisions about what part to add, how to (immediately) check it for constraints, and how to recover from those violated constraints.

One can view SALT's design task and ASK's action-selection task as varieties of planning, where configured parts and diagnostic actions correspond to plan steps. This view reveals an important difference between the two architectures. SALT's planning method provides for a backtracking search, whereas ASK's planning method is purely reactive, with no projection (lookahead) and no possibility to undo actions. This may prove to be an important variable in the question of whether knowledge of local decisions can add up to a global strategy.

## 8. Conclusion

The immediate outcome of this research is a method for partially automating the acquisition of strategic knowledge from experts. The issues that are raised, however, are more significant than the ASK program itself. Strategic knowledge was chosen for the study of knowledge acquisition because it illuminates the problems of representation mismatch. Furthermore, an extreme solution was selected—a declarative representation of reactive control knowledge—to test conjectures about sources of power for knowledge acquisition. The results have been analyzed in the preceding discussions of the scope of applicability, assumptions, limitations, and design decisions. This section concludes with a more general point brought out by this work and the future research it suggests.

If representation mismatch describes the problem of knowledge acquisition, then solutions should offer some way to bridge the representational gap between the domain expert and the implementation. This suggests that the design of knowledge representations is central to addressing the knowledge acquisition problem. This article has emphasized the motivations for and implications of ASK's representation of strategic knowledge in an effort to elucidate principles of *design for acquisition*: how to design knowledge systems to facilitate the acquisition of the knowledge they need.

Earlier reports [Bylander and Chandrasekaran 1987; Gruber and Cohen 1987] describe how knowledge representations and methods for task-level architectures can facilitate *manual* knowledge acquisition (i.e., mediated by tools that are passive). The design of representations can reduce representation mismatch from the implementation side by providing (generic) task-level primitives which enable experts to work directly with the knowledge base.

The ASK research illustrates how *automated* knowledge acquisition can help overcome representation mismatch by eliciting knowledge in a form that is available from experts and yet is very close to an operational, generalizable representation. Again, the design of representations plays a central role in the success of the knowledge acquisition process. The major contributions of ASK to the process—active elicitation of justifications, credit assignment, and syntactic generalization—are enabled by the declarative, role-restricted rule representation. At the same time, the kind of strategic knowledge that can be acquired—opportunistic and reactive rather than goal-directed and plan-driven—is a function of what can be naturally represented in strategy rules.

A similar power/generality tradeoff can be found in most knowledge acquisition tools. At the power end of the continuum lie OPAL-class elicitation tools [Freiling and Alexander 1984; Gale 1987; Musen, et al. 1987], which acquire knowledge in representations customized to a problem-solving method and a particular domain. OPAL employs elicitation techniques that are customized for both the skeletal-plan refinement method used in ONCOCIN and the domain of cancer therapy. As a result, OPAL can be used by domain experts. At the generality end lie TEIRESIAS-class tools [Davis 1976; Boose and Bradshaw 1987; Shachter and Heckerman 1987], which acquire knowledge at the symbol-level for formalisms that are not committed to particular tasks or domains. TEIRESIAS makes it easy to enter and modify rules but requires the user to bridge the representational gap from the domain- and problem-specific description to the backward-chaining architecture. Somewhere in the middle are the MOLE-class tools [Eshelman 1988; Klinker 1988; Marcus 1988], which acquire knowledge in representations that are method-specific and domain-independent. This article has shown several ways in which the design of ASK trades the generality of a representation useful for knowledge engineering for the power of a restricted representation suitable for automated knowledge acquisition.

Further research is needed to investigate how knowledge representations and reasoning methods can be designed to make the task of knowledge acquisition more amenable to computer-assisted techniques for elicitation and learning.

## Acknowledgments

This article reports on the author's doctoral research directed by Paul Cohen at the University of Massachusetts, Department of Computer and Information Science. The work was supported by DARPA-RADC contract F30602-85-C0014 and ONR University Research Initiative contract N00014-86-K-1764. The paper was written at the Stanford Knowledge Systems Laboratory with funding from Tektronics, Inc. Computing facilities were provided by the SUMEX-AIM resource under NIH grant RR-00785.

Discussions with many colleagues have contributed to the ideas in this paper, including Kevin Ashley, Jim Bennett, B. Chandrasekaran, Bill Clancey, David Day, Larry Fagan, Richard Fikes, Michael Freiling, Victor Lesser, John McDermott, Mark Musen, Paul Utgoff, and especially Paul Cohen. I am very grateful to Ray Bareiss, Tilda Brown, Paul Cohen, Richard Keller, Sandra Marcus, Mark Musen, Bruce Porter, and Nancy Wogrin for thoughtful and careful reviews of earlier drafts of this paper.

## Notes

1. Dietterich and Bennett [1988] refer to "making goals achievable" and "making goals more useful."
2. Control features correspond to the *metarelations* in Clancey's tasks-and-metarules representation [Clancey and Bock 1988].
3. Thanks to Lawrence Fagan, Mark Musen, and Samson Tu for their help with this analysis.
4. Getting the right primitive features has always been essential to getting a machine learning program to find useful generalizations. For example, Quinlan [1983] reports having spent three months devising a good set of attributes (board position features for chess) so that the learning program ID3 could produce a decision tree in seconds.
5. This is an oversimplification. In actuality, the shadowing relations among strategy rules are not reflected in the explanation. Not surprisingly, they are a source of confusion for users, possibly because they do not fit the simple conceptual model of situation-action.

# References

Agre, P.E., and Chapman. D. 1987. Pengi: An implementation of a theory of activity. *Proceedings of the Sixth National Conference on Artificial Intelligence* (pp. 268–272). Seattle. Washington: Morgan Kaufmann.

Anderson, J.R. 1986. Knowledge compilation: the general learning mechanism. In R.S. Michalski, J.G. Carbonell, and T.M. Mitchell (Eds.), *Machine learning: An artificial intelligence approach.* (Vol. 2). San Mateo, CA: Morgan Kaufmann.

Ashley, K.D. 1989. *Modelling legal argument: Reasoning with cases and hypotheticals.* Cambridge. MA: MIT Press. Based on doctoral dissertation. Department of Computer and Information Science. University of Massachusetts. Amherst.

Bareiss, E.R. 1989. *Exemplar-based knowledge acquisition: A unified approach to concept representation, classification, and learning.* Boston: Academic Press. Based on doctoral dissertation, Department of Computer Science. University of Texas. Austin.

Benjamin, D.P. 1987. Learning strategies by reasoning about rules. *Proceedings of the Tenth International Joint Conference on Artificial Intelligence* (pp. 256–259). Milan, Italy: Morgan Kaufmann.

Bennett, J.S. 1985. ROGET: A knowledge-based system for acquiring the conceptual structure of a diagnostic expert system. *Journal of Automated Reasoning, 1,* 49–74.

Boose, J.H. 1986. *Expertise Transfer for Expert System Design.* New York: Elsevier.

Boose, J.H., and Bradshaw, J.M. 1987. Expertise transfer and complex problems: Using AQUINAS as a knowledge acquisition workbench for expert systems. *International Journal of Man-Machine Studies, 26,* 21–25.

Buchanan, B.G., Barstow, D.K., Bechtel, R., Bennett, J., Clancey, W., Kulikowski, C., Mitchell, T., and Waterman, D.A. 1983. Constructing an expert system. In F. Hayes-Roth, D.A. Waterman, and D.B. Lenat (Eds.), *Building expert systems.* Reading, MA.: Addison-Wesley.

Buchanan, B.G., and Shortliffe, E.H. 1984. *Rule-Based Expert Systems: The MYCIN Experiments of the Stanford Heuristic Programming Project.* Reading, MA: Addison-Wesley.

Bylander, R., and Chandrasekaran. B. 1987. Generic tasks for knowledge-based reasoning: The "right" level of abstraction for knowledge acquisition. *International Journal of Man-Machine Studies, 26,* 231–244.

Chandrasekaran, B. 1983. Toward a taxonomy of problem-solving types. *AI Magazine, 4,* 9–17.

Chandrasekaran, B. 1986. Generic tasks in knowledge-based reasoning: High-level building blocks for expert system design. *IEEE Expert, 1,* 23–30.

Chandrasekaran, B. 1987. Towards a functional architecture for intelligence based on generic information processing tasks. *Proceedings of the Tenth International Joint Conference on Artificial Intelligence* (pp. 1183–1192). Milan. Italy: Morgan Kaufmann.

Chapman, D. and Agre. P.E. 1987. Abstract reasoning as emergent from concrete activity. In M.P. Georgeff and A.L. Lansky (Eds.), *Reasoning about Actions and Plans, Proceedings of the 1986 Workshop at Timberline. Oregon* (pp. 411–424).

Clancey, W.J. 1983a. The epistemology of a rule-based expert system—A framework for explanation. *Artificial Intelligence, 20,* 215–251.

Clancey, W.J. 1983b. The advantages of abstract control knowledge in expert system design. *Proceedings of the Third National Conference on Artificial Intelligence* (pp. 74–78). Washington, D.C.: Morgan Kaufmann.

Clancey, W.J. 1984. Details of the revised therapy algorithm. In B.G. Buchanan and E.H. Shortliffe (Eds.), *Rule-based expert systems: The MYCIN experiments of the Stanford Heuristic Programming Project.* Reading, MA: Addison-Wesley.

Clancey, W.J. 1985. Heuristic classification. *Artificial Intelligence. 27,* 289–350.

Clancey, W.J. 1988. Acquiring, representing, and evaluating a competence model of diagnosis. In Chi. Glaser. and Farr (Eds.), *Contributions to the nature of expertise* (pp. 343–418). Hillsdale, N.J.: Lawrence Erlbaum. Previously published as KSL Memo 84-2, Stanford University, February, 1984.

Clancey, W.J. 1989. Viewing knowledge bases as qualitative models. *IEEE Expert. 4,* 9–23. Previously published as Technical Report KSL-86-27. Stanford University.

Clancey, W.J., and Bock. C. 1988. Representing control knowledge as abstract tasks and metarules. In L. Bolc and M. Coombs (Eds.), *Expert system applications* (pp. 1–77). New York: Springer-Verlag.

Cohen, P.R., Day, D.S., Delisio, J., Greenberg, M., Kjeldsen. R., Suthers, D., and Berman, P. 1987. Management of uncertainty in medicine. *International Journal of Approximate Reasoning, 1,* 103–116.

Cohen, P.R., Greenberg, M., and Delisio, J. 1987. MU: A development environment for prospective reasoning systems. *Proceedings of the Sixth National Conference on Artificial Intelligence* (pp. 783–788). Seattle. Washington: Morgan Kaufmann.

Davis, R. 1976. *Applications of meta-level knowledge to the construction, maintenance, and use of large knowledge bases.* Doctoral dissertation. Computer Science Department. Stanford University. Reprinted in R. Davis and D.B. Lenat (Eds.), *Knowledge-based systems in artificial intelligence.* New York: McGraw-Hill. 1982.

DeJong, G., and Mooney, R.J. 1986. Explanation-based learning: An alternative view. *Machine Learning, 1,* 145–176.

Dietterich. T.G. and Bennett. J.S. 1988. Varieties of operationality. (Technical Report). Department of Computer Science, Oregon State University.

Dietterich. T.G., London, B., Clarkson. K., and Dromey, G. 1982. Learning and inductive inference. In P.R. Cohen and E. Feigenbaum (Eds.), *The handbook of artificial intelligence (Vol. 3).* Menlo Park, CA: Addison-Wesley.

Dietterich. T.G.. and Michalski. R.S. 1983. A comparative review of selected methods for learning from examples. In R.S. Michalski. J.G. Carbonell. and T.M. Mitchell (Eds.), *Machine learning: An artificial intelligence approach.* San Mateo, CA: Morgan Kaufmann.

Dietterich. T.G.. and Michalski. R.S. 1986. Learning to predict sequences. In R. Michalski. J. Carbonell, and T. Mitchell (Eds.), *Machine learning: An artificial intelligence approach (Vol. 2).* San Mateo, CA: Morgan Kaufmann.

Erman, L.D., Scott, A.C., and London. P.E. 1984. Separating and integrating control in a rule-based tool. *Proceedings of the IEEE Workshop of Knowledge-base Systems* (pp. 37–43). Denver, Colorado.

Eshelman, L. 1988. MOLE: A knowledge-acquisition tool for cover-and-differentiate systems. In S. Marcus (Ed.), *Automating knowledge acquisition for expert systems.* Boston: Kluwer Academic Publishers.

Firby, R.J. 1987. An investigation into reactive planning in complex domains. *Proceedings of the Sixth National Conference on Artificial Intelligence* (pp. 202–206). Seattle. Washington: Morgan Kaufmann.

Freiling, M.J., and Alexander. J.H. 1984. Diagrams and grammars: Tools for mass producing expert systems. *Proceedings of the First Conference on Artificial Intelligence Applications* (pp. 537–543). Denver, Colorado: IEEE Computer Society Press.

Friedland, P.E., and Iwasaki. Y. 1985. The concept and implementation of skeletal plans. *Journal of Automated Reasoning, 1,* 161–208.

Gale, W.A. 1987. Knowledge-based knowledge acquisition for a statistical consulting system. *International Journal of Man-Machine Studies, 13,* 81–116.

Golding, A., Rosenbloom, P.S., and Laird. J.E. 1987. Learning general search control from outside guidance. *Proceedings of the Tenth International Joint Conference on Artificial Intelligence* (pp. 334–337). Milan, Italy: Morgan Kaufmann.

Gruber, T.R. 1989. *The Acquisition of Strategic Knowledge.* Boston: Academic Press. Based on doctoral dissertation, Department of Computer and Information Science, University of Massachusetts.

Gruber, T.R., and Cohen. P.R. 1987. Design for acquisition: Principles of knowledge system design to facilitate knowledge acquisition. *International Journal of Man-Machine Studies, 26,* 143–159.

Hammond, K.J. 1989. *Case-based Planning: Viewing Planning as a Memory Task.* Boston: Academic Press. Based on doctoral dissertation, Computer Science Department, Yale University.

Hannan, J., and Politakis. P. 1985. ESSA: An approach to acquiring decision rules for diagnostic expert systems. *Proceedings of the Second Conference on Artificial Intelligence Applications* (pp. 520–525). Orlando, Florida: IEEE Computer Society Press.

Hayes-Roth, B. 1985. A blackboard architecture for control. *Artificial Intelligence. 26,* 251–321.

Hayes-Roth, B., Garvey, A., Johnson. M., and Hewett, M. 1987. *A layered environment for reasoning about action.* (Technical Report KSL 86-38). Stanford, CA: Computer Science Department, Stanford University.

Hayes-Roth, B., and Hewett. M. 1985. *Learning control heuristics in a blackboard environment.* (Technical Report HPP-85-2). Stanford, CA: Computer Science Department, Stanford University.

Hutchins, E.L., Hollan, J.D., and Norman, D.A. 1986. Direct manipulation interfaces. In D.A. Norman, and S.W. Draper (Eds.), *User centered system design.* Hillsdale, NJ: Lawrence Erlbaum Associates.

Johnson, N.E., and Tomlinson. C.M. 1988. Knowledge representation for knowledge elicitation. *Proceedings of the Third AAAI Knowledge Acquisition for Knowledge-based Systems Workshop,* Banff, Canada, November. Calgary. Alberta: SRDG Publications. Department of Computer Science, University of Calgary.

Kaelbling, L.P. 1987. An architecture for intelligent reactive systems. In M.P. Georgeff and A.L. Lansky (Eds.), *Reasoning About Actions and Plans. Proceedings of the 1986 Workshop at Timberline, Oregon* (pp. 411-424). Morgan Kaufmann.

Kassirer, J.P., and Gorry, G.A. 1978. Clinical problem solving: A behavioral analysis. *Annals of Internal Medicine. 89.* 245-255.

Kay, A. 1984. Computer software. *Scientific American. 251.* 52-59. September.

Keeney, R.L., and Raiffa, H. 1976. *Decisions with Multiple Objectives: Preferences and Value Tradeoffs.* John Wiley and Sons.

Keller, R.M. 1988. Defining operationality for explanation-based learning. *Artificial Intelligence. 35.* 227-241.

Klinker, G. 1988. KNACK: Sample-driven knowledge acquisition for reporting systems. In S. Marcus (Ed.), *Automating knowledge acquisition for expert systems.* Boston: Kluwer Academic Publishers.

Laird, J.D., Newell, A., and Rosenbloom, P.S. 1987. SOAR: An architecture for general intelligence. *Artificial Intelligence. 33.* 1-64.

Lenat, D.B., and Brown, J.S. 1984. Why AM and EURISKO appear to work. *Artificial Intelligence. 23.* 269-294.

Marcus, S. 1987. Taking backtracking with a grain of SALT. *International Journal of Man-Machine Studies. 24.* 383-398.

Marcus, S. 1988. SALT: A knowledge acquisition tool for propose-and-refine systems. In S. Marcus (Ed.), *Automating knowledge acquisition for expert systems.* Boston: Kluwer Academic Publishers.

McDermott, J. 1988. Preliminary steps toward a taxonomy of problem-solving methods. In S. Marcus (Ed.), *Automating knowledge acquisition for expert systems.* Boston: Kluwer Academic Publishers.

Minton, S., and Carbonell, J.G. 1987. Strategies for learning search control rules: An explanation-based approach. *Proceedings of the Tenth International Joint Conference on Artificial Intelligence.* Milan, Italy: Morgan Kaufmann.

Mitchell, T.M. 1982. Generalization as search. *Artificial Intelligence. 18.* 203-226.

Mitchell, T.M., Keller, R.M., and Kedar-Cabelli, S.T. 1986. Explanation-based generalization: A unifying view. *Machine Learning. 1.* 56-80.

Mitchell, T.M., Mahadevan, S., and Steinberg, L.I. LEAP: A learning apprentice for VLSI design. *Proceedings of the Ninth International Conference on Artificial Intelligence* (pp. 573-580). Los Angeles, CA: Morgan Kaufmann.

Mitchell, T.M., Utgoff, P.E., and Banerji, R.B. 1983. Learning by experimentation: Acquiring and refining problem-solving heuristics. In R.S. Michalski, J.G. Carbonell, and T.M. Mitchell (Eds.), *Machine Learning: An Artificial Intelligence Approach.* San Mateo, CA: Morgan Kaufmann.

Mostow, D.J. 1983. Machine transformation of advice into a heuristic search procedure. In R. Michalski, J. Carbonell, and T.M. Mitchell (Eds.), *Machine learning: An artificial intelligence approach.* San Mateo, CA: Morgan Kaufmann.

Morik, K. 1988. Sloppy modeling. In K. Morik (Ed.), *Knowledge representation and organization in machine learning.* Berlin: Springer-Verlag, in press.

Musen, M.A. 1989. *Automated Generation of Model-based Knowledge-Acquisition Tools,* London: Pitman. Based on doctoral dissertation. Computer Science Department, Stanford University.

Musen, M.A., Fagan, L.M., and Shortliffe, E.H. 1986. Graphical specification of procedural knowledge for an expert system. *Proceedings of the 1986 IEEE Computer Society Workshop in Visual Languages* (pp. 167-178). Dallas, Texas.

Musen, M.A., Fagan, L.M., Combs, D.M., and Shortliffe, E.H. 1987. Use of a domain model to drive an interactive knowledge editing tool. *International Journal of Man-Machine Studies. 26.* 105.

Neches, R., Swartout, W., and Moore, J. 1985. Enhanced maintenance and explanation of expert systems through explicit models of their development. *IEEE Transactions on Software Engineering. SE-11* (11). 1337-1351.

Newell, A. 1982. The knowledge level. *Artificial Intelligence. 18.* 87-127.

Nisbett, R., and Wilson, T. 1977. Telling more than we can know: Verbal reports on mental processes. *Psychological Review. 84.* 231-259.

Pauker, S.G., and Kassirer, J.P. 1981. Clinical decision analysis by personal computer. *Archives of Internal Medicine. 141.* 1831-1837.

Quinlan, J.R. 1983. Learning efficient classification procedures and their application to chess end games. In R. Michalski, J. Carbonell, and T. Mitchell (Eds.), *Machine learning: An artificial intelligence approach.* San Mateo, CA: Morgan Kaufmann.

Quinlan, J.R. 1986. Induction of decision trees. *Machine Learning. 1* (1). 81-106.

Sacerdoti, E.D. 1974. Planning in a hierarchy of abstraction spaces. *Artificial Intelligence. 5.* 115-135.

Shachter, R.D. and Heckerman, D.E. 1987. Thinking backward for knowledge acquisition. *AI Magazine 8.* 55-61.

Shaw, M.L.G., and Gaines, B. 1987. Techniques for knowledge acquisition and transfer. *International Journal of Man-Machine Studies. 27.*

Shortliffe, E.H., Scott, A.C., Bischoff, M.B., van Melle, W., and Jacobs, C.D. 1981. ONCOCIN: An expert system for oncology protocol management. *Proceedings of the Seventh International Joint Conference on Artificial Intelligence* (pp. 876-881). Vancouver, British Columbia: Morgan Kaufmann.

Silver, B. 1986. *Meta-level Inference: Representing and Learning Control Information in Artificial Intelligence.* New York: North-Holland.

Sticklen, J., Chandrasekaran, B., and Josephson, J.R. 1985. Control issues in classificatory diagnosis. *Proceedings of the Ninth International Joint Conference on Artificial Intelligence* (pp. 300-306). Los Angeles, CA: Morgan Kaufmann.

Swartout, W. 1983. XPLAIN: A system for creating and explaining expert consulting systems. *Artificial Intelligence. 11.* 115-144.

Tu, S.W., Kahn, M.G., Musen, M.A., Ferguson, J.C., Shortliffe, E.H., and Fagan, L.M. 1989. Episodic monitoring of time-oriented data for heuristic skeletal-plan refinement. *Communications of the ACM.* in press.

Utgoff, P. 1986. *Machine Learning of Inductive Bias.* Boston: Kluwer Academic Publishers. Based on doctoral dissertation, Department of Computer Science, Rutgers University.

Waterman, D.A. 1970. Generalization learning techniques for automating the learning of heuristics. *Artificial Intelligence. 1.* 121-170.

Winograd, T., and Flores, F. 1987. *Understanding Computers and Cognition.* Reading, MA: Addison-Wesley.

Winston, P.H. 1985. Learning structural descriptions from examples. In P.H. Winston (Ed.), *The Psychology of Computer Vision.* New York: McGraw Hill.

# Chapter 4

# Inductive Generalization Methods

Inductive generalization has always been a core concern in artificial intelligence, because intelligence and learning from experience are so closely linked. Statistical methods provide the means for inductive generalizations whenever the pattern to be learned can be expressed mathematically. For patterns without a mathematical representation, inductive generalization had to await the development of AI techniques.

Arthur Samuel programmed an IBM 701 to play checkers in 1952 and subsequently programmed an IBM 704 to *learn* to play checkers in 1954. His tour de force was motivated by his interest in studying machine learning (Samuel, 1959). Because of computer memory limitations, Samuel's representations and operations were all at the level of bit strings. In his studies of learning, however, Samuel was ahead of his time. First, he focused on a specific performance program with an objective measure of performance. Second, he developed creative and novel methods for dealing with the credit assignment problem through look-ahead. Third, he developed creative methods for accumulating extensive experience by having two copies of the program play against each other. Fourth, he recognized difficulties in using an incomplete and redundant set of parameters

in machine learning. Fifth, he implemented techniques for introducing new terms, Sixth, he valued systematic studies based on extensive data. For years, few researchers attempted work in machine learning because Samuel's work was so complete.

Another early foundation for much AI work in inductive learning was the psychologically motivated work of Simon and Feigenbaum (Feigenbaum, 1961), Hunt (Hunt and Hovland, 1961; Hunt, 1962; Hunt et al., 1966), and others. Feigenbaum's EPAM program was a model of how humans learn and forget associations in a classical psychological task of learning paired associations of nonsense syllables. EPAM grew a decision tree as its internal knowledge structure, and its learning process provided a psychologically interesting model of human learning. Hunt's work also provided evidence for the information processing model of psychology, while offering a specific model of concept formation that Quillian and others have programmed into useful induction tools independently of the psychology.

Another important foundational block for AI work in learning comes from the mathematics of control theory, reinforcement learning, and adaptive systems. For references to the rather extensive early literature on the use of computers as hypothetical or real vehicles for exploring these ideas, one might begin with the citations in Minsky and Papert (1969), Minsky (1961b), and Nilsson (1965). This early work on biologically related neural networks laid the foundation for the resurgence of interest in neural networks that is much in evidence today.

All of the issues addressed in current work on induction were known decades ago. Techniques and issues have been refined, and the power of computers has grown so much, that problems of greater complexity can now be addressed. The papers in this chapter present a cutting-edge view of inductive methods.

# Section 4.1

# Learning Classification Knowledge

Classification underlies many, if not all, intelligent activities. Classification is involved in our abilities to take appropriate actions in everyday situations, to make appropriate decisions, to issue appropriate commands. The appropriateness in every case is determined by the patterns, rules, guidelines, policies, conventions, and commandments that each society or individual formulates as definitions of the boundaries of acceptable behavior. Very few are categorical rules that apply in every situation; nearly all are conditional. While some of our pattern recognition ability may be "hard-wired" in the circuitry of our brains, there is no question that humans also learn how to classify new objects and new situations in order to act appropriately in their presence.

This section overlaps with others in the book in which classification tasks are addressed. In particular, Sections 3.1, 5.3, 6.1, 7.2, and 8.1.2 deal directly with classification.

Learning classification knowledge can be seen as one style of inductive learning in which objects or situations that are described in terms of attributes and values ("features") provide examples of items that are or are not members of the concept class. The learning task is to generalize the descriptions of the instances in order to learn a definition of the concept (the "boundary" of the concept) which correctly includes the positive instances and excludes the negative instances in the training set of examples. Concept learning is called "supervised learning" when the training instances are presented to a learner with feedback as to whether each item is "in" or "out" of the concept class. Inductive learning is usually supervised.

This section starts with Michalski's excellent overview of inductive learning, which gives the reader useful definitions of the many terms that appear in the literature. Michalski's INDUCE system is then described. A central part of INDUCE is the STAR methodology, which is used to bias the induction system to prefer simple expressions in disjunctive normal form. A learning system for a complete language, i.e., one containing conjunction, disjunction and negation, always requires a strong bias, and the STAR methodology has been shown to provide excellent results in practice.

The Michalski paper introduces the idea of constructive induction, which refers to the creation of new terms and features during the inductive learning process. Many real-world problems are not intrinsically difficult. They can be solved quite easily if an appropriate representation of the problem is employed. By constructing new features, constructive induction can change the representation of the problem and reduce the difficulty for subsequent inductive learning tasks. To learn more about constructive induction, see Rendell and Seshu (1990).

Quinlan's work on induction of decision trees, presented in Section 4.1.2, has been very influential in moving machine learning into a knowledge engineer's tool kit. His ID3 program, itself influenced by Hunt's work on concept learning, learns decision trees from a collection of examples. The decision trees may then be interpreted by performance programs for classification of new objects or situations. ID3 has been the model for several commercial knowledge acquisition programs and the vehicle for many extensions and refinements.

In Section 4.1.3, Hinton presents an overview of neural net, or connectionist, learning methods. Work on neural nets was largely curtailed after Minsky and Papert showed the impossibil-

ity of perceptron learning of some simple concepts (Minsky and Papert, 1969). Extensions to the formalism overcome those limitations and connectionism is currently one of the fastest moving areas of AI. The methods are most attractive when there is little prior knowledge of a domain to be exploited by a learner; they are least attractive where there is little data from which to learn.

The SEEK program for knowledge base refinement is presented in Section 4.1.4. Once a classification program has been constructed, SEEK's refinement techniques suggest ways of modifying rules in the knowledge base in order to correct errors in classification. Knowledge engineers would use a tool like SEEK to suggest ways to maintain a knowledge base of rules as new information becomes available. Symbolic rule learning systems like META-DENDRAL (Buchanan and Mitchell, 1978) and its extensions need to incorporate techniques for rule refinement much like these, but of course they will differ slightly in the syntax and semantics of the rules formed.

# A Theory and Methodology of Inductive Learning

**Ryszard S. Michalski**

*Department of Computer Science, University of Illinois, Urbana, IL 61801, U.S.A.*

Recommended Bruce Buchanan

ABSTRACT

*A theory of inductive learning is presented that characterizes it as a heuristic search through a space of symbolic descriptions, generated by an application of certain inference rules to the initial observational statements (the teacher-provided examples of some concepts, or facts about a class of objects or a phenomenon). The inference rules include generalization rules, which perform generalizing transformations on descriptions, and conventional truth-preserving deductive rules (specialization and reformulation rules). The application of the inference rules to descriptions is constrained by problem background knowledge, and guided by criteria evaluating the 'quality' of generated inductive assertions.*

*Based on this theory, a general methodology for learning structural descriptions from examples, called* STAR, *is described and illustrated by a problem from the area of conceptual data analysis.*

> "...scientific knowledge through demonstration[1] is impossible unless a man knows the primary immediate premises...," "...we must get to know the primary premises by induction; for the method by which even sense-perception implants the universal is inductive..."
>
> (circa 330 B.C.)
>
> Aristotle, Posterior Analytics, Book II, Ch. 19.

## 1. Introduction

The ability of people to make accurate generalizations from few scattered facts or to discover patterns in seemingly chaotic collections of observations is a

---

[1]I.e., what we now call 'deduction'.

0004-3702/83/0000−0000/$03.00 © 1983 North-Holland

*Artificial Intelligence* **20** (1983) 111–161

This paper originally appeared in the journal, *Artificial Intelligence*, Vol. 20, No. 2, and is reprinted here with permission of the publisher, Elsevier, Amsterdam.

genetics. Here they could assist a user in detecting interesting conceptual patterns or in revealing structure in collections of observations. The widely used traditional mathematical and statistical data analysis techniques, such as regression analysis, numerical taxonomy, or factor analysis, are not sufficiently powerful for this task. Methods for *conceptual* data analysis are needed, whose results are not merely mathematical formulas but logic-style descriptions, characterizing data in terms of high-level, human-oriented concepts and relationships. An early example of such an application is the Meta-Dendral program [9] which infers cleavage rules for mass-spectrometer simulation (see its analysis in [20]).

There are two basic modes in which inductive programs can be utilized: as interactive tools for acquisition of knowledge from specific facts or examples, or as parts of machine-learning systems. In the first mode, a user supplies learning examples and exercises strong control over the way the program is used (e.g., [51, 70]).

In the second mode, an inductive program is a component of an integrated learning system whose other components generate the needed learning examples [10]. Such examples—positive and negative—constitute the feedback from the system's attempts to perform a desired task. An example of the second mode is the learning system LEX for symbolic integration [57], where a 'generalizer' module performs inductive inference on instances provided by a 'critic' module.

From the viewpoint of applications, such as aiding the construction of expert systems or conceptual analysis of experimental data, the most relevant is *conceptual inductive learning*. We use this term to designate a type of inductive learning whose final products are symbolic descriptions expressed in high-level, human-oriented terms and forms (more details are given in Section 3.1). The descriptions typically apply to real world objects or phenomena, rather than abstract mathematical concepts or computations. This paper is concerned specifically with conceptual inductive learning.

The most frequently studied type of such learning is *concept learning from examples* (called also *concept acquisition*), whose task is to induce general descriptions of concepts from specific instances of these concepts. The early studies of this subject go back to the fifties, e.g., those by Hovland [33], Bruner, Goodnow and Austin [8], Newell, Shaw and Simon [60], Amarel [1], Feigenbaum [21], Kochen [38], Banerji [2], Hunt [34], Simon and Kotovsky [76], Hunt, Marin and Stone [35], Hájek, Havel and Chytil [26] and Bongard [6]. Among more recent contributions there are those, for instance, by Winston [87], Waterman [86], Michalski [45], Hayes-Roth [28], Simon and Lea [77], Stoffel [83], Vere [85], Larson [40], Larson and Michalski [41], Mitchell [56], Quinlan [70] and Moraga [58]. An important variant of concept learning from

fascinating research topic of long-standing interest. The understanding of this ability is now also of growing practical importance, as it holds the key to an improvement of methods by which computers can acquire knowledge. A need for such an improvement is evidenced by the fact that knowledge acquisition is presently the most limiting 'bottleneck' in the development of modern knowledge-intensive artificial intelligence systems.

The above ability is achieved by a process called *inductive learning* i.e., inductive inference from facts provided by a teacher or the environment. The study and modeling of this form of learning is one of the central topics of machine learning. This paper outlines a theory of inductive learning and then presents a methodology for acquiring general concepts from examples.

Before going further into this topic, let us first discuss the potential for applications of inductive learning systems. One such application is an automated construction of knowledge bases for expert systems. The present approach to constructing knowledge bases involves a tedious process of formalizing experts' knowledge and encoding it in some knowledge representation system, such as production rules [75, 17] or a semantic network [7, 24]. Inductive learning programs could provide both an improvement of the current techniques and a basis for developing alternative knowledge acquisition methods.

In appropriately selected small domains, inductive programs are already able to determine decision rules by induction from examples of expert decisions. This process greatly simplifies the transfer of knowledge from an expert into a machine. The feasibility of such inductive knowledge acquisition has been demonstrated in the expert system PLANT/ds, for the diagnosis of soybean diseases. In this system, the diagnostic rules were developed in two ways: by formalizing experts' diagnostic processes and by induction from examples. In an experiment where both types of diagnostic rules were tested on a few hundred disease cases, the inductively derived rules outperformed the expert-derived ones [51]. Another example is an inductive acquisition of decision rules for a chess end-game [53, 61, 63].

A less direct, but potentially promising use of inductive learning is for the refinement of knowledge bases initially developed by human experts. Here, inductive learning programs could be used to detect and rectify inconsistencies, to remove redundancies, to cover gaps, and to simplify expert-derived decision rules. By applying an inductive inference program to the data consisting of original rules and examples of correct and incorrect results of these rules' application to new situations, the rules could be incrementally improved with little or no human assistance.

Another important application of inductive programs is in various experimental sciences, such as biology, chemistry, psychology, medicine, and

examples is the *incremental concept refinement*, where the input information includes, in addition to the training examples, previously learned hypotheses, or human-provided initial hypotheses that may be partially incorrect or incomplete (e.g., [52]). The paper by Dietterich and Michalski [20] discusses various evaluation criteria and several methods for concept learning from examples.

Another type of conceptual inductive learning is *concept learning from observation* (or *descriptive generalization*), concerned with establishing new concepts or theories characterizing given facts. This area includes such topics as automated theory formation (e.g., [9, 42, 43]), discovery of relationships in data (e.g., [27, 66, 39]), or an automatic construction of taxonomies (e.g., [50, 54]). Differences between concept learning from examples and concept learning from observation are discussed in more detail in the next section.

Conceptual inductive learning has a strong cognitive science flavor. Its emphasis on inducing human-oriented, rather than machine-oriented descriptions, and its primary interest in nonmathematical domains distinguishes it from other types of inductive learning, such as grammatical inference and program synthesis. In grammatical inference, the task is to determine a formal grammar that can generate a given set of symbol strings (e.g., [80, 4, 89, 23]). In program synthesis the objective is to construct a computer program from I/O pairs or computational traces, or to transform a program from one form to another by applying correctness-preserving transformation rules (e.g., [74, 11, 5, 13, 36, 79, 64]). The final result of such learning is a computer program, in an assumed programming language, destined for machine rather than human 'consumption'. For example, the method of 'model inference' by Shapiro [73] constructs a PROLOG program characterizing a given set of mathematical facts.

Recent years have witnessed the development of a number of task-oriented inductive learning systems that have demonstrated an impressive performance in their specific domain of application. Major weaknesses, however, persist in much of the research in this area. Most systems lack generality and extensibility. The theoretical principles upon which they are built are rarely well explained. Lack of common terminology and an adequate formal theory makes it difficult to compare different learning methods.

In the following sections we formulate logical foundations of inductive learning, define various types of such learning, present inference rules for generalizing concept descriptions, and finally describe a general methodology, called STAR, for learning structural descriptions from examples. To improve the readability of this chapter, below is presented a table of used symbols. Appendix A gives the details of the description language used (the annotated predicate calculus).

### 1.1. Symbols and notation

| | |
|---|---|
| $\sim$ | negation, |
| & | conjunction (logical product), |
| v | disjunction (logical sum), |
| $\Rightarrow$ | implication, |
| $\Leftrightarrow$ | logical equivalence, |
| $\leftrightarrow$ | term rewriting, |
| $\veebar$ | exception (symmetric difference), |
| $F$ | a set of facts (formally, a predicate that is true for all the facts), |
| $H$ | a hypothesis (an inductive assertion), |
| $\triangle$ | specialization, |
| $K$ | generalization, |
| $\models$ | reformulation, |
| $\exists v_i$ | existential quantifier over $v_i$, |
| $\exists(I)v_i$ | numerical quantifier over $v_i$, ($I$ is a set of integers), |
| $\forall v_i$ | universal quantifier over $v_i$, |
| $D_i$ | a concept description, |
| $K_i$ | a predicate asserting a concept name (a class) of objects, |
| $::>$ | the implication linking a concept description with a concept name, |
| $e_i$ | an event (a description of an object), |
| $E_i$ | a predicate that is true only for the training events of the concept, |
| $x_i$ | an attribute (zero or one argument descriptor), |
| LEF | a lexicographic evaluation functional, |
| $DOM(p)$ | the domain of descriptor $p$. |

## 2. Types of Inductive Learning

### 2.1. Inductive paradigm

As mentioned before, inductive learning is a process of acquiring knowledge by drawing inductive inferences from teacher- or environment-provided facts. Such a process involves operations of generalizing, transforming, correcting and refining knowledge representations. Although it is one of the most common forms of learning, it has one fundamental weakness: except for special cases, the acquired knowledge cannot, in principle, be completely validated. This predicament, observed early on by Scottish philosopher David Hume (18th century), is due to the fact that inductively acquired assertions are hypotheses with a potentially infinite number of consequences, while only a finite number of confirming tests can be performed.

Traditional inquiries into inductive inference have therefore dealt with questions of what are the best criteria for guiding the selection of inductive assertions, and how can these assertions be confirmed. These are difficult problems, permeating all scientific activities. The search for answers has turned inductive inference into a battlefield of philosophers and logicians. There was even doubt whether it would ever be possible to formalize inductive inference and perform it on a machine. For example, philosopher Karl Popper [68] believed that inductive inference requires an irrational element. Bertrand

Russell in "History of Western Philosophy" [71] stated: "...so far no method has been found which would make it possible to invent hypotheses by rule". George Polya [67] in his pioneering and now classic treatise on plausible inference (of which inductive inference is a special case) observed: "A person has a background, a machine has not; indeed, you can build a machine to draw demonstrative conclusions for you, but I think you can never build a machine that will draw plausible inferences".

The above pessimistic prospects are now being revised. With the development of modern computers and subsequent advances in artificial intelligence research, it is now possible to provide a machine with a significant amount of background information. Also, the problem of automating inductive inference can be simplified by concentrating on the subject of hypothesis generation, while ascribing to humans the question of how to adequately validate them. Some successful inductive inference systems have already been built and a body of knowledge is emerging about the nature of this inference. The rest of this section will analyze the logical basis for inductive inference, and then Section 5 will present various generalization rules, which can be viewed as inductive inference rules.

In contrast to deduction, the starting premises of induction are specific facts rather than general axioms. The goal of inference is to formulate plausible general assertions that explain the given facts and are able to predict new facts. In other words, inductive inference attempts to derive a complete and correct description of a given phenomenon from specific observations of that phenomenon or of parts of it. As we mentioned earlier, of the two aspects of inductive inference—the generation of plausible hypotheses and their validation (the establishment of their truth status)—only the first is of primary interest to inductive learning research. The problem of hypothesis validation, a subject of various philosophical inquiries (e.g., [12]) is considered to be of lesser importance, because it is assumed that the generated hypotheses are judged by human experts, and tested by known methods of deductive inference and statistics.

To understand the role of inductive inference in learning, let us consider several different ways in which a system can acquire a description of a class of objects (situations, decisions, etc.).

(1) By receiving the description from a teacher and incorporating it within the system's existing knowledge structures (e.g., [25]). This way is called 'learning by being told'.

(2) By inferring the description from characteristics of a superset of the object class. This way is called 'learning by deductive inference'.

(3) By modifying the description already possessed about a similar class of objects (e.g., [88]). This way is called 'learning by analogy'.

(4) By generalizing teacher-provided examples and counter-examples of objects from this class. This way is called 'learning from examples'.

(5) By experimenting, discovering regularities, formulating useful concepts and structuring observations about the objects. This way is called 'learning from observation' (or 'learning by discovery').

Although all of these ways, except for the first one, involve some amount of inductive inference, in the last two, i.e., in learning from examples and in learning from observation, this inference is the central operation. These two forms are therefore considered to be the major forms of inductive learning. In order to explain them, let us formulate a general paradigm for inductive inference.

*Given:*

(a) *observational statements (facts)*, F, that represent specific knowledge about some objects, situations, processes, etc.,

(b) a *tentative inductive assertion* (which may be null),

(c) *background knowledge* that defines the assumptions and constraints imposed on the observational statements and generated candidate inductive assertions, and any relevant problem domain knowledge. The last includes the *preference criterion* characterizing the desirable properties of the sought inductive assertion.

*Find:*

An *inductive assertion (hypothesis)*, H, that tautologically or weakly implies the observational statements, and satisfies the background knowledge.

A hypothesis H tautologically implies facts F if F is a logical consequence of H, i.e., if the expression $H \Rightarrow F$ is true under all interpretations ('$\Rightarrow$' denotes logical implication). This is expressed as follows.

$$H \triangleright F \quad \text{(read: } H \text{ specializes to } F) \tag{1}$$

or

$$F \triangleleft H \quad \text{(read: } F \text{ generalizes to } H). \tag{2}$$

Symbols $\triangleright$ and $\triangleleft$ are called the *specialization* and *generalization* symbols, respectively. If $H \Rightarrow F$ is valid, and H is true, then by the law of detachment (modus ponens) F must be true. Deriving F from H (deductive inference), is, therefore, truth-preserving. In contrast, deriving H from F (inductive inference) is not truth-preserving, but falsity-preserving, i.e., if some facts falsify F then they also must falsify H. (More explanation on this topic is given in Section 5.)

The condition that *H weakly implies F* means that facts F are not certain but only plausible or partial consequences of H. By allowing weak implication, this paradigm includes methods for generating 'soft' hypotheses, which hold only probabilistically, and partial hypotheses, which account for some but not all of the facts (e.g., hypotheses representing 'dominant patterns' or characterizing inconsistent data). In the following we will limit our attention to hypotheses that tautologically imply facts.

(c) Inferring *sequence extrapolation rules* (e.g., [76, 19]) are able to predict the next element (a symbol, a number, an object, etc.) in a given sequence.

*Descriptive generalization*
(a) Formulating a theory characterizing a collection of entities (e.g., chemical compounds, as in [9], or numbers, as in [42, 43]).
(b) Discovering patterns in observational data (e.g., [26, 81, 27, 39, 66, 90]).
(c) Determining a taxonomic description (a classification) of a collection of objects (e.g., [49, 54]).

This paper is concerned primarily with problems of concept acquisition. In this case, the set of observational statements $F$ can be viewed as a collection of implications:

$$F: \{e_{ik} ::> K_i\}, \quad i \in I, \qquad (3)$$

where $e_{ik}$ (a *training event*) denotes a description of the $k$th example of *concept* (*class*) asserted by predicate $K_i$ (for short, *class* $K_i$) and $I$ is a set indexing classes $K_i$. It is assumed here that any given event represents only one concept. Symbol $::>$ is used here, and will be used henceforth, to denote the *implication* linking a *concept description* with a predicate asserting the *concept name* (in order to distinguish this implication from the implication between arbitrary descriptions). The inductive assertion, $H$, can be characterized as a set of concept recognition rules:

$$H: \{D_i ::> K_i\}, \quad i \in I, \qquad (4)$$

where $D_i$ is a concept description of class $K_i$, i.e., an expression of conditions such that when they are satisfied by an object, then this object is considered an instance of class $K_i$.

According to the definition of inductive assertion, we must have

$$H \vdash F. \qquad (5)$$

By substituting (3) and (4) for $F$ and $H$, respectively, in (5), and making appropriate transformations, one can derive the following conditions to be satisfied in order that (5) holds

$$\forall i \in I \, (E_i \Rightarrow D_i) \qquad (6)$$

and

$$\forall i, j \in I \, (D_i \Rightarrow \sim E_j), \quad \text{if } j \neq i, \qquad (7)$$

where $E_i$, $i \in I$, is a description satisfied by all training events of class $K_i$, and only by such events (the logical disjunction of training events). Expression (6) is called the *completeness condition*, and (7) the *consistency*

For any given set of facts, a potentially infinite number of hypotheses can be generated that imply these facts. Background knowledge is therefore necessary to provide the constraints and a preference criterion for reducing the infinite choice to one hypothesis or a few most preferable ones.

A typical way of defining such a criterion is to specify the preferable properties of the hypothesis—for example, to require that the hypothesis is the shortest or the most economical description consistent with all the facts (as, e.g., in [46]). Such a 'biased choice' criterion is necessary when the description language is complete, i.e., able to express any possible hypothesis. An alternative is to use a 'biased language' criterion [57], restricting the description language in which hypotheses are expressed (i.e., using an incomplete description language). Although in many methods the background knowledge is not explicitly stated, the authors make implicit assumptions serving the same purpose. More details on the criteria for selecting hypotheses are given in Section 4.7.

## 2.2. Concept acquisition vs. descriptive generalization

As mentioned in the introduction, one can distinguish between two major types of inductive learning: *learning from examples* (*concept acquisition*) and *learning from observation* (*descriptive generalization*). In concept acquisition, the observational statements are characterizations of some objects (situations, processes, etc.) preclassified by a teacher into one or more classes (concepts). The induced hypothesis can be viewed as a concept recognition rule, such that if an object satisfies this rule, then it represents the given concept. For example, a recognition rule for the concept 'philosopher' might be: 'A person who pursues wisdom and gains the knowledge of underlying reality by intellectual means and moral self-discipline is a philosopher'.

In descriptive generalization the goal is to determine a general description (a law, a theory) characterizing a collection of observations. For example, observing that philosophers Aristotle, Plato and Socrates were Greek, but that Spencer was British, one might conclude: 'Most philosophers were Greek'.

Thus, in contrast to concept acquisition that produces descriptions for classifying objects into classes on the basis of the objects' properties, descriptive generalization produces descriptions specifying properties of objects belonging to a certain class. Here are some example problems belonging to the above two categories:

*Concept acquisition*
(a) Learning *characteristic descriptions* of a class of objects, which specify one or more common properties of all known objects in the class. A logical product of all such properties defines the class in the context of an unlimited number of other object classes (e.g., [6, 87, 83, 85, 15, 29, 56, 82, 49, 20]).
(b) Learning *discriminant descriptions* of a class of objects that singly distinguish the given class from a limited number of other classes (e.g., [35, 6, 46—49, 70]).

*condition.* These two conditions are the requirements that must be satisfied for an inductive assertion to be acceptable as a concept recognition rule. The completeness condition states that every training event of some class must satisfy the description $D_i$ of the same class (since the opposite does not have to hold, $D_i$ is equivalent to or more general than $E_i$). The consistency condition states that if an event satisfies a description of some class, then it cannot be a member of a training set of any other class. In learning a concept from examples and counterexamples, the latter constitute the 'other' class.

The completeness and consistency conditions provide the logical foundation of algorithms for concept learning from examples. We will see in Section 4 that to derive $D_i$ satisfying the completeness condition one can adopt some inference rules of formal logic.

### 2.3. Characteristic vs. discriminant descriptions

The completeness and consistency conditions allow us to clearly explain the distinction between the previously mentioned characteristic and discriminant descriptions. A characteristic description of a class of objects (also known as *conjunctive generalization*) is an expression that satisfies the completeness condition or is the logical product of such expressions. It is typically a conjunction of some simple properties common to all objects in the class. From the applications viewpoint, the most interesting are *maximal characteristic descriptions* (maximal conjunctive generalizations or MCG) that are the most specific (i.e., longest) logical products characterizing all objects in the given class, using terms of the given language. Such descriptions are intended to discriminate the given class from all other possible classes (for illustration see Section 7).

A discriminant description is an expression that satisfies the completeness and consistency condition, or is the logical disjunction of such expressions. It specifies a single way or various alternative ways to distinguish the given class from a fixed number of other classes. The most interesting are *minimal discriminant descriptions* that are the shortest (i.e., with the minimum number of descriptors) expressions distinguishing all objects in the given class from objects of the other classes. Such descriptions are intended to specify the minimum information sufficient to identify the given class among a fixed number of other classes (for illustration see Section 7).

### 2.4. Single- vs. multiple-concept learning

It is instructive to distinguish between learning a single concept, and learning a collection of concepts. In *single-concept learning*, one can distinguish two cases: (1) when observational statements are just examples of the concept to be learned (learning from 'positive' instances only), and (2) when they are examples and counter-examples of the concept (learning from 'positive' and 'negative' instances).

In the first case, because of the lack of counter-examples, the consistency condition (7) is not applicable, and there is no natural limit to which description $D_i$ (here, $i = 1$) can be generalized. One way to impose such a limit is to specify restrictions on the form and properties of the sought description. For example, one may require that it be the longest (most specific) conjunctive statement satisfying the completeness condition (e.g., [85, 29]). Another way is to require that the description not exceed a given degree of generality, measured, for example, by the ratio of the number of all distinct events which could potentially satisfy the description to the number of training instances [82].

In the second case, when the teacher also provides counter-examples of the given concept, the learning process is considerably simplified. These counter-examples can be viewed as representing a 'different class', and the consistency condition (7) provides an obvious limit on the extent to which the hypothesis can be generalized. The most useful counter-examples are the so-called 'near misses' that only slightly differ from positive examples [87, 88]. Such examples place stronger constraints on the generalization process than randomly generated examples.

In *multiple-concept learning* one can also distinguish two cases: (1) when descriptions $D_i$ of different classes are required to be mutually disjoint, i.e., no event can satisfy more than one description, and (2) when they are overlapping. In an overlapping generalization an event may satisfy more than one description. In some situations this is desirable. For example, if a patient has two diseases, his symptoms should satisfy the descriptions of both diseases, and in this case the consistency condition is not applicable.

An overlapping generalization can be interpreted in such a way that it always indicates only one decision class. In this special case, the concept recognition rules, $D_i::>K_i$, are applied in a linear order, and the first rule satisfied generates the decision. In this case, if a concept description $D_i$ for class $K_i$ contains a conjunctively linked condition $A$, and precedes the rule for class $K_j$ that contains condition $\sim A$, then the condition $\sim A$ is superfluous and can be removed. As a result, the linearly ordered recognition rules can be significantly simplified. For example, the set of linearly ordered rules

$$D_1::>K_1, \qquad D_2::>K_2, \qquad D_3::>K_3$$

is logically equivalent to the set of (unordered) rules

$$D_1::>K_1, \qquad \sim D_1\&D_2::>K_2, \qquad \sim D_1\&\sim D_2\&D_3::>K_3.$$

There are also other ways for deriving a single decision from overlapping rules (e.g., [17]). The above forms of multiple-concept learning have been implemented in inductive programs AQVAL/1 [46] and AQ11 [52].

## 3. Description Language

### 3.1. Bias toward comprehensibility

In concept acquisition, the main interest is in derivation of symbolic descriptions that are human-oriented, i.e., that are easy to understand and easy to use for creating mental models of the information they convey. A tentative criterion for judging inductive assertions from such a viewpoint is provided by the following *comprehensibility postulate*.

The results of computer induction should be symbolic descriptions of given entities, semantically and structurally similar to those a human expert might produce observing the same entities. Components of these descriptions should be comprehensible as single 'chunks' of information, directly interpretable in natural language, and should relate quantitative and qualitative concepts in an integrated fashion.

As a practical guide, one can assume that the components of descriptions (single sentences, rules, labels on nodes in a hierarchy, etc.) should be expressions that contain only a few (say, less than five) conditions in a conjunction, at most one single conditions in a disjunction, at most one level of bracketing, at most two quantifiers, and no recursion (the exact numbers may be disputed,[2] but the principle is clear). Sentences are kept within such limits by substituting names for appropriate subcomponents. Any operators used in descriptions should have a simple intuitive interpretation. Conceptually related sentences are organized into a simple data structure, preferably a shallow hierarchy or a linear list, such as a frame [55, 42].

The rationale behind this postulate is to ensure that descriptions generated by inductive inference bear similarity to human knowledge representations [31], and therefore, are easy to comprehend. This requirement is very important for many applications. For example, in developing knowledge bases for expert systems, it is important that human experts can easily and reliably verify the inductive assertions and relate them to their own domain knowledge. Satisfying the comprehensibility postulate will also facilitate debugging or improving the inductive programs themselves. When the complexity of problems undertaken by computer induction becomes very great, the comprehensibility of the generated descriptions will likely be a crucial criterion. This research orientation fits well within the role of artificial intelligence envisaged by Michie [44] to study and develop methods for man-machine conceptual interface and knowledge refinement.

### 3.2. Language of assertions

One of the difficulties with inductive inference is its open-endedness. This means that when one makes an inductive assertion about some aspect of reality there is no natural limit to the level of detail in which this reality may be described, or to the richness of forms in which this assertion can be expressed. Consequently, when conducting research in this area, it is necessary to circumscribe very carefully the goals and the problem to be solved. This includes defining the language and the scope of allowed forms in which assertions will be expressed, as well as the modes of inference which will be used. The description language should be chosen so that crucial features are easily representable, while peripheral or irrelevant information are ignored.

An instructive criterion for classifying inductive learning methods is therefore the type of language used to express inductive assertions. Many authors use a restricted form of predicate calculus or closely related notation (e.g., [65, 22, 59, 85, 3, 50, 90, 72]). Some other formalisms include decision trees [35, 70], production rules (e.g., [86, 30]), semantic nets (e.g., [25]), and frames [42]. In earlier work (e.g., [45-48]) this author used a multiple-valued logic propositional calculus with typed variables, called $VL_1$ (the variable-valued logic system one). Later on an extension of the predicate calculus, called $VL_2$, was developed that was especially oriented to facilitate inductive inference [49].

Here we will use a somewhat modified and extended version of the latter language, to be called the *annotated predicate calculus* (APC). The APC adds to predicate calculus additional forms and new concepts that increase its expressive power and facilitate inductive inference. The major differences between the annotated predicate calculus and the conventional predicate calculus can be summarized as follows.

(1) Each predicate, variable and function (referred to collectively as a *descriptor*) is assigned an *annotation* that contains relevant problem-oriented information. The annotation may contain the definition of the concept represented by a descriptor, a characterization of its relationship to other concepts, a specification of the set over which the concept represented by a descriptor, a characterization of its relationship to other concepts, a specification of the set over which the descriptor ranges (when it is a variable or a functor) and a characterization of the structure of this set, etc. (see Section 4).

(2) In addition to predicates, the APC also includes *compound predicates*. Arguments of such predicates can be *compound terms*, composed of two or more ordinary terms.

(3) Predicates that express relations =, ≠, ≥, >, ≤ and < between terms or between compound terms are expressed explicitly as *relational statements*, also called *selectors*.

(4) In addition to the universal and existential quantifiers, there is also a

---

[2] The numbers mentioned seem to apply to the majority of human descriptive sentences.

*numerical quantifier* that expresses quantitative information about the objects satisfying an expression.

The concept of annotation is explained more fully in the next section. Other aspects of the language are described in Appendix A. (The reader interested in a thorough understanding of this work is encouraged to read Appendix A at this point.)

## 4. Problem Background Knowledge

### 4.1. Basic components

As mentioned earlier, given a set of observational statements, one may construct a potentially infinite number of inductive assertions that imply these statements. It is therefore necessary to use some additional information, *problem background knowledge*, to constrain the space of possible inductive assertions and locate the most desirable one(s). In this section we shall look at various components of the problem background knowledge employed in the inductive learning methodology called STAR, described in Section 6. These components include the following.

- Information about descriptors (i.e., predicates, variables, and functions) used in observational statements. This information is provided by an *annotation* assigned to each descriptor (Section 4.3).

- Assumptions about the form of observational and inductive assertions.

- A preference criterion that specifies the desirable properties of inductive assertions sought.

- A variety of inference rules, heuristics, and specialized procedures, general and problem-dependent, that allow a learning system to generate logical consequences of given assertions and new descriptors.

Before we examine these components in greater detail, let us first consider the problem of how the choice of descriptors in the observational statements affects the generated inductive assertions.

### 4.2. Relevance of the initial descriptors

A fundamental problem underlying any machine inductive learning task is that of what information is provided to the machine and what information the machine is expected to produce or learn. As specified in the inductive paradigm, the major component of the input to a learning system is a set of observational statements. The descriptors used in those statements are observable characteristics and available measurements of objects under consideration. These descriptors are selected as relevant to the learning task by a teacher specifying the problem.

Determining these descriptors is a major part of any inductive learning problem. If they capture the essential properties of the objects, the role of the learning process is simply to arrange these descriptors into an expression constituting an appropriate inductive assertion. If the selected descriptors are completely irrelevant to the learning task (as the color, weight, or shape of men in chess is irrelevant to deciding the right move), no learning system will be able to construct a meaningful inductive assertion.

There is a range of intermediate possibilities between the above two extremes. Consequently, learning methods can be characterized on the basis of the degree to which the initial descriptors are relevant to the learning problem.

Three cases can be distinguished.

(1) *Complete relevance*. In this case all descriptors in the observational statements are assumed to be directly relevant to the learning task. The task of the learning system is to formulate an inductive assertion that is a mathematical or logical expression of some assumed general form that properly relates these descriptors (e.g., a regression polynomial).

(2) *Partial relevance*. Observational statements may contain a large number of irrelevant or redundant descriptors. Some of the descriptors, however, are relevant. The task of the learning system is to select the most relevant ones and construct from them an appropriate inductive assertion.

(3) *Indirect relevance*. Observational statements may contain no directly relevant descriptors. However, among the initial descriptors there are some that can be used to construct derived descriptors that are directly relevant. The task of the learning system is to construct those derived descriptors and formulate an appropriate inductive assertion. A simple form of this case occurs, e.g., when a relevant descriptor is the volume of an object, but the observational statements contain only the information about the object's dimensions (and various irrelevant facts).

The above three cases represent problem statements that put progressively less demand on the relevance of the initial descriptors (i.e., that require less work from the person defining the problem) and more demand on the learning system. Early work on adaptive control systems and concept formation represents case (1). More recent research has dealt with case (2), which is addressed in *selective inductive learning*. A method of such learning must possess efficient mechanisms for determining combinations of descriptors that are relevant and sufficient for the learning task. Formal logic provides such mechanisms, and therefore it has become the major underlying formalism for selective methods.

An example of a selective learning method is the one implemented in program AQ11 [52] that inductively determined soybean disease diagnostic rules for the system PLANT/ds, mentioned in the introduction. A different type of selective method was implemented in program ID3 [70] that determines a decision tree for classifying a large number of events. A comparison between these two programs is described by O'Rorke [63].

Case (3) represents the task of *constructive inductive learning*. Here, a method must be capable of formulating new descriptors (i.e., new concepts, new variables, etc.), of evaluating their relevance to the learning task, and of using them to construct inductive assertions. There has been relatively little done in this area. The 'automated mathematician' program AM [42] can be classified as a domain-specific system of this category. Some constructive learning capabilities have been incorporated in system BACON that automatically formulates mathematical expressions encapsulating chemical and other laws [39]. The general-purpose INDUCE program for learning structural descriptions from examples has implemented several general purpose constructive generalization techniques [40, 49]. Section 5 and 6 give more details on this subject.

### 4.3. Annotation of descriptors

An *annotation* of a descriptor (i.e., of a predicate, a variable or a function) is a store of background information about this descriptor tailored to the learning problem under consideration. It may include:
- a specification of the *domain* and the *type* of the descriptor (see below),
- a specification of operators applicable to it,
- a specification of the constraints and the relationships between the descriptor and other descriptors,
- for numerical descriptors, the mean, the variance, or the complete probability distribution of values for the problem under consideration,
- a characterization of objects to which the descriptor is applicable (i.e., a characterization of its possible arguments),
- a specification of a descriptor class containing the given descriptor that is the parent node in a generalization hierarchy of descriptors (for example, for descriptors 'length', 'width' and 'height', the parent node would be the 'dimensions'),
- synonyms that can be used to denote the descriptor,
- a definition of a descriptor (when it is derived from some other descriptors),
- if a descriptor denotes a class of objects, typical examples of this class can be specified.

Let us consider some of the above components of the annotation in greater detail.

### 4.4. The domain and type of a descriptor

Given a specific problem, it is usually possible to specify the set of values each descriptor could potentially adopt in characterizing any object in the population under consideration. Such a set is called the *domain* (or the *value set*) of the descriptor. The domain is used to constrain the extent to which a descriptor can be generalized. For example, the information that the temperature of a living human being may very, say, only between 34°C and 44°C prevents the system from considering inductive assertions in which the descriptor 'body temperature' would assume values beyond these limits.

Other important information for conducting the generalization process is concerned with the structure of the domain, that is, with the relationship existing among the elements of the domain. For numerical descriptors, such relationships are specified by the measurement scale. Depending on the structure of the descriptor domain, we distinguish among three basic types of descriptors.

(1) *Nominal (categorical) descriptors*. The value set of such descriptors consists of independent symbols or names, i.e., no structure is assumed to relate the values in the domain. For example, 'blood-type(person)' and 'name(person)' are unary nominal descriptors. Predicates, i.e., descriptors with the value set {True, False}, and $n$-ary functions whose ranges are unordered sets, are also nominal descriptors. An example of a two-argument nominal descriptor is 'license-plate-number(car, owner)', which denotes a function assigning to a specific car of the given owner a license plate number.

(2) *Linear descriptors*. The value set of linear descriptors is a totally ordered set. For example, a person's military rank or the temperature, weight or number of items in a set is such a descriptor. Variables measured on ordinal, interval, ratio, and absolute scales are special cases of a linear descriptor. Functions that map a set into a totally ordered set are also linear descriptors, e.g., 'distance($P_1$, $P_2$)'.

(3) *Structured descriptors*. The value set of such descriptors has a tree or oriented graph structure that reflects the generalization relation between the values, i.e., is a generalization hierarchy. A parent node in such a structure represents a more general concept than the concepts represented by its children nodes. For example, in the value set of descriptor 'place', 'U.S.A.' would be a parent node of the nodes 'Indiana', 'Illinois', 'Iowa', etc. The domain of structured descriptors is defined by a set of inference rules specified in the problem background knowledge (see, e.g., descriptor 'shape($B_i$)', in Section 6).

Structured descriptors can be further subdivided into ordered and unordered structured descriptors. Sometimes descriptors themselves can also be organized into a generalization hierarchy. For example, descriptors' length, width, and depth belong to a class of 'dimensions'. Information about the type of a descriptor is useful, as it determines the operations applicable to a descriptor.

### 4.5. Constraints on the description space

For a given induction problem there may exist a variety of constraints on the space of the acceptable concept descriptions, due to the specific properties and relationships among descriptors. Here are a few examples of such relationships.
- *Interdependence among values*. In many practical problems some variables specify a state of an object, and some other variables characterize the state. Depending on the values of the state-specifying variables, the variables charac-

An object $P_0$ contains parts $P_1$, $P_2$ and $P_3$ and only these parts. Parts $P_1$ & $P_2$ are on top of part $P_3$, length of $P_1$ is between 3 and 8, the color of $P_1$ is red or blue, the weight of $P_1$ is greater than that of $P_2$, and the shape of all three parts is box.

An important special case of a c-expression is an *a-expression* (an *atomic expression*), in which there is no 'internal disjunction' (see Appendix A).

Note that due to the use of internal disjunction a c-expression represents a more general concept than a universally quantified conjunction of predicates, used in typical production rules.

Progressively more complex forms of expressions are described below.

- A *case expression* is a logical product of implications:

$$[L = a_i] \Rightarrow \text{Exp}_i, \quad i = 1, 2, \ldots$$

where $a_i$ are single elements or disjoint subsets of elements from the domain of descriptor $L$, and $\text{Exp}_i$ are c-expressions.

A case expression describes a class of objects by splitting it into separate cases, each represented by a different value of a certain descriptor.

- An *implicative expression* (i-expression)

$$C \& (C_1 \Rightarrow C_2), \quad (9)$$

where $C$, $C_1$ and $C_2$ are c-expressions.

This form of description is very useful when the occurrence of some properties (defined in $C_2$) depends on the occurrence of some other properties (defined in $C_1$). Typical production rules used in expert systems are a special case of (9), where $C$ is omitted and no internal logical operators are used. When $(C_1 \Rightarrow C_2)$ is omitted, then the conditional expression becomes a c-expression.

- A *disjunctive expression* (d-expression) defined as a disjunction of implicative expressions.

- An *exception-based expression* (e-expression).

In some situations it is simpler to formulate a somewhat overgeneralized statement and indicate exceptions than to formulate a precise statement. The following form is used for such purposes:

$$D_1 \vee D_2$$

where $D_1$ and $D_2$ are d-expressions. This expression is equivalent to $(\sim D_2 \Rightarrow D_1)$ & $(D_2 \Rightarrow \sim D_1)$. Observational assertions are formulated as a set of rules

$$\{\text{a-expression} :: > K_j^i\}. \quad (10)$$

terizing a state may be needed or not. For example, if a descriptor 'state(plant's leaf)' takes on value 'diseased', then a descriptor 'leaf discoloration' will be used to characterize the change of the leaf's color. When the descriptor 'state(plant's leaf)' takes on value 'normal', then obviously the 'leaf discoloration' descriptor is irrelevant. Such information can be represented by an implication:

$$[\text{state(plant's leaf)} = \text{normal}] \Rightarrow [\text{discoloration(plant's leaf)} = NA],$$

where NA is a special value meaning 'not applicable'.

- *Properties of descriptors.* Descriptors that are relations between objects may have certain general properties—they can be reflexive, symmetric, transitive, etc. All such properties are defined as assertions in the annotated predicate calculus (see Appendix A). For example, the transitivity of relation 'above($P_1,P_2$)' can be defined as

$$\forall P_1, P_2, P_3, \quad (\text{above}(P_1, P_2)) \& \text{above}(P_2, P_3)) \Rightarrow \text{above}(P_1, P_3).$$

- *Interrelationships among descriptors.* In some problems there may exist relationships between descriptors that constrain their values. For example, the length of an object is assumed always to be greater than or equal to its width:

$$\forall P, \quad \text{length}(P) \geq \text{width}(P).$$

Also, descriptors may be related by known equations. For example, the area of a rectangle is the arithmetic product of its length and width:

$$\forall P, \quad ([\text{shape}(P) = \text{rectangle}] \Rightarrow [\text{area}(P) = \text{length}(P) \cdot \text{width}(P)]).$$

(The infix operator '·' is used to simplify notation of the term multiply(length(P), width(P)).)

### 4.6. The form of observational and inductive assertions

The basic form of assertions in the STAR methodology is a *c-expression*, defined as a conjunctive statement:

$$\langle \text{quantifier form}\rangle\langle \text{conjunction of relational statements}\rangle, \quad (8)$$

where ⟨quantifier form⟩ stands for zero or more quantifiers, and ⟨relational statements⟩ are predicates in a special form, as defined in Appendix A. The following is an example of a c-expression:

$$\exists P_0, P_1, P_2, P_3 [[\text{contains}(P_0, P_1, P_2, P_3)][\text{ontop}(P_1 \& P_2, P_3)] \\ [\text{length}(P_1) = 3..8][\text{weight}(P_1) \geq \text{weight}(P_2)] \\ [\text{color}(P_1) = \text{red} \vee \text{blue}][\text{shape}(P_1 \& P_2 \& P_3) = \text{box}])$$

that can be paraphrased in English as follows.

Inductive assertions are expressed as a set of rules

$$\{EXP ::> \text{c-expression}\},$$          (11)

where EXP is a c-expression or any of the more complex expressions described above. It is also assumed that the left side and the right side of (11) satisfy the principle of comprehensibility described in Section 2.

### 4.7. The preference criterion

In spite of the constraints imposed by the above components of the background knowledge, the number of inductive assertions consistent with observational statements may still be unlimited. The problem then arises of choosing the most desirable inductive assertion(s). In making such a choice one must take into consideration the aspects of the particular inductive learning problem, and therefore the definition of a 'preference criterion' for selecting a hypothesis is a part of the problem background knowledge. Typically, the inductive assertions are chosen on the basis of some simplicity criterion (e.g., [37, 69]).

In the context of scientific discovery, philosopher Karl Popper [68] has advocated constructing hypotheses that are both simple and easy to refute. By generating such hypotheses and conducting experiments aimed at refuting them, he argues, one has the best chance of ultimately formulating the true hypothesis. In order to use this criterion for automated inductive inference it is necessary to define it formally. This, however, is not easy because there does not seem to exist any universal measure of hypothesis simplicity and refutability.

Among more specific measures for evaluating the 'quality' of inductive assertions one may list:

- An overall simplicity for human comprehension, measured, for example, by the number of descriptors and number of operators used in an inductive assertion.

- The degree of 'fit' between the inductive and observational assertions (measured, for example, by the degree of generalization, defined as the amount of uncertainty that any given description satisfying the inductive assertion corresponds to some observational statement [49]).
- The cost of measuring values of descriptors used in the inductive assertion.
- The computational cost of evaluating the inductive assertion.
- The memory required for storing the inductive assertion.
- The amount of information needed for encoding the assertion using a priori defined operators [16].

The importance given to each such measure depends on the ultimate purpose of constructing the inductive assertions. For that reason, the STAR methodology allows a user to build a global preference criterion as a function of such measures, tailored to a specific inductive problem. Since some of the above measures are computationally costly, simpler measures are used, called *elementary criteria*. Among such criteria are the number of c-expressions in the assertion, the total number of relational statements, the ratio of possible but unseen events implied by an assertion to the total number of training events (a simple measure of generalization [50]), and the total number of different descriptors. The global preference criterion is formulated by selecting from the above list those elementary criteria that are most relevant to the problem, and then arranging them into a *lexicographic evaluation functional* (LEF). A LEF is defined as a sequence of criterion-tolerance pairs

$$LEF: (c_1, \tau_1), (c_2, \tau_2) \cdots,$$          (12)

where $c_i$ is an elementary criterion selected from the available 'menu', and $\tau_i$ is a *tolerance threshold* for criterion $c_i$ ($\tau_i \in [0 .. 100\%]$).

Given a set of inductive assertions, the LEF determines the most preferable one(s) in the following way.

In the first step, all assertions are evaluated from the viewpoint of criterion $c_1$, and those which score best, or within the range defined by the threshold $\tau_1$ from the best, are retained. Next, the retained assertions are evaluated from the viewpoint of criterion $c_2$ and reduced similarly as above, using tolerance $\tau_2$. This process continues until either the subset of retained assertions contains only one assertion (the 'best' one) or the sequence of criterion-tolerance pairs is exhausted. In the latter case, the retained set contains assertions that are equivalent from the viewpoint of the LEF.

An important and somewhat surprising property of such an approach is that by properly defining the preference criterion, the same learning system can generate either characteristic or discriminant descriptions of object classes (see Section 7).

## 5. Generalization Rules

### 5.1. Definitions and an overview

Constructing an inductive assertion from observational statements can be conceptually characterized as a heuristic state-space search [62], where

- *states* are symbolic descriptions; the initial state is the set of observational statements;

- *operators* are inference rules, specifically, generalization, specialization and reformulation rules, as defined below;

- the *goal* state is an inductive assertion that implies the observational statements, satisfies the problem background knowledge and maximizes the given preference criterion.

A *generalization rule* is a transformation of a description into a more general description, one that tautologically implies the initial description. A *specializa-*

tion rule makes an opposite transformation: given a description, it generates a logical consequence of it. A *reformulation rule* transforms a description into another, logically equivalent description. A reformulation rule can be viewed as a special case of a generalization and a specialization rule.

Specialization and reformulation rules are the conventional truth-preserving inference rules used in deductive logic. In contrast to them, the generalization rules are not truth-preserving but falsity preserving. This means that if an event falsifies some description, then it also falsifies a more general description. This is immediately seen by observing that $H \Rightarrow F$ is equivalent to $\sim F \Rightarrow \sim H$ (the law of contraposition). To illustrate this point, suppose that a statement 'some water birds in this lake are swans' has been generalized to 'all water birds in this lake are swans'. If there are no water birds in the lake that are swans, then this fact falsifies not only the first statement but also the second. Falsifying the second statement, however, does not imply the falsification of the first.

In concept acquisition, as explained in Section 2, transforming a rule $E ::> K$ into a more general rule $D ::> K$ means that description $E$ must imply description $D$:

$$E \Rightarrow D \tag{13}$$

(recall expression (6)). Thus, to obtain a generalization rule for concept acquisition, one may use a tautological implication of formal logic. The premise and consequence of such an implication must, however, be interpretable as a description of a class of objects. For example, the known law of simplification

$$P \& Q \Rightarrow P \tag{14}$$

can be turned into a generalization rule:

$$P \& Q ::> K \vdash P ::> K. \tag{15}$$

If $P$ stands for 'round objects', $Q$ for 'brown objects' and $K$ for 'balls', then rule (15) states that the expression 'round and brown objects are balls' can be generalized to 'round objects are balls'. Thus, in concept acquisition, the generalization operation has a simple set-theoretical interpretation: a description is more general if it is satisfied by a larger number of objects. (Such an interpretation does not apply, however, to descriptive generalization, as shown below.)

In order to obtain a rule for descriptive generalization, implication (14) is reversed, and $P$ and $Q$ are interpreted as properties of objects of some class $K$

$$P(K) \vdash P(K) \& Q(K). \tag{16}$$

If $P(K)$ stands for 'balls are round' and $Q(K)$ for 'balls are brown', then

according to rule (16), the statement 'balls are round and brown' is a generalization of the statement 'balls are round' (because from the former one can deduce the latter). We can see that the notion 'the number of objects satisfying a description' is not applicable here. Generalizing means here adding (hypothesizing) properties that are ascribed to a class of objects.

After this informal introduction we shall now present various types of generalization rules, concentrating primarily on the rules for concept acquisition. These rules will be expressed using the notation of the annotated predicate calculus (see Appendix A). The reverse of these rules are specialization rules or reformulation rules in special cases. With regard to other specialization and reformulation rules we shall refer the reader to a standard book on predicate calculus (e.g., [84]). Some reformulation rules of the annotated predicate calculus that do not occur in ordinary predicate calculus are given in Appendix A.

We will restrict our attention to generalization rules that transform one or more statements into a single more general statement:

$$\{D_i ::> K\}_{i \in I} \vdash D ::> K. \tag{17}$$

Such a rule states that if an event (a symbolic description of an object or situation) satisfies any description $D_i$, $i \in I$, then it also satisfies description $D$ (the reverse may not be true). A basic property of the generalization transformation is that the resulting description has 'unknown' truth-status, i.e., is a hypothesis that must be tested on new data. A generalization rule does not guarantee that the obtained description is useful or plausible.

We distinguish between two types of generalization rules: *selective* and *constructive*. If every descriptor used in the generated concept description $D$ is among descriptors occurring in the initial concept descriptions $D_i$, $i = 1, 2, \ldots$, then the rule is selective, otherwise it is constructive.

## 5.2. Selective generalization rules

In the rules presented below, CTX, CTX$_1$ and CTX$_2$ stand for some arbitrary expressions (context descriptions) that are augmented by additional components to formulate a concept description.

- The *dropping condition rule* is a generalized version of the previously described rule (15)

$$CTX \& S ::> K \vdash CTX ::> K, \tag{18}$$

where $S$ is an arbitrary predicate or logical expression.

This rule states that a concept description can be generalized by simply removing a conjunctively linked expression. This is one of the most commonly used rules for generalizing information.

- The *adding alternative rule*

$$CTX_1 ::> K \vdash CTX_1 \vee CTX_2 ::> K. \qquad (19)$$

A concept description can be generalized by adding, through the use of logical disjunction, an alternative to it. An especially useful form of this rule is when the alternative is added by extending the scope of permissible values of one specific descriptor. Such an operation can be expressed very simply by using the internal disjunction operator of the annotated predicate calculus. For example, suppose that a concept description is generalized by allowing objects to be not only red but also blue. This can be expressed as follows.

$$CTX \,\&\, [color = red] ::> K \vdash CTX \,\&\, [color = red \vee blue] ::> K \qquad (20)$$

(forms in brackets are selectors; the expressions on the right of '=' are called references (see Appendix A)).

Because of the importance of this special case, it will be presented as a separate general rule.

- The *extending reference rule*

$$CTX \,\&\, [L = R_1] ::> K \vdash CTX \,\&\, [L = R_2] ::> K, \qquad (21)$$

where $R_1 \subseteq R_2 \subseteq DOM(L)$ and $DOM(L)$ denotes the domain of $L$.

In this rule, $L$ is a term, and $R_1$ and $R_2$ (references) are internal disjunctions of values of $L$. References $R_1$ and $R_2$ can be interpreted as sets of values that descriptor $L$ can take in order to satisfy the concept description.

The rule states that a concept description can be generalized by enlarging the reference of a descriptor ($R_2 \supseteq R_1$). The elements added to $R_2$ must, however, be from the domain of $L$.

If $R_2$ is extended to be the whole domain, i.e., $R_2 = DOM(L)$, then the selector $[L = DOM(L)]$ is always true, and therefore can be removed. In this case, the extending reference rule becomes the dropping condition rule. They take into consideration the type of the descriptor $L$ (defined by the structure of $DOM(L)$). They are presented as separate rules below.

- The *closing interval rule*

$$\left.\begin{array}{c} CTX \,\&\, [L = a] ::> K \\ CTX \,\&\, [L = b] ::> K \end{array}\right| \vdash CTX \,\&\, [L = a .. b] ::> K, \qquad (22)$$

where $L$ is a linear descriptor, and $a$ and $b$ are some specific values of descriptor $L$. The two premises are assumed to be connected by the logical conjunction (this convention holds for the remaining rules, as well).

The rule states that if two descriptions of the same class (the premises of the rule) differ in the values of only one linear descriptor, then the descriptions can be replaced by a single description in which the reference of the descriptor is the interval linking these two values.

To illustrate this rule, consider as objects two states of a machine, and $K$ as a class of *normal* states. The rule says that if a machine is in the normal state for two different temperatures, say, $a$ and $b$, then a hypothesis is made that all states in which the temperature falls into the interval $[a, b]$ are also normal. Thus, this rule is not only a logically valid generalization rule, but expresses also some aspect of plausibility.

- The *climbing generalization tree rule*

$$\left.\begin{array}{c} CTX \,\&\, [L = a] ::> K \\ CTX \,\&\, [L = b] ::> K \\ \text{(one or more statements)} \\ CTX \,\&\, [L = i] ::> K \end{array}\right| \vdash CTX \,\&\, [L = s] ::> K, \qquad (23)$$

where $L$ is a structured descriptor, and $s$ represents the lowest parent node whose descendants include nodes $a, b, \ldots$ and $i$ in the generalization tree domain of $L$.

The rule is applicable only to descriptions involving structured descriptors, and is used in various forms by, e.g., Winston [88], Hedrick [30], Lenat [42], Michalski [49], Michalski, Stepp and Diday [54], Mitchell [56, 57]. The following example illustrates the rule

$$\left.\begin{array}{c} \exists P, CTX \,\&\, [shape(P) = triangle] ::> K \\ \exists P, CTX \,\&\, [shape(P) = pentagon] ::> K \end{array}\right| \vdash \exists P, CTX \,\&\, [shape(P) = polygon] ::> K.$$

Paraphrasing this rule in English: if an object of class $K$ is triangular and another object of this class is pentagonal, then the rule generates a statement that objects of class $K$ are polygonal.

- The *turning constants into variables rule* is best known for the case of descriptive generalization

$$\left.\begin{array}{c} F[a] \\ F[b] \\ \text{(one or more statements)} \\ F[i] \end{array}\right| \vdash \forall v, F[v], \qquad (24)$$

where $F[v]$ stands for some description (formula) dependent on variable $v$, and $a, b, \ldots$ are constants.

some description $F[v]$ holds for $v$'s being a constant a or constant b, etc., then the rule generalizes these observations into a statement that $F[v]$ holds for every value of $v$. This is the most often used rule in methods of inductive inference employing predicate calculus.

A corresponding rule for concept acquisition is

$$F[a] \& F[b] \& \cdots ::> K \vdash \exists v, F[v] ::> K. \qquad (25)$$

To illustrate this version, assume that a, b, etc. are parts of an object of class $K$ that have a property $F$. Rule (25) generalizes these facts into an assertion that if any part of an object has property $F$, then the object belongs to class $K$.

- The *turning conjunction into disjunction rule*

$$F_1 \& F_2 ::> K \vdash F_1 \vee F_2 ::> K, \qquad (26)$$

where $F_1$ and $F_2$ are arbitrary descriptions.

A concept description can be generalized by replacing the conjunction operator by the disjunction operator.

- The *extending the quantification domain rule*, in the simplest case, changes the universal quantifier into the existential quantifier

$$\forall v, F[x] ::> K \vdash \exists x, F[v] ::> K. \qquad (27)$$

This rule can be viewed as a generalization of the previous rule (26). Using the concept of numerical quantifier (see Appendix A) this rule can be expressed in an even more general way:

$$\exists(I_1)v, F[v] ::> K \vdash \exists(I_2)v, F[v] ::> K, \qquad (28)$$

where $I_1, I_2$ are the quantification domains (sets of integers) satisfying relation $I_1 \subseteq I_2$.

For example, the statement 'if an object has two parts ($I_1 = \{2\}$) with property $F$, then it belongs to class $K$' can be generalized by rule (28) to a statement 'if an object has two or more parts ($I_2 = \{2, 3, \ldots\}$) with property $F$, then it belongs to class $K$'.

- The *inductive resolution rule*:
(a) As applied to concept acquisition. The deductive inference rule, called the resolution principle, widely used in automatic theorem proving, can be adopted as a rule of generalization for concept acquisition. In propositional form, the resolution principle can be expressed as

$$(P \Rightarrow F_1) \& (\sim P \Rightarrow F_2) \vdash F_1 \vee F_2, \qquad (29)$$

where $P$ is a predicate and $F_1$ and $F_2$ are arbitrary formulas. By interpreting both sides of (29) as concept descriptions, and making appropriate transformations, we obtain

$$\begin{array}{l} P \& F_1 ::> K \\ \sim P \& F_2 ::> K \end{array} \vdash F_1 \vee F_2 ::> K. \qquad (30)$$

To illustrate this rule, assume that $K$ is the set of situations when John goes to a movie. Suppose that it has been observed that he goes to a movie when he has company ($P$) and the movie has high rating ($F_1$), or when he does not have company ($\sim P$), but has plenty of time ($F_2$). Rule (30) generalizes these two observations to a statement 'John goes to a movie either when the movie has high rating or he has plenty of time'.

(b) As applied to descriptive generalization. By applying the logical equivalence $(Q \vdash P) \Leftrightarrow (\sim P \vdash \sim Q)$ (the law of contraposition) to expression (29), then reversing the obtained rule and substituting the negative literals by the positive, we obtain

$$P \& F_1 \vee \sim P \& F_2 \vdash F_1 \& F_2. \qquad (31)$$

This version has been formulated by Morgan[59].

Both versions, (a) and (b), can be generalized by applying the full-fledged resolution principle that uses predicates with arguments, and the unification algorithm to unify these predicate arguments (e.g., [14]).

- The *extension against rule*

$$\begin{array}{l} CTX_1 \& [L = R_1] ::> K \\ CTX_2 \& [L = R_2] ::> \sim K \end{array} \vdash [L \neq R_2] ::> K, \qquad (32)$$

where sets $R_1$ and $R_2$ are assumed to be disjoint.

Given a description of an object belonging to class $K$ (a positive example), and a description of an object not belonging to this class (a negative example), the rule produces the most general statement consistent with these two descriptions. It is an assertion that classifies an object as belonging to class $K$ if descriptor $L$ does not take any value from the set $R_2$, thus ignoring context descriptions $CTX_1$ and $CTX_2$. This rule is the basic rule for learning context-discriminant descriptions from examples used in the previously mentioned inductive program AQ11 [52]. Various modifications of this rule can be obtained by replacing reference $R_2$ in the output assertion by some superset of it (that does not intersect with $R_1$).

### 5.3. Constructive generalization rules

Constructive generalization rules generate inductive assertions that use descriptors not present in the original observational statements. This means that the rules perform a transformation of the original representation space. The following is a general constructive rule that makes such a transformation by applying the knowledge of a relationship between different concepts. It is assumed that this relationship is known to the learning system as background knowledge, as a previously learned concept, or that it is computed according to user-defined procedures.

The rule states that if a concept description contains a part $F_1$ (a concept, a subdescription, etc.) that is known to imply some other concept $F_2$, then a more general description is obtained by replacing $F_1$ by $F_2$. For example, suppose a learning system is told that if an object is black, wide, and long, then it belongs to class $K$ (e.g., is a blackboard). This can be expressed in the annotated predicate calculus:

$$\exists P, [\text{color}(P) = \text{black}][\text{width}(P) \& \text{length}(P) = \text{large}] ::> K.$$

Suppose the learner already knows that

$$\forall P, ([\text{width}(p) \& \text{length}(P) = \text{large}] \Rightarrow [\text{area}(P) = \text{large}]) .$$

Then rule (33) produces a generalization

$$\exists P, [\text{color}(P) = \text{black}][\text{area}(P) = \text{large}] ::> K.$$

As another example, suppose the system is given a description of an object classified as an arch. This description states that a horizontal bar is on top of two equal objects placed apart, $B_1$ and $B_2$, having certain color, weight, shape, etc. Suppose now that characterizations of $B_1$ and $B_2$ in this description satisfy a previously learned concept of a block. Then rule (33) generates an assertion that an arch is a bar on top of two placed-apart blocks. This rule is the basis for an interactive concept learning system developed by Sammut [72].

Specific constructive generalization rules can be obtained from (55) by evoking procedures computing new descriptors in expression $F_2$ as functions of initial or previously derived descriptors (contained in $F_1$). Here are some examples of rules for generating new descriptors.

- *Counting arguments rules.*

(a) The CQ rule (count quantified variables). If a concept description is in the form

$$\exists v_1, v_2, \ldots, v_k, F[v_1, v_2, \ldots, v_k],$$

then the rule generates descriptors '#$v$_COND' representing the number of $v_i$'s that satisfy some condition COND. This condition expresses selected properties of $v_i$'s specified in the concept description. Since many such CONDs can usually be formulated, the rule allows the system to generate a large number of such descriptors.

For example, if the COND is '[attribute$_i(v_i) = R$]', then the generated descriptor will be '#$_i$\_attribute$_i$\_$R$' counting the number of $v_i$'s that satisfy this condition. If the attribute, is, for instance, length, and $R$ is [2..4], then the derived descriptor is '#$v_i$\_length\_2..4' (i.e., it measures the number of $v_i$'s whose length is between 2 and 4, inclusively).

(b) The CA-rule (count arguments of a predicate). If a descriptor in a description is a relation with several arguments, REL$(v_1, v_2, \ldots)$, the rule generates descriptors '#$v$_COND', measuring the number of arguments in REL that satisfy some condition COND. Similar to the above, many such descriptors can be generated, each with different COND.

The annotation of a descriptor provides information about its properties. Such a property may be that a descriptor is, for example, a transitive relation, such as relations 'above', 'inside', 'left-of', and 'before'. For example, if the relation is 'contains$(A, B_1, B_2, \ldots)$', stating that object $A$ contains objects $B_1$, $B_2, \ldots$, and COND is 'large and red', then the derived descriptor '#$B$\_large\_red\_$A$\_contained' measures the number of $B_i$'s contained in $A$ that are large and red.

- *The generating chain properties rule.* If the arguments of different occurrences of a transitive relation in a concept description form a chain, that is, form a sequence of consecutive objects ordered by this relation, the rule generates descriptors characterizing some specific objects in the chain. Such objects may be

LST-object—the 'least object', i.e., the object at the beginning of the chain (e.g., the bottom object in the case of the relation 'above'),

MST-object—the object at the end of the chain (e.g., the top object),

MID-object—the objects in the middle of the chain,

$N$th-object—the object at the $N$th position in the chain (starting from LST-object).

After identifying these objects, the rule investigates all known properties of them (as specified in the observational statements) in order to determine potentially relevant new descriptors. The rule also generates a descriptor characterizing the chain itself, namely, REL-chain-length—the length of the chain defined by relation REL.

For example, if the REL is ON-TOP, then descriptor ON-TOP-chain-length would specify the height of a stack of objects. When a new description is generated and adopted, an annotation for it is also generated and filled out, as in Lenat [42]. This rule can be extended to a partial order relation. In such a case it becomes the 'find extrema of a partial order' rule.

The *detecting descriptor interdependence rule*. Suppose that given is a set of objects exemplifying some concept, and that attribute descriptions are used to characterize these objects. Such descriptions specify only attribute values of the objects; they do not characterize the objects' structure. Suppose that the values a linear descriptor $x$ takes on in all descriptions (events) are ordered in increasing order. If the corresponding values of another linear descriptor $y$ exhibit an increasing or decreasing order, then a two-place descriptor $M(x, y)$ is created, signifying that $x$ and $y$ have a *monotonic relationship*. This descriptor has value $\uparrow$ when $y$ values are increasing and value $\downarrow$ when they are decreasing.

The idea of the above $M$-descriptor can be extended in two directions. The first is to create $M$-descriptors dependent on some condition COND that must be satisfied by the events under consideration:

$$M(x, y)\_COND .$$

For example, descriptor

$$M(length, weight)\_red$$

states that length and weight have a monotonic relationship for red objects.

The second direction of extension is to relax the requirement for the monotonic relationship, i.e., not to require that the order of $y$ values is strictly increasing (or decreasing), but only approximately increasing (or decreasing). For example, the coefficient of statistical correlation between $x$ and $y$ can be measured, and when its absolute value is above a certain threshold, a descriptor $R(x, y)$ is created. The domain of this $R$-descriptor can also be $\{\uparrow, \downarrow\}$, indicating the positive or negative correlation, respectively, or it can have values representing several subranges of the correlation coefficient. Similarly, as in the case of $M$-descriptors, $R$-descriptors can be extended to $R$-COND descriptors.

The $M$- or $R$-descriptors can be used to generate new descriptors. For example, if $[M(x, y) = \uparrow]$, then a new descriptor $z = x/y$ can be generated. If $z$ assumes a constant or a nearly constant value, then an important relationship has been discovered. Similarly, if $[M(x, y) = \downarrow]$, then a new descriptor $z = x \cdot y$ can be generated. These two techniques for generating new descriptors have been successfully used in the BACON system for discovering mathematical expressions representing physical or chemical laws [39].

The above ideas can be extended to structural descriptions. Such descriptions involve not only global properties of objects, but also properties of objects' parts and the relationships among the parts. Suppose that in a structural description of an object, existentially quantified variables $P_1, P_2, \ldots, P_m$ denote its parts. If $x(P_i)$ and $y(P_i)$ are linear descriptors of $P_i$ (e.g.,

numerical attributes characterizing parts $P_i$, $i = 1, 2 \ldots$), the above described techniques for generating $M$- and $R$-descriptors can be applied.

## 6. The STAR Methodology

### 6.1. The concept of a star

The methodology presented here for learning structural descriptions from examples receives its name from the major concept employed in it, that of a *star*. In the most general sense, a *star of an event e* (a description of a single object or situation) *under constraints F*, is a set of all possible alternative nonredundant descriptions of event $e$ that do not violate constraints $F$. A somewhat more restrictive definition of a star will be used here. Let $e$ be an example of a concept to be learned and $F$ be a set of some counterexamples of this concept. A star of the *event e against* the event set $F$, denoted $G(e|F)$, is defined as the set of all maximally general c-expressions that cover (i.e., are satisfied by) event $e$ and that do not cover any of the negative events in $F$.

The c-expressions in a star may contain *derived* descriptors, i.e., descriptors not present in the observational statements. In such a case, testing whether event $e$ satisfies a given description requires that appropriate transformations be applied to the event. Such a process can be viewed as proving that the event implies the description, and therefore methods of automatic theorem proving could be used.

In practical problems, a star of an event may contain a very large number of descriptions. Consequently, such a theoretical star is replaced by a *reduced star* $RG(e|F, m)$ that contains no more than a fixed number, $m$, of descriptions. These $m$ descriptions are selected as the $m$ most preferable descriptions among the remaining ones according to the preference criterion defined in the problem background knowledge. Variable $m$ is a parameter of the learning program, defined either by the user or by the program itself, as a function of the variable computational resources.

Papers [50, 54] give an illustration and an algorithm for generating a reduced star with c-expressions restricted to attribute expressions (i.e., expressions involving only object attributes). Section 6.3 presents an algorithm for generating a reduced star consisting of regular c-expressions. The concept of a star is useful because it reduces the problem of finding a complete description of a concept to subproblems of finding consistent descriptions of single positive examples of the concept.

Since any single example of a concept can always be characterized by a conjunctive expression (a logical product of some predicates), elements of a star can always be represented by conjunctive descriptions. One should also notice that if the concept to be learned is describable by a c-expression, then this description clearly will be among the elements of a (nonreduced) star of *any* single positive example of the concept. Consequently, if there exists a positive example not covered by any description of such a star, then the complete concept description must be disjunctive, i.e., must include more than one c-expression.

## 6.2. Outline of the general algorithm

It is assumed that every observational statement is in the form

$$a\text{-expression} ::> K, \qquad (34)$$

where a-expression is an atomic expression describing an object (recall Section 4.6) and $K$ is the concept exemplified by this object.

It is also assumed that inductive assertions are in the form of a single c-expression or the disjunction of c-expressions. For simplicity we will restrict our attention to only single-concept learning. In the case of multiple-concept learning, the algorithm is repeated for each concept with modifications depending on the assumed interdependence among the concept descriptions (Section 2.3).

Let POS and NEG denote sets of events representing positive and negative examples of a concept, respectively. A general and simplified version of the STAR algorithm can be described as follows.

*Step* 1. Select randomly an event $e$ from POS.

*Step* 2. Generate a reduced star, $RG(e|\text{NEG}, m)$, of the event $e$ against the set of negative examples NEG, with no more than $m$ elements. In the process of star generation apply generalization rules (both selective and constructive), task-specific rules, and heuristics for generating new descriptors supplied by problem background knowledge, and definitions of previously learned concepts.

*Step* 3. In the obtained star, find a description $D$ with the highest preference according to the assumed preference criterion LEF.

*Step* 4. If description $D$ covers set POS completely, then go to Step 6.

*Step* 5. Otherwise, reduce the set POS to contain only events not covered by $D$, and repeat the whole process from Step 1.

*Step* 6. The disjunction of all generated descriptions $D$ is a complete and consistent concept description. As a final step, apply various reformulation rules (defined in the problem background knowledge) and 'contracting' rules ((A.8) and (A.9)) in order to obtain a possibly simpler expression.

This algorithm is a simplified version of the general covering algorithm $A^q$ [47,48]. The main difference is that algorithm $A^q$ selects the initial events (if possible) from events not covered by any of the descriptions of generated stars, rather than not covered by only the selected descriptions $D$. This way the algorithm is able to determine a bound on the maximum number of separate descriptions in a disjunction needed to define the concept. Such a process may, however, be computationally very costly.

The above algorithm describes only single-step learning. If after generating a concept description, a newly presented training event contradicts it, specialization or generalization rules are applied to generate a new, consistent concept description. A method for such incremental learning is described by Michalski and Larson [52].

The central step in the above algorithm is the generation of a reduced star. This can be done using a variety of methods. Thus, the above STAR algorithm can be viewed as a general schema for implementing various learning methods and strategies. The next section describes one specific method of star generation.

## 6.3. Star generation: the INDUCE method

This method generates a reduced star $RG(e|\text{NEG}, m)$ by starting with a set of single selectors, which are either extracted from the event for which the star is generated or inferred from the event by applying constructive generalization rules or inference rules provided by background knowledge. These selectors are then specialized by adding other selectors until consistency is achieved (i.e., until each expression does not intersect with set NEG). Next, the obtained consistent expressions are generalized so that each achieves the maximum coverage of the remaining positive training examples. The best $m$ so-obtained consistent and generalized c-expressions (if some are also complete, then they are alternative solutions) constitute the sought reduced star $RG(e|\text{NEG}, m)$. Specifically, the steps of the procedure are as follows.

(1) In the first step individual selectors of event $e$ are put on the list called PS. This list is called a *partial star*, because its elements may cover some events in NEG. These initial elements of PS (single selectors from $e$) can be viewed as generalizations of event $e$ obtained by applying in all possible ways the dropping condition generalization rule (each application drops all selectors except one). Elements of the partial star PS are then ordered from the most to the least preferred according to a preference criterion

$$\text{LEF}_1 = ((-\text{negcov}, \tau_1), (\text{poscov}, \tau_2)), \qquad (35)$$

where negcov and poscov are numbers of positive and negative examples, respectively, covered by an expression in the star, and $\tau_1$, $\tau_2$ are tolerances (recall Section 4.7). The $\text{LEF}_1$ minimizes the negcov (by maximizing the $-\text{negcov}$) and maximizes poscov.

(2) The list PS is then expanded by adding new selectors obtained by applying the following inference rules to the event $e$:

(a) the constructive generalization rules (Section 5.3),

(b) the problem-specific heuristics defined in the background knowledge,

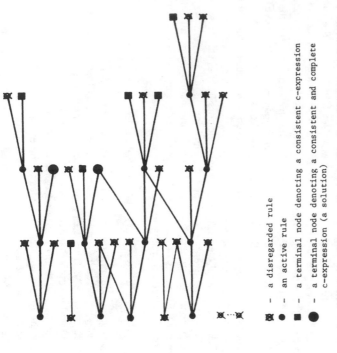

FIG. 1. Illustration of the process of generating a reduced star $RG(e/\text{NEG}, m)$. The nodes in the first column are selectors extracted from the event $e$ or derived from $e$ by applying inference rules. Each arc represents an operation of adding a new selector to the current c-expression.

- ⊠ — a disregarded rule
- ● — an active rule
- ■ — a terminal node denoting a consistent c-expression
- ⬤ — a terminal node denoting a consistent and complete c-expression (a solution)

(c) the definitions of the previously learned concepts (to determine whether parts of $e$ satisfy some already known concepts).

(3) Each new selector is inserted in the appropriate place in list PS, according to preference criterion $\text{LEF}_1$. The size of PS is kept within the limit defined by parameter $m$ by removing from PS all but the $m$ most preferred selectors.

(4) Descriptions in PS are tested for consistency and completeness. A description is consistent if negcov = 0 (i.e., if it covers no events in NEG), and is complete if poscov is equal to the total number of positive examples. Consistent and complete descriptions are removed from PS and put on the list called SOLUTIONS. If the size of the list SOLUTIONS is greater than a parameter #SOL, then the algorithm stops. Parameter #SOL determines the number of desired alternative concept descriptions. Incomplete but consistent descriptions are removed from the list PS and put on the list called CONSISTENT. If the size of the CONSISTENT list is greater than a parameter #CONS, then control is transferred to Step 6.

(5) Each expression in PS is specialized in various ways by appending to it a single selector from the original list PS. Appended selectors must be of lower preference than the last selector in the conjunctive expression (initially, the expression has only one selector). Parameter %BRANCH specifies the percentage of the selectors ranked lower (by the preference criterion) than the last selector in the current conjunction. If %BRANCH = 100%, all lower preference selectors are singly appended—that is, the number of new expressions generated from this conjunction will be equal to the total number of selectors having lower preference than the last selector in the conjunction. All new obtained expressions are ranked by $\text{LEF}_1$ and only the $m$ best are retained. This 'expression growing' process is illustrated in Fig. 1.

Steps 4 and 5 are repeated until the CONSISTENT list contains the number of expressions specified by parameter #CONS, or until the time allocated for this process is exhausted.

(6) Each expression on the CONSISTENT list is generalized by applying the extension against, closing the interval, and climbing generalization tree generalization rules. An efficient way to implement such a process is to transform the original structural description space into an attribute description space. Attributes (i.e., descriptions with zero arguments) defining this space are created from the descriptors in the given expression on the CONSISTENT list in a manner such as that described in [20]. The generalization of the obtained attribute descriptions is accomplished by the attribute star generation procedure, analogous to the one described by Michalski, Stepp and Diday [54]. Details of this process of transforming structural descriptions into attribute descriptions are described by Larson [40]. The reason for such a transformation is that structural descriptions are represented as labeled graphs, while attribute descriptions are represented as binary strings. It is computationally much more economical to handle binary strings than labeled graphs.

(7) The obtained generalizations are ranked according to the global preference criterion LEF defined in the background knowledge. A typical LEF is to maximize the number of events covered in POS set and to minimize the complexity of the expression (measured, for example, by the number of selectors it contains). The $m$ best expressions so determined constitute the reduced star $RG(e|\text{NEG}, m)$.

A somewhat restricted version of the above-described INDUCE method and STAR algorithm has been implemented in various versions of the INDUCE learning program [40, 18, 49, 32].

## 7. An Example

To illustrate the inductive learning methodology just presented, let us consider a simple problem in the area of conceptual data analysis. Suppose we are given examples of 'cancerous' and 'normal' cells, denoted DNC and DNN, respectively, in Fig. 2, and the task of the analysis is

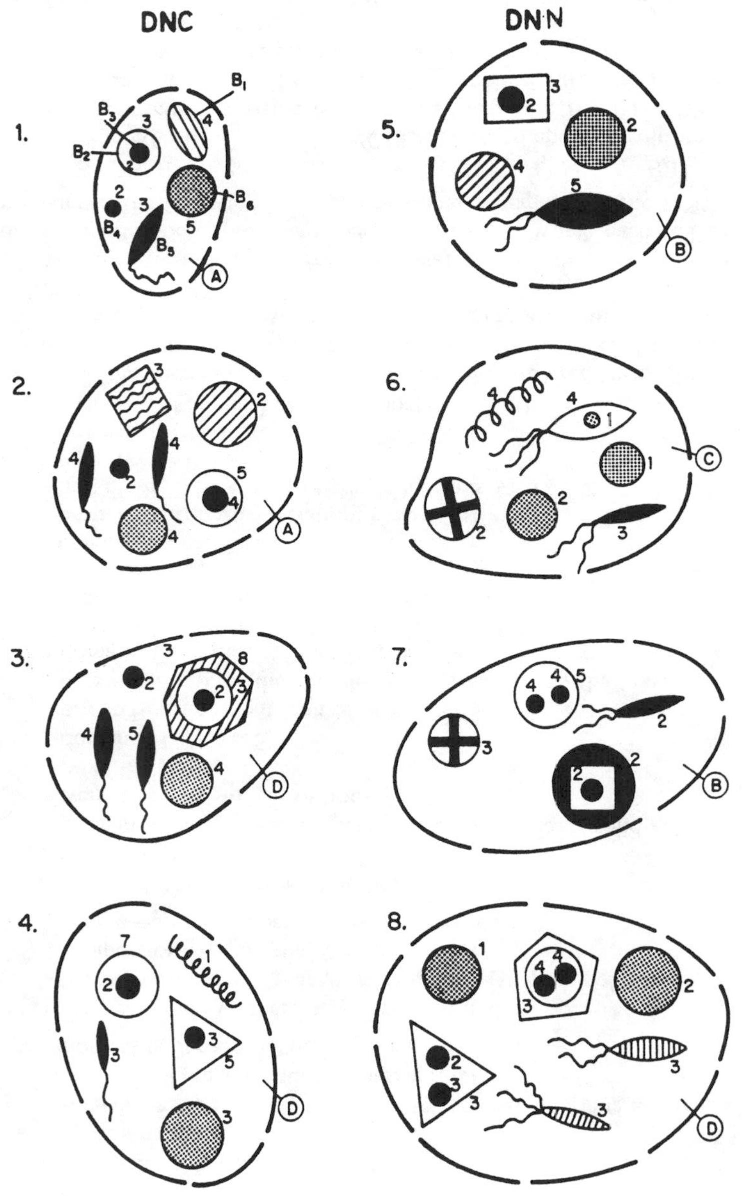

(1) to determine properties differentiating the two classes of cells (i.e., to find discriminant descriptions of each class),

(2) to determine important common properties of the cancerous and the normal cells (i.e., to find a characteristic description of each class).

An assumption is made that the properties to be discovered may involve both quantitative information about the cells and their components, and qualitative information, which includes nominal variables and relationships existing among the components.

The solution to the problem posed (or similar problems) can be obtained by a successive repetition of the 'focus attention→hypothesize→test' cycle described below.

The 'focus attention' phase is concerned with defining the scope of the problem under consideration. This includes selecting descriptors appearing to be relevant, specifying underlying assumptions, and formulating the relevant problem knowledge. This first phase is performed by a researcher; it involves his/her technical knowledge and informal intuitions. The third, the 'test' phase, examines the hypotheses and tests them on new data. This phase may require collecting new samples, performing laboratory experiments, and/or critically analyzing the hypotheses. This phase is likely to involve knowledge and abilities that go beyond currently feasible computer systems.

It is the second, the 'hypothesize' phase, in which an inductive learning system may play a useful role: the role of an assistant for conducting a search for the most plausible and/or most interesting hypotheses. This search may be a formidable combinatorial task for a researcher, if the data sample is large and if each item of the data (in this case, a cell) is described by many variables and/or relations.

Individual steps are as follows.

(1) The user determines the set of initial descriptors and provides an annotation for each descriptor. We will assume that the annotation specifies the type, the domain, and any special properties of each descriptor (e.g., the transitivity of a relation). In the case of structured descriptors, the annotation also specifies the structure of the domain. The specification of the annotation constitutes the first part of the problem background knowledge.

Suppose that for our simple example problem, the following descriptors are selected.

*Global descriptors* (descriptors characterizing a whole cell):
- circ: the number of segments in the circumference of the cell,
  type: linear,
  domain: {1 .. 10};
(II) - pplasm: the type of protoplasm in the cell (marked by encircled capital letters in Fig. 2),
  type: nominal,
  domain: {A, B, C, D};

Fig. 2.

(II) *Local descriptors* (those characterizing cell bodies and their relationships:

- shape($B_i$): the shape of body $B_i$,
type: structured,
domain: a tree structure with a set of leaves {triangle, circle, ellipse, heptagon, square, boat, spring}, nonleaf nodes are defined by rules:

[shape = circle ∨ ellipse] ⇒ [shape = oval],
[shape = triangle ∨ square ∨ heptagon] ⇒ [shape = polygon],
[shape = oval ∨ polygon] ⇒ [shape = regular],
[shape = spring ∨ boat] ⇒ [shape = irregular];

- texture($B_i$): the texture of body $B_i$,
type: nominal,
domain: {blank, shaded, crossed, wavy, solid-black, solid-grey, stripes};
- weight($B_i$): the weight of body $B_i$,
type: linear,
domain: {1, 2, ..., 5};
- orient($B_i$): the orientation of $B_i$,
type: linear-cyclic (the last element is followed by the first),
domain: {N, NE, E, SE, S, SW, W, NW};
condition of applicability: if [shape($B_i$) = boat];
- contains (C, $B_1$, $B_2$, ...) – C contains $B_1$, $B_2$, ...
type: nominal,
domain: {True, False},
properties: transitive relation;
- hastails(B, $L_1$, $L_2$, ...): a body B has tails $L_1$, $L_2$, ...
type: nominal,
domain: {True, False},
condition of applicability: if [shape(B) = boat].

Note that the descriptors 'contains' and 'hastails' are predicates with variable number of arguments. Descriptor 'contains' is characterized as a transitive relation. Descriptors 'hastails' and 'orient' are applicable only under a certain condition.

(2) The user formulates observational statements, which describe cells in terms of selected descriptors and specify the class to which each cell belongs. For example, the following is an observational statement for the DNC cell 1.

∃. CELL, $B_1$, $B_2$, ..., $B_6$ [contains(CELL$_1$, $B_1$, $B_2$, ..., $B_6$)]
[circ(CELL$_1$) = 8][pplasm(CELL$_1$) = A][shape($B_1$) = ellipse] &
[texture($B_1$) = stripes][weight($B_1$) = 4][orient($B_1$) = NW] &
[contains($B_2$, $B_3$)][texture($B_2$) = blank][weight($B_2$) = 3] ··· &
[shape($B_6$) = circle][texture($B_6$) = shaded][weight($B_6$) = 5]
:: > [class = DNC].

(3) To specify the second part of the problem background knowledge the
user indicates which general rules of constructive induction (Section 5.3) are applicable, and also formulates any problem-specific rules.

The constructive rules will generate various new derived descriptors. For example, the counting rule CQ will generate, among others, a descriptor:
- #B-black-boat: the number of bodies whose shape is 'boat' and texture is 'solid-black', i.e., assuming COND

[shape(B) = boat][texture(B) = solid-black].

(For simplicity of notation, the name of this descriptor, as well as other descriptors below, has been abbreviated, so it does not follow strictly the naming convention described in Section 5.3.) The counting rule CA will generate such descriptors as

- total-B: the total number of bodies in a cell (no COND is used);
- indep-B: the number of independent bodies in a cell, assuming the COND 'bodies not contained in another body';
- #contained-in-B: the number of smaller bodies contained in the body B;
- #tails-boat-B: the number of tails in a body B, whose shape is 'boat'.

As advice to the system, the user may formulate arbitrary arithmetic expressions for generating possibly relevant descriptors. For example, the user may suggest a descriptor:

$$weight(CELL) = \sum_i weight(B_i),$$

where $B_i$, i = 1, 2, ... denote bodies in a cell.

The background knowledge may also contain special concepts—even or odd number, the definitions of the area and perimeter of a circle or rectangle, etc.

(4) Finally, as the last part of the background knowledge, the user specifies the type of description sought and the hypothesis preference criterion. Let us assume that both maximal characteristic descriptions and minimal discriminant descriptions are sought. We therefore choose as the preference criterion for constructing characteristic descriptions: 'maximize the length of generated complete c-expressions', and for constructing discriminant descriptions: 'minimize the length of consistent and complete c-expressions'.

For illustration, we shall present here samples of discriminant descriptions and selected components of a characteristic description of the DNC 'cells', obtained by the INDUCE program[2].

*Discriminant descriptions of DNC cells.* Each of these descriptions is sufficient to discriminate all DNC cells from DNN cells. A concept description for class DNC can thus be any one of these descriptions or the disjunction of two or more of these descriptions.

$$\exists(1)B [texture(B) = shaded][weight(B) \geq 3].$$

[2]It may be instructive to the reader to try at this point to formulate his/her own descriptions.

'Every DNC cell, as opposed to DNN, has exactly one body with 'shaded' texture and weight at least 3'. (Paraphrasing in English.)

$$\exists[\text{circ} = \text{even}].$$

'The number of segments in the circumference of every DNC cell is even'. (The concept of 'even' was determined by 'climbing the generalization tree' rule.)

$$\exists(\geq 1)B\;[\text{shape}(B) = \text{boat}][\text{orient}(B) = N \vee NE].$$

'Every DNC cell has at least one 'boat' shape body with orientation N or NE'.

$$\exists(\geq 1)B\,[\#\underline{\text{tails-boat-}B} = 1].$$

'Every DNC cell has at least one body with number of tails equal to 1.'

$$\exists(1)B[\text{shape}(B) = \text{circle}][\#\underline{\text{contains-}B} = 1].$$

'Every DNC cell has a circle containing a single object.' (A related and somewhat redundant description is that every cell contains a circle that has another solid black circle inside it.)

Underscored descriptors are derived descriptors obtained through constructive generalization rules.

*Characteristic descriptions of DNC cells.* Every description below is a characterization of some pattern common to all DNC cells. Some of these patterns taken separately may cover one or more DNN cells (unlike the discriminant descriptions). In contrast to discriminant descriptions, the length of each description has been maximized rather than minimized.

$$\forall(1)B\;[\text{weight}(B) = 5].$$

'In every DNC cell there is one and only one body with weight 5.' (Paraphrasing in English.)

$$\exists(2)B_1, B_2\,[\text{contains}(B_1, B_2)][\text{shape}(B_1)\text{shape}(B_2) = \text{circle}]$$
$$[\text{texture}(B_1) = \text{blank}][\text{weight}(B_1) = \text{odd}]$$
$$[\text{texture}(B_2) = \text{solid\_black}][\text{weight}(B_2) = \text{even}]$$
$$[\#\underline{\text{contained\_in\_}B_1} = 1].$$

'In every cell there are two bodies of circle shape, one contained in another, of which the outside circle is blank, and has 'odd' weight, the inside circle is solid black and has 'even' weight. The number of bodies in the outside circle is only one'. (This is also a discriminant description but is not minimal.)

$$\exists(1)B\;[\text{shape}(B) = \text{circle}][\text{texture}(B) = \text{shaded}][\text{weight}(B) \geq 3].$$

'Every cell contains a circle with 'shaded' texture, whose weight is at least 3'. (This is also a non-minimal discriminant description.)

$$\exists(i>1)B\;[\text{shape}(B) = \text{boat}][\text{orient}(B) = N \vee NE][\#\underline{\text{tails-boat}}(B) = 1].$$

'Every cell has at least one body of 'boat' shape with N or NE orientation, which has one tail.' (This is also a non-minimal discriminant description.)

$$\exists(2)B\;[\text{shape}(B) = \text{circle}][\text{texture}(B) = \text{solid\_black}]$$

or alternatively

$$[\#\underline{B\_\text{circle\_solid\_black}} = 2].$$

'Each cell has exactly two bodies that are solid black circles.'

$$[\text{pplasm} = A \vee D]$$

'The protoplasm of every cell is of type A or D.'

The above example is too simple for really unexpected patterns to be discovered. But it illustrates well the potential of the learning program as a tool for searching for patterns in complex data, especially when the relevant properties involve both numerical and structural information about the objects under consideration. An application of this program to a more complex problem [49] did generate unexpected patterns.

## 8. Conclusion

A theory of inductive learning has been presented that views such learning as a heuristic search through a space of symbolic descriptions, generated by an application of certain inference rules to the initial observational statements (teacher-generated examples of some concepts or environment-provided facts). The process of generating the goal description—the most preferred inductive assertion—relies on the universally intertwined and complementary operations of specializing or generalizing the currently held assertion in order to accommodate new facts. The domain background knowledge has been shown to be a necessary component of inductive learning, which provides constraints, guidance and a criterion for selecting the most preferred inductive assertion.

Such characterization of inductive learning is conceptually simple, and constitutes a theoretical framework for describing and comparing learning methods, as well as developing new methods. The STAR methodology for learning structural descriptions from examples, described in the second part of the chapter, represents a general approach to concept acquisition which can be implemented in a variety of ways and applied to different problem domains.

There are many important topics of inductive learning that have not been covered here. Among them are learning from incomplete or uncertain information, multistage learning, learning from descriptions containing errors, learning with a multitude of forms of given observational statements, as well as multimodel-based inductive assertions, and learning general rules with exceptions. The problem of discovering new concepts, descriptors and, generally, various many-level transformations of the initial description space (the problem of constructive inductive learning) has been covered only very superficially.

These and related topics have been given little attention so far in the field of machine learning. There is no doubt, however, that as the understanding of the fundamental problems in the field matures, these challenging topics will be given increasing attention.

## Appendix A. Annotated Predicate Calculus (APC)

This appendix presents definitions of the basic components of the annotated predicate calculus and some rules for equivalence-preserving transformations of APC expressions (rules that are nonexistent in the ordinary calculus) follow.

### A.1. Elementary and compound terms

*Terms* can be elementary or compound. An *elementary term* (an e-term) is the same as a term in predicate calculus, i.e., a constant, a variable, or a function symbol followed by a list of arguments that are e-terms. A *compound term* (c-term) is a *composite* of elementary terms or is an e-term in which one or more arguments are such composites. The composite of e-terms is defined as the *internal conjunction* ($\&$) or *internal disjunction* ($v$) of e-terms. (The meaning of these operators is explained later.) The following are examples of compound terms:

$$RED \lor BLUE \tag{A.1}$$

$$height(BOX_1 \& BOX_2), \tag{A.2}$$

where RED, BLUE, $BOX_1$, $BOX_2$ are constants. Expression (A.1) and the form in parentheses in (A.2) are composites. Note that expressions (A.1) and (A.2) are not logical expressions that have a truth status (i.e., that can be true or false); they are to be used only as arguments of predicates. A compound term in which arguments are composites can be transformed (expanded) into a composite of elementary terms. Let $f$ be an $n$-argument function whose $n - 1$ arguments are elementary terms. Let $f$ be an $n$-argument function whose $n - 1$ arguments are represented by list $A$, and let $t_1$ and $t_2$ be elementary terms. The rules for

performing such a transformation, expressed as term-rewriting rules, are

$$f(t_1 \lor t_2, A) \leftrightarrow f(t_1, A) \lor f(t_2, A), \tag{A.3}$$

$$f(t_1 \& t_2, A) \leftrightarrow f(t_1, A) \& f(t_2, A). \tag{A.4}$$

If list $A$ itself contains composites, then it is assumed that the internal disjunction is expanded first, followed by the internal conjunction (i.e., the conjunction binds stronger than the disjunction). Thus, term (A.2) can be transformed into a composite

$$height(BOX_1) \& height(BOX_2). \tag{A.5}$$

### A.2. Elementary and compound predicates

Predicates also can be elementary or compound. An *elementary predicate* is the same as a predicate in the predicate calculus, i.e., a predicate symbol followed by a list of arguments that are e-terms. In a *compound predicate* one or more arguments is a compound term. For example, the following are compound predicates

$$Went(Mary \& Mother(Stan), Movie \lor Theatre), \tag{A.6}$$

$$Inside(Key, Drawer(Desk_1 \lor Desk_2)). \tag{A.7}$$

The meaning of a compound predicate is defined by rules for transforming it into an expression made of elementary predicates and ordinary 'external' logic operators of conjunction ($\&$) and disjunction ($v$). We denote the internal and external operators identically, because they can be easily distinguished by the context (note that there is no distinction between them in natural language). If an operator connects predicates, then it is an external operator; if it connects terms, then it is an internal operator.

Let $t_1$ and $t_2$ be e-terms and $P$ an $n$-ary predicate whose last $n - 1$ arguments are represented by a list $A$. We have the following reformulation rules (i.e., equivalence preserving transformations of descriptions)

$$P(t_1 \lor t_2, A) \models P(t_1, A) \lor P(t_2, A), \tag{A.8}$$

$$P(t_1 \& t_2, A) \models P(t_1, A) \& P(t_2, A). \tag{A.9}$$

If an argument of a predicate is a compound term that is not a composite of elementary terms, then it is transformed first into a composite by rules (A.3) and (A.4). If $A$ contains a composite of terms, then the disjunction is expanded first before conjunction (similarly as in expanding compound terms).

Rules (A.3), (A.4), (A.8) and (A.9) can be used as bidirectional transformation rules. By applying them forward (from left to right), a compound predicate can be expanded into an expression containing only elementary predicates, and by applying them backward, an expression with elementary predicates can be contracted into a compound predicate.

For example, by applying forward rule (A.8) and then (A.9), one can expand the compound predicate (A.6) into

$$\text{Went(Mary, movie)} \ \& \ \text{Went(Mother(Stan), movie)} \ \vee$$
$$\text{Went(Mary, theatre)} \ \& \ \text{Went(Mother(Stan), theatre)} . \qquad (A.10)$$

Comparing logically equivalent expressions (A.6) and (A.10), one can notice that (A.6) is considerably shorter than (A.10), and in contrast to (A.10), represents explicitly the fact that Mary & Mother(Stan) went to the same place. Also, the structure of (A.6) is more similar to the structure of the corresponding natural language expression.

## A.3. Relational statements

A simple and often used way of describing objects or situations is to state the values of selected attributes applied to these objects or situations. Although such information can be represented by predicates, this is not the most readable or natural way. The APC uses for this purpose a statement

$$\text{eterm}_i = a , \qquad (A.11)$$

stating that e-term$_i$ evaluates to a constant $a$. Such a statement is called an *atomic relational statement* (or an *atomic selector*). Expression (A.11) is a special case of a *relational statement* (also called *selector*), defined as

$$\text{Term}_1 \ \text{rel} \ \text{Term}_2 , \qquad (A.12)$$

where Term$_1$ and Term$_2$ are elementary or compound terms, and rel stands for one of the relational symbols: $=, \geq, >, <, \leq$.

If Term$_1$ and Term$_2$ are both elementary, then (A.12) states that the value of the function represented by Term$_1$ is in relation rel to the value of function represented by Term$_2$. For example, the expression

$$\text{distance(Boston, Tampa)} = \text{distance(Washington, Dallas)} \qquad (A.13)$$

states that the distance between Boston and Tampa is the same as the distance between Washington and Dallas. If Term$_2$ is a constant, then it evaluates to itself.

Expression (A.12) can be represented by a predicate

$$\text{rel(Term}_1, \text{Term}_2) . \qquad (A.14)$$

If Term$_1$ or Term$_2$ is compound, or if both are, then the meaning of (A.12) is defined by expanding it into a form containing only relational statements with elementary terms. The expansion is performed by transforming (A.12) into (A.14), applying transformation rules (A.3), (A.4), (A.8) and (A.9), and then converting the elementary predicates into relational statements. For example, a relational statement

$$\text{color}(P_1 \vee P_2) = \text{Red} \vee \text{Blue} \qquad (A.15)$$

can be expanded into an expression

$$(\text{color}(P_1) = \text{Red} \vee \text{Blue}) \vee (\text{color}(P_2) = \text{Red} \vee \text{Blue}) \qquad (A.16)$$

and finally to an expression consisting of only atomic selectors:

$$(\text{color}(P_1) = \text{Red} \vee \text{color}(P_1) = \text{Blue}) \vee$$
$$(\text{color}(P_2) = \text{Red} \vee \text{color}(P_2) = \text{Blue}). \qquad (A.17)$$

The two selectors in the disjunction (A.16) are examples of a *referential selector*, defined as a form

$$\text{Term}_1 \ \text{rel} \ \text{Term}_2 , \qquad (A.18)$$

where Term$_1$ (called *referee*) is a nonconstant elementary term and Term$_2$ (called *reference*) is a constant or the disjunction of constants from the domain of Term$_1$. If relation rel is '=' and Term$_2$ is the disjunction of some constants, then the referential selector (A.18) states that the function represented by Term$_1$ evaluates to one of the constants in Term$_2$. The referential selector is very useful for representing concept descriptions.

If the reference of a referential selector contains a sequence of consecutive constants from the domain of a linear descriptor, then the range operator '..' is used to simplify the expression. For example,

$$\text{size}(P) = 2 \vee 3 \vee 4$$

can be written

$$\text{size}(P) = 2 .. 4 .$$

The negation of a selector,

$$\sim(\text{Term}_1 = \text{Term}_2),$$

can be equivalently written

$$\text{Term}_1 \neq \text{Term}_2. \tag{A.19}$$

An arbitrary predicate $P(t_1, t_2, \ldots)$ can be written in the form of a referential selector

$$P(t_1, t_2, \ldots) = \text{True}. \tag{A.20}$$

Therefore, for the uniformity of terminology, a predicate will be considered a special form of a selector.

To facilitate the interpretation and readability of individual selectors in expressions, they are usually surrounded with square brackets and their conjunction is expressed by concatenating the bracketed forms (see Section 7).

APC expressions are created from selectors (relational statements) in the same way as predicate calculus expressions are created from predicates, i.e., by using logic connectives ($\sim$, $\&$, $\vee$, $\Rightarrow$, $\Leftrightarrow$) and quantifiers. One additional useful connective is the *exception operation* ($\diagdown$), defined as

$$S_1 \diagdown S_2 \models (\sim S_2 \Rightarrow \sim S_1), \tag{A.21}$$

where $S_1$ and $S_2$ are APC expressions. ($S_1 \diagdown S_2$ reads: $S_1$ *except when* $S_2$). It is easy to see that the exception operator is equivalent to the symmetrical difference. In addition to ordinary quantifiers there is also a *numerical quantifier*, expressed in the form

$$\exists(I)v, S[v], \tag{A.22}$$

where $I$, the *index set*, denotes a set of integers, and $S[v]$ is an APC expression having $v$ as a free variable.

Sentence (A.22) evaluates as true if the number of values of $v$ for which expression $S[v]$ is true is an element of the set $I$. For example, formula

$$\exists(2..8)v, S[v] \tag{A.23}$$

states that there are two to eight values of $v$ for which the expression $S[v]$ is true. The following equivalences hold

$$\exists v, S[v] \quad \text{is equivalent to} \quad \exists(\geq 1)v, S[v]$$

and

$$\forall v, S[v] \quad \text{is equivalent to} \quad \exists(k)v, S[v],$$

where $k$ is the number of possible values of variable $v$.

To state that there are $k$ and only $k$ distinct values for variables $v_1, v_2, \ldots, v_k$ for which expression $S(v_1, v_2, \ldots, v_k)$ is true we write:

$$\exists.v_1, v_2, \ldots, v_k, S(v_1, \ldots, v_k). \tag{A.24}$$

For example, the expression

$$\exists.P_0, P_1, P_2, [\text{contains}(P_0, P_1, \& P_2)] \& [\text{color}(P_1 \& P_2) = \text{red}]$$
$$\Rightarrow [\text{two\_red\_parts}(P_0)]$$

states that predicate two_red_parts($P_0$) holds if $P_0$ has two and only two distinct parts in it that are red.

Section 7 presents an example of the usage of the APC for formulating ovservational statements and concept descriptions.

ACKNOWLEDGMENT

In the development of the ideas presented here the author benefited from discussions with Tom Dietterich and Robert Stepp. Proofreading and comments of Jaime Carbonell, Bill Hoff, and Tom Mitchell were helpful in shaping up the final version of the paper.

The author gratefully acknowledges the partial support of the research by the National Science Foundation under grants MCS 79-06614 and MCS 82-05166.

REFERENCES

1. Amarel, F., An approach to automatic theory formation, in: von Foerster, H., Ed., *Illinois Symposium on Principles of Self-Organization* (1960).
2. Banerji, R.B., The description list of concepts, *Comm. ACM* **5** (1962) 426-431.
3. Banerji, R.B., *Artificial Intelligence: A Theoretical Perspective* (North-Holland, Amsterdam, 1980).
4. Bierman, A.W. and Feldman, J., Survey of results in grammatical inference, in: *Frontiers of Pattern Recognition* (Academic Press, New York, 1972) 32-54.
5. Bierman, A.W., The inference of regular LISP programs from examples, *IEEE Trans. Systems Man Cybernet.* **8**(8) (1978) 585-600.
6. Bongard, M.M., *Pattern Recognition* (Spartan Books, Washington, DC, 1970) [in Russian].
7. Brachman, R.T., On the epistemological status of semantic networks, Rept. No. 3807, AI Department, Bolt, Beranek and Newman, 1978.
8. Bruner, J.S., Goodnow, J. and Austin, G., *A Study of Thinking* (Wiley, New York, 1956).
9. Buchanan, G.B. and Feigenbaum, E.A., "Dendral and Meta-Dendral, their applications dimension, *Artificial Intelligence* **11** (1978) 5-24.

10. Buchanan, B.G., Mitchell, T.M., Smith, R.G. and Johnson, C.R., Jr., Models of learning systems, Tech. Rept. STAN-CS-79-692, Computer Science Department, Stanford University, 1979.

11. Burstall, R.M. and Darlington, J., A transformation system for developing recursive programs, J. ACM 24(1) (1977) 44-67.

12. Carnap, R., The aim of inductive logic, in: Nagel, E., Suppes, P. and Tarski, A., Eds., Logic, Methodology and Philosophy of Science (Stanford University Press, Stanford, 1962) 303-318.

13. Case J. and Smith, C., Comparison of identification criteria for mechanized inductive inference. Tech. Rept. No. 154, State University of New York at Buffalo, 1979.

14. Chang, C. and Lee, R.C., Symbolic Logic and Mechanical Theorem Proving (Academic Press, New York, 1973).

15. Cohen, B.L., A powerful and efficient structural pattern recognition system, Artificial Intelligence 9(3) (1977) 233-255.

16. Coulon, D. and Kayser, D., Learning criterion and inductive behavior, Pattern Recognition 10(1) (1978) 19-25.

17. Davis, R. and Lenat, D., Knowledge-based Systems in Artificial Intelligence (McGraw-Hill, New York, 1982).

18. Dietterich, T., Description of inductive program INDUCE 1.1, Internal Rept., Department of Computer Science, University of Illinois at Urbana-Champaign, 1978.

19. Dietterich, T., A methodology of knowledge layers for inducing descriptions of sequentially ordered events, Rept. No. 80-1024, Department of Computer Science, University of Illinois at Urbana-Champaign, 1980.

20. Dietterich, T. and Michalski, R.S., Inductive learning of structural descriptions: evaluation criteria and comparative review of selected methods, Artificial Intelligence 16(3) (1981) 257-294.

21. Feigenbaum, E.A., The simulation of verbal learning behavior, in: Feigenbaum, E.A. and Feldman, J., Eds., Computers and Thought (McGraw-Hill, New York, 1963).

22. Fikes, R.E., Hart, R.E. and Nilsson, N.J., Learning and executing generalization robot plans, Artificial Intelligence 3 (1972) 251-288.

23. Gaines, B.R., Maryanski's grammatical inferences. IEEE Trans. Comput. 28 (1979) 62-64.

24. Gaschnig, J., Development of uranium exploration models for prospector consultant system, Artificial Intelligence Center, SRI Intern., 1980.

25. Hass, N. and Hendrix, G.G., An approach to applying and acquiring knowledge, Proc. First Amer. Assoc. for AI Conference (1980) 235-239.

26. Hájek, P., Havel, I. and Chytil, M., The GUHA method of automatic hypothesis determination, Computing 1 (1966) 293-308.

27. Hájek, P. and Havránek, T., Mechanizing Hypothesis Formation, Mathematical Foundations for a General Theory (Springer, Berlin, 1978).

28. Hayes-Roth, F., A structural approach to pattern learning and the acquisition of classificatory power, Proc. First Internat. Joint Conference on Pattern Recognition, Washington, DC, October 30-November 1 (1973) 343-355.

29. Hayes-Roth, F. and McDermott, J., An interference matching technique for inducing abstractions, Comm. ACM 21(5) (1978) 401-411.

30. Hedrick, C.L., A computer program to learn production systems using a semantic net, Ph.D. Thesis, Department of Computer Science, Carnegie-Mellon University, Pittsburgh, PA, 1974.

31. Hintzman, D.L., The Psychology of Learning and Memory (Freeman, San Francisco, CA, 1978).

32. Hoff, B., Michalski, R.S. and Stepp, R., INDUCE 2—a program for learning structural descriptions from examples, Intelligent Systems Group Rept. No. 83-1, Department of Computer Science, University of Illinois at Urbana-Champaign, 1983.

33. Hovland, C.I., A 'communication analysis' of concept learning, Psychol. Rev. (1952) 461-472.

34. Hunt, E.B., Concept Learning: An Information Processing Problem (Wiley, New York, 1962).

35. Hunt, E.B., Marin, J. and Stone, P.T., Experiments in Induction (Academic Press, New York, 1966).

36. Jouannaud, J.P. and Kodratoff, Y., An automatic construction of LISP programs by transformations of functions synthesized from their input-output behavior, Internat. J. Policy Anal. Inform. Systems 4(4) (1980) 331-358.

37. Kemeni, T.G., The use of simplicity in induction, Psychol. Rev. 62(3) (1953) 391-408.

38. Kochen, M., Experimental study of hypothesis-formation by computer, in: Cherry, C., Ed., Information Theory, 4th London Symposium (Butterworth, London, 1961).

39. Langley, P., Neches, R., Neves, D. and Anzai, Y., A domain-independent framework for learning procedures, Internat. J. Policy Anal. Inform. Systems 4(2) (1980) 163-198.

40. Larson, J., Inductive inference in the variable-valued predicate logic system VL21: methodology and computer implementation, Ph.D. Thesis, Rept. No. 869, Department of Computer Science, University of Illinois, Urbana, Illinois, 1977.

41. Larson, J. and Michalski, R.S., Inductive inference of VL decision rules, Proc. Workshop on Pattern-Directed Inference Systems, Honolulu, Hawaii, May 23-27, 1977, SIGART Newsletter 63 (1977)

42. Lenat, D., AM: an artificial intelligence approach to discovery in mathematics as heuristic search, Computer Science Department, Rept. STAN-CS-76-570, Stanford University, Stanford, CA, 1976.

43. Lenat, D. and Harris, G., Designing a rule system that searches for scientific discovery, in: Waterman D.A. and Hayes-Roth, F., Eds., Pattern-Directed Inference Systems (Academic Press, New York, 1978) 25-51.

44. Michie, D. New face of artificial intelligence, Informatics 3 (1977) 5-11.

45. Michalski, R.S., A variable-valued logic system as applied to picture description and recognition, in: Nake F. and Rosenfeld, A., Eds., Graphic Languages (North-Holland, Amsterdam 1972) 20-47.

46. Michalski, R.S., AQVAL/1—computer implementation of a variable-valued logic system and its application to pattern recognition, Proc. First Internat. Joint Conf. on Pattern Recognition, Washington. DC, October 30-November 1 (1973).

47. Michalski, R.S., Variable-valued logic and its applications to pattern recognition and machine learning, in: Rine, D., Ed., Multiple-Valued Logic and Computer Science (North-Holland, Amsterdam, 1975).

48. Michalski, R.S., Synthesis of optimal and quasi-optimal variable-valued logic formulas, Proc. 1975 Intern. Symposium on Multiple-Valued Logic, Bloomington, IN, May 13-16, (1975) 76-87.

49. Michalski, R.S., Pattern recognition as rule-guided inductive inference, IEEE Trans. Pattern Anal. Machine Intelligence (1980).

50. Michalski, R.S., Knowledge acquisition through conceptual clustering: a theoretical framework and an algorithm for partitioning data into conjunctive concepts, Internat. J. Policy Anal. Inform. Systems 4(3) (1980) 219-244.

51. Michalski, R.S. and Chilausky, R.L., Learning by being told and learning from examples, Internat. J. Policy Anal. Inform. Systems 4(2) (1980) 125-160.

52. Michalski, R.S. and Larson, J.B., Selection of most representative training examples and incremental generation of VL1 hypotheses: the underlying methodology and the description of programs ESEL and AQ11, Rept. No. 78-867, Department of Computer Science, University of Illinois a: Urbana-Champaign, 1978.

53. Michalski, R.S. and P. Negri, An experiment on inductive learning in chess end games, in: Elcock, E.W. and Michie D., Eds., Machine Representation of Knowledge, Machine intelligence 8 (Ellis Horwood, 1977) 175-192.

54. Michalski, R.S., Stepp, R. and Diday, E., A recent advance in data analysis: clustering objects into classes characterized by conjunctive concepts, in: Kanal, L. and Rosenfeld, A., Eds., Progress in Pattern Recognition, Vol. 1 (North-Holland, Amsterdam, 1981).

55. Minsky, M., A framework for representing knowledge. MIT AI Memo 306, 1974.

56. Mitchell, T.M., Version spaces: an approach to concept learning, Ph.D. Thesis, Stanford University, Stanford, CA 1978.
57. Mitchell, T.M., Generalization as search, *Artificial Intelligence* **18** (2) (1982) 203–226.
58. Moraga, C., A didactic experiment in pattern recognition, Rept. AIUD-PR-8101, Department of Informatics, Dartmund University, 1981.
59. Morgan, C.G., Automated hypothesis generation using extended inductive resolution, *Advance Papers 4th Internat. Joint Conf. on Artificial Intelligence*, Tbilisi, G.A., Vol. I (1975) 352–356.
60. Newell, A., Shaw, J.C. and Simon, H.A., A variety of intelligent learning in the general problem solver, Rand Corp. Tech. Rept. (1959) 1791.
61. Niblett, T. and Shapiro, A., Automatic induction of classification rules for a chess endgame, MIP-R-129, Machine Intelligence Research Unit, University of Edinburgh, 1981.
62. Nilsson, N.T., *Principles of Artificial Intelligence* (Tioga, Palo Alto, CA, 1980).
63. O'Rorke, P., A comparative study of inductive learning systems AQ11 and ID3, Intelligent Systems Group Rept. No. 81-14, Department of Computer Science, University of Illinois at Urbana-Champaign, 1981.
64. Pettorossi, A., An algorithm for reducing memory requirements in recursive programs using annotations, Internat. Workshop on Program Construction, Bonas, September 8–12, 1980.
65. Plotkin, G.D., A further note on inductive generalization, in: Beltzer, B. and Michie, D., Eds., *Machine Intelligence 6* (Elsevier, New York, 1971).
66. Pokorny, D., Knowledge acquisition by the GUHA method, *Internat. J. Policy Anal. Inform. Systems* 4(4) (1980) 379–399.
67. Polya, G., Mathematics and plausible reasoning, vol. I: induction and analogy in mathematics, Vol. II: patterns of plausible inference, (Princeton University Press, Princeton, NJ, 1954).
68. Popper, K.R., *The Logic of Scientific Discovery* (Basic Books, New York, 1959).
69. Post, H.R., Simplicity of scientific theories, *British J. Philos. Sci.* 11(41) (1960).
70. Quinlan, J.R., Discovering rules by induction from large collections of examples, in: Michie, D., Ed., *Expert Systems in the Microelectronic Age* (Edinburgh University Press, Edinburgh, 1979).
71. Russell, B., *History of Western Philosophy* (Allen and Unwin, London, 1946) 566.
72. Sammut, C., Learning concepts by performing experiments, Ph.D. Thesis, Department of Computer Science, University of South Wales. Australia, 1981.
73. Shapiro, E.Y., Inductive inferences of theories from facts, Research Rept. 192, Department of Computer Science, Yale University, New Haven, CT, 1981.
74. Shaw, D.E., Swartout, W.R. and Green, C.C., Inferring LISP programs from examples, *Proc. 4th Internat. Joint Conf. on Artificial Intelligence*, Tbilisi, GA, Vol. I (1975) 351–356.
75. Shortliffe, E.H., *Computer-based Medical Consultations: MYCIN* (American Elsevier, New York, 1979).
76. Simon, H.A. and Kotovsky, Human acquisition for sequential patterns, *Psychol. Rev.* **10**(6) (1963) 534–546.
77. Simon, H. A. and Lea, G., Problem solving and rule induction: a unified view, in: Gregg. L.W., Ed., *Knowledge and Cognition*, Erlbaum, Potomac, MD, 1974).
78. Simon, H.A., *Models of Discovery* (Reidel, Dordrecht, 1977).
79. Smith, D.R., A survey of the synthesis of LISP programs from examples, Internat. Workshop on Program Construction, Bonas, September 8–12, 1980.
80. Solomonoff, R.J., A formal theory of inductive inference, *Inform. and Control* 7, (1964) 1–22, 224–254.
81. Soloway, E.M. and Riseman, E.M., Levels of pattern description in learning, *Papers 5th Internat. Joint Conf. on Artificial Intelligence*, Cambridge, MA (1977) 801–811.
82. Stepp, R., The investigation of the UNICLASS inductive program AQ7UNI and user's guide, Rept. No. 949, Department of Computer Science, University of Illinois at Urbana-Champaign, 1978.
83. Stoffel, J.C., The theory of prime events: data analysis for sample vectors with inherently discrete variables, *Information Processing 74* (North-Holland, Amsterdam, 1974) 702–706.
84. Suppes, P., *Introduction to Logic* (Van Nostrand, Princeton, NJ, 1957).
85. Vere, S.A., Induction of concepts in the predicate calculus, *Advance Papers 4th Internat. Joint Conf. on Artificial Intelligence*, Tbilisi, GA, Vol. I (1975) 351–356.
86. Waterman, DA., Generalization learning techniques for automating the learning of heuristics, *Artificial Intelligence* I(1/2) (1970) 121–170.
87. Winston, P.H., Learning structural descriptions from examples, Tech. Rept. AI TR-231, MIT AI Lab, Cambridge, MA, 1970.
88. Winston, P.H., *Artificial Intelligence* (Addison-Wesley, Reading, MA, 1977).
89. Yau K.C. and Fu, K.S., Syntactic shape recognition using attributed grammars, *Proc. 8th Annual EIA Symposium on Automatic Imagery Pattern Recognition*, 1978.
90. Zagoruiko, N.G., Methods for revealing regularities in data, *Izd. Nauka* (1981) [in Russian].

*Received August 1980; revised version received July 1982*

Machine Learning 1: 81–106, 1986
© 1986 Kluwer Academic Publishers, Boston – Manufactured in The Netherlands

# Induction of Decision Trees

J.R. QUINLAN                                                    (munnari!nswitgould.oz!quinlan@seismo.css.gov)
*Centre for Advanced Computing Sciences, New South Wales Institute of Technology, Sydney 2007, Australia*

(Received August 1, 1985)

**Key words:** classification, induction, decision trees, information theory, knowledge acquisition, expert systems

**Abstract.** The technology for building knowledge-based systems by inductive inference from examples has been demonstrated successfully in several practical applications. This paper summarizes an approach to synthesizing decision trees that has been used in a variety of systems, and it describes one such system, ID3, in detail. Results from recent studies show ways in which the methodology can be modified to deal with information that is noisy and/or incomplete. A reported shortcoming of the basic algorithm is discussed and two means of overcoming it are compared. The paper concludes with illustrations of current research directions.

## 1. Introduction

Since artificial intelligence first achieved recognition as a discipline in the mid 1950's, machine learning has been a central research area. Two reasons can be given for this prominence. The ability to learn is a hallmark of intelligent behavior, so any attempt to understand intelligence as a phenomenon must include an understanding of learning. More concretely, learning provides a potential methodology for building high-performance systems.

Research on learning is made up of diverse subfields. At one extreme there are adaptive systems that monitor their own performance and attempt to improve it by adjusting internal parameters. This approach, characteristic of a large proportion of the early learning work, produced self-improving programs for playing games (Samuel, 1967), balancing poles (Michie, 1982), solving problems (Quinlan, 1969) and many other domains. A quite different approach sees learning as the acquisition of structured knowledge in the form of concepts (Hunt, 1962; Winston, 1975), discrimination nets (Feigenbaum and Simon, 1963), or production rules (Buchanan, 1978).

The practical importance of machine learning of this latter kind has been underlin-

ed by the advent of knowledge-based expert systems. As their name suggests, these systems are powered by knowledge that is represented explicitly rather than being implicit in algorithms. The knowledge needed to drive the pioneering expert systems was codified through protracted interaction between a domain specialist and a knowledge engineer. While the typical rate of knowledge elucidation by this method is a few rules per man day, an expert system for a complex task may require hundreds or even thousands of such rules. It is obvious that the interview approach to knowledge acquisition cannot keep pace with the burgeoning demand for expert systems; Feigenbaum (1981) terms this the 'bottleneck' problem. This perception has stimulated the investigation of machine learning methods as a means of explicating knowledge (Michie, 1983).

This paper focusses on one microcosm of machine learning and on a family of learning systems that have been used to build knowledge-based systems of a simple kind. Section 2 outlines the features of this family and introduces its members. All these systems address the same task of inducing decision trees from examples. After a more complete specification of this task, one system (ID3) is described in detail in Section 4. Sections 5 and 6 present extensions to ID3 that enable it to cope with noisy and incomplete information. A review of a central facet of the induction algorithm reveals possible improvements that are set out in Section 7. The paper concludes with two novel initiatives that give some idea of the directions in which the family may grow.

## 2. The TDIDT family of learning systems

Carbonell, Michalski and Mitchell (1983) identify three principal dimensions along which machine learning systems can be classified:

- the underlying learning strategies used;
- the representation of knowledge acquired by the system; and
- the application domain of the system.

This paper is concerned with a family of learning systems that have strong common bonds in these dimensions.

Taking these features in reverse order, the *application domain* of these systems is not limited to any particular area of intellectual activity such as Chemistry or Chess; they can be applied to any such area. While they are thus general-purpose systems, the applications that they address all involve *classification*. The product of learning is a piece of procedural knowledge that can assign a hitherto-unseen object to one of a specified number of disjoint classes. Examples of classification tasks are:

1. the diagnosis of a medical condition from symptoms, in which the classes could be either the various disease states or the possible therapies;

2. determining the game-theoretic value of a chess position, with the classes *won for white*, *lost for white*, and *drawn*; and

3. deciding from atmospheric observations whether a severe thunderstorm is unlikely, possible or probable.

It might appear that classification tasks are only a minuscule subset of procedural tasks, but even activities such as robot planning can be recast as classification problems (Dechter and Michie, 1985).

The members of this family are sharply characterized by their *representation of acquired knowledge* as decision trees. This is a relatively simple knowledge formalism that lacks the expressive power of semantic networks or other first-order representations. As a consequence of this simplicity, the learning methodologies used in the TDIDT family are considerably less complex than those employed in systems that can express the results of their learning in a more powerful language. Nevertheless, it is still possible to generate knowledge in the form of decision trees that is capable of solving difficult problems of practical significance.

The *underlying strategy* is non-incremental learning from examples. The systems are presented with a set of cases relevant to a classification task and develop a decision tree from the top down, guided by frequency information in the examples but not by the particular order in which the examples are given. This contrasts with incremental methods such as that employed in MARVIN (Sammut, 1985), in which a dialog is carried on with an instructor to 'debug' partially correct concepts, and that used by Winston (1975), in which examples are analyzed one at a time, each producing a small change in the developing concept; in both of these systems, the order in which examples are presented is most important. The systems described here search for patterns in the given examples and so must be able to examine and re-examine all of them at many stages during learning. Other well-known programs that share this data-driven approach include BACON (Langley, Bradshaw and Simon, 1983) and INDUCE (Michalski, 1980).

In summary, then, the systems described here develop decision trees for classification tasks. These trees are constructed beginning with the root of the tree and proceeding down to its leaves. The family's palindromic name emphasizes that its members carry out the *Top-Down Induction of Decision Trees*.

The example objects from which a classification rule is developed are known only through their values of a set of properties or attributes, and the decision trees in turn are expressed in terms of these same attributes. The examples themselves can be assembled in two ways. They might come from an existing database that forms a history of observations, such as patient records in some area of medicine that have accumulated at a diagnosis center. Objects of this kind give a reliable statistical picture but, since they are not organized in any way, they may be redundant or omit

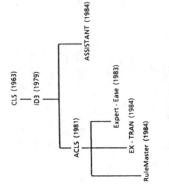

*Figure 1.* The TDIDT family tree.

uncommon cases that have not been encountered during the period of record-keeping. On the other hand, the objects might be a carefully culled set of tutorial examples prepared by a domain expert, each with some particular relevance to a complete and correct classification rule. The expert might take pains to avoid redundancy and to include examples of rare cases. While the family of systems will deal with collections of either kind in a satisfactory way, it should be mentioned that earlier TDIDT systems were designed with the 'historical record' approach in mind, but all systems described here are now often used with tutorial sets (Michie, 1985).

Figure 1 shows a family tree of the TDIDT systems. The patriarch of this family is Hunt's Concept Learning System framework (Hunt, Marin and Stone, 1966). CLS constructs a decision tree that attempts to minimize the cost of classifying an object. This cost has components of two types: the measurement cost of determining the value of property A exhibited by the object, and the misclassification cost of deciding that the object belongs to class J when its real class is K. CLS uses a lookahead strategy similar to minimax. At each stage, CLS explores the space of possible decision trees to a fixed depth, chooses an action to minimize cost in this limited space, then moves one level down in the tree. Depending on the depth of lookahead chosen, CLS can require a substantial amount of computation, but has been able to unearth subtle patterns in the objects shown to it.

ID3 (Quinlan, 1979, 1983a) is one of a series of programs developed from CLS in response to a challenging induction task posed by Donald Michie, *viz.* to decide from pattern-based features alone whether a particular chess position in the King-Rook vs King-Knight endgame is lost for the Knight's side in a fixed number of ply. A full description of ID3 appears in Section 4, so it is sufficient to note here that it embeds a tree-building method in an iterative outer shell, and abandons the cost-driven lookahead of CLS with an information-driven evaluation function.

ACLS (Paterson and Niblett, 1983) is a generalization of ID3. CLS and ID3 both require that each property used to describe objects has only values from a specified set. In addition to properties of this type, ACLS permits properties that have unrestricted integer values. The capacity to deal with attributes of this kind has allowed ACLS to be applied to difficult tasks such as image recognition (Shepherd, 1983). ASSISTANT (Kononenko, Bratko and Roskar, 1984) also acknowledges ID3 as its direct ancestor. It differs from ID3 in many ways, some of which are discussed in detail in later sections. ASSISTANT further generalizes on the integer-valued attributes of ACLS by permitting attributes with continuous (real) values. Rather than insisting that the classes be disjoint, ASSISTANT allows them to form a hierarchy, so that one class may be a finer division of another. ASSISTANT does not form a decision tree iteratively in the manner of ID3, but does include algorithms for choosing a 'good' training set from the objects available. ASSISTANT has been used in several medical domains with promising results.

The bottom-most three systems in the figure are commercial derivatives of ACLS. While they do not significantly advance the underlying theory, they incorporate many user-friendly innovations and utilities that expedite the task of generating and using decision trees. They all have industrial successes to their credit. Westinghouse Electric's Water Reactor Division, for example, points to a fuel-enrichment application in which the company was able to boost revenue by 'more than ten million dollars per annum' through the use of one of them.[1]

## 3. The induction task

We now give a more precise statement of the induction task. The basis is a universe of *objects* that are described in terms of a collection of *attributes*. Each attribute measures some important feature of an object and will be limited here to taking a (usually small) set of discrete, mutually exclusive values. For example, if the objects were Saturday mornings and the classification task involved the weather, attributes might be

outlook, with values {sunny, overcast, rain}
temperature, with values {cool, mild, hot}
humidity, with values {high, normal}
windy, with values {true, false}

Taken together, the attributes provide a zeroth-order language for characterizing objects in the universe. A particular Saturday morning might be described as

outlook: overcast
temperature: cool
humidity: normal
windy: false

[1] Letter cited in the journal *Expert Systems* (January, 1985), p. 20.

Each object in the universe belongs to one of a set of mutually exclusive *classes*. To simplify the following treatment, we will assume that there are only two such classes denoted *P* and *N*, although the extension to any number of classes is not difficult. In two-class induction tasks, objects of class P and N are sometimes referred to as *positive instances* and *negative instances*, respectively, of the concept being learned.

The other major ingredient is a *training set* of objects whose class is known. The induction task is to develop a *classification rule* that can determine the class of any object from its values of the attributes. The immediate question is whether or not the attributes provide sufficient information to do this. In particular, if the training set contains two objects that have identical values for each attribute and yet belong to different classes, it is clearly impossible to differentiate between these objects with reference only to the given attributes. In such a case attributes will be termed *inadequate* for the training set and hence for the induction task.

As mentioned above, a classification rule will be expressed as a decision tree. Table 1 shows a small training set that uses the 'Saturday morning' attributes. Each object's value of each attribute is shown, together with the class of the object (here, class P mornings are suitable for some unspecified activity). A decision tree that correctly classifies each object in the training set is given in Figure 2. Leaves of a decision tree are class names, other nodes represent attribute-based tests with a branch for each possible outcome. In order to classify an object, we start at the root of the tree, evaluate the test, and take the branch appropriate to the outcome. The process continues until a leaf is encountered, at which time the object is asserted to belong to

Table 1. A small training set

| No. | Attributes | | | | Class |
|-----|---------|-------------|----------|-------|-------|
|     | Outlook | Temperature | Humidity | Windy |       |
| 1   | sunny    | hot   | high   | false | N |
| 2   | sunny    | hot   | high   | true  | N |
| 3   | overcast | hot   | high   | false | P |
| 4   | rain     | mild  | high   | false | P |
| 5   | rain     | cool  | normal | false | P |
| 6   | rain     | cool  | normal | true  | N |
| 7   | overcast | cool  | normal | true  | P |
| 8   | sunny    | mild  | high   | false | N |
| 9   | sunny    | cool  | normal | false | P |
| 10  | rain     | mild  | normal | false | P |
| 11  | sunny    | mild  | normal | true  | P |
| 12  | overcast | mild  | high   | true  | P |
| 13  | overcast | hot   | normal | false | P |
| 14  | rain     | mild  | high   | true  | N |

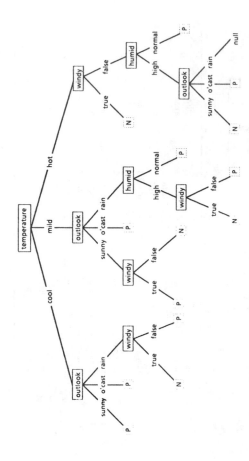

*Figure 3.* A complex decision tree.

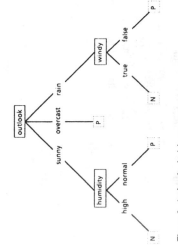

*Figure 2.* A simple decision tree

the class named by the leaf. Taking the decision tree of Figure 2, this process concludes that the object which appeared as an example at the start of this section, and which is not a member of the training set, should belong to class P. Notice that only a subset of the attributes may be encountered on a particular path from the root of the decision tree to a leaf; in this case, only the outlook attribute is tested before determining the class.

If the attributes are adequate, it is always possible to construct a decision tree that correctly classifies each object in the training set, and usually there are many such correct decision trees. The essence of induction is to move beyond the training set, i.e. to construct a decision tree that correctly classifies not only objects from the training set but other (unseen) objects as well. In order to do this, the decision tree must capture some meaningful relationship between an object's class and its values of the attributes. Given a choice between two decision trees, each of which is correct over the training set, it seems sensible to prefer the simpler one on the grounds that it is more likely to capture structure inherent in the problem. The simpler tree would therefore be expected to classify correctly more objects outside the training set. The decision tree of Figure 3, for instance, is also correct for the training set of Table 1, but its greater complexity makes it suspect as an 'explanation' of the training set.[2]

## 4. ID3

One approach to the induction task above would be to generate all possible decision trees that correctly classify the training set and to select the simplest of them. The

[2] The preference for simpler trees, presented here as a commonsense application of Occam's Razor, is also supported by analysis. Pearl (1978b) and Quinlan (1983a) have derived upper bounds on the expected error using different formalisms for generalizing from a set of known cases. For a training set of predetermined size, these bounds increase with the complexity of the induced generalization.

number of such trees is finite but very large, so this approach would only be feasible for small induction tasks. ID3 was designed for the other end of the spectrum, where there are many attributes and the training set contains many objects, but where a reasonably good decision tree is required without much computation. It has generally been found to construct simple decision trees, but the approach it uses cannot guarantee that better trees have not been overlooked.

The basic structure of ID3 is iterative. A subset of the training set called the *window* is chosen at random and a decision tree formed from it; this tree correctly classifies all objects in the window. All other objects in the training set are then classified using the tree. If the tree gives the correct answer for all these objects then it is correct for the entire training set and the process terminates. If not, a selection of the incorrectly classified objects is added to the window and the process continues. In this way, correct decision trees have been found after only a few iterations for training sets of up to thirty thousand objects described in terms of up to 50 attributes. Empirical evidence suggests that a correct decision tree is usually found more quickly by this iterative method than by forming a tree directly from the entire training set. However, O'Keefe (1983) has noted that the iterative framework cannot be guaranteed to converge on a final tree unless the window can grow to include the entire training set. This potential limitation has not yet arisen in practice.

The crux of the problem is how to form a decision tree for an arbitrary collection C of objects. If C is empty or contains only objects of one class, the simplest decision tree is just a leaf labelled with the class. Otherwise, let T be any test on an object with possible outcomes $O_1, O_2, \ldots O_w$. Each object in C will give one of these outcomes for T, so T produces a partition $\{C_1, C_2, \ldots C_w\}$ of C with $C_i$ containing those ob-

information required for the subtree for $C_i$ is $I(p_i, n_i)$. The expected information required for the tree with A as root is then obtained as the weighted average

$$E(A) = \sum_{i=1}^{v} \frac{p_i+n_i}{p+n} I(p_i, n_i)$$

where the weight for the ith branch is the proportion of the objects in C that belong to $C_i$. The information gained by branching on A is therefore

$$gain(A) = I(p, n) - E(A)$$

A good rule of thumb would seem to be to choose that attribute to branch on which gains the most information.[3] ID3 examines all candidate attributes and chooses A to maximize gain(A), forms the tree as above, and then uses the same process recursively to form decision trees for the residual subsets $C_1, C_2, \ldots C_v$.

To illustrate the idea, let C be the set of objects in Table 1. Of the 14 objects, 9 are of class P and 5 are of class N, so the information required for classification is

$$I(p, n) = -\frac{9}{14} \log_2 \frac{9}{14} - \frac{5}{14} \log_2 \frac{5}{14} = 0.940 \text{ bits}$$

Now consider the outlook attribute with values {sunny, overcast, rain}. Five of the 14 objects in C have the first value (sunny), two of them from class P and three from class N, so

$$p_1 = 2 \quad n_1 = 3 \quad I(p_1, n_1) = 0.971$$

and similarly

$$p_2 = 4 \quad n_2 = 0 \quad I(p_2, n_2) = 0$$
$$p_3 = 3 \quad n_3 = 2 \quad I(p_3, n_3) = 0.971$$

The expected information requirement after testing this attribute is therefore

$$E(outlook) = \frac{5}{14} I(p_1, n_1) + \frac{4}{14} I(p_2, n_2) + \frac{5}{14} I(p_3, n_3)$$
$$= 0.694 \text{ bits}$$

[3] Since I(p,n) is constant for all attributes, maximizing the gain is equivalent to minimizing E(A), which is the mutual information of the attribute A and the class. Pearl (1978a) contains an excellent account of the rationale of information-based heuristics.

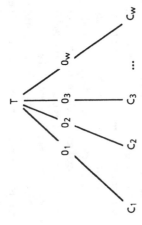

Figure 4. A tree structuring of the objects in C.

jects having outcome $O_i$. This is represented graphically by the tree form of Figure 4. If each subset $C_i$ in this figure could be replaced by a decision tree for $C_i$, the result would be a decision tree for all of C. Moreover, so long as two or more $C_i$'s are non-empty, each $C_i$ is smaller than C. In the worst case, this divide-and-conquer strategy will yield single-object subsets that satisfy the one-class requirement for a leaf. Thus, provided that a test can always be found that gives a non-trivial partition of any set of objects, this procedure will always produce a decision tree that correctly classifies each object in C.

The choice of test is crucial if the decision tree is to be simple. For the moment, a test will be restricted to branching on the values of an attribute, so choosing a test comes down to selecting an attribute for the root of the tree. The first induction programs in the ID series used a seat-of-the-pants evaluation function that worked reasonably well. Following a suggestion of Peter Gacs, ID3 adopted an information-based method that depends on two assumptions. Let C contain p objects of class P and n of class N. The assumptions are:

(1) Any correct decision tree for C will classify objects in the same proportion as their representation in C. An arbitrary object will be determined to belong to class P with probability p/(p+n) and to class N with probability n/(p+n).

(2) When a decision tree is used to classify an object, it returns a class. A decision tree can thus be regarded as a source of a message 'P' or 'N', with the expected information needed to generate this message given by

$$I(p, n) = -\frac{p}{p+n} \log_2 \frac{p}{p+n} - \frac{n}{p+n} \log_2 \frac{n}{p+n}$$

If attribute A with values $\{A_1, A_2, \ldots A_v\}$ is used for the root of the decision tree, it will partition C into $\{C_1, C_2, \ldots C_v\}$ where $C_i$ contains those objects in C that have value $A_i$ of A. Let $C_i$ contain $p_i$ objects of class P and $n_i$ of class N. The expected

The gain of this attribute is then

gain(outlook) = 0.940 − E(outlook) = 0.246 bits

Similar analysis gives

gain(temperature) = 0.029 bits
gain(humidity) = 0.151 bits
gain(windy) = 0.048 bits

so the tree-forming method used in ID3 would choose outlook as the attribute for the root of the decision tree. The objects would then be divided into subsets according to their values of the outlook attribute and a decision tree for each subset would be induced in a similar fashion. In fact, Figure 2 shows the actual decision tree generated by ID3 from this training set.

A special case arises if C contains no objects with some particular value $A_j$ of A, giving an empty $C_j$; ID3 labels such a leaf as 'null' so that it fails to classify any object arriving at that leaf. A better solution would generalize from the set C from which $C_j$ came, and assign this leaf the more frequent class in C.

The worth of ID3's attribute-selecting heuristic can be assessed by the simplicity of the resulting decision trees, or, more to the point, by how well those trees express real relationships between class and attributes as demonstrated by the accuracy with which they classify objects other than those in the training set (their *predictive accuracy*). A straightforward method of assessing this predictive accuracy is to use only part of the given set of objects as a training set, and to check the resulting decision tree on the remainder.

Several experiments of this kind have been carried out. In one domain, 1.4 million chess positions described in terms of 49 binary-valued attributes gave rise to 715 distinct objects divided 65%:35% between the classes. This domain is relatively complex since a correct decision tree for all 715 objects contains about 150 nodes. When training sets containing 20% of these 715 objects were chosen at random, they produced decision trees that correctly classified over 84% of the unseen objects. In another version of the same domain, 39 attributes gave 551 distinct objects with a correct decision tree of similar size; training sets of 20% of these 551 objects gave decision trees of almost identical accuracy. In a simpler domain (1,987 objects with a correct decision tree of 48 nodes), randomly-selected training sets containing 20% of the objects gave decision trees that correctly classified 98% of the unseen objects. In all three cases, it is clear that the decision trees reflect useful (as opposed to random) relationships present in the data.

This discussion of ID3 is rounded off by looking at the computational requirements of the procedure. At each non-leaf node of the decision tree, the gain of each untested attribute A must be determined. This gain in turn depends on the values $p_i$

and $n_i$ for each value $A_i$ of A, so every object in C must be examined to determine its class and its value of A. Consequently, the computational complexity of the procedure at each such node is $O(|C| \cdot |A|)$, where $|A|$ is the number of attributes above. ID3's total computational requirement per iteration is thus proportional to the product of the size of the training set, the number of attributes and the number of non-leaf nodes in the decision tree. The same relationship appears to extend to the entire induction process, even when several iterations are performed. No exponential growth in time or space has been observed as the dimensions of the induction task increase, so the technique can be applied to large tasks.

## 5. Noise

So far, the information supplied in the training set has been assumed to be entirely accurate. Sadly, induction tasks based on real-world data are unlikely to find this assumption to be tenable. The description of objects may include attributes based on measurements or subjective judgements, both of which may give rise to errors in the values of attributes. Some of the objects in the training set may even have been misclassified. To illustrate the idea, consider the task of developing a classification rule for medical diagnosis from a collection of patient histories. An attribute might test for the presence of some substance in the blood and will almost inevitably give false positive or negative readings some of the time. Another attribute might assess the patient's build as slight, medium, or heavy, and different assessors may apply different criteria. Finally, the collection of case histories will probably include some patients for whom an incorrect diagnosis was made, with consequent errors in the class information provided in the training set.

What problems might errors of these kinds pose for the tree-building procedure described earlier? Consider again the small training set in Table 1, and suppose now that attribute outlook of object 1 is incorrectly recorded as overcast. Objects 1 and 3 will then have identical descriptions but belong to different classes, so the attributes become inadequate for this training set. The attributes will also become inadequate if attribute windy of object 4 is corrupted to true, because that object will then conflict with object 14. Finally, the initial training set can be accounted for by the simple decision tree of Figure 2 containing 8 nodes. Suppose that the class of object 3 were corrupted to N. A correct decision tree for this corrupted training set would now have to explain the apparent special case of object 3. The smallest such tree contains twelve nodes, half again as complex as the 'real' tree. These illustrations highlight two problems: errors in the training set may cause the attributes to become inadequate, or may lead to decision trees of spurious complexity.

Non-systematic errors of this kind in either the values of attributes or class information are usually referred to as *noise*. Two modifications are required if the tree-building algorithm is to be able to operate with a noise-affected training set.

(1) The algorithm must be able to work with inadequate attributes, because noise can cause even the most comprehensive set of attributes to appear inadequate.

(2) The algorithm must be able to decide that testing further attributes will not improve the predictive accuracy of the decision tree. In the last example above, it should refrain from increasing the complexity of the decision tree to accommodate a single noise-generated special case.

We start with the second requirement of deciding when an attribute is really relevant to classification. Let C be a collection of objects containing representatives of both classes, and let A be an attribute with random values that produces subsets $\{C_1, C_2, \ldots C_V\}$. Unless the proportion of class P objects in each of the $C_i$ is exactly the same as the proportion of class P objects in C itself, branching on attribute A will give an apparent information gain. It will therefore appear that testing attribute A is a sensible step, even though the values of A are random and so cannot help to classify the objects in C.

One solution to this dilemma might be to require that the information gain of any tested attribute exceeds some absolute or percentage threshold. Experiments with this approach suggest that a threshold large enough to screen out irrelevant attributes also excludes attributes that are relevant, and the performance of the tree-building procedure is degraded in the noise-free case.

An alternative method based on the chi-square test for stochastic independence has been found to be more useful. In the previous notation, suppose attribute A produces subsets $\{C_1, C_2, \ldots C_V\}$ of C, where $C_i$ contains $p_i$ and $n_i$ objects of class P and N, respectively. If the value of A is irrelevant to the class of an object in C, the expected value $p'_i$ of $p_i$ should be

$$p'_i = p \cdot \frac{p_i + n_i}{p + n}$$

If $n'_i$ is the corresponding expected value of $n_i$, the statistic

$$\sum_{i=1}^{v} \frac{(p_i - p'_i)^2}{p'_i} + \frac{(n_i - n'_i)^2}{n'_i}$$

is approximately chi-square with $v$-1 degrees of freedom. Provided that none of the values $p'_i$ or $n'_i$ are very small, this statistic can be used to determine the confidence with which one can reject the hypothesis that A is independent of the class of objects in C (Hogg and Craig, 1970). The tree-building procedure can then be modified to prevent testing any attribute whose irrelevance cannot be rejected with a very high (e.g. 99%) confidence level. This has been found effective in preventing over-

complex trees that attempt to 'fit the noise' without affecting performance of the procedure in the noise-free case.[4]

Turning now to the first requirement, we see that the following situation can arise: a collection of C objects may contain representatives of both classes, yet further testing of C may be ruled out, either because the attributes are inadequate and unable to distinguish among the objects in C, or because each attribute has been judged to be irrelevant to the class of objects in C. In this situation it is necessary to produce a leaf labelled with class information, but the objects in C are not all of the same class.

Two possibilities suggest themselves. The notion of class could be generalized to allow the value $p/(p+n)$ in the interval (0,1), a class of 0.8 (say) being interpreted as 'belonging to class P with probability 0.8'. An alternative approach would be to opt for the more numerous class, i.e. to assign the leaf to class P if $p > n$, to class N if $p < n$, and to either if $p = n$. The first approach minimizes the sum of the squares of the error over objects in C, while the second minimizes the sum of the absolute errors over objects in C. If the aim is to minimize expected error, the second approach might be anticipated to be superior, and indeed this has been found to be the case.

Several studies have been carried out to see how this modified procedure holds up under varying levels of noise (Quinlan 1983b, 1985a). One such study is outlined here, based on the earlier-mentioned task with 551 objects and 39 binary-valued attributes. In each experiment, the whole set of objects was artificially corrupted as described below and used as a training set to produce a decision tree. Each object was then corrupted anew, classified by this tree and the error rate determined. This process was repeated twenty times to give more reliable averages.

In this study, values were corrupted as follows. A noise level of $n$ percent applied to a value meant that, with probability $n$ percent, the true value was replaced by a value chosen at random from among the values that could have appeared.[5] Table 2 shows the results when noise levels varying from 5% to 100% were applied to the values of the most noise-sensitive attribute, to the values of all attributes simultaneously, and to the class information. This table demonstrates the quite different forms of degradation observed. Destroying class information produces a linear increase in error so that, when all class information is noise, the resulting decision tree classifies objects entirely randomly. Noise in a single attribute does not have a dramatic effect. Noise in all attributes together, however, leads to a relatively rapid increase in error which reaches a peak and declines. The peak is somewhat inter-

esting in that noise can enable an information-based measure to perform much the same function, but no comparative results are available to date.

---

[4] ASSISTANT uses an information-based measure to perform much the same function, but no comparative results are available to date.

[5] It might seem that the value should be replaced by an incorrect value. Consider, however, the case of a two-valued attribute corrupted with 100% noise. If the value of each object were replaced by the (only) incorrect value, the initial attribute will have been merely inverted with no loss of information.

noise level in class information results in a 3% degradation. Comparable figures have been obtained for other induction tasks.

One interesting point emerged from other experiments in which a correct decision tree formed from an uncorrupted training set was used to classify objects whose descriptions were corrupted. This scenario corresponds to forming a classification rule under controlled and sanitized laboratory conditions, then using it to classify objects in the field. For higher noise levels, the performance of the correct decision tree on corrupted data was found to be inferior to that of an imperfect decision tree formed from data corrupted to a similar level! (This phenomenon has an explanation similar to that given above for the peak in Table 2.) The moral seems to be that it is counter-productive to eliminate noise from the attribute information in the training set if these same attributes will be subject to high noise levels when the induced decision tree is put to use.

## 6. Unknown attribute values

The previous section examined modifications to the tree-building process that enabled it to deal with noisy or corrupted values. This section is concerned with an allied problem that also arises in practice: unknown attribute values. To continue the previous medical diagnosis example, what should be done when the patient case histories that are to form the training set are incomplete?

One way around the problem attempts to fill in an unknown value by utilizing information provided by context. Using the previous notation, let us suppose that a collection C of objects contains one whose value of attribute A is unknown. ASSISTANT (Kononenko et al, 1984) uses a Bayesian formalism to determine the probability that the object has value $A_i$ of A by examining the distribution of values of A in C as a function of their class. Suppose that the object in question belongs to class P. The probability that the object has value $A_i$ for attribute A can be expressed as

$$\text{prob}(A = A_i \mid \text{class} = P) = \frac{\text{prob}(A = A_i \ \& \ \text{class} = P)}{\text{prob}(\text{class} = P)} = \frac{p_i}{p}$$

where the calculation of $p_i$ and p is restricted to those members of C whose value of A is known. Having determined the probability distribution of the unknown value over the possible values of A, this method could either choose the most likely value or divide the object into fractional objects, each with one possible value of A, weighted according to the probabilities above.

Alen Shapiro (private communication) has suggested using a decision-tree approach to determine the unknown values of an attribute. Let C' be the subset of C consisting of those objects whose value of attribute A is defined. In C', the original

Table 2. Error rates produced by noise in a single attribute, all attributes, and class information

| Noise level | Single attribute | All attributes | Class information |
|---|---|---|---|
| 5% | 1.3% | 11.9% | 2.6% |
| 10% | 2.5% | 18.9% | 5.5% |
| 15% | 3.3% | 24.6% | 8.3% |
| 20% | 4.6% | 27.8% | 9.9% |
| 30% | 6.1% | 29.5% | 14.8% |
| 40% | 7.6% | 30.3% | 18.1% |
| 50% | 8.8% | 29.2% | 21.8% |
| 60% | 9.4% | 27.5% | 26.4% |
| 70% | 9.9% | 25.9% | 27.2% |
| 80% | 10.4% | 26.0% | 29.5% |
| 90% | 10.8% | 25.6% | 34.1% |
| 100% | 10.8% | 25.9% | 49.6% |

esting, and can be explained as follows. Let C be a collection of objects containing p from class P and n from class N, respectively. At noise levels around 50%, the algorithm will still find relevant attributes to branch on, even though the performance of this tree on unseen but equally noisy objects will be essentially random. Suppose the tree for C classifies objects as class P with probability p/(n + p). The expected error if objects with a similar class distribution to those in C were classified by this tree is given by

$$\frac{p}{p+n} \cdot (1 - \frac{p}{p+n}) + \frac{n}{p+n} \cdot (1 - \frac{n}{p+n}) = \frac{2pn}{(p+n)^2}$$

At very high levels of noise, however, the algorithm will find all attributes irrelevant and classify everything as the more frequent class; assume without loss of generality that this class is P. The expected error in this case is

$$\frac{p}{p+n} \cdot 0 + \frac{n}{p+n} \cdot 1 = \frac{n}{p+n}$$

which is less than the above expression since we have assumed that p is greater than n. The decline in error is thus a consequence of the chi-square cutoff coming into play as noise becomes more intense.

The table brings out the point that low levels of noise do not cause the tree-building machinery to fall over a cliff. For this task, a 5% noise level in a single attribute produces a degradation in performance of less than 2%; a 5% noise level in all attributes together produces a 12% degradation in classification performance; while a similar

class (P or N) is regarded as another attribute while the value of attribute A becomes the 'class' to be determined. That is, C' is used to construct a decision tree for determining the value of attribute A from the other attributes and the class. When constructed, this decision tree can be used to 'classify' each object in C − C' and the result assigned as the unknown value of A.

Although these methods for determining unknown attribute values look good on paper, they give unconvincing results even when only a single value of one attribute is unknown; as might be expected, their performance is much worse when several values of several attributes are unknown. Consider again the 551-object 39-attribute task. We may ask how well the methods perform when asked to fill in a single unknown attribute value. Table 3 shows, for each of the three most important attributes, the proportion of times each method fails to replace an unknown value by its correct value. For comparison, the table also shows the same figure for the simple strategy: always replace an unknown value of an attribute with its most common value. The Bayesian method gives results that are scarcely better than those given by the simple strategy and, while the decision-tree method uses more context and is thereby more accurate, it still gives disappointing results.

Rather than trying to guess unknown attribute values, we could treat 'unknown' as a new possible value for each attribute and deal with it in the same way as other values. This can lead to an anomalous situation, as shown by the following example. Suppose A is an attribute with values $\{A_1, A_2\}$ and let C be a collection of objects such that

$$p_1 = 2 \quad p_2 = 2$$
$$n_1 = 2 \quad n_2 = 2$$

giving a value of 1 bit for E(A). Now let A' be an identical attribute except that one of the objects with value $A_1$ of A has an unknown value of A'. A' has the values $\{A'_1, A'_2, A'_3 = $ unknown$\}$, so the corresponding values might be

$$p'_1 = 1 \quad p'_2 = 2 \quad p'_3 = 1$$
$$n'_1 = 2 \quad n'_2 = 2 \quad n'_3 = 0$$

*Table 3.* Proportion of times that an unknown attribute value is replaced by an incorrect value

| Replacement method | Attribute | | |
|---|---|---|---|
| | 1 | 2 | 3 |
| Bayesian | 28% | 27% | 38% |
| Decision tree | 19% | 22% | 19% |
| Most common value | 28% | 27% | 40% |

resulting in a value of 0.84 bits for E(A'). In terms of the selection criterion developed earlier, A' now seems to give a higher information gain than A. Thus, having unknown values may apparently increase the desirability of an attribute, a result entirely opposed to common sense. The conclusion is that treating 'unknown' as a separate value is not a solution to the problem.

One strategy which has been found to work well is as follows. Let A be an attribute with values $\{A_1, A_2, \ldots A_V\}$. For some collection C of objects, let the numbers of objects with value $A_i$ of A be $p_i$ and $n_i$, and let $p_u$ and $n_u$ denote the numbers of objects of class P and N respectively that have unknown values of A. When the information gain of attribute A is assessed, these objects with unknown values are distributed across the values of A in proportion to the relative frequency of these values in C. Thus the gain is assessed as if the true value of $p_i$ were given by

$$p_i + p_u \cdot ratio_i$$

where

$$ratio_i = \frac{p_i + n_i}{\sum_i (p_i + n_i)}$$

and similarly for $n_i$. (This expression has the property that unknown values can only decrease the information gain of an attribute.) When an attribute has been chosen by the selection criterion, objects with unknown values of that attribute are discarded before forming decision trees for the subsets $\{C_j\}$.

The other half of the story is how unknown attribute values are dealt with during classification. Suppose that an object is being classified using a decision tree that wishes to branch on attribute A, but the object's value of attribute A is unknown. The correct procedure would take the branch corresponding to the real value $A_i$; but, since this value is unknown, the only alternative is to explore all branches without forgetting that some are more probable than others.

Conceptually, suppose that, along with the object to be classified, we have been passed a *token* with some value T. In the situation above, each branch of $A_i$ is then explored in turn, using a token of value

$$T \cdot ratio_i$$

i.e. the given token value is distributed across all possible values in proportion to the ratios above. The value passed to a branch may be distributed further by subsequent tests on other attributes for which this object has unknown values. Instead of a single path to a leaf, there may now be many, each qualified by its token value. These token values at the leaves are summed for each class, the result of the classification being

## 7. The selection criterion

Attention has recently been refocussed on the evaluation function for selecting the best attribute-based test to form the root of a decision tree. Recall that the criterion described earlier chooses the attribute that gains most information. In the course of their experiments, Bratko's group encountered a medical induction problem in which the attribute selected by the gain criterion ('age of patient', with nine value ranges) was judged by specialists to be less relevant than other attributes. This situation was also noted on other tasks, prompting Kononenko *et al* (1984) to suggest that the gain criterion tends to favor attributes with many values.

Analysis supports this finding. Let A be an attribute with values $A_1, A_2, \ldots A_v$ and let A' be an attribute formed from A by splitting one of the values into two. If the values of A were sufficiently fine for the induction task at hand, we would not expect this refinement to increase the usefulness of A. Rather, it might be anticipated that excessive fineness would tend to obscure structure in the training set so that A' was in fact less useful than A. However, it can be proved that gain(A') is greater than or equal to gain(A), being equal to it only when the proportions of the classes are the same for both subdivisions of the original value. In general, then, gain(A') will exceed gain(A) with the result that the evaluation function of Section 4 will prefer A' to A. By analogy, attributes with more values will tend to be preferred to attributes with fewer.

As another way of looking at the problem, let A be an attribute with random values and suppose that the set of possible values of A is large enough to make it unlikely that two objects in the training set have the same value for A. Such an attribute would have maximum information gain, so the gain criterion would select it as the root of the decision tree. This would be a singularly poor choice since the value of A, being random, contains no information pertinent to the class of objects in the training set. ASSISTANT (Kononenko *et al*, 1984) solves this problem by requiring that all tests have only two outcomes. If we have an attribute A as before with v values $A_1, A_2, \ldots A_v$, the decision tree no longer has a branch for each possible value. Instead, a subset S of the values is chosen and the tree has two branches, one for all values in the set and one for the remainder. The information gain is then computed as if all values in S were amalgamated into one single attribute value and all remaining values into another. Using this selection criterion (the *subset* criterion), the test chosen for the root of the decision tree uses the attribute and subset of its values that maximizes the information gain. Kononenko *et al* report that this modification led to smaller decision trees with an improved classification performance. However, the trees were judged to be less intelligible to human beings, in agreement with a similar finding of Shepherd (1983).

Limiting decision trees to a binary format harks back to CLS, in which each test was of the form 'attribute A has value $A_i$', with two branches corresponding to true and false. This is clearly a special case of the test implemented in ASSISTANT, which

---

that class with the higher value. The distribution of values over the possible classes might also be used to compute a confidence level for the classification.

Straightforward though it may be, this procedure has been found to give a very graceful degradation as the incidence of unknown values increases. Figure 5 summarizes the results of an experiment on the now-familiar task with 551 objects and 39 attributes. Various 'ignorance levels' analogous to the earlier noise levels were explored, with twenty repetitions at each level. For each run at an ignorance level of m percent, a copy of the 551 objects was made, replacing each value of every attribute by 'unknown' with m percent probability. A decision tree for these (incomplete) objects was formed as above, and then used to classify a new copy of each object corrupted in the same way. The figure shows that the degradation of performance with ignorance level is gradual. In practice, of course, an ignorance level even as high as 10% is unlikely — this would correspond to an average of one value in every ten of the object's description being unknown. Even so, the decision tree produced from such a patchy training set correctly classifies nearly ninety percent of objects that also have unknown values. A much lower level of degradation is observed when an object with unknown values is classified using a correct decision tree.

This treatment has assumed that no information whatsoever is available regarding an unknown attribute. Catlett (1985) has taken this approach a stage further by allowing partial knowledge of an attribute value to be stated in Shafer notation (Garvey, Lowrance and Fischler, 1981). This notation permits probabilistic assertions to be made about any subset or subsets of the possible values of an attribute that an object might have.

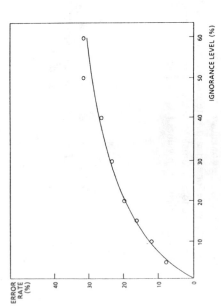

*Figure 5.* Error produced by unknown attribute values.

permits a set of values, rather than a single value, to be distinguished from the others.

It is also worth noting that the method of dealing with attributes having continuous values follows the same binary approach. Let A be such an attribute and suppose that the distinct values of A that occur in C are sorted to give the sequence $V_1, V_2, \ldots, V_k$. Each pair of values $V_i, V_{i+1}$ suggests a possible threshold

$$\frac{V_i + V_{i+1}}{2}$$

that divides the objects of C into two subsets, those with a value of A above and below the threshold respectively. The information gain of this division can then be investigated as above.

If all tests must be binary, there can be no bias in favor of attributes with large numbers of values. It could be argued, however, that ASSISTANT's remedy has undesirable side-effects that have to be taken into account. First, it can lead to decision trees that are even more unintelligible to human experts than is ordinarily the case, with unrelated attribute values being grouped together and with multiple tests on the same attribute.

More importantly, the subset criterion can require a large increase in computation. An attribute A with v values has $2^v$ value subsets and, when trivial and symmetric subsets are removed, there are still $2^{v-1} - 1$ different ways of specifying the distinguished subset of attribute values. The information gain realized with each of these must be investigated, so a single attribute with v values has a computational requirement similar to $2^{v-1} - 1$ binary attributes. This is not of particular consequence if v is small, but the approach would appear infeasible for an attribute with 20 values.

Another method of overcoming the bias is as follows. Consider again our training set containing p and n objects of class P and N respectively. As before, let attribute A have values $A_1, A_2, \ldots A_v$ and let the numbers of objects with value $A_i$ of attribute A be $p_i$ and $n_i$ respectively. Enquiring about the value of attribute A itself gives rise to information, which can be expressed as

$$IV(A) = -\sum_{i=1}^{v} \frac{p_i + n_i}{p + n} \log_2 \frac{p_i + n_i}{p + n}$$

IV(A) thus measures the information content of the answer to the question, 'What is the value of attribute A?' As discussed earlier, gain(A) measures the reduction in the information requirement for a classification rule if the decision tree uses attribute A as a root. Ideally, as much as possible of the information provided by determining the value of an attribute should be useful for classification purposes or, equivalently, as little as possible should be 'wasted'. A good choice of attribute would then be one for which the ratio

$$gain(A) / IV(A)$$

is as large as possible. This ratio, however, may not always be defined − IV(A) may be zero − or it may tend to favor attributes for which IV(A) is very small. The *gain ratio* criterion selects, from among those attributes with an average-or-better gain, the attribute that maximizes the above ratio.

This can be illustrated by returning to the example based on the training set of Table 1. The information gain of the four attributes is given in Section 4 as

gain(outlook) = 0.246 bits
gain(temperature) = 0.029 bits
gain(humidity) = 0.151 bits
gain(windy) = 0.048 bits

Of these, only outlook and humidity have above-average gain. For the outlook attribute, five objects in the training set have the value sunny, four have overcast and five have rain. The information obtained by determining the value of the outlook attribute is therefore

$$IV(outlook) = -\frac{5}{14} \log_2 \frac{5}{14} - \frac{4}{14} \log_2 \frac{4}{14} - \frac{5}{14} \log_2 \frac{5}{14}$$
$$= 1.578 \text{ bits}$$

Similarly,

$$IV(humidity) = -\frac{7}{14} \log_2 \frac{7}{14} - \frac{7}{14} \log_2 \frac{7}{14} = 1 \text{ bit}$$

So,

gain ratio(outlook) = 0.246 / 1.578 = 0.156
gain ratio(humidity) = 0.151 / 1.000 = 0.151

The gain ratio criterion would therefore still select the outlook attribute for the root of the decision tree, although its superiority over the humidity attribute is now much reduced.

The various selection criteria have been compared empirically in a series of experiments (Quinlan, 1985b). When all attributes are binary, the gain ratio criterion has been found to give considerably smaller decision trees: for the 551-object task, it produces a tree of 143 nodes compared to the smallest previously-known tree of 175 nodes. When the task includes attributes with large numbers of values, the subset criterion gives smaller decision trees that also have better predictive performance, but can require much more computation. However, when these many-valued attributes are augmented by redundant attributes which contain the same information at a lower level of detail, the gain ratio criterion gives decision trees with the greatest predictive accuracy. All in all, these experiments suggest that the gain ratio criterion does pick a good attribute for the root of the tree. Testing an attribute with many values, however, will fragment the training set C into very small subsets $\{C_i\}$ and the decision trees for these subsets may then have poor predictive accuracy. In such cases, some mechanism such as value subsets or redundant attributes is needed to prevent excessive fragmentation.

The three criteria discussed here are all information-based, but there is no reason to suspect that this is the only possible basis for such criteria. Recall that the gain ratio criterion suggests that the gain ratio criterion pick a good attribute for the root of the tree unless it could be shown to be relevant to the class of objects in the training set. For any attribute A, the value of the statistic presented in Section 5, together with the number $v$ of possible values of A, determines the confidence with which we can reject the null hypothesis that an object's value of A is irrelevant to its class. Hart (1985) has proposed that this same test could function directly as a selection criterion: simply pick the attribute for which this confidence level is highest. This measure takes explicit account of the number of values of an attribute and so may not exhibit bias. Hart notes, however, that the chi-square test is valid only when the expected values of $p'_i$ and $n'_i$ are uniformly larger than four. This condition could be violated by a set C of objects either when C is small or when few objects in C have a particular value of some attribute, and it is not clear how such sets would be handled. No empirical results with this approach are yet available.

## 8. Conclusion

The aim of this paper has been to demonstrate that the technology for building decision trees from examples is fairly robust. Current commercial systems are powerful tools that have achieved noteworthy successes. The groundwork has been done for advances that will permit such tools to deal even with noisy, incomplete data typical of advanced real-world applications. Work is continuing at several centers to improve the performance of the underlying algorithms.

Two examples of contemporary research give some pointers to the directions in which the field is moving. While decision trees generated by the above systems are fast to execute and can be very accurate, they leave much to be desired as representations of knowledge. Experts who are shown such trees for classification tasks in their own domain often can identify little familiar material. It is this lack of familiarity (and perhaps an underlying lack of modularity) that is the chief obstacle to the use of induction for building large expert systems. Recent work by Shapiro (1983) offers a possible solution to this problem. In his approach, called *Structured Induction*, a rule-formation task is tackled in the same style as structured programming. The task is solved in terms of a collection of notional super-attributes, after which the subtasks

of inducing classification rules to find the values of the super-attributes are approached in the same top-down fashion. In one classification problem studied, this method reduced a totally opaque, large decision tree to a hierarchy of nine small decision trees, each of which 'made sense' to an expert.

ID3 allows only two classes for any induction task, although this restriction has been removed in most later systems. Consider, however, the task of developing a rule from a given set of examples for classifying an animal as a monkey, giraffe, elephant, horse, etc. A single decision tree could be produced in which these various classes appeared as leaves. An alternative approach taken by systems such as INDUCE (Michalski, 1980) would produce a collection of classification rules, one to discriminate monkeys from non-monkeys, another to discriminate giraffes from non-giraffes, and so on. Which approach is better? In a private communication, Marcel Shoppers has set out an argument showing that the latter can be expected to give more accurate classification of objects that were not in the training set. The multi-tree approach has some associated problems – the separate decision trees may classify an animal as both a monkey and a giraffe, or fail to classify it as anything, for example – but if these can be sorted out, this approach may lead to techniques for building more reliable decision trees.

## Acknowledgements

It is a pleasure to acknowledge the stimulus and suggestions provided over many years by Donald Michie, who continues to play a central role in the development of this methodology. Ivan Bratko, Igor Kononenko, Igor Mosetic and other members of Bratko's group have also been responsible for many insights and constructive criticisms. I have benefited from numerous discussions with Ryszard Michalski, Alen Shapiro, Jason Catlett and other colleagues. I am particularly grateful to Pat Langley for his careful reading of the paper in draft form and for the many improvements he recommended.

## References

Buchanan, B.G., & Mitchell, T.M. (1978). Model-directed learning of production rules. In D.A. Waterman, F. Hayes-Roth (Eds.), *Pattern directed inference systems*. Academic Press.

Carbonell, J.G., Michalski, R.S., & Mitchell, T.M. (1983). An overview of machine learning, In R.S. Michalski, J.G. Carbonell and T.M. Mitchell, (Eds.), *Machine learning: An artificial intelligence approach*. Palo Alto: Tioga Publishing Company.

Catlett, J. (1985). *Induction using the shafer representation* (Technical report). Basser Department of Computer Science, University of Sydney, Australia.

Dechter, R., & Michie, D. (1985). *Structured induction of plans and programs* (Technical report). IBM Scientific Center, Los Angeles, CA.

Feigenbaum, E.A., & Simon, H.A. (1963). Performance of a reading task by an elementary perceiving and memorizing program. *Behavioral Science, 8.*

Feigenbaum, E.A. (1981). Expert systems in the 1980s. In A. Bond (Ed.), *State of the art report on machine intelligence.* Maidenhead: Pergamon-Infotech.

Garvey, T.D., Lowrance, J.D., & Fischler, M.A. (1981). An inference technique for integrating knowledge from disparate sources. *Proceedings of the Seventh International Joint Conference on Artificial Intelligence.* Vancouver, B.C., Canada: Morgan Kaufmann.

Hart, A.E. (1985). Experience in the use of an inductive system in knowledge engineering. In M.A. Bramer (Ed.), *Research and development in expert systems.* Cambridge University Press.

Hogg, R.V., & Craig, A.T. (1970). *Introduction to mathematical statistics.* London: Collier-Macmillan.

Hunt, E.B. (1962). *Concept learning: An information processing problem.* New York: Wiley.

Hunt, E.B., Marin, J., & Stone, P.J. (1966). *Experiments in induction.* New York: Academic Press.

Kononenko, I., Bratko, I., & Roskar, E. (1984). *Experiments in automatic learning of medical diagnostic rules* (Technical report). Jozef Stefan Institute, Ljubljana, Yugoslavia.

Langley, P., Bradshaw, G.L., & Simon, H.A. (1983). Rediscovering chemistry with the BACON system. In R.S. Michalski, J.G. Carbonell and T.M. Mitchell (Eds.), *Machine learning: An artificial intelligence approach.* Palo Alto: Tioga Publishing Company.

Michalski, R.S (1980). Pattern recognition as rule-guided inductive inference. *IEEE Transactions on Pattern Analysis and Machine Intelligence 2.*

Michalski, R.S., & Stepp, R.E. (1983). Learning from observation: conceptual clustering. In R.S. Michalski, J.G. Carbonell & T.M. Mitchell (Eds.), *Machine learning: An artificial intelligence approach.* Palo Alto: Tioga Publishing Company.

Michie, D. (1982). Experiments on the mechanisation of game-learning 2 – Rule-based learning and the human window. *Computer Journal 25.*

Michie, D. (1983). Inductive rule generation in the context of the Fifth Generation. *Proceedings of the Second International Machine Learning Workshop.* University of Illinois at Urbana-Champaign.

Michie, D. (1985). Current developments in Artificial Intelligence and Expert Systems. In *International Handbook of Information Technology and Automated Office Systems.* Elsevier.

Nilsson, N.J. (1965). *Learning machines,* New York: McGraw-Hill.

O'Keefe, R.A. (1983). Concept formation from very large training sets. In *Proceedings of the Eighth International Joint Conference on Artificial Intelligence.* Karlsruhe, West Germany: Morgan Kaufmann.

Patterson, A., & Niblett, T. (1983). *ACLS user manual.* Glasgow: Intelligent Terminals Ltd.

Pearl, J. (1978a). *Entropy, information and rational decisions* (Technical report). Cognitive Systems Laboratory, University of California, Los Angeles.

Pearl, J. (1978b). On the connection between the complexity and credibility of inferred models. *International Journal of General Systems, 4.*

Quinlan, J.R. (1969). A task-independent experience gathering scheme for a problem solver. *Proceedings of the First International Joint Conference on Artificial Intelligence.* Washington, D.C.: Morgan Kaufmann.

Quinlan, J.R. (1979). Discovering rules by induction from large collections of examples. In D. Michie (Ed.), *Expert systems in the micro electronic age.* Edinburgh University Press.

Quinlan, J.R. (1982). Semi-autonomous acquisition of pattern-based knowledge. In J.E. Hayes, D Michie & Y-H. Pao (Eds.), *Machine intelligence 10.* Chichester: Ellis Horwood.

Quinlan, J.R. (1983a). Learning efficient classification procedures and their application to chess endgames. In R.S. Michalski, J.G. Carbonell & T.M. Mitchell, (Eds.), *Machine learning: An artificial intelligence approach.* Palo Alto: Tioga Publishing Company.

Quinlan, J.R. (1983b). Learning from noisy data, *Proceedings of the Second International Machine Learning Workshop.* University of Illinois at Urbana-Champaign.

Quinlan, J.R. (1985a). The effect of noise on concept learning. In R.S. Michalski, J.G. Carbonell & T.M.

Mitchell (Eds.), *Machine learning.* Los Altos: Morgan Kaufmann (in press).

Quinlan, J.R. (1985b). Decision trees and multi-valued attributes. In J.E. Hayes & D. Michie (Eds.), *Machine intelligence 11.* Oxford University Press (in press).

Sammut, C.A. (1985). Concept development for expert system knowledge bases. *Australian Computer Journal 17.*

Samuel, A. (1967). Some studies in machine learning using the game of checkers II: Recent progress. *IBM J. Research and Development 11.*

Shapiro, A (1983). *The role of structured induction in expert systems.* Ph.D. Thesis, University of Edinburgh.

Shepherd, B.A. (1983). An appraisal of a decision-tree approach to image classification. *Proceedings of the Eighth International Joint Conference on Artificial Intelligence.* Karlsruhe, West Germany: Morgan Kaufmann.

Winston, P.H. (1975). Learning structural descriptions from examples. In P.H. Winston (Ed.), *The psychology of computer vision.* McGraw-Hill.

# Connectionist Learning Procedures

**Geoffrey E. Hinton**

*Computer Science Department, University of Toronto,
10 King's College Road, Toronto, Ontario, Canada M5S 1A4*

ABSTRACT

*A major goal of research on networks of neuron-like processing units is to discover efficient learning procedures that allow these networks to construct complex internal representations of their environment. The learning procedures must be capable of modifying the connection strengths in such a way that internal units which are not part of the input or output come to represent important features of the task domain. Several interesting gradient-descent procedures have recently been discovered. Each connection computes the derivative, with respect to the connection strength, of a global measure of the error in the performance of the network. The strength is then adjusted in the direction that decreases the error. These relatively simple, gradient-descent learning procedures work well for small tasks and the new challenge is to find ways of improving their convergence rate and their generalization abilities so that they can be applied to larger, more realistic tasks.*

## 1. Introduction

Recent technological advances in VLSI and computer aided design mean that it is now much easier to build massively parallel machines. This has contributed to a new wave of interest in models of computation that are inspired by neural nets rather than the formal manipulation of symbolic expressions. To understand human abilities like perceptual interpretation, content-addressable memory, commonsense reasoning, and learning it may be necessary to understand how computation is organized in systems like the brain which consist of massive numbers of richly interconnected but rather slow processing elements.

This paper focuses on the question of how internal representations can be learned in "connectionist" networks. These are a recent subclass of neural net models that emphasize computational power rather than biological fidelity. They grew out of work on early visual processing and associative memories [28, 40, 79]. The paper starts by reviewing the main research issues for connectionist models and then describes some of the earlier work on learning procedures for associative memories and simple pattern recognition devices. These learning procedures cannot generate internal representations: They are

*Artificial Intelligence* **40** (1989) 185–234
0004-3702/89/$3.50 © 1989, Elsevier Science Publishers B.V. (North-Holland)

This paper originally appeared in the journal, *Artificial Intelligence*, Vol. 40, Nos. 1-3, and is reprinted here with permission of the publisher, Elsevier, Amsterdam.

limited to forming simple associations between representations that are specified externally. Recent research has led to a variety of more powerful connectionist learning procedures that can discover good internal representations and most of the paper is devoted to a survey of these procedures.

## 2. Connectionist Models

Connectionist models typically consist of many simple, neuron-like processing elements called "units" that interact using weighted connections. Each unit has a "state" or "activity level" that is determined by the input received from other units in the network. There are many possible variations within this general framework. One common, simplifying assumption is that the combined effects of the rest of the network on the $j$th unit are mediated by a single scalar quantity, $x_j$. The quantity, which is called the "total input" of unit $j$, is usually taken to be a *linear* function of the activity levels of the units that provide input to $j$:

$$x_j = -\theta_j + \sum_i y_i w_{ji} \,,\tag{1}$$

where $y_i$ is the state of the $i$th unit, $w_{ji}$ is the weight on the connection from the $i$th to the $j$th unit and $\theta_j$ is the threshold of the $j$th unit. The threshold term can be eliminated by giving every unit an extra input connection whose activity level is fixed at 1. The weight on this special connection is the negative of the threshold. It is called the "bias" and it can be learned in just the same way as the other weights. This method of implementing thresholds will generally be assumed in the rest of this paper. An external input vector can be supplied to the network by clamping the states of some units or by adding an input term, $I_j$, that contributes to the total input of some of the units. The state of a unit is typically defined to be a nonlinear function of its total input. For units with discrete states, this function typically has value 1 if the total input is positive and value 0 (or $-1$) otherwise. For units with continuous states one typical nonlinear input-output function is the logistic function (shown in Fig. 1):

$$y_j = \frac{1}{1 + e^{-x_j}} \,.\tag{2}$$

All the long-term knowledge in a connectionist network is encoded by where the connections are or by their weights, so learning consists of changing the weights or adding or removing connections. The short-term knowledge of the network is normally encoded by the states of the units, but some models also have fast-changing temporary weights or thresholds that can be used to encode temporary contexts or bindings [44, 96].

There are two main reasons for investigating connectionist networks. First, these networks resemble the brain much more closely than conventional computers. Even though there are many detailed differences between connectionist units and real neurons, a deeper understanding of the computational properties of connectionist networks may reveal principles that apply to a whole class of devices of this kind, including the brain. Second, connectionist networks are massively parallel, so any computations that can be performed efficiently with these networks can make good use of parallel hardware.

## 3. Connectionist Research Issues

There are three main areas of research on connectionist networks: Search, representation, and learning. This paper focuses on learning, but a very brief introduction to search and representation is necessary in order to understand what learning is intended to produce.

### 3.1. Search

The task of interpreting the perceptual input, or constructing a plan, or accessing an item in memory from a partial description can be viewed as a constraint satisfaction search in which information about the current case (i.e. the perceptual input or the partial description) must be combined with knowledge of the domain to produce a solution that fits both these sources of constraint as well as possible [12]. If each unit represents a piece of a possible solution, the weights on the connections between units can encode the degree of consistency between various pieces. In interpreting an image, for example, a unit might stand for a piece of surface at a particular depth and surface orientation. Knowledge that surfaces usually vary smoothly in depth and orientation can be encoded by using positive weights between units that represent nearby pieces of surface at similar depths and similar surface

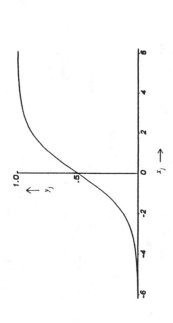

Fig. 1. The logistic input-output function defined by equation (2). It is a smoothed version of a step function.

orientations, and negative weights between nearby pieces of surface at very different depths or orientations. The network can perform a search for the most plausible interpretation of the input by iteratively updating the states of the units until they reach a stable state in which the pieces of the solution fit well with each other and with the input. Any one constraint can typically be overridden by combinations of other constraints and this makes the search procedure robust in the presence of noisy data, noisy hardware, or minor inconsistencies in the knowledge.

There are, of course, many complexities: Under what conditions will the network settle to a stable solution? Will this solution be the optimal one? How long will it take to settle? What is the precise relationship between weights and probabilities? These issues are examined in detail by Hummel and Zucker [52], Hinton and Sejnowski [45]. Geman and Geman [31], Hopfield and Tank [51] and Marroquin [65].

### 3.2. Representation

For tasks like low-level vision, it is usually fairly simple to decide how to use the units to represent the important features of the task domain. Even so, there are some important choices about whether to represent a physical quantity (like the depth at a point in the image) by the state of a single continuous unit, or by the activities in a set of units each of which indicates its confidence that the depth lies within a certain interval [10].

The issues become much more complicated when we consider how a complex, articulated structure like a plan or the meaning of a sentence might be represented in a network of simple units. Some preliminary work has been done by Minsky [67] and Hinton [37] on the representation of inheritance hierarchies and the representation of frame-like structures in which a whole object is composed of a number of parts each of which plays a different role within the whole. A recurring issue is the distinction between local and distributed representations. In a local representation, each concept is represented by a single unit [13, 27]. In a distributed representation, the kinds of concepts that we have words for are represented by patterns of activity distributed over many units, and each unit takes part in many such patterns [42]. Distributed representations are usually more efficient than local ones in addition to being more damage-resistant. Also, if the distributed representation allows the weights to capture important underlying regularities in the task domain, it can lead to much better generalization than a local representation [78, 80]. However, distributed representations can make it difficult to represent several different things at the same time and so to use them effectively for representing structures that have many parts playing different roles it may be necessary to have a separate group of units for each role so that the assignment of a filler to a role is represented by a distributed pattern of activity over a group of "role-specific" units.

Much confusion has been caused by the failure to realize that the words "local" and "distributed" refer to the *relationship* between the terms of some descriptive language and a connectionist implementation. If an entity that is described by a single term in the language is represented by a pattern of activity over many units in the connectionist system, and if each of these units is involved in representing other entities, then the representation is distributed. But it is always possible to invent a new descriptive language such that, relative to this language, the very same connectionist system is using local representations.

### 3.3. Learning

In a network that uses local representations it may be feasible to set all the weights by hand because each weight typically corresponds to a meaningful relationship between entities in the domain. If, however, the network uses distributed representations it may be very hard to program by hand and so a learning procedure may be essential. Some learning procedures, like the perceptron convergence procedure [77], are only applicable if the desired states of all the units in the network are already specified. This makes the learning task relatively easy. Other, more recent, learning procedures operate in networks that contain "hidden" units [46] whose desired states are not specified (either directly or indirectly) by the input or the desired output of the network. This makes learning much harder because the learning procedure must (implicitly) decide what the hidden units should represent. The learning procedure is therefore constructing new representations and the results of learning can be viewed as a numerical solution to the problem of whether to use local or distributed representations.

Connectionist learning procedures can be divided into three broad classes: Supervised procedures which require a teacher to specify the desired output vector, reinforcement procedures which only require a single scalar evaluation of the output, and unsupervised procedures which construct internal models that capture regularities in their input vectors without receiving any additional information. As we shall see, there are often ways of converting one kind of learning procedure into another.

### 4. Associative Memories without Hidden Units

Several simple kinds of connectionist learning have been used extensively for storing knowledge in simple associative networks which consist of a set of input units that are directly connected to a set of output units. Since these networks do not contain any hidden units, the difficult problem of deciding what the hidden units should represent does not arise. The aim is simply to store a set of associations between input vectors and output vectors by modifying the weights on the connections. The representation of each association is typically distrib-

uted over many connections and each connection is involved in storing many associations. This makes the network robust against minor physical damage and it also means that weights tend to capture regularities in the set of input-output pairings, so the network tends to generalize these regularities to new input vectors that it has not been trained on [6].

### 4.1. Linear associators

In a linear associator, the state of an output unit is a linear function of the total input that it receives from the input units (see (1)). A simple, Hebbian procedure for storing a new association (or "case") is to increment each weight, $w_{ji}$, between the $i$th input unit and the $j$th output unit by the product of the states of the units

$$\Delta w_{ji} = y_i y_j, \tag{3}$$

where $y_i$ and $y_j$ are the activities of an input and an output unit. After a set of associations have been stored, the weights encode the cross-correlation matrix between the input and output vectors. If the input vectors are orthogonal and have length 1, the associative memory will exhibit perfect recall. Even though each weight is involved in storing many different associations, each input vector will produce exactly the correct output vector [56].

If the input vectors are not orthogonal, the simple Hebbian storage procedure is not optimal. For a given network and a given set of associations, it may be impossible to store all the associations perfectly, but we would still like the storage procedure to produce a set of weights that minimizes some sensible measure of the differences between the desired output vectors and the vectors actually produced by the network. This "error measure" can be defined as

$$E = \frac{1}{2} \sum_{j,c} (y_{j,c} - d_{j,c})^2,$$

where $y_{j,c}$ is the actual state of output unit $j$ in input-output case $c$, and $d_{j,c}$ is its desired state. Kohonen [56] shows that the weight matrix that minimizes this error measure can be computed by an iterative storage procedure that repeatedly sweeps through the whole set of associations and modifies each weight by a small amount in the direction that reduces the error measure. This is a version of the least squares learning procedure described in Section 5. The cost of finding an optimal set of weights (in the least squares sense of optimal) is that storage ceases to be a simple "one-shot" process. To store one new association it is necessary to sweep through the whole set of associations many times.

Hopfield nets store vectors whose components are all $+1$ or $-1$ using the simple storage procedure described in equation (3). To retrieve a stored vector from a partial description (which is a vector containing some 0 components), we start the network at the state specified by the partial description and then repeatedly update the states of units one at a time. The units can be chosen in random order or in any other order provided no unit is ever ignored for more than a finite time. Hopfield [49] observed that the behavior of the network is governed by the global energy function[1]

$$E = -\sum_{i<j} s_i s_j w_{ij} + \sum_j s_j \theta_j, \qquad (4)$$

where $s_i$ and $s_j$ are the states of two units. Each time a unit updates its state, it adopts the state that minimizes this energy function because the decision rule used to update a unit is simply the derivative of the energy function. The unit adopts the state $+1$ if its "energy gap" is positive and the state $-1$ otherwise, where the energy gap of the $j$th unit, $\Delta E_j$, is the increase in the global energy caused by changing the unit from state $+1$ to state $-1$.

$$\Delta E_j = E(s_j = -1) - E(s_j = +1) = -2\theta_j + 2\sum_i s_i w_{ij}. \qquad (5)$$

So the energy must decrease until the network settles into a local minimum of the energy function. We can therefore view the retrieval process in the following way: The weights define an "energy landscape" over global states of the network and the stored vectors are local minima in this landscape. The retrieval process consists of moving downhill from a starting point to a nearby local minimum.

If too many vectors are stored, there may be spurious local minima caused by interactions between the stored vectors. Also, the basins of attraction around the correct minima may be long and narrow instead of round, so a downhill path from a random starting point may not lead to the nearest local minimum. These problems can be alleviated by using a process called "unlearning" [20, 50].

A Hopfield net with $N$ totally interconnected units can store about $0.15N$ random vectors.[2] This means that it is storing about 0.15 bits per weight, even though the weights are integers with $m+1$ different values, where $m$ is the number of vectors stored. The capacity can be increased considerably by

[1] The energy function should not be confused with the error function described earlier. Gradient descent in the energy function is performed by changing the *states* of the units, not the *weights*.

[2] There is some confusion in the literature due to different ways of measuring storage capacity. If we insist on a fixed probability of getting *each* component of *each* vector correct, the number of vectors that can be stored is O($N$). If we insist on a fixed probability of getting *all* components of *all* vectors correct, the number of vectors that can be stored is O($N/\log N$).

## 4.2. Nonlinear associative nets

If we wish to store a small set of associations which have nonorthogonal input vectors, there is no simple, one-shot storage procedure for linear associative nets that guarantees perfect recall. In these circumstances, a nonlinear associative net can perform better. Willshaw [102] describes an associative net in which both the units and the weights have just two states: 1 and 0. The weights are all start at 0, and associations are stored by setting a weight to 1 if ever its input and output units are both on in any association (see Fig. 2). To recall an association, each output unit must have its threshold dynamically set to be just less than $m$, the number of active input units. If the output unit should be on, the $m$ weights coming from the active input units will have been set to 1 during storage, so the output unit is guaranteed to come on. If the output unit should be off, the probability of erroneously coming on is given by the probability that all $m$ of the relevant weights will have been set to 1 when storing other associations. Willshaw showed that associative nets can make efficient use of the information capacity of the weights. If the number of active input units is the log of the total number of input units, the probability of incorrectly activating an output unit can be made very low even when the network is storing close to 0.69 of its information-theoretic capacity.

An associative net in which the input units are identical with the output units can be used to associate vectors with themselves. This allows the network to complete a partially specified input vector. If the input vector is a very degraded version of one of the stored vectors, it may be necessary to use an iterative retrieval process. The initial states of the units represent the partially specified vector, and the states of the units are then updated many times until they settle on one of the stored vectors. Theoretically, the network could oscillate, but Hinton [37] and Anderson and Mozer [7] showed that iterative retrieval normally works well. Hopfield [49] showed that if the weights are symmetrical and the units are updated one at a time the iterative retrieval process can be viewed as a form of gradient descent in an "energy function".

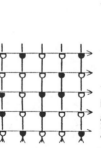

Fig. 2. An associative net (Willshaw [102]). The input vector comes in at the left and the output vector comes out at the bottom (after thresholding). The solid weights have value 1 and the open weights have value 0. The network is shown after it has stored the associations 01001 → 10001, 10100 → 01100, 00010 → 00110.

set of weights is:

$$E = \frac{1}{2} \sum_{j,c} (y_{j,c} - d_{j,c})^2, \tag{6}$$

where $y_{j,c}$ is the actual state of output unit $j$ in input-output case $c$, and $d_{j,c}$ is its desired state.

We can minimize the error measure given in (6) by starting with any set of weights and repeatedly changing each weight by an amount proportional to $\partial E / \partial w$.

$$\Delta w_{ji} = - \varepsilon \frac{\partial E}{\partial w_{ji}}. \tag{7}$$

In the limit, as $\varepsilon$ tends to 0 and the number of updates tends to infinity, this learning procedure is guaranteed to find the set of weights that gives the least squared error. The value of $\partial E / \partial w$ is obtained by differentiating (6) and (1).

$$\frac{\partial E}{\partial w_{ji}} = \sum_{\text{cases}} \frac{\partial E}{\partial y_j} \frac{\mathrm{d} y_j}{\mathrm{d} x_j} \frac{\partial x_j}{\partial w_{ji}} = \sum_{\text{cases}} (y_j - d_j) \frac{\mathrm{d} y_j}{\mathrm{d} x_j} y_i . \tag{8}$$

If the output units are linear, the term $\mathrm{d} y_j / \mathrm{d} x_j$ is a constant.

The least squares learning procedure has a simple geometric interpretation. We construct a multi-dimensional "weight space" that has an axis for each weight and one extra axis (called "height") that corresponds to the error measure. For each combination of weights, the network will have a certain error which can be represented by the height of a point in weight space. These points form a surface called the "error surface". For networks with linear output units and no hidden units, the error surface always forms a bowl whose horizontal cross-sections are ellipses and whose vertical cross-sections are parabolas. Since the bowl only has one minimum,[4] gradient descent on the error surface is guaranteed to find it.

The error surface is actually the sum of a number of parabolic troughs, one for each training case. If the output units have a nonlinear but monotonic input-output function, each trough is deformed but no new minima are created in any one trough because the monotonic nonlinearity cannot reverse the sign of the gradient of the trough in any direction. When many troughs are added together, however, it is possible to create local minima because it is possible to change the sign of the total gradient without changing the signs of any of the conflicting case-wise gradients of which it is composed. But local minima cannot be created in this way if there is a set of weights that gives zero error for all training cases. If we consider moving away from this perfect point, the error must increase (or remain constant) for each individual case and so it must

---

[4] This minimum may be a whole subspace.

---

abandoning the one-shot storage procedure and explicitly training the network on typical noisy retrieval tasks using the threshold least squares or perceptron convergence procedures described below.

### 4.3. The deficiencies of associators without hidden units

If the input vectors are orthogonal, or if they are made to be close to orthogonal by using high-dimensional random vectors (as is typically done in a Hopfield net), associators with no hidden units perform well using a simple Hebbian storage procedure. If the set of input vectors satisfy the much weaker condition of being linearly independent, associators with no hidden units can learn to give the correct outputs provided an iterative learning procedure is used. Unfortunately, linear independence does not hold for most tasks that can be characterized as mapping input vectors to output vectors because the number of relevant input vectors is typically much larger than the number of components in each input vector. The required mapping typically has a complicated structure that can only be expressed using multiple layers of hidden units.[3] Consider, for example, the task of identifying an object when the input vector is an intensity array and the output vector has a separate component for each possible name. If a given type of object can be either black or white, the intensity of an individual pixel (which is what an input unit encodes) cannot provide any direct evidence for the presence or absence of an object of that type. So the object cannot be identified by using weights on direct connections from input to output units. Obviously, it is necessary to explicitly extract relationships among intensity values (such as edges) before trying to identify the object. Actually, extracting edges is just a small part of the problem. If recognition is to have the generative capacity to handle novel images of familiar objects the network must somehow encode the systematic effects of variations in lighting and viewpoint, partial occlusion by other objects, and deformations of the object itself. There is a tremendous gap between these complex regularities and the regularities that can be captured by an associative net that lacks hidden units.

### 5. Simple Supervised Learning Procedures

Consider a network that has input units which are directly connected to output units whose states (i.e. activity levels) are a continuous smooth function of their total input. Suppose that we want to train the network to produce particular "desired" states of the output units for each member of a set of input vectors. A measure of how poorly the network is performing with its current

---

[3] It is always possible to redefine the units and the connectivity so that multiple layers of simple units become a single layer of much more complicated units. But this redefinition does not make the problem go away.

increase (or remain constant) for the sum of all these cases. So gradient descent is still guaranteed to work for monotonic nonlinear input-output functions provided a perfect solution exists. However, it will be very slow at points in weight space where the gradient of the input-output function approaches zero for the output units that are in error.

The "batch" version of the least squares procedure sweeps through all the cases accumulating $\partial E/\partial w$ before changing the weights, and so it is guaranteed to move in the direction of steepest descent. The "online" version, which requires less memory, updates the weights after each input-output case [99].[5] This may sometimes increase the total error, $E$, but by making the weight changes sufficiently small the total change in the weights after a complete sweep through all the cases can be made to approximate steepest descent arbitrarily closely.

### 5.1. A least squares procedure for binary threshold units

Binary threshold units use a step function, so the term $dy_j/dx_j$ is infinite at the threshold and zero elsewhere and the least squares procedure must be modified to be applicable to these units. In the following discussion we assume that the threshold is implemented by a "bias" weight on a permanently active input line, so the unit turns on if its total input exceeds zero. The basic idea is to define an error function that is large if the total input is far from zero and the unit is in the wrong state and is 0 when the unit is in the right state. The simplest version of this idea is to define the error of an output unit, $j$ for a given input case to be

$$E^*_{j,c} = \begin{cases} 0, & \text{if output unit has the right state}, \\ \tfrac{1}{2}x^2_{j,c}, & \text{if output unit has the wrong state}. \end{cases}$$

Unfortunately, this measure can be minimized by setting all weights and biases to zero so that units are always exactly at their threshold (Yann Le Cun, personal communication). To avoid this problem we can introduce a margin, $m$, and insist that for units which should be *on* the total input is at least $m$ and for units that should be *off* the total input is at most $-m$. The new error measure is then

$$E^*_{j,c} = \begin{cases} 0, & \text{if output unit has the right state by at least } m, \\ \tfrac{1}{2}(m - x_{j,c})^2, & \text{if output unit should be on but has } x_{j,c} < m, \\ \tfrac{1}{2}(m + x_{j,c})^2, & \text{if output unit should be off but has } x_{j,c} > -m. \end{cases}$$

[5] The online version is usually called the "least mean squares" or "LMS" procedure.

The derivative of this error measure with respect to $x_{j,c}$ is

$$\frac{\partial E^*_{j,c}}{\partial x_{j,c}} = \begin{cases} 0, & \text{if output unit has the right state by at least } m, \\ x_{j,c} - m, & \text{if output unit should be on but has } x_{j,c} < m, \\ x_{j,c} + m, & \text{if output unit should be off but has } x_{j,c} > -m. \end{cases}$$

So the "threshold least squares procedure" becomes:

$$\Delta w_{ji} = -\varepsilon \sum_c \frac{\partial E^*_{j,c}}{\partial x_{j,c}} y_{i,c}.$$

### 5.2. The perceptron convergence procedure

One version of the perceptron convergence procedure is related to the online version of the threshold least squares procedure in the following way: The magnitude of $\partial E^*_{j,c}/\partial x_{j,c}$ is ignored and only its sign is taken into consideration. So the weight changes are:

$$\Delta w_{ji,c} = \begin{cases} 0, & \text{if output unit behaves correctly by at least } m, \\ +\varepsilon y_{i,c}, & \text{if output unit should be on but has } x_{j,c} < m, \\ -\varepsilon y_{i,c}, & \text{if output unit should be off but has } x_{j,c} > -m. \end{cases}$$

Because it ignores the magnitude of the error, this procedure changes weights by at least $m$ even when the error is very small. The finite size of the weight steps eliminates the need for a margin so the standard version of the perceptron convergence procedure does not use one.

Because it ignores the magnitude of the error this procedure does not even stochastically approximate steepest descent in $E$, the sum squared error. Even with very small $\varepsilon$, it is quite possible for $E$ to rise after a complete sweep through all the cases. However, each time the weights are updated, the perceptron convergence procedure is guaranteed to reduce the value of a different cost measure that is defined solely in terms of weights.

To picture the least squares procedure we introduced a space with one dimension for each weight and one extra dimension for the sum squared error in the output vectors. To picture the perceptron convergence procedure, we do not need the extra dimension for the error. For simplicity we shall consider a network with only one output unit. Each case corresponds to a constraint hyperplane in weight space. If the weights are on one side of this hyperplane, the output unit will behave correctly and if they are on the other side it will behave incorrectly (see Fig. 3). To behave correctly for all cases, the weights

## 5.3. The deficiencies of simple learning procedures

The major deficiency of both the least squares and perceptron convergence procedures is that most "interesting" mappings between input and output vectors cannot be captured by any combination of weights in such simple networks, so the guarantee that the learning procedure will find the best possible combination of weights is of little value. Consider, for example, a network composed of two input units and one output unit. There is no way of setting the two weights and one threshold to solve the very simple task of producing an output of 1 when the input vector is (1, 1) or (0, 0) and an output of 0 when the input vector is (1, 0) or (0, 1). Minsky and Papert [68] give a clear analysis of the limitations on what mappings can be computed by three-layered nets. They focus on the question of what preprocessing must be done by the units in the intermediate layer to allow a task to be solved. They generally assume that the preprocessing is fixed, and so they avoid the problem of how to make the units in the intermediate layer learn useful predicates. So, from the learning perspective, their intermediate units are not true hidden units.

Another deficiency of the least squares and perceptron learning procedures is that gradient descent may be very slow if the elliptical cross-section of the error surface is very elongated so that the surface forms a long ravine with steep sides and a very low gradient along the ravine. In this case, the gradient at most points in the space is almost perpendicular to the direction towards the minimum. If the coefficient $\varepsilon$ in (7) is large, there are divergent oscillations across the ravine, and if it is small the progress along the ravine is very slow. A standard method for speeding the convergence in such cases is recursive least squares [5, 71, 75]. Various other methods have also been suggested [100].

We now consider learning in more complex networks that contain hidden units. The next five sections describe a variety of supervised, unsupervised, and reinforcement learning procedures for these nets.

## 6. Backpropagation: A Multi-layer Least Squares Procedure

The "backpropagation" learning procedure [80, 81] is a generalization of the least squares procedure that works for networks which have layers of hidden units between the input and output units. These multi-layer networks can compute much more complicated functions than networks that lack hidden units, but the learning is generally much slower because it must explore the space of possible ways of using the hidden units. There are now many examples in which backpropagation constructs interesting internal representations in the hidden units, and these representations allow the network to generalize in sensible ways. Variants of the procedure were discovered independently by Werbos [98], Le Cun [59] and Parker [70].

In a multi-layer network it is possible, using (8), to compute $\partial E/\partial w_{ji}$ for *all*

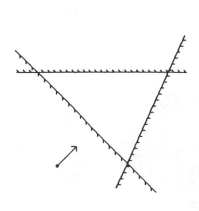

Fig. 3. Some hyperplanes in weight space. Each plane represents the constraint on the weights caused by a particular input-output case. If the weights lie on the correct (unshaded) side of the plane, the output unit will have the correct state for that case. Provided the weight changes are proportional to the activities of the input lines, the perceptron convergence procedure moves the weights perpendicularly towards a violated constraint plane.

must lie on the correct side of all the hyperplanes, so the combinations of weights that give perfect performance form a convex set. *Any* set of weights in this set will be called "ideal."

The perceptron convergence procedure considers the constraint planes one at a time, and whenever the current combination of weights is on the wrong side, it moves it perpendicularly towards the plane. This reduces the distance between the current combination of weights and *any* of the ideal combinations. So provided the weights move by less than twice the distance to the violated constraint plane, a weight update is guaranteed to reduce the measure

$$\sum_i (w_{i,\text{actual}} - w_{i,\text{ideal}})^2 .$$

The perceptron convergence procedure has many nice properties, but it also has some serious problems. Unlike the threshold least squares procedure, it does not necessarily settle down to a reasonable compromise when there is no set of weights that will do the job perfectly. Also, there are obvious problems in trying to generalize to more complex, multi-layered nets in which the ideal combinations of weights do not form a single convex set, because the idea of moving towards *the* ideal region of weight space breaks down. It is therefore not surprising that the more sophisticated procedures required for multi-layer nets are generalizations of the least squares procedure rather than the perceptron convergence procedure: They learn by decreasing a squared performance error, not a distance in weight space.

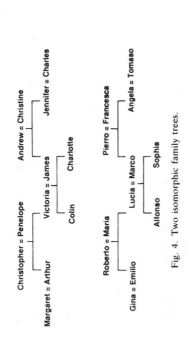

Fig. 4. Two isomorphic family trees.

Fig. 5. The activity levels in a five-layer network after it has learned. The bottom layer has 24 input units on the left for representing person1 and 12 units on the right for representing the relationship. The white squares inside these two groups show the activity levels of the units. There is one active unit in the first group (representing Colin) and one in the second group (representing has-aunt). Each of the two groups of input units is totally connected to its own group of 6 units in the second layer. These two groups of 6 units must learn to encode the input terms as distributed patterns of activity. The second layer is totally connected to the central layer of 12 units, and this layer is connected to the penultimate layer of 6 units. The activity in the penultimate layer must activate the correct output units, each of which stands for a particular person2. In this case, there are two correct output units (marked by black dots) because Colin has two aunts. Both the input and output units are laid out spatially with the English people in one row and the isomorphic Italians immediately below.

the weights in the network provided we can compute $\partial E/\partial y_j$ for all the units that have modifiable incoming weights. In a system that has no hidden units, this is easy because the only relevant units are the output units, and for them $\partial E/\partial y_j$ is found by differentiating the error function in (6). But for hidden units, $\partial E/\partial y_j$ is harder to compute. The central idea of backpropagation is that these derivatives can be computed efficiently by starting with the output layer and working backwards through the layers. For each input-output case, $c$, we first use a forward pass, starting at the input units, to compute the activity levels of all the units in the network. Then we use a backward pass, starting at the output units, to compute $\partial E/\partial y_j$ for all the hidden units. For a hidden unit, $j$, in layer $J$ the only way it can affect the error is via its effects on the units, $k$, in the next layer, $K$ (assuming units in one layer only send their outputs to units in the layer above). So we have

$$\frac{\partial E}{\partial y_j} = \sum_k \frac{\partial E}{\partial y_k}\frac{dy_k}{dx_k}\frac{dx_k}{dy_j} = \sum_k \frac{\partial E}{\partial y_k}\frac{dy_k}{dx_k}w_{kj}, \qquad (9)$$

where the index $c$ has been suppressed for clarity. So if $\partial E/\partial y_k$ is already known for all units in layer $K$, it is easy to compute the same quantity for units in layer $J$. Notice that the computation performed during the backward pass is very similar in form to the computation performed during the forward pass (though it propagates error derivatives instead of activity levels, and it is entirely linear in the error derivatives).

### 6.1. The shape of the error surface

In networks without hidden units, the error surface only has one minimum (provided a perfect solution exists and the units use smooth monotonic input-output functions). With hidden units, the error surface may contain many local minima, so it is possible that steepest descent in weight space will get stuck at poor local minima. In practice, this does not seem to be a serious problem. Backpropagation has been tried for a wide variety of tasks and poor local minima are rarely encountered, provided the network contains a few more units and connections than are required for the task. One reason for this is that there are typically a very large number of qualitatively different perfect solutions, so we avoid the typical combinatorial optimization task in which one minimum is slightly better than a large number of other, widely separated minima.

In practice, the most serious problem is the speed of convergence, not the presence of nonglobal minima. This is discussed further in Section 12.

### 6.2. Backpropagation for discovering semantic features

To demonstrate the ability of backpropagation to discover important underlying features of a domain, Hinton [38] used a multi-layer network to learn the

family relationships between 24 different people (see Fig. 4). The information in a family tree can be represented as a set of triples of the form $(\langle\text{person1}\rangle, \langle\text{relationship}\rangle, \langle\text{person2}\rangle)$, and a network can be said to "know" these triples if it can produce the third term of any triple when given the first two terms as input. Figure 5 shows the architecture of the network that was used to learn the triples. The input vector is divided into two parts, one of which specifies a person and the other a relationship (e.g. has-father). The network is trained to produce the related person as output. The input and output encoding use a different unit to represent each person and relationship, so all pairs of people are equally similar in the input and output encoding: The encodings do not give any clues about what the important features are. The architecture is designed so that all the information about an input person must be squeezed through a narrow bottleneck of 6 units in the first hidden layer. This forces the network

### 6.3. Backpropagation for mapping text to speech

Backpropagation is an effective learning technique when the mapping from input vectors to output vectors contains both regularities and exceptions. For example, in mapping from a string of English letters to a string of English phonemes there are many regularities but there are also exceptions such as the word "women." Sejnowski and Rosenberg [84] have shown that a network with one hidden layer can be trained to pronounce letters surprisingly well. The input layer encodes the identity of the letter to be pronounced using a different unit for each possible letter. The input also encodes the local context which consists of the three previous letters and three following letters in the text (space and punctuation are treated as special kinds of letters). This seven-letter window is moved over the text, so the mapping from text to speech is performed sequentially, one letter at a time. The output layer encodes a phoneme using 21 articulatory features and 5 features for stress and syllable boundaries. There are 80 hidden units each of which receives connections from all the input units and sends connections to all the output units (see Fig. 7). After extensive training, the network generalizes well to new examples which demonstrates that it captures the regularities of the mapping. Its performance on new words is comparable to a conventional computer program which uses a large number of hand-crafted rules.

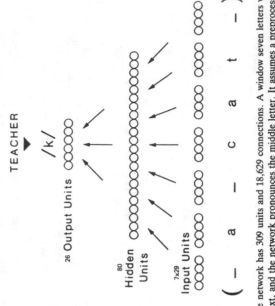

Fig. 7. The network has 309 units and 18,629 connections. A window seven letters wide is moved over the text, and the network pronounces the middle letter. It assumes a preprocessor to identify characters, and a postprocessor to turn phonemes into sounds.

to represent people using distributed patterns of activity in this layer. The aim of the simulation is to see if the components of these distributed patterns correspond to the important underlying features of the domain.

After prolonged training on 100 of the 104 possible relationships, the network was tested on the remaining 4. It generalized correctly because during the training it learned to represent each of the people in terms of important features such as age, nationality, and the branch of the family tree that they belonged to (see Fig. 6), even though these "semantic" features were not at all explicit in the input or output vectors. Using these underlying features, much of the information about family relationships can be captured by a fairly small number of "micro-inferences" between features. For example, the father of a middle-aged person is an old person, and the father of an Italian person is an Italian person. So the features of the output person can be derived from the features of the input person and of the relationship. The learning procedure can only discover these features by searching for a set of features that make it easy to express the associations. Once these features have been discovered, the *internal* representation of each person (in the first hidden layer) is a distributed pattern of activity and similar people are represented by similar patterns. Thus the network constructs its own internal similarity metric. This is a significant advance over simulations in which good generalization is achieved because the experimenter chooses representations that already have an appropriate similarity metric.

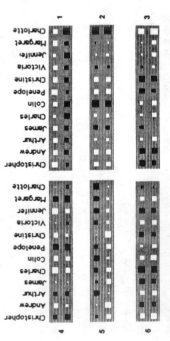

Fig. 6. The weights from the 24 input units that represent people to the 6 units in the second layer that learn distributed representations of people. White rectangles stand for excitatory weights, black for inhibitory weights, and the area of the rectangle encodes the magnitude of the weight. The weights from the 12 English people are in the top row of each unit. Beneath each of these weights is the weight from the isomorphic Italian. Unit 1 learns to encode nationality, unit 2 encodes generation (using three values), and unit 4 encodes the branch of the family tree to which a person belongs. During the learning, each weight was given a tendency to decay towards zero. This tendency is balanced by the error gradient, so the final magnitude of a weight indicates how useful it is in reducing the error.

### 6.4. Backpropagation for phoneme recognition

Speech recognition is a task that can be used to assess the usefulness of backpropagation for real-world signal-processing applications. The best existing techniques, such as hidden Markov models [9], are significantly worse than people, and an improvement in the quality of recognition would be of great practical significance.

A subtask which is well-suited to backpropagation is the bottom-up recognition of highly confusable consonants. One obvious approach is to convert the sound into a spectrogram which is then presented as the input vector to a multi-layer network whose output units represent different consonants. Unfortunately, this approach has two serious drawbacks. First, the spectrogram must have many "pixels" to give reasonable resolution in time and frequency, so each hidden unit has many incoming weights. This means that a very large number of training examples are needed to provide enough data to estimate the weights. Second, it is hard to achieve precise time alignment of the input data, so the spatial pattern that represents a given phoneme may occur at many different positions in the spectrogram. To learn that these shifts in position do not change the identity of the phoneme requires an immense amount of training data. We already know that the task has a certain symmetry—the same sounds occurring at different times mean the same phoneme. To speed learning and improve generalization we should build this a priori knowledge into the network and let it use the information in the training data to discover structure that we do not already understand.

An interesting way to build in the time symmetry is to use a multi-layer, feed-forward network that has connections with time delays [88]. The input units represent a single time frame from the spectrogram and the whole spectrogram is represented by stepping it through the input units. Each hidden unit is connected to each unit in the layer below by several different connections with different time delays and different weights. So it has a limited temporal window within which it can detect temporal patterns in the activities of the units in the layer below. Since a hidden unit applies the same set of weights at different times, it inevitably produces similar responses to similar patterns that are shifted in time (see Fig. 8).

Kevin Lang [58] has shown that a time delay net that is trained using a generalization of the backpropagation procedure compares favorably with hidden Markov models at the task of distinguishing the words "bee", "dee", "ee", and "vee" spoken by many different male speakers in a very noisy environment. Waibel et al. [97] have shown that the same network can achieve excellent speaker-dependent discrimination of the phonemes "b", "d", and "g" in varying phonetic contexts.

An interesting technical problem arises in computing the error derivatives for the output units of the time delay network. The adaptive part of the

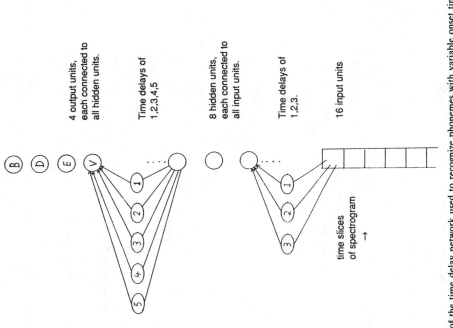

4 output units, each connected to all hidden units.

Time delays of 1,2,3,4,5

8 hidden units, each connected to all input units.

Time delays of 1,2,3.

16 input units

time slices of spectrogram →

Fig. 8. Part of the time delay network used to recognize phonemes with variable onset times. A unit in one layer is connected to a unit in the layer below by several different connections which have different time delays and learn to have different weights.

network contains one output unit for each possible phoneme and these units respond to the input by producing a sequence of activations. If the training data is labeled with the exact time of occurrence of each phoneme, it is possible to specify the exact time at which an output unit should be active. But in the absence of precisely time-aligned training data, it is necessary to compute error derivatives for a sequence of activations without knowing when the phoneme occurred. This can be done by using a fixed postprocessing layer to integrate the activity of each output unit over time. We interpret the

### 6.7. Iterative backpropagation

Rumelhart, Hinton, and Williams [80] show how the backpropagation procedure can be applied to iterative networks in which there are no limitations on the connectivity. A network in which the states of the units at time $t$ determine the states of the units at time $t+1$ is equivalent to a net which has one layer for each time slice. Each weight in the iterative network is implemented by a whole set of identical weights in the corresponding layered net, one for each time slice (see Fig. 9). In the iterative net, the error is typically the difference between the actual and desired final states of the network, and to compute the error derivatives it is necessary to backpropagate through time, so the history of states of each unit must be stored. Each weight will have many different error derivatives, one for each time step, and the sum of all these derivatives is used to determine the weight change.

Backpropagation in iterative nets can be used to train a network to generate sequences or to recognize sequences or to complete sequences. Examples are given by Rumelhart, Hinton and Williams [81]. Alternatively, it can be used to store a set of patterns by constructing a point attractor for each pattern. Unlike the simple storage procedure used in a Hopfield net, or the more sophisticated storage procedure used in a Boltzmann machine (see Section 7), backpropagation takes into account the path used to reach a point attractor. So it will not construct attractors that cannot be reached from the normal range of starting points on which it is trained.[6]

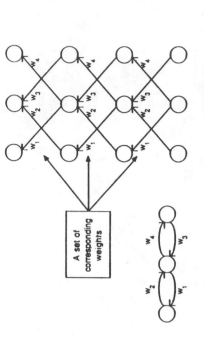

A set of corresponding weights

Fig. 9. On the left is a simple iterative network that is run synchronously for three iterations. On the right is the equivalent layered network.

[6] A backpropagation net that uses asymmetric connections (and synchronous updating) is not guaranteed to settle to a single stable state. To encourage it to construct a point attractor, rather than a limit cycle, the point attractor can be made the desired state for the last few iterations.

instantaneous activity of an output unit as a representation of the probability that the phoneme occurred at exactly that time. So, for the phoneme that really occurred, we know that the time integral of its activity should be 1 and for the other phonemes it should be 0. So at each time, the error derivative is simply the difference between the desired and the actual integral. After training, the network localizes phonemes in time, even though the training data contains no information about time alignment.

### 6.5. Postprocessing the output of a backpropagation net

Many people have suggested transforming the raw input vector with a module that uses unsupervised learning before presenting it to a module that uses supervised learning. It is less obvious that a supervised module can also benefit from a nonadaptive postprocessing module. A very simple example of this kind of postprocessing occurs in the time delay phoneme recognition network described in Section 6.4.

David Rumelhart has shown that the idea of a postprocessing module can be applied even in cases where the postprocessing function is initially unknown. In trying to imitate a sound, for example, a network might produce an output vector which specifies how to move the speech articulators. This output vector needs to be postprocessed to turn it into a sound, but the postprocessing is normally done by physics. Suppose that the network does not receive any direct information about what it should do with its articulators but it does "know" the desired sound and the actual sound, which is the transformed "image" of the output vector. If we had a postprocessing module which transformed the activations of the speech articulators into sounds, we could backpropagate through this module to compute error derivatives for the articulator activations.

Rumelhart uses an additional network (which he calls a mental model) that first learns to perform the postprocessing (i.e. it learns to map from output vectors to their transformed images). Once this mapping has been learned, backpropagation through the mental model can convert error derivatives for the "images" into error derivatives for the output vectors of the basic network.

### 6.6. A reinforcement version of backpropagation

Munro [69] has shown that the idea of using a mental model can be applied even when the image of an output vector is simply a single scalar value—the reinforcement. First, the mental model learns to predict expected reinforcement from the combination of the input vector and the output vector. Then the derivative of the expected reinforcement can be backpropagated through the mental model to get the reinforcement derivatives for each component of the output vector of the basic network.

## 6.8. Backpropagation as a maximum likelihood procedure

If we interpret each output vector as a specification of a conditional probability distribution over a set of output vectors given an input vector, we can interpret the backpropagation learning procedure as a method of finding weights that maximize the likelihood of generating the desired conditional probability distributions. Two examples of this kind of interpretation will be described.

Suppose we only attach meaning to binary output vectors and we treat a real-valued output vector as a way of specifying a probability distribution over binary vectors. We imagine that a real-valued output vector is stochastically converted into a binary vector by treating the real values as the probabilities that individual components have value 1, and assuming independence between components. For simplicity, we can assume that the desired vectors used during training are binary vectors, though this is not necessary. Given a set of training cases, it can be shown that the likelihood of producing *exactly* the desired vectors is maximized when we minimize the cross-entropy, $C$, between the desired and actual conditional probability distributions:

$$C = -\sum_{j,c} d_{j,c} \log_2(y_{j,c}) + (1 - d_{j,c}) \log_2(1 - y_{j,c}),$$

where $d_{j,c}$ is the desired probability of output unit $j$ in case $c$ and $y_{j,c}$ is its actual probability.

So, under this interpretation of the output vectors, we should use the cross-entropy function rather than the squared difference as our cost measure. In practice, this helps to avoid a problem caused by output units which are firmly off when they should be on (or vice versa). These units have a very small value of $\partial y / \partial x$ so they need a large value of $\partial E / \partial y$ in order to change their incoming weights by a reasonable amount. When an output unit that should have an activity level of 1 changes from a level of 0.0001 to level of 0.001, the squared difference from 1 only changes slightly, but the cross-entropy decreases a lot. In fact, when the derivative of the cross-entropy is multiplied by the derivative of the logistic activation function, the product is simply the difference between the desired and the actual outputs, so $\partial C_{j,c} / \partial x_{j,c}$ is just the same as for a linear output unit (Steven Nowlan, personal communication).

This way of interpreting backpropagation raises the issue of whether, under some other interpretation of the output vectors, the squared error might not be the correct measure for performing maximum likelihood estimation. In fact, Richard Golden [32] has shown that minimizing the squared error is equivalent to maximum likelihood estimation if both the actual and the desired output vectors are treated as the centers of Gaussian probability density functions over the space of all real vectors. So the "correct" choice of cost function depends on the way the output vectors are most naturally interpreted.[7]

---

[7] Both the examples of backpropagation described above fit this interpretation.

## 6.9. Self-supervised backpropagation

One drawback of the standard form of backpropagation is that it requires an external supervisor to specify the desired states of the output units (or a transformed "image" of the desired states). It can be converted into an unsupervised procedure by using the input itself to do the supervision, using a multi-layer "encoder" network [2] in which the desired output vector is identical with the input vector. The network must learn to compute an approximation to the identity mapping for all the input vectors in its training set, and if the middle layer of the network contains fewer units than the input layer, the learning procedure must construct a compact, invertible code for each input vector. This code can then be used as the input to later stages of processing.

The use of self-supervised backpropagation to construct compact codes resembles the use of principal components analysis to perform dimensionality reduction, but it has the advantage that it allows the code to be a nonlinear transform of the input vector. This form of backpropagation has been used successfully to compress images [19] and to compress speech waves [25]. A variation of it has been used to extract the underlying degrees of freedom of simple shapes [83].

It is also possible to use backpropagation to predict one part of the perceptual input from other parts. For example, in predicting one patch of an image from neighboring patches it is probably helpful to use hidden units that explicitly extract edges, so this might be an unsupervised way of discovering edge detectors. In domains with sequential structure, one portion of a sequence can be used as input and the next term in the sequence can be the desired output. This forces the network to extract features that are good predictors. If this is applied to the speech wave, the states of the hidden units will form a nonlinear predictive code. It is not yet known whether such codes are more helpful for speech recognition than linear predictive coefficients.

A different variation of self-supervised backpropagation is to insist that all or part of the code in the middle layer change as slowly as possible with time. This can be done by making the desired state of each of the middle units be the state it actually adopted for the previous input vector. This forces the network to use similar codes for input vectors that occur at neighboring times, which is a sensible principle if the input vectors are generated by a process whose underlying parameters change more slowly than the input vectors themselves.

## 6.10. The deficiencies of backpropagation

Despite its impressive performance on relatively small problems, and its promise as a widely applicable mechanism for extracting the underlying structure of a domain, backpropagation is inadequate, in its current form, for larger tasks because the learning time scales poorly. Empirically, the learning time on a serial machine is very approximately $O(N^3)$ where $N$ is the number of weights in the network. The time for one forward and one backward pass is $O(N)$. The number of training examples is typically $O(N)$, assuming the amount of information per output vector is held constant and enough training cases are used to strain the storage capacity of the network (which is about 2 bits per weight). The number of times the weights must be updated is also approximately $O(N)$. This is an empirical observation and depends on the nature of the task.[8] On a parallel machine that used a separate processor for each connection, the time would be reduced to approximately $O(N^2)$. Backpropagation can probably be improved by using the gradient information in more sophisticated ways, but much bigger improvements are likely to result from making better use of modularity (see Section 12.4).

As a biological model, backpropagation is implausible. There is no evidence that synapses can be used in the reverse direction, or that neurons can propagate error derivatives backwards (using a linear input-output function) as well as propagating activity levels forwards using a nonlinear input-output function. One approach is to try to backpropagate the derivatives using separate circuitry that *learns* to have the same weights as the forward circuitry [70]. A second approach, which seems to be feasible for self-supervised backpropagation, is to use a method called "recirculation" that approximates gradient descent and is more biologically plausible [41]. At present, backpropagation should be treated as a mechanism for demonstrating the kind of learning that can be done using gradient descent, without implying that the brain does gradient descent in the same way.

## 7. Boltzmann Machines

A Boltzmann machine [2, 46] is a generalization of a Hopfield net (see Section 4.2) in which the units update their states according to a *stochastic* decision rule. The units have states of 1 or 0,[9] and the probability that unit $j$ adopts the state 1 is given by

$$p_j = \frac{1}{1 + e^{-\Delta E_j / T}}, \qquad (10)$$

where $\Delta E_j = x_j$ is the total input received by the $j$th unit and $T$ is the "temperature." It can be shown that if this rule is applied repeatedly to the units, the network will reach "thermal equilibrium." At thermal equilibrium the units still change state, but the *probability* of finding the network in any

---

[8] Tesauro [90] reports a case in which the number of weight updates is roughly proportional to the number of training cases (it is actually a 4/3 power law). Judd shows that in the worst case it is exponential [53].

[9] A network that uses states of 1 and 0 can always be converted into an equivalent network that uses states of +1 and −1 provided the thresholds are altered appropriately.

---

global state remains constant and obeys a Boltzmann distribution in which the probability ratio of any two global states depends solely on their energy difference:

$$\frac{P_A}{P_B} = e^{-(E_A - E_B)/T}.$$

At high temperature, the network approaches equilibrium rapidly but low energy states are not much more probable than high energy states. At low temperature the network approaches equilibrium more slowly, but low energy states are much more probable than high energy states. The fastest way to approach low temperature equilibrium is generally to start at a high temperature and to gradually reduce the temperature. This is called "simulated annealing" [55]. Simulated annealing allows Boltzmann machines to find low energy states with high probability. If some units are clamped to represent an input vector, and if the weights in the network represent the constraints of the task domain, the network can settle on a very plausible output vector given the current weights and the current input vector.

For complex tasks there is generally no way of expressing the constraints by using weights on pairwise connections between the input and output units. It is necessary to use hidden units that represent higher-order features of the domain. This creates a problem: Given a limited number of hidden units, what higher-order features should they represent in order to approximate the required input-output mapping as closely as possible? The beauty of Boltzmann machines is that the simplicity of the Boltzmann distribution leads to a very simple learning procedure which adjusts the weights so as to use the hidden units in an optimal way.

The network is "shown" the mapping that it is required to perform by clamping an input vector on the input units and clamping the required output vector on the output units. If there are several possible output vectors for a given input vector, each of the possibilities is clamped on the output units with the appropriate frequency. The network is then annealed until it approaches thermal equilibrium at a temperature of 1. It then runs for a fixed time at equilibrium and each connection measures the fraction of the time during which both the units it connects are active. This is repeated for all the various input-output pairs so that each connection can measure $\langle s_i s_j \rangle^+$, the expected probability, averaged over all cases, that unit $i$ and unit $j$ are simultaneously active at thermal equilibrium when the input and output vectors are both clamped.

The network must also be run in just the same way but without clamping the output units. Again, it reaches thermal equilibrium with each input vector clamped and then runs for a fixed additional time to measure $\langle s_i s_j \rangle^-$, the expected probability that both units are active at thermal equilibrium when the output vector is determined by the network. Each weight is then updated by an amount proportional to the difference between these two quantities

$$\Delta w_{ij} = \varepsilon(\langle s_i s_j \rangle^+ - \langle s_i s_j \rangle^-).$$

It has been shown [2] that if $\varepsilon$ is sufficiently small this performs gradient descent in an information-theoretic measure, $G$, of the difference between the behavior of the output units when they are clamped and their behavior when they are not clamped.

$$G = \sum_{\alpha,\beta} P^+(I_\alpha, O_\beta) \log \frac{P^+(O_\beta|I_\alpha)}{P^-(O_\beta|I_\alpha)}, \tag{11}$$

where $I_\alpha$ is a state vector over the input units, $O_\beta$ is a state vector over the output units, $P^+$ is a probability measured when both the input and output units are clamped, and $P^-$ is a probability measured at thermal equilibrium when only the input units are clamped.

$G$ is called the "asymmetric divergence" or "Kullback information," and its gradient has the same form for connections between input and hidden units, connections between pairs of hidden units, connections between hidden and output units, and connections between pairs of output units. $G$ can be viewed as the difference of two terms. One term is the cross-entropy between the "desired" conditional probability distribution that is clamped on the output units and the "actual" conditional distribution exhibited by the output units when they are not clamped. The other term is the entropy of the "desired" conditional distribution. This entropy cannot be changed by altering the weights, so minimizing $G$ is equivalent to minimizing the cross-entropy term, which means that Boltzmann machines use the same cost function as one form of backpropagation (see Section 6.8).

A special case of the learning procedure is when there are no input units. It can then be viewed as an unsupervised learning procedure which learns to model a probability distribution that is specified by clamping vectors on the output units with the appropriate probabilities. The advantage of modeling a distribution in this way is that the network can then perform completion. When a partial vector is clamped over a subset of the output units, the network produces completions on the remaining output units. If the network has learned the training distribution perfectly, its probability of producing each completion is guaranteed to match the environmental conditional probability of this completion given the clamped partial vector.

The learning procedure can easily be generalized to networks where each term in the energy function is the product of a weight, $w_{i,j,k...}$, and an arbitrary function, $f(i, j, k, \ldots)$, of the states of a subset of the units. The network must be run so that it achieves a Boltzmann distribution in the energy function, so each unit must be able to compute how the global energy would change if it

were to change state. The generalized learning procedure is simply to change the weight by an amount proportional to the difference between $\langle f(i, j, k, \ldots)\rangle^+$ and $\langle f(i, j, k, \ldots)\rangle^-$.

The learning procedure using simple pairwise connections has been shown to produce appropriate representations in the hidden units [76]. However, it is considerably slower than backpropagation because of the time required to reach equilibrium in large networks. Also, the process of estimating the gradient introduces several practical problems. If the network does not reach equilibrium the estimated gradient has a systematic error, and if too few samples are taken to estimate $\langle s_i s_j \rangle^+$ and $\langle s_i s_j \rangle^-$ accurately the estimated gradient will be extremely noisy because it is the difference of two noisy estimates. Even when the noise in the estimate of the difference has zero mean, its variance is a function of $\langle s_i s_j \rangle^+$ and $\langle s_i s_j \rangle^-$. When these quantities are near zero or one, their estimates will have much lower variance than when they are near 0.5. This nonuniformity in the variance gives the hidden units a surprisingly strong tendency to develop weights that cause them to be on all the time or off all the time. A familiar version of the same effect can be seen if sand is sprinkled on a vibrating sheet of tin. Nearly all the sand clusters at the points that vibrate the least, even though there is no bias in the direction of motion of an individual grain of sand.

One interesting feature of the Boltzmann machine is that it is relatively easy to put it directly onto a chip which has dedicated hardware for each connection and performs the annealing extremely rapidly using analog circuitry that computes the energy gap of a unit by simply allowing the incoming charge to add itself up, and makes stochastic decisions by using physical noise. Alspector and Allen [3] are fabricating a chip which will run about 1 million times as fast as a simulation on a VAX. Such chips may make it possible to apply connectionist learning procedures to practical problems, especially if they are used in conjunction with modular approaches that allow the learning time to scale better with the size of the task.

There is another promising method that reduces the time required to compute the equilibrium distribution and eliminates the noise caused by the sampling errors in $\langle s_i s_j \rangle^+$ and $\langle s_i s_j \rangle^-$. Instead of directly simulating the stochastic network it is possible to estimate its mean behavior using "mean field theory" which replaces each stochastic binary variable by a deterministic real value that represents the expected value of the stochastic variable. Simulated annealing can then be replaced by a deterministic relaxation procedure that operates on the real-valued parameters [51] and settles to a single state that gives a crude representation of the whole equilibrium distribution. The product of the "activity levels" of two units in this settled state can be used as an approximation of $\langle s_i s_j \rangle$ so a version of the Boltzmann machine learning procedure can be applied. Peterson and Anderson [74] have shown that this works quite well.

### 7.1. Maximizing reinforcement and entropy in a Boltzmann machine

The Boltzmann machine learning procedure is based on the simplicity of the expression for the derivative of the asymmetric divergence between the conditional probability distribution exhibited by the output units of a Boltzmann machine and a desired conditional probability distribution. The derivatives of certain other important measures are also very simple if the network is allowed to reach thermal equilibrium. For example, the entropy of the states of the machine is given by

$$H = -\sum_a P_a \log_e P_a ,$$

where $P_a$ is the probability of a global configuration, and $H$ is measured in units of $\log_2 e$ bits. Its derivative is

$$\frac{\partial H}{\partial w_{ij}} = \frac{1}{T} \left( \langle E s_i s_j \rangle - \langle E \rangle \langle s_i s_j \rangle \right) . \qquad (12)$$

So if each weight has access to the global energy, $E$, it is easy to manipulate the entropy.

It is also easy to perform gradient ascent in expected reinforcement if the network is given a global reinforcement signal, $R$, that depends on its state. The derivative of the expected reinforcement with respect to each weight is

$$\frac{\partial R}{\partial w_{ij}} = \frac{1}{T} \left( \langle R s_i s_j \rangle - \langle R \rangle \langle s_i s_j \rangle \right) . \qquad (13)$$

A recurrent issue in reinforcement learning procedures is how to trade off short-term optimization of expected reinforcement against the diversity required to discover actions that have a higher reinforcement than the network's current estimate. If we use entropy as a measure of diversity, and we assume that the system tries to optimize some linear combination of the expected reinforcement and the entropy of its actions, it can be shown that its optimal strategy is to pick actions according to a Boltzmann distribution, where the expected reinforcement of a state is the analog of negative energy and the parameter that determines the relative importance of expected reinforcement and diversity is the analog of temperature. This result follows from the fact that the Boltzmann distribution is the one which maximizes entropy (i.e. diversity) for a given expected energy (i.e. reinforcement).

This suggests a learning procedure in which the system represents the expected value of an action by its negative energy, and picks actions by allowing a Boltzmann machine to reach thermal equilibrium. If the weights are updated using equations (12) and (13) the negative energies of states will tend to become proportional to their expected reinforcements, since this is the way to make the derivative of $H$ balance the derivative of $R$. Once the system has learned to represent the reinforcements correctly, variations in the temperature can be used to make it more or less conservative in its choice of actions whilst always making the optimal tradeoff between diversity and expected reinforcement. Unfortunately, this learning procedure does not make use of the most important property of Boltzmann machines which is their ability to compute the quantity $\langle s_i s_j \rangle$ *given* some specified state of the output units. Also, it is much harder to compute the derivative of the entropy if we are only interested in the entropy of the state vectors over the output units.

### 8. Maximizing Mutual Information: A Semisupervised Learning Procedure

One "semisupervised" method of training a unit is to provide it with information about what category the input vector came from, but to refrain from specifying the state that the unit ought to adopt. Instead, its incoming weights are modified so as to maximize the information that the state of the unit provides about the category of the input vector. The derivative of the mutual information is relatively easy to compute and so it can be maximized by gradient ascent [73]. For difficult discriminations that cannot be performed in a single step this is a good way of producing encodings of the input vector that allow the discrimination to be made more easily. Figure 10 shows an example of a difficult two-way discrimination and illustrates the kinds of discriminant function that maximize the information provided by the state of the unit.

If each unit within a layer independently maximizes the mutual information between its state and the category of the input vector, many units are likely to discover similar, highly correlated features. One way to force the units to diversify is to make each unit receive its inputs from a different subset of the units in the layer below. A second method is to ignore cases in which the input vector is correctly classified by the final output units and to maximize the

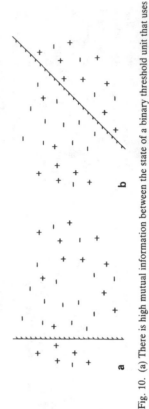

Fig. 10. (a) There is high mutual information between the state of a binary threshold unit that uses the hyperplane shown and the distribution (+ or −) that the input vector came from. (b) The probability, given that the unit is on, that the input came from the "+" distribution is not as high using the diagonal hyperplane. However, the unit is on more often. Other things being equal, a unit conveys most mutual information if it is on half the time.

mutual information between the state of each intermediate unit and the category of the input *given that the input is incorrectly classified.*[10]

If the two input distributions that must be discriminated consist of examples taken from some structured domain and examples generated at random (but with the same first-order statistics as the structured domain), this semisupervised procedure will discover higher-order features that characterize the structured domain and so it can be made to act like the type of unsupervised learning procedure described in Section 9.

## 9. Unsupervised Hebbian Learning

A unit can develop selectivity to certain kinds of features in its ensemble of input vectors by using a simple weight modification procedure that depends on the correlation between the activity of the unit and the activity on each of it input lines. This is called a "Hebbian" learning rule because the weight modification depends on both presynaptic and postsynaptic activity [36]. Typical examples of this kind of learning are described by Cooper, Liberman and Oja [18] and by Bienenstock, Cooper, and Munro [16]. A criticism of early versions of this approach, from a computational point of view, was that the researchers often postulated a simple synaptic modification rule and then explored its consequences rather than rigorously specifying the computational goal and then deriving the appropriate synaptic modification rule. However, an important recent development unifies these two approaches by showing that a relatively simple Hebbian rule can be viewed as the gradient of an interesting function. The function can therefore be viewed as a specification of what the learning is trying to achieve.

### 9.1. A recent development of unsupervised Hebbian learning

In a recent series of papers Linsker has shown that with proper normalization of the weight changes, an unsupervised Hebbian learning procedure in which the weight change depends on the correlation of presynaptic and postsynaptic activity can produce a surprising number of the known properties of the receptive fields of neurons in visual cortex, including center-surround fields [61], orientation-tuned fields [62] and orientation columns [63]. The procedure operates in a multi-layer network in which there is innate spatial structure so that the inputs to a unit in one layer tend to come from nearby locations in the layer below. Linsker demonstrates that the emergence of biologically suggestive receptive fields depends on the relative values of a few generic parameters. He also shows that for each unit, the learning procedure is performing gradient ascent in a measure whose main term is the ensemble average (across all the

various patterns of activity in the layer below) of

$$\sum_{i,j} w_i s_i w_j s_j,$$

where $w_i$ and $w_j$ are the weights on the $i$th and $j$th input lines of a unit and $s_i$ and $s_j$ are the activities on those input lines.

It is not initially obvious why maximizing the pairwise covariances of the weighted activities produces receptive fields that are useful for visual information processing. Linsker does not discuss this question in his original three papers. However, he has now shown [64] that the learning procedure maximizes the variance in the activity of the postsynaptic unit subject to a "resource" constraint on overall synaptic strength. This is almost equivalent to maximizing the ratio of the postsynaptic variance to the sum of the squares of the weights, which is guaranteed to extract the first principal component (provided the units are linear). This component is the one that would minimize the sum-squared reconstruction error if we tried to reconstruct the activity vector of the presynaptic units from the activity level of the postsynaptic unit. Thus we can view Linsker's learning procedure as a way of ensuring that the activity of a unit conveys as much information as possible about its presynaptic input vector. A similar analysis can be applied to competitive learning (see Section 10).

## 10. Competitive Learning

Competitive learning is an unsupervised procedure that divides a set of input vectors into a number of disjoint clusters in such a way that the input vectors within each cluster are all similar to one another. It is called competitive learning because there is a set of hidden units which compete with one another to become active. There are many variations of the same basic idea, and only the simplest version is described here. When an input vector is presented to the network, the hidden unit which receives the greatest total input wins the competition and turns on with an activity level of 1. All the other hidden units turn off. The winning unit then adds a small fraction of the current input vector to its weight vector. So, in future, it will receive even more total input from this input vector. To prevent the same hidden unit from being the most active in all cases, it is necessary to impose a constraint on each weight vector that keeps the sum of the weights (or the sum of their squares) constant. So when a hidden unit becomes more sensitive to one input vector it becomes less sensitive to other input vectors.

Rumelhart and Zipser [82] present a simple geometrical model of competitive learning. If each input vector has three components and is of unit length it can be represented by a point on the surface of the unit sphere. If the weight vectors of the hidden units are also constrained to be of unit length, they too can be represented by points on the unit sphere as shown in Fig. 11. The

---

[10] This method of weighting the statistics by some measure of the overall error or importance of a case can often be used to allow global measures of the performance of the whole network to influence local, unsupervised learning procedures.

One major theme has been to show that competitive learning can produce topographic maps [57]. The hidden units are laid out in a spatial structure (usually two-dimensional) and instead of just updating the weight vector of the hidden unit that receives the greatest total input, the procedure also updates the weight vectors of adjacent hidden units. This encourages adjacent units to respond to similar input vectors, and it can be viewed as a way of performing gradient descent in a cost function that has two terms. The first term measures how inaccurately the weight vector of the most active hidden unit represents the input vector. The second term measures the dissimilarity between the input vectors that are represented by adjacent hidden units. Kohonen has shown that this version of competitive learning performs dimensionality reduction, so that surplus degrees of freedom are removed from the input vector and it is represented accurately by a point in a lower-dimensional space [57]. It is not clear how this compares in efficiency with self-supervised backpropagation (see Section 6.9) for dimensionality reduction.

Fukushima and Miyake [30] have demonstrated that a version of competitive learning can be used to allow a multi-layer network to recognize simple two-dimensional shapes in a number of different positions. After learning, the network can recognize a familiar shape in a novel position. The ability to generalize across position depends on using a network in which the layers of units that learn are interleaved with layers of nonlearning units which are prewired to generalize across position. Thus, the network does not truly learn translation invariance. By contrast, it is possible to design a backpropagation network that starts with no knowledge of the effects of translation and no knowledge of which input units are adjacent in the image. After sufficient experience, the network can correctly identify familiar, simple shapes in novel positions [39].

## 10.1. The relationship between competitive learning and backpropagation

Because it is performing gradient descent in a measure of how accurately the input vector could be reconstructed, competitive learning has a close relationship to self-supervised backpropagation. Consider a three-layer encoder network in which the desired states of the output units are the same as the actual states of the input units. Suppose that each weight from an input unit to a hidden unit is constrained to be identical to the weight from that hidden unit to the corresponding output unit. Suppose, also, that the output units are linear and the hidden units, instead of using the usual nonlinear input-output function, use the same "winner-take-all" nonlinearity as is used in competitive learning. So only one hidden unit will be active at a time, and the actual states of the output units will equal the weights of the active hidden unit. This makes it easy to compute the error derivatives of the weights from the hidden units to the output units. For weights from the active hidden unit the derivatives are

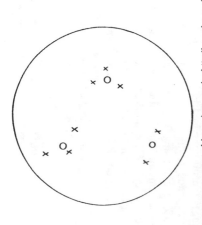

Fig. 11. The input vectors are represented by points marked "×" on the surface of a sphere. The weight vectors of the hidden units are represented by points marked "O." After competitive learning, each weight vector will be close to the center of gravity of a cluster of input vectors.

learning procedure is equivalent to finding the weight vector that is closest to the current input vector, and moving it closer still by an amount that is proportional to the distance. If the weight changes are sufficiently small, this process will stabilize when each weight vector is at the center of gravity of a cluster of input vectors.

We can think of the network as performing the following task: Represent the current input vector, $y_c$, as accurately as possible by using a single active hidden unit. The representation is simply the weight vector, $w_c$, of the hidden unit which is active in case $c$. If the weight changes are sufficiently small, this version of competitive learning performs steepest descent in a measure of the sum-squared inaccuracy of the representation. The solutions it finds are minima of the function

$$E = \frac{1}{2} \sum_c (w_c - y_c)^2 .$$

Although they use the geometrical analogy described above, Rumelhart and Zipser actually use a slightly different learning rule which cannot be interpreted as performing steepest descent in such a simple error function.

There are many variations of competitive learning in the literature [4, 29, 33, 95] and there is not space here to review them all. A model with similarities to competitive learning has been used by Willshaw and von der Malsburg [103] to explain the formation of topographic maps between the retina and the tectum. Recently, it has been shown that a variation of this model can be interpreted as performing steepest descent in an error function and can be applied to a range of optimization problems that involve topographic mappings between geometrical structures [23].

simply proportional to the difference between the actual and desired outputs (which equals the difference between the weight and the corresponding component of the input vector). For weights from inactive hidden units the error derivatives are all zero. So gradient descent can be performed by making the weights of the active hidden unit regress towards the input vector, which is precisely what the competitive learning rule does.

Normally, backpropagation is needed in order to compute the error derivatives of the weights from the input units to the hidden units, but the winner-take-all nonlinearity makes backpropagation unnecessary in this network because all these derivatives are equal to zero. So long as the same hidden unit wins the competition, its activity level is not changed by changing its input weights. At the point where a small change in the weights would change the winner from one hidden unit to another, both hidden units fit the input vector equally well, so changing winners does not alter the total error in the output (even though it may change the output vector a lot). Because the error derivatives are so simple, we can still do the learning if we omit the output units altogether. This removes the output weights, and so we no longer need to constrain the input and output weights of a hidden unit to be identical. Thus the simplified version of competitive learning is a degenerate case of self-supervised backpropagation.

It would be interesting if a mechanism as simple as competitive learning could be used to implement gradient descent in networks that allow the *m* most activated hidden units to become fully active (where *m* > 1). This would allow the network to create more complex, distributed representations of the input vectors. Unfortunately the implementation is not nearly as simple because it is no longer possible to omit the output layer. The output units are needed to combine the effects of all the active hidden units and compare the combined effect with the input vector in order to compute the error derivatives of the output weights. Also, at the point at which one hidden unit ceases to be active and another becomes active, there may be a large change in the total error, so at this point there are infinite error derivatives for the weights from the input to the hidden units. It thus appears that the simplicity of the mechanism required for competitive learning is crucially dependent on the fact that only one hidden unit within a group is active.

## 11. Reinforcement Learning Procedures

There is a large and complex literature on reinforcement learning procedures which is beyond the scope of this paper. The main aim of this section is to give an informal description of a few of the recent ideas in the field that reveals their relationship to other types of connectionist learning.

A central idea in many reinforcement learning procedures is that we can assign credit to a local decision by *measuring* how it correlates with the global

reinforcement signal. Various different values are tried for each local variable (such as a weight or a state), and these variations are correlated with variations in the global reinforcement signal. Normally, the local variations are the result of independent stochastic processes, so if enough samples are taken each local variable can average away the noise caused by the variation in the other variables to reveal its own effect on the global reinforcement signal (given the current *average* behavior of the other variables). The network can then perform gradient ascent in the expected reinforcement by altering the probability distribution of the value of each local variable in the direction that increases the expected reinforcement. If the probability distributions are altered after each trial, the network performs a stochastic version of gradient ascent.

The main advantage of reinforcement learning is that it is easy to implement because, unlike backpropagation which *computes* the effect of changing a local variable, the "credit assignment" does not require any special apparatus for *computing* derivatives. So reinforcement learning can be used in complex systems in which it would be very hard to analytically compute reinforcement derivatives. The main disadvantage of reinforcement learning is that it is very inefficient when there are more than a few local variables. Even in the trivial case when all the local variables contribute independently to the global reinforcement signal, $O(NM)$ trials are required to allow the measured effects of each of the $M$ possible values of a variable to achieve a reasonable signal-to-noise ratio by averaging away the noise caused by the $N$ other variables. So reinforcement learning is very inefficient for large systems unless they are divided into smaller modules. It is as if each person in the United States tried to decide whether he or she had done a useful day's work by observing the gross national product on a day-by-day basis.

A second disadvantage is that gradient ascent may get stuck in local optima. As a network concentrates more and more of its trials on combinations of values that give the highest expected reinforcement, it gets less and less information about the reinforcements caused by other combinations of values.

### 11.1. Delayed reinforcement

In many real systems, there is a delay between an action and the resultant reinforcement, so in addition to the normal problem of deciding how to assign credit to decisions about hidden variables, there is a temporal credit assignment problem [86]. If, for example, a person wants to know how their behavior affects the gross national product, they need to know whether to correlate today's GNP with what they did yesterday or with what they did five years ago. In the iterative version of backpropagation (Section 6.7), temporal credit assignment is performed by explicitly computing the effect of each activity level on the eventual outcome. In reinforcement learning procedures, temporal credit assignment is typically performed by learning to associate "secondary" reinforcement values with the states that are intermediate in time between the action and the external reinforcement. One important idea is to make the weighted average of the reinforcement values of its successors, where the weightings reflect the conditional probabilities of the successors. In the limit, this causes the reinforcement value of each state to be equal to the expected reinforcement of its successor, and hence equal to the expected final reinforcement.[11] Sutton [87] explains why, in a stochastic system, it is typically more efficient to regress towards the reinforcement value of the next state rather than the reinforcement value of the final outcome. Barto, Sutton and Anderson [15] have demonstrated the usefulness of this type of procedure for learning with delayed reinforcement.

### 11.2. The $A_{R-P}$ procedure

One obvious way of mapping results from learning automata theory onto connectionist networks is to treat each unit as an automaton and to treat the states it adopts as its actions. Barto and Anandan [14] describe a learning procedure of this kind called "associative reward-penalty," or $A_{R-P}$ which uses stochastic units like those in a Boltzmann machine (see (10)). They prove that if the input vectors are linearly independent and the network only contains one unit, $A_{R-P}$ finds the optimal values of the weights. They also show empirically that if the same procedure is applied in a network of such units, the hidden units develop useful representations. Williams [101] has shown that a limiting case of the $A_{R-P}$ procedure performs stochastic gradient ascent in expected reinforcement.

### 11.3. Achieving global optimality by reinforcement learning

Thatachar and Sastry [91] use a different mapping between automata and connectionist networks. Each *connection* is treated as an automaton and the weight values that it takes on are its actions. On each trial, each connection chooses a weight (from a discrete set of alternatives) and then the network maps an input vector into an output vector and receives positive reinforcement if the output is correct. They present a learning procedure for updating the probabilities of choosing particular weight values. If the probabilities are changed slowly enough, the procedure is guaranteed to converge on the globally optimal combination of weights, even if the network has hidden layers. Unfortunately their procedure requires exponential space because it involves

storing and updating a table of estimated expected reinforcements that contains one entry for every combination of weights.

### 11.4. The relative payoff procedure

If we are content to reach a local optimum, it is possible to use a very simple learning procedure that uses yet another way of mapping automata onto connectionist networks. Each connection is treated as a stochastic switch that has a certain probability of being closed at any moment [66]. If the switch is open, the "postsynaptic" unit receives an input of 0 along that connection, but if the switch is closed it transmits the state of the "presynaptic" unit. A real synapse can be modeled as a set of these stochastic switches arranged in parallel. Each unit computes some fixed function of the vector of inputs that it receives on its incoming connections. Learning involves altering the switch probabilities to maximize the expected reinforcement signal.

A learning procedure called $L_{R-I}$ can be applied in such networks. It is only guaranteed to find a local optimum of the expected reinforcement, but it is very simple to implement. A "trial" consists of four stages:

(1) Set the switch configuration. For each switch in the network, decide whether it is open or closed on this trial using the current switch probability. The decisions are made independently for all the switches.

(2) Run the network with this switch configuration. There are no constraints on the connectivity so cycles are allowed, and the units can also receive external inputs at any time. The constraint on the external inputs is that the probability distribution over patterns of external input must be stationary.

(3) Compute the reinforcement signal. This can be any nonnegative, stationary function of the behavior of the network and of the external input it received during the trial.

(4) Update the switch probabilities. For each switch that was closed during the trial, we increment its probability by $\varepsilon R(1-p)$, where $R$ is the reinforcement produced by the trial, $p$ is the switch probability and $\varepsilon$ is a small coefficient. For each switch that was open, we decrement its probability by $\varepsilon Rp$.

If $\varepsilon$ is sufficiently small this procedure stochastically approximates hill climbing in expected reinforcement. The "batch" version of the procedure involves observing the reinforcement signal over a large number of trials before updating the switch probabilities. If a sufficient number of trials are observed, the following "relative payoff" update procedure always increases expected reinforcement (or leaves it unchanged): Change the switch probability to be equal to the fraction of the total reinforcement received when the switch was closed. This can cause large changes in the probabilities, and I know of no proof that it hill-climbs in expected reinforcement, but in practice it always works. The direction of the jump in switch probability space caused by the

---

[11] There may also be a "tax" imposed for failing to achieve the external reinforcement quickly. This can be implemented by reducing the reinforcement value each time it is regressed to an earlier state.

batch version of the procedure is the same as the expected direction of the small change in switch probabilities caused by the "online" version.

A variation of the relative payoff procedure can be used if the goal is to make the "responses" of a network match some desired probability distribution rather than maximize expected reinforcement. We simply define the reinforcement signal to be the desired probability of a response divided by the network's current probability of producing that response. If a sufficient number of trials are made before updating the switch probabilities, it can be shown (Larry Gillick and Jim Baker, personal communication) that this procedure is guaranteed to decrease an information-theoretic measure of the difference between the desired probability distribution over responses and the actual probability distribution. The measure is actually the $G$ measure described in (11) and the proof is an adaptation of the proof of the EM procedure [22].

## 11.5. Genetic algorithms

Holland and his co-workers [21, 48] have investigated a class of learning procedures which they call "genetic algorithms" because they are explicitly inspired by an analogy with evolution. Genetic algorithms operate on a population of individuals to produce a better adapted population. In the simplest case, each individual member of the population is a binary vector, and the two possible values of each component are analogous to two alternative versions (alleles) of a gene. There is a fitness function which assigns a real-valued fitness to each individual and the aim of the "learning" is to raise the average fitness of the population. New individuals are produced by choosing two existing individuals as parents (with a bias towards individuals of higher than average fitness) and copying some component values from one parent and some from the other. Holland [48] has shown that for a large class of fitness functions, this is an effective way of discovering individuals that have high fitness.

## 11.6. Genetic learning and the relative payoff rule

If an entire generation of individuals is simultaneously replaced by a generation of their offspring, genetic learning has a close relationship to the batch form of the $L_{R-I}$ procedure described in Section 11.4. This is most easily understood by starting with a particularly simple version of genetic learning in which every individual in generation $t+1$ has many different parents in generation $t$. Candidate individuals for generation $t+1$ are generated from the existing individuals in generation $t$ in the following way: To decide the value of the $i$th component of a candidate, we randomly choose one of the individuals in generation $t$ and copy the value of its $i$th component. So the probability that the $i$th component of a candidate has a particular value is simply the relative frequency of that value in generation $t$. A selection process then operates on

the candidates: Some are kept to form generation $t+1$ and others are discarded. The fitness of a candidate is simply the probability that it is not discarded by the selection process. Candidates that are kept can be considered to have received a reinforcement of 1 and candidates that are discarded receive a reinforcement of 0. After selection, the probability that the $i$th component has a particular value is equal to the fraction of the successful candidates that have that value. This is exactly the relative payoff rule described in Section 11.4. The probabilities it operates on are the relative frequencies of alleles in the population instead of switch probabilities.

If the value of every component is determined by an independently chosen parent, information about the correlations between the values of different components is lost when generation $t+1$ is produced from generation $t$. If, however, we use just two parents we maximize the tendency for the pairwise and higher-order correlations to be preserved. This tendency is further increased if components whose correlations are important are near one another and the values of nearby components are normally taken from the same parent. So a population of individuals can effectively represent the probabilities of small combinations of component values as well as the probabilities of individual values. Genetic learning works well when the fitness of an individual is determined by these small combinations, which Holland calls critical schemas.

## 11.7. Iterated genetic hill climbing

It is possible to combine genetic learning with gradient descent (or hill climbing) to get a hybrid learning procedure called "iterated genetic hill climbing" or "IGH" that works better than either learning procedure alone [1, 17]. IGH is as a form of multiple restart hill climbing in which the starting points, instead of being chosen at random, are chosen by "mating" previously discovered local optima. Alternatively, it can be viewed as genetic learning in which each new individual is allowed to perform hill climbing in the fitness function before being evaluated and added to the population. Ackley [1] shows that a stochastic variation of IGH can be implemented in a connectionist network that is trying to learn which output vector produces a high enough payoff to satisfy some external criterion.

## 12. Discussion

This review has focused on a small number of recent connectionist learning procedures. There are many other interesting procedures which have been omitted [24, 26, 34, 35, 47, 54, 94]. In particular, there has been no discussion of a large class of procedures which dynamically allocate new units instead of simply adjusting the weights in a fixed architecture. Rather than attempting to cover all of these I conclude by discussing two major problems that plague most of the procedures I have described.

## 12.1. Generalization

A major goal of connectionist learning is to produce networks that generalize correctly to new cases after training on a sufficiently large set of typical cases from some domain. In much of the research, there is no formal definition of what it means to generalize correctly. The network is trained on examples from a domain that the experimenter understands (like the family relationships described in Section 6) and it is judged to generalize correctly if its generalizations agree with those of the experimenter. This is sufficient as an informal demonstration that the network can indeed perform nontrivial generalization, but it gives little insight into the reasons why the generalizations of the network and the experimenter agree, and so it does not allow predictions to be made about when networks will generalize correctly and when they will fail.

What is needed is a formal theory of what it means to generalize correctly. One approach that has been used in studying the induction of grammars is to define a hypothesis space of possible grammars, and to show that with enough training cases the system will converge on the correct grammar with probability 1 [8]. Valiant [93] has recently introduced a rather more subtle criterion of success in order to distinguish classes of boolean function that can be induced from examples in polynomial time from classes that require exponential time. He assumes that the hypothesis space is known in advance and he allows the training cases to be selected according to *any* stationary distribution but insists that the same distribution be used to generate the test cases. The induced function is considered to be good enough if it differs from the true function on less than a small fraction, $1/h$, of the test cases. A class of boolean functions is considered to be learnable in polynomial time if, for any choice of $h$, there is a probability of at least $(1 - 1/h)$ that the induced function is good enough after a number of training examples that is polynomial in both $h$ and the number of arguments of the boolean function. Using this definition, Valiant has succeeded in showing that several interesting subclasses of boolean function are learnable in polynomial time. Our understanding of other connectionist learning procedures would be considerably improved if we could derive similar results that were as robust against variations in the distribution of the training examples.

The work on inducing grammars or boolean functions may not provide an appropriate framework for studying systems that learn inherently stochastic functions, but the general idea of starting with a hypothesis space of possible functions carries over. A widely used statistical approach involves maximizing the a posteriori likelihood of the model (i.e. the function) given the data. If the data really is generated by a function in the hypothesis space and if the amount of information in the training data greatly exceeds the amount of information required to specify a point in the hypothesis space, the maximum likelihood function is very probably the correct one, so the network will then generalize correctly. Some connectionist learning schemes (e.g. the Boltzmann machine learning procedure) can be made to fit this approach exactly. If a Boltzmann machine is trained with much more data than there are weights in the machine, and if it really does find the global minimum of $G$, and if the correct answer lies in the hypothesis space (which is defined by the architecture of the machine),[12] then there is every reason to suppose that it will generalize correctly, even if it has only been trained on a small fraction of the *possible* cases. Unfortunately, this kind of guarantee is of little use for practical problems where we usually know in advance that the "true" model does not lie in the hypothesis space of the network. What needs to be shown is that the best available point within the hypothesis space (even though it is not a perfect model) will also generalize well to test cases.

A simple thought experiment shows that the "correct" generalization from a set of training cases, however it is defined, must depend on how the input and output vectors are encoded. Consider a mapping, $M_O$, from entire input vectors onto entire output vectors. If we introduce a precoding stage that uses $M_I$ and a postcoding stage that uses $M_O$ we can convert a network that generalizes in one way into a network that generalizes in any other way we choose simply by choosing $M_I$ and $M_O$ appropriately.

## 12.2. Practical methods of improving generalization

One very useful method of improving the generalization of many connectionist learning procedures is to introduce an extra term into the error function. This term penalizes large weights and it can be viewed as a way of building in an a priori bias is favor of simple models (i.e. models in which there are not too many strong interactions between the variables). If the extra term is the sum of the squares of the weights, its derivative corresponds to "weight decay"—each weight continually decays towards zero by an amount proportional to its magnitude. When the learning has equilibrated, the magnitude of a weight is equal to its error derivative because this error derivative balances the weight decay. This often makes it easier to interpret the weights. Weight decay tends to prevent a network from using table lookup and forces it to discover regularities in the training data. In a simple linear network without hidden units, weight decay can be used to find the weight matrix that minimizes the effect of adding zero-mean, uncorrelated noise to the input units [60].

Another useful method is to impose equality constraints between weights that encode symmetries in the task. In solving any practical problem, it is

[12] One popular idea is that evolution implicitly chooses an appropriate hypothesis space by constraining the architecture of the network and learning then identifies the most likely hypothesis within this space. How evolution arrives at sensible hypothesis spaces in reasonable time is usually unspecified. The evolutionary search for good architectures may actually be guided by learning [43].

wasteful to make the network learn information that is known in advance. If possible, this information should be encoded by the architecture or the initial weights so that the training data can be used to learn aspects of the task that we do not already know how to model.

## 12.3. The speed of learning

Most existing connectionist learning procedures are slow, particularly procedures that construct complicated internal representations. One way to speed them up is to use optimization methods such as recursive least squares that converge faster. If the second derivatives can be computed or estimated they can be used to pick a direction for the weight change vector that yields faster convergence than the direction of steepest descent [71]. It remains to be seen how well such methods work for the error surfaces generated by multi-layer networks learning complex tasks.

A second method of speeding up learning is to use dedicated hardware for each connection and to map the inner-loop operations into analog instead of digital hardware. As Alspector and Allen [3] have demonstrated, the speed of one particular learning procedure can be increased by a factor of about a million if we combine these techniques. This significantly increases our ability to explore the behavior of relatively small systems, but it is not a panacea. By using silicon in a different way we typically gain a *large* but constant factor (optical techniques may eventually yield a *huge* constant factor), and by dedicating a processor to each of the $N$ connections we gain at most a factor of $N$ in time at the cost of at least a factor of $N$ in space. For a learning procedure with a time complexity of, say, $O(N \log N)$ a speed up of $N$ makes a very big difference. For a procedure with a complexity of, say, $O(N^3)$ alternative technologies and parallelism will help significantly for small systems, but not for large ones. [13]

## 12.4. Hardware modularity

One of the best and commonest ways of fighting complexity is to introduce a modular, hierarchical structure in which different modules are only loosely coupled [85]. Pearl [72] has shown that if the interactions between a set of probabilistic variables are constrained to form a tree structure, there are efficient parallel methods for estimating the interactions between "hidden" variables. The leaves of the tree are the observables and the higher-level nodes are hidden. The probability distribution for each variable is constrained by the values of its immediate parents in the tree. Pearl shows that these conditional probabilities can be recovered in time $O(N \log N)$ from the pairwise correlations between the values of the leaves of the tree. Remarkably, it is also possible to recover the tree structure itself in the same time.

[13] Tsotsos [92] makes similar arguments in a discussion of the space complexity of vision.

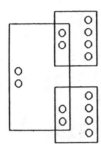

Fig. 12. The lower-level variables of a high-level module are the higher-level variables of several low-level modules.

Self-supervised backpropagation (see Section 6.9) was originally designed to allow efficient bottom-up learning in domains where there is hierarchical modular structure. Consider, for example, an ensemble of input vectors that are generated in the following modular way: Each module has a few high-level variables whose values help to constrain the values of a larger number of low-level variables. The low-level variables of each module are partitioned into several sets, and each set is identified with the high-level variables of a lower module as shown in Fig. 12.

Now suppose that we treat the values of all the low-level variables of the leaf modules as a single input vector. Given a sufficiently large ensemble of input vectors and an "innate" knowledge of the architecture of the generator, it should be possible to recover the underlying structure by using self-supervised backpropagation to learn compact codes for the low-level variables of each leaf module. It is possible to learn codes for all the lowest-level modules in parallel. Once this has been done, the network can learn codes at the next level up the hierarchy. The time taken to learn the whole hierarchical structure (given parallel hardware) is just proportional to the depth of the tree and hence it is $O(\log N)$ where $N$ is the size of the input vector. An improvement on this strictly bottom-up scheme is described by Ballard [11]. He shows why it is helpful to allow top-down influences from more abstract representations to less abstract ones, and presents a working simulation.

## 12.5. Other types of modularity

There are several other helpful types of modularity that do not necessarily map so directly onto modular hardware but are nevertheless important for fast learning and good generalization. Consider a system which solves hard problems by creating its own subgoals. Once a subgoal has been created, the system can learn how best to satisfy it and this learning can be useful (on other occasions) even if it was a mistake to create that subgoal on this particular occasion. So the assignment of credit to the decision to create a subgoal can be decoupled from the assignment of credit to the actions taken to achieve the subgoal. Since the ability to achieve the subgoals can be learned separately from the knowledge about when they are appropriate, a system can use achievable subgoals as building blocks for more complex procedures. This avoids the problem of learning the complex procedures from scratch. It may also constrain the way in which the complex procedures will be generalized to new cases, because the knowledge about how to achieve each subgoal may already include knowledge about how to cope with variations. By using subgoals we can increase modularity and improve generalization even in systems which use the very same hardware for solving the subgoal as was used for solving the higher-level goal. Using subgoals, it may even be possible to develop reasonably fast reinforcement learning procedures for large systems.

There is another type of relationship between easy and hard tasks that can facilitate learning. Sometimes a hard task can be decomposed into a set of easier constituents, but other times a hard task may just be a version of an easier task that requires finer discrimination. For example, throwing a ball in the general direction of another person is much easier than throwing it through a hoop, and a good way to train a system to throw it through a hoop is to start by training it to throw in the right general direction. This relation between easy and hard tasks is used extensively in "shaping" the behavior of animals and should also be useful for connectionist networks (particularly those that use reinforcement learning). It resembles the use of multi-resolution techniques to speed up search in computer vision [89]. Having learned the coarse task, the weights should be close to a point in weight space where minor adjustments can tune them to perform the finer task.

One application where this technique should be helpful is in learning filters that discriminate between very similar sounds. The approximate shapes of the filters can be learned using spectrograms that have low resolution in time and frequency, and then the resolution can be increased to allow the filters to resolve fine details. By introducing a "regularization" term that penalizes filters which have very different weights for adjacent cells in the high resolution spectrogram, it may be possible to allow filters to "attend" to fine detail when necessary without incurring the cost of estimating all the weights from scratch. The regularization term encodes prior knowledge that good filters should generally be smooth and so it reduces the amount of information that must be extracted from the training data.

## 12.6. Conclusion

There are now many different connectionist learning procedures that can construct appropriate internal representations in small domains, and it is likely that many more variations will be discovered in the next few years. Major new advances can be expected on a number of fronts: Techniques for making the learning time scale better may be developed; attempts to apply connectionist procedures to difficult tasks like speech recognition may actually succeed; new technologies may make it possible to simulate much larger networks; and finally the computational insights gained from studying connectionist systems may prove useful in interpreting the behavior of real neural networks.

## ACKNOWLEDGMENT

This research was funded by grant IS8520359 from the National Science Foundation and by contract N00014-86-K-00167 from the Office of Naval Research. I thank Dana Ballard, Andrew Barto, David Rumelhart, Terry Sejnowski, and the members of the Carnegie-Mellon Boltzmann Group for many helpful discussions. Geoffrey Hinton is a fellow of the Canadian Institute for Advanced Research.

## REFERENCES

1. Ackley, D.H., Stochastic iterated genetic hill-climbing, Ph.D. Thesis, Carnegie-Mellon University, Pittsburgh, PA (1987).
2. Ackley, D.H., Hinton, G.E. and Sejnowski, T.J., A learning algorithm for Boltzmann machines, *Cognitive Sci.* 9 (1985) 147-169.
3. Alspector, J. and Allen, R.B., A neuromorphic VLSI learning system, in: P. Loseleben (Ed.), *Advanced Research in VLSI: Proceedings of the 1987 Stanford Conference* (MIT Press, Cambridge, MA, 1987).
4. Amari, S.-I., Field theory of self-organizing neural nets, *IEEE Trans. Syst. Man Cybern.* 13 (1983) 741-748.
5. Amari, S.-I., A theory of adaptive pattern classifiers, *IEEE Trans. Electron. Comput.* 16 (1967) 299-307.
6. Anderson, J.A. and Hinton, G.E., Models of information processing in the brain, in: G.E. Hinton and J.A. Anderson (Eds.), *Parallel Models of Associative Memory* (Erlbaum, Hillsdale, NJ, 1981).
7. Anderson, J.A. and Mozer, M.C., Categorization and selective neurons, in: G.E. Hinton and J.A. Anderson (Eds.), *Parallel Models of Associative Memory* (Erlbaum, Hillsdale, NJ, 1981).
8. Angluin, D. and Smith, C.H., Inductive inference: Theory and methods, *Comput. Surv.* 15 (1983) 237-269.
9. Bahl, L.R., Jelinek, F. and Mercer, R.L., A maximum likelihood approach to continuous speech recognition, *IEEE Trans. Pattern Anal. Mach. Intell.* 5 (1983) 179-190.
10. Ballard, D.H., Cortical connections and parallel processing: Structure and function, *Behav. Brain Sci.* 9 (1986) 67-120.
11. Ballard, D.H., Modular learning in neural networks, in: *Proceedings AAAI-87*, Seattle, WA (1987) 279-284.
12. Ballard, D.H., Hinton, G.E. and Sejnowski, T.J., Parallel visual computation, *Nature* 306 (1983) 21-26.
13. Barlow, H.B., Single units and sensation: A neuron doctrine for perceptual psychology? *Perception* 1 (1972) 371-394.
14. Barto, A.G. and Anandan, P., Pattern recognizing stochastic learning automata, *IEEE Trans. Syst. Man Cybern.* 15 (1985) 360-375.
15. Barto, A.G., Sutton, R.S. and Anderson, C.W., Neuronlike elements that solve difficult learning control problems, *IEEE Trans. Syst. Man Cybern.* 13 (1983).
16. Bienenstock, E.L., Cooper, L.N. and Munro, P.W., Theory for the development of neuron selectivity: Orientation specificity and binocular interaction in visual cortex, *J. Neurosci.* 2 (1982) 32-48.
17. Brady, R.M., Optimization strategies gleaned from biological evolution, *Nature* 317 (1985) 804-806.
18. Cooper, L.N., Liberman, F. and Oja, E., A theory for the acquisition and loss of neuron specificity in visual cortex, *Biol. Cybern.* 33 (1979) 9-28.

19. Cottrell, G.W., Munro, P. and Zipser, D., Learning internal representations from gray-scale images: An example of extensional programming, in: *Proceedings Ninth Annual Conference of the Cognitive Science Society* Seattle, WA (1987) 461–473.

20. Crick, F. and Mitchison, G., The function of dream sleep, *Nature* 304 (1983) 111–114.

21. Davis, L. (Ed.) *Genetic Algorithms and Simulated Annealing* (Pitman, London, 1987).

22. Dempster, A.P., Laird, N.M. and Rubin, D.B., Maximum likelihood from incomplete data via the EM algorithm, *Proc. Roy. Stat. Soc.* (1976) 1–38.

23. Durbin, R. and Willshaw, D., The elastic net method: An analogue approach to the traveling salesman problem, *Nature* 326 (1987) 689–691.

24. Edelman, G.M. and Reeke, G.N., Selective networks capable of representative transformations, limited generalizations, and associative memory, *Proc. Nat. Acad. Sci. USA* 79 (1982) 2091–2095.

25. Elman, J.L. and Zipser, D., Discovering the hidden structure of speech, Tech. Rept. No. 8701, Institute for Cognitive Science, University of California, San Diego, CA (1987).

26. Feldman, J.A., Dynamic connections in neural networks, *Biol. Cybern.* 46 (1982) 27–39.

27. Feldman, J.A., Neural representation of conceptual knowledge, Tech. Rept. TR189, Department of Computer Science, University of Rochester, Rochester, NY (1986).

28. Feldman, J.A. and Ballard, D.H., Connectionist models and their properties, *Cognitive Sci.* 6 (1982) 205–254.

29. Fukushima, K., Cognitron: A self-organizing multilayered neural network, *Biol. Cybern.* 20 (1975) 121–136.

30. Fukushima, K. and Miyake, S., Neocognitron: A new algorithm for pattern recognition tolerant of deformations and shifts in position, *Pattern Recogn.* 15 (1982) 455–469.

31. Geman, S. and Geman, D., Stochastic relaxation, Gibbs distributions, and the Bayesian restoration of images, *IEEE Trans. Pattern Anal. Mach. Intell.* 6 (1984) 721–741.

32. Golden, R.M., A unified framework for connectionist systems, Manuscript, Learning Research and Development Center, University of Pittsburgh, Pittsburgh, PA (1987).

33. Grossberg, S., Adaptive pattern classification and universal recoding, I: Parallel development and coding of neural feature detectors, *Biol. Cybern.* 23 (1976) 121–134.

34. Grossberg, S., How does the brain build a cognitive code? *Psychol. Rev.* 87 (1980) 1–51.

35. Hampson, S.E. and Volper, D.J., Disjunctive models of boolean category learning, *Biol. Cybern.* 55 (1987) 1–17.

36. Hebb, D.O., *The Organization of Behavior* (Wiley, New York, 1949).

37. Hinton, G.E., Implementing semantic networks in parallel hardware, in: G.E. Hinton and J.A. Anderson (Eds.), *Parallel Models of Associative Memory* (Erlbaum, Hillsdale, NJ, 1981).

38. Hinton, G.E., Learning distributed representations of concepts, in: *Proceedings Eighth Annual Conference of the Cognitive Science Society,* Amherst, MA (1986).

39. Hinton, G.E., Learning translation invariant recognition in a massively parallel network, in: *PARLE: Parallel Architectures and Languages Europe* 1 (Springer, Berlin, 1987) 1–14.

40. Hinton, G.E. and Anderson J.A., (Eds.), *Parallel Models of Associative Memory* (Erlbaum, Hillsdale, NJ, 1981).

41. Hinton, G.E. and McClelland, J.L., Learning representations by recirculation, in: D.Z. Anderson (Ed.), *Neural Information Processing Systems* (American Institute of Physics, New York, 1988).

42. Hinton, G.E., McClelland, J.L. and Rumelhart, D.E., Distributed representations, in: D.E. Rumelhart, J.L. McClelland and the PDP Research Group (Eds.), *Parallel Distributed Processing: Explorations in the Microstructure of Cognition, I: Foundations* (MIT Press, Cambridge, MA, 1986).

43. Hinton, G.E. and Nowlan, S.J., How learning can guide evolution, *Complex Syst.* 1 (1987) 495–502.

44. Hinton, G.E. and Plaut, D.C., Using fast weights to deblur old memories, in: *Proceedings Ninth Annual Conference of the Cognitive Science Society,* Seattle, WA (1987).

45. Hinton, G.E. and Sejnowski, T.J., Optimal perceptual inference, in: *Proceedings IEEE Conference on Computer Vision and Pattern Recognition,* Washington, DC (1983) 448–453.

46. Hinton, G.E. and Sejnowski, T.J., Learning and relearning in Boltzmann machines, in: D.E. Rumelhart, J.L. McClelland and the PDP Research Group (Eds.), *Parallel Distributed Processing: Explorations in the Microstructure of Cognition, I: Foundations* (MIT Press, Cambridge, MA, 1986).

47. Hogg, T. and Huberman, B.A., Understanding biological computation: Reliable learning and recognition, *Proc. Nat. Acad. Sci. USA* 81 (1984) 6871–6875.

48. Holland, J.H., *Adaptation in Natural and Artificial Systems* (University of Michigan Press, Ann Arbor, MI, 1975).

49. Hopfield, J.J., Neural networks and physical systems with emergent collective computational abilities *Proc. Nat. Acad. Sci. USA* 79 (1982) 2554–2558.

50. Hopfield, J.J., Feinstein, D.I. and Palmer, R.G., "Unlearning" has a stabilizing effect in collective memories, *Nature* 304 (1983).

51. Hopfield, J.J. and Tank, D.W., "Neural" computation of decisions in optimization problems, *Biol. Cybern.* 52 (1985) 141–152.

52. Hummel, R.A. and Zucker, S.W., On the foundations of relaxation labeling processes, *IEEE Trans. Pattern Anal. Mach. Intell.* 5 (1983) 267–287.

53. Judd, J.S., Complexity of connectionist learning with various node functions, COINS Tech. Rept. 87-60, University of Amherst, Amherst, MA (1987).

54. Kerszberg, M. and Bergman, A., The evolution of data processing abilities in competing automata, in: *Proceedings Conference on Computer Simulation in Brain Science,* Copenhagen, Denmark (1986).

55. Kirkpatrick, S., Gelatt, C.D. and Vecchi, M.P., Optimization by simulated annealing, *Science* 220 (1983) 671–680.

56. Kohonen, T., *Associative Memory: A System-Theoretical Approach* (Springer, Berlin, 1977).

57. Kohonen, T., Clustering, taxonomy, and topological maps of patterns, in: *Proceedings Sixth International Conference on Pattern Recognition,* Munich, F.R.G. (1982).

58. Lang, K.J., Connectionist speech recognition. Thesis proposal, Carnegie-Mellon University, Pittsburgh, PA (1987).

59. Le Cun, Y., A learning scheme for asymmetric threshold networks, in: *Proceedings Cognitiva 85,* Paris, France (1985) 599–604.

60. Le Cun, Y., Modèles connexionnistes de l'apprentissage, Ph.D. Thesis, Université Pierre et Marie Curie, Paris, France (1987).

61. Linsker, R., From basic network principles to neural architecture: Emergence of spatial opponent cells, *Proc. Nat. Acad. Sci. USA* 83 (1986) 7508–7512.

62. Linsker, R., From basic network principles to neural architecture: Emergence of orientation-selective cells, *Proc. Nat. Acad. Sci. USA* 83 (1986) 8390–8394.

63. Linsker, R., From basic network principles to neural architecture: Emergence of orientation columns, *Proc. Nat. Acad. Sci. USA* 83 (1986) 8779–8783.

64. Linsker, R., Development of feature-analyzing cells and their columnar organization in a layered self-adaptive network, in: R. Cotterill (Ed.), *Computer Simulation in Brain Science* (Cambridge University Press, Cambridge, 1987).

65. Marroquin, J.L., Probabilistic solution of inverse problems, Ph.D. Thesis, MIT, Cambridge, MA (1985).

66. Minsky, M.L., Theory of neural-analog reinforcement systems and its application to the brain-rnodel problem, Ph.D. Dissertation, Princeton University, Princeton, NJ (1954).

67. Minsky, M.L., Plain talk about neurodevelopmental epistemology, in: *Proceedings IJCAI-77,* Cambridge, MA (1977) 1083–1092.

68. Minsky, M.L. and Papert, S., *Perceptrons* (MIT Press, Cambridge, MA, 1969).

69. Munro, P.W., A dual back-propagation scheme for scalar reinforcement learning, in: *Proceedings Ninth Annual Conference of the Cognitive Science Society,* Seattle, WA (1987).

70. Parker, D.B., Learning-logic, Tech. Rept. TR-47, Sloan School of Management, MIT, Cambridge, MA (1985).

71. Parker, D.B., Second order back-propagation: An optimal adaptive algorithm for any adaptive network, Unpublished manuscript (1987).

72. Pearl, J., Fusion, propagation, and structuring in belief networks, Artificial Intelligence 29 (1986) 241-288.

73. Pearlmutter, B.A. and Hinton, G.E., G-maximization: An unsupervised learning procedure for discovering regularities, in: J.S. Denker (Ed.), Neural Networks for Computing: American Institute of Physics Conference Proceedings 151 (American Institute of Physics, New York, 1986) 333-338.

74. Peterson, C. and Anderson, J.R., A mean field theory learning algorithm for neural networks, MCC Tech. Rept. EI-259-87, Microelectronics and Computer Technology Corporation, Austin, TX (1987).

75. Plaut, D.C. and Hinton, G.E., Learning sets of filters using back-propagation, Comput. Speech Lang. 2 (1987) 36-61.

76. Prager, R., Harrison, T.D. and Fallside, F., Boltzmann machines for speech recognition, Comput. Speech Lang. 1 (1986) 1-20.

77. Rosenblatt, F., Principles of Neurodynamics (Spartan Books, New York, 1962).

78. Rumelhart, D.E. and McClelland, J.L., On the acquisition of the past tense in English, in: J.L. McClelland, D.E. Rumelhart and the PDP Research Group (Eds.), Parallel Distributed Processing: Explorations in the Microstructure of Cognition, II: Applications (MIT Press, Cambridge, MA, 1986).

79. Rumelhart, D.E., McClelland, J.L. and the PDP Research Group (Eds.), Parallel Distributed Processing: Explorations in the Microstructure of Cognition, I: Foundations (MIT Press, Cambridge, MA, 1986).

80. Rumelhart, D.E., Hinton, G.E. and Williams, R.J., Learning internal representations by back-propagating errors, Nature 323 (1986) 533-536.

81. Rumelhart, D.E., Hinton, G.E. and Williams, R.J., Learning internal representations by error propagation, in: D.E. Rumelhart, J.L. McClelland and the PDP Research Group (Eds.), Parallel Distribued Processing: Explorations in the Microstructure of Cognition, I: Foundations (MIT Press, Cambridge, MA, 1986).

82. Rumelhart, D.E. and Zipser, D., Competitive learning, Cognitive Sci. 9 (1985) 75-112.

83. Saund, E., Abstraction and representation of continuous variables in connectionist networks, in: Proceedings AAAI-86, Philadelphia, PA (1986) 638-644.

84. Sejnowski, T.J. and Rosenberg, C.R., Parallel networks that learn to pronounce English text, Complex Syst. 1 (1987) 145-168.

85. Simon, H.A., The Sciences of the Artificial (MIT Press, Cambridge, MA, 1969).

86. Sutton, R.S., Temporal credit assignment in reinforcement learning, Ph.D. Thesis, COINS Tech. Rept. 84-02, University of Massachusetts, Amherst, MA (1984).

87. Sutton, R.S., Learning to predict by the method of temporal differences, Tech. Rept. TR87-509.1, GTE Laboratories, Waltham, MA (1987).

88. Tank, D.W. and Hopfield, J.J., Neural computation by concentrating information in time, Proc. Nat. Acad. Sci. USA 84 (1987) 1896-1900.

89. Terzopoulos, D., Multiresolution computation of visible surface representations., Ph.D. Dissertation, Department of Electrical Engineering and Computer Science, MIT, Cambridge MA (1984).

90. Tesauro, G., Scaling relationships in back-propagation learning: Dependence on training set size, Complex Syst. 2 (1987) 367-372.

91. Thatachar, M.A.L. and Sastry, P.S., Learning optimal discriminant functions through a cooperative game of automata, Tech. Rept. EE/64/1985, Department of Electrical Engineering, Indian Institute of Science, Bangalore, India (1985).

92. Tsotsos, J.K., A "complexity level" analysis of vision, in: Proceedings First International Conference on Computer Vision, London (1987) 346-355.

93. Valiant, L.G., A theory of the learnable, Commun. ACM 27 (1984) 1134-1142.

94. Volper, D.J. and Hampson, S.E., Connectionist models of boolean category representation, Biol. Cybern. 54 (1986) 393-406.

95. von der Malsburg, C., Self-organization of orientation sensitive cells in striate cortex, Kybernetik 14 (1973) 85-100.

96. von der Malsburg, C., The correlation theory of brain function. Internal Rept. 81-2, Department of Neurobiology, Max-Plank Institute for Biophysical Chemistry, Göttingen, F.R.G. (1981).

97. Waibel, A., Hanazawa, T., Hinton, G., Shikano, K. and Lang, K., Phoneme recognition using time-delay neural networks, Tech. Rept. TR-1-0006, ATR Interpreting Telephony Research Laboratories, Japan (1987).

98. Werbos, P.J., Beyond regression: New tools for prediction and analysis in the behavioral sciences, Ph.D. Thesis, Harvard University, Cambridge, MA (1974).

99. Widrow, B. and Hoff, M.E., Adaptive switching circuits, in: IRE WESCON Conv. Record 4 (1960) 96-104.

100. Widrow, B. and Stearns, S.D., Adaptive Signal Processing (Prentice-Hall, Englewood Cliffs, NJ, 1985).

101. Williams, R.J., Reinforcement learning in connectionist networks: A mathematical analysis, Tech. Rept. Institute for Cognitive Science, University of California San Diego, La Jolla, CA (1986).

102. Willshaw, D., Holography, associative memory, and inductive generalization, in: G.E. Hinton and J.A. Anderson (Eds.), Parallel Models of Associative Memory (Erlbaum, Hillsdale, NJ, 1981).

103. Willshaw, D.J. and von der Malsburg, C., A marker induction mechanism for the establishment of ordered neural mapping: Its application to the retino-tectal connections, Philos. Trans. Roy. Soc. Lond. B 287 (1979) 203-243.

# Automatic Knowledge Base Refinement for Classification Systems[†]

**Allen Ginsberg,\* Sholom M. Weiss and Peter Politakis\*\***

*Department of Computer Science, Rutgers University, New Brunswick, NJ 08903, U.S.A.*

Recommended by William Clancey

ABSTRACT

*An automated approach to knowledge base refinement, an important aspect of knowledge acquisition is described. Using empirical performance analysis, SEEK2 extends the capabilities of its predecessor rule refinement system, SEEK [17]. In this paper, the progress made since the original SEEK program is described: (a) SEEK2 works with a more general class of knowledge bases than SEEK. (b) SEEK2 has an automatic refinement capability, it can perform many of the basic tasks involved in knowledge base refinement without human interaction. (c) a metalanguage for knowledge base refinement has been specified which describes knowledge about the refinement process. Methods for estimating the expected gain in performance for a refined knowledge base and prospective test cases are described and some results are reported. An approach to justifying refinement heuristics is discussed.*

## 1. Knowledge Acquisition and the Knowledge Base Refinement Problem

The problem of summarizing an expert's domain knowledge in an *efficient* formal representation, the *knowledge acquisition problem*, is a key problem in artificial intelligence research. As a practical matter, the most difficult aspect of expert system development is usually the construction of the knowledge base. The rate of progress in developing useful expert systems is directly related to the rate at which expert knowledge bases can be assembled.

The knowledge acquisition problem can be divided into two phases. In phase one the knowledge engineer extracts an initial rough knowledge base from the

expert, rough in the sense that the overall level of performance of this knowledge base is usually not comparable to that of the expert. In the second phase, the *knowledge base refinement phase*, the initial knowledge base is progressively refined into a high performance knowledge base. In terms of a rule-based knowledge base, phase one involves the acquisition of entire rules, indeed entire sets of rules, for concluding various hypotheses. The refinement phase, on the other hand, is characterized not so much by the acquisition of entire rules but by the addition, deletion, and alteration of rule-components in certain rules in the existing knowledge base, in an attempt to improve the system's *empirical adequacy*, i.e., its ability to reach the correct conclusions in the problems it is intended to solve. Obviously the foregoing description of knowledge base construction is an idealization. In practice the line between these two phases is not as sharply drawn.[1]

A knowledge base refinement problem can be thought of as an optimization problem in which we start with a proposed general solution to a given set of domain problems and the goal is to refine it so that a superior solution is obtained. The proposed solution is a working knowledge base that is in need of minor adjustments, but not a major overhaul, i.e., one assumes that the rules given by the expert are basically sensible propositions concerning the problem domain. The refinements applied to the rules of this knowledge base must not only meet the obvious requirements of being syntactically and semantically admissible, they must also be conservative, in the sense that they tend to preserve, as far as possible, the expert's given version of the rules. Employing rule refinements that meet these requirements makes it more likely that the construction of a refined knowledge base will not simply be a matter of curve fitting, but will result in a knowledge base with genuinely improved empirical adequacy, that at the same time remains close to the actual knowledge of the expert. Thus when we speak of optimizing the performance of a knowledge base, we mean improving performance on sample case data as much as possible, subject to constraints of conservatism.

## 2. Related Work

In this section we briefly consider the relationship of this work to other work on classification systems in statistical pattern recognition, traditional empirical machine learning, and the more recent explanation-based machine learning techniques.

Statistical pattern recognition and empirical machine learning classification

---

[1] In this paper we limit our concern to knowledge bases that are structured collections of production rules. By the term expert system, we mean a *production rule based classification* expert system [1, 20] Furthermore we confine our attention to refinements of production rules that can be achieved as the result of the sequential application of certain generic refinement operations that are either generalization or specialization operations.

† This research was supported in part by the Division of Research Resources, National Institutes of Health, Public Health Service, Department of Health, Education, and Welfare, Grant P41 RR02230.

\* Present address: AT&T Bell Laboratories, Holmdel, NJ.

\*\* Present address: Digital Equipment Co., Hudson, MA.

*Artificial Intelligence* **35** (1988) 197–226
0004-3702/88/$3.50 © 1988, Elsevier Science Publishers B.V. (North-Holland)

This paper originally appeared in the journal, *Artificial Intelligence*, Vol. 35, No. 2, and is reprinted here with permission of the publisher, Elsevier, Amsterdam.

systems both learn from case data. Statistical techniques assume a statistical distribution or a mathematical formalism; empirical machine learning classifiers are characterized by relatively simple sets of rules with logical AND/OR operators. While machine learning approaches usually attempt to completely cover the sample cases, empirically derived estimates of error rates on new cases can be relatively large [13].

Designers of rule-based expert systems recognize the limits of learning directly from case data and rely on experts to provide summarizing rules of their experience. These rules can have intermediate hypotheses and sometimes heuristic procedures for combining uncertainty measures. Because these expert systems rely on knowledge and experience, they potentially can operate in relatively large dimensions, far exceeding what could be extracted from even representative sample cases. Thus, case data have been traditionally limited to validation tests for rule-based expert systems.

Our approach makes significant use of some of the key features of statistical pattern recognition work, namely, an emphasis on optimizing the *overall performance* of the classification system, and the use of disjoint sets of cases for training and testing [5]. Train and test techniques have been applied to rules that have been learned directly from sample case data [13]. In our work, we show how a system with a knowledge base acquired from experts can use case data for validation, estimation of error rates, and knowledge base refinement.

*Explanation-based* approaches to machine learning assume that it is possible to prove that an instance falls under a concept using a *domain theory* [15]. This proof may then be generalized to yield a general concept description. While there have been many variations on this basic idea [4, 9, 18], explanation-based approaches share one feature: they depend upon knowledge—the domain theory—over and above the known instances (cases), the primitive concepts of the domain, and the experiential rules that can be acquired from domain experts.

Our approach to knowledge base refinement is designed to be used in applications where such domain theories are either unknown, inherently uncertain or statistical in nature, too time-consuming to specify, or too complex to be useful given current technology. For such domains it is either impractical or simply impossible to design a refinement mechanism that generates refinements that are guaranteed to be correct or lead to an improvement in overall performance. This is why we employ a heuristic refinement generation procedure, and why we test a candidate refinement for its effect on the overall performance of the classification system. However, our approach is compatible with, and can be improved through, the use of a domain theory when additional knowledge is available (see Section 9).

Previous research on knowledge base refinement, in the sense defined here, has been limited. Refining a large scale knowledge base is clearly a complex undertaking. Related empirical machine learning work in concept learning has

concentrated on the learning of entire rules from case data and hierarchical descriptions [12], rather than the incremental refinement of rules acquired from a human expert. Because numerous expert systems are actively under development, in recent years there has been increased interest in immediate results to ease the knowledge acquisition task. While restricted to relatively simple knowledge bases and representations, a few papers have appeared on empirical refinement [11, 21]. Wilkins and Buchanan emphasize the need for a more complex form of analysis, similar to the optimization procedures used in SEEK2.

The form of empirical analysis that is described in this paper does not exclude other forms of analysis that are useful in knowledge acquisition. For example, systems that employ concepts and strategies for extracting domain knowledge via interaction with an expert have seen renewed interest among researchers [3, 6, 10]. In addition, researchers working on the Programmer's Apprentice have reported some progress in improving knowledge acquisition in programming tasks by combining algorithmic fragments stored in software libraries with intelligent editing facilities [19]. While these efforts may be viewed as alternative techniques for knowledge acquisition, they may also be viewed as complementary to an empirical approach to refinement.

## 3. The Basic Approach: Empirical Analysis of Rule Behavior Using Case Knowledge

### 3.1. Overview

In this section we briefly review the basic approach to knowledge base refinement taken by SEEK [17]—an approach that we have continued to employ in SEEK2. A fundamental assumption of this approach is that case knowledge can be used in an empirical analysis of rule behavior in order to generate *plausible* suggestions for rule refinement (see Fig. 1). Case knowledge is given in the form of a data base of cases with known conclusions, i.e., each case contains not only a record of the case observations but also a record of the expert's conclusion for the case. Empirical analysis of rule behavior involves gathering certain statistics concerning rule behavior with respect to the data base of cases; suggestions for rule refinements are generated by the application of refinement heuristics that relate the statistical behavior and structural properties of rules to appropriate classes of rule refinements. We will shortly explicate the nature of the statistical evidence gathered and give an example of these heuristics.

We have said that the goal of our heuristic analysis is to suggest plausible refinements. This is a term that could have a number of legitimate meanings in this context (for example, see [18]), and therefore, we need to clarify exactly what we mean. For us plausibility is a three-place relation holding among a contemplated refinement $\gamma$, a set of misdiagnosed cases $M$, and a body of

ing pattern of the rules in the knowledge base, serves to constrain the refinement generation process. If our chosen endpoint is Systemic Lupus, for example, we begin by applying the heuristics to all the rules in the knowledge base that directly conclude Systemic Lupus, i.e., rules whose right-hand side is this conclusion. A rule that directly concludes some endpoint will, in general, have components on its left-hand side that themselves are the conclusions of some other rules; such components are called *intermediate hypotheses*. The rules that conclude intermediate hypotheses may themselves include components that are intermediate hypotheses. Whenever the refinement heuristics suggest modifying an intermediate hypothesis IH, such as deleting it from some rule, the rules that conclude IH are thereby implicated as candidates for refinement.

### 3.2. Some statistics and a heuristic

At the highest level, many refinements of production rules may be thought of as falling in one of two possible classes: *generalizations* and *specializations* [14, 17]. By a rule generalization we mean any modification to a rule that makes it easier for the rule's conclusion to be accepted in any given case. A generalization refinement is usually accomplished by deleting or altering a component on the left-hand side of the rule or by raising the confidence factor associated with the rule's conclusion. By a rule specialization we mean modifications to a rule that make it harder for the rule's conclusion to be accepted in any given case. A rule specialization is usually accomplished by adding or altering a component on the left-hand side or by lowering the confidence factor associated with the rule's conclusion.[2]

On the size of evidence for rule generalization, one of the concepts we have employed in both SEEK and SEEK2 is a statistical property of a rule computed by a function that we call *Gen(rule)*. *Gen(rule)* is the number of cases in which

(a) this rule's conclusion *should have been reached but wasn't*,

(b) had this rule been satisfied, the conclusion would have been reached,

and

(c) of all the rules for which the preceding clauses hold in the case, this one is the *closest to being satisfied*.[3]

For example during the processing of a case, the Gen($r_i$) measure is incremented in the following hypothetical situation for rule $r_i$: Findings $f_1$ & $f_2$

---

[2] Confidence factors are *combined* according to the following rule: when two or more rules for the same conclusion are both satisfied, the maximum (absolute) confidence is used.

[3] A measure of how close a rule is to being satisfied in a case, based on the minimal number of additional findings required for the rule to fire, is easily computed from the case data. Speaking figuratively, one may think in terms of paths through the knowledge base that would have led to the rule's being satisfied. Since the rule is unsatisfied, all these paths are blocked. We look for the path that would require the least number of changes in the case data to become unblocked. For details of the algorithm used by SEEK see [16]; SEEK2's closeness measure is essentially the same.

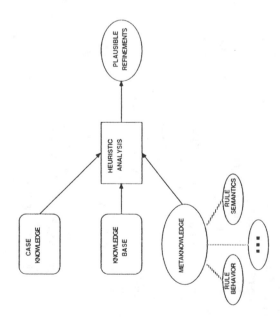

Fig. 1. Basic approach to refinement.

evidence E regarding the behavior of various rules in the current knowledge base. Since we are using *heuristic* analysis, we do not, in general, expect the evidence to be so complete that we are able to determine whether γ will actually correct any of the misdiagnosed cases in M. Rather, our goal is to generate refinements that, given our evidence E, can be determined to have a chance of correcting one or more of the cases in M. The more cases γ has a chance of correcting, the greater its plausibility [7].

Given that a knowledge base can be expected to have a large number of rules, a refinement system must have a mechanism for focusing its attention on small subsets of rules as potential candidates for correcting certain misdiagnosed cases. The focus-of-attention mechanism employed in SEEK and SEEK2 is a *divide-and-conquer* strategy and depends upon certain reasonable assumptions concerning the logical structure of the knowledge base. We assume that the expert and knowledge engineer can identify a finite set of *final diagnostic conclusions* or *endpoints*; these are the conclusions that the expert uses to classify the given cases. We also assume that every rule has only a single conclusion. One can then confine one's attention to the refinement of rules that are involved in concluding a particular endpoint. e.g., if the domain is rheumatology one may decide to work on refining those rules involved in concluding the single final diagnosis Systemic Lupus. Thus at any given moment the system is applying the refinement heuristics only to a proper subset of the rules in the domain knowledge base. Even within this chosen subset, however, another focus-of-attention mechanism, based upon the chain-

& $f_3$ imply $H_1$ with confidence 0.9; $H_1$ is the correct answer; $f_2$ and $f_3$ are satisfied, but $f_1$ is not: and the incorrect computer conclusion has a confidence of 0.5.

On the side of evidence for rule specialization, one of the concepts we have defined is a statistical property of a rule that is computed by a function we call $SpecA(rule)$. $SpecA(rule)$ is the number of cases in which

(a) this rule's conclusion *should not have been reached but was*, and

(b) if this rule had *failed to fire*. the correct conclusion would have been reached.[4]

For example during the processing of a case, the $SpecA(r_i)$ measure is incremented in the following hypothetical situation: Findings $f_1$ & $f_2$ & $f_3$ imply $H_1$ with confidence 0.9: the rule is satisfied, but $H_1$ is the wrong conclusion. $SpecA(r_i)$ will be incremented when the second choice for the computer conclusion is the correct answer.

If there is *more than one satisfied rule* that concludes the incorrect first choice, then none of these rules has its SpecA measure incremented; instead we have defined an additional concept to cover this situation called *SpecB(rule)*: each of these rules has its SpecB measure incremented.

To get a feeling for the sort of heuristics employed by these systems, suppose that for a certain rule $r$ it has been found that $Gen(r) > [SpecA(r) + SpecB(r)]$, in other words the evidence suggests that it is more appropriate to generalize than specialize $r$. Another piece of information would help us decide which component of $r$ should be deleted or altered, viz., the *most frequently missing component*, i.e., the component of $r$ that has the lowest frequency of satisfaction relative to the cases that contribute to Gen($r$). The function that computes this statistic is called *Mfmc(rule)*. Mfmc(rule) also tells us the syntactic category of this most frequently missing component. For example, one sort of component often used in medical diagnostic systems is called a *choice-component*. These have the form $k: C_1, \ldots, C_n$, where $k$, *the choice-number* is a positive integer and the $C_i$ are findings or hypotheses.[5] A choice-component is satisfied *iff* at least $k$ of its $C_i$ are satisfied. If we know that the rule $r$ should be generalized and that Mfmc($r$) is a particular choice-component, then a natural thing to do is to decrease the choice-number of that choice-component. Being conservative we decrease the choice-number by 1.

To summarize the discussion so far we now display in full the particular heuristic we have described.

If: $Gen(rule) > [SpecA(rule) + SpecB(rule)]$ & Mfmc(rule) is CHOICE-COMPONENT $C$,

Then: Decrease the choice-number of CHOICE-COMPONENT $C$ in *rule*.

Reason: This would generalize the rule so that it will be easier to satisfy.

A complete list of the refinement concepts and heuristics currently used in SEEK2 is given in Appendix A. Both generalization and specialization refinements are accomplished by modifying choice-numbers, confidence measures, or numerical ranges. Generalization heuristics may delete rule-components. For specialization, SEEK2 does not yet add components to rules. Our objective has been to explore the limits of a strictly conservative strategy of refinement.

## 4. The SEEK Experience

A salient feature of the original SEEK program [17] is that it was not designed to solve the entire knowledge base refinement problem on its own, rather it was intended to help, interactively, an expert or knowledge engineer solve the overall problem by offering potential solutions to various subproblems that arise along the way. SEEK helps its user in the following ways: (a) it provides a performance evaluation of the knowledge base relative to the case data base, (b) using its statistical concepts and heuristics it identifies rules that are plausible candidates for refinement and suggests appropriate refinements, (c) a user can instruct SEEK to calculate what the actual performance results of a particular refinement to the knowledge base would be, and if the user desires, SEEK will incorporate the change in the knowledge base.

### 4.1. Basic cycle of operation

Although control in SEEK always resides with the user, and there are a number of paths and facilities available to the user at almost every point, SEEK can be thought of as having a basic cycle of operation. The system is given an initial knowledge base and the case knowledge data base. SEEK first obtains a performance evaluation of the initial knowledge base on the data base of cases. This is done by running the initial knowledge base on each of the cases in the data base, and then comparing the knowledge base's conclusion with the stored expert's conclusion. The performance evaluation consists primarily of an overall score, e.g. 75% of cases diagnosed correctly, as well as a breakdown by final diagnostic category of the number of cases in which the system agrees with the expert in reaching a particular diagnosis, i.e., *true positives*, and the number of cases in which the system reaches that diagnosis but the expert does not, i.e., *false positives*.

[4] The correct conclusion was the second choice in the case (due to its having the second highest confidence), and the only circumstance preventing its being the first choice is the fact that this rule is satisfied.

[5] Findings are observations that are true, false or have a numerical value (such as age). Hypotheses are conclusions that may be assigned confidence values in the range of −1 to 1.

The user must decide on a diagnosis for which he would like to see refinements in the knowledge base in order to obtain better performance, e.g., if the domain is rheumatology the user may decide to try to upgrade the system's performance in diagnosing Systemic Lupus. For the sake of brevity, we call this user-specified diagnosis the GDX for the current cycle of operation, where the G stands for *given*, since this is a directive that the user must give the system. The next part of the cycle involves computing statistical properties concerning the rules of the knowledge base that conclude the GDX. Plausible refinements are then generated by evaluating a set of heuristics, similar to the one presented above for each of these rules, as well as any rule that becomes implicated via an intermediate hypothesis (see Section 3.1 above).

Once SEEK has given its advice—we think of each piece of advice as a possible experiment to improve the knowledge base—the user will initiate an experimentation phase. This is a subcycle in which the user, interacting with SEEK, determines the exact effect of incorporating any one of the proposed experiments. The user will then decide which, if any, of these refinements should be accepted, and instructs SEEK accordingly. This ends the basic cycle, which can now be repeated starting with the modified knowledge base. This process continues until the user is satisfied with the overall performance evaluation.

## 4.2. Limitations

One of SEEK's limitations has already been mentioned: it does not have the capability to attempt to solve a refinement problem on its own. We discuss how SEEK2 removes this limitation in Section 5.1 below.

Another important limitation of SEEK is that it does not work with a general production rule system, rather it expects that the domain knowledge base will be written in a form known as the *criteria table representation*. This mode of representation requires the knowledge engineer to specify a list of *major* observations and a list of *minor* observations for each possible (diagnostic) conclusion in the knowledge base. Rules for reaching particular conclusions are then stated in terms of the number of majors and minors for the conclusion, *requirements* and *exclusions*. The latter are additional observations or conclusions, or conjunctions of such, that are relevant to the diagnosis: a requirement is some condition that must be satisfied to reach the conclusion; an exclusion is some condition that rules out the conclusion. Furthermore, any rule can reach its conclusion at one of only three possible confidence levels: possible, probable, definite. As an example, assuming that a list of majors and minors for the conclusion Systemic Lupus has been specified, a rule for concluding the latter might state that if (at least) two of the majors and two of the minors are present then the conclusion is warranted at the definite level.

While this mode of representation has proven to be useful in the rheumatology domain [16] and other medical applications, it is in fact not as powerful a representation language as that of EXPERT [20] or similar production rule systems, in the sense that one can write knowledge bases in general production rule languages that are not translatable into the criteria table format. However, any criteria table can be translated into production rule syntax. Thus the set of criteria table knowledge bases is a proper subset of the set of production rule knowledge bases.

SEEK's knowledge engineering knowledge, i.e., its statistics and heuristics, was formulated with reference to the criteria table representation scheme, and criteria table concepts also were embedded in the control structure of the program. As a consequence, certain forms of rule refinement were not available or were restricted in SEEK, e.g., changing a rule's confidence factor was limited to making jumps from one level to another, such as probable to possible. In general, SEEK could do very little with a knowledge base that was not written in a criteria table format.

SEEK2, on the other hand, is a refinement system that will work with any knowledge base written in EXPERT's rule representation language.[6] In designing SEEK2, we found it was possible to decouple SEEK's knowledge engineering concepts from the criteria table representation; we were able to apply many of these concepts in relation to features of more general types of production rules. For example, criteria table rule-components using the notion of majors and minors are special cases of rule-components using choice-functions. Decreasing or increasing the number of majors or minors required by a rule, is a special case of decreasing or increasing the choice-number of a choice-function. Thus the example heuristic given above in Section 3.2 is a generalization in SEEK2 of the two separate similar heuristics originally stated in SEEK, one for majors, one for minors.

In moving to a more general representation language as the target language for knowledge base refinement, we broadened the scope of the set of generic refinement operations available to the system. For example, confidence factors for generalization experiments may be increased based on an average of the highest-weighted (erroneous) conclusion for a set of misclassified cases.[7]

From the programmer's point of view, SEEK's *own knowledge base*, the representation of its knowledge engineering statistics and heuristics, was strictly separate from its control structure. However, this was not the case from the point of view of the user, since there was no facility by which the user, qua

---

[6] This language is tailored to a classification system. Unlike OPS5, where rules fire one at a time, all rules that match are evaluated, and a relatively simple confidence scoring system is employed. The current design of SEEK2 assumes a single correct conclusion.

[7] Changing the confidence measure of a conclusion is usually considered more *radical* than minor changes to the left-hand side of rules.

user and not qua programmer, could access and modify SEEK's own knowledge base, in the way that a user can modify the domain knowledge base. Our approach to this issue forms part of a broader project which we describe in Section 8.1 below.

## 5. The SEEK2 Refinement System

### 5.1. Automatic refinement capability

Unlike SEEK, SEEK2 is a system that can present plausible solutions to the overall refinement problem *without* the need for interaction with an expert. The output of SEEK2 running in automatic mode is not a list of suggested rule refinements for a particular GDX (Given DX), rather it is a refined version of the entire knowledge base, i.e., a set of rule refinements to the initial knowledge base which yield an improvement in overall performance. In this section we describe SEEK2's current automatic refinement capability. Figure 2 is an overview of SEEK2's automatic refinement control strategy.

The attempt to find a sequence of refinements that optimizes performance is a search problem. Where there is a search problem of sufficient complexity, good heuristics must be found to guide the search. As we will see, SEEK2's current automatic refinement algorithm is a heuristic search algorithm, in the sense that it uses a classic weak method, hill-climbing.

When running in automatic mode SEEK2 makes three types of decisions that were previously made by the user of SEEK: (a) choice of GDX for the current cycle. (b) which rule refinement experiments to try, (c) which refinements to incorporate in the knowledge base given the results of the experiments (see Fig. 3). Additionally SEEK2 has to know when to stop.

In the current implementation, SEEK2 orders the potential GDXs in descending order according to a simple measure on the number of false negatives and false positives, information that is given by the performance evaluation phase. Potential rule refinement experiments for a GDX are ordered by simple measures on the statistics used in generating the refinement, e.g., if the generalization heuristic given in Section 3.2 fires, the quantity $\text{Gen}(rule) - [\text{SpecA}(rule) + \text{SpecB}(rule)]$ is used as an estimate of the *expected net gain* to be derived by performing the experiment.

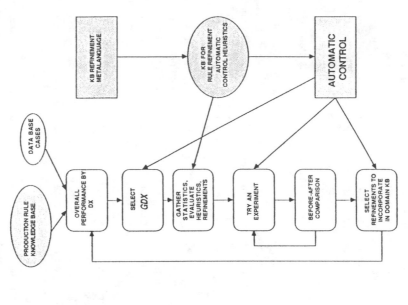

FIG. 3. Overview of SEEK2: shaded portions indicate extensions to SEEK.

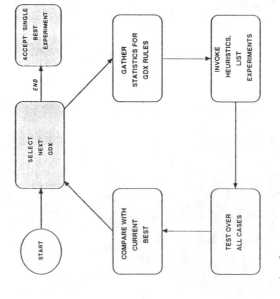

FIG. 2. Automatic refinement control strategy.

Information of this sort could be used to limit the number of experiments performed in a cycle. However, in the current implementation, the information is used only to determine the order in which GDXs are chosen and experiments attempted: ultimately *every* potential GDX (for which perfect performance has not been obtained) is chosen, and every experiment suggested by the heuristics is performed. In other words, an automatic refinement cycle involves attempting, according to the ordering just given, every proposed refinement experiment for every potential final diagnostic conclusion in the knowledge base. (Of course, the number of experiments generated by the heuristics represents a small fraction of the total number of logically admissible refinements.) Of all these attempted experiments, SEEK2 accepts only one, the one that gives the greatest *net gain* in knowledge base performance for *all* final diagnostic conclusions, not just for one GDX.[8] An internal record of the accepted refinement is kept; and then the next automatic refinement cycle begins. If the current automatic refinement cycle is such that no attempted experiment leads to an actual net gain, SEEK2 stops.

We present a simplified example in order to illustrate these concepts. Let us suppose that we have a rheumatology knowledge base dealing only with the two final diagnoses Systemic Lupus and Rheumatoid Arthritis, that a data base of 20 cases is available, and that our human expert has diagnosed 10 of these cases as Systemic Lupus and the other 10 as Rheumatoid Arthritis. Suppose that the initial performance evaluation computed by SEEK2 is as shown in Table 1.

The measure SEEK2 uses to compute GDX order is the maximum of the false negatives and false positives. Thus in our example Systemic Lupus would be the first diagnosis in the GDX ordering since it has 7 false negatives, i.e., 7 out of the 10 cases that should have been diagnosed as Systemic Lupus were not. Therefore SEEK2 will first generate refinement experiments for systemic Lupus.

Continuing the example, suppose that rule $r$ concludes Systemic Lupus, and SEEK2 finds that $Gen(r) = 6$, $SpecA(r) = 1$, $SpecB(r) = 0$, and $Mfmc(r) =$ CHOICE-COMPONENT C. These findings would satisfy the antecedent of the refinement heuristic presented in Section 3.2. Therefore SEEK2 will post the decreasing of $C$'s choice-number as a refinement experiment. SEEK2's estimate of the expected net gain of performing this experiment is given by $Gen(r) - [SpecA(r) + SpecB(r)] = 5$. (This is an estimate; the only way to know what the precise effect of decreasing the choice-number of $C$ will be, is to decrease it, and then recompute the system's performance on *all* cases in the data base.) Once all the refinement experiments for Systemic Lupus have been posted and ordered according to their expected net gain, SEEK2 performs *all* the experiments on this list as ordered. If SEEK2 finds that decreasing the choice-number of component $C$ in rule $r$ leads to an overall performance gain of 3 cases, i.e., the bottom line performance total for *both* Rheumatoid Arthritis and Systemic Lupus improves from 12 to 15 / 20, and this turns out to be the maximum net gain of all the experiments for Systemic Lupus, SEEK2 records this fact.

Next, it will select Rheumatoid Arthritis as the GDX, and repeat the process. Suppose that the aforementioned experiment for rule $r$ yields a greater net gain than the best refinement experiment for Rheumatoid Arthritis. Then SEEK2 will accept the refinement to rule $r$, i.e., it will modify its internal copy of the domain knowledge base to reflect this refinement, and a new cycle will commence.

The automatic refinement algorithm is a hill-climbing procedure: at each step SEEK2 is guided totally by local information as to which proposed refinement of the current knowledge base results in the best improvement. SEEK2 stops when none of the experiments suggested by the heuristics leads to a net gain. Because SEEK2 does not examine all possible combinations of refinement experiments, the accepted experiments may fail to achieve a global maximum. Moreover, because SEEK2's heuristics are estimators that do not consider every possible refinement, the accepted experiments may also fall short of a local maximum. SEEK2's optimization goal is tempered by constraints of conservatism and computational efficiency.

### 5.2. Using disjoint training and testing sets

The best evidence for the validity of an approach can come only from actual examples of its successful use. On this score, we can say that with respect to the rheumatology knowledge base we have used as a test case, SEEK2 has generated refinements that are similar to those produced by SEEK, some of which were found to be acceptable to the experts [16].[9]

However, some evidence of the reliability of the approach in producing refinements that improve the general empirical adequacy of a knowledge base (not just its empirical adequacy with respect to the given data base of cases) can be obtained via experimentation with a single knowledge base by using

TABLE 1. Initial performance evaluation computed by SEEK2

| DX | True positives | False positives |
| --- | --- | --- |
| Rheumatoid Arthritis | 9 / 10 | 6 |
| Systemic Lupus | 3 / 10 | 1 |
| None | 0 / 0 | 1 |
| Total | 12 / 20 | 8 |

[8] While the overall performance must increase, it is possible that the performance of some conclusions may decrease.

[9] While the SEEK refinements required human intervention during many of the refinement cycles, SEEK2 used automatic refinement procedures.

reliable estimate of the probability of error. In all, 15 train-and-test runs were conducted. In 6 runs, the size of the training sample was 50% of the cases; 3 runs each with training sample sizes of 33%, 67%, and 75%, respectively, were also conducted. The average performance increase observed in the test cases in these 15 runs was 21.2%. The average total performance over the test cases was 94.5%, which gives an estimate of probability of error of 0.055. The lowest overall performance over a test set obtained in any of these runs was 90% (this occurred in a run with training sample size 67%), which yields a 0.1 point estimate of probability of error. The highest overall performance over a test set obtained in any of these runs was 100% (this occurred in a run with training sample size 75%). The average number of rule refinements to the knowledge base was 8.

As is shown in the sample session below (see Section 6), a recent implementation of SEEK2 allows the user to perform such train-and-test experiments.

## 6. A Sample Session

A sample session is abstracted below. Annotations are italicized; user inputs are boxed.

**Enter knowledge base name:**  `RHEUM`

*The following option allows the user to establish a confidence threshold, $\Theta$, to determine whether a case is to be considered correctly diagnosed when a tie occurs. If the knowledge base reaches the correct conclusion as well as an additional erroneous conclusion at confidence level $\alpha \geq \Theta$, the case will be considered misdiagnosed. If $\alpha < \Theta$ the case will be considered correctly diagnosed.*

**Enter threshold below which ties are wins (1.1):**  `0.5`

*The user has the option of dividing the data base of cases into disjoint, randomly selected, training and testing sets, and can specify the percentage to be used for training versus testing. In this example the training sample size is 50%.*

**Would you like to set up a training sample? \***  `Y`

**Enter percentage of cases to be in training sample (1:99):**  `50`

*SEEK2 now prints out the PDX (expert's conclusion) and the CDXs (knowledge base's current conclusions) for each case. Mnemonics are used to reference specific conclusions. This output can be suppressed.*

---

various statistical techniques. In this section we describe the results of such an experiment.

The experiment will be called a *train-and-test* experiment, and is actually a series of similar experiments or runs. In a single typical train-and-test run the given data base of cases is divided into two randomly selected disjoint subsets (not necessarily of equal size) preserving the distribution of cases by endpoint. Let us call these sets $\sigma_1$ and $\sigma_2$. The first phase of a train-and-test experiment involves running SEEK2 using $\sigma_1$ as case knowledge, or as the training set. SEEK2's refined version of the knowledge base is then tested over $\sigma_2$ (and the combined set $\sigma_1 \cup \sigma_2$). In the second phase of the experiment the roles of $\sigma_1$ and $\sigma_2$ are interchanged.

Table 2 gives the results of such a run with training and test samples of equal size. Training over $\sigma_1$ led to a performance increase of 29% (69% to 98%). When tested over the new set of cases in $\sigma_2$, there was an increase in performance of 15% (78% to 93%). The results of the second run are similar. While there was often less improvement observed over the test sets than in the training sets in these runs, the fact is that the experiment shows that refinements that were learned by SEEK2 with respect to one set of cases also improved empirical adequacy with respect to a new set of cases.

This experiment has a more precise interpretation. A single train-and-test experiment can be viewed as giving an *estimate* of the *probability of error*—i.e., the probability that the refined knowledge case (classifier) misdiagnoses a case [5]. Under this interpretation, the total performance ratio obtained in the test run, e.g., the 93% figure in testing set 1, estimates the probability of error to be 0.07. While this figure is certainly more conservative than the 0.02 estimate that would be obtained by using the results of the training run as an estimate, it is only a point-estimate. To obtain a more reliable estimate, one needs to average over the results of many train-and-test experiments. Alternatively, a more accurate figure could also be obtained by employing a *leaving-one-out* or *jackknifing* technique for error estimation [5]. Unfortunately, the general application of these techniques in knowledge base refinement would appear to be computationally prohibitive for large scale problems.

However, additional train-and-test runs for the rheumatology knowledge base have been performed and these results can be used to derive a more

TABLE 2. Train-and-test experiment

| | Train-and-test experiment 1 | | Train-and-test experiment 2 | |
|---|---|---|---|---|
| | Training set 1 | Testing set 1 | Training set 2 | Testing set 2 |
| Start | 42 / 62 (69%) | 46 / 59 (78%) | 46 / 59 (78%) | 42 / 62 (69%) |
| Finish | 61 / 62 (98%) | 55 / 59 (93%) | 59 / 59 (100%) | 59 / 62 (95%) |
| Overall | 116 / 121 (96%) | | 118 / 121 (98%) | |

The system now prints the current performance breakdown by endpoint for the training set, the test sets, and the union of these sets.

| | | | | | |
|---|---|---|---|---|---|
| 1. | Pdx: MCTD | Cdx: MCTD | PSS (.4) | SLE (.4) | RA (.4) |
| 2. | Pdx: RA | Cdx: RA (.9) | SLE (.4) | | |
| • • • | | | | | |
| 121. | Pdx: RA | Cdx: RA (.7) | | | |

**TRAINING SAMPLE**

| | True Positives | False Positives |
|---|---|---|
| RA | 21/21 (100%) | 7 |
| MCTD | 4/16 (25%) | 0 |
| SLE | 6/9 (67%) | 1 |
| PSS | 11/11 (100%) | 3 |
| PM | 1/2 (50%) | 1 |
| NONE | 0/0 (0%) | 4 |
| Total | 43/59 (73%) | 16 |

**TEST CASES**

| | True Positives | False Positives |
|---|---|---|
| RA | 21/21 (100%) | 4 |
| MCTD | 5/17 (29%) | 0 |
| SLE | 6/9 (67%) | 3 |
| PSS | 11/12 (92%) | 1 |
| PM | 2/3 (67%) | 0 |
| NONE | 0/0 (0%) | 9 |
| Total | 45/62 (73%) | 17 |

**ALL CASES**

| | True Positives | False Positives |
|---|---|---|
| RA | 42/42 (100%) | 11 |
| MCTD | 9/33 (27%) | 0 |
| SLE | 12/18 (67%) | 4 |
| PSS | 22/23 (96%) | 4 |
| PM | 3/5 (60%) | 1 |
| NONE | 0/0 (0%) | 13 |
| Total | 88/121 (73%) | 33 |

*Because performance on the MCTD cases is the weakest, SEEK2 chooses to refine rules for MCTD first. It lists the relevant cases; a case number with an X after it indicates that this case is not part of the training sample.*

**GDX: MCTD**

Relevant cases for this DX:

| | | | | | | | |
|---|---|---|---|---|---|---|---|
| 1.X | Pdx: MCTD | CDX: MCTD | PSS (.4) | SLE (.4) | RA (.4) | | |
| 4.X | Pdx: MCTD | CDX: MCTD | SLE (.4) | PSS (.7) | MCTD (.4) | SLE (.4) | RA (.4) |
| 11. | Pdx: MCTD | CDX: MCTD | PSS (.7) | | | | |
| 12. | Pdx: MCTD | CDX: MCTD | RA (.4) | | | | |

*The system now evaluates its refinement concepts and heuristics with respect to the relevant cases and rules, and posts the refinement experiments generated. It then attempts each experiment in order of decreasing probable gain. In the following example, the system is on the first cycle of refinements; no experiments have been accepted. MCTD is ranked as the top candidate for refinement.*

Suggested Experiments:

Cycle: 1; GDX rank: 1; Number of GDX experiments: 1; Total experiments: 1

1. In rule 3.7, decrease the choice number of component-1 from 3 to 2
   Probable gain: 8

## Rule 3.7

Choose 3 or more of the following:

Hypothesis RAYES has confidence between .9 and 1
Finding SWOLH is true
Finding SCLDY is true
Finding DCO is less than 70
Hypothesis MYOSS has confidence between .9 and 1

CONCLUDE Hypothesis MCTD with confidence .4

*The system prints the result, on a case-by-case basis, of performing this experiment. The net gain of the experiment over the training cases is also given.*

| | | | | | | |
|---|---|---|---|---|---|---|
| 1.X | Pdx: MCTD | CDX: MCTD (.4) | PSS (.4) | SLE (.4) | RA (.4) | |
| 2. | Pdx: RA | CDX: RA (.9) | SLE (.4) | | | |
| • • • | | | | | | |
| 121. | Pdx: RA | CDX: RA (.7) | | | | |

Net gain for experiment: 5 cases.

*After considering 13 experiments, SEEK2 determines that the first experiment is the best. The knowledge base is modified, and the first cycle of experimentation is complete. With the newly modified knowledge base, a new cycle of experimentation begins. SEEK2 prints the the following performance summary of the accepted experiment.*

EXPERIMENT 1 ACCEPTED. CYCLE 1 completed.

**TRAINING SAMPLE**

BEFORE

| | True Positives | False Positives |
|---|---|---|
| RA | 21/21 (100%) | 7 |
| MCTD | 4/16 (25%) | 0 |
| SLE | 6/9 (67%) | 1 |
| PSS | 11/11 (100%) | 3 |
| PM | 1/2 (50%) | 1 |
| NONE | 0/0 (0%) | 4 |
| Total | 43/59 (73%) | 16 |

AFTER

| | True Positives | False Positives |
|---|---|---|
| RA | 21/21 (100%) | 6 |
| MCTD | 9/16 (56%) | 0 |
| SLE | 6/9 (67%) | 1 |
| PSS | 11/11 (100%) | 1 |
| PM | 1/2 (50%) | 1 |
| NONE | 0/0 (0%) | 2 |
| Total | 48/59 (81%) | 11 |

number, the statistical comparisons used in these heuristics may require some explanation.

We can view the basic goal of heuristic refinement generation as being the generation of refinements that maximize expected gains in performance with respect to a given set of misdiagnosed cases $M$. Or we can view it as being tempered by the desire not to degrade performance over the set, $C$, of cases currently diagnosed correctly; the goal is to generate refinements that maximize expected gains over the misdiagnosed cases in $M$, but at the same time minimize the expected losses over $C$. Let us call the first policy $Max\_Gain$, and the second $Max\_Gain+Min\_Loss$. SEEK and SEEK2 adopt the latter policy, and this is why all their heuristics contain a clause that is intended to compare expected gain with expected loss.

To elaborate on this point, we need to define some terms. We say that a knowledge base has made a *true positive* (TP) judgment whenever (the expert system using) it reaches an endpoint that was also reached by the expert; we say that it has made a *false positive* (FP) judgment whenever it reaches an endpoint that was not reached by the expert; we say that it has made a *true negative* (TN) judgment whenever it refrains from reaching an endpoint that the expert also did not reach; and, finally, we say that the knowledge base has made a *false negative* (FN) judgment whenever it refrains from reaching an endpoint that the expert did reach.

The goal of the overall knowledge base refinement process is to minimize the number of FP and FN judgments of the knowledge base, consistent with the constraints of conservatism. (Minimizing FPs is equivalent to maximizing TNs and minimizing FNs is equivalent to maximizing TPs.) Given this overall goal, a generalization refinement may be seen as an attempt to contribute to it by *increasing the number of TPs* for an endpoint (equivalently, decreasing the number of FNs for that endpoint). A specialization refinement is an attempt to contribute to the overall goal by *decreasing the number of FPs* for an endpoint (equivalently, increasing the number of TNs for that endpoint).

However, anytime a generalization is made there is a possibility that the refinement will lead to an increase in the number of FPs for the endpoint in question as well, which is clearly at odds with our goal. Anytime a specialization is made there is a possibility that the refinement will lead to an increase in the number of FNs (equivalently, a decrease in the number of TPs) for the endpoint in question as well, which is also at odds with our goal.

The role of the refinement generator is to produce refinements that not only have the chance of reducing the number of FPs and FNs over the misdiagnosed cases in $M$, but that also have the least chance of generating new FPs and FNs over other currently correctly diagnosed cases in $C$. We now formulate two general criteria, for generalization and specialization refinements respectively, that characterize this point of view.

Let $\Delta TP$ represent the total net change (over all cases and all endpoints) in

---

*The following sequence of experiments illustrates the way in which SEEK2 attempts to find less radical alternatives to certain classes of refinements, and it also illustrates the use of the logical structure of the knowledge base to control the refinement process.*

**Cycle: 2; GDX rank: 3; Number of GDX experiments: 4; Total experiments: 26**

4. In rule 4.11, delete component-3 referencing hypothesis RD203
Probable gain: 1

### Rule 4.11

Choose 2 or more of the following:

Hypothesis NEPH has confidence between .9 and 1
Finding MALAR is true
Hypothesis SEROS has confidence between .9 and 1
Hypothesis CNS has confidence between .9 and 1
Finding HEMAN is true

AND

Choose 2 or more of the following:

Finding FEV is true
Finding ARTH is true
Finding GGLOB is greater than 1.8
Hypothesis HCMP has confidence between .9 and 1
Finding PLAT is less than 100

AND

Hypothesis RD203 has confidence between .9 and 1

AND

Hypothesis EX1SL has confidence between -1 and .05

CONCLUDE Hypothesis SLE with confidence .9

Net gain for experiment: 1 cases.

*Since the component considered for deletion has an associated confidence range, SEEK2 goes on to suggest generalizing the range as an alternative to deletion. Because the component being considered for deletion is an intermediate hypothesis, SEEK2 also will suggest ways of modifying the rules that conclude this intermediate hypothesis as an alternative to modifying rule 4.11.*

. . .

## 7. Justification of the Heuristics

While certain parts of the heuristics used in SEEK and SEEK2 are obviously reasonable, e.g., to generalize a choice-component one may decrease its choice

TPs that will occur due to a generalization refinement $R_g$; let $\Delta FP$ represent the total net change in FPs that will occur due to $R_g$. Then the refinement $R_g$ contributes to our overall goal if:

$$\Delta TP > 0 \quad \text{and} \quad \Delta TP > \Delta FP . \tag{1}$$

Similarly, let $\Delta TN$ represent the total net change (over all cases and all endpoints) in TNs that will occur due to a specialization refinement $R_s$; let $\Delta FN$ represent the total net change in FNs that will occur due to $R_s$. Then the refinement $R_s$ contributes to our overall goal if:

$$\Delta TN > 0 \quad \text{and} \quad \Delta TN > \Delta FN . \tag{2}$$

An optimal heuristic for generating generalization refinements would be one that never suggested a refinement that violates condition (1), and, an optimal heuristic for generating specializations would never suggest a refinement that violates condition (2). It is doubtful that there are any truly heuristic principles that are optimal in this sense. One has to settle for something that is less than optimal, and computationally feasible as well.

This is where refinement concepts such as Gen, SpecA, and SpecB, come into the picture. These functions have a twofold character: they can be used as indicators of problematic rule behavior, but they can also be used as estimators of expected gains due to refinements. Thus Gen can be used as an estimator of $\Delta TP$ for appropriate generalization refinement operations, and, intuitively, this seems plausible. Therefore, it we can find a plausible estimator of $\Delta FP$ for generalization refinements then we will be able to construct heuristics for generating generalizations that use these estimators as an approximation to condition (1). A seemingly good concept for this role would be something like the following:

AntiGen(*r*)
= the number of *correctly diagnosed cases* in which:

  (a) *r* is not satisfied.
  (b) if *r had been satisfied* the case would have been misdiagnosed, and
  (c) *r* is the closest to being satisfied of all the rules for which (a) and (b) are true.

The problem with AntiGen(*r*) is that from a computational point of view it is not consistent with the general refinement strategy adopted in SEEK2. When attempting to refine rules involved in reaching endpoint DX. SEEK2 gathers information concerning cases in which either DX is reached by the expert or knowledge DX is concluded by the knowledge base. It does not gather information from

cases in which DX does not figure as either the expert's or knowledge base's conclusion. Aside from the fact that the former cases are clearly most relevant to the discovery of useful refinements for these rules, there is also a computational rationale for this policy. On the average we expect that for any endpoint there will be far fewer cases in which it is reached by the expert or knowledge base, than cases in which it is not reached by the expert or knowledge base, especially if there are several a priori equally probable endpoints. To compute AntiGen(*r*) requires one to analyze every correctly diagnosed case in the data base of cases having a stored expert conclusion that does *not* match the conclusion of *r* (to see whether the satisfaction of *r* would lead to a new false positive). Thus AntiGen(*r*) does not conform to the policy adopted in SEEK2. SEEK2 uses the quantity $[SpecA(r) + SpecB(r)]$ as an estimator of $\Delta FP$ due to a generalization refinement, and therefore the condition

$$Gen(r) > [SpecA(r) + SpecB(r)]$$

that appears in some of SEEK2's generalization heuristics are approximations to condition (1). Although in this context we are using $[SpecA(r) + SpecB(r)]$ as an estimator of $\Delta FP$, the main role of this quantity is as an estimator of $\Delta TN$ due to a specialization refinement.[10]

A similar account of the role of the conditions used in SEEK2's specialization heuristics can be given. For example the comparison:

$$SpecA(r) > Signif(r)$$

is used as an approximation to condition (2). In this case, $SpecA(r)$ is an estimator of $\Delta TN$ due to a specialization refinement, and $Signif(r)$ is an estimator of $\Delta FN$ for the same refinement. These correspondences are intuitively plausible, as the reader can verify by scanning the appropriate definitions in Appendix A.

## 8. A Metalanguage for Knowledge Base Refinement

In this section we briefly describe some of the important primitives of a metalanguage designed specifically for the refinement task [7, 8]. Using this metalanguage one can define general knowledge engineering concepts and heuristics, such as *Gen(rule)*, as well as domain-specific metaknowledge in terms of a set of primitive concepts and operations.

### 8.1. General and domain-specific metaknowledge in knowledge base refinement

Refinement concepts such as Gen, Mfmc, SpecA, and SpecB and the heuristics

---

[10] It is a measure of current false positives that might be corrected.

that employ them, are examples of *general metaknowledge*, i.e., general knowledge about the conditions under which rules should be considered for refinement. Other examples of general metaknowledge would include concepts and strategies for extracting domain knowledge via interaction with an expert [3, 10], as well as concepts needed to encode knowledge concerning the strategic role of rules within the overall classification or diagnostic process [2]. An example of *domain-specific metaknowledge* [2, 18] is that certain rules in a knowledge base are definitional and should never be modified. Such knowledge involves properties of a knowledge base that are not ascertainable by means of a general a priori procedure.

## 8.2. Motivation for a metalanguage

While SEEK2 is currently based on general metaknowledge, there are ways in which domain-specific metaknowledge could be used in this system. For example, the knowledge that certain rules in a knowledge base are definitely in their correct form could be used to prevent rules from gathering data and attempting refinement experiments for such rules. By specifying refinement systems in a flexible metalinguistic fashion it may be possible to capture and incorporate such knowledge in the refinement process as the need and opportunity arise.

Another motivation for a metalanguage was alluded to in Section 4.2, where we mentioned that SEEK's knowledge base of heuristics and statistics was inaccessible to the user of the system. The ability to access and modify this knowledge base is quite desirable for designing and experimenting with refinement concepts. For example, some of the current statistics for SEEK2 may not be as useful with respect to an expert system that employs a scoring scheme for combining confidence factors. Useful variants of these statistics could be defined within the same metalanguage that we have developed for SEEK2. A high-level framework for the specification of refinement systems thus provides an environment for conducting research in knowledge base refinement.

Finally, another motivation for a refinement metalanguage is the issue of customization. In general, even within one expert system framework, different styles of knowledge bases are possible; it is likely therefore that different styles of refinement will be needed. For example, some knowledge bases employ a taxonomic ordering of hypotheses. Such an ordering provides knowledge that could be used, together with appropriate control heuristics, to formulate a more efficient version of SEEK2's automatic refinement algorithm. A knowledge base refinement metalanguage allows for the representation of such control heuristics (see Fig. 3). Indeed, the experimental metalanguage that is being developed allows a user to specify different control strategies from the hill-climbing strategy employed in SEEK2. Several alternative control strategies are mentioned briefly in Section 9.

## 8.3. Some metalinguistic primitives

SEEK2's statistical concepts can be specified in a set-theoretic metalanguage that employs only a small number of refinement primitives together with some appropriate notions from simple set theory, arithmetic, and logic. Using these primitives it is possible to experiment with variations on SEEK2's statistics and define domain specific statistics as well.

A set-theoretic definition of concepts such as *Gen(rule)* (see Section 3.2) requires refinement primitives of the following sorts. Some primitive variables are needed to provide the system or a user with the ability to access various objects in the domain knowledge base and the data base of cases. For example, *rule* is a variable whose range is the set of rules in the domain knowledge base, *case* is a variable whose range is the set of cases in the data base of cases, and *dx* is a variable whose range is the set of possible final diagnostic conclusions in the knowledge base. In addition some primitive functions are needed to allow one to refer to selected parts or aspects of a rule or a case, e.g., *RuleCF(rule)* is a function whose value is the confidence factor associated with *rule*, *PDX(case)* is a function whose value is the expert's conclusion in *case*,[11] and *CDX(case)* is a function whose value is the conclusion reached for the current knowledge base in *case*. As an example of the way in which these primitives can be used, note that using the notions of PDX(*case*) and CDX(*case*) one may define a *misdiagnosed case* as any *case* for which PDX(*case*) $\neq$ CDX(*case*).

Certain special sets of objects are of importance in the knowledge base refinement process, and it is therefore useful to have primitives that refer to them, e.g., *Rules-For(dx)* is a function whose value is the set of rules that have *dx* as their conclusion. Finally various primitives that in some way involve semantic properties of rules, or the performance characteristics of the knowledge base as a whole are useful, e.g., *Satisfied(kb-item, case)* is a predicate that is true iff *kb-item* is satisfied by the findings in *case*, and false otherwise, where *kb-item* can be an identifier for a rule, a rule-component or subcomponent; *ModelCF(dx, case)* is a function whose value is the system's confidence factor accorded to *dx* in *case*.

The current heuristic rules in Appendix A can be described in this metalanguage. For further details on the metalanguage see [7, 8].

## 9. Discussion

SEEK2 currently has ten statistical concepts and nine heuristics for generating refinements. Working in automatic mode on a rheumatology knowledge base of approximately 140 rules with 5 final diagnostic categories, and using a data base of 121 cases, SEEK2 was able to increase the overall performance of the system from a value of 73% (88 / 121) to a value of 100% (121 / 121). It used

---

[11] PDX stands for Physician's Diagnosis and CDX stands for Computer's Diagnosis.

approximately 32 minutes of VAX-785 CPU time. The total number of experiments tried was 199, out of which 10 were accepted.

In evaluating the usefulness of SEEK2's automatic refinement capability it is important to keep in mind that the expert is still the final judge. Despite the assured gain in performance with respect to the *given* data base of cases, and the reasonable expectation of performance enhancement with respect to *new* cases, the expert may agree with only a subset of the total number of refinements suggested by SEEK2.[12] The measure of SEEK2's usefulness is not, however, simply how many of its experiments the expert accepts; even rejected experiments have value: they point out areas of the knowledge base that need to be examined if enhanced performance is to be achieved.

While we believe that we have demonstrated useful empirical refinement capabilities for expert classification systems, we recognize that this approach is not complete and that there are numerous avenues for further research. We briefly mention several areas where further work is warranted:

- *Generalization of problem types covered by refinement.* The current SEEK2 world is limited to production rules and classification systems.

- *Development of an extended knowledge base metalanguage.* A prototype system has been developed [7] in which the current heuristics can be specified. With an appropriate description, the efficacy of the heuristics would be subject to experimentation. This would provide a means to evaluate the performance of heuristics and statistical assessment measures, and allow for comparative study of alternative policies regarding the conservatism vs. optimization trade-off. The language would also allow for the representation of domain-specific and alternative sources of knowledge.

- *Incorporation of domain-specific heuristics.* This could include relatively simple forms of knowledge about rule sets that should never be modified, classes of cases that should never be misdiagnosed, or findings and rule-components that should be modified first. More complicated knowledge about domain principles, such as cause and effect knowledge, could be used to verify knowledge base consistency.[13]

- *Experimentation with the larger knowledge bases.* While SEEK2 performs well on the cited knowledge base, many typical expert systems have much larger dimensions.[13]

- *Exploitation of parallelism in certain refinement operations.* Larger knowledge base dimensions significantly increase CPU times.[14] This time may be cut

dramatically by a parallel algorithm, for example each GDX could be pursued in parallel.

- *Elucidation of alternative strategies for validation and refinement.* There are many alternative strategies that may be employed. These include strategies that consider ties, multiple conclusions, disagreement among experts. More complex search strategies may be specified that pursue multiple refinement paths. For example, when two refinements yield approximately the same improvement, we might want to postpone selecting just one until further derived refinements are pursued.

- *Inclusion of automatic learning heuristics.* Some forms of learning can be viewed as an extension of refinement. Although SEEK2 has several specialization heuristics, SEEK2 never adds a component to a rule. Domain knowledge or empirical analysis could prove helpful in allowing for these types of rule modifications.

Validity and consistency are important goals in developing expert systems. Yet the design of these systems is often lacking in a coherent formal approach for achieving these goals. The approach to knowledge base refinement described here can lead to a more solid foundation for designing and validating expert classification system knowledge bases.

## Appendix A. SEEK2's Refinement Concepts and Heuristics

### A.1. Refinement concepts

**Signif(rule):**
The number of cases in which PDX = CDX and this rule is the only rule that concludes CDX with confidence $\geq$ the model's confidence in the 2nd highest ranked conclusion. The set of cases counted by Signif(rule) is denoted by **Signif-Cases(rule)**.

**Signif-level(rule, x):**
The number of the Signif-Cases(rule) cases with the property that the 2nd highest confidence in the case is greater than x.

**Gen(rule):**
The number of cases in which PDX $\neq$ CDX and this rule would correct the case if it had fired, and this rule is the closest to being satisfied of all rules that would correct the case. The set of cases counted by Gen(rule) is denoted by **Gen-Cases(rule)**.

**SpecA(rule):**
The number of cases in which PDX $\neq$ CDX and if this rule had not fired the case would have been correct. The set of cases counted by SpecA(rule) is denoted by **SpecA-Cases(rule)**.

---

[12] The incorporation of domain-specific metaknowledge in SEEK2 might enable the system itself to sometimes reject a refinement that in some way violates the expert's understanding of the domain, even though it may improve performance.

[13] A more recent version of the rheumatology knowledge base has 26 diagnoses, 400 intermediate hypotheses, 880 observations, and over 1000 rules.

[14] The more recent rheumatology knowledge base should take 2-3 days of CPU time for a 300 case data base.

**SpecB(rule):**
The number of cases in which PDX ≠ CDX and this rule is a member of a set of two or more rules concluding CDX such that if all the members of this set had failed to fire the case would have been correct. The set of cases counted by SpecB(rule) is denoted by **SpecB-Cases(rule).**

**Mfmc(rule):**
The most frequently missing (i.e., unsatisfied) component of this rule, relative to a set of cases in which the rule is unsatisfied. usually those cases in which this rule has been chosen as the candidate for generalization.

**GenCF(rule):**
The number of cases in which PDX ≠ CDX and this rule concludes PDX and is satisfied and has confidence closest to the model's confidence in CDX of all the rules satisfied for PDX. The set of cases counted by GenCF(rule) is denoted by **GenCF-Cases(rule).**

**Mean-Cdx-CF[GenCF-Cases(rule)]:**
The mean value of the knowledge base's confidence in CDX in the cases denoted by GenCF-Cases(rule).

**Mean-Pdx-CF[SpecA-Cases(rule) ∪ SpecB-Cases(rule)]:**
The mean value of the model's confidence in PDX in the cases denoted by (SpecA-Cases(rule) ∪ SpecB-Cases(rule)).

### A.2. Generalization heuristics

**If:** Gen(rule) > [SpecA(rule) + SpecB(rule)] & Mfmc(rule) is equal to CHOICE-COMPONENT $C$.

**Then:** Decrease the choice-number of $C$ in rule.

**If:** Gen(rule) > [SpecA(rule) + SpecB(rule)] & Mfmc(rule) is some NON-CHOICE-COMPONENT $C$.

**Then:** Delete this NON-CHOICE-COMPONENT in rule.

**If:** GenCF(rule) > [SpecA(rule) + SpecB(rule)].

**Then:** Raise the confidence level of rule to Mean-CDX-CF(GenCF-Cases(rule)) + 0.5 * (Standard-Deviation).

**If:** The NON-CHOICE-COMPONENT that has been suggested to be deleted from the rule $r_1$ is an INTERMEDIATE-HYPOTHESIS & $r_2$ is a rule that concludes the INTERMEDIATE-HYPOTHESIS (at the indicated confidence range) & $r_2$ is closest to being satisfied in a plurality of the cases in which $r_1$ was chosen to be generalized.

**Then:** Identify the most frequently missing component of $r_2$ relative to the cases in which $r_1$ was chosen to be generalized; if it is a CHOICE, lower the choice-number; if it is a NON-CHOICE, delete it, or change its range if possible; if it is an INTERMEDIATE-HYPOTHESIS, apply this heuristic again.

**If:** The NON-CHOICE-COMPONENT that has been suggested to be deleted from rule $r_1$ is an INTERMEDIATE-HYPOTHESIS $H$ with associated confidence range $(L:U)$ & the majority of Gen-Cases($r_1$) in which $H$'s confidence is not in the range $(L:U)$ are ones in which $H$'s confidence factor is below $L$.

**Then:** Lower the value of $L$ in the range $(L:U)$ in $r_1$ to Mean-Value(confidence of $H$, {$case$ | $case$ is in Gen-Cases($r_1$) & the confidence for $H$ in $case$ is less than $L$}).

**If:** The NON-CHOICE-COMPONENT that has been suggested to be deleted from rule $r_1$ is an INTERMEDIATE-HYPOTHESIS $H$ with associated confidence range $(L:U)$ & the majority of Gen-Cases($r_1$) in which $H$'s confidence is not in the range $(L:U)$ are ones in which $H$'s confidence factor is above $U$.

**Then:** Raise the value of $U$ in the range $(L:U)$ in $r_1$ to Mean-Value(confidence of $H$, {$case$ | $case$ is in Gen-Cases($r_1$) & the confidence for $H$ is greater than $L$}).

**If:** The NON-CHOICE-COMPONENT that has been suggested to be deleted from rule $r_1$ is an NUMERICAL-FINDING $F$ with associated value range $(L:U)$ & the majority of Gen-Cases($r_1$) in which $F$'s value is not in the range $(L:U)$ are ones in which $F$'s value is below $L$.

**Then:** Lower the value of $L$ in the range $(L:U)$ in $r_1$ to Mean-Value(value of $F$, {$case$ | $case$ is in Gen-Cases($r_1$) & the value of $F$ in $case$ is less than $L$}).

**If:** The NON-CHOICE-COMPONENT that has been suggested to be deleted from rule $r_1$ is a NUMERICAL-FINDING $F$ with associated value range $(L:U)$ & the majority of Gen-Cases($r_1$) in which $F$'s value is not in the range $(L:U)$ are ones in which $F$'s value is above $U$.

**Then:** Raise the value of $U$ in the range $(L:U)$ in $r_1$ to Mean-Value(value of $F$, {$case$ | $case$ is in Gen-Cases($r_1$) & the value of $F$ in $case$ is greater than $L$}).

### A.3. Specialization heuristics

**If:** SpecA(*rule*) > Signif(*rule*) & there is a CHOICE in *rule*.

**Then:** Increase the choice-number of CHOICE in *rule*.

**If:** [SpecA(*rule*) + SpecB(*rule*)] > Signif-level(*rule*.
Mean-Pdx-CF(SpecA-Cases(*rule*) ∪ SpecB-Cases(*rule*)).

**Then:** Lower the confidence level of *rule* to
Mean-Pdx-CF(SpecA-Cases(*rule*) ∪ SpecB-Cases(*rule*))
$-0.5*$(Standard-Deviation).

**If:** SpecA(*rule*) > Signif(*rule*) > 0.

**Then:** For every component $C$ in *rule* with associated range $(L:H)$ do the following:

calculate:

$L' = $ Mean-Value($C$, Signif-Cases(*rule*)) $- 2*$(Standard-Deviation),
$H' = $ Mean-Value($C$, Signif-Cases(*rule*)) $+ 2*$(Standard-Deviation);
if $L' > L$. raise $L$ to $L'$; if $H' < H$. lower $H$ to $H'$.

## ACKNOWLEDGMENT

We would like to thank Casimir Kulikowski for his many helpful suggestions concerning this work, and Kevin Kern for programming assistance.

## REFERENCES

1. Clancey, W.J.. Heuristic classification. *Artificial Intelligence* **27** (1985) 289–350.
2. Clancey, W.J.. The epistemology of a rule-based expert system—a framework for explanation, *Artificial Intelligence* **20** (3) (1983) 215–251.
3. Davis, R.. Interactive transfer of expertise: Acquisition of new inference rules. *Artificial Intelligence* **12** (1979) 121–157.
4. Doyle, R.. Constructing and refining causal explanations from an inconsistent domain theory, in: *Proceedings AAAI-86*. Philadelphia. PA (1986) 538–544.
5. Duda. R. and Hart. P. *Pattern Classification and Scene Analysis* (Wiley. New York. 1973).
6. Eshelman. L. and McDermott. J.. MOLE: A knowledge acquisition tool that uses its head, in: *Proceedings AAAI-86*. Philadelphia. PA (1986) 950–955.
7. Ginsberg. A.. Refinement of expert system knowledge bases: A metalinguistic framework for heuristic analysis. Ph.D. Thesis. Department of Computer Science. Rutgers University. New Brunswick. NJ. 1986.
8. Ginsberg. A.. A metalinguistic approach to the construction of knowledge base refinement systems, in: *Proceedings AAAI-86*. Philadelphia. PA. 1986.
9. Hall. R.. Learning by failing to explain. in: *Proceedings AAAI-86*. Philadelphia, PA (1986) 568–572.
10. Kahn. G.. Nowlan. S. and McDermott. J.. MORE: An intelligent knowledge acquisition tool. in: *Proceedings IJCAI-85*. Los Angeles. CA (1985) 581–584.
11. Lee. W. and Ray. S.. Rule refinement using the probabilistic rule generator. in: *Proceedings AAAI-86*. Philadelphia. PA (1986) 442–447.
12. Michalski. Q.S.. Carbonell. J. and Mitchell. T.M. (Eds.). *Machine Learning* (Tioga. Palo Alto. CA. 1983).
13. Michalski. R.S. Mozetic. I.. Hong. J. and Lavrac. N. The multi-purpose incremental learning system AQ15 and its testing application to three medical domains. in: *Proceedings AAAI-86*. Philadelphia. PA (1986) 1041–1045.
14. Mitchell. T.M.. Generalization as search. *Artificial Intelligence* **18** (1982) 203–226.
15. Mitchell. T.. Keller. R. and Kedar-Cabelli. S.. Explanation-based generalization: A unifying view. *Machine Learning* **1** (1986) 47–80.
16. Politakis. E. Using empirical analysis to refine expert system knowledge bases, Ph.D. Thesis. Department of Computer Science. Rutgers University. New Brunswick. NJ. 1982.
17. Politakis. P. and Weiss. S.M.. Using empirical analysis to refine expert system knowledge bases. *Artificial Intelligence* **22** (1984) 23–48.
18. Smith. R.. Winston. P.H. Mitchell. T. and Buchanan. B.G.. Representation and use of explicit justification for knowledge base refinement. in: *Proceedings IJCAI-85*. Los Angeles. CA (1985) 673–680.
19. Waters. R.. KBEmacs: A step toward the programmer's apprentice. *IEEE Trans. Softw. Eng.* **11** (1985) 296–1320.
20. Weiss. S. and Kulikowski. C.. *A Practical Guide to Designing Expert Systems* (Rowman and Allanheld. Totowa. NJ. 1984).
21. Wilkins. D and Buchanan. B.. On debugging rule sets when reasoning under uncertainty. in: *Proceedings AAAI-86*. Philadelphia. PA (1986) 448–454.

*Received November 1986; revised version received July 1987*

# Section 4.2

# Learning Classes Via Clustering

The previous section focused on the problem of learning general definitions of one or more concept classes. In clustering, the number of concept classes is not necessarily fixed in advance and the goal of a clustering program is to find class boundaries that provide the "best" separation among several classes.

The CLASSIT system described in the article by Gennari, Langley, and Fisher in Section 4.2.1 performs incremental concept formation; it deals with learning tasks in which it is not feasible for a program to review all the available data at once. Therefore, the program is required to update its partial definitions of the boundaries of concept classes when new instances become available, without being able to review the old data from which those partial definitions were formed.

Statistical clustering programs use some measure of distance in the feature space (e.g., Euclidean distance) as a way of defining the best separation rules. Cheeseman et al.'s AUTOCLASS program, described in Section 4.2.2, uses a Bayesian rule (i.e., one that uses prior probabilities of class membership) to cluster objects in a set of data. AUTOCLASS has demonstrated its success in making sense of complex astronomy data.

# Models of Incremental Concept Formation

**John H. Gennari, Pat Langley and Doug Fisher***

*Irvine Computational Intelligence Project,*
*Department of Information and Computer Science,*
*University of California, Irvine, CA 92717, U.S.A.*

ABSTRACT

*Given a set of observations, humans acquire concepts that organize those observations and use them in classifying future experiences. This type of concept formation can occur in the absence of a tutor and it can take place despite irrelevant and incomplete information. A reasonable model of such human concept learning should be both incremental and capable of handling the type of complex experiences that people encounter in the real world. In this paper, we review three previous models of incremental concept formation and then present CLASSIT, a model that extends these earlier systems. All of the models integrate the process of recognition and learning, and all can be viewed as carrying out search through the space of possible concept hierarchies. In an attempt to show that CLASSIT is a robust concept formation system, we also present some empirical studies of its behavior under a variety of conditions.*

## 1. Introduction

Much of human learning can be viewed as a gradual process of *concept formation*. In this view, the agent observes a succession of objects or events from which he induces a hierarchy of concepts that summarize and organize his experience This task is very similar to the problem of *conceptual clustering* as defined by Michalski and Stepp [30], with the added constraint that learning be incremental. More formally:

- *Given*: a sequential presentation of instances and their associated descriptions;
- *Find*: clusterings that group those instances in categories;
- *Find*: an intensional definition for each category that summarizes its instances;
- *Find*: a hierarchical organization for those categories.

*Current address: Department of Computer Science, Vanderbilt University, Nashville, TN, U.S.A.

0004-3702/89/$3.50 © 1989, Elsevier Science Publishers B.V. (North-Holland)

*Artificial Intelligence* **40** (1989) 11–61

This paper originally appeared in the journal, *Artificial Intelligence*, Vol. 40, Nos. 1-3, and is reprinted here with permission of the publisher, Elsevier, Amsterdam.

The goals of conceptual clustering are straightforward: to help one better understand the world and to make predictions about its future behavior. Concept formation has essentially the same goals, and differs mainly in the constraints it places on achieving them.

In this paper, we focus on the concept formation task and examine some methods for incrementally forming clusters, concept descriptions, and concept hierarchies. We begin by attempting to abstract the features that are common to the existing work on concept formation and that set it apart from other approaches. After this, we review in some detail three models of the concept formation process—Feigenbaum's [9] EPAM, Lebowitz's [24, 26] UNIMEM, and Fisher's [12] COBWEB. Next we describe CLASSIT, an extension of Fisher's system, and report some experimental studies of the program's learning behavior. We close with some suggestions for future research and a summary of our main observations.

## 2. Methods for Concept Formation

The majority of machine learning research has focused on the broad area of concept learning. To many readers, the work on concept formation may seem a minor variation on better-known approaches, and it certainly has close ties to other work. However, methods for concept formation share a number of important features that, taken together, distinguish them from other efforts. In this section we identify those features that are common to the approach and that serve to separate it from alternative paradigms, particularly other methods for conceptual clustering. In some sense, one can also view these features as "defining" the term *concept formation*.

### 2.1. Representing knowledge in a concept hierarchy

The most obvious common feature of concept formation methods is their organization of knowledge into a *concept hierarchy*. This type of data structure contains a set of nodes partially ordered by generality, and thus is similar to the *is-a* hierarchies used by some machine learning systems (Michalski [29], Mitchell, Utgoff and Banerji [32]). Each node in a concept hierarchy represents a concept, but unlike most *is-a* hierarchies, each node also contains an intensional description of that concept.

The hierarchical organization of acquired concepts is one distinctive feature of methods for concept formation (and conceptual clustering). In contrast, most work on learning from examples (Mitchell [31], Michalski [29]) focuses on learning one or a few concepts at a single level of abstraction. Methods for constructing decision trees (Quinlan [34]) are closer in spirit, but lack any explicit descriptions on the nodes themselves.

### 2.2. Top-down classification of instances

The presence of a concept hierarchy suggests a natural approach for classifying new instances that is shared by all concept formation systems. One simply begins at the most general (top) node and sorts the instance down through the hierarchy. This classification method is very similar to that used by decision-tree systems. However, the scheme for determining which branch to follow need not be based on the result of a single attribute's value, and some concept formation systems allow the instance to follow more than one branch. Nor must the instance always be sorted to a terminal node; in principle, the sorting process may stop at a node higher in the hierarchy.

Once the instance has finished its descent, one can use the concept description at the selected node to make predictions about unseen aspects of the instance. Decision-tree systems typically make predictions about the class of the instance, but concept formation systems can make predictions about a wider range of features. This suggests measuring the performance of an acquired hierarchy in terms of its ability to make predictions about unseen attributes.[1] In principle, other methods for conceptual clustering could be evaluated along the same dimension, but few researchers have taken this approach.

### 2.3. Unsupervised nature of the learning task

The unsupervised nature of the learning task leads to another common feature of concept formation systems—they must cluster instances without advice from a teacher. In other words, they must decide not only which instances each class should contain, but also the number of such classes. This is the most important feature separating work on concept formation (and conceptual clustering) from research on learning conjunctive concepts from examples (Winston [44], Mitchell [31]).

Techniques for inducing decision trees (e.g., Quinlan [34]) come much closer to concept formation methods on this dimension. Although supervised in the sense that they are given teacher-specified class information, these systems must determine their own subclasses, which equates to forming instance clusters. Rendell, Seshu and Tcheng's [35] work on probabilistic concept learning has a similar flavor.

### 2.4. Integrating learning and performance

We have defined the concept formation task to be incremental in nature. By *incremental*, we mean not only that the agent accepts instances one at a time,

[1] Although all of the concept formation systems we will examine assume attribute-value representations, the framework we outline can handle relational or structural descriptions as well. See Levinson [27] for some initial work along these lines.

but also that it does not extensively reprocess previously encountered instances while incorporating the new one. Without this constraint, one could make any nonincremental method "incremental" simply by adding the new instance to an existing set and reapplying the nonincremental method to the extended set. Note that our definition of incremental does *not* forbid retaining all instances in memory, only the extensive reprocessing of those instances. In fact, most existing methods for concept formation retain at least some instances as terminal nodes in the concept hierarchy.

This focus on incremental learning leads naturally to the integration of learning with performance. In any incremental system (Winston [44], Mitchell [31], Schlimmer and Fisher [38]), action by the performance component (e.g., classifying an instance) drives the learning element (e.g., modifying a concept hierarchy). In contrast, nonincremental schemes (Michalski [29], Quinlan [34]) isolate the processes of learning and performance. Most research on both numerical taxonomy (Everitt [8]) and conceptual clustering (Michalski and Stepp [30], Fisher [11]) has taken a nonincremental approach. Thus, this dimension constitutes one major distinction between earlier approaches to clustering and concept formation as we have defined it.

The role of classification in concept formation systems exerts a strong influence on the nature of learning. We noted above that the performance component of these methods sort instances down through a concept hierarchy. As a result, it seems natural to acquire the concept hierarchies in a top-down fashion as well. Thus, concept formation methods typically construct their hierarchies in a *divisive* manner, rather than using the *agglomerative* approach more common within the statistical clustering community.[2]

### 2.5. Learning as incremental hill climbing

The features described above seem almost to follow from the task of concept formation itself, but the final commonality has a different flavor. The models we describe in the following pages can all be characterized as *incremental hill-climbing learners*. We have elaborated on this notion elsewhere (Langley, Gennari and Iba [21], Fisher [12]), and Schlimmer and Fisher [38] described the basic idea (without using this term) even earlier. One can view concept formation as a search through a space of concept hierarchies, and hill climbing is one possible method for controlling that search.

Hill climbing is a classic AI search method in which one applies all operator instantiations, compares the resulting states using an evaluation function, selects the best state, and iterates until no more progress can be made. There are many variants on the basic algorithm, but these do not concern us here. The main advantage of hill climbing is its low memory requirement; since here

[2] For one exception, see Hanson and Bauer's work on WITT [16], an agglomerative clustering system that can operate incrementally.

are never more than a few states in memory, it sidesteps the combinatorial memory requirements associated with search-intensive methods. However, it also suffers from well-known drawbacks, such as the tendency to halt at local optima and a dependence on step size.

We are using the term *hill climbing* in a nontraditional sense, focusing on some features and ignoring others. For instance, we do not require an incremental hill-climbing learner to have an explicit evaluation function, or even that it carry out a one-step lookahead. One can replace this approach with a strong generator that computes the successor state from new input, such as an observed instance. For our purposes, the main feature of a hill-climbing system is its limited memory. At each point in learning, the system may retain only one knowledge structure, even though this structure may itself be quite complex. Thus, hill-climbing learners cannot carry out a breadth-first search (Mitchell [3]) or a beam search (Michalski [29]) through the space of hypotheses, nor can they carry out explicit backtracking (Winston [44]). They can only move "forward," revising their single knowledge structure in the light of new experience.[3]

The most important difference between incremental hill-climbing learners and their traditional cousins lies in the role of input. As we have seen, incremental learning methods are driven by new instances, and in the case of incremental hill-climbing systems, this means that each step through the hypothesis space occurs in response to (and takes into account) some new experience. More generally, each instance may lead to a number of learning steps (e.g., one for each level in the concept hierarchy). In other words, the learner does not move through the space of hypotheses until it obtains a new datum, and this alters the nature of the hill-climbing task.

Recall that hill-climbing methods search an $n$-dimensional space over which some function $f$ is defined. This function determines the shape of an $n$-dimensional surface, and the agent attempts to find that point with the highest $f$ score. In traditional hill-climbing approaches, the shape of the surface is constant. In contrast, for systems that learn through incremental hill climbing, each new instance modifies the contours of the surface. Like Simon's [41] wandering ant, the learner's behavior is controlled by the shape of its world. However, the hills and valleys of the hill-climbing learner's space are constantly changing as it gathers more information, altering the path it follows.[4] This

[3] Some "strength-based" methods retain competing hypotheses in memory, gradually deleting some and adding others on the basis of their performance. Genetic algorithms (Holland [17], Grefenstette [15]) follow this approach, as do Anderson and Kline's [2] and Langley's [20] work on production system learning. One could view these methods as incremental hill-climbing learners, provided one treats the entire set of rules as a single "state." However, we believe this violates the spirit of our limited memory assumption.

[4] Note that this feature does *not* hold for nonincremental learners that use hill-climbing methods (Michalski and Stepp [34]); the shape of the surface over which these systems travel remains constant throughout the learning process.

feature of incremental hill climbing is novel enough that it becomes unclear whether the limitations of traditional hill-climbing methods still hold. It also gives the potential for dealing with *concept drift* (Schlimmer and Granger [39]), in which the environment actually changes over time.

However, this dependence on new instances to control the search process can make memory-limited incremental learning methods sensitive to the order of instance presentation. Initial nonrepresentative data may lead a learning system astray, and one would like it to recover when later data point the way to the correct knowledge structure. Thus, Schlimmer and Fisher [38] have argued for including *bidirectional* learning operators that can reverse the effects of previous learning should new instances suggest the need. In the context of concept formation, one might include an operator not only for creating new subcategories, but also for deleting them should they not prove useful. Similarly, one might desire an operator not only for creating new disjunctive classes, but also one for combining classes if the distinction fares poorly. Such bidirectional operators can give incremental hill-climbing learners the *effect of* backtracking search without the memory required by true backtracking. Whether this approach works or not is an empirical question, but in Section 5 we will see evidence that it can help significantly.

## 2.6. Summary

In this section we identified some common threads that run through a number of research efforts, and we borrowed the term *concept formation* to refer to this research area. The basic approach can be viewed as a form of conceptual clustering, but it also differs from "traditional" work in this area. The common features of concept formation methods include the hierarchical organization of concepts, top-down classification, and an unsupervised, incremental, hill-climbing approach to learning.

We should emphasize that none of these features by itself makes work on concept formation unique. It shares many of these features with other methods for conceptual clustering, and there exist many supervised learning methods that process instances incrementally. Even the incremental hill-climbing approach has been widely used within the machine learning community, though it has not been labeled as such.[5] However, when one takes all these features together, what emerges is a distinctive and promising approach to concept learning.

[5] For example, recent work on supervised concept learning (Schlimmer and Fisher [38], Iba, Wogulis and Langley [18]) has been within this paradigm, as has recent work on theory formation (Shrager [40], Rose and Langley [36]). Much of the work on grammar acquisition (Anderson [1], Berwick [3]) has also occurred within the incremental hill-climbing framework. Even such diverse paradigms as neural networks and explanation-based learning share incremental hill climbing as an unstated assumption.

## 3. Earlier Research on Concept Formation

Before describing our own research on concept formation, we should review previous work on the problem. In this section we review three models of this process—Feigenbaum's EPAM, Lebowitz's UNIMEM, and Fisher's COBWEB. We will see that, with minor exceptions, each system operates within the common framework described in the previous section. We will also see that each system addresses issues that its predecessor ignored. This does not mean later systems are superior to earlier ones, since they also ignore some issues addressed by their precursors. However, there has been clear progress on certain fronts, and we will focus on these. We describe each model in terms of its representation and organization of knowledge, its classification and learning methods, and its metric for evaluating the resulting concepts and hierarchies.

### 3.1. Feigenbaum's EPAM

Feigenbaum's EPAM [9] can be viewed as an early model of incremental concept formation.[6] The system was intended as a psychological model of human learning on verbal memorization tasks, and it successfully explained a variety of well-established learning phenomena. These included the serial position effect, the conditions for multi-trial versus one-trial learning, forgetting through oscillation and retroactive inhibition, and a number of other empirical generalizations.

### 3.1.1. *Representation and organization in EPAM*

EPAM represents each instance as a conjunction of attribute-value pairs, along with an optional ordered list of component objects. Each component is in turn described as a conjunction of attribute-value pairs, with its own optional components, and so forth. For instance, the system might represent the nonsense syllable GAK as a list of three component objects—the first letter, the second letter, and the third letter. Each letter might itself be described in terms of lower-level components (e.g., the lines making it up), or it might be viewed as a primitive object having only attributes and no components. For simplicity, we will avoid examples that involve components and focus on single-level instances that can be described purely in terms of attribute-value pairs.

EPAM represents and organizes its acquired knowledge in a *discrimination network*. Each nonterminal node in this network specifies some *test*, and each link emanating from this node corresponds to one possible result of that test. Some tests involve examining the value of an attribute, whereas others involve examining the category of a subobject, which can itself be learned. Each

[6] For a more comprehensive treatment of EPAM and its extensions, see Feigenbaum and Simon [10].

nonterminal node also includes a branch marked OTHER, which lets EPAM avoid specifying all possible results of the test at the outset. Each terminal node contains an *image*—a partial set of attribute values (and component categories) expected to hold for instances sorted to that node.

Consider the example discrimination network in Fig. 1, which includes only attribute tests. This domain assumes instances composed of a single cell with three attributes—surface color, number of nuclei, and number of tails. The root node in Fig. 1(a) contains a test on the attribute NUCLEI, and the two links emanating from this node are labeled ONE and OTHER. The leftmost successor is a terminal node and thus has an associated image; this contains the partial description NUCLEI = ONE ∧ TAILS = ONE. (Note that color is unspecified.) The rightmost successor is nonterminal and thus has an associated test, this one involving the attribute COLOR. One link (labeled LIGHT) points to a successor node with image COLOR = LIGHT ∧ NUCLEI = TWO. The other (labeled OTHER) leads to a successor node with image COLOR = DARK.

### 3.1.2. *Classification and learning in* EPAM

As with all the concept formation systems we will examine, EPAM's classification process is completely integrated with its learning method. Table 1 presents the top-level EPAM algorithm, which focuses on performance. As the system encounters each instance, it sorts that instance through the discrimination network, starting at the top (root) node and proceeding until it reaches a

terminal node. At each node, EPAM examines the instance's value on the test specified for that node. In the case of tests examining the category of a subobject, the model calls on itself recursively to determine the appropriate category; we have omitted this option from the table for the sake of clarity. If the category or attribute value equals that on one of the emanating branches, EPAM sends the instance down that branch; otherwise it goes down the OTHER branch. Eventually, the instance reaches a terminal node. For example, in Fig. 1(a) a dark cell with one nucleus and two tails would reach the leftmost terminal node, whereas a dark cell with two nuclei and two tails would reach the rightmost one.

Once EPAM has "recognized" an object as an instance of a terminal node, it "recalls" the image associated with that node. At this point, the algorithm invokes one of two learning mechanisms. If the image matches the instance (i.e., if no attribute-value pairs differ), then *familiarization* occurs. As summarized in Table 2, this process selects an attribute that occurs in the instance but not in the image, and then adds the attribute (along with the instance's value) to the image. In this way, EPAM gradually makes its images more specific as it encounters more instances. Eventually, a given image may become so detailed that it effectively becomes equivalent to a particular instance. Given the

Table 1
The top-level EPAM algorithm

Input: The current node $N$ in the discrimination network.
     An unclassified (attribute-value) instance $I$.
Results: A discrimination net that classifies the instance.
Top-level call: EPAM(Top-node, $I$).
Variables: $N$ and $S$ are nodes in the hierarchy.
     $M$ is an image associated with a terminal node.
     $A$ is an attribute test.
     $V$ is the value of an attribute.
     $D$ is a set of attributes.

EPAM($N$, $I$)
  **If** $N$ is a terminal node,
  **Then** let $M$ be the image associated with $N$.
       Let $D$ be the set of tests on which $I$ and $M$ differ.
       **If** $D$ is the empty set,
       **Then** Familiarize($M$, $I$).
       **Else** Discriminate(Top-node, $I$, $M$, $D$, empty set).
  **Else** let $A$ be the test associated with $N$.
       Let $V$ be the value of instance $I$ on test $A$.
       **If** $N$ has a branch labeled $V$,
       **Then** let $S$ be the successor of $N$ by branch $V$.
       **Else** let $S$ be the successor of $N$ by branch OTHER.
       EPAM($S$, $I$)

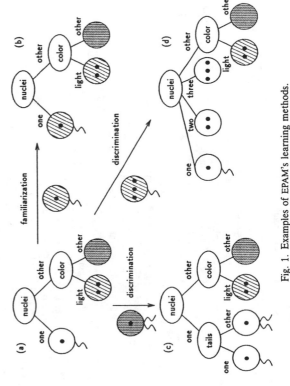

Fig. 1. Examples of EPAM's learning methods.

nonterminal node only if the instance was sorted down the OTHER branch leading from that node. If EPAM finds such a node, it creates two new branches, one based on the instance's value for the test and the other based on the image's value.[7] Each branch points to a new terminal node, and each image consists of the results of tests that lead to the node. In this way, EPAM gradually increases the breadth of its discrimination network. The transition between Fig. 1(a) and (d) gives an example of this type of discrimination, in this case invoked by the instance COLOR = LIGHT ∧ NUCLEI = THREE ∧ TAILS = ONE.

If no such node exists, the system eventually sorts the instance back down to the terminal node where the mismatch originally occurred. EPAM creates two new branches in this case as well, along with corresponding terminal nodes. The discrimination process selects a test on which the image and instance differ and which has not yet been examined. This test's value for the instance becomes the label on one branch and OTHER becomes the label for the other. The image for the instance-based node contains the results of all tests leading to that node; the image for the image-based node contains the original image plus the value for the discriminating test. In this way, EPAM gradually increases the depth of its discrimination network. The transition between Fig. 1(a) and (c) shows this type of learning in action, this time produced by the instance COLOR = DARK ∧ NUCLEI = ONE ∧ TAILS = TWO. Table 2 summarizes the overall discrimination process.

### 3.1.3. *Search control in EPAM*

In line with our discussion in Section 2, we can summarize EPAM's learning method in terms of search through a space of discrimination networks. Three basic operators make up this search:

- adding features to an image through familiarization;
- creating new disjunctive branches through discrimination;
- extending the network downward through discrimination.

Although the search-based view has its advantages, it provides little insight when one examines EPAM's control scheme. The classification method is completely deterministic, and the learning algorithm has only two choice points. One of these occurs during familiarization, when EPAM must decide which attribute to add to the image. The other occurs when discrimination must deepen the network to avoid a mismatch, when it must decide which attribute to select. One version of EPAM [9] preferred tests that had proven useful in previous discriminations. Other versions simply selected tests in a prespecified order. However, these decisions are minor in comparison to the choice between familiarization and discrimination, and between the branching

---

[7] The reason for this second branch is not clear, since the branch based on the instance's value is enough to avoid repeating the misclassification. However, we have attempted to faithfully reconstruct Feigenbaum's model as he describes it.

---

Table 2
Familiarization and discrimination in EPAM

Variables: *I* is an (attribute-value) instance.
  *N* and *S* are nodes in the hierarchy.
  *M* is an image associated with a terminal node.
  *A* is an attribute test.
  *U* and *V* are the values of attributes.
  *D* and *L* are sets of attributes.
  *T* is a set of attribute-values ((*A*, *V*), . . .).

Familiarize(*M*, *I*)
  Let *L* be those attributes in instance *I* not in image *M*.
  Select an attribute *A* from *L*.
  Let *V* be the value of *A* for *I*.
  Add the attribute-value pair (*A*, *V*) to the image *M*.

Discriminate(*N*, *I*, *M*, *D*, *T*)
  If *N* is a terminal node,
    Then Deepen(*N*, *I*, *M*, *D*, *T*).
  Else let *A* be the attribute associated with node *N*.
    Let *U* be the value of *A* for instance *I*.
    Let *V* be the value of *A* for image *M*.
    If *U* does not equal *V*,
      Then Add-branch(*N*, *U*, Union(*T*, (*A*, *U*))).
        Add-branch(*N*, *V*, Union(*T*, (*A*, *V*))).
    Else if *N* has a branch labeled *V*,
      Then let *S* be the successor of *N* by branch *V*.
      Else let *S* be the successor of *N* by branch OTHER.
      Discriminate(*S*, *I*, *M*, *D*, Union(*T*, (*A*, *U*))).

Deepen(*N*, *I*, *M*, *D*, *T*)
  Select an attribute *A* from *D*.
  Remove the image *M* from node *N*.
  Associate the attribute *A* with node *N*.
  Let *U* be the value of *A* for instance *I*.
  Let *V* be the value of *A* for image *M*.
  Add-branch(*N*, *U*, Union(*T*, (*A*, *U*))).
  Add-branch(*N*, OTHER, Union(*M*, (*A*, *U*))).

Add-branch(*N*, *V*, *I*)
  Create a successor node of *N* called *S*.
  Connect *N* to *S* with a branch having value *V*.
  Store the image *I* on *S*.

---

network in Fig. 1(a) and the instance COLOR = DARK ∧ NUCLEI = ONE ∧ TAILS = ONE, familiarization would produce the network shown in Fig. 1(b). If the image fails to match the instance (i.e., if any attribute-value pairs differ), then *discrimination* occurs instead. This process sorts the instance through the discrimination network a second time, looking for the first node at which the image and instance differ on a stored test. This can occur at a

and deepening variants of discrimination. These are completely determined by the data and the existing network.

### 3.1.4. Comments on EPAM

The EPAM model introduced some very important ideas into the machine learning literature. First, it set forth the notion of a discrimination network, and it specified an incremental method that integrated classification and learning. Second, it introduced the distinction between tests (for use in sorting) and images (for use in making predictions). One can view discrimination networks as precursors of the concept hierarchies used in later work, and images as the precursors of concept descriptions. EPAM's distinction between the process of recognition (classification) and recall (prediction) was also an important insight. Finally, it introduced the two learning mechanisms of discrimination and familiarization, which it successfully used to explain aspects of human learning and memory.

Despite its successes, EPAM also had some significant shortcomings. For instance, the system's method for selecting among attributes during discrimination and familiarization was somewhat ad hoc. Moreover, the model retained concept descriptions (images) only at terminal nodes, and so lacked a true concept hierarchy. Finally, it assumed that concepts (images) were "all or none" entities, rather than the more fluid structures suggested by recent psychological studies (Rosch [37]). The last two criticisms are not really appropriate, since EPAM's goal was to model human memorization and not the broader area of concept formation. However, our concern here is with models of the latter process, and so we have evaluated Feigenbaum's work in those terms.

### 3.2. Lebowitz's UNIMEM

One can view Lebowitz's UNIMEM [24, 25] as a successor to EPAM,[8] since it shares many features with the earlier model, but also introduces some novel ideas. The motivation behind the two systems was also quite different. EPAM modeled empirical results from verbal learning experiments, whereas Lebowitz focused on the acquisition and use of concepts for more complex tasks such as natural language understanding and inference. In addition, UNIMEM was cast within a broader framework called *generalization-based memory*. Another system that independently incorporated many of the same advances as UNIMEM, is Kolodner's [19] CYRUS. We will highlight similarities and differences between these systems as they become relevant. Our stress on UNIMEM is due primarily to Lebowitz's [26] treatment of his system as conceptual clustering, a topic of primary interest for this paper.

[8] Actually, UNIMEM is a direct descendant of Lebowitz's [22, 23] IPP system. For a discussion of the differences between these two models, see Lebowitz [26].

### 3.2.1. Representation and organization in UNIMEM

UNIMEM represents instances in the same manner as EPAM—as a conjunction of features or attribute-value pairs. In one sense, it is less general than the earlier model, since it cannot handle objects with components, though Wasserman [43] has addressed this issue within the UNIMEM framewok. However, Lebowitz's system is more general than Feigenbaum's in that it can handle numeric attributes in addition to nominal (symbolic) ones. Thus, an instance that describes a university would have some nominal attributes (e.g., location, academic-emphasis) and some numeric attributes (e.g., male/female ratio, average SAT score). In addition, nominal attributes can take on more than one value, letting the system represent sets.

Lebowitz's approach diverges even more from Feigenbaum's in its representation and organization of concepts. In EPAM's network, only terminal nodes have associated images, but in UNIMEM both terminal and nonterminal nodes have concept descriptions. Each description consists of a conjunction of attribute-value pairs, with each value having an associated integer. This number measures what Lebowitz refers to as the *confidence* in that feature. Later, we will see that this corresponds to the idea of *predictability*, i.e., how well the feature can be predicted given an instance of the concept. In order to use consistent terminology, we refer to this count as the "predictability score" for a feature.[9]

Like its precursor, UNIMEM organizes knowledge into a concept hierarchy through which it sorts new instances. However, the details of this hierarchy differ from EPAM's discrimination network. We have mentioned that Lebowitz's system stores concept descriptions with each node in the hierarchy. Nodes high in the hierarchy represent general concepts, with their children representing more specific concepts, their children still more specific concepts, and so on. Each concept has an associated set of instances stored with it; these can be viewed as terminal nodes in the hierarchy, though Lebowitz does not describe them in this fashion. Thus UNIMEM's terminal nodes are quite specific from the outset;[10] this contrasts with EPAM's images, which converge on completely specified instances only after considerable learning. Another difference is that, unlike EPAM, each instance may be stored with multiple nodes, so that categories need not be disjoint.

As in Feigenbaum's system, UNIMEM's network consists of nodes and links, with each of a node's links leading to a different child. However, in EPAM each link was labeled with the result of a single test. In contrast, UNIMEM allows

[9] Kolodner's [19] CYRUS uses a similar concept representation scheme, but maintains a probability rather than an integer with each attribute value. We argue in the context of our COBWEB discussion that this is an important distinction.

[10] Actually, the system stores only those features not inherited from nodes higher in the hierarchy, but the effect is the same as storing completely specified instances.

each link to specify the results of multiple tests (i.e., to specify multiple features). This redundant indexing lets the system handle instances with missing attributes and, as we describe below, it allows a very flexible sorting strategy. In addition, each feature on a link has an associated integer score, specifying the number of links on which that feature occurs. This second score measures the *predictiveness* of the feature, i.e., how well it can be used to predict instances of the various children.

Figure 2 presents a simple UNIMEM hierarchy after the system has created three concept nodes from six instances. For each node, we have shown its feature list and associated predictability scores. (For simplicity, we have omitted the predictability scores.) These scores represent the number of times a feature has been reinforced by successive instances. Note that one instance is indexed into both top-level nodes. This instance affects the predictability scores for both level-one nodes, although it is only incorporated into one of them.

### 3.2.2. *Classification and learning in UNIMEM*

Like other concept formation systems, UNIMEM integrates the processes of classification and learning. It sorts each instance through its concept hierarchy, modifying this hierarchy in the process. Table 3 summarizes the main steps in the algorithm.

As UNIMEM descends through its hierarchy, it uses the features (i.e., the attribute-value pairs) on each node and its emanating links to sort the instance. If the instance matches the description on the node closely enough, then it sends the instance down those links that contain features in the instance, and it continues the process with the relevant children. Both the number of features

necessary for this match and the closeness of each value (for numeric attributes) are system parameters.[11] Whether or not the instance successfully matches, UNIMEM calls on EVALUATE (which we discuss in Section 3.2.3) to modify the node's scores. Note that, in some cases, the system may sort an instance down multiple paths in the hierarchy.

Eventually UNIMEM reaches a node that matches the instance but none of whose children match. In this case, the system examines all instances currently stored with the node, comparing each of them in turn to the new instance. If an old instance shares enough features with a new one (another system parameter), the model creates a new, more general node based on these features and stores both instances as its children. When this occurs, the system increments the predictiveness count for each feature indexing the new node.

[11] UNIMEM uses a distance metric to determine the degree of match between two numeric values. This is an important issue, to which we will return in Section 4.

---

Table 3
The basic UNIMEM algorithm

Input: The current node $N$ of the concept hierarchy.
  The name of an unclassified instance $I$.
  The set of $I$'s unaccounted features $F$.
Results: The concept hierarchy that classifies the instance.
Top-level call: Unimem(Top-node, $I$, $F$).
Variables: $N$ and $C$ are nodes in the hierarchy.
  $G$, $H$, and $K$ are sets of features (attribute values).
  $J$ is an instance stored on a node.
  $S$ is a list of nodes.

Unimem($N$, $I$, $F$).
  Let $G$ be the set of features stored on $N$.
  Let $H$ be the features in $F$ that match features in $G$.
  Let $K$ be the features in $F$ that do not match features in $G$.
  If $N$ is not the root node,
    Then If Evaluate($N$, $H$, $K$) returns TRUE or there are too few features in $H$,
      Then return the empty list.
  Let $S$ be the empty list.
  For each child $C$ of node $N$,
    If $C$ is indexed by a feature in $K$,
      Then let $S$ be Union($S$, Unimem($C$, $I$, $K$)).
  If $S$ is the empty list,
    Then for each instance $J$ of node $N$,
      Let $S$ be Union($S$, Generalize($N$, $J$, $I$, $F$)).
  If $S$ is the empty list,
    Then store $I$ as an instance of node $N$ with features $K$.
      For each feature $J$ in $F$ serving as in index to $N$,
        Increment the predictiveness score $R$ of $J$ by 1.
        If $R$ is high enough,
          Then remove $J$ as an index leading to $N$.

  Return $N$.

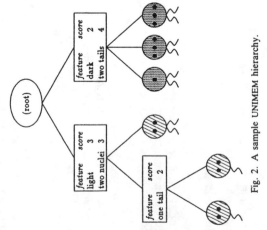

Fig. 2. A sample UNIMEM hierarchy.

Note that when UNIMEM places an instance into more than one category, these categories overlap: they do not form disjoint partitions over the instances. In the literature on cluster analysis (Everitt [8]), this approach has been called *clumping*. Lebowitz [26] has argued that in some domains, overlapping concepts may describe the data more accurately than disjoint partitions. In addition, clumping introduces flexibility into the search for useful categories. UNIMEM may initially decide to retain multiple categories and later decide to remove one or more of them. This gives the effect of a beam search while still working within the hill-climbing metaphor described in Section 2. The clumping strategy and its associated advantages are shared by CYRUS.

### 3.2.3. Evaluation and pruning in UNIMEM

We have noted that UNIMEM retains two counts on nodes' features. The EVALUATE procedure shown in Table 4 updates these scores each time the system attempts to match an instance to a node's description. If a given feature in the instance matches a feature on the node, UNIMEM increments the predictability score for that feature. The increment for nominal attributes is one; the increment for numeric attributes is a function of the distance between the stored and observed values. If a given instance feature fails to match a node feature, the system decrements that feature's predictability score in a similar fashion.

When the predictability score for a feature exceeds a (user-specified) threshold, UNIMEM permanently fixes that feature as part of the node's description, so that future instances no longer affect it. More important, when a feature's score drops below another (user-specified) threshold, the system removes that feature from the concept description. In this way, an initially specific concept may gradually become more and more general. However, it may also become so general that it has little usefulness in making predictions. Thus, when the number of features stored on a node becomes low enough (another parameter), UNIMEM removes the node from memory along with all links to its children.

When the predictiveness score for a node's feature becomes too high (i.e., when the feature indexes too many children), UNIMEM removes that feature from links emanating from the node. In this way, concepts that were originally retrieved often may become accessed more selectively. However, if the system removes all indices to a child, that node is effectively forgotten, since there is no longer any way to sort instances to it. This is another way in which UNIMEM prunes its concept hierarchy.

### 3.2.4. Comments on UNIMEM

To summarize, UNIMEM can be viewed as carrying out a hill-climbing search through a space of concept hierarchies. This search process involves six basic operators:

Since UNIMEM compares the new instance to each of the stored instances, it can form multiple nodes in this manner. Table 4 summarizes the steps in this GENERALIZE process. [12] If none of the existing instances are similar enough to the new one, the system simply stores it with the current node, effectively creating a new disjunct.

[12] Our description of the UNIMEM algorithm (Tables 3 and 4) differs syntactically from that given by Lebowitz [24, 26]. Our somewhat different view of his algorithm produced a different organization to the specification. We believe that our description is clearer and functionally equivalent to Lebowitz's.

Table 4
UNIMEM's update and evaluation processes

Variables: $N$ and $C$ are nodes in the hierarchy.
$F, G, H,$ and $K$ are sets of features (attribute values).
$I$ and $J$ are the names of instances.
$S$ and $T$ are predictability scores of nodes' features.
$R$ is the predictiveness score of a node's feature.

Generalize($N, J, I, F$)
  Let $G$ be the features in instance $J$.
  Let $H$ be the features in $F$ that match features in $G$.
  If $H$ contains enough features,
    Then create a new child $C$ of node $N$.
      Index and describe $C$ by the features in $H$.
      For each feature $K$ serving as index to $C$,
        Increment the predictiveness score $R$ of $K$ by 1.
        If $R$ is high enough,
          Then remove $K$ as an index.
      Remove $J$ as an instance of $N$.
      Let $G'$ be the features in $G$ that are not in $H$.
      Let $F'$ be the features in $F$ that are not in $H$.
      Store $J$ as an instance of $C$ with features $G'$.
      Store $I$ as an instance of $C$ with features $F'$.
      Return $C$.

Evaluate($N, H, K$)
  For each nonpermanent feature $F$ in $H$,
    Raise the predictability score $S$ for $F$ on $N$.
    If $S$ is high enough,
      Then make $F$ a permanent feature of $N$.
  For each nonpermanent feature $G$ in $K$,
    Lower the predictability score $T$ for $G$ on $N$.
    If $T$ is low enough,
      Then remove the feature $G$ from $N$.
      If $N$ has too few features,
        Then remove $N$ from its parent's list of children.
          Remove all indices serving $N$.
          Return TRUE

  Return FALSE

– storing a new instance with a node (creating a new disjunct);
– creating a more general node based on the features shared by two instances;

– permanently fixing a feature in a node's description;
– deleting an unreliable feature from a node's description;
– deleting an overly general node (and its children);
– deleting a nonpredictive index to a node's children.

Lebowitz's approach to concept formation introduces a number of advances over EPAM. Each node in the UNIMEM hierarchy has an associated concept description, rather than just the terminal nodes. Moreover, each feature in these descriptions has associated weights; thus concepts are less "all or none." There is a clear evaluation of concepts and their components, and the notions of predictiveness and predictability further clarify the distinction between recognition (classification) and recall (prediction). The system also introduced the possibility of multiple indices to a given concept, and provided one method for constructing nondisjoint hierarchies. Each of these general advances is also true of CYRUS, although their realization differs in some important respects from UNIMEM.

However, UNIMEM also has significant drawbacks as a model of concept formation. The measures of predictiveness and predictability are informal and have no clear semantics. The system also lacks a principled method for deciding between learning operators, being dependent on user-specified parameters to make such decisions. Lebowitz [26] has carried out initial studies on how these parameters affect the system's behavior, but much work remains before their full impact becomes clear.

### 3.3. Fisher's COBWEB

Fisher's [12, 13] COBWEB constitutes another algorithm for incremental concept formation. As we will see below, this research builds heavily on Lebowitz's earlier approach, and it also borrows from Kolodner's [19] work on CYRUS. Although Fisher does not present COBWEB itself as a psychological model, it has been heavily influenced by research in cognitive psychology on basic-level and typicality effects (Rosch [37]). Briefly, experiments with humans suggest that some categories are more "basic" than others, being retrieved more rapidly and named more frequently. In addition, there is evidence that for a given category, some members are more "typical" than others, being retrieved more quickly and rated as better examples. Fisher [13] describes COBWEB/2, a related system that models these effects, but we will focus on the simpler COBWEB instead.

### 3.3.1. Representation and organization in COBWEB

Like its predecessors, Fisher's system represents each instance as a set of attribute-value pairs. The mapping is closest to EPAM, since each attribute takes on only one value and since only nominal attributes are allowed.[13] As in UNIMEM, each concept node is described in terms of attributes, values, and associated weights, but here the similarity ends. One difference is that COBWEB stores the probability of each concept's occurrence. Another is that each node, from the most specific to the most general, includes every attribute observed in the instances. Moreover, associated with each attribute is every possible value for that attribute. Each such value has two associated numbers, which roughly correspond to Lebowitz's predictiveness and predictability scores. However, in COBWEB these scores have a formal grounding in probability theory.

Fisher defines the *predictiveness* of a value $v$ for category $c$ as the conditional probability that an instance $i$ will be a member of $c$, given that $i$ has value $v$, or $P(c|a = v)$. Similarly, he defines the *predictability* of a value $v$ for category $c$ as the conditional probability that an instance $i$ will have value $v$, given that $i$ is a member of $c$, or $P(a = v|c)$. Actually, COBWEB does not explicitly store predictiveness scores, since it can derive them from predictability and node probability using Bayes' rule. Smith and Medin [42] have used the term *probabilistic concepts* to refer to concept representations that incorporate such conditional probabilities.

Figure 3 presents a sample concept hierarchy, including the probabilities associated with each concept and with its attribute values. For instance, the top node ($N_1$) has an associated probability of 1.0. It also states that its members have an equal chance of having one or two tails and an even chance of being light or dark. Concept $N_3$ has a 50% chance of occurring, and its members so far have always had one tail and two nuclei, but have been evenly split among light and dark colors. The terminal nodes in the hierarchy—$N_2$, $N_4$, $N_5$, and $N_6$—have less interesting probabilistic descriptions, since each is based on a single instance. However, note that the probability of each node's occurrence is specified relative to its parent, rather than with respect to the entire distribution.

COBWEB's concept hierarchy is similar to UNIMEM's in that each node has an associated "image," with more general nodes higher in the hierarchy and more specific ones below their parents. However, the system's terminal nodes are always specific instances that it has encountered; unlike UNIMEM, it never deletes instances. In addition, the hierarchy divides instances into disjoint classes. More important, COBWEB links parents to their children only through *is-a* links. The system differs from both EPAM and UNIMEM in that it avoids explicit indices stated as tests on attribute values. Thus, the sample hierarchy shown in Fig. 3 has a different semantics than those we have seen earlier. This assumption leads to a novel method for sorting instances through the concept hierarchy.

[13] In Section 4, we will see how COBWEB can be extended to handle both numeric attributes and instances involving multiple components.

Table 5
The COBWEB algorithm

Input: The current node $N$ of the concept hierarchy.
       An unclassified (attribute-value) instance $I$.
Results: A concept hierarchy that classifies the instance.
Top-level call: Cobweb(Top-node, $I$).
Variables: $C$, $P$, $Q$, and $R$ are nodes in the hierarchy.
           $U$, $V$, $W$, and $X$ are clustering (partition) scores.

Cobweb($N$, $I$)
  **If** $N$ is a terminal node,
    **Then** Create-new-terminals($N$, $I$)
         Incorporate ($N$, $I$).
  **Else** Incorporate($N$, $I$).
    **For** each child $C$ of node $N$,
      Compute the score for placing $I$ in $C$.
    Let $P$ be the node with the highest score $W$.
    Let $R$ be the node with the second highest score.
    Let $X$ be the score for placing $I$ in a new node $Q$.
    Let $Y$ be the score for merging $P$ and $R$ into one node.
    Let $Z$ be the score for splitting $P$ into its children.
    **If** $W$ is the best score,
      **Then** Cobweb($P$, $I$) (place $I$ in category $P$).
    **Else if** $X$ is the best score,
      **Then** initialize $Q$'s probabilities using $I$'s values
           (place $I$ by itself in the new category $Q$).
    **Else if** $Y$ is the best score,
      **Then** let $O$ be Merge($P$, $R$, $N$).
           Cobweb($O$, $I$).
    **Else if** $Z$ is the best score,
      **Then** Split($P$, $N$).
           Cobweb($N$, $I$).

Fig. 3. A sample COBWEB hierarchy with nodes numbered in order of creation.

$P(N_1)=4/4$

| | | P(v\|c) |
|---|---|---|
| TAILS | ONE | 0.50 |
| | TWO | 0.50 |
| COLOR | LIGHT | 0.50 |
| | DARK | 0.50 |
| NUCLEI | ONE | 0.25 |
| | TWO | 0.50 |
| | THREE | 0.25 |

$P(N_2)=1/4$

| | | P(v\|c) |
|---|---|---|
| TAILS | ONE | 1.0 |
| | TWO | 0.0 |
| COLOR | LIGHT | 1.0 |
| | DARK | 0.0 |
| NUCLEI | ONE | 1.0 |
| | TWO | 0.0 |
| | THREE | 0.0 |

$P(N_3)=2/4$

| | | P(v\|c) |
|---|---|---|
| TAILS | ONE | 0.0 |
| | TWO | 1.0 |
| COLOR | LIGHT | 0.5 |
| | DARK | 0.5 |
| NUCLEI | ONE | 0.0 |
| | TWO | 1.0 |
| | THREE | 0.0 |

$P(N_6)=1/4$

| | | P(v\|c) |
|---|---|---|
| TAILS | ONE | 1.0 |
| | TWO | 0.0 |
| COLOR | LIGHT | 0.0 |
| | DARK | 1.0 |
| NUCLEI | ONE | 0.0 |
| | TWO | 0.0 |
| | THREE | 1.0 |

$P(N_4)=1/2$

| | | P(v\|c) |
|---|---|---|
| TAILS | ONE | 0.0 |
| | TWO | 1.0 |
| COLOR | LIGHT | 1.0 |
| | DARK | 0.0 |
| NUCLEI | ONE | 0.0 |
| | TWO | 1.0 |
| | THREE | 0.0 |

$P(N_5)=1/2$

| | | P(v\|c) |
|---|---|---|
| TAILS | ONE | 0.0 |
| | TWO | 1.0 |
| COLOR | LIGHT | 1.0 |
| | DARK | 0.0 |
| NUCLEI | ONE | 0.0 |
| | TWO | 1.0 |
| | THREE | 0.0 |

### 3.3.2. *Classification and learning in* COBWEB

The basic COBWEB algorithm is quite simple, as can be seen from the summaries in Tables 5 and 6. Again classification and learning are intertwined, with each instance being sorted down through a concept hierarchy and altering that hierarchy in its passage. The system initializes its hierarchy to a single node, basing the values of this concept's attributes on the first instance. Upon encountering a second instance, COBWEB averages its values into those of the concept and creates two children, one based on the first instance and another based on the second.

Unlike EPAM and UNIMEM, Fisher's model does not use explicit tests or indices to retrieve potential categories. Instead, at each node COBWEB retrieves all children and considers placing the instance in each of these categories. Each of these constitutes an alternative *clustering* (a set of clusters with a common parent) that incorporates the new instance. Using an evaluation function that we describe in Section 3.3.3, it then selects the best such clustering. COBWEB also considers creating a new category that contains only the new instance, and compares this clustering to the best clustering that uses only existing categories. If the clustering based on existing classes wins the competition, COBWEB modifies the probability of the selected category and the conditional prob-

abilities for its attribute values. Thus, predictability scores for values occurring in the instance will increase, whereas those for values not occurring will decrease. Predictiveness scores change as well, but since the system does not actually store these, it does not update them explicitly. In addition, COBWEB continues to sort the instance down through the hierarchy, recursively considering the children of the selected category. Node $N_3$ in Fig. 3 shows the result of incorporating a new instance into an existing node. At an earlier stage, this had been a terminal node based on a single instance. However, the act of hosting a new instance has left its COLOR probabilities evenly divided and given it two children.

If the clustering with the singleton class emerges as the winner, COBWEB creates this new category and makes it a child of the current parent node. The system bases the values for this new concept's attributes on those found in the instance, giving them each predictability scores of one. In this case, classification halts at this step, since the new concept is a terminal node. Node $N_6$ in

resulting clustering is better (according to the function described in Section 3.3.3) than the original, it combines the two nodes into a single category, though still retaining the original nodes as its children. This transforms a clustering of $N$ nodes into one having $N-1$ nodes, as in the transition shown by Fig. 4.

The system also incorporates the inverse operation of *splitting* nodes. At each level, if COBWEB decides to classify an instance as a member of an existing category, it also considers removing this category and elevating its children. If this action leads to an improved clustering, the system changes the structure of its hierarchy accordingly. Thus, if one of $N$ nodes at a given level has $M$ children, splitting this node would give $N+M-1$ nodes at this level, as depicted by the transition in Fig. 5.

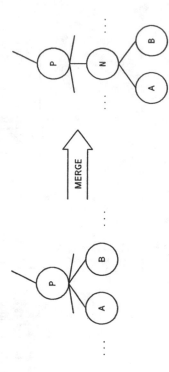

Fig. 4.  Merging categories in COBWEB.

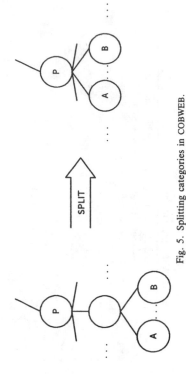

Fig. 5.  Splitting categories in COBWEB.

Table 6
Auxiliary COBWEB operations

Variables: $N$, $O$, $P$, and $R$ are nodes in the hierarchy.
          $I$ is an unclassified instance
          $A$ is a nominal attribute.
          $V$ is a value of an attribute.

Incorporate($N$, $I$)
    Update the probability of category $N$.
    **For** each attribute $A$ in instance $I$,
        **For** each value $V$ of $A$,
            Update the probability of $V$ given category $N$.

Create-new-terminals($N$, $I$)
    Create a new child $M$ of node $N$.
    Initialize $M$'s probabilities to those for $N$.
    Create a new child $O$ of node $N$.
    Initialize $O$'s probabilities using $I$'s values.

Merge($P$, $R$, $N$)
    Make $O$ a new child of $N$.
    Set $O$'s probabilities to be $P$ and $R$'s average.
    Remove $P$ and $R$ as children of node $N$.
    Add $P$ and $R$ as children of node $O$.
    Return $O$.

Split($P$, $N$)
    Remove the child $P$ of node $N$.
    Promote the children of $P$ to be children of $N$.

Fig. 3 was created in this fashion, since the instance it summarizes was sufficiently different from node $N_2$ and $N_3$.

Although in principle the above method provides everything needed to construct hierarchies of probabilistic concepts, it can be sensitive to the order of instance presentation, creating different hierarchies from different orders of the same data. In particular, if the initial instances are nonrepresentative of the entire population, one may get hierarchies with poor predictive ability. For example, if the first instances are all conservative congressmen, the algorithm would create subcategories of these at the top level. When it finally encountered instances of liberal congressmen, it would create one category for them at the top level. However, it would still have all the conservative instances at this same level, when one would prefer them grouped under a separate category.

COBWEB includes two additional operators to help it recover from such nonoptimal hierarchies. At each level of the classification process, the system considers *merging* the two[14] nodes that best classify the new instance. If the

[14] Although one could consider merging all possible node pairs, such a strategy would be costly and unlikely to improve the resulting hierarchy.

### 3.3.3. *Evaluation in* COBWEB

We have made numerous references to COBWEB's evaluation function, but we have yet to define this metric. We have also mentioned Fisher's concern with the basic-level phenomena, but we have yet to show how the system has been influenced by these phenomena. The key to both issues involves *category utility*, a measure that Gluck and Corter [14] have shown predicts the basic level found in psychological experiments. They derive this function by two paths, one using information theory and the other using game theory.

COBWEB uses a slightly generalized version of Gluck and Corter's function to control its classification and learning behavior. Category utility favors clusterings that maximize the potential for inferring information (Fisher [13]). In doing this, it attempts to maximize intra-class similarity and inter-class differences, and it also provides a principled tradeoff between predictiveness and predictability. The basic measure assumes that concept descriptions are probabilistic in nature. We do not have space to rederive this metric, but we can consider some of its characteristics.

For any set of instances, any attribute-value pair, $A_i = V_{ij}$, and any class, $C_k$, one can compute $P(A_i = V_{ij}|C_k)$, the conditional probability of the value given membership in the class, or its predictability. One can also compute $P(C_k|A_i = V_{ij})$, the conditional probability of membership in the class given this value, or its predictiveness. One can combine these measures of individual attributes and values into an overall measure of clustering quality. Specifically,

$$\sum_i \sum_j P(A_i = V_{ij}) P(C_k|A_i = V_{ij}) P(A_i = V_{ij}|C_k) \qquad (1)$$

represents a tradeoff between predictability $P(A_i = V_{ij}|C_k)$ and predictiveness $P(C_k|A_i = V_{ij})$ that has been summed across all classes ($k$), attributes ($i$), and values ($j$). The probability $P(A_i = V_{ij})$ weights the individual values, so that frequently occurring values play a more important role than those occurring less frequently.

Using Bayes' rule, we have $P(A_i = V_{ij})P(C_k|A_i = V_{ij}) = P(C_k)P(A_i = V_{ij}|C_k)$, letting us transform expression (1) into the alternative form

$$\sum_k P(C_k) \sum_i \sum_j P(A_i = V_{ij}|C_k)^2. \qquad (2)$$

Gluck and Corter have shown that the subexpression $\sum_i \sum_j P(A_i = V_{ij}|C_k)^2$ is the *expected* number of attribute values that one can correctly guess for an arbitrary member of class $C_k$. This expectation assumes a *probability matching* strategy, in which one guesses an attribute value with a probability equal to its probability of occurring. Thus, it assumes that one guesses a value with probability $P(A_i = V_{ij}|C_k)$ and that this guess is correct with the same probability.

Gluck and Corter build on expression (2) in their derivation. They define category utility as the *increase* in the expected number of attribute values that can be correctly guessed, given a set of $n$ categories, over the expected number of correct guesses without such knowledge. The latter term is simply ($\sum_i \sum_j P(A_i = V_{ij})^2$), so one must subtract this from expression (2). The complete expression for category utility is thus

$$\frac{\sum_{k=1}^{K} P(C_k) \sum_i \sum_j P(A_i = V_{ij}|C_k)^2 - \sum_i \sum_j P(A_i = V_{ij})^2}{K}. \qquad (3)$$

Note that the difference between the two expected numbers is divided by $K$, the number of categories. This division lets one compare different size clusterings, which must occur whenever one considers merging, splitting, or creating a new category.

Since category utility is based on expected numbers of correct guesses about attribute values, it suggests predictive ability as the natural measure of behavior. Fisher has tested COBWEB on both natural and artificial domains, measuring its performance by asking it to predict missing attribute values on test instances. This approach is similar to Quinlan's [34] methodology for evaluating supervised learning systems, except that one averages across many attributes rather than predicting a single one (the class name). In Section 4, we will extend this notion of prediction (and category utility) to domains involving numeric attributes.

COBWEB is not the first inductive learning system that has employed an evaluation function based on information theory. The best-known work of this type is Quinlan's [34] ID3 method for constructing decision trees. Machine learning researchers have explored many extensions and variations of the basic technique, including incremental versions (Schlimmer and Fisher [38]). Rendell et al.'s [35] PLS system also uses an information-theoretic metric to direct its divisive construction of disjunctive concept descriptions. In addition, Hanson and Bauer [16] have used an information-based function in their WITT clustering system, Cheeseman et al. [6] have used a Bayesian approach in their nonincremental clustering system AUTOCLASS, and Anderson (personal communication) has used conditional probabilities in his recent work on incremental clustering.

### 3.3.4. *Comments on* COBWEB

Like its predecessors, one can view COBWEB as carrying out a hill-climbing search through a space of concept hierarchies. In this case, there are four main operators

- classifying the object into an existing class;
- creating a new class (a new disjunct);

– combining two classes into a single class (merging);
– dividing a class into several classes (splitting).

The system employs an evaluation function—category utility—to determine which operator (and which instantiation) to employ at each point in the classification process.

The use of a well-defined evaluation function constitutes an advance over previous work on concept formation, as does Fisher's reformulation of predictiveness and predictability in terms of conditional probabilities. The explicit inclusion of merging and splitting also seems desirable, since they should let COBWEB recover from nonrepresentative samples without losing its incremental, memory-limited flavor.

However, Fisher's work also has some limitations. As implemented, COBWEB can handle only nominal attributes, whereas UNIMEM dealt with both symbolic and numeric data. The system also assumes that each instance consists of a single "object," and thus avoids issues of finding mappings between analogous components. Finally, COBWEB retains all instances ever encountered as terminal nodes in its concept hierarchy. Although this approach works well in noise-free, symbolic domains, it can lead to "overfitting the data" in noisy or numeric domains. In these cases, some form of pruning or cutoff seems in order. These and other concerns led us to carry out the research described in the following section.

## 4. Modeling the Formation of Object Concepts

With these systems as background, we can turn to CLASSIT, a model of concept formation that attempts to improve upon earlier work. This system has been most strongly influenced by COBWEB, differing mainly in its representation of instances, its representation of concepts, and its evaluation function. However, CLASSIT uses the same basic operators and the same control strategy that Fisher's system employs. Below we describe the new model, stressing its differences from earlier systems, and explaining our motivations for introducing these differences.

### 4.1. Representation and organization in CLASSIT

Although symbolic or nominal attributes occupy an important role in natural language, they are less useful for describing the physical world. When describing a stick in English, one might say that stick is short or long, but our perceptual system can also distinguish two sticks that differ only slightly in length. This latter capability suggests that humans' representation of real-world objects can include detailed information about the quantitative features of those objects. A variety of real-world attributes can be described using real numbers, including features such as color, which are usually treated symboli-

cally. Since we are concerned with the formation of physical object concepts, CLASSIT currently only accepts real-valued attributes as input.[15] In Section 6, we will discuss combining real-valued and symbolic attributes.

Physical objects can be represented with numeric attributes by describing each object as a set of components, each with a list of attributes such as height and width. Although this approach represents some relation information implicitly (such as the adjacency of components), it does not restrict the types of objects that can be described. Furthermore, this form of numeric representation seems a more plausible output from a perception system.

The introduction of real-valued data requires an analogous extension in one's representation of concepts. There are two obvious approaches to this problem. First, one can divide each numeric attribute into ranges; by "discretizing" the continuous values, one can retain the symbolic concept representation used in COBWEB. Lebowitz [24] has taken this approach in one version of UNIMEM. Alternatively, one can represent concepts directly in terms of real-valued attributes.

CLASSIT takes the second approach, retaining COBWEB's notion of storing a probability distribution with each attribute occurring in a concept. However, instead of storing a probability for each attribute value (e.g., for a given concept C, $P(small|C) = 0.3$; $P(large|C) = 0.7$), our model stores a continuous normal distribution (bell-shaped curve) for each attribute. CLASSIT expresses each distribution in terms of a mean (average) value and a standard deviation.[16] For instance, it might believe that the average length of a dog's tail is 1.1 feet and that its standard deviation is 0.65 feet. Attributes with low standard deviations have narrow, tall distributions, whereas those with high standard deviations have wide, shallow distributions.

CLASSIT organizes concepts into a hierarchy in the same manner as do UNIMEM and COBWEB. General concepts representing many instances are near the top of the tree, with more specific concepts below them. In general, concepts lower in the hierarchy will have attributes with lower standard deviations, since they represent more specific classes with greater within-group regularity.

### 4.2. Classification and learning in CLASSIT

This new representation scheme requires no modification to COBWEB's learning operators or basic control structure. Thus, CLASSIT includes the same four

[15] Statisticians have developed methods for clustering objects described in terms of real-valued attributes; these are known as *cluster analysis* and *numerical taxonomy* (Everitt [8]). Unfortunately, these methods are usually nonincremental.

[16] Standard deviation is defined as the square root of $\sum_{i=1}^{N}(x_i - \bar{x})^2/N$. Note that this equation as written cannot be computed incrementally; all $x_i$ values need to be present. However, one can transform this expression for incremental computation by expanding the squared term and storing the sum of squares. Specifically, each concept contains a count, a sum of values, and a sum of squares. From these, we compute the mean and the standard deviation when needed.

basic operators as its predecessor—one for incorporating an instance into a existing concept, another for creating a new disjunctive concept, a third operator for merging two classes, and a final one for splitting classes. As described in Tables 5 and 6, for every new instance, the algorithm considers all four operators, computes the score of the evaluation function in each case, and selects that choice with the highest score. In Section 4.4, we will step through a detailed example of this procedure.

However, CLASSIT makes a few important additions to the basic algorithm. For example, rather than always descending to the leaves of the hierarchy as it classifies an instance, our system may decide to halt at some higher-level node. When this occurs, the system has decided that the instance is similar enough to an existing concept that further descent is unnecessary and that it should throw away specific information about that instance. We define "similar enough" with a system parameter, *cutoff*, that is based on our evaluation function.

There are two advantages of this modification. First, Quinlan [34] has shown that methods for building exhaustive decision trees tend to "overfit" the data in noisy domains, leading to decreased performance. The same effect should occur with concept formation systems, unless they employ some form of cutoff. Second, a system that retains every instance builds too large a data structure for real applications. Forgetting certain instances should lead to both better performance and to greater efficiency.

The representation of objects that CLASSIT uses requires another addition to the COBWEB algorithm. If instances are described as a set of components, how can the system correctly match instance components to concept components? For example, how can it know that the right front leg in the instance corresponds to the right front leg in the "dog" concept? In general terms, this problem is that of finding an optimal match in a weighted bipartite graph.

The brute force solution to this problem is far too expensive for practical use: to calculate the worth of every possible correspondence for $n$ components has an $O(n!)$ time cost. Instead we have used a cheaper $O(n^2)$ time complexity heuristic algorithm. Using the variances for each attribute in the concept description, CLASSIT finds a match for that component with the least associated variation. Using this as a constraint, the system then finds a match for the next most constrained component and so forth, continuing this process until all components in the concept description have been matched against components in the instance. This "greedy" approach is not assured of finding the best match, but it is likely to find an acceptable one with minimal cost.[17]

We have chosen to retain COBWEB's learning operators because we believe they provide a good framework for concept formation. The hill-climbing search organization provides a robust method for learning while making minimal demands on memory. Rather than formulating new algorithms, our goal has

---

[17] There also exists an $O(n^3)$ guaranteed algorithm for this problem, which we will describe in Section 6.

been to extend the existing program to work in new domains and with a more general representational scheme.

### 4.3. CLASSIT's evaluation function

CLASSIT's use of real-valued attributes in both instances and concepts requires a generalization of category utility, COBWEB's evaluation function. In particular, the two innermost summations in category utility (equation (3)) need to be generalized for real-valued attributes:

$$\sum_j^{values} P(A_i = V_{ij}|C_k)^2 \quad \text{and} \quad \sum_j^{values} P(A_i = V_{ij})^2.$$

Both of these terms are a sum of squares of the probabilities of all values of an attribute. The former uses probabilities given membership in a particular class, $C_k$, while the latter is without any class information. The second term is equivalent to the probability at the parent, since that node includes all instances for the clustering and therefore has no information about class membership.

In order for these terms to be applied to a continuous domain, summation must be changed to integration, and some assumption must be made about the distribution of values. Without any prior knowledge about the distribution of an attribute, the best assumption is that the distribution of values for each attribute follows a normal curve. Thus, the probability of a particular attribute value is the height of the curve at that value and the summation of the square of all probabilities becomes the integral of the normal distribution squared. For the first summation, the distribution is for a particular class, while the second must use the distribution at the parent. In either case, the integral evaluates to a simple expression:

$$\sum_j^{values} P(A_i = V_{ij})^2 \Leftrightarrow \int \frac{1}{\sigma^2 2\pi} \exp\left(\frac{x-\mu}{\sigma}\right)^2 \, dx = \frac{1}{\sigma}\frac{1}{2\sqrt{\pi}},$$

where $\mu$ is the mean and $\sigma$ is the standard deviation. Finally, since the expression is used for comparison only (see the COBWEB algorithm), the constant term $1/2\sqrt{\pi}$ can be discarded.

In summary, one can replace the innermost summations from category utility with the term $1/\sigma$. The revised evaluation function used by CLASSIT is:

$$\frac{\sum_k^K P(C_k) \sum_i^I 1/\sigma_{ik} - \sum_i^I 1/\sigma_{ip}}{K},$$

where $I$ is the number of attributes, $K$ is the number of classes in the partition, $\sigma_{ik}$ is the standard deviation for a given attribute in a given class, and $\sigma_{ip}$ is the standard deviation for a given attribute in the parent node.[18]

---

[18] In our implementation, the attribute summations are divided by $I$. This is necessary because CLASSIT allows instances to have some missing attributes.

This evaluation function is equivalent to the function used by COBWEB; it is a transformation of category utility. Unfortunately, this transformation introduces a problem when the standard deviation is zero for a concept. For any concept based on a single instance, the value of $1/\sigma$ is therefore infinite.

In order to resolve this problem, we have introduced the notion of *acuity*, a system parameter that specifies the minimum value for $\sigma$. This limit corresponds to the notion of a "just noticeable difference" in psychophysics—the lower limit on our perception ability. Because acuity strongly affects the score of new disjuncts, it indirectly controls the breadth, or branching factor of the concept hierarchy produced, just as the cutoff parameter controls the depth of the hierarchy.

### 4.4. A detailed example

Now that we have examined CLASSIT's representation, control structure, and evaluation function, we will demonstrate the system's behavior in more detail by stepping through a sample execution. For this example, we have constructed a very simple input domain. Imagine a set of rectangles that naturally divides into three classes: small, medium, and large. Each instance has only one component and is described with only three attributes; height, width, and a texture attribute. For this domain, the texture attribute is irrelevant to classification. Small rectangles have a mean height of 12.5 and width of 6.5; medium rectangles average 30 by 14 and large rectangles average 41 by 35. The texture attribute is allowed to vary over the range 5 to 40, independent of class. Note that the system is not given any class information—it is not told whether a given instance is small, medium, or large. Instead, these concepts must be induced from regularity in the data. This is precisely the task of unsupervised concept formation.

We will now step through an execution as CLASSIT encounters the first six rectangles. The system begins with an empty concept hierarchy. Suppose the first instance is a small rectangle with values of 14 for height, 7 for width and 8 for texture. This instance is used to create the root node of the hierarchy, as shown in Fig. 6(a). Since this initial concept is based on a single instance, it has the minimum value for its $\sigma$ values. For this execution the acuity parameter specifies this minimum to be 1.0 for all attributes.

For each concept created by the system, we have shown the mean and standard deviation ($\sigma$) for all attributes, as well as $P(C_k)$, the probability of that concept within the clustering. As noted earlier, concepts store cumulative sums and sum of squares in order to recompute the standard deviation incrementally. Similarly, $P(C_k)$ is computed on demand by using counts stored at each concept. In order to make clear the semantics of our concepts, we have not shown these computational values in our figures.

Figure 6(b) shows the entire concept hierarchy after the system classifies the

second instance. Since every instance encountered is incorporated into the root node, there is only one decision point as the system classifies this instance: is it different enough from the first to warrant extending the hierarchy down a level and creating separate concepts for each instance? In this case, although the second instance is also a "small" rectangle, the texture attribute is different enough from the first instance that CLASSIT creates a new level. Note that the $\sigma$ scores for height and width at the root node are unchanged; this is because the standard deviations of these attributes remain lower than acuity.

Figure 7 shows the concept hierarchy after the system observes a third instance. After incorporating the instance into the root, the system must decide whether to add the instance into an existing child concept, or to make a new disjunct at level one. In this case, the choice with the highest category quality score is to create a new disjunct. Intuitively, this occurs because the instance is

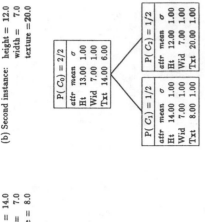

(a) First instance:  height = 14.0
                     width = 7.0
                     texture = 8.0

| P(C₀) = 1/1 | | |
|---|---|---|
| *attr* | *mean* | *σ* |
| Ht | 14.00 | 1.00 |
| Wid | 7.00 | 1.00 |
| Txt | 8.00 | 1.00 |

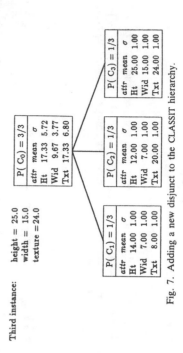

(b) Second instance:  height = 12.0
                      width = 7.0
                      texture = 20.0

| P(C₀) = 2/2 | | |
|---|---|---|
| *attr* | *mean* | *σ* |
| Ht | 13.00 | 1.00 |
| Wid | 7.00 | 1.00 |
| Txt | 14.00 | 6.00 |

| P(C₁) = 1/2 | | |
|---|---|---|
| *attr* | *mean* | *σ* |
| Ht | 14.00 | 1.00 |
| Wid | 7.00 | 1.00 |
| Txt | 8.00 | 1.00 |

| P(C₂) = 1/2 | | |
|---|---|---|
| *attr* | *mean* | *σ* |
| Ht | 12.00 | 1.00 |
| Wid | 7.00 | 1.00 |
| Txt | 20.00 | 1.00 |

Fig. 6. Extending the CLASSIT hierarchy downward.

Third instance:  height = 25.0
                 width = 15.0
                 texture = 24.0

| P(C₀) = 3/3 | | |
|---|---|---|
| *attr* | *mean* | *σ* |
| Ht | 17.33 | 5.72 |
| Wid | 9.67 | 3.77 |
| Txt | 17.33 | 6.80 |

| P(C₁) = 1/3 | | |
|---|---|---|
| *attr* | *mean* | *σ* |
| Ht | 14.00 | 1.00 |
| Wid | 7.00 | 1.00 |
| Txt | 8.00 | 1.00 |

| P(C₂) = 1/3 | | |
|---|---|---|
| *attr* | *mean* | *σ* |
| Ht | 12.00 | 1.00 |
| Wid | 7.00 | 1.00 |
| Txt | 20.00 | 1.00 |

| P(C₃) = 1/3 | | |
|---|---|---|
| *attr* | *mean* | *σ* |
| Ht | 25.00 | 1.00 |
| Wid | 15.00 | 1.00 |
| Txt | 24.00 | 1.00 |

Fig. 7. Adding a new disjunct to the CLASSIT hierarchy.

a medium-sized rectangle; attributes height and width are sufficiently different from the existing classes to cause the creation of a new concept.

Figure 8 shows the hierarchy after the system classifies a second medium-sized rectangle. In this case, adding to an existing concept has a higher score than creating a new disjunct. This instance is therefore added to the existing "medium rectangle" concept ($C_3$) at level one. The system also decides that the new instance is different enough from concept $C_3$ to continue and extend the hierarchy to level two, creating a concept for each instance at that level.

The fifth instance is a large rectangle, and the system chooses to create another disjunct at level one. Figure 9 presents the hierarchy at this stage in the learning process. Remember that CLASSIT does not label this node as "large" nor does it know that the fifth instance belongs to the large class. The system incorporates each instance into its hierarchy without the benefit of class information.

Figure 10 shows the hierarchy after CLASSIT incorporates the final instance, a third "small" rectangle. This instance allows the system to merge two level-one concepts into a more general concept describing all three "small" rectangles. In more detail, the system proceeds as follows: It first considers adding the new instance to each of the four existing classes. In this case, the concept $C_1$ in Fig. 9 is the best candidate. CLASSIT then compares this score to that of making another level-one disjunct. Finally, the system considers merging the best and

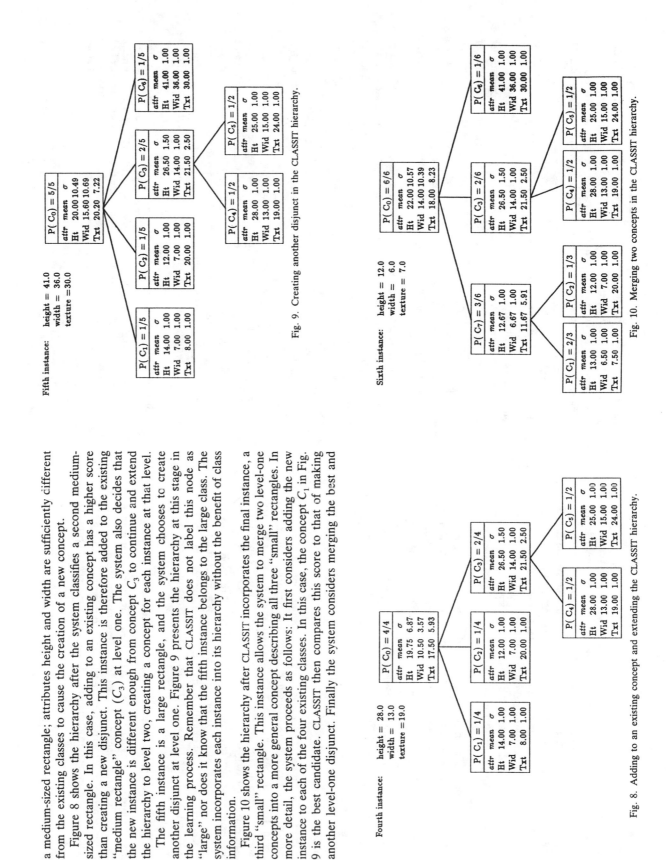

Fig. 9. Creating another disjunct in the CLASSIT hierarchy.

Fig. 10. Merging two concepts in the CLASSIT hierarchy.

Fig. 8. Adding to an existing concept and extending the CLASSIT hierarchy.

the second-best concepts into a new node; in our example, this last option has the best score.[19]

The merge operator merely pushes existing categories down a level. CLASSIT must also consider what to do with the new instance at level two. In this execution, the system decides to incorporate it into an existing child concept, $C_1$. At this point the cutoff parameter comes into play and the system decides that the new instance does not warrant its own concept at level three. This is hardly surprising, since the new instance is so close to the existing concept description that the standard deviations do not rise above acuity. In fact, the standard deviations for attributes height and width remain at acuity even for the new level-one concept, $C_7$.

CLASSIT continues processing new instances in this manner, incrementally modifying both its concept descriptions and the structure of its concept hierarchy as it encounters new data. Unlike some incremental learning systems—such as Mitchell's [31] version space method—CLASSIT never achieves a final knowledge state; the system continues to learn as long as new instances are available. This behavior is the strength of an incremental model. For example, it allows a system to recover from *concept drift*; if the environment changes over time, the learner must continue to modify his conceptual structures in response to new data.

### 4.5. A summary of CLASSIT

A principle motivation for the CLASSIT system was to model concept formation in the domain of real-valued inputs. This has affected our representation and our evaluation function. As yet, we have worked only with real-valued attributes since we feel that this type of input more closely models the output of the human perceptual system.

Since the same algorithm and four learning operators are used, CLASSIT retains the advantages of COBWEB. Both are incremental systems that integrate learning (concept formation and modification) and performance (classification), while carrying out a hill-climbing search for an optimal concept hierarchy.

## 5. Experimental Studies of CLASSIT's Behavior

One important approach to evaluating any AI system involves experimentation—studying the system's behavior under a variety of conditions. In this section, we present some experimental results that demonstrate CLASSIT's learning ability. We begin by introducing the domain we have used in most of

19 The split operator is only considered when CLASSIT is about to add to a concept that already has children.

these studies. After this, we report three experiments in which we vary aspects of CLASSIT, followed by another study in which we vary the regularity in the domain. In each case, we describe the independent and dependent variables used in the experiment, summarizing the results in graphs. We close by reporting the system's behavior on a real-world domain that involves numeric attributes.

### 5.1. The domain of quadruped mammals

For our initial experiments, we designed an artificial domain involving four-legged mammals, each described as a set of eight cylinders. This approach let us control the environment while still retaining a reasonable approximation of physical objects. One can view our representation of objects as a simplification of Binford's [5] generalized cylinders, which have received wide attention within the machine vision community. Also, Marr [28] has argued that such representations are reasonable approximations of the output of the human visual system.[20]

As discussed earlier, CLASSIT assumes that each instance consists of a set of component objects, each described by a set of real-valued attributes. In the domain of quadruped mammals, each instance consists of eight cylindrical components: a head, a neck, a torso, a tail, and four legs. Each cylinder includes attributes such as height, radius, and location; there are a total of nine attributes per component, hence 72 attribute-value pairs per instance. We believe that real-world objects have at least this order of complexity and that a robust concept formation system should be able to handle instances of this form.[21]

In the runs described below, we assumed four basic categories that differed systematically only in the sizes of their cylinders. We will refer to these classes as *cats*, *dogs*, *horses*, and *giraffes*, since their relative sizes are roughly the same as those occurring for these real-world categories. Figure 11 shows a typical instance for each of these classes. One can view the prototype for a class as the "Platonic form" or ideal for that class. To generate instances from a particular class, we use a template that defines the prototypical value for each attribute

20 We have developed CLASSIT within the context of the World Modeler's Project, a joint research effort between the University of California, Irvine, and Carnegie Mellon University. This project incorporates a simulated three-dimensional world, representing physical objects in terms of cylinders, spheres, circles, and polygons. Agents that interact with this environment perceive their surroundings directly in terms of such primitive shapes, along with their size, location, and orientation. Of course, CLASSIT need not assume such representations; it can be applied to any domain that one can express using numeric attributes.

21 A more realistic description would represent physical objects at different levels of aggregation, as Marr [28] has proposed. Thus, an animal might have four legs, with each leg having three components, etc. However, such multi-level representations introduce some difficult problems, which we discuss in Section 6.

ideal than others and some attributes tend to vary more than others. Later we will examine CLASSIT's behavior on another artificial domain, but we will use the same basic method for generating data.

### 5.2. Learning and component matching

We have claimed that CLASSIT is a learning system, and learning is usually defined as some improvement in performance. Following Fisher [12], our first experiment examined the incremental improvement in the system's ability to make predictions. The dashed line in Fig. 12 presents CLASSIT's learning curve as it incorporates instances from the domain of quadruped mammals into its concept hierarchy.

The independent variable here is simply the number of instances seen. The dependent variable is the system's ability to predict a single missing attribute from all the other attributes in an instance. We measured this variable after every five instances by "turning off" the learning component and presenting CLASSIT with five randomly selected test instances, each missing a single attribute. After classifying each instance, the system uses the selected category to predict the value of the missing attribute. The graph measures the percentage error between the predicted value and the ideal value for the instance's actual class.[22] The percentage error describes the absolute prediction error relative to the other categories present in the hierarchy. One hundred percent indicates that the system has confused the instance with the wrong category.

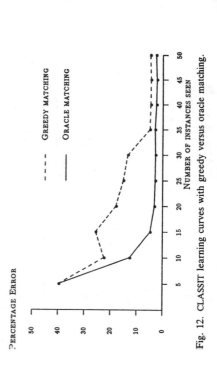

Fig. 12. CLASSIT learning curves with greedy versus oracle matching.

[22] Obviously, this measurement of error only makes sense for attributes that are relevant to classification; those attributes whose values differ across different classes. One cannot expect the system to correctly predict the value of an attribute that is irrelevant with respect to classification. Thus, we omitted only relevant attributes in measuring CLASSIT's improvement in predictive ability.

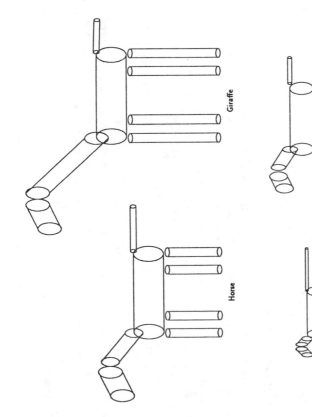

Fig. 11. Typical instances for four categories of quadruped mammals.

and a variance, specifying the degree to which that attribute will vary in the actual distribution of instances. Finally, each category has a probability that it will occur; some classes can be more common than others.

In producing data for our experiments, we used the prototype for each basic category to generate each instance according to the following procedure:

Randomly select a template C with probability P(C).
**For** each component O in the prototype for C,
  **For** each attribute A of component O,
    Let M be the typical value of A for O in template C.
    Let S be the variance of A for O in template C.
    Randomly select a value V for A according to a
      normal distribution with mean M and variance S.

Thus, every instance is a member of one of the four categories, although CLASSIT is told neither the class name nor the number of classes. Each instance diverges from the ideal for that category, though some diverge more from this

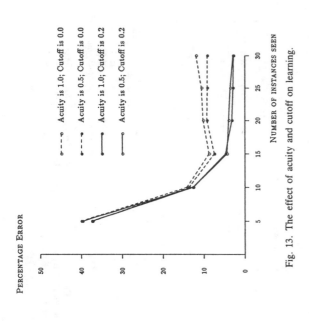

Fig. 13. The effect of acuity and cutoff on learning.

Clearly, the system's performance improves with experience, starting at 40% error and moving down to less than 5% error after 35 instances.

As described earlier, incremental algorithms tend to be sensitive to instance ordering. Although CLASSIT's split and merge operators allow some recovery from initial nonrepresentative orderings, learning curves still vary with different orderings. In order to minimize this effect, the measures in Fig. 12 have been averaged over 15 runs involving different random orderings. Also, since the data are produced randomly from templates, different instances are used for each ordering. We have followed this procedure in all our experiments.

In Section 4.2 we discussed CLASSIT's use of a greedy algorithm to match components in an instance to components in its concept descriptions, and it is this version that is summarized by the dashed line in Fig. 12. Given the heuristic nature of this matching scheme, we were interested in how it would fare against a version that had the optimal match available. The solid line in the figure shows the learning curve for such a system, in which we supplied CLASSIT with the correct correspondence between concept and instance components. This "oracle"-based variant improves its performance more quickly than the greedy version, reaching an asymptotic level after only 20 instances. However, despite some major errors early on (due to mismatched components), the greedy algorithm gradually narrows the gap, converging on nearly the same performance as the oracle version after 35 instances. This is a fairly impressive result for objects involving eight distinct components. In the remaining experiments, we report results only for the oracle version of CLASSIT, in order to factor out errors due to mismatches.

### 5.3. The effect of system parameters

We introduce the parameters for acuity and cutoff into CLASSIT only reluctantly, since such parameters encourage fine-tuning to achieve desirable behavior. To determine the effect of such tuning, we carried out the second experiment summarized in Fig. 13. As in the previous study, the horizontal axis specifies the number of instances and the vertical (dependent) axis shows the average percentage error. However, this time there are four learning curves, one for each setting of the acuity and cutoff parameters. We have repeated the oracle curve from Fig. 12, which was based on an acuity setting of 1.0 and cutoff setting of 0.2.

In this experiment we examined two levels of the cutoff parameter—0.2 and zero. The latter is the lowest possible setting, and effectively forces CLASSIT to retain all instances it has ever seen as terminal nodes in the hierarchy. Since the system always sorts a new instance as far down the hierarchy as possible, it will base its predictions on the values for a singleton concept. Unless each instance actually represents a distinct category, this strategy should lead to an

*overfitting* effect, similar to that Quinlan [34] has observed with decision trees in noisy domains.

Since we designed our quadruped data set to have only four generic categories, we would expect such overfitting on this domain as well. Indeed, the curves in Fig. 13 confirm this prediction. Both learning curves for the no-cutoff condition appear to asymptote at a higher error rate than the curves in the cutoff condition. With a higher setting for this parameter (i.e., with cutoff in operation), the system constructs simpler hierarchies with more general concepts as terminal nodes, and thus is able to make better predictions.

We also examined the effect of acuity, using two settings in this case as well. Unfortunately, the role of acuity is not as clear. In principle, one would expect overfitting to occur for low values of this parameter since this encourages CLASSIT to form many disjuncts. This should lead to a larger number of singleton classes, and thus to idiosyncratic predictions. However, this seems to occur only for extreme settings of the acuity parameter. Modifying the breadth of the hierarchy slightly does not have as strong an effect on prediction as does changing the depth of the tree with the cutoff parameter. Clearly, we need to carry out further studies to clarify the effect of this parameter.

In principle, one can get underfitting as well as overfitting effects. This should result in cases where CLASSIT constructs too shallow a hierarchy or creates too few disjunctive categories. However, the former can occur only if the "true" hierarchy contains multiple levels, and our quadruped data contains only one level of categories. For both parameters, one would expect a U-shaped curve, with high error from overfitting at one end of the spectrum and high error from underfitting at the other end, but we have not yet tested this prediction.

### 5.4. The effect of merging

We have discussed both COBWEB's and CLASSIT's potential sensitivity to the ordering of instances, and their use of merging and splitting operators to alleviate this effect. Our third experiment verifies that the merge operator has this predicted beneficial effect. Our technique was to "lesion" the system: that is, create a version of CLASSIT that cannot apply the merge operator, and compare its performance to the complete system. Recall that these "backtracking" operators are most useful when the system initially receives nonrepresentative instances. Therefore, for this experiment we arranged the order of instances by hand.

Figure 14 shows the results of an experiment in which two versions of CLASSIT—one with merging and the other without—were given a very skewed ordering of instances from the quadruped domain. First we presented five instances of the "horse" category, then five "giraffes," then five "cats," then five "dogs," then five more "horses," and finally five more "giraffes." Given such data, CLASSIT splits the initial horses into several classes at the top level, then creates new categories upon seeing the giraffes, cats, and dogs. The result is a skewed hierarchy, in which different types of horses are given the same status as the general classes of giraffes, cats, and dogs. The merge operator is designed to restructure such a hierarchy, creating a new category for horses and bringing particular horses down to an appropriate (lower) level.

Since CLASSIT sorts an instance as far down the hierarchy as possible, the internal structure of the hierarchy will have little if any effect on prediction. For this reason, we have used a different dependent measure in Fig. 14—the number of top-level categories. This measure demonstrated precisely what one would expect. The number of categories at the top level continues to increase through instance 20. At this point, the new instances of "horse" lead the merging version of CLASSIT to combine the horse nodes at the top level into a single category. By instance 25, the number of top-level horse classes has decreased to around six, and by instance 30 it has reached four, the "correct" number. Note that merging combines only two nodes at a time, so this decrease is due to a sequence of merge operations. In contrast, the nonmerging version of CLASSIT incorporates the new horses into its existing categories, but retains the same top-level classes that the initially skewed data led it to create.

### 5.5. The effect of overlap and redundancy

Having considered the effect of varying CLASSIT's components on its learning behavior, let us examine the influence of two interesting domain characteristics. The first involves the number of attributes that are *relevant* in the sense that their values vary systematically with category membership. Intuitively, the more relevant attributes, the more *redundant* the data. The second variable involves the degree to which there is overlap between categories' values on an attribute; this corresponds to the percentage area that an attribute's probability distribution shares with the distribution from a neighboring class. Intuitively, the less overlap between two categories' values on an attribute, the more *distinguishable* those classes are on that attribute.

One would expect CLASSIT to have more difficulty in forming useful categories in the presence of highly overlapping attributes. The overlap between two distributions determines the probability that, on any given instance, the attribute value will fall in the region shared by both categories. In such cases, the attribute cannot be effectively used to determine the category to which the instance should be assigned. However, one would also expect highly redundant data to mitigate this effect. The more relevant attributes, the more attributes are likely to have values falling outside the area of overlap. Thus, we can predict an interaction effect, with CLASSIT's learning behavior worsening with increased overlap between categories, but with increased numbers of relevant attributes lessening this effect.

We tested this prediction in a fourth experiment. In this case we used a somewhat simpler artificial domain that let us independently control the two domain variables. Each instance consisted of five components with six attributes each, giving a total of 30 attributes, and instances were generated from only three category templates. (Hence, we assume there should be only three top-level categories). We varied the number of relevant attributes from two to ten. This represents a large amount of irrelevant information; two thirds or more of the attributes are irrelevant to predicting an instance's class. In contrast, an instance from the quadruped domain had two thirds of its attributes relevant. We also varied the amount of overlap between zero and fifty percent.

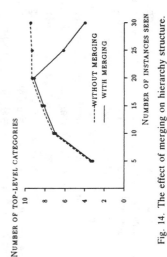

NUMBER OF TOP-LEVEL CATEGORIES

NUMBER OF INSTANCES SEEN

—— WITHOUT MERGING
——— WITH MERGING

Fig. 14. The effect of merging on hierarchy structure.

independently. This is an important direction for future work, and it may ultimately let us predict CLASSIT's behavior from domain characteristics.

### 5.6. CLASSIT in a natural domain

Our final study examined CLASSIT's behavior on a real-world domain, using data on cardiology patients (Detrano [7]). In this data set, each patient has 13 measured or derived numeric attributes, along with a "class" attribute—whether or not the patient has heart disease. Unfortunately, Detrano indicates that this class information does not have a high accuracy; he estimates a 20% error rate.

Since CLASSIT is an unsupervised learning system, we discarded the class name and presented the system only with the numeric attributes for each instance. We then measured performance in terms of whether the system created concepts that corresponded to the prespecified classes. In effect, we asked the system to rediscover the class information from regularity in the numeric data. After seeing only ten of the total 303 instances, CLASSIT created three top-level concepts, and it retained this structure for the entire learning run.

Upon inspection, we found that one of these categories clearly corresponded to patients without heart disease; some 86.1% of its members had this label in the original data. The other two classes corresponded to patients with heart disease, one more consistently than the other; the accuracy was 79.7% and 66.6% for these groups. Overall, this represents a weighted average of 78.9% accuracy, which matches very well with the expected error rate of 20%. This is impressive, given that CLASSIT arrived at these categories without benefit of the class information.

### 6. Directions for Future Research

We believe that CLASSIT constitutes a promising framework for concept formation, and that it incorporates significant advances of earlier models. However, the existing system has a number of limitations that should be remedied in future efforts, and we discuss these below. We divide our treatment into issues of representation, matching, and learning.

### 6.1. Extending CLASSIT's representation

CLASSIT is designed to operate on numeric attributes, and we feel this is appropriate for domains based on visual input. However, symbolic or nominal attributes also have their uses, and we need to extend the system to handle this form of data. Recall that Fisher designed COBWEB to operate on nominal representations, and that CLASSIT uses a nearly identical algorithm for classification and learning. Moreover, our system's evaluation function is equivalent

Figure 15 presents the results of this experiment. For simplicity, we have not reported learning curves in this case. Instead, the dependent variable shows predictive ability (average percentage error) after CLASSIT has viewed 30 instances. In all runs, we set acuity at 1.0 and cutoff at 0.2. As before, we averaged each point over 15 different random orderings.

The results are surprising. For higher numbers of relevant attributes, we see the expected interaction: increasing the number of relevant features helps more for higher levels of overlap, since they are worse to begin with. However, unexpected effects occur for lower redundancy settings, where even data with zero overlap leads to high error rates. Closer inspection suggests an explanation for this phenomenon. When there are only two relevant attributes (only one of which can be used on test instances), there are some 28 irrelevant ones that vary independently of category. Even when the relevant attributes never fall into the overlap areas, the irrelevant ones almost certainly do; despite their small individual contributions to category utility, their numbers overwhelm the small set of relevant features.

Unfortunately, this experiment confounds the total number of relevant attributes with the *percentage* of relevant attributes. To test our explanation, we must carry out further experiments in which we vary these two factors

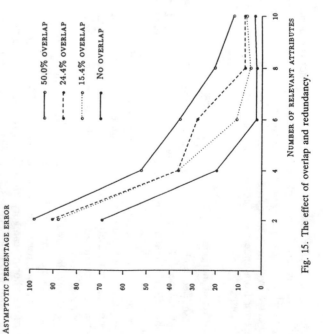

Fig. 15. The effect of overlap and redundancy.

to Fisher's category utility metric, though we have modified it to work with numeric attributes. Thus, we hope to use a mixed evaluation function that includes discrete conditional probabilities for symbolic attributes and variances for numeric ones.[23] This should result in an integrated system that supports mixed forms of data.

In our work to date, we have used a simple set of primitives for describing objects, including cylinders and polygons. Clearly, we need to extend our framework to more realistic representations of the physical world. One approach would employ arbitrary polygons, which can be used to describe the surface characteristics on any three-dimensional object in arbitrary detail. However, this approach quickly leads to an unmanageable number of components for moderately complex objects. Alternatively, one might use Binford's [5] generalized cylinders to describe the volumetric aspects of objects. These require fewer components, but they introduce complex functional expressions to describe variations from a simple cylinder, and it would be difficult to extend CLASSIT to handle this scheme.

A more promising approach involves Biederman's [4] theory of *geons*, a set of 36 primitive shapes that can represent a wide range of complex objects. We see no difficulty in replacing our cylinders and polygons with geons, combining them to form more complex structures just as we currently do with simpler shapes. As before, each primitive component would be described in terms of its basic shape, along with numeric parameters specifying its size, location, and orientation. Some geons would require additional attributes to specify relative lengths of edges, but this would not be a problem for CLASSIT. Biederman has presented evidence that humans use geons in recognizing physical objects, and we hope that our revised system would make predictions about the human classification process.

### 6.2. Improving the matching process

The process of matching components between instance and concept is central to CLASSIT's behavior. Although the "oracle" approach was useful for experimental studies, it is not appropriate for normal operation. The greedy algorithm works reasonably well, but it leads to slower learning than the oracle method. We need additional studies to determine the robustness of the greedy scheme but we should also look for improvements on this method.

One approach involves making the greedy technique more heuristic in nature. The current version selects a component from the concept at random, finds the best matching component from the instance, selects another concept component at random, and so on. However, some components may have more diagnostic attributes than others, and matching against these components first

should improve the greedy method's chances for finding the optimal correspondences.

We also plan to examine the Hungarian algorithm (Papademetriou and Steiglitz [33]), a more expensive matching process that is guaranteed to find the optimal match. Given a bipartite graph with $2n$ nodes, along with some function for evaluating the quality of a match, the Hungarian method finds the best match in $O(n^3)$ time, as compared with $O(n^2)$ time for the greedy method. The algorithm works by creating an $n \times n$ cost matrix for all possible pairs of components and then solving an "$n$ rooks" problem over this matrix. In general, we would expect this approach to perform better than the greedy algorithm. However, although it is guaranteed to find the optimal match according to CLASSIT's evaluation function, this need not agree with the "correct" match. Thus, we expect the resulting learning curve for this algorithm to fall somewhere between the two curves of Fig. 12. Whether the $n^3$ cost is prohibitive is an empirical question, but we guess that it is not, since $n$ (the number of components) should seldom exceed ten for physical objects.

### 6.3. Handling missing attributes and components

Another aspect of matching involves dealing with instances having missing attributes. The current version of CLASSIT already takes this possibility into account, dividing the summed $1/\sigma$ scores by the number of attributes present. We used this scheme in classifying instances with a single missing attribute in our experiments, but we need further studies of its behavior when many attributes have been omitted.

In addition, entire components may be missing from an instance description. If we assume that CLASSIT's input is generated by a vision system, then components may be omitted because they are not visible. We may be able to use the same evaluation function in this case, simply treating the missing components as a set of missing attributes. However, we must still modify the component matching process to find a *partial* match between components in the instance and the concept. Although we do not have a complete specification, this modification seems feasible for either the greedy matching algorithm or the Hungarian algorithm.

### 6.4. Multiple levels of aggregation

Another research issue relates to the organization of complex objects with multiple components. Marr [28] has argued that the human visual system can generate descriptions of physical objects at different levels of aggregation. Thus, a dog might be viewed as a single cylinder at one level, as eight connected cylinders for (torso, neck, head, tail, and legs) at a lower level, with each leg described as three cylinders (thigh, calf, and foot) at a still lower level.

---

[23] This means that the $1/2\sqrt{\pi}$ term from Section 4.3 must be retained.

One difficulty with such a *part-of* hierarchy of objects lies in specifying the relation between different levels. We need to specify algorithms for moving from lower to higher levels that minimize information loss.

Once we have extended CLASSIT's representation in this direction, we will also need to alter its evaluation function and its matcher. CLASSIT can deal with two levels (a composite object and its components), but it cannot handle the general *n*-level case. Although EPAM was designed to handle composite, multi-level instances, neither UNIMEM nor COBWEB retained this ability. Wasserman [43] has described an extension to UNIMEM that takes a similar approach to EPAM, recursively sorting each component (and its components) through the concept hierarchy. However, EPAM does not address the problem of matching components at all (i.e., each component fills a unique slot), and Wasserman's extension uses a "greedy" matching strategy, the performance characteristics of which are not systematically evaluated.

Adding multiple levels of description to the CLASSIT framework raises a number of questions. Should the system use all levels in classification or only some? EPAM preferred to use attributes of composite objects when these were sufficient for avoiding errors. If we represent different levels in the same language, how can CLASSIT determine analogous levels between an instance and a concept description? How can one adapt the component matching process to work at multiple levels? Finally, how can one match a complex instance to a complex concept when its components are structurally different (e.g., a cylinder versus a block)? We must find at least tentative answers to these questions before we can extend CLASSIT in this direction.

### 6.5. Matching and normalization

We have designed CLASSIT with the domain of physical objects in mind, and this has led to our focus on composite instances and numeric attributes. In our experiments with the system, we have assumed that instances have the same location, orientation, and scale, but we must clearly abandon this simplification in future versions. Upon seeing a cat from a different angle than normal, one still recognizes it as a cat. Similarly, if one sees a cat in a different location, or even a cat of unusually large or small size, there is no recognition problem. Apparently, recognition focuses not on the absolute values of attributes, but on their *relative* values.

One might store in a concept description all pairwise relations between component objects, but this is neither space-efficient nor very plausible. A better approach involves selecting some scale, origin, and set of axes for the overall object concept, and then specify the scale, origin, and axes for each component relative to them. However, this raises a new issue: how can one determine these parameters for a new complex instance before it has been

classified? We have not been able to devise a general algorithm that generates a canonical representation regardless of viewing angle, location, and size.

Instead, we hope to solve this *normalization* problem during the act of matching concept to instance. Upon observing an instance with multiple components, an extended CLASSIT would first match one of these components and use it to hypothesize the scale, origin, and axes for the composite object. This will lead to predictions about the locations of other components, which may or may not be correct. Hypothesized coordinate systems would be rejected, and those with better predictive ability would be extended, eventually leading to a completely normalized match. We plan to implement this normalization process in future versions of CLASSIT, though many details must still be specified.

### 6.6. Abstract descriptions and selective attention

Like Fisher's COBWEB, our system stores all known attributes on every concept description, even when they are neither predictive nor predictable. Earlier models of concept formation were more selective. Feigenbaum's EPAM starts with very general descriptions and gradually makes its images more specific through a process of familiarization. Lebowitz's UNIMEM and Kolodner's CYRUS gradually make their descriptions less specific through a generalization process. We need to explore variants on our basic algorithm that let it generate more abstract concept summaries, though the exact method is an open question.

A closely related problem is that CLASSIT inspects every attribute during the classification process, even if they have no predictive value. An improved system would incorporate the idea of selective attention, in which one focuses only on some features, presumably the useful ones. Earlier models of concept formation have this ability, including EPAM, UNIMEM, and CYRUS, as well as Fisher's COBWEB/2. The latter is encouraging, since it gives one path for incorporating attention into COBWEB, and thus into CLASSIT.

Ideally, the modified system would learn to prefer some attributes over others. In the early stages this selection would be random, since it would not know a priori which features would be diagnostic. However, as the system gained experience, it would come to prefer some attributes to others. Actually, CLASSIT already keeps statistics that would support this process. Using Bayes' rule, one can compute the predictiveness of each attribute from the existing scores. For example, the attribute "height" in Fig. 10 is clearly more predictive than "texture" at the first level. This is reflected by the fact that the difference between the average $1/\sigma$ score and the parent's $1/\sigma$ score is much larger for height than for texture.

In other words, CLASSIT's learning mechanism already supports such a focusing mechanism, and we need modify only the performance algorithm. The revised system would select only those attributes necessary to determine category membership with high probability. We could make this selection a deterministic function of predictiveness scores, but there is danger in this approach. If the initial instances are nonrepresentative or if the environment changes, the system might come to ignore attributes that later proved relevant. For this reason we prefer a probabilistic scheme, with more predictive attributes being selected more often, but even those with very low scores occasionally being sampled. We believe the addition of selective attention will make CLASSIT a more accurate model of human categorization and concept formation.

## 7. Summary

In this paper, we proposed a unifying framework for concept formation. We identified five features common to work on this task: that knowledge is represented in a concept hierarchy, that classification occurs in a top-down manner, that learning is unsupervised, integrated with performance, and employs an incremental hill-climbing search. We feel the search metaphor is especially important in understanding concept formation; it suggests both operators for learning and heuristics for controlling those operators.

We reviewed three concept formation systems (EPAM, UNIMEM, and COBWEB) that fit within our framework, along with a new system (CLASSIT) that builds on the earlier work. We have tried to emphasize the close relation between the systems, as well as the additions each makes over its predecessor. In particular, CLASSIT extends Fisher's approach to numeric attributes, can handle instances with multiple (unordered) components, and retains only some of the instances it encounters.

Finally, we presented some experimental studies of CLASSIT's behavior. We found that for the artificial domain of quadruped mammals, the system significantly improved its performance with experience, and that the greedy matching algorithm slowed down learning but did not seem to affect asymptotic performance. CLASSIT showed some sensitivity to its parameter settings, with low values for cutoff giving overfitting effects. We also presented evidence that the merge operator leads to more balanced hierarchies when the initial data is nonrepresentative. In examining the effects of domain characteristics, we found that more overlap between categories led to reduced improvement, and that more redundancy alleviated this effect. However, the relationship was more complex than we expected, and we need further experiments along these lines. Finally, we showed that when given real-world data on heart disease, CLASSIT was able to formulate diagnostically useful categories even without class information.

The representation, use, and acquisition of concepts is a complex, interconnected set of problems, and we cannot claim to have solved these problems in any absolute sense. However, we believe the basic approach we have

described, and which is reflected in EPAM, UNIMEM, CYRUS, COBWEB, and CLASSIT, constitutes a promising thrust towards the computational understanding of categorization. We encourage other researchers to join in the effort, and to construct incremental models of concept formation that extend the initial results that have been achieved to date.

## ACKNOWLEDGMENT

The ideas in this paper have resulted from many fruitful discussions with members of the UCI World Modelers Group. We would like to particularly acknowledge the criticism and encouragement provided by our work with Wayne Iba, Kevin Thompson, Patrick Young, and David Benjamin. Dennis Kibler, David Nicholas, Rick Granger and Jaime Carbonell also contributed important ideas. This research was supported by Contract MDA 903-85-C-0324 from the Army Research Institute.

## REFERENCES

1. Anderson, J.R., Induction of augmented transition networks, *Cognitive Sci.* **1** (1977) 125–157.
2. Anderson, J.R. and Kline, P.J., A learning system and its psychological implications, in: *Proceedings IJCAI-79*, Tokyo (1979) 16–21.
3. Berwick, R., Learning structural descriptions of grammar rules from examples, in: *Proceedings IJCAI-79* Tokyo (1979) 56–58.
4. Biederman, I., Matching image edges to object memory, in: *Proceedings IEEE First International Conference on Computer Vision*, London (1987) 384–392.
5. Binford, T.O., Visual perception by computer, Presented at IEEE Conference on Systems and Control, Miami, FL (1971).
6. Cheeseman, P., Kelly, J., Self, M., Taylor, W. and Freeman, D., Autoclass: A Bayesian classification system, in: *Proceedings Fifth International Conference on Machine Learning*, Ann Arbor, MI (1988) 65–64.
7. Detrano, R., International application of a new probability algorithm for the diagnosis of coronary artery disease, VA Medical Center, Long Beach, CA.
8. Everitt, E., *Cluster Analysis* (Heinemann Educational, London, 1974).
9. Feigenbaum, E.A., The simulation of verbal learning behavior, in: E.A. Feigenbaum and J. Feldman (Eds.), *Computers and Thought* (McGraw-Hill, New York, 1963).
10. Feigenbaum, E.A. and Simon, H., EPAM-like models of recognition and learning, *Cognitive Sci.* **8** (1984) 305–336.
11. Fisher, D., A hierarchical conceptual clustering algorithm, Tech. Rept. No. 85-21, Department of Information and Computer Science, University of California, Irvine, CA (1984).
12. Fisher, D., Knowledge acquisition via incremental conceptual clustering, *Mach. Learning* **2** (1987) 139–172.
13. Fisher, D., Knowledge acquisition via incremental conceptual clustering, Tech. Rept. No. 87-22 (Doctoral Dissertation), Department of Information and Computer Science, University of California, Irvine, CA (1987).
14. Gluck, M. and Corter, J., Information, uncertainty and the utility of categories, in: *Proceedings Seventh Annual Conference of the Cognitive Science Society*, Irvine, CA (1985) 283–287.
15. Grefenstette, J., Multilevel credit assignment in a genetic learning system, in: *Proceedings Second International Conference on Genetic Algorithms* (1987) 202–209.
16. Hanson, S.J. and Bauer, M., Conceptual clustering, categorization, and polymorphy, *Mach. Learning* **3** (1989) 343–372.
17. Holland, I., Escaping brittleness: The possibilities of general purpose algorithms applied to parallel rule-based systems, in: R.S. Michalski, J.G. Carbonell and T.M. Mitchell (Eds.),

39. Schlimmer, J. and Granger, R., Beyond incremental processing: Tracking concept drift, in: *Proceedings AAAI-86*, Philadelphia, PA (1986) 502–507.
40. Shrager, J., Theory change via application in instructionless learning, *Mach. Learning* **2** (1987) 247–276.
41. Simon, H.A., *The Sciences of the Artificial* (MIT Press, Cambridge, MA, 1969).
42. Smith, E.E. and Medin, D.L., *Categories and Concepts* (Harvard University Press, Cambridge, MA, 1981).
43. Wasserman, K., Unifying representation and generalization: Understanding hierarchically structured objects, Doctoral Dissertation, Columbia University, New York (1985).
44. Winston, P.H., Learning structural descriptions from examples, in: P.H. Winston (Ed.), *The Psychology of Computer Vision* (McGraw-Hill, New York, 1975).

*Machine Learning: An Artificial Intelligence Approach 2* (Morgan Kaufmann, Los Altos, CA, 1986).
18. Iba, W., Wogulis, J. and Langley, P., Trading off simplicity and coverage in incremental learning, in: *Proceedings Fifth International Conference on Machine Learning*, Ann Arbor, MI (1988) 73–79.
19. Kolodner, J., Maintaining organization in a dynamic long-term memory, *Cognitive Sci.* **7** (1983) 243–280.
20. Langley, P., A general theory of discrimination learning, in: D. Klahr, P. Langley and R. Neches (Eds.), *Production System Models of Learning and Development* (MIT Press, Cambridge, MA, 1987).
21. Langley, P., Gennari, J. and Iba, W., Hill climbing theories of learning, in: *Proceedings Fourth International Workshop on Machine Learning*, Irvine, CA (1987) 312–323.
22. Lebowitz, M., Generalization and memory in an integrated understanding system, Tech. Rept. No. 186 (Doctoral Dissertation), Department of Computer Science, Yale University, New Haven, CT (1980).
23. Lebowitz, M., Generalization from natural language text, *Cognitive Sci.* **7** (1983) 1–40.
24. Lebowitz, M., Categorizing numeric information for generalization, *Cognitive Sci.* **9** (1985) 285–309.
25. Lebowitz, M., Concept learning in a rich input domain: Generalization based memory, in: R.S. Michalski, J.G. Carbonell and T.M. Mitchell (Eds.), *Machine Learning: An Artificial Intelligence Approach 2* (Morgan Kaufmann, Los Altos, CA, 1986).
26. Lebowitz, M., Experiments with incremental concept formation: UNIMEM, *Mach. Learning* **2** (1987) 103–138.
27. Levinson, R., A self-organizing retrieval system for graphs, in: *Proceedings AAAI-84*, Austin, TX (1984) 203–206.
28. Marr, D., *Vision: A Computational Investigation into the Human Representation and Processing of Visual Information* (Freeman, San Francisco, CA, 1982).
29. Michalski, R.S., A theory and methodology of inductive learning, in: R.S. Michalski, J.G. Carbonell and T.M. Mithcell (Eds.), *Machine Learning: An Artificial Intelligence Approach* (Tioga, Palo Alto, CA, 1983).
30. Michalski, R.S. and Stepp, R., Learning from observation: Conceptual clustering, in: R.S. Michalski, J.G. Carbonell and T.M. Mitchell (Eds.), *Machine Learning: An Artificial Intelligence Approach* (Tioga, Palo Alto, CA, 1983).
31. Mitchell, T.M., Generalization as search, *Artificial Intelligence* **18** (1982) 203–226.
32. Mitchell, T.M., Utgoff, P. and Banerji, R., Learning by experimentation: Acquiring and refining problem-solving heuristics, in: R.S. Michalski, J.G. Carbonell and T.M. Mitchell (Eds.), *Machine Learning: An Artificial Intelligence Approach* (Tioga, Palo Alto, CA, 1983) 163–190.
33. Papademetriou, C. and Steiglitz, K., *Combinatorial Optimization* (Prentice-Hall, Englewood Cliffs, NJ, 1982).
34. Quinlan, J.R., Induction of decision trees, *Mach. Learning* **1** (1986) 81–106.
35. Rendell, L., Seshu, R. and Tcheng, D., More robust concept learning using dynamically-variable bias, in: *Proceedings Fourth International Workshop on Machine Learning*, Irvine, CA (1987) 66–78.
36. Rose, D. and Langley, P., A hill-climbing approach to machine discovery, in: *Proceedings Fifth International Conference on Machine Learning*, Ann Arbor, MI (1988) 367–373.
37. Rosch, E., The principles of categorization, in: E. Rosch and B.B. Lloyd (Eds.), *Cognition and Categorization* (Erlbaum, Hillsdale, NJ, 1978).
38. Schlimmer, J. and Fisher, D., A case study of incremental concept induction, in: *Proceedings AAAI-86*, Philadelphia, PA (1986) 496–501.

# AutoClass: A Bayesian Classification System

PETER CHEESEMAN*  (CHEESEMAN@PLUTO.ARC.NASA.GOV)
JAMES KELLY[†]  (KELLY@PLUTO.ARC.NASA.GOV)
MATTHEW SELF[†]  (SELF@PLUTO.ARC.NASA.GOV)
JOHN STUTZ[‡]  (STUTZ@PLUTO.ARC.NASA.GOV)
WILL TAYLOR[†]  (TAYLOR@PLUTO.ARC.NASA.GOV)
DON FREEMAN[†]

*NASA Ames Research Center*
*Mail Stop 244-17, Moffett Field, CA 94035 U.S.A.*

## Abstract

This paper describes AutoClass II, a program for automatically discovering (inducing) classes from a database, based on a Bayesian statistical technique which automatically determines the most probable number of classes, their probabilistic descriptions, and the probability that each object is a member of each class. AutoClass has been tested on several large, real databases and has discovered previously unsuspected classes. There is no doubt that these classes represent new phenomena.

## 1  Introduction

The standard approach in much of AI and statistical pattern recognition research is that a classification consists of a partitioning of the data into separate subsets, and that these subsets *are* the classes. In the Bayesian approach classes are described by probability distributions over the attributes of the objects, specified by a model function and its parameters. To define a class is to describe (not list) the objects which belong to it. This approach appears in the statistical literature as the theory of finite mixtures [5].

The Bayesian approach has several advantages over other methods:

- **The number of classes is determined automatically.**

  Deciding when to stop forming classes is a fundamental problem in classification. More classes can always explain the data better, so what should limit the number of classes the program finds? Many systems rely on an *ad hoc* stopping criterion. The Bayesian solution to the problem lies in the use of prior knowledge. We believe simpler class hypotheses (e.g., those with fewer classes) to be more likely

---

*RIACS. This work partially supported by NASA grant NCC2–428.
[†]Sterling Software (Don Freeman is now at the University of Pittsburgh)
[‡]NASA Ames Research Center

than complex ones, in advance of seeing any data, and the *prior probability* of the hypothesis reflects this preference. The prior probability term prefers fewer classes, the likelihood of the data prefers more, and the two effects balance at the most probable number of classes. As a result, AutoClass finds only one class in random data.

- **Objects are not assigned to classes absolutely.**

  AutoClass calculates the probability of each object's membership in each class, providing a more intuitive classification than absolute partitioning techniques. An object described equally well by two class descriptions should not be assigned to either class with certainty, because the evidence cannot support such an assertion.

- **All attributes are potentially significant.**

  Classification can be based on any or all attributes simultaneously, not on just the most important one. This represents an advantage of the Bayesian method over human classification. In many applications, classes are distinguished not by one or even by several attributes, but by small differences in many. Humans often have difficulty taking more than a few attributes into account. The Bayesian approach utilizes all attributes simultaneously, permitting uniform consideration of all the data.

- **Data can be real or discrete.**

  Many previous methods have difficulty analyzing mixed data. Some methods insist on real valued data [2], while others accept only discrete data [6]. There have been attempts to reconcile the two types of data by coercing real data into discrete form [13] or by incorporating flexible thresholds into categorical classification [11]. Coercion of heterogeneous data to a single type destroys information and is done purely to meet the needs of the particular classification procedure. The Bayesian approach can utilize the data exactly as they are given.

# 2    Overview of Bayesian Classification

AutoClass is based on Bayes's theorem, a formula for combining probabilities. Given observed data $D$ and a hypothesis $H$, it states that the probability that the hypothesis explains the data $p(H \mid D)$, (called the *posterior* probability of the hypothesis given the data) is proportional to the probability of observing the data if the hypothesis were known to be true $p(D \mid H)$ (the *likelihood* of the data) times the inherent probability of the hypothesis regardless of the data ($p(H)$, the *prior* probability of the hypothesis). Bayes's theorem is commonly expressed

$$p(H \mid D) = \frac{p(H)\, p(D \mid H)}{p(D)}. \tag{1}$$

For our purposes, the hypothesis $H$ is the number and descriptions of the classes from which we believe the data $D$ to have been drawn. Given $D$, we must select $H$ to maximize the posterior $p(H \mid D)$.

For a specific classification hypothesis, calculation of the likelihood of the data involves a straightforward application of statistics. The prior probability of the hypothesis is less transparent and is taken up in section 2.3. Finally, the prior probability of the data, $p(D)$ in the denominator above, need not be calculated directly. It can be derived as a normalizing constant or ignored so long as we seek only the relative probabilities of hypotheses.

## 2.1   Application to Classification

In the theory of finite mixtures (the mathematical foundation of AutoClass) each datum in a database containing $I$ objects is assumed to be drawn from one of $J$ classes. Each class is described by a *class distribution* function, $p(x_i \mid x_i \in C_j, \vec{\theta}_j)$, which gives the probability distribution of the attributes of a datum if it were known to belong to class $C_j$. These class distributions are described by a *class parameter vector*, $\vec{\theta}_j$, which for a single attribute normal distribution would consist of the class mean, $\mu_j$, and variance, $\sigma_j^2$.

The probability of an object being drawn from class $j$ is called the *class probability* $\pi_j$. Thus, the probability of a given datum coming from a set of classes is the sum of the probabilities that it came from each class separately, weighted by the class probabilities.

$$p(x_i \mid \vec{\theta}, \vec{\pi}, J) = \sum_{j=1}^{J} \pi_j \, p(x_i \mid x_i \in C_j, \vec{\theta}_j). \tag{2}$$

We assume that the data are drawn from an exchangeable (static) process—that is, the data are unordered and independent of each other given the model. Thus the *likelihood* of measuring an entire database is the product of the probabilities of measuring each object.

$$p(\vec{x} \mid \vec{\theta}, \vec{\pi}, J) = \prod_{i=1}^{I} p(x_i \mid \vec{\theta}, \vec{\pi}, J) \tag{3}$$

For a given value of the class parameters, we can calculate the probability that object $i$ belongs to class $j$ using Bayes's theorem.

$$p(x_i \in C_j \mid x_i, \vec{\theta}, \vec{\pi}, J) = \frac{\pi_j \, p(x_i \mid x_i \in C_j, \vec{\theta}_j)}{p(x_i \mid \vec{\theta}, \vec{\pi}, J)} \tag{4}$$

These classes are "fuzzy" in the sense that even with perfect knowledge of an object's attributes, it will be possible to determine only the probability that it is a member of a given class.

We break the problem of identifying a finite mixture into two parts: determining the classification parameters for a given number of classes, and determining the number of classes. Rather than seeking an *estimator* of the classification parameters (the class parameter vectors, $\vec{\theta}$, and the class probabilities, $\vec{\pi}$), we seek their full *posterior* probability distribution. The posterior distribution is proportional to the product of the prior distribution of the parameters $p(\vec{\theta}, \vec{\pi} \mid J)$ and the likelihood function $p(\vec{x} \mid \vec{\theta}, \vec{\pi}, J)$.

$$p(\vec{\theta}, \vec{\pi} \mid \vec{x}, J) = \frac{p(\vec{\theta}, \vec{\pi} \mid J) \, p(\vec{x} \mid \vec{\theta}, \vec{\pi}, J)}{p(\vec{x} \mid J)} \tag{5}$$

The pseudo-likelihood $p(\vec{x} \mid J)$ is simply the normalizing constant of the posterior distribution, obtained by marginalizing (integrating) out the classification parameters—in effect, treating them as "nuisance" parameters:

$$p(\vec{x} \mid J) = \iint p(\vec{\theta}, \vec{\pi} \mid J) \, p(\vec{x} \mid \vec{\theta}, \vec{\pi}, J) \, d\vec{\theta} \, d\vec{\pi}. \tag{6}$$

To solve the second half of the classification problem (determining the number of classes) we calculate the posterior distribution of the number of classes $J$. This is proportional to the product of the prior distribution $p(J)$ and the pseudo-likelihood function $p(\vec{x} \mid J)$.

$$p(J \mid \vec{x}) = \frac{p(J) \, p(\vec{x} \mid J)}{p(\vec{x})} \tag{7}$$

In principle we can determine the most probable number of classes by evaluating $p(J \mid \vec{x})$ over the range of $J$ for which our prior $p(J)$ is significant. In practice, the multi-dimensional integrals of equation 6 are computationally intractable, and we must search for the maximum of the function and approximate it about that point. Details of the AutoClass algorithm appear in section 3.

## 2.2    Assumptions

We cannot attempt classification without making some assumptions. Our mathematical formulation of the problem permits us to state our assumptions precisely and to assess their validity. The derivation above incorporates two:

1. The data are independent given the model. That is, the data are unordered. This is a fundamental assumption intrinsic to all classification systems.

2. The model functions—*class distributions* of page 3—are appropriate descriptors of the classes. The model functions themselves may incorporate additional assumptions, such as independence of attribute values (as AutoClass currently does).

## 2.3    Prior Probabilities

The prior probability term $p(\vec{\theta}, \vec{\pi} \mid J)$ in equation 5 constitutes the fundamental difference between Bayesian and classical statistics and still fuels debate. We will not attempt to defend the use of priors herein but refer the skeptical reader to Jaynes [8] for a full explanation of the Bayesian approach.

Introduction of the prior probability solves two problems. First, it permits mathematical determination of the number of classes by introducing a preference for fewer classes. We believe *a priori* that complex hypotheses are less likely than simple ones, those with fewer classes, for example, and any reasonable prior implants this belief in the equations. A more complex hypothesis will incur a penalty in the prior and will be disfavored unless it explains the data significantly better. Second, the likelihood contains singularities that would complicate analysis if it were used alone. The prior tames the likelihood by damping out the singularities, and the resulting posterior is much better behaved.

However, the prior probability distribution is not completely arbitrary. There are two basic approaches to prior distributions. A prior may be sought which captures some prior knowledge which is available, or an *uninformative* prior distribution may be sought. Uninformative priors which are invariant to changes of scale or origin are available, but the AutoClass II program does not as yet use these priors. Rather, AutoClass uses a weak informative prior. The actual values used do not appreciably affect the classifications found by AutoClass. The actual priors used are discussed in Section 3.2

# 3   The AutoClass II Program

Section 2 described the theory behind the Bayesian approach to classification. We now outline its implementation, AutoClass II.

## 3.1   The AutoClass II Class Model

In AutoClass II, we assume the data are in an attribute-value vector form. That is, the database contains $I$ objects $x_i$, each described by $K$ attribute values $x_{ik}$, $k \in \{1 \ldots K\}$. Attributes may be either real or discrete variables. In AutoClass II we currently make the further strong assumption that the attributes are independent in each class. This permits an extremely simple form for the class distributions used in equation 2.

$$p(x_i \mid x_i \in C_j, \vec{\theta}_j) = \prod_{k=1}^{K} p(x_{ik} \mid x_i \in C_j, \vec{\theta}_{jk}) \qquad (8)$$

where $\vec{\theta}_{jk}$ is the parameter vector describing the $k$th attribute in the $j$th class $C_j$. We plan to extend AutoClass to model covariance of the attributes within a class in the near future.

AutoClass models real valued attributes with a Gaussian normal distribution, parameterized by a mean and a standard deviation, and thus $\vec{\theta}_{jk}$ takes the form

$$\vec{\theta}_{jk} = \begin{bmatrix} \mu_{jk} \\ \sigma_{jk} \end{bmatrix}.$$

The class distribution is thus

$$p(x_{ik} \mid x_i \in C_j, \mu_{jk}, \sigma_{jk}) = \frac{1}{\sqrt{2\pi}\sigma_{jk}} \exp\left[-\frac{1}{2}\left(\frac{x_{ik} - \mu_{jk}}{\sigma_{jk}}\right)^2\right]. \qquad (9)$$

For discrete attributes the class distribution is specified by the probability $\rho_{jkl}$ of getting each possible value $l$. The elements of $\vec{\theta}_{jk}$ are the probabilities themselves. If there are $L$ possible values, labeled 1 to $L$, then the class distribution is

$$p(x_{ik} = l \mid x_i \in C_j, \vec{\rho}_{jk}) = \rho_{jkl}. \qquad (10)$$

## 3.2   Informative Priors

Although uninformative priors can be derived for use in Bayesian classification, AutoClass II currently uses informative priors. This is due mostly to the history of the program, and the fact that we have obtained excellent results using these priors. The prior information we use has only a small effect on the classification estimates.

AutoClass II employs *conjugate* priors, that is, prior information in the same form as the data. In effect, the prior information for attribute $k$ in class $j$ consists of a set of $w'$ fictitious data points, described by the same summary statistics as are used for the actual data. The larger the value of $w'$, the stronger the influence of the prior relative to the data. AutoClass II currently treats all classes symmetrically, using the same conjugate points for every class and for each attribute of the same type.

## 3.3   Search Algorithm

As mentioned in section 2, AutoClass breaks the classification problem into two parts: determining the number of classes and determining the parameters defining them. Equation 7 gives the probability distribution over the number of classes. For each possible number of classes the multi-dimensional integral of equation 6 must be performed. Rather than attempt the integration the posterior distribution of the classification parameters directly, AutoClass performs a search over $\vec{\theta}_j$ and $\pi_j$ to find the maximum of the posterior distribution (equation 5), and then approximates the integral around that point.

The complete problem involves starting with more classes than are beleieved to be present (as specified by the user), searching to find the best class parameters for that number of classes, approximating the integral to find the relative probability of that number of classes, and then decreasing the number of classes and repeating the procedure.

AutoClass uses a Bayesian variant of Dempster and Laird's EM algorithm [1] to find the best class parameters for a given number of classes (the maximum of equation 5). To derive the algorithm, we differentiate the posterior distribution with respect to the class parameters and equate with zero. This yields a system of nonlinear equations which hold at the maximum of the posterior:

$$\hat{\pi}_j = \frac{W_j + w' - 1}{I + J(w' - 1)} \tag{11}$$

$$\frac{\partial}{\partial \theta_j} \ln p(\hat{\theta}_j) + \sum_{i=1}^{I} w_{ij} \frac{\partial}{\partial \theta_j} \ln p(x_i \mid \hat{\theta}_j) = 0, \tag{12}$$

where $w_{ij}$ is the probability that the datum $x_i$ was drawn from class $j$ (previously given in equation 4), and $W_j$ is the total weight in class $j$:

$$w_{ij} = p(x_i \in C_j \mid x_i, \hat{\theta}, \hat{\pi})$$
$$W_j = \sum_{i=1}^{I} w_{ij}.$$

To find a solution to this system of equations, we iterate between equations 11 and 12 (treating $\vec{w}$ as a constant ) and equation 4 (treating $\vec{\pi}$ and $\vec{\theta}$ as constants).

On any given iteration, the membership probabilities are constant, so equation 12 can be simplified by bringing $w_{ij}$ through the derivative, giving

$$\frac{\partial}{\partial \theta_j} \left[ p(\hat{\theta}_j) \prod_{i=1}^{I} p(x_i \mid \hat{\theta}_j, x_i \in C_j)^{w_{ij}} \right] = 0. \tag{13}$$

Thus far, our discussion of the search algorithm has related to a general class model with an arbitrary $\vec{\theta}_{jk}$. We now apply equation 13 to the specific AutoClass II model of equations 8 through 10. For discrete attributes, the values of the updated parameters $\hat{\theta}_{jkl}$ derived from the class probabilities $w_{ij}$ and prior weight $w'$ are

$$\hat{\rho}_{jkl} = \frac{\sum_{i=1}^{I} w_{ij} \delta(l, x_{ik}) + w' - 1}{W_j + L(w' - 1)} \qquad \delta(l, x_{ik}) \equiv \begin{cases} 1, & x_{ik} = l \\ 0, & \text{otherwise} \end{cases} \tag{14}$$

This is simply the weighted proportion of objects in class $j$ for which attribute $k$ had value $l$.

For real valued attributes, the equations for the updated $\hat{\mu}_{jk}$ and $\hat{\sigma}_{jk}$ are a function of the prior information and the empirical mean, $\bar{x}_{jk}$, and variance, $s_{jk}^2$, of the $k$th attribute in class j, weighted by $w_{ij}$:

$$\bar{x}_{jk} = \frac{\sum_{i=1}^{I} w_{ij} x_{ik}}{W_j},$$
$$s_{jk}^2 = \frac{\sum_{i=1}^{I} w_{ij} x_{ik}^2}{W_j} - \bar{x}_{jk}^2.$$

The update formulas are then:

$$\hat{\mu}_{jk} = \frac{w' \bar{x}_k' + W_j \bar{x}_{jk}}{w' + W_j} \tag{15}$$

$$\hat{\sigma}_{jk}^2 = \frac{w'(s_k')^2 + W_j s_{jk}^2}{w' + W_j + 1} + \frac{w' W_j}{(w' + W_j)(w' + W_j + 1)} (\mu_k' - \bar{x}_{jk})^2. \tag{16}$$

The computational cost of a single iteration is of order $I \cdot J \cdot K$. Typically the procedure converges in about twenty iterations, depending upon the strength of the actual classes. A search in data having many weak classes takes longer than one having few strong classes. The search may be speeded up by over-relaxation techniques. Of course, the procedure may converge to local maxima depending on the starting point chosen for the iteration, so we employ heuristic methods to jump away from local maxima. Even so, many searches may be necessary to establish the global maximum.

## 3.4   Determining the Number of Classes

We previously outlined the theory for the determination of the number of classes present, but integration over the full parameter space is clearly infeasible. AutoClass II uses a crude but very effective approximation based solely on the results of the iteration algorithm. If a class has negligible posterior probability $\pi_j$, then including that class in the model cannot improve the likelihood of the data at all. At the same time, the prior probability of one class probability being near zero is very low. Thus models in which a class has negligible probability will always be less probable than models which simply omit that class. The user runs AutoClass with $J$ larger than the expected number of classes. If all resulting classes have significant probability then the user increases $J$ until some classes are empty. AutoClass then ignores the empty classes, and the populated classes represent an optimal classification of the data given the assumed class model function.

The utility of this approach has been experimentally confirmed on a number of prepared data bases. Specifically, when AutoClass runs with $J$ greater than the actual number of classes present, the iteration converges with negligible probability for the extra classes. This behavior differs qualitatively from the behavior of maximum likelihood methods, which will continue to partition the classes until eventually there is only one object in each class.

# 4   Extensions to the Model

## 4.1   Hierarchical Classification

After a database has been analyzed, many classes frequently have many attributes in common. For instance, in a database of mammals, the "dog" class and the "cat" class will be described by the same values for many attributes (fur, four legs, etc.). In this case, a description of all the attributes of all the classes separately is not as useful as a *hierarchical* classification scheme which identifies the common attributes and the distinguishing attributes between classes.

The Bayesian method can accomodate hierarchical classification by considering a model in which some attributes are common to a group of sub-classes. This amounts to a significance test of the equality of two attribute's parameter vectors in the non-hierarchical classification. If there is no significant difference between some attributes of a group of classes, then these attributes may be estimated jointly.

## 4.2 Supervised Classification

Although AutoClass was designed for automatic unsupervised classification, the prior information in equation 5 permits supervised classification as well. If the user wishes to assert that certain objects are in certain classes, a prior probability can be used which favors class descriptions reflecting this. See Duda and Hart [4] for a discussion of supervised Bayesian inference.

## 4.3 Missing Data

Consistent probability calculations require that 'unknown' be treated as a valid data value. This is not merely a computational convenience. Failure to determine a value is just as valid an observation as any other, and must be allowed for in any predictive model. There may be physical reasons that a value is unknown, and discarding that fact (by interpolating a value or, even worse, discarding the object completely) destroys potentially valuable information.

A straightforward extension of the class model allows AutoClass to accept objects with unknown values. For discrete attributes it can be shown that the correct procedure for treating an unknown value is equivalent to adding an 'unknown' category to the value set. For real-valued attributes we condition our Gaussian normal model with discrete 'unknown' and 'known' categories:

$$\vec{\theta}_{jk} = [\rho_{jk}, \mu_{jk}, \sigma_{jk}] \tag{17}$$

$$p(x_{ik} \mid x_i \in C_j, \rho_{jk}, \mu_{jk}, \sigma_{jk}) = \begin{cases} \rho_{jk} \frac{1}{\sqrt{2\pi}\sigma_{jk}} \exp\left[-\frac{1}{2}\left(\frac{x_{ik}-\mu_{jk}}{\sigma_{jk}}\right)^2\right], & x_{ik} \text{ known} \\ 1-\rho_{jk}, & x_{ik} \text{ unknown} \end{cases} \tag{18}$$

The mean and variance are updated as before, but the proportion of data for which $x_k$ is known is also updated just like any other discrete variable.

## 5 Results

AutoClass has classified data supplied by researchers active in various domains and has yielded some new and intriguing results:

- **Iris Database** Fisher's data on three species of iris [7] are a classic test for classification systems. AutoClass discovers the three classes present in the data with very high confidence, despite the fact that not all of the cases can be assigned to their classes with certainty. Wolfe's NORMIX and NORMAP [12] both incorrectly found four classes, and Dubes's MH index [3] offers only weak evidence for three clusters.

- **Soybean Disease Database**  AutoClass found the four known classes in Stepp's soybean disease data, providing a comparison with Michalski's CLUSTER/2 system [10]. AutoClass's class assignments exactly matched Michalski's—each object belonged overwhelmingly to one class, indicating exceptionally well separated classes for so small a database (47 cases, 35 attributes).

- **Horse Colic Database**  AutoClass analyzed the results of 50 veterinary tests on 259 horses and extracted classes which provided reliable disease diagnoses, despite the fact that almost 40% of the data were missing.

- **Infrared Astronomy Database**  The Infrared Astronomical Satellite tabulation of stellar spectra is not only the largest database Autoclass has assayed (5,425 cases, 94 attributes) but the least thoroughly understood by domain experts. AutoClass discovered classes which differed significantly from NASA's previous analysis but clearly reflect physical phenomena in the data.

  Note that AutoClass knows nothing about spectra—the current model treats the intensity at each wavelength as an independent quantity. As a result AutoClass would find exactly the same classes if the order of the wavelengths were scrambled. The AutoClass infrared source classification is the basis of a new star catalog to appear shortly.

We are actively collecting and analyzing other databases which seem appropriate for classification, including an AIDS database and a second infrared spectral database.

# 6    Conclusion

This paper has described the Bayesian approach to the problem of classification and AutoClass, a simple implementation of it. Bayesian probability theory provides a simple and extensible approach to problems such as classification and general mixture separation. Its theoretical basis is free of *ad hoc* quantities, and in particular free of any measures which alter the data to suit the needs of the program. As a result, the elementary classification model we have described lends itself easily to extensions.

# References

[1]  A. P. Dempster, N. M. Laird, and D. B. Rubin. Maximum likelihood from incomplete data via the EM algorithm. *Journal of the Royal Statistical Society, Series B*, 39(1):1–38, 1977.

[2]  W. Dillon and M. Goldstein. *Multivariate Analysis: Methods and Applications*, chapter 3. Wiley, 1984.

[3]  Richard C. Dubes. How many clusters are best? — an experiment. *Pattern Recognition*, 20(6):645–663, 1987.

[4] Richard O. Duda and Peter E. Hart. *Pattern Recognition and Scene Analysis.* Wiley-Interscience, 1973.

[5] B. S. Everitt and D. J. Hand. *Finite Mixture Distributions. Monographs on Applied Probability and Statistics,* Chapman and Hall, London, England, 1981. Extensive Bibliography.

[6] D. H. Fisher. Conceptual clustering, learning from examples, and inference. In *Proceedings of the Fourth International Workshop on Machine Learning,* pages 38–49, Morgan Kaufmann, 1987.

[7] R. A. Fisher. Multiple measurments in taxonomic problems. *Annals of Eugenics,* VII:179–188, 1936.

[8] Edwin T. Jaynes. Bayesian methods: general background. In James H. Justice, editor, *Maximum Entropy and Bayesian Methods in Applied Statistics,* pages 1–25, Cambridge University Press, Cambridge, Massachusetts, 1986.

[9] Edwin T. Jaynes. *Papers on Probability, Statistics and Statistical Physics.* Volume 158 of *Synthese Library,* D. Reidel, Boston, 1983.

[10] Ryszard S. Michalski and Robert. E. Stepp. Automated construction of classifications: conceptual clustering versus numerical taxonomy. *IEEE Transactions on Pattern Analysis and Machine Intelligence,* PAMI-5:396–410, 1983.

[11] J. R. Quinlan. Decision trees as probabilistic classifiers. *Proceedings of the Fourth International Workshop on Machine Learning,* 31–37, 1987.

[12] John H. Wolfe. Pattern clustering by multivariate mixture analysis. *Multivariate Behavioural Research,* 5:329–350, July 1970.

[13] A. Wong and D. Chiu. Synthesizing statistical knowledge from incomplete mixed-mode data. *IEEE Transactions on Pattern Analysis and Machine Intelligence,* PAMI-9:796–805, 1987.

# Section 4.3

# Measurement and Evaluation of Learning Systems

Two fundamental questions can be asked about any method or program: How good is it? How does it compare with alternative methods? The articles in this section address these questions for machine learning methods.

The article in Section 4.3.1 underscores the fact that symbolic learning systems and neural net systems build structures that will be interpreted by performance programs for the same kinds of tasks. The article also shows that there is little difference in the level of performance of the resulting systems.

That is to say, many approaches and architectures can be used for solving the same kinds of problems. Therefore choices among methods will be made on other grounds, such as the availability of data, the amount of prior knowledge available, the extent to which knowledge needs to be distributed over a large structure (e.g., distributed over a network instead of being made explicit in discrete rules), and the need for human-comprehensible knowledge structures.

The article by Gaines in Section 4.3.2 quantifies the cost tradeoff between the use of knowledge supplied by an expert and knowledge supplied by an induction program. The article shows that expert-supplied knowledge can reduce the amount of data required by an inductive learning system by several orders of magnitude. The article makes a powerful case for using both machine learning and expertise transfer when creating a knowledge-based system.

The last article in this section, by Dietterich, is a theoretical analysis of some limits of inductive learning systems. Theoretical limitations derived from probably-approximately-correct (PAC) learning theory have been influential. But they are of marginal utility for guiding the construction of knowledge-based systems because PAC learning deals with worst-case analysis, and knowledge engineers and AI researchers use as many heuristics as can be articulated to avoid worst cases.

Machine Learning, 6, 111–143 (1991)
© 1991 Kluwer Academic Publishers, Boston. Manufactured in The Netherlands.

# Symbolic and Neural Learning Algorithms: An Experimental Comparison

JUDE W. SHAVLIK                                    (SHAVLIK@CS.WISC.EDU)
*Computer Sciences Department, University of Wisconsin, 1210 West Dayton Street, Madison, WI 53706*

RAYMOND J. MOONEY                                  (MOONEY@CS.UTEXAS.EDU)
*Department of Computer Sciences, Taylor Hall 2.124, University of Texas, Austin, TX 78712*

GEOFFREY G. TOWELL                                 (TOWELL@CS.WISC.EDU)
*Computer Sciences Department, University of Wisconsin, Madison, WI 53706*

Editor: J.R. Quinlan

**Abstract.** Despite the fact that many symbolic and neural network (connectionist) learning algorithms address the same problem of learning from classified examples, very little is known regarding their comparative strengths and weaknesses. Experiments comparing the ID3 symbolic learning algorithm with the perceptron and backpropagation neural learning algorithms have been performed using five large, real-world data sets. Overall, backpropagation performs slightly better than the other two algorithms in terms of classification accuracy on new examples, but takes much longer to train. Experimental results suggest that backpropagation can work significantly better on data sets containing numerical data. Also analyzed empirically are the effects of (1) the amount of training data, (2) imperfect training examples, and (3) the encoding of the desired outputs. Backpropagation occasionally outperforms the other two systems when given relatively small amounts of training data. It is slightly more accurate than ID3 when examples are noisy or incompletely specified. Finally, backpropagation more effectively utilizes a "distributed" output encoding.

**Keywords.** Empirical learning, connectionism, neural networks, inductive learning, ID3, perceptron, backpropagation

## 1. Introduction

The division between symbolic and neural network approaches to artificial intelligence is particularly evident within machine learning. Both symbolic and artificial neural network (or connectionist) learning algorithms have been developed; however, until recently (Fisher & McKusick, 1989; Mooney, Shavlik, Towell, & Gove, 1989; Weiss & Kapouleas, 1989; Atlas, et al., 1990; Dietterich, Hild, & Bakiri, 1990) there has been little direct comparison of these two basic approaches to machine learning. Consequently, despite the fact that symbolic and connectionist learning systems frequently address the same general problem, very little is known regarding their comparative strengths and weaknesses.

The problem most often addressed by both neural network and symbolic learning systems is the inductive acquisition of concepts from examples. This problem can be briefly defined as follows: given descriptions of a set of examples each labeled as belonging to a particular class, determine a procedure for correctly assigning new examples to these classes. In the neural network literature, this problem is frequently referred to as *supervised* or *associative* learning.

For associative learning, symbolic and neural systems generally require the same input; namely, classified examples represented as feature vectors. In addition, the performance of both type of learning systems is usually evaluated by testing their ability to correctly classify novel examples. Within symbolic machine learning, numerous algorithms have been developed to perform associative learning. Systems exist for learning decision trees (e.g., Quinlan, 1986a) and logical concept definitions (Mitchell, 1982; Michalski, 1983) from examples, which can be used to classify subsequent examples. These algorithms have been tested on problems ranging from soybean disease diagnosis (Michalski & Chilausky, 1980) to classifying chess end games (Quinlan, 1983). Within neural networks, several algorithms have been developed for training a network to respond correctly to a set of examples by appropriately modifying its connection weights (e.g., Rosenblatt, 1962; Rumelhart, Hinton, & Williams, 1986; Hinton & Sejnowski, 1986). After training, a network can be used to classify novel examples. Neural learning algorithms have been tested on problems ranging from converting text to speech (Sejnowski & Rosenberg, 1987; Dietterich, et al., 1990) to evaluating moves in backgammon (Tesauro & Sejnowski, 1989).

This article presents the results of several experiments comparing the performance of the *ID3* symbolic learning algorithm (Quinlan, 1986a) with both the *perceptron* (Rosenblatt, 1962) and *backpropagation* (Rumelhart, et al. 1986) neural algorithms. All three systems are tested on five large data sets from previous symbolic and connectionist experiments, and their learning times and accuracies on novel examples are measured. In two cases, backpropagation's classification accuracy was statistically significantly better than ID3's. In the other three, they perform roughly equivalently. However, in all cases, backpropagation took much longer to train. Given its well-known limitations, the perceptron performed surprisingly well; it usually performed within a few percentage points of the other methods.

Besides accuracy and learning time, this paper investigates three additional aspects of empirical learning: (1) the dependence on the amount of training data; (2) the ability to handle imperfect data of various types; (3) the ability to utilize "distributed" output encodings. These investigations shed further light on the relative merits of the different approaches to inductive learning.

Three types of imperfect data sets are studied. The first type (random noise) occurs when feature values and example categorizations are incorrectly recorded, the second results from missing feature values, while the third occurs when an insufficient number of features are used to describe examples.

The output encoding issue arises because symbolic learning algorithms usually are trained to learn category names. A direct translation of this approach yields a "local" connectionist representation of each category as the output to be learned. That is, each possible category would be represented by a single output unit. However, the backpropagation algorithm is often trained with more complicated output encodings that use information upon which the category naming is based. These "distributed" encodings of the output are more compact than the local encodings and may have aspects that neurally-based algorithms can exploit during learning.

Results of the experiments described in the following sections indicate that the neural methods occasionally perform better than ID3 when given relatively small amounts of training data. The experiments also indicate that backpropagation is slightly more accurate than ID3 when data sets contain imperfections. Finally, the results suggest that backpropagation takes greater advantage of domain-specific distributed output encodings, although ID3 is able to successfully use distributed encodings.

The next section describes the five data sets and their representation, plus the three algorithms and their implementations. Following that, the experiments are described and their results reported and analyzed. A fourth section discusses general issues concerning the relationships between symbolic and neural approaches to inductive learning.

## 2. General experimental setup

This section first describes the data sets used to compare the different learning systems. Next, it motivates the choice of algorithms used in the study and briefly describes these algorithms. Finally, it describes the representation language used to encode examples.

### 2.1. Data sets

These experiments use five different data sets. Four have been previously used to test different symbolic learning systems and one has been used to test backpropagation.

The *soybean* data set has 17 different soybean diseases described by 50 features, such as weather, time of year, and descriptions of leaves and stems. Each disease has 17 examples, for a total of 289 examples. This domain was popularized by Michalski & Chilausky (1980); however, the exact data is that used in Reinke (1984). It should be noted that several soybean data sets exist. The full set used here should not be confused with the simpler, purely conjunctive, four-disease data used to test clustering systems (Stepp, 1984; Fisher, 1987).

The *chess* data set (Shapiro, 1987) consists of examples of a "king and rook versus king and pawn" end game (KPa7KR). There are two categories (*Win* and *Not Win*) and 36 high-level features. There are a total of 591 examples randomly selected from the original 3196 examples; these examples are approximately evenly divided between the two categories. Similar chess end game data sets have been previously used to test ID3 (Quinlan, 1983).

The *audiology* data (Bareiss, 1989) consist of cases from the Baylor College of Medicine. There are 226 examples of 24 categories of hearing disorders involving 58 features. This data set has a large amount of missing information; an average of only about 11 features have known values for each example (Bareiss, 1989).

The *heart disease* data set contains medical cases from the Cleveland Clinic Foundation (Detrano, unpublished manuscript). It is the only one of the five data sets that contains numerically-valued features; there are eight nominally-valued (i.e., possible values form a finite, unordered set) and six numerically-valued features. There are two categories: healthy and diseased heart. The full data set contains 303 examples, roughly evenly divided between the two categories. However, seven examples were missing feature values, and we did not use these seven in our experiments.

The *NETtalk* (Sejnowski & Rosenberg, 1987) data set involves text-to-speech conversion. It consists of a 20,012 word dictionary in which every letter of each word is associated with a phoneme/stress pair. Training examples in NETtalk are formed by passing one word at a time through a seven-letter window. The phoneme/stress pair of the middle letter in the window constitutes the category of the example. Thus, the number of training examples for each word is equal to the number of letters in that word; the 20,012 word dictionary has more than 143,000 possible training examples.

A seven-letter window is insufficient to uniquely identify the phoneme/stress pair attributable to the central letter of that window. For instance, the sound on the first letter of *asset* and *assess* is different. However, the two words have identical seven-letter windows for the first letter: ---*asse*. As a result, the data can be considered to have low levels of noise.

Unfortunately, the full dictionary is too extensive to analyze tractably in a manner equivalent to the other domains. Instead, a small training set is extracted by looking at the 1000 most common English words (as reported in Kuchera, 1967) and keeping those that appear in the NETalk dictionary. This training set—called *NETalk-full* or, simply, *NETalk*—contains 808 words, which produce 4,259 examples classified into 115 phoneme/stress categories. (In the whole NETalk corpus, there are 166 categories. The 41 categories not represented in the training set constitute less than 0.5% of the examples in the corpus.) The standard test set for NETalk-full consists of 1,000 words (7,241 examples) randomly selected from the remainder of the dictionary. For one experiment, the NETalk-full data set is further pruned by keeping only the examples involving "A" sounds. This produces 444 examples that fall into 18 sound/stress categories; this data set is called *NETalk-A*.

## 2.2. Learning algorithms

In order to experimentally compare neural-net and symbolic learning algorithms, we chose the ID3, perceptron, and backpropagation algorithms as representative algorithms. This section briefly describes the systems used and our reasons for choosing them as representatives.

### 2.2.1. ID3

We chose ID3 because it is a simple and widely used symbolic algorithm for learning from examples. It has been extensively tested on a number of large data sets (Quinlan, 1983; Wirth & Catlett, 1988) and is the basis of several commercial rule-induction systems. In addition, ID3 has been augmented with techniques for handling numerically-valued features, noisy data, and missing information (Quinlan, 1986a). Finally, in experimental comparisons with other symbolic learning algorithms, ID3 generally performs about as well or better than other systems (O'Rorke, 1982; Rendell, Cho, & Seshu, 1989).

ID3 uses the training data to construct a *decision tree* for determining the category of an example. At each step, a new node is added to the decision tree by partitioning the training examples based on their value along a single, most-informative attribute. The attribute chosen is the one which minimizes the following function:

$$E(A) = - \sum_{i=1}^{V} \frac{S_i}{S} \sum_{j=1}^{N} \frac{k_{ji}}{S_i} \log_2 \frac{k_{ji}}{S_i}$$

where $V$ is the number of values for attribute $A$, $k_{ji}$ is the number of examples in the $j$th category with the $i$th value for attribute $A$, $S$ is the total number of examples, $S_i$ is the number of examples with the $i$th value for attribute $A$, and $N$ is the number of categories. Each resulting partition is processed recursively, unless it contains examples of only a single category, in which case a leaf is created and labeled with this category. The information-gain criterion that determines the "splitting" attribute acts as a hill-climbing heuristic, which tends to minimize the size of the resulting decision tree.

Following Quinlan (1986b), we used *chi-squared pruning* to handle noisy data and prevent overfitting the data. This method terminates the growth of a branch of the decision tree when no remaining attribute improves prediction in a statistically significant manner. In this case, a leaf is created and labeled with the most common category in the partition. Missing feature values are handled using techniques recommended by Quinlan (1989); see Section 3.3.2 for more details. Numerically-valued features are handled by examining all thresholds (e.g., *height* < 5) that split the data into two partitions (with $N$ examples there are up to $N - 1$ distinct splits for each numerical feature). Each such split is then treated the same in the information-gain calculation as a split on a nominal feature (Quinlan, 1986a).

### 2.2.2. Perceptron

As is well known, the perceptron learning procedure is incapable of learning concepts that are not linearly separable (Minsky & Papert, 1988). Despite this fact, it performs quite well on several large data sets used to test recent learning systems. Therefore, we included the perceptron, one of the first neural network learning algorithms, in this study as an example of a simple, fast neural learning algorithm.

The perceptron learning procedure is a method for adjusting the weights of a single linear threshold unit so that it produces the correct outputs for a set of training examples. The procedure performs gradient descent (i.e., hill climbing) in weight space in an attempt to minimize the sum of the squares of the errors across all of the training examples. The following specifies how the weights should be changed after each presentation of an input/output pair $p$:

$$\Delta_p w_i = a_{pi} (t_p - o_p)$$

where $w_i$ is the weight for input feature $i$, $t_p$ is the target output for pattern $p$, $o_p$ is the current output for pattern $p$, and $a_{pi}$ is the value of input feature $i$ for pattern $p$. If the training data are linearly separable, this procedure is guaranteed to converge on a correct set of weights after a finite number of input presentations (Minsky & Papert, 1988).

The implementation of the perceptron we used in our experiments includes cycle detection so that, once a set of weights repeats, the system stops and indicates that the data is not linearly separable. The *perceptron cycling theorem* (Minsky & Papert, 1988) guarantees this will eventually happen if and only if the data are not linearly separable. (However, due to simulation time restrictions, the perceptron is also stopped if it cycles through the training data 100 times on the NETalk-full data set and 5000 times on the other data sets.) A single perceptron is trained for each possible category to distinguish members of that category from all other categories. A test example is classified by passing it through all the perceptrons and assigning it to the category whose perceptron's output exceeds its threshold by the largest amount.

### 2.2.3. *Backpropagation*

Over the past several years, a few neural learning algorithms have been developed that are capable of learning concepts that are not linearly separable (e.g., Rumelhart, et al., 1986; Hinton & Sejnowski, 1986; Barnard & Cole, 1989). Backpropagation (also called the *generalized delta rule*, Rumelhart, et al., 1986) is a well-known procedure and has been tested on several large-scale problems (e.g., Sejnowski & Rosenberg, 1987; Tesauro & Sejnowski, 1989). Consequently, we chose backpropagation to represent the new neural learning algorithms.

Like the perceptron, backpropagation uses gradient descent in an attempt to minimize the sum of the squares of the errors across all of the training inputs. However, it is capable of doing this for multi-layer networks with hidden units (units that neither directly receive external input nor produce external output). For the method to work, the thresholding function of each unit must be altered so that it is everywhere differentiable. The most common output function is presented below. For each unit $j$, its output $o_{pj}$ for an input/output pair $p$ is:

$$o_{pj} = \frac{1}{1 + e^{-(\sum_i w_i o_{pi} + \theta_j)}}$$

where $w_{ji}$ is the weight from unit $i$ to unit $j$ and $\theta_j$ is a tunable "threshold" or bias for unit $j$. The weights (and bias) of each unit are changed after the presentation of each pattern $p$ by backpropagating error measures layer by layer from the output back to the input according to the following equations:

$$\Delta_p w_{ji} = \eta \delta_{pj} o_{pi} + \alpha \Delta_{p-1} w_{ji}$$

where

$$\delta_{pj} = o_{pj}(1 - o_{pj})(t_{pj} - o_{pj}) \quad \text{if } j \text{ is an output unit}$$

and

$$\delta_{pj} = o_{pj}(1 - o_{pj}) \sum_k \delta_{pk} w_{kj} \quad \text{if } j \text{ is a hidden unit.}$$

Parameter $\eta$ is called the *learning rate*; $\alpha$ is a parameter called the *momentum term* (which reduces fluctuations during hill climbing); $t_{pj}$ is the target output for the output unit $j$ for pattern $p$; and $\delta_{pj}$ measures the error of the output of unit $j$ for pattern $p$. Unlike the perceptron, backpropagation may get stuck at a local minima and therefore is not guaranteed to

converge to 100% correctness on the training data. In addition, it may get trapped in an oscillation; however, the momentum term helps prevent oscillations.

The version of backpropagation used in the experiments is that supplied with the third volume of the PDP series (McClelland & Rumelhart, 1987). We set the learning rate to 0.25 and the momentum term to 0.9, both of which are standard values. Except as described in Section 3.4, networks contain one hidden layer which is totally connected to the input and output layers. The number of hidden units used is 10% of the total number of input and output units, a value we empirically found to work well. During testing, an example is assigned to the category whose output unit has the highest value. Training terminates when the network correctly classifies at least 99.5% of the training data or when the number of passes through the data (i.e., the number of *epochs*) reaches 5000. Training on the NETtalk-full data is terminated after 100 epochs due to time restrictions.

### 2.3. *Representation of examples*

We represented the examples in the data sets as bit vectors[1] rather than multi-valued feature vectors (with a slight modification for the numerically-valued features in the heart-disease data). Each input bit corresponds to a possible value of a particular feature and is on or off depending on whether an example has that value for that feature. Normally, exactly one bit in the set of bits representing a single feature will be on. However, if the feature value is missing in the original data (which only occurs in the audiology data), then all the bits in the set are off, and no special processing for missing features is required. (The issue of the representation of missing feature values is further discussed in Section 3.3.2.) The numerically-valued features in the heart-disease data set are treated differently. The values for these numeric features are normalized to be real numbers in the range [0, 1]; the minimum value for each feature is mapped to zero and the maximum to one.

Binary encodings are a natural representation for neural learning algorithms. We found that binary encoding slightly improved classification performance of ID3, and therefore we used it for all of the learning algorithms. Since bit vectors are usable by all three systems, their use helps standardize the experimental setup.

ID3's improved performance with the binary encoding may be due to several factors. First, since every feature has only two values, the binary encoding eliminates the gain criterion's undesirable preference for many-valued features (Quinlan, 1986a). Second, it allows for more general branching decisions such as *red* vs. *non-red* instead of requiring nodes to branch on all values of a feature. This may help overcome the *irrelevant values problem* (Cheng, Fayyad, Irani, & Qian, 1988) and result in more general and therefore better decision trees. However, since the binary-encoded examples have more features, ID3's run time is increased somewhat under this approach.

### 3. Experiments and results

We report four experiments in this section. The first experiment compares the learning times and accuracies of the three algorithms. Relative performance as a function of the

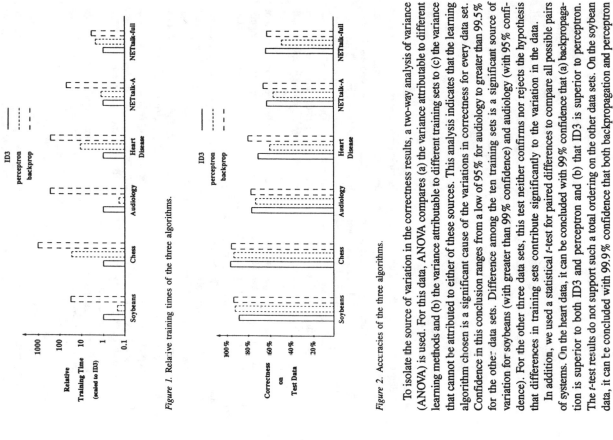

*Figure 1.* Relative training times of the three algorithms.

*Figure 2.* Accuracies of the three algorithms.

amount of training data is studied in the second experiment. The third experiment investigates the performance of the learning algorithms in the presence of three types of imperfect data. In the final experiment, we investigate the value of distributed output encodings.

To perform the experiments, we separated each data set into a collection of training and testing sets. After each system processes a training set, its performance is measured on the corresponding test set. To reduce statistical fluctuations, except for NETtalk-full, results are averaged over several different training and testing sets. In all of our experiments, two-thirds of the examples in each category are randomly placed in the training set, and the others are placed in the corresponding test set. Again to reduce statistical fluctuations, each run of backpropagation uses a different seed random number when determining the initial random network weights.

For NETtalk-full, we only used a single training set. However, for all runs where backpropagation processes the NETtalk-full data, we ran backpropagation five times, with a different seed random number for each run. The network that performs the best on the training set is used to classify the corresponding test set.

The initial random choice of weights can effect the performance of backpropagation. In our tests with the domains other than NETtalk, local minima problems were not found to occur. Rather, there often are long plateaus where correctness remains constant before again rising. Since only a small number of training epochs are possible with the NETtalk data, we used five randomly chosen initial states in order to minimize the effect of starting out in a bad state.

### 3.1. Experiment one: Learning time and correctness

Two major issues in inductive learning are the time spent learning and the classification accuracy on novel examples. Except for NETtalk-full, each data set is randomly permuted and divided into training and test sets ten times for this experiment. The training sets are processed until the learning algorithms terminate and then correctness is measured on the corresponding test sets.

### 3.1.1. Results

Figures 1 and 2 contain the experimental results. The first figure reports the training times of the three systems (normalized to the time taken by ID3). Correctness on the test data is reported in Figure 2. The numbers reported are the means over the ten partitionings of the data sets; the actual numbers, their standard deviations, and several other statistics appear in the appendix. The geometric means of the training times for soybeans, chess, audiology, heart disease, and NETtalk-A are 98 seconds (ID3), 130 seconds (perceptron), and 15,100 seconds (backpropagation). For correctness, the geometric means are 78.5% (ID3), 73.8% (perceptron), and 82.2% (backpropagation). The backpropagation time for NETtalk-full is for *one* run, although the test set correctness is that of the network (out of five) that performed best on the training set.

To isolate the source of variation in the correctness results, a two-way analysis of variance (ANOVA) is used. For this data, ANOVA compares (a) the variance attributable to different learning methods and (b) the variance attributable to different training sets to (c) the variance that cannot be attributed to either of these sources. This analysis indicates that the learning algorithm chosen is a significant cause of the variations in correctness for every data set. Confidence in this conclusion ranges from a low of 95% for audiology to greater than 99.5% for the other data sets. Difference among the ten training sets is a significant source of variation for soybeans (with greater than 99% confidence) and audiology (with 95% confidence). For the other three data sets, this test neither confirms nor rejects the hypothesis that differences in training sets contribute significantly to the variation in the data.

In addition, we used a statistical *t*-test for paired differences to compare all possible pairs of systems. On the heart data, it can be concluded with 99% confidence that (a) backpropagation is superior to both ID3 and perceptron and (b) that ID3 is superior to perceptron. The *t*-test results do not support such a total ordering on the other data sets. On the soybean data, it can be concluded with 99.9% confidence that both backpropagation and perceptron are superior to ID3. On the chess, audiology, and NETalk-A data, it can be concluded with at least 95% confidence that both backpropagation and ID3 are superior to perceptron. All other pair-wise differences are not statistically significant.

### 3.1.2. Discussion

In this experiment, for the most part all three learning systems are similar with respect to accurately classifying novel examples. Accuracy shortcomings occur for perceptron on the heart disease and NETalk data sets, which are not even close to being linearly separable.

Compared to backpropagation, ID3 performs poorly on the heart-disease data set, which contains many numerically-valued features. Otherwise all of the systems are within five percentage points of each other. However, ID3 and perceptron train much faster than backpropagation. Despite the obvious differences between decision trees and neural networks, their ability to accurately represent concepts and correctly classify novel instances is often quite comparable. Data from other recent experiments supports this conclusion.

Fisher and McKusick (1989) compared ID3 and backpropagation on two natural domains. In both cases they found backpropagation was about three percentage points more accurate. Weiss and Kapouleas (1989) compared backpropagation to CART (Breiman, Friedman, Olshen, & Stone, 1984), an algorithm similar to ID3 that also produces decision trees. They studied four data sets; CART outperformed backpropagation on two data sets and on the other two, backpropagation worked better. They also considered their PVM algorithm (Weiss, Galen, & Tadepalli, 1987), which produces classification rules. PVM beat backpropagation on three of the four domains, but never by more than a few percentage points. Atlas, et al. (1990) also compared CART to backpropagation on three data sets. In all three cases, backpropagation was more accurate. However, only once was the difference statistically significant. As noted previously, we found that ID3 can improve slightly when examples are converted to a binary representation. As best we can tell, these other studies did not use a binary representation with their decision-tree builders; hence, the differences they found may well be reduced by doing so. Finally, all of these studies mention the slowness of backpropagation.

One possible explanation for the similarity in performance is that most reasonable generalization procedures that correctly classify a particular set of training instances (possibly allowing for some noise) are about equally likely to classify a novel instance correctly. This is consistent with recent work in computational learning theory (Blumer, Ehrenfeucht, Haussler, & Warmuth, 1987) which states, roughly, that any polynomial algorithm that compresses the training data is a polynomial learner in the sense of Valiant (1984). That is, any algorithm guaranteed to compress the information present in the training set is guaranteed to learn a probably approximately correct (PAC) concept and therefore, on average, will perform well on novel test data.

Another possible explanation is that the inductive biases inherent in connectionist and symbolic representations and algorithms reflect implicit biases in real categories equally well. For example, all three systems share some form of an "Occam's Razor" bias and, at least to some degree, prefer simpler hypotheses. However, for standard neural network approaches, the complexity of the hypothesis is constrained by the user who must initially select an appropriate network for the problem. Unlike most symbolic learning systems which explicitly search for a simple hypothesis, neural systems simply search for a correct hypothesis which fits into a user-specified network. Although both generally use hill-climbing search to guide learning, neural systems hill climb in "correctness space," while symbolic systems also hill climb in "simplicity space." There are recent interesting developments involving neural learning algorithms that explicitly try to learn simple networks, for example by eliminating unnecessary hidden units or slowly adding hidden units as they are needed (e.g., Hanson & Pratt, 1988; Honavar & Uhr, 1988; Ash, 1989; Le Cun, Denker, and & Solla, 1990). Such systems help ease the burden of having to initially specify an appropriate network for a problem.

On the heart-disease data set, backpropagation performed substantially more accurately than ID3. As previously mentioned, this is the only data set in our study that contains numerically-valued features. Hence, our results suggest that backpropagation works better than ID3 when the training examples contain numeric values. This conclusion is corroborated by the study of Atlas, et al. (1990). Two of their three data sets contain numeric features, including the one where the accuracy superiority of backpropagation over CART is statistically significant. However, Weiss and Kapouleas' (1989) study also involved numeric features. Each of their four data sets contains numeric values, but twice the decision tree-building CART algorithm produced a more accurate result than did backpropagation. Thus, more detailed study is required to understand the relative merits of the symbolic and connectionist approaches to learning in the presence of numeric features. Quinlan (1987a) proposed a method for learning "soft thresholds" for decisions involving numerically-valued features. We briefly investigated the use of soft thresholds in ID3 and found no statistically significant differences on the heart-disease data.

Another recent study found a substantial accuracy difference between backpropagation and ID3. Towell, Shavlik, and Noordewier (1990) investigate learning how to recognize a biologically-interesting class of DNA sequences called *promoters*. In their experiment, which did not involve numeric features, backpropagation's test set accuracy was 92%, while ID3's accuracy was only 82%. As their DNA data set contained only 106 examples, one explanation of the accuracy difference is that backpropagation outperforms ID3 on "small" data sets; we investigate this issue of training set size in our next experiment. A second, and more compelling, explanation is that the DNA task involves learning a concept of the form $X$ *of these* $N$ *predicates must be true*. Fisher and McKusick (1989) report that backpropagation performs better than ID3 on problems containing $X$ *of* $N$ functions. Some aspects of the promoter task fit this format. For example, there are several potential sites where hydrogen bonds can form between the DNA and a protein; if enough of these bonds form, promoter activity can occur.

A final point of discussion concerns the performance of backpropagation on the NETalk-full data set. On this data set, backpropagation learns the training set less well than on the other four data sets. It is possible that with a different number of hidden units or if allowed more than 100 training epochs, backpropagation would have done better on the NETalk-full test set. However, between epochs 75 and 100, the training set performance of backpropagation never improved more than one percentage point; hence, it may require a prohibitive amount of training to substantially improve backpropagation's performance on NETalk-full.

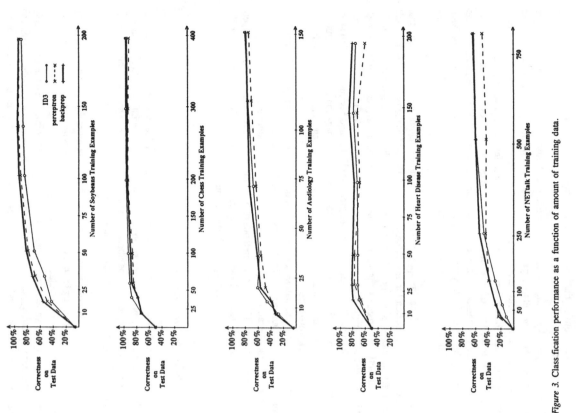

*Figure 3.* Classfication performance as a function of amount of training data.

## 3.2. Experiment two: *Effect of the number of training examples*

It is possible that some learning methods perform relatively better with a small amount of training data while others perform relatively better on large training sets. To address this issue, this experiment presents graphs that plot correctness as a function of training set size. These "learning curves" are generated by performing batch training on the first $N$ examples in each training set as $N$ is gradually increased. Hence, subsequent training sets of increasing size subsume one another. Learning is non-incremental; for example, there is no carryover from the learning on 50 training examples to the learning on 100 training examples. Although learning in this experiment is not incremental, the results provide an upper bound on the performance, in terms of correctness, that can be expected from incremental algorithms. Fisher, McKusick, Mooney, Shavlik, and Towell (1989) provide a discussion of several ways to apply backpropagation in an incremental setting.

### 3.2.1. Results

Figure 3 presents correctness as a function of the amount of training data. Each data point represents the average of three (rather than ten, due to simulation time restrictions) randomly chosen training sets, except the NETtalk curve represents training on only a single data set. The correctness expected from random guessing is plotted when there are zero training examples.

On the soybean and NETtalk data, both backpropagation and the perceptron perform better than ID3 when given only a small amount of training data. Backpropagation consistently outperforms the other two systems on the heart-disease data set. Finally, there is little difference among the three systems on the chess and audiology data.

### 3.2.2. Discussion

The results indicate that for small amounts of training data backpropagation is perhaps a better choice. With small training sets, the slower speed of backpropagation is much less of a problem, and on the five sample domains studied backpropagation did about the same as or better than ID3. The results also suggest that if ID3 does relatively well on a small sample, then the faster ID3 should be used on the full training set. Since backpropagation takes so long to run, this technique can have value in practical systems.

Perceptron's accuracy on the heart-disease data declines slightly as the number of examples increases. This can be attributed to the fact that perceptron terminates once it decides that the data set is not linearly separable. Perceptron's performance on both the heart-disease and NETtalk data could be improved by having it, once it detects an inseparable data set, search for the hyperplane that best separates the training examples.

ID3's tendency to perform worse on small training sets may be related to the *problem of small disjuncts* (Holte, Acker, & Porter, 1989). Holte et al. have shown that it leaves in a decision tree (or disjuncts in a DNF rule) that cover only a small number of training examples tend to have much higher error rates than those that cover a large number of

examples. They present evidence that this higher error rate is due to the *maximum generality bias* used by most symbolic induction systems. The basic problem is that the simplest conjunction that covers a small set of examples is frequently an overgeneralization. Given a small training set, ID3 will build trees composed primarily of small disjuncts with high error rates. Unlike most symbolic systems, backpropagation and the perceptron do not build explicit disjuncts and do not have a maximum generality bias; therefore, they may be less susceptible to the problem of small disjuncts. Also, note that data with a large number of categories will have fewer examples per category and therefore generate smaller disjuncts. This would explain why ID3 does better on the chess data, which has only two classes. It also explains why ID3 performs as well as backpropagation on the audiology data; although there are 24 audiology categories, about three-fourths of the examples fall into one of five classes.

Fisher and McKusick (1989) suggest that ID3 may be more effective than backpropagation on relatively small training sets, but as the size of the training set increases, backpropagation eventually outperforms ID3. This discrepancy results from a procedural difference. When generating learning curves, Fisher and McKusick use backpropagation in an incremental fashion and update the weights only once for each new training example. In the learning curves presented in Figure 3, backpropagation is allowed to converge on all of the training examples so far encountered before it is run on the test set. Running backpropagation to convergence leads to much better performance on small amounts of training data.

### 3.3. Experiment three: Effect of imperfect data sets

An important aspect of inductive learning systems is their sensitivity to imperfections in the data. Improperly represented examples can occur for several reasons. Mistakes may be made when recording feature values or when judging the class of an example. Some feature values may be missing or an insufficient collection of features may be used to describe examples.

Experiments described in this section investigate various types of imperfections and report their effect on the three learning algorithms. Noisy, incomplete, and reduced data sets are produced and the performance of the three learning algorithms compared. Classification performance after learning on corrupted data is measured using test sets that have the same types and rates of imperfections as the training data.[2] This is consistent with work on the theoretical basis of learning (Valiant, 1984), which assumes that the distribution of examples is the same during training and testing.

Due to processing limitations, in these experiments we used a reduced version of the NETtalk-full training set. Rather than using the 808-word training set, only the first 256 words (1099 examples) are used in training. Except for this data set, called NETtalk256, all the curves in this experiment are the result of averaging performance on three random training/test divisions.

### 3.3.1. Random noise

The first type of imperfection investigated will be called *random noise*. This is the noise produced when feature values and example classifications are mistakenly recorded. With probability $p$, a given feature value is randomly changed to another legal value for that feature. With the same probability, the classification of the example is randomly changed to a different category. We replaced heart disease's numeric features by randomly choosing uniformly from the interval [0, 1].

Note that noise is introduced at the feature level. That is, noise is added to data sets before they are converted to the binary representation. For instance, at a 75% noise level in the NETtalk data, 75% of the feature values are different but less than 6% of the bits actually change (each feature comprises 27 bits, all but one of which are zero, so to change a feature value requires that only two bits change their values).

*Results.* Figure 4 presents the effect of the amount of random noise on classification performance. (The same relative performance is obtained when there is only feature noise, i.e., when no classification errors are introduced.) The thin dotted lines on each of these graphs represents the frequency of the most common item in the training set. Thus, this line represents the level of performance obtainable by merely guessing the most common category in the training set. While in one domain (audiology) ID3 outperforms the other two systems, in two others (soybeans and chess) backpropagation is the best. ID3 and backpropagation degrade at roughly the same rate in the heart-disease and NETtalk domains.

*Discussion.* Overall, backpropagation appears to handle random noise slightly better than ID3 does. An explanation for this difference between ID3 and backpropagation is that backpropagation makes its decisions by simultaneously weighing all the input features, while ID3 sequentially considers the values of input features as it traverses the decision trees it learns. Hence, a single noisy feature value early in an ID3 decision tree could significantly impact classification. Our results mildly disagree with Fisher and McKusick's (1989) study of the comparative effect of noise. They report that backpropagation *consistently* outperforms ID3, while our results indicate that sometimes ID3 can handle noise as well as or better than backpropagation.

Recently, several alternatives to chi-squared pruning have been proposed for handling noisy data in ID3 (Quinlan, 1987b; Mingers, 1989). These are generally referred to as *post-pruning* methods because they prune the tree after it is built rather than terminating growth during construction. These newer methods of handling noise in ID3 may be more competitive with backpropagation. However, backpropagation has the advantage that it handles noise naturally without requiring such special-purpose procedures.

### 3.3.2. Missing feature values

A second type of data set imperfections occurs when feature values are missing. The presence of incompletely described examples complicates learning, as the information necessary to distinguish two examples may be absent. To build data sets with missing feature values, with probability $p$ a given feature value is deleted.

*Methods for handling missing values.* Learning from incomplete data requires an effective method for handling missing feature values. Several techniques have been developed for dealing with unknown attribute values in ID3. Quinlan (1989) presents a thorough set of experiments comparing the various approaches. Our version of ID3 uses a method that is arguably the best according to the results of these experiments. When evaluating a potential splitting feature, the system adjusts its information gain by distributing examples with unknown

When classifying a new case with an unknown value for the attribute being tested, all branches are explored and the results are combined to reflect the relative probabilities of the different outcomes (Quinlan, 1986b). Our own experimental results confirm that this approach is superior to other methods such as replacing unknown values with the most common value or discarding examples with unknown values during partitioning.

However, while this method leads to higher accuracies on novel examples, it has one drawback; processing time grows exponentially as a function of the number of missing feature values. One approach to reducing ID3's run time is to prevent splitting on features that create a partition containing less than a total of one example (Quinlan, personal communication). This frequently (although not always) decreases run time a substantial amount but also tends to reduce accuracy by a few percentage points. Even with this addition, run time grows exponentially in the number of missing values and becomes intractable for large data sets with large amounts of missing data. Unfortunately, for this reason this technique could not be applied to the NETtalk256 data set. Hence, to apply ID3 to the NETtalk data, we replaced unknown values with the most common value for an attribute, given the example's classification. In our experiments we found that on the other data sets this method led to only a small degradation in test set accuracy.

To the best of our knowledge, the issue of representing missing values in neural networks has not been investigated previously. We evaluated three representations of missing features for backpropagation. Assume that there are $N$ possible values for some feature; hence, we used $N$ inputs to represent the value of this feature. If the value is missing, these inputs could all be zero, all be 0.5, or all be $1/Nth$. The first representation reflects the fact that none of the possible values are known to be present. The second uses the intermediate input value of 0.5 to represent unspecified inputs, while the third reflects the *a priori* probability that a given input is a one. In a sense, the third approach "spreads" across all $N$ inputs the single "one" used to indicate the feature value. (This third approach could be extended by distributing the single "one" according to the distribution of the feature's values in the training set; however, we did not investigate this approach.)

Performance of these three approaches, averaged over the soybeans, chess, and audiology data sets, is reported in Figure 5. The reason that $1/Nth$ works best may be that the other two techniques provide too little or too much input "activity" at features whose value is

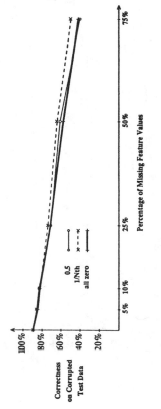

*Figure 5.* Effect of representation of missing features on backpropagation performance.

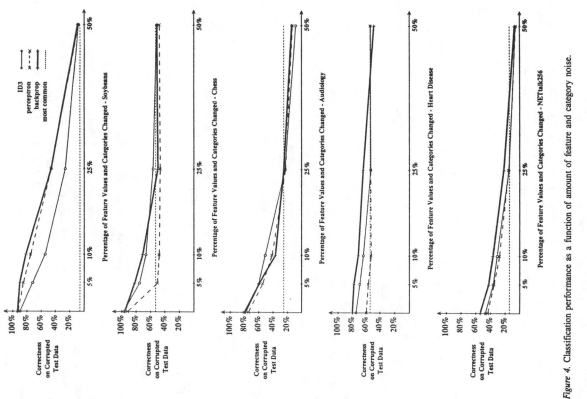

*Figure 4.* Classification performance as a function of amount of feature and category noise.

values across the possible values according to their frequency (Quinlan, 1986b). When considering partitioning the training set along a particular attribute if a training example has an unknown value for this attribute, a fraction of the example is assigned to each subset based on the frequency of its corresponding value (Kononenko, Bratko, & Roskar, 1984).

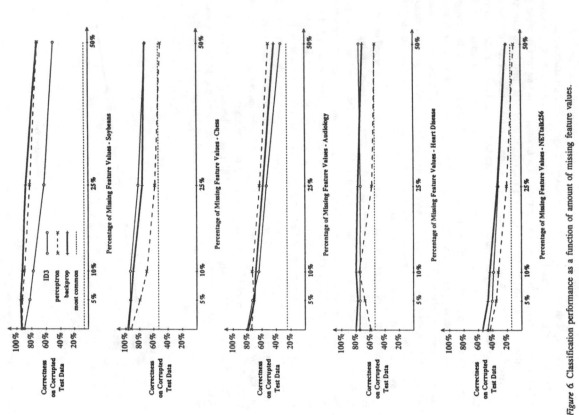

*Figure 6* Classification performance as a function of amount of missing feature values. of features are discarded. (When an odd number of features are discarded, two training sets are produced. In one case the extra letter is dropped from the front and in the other it is dropped from the back. The results are then averaged.)

missing. Since *1/Nth* works best, we used it for backpropagation in the remainder of this experiment. For heart disease's numeric features, we replaced missing features with the value 0.5.

We also tested perceptron with the same three approaches and the *1/Nth* approach works best. Therefore, this method is also used with the perceptron.

Earlier we mentioned that the audiology data set contains many missing feature values. However, these features are not missing because they were "lost." Rather, "missing" in this domain means that the expert producing the example decided that the feature was *irrelevant*, given the other details of the case (Duran, 1988). Our experiments indicated that it is best to represent this type of absent feature value by all zeroes. To produce the curves below, we represented only the *randomly* discarded feature values using the techniques described above.

*Results.*   Figure 6 contains the performance of the three learning algorithms as a function of the percentage of missing features values. ID3 and perceptron perform poorly on some of the data sets, while backpropagation performs well across all five domains. Once again, ID3 performs substantially worse than the other methods on the soybean data. Perceptron performs poorly on the chess data. Surprisingly, perceptron outperforms the other two systems on the audiology data.

*Discussion.*   The results indicate that backpropagation handles missing feature values better than ID3 and perceptron. Perceptron frequently does poorly because complicated representation of missing values lead to concepts that are not linearly separable. The reason for backpropagation outperforming ID3 may be that backpropagation naturally supports the representation of partial evidence for a feature's value. As discussed in the analysis of performance on noisy data, backpropagation makes decisions by summing weighted evidence across many features, while ID3 locally bases its decisions on the value of a single feature. It appears missing feature values are most naturally matched by the inductive biases inherent in backpropagation.

An interesting question is why ID3 consistently does poorly on the soybean data. Possibly its high number of input features (more than that of any other domain), large number of categories, and even distribution of examples across categories interacts poorly with ID3's information gain measurement. In each training set there are only 11 examples for each of 17 categories.

### 3.3.3. *Completely dropped features*

A third type of imperfection arises when an insufficiently rich vocabulary is used to represent examples. Features that would simplify classification may not have been included when the examples were produced. We investigate sensitivity of the learning algorithms to the number of features by randomly dropping a percentage of the features; if a feature is dropped, it is dropped from *all* examples in the training set and in the corresponding test set. Except for NETtalk256, we used three different training sets and chose a different random collection of dropped features for each set. For NETalk 256, which has a clear ordering on its features, letters are dropped from both ends of the example window until a sufficient number

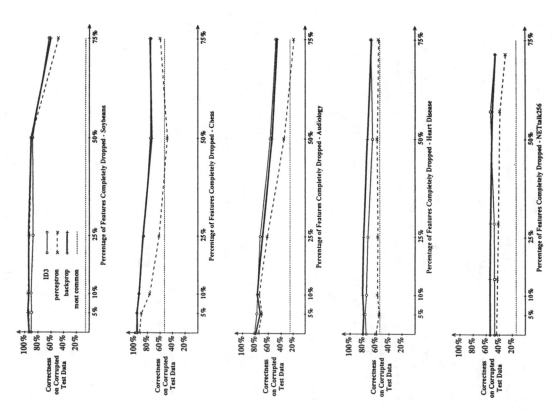

Figure 7. Classification performance as a function of number of features totally dropped.

*Discussion.* Both ID3 and backpropagation do surprisingly well as the number of features is reduced. Perceptron's poor performance is due to the training sets becoming linearly inseparable. One interesting aspect of Figure 7 is the apparent redundancies in several of the domains. Randomly dropping half the features only slightly impairs performance. Also interesting are the occasions where performance *improves* when a small number of features are dropped, illustrating that extra features can degrade inductive learning algorithms. For example, on the NETtalk256 data set, ID3 performs best when it only considers a three-letter window.

### 3.4. Experiment four: Effect of output encoding of NETtalk examples

Often in neural network systems, concept representations are distributed over a collection of units. For example, Sejnowski and Rosenberg (1987) encode the phoneme/stress outputs in NETtalk-full as a sequence of 26 bits (as opposed to one bit for each of the 115 categories). The first 21 bits are a distributed encoding of the 51 phonemes contained in the dictionary. Each bit is a unary feature describing one of: position of the tongue in the mouth, phoneme type, vowel height, or punctuation. The remaining five bits form a local encoding of the five types of stresses used in the dictionary.

In our final experiment, we repeat Sejnowski's methodology with the NETtalk-full data set to investigate the merits of distributed output encodings and to ascertain which learning algorithms can best utilize this type of output representation. This experiment compares classification performance after learning using the localized method of output encoding to the distributed encoding. The output encoding experiment only involves the NETtalk data set, as this is the only data set whose producers rendered a distributed output encoding. Hence, note that using a distributed output vector requires more information about the data sets

### 3.4.1. Methodology

The backpropagation algorithm easily handles this distributed encoding of the output. For the backpropagation tests involving distributed outputs, we used 120 hidden units, 26 output units, and 30 training epochs, following Sejnowski and Rosenberg (1987). While backpropagation handles the distributed output representation naturally, to implement this representation in ID3 requires building a separate decision tree for each of the 26 output bits. Similarly, to implement this representation in perceptron, one perceptron is learned for each of the 26 output bits.

To categorize a test example, a string of 26 outputs is formed by either a single pass through a backpropagation network or by passes through each of the 26 decision trees or perceptrons. Backpropagation produces a vector containing numbers between 0 and 1. Perceptron produces a vector of numbers, where each entry is a perceptron's output minus its threshold. As we discuss in the next section, ID3 produces either a binary vector or a vector of numbers between 0 and 1. The specified category is then determined by finding the phoneme/stress pair encoding that has the smallest angle with the 26 outputs. (This is the "best guess" metric used by Sejnowski and Rosenberg (1987).)

*Results.* Figure 7 presents the results of the experiment where some fraction of the features are completely dropped. ID3 and backpropagation degrade at roughly the same rate as the number of features is reduced, while for large numbers of dropped features perceptron degrades more drastically.

### 3.4.2. Results

Figure 8 compares the classification performance of the learning systems on the NETtalk data using the local output encoding and the distributed output encoding. All training for this table is done using the 808-word set. Classification accuracy is measured using the 1000-word test set described previously.

In this experiment, we initially used the chi-squared version of ID3 and got poor performance (82% correctness on the training set and 49% correctness on the test set). We next investigated the hypothesis that producing a binary vector before making a best guess led to a loss of useful information; knowing the amount of evidence for each output value may be advantageous. To answer this question, we applied Buntine's (1989) method for giving a probabilistic interpretation of the outputs. Using, as input to the "best guess" routine, the 26 probabilities produced by this method results in a training set correctness of 89% and a test set correctness of 56%. Next, we turned off ID3's chi-squared pruning and fitted the data as closely as possible, getting 97% correctness on the training set and 62% on the test set. Using Buntine's classification method with these trees (i.e., those built without using chi-squared pruning) produced the best results. With this configuration, we got a training set accuracy of 98% and a test set accuracy of 65%; Figure 8's statistics refer to this final method.

### 3.4.3. Discussion

The use of a distributed encoding of the output substantially improves the performance of backpropagation. For the distributed encoding, backpropagation's correctness is 96% on the training set and 72% on the testing set. Using the local encoding—one output bit for each category—results in a backpropagation correctness of 88% percent on the training set and 63% on the testing set. ID3 is also able to successfully use the distributed encoding, but its performance with the two encoding styles are roughly equivalent (at about a 65% test-set accuracy). With the distributed encoding, backpropagation performs substantially better than ID3 on the NETtalk task. Dieterich, et al. (1990) report similar results for their comparison of ID3 and backpropagation on the NETtalk data.

Perceptron has no similar improvement in performance and, instead, degrades. This occurs because the 115 individual concepts are easier to learn than the 26 concepts. With the local encoding, perceptron converged on 60 out of the 115 bits, while on the distributed encoding it converged on only four.

There is a cost of using the distributed encoding with backpropagation. The range of correctness varies widely when the training data is imperfect. Using the NETtalk256 data corrupted with 10% noise, backpropagation's correctness on three runs ranged from 27% to 44% when we only varied the seed random number. With 25% noise, the accuracy on three runs ranged from 0.1% to 19%. The problem became worse as we increased the noise level. On all other data sets, and on NETtalk using the local output encoding, there was only a little variation in classification performance between different randomly-initialized networks. The use of the distributed encoding seems to introduce problems with local minima that are absent with the local encoding.

Dieterich, et al. (1990) performed an extensive series of tests in an attempt to isolate the reasons for the superiority of backpropagation over ID3 under the distributed output encoding. They considered three hypotheses that could, individually or jointly, account for the differences between ID3 and backpropagation. Their experiments indicate that neither of the following hypotheses account for the observed differences between ID3 and backpropagation: (a) ID3 overfits the training data; (b) backpropagation's ability to share intermediate conclusions in its hidden units is a factor. They concluded that the primary difference was that backpropagation's numerical parameters (e.g., its continuous output values) allow it to capture statistical information missed by ID3. They propose a "block decoding" scheme for ID3 that substantially reduces the accuracy difference between ID3 and backpropagation.

### 4. General discussion

This study investigates the relative performance of symbolic and neural approaches to learning. The first experiment shows that backpropagation performs slightly better than the other two algorithms in terms of classification correctness on novel examples, but takes much longer to train. Results on the heart-disease data set suggest that backpropagation may perform substantially better than ID3 when there are numerically-valued features. The result of the second experiment is that the neural algorithms tend to perform more accurately than ID3 when given relatively small amounts of training data. The third experiment, which investigates the handling of imperfect data sets, indicates that backpropagation handles noisy and missing feature values slightly better than ID3 and perceptron do. ID3 and backpropagation perform about the same in the presence of reduced numbers of features. In the fourth experiment, backpropagation is better able to utilize a distributed output encoding, although ID3 is also able to take advantage of this representation style. We discuss several additional aspects of the experiments in this section.

### 4.1. The symbolic/subsymbolic distinction

A supposed difference between traditional symbolic and neural-net learning systems is that the latter operate at a distinct "subsymbolic" level (Smolensky, 1988). The experiments

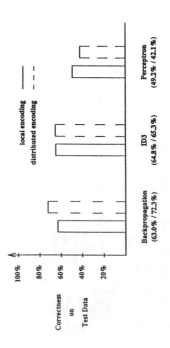

*Figure 8.* Classification correctness on the NETtalk data set for two output encoding methods.

reported in the previous section demonstrate that this distinction can be misleading (Fodor and Pylyshyn (1988) and Langley (1989) also discuss this issue). "Symbolic" systems like ID3 and "subsymbolic" systems like backpropagation are essentially solving the same learning problem and each can be applied to problems typically used to test the other. They both take a set of input vectors and produce a classification function. Both accept input features of any grain size; the ability to use "microfeatures" is not unique to neural nets. As demonstrated in Section 3.4, both can also use distributed representations; however, current neural-net methods such as backpropagation seem to be able to take greater advantage of distributed representations than current symbolic systems like ID3.

It is important to note that, assuming the initial inputs and final outputs are finite-valued, different concept representations such as decision trees, disjunctive normal form (DNF) expressions, and multi-layer neural nets are all equivalent in terms of representational power. Each of these formalisms can represent all $2^{2^N}$ functions on $N$ binary inputs. This is a well-known property of DNF expressions (i.e., two-layer $AND$–$OR$ networks; Muroga, 1979) and any DNF expression can be easily converted into an equivalent decision tree. Since the weights of a linear threshold unit can be set to model $AND$, $OR$, and $NOT$ gates, assuming a sufficient number of hidden units are available, any DNF expression can also be converted into an equivalent neural net. Consequently, every neural net implicitly represents some logical rule (i.e., one of the possible $2^{2^N}$ functions); decision trees and DNF formulae are simply more explicit representations of such rules.

The difference between symbolic and connectionist systems lies in their inherent inductive biases, which determine which of the many logical rules consistent with a set of data is actually chosen as the concept definition. Most symbolic learning systems prefer syntactically simple rules, while many functions that are easily learned by neural nets correspond to relatively complex DNF formulae or decision trees (e.g., $X$ of $N$ functions which output 1 if and only if at least $X$ of the $N$ inputs are 1). Not surprisingly, experiments with artificial data show that backpropagation performs better than ID3 on problems which fit its natural bias, like $X$ of $N$ functions (Fisher & McKusick, 1989). However, the current experiments indicate that the inductive biases of symbolic and neural net systems are equally suitable for many "real world" problems.

### 4.2. Perceptron performance and problem difficulty

One surprising result of these experiments is how well the simple perceptron algorithm performs. The perceptron was largely abandoned as a general learning mechanism over twenty years ago because of its inherent limitations, such as its inability to learn concepts that are not linearly separable (Minsky & Papert, 1988). Nevertheless, it performs quite well in these experiments. Except on the heart-disease and NETtalk data sets, and in the presence of imperfect training data, the accuracy of the perceptron is hardly distinguishable from the more complicated learning algorithms. In addition, it is very efficient; perceptron's training time is comparable to ID3's.

These results indicate the presence of a large amount of regularity in the training sets chosen as representative of data previously used to test symbolic learning systems. The categories present in both the soybean and audiology data are linearly separable for all

---

ten randomly chosen training sets. The two categories in the chess data are linearly separable for four of the ten training sets and almost linearly separable on the rest (average correctness on the training sets is 97.5%). Despite the fact that the data sets are large and represent real categories, their regularity makes them relatively "easy" for even simple learning algorithms like the perceptron.

One possible explanation for the regularity in the data is that it is reflecting regularity in the real-world categories. In other words, members of a real category naturally have a great deal in common and are relatively easy to distinguish from examples of other categories. Another more likely explanation is that the features present in the data have been very carefully engineered to reflect important differences in the categories. For example, formulating features for chess end games which were appropriate for learning required considerable human effort (Quinlan, 1983). More difficult problems need to be studied in order to determine the true power of current inductive learning systems. The NETtalk data set is one of the most difficult ones studied so far and other researchers in machine learning are beginning to use it as a benchmark (e.g., Dietterich, et al., 1990).

Regardless of the reason, data for a number of "real" problems seems to consist of linearly separable categories. Since the perceptron is a simple and efficient learning algorithm in this case, using a perceptron as an initial test system is probably a good idea. If a set of categories are not linearly separable, the *perceptron cycling theorem* (Minsky & Papert, 1988) guarantees that the algorithm will eventually repeat the same set of weights and can be terminated. In this case, a more complicated algorithm such as ID3 or backpropagation can be tried. The *perceptron tree error correction procedure* (Utgoff, 1988) is an example of such a hybrid approach. This algorithm first tries the perceptron learning procedure, and if it fails splits the data into subsets using ID3's information-theoretic measure and applies itself recursively to each subset.

### 4.3. Slowness of backpropagation

Although backpropagation performs about as well or better than the other systems at classifying novel examples, it consistently takes a lot more time to train. Averaged across all five data sets, in the first experiment backpropagation takes about 150 times as long to train as ID3. (Testing in backpropagation takes about 10 times longer than the other two systems.) These factors would probably increase if we optimized our Common Lisp versions of ID3 and perceptron, which are not coded efficiently compared to the C version of backpropagation.

Researchers are developing faster methods for neural network training (e.g., Fahlman, 1988; Barnard & Cole, 1989). For example, Fahlman's *quickprop* algorithm ran almost an order of magnitude faster than backpropagation on one sample task. Unfortunately, Fahlman does not report how well his algorithm performs relative to backpropagation in terms of accuracy on novel examples.

Another obvious way backpropagation can be made faster is to exploit its intrinsic parallelism. The networks used in these experiments contained an average of about 150 units. Consequently, assuming one processor per unit and perfect speedup, the training time for backpropagation could possibly be made competitive with ID3's. However, ID3 is a recursive

are inappropriately set or if initial weights are unfavorable, backpropagation may fail to converge efficiently. However, it should also be noted that many symbolic learning systems have parameters which one must appropriately set to insure good performance (Rendell, et al., 1989).

Another issue is the human interpretability of the acquired rules. Symbolic learning can produce interpretable rules while networks of weights are harder to interpret. However, large decision trees can also be very difficult to interpret (Shapiro, 1987). If the learned classifiers are implemented using unreliable components, sensitivity to component failure can be a concern. Neural models, which sum partial evidence, are robust in the presence of component failure (McClelland, 1986). Sensitivity to component failure is seldom addressed in symbolic systems. Finally, connectionist models are intended to be neurally-plausible models, while symbolic models are not. Hence, connectionist models may shed more light on neurophysiology.

## 5. Future research issues

Our experiments suggest a number of issues for future research. We have already mentioned several interesting research topics: comparing parallel implementations; comparing incremental learning approaches; understanding why ID3 does poorly on the soybean data; further investigating the hypothesis that backpropagation better addresses the problem of *small disjuncts* (Holte, et al., 1989). The remainder of this section describes additional topics involving empirical, theoretical, and psychological comparison of symbolic and connectionist learning.

An obvious extension is comparison of additional algorithms and domains. Besides other connectionist and rule-based algorithms, instance-based, genetic, and probabilistic algorithms could be included. Such experiments would hopefully give additional insight into which algorithms are suitable for different types of problems.

Also of interest would be detailed experiments that isolate the algorithmic differences between backpropagation and ID3 that cause the observed performance differences. Each inductive learning algorithm contains some sort of inductive bias, and it is of interest how well these biases work on real-world learning tasks. As mentioned in Section 3.4.3, Dietterich, et al. (1990) performed a comparative analysis on the NETtalk data, represented in the distributed encoding. Similar analysis of numerical data, noisy data, data with missing values, and small data sets could lead to additional insights and the development of better learning algorithms for these types of data. The relative performance of ID3 and backpropagation in the presence of numerical data is of particular interest, since the results of our experiments and those of Atlas, et al. (1990) and Weiss and Kapouleas (1989) do not provide a clear answer to this question.

The effect of parameter settings on the relative performance of algorithms such as backpropagation is another area for research. Manually tuning parameters to fit a particular set of data can give an algorithm an unfair advantage. Consequently, we did not carefully tune backpropagation's parameters to each data set, but rather adopted a uniform parameter-setting policy after some initial experimentation. Improved policies for setting parameters could result in better performance.

divide-and-conquer algorithm and therefore also has a great deal of intrinsic parallelism. In addition, in perceptron each output bit is learned independently, one simple source of parallelism for this method. Comparing the training time for parallel implementations of all three algorithms would be the only fair way to address this issue.

### 4.4. Scalability

The computational complexity of a learning algorithm is an important theoretical and practical issue. This issue is generally more important than parallelism since a fixed number of processors can at most decrease run time by a constant factor while increasing the size of a problem can increase run time an arbitrary amount depending on the computational complexity of the algorithm.

Learning time for ID3 grows linearly with the number of examples and, in the worst case, quadratically with the number of features (Schlimmer & Fisher, 1986; Utgoff, 1989). However, our learning times for the "dropped features" experiment (Section 3.4.3) support the hypothesis that on average ID3's learning time grows linearly with the number of features. Therefore, ID3 seems to scale quite well.

There have been speculations that neural networks scale poorly (Minsky & Papert, 1988). Recent theoretical work shows that neural network learning can be NP-complete (Blum & Rivest, 1988; Judd, 1988). There is empirical evidence that, on average, backpropagation's time to reach asymptotic performance grows as the cube of the number of weights (Hinton, 1989). However, as evidenced on the NETtalk-full data, backpropagation can still produce impressive results even when training is terminated before the training set is fully learned.

### 4.5. Incremental learning

One issue we did not investigate is learning incrementally. Incremental versions of ID3 have been proposed (Schlimmer & Fisher, 1986; Utgoff, 1989) and backpropagation can be performed by processing each new example some number of times before discarding it. Comparison of various incremental approaches is another area for future research (Fisher, et al., 1989).

### 4.6. Other issues

There are several other differences between the three learning algorithms and between symbolic and connectionist approaches in general. For example, if one has a collection of input/output training pairs, one can directly run ID3 and perceptron. On the other hand, in order to run backpropagation, a network architecture must be chosen, currently much more of an art than a science. Not only must one choose the number of hidden units, but the number of hidden layers must also be specified. In addition, one must choose settings for the learning rate and the momentum term. Performance may depend greatly on the initial randomly-selected weights and several runs with different initial weights may be necessary to get a good final result. Finally, a criterion for stopping training must be chosen. If parameters

Theoretical analysis of the relative performance of different approaches to concept learning is also warranted. A particularly relevant result would provide a formal characterization of classes of concepts that different types of algorithms are probabilistically guaranteed to learn with high accuracy from few examples. Most theoretical work has focused on which classes are learnable or unlearnable in polynomial time, rather than on detailed analysis of the relative sample complexity of practical algorithms.

Finally, this paper focuses on evaluating algorithms based on training time and predictive accuracy. Psychological plausibility is another interesting evaluation metric. For example, Pazzani and Dyer (1987) found that backpropagation does not adequately model human data on learning simple conjunctive and disjunctive concepts. Further investigation is needed on the relative ability of symbolic and neural learning algorithms to model various aspects of human learning.

## 6. Conclusion

A current controversy is the relative merits of symbolic and neural network approaches to artificial intelligence. Although symbolic and connectionist learning systems often address the same task of inductively acquiring concepts from classified examples, their comparative performance has not been adequately investigated. In this article, the performance of a symbolic learning system (ID3) and two connectionist learning systems (perceptron and backpropagation) are compared on five real-world data sets. These data sets have been used in previous experiments. Four in symbolic learning research (soybeans, chess, audiology, and heart-disease) and one in neural network research (NETtalk). There are several contributions of the reported experiments:

• Experimental results indicate that ID3 and perceptron run significantly faster than does backpropagation, both during learning and during classification of novel examples. Except for ID3 and perceptron on the heart-disease data and perceptron on the NETtalk data, the probability of correctly classifying new examples is about the same for the three systems.

• Backpropagation's performance on the heart-disease data set suggests it outperforms ID3 on data sets that contain numerically-valued features. This conclusion is supported by the experiments of Atlas et al. (1990) and contradicted by the results of Weiss and Kapouleas (1989).

• Empirical evidence indicates that, when given "small" amounts of training data, backpropagation occasionally learns more accurate classifiers than ID3 does. Also, backpropagation's slowness is less of a concern on small data sets.

• Additional experiments, in which the sample data sets are carefully corrupted, suggest that with noisy data sets backpropagation slightly outperforms ID3. However, in one domain (audiology) ID3 was more robust to noise.

• When examples are incompletely specified, backpropagation also performs slightly better than the other two approaches. A technique for representing missing feature values in neural networks is proposed and shown effective.

• ID3 and backpropagation appear to be equally sensitive to reductions in the number of features used to express examples. Surprisingly, often *half* the features could be randomly dropped without substantially impacting classification accuracy.

• One claimed advantage of neural approaches to learning is that they are able to profitably use distributed encodings. Empirical study of the NETtalk data set suggests that backpropagation is able to take advantage of domain-specific distributed output encodings better than the two other systems, although ID3 is able to successfully use distributed output encodings.

In conclusion, this study provides the beginnings of a better understanding of the relative strengths and weaknesses of the symbolic and neural approaches to machine learning. We hope it provides results against which future learning algorithms can be evaluated.

## Acknowledgments

The comments and suggestions of editor Ross Quinlan and an anonymous reviewer are gratefully acknowledged. The authors would also like to thank the following people for supplying data sets: Bob Stepp and Bob Reinke for the soybean data; Ray Bareiss, Bruce Porter, and Craig Wier for the audiology data which was collected with the help of Professor James Jerger of the Baylor College of Medicine; Dr. Robert Detrano of the Cleveland Clinic Foundation for the heart disease data set (which was obtained from the University of California—Irvine's repository of machine learning data bases, managed by David Aha); Rob Holte and Peter Clark for Alen Shapiro's chess data; and Terry Sejnowski for the NETtalk data. Alan Gove ran many of the preliminary experiments and assisted in converting the data sets into a common format. Elizabeth Towell assisted with the analysis of variance. Rita Duran, Wan Yik Lee, and Richard Maclin contributed to the implementations. The Condor system (Litzkow, Livny, & Mutka, 1988), which runs Unix jobs on idle workstations, provided many of the large number of cycles needed for these experiments. The equivalent of over two Sun-4/110 CPU *years* was provided by Condor.

This research was partially supported by the University of Wisconsin Graduate School, the University of Texas at Austin's Department of Computer Sciences and Artificial Intelligence Laboratory, Office of Naval Research Grant N00014-90-J-1941 to Shavlik, and NASA-Ames Grant NCC-2-629 to Mooney.

This paper's results extend and supercede those previously reported at the Eleventh International Conference on Artificial Intelligence and in University of Wisconsin Technical Report #857.

## Notes

1. The numbers of input and output bits for each domain are as follows: soybeans—208 and 17; chess—73 and 2; audiology—86 and 24; heart disease—26 and 2; NETtalk—189 and 115.

2. There is one exception to this. In one experiment's training set (Section 3.3.1), the classifications of examples are randomly corrupted. The classifications in the corresponding test sets, against which the accuracies of the learning algorithms are measured, are *not* corrupted.

## Appendix

Table 1 contains the arithmetic means and standard deviations of the results produced on the ten data sets for each domain (Section 3.1). For perceptron, the number of epochs refers

## References

Ash, T. (1989). *Dynamic node creation in backpropagation networks* (Technical Report ICS-8901). San Diego, CA: University of California, Institute for Cognitive Science.

Atlas, L., Cole, R., Connor, J., El-Sharkawi, M., Marks II, R.J., Muthusamy, Y., & Barnard, E. (1990). Performance comparisons between backpropagation networks and classification trees on three real-world applications. *Advances in neural information processing systems* (Vol. 2). Denver, CO.

Bareiss, E.R. (1989). *Exemplar-based knowledge acquisition: A unified approach to concept representation, classification, and learning.* Boston: Academic Press.

Barnard, E., & Cole, R.A. (1989). *A neural-net training program based on conjugate-gradient optimization* (Technical Report CSE 89-014). Beaverton, OR: Oregon Graduate Institute.

Blum, A., & Rivest, R.L. (1988). Training a 3-node neural network is NP-complete. *Proceedings of the 1988 Workshop on Computational Learning Theory* (pp. 9–18). Cambridge, MA.

Blumer, A., Ehrenfeucht, A., Haussler, D., & Warmuth, M.K. (1987). Occam's razor. *Information Processing Letters, 24,* 377–380.

Breiman, L., Friedman, J.H., Olshen, R.A., & Stone, C.J. (1984). *Classification and regression trees.* Monterey, CA: Wadsworth and Brooks.

Buntine, W. (1989). Decision tree induction systems: A Bayesian analysis. In L.N. Kanal, T.S. Levitt, & I.F. Lemmer (Eds.), *Uncertainty in artificial intelligence* (Vol. 3). Amsterdam: North-Holland.

Cheng, J., Fayyad, U.M., Irani, K.B., & Qian, A. (1988). Improved decision trees: A generalized version of ID3. *Proceedings of the Fifth International Conference on Machine Learning* (pp. 100–106). Ann Arbor, MI.

Detrano, R. (unpublished manuscript). International application of a new probability algorithm for the diagnosis of coronary artery disease. (V.A. Medical Center. Long Beach, CA).

Dietterich, T.G., Hild, H., & Bakiri, G. (1990). A comparative study of ID3 and backpropagation for English text-to-speech mapping. *Proceedings of the Seventh International Conference on Machine Learning* (pp. 24–31). Austin, TX.

Duran, R.I. (1988). *Concept learning with incomplete datasets* (Technical Report AI88-82). Austin, TX: University of Texas, Department of Computer Sciences.

Fahlman, S.E. (1988). Faster learning variations on back-propagation: An empirical study. *Proceedings of the 1988 Connectionist Models Summer School* (pp. 38–51). San Mateo, CA: Morgan Kaufmann.

Fisher, D.H. (1987). *Knowledge acquisition via incremental conceptual clustering.* Ph.D. thesis, Department of Information and Computer Science, University of California, Irvine, CA. (Available as Technical Report 87-22).

Fisher, D.H., & McKusick, K.B. (1989). An empirical comparison of ID3 and back-propagation. *Proceedings of the Eleventh International Joint Conference on Artificial Intelligence* (pp. 788–793). Detroit, MI.

Fisher, D., McKusick, K., Mooney, R.J., Shavlik, J.W., & Towell, G.G. (1989). Processing issues in comparison of symbolic and connectionist learning systems. *Proceedings of the Sixth International Machine Learning Workshop* (pp. 169–173). Ithaca, NY.

Fodor, J.A., & Pylyshyn, Z.W. (1988). Connectionism and cognitive architecture: A critical analysis. In S. Pinker, & J. Mehler (Eds.), *Connections and symbols.* Cambridge, MA: MIT Press.

Hanson, S.J., & Pratt, L.Y. (1989). Comparing biases for minimal network construction with back-propagation. *Advances in neural information processing systems* (Vol. 1). Denver, CO.

Hinton, G.E. (1989). Connectionist learning procedures. *Artificial Intelligence, 40,* 185–234.

Hinton, G.E., & Sejnowski, T.J. (1986). Learning and relearning in Boltzmann machines. In D.E. Rumelhart, & J.L. McClelland (Eds.), *Parallel distributed processing: Explorations in the microstructure of cognition. Volume 1: Foundations.* Cambridge, MA: MIT Press.

Holte, R.C., Acker, L.E., & Porter, B.W. (1989). Concept learning and the problem of small disjuncts. *Proceedings of the Eleventh International Joint Conference on Artificial Intelligence* (pp. 813–819). Detroit, MI.

Honavar, V., & Uhr, L. (1988). A network of neuron-like units that learns to perceive by generation as well as a reweighting of its links. *Proceedings of the 1988 Connectionist Models Summer School* (pp. 472–484). San Mateo, CA: Morgan Kaufmann.

Judd, J.S. (1988). On the complexity of loading shallow neural networks. *Journal of Complexity, 4,* 177–192.

Kononenko, I., Bratko, I., & Roskar, E. (1984). *Experiments in automatic learning of medical diagnostic rules* (Technical Report), Ljubljana, Yugoslavia: Jozef Stefan Institute.

to the mean number of cycles taken per category. NETtalk-full only involves one training set and, hence, no standard deviations are reported. Statistically significantly different test set accuracies are reported; all other pair-wise comparisons between test set accuracies are not statistically significant.

*Table 1.* Results of experiment 1 (means and standard deviations).

| Domain/System | Training Time (sec) | Training Epochs | Testing Time (sec) | Correctness (%) Training Set | Correctness (%) Test Set |
|---|---|---|---|---|---|
| **Soybeans** | | | | | |
| ID3 | 161.0 ± 8.9 | | 0.1 ± 0.0 | 100.0 ± 0.0 | 89.0 ± 2.0 |
| perceptron | 35.8 ± 5.2 | 11.9 ± 0.7 | 0.8 ± 0.1 | 100.0 ± 0.0 | 92.9 ± 2.1 |
| backprop | 5,260.0 ± 7,390.0 | 158.0 ± 175.0 | 7.9 ± 0.3 | 99.9 ± 0.2 | 94.1 ± 2.5 |

*t*-test (on test set accuracy) indicates, with 99.9% confidence, that backpropagation and perceptron are superior to ID3 on soybeans.

| Domain/System | Training Time (sec) | Training Epochs | Testing Time (sec) | Correctness (%) Training Set | Correctness (%) Test Set |
|---|---|---|---|---|---|
| **Chess** | | | | | |
| ID3 | 33.1 ± 2.8 | | 0.1 ± 0.0 | 100.0 ± 0.0 | 97.0 ± 1.6 |
| perceptron | 970.0 ± 554.0 | 3,460.0 ± 1,910.0 | 0.1 ± 0.0 | 97.6 ± 2.4 | 93.9 ± 2.2 |
| backprop | 34,700.0 ± 15,000.0 | 4,120.0 ± 1,770.0 | 1.8 ± 0.0 | 99.3 ± 0.4 | 96.3 ± 1.0 |

*t*-test indicates, with 95% confidence, that backpropagation and ID3 are superior to perceptron on chess.

| Domain/System | Training Time (sec) | Training Epochs | Testing Time (sec) | Correctness (%) Training Set | Correctness (%) Test Set |
|---|---|---|---|---|---|
| **Audiology** | | | | | |
| ID3 | 66.0 ± 2.5 | | 0.1 ± 0.0 | 100.0 ± 0.0 | 75.5 ± 4.4 |
| perceptron | 12.5 ± 0.5 | 9.6 ± 0.5 | 0.3 ± 0.0 | 100.0 ± 0.0 | 73.5 ± 3.9 |
| backprop | 19,000.0 ± 13,100.0 | 2,880.0 ± 1,980.0 | 1.8 ± 0.1 | 99.8 ± 0.3 | 77.7 ± 3.8 |

*t*-test indicates, with 95% confidence, that backpropagation and ID3 are superior to perceptron on audiology.

| Domain/System | Training Time (sec) | Training Epochs | Testing Time (sec) | Correctness (%) Training Set | Correctness (%) Test Set |
|---|---|---|---|---|---|
| **Heart Disease** | | | | | |
| ID3 | 69.1 ± 5.0 | | 0.2 ± 0.0 | 100.0 ± 0.0 | 71.2 ± 5.2 |
| perceptron | 771.0 ± 1,450.0 | 767.0 ± 1,430.0 | 0.2 ± 0.0 | 63.1 ± 8.3 | 60.5 ± 7.9 |
| backprop | 4,060.0 ± 424.0 | 5,000.0 ± 0.0 | 1.1 ± 0.1 | 96.0 ± 1.0 | 80.6 ± 3.1 |

*t*-test indicates, with 99% confidence, that (a) backpropagation is superior to ID3 and perceptron and (b) ID3 is superior to perceptron on heart disease.

| Domain/System | Training Time (sec) | Training Epochs | Testing Time (sec) | Correctness (%) Training Set | Correctness (%) Test Set |
|---|---|---|---|---|---|
| **NETtalk-A** | | | | | |
| ID3 | 378.0 ± 43.4 | | 0.1 ± 0.0 | 98.3 ± 0.4 | 63.1 ± 3.0 |
| perceptron | 472.0 ± 30.4 | 108.0 ± 28.4 | 1.2 ± 0.0 | 88.9 ± 1.8 | 57.2 ± 2.0 |
| backprop | 234,000.0 ± 27,600.0 | 5,000.0 ± 0.0 | 10.1 ± 1.5 | 96.7 ± 0.9 | 66.4 ± 2.4 |

*t*-test indicates, with 95% confidence, that backpropagation and ID3 are superior to perceptron on NETtalk-A.

| Domain/System | Training Time (sec) | Training Epochs | Testing Time (sec) | Correctness (%) Training Set | Correctness (%) Test Set |
|---|---|---|---|---|---|
| **NETtalk-Full** | | | | | |
| ID3 | 5,410 | | 278 | 98.5 | 64.8 |
| perceptron | 12,300 | 38.4 | 5,640 | 67.7 | 49.2 |
| backprop | 168,000 | 100.0 | 24,300 | 88.5 | 63.0 |

Kuchera, H., & Francis, W.N. (1967). *Computational analysis of modern-day American English.* Providence, RI: Brown University Press.

Langley, P. (1989). Editorial: Toward a unified science of machine learning. *Machine Learning, 3,* 253–259.

Le Cun, Y., Denker, J.S., & Solla, S.A. (1990). Optimal brain damage. *Advances in neural information processing systems* (Vol. 2). Denver, CO.

Litzkow, M., Livny, M., & Mutka, M.W. (1988). Condor—a hunter of idle workstations. *Proceedings of the Eighth International Conference on Distributed Computing Systems.*

McClelland, J.L. (1986). Resource requirements of standard and programmable nets. In D.E. Rumelhart, & J.L. McClelland (Eds.), *Parallel distributed processing: Explorations in the microstructure of cognition. Volume 1: Foundations.* Cambridge, MA: MIT Press.

McClelland, J.L., & Rumelhart, D.E. (1987). *Explorations in parallel distributed processing: A handbook of models, programs, and exercises.* Cambridge, MA: MIT Press.

Michalski, R.S. (1983). A theory and methodology of inductive learning. *Artificial Intelligence, 20,* 111–161.

Michalski, R.S., & Chilausky, R.L. (1980). Learning by being told and learning from examples: An experimental comparison of two methods of knowledge acquisition in the context of developing an expert system for soybean disease diagnosis. *Policy Analysis and Information Systems, 4,* 125–160.

Mingers, J. (1989). An empirical comparison of pruning methods for decision tree induction. *Machine Learning, 4,* 227–243.

Minsky, M.L., & Papert, S. (1988). *Perceptrons: Expanded edition.* Cambridge, MA: MIT Press. (Original edition published in 1969).

Mitchell, T.M. (1982). Generalization as search. *Artificial Intelligence, 18,* 203–226.

Mooney, R.J., Shavlik, J.W., Towell, G.G., & Gove, A. (1989). An experimental comparison of symbolic and connectionist learning algorithms. *Proceedings of the Eleventh International Joint Conference on Artificial Intelligence* (pp. 775–780). Detroit, MI.

Muroga, S. (1979). *Logic design and switching theory.* New York: Wiley.

O'Rorke, P. (1982). *A comparative study of inductive learning systems AQ15 and ID3 using a chess endgame test problem* (Technical Report UIUCDCS-F-82-899). Urbana, IL: University of Illinois, Department of Computer Science.

Pazzani, M., & Dyer, M. (1987). A comparison of concept identification in human learning and network learning with the generalized delta rule. *Proceedings of the Tenth International Joint Conference on Artificial Intelligence* (pp. 147–150). Milan, Italy.

Quinlan, J.R. (1983). Learning efficient classification procedures and their application to chess end games. In R.S. Michalski, J.G. Carbonell, & T.M. Mitchell (Eds.), *Machine learning: An artificial intelligence approach* (Vol. 1). Palo Alto, CA: Tioga.

Quinlan, J.R. (1986a). Induction of decision trees. *Machine Learning, 1,* 81–106.

Quinlan, J.R. (1986b). The effect of noise on concept learning. In R.S. Michalski, J.G. Carbonell, & T.M. Mitchell (Eds.), *Machine learning: An artificial intelligence approach* (Vol. 2). San Mateo, CA: Morgan Kaufmann.

Quinlan, J.R. (1987a). Decision trees as probabilistic classifiers. *Proceedings of the Fourth International Machine Learning Workshop* (pp. 31–37). Irvine, CA.

Quinlan, J.R. (1987b). Simplifying decision trees. *International Journal of Man-Machine Studies, 27,* 221–234.

Quinlan, J.R. (1989). Unknown attribute values in induction. *Proceedings of the Sixth International Machine Learning Workshop* (pp. 164–168). Ithaca, NY.

Reinke, R. (1984). *Knowledge acquisition and refinement tools for the ADVISE meta-expert system.* Master's thesis, Department of Computer Science, University of Illinois, Urbana, IL.

Rendell, L.A., Cho, H.H., & Seshu, R. (1989). Improving the design of similarity-based rule-learning systems. *International Journal of Expert Systems, 2,* 97–133.

Rosenblatt, F. (1962). *Principles of neurodynamics: Perceptrons and the theory of brain mechanisms.* New York: Spartan.

Rumelhart, D.E., Hinton, G.E., & Williams, R.J. (1986). Learning internal representations by error propagation. In D.E. Rumelhart, & J.L. McClelland (Eds.), *Parallel distributed processing: Explorations in the microstructure of cognition. Volume 1: Foundations.* Cambridge, MA: MIT Press.

Schlimmer, J.C., & Fisher, D. (1986). A case study of incremental concept induction. *Proceedings of the National Conference on Artificial Intelligence* (pp. 496–501). Philadelphia, PA.

Sejnowski, T.J., & Rosenberg, C. (1987). Parallel networks that learn to pronounce English text. *Complex Systems, 1,* 145–168.

Shapiro, A. (1987). *Structured induction in expert systems.* Reading, MA: Addison Wesley.

Smolensky, P. (1988). On the proper treatment of connectionism. *Behavioral and Brain Sciences, 11,* 1–23.

Stepp, R.E. (1984). *Conjunctive conceptual clustering: A methodology and experimentation.* Ph.D. thesis, Department of Computer Science, University of Illinois, Urbana, IL.

Tesauro, G., & Sejnowski, T.J. (1989). A parallel network that learns to play backgammon. *Artificial Intelligence, 39,* 357–390.

Towell, G.G., Shavlik, J.W., & Noordewier, M.O. (1990). Refinement of approximately correct domain theories by knowledge-based neural networks. *Proceedings of the Eighth National Conference on Artificial Intelligence* (pp. 861–866), Boston, MA.

Utgoff, P.E. (1988). Perceptron trees: A case study in hybrid concept representations. *Proceedings of the National Conference on Artificial Intelligence* (pp. 601–606). St. Paul, MN.

Utgoff, P.E. (1989). Incremental induction of decision trees. *Machine Learning, 4,* 161–186.

Valiant, L.G. (1984). A theory of the learnable. *Communications of the ACM, 27,* 1134–1142.

Weiss, S.M., Galen, R., & Tedepalli, P. (1987). Optimizing the predictive value of diagnostic decision rules. *Proceeding of the National Conference on Artificial Intelligence* (pp. 521–526). Seattle, WA.

Weiss, S.M., & Kapouleas, I. (1989). An empirical comparison of pattern recognition, neural nets, and machine learning classification methods. *Proceedings of the Eleventh International Joint Conference on Artificial Intelligence* (pp. 688–693). Detroit, MI.

Wirth, J., & Catlett, J. (1988). Experiments on the costs and benefits of windowing in ID3. *Proceedings of the Fifth International Machine Learning Conference* (pp. 87–99). Ann Arbor, MI.

# THE QUANTIFICATION OF KNOWLEDGE—
# FORMAL FOUNDATIONS FOR ACQUISITION METHODOLOGIES

Brian R Gaines
Knowledge Science Institute
Department of Computer Science, University of Calgary
Calgary, Alberta, Canada T2N 1N4
(gaines@cpsc.ucalgary.ca, (403) 220-5901)

## ABSTRACT

The next generation of intelligent systems methodologies must give priority to the integration of the increasingly fragmented artificial intelligence research literature. What are the relations between work on machine vision and robotics and that on logic programming and the emulation of cognition? How can the amorphous chaos of a neural net and the axiomatic structure of a predicate calculus both provide appropriate solutions to the same problems in knowledge-based systems? For example, there is currently a major paradigm split in knowledge acquisition research and practice between techniques for the transfer of existing knowledge from human experts through "expertise transfer" and those for the creation of new expertise through empirical induction or "machine learning". There is, however, a fundamental relation between the two paradigms in that existing expertise was at some time derived through empirical induction. There is also continuity between the two paradigms in that existing expertise may be partial, erroneous, and of various forms, such that it cannot completely replace empirical induction but may serve to to guide and expedite it. This paper provides a quantitative framework for knowledge acquisition that encompasses machine learning and expertise transfer as related paradigms within a single spectrum. It shows that the development of practical knowledge-based systems generally lies between these extremes, and suggests system architectures that combine the underlying paradigms. It extends these to a framework integrating other intelligent systems technologies and methodologies.

## INTRODUCTION

Research and practice in intelligent systems methodologies has developed major technologies for "knowledge-based systems" without very strongly founded concepts of the nature of "knowledge" itself. In the economic literature the notion that "knowledge" in general is an abstract term for a concrete economic entity similar in status to other "goods" was extensively developed by Machlup (1980, 1982, 1984), and has found increasing acceptance in both professional (Machlup & Mansfield 1983) and popular literature (Sveiby & Lloyd 1987). It underlies the powerful metaphor that Hayes-Roth (1984) used to explain the significance of expert systems in the early 1980s, that:

> "The power is in the knowledge. Mining, molding, assembling and refining expert knowledge are the main problems."

There are strong analogies between the classical resource management and extraction industries and the new knowledge management and extraction industries which serve to guide us in developing knowledge-based industries.

There are also differences which we do not yet fully comprehend and which may mislead us if we stretch the analogies too far. One of these is the essential human role in knowledge production and application as a by-product of our social existence. The knowledge sources that we mine are already partially processed by prior human activity and will continue to be further processed in use. There are parallels in classical resource extraction and manufacturing, but the ongoing dynamics of knowledge processing dominate knowledge-based industries in such a way as to typify them. Knowledge is an essentially dynamic resource which requires active management to maintain its existence.

Copyright 1989 by Elsevier Science Publishing Co., Inc.
Methodologies for Intelligent Systems, 4
Zbigniew W. Ras, Editor

This paper focuses on the analogy underlying Hayes Roth's metaphor, attempting to develop a framework for knowledge acquisition that encompasses the partial processing and dynamic aspects of knowledge resources. In particular, the framework developed encompasses knowledge acquisition through both machine learning and expertise transfer.

## EXPERTISE TRANSFER AND EMPIRICAL INDUCTION

There is currently a major paradigm split in knowledge acquisition research and practice between techniques for the transfer of existing knowledge from human experts and those for the creation of new expertise through empirical induction or "machine learning" (Gaines & Boose 1988, Boose & Gaines 1988). There is, however, a fundamental relation between the two paradigms in that existing expertise was at some time derived through empirical induction. There is also continuity between the two paradigms in that existing expertise may be partial, erroneous, and of various forms, such that it cannot completely replace empirical induction but may serve to to guide and expedite it (Gaines 1987a).

Figure 1 makes these relations explicit:

At the top, some "world" acts as a source from which data may be acquired.

On the left the acquisition is by a person who models the data and becomes an "expert" about some aspect of the world. In developing a knowledge-based system such experts may be interviewed using expertise transfer tools (Boose 1986) and their "knowledge" (model of part the world) may be transferred to a computer-based knowledge base.

On the right the acquisition loads a computer-based database. In developing a knowledge-based system such a database may be modeled using empirical induction tools (Quinlan 1986) and the resultant "knowledge" (model of part the world) may be transferred to a computer-based knowledge base.

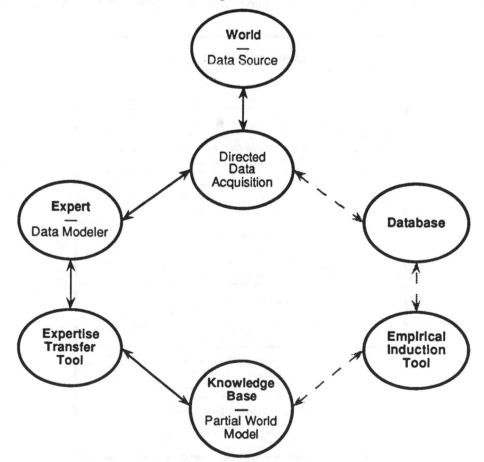

**Figure 1 Expertise transfer and empirical induction**

Figure 1 neatly captures the relation between expertise transfer and empirical induction. However, it over-emphasizes the separation between the two approaches:

On the left, the "expert" rarely makes available pure knowledge, that is, a minimal correct model of part of the world. Experts provide a mixture of relevant and irrelevant viewpoints, correct and incorrect modeling rules, case histories with partially known outcomes, and so on. The current generation of "expertise transfer" and "knowledge support" systems, such as Aquinas (Boose & Bradshaw 1987) and KSS0 (Gaines & Shaw 1987) provide a wide range of tools to cope with, integrate, and clean up, this variety of forms and qualities of knowledge.

On the right, the "database" is not a complete or unselective collection of information about the world. It has been structured and collected by people for a purpose, and this structuring and collection already involves substantial expertise. Figure 1 emphasizes that the data used in both expertise and database formation is obtained by *directed* data acquisition. The provision of that direction is itself a task for experts.

Thus, an expert provides a mixture of knowledge, data, and garbage (incorrect or irrelevant knowledge and data), and so does a database. There is much in common between both the left- and right-hand paths in Figure 1—both expertise transfer and empirical induction involve the extraction of knowledge from partial mixes of knowledge, data, and garbage.

The following section provides a qualitative analysis of the various qualities of information between knowledge and data, and later sections provide quantitative measures of the resultant trade-off.

## LEVELS OF EXPERTISE

Consider a practical knowledge-based system development in which both human experts and various sources of case histories are available, for example, Quinlan's development of thyroid diagnosis rules (Quinlan, Compton, Horn & Lazarus 1987). The experts might know:

---

**Levels of Knowledge**

**1 Minimal Rules**
a complete, minimal set of correct decision rules

**2 Adequate Rules**
a set of decision rules that is complete in giving correct decisions but not minimal in containing redundant rules and references to irrelevant attributes

**3 Critical Cases**
a critical set of cases described in terms of a minimal set of relevant attributes with correct decisions

**4 Source of Cases**
a source of cases that contains such critical examples described in terms of a minimal set of relevant attributes with correct decisions

**5 Irrelevant Attributes**
a source of cases as in 4 with correct decisions but described in terms of attributes among which are those relevant to the decision

**6 Incorrect Decisions**
a source of cases as in 4 but with only a greater than chance probability of correct decisions

**7 Irrelevant Attributes & Incorrect Decisions**
a source of cases as in 5 but with only a greater than chance probability of correct decisions

---

**Figure 2 Levels of expert knowledge**

This is a continuum of decreasing knowledge on the part of the human expert. It encompasses a range of situations met in practice, and it raises the question of how the amount of knowledge available from the expert affects the amount of data required for effective empirical induction. For case 1 no data is required for empirical induction since the correct answer is available. For case 7 the 'expert' has provided little except access to a source of data from which the correct answer might be derived. How much data is required for an optimal empirical induction procedure to derive 1 given 7, and how much less data is required for cases 2 through 6?

The following section report some studies that give quantitative answers to these questions. The studies are empirical rather than analytic so that it is not apparent yet how the answers generalize to arbitrary situations. However, they establish some base-line data which is interesting in its own right, a possible guide to practitioners of knowledge acquisition, and a test case for potential analytic estimates of the ratios involved.

## THE TRADE-OF BETWEEN KNOWLEDGE AND DATA

INDUCT (Gaines 1989) is part of a knowledge acquisition tool KSS0 (Gaines 1987b) which uses entity-attribute grid techniques (Shaw 1980, Shaw & Gaines 1983, Boose 1984) to elicit relevant attributes and critical entities from experts, and empirical induction based on these to build a knowledge base in terms of classes, objects, properties, values and methods (rules). The tool also accepts rules entered by experts and entity-attribute data from databases, so that its range of knowledge/data combinations encompasses all those listed in the previous section.

INDUCT is comparable in its approach and performance to other empirical induction algorithms (Quinlan 1987), having a particularly high noise rejection—technical details are given in the Appendix. However, we believe that the experimental results on the trade-offs between knowledge and data given below are fairly independent of the empirical induction algorithm used—they are systemic consequences of the quality of knowledge available rather than side-effects of a particular approach to inductive modeling.

Cendrowska's (1987) contact lens data (Figure 3) used in her exposition of PRISM has been taken as a starting point for our trade-off studies since it is well-defined, previously analyzed and results in a range of rules of varying complexity, some of which are supported by a high proportion of the data set and others of which are supported by only single cases. The deterministic, complete data set involves 24 cases described in terms of 3 binary attributes, 1 ternary attribute and 1 ternary decision attribute. PRISM gives a solution based on 9 rules, but using default logic correct solutions with only 6 rules are available.

| Age | Prescription | Astigmatism | Tear Production | Lens |
|---|---|---|---|---|
| young | myope | not astigmatic | reduced | none |
| young | myope | not astigmatic | normal | soft |
| young | myope | astigmatic | reduced | none |
| young | myope | astigmatic | normal | hard |
| young | hypermetrope | not astigmatic | reduced | none |
| young | hypermetrope | not astigmatic | normal | soft |
| young | hypermetrope | astigmatic | reduced | none |
| young | hypermetrope | astigmatic | normal | hard |
| pre-presbyopic | myope | not astigmatic | reduced | none |
| pre-presbyopic | myope | not astigmatic | normal | soft |
| pre-presbyopic | myope | astigmatic | reduced | none |
| pre-presbyopic | myope | astigmatic | normal | hard |
| pre-presbyopic | hypermetrope | not astigmatic | reduced | none |
| pre-presbyopic | hypermetrope | not astigmatic | normal | soft |
| pre-presbyopic | hypermetrope | astigmatic | reduced | none |
| pre-presbyopic | hypermetrope | astigmatic | normal | none |
| presbyopic | myope | not astigmatic | reduced | none |
| presbyopic | myope | not astigmatic | normal | none |
| presbyopic | myope | astigmatic | reduced | none |
| presbyopic | myope | astigmatic | normal | hard |
| presbyopic | hypermetrope | not astigmatic | reduced | none |
| presbyopic | hypermetrope | not astigmatic | normal | soft |
| presbyopic | hypermetrope | astigmatic | reduced | none |
| presbyopic | hypermetrope | astigmatic | normal | none |

**Fig.3 Cendrowska's (1987) contact lens data**

On this data set INDUCT generates both the 9 rule and 6 rule solutions dependent on whether default logic is allowed (exception rules are given higher priority than partially-correct default rules). Figure 4 shows the 9 rule solution—the first number after each rule is the percentage correct on the test data—it would be lower if the data were noisy—the second number is the statistical significance of the rule in terms of the percentage probability that it has arisen by chance.

prescription=hypermetrope & astigmatism=not astigmatic & tear production=normal -> lens recommendation=soft 100% 0.904%

age=young & astigmatism=not astigmatic & tear production=normal -> lens recommendation=soft 100% 4.34%

age=pre-presbyopic & astigmatism=not astigmatic & tear production=normal -> lens recommendation=soft 100% 4.34%

tear production=reduced -> lens recommendation=none 100% 0.355%

age=presbyopic & prescription=myope & astigmatism=not astigmatic -> lens recommendation=none 100% 39.1%

age=pre-presbyopic & prescription=hypermetrope & astigmatism=astigmatic -> lens recommendation=none 100% 39.1%

age=presbyopic & prescription=hypermetrope & astigmatism=astigmatic -> lens recommendation=none 100% 39.1%

prescription=myope & astigmatism=astigmatic & tear production=normal -> lens recommendation=hard 100% 0.463%

age=young & astigmatism=astigmatic & tear production=normal -> lens recommendation=hard 100% 2.78%

**Fig.4 Decision rules derived from the dataset of Figure 3**

This data set is used as a kernel from which to generate corrupted data with varying probabilities of errors and with varying numbers of irrelevant attributes as shown in Figure 5. The generator selects an entity at random from the 24 cases, randomly changes the decision according to a prescribed probability, and adds a prescribed number of irrelevant binary attributes with random values. The corrupted data sets are run incrementally on INDUCT to determine the minimum amount of data necessary for a correct solution. This quantity is itself a random variable and 10 data sets generated with the same parameters are run to obtain more robust estimates of the data requirement.

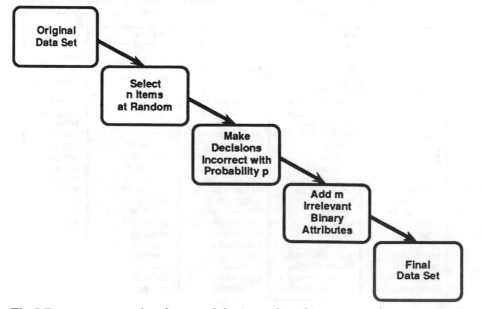

**Fig.5 Dataset generation for empirical studies of knowledge/data tradeoff**

Figure 6 shows the results obtained to date with a variation from 6 to over 1000 data items being needed to cover the spectrum of knowledge availability specified in cases 1 through 7 in Figure 2. It is interesting to note that very high levels of noise can be tolerated—the expert by no means has to be 100% correct, only better than chance. Noisy irrelevant attributes cause similar effects to noise in the decision—this seems to validate claims that knowledge acquisition tools targeted on eliciting relevant attributes are in themselves worthwhile. There is strong interaction between errors and irrelevancy—much more data is required to eliminate both than either alone.

| Knowledge | Data Required | |
|---|---|---|
| | Mean | S.D. |
| Exact rules | 6 | 0 |
| Critical cases | 18 | 0 |
| Correct cases | 90 | 43 |
| 10% Errors | 123 | 49 |
| 25% Errors | 326 | 159 |
| 1 Irrelevant Att. | 160 | 77 |
| 2 Irrelevant Atts. | 241 | 125 |
| 5 Irrelevant Atts. | 641 | 352 |
| 10% Err. + 1 Irr.Att. | 1970 | 1046 |

**Fig.6 Data/knowledge tradeoff**

## COMBINING EXPERTISE TRANSFER AND EMPIRICAL INDUCTION

Current systems for expertise transfer generally also provide empirical induction tools for modeling cases and deriving rules from, for example, entity-attribute grid data. The studies reported in this paper give a formal framework within which the relative roles of these tools, and their interplay and integration, can be analyzed. The seven levels of expertise defined in Figure 2 are those we actually find in the "experts" typically available to us in the development of knowledge-based systems. Our "expertise transfer" methodologies give us problem-solving attributes and exemplary cases expressed in terms of those attributes. There are no guarantees that the attributes elicited are all necessary or that the cases elicited all have correct decisions. The results of the previous section show that we can eliminate irrelevant attributes and incorrect decisions providing:

(a) A sufficient set of relevant attributes for problem-solving has been elicited;

(b) an adequate number of cases has been elicited in relation to the number of irrelevant attributes and probability of error in exemplary cases.

Achieving condition (a) has been a major design requirement in even the earliest personal construct elicitation systems. Shaw's (1980) original design for a computer-based grid elicitation system emphasized features aimed at stimulating the user to add complementary attributes through feedback about those already elicited, and these have been further refined and developed in later systems.

The difficulty with achieving condition (b) is that estimates of the number of irrelevant attributes and the error rates in case data may be difficult to obtain. However, even coarse estimates make it possible to use studies such as that reported above to obtain lower bounds on data requirements.

What is interesting in considering requirement (b), however, is to note that additional case history data and improving estimates of error rates become available through the application of the knowledge-based system being developed. Whatever initial expertise is available can be used to prime an expert system that then, through use, acquires more case data on which to base improved empirical induction.

Additional cases that conform to, and hence confirm, existing rules present no problems. However, those which induce learning, that is a change in rules, also suggest that the decisions being recommended by the system are suspect. As in human behavior, the detection of anomalies between knowledge and data is critical to both action and learning.

I have previously suggested that rules based on empirical induction, such as those shown in Figure 4, should be coupled with anomaly detection rules that trigger "surprise" if their premises are true but their conclusions are false (Gaines 1988b). In such cases, further empirical induction on the enhanced data set will result in either the rule being changed or the new data rejected as in error. This is precisely the process that Stich and Nisbett (1984) have termed the expert's management of "reflective equilibrium" in their analysis of expertise using Goodman's (1973) model of induction.

The current generation of expert systems, based on taking static snapshots of expertise, will become obsolete very rapidly and present major problems of maintenance. We will be forced to move very rapidly toward what Steels (1986) has termed "second generation" systems able to learn from experience (Gaines 1988a). However, we have also to remember that the associated human experts will also be acquiring new knowledge from many sources not necessarily accessible to the knowledge-based system. Our system architectures must accomplish a long-term integration of expertise transfer and machine learning methodologies.

## WHAT MAY BE ACQUIRED THROUGH COMBINED EXPERTISE TRANSFER AND EMPIRICAL INDUCTION?

The model of Figure 1 can be extended to encompass other aspects of knowledge acquisition, notably the roles of neural networks and text processing. The "directed data acquisition" at the top of the model is not readily emulated using current knowledge acquisition technologies. We may obtain labels for attributes from an experts and have them characterize cases in terms of these, but our methodologies do not capture the way in which the expert does this, the procedures for measuring the values of attributes. Thus, our knowledge-based systems cannot describe cases themselves but must question clients. In practice we assume that the clients themselves are already sufficiently expert to understand the expert's terminology and are able to supply valid characterizations of cases within the expert's conceptual framework. These are strong assumptions.

Figure 7 summarizes the levels and types of knowledge that we may regenerate given sufficient data based on lower levels of knowledge. A combination of expertise transfer and empirical induction enables us to regenerate the *prescriptive* knowledge of the expert in the form of decision-making models, the *descriptive* knowledge in the form of relevant attributes and their critical values, and the *ecological* knowledge in the form of cleaned-up case histories. What remains inaccessible is the role of the expert as an *interactive* transducer providing measurements of the world.

Speculatively, we suggest that the role of neural network research within knowledge acquisition is to emulate the human capabilities of perceptual learning that enable us to form new cognitive constructs using the mass of available data to our sensations (Grossberg 1988, Eckmiller & Malsburg 1988). The lowest level of "directed data acquisition" in Figure 1 requires the formation of measurements, the recognition of new patterns, that provide values for attributes appropriate to problem solving.

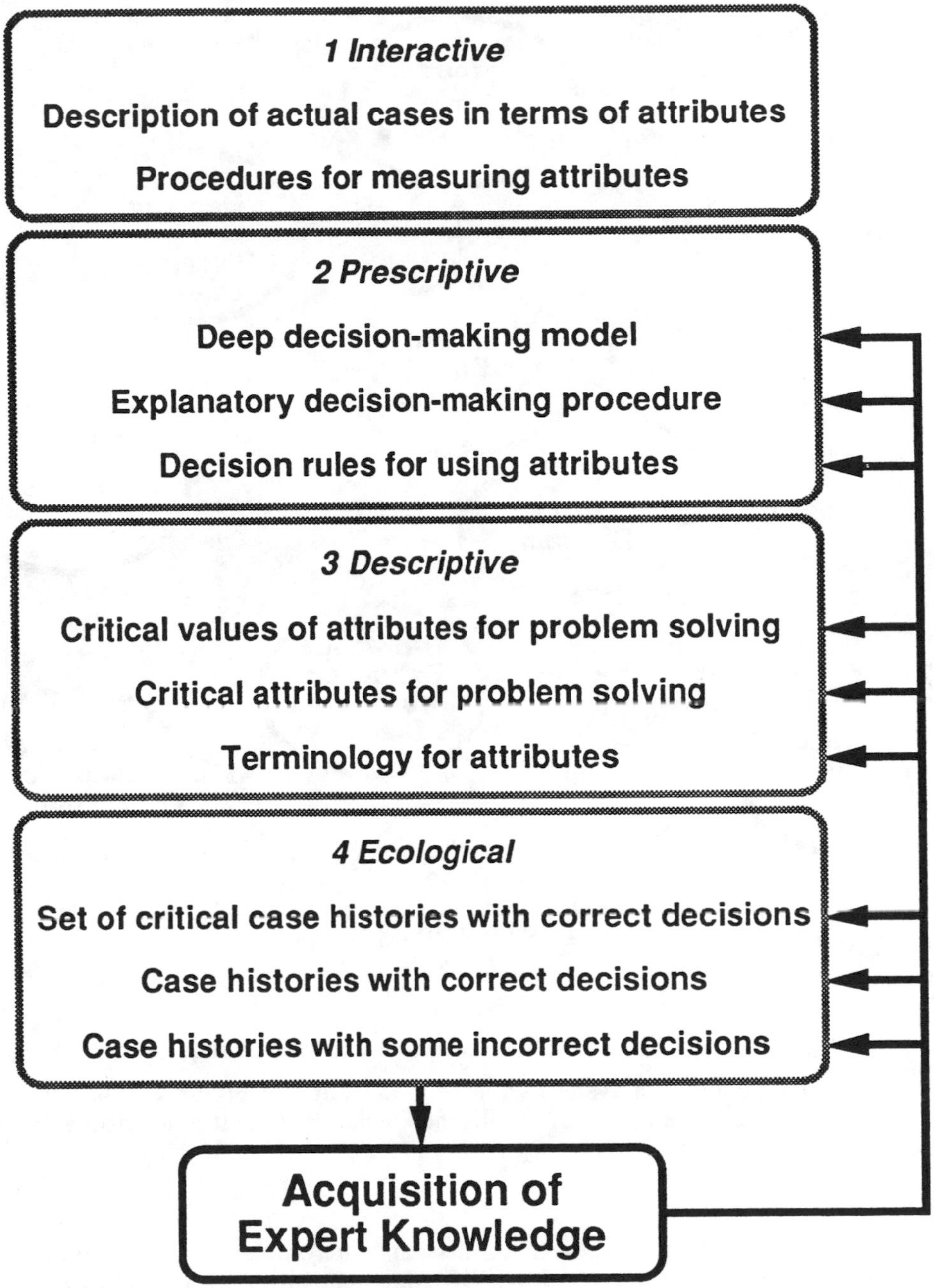

**Fig.7 Regeneration of knowledge**

This is not a new concept in terms of the direction of much research on neural networks. However, it is novel in the expertise transfer community because, so far, the emphasis has been on transferring the high level knowledge, not the perceptual capabilities. As knowledge-based systems develop it is reasonable to expect more emphasis of complete functionality, including the emulation of perceptual capabilities. It is reasonable to aim for these to be an enhancement of existing approaches rather than a complete change to radically different technologies.

Figure 8 shows Figure 1 extended with a neural network learning to emulate the directed data acquisition through perceptual learning. It also shows a second extension in that expertise is conventionally externalized and communicated through encoding in media such as text and diagrams. This provides yet another path into the knowledge base through tools that extract knowledge from such material.

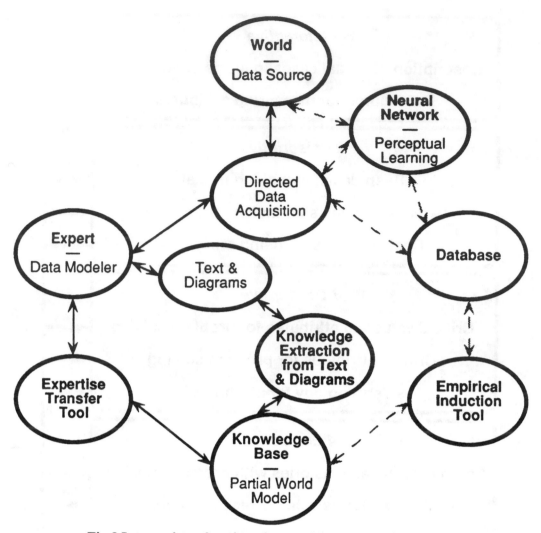

**Fig.8 Integration of various forms of knowledge acquisition**

A knowledge acquisition system with the architecture of Figure 8 would integrate the state of the art of four diverse artificial intelligence technologies. It is a reasonable objective for next generation research.

## CONCLUSIONS

At one level the studies reported in this paper may be seen as legitimating current practice in research and development for knowledge acquisition systems. Most applicable systems are providing tools for both expertise transfer and empirical induction, and for using thse in closely coupled combinations. However, some of the tutorial literature presents them as almost competetive approaches rather than as extremes along a continuum of possibilities that match a continuum of types and levels of expertise.

In architectural terms, the analysis leading to Figure 8 provides a integrative structure for four of the major technologies supporting knowledge acquisition processes in artificial intelligence research. A practical system with such an architecture will involve many paths not shown in the figure which support the meta-tasks of managing the acquisition process, and it will involve multiple experts in different roles.

In practical terms, the studies reported in this paper provide a principled, quantitative approach to many of the different techniques being used for knowledge acquisition, from those based on expert interviews to those based on empirical induction. The trade-off data is a guide to practitioners as to the appropriate approach and data requirements in their situations—it needs testing with other data sets but that is now a matter of sheer number crunching.

In theoretical terms, the approach taken in this paper seems to offer the possibility of developing a quantitative science of knowledge in terms of the amount of data reduction that knowledge buys us when carrying out empirical induction. This can be seen as a reasonably principled economic evaluation of the knowledge.

Figure 9 shows the results of Figure 6 used to define a measure of knowledge in terms of the logarithm of the data required to achieve it. This gives a basis for an economic measure of the "value" of different forms and levels of knowledge if we assume, for example, that obtaining each item of data incurs equal cost. The studies in this paper are empirical using a particular situation. It should be possible to obtain some analytic results for more general cases.

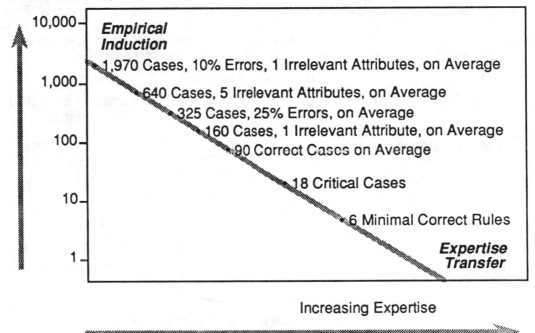

**Fig.9 Knowledge/data tradeoff in expertise transfer and empirical induction**

In design terms, the most important results obtained are that a single inductive algorithm is adequate to cover the complete spectrum of cases 1 through 7 of "levels of expertise" defined at the beginning of this paper, from rule simplification, to noise reduction and relevancy determination, and that it is possible to generate an integrated system that ranges across that spectrum, from the transfer of expertise from experts to the creation of equivalent expertise through empirical induction.

## ACKNOWLEDGEMENTS

Financial assistance for this work has been made available by the Natural Sciences and Engineering Research Council of Canada. I am grateful to many colleagues for discussions over the years that have influenced this paper. In particular I would like to thank John Boose, Jeff Bradshaw, Mildred Shaw, and Ross Quinlan, for access to their own research and many stimulating discussions.

## APPENDIX: THE INDUCT ALGORITHM

It is relevant to the assessment of the results in this paper to understand the method used to derive decision rules from data, and this section outlines the INDUCT algorithm, linking it to previous approaches, clarifying enhancements made and their roles in the studies, and comparing performance with the best known methods.

Cendrowska (1987) has shown that empirical induction through decision trees and direct conversion to rules, even with pruning, leads to rule sets that test the values of irrelevant attributes and are much larger than is necessary. Her PRISM algorithm goes from entity-attribute data direct to rules but does not address the problems of noisy data or missing values. Quinlan (1987) has developed extended pruning techniques in a way that are effective in coping with noisy data but still involve decision tree production with problems of irrelevant attributes and missing values.

INDUCT extends the PRISM algorithm to control direct rule generation through statistical tests that are effective in dealing with both noisy data and missing values. Figure 10 shows the basis for these statistical tests. Given a universe of entities, E, a target predicate, **Q**, and a set of possible test predicates of the form, **S**, on entities in E, use them to construct a set of rules from which the target predicate may be inferred given the values of the test predicates.

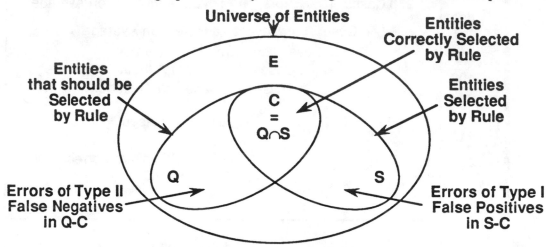

**Fig.10 Problem of empirical induction**

For the purposes of the statistical analysis the forms of S and **Q** do not matter. One may regard S as a *selector* choosing those e out of some subset of E for which to assert **Q**(e), and compare the selection process of the rule with that of random selection, asking "what is the probability that random selection of the same degree of generality would achieve the same accuracy or greater."

This probability is easily calculated, let Q be the relevant entities in E for which **Q**(e) holds, S be the selected entities in E for which $\bar{S}$(e) holds, C be the correct entities in E for which both S(e) and **Q**(e) hold:

$$Q \equiv \{e: e \in E \wedge Q(e)\} \tag{1}$$

$$S \equiv \{e: e \in E \wedge S(e)\} \tag{2}$$

$$C \equiv \{e: e \in E \wedge S(e) \wedge Q(e)\} \tag{3}$$

Let the cardinalities of E, Q, S and C be e, q, s and c respectively. The probability of selecting an entity from E for which **Q** holds at random is:

$$p = q/e \tag{4}$$

The probability of selecting s and getting c or more correct at random is:

$$r = \sum_{i=c}^{s} {}^sC_i \, p^i \, (1-p)^{s-i} \tag{5}$$

The advantage of using r as a measure of the correctness of a rule is that is easily understood, as the probability that the rule could be this good at random, and that it involves no assumptions about the problem such as sampling distributions. Note that if c=s (all correct) then log(p) = s log(q/u) which seems to be the basis of 'information-theoretic' measures.

The probability that the performance of an isolated rule could be obtained by random selection is not adequate in itself to evaluate a rule that has itself been selected as best after a search through many possible rules. If n different rules have been searched then we may ask "what is the probability that the rule found by search achieved its performance by chance," that is the probability that a rule will have been found that in itself has a probability of being selected at random of r. This probability is:

$$t = 1 - (1-r)^n \tag{6}$$

As one would expect this approximates to nr if this term is substantially less than 1.

To obtain a value for t one needs to estimate n, the number of rules in the search space, and this requires information about the forms of possible rules. If the rules are conjunctions of value tests of attributes as illustrated in (3) then $n_1$ can be estimated for rules with one clause, $n_2$ for rules with two or less clauses, and so on. For example if there are m attributes the i'th of which can be tested in $m_i$ possible ways, then:

$$n_1 = \sum_{i=1}^{m} m_i \tag{7}$$

$$n_2 = (n_1)^2 - \sum_{i=1}^{m} (m_i)^2 \tag{8}$$

Missing values are taken into account by assuming that they might have any value. When the selection of an entity is tested a missing value is assumed to have the required value for selection. In the statistics a selection based on missing values is allowed to contribute to false positives but not to correct positives. This has important consequence in knowledge acquisition since it allows the expert to enter conjunctive rules as if they were entities with missing values. INDUCT then generates the same or an equivalent smaller rule set. It is reasonable to test the consistency of an inductive procedure by requiring the rule-set produced by it to be 'fixed-point' if re-entered as data.

INDUCT has been tested on a wide range of data sets in the literature together with many artificial data sets with known degrees of noise, missing values and irrelevant attributes, and found to perform consistently at least as well as the previously published best results. For example, with Quinlan's (1987) very noisy data sets, Prob-Disj (disjunction of three terms in three attributes, one irrelevant attribute, 10% noise), and Digits (7-segment display, 10% noise in attributes, Bayes optimal solution 26% errors) the comparisons are shown in Figure 11.

**Results on Prob-Disj Data (3-term disjunct)**

| Data | ID3 to Pruned Rules | INDUCT |
|------|------|------|
| | Error Rate (Type I + Type II) | |
| Sample | 4.2 rules | 3 rules |
| Test1 | 10.0% | 10.0% |
| Test2 | 10.0% | 10.0% |

**Results on Digits Data**

| Data | Rules | ID3 to Pruned Rules | INDUCT |
|------|------|------|------|
| | | Error Rate (Type I + Type II) | |
| Sample | 10 | | 31.05% |
| | 16 | | 26.8% |
| Test1 | 10 | | 32.0% |
| | 16 | 31.3% | 29.0% |
| Test2 | 10 | | 31.4% |
| | 16 | 28.3% | 27.8% |

**Fig.11 Comparison of INDUCT and optimally-pruned ID3**

## REFERENCES

Boose, J.H. (1984). Personal construct theory and the transfer of human expertise. **Proceedings AAAI-84**, 27-33. California: American Association for Artificial Intelligence.

Boose, J H. (1986) **Expertise Transfer for Expert System Design**. New York: Elsevier.

Boose, J.H. & Gaines, B.R., Eds. (1988). **Knowledge Acquisition Tools for Expert Systems**. London, Academic Press.

Boose, J.H. & Bradshaw, J.M. (1987) Expertise transfer and complex problems: using AQUINAS as a knowledge acquisition workbench for knowledge-based systems. **International Journal of Man-Machine Studies 26**, 3-28.

Cendrowska, J. (1987) An algorithm for inducing modular rules. **International Journal of Man-Machine Studies 27** (4), 349-370 (October).

Eckmiller, R. & Malsburg, C., Eds. (1988). **Neural Computers**. Berlin: Springer.

Gaines, B.R. (1987a) An overview of knowledge acquisition and transfer. **International Journal of Man-Machine Studies 26** (4), 453-472 (April).

Gaines, B.R. (1987b). Rapid prototyping for expert systems. Oliff, M., Ed. **Proceedings of International Conference on Expert Systems and the Leading Edge in Production Planning and Control**. pp.213-241. University of South Carolina.

Gaines, B.R. (1988a). Second generation knowledge acquisition systems. **Proceedings of the Second European Workshop on Knowledge Acquisition for Knowledge-Based Systems (EKAW'88)**. GMD-Studien Nr.143. pp.17-1-17-14. Bonn, Germany: Gellsellschaft für Mathematik und Datenverarbeitung (June).

Gaines, B.R. (1988b). Positive feedback processes underlying the formation of expertise. **IEEE Transactions on Systems, Man & Cybernetics**, SMC-18(6), 1016-1020 (November).

Gaines, B.R. (1989) An Ounce of Knowledge is Worth a Ton of Data: Quantitative Studies of the Trade-Off between Expertise and Data based on Statistically Well-Founded Empirical Induction. **Proceedings of 6th International Workshop on Machine Learning**, Cornell University, Ithaca.

Gaines, B.R. & Boose, J.H., Eds. (1988). **Knowledge Acquisition for Knowledge-Based Systems**. London, Academic Press.

Gaines, B.R. & Shaw, M.L.G. (1987). Knowledge support systems. **ACM MCC-University Research Symposium**. Austin, Texas: MCC. pp.47-66.

Goodman, N. (1973). **Fact, Fiction and Forecast**. Indianapolis: Bobbs-Merrill.

Grossberg, S., Ed. (1988). **Neural Networks and Natural Intelligence**. Cambridge, Massachusetts: MIT Press.

Hayes-Roth, F. (1984). The industrialization of knowledge engineering. Reitman, W., Ed. **Artificial Intelligence Applications for Business**. pp. 159-177. Norwood, New Jersey: Ablex.

Machlup, F. (1980). **Knowledge and Knowledge Production**. Princeton University Press.

Machlup, F. (1982). **The Branches of Learning**. Princeton University Press.

Machlup, F. (1984). **The Economics of Information and Human Capital**. Princeton University Press.

Machlup, F. & Mansfield, U. (Eds.) (1983). **The Study of Information**. New York: Wiley.

Quinlan, J.R. (1986) Induction of decision trees. **Machine Learning 1**(1) 81-106 (March).

Quinlan, J.R. (1987) Simplifying decision trees. **International Journal of Man-Machine Studies 27** (3), 221-234 (September).

Quinlan, J.R., Compton, P.J., Horn, K.A. & Lazarus, L. (1987) Inductive knowledge acquisition: a case study. Quinlan, J.R. (Ed.), **Artificial Intelligence and Expert Systems**. pp.157-173. Sydney: Addison-Wesley.

Shaw, M.L.G. (1980). **On Becoming a Personal Scientist**. London: Academic Press.

Shaw, M.L.G. & Gaines, B.R. (1983). A computer aid to knowledge engineering. **Proceedings of British Computer Society Conference on Expert Systems**, 263-271 (December). Cambridge.

Steels, L. (1986). Second generation expert systems. Bramer, M.A. (Ed). **Research and Development in Expert Systems III**. pp.175-183. Cambridge: University Press.

Stich, S.P. & Nisbett, R.E. (1984). Expertise, justification and the psychology of inductive reasoning. Haskell, T.L., Ed. **The Authority of Experts**. pp. 226-241. Bloomington, Indiana: Indiana University Press.

Sveiby, K.E. & Lloyd, T. (1987). **Managing Knowhow**. London: Bloomsbury.

# LIMITATIONS ON INDUCTIVE LEARNING*
## (Extended Abstract)

Thomas G. Dietterich
Department of Computer Science
Oregon State University
Corvallis, OR 97331
*tgd@cs.orst.edu*

## ABSTRACT

This paper explores the proposition that inductive learning from examples is fundamentally limited to learning only a small fraction of the total space of possible hypotheses. We begin by defining the notion of an algorithm *reliably* learning a good approximation to a concept $C$. An empirical study of three algorithms (the classical algorithm for maximally specific conjunctive generalizations, ID3, and back-propagation for feed-forward networks of logistic units) demonstrates that each of these algorithms performs very poorly for the task of learning concepts defined over the space of Boolean feature vectors containing 3 variables. Simple counting arguments allow us to prove an upper bound on the maximum number of concepts reliably learnable from $m$ training examples.

## INTRODUCTION

How good are current inductive learning algorithms? How well can any inductive learning algorithm perform? This paper addresses these questions for the case of learning concepts defined over the universe of Boolean $n$-tuples.

Most work in the probably-approximately correct (PAC) learning theory yields results of the form "If the learning algorithm searches a space of hypotheses $H$ and finds an hypothesis $\hat{h} \in H$ consistent with all $m$ given training examples, and if $m$ is large enough, then $\hat{h}$ is probably approximately correct." The goal of this paper is to turn these results around and ask "Suppose we are given $m$ training examples, what is the size of the largest space of concepts $H$ such that if $h \in H$ is the correct hypothesis, a given learning algorithm will find an hypothesis $\hat{h}$ that is probably approximately correct?"

We approach this question by first defining a new notion, frequently approximately correct (FAC) learning, that assumes the uniform probability distribution over the space of training examples (sampling without replacement). Then, we report the results of an experiment on three existing learning algorithms to determine the number of hypotheses that each algorithm can FAC-learn. Finally, we derive an upper bound on the maximum number of concepts FAC-learnable by any algorithm. The results suggest either that the upper bound is not tight or else that current algorithms are not very good. In either case, the upper bound demonstrates that only a small fraction of the space of possible hypotheses is FAC-learnable by any inductive learning algorithm.

## NOTATION

Following the usual practice in PAC-learning theory, we define the set $U$ to be the space of all Boolean $n$-tuples. A *concept $h$* is a subset of $U$, so there are $2^{|U|} = 2^{2^n}$ possible concepts definable over $U$. An

---

*This work was supported in part by NSF under grant numbers IRI-86-57316 (Presidential Young Investigator Award) and CCR-87-16748 and by gifts from Tektronix and SUN Microsystems. Thanks also to Hussein Almuallim for assisting with Corollary 1.

*example* of a concept $h$ is a pair of the form $(u, +)$ if $u \in h$ and $(u, -)$ otherwise. A training sample of size $m$ is a set $S$ of $m$ distinct examples.

Suppose a learning algorithm is given a sample $S$ and produces as output the hypothesis $\hat{h}$. We say that the error of $\hat{h}$ is the fraction of $U$ that is incorrectly classified by $\hat{h}$. This is equal to $\frac{|h \oplus \hat{h}|}{2^n}$, where $\oplus$ denotes the disjoint union. This error measure is a special case of the PAC error measure for learning problems where the examples are drawn without replacement according to the uniform distribution.

Let $T$ be the total number of possible training sets of size $m$ for a given concept $h$. Since there are $2^n$ possible training examples, there are $T = \binom{2^n}{m}$ possible training sets.

We say that an algorithm *frequently approximately correctly* (FAC) learns a concept $h$ if for $(1 - \delta)T$ training sets, the guess $\hat{h}$ returned by the algorithm has error at most $\epsilon$. Let $F_A(m, \epsilon, \delta)$ be number of distinct concepts FAC learnable by learning algorithm $A$. One goal of inductive learning research is to find an algorithm $A$ that maximizes $F_A(m, \epsilon, \delta)$ for typical values of $\epsilon$ and $\delta$.

## EXPERIMENTAL RESULTS

We have experimentally measured the $F_A$ of three popular learning algorithms for the case $n = 3$, $\epsilon = \frac{1}{8}$, and $\delta = \frac{1}{10}$. This case is admittedly small, since there are only 8 possible training examples and 256 possible hypotheses. However, it is the largest case that it has thus far been practical to compute. The three algorithms are

**CONJ:** the classical algorithm for computing the maximally specific conjunctive Boolean formula consistent with the training set. If there are no positive examples in the training sample, then the algorithm returns the concept NIL (the empty set). If there is no conjunctive concept, the algorithm is considered to have returned a concept with error greater than $\epsilon$.

**ID3:** a version of Quinlan's popular algorithm for constructing decision trees (Quinlan, 1986). This version employs the information gain criterion to select the root feature for each decision (subtree). Windowing is not performed.

**BACK:** the version of the error back-propagation algorithm described in (Rumelhart, Hinton, and Williams, 1986). This version employs a learning rate of 0.25 and a momentum term of 0.9. An architecture consisting of 2 hidden units (fully connected to the 3 inputs) and 1 output unit (fully connected to the hidden units) is trained until minimum error is attained (change in total error of less than .0001 after a complete pass over the training set) and no classification errors are made on the training set. Each unit computes the logistic function. For training purposes, an output value of .9 or greater is considered a one; an output .1 or less is considered a zero; and all other output values are indeterminate. For testing purposes, an output is a one if it is greater than .5 and a zero otherwise. If the algorithm is unable to find a consistent network after 10 attempts (each attempt starting with randomized weights), then the algorithm is considered to have returned a concept with error greater than $\epsilon$.

For each possible concept $h$ defined over 3 Boolean features, all $\binom{2^3}{4} = 70$ training sets of size 4 were generated and processed by each algorithm. If on at least 63 of those training sets the algorithm returned an hypothesis that incorrectly classified at most one of the 8 possible examples, then the concept $h$ was FAC-learned by the algorithm. The results are summarized in Table 1.

The results show that only a very small fraction of the 256 possible concepts are FAC-learned by these algorithms. The relative order of the three algorithms is probably not generalizable to larger $n$, and the reader should not conclude from this experiment that CONJ is superior to ID3 or that ID3 is superior to BACK. The surprising result is that *none* of the algorithms performs very well.

Table 1: Number of concepts FAC-learnable when $n = 3, m = 4, \epsilon = \frac{1}{8}$, and $\delta = \frac{1}{10}$.

| Algorithm | Number of FAC-learned concepts |
|-----------|-------------------------------|
| ID3 | 8 |
| BACK | 2 |
| CONJ | 10 |

This demonstrates the fallacy of the following argument: (a) ID3 learns decision trees, (b) any Boolean concept can be represented by a decision tree, therefore (c) ID3 can learn any Boolean concept. This is true only if all of the possible training examples are given to the algorithm. In practice, it is rare for a learning algorithm to have even 50% of the possible training examples available for learning. Similar arguments have been put forward concerning the learning power of back propagation. It should be clear that the expressive power of the hypothesis space is not the only factor to consider in assessing the ability of a learning algorithm to FAC-learn an unknown concept.

To obtain the data for Table 1, each learning algorithm was executed 1,120 times. Unfortunately, to obtain data for the analogous case where $n = 4$ and $m = 8$ would require executing each algorithm 3,294,720 times. Statistical approximations do not substantially decrease this number. We are currently reimplimenting our code on a connection machine to perform these runs.

## AN UPPER BOUND

To determine how well any algorithm could do, it is useful to view a learning algorithm as a mapping from training sets to concepts. For a given training set of size $m$, there are $2^{2^n-m}$ possible consistent concepts. This is because there are $2^n - m$ remaining examples in $U$, and each one of them could be classified in 2 possible ways. A learning algorithm must choose one of these consistent concepts (or possibly some inconsistent concept!) as its guess $\hat{h}$.

Now the $\hat{h}$ that it guesses will be a good approximation (error $\leq \epsilon$) for some of the $2^{2^n-m}$ hypotheses and a bad approximation for the others. From the definition of FAC learning, we see that a concept $h$ is FAC-learnable only if for most of the training sets consistent with $h$, the guess $\hat{h}$ is a good approximation to $h$. An algorithm will perform badly if it tends to "scatter" its guesses, so that for some training sets consistent with $h$, the guess $\hat{h}$ is good and for others it is bad. An algorithm will perform well if it can more-or-less concentrate its guesses on a subset of the possible hypotheses. This perspective allows us to prove the following theorem.

**Theorem 1** *If $m \leq (1 - \epsilon)2^n$, then no learning algorithm can FAC-learn more than*

$$\frac{2^m \sum_{i=0}^{\epsilon 2^n} \binom{2^n-m}{i}}{1 - \delta}$$

*concepts from $m$ training examples, for error parameter $\epsilon$ and confidence parameter $\delta$.*

**Proof:**

For a training set $S$, when a learning algorithm $A$ makes a guess, $\hat{h}$, there are at most

$$Ball(\epsilon) = \sum_{i=0}^{\epsilon 2^n} \binom{2^n - m}{i}$$

concepts that are within $\epsilon$ of $\hat{h}$ and consistent with $S$. This is because there are exactly $\binom{2^n-m}{i}$ concepts at Hamming distance $i$ from $\hat{h}$, and we sum for Hamming distances from 0 up to $\epsilon 2^n$. The binomial coefficient is well-defined only when $2^n - m \geq \epsilon 2^n$, or $m \leq (1-\epsilon)2^n$. Let us call these $\epsilon$-close concepts "wins." Similarly, there are at least

$$2^{2^n - m} - Ball(\epsilon)$$

concepts that have error more than $\epsilon$ from $\hat{h}$. Let us call these "losses."

Because there are $\binom{2^n}{m}2^m$ training sets, no learning algorithm can create more than $\binom{2^n}{m}2^m Ball(\epsilon)$ wins. We will call a concept $h$ a winner if in at least $(1-\delta)\binom{2^n}{m}$ of the training sets with which it is consistent, it receives a "win". A winner is therefore FAC-learnable. An optimal FAC algorithm can do no better than to allocate exactly $(1-\delta)\binom{2^n}{m}$ wins to each winner. This spreads the wins as widely as possible and therefore maximizes the number of winners. Let $W$ be the maximum number of winners created by any FAC-learning algorithm. By dividing the maximum number of wins by the minimum number of wins needed to create a winner, we obtain the following bound:

$$W \leq \frac{\binom{2^n}{m}2^m Ball(\epsilon)}{(1-\delta)\binom{2^n}{m}}.$$

Simplifying, this gives us

$$W \leq \frac{2^m Ball(\epsilon)}{1-\delta} = \frac{2^m \sum_{i=0}^{\epsilon 2^n} \binom{2^n-m}{i}}{1-\delta}. \quad \Box$$

When $m = 4, n = 3, \epsilon = \frac{1}{8}$, and $\delta = \frac{1}{10}$, this quantity is 88. Comparison with Table 1 suggests either that our bound is too high or else that existing learning algorithms could stand significant improvement. In either case, however, this theorem puts a bound on the fraction of the $2^{2^n}$ concepts that can be FAC-learned from examples.

While Theorem 1 gives useful answers for small values of $n$, it is surely an overestimate for large $n$, since it grows as $O(2^{n2^n})$. Another way of deriving a bound is to apply the following theorem proved by Ehrenfeucht, Haussler, Kearns, and Valiant (1988):

**Theorem 2** *Assume* $0 < \epsilon \leq \frac{1}{8}, 0 < \delta \leq \frac{1}{100}$, *and* $VCdim(H) \geq 2$. *Then any learning algorithm $A$ that PAC learns every concept in $H$ for any probability distribution $P$ over $U$ must use sample size*

$$m \geq \frac{VCdim(H) - 1}{32\epsilon}.$$

Here the $VCdim(H)$ is the Vapnik-Chervonenkis dimension of $H$ (Blumer, Ehrenfeucht, Haussler, and Warmuth, in press). Natarajan (in press) has proved that $VCdim(H) \geq \left\lceil \frac{1}{n+2} \lg |H| \right\rceil$. Hence, by combining these results and solving for $|H|$, we obtain the following bound:

**Corollary 1** *Assume* $0 < \epsilon \leq \frac{1}{8}, 0 < \delta \leq \frac{1}{100}$, *and* $VCdim(H) \geq 2$. *Then given $m$ training examples, the number of hypotheses any algorithm $A$ can PAC learn is bounded by*

$$|H| \leq 2^{(n+2)(32\epsilon m)}.$$

For practical cases, $m$ will be a polynomial function of $n$, $\frac{1}{\epsilon}$, and $\frac{1}{\delta}$. Hence, Corollary 1 states that $|H|$ can only grow as $2^{poly(n)}$ for some polynomial. Since there are $2^{2^n}$ possible concepts, this means that for reasonable sample sizes, only a small fraction of the possible concepts can be learned from examples under arbitrary distributions.

It is important to realize that the bound in Corollary 1 is not directly comparable to Theorem 1, because Corollary 1 requires that every concept in $H$ be learnable from any probability distribution $P$ over $U$. Theorem 1, on the other hand, is only concerned with the case where the probability distribution $P$ is uniform. It is likely that fewer examples are required to learn under a fixed distribution than under an unknown distribution. Hence, for a given number of training examples $m$, it is likely that a larger number of concepts is learnable from a fixed distribution.

## IMPLICATIONS

The fact that inductive learning methods are fundamentally limited to learning only a small fraction of all possible hypotheses has many implications.

First, it means that there are no general purpose learning methods that can learn any concept (from a sample of reasonable size). Instead, different classes of learning problems may call for different learning algorithms. An important problem for future research is to attempt to identify relationships between types of learning problems (e.g., problems in speech understanding) and types of hypothesis spaces (e.g., decision trees, neural nets, etc.).

Second, the results suggest that human learning involves much more than learning from positive and negative training examples. It is unlikely that human learning is limited in the way that these inductive learning algorithms are limited, since people seem to be able to learn well in a wide variety of domains. If these results accurately modeled human learning situations, one would expect that people would only succeed in learning a small proportion of the "concepts" that they face in daily life.

Third, these results underline the importance of studying actual learning situations to determine what prior knowledge and sources of information (including training examples) are available to the learner. Research aimed at understanding how prior knowledge and other sources of information can be exploited by the learning process is also very important.

Fourth, if the upper bounds can be tightened, and I believe they can, then the results would indicate that further work on inductive learning methods—including methods that construct "new terms"—is unlikely to produce significant improvements in learning performance. In any case, algorithms that introduce new terms cannot overcome these upper bounds.

Future work must focus on reducing the difference between the performance of existing algorithms and the upper bound.

## BIBLIOGRAPHY

Blumer, A., Ehrenfeucht, A., Haussler, D., and Warmuth, M. K., (in press). Learnability and the Vapnik-Chervonenkis dimension. To appear in *Journal of the ACM*.

Ehrenfeucht, A., Haussler, D., Kearns, M., and Valiant, L., (1988). A general lower bound on the number of examples needed for learning. *COLT 88: Proceedings of the Conference on Learning Theory*, Los Altos, CA: Morgan-Kaufmann. 110–120.

Natarajan, B. K. (In press). On learning sets and functions. Unpublished manuscript.

Quinlan, J. R. (1986). Induction of Decision Trees, *Machine Learning,* 1(1), 81–106.

Rumelhart, D. E., Hinton, G. E., and Williams, R. J. (1986). Learning internal representations by error propagation. In Rumelhart, D. E., and McClelland, J. L., (eds.) *Parallel Distributed Processing*, Vol 1. 318–362.

# Chapter 5

# Compilation and Deep Models

The last two chapters presented two major methods that have been developed to create expert systems: elicitation and induction. The compilation approach presented in this chapter is another major method. It is useful to distinguish two different types of compilation. The first of these is *speed-up learning*. The second is compilation that involves *synthesis of a deep model* into a compiled problem-solving program.

The importance of speed-up learning has mostly been in AI domains other than expert systems, for example, planning and formal domains, such as mathematics (e.g., symbolic integration) and game playing (e.g., eight puzzle). Part of the reason for the lack of wider use of compilation is that most existing expert systems are for analysis problems, such as classification, monitoring and data interpretation. Speed is not a bottleneck for these systems, so speed-up learning has not been that crucial. On the other hand, expert systems for synthesis problems do usually involve search over a large problem space. As methods are created to allow automated knowledge acquisition to create a working but overly slow synthesis expert system, the need for speed-up learning is sure to increase.

The papers in this chapter deal with deductive learning. The necessary knowledge to be learned is provided at the start, and the learning consists of compiling that knowledge either for efficiency or operationality.

Section 5.1 of this chapter deals with compilation for efficiency. Compilation is most germane when the solution search space can be completely defined and the key element to successful problem-solving performance is efficient search of this search space. For knowledge-based systems that are very inefficient, compilation of the problem solver into a more efficient form is a worthwhile goal in and of itself.

Section 5.2 focuses on explanation-based learning of concepts, which has been a very active area of research in recent years. Learning takes place by compiling background knowledge to create or refine a concept definition.

Section 5.3 focuses on synthesizing a problem solver from a first-principles or deep model. Often the initial knowledge is in a non-operationalized form and the process of synthesis creates an operational problem solver.

# Section 5.1

# Compilation of Knowledge for Efficiency

Search is a major problem-solving technique in artificial intelligence. When given a completely defined search space, the key information needed to create a useful problem solver is knowledge of how to search the solution space efficiently.

All three papers in this section take the same approach to compilation: a solution sequence of operators is found and then the sequence is generalized and saved. Each system described in this section is potentially capable of learning whenever the performance element is solving problems (although usually nothing new is learned if the same problem is solved twice). Problems that are typically encountered when doing compilation are overgeneralization, overspecialization, and the generation of too much compiled knowledge which slows the system down due to an excess of information. For all three systems, the limitations in problem-solving performance are as much due to the design of the performance elements as to the learning method.

The article by Fikes, Hart and Nilsson in Section 5.1.1 describes the STRIPS program designed for the domain of robot planning; over the last twenty years, the ideas in STRIPS have had great influence on AI learning and planning research.

STRIPS' introduction of macro operators laid the foundation for the development of explanation-based learning (Section 5.2) a decade later. The creation of macro operators that it describes is very basic.

The article by Mitchell, Utgoff and Banerji in Section 5.1.2 presents the LEX system, which operates in the domain of symbolic integration; LEX formulates the problem of symbolic integration as the question of which integration operator to apply next to a partial solution. LEX defines a version space for each of the preconditions of approximately twenty symbolic integration operators, and all the learned knowledge is stored in the preconditions. By defining and updating a version space for each of the symbolic operators, the system can incrementally refine and integrate its search control knowledge. The LEX work emphasizes the importance of example selection to learning; a good example will reduce the size of the version space of an operator precondition.

The article by Laird, Rosenbloom and Newell in Section 5.1.3 presents the SOAR system. Unlike STRIPS and LEX, SOAR was not developed for a specific application domain; instead SOAR is intended as an architecture for general intelligence, where learning occurs by chunking or caching of the search trees that lead to successful solutions. A learning opportunity occurs when SOAR has more than one rule that applies in a problem-solving situation. SOAR creates a subgoal to resolve the impasse, and chunking summarizes the processing of the subgoal. Learning is automatic in those situations where SOAR can resolve the impasse itself; otherwise manual human intervention is required.

# Learning and Executing Generalized Robot Plans[1]

**Richard E. Fikes, Peter E. Hart and Nils J. Nilsson**

*Stanford Research Institute, Menlo Park, California 94025*

Recommended by D. Michie

ABSTRACT

*In this paper we describe some major new additions to the STRIPS robot problem-solving system. The first addition is a process for generalizing a plan produced by STRIPS so that problem-specific constants appearing in the plan are replaced by problem-independent parameters.*

*The generalized plan, stored in a convenient format called a triangle table, has two important functions. The more obvious function is as a single macro action that can be used by STRIPS— either in whole or in part—during the solution of a subsequent problem. Perhaps less obviously, the generalized plan also plays a central part in the process that monitors the real-world execution of a plan, and allows the robot to react "intelligently" to unexpected consequences of actions.*

*We conclude with a discussion of experiments with the system on several example problems.*

## 1. Introduction

In this paper we describe a system of computer programs for controlling a mobile robot. This system can conceive and execute plans enabling the robot to accomplish certain tasks such as pushing boxes from one room to another in a simple but real environment. Although these sorts of tasks are commonly thought to demand little skill or intelligence, they pose important conceptual problems and can require quite complex planning and execution strategies.

In previous papers, we described two important components of our robot system, namely, STRIPS [1] and PLANEX [2]. When a task statement is given to the robot, STRIPS produces a plan consisting of a sequence of preprogrammed actions, and PLANEX supervises the execution of this sequence to accomplish the task. In this paper we present a major new addition to the original capabilities of STRIPS and PLANEX that enables the system to generalize and then save a solution to a particular problem. This generalization capability is used in two ways. The more obvious use of a generalized plan is as a "macro action" that can be used as a single component of a new plan to solve a new problem. When used in this fashion, generalization becomes a powerful form of learning that can reduce the planning time for similar tasks as well as allow the formation of much longer plans, previously beyond the combinatoric capabilities of STRIPS.

The second use of generalized plans involves the supervision or monitoring of plan execution. Often, a real-world robot must reexecute a portion of its plan because of some failure that occurred during the first attempt at execution. At such a time, the system has more flexibility if it is not restricted to repeating identically the unsuccessful portion of the plan, but instead can reexecute the offending actions with different arguments.

Before getting into details (and defining just what we mean by *generalize*), we present in outline form a scenario that illustrates some of the capabilities of the system. Suppose we give a robot the task "Close window WIND1 and turn off light LITE1."[2] To accomplish this, let us say that the robot decides to push box BOX1 to window WIND1, climb BOX1 in order to close the window, and then proceed to turn off light LITE1. First, the system generalizes this specific plan to produce a plan that can, under certain specified conditions, close an arbitrary window (not just WIND1) and turn off an arbitrary light. Next, the system applies the appropriate version of this generalized plan to the specific problem at hand, namely, "close WIND1 and turn off LITE1." While executing the appropriate version, let us suppose that the robot fails to push BOX1 to the window because, say, it discovers another box is already under the window. The PLANEX supervisor will recognize that this new box will serve the purpose that BOX1 was to serve, and the plan execution will proceed.

Now let us suppose that, after finishing the first task, the robot is given a new problem, "Close window WIND5 and lock door DOOR1." The system is capable of recognizing that a portion of the old generalized plan can help solve the new task. Thus, the sequence of several component actions needed to close the window can be readily obtained as a single macro action, and the planning time required to solve the new problem thereby reduced.

We shall begin with a brief review of the problem-solving program STRIPS. Then we shall review a novel format for storing plans that conveniently

---

[1] The research reported herein was supported at SRI by the Advance Research Projects Agency of the Department of Defense, monitored by the U.S. Army Research Office-Durham under Contract DAHC04 72 C 0008.

[2] The scenario is imaginary; our robot cannot actually turn off light switches or close windows.

*Artificial Intelligence* 3 (1972), 251–288

Copyright © 1972 by North-Holland Publishing Company

This paper originally appeared in the journal, *Artificial Intelligence*, Vol. 3, No. 4, and is reprinted here with permission of the publisher, Elsevier, Amsterdam.

allows most of the legitimate $2^n - 1$ subsequences of an $n$-step plan to be extracted as a unit in a subsequent planning activity. We then describe a process by which constants appearing in the plan can be converted to parameters so that each plan can handle a family of different tasks. Thus generalized, the plan can be stored (i.e., learned) for future use. Next, we review the operation of PLANEX and discuss how generalized plans are used during execution to increase the system's capabilities for responding to unplanned-for situations. Finally, we discuss how STRIPS uses stored plans to compose more complex ones and describe some experiments with a sequence of learning tasks.

## 2. Summary of Strips

### 2.1. Description

Because STRIPS is basic to our discussion, let us briefly outline its operation. (For a complete discussion and additional examples, see [1].) The primitive actions available to the robot vehicle are preceded in a set of action routines. For example, execution of the routine GOTHRU(D1,R1,R2) causes the robot vehicle actually to go through the doorway D1 from room R1 to room R2. The robot system keeps track of where the robot vehicle is and stores its other knowledge of the world in a model [3] composed of well-formed formulas (wffs) in the predicate calculus. Thus, the system knows that there is a doorway D1 between rooms R1 and R2 by the presence of the wff CONNECTS-ROOMS(D1,R1,R2) in the model.

Tasks are given to the system in the form of predicate calculus wffs. To direct the robot to go to room R2, we pose for it the goal wff INROOM(ROBOT,R2). The planning system, STRIPS, then attempts to find a sequence of primitive actions that would change the world in such a way that the goal wff is true in the correspondingly changed model. In order to generate a plan of actions, STRIPS needs to know about the effects of these actions; that is, STRIPS must have a model of each action. The model actions are called *operators* and, just as the actions change the world, the operators transform one model into another. By applying a sequence of operators to the initial world model, STRIPS can produce a sequence of models (representing hypothetical worlds) ultimately ending in a model in which the goal wff is true. Presumably then, execution of the sequence of actions corresponding to these operators would change the world to accomplish the task.

Each STRIPS operator must be described in some convenient way. We characterize each operator in the repertoire by three entities: an *add list*, a *delete list*, and a *precondition wff*. The meanings of these entities are straightforward. An operator is applicable to a given model only if its precondition

³ Our use of the word "model" is consistent with customary terminology in Artificial Intelligence. We hope there will be no confusion between our use of the word and its technical definition in logic, namely an interpretation for a set of formulas.

wff is satisfied in that model. The effect of applying an (assumed applicable) operator to a given model is to delete from the model all those clauses specified by the delete list and to add to the model all those clauses specified by the add list. Hence, the add and delete lists prescribe how an operator transforms one state into another.

Within this basic framework STRIPS operates in a GPS-like manner [6]. First, it tries to establish that a goal wff is satisfied by a model. (STRIPS uses the QA3 resolution-based theorem prover [3] in its attempts to prove goal wffs.) If the goal wff cannot be proved, STRIPS selects a "relevant" operator that is likely to produce a model in which the goal wff is "more nearly" satisfied. In order to apply a selected operator the precondition wff of that operator must of course be satisfied; this precondition becomes a new subgoal and the process is repeated. At some point we expect to find that the precondition of a relevant operator is already satisfied in the current model. When this happens the operator is *applied*; the initial model is transformed on the basis of the add and delete lists of the operator, and the model thus created is treated in effect as a new initial model of the world.

To complete our review of STRIPS we must indicate how relevant operators are selected. An operator is needed only if a subgoal cannot be proved from the wffs defining a model. In this case the operators are scanned to find one whose effects would allow the proof attempt to continue. Specifically, STRIPS searches for an operator whose add list specifies clauses that would allow the proof to be successfully continued (if not completed). When an add list is found whose clauses do in fact permit an adequate continuation of the proof, then the associated operator is declared relevant; moreover, the substitutions used in the proof continuation serve to instantiate at least partially the arguments of the operator. Typically, more than one relevant operator instance will be found. Thus, the entire STRIPS planning process takes the form of a tree search so that the consequences of considering different relevant operators can be explored. In summary, then, the "inner loop" of STRIPS works as follows:

(1) Select a subgoal and try to establish that it is true in the appropriate model. If it is, go to Step 4. Otherwise:

(2) Choose as a relevant operator one whose add list specifies clauses that allow the incomplete proof of Step 1 to be continued.

(3) The appropriately instantiated precondition wff of the selected operator constitutes a new subgoal. Go to Step 1.

(4) If the subgoal is the main goal, terminate. Otherwise, create a new model by applying the operator whose precondition is the subgoal just established. Go to Step 1.

The final output of STRIPS, then, is a list of instantiated operators whose corresponding actions will achieve the goal.

## 2.2. An Example

An understanding of STRIPS is greatly aided by an elementary example. The following example considers the simple task of fetching a box from an adjacent room. Let us suppose that the initial state of the world is as shown below:

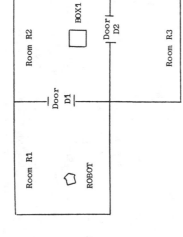

*Initial Model*

$M_0$: INROOM(ROBOT,R1)
    CONNECTS(D1,R1,R2)
    CONNECTS(D2,R2,R3)
    BOX(BOX1)
    INROOM(BOX1,R2)
        .
        .

$(\forall x \forall y \forall z)[\text{CONNECTS}(x,y,z) \Rightarrow \text{CONNECTS}(x,z,y)]$

*Goal wff*

$G_0$: $(\exists x)[\text{BOX}(x) \wedge \text{INROOM}(x,R1)]$

We assume for this example that models can be transformed by two operators GOTHRU and PUSHTHRU, having the descriptions given below. Each description specifies an *operator schema* indexed by schema variables. We will call schema variables *parameters*, and denote them by strings beginning with lower-case letters. A particular member of an operator schema is obtained by instantiating all the parameters in its description to constants. It is a straightforward matter to modify a resolution theorem prover to handle wffs containing parameters [1], but for present purposes we need only know that the modification ensures that each parameter can be bound only to one constant; hence, the operator arguments (which may be parameters) can assume unique values. (In all of the following we denote constants by strings beginning with capital letters and quantified variables by $x$, $y$ or $z$):

*GOTHRU(d,r1,r2)*
(Robot goes through Door d from Room r1 into Room r2.)
*Precondition wff*
    INROOM(ROBOT,r1) ∧ CONNECTS(d,r1,r2)
*Delete List*
    INROOM(ROBOT,$)
(Our convention here is to delete any clause containing a predicate of the form INROOM(ROBOT,\$) for any value of \$.)
*Add List*
    INROOM(ROBOT,r2)

*PUSHTHRU(b,d,r1,r2)*
(Robot pushes Object b through Door d from Room r1 into Room r2.)
*Precondition wff*
    INROOM(b,r1) ∧ INROOM(ROBOT,r1) ∧ CONNECTS(d,r1,r2)
*Delete List*
    INROOM(ROBOT,$)
    INROOM(b,$)
*Add List*
    INROOM(ROBOT,r2)
    INROOM(b,r2).

When STRIPS is given the problem it first attempts to prove the goal $G_0$ from the initial model $M_0$. This proof cannot be completed; however, were the model to contain other clauses, such as INROOM(BOX1,R1), the proof attempt could continue. STRIPS determines that the operator PUSHTHRU can provide the desired clause; in particular, the partial instance PUSHTHRU (BOX1,d,r1,R1) provides the wff INROOM(BOX1,R1).
The precondition $G_1$ for this instance of PUSHTHRU is

$G_1$: INROOM(BOX1,r1)
    ∧ INROOM(ROBOT,r1)
    ∧ CONNECTS(d,r1,R1).

This precondition is set up as a subgoal and STRIPS tries to prove it from $M_0$. Although no proof for $G_1$ can be found, STRIPS determines that if r1 = R2 and d = D1, then the proof of $G_1$ could continue were the model to contain INROOM(ROBOT,R2). Again STRIPS checks operators for one whose effects could continue the proof and settles on the instance GO-THRU(d,r1,R2). Its precondition is the next subgoal, namely:

$G_2$: INROOM(ROBOT,r1)
    ∧ CONNECTS(d,r1,R2).

STRIPS is able to prove $G_2$ from $M_0$, using the substitutions r1 = R1 and d = D1. It therefore applies GOTHRU(D1,R1,R2) to $M_0$ to yield:

$M_1$: INROOM(ROBOT,R2)
CONNECTS(D1,R1,R2)
CONNECTS(D2,R2,R3)
BOX(BOX1)
INROOM(BOX1,R2)
.
.

$(\forall x)(\forall y)(\forall z)[CONNECTS(x,y,z) \Rightarrow CONNECTS(x,z,y)]$.

Now STRIPS attempts to prove the subgoal $G_1$ from the new model $M_1$. The proof is successful with the instantiations r1 = R2, d = D1. These substitutions yield the operator instance PUSHTHRU(BOX1,D1,R2,R1), which applied to $M_1$ yields

$M_2$: INROOM(ROBOT,R1)
CONNECTS(D1,R1,R2)
CONNECTS(D1,R2,R3)
BOX(BOX1)
INROOM(BOX1,R1)
.
.

$(\forall x)(\forall y)(\forall z)[CONNECTS(x,y,z) \Rightarrow CONNECTS(x,z,y)]$.

Next, STRIPS attempts to prove the original goal, $G_0$, from $M_2$. This attempt is successful and the final operator sequence is

GOTHRU(D1,R1,R2)
PUSHTHRU(BOX1,D1,R2,R1).

We have just seen how STRIPS computes a specific plan to solve a particular problem. The next step is to generalize the specific plan by replacing constants by new parameters. In other words, we wish to elevate our particular plan to the status of a plan schema, or macro operator, analogous to the primitive operators we were given initially. Moreover, we would like to store a macro operator in such a way as to make any of its legitimate subsequences also available to STRIPS. In the next section we describe a storage format, called a triangle table, that has this property. Our procedure for plan generalization will be explained after we have discussed triangle tables and their properties.

## 3. Triangle Tables

Suppose STRIPS has just computed a plan consisting of the sequence of $n$ operators $OP_1, OP_2, ..., OP_n$. In what form should this plan be presented to

PLANEX, the system responsible for monitoring the execution of plans? In what form should it be saved? For purposes of monitoring execution, PLANEX needs at every step to be able to answer such questions as

(a) Has the portion of the plan executed so far produced the expected results?

(b) What portion of the plan needs to be executed next so that after its execution the task will be accomplished?

(c) Can this portion be executed in the current state of the world?

Also, for purposes of saving plans, we need to know the preconditions and effects of any portion of the plan.

If we are to have efficient methods for answering Questions (a)–(c), we must store a plan in a way that plainly reveals its internal structure. In particular, we must be able to identify the role of each operator in the overall plan: what its important effects are (as opposed to side effects) and why these effects are needed in the plan. To accomplish this, we decided to store plans in a tabular form called a triangle table.[4]

A triangle table is a lower triangular array where rows and columns correspond to the operators of the plan.

An example of a triangle table is shown in Fig. 1. (The reader may temporarily ignore the heavily outlined rectangle.) The columns of the table, with the exception of Column zero, are labelled with the names of the operators of the plan, in this example $OP_1, ..., OP_4$. For each Column $i$, $i = 1, ..., 4$, we place in the top cell the add list $A_i$ of operator $OP_i$. Going down the $i$th column, we place in consecutive cells the portion of $A_i$ that survives the application of subsequent operators. Thus, $A_{1/2}$ denotes those clauses in $A_1$ not deleted by $OP_2$; $A_{1/2,3}$ denotes those clauses in $A_{1/2}$ not deleted by $OP_3$, and so forth. Thus, the $ij$th cell of the matrix contains those wffs added by the $j$th operator that are still true at the time of application of the $i$th operator.

We can now interpret the contents of the $i$th row of the table, excluding the left-most column. Since each cell in the $i$th row (excluding the left-most) contains statements added by one of the first $(i-1)$ operators but not deleted by any of those operators, we see that the union of the cells in the $i$th row (excluding the left-most) specifies the add list obtained by applying the $(i-1)$st head of the plan; i.e., by applying in sequence $OP_1, ..., OP_{i-1}$. We denote by $A_{1,...,j}$ the add list achieved by the first $j$ operators applied in sequence. The union of the cells in the bottom row of a triangle table evidently specifies the add list of the complete sequence.

The left-most column of the triangle table, which we have thus far ignored, is involved with the preconditions for the stored plan. During the formation

[4] We are indebted to John Munson who prompted us to try a tabular format.

of the plan, STRIPS produced a proof of each operator's preconditions from the model to which the operator was applied. We will define the set of clauses used to prove a formula as the support of that formula. We wish to ensure that the ith row of a triangle table contains all the wffs in the support of the preconditions for Operator i. In general, some clauses in the support for Operator i will have been added by the first i − 1 operators in the plan and will therefore be included in Row i, as described in the previous paragraphs.

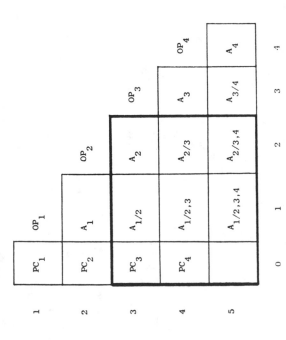

Fig. 1. A triangle table.

The remainder of the support clauses appeared in the initial model and were not deleted by any of the first i − 1 operators. These clauses, which we denote by $PC_i$, are precisely the clauses that are entered into the left-most (Column 0) cell of a triangle table. Hence, we see that Column 0 of a triangle table contains those clauses from the initial model that were used in the precondition proofs for the plan. It is convenient to flag the clauses in each Row i that are in the support for Operator i and hereafter speak of them as marked clauses; by construction, all clauses in Column 0 are marked. Note that in proving the preconditions of operators, STRIPS must save the support clauses so that the triangle table can be constructed.

As an example, we show in Fig. 2 the triangle table for the plan discussed in the previous section. The clauses that are marked by an asterisk "*" were all used in the proofs of preconditions.

We have seen how the marked clauses on Row i constitute the support of

the preconditions for the ith operator. Let us now investigate the preconditions for the ith operator—that is, the preconditions for applying the operator sequence $OP_i, OP_{i+1}, \ldots, OP_n$. The key observation here is that the ith tail is applicable to a model if the model already contains that portion of the support of each operator in the tail that is not supplied within the tail itself. This observation may be formulated more precisely by introducing the notion of a kernel of a triangle table. We define the ith kernel of a table to be the unique rectangular subarray containing the lower left-most cell and Row i. We assert now that the ith tail of a plan is applicable to a model if all the marked clauses in the ith kernel are true in that model. Let us see by example why this is so.

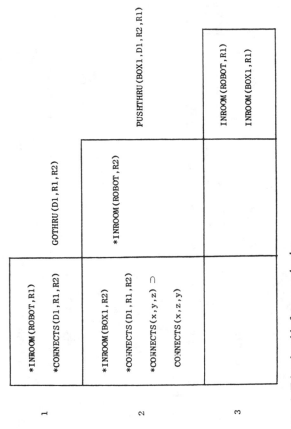

Fig. 2. Triangle table for example plan. (A "*" preceding a clause indicates a "marked" clause.)

Consider again Fig. 1, in which we have heavily outlined Kernel 3. Let us assume that all marked clauses in this kernel are true in the current model. (When all the marked clauses in a kernel are true, we shall say that the kernel is true.) Certainly, $OP_3$ is applicable; the marked clauses in Row 3 are true, and these marked clauses support the proof of the preconditions of $OP_3$. Suppose now that $OP_3$ is applied to the current model to produce a new model in which $A_3$, the set of clauses added by $OP_3$, is true. Evidently, $OP_4$ is now applicable, since all the marked clauses in Row 4 are true; those clauses within the outlined kernel were true before applying $OP_3$ (and by construction of the triangle table are still true), and those outside the kernel (that is, $A_3$)

are true because they were added by $OP_3$. Thus, the truth of the marked clauses in Kernel 3 is a sufficient condition for the applicability of the tail of the plan beginning with $OP_3$.

We have some additional observations to make about triangle tables before moving on to the matter of plan generalization. First, notice that Kernel 1—that is, the left-most column of a triangle table—constitutes a set of sufficient conditions for the applicability of the entire plan. Thus, we can take the conjunction of the clauses in Column 0 to be a precondition formula for the whole plan.

A second observation may help the reader gain a little more insight into the structure of triangle tables. Consider again the table of Fig. 1, and let us suppose this time that Kernel 2 is true. Since Kernel 2 is true, the sequence $OP_2$, $OP_3$, $OP_4$ is applicable. Upon applying $OP_2$, which is immediately applicable because the marked clauses in Row 2 are true, we effectively add Column 2 to the table. Moreover, we lose interest in Row 2 because $OP_2$ has already been applied. Thus the application of $OP_2$ transforms a true Kernel 2 into a true Kernel 3, and the application of the operators in the tail of the plan can continue.

## 4. Generalizing Plans

### 4.1. Motivation

The need for plan generalization in a learning system is readily apparent. Consider the specific plan produced in the example of Section 2:

GOTHRU(D1,R1,R2)
PUSHTHRU(BOX1,D1,R2,R1).

While this sequence solves the original task, it probably doesn't warrant being saved for the future unless, of course, we expect that the robot would often need to go from Room R1 through Door D1 to Room R2 to push back the specific box, BOX1, through Door D1 into Room R1. We would like to generalize the plan so that it could be free from the specific constants, D1, R1, R2, and BOX1 and could be used in situations involving arbitrary doors, rooms, and boxes.

In considering possible procedures for generalizing plans we must first reject the naive suggestion of merely replacing each constant in the plan by a parameter. Some of the constants may really need to have specific values in order for the plan to work at all. For example, consider a modification of our box-fetching plan in which the second step of the plan is an operator that *only* pushes objects from room R2 into room R1. The specific plan might then be

GOTHRU(D1,R1,R2)
SPECIALPUSH(BOX1).

When we generalize this plan we cannot replace all constants by parameters, since the plan only works when the third argument of GOTHRU is R2. We would want our procedure to recognize this fact and produce the plan

GOTHRU(d1,r1,R2)
SPECIALPUSH(b1).

Another reason for rejecting the simple replacement of constants by parameters is that there is often more generality readily available in many plans than this simple procedure will extract. For example, the form of our box-pushing plan, GOTHRU followed by PUSHTHRU, does not require that the room in which the robot begins be the same room into which the box is pushed. Hence the plan could be generalized as follows:

GOTHRU(d1,r1,r2)
PUSHTHRU(b,d2,r2,r3)

and be used to go from one room to an adjacent second room and push a box to an adjacent third room.

Our plan-generalization procedure overcomes these difficulties by taking into account the internal structure of the plan and the preconditions of each operator. The remainder of this section is a description of this generalization procedure.

### 4.2. The Generalization Procedure

The first step in our generalization procedure is to "lift" the triangle table to its most general form as follows: We first replace every occurrence of a constant in the clauses of the left-most column by a new parameter. (Multiple occurrences of the same constant are replaced by distinct parameters.) Then the remainder of the table is filled in with appropriate add clauses assuming completely uninstantiated operators (i.e., as these add clauses appear in the operator descriptions), and assuming the same deletions as occurred in the original table. As an example, Fig. 3 shows the table from Fig. 2 in its most general form.

The lifted table thus obtained is too general; we wish to constrain it so that the marked clauses in each row support the preconditions of the operator on that row, while retaining the property that the lifted table has the original table as an instance. To determine the constraints we redo each operator's precondition proof using the support clauses in the lifted table as axioms and the precondition formulas from the operator descriptions as the theorems to be proved. Each new proof is constructed as an isomorphic image of STRIPS' original precondition proof by performing at each step resolutions on the same clauses and unifications on the same literals as in the original proof. This proof process ensures that each original proof is an instance of the new

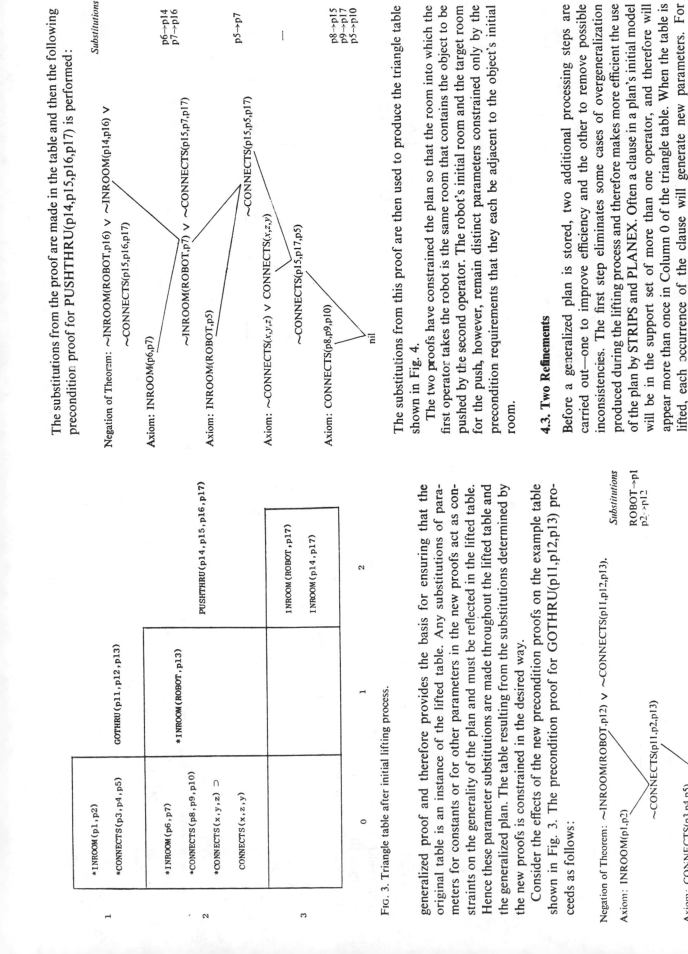

The substitutions from the proof are made in the table and then the following precondition proof for PUSHTHRU(p14,p15,p16,p17) is performed:

| | Substitutions |
|---|---|
| Negation of Theorem: ~INROOM(ROBOT,p16) ∨ ~INROOM(p14,p16) ∨ ~CONNECTS(p15,p16,p17) | |
| Axiom: INROOM(p6,p7) | p6→p14, p7→p16 |
| ~INROOM(ROBOT,p7) ∨ ~CONNECTS(p15,p7,p17) | |
| Axiom: INROOM(ROBOT,p5) | p5→p7 |
| ~CONNECTS(p15,p5,p17) | |
| Axiom: ~CONNECTS(x,y,z) ∨ CONNECTS(x,z,y) | — |
| CONNECTS(p15,p17,p5) | |
| Axiom: CONNECTS(p8,p9,p10) | p8→p15, p9→p17, p5→p10 |
| nil | |

The substitutions from this proof are then used to produce the triangle table shown in Fig. 4.

The two proofs have constrained the plan so that the room into which the first operator takes the robot is the same room that contains the object to be pushed by the second operator. The robot's initial room and the target room for the push, however, remain distinct parameters constrained only by the precondition requirements that they each be adjacent to the object's initial room.

## 4.3. Two Refinements

Before a generalized plan is stored, two additional processing steps are carried out—one to improve efficiency and the other to remove possible inconsistencies. The first step eliminates some cases of overgeneralization produced during the lifting process and therefore makes more efficient the use of the plan by STRIPS and PLANEX. Often a clause in a plan's initial model will be in the support set of more than one operator, and therefore will appear more than once in Column 0 of the triangle table. When the table is lifted, each occurrence of the clause will generate new parameters. For example, in Fig. 3, CONNECTS(D1,R1,R2) was lifted to CONNECTS-(p3,p4,p5) and to CONNECTS(p8,p9,p10). In many cases this lifting pro-

generalized proof and therefore provides the basis for ensuring that the original table is an instance of the lifted table. Any substitutions of parameters for constants or for other parameters in the new proofs act as constraints on the generality of the plan and must be reflected in the lifted table. Hence these parameter substitutions are made throughout the lifted table and the generalized plan. The table resulting from the substitutions determined by the new proofs is constrained in the desired way.

Consider the effects of the new precondition proofs on the example table shown in Fig. 3. The precondition proof for GOTHRU(p11,p12,p13) proceeds as follows:

| | Substitutions |
|---|---|
| Negation of Theorem: ~INROOM(ROBOT,p12) ∨ ~CONNECTS(p11,p12,p13) | |
| Axiom: INROOM(p1,p2) | ROBOT→p1, p2→p12 |
| ~CONNECTS(p11,p2,p13) | |
| Axiom: CONNECTS(p3,p4,p5) | p3→p11, p2→p4, p5→p13 |
| nil | |

Fig. 3. Triangle table after initial lifting process.

Triangle table (Fig. 3):

| | 0 | 1 | 2 | 3 |
|---|---|---|---|---|
| 1 | *INROOM(p1,p2)  *CONNECTS(p3,p4,p5) | GOTHRU(p11,p12,p13) | | |
| 2 | *INROOM(p6,p7)  *CONNECTS(p8,p9,p10)  *CONNECTS(x,y,z) ⊃ CONNECTS(x,z,y) | *INROOM(ROBOT,p13) | PUSHTHRU(p14,p15,p16,p17) | |
| 3 | CONNECTS(x,z,y) | | INROOM(ROBOT,p17)  INROOM(p14,p17) | |

INROOM example above, thereby making the two occurrences of the clause identical, but would not generate any constraining substitutions for the CONNECTS clause in the box-fetching example.

The second processing step that is performed before the plan is stored is needed to avoid inconsistencies that can occur in the lifted tables. The difficulty can be illustrated with the following example.

Consider a simple plan, PUSH(BOX1,LOC1), PUSH(BOX2,LOC2), for pushing two boxes to two locations. The unlifted triangle table for this plan might be as shown in Fig. 5a, where for simplicity we have not shown all clauses. When this table is lifted and the precondition proofs redone, no constraints are placed on the lifted table and it has the form shown in Fig. 5b. Suppose now that STRIPS were to use this plan with box1 and box2 instantiated to the same object and loc1 and loc2 instantiated to distinct locations. In that case STRIPS would evidently have a plan for achieving a state in which the same object is simultaneously at two different places!

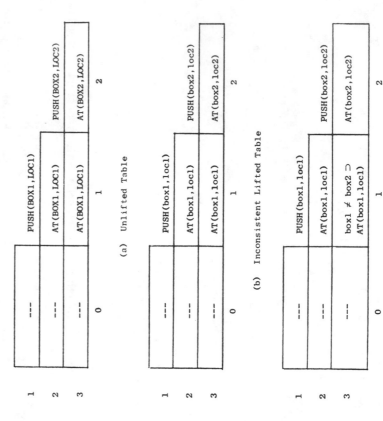

|   |     |                   | PUSH(BOX2,LOC2) |
|---|-----|-------------------|-----------------|
| 1 | --- | PUSH(BOX1,LOC1)   |                 |
| 2 | --- | AT(BOX1,LOC1)     | PUSH(BOX2,LOC2) |
| 3 | --- | AT(BOX1,LOC1)     | AT(BOX2,LOC2)   |
|   | 0   | 1                 | 2               |

(a)  Unlifted Table

|   |     |                   | PUSH(box2,loc2) |
|---|-----|-------------------|-----------------|
| 1 | --- | PUSH(box1,loc1)   |                 |
| 2 | --- | AT(box1,loc1)     | PUSH(box2,loc2) |
| 3 | --- | AT(box1,loc1)     | AT(box2,loc2)   |
|   | 0   | 1                 | 2               |

(b)  Inconsistent Lifted Table

|   |     |                   | PUSH(box2,loc2) |
|---|-----|-------------------|-----------------|
| 1 | --- | PUSH(box1,loc1)   |                 |
| 2 | --- | AT(box1,loc1)     | PUSH(box2,loc2) |
| 3 | --- | box1 ≠ box2 ⊃<br>AT(box1,loc1) | AT(box2,loc2)   |
|   | 0   | 1                 | 2               |

(c)  Correct Lifted Table

Fig. 5. Triangle table for box-pushing plan

cedure enhances the generality of the plan (as it did for the box-fetching plan by allowing the first and third rooms to be distinct), but it also produces cases of over-generalization that, while not incorrect, can lead to inefficiencies. For example, consider a case in which INROOM(BOX1,R1) appears twice in Column 0 of a triangle table. When the table is lifted, the occurrences of the clause in Column 0 might become INROOM(p1,p2) and INROOM(p3, p4). If the precondition proofs cause p1 to be substituted for p3, but do not constrain p2 and p4, then we have a plan whose preconditions include the clauses

INROOM(p1,p2) and
INROOM(p1,p4).

Therefore we have a plan whose preconditions allow Object p1 to be in two distinct rooms at the same time, even though we know that in any semantically correct model Object p1 will be in only one room.

We eliminate most cases of this overgeneralization by recognizing those cases where two parameters are produced from a single occurrence of a constant in a single clause; if both such parameters do not appear as arguments of operators in the plan, then they can be bound together and one substituted for the other throughout the table without effectively inhibiting the generality of the plan. This procedure would substitute p2 for p4 in the

|   |     |                   | PUSHTHRU(p6,p8,p5,p9) |
|---|-----|-------------------|-----------------------|
| 1 | *INROOM(ROBOT,p2)<br>*CONNECTS(p3,p2,p5) | GOTHRU(p3,p2,p5) |                 |
| 2 | *INROOM(p6,p5)<br>*CONNECTS(p8,p9,p5)<br>*CONNECTS(x,y,z) ⊃<br>CONNECTS(x,z,y) | *INROOM(ROBOT,p5) |             |
| 3 |     |                   | INROOM(ROBOT,p9)<br>INROOM(p6,p9) |
|   | 0   | 1                 | 2                     |

Fig. 4. Final form of triangle table for generalized plan.

The source of this embarrassment lies in the assumption made above that the deletions in the lifted table can be the same as in the unlifted table. In our example, the clause AT(box1,loc1) operator in the case where box1 and box2 are bound to the same object, but not deleted otherwise. Using the deletion algorithm described below, we represent this situation in the lifted table by replacing the clause AT(box1, loc1) in Row 3 by the clause form of

$$box1 \neq box2 \supset AT(box1,loc1)$$

as shown in Fig. 5(c). This implication serves us well since the theorem prover can deduce AT(box1,loc1) as being part of the plan's additions list for exactly those cases in which box1 and box2 are distinct.

We now consider in general how deletions are correctly accounted for in the lifted triangle tables. After all the precondition proofs are redone for the lifted table, the delete list of each operator is considered beginning with the first operator and continuing in sequence through the plan. The delete list of the $i$th operator is applied to the clauses in Row $i$ of the table to determine which clauses should appear in Row $i + 1$ of the table.[5] Recall that an operator's delete list is specified to STRIPS as a list of literals, and any clause that unifies with one of these literals is deleted. Application of the delete list will cause the lifted table to be modified only when a unification with a delete literal requires that a parameter p1 be replaced by another parameter p2 or by a constant C1. In that case the clause will unify with the delete literal only when p1 and p2 are instantiated to the same constant or when p1 is instantiated to C1. Hence the clause is replaced in the next row of the table by an implication as follows:

p1 ≠ p2 ⊃ clause      or

p1 ≠ C1 ⊃ clause.

This implication allows the theorem prover to deduce the clause in only those cases where the operator's delete list would not have deleted it from the model.

If the clause that is replaced by the implication in a conditional deletion is part of the support of an operator in the plan (i.e., the clause is marked), then the implication must be accompanied by another addition to the table. In particular, if a clause CL1 is part of the support for the $j$th operator of the plan and CL1 is replaced in Row $j$ of the table by the implication p1 ≠ p2 ⊃ CL1, then p1 ≠ p2 must be added as a marked clause to Cell $(j,0)$ of the table. This addition to the table ensures that the $j$th operator's preconditions can be proved from the marked clauses in Row $j$ of the table. The preconditions proof previously obtained will remain valid with the addition of a preliminary proof step in which clause CL1 is derived from p1 ≠ p2 and p1 ≠ p2 ⊃ CL1.

After these two processing steps are completed, the generalized plan is ready to be stored away as a macro operator, or *MACROP*, for later use by STRIPS and PLANEX.

## 5. Execution Strategies

### 5.1. Requirements for the Plan Executor

In this section we shall describe how a program called PLANEX uses triangle tables to monitor the execution of plans. An early version of PLANEX was described by Fikes [2]. It is now being used in conjunction with STRIPS and the MACROP generation procedures to control the SRI robot [4].

One of the novel elements introduced into artificial intelligence research by work on robots is the study of execution strategies and how they interact with planning activities. Since robot plans must ultimately be executed in the real world by a mechanical device, as opposed to being carried out in a mathematical space or by a simulator, consideration must be given by the executor to the possibility that operations in the plan may not accomplish what they were intended to, that data obtained from sensory devices may be inaccurate, and that mechanical tolerances may introduce errors as the plan is executed. Many of these problems of plan execution would disappear if our system generated a whole new plan after each execution step. Obviously, such a strategy would be too costly, so we instead seek a plan execution scheme with the following properties:

(1) When new information obtained during plan execution implies that some remaining portion of the plan need not be executed, the executor should recognize such information and omit the unneeded plan steps.

(2) When execution of some portion of the plan fails to achieve the intended results, the executor should recognize the failure and either direct reexecution of some portion of the plan or, as a default, call for a replanning activity.

### 5.2. Preparation of the MACROP for Execution

Rather than working with the specific version of the plan originally produced by STRIPS, PLANEX uses the generalized MACROP to guide execution. The generalized plan allows a modest amount of replanning by the executor should parts of the plan fail in certain ways.

Before a MACROP can be used by PLANEX, its parameters must be partially instantiated using the specific constants of the goal wff. This specializes the MACROP to the specific task at hand while it leaves as general as possible the conditions under which it can be executed. This partial instantiation process is quite simple: We put in the lower left-most cell of the triangle

[5] This characterization of the deletion applications requires that we include in Cell (1, 0) of the table all the clauses that appear anywhere in Column 0. The resulting redundant occurrences of Column 0 clauses can be edited out before the table is stored.

table those clauses from the original model that were used by STRIPS in proving the goal wff. Then we use all of the clauses in the entire last row of the MACROP to prove the goal wff. Those substitutions made during this proof are then made on the entire MACROP. In addition we mark those clauses in the last row of the MACROP that were used to support the goal wff proof. This version of the MACROP is the one used to control execution.[6]

Let us illustrate what we have said about preparing a MACROP for execution by considering our example of fetching a box. In Fig. 4, we have the MACROP for this task. In Section 2, the goal wff for this task was given as

$$(\exists x)[BOX(x) \wedge INROOM(x,R1)].$$

In the proof of this goal wff we used the clause BOX(BOX1) from the original model, $M_0$. Therefore, we insert this clause in Cell (3,0) of the triangle table. We now use the clauses in Row 3 of the MACROP in Fig. 4 (together with BOX(BOX1), just inserted) to prove the goal wff. That is, we use BOX(BOX1), INROOM(ROBOT,p9) and INROOM(p6,p9) to prove $(\exists x)[BOX(x) \wedge INROOM(x,R1)]$. The substitutions made in obtaining the proof are BOX1 for p6 and R1 for p9. When these substitutions are applied to the MACROP of Fig. 4 and the support clauses for the new proof are marked, we obtain the execution MACROP shown in Fig. 6.

## 5.3. The PLANEX Execution Strategy

Our strategy for monitoring the execution of plans makes use of the kernels of the execution MACROP. Recall that the *i*th kernel of a triangle table for an *n*-step plan is the unique rectangular subarray containing Row *i* and Cell $(n + 1, 0)$. The importance of the *i*th kernel stems from the fact that it contains (as marked clauses) the support of the preconditions for the *i*th tail of the plan—that is, for the operator sequence $\{OP_i, \ldots, OP_n\}$. Thus if at some stage of plan execution the marked clauses in the *i*th kernel are provable, then we know that the *i*th tail is an appropriate operator sequence for achieving the goal. At each state of execution we must have at least one true kernel if we are to continue execution of the plan.

At the beginning of execution we know that the first kernel is true, since the initial model was used by STRIPS when the plan was created. But at later stages, unplanned outcomes might place us either unexpectedly close to the goal or throw us off the track completely. Our present implementation adopts a rather optimistic bias. We check each kernel in turn starting with the highest numbered one (which is the last row of the MACROP) and work backwards from the goal until we find a kernel that is true. If the goal kernel (the last row) is true, execution halts; otherwise we determine if the next-to-last kernel is true, and so on, until we find a true kernel $k_i$ and a corresponding tail of the plan $\{OP_i, \ldots, OP_n\}$. The execution strategy then executes the action corresponding to $OP_i$ and checks the outcome, as before, by searching for the highest-numbered true kernel. In an "ideal" world this procedure merely executes in order each operator in the plan. On the other hand, the procedure has the freedom to omit execution of unnecessary operators and to overcome failures by repeating the execution of operators. Replanning by STRIPS is initiated when no kernels are true.[7]

When checking to see if a kernel is true, we check to see if some instance of the conjunction of marked clauses in the kernel can be proved from the present model. Once such an instance is found, we determine the corresponding instance of the first operator in the tail of the plan and execute the action corresponding to that instance. Thus the generality of representation of the execution MACROP allows a great deal of flexibility in plan execution. For example, consider a case where PLANEX is executing a plan that takes the robot from one room through a second room into a third room. If, when the robot attempts to go through the door connecting the second and third rooms, the door is found to be locked, then PLANEX may be able to

[6] Some increase in generality can be obtained by putting in the lower leftmost cell of the triangle table *generalized* versions of the original model clauses. Some of the parameters in these generalized clauses might remain unbound in the proof of the goal wff, thereby making the table more general. In our implementation we shunned this additional complication.

[7] Typically, when replanning is necessary it is sufficient to produce a short sequence of operators to "get back onto the track" of the original plan. Since STRIPS has the MACROP for the original plan in its repertoire of operators, the new plan can often be formed by composing a sequence of operators and appending it to an appropriate tail of the MACROP.

| | | | |
|---|---|---|---|
| 1 | *INROOM(ROBOT,p2) | | |
| | *CONNECTS(p3,p2,p10) | GOTHRU(p3,p2,p10) | |
| 2 | *INROOM(BOX1,p10) | | |
| | *CONNECTS(p8,R1,p10) | *INROOM(ROBOT,p10) | |
| | *CONNECTS(x,y,z) ⊃ | | |
| | CONNECTS(x,z,y) | | PUSHTHROUGH(BOX1,p8,p10,R1) |
| 3 | *BOX(BOX1) | | INROOM(ROBOT,R1) |
| | | | *INROOM(BOX1,R1) |

Fig. 6. Execution MACROP for the fetch a box task.

# 6. Planning with MACROPS

In the preceding sections, we described the construction of MACROPS and how they are used to control execution. Now let us consider how a MACROP can be used by STRIPS during a subsequent planning process.

## 6.1. Extracting a Relevant Operator Sequence from a MACROP

Recall that the $(i + 1)$st row of a triangle table (excluding the first cell) represents the add list, $A_{1,\ldots,i}$, of the $i$th head of the plan, i.e. of the sequence $OP_1,\ldots,OP_i$. An $n$-step plan presents STRIPS with $n$ alternative add lists, any one of which can be used to reduce a difference encountered during the normal planning process. STRIPS tests the relevance of each of a MACROP's add lists in the usual fashion, and the add lists that provide the greatest reduction in the difference are selected. Often a given set of relevant clauses will appear in more than one row of the table. In that case only the lowest-numbered row is selected, since this choice results in the shortest operator sequence capable of producing the desired clauses.

Suppose that STRIPS selects the $i$th add list $A_{1,\ldots,i}$, $i < n$. Since this add list is achieved by applying in sequence $OP_1,\ldots,OP_i$, we will obviously not be interested in the application of $OP_{i+1},\ldots,OP_n$, and will therefore not be interested in establishing any of the preconditions for these operators. Now in general, some steps of a plan are needed only to establish preconditions for subsequent steps. If we lose interest in a tail of a plan, then the relevant instance of the MACROP need not contain those operators whose sole purpose is to establish preconditions for the tail. Also, STRIPS will, in general, have used only some subset of $A_{1,\ldots,i}$, in establishing the relevance of the $i$th head of the plan. Any of the first $i$ operators that does not add some clause in this subset or help establish the preconditions for some operator that adds a clause in the subset is not needed in the relevant instance of the MACROP.

Conceptually, then, we can think of a single triangle table as representing a family of generalized operators. Upon the selection by STRIPS of a relevant add list, we must extract from this family an economical parameterized operator achieving the add list. In the following paragraphs, we will explain by means of an example an editing algorithm for accomplishing this task of operator extraction.

## 6.2. The Editing Algorithm

Consider the illustrative triangle table shown in Fig. 7. Each of the numbers within cells represents a single clause. The circled clauses are "marked" in the sense described earlier; that is, they are used to prove the precondition of the operator whose name appears on the same row. A summary of the structure

reinstantiate parameters so that the first part of the plan can be reexecuted to take the robot from the second room through some new fourth room and then into the target third room.

An interesting by-product of our optimistic strategy of examining kernels in backwards order is that PLANEX sometimes remedies certain blunders made by STRIPS. Occasionally, STRIPS produces a plan containing an entirely superfluous subsequence—for example, a subsequence of the form $OP$, $OP^{-1}$, where $OP^{-1}$ precisely negates the effects of $OP$. (Such a "detour" in a plan would reflect inadequacies in the search heuristics used by STRIPS.) During plan execution, however, PLANEX would effectively recognize that the state following $OP^{-1}$ is the same as the state preceding $OP$, and would therefore not execute the superfluous subsequence.

## 5.4. The PLANEX Scanning Algorithm

The triangle table is a compact way of representing the kernels of a MACROP; most cells of the table occur in more than one kernel. We have exploited this economy of representation by designing an efficient algorithm for finding the highest-numbered true kernel. This algorithm, called the *PLANEX scan*, involves a cell-by-cell scan of the triangle table. We give a brief description of it here and refer the reader to Fikes [2] for more details. Each cell examined is evaluated as either *True* (i.e., all the marked clauses are provable from the current model) or *False*. The interest of the algorithm stems from the order in which cells are examined. Let us call a kernel "potentially true" at some stage in the scan if all evaluated cells of the kernel are true. The scan algorithm can then be succinctly stated as: *Among all unevaluated cells in the highest-indexed potentially true kernel, evaluate the left-most. Break "left-most ties" arbitrarily.* The reader can verify that, roughly speaking, this table-scanning rule results in a left-to-right, bottom-to-top scan of the table. However, the table is never scanned to the right of any cell already evaluated as false. An equivalent statement of the algorithm is "Among all unevaluated cells, evaluate the cell common to the largest number of potentially true kernels. Break ties arbitrarily." We conjecture that this scanning algorithm is optimal in the sense that it evaluates, on the average, fewer cells than any other scan guaranteed always to find the highest true kernel. A proof of this conjecture has not been found.

As the cells in the table are scanned we will be making substitutions for the MACROP parameters as dictated by the proofs of the cells' clauses. It is important to note that a substitution made to establish the truth of clauses in a particular cell must be applied to the entire table. When there are alternative choices about which substitutions to make, we keep a tree of possibilities so that backtracking can occur if needed.

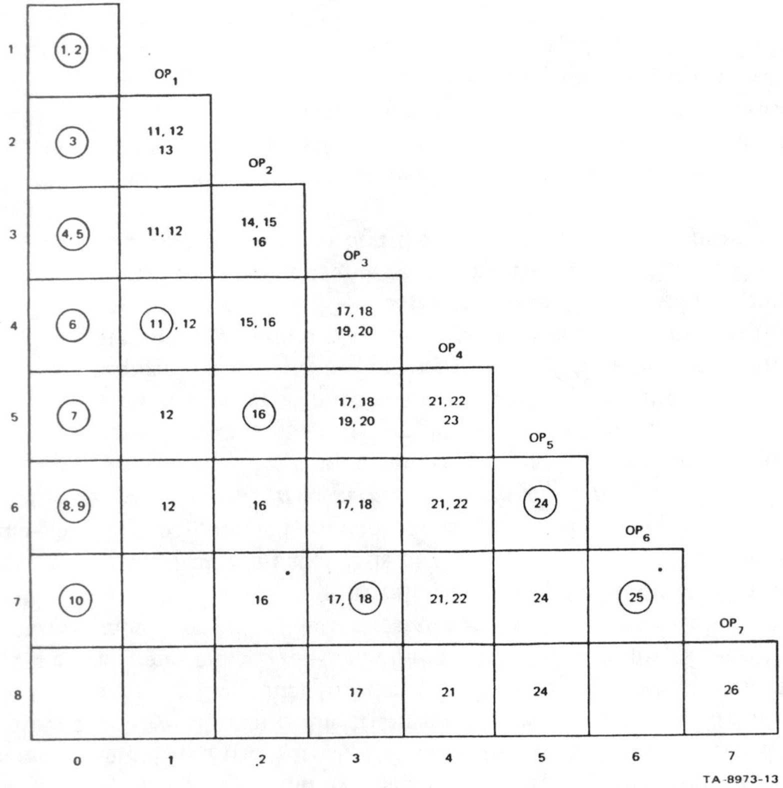

These clauses have been indicated on the table by an asterisk (*). The editing algorithm proceeds by examining the table to determine what effects of individual operators are not needed to produce Clauses 16 and 25. First, $OP_7$ is obviously not needed; we can therefore remove all circle marks from Row 7, since those marks indicate the support of the preconditions of $OP_7$. We now inspect the columns, beginning with Column 6 and going from right to left, to find the first column with no marks of either kind (circles or asterisks). Column 4 is the first such column. The absence of marked clauses in Column 4 means that the clauses added by $OP_4$ are not needed to reduce the difference and are not required to prove the pre-condition of any subsequent operator; hence $OP_4$ will not be in the edited operator sequence and we can unmark all clauses in Row 4. Continuing our right-to-left scan of the columns, we note that Column 3 contains no marked clauses. (Recall that we have already unmarked Clause 18.) We therefore delete $OP_3$ from the plan and unmark all clauses in Row 3. Continuing the scan, we note that Column 1 contains no marked entries (we have already unmarked Clause 11), and therefore we can delete $OP_1$ and the marked entries in Row 1.

The result of this editing process is to reduce the original seven-step plan to the compact three-step plan, $\{OP_2, OP_5, OP_6\}$, whose add list specifically includes the relevant clauses. The structure of this plan is shown below.

| OPERATOR | PRECONDITION SUPPORT SUPPLIED BY | PRECONDITION SUPPORT SUPPLIED TO |
| --- | --- | --- |
| $OP_2$ | $I$ | $OP_5, F$ |
| $OP_5$ | $I, OP_2$ | $OP_6, F$ |
| $OP_6$ | $I, OP_5$ | $F$ |

### 6.3. Use of Edited MACROPS as Relevant Operators

Once an edited MACROP has been constructed, we would like STRIPS to use it in the same manner as any other operator. We have some latitude though, in specifying the preconditions of the MACROP. An obvious choice would be to use the conjunction of the clauses in the left-most column, but there is a difficulty with this straightforward choice that can be made clear with the aid of a simple example. Suppose we are currently in a state in which the first kernel of an edited MACROP—that is, its left-most column—is false, but suppose further that, say, the third kernel is true. Since the third kernel is true, the tail of the MACROP beginning with $OP_3$ is immediately applicable and would produce the desired relevant additions to the model. If STRIPS were to ignore this opportunity and set up the left-most column of the MACROP as a subgoal, it would thereby take the proverbial one step backward to go two steps forward.

This example suggests that we employ a PLANEX scan on the edited table

FIG. 7. MACROP with marked clauses.

of this plan is shown below, where "$I$" refers to the initial state and "$F$" to the final state:

| OPERATOR | PRECONDITION SUPPORT SUPPLIED BY | PRECONDITION SUPPORT SUPPLIED TO |
| --- | --- | --- |
| $OP_1$ | $I$ | $OP_4$ |
| $OP_2$ | $I$ | $OP_5$ |
| $OP_3$ | $I$ | $OP_7, F$ |
| $OP_4$ | $I, OP_1$ | $F$ |
| $OP_5$ | $I, OP_2$ | $OP_6, F$ |
| $OP_6$ | $I, OP_5$ | $OP_7$ |
| $OP_7$ | $I, OP_3, OP_6$ | $F$ |

Suppose now that STRIPS selects $A_{1,\ldots,6}$ as the desired add list and, in particular, selects Clause 16 and Clause 25 as the particular members of the add list that are relevant to reducing the difference of immediate interest.

so that all tails of the relevant MACROP will be tested for applicability. If an applicable tail is found, STRIPS applies, in sequence, each operator in this tail to produce a new planning model. Each operator application is performed in the usual manner using the add and delete lists of the individual operators. If the PLANEX scan fails to find a true kernel, then no tail is applicable and the conjunction of the marked clauses in the first kernel is set up as a subgoal to be achieved by STRIPS. Actually, any kernel would constitute a perfectly good subgoal and, in principle, the disjunction of all the kernels would be better still. Unfortunately, this disjunction places excessive demands on both the theorem prover and the STRIPS executive, so we restrict ourselves to consideration of the first kernel.

We have seen that STRIPS uses a MACROP during planning by extracting a relevant subsequence of the MACROP's operators, and then including that subsequence in the new plan being constructed. When the new plan is made into a MACROP it is often the case that it will contain add lists that are subsets of add lists in already existing tables. For example, if an entire existing MACROP is used in the construction of a new plan, and the parameter substitutions in the new MACROP correspond to those in the old MACROP, then each add list in the old MACROP will be a subset of an add list in the new MACROP. To assist STRIPS in its use of MACROPS, we have designed a procedure that will remove redundant add lists from consideration during planning, and in cases where an entire MACROP is contained within another, will delete the contained MACROP from the system.

Our procedure takes the following action: If every instance of the operator sequence that is the $i$th head of some MACROP is also an instance of a sequence occurring anywhere else in the same or some other MACROP, then all the add lists in that head (i.e. Rows 2 through $i + 1$) are disallowed for consideration by STRIPS.[8] For example, consider the following two generalized plans:

Plan A: OPA(p1),OPB(p1,p2),OPC(p3),OPD(p3,C1),OPA(p3),OPB(p4,p5)
Plan B: OPC(p6),OPD(p6,C1),OPA(p7),OPF(p6,p7).

Rows 2 and 3 of Plan A are disallowed for consideration as add lists since every instance of the sequence, OPA(p1),OPB(p1,p2), is also an instance of the sequence, OPA(p3),OPB(p4,p5), that occurs at the end of Plan A. Rows 2 and 3 of Plan B are disallowed because of the sequence, OPC(p3),OPD-(p3,C1), that occurs in Plan A. Note that Row 4 of Plan B could not be disallowed for consideration by Plan A since there are instances of the sequence, OPC(p6),OPD(p6,C1),OPA(p7), that are not instances of OPC(p3),OPD(p3,C1),OPA(p3).

This procedure is applied whenever a new MACROP is added to the system. It has proved to be quite effective at minimizing the number of

[8] Note that the first row of a MACROP contains no add clauses.

MACROP add lists that STRIPS must consider during planning. (See Section 7, for examples.) A difficulty arises in the use of this procedure when the same operator appears in two MACROPs and the support sets for the precondition proofs of that operator differ markedly in the two triangle tables. This can occur, for example, when the precondition is a disjunction of two wffs and in one case the first disjunct was proven to be true and in the other case the second disjunct was proven to be true. In those situations the two occurrences of the operator should not be considered as instances of the same operator since each occurrence effectively had different preconditions. A refinement of our procedure that would include an appropriate comparison of the support sets could be employed to overcome this difficulty.

## 7. Experimental Results

The mechanisms we have described for generating and using MACROPS have been implemented as additions and modifications to the existing STRIPS and PLANEX systems. In this section we will describe the results of some of the experiments we have run with the new system. Problems were posed to the system in the SRI robot's current experimental environment of seven rooms, eight doors, and several boxes about two feet high. The robot is a mobile vehicle equipped with touch sensors, a television camera, and a push bar that allows the robot to push the boxes [4]. A typical state of this experimental environment is modeled by STRIPS using about 160 axioms.

### 7.1. Operator Descriptions

The operator descriptions given to STRIPS for these experiments model the robot's preprogrammed action routines for moving the robot next to a door in a room, next to a box in a room, to a location in a room, or through a door. There are also operators that model action routines for pushing a box next to another box in a room, to a location in a room, or through a door. In addition, we have included operator descriptions that model fictitious action routines for opening and closing doors. These descriptions are as follows:

GOTOB($bx$) *Go to object bx.*
Preconditions: TYPE($bx$,OBJECT),($\exists rx$)[INROOM($bx,rx$) $\land$ INROOM(ROBOT,$rx$)]
Deletions: AT(ROBOT,$1,$2),NEXTTO(ROBOT,$1)
Additions: *NEXTTO(ROBOT,$bx$)

GOTOD($dx$) *Go to door dx.*
Preconditions: TYPE($dx$,DOOR),($\exists rx$)($\exists ry$)[INROOM(ROBOT,$rx$) $\land$ CONNECTS($dx,rx,ry$)]
Deletions: AT(ROBOT,$1,$2),NEXTTO(ROBOT,$1)
Additions: *NEXTTO(ROBOT,$dx$)

GOTOL($x,y$) *Go to coordinate location (x,y).*
Preconditions: ($\exists rx$)[INROOM(ROBOT,$rx$) $\land$ LOCINROOM($x,y,rx$)]
Deletions: AT(ROBOT,$1,$2),NEXTTO(ROBOT,$1)
Additions: *AT(ROBOT,$x,y$)

operator applications actually occurring in the STRIPS solution. STRIPS' attention was directed to the rooms shown in the diagrams by closing the doors connecting all other rooms.

The plan for the first problem in the sequence pushes two boxes together and then takes the robot into an adjacent room. The second problem is similar to the first except that different rooms and different boxes are involved, and the robot begins in a room adjacent to the room containing the boxes. STRIPS uses a tail of MACROP1 to get the robot into the room with the boxes and then uses the entire MACROP1 to complete the plan.

The third problem involves taking the robot from one room through a second room and into a third room, with the added complication that the door connecting the second and third rooms is closed. STRIPS first decides to use MACROP2 with the box-pushing sequence edited out and then finds that the door must be opened; to get the robot next to the closed door, a head of MACROP2 is selected with the box-pushing sequence again edited out. After formation of the plan to go to the door and open it, the PLANEX scan observes that only the final operator of the first relevant instance of MAC-ROP2 is needed to complete the plan.

The fourth problem requires that three boxes be pushed together, with the robot beginning in a room adjacent to the room containing the boxes. A head of MACROP2 is used to get the robot into the room with the boxes and to push two of them together; the box-pushing sequence of MACROP2 is used to complete the plan, again with the assistance of the PLANEX scan.

The fifth problem requires the robot to go from one room into a second room, open a door that leads into a third room, go through the third room into a fourth room, and then push together two pairs of boxes. The plan, which is formed by combining all of MACROP4 with all of MACROP3, is well beyond the range of plans producible by STRIPS without the use of MACROPs. Note that although MACROP4 was created by lifting a plan that pushed three boxes together, it has enough generality to handle this form of a four-box problem. Note also that MACROP1, MACROP3, and MACROP4 have been recognized as redundant and deleted, so that the net result of this learning sequence is to add only MACROP2 and MACROP5 to the system.

In Table I we present a table showing the search tree sizes and running times for the five problems. The problems were run both with and without the use of MACROPs for comparison. Even when MACROPs were not being used for planning we include the MACROP production time since PLANEX needs the MACROP to monitor plan execution. Note that the times and the search tree sizes are all smaller when MACROPS are used and that the MACROPs allow longer plans to be formed without necessarily incurring an exponential increase in planning time.

PUSHB(bx,by) *Push bx to object by.*
Preconditions: TYPE(by,OBJECT),PUSHABLE(bx),PUSHABLE(by) ∧ INROOM(by,rx),
(∃rx)[INROOM(bx,rx) ∧ INROOM(by,rx)]
Deletions: AT(ROBOT,$1,$2),NEXTTO(ROBOT,$1),AT(bx,$1,$2),NEXTTO(bx,$1),
NEXTTO($1,bx)
Additions: *NEXTTO(bx,by),NEXTTO(ROBOT,bx)

PUSHD(bx,dx) *Push bx to door dx.*
Preconditions: PUSHABLE(bx),TYPE(dx,DOOR),NEXTTO(ROBOT,bx)
(∃rx)(∃ry)[INROOM(bx,rx) ∧ CONNECTS(dx,rx,ry)]
Deletions: AT(ROBOT,$1,$2),NEXTTO(ROBOT,$1),AT(bx,$1,$2),NEXTTO(bx,$1),
NEXTTO($1,bx)
Additions: *NEXTTO(bx,dx),NEXTTO(ROBOT,bx)

PUSHL(bx,x,y) *Push bx to coordinate location (x,y).*
Preconditions: PUSHABLE(bx),NEXTTO(ROBOT,bx),(∃rx)[INROOM(ROBOT,rx),(∃rx)[INROOM(ROBOT,rx) ∧ LOCINROOM(x,y,rx)]
Deletions: AT(ROBOT,$1,$2),NEXTTO(ROBOT,$1),AT(bx,$1,$2),NEXTTO(bx,$1),
NEXTTO($1,bx)
Additions: *AT(bx,x,y),NEXTTO(ROBOT,bx)

GOTHRUDR(dx,rx) *Go through door dx into room rx.*
Preconditions: TYPE(dx,DOOR),STATUS(dx,OPEN),TYPE(rx,ROOM),
NEXTTO(ROBOT,dx) (∃ry)[INROOM(ROBOT,ry) ∧ CONNECTS(dx,ry,rx)]
Deletions: AT(ROBOT,$1,$2),NEXTTO(ROBOT,$1),INROOM(ROBOT,$1)
Additions: *INROOM(ROBOT,rx)

PUSHTHRUDR(bx,dx,rx) *Push bx through door dx into room rx.*
Preconditions: PUSHABLE(bx),TYPE(dx,DOOR),STATUS(dx,OPEN),TYPE(rx,
ROOM),NEXTTO(bx,dx),NEXTTO(ROBOT,bx),(∃ry)[INROOM(bx,ry) ∧
CONNECTS(dx,ry,rx)]
Deletions: AT(ROBOT,$1,$2),NEXTTO(ROBOT,$1),AT(bx,$1,$2),NEXTTO(bx,$1),
NEXTTO($1,bx),INROOM(ROBOT,$1),INROOM(ROBOT,rx),NEXTTO(ROBOT,bx)
Additions: *INROOM(bx,rx),INROOM(ROBOT,rx),NEXTTO(ROBOT,bx)

OPEN(dx) *Open door dx.*
Preconditions: NEXTTO(ROBOT,dx),TYPE(dx,DOOR),STATUS(dx,CLOSED)
Deletions: STATUS(dx,CLOSED)
Additions: *STATUS(dx,OPEN)

CLOSE(dx) *Close door dx.*
Preconditions: NEXTTO(ROBOT,dx),TYPE(dx,DOOR),STATUS(dx,OPEN)
Deletions: STATUS(dx,OPEN)
Additions: *STATUS(dx,CLOSED)

*Note:* The addition clauses preceded by an asterisk are the *primary additions* of the operator. When STRIPS searches for a relevant operator is considers only these primary addition clauses.

## 7.2. Example Problems

7.2.1. SUMMARY. A sequence of five problems was designed to illustrate the various ways in which MACROPs are used during planning. We show in the next subsection an annotated trace of the system's behaviour for each problem in the sequence. Each trace is preceded by a diagram of the problem's initial and final states, and includes the sequence of subgoal generations and

TABLE I
Statistics for STRIPS behavior

| | PROBLEM 1 | PROBLEM 2 | PROBLEM 3 | PROBLEM 4 | PROBLEM 5 |
|---|---|---|---|---|---|
| **Without MACROPS** | | | | | |
| Total time (minutes) | 3 : 05 | 9 : 42 | 7 : 03 | 14 : 09 | — |
| Time to produce MACROP | 1 : 00 | 1 : 28 | 1 : 11 | 1 : 43 | — |
| Time to find unlifted plan | 2 : 05 | 8 : 14 | 5 : 52 | 12 : 26 | — |
| Total nodes in search tree | 10 | 33 | 22 | 51 | — |
| Nodes on solution path | 9 | 13 | 11 | 15 | — |
| Operators in plan | 4 | 6 | 5 | 7 | — |
| **With MACROPS** | | | | | |
| Total time (minutes) | 3 : 05 | 3 : 54 | 6 : 34 | 4 : 37 | 9 : 13 |
| Time to produce MACROP | 1 : 00 | 1 : 32 | 1 : 16 | 1 : 37 | 3 : 24 |
| Time to find unlifted plan | 2 : 05 | 2 : 22 | 5 : 18 | 3 : 00 | 5 : 49 |
| Total nodes in search tree | 10 | 9 | 14 | 9 | 14 |
| Nodes on solution path | 9 | 9 | 9 | 9 | 14 |
| Operators in plan | 4 | 6 | 5 | 6 | 11 |

STRIPS is written in BBN-LISP and runs as compiled code on a PDP-10 computer under the TENEX time-sharing system.

STRIPS could not solve Problem 5 without using MACROPs.

### 7.2.2. ANNOTATED TRACE OF SYSTEM BEHAVIOR FOR EACH EXAMPLE PROBLEM.

*Problem 1*

G1:  INROOM(ROBOT,RRAM) ∧ NEXTTO(BOX1,BOX2)
*****
     G1 is the task statement.
*****
G2:  Preconditions for PUSHB(BOX2,BOX1)
G3:  Preconditions for GOTOB(BOX2)
*Apply* GOTOB(BOX2)
*Apply* PUSHB(BOX2,BOX1)
G4:  Preconditions for GOTHRUDR(par18,RRAM)
G6:  Preconditions for GOTOD(DRAMCLK)
*****
     G5 was the precondition for an operator that did not appear in the completed plan.
*****

*Apply* GOTOD(DRAMCLK)
*Apply* GOTHRUDR(DRAMCLK,RRAM)
Solution

Form MACROP1(par29,par37,par45,par54,par33)
*****
     The parameter list for a MACROP contains all the parameters that occur in the triangle table.
*****

GOTOB(par29)
PUSHB(par29,par37)
GOTOD(par45)
GOTHRUDR(par45,par54)
*****
     The generalized plan pushes two boxes together and takes the robot into an adjacent room, given that the robot and the boxes are initially all in the same room.
*****

Set first additions row of MACROP1 to 3.
*****
     STRIPS will consider only rows numbered 3 and higher as add lists during planning. Rows 1 and 2 of a triangle table are never considered as add lists since there are no add clauses in Row 1, and the add clauses in Row 2 are redundant with respect to the operator description of the first operator in the MACROP.
*****

*Problem 2*

G1:  INROOM(ROBOT,RPDP) ∧ NEXTTO(BOX2,BOX3)
*****
     G1 is the task statement.
*****
G2:  Preconditions for MACROP1:5(BOX3,BOX2,par3,RPDP,par5)
*****
     The notation MACROP1:5 means that Row 5 of MACROP1 is selected as a relevant add list. MACROP1 is instantiated so that Row 5 contains the relevant clauses INROOM(ROBOT,RPDP) added by GOTHRUDR(par3,RPDP) and NEXTTO(BOX2,BOX3) added by PUSHB(BOX3,BOX2). All four operators in MACROP1 are needed to produce these relevant clauses. No kernels in the triangle table are satisfied. A difference consisting of the single clause INROOM(ROBOT,RCLK) is extracted from the first kernel.
*****

**G1:** INROOM(ROBOT,RPDP)
*****
G1 is the task statement.
*****

**G2:** Preconditions for MACROP2:7(par1,par2,par3,par4,RPDP,par6,par7)
*****
Row 7 of MACROP2 is selected as a relevant add list. MACROP2 is instantiated so that Row 7 contains the relevant clause INROOM-(ROBOT,RPDP) added by GOTHRUDR(par4,RPDP). Only the first, second, fifth, and sixth operators are needed to produce this relevant clause. No kernels in the triangle table are satisfied. A difference consisting of the single clause STATUS(DPDPCLK,OPEN) is extracted from the first kernel.
*****

**G5:** Preconditions for OPEN(DPDPCLK)
*****
After considering two other relevant operators for achieving G1, STRIPS returns to the solution path. OPEN(DPDPCLK) is found to be a relevant operator and a difference consisting of the single clause NEXTTO(ROBOT,DPDPCLK) is extracted from the preconditions.
*****

**G9:** Preconditions for MACROP2:6(par15,par16,par17,DPDPCLK,par19, par20,par21)
*****
After considering three other relevant operators for achieving G5, STRIPS selects Row 6 of MACROP2 as a relevant add list. MACROP2 is instantiated so that Row 6 contains the relevant clause NEXTTO-(ROBOT,DPDPCLK) added by GOTOD(DPDPCLK). Only the first, second, and fifth operators are needed to produce this relevant clause.
*****

Kernel 1 satisfied.
*Apply* GOTOD(DRAMCLK)
*Apply* GOTHRUDR(DRAMCLK,RCLK)
*Apply* GOTOD(DPDPCLK)
*Apply* OPEN(DPDPCLK)
Kernel 6 satisfied
*****
A PLANEX scan is used so that all kernels are checked. Kernel 6 is the precondition for the final operator in the relevant instance of MACROP2.
*****
*Apply* GOTHRUDR(DPDPCLK,RPDP)
Solution

Form MACROP3(par24,par59,par82,par32,par42)
GOTOD(par24)
GOTHRUDR(par24,par42)
GOTOD(par59)
OPEN(par59)
GOTHRUDR(par59,par82)

---

**G3:** Preconditions for MACROP1:5(par17,par18,par19,RCLK,par21)
*****
Row 5 of MACROP1 is again selected as a relevant add list. MACROP1 is instantiated so that Row 5 contains the relevant clause INROOM-(ROBOT,RCLK) added by GOTHRUDR(par19,RCLK). Only the last two operators in MACROP1 are needed to produce the relevant clause.
*****

Kernel 3 satisfied
*****
Kernel 3 is the precondition for the last two operators in MACROP1.
*****

Kernel 1 satisfied
*Apply* GOTOD(DRAMCLK)
*Apply* GOTHRUDR(DRAMCLK,RCLK)

*Apply* GOTOD(DPDPCLK)
*Apply* GOTHRUDR(DPDPCLK,RPDP)
Solution

*Apply* GOTOD(BOX3)
*Apply* PUSHB(BOX3,BOX2)
*Apply* GOTOD(DPDPCLK)
*Apply* GOTHRUDR(DPDPCLK,RPDP)
Solution

Form MACROP2(par27,par52,par72,par91,par111,par38,par40)
GOTOD(par27)
GOTHRUDR(par27,par40)
GOTOD(par52)
PUSHB(par52,par72)
GOTOD(par91)
GOTHRUDR(par91,par111)
*****

The generalized plan takes the robot from one room into an adjacent room, pushes two boxes together in the second room, and then takes the robot into a third room adjacent to the second.
*****

Erase MACROP1.
*****
MACROP1 is completely contained in MACROP2.
*****

Set first additions row of MACROP2 to 4.
*****
The first two operators of MACROP2 match the last two operators of MACROP2.
*****

*Problem 3*

Form MACROP4(par37,par80,par102,par123,par134,par57,par59)
GOTOD(par37)
GOTHRUDR(par37,par59)
GOTOB(par80)
PUSHB(par80,par102)
GOTOB(par123)
PUSHB(par123,par134)

The generalized plan takes the robot from one room into an adjacent room, pushes one box to a second box, and then pushes a third box to a fourth box.
*****

Set first additions row of MACROP2 to 6.
*****

The first 4 operators of MACROP2 match the first 4 operators of MACROP4.
*****

Set first additions row of MACROP4 to 4.
*****

The first 2 operators of MACROP4 match the last 2 operators of MACROP2.
*****

*****
The generalized plan takes the robot from one room into an adjacent room, then to a closed door in the second room, opens the closed door, and then takes the robot through the opened door into a third room.
*****

Set first additions row of MACROP3 to 4.
*****

The first two operators of MACROP3 match the first two operators of MACROP2.
*****

## Problem 4

G1:  NEXTTO(BOX1,BOX2) ∧ NEXTTO(BOX2,BOX3)
*****
G1 is the task statement.
*****

G2:  Preconditions for MACROP2:5(par1,BOX2,BOX1,par4,par5,par6,par7)
*****
Row 5 of MACROP2 is selected as a relevant add list. MACROP2 is instantiated so that Row 5 contains the relevant clause NEXTTO-(BOX1,BOX2) added by PUSHB(BOX2,BOX1). All of the first four operators in MACROP2 are needed to produce this relevant clause.
*****

G3:  Preconditions for MACROP2:5(par19,BOX3,BOX2,par22,par23,par24,par25)
*****
Row 5 of MACROP2 is selected as before. The instantiation is so that Row 5 contains the relevant clause NEXTTO(BOX2,BOX3) added by PUSHB(BOX3,BOX2). Again all of the first four operators are included in the relevant instance of MACROP2
*****

Kernel 1 satisfied
*Apply* GOTOD(DRAMCLK)
*Apply* GOTHRUDR(DRAMCLK,RCLK)
*Apply* GOTOB(BOX2)
*Apply* PUSHB(BOX2,BOX1)

Kernel 3 satisfied
*****
A PLANEX scan is used so that all kernels are checked. Kernel 3 is the precondition for the third and fourth operators.
*****

*Apply* GOTOB(BOX3)
*Apply* PUSHB(BOX3,BOX2)
Solution

## Problem 5

G1:  NEXTTO(BOX1,BOX2) ∧ NEXTTO(BOX3,BOX4)
*****
G1 is the task statement.
*****

G2:  Preconditions for MACROP4:7(par13,BOX2,BOX1,BOX3,BOX4,par18,par19)
*****
Row 7 of MACROP4 is selected as a relevant add list. MACROP4 is instantiated so that Row 7 contains the relevant clauses NEXTTO(BOX1,BOX2) added by PUSHB(BOX2,BOX1) and NEXTTO(BOX3,BOX4) added by PUSHB(BOX3,BOX4). All six operators in MACROP4 are needed to produce these relevant clauses. No kernels in the triangle table are satisfied. A difference consisting of the single clause INROOM(ROBOT,RCLK) is extracted from the first kernel.
*****

G3:  Preconditions for MACROP3:6(par27,par28,RCLK,par30,par31)
*****
Row 6 of MACROP3 is selected as a relevant add list. MACROP3 is instantiated so that Row 6 contains the relevant clause INROOM(ROBOT,RCLK) added by GOTHRUDR(par28,RCLK). All five

robot environment that culminated in the production of a 19-operator plan for fetching three boxes from three different rooms and then pushing the three boxes together. This final MACROP subsumed the seven earlier ones so that only one MACROP was retained by the system. Subsequences of the 19-step MACROP could be used to fetch boxes, push boxes together, move the robot from room to room, etc.

The experiments we have been discussing show the use of MACROPs during planning. We have also run experiments with PLANEX to illustrate the use of MACROPs during plan execution. One such experiment is documented in a report [4] and film [5] that illustrate how PLANEX monitors robot task execution in the seven-room experimental environment. One interesting sequence in this experiment involves the robot attempting to go from one room through a second room into a third room. After entering the second room, the robot discovers that a box is blocking the door that leads into the third room. Since PLANEX is working with a generalized plan, the difficulty can be overcome by finding a different instance of the plan's first kernel that is satisfied. This new instantiation of the plan's parameters causes the robot to be sent from the second room into a fourth room and then into the target third room.

## 8. Conclusions

We have presented in considerable detail methods by which a problem-solving program can "learn" old solutions and use them both to monitor real-world execution and to aid in the solution of new problems. We view these methods as representing only a preliminary excursion into an area that, in the long run, may hold high potential for the design of "intelligent" robots. Before such potential is realized, however, there are a number of substantial technical problems to be solved; in this final section we briefly point out a few of these.

### 8.1. Abstracting Preconditions

It is a commonplace observation that successful problem solvers (human or machine) must plan at a level of detail appropriate to the problem at hand. In typical problem-solving programs, the level of detail is set a priori by the experimenter when he carefully selects the representations employed. This situation changes when the problem solver can create its own MAC-ROPS. Now we have the possibility of creating powerful macro operators whose specification is at the same level of detail as each component operator. In terms of our system, we may create a large triangle table whose preconditions (its first kernel) is the conjunction of so many literals that the theorem prover has little hope of success. What we need is a way of appropriately

---

operators in MACROP3 are needed to produce this relevant clause.
```
*****
Kernel 1 satisfied
  Apply GOTOD(DRAMHAL)
  Apply GOTHRUDR(DRAMHAL,RRAM)
  Apply GOTOD(DRAMCLK)
  Apply OPEN(DRAMCLK)
  Apply GOTHRUDR(DRAMCLK,RCLK)
Kernel 1 satisfied
  Apply GOTOD(DPDPCLK)
  Apply GOTHRUDR(DPDPCLK,RPDP)
  Apply GOTOB(BOX2)
  Apply PUSHB(BOX2,BOX1)
  Apply GOTOB(BOX3)
  Apply PUSHB(BOX3,BOX4)
Solution
```

```
Form MACROP5(par44,par87,par151,par208,par237,par265,par294,par180,par130,
    par64,par66)
  GOTOD(par44)
  GOTHRUDR(par44,par66)
  GOTOD(par87)
  OPEN(par87)
  GOTHRUDR(par87,par130)
  GOTOD(par151)
  GOTHRUDR(par151,par180)
  GOTOB(par208)
  PUSHB(par208,par237)
  GOTOB(par265)
  PUSHB(par265,par294)
*****
```

The generalized plan takes the robot from one room into a second room, opens a door leading to a third room, takes the robot through the third room into a fourth room, and then pushes together two pairs of boxes.
```
*****
```

```
Erase MACROP3.
Erase MACROP4.
*****
MACROP3 and MACROP4 are completely contained in MACROP5.
*****
Set first additions row of MACROP5 to 4.
*****
```

The first two operators of MACROP5 match the sixth and seventh operators of MACROP5.
```
*****
```

### 7.3. Further Experiments

In another set of experiments that were run with the new system, the primary goal was to produce long plans. We ran a sequence of eight problems in our

abstracting the preconditions of a MACROP so that only its "main" preconditions remain. A plan would first be attempted using these abstract preconditions; if successful, a subsequent planning process would fill in the details (and perhaps suggest changes to the abstract plan) as needed. As a rough example of the sort of process we have in mind, suppose we have a MACROP that requires the robot to travel through several doors. An abstract precondition for the MACROP might not contain the requirement that the doors be open on the supposition that, should they be closed, the robot could easily open them at the appropriate time. In whatever manner such a scheme is ultimately implemented, it seems clear that a problem solver will be able to increase its power with experience only if it can use this experience at an appropriate level of abstraction.

## 8.2. Saving MACROPS

We discussed previously a method for discarding a MACROP when it is subsumed by another, more powerful MACROP. In general, any system that learns plans must also either incorporate a mechanism for forgetting old plans or else face the danger of being swamped by an ever-increasing repertoire of stored plans. One straightforward approach to this problem would be to keep some statistics on the frequencies with which the various MACROPS are used, and discard those that fall below some threshold. We have not, however, experimented with any such mechanisms.

## 8.3. Other Forms of Learning

The generalization scheme discussed in this paper is but one of many possible forms of machine learning. Another form of learning that would be interesting to investigate involves reconciling predicted and observed behavior. Suppose, by way of example, that an operator *OP* is originally thought to add Clause *C* whenever it is applied, but suppose we notice that the action corresponding to *OP* consistently fails to add *C*. We would like the system to remedy this situation by taking one of three steps: drop *C* from the add list of *OP*, restrict the preconditions of *OP* to those (if any) that guarantee that *C* is added by the action, or change the actual action routine so that it does in fact behave as originally advertised. While we offer no algorithms for accomplishing these forms of learning, it is interesting to note that the problem itself arises only when we deal with real, as opposed to simulated, robot systems. It is the occurrence of problems of this sort that persuades us of the continuing interest and importance of robot problem solving.

REFERENCES

1. Fikes, R. E. and Nilsson, N. J. STRIPS: A new approach to the application of theorem proving to problem solving. *Artificial Intelligence* **2** (1971), 189–208.

2. Fikes, R. E. Monitored execution of robot plans produced by STRIPS. *Proc. IFIP Congress 71*, Ljubljana, Yugoslavia (August 23–28, 1971).
3. Garvey, T. D. and Kling, R. E. User's Guide to QA3.5 Question-Answering System. Technical Note 15, Artificial Intelligence Group, Stanford Research Institute, Menlo Park, California (December 1969).
4. Raphael, B. et al. Research and Applications—Artificial Intelligence. Final Report, Contract NASW-2164, Stanford Research Institute, Menlo Park, California (December 1971).
5. Hart, P. E. and Nilsson, N. J. Shakey: Experiments in Robot Planning and Learning. Film produced at Stanford Research Institute, Menlo Park, California (1972).
6. Ernst, G. and Newell, A. *GPS: A Case Study in Generality and Problem Solving*. ACM Monograph Series. Academic Press, New York, New York, 1969.

*Received July 1972; revised version received September 1972.*

# LEARNING BY EXPERIMENTATION: ACQUIRING AND REFINING PROBLEM-SOLVING HEURISTICS

Tom M. Mitchell
Paul E. Utgoff
*Rutgers University*

Ranan Banerji
*St. Joseph's University*

## ABSTRACT

This chapter concerns learning heuristic problem-solving strategies through experience. In particular, we focus on the issue of learning heuristics to guide a forward-search problem solver, and describe a computer program called LEX, which acquires problem-solving heuristics in the domain of symbolic integration. LEX acquires and modifies heuristics by iteratively applying the following process: (i) generate a practice problem; (ii) use available heuristics to solve this problem; (iii) analyze the search steps performed in obtaining the solution; and (iv) propose and refine new domain-specific heuristics to improve performance on subsequent problems. We describe the methods currently used by LEX, analyze strengths and weaknesses of these methods, and discuss our current research toward more powerful approaches to learning heuristics.

## 6.1 INTRODUCTION

Efforts to build powerful, specialized, heuristic problem solvers have met with increasing success over the past decade. However, identifying and encoding the domain-specific heuristics necessary for high performance of these systems is a painstaking, difficult process. As the complexity of a heuristic program grows, it becomes increasingly difficult for the system builder to predict how the addition of a particular new heuristic or operator will affect overall system performance. In response to this problem, there has been increased interest over the past several years in developing semi-automated and fully-automated methods to help construct expert heuristic problem solvers [Waterman, 1970; Davis, 1981; Buchanan, 1978; Politakis, 1979] (See also Chapter 7 of this book). At the same time, in the Cognitive Psychology literature there have been several attempts to model acquisition of problem-solving skills in humans [Anzai, 1979; Neves, 1978] (See also Chapter 7 of this book).

The research presented here is directed toward devising methods by which heuristic problem-solving programs improve their problem-solving expertise through experience, by generating selected problems in the domain, solving them, and learning by analyzing their solutions. As part of this research we have designed and constructed a computer program, called LEX, that incorporates general methods for discovering domain-dependent problem-solving heuristics.

The organization of this chapter is as follows. The learning problem considered by LEX is described, followed by a discussion of the methods employed by the current system. This includes methods for (i) solving practice problems, (ii) performing the *credit assignment* task of isolating appropriate and inappropriate search steps, (iii) proposing and generalizing heuristics, and (iv) generating new practice problems with which to experiment. The final sections of the chapter discuss augmenting the system by giving it knowledge to conduct detailed analyses of problem solutions. This knowledge can be used to provide strong guidance for the generalization process, and to generate new terms in the language with which heuristics are described. Some of the material from this chapter is drawn from a collection of previously published articles, including [Mitchell, 1981; Mitchell, 1982a; Mitchell, 1982b; Utgoff, 1982].

## 6.2 THE PROBLEM

LEX begins with a heuristic search problem solver without the heuristics. It is given a set of operators for solving problems in symbolic integration, and it learns a set of heuristics that recommend in which situations the various operators should be applied. Whereas each operator given to LEX contains a set of preconditions that characterize a class of problem states to which that operator *can* validly be applied, learned heuristics characterize the more restrictive subclass of problem states to which the operator *should* be applied; that is, the subclass of problem states for which application of the operator leads to an acceptable solution. Heuristics are learned by *generalizing from examples* of problem states to which the operator is applied in solving practice problems. These training examples are generated by the program, by proposing, solving, and analyzing practice problems.

LEX operates in the domain of symbolic integration. It solves integration problems by searching through a space of mathematical expressions containing indefinite integrals. The operators for traversing the search space are the standard rules of integration (for instance, integration by parts) as well as transformations that characterize algebraic equivalence of expressions (such as the associative and distributive laws). The problem-solving goal is to derive a problem state that contains no integrals.

| | | |
|---|---|---|
| OP1 | $\int r \cdot f(x)\,dx$ | ⟶ $r \int f(x)\,dx$ |
| OP2 | Integration by parts: |
| | $\int u\,dv$ ⟶ $uv - \int v\,du$ |
| | (the precondition is internally represented as $\int f1(x)\ f2(x)\,dx$, where $f1(x)$ corresponds to $u$ and $f2(x)\,dx$ corresponds to $dv$) |
| OP3 | $1 \cdot f(x)$ ⟶ $f(x)$ |
| OP4 | $\int f1(x)+f2(x)\,dx$ ⟶ $\int f1(x)\,dx + \int f2(x)\,dx$ |
| OP5 | $\int \sin(x)\,dx$ ⟶ $-\cos(x) + C$ |
| OP6 | $\int \cos(x)\,dx$ ⟶ $\sin(x) + C$ |
| OP7 | $\int x^r\,dx$ ⟶ $[x^{(r+1)}]/(r+1) + C$ |

**Figure 6-1:** Some of the operators for symbolic integration.

Over 40 problem-solving operators are currently provided to LEX, some of which are shown in Figure 6-1. Each operator is interpreted as follows: If the general pattern on the left hand side of the operator is found within the problem state, then that pattern may be replaced by the pattern specified on the right hand side of the operator. For example, op1 indicates that if the problem state contains a subexpression of the form "$\int r \cdot f(x)\,dx$" (here "r" stands for any real number, and "f(x)" for any function of x), then that subexpression may be rewritten with the real number outside the integral.

In addition to its problem solver, representation for problem states, and problem-solving operators, LEX also begins with a language for describing heuristics. Each heuristic learned by LEX is of the form:

IF the current problem state matches the applicability condition P,
    THEN apply operator O, with variable binding B.

Thus, the generalization task that LEX faces is that of determining the appropriate applicability condition, P, for each heuristic. Learning this applicability condition corresponds to learning the concept "situations in which operator O should be applied, with variable binding B."

The language for describing generalizations, or applicability conditions, of heuristics is based on a grammar for algebraic expressions containing indefinite integrals. The sentences derivable by this grammar are the expressions that form legal problem states. The sentential forms derivable by the grammar constitute legal generalizations. Briefly, the grammar contains non-terminal symbols that correspond to classes of functions (for example, trigonometric, polynomial) and classes of operators (such as function composition, multiplication, integration). These can be combined to form generalized algebraic expressions. Figure 6-2 shows this grammar in the form of a hierarchy. Each node in the hierarchy represents some substring of a sentential form, and each edge corresponds to a rule in the grammar.

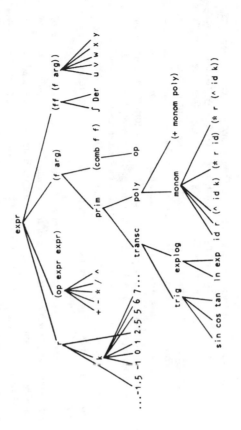

**Figure 6-2:** A grammar for a concept description language for symbolic integration.

Below is an example of the kind of heuristics that LEX can describe and learn. This heuristic may be interpreted as "*If* the current problem state contains an integrand which is the product of x and any transcendental function of x, *Then* try integration by parts, with u and dv bound to the indicated subexpressions."

$$\int x\,\mathrm{transc}(x)\,dx \Rightarrow \mathrm{op2}\ \text{(Integration by parts)},$$
$$\text{with } u = x$$
$$\text{and } dv = \mathrm{transc}(x)\,dx$$

The language used to describe applicability conditions of heuristics determines, to a great extent, the range of heuristics that can be learned by the system. In the current system, this language is fixed. Section 6.4 discusses an approach to dynamically altering the language when necessary.

## 6.3 DESIGN OF LEX

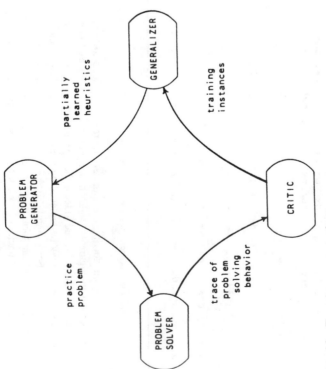

**Figure 6-3:** The major components of LEX.

LEX is based on four program modules, as shown in Figure 6-3. These modules are summarized below, and described in more detail in the following subsections.

1. **Problem Solver**—This module utilizes whatever operators and heuristics are currently available, to solve a given practice problem. The output of this module is a solution to the given problem, along with a detailed trace of the search performed in attempting to solve the problem.

2. **Critic**—This module analyzes the search performed by the Problem Solver. The output of this module is a set of positive and negative training instances from which heuristics will be inferred. Positive instances correspond to desirable search steps executed in solving the problem, whereas negative instances correspond to undesirable steps.

3. **Generalizer**—This module proposes and refines general heuristics intended to produce more effective problem-solving behavior on subsequent problems. It formulates heuristics by generalizing from the training instances provided by the Critic.

4. **Problem Generator**—This module generates practice problems to be considered by the other modules. It attempts to generate practice problems that will be informative (that is, problems that will lead to training data useful for proposing and refining heuristics), yet easy enough to be solved using existing heuristics.

### 6.3.1 Representing Incompletely-learned Heuristics

LEX learns heuristics incrementally, requiring many positive and negative training instances before converging to a final definition of any given heuristic. Therefore, at any given stage in the system's development, there are typically many partially-learned heuristics whose exact description is underdetermined by the data, knowledge, and assumptions currently held by the system. It is essential that the system have a way of describing what the system *does* and *does not* know about each such partially-learned heuristic. This information is important (*i*) to the Problem Solver, which must use the partially-learned heuristics in trying to solve problems, (*ii*) to the Generalizer, which must revise partially-learned heuristics as new training data become available, and (*iii*) to the Problem Generator, which must choose practice problems that will lead to refinements of partially-learned heuristics.

LEX represents each partially-learned heuristic by representing the range of *all alternative plausible descriptions of the heuristic*. A description is considered plausible if it applies to all the known positive instances associated with the heuristic, but to none of the negative instances. Thus, for each partially-learned heuristic, we refer to the set of all plausible descriptions of the heuristic as the *version space* of the partially-learned heuristic, relative to the observed instances and the language in which heuristics are described.

While, in principle, the version space of a partially-learned heuristic could be represented by listing all of its members, there are typically far too many plausible descriptions of a heuristic for this to be feasible. Fortunately, a much more compact method for representing version spaces is possible. Any version space can be represented compactly by storing only its maximally-specific and maximally-general elements, according to the following definition of "more specific".

amples has been used previously in the META-DENDRAL program for inferring rules of mass spectroscopy, and is described more fully in [Mitchell, 1978] and [Mitchell, 1982a]. In [Mitchell, 1978] a more formal definition of version spaces is given, along with proofs that the algorithm for incrementally updating the sets S and G is correct.

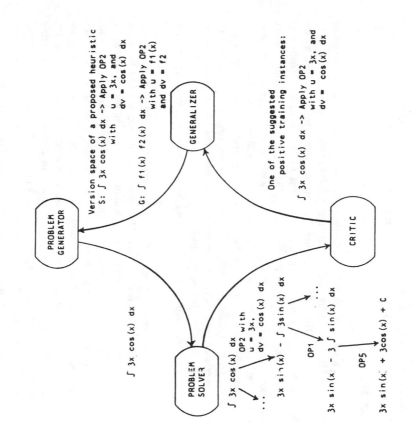

**Figure 6-5:** The learning cycle in LEX.

The remainder of this section presents the methods used by the four modules of LEX, in formulating and refining heuristics. The discussion centers around the example shown in Figure 6-5, which illustrates one particular practice problem considered by LEX, and the resulting version space of one heuristic. This figure shows the search tree generated by the Problem Solver, one of the training instances produced by the Critic, and the sets S and G computed by the Generalizer to describe the resulting proposed heuristic.

---

Heuristic H1 is **more specific than or equal to** heuristic H2 if and only if both of the following conditions hold:

1. The applicability condition of H2 matches every instance matched by the applicability condition of H1 (that is, the applicability condition of H1 is more specific than or equal to the applicability condition of H1).

2. In each case where both H1 and H2 apply, their recommendations are identical (that is, they recommend the same operator and the same binding of operator arguments).

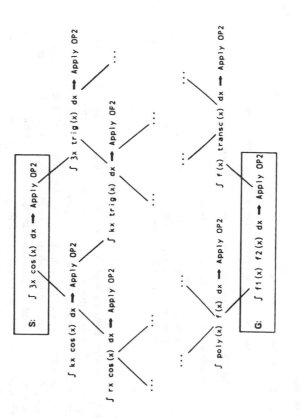

**Figure 6-4:** Representing a version space.

We will refer to the maximally-specific members of a version space as the subset S of the version space, and to the maximally-general (minimally-specific) members of the version space as the subset G. LEX represents the version space of each partially-learned heuristic by storing the subsets S and G of that version space, as illustrated in Figure 6-4. In this figure, some of the members of a particular version space are shown, with the more-specific-than relationship among them indicated. While there are very many plausible heuristic descriptions in this version space, the (singleton) sets S and G completely determine the version space by the following rule: a heuristic description is contained in the version space if and only if it is both (i) more specific than or equal to some member of G, and (ii) more general than or equal to some member of S. This representation and use of version spaces for generalizing from ex-

trol search is important in allowing it to solve problems that will provide additional training data. In experiments with LEX, it has typically been the case that the majority of available heuristics are only partially learned. Even so, it is quite common that a partially-learned heuristic will apply to a particular node with a degree of match of 1. In such cases, even though the exact identity of the heuristic is not yet determined, the applicability of the heuristic to this particular node is fully determined (that is, it does not matter which of the alternative heuristic descriptions is correct, since they all apply to the node in question). The ability to distinguish such cases from those in which there is ambiguity regarding the heuristic recommendation is an important capability in the Problem Solver's use of partially-learned heuristics.

### 6.3.2 The Problem Solver

The Problem Solver uses a forward-search strategy guided by whatever heuristics are available during the current propose-solve-criticize-generalize cycle. The Problem Solver accepts as input a problem to be solved, along with a resource limit on the CPU time and memory space that it may expend in attempting to solve that problem. If the problem is not solved within the allocated resources, the Problem Solver stops and waits for a new problem.[1] Unsolved problems do not lead to any learning, because the credit assignment strategy of the Critic depends upon obtaining the problem solution.

The Problem Solver generates a search tree, repeatedly choosing a node to expand and an operator with which to expand it, as shown below.

DO UNTIL problem is solved OR resource allocation is expended

BEGIN

IF no heuristics are applicable to any open node

THEN expand the lowest cost open node, using any applicable operator

ELSE IF exactly one heuristic applies to exactly one open node,

THEN execute the step recommended by that heuristic,

ELSE follow the recommendation of one of the applicable heuristics, choosing that heuristic which applies with the highest estimated degree of match (see explanation below).

END.

Here, the "cost" of a node refers to the sum of CPU time expended for each step leading from the root of the tree to that node. An open node refers to any node in the search tree with at least one applicable operator that has not yet been applied. The notion of "estimated degree of match" of a heuristic to a node is introduced to allow using partially-learned heuristics in a reasonable fashion. Notice that for a given partially-learned heuristic and search node, it is possible that some of the alternative plausible descriptions of the heuristic will match the node while others will not. Because of this we define the degree of match of a partially-learned heuristic to a given node as the proportion of the members of its version space that match the node. Because the degree of match is difficult to compute exactly, it is estimated by the proportion of members in the union of S and G that match the given problem state.

The ability of the Problem Solver to use partially-learned heuristics to con-

### 6.3.3 The Critic

After a solution has been determined, the Critic faces the task of assigning credit (or blame) to individual search steps for their role in leading to (or away from) a solution. The Critic examines the detailed search trace recorded by the Problem Solver, and selects certain search steps to be classified as positive or negative training instances for forming general heuristics. Each training instance corresponds to a single search step; that is, the application of a single operator to a given problem state, with a particular binding of operator arguments.

Figure 6-5 illustrates part of the search tree generated by the Problem Solver for a given practice problem, and one of the associated positive training instances produced by the Critic. The positive instance shown there corresponds to the first step along the path to the solution.

The criterion used by the Critic to produce training instances may be summarized as follows:

1. The Critic labels as a *positive instance* every search step along the lowest cost solution path found. Here, the cost of a solution is taken to be the sum of the execution times of all operators applied along the solution path.

2. The Critic labels as a *negative instance* every search step that (i) leads away from a node on the lowest cost solution path found, to a node not on this path, and (ii) when its resulting problem state is given anew to the Problem Solver, leads either to no solution or to a higher cost solution. Here a solution is considered higher cost if its cost is more than a certain factor times the cost of the lowest cost known solution (currently this factor is set to 1.15). The resource allocation given to the Problem Solver in this case is equal to the resources spent in obtaining the known solution.

Notice that the Critic is not infallible. It is possible for the Critic to produce positive training instances that are not on the minimum cost solution path, but are rather on the lowest cost solution path found by the Problem Solver. Also, it is possible for the Critic to label as negative a search step that is in fact part of the true (but never discovered) minimum cost solution path. Both

---

[1]LEX makes no distinction between problems that are unsolvable in principle, and those that are solvable in principle but unsolvable within the given resource limits.

kinds of errors can arise because the heuristic Problem Solver is not assured of finding the minimum cost solution. Criterion 2(ii) above is included in order to reduce the likelihood that such errors will occur. Here, the Critic reinvokes the Problem Solver, giving it a problem state associated with a potential negative instance, in order to explore a portion of the problem space that may not have been sufficiently considered during the solution of the original problem. If the Problem Solver is unable to find an appropriate solution from the given state within the specified resource limits, the confidence that this is a negative instance is increased. If the Problem Solver finds a lower cost solution when it is reinvoked, this new solution is used in determining positive training instances. Of course, the only completely error-free strategy for labeling training instances requires a full breadth-first or uniform-cost search, which is usually prohibitively time consuming.

The Critic typically produces between two and twenty training instances from each solved problem, depending upon the length of the problem solution and the branching factor of the search (the search trees produced by the Problem Solver typically contain from a few to a few hundred search nodes). We have found empirically that even though the Critic cannot guarantee correct classifications, it rarely produces incorrect training instances. We have also found that in a significant number of cases, when the Critic calls the Problem Solver to consider a possible negative instance (see criterion 2(ii) above) an improved solution is found. For example, in one run of LEX for a sequence of 12 training problems, this occurred 4 times. In those cases in which the Problem Solver does not find the best solution during its first attempt, the cause is usually a misleading recommendation by an incompletely-learned heuristic.

### 6.3.4 The Generalizer

The Generalizer considers the positive and negative training instances supplied by the Critic within the current learning cycle, in order to propose and refine heuristics to improve problem-solving performance. The generalization problem faced by this module is one of learning from examples. Given a sequence of training instances corresponding to search steps involving a given operator, the generalization problem here is to infer the general class of problem states for which this operator will be useful, along with the range of appropriate bindings for operator variables.

The Generalizer describes the version space for each proposed heuristic, by computing the sets S and G that delimit the plausible versions of that heuristic. For example, Figure 6-5 shows a positive training instance associated with op2 as input to the Generalizer. The output of the Generalizer in this case is a version space corresponding to a partially-learned heuristic, and represented by the (singleton) sets S and G shown in Figure 6-5. This partially-learned heuristic is proposed on the basis of the single training instance shown, and will be refined as subsequent instances become available. Below, we describe the procedures for proposing and refining problem-solving heuristics in LEX.

**Proposing a new heuristic**—When the Generalizer is given a new positive instance, it determines whether any member of the version space of any current heuristic applies to this instance. If not, a new heuristic is formed to cover the positive instance. This is the case in the example of Figure 6-5. In forming a new heuristic, the set S is initialized to the very specific version of the heuristic, that applies *only* to the current positive training instance (this is the most specific possible version consistent with the single observed training instance). G is initialized to the version of the heuristic that suggests the operator will prove useful in *every* situation where it can validly be applied; that is, it is initialized to the given precondition of the operator being recommended. Thus, in the example of Figure 6-5, G is initialized to the version whose precondition is the precondition for op2. Here, $\int f1(x) \ f2(x) \ dx$ represents the integral of the product of any two real functions of x, and corresponds to the precondition $\int u \ dv$ as it is stated in the system's generalization language.

At this point, S and G delimit a broad range of alternative versions of the proposed heuristic, corresponding to *all* the generalizations expressible in the given language that are consistent with this single training instance. As subsequent positive instances are considered, S becomes more general to include newly-observed instances in which op2 is found to be useful. Likewise, as subsequent negative instances are considered, G becomes more specific in order to exclude negative instances in which op2 may validly be applied, but in which it does not lead to an acceptable solution path. Thus, the range of alternative plausible versions of the heuristic delimited by S and G will narrow as new information is acquired through subsequent practice problems, and the uncertainty regarding the correct description of the heuristic is thereby reduced.

**Refining incompletely-learned heuristics**—If the Generalizer finds that an existing heuristic applies to a newly-presented positive or negative instance (that is, if its degree of match to the instance is nonzero), then that heuristic is revised by eliminating from its version space any version that is inconsistent with this training instance. In the current example, the next practice problem that is considered is $\int 3x \ \sin(x) \ dx$ (the following section explains why). The solution to this problem leads to both a positive and a negative training instance for the heuristic from Figure 6-5. Figure 6-6 shows these two new training instances, and the way in which they lead to a refinement of the version space of this heuristic. In the revised version space shown there, the most specific version, S, of the heuristic has been generalized just enough to allow it to apply to the new positive training instance. Here trig(x) replaces cos(x) so that the heuristic will apply to integrals containing *any* trigonometric function of x. The program determines this revision by first noting that the term cos(x) in the old S prevents the generalization from applying to the new instance. It then consults the grammar for expressing heuristics (shown in Figure 6-2) to determine the next more general term that can be substituted in order to include this new instance.[2]

The general boundary of the revised version space of Figure 6-6 has also been altered so that it does not apply to the new negative training instance. In this case, there are two maximally-general versions (g1 and g2) of the heuristic consistent with the three observed training instances. Here, "poly(x)" refers to any polynomial function of x, and "transc(x)" denotes any transcendental function of x. As with revising the set S, revisions to G depend upon the generalization language being used. For instance, g1 is computed by replacing f1(x) (which represents "any real-valued function") by the next more specific acceptable expression. Notice in the hierarchy of Figure 6-2, this expression is "poly".

As subsequent training instances are considered, this partially-learned heuristic is further refined, and S and G converge to the heuristic description shown below. Notice that this description is contained in the version space represented in Figure 6-6, since it is more general than the S boundary set and more specific than the G boundary set of the version space.

$$\int rx\ \text{transc}(x)\ dx \rightarrow \text{apply op2 with } u = rx, \text{ and } dv = \text{transc}(x)\ dx$$

Although the Generalizer attempts to form a single conjunctive heuristic for each operator known to the system, sometimes it is not possible to cover all the positive instances and exclude all the negative instances with a single conjunctive generalization. The Generalizer deals with learning disjunctions in the following straightforward manner: if a positive instance associated with operator O is not consistent with any current heuristic that recommends operator O, then it proposes a new heuristic (that is, disjunct) for operator O that covers this instance. This new heuristic will be updated by all subsequent negative instances associated with operator O, and by any subsequent positive instances with operator O and to which at least some member of its version space applies. This technique for learning disjunctive concepts is similar to several described previously (for example, [Mitchell, 1978; Iba, 1979; Vere, 1978]).

How effective is the Generalizer at producing useful heuristics? One way to answer this question is to measure the improvement in problem-solving performance due to learned heuristics. In one experiment that illustrates typical behavior of LEX, a sequence of twelve hand-selected[3] training problems was presented to the Problem Solver, Critic, and Generalizer, and performance of the Problem Solver was measured at various stages in the training sequence. Perfor-

---

[2]Although the disjunction "cos(x) OR sin(x)" would be a more specific generalization than "trig", this disjunction is not currently in the generalization language, and therefore cannot be stated by the program. Of course if this disjunction were defined *a priori* as a separate term in the language, then it would be considered by the Generalizer.

[3]At the time that this experiment was conducted, we had not implemented the Problem Generator module.

```
Version Space of Heuristic

    S: ∫ 3x cos(x) dx -> Apply OP2 with
                         u = 3x, and
                         dv = cos(x) dx

    G: ∫ f1(x) f2(x) dx -> Apply OP2 with
                           u = f1(x), and
                           dv = f2(x)dx


New Training Instances:

    Positive training instance:

        ∫ 3x sin(x) dx -> Apply OP2 with
                          u = 3x, and
                          dv = sin(x) dx

    Negative training instance:

        ∫ 3x sin(x) dx -> Apply OP2 with
                          u = sin(x), and
                          dv = 3x dx


Revised Version Space:

    S: ∫ 3x trig(x) dx -> Apply OP2 with
                          u = 3x, and
                          dv = trig(x) dx

    G:
      g1: ∫ poly(x) f2(x) dx -> Apply OP2 with
                                u = poly(x), and
                                dv = f2(x) dx

      g2: ∫ f1(x) transc(x) dx -> Apply OP2
                                  with u = f1(x), and
                                  dv = transc(x) dx
```

**Figure 6-6:** Revising the version space of a heuristic.

ing problem, only four of the test problems could be solved after the sixth training problem. This phenomenon was due to the proposal of new, partially-learned heuristics that led the Problem Solver to consider new (and not very useful) branches of the search in one of the test problems. Subsequent training refined these heuristics and the Problem Solver became able again to solve (this time more efficiently) all five test problems by the completion of the eighth training problem.

### 6.3.5 The Problem Generator

After a practice problem has been solved and analyzed, and the resulting training data has been used to propose and refine heuristics, the Problem Generator must propose a new practice problem. This module is responsible for focusing the system's efforts on useful activity, by choosing useful experiments. Its task is very different from that of a teacher of symbolic integration, or an outside trainer in most work on learning from examples. In contrast to an expert teacher, the Problem Generator must choose appropriate practice problems *without knowing* the heuristics that it is trying to teach. While the Problem Generator lacks this important information, it has other information that an expert teacher may not have: very detailed knowledge about the learner's current state (including knowledge of alternative versions of heuristics under consideration). As a result of these characteristics, the experimentation strategy of the Problem Generator is based primarily on generating problems designed to eliminate known ambiguities in LEX's heuristic knowledge.

The major criteria for generating problems are (i) to generate training problems whose solutions will provide informative new training data, and (ii) to generate training problems that can be solved using the available operators and current set of heuristics. The current implementation of the Problem Generator is based mainly on the first of these considerations, and consists of two different problem generation tactics.

The first problem generation tactic is to produce problems that will allow refinement of existing, partially-learned heuristics. This is done by selecting a partially-learned heuristic, then generating a problem state that matches some, but not all, of the members of the version space of that heuristic. For example, consider the partially-learned heuristic described by the version space at the top of Figure 6-6. The problem state $\int 3x \sin(x) \, dx$ matches some, but not all, of the alternative generalizations in this version space, and is therefore a useful problem to attempt to solve. By solving the problem, LEX will find out whether or not the heuristic should cover this problem state. If the answer is yes, a positive instance will be produced for this heuristic, and the S boundary of the version space will be generalized. If the answer is no, a negative instance will be produced, and the G boundary of the version space will be specialized. As it turns out, this problem leads to both a positive and a negative instance (corresponding to different bindings of operator arguments), and both version space boundaries are refined as shown in Figure 6-6.

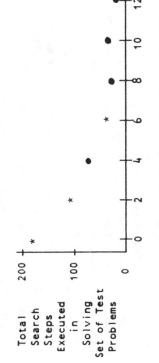

**Figure 6-7:** *Performance Results*

mance was measured by testing the Problem Solver on a set of five test problems before any training had occurred, and again after every second training problem. The five test problems were different from the set of twelve training problems, though the two sets were chosen to be similar enough that learned heuristics would be relevant to the test problems. This experiment is reported in greater detail in [Mitchell, 1981], and is summarized in Figure 6-7.

Fourteen heuristics were formed by LEX during this training session, covering thirteen of the 32 operators available to the system at that time. Twelve of these fourteen heuristics remained incompletely learned at the end of the training sequence (that is, their version space still contained multiple plausible descriptions of the heuristic).

Figure 6-7 shows the improvement in problem-solving performance (roughly two orders of magnitude) for this experiment, as measured by the total number of search steps required in attempting to solve the five test problems. At certain points during the training, the Problem Solver could not solve all five test problems within the given resource allocation.[4] Such points are shown as a "*" in Figure 6-7, and the number of search steps recorded in those cases is the number of steps executed before the solution attempt was aborted. While the exact values of the points on this curve would be different for different sets of training and test problems, the general form of the curve is quite repeatable, given reasonable test problems and a well-chosen sequence of training problems.

In addition to observing that problem-solving performance improved significantly using the learned heuristics, it is interesting to note that problem-solving performance did not improve monotonically as a function of training. In particular, while all five test problems could be solved following the fourth train-

---

[4]The Problem Solver was allowed four CPU minutes and 800,000 cons cells per test problem, running in RUCLISP on a DEC2060.

into account the reason why the current problem has been suggested, and focus their activity accordingly. For example, if a problem is suggested in order to refine a particular heuristic, then the Problem Solver and Critic should be sure to consider the search steps that become training instances for that heuristic, and the Critic might allocate greater resources to obtain a reliable classification of that training instance.

- While the tactics described above are generally successful at creating informative problems to consider, they are not always successful at creating *solvable* problems. Some problems that are generated are simply not solvable with the set of operators known to the system. Other generated problems are solvable in principle, but cannot be solved within the allocated CPU time and space resources, using existing heuristics. In our initial experiments, more than half the generated problems turned out to be solved by the Problem Solver. Both of the current tactics produce a generalization which can be instantiated in any fashion to produce an informative problem. The instantiation is then controlled by a single heuristic: try to create a problem state that is as similar as possible to a previously-solved problem. More reliable methods for creating solvable instances of problems may require that the system have (or acquire) more appropriate knowledge about the characteristics of solvable problems.

- It may be useful to introduce a new tactic that produces problems that are guaranteed to be solvable, by beginning with a goal state, then applying inverses of the known operators to produce a problem state with a known solution. While the solution produced along with the problem will not necessarily be the optimal solution, it will provide an upper bound on the cost of the optimal solution. For this tactic to be useful, there must be a way of selecting sequences of operators that produce informative as well as solvable problems.

- There are also interesting questions to be considered regarding global strategies for exploring the problem domain. For example, should the Problem Generator focus first on refining existing heuristics, and then suggest problems that lead to new heuristics? Or is it better to build up a more broad set of heuristics, focusing at each step on problem types for which no heuristics yet exist, leaving refinement of these heuristics until a broad set of incompletely-determined heuristics are proposed?

## 6.4  NEW DIRECTIONS: ADDING KNOWLEDGE TO AUGMENT LEARNING

The current LEX system, as described in the previous section, is able to learn useful problem-solving heuristics in the domain of symbolic integration, by generalizing from self-generated examples. There are several features of the design of LEX that have an important impact on its capabilities. The ability to represent incompletely-learned heuristics is crucial; to the Problem Solver that

How does the Problem Generator create a problem that matches part of a given version space? It begins by selecting a single member, s1, of the S boundary, and a more general member, g1, of the G boundary. (In the version space at the top of Figure 6-6 both boundary sets happen to be singleton sets.) It then creates, as follows, a problem state that matches g1, but does not match s1. One term in the generalization s1 is selected (in this case $\cos(x)$), and the corresponding term in g1 is found (in this case $f2(x)$). The generalization hierarchy (see Figure 6-2) is then examined to determine a sibling of the term from s1, that is more specific than the corresponding term from g1. In this case, $\sin(x)$ is a sibling of $\cos(x)$ that is more specific than $f2(x)$. This sibling is then substituted into s1, and the resulting generalization is fully instantiated to produce a problem state that matches g1, but not the original s1. In the current example, this leads to the problem state $\int 3x \sin(x)\, dx$. Notice that if the term $3x$ were chosen, rather than $\cos(x)$, as the basis for forming a new problem state, the new problem might instead be $\int 7x \cos(x)\, dx$. Furthermore, both of these terms could be replaced to produce the problem state $\int 7x \sin(x)\, dx$. Because of the need to create a problem that can be solved, the Problem Generator attempts to create a problem that is very similar to the most recently encountered positive instance for the heuristic. Therefore, only a single term from s1 is altered, and the resulting generalization is instantiated to correspond as closely as possible to the most recently encountered positive instance (a known solvable problem).

The second tactic for problem generation is to create a problem that will lead to proposing a new heuristic. This is accomplished by looking for pairs of operators whose preconditions intersect, but for which there is no current heuristic. Should a problem be encountered for which both operators apply, a heuristic will be needed to choose which of the two to apply. For example, consider op1 and op3 from Figure 6-1. The intersection of the preconditions of these operators is $\int 1 \cdot f(x)\, dx$; that is, both op1 and op3 will apply to any problem that matches this applicability condition. This applicability condition is therefore instantiated to produce a specific problem state (such as $\int 1 \cdot \cos(x)\, dx$) which is then output by the Problem Generator. When the Problem Solver, Critic, and Generalizer consider this problem, a new heuristic will be proposed which will be useful in selecting between op1 and op3 in cases where they are both applicable.

The current Problem Generator incorporates the above two tactics for creating practice problems, and can employ any of several strategies for determining which tactic to apply at any given step. One such experimentation strategy is to apply the first tactic (refine an existing heuristic) whenever possible, and to apply the second tactic only when the first cannot be applied (for example, when the system begins operation and has no heuristics at all). While we have not yet done extensive testing of this module, it has been used to generate sequences of practice problems that lead to useful heuristics. The main observations that have come out of our preliminary experiments with this module are given below.

- It will be useful to extend the other system modules so that they can take

must use these partially-learned heuristics in order to solve additional practice problems to obtain additional training data; to the Generalizer that must refine these heuristics; and to the Problem Generator that must be able to consider alternative plausible descriptions of a heuristic in order to suggest an informative practice problem. The ability of the Critic to produce reliable training instances is also crucial to system performance. In spite of the heuristic nature of the Critic's credit assignment method (following from the fact that only part of the search space is explored by the Problem Solver), the Critic in fact performs quite well in producing reliable classifications of training instances. Its ability to call the Problem Solver in a controlled manner to explore selected portions of the search space is important to increasing the reliability of its classifications of training instances. The Generalizer's use of the version space method for generalizing from examples is also a major feature of LEX, which gives it the capability to incrementally converge on heuristics consistent with a sequence of training instances observed over the course of many practice problems.

While LEX is able to learn useful heuristics, it also has significant limitations. One of the most fundamental difficulties is that learning is strongly tied to the language used to describe heuristics—the system can only learn heuristics that it can represent in the provided language. It is difficult to manually select an appropriate language before learning occurs, and LEX often fails to converge on an acceptable heuristic for a given set of training instances, simply because it does not have the appropriate vocabulary for stating the heuristic. For example, we have found that the addition of terms such as "odd integer" and "twice integrable function" to the language shown in Figure 6-2, would allow LEX to describe (and therefore learn) heuristics that it cannot currently represent. This constraint imposed by a fixed representation language is one of the most fundamental difficulties associated with current approaches to learning from examples.

A second deficiency of LEX is its failure to take advantage of an important source of information for chosing an appropriate generalization: analysis of *why* a particular search step was useful in the context of the overall problem solution. By analyzing the role of a particular search step in leading to a problem solution, it is sometimes possible for humans to determine a very good general heuristic after observing only a single training instance. If LEX were to conduct such an analysis, it would converge much more quickly on appropriate heuristics, possibly with less sensitivity to classification errors by the Critic.

In this section, we describe our current research toward giving LEX new knowledge and reasoning capabilities to overcome the above limitations. In particular, we consider how knowledge about heuristic search and about the intended purpose of learned heuristics could allow LEX to (i) derive justifiable generalizations of heuristics via analysis of individual training instances, and (ii) respond to situations in which the vocabulary for describing heuristics is insufficient to characterize a given set of training instances. More detailed discussions of this material can be found in [Mitchell, 1982b] and [Utgoff, 1982]. The kind of knowledge considered here, regarding the intended purpose of learned heuristics, is one kind of meta-knowledge that can be useful in acquiring these heuristics. The importance of meta-knowledge in acquiring problem-solving strategies is also discussed in other chapters of this book, such as Chapters 9 and 12.

### 6.4.1 Describing the Learner's Goal

In order to reason about *why* a given training instance is positive, and to determine which features of the training instance are relevant, it is necessary that the system have a definition of the criterion by which the instance is labeled as positive (that is, the criterion that determines the goal of its learning activity). LEX is intended to learn heuristics that lead the Problem Solver to minimum cost solutions of symbolic integration problems. This goal is implicit in the credit assignment procedure used by the Critic, which attempts to classify individual search steps as positive or negative according to this criterion. While this criterion is currently defined procedurally within the Critic, it is not defined declaratively, and the system therefore cannot reason symbolically about its learning goal. Here we present a declarative representation of this credit assignment criterion, then discuss in subsequent subsections how this knowledge provides the starting point for analyzing training instances, and extending the vocabulary of the language for describing heuristics.

To simplify the examples and discussion here, we assume a slightly modified credit assignment criterion, for which the goal of LEX is to learn heuristics that recommend problem-solving steps that lead to *any* solution (rather than the minimum cost solution). In this case, any search step that applies some operator, $op$, to some problem state, $state$, is a positive instance, provided it satisfies the predicate PosInst defined as follows:

$$\text{PosInst}(op, state) \Leftrightarrow$$
$$\sim\text{Goal}(state) \wedge [\,\text{Goal}(\text{Apply}(op, state)) \vee \text{Solvable}(\text{Apply}(op, state))].$$

Here, Goal is the predicate for recognizing solution states, Apply is the function for applying operators to states, and Solvable is the predicate that tests whether a state can be transformed to a Goal state with the available operators.

Solvable is defined as follows:

$$\text{Solvable}(state) \Leftrightarrow$$
$$(\exists\, op)\,[\text{Goal}(\text{Apply}(op, state)) \vee \text{Solvable}(\text{Apply}(op, state))]$$

### 6.4.2 Analyzing Training Instances to Guide Generalization

This section suggests how the declarative representation of the credit assignment criterion, PosInst, could be used by LEX to produce a justifiable generalization of a heuristic based on analysis of a single training instance. The key idea here is that by analyzing *why* the observed positive instance is classified as positive, in the context of the overall problem solution, it is possible to deter-

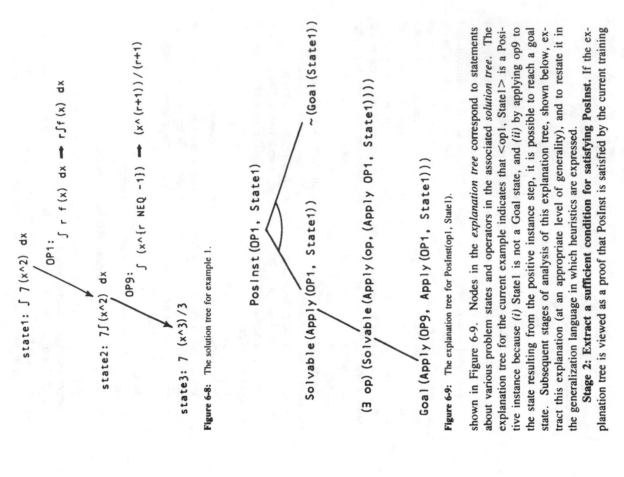

state1: $\int 7 (x^2)\, dx$

OP1: $\int r\, f(x)\, dx \;\longrightarrow\; r\int f(x)\, dx$

state2: $7\int (x^2)\, dx$

OP9: $\int (x^\wedge\{r\ NEQ\ -1\}) \;\longrightarrow\; (x^\wedge(r+1))/(r+1)$

state3: $7\ (x^3)/3$

**Figure 6-8:**  The solution tree for example 1.

PosInst(OP1, State1)

Solvable(Apply(OP1, State1))    ~(Goal(State1))

(∃ op)(Solvable(Apply(op,(Apply OP1, State1))))

Goal(Apply(OP9, Apply(OP1, State1)))

**Figure 6-9:**  The explanation tree for PosInst(op1, State1).

mine a logically sufficient condition for satisfying PosInst. Such an analysis leads to a *justifiable* generalization of the heuristic, that follows from the credit assignment criterion, together with knowledge about search and the representation of operators and problem states. This process is related to the process of operationalizing advice, as discussed by Mostow in Chapter 12 of this book and by [Hayes-Roth, 1980]. The particular method for analyzing solution traces is a generalization of the method of solution analysis presented in [Fikes *et al.*, 1972].

As an example, suppose that the system has just produced the problem solution tree shown in Figure 6-8, and the generalizer is now considering the first step along the solution path as a positive training instance for a heuristic that is to recommend op1. Assuming no heuristic yet exists for op1, the empirical generalization method described earlier will produce the following version space for the new heuristic:

S: $\int 7\,(x^2)\, dx \Rightarrow$ use op1

G: $\int r\, f(x)\, dx \Rightarrow$ use op1

In this example, analysis of how this training instance satisfies the credit assignment criterion will lead to additional information for refining the above version space of alternative hypotheses. The trace of this analysis is broken into four main stages, which attempt to determine some property of the integrand in the training instance which is *sufficient* to assure that the credit assignment criteria will be met. This sufficient condition for satisfying PosInst can then be used to further generalize the S boundary of the version space for this heuristic. The four main stages are (*i*) Generate an explanation that shows how the current positive instance satisfies PosInst, (*ii*) Extract from this explanation a sufficient condition for satisfying PosInst, (*iii*) Restate the sufficient condition in terms of the generalization language (that is, the language of applicability conditions for heuristics), as restrictions on various problem states in the solution tree, and (*iv*) Propagate the restrictions on various problem states through the solution tree, and combine them into a generalization that corresponds to a sufficient condition for assuring PosInst will be satisfied.

**Stage 1: Produce an explanation of how the current training instance satisfies PosInst.** This explanation is produced by instantiating the definition of PosInst for the positive instance in question. By determining which disjunctive clauses in the definition of PosInst are satisfied by the current training instance, and then by further expanding those clauses by instantiating predicates to which they refer, a proof is produced that PosInst(op1, State1). The result of this stage is an And/Or proof tree, which we shall call the *explanation tree* for the training instance. The tip nodes in the explanation tree are known to be satisfied because of the observed solution tree to which the training instance belongs. This explanation tree indicates how the training instance satisfies PosInst, and forms the basis for generalization by inferring sufficient conditions for satisfying PosInst.

The explanation tree for the positive training instance <op1, State1> is

shown in Figure 6-9. Nodes in the *explanation tree* correspond to statements about various problem states and operators in the associated *solution tree*. The explanation tree for the current example indicates that <op1, State1> is a Positive instance because (*i*) State1 is not a Goal state, and (*ii*) by applying op9 to the state resulting from the positive instance step, it is possible to reach a goal state. Subsequent stages of analysis of this explanation tree, shown below, extract this explanation (at an appropriate level of generality), and to restate it in the generalization language in which heuristics are expressed.

**Stage 2: Extract a sufficient condition for satisfying PosInst.** If the explanation tree is viewed as a proof that PosInst is satisfied by the current training instance, then it is clear that any set of nodes that satisfy this And/Or tree correspond to a sufficient condition for satisfying PosInst. In the current example, for instance, if all the tip nodes of the explanation tree are satisfied by a given state, s, then PosInst will be satisfied by the training instance <op1, s>. In this stage, a set of nodes that satisfy the And/Or tree is selected, and the corresponding sufficient condition for PosInst is formulated by replacing the problem state from the training instance by a universally-quantified variable. In the current example, if the tip nodes of the explanation tree are selected, then the resulting sufficient condition for PosInst may be stated as follows:

$$(\forall s)\ \text{PosInst}(op1, s) \Leftarrow (\sim\text{Goal}(s) \land \text{Goal}(\text{Apply}(op9, \text{Apply}(op1, s))))$$

Notice that there are many possible choices of sets of nodes to satisfy the And/Or tree, and correspondingly many sufficient conditions. This choice of nodes is one of the major control issues in the analysis of the training instance. Generally, nodes close to the root of the explanation tree lead to more general sufficient conditions. However, since the sufficient conditions formulated in this stage must be transformed by subsequent stages to statements in the generalization language for heuristics, the choice of covering nodes from the explanation tree must trade off (i) the generality of the corresponding sufficient condition, with (ii) the loss in generality that is likely when this sufficient condition is transformed into the generalization language for heuristics. As an example, consider the alternative choice of the two nodes at the second level of the explanation tree. This set of nodes leads to the following sufficient condition for PosInst:

$$(\forall s)\ \text{PosInst}(op1, s) \Leftarrow (\sim\text{Goal}(s) \land \text{Solvable}(\text{Apply}(op1, s)))$$

While this sufficient condition on satisfying PosInst is more general than the earlier sufficient condition, it turns out that this added generality will be lost when attempting to redescribe the sufficient condition in terms of the generalization language. The difficulty in this case stems from the fact that there is no straightforward translation from the predicate "Solvable" to a statement in the generalization language of LEX. In contrast, the sufficient condition corresponding to the tip nodes of the explanation tree involves only the predicate "Goal", which is easily characterized in terms of the generalization language.

**Stage 3: Restate the sufficient condition in terms of the generalization language, as restrictions on various problem states involved in the solution tree.** In the current example, the sufficient condition corresponding to the tip nodes of the explanation tree can be restated as follows:

$$(\forall s)\ \text{PosInst}(op1, s) \Leftarrow$$
$$(\text{Match}(\textstyle\int f(x)dx, s) \land \text{Match}(f(x), \text{Apply}(op9, \text{Apply}(op1, s))))$$

The predicate "Match" corresponds to the matching procedure used to compare applicability conditions, or generalizations, with problem states (that is, it tests whether the applicability conditions are satisfied in the problem state). The first conjunct above expresses the fact that "s" is *not* a Goal state ("s" contains an integral), and the second conjunct expresses the fact that Apply(op9,

Apply(op1, s)) *is* a goal state (it is some expression that does not contain an integral sign). This second conjunct corresponds to a restriction on the state labeled State3 in Figure 6-8.

In general, the goal of this stage is to translate the sufficient condition into a conjunctive set of statements of the form Match(<generalization>, <problem-state>), where <generalization> can be any statement in the generalization language used by the system, and <problem-state> can be any expression that corresponds to a particular problem state in the solution tree for the current example.

The translation of sufficient conditions into the generalization language requires knowledge about the correspondence between the representation language in which the analysis is being done, and the generalization language used to describe heuristics. For instance, in the current example the following knowledge is used in the translation:

$$(\forall s)\ \sim\text{Goal}(s) \Leftrightarrow \text{Match}(\textstyle\int f(x)dx, s)$$

and

$$(\forall s)\ \text{Goal}(s) \Leftrightarrow \text{Match}(f(x)dx, s)$$

Unfortunately, some expressions generated by analyzing the explanation tree may have no corresponding expression in the generalization language. For example, in the current LEX generalization language, there is no way of characterizing all "Solvable" functions. In this case, translating the sufficient condition corresponding to the second level nodes in the explanation tree may require further specializing the sufficient condition, by replacing Solvable(x) by sufficient conditions for Solvable. An example of such knowledge is the knowledge that all polynomial integrands are solvable. It is important to note that even if no such knowledge is available, it will always be possible to translate the sufficient condition into some weaker condition describable in the generalization language. This can always be accomplished by using the fact that the solution tree provides at least one problem state which satisfies the predicate, and the problem state is itself describable in the generalization language. Thus, for example, the condition Solvable(Apply(op1, s)) may, if no other relevant knowledge is available, be weakened and replaced by Match($7\int(x^2)dx$, Apply(op1, s)).

**Stage 4: Propagate the restrictions on various problem states through the solution tree to determine equivalent conditions on the problem state involved in the current training instance.** By examining the definitions of the operators involved in reaching a given state, x, it is possible to propagate restrictions on x through the solution tree to deduce the corresponding constraints on an earlier problem state. This back propagation of restrictions is necessary in order to restate the sufficient condition on PosInst in terms of a generalization that applies to the training instance. This propagation requires using the operators in a way different from the way in which they are used during forward search problem-solving, and is similar to the process of goal regression discussed in the literature on means-ends problem-solving and planning [Nilsson, 1980].

As an example, consider the second expression in the sufficient condition from stage 3: Match( f(x), Apply(op9, Apply(op1, s))). This condition, when back propagated through op9 becomes Match( f(x)$\int$f(x↑(r ≠ -1)dx), s)). Apply(op1, s)). The new generalization corresponds to the class of problem states which can be transformed using op9 into an expression that satisfies the original condition. Similarly, this new expression can be propagated back through op1 to yield an equivalent condition on State1: Match( $\int$ r(x↑{r ≠ -1})dx, s). Thus, the sufficient condition from stage 3 can be restated as:

(∀s) PosInst(op1, s) ⇐
(Match $\int$ f(x)dx, s) ∧ Match( $\int$ r(x ↑ {r ≠ -1})dx, s)

Since the second conjunct is more specific than the first, the above expression can be simplified to:

(∀s) [PosInst(op1, s) ⇐ Match $\int$ r(x ↑ {r ≠ -1})dx, s]

Finally, we have found sufficient conditions for PosInst(op1, s) which are stated as a generalization that must match State1. While the sufficient condition determined by the above analysis is not the most general sufficient condition possible, it is satisfied by the current training instance and follows naturally from analyzing that instance. If this training instance were the first instance encountered for this particular heuristic, the resulting version space would reflect the extra information extracted from analyzing this instance, as shown below.

S: $\int$ r [x ↑ (r ≠ -1)] dx ⇒ Apply op1

G: $\int$ r f(x) dx ⇒ Apply op1

### 6.4.3 Automatically Extending the Vocabulary for Describing Heuristics

One of the most fundamental difficulties associated with current approaches to machine learning is the problem of acquiring an appropriate vocabulary with which to describe learned concepts. Nearly all existing systems assume some fixed vocabulary of terms with which to represent learned concepts (for instance, the LEX terms trigonometric, polynomial, exponential, and so on, as shown in Figure 6-2). In cases where this vocabulary is inappropriate, it will be impossible to describe (and hence to learn) the desired concept. In the LEX system, we have found that there are many cases where the current language for describing heuristics is insufficient to correctly characterize sets of training instances produced by the Critic.

As an example, consider the solution path shown in Figure 6-10, and the positive training instance corresponding to the first step of this solution path. If this positive training instance is observed, together with the positive training instance $\int$cos$^7$(x)dx, and the negative training instance $\int$cos$^6$(x)dx, then LEX will be unable to produce a heuristic that matches these two positive instances, and excludes the negative instance. The problem here is that the language in Figure 6-2 for describing heuristics has no term that includes both 5 and 7 while excluding 6.

state1: $\int$cos$^7$(x)dx

op1: f$^r$(x)⇒f$^{[r-1]}$(x)f(x)

state2: $\int$cos$^6$(x)cos(x)dx

op2: f$^r$(x)⇒(f$^2$(x))$^{[r/2]}$

state3: $\int$(cos$^2$(x))$^3$cos(x)dx

op3: cos$^2$(x)⇒(1-sin$^2$(x))

state4: $\int$(1-sin$^2$(x))$^3$cos(x)dx

op4: $\int$g(f(x))f'(x)dx⇒$\int$g(u)du, u = f(x)

state5: $\int$(1-u$^2$)$^3$du, u = sin(x)

op5: poly$^k$(x)⇒[poly(x)*$_1$...*$_k$poly(x)]

state6: $\int$1-3u$^2$ + 3u$^4$-u$^6$du, u = sin(x)

**Figure 6-10:**   Solution path for $\int$cos$^7$(x)dx.

In this case, a solution analysis similar to that described in the previous section can lead to the generation of a new term to be added to the language of Figure 6-2. As in the previous case, the solution trace analysis first produces a set of statements about various nodes in the search tree, which characterize why the training instance is positive. These statements are then propagated through the problem-solving operators in the search tree to determine which features of the training instance were necessary to satisfy these statements. *It is during this propagation and combination of constraints that new descriptive terms may be suggested.*

For example, in the case of the solution path shown in Figure 6-10, suppose that the analysis first determines that the solution path leads to a solution because State6 is of the following form, which we assume satisfies the system's definition of a solvable state.

$$\int poly(x)*_1...*_k poly(x)dx$$

Then the set of states, X$_1$, for which application of op5 leads to such a solvable state can be computed as:

X$_1$ ⇐ op5$^{-1}$($\int$poly(x)*$_1$...*$_k$poly(x)dx)

giving

X$_1$ = $\int$poly$^k$(x)dx

In turn, we can compute the set of states, X$_2$, for which application of op4 leads to such a solvable state, as shown below. Here, "range(op4)" indicates the set of all problem states that can be reached by applying op4 to some other problem state.

$X_2 \leftarrow$ op4$^{-1}$(intersection(range(op4),$X_1$)).

By this repeated backward propagation of constraints through the solution tree, it can be determined that application of the solution method of Figure 6-10 leads to a solvable state when the initial state (in this case State1) is of the form $\int \cos^c(x)dx$ where c is constrained to satisfy the predicate "real(c) $\wedge$ integer((c-1)/2)", better known as "odd integer". Thus, detailed analysis of the solution path can suggest the need for new predicate terms in the language for describing heuristics. These terms (such as "odd integer") arise from combinations of existing terms, composed in a way that is determined by the particular operator sequence in the solution path being analyzed.

## 6.5 SUMMARY

The LEX system is an experiment in learning by experimentation. The current system, based on a generator of practice problems, problem solver, critic, and generalizer, indicates that useful problem-solving heuristics can be learned by employing empirical methods for generalizing from examples. It also indicates that more powerful and more general approaches to learning will be needed before practical systems can be built that improve their strategies in significant ways. One way of augmenting empirical learning methods by analytical methods has been discussed, which is based on giving the system the ability to reason about its goals, heuristic search, and the task domain. This research and the research of others (for example, that described in Chapters 8, 9, and 12 of this book) suggests that the addition of such meta-knowledge about the goals, the learner, and the problem-solving methods in the domain, is a promising area for further research.

## ACKNOWLEDGMENTS

The LEX system has been developed over the past three years with the aid of several researchers in addition to the authors. We gratefully acknowledge the aid of William Bogdan, who helped implement the Critic; Bernard Nudel, who helped implement the Critic and Problem Solver; and Adam Irgon, who implemented the Problem Generator. Richard Keller has contributed to the newer work on using the intended purpose of heuristics for analyzing training instances. This research is supported by the National Science Foundation under Grant No. MCS80-08889, and by the National Institutes of Health under Grant No. RR-64309.

## REFERENCES

Anzai, Y. and Simon, H., "The theory of learning by doing," *Psychological Review*, Vol. 36, No. 2, pp. 124-140, 1979.

Buchanan, E. G. and Mitchell, T. M., "Model-Directed Learning of Production Rules," *Pattern-Directed Inference Systems*, Waterman, D. A. and Hayes-Roth, F. (Eds.), Academic Press, New York, 1978.

Davis, R., "Applications of meta level knowledge to the construction and use of large knowledge bases," *Knowledge-based Systems in Artificial Intelligence*, Davis, R. and Lenat, D. (Eds.), McGraw-Hill, New York, 1981.

Fikes, R. E., Hart, P. E. and Nilsson, N. J., "Learning and executing generalized robot plans," *Artificial Intelligence*, Vol. 3, pp. 251-288, 1972.

Hayes-Roth, F., Klahr, P. and Mostow, D. J., "Knowledge acquisition, knowledge programming, and knowledge refinement", Technical Report R-2540-NSF, The Rand Corporation, Santa Monica, CA., May 1980.

Iba, G. A., "Learning disjunctive concepts from examples," Master's thesis, M.I.T., Cambridge, Mass , 1979, (also AI memo 548).

Mitchell, T. M., *Version Spaces: An approach to concept learning*, Ph.D. dissertation, Stanford University, December 1978, (also Stanford CS report STAN-CS-78-711, HPP-79-2).

Mitchell, T. M., Utgoff, P. E., Nudel, B. and Banerji, R., "Learning problem-solving heuristics through practice," *Proceedings of the Seventh International Joint Conference on Artificial Intelligence*, Vancouver, pp. 127-134, August 1981.

Mitchell, T. M., "Generalization as Search," *Artificial Intelligence*, Vol. 18, No. 2, pp. 203-226, March 1982.

Mitchell, T. M., "Toward Combining Empirical and Analytic Methods for Learning Heuristics," *Human and Artificial Intelligence*, Elithorn, A. and Banerji, R. (Eds.), Erlbaum, 1982.

Neves, D. M., "A computer program that learns algebraic procedures," *Proceedings of the 2nd Conference on Computational Studies of Intelligence*, Toronto, 1978.

Nilsson, N. *Principles of Artificial Intelligence*, Tioga, Palo Alto, 1980.

Politakis, P , Weiss, S. and Kulikowski, C., "Designing consistent knowledge bases for expert consultation systems", Technical Report DCS-TR-100, Department of Computer Science, Rutgers University, 1979, (also 13th Annual Hawaii International Conference on System Sciences).

Utgoff, P. E. and Mitchell, T. M., "Acquisition of Appropriate Bias for Inductive Concept Learning," *Proceedings of the 1982 National Conference on Artificial Intelligence*, Pittsburgh, August 1982.

Vere, S. A., "Inductive learning of relational productions," *Pattern-Directed Inference Systems*, Waterman, D. A. and Hayes-Roth, F. (Eds.), Academic Press, New York, 1978.

Waterman, D. A., "Generalization learning techniques for automating the learning of heuristics," *Artificial Intelligence*, Vol. 1, No. 1/2, pp. 121-170, 1970.

Machine Learning 1: 11–46, 1986

© 1986 Kluwer Academic Publishers, Boston – Manufactured in The Netherlands

# Chunking in Soar:
# The Anatomy of a General Learning Mechanism

JOHN E. LAIRD                                    (LAIRD. PA @ XEROX.ARPA)
Intelligent Systems Laboratory, Xerox Palo Alto Research Center,
3333 Coyote Hill Rd., Palo Alto, CA 94304, U.S.A.

PAUL S. ROSENBLOOM                    (ROSENBLOOM @ SUMEX-AIM.ARPA)
Departments of Computer Science and Psychology, Stanford University, Stanford, CA 94305, U.S.A.

ALLEN NEWELL                                    (NEWELL @ A.CS.CMU.EDU)
Department of Computer Science, Carnegie-Mellon University, Pittsburgh, PA 15213, U.S.A.

(Received August 1, 1985)

Key words: learning from experience, general learning mechanisms, problem solving, chunking, production systems, macro-operators, transfer

Abstract. In this article we describe an approach to the construction of a general learning mechanism based on *chunking* in *Soar*. Chunking is a learning mechanism that acquires rules from goal-based experience. *Soar* is a general problem-solving architecture with a rule-based memory. In previous work we have demonstrated how the combination of chunking and *Soar* could acquire search-control knowledge (strategy acquisition) and operator implementation rules in both search-based puzzle tasks and knowledge-based expert-systems tasks. In this work we examine the anatomy of chunking in *Soar* and provide a new demonstration of its learning capabilities involving the acquisition and use of macro-operators.

## 1. Introduction

The goal of the *Soar* project is to build a system capable of general intelligent behavior. We seek to understand what mechanisms are necessary for intelligent behavior, whether they are adequate for a wide range of tasks – including search-intensive tasks, knowledge-intensive tasks, and algorithmic tasks – and how they work together to form a general cognitive architecture. One necessary component of such an architecture, and the one on which we focus in this paper, is a general learning mechanism. Intuitively, a general learning mechanism should be capable of learning all that needs to be learned. To be a bit more precise, assume that we have a

general performance system capable of solving any problem in a broad set of domains. Then, a general learning mechanism for that performance system would possess the following three properties:[1]

- *Task generality*. It can improve the system's performance on all of the tasks in the domains. The scope of the learning component should be the same as that of the performance component.
- *Knowledge generality*. It can base its improvements on any knowledge available about the domain. This knowledge can be in the form of examples, instructions, hints, its own experience, etc.
- *Aspect generality*. It can improve all aspects of the system. Otherwise there would be a *wandering-bottleneck problem* (Mitchell, 1983), in which those aspects not open to improvement would come to dominate the overall performance effort of the system.

These properties relate to the scope of the learning, but they say nothing concerning the generality and effectiveness of what is learned. Therefore we add a fourth property.

- *Transfer of learning*. What is learned in one situation will be used in other situations to improve performance. It is through the transfer of learned material that *generalization*, as it is usually studied in artificial intelligence, reveals itself in a learning problem solver.

Generality thus plays two roles in a general learning mechanism: in the scope of application of the mechanism and the generality of what it learns.

There are many possible organizations for a general learning mechanism, each with different behavior and implications. Some of the possibilities that have been investigated within AI and psychology include:

- A *Multistrategy Learner*. Given the wide variety of learning mechanisms currently being investigated in AI and psychology, one obvious way to achieve a general learner is to build a system containing a combination of these mechanisms. The best example of this to date is Anderson's (1983a) ACT* system which contains six learning mechanisms.
- A *Deliberate Learner*. Given the breadth required of a general learning mechanism, a natural way to build one is as a problem solver that deliberately devises modifications that will improve performance. The modifications are

---

[1] These properties are related to, but not isomorphic with, the three dimensions of variation of learning mechanisms described in Carbonell, Michalski, and Mitchell (1983) – application domain, underlying learning strategy, and representation of knowledge.

human practice and used it to model the ubiquitous power law of practice — that the time to perform a task is a power-law function of the number of times the task has been performed. The model was based on the idea that practice improves performance via the acquisition of knowledge about patterns in the task environment, that is, chunks. When the model was implemented as part of a production-system architecture, this idea was instantiated with chunks relating patterns of goal parameters to patterns of goal results (Rosenbloom, 1983; Rosenbloom & Newell, 1986). By replacing complex processing in subgoals with chunks learned during practice, the model could improve its speed in performing a single task or set of tasks.

To increase the scope of the learning beyond simple practice, a similar chunking mechanism has been incorporated into the *Soar* problem-solving architecture (Laird, Newell & Rosenbloom, 1985). In previous work we have demonstrated how chunking can improve *Soar*'s performance on a variety of tasks and in a variety of ways (Laird, Rosenbloom & Newell, 1984). In this article we focus on presenting the details of how chunking works in *Soar* (Section 3), and describe a new application involving the acquisition of macro-operators similar to those reported by Korf (1985a) (Section 4). This demonstration extends the claims of generality, and highlights the ability of chunking to transfer learning between different situations.

Before proceeding to the heart of this work — the examination of the anatomy of chunking and a demonstration of its capabilities — it is necessary to make a fairly extensive digression into the structure and performance of the *Soar* architecture (Section 2). In contrast to systems with multistrategy or deliberate learning mechanisms, the learning phenomena exhibited by a system with only a simple experience-based learning mechanism is a function not only of the learning mechanism itself, but also of the problem-solving component of the system. The two components are closely coupled and mutually supportive.

## 2. Soar — an architecture for general intelligence

*Soar* is an architecture for general intelligence that has been applied to a variety of tasks (Laird, Newell, & Rosenbloom, 1985; Rosenbloom, Laird, McDermott, Newell, & Orciuch, 1985): many of the classic AI toy tasks such as the Tower of Hanoi, and the Blocks World: tasks that appear to involve non-search-based reasoning, such as syllogisms, the three-wise-men puzzle, and sequence extrapolation; and large tasks requiring expert-level knowledge, such as the *R1* computer configuration task (McDermott, 1982). In this section we briefly review the *Soar* architecture and present an example of its performance in the Eight Puzzle.

usually based on analyses of the tasks to be accomplished, the structure of the problem solver, and the system's performance on the tasks. Sometimes this problem solving is done by the performance system itself, as in Lenat's *AM* (1976) and *Eurisko* (1983) programs, or in a production system that employs a *build* operation (Waterman, 1975) — whereby productions can themselves create new productions — as in Anzai and Simon's (1979) work on learning by doing. Sometimes the learner is constructed as a separate *critic* with its own problem solver (Smith, Mitchell, Chestek, & Buchanan, 1977; Rendell, 1983), or as a set of critics as in Sussman's (1977) *Hacker* program.

• *A Simple Experience Learner.* There is a single learning mechanism that bases its modifications on the experience of the problem solver. The learning mechanism is fixed, and does not perform any complex problem solving. Examples of this approach are memo functions (Michie, 1968; Marsh, 1970), macro-operators in *Strips* (Fikes, Hart & Nilsson, 1972), production composition (Lewis, 1978; Neves & Anderson, 1981) and knowledge compilation (Anderson, 1983b).

The third approach, the simple experience learner, is the one adopted in *Soar*. In some ways it is the most parsimonious of the three alternatives: it makes use of only one learning mechanism, in contrast to a multistrategy learner; it makes use of only one problem solver, in contrast to a critic-based deliberate learner; and it requires only problem solving about the actual task to be performed, in contrast to both kinds of deliberate learner. Counterbalancing the parsimony is that it is not obvious a priori that a simple experience learner can provide an adequate foundation for the construction of a general learning mechanism. At first glance, it would appear that such a mechanism would have difficulty learning from a variety of sources of knowledge, learning about all aspects of the system, and transferring what it has learned to new situations.

The hypothesis being tested in the research on *Soar* is that *chunking*, a simple experience-based learning mechanism, can form the basis for a general learning mechanism.[2] Chunking is a mechanism originally developed as part of a psychological model of memory (Miller, 1956). The concept of a chunk — a symbol that designates a pattern of other symbols — has been much studied as a model of memory organization. It has been used to explain such phenomena as why the span of short-term memory is approximately constant, independent of the complexity of the items to be remembered (Miller, 1956), and why chess masters have an advantage over novices in reproducing chess positions from memory (Chase & Simon, 1973). Newell and Rosenbloom (1981) proposed chunking as the basis for a model of

[2] For a comparison of chunking to other simple mechanisms for learning by experience, see Rosenbloom and Newell (1986).

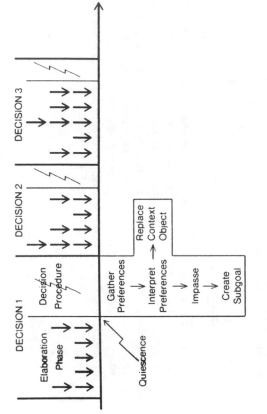

*Figure 1.* The *Soar* decision cycle.

## 2.1 The architecture

Performance in *Soar* is based on the *problem space hypothesis*: all goal-oriented behavior occurs as search in problem spaces (Newell, 1980). A problem space for a task domain consists of a set of *states* representing possible situations in the task domain and a set of *operators* that transform one state into another one. For example, in the chess domain the states are configurations of pieces on the board, while the operators are the legal moves, such as P-K4. In the computer-configuration domain the states are partially configured computers, while the operators add components to the existing configuration (among other actions). Problem solving in a problem space consists of starting at some given *initial state*, and applying operators (yielding intermediate states) until a *desired state* is reached that is recognized as achieving the goal.

In *Soar*, each goal has three slots, one each for a current problem space, state, and operator. Together these four components – comprise a *context*. Goals can have subgoals (and associated contexts), which form a strict goal-subgoal hierarchy. All objects (such as goals, problem spaces, states, and operators) have a unique *identifier*, generated at the time the object was created. Further descriptions of an object are called *augmentations*. Each augmentation has an identifier, an attribute, and a value. The value can either be a constant value, or the identifier of another object. All objects are connected via augmentations (either directly, or indirectly via a chain of augmentations) to one of the objects in a context, so that the identifiers of objects act as nodes of a semantic network, while the augmentations represent the arcs or links.

Throughout the process of satisfying a goal, *Soar* makes *decisions* in order to select between the available problem spaces, states, and operators. Every problem-solving episode consists of a sequence of decisions and these decisions determine the behavior of the system. Problem solving in pursuit of a goal begins with the selection of a problem space for the goal. This is followed by the selection of an initial state, and then an operator to apply to the state. Once the operator is selected, it is applied to create a new state. The new state can then be selected for further processing (or the current state can be kept, or some previously generated state can be selected), and the process repeats as a new operator is selected to apply to the selected state. The weak methods can be represented as knowledge for controlling the selection of states and operators (Laird & Newell, 1983a). The knowledge that controls these decisions is collectively called *search control*. Problem solving without search control is possible in *Soar*, but it leads to an exhaustive search of the problem space.

Figure 1 shows a schematic representation of a series of decisions. To bring the available search-control knowledge to bear on the making of a decision, each decision involves a monotonic *elaboration phase*. During the elaboration phase, all *directly* available knowledge relevant to the current situation is brought to bear. This is the act of retrieving knowledge from memory to be used to control problem solv-

ing. In *Soar*, the long-term memory is structured as a production system, with all directly available knowledge represented as productions.[3] The elaboration phase consists of one or more cycles of production execution in which all of the eligible productions are fired in parallel. The contexts of the goal hierarchy and their augmentations serve as the working memory for these productions. The information added during the elaboration phase can take one of two forms. First, existing objects may have their descriptions elaborated (via augmentations) with new or existing objects, such as the addition of an evaluation to a state. Second, data structures called *preferences* can be created that specify the desirability of an object for a slot in a context. Each preference indicates the context in which it is relevant by specifying the appropriate goal, problem space, state and operator.

When the elaboration phase reaches quiescence – when no more productions are eligible to fire – a fixed *decision procedure* is run that gathers and interprets the preferences provided by the elaboration phase to produce a specific decision. Preferences of type *acceptable* and *reject* determine whether or not an object is a candidate for a context. Preferences of type *better*, *equal*, and *worse* determine the relative worth of objects. Preferences of type *best*, *indifferent* and *worst* make absolute judgements about the worth of objects.[4] Starting from the oldest context, the decision procedure uses the preferences to determine if the current problem space, state,

---

[3] We will use the terms production and rule interchangeably throughout this paper.
[4] There is also a *parallel* preference that can be used to assert that two operators should execute simultaneously.

or operator in any of the contexts should be changed. The problem space is considered first, followed by the state and then the operator. A change is made if one of the candidate objects for the slot dominates (based on the preferences) all of the others, or if a set of equal objects dominates all of the other objects. In the latter case, a random selection is made between the equal objects. Once a change has been made, the subordinate positions in the context (state and operator if a problem space is changed) are initialized to **undecided**, all of the more recent contexts in the stack are discarded, the decision procedure terminates, and a new decision commences.

If sufficient knowledge is available during the search to uniquely determine a decision, the search proceeds unabated. However, in many cases the knowledge encoded into productions may be insufficient to allow the direct application of an operator or the making of a search-control decision. That is, the available preferences do not determine a unique, uncontested change in a context, causing an *impasse* in problem solving to occur (Brown & VanLehn, 1980). Four classes of impasses can arise in *Soar*: (1) *no-change* (the elaboration phase ran to quiescence without suggesting any changes to the contexts), (2) *tie* (no single object or group of equal objects was better than all of the other candidate objects), (3) *conflict* (two or more candidate objects were better than each other), and (4) *rejection* (all objects were rejected, even the current one). All types of impasse can occur for any of the three context slots associated with a goal — problem space, state, and operator — and a no-change impasse can occur for the goal. For example, a state tie occurs whenever there are two or more competing states and no directly available knowledge to compare them. An operator no-change occurs whenever no context changes are suggested after an operator is selected (usually because not enough information is directly available to allow the creation of a new state).

*Soar* responds to an impasse by creating a subgoal (and an associated context) to resolve the impasse. Once a subgoal is created, a problem space must be selected, followed by an initial state, and then an operator. If an impasse is reached in any of these decisions, another subgoal will be created to resolve it, leading to the hierarchy of goals in *Soar*. By generating a subgoal for each impasse, the full problem-solving power of *Soar* can be brought to bear to resolve the impasse. These subgoals correspond to all of the types of subgoals created in standard AI systems (Laird, Newell, & Rosenbloom, 1985). This capability to generate automatically all subgoals in response to impasses and to open up all aspects of problem-solving behavior to problem solving when necessary is called *universal subgoaling* (Laird, 1984).

Because all goals are generated in response to impasses, and each goal can have at most one impasse at a time, the goals (contexts) in working memory are structured as a stack, referred to as the *context stack*. A subgoal terminates when its impasse is resolved. For example, if a tie impasse arises, the subgoal generated for it will terminate when sufficient preferences have been created so that a single object (or set of equal objects) dominates the others. When a subgoal terminates, *Soar* pops the context stack, removing from working memory all augmentations created in that

subgoal that are not connected to a prior context, either directly or indirectly (by a chain of augmentations), and preferences whose context objects do not match objects in prior contexts. Those augmentations and preferences that are not removed are the *results* of the subgoal.

Default knowledge (in the form of productions) exists in *Soar* to cope with any of the subgoals when no additional knowledge is available. For some subgoals (those created for all types of rejection impasses and no-change impasses for goals, problem-spaces, and states) this involves simply backing up to a prior choice in the context, but for other subgoals (those created for tie, conflict and operator no-change impasses), this involves searches for knowledge that will resolve the subgoal's impasse. If additional non-default knowledge is available to resolve an impasse, it dominates the default knowledge (via preferences) and controls the problem solving within the subgoal.

### 2.2 An example problem solving task

Consider the Eight Puzzle, in which there are eight numbered, movable tiles set in a 3×3 frame. One cell of the frame is always empty (the blank), making it possible to move an adjacent tile into the empty cell. The problem is to transform one configuration of tiles into a second configuration by moving the tiles. The states of the **eight-puzzle** problem space are configurations of the numbers 1–8 in a 3×3 grid. There is a single general operator to move adjacent tiles into the empty cell. For a given state, an instance of this operator is created for each of the cells adjacent to the empty cell. Each of these operator instances is instantiated with the empty cell and one of the adjacent cells. To simplify our discussion, we will refer to these instantiated operators by the direction they move a tile into the empty cell: **up, down, left,** or **right.** Figure 2 shows an example of the initial and desired states of an Eight Puzzle problem.

To encode this task in *Soar*, one must include productions that propose the appropriate problem space, create the initial state of that problem space, implement the operators of the problem space, and detect the desired state when it is achieved. If

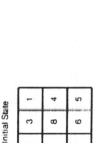

Initial State

| 2 | 3 | 1 |
|---|---|---|
| 8 |   | 4 |
| 7 | 6 | 5 |

Desired State

| 1 | 2 | 3 |
|---|---|---|
| 8 |   | 4 |
| 7 | 6 | 5 |

*Figure 2.* Example initial and desired states of the Eight Puzzle.

no additional knowledge is available, an exhaustive depth-first search occurs as a result of the default processing for tie impasses. Tie impasses arise each time an operator has to be selected. In response to the subgoals for these impasses, alternatives are investigated to determine the best move. Whenever another tie impasse arises during the investigation of one of the alternatives, an additional subgoal is generated, and the search deepens. If additional search-control knowledge is added to provide an evaluation of the states, the search changes to steepest-ascent hill climbing. As more or different search-control knowledge is added, the behavior of the search changes in response to the new knowledge. One of the properties of Soar is that the weak methods, such as generate and test, means-ends analysis, depth-first search and hill climbing, do not have to be explicitly selected, but instead emerge from the structure of the task and the available search-control knowledge (Laird & Newell, 1983a; Laird & Newell, 1983b; Laird, 1984).

Another way to control the search in the Eight Puzzle is to break it up into a set of subgoals to get the individual tiles into position. We will look at this approach in some detail because it forms the basis for the use of macro-operators for the Eight Puzzle. Means-ends analysis is the standard technique for solving problems where the goal can be decomposed into a set of subgoals, but it is ineffective for problems such as the Eight Puzzle that have *non-serializable* subgoals — tasks for which there exists no ordering of the subgoals such that successive subgoals can be achieved without undoing what was accomplished by earlier subgoals (Korf, 1985a). Figure 3 shows an intermediate state in problem solving where tiles 1 and 2 are in their desired positions. In order to move tile 3 into its desired position, tile 2 must be moved out of its desired position. Non-serializable subgoals can be tractable if they are *serially decomposable* (Korf, 1985a). A set of subgoals is serially decomposable if there is an ordering of them such that the solution to each subgoal depends only on that subgoal and on the preceding ones in the solution order. In the Eight Puzzle the subgoals are, in order: (1) have the blank in its correct position; (2) have the blank and the first tile in their correct positions; (3) have the blank and the first two tiles in their correct positions; and so on through the eighth tile. Each subgoal depends only on the positions of the blank and the previously placed tiles. Within one subgoal a previous subgoal may be undone, but if it is, it must be re-achieved before the current subgoal is completed.

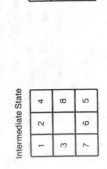

Intermediate State          Desired State

*Figure 3.* Non-serializable subgoals in the Eight Puzzle.

Adopting this approach does not result in new knowledge for directly controlling the selection of operators and states in the **eight-puzzle** problem space. Instead it provides knowledge about how to structure and decompose the puzzle. This knowledge consists of the set of serially decomposable subgoals, and the ordering of those subgoals. To encode this knowledge in *Soar*, we have added a second problem space, **eight-puzzle-sd**, with a set of nine operators corresponding to the nine subgoals.[5] For example, the operator **place-2** will place tile 2 in its desired position, while assuring that the blank and the first tile will also be in position. The ordering of the subgoals is encoded as search-control knowledge that creates preferences for the operators. Figure 4 shows a trace of the decisions for a short problem-solving episode for the initial and desired states from Figure 2. This example is heavily used in the remainder

[5] Both **place-7** and **place-8** are always no-ops because once the blank and tiles 1–6 are in place, either tiles 7 and 8 are in place, or the problem is unsolvable. They can therefore be safely ignored.

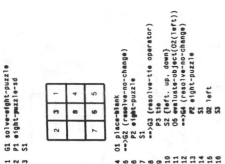
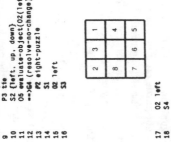

```
 1   G1 solve-eight-puzzle
 2   P1 eight-puzzle-sd
 3   S1

 4   O1 place-blank
 5   ==>G2 (resolve-no-change)
 6   P2 eight-puzzle
 7   S1
 8   ==>G3 (resolve-tie operator)
 9   P3 tie
10   S2 (left, up, down)
11   O6 evaluate-object(O2(left))
12   ==>G4 (resolve-no-change)
13   P2 eight-puzzle
14   S1
15   O2 left
16   S3

17   O2 left
18   S4
19   S4
20   O8 place-1
```

*Figure 4.* A **problem-solving** trace for the Eight Puzzle. Each line of the trace includes, from left to right, the decision **number**, the identifier of the object selected, and possibly a short description of the object.

### 3. Chunking in Soar

*Soar* was originally designed to be a general (non-learning) problem solver. Nevertheless, its problem-solving and memory structures support learning in a number of ways. The structure of problem solving in *Soar* determines when new knowledge is needed, what that knowledge might be, and when it can be acquired.

- *Determining when new knowledge is needed.* In *Soar*, impasses occur if and only if the directly available knowledge is either incomplete or inconsistent. Therefore, impasses indicate when the system should attempt to acquire new knowledge.

- *Determining what to learn.* While problem solving within a subgoal, *Soar* can discover information that will resolve an impasse. This information, if remembered, can avert similar impasses in future problem solving.

- *Determining when new knowledge can be acquired.* When a subgoal completes, because its impasse has been resolved, an opportunity exists to add new knowledge that was not already explicitly known.

*Soar*'s long-term memory, which is based on a production system and the workings of the elaboration phase, supports learning in two ways:

- *Integrating new knowledge.* Productions provide a modular representation of knowledge, so that the integration of new knowledge only requires adding a new production to production memory and does not require a complex analysis of the previously stored knowledge in the system (Newell, 1973; Waterman, 1975; Davis & King, 1976; Anderson, 1983b).

- *Using new knowledge.* Even if the productions are syntactically modular, there is no guarantee that the information they encode can be integrated together when it is needed. The elaboration phase of *Soar* brings all appropriate knowledge to bear, with no requirement of synchronization (and no conflict resolution). The decision procedure then integrates the results of the elaboration phase.

Chunking in *Soar* takes advantage of this support to create rules that summarize the processing of a subgoal, so that in the future, the costly problem solving in the subgoal can be replaced by direct rule application. When a subgoal is generated, a learning episode begins that could lead to the creation of a chunk. During problem solving within the subgoal, information accumulates on which a chunk can be based. When the subgoal terminates, a chunk can be created. Each chunk is a rule (or set of rules) that gets added to the production memory. Chunked knowledge is brought to bear during the elaboration phase of later decisions. In the remainder of this section we look in more detail at the process of chunk creation, evaluate the scope of chunking as a learning mechanism, and examine the sources of chunk generality.

of the paper, so we shall go through it in some detail. To start problem solving, the current goal is initialized to be **solve-eight-puzzle** (in decision 1). The goal is represented in working memory by an identifier, in this case G1. Problem solving begins in the **eight-puzzle-sd** problem space. Once the initial state, S1, is selected, preferences are generated that order the operators so that **place-blank** is selected. Application of this operator, and all of the **eight-puzzle-sd** operators, is complex, often requiring extensive problem solving. Because the problem-space hypothesis implies that such problem solving should occur in a problem space, the operator is not directly implemented as rules. Instead, a no-change impasse leads to a subgoal to implement **place-blank**, which will be achieved when the blank is in its desired position. The **place-blank** operator is then implemented as a search in the **eight-puzzle** problem space for a state with the blank in the correct position. This search can be carried out using any of the weak methods described earlier, but for this example, let us assume there is no additional search-control knowledge.

Once the initial state is selected (decision 7), a tie impasse occurs among the operators that move the three adjacent tiles into the empty cell (**left**, **up** and **down**). A resolve-tie-subgoal (G3) is automatically generated for this impasse, and the **tie** problem space is selected. Its states are sets of objects being considered, and its operators evaluate objects so that preferences can be created. One of these **evaluate-object** operators (O5) is selected to evaluate the operator that moves tile 8 to the left, and a resolve-no-change subgoal (G4) is generated because there are no productions that directly compute an evaluation of the **left** operator for state S1. Default search-control knowledge attempts to implement the **evaluate-object** operator by applying the **left** operator to state S1. This is accomplished in the subgoal (decisions 13–16), yielding the desired state (S3). Because the **left** operator led to a solution for the goal, a preference is returned for it that allows it to be selected immediately for state S1 (decision 17) in goal G2, flushing the two lower subgoals (G3 and G4). If this state were not the desired state, another tie impasse would arise and the **tie** problem space would be selected for this new subgoal. The subgoal combination of a resolve-tie followed by a resolve-no-change on an **evaluate-object** operator would recur, giving a depth-first search.

Applying the **left** operator to state S1 yields state S4, which is the desired result of the **place-blank** operator in goal G1 above. The **place-1** operator (O8) is then selected as the current operator. As with **place-blank, place-1** is implemented by a search in the **eight-puzzle** problem space. It succeeds when both tile 1 and the blank are in their desired positions. With this problem-solving strategy, each tile is moved into place by one of the operators in the **eight-puzzle-sd** problem space. In the subgoals that implement the **eight-puzzle-sd** operators, many of the tiles already in place might be moved out of place, however, they must be back in place for the place operator to terminate successfully.

from the outside, or when an impasse is resolved by domain-independent default knowledge.

The actions of a chunk are based on the results of the subgoal for which the chunk was created. No chunk is created if there are no results. This can happen, for example, when a result produced in a subgoal leads to the termination of a goal much higher in the goal hierarchy. All of the subgoals that are lower in the hierarchy will also be terminated, but they may not generate results.

For an example of chunking in action, consider the terminal subgoal (G4) from the problem-solving episode in Figure 4. This subgoal was created as a result of a no-change impasse for the **evaluate-object** operator that should evaluate the operator that will **move** tile 8 to the left. The problem solving within goal G4 must implement the **evaluate-object** operator. Figure 5 contains a graphic representation of part of the working memory for this subgoal near the beginning of problem solving (A) and just before the subgoal is terminated (B). The working memory that existed before the subgoal was created consisted of the augmentations of the goal to resolve the tie between the **eight-puzzle** operators, G3, and its supergoals (G2 and G1, not shown). The **tie** problem space is the current problem space of G3, while state S2 is the current state and the **evaluate-object** operator (O5) is the current operator. D1 is the desired state of having the blank in the middle, but with no constraint on the tiles in the other cells (signified by the X's in the figure). All of these objects have further descriptions, some only partially shown in the figure.

The purpose of goal G4 is to evaluate operator O2, that will move tile 8 to the left in the initial state (S1). The first steps are to augment the goal with the desired state (D1) and then select the **eight-puzzle** problem space (P2), the state to which the operator will be applied (S1), and finally the operator being evaluated (O2). To do this, the augmentations from the **evaluate-object** operator (O5) to these objects are accessed and therefore added to the referenced list (the highlighted arrows in part (A) of **Figure 5**). Once operator O2 is selected, it is applied by a production that creates a new state (S3). The application of the operator depends on the exact representation used for the states of the problem space. State S1 and desired state D1, which were shown only schematically in Figure 5, are shown in detail in Figure 6. The states are built out of *cells* and *tiles* (only some of the cells and tiles are shown in Figure 6). The nine cells (C1-C9) represent the structure of the Eight Puzzle frame. They form a $3 \times 3$ grid in which each cell points to its adjacent cells. There are eight numbered tiles (T2-T9), and one blank (T1). Each tile points to its name, 1 through 8 for the numbered tiles and 0 for the blank. Tiles are associated with cells by objects called *bindings.* Each state contains 9 bindings, each of which associates one tile with the cell where it is located. The bindings for the desired state, D1, are L1-L9, while the bindings for state S1 are B1-B9. The fact that the blank is in the center of the desired state is represented by binding L2, which points to the blank tile (T1) and the center cell (C5). All states (and desired states) in both the **eight-puzzle** and **eight-puzzle-sd** problem spaces share this same cell structure.

## 3.1 Constructing chunks

Chunks are based on the working-memory elements that are either examined or created during problem solving within a subgoal. The conditions consist of those aspects of the situation that existed prior to the goal, and which were examined during the processing of the goal, while the actions consist of the results of the goal. When the subgoal terminates,[6] the collected working-memory elements are converted into the conditions and actions of one or more productions.[7] In this subsection, we describe in detail the three steps in chunk creation: (1) the collection of conditions and actions, (2) the variabilization of identifiers, and (3) chunk optimization.

### 3.1.1 Collecting conditions and actions

The conditions of a chunk should test those aspects of the situation existing prior to the creation of the goal that are relevant to the results that satisfy the goal. In *Soar* this corresponds to the working-memory elements that were matched by productions that fired in the goal (or one of its subgoals), but that existed before the goal was created. These are the elements that the problem solving implicitly deemed to be relevant to the satisfaction of the subgoal. This collection of working-memory elements is maintained for each active goal in the goal's *referenced-list.*[8] *Soar* allows productions belonging to any goal in the context stack to execute at any time, so updating the correct referenced-list requires determining for which goal in the stack the production fired. This is the most recent of the goals matched by the production's conditions. The production's firing affects the chunks created for that goal and all of its supergoals, but because the firing is independent of the more recent subgoals, it has no effect on the chunks built for those subgoals. No chunk is created if the subgoal's results were not based on prior information; for example, when an object is input

---

[6] The default behavior for *Soar* is to create a chunk *always*; that is, every time a subgoal terminates. The major alternative to creating chunks for all terminating goals is to chunk *bottom-up*, as was done in modeling the power law of practice (Rosenbloom, 1983). In bottom-up chunking, only terminal goals – goals for which no subgoals were generated – are chunked. As chunks are learned for subgoals, the subgoals need no longer be generated (the chunks accomplish the subgoals' tasks before the impasses occur), and higher goals in the hierarchy become eligible for chunking. It is unclear whether chunking always or bottom-up will prove more advantageous in the long run, so to facilitate experimentation, both options are available in *Soar.*

[7] *Production composition* (Lewis, 1978) has also been used to learn productions that summarize goals (Anderson, 1983b). It differs most from chunking in that it examines the actual definitions of the productions that fired in addition to the working-memory elements referenced and created by the productions.

[8] If a fired production has a negated condition – a condition testing for the absence in working memory of an element matching its pattern – then the negated condition is instantiated with the appropriate variable bindings from the production's positive conditions. If the identifier of the instantiated condition existed prior to the goal, then the instantiated condition is included in the referenced-list.

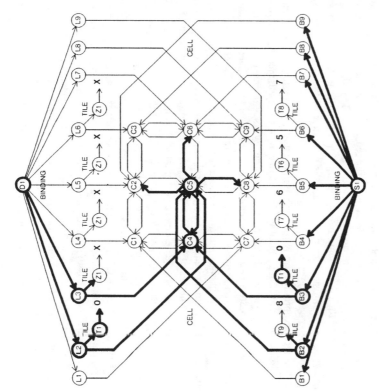

*Figure 6.* Example of working-memory elements representing the state used to create a chunk. The highlighted augmentations were referenced during the the subgoal.

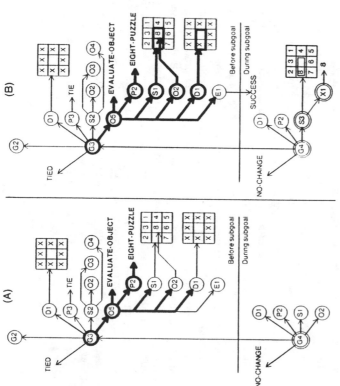

*Figure 5.* An example of the working-memory elements used to create a chunk. (A) shows working memory near the beginning of the subgoal to implement the **evaluate-object** operator. (B) shows working memory at the end of the subgoal. The circled symbols represent identifiers and the arrows represent augmentations. The identifiers and augmentations above the horizontal lines existed before the subgoal was created. Below the lines, the identifiers marked by doubled circles, and all of the augmentations, are created in the subgoal. The other identifiers below the line are not new; they are actually the same as the corresponding ones above the lines. The highlighted augmentations were referenced during the problem solving in the subgoal and will be the basis of the conditions of the chunk. The augmentation that was created in the subgoal but originates from an object existing before the subgoal (E1→SUCCESS) will be the basis for the action of the chunk.

apply to the new state. All cells that are adjacent to the blank cell (C2, C4, C6, and C8) are used to create operators. This requires testing the structure of the board as encoded in the connections between the cells. Following the creation of the operators that can apply to state S3, the operator that would undo the previous operator is rejected so that unnecessary backtracking is avoided. During the same elaboration phase, the state is tested to determine whether a tile was just moved into or out of its correct position. This information is used to generate an evaluation based on the sum of the number of tiles that do not have to be in place and the number of tiles that both have to be in place and are in place. This computation, whose result is represented by the object X1 with a value of 8 in Figure 5, results in the accessing of those aspects of the desired state highlighted in Figure 6. The value of 8 means that the goal is satisfied, so the evaluation (E1) for the operator has the value **success**. Because E1 is an identifier that existed before the subgoal was created and the **success** augmentation was created in the subgoal, this augmentation becomes an action. If

To apply the operator and create a new state, a new state symbol is created (S3) with two new bindings, one for the moved tile and one for the blank. The binding for the moved tile points to the tile (T9) and to the cell where it will be (C4). The binding for the blank points to the blank (T1) and to the cell that will be empty (C5). All the other bindings are then copied to the new state. This processing accesses the relative positions of the blank and the moved tile, and the bindings for the remaining tiles in current state (S1). The augmentations of the operator are tested for the cell that contains the tile to be moved.

Once the new state (S3) is selected, a production generates the operators that can

### 3.1.3 Chunk optimization

At this point in the chunk-creation process the semantics of the chunk are determined. However, three additional processes are applied to the chunks to increase the efficiency with which they are matched against working memory (all related to the use in *Soar* of the *Ops5* rule matcher (Forgy, 1981)). The first process is to remove conditions from the chunk that provide (almost) no constraint on the match process. A condition is removed if it has a variable in the value field of the augmentation that is not bound elsewhere in the rule (either in the conditions or the actions). This process recurses, so that a long linked-list of conditions will be removed if the final one in the list has a variable that is unique to that condition. For the chunk based on Figures 5 and 6, the bindings and tiles that were only referenced for copying (B1, B4, B5, B6, B7, B8, B9, and T9) and the cells referenced for creating operator instantiations (C2, C6, and C8) are all removed. The evaluation object, E1, in Figure 5 is not removed because it is included in the action. Eliminating the bindings does not increase the generality of the chunk, because all states must have nine bindings. However, the removal of the cells does increase the generality, because they (along with the test of cell C4) implicitly test that there must be four cells adjacent to the one to which the blank will be moved. Only the center has four adjacent cells, so the removal of these conditions does increase the generality. This does increase slightly the chance of the chunk being over-general, but in practice it has never caused a problem, and it can significantly increase the efficiency of the match by removing unconstrained conditions.

The second optimization is to eliminate potential combinatorial matches in the conditions of productions whose actions are to copy a set of augmentations from an existing object to a new object. A common strategy for implementing operators in subgoals is to create a new state containing only the new and changed information, and then to copy over pointers to the rest of the previous state. The chunks built for these subgoals contain one condition for each of the copied pointers. If, as is usually the case, a set of similar items are being copied, then the copy conditions end up differing only in the names of variables. Each augmentation can match each of these conditions independently, generating a combinatorial number of instantiations. This problem would arise if a subgoal were used to implement the **eight-puzzle** operators instead of the rules used in our current implementation. A single production would be learned that created new bindings for the moved tile and the blank, and also copied all of the other bindings. There would be seven conditions that tested for the bindings, but each of these conditions could match any of the bindings that had to be copied, generating 7! (5040) instantiations. This problem is solved by collapsing the set of similar copy conditions down to one. All of the augmentations can still be copied over, but it now occurs via multiple instantiations (seven of them) of the simpler rule. Though this reduces the number of rule instantiations to linear in the number of augmentations to be copied, it still means that the other non-copying ac-

---

success had further augmentations, they would also be included as actions. The augmentations of the subgoal (G4), the new state (S3), and its sub-object (X1) that point to objects created before the subgoal are not included as actions because they are not augmentations, either directly or indirectly, of an object that existed prior to the creation of the subgoal.

When goal G4 terminates, the initial set of conditions and actions have been determined for the chunk. The conditions test that there exists an **evaluate-object** operator whose purpose is to evaluate the operator that moves the blank into its desired location, and that all of the tiles are either in position or irrelevant for the current **eight-puzzle-sd** operator. The action is to mark the evaluation as successful, meaning that the operator being evaluated will achieve the goal. This chunk should apply in similar future situations, directly implementing the **evaluate-object** operator, and avoiding the no-change impasse and the resulting subgoal.

### 3.1.2 Identifier variabilization

Once the conditions and actions have been determined, all of the identifiers are replaced by production (pattern-match) variables, while the constants, such as **evaluate-object**, **eight-puzzle**, and **0** are left unchanged. An identifier is a label by which a particular instance of an object in working memory can be referenced. It is a short-term symbol that lasts only as long as the object is in working memory. Each time the object reappears in working memory it is instantiated with a new identifier. If a chunk that is based on working-memory elements is to reapply in a later situation, it must not mention specific identifiers. In essence the variabilization process is like replacing an 'eq' test in *Lisp* (which requires pointer identity) with an 'equal' test (which only requires value identity).

All occurrences of a single identifier are replaced with the same variable and all occurrences of different identifiers are replaced by different variables. This assures that the chunk will match in a new situation only if there is an identifier that appears in the same places in which the original identifier appeared. The production is also modified so that no two variables can match the same identifier. Basically, *Soar* is guessing which identifiers must be equal and which must be distinct, based only on the information about equality and inequality in working memory. All identifiers that are the same are assumed to require equality. All identifiers that are not the same are assumed to require inequality. Biasing the generalization in these ways assures that the chunks will not be overly general (at least because of these modifications), but they may be overly specific. The only problem this causes is that additional chunks may need to be learned if the original ones suffer from overspecialization. In practice, these modifications have not led to overly specific chunks.

tions are done more than once. This problem is solved by splitting the chunk into two productions. One production does everything the subgoal did except for the copying. The other production just does the copying. If there is more than one set of augmentations to be copied, each set is collapsed into a single condition and a separate rule is created for each.[9]

The final optimization process consists of applying a condition-recording algorithm to the chunk productions. The efficiency of the Rete-network matcher (Forgy, 1982) used in *Soar* is sensitive to the order in which conditions are specified. By taking advantage of the known structure of *Soar's* working memory, we have developed a static reordering algorithm that significantly increases the efficiency of the match. Execution time is sometimes improved by more than an order of magnitude, almost duplicating the efficiency that would be achieved if the reordering was done by hand. This reordering process preserves the existing semantics of the chunk.

### 3.2 The scope of chunking

In Section 1 we defined the scope of a general learning mechanism in terms of three properties: task generality, knowledge generality, and aspect generality. Below we briefly discuss each of these with respect to chunking in *Soar*.

*Task generality.* *Soar* provides a single formalism for all behavior – heuristic search of problem spaces in pursuit of goals. This formalism has been widely used in Artificial Intelligence (Feigenbaum & Feldman, 1963; Nilsson, 1980; Rich, 1983) and it has already worked well in *Soar* across a wide variety of problem domains (Laird, Newell, & Rosenbloom, 1985). If the problem-space hypothesis (Newell, 1980) does hold, then this should cover all problem domains for which goal-oriented behavior is appropriate. Chunking can be applied to all of the domains for which *Soar* is used. Though it remains to be shown that useful chunks can be learned for this wide range of domains, our preliminary experience suggests that the combination of *Soar* and chunking has the requisite generality.[10]

*Knowledge generality.* Chunking learns from the experiences of the problem solver. At first glance, it would appear to be unable to make use of instructions, examples, analogous problems, or other similar sources of knowledge. However, by using such information to help make decisions in subgoals, *Soar* can learn chunks that incorporate the new knowledge. This approach has worked for a simple form

[9] The inelegance of this solution leads us to believe that we do not yet have the right assumptions about how new objects are to be created from old ones.

[10] For demonstrations of chunking in *Soar* on the Eight Puzzle, Tic-Tac-Toe, and the *R1* computer-configuration task, see Laird, Rosenbloom, & Newell (1984), Rosenbloom, Laird, McDermott, Newell, & Orciuch (1985), and van de Brug, Rosenbloom, & Newell (1985).

of user direction, and is under investigation for learning by analogy. The results are preliminary, but it establishes that the question of knowledge generality is open for *Soar*.

*Aspect generality.* Three conditions must be met for chunking to be able to learn about all aspects of *Soar's* problem solving. The first condition is that all aspects must be open to problem solving. This condition is met because *Soar* creates subgoals for all of the impasses it encounters during the problem solving process. These subgoals allow for problem solving on any of the problem solver's functions: creating a problem space, selecting a problem space, creating an initial state, selecting a state, selecting an operator, and applying an operator. These functions are both necessary and sufficient for *Soar* to solve problems. So far chunking has been demonstrated for the selection and application of operators (Laird, Rosenbloom & Newell, 1984); that is, strategy acquisition (Langley, 1983; Mitchell, 1983) and operator implementation. However, demonstrations of chunking for the other types of subgoals remain to be done.[11]

The second condition is that the chunking mechanism must be able to create the long-term memory structures in which the new knowledge is to be represented. *Soar* represents all of its long-term knowledge as productions, and chunking acquires new productions. By restricting the kinds of condition and action primitives allowed in productions (while not losing Turing equivalence), it is possible to have a production language that is coextensive syntactically with the types of rules learned by chunking; that is, the chunking mechanism can create rules containing all of the syntactic constructs available in the language.

The third condition is that the chunking mechanism must be able to acquire rules with the requisite content. In *Soar*, this means that the problem solving on which the requisite chunks are to be based must be understood. The current biggest limitations on coverage stem from our lack of understanding of the problem solving underlying such aspects as problem-space creation and change of representation (Hayes & Simon, 1976; Korf, 1980; Lenat, 1983; Utgoff, 1984).

### 3.3 Chunk generality

One of the critical questions to be asked about a simple mechanism for learning from experience is the degree to which the information learned in one problem can transfer to other problems. If generality is lacking, and little transfer occurs, the learning mechanism is simply a caching scheme. The variabilization process described in Section 3.1.2 is one way in which chunks are made general. However, this process would by itself not lead to chunks that could exhibit non-trivial forms of transfer. All it does

[11] In part this issue is one of rarity. For example, selection of problem spaces is not yet problematical, and conflict impasses have not yet been encountered.

is allow the chunk to match another instance of the same exact situation. The principal source of generality is the *implicit generalization* that results from basing chunks on only those aspects of the situation that were referenced during problem solving. In the example in Section 3.1.1, only a small percentage of the augmentations in working memory ended up as conditions of the chunk. The rest of the information, such as the identity of the tile being moved and its absolute location, and the identities and locations of the other tiles, was not examined during problem solving, and therefore had no effect on the chunk.

Together, the representation of objects in working memory and the knowledge used during problem solving combine to form the *bias* for the implicit generalization process (Utgoff, 1984); that is, they determine which generalizations are embodied in the chunks learned. The object representation defines a language for the implicit generalization process, bounding the potential generality of the chunks that can be learned. The problem solving determines (indirectly, by what it examines) which generalizations are actually embodied in the chunks.

Consider the state representation used in Korf's (1985a) work on the Eight Puzzle (recall Section 2.2). In his implementation, the state of the board was represented as a vector containing the positions of each of the tiles. Location 0 contained the coordinates of the position that was blank, location 1 contained the coordinates of the first tile, and so on. This is a simple and concise representation, but because aspects of the representation are overloaded with more than one functional concept, it provides poor support for implicit generalization (or for that matter, any traditional condition-finding method). For example, the vector indices have two functions: they specify the identity of the tile, and they provide access to the tile's position. When using this state representation it is impossible to access the position of a tile without looking at its identity. Therefore, even when the problem solving is only dependent on the locations of the tiles, the chunks learned would test the tile identities, thus failing to apply in situations in which they rightly could. A second problem with the representation is that some of the structure of the problem is implicit in the representation. Concepts that are required for good generalizations, such as the relative positions of two tiles, cannot be captured in chunks because they are not explicitly represented in the structure of the state. Potential generality is maximized if an object is represented so that functionally independent aspects are explicitly represented and can be accessed independently. For example, the Eight Puzzle state representation shown in Figure 6 breaks each functional role into separate working-memory objects. This representation, while not predetermining what generalizations are to be made, defines a class of possible generalizations that include good ones for the Eight Puzzle.

The actual generality of the chunk is maximized (within the constraints established by the representation) if the problem solver only examines those features of the situation that are absolutely necessary to the solution of the problem. When the problem solver knows what it is doing, everything works fine, but generality can be lost when information that turns out to be irrelevant is accessed. For example, whenever a new state is selected, productions fire to suggest operators to apply to the state. This preparation goes on in parallel with the testing of the state to see if it matches the goal. If the state does satisfy the goal, then the preparation process was unnecessary. However, if the preparation process referenced aspects of the prior situation that were not accessed by previous productions, then irrelevant conditions will be added to the chunk. Another example occurs when false paths — searches that lead off of the solution path — are investigated in a subgoal. The searches down unsuccessful paths may reference aspects of the state that would not have been tested if only the successful path were followed.[12]

## 4. A demonstration — acquisition of macro-operators

In this section we provide a demonstration of the capabilities of chunking in *Soar* involving the acquisition of macro-operators in the Eight Puzzle for serially decomposable goals (see Section 2). We begin with a brief review of Korf's (1985a) original implementation of this technique. We follow this with the details of its implementation in *Soar*, together with an analysis of the generality of the macro-operators learned. This demonstration of macro-operators in *Soar* is of particular interest because: we are using a general problem solver and learner instead of special-purpose programs developed specifically for learning and using macro-operators; and because it allows us to investigate the generality of the chunks learned in a specific application.

### 4.1 Macro problem solving

Korf (1985a) has shown that problems that are serially decomposable can be efficiently solved with the aid of a table of *macro-operators*. A macro-operator (or *macro* for short) is a sequence of operators that can be treated as a single operator (Fikes, Hart & Nilsson, 1972). The key to the utility of macros for serially decomposable problems is to define each macro so that after it is applied, all subgoals that had been previously achieved are still satisfied, and one new subgoal is achieved. Means-ends analysis is thus possible when these macro-operators are used. Table 1 shows Korf's (1985a) macro table for the Eight Puzzle task of getting all of the tiles in order, clockwise around the frame, with the 1 in the upper left hand corner, and the blank in the middle (the desired state in Figure 3). Each column contains the macros required to achieve one of the subgoals of placing a tile. The rows give the

[12] An experimental version of chunking has been implemented that overcomes these problems by performing a dependency analysis on traces of the productions that fired in a subgoal. The production traces are used to determine which conditions were necessary to produce results of the subgoal. All of the results of this paper are based on the version of chunking without the dependency analysis.

To discover the macros, the learner started with the desired state, and performed an iterative-deepening search (for example, see Korf, 1985b) using the elementary tile-movement operators.[13] As the search progressed, the learner detected sequences of operators that left some of the tiles invariant, but moved others. When an operator sequence was found that left an initial sequence of the subgoals invariant – that is, for some tile k, the operator moved that tile while leaving tiles 1 through k-1 where they were – the operator sequence was added to the macro table in the appropriate column and row. In a single search from the desired state, all macros could be found. Since the search used iterative-deepening, the first macro found was guaranteed to be the shortest for its slot in the table.

### 4.2 Macro problem solving in Soar

Soar's original design criteria did not include the ability to employ serially decomposable subgoals or to acquire and use macro-operators to solve problems structured by such subgoals. However, Soar's generality allows it to do so with no changes to the architecture (including the chunking mechanism). Using the implementation of the Eight Puzzle described in Sections 2.2 and 3.1.1, Soar's problem solving and learning capabilities work in an integrated fashion to learn and use macros for serially decomposable subgoals.

The opportunity to learn a macro-operator exists each time a goal for implementing one of the eight-puzzle-sd operators, such as place-5, is achieved. When the goal is achieved there is a stack of subgoals below it, one for each of the choice points that led up to the desired state in the eight-puzzle problem space. As described in Section 2, all of these lower subgoals are terminated when the higher goal is achieved. As each subgoal terminates, a chunk is built that tests the relevant conditions and produces a preference for one of the operators at the choice point.[14] This set of chunks encodes the path that was successful for the eight-puzzle-sd operator. In future problems, these chunks will act as search-control knowledge, leading the problem solver directly to the solution without any impasses or subgoals. Thus, Soar learns macro-operators, not as monolithic data structures, but as sets of chunks that determine at each point in the search which operator to select next. This differs from previous realizations of macros where a single data structure contains the macro, either as a list of operators, as in Korf's work, or as a triangle table, as in Strips (Fikes, Hart & Nilsson, 1972). Instead, for each operator in the macro-operator se-

[13] For very deep searches, other more efficient techniques such as bidirectional search and macro-operator composition were used.

[14] Additional chunks are created for the subgoals resulting from no-change impasses on the evaluate-object operators, such as the example chunk in Section 3.1.1, but these become irrelevant for this task once the rules that embody preferences are learned.

Table 1. Macro table for the Eight Puzzle (from Korf, 1985, Table 1). The primitive operators move a tile one step in a particular direction; u (up), d (down), l (left), and r (right).

| Positions | Tiles | | | | | | |
|---|---|---|---|---|---|---|---|
| | 0 | 1 | 2 | 3 | 4 | 5 | 6 |
| A | | | | | | | |
| B | ul | | | | | | |
| C | u | rdlu | | | | | |
| D | ur | dlurrdlu | dlur | | | | |
| E | r | ldrurdlu | ldru | rdllurdrul | | | |
| F | dr | uldrurdldrul | lurdldru | ldrulurddlru | lurd | rdlluurddldrrul | |
| G | d | urdldrul | ulddru | urddluldrrul | uldr | urdluldr | |
| H | dl | rulddrul | druuldrdlu | ruldrdluldrrul | urdluldr | uldrurdllurd | urdl |
| I | l | drul | rulldru | rdluldrrul | rulldr | uldrruldrul | ruld |

appropriate macro according to the current position of the tile, where the positions are labeled A-I as in Figure 7. For example, if the goal is to move the blank (tile 0) into the center, and it is currently in the top left corner (location B), then the operator sequence ul will accomplish it.

Korf's implementation of macro problem solving used two programs: a problem solver and a learner. The problem solver could use macro tables acquired by the learner to solve serially decomposable problems efficiently. Using Table 1, the problem-solving program could solve any Eight Puzzle problem with the same desired state (the initial state may vary). The procedure went as follows: (a) the position of the blank was determined; (b) the appropriate macro was found by using this position to index into the first column of the table; (c) the operators in this macro were applied to the state, moving the blank into position; (d) the position of the first tile was determined; (e) the appropriate macro was found by using this position to index into the second column of the table; (f) the operators in this macro were applied to the state, moving the first tile (and the blank) into position; and so on until all of the tiles were in place.

| B | C | D |
|---|---|---|
| I | A | E |
| H | G | F |

Figure 7. The positions (A-I) in the Eight Puzzle frame.

ple problem. The figure shows the searches for which the depth is sufficient to implement each operator. The first **eight-puzzle-sd** operator, **place-blank**, moves the blank to the center. Without learning, this yields the search shown in the left column of the first row. During learning (the middle column), a chunk is first learned to avoid an operator that does not achieve the goal within the current depth limit (2). This is marked by a ' - ', and the number 1 in the figure. The unboxed numbers give the order that the chunks are learned, while the boxed numbers show where the chunks are used in later problem solving. Once the goal is achieved, signified by the darkened circle, a chunk is learned that prefers the first move over all other alternatives, marked by ' + ' in the figure. No chunk is learned for the final move to the goal since the only other alternative at that point has already been rejected, eliminating any choice, and thereby eliminating the need to learn a chunk. The right column shows that on a second attempt, chunk 2 applied to select the first operator. After the operator applied, chunk 1 applied to reject the operator that did not lead to the goal. This leaves only the operator that leads to the goal, which is selected and applied. In this scheme, the chunks control the problem solving within the subgoals that implement the **eight-puzzle-sd** operator, eliminating search, and thereby encoding a macro-operator.

The examples in the second and third rows of Figure 8 show more complex searches and demonstrate how the chunks learned during problem solving for one **eight-puzzle-sd** operator can reduce the search both within that operator and within other operators. In all of these examples, a macro-operator is encoded as a set of chunks that are learned during problem solving and that will eliminate the search the next time a similar problem is presented.

In addition to learning chunks for each of the operator-selection decisions, *Soar* can learn chunks that directly implement instances of the operators in the **eight-puzzle-sd** problem space. They directly create a new state where the tiles have been moved so that the next desired tile is in place, a process that usually involves many Eight Puzzle moves. These chunks would be ideal macro-operators if it were not necessary to actually apply each **eight-puzzle** operator to a physical puzzle in the real world. As it is, the use of such chunks can lead to illusions about having done something that was not actually done. We have not yet implemented in *Soar* a general solution to the problem posed by such chunks. One possible solution – whose consequences we have not yet analyzed in depth – is to have chunking automatically turned off for any goal in which an action occurs that affects the outside world. For this work we have simulated this solution by disabling chunking for the **eight-puzzle** problem space. Only search-control chunks (generated for the **tie** problem space) are learned.

The searches within the **eight-puzzle** problem space can be controlled by a variety of different problem solving strategies, and any heuristic knowledge that is available can be used to avoid a brute-force search. Both iterative-deepening and breadth-first

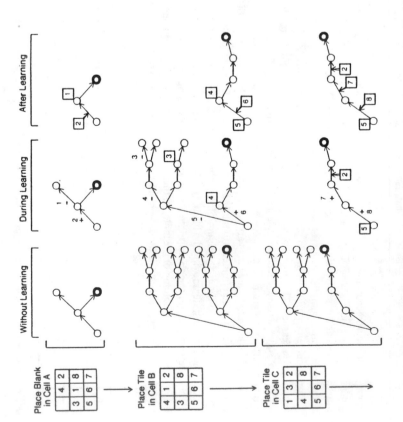

**Place Blank in Cell A**

| 4 | 2 |   |
|---|---|---|
| 3 | 1 | 8 |
| 5 | 6 | 7 |

**Place Tile in Cell B**

| 4 | 2 |   |
|---|---|---|
| 3 | 1 | 8 |
| 5 | 6 | 7 |

**Place Tile in Cell C**

| 1 | 3 | 2 |
|---|---|---|
| 4 |   | 8 |
| 5 | 6 | 7 |

*Figure 8.* Searches performed for the first three **eight-puzzle-sd** operators in an example problem. The left column shows the search without learning. The horizontal arrows represent points in the search where no choice (and therefore no chunk) is required. The middle column shows the search during learning. A ' + ' signifies that a chunk was learned that preferred a given operator: A ' - ' signifies that a chunk was learned to avoid an operator. The boxed numbers show where a previously learned chunk was applied to avoid search during learning. The right column shows the search after learning.

quence, there is a chunk that causes it to be selected (and therefore applied) at the right time. On later problems (and even the same problem), these chunks control the search when they can, giving the appearance of macro problem solving, and when they cannot, the problem solver resorts to search. When the latter succeeds, more chunks are learned, and more of the macro table is covered. By representing macros as sets of independent productions that are learned when the appropriate problem arises, the processes of learning, storing, and using macros become both incremental and simplified.

Figure 8 shows the problem solving and learning that *Soar* does while performing iterative-deepening searches for the first three **eight-puzzle-sd** operators of an exam-

be, then the chunks will also not examine them. However, this does not tap all of the possible sources of generality in the Eight Puzzle. In the remainder of this subsection we will describe two additional forms of transfer available in the *Soar* implementation.

### 4.3.1 Different goal states

One limitation on the generality of the macro table is that it can only be used to solve for the specific final configuration in Figure 3. Korf (1985a) described one way to overcome this limitation. For other desired states with the blank in the center it is possible to use the macro table by renumbering the tiles in the desired state to correspond to the ordering in Figure 3, and then using the same transformation for the initial state. In the *Soar* implementation this degree of generality occurs automatically as a consequence of implicit generalization. The problem solver must care that a tile is in its desired location, but it need not care which tile it actually is. The chunks learned are therefore independent of the exact numbering on the tiles. Instead they depend on the relationship between where the tiles are and where they should be.

For desired states that have the blank in a different position, Korf (1985a) described a three-step solution method. First find a path from the initial state to a state with the blank in the center; second, find a path from the desired state to the same state with the blank in the middle; and third, combine the solution to the first problem with the inverse of the solution to the second problem – assuming the inverse of every operator is both defined and known – to yield a solution to the overall problem. In *Soar* this additional degree of generality can be achieved with the learning of only two additional chunks. This is done by solving the problem using the following subgoals (see Figure 9): (a) get the blank in the middle, (b) get the first six tiles into their correct positions, and (c) get the blank in its final position. The first 7 moves can be performed directly by the chunks making up the macro table, while the last step requires 2 additional chunks.

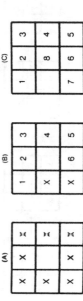

*Figure 9.* Problems with different goals states, with different positions of the blank, can be solved by: (a) moving the blank into the center, (b) moving the first six tiles into position, and (c) moving the blank into its desired position.

search[15] strategies were implemented and tested. Only one piece of search control was employed – do not apply an operator that will undo the effects of the previous operator. Unfortunately, *Soar* is too slow to be able to generate a complete macro table for the Eight Puzzle by search. *Soar* was unable to learn the eight macros in columns three and five in Figure 1. These macros require searches to at least a depth of eight.[16]

The actual searches used to generate the chunks for a complete macro table were done by having a user lead *Soar* down the path to the correct solution. At each resolve-tie subgoal, the user specified which of the tied operators should be evaluated first, insuring that the correct path was always tried first. Because the user specified which operator should be evaluated first, and not which operator should actually be applied, *Soar* proceeded to try out the choice by selecting the specified **evaluate-object** operator and entering a subgoal in which the relevant **eight-puzzle** operator was applied. *Soar* verified that the choice made by the user was correct by searching until the choice led to either success or failure. During the verification, the appropriate objects were automatically referenced so that a correct chunk was generated. This is analogous to the *explanation-based learning* approach (for example, see De Jong, 1981 or Mitchell, Keller, & Kedar-Cabelli, 1986), though the explanation and learning processes differ.

*Soar's* inability to search quickly enough to complete the macro table autonomously is the one limitation on a claim to have replicated Korf's (1985a) results for the Eight Puzzle. This, in part, reflects a trade-off between speed (Korf's system) and generality (*Soar*). But it is also partially a consequence of our not using the fastest production-system technology available. Significant improvements in *Soar's* performance should be possible by reimplementing it using the software technology developed for *Ops83* (Forgy, 1984).

### 4.3 Chunk generality and transfer

Korf's (1985a) work on macro problem solving shows that a large class of problems – for example, all Eight Puzzle problems with the same desired state – can be solved efficiently using a table with a small number of macros. This is possible only because the macros ignore the positions of all tiles not yet in place. This degree of generality occurs in *Soar* as a direct consequence of implicit generalization. If the identities of the tiles not yet placed are not examined during problem solving, as they need not

---

[15] This was actually a *parallel* breadth-first search in which the operators at each depth were executed in parallel.

[16] Although some of the macros are fourteen operators long, not every operator selection requires a choice (some are forced moves) and, in addition, *Soar* is able to make use of transfer from previously learned chunks (Section 4.3).

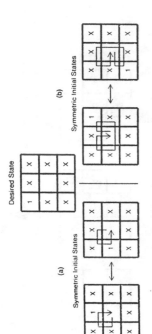

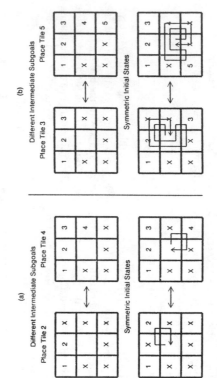

Figure 10. Two examples of within-column symmetry transfer.

Figure 11. An example of across-column symmetry transfer.

### 4.3.2 Transfer between macro-operators

In addition to the transfer of learning between desired states, we can identify four different levels of generality that are based on increasing the amount of transfer that occurs *between* the macro-operators in the table: *no transfer, simple transfer, symmetry transfer (within column)*, and *symmetry transfer (across column)*. The lowest level, *no transfer*, corresponds to the generality provided directly by the macro table. It uses macro-operators quite generally, but shows no transfer between the macro-operators. Each successive level has all of the generality of the previous level, plus one additional variety of transfer. The number of chunks required for the other cases were computed by hand. Let us consider each of them in turn.

*No transfer.* The no-transfer situation is identical to that employed by Korf (1985a). There is no transfer of learning between macro-operators. In *Soar*, a total of 230 chunks would be required for this case.[17] This is considerably higher than the number of macro-operators (35) because one chunk must be learned for each macro-operator in the table (if there is no search control) rather than for each macro-operator. If search control is available to avoid undoing the previous operator, only 170 chunks must be learned.

*Simple transfer.* Simple transfer occurs when two entries in the same column of the macro table end in exactly the same set of moves. For example, in the first column of Table 1, the macro that moves the blank to the center from the upper-right corner uses the macro-operator *ur* (column 0, row D in the table). The chunk learned for the second operator in this sequence, which moves the blank to the center from the position to the right of the center (by moving the center tile to the right), is dependent on the state of the board following the first operator, but independent of what the first operator actually was. Therefore, the chunk for the last half of this macro-operator is exactly the chunk/macro-operator in column 0, row E of the table. This type of transfer is always available in *Soar*, and reduces the number of chunks needed to encode the complete macro table from 170 to 112. The amount of simple transfer is greater than a simple matching of the terminal sequences of operators in the macros in Table 1 would predict because different macro operators of the same length as those in the table can be found that provide greater transfer.

*Symmetry transfer (within column).* Further transfer can occur when two macro-operators for the same subgoal are identical except for rotations or reflections. Figure 10 contains two examples of such transfer. The desired state for both is to move the 1 to the upper left corner. The X's represent tiles whose values are irrelevant to the specific subgoal and the arrow shows the path that the blank travels in order to achieve the subgoal. In (a), a simple rotation of the blank is all that is required, while in (b), two rotations of the blank must be made. Within both examples the

pattern of moves remains the same, but the orientation of the pattern with respect to the board changes. The ability to achieve this type of transfer by implicit generalization is critically dependent upon the representation of the states (and operators) discussed in Section 3.3. The representation allows the topological relationships among the affected cells (which cells are next to which other cells) and the operators (which cells are affected by the operators) to be examined while the absolute locations of the cells and the names of the operators are ignored. This type of transfer reduces the number of required chunks from 112 to 83 over the simple-transfer case.

*Symmetry transfer (across column).* The final level of transfer involves the carry-over of learning between different subgoals. As shown by the example in Figure 11, this can involve far from obvious similarities between two situations. What is important in this case is: (1) that a particular three cells are not affected by the moves (the exact three cells can vary); (2) the relative position of the tile to be placed with respect to where it should be; and (3) that a previously placed piece that is affected

---

[17] These numbers include only the chunks for the resolve-tie subgoals. If the chunks generated for the **evaluate-object** operators were included, the chunk counts given in this section would be doubled.

*Table 2.* Structure of the chunks that encode the macro table for the Eight Puzzle.

|  |  | Tiles | | | | | | |
|  |  | 0 | 1 | 2 | 3 | 4 | 5 | 6 |
|---|---|---|---|---|---|---|---|---|
| A |  |  |  |  |  |  |  |  |
| B |  | 2,1 |  |  |  |  |  |  |
| P o s i t i o n s | C | 1 | 4,3,1 |  |  |  |  |  |
|  | D | 2 | 7,6,5,4 | 15,14,1 |  |  |  |  |
|  | E | 1 | 10,9,8,4 | 18,17,16 | 34,33,32,31,30, 29,1 |  |  |  |
|  | F | 2 | 13,12,11,10 | 21,20,19,18 | 40,39,38,37,36, 35,30 | 15 |  |  |
|  | G | 1 | 10 | 23,22,17 | 46,45,44,43,42, 41,30 | 18 | 61,60,59,58, 56,55,29 |  |
|  | H | 2 | 7 | 26,25,24,23 | 54,53,52,51,50, 49,48,47,46,29 | 21 | 40 |  |
|  | I | 1 | 4 | 28,27,22 | 51 | 23 | 46 | 18 |

by the moves gets returned to its original position. Across-column symmetry transfer reduces the number of chunks to be learned from 83 to 61 over the within-column case.[18] Together, the three types of transfer make it possible for *Soar* to learn the complete macro table in only three carefully selected trials.

Table 2 contains the macro-table structure of the chunks learned when all three levels of transfer are available (and search control to avoid undoing the previous operator is included). In place of operator sequences, the table contains numbers for the chunks that encode the macros. There is no such table actually in *Soar* – all chunks (productions) are simply stored, unordered, in production memory. The purpose of this table is to show the actual transfer that was achieved for the Eight Puzzle.

The order in which the subgoals are presented has no effect on the collection of chunks that are learned for the macro table, because if a chunk will transfer to a new situation (a different place in the macro table) the chunk that would have been learned in the new situation would be identical to the one that applied instead.

[18] The number of chunks can be reduced further, to 54, by allowing the learning of macros that are not of minimum length. This increases the total path length by 2 for 14% of the problems, by 4 for 26% of the problems and 6 for 7% of the problems.

Though this is not true for all tasks, it is true in this case. Therefore, we can just assume that the chunks are learned starting in the upper left corner, going top to bottom and left to right. The first chunk learned is number 1 and the last chunk learned is number 61. When the number for a chunk is highlighted, it stands for all of the chunks that followed in its first unhighlighted occurrence. For example, for tile 1 in position F, the chunks listed are 13, 12, 11, *10*. However, *10* signifies the sequence beginning with chunk 10: 10, 9, 8, *4*. The terminal *4* in this sequence signifies the sequence beginning with chunk 4: 4, 3, 1. Therefore, the entire sequence for this macro is: 13, 12, 11, 10, 9, 8, 4, 3, 1.

The abbreviated macro format used in Table 2 is more than just a notational convenience; it directly shows the transfer of learning between the macro-operators. Simple transfer and within-column symmetry transfer show up as the use of a macro that is defined in the same column. For example, the sequence starting with chunk 51 is learned in column 3 row H, and used in the same column in row I. The extreme case is column 0, where the chunks learned in the top row can be used for all of the other rows. Across-column symmetry transfer shows up as the reoccurrence of a chunk in a later column. For example, the sequence starting with chunk 29 is learned in column 3 (row E) and used in column 5 (row G). The extreme examples of this are columns 4 and 6 where all of the macros were learned in earlier columns of the table.

### 4.4 Other tasks

The macro technique can also be used in the Tower of Hanoi (Korf, 1985a). The three-peg, three-disk version of the Tower of Hanoi has been implemented as a set of serially decomposable subgoals in *Soar*. In a single trial (moving three disks from one peg to another), *Soar* learns eight chunks that completely encode Korf's (1985a) macro table (six macros). Only a single trial was required because significant within and across column transfer was possible. The chunks learned for the three-peg, three-disk problem will also solve the three-peg, two-disk problem. These chunks also transfer to the final moves of the three-peg, N-disk problem when the three smallest disks are out of place. Korf (1985a) demonstrated the macro table technique on three additional tasks: the Fifteen Puzzle, Think-A-Dot and Rubik's Cube. The technique for learning and using macros in *Soar* should be applicable to all of these problems. However, the performance of the current implementation would require user-directed searches for the Fifteen Puzzle and Rubik's Cube because of the size of the problems.

## 5. Conclusion

In this article we have laid out how chunking works in *Soar*. Chunking is a learning mechanism that is based on the acquisition of rules from goal-based experience. As such, it is related to a number of other learning mechanisms. However, it obtains extra scope and generality from its intimate connection with a sophisticated problem solver (*Soar*) and the memory organization of the problem solver (a production system). This is the most important lesson of this research. The problem solver provides many things: the opportunities to learn, direction as to what is relevant (biases) and what is needed, and a consumer for the learned information. The memory provides a means by which the newly learned information can be integrated into the existing system and brought to bear when it is relevant.

In previous work we have demonstrated how the combination of chunking and operator implementation rules in both search-based puzzle tasks and knowledge-based expert systems tasks (Laird, Rosenbloom & Newell, 1984; Rosenbloom, Laird, McDermott, Newell, & Orciuch, 1985). In this paper we have provided a new demonstration of the capabilities of chunking in the context of the macro-operator learning task investigated by Korf (1985a). This demonstration shows how: (1) the macro-operator technique can be used in a general, learning problem solver without the addition of new mechanisms; (2) the learning can be incremental during problem solving rather than requiring a preprocessing phase; (3) the macros can be used for any goal state in the problem; and (4) additional generality can be obtained via transfer of learning between macro-operators, provided an appropriate representation of the task is available.

Although chunking displays many of the properties of a general learning mechanism, it has not yet been demonstrated to be truly general. It can not yet learn new problem spaces or new representations, nor can it yet make use of the wide variety of potential knowledge sources, such as examples or analogous problems. Our approach to all of these insufficiences will be to look to the problem solving. Goals will have to occur in which new problem spaces and representations are developed, and in which different types of knowledge can be used. The knowledge can then be captured by chunking.

## Acknowledgements

We would like to thank Pat Langley and Richard Korf for their comments on an earlier draft of this paper.

This research was sponsored by the Defense Advanced Research Projects Agency (DOD), ARPA Order No. 3597, monitored by the Air Force Avionics Laboratory under contracts F33615-81-K-1539 and N00039-83-C-0136, and by the Personnel and Training Research Programs, Psychological Sciences Division, Office of Naval Research, under contract number NR667-477. The views and conclusions contained in this document are those of the authors and should not be interpreted as representing the official policies, either expressed or implied, of the Defense Advanced Research Projects Agency, the Office of Naval Research, or the US Government.

## References

Anderson, J.R. (1983). *The architecture of cognition*. Cambridge: Harvard University Press.

Anderson, J.R. (1983). Knowledge compilation: The general learning mechanism. In R.S. Michalski, J.G. Carbonell, & T.M. Mitchell (Eds.). *Proceedings of the 1983 Machine Learning Workshop*. University of Illinois at Urbana-Champaign.

Anzai, Y., & Simon, H.A. (1979). The theory of learning by doing. *Psychological Review, 86*, 124–140.

Brown, J.S., & VanLehn, K. (1980). Repair theory: A generative of bugs in procedural skills. *Cognitive Science, 4*, 379–426.

Carbonell, J.G., Michalski, R.S., & Mitchell, T.M. (1983). An overview of machine learning. In R.S. Michalski, J.G. Carbonell, T.M. Mitchell (Eds.). *Machine learning: An artificial intelligence approach*. Los Altos, CA: Morgan Kaufmann.

Chase, W.G., & Simon, H.A. (1973). Perception in chess. *Cognitive Psychology, 4* 55–81.

Davis, R., & King, J. (1976). An overview of production systems. In E.W. Elcock & D. Michie (Ed.), *Machine intelligence 8*. New York: American Elsevier.

DeJong, G. (1981). Generalizations based on explanations. *Proceedings of the Seventh International Joint Conference on Artificial Intelligence* (pp. 67–69). Vancouver, B.C., Canada: Morgan Kaufmann.

Feigenbaum, E.A., & Feldman, J. (Eds.) (1963). *Computers and thought*. New York: McGraw-Hill.

Fikes, R.E., Hart, P.E. & Nilsson, N.J. (1972). Learning and executing generalized robot plans. *Artificial intelligence, 3*, 251–288.

Forgy, C.L. (1981). *OPS5 manual* (Technical Report). Pittsburgh, PA: Computer Science Department, Carnegie-Mellon University.

Forgy, C.L. (1982). Rete: A fast algorithm for the many pattern/many object pattern match problem. *Artificial intelligence, 19*, 17–37.

Forgy, C.L. (1984). *The OPS83 Report* (Tech. Rep. #84–133). Pittsburgh, PA: Computer Science Department, Carnegie-Mellon University.

Hayes, J.R., & Simon, H.A. (1976). Understanding complex task instructions. In Klahr, D.(Ed.), *Cognition and instruction*. Hillsdale, NJ: Erlbaum.

Korf, R.E. (1980). Toward a model of representation changes. *Artificial intelligence, 14*, 41–78.

Korf, R.E. (1985). Macro-operators: A weak method for learning. *Artificial intelligence, 26*, 35–77.

Korf, R.E. (1985). Depth-first iterative-deepening: An optimal admissable tree search. *Artificial intelligence, 27*, 97–110.

Laird, J.E. (1984). *Universal subgoaling*. Doctoral dissertation, Computer Science Department, Carnegie-Mellon University, Pittsburgh, PA.

Laird, J.E., & Newell, A. (1983). A universal weak method: Summary of results. *Proceedings of the Eighth International Joint Conference on Artificial Intelligence* (pp. 771–773). Karlsruhe, West Germany: Morgan Kaufmann.

Laird, J.E., & Newell, A. (1983). *A universal weak method* (Tech. Rep. #83–141). Pittsburgh, PA: Computer Science Department, Carnegie-Mellon University.

Laird, J.E., Newell, A., & Rosenbloom, P.S. (1985). Soar: An architecture for general intelligence. In preparation.

Laird, J.E., Rosenbloom, P.S., & Newell, A. (1984). Towards chunking as a general learning mechanism. *Proceedings of the National Conference on Artificial Intelligence* (pp. 188–192). Austin, TX: Morgan Kaufmann.

Langley, P. (1983). Learning Effective Search Heuristics. *Proceedings of the Eighth International Joint Conference on Artificial Intelligence* (pp. 419–425). Karlsruhe, West Germany: Morgan Kaufmann.

Lenat, D. (1976). *AM: An artificial intelligence approach to discovery in mathematics as heuristic search.* Doctoral dissertation, Computer Science Department, Stanford University, Stanford, CA.

Lenat, D.B. (1983). Eurisko: A program that learns new heuristics and domain concepts. *Artificial intelligence, 21,* 61–98.

Lewis, C.H. (1978). *Production system models of practice effects.* Doctoral dissertation, University of Michigan, Ann Arbor, Michigan.

Marsh, D. (1970). Memo functions, the graph traverser, and a simple control situation. In B. Meltzer & D. Michie (Eds.), *Machine intelligence 5.* New York: American Elsevier.

McDermott, J. (1982). R1: A rule-based configurer of computer systems. *Artificial intelligence, 19,* 39–88.

Michie, D. (1968). 'Memo' functions and machine learning. *Nature, 218,* 19–22.

Miller, G.A. (1956). The magic number seven, plus or minus two: Some limits on our capacity for processing information. *Psychological Review, 63,* 81–97.

Mitchell, T.M. (1983). Learning and problem solving. *Proceedings of the Eighth International Joint Conference on Artificial Intelligence* (pp. 1139–1151). Karlsruhe, West Germany: Morgan Kaufmann.

Mitchell, T.M., Keller, R.M., & Kedar-Cabelli, S.T. (1986). Explanation-based generalization: A unifying view. *Machine learning, 1:* 47–80.

Neves, D.M., & Anderson, J.R. (1981). Knowledge compilation: Mechanisms for the automatization of cognitive skills. In Anderson, J.R. (Ed.), *Cognitive skills and their acquisition.* Hillsdale, NJ: Erlbaum.

Newell, A. (1973). Production systems: Models of control structures. In Chase, W. (Ed.). *Visual information processing.* New York: Academic.

Newell, A. (1980). Reasoning, problem solving and decision processes: The problem space as a fundamental category. In R. Nickerson (Ed.), *Attention and performance VIII.* Hillsdale, N.J.: Erlbaum. (Also available as CMU CSD Technical Report, Aug 79).

Newell, A., & Rosenbloom, P.S. (1981). Mechanisms of skill acquisition and the law of practice. In J.R. Anderson (Ed.), *Cognitive skills and their acquisition.* Hillsdale, NJ: Erlbaum. (Also available as Carnegie-Mellon University Computer Science Tech.Rep. #80–145).

Nilsson, N. (1980). *Principles of artificial intelligence.* Palo Alto, CA: Tioga.

Rendell, L.A. (1983). A new basis for state-space learning systems and a successful implementation. *Artificial intelligence, 20,* 369–392.

Rich, E. (1983). *Artificial intelligence.* New York: McGraw-Hill.

Rosenbloom, P.S. (1983). *The chunking of goal hierarchies: A model of practice and stimulus-response compatibility.* Doctoral dissertation, Carnegie-Mellon University, Pittsburgh, PA. (Available as Carnegie-Mellon University Computer Science Tech. Rep. #83–148).

Rosenbloom, P.S., & Newell, A. (1986). The chunking of goal hierarchies: A generalized model of practice. In R.S. Michalski, J.G. Carbonell, & T.M. Mitchell (Eds.), *Machine Learning: An Artificial Intelligence Approach, Volume II.* Los Altos, CA: Morgan Kaufmann Publishers, Inc. In press (Also available in *Proceedings of the Second International Machine Learning Workshop,* Urbana: 1983).

Rosenbloom, P.S., Laird, J.E., McDermott, J., Newell, A., & Orciuch, E. (1985). R1-Soar: An experiment in knowledge-intensive programming in a problem-solving architecture. *IEEE Transactions on Pattern Analysis and Machine Intelligence, 7,* 561–569. (Also available in *Proceedings of the IEEE Workshop on Principles of Knowledge-Based Systems,* Denver: IEEE Computer Society, 1984, and as part of Carnegie-Mellon University Computer Science Tech. Rep. #85–110).

Smith, R.G., Mitchell, T.M., Chestek, R.A., & Buchanan, B.G. (1977). A model for learning systems. *Proceedings of the Fifth International Joint Conference on Artificial Intelligence.* (pp. 338–343). Cambridge, Mass.: Morgan Kaufmann.

Sussman, G.J. (1977). *A computer model of skill acquisition.* New York: Elsevier.

Utgoff, P.E. (1984). *Shift of bias for inductive concept learning.* Doctoral dissertation, Rutgers University, New Brunswick, NJ.

van de Brug, A., Rosenbloom, P.S., & Newell, A. (1985). *Some experiments with R1-Soar* (Tech. Rep.). Computer Science Department, Carnegie-Mellon University, Pittsburgh, PA. In preparation.

Waterman, D.A. (1975). Adaptive production systems. *Proceedings of the Fourth International Joint Conference on Artificial Intelligence* (pp. 296–303). Tbilisi, USSR: Morgan Kaufmann.

# Section 5.2

# Explanation-Based Learning

There has been an explosion of research in recent years in the area of explanation-based learning (EBL). Explanation-based learning is meant to be a very general term. EBL is sometimes defined as learning from a single example or even with no examples. It is sometimes defined as learning using background knowledge. In usage, it is sometimes a placeholder for any noninductive method.

Historically, the EBL approach assumed that the domain theory (knowledge base) was complete, consistent, correct, and tractable. The lack of such theories in expert system domains has generated much research in relaxing the requirements on the form of the domain theory. Another active area of EBL research relates to the integration of explanation-based and similarity-based learning systems. Most apprenticeship systems fall into this category, including the three systems described in Chapter 6.

The article by Mitchell, Keller and Kedar-Cabelli in Section 5.2.1 provides an excellent overview and introduction to EBL. Another article that was published at the same time by De-Jong and Mooney (1988) has been equally influential and is recommended to the interested reader. Mitchell et al. outline the major issues of generalization as proof and operationalization of abstract concepts as a means of improving efficiency. Their framework, now standard in the EBL literature, states that one begins with a *domain theory*, a *goal concept*, an *operationality criterion*, and a *training example*. The knowledge acquisition task is viewed as the problem of revising the domain theory.

The article by Mooney in Section 5.2.2 describes the EGGS domain-independent approach to EBL, and compares it to several other EBL systems, including STRIPS, SOAR, LEX2, and EBG. The insightful conclusion drawn from this comparison is that the types of explanation-based learning done by all these systems are essentially the same: they all find the most general unifier for the expressions in a given explanation structure.

Machine Learning 1: 47–80, 1986
© 1986 Kluwer Academic Publishers, Boston – Manufactured in The Netherlands

# Explanation-Based Generalization: A Unifying View

TOM M. MITCHELL                                    (MITCHELL @ RED.RUTGERS.EDU)
RICHARD M. KELLER                                    (KELLER @ RED.RUTGERS.EDU)
SMADAR T. KEDAR-CABELLI
                                            (KEDAR-CABELLI @ RED.RUTGERS.EDU)
Computer Science Department, Rutgers University, New Brunswick, NJ 08903, U.S.A.

(Received August 1, 1985)

**Key words:** explanation-based learning, explanation-based generalization, goal regression, constraint back-propagation, operationalization, similarity-based generalization.

**Abstract.** The problem of formulating general concepts from specific training examples has long been a major focus of machine learning research. While most previous research has focused on empirical methods for generalizing from a large number of training examples using no domain-specific knowledge, in the past few years new methods have been developed for applying domain-specific knowledge to formulate valid generalizations from single training examples. The characteristic common to these methods is that their ability to *generalize* from a single example follows from their ability to *explain* why the training example is a member of the concept being learned. This paper proposes a general, domain-independent mechanism, called EBG, that unifies previous approaches to explanation-based generalization. The EBG method is illustrated in the context of several example problems, and used to contrast several existing systems for explanation-based generalization. The perspective on explanation-based generalization afforded by this general method is also used to identify open research problems in this area.

## 1. Introduction and motivation

The ability to generalize from examples is widely recognized as an essential capability of any learning system. Generalization involves observing a set of training examples of some general concept, identifying the essential features common to these examples, then formulating a concept definition based on these common features. The generalization process can thus be viewed as a search through a vast space of possible concept definitions, in search of a correct definition of the concept to be learned. Because this space of possible concept definitions is vast, the heart of the generalization problem lies in utilizing whatever training data, assumptions and knowledge are available to constrain this search.

Most research on the generalization problem has focused on empirical, data-intensive methods that rely on large numbers of training examples to constrain the search for the correct generalization (see Mitchell, 1982; Michalski, 1983; Dietterich,

1982 for overviews of these methods). These methods all employ some kind of *inductive bias* to guide the inductive leap that they must make in order to define a concept from only a subset of its examples (Mitchell, 1980). This bias is typically built into the generalizer by providing it with knowledge only of those example features that are presumed relevant to describing the concept to be learned. Through various algorithms it is then possible to search through the restricted space of concepts definable in terms of these allowed features, to determine concept definitions consistent with the training examples. Because these methods are based on searching for features that are common to the training examples, we shall refer to them as *similarity-based* generalization methods.[1]

In recent years, a number of researchers have proposed generalization methods that contrast sharply with these data-intensive, similarity-based methods (e.g., Borgida et al., 1985; DeJong, 1983; Kedar-Cabelli, 1985; Keller, 1983; Lebowitz, 1985; Mahadevan, 1985; Minton, 1984; Mitchell, 1983; Mitchell et al., 1985; O'Rorke, 1984; Salzberg & Atkinson, 1984; Schank, 1982; Silver, 1983; Utgoff, 1983; Winston et al., 1983). Rather than relying on many training examples and an inductive bias to constrain the search for a correct generalization, these more recent methods constrain the search by relying on knowledge of the task domain and of the concept under study. After analyzing a single training example in terms of this knowledge, these methods are able to produce a valid generalization of the example *along with a deductive justification of the generalization in terms of the system's knowledge.* More precisely, these *explanation-based* methods[2] analyze the training example by first constructing an explanation of how the example satisfies the definition of the concept under study. The features of the example identified by this explanation are then used as the basis for formulating the general concept definition. The justification for this concept definition follows from the explanation constructed for the training example.

Thus, by relying on knowledge of the domain and of the concept under study, explanation-based methods overcome the fundamental difficulty associated with inductive, similarity-based methods: their inability to justify the generalizations that they produce. The basic difference between the two classes of methods is that similarity-based methods must rely on some form of inductive bias to guide generalization, whereas explanation-based methods rely instead on their domain knowledge. While explanation-based methods provide a more reliable means of

---

[1] The term *similarity-based generalization* was suggested by Lebowitz (1985). We use this term to cover both methods that search for similarities among positive examples, and for differences between positive and negative examples.

[2] The term *explanation-based generalization* was first introduced by DeJong (1981) to describe his particular generalization method. The authors have previously used the term *goal-directed generalization* (Mitchell, 1983) to refer to their own explanation-based generalization method. In this paper, we use the term explanation-based generalization to refer to the entire class of methods that formulate generalizations by constructing explanations.

generalization, and are able to extract more information from individual training examples, they also require that the learner possess knowledge of the domain and of the concept under study. It seems clear that for a large number of generalization problems encountered by intelligent agents, this required knowledge is available to the learner. In this paper we present and analyze a number of such generalization problems.

The purpose of this paper is to consider in detail the capabilities and requirements of explanation-based approaches to generalization, and to introduce a single mechanism that unifies previously described approaches. In particular, we present a domain-independent method (called EBG) for utilizing domain-specific knowledge to guide generalization, and illustrate its use in a number of generalization tasks that have previously been approached using differing explanation-based methods. EBG constitutes a more general mechanism for explanation-based generalization than these previous approaches. Because it requires a larger number of explicit inputs (i.e., the training example, a domain theory, a definition of the concept under study, and a description of the form in which the learned concept must be expressed) EBG can be instantiated for a wider variety of learning tasks. Finally, EBG provides a perspective for identifying the present limitations of explanation-based generalization, and for identifying open research problems in this area.

The remainder of this paper is organized as follows. Section 2 introduces the general EBG method for explanation-based generalization, and illustrates the method with an example. Section 3 then illustrates the EBG method in the context of two additional examples: (1) learning a structural definition of a cup from a training example plus knowledge about the function of a cup (based on Winston et al.'s (1983) work), and (2) learning a search heuristic from an example search tree plus knowledge about search and the search space (based on Mitchell et al.'s (1983) work on the LEX system). Section 4 concludes with a general perspective on explanation-based generalization and a discussion of significant open research issues in this area. The appendix relates DeJong's (1981, 1983) research on explanation-based generalization and explanatory schema acquisition to the other work discussed here.

## 2. Explanation-based generalization: discussion and an example

The key insight behind explanation-based generalization is that it is possible to form a justified generalization of a single positive training example provided the learning system is endowed with some explanatory capabilities. In particular, the system must be able to explain to itself *why* the training example is an example of the concept under study. Thus, the generalizer is presumed to possess a definition of the concept under study as well as domain knowledge for constructing the required explanation. In this section, we define more precisely the class of generalization problems covered by explanation-based methods, define the general EBG method, and illustrate it in terms of a specific example problem.

### 2.1 The explanation-based generalization problem

In order to define the generalization problem considered here, we first introduce some terminology. A *concept* is defined as a predicate over some universe of instances, and thus characterizes some subset of the instances. Each *instance* in this universe is described by a collection of ground literals that represent its features and their values. A *concept definition* describes the necessary and sufficient conditions for being an example of the concept, while a *sufficient concept definition* describes sufficient conditions for being an example of the concept. An instance that satisfies the concept definition is called an *example*, or *positive example* of that concept, whereas an instance that does not satisfy the concept definition is called a *negative example* of that concept. A *generalization* of an example is a concept definition which describes a set containing that example.[3] An *explanation* of how an instance is an example of a concept is a proof that the example satisfies the concept definition. An *explanation structure* is the proof tree, modified by replacing each instantiated rule by the associated general rule.

The generic problem definition shown in Table 1 summarizes the class of generalization problems considered in this paper. Table 2 illustrates a particular instance of an explanation-based generalization problem from this class. As indicated by these tables, defining an explanation-based generalization problem involves specifying four kinds of information:

- The *goal concept* defines the concept to be acquired. For instance, in the problem defined in Table 2 the task is to learn to recognize pairs of objects <x,y> such that it is safe to stack x on top of y. Notice that the goal concept

*Table 1.* The explanation-based generalization problem

---

*Given:*

- *Goal Concept*: A concept definition describing the concept to be learned. (It is assumed that this concept definition fails to satisfy the Operationality Criterion.)
- *Training Example*: An example of the goal concept.
- *Domain Theory*: A set of rules and facts to be used in explaining how the training example is an example of the goal concept.
- *Operationality Criterion*: A predicate over concept definitions, specifying the form in which the learned concept definition must be expressed.

*Determine:*

- A generalization of the training example that is a sufficient concept definition for the goal concept and that satisfies the operationality criterion.

---

[3] In fact, we use the term *generalization* in this paper both as a noun (to refer to a general concept definition), and as a verb (to refer to the process of deriving this generalization).

*Table 2.* The SAFE-TO-STACK generalization problem after Borgida et al. (1985)

**Given:**

- *Goal Concept:* Pairs of objects <x, y> such that SAFE-TO-STACK (x, y), where
  SAFE-TO-STACK (x, y) ⇔ NOT (FRAGILE (y)) V LIGHTER (x, y).
- *Training Example:*
  ON (OBJ1, OBJ2)
  ISA (OBJ1, BOX)
  ISA (OBJ2, ENDTABLE)
  COLOR (OBJ1, RED)
  COLOR (OBJ2, BLUE)
  VOLUME (OBJ1, 1)
  DENSITY (OBJ1, .1)
  ...
- *Domain Theory:*
  VOLUME (p1, v1) ∧ DENSITY (p1, d1) → WEIGHT (p1, v1*d1)
  WEIGHT (p1, w1) ∧ WEIGHT (p2, w2) ∧ LESS (w1, w2) → LIGHTER (p1, p2)
  ISA (p1, ENDTABLE) → WEIGHT (p1, 5) (default)
  LESS (.1, 5)
  ...
- *Operationality Criterion:* The concept definition must be expressed in terms of the predicates used to describe examples (e.g., VOLUME, COLOR, DENSITY) or other selected, easily evaluated, predicates from the domain theory (e.g., LESS).

**Determine:**

- A generalization of training example that is a sufficient concept definition for the goal concept and that satisfies the operationality criterion.

here, SAFE-TO-STACK, is defined in terms of the predicates FRAGILE and LIGHTER, whereas the training example is defined in terms of other predicates (i.e., COLOR, DENSITY, VOLUME, etc.).

- The *training example* is a positive example of the goal concept. For instance, the training example of Table 2 describes a pair of objects, a box and an endtable, where one is safely stacked on the other.
- The *domain theory* includes a set of rules and facts that allow explaining how training examples are members of the goal concept. For instance, the domain theory for this problem includes definitions of FRAGILE and LIGHTER, rules for inferring features like the WEIGHT of an object from its DENSITY and VOLUME, rules that suggest default values such as the WEIGHT of an ENDTABLE, and facts such as '.1 is LESS than 5'.
- The *operationality criterion* defines the terms in which the output concept definition must be expressed. Our use of this term is based on Mostow's (1981) definition that a procedure is *operational* relative to a given agent and task, provided that the procedure can be applied by the agent to solve the task. Similarly, we assume that the learned concept definition will be used by some agent to perform some task, and must be defined in terms operational for

that agent and task. For this problem, the operationality criterion requires that the final concept definition be described in terms of the predicates used to describe the training example (e.g., COLOR, VOLUME, DENSITY) or in terms of a selected set of easily evaluated predicates from the domain theory (e.g., LESS). Reexpressing the goal concept in these terms will make it operational with respect to the task of *efficiently recognizing examples of the concept*.

Given these four inputs, the task is to determine a generalization of the *training example* that is a sufficient concept definition for the *goal concept* and that satisfies the *operationality criterion*. Note that the notion of operationality is crucial for explanation-based generalization: if the operationality criterion were not specified, the input goal concept definition could always be a correct output concept definition and there would be nothing to learn! The operationality criterion imposes a requirement that learned concept definitions must be not only correct, but also *in a usable form* before learning is complete. This additional requirement is based on the viewpoint that concept definitions are not learned as theoretical entities, but rather as practical entities to be used by a particular agent for a particular task.

### 2.2 The EBG method

The EBG method, which is designed to address the above class of problems, is defined as follows:

*The EBG method*

1. *Explain.* Construct an explanation in terms of the *domain theory* that proves how the *training example* satisfies the *goal concept* definition.
   - This explanation must be constructed so that each branch of the explanation structure terminates in an expression that satisfies the *operationality criterion*.
2. *Generalize:* Determine a set of sufficient conditions under which the explanation structure holds, stated in terms that satisfy the *operationality criterion*.
   - This is accomplished by regressing the *goal concept* through the explanation structure. The conjunction of the resulting regressed expressions constitutes the desired concept definition.

To see more concretely how the EBG method works, consider again the problem of learning the concept SAFE-TO-STACK (x, y). The bottom of Figure 1 shows a training example for this problem, described in terms of a semantic network of objects and relations. In particular, the example consists of two physical objects, OBJ1

portion of Figure 1 is given in the top portion of the figure. As shown there, the pair of objects <OBJ1, OBJ2> satisfies the goal concept SAFE-TO-STACK because OBJ1 is LIGHTER than OBJ2. Furthermore, this is known because the WEIGHTs of OBJ1 and OBJ2 can be inferred. For OBJ1, the WEIGHT is inferred from its DENSITY and VOLUME, whereas for OBJ2 the WEIGHT is inferred based on a rule that specifies the default weight of ENDTABLEs in general.

Through this chain of inferences, the explanation structure demonstrates how OBJ1 and OBJ2 satisfy the goal concept definition. Note that the explanation structure has been constructed so that each of its branches terminates in an expression that satisfies the operationality criterion (e.g., VOLUME (OBJ1, 1), LESS (.1, 5)). In this way, the explanation structure singles out those features of the training example that are relevant to satisfying the goal concept, and that provide the basis for constructing a justified generalization of the training example. For the current example, these relevant training example features are shown shaded over in the figure, and correspond to the conjunction VOLUME (OBJ1, 1) ∧ DENSITY (OBJ1, 0.1) ∧ ISA (OBJ2, ENDTABLE).

Whereas the first step of the EBG method isolates the relevant features of the training example, it does not determine the desired generalized constraints on feature values. For instance, while the feature VOLUME (OBJ1, 1) is relevant to explaining how the present training example satisfies the goal concept, the general constraint on acceptable values for VOLUME is yet to be determined. The second step of the EBG method therefore generalizes on those feature values selected by the first step, by determining sufficient conditions on these feature values that allow each step in the explanation structure to carry through.

In order to determine general sufficient conditions under which the explanation holds, the second step of the EBG method involves regressing (back propagating) the goal concept step by step back through the explanation structure. In general, *regressing* a given formula F through a rule R is a mechanism for determining the necessary and sufficient (weakest) conditions under which that rule R can be used to infer F. We employ a slightly modified version of the goal-regression algorithm described by Waldinger (1977) and Nilsson (1980).[4] Our modified goal regression algorithm computes an expression that represents only a sufficient condition (rather than necessary and sufficient conditions) under which rule R can be used to infer formula F, but that corresponds closely to the training example under consideration. In particular, whereas the general goal regression algorithm considers all possible variable bindings (unifications) under which R can infer F, our modified algorithm considers only the specific variable bindings used in the explanation of the training example. Furthermore, if the rule R contains a disjunctive antecedent (left-hand side), then our

[4] Dijkstra (1976) introduces the related notion of *weakest preconditions* in the context of proving program correctness. The *weakest preconditions* of a program characterize the set of all initial states of that program such that activation guarantees a final state satisfying some postcondition.

EXPLANATION
STRUCTURE:

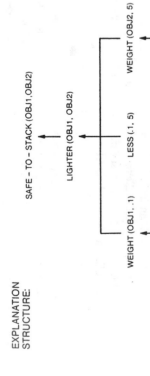

TRAINING
EXAMPLE:

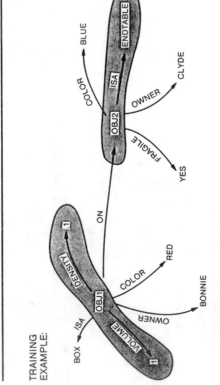

*Figure 1.* Explanation of SAFE-TO-STACK (OBJ1, OBJ2).

and OBJ2, in which OBJ1 is ON OBJ2, and for which several features of the objects are described (e.g., their OWNERs, COLORs).

Given this training example, the task is to determine which of its features are relevant to characterizing the goal concept, and which are irrelevant. To this end, the first step of the EBG method is to construct an explanation of how the training example satisfies the goal concept. Notice that the explanation constitutes a proof, and constructing such an explanation therefore may involve in general the complexities of theorem proving. The explanation for the training example depicted in the lower

the rule to yield some set of substitutions (particular variable bindings). The substitution consistent with the example is then applied to the antecedent (left-hand side) of the rule to yield the resulting regressed expression.[6] Any conjuncts of the original expression which cannot be unified with the consequent of any rule are simply added to the resulting regressed expression (with the substitutions applied to them). As illustrated in the figure, regressing the conjunct WEIGHT (x, w1) through the rule VOLUME (p1, v1) ∧ DENSITY (p1, d1) → WEIGHT (p1, v1*d1) therefore yields VOLUME (x, v1) ∧ DENSITY (x, d1). Regressing the conjunct WEIGHT (y, w2) through the rule ISA (p2, ENDTABLE) → WEIGHT (p2, 5) yields ISA (y, ENDTABLE). Finally, since no rule consequent can be unified with the conjunct LESS (w1, w2), this conjunct is simply added to the resulting regressed expression after applying the substitutions produced by regressing the other conjuncts. In this case these substitutions are {x/p1, v1*d1/w1, y/p2, 5/w2}, which yield the third conjunct LESS (v1*d1, 5). The final, operational definition for SAFE-TO-STACK (x, y) is therefore:

$$\text{VOLUME (x, v1)}$$
$$\land\ \text{DENSITY (x, d1)}$$
$$\land\ \text{LESS (v1*d1, 5)}$$
$$\land\ \text{ISA (y, ENDTABLE)} \rightarrow \text{SAFE-TO-STACK (x, y)}$$

This expression characterizes in operational terms the features of the training example that are sufficient for the explanation structure to carry through in general. As such, it represents a justified generalization of the training example, for which the explanation structure serves as justification.

### 2.3 Discussion

Several general points regarding the EBG method are illustrated in the above example. The main point of the above example is that the EBG method produces a justified generalization from a single training example in a two-step process. The first step creates an explanation that separates the relevant feature values in the examples from the irrelevant ones. The second step analyzes this explanation to determine the particular constraints on these feature values that are sufficient for the explanation structure to apply in general. Thus, explanation-based methods such as EBG overcome the main limitation of similarity-based methods: their inability to produce justified generalizations. This is accomplished by assuming that the learner has available knowledge of the domain, the goal concept, and the operationality

[6] It is correctly observed in DeJong (1986) that the substitution list used to regress expressions through previous steps in the explanation must be applied to the current expression before the next regression step.

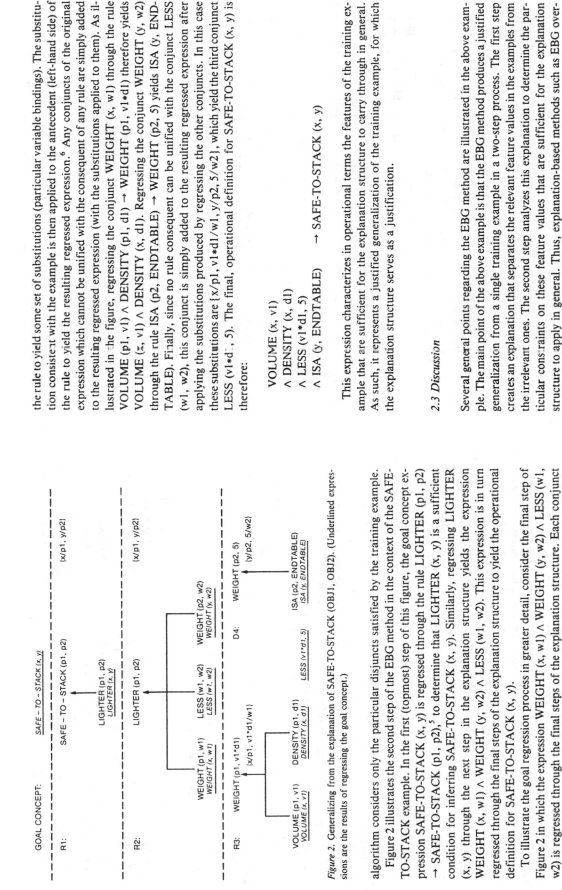

*Figure 2.* Generalizing from the explanation of SAFE-TO-STACK (OBJ1, OBJ2). (Underlined expressions are the results of regressing the goal concept.)

algorithm considers only the particular disjuncts satisfied by the training example. Figure 2 illustrates the second step of the EBG method in the context of the SAFE-TO-STACK example. In the first (topmost) step of this figure, the goal concept expression SAFE-TO-STACK (x, y) is regressed through the rule LIGHTER (p1, p2) → SAFE-TO-STACK (p1, p2),[5] to determine that LIGHTER (x, y) is a sufficient condition for inferring SAFE-TO-STACK (x, y). Similarly, regressing LIGHTER (x, y) through the next step in the explanation structure yields the expression WEIGHT (x, w1) ∧ WEIGHT (y, w2) ∧ LESS (w1, w2). This expression is in turn regressed through the final steps of the explanation structure to yield the operational definition for SAFE-TO-STACK (x, y).

To illustrate the goal regression process in greater detail, consider the final step of Figure 2 in which the expression WEIGHT (x, w1) ∧ WEIGHT (y, w2) ∧ LESS (w1, w2) is regressed through the final steps of the explanation structure. Each conjunct of the expression is regressed separately through the appropriate rule, in the following way. The conjunct is unified (matched) with the consequent (right-hand side) of

[5] Notice that the definition of SAFE-TO-STACK given in Table 2 is a disjunctive definition. As noted above, the procedure considers only the disjunct that is satisfied by the current training example (e.g., the disjunct involving the LIGHTER predicate).

criterion, whereas similarity-based generalization does not rely on any of these inputs.

A second point illustrated by the above example is that the language in which the final concept definition is stated can be quite rich. Notice in the above example that the final generalization includes a constraint that the product of the DENSITY and the VOLUME of x must be less than 5. There are very many such relations among the parts of the training example that might be considered during generalization (e.g., why not consider the fact that the OWNERs of the two objects are of different SEX?). The interesting point here is that the appropriate constraint was derived directly by analyzing the explanation, without considering the universe of possible relations among parts of the training example. This is in marked contrast with similarity-based generalization methods (e.g. Michalski, 1983; Quinlan, 1985). Such methods are typically based on a heuristic focusing criterion, such as the heuristic that 'less complex features are preferred over more complex features for characterizing concepts'. Therefore, before such methods will consider the feature LESS $(v1*d1, 5)$ as a plausible basis for generalization, they must first consider vast numbers of syntactically simpler, irrelevant features.

A final point illustrated by this example is that the final concept definition produced by EBG is typically a specialization of the goal concept rather than a direct reexpression of the concept. This is largely due to the fact that the explanation structure is created for the given training example, and does not explain every possible example of the goal concept. Thus, the generalization produced from analyzing this explanation will only cover examples for which the explanation holds. Furthermore, because the modified goal regression algorithm computes only sufficient (not necessary and sufficient) conditions under which the explanation holds, it leads to a further specialization of the concept. This limitation of explanation-based generalization suggests an interesting problem for further research: developing explanation-based methods that can utilize multiple training examples (see the discussion in Section 4).

## 3. Other examples and variations

This section discusses two additional examples of explanation-based generalization that have previously been reported in the literature. The first is Winston, Binford, Katz, and Lowry's (1983) research on learning structural definitions of concepts such as 'cup' from their functional definitions. The second is Mitchell, Keller, and Utgoff's (1983) research on learning search heuristics from examples (see also Utgoff, 1984; Keller, 1983). A common perspective on these two systems is provided by instantiating the EBG method for both problems. Differences among the two original approaches and the EBG method are also considered, in order to underscore some subtleties of the EBG method, and to suggest some possible variations.

### 3.1 An example: learning the concept CUP

In this subsection we first summarize the application of the EBG method to a second example of an explanation-based generalization problem: the CUP generalization problem, patterned after the work of Winston et al. (1983). We then discuss the relationship between the EBG method and the ANALOGY program of Winston et al., which addresses this same problem.

The CUP generalization problem, defined in Table 3, involves learning a structural definition of a cup from its functional definition. In particular, the goal concept here is the concept CUP, defined as the class of objects that are OPEN-VESSELs, LIFT-ABLE, and STABLE. The domain theory includes rules that relate these properties to the more primitive structural properties of physical objects, such as FLAT, HAN-DLE, etc. The operationality criterion requires that the output concept definition be useful for the task of visually recognizing examples of CUPs. It thus requires that the output concept definition be expressed in terms of its structural features.

Figure 3 illustrates a training example describing a particular cup, OBJ1, along with the explanation that shows how OBJ1 satisfies the goal concept CUP. In particular, the explanation indicates how OBJ1 is LIFTABLE, STABLE, and an OPEN-VESSEL. As in the SAFE-TO-STACK example, this explanation distinguishes the relevant features of the training example (e.g., its LIGHTness) from irrelevant features (e.g., its COLOR). The second step of the EBG method, regressing the goal concept through the explanation structure, results in the following general definition of the CUP concept:

$$(\text{PART-OF}(x, xc) \wedge \text{ISA}(xc, \text{CONCAVITY}) \wedge \text{IS}(xc, \text{UPWARD-POINTING})$$
$$\wedge\ \text{PART-OF}(x, xb) \wedge \text{ISA}(xb, \text{BOTTOM}) \wedge \text{IS}(xb, \text{FLAT})$$
$$\wedge\ \text{PART-OF}(x, xh) \wedge \text{ISA}(xh, \text{HANDLE}) \wedge \text{IS}(x, \text{LIGHT})) \rightarrow \text{CUP}(x)$$

*Table 3.* The CUP generalization problem after Winston et al. (1983)

*Given:*

- *Goal Concept:* Class of objects, x, such that CUP(x), where
  $\text{CUP}(x) \Leftrightarrow \text{LIFTABLE}(x) \wedge \text{STABLE}(x) \wedge \text{OPEN-VESSEL}(x)$
- *Training Example:*
  OWNER(OBJ1, EDGAR)
  PART-OF(OBJ1, CONCAVITY-1)
  IS(OBJ1, LIGHT)
  ...
- *Domain Theory:*
  $\text{IS}(x, \text{LIGHT}) \wedge \text{PART-OF}(x, y) \wedge \text{ISA}(y, \text{HANDLE}) \rightarrow \text{LIFTABLE}(x)$
  $\text{PART-OF}(x, y) \wedge \text{ISA}(y, \text{BOTTOM}) \wedge \text{IS}(y, \text{FLAT}) \rightarrow \text{STABLE}(x)$
  $\text{PART-OF}(x, y) \wedge \text{ISA}(y, \text{CONCAVITY}) \wedge \text{IS}(y, \text{UPWARD-POINTING} \rightarrow \text{OPEN-VESSEL}(x)$
  ...
- *Operationality Criterion:* Concept definition must be expressed in terms of structural features used in describing examples (e.g., LIGHT, HANDLE, FLAT, etc.).

*Determine:*

- A generalization of training example that is a sufficient concept definition for the goal concept and that satisfies the operationality criterion.

### 3.1.1 Discussion

As in the first example, the EBG method is able to produce a valid generalization from a single training example, by explaining and analyzing how the training example satisfies the definition of the goal concept. Notice that the regression step in this example is quite straightforward, and leads to generalizing the training example features effectively by replacing constants with variables (i.e., replacing OBJ1 by x). It is interesting that several earlier attempts at explanation-based generalization (e.g., Mitchell, 1983) involved the assumption that the explanation could always be generalized simply by replacing constants by variables in the explanation, without the need to regress the goal concept through the explanation structure.[7] As the earlier SAFE-TO-STACK example illustrates, this is not the case. In general, one must regress the goal concept through the explanation structure to ensure a valid generalization of the training example (which may involve composing terms from different parts of the explanation, requiring constants where no generalization is possible, and so on).

Several interesting features of this example come to light when the EBG method is compared to the method used in Winston et al.'s (1983) ANALOGY program, upon which this example problem is based. The most striking difference between the two methods is that although ANALOGY does construct an explanation, and also uses this explanation to generalize from a single example, the system has no domain theory of the kind used in the above example. Instead, Winston's program constructs its explanations by drawing analogies between the training example and a library of precedent cases (e.g., annotated descriptions of example suitcases, bricks, bowls, etc.). For example, ANALOGY explains that the FLAT BOTTOM of OBJ1 allows OBJ1 to be STABLE, by drawing an analogy to a stored description of a brick which has been annotated with the assertion that its FLAT BOTTOM 'causes' it to be STABLE. Similarly, it relies on an annotated example of a suitcase to explain by analogy why a handle allows OBJ1 to be LIFTABLE.

In general, the precedents used by ANALOGY are assumed to be annotated by links that indicate which features of the precedent account for which of its properties. Thus, for the ANALOGY program, the causal links distributed over the library of precedents constitute its domain theory. However, this theory is qualitatively different than the domain theory used in the CUP example above: it is described by examples rather than intention (i.e., by examples rather than by general rules), and is therefore a weaker domain theory. Because ANALOGY's knowledge about causality is summarized by a collection of instances of causal relations rather than by general rules of causality, its theory cannot lead *deductively to* assertions about new causal links.

---

[7] This observation is due in part to Sridhar Mahadevan.

EXPLANATION
STRUCTURE:

CUP (OBJ1)

OPEN-VESSEL (OBJ1)        STABLE (OBJ1)        LIFTABLE (OBJ1)

PART-OF (OBJ1, CONCAVITY-1)      PART-OF (OBJ1, BOTTOM-1)      IS (OBJ1, LIGHT)
ISA (CONCAVITY-1, CONCAVITY)     ISA (BOTTOM-1, BOTTOM)        PART-OF (OBJ1, HANDLE-1)
IS (CONCAVITY-1, UPWARD-POINTING) IS (BOTTOM-1, FLAT)          ISA (HANDLE-1, HANDLE)

TRAINING
EXAMPLE:

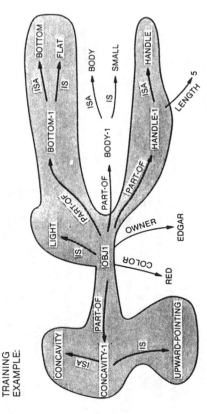

*Figure 3.* Explanation of CUP (OBJ1).

*Table 4.* The search heuristic generalization problem after Mitchell et al. (1983)

**Given:**

- *Goal Concept:* The class of integral expressions that can be solved by first applying operator OP3 (removing a constant from the integrand); that is, the class of integrals, x, such that USEFUL-OP3 (x), where

$$\text{USEFUL-OP3}(x) \Leftrightarrow \text{NOT}(\text{SOLVED}(x)) \land \text{SOLVABLE}(\text{OP3}(x))$$

and

$$\text{OP3: } \int r \cdot <any-fn> dx \rightarrow r \int <any-fn> dx.$$

- *Training Example:* $\int 7x^2 dx$.
- *Domain Theory:*

$$\text{SOLVABLE}(x) \Leftrightarrow (\exists op) (\text{SOLVED}(op(x)) \lor \text{SOLVABLE}(op(x)))$$
$$\text{MATCHES}(x, \text{'}\int <any-fn> dx\text{'}) \rightarrow \text{NOT} (\text{SOLVED}(x))$$
$$\text{MATCHES}(x, \text{'}<any-fn>\text{'}) \rightarrow \text{SOLVED}(x)$$
$$\text{MATCHES}(op(x), y) \Leftrightarrow \text{MATCHES}(x, \text{REGRESS}(y, op))$$

- *Operationality Criterion:* Concept definition must be expressed in a form that uses *easily-computable* features of the problem state, x, (e.g., features such as <polynomial-fn>, <transcendental-fn>, <any-fn>, r, k).

**Determine:**

- A generalization of training example that is a sufficient concept definition of the goal concept and that satisfies the operationality criterion.

---

Because its domain theory is weak, the ANALOGY system raises some interesting questions about explanation-based generalization. Whereas the SAFE-TO-STACK and CUP examples above show how a sufficient set of domain theory rules can provide powerful guidance for generalization, ANALOGY suggests how a weaker, extensional theory might be used to focus the generalization process in a weaker fashion. In particular, the causal links are used by ANALOGY to construct a plausible explanation, but not a proof, that the training example satisfies the goal concept definition. As discussed above, such plausible explanations can guide generalization by focusing on plausibly relevant features of the training example. But since ANALOGY lacks general inference rules to characterize the links in this explanation, it cannot perform the second (goal regression) step in the EBG method, and therefore has no valid basis for generalizing the explanation. In fact, the ANALOGY program generalizes anyway, implicitly, assuming that each causal link of the form (feature (OBJ1) → property (OBJ1)) is supported by a general rule of the form ((∀x) (feature (x) → property (x)).[8] Thus, ANALOGY represents an important step in considering the use of a weak domain theory to guide generalization, and helps to illuminate a number of open research issues (see the discussion in Section 4).

### 3.2 An example: learning a search heuristic

This section presents a third example of an explanation-based generalization problem – this one involving the learning of search heuristics. This example is based on the problem addressed by the LEX program (Mitchell et al., 1983) which learns search control heuristics for solving problems in the integral calculus. In particular, LEX begins with a set of legal operators (transformations) for solving integrals (e.g., integration by parts, moving constants outside the integrand). For each such operator, the system learns a heuristic that summarizes the class of integrals (problem states) for which it is useful to apply that operator. For example, one typical heuristic learned by the LEX system is:

IF the integral is of the form $\int <polynomial-fn> \cdot <trigonometric-fn> dx$, THEN apply Integration-by-Parts

Thus, for each of its given operators, LEX faces a generalization problem: learning the class of integrals for which that operator is useful in reaching a solution. Table 4 defines the generalization problem that corresponds to learning when it is useful to apply OP3 (moving constants outside the integrand). Here the goal concept USEFUL-OP3 (x) describes the class of problem states (integrals) for which OP3 will

be useful. This is defined to be the class of problem states that are NOT already SOLVED (i.e., algebraic expressions that contain an integral sign), and for which applying OP3 leads to a SOLVABLE problem state. The domain theory in this case contains rules that relate SOLVED and SOLVABLE to observable features of problem states (e.g., one rule states that if problem state x MATCHES the expression $\int <any-fn> dx$, then x is NOT a SOLVED state.). Notice that some of the domain theory rules constitute knowledge about search and problem solving in general (e.g., the definition of SOLVABLE), while other rules represent knowledge specific to integral calculus (e.g., that the absence of an integral sign denotes a SOLVED state). The operationality condition in this problem requires that the final concept definition be stated in terms of *easily-computable* features of the given problem state. This requirement assures that the final concept definition will be in a form that permits its effective use as a search control heuristic.[9] For the LEX program, the set of *easily-computable* features is described by a well-defined generalization language over problem states that includes features (e.g., <trigonometric-fn>, <real-constant>) which LEX can efficiently recognize using its MATCHES predicate.

[8] Winston's (1985) own work on building rule censors can be viewed as an attempt to address difficulties that arise from this implicit assumption.

[9] If the concept definition were permitted to include features that are difficult to compute (e.g., SOLVABLE), then the resulting heuristic would be so expensive to evaluate that its use would degrade, rather than improve, the problem solver's performance.

This is in turn explained by indicating that applying OP9[10] to the resulting state produces a SOLVED problem, as evidenced by the fact that the resulting state MATCHES the expression '$<any-fn>$' (i.e., that it contains no integral sign). Thus, up to this point (marked as (a) in the figure), each step in the right-hand branch of the explanation structure corresponds to some step along the solution path of the training example.

By point (a), the explanation has indicated that one relevant feature of the training example state is that the result of applying OP3 (followed by OP9, is a state that MATCHES '$<any-fn>$'. The operationality criterion requires, however, that the explanation be in terms of features of the single given training example state, rather than features of its resulting solution state. Thus, the remainder of the explanation consists of reexpressing this constraint in terms of the training example state. This is accomplished by applying the last rule in the domain theory of Table 4. This rule[11] allows back propagating the expression '$<any-fn>$' through the general definitions of OP9 and OP3, to determine the equivalent constraint on the training example state. The resulting constraint is that the training example state must MATCH the expression '$<any-fn> \int r_1 \cdot x r_2 \neq -1 \, dx$' (Here $r_1$ and $r_2$ stand for two distinct real numbers, where $r_2$ must not be equal to $-1$.). This together with the left-hand branch of the explanation structure, explains which features of $\int 7x^2 dx$ guarantee that it satisfies the goal concept USEFUL-OP3.

Given this explanation structure, the second step of the EBG method is straightforward. As in the CUP example, regressing the goal concept expression USEFUL-OP3 (x) through the explanation structure effectively results in replacing the training example state by a variable, so that the resulting generalization (taken from the leaves of the explanation tree) is:

$$\text{MATCHES (x, '} \int <any-fn> dx') \wedge$$
$$\text{MATCHES (x, '} <any-fn> \int r_1 \cdot x r_2 \neq -1 \, dx') \rightarrow \text{USEFUL-OP3}$$

which simplifies to:

$$\text{MATCHES (x, '} <any-fn> \int r_1 \cdot x r_2 \neq -1 \, dx') \rightarrow \text{USEFUL-OP3 (x)}$$

[10] OP9: $\int x^{r \neq -1} dx \rightarrow x^{r+1}/(r+1)$.

[11] The domain theory rule MATCHES (op (x), y) $\Leftrightarrow$ MATCHES (x, REGRESS (y, op)) indicates that if the result of applying operator *op* to state x MATCHES some expression y, then the state x MATCHES some expression which can be computed by REGRESSing the expression y through operator *op*. Notice that the regression here involves propagating constraints on problem states through problem solving operators. This is a different regression step from the second step of the EBG process, in which the goal concept is regressed through the domain theory rules used in the explanation structure.

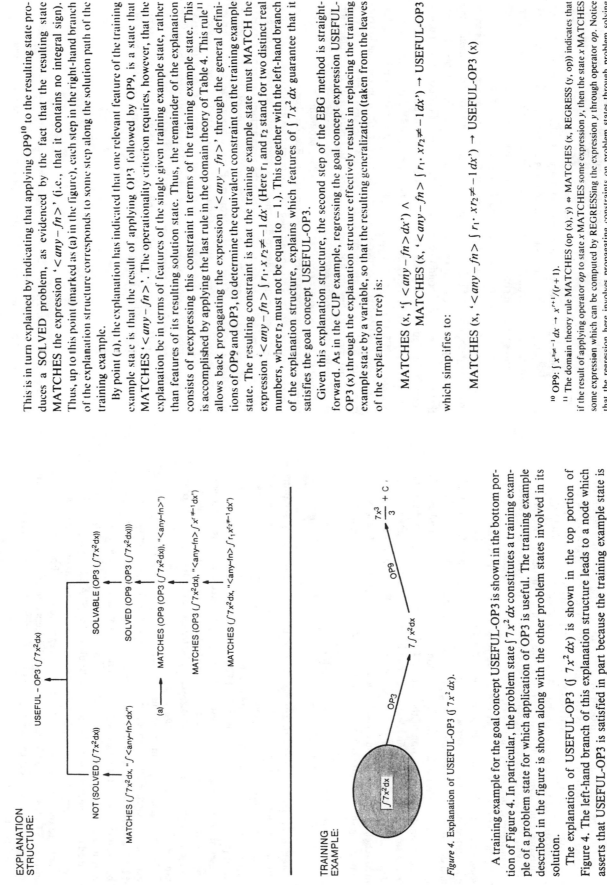

*Figure 4.* Explanation of USEFUL-OP3 ($\int 7x^2 dx$).

A training example for the goal concept USEFUL-OP3 is shown in the bottom portion of Figure 4. In particular, the problem state $\int 7x^2 dx$ constitutes a training example of a problem state for which application of OP3 is useful. The training example described in the figure is shown along with the other problem states involved in its solution.

The explanation of USEFUL-OP3 ($\int 7x^2 dx$) is shown in the top portion of Figure 4. The left-hand branch of this explanation structure leads to a node which asserts that USEFUL-OP3 is satisfied in part because the training example state is not already a SOLVED state. The right-hand branch of the explanation structure explains that applying OP3 to the example state leads to a SOLVABLE problem state.

### 3.2.1 Discussion

To summarize, this example demonstrates again the general EBG method of constructing an explanation in terms that satisfy the operationality condition, then regressing the goal concept through the explanation structure to determine a justified generalization of the training example. As in the previous examples, this process results in a generalization of the training example which is a sufficient condition for satisfying the goal concept, and which is justified in terms of the goal concept, domain theory, and operationality criterion.

In the above example, the goal concept corresponds to the precondition for a search heuristic that is to be learned. The domain theory therefore involves both domain-independent knowledge about search (e.g., the definition of SOLVABLE) and domain-dependent knowledge (e.g., how to recognize a SOLVED integral). To use this method to learn heuristics in a new domain, one would have to replace only the domain-dependent portion of the theory. To learn a different type of heuristic in the same domain, one could leave the domain theory intact, changing only the definition of the USEFUL-OP3 goal concept accordingly. For example, as suggested in Mitchell (1984), the system could be modified to learn heuristics that suggest only steps along the *minimum cost* solution path, by changing the goal concept to

USEFUL-OP3 (s) ⇔ NOT(SOLVED (s)) ∧
    MIN-COST-SOLN (SOLUTION-PATH (OP3, s))

Note that the explanation structure in this example, like the domain theory, separates into a domain-independent and a domain-dependent portion. Domain-independent knowledge about search is applied above point (a) in Figure 4, and domain-dependent knowledge about calculus problem solving operators is applied below point (a). In the implementation of the LEX2 program (Mitchell, 1983), these two phases of the explanation were considered to be two unrelated subprocesses and were implemented as separate procedures. From the perspective afforded by the EBG method, however, these two subprocesses are better seen as different portions of the same explanation-generation step.

One final point regarding the current example has to do with the ability of explanation-based methods to augment their description language of concepts. In LEX2, as in the SAFE-TO-STACK problem, this method is able to isolate fairly complex features of the training example that are directly related to the explanation of how it satisfies the goal concept. In the context of the LEX project, Utgoff (1985) studied this issue and developed the STABB subsystem. STABB is able to extend the initial vocabulary of terms used by LEX, by naming and assimilating terms that correspond to the constraints derived during the regression step. For example, in one instance STABB derived the definition of odd integers through this regression step, defining it as 'the set of real numbers, x, such that subtracting 1 then dividing by 2 produces an integer'.

### 3.2.2 Related methods for strategy learning

There are a number of additional systems that learn problem solving strategies by analyzing single examples of successful solutions.[12] These systems (e.g. Fikes et al., 1972; Utgoff, 1984; Minton, 1984; Mahadevan, 1985), which we might call STRIPS-like systems, can all be viewed as systems that learn a goal concept of the following form: 'the set of problem states such that applying a given operator sequence, OS, yields a final state matching a given solution property, P.' Since these systems are tuned to this single goal concept, and are not intended to learn other forms of concepts, they typically do not represent the goal concept and explanation declaratively. However, they do represent the solution property, P, explicitly, and regress this property through the operator sequence OS to determine an operational definition of the (implicit) goal concept. From the perspective of the above LEX example, the steps that they perform correspond to constructing the portion of the explanation below point (a) in Figure 4. It is in constructing these steps of the explanation that LEX regresses its solution property 'MATCHES (x, $<any-fn>$)' through the operator sequence $<OP3, OP9>$ to determine the equivalent constraint on the initial problem state. These STRIPS-like systems do not construct the portion of the explanation corresponding to the section above point (a) in Figure 4. Because they are tuned to a fixed goal concept, they do not need to generate this portion of the explanation explicitly for each training example.

To illustrate this point, consider Minton's (1984) program for learning search heuristics in two-person games such as Go-Moku, Tic-Tac-Toe, and Chess. This program analyzes one positive instance of a sequence of moves that leads to a winning board position, in order to determine an operational definition of the goal concept 'the class of board positions for which the given sequence of moves leads to a forced win'. But Minton's system has no explicit definition of this goal concept. It has only a definition of the solution property P that characterizes a winning position. For example, in the game of Go-Moku, (a variant of Tic-Tac-Toe) this solution property characterizes a winning board position as 'a board position with five X's in a row'. This solution property is regressed by Minton's program through the operator sequence for the given training example. In this way, the program determines that an effective definition of its implicit goal concept is 'board positions that contain three X's, with a blank space on one side, and two blank spaces on the other'.

[12] See Kibler and Porter (1985) for a thoughtful critique of analytic goal regression methods for learning search control heuristics. They discuss certain requirements for regression to succeed: that the operators be invertible, and that the representation language be able to express goal regression products.

# 4. Perspective and research issues

The previous sections presented a general method for explanation-based generalization, and illustrated its application to several generalization tasks. This section summarizes some general points regarding explanation-based generalization, and considers a number of outstanding research issues.

To summarize, explanation-based generalization utilizes a domain theory and knowledge of the goal concept to guide the generalization process. By doing so, the method is able to produce a valid generalization of the training example, along with an explanation that serves as a justification for the generalization. The EBG method introduced here unifies mechanisms for explanation-based generalization that have been previously reported for a variety of task domains. The generality of the EBG method stems from the fact that the goal concept, domain theory, and operationality criterion are made explicit inputs to the method, rather than instantiated implicitly within the method.

## 4.1 Perspectives on explanation-based generalization

Several perspectives on explanation-based generalization, and on the EBG method in particular, are useful in understanding their strengths and weaknesses:

*EBG as theory-guided generalization of training examples.* EBG can be seen as the process of interpreting or perceiving a given training example as a member of the goal concept, based on a theory of the domain. Soloway's (1978) early work on learning action sequences in the game of baseball shares this viewpoint on generalization. This is the perspective stressed in the above sections, and it highlights the centrality of the goal concept and domain theory. It also highlights an important feature of EBG: that learning depends strongly on what the learner already knows. One consequence of this is that the degree of generalization produced for a particular training example will depend strongly on the generality with which the rules in the domain theory are expressed. A second consequence is that the learning system can improve its *learning* performance to the degree that it can learn new rules for its domain theory.

*EBG as example-guided operationalization of the goal concept.* One can also view EBG as the process of reformulating the goal concept in terms that satisfy the operationality criterion, with the domain theory providing the means for reexpressing the goal concept. Given this perspective, one wonders why training examples are required at all. In principle, they are not. Mostow's (1983) FOO system operationalizes general advice about how to play the card game of Hearts, without considering specific examples that satisfy that advice. Similarly, Keller (1983) describes a process of *concept operationalization*, by which a sequence of transformations is applied to the goal concept in search of a reformulation that satisfies the operationality criterion, without the guidance of specific training examples.

However, training examples can be critical in guiding the learner to consider relevant transformations of the goal concept. For instance, consider the CUP learning task as described in Section 3.1, where a functional definition of CUP is reexpressed in structural terms for use by a vision system recognizing cups. A system that reformulates the functional definition of CUP in structural terms, without the guidance of training examples, amounts to a system for producing all possible structural definitions for classes of cups (i.e., for *designing* all possible classes of cups). Since there are so many possible designs for cups, and since so few of these are actually encountered in the world, the learning system could easily waste its effort learning structural definitions corresponding to cups that will never be seen by the vision system![13] Training examples thus provide a means of focusing the learner on formulating only concept descriptions that are relevant to the environment in which it operates.

*EBG as Reformulating/Operationalizing/Deducing from what is already known.* The above paragraph suggests that explanation-based generalization does not lead to acquiring truly 'new' knowledge, but only enables the learner to reformulate/operationalize/deduce what the learner already knows implicitly. While this statement is true, it is somewhat misleading. Consider, for example, the task of learning to play chess. Once one is told the rules of the game (e.g., the legal moves, and how to recognize a checkmate), one knows *in principle* everything there is to know about chess – even the optimal strategy for playing chess follows deductively from the rules of the game. Thus, although the EBG method is restricted to compiling the deductive consequences of its existing domain theory, this kind of learning is often nontrivial (as is the case for learning chess strategies). Nevertheless, it is a significant limitation that EBG is highly dependent upon its domain theory. As discussed below, further research is needed to extend the method to generalization tasks in which the domain theory is not sufficient to deductively infer the desired concept.

## 4.2 Research issues

### 4.2.1 Imperfect theory problems

As the above discussion points out, one important assumption of EBG is that the

---

[13] Of course information about what types of cups are to be encountered by the vision system also could be presented in the *operationality criterion*, since this information relates to the *use* of the concept definition for the recognition task. This information, however, may not be easily described in the declarative form required by the *operationality criterion*.

this theory of chess is intractable for explaining why nearly any move is good or bad. Humans tend to respond to this problem by constructing more abstract, tractable theories that are approximations to the underlying intractable theory. In chess, for example, the learner might formulate a more abstract theory that includes approximate assertions such as 'there is no threat to the king if it is surrounded by many friendly pieces' (Tadepalli, 1985). Such approximate, abstracted theories can be tractable enough and accurate enough to serve as a useful basis for creating and learning from explanations. Developing computer methods that can construct such abstracted theories, and that can judge when they can safely be applied, is a problem for further research.

*The Inconsistent Theory Problem.* A third difficulty arises in theories from which inconsistent statements can be derived. The domain theory in the SAFE-TO-STACK problem provides one example of such a theory. While this theory has a default rule for inferring the weight of an end table, it also has a rule for computing weights from the known density and volume. Thus, the theory will conclude two different weights for a given end table provided that its density and volume are known, and provided that these are inconsistent with the default assumption about its weight. In such cases, it is possible to construct inconsistent explanations for a single training example. Furthermore, if two different training examples of the same concept are explained in inconsistent terms (e.g., by utilizing one default assumption for one example, and some other assumptions for the second example), difficulties will certainly arise in merging the resulting generalizations. Because of this, and because default assumptions are commonplace in theories of many domains, the problem of dealing with inconsistent theories and inconsistent explanations is also an important one for future research.

While EBG infers concept definitions deductively from a single example, similarity-based methods infer concept definitions inductively from a number of training examples. It seems clearly desirable to develop combined methods that would utilize both a domain theory and multiple training examples to infer concept definitions. This kind of combined approach to generalization will probably be essential in domains where only imperfect theories are available.

Although few results have been achieved in combining explanation-based and similarity-based methods, a number of researchers have begun to consider this issue. Lebowitz (Lebowitz, 1985) is exploring methods for combining similarity-based methods and explanation-based methods in his UNIMEM system. UNIMEM examines a database of the voting records of congresspersons, searching for empirical, similarity-based generalizations (e.g., midwestern congresspersons vote in favor of farm subsidies). The system then attempts to verify these empirical generalizations

domain theory is sufficient to *prove* that the training example is a member of the goal concept; that is, that the inferred generalizations follow deductively (even if remotely) from what the learner already knows. Although this assumption is satisfied in each of the example problems presented above, and although there are interesting domains in which this assumption is satisfied (e.g., chess, circuit design (Mitchell et al., 1985)), for the majority of real-world learning tasks it is unrealistic to assume that the learner begins with such a strong theory. For both the SAFE-TO-STACK domain and the CUP domain, it is easy to imagine more realistic examples for which the required domain theory is extremely complex, difficult to describe, or simply unknown. For generalization problems such as inferring general rules for predicting the stock market or the weather, it is clear that available theories of economics and meteorology are insufficient to produce absolutely predictive rules. Thus, a major research issue for explanation-based generalization is to develop methods that utilize imperfect domain theories to guide generalization, as well as methods for improving imperfect theories as learning proceeds. The problem of dealing with imperfect theories can be broken down into several classes of problems:

*The Incomplete Theory Problem.* The stock market and weather prediction examples above both illustrate the incomplete theory problem. The issue here is that such theories are not complete enough to *prove* that the training example is a member of the goal concept (e.g., to prove why a particular training example stock has doubled over a twelve month period). However, even an incomplete theory might allow constructing *plausible explanations* summarizing likely links between features of the training example and the goal concept. For example, even a weak theory of economics allows one to suggest that the 'cash on hand' of the company may be relevant to the goal concept 'stocks that double over a twelve month period', whereas the 'middle initial of the company president' is probably an irrelevant feature. Thus, incomplete theories that contain only information about plausible cause-effect relations, with only qualitative rather than quantitative associations, can still provide important guidance in generalizing. Methods for utilizing and refining such incomplete theories would constitute a major step forward in understanding explanation-based generalization.

*The Intractable Theory Problem.* A second class of imperfect theories includes those which are complete, but for which it is computationally prohibitive to construct explanations in terms of the theory. For instance, quantum physics constitutes a fairly complete theory that would be inappropriate for generating explanations in the SAFE-TO-STACK problem – generating the necessary explanations in terms of quantum physics is clearly intractable. Similarly, although the rules of chess constitute a domain theory sufficient to explain why any given move is good or bad, one would never use this theory to explain why the opening move 'pawn to king four' is a member of the goal concept 'moves that lead to a win or draw for white'. In fact,

by explaining them in terms of a domain theory (e.g. explaining how midwestern congresspersons satisfy the goal concept 'people who favor farm subsidies'). This approach has the advantage that the similarity-based techniques can be used to generate a candidate set of possible generalizations from a large number of potentially noisy training examples. Once such empirical generalizations are formulated, explanation-based methods can help prune and refine them by using other knowledge in the system.

Whereas Lebowitz's approach involves applying similarity-based generalization followed by explanation-based methods, an alternative approach is to first apply explanation-based methods to each training example, then to combine the resulting generalized examples using a similarity-based generalization technique. Consider, for example, using the version space method[14] to combine the results of explanation-based generalizations of a number of training examples (Mitchell, 1984). Since the explanation-based generalization of a positive training example constitutes a sufficient condition for the goal concept, this can be used as a generalized positive example to refine (generalize) the specific boundary set of the version space. Similarly, one could imagine generalizing negative training examples using explanation-based generalization, by explaining why they are not members of the goal concept. The resulting generalized negative example could then be used to refine (specialize) the general boundary set of the version space. Thus, while this combined method still suffers the main disadvantage of similarity-based methods (i.e., it makes inductive leaps based on its generalization language, which it cannot justify), it converges more rapidly on a final concept definition because it employs EBG to generalize each training example.

Kedar-Cabelli (1984, 1985) proposes an alternative method for combining the results of explanation-based generalizations from multiple training examples. This method, Purpose-Directed Analogy, involves constructing an explanation of one example by analogy with an explanation of a familiar example, then combining the two explanations to produce a general concept definition based on both. Given explanations for two different examples, the proposed system combines the explanations as follows: Common portions of the two explanations remain unaltered in the combined explanation. Differing portions either become disjunctive subexpressions in the combined explanation, or are generalized to the next more specific common subexpression in the explanation. For example, given an explanation that a blue, ceramic mug is a CUP, and a second example of a white styrofoam cup, the explanation of the first example is used to construct by analogy an explanation for the

second example. The two resulting explanations may differ in how they explain that the two example cups are GRASPABLE (assume the first example cup is GRASPABLE because it has a handle, whereas the second is GRASPABLE because it is conical). In this case, a generalization of the two explanations would include a disjunction, that either the conical shape, or a handle, makes it graspable. That, along with the common features of the two objects in the combined explanation structure leads to the generalization that cups include objects which are concave upward, have a flat bottom, are light, and have either a conical shape or a handle. Alternatively, the combined explanation would retain only the next most-specific common subexpression, GRASPABLE, which would lead to a slightly more general, yet less operational, definition of a cup. Thus, this method of combining explanations of multiple examples provides a principled method for introducing disjunctions where needed into the common generalization of the two examples.

The three methods discussed above for combining similarity-based and explanation-based generalization offer differing advantages. The first method uses similarity-based generalization to determine empirical generalizations which may then be validated and refined by explanation-based methods. The second method involves employing a similarity-based method to combine the results of explanation-based generalizations from multiple examples. It suffers the disadvantage that this combination of methods still produces unjustified generalizations. The third method merges the explanations of multiple examples in order to produce a combined generalization that is justified in terms of the merged explanations. More research is required on these and other possible methods for employing explanation-based methods when multiple training examples are available.

### 4.2.3 Formulating generalization tasks

The above discussion focuses on research issues within the framework of explanation-based generalization. An equally important set of research issues has to do with how such methods for generalization will be used as subcomponents of larger systems that improve their performance at some given task. As our understanding of generalization methods advances, questions about how to construct performance systems that incorporate generalization mechanisms will become increasingly important.

One key issue to consider in this regard is how generalization tasks are initially formulated. In other words, where do the inputs to the EBG method (the goal concept, the domain theory, the operationality criterion) come from? Is it possible to build a system that automatically formulates its own generalization tasks, and these inputs? Is it possible to build learning systems that automatically shift their focus of attention from one learning problem to the next as required? What kind of knowledge must be transmitted between the performance system and the learning system to enable the automatic formulation of generalization tasks?

---

[14] The version space method (Mitchell, 1978) is a similarity-based generalization method based on summarizing the alternative plausible concept definitions by maintaining two sets: the 'specific' set contains the set of most specific concept definitions consistent with the observed data, and the 'general' set contains the most general concept definitions consistent with the data. All other plausible concept definitions lie between these two sets in the general-to-specific ordering over concept definitions.

### 4.2.4 Using contextual knowledge to solve the generalization task

Above we have discussed some approaches to automatically formulating learning tasks, given knowledge of the performance task for which the learning takes place. In cases where the learner formulates its own learning task, information about how and why the task was formulated can provide important guidance in solving the learning task. Keller's (1986) METALEX system provides an example of how such information can be used in guiding learning. Like LEX2, METALEX addresses the learning task of operationalizing the goal concept USEFUL-OP3. It takes as input a procedural representation of the *performance task* to be improved (the calculus problem solver), a specification of the *performance objectives* to be achieved ('minimize problem solving time') and knowledge of the *performance improvement plan* (search space pruning via filtering), which is a record of how the operationalization task was originally formulated. METALEX uses this additional knowledge about the context in which its learning task was formulated to guide its search for an operational transformation of the goal concept. Specifically, it executes the calculus problem solver using the initial (and subsequent intermediary) definitions of the goal concept to collect diagnostic information which aids in operationalizing the goal concept if performance objectives are not satisfied.

In effect, the performance task and performance objective inputs required by METALEX elaborate on the operationality criterion required by the EBG method. Instead of evaluating operationality in terms of a binary-valued predicate over concept definitions (as in EBG), METALEX evaluates the *degree* of operationality of the concept definition in relation to the performance task and objective. This ability to make a more sophisticated analysis of operationality enables METALEX to make important distinctions among alternative concept definitions. For example, because METALEX uses approximating (non truth-preserving) transforms to modify the goal concept, it can generate concept definitions that only approximate the goal concept. In such cases, METALEX is able to determine whether such an approximate concept definition is desirable based on the degree to which it helps improve the performance objectives.

As the first sections of this paper demonstrate, explanation-based generalization methods offer significant promise in attempts to build computer models of learning systems. Significant progress has been made in understanding explanation-based generalization, especially for problems in which the learner possesses a complete and correct theory. As the final section illustrates, much more remains to be discovered about how a learner can use what it already knows to guide the acquisition of new knowledge.

Again, little work has been devoted to these issues. The SOAR system (Laird et al., 1984, Laird et al., 1986) is one example of a learning system that formulates its own generalization tasks. Each time that SOAR encounters and solves a subgoal, it formulates the generalization problem of inferring the general conditions under which it can reuse the solution to this subgoal. SOAR then utilizes a technique closely related to explanation-based generalization, called *implicit generalization* (Laird et al., 1986), to infer these subgoal preconditions.

A second research effort which confronts the problem of formulating learning tasks is Keller's research on *contextual learning* (Keller, 1983, 1985, 1986). In this work, Keller suggests how a problem solving system could itself formulate generalization problems such as those addressed by the LEX2 system. In particular, he shows how the task of learning the goal concept USEFUL-OP3 arises as a subgoal in the process of planning to improve performance at solving calculus problems. By reasoning from a top-level goal of improving the efficiency of the problem solver, the method derives the subgoal of introducing a filter to prune the search moves that it considers. The definition of this filter includes the specification that it is to allow only problem solving steps that are 'useful' (i.e., that lead toward solutions). The subgoal of introducing this filter leads, in turn, to the problem of operationalizing the definition of 'useful' (i.e., to the subgoal corresponding to the LEX2 generalization task).

Recent work by Kedar-Cabelli (1985) also addresses the problem of formulating learning tasks. In this work, Kedar-Cabelli proposes a system to automatically formulate definitions of goal concepts in the domain of artifacts. In particular, the proposed system derives functional definitions of artifacts (e.g., CUP) from information about the purpose for which agents use them (e.g., to satisfy their thirst). Given two different purposes for which an agent might use a cup (e.g., as an ornament, versus to satisfy thirst), two different functional definitions can be derived.[15] To derive the functional definition of the artifact, the proposed system first computes a plan of actions that leads to satisfying the agent's goal. For example, if the agent's goal is to satisfy thirst, then this plan might be to POUR the liquids into the cup, GRASP the cup with the liquid in order to LIFT, and finally DRINK the liquids. In order to be used as part of this plan, the artifact must satisfy the preconditions of those plan actions in which it is involved. These preconditions form the functional definition of a cup: an open-vessel, which is stable, graspable, liftable. Thus, formulating functional definitions of artifacts is accomplished by analyzing the role that the artifact plays in facilitating the goal of some agent.

---

15 This extends Winston's work (see Section 3.1), in that it can derive its own goal concept from a given purpose.

It then produces as output a generalized schema for KIDNAPPING. The KIDNAPPING schema contains only the relevant details of the kidnapping (e.g., that three people are involved: Person A who wants money, Person B who has money and Person C who is valued by Person B), but none of the irrelevant details (e.g., that Person C wears blue jeans).

DeJong's system uses a generalization method that closely parallels the EBG method. Although there is no direct counterpart to the goal concept in DeJong's system, the goal concept can be thought of as 'the class of action sequences that achieve personal goal X for actor Y.' For the kidnapping story, the actor's personal goal is 'attainment of wealth.' The system constructs an explanation for how the actions in the story lead to the kidnapper's 'attainment of wealth' as a by-product of the story-understanding process. During the story parse, *data dependency links* are created to connect actions in the story with the inference rules that are used by the parser in interpreting the actions. The set of inference rules constitutes a domain theory for DeJong's system, and includes knowledge about the goals and plans of human actors, as well as causal knowledge used to set up and verify expectations for future actions. The network of all the data dependency links created during the story parse is called an *inference justification network*, and corresponds to an explanation for the action sequence.

Generalization of the inference justification network is carried out by replacing general entities for the specific objects and events referenced in the network. As with the EBG method, the entities in the inference justification network are generalized as far as possible while maintaining the correctness of the data dependency links.[16] Then a *new* schema is constructed from the network. The issue of operationality enters into the process of determining an appropriate level of generalization for the schema constructed from the network. Should, for example, a generalized schema be created to describe the KIDNAPPING action sequence or the more general action sequences representing BARGAINING-FOR-MONEY or BARGAINING-FOR-WEALTH? All of these schemata explain the actions in the example story. DeJong cites several criteria to use in determining the level of generalization at which to represent the new schema (DeJong, 1983). The criteria include such considerations as: 1) Will the generalized schema be useful in processing stories in the future, or does the schema summarize an event that is unlikely to recur? 2) Are the preconditions for schema activation commonly achievable? 3) Will the new schema represent a more efficient method of achieving personal goals than existing schemata? Note that these schema generalization criteria roughly correspond to the operationalization criteria used in the EBG method. Because the generalized schemata are subsequently used for a story-understanding task, the operationality criteria pertain to that task.

---

[16] It is unclear whether the system regresses its equivalent of the goal concept through the inference justification network.

## Acknowledgments

The perspective on Explanation-Based Generalization reported here has arisen from discussions over a period of time with a number of people in the Machine Learning Group at Rutgers and elsewhere. Discussions with the following people have been particularly useful in formulating the ideas presented here: Alex Borgida, Gerry DeJong, Thomas Dietterich, Thorne McCarty, Sridhar Mahadevan, Jack Mostow, Michael Sims, Prasad Tadepalli, Paul Utgoff, and Keith Williamson. We also thank the following people for providing useful comments on an earlier draft of this paper: Pat Langley, Sridhar Mahadevan, Jack Mostow, Louis Steinberg, Prasad Tadepalli, and Keith Williamson.

This material is based on work supported by the Defense Advanced Research Projects Agency under Research Contract N00014-81-K-0394, by the National Science Foundation under grants DCS83-51523 and MCS80-08889, by the National Institutes of Health under grant RR-64309, by GTE under grant GTE840917, and by a Rutgers University Graduate Fellowship. The views and conclusions contained in this document are those of the authors and should not be interpreted as necessarily representing the official views or policies of these sponsors.

## Appendix

The appendix describes DeJong's research on explanation-based generalization. In particular, it casts the work on learning schemata for story understanding in terms of the EBG method. In addition to this project, there has been a great deal of recent research on explanation-based generalization, including (DeJong, 1985; Ellman, 1985; Mooney, 1985; O'Rorke, 1985; Rajamoney, 1985; Schooley, 1985; Segre, 1985; Shavlik, 1985; Sims, 1985; Watanabe, 1985; Williamson, 1985).

DeJong (1981, 1983) developed one of the earliest successful explanation-based generalization systems as part of his research on *explanatory schema acquisition*. DeJong is interested in the problem of learning schemata for use in natural language story understanding. DeJong's system takes as input an example story and produces as output a generalized schema representing the stereotypical action sequence that is instantiated in the story. For example, the system can process the following story (adapted from G. DeJong, personal communication, November 16, 1984):

Fred is Mary's father. Fred is rich. Mary wears blue jeans. John approached Mary. He pointed a gun at her. He told her to get into his car. John drove Mary to the hotel. He locked her in his room. John called Fred. He told Fred he had Mary. He promised not to harm her if Fred gave him $250,000 at Treno's Restaurant. Fred delivered the money. Mary arrived home in a taxi.

*Table 5.* The wealth acquisition schema generalization problem: Learning about ways to achieve wealth (DeJong, 1983)

*Given:*

- *Goal Concept:* The class of action sequences (i.e., a general schema) by which actor x can achieve wealth:

WEALTH-ACQUISITION-ACTION-SEQUENCE (<a1, a2, ..., an>, x) ⇔
NOT (WEALTHY (x, s0)) ∧ WEALTHY (x, EXECUTE (x, <a1, a2, ... an>, s0))

where

<a1, a2, ..., an> is an action sequence; x is the actor; s0 is the actor's current state; and EXECUTE (a, b, c) returns the state resulting from the execution of action sequence b by actor a in state c:

- *Training Example:* The kidnapping story:
FATHER-OF (FRED, MARY) ∧ WEALTHY (FRED)
∧ DESPERATE (JOHN) ∧ WEARS (MARY, BLUE-JEANS)
∧ APPROACHES (JOHN, MARY, s0) ∧ POINTS-GUN-AT (JOHN, MARY, s1)
...
∧ EXCHANGES (FRED, JOHN, $250000, MARY, s12)

- *Domain Theory:* Rules about human interaction, and knowledge about human goals, intentions, desires, etc.::
FATHER-OF (person1, person2) → LOVES (person1, person 2)

WEALTHY (person) → HAS (person, $250000)
EXCHANGES (person 1, person2, object1, object2) ⇔
NOT (HAS (person1, object1)) ∧ VALUES (person1, object1)
∧ NOT (HAS (person2, object2)) ∧ VALUES (person2, object2)
∧ HAS (person1, object2) ∧ HAS (person2, object1)
...

- *Operationality Criterion:* Acquired generalization (i.e., the generalized schema) must satisfy the requirements for future usefulness in story-understanding (see text).

*Determine:*

- A generalization of training example (i.e., a generalized schema) that is a sufficient concept definition for the goal concept (i.e., that is a specialization of the wealth acquisition schema) and that satisfies the operationality criterion.

Table 5 summarizes the explanation-based generalization problem addressed by the explanatory schema acquisition research.

## References

Borgida, A., Mitchell, T. & Williamson, K.E. (1985). Learning improved integrity constraints and schemas from exceptions in data and knowledge bases. In M.L. Brodie & J. Mylopoulos (Eds.), *On knowledge base management systems.* New York, NY: Springer Verlag.

DeJong, G. (1981). Generalizations based on explanations. *Proceedings of the Seventh International Joint Conference on Artificial Intelligence* (pp. 67–69). Vancouver, B.C., Canada: Morgan Kaufmann.

DeJong, G. (1983). Acquiring schemata through understanding and generalizing plans. *Proceedings of the Eighth International Joint Conference on Artificial Intelligence* (pp. 462–464). Karlsruhe, West Germany: Morgan Kaufmann.

DeJong, G. (1985). A brief overview of explanatory schema acquisition. *Proceedings of the Third International Machine Learning Workshop.* Skytop, PA, June.

DeJong, G., & Mooney, R. (in press). Explanation-based learning: An alternative view. *Machine learning.*

Dietterich, T.G., London, B., Clarkson, K., & Dromey, G. (1982). Learning and Inductive Inference. In P.R. Cohen, & E.A. Feigenbaum (Eds.), *The handbook of artificial intelligence.* Los Altos, CA: William Kaufmann, Inc.

Dijkstra, E.W. (1976). *A discipline of programming.* Englewood Cliffs, NJ: Prentice Hall.

Ellman, T. (1985). Explanation-based learning in logic circuit design. *Proceedings of the Third International Machine Learning Workshop.* Skytop, PA, June.

Fikes, R., Hart, P., & Nilsson, N.J. (1972). Learning and executing generalized robot plans. *Artificial intelligence, 3,* 251–288. Also in B.L. Webber & N.J. Nilsson (Eds.), *Readings in artificial intelligence.*

Kedar-Cabelli, S.T. (1984). *Analogy with purpose in legal reasoning from precedents.* (Technical Report LRP-TR-17). Laboratory for Computer Science Research, Rutgers University, New Brunswick, NJ.

Kedar-Cabelli, S.T. (1985). Purpose-directed analogy. *Proceedings of the Cognitive Science Society Conference.* Irvine, CA: Morgan Kaufmann.

Keller, R.M. (1983). Learning by re-expressing concepts for efficient recognition. *Proceedings of the National Conference on Artificial Intelligence* (pp 182–186). Washington, D.C.: Morgan Kaufmann.

Keller, R.M. (1985). Development of a framework for contextual concept learning. *Proceedings of the Third International Machine Learning Workshop.* Skytop, PA, June.

Keller, R.M. (1986). *Contextual learning: A performance-based model of concept acquisition.* Unpublished doctoral dissertation, Rutgers University

Kibler, D., & Porter, B. (1985). A comparison of analytic and experimental goal regression for machine learning. *Proceedings of the Ninth International Joint Conference on Artificial Intelligence.* Los Angeles, CA: Morgan Kaufmann.

Laird, J.E., Rosenbloom, P.S., Newell, A. (1984). Toward chunking as a general learning mechanism. *Proceedings of the National Conference on Artificial Intelligence.* Austin, TX: Morgan Kaufmann.

Laird, J.E., Rosenbloom, P.S., & Newell, A. (1986). SOAR: The architecture of a general learning mechanism. *Machine learning, 1,* 11–46.

Lebowitz, M. (1985). Concept learning in a rich input domain: Generalization-based memory. In R.S. Michalski, J.G. Carbonell & T.M. Mitchell (Eds.), *Machine learning: An artificial intelligence approach,* Vol. 2. Los Altos, CA: Morgan Kaufmann.

Mahadevan, S. (1985). Verification-based learning: A generalization strategy for inferring problem-decomposition methods. *Proceedings of the Ninth International Joint Conference on Artificial Intelligence.* Los Angeles, CA: Morgan Kaufmann.

Michalski, R.S. (1983). A theory and methodology of inductive learning. *Artificial intelligence, 20,* 111–161. Also in R.S. Michalski; J.G. Carbonell & T.M. Mitchell (Eds.), *Machine learning: An artificial intelligence approach.*

Minton, S. (1984). Constraint-based generalization: Learning game-playing plans from single examples. (pp 251–254). *Proceedings of the National Conference on Artificial Intelligence.* Austin, TX: Morgan Kaufmann.

Mitchell, T.M. (1978). *Version spaces: An approach to concept learning.* PhD thesis, Department of Electrical Engineering, Stanford University. Also Stanford CS reports STAN-CS-78-711, HPP-79-2.

Mitchell, T.M. (1980). *The need for biases in learning generalizations* (Technical Report CBM-TR-117). Rutgers University, New Brunswick, NJ.

Mitchell, T.M. (1982). Generalization as search. *Artificial Intelligence*, March, *18*(2), 203–226.

Mitchell, T.M. (1983). Learning and Problem Solving. *Proceedings of the Eighth International Joint Conference on Artificial Intelligence* (pp 1139–1151). Karlsruhe, West Germany: Morgan Kaufmann.

Mitchell, T.M. (1984). Toward combining empirical and analytic methods for learning heuristics. In A. Elithorn & R. Banerji (Eds.), *Human and artificial intelligence*. Amsterdam: North-Holland Publishing Co. Also Rutgers Computer Science Department Technical Report LCSR-TR-27, 1981.

Mitchell, T.M., Utgoff, P.E., & Banerji, R.B. (1983). Learning by experimentation: Acquiring and refining problem-solving heuristics. In R.S. Michalski, J.G. Carbonell & T.M. Mitchell (Eds.), *Machine learning*. Palo Alto, CA: Tioga.

Mitchell, T.M., Mahadevan, S., & Steinberg, L. (1985). *LEAP*: A learning apprentice for VLSI design. *Proceedings of the Ninth International Joint Conference on Artificial Intelligence* (pp. 573–580). Los Angeles, CA: Morgan Kaufmann.

Mooney, R. (1985). Generalizing explanations of narratives into schemata. *Proceedings of the Third International Machine Learning Workshop*. Skytop, PA.

Mostow, D.J. (1981). *Mechanical transformation of task heuristics into operational procedures*. PhD thesis, Department of Computer Science, Carnegie-Mellon University, Pittsburgh, PA.

Mostow, D.J. (1983). Machine transformation of advice into a heuristic search procedure. In R.S. Michalski, J.G. Carbonell, & T.M. Mitchell (Eds.), *Machine learning*. Palo Alto, CA: Tioga.

Nilsson, N.J. (1980). *Principles of artificial intelligence*. Palo Alto, CA: Tioga.

O'Rorke, P. (1984). Generalization for explanation-based schema acquisition. *Proceedings of the National Conference on Artificial Intelligence* (pp 260–263). Austin, TX: Morgan Kaufmann.

O'Rorke, P. (1985). Recent progress on the 'mathematician's apprentice' project. *Proceedings of the Third International Machine Learning Workshop*. Skytop, PA.

Quinlan, J.R. (1985). The effect of noise on concept learning. In R.S. Michalski, J.G. Carbonell & T.M. Mitchell (Eds.), *Machine learning: An artificial intelligence approach*, Vol. 2. Los Altos, CA: Morgan Kaufmann. Modified, also in *Proceedings of the Second International Machine Learning Workshop*.

Rajamoney, S. (1985). Conceptual knowledge acquisition through directed experimentation. *Proceedings of the Third International Machine Learning Workshop*. Skytop, PA.

Salzberg, S., & Atkinson, D.J. (1984). Learning by building causal explanations. *Proceedings of the Sixth European Conference on Artificial Intelligence* (pp 497–500). Pisa, Italy.

Schank, R.C. (1982). Looking at learning. *Proceedings of the Fifth European Conference on Artificial Intelligence* (pp 11–18). Paris, France.

Schooley, P. (1985). Learning state evaluation functions. *Proceedings of the Third International Machine Learning Workshop*. Skytop, PA.

Segre, A.M. (1985). Explanation-based manipulator learning. *Proceedings of the Third International Machine Learning Workshop*. Skytop, PA.

Shavlik, J.W. (1985). Learning classical physics. *Proceedings of the Third International Machine Learning Workshop*. Skytop, PA.

Sims, M. (1985). An investigation of the nature of mathematical discovery. *Proceedings of the Second International Machine Learning Workshop*. Skytop, PA.

Silver, B. (1983). Learning equation solving methods from worked examples. *Proceedings of the Third International Machine Learning Workshop* (pp. 99–104). Urbana, IL.

Soloway, E.M. (1978). *Learning = interpretation + generalization: A case study in knowledge-directed learning*. PhD thesis, Department of Computer and Information Science, University of Massachusetts, Amherst. Computer and Information Science Report COINS TR-78-13.

Tadepalli, P.V. (1985). Learning in intractable domains. *Proceedings of the Third International Machine Learning Workshop*. Skytop, PA.

Utgoff, P.E. (1983). Adjusting bias in concept learning. *Proceedings of the Eighth International Conference on Artificial Intelligence* (pp. 447–449). Karlsruhe, West Germany: Morgan Kaufmann.

Utgoff, P.E. (1984). *Shift of bias for inductive concept learning*. PhD thesis, Department of Computer Science, Rutgers University, New Brunswick, NJ.

Utgoff, P.E. (1985). Shift of bias for inductive concept learning. In R.S. Michalski, J.G. Carbonell & T.M. Mitchell (Eds.), *Machine learning: An artificial intelligence approach*, Vol. 2. Los Altos, CA: Morgan Kaufmann. Modified, also in *Proceedings of the Second International Machine Learning Workshop*.

Waldinger, R. (1977). Achieving several goals simultaneously. In E. Elcock & D. Michie, D. (Eds.), *Machine intelligence 8*, London: Ellis Horwood, Limited. Also in B.L. Webber & N.J. Nilsson (Eds.), *Readings in artificial intelligence*.

Watanabe, M. (1985). Learning implementation rules in operating-conditions depending on states in VLSI design. *Proceedings of the Third International Machine Learning Workshop*. Skytop, PA.

Williamson, K. (1985). Learning from exceptions to constraints in databases. *Proceedings of the Third International Machine Learning Workshop*. Skytop, PA.

Winston, P.H. (1985). Learning by augmenting rules and accumulating censors. In R.S. Michalski, J.G. Carbonell & T.M. Mitchell (Eds.), *Machine learning: An artificial intelligence approach*, Vol. 2. Los Altos, CA: Morgan Kaufmann.

Winston, P.H. Binford, T.O., Katz, B., & Lowry, M. (1983). Learning physical descriptions from functional definitions, examples, and precedents. *National Conference on Artificial Intelligence* (pp. 433–439). Washington, D.C.: Morgan Kaufmann.

# Explanation Generalization in EGGS

Raymond J. Mooney

## 1. Introduction

Over the past few years, a number of similar explanation generalization techniques have been developed which constitute general domain-independent mechanisms for performing explanation-based learning [1–7]. Prior to the development of these techniques, a number of domain-dependent systems were built which used similar generalization techniques to learn concepts, heuristics, or plans from single examples by analyzing their underlying causal structure [8–17].

This chapter describes a particular domain-independent EBL system called EGGS which has been tested on a variety of examples from the literature on explanation-based learning. Many of these examples were originally used to demonstrate earlier, more domain-dependent systems such as STRIPS [8], LEX2 [9], CUPS [10], MA [11], and LEAP [16]. The examples from these systems come from a number of different domains including robot planning in a "blocks world," solving symbolic integration problems, learning artifact descriptions, proving theorems in logic, and designing logic circuits. Nevertheless, the same learning system can be used to generalize explanations for all of these examples. EGGS also includes performance systems which produce explanations for the learning system and in turn use the rules it generates to improve their ability to solve future problems. Currently, EGGS is capable of generalizing explanations composed of Horn clauses, term rewriting rules, and STRIPS operators.

EBG [2] is an alternative domain-independent technique for generalizing explanations which was independently developed at the same time EGGS was originally designed and implemented. The eventual implementation of EBG [4] has also been tested on several of the domains mentioned above. All of the original domain-dependent systems listed above used similar generalization techniques; however, until the development of EGGS and EBG, there was no general learning technique to generalize examples in all of these domains.

An outline of the learning process in EGGS is given in Figure 2–1, and an architectural diagram of the system is given in Figure 2–2. The tasks of constructing an explanation (step 1) and packaging a generalized explanation for future use (step 4) depend on the underlying representational formalism. Each representational formalism requires different modules for these tasks. For example, when using Horn clauses, a theorem prover is appropriate for constructing explanations, while when using STRIPS operators, a planner is appropriate. Unlike explanation construction and packaging, explanation generalization (step 3) can be

1. **Explain:** Construct a complete explanation for a specific example by either proving that an example is a member of a concept, by independently solving a problem or constructing a plan, or by understanding and explaining the actions or operators executed by an external agent.

2. **Prune:** Remove branches of the explanation that are more specific than needed for the operationality of the resulting plan or proof.

3. **Generalize:** Generalize the remaining explanation as far as possible without invalidating its underlying structure.

4. **Package:** Create a macro-operator or macro-rule that summarizes the resulting generalized explanation, and index it so that it can be used to aid future task classification, problem solving, planning, or understanding.

Figure 2–1: The Learning Process in EGGS

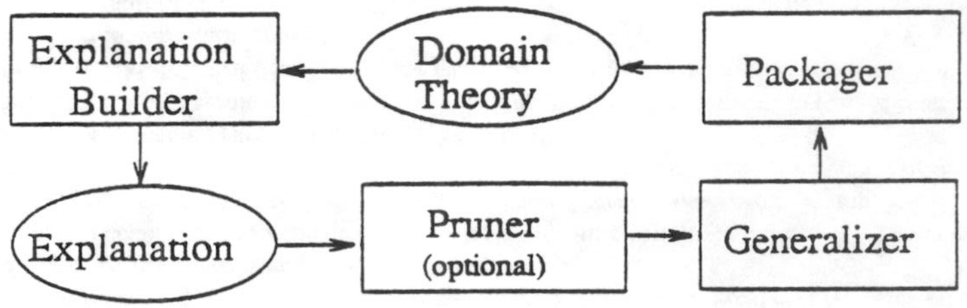

Figure 2–2: EGGS Architecture

characterized in a very general way and is discussed in detail in this chapter. The process of pruning explanations for operationality (step 2) is also discussed in this chapter; however, determining exactly what should be pruned from a particular explanation prior to generalization is primarily a domain-dependent decision.

The chapter is organized as follows. Section 2 presents a specification of how explanations are represented in EGGS. In Section 3, a number of alternative explanation generalization algorithms are presented, including the EGGS algorithm, and in Section 4, the various generalization algorithms are compared. In Sections 5 and 6, the correctness and computational complexity of the explanation generalization process is analyzed. Section 7 discusses the process of pruning explanations for operationality, and Section 8 presents some problems with integrating the generalization process with explanation construction. In Section 9, the process of explanation generalization is compared with *chunking* and *composition* methods used to learn productions in SOAR [18] and ACT* [19], respectively. Finally, in Sections 10 and 11, some examples are presented of learning *macro-rules* by generalizing Horn clause proofs and term rewritings. Examples of learning *macro-operators* using STRIPS rules are presented in Chapter 3. Many other examples of EGGS' performance were presented by Mooney [20].

## 2. Explanations, Explanation Structures, and Generalized Explanations

In different domains, various types of explanations are appropriate. Mitchell and colleagues [2] defined an explanation as a logical proof that demonstrates how an example meets a set of sufficient conditions defining a particular concept. This type of explanation is appropriate for learning classical concept definitions, such as learning a structural specification of a cup, an example introduced in [10] and discussed in [2]. However, when learning general plans in a problem-solving domain (as in STRIPS [8] or GENESIS [14]), it is more appropriate to consider an explanation to be a set of causally connected actions that demonstrate how a goal state is achieved.

Consequently, this work takes a very broad definition of the term *explanation* and considers it to be a connected set of *units*, where a unit is set of related *expressions* in predicate calculus and an expression can be either a literal or a term. Horn clause proofs, where each Horn clause is a unit, and plans composed of STRIPS operators, where each operator is a unit, are special cases of this very general representation. Formally, a unit can be defined as follows:

A unit is a connected directed acyclical graph $(V, E)$ in which the vertices in $V$ are expressions.

For example, a unit for a Horn clause rule has literals for its antecedents and its consequent, while a unit for a STRIPS operator has literals for its additions, deletions, and preconditions. An expression $a$ in a unit is said to *support* another expression $b$ in the unit if and only if there is a directed path from $a$ to $b$. For example, in the unit for a Horn clause, each antecedent *supports* the consequent through a path containing a single edge.

A *domain theory*, $\mathbf{T}$, is formally defined as a set of units. As defined by Nilsson [21], a *substitution* is a set of ordered pairs each specifying a term to be substituted for a particular variable. The form $p\theta$, where $p$ is a expression and $\theta$ is a substitution, denotes the expression resulting from applying $\theta$ to $p$. The expression $\gamma\theta$, where both $\gamma$ and $\theta$ are substitutions, denotes the substitution resulting from the *composition* of $\gamma$ and $\theta$, which is obtained by applying $\theta$ to the terms of $\gamma$ and then adding any pairs of $\theta$ having variables not occurring among the variables of $\gamma$. An *instance* of a unit, $\alpha$, is a unit obtained by applying a variable substitution to all of the expressions in $\alpha$. Two expressions are said to be *identical* if and only if all of their corresponding predicates, functions, variables, and constants are exactly the same (i.e., their most general unifier is the null substitution). Before formally defining an explanation in this representation, a few additional definitions are needed:

A unit-set is a pair $(U, R)$, where $U$ is a set of units: $\{(V_1, E_1), \ldots, (V_n, E_n)\}$ and $R$ is an equivalence relation defined on the set of expressions: $V_1 \cup V_2 \cup \cdots \cup V_n$. For each pair of expressions $(a, b)$ in $R$, where $a \in V_i$ and $b \in V_j$, it must be the case that that $i \neq j$ (i.e., equivalent expressions must be from separate units).

Given a unit-set $S = (U, R)$, where $U = \{(V_1, E_1), \ldots, (V_n, E_n)\}$, let $C_1, C_2, \ldots, C_m$ be the equivalence classes of expressions defined by $R$. Let $G$ be the graph $(V', E')$ where $V' = \{C_1, C_2, \ldots, C_m\}$ and $(C_i, C_j) \in E'$ if and only if there are expressions $a \in C_i$ and $b \in C_j$ such that $(a, b) \in E_1 \cup E_2 \cup \cdots \cup E_n$. $G$ is referred to as the *graph of $S$* and represents the directed graph obtained by "collapsing" all equivalent expressions into

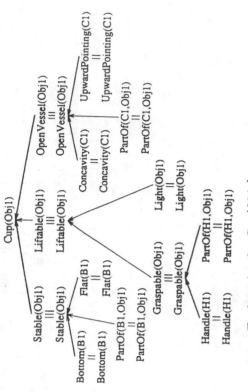

Figure 2-3:   Explanation for Cup(Obj1)

a single vertex. A formal definition of an explanation can now be stated as follows:

An explanation is a unit-set, $S = (U, R)$, where the graph of $S$ is connected and acyclic and where for each pair of expressions $(a, b) \in R$, $a$ and $b$ are identical. Furthermore, let the set $U' \subset U$ be the set of all units in $U$ that are instances of units in the domain theory, $T$, and let $R'$ be the equivalence relation such that $(a, b) \in R'$ if and only if both $a$ and $b$ are expressions from units in $U'$ and $(a, b) \in R$. In order for $S$ to be an explanation, $U'$ must be nonempty and the graph of the unit-set $S' = (U', R')$ must also be connected and acyclic.

In other words, an explanation is a combination of units that forms an even larger connected acyclic graph by means of an equivalence relation defined on their vertices. Each pair of expressions that the relation defines as equivalent must be identical. Furthermore, if all units that are not instances of units in the domain theory are removed from an explanation, the remaining explanation also defines a connected directed acyclic graph. The *goal* is a distinguished expression in the explanation that is a sink of the graph of the explanation and represents the final conclusion in an inference chain or the desired state in a plan.

A Horn clause proof in this representation is an explanation whose units are Horn clauses and whose equivalence relation matches antecedents of some clauses to consequents of others. In this case, an explanation is analogous to the *data dependency structure* maintained by a *truth maintenance system* [22]. For example, consider the following domain theory for the problem of learning a structural definition of a cup, an example originally presented by Winston and colleagues [10]:

Stable(?x) ∧ Liftable(?x) ∧ OpenVessel(?x) → Cup(?x)
Bottom(?y) ∧ PartOf(?y,?x) ∧ Flat(?y) → Stable(?x)
Graspable(?x) ∧ Light(?x) → Liftable(?x) Handle(?y)
∧ PartOf(?y,?x) → Graspable(?x) Concavity(?y) ∧
PartOf(?y,?x) ∧ UpwardPointing(?y) → OpenVessel(?x)

Additional units needed for the problem are the following individual facts:

Light(Obj1), Color(Obj1,Red), PartOf(Handle1,Obj1),
Handle(Handle1), Bottom(B1), PartOf(B1,Obj1), Flat(B1),
Concavity(C1), PartOf(C1,Obj1), UpwardPointing(C1)

A proof tree for Cup(Obj1) is shown in Figure 2-3 as an explanation whose goal is Cup(Obj1). This proof explains why Obj1 is a cup by showing how its structural properties fulfill the functional purpose of a cup. Triple edges in the graphs indicate equivalences between expressions in two units that are instances of the domain theory, and double edges indicate equivalences to expressions in units that are not instances of units in the domain theory. Specifically, for explanations using Horn clauses as units, triple edges indicate connections between instantiations of rules from the domain theory, and double edges indicate connections to initial facts about the specific example. Examples of explanations where the units are rewrite rules and STRIPS operators are presented in Section 11 and Chapter 3, respectively.

An expression $a$ is a *uniquized version* of an expression $b$ if and only if $a$ is obtained by substituting a uniquely named variable for each variable in $b$. In correspondence with the terminology in [2], an *explanation structure* is defined as an explanation with each instantiated unit from the domain theory replaced by a uniquized version of its general definition. Formally:

An explanation structure of an explanation $E = (U, R)$ is a unit-set, $S = (U'\ R')$, where for each $u_i \in U$ where $u_i$ is an instance of a unit $t_i \in T$, there is exactly one $u_i' \in U'$ such that $u_i'$ is a uniquized version of $t_i$

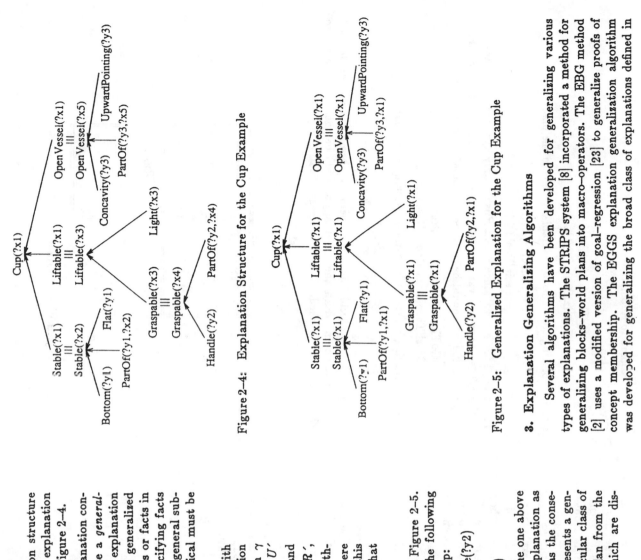

Figure 2–4:  Explanation Structure for the Cup Example

Figure 2–5:  Generalized Explanation for the Cup Example

and where $(u_i', u_j') \in R'$ if and only if $(u_i, u_j) \in R$.

The definition of an explanation ensures that an explanation structure defines a connected directed acyclic graph. For example, the explanation structure of the explanation for the cup example is shown in Figure 2–4.

The task of *explanation generalization* is to take an explanation containing instances of units from a domain theory and generate a *generalized explanation*, which is the most general instance of its explanation structure in which equivalent expressions are identical. The generalized explanation maintains matches between expressions from rules or facts in the domain theory but eliminates matches to expressions specifying facts of the particular specific example. This means that the most general substitution that results in all equivalent expressions being identical must be applied to the explanation structure. Formally:

A generalized explanation of an explanation $E$ with an explanation structure $S = (U, R)$ is an explanation $G = (U', R')$ such that there exists a substitution $\gamma$ where for each $u_i \in U$ there is exactly one $u_i' \in U'$ such that $u_i' = u_i\gamma$ and where $(u_i', u_j') \in R'$ if and only if $(u_i, u_j) \in R$. Furthermore, if $(u_i', u_j') \in R'$, then $u_i'$ and $u_j'$ must be identical. Finally, for any other substitution $\theta$, satisfying these constraints, there must exist a substitution $\theta'$ such that $U\theta = U\gamma\theta'$ (this ensures that $\gamma$ is the *most general* substitution that satisfies the constraints).

The generalized explanation of the cup example is shown in Figure 2–5. This generalized explanation can then be used to obtain the following *macro–rule* representing a general structural definition of a cup:

Bottom(?y1)∧PartOf(?y1,?x1)∧Flat(?y1)∧Handle(?y2)
∧PartOf(?y2,?x1)∧Light(?x1)∧Concavity(?y3)∧
PartOf(?y3,?x1)∧UpwardPointing(?y3) → Cup(?x1)

For explanations that are logical proofs, a macro–rule like the one above is easily obtained by taking the leaves of the generalized explanation as the antecedents and the goal of the generalized explanation as the consequent. In planning domains, the generalized explanation represents a general plan schema or macro–operator [8] for achieving a particular class of goals. Creating a new action definition for the composed plan from the generalized explanation requires a few additional steps, which are discussed in Chapter 3.

## 3. Explanation Generalizing Algorithms

Several algorithms have been developed for generalizing various types of explanations. The STRIPS system [8] incorporated a method for generalizing blocks–world plans into macro–operators. The EBG method [2] uses a modified version of goal–regression [23] to generalize proofs of concept membership. The EGGS explanation generalization algorithm was developed for generalizing the broad class of explanations defined in the previous section. This algorithm was first published by DeJong and Mooney [1] along with a description of an error found in the specification of the EBG algorithm. Kedar-Cabelli and McCarty subsequently developed a PROLOG version of EBG [4] which corrected this problem with the original algorithm.

The general technique used by STRIPS, EBG, EGGS, and PROLOG-EBG can be abstracted to apply to the class of explanations defined in the previous section. The rest of this section is devoted to presenting and comparing algorithmic descriptions of all of these methods as applied to this class of explanations. All of the algorithms rely on unification pattern matching, and the abbreviation MGU is used to refer to the substitution that is the *most general unifier* of two expressions [21, 24]. All of the generalization algorithms presented have been implemented and tested within the context of the overall EGGS system.

## 3.1. STRIPS Macrop Learning

The first work on generalizing explanations was the learning of robot plans in STRIPS [8]. STRIPS worked in a "blocks-world" domain. After its problem-solving component generated a plan for achieving a particular state, it generalized the plan into a problem-solving schema (a MACROP or macro-operator) that could be used to efficiently solve similar problems in the future. Work on the STRIPS system was the first to point out that a correct generalization of a connected set of actions or inferences *cannot* be obtained by simply replacing each constant by an independent variable. This method happens to work on the Cup example given earlier. The proper generalized explanation can be obtained by replacing Obj1 by ?x1, B1 by ?y1, H1 by ?y2, and C1 by ?y3. However, in general, such a simplistic approach can result in a structure that is either more general or more specific than what is actually supported by the system's domain knowledge.

Fikes and colleagues [8] used the following examples to illustrate that simply replacing constants with variables can result in improper generalizations. These examples assume the initial state shown in Figure 2–6 and use the following operators:

GoThru(?d,?r1,?r2): Go through door ?d from room ?r1 to room ?r2.

PushThru(?b,?d,?r1,?r2): Push box ?b through door ?d from room ?r1 to room ?r2.

SpecialPush(?b): Specific operator for pushing box ?b from Room2 to Room1.

Given the plan

GoThru(Door1,Room1,Room2)
SpecialPush(Box1)

simply replacing constants by variables results in the plan

GoThru(?d,?r1,?r2)
SpecialPush(?b)

This plan is too general since SpecialPush is only applicable when starting in Room2, so having a variable ?r2 as the destination of the GoThru is too general and ?r2 should be replaced by Room2. Given the plan

GoThru(Door1,Room1,Room2)
PushThru(Box1,Door1,Room2,Room1)

simply replacing constants by variables results in the plan

GoThru(?d,?r1,?r2)
PushThru(?b,?d,?r2,?r1)

This plan is too specific since the operators themselves do not demand that the room in which the robot begins (?r1) be the same room into which the box is pushed. The correct generalization is

GoThru(?d,?r1,?r2)
PushThru(?b,?d,?r2,?r3)

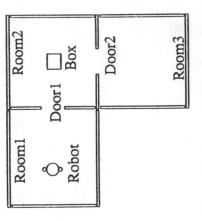

Figure 2–6: Initial World State for STRIPS Examples

The exact process STRIPS uses to avoid these problems and correctly generalize an example is dependent on its particular representations (triangle tables) and inference techniques (resolution); however, the basic technique is easily captured using the representation discussed in Section 2. A description of the basic explanation generalizing algorithm used in STRIPS is shown in Figure 2–7. It should be noted that the generalization process in STRIPS was constructed specifically for generalizing robot plans. There was no attempt to present a general learning method based on generalizing explanations in any domain. However, the algorithm in Figure 2–7 is a straightforward generalization of the basic process used in STRIPS. The basic technique is to unify each pair of equivalent expressions in the explanation structure and apply each resulting substitution to all of the expressions in the explanation structure. After all of the unifications and substitutions have been made, the result is the generalized explanation since each expression has been replaced by the most general expression that allows all of the equality matches in the explanation to be satisfied.

## 3.2. EBG

Mitchell, Keller, and Kedar–Cabelli [2] described a technique called EBG (explanation–based generalization) for generalizing a logical proof that a particular example satisfies the definition of a concept. An example concept–membership proof showing how a particular object satisfies the functional definition of a cup was given in Figure 2–3. Unlike the STRIPS MACROP learning method, EBG was intended as a general method for learning by generalizing explanations of why an example is a member of a concept. In [2], detailed examples are presented illustrating how EBG can be applied to learning an operational definition for when it is safe to stack something on an endtable, to Winston's CUP example

for each equality between expressions $x$ and $y$ in the explanation structure do

    let $\theta$ be the MGU of $x$ and $y$
    for each expression $z$ in the explanation structure do
        replace $z$ with $z\theta$

Figure 2–7:  STRIPS Explanation Generalizing Algorithm

[10], and to an example from LEX2's domain of learning heuristics for symbolic integration [9]. A much more abstract description of how it might be used to learn a kidnapping plan like that learned by the original GENESIS system is presented in an appendix to [14].

The original EBG algorithm presented in [2] is based on *goal regression* [23] and involves back–propagating constraints from the goal through the explanation structure to the leaves. Figure 2–8 presents a formal specification of the original algorithm in terms of the explanation representation introduced earlier. The global variable $R$ maintains the current set of regressed expressions and represents the most general set of antecedents necessary to prove the goal given the portion of the explanation structure already traversed. The explanation structure is traversed from the goal back to the leaves in a depth–first manner. Each time a unit (rule) is traversed, the set $R$ is updated and the substitution resulting from the unit's unification to the structure already traversed is applied to all of the expressions in $R$. After the entire explanation structure has been traversed, $R$ is the most general set of antecedents for the given

let $g$ be the goal expression in the explanation structure
let $R$ be the set of expressions supporting $g$
EBG($g$)

procedure EBG($p$)
  for each expression $z$ supporting $p$ do
    if $z$ is equivalent to some expression $e$
    then

        let $R = R - \{z\}$
        for each expression $y$ supporting $e$ do
          let $R = R \cup \{y\}$
        let $\theta$ be the MGU of $e$ and $z$
        for $y$ in $R$ do
          replace $y$ with $y\theta$
        EBG($e$)

Figure 2–8:  Original EBG Explanation Generalizing Algorithm

that anyone who is depressed and buys a gun will commit suicide is shown in Figure 2–11. The general macro–rule learned from the generalized explanation is

$$\text{Depressed}(?y1) \wedge \text{Buy}(?y1,?c1) \wedge \text{Isa}(?c1,\text{Gun}) \rightarrow \text{Kill}(?y1,?y1)$$

Goal regression, as given in [2] and Figure 2–8, computes only the most general set of antecedents that would support a proof with the same explanation structure as the training example (i.e., the weakest preconditions [12, 25]). If only goal regression is performed, the proper description of the goal concept supported by the explanation is not always determined since the explanation itself may impose constraints on the goal concept. In terms of the Suicide example, the constraint that the killer be the same as the person killed is never imposed and, as demonstrated in [1], EBG constructs the following erroneous rule:

$$\text{Depressed}(?y) \wedge \text{Buy}(?y,?c) \wedge \text{Isa}(?c,\text{Gun}) \rightarrow \text{Kill}(?x,?y)$$

This rule states that everyone kills someone who is depressed and buys a gun, which is clearly not a conclusion warranted by the domain theory. Since the abstract STRIPS algorithm applies substitutions generated by each unification to the entire explanation structure, it computes the appropriately constrained goal concept and does not make this mistake.

As suggested in [1], the proper generalized goal and generalized explanation can be obtained by starting with the generalized antecedents obtained from regression and rederiving the general proof. Rederiving the proof propagates constraints from the regressed expressions to the goal, thereby appropriately constraining the goal concept. The resulting

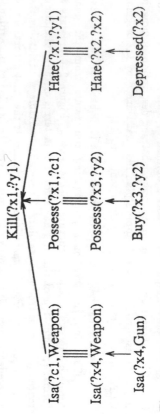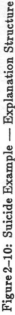

Kill(?x1,?y1)

Hate(?x1,?y1)   Possess(?x1,?c1)   Isa(?c1,Weapon)

Hate(?x2,?x2)   Possess(?x3,?y2)   Isa(?x4,Weapon)

Depressed(?x2)   Buy(?x3,?y2)   Isa(?x4,Gun)

Figure 2-10:   Suicide Example — Explanation Structure

Kill(John,John)

Hate(John,John)   Possess(John,Obj1)   Isa(Obj1,Weapon)

Hate(John,John)   Possess(John,Obj1)   Isa(Obj1,Weapon)

Depressed(John)   Buy(John,Obj1)   Isa(Obj1,Gun)

Depressed(John)   Buy(John,Obj1)   Isa(Obj1,Gun)

Figure 2-9:   Suicide Example — Specific Explanation

explanation structure.[1]

However, as DeJong and Mooney [1] initially pointed out, this algorithm is only guaranteed to determine the leaves of the generalized explanation and in certain situations fails to obtain the correct generalized goal. The "Suicide" example, originally introduced in [1], is an example for which the original EBG algorithm does not compute the correct generalized goal and as a result learns an incorrect macro-rule. This example involves inferring that an individual will commit suicide if he is depressed and buys a gun. The specific facts of the problem are

Depressed(John), Buy(John,Obj1), Isa(Obj1,Gun)

The domain rules are

Depressed(?x) → Hate(?x,?x)
Hate(?x,?y) ∧ Possess(?x,?z) ∧ Isa(?z,Weapon) → Kill(?x,?y)
Buy(?x,?y) → Possess(?x,?y),   Isa(?x,Gun) → Isa(?x,Weapon)

The proof that John will commit suicide is shown in Figure 2–9, its explanation structure is shown in Figure 2–10, and the correct general proof

---

[1]The algorithm presented in Figure 2–8 corrects problems with the BackPropagate function presented in [3]. As discussed in [3], the BackPropagate function (which was based on the informal description of this process given in [2]) does not properly propagate constraints across conjuncts and consequently in some situations does not compute the correct regressed expressions. The version in Figure 2–8 does not have this problem since each substitution is applied to all of the current regressed expressions in the set $R$.

let $\gamma$ be the null substitution {}
for each equality between expressions $x$ and $y$ in the explanation structure do

    let $\theta$ be the MGU of $x\gamma$ and $y\gamma$
    let $\gamma$ be $\gamma\theta$

for each expression $x$ in the explanation structure do
    replace $x$ with $x\gamma$

Figure 2-12: EGGS Explanation Generalizing Algorithm

step, all the substitutions are composed into one substitution, $\gamma$. After all the unifications have been performed, one sweep through the explanation applying the accumulated substitution $\gamma$ results in the generalized explanation. Table 2-1 demonstrates this technique as applied to the Cup example. It shows how $\gamma$ changes as it is composed with the substitutions resulting from each unification. Applying the final substitution $\gamma$ to the explanation structure shown in Figure 2-4 results in the generalized explanation shown in Figure 2-5. Table 2-2 shows how EGGS generalizes the Suicide example. Applying the final substitution to the explanation structure shown in Figure 2-10 results in the generalized explanation shown in Figure 2-11. In the tables, equalities are processed in the order produced by depth-first traversals of the explanation structures; however, any order will result in equivalent generalized explanations up to a change of variable names.

## 3.4. PROLOG-EBG

Kedar-Cabelli and McCarty [4] presented a PROLOG version of EBG which, unlike the original EBG, computed the proper goal concept. PROLOG-EBG integrates the generalization process with the construction of explanations by PROLOG. A generalized proof is constructed in parallel with the proof for the specific example. Any query results in both a specific and and a generalized proof being returned.

The algorithmic description presented in Figure 2-13 is an attempt to specify the generalization algorithm underlying PROLOG-EBG as an independent process (i.e., separated from the process of theorem proving). Like EGGS, PROLOG-EBG constructs a global substitution, $\gamma$, which is then applied to the complete explanation structure. However, unlike EGGS, $\gamma$ is constructed by traversing the explanation depth-first from the goal in a manner analogous to trying to prove the general goal of the

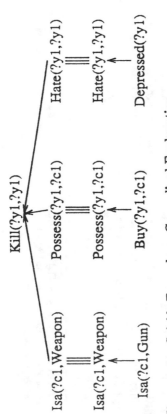

Figure 2-11: Suicide Example — Generalized Explanation

generalization algorithm is then a two-step process: goal regression (back-propagation) followed by proof reconstruction (forward-propagation). This approach was suggested based on a similar two-pass generalization process presented in [26]. A formal description of a version of EBG corrected in this manner is given in [3].[2] Kedar-Cabelli and McCarty [4] presented a PROLOG version of EBG which also corrects the problem and avoids making two separate passes through the explanation.[3] This version of EBG is considered in a subsequent section.

## 3.3. EGGS

The EGGS (explanation generalization using a global substitution) algorithm was developed for generalizing explanations of the abstract form defined and used in this chapter. The algorithm is quite similar to the abstract STRIPS algorithm and is shown in Figure 2-12. The difference between EGGS and the abstract STRIPS algorithm is that instead of applying the substitutions throughout the explanation at each

---

[2] Since, as mentioned in the previous footnote, the BackPropagate function presented in [3] does not properly propagate constraints across conjuncts, the corrected version of EBG presented in [3] required that ForwardPropagate be performed before BackPropagate. If the correct version of back-propagation presented in Figure 2-8 is used, it is not necessary to perform forward propagation first.

[3] Due to a typographical error, the EGGS algorithm presented in [3] did not include applying $\gamma$ to $x$ and $y$ prior to computing their MGU. The original publication of the algorithm in [1] did not suffer from this mistake, and the longer technical report version of [3] included a corrected version of the EGGS algorithm.

**Table 1: EGGS Applied To the Cup Example**

| Equality | θ | γ |
|---|---|---|
| Stable(?x1) ≡ Stable(?x2) | {?x1/?x2} | {?x1/?x2} |
| Liftable(?x1) ≡ Liftable(?x3) | {?x1/?x3} | {?x1/?x2, ?x1/?x3} |
| Graspable(?x3) ≡ Graspable(?x4) | {?x1/?x4} | {?x1/?x2, ?x1/?x3, ?x1/?x4} |
| OpenVessel(?x1) ≡ OpenVessel(?x5) | {?x1/?x5} | {?x1/?x2, ?x1/?x3, ?x1/?x4, ?x1/?x5} |

**Table 2: EGGS Applied To the Suicide Example**

| Equality | θ | γ |
|---|---|---|
| Isa(?c1,Weapon) ≡ Isa(?x4,Weapon) | {?c1/?x4} | {?c1/?x4} |
| Possess(?x1,?c1) ≡ Possess(?x3,?y2) | {?x1/?x3, ?c1/?y2} | {?c1/?x4, ?x1/?x3, ?c1/?y2} |
| Hate(?x1,?y1) ≡ Hate(?x2,?x2) | {?y1/?x2, ?y1/?x1} | {?c1/?x4, ?x1/?x3, ?c1/?y2, ?y1/?x2, ?y1/?x1} |

```
let g be the goal expression in the explanation structure
let (γ, E) = PROLOG-EBG(g, {})
for e in E do replace e with eγ

procedure PROLOG-EBG(x, θ)
    let S be the set of expressions supporting x
    for s in S do replace s with sθ
    let (γ, E) = PROLOG-EBG-Supporters(S, {}, ∅)
    return (γθ, E ∪ {x})

procedure PROLOG-EBG-Supporters(S, γ, E)
    if S = ∅
        then return (γ, E)
    else
        let f be the first element of S
        let R = S − {f}
        if f is equivalent to some expression e
        then
            let φ be the MGU of f and e
            let (δ, P) = PROLOG-EBG(e, φ)
            for r in R do replace r with rδ
            PROLOG-EBG-Supporters(R, γδ, E ∪ P)
        else PROLOG-EBG-Supporters(R, γ, E ∪ {f})
```

Figure 2–13: PROLOG-EBG Explanation Generalizing Algorithm

explanation structure using backward-chaining. The substitution γ is constructed by finding a substitution that allows the goal to be proved from the set of operational expressions represented by the leaves of the explanation structure. The generalization algorithm is analogous to the algorithm for a backward-chaining deductive system (like PROLOG or the deductive retrieval system in [24]). In the algorithm in Figure 2–13, the function PROLOG-EBG returns two values: the current substitution (γ) and the subset of the expressions in the explanation structure that have already been traversed (E).[4] When the top-level call to PROLOG-EBG returns, E is the set of all expressions in the explanation structure and γ is the final global substitution.

It should be noted that Hirsh [5] simultaneously developed a version of EBG for logic programming (using the MRS logic programming system [27]) that uses a generalization algorithm equivalent in operation to PROLOG-EBG's. In addition to integrating theorem proving and generalization, MRS-EBG integrates both of these with operationality checking [2] or *pruning* [1, 3], a process discussed in Section 7.

---

[4] The notation "(a, b) = F(x)" and "return (a, b)" is used to denote the fact that the function F returns two values: a and b. All variables referenced by a procedure are assumed to be local to that procedure call.

## 4. Comparison of Explanation Generalizing Algorithms

It is reasonably clear that STRIPS, EGGS, and PROLOG-EBG all compute the same desired generalized explanation. They all perform a set of unifications and substitutions that constrain the explanation structure into one in which equivalent expressions are identical. The difference between them lies in the manner and order in which the unifications and substitutions are done. As described by O'Rorke [7], explanation generalization can be viewed as a process of posting and propagating the effects of equality or co-reference constraints. Neither the STRIPS nor EGGS algorithm imposes an ordering on the assimilation of the various equality constraints in the explanation structure. On the other hand, the various EBG algorithms order the assimilation of constraints by traversing the explanation structure in a depth-first manner. Although this ordering is not required by the generalization process, it is a natural consequence of integrating generalization with a backward-chaining theorem prover.

Actually, the task of producing a global substitution ($\gamma$) for an explanation structure can be easily shown to reduce to the task of finding a single most general unifier for two expressions. A single unification algorithm for explanation generalization is shown in Figure 2-14. The two unifying expressions for the reduction are constructed by having two expressions in the explanation structure occupy corresponding equivalent positions in the two constructed expressions. For example, following are the two expressions constructed for the explanation structure of the Cup example (Figure 2-4).

P[Stable(?x2), Liftable(?x3), Graspable(?x4), OpenVessel(?x5))
P[Stable(?x1), Liftable(?x1), Graspable(?x3), OpenVessel(?x1))

An MGU for these two expressions is {?x1/?x2, ?x1/?x3, ?x1/?x4, ?x1/?x5}, which is the same as the global substitution EGGS constructed for this example (Table 2-1). The two expressions constructed for the Suicide example are:

P[Isa(?x4,Weapon), Possess(?x3,?y2), Hate(?x2,?x2))
P[Isa(?c1,Weapon), Possess(?x1,?c1), Hate(?x1,?y1))

An MGU for these two expressions is {?c1/?x4, ?x1/?x3, ?c1/?y2, ?y1/?x2, ?y1/?x1}, which is again the same as the global substitution constructed by EGGS (Table 2-2).

Consequently, in some sense the various explanation generalizing algorithms are just different ways of implementing unification. In fact, EGGS directly corresponds to the implementation of UNIFY in [24], which takes a pair of expressions and a current substitution and returns an updated substitution which includes variable bindings that unify the

let $A$ and $B$ be two expressions each containing one member of each pair of equivalent expressions in the explanation structure such that equivalent expressions occupy corresponding positions in the two expressions.
let $\gamma$ be the MGU of $A$ and $B$
for each expression $z$ in the explanation structure do
  replace $z$ with $z\gamma$

Figure 2-14: Single Unification Explanation Generalizing Algorithm

two expressions in the context of the current substitution. In EGGS, this UNIFY is simply used to update the initially empty global substitution ($\gamma$) to include the variable bindings necessary to unify each pair of equivalent expressions in the explanation structure. In fact, showing that EGGS and the single unification algorithm are equivalent would simply require a proof of correctness for the unification algorithm given in [24]. The STRIPS generalizing algorithm, on the other hand, is more similar to the implementation of UNIFY presented in [21] in which the substitution unifying the first elements of two expressions is applied to the rest of the expressions before continuing. A unification algorithm that applied each substitution to the entire expression (thereby generating the resulting unified expression as well as a unifying substitution) would be equivalent to the STRIPS generalizing algorithm.

## 5. Correctness of Explanation Generalizing Algorithms

Intuitively, for an explanation generalizing algorithm to be "correct," its output should be logically entailed by the system's existing knowledge or domain theory, and it should be as general as possible given this constraint and the constraint that it retain the "structure" of the original explanation.

One approach to proving correctness of explanation generalization, discussed by O'Rorke [7], involves demonstrating that a generalization algorithm maintains all of the equality or co-reference constraints in the explanation structure in the most general way possible. This is an attempt to formally capture the intuitive notion that an explanation should be generalized as far as possible while still maintaining its underlying structure. As described by O'Rorke [7], explanation generalization can be performed by combining the individual co-reference constraints in order to compute the most general description of each expression in the explanation that satisfies all of these constraints. More details on this approach to verification and how it specifically applies to generalizers based on unification are given in [7].

The formal definition of a generalized explanation given in Section 2 captures O'Rorke's notion of correctness since it requires the global substitution $\gamma$ to be the most general substitution that makes all equivalent expressions in the explanation structure identical. Based on known properties of unification, it is easy to prove the following theorem.

**Theorem 1:** Given an explanation and its corresponding explanation structure, the single unification algorithm produces a correct generalized explanation that is unique except for alphabetic variants.

*Proof:* Since unification produces the most general substitution that makes two expressions identical (as proved in [28]), the single unification algorithm is guaranteed to produce the most general substitution $\gamma$ which makes all of the equivalent expressions in the explanation structure identical. Therefore, by definition, applying this substitution to the explanation results in a generalized explanation. Since a most general unifier is unique except for alphabetic variants, the generalized explanation is also unique except for alphabetic variants.

A proof that any of the individual algorithms given in Section 3 produce a generalized explanation could be constructed by proving that the algorithm is equivalent to the single unification algorithm. As previously mentioned, for the EGGS algorithm, this proof would involve proving the correctness of the unification algorithm in [24].

If it is assumed that explanations are logical proofs (as in [2]), one can also easily prove *soundness*, that is, that the learned macro–rule is logically entailed by the existing domain theory.

**Theorem 2:** A macro–rule extracted from a generalized explanation composed of Horn clauses is logically entailed by the Horn clauses in the domain theory.

*Proof:* By definition, all of the equivalent expressions in a generalized explanation must be identical. Since all of the Horn clauses in the generalized explanation are instantiations of clauses in the domain theory (i.e., they are the result of applying the global substitution to the explanation structure), the logically sound inference rule of *universal instantiation* guarantees that they are entailed by the domain theory. Finally, one needs to show that computing a macro–rule is simply performing logically sound deduction on the Horn clauses in the generalized explanation. If

$$k_1 \cdots k_{i-1} \wedge k_i \wedge k_{i+1} \cdots k_n \rightarrow c$$

and

$$l_1 \wedge \cdots \wedge l_n \rightarrow d$$

are two clauses in the generalized explanation, and $d$ is equivalent to $k_i$, then $d$ and $k_i$ must be identical expressions. Assume the second clause is removed from the generalized explanation and the first clause is replaced by

$$k_1 \cdots k_{i-1} \wedge l_1 \wedge \cdots \wedge l_n \wedge k_{i+1} \cdots k_n \rightarrow c$$

Since $d$ and $k_i$ are identical expressions, the added clause is entailed by the domain theory because it is the resolvent of the two clauses and the resolution rule is sound [28]. Repeating this process for every set of equivalent expressions reduces the generalized explanation to the explanation macro–rule. Since all of the clauses in the original generalized explanation are entailed by the domain theory, and since the clause added by each step in the reduction process is entailed by the existing clauses, by induction the completely reduced generalized explanation (i.e., the learned macro–rule) is entailed by the domain theory.

If it could be proven that a generalization algorithm such as EGGS or PROLOG–EBG computes the correct global substitution and is therefore equivalent to the single unification algorithm, then it would follow that the algorithm also produced a sound macro–rule. Once again, for EGGS, this would involve proving that the unification algorithm in [24] is correct.

Recently, a couple of additional approaches to proving the correctness of algorithms for generalizing logical proofs have been developed. In [29, 30], a definition and proof of correctness is based on showing that the generalization algorithm computes the set of *weakest preconditions* of a proof. In [31], a correctness proof for explanation–based generalization as resolution theorem proving is presented. The generalization algorithm proved correct in this chapter is similar to PROLOG–EBG, but it is a separate process for generalizing resolution proof trees and is not integrated with a theorem prover.

## 6. Computational Complexity of Explanation Generalization

The single unification generalization algorithm also demonstrates that the time complexity of producing a global substitution is linear in the size of the explanation since linear time algorithms exist for unification [32]. Since unification can be performed in linear time, obviously the size of the resulting MGU must also be linear in the size of the explanation since only a linear amount of output can be produced in linear time. Therefore, if $|E|$ represents the size of the explanation, we can let $c_1|E|$ be the time required to construct the global substitution and $c_2|E|$ be the length of the global substitution. Since the time complexity of applying a substitution to an expression is also linear in the length of its inputs,[5] let $c_3(c_2|E|+|E|)$ be the time required to apply the global substitution to the explanation. Therefore, the time required for the complete process of constructing a generalized explanation is

$$c_3(c_2|E|+|E|) + c_1|E| = (c_1 + c_3(c_2 + 1))|E|$$

which is clearly linear in size of the explanation.

Although this result does not reveal the time complexity of the individual visual algorithms in Section 3, it is a constructive proof of the existence of a linear-time explanation generalizing algorithm. Since linear-time unification algorithms have apparently found limited use in practice due to large overhead, it is unlikely that a generalizing algorithm based on one would be particularly useful in practice. Nevertheless, it is an interesting theoretical result which supports the important claim that a generalized explanation can be computed very efficiently.

In practice, the generalizing algorithms given in Section 3 are quite efficient using a standard (nonlinear time) unifier. For example, one of the largest explanations upon which EGGS has been tested had 25 equalities and took only 3.6 seconds of CPU time to generalize on a Xerox 1108.

## 7. Pruning Explanations for Operationality

Often, the explanation structure for a particular example is too specific to support a reasonably useful generalization. In these cases, the *operationality criterion* [2] is met by nodes higher in the explanation tree than the leaves, and it is advisable to *prune* units from the explanation structure that are more specific than required for operationality. The goal of pruning is to make an explanation (and resulting macro-rule) as general as possible while still keeping it *operational*, that is, useful and efficient for the purpose of classifying future examples or solving future problems. If this pruning is done prior to generalization as shown in Figure 2–1, it will result in a more abstract generalized explanation which is applicable to a broader range of examples. For example, if the rule for inferring Graspable is removed from the explanation structure shown in Figure 2–4, the following more general (but less operational) definition of Cup is acquired:

Bottom(?y1) $\wedge$ PartOf(?y1,?x1) $\wedge$ Flat(?y1) $\wedge$ Graspable(?x1) $\wedge$ Light(?x1)

---

[5]The literature on linear unification does not discuss linear time substitution application; however, a linear time algorithm for this procedure is presented in [20].

$\wedge$ Concavity(?y3) $\wedge$ PartOf(?y3,?x1) $\wedge$ UpwardPointing(?y3) $\rightarrow$ Cup(?x1)

Determining the appropriate operationality criterion has been the subject of much discussion in the EBL literature [1, 2, 33–36]. For most domains, there is generally a trade-off that must be resolved between operationality and generality. A more general explanation is useful in a larger set of future situations; however, it is normally also harder to apply in those situations. A more specific explanation, on the other hand, is generally easier to apply to future situations; however, it is less applicable. In the long run, it is probably best to retain explanations at several levels of generality as suggested in [37] and as done in the PHYSICS101 system [35]. This allows a more specific explanation to be used when it is applicable while still permitting a more general explanation to be used when a more operational one is not available.

A recent suggestion for determining operationality is the one used in ARMS, an EBL system for robotics [34]. It involves pruning all of the explanation below *shared substructure*. In terms of the representations used here, this approach would prune all nodes below the point where a subgraph of the explanation becomes a tree as opposed to a general directed acyclical graph. In other words, it keeps pruning leaves of the explanation until a node is found that supports more than one other node. Although this pruning algorithm may work well for the ARMS domain, it is not a general solution to the problem of determining operationality. Many explanations that support useful generalizations do not have any shared substructure. In fact, most of the examples of explanations on which EGGS has been tested are trees and consequently do not have shared substructure. The ARMS approach to pruning would remove the entire explanation in such cases and consequently miss the opportunity to learn useful new rules and operators.

Therefore, determining which predicates or operators are operational is now generally a domain-dependent decision. Consequently, the current EGGS system simply has a hook that allows an arbitrary pruning function to be called before an explanation is generalized. In Hirsh's MRS-EBG system [5], meta-level logical deduction is used to determine operationality. This approach has the advantage of allowing operationality proofs themselves to be generalized in an explanation-based manner in order to determine the most general operational explanation.

## 8. Integrating Explanation Construction, Pruning, and Generalization

Instead of performing the first three steps in Figure 2-1 sequentially, these steps can often be integrated and performed in an interleaved fashion. As discussed in [1, 3], the EGGS generalization algorithm is easily integrated with the explanation-building process by updating the global substitution each time a new rule is added to the evolving explanation. As mentioned earlier, PROLOG-EBG elegantly integrates generalization with the theorem-proving process, and MRS-EBG elegantly integrates both of these processes with pruning the explanation for operationality.

Although integrating these processes is aesthetically appealing, there is a price associated with it. For example, the integration of theorem proving and generalization in PROLOG-EBG and MRS-EBG involves unnecessarily generalizing dead-end branches of the search tree that are eventually abandoned and never become part of the final proof. If generalization were postponed until the final proof is available, this useless computation could be avoided. However, as noted in [5], integrating generalization and theorem proving can still be useful when there are multiple possible explanations for the specific example, only some of which are operational. In this case, integrated generalization, theorem proving, and operationality checking allows theorem proving to continue until an operational proof is eventually found.

Another problem with integration is that in many cases operationality cannot be determined until the complete explanation is available. When learning by observing the problem-solving behavior of an external agent, the eventual goal to be achieved is generally unknown until all of the agent's actions have been observed. However, the pruning algorithm often requires knowledge of the goal. Consequently, in these situations, pruning must be postponed until the complete explanation has been constructed. If generalization is performed before pruning, the resulting generalization may be too specific since it may incorporate constraints introduced by the pruned parts of the explanation. Therefore, when pruning must be performed after the explanation is complete, generalization and explanation cannot be easily integrated. As discussed in [1], if generalization and explanation are integrated, additional constraints introduced by pruned portions of the explanation can later be retracted; however, retracting equality constraints is very difficult and requires the capabilities of a truth maintenance system (TMS) [22]. The MA system [7] is an example of an EBL system that uses a TMS [38] to retract co-reference constraints; however, this system is very inefficient compared to simpler systems based on unification.

A final advantage of a separate and independent generalization process is that it does not constrain the process of explanation construction. Generalizers that are integrated with theorem provers, like PROLOG-EBG and MRS-EBG, require that explanations be constructed by the theorem prover. This process prevents the use of alternative methods of explanation construction such as building explanations by understanding the actions of an external agent.

Therefore, despite the aesthetic appeal of integration, it entails a number of important problems, but they are easily resolved by requiring a separate, independent generalization process. As a result, explanation construction, pruning, and generalization are performed sequentially in the EGGS system, as shown in Figure 2-1.

## 9. Explanation Generalization Versus Chunking and Production Composition

Explanation-based learning of macro-rules and macro-operators is closely related to production system learning mechanisms that compose production rules. The *chunking* process in SOAR [18, 39, 40] and the *knowledge compilation* process of *composition* in ACT* [19, 41] are two similar production system learning models. Both processes build macro-productions based on traces of productions produced by the problem solver when solving a particular problem.

Besides the fact that these systems, unlike STRIPS, EBG, and EGGS, do not rely on a logic-based representation, their primary difference lies in their less analytical generalization process. SOAR's generalization algorithm is described in detail in [42], where it is compared and contrasted to EBG. The generalization process is basically one of changing constants to independent variables. However, due to the difference in representation language, the problem of overgeneralization mentioned in Section 3.1 is avoided. Constants in SOAR come in two types: *identifiers*, which are symbols for particular objects, and more meaningful constants such as "5" and "blue." For example, representing the logical assertion Color($\beta$,blue) requires creating an extra identifier for the constant "blue" and using the two assertions Color($\beta$,$\zeta$) and Name($\zeta$, blue). The generalization process in SOAR changes only identifiers to variables, and since production rules cannot check for particular identifiers, the over-generalization problem is avoided. The cost incurred for avoiding the problem in this manner is an extra distinction in the representation language.

However, the problem of undergeneralization mentioned in Section 3.1 remains. For example, in the SOAR formulation of the Safe-To-Stack example (an example from [2]) presented by Rosenbloom and Laird [42], the rule learned is

$$\text{Volume}(x,v) \wedge \text{Density}(x,d) \wedge \text{Name}(y,\text{endtable}) \wedge \text{Product}(v,d,d)$$
$$\wedge \text{Less}(d,w) \wedge \text{Name}(w,5) \rightarrow \text{Safe-To-Stack}(x,y)$$

As noted in [42], this rule is an undergeneralization since it requires the density and the weight of the object being stacked to be the same (i.e., *d*). Since the box in the example just happened to have the same weight and density, the simple variabilization process requires them to be the same. For the same reason, the initial and final rooms would unnecessarily be required to be the same if this technique were applied to the STRIPS example. Retaining such spurious features of the example in the generalization is a basic violation of the explanation-based approach. EBL stipulates that only those constraints required to maintain the validity of the solution should be incorporated in the generalization.

In response to the problem of undergeneralization, Rosenbloom and Laird [42] stated, "If an example were run in which the density and the weight were different, then a rule would be learned to deal with future situations in which they were different" (p. 564). However, if the more general rule were learned from the original example, this new example could be solved more quickly by using the learned rule. Also, unless a check is made to remove subsumed rules (i.e., rules that are specializations of existing rules), this solution leaves useless rules lying around that decrease performance by increasing the number of rules the system must check for application. Rosenbloom and Laird also stated "The SOAR approach to goal regression is simpler, and focuses on the information in working memory rather than the possibly complex patterns specified by the rules" (p. 564). If the problems with a simple constant to variable generalization algorithm were offset by a marked increased in efficiency of generalization, then perhaps a case could be made for the simpler generalization process. However, as shown in Section 6, the computational complexity of a unification-based generalization algorithm is linear in the size of the explanation. Since simply tracing through the complete explanation to replace each constant with a variable is also a linear process, the gain in efficiency is at most a constant factor.

Of course, SOAR could probably be modified to include a generalizer that prevents undergeneralization. This process would require retaining copies of the general parameterized productions (with unique variables) in the production traces produced during problem solving. Generalization would then require constructing the most general set of variable bindings that allows all of the left-hand sides of general productions to match the right-hand sides of the general productions that they support in the production trace. A procedure analogous to unification for matching production conditions could be used to produce the required global substitution.

Finally, regarding composition in ACT*, discussions of the underlying generalization process in *production composition* [19, 41, 43, 44] fail to give explicit details of the generalization algorithm. However, the fact that no mention is made of the subtleties of generalization, the limits of simply changing constants to variables, or the use of a generalizer that analyzes variable bindings indicates that a more analytic generalizer is not used. Also, the examples given of composition involving telephone dialing [43], geometry problem solving [19, 44], and LISP programming [19, 41, 45] can all be accomplished by simply changing constants to variables.

## 10. Horn Clause Proof Explanations in EGGS

For dealing with explanations composed of Horn clauses, the complete EGGS system is equipped with general purpose subsystems for proving theorems, understanding incomplete proofs, and generating macrorules. Figure 2-15 illustrates how these components combine with the generalizer to comprise a complete learning system. The theorem prover and proof verifier allow EGGS to construct explanations by either proving theorems itself or by filling in gaps in sketchy proofs provided by the user. These explanations can then be generalized using the EGGS generalization algorithm, resulting in macro-rules that can be used to construct and understand similar proofs more efficiently.

The Horn clause theorem prover in EGGS is a depth-first, backward-chaining system (like PROLOG) based on the deductive retriever given in [24]. The retriever can be given a depth bound, *d*, to prevent it from chaining more than *d* rules deep when attempting to retrieve a particular fact. When a macro-rule is learned, it is added to the front of the current list of rules so that the retriever attempts to use it before resorting to the initial domain theory.

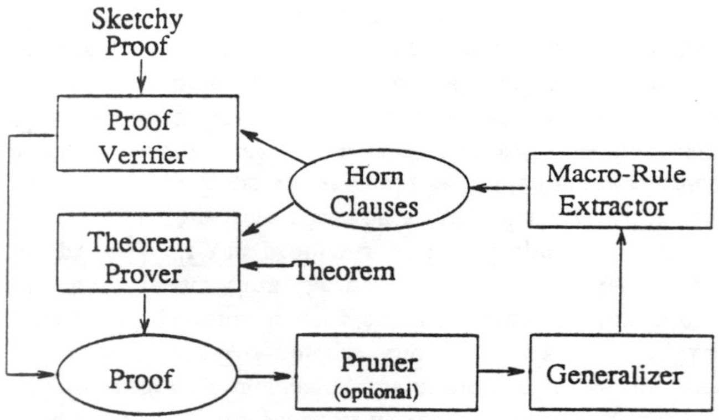

The deductive retriever can also be used to fill in gaps in sketchy proofs given to the system. Sketchy proofs are ordered sequences of subgoals or lemmas to be proven before attempting to prove the ultimate goal. The system attempts to prove that each step in the proof follows deductively from the initial facts together with the facts deduced in previous steps. If it can safely be assumed that the sketchy proof will not be missing more than $d$ inferences between steps, then the depth bound on the prover can be set to $d$ during verification. This allows proof verification to be much more efficient than theorem proving.[6]

If the EGGS system is used solely as an independent theorem prover that learns macro-rules, it closely resembles a learning PROLOG interpreter, like that described by Prieditus and Mostow [46]. If, on the other hand, it is used to analyze sample proofs and learn macro-rules from them, it behaves more like a learning apprentice system [11, 16]. The important thing to note, however, is that the same generalization algorithm underlies both approaches to learning.

EGGS has been tested on a wide variety of examples that employ explanations based on Horn clauses, including robot planning in a "blocks world" [8], solving symbolic integration problems [9], learning artifact descriptions [10], designing logic circuits [16], and proving theorems in logic [11] and geometry [44]. The following subsection presents an

---

[6]See Mooney [20] for an analysis of the computational complexity of proof verification.

**Figure 2-15: EGGS Architecture for Horn Clause Proof Explanations**

example from one of these domains.

## 10.1. MA Example

An explanation-based learning system in the domain of logic theorem proving is MA [7, 11], which learns proof schemata from sample natural deduction proofs. When the system cannot complete a proof for a particular theorem, a teacher steps in and completes the proof. MA then generalizes the teacher's proof in an explanation-based manner to generate a proof schema that can be used to solve future problems. Consider a variant of the example discussed in [11] of proving a particular case of the law of excluded middle: NIL⇒(P∧Q)∨¬(P∧Q) (i.e., (P∧Q)∨¬(P∧Q) can be deduced from the empty set of assumptions). The natural deduction proof the deductive retriever generates for this example is shown in Figure 2-16. The following rules of natural deduction [47] are employed in this proof:

*Assumption Axiom:* $(?x . ?y) \Rightarrow ?x$
*Or Introduction:* $?x \Rightarrow ?y \rightarrow ?x \Rightarrow ?y \lor ?z$
*Or Introduction:* $?x \Rightarrow ?y \rightarrow ?x \Rightarrow ?z \lor ?y$
*Elimination Of Assumption:* $(?x . ?y) \Rightarrow ?z \land (\neg ?x . ?y) \Rightarrow ?z \rightarrow ?y \Rightarrow ?z$

The expression $?x \Rightarrow ?y$ means that the wff $?y$ is deducible from the list of assumptions (wffs) $?x$. LISP *dot notation* is used to represent lists of assumptions. The generalized proof EGGS generates for this example is shown in Figure 2-17. From a specific instance of proving (P∧Q)∨¬(P∧Q) from no assumptions, a general proof is learned for proving the disjunction of any wff and its negation from any set of assumptions. Notice again that simply changing the constants P and Q to variables would have resulted in an undergeneralization. The more general fact learned by EGGS allows it to solve the test problem: NIL⇒P∨¬P in one step.

The same proof and generalization result from understanding the following sketchy proof:

$$((P\land Q)) \Rightarrow (P\land Q) \lor \neg(P\land Q)$$
$$(\neg(P\land Q)) \Rightarrow (P\land Q) \lor \neg(P\land Q)$$
$$Q.E.D.: \text{NIL} \Rightarrow (P\land Q) \lor \neg(P\land Q)$$

If the depth bound on the deductive retriever is set to two, explaining this proof takes only 4.5 CPU seconds compared to proving the theorem directly, which takes 9 CPU seconds with a depth bound of three, 18.5

$$NIL \Rightarrow (P \land Q) \lor \neg(P \land Q)$$

$$(\neg(P \land Q)) \Rightarrow (P \land Q) \lor \neg(P \land Q) \qquad ((P \land Q)) \Rightarrow (P \land Q) \lor \neg(P \land Q)$$

$$(\neg(P \land Q)) \Rightarrow \neg(P \land Q) \qquad ((P \land Q)) \Rightarrow P \land Q$$

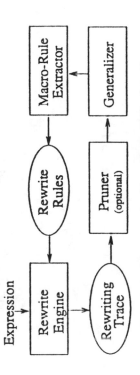

**Figure 2-16: MA Example — Specific Explanation**

$$?y17 \Rightarrow ?y16 \lor \neg ?y16$$

$$(?y16 . ?y17) \Rightarrow ?y16 \lor \neg ?y16 \qquad (\neg ?y16 . ?y17) \Rightarrow ?y16 \lor \neg ?y16$$

$$(?y16 . ?y17) \Rightarrow ?y16 \qquad (\neg ?y16 . ?y17) \Rightarrow \neg ?y16$$

**Figure 2-17: MA Example — Generalized Explanation**

CPU seconds with a depth bound of five, and 759 CPU seconds with a depth bound of ten! This simply demonstrates that, as expected, understanding a proof can be much more efficient than independently discovering one. After learning the macro-rule, the theorem can be proved in only 0.53 CPU second. Therefore, EGGS can be up to 1,432 times faster at proving a theorem after learning than before.

## 11. Rewrite Rule Explanations in EGGS

Compared to using logical deduction, many mathematical problems can be represented more concisely and solved more efficiently by using *rewrite rules* to perform term rewriting [48]. Like logical proofs, chains of rewrite rule applications can be represented as explanations. Each rewritten term is an expression in the explanation, and the chaining together of two rules is represented by a unification between the right–hand side (RHS) of the first rule and the left–hand side (LHS) of the second.

Figure 2-18 illustrates the components in EGGS that use and learn rewrite rules. The rewrite rule engine allows EGGS to construct rewrite rule explanations by solving problems itself. These explanations can then be generalized, resulting in macro–rules that can be used to solve similar problems more efficiently. EGGS has been tested on a number of examples which employ explanations based on rewrite rules. These include

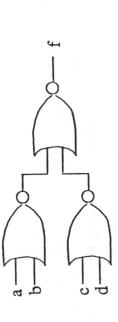

**Figure 2-18: EGGS Architecture for Rewrite Rule Explanations**

examples involving solving symbolic integration problems [9], designing logic circuits [16], and solving algebraic equations [13]. The following subsection presents an example from one of these domains.

### 11.1. LEAP Example

The LEAP system [16] is a learning apprentice in VLSI design which observes the behavior of a circuit designer. It attempts to learn in an explanation–based fashion by observing and analyzing specific examples of logic design. As an example of learning in this domain, consider the following example taken from [16]. Given the task of implementing a circuit that computes the logical function $(a \lor b) \land (c \lor d)$, a circuit designer creates a circuit consisting of three NOR gates like that shown in Figure 2-19. The system attempts to verify that the given circuit actually computes the desired function. The explanation constructed by EGGS' rewrite engine showing that the circuit computes the desired function is shown in Figure 2-20. In this example, the domain knowledge available to the

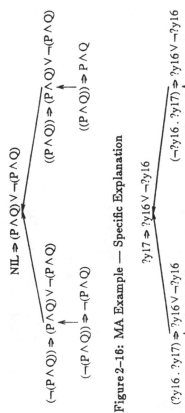

**Figure 2-19: Circuit Design Learning Problem**

system includes the following rewrite rules:

$$\neg\neg?x \rightarrow ?x$$

$$\neg(?x \vee ?y) \rightarrow \neg?x \wedge \neg?y$$

The explanation structure and generalized explanation for this example are shown in Figure 2–21 and Figure 2–22, respectively. Notice that if a rule rewrites only a subterm of an expression, "dummy variables" are added to the pattern in the explanation structure to fill out the expression so that it can be unified with the previous expression. LISP list notation is used in the illustration of the explanation structure since the technique used to add dummy variables relies on the underlying list representation. For example, after applying DeMorgan's law in the LEAP problem, the rule for eliminating a double negation is used to rewrite the first term in the resulting conjunction. In order to allow the LHS of this rule to unify with the RHS of the instance of DeMorgan's law in the explanation structure, this rule is padded with the dummy variables ?f1 and ?f2. During generalization, this unification results in the following substitution:

{and/?f1, not(?x2)/?x1, (not(?y1))/?f2}

Next, the rule for eliminating a double negation is used to rewrite the second term in the conjunction, and this instance of the rule is padded with the dummy variables ?f3, ?f4, and ?f5 in order to allow its LHS to unify with the previous instance. During generalization, this unification results in the following substitution:

{and/?f3, ?f4/?x2, not(?x3)/?y1, NIL/?f5}

Applying the composition of these two substitutions to the explanation structure results in the generalized explanation shown in Figure 2–22.

$$\neg(\neg(a \vee b) \vee \neg(c \vee d))$$
$$\downarrow$$
$$\neg(\neg(a \vee b)) \wedge \neg(\neg(c \vee d))$$
$$\downarrow$$
$$(a \vee b) \wedge \neg(\neg(c \vee d))$$
$$\downarrow$$
$$(a \vee b) \wedge (c \vee d)$$

Figure 2–20: LEAP Rewrite — Specific Explanation

The new rewrite rule macro–rule learned from the LEAP example is

$$\neg(\neg?f4 \vee \neg?x3) \rightarrow ?f4 \wedge ?x3$$

Once again, had generalization been performed by simply changing constants to variables, the result would have been overly specific. As a result of the explanation–based approach, the resulting generalization is not sensitive to the fact that the first stage of the circuit involved two NOR

$$(\text{not } (\text{or } ?x1\ ?y1))$$
$$\downarrow$$
$$(\text{and } (\text{not } ?x1)\ (\text{not } ?y1))$$
$$\equiv$$
$$(?f1\ (\text{not } (\text{not } ?x2))\ .\ ?f2)$$
$$\downarrow$$
$$(?f1\ ?x2\ .\ ?f2)$$
$$\equiv$$
$$(?f3\ ?f4\ (\text{not } (\text{not } ?x3))\ .\ ?f5)$$
$$\downarrow$$
$$(?f3\ ?f4\ ?x3\ .\ ?f5)$$

Figure 2–21: LEAP Rewrite — Explanation Structure

$$\neg(\neg(?f4) \vee \neg(?x3))$$
$$\downarrow$$
$$\neg(\neg(?f4) \wedge \neg(\neg(?x3)))$$
$$\downarrow$$
$$?f4 \wedge \neg(\neg(?x3))$$
$$\downarrow$$
$$?f4 \wedge ?x3$$

Figure 2–22: LEAP Rewrite — Generalized Explanation

gates.

## 12. Conclusions

This chapter has presented the EGGS system as a general domain-independent explanation-based learning system which has been tested on many examples in a variety of domains. Numerous other applications of EGGS as well as empirical data on the effect of learned macro-rules on future problem-solving performance are presented in Mooney [20].

The explanation generalization algorithm in EGGS was compared to generalization algorithms in other systems such as STRIPS, PROLOG-EBG, and SOAR. STRIPS, EGGS, and PROLOG-EBG were all informally shown to produce generalized explanations (as defined in Section 2); however, SOAR was shown to be susceptible to under-generalization. Unlike other generalizers that are tied to a particular representation of explanations, such as STRIPS plans (STRIPS) or Horn clause proofs (PROLOG-EBG), the EGGS system was shown to be capable of generalizing explanations composed of Horn clauses, STRIPS operators, *and* rewrite rules. Finally, several arguments were given for preferring an independent generalization process (as in EGGS) instead of integrating generalization with theorem proving (as in PROLOG-EBG). A primary advantage of an independent generalizer is that it allows learning from observed problem-solving behavior as well as internally generated problem solutions.

The chapter also analyzed the correctness and the computational complexity of explanation generalization, demonstrating the existence of a correct and sound generalization algorithm with linear time complexity. Although other research in explanation generalization has also addressed the issue of correctness [29, 31], the issue of computational complexity has not been addressed elsewhere.

The approach to explanation generalization taken in EGGS has served as a foundation for a number of explanation-based learning systems investigating advanced issues in EBL. The research presented in most of the remaining chapters of this book rely on the method of explanation generalization outlined in this chapter.

## References

1. G. F. DeJong and R. J. Mooney, "Explanation-Based Learning: An Alternative View," *Machine Learning 1*, 2 (1986), pp. 145–176.

2. T. M. Mitchell, R. M. Keller and S. Kedar-Cabelli, "Explanation-Based Generalization: A Unifying View," *Machine Learning 1*, 1 (January 1986), pp. 47–80.

3. R. J. Mooney and S. W. Bennett, "A Domain Independent Explanation-Based Generalizer," *Proceedings of the National Conference on Artificial Intelligence*, Philadelphia, PA, August 1986, pp. 551–555.

4. S. T. Kedar-Cabelli and L. T. McCarty, "Explanation-Based Generalization as Resolution Theorem Proving," *Proceedings of the Fourth International Workshop on Machine Learning*, University of California, Irvine, June 1987, pp. 383–389.

5. H. Hirsh, "Explanation-Based Generalization in a Logic-Programming Environment," *Proceedings of the Tenth International Joint Conference on Artificial Intelligence*, Milan, Italy, August 1987, pp. 221–227.

6. S. Minton and J. G. Carbonell, "Strategies for Learning Search Control Rules: An Explanation-based Approach," *Proceedings of the Tenth International Joint Conference on Artificial Intelligence*, Milan, Italy, August 1987, pp. 228–235.

7. P. V. O'Rorke, "Explanation-Based Learning Via Constraint Posting and Propagation," Ph.D. Thesis, Department of Computer Science, University of Illinois, Urbana, IL, January 1987.

8. R. E. Fikes, P. E. Hart and N. J. Nilsson, "Learning and Executing Generalised Robot Plans," *Artificial Intelligence 3*, (1972), pp. 251–288.

9. T. M. Mitchell, "Learning and Problem Solving," *Proceedings of the Eighth International Joint Conference on Artificial Intelligence*, Karlsruhe, West Germany, August 1983, pp. 1139–1151.

10. P. H. Winston, T. O. Binford, B. Katz and M. Lowry, "Learning Physical Descriptions from Functional Definitions, Examples, and Precedents," *Proceedings of the National Conference on Artificial Intelligence*, Washington, D.C., August 1983, pp. 433–439.

11. P. V. O'Rorke, "Generalization for Explanation-based Schema Acquisition," *Proceedings of the National Conference on Artificial Intelligence*, Austin, TX, August 1984, pp. 260–263.

12. S. N. Minton, "Constraint-Based Generalization: Learning Game-Playing Plans from Single Examples," *Proceedings of the National Conference on Artificial Intelligence*, Austin, TX, August 1984, pp. 251–254.

13. B. Silver, "Learning Equation Solving Methods from Worked Examples," *Proceedings of the 1983 International Machine Learning Workshop*, Urbana, IL, June 1983, pp. 99–104.

14. R. J. Mooney and G. F. DeJong, "Learning Schemata for Natural Language Processing," *Proceedings of the Ninth International Joint Conference on Artificial Intelligence*, Los Angeles, CA, August 1985, pp. 681–687.

15. J. W. Shavlik, "Learning about Momentum Conservation," *Proceedings of the Ninth International Joint Conference on Artificial Intelligence*, Los Angeles, CA, August 1985, pp. 667–669.

16. T. M. Mitchell, S. Mahadevan and L. I. Steinberg, "LEAP: A Learning Apprentice for VLSI Design," *Proceedings of the Ninth International Joint Conference on Artificial Intelligence*, Los Angeles, CA, August 1985, pp. 573–580.

17. A. M. Segre and G. F. DeJong, "Explanation Based Manipulator Learning: Acquisition of Planning Ability Through Observation," *Proceedings of the IEEE International Conference on Robotics and Automation*, St. Louis, MO, March 1985, pp. 555–560. (Also appears as Working Paper 62, AI Research Group, Coordinated Science Laboratory, University of Illinois at Urbana–Champaign.)

18. J. E. Laird, P. S. Rosenbloom and A. Newell, *Universal Subgoaling and Chunking: The Automatic Generation and Learning of Goal Hierarchies*, Kluwer Academic Publishers, Norwell, MA, 1986.

19. J. R. Anderson, *The Architecture of Cognition*, Harvard University Press, Cambridge, MA, 1983.

20. R. J. Mooney, "A General Explanation–Based Learning Mechanism and its Application to Narrative Understanding," Ph.D. Thesis, Department of Computer Science, University of Illinois, Urbana, IL, January 1988.

21. N. J. Nilsson, *Principles of Artificial Intelligence*, Tioga Publishing Company, Palo Alto, CA, 1980.

22. J. Doyle, "A Truth Maintenance System," *Artificial Intelligence 12*, 3 (1979), pp. 231–272.

23. R. Waldinger, "Achieving Several Goals Simultaneously," in *Machine Intelligence 8*, E. Elcock and D. Michie (ed.), Ellis Horwood Limited, London, 1977.

24. E. Charniak, C. Riesbeck and D. McDermott, *Artificial Intelligence Programming*, Lawrence Erlbaum and Associates, Hillsdale, NJ, 1980.

25. E. W. Dijkstra, *A Discipline of Programming*, Prentice–Hall, 1976.

26. S. Mahadevan, "Verification–Based Learning: A Generalization Strategy for Inferring Problem–Reduction Methods," *Proceedings of the Ninth International Joint Conference on Artificial Intelligence*, Los Angeles, CA, August 1985, pp. 616–623.

27. S. Russell, "The Compleat Guide to MRS," Technical Report KSL 85–12, Computer Science Department, Stanford University, June 1985.

28. J. A. Robinson, "A Machine–Oriented Logic Based on the Resolution Principle," *Journal of the Association for Computing Machinery 12*, 1 (1965), pp. 23–41.

29. S. Minton, "EBL and Weakest Preconditions," *Proceedings of the AAAI Symposium on Explanation–Based Learning*, Stanford, CA, March 1988, pp. 210–214.

30. S. Minton, "Learning Effective Search Control Knowledge: An Explanation–based Approach," Ph.D. Thesis CMU-CS-88-133, Department of Computer Science, Carnegie–Mellon University, Pittsburgh, PA, March 1988.

31. N. Bhatnagar, "A Correctness Proof of Explanation–Based Generalization as Resolution Theorem–Proving," *Proceedings of the AAAI Symposium on Explanation–Based Learning*, Stanford, CA, March 1988, pp. 220–225.

32. M. S. Paterson and M. N. Wegman, "Linear Unification," *Journal of Computer and System Sciences 16*, (1978), pp. 158–167.

33. R. M. Keller, "Defining Operationality for Explanation–Based Learning," *Proceedings of the National Conference on Artificial Intelligence*, Seattle, WA, July 1987, pp. 482–487.

34. A. M. Segre, "On the Operationality/Generality Trade–off in Explanation–Based Learning," *Proceedings of the Tenth International Joint Conference on Artificial Intelligence*, Milan, Italy, August 1987, pp. 242–248.

35. J. W. Shavlik, G. F. DeJong and B. H. Ross, "Acquiring Special Case Schemata in Explanation–Based Learning," *Proceedings of the Ninth Annual Conference of the Cognitive Science Society*, Seattle,

WA, July 1987, pp. 851–860.

36. R. Keller, "Operationality and Generality in Explanation–Based Learning: Separate Dimensions or Opposite Endpoints?," *Proceedings of the AAAI Symposium on Explanation–Based Learning*, Stanford, CA, March 1988, pp. 153–157.

37. R. J. Mooney, "Generalizing Explanations of Narratives into Schemata," M.S. Thesis, Department of Computer Science, University of Illinois, Urbana, IL, May 1985.

38. D. A. McAllester, "Reasoning Utility Package User's Manual, Version One," Memo 667, MIT AI Lab, Cambridge, MA, April 1982.

39. J. Laird, P. Rosenbloom and A. Newell, "Towards Chunking as a General Learning Mechanism," *Proceedings of the National Conference on Artificial Intelligence*, Austin, TX, August 1984, pp. 188–192.

40. J. Laird, P. Rosenbloom and A. Newell, "Chunking in Soar: The Anatomy of a General Learning Mechanism," *Machine Learning 1*, 1 (1986), pp. 11–46.

41. J. R. Anderson, "Knowledge Compilation: The General Learning Mechanism," in *Machine Learning: An Artificial Intelligence Approach, Vol. II*, R. S. Michalski, J. G. Carbonell and T. M. Mitchell (ed.), MORGAN, 1986, pp. 289–309.

42. P. Rosenbloom and J. Laird, "Mapping Explanation–Based Generalization into Soar," *Proceedings of the National Conference on Artificial Intelligence*, Philadelphia, PA, August 1986, pp. 561–567.

43. J. R. Anderson, "Acquisition of Cognitive Skill," *Psychological Review 89*, 4 (1982), pp. 369–406.

44. J. R. Anderson, "Acquisition of Proof Skills in Geometry," in *Machine Learning: An Artificial Intelligence Approach*, R. S. Michalski, J. G. Carbonell, T. M. Mitchell (ed.), Tioga Publishing Company, Palo Alto, CA, 1983, pp. 191–221.

45. J. R. Anderson and R. Thompson, "Use of Analogy in a Production System Architecture," in *Similarity and Analogical Reasoning*, S. Vosniadou and A. Ortony (ed.), Cambridge University Press, Cambridge, England, 1989.

46. A. E. Prieditis and J. Mostow, "PROLEARN: Towards a Prolog Interpreter that Learns," *Proceedings of the National Conference on Artificial Intelligence*, Seattle, WA, July 1987, pp. 494–498.

47. Z. Manna, *Mathematical Theory of Computation*, McGraw–Hill, New York, NY, 1974.

48. A. Bundy, *The Computer Modelling of Mathematical Reasoning*, Academic Press, New York, NY, 1983.

# Section 5.3

# Synthesizing Problem Solvers
# from Deep Models

Deep or first-principle knowledge is that knowledge that underlies or provides justification for compiled or shallow knowledge. Deep or first-principle models play a very important role in the development and refinement of human expertise, and so they can be expected to play an important role in the acquisition and refinement of expert system knowledge bases.

A common but understandable error made by many novices in the field of knowledge acquisition is the assumption that deep or first-principle expert systems are better or more desirable than shallow or compiled expert systems. Those familiar with human expertise know that in fact novices are the principal users of first-principle knowledge and bona-fide experts mainly use compiled knowledge. A good expert system must contain both deep and shallow knowledge of the domain, organized so that the relationships between deep and shallow knowledge are clear (Karp and Wilkins, 1989).

The term *model-based* expert systems can also be a source of confusion. Both first-principle and compiled expert systems usually assume a model of the domain. In compiled expert systems, this model is defined by the structure and inference mechanisms of the generic expert system shell. For example, the model used by SALT is revise-and-refine; the model used by NEOMYCIN and MINERVA is hypothesis-directed reasoning.

Swartout's paper in Section 5.3.1, on the XPLAIN system, introduces the idea of a justification structure. XPLAIN synthesizes a compiled expert system from a domain model (i.e., facts in the domain) and a set of domain principles (i.e., methods and heuristics), and keeps a justification structure that records their relationship. The justification structure facilitates the generation of explanations of the compiled knowledge.

Barstow's paper in Section 5.3.2 describes the ΦNIX system. The paper makes a strong case for the central role of domain-specific knowledge in automatic programming. Traditionally, automatic programming research has focused on general programming knowledge rather than domain-specific knowledge. Barstow believes that the structuring of domain knowledge being done in the expert systems community will be adequate for an automatic programming synthesizer.

Barstow's paper provides much food for thought to researchers in automatic programming and in machine learning. His paper shows the crucial need for the automatic programming system to have a large amount of domain-specific knowledge, a factor not previously taken into account in the automatic programming community, though taken for granted by machine learning researchers.

Barstow also shows how automatic programming and machine learning are tackling the same problem, with the difference that the performance elements in automatic programming are much more complex than those in machine learning. When machine learning researchers eventually address more realistic and complex performance elements, they will find the experiences of the automatic programming community very instructive.

Exploring the terrain between machine learning and automatic programming (which in recent years is referred to as knowledge-based software engineering) is an important research direction for machine learning. The three areas of automatic programming of most relevance to machine learning are program synthesis (Smith et al., 1985; Steier, 1987; Barstow, 1979), programming analysis (Harandi and Ning, 1990; Rich and Wills, 1990), and programming assistants (Waters, 1985; Smith, 1988).

Bratko's article in Section 5.3.3 describes the KARDIO system. This very elegant study shows how a qualitative simulation based on a causal model of the world (in this case, the heart) can be used to generate a knowledge base. The advantage of this approach for the creation of diagnostic expert systems is the ability to guarantee that the resulting rule-based system will be able to diagnose any disease.

# XPLAIN: a System for Creating and Explaining Expert Consulting Programs

**William R. Swartout***

*USC/Information Sciences Institute, Marina del Rey, CA 90291, U.S.A.*

Recommended by N.S Sridharan

ABSTRACT

*Traditional methods for explaining programs provide explanations by converting the code of the program or traces of its execution to English. While such methods can sometimes adequately explain program behavior, they typically cannot provide justifications for that behavior. That is, such systems cannot tell why what the system is doing is a reasonable thing to be doing. The problem is that the knowledge required to provide these justifications was used to produce the program but is itself not recorded as part of the code, and hence is unavailable.*

*The XPLAIN system uses an automatic programmer to generate a consulting program by refinement from abstract goals. The automatic programmer uses a domain model, consisting of descriptive facts about the application domain, and a set of domain principles which prescribe behavior and drive the refinement process forward. By examining the refinement structure created by the automatic programmer, XPLAIN provides justifications of the code. XPLAIN has been used to re-implement major portions of a Digitalis Therapy Advisor and provides superior explanations of its behavior.*

## 1. Introduction

Computers can be inscrutable. To the layman, the computer is often regarded as either an omniscient, fathomless device or a convenient scapegoat. In part, this situation has arisen because computer systems are designed with little provision for self-description. That is, programs cannot explain or justify what they do. Typically, the designer of a data processing system can rely on a staff

*This research was performed while the author was at the Laboratory for Computer Science of the Massachusetts Institute of Technology and was supported (in part) by the National Institutes of Health Grant No. 1 P01 LM 03374-01 from the National Library of Medicine.

*Artificial Intelligence* **21** (1983) 285–325

0004-3702/83/$3.00 © 1983, Elsevier Science Publishers B.V. (North-Holland)

This paper originally appeared in the journal, *Artificial Intelligence*, Vol. 21, No. 3, and is reprinted here with permission of the publisher, Elsevier, Amsterdam.

gies are limited to describing what they did (or the reasoning path they followed to reach a conclusion), but they are incapable of justifying their actions (or reasoning paths). By justifications, we mean explanations that tell why an expert system's actions are reasonable in terms of principles of the domain—the reasoning *behind* the system. The knowledge required to provide justifications is not represented in typical expert systems because the program can perform correctly without it. Just as one can follow a recipe and bake a cake without ever knowing why the flour or baking powder is there, so too an expert system can deliver impressive performance without any representation of the reasoning underlying its rules or methods.

The reasoning that system designers go through during the creation of an expert system is precisely what is required to produce justifications, yet it is not likely to appear in the expert system itself. This paper presents one approach for capturing that reasoning. The basic idea is to use an automatic programmer to create the expert system. As it refines the performance program from abstract goals, the programmer leaves behind a trace of its reasoning, which can then be used by explanatory routines to justify the actions of the expert system.

In creating the expert system, the automatic programmer draws on two bodies of knowledge. The first, called the *domain model*, contains the descriptive facts of the domain, such as causal relationships and classification hierarchies—the textbook knowledge of the domain. The second body of knowledge, the *domain principles*, contains the methods and heuristics of the domain—the 'how to' knowledge. The automatic programmer integrates these prescriptive principles together with the descriptive facts of the domain to produce the performance program. This process of integration is recorded and used as the justification of the expert system's behavior.

This explicit separation of prescriptive and descriptive knowledge is not made in most expert systems and has some important benefits in addition to facilitating justification. In systems where descriptive and prescriptive knowledge is implicitly intermixed, methods or rules must often be stated at an overly specific level of abstraction. This reduces the quality of the explanations the system can deliver. As we will see (in Section 6), separating these different kinds of knowledge allows methods to be stated at a higher level of abstraction resulting in superior explanations. The other primary benefit is to modifiability: the domain model and domain principles can be modified (or used) in-dependently. For example, most of the domain principles which were written to anticipate digitalis sensitivities can in fact be used to anticipate sensitivity to any drug. Only the domain model would have to change to allow these principles to be used in a new application domain. On the other hand, much of the domain model that was developed for correcting for digitalis sensitivities was also used in detecting digitalis toxicity. In expert systems that intermix descriptive and prescriptive knowledge, modification of methods can be quite difficult. The separation of the two eases that process.

of computer support personnel to deal with problems and questions as they occur. However, even in relatively simple areas such as accounting and billing this approach has not been an overwhelming success, and it becomes less appropriate as we become more ambitious and attempt to use the computer to solve more sophisticated problems in an environment where support personnel may not be available to answer inquiries.

Trust in a system is developed not only by the quality of its results, but also by clear description of how they were derived. This can be especially true when first working with an expert system. Expert systems are usually based on heuristics. While heuristics may provide good performance for most cases, there may be unusual cases where they produce erroneous results, or where the rationale for using them is faulty. If a user is suspicious of the advice he receives, he should be able to ask for a description of the methods employed and the reasons for employing them. In addition, the scope of expert systems, like that of human experts, is often quite narrow. An explanation facility can help a user discover when a system is being pushed beyond the bounds of its expertise.

As a further illustration of the need for explanation consider expert medical consultant programs.[1] In designing a consultant program, we must consider what sorts of capabilities we are trying to provide for the physician user. If we consider the interaction between a physician and a human consultant, we realize that it is not just a simple one-way exchange where the physician provides data and the consultant provides an answer in the form of a prescription or diagnosis. Rather, there is typically a lively dialog between the two. The physician may question whether some factor was considered or what effect a particular finding had on the final outcome and the expert is expected to be able to justify his answer and show that sound medical principles and knowledge were used to obtain it. Viewed in this light, we realize that a computer program which only collects data and provides a final answer will not be found acceptable by most physicians. In addition to providing diagnoses or prescriptions, a consultant program must be able to explain what it is doing and justify why it is doing it.

Researchers have recognized this, and many proposals for new expert systems have at least mentioned the need for explanation. Some systems have actually provided an explanatory facility. Yet existing approaches to explanation fail in some important ways.

## 1.1. Major points

In particular, we will argue in this paper that current explanation methodo-

---

[1] Some medical consultant programs include:: MYCIN, a program that aids physicians with antimicrobial therapy [27], INTERNIST, a program that makes diagnoses in internal medicine [25] and PIP, a program that makes diagnoses primarily in the area of renal disease [24].

## 1.2. Outline

The next section will describe the Digitalis Therapy Advisor, the program we have chosen as a testbed for our ideas about explanation, and some of the medical aspects of digitalis therapy. Section 3 discusses some of the kinds of questions that require explanation. Section 4 outlines some of the problems with previous approaches to explanation. Section 5 details how the automatic programmer works and Section 6 shows how explanations are produced, Section 7 further discusses the problems and promise of this approach.

While we have concentrated on the problem of providing explanations to medical personnel, we do not feel that the need for explanation is limited to medicine nor that the techniques we have developed for explanation and justification are limited to medical applications. Medical programs provide a good testbed for the general problem of explaining a consulting program to the audience it is intended to serve.

## 2. Digitalis Therapy and the Digitalis Advisor

The digitalis glycosides are a group of drugs that were originally derived from the foxglove, a common flowering plant. Their principal effect is to strengthen and stabilize the heartbeat. In current practice, digitalis is prescribed chiefly to patients who show signs of *congestive heart failure* (CHF) or *conduction disturbances* of the heart. Congestive heart failure refers to the inability of the heart to provide the body with an adequate blood flow. This condition causes fluid to accumulate in the lungs and outer extremities and it is this aspect that gives rise to the term 'congestive'. Digitalis is useful in treating this condition because it increases the contractility of the heart, making it a more effective pump. A conduction disturbance appears as an arrhythmia, which is an unsteady or abnormally paced heartbeat. Digitalis tends to slow the conduction of electrical impulses through the conduction system of the heart, and thus steady certain types of arrhythmias. Due to the positive effect that digitalis has on the heart, it is one of the most commonly prescribed drugs in the United States.

Like many other drugs, digitalis can also be a poison if too much is administered. For a variety of reasons, including a small difference between a therapeutic and toxic dose, subtle signs of toxicity, and high interpatient variability, digitalis is difficult to administer. The physician must deal with the possibility that his patient may be more sensitive to the drug (for whatever reason) than the average patient. If a physician knows those factors that make a patient more sensitive he can reduce the likelihood of overdosing (or underdosing) the patient by adjusting the dose depending on whether he observes the sensitizing factors or not.

One possible toxic effect of digitalis is to increase the *automaticity* of the heart. In the normal heart, there is a place in the left atrium called the sino-atrial (SA) node, which sets the pace for the heart. Under certain circumstances, other parts of the heart can take over the pace-setting function. Sometimes this can be life-saving if, for example, the SA node is damaged. But at other times it can be life-threatening, since several pace-makers operating simultaneously tend to increase the likelihood of setting up a dangerous arrhythmia, such as ventricular fibrillation. When we say that digitalis increases the automaticity of the heart, we mean that digitalis increases the tendency of other parts of the heart to take over the pace-setting function from the SA node.

Over the years, a number of factors have been identified that also increase the automaticity of the heart. These include: a low level of serum potassium (hypokalemia), a high level of serum calcium (hypercalcemia), damage to the heart muscle (cardiomyopathy), and a recent myocardial infarction. When these exist in conjunction with digitalis administration, the automaticity can be increased substantially. We will concentrate on the first two factors in this paper.

## 2.1. The Digitalis Therapy Advisor testbed

A few years ago, a Digitalis Therapy Advisor was developed at MIT by Pauker, Silverman, and Gorry [10, 28]. This program was later revised and given a preliminary explanatory capability [30]. The limitations of these explanations (and of those produced by similar techniques) will be discussed below. This program differed from earlier digitalis advisors [13, 14, 23, 26] in two important respects. First, when formulating dosage schedules, it anticipated possible toxicity by taking into account the factors that increased digitalis sensitivity and reduced the dose when those factors were present. Second, the program made assessments of the toxic and therapeutic effects which actually occurred in the patient after receiving digitalis to formulate subsequent dosage recommendations. This program worked in an interactive fashion. The program would ask the physician for data about the patient and produce recommendations after those data were entered. When the dose of digitalis was being adjusted, the physician was asked to consult with the program again to assess the patient's response. This program was used as a testbed for this work in explanation and justification. In the remainder of the paper, this program will be referred to as the 'old Digitalis Advisor'.

## 3. Kinds of Questions

In the spring of 1979, a series of informal trials was conducted in an attempt to discover what kinds of questions occurred to medical personnel as they ran the Digitalis Advisor. In this trial, medical students and fellows were asked to run the program and ask questions (verbally) as they occurred to them. I attempted to answer these questions. The interactions were tape recorded and later transcribed.

No formal analysis of the data was attempted, but examination of the transcripts did suggest three major types of questions that might arise while running a consulting program. These were:

(1) Questions about the methods the program employed:

*Subject:* "How do you calculate your body store goal? That's a little lower than I anticipated."

(2) Justifications of the program's actions:

*Subject* (perusing recommendations): "Why do we want to make a temporary reduction?

*Experimenter:* "We're anticipating surgery coming up and surgery, even non-cardiac surgery, can cause increased sensitivity to digitalis, so it wants to temporarily reduce the level of digitalis."

(3) Questions involving confusion about the meaning of questions the system asked:

IS THE RENAL FUNCTION STABLE?
THE POSSIBILITIES ARE:
    1. STABLE
    2. UNSTABLE
ENTER SINGLE VALUE ===>

*Subject:* "Now this question ... I'm not really sure ... 'renal function stable' does it mean stable abnormally or ... because I mean, the patient's renal function is not normal but it's stable at the present time."

*Experimenter:* "That's what it means."

The first type of question can be answered by any system that can produce an English description of the code it executes. This sort of question could be answered by the explanation routines of the old Digitalis Advisor and by the XPLAIN system presented here. Answering the second type of question requires not only an ability to translate code to English but also requires that the system represent and be able to express the medical knowledge upon which that code is based. This medical knowledge may not be necessary for the successful execution of code, but is necessary to be able to justify it. The third type of question requires a system that can model potential differences between a user's understanding of a term and the system's and generate an explanation which reconciles the two. The XPLAIN system does not address this type of question.

## 4. Previous Approaches to Explanation

A number of different approaches have been taken to attempt to provide programs with an explanatory capability. The major approaches are (1) using previously prepared text to provide explanations and (2) producing explanations directly from the computer code and traces of its execution.

The simplest way to get a computer to answer questions about what it is doing is to anticipate the questions and store the answers as English text. Only the text that has been stored can be displayed. This is called *canned text,* and explanations produced by displaying canned text are called canned explanations. The simplest sorts of canned explanations are error messages. For example, a medical program designed to treat adults might print the following message if someone tried to use it to treat an infant:

THE PATIENT IS TOO YOUNG TO BE TREATED BY THIS PROGRAM.

It is relatively easy to get a small program to provide English explanations of its activity using this canned text approach. After the program is written, canned text is associated with each part of the program explaining what that part of the program is doing. When the user wants to know what is going on, the computer merely displays the text associated with what it is doing at the moment.

There are several problems with the canned-text approach. The fact that the program code and the text strings that explain that code can be changed independently makes it difficult to maintain consistency between what the program does and what it claims to do. Another problem is that all questions must be anticipated in advance and the programmer must provide answers for all the questions that the user might ask. For large systems, this is a nearly impossible task. Finally, the system has no conceptual model of what it is saying. That is, to the computer, one text string looks much like any other, regardless of the content of that string. Thus, it is difficult to use this approach to provide more advanced sorts of explanations such as suggesting analogies or giving explanations at different levels of abstraction.

Another approach is to produce explanations directly from the program. That is, the explanation routines examine the program that is executed. Then by performing relatively simple transformations on the code these explanation routines can produce explanations of how the system does things. This approach has been used to produce explanations in a number of systems [8, 27, 29, 30, 34]. More recent work by Kastner, Weiss and Kulikowski [15] uses a mixture of this approach with the canned text approach to achieve good explanations in the limited domain of a precedence-based therapy selection algorithm.

The old Digitalis Advisor could examine the code it used to check for increased digitalis sensitivity caused by increased serum calcium and produce an explanation of what that code did (as shown in Fig. 1). Like most similar systems, it also maintained an execution trace. The trace could be examined by the explanation routines to tell what was done for a particular patient. Fig. 2 describes how the system checked for myxedema. The system also had a limited ability to explain why it was asking the user a question. Fig. 3 shows

```
TO CHECK SENSITIVITY DUE TO CALCIUM I DO THE FOLLOWING STEPS:

1. I DO ONE OF THE FOLLOWING:

   1.1 IF EITHER THE LEVEL OF SERUM CALCIUM IS GREATER THAN 10 OR
   INTRAVENOUS CALCIUM IS GIVEN THEN I DO THE FOLLOWING SUBSTEPS:

      1.1.1 I SET THE FACTOR OF REDUCTION DUE TO HYPERCALCEMIA TO 0.75.

      1.1.2 I ADD HYPERCALCEMIA TO THE REASONS OF REDUCTION.

   1.2 OTHERWISE, I REMOVE HYPERCALCEMIA FROM THE REASONS OF REDUCTION AND
   SET THE FACTOR OF REDUCTION DUE TO HYPERCALCEMIA TO 1.00.
```

FIG. 1. How the old Digitalis Advisor checks hypercalcemia.

```
WHAT IS THE LEVEL OF SERUM CALCIUM?

ENTER NUMERICAL VALUE ===> why? (The user types "why?" indicating that he questions
why he is being asked to supply the value of serum potassium.)

MY TOP GOAL IS TO BEGIN THERAPY. ONE STEP IN DOING THAT IS TO CHECK
SENSITIVITIES. I AM NOW TRYING TO CHECK SENSITIVITY DUE TO CALCIUM.
```

FIG. 3. A *limited* explanation telling why a question is asked.

the system's response when the user wants to know why he is being asked about serum calcium.

Since the explanation routines only perform simple transformations on the program code, the quality of the explanations produced in this manner depends to a great degree on how the system code is written. In particular, the basic structure of the program is not altered significantly, and the names of variables in the explanation are basically the same as those in the program. If the explanations are to be understandable, the expert system must be written so that its structure is easily understood by anyone familiar with its domain of expertise, and the variable and procedure names used in the program must represent concepts which are meaningful to the user.

This method of producing explanations has some advantages. It is relatively simple. If the right way of structuring the problem can be found, it does not impose too great a burden on the programmer; since the explanations reflect the code directly, consistency between explanation and code is assured.

Despite these advantages, there are some serious problems with this technique. It may be difficult or impossible to structure the program so that the user can easily understand it. The fact that every operation performed by the computer must be explicitly spelled out sometimes forces the programmer to program operations which a physician would perform without thinking about them. That problem is illustrated in Fig. 2. Steps 2.1, 2.2 and 2.4 are somewhat mystifying. In fact, these steps are needed by the system so that it can record what sensitivities the patient had that made him more likely to develop digitalis toxicity. These steps are involved more with record keeping than with medical reasoning, but they must appear in the code so that the computer will remember why it made a reduction. Since they appear in the code, they are described by the explanation routines, although they are more likely to confuse a physician-user than enlighten him. An additional problem is that it is difficult to get an overview of what is really going on here. While the system is explicit about record keeping, it is not very explicit about the fact that it is going to reduce the dose, though it hints at a reduction by saying that the 'factor of reduction' s being set to 0.67.

A serious problem, and the primary one we will address in this paper is that the system *cannot* give adequate justifications for its actions. That is, while this way of giving explanations can state *what* a system does or did, it has only a limited ability to state *why* it did what it did (see Fig. 3). Justifications are an important part of explanation. They can reveal either that a system is based on sound principles cr, equally importantly, show that a program is being pushed beyond the bounds of its expertise. In the explanations given above, the system cannot state that it reduces the dose because increased calcium causes increased automaticity. The information needed to justify the program is the information that was used by the programmer to write the program, but it does not have to be incorporated into the program for the program to perform successfully. Since it is desirable for expert programs to be able to justify what they do as well as do it, we need to find a way of capturing the knowledge and decisions that went into writing the program in the first place.

It is interesting to note that work in computer aided instruction has followed a similar path. Initially, canned text responses were employed, but these were found to be too constraining. Later attempts were made to teach the rules used by expert systems [5, 6]. Clancey [6] notes that these rule-based systems presented some explanation problems very similar to the ones described here.

```
I CHECKED SENSITIVITY DUE TO THYROID-FUNCTION BY EXECUTING THE FOLLOWING
STEPS:

1. I ASKED THE USER THE STATUS OF MYXEDEMA. THE USER RESPONDED THAT THE
STATUS OF MYXEDEMA WAS PRESENT.

2. SINCE THE STATUS OF MYXEDEMA WAS PRESENT I DID THE FOLLOWING:

   2.1 I ADDED MYXEDEMA TO THE PRESENT AND CORRECTABLE CONDITIONS. THE DEGRADABLE
   CONDITIONS THEN BECAME MYXEDEMA.

   2.2 I REMOVED MYXEDEMA FROM THE DEGRADABLE CONDITIONS. THE DEGRADABLE
   CONDITIONS THEN BECAME HYPOKALEMIA, HYPOXEMIA, CARDIOMYOPATHIES-MI, AND
   POTENTIAL POTASSIUM LOSS DUE TO DIURETICS.

   2.3 I SET THE FACTOR OF REDUCTION DUE TO MYXEDEMA TO 0.67. THE FACTOR
   OF REDUCTION DUE TO MYXEDEMA WAS PREVIOUSLY UNDETERMINED.

   2.4 I ADDED MYXEDEMA TO THE REASONS OF REDUCTION. THE REASONS OF
   REDUCTION THEN BECAME MYXEDEMA.
```

FIG. 2. Explaining how thyroid function was checked.

## 5. Providing Justifications

More advanced work recognizes that for successful teaching, the problem domain and problem solving mechanisms must be explicitly represented [3, 7].

We need a way of capturing the knowledge and decisions that went into writing the program. One way to do this is to give the computer enough knowledge so that it can write the program itself and remember what it did. While automatic programming itself has been researched considerably [1, 2, 11, 16, 18], the idea of using an automatic programmer to help in producing explanations is new. Since we are primarily interested in explanation, we have chosen not to deal with a number of problems that arise in automatic programming, including: choosing between different implementations, backup and recovery from dead-end refinements, and optimization.

XPLAIN's automatic program writer creates augmented performance programs which not only perform the intended task, but also can be explained and justified. Fig. 4 illustrates some of the kinds of explanations the system can produce. Note that the system can justify its actions in terms of causal relations in the medical domain and that it can suggest analogies with previous explanations. These explanations should be compared with those in Figs. 1–3 to appreciate the improvement.

An overview of the XPLAIN system is given in Fig. 5. The system has five parts: a Writer, a domain model, a set of domain principles, an English

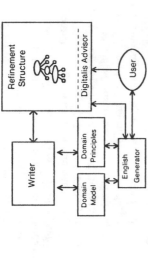

FIG. 5. System overview.

Generator and a generated refinement structure. The Writer is an automatic programmer. It has been used to write new code which captures the functionality of major portions of the old Digitalis Advisor. The domain model and the domain principles contain knowledge about the domain of expertise—in this case, digitalis and digitalis therapy. They provide the Writer with the knowledge it needs to write the code for the Digitalis Advisor. The refinement structure can be thought of as a trace left behind by the Writer. It shows how the Writer develops the Digitalis Advisor. When a physician-user runs the Digitalis Advisor, he can ask the system to justify why the program is doing what it is doing. The Generator gives him an answer by examining the refinement structure and the step of the Advisor currently being executed. If we wanted to write a new program covering a new medical domain, we would have to change the domain model and the domain principles, but we should not have to change the Writer or the English Generator. (The refinement structure would be generated by the Writer.)

### 5.1. The refinement structure

The refinement structure is created by the Writer from the top level goal (in this case 'Administer Digitalis') as it writes the Digitalis Advisor. The refinement structure is a tree of goals, each being a refinement of the one above it (see Fig. 6). Here, 'refining a goal' means turning it into more specific subgoals. As Fig. 6 shows, the top of the tree is a very abstract goal: in this case, 'Administer Digitalis'. This goal is refined into less abstract steps by the Writer. These more specific steps are steps the system executes to administer digitalis. For example, one such subgoal is to 'Anticipate Toxicity'; that is, to anticipate whether the patient may become toxic due to increased digitalis sensitivity. The Writer then refines this more specific goal to a still more specific goal. Eventually, the level of system primitives is reached. System primitives are built-in operations. Normally they are very basic, simple opera-

---

Please enter the value of serum potassium: why?

**The system is anticipating digitalis toxicity. Decreased serum potassium toxicity. Decreased serum potassium causes increased automaticity, which may cause a change to ventricular fibrillation. Increased digitalis also causes increased automaticity. Thus, if the system observes decreased serum potassium, it reduces the dose of digitalis due to decreased serum potassium.**

Please enter the value of serum potassium: 3.7

Please enter the value of serum calcium: why?

*(The system produces a shortened explanation, reflecting the fact that it has already explained several of the causal relationships in the previous explanation. Also, since the system remembers that it has already told the user about serum potassium, it suggests the analogy between the two here.)*

**The system is anticipating digitalis toxicity. Increased serum calcium also causes increased automaticity. Thus, (as with decreased serum potassium) if the system observes increased serum calcium, it reduces the dose of digitalis due to increased serum calcium.**

Please enter the value of serum calcium: 9

FIG. 4. Justifications from a program created with XPLAIN.

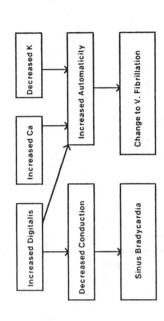

Fig. 6. A sample refinement structure.

tions, so the fact that they cannot be explained is usually not a problem. Typical primitives include arithmetic operations like PLUS and TIMES and those that set variables to a particular value. The leaves of the refinement structure constitute the basic operations performed by the Digitalis Advisor, the program that we wanted the automatic programmer to produce.

## 5.2. The domain model

The domain model represents the facts of the domain. In this case, it is a model of the causal relationships important in digitalis therapy. The model is similar in character to the causal networks of CASNET [33], with two differences. First, the causal links are not numerically weighted. Weights could easily be added, but for this domain, most of the reasoning does not require them.[2] Second, inter-relationships between casual paths which impinge on the same state are explicitly represented.

A simplified portion of the model is shown in Fig. 7. The boxes are states and the arrows represent casuality. This model shows some of the effects of increased digitalis. It also shows that increased serum Ca and decreased serum K each can cause increased automaticity. These facts correspond to the sorts of facts that a medical student learns in class during the first two years of medical school. They are descriptive. While they tell what happens in the domain, they do not indicate what the Advisor's behavior should be to achieve its goal of

[2] When numerical weighting is required, XPLAIN asks the system developer for the appropriate constants during creation of the performance program.

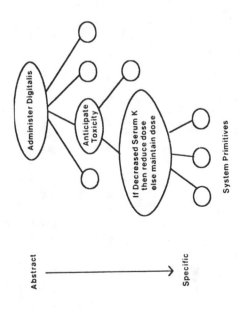

FIG. 7. A simplified portion of the domain model.

administering digitalis. For example, the model says that increased digitalis can cause a change from a normal heart rhythm to ventricular fibrillation and it notes that that is dangerous, but it does not say what should be done to prevent such a change. Medical students go to medical school for an additional two years and acquire these procedures by observing experienced practitioners at work. The set of domain principles provides the Writer with this sort of procedural knowledge.

## 5.3. Domain principles

Domain principles tell the Writer how something (such as prescribing a drug or analyzing symptoms) should be done. They can be thought of as abstract procedural schema which are filled in with facts from the domain model to yield specific procedures. A (somewhat simplified) domain principle appears in Fig. 8. Domain principles are composed of variables and constants. Variables appear in boldface in Fig. 8. Pattern variable matching uses the kind hierarchy imposed by XLMS, the knowledge representation language used by XPLAIN. For an object to match a pattern variable, it must be at the same level as or beneath the pattern variable in the hierarchy. Thus, the variable **finding** matches increased serum calcium or decreased serum potassium, since increased serum calcium and decreased K are both kinds of findings. The principle appearing in Fig. 8 is used to anticipate digitalis toxicity. It represents the common sense notion that if one is considering administering a drug, and there is some factor that enhances the deleterious effects of that drug, then if that factor is present in the patient, less drug should be given. This principle has three parts: a *goal*, a *domain rationale*, and a *prototype method*. In general, a principle may also have a set of constraints associated with it which must be satisfied if the principle is to be used.

The goal tells the Writer what the principle can accomplish. In this case, the principle can help the Writer in anticipating toxicity. Domain principles are

the single abstract problem of how to anticipate toxicity into several more specific ones, such as how to determine whether increased serum K exists, how to reduce the dose, and how to maintain it.

After instantiation, the goals of the prototype method are placed in the refinement structure as sons of the goal being resolved. If we look at Fig. 6, we can see that the instantiated prototype method that checks for decreased serum K has been placed below the Anticipate Toxicity goal. Once they have been placed in the refinement structure, the newly instantiated goals become goals for the writer to resolve. For example, after the Writer applied this domain principle, it would have to find ways of determining whether increased calcium existed in the patient, whether decreased potassium existed, and ways of reducing and maintaining the dose. The system continues in this fashion, refining goals at the bottom of the structure and growing the tree down and down until eventually the level of system primitives is reached (see Fig. 9).

### 5.4. The domain rationale: more detail

As was mentioned above, the domain rationale is a pattern which is matched against the domain model. It server two purposes. First, it is a constraint on the acceptability of the domain principle, because if no matches are found, the domain principle is rejected. Second, it can also be thought of as a further specification of the performance program.

To place further restrictions on the match that would be difficult to express as a pattern, the domain rationale can have predicates associated with it which filter out unacceptable matches. The domain rationale we have been using as an example has three predicates. (These are not shown in Fig. 8.) The first predicate specifies that the **finding** cannot be the increased drug level. We cannot allow that match because we are looking for *other* factors which increase the danger of giving the drug. The second predicate fails if the current value of **finding** is the same as the value it had on a previous match. This requirement ensures that for each successful match, the value of **finding** will be different from its value in all other successful matches. This predicate is necessary because a particular finding may cause more than one dangerous deviation. For the purposes of this principle it is sufficient that it cause one dangerous deviation. The third predicate requires that the causal effects of the increased drug level and **finding** must be at least causally additive. This predicate checks to see whether the causal links in the causal chains between **finding** and **dangerous deviation** and between **increased drug** and **dangerous deviation** are at least additive[4] at the node where the two chains merge together. That is, the combined dangerous deviation caused by the finding together with the increased drug must be at least as great as the sum of their individual effects.

[4] Effects which are synergistic would be considered more than additive.

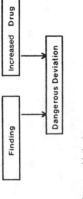

Goal: Anticipate  Drug  Toxicity

Domain Rationale:

Finding    →    Dangerous Deviation   ←   Increased  Drug

Prototype Method:
If the Finding exists
   then: reduce the  drug dose
   else: maintain the  drug dose

FIG. 8. An example of a domain principle.

organized into a hierarchy based on the specificity of their goals. The Writer selects the principle whose goal matches the step to be refined and whose constraints (if any) are satisfied.[3] The domain rationale is a pattern which is matched against the domain model. It provides, in the context a particular method for achieving a goal, additional information necessary for achieving the goal. In this example, the domain rationale describes which findings should be checked in anticipating toxicity. Essentially, this domain rationale defines the characteristics that a finding must have if it is to be considered when checking for digitalis sensitivities. The system looks in the domain model for every **dangerous deviation** (e.g. change to ventricular fibrillation) caused by the combination of a **finding** (e.g. increased Ca) and an increased **drug** level. It finds two matches: a change to ventricular fibrillation can be caused by an increased level of digitalis when combined with either increased calcium or decreased potassium.

The prototype method is an abstract method which tells how to accomplish the goal. Once the domain rationale has been matched, the prototype method is instantiated for each match of the domain rationale. Instantiating the prototype method means creating a new structure by replacing the variables in the prototype method with the things they matched. In this case, two structures are created. In the first, **finding** is replaced by increased serum Ca and **drug** is replaced by digitalis. In the second, **finding** is replaced by decreased serum K and **drug** is again replaced by digitalis. Note that these new structures, change

[3] If more than one principle matches the most specific one is selected. Thus, the Writer can handle special cases cleanly. For example, a general method for obtaining the value of a variable $x$ from the user would be to ask "What is the value of $x$?". If the variable were boolean, a more appropriate question would be to ask "Is $x$ present?" and expect a yes or no answer. The goal for the first method would be "Determine the value of a variable", while the goal for the second would be the more specific "Determine the value of a boolean variable".

When the domain rationale is matched against the digitalis domain model, there are two matches, corresponding to the two sensitivities that are described above—increased serum calcium and decreased serum potassium. When the pattern matcher returns the matches, the matched structure and variable bindings are saved for use in producing explanations. Once all the matches have been obtained, the Writer instantiates the prototype method.

### 5.5. Intertwining specification and implementation

The notion of the domain rationale as a partial program specification is something that seems to be unique to the XPLAIN system. Generally, in other automatic programming systems, the complete specifications for the program must be given before the implementation of the program begins. Here, the specifications for the program are elaborated by matching the domain rationale against the domain model as the refinement of the program progresses. Thus, the nature of the specification will be affected by which particular domain principles are chosen for the implementation so that the process of elaborating the specification of the performance program is intertwined with its implementation [32].

This approach permits considerable flexibility and generality. The creator of the domain model has to encode only the descriptive knowledge of the domain. He does not have to worry about how that knowledge will be used in the creation of a program or worry about what that program should do (as he might if he were trying to create program specifications). New information can be added to this model and incorporated into a new version of the performance program by re-running the automatic programmer. A particular piece of knowledge might be used for several purposes (or not at all). For example, information about the effects of increased digitalis levels is used by the system both in anticipating toxicity and in assessing toxic and therapeutic reactions.

Davis [8] introduced the notion of meta-rules, which bear some similarity to domain principles. However, meta-rules were used only for ordering and pruning the application of lower level rules within the context of a standard rule interpreter. Domain principles can control program refinement to a much greater degree.

The domain rationale is one of the mechanisms used in the XPLAIN system for tying the independent domain model into the specification of the performance program. Yet, the domain rationales themselves can be quite general, and are really independent of the particular domain model. The domain principle used by the system for anticipating digitalis toxicity could be used with different domain models to accomplish the same task for a number of other drugs.

### 5.6. Integrating program fragments

The Writer must also take into account interactions between the actions it takes. For example, the individual instantiations above indicate that if increased serum calcium exists the dose should be reduced, and if decreased serum potassium exists the dose should be reduced, but they do not tell what should happen if *both* increased calcium *and* decreased serum potassium co-occur. Thus, the Writer is confronted with the problem of integrating these individual instantiations into a whole. (See Fig. 10.)

Exactly what should happen depends on the characteristics of the domain. It could be that the occurrence of either sensitivity 'covers' for the other, so that only one reduction should be made and the predicate of the IF should be made

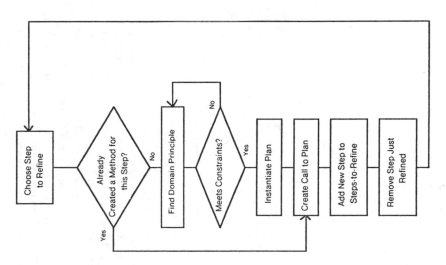

FIG. 9. Overview of the program writer.

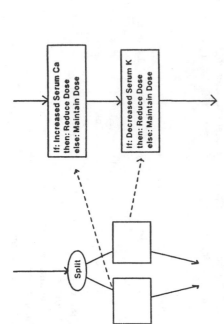

Note: To keep the figure simple, only 2 sensitivities are shown

FIG. 11. Resolving a split by serialization.

The goal of the domain principle matches an arbitrary number of program fragments of the form:

> If Exists(**finding**)
>    then **adjust1**
>    else **adjust2**

(Note: boldface represents pattern variables)

Although the goal matches, there are some constraints associated with this domain principle which must be satisfied before it can be used to transform the program structure. The constraints check whether this serialization is a reasonable sort of resolution. There are two general types of constraints: *domain constraints* and *refinement constraints.*

Domain constraints are tests to see whether a domain principle is applicable given the characteristics of the domain. The first constraint checks that all the deviations (e.g. increased serum calcium, decreased serum potassium and cardiomyopathy) are causally independent in the sense that none of them causes the other. This is done by examining the domain model to see if there is a causal chain leading from any of the deviations to any other. If one finding causes another, serialization would be inappropriate because if both findings appeared a double reduction would be made when only the reduction for the underlying cause was appropriate.

The second constraint checks to see whether the effects of the causal chains are additive. That is, before making multiple reductions for multiple sensitivities, it must be the case that the occurrence of multiple deviations is worse than just one by itself. The domain model supplies this information.

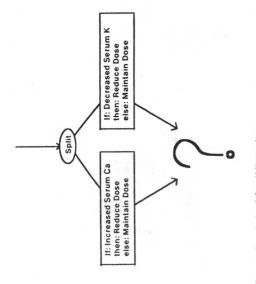

Note: To keep the figure simple, only 2 sensitivities are shown

FIG. 10. A split to be resolved.

into a disjunction. Or (as is actually the case), it could be that when multiple sensitivities appear, multiple reductions should be made.

Interaction problems of this sort are handled by setting them up as explicit goals to be refined. For each of the matches of the domain rationale, the Writer instantiates the prototype method. It then places each of these instantiations into a larger structure called a *split-join.* The split-join is placed in the refinement structure and domain principles are used to transform it into executable program structure. If only one match is found for the domain rationale, or if there is no domain rationale at all in the domain principle, the Writer just instantiates the prototype method and does not make up a split-join.

### 5.6.1. *Refining a split-join*

The system chooses to refine the split-join next because it will result in a transformation of the program structure. It is necessary to refine transformations first because they may impose constraints on the way other steps will be refined.

The domain principle that will be used produces an executable piece of code by serializing the parts of the split join (see Fig. 11). That is, the checks for increased serum calcium and decreased serum potassium will be performed in turn and the outputs for the first reduction will be connected to the second, so that if multiple sensitivities exist, multiple reductions will be performed.

Refinement constraints are the other type of constraints used in this domain principle. Like domain constraints, refinement constraints determine whether or not a particular domain principle is applicable, but if it is found to be applicable, they also constrain the way in which further refinements may be made.

In this particular case, we are resolving the split-join by serializing the reductions. Whether or not this is a valid way to proceed depends in part on how the reductions themselves are refined. If the reductions are to be performed by subtracting some quantity from the dose, then there is some possibility that the dose will eventually become negative. That, of course, does not make sense. So the principle for resolving the split-join would have to insert a step at the end which would check for a negative dose and do whatever was proper. On the other hand, if the dose is reduced by multiplying the original dose by some constant less than one to produce a new dose, then the dose can never become negative, and no check is required. To resolve the split-join now, the Writer needs to be able to constrain the resolution of the steps that perform the reduction.

The domain principle for refining the split-join specifies that the Writer must find domain principles for refining the two instances of [adjust1] and [adjust2] (which are the calls to reduce and maintain the dose respectively) so that that the method of the principle is described as a multiplicative operator. If a principle is found for each of the calls, the refinement constraint is satisfied. As the principles are found, the system remembers them by associating them with the appropriate energy in the list of steps to be refined.

### 5.7. Assessing toxicity

Whenever the dosage of digitalis is being adjusted, it is necessary to monitor the patient closely to determine the effect (if any) of the change. In the old Digitalis Advisor, there were two sets of routines for assessing the drug's effects. One set was concerned with the harmful toxic effects of digitalis, while the other dealt with the therapeutic effects. Each set of routines produced an assessment of the degree to which the patient was showing either toxic or therapeutic effects. Based on these assessments, the system recommended corrective actions if needed. This section briefly describes how the portion of the Digitalis Advisor that assesses toxicity was implemented using the XPLAIN system. A more complete discussion may be found in [31].

To assess toxicity, the user is asked whether the various toxic effects that digitalis may cause have been observed in the patient. The assessments of these individual findings are then combined into an overall assessment of toxicity. The assessment is a number representing the degree of toxicity and the individual assessments are combined together using numerical techniques.

The cardiologists we consulted felt that when assessing digitalis toxicity they looked for signs in three general classes: highly specific signs of digitalis toxicity, moderately specific signs, and signs with low specificity (also called non-specific signs). The original Digitalis Advisor adopted these classifications and weighted the various findings according to their classification to produce an assessment to digitalis toxicity. To implement this algorithm, the domain model had to be augmented to indicate the various types of findings that could result from digitalis toxicity, and the specificity of those findings. The domain model used by the implementation appears in Fig. 12.

It was also necessary to add a number of new domain principles. The top level principle to assess digitalis toxicity just sets up the goals to assess the highly specific signs, moderately specific signs and non-specific signs and to then combine them together. The three different assessment steps are all refined by the same domain principle because that principle has the degree of specificity as a variable in its goal[5]:

Assess **specific** findings of **drug** toxicity.

The domain rationale looks for all findings caused by increased digitalis that have the degree of specificity specified in the call. For example, when the call is 'Assess highly specific findings of digitalis toxicity' the domain rationale will find paroxysmal atrial tachycardia with block, double tachycardia, and av dissociation, because these are all highly specific signs of digitalis toxicity.

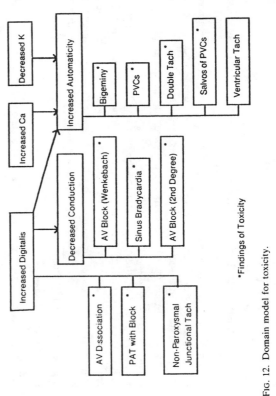

*Findings of Toxicity

FIG. 12. Domain model for toxicity.

[5] This is the English translation of the goal used in the system. Again, variables appear in boldface. Here, **specific** is a variable which can take on the values *highly specific*, *moderately specific* or *non-specific*.

The prototype method then sets up calls to assess these various findings. For most of the findings, the system just asks the user whether the finding is present or not. Some findings, such as premature ventricular contractions (PVCs), are properly assessed by comparing their current level to a patient-specific baseline. A special purpose domain principle is provided for assessing PVCs. Since the Writer always picks the most specific principle for the call being refined, this special-case knowledge is automatically employed at the appropriate time. The code for assessing findings is not normally explained to physicians, because it is unlikely to interest them. The viewpoint mechanism (described below) is used to encode that fact.

It is encouraging to note that little additional mechanism needs to be added to deal with assessing toxicity, a problem which seems quite different from the earlier examples. The algorithm of the program writer was not altered, and much of the domain model needed for dealing with sensitivities was applicable in assessing toxicity.

## 6. Generating Explanations

We have described how XPLAIN creates the refinement structure and the characteristics of the domain principles and the domain model. These are used by the explanation generator to provide English justifications of the program's behavior and descriptions of what the program does and how it does it.

This section describes how XPLAIN produces explanations. By design, the knowledge structures left behind by the automatic programmer make it possible to achieve quite high quality English output with a simple generator. The generator is an engineering effort aimed at producing acceptable English. The main thrust of the work described in this paper has been to investigate ways of representing the knowledge necessary to justify the behavior of expert consulting systems. A generator is necessary to demonstrate the capabilities of the approach espoused here, but is not the focus of the research. (See [17, 21] for a discussion of current work in generation.)

The generator is really composed of two types of generators. The low level *phrase generator* constructs phrases directly from XPLAIN's knowledge base. Higher level *answer generators* determine what to say—they select the parts of the knowledge representation to be translated into English by the phrase generator in response to specific questions. The answer generators must deal with the issue of determining at what level an explanation should be given. In making this determination, it employs knowledge of the state of the program execution, knowledge of what has already been said, and knowledge of what the user is likely to be interested in. Other issues the answer generators confront include deciding whether to omit information the user can be presumed to know from the explanation and determining whether analogies can be suggested to previous explanations. The phrase generator and the knowledge representation language used by XPLAIN, called XLMS, will be

briefly discussed in the next section, followed by a discussion of the answer generators. For a more detailed discussion, see [31].

### 6.1. XLMS notation and the phrase generator

The XPLAIN system uses XLMS to manage its knowledge base. XLMS (which stands for eXperimental Linguistic Memory System) was developed by Lowell Hawkinson, William Martin, Peter Szolovits and members of the Clinical Decision Making and Automatic Programming Groups at MIT. Since a complete understanding of the intricacies of XLMS is not needed to understand the XPLAIN system, this section is only intended to give the reader a brief overview of XLMS. For a more complete discussion of the design goals and implementation of XLMS, see [12, 20].

For the purposes of this paper, perhaps the best way to think of XLMS is that it is an extension of LISP that allows one to use *structured names*. In LISP, atoms are used to name variables and functions. In the XPLAIN system, variables and procedures are named by XLMS concepts—the difference is that these concepts can have a substructure which can be taken apart and examined, while LISP atoms are indivisible.

#### 6.1.1. XLMS concepts

In XLMS, every concept is composed of an ilk, a tie and a cue and is written as:

[((ilk)*(tie)) (cue)]

or, to pick an actual example from the XPLAIN system:

[(LEVEL*R DIGITALIS)]

The *ilk* of a concept is itself a concept. It tells what kind of a concept this is. Thus, the example concept is a kind of level. The *cue* of a concept is either a concept or a LISP atomic symbol. It indicates what it is that makes this concept different from others with the same ilk. The example represents the 'level of digitalis': a particular kind of level. Finally, the *tie* of a concept indicates the relationship between the ilk and the cue. In this case, the tie is R for 'role'. Role ties are used to indicate slots in concepts. Thus this concept represents the 'level' slot in the concept 'digitalis'. This is one implementation of the notion of slots and frames as described by Minsky [22]. There are several ties that are used extensively in the XPLAIN system. Some of these are listed in Table 1 together with examples of their use.

Concepts of XLMS are organized into a kind hierarchy. The root concept is [summum-genus] (see Fig. 13) and is pre-defined in XLMS. *'s ties create a strict taxonomy of mutually exclusive subclasses. Like atomic symbols in LISP, concepts in XLMS are unique.

In LISP, it is possible to associate lists and atoms relating to a particular

into the English phrase:

Assess the level of digitalis

The phrase generators are completely described in [31]. The next section discusses the more interesting question of how XPLAIN chooses what to say.

### 6.2. The answer generators: determining what to say

6.2.1. *Viewpoints.*

The reader may recall that one problem with previous explanation systems has been the problem of *computer artifacts.* Computer artifacts are parts of the program which appear mainly because we are implementing an algorithm on a computer. If these steps are described by physicians, they are likely to be uninteresting and potentially confusing. The introductory section gave some examples of these computer artifacts. In the XPLAIN system, we can attach viewpoints to steps in prototype methods (described more fully below) to indicate to whom the step should be explained. [6] When a prototype method is instantiated, the instantiated steps will share these viewpoints. As the XPLAIN system is generating an explanation for a step it compares the viewpoint(s) of the step (if any) against a list of viewpoints which should be filtered out and another list of viewpoints which should be included. If one of the step's viewpoints appears on the include list, that step is included in the English explanation. If not, and one of the viewpoints appears on the exclude list, the step is excluded from the explanation. If the step has no viewpoint, it is included in the explanation. This approach allows us to separate those steps that are appropriate for a particular audience from those that are not. Of course, the exclude and include lists may be changed to reflect a change in the user's viewpoint.

While this is a simple solution from the standpoint of generation, it is a feasible one because we are employing an automatic programmer. In the domain principles, we bring together and define for the system to use, computer implementation knowledge and medical reasoning knowledge. A domain principle is thus the appropriate place to indicate what viewpoint should be taken on the knowledge that it is composed of. By placing a viewpoint on a step in a prototype method, we cause all the instantiations of that step (and there are usually several) to share that viewpoint. If we were to try to do the same thing at the level of the performance program (without an automatic programmer) we would have to annotate each individual step—we could not capture as high a level of abstraction.

This result is consistent with the observation we made in the introduction: improvements in the quality of the explanations generated resulted more from

6 This can occur either during the refinement of a step from a higher goal, or during a transformational refinement.

---

TABLE 1. Types of ties (partial list)

| Tie | Name | Example use | English form | purpose |
|---|---|---|---|---|
| *f | function | [[ball*f red]] | (the) red ball | modifies |
| *r | role-in | [[color*r ball]] | (the) color of (the) ball | slot-filling |
| *i | individual | [[ball*i 1]] | ball | instantiates individual |
| *o | object | [[treat*o patient]] | treat (the) patient | verb-object |
| *s | species | [dog = (animal*s 'dog')] | dog | (see text) |

atomic symbol with that symbol by placing them on that symbol's property list. In XLMS, one can associate concepts relating to a concept, with that concept, by *attaching* them. The viewpoint mechanism (described more fully below) uses attachments placed on concepts by the Writer to determine whether or not the concept should be explained.

In the XPLAIN system, a phrase generator is associated with each kind of tie. To generate English for a particular concept, the tie of the concept is examined and control is passed to the corresponding phrase generator. The structured nature of XLMS concepts and the fact that XLMS is a linguistically oriented representation language makes it relatively straightforward to construct a phrase generator that can turn an XLMS concept such as:

[[assess*o (level*r digitalis)]]

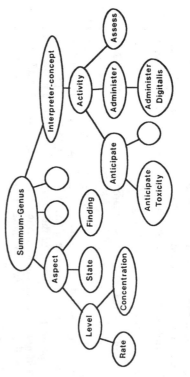

This figure only shows a portion of the hierarchy

FIG. 13. The kind hierarchy.

the use of an automatic programmer than from increases in the sophistication of the generation routines. It should be pointed out, however, that while this solution allows the system to customize its explanations based on a particular viewpoint or set of viewpoints, the problem of deciding which viewpoint to present to a particular user remains open and is beyond the scope of this paper.

### 6.2.2. *Answering 'why' questions*

One of the chief goals in this research was to have the XPLAIN system explain why the performance program was doing what it was doing. In producing answers to such questions, the system makes use of the knowledge in the domain model and the domain principles as well as traces left behind by the automatic programmer resulting from creation of the performance program. Some of the capabilities of the system were illustrated in Section 5 where the performance program was anticipating digitalis toxicity. Additional capabilities are illustrated below from those portions of the advisor that anticipate toxicity and assess toxicity.

Is the patient showing signs of cardiomyopathy? (yes or no): *why?*

The system is anticipating digitalis toxicity. Cardiomyopathy causes increased automaticity, which may cause a change to ventricular fibrillation. Increased digitalis also causes increased automaticity. Thus, if the system determines that cardiomyopathy exists, it reduces the dose of digitalis due to cardiomyopathy.

This explanation is similar to those in Section 5.

The remaining explanations are produced while assessing toxicity.

Is the patient showing signs of paroxysmal atrial tachycardia with block? (yes or no): *why?*

The system is assessing the highly specific findings of digitalis toxicity. Increased digitalis may cause paroxysmal atrial tachycardia with block which is a highly specific finding of digitalis toxicity.

Is the patient showing signs of paroxysmal atrial tachycardia with block? (yes or no): *overview*

The system repeats the question, but the user wants an overview. This is produced by describing the method for assessing highly specific findings which was mentioned in the previous explanation.

To assess the highly specific findings of digitalis toxicity:
(1) The system assesses paroxysmal atrial tachycardia with block.
(2) It assesses double tachycardia.
(3) It assesses av-dissociation.
(4) It combines the assessments of paroxysmal atrial tachycardia with block, double tachycardia and av-dissociation.

This produces the assessment of the highly specific findings of digitalis toxicity, which is used when the system combines the assessments of the highly specific findings of digitalis toxicity, the moderately specific findings of digitalis toxicity and the non-specific findings of digitalis toxicity.

To avoid leaving the user hanging, the system describes how the output of the method will be used in a higher context. This is done whenever the output of the method is something which is not likely to be familiar to the user. Thus, if the output of a method were a drug dose, no additional explanation would be generated (at least for a medical audience) because the user would be presumed to be familiar with the notion of a drug dose.

Is the patient showing signs of paroxysmal atrial tachycardia with block? (yes or no): *why?*

Still curious, the user asks 'why?' again. This causes the system to give an explanation of the procedure that calls the procedure for assessing the highly specific findings. This explanation is much shorter, because the domain principle used to refine the higher level procedure had no domain rationale.

The system is assessing digitalis toxicity. One step in doing that is to assess the highly specific findings of digitalis toxicity.

Is the patient showing signs of paroxysmal atrial tachycardia with block? (yes or no): *overview*

This time the description is offered at the level of the higher procedure.

To assess digitalis toxicity:
(1) The system assesses the highly specific findings of digitalis toxicity.
(2) It assesses the moderately specific findings of digitalis toxicity.
(3) It assesses the non-specific findings of digitalis toxicity.
(4) It combines the assessments of the highly specific findings of digitalis toxicity, the moderately specific findings of digitalis toxicity and the non-specific findings of digitalis toxicity.

This produces the assessment of digitalis toxicity, which is used when the system adjusts the dose of digitalis.

When a 'why' question is entered, control passes to the routine that produces justifications. This routine determines at what level the description should be given, states what is going on in general, describes the domain rationale (if any) used in refining the step being described, and finally describes the step. Each of these four stages will be outlined below.

### 6.2.2.1. *Choosing the level of description*

The system uses the viewpoint attachments to determine where to start the explanation. The control stack of the interpreter executing the performance program is available to the explanation modules. The justification routine goes up the stack looking for the first procedure which is not an excluded viewpoint and which has no procedure that has an excluded viewpoint above it. If that procedure happens to be a system primitive[7] with a system primitive above it, then the system keeps going up the stack until it finds a procedure which does not have a system primitive above it.

Consider the situation presented in the sample interaction above where the

[7] System primitives include assignment statements, conditionals, arithmetic operators and the like.

system first queries the user about the 'signs of paroxysmal atrial tachycardia' and the user responds 'why?'. As was mentioned earlier, the procedures for assessing findings, like paroxysmal atrial tachycardia, have computer-viewpoints, indicating that physicians will not be interested in them. Therefore, the system will start giving its explanation at the next level up, at the level of the next call to that procedure. This will be referred to as the *current description level*. In contrast, if the exclude list had not contained computer-viewpoint, explanation would have begun at a lower level, producing the following explanation:

> Is the patient showing signs of paroxysmal atrial tachycardia with block? (yes or no): why?

> The system is assessing paroxysmal atrial tachycardia with block. If the status of paroxysmal atrial tachycardia with block is equal to present, the assessment of paroxysmal atrial tachycardia with block is set to the assessment level for present findings (1), otherwise the assessment of paroxysmal atrial tachycardia with block is set to the assessment level for absent findings (0)

This is the sort of information a person maintaining the advisor might wish to know, but that a medical audience certainly would not.

### 6.2.2.2. Stating what's going on in general

To give the user an overview of what the system is trying to accomplish, the system finds the next procedure above the current description level in the control stack. This will be called the *higher level procedure*. It then generates a phrase using the name of the procedure to describe what is going on:

> The system is assessing the highly specific findings of digitalis toxicity.

### 6.2.2.3. Explaining the domain rationale

If the higher level procedure was refined using a domain principle which had a domain rationale, then the procedure at the current description level must be the result of one of the matches of the domain rationale. The system finds the domain rationale and the particular match of it that resulted in the procedure at the current description level. Flags are set to indicate to the phrase generator that it should replace occurrences of pattern variables with the objects they matched. After this environment has been set up, the complete pattern is found and converted to English using the phrase generator. For example, the phrase generator produced the following description of the domain rationale of the domain principle that refined the procedure to assess highly specific toxic findings:

> Increased digitalis may cause paroxysmal atrial tachycardia with block which is a highly specific finding of digitalis toxicity.

### 6.2.2.4. Finishing up the explanation

Finally, the system uses the phrase generator to produce a description of the step at the current level of description. So when the user replies 'why?' to the program's question about cardiomyopathy, XPLAIN generates the following description of the current step:

> Thus, if the system determines that cardiomyopathy exists, it reduces the dose of digitalis due to cardiomyopathy.

The system then re-iterates its original question. If the user asks 'why?' again, the system moves the current description level up to the level of the next higher level procedure and repeats the explanation process.

Sometimes this description is omitted. When the user types 'why?' in response to the program's first question about paroxysmal atrial tachycardia, the current level of description is 'assess paroxysmal atrial tachyacrdia with block'. Yet, XPLAIN does not produce the sentence:

> "Thus, the system assesses paroxysmal atrial tachycardia with block."

as the last sentence of its answer to the second question. The reason is that such a sentence would have been redundant. The user already knows that the system is assessing paroxysmal atrial tachycardia with block, because he has just been asked a question about it. Following the general principle that the user should not be told something he already knows, the system deletes this part of the explanation if the step about to be described is a type of assessing step and the object of that step is the same as the thing the user has been asked about.

Given the system described so far, it is relatively easy to get it to generate descriptions of methods by translating them directly into English. The explanations given by the 'overview' command in the previous section were produced by passing the current higher level procedure to the function that describes methods. However, as we pointed out in the introduction, this particular style of explanation has some limitations. In the next section, we present a different way of explaining methods which provides a richer sort of abstraction which cannot be done in explanations produced directly from the code.

### 6.2.3. Domain principle explanations

In the original version of the Digitalis Advisor, when we wanted to give a more abstract view of what was going on, we just described a higher level procedure [29,30]. In this regard, we were following the principles of structured programming. While this approach was often reasonable, there were times when it was considerably less than illuminating. The general method for anticipating digitalis toxicity was called 'Check Sensitivities' in the old version of the Digitalis Advisor. An explanation of it appears in Fig. 14. While this explanation does not tell the user what sensitivities are being checked,[8] it does not say what

[8] The reader may notice that there were more sensitivities checked in the original version of the program than in the current version. We now feel that some of these, such as thyroid function and advanced age, should not be treated as sensitivities per se because they tend to have an effect on reducing renal function and hence slowing excretion, rather than on increasing sensitivity to digitalis. The other sensitivities would be easy to add by including the appropriate causal links in the domain model.

```
(describe-method [(check sensitivities)])

TO CHECK SENSITIVITIES I DO THE FOLLOWING STEPS:
1. I CHECK SENSITIVITY DUE TO CALCIUM.
2. I CHECK SENSITIVITY DUE TO POTASSIUM.
3. I CHECK SENSITIVITY DUE TO CARDIOMYOPATHY-MI.
4. I CHECK SENSITIVITY DUE TO HYPOXEMIA.
5. I CHECK SENSITIVITY DUE TO THYROID-FUNCTION.
6. I CHECK SENSITIVITY DUE TO ADVANCED AGE.
7. I COMPUTE THE FACTOR OF ALTERATION.
```

FIG. 14. An explanation from the old Digitalis Therapy Advisor.

will be done if sensitivities are discovered nor does it say why the system considers these particular factors to be sensitivities. Finally, it is much too redundant and verbose. The first objection can be dealt with by removing the calls to lower procedures and substituting the code of those procedures in-line. This results in the somewhat improved explanation produced by XPLAIN when it is asked to describe the method for anticipating digitalis toxicity (see Fig. 15). However, while this explanation shows what the system does, it does not say why things like increased calcium, cardiomyopathy and decreased potassium are sensitivities, and if anything, it is even more verbose when the original explanation.

The reason we cannot get the sorts of explanations we want by producing explanations directly from the code is that much of the sort of reasoning we want to explain has been 'compiled out'. Thus, we are forced into explaining at a level that is either too abstract or too specific. The intermediate reasoning which we would like to explain was done by a human programmer in the case of the old Digitalis Advisor. However, because this performance program was produced by an automatic programmer, we have a handle on that reasoning. For example, if we were to explain the domain principle that produced the code for anticipating digitalis toxicity rather then the code itself we would get the explanation that appears in Fig. 16. This explanation is produced by first describing the domain rationale with the refinement pattern variables[9] replaced by what they matched, but with the domain pattern variables described as themselves rather than as what they matched. Thus while the system says 'finding' rather than 'increased drug', it nevertheless says 'finding' rather than 'increased serum potassium'. The next part of the explanation is produced by describing the prototype method. Finally, the set of the values is given for the domain variable used in the prototype method. Thus, the use of an automatic programmer not only allows us to justify the performance program, but it also allows us to give better descriptions of methods by making

---

[9] Those are the variables in the head of the domain principle that were bound during plan finding by the automatic program writer.

---

```
(describe-method [((ANTICIPATE*O (TOXICITY*F DIGITALIS))*1)])

To anticipate digitalis toxicity:
1. If the system determines that cardiomyopathy exists, it reduces
   the dose of digitalis due to cardiomyopathy.
2. If the system determines that decreased serum potassium exists, it reduces
   the dose of digitalis due to decreased serum potassium.
3. If the system determines that increased serum calcium exists, it
   reduces the dose of digitalis due to increased serum calcium.
```

FIG. 15. An explanation from the code for anticipating toxicity.

available intermediate levels of abstraction which were not previously available.

### 6.2.4. The domain rationale: its role in explanation

The above example also illustrates the role that the domain rationale plays in allowing us to provide better quality explanations. Programming in the top-down structured programming methodology can be thought of as moving between levels of language. Nodes higher in the development structure are stated in a higher level language than those that are lower down. However, as Fig. 14 illustrates, the correspondences (or 'translations') between those language levels are implicit. In the example, the method [(check sensitivities)] is at a higher level than the methods it calls which check individual sensitivities. Yet, the reasons why those sensitivities are sensitivities are not represented. The domain rationale is used to indicate those correspondences. For example, the domain rationale of the domain principle used for anticipating toxicity essentially defines what it means for a finding to be a sensitizing factor in digitalis therapy. Paraphrasing the description given in Fig. 16, it is a finding that causes a dangerous deviation that is also caused by increased digitalis. It should be noted that the current implementation should be more explicit about exactly which terms in the higher level language are being redefined at a lower level by the domain rationale. This limitation could impair the quality of explanations in more complex situations than were encountered in the Digitalis Advisor. For

```
(describe-proto-method [(anticipate*o (toxicity*f digitalis))])

The system considers those cases where a finding causes a dangerous deviation and increased
digitalis also causes the dangerous deviation. If the system determines that the finding exists, it
reduces the dose of digitalis due to the finding.

The findings considered are increased serum calcium, decreased serum potassium and
cardiomyopathy.
```

FIG. 16. Explanation of a domain principle.

example, if multiple terms were being re-defined, the current implementation would have trouble sorting everything out. That limitation aside, the major point here is that the domain rationale allows us to be much more explicit about how moves between levels of language are being made. This, in turn, makes it possible to provide substantially better explanations.

### 6.2.5. Explaining events

The interpreter of the performance program can be set up to leave behind a trace of its execution. As it executes a procedure, it creates an *event object*, which records the call and method used, the variable environments on entrance and exit, and the value returned if the procedure is a functional subroutine. These events can be examined by the system after execution is completed to produce an explanation of what the system did for a particular patient.

Once we have the mechanisms in place to explain methods, it turns out to be quite easy to explain events. Basically, it is done by having the system examine the event to be explained, generate a heading sentence using the call that caused the event, and then generate phrases for the immediate subevents of the event. As when explaining methods, the subevents are filtered by their viewpoints.

The major changes in the explanation routines that have to be made are that a flag has to be set so that verbs are generated in the past tense, and the generator for conditionals has to be modified to indicate the choice taken. This is done by first having the generator check that there was an action taken by the conditional and then having it generate English for the predicate and the action taken. For example, the conditional does not take an action if its predicate evaluated to false and there was no 'else' clause, or if the action taken was of a viewpoint that was filtered out. If no action was taken, or the action taken is filtered out, the system just generates English for the predicate (for example, see steps 1 and 2 in Fig. 17.) Finally, the system generates a phrase indicating the final output values of the routine.

*"How did the system anticipate digitalis toxicity?"*

(describe-event [(event*i "e0002")])

To anticipate digitalis toxicity:
1. The system determined that cardiomyopathy did not exist.
2. The system determined that decreased serum potassium did not exist.
3. Since the system determined that increased serum calcium existed, the system reduced the dose of digitalis due to increased serum calcium.

The adjusted dose of digitalis was set to 0.20.

*"How did the system determine that serum calcium was increased?"*

(describe-event [(event*i "e0016")])

Since serum calcium (13) was greater than the threshold of increased serum calcium (11) the system determined that increased serum calcium existed.

FIG. 17. Examples of event explanations.

*"How d'd you reduce the dose for increased serum calcium?"*

The dose after adjusting for increased serum calcium was set according to the following formula:

$$D2 = D1\ C$$

where:
C = the reduction constant for increased serum calcium (0.8)
D1 = the dose before adjusting for increased serum calcium (0.25)
D2 = the dose after adjusting for increased serum calcium (0.20).

The dose of digitalis adjusted for the condition of the heart muscle, serum potassium and serum calcium was set to 0.20.

FIG. 18. Describing events with arithmetic expressions.

*"How does the system combine the assessments of highly specific, moderately specific, and non-specific findings of toxicity?"*

The combined assessment of the highly specific findings of digitalis toxicity, the moderately specific findings of digitalis toxicity and the non-specific findings of digitalis toxicity is set according to the following formula:

$$C = F1\ A1 + F2\ A2 + F3\ A3$$

where:
A1 = the assessment of the highly specific findings of digitalis toxicity
A2 = the assessment of the moderately specific findings of digitalis toxicity
A3 = the assessment of the non-specific findings of digitalis toxicity
C = the combined assessment of the highly specific findings of digitalis toxicity, the moderately specific findings of digitalis toxicity and the non-specific findings of digitalis toxicity
F1 = the weighting factor of the highly specific findings of digitalis toxicity (4)
F2 = the weighting factor of the moderately specific findings of digitalis toxicity (2)
F3 = the weighting factor of the non-specific findings of digitalis toxicity (1).

FIG. 19. Describing methods with arithmetic expressions.

### 6.2.6. Non-English explanation

There are many situations in which English is not the only or best way to give an explanation. Many times, explanations are much more effective when English text is supplemented with figures, charts, drawings and so forth.

A case in point is explaining mathematical formulas. Mathematical formulas expressed in English are not only verbose; they are ambiguous as well [29]. As a small step in moving toward a larger investigation of non-English explanations, the XPLAIN system describes arithmetic expressions using mathematical notation. This is done by choosing shortened variable names for the variables and converting the prefix XLMS form for arithmetic expressions to an infix form which is printed. Figs. 18 and 19 show some examples.

## 7. A Discussion of the Automatic Programming Approach to Explanation

This section addresses several issues that arose while implementing the system. Most of these deal with the interrelationships between the automatic programmer, the performance program, and the explanations that can be produced.

### 7.1. Does automatic programming affect the performance program?

We attempted to get the XPLAIN system to write procedures that captured the intent of the corresponding sections of the original Digitalis Advisor as much as possible. However, there were situations where we decided to adopt different strategies. Usually this occurred because the attempt to find domain principles forced us to look more closely at the methods we were adopting, and occasionally we discovered that the original program was flawed or inconsistent.

For example, in the original Digitalis Advisor, myxedema[10] was considered as one of the digitalis sensitivities (like increased calcium or decreased potassium). In creating the domain model and domain principle to anticipate toxicity in the new system, we realized that a problem existed because myxedema was not causally additive with the other sensitivities and hence would not meet all the refinement constraints required by the domain principles in refining the program. To resolve the problem, we dug deeper into the medical literature and discovered that myxedema should not really be considered a sensitivity at all! In fact, myxedema reduces the excretion of digitalis through the kidneys and thus tends to make digitalis accumulate in the body rather than making the patient more sensitive to digitalis. Therefore, the appropriate way to handle

[10] Myxedema is a disease caused by decreased thyroid function. Signs of the disease include dry skin, swellings around the lips and nose, mental deterioration, and a subnormal basal metabolic rate.

myxedema is not as a sensitivity, but as a factor which modifies the excretion rate in the pharmacokinetic model.

One of the advantages of the automatic programming approach is that it forces the user to think harder about the performance program and its implementation. Just as the implementation of any theory on a computer forces one to work out the details and think about the consistency of the theory, working out the implementation of the implementation carries the process one step further and forces one to think that much harder about the entire undertaking.

### 7.2. Is this approach to explanation compatible with others?

The approach to explanation espoused in this thesis is compatible with other approaches such as using canned text or producing explanations by translating the program code. It should be regarded as an extension of these earlier approaches rather than a replacement for them. This is important because there may be times when it is not feasible to get an automatic programmer to produce the code. The XPLAIN system allows the user to hand code parts of the system and can generate the remainder automatically. Those parts of the system that are hand-coded can be translated to English just like the parts that are automatically generated. The current implementation of the XPLAIN system does not support canned-text explanations (mainly because they have not been needed) but could easily be modified to do so.

### 7.3. Is automatic programming too hard?

One possible objection to the whole approach to explanation advocated here is that it is just too difficult to get an automatic programmer to write the performance program. When I first began this research, I thought that was the case. The original plan for producing better explanations was to create structures detailing the development of the performance program, but these structures would be created by hand rather than automatically. It was feared that automatic programming was just too hard. However, as the research progressed, it became clear that if we had sufficiently powerful representations available so that it could be said that in some sense explanations were being produced from an understanding of the program, then actually writing the program in the first place would not be much more difficult. I suspect this is true in general. It seems that the primary difficulty in both explanation and automatic programming is a knowledge representation problem, and that the kinds of knowledge to be represented in both cases are similar so that a solution to one case makes the other much easier. Furthermore, if this conjecture is correct, it implies that we are not likely to find easier approaches to explanation than the one presented here (if we require that our explanations be based on an understanding of the program as opposed to, say, canned text.)

### 7.4. Is a top-down approach really necessary?

The XPLAIN system can produce good justifications in part because it has access to the refinement structure produced by the automatic programmer in a top-down fashion. A natural question to ask is whether a bottom-up approach might not work equally well. In other words, one could envision a system that analyzed an existing program structure into higher principles, and explained it at that level. This system would need to employ knowledge structures much like the domain principles and domain model, but they would be used in reverse to parse the existing performance program into a parse tree (which would correspond to XPLAIN's refinement structure).[11] This approach is enticing: it seems that if it can be made to work in general then any program can be explained whether or not it was written with explanation in mind. While such an approach might be attractive in principle, I feel there are several obstacles that make its implementation difficult. First, as was pointed out earlier, the process of writing a program is a process that distills 'how-to-do' something out of a much larger body of knowledge. Given that, the analyzer will not be able to explain a program without knowledge structures similar to the domain principles and domain model used by XPLAIN, and furthermore, these structures will have to be similar in both size and scope to those used by XPLAIN. While XPLAIN works deductively this recognizer would have to work by induction and the possibility of ambiguity would exist. In the XPLAIN system, a major effort involved figuring out how the domain principles and domain model should be represented. Once they existed, it was relatively easy to get the program writer to use them to write the performance program. Since both require similar knowledge structures, and once they exist it is easy to synthesize the performance program, the top-down approach would appear to have the edge.

### 7.5. Limitations and extensions of the XPLAIN system

While the explanations presented in this paper provide an indication of the power of the automatic programming approach to explanation, they do not exhaust its possibilities. The current system can be extended in several areas.

#### 7.5.1. What can the current implementation do?

The current domain model and domain principles contain enough knowledge to generate all the examples within this paper. They can also produce additional examples, although these are quite similar to those that appear here. There are three things that would have to be done to complete the implementation of the Digitalis Advisor. First, it would be necessary to implement routines to assess therapeutic improvement. These should not be too difficult

[11] See also [6] for a discussion of this approach.

because they can be very similar to the routines that assess toxicity. Second, it would be necessary to recapture from the old Digitalis Advisor domain principles to adjust the dose based on the therapeutic and toxic assessments. Third, it would be necessary to implement various utility functions for gathering data and the pharmacokinetic model of digitalis excretion. While there would be a fair amount of programming involved, I do not foresee any major conceptual hurdles. Once this implementation was completed, the domain principles of that program could be used with different domain models to develop similar consulting programs (i.e. programs that offered advice about therapy with various drugs).

#### 7.5.2. Improved answer generators

Additional answer generators could be employed to provide the user with: (1) improved access to the domain model so that the domain model itself could be explained as well as its use in the development of the program; (2) improved explication of the decisions made by the automatic programmer; (3) an ability to assess the significance of the program's recommendations.

(1) Currently, the explanation routines make use of the domain model to justify a piece of program structure. It would be nice (particularly in a teaching environment) to have answer generators which focused on the domain model so that a user could enhance his understanding of the domain. In addition, it would not be particularly difficult to cross-reference the domain model with the refinement structure to indicate where the domain knowledge was used in the program. This would allow the system to answer questions such as, 'How does the system take increased calcium into account?' The answer would be produced by finding those places in the system where the concept increased calcium was used[12] and then displaying the appropriate pieces of code (see also [29]).

(2) The current system has no ability to explain domain or refinement constraints In part, this is because the implementation of the XPLAIN system has concentrated on offering explanations to medical users and it was felt that the constraints have more of a computer than medical viewpoint. But that is not entirely correct. Recall that when the system was refining the split-join associated with anticipating toxicity it was necessary to assure that all the factors involved were at least causally additive. Whether or not the factors are additive is a question that clearly involves medical knowledge, and it is something which should be explainable to a medical audience in terms of its medical significance.

(3) The system should also be able to explain the advice of the performance program in terms of its medical significance. For example, the advisor might conclude that no digitalis should be given for 3 hours and then 0.25 mg should

[12] For example, increased calcium could be a match for a pattern variable used in a domain rationale or as an argument to a domain constraint.

be administered. If the advice was given at 11 pm, the patient would have to be awakened at two in the morning if the attending physician wished to follow the program's recommendation to the letter. However, since digitalis has a relatively long half-life, the precise timing of doses (within a few hours) is not thought to be terribly important. In this case, the inconvenience and discomfort involved in waking the patient would probably dictate that the patient receive the drug at an earlier time. While we could program the system so that it does not give drugs during sleeping hours, it seems that that approach might eventually result in a program which knew substantially more about hospital procedure than about digitalis therapy. A better approach might be one where the system could indicate to the user the importance of its recommendations. For example, in this case, the system could mention that a variation of a few hours in drug administration would not be significant.

### 7.5.3. Telling white lies

Currently, XPLAIN can describe what a performance program it creates does and why it does it at various levels of abstraction by describing the methods it uses, the refinement structure, the domain principles and the domain model. While it can leave out details based on viewpoint or by a higher abstraction, it does not deliberately distort its explanations. Yet sometimes human teachers do exactly that to make their explanations easier to understand. That is, to introduce a new concept, a teacher may deliberately over-simplify things and give an explanation which is in fact wrong but easier to understand and close enough to the truth that the student can easily understand the approximation the teacher presents. These 'white lies' represent a kind of explanation that cannot be delivered by systems that just present (at some level of detail) the reasoning paths followed by a problem solver (or automatic programmer).

But where do white lies come from? Sometimes a teacher may create them from scratch, but often they are just earlier versions of what was though at the time to be the complete, final version of the theory, program or whatever. For example, the old Digitalis Advisor used to adjust the dose for sensitivities using a simple threshold model: if the level of serum potassium (say) was below a certain threshold, the dose was reduced by a fixed percentage. The most recent version of the Digitalis Advisor makes a sliding reduction depending on how depressed the serum potassium is. Since the threshold model is more understandable, when describing the Digitalis Advisor, one might present it first to give the user a general idea of what happens before describing the sliding reduction that is actually used.

It seems that it could be very helpful in providing better explanations if the XPLAIN system adopted a similar technique. That is, suppose that someone discovered that a domain principle had to be modified to give better results. Currently, he would make the modification and re-run the program writer to get a new performance program which incorporated the change. The old version of the domain principle and performance program would be discarded. What we are suggesting here is that rather than throwing away old versions of the performance program, it might be useful if the program writer kept them around and noted the differences between the refinement of the old program and the new and where these differences arose (i.e. new principle, different domain model, etc.). The explanation routines could then use the old program fragments as a source for white lies and after the old version was understood, the difference links could be used to indicate how things really worked. Additionally, recording the changes between versions would allow the system to offer effective explanations about those changes to a user who had not used the system for a while. To continue the example above, suppose a user who had last used the performance program when it made reductions by a threshold used the new version with sliding reductions. If his patient were only slightly hypokalemic, he might wonder why the reduction for decreased potassium was much smaller than before. The system could justify the difference only if it has access to the differences between the two versions and the reasons for those differences. Of course, the system would have to be careful. Sometimes new program fragments would result from new insights into the problem, leading to a better and simpler program. In that case, referring to the old program would gain nothing for expository purposes, although it could still be used for explaining differences between the old and new versions.

### 7.5.4. Telling the user what he wants to know

While the current system has a limited ability to tailor the explanation to the interests of the user and to model what has been explained to him, the quality of the explanations could be substantially improved if the results of other research efforts could be integrated with the XPLAIN system. These include: (1) having the system model what it believes the user knows [9], (2) developing tutorial strategies giving the system a more global view of its interaction with the user and allowing it to take part in directing it [5,6], (3) on the opposite end of the scale, improving the low level English generators so they are more firmly grounded on linguistic principles [17, 21] and (4) improving the system's understanding of its own explanatory capabilities and the user's question so that it can reformulate the user's request into what it can deliver [19].

## 8. A Summary of Major Points

First, we have argued that to be acceptable, consultant programs must be able to explain what they do and why. Second, we have described the various ways that traditional approaches fail to provide adequate explanations and justifications. Major failings include: (1) the inability of such approaches to justify what the system is doing because the knowledge required to produce justifications is not represented within the system, and (2) a lack of distinction between steps required just to get the computer-based implementation to work, and those that are motivated by the application domain. Third, we have outlined an approach which captures the knowledge necessary to improve explanations. This involves using an automatic programmer to generate the performance program. As the program is generated, a refinement structure is created which gives the explanation routines access to decisions made during the creation of the program. The improvement in explanatory capabilities that is achieved is due more to the availability of this refinement structure than to the use of more sophisticated English generation functions.

## ACKNOWLEDGMENT

I would like to thank the members of the MIT Clinical Decision Making Group, particularly Ramesh Patil, Ken Church, Bill Long, Harold Goldberger, and especially my advisor, Peter Szolovits, for insightful comments and suggestions that greatly aided this research. I would also like to thank Bob Balzer, Lee Erman, Mike Fehling, Jack Mostow and Norm Sondheimer, all of ISI, for their suggestions which facilitated the writing of this paper.

## REFERENCES

1. Balzer, R., Goldman, N. and Wile, D., Informality in program specifications, *Proceedings of the Fifth International Conference on Artificial Intelligence* (IJCAI, Cambridge, MA, 1977).
2. Barstow, D., A knowledge-based system for automatic program construction, *Proceedings of the Fifth International Conference on Artificial Intelligence* (IJCAI, Cambridge, MA, 1977).
3. Brown, J.S., Burton, R.R. and Zydbel, F., Multiple representations of knowledge for tutorial reasoning, in: D.G. Bobrow and A. Collins (Eds.), *Representation and Understanding* (Academic Press, New York, 1975).
4. Carr, B. and Goldstein, I.P., Overlays: a theory of modelling for computer aided instruction, MIT AI Laboratory Memo 406, Cambridge, MA, February 1977.
5. Carr, B., Wusor II: a computer aided instruction program with student modelling capabilities, MIT Artificial Intelligence Laboratory Memo 417, Cambridge, MA, May 1977.
6. Clancey, W.J., Transfer of rule-based expertise through a tutorial dialogue, Stanford University, Department of Computer Science, STAN-CS-79-769, Stanford, CA, 1979.
7. Clancey, W.J., Neomycin: reconfiguring a rule-based expert system for application to teaching, *Proceedings of the Seventh International Conference on Artificial Intelligence* (IJCAI, Cambridge, MA, 1981).
8. Davis, R., Applications of meta level knowledge to the construction, maintenance and use of large knowledge bases, Ph.D. Thesis, Stanford Artificial Intelligence Laboratory Memo 283 Stanford, CA, 1976.
9. Genesereth, M.R., The role of plans in automated consultation, *Proceedings of the Sixth International Conference on Artificial Intelligence* (IJCAI, Cambridge, MA, 1979).
10. Gorry, G.A., Silverman, H. and Pauker, S.G., Capturing clinical expertise: a computer program that considers clinical responses to digitalis, *Amer. J. Medicine* **64** (1978) 452–460.
11. Green, C.C., Gabriel, R.P., Kant, E., Kedzierski, B.I., McCune, B.P., Phillips, J.V., Tappel, S.T. and Westfold, S.J., Results in knowledge based program synthesis, *Proceedings of the Sixth International Joint Conference on Artificial Intelligence* (IJCAI, Cambridge, MA, 1979).
12. Hawkinson, L.B., XLMS: a linguistic memory system, MIT Laboratory for Computer Science TM-173, Cambridge, MA, 1980.
13. Jelliffe, R.W., Buell, J., Kalaba. R. et al., A computer program for digitalis dosage regimens, *Math. Biosci.* **9** (1970) 179–193.
14. Jelliffe, R.W., Buell, J. and Kalaba, R., Reduction of digitalis toxicity by computer-assisted glycoside dosage regimens, *Ann. Intern. Med.* **77** (1972) 891–906.
15. Kastner, J.K., Weiss, S.M. and Kulikowski, C.A., Treatment selection and explanation in expert medical consultation application to a model of ocular herpes simplex, *Proceedings of MEDCOMP82* (1982) 420–427.
16. Long, W.J., A program writer, MIT Laboratory for Computer Science, TR-187, Cambridge, MA, 1977.
17. Mann, W.C. and Moore, J.A., Computer as author—results and prospects, USC Information Sciences Institute ISI/RR-79-82, Marina del Rey, CA, 1980.
18. Manna, Z. and Waldinger, R., The automatic synthesis of systems of recursive programs, *Proceedings of the Fifth International Conference on Artificial Intelligence* (IJCAI, Cambridge, MA, 1977.
19. Mark, W., Rule-based inference in large knowledge bases, *Proceedings of the First Annual National Conference on Artificial Intelligence*, 1980.
20. Martin, W.A., Roles, co-descriptors and the formal representation of quantified english expressions, MIT Laboratory for Computer Science TM-139, Cambridge, MA, 1979.
21. McDonald, D.D., Natural language production as a process of decision-making under constraints, MIT Ph.D. Thesis, Cambridge, MA, 1980.
22. Minsky, M., A framework for representing knowledge, in: P.H. Winston (Ed.). *The Psychology of Computer Vision* (McGraw-Hill, New York, 1975).
23. Peck, C.C., Sheiner, L.B. et al., Computer-assisted digoxin therapy, *New England J. Medicine* **289** (1973) 441–446.
24. Pauker, S.G., Gorry, G.A., Kassirer, J.P. and Schwartz, W.B., Toward the simulation of clinical cognition: taking a present illness by computer, *Amer. J. Medicine* **60** (1976) 981–995.
25. Pople, Jr., H.E., The formation of composite hypotheses in diagnostic problem solving: an exercise in synthetic reasoning, *Proceedings of the Fifth International Joint Conference on Artificial Intelligence* (IJCAI, Cambridge, MA, 1977).
26. Sheiner, L.B., Rosenberg, B. and Melmon, K., Modelling of individual pharmacokinetics for computer-aided drug dosage, *Comput. Biomedical Res.* **5** (1972) 441–459.
27. Shortliffe, E.H., *Computer Based Medical Consultations: MYCIN* (North-Holland, Amsterdam, 1976).
28. Silverman. H., A Digitalis Therapy Advisor. MIT Project MAC TR-143. Cambridge, MA, 1975.
29. Swartout W.R., A Digitalis Therapy Advisor with explanations, MIT Laboratory for Computer Science TR-176, Cambridge, MA, 1977.
30. Swartout. W.R., A Digitalis Therapy Advisor with explanations, *Proceedings of the Fifth International Joint Conference on Artificial Intelligence* (IJCAI, Cambridge, MA, 1977).
31. Swartout, W.R., Producing explanations and justifications of expert consulting systems, MIT Laboratory for Computer Science Tech. Rept. TR-251, Cambridge, MA, 1981.
32. Swartout, W.R. and Balzer, R., On the inevitable intertwining of specification and implementation, *Comm. ACM* **25**(7) (1982) 438–439.
33. Weiss, S.M., Kulikowski, C.A., Amarel, S. and Safir, A., A model-based method for computer-aided medical decision-making, *Artificial Intelligence* **11**(1,2) (1978) 145–172.
34. Winograd T., A computer program for understanding natural language, MIT Artificial Intelligence Laboratory TR-17, Cambridge, MA, 1971.

*Received March 1982; revised version received December 1982*

# Domain-Specific Automatic Programming

DAVID R. BARSTOW

*(Invited Paper)*

*Abstract*—Domain knowledge is crucial to an automatic programming system and the interaction between domain knowledge and programming at the current time. The ΦNIX project at Schlumberger-Doll Research has been investigating this issue in the context of two application domains related to oil well logging. Based on these experiments, we have developed a framework for domain-specific automatic programming. Within the framework, programming is modeled in terms of two activities, formalization and implementation, each of which transforms descriptions of the program as it proceeds through intermediate states of development. The activities and transformations may be used to characterize the interaction of programming knowledge and domain knowledge in an automatic programming system.

*Index Terms*—Automatic programming, programming knowledge, program transformations.

## I. INTRODUCTION

DURING the past few years the ΦNIX ("phi-nix") project at Schlumberger-Doll Research has been investigating the use of automatic programming techniques in two application domains related to oil well logging [1]–[5]. In the course of this work, we have been using the following informal definition of an automatic programming system:

*An automatic programming system allows a computationally naive user to describe problems using the natural terms and concepts of a domain with informality, imprecision and omission of details. An automatic programming system produces programs that run on real data to effect useful computations and that are reliable and efficient enough for routine use.*

One of the interesting implications of this definition is that an automatic programming system must be domain-specific, both in order to interact effectively with the user and to draw upon domain-specific knowledge during the implementation process.

It might be argued that a general purpose automatic programming system would suffice because the domain-specific knowledge would simply be part of a program's specification. That is, a program specification would consist of not only a description of what the software is to do, but also a set of definitions that enable the program description to be understood. This seems to fall short in several ways. First, the required domain knowledge is much more diverse than just definitions—it ranges from problem-solv-

Manuscript received June 3, 1985; revised July 2, 1985.
The author is with Schlumberger-Doll Research, Ridgefield, CT 06877.

©1985 IEEE. Reprinted, with permission, from *IEEE Transactions on Software Engineering*; 11:11, pp. 1321-1336; November 1985.

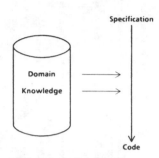

Fig. 1. Domain knowledge base and program specification.

ing heuristics to expectations about the run-time characteristics of the data. Second, most of the domain knowledge is relevant for many different programs—coupling it too tightly to the specification of a single program restricts the reusability of the knowledge. Third, it would be difficult for a computationally naive user to express the domain knowledge unless the automatic programming system knew a significant amount already. For these reasons, there is a useful distinction to be made between the specification of a program and the domain-specific definitions, facts, and heuristics that provide the context for understanding the specification and the knowledge to permit its efficient implementation (see Fig. 1).

It might also be argued that providing the domain-specific knowledge could be part of an interactive specification process. That is, the automatic programming sytem would initially be ignorant of the domain and the user would provide the necessary domain knowledge during the process of specifying a program; after several programs have been specified, the system's knowledge of the domain would have grown substantially. This seems to be much closer to the mark: it solves the reusability problem and helps cope with the diversity of domain knowledge. It still falls short of what is needed for a computationally naive user, but presumably the first users could be more sophisticated, with the naive users waiting until the system's domain knowledge had grown sufficiently. In the long run, this situation is probably what we should aim for. However, this approach is not yet feasible because too little is known about how to organize and structure the domain knowledge and about how domain knowledge and programming knowledge interact. In fact, these seem to me to be the key research issues in automatic programming at this time:

*How should domain knowledge be represented for use by an automatic programming system?*

*How do domain knowledge and programming knowledge interact during the programming process?*

Addressing these issues requires experimentation in the context of specific domains. In the rest of this paper, I will discuss some of the preliminary results of our experimentation in two domains. I will first describe the domains briefly, then present hypothetical syntheses that illustrate the knowledge required to write programs in each domain. I will then describe a framework that provides preliminary answers to the questions posed above. Although it has not been tested in the form of an implementation, the framework provides a model of the interaction between domain knowledge and programming knowledge that seems appropriate for these two application domains.

## II. APPLICATION DOMAINS

Our two application domains are both related to oil well logging. As illustrated in Fig. 2, oil well logs are made by lowering instruments (called tools) into a borehole and recording the measurements made by the tools as they are raised to the surface. The resulting logs are sequences of values indexed by depth. Logging tools measure a variety of basic petrophysical properties, such as the resistivity of the rock surrounding the borehole. Petroleum engineers, geophysicists, and geologists interpret these logs to determine properties that cannot be measured directly, such as the relative volumes of the minerals and fluids that make up the formation. For example, Fig. 3(b) shows the relative volumes of several minerals as calculated from the measured logs shown in Fig. 3(a). Specifically, we have been concerned with the following domains.

### Interpretation Software

Our work on interpretation software has focused primarily on quantitative log interpretation. Quantitative interpretation relies on numerical relationships between the measured data and the desired information. For example, the following equation relates the fractional volume of fluid, water saturation (the proportion of the fluid that is water), the electrical resistivity of the water and of the rock formation [6]:

$$SaturationWater^2 = \frac{A * ResistivityWater}{VolumeFluid^2 * ResistivityFluid}.$$

Since the fluid must be either water or hydrocarbons, a low water saturation indicates the presence of oil or gas. Quantitative interpretation often requires that qualitative assumptions be made. For example, the appropriate value of $A$ in the equation above depends on what minerals are assumed to be present in the rock formation.

### Tool Software

The logging process itself is controlled by computers on the surface that communicate with the downhole logging tools. It is convenient to think of the tools both as remote sensors whose measurements must be recorded and as remote devices that must be controlled. Corresponding to these two views are two qualitatively different activities that tool software must perform: data acquisition and process control. Data acquisition includes decoding the sig-

Fig. 2. Logging an oil well.

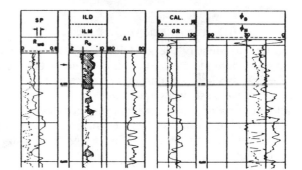

(a)

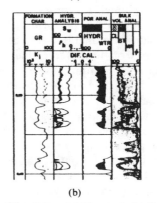

(b)

Fig. 3. Oil well logs. (a) Measured. (b) Computed.

nals from the tool, performing mathematical calculations on the signals, determining the depths at which the signals were measured, and recording the resulting logs. Process control includes monitoring the state of the tool and sending commands to alter its state when appropriate. Typical process control activities include feedback loops to adjust tool settings and sequences of commands directing the tool through a predefined sequence of actions. One interesting aspect of the software is that it must perform both activities within real-time constraints; thus, efficiency is a critical issue.

The greatest similarity between these two domains is that they both involve the manipulation of large amounts of quantitative data. The two greatest differences are that interpretation software does not have the same real-time constraints as tool software, and that interpretation software involves qualitative inferences that must sometimes be made on the basis of relatively little quantitative information.

Both types of software could be considered to be programming-in-the-small: programs range in size from a few hundred lines to a few thousand. However, the context in which they are used is closer to programming-in-the-large: there are several hundred thousand lines of system code that support both tool and interpretation software, the result of many person-years of effort. These two domains are instances of fairly broad classes of software: interpretation software is an example of data manipulation and analysis software; tool software is an example of real-time process control software. Thus, there is some hope that a framework for automatic programming that applies to these domains would generalize to much larger classes of software.

### III. HYPOTHETICAL SYNTHESES

One way to identify the knowledge that would be required by an automatic programming system is to develop hypothetical syntheses of particular programs [7], [8]. A hypothetical synthesis is a sequence of reasoning steps that an automatic programming system might follow in writing the program. In this section, I will present two such syntheses, one for an interpretation program, one for a tool control program.

### A. An Interpretation Software Problem

For the first hypothetical synthesis, we will consider an interpretation program that performs a task generally referred to as volumetric analysis—the computation of the fractional volumes of the different materials (solids and fluids) in the formation around the borehole. The number of possible materials is typically much larger than the number of available logs. Therefore, it is necessary to determine (or to make assumptions about) what materials are in the formation before computing their relative volumes. For example, a simple set of assumptions might be that the solid part of the formation consists solely of sandstone and that the fluid part consists of water and hydrocarbon. For this hypothetical synthesis, we will consider the problem of computing the amount of hydrocarbon in the formation under these assumptions, given that we have logs of the sonic transit time (the measured speed of a sonic wave in the formation) and the resistivity of the formation.

The hypothetical synthesis involves two major activities. The first, formalization, begins with an imprecise and incomplete specification and ends with a precise formal specification. The informal specification describes, in domain-specific terms, the major purpose of the program and the assumptions that may be made when implementing it. The formal specification describes, in mathematical terms, the constraints (called postconditions) that must be satisfied by the outputs. The postconditions should be sufficiently restrictive to ensure that any given set of inputs uniquely determines a set of outputs. The second activity,

implementation, begins with the formal specification and produces code that computes the appropriate outputs for given inputs.

*1) Specification:* The informal specification of the problem is as follows.

*Informal Specification 1:*
> Given logs of the sonic transit time and resistivity, compute a log of the fractional volume of hydrocarbon in the formation, assuming the solid part of the formation consists of sandstone and the fluid part consists of water and hydrocarbon.

This may be represented in a schema-like fashion:

*Informal Specification 1:*
| | |
|---|---|
| Inputs: | *Sonic : Log (Real)* |
| Outputs: | *VolumeHydrocarbon : Log (Real)* |
| Assumptions: | Solid is sandstone. |
| | Fluid is water and hydrocarbon. |

(Throughout this synthesis, *Log (Real)* denotes a well log whose values are real numbers.)

*2) Formalization:* The general strategy in a quantitative problem such as this is to find a quantitative relationship on the inputs and outputs that constrains the outputs to unique values. A log interpreter knows dozens of such relationships and knows where to find a few hundred more, and an automatic programming system would have a relatively complete catalogue of these relationships. The best situation would be if there were a single relationship that sufficiently constrained the outputs, given the inputs. However, in this case, there is not such a single relationship, so the system must try to find some set of relationships. Unfortunately, the space of possible sets of relationships is quite large. In order to cope with this complexity of size, domain-specific problem-solving heuristics are used, such as the following:

*In a volumetric analysis problem, separate the solid and fluid analysis parts.*

That is, determine the relative amounts of solid and fluid before analyzing the fluids. Applying this rule allows the specification to be decomposed into two subspecifications:

*Informal Specification 1.1:*
| | |
|---|---|
| Inputs: | *Sonic : Log (Real)* |
| | *Resistivity : Log (Real)* |
| Outputs: | *VolumeFluid : Log (Real)* |
| Assumptions: | Solid is sandstone. |
| | Fluid is water and hydrocarbon. |

*Informal Specification 1.2:*
| | |
|---|---|
| Inputs: | *Sonic : Log (Real)* |
| | *Resistivity : Log (Real)* |
| | *VolumeFluid : Log (Real)* |
| Outputs: | *VolumeHydrocarbon : Log (Real)* |
| Assumptions: | Solid is sandstone. |
| | Fluid is water and hydrocarbon. |

In the case of Informal Specification 1.1, there is a single relationship involving the inputs and outputs, an empirically determined formula relating sonic transit time and the fractional volume of fluid in a formation [9]

$$Sonic = VolumeFluid * SonicFluid$$
$$+ (1 - VolumeFluid) * SonicSolid$$

where *SonicFluid* and *SonicSolid* are parameters that represent the sonic transit time in pure solid and pure fluid, respectively. Given this relationship, we may apply the following rule:

*If a relationship is known that constrains the inputs and outputs and is consistent with the assumptions, use that relationship as a postcondition for the specification; if that relationship includes additional terms, add them as inputs.*

This yields the following specification.

*Informal Specification 1.1a:*

| | |
|---|---|
| Inputs: | *Sonic : Log (Real)* |
| | *Resistivity : Log (Real)* |
| | *SonicFluid : Real* |
| | *SonicSolid : Real* |
| Outputs: | *VolumeFluid : Log (Real)* |
| Assumptions: | Solid is sandstone. |
| | Fluid is water and hydrocarbon. |

Postconditions:
$$Sonic = VolumeFluid * SonicFluid$$
$$+ (1 - VolumeFluid) * SonicSolid$$

The values of terms such as *SonicFluid* and *SonicSolid* generally depend on characteristics of the formation. In this case, the sonic transit time in water or hydrocarbon is 189 $\mu$s/ft and in sandstone is 55 $\mu$s/ft. Given these facts, we may use the following rule to simplify the specification:

*If an input term has a constant value, consider the term to be a local, and add its value to the postconditions.*

Applying this rule yields the following:

*Informal Specification 1.1b:*

| | |
|---|---|
| Inputs: | *Sonic : Log (Real)* |
| | *Resistivity : Log (Real)* |
| Outputs: | *VolumeFluid : Log (Real)* |
| Locals: | *SonicFluid : Real* |
| | *SonicSolid : Real* |
| Assumptions: | Solid is sandstone. |
| | Fluid is water and hydrocarbon. |

Postconditions:
$$Sonic = VolumeFluid * SonicFluid$$
$$+ (1 - VolumeFluid) * SonicSolid$$
$$SonicFluid = 189$$
$$SonicSolid = 55$$

Finally, we may simplify the specification one more time by applying the following domain-independent rule.

*If the output terms are uniquely determined by the postconditions and a subset of the input terms, remove the extra input terms.*

This yields the following:

*Informal Specification 1.1c:*

| | |
|---|---|
| Inputs: | *Sonic : Log (Real)* |
| Outputs: | *VolumeFluid : Log (Real)* |
| Locals: | *SonicFluid : Real* |
| | *SonicSolid : Real* |

| | |
|---|---|
| Assumptions: | Solid is sandstone. |
| | Fluid is water and hydrocarbon. |

Postconditions:
$$Sonic = VolumeFluid * SonicFluid$$
$$+ (1 - VolumeFluid) * SonicSolid$$
$$SonicFluid = 189$$
$$SonicSolid = 55$$

Now the postconditions uniquely determine a value for the output given a value for the input, and thus Informal Specification 1.1 has been formalized.

In considering Informal Specification 1.2, we are not as fortunate, because there is no single relationship that we may use to constrain the inputs and outputs. Again, we must rely on a domain-specific problem-solving heuristic:

*In a fluid analysis problem, a useful intermediate step is to compute water saturation.*

Thus, the specification is decomposed.

*Informal Specification 1.2.1:*

| | |
|---|---|
| Inputs: | *Sonic : Log (Real)* |
| | *Resistivity : Log (Real)* |
| | *VolumeFluid : Log (Real)* |
| Outputs: | *SaturationWater : Log (Real)* |
| Assumptions: | Solid is sandstone. |
| | Fluid is water and hydrocarbon. |

*Informal Specification 1.2.2:*

| | |
|---|---|
| Inputs: | *Sonic : Log (Real)* |
| | *Resistivity : Log (Real)* |
| | *VolumeFluid : Log (Real)* |
| | *SaturationWater : Log (Real)* |
| Outputs: | *VolumeHydrocarbon : Log (Real)* |
| Assumptions: | Solid is sandstone. |
| | Fluid is water and hydocarbon. |

In the case of Informal Specification 1.2.1, there is a well-known empirical relationship between resistivity and water saturation [6]:

$$SaturationWater^2 = \frac{A * ResistivityWater}{VolumeFluid^2 * Resistivity}$$

where the value of *A* depends on the nature of the solid part of the formation, and the value of *ResistivityWater* depends on local geological conditions. The specification has now been transformed into

*Informal Specification 1.2.1a:*

| | |
|---|---|
| Inputs: | *Sonic : Log (Real)* |
| | *Resistivity : Log (Real)* |
| | *VolumeFluid : Log (Real)* |
| | *A : Real* |
| | *ResistivityWater : Real* |
| Outputs: | *SaturationWater : Log (Real)* |
| Assumptions: | Solid is sandstone. |
| | Fluid is water and hydrocarbon. |

Postconditions:
$$SaturationWater^2 = \frac{A * ResistivityWater}{VolumeFluid^2 * Resistivity}$$

The *ResistivityWater* term depends on run-time conditions, but the *A* term may be determined from the assumptions (*A* = 0.81 in sandstone). Therefore we may apply the same rule used earlier:

*If an input term has a constant value, consider the term to be a local, and add its value to the postconditions.*
This yields:

*Informal Specification 1.2.1b:*

| | |
|---|---|
| Inputs: | *Sonic : Log (Real)* |
| | *Resistivity : Log (Real)* |
| | *VolumeFluid : Log (Real)* |
| | *ResistivityWater : Real* |
| Outputs: | *SaturationWater : Log (Real)* |
| Locals: | *A : Real* |
| Assumptions: | Solid is sandstone. |
| | Fluid is water and hydrocarbon. |

Postconditions:

$$SaturationWater^2 = \frac{A * ResistivityWater}{VolumeFluid^2 * Resistivity}$$

$$A = .81$$

Again, extra inputs may be eliminated.

*Informal Specification 1.2.1c:*

| | |
|---|---|
| Inputs: | *Resistivity : Log (Real)* |
| | *VolumeFluid : Log (Real)* |
| | *ResistivityWater : Real* |
| Outputs: | *SaturationWater : Log (Real)* |
| Assumptions: | Solid is sandstone. |
| | Fluid is water and hydrocarbon. |

Postconditions:

$$SaturationWater^2 = \frac{A * ResistivityWater}{VolumeFluid^2 * Resistivity}$$

$$A = .81$$

And Informal Specification 1.2.1 has been formalized.

In considering Informal Specification 1.2.2, there is again no single relationship that constrains the inputs and outputs, but there are two definitional relationships that will be used:

$$SaturationWater = \frac{VolumeWater}{VolumeFluid}$$

$$VolumeWater + VolumeHydrocarbon = VolumeFluid.$$

Incorporating these two relationships yields the following specification:

*Informal Specification 1.2.2.a:*

| | |
|---|---|
| Inputs: | *Sonic : Log (Real)* |
| | *Resistivity : Log (Real)* |
| | *VolumeFluid : Log (Real)* |
| | *SaturationWater : Log (Real)* |
| Outputs: | *VolumeHydrocarbon : Log (Real)* |
| Locals: | *VolumeWater : Log (Real)* |
| Assumptions: | Solid is sandstone. |
| | Fluid is water and hydrocarbon. |

Postconditions:

$$SaturationWater = \frac{VolumeWater}{VolumeFluid}$$

$$VolumeWater + VolumeHydrocarbon = VolumeFluid$$

Eliminating extra inputs now yields the following formalized specification.

*Informal Specification 1.2.2b:*

| | |
|---|---|
| Inputs: | *VolumeFluid : Log (Real)* |
| | *SaturationWater : Log (Real)* |
| Outputs: | *VolumeHydrocarbon : Log (Real)* |
| Locals: | *VolumeWater : Log (Real)* |
| Assumptions: | Solid is sandstone. |
| | Fluid is water and hydrocarbon. |

Postconditions:

$$SaturationWater = \frac{VolumeWater}{VolumeFluid}$$

$$VolumeWater + VolumeHydrocarbon = VolumeFluid$$

Thus, at this point the original informal specification has been transformed into three formalized specifications. One final step is required for each of the three subspecifications. Implicit in the original specification was the fact that the program is to be applied to some range of depths in a well. Thus, to each formalized specification, we must add another input (*Depths*, an interval of real numbers) and postconditions must be quantified over all elements of *Depths*. (Note that *Depths* is an infinite set—this is acceptable at the level of postconditions in a formal specification, since it defines a constraint without implying that an infinite amount of computation must be done.)

*Formal Specification 1.1:*

| | |
|---|---|
| Inputs: | *Depths : Interval (Real)* |
| | *Sonic : Log (Real)* |
| Outputs: | *VolumeFluid : Log (Real)* |
| Locals: | *SonicFluid : Real* |
| | *SonicSolid : Real* |

Postconditions:

$\forall d \in Depths:$

$$Sonic(d) = VolumeFluid(d) * SonicFluid + (1 - VolumeFluid(d)) * SonicSolid$$

$$SonicFluid = 189$$

$$SolidSolid = 55$$

*Formal Specification 1.2.1:*

| | |
|---|---|
| Inputs: | *Depths : Interval (Real)* |
| | *Resistivity : Log (Real)* |
| | *VolumeFluid : Log (Real)* |
| | *ResistivityWater : Real* |
| Outputs: | *SaturationWater : Log (Real)* |
| Locals: | *A : Real* |

Postconditions:

$\forall d \in Depths:$

$$SaturationWater(d)^2 = \frac{A * ResistivityWater}{VolumeFluid(d)^2 * Resistivity(d)}$$

$$A = 0.81$$

*Formal Specification 1.2.2:*

| | |
|---|---|
| Inputs: | *Depths : Interval (Real)* |
| | *VolumeFluid : Log (Real)* |
| | *SaturationWater : Log (Real)* |
| Outputs: | *VolumeHydrocarbon : Log (Real)* |
| Locals: | *VolumeWater : Log (Real)* |

Postconditions:

$\forall d \in Depths:$

$$SaturationWater(d) = \frac{VolumeWater(d)}{VolumeFluid(d)}$$

$\forall d \in Depths :$

$$VolumeWater(d) + VolumeHydrocarbon(d) = VolumeFluid(d)$$

The formalization activity is now complete: we have formal specifications for the three subspecifications. Note that in the process of formalizing the problem, we have changed the input/output characteristics of the informal specification by adding an input (*ResistivityWater*) whose value can only be determined at run-time.

*3) Implementation:* The three formal specifications may now be implemented as code in the target language. The general strategy is to apply two different types of rules: refinement rules replace abstract concepts by more concrete concepts; reformulation rules rearrange descriptions into forms that may be more easily refined. Most of the rules are domain-independent, although a few are domain-specific.

In the case of Formal Specification 1.1, the first step involves reformulation through algebraic manipulation, simplifying and solving for the output term:

*Formal Specification 1.1a:*

Inputs:    *Depths : Interval(Real)*
           *Sonic : Log(Real)*
Outputs:   *VolumeFluid : Log(Real)*
Postconditions:
  $\forall d \in Depths:$
  $$VolumeFluid(d) = \frac{Sonic(d) - 55}{134}$$

The next step involves reformulating the postcondition into an algorithm by changing the quantifier to an enumeration and the equality to an assignment:

*Algorithm 1.1:*

Inputs:    *Depths : Interval(Real)*
           *Sonic : Log(Real)*
Outputs:   *VolumeFluid : Log(Real)*
Algorithm:
  *for d in Depths do*
  $$VolumeFluid(d) \leftarrow \frac{Sonic(d) - 55}{134}$$

Formal Specification 1.2.1 and Formal Specification 1.2.2 are handled in a similar fashion:

*Algorithm 1.2.1:*

Inputs:    *Depths : Interval(Real)*
           *Resistivity : Log(Real)*
           *VolumeFluid : Log(Real)*
           *ResistivityWater : Real*
Outputs:   *SaturationWater : Log(Real)*
Algorithm:
  *for d in Depths do*
  $$SaturationWater(d) \leftarrow \left( \frac{.81 * ResistivityWater}{VolumeFluid(d)^2 * Resistivity(d)} \right)^{1/2}$$

*Algorithm 1.2.2:*

Inputs:    *Depths : Interval(Real)*
           *VolumeFluid : Log(Real)*
           *SaturationWater : Log(Real)*
Outputs:   *VolumeHydrocarbon : Log(Real)*
Algorithm:
  *for d in Depths do*
  $VolumeHydrocarbon(d) \leftarrow VolumeFluid(d)$
  $- SaturationWater(d)*VolumeFluid(d)$

At this point, Algorithm 1.2.1 and Algorithm 1.2.2 may be combined.

*Algorithm 1.2:*

Inputs:    *Depths : Interval(Real)*
           *Resistivity : Log(Real)*
           *VolumeFluid : Log(Real)*
           *ResistivityWater : Real*
Outputs:   *VolumeHydrocarbon : Log(Real)*
Algorithm:
  *for d in Depths do*
  $$VolumeHydrocarbon(d) \leftarrow VolumeFluid(d) - \left( \frac{.81 * ResistivityWater}{Resistivity(d)} \right)^{1/2}$$

In a similar fashion, Algorithm 1.1 and Algorithm 1.2 may be combined.

*Algorithm 1:*

Inputs:    *Depths : Interval(Real)*
           *Sonic : Log(Real)*
           *Resistivity : Log(Real)*
           *ResistivityWater : Real*
Outputs:   *VolumeHydrocarbon : Log(Real)*
Algorithm:
  *for d in Depths do*
  $$VolumeHydrocarbon(d) \leftarrow \frac{Sonic(d) - 55}{134} - \left( \frac{.81 * ResistivityWater}{Resistivity(d)} \right)^{1/2}$$

Note that this algorithm is still quite abstract. In fact, it is not directly computable, since the enumeration is over an infinite set. In reality, of course, logs are finite data structures, containing values sampled at regularly spaced depths in the well. This knowledge is embodied in the following two domain-specific refinement rules:

*A log should be refined into a mapping of integers to values, where successive indexes correspond to 6" depth intervals.*

*An interval of depths should be refined into a pair of indexes.*

Applying these two rules yields the following algorithm, which is more concrete than Algorithm 1, but not yet refined to the level of the target language:

*Algorithm 1a:*

Inputs:  *TopDepthIndex : Integer*
         *BottomDepthIndex : Integer*
         *Sonic : Mapping(Integer, Real)*
         *Resistivity : Mapping(Integer, Real)*
         *ResistivityWater : Real*
Outputs: *VolumeHydrocarbon : Mapping(Integer, Real)*
Algorithm:
  *for d from TopDepthIndex to BottomDepthIndex do*
  $$VolumeHydrocarbon(d) \leftarrow \frac{Sonic(d) - 55}{134} - \left( \frac{.81 * ResistivityWater}{Resistivity(d)} \right)^{1/2}$$

We may now refine this algorithm by applying the following rule:

*A mapping whose domain is a range of integers may be refined into an array.*

This results in the following concrete algorithm:

*Algorithm 1b:*

Inputs:     *TopDepthIndex : Integer*
            *BottomDepthIndex : Integer*
            *Sonic : Array[TopDepthIndex, BottomDepthIndex] of Real*
            *Resistivity : Array[TopDepthIndex, BottomDepthIndex] of Real*
            *ResistivityWater : Real*

Outputs:    *VolumeHydrocarbon : Array[TopDepthIndex, BottomDepthIndex] of Real*

Algorithm:

*for d from TopDepthIndex to BottomDepthIndex do*

$$VolumeHydrocarbon[d] \leftarrow \frac{Sonic[d] - 55}{134} - \left(\frac{.81 * ResistivityWater}{Resistivity[d]}\right)^{1/2}$$

This algorithm is now suitable for direct translation into code in the target language. For example, a Pascal implementation would be as follows:

```
procedure HYDRO (TOP, BOTTOM: integer; RW: real;
              var S, R, VH: array[TOP..BOTTOM] of real);
var D: integer;
begin
   for D := TOP to BOTTOM do
      VH[D] := ((S[D]-55)/134) − sqrt (.81*RW/R[D])
   end;
```

## B. A Tool Software Problem

In this section we will consider a hypothetical synthesis of a tool software program. It will be similar in style to the hypothetical synthesis of the interpretation program, but in the interest of brevity will be presented in somewhat less detail. This hypothetical synthesis involves the same activities, formalization and implementation, that were involved in the previous one. In fact, many of the reasoning steps are quite similar. However, the basic underlying facts about the domain are quite different.

Imagine a logging tool with a sensor that measures the time required for a sound wave to travel a fixed distance through the formation around the borehole. Upon receiving a command from the surface, it emits a sound wave, measures the sonic transit time, and sends a signal to the surface. The strength of that signal is controlled by an amplifier in the tool, and the amplifier's gain is specified with each command.

As illustrated in Fig. 4, there are two hardware components: the downhole tool, including the amplifier; and the surface controller, which sends control signals to the tool and receives electrical encodings of the sonic measurement from the tool. The surface controller outputs data to be recorded (the sonic log) and also the amplitude of the signal that was received at the surface. The amplitude at the surface depends on the amplitude at the downhole tool and the amount of attenuation in the transmission from the tool to the surface. The amplitude at the downhole tool depends in turn on the gain in the amplifier. The quality of the measurement is best when the signal's amplitude at the surface is close to 5 V.

The problem is to write a program (the Sonic Software in Fig. 4) that adjusts the gain to ensure a high quality signal, i.e., a feedback loop to control the sonic tool. From this point of view, we may use a somewhat simpler model of the tool. As illustrated in Fig. 5. we may consider the

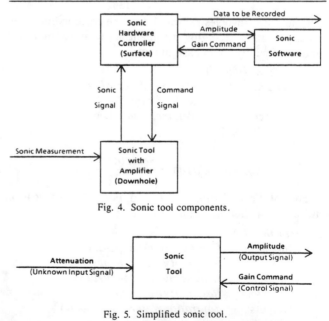

Fig. 4. Sonic tool components.

Fig. 5. Simplified sonic tool.

tool to be a device with an input signal with unknown value, a control signal whose value may be set by the software, and an output signal whose value is available to the software. The unknown input corresponds to the attenuation during transmission to the surface; the control signal is the gain command; the output signal is the amplitude at the surface.

*1) Specification:* An informal specification for this problem is as follows:

*Informal Specification 2:* Given the current amplitude, compute the next gain command so that the next amplitude will be as close as possible to 5 V.

We may express this in the following schema.

*Informal Specification 2:*
    Inputs:            *CurrentAmplitude : Real*
    Outputs:          *NextGainCommand : Integer*
    Postconditions:
        *NextAmplitude* $\approx$ 5

(Throughout this synthesis, terms beginning with *Current...* will refer to values of the most recently sent and received signals; terms beginning with *Next...* will refer to values of the next send/receive cycle. Thus, in Informal Specification 2, *CurrentAmplitude* refers to the amplitude of the most recently received signal from the tool; *NextGainCommand* refers to the next gain command to be sent to the tool; *NextAmplitude* refers to the amplitude of the signal sent from the tool upon receipt of the *NextGainCommand*.)

*2) Formalization:* One of the interesting aspects of this problem is the fact that the gain command to the hardware controller is a four-bit integer, so the amplifier's gain may only be set to one of sixteen possible values. The following rule allows us to separate this consideration from the problem of computing the value that would be sent if the hardware controller's command interpreter allowed arbitrary gain values:

*If a command can only approximate the desired command value, first compute the ideal value, then compute the encoding that corresponds as closely as possible to the ideal value.*

This yields the following two subspecifications:

*Informal Specification 2.1:*
    Inputs:            *CurrentAmplitude : Real*
    Outputs:          *IdealNextGainValue : Real*
    Postconditions:
        *NextAmplitude* $\approx$ 5

*Informal Specification 2.2:*
    Inputs:            *IdealNextGainValue : Real*
    Outputs:          *NextGainCommand : Integer*
    Postconditions:
        *IdealNextGainValue* $\approx$ *Gain (NextGainCommand)*

Here, *Gain (i)* is the function that specifies the gain to be applied by the tool when it receives the command *i*.

We may decompose Informal Specification 2.1 by applying the following rule:

*If there is a known relationship between the input, control, and output signals, first compute a predicted value for the next input signal, then compute the value for the ideal control signal.*

In this case, we know the following fact about the sonic tool.

*The uphole amplitudeof the sonic signal is the product of the downhole gain and the signal attenuation.*

Thus, applying the rule yields the following:

*Informal Specification 2.1.1:*
    Inputs:            *CurrentAmplitude : Real*
    Outputs:          *PredictedAttenuation : Real*

*Informal Specification 2.1.2:*
    Inputs:            *PredictedAttenuation : Real*
    Outputs:          *IdealNextGainValue : Real*

Postconditions:
    *PredictedAttenuation \* IdealNextGainValue* = 5

Informal Specification 2.1.2 is already fully formalized. The first step in formalizing Informal Specification 2.1.1 involves applying the following rule.

*If the unknown input signal changes slowly, then the current value of the unknown is a good prediction of the next value of the unknown.*

To apply this rule, we also require the following domain-specific fact.

*At normal logging speeds, the attenuation of the sonic signal changes slowly.*

The result is the following:

*Informal Specification 2.1.1a:*
    Inputs:            *CurrentAmplitude : Real*
    Outputs:          *PredictedAttenuation : Real*
    Locals:           *CurrentAttenuation : Real*
    Postconditions:
        *PredictedAttenuation = CurrentAttenuation*

Informal Specification 2.1.1a may be further formalized by applying the following rule.

*If there is a known relationship between the input, control, and output signals, use it to compute the current value of the input signal, given the current values for the output and control signals.*

Again, the output signal is simply the product of the unknown signal and the control signal:

*Informal Specification 2.1.1b:*
    Inputs:            *CurrentAmplitude : Real*
                      *CurrentGainValue : Real*
    Outputs:          *PredictedAttenuation : Real*
    Locals:           *CurrentAttenuation : Real*
    Postconditions:
        *PredictedAttenuation = CurrentAttenuation*
        *CurrentAttenuation \* CurrentGainValue*
            = *CurrentAmplitude*

Note that we have added another input, namely the actual value of the gain applied by the tool. With this change, Informal Specification 2.1.1 has been fully formalized. Since Informal Specification 2.1.2 was already formalized, all of Informal Specification 2.1 has now been fully formalized.

In considering Informal Specification 2.2, we must first add *NextGainValue* as an output, which will be used as *CurrentGainValue* (required by Informal Specification 2.1.1b) on the next execution of the feedback loop:

*Informal Specification 2.2a:*
    Inputs:            *IdealNextGainValue : Real*
    Outputs:          *NextGainCommand : Integer*
                      *NextGainValue : Real*
    Postconditions:
        *IdealNextGainValue* $\approx$ *Gain (NextGainCommand)*
        *Gain (NextGainCommand) = NextGainValue*

Informal Specification 2.2a is concerned with the details of the commands that may be sent to the tool. In this case, the gain command must be an integer in the range [0,15]:

*The gain applied by the sonic tool's amplifier is $2^{i-5}$, where i is the four bit command.*

Our specification is then:

*Informal Specification 2.2b:*

| | |
|---|---|
| Inputs: | *IdealNextGainValue : Real* |
| Outputs: | *NextGainCommand : Integer* |
| | *NextGainValue : Real* |
| Locals: | *Gain : Mapping (Integer, Real)* |
| Postconditions: | |

$IdealNextGainValue \approx Gain (NextGainCommand)$
$Gain (NextGainCommand) = NextGainValue$
$0 \leq NextGainCommand \leq 15$
$\forall i \in [0,15] : Gain (i) = 2^{i-5}$

Since the tool only accepts a finite set of gain values, we must discretize the range of possible gain values, which we may do by applying the following rule:

*If an interval of real values is approximated by a geometric series, the interval should be discretized with boundaries at the geometric means of neighboring approximations.*

This yields the following formalized specification.

*Informal Specification 2.2c:*

| | |
|---|---|
| Inputs: | *IdealNextGainValue : Real* |
| Outputs: | *NextGainCommand : Integer* |
| | *NextGainValue : Real* |
| Locals: | *Gain : Mapping (Integer, Real)* |
| | *LowerBound : Mapping (Integer, Real)* |

Postconditions:

$IdealNextGainValue \approx Gain (NextGainCommand)$
$Gain (NextGainCommand) = NextGainValue$
$0 \leq NextGainCommand \leq 15$
$\forall i \in [0,15] : Gain (i) = 2^{i-5}$
$0 \leq i \leq 15 : LowerBound (i) = (Gain (i-1)*Gain (i))^{1/2}$
$LowerBound (0) = 0$
$LowerBound (16) = \infty$
$LowerBound (NextGainCommand) \leq NextGainValue$
$\quad < LowerBound (NextGainCommand + 1)$

At this point, we have three subspecifications, all of which are fully formalized:

*Formal Specification 2.1.1:*

| | |
|---|---|
| Inputs: | *CurrentAmplitude : Real* |
| | *CurrentGainValue : Real* |
| Outputs: | *PredictedAttenuation : Real* |
| Locals: | *CurrentAttenuation : Real* |
| Postconditions: | |

$PredictedAttenuation = CurrentAttenuation$
$CurrentAttenuation * CurrentGainValue$
$\quad = CurrentAmplitude$

*Formal Specification 2.1.2:*

| | |
|---|---|
| Inputs: | *PredictedAttenuation : Real* |
| Outputs: | *IdealNextGainValue : Real* |
| Postconditions: | |

$PredictedAttenuation * IdealNextGainValue = 5$

*Formal Specification 2.2:*

| | |
|---|---|
| Inputs: | *IdealNextGainValue : Real* |
| Outputs: | *NextGainCommand : Integer* |
| | *NextGainValue : Real* |

| | |
|---|---|
| Locals: | *Gain : Mapping (Integer, Real)* |
| | *LowerBound : Mapping (Integer, Real)* |
| Postconditions: | |

$IdealNextGainValue \approx Gain (NextGainCommand)$
$Gain (NextGainCommand) = NextGainValue$
$0 \leq NextGainCommand \leq 15$
$\forall i \in [0,15] : Gain (i) = 2^{i-5}$

$0 < i \leq 15 : LowerBound (i) = (Gain (i-1) * Gain (i))^{1/2}$
$LowerBound (0) = 0$
$LowerBound (16) = \infty$
$LowerBound(NextGainCommand) \leq NextGainValue$
$\quad < LowerBound(NextGainCommand + 1)$

*3) Implementation:* The implementation activity is somewhat more complicated than it was with the interpretation program. In the interest of brevity, I will summarize the main steps.

Through algebraic manipulation techniques similar to those involved in the previous hypothetical synthesis, the first two specifications may be translated into algorithmic form and combined.

*Algorithm 2.1:*

| | |
|---|---|
| Inputs: | *CurrentAmplitude : Real* |
| | *CurrentGainValue : Real* |
| Outputs: | *IdealNextGainValue : Real* |
| Algorithm: | |

$$IdealNextGainValue \leftarrow \dfrac{5}{CurrentAmplitude} * CurrentGainValue$$

In implementing Formal Specification 2.2, three major steps are made. The first involves determining a technique for finding the gain command that corresponds to the ideal gain value. This will be done by finding the appropriate index in the *LowerBound* mapping. Several search techniques might be reasonable, including linear and binary search. In this case, a third technique will be used, namely proposing a candidate and searching linearly in the appropriate direction if the candidate is too high or too low.

*If a problem involves finding an element in a discrete ordered set and a test is known for determining whether a candidate is too high or too low, one implementation technique is to propose a candidate and to increment or decrement it until an appropriate element is found.*

The selection of this technique over binary and linear search is based on the following efficiency rule.

*If the set is small and an initial candidate with high probability is known, the "propose candidate with linear search" is the most efficient.*

In order to apply these rules, we also need the following fact:

*If the unknown input to a device changes slowly, then the control signal will also change slowly.*

Thus, *CurrentGainCommand* is a good candidate for *NextGainCommand*.

The second major step concerns the fact that the computation must keep a record of its history, namely the value of the previously computed gain command. The appropriate technique depends on the software architecture of the system on which the program is to be executed. If that architecture supports multiple processes, the history could be stored in the state of the process. For this exercise, however, we will assume that multiple processes are not supported. In this case, we will apply the following rule.

*A process may be implemented as a sequence of function calls with the process state stored in global variables.*

We will assume that such global state variables are appropriately initialized elsewhere.

The third major step involves applying a rule used in the first hypothetical synthesis:

*A mapping whose domain is a range of integers may be refined into an array.*

---

Algorithm:

$$Candidate \leftarrow CurrentGainCommand;$$
$$NotYet \leftarrow True;$$
while NotYet do
    if $Candidate > 0 \wedge LowerBound[Candidate] < IdealNextGainValue$
        then $Candidate \leftarrow Candidate - 1$
    elseif $Candidate < 15 \wedge LowerBound[Candidate + 1] \leq IdealNextGainValue$
        then $Candidate \leftarrow Candidate + 1$
    else $NotYet \leftarrow False;$
$NextGainCommand \leftarrow Candidate;$
$NextGainValue \leftarrow Gain[NextGainCommand];$
$CurrentGainCommand \leftarrow NextGainCommand$

---

both are stored in global variables that are initialized elsewhere.

The result of these steps is the following algorithm:

Algorithm 2.2:
| | |
|---|---|
| Inputs: | *IdealNextGainValue : Real* |
| Outputs: | *NextGainCommand : Integer* |
| | *NextGainValue : Real* |
| Locals: | *Candidate : Integer* |
| | *NotYet : Boolean* |
| Globals: | *CurrentGainCommand : Integer* |
| | *LowerBound : Array[0,15] of Real* |
| | *Gain : Array[0,15] of Real* |

Finally, the two algorithms may be combined into one, in which case the *CurrentGainValue* is also retained between calls as the value of a global variable, and *NextGainValue* is not needed.

Algorithm 2:
| | |
|---|---|
| Inputs: | *CurrentAmplitude : Real* |
| Outputs: | *NextGainCommand : Integer* |
| Locals: | *IdealNextGainValue : Real* |
| | *Candidate : Integer* |
| | *NotYet : Boolean* |
| Globals: | *CurrentGainCommand : Integer* |
| | *CurrentGainValue : Real* |
| | *LowerBound : Array[0,15] of Real* |
| | *Gain : Array[0,15] of Real* |

Algorithm:

$$IdealNextGainValue \leftarrow \frac{5}{CurrentAmplitude} * CurrentGainValue$$
$$Candidate \leftarrow CurrentGainCommand;$$
$$NotYet \leftarrow True;$$
while NotYet do
    if $Candidate > 0 \wedge LowerBound[Candidate] < IdealNextGainValue$
        then $Candidate \leftarrow Candidate - 1$
    elseif $Candidate < 15 \wedge LowerBound[Candidate + 1] \leq IdealNextGainValue$
        then $Candidate \leftarrow Candidate + 1$
    else $NotYet \leftarrow False;$
$NextGainCommand \leftarrow Candidate;$
$CurrentGainValue \leftarrow Gain[NextGainCommand];$
$CurrentGainCommand \leftarrow NextGainCommand$

---

In fact, this rule is applied twice, once to *Gain* and once to *LowerBound*. For this exercise, we will assume that

Finally, this concrete algorithm may be translated into code (e.g., in Pascal):

```
procedure SONIC (AMP: real;
var GAINCOM: integer);
var IDEAL: REAL;
    CAND: integer;
    NOTYET: boolean;
/ *
globals declared elsewhere:
    GAIN, LOWER: array[0 .. 15] of real;
    CURGAIN: real;
    CURCOM: integer;
* /
begin
    IDEAL := (5. /AMP) * CURGAIN;
    CAND := CURCOM;
    NOTYET := True;
    while NOTYET do
        if CAND > 0 and LOWER[CAND] > IDEAL
            then CAND := CAND − 1
        elseif CAND < 15 and
                LOWER[CAND + 1] <= IDEAL
            then CAND := CAND + 1
        else NOTYET := False;
    GAINCOM := CAND;
    CURGAIN := GAIN[GAINCOM];
    CURCOM := GAINCOM
    end;
```

### C. Knowledge Required for the Hypothetical Syntheses

In reviewing the knowledge that was required for the two hypothetical syntheses, we can see that it can be classified into four general areas: programming, the application domain, mathematics, and the target architecture and language. In this section, these areas will be reviewed with examples of the required knowledge.

*1) Knowledge of Programming:* The syntheses relied on several different types of knowledge about programming. The formalization activity required domain-independent problem-solving heuristics, such as the following:

*If a relationship is known that constrains the inputs and outputs and is consistent with the assumptions, use that relationship as a postcondition for the problem; if that relationship includes additional terms, add them as inputs.*

The implementation activity involved knowledge of abstract data types and the associated refinement rules, such as:

*A mapping whose domain is a range of integers may be refined into an array.*

Knowledge of specific programming techniques and algorithms was also used. For example:

*If a problem involves finding an element in a discrete ordered set and a test is known for determining whether a candidate is too high or too low, one implementation technique is to propose a candidate and to increment or decrement it until an appropriate element is found.*

Knowledge of the efficiency of alternative techniques was also required.

*If the set is small and an initial candidate with high probability is known, the "propose candidate with linear search" is the most efficient.*

*2) Knowledge of the Application Domain:* Knowledge of the application domain included basic facts about the subject matter, such as:

*The sonic transit time of sandstone is 55 μs/ft.*

*The gain applied by the sonic tool's amplifier is $2^{i-5}$, where i is the four bit command*

In addition, the syntheses required a variety of relationships. Some were empirically determined quantitative relationships, such as:

*The relationship among water saturation, fluid volume, and resistivity is given by the following formula:*

$$SaurationWater^2 = \frac{A * ResistivityWater}{VolumeFluid^2 * Resistivity}$$

*where A depends on characteristics of the formation.*

Others were definitional quantitative realationships, such as the following:

*The relationship among water saturation, fluid volume, and water volume is defined by the following formula:*

$$SaturationWater = \frac{VolumeWater}{VolumeFluid}$$

Finally, there were qualitative relationships.

*At normal logging speeds, the attenuation of the sonic signal changes slowly.*

In addition to this factual type of knowledge, the syntheses also required the use of domain-specific problem-solving heuristics, such as

*In a volumetric analysis problem, separate the solid and fluid analysis parts.*

*If a command can only approximate the desired command value, first compute the ideal value, then compute the encoding that corresponds as closely as possible to the ideal value.*

Finally, the synthesis required the use of domain-specific data types and their associated refinement rules, such as the following:

*A log should be refined into a mapping of integers to values, where successive indexes correspond to 6 inch depth intervals.*

*3) Knowledge of Mathematics:* The mathematical knowledge used in the syntheses consisted primarily of techniques for manipulating mathematical expressions, in particular, for solving an equation or a system of equations, and for simplifying an expression.

*4) Knowledge of the Target Architecture and Language:* The tool software synthesis required knowledge of the target architecture:

*The target architecture does not support multiple processes.*

Finally, knowledge of the syntax of the target language was required:

*The Pascal syntax of an iteration over an integer variable is*

```
for I := X to Y do ...
```

## IV. A FRAMEWORK FOR DOMAIN-SPECIFIC AUTOMATIC PROGRAMMING

The hypothetical syntheses of the previous section illustrated the steps that an automatic programming system might go through in the process of producing code from informal specifications. That process involves two activities, formalization and implementation, each of which manipulates and transforms descriptions of the program as it proceeds through various intermediate stages of development. In this section, I will describe in more detail a framework for domain-specific automatic programming systems, based on these activities and the descriptions that they manipulate.

## A. Programming Activities

As illustrated in the hypothetical syntheses, programming in our domains involves two qualitatively different activities.

*Formalization* begins with some informal idea about what the program should do and ends with a formal description of precisely what the program should do but not how it should do it.

*Implementation* begins with a formal description of the required behavior and ends with code in the target language.

In our application domains, the difficulty of the formalization activity is due to the large amount of knowledge that is potentially applicable to solving any given problem. The formalization activity must select the relevant knowledge and organize it into a precise description. The best strategy for this activity seems to involve two components: if a problem can be recognized as one for which a simple formal representation is known (e.g., a quantitative relationship stored in a data base of relationships), then use that relationship; otherwise, try to apply a problem-solving heuristic to decompose the problem into smaller, hopefully simpler, ones. Note that this strategy was used in both of the hypothetical syntheses, although there were substantial differences in the detailed facts and relationships upon which the strategy relied. One interesting aspect of the formalization activity in our domains is that it seems more concerned with incompleteness than with inconsistency in the original informal specification. This seems to be because individual programs in our domains are relatively small and inconsistencies in the specifications are less likely to occur. On the other hand, issues of inconsistency do arise with respect to the domain knowledge base, especially because of the empirical nature of much of the knowledge. During the formalization activity, this would be reflected in alternative relationships that could be used in the postconditions. The selection among such alternatives must be made on the basis of assumptions or preferences expressed by the user.

The implementation activity is largely concerned with computational tractability and efficiency. The basic goal is to determine a program that performs a precisely defined task. In trying to determine such a program, knowledge of programming techniques and mathematics plays a central role, although knowledge of the domain is occasionally required. The overall process is one of gradual refinement, ending when the program description involves only concepts that are available in the target language. The basic strategy involves considering each of the components of the specification. If the component is already in an algorithmic form, then refine the algorithm by using refinement rules, selecting among alternative rules on the basis of efficiency considerations. If the component is not yet an algorithm, try to use mathematical rules or techniques to find a different but equivalent description, with the hope that it will be more amenable to direct translation into an algorithmic form. At various times during the implementation activity, it may also be advantageous to apply optimizing transformations to the algorithm.

## B. Program Descriptions

Formalization and implementation manipulate descriptions of partially written programs. There are three qualitatively different types of descriptions.

An *Informal Specification* is an imprecise, incomplete description of the program to be written.

A *Formal Specification* is a precise description of the program's inputs and outputs and the relationship that they must satisfy.

An *Algorithm*, either abstract or concrete, is a procedural description of a technique for computing the outputs from the inputs.

An informal specification is a description of the problem to be solved, including inputs, outputs, assumptions, and some of the constraints that must be satisfied. Such a description is informal in that it may be incomplete (e.g., not enough information to compute the outputs from the inputs) or not quite correct (e.g., some inputs may be missing, others unnecessary). Such a description may involve many domain-specific concepts. The formalization activity manipulates such descriptions; for example, it may add more information, such as the fact that an additional input is required. Some of the manipulations may be domain-specific; for example, the system may determine that a desired log can be computed only if an additional assumption is made (e.g., that the rock formation consists of a specific set of minerals).

A formal specification consists of inputs, outputs, preconditions, and postconditions. The pre- and postconditions are formal statements, generally in mathematical terms, of the relationships that may be assumed about the inputs and that must be satisfied by the outputs. Formal specifications are produced by the formalization activity when problem statements have been made complete and precise enough to be rendered in a mathematical style. During the implementation activity, a formal specification may be reformulated several times in order to find a formal specification that may be translated directly into an algorithm. Our approach to formal specification is quite similar to that of traditional automatic programming work in the use of preconditions and postconditions. However, our approach differs from recent nontraditional specification languages (e.g., GIST [10]) in that we do not include constructs with side-effects.

An algorithm consists of inputs, outputs, and a procedure for computing the outputs from the inputs. It includes control structures and imperative operations, as well as applicative ones. During the implementation activity, an algorithm may range from abstract to concrete: the formal specification is initially transformed into an abstract algorithm which is then refined into a concrete algorithm. The difference between the abstract and concrete levels lies in the data types and operators. In fact, there is a spectrum of data types, ranging from the most abstract (e.g., sets and mappings) to the most concrete (e.g., lists and arrays), with intermediate levels in between (e.g., sequences). The implementation activity replaces the abstract concepts by slightly more refined ones (e.g., refine a set into a sequence) until concrete data structures and operators are determined. This part of the implementation activity would be similar to the algorithm refinement techniques used by PSISYN [11]. The implementation activity continues until the description is expressed solely in terms of concepts available in the target language. There may be considerable variation in the concepts used at this level, since different languages support different constructs (e.g., lists are available in Lisp, but not in Pascal). Although most of the data types are relatively general, some may be domain-specific (e.g., a well log). The domain-specific data types are primarily used early in the implementation activity.

Although we may distinguish among these three types of program description, it seems important to have a notation that spans all of them. That is, an automatic programming system should manipulate program descriptions in a wide-spectrum language [12]. There are two major reasons. First, the system must be able to develop different components of the program at different rates. For example, it may be wise to implement one component, in order to ensure that it is possible to do so, before attempting to work on another. Second, the system must include a variety of mechanisms that operate on program descriptions, for example, to perform efficiency analysis or symbolic execution. These are most easily built if there is a single coherent language upon which they can operate. Since all three types of program descriptions include typed inputs and outputs, one way to combine the levels into a wide-spectrum language would be to connect the components together through the flow of data values from one component to another. That is, the description of a partially developed program would consist of a data flow network whose components may be descriptions at any of the three levels. Our use of data flow links is similar to that of the plan calculus used in the Programmer's Apprentice [13], except that we restrict the use of operations with side-effects and that we have not yet found a need for purpose links.

## C. Representing the Knowledge

Given the two programming activities and the three types of program descriptions, it is now possible to state more precisely how the various areas of knowledge might be represented for use by an automatic programming system.

Programming knowledge would be represented in several different ways. Domain-independent problem-solving heuristics would be represented as pattern-action rules, where the patterns are informal specifications and the actions are decompositions into other specifications. Knowledge about the relationship between formal specifications and algorithms would be represented as rules whose patterns are formal specifications and whose actions produce abstract algorithms that compute outputs from inputs. Knowledge about data types and operators would be represented in a hierarchically structured knowledge base (e.g., in a language like STROBE [14]). Knowledge about implementing the data types and operators would be represented as refinement rules whose patterns are expressions involving the data types and operators and whose actions are expressions involving more concrete or rearranged constructs. The data types and rules would be quite similar to the rules used by PECOS [15], [16] or the plan equivalences used by the Programmer's Apprentice [17]. Although not required for the hypothetical syntheses given earlier, additional knowledge about programming would include algorithms to perform efficiency analysis [18] or symbolic execution [19], [20].

Domain knowledge would also be represented in several ways. Basic facts and relationships would be represented as structured objects, and stored in a knowledge base. Domain-specific problem-solving heuristics would be represented in a fashion similar to the domain-independent problem-solving heuristics. Finally, knowledge of domain-specific data types would be represented as extensions to the system's knowledge of domain-independent data types and refinement rules. Although we can identify these specific representations for domain knowledge, it seems likely that, in addition, a more general facility (e.g., RML [21]) will also be required.

Mathematical knowledge would be represented primarily in a procedural fashion, as algorithms that perform the desired manipulations, such as solving equation systems or simplifying expressions.

Finally, knowledge about the target language would be represented essentially as a filter on the allowability of refinements into data types and operators. That is, different programming languages support different base level data types and operators; those that are inappropriate for a given target language would simply be tagged as such. Knowledge about the syntax of the target language would be represented as a translator from the lower levels of the wide-spectrum language into the textual form required by the target language's compiler or interpreter. Finally, knowledge about the execution costs of the various operators in different languages would be stored in the operator hierarchy. Knowledge about the software architecture would be represented in a way similar to knowledge of the target language. For example, processes would be tagged as an inappropriate implementation technique for programs intended for use on an architecture that does not support multiple processes.

## D. Using the Knowledge

Based on the representations just described, it is now possible to describe how each of the programming activities, formalization and implementation, would use the knowledge to write programs. Both activities are best modeled in terms of transformations on program descriptions. That is, each starts with a program description and transforms it gradually into the desired result of that activity.

Given an informal specification, the formalization activity would first search through its knowledge base of relationships to find one (or several) that could be used to constrain the inputs and outputs. If suitable relationships could not be found (perhaps because of resource limitations on the search), the system would search through a presumably smaller set of problem-solving heuristics, looking for one whose pattern matched the informal specification. If successful, the specification would be decomposed and the parts considered separately. If unsuccessful, the system would be forced to abandon this path.

Given a formal specification, the implementation activity would search its body of rules for translating specifications into algorithms. If none are found, the system would try to use its repertoire of mathematical techniques to rearrange the program description in order to find a description that would be more amenable to translation into algorithmic form. Once an abstract algorithm has been determined, the system would search through its body of refinement rules for those that match various components of the algorithm (instances of data types or operators) and that are on paths toward concrete concepts that are appropriate for the given target language. If none are found, the system would have to abandon this approach and consider an alternative path; if one is found, it would be applied; if several are found, efficiency analysis or heuristics would be invoked in order to choose among them. The refinement process would continue until the program description consisted solely of concepts that are appropriate to the target language, at which point a translator from the program description language into the syntax of the target language would be used to produce the final code that implements the original informal specification.

As suggested by the above descriptions, there is actually a tree of program descriptions to be explored. The successors of a node in the tree are determined by the transformations that are applicable to that node. An interesting point of comparison between the two activities is that the trees associated with them are qualitatively different. The formalization tree is broad and shallow with many dead-ends; the implementation tree is narrow and deep with relatively few dead-ends. Thus, the strategy for formalization is aimed at finding any successful path, while the strategy for implementation is aimed at eliminating as soon as possible paths that lead to inefficient implementations. An extended discussion of the issues that arise when considering the entire tree of descriptions is available elsewhere [11], as are discussions of other transformation systems [22]–[24].

### E. Evolution of Knowledge

One of the interesting characteristics of our application domains, as well as most other domains, is that the knowledge of the domains evolves over time. One consequence of the separation of the programming process into the formalization and implementation activities is that different types of changes in the knowledge lead to changes in different activities. For example, recent experiments suggest that a different sonic transit time equation would be more accurate than that used in the first hypothetical synthesis. This would be reflected by a change in one of the postconditions of the formal specification, followed by a rederivation of the program. Thus, both formalization and implementation would be affected. Another interesting source of change relates to the computer systems on which the software runs: as more advanced computer systems become available, software written for the one system must be converted to run under another. For example, if the new system supported multiple processes, the feedback loop in the second hypothetical synthesis would be implemented as a separately executing process with an internal state. Thus, the formal specification would not be changed, so only the implementation activity would be affected. In both of these cases, the framework described earlier lends itself to recording the various decisions that were made initially during either activity, which would in turn support the selective rederivation of a program to reflect either type of change. More detailed discussions of the rederivation issue are available elsewhere [25].

### V. Discussion

One of the central aspects of the framework described in Section IV is the characterization of two programming activities, formalization and implementation. Traditionally, research in automatic programming has focused on the second of these activities. For example, most work in the deductive paradigm (e.g., the work of Manna and Waldinger and others [26], [27]) addresses primarily the early part of the implementation activity. Work within the knowledge-based paradigm (e.g., PSISYN [11]) has generally focused on refining abstract algorithms into concrete algorithms. However, it seems clear that the formalization activity is also necessary if we are to build an automatic programming system satisfying the definition given in the first section of this paper. There are several reasons. First, a formal specification by its very definition must be complete and precise. Second, a formal specification language would probably not be considered natural to a computationally naive user. Finally, most formal specification languages require the same sort of care and attention to detail that traditional programming requires: "No matter how high the level, its's still programming" [28]. Thus, the amount of work required to produce a formal specification is likely to be comparable to that required to write a traditional program. Although formal specifications would free the user from excessive concern with efficiency, and would relieve some of the burdens of maintenance, the overall productivity gain would not approach the gains that would be achieved by building an automatic programming system that performs formalization as well as implementation. Thus, our motivation for using an informal specification is similar to that of the SAFE project [29], which included a pseudonatural language informal specification language, and a procedural formal specification language.

It has been argued elsewhere (e.g., by Swartout and Balzer [30]) that the two activities are inevitably mixed together. In fact, there is a growing belief in the software engineering community that formalization in the absence of implementation is not possible because of the difficulty of formalizing the right set of requirements. Without feedback from experimenting with an implementation, it is impossible to be certain that the specification specifies the program that the user really wants. Why then do we make the distinction? The primary reason is that it seems important to preserve a precise description of the software that is independent of the software itself. As a simple example, the problem of converting a body of software from one computational environment to another would be simplified considerably by the existence of a high-level description of the software. Therefore, the use of a formal specification seems important enough to single it out during the development process. A secondary reason is that the two activities of formalization and implementation are qualitatively different. Formalization is concerned with determining a precise description of what the software should do. Implementation is concerned with determining an efficient way to do it. Thus, the characterization of the two activities seems appropriate and useful. For similar reasons, a comparable distinction is also made in the proposal for a Knowledge-Based Software Assistant [31] that is intended for use in many different domains. Note, however, that the use of a wide-spectrum language actually permits the two activities to be mixed together: one component of an informal specification could be fully implemented before another component is even fully specified. Therefore, the distinction does not prevent the intertwining.

In many ways, the formalization activity is analogous to recent work in algorithm design [27], [32], [33]. For example, the Designer system also deals with intermediate states that are informal and imprecise. The greatest difference seems to be that the source of difficulty in our domains is somewhat different from that in the mathematical domains that are usually the subject of algorithm design work. In the case of the mathematical domains, there usually seems to be a need for some creative insight or discovery, some kind of "Eureka!" In our domains, the major difficulty is simply the large amount of domain knowledge that must be understood and applied.

Another automatic programming issue that has received considerable attention involves the interaction between the implementations of different components of a program [11], [34], [35]. Different components must be implemented in such a way that they do not interfere with each other, and cooperate when necessary. To date, this appears not to be a major issue in our domains. There seem to be two reasons for this. First, for the types of abstract algorithms with which we are concerned, there are often relatively few choices to be considered and their implications seem to be within a component more than outside of it. For example, the selection of a search algorithm for the command encoder of the sonic feedback loop could be made without concern about interference with the computation of the ideal gain value. Second, there are standard representations of the data (e.g., logs) to be passed between components. This further reduces the possibilities for unplanned interactions. A related automatic programming issue involves constraint propagation. In our domains, it seems likely that some form of constraint propagation will be important, especially for dealing with exceptional conditions. One form in which it might be incorporated would be in a mechanism for symbolic execution [20]. Both of these issues, interaction among components and constraint propagation arise, not only in software design, but also in other types of design [36].

Recent work in application program generators has also been aimed at domain-specific special-purpose automatic programming systems [37]. These are generally characterized by domain-specific specification languages, usually with a simple syntax, and algorithmic techniques for producing code from these languages. In such a generator, the language and algorithms amount to an implicit embodiment of the required domain and programming knowledge. In our domain, such an approach is inadequate for two reasons. First, there is considerable variability in the programs that must be written. Even programs whose specifications are superficially similar may be implemented in significantly different ways. The reasons for this variability include mathematical considerations (e.g., not all systems of equations can be solved explicitly), domain considerations (e.g., light hydrocarbons should be treated differently from heavy hydrocarbons), and programming considerations (e.g., different implementations may be more or less efficient in different circumstances). Such variability is often a difficulty for algorithmic techniques in which assumptions about the domain are implicit in procedure bodies. Second, our domains require qualitative reasoning. For example, a volumetric analysis program generally presupposes assumptions about what materials are present in the formation. This is especially important for dealing with exceptional conditions, as illustrated by $\varphi_0$ ("phi-naught"), an application generator for certain classes of interpretation programs [2]. $\varphi_0$ worked quite well for single interpretation models, but was less helpful when the model was not applicable or produced implausible results.

Work on DRACO [38] has also emphasized the use of domain knowledge. DRACO includes a mechanism for defining models of new domains in terms of previously defined domains. In particular, DRACO enables the definition of domain-specific constructs and the description of refinements of those constructs in other domains. Experience with DRACO supports the belief that realistic real-world domains require substantial amounts of domain-knowledge; for example, the domain model for one rather specific domain (tactical display systems) was over 100 pages long. In terms of the distinction between the formalization and implementation activities, DRACO seems to be focused primarily on the second.

A final point of comparison is with the PSI project [39]. PSI's distinction between acquisition and synthesis was similar to our distinction between formalization and implementation except that PSI's intermediate level was more algorithmic than our formal specification language. PSI also included a "domain expert" in its initial design, but this was eventually absorbed into the Program Model Builder [40], one of the components of PSI's acquisition phase. Thus, PSI placed considerably less emphasis on domain knowledge.

In conclusion, the ΦNIX effort has some similarities with previous work in automatic programming, but the domains in which we have pursued our research have led to some substantial differences. The key distinction of our domains seems to be that the complexity is due to the sheer volume of domain knowledge that is involved, rather than to the domain-independent algorithm and data structure choices that the software embodies. A second important characteristic is that much of that knowledge seems to be important for many different programs within the domain. These both seem to be characteristics of many real-world domains, so there is some reason to hope that the domain-specific directions being pursued by the ΦNIX project will have relevance outside of our domains.

### ACKNOWLEDGMENT

This paper reflects the individual and collective insights of many people. I would especially like to acknowledge the contributions of the current members of the Software Research group at SDR: P. Barth, P. Dietz, R. Dinitz, S. Greenspan, and E. Kant.

### REFERENCES

[1] D. Barstow, R. Duffey, S. Smoliar, and S. Vestal, "An overview of ΦNIX," *Amer. Ass. Artificial Intell.*, Pittsburgh, PA, Aug. 1982.

[2] D. Barstow, R. Duffey, S. Smoliar, and S. Vestal, "An automatic programming system to support an experimental science," in *Proc. 6th Int. Conf. Software Eng.*, Tokyo, Japan, Sept. 1982, pp. 360–366.

[3] R. Duffey and S. Smoliar, "From geological knowledge to computational relationships: A case study of the expertise of programming," in *Proc. Workshop Program Transformation and Programming Environments*, Munich, West Germany, Sept. 1983.

[4] D. Barstow, "A perspective on automatic programming," *Artificial Intell. Mag.*, vol. 5, no. 1, pp. 5–27, Spring 1984.

[5] ——, "Automatic programming for streams," in *Proc. 9th Int. Joint Conf. Artificial Intell.*, Los Angeles, CA, Aug. 1985.

[6] G. Archie, "The electrical resistivity log as an aid in determining some reservoir characteristics," *Petroleum Technol.*, vol. 5, no. 1, Jan. 1942.

[7] R. Floyd, "Toward interactive design of correct programs," *Inform. Processing 71*, Int. Federation Inform. Processing Soc., 1971.

[8] C. Green and D. Barstow, "A hypothetical dialogue exhibiting a knowledge base for a program understanding system," in *Machine Intelligence 8*, E. Elcock and D. Michie, Eds. New York: Ellis Horwood and Wiley, 1976, pp. 335–359.

[9] M. Wylie, A. Gregory, and G. Gardner, "An experimental investigation of factors affecting elastic wave velocities in porous media," *Geophys.*, vol. 23, no. 3, July 1958.

[10] R. Balzer, N. Goldman, and D. Wile, "Final report on GIST," Inform. Sci. Inst., Univ. Southern California, Los Angeles, Tech. Rep., 1981.

[11] E. Kant and D. Barstow, "The refinement paradigm: the interaction of coding and efficiency knowledge in program synthesis," *IEEE Trans. Software Eng.*, vol. 7, pp. 458–471, Sept. 1981; reprinted in *Interactive Programming Environments*, D. Barstow, H. Shrobe, and E. Sandewall, Eds. New York: McGraw-Hill, 1984.

[12] CIP Language Group, *The Munich Project CIP. Volume I: The Wide Spectrum Language CIP-L* (Lecture Notes in Computer Science, Vol. 183). New York: Springer-Verlag, 1985.

[13] C. Rich, "Inspection methods in programming," Massachusetts Inst. Technol., Cambridge, Tech. Rep. MIT/AI/TR-604, Aug. 1981.

[14] R. Smith, "Structured object programming in Strobe," Research Note, Schlumberger-Doll Res., Ridgefield, CT, Mar. 1984.

[15] D. Barstow, "An experiment in knowledge-based automatic programming," *Artificial Intell. J.*, vol. 12, no. 2, pp. 73–119, Aug. 1979.

[16] ——, *Knowledge-Based Program Construction*. New York: Elsevier-North-Holland, 1979.

[17] C. Rich and H. Shrobe, "Initial report on a LISP programmer's apprentice," *IEEE Trans. Software Eng.*, vol. 4, pp. 456–467, Nov. 1978; reprinted in *Interactive Programming Environments*, D. Barstow, H. Shrobe, and E. Sandwell, Eds. New York: McGraw-Hill, 1984.

[18] E. Kant, *Efficiency in Program Synthesis*. Ann Arbor, MI: UMI Research Press, 1981.

[19] D. Cohen, "A forward inference engine to aid in understanding specifications," *Amer. Ass. Artificial Intell.*, Austin, TX, Aug. 1984, pp. 56–60.

[20] D. Steier and E. Kant, "Symbolic execution in algorithm design," in *Proc. 9th Int. Joint Conf. Artificial Intell.*, Los Angeles, CA, Aug. 1985.

[21] A. Borgida, S. Greenspan, and J. Mylopoulos, "Knowledge representation as the basis for requirements specifications," *Computer*, vol. 18, no. 4, pp. 82–91, Apr. 1985.

[22] R. Balzer, "Transformational programming: An example," *IEEE Trans. Software Eng.*, vol. 7, pp. 3–14, Jan. 1981.

[23] S. Fickas, "Automating the transformational development of software," Dep. Comput. Sci., Univ. California, Tech. Rep., 1982.

[24] H. Partsch and R. Steinbruggen, "Program transformation systems," *ACM Comput. Surveys*, vol. 15, no. 3, pp. 199–236, Sept. 1983.

[25] D. Wile, "Program developments as formal objects," Inform. Sci. Inst., Univ. Southern California, Los Angeles, Tech. Rep., 1981.

[26] A. Biermann, G. Guiho, and Y. Kodratoff, Eds., *Automatic Program Construction Techniques*. New York: Macmillan, 1984.

[27] D. Smith, "Top-down synthesis of divide and conquer algorithms," *Artificial Intell. J.*, to be published.

[28] S. Smoliar and D. Barstow, "Who needs languages and why do they need them? Or: no matter how high the level, it's still programming," *SIGPLAN Notices*, vol. 18, no. 6, pp. 149–157, June 1983.

[29] R. Balzer, N. Goldman, and D. Wile, "Informality in program specifications," *IEEE Trans. Software Eng.*, vol. 4 pp. 94–103, Mar. 1978.

[30] W. Swartout and R. Balzer, "On the inevitable intertwining of specification and implementation," *Commun. ACM*, vol. 25, no. 7, pp. 438–440, July 1982.

[31] R. Balzer, T. Cheatham, and C. Green, "Software technology in the 1990's: Using a new paradigm," *Computer*, vol. 16, no. 11, pp. 39–45, Nov. 1983.

[32] D. Barstow, "The roles of knowledge and deduction in algorithm design," in *Machine Intelligence 10*, J. Hayes, D. Michie, and Y.-H. Pao, Eds. New York: Ellis Horwood and Wiley, 1982, pp. 361–381; reprinted in *Automatic Program Construction Techniques*, A. Biermann, G. Guihon, and Y. Kodratoff, Eds. New York: Macmillan, 1984.

[33] E. Kant, "Understanding and automating algorithm design," in *Proc. 9th Int. Conf. Artificial Intell.*, Los Angeles, CA, Aug. 1985.

[34] H. Shrobe, "Dependency directed reasoning for complex program understanding," Massachusetts Inst. Technol., Cambridge, Tech. Rep. MIT/AI/TR-503, Apr. 1979.

[35] G. Sussman, *A Computer Model of Skill Acquisition*. New York: Elsevier-North-Holland, 1975.

[36] J. Mostow, "Toward better models of the design process," *Artificial Intell. Mag.*, vol. 6, no. 1, pp. 44–57, Spring 1985.

[37] J. Rice, *Build Program Technique: A Practical Approach for the Development of Automatic Software Generation Systems*. New York: Wiley-Interscience, 1981.

[38] J Neighbors, "The DRACO approach to constructing software from reusable components," in *Proc. Workshop Reusability in Programming*, Newport, RI, Sept. 1983, pp. 167–178.

[39] C. Green, "A summary of the PSI program synthesis system," in *Proc. 5th Int. Joint Conf. Artificial Intell.*, Cambridge, MA, Aug. 1977.

[40] B. McCune, "Building program models incrementally from informal specifications," Dep. Comput. Sci., Stanford Univ., Stanford, CA, Tech. Rep., 1979.

[41] D. Barstow, H. Shrobe, and E. Sandewall, Eds., *Interactive Programming Environments*. New York: McGraw-Hill, 1984.

**David R. Barstow** received the B.A. degree in mathematics from Carleton College, Northfield, MN, in 1969 and the M.S. and Ph.D. degrees in computer science from Stanford University, Stanford, CA, in 1971 and 1977, respectively.

From 1977 to 1980 he was on the faculty of the Department of Computer Science, Yale University, New Haven, CT. Since 1980 he has been a member of the Professional Staff of Schlumberger-Doll Research, Ridgefield, CT. His research interests are in the areas of artificial intelligence and programming environments, with a focus on automatic programming.

Dr. Barstow is a member of the Association for Computing Machinery, the IEEE Computer Society, and the American Association for Artificial Intelligence.

# Qualitative modelling and learning in KARDIO

Ivan Bratko

Faculty of Electrical Engineering and Computer Science,
and J. Stefan Institute
Ljubljana, Yugoslavia

## Abstract

Deep knowledge and machine learning are usually considered to be the distinguishing features of second generation expert systems. This paper reviews the use of deep qualitative knowledge and machine learning in the context of the KARDIO system for ECG diagnosis of cardiac arrhythmias. Techniques applied to construct and manipulate a complex knowledge base in KARDIO are discussed in the view of the following themes: use of logic-based formalisms for qualitative modelling, transformations between deep model and surface representations, transformations aiming at improved transparency, 'knowledge-acquisition cycle' based on these transformations, introducing hierarchy into a qualitative model, machine learning to aid the construction of a qualitative model.

## 1 Introduction

KARDIO is an expert system for electrocardiographic (ECG) diagnosis of cardiac arrhythmias. More precisely, the problem is stated as: given a symbolic, *qualitative description* of the patient's ECG, find the disorders in the patient's heart that could have causesd this ECG.

From the research point of view, KARDIO has become more interesting as an experimental testbed for techniques and ideas that are usually associated with second generation expert systems. According to Steels (1985) deep knowedge and machine learning are the distinguishing features of second generation expert systems. The most important vehicles in the KARDIO project were the use of deep, qualitative knowledge, and machine learning. In particular, qualitative modelling in association with the 'knowledge-acquisition cycle' in KARDIO, discussed later, is applicable as a knowledge acquisition paradigm to many other problem areas. This KARDIO paradigm has been, for example, adapted in the development of expert systems for the diagnosis of a satellite power system (Pearce 1988), and the diagnosis of a robot hardware/software environment (Pearce, 1989).

The paper reviews the following themes from KARDIO:

- Use of logic-based formalisms for qualitative modelling
- Transformations between deep model and surface representations
- Knowledge transformations aiming at improved transparency
- 'Knowledge-acquisition cycle' based on these transformations
- Introducing hierarchy into a qualitative model
- Machine learning to aid the construction of a qualitative model

Various points of interest are discussed and illustrated by simplified examples from KARDIO. A description of the full technical details will appear in (Bratko, Mozetic and Lavrac 1989).

## 2 KARDIO knowledge-acquisition cycle

The main difficulty in diagnosing heart disorders, called arrhythmias, lies in their combinatorial nature. The situation is similar to the diagnosis of technical systems where the problem is much easier if single faults only are assumed. Usually the problem becomes much more difficult if multiple faults can be present simultaneously because it is difficult to take into account the interactions between all possible combinations of faults.

*Fifth Australian Conference on Applications of Expert Systems*
*Sydney, May 1989*

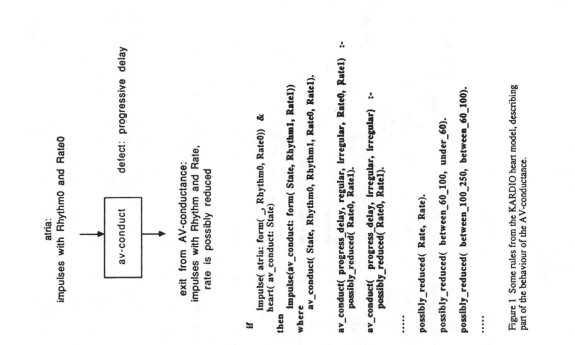

atria:
impulses with Rhythm0 and Rate0

av-conduct          defect: progressive delay

exit from AV-conductance:
impulses with Rhythm and Rate,
rate is possibly reduced

```
if
    Impulse( atria: form(_, Rhythm0, Rate0)) &
    heart( av_conduct: State)
then
    Impulse(av_conduct: form( State, Rhythm1, Rate1))
where
    av_conduct( State, Rhythm0, Rhythm1, Rate0, Rate1).

av_conduct( progress_delay, regular, irregular, Rate0, Rate1) :-
    possibly_reduced( Rate0, Rate1).
av_conduct( progress_delay, irregular, irregular) :-
    possibly_reduced( Rate0, Rate1).
.....
possibly_reduced( Rate, Rate).
possibly_reduced( between_60_100, under_60).
possibly_reduced( between_100_250, between_60_100).
.....
```

Figure 1 Some rules from the KARDIO heart model, describing part of the behaviour of the AV-conductance.

There are 30 single disorders in KARDIO. They can combine and the combinatorial number of possible situations grows exponentially with the number of simultaneous disorders. To cope with these numerous potentially possible situations, KARDIO uses a deep qualitative model of the heart that allows the simulation of any combination of basic disorders.

The model is represented essentially in logic. Figure 1 shows some example rules from the heart model, together with a schematic illustration of part of the electrical system of the heart that these rules are concerned with. The syntax is that of Edinburgh Prolog. The symbols 'if', 'then' etc. are assumed to be defined as operators.

The model can be used for predicting the consequences of defects in the heart, and also, although less efficiently, for ECG diagnosis. The model was compiled into other representations that are advantageous from certains points of view (transparency, explicitness, diagnostic efficiency). These transformations form the 'knowledge- acquisition cycle' shown in Figure 2.

The arrhytmia-ECG base is a direct, surface relation between (combinations of) arrhythmias and their ECG manifestations. This relation can be viewed as an extensional representation of the model, and was derived from the model by exhaustive simulation. It is represented as a Prolog program consisting of 8314 clauses. These cover all physiologically possible and 'medically interesting' combinations of defects and their possible ECG manifestations. The word 'possible' here is meant relative to the scope of the KARDIO deep model. Of course, there exist details that are not covered by the model. It was found by exhaustive simulation that there are about 2400 combinations of disorders possible at the model's level of detail. These combinations of disorders are manifested in about 140 000 ECG descriptions. Several different ECGs can be caused by the same combination of disorders - a consequence of the fact that the model is non-deterministic.

The arrhythmia-ECG base can be efficiently used for diagnosis and prediction, but it falls short of conceptual structure. With its 8314 Prolog clauses which, if stored as a text file, occupy 5 MB on disk it is a bit impractical for some applications requirements. But more important, its mere complexity renders the contents of this knowledge-base difficult to study and understand as a whole by a human because it is too much just a flat mass of facts. This knowledge base is therefore also difficult to compare with the conventional medical codifications of the electrocardiographic knowledge.

Therefore an attempt was made to find a more compact representation of the arrhythmia-ECG base that would still allow efficient ECG diagnosis. This corresponds to the induction step in Figure 2 which aims at conceptualising the contents of the arrhythmia-ECG base so that it would become mentally manageable by a human expert. The expert would then be able to see not only individual facts, but also the 'whole'. The result of transformation is a largely compressed and still equivalent representation. Among the representations in Figure 2, this representation is the most suitable for human experts to study and compare with the existing human codifications of the same knowledge. Such comparison offers a powerful possibility for knowledge validation. At this point errors in the **deep model** or slips in the medical literature are easiest to catch. Therefore this representation closes our '**knowledge-acquisition cycle**', providing a feedback loop for verifying and correcting the **deep model**, and helps to **expose blemishes in the corresponding literature. It can thus help to improve the exist-ing, human codifications of knowledge.**

## 3 Compression aiming at improved comprehensibility

The main idea for compression (induction step in Figure 2) was to use the arrhythmia-ECG base as a source of examples and to use inductive learning program to obtain their compact descriptions. Various inductive learning programs were used in this and final results were obtained with NEWGEM (Mozetic 1985) that learns attribute-based descriptions (propositional logic level).

By leaving out here considerable technical detail, the compression procedure was roughly as follows. The arrhythmia-ECG base comprises rules of the form:

**Combined_arrhythmia ⟹ ECG_description**

The goal of learning was to convert this information into rules of two forms:

(1) Compressed *prediction rules* that answer the question: What ECGs may be caused by a given disorder in a heart's component?

(2) Compressed *diagnostic rules* that answer the question: What heart disorders are indicated by a given ECG feature?

For synthesising prediction rules, the learning examples were pairs of the form:

**(Selected_disorder, ECG_description)**

Such pairs ware obtained from the arrhythmia-ECG base as an abstraction of the arrhythmia-ECG relation: omiting all but one of the disorders in a combination of disorders. A 'selected disorder' (the one that is *not* omitted) is for example: atrial focus is in the tachycardic state. From the point of view of the learning program, the disorder is the class, and the ECG desription is the vector of attribute values. For the synthesis of diagnostic rules, the learning examples were pairs of the form:

**(Selected_ECG_feature, Combined_arrhythmia)**

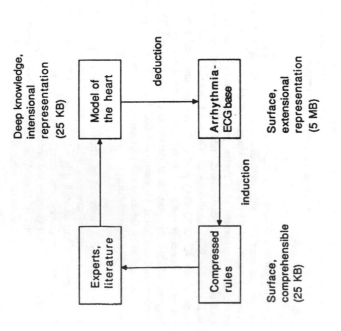

Figure 2  Knowledge-acquisition cycle in KARDIO

Deep knowledge, intensional representation (25 KB)

Model of the heart

deduction

Arrhythmia-ECG base

Surface, extensional representation (5 MB)

induction

Experts, literature

Compressed rules

Surface, comprehensible (25 KB)

where a 'selected ECG feature' is for example: P wave has abnormal shape.

As the result of learning from examples of the forms above, representations for diagnosis and prediction were obtained, each of size 25 KB. This gives the compression factor of 200 with respect to the original representation. It should be noted that learning was only used here as a representation compression technique in which no generalisation actually occurred. Therefore the resulting compressed representations are completely equivalent to the original representation.

The most interesting question now is, how comprehensible these new representations are, and how easily they compare with the medical descriptions. Here is an example of a synthesised predictions rule which tells what are the characteristic features in the ECG signal in the case of the disorder called AV block of the third degree (avb3 for short, possibly combined with any number of other defects in the heart):

```
[av_conduct = avb3]  is characterised by
[rhythm_QRS = regular] &
[relation_P_QRS = independent_P_QRS]
```

This rule is in the VL1 formalism, normally used in the AQ family of programs (Michalski 1983). The propositions have the form *[attribute = value]*. Figure 3 illustrates what essentially happens in the case of the avb3 defect. For comparison, one of the classical books on ECG (Goldman 1976) describes this arrhythmia as follows:

In this condition the atria and ventricles beat entirely *independently* of one another. ... The ventricular *rhythm* is usually quite *regular* but at a much slower rate (20-60).

Some words here are in italics to help the comparison between Goldman's description and the machine synthesised description. It is easy to notice strong similarities between both descriptions. It is nice that even the same qualitative descriptors, such as *independent* or *regular* appear in both descriptions. Goldman notices that the ventricular rate is usually much lower (20-60) which is not mentioned in the machine description. This is in fact the only essential difference between both descriptions. The reason that the ventricular rate is not mentioned in the machine description is that it is redundant with respect to distinguishing between those conditions of the heart in which avb3 appears, and those in which it does not. Another authority on ECG, Phibbs (1973) describes avb3 as:

1. The atrial and ventricular *rates are different*: the atrial rate is faster; the ventricular rate is slow and *regular*. 2. There is *no consistent relation between P waves and QRS complexes*.

Again, some descriptors are in italics to facilitate comparison that is also in this case rather straightforward.

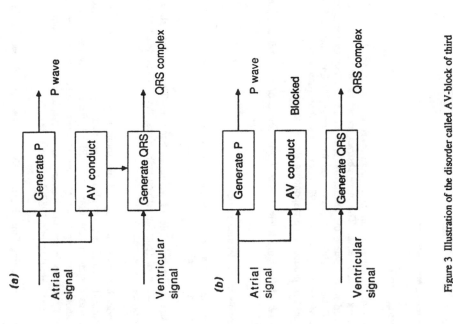

*(a)*

Atrial signal → Generate P → P wave
AV conduct
Ventricular signal → Generate QRS → QRS complex

*(b)*

Atrial signal → Generate P → P wave
AV conduct → Blocked
Ventricular signal → Generate QRS → QRS complex

**Figure 3** Illustration of the disorder called AV-block of third degree. (a) In the normal heart, the atrial signal reaches the ventricles through the AV-conductance and thus affects the QRS complex. (b) AV-conductance is totally blocked and the atrial signal does not reach the ventricles.

The examples above show how well some of the synthesised descriptions correspond to those in the standard medical literature. On the other hand, some of the synthesised descriptions are considerably more complex than those in the literature. Machine-generated descriptions in such cases give much more detail that may not be necessary for an intelligent reader with a physiological background. Such a reader can usually infer the missing detail from his or her background knowledge. However, the additional details must still be made explicit in the case of computer application in the form of a diagnostic expert system. Otherwise a lot of background knowledge and inference would have to be added.

Below is an example of a synthesised diagnostic rule that corresponds to a particular feature in the ECG, characterised by that some P waves are not followed (as normally) by the corresponding QRS complexes.

[relation_P_QRS = after_P_some QRS_missing]    is characterised by
[av_conduct = wenkebach v mobitz2]
v
[av_conduct = normal] &
[atrial_focus = atrial_flutter v atrial_fibrillation]

The rule states that this abnormal ECG feature is indicative of the defects in the AV conductance, called Wenkebach or Mobitz 2, or, when the AV conductance is normal, of the atrial flutter or fibrillation. The rule thus indicates what kinds of disorders the diagnostic system should be looking for in the case that this abnormality is detected in the ECG. Such rules thus suggest a goal-oriented strategy for investigating ECG features in the ECG interpretation processs.

## 4  Hierarchical model

The model of the heart can be viewed as a relation

model( Disorders, Manifestations)

The prediction task is: given disorders, find the corresponding manifestations. The corresponding execution of the model amounts essentially to simulation. The diagnostic task is the inverse: given manifestations, find the corresponding disorders. As the model is stated in logic, it is in principle possible to execute it in this inverse direction. However, the combinatorial complexity of running the model in the inverse direction, from manifestations to diagnoses, is much higher than in the forward, simulation mode. The difficulty stems from the fact that the branching factor when searching backward is much higher than when searching forward. Straightforward execution of the model for the diagnostic task is very much like the generate-and-test: for given

manifestations, hypothesise disorders and simulate the model to check if their manifestations match the given ones; repeat this until a hypothesis is found that produces the given manifestations.

One way to circumvent this difficulty was the compilation of the model as described earlier. Another idea is to improve the search performance by introducing a hierarchy into the model. So instead of only one model relation, we have several, indexed by their level of abstraction:

model( Level, Disorders, Manifestations)

where Level is an integer 1, 2, ... . The convention adapted is that the lower the level is, the more abstract the model is. So

model( 1, Disorders, Manifestations)

is the most abstract model.

Two models of the same system at adjacent levels of abstraction of course have to be consistent in a certain sense. The more abstract model has to be an abstraction of the more detailed model where the abstraction is obtained by applying some transformation rules. These principles of abstraction (or inversely: refinement) in KARDIO (developed by Mozetic, e.g. Mozetic 1988) can be stated as allowed abstraction operations on a model that produce a corresponding abstracted model:

(1) Replace a set of (possibly interconnected) components of the detailed model by a single component.

(2) Omit a variable in the detailed model.

(3) Replace the value of a variable at the detailed level by a more abstract (coarser) value; this entails a hierarchy of domain values of variables.

Figure 4 illustrates the principle of value abstraction. This example shows how through the abstraction of (possibly structured) values, the level of detail of the ECG signal description can be varied.

Such a model hierarchy can be used in various respects. For example, it can be used for adjusting the detail in the explanation generated by the system, and focussing the explanation as desired by the user. In KARDIO, the hierarchy has been used to make the diagnostic reasoning more efficient (Mozetic 1988; Mozetic, Bratko and Urbancic 1987), and to make the learning of a qualitative model from example behaviours more efficent (Mozetic 1987; Mozetic 1988).

In diagnostic reasoning, the hierarchy is exploited as follows: to solve the diagnostic task at some level L, the given manifestations are abstracted to level L-1. Then the simpler diagnostic task is solved at level L-1. The resulting solution at this level is then used to guide the search at level L. Of course, in solving the task at level L-1, further abstractions (if they exist) can be used. In Prolog this can be stated as:

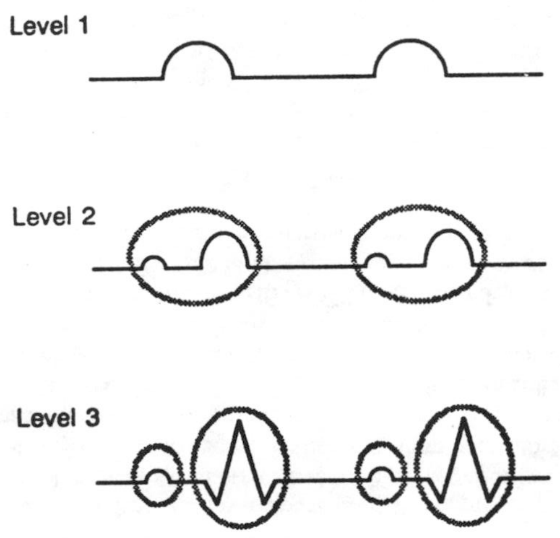

```
diagnose( Level, Manifest, Disorders) :-
    no_abstraction( Level, Manifest),          % Cannot be abstracted
    model( Level, Disorders, Manifest).

diagnose( Level, Manifest, Disorders) :-
    UpperLevel is Level - 1,
    type( model( DisType, ManType)),            % Type of arguments
    hierarchy( UpperLevel, ManType, AbstractManifest, Manifest),   %Level up
    diagnose( UpperLevel, AbstractManifest, AbstractDisorders),
    hierarchy( UpperLevel, DisType, AbstractDisorders, Disorders),  %Level down
    model( Level, Disorders, Manifest).
```

The relation

```
hierarchy( Level, Type, Value, RefinedValue)
```

specifies how a term Value of type Type at level Level is detailed at the next lower level of abstraction. It is important to notice that an item at the detailed level may have no abstract counterpart at the abstract level. This is not only the case when Level = 1, but is also possible at Level > 1. The first clause above handles such cases which are reduced to executing the naive model procedure.

The use of hierarchy for diagnosis is in the KARDIO domain experimentally compared with naive non-hierarchical diagnosis in Mozetic, Bratko and Urbancic (1987). In that paper, it is also shown how this hierarchical formalism can be applied as a generally applicable technique of logic programming to reduce combinatorial search in problems that render themselves to useful abstraction.

## 5 Learning qualitative models

Mozetic (1987; 1988) developed an integrated system (now called QuMAS) for machine-aided construction of qualitative models. It is integrated in that it combines a propositional type learning program as a basic induction machine, a logic debugging algorithm, and an interpreter for qualitative models. Using this system, he was able to interactively construct from examples the essential part of the KARDIO model of the heart. This is an illustration of potential usefulness of such a machine learning tool,

Level 1

Level 2

Level 3

Figure 4  Abstractions of a signal.

(1) *Initial stage*: initial hypotheses about the components are induced from initial examples; these hypotheses, the structure and background predicates constitute the current *model hypothesis*.

(2) *Debugging stage*: the current model hypothesis is executed on example inputs to the model. The hypothesis is then updated whenever this execution produces results different from those expected by the teacher. This process of gradual debugging continues until the designer feels confident about the model.

In the initial stage, the teacher provides the system with a set of examples of detailed causal traces, specifying exactly what happens in these examples with each component in the model. This is like introducing the problem through a number of selected detailed case studies, to give the learner some initial ideas about the targetted model. From these detailed traces the system extracts examples of behaviour of individual components. These examples are used for non-incremental learning that results in the initial hypothesis for each component.

In the debugging stage, the teacher does not provide detailed traces any more. Instead, only the input-output behaviour is monitored on new examples of input to the model. Whenever the current model hypothesis produces unexpected results, the teacher signals that an error has occurred. Then the system tries to locate the component responsible for the error. Once a possibly faulty component has been located, the system itself proposes ways to repair the component so that the new component hypothesis produces the correct result, and the behaviour of the new model is still consistent with all the previous examples. Alternative repair actions are checked with the teacher in a way that minimises the teacher's effort: the system generates a critical example of the newly hypothesised behaviour of the component. The teacher is asked to confirm or reject the proposed example behaviour. If this new hypothesised behaviour is confirmed then the corresponding correction is carried out. If the teacher rejects the proposal then a new repair action is considered. Confirmed critical behaviours are used as new learning examples to modify the current component hypothesis through (possibly incremental) learning.

Thus in debugging, the system itself generates corrective actions and requests confirmation from the teacher by asking only yes/no questions about the behaviour of the component in question. This style of debugging that greatly alleviates the teacher's task is facilitated by the use of typed logic.

Another feature that reduces the burden on the teacher is the use of hierarchy of models as explained in the previous section. Referring to a more abstract model also speeds up the learning process in a similar way as it helps diagnostic reasoning. More abstract models are learned first. As they are simpler, they are easier to learn. Then, when learning a more detailed model, the already learned abstract model is used to guide the debugging process at the detailed level. In particular, the abstract model is used to guide the generation of candidate critical examples of component behaviour

although in this particular case it was not of practical value because in this process nothing new was discovered that did not already exist in the original KARDIO model (although the representation was different from the one in the original model).

In Mozetic's system, the targeted model is represented as a set of logic clauses of *deductive hierarchical database* type (DHDB for short; Lloyd and Topor 1985). Such a clause is a Horn clause where the arguments of predicates are typed. The attribute 'hierarchical' here means that the calling relation between predicates is hierarchical, that is, predicates cannot be defined recursively. To avoid confusion with hierarchical models in KARDIO, we will be here referring to hierarchical database as *non-recursive database*.

This particular logic formalism was chosen for two reasons:

(1) The fact that the arguments are typed and their domains are finite enables correct implementation of negation (unlike Prolog).

(2) Non-recursiveness makes it possible that clauses are learned from examples essentially by a system that uses attribute descriptions and propositional logic.

The typing of arguments did not in any respect limit the expressiveness needed for the heart model. On the other hand, the correct handling of negation was important. It was also important that a propositional level learning system was possible to use as the basic induction machine because of computational efficiency of immediately available such systems. Mozetic used the NEWGEM program (Mozetic 1985) for this purpose, which was later developed into the better known AQ15 (Michalski et al. 1986). But other systems could be easily used instead, for example those of the TDIDT family (Quinlan 1986). One of this family, ASSISTANT (e.g. Cestnik et al. 1987) was in fact later plugged in instead of NEWGEM. The translation between attribute vectors, propositional descriptions and non-recursive database clauses is rather straightforward.

A *model* in the non-recursive database formalism is defined as a *set of components* that constitute the model, and *connections* between the components. The connections specify the *structure* of the model.

A model is with QuMAS constructed gradually through interaction between the model designer (teacher) and the system. Initially the system is provided with the structure of the model and, as background knowledge, a set of utility predicate definitions that it can use in the definitions of the components. In the structure, the components of the model are only mentioned, but their behaviour is not defined. Formally, each component is a predicate. The task of learning a model with QuMAS is to learn these predicates.

The learning of components progresses through two stages:

when reparing components. This again reduces the number of relevant yes/no questions asked of the teacher.

The effectiveness of learning is illustrated by the following figures from Mozetic's experiment. The target model had seven components. 25 detailed examples of traces were given to the system in the initial learning stage. When the initial learning was completed, the current model was able to correctly handle 65% of all possible inputs. In the debugging stage, 19 examples of inputs were needed before the target model (100%) emerged.

This indicates practical effectiveness of such machine-aided development of models. There are, however, two aspects of the modelling task in which the present system seems to be of little help. Before the learning can start the model designer has precisely to specify the following:

(1) the structure of the model, and

(2) all the details of the description language (domains of arguments of components).

In the case of KARDIO, it is realistic to expect that the model designer would have a sensible idea of the structure of the model because the medical literature is quite indicative in this respect. The second requirement, however, all the details of the description language, seems a much more difficult task. Of course, all this has to be done in traditional model development as well, but automating it would seem to be a very important improvement over Mozetic's system. A more powerful learning framework would be necessary for that. For example, the CIGOL program (Muggleton and Buntine 1988) that constructs new predicates could be used to help in the elicitation of the model structure (propose new components to be introduced into the structure).

## 6 Comparison with other approaches to qualitative modelling

The process modelled in KARDIO is among the most complex (if not *the* most complex) til now modelled qualitatively. Traditional exercises in qualitative physics are typically concerned with simpler processes, and as the complexity of the modelled process increases, the complexity of the associated computations soon becomes critical. In this section I will compare the KARDIO approach with some well known approaches to qualitative modelling. I will in particular try to identify differences that make the KARDIO approach comparatively effective in areas such as physiology. It will follow from this comparison that the essential difference lies in the representation: the effectiveness in KARDIO is achieved through using, as the primitives of the representation, higher level concepts than in other approaches. These higher level concepts are

in KARDIO represented essentially in logic. In this way the computation between more basic primitives and these higher level concepts is saved. It may be argued that other approaches are concerned with deeper models and that the effectiveness in KAR-DIO is then simply achieved at the expense of the depth of the model. However, a good general principle is to adjust the representation level to the task. In KARDIO, the representation level of the model was carefully chosen so that it is flexible (deep) enough for the targetted task of ECG diagnosis, and not deeper than necessary (to avoid unnecessary complexity). It seems that the representational primitives postulated in other best known approaches to qualitative modelling simply do not allow enough flexibility in choosing a more effective representation for areas such as physiology.

Let us briefly look at three most known approaches to qualitative modelling and make a short comparison with respect to their application in physiology. The three approaches are Kuipers (1986), de Kleer and Brown (1984), and Forbus (1984).

Kuipers' approach, called QSIM, can be viewed as an abstraction of ordinary differential equations. QSIM is very attractive because of its solid mathematical basis. A model is defined by a set of *functions* of time and a set of *constrains* on these functions. For each function we have an ordered set of distinguished symbolic values, called *landmarks*. The current value is expressed in terms of these values: the current value of a function can be either a landmark or an interval between two adjacent landmarks. Constraints on functions formalize their interdependencies in terms of arithmetic operations and time derivatives. In addition to these we can also use a more interesting relation: *monotonically increasing* (or *decreasing*) function. Using this type of constraint it is possible to express qualitative relation between two functions when the exact relationship between them is not known. Time in QSIM is treated as a sequence of symbolic time points that are associated with 'interesting events'. Such events occur when a function crosses its landmark value or the derivative of a function becomes equal to zero. A distinguishing feature of QSIM is that during qualitative simulation new landmarks are discovered.

QSIM has been applied in modelling of physiological processes: hormone control of water balance in the body (Kuipers and Kassirer 1985; Kuipers 1987), compartmental systems (Nicolosi and Leaning 1988), and acid-base base regulation (Coiera 1989). It is straightforward to define a QSIM model when a traditional mathematical model based on differential equations is already known. Also, it is possible to construct a QSIM model in a less formal and more intuitive way. There are two serious limitations of QSIM, however. First, it seems to be very difficult to express in QSIM models that are not susceptible to differential equations. This is often the case in medicine and it seems that a QSIM model of the heart that would correspond to the KARDIO model would be extremely complex. Second, even when a QSIM model is derived from corresponding differential equations, the QSIM qualitative simulation algorithm may non-deterministically generate numerous behaviours. Some of the generated behaviours can be justified simply by lack of information in a qualitative model. Unfortunately QSIM also generates unreal behaviours that are not justified by the lack

valuable. Let us illustrate this by representations used in KARDIO. One example is the treatment of time. Although the modelling of the electrical activity of the heart involves processes in time, time is not explicitly mentioned in the KARDIO model at all. Instead, repetitive processes in time are described in terms of features, such as the rate of a repetitive event, regularity of its rhythm, and shape of a waveform. The qualitative values of these features can be for example as follows:

rate: slow, normal, fast
rhythm: regular, irregular
shape: normal, distorted

Figure 5 indicates the style of defining relations between processes in KARDIO. For two sequences of events, generated by two asynchronous processes, we simply say that they are 'independent'; or if two periodic processes are synchronised, we may say that one of them is delayed with respect to the other which may reflect their causal interdependence.

The domains of parameters in KARDIO can contain structured values whereas in other approaches to qualitative modelling the elements of 'quantity spaces' are unstructured. We also define the operations on such descriptions so as to best suit the domain. For example, we may choose to define that the sum of one process with regular rhythm and another one with irregular rhythm will give a process with irregular rhythm (third example in Figure 5).

On the more cautious side, the flexibility to choose a powerful description language and define own laws (to be used as constraints in the model) in the style of KARDIO usually requires the programming of a new interpreter for a new model. In other approaches the model designer can normally apply a ready-to-use implementation. But as our experience powerfully showed, Prolog as an implementation language enormously facilitates the programming of specialized interpreters needed for a chosen description language and corresponding user-defined operations or laws of inference. In the case of KARDIO at least, the programming itself occupied a very minor part of the total effort in the project.

One broad strategy of qualitative modelling in medicine, aiming to combine the representational flexibility of the KARDIO approach with the qualitative versions of other approaches to modelling in physics would be: use logic as a description language in the style of KARDIO, use the concepts of *process* and *individual view* from Qualitative Process Theory for structuring the model and for generating explanations, and use an improved QSIM-like theory as a basis for qualitative differential equations in cases that the physiological process is amenable to such a description.

of information. This problem with QSIM is known as excessive branching which generates spurious behaviours and has been studied by several authors (e.g. Lee, Chiu and Kuipers 1987; Struss 1988).

The approach to qualitative simulation by de Kleer and Brown (1984) is centred around the concept of *confluence*, that is a qualitative differential equation. It seems that it would, as a candidate for physiological modelling, suffer from similar limitations as QSIM. Similar to KARDIO, and unlike QSIM, the approach of de Kleer and Brown explicitly involves the structure of a model. The structure consists of components and their interconnections. As in KARDIO, the qualitative behaviour of the system is derived from the behaviour of the components and connections between them.

The third approach in this comparison, QPT (Qualitative Process Theory, by Forbus 1984), is the most complicated of all three and its execution requires substantial computation. QPT has not been applied to physiological domains although it does offer some valuable concepts that cannot be found in any other approach. In particular, QPT explicitly formalizes the concept of *process*. This clearly offers a new way of diagnostic reasoning about a system whose normal or abnormal behaviour can be explained in terms of what processes are going on, or should be going on.

Other studies in qualitative modelling of cardiac arrhythmias are (Shibahara 1985) and (Hunter, Gotts and Hamlet 1988). Their work was basically concerned with a more narrow domain, namely the behaviour of the AV node. In comparison with KARDIO, their models of the AV node are more detailed (and deeper), but do not cover other arrhythmias. The KARDIO model level was chosen mainly with the view to practical diagnostic needs, and in this respect the other two model levels are probably unnecessarily detailed. They can, on the other hand, explain some interesting physiological phenomena that are beyond the level of detail in KARDIO.

Let us now try to identify those features that contribute to the practicality of the KARDIO approach in physiological modelling. The main feature is the use of logic as the representation formalism. KARDIO is not rooted in any traditional theory for modelling, based on describing processes with numbers and differential equations. In comparison with other approaches, the main advantage of KARDIO applied to physiology lies in the power of the description language used. The model designer has the freedom to choose the most suitable description language and define the laws of the domain in a most natural way. The description language is thus hardly constrained by any traditional mathematical notions. In general, this has of course also a disadvantage: no existing mathematical theory is assumed and automatically available to the model designer. Instead, if such a theory is useful, it has to be explicitly stated in the model. It really depends on the problem whether the flexibility is more precious than the immediate availability of some established mathematical theory. The latter is probably more important when the problem is susceptible to some traditional approach, such as differential equations, but in physiology, the flexibility and freedom is probably more

## 7 Conclusions

In our view KARDIO's main contribution is as a demonstration of the use of deep knowledge in the form of a qualitative model in building a complex knowledge base. The KARDIO knowledge base would be practically impossible to construct as surface knowledge in the conventional dialogue style of knowledge acquisition. The basic exercise in qualitative modelling for ECG diagnosis was extended in several directions: extraction of compact and comprehensible rules, hierarchical modelling, and machine learning supported construction of qualitative models. Further research themes that seem important are:

(1) Extension of the model learning system to be able to construct new terms of the model description language (constructive induction within logic).

(2) Extension of this system to learn dynamic models where time is explicitly represented.

(3) Identification of physiological background knowledge to further simplify compressed rules.

Regarding the last item, in extraction of compact and comprehensible rules the system often generates descriptions that are, although logically correct and minimal, still much more complicated than human-generated descriptions intended for communication of knowledge between humans. Human experts' descriptions are often largely incomplete, but they are still usually correctly interpreted by a human. This is possible because in this communication between humans some shared background knowledge is assumed. It would be most interesting to identify this background knowledge through systematic processing of differences between machine-generated and human-generated descriptions.

## References

Bratko, I., Mozetic, I., Lavrac, N. (1989) *KARDIO: a Study in Deep and Qualitative Knowledge for Expert Systems*. (MIT Press, to appear).

Cestnik, B., Kononenko, I., Bratko, I. (1987) ASSISTANT 86: a knowledge elicitation tool for sophisticated users. In: *Progress in Machine Learning* (eds. I.Bratko, N. Lavrac). Wilmslow, England: Sigma Press.

Coiera, R. (1989) Intelligent patient monitoring: a qualitative technique for tracking multiple interacting and progressive diseases. *Fifth Australian Conference on*

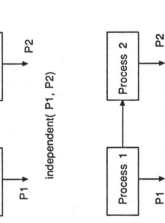

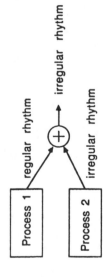

Figure 5   Examples of modelling relations between processes in KARDIO.

Mozetic, I., Bratko, I., Urbancic, T. (1987) Varying level of abstraction in qualitative modelling. Machine Intelligence Workshop 12, Tallin. To appear in *Machine Intelligence 12* (eds. D.Michie, J.Hayes, E.Tyugu).

Muggleton, S., Buntine, W. (1988) Machine invention of first-order predicates by inverting resolution. *Proc. Fifth Int. Conf. Machine Learning*, Ann Arbor, Michigan, June 1988.

Nicolosi, E., Leaning, M.S. (1988) Qualitative simulation of compartmental models. *IFAC Conf. Modeling and Control in Biomedical Systems*. Venice, April 1988.

Pearce, D. (1988) The induction of fault diagnosis systems from qualitative models. *Proc. AAAI-88 Conf.*, Saint Paul, Minnesota, August 1988.

Pearce, D. (1989) A qualitative modelling environment for design and diagnosis of automation. *Proc. 2nd Int. Conf. Industrial and Eng. Applications of Expert Systems* (IEA/AIE-89), Tullohama, Tenn., June 1989.

Phibbs, B. (1973) *The Cardiac Arrhythmias*. St. Luis: The C.V. Mosby Co.

Quinlan, J.R. (1986) Induction of decision trees. *Machine Learning Journal*, Vol. 1, 81-106.

Shibahara, T. (1985) On using causal knowledge to recognize vital signals: knowledge-based interpretation of arrhythmias. *Proc. 9th Int. Joint Conf. on Artificial Intelligence*, Los Angeles, CA, August 1985.

Steels, L. (1985) Second generation expert systems. *Future Generations Expert Systems*, Vol. 1, 213-221.

Struss, P. (1988) Global filters for qualitative behaviours. *Proc. AAAI-88 Conf.*, Saint Paul, Minnesota, August 1988.

*Applications of Expert Systems*, Sydney, May 1989.

de Kleer, J., Brown, J.S. (1984) A qualitative physics based on confluences. *Artificial Intelligence*, Vol. 24, 7-83.

Forbus, K.D. (1984) Qualitative process theory. *Artificial Intelligence*, Vol. 24, 85-168.

Goldman, M.J. (1976) *Principles of Clinical Electrocardiography*. Los Altos: Lange Medical Publications.

Hunter, J., Gotts, N., Hamlet, I. (1988) Qualitative spatial and temporal reasoning in cardiac electrophysiology. *Second Workshop on Qualitative Physics*, Paris, July 1988.

Kuipers, B.J. (1986) Qualitative simulation. *Artificial Intelligence*, Vol. 29, 289-338.

Kuipers, B., Kassirer, J.P. (1985) Qualitative simulation in medical physiology: a progress report. Mass. Institute of Technology: Laboratory for Computer Sc., Memorandum MIT/LCS/TM-280.

Kuipers, B.J. (1987) Qualitative simulation as causal explanation. *IEEE Trans. Systems, Man and Cybernetics*, SMC-17, 432-444.

Lee, W.W., Chiu, C., Kuipers, B.J. (1987) Developments toward constraining qualitative simulation. Univ. of Texas at Austin: AI Lab, Technical Report AI TR87-44.

Lloyd, J.W., Topor, R.W. (1985) A basis for deductive database systems. *Journal of Logic Programming*, Vol. 2, 93-109.

Michalski, R. (1983) A theory and methodology of inductive learning. In: *Machine Learning: an Artificial Intelligence Approach* (Michalski, Carbonel, Mitchell, eds.) Palo Alto: Tioga.

Michalski, R.S., Mozetic, I., Hong, J., Lavrac, N. (1986) The multipurpose learning system AQ15 and its testing application to three medical domains. *AAAI Conf. 86*, Philadelphia.

Mozetic, I. (1985) NEWGEM: program for learning from examples, technical documentaion and user's guide. Univ. of Illinois at Urbana-Cahmpaign: Dept. of Computer Sc. Also IIS Report DP-4390, Ljubljana: J. Stefan Institute.

Mozetic, I. (1987) The role of abstractions in learning qualitative models. *Proc. 4th Int. Workshop on Machine Learning*. Irvine, CA, June 1987. Morgan Kauffman.

Mozetic, I. (1988) *Learning of Qualitative Models*. Ljubljana: Faculty of Electr. Eng., Ph.D. Thesis (in Slovenian).

# Chapter 6

# Apprenticeship Learning Systems

Apprenticeship learning systems refine and debug the knowledge base of an expert system during the course of problem solving. The problem solving may done by the expert system itself (learning by doing), by another expert (learning by watching), or by being instructed by another expert (learning by accepting advice).

Apprenticeship learning by doing, watching and accepting advice is an essential step in the creation of human experts in many knowledge-intensive expert domains, such as medical diagnosis. This provides strong motivation to give such learning capabilities to an expert system. Apprenticeship systems are particularly valuable during end-game knowledge acquisition, that period after an initial rudimentary knowledge base has been created that allows an expert system to adequately solve one problem.

Another motivation for automating apprenticeship learning by watching is that human experts are often inarticulate when it comes to explaining how they solve problems. An apprenticeship system takes as its input the normal problem-solving actions of experts, without a need for articulate explanation.

Another motivation for apprenticeship systems is that they address the problem of knowledge base evaluation over time in expert domains. Thus they provide a means of knowledge base maintenance of the type that is needed to deal with an ever-changing and evolving world.

All of the apprentice systems discussed in this chapter focus on expanding an incomplete knowledge base. They assume that the knowledge that is initially present is correct, or else use a deep theory of the domain to validate the initial knowledge. Although none of the systems discussed in this chapter learn control knowledge, the PRODIGY system can be viewed as such an apprentice.

Work on apprenticeship learning has shown the importance of the design of the performance element. Crucial to the design of all apprentice systems mentioned in this chapter is an expert system whose mode of problem solving approximates that of human experts.

# Section 6.1

# Apprentice Systems for Classification Knowledge

Two apprentice systems for heuristic classification problem solving are described in this book. The ODYSSEUS system of Wilkins, described in Section 6.1.1, refines knowledge bases of advanced rule-based systems. The PROTOS system of Porter, Bareiss and Holte, described in Section 7.2, refines the knowledge base of a case-based reasoning system. Both of these systems operate in the domain of medical diagnosis. They each have an initial automatic learning phase to generate an initial knowledge base from scratch from a set of solved cases provided by an expert. Then they each have a apprenticeship phase for knowledge base refinement.

ODYSSEUS is a learning by watching apprentice: learning opportunities arise when the apprentice program fails to construct an explanation of an observed problem-solving action of a human expert. An explanation failure occurs when the apprentice program cannot construct an explanation chain between the observed expert action and a high-level problem-solving goal. The context of the explanation failure allows the learning system to generate candidate knowledge base repairs. Like the LEAP apprentice,

ODYSSEUS uses underlying domain theories to test these candidate repairs. For example, when a candidate repair is a heuristic rule, it is tested by an induction program. When a candidate repair is successfully validated, it is added to the knowledge base. Note that in the ODYSSEUS paper, the empirical comparison against case-based learning refers to rule induction over a library of classified cases, not to exemplar-based learning.

PROTOS is a learning by advice-taking apprentice. An expert informs the system when it incorrectly solves a problem, whereupon the system initiates an interactive elicitation dialogue to extract the missing knowledge from the expert. A strength of this approach is the learning system's ability to understand and operationalize the explanations of the expert.

All apprentices require that the problem-solving method be in place. ODYSSEUS is designed for use with heuristic classification using hypothesis-directed reasoning, PROTOS expects heuristic classification using exemplar-based reasoning, and the LEAP and DISCIPLE design apprentices described in Section 6.2 expect top-down refinement.

# KNOWLEDGE BASE REFINEMENT AS
# IMPROVING AN INCORRECT AND
# INCOMPLETE DOMAIN THEORY

David C. Wilkins
(*University of Illinois*)

## Abstract

The ODYSSEUS program automates knowledge-base refinement by improving a domain theory. This chapter describes the techniques used by ODYSSEUS to address three types of domain theory pathologies: incorrectness, inconsistency, and incompleteness.

In ODYSSEUS, an incomplete domain theory is extended by the *metarule chain completion method*. This method exploits the use of an explicit metalevel representation of the strategy knowledge for a generic problem class (e.g., heuristic classification) that is separate from the domain theory (e.g., medicine) to be improved. Our work implements and compares the extension of an incomplete domain theory using case-based inductive learning and explanation-based apprenticeship learning; in the latter, learning occurs by completing failed explanations of observed human problem-solving actions. Extending an incomplete domain theory and correcting an incorrect domain theory both use of the *confirmation decision procedure method*, which validates arbitrary instantiated tuples of the knowledge base by the use of an underlying domain theory. Lastly, the consistency of the knowledge base is improved by use of a *sociopathic reduction algorithm*.

## 18.1 INTRODUCTION

A central problem of expert systems is knowledge-base refinement [Buchanan and Shortliffe, 1984]. Numerous research efforts have addressed the problem of im-

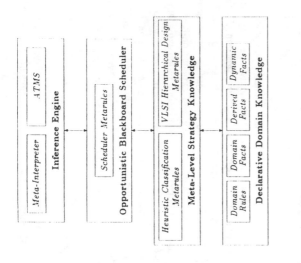

**Figure 18–1:**    MINERVA system architecture

*Domain knowledge* consists of MYCIN-like rules and simple frame knowledge for an application domain (e.g., medicine, geology). An example of rule knowledge in Horn clause format is

```
conclude(migraine-headache, yes, .5) :- finding(photophobia,
yes)
```

meaning "to conclude the patient has a migraine headache with a certainty .5, determine if the patient has photophobia." An example of frame knowledge is

```
subsumed-by(viral-meningitis, meningitis)
```

meaning "hypothesis viral meningitis is subsumed by the hypothesis meningitis." *Problem-state knowledge* is generated during execution of the expert system. Examples of problem-state knowledge are rule-applied(rule163), which says that rule 163 has been applied during this consultation, and

```
differential(migraine-headache, tension-headache)
```

which says that the expert system's active hypotheses are migraine headache and tension headache.

proving an expert system that solves heuristic classification problems. The major research projects that have directly confronted this problem include TEIRESIAS [Davis, 1982], AQUINAS [Boose, 1984], and MORE [Kahn, *et al.*, 1985]. They also include the automatic case-based inductive methods of INDUCE [Michalski, 1983], ID3 [Quinlan, 1983], SEEK2 [Ginsberg, *et al.*, 1985], and RL [Fu and Buchanan, 1985], which perform empirical induction over a library of test cases. This chapter describes a new approach to the refinement problem is described that involves a combination of failure-driven explanation-based learning and the use of underlying domain theories. Our approach is embodied in the ODYSSEUS learning program; ODYSSEUS contains specific (and separate) methods to address automatically three types of knowledge base pathologies: incorrectness, inconsistency, and incompleteness [Wilkins, 1987].

The remainder of this paper is organized as follows: Section 18.2 describes the MINERVA expert system shell that was specifically designed to facilitate failure-driven explanation-based learning. Our experience has shown that a sophisticated expert system architecture can provide an enormous amount of leverage to a learning program. Section 18.3 describes the apprenticeship learning methods used by ODYSSEUS to extend an incomplete domain theory; the key idea used to extend an incomplete domain theory is called the *metarule chain completion method*. Section 18.4 describes the methods used by ODYSSEUS to correct an incomplete domain theory; our approach to dealing with an incorrect domain theory is called the *confirmation decision procedure method*. Section 18.5 discusses the method used to remove certain types of inconsistencies from a correct but inconsistent domain theory; this method is called the *sociopathic reduction algorithm*. Section 18.6 presents results of a wide range of evaluation experiments that have been carried out, and Section 18.7 describes related research.

## 18.2  MINERVA CLASSIFICATION AND DESIGN SHELL

The ODYSSEUS learning program can improve any knowledge base crafted for the MINERVA expert system shell [Park, *et al.*, 1989]; its overall organization is shown in Figure 18–1. MINERVA is a refinement of HERACLES, based on the experience gained in creating the ODYSSEUS apprenticeship learning program for HERACLES [Wilkins, 1987]. HERACLES is itself a refinement of EMYCIN, based on the experience gained in creating the GUIDON case-based tutoring program for EMYCIN [Clancey, 1986]. These shells use a problem-solving method called *heuristic classification*, which is the process of selecting a solution out of a pre-enumerated solution set, using heuristic techniques [Clancey, 1985]. The primary approach is the NEOMYCIN medical knowledge base for diagnosis of meningitis and similar neurological disorders [Clancey, 1984]. This section describes the types of knowledge encoded in MINERVA and HERACLES, and how MINERVA differs from HERACLES.

*Strategy knowledge* is contained in the shell, and it approximates a cognitive model of problem solving. For heuristic classification problems, this model is often referred to as hypothesis-directed reasoning [Elstein, 1978]. The different problem-solving strategies that can be employed during problem solving are explicitly represented, which facilitates use of the model to follow the line of reasoning of a human problem solver. The strategy knowledge determines what domain knowledge is relevant at any given time, and what additional information is needed to solve the problem. The problem-state and domain knowledge, including rules, are represented as tuples, and strategy metarules are quantified over these tuples.

The strategy knowledge needs to access the domain and problem-state knowledge. To achieve this, the domain and problem-state knowledge is represented as tuples. Even rules are translated into tuples. For example, if rule 160 is

```
conclude(hemorrhage yes .5) :- finding (diplopia, yes) ∧
finding(aphasia, yes)
```

it would be translated into the following four tuples:

```
evidence.for(diplopia hemorrhage rule160 .5),
evidence.for(aphasia hemorrhage rule160 .5),
antecedent(diplopia rule160),
antecedent(aphasia, rule160).
```

Strategy metarules are quantified over the tuples. Figure 18-4 (page 501) presents four strategy metarules in Horn clause form; the tuples in the body of the clause quantify over the domain and problem-state knowledge. The rightmost metarule in Figure 18-4 encodes the strategy to find out about a symptom by finding out about a symptom that subsumes it. The metarule applies when the goal is to find out symptom P1, and there is a symptom P2 that is subsumed by P1, and P2 takes Boolean values, and it is currently unknown, and P2 should be asked about instead of being derived from first principles. This is one of eight strategies in HERACLES that is also used in MINERVA for finding out the value of a symptom; this particular strategy of asking a more general question has the advantage of cognitive economy: a "no" answer provides the answer to a potentially large number of questions, including the subsumed question.

### 18.2.1 The Evolution from HERACLES to MINERVA

MINERVA is a reworking of HERACLES, similar to the way that HERACLES is a reworking of EMYCIN. The ultimate objective in both these efforts has been a more declarative and modular representation of knowledge. This facilitates construction of a learning program to examine and reason about the knowledge structures of the metalevel strategy in the expert system, to interpret better a user's strategy in terms of the metalevel strategy knowledge in the expert system, and to allow the same shell to encode strategy knowledge for the generic problem tasks of analysis (e.g., heuristic classification) and synthesis (e.g., VLSI circuit design).

There are four principal differences between MINERVA and HERACLES at the strategy level. In determining which task to perform next, HERACLES uses a fixed order goal tree; by contrast MINERVA employs an opportunistic blackboard scheduler. This facilitates interpreting a user's strategy in terms of the expert system's strategies, and better integrates top-down and bottom-up strategic reasoning. Second, in controlling metalevel reasoning, HERACLES uses dynamic control flags and variables, such as task end conditions. In MINERVA a pure, functional programming style and a deliberation-action loop have been used; this eliminates all flags and variables at the strategy level. So, in MINERVA the system state is completely determined by the state of the domain-level static and dynamic knowledge. Third, in Heracles, strategy metarule premises sometimes change the state of the system, invoke subgoals, and use procedural attachment to LISP code; and HERACLES strategy metarule actions can invoke several goals. In contrast, MINERVA metarules do not follow any of these practices, which allows a pure deliberation-action cycle for strategic reasoning. The MINERVA style of metarules reduces side effects, thus making it easier for the learning program to reason about the strategy knowledge. Fourth, in MINERVA, more of the expert system's reasoning, such as the rule interpreter code, has been encoded in strategy metarules.

Other changes are as follows: The MINERVA system has been completely implemented in PROLOG; by contrast, HERACLES uses a combination of PROLOG-like clauses with procedural attachment to LISP for each of the PROLOG clause predicates in metarules. The more uniform representation in MINERVA moves us toward our long-term goal of allowing a learning program to reason about all knowledge structures in the expert system shell. MINERVA incorporates an ATMS to maintain consistency of the knowledge base, uses a logic metainterpreter, and supports both certainty factors and Pearl's method to represent rule uncertainty and for propagation of information in a hierarchy of diagnostic hypotheses [Pearl, 1986a; 1986b]. As can be seen, all of the changes mentioned have resulted in a more declarative and functional knowledge representation.

### 18.3 ODYSSEUS'S METHOD FOR EXTENDING AN INCOMPLETE DOMAIN THEORY

We have developed two methods for extending an incomplete domain theory: an apprenticeship learning approach and a case-based reasoning approach. This section will only describe the former approach. Table 18-1 shows the major refinement steps and the method of achieving them for apprenticeship and case-based learning. The techniques will be elaborated below.

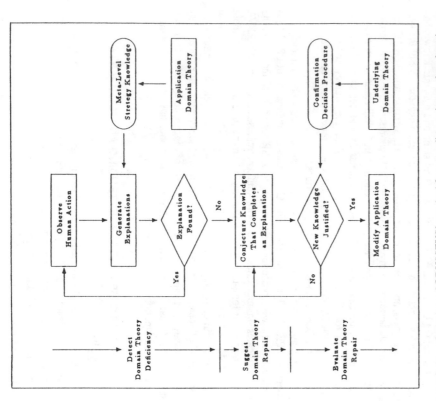

**Figure 18–2:** Overview of ODYSSEUS's method for extending an incomplete domain theory in a learning-by-watching apprentice situation. This chapter describes techniques that permit automation of each of the three stages of learning shown on the left edge of the figure. An explanation is a proof that shows how the expert's action achieves a problem-solving goal.

such as diagnosis, can provide a basis for learning the knowledge that is specific to a particular domain, such as medicine.

### 18.3.1 Detection of Knowledge Base Deficiency

The first stage of learning involves the detection of a knowledge base deficiency. An expert's problem solving is observed and explanations are constructed for

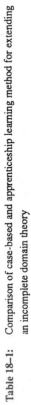

**Table 18–1:** Comparison of case-based and apprenticeship learning method for extending an incomplete domain theory

| Learning method | Case-based learning (similarity-based) | Apprenticeship learning (explanation-based) |
|---|---|---|
| Scope | Heuristic rules. | Heuristic rules. 4 types of frame knowledge. |
| Detect knowledge-base deficiency | Select and run a case. Deficiency exists if case is misdiagnosed. | Observe expert solving a case. Deficiency exists if action of expert cannot be explained. |
| Suggest knowledge-base deficiency | Generalize or specialize rules. Induce new rules. | Find tuples that allow explanation to be completed under single fault assumption. |
| Validate knowledge-base repair | Use underlying domain theory to validate repairs. | Use underlying domain theory to validate repairs. |

The solution approach of the ODYSSEUS apprenticeship program for extending an incomplete domain theory in a learning-by-watching scenario is illustrated in Figure 18–2. As Figure 18–2 shows, the learning process involves three distinct steps: detect domain theory deficiency, suggest domain theory repair, and validate domain theory repair. This section defines the concept of an explanation and then describes the three learning steps.

The main observable problem-solving activity in a diagnostic session is finding out values of features of the artifact to be diagnosed—we refer to this activity as asking *findout questions*. An *explanation* in ODYSSEUS is a proof that demonstrates how an expert's findout question is a logical consequence of the current problem-state, the domain and strategy knowledge, and one of the current high-level strategy goals. An explanation is created by backchaining the metalevel strategy metarules; Figure 18–4 provides examples of these metarules represented in Horn clause form. The backchaining starts with the findout metarule and continues until a metarule is reached whose head represents a high-level problem-solving goal. To backchain a metarule requires unification of the body of the Horn clause with domain and problem-state knowledge. Examples of high-level goals are: to test a hypothesis, to differentiate between several plausible hypotheses, to ask a clarifying question, and to ask a general question.

Apprenticeship learning is a form of learning by watching, in which learning occurs as a by-product of building explanations of human problem-solving actions. An apprenticeship is the most powerful method that human experts use to refine and debug their expertise in knowledge-intensive domains such as medicine. The major accomplishment of our method of apprenticeship learning is a demonstration of how an explicit representation of the strategy knowledge for a general problem class,

| Group Hypotheses Strategy Metarule | Test Hypothesis Strategy Metarule | Applyrule Strategy Metarule | Findout Strategy Metarule |
|---|---|---|---|
| goal(group-hyp(H1,H2)) :- differential(H1), taxonomic(H1), parent(H2,H1), not pursued(H2), closest-common-ancestor(H2,H1), not(root(H2)), goal(test-hyp(H2)). | goal(test-hyp(H2)) :- concluded-by(H1,R1), not(pursued(R1)), inpremise(P1 R1), goal(applyrule(R1)). | goal(applyrule(R1)) :- not(rule-applied(R1)), inpremise(P1,R1), evid-for(P1,H2,R1,S1), soft-datum(P1), not(concluded(P1)), goal(findout(P1)), applyrule-forward(R1). | goal(findout(P1)) :- subsumes(P2,P1), not(concluded(P1)), boolean(P2), not(concluded(P2)), ask-user(P1). |

**Figure 18–4:** Learning by completing failed explanations. The illustrated strategy-level Horn clause metarules can chain together to form an explanation of how the findout action of ask-user(P1) relates to the high-level goal of group-hypoth(H1,H2). In this particular case, all the tuples in the chain cannot be instantiated with domain knowledge. ODYSSEUS attempts to complete this and other failed explanation chains by adding domain knowledge to the knowledge base so that all the tuples unify.

## 18.3.2 Suggesting a Knowledge Base Repair

The second step of apprenticeship learning is to conjecture a knowledge base repair. A confirmation theory (which will be described in the discussion of the third stage of learning) can judge whether an arbitrary tuple of domain knowledge is erroneous, independent of the other knowledge in the knowledge base.

The search for the missing knowledge begins with the single fault assumption. It should be noted that the missing knowledge is conceptually a single fault, but because of the way the knowledge is encoded, we can learn more than one tuple when we learn rule knowledge. For ease of presentation, this feature is not shown in the following examples. Conceptually, the missing knowledge could be eventually identified by adding a random domain knowledge tuple to the knowledge base and seeing whether an explanation of the expert's findout request can be constructed. How can a promising piece of such knowledge be effectively found? Our approach is to apply backward chaining to the findout question metarule, trying to construct a proof that explains why it was asked. When the proof fails, it is because a tuple of domain or problem-state knowledge needed for the proof is not in the knowledge base. If the proof fails because of problem-state knowledge, we look for a different proof of the findout question. If the proof fails because of a missing piece of domain knowledge, we temporarily add this tuple to the domain knowledge base. If the proof then goes through, the temporary piece of knowledge is our conjecture of how to refine the knowledge base.

---

Patient's Complaint and Volunteered Information:
1. Alice Ecila, a 41 year old black female.
2. Chief complaint is a headache.

Physician's Data Requests:
3. Headache duration?
   focus=tension headache.   7 days.
4. Headache episodic?
   focus=tension headache.   No.
5. Headache severity?
   focus=tension headache.   4 on 0-4 scale.
6. Visual problems?
   focus=subarachnoid hemorrhage.   Yes.
7. Double vision?
   focus=subarachnoid hemorrhage, tumor.   Yes.
8. Temperature?
   focus=infectious process.   98.7 Fahrenheit.

......

Physician's Final Diagnosis:
25. Migraine Headache.

**Figure 18–3:** An example of what the ODYSSEUS apprentice learner sees. The data requests in this problem-solving protocol were made by John Sotos, MD. The physician also provides information on the focus of the data requests. The answers to the data requests were obtained from an actual patient file from the Stanford University Hospital, extracted by Edward Herskovits, MD.

each of the observed problem-solving actions. An example will be used to illustrate our description of the three stages of learning, based on the NEOMYCIN knowledge base for diagnosing neurology problems. The input to ODYSSEUS is the problem-solving behavior of a physician, John Sotos, as shown in Figure 18–3. In our terminology, Dr. Sotos asks findout questions and concludes with a final diagnosis. For each of his actions, ODYSSEUS generates one or more explanations of his behavior.

When ODYSSEUS observes the expert asking a findout question, such as asking if the patient has visual problems, it finds all explanations for this action. When none can be found, an explanation failure occurs. This failure suggests that there is a difference between the knowledge of the expert and the expert system, and it provides a learning opportunity. The knowledge difference may lie in any of the three types of knowledge that we have described: strategy knowledge, domain knowledge, or problem-state knowledge. Currently, ODYSSEUS assumes that the cause of the explanation failure is that the domain knowledge is deficient. In the current example, no explanation can be found for findout question number 7 in Figure 18–3 (asking about visual problems), and an explanation failure occurs.

Figure 18-4 illustrates one member of the set of failed explanations that ODYSSEUS examines in connection with the unexplained action

```
ask-user(visual problems)
```

that is contained in the tail of the rightmost metarule. These strategy metarules create a chain between the high-level goal in the head of the leftmost metarule,

```
group-hypotheses (Hypothesis1, Hypothesis2)
```

and the low-level observable action in the tail of the rightmost metarule

```
ask-user (visual problems).
```

Note that this chain is but one path is a large explanation graph that connects the observable action of asking about visual problems to all high-level goals. Each path in the graph is a potential explanation, and each node in a path is a strategy metarule. The failed explanation that ODYSSEUS is examining consists of the four metarules shown in Figure 18-4: Group Hypothesis, Test Hypothesis, Applyrule, and Findout. For a metarule to be used in a proof, its variables must be instantiated with domain or problem-state tuples that are present in the knowledge base. In this example, the evidence.for tuple is responsible for the highlighted chain not forming a proof. It forms an acceptable proof if the tuple

```
evidence.for (photophobia acute.meningitis $rule $cf)
```

is added to the knowledge base. During the step that generates repairs, neither the form of the left-hand side of the rule (e.g., number of conjuncts) or the strength is known. In the step to evaluate repairs, the exact form of the rule is produced in the process of evaluation of the worth of the tuple.

### 18.3.3 Validation of Knowledge Base Repair

The task of the third step of apprenticeship learning is to evaluate the proposed repair. To do this, we use the *confirmation decision procedure* (CDP) method. CDPs are constructed for each type of tuple in the domain and can determine if the tuple is an acceptable tuple. Of the 19 different types of tuples in the NEOMYCIN knowledge base, we have implemented CDPs for three of them:

```
evidence.for, clarifying.question, and ask.general.question
```

tuples. In addition to their use for validating knowledge base repairs, CDPs are also used to modify or delete incorrect parts of the initial domain theory; they are described in greater detail in Section 18.4.

Evidence.for tuples were generated in the visual problems example. In order to confirm the first candidate tuple, ODYSSEUS uses an empirical induction system that generates and evaluates rules that have photophobia in their premise and

acute meningitis in their conclusion. A rule is found that passes the rule "goodness" measures, and it is automatically added to the object-level knowledge base. All the tuples that are associated with the rule are also added to the knowledge base. This completes our example.

The CDP method also validates frame-like knowledge. An example of how this is accomplished will be described for clarify question tuples, such as

```
clarify-questions (headache-duration headache).
```

This tuple means that if the physician discovers that the patient has a headache, she should always ask how long the headache has lasted. The confirmation theory must determine whether headache duration is a good clarifying question for the "headache" symptom. To achieve this, ODYSSEUS first checks to see if the question to be clarified is related to many hypotheses (the ODYSSEUS explanation generator allows it to determine this), and then tests whether the clarifying question can potentially eliminate a high percentage of these hypotheses. If these two criteria are met, then the clarify questions tuple is accepted.

## 18.4 ODYSSEUS'S METHOD FOR IMPROVING AN INCORRECT DOMAIN THEORY

The main focus of this chapter is on extending an incomplete domain theory via apprenticeship learning. However, it is clearly helpful if we are extending a domain theory that is correct and consistent. This section describes the methods that we have developed to improve the correctness of the domain theory. These methods are applied to the domain theory prior to the use of apprenticeship learning.

The key to addressing the problem of incorrect knowledge is the use of the *confirmation decision procedure* (CDP) method, which connects tuples in the domain theory to underlying theories of the domain that are capable of judging their correctness. In this approach, a CDP is created for each type of domain theory tuple in the knowledge base. Given an arbitrary instantiated tuple, the CDP calculates whether the tuple is true or false. In some cases the CDP can suggest how the tuple can be modified so as to make it true.

Of the 19 different types of domain theory tuples in the NEOMYCIN domain theory, we have created CDPs for three types of tuples. These tuples comprise approximately 70% of all tuples in the domain theory. For example, a CDP has been implemented for evidence.for tuples. These tuples are derived from the heuristic domain rules provided by a user that relate evidence to hypotheses. Validating evidence.for tuples therefore consists of validating the heuristic associational rules in the knowledge base.

The CDP evidence.for consists of an induction system, a set of rule biases, and a representative case library for the application domain. It accepts or rejects heuristic rules, whether they are rules in the initial knowledge base or rules conjectured during apprenticeship learning. In addition to accepting or rejecting rules, the CDP for evidence.for can modify a given rule to make it correct; it does this by adding conjuncts or modifying the rule strength. A rule can be modified to be "correct" by using probability and decision theory and representative sets of cases to determine its correct weight or strength (in contrast to trusting the weight provided by the user). If a rule lacks sufficient strength, the CDP will try to add conjuncts to the rule to increase its specificity.

When given an evidence.for tuple, its corresponding heuristic associational rule, which is indicated by the third argument of the evidence.for relation, is tested in five ways by the evidence.for CDP. A test for *simplicity* ensures that the number of antecedent conditions of the rules are less than the specified number. The test for *strength* accepts rules whose certainty factors (CF) are greater than a threshold value. The third bias is to test the *generality* of the rules. It succeeds only if the rules cover a certain percentage of the cases in a representative case library. The test for *colinearity* ensures that the proposed rules are not similar to any existing rules in performing classification of the induction set of cases. Finally the bias for *uniqueness* will check that the rules fire on a training case and that there exist no rules in the current domain rule set that also succeed for that case. Good rules are those recommendations that pass the verification process. This rule may then be added into the system.

It is often difficult to create CDPs for some types of tuples in the domain theory. For example, consider the tuple type askfirst(PARM). This tuple says that a particular feature of the system being diagnosed should be obtained from a user instead of derived from first principles. It is difficult to imagine how to do this for an arbitrary feature, although eventually a way must be found if knowledge acquisition is to be completely automated.

Note that most knowledge bases are much more heterogeneous than LEAP, a learning apprentice for acquiring a domain theory that consists of VLSI circuit implementation rules. In this system, the domain theory only contains implementation rules (in our parlance, only contains one type of domain tuple). LEAP can verify the implementation rules using Kirkhoff's laws as its underlying domain theory. The challenge of using this idea for knowledge-base systems is that most domain theories contain many different types of domain knowledge, not just one type as in LEAP.

The CDPs were originally constructed to validate repairs during apprenticeship learning. However, they nicely allow the initial knowledge base to be validated prior to apprenticeship learning. As will be reported in Section 18.6, about half of the existing knowledge base is modified during the processing stage that focuses on ensuring that the domain theory contains correct knowledge.

## 18.5 ODYSSEUS'S METHOD FOR IMPROVING AN INCONSISTENT DOMAIN THEORY

A processing stage prior to apprenticeship learning also removes a form of inconsistent knowledge from the domain theory, which is responsible for deterioration of the performance of the system due to sociopathic interactions between elements of the domain theory. A domain theory is *sociopathic* if and only if (1) all the rules in the knowledge base individually meet some "goodness" criteria; and (2) a subset of the knowledge base gives better performance than the original knowledge base. The five biases described in Section 18.4 provide an example of goodness criteria for heuristic rules in the domain theory.

The significance of the phenomena of sociopathicity is as follows. First, most extant expert systems have sociopathic knowledge bases. Second, traditional methods to correct missing and wrong rules, e.g., the general TEIRESIAS approach [Davis, 1982], cannot handle the problem. Third, sociopathicity imposes a limit on the quality of knowledge base performance. And last, it implies that some kind of global refinement for the acquired knowledge is essential for machine learning systems.

The phenomena of sociopathicity is addressed at length in another paper, [Wilkins and Ma, 1989], wherein we show that the best method for dealing with this form of inconsistency is to find a subset of the original domain theory that is not sociopathic (which must exist by our definition of sociopathicity). A summary of our results are as follows: The process of finding an optimal subset of a sociopathic knowledge base is modeled as a bipartite graph minimization problem and shown to be NP-hard. A heuristic method, the *sociopathic reduction algorithm*, has been developed to find a suboptimal solution for sociopathic domain theories. The heuristic method has been experimentally shown to give good results.

## 18.6 RELATED RESEARCH

### 18.6.1 ODYSSEUS and Explanation-based Learning

The ODYSSEUS apprenticeship learning method involves the construction of explanations, but it is different from explanation-based learning as formulated in EBG [Mitchell, *et al.*, 1986] and EBL [DeJong, 1986]; it is also different from explanation-based learning in LEAP [Mitchell, *et al.*, 1989], even though LEAP also focuses on the problem of improving a knowledge-based expert system. In EBG, EBL, and LEAP, the domain theory is capable of explaining a training instance, and learning occurs by generalizing an explanation of the training instance. In contrast, in our apprenticeship research, a learning opportunity occurs when the domain theory, which is the domain knowledge base, is incapable of producing an explanation of a training instance. The domain theory is incomplete or erroneous, and all learning occurs by making an improvement to this domain theory.

### 18.6.2    Case-based versus Apprenticeship Learning

In empirical induction from cases, a training instance consists of an unordered set of feature-value pairs for an entire diagnostic session and the correct diagnosis. In contrast, a training instance in apprenticeship learning is a single feature-value pair given within the context of a problem-solving session. This training instance is therefore more fine-grained, can exploit the information implicit in the order in which the diagnostician collects information, and allows obtaining many training instances from a single diagnostic session. Our apprenticeship learning program attempts to construct an explanation of each training instance; an explanation failure occurs if none is found. The apprenticeship program then conjectures and tests modifications to the knowledge base that allow an explanation to be constructed. If an acceptable modification is found, the knowledge base is altered accordingly. This is a form of learning by completing failed explanations.

The case-based learning approach currently modifies or adds heuristic rules to the knowledge base. It runs all the cases in the library and locates those that are misdiagnosed. Given a misdiagnosed case, the local credit assignment problem is solved as follows: The premises of the rules that concluded the wrong final diagnosis are weakened by specialization, and the premises of the rules that concluded the correct diagnosis are strengthened. If this does not solve the problem, new rules will be induced from the patient case library that apply to the misdiagnosed case and that conclude the correct final diagnosis. The verification procedure used to test all knowledge-base modifications is identical to that described for apprenticeship learning.

### 18.7    EXPERIMENTAL RESULTS

Our knowledge-acquisition experiments centered on improving the knowledge base of the NEOMYCIN expert system for diagnosing neurology problems. The initial NEOMYCIN knowledge base was constructed manually over a 7-year period; the first test of this system on a representative suite of test cases was performed in conjunction with the ODYSSEUS system. The NEOMYCIN vocabulary includes 60 diseases; our physician, Dr. John Sotos, determined that the existing data request vocabulary of 350 manifestations only allowed diagnosis of 10 of these diseases. Another physician, Dr. Edward Herskovits, constructed a case library of 115 cases for these 10 diseases from actual patient cases from the Stanford Medical Hospital, to be used for testing ODYSSEUS. The validation set consisted of 112 of these cases.

Let us begin our performance analysis by considering the baseline system performance prior to any ODYSSEUS knowledge base refinement. The expected diagnostic performance that would be obtained by randomly guessing diagnoses is 10%,

and the performance expected by always choosing the most common disease is 18%. Version 2.3 of HERACLES with the NEOMYCIN knowledge base initially diagnosed 31% of the cases correctly, which is 3.44 standard deviations better than always selecting the disease that is *a priori* the most likely. On a student t-test, this is significant at a $t = .001$ level of significance. Thus we can conclude that NEOMYCIN's initial diagnostic performance is significantly better than guessing. Version 3.1 of MINERVA, with the manually constructed NEOMYCIN knowledge base gave almost identical performance results; it initially diagnosed 32 of the 112 cases correctly (28.5% accuracy).

Table 18–2 shows the various diseases and their sample sizes in the evaluation set. The result of each test suite are described along three dimensions. TP (true-positive) refers to the number of cases that the expert system correctly diagnosed as present, FN (false-negative) to the number of times a disease was not diagnosed as present but was indeed present, and FP (false-positive) to the number of times a disease was incorrectly diagnosed as present.

**Table 18–2:**  Summary of MINERVA experiments. The KB1 column is the performance using the manually constructed domain theory. KB2 shows performance after use of methods that correct an incorrect domain theory.

| Disease | Number of cases | KB1 | | | KB2 | | |
|---|---|---|---|---|---|---|---|
| | | TP | FN | FP | TP | FN | FP |
| Bacterial meningitis | 16 | 14 | 2 | 49 | 14 | 2 | 21 |
| Brain abscess | 7 | 0 | 7 | 1 | 0 | 7 | 1 |
| Cluster headache | 10 | 1 | 9 | 0 | 7 | 3 | 4 |
| Fungal meningitis | 8 | 0 | 8 | 0 | 4 | 4 | 0 |
| Migraine | 10 | 4 | 6 | 6 | 1 | 9 | 0 |
| Myco-TB meningitis | 4 | 0 | 4 | 2 | 4 | 0 | 0 |
| Primary brain tumor | 16 | 0 | 16 | 0 | 0 | 16 | 0 |
| Subarach hemorrhage | 21 | 1 | 20 | 0 | 15 | 6 | 0 |
| Tension headache | 9 | 7 | 2 | 5 | 7 | 2 | 6 |
| Viral meningitis | 11 | 5 | 6 | 11 | 10 | 1 | 12 |
| None | 0 | 0 | 0 | 6 | 0 | 0 | 6 |
| Totals | 112 | 32 | 80 | 80 | 62 | 50 | 50 |

**Table 18–3:** Summary of MINERVA experiments. KB3 and KB4 show the performance after using case-based learning and apprenticeship learning, respectively, to extend the incomplete domain theory.

| Disease | Number of cases | KB3 | | | KB4 | | |
|---|---|---|---|---|---|---|---|
| | | TP | FN | FP | TP | FN | FP |
| Bacterial meningitis | 21 | 12 | 4 | 4 | 14 | 2 | 13 |
| Brain abscess | 7 | 5 | 2 | 15 | 1 | 6 | 0 |
| Cluster headache | 10 | 7 | 3 | 4 | 8 | 2 | 0 |
| Fungal meningitis | 8 | 3 | 5 | 0 | 3 | 5 | 0 |
| Migraine | 10 | 4 | 6 | 0 | 6 | 4 | 0 |
| Myco-TB meningitis | 4 | 4 | 0 | 0 | 4 | 0 | 1 |
| Primary brain tumor | 16 | 0 | 16 | 0 | 3 | 13 | 0 |
| Subarach hemorrhage | 21 | 16 | 5 | 2 | 16 | 5 | 3 |
| Tension headache | 9 | 7 | 2 | 6 | 8 | 1 | 3 |
| Viral meningitis | 11 | 10 | 1 | 6 | 10 | 1 | 12 |
| None | 0 | 0 | 0 | 7 | 0 | 0 | 7 |
| Totals | 112 | 68 | 44 | 44 | 73 | 39 | 39 |

### 18.7.1 Improving an Incorrect and Inconsistent Domain Theory

The first stage of improvement involves locating and modifying *incorrect* domain knowledge tuples. Our method modified 48% of the heuristic rules in the knowledge base. The improvement obtained using the refined knowledge base is shown in column KB2 of Table 18–2; MINERVA diagnosed 62 cases correctly (55.3% accuracy), showing an improvement of about 27%. The second stage of improvement involves correcting inconsistent domain knowledge. No experimental results are reported here, although our methods have been previously shown to lead to significant improvement [Wilkins and Ma, 1989].

### 18.7.2 Extending Incomplete Domain Theory via Case-based Reasoning

The third stage of improvement involves extending a correct but incomplete domain knowledge base. Two experiments were conducted. The first used case-based learning. All the cases were run, and two misdiagnosed cases in areas where the knowledge base was weak were selected. The case-based learning approach was applied to these two cases. This refinement, shown in column KB3 of Table 18–3, enabled the system to diagnose 68 cases correctly (60.7% accuracy), showing an aggregate improvement of 32%.

### 18.7.3 Extending Incomplete Knowledge Base via Apprenticeship Learning

The second experiment used apprenticeship learning. For use as a training set, problem-solving protocols were collected by Dr. Sotos's solving two cases, consisting of approximately 30 questions each. ODYSSEUS discovered 10 pieces of knowledge by watching these two cases being solved; eight of these were domain rule knowledge. These eight pieces of information were added to the NEOMYCIN knowledge base of 152 rules, along with two pieces of frame knowledge that classified two symptoms as "general questions"; these are questions that should be asked of every patient. This refinement, shown in column KB4 of Table 18–3, enabled the system to diagnose 73 cases correctly (65.2% accuracy), an aggregate improvement of about 37%. Compared to NEOMYCIN's original performance, the performance of NEOMYCIN after improvement by ODYSSEUS is 2.86 standard deviations better. On a student t-test, this is significant for t = .006. One would expect the improved NEOMYCIN to perform better than the original NEOMYCIN in better than 99 out of 100 sample sets.

It is important to note that the improvement occurred despite the physician's only diagnosing one of the two cases correctly. The physician correctly diagnosed a cluster headache case and misdiagnosed a bacterial meningitis case. As is evident from examining Tables 18–2 and 18–3, the improvement was over a wide range of cases. And the accuracy of diagnosing bacterial meningitis cases actually decreased. These counterintuitive results confirm our hypothesis that the power of our learning method derives from following the line of reasoning of a physician on individual findout question and is not sensitive to the final diagnosis as is the case in learning by empirical induction from examples.

All of this new knowledge learned by apprenticeship learning was judged by Dr. Sotos as plausible medical knowledge, except for a domain rule linking aphasia to brain abscess. Importantly, the new knowledge was judged by our physicians to be of much higher quality than when straight empirical induction was used to expand the knowledge base, without the use of explanation-based learning.

More experimental work remains. Our previous experiments with ODYSSEUS suggest that the apprenticeship learning approach is better than a case-based approach for producing a user-independent knowledge base to support multiple problem-solving goals such as learning, teaching, problem-solving, and explanation generation.

## 18.8  CONCLUSIONS

In this chapter, we presented three distinct methods used by ODYSSEUS to improve a domain theory.

Our method of extending an incomplete domain theory is a form of failure-driven explanation-based learning, which we refer to as apprenticeship learning. Apprenticeship is the most effective means for human problem solvers to learn domain-specific problem-solving knowledge in knowledge-intensive domains. This observation provides motivation to give apprenticeship learning abilities to knowledge-based expert systems. The paradigmatic example of an apprenticeship period is medical training, in which we have performed our investigations.

With respect to the incomplete theory problem, the research described illustrates how an explicit representation of the strategy knowledge for a general problem class, such as diagnosis, provides a basis for learning the domain-level knowledge that is specific to a particular domain, such as medicine, in an apprenticeship setting. Our approach uses a given body of strategy knowledge that is assumed to be complete and correct with the goal of learning domain-specific knowledge. This contrasts with learning programs such as LEX and LP where the domain-specific knowledge (e.g., integration formulas) is completely given at the start, and the goal is to learn strategy knowledge (e.g., preconditions of operators) [Mitchell, *et al.*, 1983]. Two sources of power of the ODYSSEUS approach are the method of completing failed explanations, called the *metarule chain completion method*, and the use of underlying domain theories to evaluate domain-knowledge changes via the *confirmation decision procedure method*. Our approach complements the traditional method of empirical induction from examples for refining a knowledge base for an expert system for heuristic classification problems. With respect to learning certain types of heuristic rule knowledge, empirical induction from examples plays a significant role in our work. In these cases, an apprenticeship approach can be viewed as a new method of biasing selection of which knowledge is learned by empirical induction.

An apprenticeship learning approach, such as described in this chapter, is perhaps the best possible bias for automatic creation of large "user-independent" knowledge bases for expert systems. We desire to create knowledge bases that will support the multifaceted dimensions of expertise exhibited by some human experts, dimensions such as diagnosis, design, teaching, learning, explanation, and critiquing the behavior of another expert.

The long-term objectives of this research are the creation of learning methods that can harness an explicit representation of generic shell knowledge and that can lead to the creation of a user-independent knowledge base that rests on deep underlying domain models. Within this framework, this chapter described specialized methods that address three major types of knowledge base pathologies: incorrect, inconsistent, and incomplete domain knowledge. We believe that the use of *specialized methods* for different domain knowledge pathologies minimizes the interactions between pathologies, thereby making the problem much more tractable.

## ACKNOWLEDGMENTS

Many people have greatly contributed to the evolution of the ideas presented in this chapter. We would especially like to thank Bruce Buchanan, Bill Clancey, Tom Dietterich, Haym Hirsh, John Holland, John Laird, Pat Langley, Bob Lindsay, John McDermott, Ryszard Michalski, Roy Rada, Tom Mitchell, Paul Rosenbloom, Ted Shortliffe, Paul Scott, Devika Subramanian, Marianne Winslett, the members of the Grail learning group, and the Guidon tutoring group. This work would not have been possible without the help of physicians Eddy Herskovits, Kurt Kapsner, and John Sotos.

We would also like to express our deep gratitude to Lawrence Chachere, Ziad Najem, Young-Tack Park, and Kok-Wah Tan, and other members of the Knowledge-based Systems group at the University of Illinois for their major role in the design and implementation of the MINERVA shell and for many fruitful discussions. This research was principally supported by NSF grant MCS-83-12148, and ONR grants N00014-79C-0302 and N00014-88K0124.

## References

Boose, J.H. 1984. Personal construct theory and the transfer of human expertise. In *Proceedings of the 1983 National Conference on Artificial Intelligence*, pp. 27–33, Washington, D.C.

Buchanan, B.G. and Shortliffe, E.H. 1984. *Rule-Based Expert Systems: The MYCIN Experiments of the Stanford Heuristic Programming Project*. Reading, MA: Addison-Wesley.

Clancey, W.J. 1984. NEOMYCIN: Reconfiguring a rule-based system with application to teaching. In Clancey, W.J. and Shortliffe, E.H., editors, *Readings in Medical Artificial Intelligence*, Chapter 15, pp. 361–381. Reading, MA: Addison-Wesley.

Park, Y.T., Tan, K.W., and Wilkins, D.C. 1989. ProHCD: A knowledge based system shell with declarative representation and flexible control: For heuristic classification and VLSI design tasks. Working Paper KBS-89-01, Department of Computer Science, University of Illinois, Urbana-Champaign, Illinois.

Pearl, J. 1986a. Fusion, propagation, and structuring in belief networks. *Artificial Intelligence*, 29(3):241–288.

Pearl, J. 1986b. On evidential reasoning in a hierarchy of hypotheses. *Artificial Intelligence*, 28(1):9–15.

Quinlan, J.R. 1983. Learning efficient classification procedures and their application to chess end games. In Michalski, R.S., Carbonell, J.G., and Mitchell, T.M., editors. *Machine Learning: An Artificial Intelligence Approach*, pp. 463–482. San Mateo, CA: Morgan Kaufmann.

Tecuci, G. and Kodratoff, Y. 1990. Apprenticeship learning in imperfect domain theories. In Kodratoff, Y. and Michalski, R.S., (eds), *Machine Learning: An Artificial Intelligence Approach, Volume III*, pp. 514–551. San Mateo: CA, Morgan Kaufmann.

Wilkins, D.C. 1987. *Apprenticeship Learning Techniques For Knowledge Based Systems*. PhD Thesis, University of Michigan. Also, Report No. STAN-CS-88-1242, Dept. of Computer Science, Stanford University, 1988.

Wilkins, D.C. and Ma, Y. 1989. Sociopathic knowledge bases. Technical Report UIUCDCS-R-89-1538, Department of Computer Science, University of Illinois. Submitted to *Artificial Intelligence*.

Clancey, W.J. 1985. Heuristic classification. *Artificial Intelligence*, 27:289–350.

Clancey, W.J. 1986. From GUIDON to NEOMYCIN to HERACLES in twenty short lessons. *AI Magazine*, 7:40–60.

Davis, R. 1982. Application of meta level knowledge in the construction, maintenance and use of large knowledge bases. In Davis, R. and Lenat, D.B., editors, *Knowledge-Based Systems in Artificial Intelligence*, pp. 229–490. NY: McGraw-Hill.

DeJong, G. 1986. An approach to learning from observation. In Michalski, R.S., Carbonell, J.G., and Mitchell, T.M., editors, *Machine Learning: An Artificial Intelligence Approach, Volume II*, pp. 571–590. San Mateo, CA: Morgan Kaufmann.

Elstein, A.A., Shulman, L.S., and Sprafka, S.A. 1978. *Medical Problem Solving: An Analysis of Clinical Reasoning*. Cambridge: Harvard University Press.

Fu, L.M. and Buchanan, B.G. 1985. Learning intermediate concepts in constructing a hierarchical knowledge base. In *Proceedings of the 1985 IJCAI*, pp. 659–666, Los Angeles, CA.

Ginsberg, A., Weiss, S., and Politakis, P. 1985. SEEK2: A generalized approach to automatic knowledge base refinement. In *Proceedings of the 1985 IJCAI*, pp. 367–374, Los Angeles, CA.

Kahn, G., Nowlan, S., and McDermott, J. 1985. MORE: An intelligent knowledge acquisition tool. In *Proceedings of the 1985 IJCAI*, pp. 573–580, Los Angeles, CA.

Michalski, R.S. 1983. A theory and methodology of inductive inference. In Michalski, R.S., Carbonell, J.G., and Mitchell, T.M., editors, *Machine Learning: An Artificial Intelligence Approach*, pp. 83–134. San Mateo, CA: Morgan Kaufmann.

Mitchell, T., Utgoff, P.E., and Banerji, R.S. 1983. Learning by experimentation: Acquiring and refining problem-solving heuristics. In Michalski, T.M., Carbonell, J.G., and Mitchell, T.M., editors, *Machine Learning: An Artificial Intelligence Approach*, pp. 163–190. San Mateo, CA: Morgan Kaufmann.

Mitchell, T.M., Keller, R.M., and Kedar-Cabelli, S.T. 1986. Explanation-based generalization: A unifying view. *Machine Learning*, 1(1):47–80.

Mitchell, T.M., Mahadevan, S., and Steinberg, L.I. 1989. LEAP: A learning apprentice for VLSI design. In Kodratoff, Y. and Michalksi, R.M., editors, *Machine Learning: An Artificial Intelligence Approach, Volume III*, pp. 271–289. San Mateo, CA: Morgan Kaufmann.

# Section 6.2

# Apprentice Systems for Design Knowledge

Automation of knowledge acquisition for design expert systems is a very difficult problem. The two most promising approaches to date are interactive elicitation and design apprentices.

LEAP is a learning apprentice in the domain of VLSI circuit design. The apprentice program improves the knowledge base of the VEXED intelligent editor for VLSI design. The VEXED editor is not an expert system for design, but rather a design aid that can be used by experts. As such, the need to learn or handle procedural and control knowledge is minimized.

When VEXED is augmented with LEAP, the combined system can be viewed as a smart elicitation tool. LEAP goes beyond the intelligent elicitation tools discussed in Chapter 3, such as AQUINAS, MOLE, SALT, and PROTEGE, because it is able to verify and generalize the training examples given by the user.

DISCIPLE is a design aid that assumes a top-down refinement approach to design, and uses an explain-and-generalize cycle and performs constraint propagation. DISCIPLE is distinguished by its use of many different learning methods. When there is a strong domain theory for the knowledge it is learning, it generalizes this knowledge using EBL. When the knowledge is weak, it uses multiple learning strategies including EBL, learning by analogy, and empirical learning.

Much of the human intelligence in design relates to knowing what refinement to make next. Neither LEAP nor DISCIPLE learns such control knowledge.

# LEAP:
## A LEARNING APPRENTICE
## FOR VLSI DESIGN

Tom M. Mitchell
(*Carnegie Mellon University*)

Sridhar Mahadevan
Louis I. Steinberg
(*Rutgers University*)

**Abstract**

It is by now well recognized that a major impediment to developing knowledge-based systems is the knowledge-acquisition bottleneck: The task of building up a complete enough and correct enough knowledge base to provide high-level performance. This chapter proposes a new class of knowledge-based systems designed to address this knowledge-acquisition bottleneck by incorporating a learning component to acquire new knowledge through experience. In particular, we define *learning apprentice systems* as the class of *interactive*, knowledge-based consultants that directly assimilate new knowledge by observing and analyzing the problem-solving steps contributed by their users through their *normal* use of the system. This chapter describes a specific learning apprentice system, called LEAP, which is currently being developed in the domain of VLSI design. We also discuss design issues for learning apprentice systems more generally, as well as restrictions on the generality of our current approach.

## 10.1 LEARNING APPRENTICE SYSTEMS

It is by now well recognized that a major impediment to developing knowledge-based systems is the knowledge-acquisition bottleneck: The task of building up a complete enough and correct enough knowledge base to provide high-level performance. In an effort to reduce the cost and increase the level of performance of current knowledge-based systems, a number of researchers have developed semi-automated tools for aiding in the knowledge-acquisition process. These tools include interactive aids to help pinpoint and correct weaknesses in existing sets of rules (e.g., [Davis, 1981; Politikas, 1982]), as well as aids for the acquisition of new rules (e.g., [Kahn, et al., 1984]). Others have studied automated learning of rules from databases of stored cases, but with few exceptions (e.g., [Buchanan and Mitchell, 1978; Michalski and Chilauskym, 1980]), work on machine learning has not yet led to useful knowledge-acquisition tools.

This chapter proposes a new class of knowledge-based consultant systems designed to overcome the knowledge-acquisition bottleneck, by incorporating recently developed machine learning methods to automate the acquisition of new rules. In particular, we define *learning apprentice systems* as the class of *interactive* knowledge-based consultants that directly assimilate new knowledge by observing and analyzing the problem-solving steps contributed by their users through their *normal* use of the system. This chapter discusses issues related to the development of such learning apprentice systems, focusing on the design of a particular learning apprentice system (called LEAP) for VLSI circuit design.

One key aspect of learning apprentice systems as we define them is that they are designed to continually acquire new knowledge without an explicit "training mode." For example, the LEAP system provides advice on how to refine the design of a VLSI circuit, while allowing the user to override this advice and to manually refine the circuit when he so desires. In those cases where the user manually refines the circuit, LEAP records this problem-solving step as a training example of some new rule that it should have had. LEAP then generalizes from this example to form a new rule summarizing this refinement tactic.

In task domains for which learning apprentice systems are feasible, we expect that they will offer strong advantages over current architectures for knowledge-based systems. Many copies of a learning apprentice system distributed to a broad community of users could acquire a base of problem-solving experience very large compared to the experience from which a human expert learns. For example, by distributing copies of LEAP to a thousand circuit designers, the system (collection) would quickly be exposed to a larger number of example circuit designs than a human designer could hope to see during a lifetime. Such a large experience base would offer the potential for acquiring a very strong knowledge base, provided effective learning methods can be developed.

The following section describes the design of the LEAP learning apprentice system for VLSI design, focusing on its mechanism for capturing training examples, and on its methods for generalizing from these examples to form new rules. The final

section discusses some of the major choices made in the initial design of LEAP, limitations on the applicability of our initial approach, and several basic issues that we see as central to developing learning apprentice systems in a variety of task domains.

## 10.2  LEAP: A LEARNING APPRENTICE FOR VLSI DESIGN

LEAP is currently being constructed as an augmentation to a knowledge-based VLSI design assistant called VEXED [Mitchell, *et al.*, 1985]. VEXED provides interactive aid to the user in implementing a circuit given its functional specifications, by suggesting and carrying out possible refinements to the design. A large part of its knowledge about circuit design is composed of a set of *implementation rules*, each of which suggests some legal method for refining a given function. For example, one implementation rule states that *IF the required function is to convert a parallel signal to a serial signal, THEN one possible implementation is to use a shift register*. It is these rules that LEAP is designed to learn. This section describes the VEXED system, the type of training examples that it can capture from its users, and two generalization methods that allow LEAP to form general rules from these examples.

### 10.2.1  The VEXED Design Consultant

VEXED is a prototype knowledge-based design consultant that provides a convenient editor and user interface that helps the user design digital circuits beginning with functional specifications and leading to implementation. VEXED maintains an agenda of design subtasks (e.g., "implement the module that must multiply two numbers"), which initially contains the top-level task of implementing the entire circuit. VEXED repeatedly selects a subtask from the agenda, examines its implementation rules to determine whether it can suggest possible implementations for the corresponding circuit module, then presents any such suggestions to the user. The user may select one of the suggested implementation rules—in which case that rule is executed to refine the module. Alternatively, the user may disregard VEXED's suggestions and instead use the editor to refine the circuit module manually. It is in this latter case that LEAP will add to its knowledge of circuit design, by generalizing from the implementation step contributed by the user to formulate a new rule that summarizes a previously uncatalogued implementation method.

As an example of this kind of learning scenario, suppose that at some point during the design VEXED and the user are considering the task of implementing a particular circuit module. In the example, this circuit module must compute the Boolean product of sums of four particular input signals that appear in the context of the larger circuit. Assume further that these input signals are regular streams of Boolean values arriving every 100 nanoseconds, remaining stable for approximately 70 nanoseconds, and encoded in positive logic.[1] Assume furthermore, that the stream of input values for Input1 is known to be an alternating stream of logical ones and zeros. The exact definitions of the function to be implemented and of the signals for which it must work are given in the top half of Figure 10–1.[2]

Given this information about the module to be implemented, the system searches its set of implementation rules for advice regarding possible refinements of this circuit. In this case, the system may have a rule that suggests implementing the circuit module using an AND gate and two OR gates. Suppose, however, that the user disregards the advice of the system in this case, choosing instead to implement the module using the circuit shown in Figure 10–1. This implementation contributed by the user provides the system with precisely the kind of training example that LEAP needs for learning a new implementation rule. In general, then, each training example consists of

1. a description of the function to be implemented,

2. a description of the known characteristics of the input signals, and

3. a circuit entered by the user to implement the given function for the given input signals.[3]

Given such a training example, there are two kinds of changes that one might expect the system to make to its knowledge base. First, LEAP has the opportunity to acquire a new implementation rule that can be used in subsequent cases to suggest the user's NOR-gate circuit where it is a *possible* implementation. Second, the system also has an opportunity to learn a fragment of control knowledge for selecting between the NOR–gate implementation and the previously known AND-OR-gate implementation, depending on which is *preferred* according to some cost criterion. In VEXED, we have cleanly separated out these two kinds of knowledge. Implementation rules characterize only the *possible* correct implementations, while a separate body of control knowledge will be used to select the *preferred* implementation from among several possible alternatives. In our work to date and in this chapter, we consider only learning of new implementation rules that characterize the general conditions under which the user's circuit can be correctly used.

---

[1] That is, a logical one is encoded as five volts, and a logical zero as zero volts.

[2] Signals or "datastreams" in VEXED are described as an array of data elements, each defined in terms of its value, start-time, duration, data type, and encoding.

[3] Although in this example the user's circuit has been refined down to the gate level, in general it need only be one step more refined than the submodule it is implementing.

**Function to be Implemented:**
Inputs: Input1. Input2. Input3. Input4
Outputs: Output.
Function: (Equals (Value Output(i))
    (And (Or (Value Input1(i)) (Value Input2(i)))
         (Or (Value Input3(i)) (Value Input4(i)))))

**Where Input Signals Satisfy:**
(Datatype Input1(i)) = Boolean
(Value Input1(i)) = i Mod 2
(Encoding Input1(i)) = Positive-Logic
(Start-Time Input1(i)) = $i \cdot 100 + t_0$
(Duration Input1(i)) = 75 nsec.
(Datatype Input2(i)) = Boolean
(Value Input2(i)) = unknown
(Encoding Input2(i)) = Positive-Logic
(Start-Time Input2(i)) = $i \cdot 100 + t_0$
(Duration Input2(i)) = 65 nsec.
(Datatype Input3(i)) = Boolean
(Value Input3(i)) = unknown
(Encoding Input3(i)) = Positive-Logic
(Start-Time Input3(i)) = $i \cdot 100 + t_0$
(Duration Input3(i)) = 58 nsec.
(Datatype Input4(i)) = Boolean
(Value Input4(i)) = unknown
(Encoding Input4(i)) = Positive-Logic
(Start-Time Input4(i)) = $i \cdot 100 + t_0$
(Duration Input4(i)) = 75 nsec.

**User's Solution:**

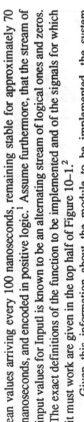
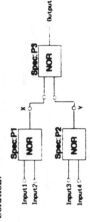

**Figure 10–1:**    A training example for LEAP

Given this training example, the most straightforward method of acquiring a new implementation rule is to create a rule that suggests the given circuit can be used to implement the given module function in precisely this context (e.g., whenever the input signals are precisely the same as in the training example). Such a rule would clearly be so specific that it would add little of general use to the system's knowledge of implementation methods. A better approach would be to generalize the pre-

IF the Function to be Implemented is of the form:
    Inputs: Input1, Input2, Input3, Input4
    Outputs: Output
    Function: (Equals (Value Output(i))
                (And (Or (Value Input1(i)) (Value Input2(i)))
                     (Or (Value Input3(i)) (Value Input4(i)))))

Where Input Signals Satisfy:
    ((Datatype Input1(i) = Boolean)
    ((Encoding Input1(i)) = Positive-Logic)
    ((Datatype Input2(i) = Boolean)
    ((Encoding Input2(i)) = Positive-Logic)
    ((Datatype Input3(i) = Boolean)
    ((Encoding Input3(i)) = Positive-Logic)
    ((Datatype Input4(i) = Boolean)
    ((Encoding Input4(i)) = Positive-Logic)
    (Length (Intersection (Interval Input1(i))
             (Interval Input2(i))
             (Interval Input3(i))
             (Interval Input4(i)))) > 3 nsec.

THEN one possible implementation is:

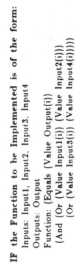

**Figure 10–2:**   Inferred rule with generalized left-hand side

IF the Function to be Implemented is of the form:
    Inputs: · inputs
    Outputs: <out·
    Function: (Equals (Value <out>(i))
                (And <bool-fn2> <bool-fn1·>) )

THEN one possible implementation is:

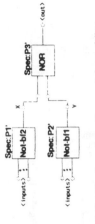

With Specifications of the three modules as follows:

P1': (Equals (Value X(i)) (Not <bool-fn2>))

P2': (Equals (Value Y(i)) (Not <bool-fn1>))

P3': (Equals (Value <out>(i)) (Not (Or X(i) Y(i))))

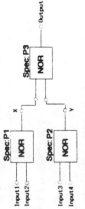

**Figure 10–3:**   Inferred rule with generalized right-hand side

conditions (left-hand side) of the implementation rule, so that it characterizes the general class of input signals for which the given circuit correctly implements the specified function. Such a generalized rule is shown in Figure 10–2 and the method for producing such generalizations in LEAP is described in the following subsection.

A further step in generalizing the implementation rule would be to generalize the user's circuit as well as the function it implements. (e.g., the essential idea behind the NOR-gate implementation can be used to implement a class of functions related to the one encountered in this training example). Such a generalization of the implementation rule is shown in Figure 10–3, and the method used by LEAP for generalizing the rule in this fashion is described in Section 10.2.3.

LEAP computes a justifiably general rule precondition by using its theory of digital circuits to analyze the single training example. In particular, LEAP first explains (verifies) for itself that the circuit does in fact work for the example input signals, then generalizes from this example by retaining only those features of the signals that were mentioned in this explanation. It is this set of signal features that is required for the explanation to hold in general, and which therefore characterizes the class of input signals for which the circuit will correctly implement the desired function. This explain-then-generalize method for producing justifiable generalizations from single examples is based on our previous work on goal-directed generalization [Mitchell, 1983], and is also similar to the generalization methods employed in [De-Jong, 1982; Salzberg and Atkinson, 1984; Minton, 1984].

To illustrate this generalization method, consider again the training example introduced in Figure 10–1. LEAP begins by verifying that the example circuit will operate correctly for the example input signals. In order to do this, it examines its definitions of the primitive components that make up the example circuit. Figure 10–4 shows the description of the primitive NOR gate used in the present example circuit. The *Operating Conditions* in this description summarize characteristics of the input signals that are required for the component to have a well-defined output. For example, the constraint

(Length (Intersection (Interval Input1(i)) (Interval Input2(i)))) > 3 nsec.

which follows from the operating conditions of the rightmost NOR gate, is re-expressed in terms of the four global circuit inputs to produce the equivalent constraint

*(Length (Intersection (Interval Input1(i))(Interval Input2(i)) (Interval Input3(i)) (Interval Input4(i)))) > 3 nsec.*[5]

By propagating the constraints arising from the operating conditions of the circuit components, as well as the original constraint on the circuit output (e.g., that it produces the Boolean sum of products of the input, LEAP can then verify that the user-introduced circuit will correctly implement the desired function for the given inputs. More importantly, the constraints that are propagated to the inputs of the circuit network characterize precisely the class of inputs for which the circuit will operate correctly, and therefore constitute the desired general preconditions for the newly acquired implementation rule.

In summary, the procedure for computing the generalized preconditions for the new rule is

1. to propagate each constraint derived from the operating conditions of each primitive circuit component, along with constraints on the global circuit output, back to the global inputs to the circuit network, then

2. to record the resulting constraints on the global inputs, with appropriate substitution of variable names, as the generalized preconditions for the new implementation rule.

Figure 10–2 illustrates the resulting generalization for the training example from Figure 10–1. Notice that in comparing this generalized rule with the original training example, values of several features of the circuit inputs have been generalized. Only the constraints on data type and on signal encodings remain intact, while the detailed values for the signal start-times and durations have been replaced by the general constraint on overlapping time intervals.

### 10.2.3 Generalizing Rule Right-Hand Side

The previous section describes how LEAP is able to generalize the left-hand side (LHS) of the rule by determining the class of input signals for which the given circuit will work. This section describes how LEAP can also generalize the right-hand side (RHS) of the rule; that is, generalize the circuit schematic along with the functional specifications to be implemented.

---

[5] This constraint propagation step is performed in the VEXED system by a set of routines called CRITTER [Kelly, 1984] which is able to propagate and check signal constraints in loop-free digital circuits by examining the function definition of the primitive circuit elements.

---

Inputs: Input1, Input2
Outputs: Output

Operating Conditions:
(Equals (**Datatype** Input1(i)) Boolean)
(Equals (**Encoding** Input1(i)) Positive-Logic)
(Equals (**Datatype** Input2(i)) Boolean)
(Equals (**Encoding** Input2(i)) Positive-Logic)
(Length (Intersection (Interval Input1(i))
                (Interval Input2(i)))) > 3 nsec.

Mapping:
(Equals (Value Output(i))
    (Not (Or (Value Input1(i)) (Value Input2(i)))))

(Equals (Encoding Output(i)) Positive-Logic)
(Equals (Start-Time Output(i))
    (+ 10 (Latest (Start-Time Input1(i))
                (Start-Time Input2(i)))))

(Equals (Duration Output(i))
    (Length (Intersection (Interval Input1(i))
                (Interval Input2(i)))))

The *Operating Conditions* describe minimum requirements on input signals to assure the component will produce a well-defined output. The *Mapping* describes how features of the output signal depend on the inputs.

**Figure 10–4:**   Known behavior of a NOR gate

indicates that for the NOR gate to operate correctly, its inputs must overlap in time by at least 3 nanoseconds.[4]

These operating conditions of the individual circuit components are constraints that must be verified for the example circuit and the given input signals. Some of these operating conditions can be tested directly against the descriptions of the global circuit inputs (e.g., the operating conditions for the leftmost NOR gates in the example circuit can be tested against the known characteristics of the circuit inputs). The operating conditions associated with components internal to the example circuit must be restated in terms of the equivalent constraints on the global circuit inputs. These constraints are therefore *propagated* to (reexpressed in terms of) the global inputs of the circuit network, then tested to see that they are satisfied by the example input signals. For instance, the constraint

*(Length (Intersection (Interval X(i)) (Interval Y(i)))) > 3 nsec.*

---

[4] The *Interval* of a data element is defined here as the time interval beginning at the *Start-time* of the data element, and continuing for the *Duration* of that element.

The key to generalizing the RHS is to first verify that the circuit correctly implements the desired function. This verification can then be examined to determine the general class of circuits and functional specifications to which the same verification steps will apply. This method, which we call *verification-based learning*, is described more generally in [Smith, *et al.*, 1988]. That paper discusses the general applicability of this method to learning problem decomposition rules, or planning schema. Here we discuss the application of this method to generalizing circuit implementation rules and illustrate the method using the training example and rule discussed above.

### 10.2.3.1 Step 1: Forming the Composed Specification from Rule RHS

The first step in the process of inferring a general circuit design rule from a training example is verification—ensuring that the function computed by the user's circuit meets the original circuit specification.

We can derive a description of the circuit's function from its structure by composing the functions of the submodules constituting the circuit, according to the configuration in which they are interconnected. For the user's NOR-gate circuit, this *composed specification* is given as

```
(EQUALS (VALUE Output (i))
        (NOT (OR (NOT (OR (VALUE Input1 (i))
                          (VALUE Input2 (i))))
                 (NOT (OR (VALUE Input3 (i))
                          (VALUE Input4 (i))))
)))
```

Note that, in general, the composed specification will be a *syntactically re-expressed* version of the original specification. For example, the above composed specification is not syntactically identical to the functional specifications in the training example, even though it does represent the same Boolean function. This frequently occurs in VLSI circuits in which, for example, functional specifications in terms of AND and OR Boolean expressions are often implemented in terms of NAND and NOR gates.

### 10.2.3.2 Step 2: Verifying the Circuit Function

To verify the correctness of the user-suggested NOR-gate circuit, LEAP must show the equivalence between the *composed specification* for this circuit and the *original specification* of the circuit being implemented. Thus, it seeks to verify that

```
(IMPLIES <composed-spec> <original-spec>)
```

or in this case

```
(IMPLIES
  (NOT (OR (NOT (OR (VALUE Input1 (i))
                    (VALUE Input2 (i))))
           (NOT (OR (VALUE Input3 (i))
                    (VALUE Input4 (i))))))
  (AND (OR (VALUE Input1 (i))
           (VALUE Input2 (i)))
       (OR (VALUE Input3 (i))
           (VALUE Input4 (i)))))
```

LEAP verifies that the composed specification meets the original specification by determining a sequence of algebraic transformations which, when applied to the composed specification, will yield the original specification. Each transform has a *precondition*, which describes the class of situations to which it can be applied, and a *postcondition*, which specifies the result of the transformation. The two transforms that will be used for the current example in the circuit domain are given below.

de Morgan's Law
Precondition:
```
(NOT (OR <bool-fn1> <bool-fn2>))
```
Postcondition:
```
(AND (NOT <bool-fn1>) (NOT <bool-fn2>))
```

Remove-Double-Negation:
Precondition:
```
(NOT (NOT <bool-fn>))
```
Postcondition:
```
<bool-fn>
```

Here "<bool-fn>" represents an arbitrary Boolean function. Shown below is the verification as a sequence of transformations.

Verification

```
(NOT (OR (NOT (OR (VALUE Input1(i))
                  (VALUE Input2(i))))
         (NOT (OR (VALUE Input3(i))
                  (VALUE Input4(i))))))
```
↓
de Morgan
↓
```
(AND (NOT (NOT (OR (VALUE Input1(i))
                   (VALUE Input2(i)))))
     (NOT (NOT (OR (VALUE Input3(i))
                   (VALUE Input4(i))))))
```

### Remove-Double-Negation

```
→
→
(AND (OR (VALUE Input1(i))
         (VALUE Input2(i)))
    (NOT (NOT (OR (VALUE Input3(i))
                  (VALUE Input4(i))))))
→
```

### Remove-Double-Negation

```
→
(AND (OR (VALUE Input1(i))
         (VALUE Input2(i)))
    (OR (VALUE Input3(i))
        (VALUE Input4(i))))
```

## 10.2.3.3 Step 3: Determining the Generalized Composed Specification

Given the verification tree shown above, the next step is to determine the general class of expressions for which this sequence of verification steps will correctly apply. This is essentially a problem of viewing the transformation sequence as an operator and of determining the necessary preconditions for the operator sequence. LEAP accomplishes this by back-propagating the precondition of each transform in the sequence, to determine the necessary conditions on the starting expression. This process is described in greater detail in [Mahadevan, 1985]. The sequence shown below illustrates this back-propagation and indicates the resulting generalization of the composed specification.

### Computing the Generalized Composed Specification

```
(AND (OR (VALUE Input1(i))
         (VALUE Input2(i)))
    (OR (VALUE Input3(i))
        (VALUE Input4(i))))
→
```

### Remove-Double-Neg

```
→
→
(AND (OR (VALUE Input1(i))
         (VALUE Input2(i)))
    (NOT (NOT <bool-in1>)))
→
```

### Remove-Double-Neg

```
→
→
(AND (NOT (NOT <bool-fn2>))
    (NOT (NOT <bool-fn1>)))
→
```

### de Morgan

```
→
(NOT (OR (NOT <bool-fn2>)
         (NOT <bool-fn1>)))
```

Notice that the final expression in the above sequence describes the generalized composed specification for which the verification will correctly apply. From it, we see that the important feature of the two submodule specifications $P_1$ and $P_2$ (the two leftmost NOR gates in Figure 10-1) is that they both compute the *negation of some Boolean function*, while the specifications of the third component cannot be generalized.

### Generalized Specifications of Submodules

```
P₁': (EQUALS (VALUE X(i)) (NOT <bool-fn2>))
P₂': (EQUALS (VALUE Y(i)) (NOT <bool-fn1>))
P₃ : (EQUALS (VALUE <out>(i))
             (NOT (OR X(i) Y(i))))
```

## 10.2.3.4 Step 4: Determining the Generalized Original Specification

Having determined the generalized specifications of the circuit submodules, the RHS of the new rule can now be formed. However, LEAP must also produce a corresponding generalization of the original functional specification in the rule LHS. This generalized original specification can be computed in a relatively straightforward manner, either by reapplying the sequence of verification transforms or by using the variable bindings generated when computing the generalized composed specification. Following either of these two approaches, the result is that the new, original specification becomes

```
(EQUALS (VALUE Output(i))
        (AND <bool-fn2> <bool-fn1>))
```

Comparing the generalized original specification above with the original specification of the circuit implementation in Figure 10-1, it is seen that a generalization of the original specification has been achieved from a conjunction of disjunctions to a *conjunction of any Boolean functions*.

## 10.2.3.5 Step 5: Forming the New Implementation Rule

We have shown in the last few paragraphs how the original specification of a circuit module as well as the functional specifications of each of the submodules $P_i$ in its implementation could be generalized. The final step is to form the new implementation rule, which is based on these generalized specifications. The preconditions for this new rule are formulated to require (1) that the function to be implemented match the generalized original specification, and (2) that the input signals satisfy the constraints that are determined as shown in the previous subsection. The right-hand side of the new rule is formulated so that it produces the submodules with their corresponding submodule specifications $P'_i$. For the present example, the new implementation rule formed in this fashion is shown in Figure 10–3.[6]

## 10.3 DISCUSSION

The previous section describes in some detail how LEAP captures training examples from its users, and how it forms general rules from these examples. This section discusses more broadly the architectural issues involved in designing knowledge-based systems that can incorporate such learning methods. In particular, we discuss the major design features of LEAP that appear important to the design of learning apprentice systems more generally. Three design features that have a major impact on the capabilities of LEAP are:

1. the interactive nature of the problem solving system,

2. the use of analytic methods for generalizing from examples, and

3. the separation of knowledge about when an implementation technique can be used from knowledge about when it *should* be used.

### 10.3.2 Interactive Nature of the Apprentice Consultant

A fundamental feature of LEAP is that it embeds a learning component within an *interactive* problem-solving consultant. This allows it to collect training examples that are closely suited to refining its rule base. In particular, training examples collected by a learning apprentice have two attractive properties:

1. Training examples focus only on knowledge that is missing from the system. The need for the user to intervene in problem solving occurs only when the system is missing knowledge relevant to the task at hand, and the resulting training examples therefore focus specifically on this missing knowledge.

2. The training examples correspond to single problem-solving steps. This is in contrast to the type of training examples used by other rule learning systems such as Meta-DENDRAL [Buchanan and Mitchell, 1978] and INDUCE-PLANT [Michalski and Chilausky, 1980], in which training examples are complete problem solutions. By working with training examples that are single steps, LEAP circumvents many difficult issues of credit assignment that arise in cases where the training example corresponds to a chain of several rules.

While to first order, LEAP acquires training examples that correspond to single-rule inferences, this is only approximately true. We expect that LEAP will encounter training examples in which its existing rules will correspond to finer grained decisions than the user thinks of as a single step. For instance, the system may have a sequence of rules to implement a serial–parallel converter by first selecting a shift register, then a general class of shift registers (e.g., dynamic), and only then a specific circuit, while the user may think of the whole series of decisions as a single step, implementing the converter with a specific circuit.

In such cases, LEAP could just go ahead and learn the larger grained rule that will follow from the user's training example, but doing so could cause a number of problems. One problem is that it will result in a ruleset with rules of greatly varying grain. Such inconsistency in grain is likely to lead to redundancy and lack of generality in the rules. A second potential problem associated with large-grain training examples is that our analytical methods of generalization may be too expensive to use on steps of large grain. Since the methods depend on constructing a verification of the step, there is reason to fear the cost may grow very quickly as the size of the step gets large compared to the size of the transformations used in the verification process.

Thus, the question of how to handle grain-size mismatch may be an important issue for future research. One possible direction would be to develop methods for examining a training example that corresponds to a large step, then determining which existing rules correspond to parts of this inference step, leaving only the task of acquiring the missing finer grain rules.

### 10.3.2 Use of Analytical Methods for Generalization

A second significant feature of the design of LEAP is that it uses analytical methods to form general rules from specific training examples, rather than more traditional empirical, data-intensive methods. LEAP's explain-then-generalize method, based on having an initial domain theory for constructing the explanation of the example, allows LEAP to produce justifiable generalizations from single training examples. This capability is particularly important for LEAP since it is not at all clear how LEAP could tell that two different training examples involving different circuit specifications and different resulting circuits, were in fact two examples of the same rule.

One significant advantage of the analytical methods involves learning in the presence of error-prone training data. An issue that seems central to research on learning apprentice systems, and one that LEAP must confront immediately, is that the users who (unwittingly) supply its training examples are likely to make mistakes. In particular, since we hope to first introduce LEAP to a user community of university students who are themselves learning about VLSI design, the issue of dealing with error-prone examples is a major one. Our initial plan for dealing with this prob-

---

[6]Notice that in this rule, there are no final constraints that must be satisfied by the input signal. This is because the leftmost circuit modules in the figure are defined so abstractly that they pose no constraints on the signal formats of their inputs.

lem is straightforward. LEAP will form general rules *only* from the training example circuits that it can verify in terms of its knowledge of circuits. Since its generalization method requires that it explain an example circuit before it can generalize it, LEAP will be a very conservative learner. Since it will be unable to verify incorrect circuit examples that it encounters, there is little danger of its learning from incorrect examples.[7] This method of dealing with errorful data is attractive, but may be insufficient if we need to include empirical learning methods along with analytical methods for generalization.

While analytical generalization methods offer a number of advantages, they require that the system begin with a domain theory to explain/validate the training examples. This requirement, then, constrains the kind of domain for which our approach can be used. In the domain of digital circuit design, the required domain theory corresponds to a theory for verifying the correctness of circuits. In certain other domains, such a theory may be difficult to come by. For example, in domains such as medical diagnosis the underlying theory to explain/verify an inference relating symptoms to diseases is often unknown even to the domain experts. In such domains, the system would lack a domain theory to guide the analytical generalization methods, and would have to rely instead on empirical generalization methods that generalize by searching for similarities among a large number of training examples. In fact, our current methods for utilizing domain theories to guide generalization are limited to cases where there is a strong enough theory to "prove" the training example is correct. One important research problem is thus to develop methods for utilizing more approximate, incomplete domain theories to guide generalization, and for combining analytical and empirical generalization methods in such cases. One new research project that is interesting in this light is an attempt to construct a learning apprentice for well-log interpretation [Smith, *et al.*, 1985]. In this domain, the underlying theory necessary to learn new rules involves geology and response of well-logging tools. Since these theories are inherently approximate and incomplete, that research project must face the issue of generating and utilizing approximate explanations of training examples to infer general rules.

### 10.3.3 Partitioning of Control and Basic Domain Knowledge

A third significant feature in the design of LEAP is the partitioning of its knowledge base into (1) implementation rules that characterize *correct* (though not necessarily preferred) circuit implementations, and (2) control knowledge for selecting the *preferred* implementation from multiple legal options. This partitioning is

important because it helps deal with the common problem that when one adds a new rule to a knowledge base one must often adjust existing rules as well.

The first of these two parts of the knowledge base has the convenient property that its rules are logically independent; that is, when one adds a new implementation rule characterizing a new implementation method, it does not alter in any way the correctness of the existing implementation rules. Thus, when a new implementation rule is added, the only portion of the knowledge base that might require an update is the control knowledge for selecting among alternative implementations. This logical independence of implementation rules is also important when combining sets of rules that may have been learned from various users by different copies of the learning apprentice. While the problem of combining multiple rulesets learned from different sources is in principle simply a matter of forming the union of the rulesets, in fact the resulting set of correct rules may be overly redundant and disorganized. Thus, we anticipate that we may have to develop methods for merging and reorganizing sets of correct rules to make them more manageable.

To date, we have only considered learning the first type of knowledge. In some sense, learning these rules is easier than learning the control knowledge, because the complexity of explaining a training example is much less for implementation rules than for control rules. To explain/verify an example of an implementation rule, the system need only verify the correctness of the circuit fragment mentioned in the training example. However, to learn a control rule that characterizes when some implementation is *preferred*, it is necessary to compare this implementation with all the alternative possibilities. Thus, the complexity of constructing the explanations is quite different in these two cases. In the longer term, we see learning of control knowledge as an important task for LEAP, and a task for which it can easily capture useful training examples.

### 10.4 CONCLUSION

We have presented the notion of a learning apprentice system as a framework for automatically acquiring new knowledge in the context of an interactive knowledge-based consultant. The initial design of a learning apprentice for VLSI design has been described. In particular, we have detailed the methods that LEAP employs for learning new implementation rules, and for generalizing both the left- and right-hand side of these rules. Whereas, previous attempts at automatic knowledge acquisition have met with little success, the proposed learning apprentice system differs in two important respects: It utilizes more powerful analytical learning methods, and it is restricted to interactive knowledge-based systems that can easily capture useful training examples.

---

[7] Even this is not quite true. Since the domain theory is only approximate (as will probably be true for learning apprentice systems in general), there may be incorrect circuits that it succeeds in verifying (say, because it overlooks parasitic capacitances).

# ACKNOWLEDGMENTS

We thank several people who provided useful criticisms of earlier drafts of this chapter: Rich Keller, Yves Kodratoff, John McDermott, Jack Mostow, Reid Smith, and Timothy Weinrich. We also thank the members of the Rutgers AI/VLSI project for many useful discussions regarding the design of LEAP, and for creating the VEXED system on top of which LEAP is being constructed. Schlumberger-Doll Research has made the STROBE system available as a representation framework in which VEXED and LEAP are being implemented. This chapter was reprinted from *Proceedings of the International Conference on Artificial Intelligence*, 1985, with permission of IJCAI, Inc. This material is based on work supported by the Defense Advanced Research Project Agency under Research Contract N00014-81-K-0394, and by the National Science Foundation under grant DCS83-51523. The views and conclusions in this document are those of the authors and should not be interpreted as necessarily representing the official policies, either expressed or implied, of the Defense Advanced Research Projects Agency, the National Science Foundation, or the U.S. Government.

## References

Davis, R. 1981. "Application of meta level knowledge to the construction and use of large knowledge bases." In *Knowledge-based Systems in Artificial Intelligence*, Davis, R. and Lenat, D., eds., McGraw-Hill, NY.

Politakis, P. 1982. *Using Empirical Analysis to Reline Expert System Knowledge Bases*, PhD Dissertation, Rutgers University, August 1982.

Kahn, G., Nowlan, S., and McDermott, J. 1984. "A Foundation for Knowledge Acquisition." In *Proceedings of the IEEE Workshop of Principles of Knowledge-based Systems*. IEEE, December 1984, pp. 89–96.

Buchanan, B.G. and Mitchell, T.M. 1978. "Model-directed learning of production rules," in *Pattern-directed Inference Systems*, Waterman, D, A. and Hayes-Roth, F., eds., Academic Press, NY.

Michalski, R.S. and Chilausky R.L. 1980. "Knowledge Acquisition by Encoding Expert Rules Versus Computer Induction from Examples: A Case Study using Soybean Pathology." *Intl. Jrnl. for Man-Machine Studies* 12:63.

Mitchell, T.M., Steinberg, L.I., and Shulman, J.S. 1984. "A Knowledge-based Approach to Design." In *Proceedings of the IEEE Workshop of Principles of Knowledge-based Systems*, IEEE, December 1984, pp. 27–34. Revised version

appeared *IEEE Transactions on Pattern Analysis and Machine Intelligence*, September 1985.

Mitchell, T. 1983. "Learning and Problem-Solving." In *IJCAI-83*, August 1983, pp. 1139–1151.

DeJong, G. 1982. "Automatic Schema Acquisition in a Natural Language Environment." In *Second National Conference on Artificial Intelligence*. Pittsburgh, PA, August 1982, pp. 410–413.

Salzberg, S. and Atkinson, D.J. 1984. "Learning by Building Causal Explanations." In *ECAI-84*. September 1984, pp. 497–500.

Minton, S. 1984. "Constraint-based Generalization." In *AAAI-84*. Austin, Texas, August 1984, pp. 251–254,

Kelly, Van E. 1984. "The CRITTER System—Automated Critiquing of Digital Circuit Designs." In *Proceedings of the elat Design Automation Conference.* IEEE, June 1984, pp. 419–425. Also Rutgers AI/VLSI Project Working Paper No. 13

Mahadevan, S. 1985. "Verification-based Learning: A Generalization Strategy for Inferring Problem Decomposition Methods." In *Proceedings of the Ninth International Joint Conference on Artificial Intelligence*, August 1985.

Smith, R.G., Winston, H.A., Mitchell, T.M., and Buchanan, B.G. 1985. "Representation, Use and Generation of Explicit Justifications for Knowledge Base Refinement." In *Proceedings of the Ninth International Joint Conference on Artificial Intelligence*, August 1985.

# Techniques of Design and DISCIPLE Learning Apprentice

YVES KODRATOFF
Université de Paris-Sud, France

AND

GHEORGHE TECUCI
Research Institute for Computers and Informatics, Bucharest

ABSTRACT: Recent machine learning achievements have given expert systems the ability to acquire knowledge automatically. Our system, DISCIPLE, is part of this effort. DISCIPLE contains an interactive problem solver that integrates new knowledge by observing, analyzing, and questioning its user, as a normal way of functioning. This article presents an account of the DISCIPLE learning apprentice system (its knowledge representation, problem solving, and learning mechanisms) from the user's point of view. The emphasis is on the system's external behavior and not on its internal mechanisms. The article is a case study of the application of DISCIPLE to a domain with weak theory: techniques of design for the manufacturing of loudspeakers.

KEYWORDS: expert systems, machine learning, planning, explanation-based learning, generalization

## INTRODUCTION

If expert systems have proven useful in many domains, their applications are limited by their difficulty (or inability) to acquire and to update their knowledge. This problem is largely recognized as the *knowledge acquisition bottleneck* of expert systems.[5]

Recent machine learning achievements[15,17,19] offer new solutions to the knowledge acquisition problem and open a new area in the evolution of expert

*International Journal of Expert Systems*      Pp. 39–66. Volume 1, Number 1, 1987. ISSN 0894-9077.
Copyright © 1987 by JAI PRESS INC.                        All rights of reproduction in any form reserved.

systems: the second generation expert systems,[23] that is, expert systems able to automatically acquire knowledge and learn. Learning apprentice systems (LAS)[20] are examples of such second generation expert systems. A learning apprentice system incorporates a traditional expert system and a learning system as follows.

The user gives the system a problem to solve and the expert subsystem starts solving this problem by showing the user all the problem-solving steps. The user may agree or reject them. Therefore, during the course of its functioning as an expert system, a LAS may encounter two situations: (1) the current problem-solving step (which we shall call *partial solution*) is accepted by the user, in which case, the current state of the knowledge base is judged as satisfactory, and no learning will take place; or (2) it is unable to propose any partial solution (or the solution it proposes is rejected by the user), in which case the user is compelled to give his/her own solution. Once this solution is given, a learning process will take place. The LAS will try to learn a general rule so that, when faced with problems similar to the current one (which it has been unable to solve thus far), will be able to propose a solution similar to the solution given by the user.

From this general presentation one could notice the following important features of a LAS: (1) it is an interactive problem solver, and (2) it continually acquires and improves its knowledge. One consequence of the first feature is that a LAS should be able to solve problems that are ahead of its implemented capabilities. One consequence of the second feature is that we can start using a LAS even if its knowledge is very limited because it will be developed during problem solving. This is not possible with the traditional expert systems, which, before being used, require a long and difficult process of knowledge-base construction.

Another consequence of the second feature is that a LAS seems to be, as Mitchell et al[20] pointed out, a means of acquiring a social expertise. Indeed, many copies of a LAS, distributed to a broad community of users, could acquire the problem-solving experience of this community, that is, a base of problem-solving experience very large compared to the experience from which a human expert learns.

In principle, the knowledge base should keep a reasonable size and stay consistent, because any new chunk of knowledge must be proven useful and consistent before being added. Nevertheless, because in this article we are concerned with the domains having a weak theory, it is hopeless to believe we can avoid these drawbacks. The worse the domain, the more the system, in its learning mode, calls for interactions with a few selected experts.

One such LAS is LEAP,[20] which was developed in the domain of VLSI design. LEAP utilizes explanation-based generalization: (1) it produces justifiable generalization from a single example, (2) it is able to reject incorrect training examples, and (3) it relies on a strong domain theory.

**Figure 1:** Problem-Solving Operations: Decomposition of Problems into Simpler Subproblems

*In order to achieve the goal:*
    **manufacture** loudspeaker
*achieve in sequence the subgoals:*

1.  **make** chassis-assembly

    *In order to achieve this subgoal, achieve in sequence the sub-subgoals:*

    1.1. **fix** upper-flange **on** chassis
    1.2. **mount** magnet lower-flange **and** bolt

2.  **make** membrane-assembly

3.  **assemble** chassis-assembly **and** membrane-assembly

4.  **perform** final-operations **for** loudspeaker

**Figure 2:** Problem-Solving Operations: Successive Specializations of a Problem

*In order to achieve the goal:*
    **fix** upper-flange **on** chassis
*achieve the more specialized goal:*
    **fix** upper-flange **on** chassis **with** an automatic press

*In order to achieve the goal:*
    **fix** upper-flange **on** chasses **with** an automatic press
*achieve the more specialized goal:*
    **fix** upper-flange **on** chassis **with** an automatic press **and** Aloorex-C107 adhesive

We are developing another type of learning apprentice, called DISCIPLE, which could be contrasted with LEAP in that it utilizes a combination of explanation-based learning and similarity-based learning: (1) it relies on incomplete and/or weak domain theory, (2) it relies on user to reject incorrect training instances; and (3) it produces justifiable generalizations from examples.

While DISCIPLE is presented in detail by Kodratoff and Tecuci,[12] and Tecuci,[25] in this article we present an account of DISCIPLE from the user's point of view. To this purpose we use examples from a technology design domain.

## AN INTUITIVE VIEW OF DISCIPLE[1]

While there are many different types of techniques, we shall restrict our discussion here to assembling techniques. More precisely, we shall consider examples of designing manufacturing techniques for loudspeakers. The technique design problem could then be characterized as follows: given the constructive design of a loudspeaker, design the actions needed to manufacture the loudspeaker. This problem is similar to several others, for instance, robot action planning,[4,21,25] acquisition of procedural knowledge,[13] or configuration design,[7] or reasoning about devices.[2] The so-called blackboard architecture is also a solution to the kind of problems we are dealing with.[9]

Before presenting this domain in more detail, we stress two of its important features: (1) the domain is usually too complex for an autonomous system, and (2) small technical improvements have important outcomes, since a technology is usually used for a large number of products. Therefore the best solution is sought. One consequence of these features is that such a domain is most appropriately handled with an interactive system, as the consultant subsystem of a LAS.

The design of technologies is viewed here as a successive decomposition of complex operations into simpler ones, and better defining these simpler operations by choosing tools, materials, or verifiers, which are in turn successively refined.

### The Problem-Solving Method: Decomposition and Specialization Rules

Let us consider designing the manufacturing of some given loudspeaker. We start with the following top-level operation, which can be seen as the current goal:

    **manufacture** loudspeaker

DISCIPLE will try to solve this problem by successive decompositions and specializations, as illustrated in Figure 1 and Figure 2. DISCIPLE will combine the decompositions and the specialization, thus constructing a problem-solving tree, as shown in Figure 3.

**2. Output.** *The following is issued by the system:* A general rule indicating how to decompose or specialize problems similar to the given one.

## The Typical Acquisition of Knowledge

Let us suppose that while planning the manufacturing of the loudspeaker, DISCIPLE encounters the following problem:

> **clean** entrefer **from** dust

For which it is unable to propose a satisfactory specialization of the cleaning operation. Let us further suppose that the user indicated the following solution to DISCIPLE:

> **clean** entrefer **from** dust **with** air-sucker

Now DISCIPLE knows a solution of the current problem. This solution will be considered farther as an instance of a general rule to be learned:

> *In order to achieve* **clean** entrefer **from** dust
> *achieve the specialization* **clean** entrefer **from** dust **with** air-sucker

From the above example, DISCIPLE is able to learn the following specialization rule:

> **If:**     ($z$ **isa** cleaner) & ($z$ **removes** $y$)
> **Then:**   *achieve*      **clean** $x$ **from** $y$
>           *by achieving*   **clean** $x$ **from** $y$ **with** $z$

Further, this rule will enable DISCIPLE to make new specializations as for instance:

> *In order to achieve* **clean** membrane-assembly **from** surplus-glue
> *achieve the specialization* **clean** membrane-assembly **from** surplus-glue **with** solvent

This way DISCIPLE acquires new knowledge and improves its problem-solving abilities.

## Interactions Between DISCIPLE and Its User

The context for using DISCIPLE can be described by the interaction among DISCIPLE and its user. DISCIPLE, the human expert (i.e., the user of DISCIPLE), the background knowledge about the concerned technology (further called *domain theory*), and the current application of DISCIPLE.

DISCIPLE and its user are in constant interaction, both proposing solutions and explanations to the other. DISCIPLE has access to a database containing the domain theory, but its user does not. The user has access to the features of the current application, but DISCIPLE does not.

---

## Inputs and Outputs of DISCIPLE

When DISCIPLE is unable to solve a problem satisfactorily, it will ask for a solution from the user. Once this solution is given, a learning process will take place, which can be described by its inputs and its output.

**1. Inputs.** *The following are given to the system:* An incomplete domain theory (types of objects with properties, inference rules, and problem-solving operators, i.e., decomposition and specialization rules), a problem to be solved, and a partial solution to the problem (i.e., a decomposition or a specialization).

---

**Figure 3:** A Problem-Solving Tree*

*In order to achieve the goal*
    **manufacture** loudspeaker
*achieve in sequence the subgoals*
1.  **make** chassis-assembly
    *In order to achieve this subgoal,*
    *achieve in sequence the sub-subgoals*
    1.1.  **fix** upper-flange **on** chassis
          *In order to achieve the sub-subgoal*
          **fix** upper-flange **on** chassis
          *achieve the specialization*
          **fix** upper-flange **on** chassis **with** an
          automatic press

          *In order to achieve*
          **fix** upper-flange **on** chassis **with** an
          automatic press

          *achieve the specialization*
          **fix** upper-flange **on** chassis **with** an
          automatic press **and** Alorex-C107
          adhesive
    1.2.  **mount** magnet lower-flange **and** bolt
2.  **make** membrane-assembly
3.  **assemble** chassis-assembly **and** membrane-
    assembly
4.  **perform** final-operations **for** loudspeaker

*The tree was built by using the decompositions from Figure 1 and the specializations from Figure 2.

This last feature may be felt as a serious drawback. This is wrong, because while needing to know if the current loudspeaker has a certain feature, DIS-CIPLE will simply ask the user, waiting for one of the following answers: yes, no, irrelevant, as exemplified in "Problem Reduction Rules" below. This is similar to the approach taken in robot action planning systems when the system has to take care of execution errors.

DISCIPLE starts with a very general specification of the problem (plan the manufacturing of a loudspeaker, in our example) and the system will start solving this problem without knowing the specific features of the current loud-speaker. Only when the known technological solution depends on the presence (or absence) of certain features, will DISCIPLE ask the user if the loudspeaker has the respective feature.

The set of all questions asked during a session, together with their answers, provides a complete consistent description of the current loudspeaker, as opposed to the class of loudspeakers so far designed. In other words, the current loudspeaker is described, and one can notice the features that make it different from the already known loudspeakers.

In order to be able to build a technique of design of loudspeakers, DISCIPLE needs some knowledge about the components of the loudspeakers, about the technological solutions for the manufacturing of loudspeakers, and about the tools and the materials one can use to manufacture loudspeakers. All this knowledge constitutes the *domain theory*. This domain theory is inherently incomplete since one cannot suppose that DISCIPLE knows:

- all the objects of the domain,
- all the properties of a given object,
- all the actions that can be performed for manufacturing loudspeakers,
- all the properties of the known actions (preconditions, effects),
- all the ways of decomposing or specializing a given action.

During problem solving, DISCIPLE will learn new knowledge and will develop its domain theory.

The utility of DISCIPLE to design techniques results from the fact that there are many types of products (belonging to a certain family, for instance, the loudspeaker family) that are not very different from each other. As a conse-quence, many of the technological solutions used to manufacture a certain type of loudspeaker are also applicable to a new type.

## KNOWLEDGE REPRESENTATION IN DISCIPLE, AND THE EXPERT SUBSYSTEM

DISCIPLE is aimed both at acquiring knowledge from an expert and at auto-matically inferring new rules from this knowledge. This section describes the organization of knowledge obtained by, so to say, rote learning, directly from the expert, without any automatic learning. The section "The Learning Subsystem," will describe how inferences are performed.

The knowledge base of DISCIPLE consists of objects with properties and relations, goals (which are always actions in the present version of DISCIPLE), rules for decomposing actions, and rules for specializing actions. In the follow-ing, objects, actions, and goals are all generically called *concepts*.

One of our prime concerns was to design a knowledge representation and organization in which the main operations involved in learning (that is, generali-zations and particularizations,[14,10]) must be easily done. It was inspired by Kodratoff,[11] by Sridharan and Bresina,[22] and by Tecuci.[24]

### Objects

DISCIPLE uses hierarchical semantic networks to represent the objects (con-cepts). An object (concept) is represented as belonging to a superconcept (thus inheriting all the properties of the superconcept) and having additional proper-ties. The value of a property may be a constant (5 or ANALOGICAL, for instance) or a definite concept (the name of a tool, for instance). A concept may be a son of several superconcepts (that is, it may belong to several hierarchies). An example of an object hierarchy is shown in Figure 4. Externally, these objects are represented as follows:

(superconcept   concept   (property-1 value 1)...(property-n value-n))

For instance:

```
(CLEANER     AIR-MOVER    (REMOVES DUST))
(AIR-MOVER   AIR-SUCKER   (ABSORBS DUST))
(COLLECTOR   AIR-SUCKER)
```

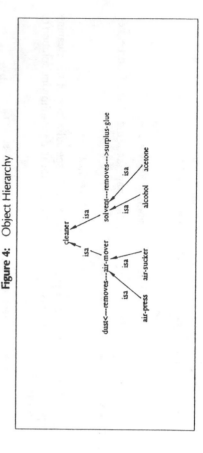

**Figure 4:**   Object Hierarchy

The following, for instance, is a decomposition rule:

```
If:     (preconditions)     (ADHESIVE z
                            (GLUES x)
                            (GLUESy))
Then:   achieve goal        ATTACH OBJECT x ON y
        by achieving        |-
        the sequence of subgoals:  APPLY SUBSTANCE z ON x.
                            PRESS OBJECT x ON y.
```

This rule says that if $z$ is an adhesive that glues $x$ and $y$, then, in order to attach $x$ on $y$, one might apply $z$ on $x$ and then press $x$ on $y$. In the current implementation of DISCIPLE it is assumed that the subgoals are to be achieved sequentially. This restriction should disappear in future versions, allowing the user to describe a strategy for the achievement of the subgoals.

The decomposition rules are one of the means by which DISCIPLE represents technological solutions. Recall from section 2 that DISCIPLE starts designing the manufacturing of a loudspeaker without requiring a description of it. It should be evident, however, that certain technological solutions depend on the loudspeaker's features. Then, if needed, it will ask the user whether the loudspeaker has some given feature. The origin of the system's questions is a certain type of precondition (called here *question precondition*), which is associated with certain rules.[8]

The following, for instance, is a decomposition rule with a question precondition:

```
If:     LOUDSPEAKER HAS SCREENING-CAP?   YES
Then:   FINAL-OPERATIONS OBJECT LOUDSPEAKER.
        |-
        VERIFY OBJECT LOUDSPEAKER.
        ATTACH OBJECT SCREENING-CAP TO LOUDSPEAKER.
        MARK OBJECT LOUDSPEAKER.
```

That is, when designing the final operations for the loudspeaker, DISCIPLE will ask the user the following questions:

LOUDSPEAKER HAS SCREENING-CAP?   [Yes, No, Irrelevant]

If the answer is yes, DISCIPLE will propose to verify the loudspeaker, to attach the screening-cap, and to mark the loudspeaker. If the answer is no, this rule will not be applicable and DISCIPLE will look for another one, in which the loudspeaker has no screening-cap.

These question preconditions refer only to the features of the current application, which, as said in the section "Interactions Between DISCIPLE and Its User," may be unknown to DISCIPLE. They avoid forcing the user to provide beforehand a complete description of the application. These questions single out the features that are relevant to the manufacturing process. During the design session, the questions and their answers are recorded, and help to construct, step by step, a relevant description of the current application.

## Actions

Generally speaking, actions are described by specifying operators (as CLEAN in the example below) and objects representing the parameters of these operators (as ENTREFER in the example below). The external representation of an action is:

```
name     property-1    value-1
         :
         property-n    value-n
```

For instance:

```
CLEAN   OBJECT    ENTREFER
        FROM      DUST
        WITH      AIR-SUCKER
```

Very important additional features of an action are its preconditions (or simply conditions) and postconditions (or effects). The traditional action planning systems make intensive use of these features. Nevertheless, when acquiring knowledge from an expert, requiring from him/her a complete description of the conditions and effects of an action may quickly lead to a dead end in the relationships between system and human. This is why the conditions and the effects of an action are only optional features of the action at this stage. As we shall see, DISCIPLE is precisely built in order to overcome this problem. When the expert provides a totally instantiated rule, its pre- and postconditions are implicit in the properties of the instances. When some generalization takes place (by means described in "The Learning Subsystem"), one has to explicitly find these conditions, which is DISCIPLE's job, performed at the learning step.

## Problem Reduction Rules

There are two types of problem reduction rules: decomposition rules and specialization rules. It must be understood that specialization rules are nothing but a special type of decomposition rule. Nevertheless, they are usually thought of as different by users, which forces us to differentiate them.

### Decomposition Rules

A decomposition has the following form:

```
If:     preconditions      PC
Then:   Achieve goal       A
        by achieving       |-
        the sequence of goals   (A₁, . . . Aₙ)
```

It indicates a decomposition of an action $A$ into a set of subactions $A_1, . . . , A_n$. The preconditions are a conjunction of predicates indicating the conditions under which this decomposition is applicable. Usually these predicates represent constraints on the objects referred to in the rule.

In the technique design domain, we found it useful to isolate three successive stages in the development of a design: (1) design of the detailed (elementary) operations of the technique; (2) design (choice of the tools, devices, or verifiers for each elementary operation; and (3) design (choice) of the materials needed for each operation. Depending on the implemented control strategy, the system may decide itself which problem to reduce next and what type of rule to look for. However, before deciding on the next problem to reduce, DISCIPLE gives control to the user. The user may return control to the system or may give a command. Some of the available user commands are: (1) decompose the current problem, (2) specialize the current problem to another problem from the system's hierarchies, (3) specialize an object from the current problem, (4) print the current partial solution (the leaves of the current problem-solving tree); or (5) delete the subtree of the current problem (that is, disregard the partial solution of the problem).

## Specialization Rules

Note that these specializations concern only the actions. When the specialization of an object is needed, this is taken into account in the knowledge base provided by the user. A specialization rule has the following form:

```
If:    preconditions     PC
Then:  Achieve goal       A
       by achieving       |-
       goal               A_i
```

This simply indicates that if the preconditions are true then $A_i$ is a possible specialization of the action A. Therefore, a specialization rule is a subcase of a decomposition rule, where only one action is allowed in the "decomposition."

The specialization rule whose learning has been informally presented in the introduction is shown below.

```
If:    (CLEANER z (REMOVES y))
Then:  CLEAN OBJECT x FROM y
       |-
       CLEAN OBJECT x FROM y WITH z
```

The specialization rules proved very useful in the technical design domain, allowing the introduction of information concerning tools, devices, verifiers, or materials, into an action description.

The decomposition and the specialization rules model in fact the main operations used in design, where we usually start with a very general specification of an object and successively impose different constraints on the specification and reduce object design to subparts design.

## Knowledge Utilization

In this section we intuitively describe the way DISCIPLE uses its knowledge to solve problems. The way DISCIPLE uses its knowledge to learn will be presented in the section, "The Learning Subsystem."

Recall from "An Intuitive View of DISCIPLE" that, after receiving a problem, DISCIPLE builds a problem-solving tree, such as the one shown in Figure 3, by applying successive decompositions and specializations. Let us consider, for instance, the problem of achieving the goal:

ATTACH OBJECT CENTERING-DEVICE ON CHASSIS-ASSEMBLY

DISCIPLE will look in its knowledge base for the rules that could indicate decompositions of this goal. Recall the form of a decomposition rule shown previously. If its left-hand side (A, i.e., the goal to be decomposed) is more general than the current goal (according to the syntactic rules of generalization we shall give in "Syntactic Generalization Rules"), and the preconditions of the rule are not known to be false, then the right-hand side of the rule $(A_1, \ldots, A_n)$ indicates a decomposition of the current goal.

Consider, for instance, the first rule on page 48. Its right-hand side is AT-TACH OBJECT x ON y, which is more general than our current goal (see "Turning Constants into Variables"). Therefore, DISCIPLE looks in its knowledge base to find out if the condition of the rule is satisfiable. That is, it tries to find out if there are adhesives which glue the centering-device and the chassis-assembly, and finds out that mowicoll, neoprene, prenadez, etc., are such adhesives. It therefore concludes that the decomposition indicated by the rule is feasible, and will propose it to the user as follows:

## Management of the Interactions Between the System and Its User

DISCIPLE communicates with the user by means of an interface, which of course gives the dialog a natural language appearance, but more important, allows the user to get involved in the problem solving and learning processes. The expert subsystem maintains an agenda of problems, which initially contains the top-level problem proposed by the user. This initial problem evolves in a problem-solving tree, while decomposition and specialization rules are applied, as shown in Figure 3.

DISCIPLE uses a certain control strategy to choose the next problem (among the leaves of the current tree) to reduce and what type of rule (decomposition or specialization) to look for. Although such a control strategy may itself be learned, we have not yet considered this learning task. Instead, several control strategies (depending on the application domain) are easily implementable into the system.

APPLY SUBSTANCE (ADHESIVE x (GLUES CENTERING-DEVICE)
                            (GLUES CHASSIS-ASSEMBLY))

ON CENTERING-DEVICE.
PRESS OBJECT CENTERING-DEVICE ON CHASSIS-ASSEMBLY.

Note that although DISCIPLE knows the adhesives that could be used, choosing an adhesive is a problem that will be addressed later.

Recall, however, that DISCIPLE is a learning apprentice and that it is "aware" that it does not know everything. Therefore, if it is not able to prove that the precondition of the rule is true, then it will ask the user if there exist adhesives gluing the centering-device and the chassis-assembly. If the user answers yes, then DISCIPLE will propose the above decomposition. Later on, when the user chooses an adhesive, the system will not only use it in the current problem solving, but will also introduce it into its knowledge base.

The specialization rules are used in a similar way, for specializing goals. But using specialization rules is not the only means DISCIPLE has for specializing goals. It might also specialize goals by using its object hierarchies. Let us consider, for instance, the object hierarchy in Figure 4, and the following goal: GET OBJECT CLEANER (REMOVES t). This goal could be specialized by replacing the concept CLEANER (REMOVES t) (which is not present in the hierarchy) with any of the most general concepts from Figure 4, which are less general than this concept. That is, the above concept may be replaced with AIR-MOVER (by turning the variable t into the constant DUST) or with SOL-VENT (by turning t to SURPLUS-GLUE).

In the first case, the goal is specialized to GET OBJECT AIR-MOVER. Further possible specializations consist in replacing AIR-MOVER with AIR-PRESS or with AIR-SUCKER, obtaining, for instance, GET OBJECT AIR-SUCKER.

## Metarules

In a given situation, more than one rule may be applicable and the system has to choose one of them to fire. The expert systems literature calls this "the conflict resolution problem." As in OPS,[6] for instance, we need a strategy (optimization criterion) that establishes the order of firing for the rules.

The conflict resolution problem is solved in DISCIPLE by using metarules of the form

A, OC → R₁, ..., Rₙ

$$A,\ OC \rightarrow R_1, \ldots, R_n$$

where A is the goal to be solved, OC an optimization criterion, and $R_1, \ldots, R_n$ are the applicable rules, ranked according to OC ($R_1$ being the best, according to OC). In the present version of DISCIPLE, each conflict set is split in several parts, because of the following problem-solving strategy:

1. When trying to solve a goal A, DISCIPLE first looks for solutions in more general goals, that is, it looks for decomposition rules.
2. Failing to find an acceptable solution, DISCIPLE looks at less general goals for specializations of A, that is, it looks for specialization rules.
3. Failing to specialize A by means of specialization rules, DISCIPLE searches the object hierarchies, trying to specialize an object from A.

Therefore, the decomposition and specialization rules are never mixed in the present version of the system. The reason for this approach is that the metarules can now be associated with the concepts (goals or objects) in the system hierarchies.

Let us consider, for instance, the object hierarchy in Figure 4. The conflict set associated with the concept **AIR-MOVER** is {**AIR-SUCKER, AIR-PRESS**}, since each element of this set may specialize the AIR-MOVER concept in a problem description containing it. In general, the conflict set associated with an object is formed by all the sons of the object (or the set of all sons, if the object belongs to several hierarchies).

A metarule, for instance, associated with the object AIR-MOVER, in the hierarchy from Figure 4, could be as shown in Figure 5. That is, if we want to increase the work-safety, then it is better to specialize AIR-MOVER to AIR-SUCKER than to AIR-PRESS.

Similarly, there are metarules associated with goals in system goal hierarchies. A metarule associated with a goal could indicate an ordering on the rules applicable for decomposing the goal or an ordering on the rules applicable for specializing the goal.

## THE LEARNING SUBSYSTEM

The aim of the learning subsystem is to learn more general concepts than the ones provided by the user. Classically, a concept $C_i$ is said to be more general than another concept $C_j$ if $C_i$ applies in all situations in which $C_j$ applies and in some other situations. Or, otherwise stated, the set of instances of $C_i$ includes the set of instances of $C_j$. The system considers that $C_i$ is more general than $C_j$ if it can transform $C_j$ into $C_i$ by applying generalization rules (replacing a concept from $C_i$ by a more general concept, for instance). The syntactic rules of generalizations used in DISCIPLE are presented in the following sections.

**Figure 5:** A Metarule

| | |
|---|---|
| object: | AIR-MOVER |
| criterion: | INCREASE FEATURE WORK-SAFETY |
| ordering: | 1. AIR-SUCKER |
| | 2. AIR-PRESS |

## Syntactic Generalization Rules

### Turning Constants into Variables

CLEANER (REMOVES DUST) > CLEANER (REMOVES x)

This rule consists in generalizing an expression by replacing a constant (DUST) with a variable $(x)$.[14] A slightly different rule is that of turning several occurrences of a variable into different variables.

### Climbing the Generalization Hierarchies

SECTORS (GLUED-BY MOWICOLL) > SECTORS (GLUED-BY ADHESIVE)

**Figure 6**

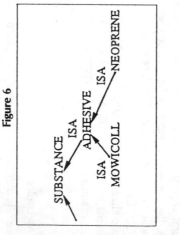

This rule consists in replacing a concept (MOWICOLL) with a more general one (ADHESIVE), according to a generalization hierarchy (shown in Figure 6). This rule is the most used one since the system's knowledge is organized as generalization hierarchies. If a child of SUBSTANCE, other than ADHESIVE, is met, then one would have to climb the generalization tree up to SUBSTANCE. In other words, the tree is climbed up to the first common parent of all the instances met.

### Climbing Goal Hierarchies

This generalization rule consists of replacing a goal with a more general one:

CLEAN OBJECT ENTREFER FROM DUST WITH AIR-SUCKER > CLEAN OBJECT ENTREFER FROM DUST

This rule is, in fact, a variant of the preceding one, but we mention it here because the climbing generalization hierarchies rule is usually used for generalizing object concepts only.

### Structural Generalization

This rule consists in the reverse application of a decomposition rule $A_i \rightarrow (A_{i1}, \ldots, A_{im})$, that is, in replacing $(A_{i1}, \ldots, A_{in})$ with $A'_i$, where $A'_i$ is obtained from $A_i$ by applying to $A_i$ the same particularizations needed to transform $A_{i1}, \ldots, A_{in}$ into $A'_{i1}, \ldots, A'_{in}$, respectively. For instance, the rule for decomposing the ATTACH action previously shown suggests that we should generalize:

APPLY SUBSTANCE NEOPRENE ON CENTER-DEVICE.
PRESS OBJECT CENTERING-DEVICE ON CHASSIS-ASSEMBLY.

into

ATTACH OBJECT CENTERING-DEVICE ON CHASSIS-ASSEMBLY.

### Dropping Conditions

ADHESIVE (TYPE FLUID) > ADHESIVE

This rule consists in removing a constraint from a description (in this case the constraint on the adhesive to be of fluid type). Although very risky,[11] this rule actualizes inductive hypotheses on what must be forgotten. One should use it only once one is sure that the domain theory does not forbid it.

### The Learning Problem

Let us suppose that, during planning the manufacturing of the loudspeaker, DISCIPLE encounters the problem of achieving the following goal for which it is unable to propose a satisfactory solution.

ATTACH OBJECT SECTORS ON CHASSIS-MEMBRANE-ASSEMBLY.

Let us further suppose that the user indicated the following solution to DISCIPLE:

APPLY SUBSTANCE MOWICOLL ON SECTORS.
PRESS OBJECT SECTORS ON CHASSIS-MEMBRANE-ASSEMBLY.

Now DISCIPLE knows a solution of the current problem, which it will further consider as an instance of the rule to be learned, even if APPLY and PRESS were previously unknown actions (in this last case, it only knows that they are a means of ATTACHING). Therefore the following illustrates an instance of a rule to be learned:

ATTACH OBJECT SECTORS ON CHASSIS-MEMBRANE-ASSEMBLY.
|-
APPLY SUBSTANCE MOWICOLL ON SECTORS.
PRESS OBJECT SECTORS ON CHASSIS-MEMBRANE-ASSEMBLY.

The rule DISCIPLE will try to learn has the following form:

If:   $x$, $y$, and $z$ satisfy < constraints >
Then:  ATTACH OBJECT $x$ ON $y$.
|-
APPLY SUBSTANCE $z$ ON $x$.
PRESS OBJECT $x$ ON $y$.

Rule learning is reduced to discovering the constraints on the $x$, $y$, and $z$ variables or, otherwise stated, to discovering the valid domains of the $x$, $y$, and $z$ variables.

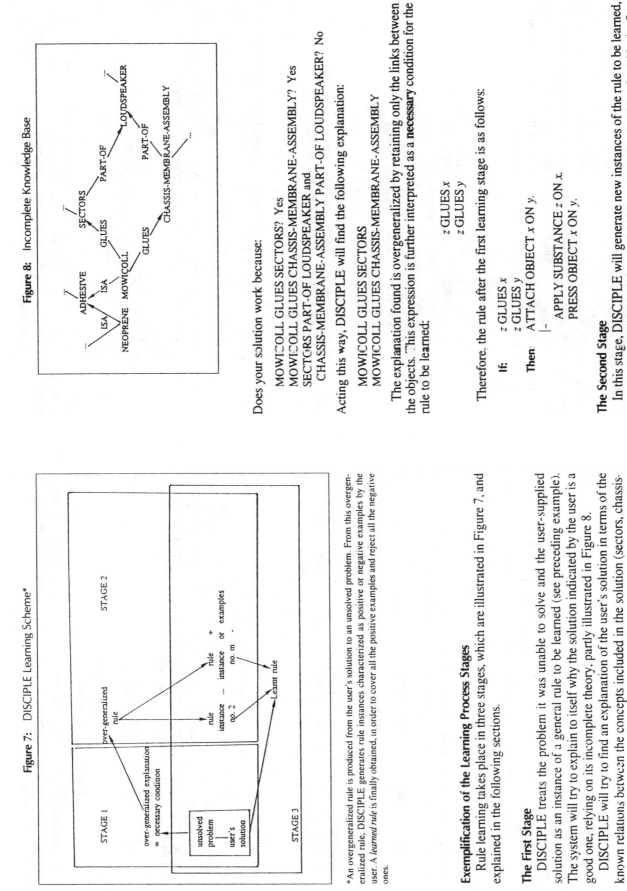

**Figure 8:**   Incomplete Knowledge Base

**Figure 7:**   DISCIPLE Learning Scheme*

Does your solution work because:

MOWICOLL GLUES SECTORS? Yes
MOWICOLL GLUES CHASSIS-MEMBRANE-ASSEMBLY?  Yes
SECTORS PART-OF LOUDSPEAKER and
CHASSIS-MEMBRANE-ASSEMBLY PART-OF LOUDSPEAKER?  No

Acting this way, DISCIPLE will find the following explanation:

MOWICOLL GLUES SECTORS
MOWICOLL GLUES CHASSIS-MEMBRANE-ASSEMBLY

The explanation found is overgeneralized by retaining only the links between the objects. This expression is further interpreted as a **necessary** condition for the rule to be learned:

$$z \text{ GLUES } x$$
$$z \text{ GLUES } y$$

Therefore, the rule after the first learning stage is as follows:

**If:**   $z$ GLUES $x$
          $z$ GLUES $y$

**Then:** ATTACH OBJECT $x$ ON $y$.
          |—  APPLY SUBSTANCE $z$ ON $x$.
               PRESS OBJECT $x$ ON $y$.

### The Second Stage

In this stage, DISCIPLE will generate new instances of the rule to be learned, by looking for all the objects satisfying the necessary condition found in the first stage. Let us suppose, for instance, that Figure 9 represents another fragment of DISCIPLE's knowledge base.

*An overgeneralized rule is produced from the user's solution to an unsolved problem. From this overgeneralized rule, DISCIPLE generates rule instances characterized as positive or negative examples by the user. A *learned rule* is finally obtained, in order to cover all the positive examples and reject all the negative ones.

### Exemplification of the Learning Process Stages

Rule learning takes place in three stages, which are illustrated in Figure 7, and explained in the following sections.

### The First Stage

DISCIPLE treats the problem it was unable to solve and the user-supplied solution as an instance of a general rule to be learned (see preceding example). The system will try to explain to itself why the solution indicated by the user is a good one, relying on its incomplete theory, partly illustrated in Figure 8.

DISCIPLE will try to find an explanation of the user's solution in terms of the known relations between the concepts included in the solution (sectors, chassis-membrane-assembly, and mowicoll, in our example). It will ask the user questions in order to distinguish between the relevant and the irrelevant links of the network.

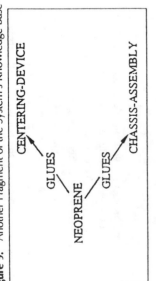

**Figure 9:** Another Fragment of the System's Knowledge Base

Because neoprene, centering-device, and chassis-assembly satisfy the rules condition, DISCIPLE will generate the following rule instance:

ATTACH OBJECT CENTERING-DEVICE ON CHASSIS—ASSEMBLY.
|-
    APPLY SUBSTANCE NEOPRENE ON CENTERING-DEVICE.
    PRESS OBJECT CENTERING-DEVICE ON CHASSIS-ASSEMBLY.

The user has to characterize such system-generated instances as examples or counterexamples of the rule to be learned. In this way, DISCIPLE discovers new examples and counterexamples of the rule.

### The Third Stage

If the instance shown above is a positive example of the rule to be learned, then neoprene (like mowicoll) is a positive example of the $x$ variable. Otherwise, neoprene is a negative example. In this third stage, DISCIPLE looks for the generalizations of the positive examples of $x$ $(y, z)$ that do not cover the negative examples. In this way it will discover the concept represented by $x$ $(y, z)$, that is the domain of $x$ $(y, z)$. Therefore, the learned rule is as follows:

If:     (ADHESIVE $z$ (GLUES $x$) (GLUES $y$)
Then:  ATTACH OBJECT $x$ ON $y$.
       |-
          APPLY SUBSTANCE $z$ ON $x$.
          PRESS OBJECT $x$ ON $y$.

The idea behind the use of the explanations for learning is that an explanation points to the main features of the objects, that is, to the features that have to be kept into the generalization.

## A SAMPLE DESIGN SESSION

In this section we present a sample session with DISCIPLE. The session is put between the delimiters /* ... */, and our comments are outside the delimiters. To differentiate between the user and the system, the user's replies are in italics. The session starts with the user indicating the top-level goal of manufacturing a loudspeaker. The system will present the possible reductions of the current operation (in this case MANUFACTURE), ordered by preference. Each reduction is prefixed by a number. The user may accept the system's suggestion, may prefer a lower ranked reduction—if any, may reject all the systems suggestions, or may wish to correct one of the system's suggestions.

/*
MANUFACTURE OBJECT LOUDSPEAKER.

1.  MAKE OBJECT CHASSIS-ASSEMBLY.
    MAKE OBJECT MEMBRANE-ASSEMBLY
    ASSEMBLE OBJECT CHASSIS-ASSEMBLY
       WITH MEMBRANE-ASSEMBLY.
    ATTACH OBJECT SECTORS
       ON CHASSIS-MEMBRANE-ASSEMBLY.
    ULTIMATE-OPERATIONS ON LOUDSPEAKER.
    Do you agree? [Yes, No, Modify]: *Yes*

1.  FIX OBJECTS CONTACTS ON CHASSIS.
    MAKE OBJECT MECHANICAL-CHASSIS-ASSEMBLY.
    CLEAN OBJECT ENTREFER FROM DUST.
    Do you agree? *Yes*
*/

DISCIPLE indicated a possible decomposition of the MANUFACTURE operation into simpler operations and the user agreed with the system's suggestion. Further on, following the implicit control strategy, DISCIPLE proposed a decomposition of the goal: MAKE OBJECT CHASSIS-ASSEMBLY. This decomposition was also accepted by the user. Now, DISCIPLE is trying to decompose the operation FIX OBJECTS CONTACTS ON CHASSIS.

/*
LOUDSPEAKER HAS TERMINAL-BLOCK? *Yes*
1.  * CRIMP OBJECTS CONTACTS ON SUPPORT.
    * CONNECT OBJECT TERMINAL-BLOCK ON CHASSIS.
    Do you agree? *Yes*
*/

DISCIPLE tried to decompose the FIX operation but the known rules are dependent on the loudspeaker features. Therefore, DISCIPLE asked the user a question and the answer received allowed it to choose the right rule. It is by means of such questions that DISCIPLE becomes progressively aware of loudspeaker features. Describing the loudspeaker in advance would not only be too cumbersome, but even impractical, since we do not know in advance which features are important and which are not important for the technique design.

The system prints an asterisk before each goal that may no longer be decomposed into simpler ones (CRIMP and CONNECT, in this case).

/*

    ..

    MAKE OBJECT MEMBRANE-ASSEMBLY.

1.  CONNECT OBJECTS TERMINAL-WIRES ON COIL.
    ASSEMBLE OBJECT MEMBRANE WITH COIL.
    ASSEMBLE OBJECT MEMBRANE WITH
       CENTERING-DEVICE.
    Do you agree? Yes

1.  TIN OBJECTS TERMINAL-WIRES.
    SHORTEN OBJECTS COIL-ENDS.
    TIN OBJECTS COIL-ENDS.
    TIN OBJECTS TERMINAL-WIRES WITH COIL-ENDS.
    Do you agree? No
    Could you indicate a solution? Yes
    *SHORTEN OBJECTS COIL-ENDS.*
    *SOLDER OBJECTS TERMINAL-WIRES WITH COIL-ENDS.*
    Does your solution work because:
    COIL-ENDS PART-OF COIL? No
    COIL-ENDS ISA TERMINALS and TERMINAL-WIRES
       ISA TERMINALS? No
    Could you give me an explanation? No

    I cannot make any generalization.
    I learned the following rule:
    problem:
    CONNECT OBJECTS TERMINAL-WIRES ON COIL.
    decomposition:
    SHORTEN OBJECTS COIL-ENDS.
    SOLDER OBJECTS TERMINAL-WIRES WITH COIL-ENDS.
    Do you agree? Yes

*/

As stated in "Management of the Interactions Between the System and Its User," the system has an implicit control strategy to choose the next problem to solve. Nevertheless, the user can direct the system to solve another problem. To this purpose it uses commands for traversing the problem-solving tree. Using such commands (not shown in our example) the user positioned DISCIPLE on the problem:

MAKE OBJECT MEMBRANE-ASSEMBLY.

Then, the implicit control strategy was resumed. Therefore, DISCIPLE proposed a decomposition of the MAKE operation. Then it automatically chose to decompose the first operation of this reduction (i.e., CONNECT) and proposed a possible decomposition of it. The user rejected this decomposition because he had in mind another technological solution. DISCIPLE tried to learn a general rule from user's solution. Therefore it started by looking for an explanation of this solution (as presented in "The Learning Subsystem"). Because neither DISCIPLE nor the user was able to provide an explanation, no generalization was possible. Nevertheless, DISCIPLE retained the specific rule indicated by the user because it was told to do so. This example shows that generalization is not always possible or desirable.

/*

    ..

ATTACH OBJECT SECTORS
   ON CHASSIS-MEMBRANE-ASSEMBLY.
Could you indicate a solution? Yes
*APPLY SUBSTANCE MOWICOLL ON SECTORS.*
*PRESS OBJECT SECTORS*
   *ON CHASSIS-MEMBRANE-ASSEMBLY.*
Does your solution work because:
MOWICOLL GLUES SECTORS? Yes
MOWICOLL GLUES
   CHASSIS-MEMBRANE-ASSEMBLY? Yes
CHASSIS-MEMBRANE-ASSEMBLY PART-OF
   LOUDSPEAKER and
SECTORS PART-OF LOUDSPEAKER? No
Do you agree with the explanation:
MOWICOLL GLUES SECTORS and MOWICOLL GLUES
   CHASSIS-MEMBRANE-ASSEMBLY? Yes

*/

Since DISCIPLE did not know any reduction of the ATTACH operation, it asked the user for one and proposed an explanation of it, as described in "The First Stage." Note that the explanation says why the decomposition is good and not why the ATTACH operation should be done. Therefore the user's answer to the third question was No.

/*

APPLY SUBSTANCE NEOPRENE ON SECTORS.
PRESS OBJECT SECTORS
   ON CHASSIS-MEMBRANE-ASSEMBLY.
Is it also a solution of the current problem? Yes

```
/*
    CLEAN OBJECT ENTREFER FROM DUST.
    Could you indicate a solution? Yes
    CLEAN OBJECT ENTREFER FROM DUST
        WITH AIR-SUCKER

    Does your solution work because:
    ENTREFER HAS DUST? No
    AIR-SUCKER ISA AIR-MOVER and AIR-MOVER
        REMOVES DUST? Yes
    Do you agree with the explanation
    AIR-SUCKER ISA AIR-MOVER and AIR-MOVER
        REMOVES DUST? Yes
*/
```

DISCIPLE was unable to propose any tool for the CLEAN operation, therefore it asked for a solution from the user. Then it found an explanation.

```
/*
    problem:
    CLEAN OBJECT MEMBRANE-ASSEMBLY
        FROM SURPLUS-GLUE.
    specialization:
    CLEAN OBJECT MEMBRANE-ASSEMBLY
        FROM SURPLUS-GLUE WITH SOLVENT.
    Is this specialization valid? Yes

    I learned the following rule:
    problem:
    CLEAN OBJECT x
        FROM y.
    condition:
    (CLEANER z (REMOVES y))
    specialization:
    CLEAN OBJECT x
        FROM y
        WITH z.
    Do you agree? Yes
*/
```

DISCIPLE proposed another specialization (consistent with the explanation) and synthesized a general specialization rule:

```
    problem:
    ATTACH OBJECT CENTERING-DEVICE
        ON CHASSIS-ASSEMBLY.
    decomposition:
    APPLY SUBSTANCE MOWICOLL
        ON CENTERING-DEVICE.
    PRESS OBJECT CENTERING-DEVICE
        ON CHASSIS-ASSEMBLY.
    Is this decomposition valid? Yes

    I learned the following rule:
    problem:
    ATTACH OBJECT x
        ON y.
    conditions:
    (ADHESIVE z (GLUES x)
        (GLUES y))

    decomposition:
    APPLY SUBSTANCE z
        ON x.
    PRESS OBJECT x
        ON y.
    Do you agree? Yes
*/
```

DISCIPLE proposed two other decompositions (consistent with the found explanation), which were validated by the user. This allowed the system to learn a general rule, validated by the user.

During the second stage of technique design, the system will try to propose tools for the established operations, by using specialization rules.

```
/*
    FIX OBJECT UPPER-FLANGE ON CHASSIS TOOL PRESS.
    Specialize PRESS
    Could you indicate a solution? Yes
    PRESS (TYPE AUTOMATIC)
*/
```

After DISCIPLE proposed a PRESS for the FIX operation, the user wanted to specialize it, but the system was unable to do this since it knew no press sub-concepts. Therefore, the user had to indicate a specialized press, which was also introduced into system's object hierarchies, under the press concept. In the future sessions the system will, of course, be able to specialize a press.

/*

DRY OBJECT LOUDSPEAKER DEVICE DRYER.
Trying to constrain the dryer.
1. DECREASE FEATURE COST.
2. DECREASE FEATURE TIME.
Choose the optimization criterion [Number, No]: 2
1. TUNNEL-KILN
2. CARROUSEL
3. DRYING-SHELF

*/

The system knows several specialized dryers. It also knows two metarules corresponding to the specializations of dryers: one for minimizing the cost and the other for minimizing the time. The system is unable to choose among the dryers until the user expresses his/her preference for one of the above optimization criteria.

/*

PRINT

problem:
MANUFACTURE OBJECT LOUDSPEAKER

loudspeaker's features:
LOUDSPEAKER HAS TERMINAL-BLOCK

optimization criteria:
DECREASE FEATURE TIME.

partial technique:
*CRIMP OBJECTS CONTACTS ON SUPPORT.
*CONNECT OBJECT TERMINAL-BLOCK ON CHASSIS.
*FIX OBJECT UPPER-FLANGE ON CHASSIS
      TOOL PRESS (TYPE AUTOMATIC).
CLEAN OBJECT ENTREFER FROM DUST
      WITH AIR-SUCKER.
SHORTEN OBJECTS COIL-ENDS.
SOLDER OBJECTS TERMINAL-WIRES
      WITH COIL-ENDS.
ASSEMBLE OBJECT MEMBRANE WITH COIL.
ASSEMBLE OBJECT MEMBRANE
      WITH CENTERING-DEVICE.
ASSEMBLE OBJECT CHASSIS-ASSEMBLY
      WITH MEMBRANE-ASSEMBLY.

*APPLY SUBSTANCE MOWICOLL ON SECTORS.
*PRESS OBJECT SECTORS ON
      CHASSIS-MEMBRANE-ASSEMBLY.

      ...

      *DRY OBJECT LOUDSPEAKER
            DEVICE TUNNEL-KILN.

      ...

*/

The user asked for a printout of the technique designed thus far. The session continued until a detailed technique was designed.

The performance of DISCIPLE in the technique-design domain is very encouraging. At present, the knowledge base for the design of loudspeakers contains several hundred rules and objects.

## DISCUSSION AND CONCLUSIONS

It is still a widely accepted opinion that machine learning is a remote research topic when it comes to applications to real expert systems. This opinion appears wrong to us in several respects. It is true that similarity-based learning (SBL) leads to complicated rules and asks for huge amounts of information[14] but this state has already been very much improved.[16,18] If this approach can allow even one entirely new rule to be found, it is worth using in present systems due to the actual price of the noncontradictory additional rule in an expert system.

It is also true that explanation-based learning (EBL) has been used only in domains having a well-defined underlying theory, such as VLSI design[20] and "robotics."[3] This explains why one can always believe that one's own problem is not suited to machine learning techniques. Our methodology for weak-theory domains, combining SBL and EBL, as illustrated by DISCIPLE, contradicts this opinion. DISCIPLE is able to build up a knowledge base in such a way that interactive machine learning takes place, which contains some simple rote learning from the user's data. We cannot claim that consistency will always be conserved, because contradictory answers to the system's questions will lead to contradictory rules. Nevertheless, DISCIPLE will favor consistency conservation by asking questions only when unknown new knowledge is necessary, and also by seeking to derive the new knowledge from the old.

In other words, if two experts have opposite opinions on a diagnosis for a given situation, we have no way to prevent them from introducing contradictions into the database. When their disagreement is less strong, e.g., the experts agree on the diagnosis but disagree on their justification for it (which is often the case), then DISCIPLE will not generate contradictory rules, but sets of different explanations. From the machine learning point of view, one must stress that implicit information is also conserved when it has proved important for the present state of the knowledge base.

In its present state, DISCIPLE is still much closer to a simple expert system shell for building practical expert systems than to a really clever "knowledge extractor." Its means of extracting knowledge are, as yet, rather stereotyped and too inefficient. They are perfectly fitted for interaction with an everyday user who has a good, but not deep knowledge of his/her field. Nevertheless, the very fact that DISCIPLE has been built using machine learning techniques will allow separate and continuous improvement of its EBL and SBL components, thus reaching a level of sophistication in the learning processes that may require the best experts in the field to answer its questions. This feature is far from negative because one must first build a knowledge base that is not too far from the desired one and that contains most of the trivial information. Only on this base can a really intelligent one begin to be built, containing subtle concepts and able to do deep reasoning similar to that of a good human expert.

DISCIPLE has been implemented in LE_LISP[1] and is being run on VAX-750, APPOLO, and MACINTOSH computers. Implementations in COMMON-LISP on SUN stations and EXPLORER LISP machines are underway.

*ACKNOWLEDGMENTS:* This work has been sponsored by PRC-GRECO 'Intelligence Artificielle' and the Romanian CNST. The paper has been written while one of the authors (Gheorghe Tecuci) was at LRI, on leave from his institute. His travel and living expenses have been taken in charge through an agreement between the French CNRS and the Romanian Academy of Sciences. We wish to express our gratitude to both these institutions. We also wish to thank Mr. Zani Bodnaru, for his indispensable contribution as domain expert. Mr. Stephen Thorp for help with the English, and the referees for their detailed and helpful comments.

## NOTE

1. In this section, all descriptions are informal.

## REFERENCES

(1) Chailloux, J. "LE_LISP de l'INRIA, Le Manuel de référence" (Rocquencourt, France: INRIA. February 1985).

(2) Bylander, T., and B. Chandrasekaran. "Understanding Behavior Using Consolidation." *Proc. IJCAI-85*, Los Angeles 1985, 450-454.

(3) DeJong, G., and R. Mooney. "Explanation-Based Learning: An Alternative View." *Machine Learning* 1986 1(2): 145-176.

(4) Fahlman, S.E. "A Planning System for Robot Construction Tsks." *Artificial Intelligence* 1974 5:1-49.

(5) Feigenbaum, E. "The Art of Artificial Intelligence: Themes and Case Studies in Knowledge Engineering." *Proc. IJCAI* 1977 5:1014-1029.

(6) Forgy, C.L. *OPS5 User's Manual* (Pittsburgh, PA: Carnegie-Mellon University, CMU-CS-78-116, 1981).

(7) Friedland, P. "Acquisition of Procedural Knowledge from Domain Experts." *Proc. IJCAI-81*, Vancouver 1981: 856-861.

(8) Ganascia, J.-G. "Détection de Pannes par Systè Expert." Internal Paper. Univ. Paris-Sud, Orsay, 1983.

(9) Hayes-Roth, B. "A Blackboard Architecture for Control." *Artificial Intelligence* 1985 26: 251-321.

(10) Kodratoff, Y. "Generalizing and Particularizing as the Techniques of Learning." *Computers and Artificial Intelligence* 1983 4:417-441.

(11) Kodratoff, Y. "Une theorie et une methodologie de l'apprentissage symbolique." *Actes COGNITIVA 85* 1985 (June): 639-651.

(12) Kodratoff, Y., and G. Tecuci. "DISCIPLE: An Interactive Approach to Learning Apprentice Systems." LRI Research Report No. 293 (Univ. Paris-Sud, Orsay, August 1986).

(13) McDermott, J. "XSEL A Computer Sales Person's Assistant. Pp. 325–337 in *Machine Intelligence*, Vol. 10, edited by J.E. Hayes, D. Michie, and Y.H. Pao (Chichester: Ellis Horwood).

(14) Michalski, R.S. "A Theory and a Methodology of Inductive Learning." *Artificial Intelligence* 1983 20:111-161.

(15) Michalski, R.S., J.G. Carbonell, and T.M. Mitchell, eds. *Machine Learning: An Artificial Intelgence Approach* (Palo Alto, CA: Tioga, 1983).

(16) Michalski, R.S. "Inference-based Theory of Learning." *Proc. Int. Mtg. Advances in Learning* (Les Arcs, July 28-August 1, 1986).

(17) Michalski, R.S., J.G. Carbonell, and T.M. Mitchell, eds. *Machine Learning: An Artificial Intelligence Approach* Vol. II (Los Altos, CA: Morgan Kaufmann, 1986).

(18) Michalski, R.S., I. Mozetic, J. Hong, and N. Lavrac. "The AQ15 Inductive Learning System: An Overview and Experiments" (Internal Paper, Univ. of Illinois at Urbana-Champaign, July 1986).

(19) Mitchell, T.M., J.G. Carbonell, and R.S. Michalski, eds. *Machine Learning: A Guide to Current Research* (Amsterdam: Kluwer Academic Publishers, 1985).

(20) Mitchell, T., S. Mahadevan, and L. Steinberg. "LEAP: A Learning Apprentice System for VLSI Design." *Proc. IJCAI-85*, Los Angeles 1985, 573–580.

(21) Sridharan, N., and J. Bresina. "Plan Formation in Large Realistic Domains." *Proc. CSCSI Conference* (Saskatoon, Saskatchewan, 1982: 12–18).

(22) Sridharan, N., and J. Bresina. "A Mechanism for the Management of Partial and Indefinite Descriptions" (Technical Report CBM-TR-134, Rutgers, NJ: Rutgers University, 1983).

(23) Steels, L., and W. Van de Welde. "Learning in Second Generation Expert Systems." In *Knowledge-Based Problem Solving*, edited by A.S. Kowalik (Englewood Cliffs: NJ: Prentice-Hall, 1985).

(24) Tecuci, G. "Learning Hierarchical Descriptions from Examples." *Computers and Artificial Intelligence* 1984 3:211-222.

(25) Tecuci, G. "DISCIPLE: Integrated Learning for Weak Theory Domains," Ph.D. Thesis, Université de Paris-Sud, forthcoming 1988.

(26) Wilkins, D. "Domain Independent Planning: Representation and Plan Generation." *Artificial Intelligence* 1984 22:269-301.

Manuscript received September 1986: Revised January 1987.

*Address correspondence to Y. Kodratoff, Laboratoire de Recherché en Informatique, Université de Paris-Sud, 91-405 Orsay Cedex, France.*

# Chapter 7

# Analogical and Case-Based Reasoning

Problem-solving using analogical and case-based learning approaches involves selecting and mapping an explicit representation of past experience to a current problem. In some areas of expertise, such as legal reasoning from prior precedents, this is a dominant form of reasoning (Ashley, 1990). For other knowledge-based systems tasks, its role is less central. Analogical and case-based learning contrast with the generalization methods of Chapters 4 and 5, which are concerned with generalizing past experience using inductive and deductive methods.

Analogical reasoning between domains presupposes the existence of large knowledge bases for multiple domains. But constructing large, usable knowledge bases for any domain is still slightly beyond the state of the art. So although analogical reasoning is a pervasive mode of human reasoning, its use in knowledge-based expert systems has been limited to date.

Another issue that eventually must be confronted is the relationship between analogical learning and other forms of learning. An expert system in the domain of electronic circuits might resolve a problem-solving impasse by mapping knowledge from hydrodynamic flows. But this requires that the common mode of problem solving reach a failure point, and that the AI program realize that a good way to resolve the failure is by analogy, instead of, say, induction or explanation-based learning.

# Section 7.1

# Analogical Reasoning

The article by Gentner in Section 7.1.1 provides a lucid overview of the computational stages of analogical learning and distinguishes analogy from other similar forms of domain comparison. Under Gentner's structure mapping theory of analogy, analogy depends on similarities of structure (syntax) rather than similarities of interpretation (semantics).

The article by Falkenhainer et al. in Section 7.1.2 describes the structure-mapping engine (SME), which is a computational realization of Gentner's structure-mapping theory of analogical reasoning and learning. SME is not a general theory of analogy, but carefully models the central problem of analogy, which is mapping. SME represents the most complete implementation of a theory of analogy to date.

PHINEAS is a machine learning program based on SME (Falkenhainer, 1990). The goal of this system is to explain and predict phenomena like the evaporation of alcohol from an open container by discovering its relationship with the dissolving of salt in water.

The third article in this section describes Carbonell's theory of derivational analogy. The method of derivational analogy is to reuse and replay previously determined solution plans and modify them as needed to fit the current problem. A similar approach is sometimes used in case-based reasoning. Derivational analogy can be contrasted with speedup learning methods; systems such as STRIPS, LEX, and PRODIGY examine and then generalize their solution traces, whereas derivational analogy keeps the trace as is. Carbonell's derivational analogy approach has been applied to expertise acquisition for a diagnostic expert system.

# The mechanisms of analogical learning

DEDRE GENTNER

It is widely accepted that similarity is a key determinant of transfer. In this chapter I suggest that both of these venerable terms – *similarity* and *transfer* – refer to complex notions that require further differentiation. I approach the problem by a double decomposition: decomposing similarity into finer subclasses and decomposing learning by similarity and analogy into a set of component subprocesses.

One thing reminds us of another. Mental experience is full of moments in which a current situation reminds us of some prior experience stored in memory. Sometimes such remindings lead to a change in the way we think about one or both of the situations. Here is an example reported by Dan Slobin (personal communication, April 1986). His daughter, Heida, had traveled quite a bit by the age of 3. One day in Turkey she heard a dog barking and remarked, "Dogs in Turkey make the same sound as dogs in America.... Maybe all dogs do. Do dogs in India sound the same?" Where did this question come from? According to Slobin's notebook, "She apparently noticed that while the people sounded different from country to country, the dogs did not." The fact that only humans speak different languages may seem obvious to an adult, but for Heida to arrive at it by observation must have required a series of insights. She had to compare people from different countries and note that they typically sound different. She also had to compare dogs from different countries and note that they sound the same. Finally, in order to attach significance to her observation about dogs, she must have drawn a parallel – perhaps implicitly – between dogs making sounds and humans making sounds so that she could contrast: "As you go from country to country, people sound different, but dogs sound the same." Thus her own experiential comparisons led her to the beginnings of a major insight about the difference between human language and animal sounds.

This example illustrates some of the power of spontaneous remindings. Spontaneous remindings can lead us to make new inferences, to discover a common abstraction, or, as here, to notice an important difference between two partly similar situations (e.g., Ross, 1984, this volume). The ultimate aim of this chapter is to trace learning by analogy and similarity from the initial reminding to the final storage of some new information. Spontaneous analogical learning[1] can be decomposed into subprocesses of (a) accessing the base* system; (b) performing the mapping between base and target; (c) evaluating the match; (d) storing inferences in the target; and sometimes, (e) extracting the commonalties (Clement, 1981, 1983; Gentner, 1987; Gentner & Landers, 1985; Hall, in press; Kedar-Cabelli, 1988).

This breakdown suggests that we examine the subprocesses independently. Once this is done, it will become clear that different subprocesses involved in analogical learning are affected by very different psychological factors. Although the chronological first step in an experiential learning sequence is *accessing the potential analog*, I shall postpone the discussion of access until later in this chapter. Instead, I begin with steps 2 and 3: *analogical mapping and judging analogical soundness*. This is the logical place to start, because it is these processes that uniquely define analogy and allow us to see distinctions among different kinds of similarity. It turns out that the theoretical distinctions necessary for talking about analogical mapping are also useful for talking about other analogical subprocesses.

The plan of the chapter is, first, to describe the core structure-mapping theory of analogical mapping, using a computer simulation to make the points clear; second, to offer psychological evidence for the core theory of analogical mapping; and, finally, to discuss research that extends the framework to the larger situation of analogical learning.

## Analogical mapping

The theoretical framework for this chapter is the structure-mapping theory of analogy (Gentner, 1980, 1982, 1983, 1987; Gentner & Gentner, 1983).[2] As Stephen Palmer (this volume) states, structure-mapping is concerned, first, with what Marr (1982) called the "computational level" and what Palmer and Kimchi (1985) call the "informational constraints" that define analogy. That is, structure-mapping aims to capture the essential elements that constitute analogy and the operations that are computationally necessary in processing

analogy. The question of how analogies are processed in real time – that is, the question of which algorithms are used, in Marr's terminology, or which behavioral constraints apply, in Palmer and Kimchi's terminology – will be deferred until later in the chapter.

The central idea in structure-mapping is that an analogy is a mapping of knowledge from one domain (the base) into another (the target), which conveys that a system of relations that holds among the base objects also holds among the target objects. Thus an analogy is a way of focusing on relational commonalties independently of the objects in which those relations are embedded. In interpreting an analogy, people seek to put the objects of the base in one-to-one correspondence with the objects in the target so as to obtain the maximum structural match. Objects are placed in correspondence by virtue of their like roles in the common relational structure; there does not need to be any resemblance between the target objects and their corresponding base objects. Central to the mapping process is the principle of systematicity: People prefer to map connected *systems of relations* governed by higher-order relations with inferential import, rather than isolated predicates.

Analogical mapping is in general a combination of matching existing predicate structures and importing new predicates (carry-over). To see this, first consider the two extremes. In *pure matching*, the learner already knows something about both domains. The analogy conveys that a relational system in the target domain matches one in the base domain. In this case the analogy serves to focus attention on the matching system rather than to convey new knowledge. In *pure carry-over*, the learner initially knows something about the base domain but little or nothing about the target domain. The analogy specifies the object correspondences, and the learner simply carries across a known system of predicates from the base to the target. This is the case of maximal new knowledge. Whether a given analogy is chiefly matching or mapping depends, of course, on the state of knowledge in the learner. For example, consider this analogy by Oliver Wendell Holmes, Jr.: "Many ideas grow better when transplanted into another mind than in the one where they sprang up." For some readers, this might be an instance of pure mapping: By importing the knowledge structure from the domain of plant growing to the domain of idea development they receive a completely new thought about the latter domain. But for readers who have entertained similar thoughts the process is more one of matching. The effect of the analogy is then not so much to import new knowledge as to focus attention on certain portions of the existing knowledge. Most explanatory analogies are a

---

* *Editors' note:* The terms "base" and "source" are used interchangeably both in the field in general and in this volume in particular.

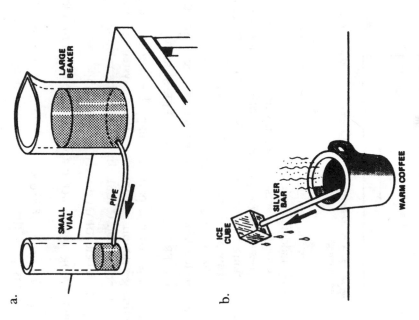

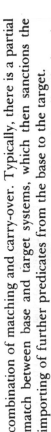

*Figure 7.1.* Examples of physical situations involving (*a*) water flow and (*b*) heat flow (adapted from Buckley, 1979. pp. 15–25).

flow, with temperature in the heat situation playing the role of pressure in the water situation. The learner is also given the object correspondences

water → heat; pipe → metal bar;
beaker → coffee; vial → ice

as well as the function correspondence

PRESSURE → TEMPERATURE

Now the learner is in a position to interpret the analogy. Even with the correspondences given, there is still some active processing required. In order to comprehend the analogy, the learner must

combination of matching and carry-over. Typically, there is a partial match between base and target systems, which then sanctions the importing of further predicates from the base to the target.

A clarification may be useful here. The systematicity principle implies that the same set of predicates should always be mapped from a given base domain, regardless of the target (Holyoak, 1985). But, by this construal, the interpretation of an analogy would depend only on the base domain, which is patently false, except in the case when nothing is known about the target (the pure carry-over case). In the normal case, when there is information about both base and target, a given base–target pair produces a set of matching predicates. Changing either member of the pair produces a different set of matching predicates. Thus, systematicity operates as a selection constraint: Among the many possible predicate matches between a given base and target, it favors those that form coherent systems of mutually interconnecting relations (see Clement & Gentner, 1988; Gentner & Clement, in press).

To illustrate the structure-mapping rules, we turn to a specific example: the analogy between heat flow and water flow. (See Gentner & Jeziorski, in press, for a discussion of Carnot's use of this analogy in the history of heat and temperature.) Figure 7.1 shows a water-flow situation and an analogous heat-flow situation.

I will go through this analogy twice. The first time I give the analogy as it might occur in an educational setting in which the learner knows a fair amount about water and almost nothing about heat flow. Here the learner is given the object correspondences between water and heat and simply imports predicates from the water domain to the heat domain. This is a case of pure carry-over. The second time, to illustrate the computer simulation, I give the analogy as it might occur with the learner having a good representation of the water domain and a partial representation of the heat domain. Here the analogy process is a combination of matching existing structures and importing new predicates (carry-over).

*The heat/water analogy, Pass 1: pure carry-over.* Figure 7.2 shows the representation a learner might have of the water situation. We assume that the learner has a very weak initial representation of the heat situation and perhaps even lacks a firm understanding of the difference between heat and temperature. This network represents a portion of what a person might know about the water situation illustrated in Figure 7.1.[3]

The learner is told that heat flow can be understood just like water

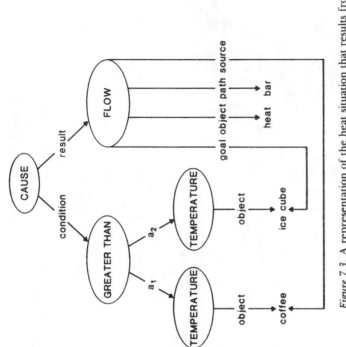

*Figure 7.3.* A representation of the heat situation that results from the heat/water analogy.

Figure 7.3 shows the resulting causal representation of heat flow induced by the analogical mapping.

There are several points to note in this example. First, the object correspondences – heat/water, beaker/coffee, vial/ice, and pipe/bar – and the function correspondence PRESSURE/TEMPERATURE[4] are determined not by any intrinsic similarity between the objects but by their role in the systematic relational structure. Systematicity also determines which relations get carried across. The reason that

GREATER [PRESSURE (beaker), PRESSURE (vial)]

is preserved is that it is part of a mappable system of higher-order constraining relations: in this case, the subsystem governed by the higher-order relation CAUSE. In contrast, the relation

GREATER [DIAM (beaker), DIAM (vial)]

does not belong to any such mappable system and so is less favored in the match.

Second, the order of processing is probably variable. Even when the learner is given the object correspondences first, there is no ob-

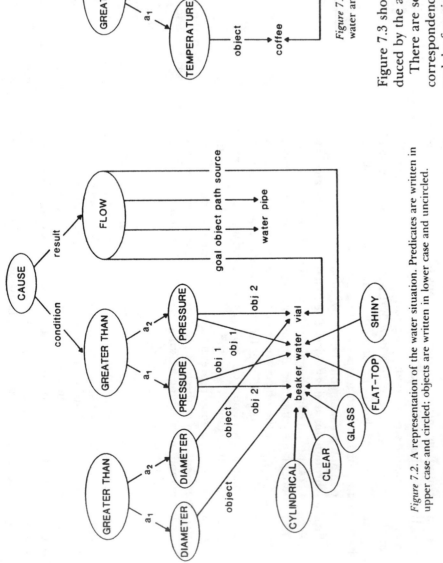

*Figure 7.2.* A representation of the water situation. Predicates are written in upper case and circled; objects are written in lower case and uncircled.

- ignore object attributes; e.g., CYLINDRICAL (beaker) or LIQUID (coffee)
- find a set of systematic base relations that can apply in the target, using the correspondences given. Here, the pressure-difference structure in the water domain

  CAUSE {GREATER [PRESSURE (beaker), PRESSURE (vial)], [FLOW (water, pipe, beaker, vial)]}

  is mapped into the temperature-difference structure in the heat domain

  CAUSE {GREATER [TEMP (coffee), TEMP (ice)], [FLOW (heat, bar, coffee, ice)]}

- and discard isolated relations, such as

  GREATER [DIAM (beaker), DIAM (vial)]

Table 7.1. *Kinds of domain comparisons*

|  | Attributes | Relations | Example |
|---|---|---|---|
| Literal similarity | Many | Many | Milk is like water |
| Analogy | Few | Many | Heat is like water |
| Abstraction | Few | Many | Heat flow is a through-variable |
| Anomaly | Few | Few | Coffee is like the solar system |
| Mere appearance | Many | Few | The glass tabletop gleamed like water |

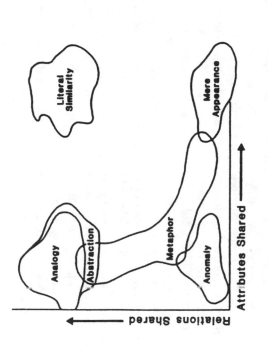

*Figure 7.4.* Similarity space: classes of similarity based on the kinds of predicates shared.

vious constraint on the order in which predicates should be mapped. This is even more the case when the learner is not told the object correspondences in advance. In this case, as exemplified in the next pass through this analogy, the object correspondences are arrived at by first determining the best predicate match – that is, the most systematic and consistent match. I suspect that the order in which matches are made and correspondences tried is extremely opportunistic and variable. It seems unlikely that a fixed order of processing stages will be found for the mapping of complex analogies (see Grudin, 1980; Sternberg, 1977).

Third, applying the structural rules is only part of the story. Given a potential interpretation, the candidate inferences must be checked for validity in the target. If the predicates of the base system are not valid in the target, then another system must be selected. In goal-driven contexts, the candidate inferences must also be checked for relevance to the goal.

## Kinds of similarity

Distinguishing different kinds of similarity is essential to understanding learning by analogy and similarity. Therefore, before going through the heat/water analogy a second time, I lay out a decomposition of similarity that follows from what has been said. Besides analogy, other kinds of similarity can be characterized by whether the two situations are alike in their relational structure, in their object descriptions, or in both. In *analogy*, only relational predicates are mapped. In *literal similarity*, both relational predicates and object attributes are mapped. In *mere-appearance matches*, it is chiefly object attributes that are mapped. Figure 7.4 shows a similarity space that summarizes these distinctions. Table 7.1 shows examples of these different kinds of similarity. The central assumption is that it is not merely the relative *numbers* of shared versus nonshared predicates that matter – although that is certainly important, as Tversky (1977) has shown – but also the *kinds* of predicates that match.

*Analogy* is exemplified by the water/heat example discussed above, which conveys that a common relational system holds for the two domains: Pressure difference causes water flow, and temperature difference causes heat flow. *Literal similarity* is exemplified by the comparison "Milk is like water," which conveys that much of the water description can be applied to milk. In literal similarity, both object attributes, such as FLAT TOP (water) and CYLINDRICAL (beaker), and relational predicates, such as the systematic causal structure discussed above, are mapped over. A *mere-appearance match* is one with overlap in lower-order predicates – chiefly object attributes[5] – but not in higher-order relational structure as in "The glass tabletop gleamed like water." Mere-appearance matches are in a sense the opposite of analogies. Such matches are sharply limited in their utility. Here, for example, little beyond physical appearance is shared between the tabletop and water. These matches, however, cannot be ignored in a theory of learning, because they often occur among novice learners. One further type of match worth discussing is *relational abstraction*.

which represent individuals and constants, and three types of predicates. Predicates are further subdivided into truth-functional predicates (*relations* and *attributes*) and *functions. Entities* (e.g., *Eddie, side pocket*) are logical individuals: the objects and constants of a domain. Typical entities include pieces of stuff, individual objects or beings, and logical constants. *Attributes* and *relations* are predicates that range over truth values; for example, the relation HIT(cue ball, ball) can be evaluated as true or false. The difference is that attributes take one argument and relations take two or more arguments. Informally, attributes describe properties of entities, such as RED or SQUARE. Relations describe events, comparisons, or states applying to two or more entities or predicates. First-order relations take objects as arguments: for example, HIT(ball, table) and INSIDE (ball, pocket). Higher-order relations such as IMPLIES and CAUSE take other predicates as their arguments: for example, CAUSE [HIT (cue stick, ball), ENTER (ball, pocket)]. *Functions* map one or more entities into another entity or predicate. For example, SPEED(ball) does not have a truth value; instead, it maps the physical object *ball* into the quantity that describes its speed. Functions are a useful representational device because they allow either (a) evaluating the function to produce an object descriptor, as in HEIGHT (Sam) = 6 feet, or (b) using the unevaluated function as the argument of other predicates, as in GREATER THAN [HEIGHT(Sam), HEIGHT(George)].

These four constructs are all treated differently in the analogical mapping algorithm. Relations, including higher-order relations, must match identically. Entities and functions are placed in correspondence with other entities and functions on the basis of the surrounding relational structures. Attributes are ignored. Thus there are three levels of preservation: identical matching, placing in correspondence, and ignoring.[6] For example, in the analogy "The wrestler bounced off the ropes like a billiard ball off the wall," the *relations*, such as CAUSE [HIT(wrestler1, wrestler2), COLLIDE(wrestler2, ropes)] must match identically. For *objects* and for *functions*,[7] we attempt to find corresponding objects and functions, which need not be identical: for example, cue ball/wrestler and SPEED(cue ball)/FORCE(wrestler1). Attributes are ignored; we do not seek identical or even corresponding attributes in the billiard ball for each of the wrestler's attributes. To sum up, relations must match, objects and functions must correspond, and attributes are ignored.

It is important to note that these representations, including the distinctions between different kinds of predicates, are intended to reflect the way situations are construed by people. Logically, an *n*-

An example is the abstract statement, "Heat is a through-variable," which might be available to a student who knew some system dynamics. This abstraction, when applied to the heat domain, conveys much the same relational structure as is conveyed by the analogy: that heat (a through-variable) can be thought of as a flow across a potential difference in temperature (an across-variable). The difference is that the base domain contains only abstract principles of through-variables and across-variables and variables; there are no concrete properties of objects to be left behind in the mapping.

These contrasts are continua, not dichotomies. Analogy and literal similarity lie on a continuum of degree-of-attribute-overlap. In both cases, the base and target share common relational structure. If that is *all* they share, then the comparison is an analogy (assuming, of course, that the domains are concrete enough to have object descriptions). To the extent that the domains also share common object descriptions, the comparison becomes one of literal similarity. Another continuum exists between analogies and relational abstractions. In both cases, a relational structure is mapped from base to target. If the base representation includes concrete objects whose individual attributes must be left behind in the mapping, the comparison is an analogy. As the object nodes of the base domain become more abstract and variable-like, the comparison becomes a relational abstraction.

We turn now to the second pass through the analogy. There are two innovations. First, in this pass I describe the way our computer simulation processes the heat/water example. Here we move from informational constraints to behavioral constraints. (See Palmer, this volume.) Second, in this pass I assume that there is some prior knowledge of *both* base and target; thus this pass illustrates a combination of matching and carry-over. Before giving the algorithm, I describe the representational conventions.

*Representation conventions.* The order of an item in a representation is as follows: Objects and constants are order 0. The order of a predicate is 1 plus the maximum of the order of its arguments. Thus, if *x* and *y* are objects, then GREATER THAN (*x*, *y*) is first-order. and CAUSE [GREATER THAN (*x*, *y*), BREAK(*x*)] is second-order. Typical higher-order relations include CAUSE and IMPLIES. On this definition, the order of an item indicates the depth of structure below it. Arguments with many layers of justifications will give rise to representation structures of high order.

A typed predicate calculus is used in the representation. There are four representational constructs that must be distinguished: *entities*,

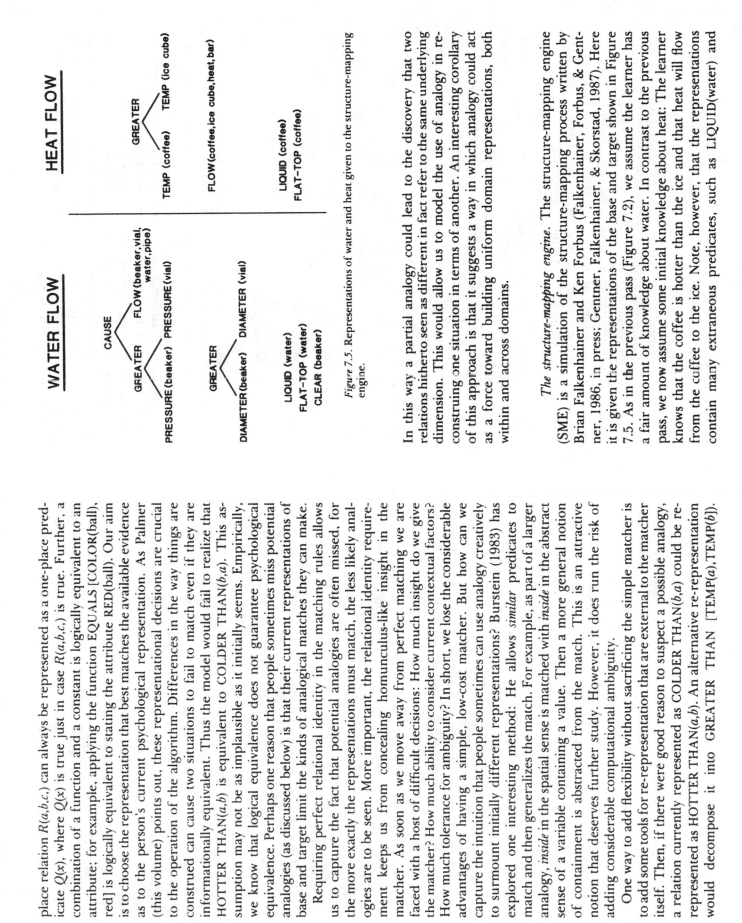

*Figure 7.5.* Representations of water and heat given to the structure-mapping engine.

place relation $R(a,b,c)$ can always be represented as a one-place predicate $Q(x)$, where $Q(x)$ is true just in case $R(a,b,c)$ is true. Further, a combination of a function and a constant is logically equivalent to an attribute; for example, applying the function EQUALS [COLOR(ball), red] is logically equivalent to stating the attribute RED(ball). Our aim is to choose the representation that best matches the available evidence as to the person's current psychological representation. As Palmer (this volume) points out, these representational decisions are crucial to the operation of the algorithm. Differences in the way things are construed can cause two situations to fail to match even if they are informationally equivalent. Thus the model would fail to realize that HOTTER THAN($a,b$) is equivalent to COLDER THAN($b,a$). This assumption may not be as implausible as it initially seems. Empirically, we know that logical equivalence does not guarantee psychological equivalence. Perhaps one reason that people sometimes miss potential analogies (as discussed below) is that their current representations of base and target limit the kinds of analogical matches they can make.

Requiring perfect relational identity in the matching rules allows us to capture the fact that potential analogies are often missed, for the more exactly the representations must match, the less likely analogies are to be seen. More important, the relational identity requirement keeps us from concealing homunculus-like insight in the matcher. As soon as we move away from perfect matching we are faced with a host of difficult decisions: How much insight do we give the matcher? How much ability to consider current contextual factors? How much tolerance for ambiguity? In short, we lose the considerable advantages of having a simple, low-cost matcher. But how can we capture the intuition that people sometimes can use analogy creatively to surmount initially different representations? Burstein (1983) has explored one interesting method: He allows *similar* predicates to match and then generalizes the match. For example, as part of a larger analogy, *inside* in the spatial sense is matched with *inside* in the abstract sense of a variable containing a value. Then a more general notion of containment is abstracted from the match. This is an attractive notion that deserves further study. However, it does run the risk of adding considerable computational ambiguity.

One way to add flexibility without sacrificing the simple matcher is to add some tools for re-representation that are external to the matcher itself. Then, if there were good reason to suspect a possible analogy, a relation currently represented as COLDER THAN($b,a$) could be re-represented as HOTTER THAN($a,b$). An alternative re-representation would decompose it into GREATER THAN [TEMP($a$),TEMP($b$)].

In this way a partial analogy could lead to the discovery that two relations hitherto seen as different in fact refer to the same underlying dimension. This would allow us to model the use of analogy in re-construing one situation in terms of another. An interesting corollary of this approach is that it suggests a way in which analogy could act as a force toward building uniform domain representations, both within and across domains.

*The structure-mapping engine.* The structure-mapping engine (SME) is a simulation of the structure-mapping process written by Brian Falkenhainer and Ken Forbus (Falkenhainer, Forbus, & Gentner, 1986, in press; Gentner, Falkenhainer, & Skorstad, 1987). Here it is given the representations of the base and target shown in Figure 7.5. As in the previous pass (Figure 7.2), we assume the learner has a fair amount of knowledge about water. In contrast to the previous pass, we now assume some initial knowledge about heat: The learner knows that the coffee is hotter than the ice and that heat will flow from the coffee to the ice. Note, however, that the representations contain many extraneous predicates, such as LIQUID(water) and

LIQUID(coffee). These are included to simulate a learner's uncertainty about what matters and to give SME the opportunity to make erroneous matches, just as a person might.

In addition to modeling analogy, SME can be used with literal similarity rules or mere-appearance rules. Both analogy rules and literal similarity rules seek matches in relational structure; the difference is that literal similarity rules also seek object-attribute matches. Mere-appearance rules seek only object-attribute matches. I will describe the process using literal similarity rules, rather than pure analogy, because this offers a better demonstration of the full operation of the simulation, including the way conflicts between surface and structural matches are treated.

*The heat/water analogy, Pass 2: matching plus carry-over.* Given the comparison "Heat is like water," SME uses systematicity of relational structure and consistency of hypothesized object correspondences to determine the mapping. The order of events is as follows:

*1. Local matches.* SME starts by looking for identical relations in base and target and using them to postulate potential matches. For each entity and predicate in the base, it finds the set of entities or predicates in the target that could plausibly match that item. These potential correspondences (*match hypotheses*) are determined by a set of simple rules: for example,

1. If two relations have the same name, create a match hypothesis.
2. For every match hypothesis between relations, check their corresponding arguments; if both are entities, or if both are functions, then create a match hypothesis between them.

For example, in Figure 7.5, Rule 1 creates match hypotheses between the GREATER-THAN relations occurring in base and target. Then Rule 2 creates match hypotheses between their arguments, since both are functions. Note that at this stage the system is entertaining two different, and inconsistent, match hypotheses involving GREATER THAN: one in which PRESSURE is matched with TEMPERATURE and one in which DIAMETER is matched with TEMPERATURE. Thus, at this stage, the program will have a large number of local matches. It gives these local matches *evidence scores*, based on a set of local evidence rules. For example, evidence for a match increases if the base and target predicates have the same name. More interestingly, the evidence rules also invoke systematicity, in that the evidence for a given match increases with the evidence for a match among the parent relations – that is, the immediately governing higher-order relations.

*2. Constructing global matches.* The next stage is to collect systems of matches that use consistent entity pairings. SME first propagates entity correspondences up each relational chain to create systems of match hypotheses that use the same entity pairings. It then combines these into the largest possible systems of predicates with consistent object mappings. These global matches (called Gmaps) are SME's possible interpretations of the comparison.

An important aspect of SME is that the global matches (Gmaps) sanction *candidate inferences*: predicates from the base that get mapped into the target domain. These are base predicates that were not originally present in the target, but which can be imported into the target by virtue of belonging to a system that is shared by base and target. Thus, associated with each Gmap is a (possibly empty) set of *candidate inferences*. For example, in the "winning" Gmap (as discussed below), the pressure-difference causal chain in water is matched with the temperature-difference causal chain in heat, and water flow is matched with heat flow. However, you may recall that the initial heat representation lacked any causal link between the temperature difference and the heat flow (see Figure 7.5). In this case, the system brings across the higher-order predicate CAUSE from the water domain to the heat domain. In essence, it postulates that there may be more structure in the target than it initially knew about. Thus the resulting candidate inference in the heat domain is

> CAUSE {GREATER [TEMP(coffee), TEMP(ice)], FLOW(heat, bar, coffee, ice)}.

*3. Evaluating global matches.* The global matches are then given a structural evaluation, which can depend on their local match evidence, the number of candidate inferences they support, and their graph-theoretic structure – for example, the depth of the relational system.[x] In this example, the winning Gmap is the pressure–temperature match discussed above, with its candidate inference of a causal link in the heat domain. Other Gmaps are also derived, including a Gmap that matches diameter with temperature and another particularly simple Gmap that matches LIQUID (water) with LIQUID (coffee). But these are given low evaluations. They contain fewer predicates than the winning Gmap and, at least equally important, they have shallower relational structures.

A few points should be noted about the way the structure-mapping engine works. First, SME's interpretation is based on selecting the deepest – that is, most systematic – consistent mappable structure. Computing a structurally consistent relational match precedes and determines the final selection of object correspondences.

Second, SME's matching process is entirely structural. That is, it attends only to properties such as identity of predicates, structural consistency (including 1–1 object pairings), and systematicity, as opposed to seeking specific kinds of content. Thus, although it operates on semantic representations, it is not restricted to any particular pre-specified content. This allows it to act as a domain-general matcher. By promoting deep relational chains, the systematicity principle operates to promote predicates that participate in any mutually constraining system, whether causal, logical, or mathematical.

Third, as discussed above, different interpretations will be arrived at depending on which predicates match between two domains. For example, suppose that we keep the same base domain – the water system shown in Figure 7.5 – but change the target domain. Instead of two objects differing in *temperature*, let the target be two objects differing in their *specific heats*; say, a metal ball bearing and a marble. Assuming equal mass, they will also have different *heat capacities*. Now, the natural analogy concerns capacity differences in the base, rather than height differences. This is because the deepest relational chain that can be mapped to the target is, roughly, "Just as the container with greater diameter holds more water (levels being greater than or equal), so the object with greater heat capacity holds more heat (temperatures being greater than or equal)."

        IMPLIES {AND (GREATER [DIAM (beaker), DIAM (vial)],
                GREATER [LEVEL (beaker), LEVEL (vial)]),
                GREATER [AMT-WATER (beaker), AMT-WATER (vial)]}

where AMT stands for the amount. This maps into the target as

        IMPLIES {AND (GREATER [H-CAP (marble), H-CAP (ball)],
                GREATER [TEMP (marble), TEMP (ball)]),
                GREATER [AMT-HEAT (marble), AMT-HEAT (ball)]}

where H-CAP stands for heat capacity. This illustrates that the same base domain can yield different analogical mappings, depending on how it best matches the target.

Fourth, SME is designed as a general-purpose tool kit for similarity matching. It can operate with analogy rules, mere-appearance rules, or literal similarity rules, as discussed above.

Fifth, the matching process in SME is independent of the system's problem-solving goals, although the learner's goals can influence the matcher indirectly, by influencing the domain representations present in working memory. Again, this represents a commitment to generality. The view is that analogy in problem solving is a special case of analogy.

## An architecture for analogical reasoning

A complete model of analogical problem solving must take account of the context of reasoning, including the current plans and goals of the reasoner (Burstein, 1986; Carbonell, 1983; Holyoak, 1985; Kedar-Cabelli, 1985; Miller, Gallanter, & Pribram, 1960; Schank, 1982; Schank & Abelson, 1977). Indeed, as I discuss in the next section, some researchers have argued that plans and goals are so central in analogical reasoning that the analogy mechanism is built around them. However, analogies can occur outside of a goal-driven context. Further, the very fact that plans and goals influence all kinds of human thought processes, from transitive inference to the use of deductive syllogism, shows that they are not in themselves definitive of analogy. Somehow we need to capture the fact that analogy can be influenced by the goals of the problem solver while at the same time capturing what is specific about analogy.

I propose the architecture shown in Figure 7.6 for analogical reasoning. In this account, plans and goals influence our thinking *before* and *after* the analogy engine but not during its operation. Plans and goals and other aspects of current context influence the analogy process *before* the match by determining the working-memory representation of the current situation. This in turn influences what gets accessed from long-term memory. So, in the heat example, there are many aspects of the heat domain, but only the aspects currently represented in working memory are likely to influence remindings. Once a potential analog is accessed from long-term memory, the analogy processor runs its course. Here too the initial domain representation has strong effects, because it defines one input to the processor; thus it constrains the set of matches that will be found. This leads to "set" effects in problem solving; it is an advantage if we are thinking about the problem correctly and a disadvantage if we are not.

The analogy processor produces an interpretation, including candidate inferences and a structural evaluation. If the evaluation is too low – that is, if the depth and size of the system of matching predicates are too low – then the analogy will be rejected on structural grounds. If the analogy passes the structural criterion, then its candidate in-

postulated semiautonomous interacting subsystems for syntax, semantics, and pragmatics (e.g., Reddy, Erman, Fennell, & Neely, 1973). This allows us to capture the fact that analogy must satisfy *both* a structural and a pragmatic criterion.

Separating the planning context from the actual analogy processor represents a commitment to identifying processes common to analogy across different pragmatic contexts. It suggests that when comprehending an analogy in isolation, people use many of the same processes as they do to comprehend analogy in a problem-solving context. That is, they use the same structurally guided processor for both situations, simply adding or removing pragmatic context.[10] An advantage of modeling the matching process as structure-driven rather than goal-driven is that it allows for the possibility of finding unexpected matches, even perhaps matches that contradict the learner's initial problem-solving goals. Such unexpected outcomes are important in scientific discovery. For example, the mathematician Poincaré writes about an occasion on which he set out to prove a certain theorem and ended by discovering a class of functions that proved the theorem wrong. If we are ever to model such cases of unexpected creative discovery, the analogy process must be capable of finding matches that do not depend on — and may even contradict — the learner's current goals.

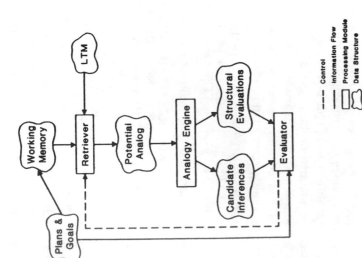

*Figure 7.6.* An architecture for analogical processing.

ferences must be evaluated to determine whether they are appropriate with respect to the goals of the reasoner. In terms of the computer model, this suggests adding a context-sensitive, expectation-driven module to evaluate the output of SME (Falkenhainer, Forbus, & Gentner, 1986; Falkenhainer, 1987a). This extension is compatible with the combination models proposed by Burstein (1983) and Kedar-Cabelli (1985). Thus the key points of this proposed treatment of plans and goals are that (a) plans and goals constrain the inputs to the matcher, which is where they have their largest effect; (b) after the match three separate evaluation criteria must be invoked: structural soundness, relevance, and validity in the target; and (c) the match itself does not require a prior goal statement.

In the model proposed here, both structural properties and contextual-pragmatic considerations enter into analogical problem-solving, but they are not equated. The analogy processor is a well-defined, separate cognitive module" whose results interact with other processes, analogous to the way some natural-language models have

## Competing views and criticisms of structure-mapping

Some aspects of structure-mapping have received convergent support in artificial intelligence and psychology. Despite differences in emphasis, there is widespread agreement on the basic elements of one-to-one mapping of objects and carry-over of predicates (Burstein, 1986; Carbonell, 1983; Hofstadter, 1984; Indurkhya, 1986; Kedar-Cabelli, 1985; Miller, 1979; Reed, 1987; Rumelhart & Norman, 1981; Tourangeau & Sternberg, 1981; Van Lehn & Brown, 1980; Verbrugge & McCarrell, 1977; and Winston, 1980, 1982). Further, all these researchers have some kind of selection principle — of which systematicity is one example — to filter which predicates matter in the match. But accounts differ on the nature of the selection principle. Many researchers use specific content knowledge or pragmatic information to guide the analogical selection process, rather than structural principles like systematicity. For example, Winston's (1980, 1982) system favors causal chains in its *importance-guided* matching algorithm. Winston (personal communication, November 1985) has also investigated goal-driven importance algorithms. Hofstadter and his colleagues have developed a connectionist like model of analogical mapping, in which systematicity is one of several parallel influences on the mapping process (Hofstadter, 1984; Hofstadter, Mitchell, & French 1987).

Many accounts emphasize the role of plans and goals as part of the analogical mapping process. For example, some models combine a structure-mapping component with a plans-and-goals component in order to choose the most contextually *relevant* interpretation (e.g., Burstein, 1986; Kedar-Cabelli, 1985). These models use pragmatic context to select and elaborate the relevant predicates and to guide the mapping process. However, although these models have the ability to take contextual relevance into account, they also postulate a set of relatively constant structural processes that characterize analogical mapping. This view contrasts with a very different position, namely, that analogy should be seen as fundamentally embedded in a goal-driven problem-solving system. I now turn to a discussion of this second position.

*The pragmatic account: an alternative to structure mapping*

Holyoak (1985) proposed an alternative, *pragmatic,* account of analogical processing. Stating that analogy must be modeled as part of a goal-driven processing system, he argued that the structure-mapping approach is "doomed to failure" because it fails to take account of goals. In his proposed account, structural principles played no role; matching was governed entirely by the relevance of the predicates to the current goals of the problem solver. Because of the appeal of such a goal-centered position, I will discuss his arguments in some detail, even though Holyoak and his collaborators are now much less pessimistic concerning the utility of structural principles. I first present Holyoak's pragmatic account of analogy and then consider his critique of structure mapping.[11]

Holyoak states that "Within the pragmatic framework, the structure of analogy is closely tied to the mechanisms by which analogies are actually used by the cognitive system to achieve its goals" (Holyoak, 1985, p. 76). In the pragmatic account, the distinction between structural commonalities and surface commonalities is based solely on relevance. Holyoak's (1985, p. 81) definitions of these terms are as follows:

It is possible, based on the taxonomy of mapping relations discussed earlier, to draw a distinction between *surface* and *structural* similarities and dissimilarities. An identity between two problem solutions to one or the other analog constitutes a surface similarity. Similarly, a structure-preserving difference, as defined earlier constitutes a surface dissimilarity. In contrast, identities that influence goal attainment constitute structural similarities, and structure-violating differences constitute structural dissimilarities. Note that the distinction between surface and structural similarities, as used here, hinges on the relevance of the property in question to attainment of a successful solution. The distinction thus crucially depends on the goal of the problem solver.

Thus a *surface similarity* is defined as "an identity between two problem situations that plays no causal role in determining the possible solutions to one or the other analog," and *structural similarities* are "identities that influence goal attainment." The distinction between surface and structural similarities "hinges on the relevance of the property in question to attainment of a successful solution. The distinction thus crucially depends on the goal of the problem solver."

Holyoak's emphasis on plans and goals has some appealing features. This account promises to replace the abstract formalisms of a structural approach with an ecologically motivated account centered around what matters to the individual. Further, whereas structure-mapping requires both structural factors within the matcher and (in a complete account) pragmatic factors external to the matcher, Holyoak's account requires only pragmatic factors. But there are severe costs to this simplification. First, since structural matches are defined only by their relevance to a set of goals, the pragmatic account requires a context that specifies what is relevant before it can operate. Therefore, it cannot deal with analogy in isolation, or even with an analogy whose point is irrelevant to the current context. By this account, Francis Bacon's analogy "All rising to a great place is by a winding stair," should be uninterpretable in the present context. I leave it to the reader to judge whether this is true.

Holyoak (1985) seems aware of this limitation and states that his pragmatic account is meant to apply only to analogy in problem solving. But this means having to postulate separate analogy processors for analogy in context and analogy in isolation, which seems inconvenient at best. But there are further difficulties with the pragmatic account. Because the interpretation of an analogy is defined in terms of relevance to the initial goals of the problem solver, the pragmatic view does not allow for unexpected outcomes in an analogical match. This means that many creative uses of analogy – such as scientific discovery – are out of bounds. Finally, the pragmatic account lacks any means of capturing the important psychological distinction between an analogy that fails because it is irrelevant and an analogy that fails because it is unsound. In short, a good case can be made for the need to *augment* structural considerations with goal-relevant considerations (though I would argue that this should be done externally to the matcher, as shown in Figure 7.6, for example). However, the attempt to *replace* structural factors like systematicity with pragmatic factors like goal-relevance does not appear tenable.

Holyoak raises three chief criticisms of structure-mapping (Holyoak, 1985, pp. 74, 75). First, as discussed above, Holyoak argues that structural factors are epiphenomenal: What really controls analogical matching is the search for goal-relevant predicates. The higher-order relations that enter into systematic structures "typically are such predicates as 'causes,' 'implies,' and 'depends on,' that is, causal elements that are pragmatically important to goal attainment. Thus, the pragmatic approach readily accounts for the phenomena cited as support for Gentner's theory." There are two problems with this argument. First, as discussed above, people are perfectly capable of processing analogy without any prior goal context, and of interpreting analogies whose point runs contrary to our expectations. Second, it is not correct to state that all higher-order relations are "causal elements pragmatically relevant to goal attainment." For example, *implies* (used in its normal logical sense) is not causal. Mathematical analogies, such as Polya's (1954) analogy between a triangle in a plane and a tetrahedron in space, are clear cases of shared relational structure that is not causal, and that need not be goal-relevant to be appreciated. Hofstadter (1984) provides many examples of analogies based on purely structural commonalities: for example, if $abc \longrightarrow abd$, then $pqr \longrightarrow pqs$.

Holyoak's second point is one of definition. In structure-mapping the distinction between analogy and literal similarity is based on the kinds of predicates shared: Analogy shares relational structure only, whereas literal similarity shares relational structure plus object descriptions. Holyoak proposes a different distinction: that analogy is similarity with reference to a goal. Thus "Even objects that Gentner would term 'literally similar' can be analogically related if a goal is apparent." The problem with this distinction is that although it captures analogy's role as a focusing device, it classifies some things as analogy that intuitively seem to be literal similarity. For example, consider the comparison "This '82 Buick is like this '83 Buick: You can use it to drive across town." By Holyoak's criterion this is an analogy, because a specific goal is under consideration; yet to my ear the two Buicks are literally similar whether or not a goal is involved. But since this is essentially a question of terminology, it may be undecidable.

Holyoak's third set of criticisms is based on the misinterpretation discussed earlier: namely, that in structure-mapping the systematicity of the base domain *by itself* determines the interpretation of an anal-

ogy, so that "the mappable propositions can be determined by a syntactic [structural] analysis of the source analog alone." This is false except in the rare case where nothing at all is known about the target (the "pure carry-over" case discussed earlier). This can be seen in the operation of SME, in which the interpretation arises out of a detailed *match* between base and target and not from "a syntactic analysis of the source analog alone." (See Skorstad, Falkenhainer, & Gentner, 1987, for examples of how SME yields different interpretations when the same base domain is paired with different targets.) At the risk of belaboring the point, let us recall that, in structure-mapping, analogy is seen as a subclass of similarity, and therefore, as with any other kind of similarity comparison, its interpretation is based on the best match between base and target. What distinguishes analogy from other kinds of similarity is that, for analogy, the *best match* is defined as the maximally systematic and consistent match of relational structure.

In summary, Holyoak's pragmatic account must be considered a failure insofar as it seeks to replace structure with relevance. Though one may sympathize with the desire to take plans and goals into account, discounting structure is the wrong way to go about it. Nonetheless, this work, like that of Burstein (1986), Carbonell (1981, 1983), and Kedar-Cabelli (1985), has the merit of calling attention to the important issue of how plans and goals can be integrated into a theory of analogy.

Separating structural rules from pragmatics has some significant advantages: It allows us to capture the commonalities among analogy interpretation across different pragmatic contexts, including analogy in isolation; it allows for creativity, since the processor does not have to know in advance which predicates are going to be shared; and it allows us to capture the difference between relevance and soundness. However, if the two-factor scheme I propose in Figure 7.6 is correct, there is still much work to be done in specifying exactly how plans and goals affect the initial domain representations that are given to the analogy processor and how they are compared with the output of this processor in the postprocessing stage.

## Psychological evidence for structure-mapping

*Ideal mapping rules.* Structure-mapping claims to characterize the implicit competence rules by which the meaning of an analogy is derived. The first question to ask is how successfully it does so –

many responses based on common object attributes (Gentner, 1980, 1988; Gentner & Stuart, 1983). The same developmental shift holds for choice tasks and rating tasks (Billow, 1975; Gentner, 1988). Thus there is evidence for a developmental shift from a focus on common object attributes to a focus on common relations in analogical processing.

### Performance factors in analogical mapping

As Palmer (this volume) points out, structure-mapping aims first and foremost to capture the essential nature of analogy: what constitutes an analogy and which distinctions are necessary to characterize analogy – what Marr (1982) calls the "computational level" and Palmer and Kimchi (1985) call "informational constraints." Thus structure-mapping is in part a competence theory in that it attempts to capture people's implicit understanding of which commonalities should belong to analogy and which should not. The research described above suggests that under ordinary conditions structure-mapping is also a good approximation to a performance theory, for people's actual interpretations of analogies fit the predictions rather well. But what happens if we make it harder for people to perform according to the rules? Given that the ideal in analogy is to discover the maximal common higher-order relational structure, here we ask how closely people approach the *ideal* under difficult circumstances and what factors affect people's *performance* in carrying out a structure mapping.

*Transfer performance.* Gentner and Toupin (1986) posed this question developmentally. We asked children of 4–6 and 8–10 years of age to transfer a story plot from one group of characters to another. Two factors were varied: (a) the *systematicity* of the base domain (the original story); and (b) the *transparency* of the mapping (that is, the degree to which the target objects resembled their corresponding base objects). The systematicity of the original story was varied by adding beginning and ending sentences that expressed a causal or moral summary. Otherwise, the stories in the systematic condition were the same as those in the nonsystematic condition. Transparency was manipulated by varying the similarity of corresponding characters. For example, the original story might involve a *chipmunk* helping his friend the *moose* to escape from the villain *frog*.

After acting out the story with the base characters, the child was told to act out the story again, but with new characters. In the high-

whether people do indeed follow the rules of structure-mapping in interpreting analogies. The prediction is that people should include relations and omit object descriptions in their interpretations of analogy. To test this, subjects were asked to write out descriptions of objects and then to interpret analogical comparisons containing these objects. (Gentner, 1980, 1988; Gentner & Clement, in press). They also rated how apt (how interesting, clever, or worth reading) the comparisons were.

The results showed that, whereas object descriptions tended to include both relational and object-attribute information, the interpretations of comparisons tended to include relations and omit object attributes. For example, a subject's description of "cigarette" was as follows:

chopped cured tobacco in a paper roll / with or without a filter at the end / held in the mouth / lit with a match and breathed through to draw smoke into the lungs / found widely among humans / known by some cultures to be damaging to the lungs / once considered beneficial to health.

Note that this description contains both relational and attributional information. Yet, when the same subject is given the metaphor "Cigarettes are like time bombs," his interpretation is purely in terms of common relational information: "They do their damage after some period of time during which no damage may be evident." A second finding was that the comparisons were considered more apt to the degree that subjects could find relational interpretations. There was a strong positive correlation between rated aptness and relationality but no such correlation for attributionality. Adults thus demonstrate a strong relational focus in interpreting metaphor. They emphasize relational commonalities in their interpretations when possible, and they prefer metaphors that allow such interpretations (Gentner & Clement, in press).

*Development of mapping rules.* The implicit focus on relations in interpreting analogy can seem so natural to us that it seems to go without saying. One way to see the effects of the competence rules is to look at cases in which these rules are not followed. Children do not show the kind of relational focus that adults do in interpreting analogy and metaphor.[12] A 5 year-old, given the figurative comparison "A cloud is like a sponge," produces an attributional interpretation, such as "Both are round and fluffy." A typical adult response is "Both can hold water for some time and then later give it back." Nine-year-olds are intermediate, giving some relational interpretations but also

systematic condition, 9-year-olds found the cross-mapping condition quite difficult. Yet, given a systematic relational structure to hold onto, they could keep their mappings straight. In contrast, the 5-year-olds were affected only by transparency; they showed no significant benefit from systematic relational structure.

How does this happen? Gentner and Toupin (1986) speculated that the benefit comes in part from the way shared systems of relations help guide the mapping of lower-order relations. An error made in mapping a particular relation from base to target is more likely to be detected if there is a higher-order relation that constrains that lower-order relation. Informal observations in our study support this view. The older children, in the systematic condition, would sometimes begin to make an object-similarity-based error and then correct themselves, saying something like "Oh no, it's the *bad* one who got stuck in the hole, because he ate all the food." They were using the systematic causal structure of the story to overcome their local mapping difficulties.

Research with adults suggests that both systematicity and transparency continue to be important variables. Both Ross (1984; this volume) and Reed (1987) have shown that subjects are better at transferring algebraic solutions when corresponding base and target objects are similar. Reed (1987) measured the transparency of the mapping between two analogous algebra problems by asking subjects to identify pairs of corresponding concepts. He found that transparency was a good predictor of their ability to notice and apply solutions from one problem to the other. Ross (1987) has investigated the effects of cross-mappings in remindings during problem solving. He found that, even though adults could often *access* the prior problem, their ability to *transfer* the solution correctly was disrupted when cross-mapped correspondences were used. Robert Schumacher and I found benefits of both systematicity and transparency in transfer of device models, using a design similar to that of Gentner and Toupin (1986), in which subjects transfer an operating procedure from a base device to a target device (Gentner & Schumacher, 1986; Schumacher & Gentner, in press).

The evidence is quite strong, then, that transparency makes mapping easier. Thus literal similarity is the easiest sort of mapping and the one where subjects are least likely to make errors. The evidence also shows that a systematic base model promotes accurate mapping. This means that systematicity is a performance variable as well as a competence variable. Not only do people *believe* in achieving systematic mappings; they *use* systematic structure to help them perform the mapping.

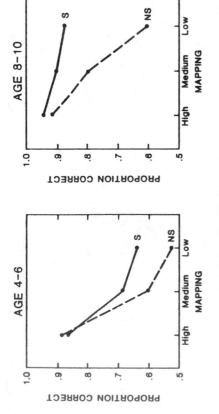

*Figure 7.7.* Results of the cross-mapping experiment: proportion correct on transfer story given systematic (S) or nonsystematic (NS) original stories, across mappings varying from high transparency to low transparency (Gentner & Toupin, 1986). *High* transparency means similar characters in corresponding roles; *medium,* different characters; and *low,* similar characters in different roles (the cross-mapped condition).

transparency mapping, the new characters would resemble the original characters: for example, a *squirrel,* an *elk,* and a *toad,* respectively. In the medium-transparency condition, three new unrelated animals were used. In the low-transparency (*cross-mapped*) condition, the characters were similar to the original characters but occupied noncorresponding roles: For example, the *chipmunk, moose,* and *frog* of the original story would map onto an *elk,* a *toad,* and a *squirrel,* respectively. We expected the cross-mapped condition to be very difficult. More interestingly, we wanted to know how robust the mapping rules are: How firmly can people hold to a systematic mapping when surface similarity pushes them toward a nonsystematic solution?

Both systematicity and transparency turned out to be important in determining transfer accuracy. However the two age groups showed different patterns. Transparency affected both age groups, whereas systematicity affected only the older group. For both ages, transfer accuracy was nearly perfect with highly similar corresponding characters (high transparency), lower when corresponding characters were quite different (medium transparency), and lower still in the cross-mapped condition (low transparency). For the older group, systematicity also had strong effects. As Figure 7.7 shows, 9-year-olds performed virtually perfectly, even in the most difficult mapping conditions, when they had a systematic story structure. This is noteworthy because, as can be seen from their performance in the non-

Table 7.2. *Sample story set for the access experiment (Gentner & Landers, 1985)*

**BASE story**
Karla, an old hawk, lived at the top of a tall oak tree. One afternoon, she saw a hunter on the ground with a bow and some some crude arrows that had no feathers. The hunter took aim and shot at the hawk but missed. Karla knew the hunter wanted her feathers so she glided down to the hunter and offered to give him a few. The hunter was so grateful that he pledged never to shoot at a hawk again. He went off and shot deer instead.

**True-analogy TARGET**
Once there was a small country called Zerdia that learned to make the world's smartest computer. One day Zerdia was attacked by its warlike neighbor, Gagrach. But the missiles were badly aimed and the attack failed. The Zerdian government realized that Gagrach wanted Zerdian computers so it offered to sell some of its computers to the country. The government of Gagrach was very pleased. It promised never to attack Zerdia again.

**Mere-appearance TARGET**
Once there was an eagle named Zerdia who donated a few of her tailfeathers to a sportsman so he would promise never to attack eagles. One day Zerdia was nesting high on a rocky cliff when she saw the sportsman coming with a crossbow. Zerdia flew down to meet the man, but he attacked and felled her with a single bolt. As she fluttered to the ground Zerdia realized that the bolt had her own tailfeathers on it.

**False-analogy TARGET**
Once there was a small country called Zerdia that learned to make the world's smartest computer. Zerdia sold one of its supercomputers to its neighbor, Gagrach, so Gagrach would promise never to attack Zerdia. But one day Zerdia was overwhelmed by a surprise attack from Gagrach. As it capitulated the crippled government of Zerdia realized that the attacker's missiles had been guided by Zerdian supercomputers.

Subjects were told that if any of the new stories reminded them of any of the original stories, they were to write out the original story (or stories) as completely as possible. There were three kinds of similarity matches between base and target:

- *mere appearance* (MA): object attributes and first-order relations match
- *true analogy* (TA): first-order relations and higher-order relations match
- *false analogy* (FA): only the first-order relations match

In all three cases, the base and target shared first-order relations. Other commonalities were added to create the different similarity

*Developmental implications: the relational shift.* Like adults, the 9-year-olds in the Gentner and Toupin (1986) study were affected by both systematicity and transparency. But the 5-year-olds showed no significant effects of systematic base structure. All that mattered to this younger group was the transparency of the object correspondences. These results are consistent with the results reported earlier, and with the general developmental finding that young children rely on object-level similarities in transfer tasks (DeLoache, in press; Holyoak, Junn, & Billman, 1984; Keil & Batterman 1984; Kemler, 1983; Shepp, 1978; L. Smith, this volume; Smith & Kemler, 1977) and in metaphor tasks (Asch & Nerlove, 1960; Billow, 1975; Dent, 1984; Gardner, Kircher, Winner, & Perkins, 1975; Kogan, 1975). These findings suggest a developmental shift from reliance on surface similarity, and particularly on transparency of object correspondences, to use of relational structure in analogical mapping.[13]

### Access processes

Now we are ready to tackle the issue of *access* to analogy and similarity. Before doing so, let us recapitulate briefly. I proposed at the start of this chapter a set of subprocesses necessary for spontaneous learning by analogy: (a) accessing the base system; (b) performing the mapping between base and target; (c) evaluating the match; (d) storing inferences in the target; and (e) extracting the common principle. So far we have considered mapping, evaluating, and making inferences. A major differentiating variable in the research so far is *similarity class*: whether the match is one of mere appearance, analogy, or literal similarity. Now we ask how similarity class affects memorial *access* to analogy and similarity.

*Accessing analogy and similarity.* What governs spontaneous access to similar or analogous situations? Gentner & Landers (1985) investigated this question, using a method designed to resemble natural long-term memory access. (For details of this and related studies, see Gentner & Landers, 1985; Gentner & Rattermann, in preparation; Rattermann & Gentner, 1987.) We first gave subjects a large set of stories to read and remember (18 key stories and 14 fillers). Subjects returned about a week later and performed two tasks: (a) a *reminding* task; and (b) a *soundness-rating* task.

In the reminding task, subjects read a new set of 18 stories, each of which matched one of the 18 original stories, as described below.

Ross (1984, 1987; Ross & Sofka, 1986). In this research it has reliably been demonstrated that subjects in a problem-solving task often fail to access prior material that is analogous to their current problem. For example, in Gick and Holyoak's (1980, 1983) studies, a substantial number of subjects failed to access a potential analog – and therefore could not solve the problem – yet, when the experimenter suggested that the prior material was relevant, they could readily apply it to solve the problem. This means that (a) they had clearly stored the prior analog; (b) the prior analog contained sufficient information to solve their current problem; but (c) they could not access the prior analog solely on the basis of the current (analogous) problem structure. Thus there is converging evidence for the gloomy finding that relational commonalities often fail to lead to access.

There is also confirmation for the other side of the coin: that surface commonalities do promote access (Holyoak & Thagard, this volume; Novick, 1988; Reed & Ackinclose, 1986; Ross, 1984, 1987, this volume; Ross & Sofka, 1986; Schumacher, 1987). For example, Ross (1984) found clear effects of surface similarity in determining which earlier algebra problems subjects would be reminded of in trying to solve later problems. Reed and Ackinclose (1986) found that perceived similarity, rather than structural isomorphism, was the best predictor of whether subjects solving algebra problems would apply the results of a previous problem to a current problem.[14] Overall similarity, especially surface similarity, appears to be a major factor in accessing material in long-term memory.

Having said all this, we must remember that purely relational reminding does occur. Even young children sometimes experience analogical insights, as attested by Heida's analogy at the beginning of this chapter. As Johnson-Laird (this volume) points out, though remindings between remote domains are relatively rare, their occurrence sometimes sparks important creative advances (Falkenhainer, 1987b; Gentner, 1982; Hesse, 1966; Waldrop, 1987). A correct model of access will have to capture both the fact that relational remindings are comparatively rare and the fact that they occur.

## Decomposing similarity

I began this chapter by noting that similarity is widely considered to be an important determinant of transfer (Thorndike, 1903; see Brown, this volume, and Brown & Campione, 1984, for discussions of this issue). The research reviewed here suggests that both *similarity*

conditions. Table 7.2 shows an example set of four stories: a base story plus one example of each of the three kinds of matches. Each subject received one-third MA, one-third TA, and one-third FA matches, counterbalanced across three groups. After the subjects had completed the reminding task, they performed the soundness-rating task. They were shown their 18 pairs of stories side by side and asked to rate each pair for the soundness or inferential power of the match (with 5 being "sound" and 1 being "spurious").

In the soundness-rating task, subjects showed the predicted preference for true analogies. The mean soundness ratings were 4.4 for true analogies, 2.8 for mere appearance, and 2.0 for false analogy, with the only significant difference being between true analogy and the other two match types. This aspect of the study provides further evidence for the systematicity principle: Common higher-order relational structure is an important determinant of the subjective goodness of an analogy.

The results for access were surprising. Despite subjects' retrospective agreement that only the analogical matches were sound, their natural remindings did not produce analogies. Instead, they were far more likely to retrieve superficial mere-appearance matches. Given mere-appearance matches, subjects were able to access the original story 78% of the time, whereas the true analogies were accessed only 44% of the time, and the false analogies 25% of the time. All three differences were significant, suggesting that (a) surface commonalities have the most important role in access but that (b) higher-order relational commonalities – present in the true analogies but not in the false analogies – also promote access.

We have recently replicated these results, adding a literal similarity condition, and the results show the same pattern (Gentner & Rattermann, in preparation; Rattermann & Gentner, 1987). In access, surface similarity seems to be the dominant factor. Literal similarity and mere-appearance matches are more accessible than true analogies and false analogies. In soundness, systematicity of relational structure is the dominant factor. True analogy and literal similarity are considered sound, and false analogies and mere-appearance matches are not. Interestingly, surface information is superior in access even for subjects who clearly believe that only structural overlap counts toward soundness. It appears that analogical *access* and analogical *soundness* – or at least our subjective estimates of soundness – are influenced in different degrees by different kinds of similarity.

These access results accord with the findings of Gick and Holyoak (1980, 1983) of Reed (1987; Reed, Ernst, & Banerji, 1974), and of

ing soundness are more like discretionary processes. In any case, as we move from access to mapping and judging soundness there is a sense of increasing volitional control over the processes. To use an analogy, gaining access to long-term memory is a bit like fishing: The learner can bait the hook – that is, set up the working memory probe – as he or she chooses, but once the line is thrown into the water it is impossible to predict exactly which fish will bite.

The access bias for overall-similarity and surface-similarity matches rather than abstract analogical remindings may seem like a poor design choice from a machine-learning standpoint. But there may be good reasons for a bias toward overall similarity. First, a conservative, overall-similarity bias may be reasonable given the large size of human data bases relative to current artificial intelligence systems. For large data bases, the costs of checking all potential relational matches may well be prohibitive. Second, a conservative matching strategy might be prudent for mobile biological beings, for whom a false positive might be perilous. Third, by beginning with overall similarity the learner allows the relational vocabulary to grow to fit the data. This may be one reason children are better language learners than are adults; paradoxically, their initial conservatism and surface focus may allow the correct relational generalizations slowly to emerge (cf. New-port, 1984; see Forbus & Gentner, 1983; Murphy & Medin, 1985).

These arguments suggest that human access is geared toward literal similarity. But what about the fact that our access mechanisms also retrieve mere-appearance matches? Possibly, this comes about as a by-product of the overall-similarity bias. By this account, it is a design flaw, but perhaps a fairly minor one for concrete physical domains, where appearances tend not to be very deceiving. Very often, things that look alike *are* alike. (See Gentner, 1987; Medin & Ortony, this volume; Wattenmaker, Nakamura, & Medin, 1986.) Where surface matches become least reliable is in abstract domains such as algebra or Newtonian mechanics. The novice who assumes that any new pulley problem should be solved like the last pulley problem will often be wrong (Chi, Feltovich, & Glaser, 1981). Thus our surface-oriented accessor can be an obstacle to learning in abstract domains, where the correlation between surface features and structural features is low.

## Implications for learning

Now let's put together these findings and ask how they bear on experiential learning. This discussion is based on that given by Forbus

and *transfer* may be too coarse as variables. A strong theme in this chapter, and indeed a convergent theme across this volume, has been the need to make finer differentiations in the notion of similarity (Collins & Burstein, this volume; Medin & Ortony, this volume; Rips, this volume; Ross, this volume; L. Smith, this volume). The research discussed in this chapter further suggests that *transfer* must be decomposed into different subprocesses that interact differently with different kinds of similarity. Thus the simple statement "Similarity is important in transfer" may conceal an intricate set of interactions between different varieties of similarity and different subprocesses in transfer.

Based on the research presented so far, it appears that different subprocesses are affected by different kinds of similarity. *Access* is strongly influenced by surface similarity and only weakly influenced by structural similarity. *Analogical mapping* is strongly influenced by structural similarity, including shared systematicity; it may also be weakly influenced by surface similarity. *Judging soundness* is chiefly influenced by structural similarity and systematicity. Finally, *extracting and storing the principle* underlying an analogy seems likely to be governed by structural similarity and systematicity. There is thus a relational shift in processing analogy and similarity from surface to structural commonalities.[15]

Similarity-based access may be a rather primitive mechanism, a low-cost low-specificity, high-quantity process, requiring little conscious effort. Analogical mapping and judging soundness are rather more sophisticated. They are often somewhat effortful, they often involve conscious reasoning, and, unlike access, they can be specifically tailored to different kinds of similarity. One can choose whether to carry out a mapping as an analogy or as a mere-appearance match, for example; but one cannot choose in advance whether to *access* an analogy or a mere-appearance match. Access has the feel of a passive process that simply produces some number of potential matches that the reasoner can accept or reject. Finally, one suspects that the processes of mapping and judging soundness are heavily influenced by culturally learned strategies (see Gentner & Jeziorski, in press). In contrast, access processes seem less amenable to cultural influence and training.[16] To the extent that experts differ from novices in their access patterns, I suspect this results chiefly from experts' having different domain representations (e.g., possessing relational abstractions) rather than from their having different access processes.

It is tempting to speculate that similarity-driven access involves something rather like a ballistic process, whereas mapping and judg-

and Gentner (1983). Forbus and Gentner examined the role of similarity comparisons in the progression from early to later representations. A key assumption here is that implicit comparisons among related knowledge structures are important in learning (Brooks, 1978; Jacoby & Brooks, 1984; Medin & Schaffer, 1978; Wattenmaker et al., 1986). We conjecture that much of experiential learning proceeds through spontaneous comparisons – which may be implicit or explicit – between a current situation and prior similar or analogous situations that the learner has stored in memory. We also assume that early representations are characteristically rich and perceptually based. That is, early domain representations differ from more advanced representations of the same domain in containing more perceptual information specific to the initial context of use. What does this predict? First, in terms of *access*, the greater the surface match the greater the likelihood of access. Thus the matches that are likely to occur most readily are literal similarity matches and mere-appearance matches.

Once the base domain has been accessed, the mapping process occurs. To transfer knowledge from one domain to another, a person must not only access the base domain but also set up the correct object correspondences between the base and target and map predicates across. At this level, a mix of deep and surface factors seems to operate. Systematicity and structural similarity become crucial, but so does the transparency of the object correspondences (Gentner & Toupin, 1986; Reed, 1987; Ross, 1987). It appears that, for adults and/or experts, systematicity can to some extent compensate for lack of transparency. The rules of analogy are clear enough and the relational structures robust enough to allow accurate mapping without surface support. But for children and novices surface similarity is a key determinant of success in analogical mapping.

To the extent that children and novices rely on object commonalities in similarity-based mapping, they are limited to literal similarity matches and mere-appearance matches. The disadvantage of mere-appearance matches is obvious: They are likely to lead to wrong inferences about the target. But even literal similarity matches have their limitations. Although adequate for prediction, literal similarity matches are probably less useful than analogies for purposes of explicitly extracting causal principles. In an analogical match, the shared data structure is sparse enough to permit the learner to isolate the key principles. In literal similarity, there are too many common predicates to know which are crucial (Forbus & Gentner, 1983; Ross, this volume; Wattenmaker et al., 1986).

How do learners escape the confines of literal similarity? One way, of course, is through explicit instruction about the relevant abstractions. But there may be ways within experiential learning as well. If we speculate that the results of a similarity comparison become slightly more accessible (Elio & Anderson, 1981, 1984; Gick & Holyoak, 1983; Ortony, 1979; Skorstad, Gentner, & Medin, 1988), then repeated instances of near-literal similarity could gradually increase the salience of the relational commonalities. At some point the relational structures become sufficiently salient to allow analogy to occur. Once this happens, there is some likelihood of noticing the relational commonalities and extracting them for future use. (This conjectural sequence, which is essentially that proposed in Forbus and Gentner, 1983, hinges on the claim that the results of an analogy are sparser and therefore more inspectable than the results of a literal similarity comparison. Hence, the probability of noticing and extracting the common relational structure is greater.) The extracted relational abstractions can then influence domain knowledge, the set of known abstractions – such as *flow rate* or *positive feedback situation* – becomes firm enough to allow relational encoding and retrieval.

The post-access processes can be influenced both by individual training and by local strategies. I suspect that this is the area in which training in thinking skills can be of most benefit. For example, people may learn better skills for checking potential matches and rejecting bad matches, and perhaps also skills for tinkering with potential matches to make them more useful (Clement, 1983, 1986). However, I suspect that some parts of the system will always remain outside direct volitional control. To return to the fishing analogy, we can learn to bait the hook better, and once the fish bites we can learn better skills for landing it, identifying it, and deciding whether to keep it or throw it back. But no matter how accurate the preaccess and post-access processes, there is always uncertainty in the access itself. When we throw the hook into the current we cannot determine exactly which fish will bite. A strategically managed interplay between discretionary and automatic processes may be the most productive technique for analogical reasoning.

## Conclusion

In this chapter I have suggested that different kinds of similarity participate differently in transfer. In particular, I have proposed decomposing similarity into subclasses of *analogy, mere-appearance, and literal similarity* and transfer into subprocesses of *access, mapping, storing inferences,* and *extracting commonalities.* Although many issues remain to be worked out, it seems clear that this finer-grained set of distinctions will allow a more fruitful discussion of similarity based learning.

## NOTES

This research was supported by the Office of Naval Research under Contract N00014-5-K-0559, NR667-551. The developmental studies were supported by the National Institute of Education under Contract 400-80-0031 awarded to the Center for the Study of Reading. I thank Ann Brown, Allan Collins, Judy DeLoache, Ken Forbus, Doug Medin, and Brian Ross for many insightful discussions of these issues, and Cathy Clement, Rogers Hall, Mike Jeziorski, Doug Medin, Andrew Ortony, Mary Jo Rattermann, Bob Schumacher, and Janice Skorstad for their helpful comments on a draft of this paper.

1 For now, I will use the term *analogical learning* to refer to both learning by analogy and learning by literal similarity. Later in the chapter I will distinguish between analogy and similarity.

2 This account has benefited from the comments and suggestions of my colleagues since my first proposal in 1980. Here and there I will indicate some ways in which the theory has changed.

3 The notation in Figure 7.2 is equivalent to a predicate calculus representation; I use it because it emphasizes structural relationships (see Norman & Rumelhart, 1975; Palmer, 1978).

4 In this analogy, the function PRESSURE in the water domain must be mapped onto TEMPERATURE in the heat domain. Like objects, functions on objects in the base can be put in correspondence with different functions in the target in order to permit mapping a larger systematic chain.

5 An ongoing question in our research is whether mere-appearance matches should be viewed as including first-order relations as well as object attributes.

6 The reason that attributes are ignored, rather than being placed in correspondence with other attributes, is to permit analogical matches between rich objects and sparse objects.

7 Adding functions to the representation is a change from my former position, which distinguished only between object attributes (one-place predicates) and relations (two-or-more-place predicates). I thank Ken Forbus, Brian Falkenhainer, and Janice Skorstad for discussions on this issue.

8 Currently, the global evaluation is extremely simple: The match-hypothesis evidence scores are simply summed for each Gmap. Although we have developed more elaborate schemes for computing the goodness of the Gmaps, this simple summation has proved extremely effective. We have tried SME on over 40 analogies, and in every case its highest-ranked Gmap is the one humans prefer.

9 The term *module* here should not be taken in the Fodorian sense. I assume that analogical processing is not innate or hard-wired but, at least in part, learned; nor do I assume that the analogy processor is impenetrable, although its workings may be opaque.

10 As in all top-down expectation situations, comprehension should be easier with a supporting context and harder when context leads to the wrong expectations; but the basic analogy processes do not *require* a context.

11 It should be noted that since this chapter was written Holyoak has revised his position. His recent work incorporates many of the structural constraints discussed here while still postulating a central role for contextual goals (Thagard & Holyoak, 1988).

12 Much of the developmental literature has been couched in terms of *metaphor* rather than *analogy.* Often, the items called *metaphors* are figurative comparisons that adults would treat as analogies.

13 It is not clear whether this shift is due to a developmental change in analytical reasoning skills or simply to an increase in domain knowledge, especially relational knowledge (Brown, this volume; Brown & Campione, 1984; Carey, 1984; Chi, 1978; Crisafi & Brown, 1986; Gentner, 1977a,b, 1988; Larkin, McDermott, Simon, & Simon, 1980; Reynolds & Ortony, 1980; Siegler, 1988; Vosniadou & Ortony, 1986).

14 These results, especially in problem-solving contexts, are problematic for the plan-based indexing view held by many researchers in artificial intelligence. See Gentner (1987) for a discussion.

15 This echoes the relational shift in the development of analogy from an early focus on surface commonalities to the adult focus on relational commonalities. How much we should make anything of this parallel is unclear.

16 We may perhaps learn to guide access by the indirect route of changing the contents of working memory so that a different set of matches arises. However, this is not a very fine-tuned method. I thank Brian Ross for discussions of this issue.

## REFERENCES

Asch, S. E., & Nerlove, H. (1960). The development of double function terms in children: An exploratory investigation. In B. Kaplan & S. Wapner (Eds.), *Perspectives in psychological theory.* New York: International Universities Press.

Billow, R. M. (1975). A cognitive development study of metaphor comprehension. *Developmental Psychology, 11,* 415–423.

Brooks, L. (1978). Nonanalytic concept formation and memory for instances. In E. Rosch & B. B. Lloyd (Eds.), *Cognition and categorization* (pp. 169–211). Hillsdale, NJ: Erlbaum.

Brown, A. L., & Campione, J. C. (1984). Three faces of transfer: Implications for early competence, individual differences, and instruction. In M. Lamb, A. Brown, & B. Rogoff (Eds.), *Advances in developmental psychology* (Vol. 3, pp. 143–192). Hillsdale, NJ: Erlbaum.

Buckley, S. (1979). *Sun up to sun down.* New York: McGraw-Hill.

Burstein, M. H. (1986). Concept formation by incremental analogical rea-

Falkenhainer, B. (1987b). Scientific theory formation through analogical inference. *Proceedings of the Fourth International Machine Learning Workshop* (pp. 218–229). Los Altos, CA: Kaufmann.

Falkenhainer, B., Forbus, K. D., & Gentner, D. (1986). The structure-mapping engine. *Proceedings of the American Association for Artificial Intelligence* (pp. 272–277). Philadelphia.

Falkenhainer, B., Forbus, K. D., & Gentner, D. (in press). The structure-mapping engine. *Artificial Intelligence.*

Forbus, K. D., & Gentner, D. (1983, June). Learning physical domains: Towards a theoretical framework. *Proceedings of the 1983 International Machine Learning Workshop* (pp. 198–202), Monticello, IL. Also in R. S. Michalski, J. G. Carbonell, & T. M. Mitchell (Eds.), *Machine learning: An artificial intelligence approach* (Vol. 2). Los Altos, CA: Kaufmann, 1986.

Gardner, H., Kircher, M., Winner, E., & Perkins, D. (1975). Children's metaphoric productions and preferences. *Journal of Child Language, 2,* 1–17.

Gentner, D. (1977a). Children's performance on a spatial analogies task. *Child Development, 48,* 1034–1039.

Gentner, D. (1977b). If a tree had a knee, where would it be? Children's performance on simple spatial metaphors. *Papers and Reports on Child Language Development, 13,* 157–164.

Gentner, D. (1980). *The structure of analogical models in science* (BBN Tech. Rep. 4451). Cambridge, MA: Bolt, Beranek & Newman.

Gentner, D. (1982). Are scientific analogies metaphors? In D. Miall (Ed.), *Metaphor: Problems and perspectives.* Brighton: Harvester Press.

Gentner, D. (1983). Structure-mapping: A theoretical framework for analogy. *Cognitive Science, 7,* 155–170.

Gentner, D. (1987). Analogical inference and analogical access. In A. Prieditis (Ed.), *Analogica: Proceedings of the First Workshop in Analogical Reasoning.* London: Pitman.

Gentner, D. (1988). Metaphor as structure-mapping: The relational shift. *Child Development, 59,* 47–59.

Gentner, D., & Clement, C. A. (in press). Evidence for relational selectivity in the interpretation of analogy and metaphor. In G. H. Bower (Ed.), *The psychology of learning and motivation.* New York: Academic Press.

Gentner, D., Falkenhainer, B., & Skorstad, J. (1987, January). Metaphor: The good, the bad, and the ugly. *Proceedings of the Third Conference on Theoretical Issues in Natural Language Processing* (pp. 155–159), Las Cruces, NM.

Gentner, D., & Gentner, D. R. (1983). Flowing waters or teeming crowds: Mental models of electricity. In D. Gentner & A. L. Stevens (Eds.), *Mental models* (pp. 99–129). Hillsdale, NJ: Erlbaum.

Gentner, D., & Jeziorski, M. (in press). Historical shifts in the use of analogy in science. In B. Gholson, W. R. Shadish, & A. Graesser (Eds.) *Psychology of Science.* Cambridge: Cambridge University Press.

Gentner, D., & Landers, R. (1985, November). Analogical reminding: A good match is hard to find. *Proceedings of the International Conference on Systems, Man, and Cybernetics.* Tucson, AZ.

Gentner, D., & Rattermann, M. J. (in preparation). Analogical access: A good match is hard to find.

soning and debugging. In R. S. Michalski, J. G. Carbonell, & T. M. Mitchell (Eds.), *Machine learning: An artificial intelligence approach* (Vol. 2, pp. 351–370). Los Altos, CA: Kaufmann.

Carbonell, J. G. (1981, August). Invariance hierarchies in metaphor interpretation. *Proceedings of the Third Annual Conference of the Cognitive Science Society* (pp. 292–295), Berkeley, CA.

Carbonell, J. G. (1983). Learning by analogy: Formulating and generalizing plans from past experience. In R. S. Michalski, J. G. Carbonell, and T. M. Mitchell (Eds.), *Machine learning: An artificial intelligence approach* (Vol. 1, pp. 137–161). Palo Alto, CA: Tioga.

Carey, S. (1984). Are children fundamentally different kinds of thinkers and learners than adults? In S. F. Chipman, J. W. Segal, & R. Glaser (Eds.), *Thinking and learning skills: Current research and open questions* (Vol. 2, pp. 485–517). Hillsdale, NJ: Erlbaum.

Chi, M. T. H. (1978). Knowledge structures and memory development. In R. Siegler (Ed.), *Children's thinking: What develops?* Hillsdale, NJ: Erlbaum.

Chi, M. T. H., Feltovich, P. J., & Glaser, R. (1981). Categorization and representation of physics problems by experts and novices. *Cognitive Science, 5,* 121–152.

Clement, J. (1981). Analogy generation in scientific problem solving. *Proceedings of the Third Annual Conference of the Cognitive Science Society* (pp. 137–140), Berkeley, CA.

Clement, J. (1983, April). *Observed methods for generating analogies in scientific problem solving.* Paper presented at the annual meeting of the American Educational Research Association, Montreal.

Clement, J. (1986, August). Methods for evaluating the validity of hypothesized analogies. *Proceedings of the Eighth Annual Conference of the Cognitive Science Society,* Amherst, MA.

Clement, C. A., & Gentner, D. (1988). Systematicity as a selection constraint in analogical mapping. *Proceedings of the Tenth Annual Conference of the Cognitive Science Society,* Montreal.

Crisafi, M. A., & Brown, A. L. (1986). Analogical transfer in very young children: Combining two separately learned solutions to reach a goal. *Child Development, 57,* 953–968.

DeLoache, J. S. (in press). The development of representation in young children. In H. W. Reese (Ed.), *Advances in child development and behavior* (Vol. 21). New York: Academic Press.

Dent, C. H. (1984). The developmental importance of motion information in perceiving and describing metaphoric similarity. *Child Development, 55,* 1607–1613.

Elio, R., & Anderson, J. R. (1981). The effects of category generalizations and instance similarity on schema abstraction. *Journal of Experimental Psychology: Human Learning and Memory, 7,* 397–417.

Elio, R., & Anderson, J. R. (1984). The effects of information and learning mode on schema abstraction. *Memory & Cognition, 12,* 20–30.

Falkenhainer, B. (1987a). *An examination of the third stage in the analogy process: Verification-based analogical reasoning* (Tech. Rep. UIUCDCS-R86-1302). Urbana-Champaign: University of Illinois, Department of Computer Science.

Gentner, D., & Schumacher, R. M. (1986, October). Use of structure-mapping theory for complex systems. *Proceedings of the IEEE International Conference on Systems, Man, and Cybernetics* (pp. 252–258), Atlanta, GA.

Gentner, D., & Stuart, P. (1983). *Metaphor as structure-mapping: What develops* (Tech. Rep. 5479). Cambridge, MA: Bolt, Beranek & Newman.

Gentner, D., & Toupin, C. (1986). Systematicity and surface similarity in the development of analogy. *Cognitive Science, 10,* 277–300.

Gick, M. L., & Holyoak, K. J. (1980). Analogical problem solving. *Cognitive Psychology, 12,* 306–355.

Gick, M. L., & Holyoak, K. J. (1983). Schema induction and analogical transfer. *Cognitive Psychology, 15,* 1–38.

Grudin, J. (1980). Processes in verbal analogy solution. *Journal of Experimental Psychology: Human Perception and Performance, 6,* 67–74.

Hall, R. (in press). Computational approaches to analogical reasoning: A comparative analysis. *Artificial Intelligence.*

Hesse, M. B. (1966). *Models and analogies in science.* Notre Dame, IN: University of Notre Dame Press.

Hofstadter, D. R. (1984). *The Copycat project: An experiment in nondeterministic and creative analogies* (Memo 755). Cambridge, MA: MIT, Artificial Intelligence Laboratory.

Hofstadter, D. R., Mitchell, T. M., & French, R. M. (1987). *Fluid concepts and creative analogies: A theory and its computer implementation* (Tech. Rep. 87–1). Ann Arbor: University of Michigan, Fluid Analogies Research Group.

Holyoak, K. J. (1985). The pragmatics of analogical transfer. In G. H. Bower (Ed.), *The psychology of learning and motivation* (Vol. 19, pp. 59–87). New York: Academic Press.

Holyoak, K. J., Junn, E. N., & Billman, D. O. (1984). Development of analogical problem-solving skill. *Child Development, 55,* 2042–2055.

Indurkhya, B. (1986). Constrained semantic transference: A formal theory of metaphors. *Synthese, 68,* 515–551.

Jacoby, L. L., & Brooks, L. R. (1984). Nonanalytic cognition: Memory, perception and concept learning. In G. H. Bower (Ed.), *The psychology of learning and motivation* (Vol. 18, pp. 1–47). New York: Academic Press.

Kedar-Cabelli, S. (1985, August). Purpose-directed analogy. *Proceedings of the Seventh Annual Conference of the Cognitive Science Society* (pp. 150–159), Irvine, CA.

Kedar-Cabelli, S. (1988). Analogy: From a unified perspective. In D. H. Helman (Ed.), *Analogical reasoning: Perspectives of artificial intelligence, cognitive science, and philosophy.* Boston: Reidel.

Keil, F., & Batterman, N. A. (1984). A characteristic-to-defining shift in the development of word meaning. *Journal of Verbal Learning and Verbal Behavior, 23,* 221–236.

Kemler, D. G. (1983). Holistic and analytical modes in perceptual and cognitive development. In T. J. Tighe & B. E. Shepp (Eds.), *Perception, cognition, and development: Interactional analysis* (pp. 77–102). Hillsdale, NJ: Erlbaum.

Kogan, N. (1975, April). *Metaphoric thinking in children: Developmental and*

individual-difference aspects. Paper presented at the meeting of the Society for Research in Child Development, Denver, CO.

Larkin, J., McDermott, J., Simon, D. P., & Simon, H. A. (1980). Expert and novice performance in solving physics problems. *Science, 208,* 1335–1342.

Marr, D. (1982). *Vision.* San Francisco: Freeman.

Medin, D. L. & Schaffer, M. M. (1978). Context theory of classification learning. *Psychological Review, 85,* 207–238.

Miller, G. A. (1979). Images and models, similes and metaphors. In A. Ortony (Ed.), *Metaphor and thought* (pp. 202–250). Cambridge: Cambridge University Press.

Miller, G. A., Gallanter, E., & Pribram, K. H. (1960). *Plans and the structure of behavior.* New York: Holt, Rinehart & Winston.

Murphy, G. L., & Medin, D. L. (1985). The role of theories in conceptual coherence. *Psychological Review, 92,* 289–316.

Newport, E. L. (1984). Constraints on learning: Studies in the acquisition of American Sign Language. *Papers and Reports on Child Language Development, 23,* 1–22.

Norman, D. A., Rumelhart, D. E., & LNR Research Group (1975). *Explorations in cognition.* San Francisco: Freeman.

Novick, L. R. (1988). Analogical transfer, problem similarity, and expertise. *Journal of Experimental Psychology: Learning, Memory, and Cognition, 14,* 510–520.

Ortony, A. (1979). Beyond literal similarity. *Psychological Review, 86,* 161–180.

Palmer, S. E. (1978). Fundamental aspects of cognitive representation. In E. Rosch & B. B. Lloyd (Eds.), *Cognition and categorization* (pp. 259–302). Hillsdale, NJ: Erlbaum.

Palmer, S. E., & Kimchi, R. (1985). The information processing approach to cognition. In T. Knapp & L. C. Robertson (Eds.), *Approaches to cognition: Contrasts and controversies* (pp. 37–77). Hillsdale, NJ: Erlbaum.

Polya, G. (1954). *Induction and analogy in mathematics: Vol. 1. Of mathematics and plausible reasoning.* Princeton, NJ: Princeton University Press.

Rattermann, M. J., & Gentner, D. (1987). Analogy and similarity: Determinants of accessibility and inferential soundness. *Proceedings of the Ninth Annual Meeting of the Cognitive Science Society* (pp. 23–34), Seattle.

Reddy, D. R., Erman, L. D., Fennell, R. D., & Neely, R. B. (1973, August). HEARSAY Speech understanding system: An example of the recognition process. *Proceedings of the Third International Joint Conference on Artificial Intelligence* (pp. 185–193), Stanford University.

Reed, S. K. (1987). A structure-mapping model for word problems. *Journal of Experimental Psychology: Learning, Memory, and Cognition, 13,* 124–139.

Reed, S. K., & Ackinclose, C. C. (1986). *Selecting analogous solutions: Similarity vs. inclusiveness.* Unpublished manuscript, Florida Atlantic University, Boca Raton.

Reed, S. K., Ernst, G. W., & Banerji, R. (1974). The role of analogy in transfer between similar problem states. *Cognitive Psychology, 6,* 436–450.

Reynolds, R. E., & Ortony, A. (1980). Some issues in the measurement of children's comprehension of metaphorical language. *Child Development, 51,* 1110–1119.

Van Lehn, K., & Brown, J. S. (1980). Planning nets: A representation for formalizing analogies and semantic models of procedural skills. In R. E. Snow, P. A. Federico, & W. E. Montague (Eds.), *Aptitude, learning, and instruction: Cognitive process analyses* (Vol. 2, pp. 95–137). Hillsdale, NJ: Erlbaum.

Verbrugge, R. R., & McCarrell, N.S. (1977). Metaphoric comprehension: Studies in reminding and resembling. *Cognitive Psychology, 9,* 494–533.

Vosniadou, S. & Ortony, A. (1986). Testing the metaphoric competence of the young child: Paraphrase versus enactment. *Human Development, 29,* 226–230.

Waldrop, M. (1987). Causality, structure, and common sense. *Science, 237,* 1297–1299.

Wattenmaker, W. D., Nakamura, G. V., & Medin, D. L. (1986). *Relationships between similarity-based and explanation-based categorization.* Unpublished manuscript, University of Illinois, Department of Psychology, Urbana-Champaign.

Winston, P. H. (1980). Learning and reasoning by analogy. *Communications of the Association for Computing Machinery, 23,* 689–703.

Winston, P. H. (1982). Learning new principles from precedents and exercises. *Artificial Intelligence, 19,* 321–350.

Ross, B. H. (1984). Remindings and their effects in learning a cognitive skill. *Cognitive Psychology, 16,* 371–416.

Ross, B. H. (1987). This is like that: The use of earlier problems and the separation of similarity effects. *Journal of Experimental Psychology: Learning, Memory, and Cognition, 13,* 629–639.

Ross, B. H., & Sofka, M. D. (1986). *Remindings: Noticing, remembering, and using specific knowledge of earlier problems.* Unpublished manuscript, University of Illinois, Department of Psychology, Urbana-Champain.

Rumelhart, D. E., & Abrahamson, A. A. A. (1973). A model for analogical reasoning. *Cognitive Psychology, 5,* 1–28.

Rumelhart, D. E., & Norman, D. A. (1981). Analogical processes in learning. In J. R. Anderson (Ed.) *Cognitive skills and their acquisition* (pp. 335–339). Hillsdale, NJ: Erlbaum.

Schank, R. C. (1982). *Dynamic memory.* Cambridge: Cambridge University Press.

Schank, R. C., & Abelson, R. P. (1977). *Scripts, plans, goals, and understanding: An inquiry into human knowledge structures.* Hillsdale, NJ: Erlbaum.

Schumacher, R. M. (1987). *Similarity-based reminding: Effects of distance and encoding on retrieval.* Unpublished master's thesis, University of Illinois, Urbana-Champaign.

Schumacher, R., & Gentner, D. (in press). Transfer of training as analogical mapping. *Communications of the IEEE.*

Shepp, B. E. (1978). From perceived similarity to dimensional structure: A new hypothesis about perceptual development. In E. Rosch & B. B. Lloyd (Eds.) *Cognition and categorization* (pp. 135–167). Hillsdale, NJ: Erlbaum.

Seigler, R. S. (1988). Mechanisms of cognitive growth: Variation and selection. In R. J. Sternberg (Ed.), *Mechanisms of cognitive development.* Prospect Heights, IL: Waveland Press.

Skorstad, J., Falkenhainer, B., & Gentner, D. (1987). Analogical processing: A simulation and empirical corroboration. *Proceedings of the American Association for Artificial Intelligence.* Seattle.

Skorstad, J., Gentner, D., & Medin, D. (1988). Abstraction processes during concept learning: A structural view. *Proceedings of the Tenth Annual Conference of the Cognitive Science Society,* Montreal.

Smith, L. B., & Kemler, D. G. (1977). Developmental trends in free classification: Evidence for a new conceptualization of perceptual development. *Journal of Experimental Child Psychology, 24,* 279–298.

Sternberg, R. J. (1977). Component processes in analogical reasoning. *Psychological Review, 84,* 353–378.

Thagard, P., & Holyoak, K. (1988, August). Analogical problem solving: A constraint satisfaction approach. *Proceedings of the Tenth Annual Conference of the Cognitive Science Society,* Montreal.

Thorndike, E. L. (1903). *Educational psychology.* New York: Lemcke & Buechner.

Tourangeau, R., & Sternberg, R. J. (1981). Aptness in metaphor. *Cognitive Psychology, 13,* 27–55.

Tversky, A. (1977). Features of similarity. *Psychological Review, 84,* 327–352.

# The Structure-Mapping Engine: Algorithm and Examples

**Brian Falkenhainer\* and Kenneth D. Forbus**

*Qualitative Reasoning Group, Department of Computer Science, University of Illinois, 1304 West Springfield Avenue, Urbana, IL 61801, USA*

**Dedre Gentner**

*Psychology Department, University of Illinois, Urbana, IL, USA*

ABSTRACT

*This paper describes the structure-mapping engine (SME), a program for studying analogical processing. SME has been built to explore Gentner's structure-mapping theory of analogy, and provides a "tool kit" for constructing matching algorithms consistent with this theory. Its flexibility enhances cognitive simulation studies by simplifying experimentation. Furthermore, SME is very efficient, making it a useful component in machine learning systems as well. We review the structure-mapping theory and describe the design of the engine. We analyze the complexity of the algorithm, and demonstrate that most of the steps are polynomial, typically bounded by $O(N^2)$. Next we demonstrate some examples of its operation taken from our cognitive simulation studies and work in machine learning. Finally, we compare SME to other analogy programs and discuss several areas for future work.*

## 1. Introduction

In analogy, a given situation is understood by comparison with another similar situation. Analogy may be used to guide reasoning, to generate conjectures about an unfamiliar domain, or to generalize several experiences into an abstract schema. Consequently, analogy is of great interest to both cognitive psychologists and artificial intelligence researchers. Psychologists aim to clarify the mechanisms underlying analogy in order to understand human learning and reasoning. Artificial intelligence researchers aim to emulate analogical processing on computers to produce more flexible reasoning and learning systems. This paper describes the *structure-mapping engine* (SME), a program built to

\* Current address: Xerox Palo Alto Research Center, 3333 Coyote Hill Road. Palo Alto, CA 94304, USA

0004-3702/89/\$3.50 © 1989, Elsevier Science Publishers B.V. (North-Holland)

*Artificial Intelligence* **41** (1989/90) 1–63

This paper originally appeared in the journal, *Artificial Intelligence*, Vol. 41, No. 1, and is reprinted here with permission of the publisher, Elsevier, Amsterdam.

explore the computational aspects of Gentner's *structure-mapping theory* of analogical processing [28, 30]. SME constructs all consistent ways to interpret a potential analogy and does so without backtracking. It is both flexible and efficient. Beyond this, SME provides a "tool kit" for building matchers that satisfy the structural consistency constraint of Gentner's theory. Additional constraints defining a matcher are specified by a collection of rules, which indicate local, partial matches and estimate how strongly they should be believed. The program uses these estimates and a novel procedure for combining the local matches to efficiently produce and evaluate all consistent global matches.

Cognitive simulation studies can offer important insights for understanding the human mind. They serve to verify psychological theories and supply a detailed vocabulary for describing cognitive processes. Cognitive simulations can provide "idealized subjects," whose prior knowledge and set of available processes is completely known to the experimenter. Unfortunately, cognitive simulations tend to be complex and computationally expensive (cf. [2, 72]). Complexity can obscure the relationship between the theory and the program. While all design decisions affect a program's performance, not all of them are directly motivated by the theory being tested. To assign credit properly (or to model performance in detail) requires exploring a space of similar architectures. Such explorations are very difficult if the major way to change the program's operation is surgery on the code. Complex programs also tend to be computationally expensive, which usually means fewer experiments are performed and fewer possibilities are explored. While there have been several important AI programs that study computational aspects of analogy (e.g., [5, 78, 79]), they were not designed to satisfy the above criteria.

Over the last decade there have been a variety of programs that simulate different aspects of analogical processing (as reviewed in Section 6). However, the progress to date has been disappointingly slow. Often papers describe programs that work on only a handful of carefully chosen examples, and do not specify the algorithms in a replicable fashion. We believe the difficulty has been due in part to the lack of a good problem decomposition. Without some theoretically motivated decomposition of analogy, it is easy to conflate distinct problems, and become lost in the space of possible mechanisms. Our decomposition, described in the next section, is psychologically motivated. Roughly, SME focuses on the *mapping* process in analogy, leaving the *access* and *application* aspects to future studies. The power of the program and its success on a wide variety of examples (over 40 as of this writing) provides additional evidence that the decomposition is a good one.

This paper examines the architecture of the structure-mapping engine and how it has been used for machine learning and cognitive simulation. First, we review Gentner's structure-mapping theory and some of the psychological evidence for it. Next we discuss the organization of SME, including knowledge representation conventions and the algorithm. After a complexity analysis, we

then illustrate SME's operation on several examples drawn from machine learning and cognitive simulation studies. Related work in both AI and psychology is reviewed next, followed by a discussion of future work.

## 2. Structure-Mapping Theory

The theoretical framework for this research is Gentner's structure-mapping theory of analogy [28–32, 34]. Structure-mapping describes the set of implicit constraints by which people interpret analogy and similarity. The central idea is that an analogy is a mapping of knowledge from one domain (the *base*) into another (the *target*) which conveys that a system of relations known to hold in the base also holds in the target. The target objects do not have to resemble their corresponding base objects. Objects are placed in correspondence by virtue of corresponding roles in the common relational structure.

This structural view of analogy is based on the intuition that analogies are about relations, rather than simple features. No matter what kind of knowledge (causal models, plans, stories, etc.), it is the structural properties (i.e., the interrelationships between the facts) that determine the content of an analogy. For example, consider the water flow and heat flow situations shown in Fig. 1. These situations are thought to be analogous because they share the complex relationship known as "flow." In each, we have a notion of something flowing downhill, from a source to a destination. We prefer to ignore the appearances and even specific defining properties of the objects, such as the fact that water and coffee are both liquids. Indeed, focusing on these attributes tends to confuse our picture of the analogy.

### 2.1. Subprocesses in analogy

Structure-mapping decomposes analogical processing into three stages ([27, 31, 35], see also [10, 11, 42, 51]):

(1) *Access*: Given a current *target* situation, retrieve from long-term memory another description, the *base*, which is analogous or similar to the target.

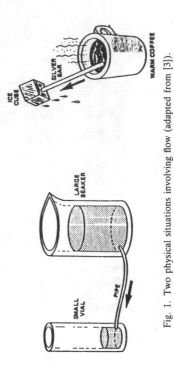

Fig. 1. Two physical situations involving flow (adapted from [3]).

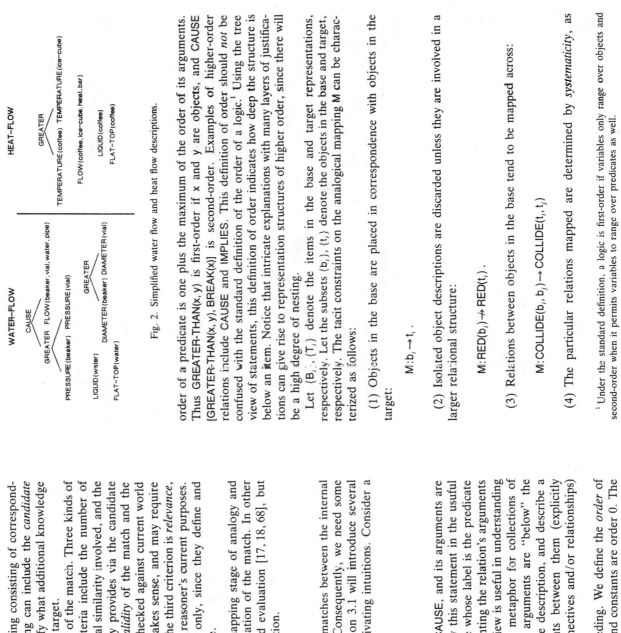

Fig. 2. Simplified water flow and heat flow descriptions.

(2) *Mapping and inference:* Construct a mapping consisting of correspondences between the base and target. This mapping can include the *candidate inferences* sanctioned by the analogy, which specify what additional knowledge in the base can potentially be transferred to the target.

(3) *Evaluation and use:* Estimate the "quality" of the match. Three kinds of criteria are involved [31, 32]. The *structural* criteria include the number of similarities and differences, the degree of structural similarity involved, and the amount and type of new knowledge the analogy provides via the candidate inferences. The second criterion concerns the *validity* of the match and the inferences it sanctions. The inferences must be checked against current world knowledge to ensure that the analogy at least makes sense, and may require additional inferential work to refine the results. The third criterion is *relevance*, i.e., whether or not the analogy is useful to the reasoner's current purposes. Structure-mapping focuses on structural criteria only, since they define and distinguish analogy from other kinds of inference.

The structure-mapping engine emulates the mapping stage of analogy and provides a structural, domain-independent evaluation of the match. In other work we have used SME in modeling access and evaluation [17, 18, 68], but here we focus on mapping and structural evaluation.

## 2.2. Constraints on analogy

Structure-mapping defines similarity in terms of matches between the internal structures of the descriptions being compared. Consequently, we need some terminology for describing such structures. Section 3.1 will introduce several formal descriptions. Here we provide some motivating intuitions. Consider a propositional statement, like

CAUSE[GREATER-THAN(x, y), BREAK(x)]

The chief relation involved in this statement is CAUSE, and its arguments are GREATER-THAN(x, y) and BREAK(x). We can view this statement in the usual way as a tree, i.e., the root of the tree is a node whose label is the predicate CAUSE and the root's children are nodes representing the relation's arguments (Fig. 2 provides an example of this view). This view is useful in understanding structure-mapping because it provides a spatial metaphor for collections of statements. For instance, we can say that the arguments are "below" the CAUSE statement in the internal structure of the description, and describe a collection of statements with logical constraints between them (explicitly represented by statements involving logical connectives and/or relationships) as a "connected" system of relations.

One formal definition is needed before proceeding. We define the *order* of an item in a representation as follows: Objects and constants are order 0. The order of a predicate is one plus the maximum of the order of its arguments. Thus GREATER-THAN(x, y) is first-order if x and y are objects, and CAUSE [GREATER-THAN(x, y), BREAK(x)] is second-order. Examples of higher-order relations include CAUSE and IMPLIES. This definition of order should *not* be confused with the standard definition of the order of a logic.[1] Using the tree view of statements, this definition of order indicates how deep the structure is below an item. Notice that intricate explanations with many layers of justifications can give rise to representation structures of higher order, since there will be a high degree of nesting.

Let $\{B_i\}$, $\{T_j\}$ denote the items in the base and target representations, respectively. Let the subsets $\{b_i\}$, $\{t_j\}$ denote the objects in the base and target, respectively. The tacit constraints on the analogical mapping M can be characterized as follows:

(1) Objects in the base are placed in correspondence with objects in the target:

$$M:b_i \rightarrow t_j.$$

(2) Isolated object descriptions are discarded unless they are involved in a larger relational structure:

$$M:RED(b_i) \nrightarrow RED(t_j).$$

(3) Relations between objects in the base tend to be mapped across:

$$M:COLLIDE(b_i, b_j) \rightarrow COLLIDE(t_i, t_j).$$

(4) The particular relations mapped are determined by *systematicity*, as

[1] Under the standard definition, a logic is first-order if variables only range over objects and second-order when it permits variables to range over predicates as well.

defined by the existence of higher-order constraining relations which can themselves be mapped:

M:CAUSE[PUSH($b_i$, $b_j$), COLLIDE($b_j$, $b_k$)]
→CAUSE[PUSH($t_i$, $t_j$), COLLIDE($t_j$, $t_k$)]

We require M to be *one-to-one*: that is, no base item maps to two target items and no target item maps to two base items. Furthermore, we require M to be *structurally consistent*. This means that, in addition to being 1:1, if M maps $B_i$ onto $T_j$, then it must also map the arguments of $B_i$ onto the corresponding arguments of $T_j$.

Consider for example a simple analogy between heat flow and water flow. Figure 2 shows a simplified version of what a learner might know about the situations pictured in Fig. 1. In order to comprehend the analogy "heat is like water" a learner must do the following (although not necessarily in this order):

(1) Set up the object correspondences between the two domains:

water → heat,        pipe → bar,
beaker → coffee,     vial → ice-cube

(2) Discard object attributes, such as LIQUID(water).
(3) Map base relations such as

GREATER-THAN[PRESSURE(beaker), PRESSURE(vial)]

to the corresponding relations in the target domain.
(4) Observe systematicity, i.e., keep relations belonging to a systematic relational structure in preference to isolated relationships. In this example,

CAUSE[GREATER-THAN[PRESSURE(beaker), PRESSURE(vial)],
FLOW(beaker, vial, water, pipe)]

is mapped into

CAUSE(GREATER-THAN[TEMPERATURE(coffee),
TEMPERATURE (ice-cube)],
FLOW(coffee, ice-cube, heat, bar)

while isolated relations, such as

GREATER-THAN[DIAMETER(beaker), DIAMETER(vial)]

are discarded.

---

The *systematicity* principle is central to analogy. Analogy conveys a system of connected knowledge, not a mere assortment of independent facts. Preferring systems of predicates that contain higher-order relations with inferential import is a structural expression of this tacit preference for coherence and deductive power in analogy. Thus, it is the amount of common higher-order relational structure that determines which of several possible matches is preferred. For example, suppose in the previous example we were concerned with objects differing in specific heat, such as a metal ball-bearing and a marble of equal mass, rather than temperatures. Then DIAMETER would enter the mapping instead of (or in addition to) PRESSURE, since DIAMETER affects the capacity of a container, the analogue to specific heat.

## 2.3. Other types of similarity

In addition to analogy, the distinctions introduced by structure-mapping theory provide definitions for several other kinds of similarity. In all cases, we require one-to-one, structurally consistent mappings. As we have seen, in *analogy* only relational structures are mapped. Aspects of object descriptions which play no role in the relational structure are ignored. By contrast, in *literal similarity* both relational predicates and object descriptions are mapped.[2] Literal similarity typically occurs in within-domain comparisons, in which the objects involved look alike as well as act alike. An example of a literal similarity is the comparison "Kool-Aid is like juice." In *mere-appearance* matches, it is primarily the object descriptions which are mapped, as in the metaphor

"The road is like a silver ribbon."

A fourth kind of mapping is the *abstraction mapping*. Here, the entities in the base domain are variables, rather than objects. Few, if any, attributes exist that do not contribute to the base's relational structure. Applying an abstraction match is very close to the instantiation of a rule. The difference is that only entities may be variables, whereas in many pattern-directed rule systems predicates may be used in substitutions as well.

## 2.4. Empirical evidence

Although the focus of this paper is on computational modeling, two sets of psychological findings are particularly relevant. First, empirical psychological studies have borne out the prediction that systematicity is a key element of people's implicit rules for analogical mapping. Adults focus on shared systematic relation structure in interpreting analogy. They tend to include rela-

---

[2] Notice that our structural characterization of literal similarity differs from some other psychological approaches (e.g., [70]).

tions and omit attributes in their interpretations of analogy, and they judge analogies as more sound and more apt if base and target share systematic relational structure [9, 28, 33, 35, 36]. In developmental work, it has been found that eight-year olds (but not five-year olds) are better at performing difficult mappings when the base structure is systematic [37]. Second, there is also empirical evidence that the different types of similarity comparisons defined by structure-mapping have different psychological properties [30–32].

## 3. The Structure-Mapping Engine

A simulation of Gentner's theory has been implemented in the structure-mapping engine (SME). Given descriptions of a base and target, SME constructs all structurally consistent mappings between them. The mappings consist of pairwise matches between statements and entities in the base and target, plus the set of analogical inferences sanctioned by the mapping. SME also provides a structural evaluation score for each mapping according to the constraints of systematicity and structural consistency. For example, given the descriptions of water flow and heat flow shown in Fig. 2, SME would offer several alternative interpretations. In one interpretation, the central inference is that water flowing from the beaker to the vial corresponds to heat flowing from the coffee to the ice cube. Alternatively, one could map water to coffee, since they are both liquids. The first interpretation has a higher structural evaluation score than the second, since a larger relational structure can be mapped.

Importantly, SME is not a single matcher, but a simulator for a class of matchers. The structure-mapping notion of structural consistency is built into the system. However, which local elements can match and how these combinations are scored can be changed by implementing new *match rules* that govern what pairwise matches between predicates are allowable and provide local measures of evidence. Thus, for example, SME can be used to simulate all the similarity comparisons sanctioned by structure-mapping theory, not just analogy. Since the match rules can include arbitrary LISP code, it is possible to implement many other kinds of matchers as well.

This section describes the SME algorithm in sufficient detail to allow replication. We start by specifying some simple conventions for knowledge representation which are essential to understanding the algorithm.

### 3.1. Representation conventions

We make as few representational assumptions as possible so that SME remains domain-independent. We use a typed (higher-order, in the standard sense) predicate calculus to represent facts. The constructs of this language are:

– *Entities*: Individuals and constants.
– *Predicates*: There are three types: *functions*, *attributes*, and *relations*. Each is described below.

– *Dgroup*: A *description group* is a collection of entities and facts about them, considered as a unit.

We examine each construct in turn.

#### 3.1.1. *Entities*

Entities are logical individuals, i.e., the objects and constants of a domain. Typical entities include physical objects, their temperature, and the substance they are made of. Primitive entities are the tokens or constants of a description and are declared with the defEntity form:

```
(defEntity ⟨name⟩
    [:type ⟨EntityType⟩]
    [:constant? {t|nil}])
```

Entities can also be specified in the usual way by compound terms, i.e. the term (pressure Well32) refers to a quantity.

The :type option establishes a hierarchy of entity types. For example, we state that our sun is a particular instance of a star with

```
(defEntity sun :type Star)
```

Constants are declared by using the :constant? option, as in

```
(defEntity zero :type number :constant? t)
```

#### 3.1.2. *Predicates*

Classically, "predicate" refers to any functor in a predicate calculus statement. We divide predicates into three categories: *functions*, *attributes*, and *relations*. Each is treated differently under structure-mapping.

– *Functions*: Functions map one or more entities into another entity or constant. For example, (PRESSURE piston) maps the physical object piston into the quantity which describes its pressure. We treat boolean predicates as attributes or relations (see below), rather than functions. Structure-mapping allows substitution of functions to acknowledge their role as an indirect way of referring to entities. All other predicates must be matched identically.

– *Attributes*: An attribute describes some property of an entity. Examples of attributes include RED and CIRCLE. We restrict attributes to take only one argument—if there are multiple arguments we classify the predicate as a relation. It is well-known that a combination of a function and a constant can be logically equivalent to an attribute. For example,

```
(RED BlockA)
```

and

(= (COLOR BlockA) RED)

are logically equivalent. However, these two forms do not behave identically under structure-mapping. In analogy, attributes are ignored unless they are part of some higher-order structure. When attributes are matched (e.g., literal similarity and mere-appearance comparisons), they must match identically. We assume that a reasoner has a particular piece of information represented in one form or another, but not both, at any particular time (we return to this issue in Section 7.1).

– *Relations*: Like attributes, relations range over truth values. Relations always have multiple arguments, and the arguments can be other predicates as well as entities. (However, we classify logical connectives, regardless of the number of arguments, as relations.) Examples of relations include CAUSE, GREATER-THAN, and IMPLIES. In structure-mapping, relations must always match identically.

Predicates are declared with the defPredicate form. It has several options:

```
(defPredicate ⟨Name⟩ ⟨ArgumentDeclarations⟩ ⟨PredicateType⟩
  :expression-type ⟨DefinedType⟩
  [:commutative? {t|nil}]
  [:n-ary? {t|nil}])
```

⟨*Predicate Type*⟩ is either function, attribute, or relation, according to what kind of predicate ⟨*Name*⟩ is. The ⟨*ArgumentDeclarations*⟩ specifies the predicate's arity and allows the arguments to be named and typed. For example, the declaration:

```
(defPredicate CAUSE ((antecedent sevent) (consequent sevent)) relation)
```

states that CAUSE is a two-place relational predicate. Its arguments are called antecedent and consequent, both of type sevent. (We use sevent to mean the union of states and events.) The names and types of arguments are for the convenience of the representation builder, and are not currently used by SME. However, the predicate type is very important to the algorithm, as we will see below.

The optional declarations :commutative? and :n-ary? provide SME with important syntactic information. :commutative? indicates that the predicate is commutative, and thus the order of arguments is unimportant when matching. :n-ary? indicates that the predicate can take any number of arguments. Declaring *n*-ary predicates reduces the need for applying associativity to binary predicates [69], allowing SME to avoid explicitly encoding associative laws in the matcher. Examples of commutative *n*-ary predicates include AND, OR, and SUM.

### 3.1.3. *Expressions and dgroups*

For simplicity, predicate instances and compound terms are called **expressions**. A *description group*, or *dgroup*, is a collection of primitive entities and expressions concerning them. Dgroups are defined with the **defDescription** form:

```
(defDescription ⟨DescriptionName⟩
  entities (⟨Entity₁⟩, ⟨Entity₂⟩,..., ⟨Entityᵢ⟩)
  expressions (⟨ExpressionDeclarations⟩))
```

where ⟨*ExpressionDeclarations*⟩ take the form

$$⟨expression⟩ \quad \text{or} \quad (⟨expression⟩ \ :name \ ⟨ExpressionName⟩)$$

The :name option is provided for convenience; ⟨*expression*⟩ will be substituted for every occurrence of ⟨*ExpressionName*⟩ in the dgroup's expressions when the dgroup is created. For example, the description of water flow depicted in Fig. 2 was given to SME as

```
(defDescription simple-water-flow
  entities (water beaker vial pipe)
  expressions (((flow beaker vial water pipe) :name wflow)
    ((pressure beaker) :name pressure-beaker)
    ((pressure vial) :name pressure-vial)
    ((greater pressure-beaker pressure-vial) :name >pressure)
    ((greater (diameter beaker) (diameter vial))
      :name >diameter)
    ((cause >pressure wflow) :name cause-flow)
    (flat-top water)
    (liquid water)))
```

The description of heat flow depicted in Fig. 2 was given to SME as

```
(defDescription simple-heat-flow
  entities (coffee ice-cube bar heat)
  expressions (((flow coffee ice-cube heat bar) :name hflow)
    ((temperature coffee) :name temp-coffee)
    ((temperature ice-cube) :name temp-ice-cube)
    ((greater temp-coffee temp-ice-cube) :name >temperature)
    (flat-top coffee)
    (liquid coffee)))
```

Notice that each expression does not need to be declared explicitly; for example, SME will automatically create and name expressions corresponding to (diameter beaker) and (diameter vial) in the water flow description.

We will refer to the expressions and entities in a dgroup collectively as *items*. To describe the SME algorithm we need some terminology to express the structural relations between items. These relationships form directed acyclic graphs, so we adopt some standard graph-theory terminology. Each item corresponds to a vertex in a graph. When item $\mathcal{I}_i$ has $\mathcal{I}_j$ as an argument, there will be a directed arc from the node corresponding to $\mathcal{I}_i$ to the node corresponding to $\mathcal{I}_j$. The *offspring* of an expression are its arguments. By definition, primitive entities (i.e., those denoted by constants) have no offspring. Expressions which name entities by compound terms are treated like any other item. An item $\mathcal{I}_1$ which is in the transitive closure (arguments of arguments, etc.) of another item $\mathcal{I}_2$ is said to be a *descendant* of $\mathcal{I}_2$, while $\mathcal{I}_2$ is said to be an *ancestor* of $\mathcal{I}_1$. An item with no ancestors is called a *root*. The term $Reachable(\mathcal{I})$ refers to the transitive closure of the subgraph starting at $\mathcal{I}$. We define the *depth* of an item with respect to $Reachable(\mathcal{I})$ by the minimum number of arcs it takes to reach the item starting from $\mathcal{I}$.

## 3.2. The SME algorithm: Overview

Given descriptions of a base and a target, represented as dgroups, SME builds all structurally consistent interpretations of the comparison between them. Each interpretation of the match is called a *global mapping*, or *gmap*.[3] Gmaps consist of three parts:

(1) *Correspondences*: A set of pairwise matches between the expressions and entities of the two dgroups.

(2) *Candidate inferences*: A set of new expressions (called SES for brevity) which the comparison suggests holds in the target dgroup.

(3) *Structural evaluation score* (called SES for brevity): A numerical estimate of match quality based on the gmap's structural properties.

Following the structure-mapping theory, we use only purely structural criteria to construct and evaluate the mapping. SME has no other knowledge of either base or target domain. Neither rules of inference nor even logical connectives themselves are built into the algorithm. Each candidate inference must be interpreted as a surmise, rather than a logically valid conclusion. The SES reflects the aesthetics of the particular type of comparison, not validity or

potential usefulness. Testing the validity of candidate inferences and determining the utility of a match are left to other modules, as described in Section 2.

*Match rules* specify which pairwise matches are possible and provide local measures of quality used in computing the SES. These rules are the key to SME's flexibility. To build a new matcher one simply loads a new set of match rules. This has several important advantages. First, we can simulate all of the similarity comparisons sanctioned by structure-mapping theory with one program. Second, we could in theory "tune" the rules if needed to simulate particular kinds of human performance (although, importantly, this flexibility has not been needed so far!). Third, we can also simulate a number of other analogy systems (including [43, 78], as described below) for comparison purposes.

Conceptually, the SME algorithm is divided into four stages:

(1) *Local match construction*: Finds all pairs of ⟨⟨*BaseItem*⟩, ⟨*TargetItem*⟩⟩ that can potentially match. A *match hypothesis* is created for each such pair to represent the possibility that this local match is part of a global match.

(2) *Gmap construction*: Combines the local matches into maximal consistent collections of correspondences.

(3) *Candidate inference construction*: Derives the inferences suggested by each gmap.

(4) *Match evaluation*: Attaches evidence to each local match hypothesis and uses this evidence to compute structural evaluation scores for each gmap.

We now describe each computation in detail, using a simple example to illustrate their operation.

### 3.2.1. *Local match construction (Step 1)*

Given two dgroups, SME begins by finding potential matches between items in the base and target (see Fig. 3). Allowable matches are specified by *match constructor* rules, which take the form:

(MHCrule (⟨*Trigger*⟩ ⟨*BaseVariable*⟩ ⟨*TargetVariable*⟩)
    [:test ⟨*TestForm*⟩])
  ⟨*Body*⟩)

In all match constructor rules, ⟨*Body*⟩ will be executed in an environment in which ⟨*BaseVariable*⟩ and ⟨*TargetVariable*⟩ are bound to items from the base and target dgroups, respectively. If ⟨*TestForm*⟩ is present, the bindings must satisfy the test (i.e., the form when evaluated must return non-NIL). There are two possible values for ⟨*Trigger*⟩. A filter trigger indicates that the rule is applied to each pair of items from the base and target. These rules create an initial set of match hypotheses between individual base and target expressions. For example, the following rule hypothesizes a match between any two

---

[3] The definition of gmap is inspired in part by de Kleer's work on assumption-based truth maintenance, although we do not use an ATMS in the actual code. The idea of combining local solutions by constructing maximally consistent sets is analogous to the process of *interpretation construction* in an ATMS. We also find bit-vectors a useful implementation technique for the set of operations needed to maintain structural consistency.

is the filter rule shown above. The other two are intern rules. The content of the first is, roughly,

> If the match hypothesis concerns two expressions, then create match hypotheses between any corresponding arguments that are both functions or entities.

The second is a specialization of this which runs only on commutative predicates (i.e., the "corresponding arguments" condition is removed). The analogy rule set differs in that matches are created between attributes only when they are part of some higher-order structure. The mere-appearance rule set differs by completely ignoring higher-order structure.

The result of running the match constructor rules is a collection of match hypotheses. We denote the hypothesis that $b_i$ and $t_j$ match by $MH(b_i, t_j)$. When no ambiguity will result, we will simply say $MH$. We will use the same terminology to refer to the structural properties of graphs of match hypotheses (offspring, descendants, ancestors, root) as we use for describing items in dgroups. As with dgroups, the collection of match hypotheses can be viewed as a directed acyclic graph, with at least one (and possibly many) roots.

**Example** (*Simple analogy between heat and water*). In this example we will use the *literal similarity* rule set, rather than *analogy*, in order to better illustrate the algorithm. The result of running these rules on the water flow and heat flow dgroups of Fig. 2 is shown in Fig. 3 (see also Fig. 4). Each match hypothesis locally pairs an item from the base dgroup with an item from the target dgroup.

There are several points to notice in Fig. 4. First, there can be more than one match hypothesis involving any particular base or target item. Here, TEMPERATURE can match with both PRESSURE and DIAMETER, since there are corresponding matches between the GREATER-THAN expressions in both dgroups (MH-1 and MH-6). Second, note that all predicates which are not functions must match identically. Entities, on the other hand, are matched on the basis of their roles in the predicate structure. Thus while TEMPERATURE can match either PRESSURE or DIAMETER, GREATER cannot match anything but GREATER. This distinction reflects the fact that functions are often used to refer to objects or constants, which are fair game for substitution under analogy. Third, not every possible correspondence is created. We do not, for example, attempt to match TEMPERATURE with water or heat with beaker. Functions only match with other functions: and local matches between entities are only created when justified by some other match. In general, this significantly constrains the number of possible matches.

### 3.2.2. Global match construction (Step 2)

The second step in the SME algorithm combines local match hypotheses into collections of global matches (gmaps). Intuitively, each global match is the

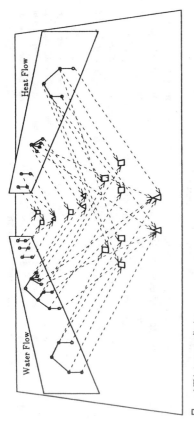

Water Flow   Heat Flow

□ - MH between predicates
△ - MH between entities (Emap)

Fig. 3. Local match construction. The graphs corresponding to the water flow and heat flow descriptions of Fig. 2 are depicted on the left and right panels, respectively. The squares and triangles in the middle represent the match hypotheses created by the literal similarity rules for these dgroups. The dashed arrows indicate which base and target items are conjectured as matching by each match hypothesis. The squares represent match hypotheses involving expressions, while the triangles represent match hypotheses involving entities. Notice how sparse the match is. Expression matches are only created when relations are identical, and matches between functions and entities are only created to support expression matches. This "middle out" local match computation provides SME with much of its power.

expressions that have the same functor:

```
(MHCrule (:filter ?b ?t :test (equal (expression-functor ?b)
                                     (expression-functor ?t)))

         (install-MH ?b ?t))
```

An :intern trigger indicates that the rule should be run on each newly created match hypothesis, binding the variables to its base and target items. These rules create additional matches suggested by the given match hypothesis. For example, hypothesizing matches between every pair of entities would lead to combinatorial explosions. Instead, we can use an :intern rule to create match hypotheses between entities in corresponding argument positions of other match hypotheses, since these correspondences will be required for structural consistency.

Appendix A lists the rule sets used to implement each similarity comparison of structure-mapping (*analogy, literal similarity,* and *mere appearance*). Notice that each rule set is small and simple (we describe the evidence rules below). The literal similarity rule set uses only three match constructor rules. One rule

collections and helps preserve the soundness and plausibility of the candidate inferences. Without it, every collection of local matches would need to be considered, and effort would be wasted on degenerate many-to-one mappings without any possible inferential value. The maximality condition also serves to reduce the number of gmaps, since otherwise every subset of a gmap could itself be a gmap.

Global matches are built in two steps:

(1) *Compute consistency relationships*: For each match hypothesis, generate (a) the set of entity mappings it entails, (b) which match hypotheses it locally conflicts with, and (c) which match hypotheses it is structurally inconsistent with.

(2) *Merge match hypotheses*: Compute gmaps by successively combining match hypotheses as follows:

(a) *Form initial combinations*: Combine the descendants of the highest-order structurally consistent match hypotheses into an initial set of gmaps.

(b) *Combine dependent gmaps*: Merge initial gmaps that have overlapping base structure, subject to structural consistency.

(c) *Combine independent collections*: Form complete gmaps by merging the partial gmaps from the previous step, subject to structural consistency, keeping only the maximal results.

Importantly, the process of gmap *construction* is independent of gmap *evaluation*. Which gmaps are constructed depends solely on structural consistency. Numerical evidence, described below, is used only to compare their relative merits.

We now describe the algorithm in detail.

*Computing consistency relationships*

Consistency checking is the crux of gmap construction. To do this we compute for each match hypothesis (a) the entity mappings it entails and (b) the set of match hypotheses it is inconsistent with.

Consider a particular match hypothesis $MH(b_i, t_j)$ involving base item $b_i$ and target item $t_j$. If $b_i$, $t_j$ are expressions, then by the support constraint the match hypotheses linking their arguments must also be in any collection that $MH(b_i, t_j)$ is in. Applying this constraint recursively, all descendants of $MH(b_i, t_j)$ must be in the same collection if it is structurally consistent (see Fig. 5). Since the chain of descendants ends with match hypotheses involving entities, each match hypothesis implies a specific set of entity correspondences:

**Definition 3.1.** An *emap* is a match hypothesis between entities. $Emaps(MH(b_i, t_j))$ represents the set of emaps implied by a match hypothesis $MH(b_i, t_j)$. $Emaps(MH(b_i, t_j))$ is simply the union of the emaps supported by

largest possible set of match hypotheses that depend on the same one-to-one object correspondences.

More formally, gmaps consist of *maximal, structurally consistent* collections of match hypotheses. A collection of match hypotheses is *structurally consistent* if it satisfies two constraints:

(1) *One-to-oneness*: The match hypotheses in the collection do not assign the same base item to multiple target items or any target item to multiple base items.

(2) *Support*: If a match hypothesis MH is in the collection, then so are match hypotheses which pair the arguments of MH's base and target items.

The one-to-one constraint allows straightforward substitutions in candidate inferences. The support constraint preserves connected predicate structure. A collection is maximal if adding any additional match hypothesis would render the collection structurally inconsistent.

Requiring structural consistency both reduces the number of possible global

MH-13
B: Liquid-3
T: Liquid-5

MH-12
B: Flat-top-4
T: Flat-top-6

MH-14
B: water
T: coffee

MH-9
B: Wflow
T: Hflow

MH-11
B: pipe
T: bar

MH-10
B: water
T: heat

MH-6
B: >Diameter
T: >Temperature

MH-8
B: Diameter-2
T: Temp-ice-cube

MH-1
B: >Pressure
T: >Temperature

MH-3
B: Pressure-vial
T: Temp-ice-cube

MH-7
B: Diameter-1
T: Temp-coffee

MH-2
B: Pressure-beaker
T: Temp-coffee

MH-4
B: beaker
T: coffee

MH-5
B: vial
T: ice-cube

Fig. 4. Water flow/heat flow analogy after local match construction. Here we show the graph of match hypotheses depicted schematically in Fig. 3, augmented by links indicating expression-to-arguments relationships. Match hypotheses which are not descended from others are called *roots* (e.g., the matches between the GREATER predicates, MH-1 and MH-6, and the match for the predicate FLOW, MH-9). Match hypotheses between entities are called *emaps* (e.g., the match between beaker and coffee, MH-4). Emaps play an important role in algorithms based on structural consistency.

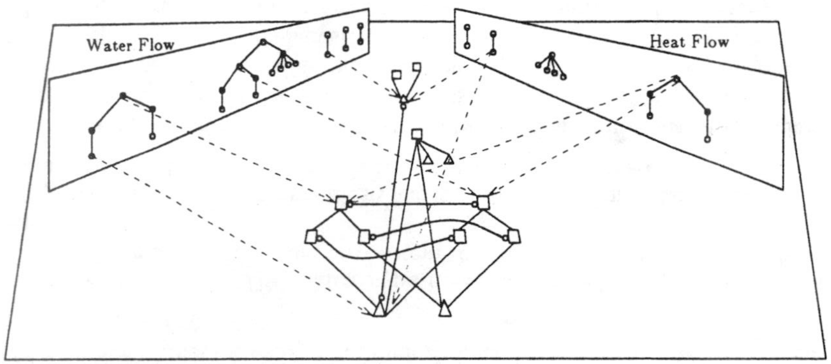

wise, $NoGood(MH_i)$ is the union of $MH_i$'s *Conflicting* set with the *NoGood* sets for all of its descendants, i.e.,

$$NoGood(MH_i) = Conflicting(MH_i) \cup \bigcup_{MH_j \in Args(MH_i)} NoGood(MH_j).$$

We compute *Conflicting*, *Emaps*, and *NoGood* sets as follows. First, *Conflicting* is computed for each match hypothesis, since it requires only local information. Second, *Emaps* and *NoGood* are computed for each emap. Third, *Emaps* and *NoGood* sets are computed for all other match hypotheses by propagating the results from *Emaps* upwards to their ancestors.

We make two observations about this computation. First, these operations can be efficiently implemented via bit vectors. For example, SME assigns a unique bit position to each match hypothesis, and carries out union and intersection operations by using OR and AND bit operations. Second, it is important to look for *justification holes* in the match hypothesis graph—match hypotheses whose arguments fail to match. Such match hypotheses will always violate the support constraint, and hence should be removed. For example, if one of the PRESSURE-TEMPERATURE match hypotheses had not been formed (see Fig. 4), then the match between their governing GREATER predicates would be removed. Notice that removing justification holes eliminates many blatantly incorrect matches, such as trying to place an eighth-order IMPLIES in correspondence with a second-order IMPLIES.

The next step in gmap construction is to identify those match hypotheses which are internally inconsistent, and thus cannot be part of any gmap. This can happen when the descendants of a match hypothesis imply mutually incompatible bindings.

**Definition 3.4.** A match hypothesis is *inconsistent* if the emaps entailed by one subgraph of its descendants conflicts with the emaps entailed by another subgraph of its descendants:

$$Inconsistent(MH_i) \Leftrightarrow Emaps(MH_i) \cap NoGood(MH_i) \neq \emptyset .$$

Clearly, every ancestor of an inconsistent match hypothesis is also inconsistent. By caching the *NoGood* sets, inconsistent match hypotheses can be identified easily.

Global match construction proceeds by collecting sets of consistent match hypotheses. Since gmaps are defined to be maximal, we begin from roots and work downward rather than starting bottom-up. If a root is consistent, then the entire structure under it must be consistent, and thus forms an initial gmap. If the graph of match hypotheses had only a single consistent root, this step

Fig. 5. Water flow/heat flow analogy after computation of *Conflicting* relationships. Simple lines show the tree-like graph that the support constraint imposes upon match hypotheses. Lines with circular endpoints indicate the *Conflicting* relationships between matches. Some of the original lines from match hypothesis construction have been left in to show the source of a few *Conflicting* relations.

□ - MH between predicates
△ - MH between entities (Emap)

$MH(b_i, t_j)$'s descendants. We also include match hypotheses involving functions in $Emaps(MH(b_i, t_j))$.

To enforce one-to-one mappings we must associate with each $MH(b_i, t_j)$ the set of match hypotheses that provide alternate mappings for $b_i$ and $t_j$. Clearly, no member of this set can be in the same gmap with $MH(b_i, t_j)$.

**Definition 3.2.** Given a match hypothesis $MH(b_i, t_j)$, the set *Conflicting* $(MH(b_i, t_j))$ consists of the set of match hypotheses that represent the alternate mappings for $b_i$ and $t_j$:

$Conflicting(MH(b_i, t_j))$
$$\equiv \left[ \bigcup_{b_k \in base} \{MH(b_k, t_j) \mid b_k \neq b_i\} \right] \cup \left[ \bigcup_{t_k \in target} \{MH(b_i, t_k) \mid t_k \neq t_j\} \right].$$

The set $Conflicting(MH(b_i, t_j))$ only notes local inconsistencies (see Fig. 5). However, we can use it and $Emaps(MH(b_i, t_j))$ to recursively define the set of all match hypotheses that can never be in the same gmap as $MH(b_i, t_j)$.

**Definition 3.3.** The set $NoGood(MH_i)$ is the set of all match hypotheses which can never appear in the same gmap as $MH_i$. This set is recursively defined as follows: if $MH_i$ is an emap, then $NoGood(MH_i) = Conflicting(MH_i)$. Other-

with one another must be merged. Consistency between two gmaps can be defined as follows:

$$Consistent(GMap_i, GMap_j)$$
$$\text{iff } Elements(GMap_i) \cap NoGood(GMap_j) = \emptyset$$
$$\wedge NoGood(GMap_i) \cap Elements(GMap_j) = \emptyset.$$

*Merge step 2: Combine connected gmaps.* Consider two elements of $Gmaps_1$ which share base structure, i.e., whose roots in the base structure are identical. Since we are assuming distinct elements, either (a) their correspondences are structurally inconsistent or (b) there is some structure in the base which connects them that does not appear in the target (if it did, match hypotheses would have been created which would bring the two elements under a common match hypothesis root; hence they would not be distinct). Combining such elements, when consistent, leads to potential support for candidate inferences. We call the partial gmaps resulting from this merge $Gmaps_2$ (Fig. 6(b)).

*Merge step 3: Combine independent collections.* Consider two elements of $Gmaps_2$ which have no overlap between their relational correspondences. Clearly, any such pair could be merged without inconsistency, if they sanction consistent sets of emaps. This final step generates all consistent combinations of gmaps from $Gmaps_2$ by successive unions, keeping only those combinations that are maximal (Fig. 6(c)).

**Example** (*Simple analogy between heat and water*). Figure 6 shows how the gmaps are formed from the collection of match hypotheses for the simple water flow/heat flow example. After merge step 1, only isolated collections stemming from common roots exist. Merge step 2 combines the PRESSURE to TEMPERATURE mapping with the FLOW mapping, since they have common base structure (i.e., the base structure root is the CAUSE predication). Finally, merge step 3 combines the isolated water and coffee attributes (see Fig. 7). Notice that the FLOW mapping is structurally consistent with the DIAMETER to TEMPERATURE mapping. However, because merge step 2 placed the FLOW mapping into the same gmap as the PRESSURE to TEMPERATURE mapping, merge step 3 was unable to combine the FLOW mapping with the DIAMETER to TEMPERATURE gmap.

### 3.2.3. Compute candidate inferences (Step 3)

Each gmap represents a set of correspondences that can serve as an interpretation of the match. For new knowledge to be generated about the target, there must be information from the base which can be carried over into the target. Not just any information can be carried over—it must be consistent with the substitutions imposed by the gmap, and it must be *structurally grounded* in the gmap. By structural grounding, we mean that its subexpressions must at some

would suffice. However, typically there are several roots, and hence several initial gmaps. To obtain true gmaps, that is, *maximal* collections of match hypotheses, these initial gmaps must then be merged into larger, structurally consistent collections.

*Merge step 1: Form initial combinations.* The first step is to combine interconnected and consistent structures (Fig. 6(a)). Each consistent root, and its descendants, forms an initial gmap. If a root is inconsistent, then the same procedure is applied recursively to each descendant (i.e., each immediate descendant is now considered as a root). The resulting set will be called $Gmaps_1$. The procedure is:

(1) Let $Gmaps_1 = \emptyset$.
(2) For every root $MH(b_i, t_i)$
  (a) if $\neg Inconsistent(MH(b_i, t_i))$, then create a gmap $GM$ such that $Elements(GM) = Reachable(MH(b_i, t_i))$;
  (b) if $Inconsistent(MH(b_i, t_i))$, then recurse on *Offspring* $(MH(b_i, t_i))$.
(3) For every $GM \in Gmaps_1$
  (a) $NoGood(GM) = \bigcup_{MH(b_i,t_i) \in Roots(GM)} NoGood(MH(b_i, t_i));$
  (b) $Emaps(GM) = \bigcup_{MH(b_i,t_i) \in Roots(GM)} Emaps(MH(b_i, t_i)).$

In this step inconsistent match hypotheses have been completely eliminated. However, we do not yet have true gmaps, since the sets of correspondences are not maximal. To obtain maximality, elements of $Gmaps_1$ that are consistent

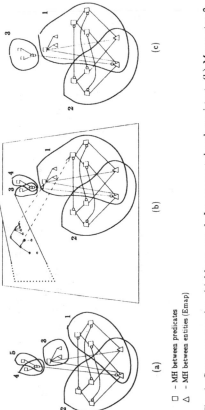

□ – MH between predicates
△ – MH between entities (Emap)

Fig. 6. Gmap construction. (a) Merge step 1: Interconnected and consistent. (b) Merge step 2: Consistent members of the same base structure. (c) Merge step 3: Any further consistent combinations.

point intersect the base information belonging to the gmap. Such structures form the *candidate inferences* of a gmap.

To compute the candidate inferences for a gmap *GM*, SME begins by examining each root $B_R$ in the base dgroup to see if it is an ancestor of any match hypothesis roots in the gmap. If it is, then any elements in *Descendants*($B_R$) which are not in *BaseItems*(*GM*) are included in the set of candidate inferences.

The candidate inferences often include entities. Whenever possible, SME replaces all occurrences of base entities with their corresponding target entities. Sometimes, however, there will be base entities that have no corresponding target entity; i.e., the base entity is not part of any match hypothesis for that gmap. What SME does depends on the type of entity. If the base entity is a constant, such as zero, it can be brought directly into the target unchanged (a flag is provided to turn on this behavior). Otherwise, SME introduces a new, hypothetical entity into the target which is represented as a skolem function of the original base entity. Such entities are represented as (:skolem base-entity). Recall that structure-mapping does not guarantee that any candidate infer-

ence is valid. Each candidate inference is only a surmise, which must be tested by other means. By theoretical assumption, general testing for validity and relevance is the province of other modules which use SME's output.[4] However, SME does provide a weak consistency check based on purely structural considerations. In particular, it discards a candidate inference when (a) the predicate is noncommutative and (b) its arguments are simply a permuted version of the arguments to another expression involving that predicate in the target domain. For example, if (GREATER (MASS sun) (MASS planet)) existed in the target, (GREATER (MASS planet) (MASS sun)) would be discarded as a candidate inference.

**Example** (*Simple analogy between heat and water*). In Fig. 7, gmap #1 has the top-level CAUSE predicate as its sole candidate inference. In other words, this gmap suggests that the cause of the flow in the heat dgroup is the difference in temperatures.

Suppose the FLOW predicate was missing in the target dgroup. Then the candidate inferences for a gmap corresponding to the pressure inequality would include expressions involving both CAUSE and FLOW, as well as conjectured target entities corresponding to water (heat) and pipe (bar). The two skolemized entities would be required because the FLOW match provides the match from water and pipe to heat and bar, respectively. Note also that GREATER-THAN[DIAMETER(coffee), DIAMETER(ice-cube)] is not a valid candidate inference for the first gmap because it does not intersect the existing gmap structure.

### 3.2.4. *Compute structural evaluation scores* (*Step 4*)

Typically a particular base and target pair will give rise to several gmaps, each representing a different interpretation. Selecting the "best" interpretation of an analogy, as mentioned previously, can involve nonstructural criteria. However, as the psychological results indicated, evaluation includes an important structural component. SME provides a programmable mechanism for computing a *structural evaluation score* (*SES*) for each gmap. This score can be used to rank-order the gmaps or as a factor in some external evaluation procedure.

The structural evaluation score is computed in two phases, each using *match evidence rules* to assign and manage numerical scores. The first phase assigns weights to individual match hypotheses, and the second phase computes a score for each gmap by combining the evidence for the match hypotheses comprising its correspondences. After a brief introduction to the evidence processing mechanism, we describe each phase in turn.

The management of numerical evidence is performed by a *belief maintenance system* (BMS) [16]. The BMS is much like a standard TMS, using Horn clauses as justifications. However, the justifications are annotated with evidential

[4] One such module is described in [17, 20].

```
Rule File: literal-similarity.rules    Number of Match Hypotheses: 14

Match Hypotheses:

(0.6500  0.0000)    (>PRESSURE >TEMP)
(0.7120  0.0000)    (PRESS-BEAKER TEMP-COFFEE)
(0.7120  0.0000)    (PRESS-VIAL TEMP-ICE-CUBE)
(0.9318  0.0000)    (BEAKER-6 COFFEE-1)
(0.6320  0.0000)    (PIPE-8 BAR-3)

Global Mappings:

Gmap #1: (>PRESSURE >TEMPERATURE) (PRESSURE-BEAKER TEMP-COFFEE)
         (PRESSURE-VIAL TEMP-ICE-CUBE) (WFLOW HFLOW)
         (beaker coffee) (vial ice-cube) (water heat)  (pipe bar)
  Emaps: (beaker coffee) (vial ice-cube)
  Weight: 5.99
  Candidate Inferences: (CAUSE >TEMPERATURE HFLOW)

Gmap #2: (>DIAMETER >TEMPERATURE) (DIAMETER-1 TEMP-COFFEE)
         (DIAMETER-2 TEMP-ICE-CUBE)
  Emaps: (beaker coffee) (vial ice-cube)
  Weight: 3.94
  Candidate Inferences:

Gmap #3: (LIQUID-3 LIQUID-5)  (FLAT-TOP-4 FLAT-TOP-6)
  Emaps: (water coffee)
  Weight: 2.44
  Candidate Inferences:
```

Fig. 7. Complete SME interpretation of water flow/heat flow analogy.

implement this preference by passing evidence from a match involving a relationship to the matches involving its arguments. The following rule accomplishes this, propagating 80% of a match hypothesis' belief to its offspring:

```
(rule ((:intern (MH ?b1 ?t1))
       (:intern (MH ?b2 ?t2) :test (children-of? ?b2 ?t2 ?b1 ?t1)))
  (assert! (implies (MH ?b2 ?t2) (MH ?b1 ?t1) (0.8 . 0.0))))
```

The more matched structure that exists above a given match hypothesis, the more that hypothesis will be believed. The effect cascades, so that entity mappings involved in a large systematic structure receive much higher scores than those which are not. Thus this ''trickle down'' effect provides a local encoding of the systematicity principle.

*Computing the structural evaluation score*

The structural evaluation score for a gmap is simply the sum of the evidence of its match hypotheses. This simplistic summation rule has sufficed for most of the examples encountered so far. There are a number of other factors that are potentially relevant as well, which we discuss in Section 7.3.1. In order to provide maximum flexibility, evidence rules are used to compute the evidence of gmaps as well.

Originally we combined evidence for gmaps according to Dempster's rule, so that the sum of beliefs for all the gmaps equaled 1 [21]. We discovered two problems with this scheme. First, Demster's rule is susceptible to roundoff, which caused stability problems when a large number of match hypotheses supported a gmap. Second, normalizing gmap evidence prevents us from comparing matches using different base domains (as needed for access experiments, see Section 4.4), since the score would be a function of the other gmaps for a particular base and target pair.

**Example** (*Simple analogy between heat and water*). Returning to Fig. 7, note that the best interpretation (i.e., the one which has the highest structural evaluation score) is the one we would intuitively expect. In this interpretation, beaker maps to coffee, vial maps to ice-cube, water maps to heat, pipe maps to bar, and PRESSURE maps to TEMPERATURE. Furthermore, we have the candidate inference that the temperature difference is what causes the flow of heat.

### 3.3. Complexity analysis

Here we analyze the complexity of the SME algorithm. Because it depends critically on both the input descriptions and the match rules, strict bounds are hard to determine. However, we give both best- and worst-case analyses for each step, and provide estimates of typical performance based on our ex-

weights, so that ''degrees of belief'' may be propagated. A modified version of Dempster–Shafer formalism is used for expressing and combining evidence. Belief in a proposition is expressed by the pair $(s(A), s(\neg A))$, where $s(A)$ represents the current amount of support for A and $s(\neg A)$ is the current support against A. A simplified form of Dempster's rule of combination [16, 39, 57, 64] allows combining evidence from multiple justifications. For example, given that $\text{Belief}(A) = (0.4, 0)$ and $\text{Belief}(B) = (0.6, 0)$, together with $(\text{IMPLIES A C})_{(0.8,0)}$ and $(\text{IMPLIES B C})_{(1.0)}$, Dempster's rule provides a belief in C equal to $(0.728, 0.0)$. In addition to providing evidence combination, these justifications provide useful explanations about the structural evaluation (see [16]).

We note two points about the role of numerical evidence in SME:

(1) While we have found Dempster–Shafer useful, our algorithms are independent of its details, and should work with any reasonable formalism for combining evidence.

(2) We use numerical evidence to provide a simple way to combine local information concerning match quality. These weights have nothing to do with any probabilistic or evidential information about the base or target per se.

*Assigning local evidence*

Each match hypothesis and gmap has an associated BMS node to record evidential information. The match evidence rules can add evidence directly to a match hypothesis based on its local properties or indirectly by installing relationships between them. Syntactically, these rules are similar to the match constructor rules. For example,

```
(assert! 'same-functor)
(rule ((:intern (MH ?b ?t)
        :test (and (expression? ?b) (expression? ?t)
                   (eq (expression-functor ?b)
                       (expression-functor ?t)))))
  (assert! (implies same-functor (MH ?b ?t) (0.5 . 0.0)))))
```

states that ''if the base item and target item of a match hypothesis are expressions with the same functors, then supply 0.5 evidence in favor of the match hypothesis.'' (The assertion of same-functor provides a global record for explanatory purposes that this factor was considered in the structural evaluation.) The complete set of evidence rules used in this paper are provided in Appendix A.

The ability to install relationships between match hypotheses allows a simple, local implementation of the systematicity constraint. Recall that the systematicity constraint calls for preferring expressions involving higher-order relationships belonging to a systematic structure over isolated relationships. We

1. Run MHC rules to construct match hypotheses.
2. Calculate the *Conflicting* set for each match hypothesis.
3. Calculate the *EMaps* and *NoGood* sets for each match hypothesis by upward propagation from entity mappings.
4. Merge match hypotheses into gmaps.
   (a) Interconnected and consistent.
   (b) Consistent members of same base structure.
   (c) Any further consistent combinations.
5. Calculate the candidate inferences for each gmap.
6. Score the matches
   (a) Local match scores.
   (b) Global structural evaluation scores.

Fig. 8. Summary of SME algorithm.

perience. The decomposition used in the analysis is shown in Fig. 8. We use the following notation in the analysis:

$\mathscr{E}_b$ = number of entities in the base dgroup,
$\mathscr{E}_t$ = number of entities in the target dgroup,
$\mathscr{F}_b$ = number of expressions in the base dgroup,
$\mathscr{F}_t$ = number of expressions in the target dgroup,
$\mathscr{M}$ = number of match hypotheses,
$\mathscr{G}$ = number of gmaps,
$N_b \equiv \mathscr{E}_b + \mathscr{F}_b,$   $N_t \equiv \mathscr{E}_t + \mathscr{F}_t,$   $N \equiv \tfrac{1}{2}(N_b + N_t).$

### 3.3.1. Analysis of Step 1: Local match construction

SME does not restrict either the number of match rules or their complexity. There is nothing to prevent one from writing a rule that examines extensive information from external sources (e.g., a knowledge base, plans, goals, etc.). However, the rule sets which implement the comparisons of structure-mapping theory consist of only a few simple rules each. This reduction of computational complexity is one of the advantages of the structure-mapping account, since it restricts the tests performed in rules to local properties of the representation. Consequently, we assume rule execution takes unit time, and focus on the total number of rules executed. The filter rules are run once for each pair of base and target predicates. Consequently, they will always require $O(N_b \cdot N_t)$. Each :intern rule is run once on every match hypothesis. In the worst case, $\mathscr{M} = N_b \cdot N_t$, or roughly $N^2$. But in practice, the actual number of match hypotheses is substantially less, usually on the order of $cN$, where $c$ is less than 5 and $N$ is the average of $N_b$ and $N_t$. Thus, in practice, :intern rules have a run time of approximately $O(N)$.

### 3.3.2. Analysis of Step 2: Calculating Conflicting

Recall that SME assigns a *Conflicting* set to each match hypothesis, $MH(b_i, t_j)$, which represents the alternate mappings for $b_i$ and $t_j$. The conflicting sets are calculated by examining each base and target item to gather the match hypotheses which mention them. Let $\mathscr{C}$ be the average number of alternative matches each item in the base and target appears in. SME loops through the $\mathscr{C}$ match hypotheses twice: once to form the bitwise union of these match hypotheses and once to update each hypothesis' *Conflicting* set. Thus, the entire number of bit vector operations is

$$(\mathscr{F}_b \cdot 2\mathscr{C}) + (\mathscr{E}_b \cdot 2\mathscr{C}) + (\mathscr{F}_t \cdot 2\mathscr{C}) + (\mathscr{E}_t \cdot 2\mathscr{C}).$$

The worst case is when a match hypothesis is created between every base and target item. If we also assume $N_b = N_t$, then $\mathscr{C} = N_t$ in that case. The number of operations becomes $4N_t^2$ or approximately $O(N^2)$. Conversely, the best-case performance occurs when $\mathscr{C}$ is 1, producing $O(\max(N_b, N_t))$ operations. In our experiments so far, we find that $\mathscr{C}$ is typically quite small, and so far has always been less than 10. Consequently, the typical performance lies between $O(N)$ and $O(N^2)$.

### 3.3.3. Analysis of Step 3: Emaps and NoGood calculation

Recall that once the *Conflicting* sets are calculated, the *Emaps* and *NoGood* sets are propagated upwards from the entity mappings through the match hypotheses. By caching which $MH(b_i, t_j)$'s correspond to emaps and using a queue, we only operate on each node once. Hence the worst- and best-case performance of this operation is $O(\mathscr{M})$, which in the worst case is $O(N^2)$.

### 3.3.4. Analysis of Step 4: Gmap construction

Global matches are formed in three steps. The first step collects all of the consistent connected components of match hypotheses by starting at the match hypothesis roots, walking downwards to find consistent structures. Each graph walk takes at most $O(N_i)$, where $N_i$ is the number of nodes *Reachable* from the current match hypothesis root. If there are $N_R$ roots, then the first merge step (Step 4(a)) takes $O(N_R \cdot N_i)$. Assuming that most of the match hypotheses will appear in only one or two subgraphs (some roots may share substructure), we can approximate this by saying that the first merge step is $O(\mathscr{M})$. Call the number of partial gmaps formed at this stage $\mathscr{G}_{P1}$.

Perhaps surprisingly, the complexity of the previous steps has been uniformly low. Sophisticated matching computations usually have much worse performance, and SME cannot completely escape this. In particular, the worst case for Steps 4(b) and 4(c) is $O(N!)$ (although worst case for one implies best case for the other).

Step 4(b) combines partial gmaps from Step 4(a) that intersect the same base structure. This requires looping through each base description root to find which partial gmaps intersect it, and then generating every consistent, maximal combination of them. In the worst case, every gmap could intersect the same base structure. This would mean generating all possible consistent, maximal sets of gmaps, which is equivalent to Step 4(c), so we defer this part of the analysis until then. In the other extreme, none of the gmaps share a common base structure, and so Step 4(b) requires $O(\mathcal{G}_{P1}^2)$ operations, although this is not the best-case performance (see below). Typically, the second merge step is very quick and displays near best-case performance.

Step 4(c) completes gmap construction by generating all consistent combinations of the partial gmaps, discarding those which are not maximal. The complexity of this final merge step is directly related to the degree of structure in the base and target domains and how many different predicates are in use. Worst-case performance occurs when the description language is flat (i.e., no higher-order structure) and the same predicate occurs many times in both the base and the target. Consider a language with a single, unary predicate, and base and target dgroups each consisting of $N$ distinct expressions. In this case every base expression can match with every target expression, and each such match will suggest matching in turn the entities that serve as their arguments. This reduces to the problem of finding all isomorphic mappings between two equal size sets, which is $O(N!)$.

Now let us consider the best case. If the base and target dgroups give rise to a match hypothesis graph that has but one root, and that root is consistent, then there is only one gmap! The second and third merge steps in this case are now independent of $N$. i.e., constant-time.

Of course, the typical case is somewhere between these two extremes. Typically the vocabulary of predicates is large, and the relationships between entities diverse. Structure provides a strong restriction on the number of possible interpretations for an analogy. By the time SME gets to Step 4, many of the match hypotheses have been filtered out as being structurally impossible. Steps 4(a) and 4(b) have already merged many partial gmaps, reducing the number of elements which may be combined. The identicality constraint of structure-mapping (encoded in the match rules) also reduces typical-case complexity, since match hypotheses are only created between relations when functors are identical. Thus, SME will perform badly on large descriptions with no structure and extensive predicate repetition, but will perform well on large descriptions with deep networks of diverse higher-order relationships. Semantically, the former case roughly corresponds to a jumble of unconnected expressions, and the latter case to a complex argument or theory. The better organized and justified the knowledge, the better SME will perform.

While the potential complexity of Step 4(b) is $O(N!)$, our experience is that this step is very quick and displays near best-case performance in practice. We suspect the worst-case behavior is very unlikely to occur, since it requires that all members of $Gmaps_1$ intersect the same base structure and so must be merged in all possible ways. However, partial gmaps intersecting the same base structure are almost always consistent with one another, meaning that Step 2 would usually merge $Gmaps_1$ into one gmap in $O(\mathcal{G}_{P1})$ time. On the other hand, we have on occasion experienced worst-case performance for Step 4(c).

### 3.3.5. Analysis of Step 5: Finding candidate inferences

The candidate inferences are gathered by looping through the base description roots for each gmap, collecting missing base expressions whenever their structure intersects a match hypothesis in the gmap. Each expression is tested to ensure that (1) it is not already matched with part of the target description, and (2) that it does not represent a syntactic contradiction of an existing target expression. The size of the typical candidate inference is inversely related to the percentage of base structure roots: more roots implies less structure to infer, and vice versa. Thus in the worst case we have $O(\mathcal{G} \cdot \mathcal{F}_b \cdot \mathcal{F}_t)$, or roughly $O(N^3)$. However, this is an extreme worst case. First, the $\mathcal{F}_t$ term implies that we check every target expression on each iteration. The algorithm actually only checks the pertinent target expressions (i.e., those with the same predicate), giving a tighter bound of $O(N^2)$. In the best case, there will only be one gmap and no candidate inferences, producing constant-time behavior.

### 3.3.6. Analysis of Step 6: SES computation

The complexity of the BMS is difficult to ascertain. Fortunately it is irrelevant to our analysis since the BMS can be eliminated if detailed justification of evidential results are not required. For example, the first version of SME [21] used specialized evidence rules which had most of the flexibility of the BMS-based rules yet ran in $O(M)$ time.

Although the flexibility of the BMS can be valuable, in fact the majority of SME's processing time takes place within it—typically 70 to 80%. So far this has not been a serious performance limitation, since on the examples in this paper (and most of the examples we have examined), SME takes only a few seconds on a Symbolics machine.

## 4. Examples

The structure-mapping engine has been applied to a variety of domains and tasks. It is being used in psychological studies, comparing human responses with those of SME for both short stories and metaphors. SME is serving as a module in a machine learning program called PHINEAS, which uses analogy to discover and refine qualitative models of physical processes such as water flow and heat flow. SME is also used in a concept-learning program called SEQL, which induces structural descriptions from examples [66, 68]. Here we discuss a few representative examples to demonstrate SME's flexibility and generality.

## 4.1. Methodological constraints

Flexibility is a two-edged sword. The danger in using a program like SME is that one could imagine tailoring the match construction and evidence rules for each new example. Little would be learned by using the program in this way—we would have at best a series of "wind-up toys," a collection of ad hoc programs which shed little theoretical light. Here we describe our techniques for reducing tailorability.

First, all the cognitive simulation experiments were run with a fixed collection of rule sets, listed in Appendix A. Each rule set represents a particular type of comparison sanctioned by the structure-mapping theory (i.e., analogy, literal similarity, and mere appearance). The mere-appearance rules (MA) match only low-order items: attributes and first-order relations. The analogy rules (AN) match systems of relations and higher-order relations, while the literal similarity rules (LS) match both low-order and higher-order structure. The first two examples in this section use the AN rules, and the third uses both AN and MA rules, as indicated.

While the choice of match construction rules is dictated by structure-mapping, the particular values of evidence weights are not. Although we have not performed a sensitivity analysis, in our preliminary explorations it appears that the gmap rankings are not overly sensitive to the particular values of evidence weights. (Recall that which gmaps are constructed is *independent* of the weights, and is determined only by the construction rules and structural consistency.)

Second, we have accumulated a standard description vocabulary which is used in all experiments. This is particularly important when encoding natural language stories, where the translation into a formal representation is underconstrained. By accumulating representation choices across stories, we attempt to free ourselves from biasing the description for particular examples.

Third, we have tested SME with descriptions generated automatically by other AI programs. A representation developed to perform useful inferences has fewer arbitrary choices than a representation developed specifically for learning research. So far, we have used descriptions generated by two different qualitative simulation programs with encouraging results. For example, SME actually performs better (in the sense of producing fewer spurious interpretations) on a water flow/heat flow comparison using more complex descriptions generated by GIZMO [24] than it does on many hand-generated descriptions. We are working on interfacing SME to other inference systems, as described in Section 7.3.1.

## 4.2. Solar system/Rutherford atom analogy

The Rutherford model of the hydrogen atom was a classic use of analogy in science. The hydrogen atom was explained in terms of the better understood behavior of the solar system. We illustrate SME's operation on this example with a simplified representation, shown in Fig. 9.

SME constructed three possible interpretations. The highest-ranked mapping (SES = 6.03) pairs the nucleus with the sun and the planet with the electron. This mapping is based on the mass inequality in the solar system playing the same role as the mass inequality in the atom. It sanctions the inference that the differences in masses, together with the mutual attraction of the nucleus and the electron, causes the electron to revolve around the nucleus. This is the standard interpretation of this analogy.

The other major gmap (SES = 4.04) has the same entity correspondences, but maps the temperature difference between the sun and the planets onto the mass difference between the nucleus and the electron. The SES for this gmap is low for two reasons. First, temperature and mass are different functions, and hence they receive less local evidence. The second, and more important reason is that there is no mappable systematic structure associated with temperature in the base dgroup. Thus other relations, such as the match for ATTRACTS, do not enter into this gmap. We could in theory know a lot more about the thermal properties of the solar system than its dynamics, yet unless there is some relational group in the target description there will not be a set of *mappable* systematic relations. (If we instead were explaining a home heating system in terms of the solar system the situation would be the reverse.)

The third gmap is a spurious collection of match hypotheses which imply that the mass of the sun should correspond to the mass of the electron, and the mass of the planet should correspond to the mass of the nucleus. There is even less structural support for this interpretation (SES = 1.87).

This example demonstrates an important aspect of the structure-mapping

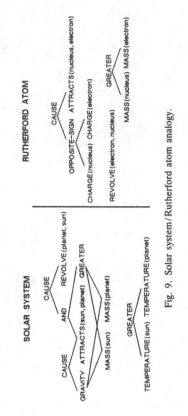

Fig. 9. Solar system/Rutherford atom analogy.

| Water-Flow History | Heat-Flow History |
|---|---|
| (Situation S0) | (Situation S0) |
| (Decreasing (Pressure (At beaker S0))) | (Decreasing (Temp (At horse-shoe S0))) |
| (Increasing (Pressure (At vial S0))) | (Increasing (Temp (At water S0))) |
| (Decreasing (Amount-of (At beaker S0))) | (Greater (Temp (At horse-shoe S0)) |
| (Increasing (Amount-of (At vial S0))) | (Temp (At water S0))) |
| (Greater (Pressure (At beaker S0)) | |
| (Pressure (At vial S0))) | |
| | |
| (Situation S1) | (Situation S1) |
| (Meets S0 S1) | (Meets S0 S1) |
| (Constant (Pressure (At beaker S1))) | (Constant (Temp (At horse-shoe S1))) |
| (Constant (Pressure (At vial S1))) | (Constant (Temp (At water S1))) |
| (Constant (Amount-of (At beaker S1))) | (Equal-To (Temp (At horse-shoe S1)) |
| (Constant (Amount-of (At vial S1))) | (Temp (At water S1))) |
| (Equal-To (Pressure (At beaker S1)) | |
| (Pressure (At vial S1))) | |
| | |
| (Function-Of (Pressure ?x) | (Function-Of (Temp ?x) |
| (Amount-of ?x)) | (Heat ?x)) |

Behavioral Correspondences

| Pressure | → | Temperature |
|---|---|---|
| Amount-of | → | Heat |
| S0 | → | S0 |
| S1 | → | S1 |
| beaker | → | horse-shoe |
| vial | → | water |

Fig. 11. Analogical match between water flow history and heat flow history.

correspondences that provide a mapping between entities or between their quantities (e.g., Pressure and Temperature) for later reference.

When it is satisfied that the chosen water flow history is sufficiently analogous to the current situation, PHINEAS begins a deeper analysis of the analogy. It fetches the domain used to generate its prior understanding of the base (water flow) experience. Its description of water flow, shown in Fig. 12, is a straightforward qualitative model similar to that used in other projects [24, 27]. This model states that if we have an aligned fluid path between the beaker and the vial (i.e., the path either has no valves or if it does, they are all open), and the pressure in the beaker is greater than the pressure in the vial, then a liquid flow process will be active. This process has a flow rate which is proportional to the difference between the two pressures. The flow rate has a positive influence on the amount of water in the vial and a negative influence on the amount of water in the beaker.

Using SME a second time, this theory is matched to the current heat flow situation using the correspondences established with the behavioral analogy. The output is shown in Fig. 13. The entity and function correspondences

account of analogy. The interpretation preferred on structural grounds is also the one with the most inferential import. This is not an accident; the systematicity principle captures the structural features of well-supported arguments. Using the structure-mapping analogy rules (AN), SME prefers interpretations based on a deep theory (i.e., a subset of a dgroup containing a system of higher-order relations) to those based on shallow associations (i.e., a subset of a dgroup containing an assortment of miscellaneous facts).

### 4.3. Discovering heat flow

The PHINEAS program [17, 18, 20] learns by observation. When presented with a new behavior, it attempts to explain it in terms of its theories of the world. These theories are expressed as qualitative models of physical processes using Forbus' *qualitative process theory* [22, 23]. When it is given a behavior that it cannot explain, an analogical learning module is invoked which attempts to generate a new or revised model that can account for the new observation. This module uses SME in two ways.[5] First SME is used to form a match between a previous experience which has been explained and the current behavior. These correspondences provide the foundation for constructing a model that can explain the new observation based on the model for the previous behavior.

For example, suppose that the program was presented with measurements of the heat flow situation depicted in Fig. 10 and described in Fig. 11. If the domain model does not include a theory of heat flow, PHINEAS will be unable to interpret the new observation.[6] Using SME, PHINEAS constructs an analogy with the previously encountered water flow experience also shown in Figs. 10 and 11. This match establishes that certain properties from the two situations behave in the same way. As shown in Fig. 11, the roles of the beaker and the vial in the water flow history are found to correspond to the roles of the horse-shoe and water in the heat flow history, respectively. PHINEAS stores the

Fig. 10. Two examples of water flow and heat flow.

[5] In this example PHINEAS is using the structure-mapping analogy rules. In normal operation, it uses a more knowledge-intensive rule set that relaxes the identicality constraint and includes goal-sensitive match evaluation criteria [20].

[6] PHINEAS uses the ATMI theory of measurement interpretation to explain observations. See [25] for details.

any alternate matches for these quantities (e.g., AMOUNT-OF and TEM-PERATURE).

This example demonstrates several points. First, the second analogy, which imports the theoretical explanation of the new phenomena, is composed almost entirely of candidate inferences, since the system had no prior model of heat flow. It is largely a *carryover* analogy [31]. Hence, the model was *constructed* by analogy rather than augmented by analogy. This shows the power of SME's candidate inference mechanism. Second, the example illustrates how SME's rule-based architecture can support tasks in which the entity correspondences are given prior to the match, rather than derived as a result of the match. Finally, it shows the utility of introducing skolemized entities into the candidate inferences. The results produced by SME (Fig. 13) contain the entity (:skolem pipe). This indicates that, at the moment, the heat path is a conjectured entity. At this time, the system inspects its knowledge of paths to infer that immersion or physical contact is a likely heat path. However, we note that much knowledge gathering and refinement may still take place while leaving the heat path as a conjectured entity. For example, in the history of science *ether* was postualted to provide a medium for the flow of light waves because other kinds of waves require a medium.

## 4.4. Modeling human analogical processing

SME is being used in several cognitive simulation studies. Our goal is to compare SME's responses with those of humans for a variety of tasks and problems. For example, two psychological studies [35, 59] have explored the variables that determine the *accessibility* of a similarity match and the *inferential soundness* of a match. Structure-mapping predicts that soundness is determined by the degree of systematic relational overlap [30]. In contrast, Gentner [31, 32] has suggested that the accessibility of potential matches in long-term memory is heavily influenced by surface similarity. Psychological studies have supported both hypotheses [35, 59, 62]. In order to verify the computational assumptions we ran SME on the same examples that had been given to human subjects. Here we briefly summarize the simulation methodology and the results; for details see [67].

The hypotheses were tested psychologically as follows. Pairs of short stories were constructed which were similar in different ways: in particular, some pairs embodied mere appearance and some analogy.[7] Subjects read a large set of stories, which were the base members of each pair. Then, in a second session, subjects saw the similar stories and tried to retrieve the original stories (the access measure). After that, the subjects were then asked to judge the inferential soundness of each of the story pairs. For the cognitive simulation

---

provided by the behavioral analogy provide significant constraint for carrying over the explanation. SME's rule-based architecture is critical to this operation: PHINEAS imposes these constraints by using a special set of match constructor rules that only allow hypotheses consistent with the specific entity and function correspondences previously established. Entities and functions left without a match after the accessing stage are still allowed to match other unmatched entities and functions. For example, the rule

```
(MHC-rule (:filter ?b ?t
    :test (sanctioned-pairing? (expression-functor ?b)
                              (expression-functor ?t)))
    (install-MH ?b ?t))
```

forces a match between those quantities which were found to be analogous in the behavioral analogy (e.g., PRESSURE and TEMPERATURE) and prevents

---

[7] Other kinds of matches, including literal similarity, were also used. Here we discuss only analogy and mere appearance.

---

Fig. 12. Qualitative process theory model of liquid flow.

```
Gmap #1: { (AMOUNT-OF-35 HEAT-WATER) (AMOUNT-OF-33 HEAT-HSHOE)
           (PRESSURE-BEAKER TEMP-HSHOE) (PRESSURE-VIAL TEMP-WATER) }
   Emaps: { (beaker horse-shoe) (vial water) }
   Weight: 2.675
   Candidate Inferences: (IMPLIES
                           (AND (ALIGNED (:skolem pipe))
                                (GREATER-THAN (A TEMP-HSHOE) (A TEMP-WATER)))
                           (AND (q= (FLOW-RATE pi) (- TEMP-HSHOE TEMP-WATER))
                                (GREATER-THAN (A (FLOW-RATE pi) zero)
                                (I+ HEAT-WATER (A (FLOW-RATE pi)))
                                (I- HEAT-HSHOE (A (FLOW-RATE pi))))))
```

Fig. 13. An analogically inferred model of heat flow.

study, five triads of stories—a base, a mere-appearance match, and an analogy match were encoded (15 in all). The pairs of stories were presented to SME, using different rule sets corresponding to analogy (the AN rules) and mere appearance (the MA rules). The results from the AN rules were used to estimate soundness, while the results from the MA rules were used to estimate accessibility. One of these story groups will be discussed in detail, showing how SME was used to simulate a test subject.

In the story set shown in Fig. 14, the original story concerned a hawk named Karla who survives an attack by a hunter. Two target stories were used as potential analogies for the Karla narration. One was designed to be truly analogous (TA5) and described a small country named Zerdia that survives an attack by another country. The other story (MA5) was designed to be only superficially similar and described an eagle named Zerdia who is killed by a sportsman. The representation of the Karla story given to SME was:

```
(CAUSE (EQUALS (HAPPINESS HUNTER) HIGH)
       (PROMISE HUNTER KARLA (NOT (ATTACK HUNTER KARLA))))
(CAUSE (OBTAIN HUNTER FEATHERS) (EQUALS (HAPPINESS HUNTER) HIGH))
(CAUSE (OFFER KARLA FEATHERS HUNTER) (OBTAIN HUNTER FEATHERS))
(CAUSE (REALIZE KARLA (DESIRE HUNTER FEATHERS))
       (OFFER KARLA FEATHERS HUNTER))
(FOLLOW (EQUALS (SUCCESS (ATTACK HUNTER KARLA)) FAILED)
        (REALIZE KARLA (DESIRE HUNTER FEATHERS)))
(CAUSE (NOT (USED-FOR FEATHERS CROSS-BOW))
       (EQUALS (SUCCESS (ATTACK HUNTER KARLA)) FAILED))
(FOLLOW (SEE KARLA HUNTER) ATTACK HUNTER KARLA))
(WEAPON CROSS-BOW)
(KARLAS-ASSET FEATHERS)
(WARLIKE HUNTER)
(PERSON HUNTER)
(BIRD KARLA)
```

The results from human subjects showed that (1) in the soundness evaluation task, as predicted by Gentner's systematicity principle, people judged analogies as more sound than mere-appearance matches; and (2) in the memory access task, people were more likely to retrieve surface similarity matches than analogical matches.

To test SME as a cognitive simulation of how people determine the soundness of an analogy, SME was run using its analogy (AN) match rules on each base-target pair of stories—that is, base/mere-appearance story and base/analogical story. Figure 15 shows the output of SME for the AN task. For

```
Analogical Match from Karla to Zerdia the country (TA5).

Rule File: analogy.rules    Number of Match Hypotheses: 54    Number of GMaps: 1

Gmap #1:
  (CAUSE-PROMISE CAUSE-PROMISE) (SUCCESS-ATTACK SUCCESS-ATTACK) (HAPPY-HUNTER HAPPY-GAGRACH)
  (HAPPINESS-HUNTER HAPPINESS-GAGRACH) (REALIZE-DESIRE REALIZE-DESIRE) (CAUSE-TAKE CAUSE-BUY)
  (ATTACK-HUNTER ATTACK-GAGRACH) (DESIRE-FEATHERS DESIRE-SUPERCOMPUTER) (FAILED-ATTACK FAILED-ATTACK)
  (TAKE-FEATHERS BUY-SUPERCOMPUTER) (CAUSE-FAILED-ATTACK CAUSE-FAILED-ATTACK)
  (CAUSE-OFFER CAUSE-OFFER) (FOLLOW-REALIZE FOLLOW-REALIZE) (HAS-FEATHERS USE-SUPERCOMPUTER)
  (CAUSE-HAPPY CAUSE-HAPPY) (NOT-ATTACK NOT-ATTACK) (PROMISE-HUNTER PROMISE)
  (NOT-HAS-FEATHERS NOT-USE-SUPERCOMPUTER) (OFFER-FEATHERS OFFER-SUPERCOMPUTER)
  Emaps:   (HIGH23 HIGH17) (FEATHERS20 SUPERCOMPUTER14) (CROSS-BOW21 MISSILES15)
           (HUNTER19 GAGRACH13) (KARLA18 ZERDIA12) (FAILED22 FAILED16)
  Weight: 22.362718


Analogical Match from Karla to Zerdia the eagle (MA5).

Rule File: analogy.rules    Number of Match Hypotheses: 47    Number of GMaps: 1

Gmap #1:
  (PROMISE-HUNTER PROMISE) (DESIRE-FEATHERS DESIRE-FEATHERS) (TAKE-FEATHERS TAKE-FEATHERS)
  (CAUSE-OFFER CAUSE-OFFER) (OFFER-FEATHERS OFFER-FEATHERS) (HAS-FEATHERS HAS-FEATHERS)
  (REALIZE-DESIRE REALIZE-DESIRE) (ATTACK-HUNTER ATTACK-SPORTSMAN) (NOT-ATTACK NOT-ATTACK)
  (SUCCESS-ATTACK SUCCESS-ATTACK) (FOLLOW-SEE-ATTACK FOLLOW-SEE) (SEE-KARLA SEE-ZERDIA)
  (FAILED-ATTACK SUCCESSFUL-ATTACK) (CAUSE-TAKE CAUSE-TAKE)
  Emaps:   (FAILED22 TRUE11) (KARLA18 ZERDIA7) (HUNTER19 SPORTSMAN8)
           (FEATHERS20 FEATHERS9) (CROSS-BOW21 CROSS-BOW10)
  Weight: 16.816530
```

Fig. 15. SME's analysis of story set 5, using the TA rules.

### Base Story

Karla, an old hawk, lived at the top of a tall oak tree. One afternoon, she saw a hunter on the ground with a bow and some crude arrows that had no feathers. The hunter took aim and shot at the hawk but missed. Karla knew that hunter wanted her feathers so she glided down to the hunter and offered to give him a few. The hunter was so grateful that he pledged never to shoot at a hawk again. He went off and shot deer instead.

### Target Story: Analogy

Once there was a small country called Zerdia that learned to make the world's smartest computer.
  One day Zerdia was attacked by its warlike neighbor, Gagrach. But the missiles were badly aimed and the attack failed. The Zerdian government realized that Gagrach wanted Zerdian computers so it offered to sell some of its computers to the country. The government of Gagrach was very pleased. It promised never to attack Zerdia again.

### Target Story: Mere Appearance

Once there was an eagle named Zerdia who donated a few of her tailfeathers to a sportsman so he would promise never to attack eagles.
  One day Zerdia was nesting high on a rocky cliff when she saw the sportsman coming with a crossbow. Zerdia flew down to meet the man, but he attacked and felled her with a single bolt. As she fluttered to the ground Zerdia realized that the bolt had had her own tailfeathers on it.

Fig. 14. Story set 5.

architecture provides. We know of no other general-purpose matcher which successfully models two *distinct* kinds of human similarity comparisons. Second, the short story analogies show that SME is capable of matching large structures as well as the smaller, simpler structures shown previously.

### 4.5. Testing structure-mapping constraints

While structural consistency is built into the SME algorithm, the other constraints of structure-mapping are not. This allows us to emulate a space of matchers and explore extensions and variations of structure-mapping. It also provides a means to determine just how much work the various theoretical constraints contribute, by modifying or deleting the rules which implement them. Recall that identicality is implemented by the match constructor rules, and systematicity is implemented by match evidence rules. We could determine how much work identicality does, say, by changing the rules to allow arbitrary predicates to match.

We constructed the *free-for-all* (*FFA*) rule set to explore just that question. The FFA rule set builds a match hypothesis for every pair of predicates and every pair of entities, regardless of identity, type, or number of arguments. The only constraint still enforced is commutativity—the current implementation will not allow a commutative predicate to match a noncommutative one. Every match hypothesis receives an initial score of 0.2. Gmap selection is based strictly on systematicity. This rule set has been successfully tested on several graph isomorphisms taken from [54], as well as a few hand-crafted examples.

It is interesting to examine SME's performance with the FFA rules on the simple water flow/heat flow example of Fig. 2. SME constructed 74 match hypotheses, which were combined into 26 gmaps. Four gmaps were tied for the highest ranking (SES = 3.71). Two of these gmaps were supersets of the standard interpretation (i.e., Gmap #1, where PRESSURE maps to TEMPERATURE, as shown in Fig. 7). The new correspondences involved attributes of the beaker–coffee pair. In one gmap, (DIAMETER beaker) was mapped to (LIQUID coffee) and (CLEAR beaker) was mapped to (FLAT-TOP coffee), and the other reversed these attribute mappings. The other two gmaps were supersets of Gmap #2 from Fig. 7, which paired the diameter inequality from the water flow base domain to the temperature inequality in the heat flow target domain. The new correspondences in these gmaps included matches from (PRESSURE beaker) and (CLEAR beaker) to (LIQUID coffee) and (FLAT-TOP coffee).

Our experiments with the FFA rules suggest two conclusions. First, while structural consistency is a powerful guide to matching, it is not by itself sufficient to constrain a matcher. In our simple heat/water analogy, for example, the number of match hypotheses increased by a factor of 5 and the gmaps increased by a factor of 8. Larger examples will provide even worse

example, "Zerdia the country" (the analogy) was found to be a better analogical match (SES = 22.4) to the original Karla story than "Zerdia the eagle" (SES = 16.8). Overall, SME as an analogical mapping engine agrees quite well with the soundness rating of human subjects.

We also used SME to test the claim that the human access patterns result from access depending on surface similarity matches (objects and object-attribute overlap). SME was run on each of the pairs using its mere-appearance (MA) match rules. This measured their degree of superficial overlap. Again, over the five stories SME's rankings match those of human subjects. For example, the output of SME for the MA task is given in Fig. 16, which shows that the eagle story (SES = 7.7) has a higher MA rating than the country story (SES = 6.4).

It should be noted that, unlike the soundness rating task, the access mimicking task is not a true simulation. To do this would require finding and selecting the prior story from a large set of potential matches. Rather, SME is acting as a bookkeeper to count the variable (here, degree of surface overlap) being claimed as causally related to the variable being measured (accessibility of matches). The results demonstrate that surface similarity, as strictly defined and used in SME's match rules, matches well with people's retrieval patterns in an access task. In contrast, in the soundness rating simulation, SME's analogy processes constitute a psychologically viable model.

This study illustrates the viability of SME as a cognitive simulation of human processing of analogy. We make two additional observations. First, the results demonstrate the considerable leverage for cognitive modeling that SME's

---

```
Analogical Match from Karla to Zerdia the country (TA5).

Rule File: appearance-match.rules   Number of Match Hypotheses: 12   Number of GMaps: 1

Gmap #1:
(HAPPINESS-HUNTER HAPPINESS-GAGRACH) (ATTACK-HUNTER ATTACK-GAGRACH) (TAKE-FEATHERS BUY-SUPERCOMPUTER)
(WARLIKE-HUNTER WARLIKE-GAGRACH) (DESIRE-FEATHERS DESIRE-SUPERCOMPUTER)
(HAS-FEATHERS USE-SUPERCOMPUTER) (OFFER-FEATHERS OFFER-SUPERCOMPUTER) (WEAPON-BOW WEAPON-BOW)
Emaps: (KARLA1 ZERDIA12) (FEATHERS3 SUPERCOMPUTER14) (CROSS-BOW4 MISSILES15) (HUNTER2 GAGRACH13)
Weight: 6.411572
```

---

```
Analogical Match from Karla to Zerdia the eagle (MA5).

Rule File: appearance-match.rules   Number of Match Hypotheses: 14   Number of GMaps: 1

Gmap #1:
(OFFER-FEATHERS OFFER-FEATHERS) (TAKE-FEATHERS TAKE-FEATHERS) (ATTACK-HUNTER ATTACK-SPORTSMAN)
(SEE-KARLA SEE-ZERDIA) (HAS-FEATHERS HAS-FEATHERS) (BIRD-KARLA BIRD-ZERDIA) (WEAPON-BOW WEAPON-BOW)
(DESIRE-FEATHERS DESIRE-FEATHERS) (WARLIKE-HUNTER WARLIKE-SPORTSMAN) (PERSON-HUNTER PERSON-SPORTSMAN)
Emaps: (FEATHERS3 FEATHERS9) (CROSS-BOW4 CROSS-BOW10) (HUNTER2 SPORTSMAN8) (KARLA1 ZERDIA7)
Weight: 7.703568
```

Fig. 16. SME's analysis of story set 5, using the MA rules.

combinatorial explosions. Second, the identicality constraint plays an important role by assuring that the structures being compared are semantically similar. Without it, a matcher can generate many spurious inferences which must then be filtered by external systems. For example, the FFA rules led SME to propose the candidate inference (GREATER (LIQUID coffee) (DIAMETER ice-cube)), which is clearly nonsense. This does not mean that only a constraint as strong as identicality can play this role, of course. We describe some alternatives being explored in Section 7.1.

## 5. Performance Evaluation

SME is written in COMMON LISP. The examples in this paper were run on a Symbolics 3640 with 8 megabytes of RAM. Table 1 shows SME's performance for each example in this paper. All run times are in seconds. We have separated the BMS run time from the total run time to give a more accurate account of SME's speed, since the computational cost of the BMS can be removed if necessary. This data indicates that SME is extremely fast at producing unevaluated gmaps. In fact, it seems to be close to linear in the number of match hypotheses and in the number of base and target expressions. The majority of the run time is spent within the BMS, producing structural evaluation scores. However, the total run times are short enough that we have opted to continue using the BMS for now, since it has proven to be a valuable analysis tool.

The longest runtime occurred for the behavioral match between the water flow and heat flow observations (PHINEAS behavioral). While the descriptions for this example were the largest, the primary source of slowdown was the flat representations used to describe the situations.

## 6. Comparison with Other Work

The structure-mapping theory has received a greater deal of convergent theoretical support in artificial intelligence and psychology. Although there are differences in emphasis, there is now widespread agreement on the basic elements of one-to-one mapping of objects with carryover of predicates ([5, 6, 41, 44, 49, 50, 61, 63, 71, 78, 79]). Moreover, several of these researchers have used selection constraints that are specializations of the systematicity principle. For example, Carbonell focuses on plans and goals as the high-order relations that give constraint to a system, while Winston focuses on causality. Structure-mapping theory is more general in three respects. First, it defines mapping rules which are independent of particular domains or primitives. Second, the structure-mapping characterization applies across a range of applications of analogy, including problem solving, understanding explanations, etc. Third, the structure-mapping account treats analogy as one of a family of similarity comparisons, each with particular psychological privileges, and thus explains more phenomena.

Table 1
SME performance on described examples

| Example | Number base expressions/entities | Number target expressions/entities | # MHs | # Gmaps | Total BMS run time[a] | Total match run time[a] |
|---|---|---|---|---|---|---|
| Simple water/heat | 11/4 | 6/4 | 14 | 3 | 0.70 | 0.23 |
| Solar system/atom | 12/2 | 9/2 | 16 | 3 | 0.91 | 0.28 |
| PHINEAS behavioral | 40/8 | 27/6 | 69 | 6 | 9.68 | 1.92 |
| PHINEAS theory | 19/11 | 13/6 | 10 | 1 | 0.17 | 0.66 |
| Base5/TA5 (AN) | 26/6 | 24/6 | 54 | 1 | 5.34 | 0.87 |
| Base5/MA5 (AN) | 26/6 | 24/5 | 47 | 1 | 4.55 | 0.98 |
| Base5/TA5 (MA) | 26/6 | 24/6 | 12 | 1 | 0.38 | 0.36 |
| Base5/MA5 (MA) | 26/6 | 24/5 | 14 | 1 | 0.73 | 0.46 |
| Water/Heat (FFA) | 11/4 | 6/4 | 74 | 26 | 2.81 | 1.76 |

[a] Note. All times are given in seconds. Total match time is total SME run time minus BMS run time.

A limitation of structure-mapping is that the mapping process (as opposed to access or evaluation, see Section 2.1) ignores all nonstructural factors. Some models have combined an explicit structure-mapping component to generate potential interpretations of a given analogy with a pragmatic component to select and refine the relevant interpretation (e.g., [5, 20, 50]). Given our experience with PHINEAS, we believe SME will prove to be a useful tool for such systems.

A very different approach is taken by Holyoak [47]. In this account, there is no separate stage of structural matching. Instead, analogy is completely driven by the goals of the current problem-solving context. Retrieval of the base domain is driven by an abstract scheme of current problem-solving goals. Creating the mapping is interleaved with other problem-solving activities. This "pragmatic" account, while appealing in some ways, has several crucial limitations [31, 32]. First, the pragmatic model has no account of soundness in terms of systematicity. Without structural consistency, the search space for matching explodes (see below). Second, the pragmatic account can only be defined in problem-solving contexts. Yet analogy is used for purposes other than problem solving, including many contexts in which relevance does not apply. Analogy can be used to explain a new concept and to focus attention on a particular aspect of a situation. Analogy can result in noticing commonalities and conclusions that are totally irrelevant to the purpose at hand. Thus an analogy interpretation algorithm that requires relevance cannot be a general solution [31, 32]. Third, psychological data indicates that access is driven by surface similarity, not relevance, as described previously.

We believe the modularity imposed by the structure-mapping account has several desirable features over the pragmatic account. In the structure-mapping account, the same match procedure is used for all applications of analogy. For example, in a problem-solving environment, current plans and goals influence what is accessed. Once base and target are both present, the analogy mapping is performed, independently of the particular context. Its results can then be examined and tested as part of the problem-solving process (see [31, 32]).

SME demonstrates that an independent, structural matcher can be built which is useful in several tasks and for a variety of examples (over 40 at this writing). By contrast, no clear algorithms have been presented based on the pragmatic account, and published accounts so far [46] describe only two running examples. Another issue is that of potential complexity. The "typical-case" bounds we have been able to derive so far are not very precise, and a more complete complexity analysis would certainly be desirable. However, the analysis so far indicates reasonable typical-case performance (roughly, $O(N^2)$), and the empirical results bear this out. Our excellent performance arises from the fact that SME focuses on local properties of the representation. On the other hand, the pragmatic account appears to involve arbitrary inference, and arbitrary amounts of knowledge, in the mapping process. Thus we would expect that the average-case computational complexity of a pragmatically oriented matcher will be dramatically worse than SME.

## 6.1. Matching algorithms

To our knowledge, SME is unique in that it generates all structurally consistent analogical mappings without search. Previous partial matchers have utilized heuristic search through the space of possible matches, typically returning a single, best match (e.g., [15, 43, 52, 55, 73, 74, 77–79]). Some researchers on analogy have suggested that generating all possible interpretations is computationally intractable [43, 52, 78]. Our analysis and empirical results indicate that this conclusion must be substantially modified. Only when structural constraints do not exist, or are ignored, does the computation become intractable. For instance, in [52] the knowledge base was uniform and had no higher-order structure. In such cases exponential explosions are unavoidable.

Winston [78, 79] did some of the earliest, ground-breaking work in analogy. His system was the first to be tested on a wide variety of examples from several domains, thus setting an important methodological example. It still stands today as the most complete analogical reasoning and learning system, incorporating a model of access, reasoning via precedents, and learning new rules from examples. His importance-dominated matcher heuristically searched for a single best match. It begins by enumerating all entity pairings and works upward to match relations, thus generating all $N_{Eb}!/(N_{Eb} - N_{Et})!$ possible entity pairings. Because SME only introduces entity pairings when suggested by potential shared relational structure, it typically generates many fewer entity pairings. Some limited amount of pruning due to domain-specific category information was also available on demand, such as requiring that males match with males. By contrast, SME ignores attributes when in analogy mode, unless they play a role in a larger systematic structure. Winston's scoring scheme would attribute one point for each shared relation (e.g., LOVE, CAUSE), property (e.g., STRONG, BEAUTIFUL), and class classification (e.g., A-KIND-OF(?x, woman)). Unlike SME's analogy rules, this scheme makes no distinction between a single, systematic relational chain and a large collection of independent facts.

Kline's RELAX system [52] focused on matching relations rather than entities. RELAX did not attempt to maintain structural consistency, allowing many-to-one mappings between entities or predicate instances. In conjunction with a semantic network, RELAX was able to match items having quite different syntax (e.g., (Segment A1 A2) matching (Angle A1 X A2)). However, there was no guarantee that the best match would be found due to local pruning during search.

SME computes a structural match first, and then uses this structural match to derive candidate inferences. The implementations of Winston [78, 79] and

### 6.2. Other pattern-matching systems

Structure-mapping is a form of pattern-matching, but it is different than previous pattern-matchers. For example, it should be clear that structure-mapping neither subsumes unification nor is subsumed by it. Consider the pair of statements

(CAUSE (FLY PERSON1) (FALL PERSON1))
(CAUSE (FLY PERSON2) (FALL PERSON2))

These could be part of a legitimate analogy, with PERSON1 being mapped to PERSON2, but these two statements do not unify since PERSON1 and PERSON2 are distinct constants. Conversely,

(CAUSE (?X PERSON1) (FALL PERSON1))
(CAUSE (FLY ?Y) (FALL ?Z))

will unify, assuming ? indicates variables, with the substitutions:

?X ↔ FLY
?Y ↔ PERSON1
?Z ↔ PERSON1

However, since structure-mapping treats variables as constants, these statements fail to be analogous in two ways. First, FLY and ?X are treated as distinct relations, and thus cannot match. Second, ?Y and ?Z are considered to be distinct entities, and thus are forbidden to map to the same target item (i.e., PERSON1).

Most importantly, the goals of structure-mapping and unification are completely different. Unification seeks a set of substitutions which makes two statements identical. Structure-mapping seeks a set of correspondences between two descriptions which can suggest additional inferences. Unlike unification, partial matches are perfectly acceptable.

Several of the implementation techniques used in SME are however similar in spirit to those used in *axiomatized unifiers* [4, 56, 60], which use equational theories (such as associativity and commutativity) to extend equality beyond identicality.

### 7. Discussion

We have described the structure-mapping engine, a simulation of Gentner's structure-mapping theory of analogy and similarity, and a tool-kit for building matchers consistent with the structural consistency constraint. We have de-

Burstein [5] are similar to SME in this respect. An alternate strategy is used by Kedar-Cabelli [50], Carbonell [6, 7], and Greiner [41]. These programs do not perform a match per se, but instead attempt to carry over relevant structure first and modify it until it applies to the target domain. The match arises as an implicit result of the structure modification. We know of no complexity results available for the technique, but we suspect it is much worse than SME. It appears that there is great potential for extensive search in the modification method. Furthermore, the modification method effectively requires that the access mechanism is able to provide only salient structures (e.g., *purpose-directed* [50]) since the focusing mechanism of a partial match is not present. This means these systems are unlikely to ever derive a surprising result from an analogy. See [31] for details.

Programs for forming inductive generalizations have also addressed the partial matching problem. These systems use a heuristically pruned search to build up sets of correspondences between terms which are then variablized to form generalized concept descriptions. Since these systems were not designed for analogy, they resemble the operation of SME programmed as a literal graph matcher (e.g., they could not match Pressure to Temperature). Hayes-Roth and McDermott's SPROUTER [43] and Dietterich and Michalski's INDUCE 1.2 [15] utilize one-to-one consistency in matching. Vere's THOTH system [73, 74] uses less stringent match criteria. Once the initial sets of matched terms are built, previously unmatched terms may be added to the match if their constants are in related positions. In the process, THOTH may allow many-to-one mappings between terms.

The usefulness of many-to-one mappings in matches has been discussed in the literature [43, 52]. Hayes-Roth and McDermott [43] advocate the need for many-to-one mappings among entities. Kline [52] calls for many-to-one mappings between propositions as well. For example, Kline points out that in trying to match a description of National League baseball to American League baseball, the statement (male NLpitcher) should match both (male ALpitcher) and (male ALdesignatedhitter).

Allowing many-to-one mappings undercuts structural consistency, which in our view is central to analogy. Many-to-one mappings appear to be permitted in artistic metaphor, but are not viewed as acceptable by subjects in explanatory, predictive analogies [29, 38]. However, we agree that multiple mappings should be viewed as multiple analogies between the same base and target. Since SME produces all of the interpretations of an analogy, a postprocessor could keep more than one of them to achieve the advantages of many-to-one mappings, without sacrificing consistency and structural clarity. Thus in the baseball example, SME would produce an *offense* interpretation and a *defense* interpretation.

scribed SME's algorithm in sufficient detail to allow replication by other researchers.[8] SME is both efficient and flexible. A particular matching algorithm is specified by a set of *constructor rules* and *evidence rules*. It produces all structurally consistent interpretations of a match, without backtracking. The interpretations include the candidate inferences suggested by the match and a structural evaluation score, which gives a rough measure of quality. SME has been used both in cognitive simulation studies and a machine learning project. In the cognitive simulation studies, the results so far indicate that SME, when guided with analogy rules, replicates human performance. In the machine learning project (PHINEAS), SME's flexibility provides the means for constructing new qualitative theories to explain observations.

While our complexity analysis indicates that SME's worst-case performance is factorial, our empirical experience is that the typical behavior is much better than that. Importantly, the characteristic which determines efficiency is not size, but the degree of structure of the knowledge. Unlike many AI systems, SME performs better with systematic, deeply nested descriptions.

In this section we discuss some broader implications of the project, and sketch some of our plans for future work.

## 7.1. Representational issues

The SME algorithm is of necessity sensitive to the detailed form of the representation, since we are forbidding domain-specific inference in the matching process. Existing AI systems rarely have more than one or two distinct ways to describe any particular situation or theory. But as our programs grow more complex (or as we consider modeling the range and depth of human knowledge) the number of structurally distinct representations for the same situation is likely to increase. For example, a story might be represented at the highest level by a simple classification (i.e., GREEK-MYTH), at an intermediate level by relationships involving the major characters (i.e., (CAUSE (MELTING WAX) FALL(ICARUS))), and at the lowest level by something like conceptual dependencies. An engineer's knowledge of a calculator might include its functional description, the algorithms it uses, and the axioms of arithmetic expressed in set theory. Unless there is some window of overlap between the levels of description for base and target, no analogy will be found. When our representations reach this complexity, how could SME cope?

There are several possible approaches to this problem. Consider the set of possible representations for a description. Assume these representations can be ordered (at least partially) in terms of degree of abstraction. If two descriptions are too abstract, there will either be no predicate overlap (e.g., GREEK-MYTH versus NORSE-MYTH) or identity (e.g., MYTH versus MYTH). On the other

[8] SME is publically available for interested researchers. There is a manual available [19] which provides extensive implementation-level details and interface information.

hand, if two descriptions are greatly detailed, there can be too many spurious, inconsequential matches (e.g., describing the actions of characters every microsecond). The problem is to find levels of description which provide useful analogies. We believe one solution is to invoke SME repeatedly, using knowledge of the definitions of predicates to shift the base or target descriptions up or down in the space of possible representations until a useful size match is found.

The structure-mapping identicality constraint (i.e., requiring that relational predicates match only if they are identical) is another source of representation-sensitivity. This constraint is important in that it ensures the structures being compared are semantically similar. However, it can be overly restrictive. We are currently exploring ways to relax the identicality requirement while still maintaining semantic similarity. One approach, called the *minimal ascension principle*, allows relations to match if they share a common ancestor in a multi-root is-a hierarchy of expression types [20]. The local evidence score for their match is inversely proportional (exponentially) to the relations' distance in the hierarchy. This enables SME to match nonidentical relations if such a match is supported by the surrounding structure, while still maintaining a strong preference for matching semantically close relations. This approach is similar to [5, 41, 78].

An orthogonal consideration is the degree of systematicity. Worst-case behavior tends to occur when representations are large and relatively flat. For example, SME is unable to duplicate Kline's baseball analogy [52] within a reasonable amount of time (i.e., hours). This is due to his flat description of the domain (e.g., (MALE catcher), (BATS center-fielder), etc.). Changes in representation can make large differences. For example, a PHINEAS problem which took SME 53 minutes was reduced to 34 seconds by imposing more systematic structure [20]. We are currently exploring these trade-offs to formulate more precise constraints on useful representations for analogical reasoning and learning.

## 7.2. Addressing the combinatorics

As we have shown, SME is $O(N^2)$ except for the last critical merge step, which has $O(N!)$ worst-case performance. Our experience with both small (11 expressions) and large (71 expressions) domain descriptions indicates that performance is more a function of representation and repetitiveness rather than a function of size. We have found that even moderately structural domain descriptions produce excellent performance. However, in practice it is not always convenient to avoid traditional, flat domain representations. For such cases generating all possible interpretations of an analogy may be prohibitive. A simple modification of the SME algorithm offers a natural way to deal with this problem. In particular, if we stop after the first merge step, SME provides an $O(N^2)$ algorithm for generating the complete set of initial gmaps! The subsequent merge steps could then be heuristically driven through a limited search procedure (e.g., beam-search, best-first, etc.) to produce the best or $N$ best maximal interpretations. Alternatively, we could retain the current SME design (recall that the second merge step is required to support candidate inference generation and is almost always $O(N^2)$ or better) and simply drop the troublesome third merge step. This is an (unused) option that the current implementation provides. We have not yet explored the ramifications of dropping merge step 3, although work with PHINEAS has indicated the need for the maximality criterion in practice.

In the next sections, we discuss the potential for parallel versions of the SME algorithm. In particular, we argue that (1) there are many opportunities for parallel speedup, and (2) the expensive merge steps can be eliminated in principle.

### 7.2.1. Medium-grained parallel architectures

We begin by examining each stage of the algorithm to see how it might be decomposed into parallel operations, and what kinds of speedups might result. First we assume a software architecture that allows tasks to be spawned for parallel execution (such as [1]), and we ignore communications and setup costs.

*Constructing match hypotheses.* All filter rules can be run independently, giving rise to $O(N^2)$ tasks. With enough processors this could be done in constant time, assuming the structure-mapping match constructor rules. Each intern rule can be run on every match hypothesis as it gets created. Since these rules can in turn create new match hypotheses, but only involving an expression's arguments, the best speedup would be roughly the log of the input.

*Computing Conflicting, Emaps, and NoGood sets.* The Conflicting set computation is completely local. It could either be organized around each base or target item, or around pairs of match hypotheses. Finding the Emaps and NoGood sets require propagation of results upwards, and hence again will take log time.

*Merge step 1: Form initial combinations.* Recall that this step starts from the roots of the match hypothesis graph, adding the subgraph to the list of gmaps if the hypothesis is not inconsistent and recursing on its offspring otherwise. The results from each root are independent, and so may be done as separate tasks. If each recursive step spawns a new process to handle each offspring, then the minimum time is proportional again to the order of the highest root in the graph.

*Merge step 2: Combine dependent but unconnected gmaps.* Recall that this step combines initial gmaps which share common base structure and are not inconsistent when taken together. This procedure can be carried out bottom-up, merging pairs which share base structure and are consistent together and then recursing on the results. The computation time will be logarithmic in the number of gmaps.

*Merge step 3: Combine independent collections.* This can be performed like the previous step, but skipping pairs of gmaps that have common structure (since they would have been merged previously and hence must be inconsistent). Again, with enough processors the time is bounded by the log of the number of gmaps. However, since the number of gmaps is in the worst case factorial, the number of tasks required could become rather large.

This cursory analysis no doubt glosses over several problems lurking in creating a highly parallel version of the SME algorithm. However, we believe such algorithms could be very promising.

SME's simplicity also raises another interesting experimental possibility. Given that currently many medium-grain parallel computers are being built with reasonable amounts of RAM and a LISP environment on each machine, one can imagine simply loading a copy of SME into each processor. Access experiments involving very large knowledge bases, for example, would be greatly sped up by allowing a pool of SMEs to work over the knowledge base in a distributed fashion.

### 7.2.2. Connectionist architectures

Another interesting approach would be to only generate a single, best gmap while still maintaining SME's "no search" policy. The problem of choosing among all possible interpretations in analogy processing is very much like choosing among possible interpretations of the sentence "John shot two bucks" in natural language processing. A "no search" solution to this natural language problem was provided by the connectionist work of Waltz and Pollack [76]. Rather than explicitly constructing all possible sentence interpretations and then choosing the best one, Waltz and Pollack used their networks to implicitly represent all of the possible choices. Given a particular network, spreading activation and lateral inhibition were used to find the single best interpretation. This work in fact inspired the use of the BMS for representing evidential relationships and helped motivate the decomposition of the processing into the local/global steps.

Consider the network produced by SME prior to the gmap merge steps (shown in Fig. 5). Some match hypotheses support each other (grounding criterion) while others inhibit each other (*Conflicting* relations). Viewing this as a spreading activation, lateral inhibition network, it appears that standard connectionist relaxation techniques could be used to produce a "best" interpretation without explicitly generating all gmaps. Furthermore, it may be possible to generate the second-best, third-best, etc. interpretations on demand by inhibiting the nodes of the best interpretation, forcing the second-best to rise. Thus SME would be able to establish a global interpretation simply as an indirect consequence of the establishment of local structural consistency and systematicity. This would eliminate the single most expensive computation of the SME algorithm. By eliminating explicit generation of all gmaps, the complexity of the algorithm could drop to the $O(N^2)$ required to generate the connectionist network.

### 7.3. Future work

#### 7.3.1. Cognitive simulation

We are conducting additional cognitive simulation studies of analogical reasoning, memory, and learning involving SME. One line of experiments concerns the development of analogical reasoning. Psychological research shows a marked developmental shift in analogical processing. Young children rely on surface attribute information in mapping; at older ages, systematic relational mappings are preferred [36, 37, 48, 75]. Further, there is some evidence that a similar shift from surface to systematic mappings occurs in the novice–expert transition in adults [8, 53, 61, 62].

There are two very different interpretations for the analogical shift: (1) acquisition of knowledge; or (2) a change in the analogy algorithm. The knowledge-based interpretation is that children and novices lack the necessary relational structures to guide their analogizing. The second explanation is that the algorithm for analogical mapping changes, either due to maturation or learning. In human learning it is difficult to decide this issue, since exposure to domain knowledge and practice in analogy and reasoning tend to occur simultaneously. SME gives us the capability to vary independently the analogy algorithm and the amount and kind of domain knowledge. For example, we can compare identical evaluation algorithms operating on novice versus expert representations, or we can compare different analogy evaluation rules operating on the same representation.

Another line of future development is exploring alternate versions of structural evaluation. Recall that our current structural evaluation score is simply the sum of all the match hypothesis weights in the gmap's correspondences. There are two problems with the computation. First, there are several other structural properties which should enter into the SES, such as the number and size of connected components, the existence and structure of the candidate inferences. Second, it is not normalized with respect to the sizes of the base and target domains. The current SES can be used to compare matches of different bases to the same target, or different targets to the same base. But it cannot be used to compare two completely different analogies (i.e., different bases and different targets). Janice Skorstad is building a programmable *structural evaluator* module that will let us experiment with these factors and different normalization schemes [66]. We suspect that being able to tune the structural evaluation criteria might allow us to model individual and task

differences in analogical processing. For example, a conservative strategy might favor taking gmaps with some candidate inferences but not too many, in order to maximize the probability of being correct.

We are also exploring ways to reduce the potential for tailorability in the process of translating descriptions provided as experimental stimuli for human subjects into formal representations for SME input. For example, Janice Skorstad is creating a graphical editor for producing graphical figures for experimental stimuli. One output of the editor is a picture which can be used as a stimulus for psychological experiments. The other output is a set of symbolic assertions with numerical parameters, which is expanded into SME input by a simple inference engine that calculates spatial relationships, such as INSIDE or LEFT-OF. These combined outputs will enable us to cleanly simulate the recent results of Goldstone, Medin, and Gentner [40], who found a preference for relational information even in perceptual similarity judgements. Inspired by Winston's used of a pidgin-English parser for input [79], we are also seeking a parser that, perhaps in conjunction with a simple inference engine, can produce useful descriptions of stories.

#### 7.3.2. Machine learning studies

Falkenhainer's PHINEAS program is part of the *Automated Physicist Project* at the University of Illinois. This project, led by Forbus and Gerald DeJong, is building a collection of programs that use qualitative and quantitative techniques for reasoning and learning about the physical world. DeJong and his students have built several programs that use explanation-based learning [13, 14] to acquire knowledge of the physical world [58, 65]. Forbus' group has developed a number of useful qualitative reasoning programs [25, 26, 45] which can be used in learning projects (as PHINEAS demonstrates). By combining these results, we hope to build systems that can reason about a wide range of physical phenomena and learn both from observation and by being taught.

## Appendix A. SME Match Rules

The construction of a match is guided by a set of *match rules* that specify which expressions and entities in the base and target might match and estimate the believability of each possible component of a match. In our experiments using SME, we currently use three types of rule sets, *literal similarity*, *analogy*, and *mere appearance*.

### A.1. Literal similarity (LS) rules

The *literal similarity* rules look at both relations and object descriptions.

```
;;;; Define MH constructor rules

;; If predicates are the same, match them
```

```
(MHC-rule (:filter ?b ?t :test (eq (expression-functor ?b) (expression-functor ?t)))
  (install-MH ?b ?t))

;; Intern rule for noncommutative predicates—corresponding arguments only.
;; Match compatible arguments of already matched items

(MHC-rule (:intern ?b ?t :test (and (expression? ?b) (expression? ?t)
                                     (not (commutative? (expression-functor ?b)))
                                     (not (commutative? (expression-functor ?t)))))
  (do ((bchildren (expression-arguments ?b) (cdr bchildren))
       (tchildren (expression-arguments ?t) (cdr tchildren)))
      ((or (null bchildren) (null tchildren)))
    (cond ((and (entity? (first bchildren)) (entity? (first tchildren)))
           (install-MH (first bchildren) (first tchildren)))
          ((and (function? (expression-functor (first tchildren)))
                (function? (expression-functor (first tchildren))))
           (install-MH (first bchildren) (first tchildren))))))

;; Intern rule for commutative predicates—any "compatible" arguments,
;; regardless of order.
;; Match compatible arguments of already matched items

(MHC-rule (:intern ?b ?t :test (and (expression? ?b) (expression? ?t)
                                     (commutative? (expression-functor ?b))
                                     (commutative? (expression-functor ?t))))
  (dolist (bchild (expression-arguments ?b))
    (dolist (tchild (expression-arguments ?t))
      (cond ((and (entity? bchild) (entity? tchild))
             (install-MH bchild tchild))
            ((and (function? (expression-functor bchild))
                  (function? (expression-functor tchild)))
             (install-MH bchild tchild))))))

;;;; Define MH evidence rules

;; having the same functor is a good sign
;;

(assert! 'same-functor)

(rule ((:intern (MH ?b ?t) :test (and (expression? ?b) (expression? ?t)
                                      (eq (expression-functor ?b)(expression-functor ?t))))
  (if (function? (expression-functor ?b))
      (assert! (implies same-functor (MH ?b ?t) (0.2 . 0.0)))
      (assert! (implies same-functor (MH ?b ?t) (0.5 . 0.0)))))

;; check children (arguments) match potential
;;

(assert! 'arguments-potentially-match)

(rule ((:intern (MH ?b ?t) :test (and (expression? ?b) (expression? ?t)))
  (if (children-match-potential ?b ?t)
      (assert! (implies arguments-potentially-match (MH ?b ?t) (0.4 . 0.0)))
      (assert! (implies arguments-potentially-match (MH ?b ?t) (0.0 . 0.8)))))

;; if their order is similar, this is good. If the item is a function,
;; ignore since order comparisons give false support here.
```

```
(assert! 'order-similarity)

(rule ((:intern (MH ?b ?t) :test (and (expression? ?b) (expression? ?t)
                                      (not (function? (expression-functor ?b)))
                                      (not (function? (expression-functor ?t)))))
  (cond ((= (expression-order ?b) (expression-order ?t))
         (assert! (implies order-similarity (MH ?b ?t) (0.3 . 0.0))))
        ((or (= (expression-order ?b) (1+ (expression-order ?t)))
             (= (expression-order ?t) (1- (expression-order ?b))))
         (assert! (implies order-similarity (MH ?b ?t) (0.2 . 0.05)))))))

;; propagate evidence down—systematicity
;; support for the arg will be 0.8 of the current support for the parent

(rule ((:intern (MH ?b1 ?t1) :test (and (expression? ?b1) (expression? ?t1)
                                        (not (commutative? (expression-functor ?b1)))))
  (:intern (MH ?b2 ?t2) :test (children-of? ?b2 ?t2 ?b1 ?t1))
  (sme:assert! (implies (MH ?b1 ?t1) (MH ?b2 ?t2) (0.8 . 0.0))))

(rule ((:intern (MH ?b1 ?t1) :test (and (expression? ?b1) (expression? ?t1)
                                        (commutative? (expression-functor ?b1))))
  (:intern (MH ?b2 ?t2) :test (and (member ?b2 (expression-arguments ?b1) :test #'eq)
                                   (member ?t2 (expression-arguments ?t1) :test #'eq)))
  (sme:assert! (implies (MH ?b1 ?t1) (MH ?b2 ?t2) (0.8 . 0.0))))

;;;; Gmap rules

;; Support from its MHs. At this time we ignore other expressions such as number
;; of candidate inferences, etc.

(rule ((:intern (GMAP ?gm))
  (dolist (mh (gm-elements ?gm))
    (assert! '(implies, (mh-form mh) (GMAP ?gm))))))
```

## A.2. Analogy (AN) rules

The *analogy* rules prefer systems of relations and discriminate against object descriptions. The analogy evidence rules are identical to the literal similarity evidence rules and are not repeated here. The match constructor rules only differ in their check for attributes:

```
;;;; Define MH constructor rules

;;; If predicates are the same, match them

(MH-C-rule (:filter ?b ?t :test (and (eq (expression-functor ?b) (expression-functor ?t))
                                     (not (attribute? (expression-functor ?t)))))
  (install-MH ?b ?t))

;; Match compatible arguments of already matched items.
;; Notice attributes are allowed to match here, since they are part of some
;; higher relation that matched.

;; Intern rule for noncommutative predicates—corresponding arguments only.

(MHC-rule (:intern ?b ?t :test (and (expression? ?b) (expression? ?t)
                                     (not (commutative? (expression-functor ?b)))
                                     (not (commutative? (expression-functor ?t)))))
```

```
(do ((bchildren (expression-arguments ?b) (cdr bchildren))
     (tchildren (expression-arguments ?t) (cdr tchildren)))
    ((or (null bchildren) (null tchildren))
     (cond ((and (entity? (first bchildren)) (entity? (first tchildren)))
            (install-MH (first bchildren) (first tchildren)))
           ((and (function? (expression-functor (first bchildren)))
                 (function? (expression-functor (first tchildren))))
            (install-MH (first bchildren) (first tchildren)))
           ((and (attribute? (expression-functor (first bchildren)))
                 (eq (expression-functor (first bchildren))
                     (expression-functor (first tchildren))))
            (install-MH (first bchildren) (first tchildren)))))))
```

## A.3. Mere-appearance (MA) rules

The *mere-appearance* rules focus on object description and prevent matches between functions or relations. As a result, the number of evidence rules is greatly reduced.

```
;;;; Define MH constructor rules

(MHC-rule (:filter ?b ?t :test (and (eq (expression-functor ?b) (expression-functor ?t))
                 (<= (expression-order ?b) 1)
                 (<= (expression-order ?t) 1)))

  (install-MH ?b ?t))

(MHC-rule (:intern ?b ?t :test (and (expression? ?b) (expression? ?t)
                 (not (commutative? (expression-functor ?b)))
                 (not (commutative? (expression-functor ?t)))))

  (do ((bchildren (expression-arguments ?b) (cdr bchildren))
       (tchildren (expression-arguments ?t) (cdr tchildren))
       ((or (null bchildren) (null tchildren))
        (if (and (entity? (first bchildren)) (entity? (first tchildren)))
            (install-MH (first bchildren) (first tchildren)))))

(MHC-rule (:intern ?b ?t :test (and (expression? ?b) (expression? ?t)
                 (commutative? (expression-functor ?b))
```

;; Intern rule for commutative predicates—any "compatible" arguments,
;; not necessarily corresponding.

```
(MHC-rule (:intern ?b ?t :test (and (expression? ?b) (expression? ?t)
                 (commutative? (expression-functor ?b))
                 (commutative? (expression-functor ?t))))

  (dolist (bchild (expression-arguments ?b))
  (dolist (tchild (expression-arguments ?t))
    (cond ((and (entity? bchild) (entity? tchild))
           (install-MH bchild tchild))
          ((and (function? (expression-functor bchild))
                (function? (expression-functor tchild)))
           (install-MH bchild tchild))
          ((and (attribute? (expression-functor bchild))
                (eq (expression-functor bchild) (expression-functor tchild)))
           (install-MH bchild tchild)))))))
```

```
(do ((bchildren (expression-arguments ?b)) (cdr bchildren))
    (tchild (tchild (expression-arguments ?t) (cdr tchild)))
    ((or (null bchildren) (null tchildren))
     (if (and (entity? bchild) (entity? tchild))
         (install-MH bchild tchild)))))

;;;; Define MH evidence rules

;; having the same functor is a good sign
(initial-assertion (assert! 'same-functor))

(rule ((:intern (MH ?b ?t) :test (and (expression? ?b) (expression? ?t)
   (cond ((attribute? (expression-functor ?b))
          (assert! (implies same-functor (MH ?b ?t) (0.5 . 0.0))))
         ((=1 (max (expression-order ?b) (expression-order ?t))
          (assert! (implies same-functor (MH ?b ?t) (0.4 . 0.0)))))))

;; propagate evidence down—only for entity MHs caused by attribute pairings
;; support for the arg will be 0.9 of the current support for the parent
(rule ((:intern (MH ?b1 ?t1) :test (and (expression? ?b1) (expression? ?t1)
        (<= (max (expression-order ?b1) (expression-order ?t1)) 1)
        (not (commutative? (expression-functor ?b1))))

  (:intern (MH ?b2 ?t2) :test (children-of? ?b2 ?t2 ?b1 ?t1)))
  (sme:assert! (implies (MH ?b1 ?t1) (MH ?b2 ?t2) (0.9 . 0.0))))

(rule ((:intern (MH ?b1 ?t1) :test (and (expression? ?b1) (expression? ?t1)
        (<= (max (expression-order ?b1) (expression-order ?t1)) 1)
        (commutative? (expression-functor ?b1)))
  (:intern (MH ?b2 ?t2) :test (and (member (expression-arguments ?b1) :test #'eq)
        (member ?t2 (expression-arguments ?t1) :test #'eq))))
  (sme:assert! (implies (MH ?b1 ?t1) (MH ?b2 ?t2) (0.9 . 0.0))))

;;;; Gmap rules

;;; Support from its MHs. At this time we ignore other expressions such as number of
;;; candidate inferences
(rule ((:intern (GMAP ?gm)))
  (dolist (mh (gm-elements ?gm))
    (assert! '(implies ,(mh-form mh) (GMAP ?gm)))))
```

## Appendix B.   Sample Domain Descriptions

In this section we show the domain description given to SME for the described examples.

### B.1.   Simple water flow/heat flow

#### B.1.1.   *Water flow*

```
(defEntity water :type inanimate)
(defEntity beaker :type inanimate)
(defEntity vial :type inanimate)
(defEntity pipe :type inanimate)
```

### B.2.2. Rutherford atom

```
(defEntity nucleus :type inanimate)
(defEntity electron :type inanimate)

(defDescription rutherford-atom
  entity (nucleus electron)
  expressions
    (((mass nucleus) :name mass-n)
     ((mass electron) :name mass-e)
     ((greater mass-n mass-e) :name >mass)
     ((attracts nucleus electron) :name attracts)
     ((revolve-around electron nucleus) :name revolve)
     ((charge electron) :name q-electron)
     ((charge nucleus) :name q-nucleus)
     ((opposite-sign q-nucleus q-electron) :name >charge)
     ((cause >charge attracts) :name why-attracts)))
```

## B.3. Karla stories

### B.3.1. Zerdia the eagle: Base story

```
(defEntity Karla)
(defEntity hunter)
(defEntity feathers)
(defEntity cross-bow)
(defEntity Failed)
(defEntity high)

(defDescription base-5
  entities (Karla hunter feathers cross-bow Failed high)
  expressions
    (((bird Karla) :name bird-Karla)
     ((person hunter) :name person-hunter)
     ((warlike hunter) :name warlike-hunter)
     ((Karlas-asset feathers) :name feathers-asset)
     ((weapon cross-bow) :name weapon-bow)
     ((used-for feathers cross-bow) :name has-feathers)
     ((not has-feathers) :name not-has-feathers)
     ((attack hunter Karla) :name attack-hunter)
     ((not attack-hunter) :name not-attack)
     ((see Karla hunter) :name see-Karla)
     ((follow see-Karla attack-hunter) :name follow-see-attack)
     ((success attack-hunter) :name success-attack)
     ((equals success-attack Failed) :name failed-attack)
     ((cause not-has-feathers failed-attack) :name cause-failed-attack)
     ((desire hunter feathers) :name desire-feathers)
     ((realize Karla desire-feathers) :name realize-desire)
     ((follow failed-attack realize-desire) :name follow-realize)
     ((offer Karla feathers hunter) :name offer-feathers)
     ((cause realize-desire offer-feathers) :name cause-offer)
     ((obtain hunter feathers) :name take-feathers)
     ((cause offer-feathers take-feathers) :name cause-take)))
```

```
(defDescription simple-water-flow
  entities (water beaker vial pipe)
  expressions
    (((flow beaker vial water pipe) :name wflow)
     ((pressure beaker) :name pressure-beaker)
     ((pressure vial) :name pressure-vial)
     ((greater pressure-beaker pressure-vial) :name >pressure)
     ((greater (diameter beaker) (diameter vial)) :name >diameter)
     ((cause >pressure wflow) :name cause-flow)
     (flat-top water)
     (liquid water)))
```

### B.1.2. Heat flow

```
(defEntity coffee :type inanimate)
(deEntity ice-cube :type inanimate)
(defEntity bar :type inanimate)
(defEntity heat :type inanimate)

(defDescription simple-heat-flow
  entities (coffee ice-cube bar heat)
  expressions
    (((flow coffee ice-cube heat bar) :name hflow)
     ((temperature coffee) :name temp-coffee)
     ((temperature ice-cube) :name temp-ice-cube)
     ((greater temp-coffee temp-ice-cube) :name >temperature)
     (flat-top coffee)
     (liquid coffee)))
```

## B.2. Solar system/Rutherford atom

### B.2.1. Solar system

```
(defEntity sun :type inanimate)
(defEntity planet :type inanimate)

(defDescription solar-system
  entities (sun planet)
  expressions
    (((mass sun) :name mass-sun)
     ((mass planet) :name mass-planet)
     ((greater mass-sun mass-planet) :name >mass)
     ((attracts sun planet) :name attracts)
     ((revolve-around planet sun) :name revolve)
     ((and >mass attracts) :name and1)
     ((cause and1 revolve) :name cause-revolve)
     ((temperature sun) :name temp-sun)
     ((temperature planet) :name temp-planet)
     ((greater temp-sun temp-planet) :name >temp)
     ((gravity mass-sun mass-planet) :name force-gravity)
     ((cause force-gravity attracts) :name why-attracts)))
```

(happiness hunter) :name happiness-hunter)
(equals happiness-hunter high) :name happy-hunter)
(cause take-feathers happy-hunter) :name cause-happy)
(promise hunter Karla not-attack) :name promise-hunter)
(cause happy-hunter promise-hunter) :name cause-promise))))

## B.3.2. *Zerdia the country: TA5*

(defEntity Zerdia)
(defEntity Gagrach)
(defEntity supercomputer)
(defEntity missiles)
(defEntity failed)
(defEntity high)

(defDescription ta-5
entities (Zerdia Gagrach supercomputer missiles failed high)
expressions
(((country Zerdia) :name country-Zerdia)
((country Gagrach) :name country-Gagrach)
((warlike Gagrach) :name warlike-Gagrach)
((Zerdias-asset supercomputer) :name supercomputer-asset)
((weapon missiles) :name weapon-bow)
((use-for supercomputer missiles) :name use-supercomputer)
((not use-supercomputer) :name not-use-supercomputer)
((attack Gagrach Zerdia) :name attack-Gagrach)
((not attack-Gagrach) :name not-attack)
((success attack-Gagrach) :name success-attack)
((equals success-attack failed) :name failed-attack)
((cause not-use-supercomputer failed-attack) :name cause-failed-attack)
((desire Gagrach supercomputer) :name desire-supercomputer)
((realize Zerdia desire-supercomputer) :name realize-desire)
((follow failed-attack realize-desire) :name follow-realize)
((offer Zerdia supercomputer Gagrach) :name offer-supercomputer)
((cause realize-desire offer-supercomputer) :name cause-offer)
((obtain Gagrach supercomputer) :name buy-supercomputer)
((cause offer-supercomputer buy-supercomputer) :name cause-buy)
((happiness Gagrach) :name happiness-Gagrach)
((equals happiness-Gagrach high) :name happy-Gagrach)
((cause buy-supercomputer happy-Gagrach) :name cause-happy)
((promise Gagrach Zerdia not-attack) :name promise)
((cause happy-Gagrach promise) :name cause-promise))))

## B.3.3. *Zerdia the hawk: MA5*

(defEntity Zerdia)
(defEntity sportsman)
(defEntity feathers)
(defEntity cross-bow)
(defEntity true)

(defDescription ma-5
entities (Zerdia sportsman feathers cross-bow true)
expressions
(((bird Zerdia) :name bird-Zerdia)
((person sportsman) :name person-sportsman)
((warlike sportsman) :name warlike-sportsman)
((Zerdias-asset feathers) :name feathers-asset)
((weapon cross-bow) :name weapon-bow)
((used-for feathers cross-bow) :name has-feathers)
((desire sportsman feathers) :name desire-feathers)
((realize Zerdia desire-feathers) :name realize-desire)
((offer Zerdia feathers sportsman) :name offer-feathers)
((cause realize-desire offer-feathers) :name cause-offer)
((obtain sportsman feathers) :name take-feathers)
((cause offer-feathers take-feathers) :name cause-take)
((attack sportsman Zerdia) :name attack-sportsman)
((not attack-sportsman) :name not-attack)
((promise sportsman Zerdia not-attack) :name promise)
((cause take-feathers promise) :name cause-promise)
((see Zerdia sportsman) :name see-Zerdia)
((follow promise see-Zerdia) :name follow-promise)
((follow see-Zerdia attack-sportsman) :name follow-see)
((success attack-sportsman) :name success-attack)
((equals success-attack true) :name successful-attack)
((cause has-feathers successful-attack) :name cause-success-attack)
((realize Zerdia has-feathers) :name realize-Zerdia)
((follow successful-attack realize-Zerdia) :name follow-succ-attack))))

## ACKNOWLEDGMENT

The authors wish to thank Janice Skorstad, Danny Bobrow, and Steve Chien for helpful comments on prior drafts of this paper. Janice Skorstad provided invaluable assistance in encoding domain models. Alan Frisch provided pointers into the unification literature.

This research is supported by the Office of Naval Research. contract no. N00014-85-K-0559. Additional support has been provided by IBM. both in the form of a Graduate Fellowship for Falkenhainer and a Faculty Development award for Forbus. The equipment used in this research was provided by an equipment grant from the Information Sciences Division of the Office of Naval Research, and by a gift from Texas Instruments.

## REFERENCES

1. Allen, D., Steinberg, S. and Stabile, L., Recent developments in Butterfly Lisp, *Proceedings AAAI-87*, Seattle, WA (1987).
2. Anderson, J., *The Architecture of Cognition* (Harvard University Press, Cambridge, MA 1983).
3. Buckley, S., *Sun up to Sun down* (McGraw-Hill, New York, 1979).
4. Bundy, A., *The Computer Modelling of Mathematical Reasoning* (Academic Press, New York, 1983).
5. Burstein, M., Concept formation by incremental analogical reasoning and debugging, in: *Proceedings Second International Workshop on Machine Learning*, Monticello, IL (1983); revised version in: R.S. Michalski, J.G. Carbonell and T.M. Mitchell (Eds.), *Machine Learning: An Artificial Intelligence Approach II* (Morgan Kaufmann, Los Altos, CA, 1986).
6. Carbonell, J.G., Learning by analogy: Formulating and generalizing plans from past ex-

perience, in: R.S. Michalski, J.G. Carbonell, and T.M. Mitchell (Eds.), Machine Learning: An Artificial Intelligence Approach (Morgan Kaufmann, Los Altos, CA, 1983).

7. Carbonell, J.G., Derivational analogy in problem solving and knowledge acquisition, in: Proceedings Second International Machine Learning Workshop, Monticello, IL (1983); revised version in: R.S. Michalski, J.G. Carbonell, and T.M. Mitchell (Eds.), Machine Learning: An Artificial Approach II (Morgan Kaufmann, Los Altos, CA, 1986).

8. Chi, M.T.H., Glaser, R. and Reese, E. Expertise in problem solving, in: R. Sternberg (Ed.), Advances in the Psychology of Human Intelligence (Erlbaum, Hillsdale, NJ., 1982).

9. Clement, C. and Gentner, D., Systematicity as a selection constraint in analogical mapping, in: Proceedings Tenth Annual Meeting of the Cognitive Science Society, Montreal, Que. (1988).

10. Clement, J., Analogy generation in scientific problem solving, in: Proceedings Third Annual Meeting of the Cognitive Science Society, Berkeley, CA (1981).

11. Clement, J., Analogical reasoning patterns in expert problem solving, in: Proceedings Fourth Annual Meeting of the Cognitive Science Society (1982).

12. Collins, A.M. and Gentner, D., How people construct mental models, in: D. Holland and N. Quinn (Eds.), Cultural Models in Language and Thought (Cambridge University Press, Cambridge, England, 1987).

13. DeJong, G., Generalizations based on explanations, in: Proceedings IJCAI-81, Vancouver, BC (1981).

14. DeJong, G. and Mooney, R., Explanation-based learning: An alternative view, Mach. Learning 1 (2) (1986).

15. Dietrich, T. and Michalski. R.S., Inductive learning of structural descriptions: evolution criteria and comparative review of selected methods. Artificial Intelligence 16 (1981) 257–294.

16. Falkenhainer, B., Towards a general-purpose belief maintenance system, in: J.F. Lemmer and L.N. Kanal (Eds.), Uncertainty in Artificial Intelligence 2 (North-Holland, Amsterdam, 1988); also Tech. Rept. UIUCDCS-R-87-1717, Department of Computer Science, University of Illinois, Urbana, IL (1987).

17. Falkenhainer, B., An examination of the third stage in the analogy process: Verification-based analogical learning, Tech. Rept. UIUCDCS-R-86-1302, Department of Computer Science, University of Illinois, Urbana, IL (1986); summary in: Proceedings IJCAI-87, Milan, Italy (1987).

18. Falkenhainer, B., Scientific theory formation through analogical inference, in: Proceedings Fourth International Machine Learning Workshop, Irvine, CA (1987).

19. Falkenhainer, B., The SME user's manual, Tech. Rept. UIUCDCS-R-88-1421, Department of Computer Science, University of Illinois, Urbana, IL (1988).

20. Falkenhainer, B., Learning from physical analogies: A study in analogy and the explanation process, Ph.D. Thesis, University of Illinois, Urbana, IL (1988).

21. Falkenhainer, B., Forbus, K.D. and Gentner, D., The structure-mapping engine, in: Proceedings AAAI-86, Philadelphia, PA (1986).

22. Forbus, K.D., Qualitative reasoning about physical processes, in: Proceedings IJCAI-81, Vancouver, BC (1981).

23. Forbus, K.D., Qualitative process theory, Artificial Intelligence 24 (1984) 85–168.

24. Forbus, K.D., Qualitative process theory, Tech. Rept. No. 789, MIT Artificial Intelligence Laboratory, Cambridge, MA (1984).

25. Forbus, K.D., Interpreting measurements of physical systems, in: Proceedings AAAI-86, Philadelphia, PA (1986).

26. Forbus, K., The qualitative process engine, Tech. Rept. UIUCDCS-R-86-1288, Department of Computer Science, University of Illinois, Urbana, IL (1986).

27. Forbus, K.D. and Gentner, D., Learning physical domains: Towards a theoretical famework, in: Proceedings Second International Machine Learning Workshop, Monticello, IL (1983); revised version in: R.S. Michalski, J.G. Carbonell, and T.M. Mitchell (Eds.), Machine Learning: An Artificial Approach II (Morgan Kaufmann, Los Altos, CA, 1986).

28. Gentner, D., The structure of analogical models in science, BBN Tech. Rept. No. 4451, Bolt Beranek and Newman Inc., Cambridge, MA (1980).

29. Gentner, D., Are scientific analogies metaphors?, in: D. Miall (Ed.), Metaphor: Problems and Perspectives (Harvester Press, Brighton, England, 1982).

30. Gentner, D., Structure-mapping: A theoretical framework for analogy, Cognitive Sci. 7 (2) (1983).

31. Gentner, D., Mechanisms of analogy, in: S. Vosniadou and A. Ortony (Eds.), Similarity and Analogical Reasoning (to appear).

32. Gentner, D., Analogical inference and analogical access, in: A. Prieditis (Ed.), Analogical: Proceedings of the First Workshop on Analogical Reasoning (Pitman, London, 1988).

33. Gentner, D. and Clement, C., Evidence for relational selectivity in the interpretation of analogy and metaphor, in: G.H. Bower (Ed.), The Psychology of Learning and Motivation, Advances in Research and Theory 22 (Academic Press, New York, to appear).

34. Gentner, D. and Gentner, D.R., Flowing waters or teeming crowds: Mental models of electricity, in: D. Gentner and A.L. Stevens (Eds.), Mental Models (Erlbaum, Hillsdale, NJ, 1983).

35. Gentner, D. and Landers, R., Analogical reminding: A good match is hard to find, in: Proceedings International Conference on Systems, Man and Cybernetics, Tucson, AZ (1985).

36. Gentner, D., Metaphor as structure-mapping: The relational shift, Child Dev. 59 (1988) 47–59.

37. Gentner, D. and Toupin, C., Systematicity and surface similarity in the development of analogy, Cognitive Sci. (1986).

38. Gentner, D., Falkenhainer, B. and Skorstad, J., Metaphor: The good, the bad and the ugly, Proceedings Third Conference on Theoretical Issues in Natural Language Processing, Las Cruces, NM (1987).

39. Ginsberg, M.L., Non-monotonic reasoning using Dempster's rule, in: Proceedings AAAI-84, Austin, TX (1984).

40. Goldstone, R., Medin, D. and Gentner, D., Relational similarity and the non-independence of features in similarity judgements, Presented at the Meeting of the Midwestern Psychological Association (1988).

41. Greiner, E., Learning by understanding analogies, Artificial Intelligence 35 (1988) 81–125.

42. Hall, R. Computational approaches to analogical reasoning: A comparative analysis, Artificial Intelligence 39 (1989) 39–120.

43. Hayes-Roth, F. and McDermott, J., An interference matching technique for inducing abstractions, Commun. ACM 21 (5) (1978) 401–411.

44. Hofstadter, D.R., The Copycat project: An experiment in nondeterministic and creative analogies, MIT AI Laboratory Memo 755, Cambridge, MA (1984).

45. Hogge, J., Compiling plan operators from domains expressed in qualitative process theory, in: Proceedings IJCAI-87, Seattle, WA (1987).

46. Holland, J.H., Holyoak, K.J., Nisbett, R.E. and Thagard, P., Induction: Processes of Inference, Learning, and Discovery (1987).

47. Holyoak, K.J., The pragmatics of analogical transfer, in: G.H. Bower (Ed.), The Psychology of Learning and Motivation 1 (Academic Press, New York, 1984).

48. Holyoak, K.J., Juin, E.N. and Billman, D.O., Development of analogical problem-solving skill, Child Dev. (to appear).

49. Indurkhya, B., Constrained semantic transference: A formal theory of metaphors, Synthese 68 (1986) 515–551.

50. Kedar-Cabelli, S., Purpose-directed analogy, in: Proceedings Seventh Annual Conference of the Cognitive Science Society, Irvine, CA (1985).

51. Kedar-Cabelli, S.T. Analogy: From a unified perspective, in: D.H. Helman (Ed.), Analogical Reasoning: Perspectives of Artificial Intelligence, Cognitive Science, and Philosophy (Reidel, Dordrecht, Netherlands, to appear).

52. Kline, P.J., Computing the similarity of structured objects by means of a heuristic search for correspondences, Ph.D. Thesis, Department of Psychology, University of Michigan, Ann Arbor, MI (1983).

53. Larkin, J.H., Problem representations in physics, in: D. Gentner and A.L. Stevens (Eds.), *Mental Models* (Erlbaum, Hillsdale, NJ, 1983).

54. Liu, C.L. *Elements of Discrete Mathematics* (McGraw-Hill, New York, 1977).

55. Michalski, R.S., Pattern recognition as rule-guided inductive inference, *IEEE Trans. Pattern Anal. Mach. Intell.* **2** (1980) 349–361.

56. Plotkin, G.D., Building in equational theories, in: B. Meltzer and D. Michie (Eds.), *Machine Intelligence 7* (Wiley, New York, 1972).

57. Prade, H., A synthetic view of approximate reasoning techniques, in: *Proceedings IJCAI-83*, Karlsruhe, F.R.G. (1983).

58. Rajamoney, S., DeJong, G. and Faltings, B., Towards a model of conceptual knowledge acquisition through directed experimentation, in: *Proceedings IJCAI-85*, Los Angeles, CA (1985).

59. Rattermann, M.J. and Gentner, D., Analogy and similarity: Determinants of accessibility and inferential soundness, in: *Proceedings Ninth Annual Meeting of the Cognitive Science Society*, Seattle, WA (1987).

60. Reed, S.K., A short survey on the state of the art in matching and unification problems, *ACM SIGSAM Bull.* **13** (2) (1979) 14–20.

61. Reed, S.K., Ernst, G.W. and Banerji, R., A structure-mapping model for word problems, *J. Experimental Psychol. Learning, Memory Cognition* **13** (1) (1987) 124–139.

62. Ross, B.H., Remindings and their effects in learning a cognitive skill, *Cognitive Psychol.* **16** (1984) 371–416.

63. Rumelhart, D.E. and Norman, D.A., Analogical processes in learning, in: J.R. Anderson (Ed.), *Cognitive Skills and Their Acquisition* (Erlbaum, Hillsdale, NJ, 1981).

64. Shafer, G., *A Mathematical Theory of Evidence* (Princeton University Press, Princeton, NJ 1976).

65. Shavlik, J.W., Learning about momentum conservation, in: *Proceedings IJCAI-85*, Los Angeles, CA (1985).

66. Skorstad, J., A structural approach to abstraction processes during concept learning, Master's Thesis (1989).

67. Skorstad, J., Falkenhainer, B. and Gentner, D., Analogical processing: A simulation and empirical corroboration, in: *Proceedings AAAI-87*, Seattle, WA (1987).

68. Skorstad, J., Gentner, D. and Medin, D., Abstraction processes during concept learning: A structural view, in: *Proceedings Tenth Annual Meeting of the Cognitive Science Society*, Montreal, Que. (1988).

69. Stickel, M., A complete unification algorithm for associative-commutative functions, in: *Proceedings IJCAI-75*, Tbilisi, USSR (1975) 71–76.

70. Tversky, A., Representation of structure in similarity data: Problems and prospects, *Psychometrika* **39** (1974) 373–421.

71. van Lehn, K. and Brown, J.S., Planning nets: A representation for formalizing analogies and semantic models of procedural skills, in: R.E. Snow, P.A. Federico and W.E. Montague (Eds.), *Aptitude, Learning and Instruction: Cognitive Process Analyses* (Erlbaum, Hillsdale, NJ, 1980).

72. van Lehn, K., Felicity conditions for human skill acquisition: Validating an AI-based theory Xerox Palo Alto Research Center Tech. Rept. CIS-21, Palo Alto, CA (1983).

73. Vere, S., Induction of concepts in the predicate calculus, in: *Proceedings IJCAI-75*, Tbilisi, USSR (1975).

74. Vere, S., Inductive learning of relational productions, in: D.A. Waterman and F. Hayes-Roth (Eds.), *Pattern-Directed Inference Systems* (1978).

75. Vosniadou, S., On the development of metaphoric competence, University of Illinois, Urbana, IL (1985).

76. Waltz, D.L. and Pollack, J.B., Massively parallel parsing: A strongly interactive model of natural language interpretation, *Cognitive Sci.* **9** (1985) 51–74.

77. Winston, P.H., Learning structural descriptions from examples, Ph.D. Thesis, Rept. AI-TR-231, MIT Artificial Intelligence Laboratory, Cambridge, MA (1970).

78. Winston, P.H., Learning and reasoning by analogy, *Commun. ACM* **23** (12) (1980).

79. Winston, P.H., Learning new principles from precedents and exercises. *Artificial Intelligence* **19** (1982) 321–350.

*Received July 1987; revised version received June 1988*

# DERIVATIONAL ANALOGY:

## A Theory of Reconstructive Problem Solving and Expertise Acquisition

Jaime G. Carbonell
*Carnegie-Mellon University*

### Abstract

Derivational analogy, a method of solving problems based on the transfer of past experience to new problem situations, is discussed in the context of other general approaches to problem solving. The experience transfer process consists of recreating lines of reasoning, including decision sequences and accompanying justifications, that proved effective in solving particular problems requiring similar initial analysis. The role of derivational analogy in case-based reasoning and in automated expertise acquisition is discussed.

## 14.1 INTRODUCTION: THE ROLE OF ANALOGY IN PROBLEM SOLVING

The term *problem solving* in artificial intelligence has been used to denote disparate forms of intelligent action to achieve well-defined goals. Perhaps the most common usage stems from the work of Newell and Simon (1972) in which problem solving consists of selecting a sequence of operators (from a preanalyzed finite set) that transforms an initial problem state into a desired goal state. Intelligent behavior consists of a focused search for a suitable operator sequence involving analysis of the

equilibrium of forces at the point of interest (the vector sum of the forces = 0). But the application of this plan only reduces the original problem to one of finding and combining the appropriate forces, without hinting at how that may be accomplished in a specific problem (Carbonell, Larkin, and Reif, 1983; Larkin, Reif, and Carbonell, 1985).

- If no specific plans apply but the problem resembles one solved previously, analogical transformation can be applied to adapt the solution of that similar past problem to the new situation. For instance, in some studies it has proven easier for students to solve mechanics problems by analogy to simpler, solved problems than by appealing to first principles or by applying general procedures presented in a physics text (Clements, 1982). As an example of analogy involving composite skills rather than pure cognition, consider a person who knows how to drive a car and is asked to drive a truck. Such a person may have no general plan or procedure for driving trucks but is likely to perform most of the steps correctly by transferring much of his or her automobile-driving knowledge. Would that we had robots that were so self-adaptable to new, if recognizably related, tasks!

Clearly, these problem-solving approaches, illustrated in figure 14-1, are not mutually exclusive; for instance, a "first-principles" approach can be used to reduce a problem to simpler subproblems, which in turn can be solved by analogy to recognizably similar past problems or by any of the other methods. In fact, a general inference engine for problem solving in the natural sciences that combines all four

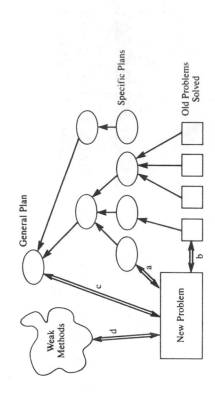

**Figure 14-1:** Problem solving may involve the following: (a) instantiating specific plans, (b) using analogical transformation to a known solution of a similar problem, (c) applying general plans to reduce the problem, (d) applying weak methods to search heuristically for a possible solution, or (e) using a combination of these approaches.

states resulting from the application of different operators to earlier states.[1] Many researchers have adopted this viewpoint (Fikes and Nilsson, 1971; Sacerdoti, 1974; Nilsson, 1980).

However, a totally different approach has been advocated by McDermott (1967) and by Wilensky (1978, 1983) that views problem solving as plan instantiation. For each problem posed there are one or more plans that outline a solution, and problem solving consists of identifying and instantiating these plans. In order to select, instantiate, or refine plans, additional plans that tell how to instantiate other plans or how to solve subproblems are brought to bear in a recursive manner. Traditional notions of search are totally absent from this formulation. Some systems, such as the counterplanning mechanism in POLITICS (Carbonell, 1981b, 1981c), provide a hybrid approach, instantiating plans whenever possible and searching to construct potential solutions in the absence of applicable plans.

A third approach is to solve a new problem by analogy to a previously solved similar problem. This process entails searching for related past problems and transforming their solutions into solutions potentially applicable to the new problem (Pólya, 1945). Such a method was developed and advocated by the author (Carbonell, 1982, 1983) primarily as a means of bringing to bear problem-solving expertise acquired from past experience. The analogical transformation process itself may require search, as it is seldom immediately clear how a solution to a similar problem can be adapted to a new situation.

A useful means of classifying different problem-solving methods is to compare them in terms of the amount and specificity of domain knowledge they require.

- If no structuring domain knowledge is available and there is no useful past experience to draw upon, weak methods such as heuristic search and means-end analysis are the only tools that can be brought to bear. Even in these knowledge-poor situations, information about goal states, possible actions, their known preconditions, and their expected outcomes is required.

- If specific domain knowledge in the form of plans or procedures exists, such plans may be instantiated directly, recursively solving any subproblems that arise in the process.

- If general plans apply but no specific ones do, the general plans can be used to reduce the problem (by partitioning the problem or providing islands in the search space). For instance, in computing the pressure at a particular point in a fluid statics problem, one may use the general plan of applying the principle of

---

[1]In means-ends analysis, the current state is compared to the goal state, and one or more operators that reduce the difference are selected, whereas in heuristic search, the present state is evaluated in isolation and compared to alternate states resulting from the application of different operators (to states generated earlier in the search), and the search for a solution continues from the highest-rated state.

approaches is being developed (Carbonell, Larkin, and Reif, 1983; Larkin, Reif, and Carbonell, 1985).

As discussed earlier, only direct plan instantiation and weak methods have received substantial attention by AI practitioners. For instance, Laird and Newell's recent formulation of a universal weak method (Laird and Newell, 1983) as a general problem-solving engine is developed completely within the search paradigm. Expert systems, for the most part, combine aspects of plan instantiation (often broken into small rule-size chunks of knowledge) and heuristic search in whatever manner best exploits the explicit and implicit constraints of the specific domain (Feigenbaum, Buchanan, and Lederberg, 1971; Shortliffe, 1976; Duda et al., 1979; McDermott, 1980, 1982). The author is more concerned with the other two approaches, as they could conceivably provide powerful reasoning mechanisms not heretofore analyzed in the context of automating problem-solving processes and of allowing the problem solver to learn from experience. The rest of this chapter focuses on a new formulation of the analogical problem-solving approach and its role in automating the knowledge acquisition process.

## 14.2 ANALOGY AND EXPERIENTIAL REASONING

The term *analogy* often conjures up recollections of artificially contrived problems in various psychometric exams, such as, "X is to Y as Z is to?" This aspect of analogy is far too narrow and independent of context to be useful in general problem-solving domains. Instead, the following operational definition of analogical problem solving is proposed consistent with past AI research efforts (Kling, 1971; Winston, 1978, 1979; Gentner, 1980; Carbonell, 1980; Carbonell, 1981a, 1983):

**Definition:** *Analogical problem solving consists of transferring knowledge from past problem-solving episodes to new problems that share significant aspects with corresponding past experience and using the transferred knowledge to construct solutions to the new problems.*

In order to make this definition operational, the problem-solving method must specify the following:

• What it means for problems to "share significant aspects"
• What knowledge is transferred from past experience to the new situation
• Precisely how the knowledge transfer process occurs
• How analogically related experiences are selected from a potentially vast long-term memory of past problem-solving episodes.

There are two distinct approaches to analogical problem solving. The first approach, called *transformational analogy*, has been successfully implemented in ARIES (Analogical Reasoning and Inductive Experimentation System) (Carbonell, 1983). The second approach, called *derivational analogy*, is a reconstructive rather than a transformational method, and it is the topic of this chapter. Both methods are analyzed with respect to the four criteria listed above.

### 14.2.1 Analogical Transformation of Past Solutions

If a particular solution has been found to work on a problem similar to the one at hand, perhaps it can be used, with minor modification, for the present problem. By *solution* is meant only a sequence of actions that if applied to the initial state of a problem brings about its goal state. Simple though this process may appear, an effective computer implementation requires that many difficult issues be resolved, namely:

1. Descriptions of past problems and of their solutions must be remembered and indexed for later retrieval.

2. The new problem must be matched against a large number of potentially relevant past problems to find closely related ones, if any. An operational similarity metric is required as a basis for selecting the most suitable past experiences.

3. The solution to a selected old problem must be transformed to satisfy the requirements of the new problem statement.

In order to achieve these objectives, the initial analogical problem solver (Carbonell, 1983) required a partial matcher with a built-in similarity criterion, a set of possible transformations to map the solution of one problem into the solution to a closely related problem, and a memory-indexing mechanism based on a MOPs-like memory encoding of events and actions (Schank, 1982). The solution transformation process was implemented as a set of atomic transform operators and a means-ends process that searched for sequences of atomic transformations that, when applied to the retrieved solution, yielded a solution to the new problem. The resultant system, called ARIES, turned out to be far more complex than was originally envisioned. Partial pattern matching of problem descriptions and searching in the space of solution transformations are difficult tasks in themselves. Figure 14-2 illustrates the transformational analogy process.

In terms of the four criteria, the solution transformation process may be classified as follows:

1. Two problems share significant aspects if they match within a certain preset threshold in the initial partial matching process, according to the built-in similarity metric.

2. The knowledge transferred to the new situation is the sequence of actions from the retrieved solution, whether or not that sequence is later modified in the analogical mapping process.

3. The knowledge transfer process is accomplished by copying the retrieved solution and perturbing it incrementally according to the primitive transformation

and disregarding the reasons for selecting those actions. Why should one take such extra information into account? It would certainly complicate the analogical problem-solving process; nevertheless, what benefits would accrue from such an endeavor? Perhaps the best way to answer this question is by analysis of the shortcomings of the simple solution transformation process and of ways that such problems may be alleviated or circumvented by preserving more information from which qualitatively different analogies may be drawn. The general idea of derivational analogy is depicted in figure 14-3 and examined in greater detail below.

### 14.3.1  The Need for Preserving Derivation Histories

Consider, for instance, the domain of constructing computer programs to meet a set of predefined specifications. In the automatic programming literature, perhaps the most widely used technique is one of progressive refinement (Barstow, 1977; Balzer, 1975; Kant, 1981). In brief, progressive refinement is a multistage process that starts from abstract specifications stated in a high-level language (typically English or some variant of first-order logic) and produces progressively more operational or algorithmic descriptions of the specification committing to control decisions, data structures, and eventually specific statements in the target computer language. However, humans (at least this writer) seldom follow such a long and painstaking process, unless perhaps the specifications call for a truly novel program

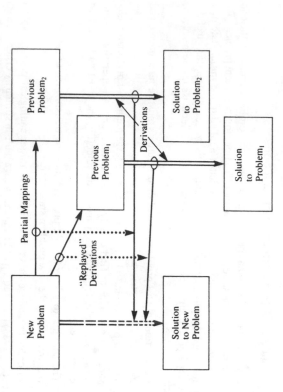

**Figure 14-3:**   The derivational analogy process. The derivational traces of similar past problems are replayed and where necessary modified to construct a solution to a similar new problem.

steps in the heuristically guided manner until it satisfies the requirements of the new problem. (See Carbonell, 1983, for details.)

4.  The selection of relevant past problems is constrained by the memory-indexing scheme and the partial pattern matcher.

Since a significant fraction of problems encountered in mundane situations and in areas requiring substantial domain expertise (but not in abstract mathematical puzzles) bears close resemblance to past solved problems, the **ARIES** method proved effective when tested in various domains, including algebra problems and route-planning tasks. An experiential learning component was added to **ARIES** that constructed simple plans (generalized sequences of actions) for recurring classes of problems, hence allowing the system to solve new problems in this class by the direct plan instantiation approach. However, no sooner was the solution transformation method implemented and analyzed than some of its shortcomings became strikingly apparent. In response to these deficiencies, more sophisticated methods of drawing analogies were analyzed, as discussed in the following section.

### 14.3  THE DERIVATIONAL ANALOGY METHOD

In formulating plans and solving problems, a considerable amount of intermediate information is produced in addition to the resultant plan or specific solution. For instance, formulation of subgoal structures, generation and subsequent rejection of alternatives, and access to various knowledge structures all typically take place in the problem-solving process. But the solution transformation method outlined above ignores all such information, focusing only upon the resultant sequence of actions

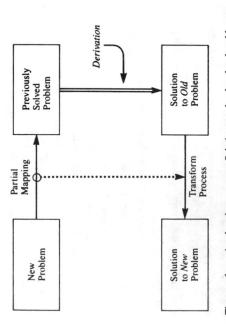

**Figure 14-2:**   The transformational analogy process. Solutions to closely related problems are retrieved and modified to satisfy the requirements of the new problem.

advantages of the derivational analogy approach are quite evident in programming because of the frequent inappropriateness of direct solution transformation; but even in domains in which the latter is useful, one can envision problems that demonstrate the need for preserving or reconstructing past reasoning processes.

### 14.3.2 The Process of Drawing Analogies by Derivational Transformation

Let us examine in greater detail the process of drawing analogies from past reasoning processes. The essential insight is that useful experience is encoded in the reasoning process used to derive solutions to similar problems, rather than just in the resultant solution. Additionally, a method of bringing that experience to bear in the problem-solving process is required in order to make this form of analogy a computationally tractable approach. Here we outline such a method:

1. When solving a problem by any means, store each step taken in the solution process, as illustrated in figure 14-4, including the following:

   • The subgoal structure of the problem

   • Each decision made (whether a decision to take action, to explore new possibilities, or to abandon present plans), including the following:

     ○ Alternatives considered and rejected

     ○ The reasons for the decisions taken (with dependency links to the problem description or information derived therefrom)

     ○ The start of a false path taken (with the reason why it proved otherwise, again with dependency links to the problem description. Note that the body of the false path and other resultant information need not be preserved).

     ○ Dependencies of later decisions on earlier ones in the derivation.

   • Pointers to the knowledge that was accessed and that proved useful in the eventual construction of the solution

   • The resultant solution itself

     ○ In the event that the problem solver proved incapable of solving the problem, store the closest approach to a solution, along with the reasons why no further progress could be made (e.g., a conjunctive subgoal that could not be satisfied).

     ○ In the event that the solution depends, perhaps indirectly, on volatile assumptions not stated in the problem description (such as the cooperation of another agent or time-dependent states), store the appropriate dependencies.

unlike anything in their past experience. Instead, a common practice is to recall similar past programs and reconstruct the new programming problem along the same lines. For instance, one should be able to program a quicksort algorithm in LISP quite easily if one has recently implemented quicksort in Pascal. Similarly, writing LISP programs that perform tasks centered around depth-first tree traversal (such as testing equality of S-expressions or finding the node with maximal value) are rather trivial for LISP programmers but surprisingly difficult for those who lack the appropriate experience.

The solution transformation process proves singularly inappropriate as a means of exploiting past experiences in such problems. A Pascal implementation of quicksort may look very different from a good LISP implementation. In fact, attempting to transfer corresponding steps from the Pascal program into LISP is clearly not a good way to produce any reasonable LISP program, let alone an elegant or efficient one. Although the two problem statements may have been similar, and although the problem-solving processes may preserve much of the inherent similarity, the resultant solutions (i.e., the Pascal and LISP programs) may bear little if any direct similarities.

The useful similarities lie in the algorithms implemented and in the set of decisions and internal reasoning steps required to produce the two programs by successively refining the general specification of the problem. Therefore, the analogy must take place starting at earlier stages of the original Pascal implementation, and it must be guided by a reconsideration of the key decisions in light of the new situation. In particular, the derivation of the LISP quicksort program starts from the same specifications, retaining the same divide-and-conquer strategy, but it may diverge in the selection of data structures (e.g., lists versus arrays) or in the method of choosing the comparison element, depending on the tools available in each language and their expected efficiency. However, future decisions (e.g., whether to recurse or iterate, what mnemonics to use as variable names, and so on) that do not depend on earlier divergent decisions can still be transferred to the new domain rather than recomputed. Thus, the derivational analogy method walks through the reasoning steps in the construction of the past solution and considers whether they are still appropriate in the new situation or whether they should be reconsidered in light of significant differences between the two situations.

The difference between the solution transformation approach and the derivational analogy approach just outlined can be stated in terms of the operational knowledge that can be brought to bear. The former corresponds to a person who has never before programmed quicksort and is given the Pascal code as an aid in constructing the LISP implementation; whereas the latter is akin to a person who has programmed the Pascal version and therefore has a better understanding of the issues involved before undertaking the LISP implementation. Swartout and Balzer (1982) and Reif and Scherlis (1982) have argued independently in favor of working with program derivations as the basic entities in tasks relating to automatic programming. The

*derivations*) are retrieved if their initial segment matches that of the first stages of the analysis of the present problem.

• The retrieved reasoning processes are then used much as individual relevant cases in medicine are used to generate expectations and drive the diagnostic analysis. Reasoning from individual cases has been recognized as an important component of expertise (Schank, 1983), but little has been said of the necessary information that each case must contain, let alone providing a simple method of retrieving the appropriate cases in a manner that does not rely on arbitrary similarity metrics. The stand is taken here that cases must contain the reasoning process used to yield an answer, together with dependencies to the particular circumstances of the problem, pointers to data that proved useful, a list of alternative reasoning paths not taken, and failed attempts (coupled with both reasons for their failure and reasons for their having been tried). Case-based reasoning is nothing more than derivational analogy applied to domains of extensive expertise.

• It is important to know that although one may view derivational analogy as an interim step in reasoning from particular past experiences as more general plans are acquired, it is a mechanism that remains forever useful, since knowledge is always incomplete, and exceptions to the best formulated general plans require representation and use of individual reasoning episodes.

4. Apply a retrieved derivation to the current situation as follows: For each step in the derivation, starting immediately after the matched initial segment, check whether the reasons for performing that step are still valid by tracing dependencies in the retrieved derivation to relevant parts of the old problem description or to volatile external assumptions made in the initial problem solving.

• If parts of the problem statement or external assumptions on which the retrieved situation rests are also true in the present problem situation, proceed to check the next step in the retrieved derivation.

• If there is a violated assumption or problem statement, check whether the decision made would still be justified by a different derivation path from the new assumptions or statements. If so, store the new dependencies and proceed to the next step in the retrieved derivation. The idea of tracing causal dependencies and verifying past inference paths borrows heavily from TMS (Doyle, 1979) and some of the nonmonotonic logic literature (McDermott and Doyle, 1980). However, the role played by data dependencies in derivational analogy is somewhat different and more constrained than it is in maintaining global consistency in deductive data bases.

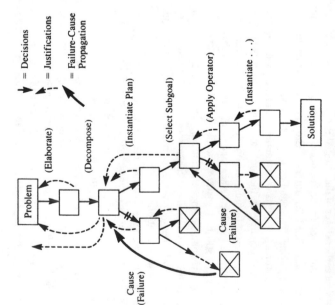

**Figure 14-4:** A derivational trace. Each reasoning step is justified in terms of previous reasoning steps or external knowledge. When a solution attempt fails, the cause of failure is propagated back to the branching point from the successful path and retained.

2. When a new problem is encountered that does not lend itself to direct plan instantiation or other direct recognition of the solution pattern, start to analyze the problem by applying general plans or weak methods, whichever is appropriate to the situation.

3. If after the analysis of the problem is commenced, the reasoning process (the initial decisions made and the information taken into account) parallels that of past problem situations, retrieve the full reasoning traces and proceed with the derivational transformation process. If not, consider the possibility of solution transformation analogy or, failing that, proceed with the present line of nonanalogical reasoning.

• Two problems are considered similar if their analysis results in equivalent reasoning processes, at least in its initial stages. This replaces the more arbitrary context-free similarity metric required for partial matching among problem descriptions in drawing analogies by direct solution transformation. Hence, past reasoning traces (henceforth called

- If the old decision cannot be justified by the new problem situation, proceed as follows:

  o Evaluate the alternatives not chosen at that juncture and select an appropriate one in the usual problem-solving manner, storing it along with its justifications, or

  o Initiate the subgoal of establishing the right supports in order for the old decision to apply in the new problem[2] (clearly, any problem-solving method can be brought to bear in achieving the new subgoal), or

  o Abandon this derivational analogy in favor of another, more appropriate problem-solving experience from which to draw the analogy or in favor of other means of problem solving.

- If one or more failure paths are associated with the current decision, check the cause of failure and the reasons these alternatives appeared viable in the context of the original problem (by tracing dependency links when required). In the case that their reasons for failure no longer apply but the initial reasons for selecting these alternatives are still present, consider reconstructing this alternate solution path in favor of continuing to apply and modify the present derivation (especially if quality of solution is more important than problem-solving effort).

- In the event that a different decision is taken at some point in the rederivation, do not abandon the old derivation, since future decisions may be independent of some past decisions or may still be valid (via different justifications) in spite of the somewhat different circumstances. This requires that dependency links be kept between decisions at different stages in the derivation.

- In the event that a preponderance of the old decisions are invalidated in the new problem situation, abandon the derivational analogy. Exactly what the perseverance threshold should be is a topic for empirical investigation, as it depends on whether there are other tractable means of solving this problem and on the overhead cost of reevaluating individual past decisions that are no longer supported and that may or may not have independent justification.

[2]This approach works only if the missing or violated premise relates to that part of the global state under control of the problem solver, such as acquiring a missing tool or resource, rather than that part under the control of an uncooperative external agent or a recalcitrant environment. The discussion of strategy-based counterplanning gives a more complete account of subgoaling to rectify unfulfilled expectations (Carbonell, 1981b, 1981c).

5. After an entire derivation has been found to apply to the new problem, store its divergence from the parent derivation as another potentially useful source of analogies and as an instance from which more general plans can be formulated if a large number of problems share a common solution procedure (Carbonell, 1983).

## 14.3.3 Efficiency Concerns

An important aspect of the derivational analogy approach is the ability to store and trace dependency links. It should be noted that some of the inherent inefficiencies in maintaining global consistency in a large deductive database do not apply, as the dependency links are internal to each derivation with external pointers only to the problem description and to any volatile assumptions necessitated in constructing the resultant solution. Hence, the size of each dependency network is quite small compared to a dependency network spanning all memory. Dependencies are also stored among decisions taken at different stages in the temporal sequence of the derivation, thus providing the derivational analogy process access to causal relations computed at the time the initial problem was solved.

The analogical rederivation process is not inherently space inefficient, although it may so appear at first glance. The sequence of decisions in the solution path of a problem is stored, together with necessary dependencies, the problem description, the resultant solution, and alternative reasoning paths not chosen. Failed paths are not stored; only the initial decision that was taken to embark upon that path and the eventual reason for failure (with its causal dependencies) are remembered. Hence, the size of the memory for derivational traces is proportional to the depth of the search tree rather than to the number of nodes visited. Problems that share large portions of their derivational structure can be so represented in memory, saving space and allowing similarity-based indexing. Moreover, when a generalized plan is formulated for recurring problems that share a common derivational structure, the individual derivations that are totally subsumed by the more general structure can be permanently masked or deleted. Those derivations that represent exceptions to the general rule, however, are precisely the instances that should be saved and indexed accordingly for future problem solving (Hayes-Roth, 1983).

## 14.3.4 Summarizing the Derivational Process

Derivational analogy bears closer resemblance to Schank's reconstructive memory (1980, 1982) and Minsky's K-lines (1980) than to traditional notions of analogy. Although derivational analogy is less ambitious in scope than either of these theories, it is a more precisely defined inference process that can lead to an operational method of reasoning from particular experiential instances. The key notion is to reconstruct the relevant aspects of past problem-solving situations and thereby transfer knowledge to the new scenario, where that knowledge consists of decision

context-independent rules is proving to be only an early engineering decision, and a very limiting one at that. The knowledge must be captured, but the question of the best means of acquiring and representing it in a computationally effective manner remains.

What then would be an alternative means of representing and acquiring domain knowledge? In order to address this question, the author set out to build an expert system and gain first-hand experience, keeping in perspective all the different problem-solving methods and machine learning paradigms. In less than a year, with the help of one programmer and two domain experts, SMOKEY (Carbonell, 1985), a prototype fire diagnosis expert system, was produced. In essence, SMOKEY polls multiple remote sensors (heat detectors, smoke detectors, air pressure detectors, and so on), and calculates the location, expected spread, and critical nature of a fire on a building or a ship. From this assessment it recommends actions, such as signaling safe exit routes free of smoke, closing down air circulation ducts before they spread toxic smoke to unaffected areas, selecting equipment for the fire-fighting team appropriate to the nature of the fire, and so on. Several lessons were learned from this endeavor, and here the focus will be on the central one: the utility of case-based reasoning.

When naval experts were interviewed about on-board fire diagnosis situations, it was found that for sizable fires, they are swamped with too much information coming from all the potentially relevant sensors. Therefore, videotape simulations of several fires were played at much-reduced speeds. The results were amazing: previously sloppy decisions ignoring crucial information vanished, and elaborate problem-solving protocols were recorded, including fairly complete justifications for each action or decision taken. Unfortunately, real fires cannot be played in slow motion to allow for human reaction time and memory limitations. Thus, the need for a SMOKEY-like system on a fast processor was established. Now the question remained of how the excellent (slow-motion) problem-solving traces could be converted into the knowledge base of an expert system. The key insight was that perhaps they need not be converted—only encoded appropriately and fed to a derivational analogy problem solver and learning module. SMOKEY was built concurrently with the development of the derivational analogy method, so the expertise acquisition steps discussed below were carried out largely by hand, rather than in a completely automated fashion.

Human experts are incredibly poor at producing general deductive rules that account for their behavior. When forced to do so by insistent knowledge engineers, they try hard and produce faulty rules. When they are later faced with a problem in which the rule fails, the typical response is: "Well, I didn't think of *that* situation, but perhaps I can fix the rule . . . or add a new one . . ." This ad hoc iterative process, slow and frustratingly inefficient as it may be, usually converges upon an acceptable knowledge base. However, a much more efficient and humane approach is to let the experts do what they do best: solve problems in their domain of expertise. The only added burden is a reporting requirement. Each problem-solving step, including

sequences and their justifications rather than individual declarative assertions. In summary, consider how the process of derivational analogy can be described in terms of the four criteria for analogical reasoning presented in the previous section:

1. Two problems share significant aspects if their initial analysis yields the same reasoning steps, that is, if the initial segments of their respective derivations start by considering the same issues and making the same decisions.

2. The earlier derivation may be transferred to the new situation, in essence recreating the significant aspects of the reasoning process that solved the past problem.

3. Knowledge transfer is accomplished by reconsidering old decisions in light of the new problem situation, preserving those that apply, and replacing or modifying those whose supports are no longer valid in the new situation.

4. Problems and their derivations are stored in a large episodic memory along the line of Schank's MOPs (1982), and retrieval occurs by replication of initial segments of decision sequences recalling the past reasoning process.

## 14.4 INCREMENTAL EXPERTISE ACQUISITION

Derivational analogy is a fertile computational paradigm that supports various knowledge acquisition and skill refinement strategies. Thus far the focus here has been on the basic problem-solving aspects, but a major motivation behind the reconstructive derivational strategy is the natural manner in which it can be extended to include incremental acquisition of domain expertise. First, case-based reasoning as a major component of human expertise will be briefly considered. Then, some concrete methods for acquiring and refining expertise from experience will be examined, based upon the derivational analogy model.

### 14.4.1 Case-Based Reasoning as a Model of Human Expertise

The vast majority of present-day expert systems encode their knowledge as a large, amorphous set of domain-specific rules (Feigenbaum, Buchanan, and Lederberg, 1971; McDermott, 1980, 1982; Shortliffe, 1976; Waterman, Hayes-Roth, and Lenat, 1983). The "knowledge engineering" task is defined as one of extracting from the human expert the set of rules that comprise his or her expertise in particular, well-defined domains. The task is by no means easy—quite the contrary. It can take years of laborious efforts by teams of domain experts and AI researchers in an iterative process of formulating, evaluating, reformulating, discarding, and refining a set of rules to develop the knowledge base of a particular expert system. Observing this phenomenon, Edward Feigenbaum uttered his now-famous proclamation, "In the knowledge lies the power." How right he was! Fortunately, however, the tacit assumption that domain knowledge must necessarily be represented as large sets of

references to static domain knowledge or to heuristics of the domain, must be reported explicitly, along with the reason why such knowledge was used. This process provides external derivational traces that a derivational analogy inference engine can use to solve similar future problems in an effective manner. Although the derivational method was originally conceived as a means to reason and learn from one's own past experience, a more knowledgeable external source, such as a human expert or a worked-out problem example in a textbook, can prove even more effective.

Case-based reasoning is particulary prevalent in law—at least in the British and American systems of jurisprudence—and in medical diagnosis and treatment. The idea of case-based reasoning in expert systems is not new. Schank (1983), for instance, advocates this method as superior and closer to human reasoning than present expert systems. Doyle (1984) proposes the notion of emulating the human master-apprentice process as a means whereby the latter (human or computer) can acquire expertise by replicating the reasoning processes of the former. Here, a concrete computational mechanism—the derivational analogy process—is proposed as a means of providing expert systems with the ability to reason from cases, whether the cases be past experience or externally acquired knowledge. However, human experts can solve problems progressively more quickly and effectively with repeated experience. Whereas case-based reasoning may reflect accurately a crucial intermediate stage in the learning process and may account for problem-solving behavior in infrequently recurring situations, some knowledge is gradually compiled into more general processes abstracted from the concrete cases. That is to say, for the most routine, recurring problems, the derivational analogy process should produce general plans that can be instantiated directly. The following section explores learning techniques in derivational analogy.

### 14.4.2 Automatic Acquisition of Plans and Strategies

The standard behavioral definition for learning can be paraphrased as follows:

**Definition:** *A system (biological or mechanical) is said to learn if it can modify its behavior after a set of experiences such that it can perform a task more accurately or more efficiently than before or perform a new task beyond its previous capabilities.*

What can be learned in the derivational analogy process, according to this definition? Learning can occur at many levels and in many forms.

### 14.4.2.1 Enrichment of Case-Based Memory

As a system solves problems or is presented with fully annotated derivations of solutions, its repertoire of cases increases. Thus it will be able to derive analogical solutions from these new experiences. This incremental, monotonic increase in its

experiential knowledge base provides a powerful argument in favor of a method such as derivational analogy, which can utilize the experience directly to solve new problems.

### 14.4.2.2 Generalized Plans

If only the resultant solutions to a large set of analogically related problems are used (rather than the entire derivations), generalized operator sequence plans can be abstracted. This process requires that solutions derived from a common analogical parent form a set of positive exemplars, and unrelated or failed solutions form a set of negative exemplars. These sets are given to a general inductive engine (Michalski, 1983) or to an incremental one such as Mitchell's version space method (Mitchell, 1978; Mitchell, Utgoff, and Banerji, 1983), which abstracts a generalized plan from the recurring common aspects of these solutions. Later, the generalized plan can be instantiated directly—or refined further if more instance solutions are derived. Figure 14-5 summarizes this process. (For a longer discussion, see Carbonell, 1983.)

### 14.4.2.3 Strategy Acquisition

The same method for inducing generalized plans from positive and negative exemplars can be applied to different parts of the full derivational trace.

Considerations of alternate decision points in derivationally related solutions can lead to the compilation of domain-specific heuristics for making future choices

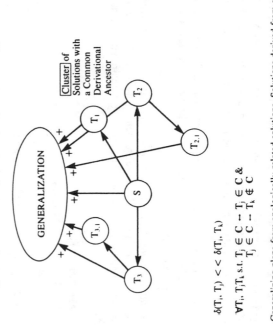

$$\delta(T_i, T_j) << \delta(T_i, T_k)$$

$$\forall T_i, T_j, T_k \text{ s.t. } T_j \in C \sim T_i \in C \ \& \ T_j \in C \sim T_k \notin C$$

**Figure 14-5:** Generalizing plans from analogically related solutions. Solutions derived from common transformational ancestors form a cluster of positive exemplars. Failed attempts and members of other clusters provide the negative exemplars to an induction engine.

of the same nature. If a particular decision was part of a successful derivation in several related solutions but led to a false path under other problem solutions, the requisite grist for the induction engine again exists: a set of positive exemplars in the justifications of the successful decision and a set of near-miss negative exemplars in the cases where the same decision proved ineffective. In fact, the cause of failure (propagated back to the causally related decision point and retained in the derivational trace, as discussed earlier) provides a set of necessary—but perhaps not sufficient—conditions to discriminate between the positive and negative instances of the decision.

Consider, for instance, the selection of a means of transportation in various problem-solving situations that involve travel. If an automobile was successfully selected three times to travel between cities in the continental United States but was erroneously suggested as a means of traveling between Boston and London, the strategy for selecting a means of transportation can be refined. The cause of failure (no land route between the source and destination) serves to add a necessary condition to the strategy, and the fact that automobile travel proved successful independent of the exact compass orientation or identity of the cities within the United States serves to assert the independence of the strategy from such considerations. In fact, a trial implementation in the route-finding domain has yielded planning strategies increasingly more appropriate to the task domain.

Applying the same technique to problem decomposition tasks, plan selection tasks (when multiple generalized plans exist for a given subproblem), and methods of avoiding the causes of failure under similar circumstances can also yield automated refinement of the system's behavior. In all cases, the internal and external justifications provide the means for the system to focus on the functionally relevant aspects of the phase in the derivation from which it is attempting to learn. However, in contrast to the strategy selection task above, there is no empirical validation of the utility or feasibility of attempting to produce better problem decomposition criteria, plan selection methods, or generalized avoidance of recurring pitfalls. This is currently an active area of exploration.

### 14.4.2.4   Fractioning Derivations into Rules

A process akin to "decomposition" is the formulation of generally applicable rules from more problem-specific derivational sequences. Contrary to Anderson (1983) and others who view knowledge compilation as perhaps the most significant learning strategy, this author considers the decompilation process to be at least as important. Recall that in case-based reasoning one is given compiled but fully annotated audit trails of the reasoning process—the derivational traces. The fractioning task is one of axiomatizing the long, problem-specific traces into individual rules that are applicable to a much wider range of situations, although each rule solves only part of the new problem. The difficult aspect of the task is to bundle the derivationally

related steps into useful rules, insuring that the necessary (and only the necessary) preconditions are associated with each rule. But its utility lies in its ability to permit the learning of more generally applicable knowledge from specific experiences. **The knowledge engineers may yet have their precious rule sets, but they will be rule sets generated automatically after extended experience with derivational traces** rather than rules produced and gradually refined by hand at the cost of much time and frustration.

Let us see how rules would be fractioned off from longer derivational traces. The process described below has been tested only in the route-finding domain thus far, but there it has proven useful.

1. *Find relevant candidates.* The first step in the formulation of rules from derivational traces is to search for candidate subsequences of actions that recur in different, possibly unrelated, derivational traces in the domain. For instance, the sequence

   ```
   LOCATE(bridge),
   PLAN-ROUTE(here,bridge),
   PLAN-ROUTE(bridge,destination)
   ```

   occurred with high frequency and it was proposed as a rule kernel.

2. *Trace justifications.* Why must one plan a route or locate a bridge? The justification for the former comes from the supergoal goal PLAN-ROUTE (here, destination), and the justification for the latter comes from the fact that the presence of a river between "here" and "destination" violates a precondition for land travel.

3. *Formulate rule.* Computable predicates must first be found to establish the justifications. These become the condition side of the rule. Then the justified subsequences of actions, parameterized to the most general justifiable class of actions or objects, becomes the action side of the rule. In the present example, the resultant rule is:

   ```
   IF  GOAL(x) is LOC(x,time-2) = destination
      & LOC(x,time-1) = here
      & BETWEEN (here,destination) = river
      & TRANSPORTATION(x) = land-vehicle
   THEN FIND(bridge,river)
        PLAN-ROUTE(here,bridge)
        PLAN-ROUTE(bridge,destination)
   ```

Thus it can be seen that from multiple planning episodes the following rule can be induced: If one must cross a river, then one should first worry about finding a bridge and plan the route according to this constraint. The rule-fractioning process truly requires all three phases: finding relevant sequences, determining the justifications for these sequences, and actually formulating the rule from this information. Without a derivational trace it would not be possible to fraction rules reliably, because the justifications provided in the trace are needed for searching out the *necessary and useful* conditions for the left-hand side of the rule. Otherwise, one would have to postulate that the recurrent subsequence was either totally independent of context (a terrible assumption—the system would be searching for bridges when there were no rivers to cross) or completely dependent on context, requiring that the entire trace up to that point be included in the condition side, rather than just the causally relevant conditions indicated by the justifications.

## 14.5 CONCLUDING REMARK

Derivational analogy is a powerful reasoning mechanism, one that provides the information necessary for learning to occur in many different forms, from accumulation of cases to formulation of domain-oriented strategies and sets of deductive rules. It has been remarked that heuristics are "compiled hindsight" and as such can prove useful in guiding future behavior. But how can one take advantage of hindsight unless one recalls past experiences, including aspects of one's state of mind that are necessary in order to reconstruct past problem-solving behaviors in new situations? There must be a retrospective process capable of exploiting past experience and a gradual, incremental learning process that abstracts more generally applicable chunks of knowledge from that experience. The derivational analogy process is one concrete method for realizing the former, and the strategy and rule acquisition process are a means of implementing the latter. Together they form a computational theory of incremental expertise acquisition, a theory that is still in the process of being implemented, tested, refined, and reformulated.

## ACKNOWLEDGMENTS

This research was supported in part by the Office of Naval Research (ONR) under grants Nos. N00014-79-C-0661 and N00014-82-C-50767 and in part by a grant from IBM. The author thanks the following colleagues for their enlightening discussions that helped to clarify the ideas presented in this chapter: Jon Doyle, Jill Larkin, Steve Minton, and Allen Newell.

## References

Anderson, J. A., "Acquisition of Proof Skills in Geometry," in *Machine Learning: An Artificial Intelligence Approach*, R. S. Michalski, J. G. Carbonell, and T. M. Mitchell (Eds.), Tioga, Palo Alto, Calif., 1983.

Balzer, R., "Imprecise Program Specification," Technical Report RR-75-36, USC/Information Sciences Institute, 1975.

Barstow, D. R., "Automatic Construction of Algorithms and Data Structures Using a Knowledge Base of Programming Rules," Ph.D. diss., Stanford University, 1977.

Carbonell, J. G., "Counterplanning: A Strategy-Based Model of Adversary Planning in Real-World Situations," *Artificial Intelligence*, Vol. 16, pp. 295–329, 1981a.

——, "A Computational Model of Problem Solving by Analogy," *Proceedings of the Seventh IJCAI*, Vancouver, B.C., pp. 147–52, 1981b.

——, *Subjective Understanding: Computer Models of Belief Systems*, UMI Research Press, Ann Arbor, Mich., 1981c.

——, "Experiential Learning in Analogical Problem Solving," *Proceedings of AAAI-82*, Pittsburgh, Pa., pp. 168–71, 1982.

——, "Learning by Analogy: Formulating and Generalizing Plans from Past Experience," in *Machine Learning: An Artificial Intelligence Approach*, R. S. Michalski, J. G. Carbonell, and T. M. Mitchell (Eds.), Tioga, Palo Alto, Calif., 1983.

——, "The SMOKEY Fire-Diagnosis System," Technical Report, Computer Science Department, Carnegie-Mellon University, 1985.

Carbonell, J. G., Larkin, J. H., and Reif, F., "Towards a General Scientific Reasoning Engine," Technical Report, CIP No. 445, Computer Science Department, Carnegie-Mellon University, 1983.

Clements, J., "Analogical Reasoning Patterns in Expert Problem Solving," *Proceedings of the Fourth Annual Conference of the Cognitive Science Society*, 1982.

Doyle, J., "A Truth Maintenance System," *Artificial Intelligence*, Vol. 12, pp. 231–72, 1979.

——, "Expert Systems Without Computers," *AI Magazine*, Vol. 5, No. 2, pp. 59–63, 1984.

Duda, R. O.; Hart, P. E.; Konolige, K.; and Reboh, R., "A Computer-Based Consultant for Mineral Exploration," Technical Report 6415, SRI, 1979.

Feigenbaum, E. A., Buchanan, B. G., and Lederberg, J., "On Generality and Problem Solving: A Case Study Using the DENDRAL Program," in *Machine Intelligence 6*, D. Michie (Ed.), Edinburgh University Press, Edinburgh, 1971.

Fikes, R. E., and Nilsson, N. J., "STRIPS: A New Approach to the Application of Theorem Proving to Problem Solving," *Artificial Intelligence*, Vol. 2, pp. 189–208, 1971.

Gentner, D., "The Structure of Analogical Models in Science," Technical Report 4451, Bolt Beranek and Newman, 1980.

Hayes-Roth, F., "Using Proofs and Refutations to Learn from Experience," in *Machine Learning: An Artificial Intelligence Approach*, R. S. Michalski, J. G. Carbonell, and T. M. Mitchell (Eds.), Tioga, Palo Alto, Calif., 1983.

Kant, E., *Efficiency in Program Synthesis*, UMI Research Press, Ann Arbor, Mich., 1981.

Kling, R. E., "A Paradigm for Reasoning by Analogy," *Artificial Intelligence*, Vol. 2, pp. 147–78, 1971.

Laird, J. E., and Newell, A., "A Universal Weak Method," *Proceedings of the Eighth IJCAI*, Karlsruhe, W. Ger., pp. 771–73, 1983.

Larkin, J., Reif, F., and Carbonell, J. G., "FERMI: A Flexible Expert Reasoner with Multi-Domain Inference," *Cognitive Science*, Vol. 9, 1985, submitted.

McDermott, D. V., "Planning and Acting," *Cognitive Science*, Vol. 2, No. 2, pp. 71–109, 1967.

McDermott, D. V., and Doyle, J., "Non-Monotonic Logic I," *Artificial Intelligence*, Vol. 13, pp. 41–72, 1980.

McDermott, J., "R1: A Rule-Based Configurer of Computer Systems," Technical Report, Computer Science Department, Carnegie-Mellon University, 1980.

———, "XSEL: A Computer Salesperson's Assistant," in *Machine Intelligence 10*, J. Hayes, D. Michie, and Y-H. Pao (Eds.), Ellis Horwood Ltd., Chichester, U.K., 1982.

Michalski, R. S., "A Theory and Methodology of Learning from Examples," in *Machine Learning: An Artificial Intelligence Approach*, R. S. Michalski, J. G. Carbonell, and T. M. Mitchell (Eds.), Tioga, Palo Alto, Calif., 1983.

Minsky, M., "K-Lines: A Theory of Memory," *Cognitive Science*, Vol. 4, No. 2, pp. 117–33, 1980.

Mitchell, T. M., "Version Spaces: An Approach to Concept Learning," Ph.D. diss., Stanford University, 1978.

Mitchell, T. M., Utgoff, P. E., and Banerji, R. B., "Learning by Experimentation: Acquiring and Refining Problem-Solving Heuristics," in *Machine Learning: An Artificial Intelligence Approach*, R. S. Michalski, J. G. Carbonell, and T. M. Mitchell (Eds.), Tioga, Palo Alto, Calif., 1983.

Newell, A., and Simon, H. A., *Human Problem Solving*, Prentice-Hall, Englewood Cliffs, N. J., 1972.

Nilsson, N. J., *Principles of Artificial Intelligence*, Tioga, Palo Alto, Calif., 1980.

Pólya, G., *How to Solve It*, Princeton University Press, Princeton, N. J., 1945.

Reif, J. H., and Scherlis, W. L., "Deriving Efficient Graph Algorithms," Technical Report, Computer Science Department, Carnegie-Mellon University, 1982.

Sacerdoti, E. D., "Planning in a Hierarchy of Abstraction Spaces," *Artificial Intelligence*, Vol. 5, No. 2, pp. 115–35, 1974.

Schank, R. C., "Language and Memory," *Cognitive Science*, Vol. 4, No. 3, pp. 243–84, 1980.

———, *Dynamic Memory*, Cambridge University Press, Cambridge, 1982.

———, "The Current State of AI: One Man's Opinion," *AI Magazine*, Vol. 4, No. 1, pp. 1–8, 1983.

Shortliffe, E., *Computer Based Medical Consultations: MYCIN*, American Elsevier, New York, 1976.

Swartout, W., and Balzer, R., "On the Inevitable Intertwining of Specification and Implementation," *Communications of the ACM*, Vol. 25, No. 7, pp. 438–40, 1982.

Waterman, D., Hayes-Roth, F., and Lenat, D. (Eds.), *Building Expert Systems*, Addison-Wesley, Reading, Mass., 1983.

Wilensky, R., "Understanding Goal-Based Stories," Ph.D. diss., Yale University, 1978.

———, *Planning and Understanding*, Addison-Wesley, Reading, Mass., 1983.

Winston, P., "Learning by Creating and Justifying Transfer Frames," Technical Report AIM-520, AI Laboratory, MIT, 1978.

———, "Learning and Reasoning by Analogy," *Communications of the ACM*, Vol. 23, No. 12, pp. 689–703, 1979.

# Section 7.2

# Case-Based Reasoning

In case-based reasoning for classification problem solving, the fundamental problem-solving method revolves around the indexing and matching of past cases to a current problem. This contrasts with the traditional expert system approach, wherein past cases are compiled, usually into rules, by inductive or explanation-based generalization from a set of one or more past cases, so that problem solving revolves around reasoning with these rules. Much of the intelligence of a case-based system resides in its indexing of past cases and in its creation of an exemplar case.

The PROTOS system, described in Section 7.2.1, takes an exemplar-based approach to the problem of heuristic classification problem solving. PROTOS can be viewed from many different dimensions: as an interactive elicitation tool, as a learning apprentice, and as a case-based reasoner.

The PROTOS method consists of two steps. First, an initial set of exemplars is automatically created based on analysis of previously classified cases. This step is analogous to the creation of an initial rule base for a MYCIN-like system using an induction program such as RL or AQ15. In the second step, PROTOS engages the expert in a dialogue to explain the cases that were incorrectly solved, so that PROTOS can generate refinements to its knowledge base of exemplars. This is analogous to the interactive dialogue of TEIRESIAS wherein an expert explains the cases that were incorrectly solved, thereby allowing TEIRESIAS to refine and debug the rules in the knowledge base. A major research contribution of PROTOS is its techniques to allow these two steps to occur within a case-based reasoning paradigm.

Case-based and rule-based reasoning are both fundamental to human problem solving. Their strengths are complementary, and cases appear to be particularly well suited to handling exceptions to the rule. ANAPRON, described in Section 7.2.2, provides a nice example of the use of both cases and rules in one system to achieve better performance.

The CHEF system of Hammond, described in Section 7.2.3, views planning as a memory task. Memories of past successes, failures, and modifications are used as prototypes of future successes, failures, and modifications, respectively.

# Concept Learning and Heuristic Classification in Weak-Theory Domains

**Bruce W. Porter**

*Department of Computer Sciences, University of Texas, Austin, TX 78712, USA*

**Ray Bareiss**

*Computer Science Department, Vanderbilt University, Nashville, TN 37235, USA*

**Robert C. Holte**

*Computer Science Department, University of Ottawa, Ottawa, Ontario, Canada K1N 6N5*

ABSTRACT

*This paper describes a successful approach to concept learning for heuristic classification. Almost all current programs for this task create or use explicit, abstract generalizations. These programs are largely ineffective for domains with weak or intractable theories. An exemplar-based approach is suitable for domains with inadequate theories but raises two additional problems: determining similarity and indexing exemplars. Our approach extends the exemplar-based approach with solutions to these problems. An implementation of our approach, called Protos, has been applied to the domain of clinical audiology. After reasonable training, Protos achieved a competence level equaling that of human experts and far surpassing that of other machine learning programs. Additionally, an "ablation study" has identified the aspects of Protos that are primarily responsible for its success.*

## 1. Introduction

This paper describes a successful approach to the task of concept learning for heuristic classification. This task differs from the usual concept learning task in three ways. First, classifications must be explained, not simply reported. Second, a program for this task must accommodate incomplete case descriptions. Third, the program must learn domain-specific knowledge for inferring case features needed for classification. Section 2 summarizes this learning and classification task.

*Artificial Intelligence* **45** (1990) 229–263

0004-3702/90/$03.50 © 1990 — Elsevier Science Publishers B.V. (North-Holland)

This paper originally appeared in the journal, *Artificial Intelligence*, Vol. 45, No. 3, and is reprinted here with permission of the publisher, Elsevier, Amsterdam.

Expert: *NewCase* has the features...

Protos: *NewCase*'s classification appears to be *age-induced cochlear with otitis-media* because of its similarity with *patient163*; some of the features of the cases are identical.

Expert: Wrong diagnosis.

Protos: *NewCase* is missing some of the features of *Patient163* which I thought were unimportant. Are any of *bone(mild)*, *acoustic_ref_u(absent)*,... more important than I thought?

Expert: Yes. *Acoustic_ref_u(absent)* is very important for membership in the category *age-induced cochlear with otitis-media*.

Protos: I'll remember that. Now *NewCase*'s classification appears to be *age and noise-induced cochlear* because of its similarity with *patient054*; most of the features match directly, and the *speech* feature is matched using the knowledge:

IF the category is *age and noise-induced cochlear*
THEN *speech(poor)* is usually equivalent to *speech(very_poor)*.

Expert: The category and explanation are correct.

Protos: There are two weak points in the explanation I'd like to clear up. First, the feature *bone(abnormal)* is important in *Patient054*, but is not present in *NewCase*.

Expert: *Bone(abnormal)* is sometimes equivalent to *bone(unmeasured)*, which is present in *NewCase*.

Protos: OK. The other weak point in that feature *s_neural(severe,1k)* is important in *Patient054*, but is not present in *NewCase*.

Expert: Yes, that is a genuine difference between the two cases.

Protos: Then I'll retain *NewCase* as a separate exemplar of this category. Is there anything else I should know about this case?

Expert: Yes, *acoustic_ref_c(elevated)* is spurious to *age and noise-induced cochlear*;...

Fig. 1. An abridged dialogue between Protos and a domain expert in clinical audiology. The expert presents a new case to Protos. Protos classifies the case by matching it with similar exemplars, and explains each classification by presenting the match. Protos acquires knowledge from the expert to improve the correct match, and retains the case as a new exemplar.

The traditional approach to concept learning and classification relies on generalizations. It requires a strong domain theory both to summarize training cases with concept descriptions and to classify new cases using these descriptions. Section 3 argues that this approach is ineffective for many domains.

An alternative approach relies on exemplars. Concepts are learned by retaining exemplars, and new cases are classified by matching them with exemplars. Our learning and classification program, Protos, uses the exemplar-based approach. Section 4 describes Protos' design and its appropriateness for weak-theory domains.

To evaluate the design, Protos was applied to the task in clinical audiology of identifying a patient's hearing disorder from symptoms, test results, and history. An expert clinician instructed Protos with 200 cases—a level of training comparable to that received by student clinicians. After this training, Protos' classification accuracy was compared with that of clinicians and several learning programs. Protos compared favorable with the best clinician and was significantly better than the other programs. Finally, an "ablation study" [14] identified the aspects of Protos that are primarily responsible for its success. Section 5 describes the evaluation.

Section 6 summarizes the research. We conclude that exemplar-based learning and classification is appropriate and effective for domains lacking a strong domain theory. Our current research focuses on shortcomings of Protos that became evident in these studies.

## 2. The Task: Concept Learning for Classification and Explanation

Our research addresses the task of improving competence at classification and explanation, starting at a level of utter incompetence and aiming for a level of expert competence. Improvement results from learning concepts and acquiring knowledge from cases which are classified and explained by a human expert. This section specifies this task in detail by defining classification, explanation, and knowledge acquisition, and by giving measures of competence for each. Figure 1 illustrates this task with a modestly abridged version of an actual dialogue between Protos and a domain expert (Section 4.4 is a detailed description of this scenario).

### 2.1. Classification

**Classification**[1] is assigning a given input, called a **case**, to one of the categories in a pre-enumerated list. Competence at classification is defined in terms of accuracy and efficiency.

A case is described by a collection of features. However, case descriptions differ in two significant ways from the feature-vector descriptions common in machine learning. First, a case description may be incomplete, in the sense that it does not include some of the features present in other case descriptions. Second, the features with which cases are described may not directly indicate

[1] Terms appear in boldface when they are defined.

category membership. Instead, inference using domain-specific knowledge may be necessary to determine category membership from a case description. For example, suppose a case is a configuration of pieces on a chessboard, described in terms of pieces and their positions, and the categories are *win-for-white-in-9-ply* and *no-win-for-white-in-9-ply*. There is no known way to determine membership in these categories directly from a case description, but it can be determined using knowledge-based inference, such as an exhaustive 9-ply look-ahead based on the knowledge of the rules of chess.

The "heuristic classification method" described by Clancey [11] is tailored to domains in which cases are described with features that do not directly indicate category membership. It explicitly includes "the important twist of relating concepts in different classification hierarchies by nonhierarchical, uncertain inferences" [11, p. 290]. Protos' classification method, although it differs from Clancey's, is also appropriate for domains requiring this twist (see Section 3).

## 2.2. Explanation

In this paper, classification is combined with explanation: an input case must be classified and the classification must be explained. **Explanation**, in the broadest sense, includes a variety of inference methods for reasoning, learning, and communicating [59]. However, we have adopted a simplified notion of explanation in order to concentrate on other aspects of the task. The main simplifying assumptions, similar to those made in first-generation expert systems, are as follows.

First, explanations are used for only two purposes: to justify classifying a case in a particular way and to establish the degree of similarity of two cases. Explanations are not used to teach domain knowledge or to elaborate previous explanations (see [10, 38] for recent research on these tasks).

Second, explanations are all of the same form: domain-specific terms (e.g., features, feature-values, categories) are related to one another in domain-independent ways (e.g., "*bone(abnormal)* is sometimes equivalent to *bone(un-measured)*," in Fig. 1).

Third, explaining the classification of a case only requires mentioning the evidence supporting the classification. It is not necessary to mention evidence against the classification or evidence pertaining to other possible classifications. For example, to explain how a particular conclusion was reached, MYCIN [53] lists only the satisfied rules leading to the conclusion; it does not list the rules leading, with less confidence, to different conclusions.

Finally, an explanation can be constructed by a simple transformation of the inferential path that leads to a classification. The transformation may involve suppressing certain details and rephrasing or reorganizing the remaining details, but it does not involve complex processes such as natural language generation or adaptation to a model of the person to whom explanations are targeted.

In our study, competence at explanation is defined in terms of the quality of the explanation, as assessed by a human expert.

## 2.3. Knowledge acquisition

**Knowledge acquisition** is the elicitation of knowledge from a human expert and the incorporation of this knowledge into an existing body of knowledge. In the present task, knowledge is elicited in the form of **training cases** which are classified and explained by the expert.

Knowledge acquisition is mixed initiative. The program may request particular knowledge from the expert, or the expert may take the initiative and volunteer knowledge. The knowledge provided by the program are classified and explained by the expert. New vocabulary (i.e., categories and features) can be introduced by the expert at any time.

Competence at knowledge acquisition is defined in terms of two factors. The first is the competence at classification and explanation attained after a realistic amount of training. The second factor is the degree to which the knowledge acquisition program gains **autonomy** as the knowledge base develops. Autonomy may be measured by the number and nature of program-issued requests for knowledge. For example, a program exhibits low autonomy if it asks questions of the expert that it could answer by consulting the existing knowledge base. A program's ability to gain autonomy is important because greater autonomy is required in the later stages of knowledge base development than in the early stages. Most existing concept learning and knowledge acquisition programs do not gain autonomy, and so are appropriate for only a single stage of a knowledge base's development [4]. For example, ETS [7] and ROGET [6] create a knowledge base by eliciting the basic terminology and conceptual structure of a domain. However, they are inappropriate for later stages of development such as refinement and reformulation. A full discussion of this issue and a survey of existing programs, including Protos, is given in [5].

## 3. Weaknesses of Generalization-Based Methods for Learning and Classification

Almost all programs that learn to classify are generalization-based, in the sense that they create or use explicit, abstract generalizations. Generalization-based programs are either **simple** or **theory-based**, depending on whether the language with which cases are described (called the **case language**) and the language with which generalizations are expressed (called the **generalization language**) are closely related or entirely different. Examples of simple programs are ID3 [44], CN2 [13], and connectionist programs (e.g., [49]). Examples of theory-based programs are explanation-based programs (e.g., [16, 36]) and similarity-based programs that use background knowledge (e.g., [21, 26,

35, 37]). Both types of generalization-based programs have been applied successfully.

A case language usually consists of intrinsic, readily perceivable features. Such features are called **superficial**. An intrinsic feature of a case is one that is defined without reference to the case's context, e.g., the role of the case in a particular task, or the situation in which the case occurs. For example, with intrinsic features, a desk would be described as an arrangement of structural parts (e.g., drawers, legs, top) with physical properties (weight, size, strength). With nonintrinsic features it might be described as an arrangement of functional parts (e.g., work surface, storage areas) with use-related properties (e.g., ample, ergonomic, easy to clean). Features that are not superficial are called **abstract**.

Simple programs for learning and classification are applicable when superficial features suffice to define the generalizations of interest. For example, in a simulated blocks world, the superficial features *shape, size, color*, and *relative position* suffice to define generalizations such as *arch, stack*, and *large, red block*.

In most domains, superficial features do not suffice to define generalizations. Generalizations such as *cup* [61] and *hammer* [15] are defined in terms of function, not form. Categories such as *infected by pseudomonas* [53] and *seedless grape* [2] are generalizations defined in terms that are not readily perceivable in the context of classification.

When abstract features are required to define generalizations, a **gap** exists between the case language and the generalization language. This gap may be bridged in two ways. The first is to preprocess the case descriptions to add the required abstract features. It is usually necessary for human experts to do the preprocessing, because evaluating the abstract terms (e.g., "abnormal") requires expert judgement. In this way, simple programs can be used in domains in which the relationship between abstract and superficial features is not well understood. The second way to bridge the language gap is to construct a **domain theory** describing the relationships between terms in the two languages and use theory-based programs. Note that theory-based programs provide no assistance in the difficult task of constructing a domain theory.

Theory-based programs are applicable only if the domain theory is both tractable and strong. A **tractable** domain theory is one in which the definitions of all terms can be computed efficiently from superficial features. The **strength** of a domain theory depends on the certainty associated with the relationships between terms. The strongest theories, called **perfect**, consist entirely of relationships of perfect certainty, such as standard logical and taxonomic relationships. The weakest theories consist of correlational relationships, such as "X and Y often co-occur."

Very few domains have the tractable, perfect domain theories required by current theory-based programs. Indeed, few domains have perfect domain theories, tractable or otherwise. Legal reasoning, for example, almost always involves open-textured concepts, i.e., concepts having only a weak domain theory [22, 23]. The fact that many fields of diagnostic expertise lack a perfect domain theory is indicated by the widespread use of certainty factors in expert systems. When a perfect domain theory does exist, it is often **intractable**. For example, the rules of chess constitute a perfect, but **intractable**, theory of "winning position." Even for chess endgames involving very few pieces and analyzed extensively in textbooks, the rules constitute an intractable theory, and the existing tractable theories are far from perfect [52].

The developers of theory-based programs have acknowledged this severe limitation [36], and have recently begun trying to adapt their programs to work with weak theories. We anticipate that generalization-based programs will not adapt well to weak theories.

With a weak theory, the most reliable and efficiently found chains of inference are those that are strong and involve individual steps of low uncertainty. Chains of inference bridging the language gap, which are necessary whenever a generalization is created or used, are usually long and involve steps of high uncertainty. Consequently, generalization-based programs, when used with a weak theory, can be expected to be unreliable and inefficient.

By contrast, chains of inference consisting entirely of direct matches between features are short and reliable. For example, a case can be classified with certainty if it is identical to a training case. The exemplar approach to learning and classification, described in the next section, attempts to achieve reliability and efficiency by maximizing the use of direct match. Training cases are recorded, and a case is classified by comparing it, feature by feature, with the training cases. Domain theory is used only for those features that have no direct match. The number of such features, and therefore the use of domain theory, can be minimized by retaining all training cases. However, this is only necessary when the domain theory is very weak. With a strong domain theory, very few training cases need to be retained to achieve reliable, efficient inference.

In summary, generalization-based methods are not likely to perform as well as exemplar-based methods in domains with weak theories. Furthermore, domains with weak theories are far more common, in practical applications, than domains with strong, tractable theories. Other weaknesses of generalization-based methods are given in [2, 12, 51, 55, 62].

## 4. Protos: The Exemplar-Based Alternative

This section describes the design of Protos, an exemplar-based program for concept learning and classification. Simple exemplar-based programs, although supported by psychological studies, suffer from two fundamental problems: determining similarity and indexing exemplars. Protos' design includes solutions to these two problems. The design principles are introduced with simple, familiar examples and demonstrated with a large-scale application of Protos to clinical audiology. Complete details of Protos are given in [3], and a COMMON LISP reconstruction, available for distribution, is documented in [19].

### 4.1. Simple exemplar-based concept learning and classification

Figure 2 describes the exemplar-based approach to concept learning and classification and identifies the hard problems. Concepts are represented extensionally with a collection of **exemplars** described with features in the case language. For example, the concept *chair* is represented in Fig. 3 by two exemplars, *chair1*, a metal chair with a pedestal and wheels, and *chair2*, a wooden chair with four legs. Classifying a new case involves searching for an exemplar that strongly matches the case. The simplest method is an exhaustive search for a direct match. Explaining the classification involves showing the line of reasoning used during match. The simplest explanation is a list of the common features of the case and the exemplar. Learning from a case involves adjusting the categories so that the case will be properly classified and explained. The simplest adjustment adds the case to the correct category as a new exemplar and ensures that it will be found, should this case be classified again.

In some theories of exemplar-based categories, including Protos' theory, abstract features may be defined by exemplars, just as categories are. De-termining whether such a feature is present or absent in a given case involves matching the case with the exemplars of the feature.

Psychological experiments, devised to distinguish between the generalization-based approach and the exemplar-based approach, support the exemplar-based approach. As in machine learning, early psychological research assumed that generalization was automatic; researchers focused on *what* is abstracted and *how* generalization is performed, rather than *whether* cases are generalized [32]. Recent research indicates that people resist generalization and retain cases. For example, Medin [32] and Brooks [9] found that people classify previously seen cases by direct matching. Tversky and Kahneman [57] found that people estimate the frequency of a class or the probability of an event by their ability to recall instances of the class or event. Holyoak and Glass [24] found that people reject false statements by recalling category exemplars for which the statement is untrue. For a range of cognitive tasks, these studies emphasize retaining, recalling, and matching category exemplars, rather than reasoning with category-wide abstractions. To account for this data, psychological theories propose models involving exemplar-based concept learning and classification [33, 34, 46, 50, 55].

The simple exemplar-based method uses no domain theory. However, domain theory is indispensable for solving the hard problems indicated in Fig. 2. For example, determining the strength of the match between an exemplar and a case requires knowing the basis for category membership. Murphy and Medin [39] argue that domain theory provides this basis and adds coherence to a collection of otherwise dissimilar exemplars. The following sections describe how Protos uses domain theory to determine the similarity of a case and an exemplar ard to index exemplars.

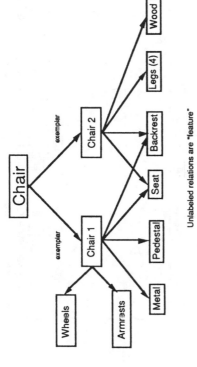

Fig. 3. A portion of the exemplar-based category *chair*.

**Given:**
a set of exemplar-based categories $C = \{c_1, c_2, \ldots, c_n\}$ and a case (*NewCase*) to classify.

REPEAT
**Classify:**
 [Find] an exemplar of $c_j \in C$ that [Strongly Matches] *NewCase* and classify *NewCase* as $c_j$.
 [Explain] the classification.

**Learn:**
If the expert disagrees with the classification or explanation then acquire classification and explanation knowledge and [adjust] $C$ so that *NewCase* is correctly classified and explained.
UNTIL the expert approves the classification and explanation.

Fig. 2. Exemplar-based learning and classification algorithm. The hard problems of the exemplar-based approach are boxed.

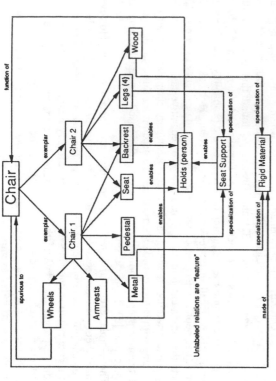
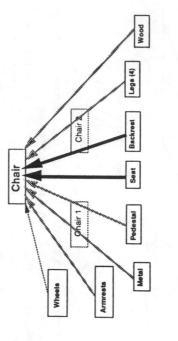
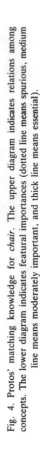

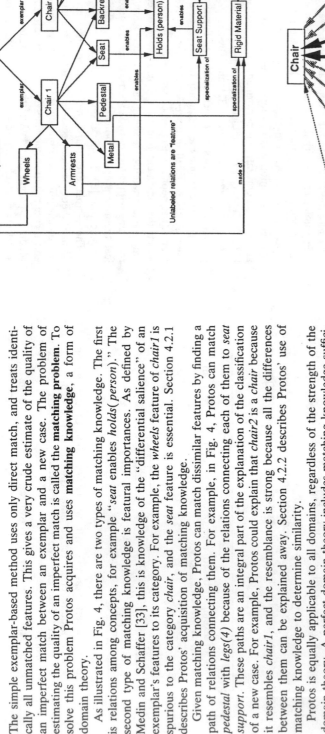

Fig. 4. Protos' matching knowledge for *chair*. The upper diagram indicates relations among concepts. The lower diagram indicates featural importances (dotted line means spurious, medium line means moderately important, and thick line means essential).

### 4.2. Determining the similarity of a case and an exemplar

The simple exemplar-based method uses only direct match, and treats identically all unmatched features. This gives a very crude estimate of the quality of an imperfect match between an exemplar and a new case. The problem of estimating the quality of an imperfect match is called the **matching problem**. To solve this problem Protos acquires and uses **matching knowledge**, a form of domain theory.

As illustrated in Fig. 4, there are two types of matching knowledge. The first is relations among concepts, for example "*seat* enables *holds*(*person*)." The second type of matching knowledge is featural importances. As defined by Medin and Schaffer [33], this is knowledge of the "differential salience" of an exemplar's features to its category. For example, the *wheels* feature of *chair1* is spurious to the category *chair*, and the *seat* feature is essential. Section 4.2.1 describes Protos' acquisition of matching knowledge.

Given matching knowledge, Protos can match dissimilar features by finding a path of relations connecting them. For example, in Fig. 4, Protos can match *pedestal* with *legs*(4) because of the relations connecting each of them to *seat support*. These paths are an integral part of the explanation of the classification of a new case. For example, Protos could explain that *chair2* is a *chair* because it resembles *chair1*, and the resemblance is strong because all the differences between them can be explained away. Section 4.2.2 describes Protos' use of matching knowledge to determine similarity.

Protos is equally applicable to all domains, regardless of the strength of the domain theory. A perfect domain theory includes matching knowledge sufficient to match all the members of a category with each other. When this is available, the category can be represented with a single exemplar, called a prototype [31, 55]. When a perfect theory is not available, the category can still be represented, fairly accurately, by using several exemplars. For example, the category *strike* in baseball can be represented with two exemplars, one in which the batter swings and fails to hit the ball into fair play, and another in which the ball crosses the plate through the strike zone. With a very weak domain theory, an accurate representation of a category may require many exemplars.

The **polymorphy** of a category is the amount of unexplained variability among its members [47]. In domains with a strong theory, the polymorphy of most categories will be low. In domains with a weak theory, the polymorphy of categories can vary considerably (e.g., see Fig. 15 in Section 5.1). Because of this, Protos has been designed to cope with categories of any degree of polymorphy. Protos retains a case as an exemplar only if the case differs from existing exemplars in significant ways that cannot be explained using existing matching knowledge. If a case does match an exemplar strongly, it is not retained. Thus, the number of exemplars that Protos retains for a category is a direct indication of the category's polymorphy.

### 4.2.1. Acquiring matching knowledge from explained cases

Protos acquires matching knowledge from explained cases. When Protos fails on a new case, the expert provides the classification and explanation. Protos installs this information in its network of matching knowledge. For example, part of the knowledge of chairs (Fig. 4) was learned when the expert classified *chair1* and explained:

*pedestal* is a specialization of *seat support* which enables *holds(person)* which is the function of *chair*.

Protos requires **feature-to-category explanations** relating each case feature to the case's classification. To explain the relationship, the expert typically introduces new concepts and relations. For example, the previous explanation introduces the category *seat support*, the function *holds(person)*, and three relations. Protos adds these concepts and relations to its current network of matching knowledge.

Protos and the expert work together to explain the relationship between case features and categories. Often the expert provides **feature-to-feature explanations** and Protos completes the explanation of the classification. For example, after the expert explains the relationship between *pedestal* and *chair*, Protos explains the relevance of *legs(4)* for *chair2* given only that "*legs(4)* is a specialization of *seat support*."

Explanations are expressed in a predefined language of relations (see Fig. 5). The relations fall into three certainty classes:

(1) Definitional relations denote invariant facts (e.g., "*adolescent* definitionally entails *minor*").
(2) Causal/functional relations denote known mechanisms (e.g., "*air pollution causes acid rain*").
(3) Correlational relations denote experimental knowledge (e.g., "*sharp teeth suggest carnivorous*").

Each relation can be strengthened or weakened with qualifiers, such as *always, usually, sometimes,* or *occasionally.*

Some explanations, called **conditional**, are restricted to members of a particular category, cases with particular features, or matches with particular exemplars. For example,

IF the category is *apples*
THEN *color(red)* is equivalent to *color(green)*

explains that the colors red and green are equivalent for the purposes of classifying apples. Conditional explanations are essential for concepts defined functionally such as *hammer*. They permit stating that a claw is spurious for a hammer *qua* nail-inserter but is essential for a hammer *qua* nail-extractor.

Protos heuristically estimates the importance of a feature to a category by analyzing a feature-to-category explanation. For example, from the explanations relating *chair1*'s features to the category *chair*, Protos estimates that *seat* is an essent al feature of a *chair*, that *pedestal* is a moderately important feature of a *chair*, and that *wheels* is a spurious feature of *chair1* (see Fig. 4). Internally, featural importances are represented as numbers between 0 (spurious) and 1 (essential). Protos' estimates of featural importances may be revised by the expert if they result in a misclassification or an unacceptable explanation.

The lower part of Fig. 6 summarizes Protos' algorithm for learning matching knowledge. As this figure indicates, the matching knowledge that is acquired depends on Protos' assessment of the similarity of a case and an exemplar, and whether the expert agrees. Protos' algorithm for assessing similarity is discussed next.

### 4.2.2. Using matching knowledge to determine similarity

Protos classifies a new case by explaining its similarity to an exemplar. This method, summarized in the upper part of Fig. 6, is called **knowledge-based**

**Definitional:**
definitionally entails
is equivalent to
requires
if and only if
has generalization
part of
is mutually exclusive with
**Causal/functional:**
causes
has function
enables
**Correlational:**
co-occurs with
is consistent with
implies
suggests
spurious to

Fig. 5. Relations in Protos' explanation language. The relations are in equivalence classes with respect to certainty. Each relation has an inverse which is not shown (e.g. the inverse of *has generalization* is *has specialization*.)

[1, 42, 58], exemplars are specific and numerous. Usually, case features and exemplar features match directly, and the range of category exemplars provides models for both typical and atypical cases.

Knowledge-based matching is a uniform-cost, heuristic search. The search begins from each unmatched exemplar feature and chains through the network of matching knowledge until reaching either a case feature or the depth bound (step 6.2 in Fig. 6). Each step of the search extends the current path with a relation. A path connecting an exemplar feature with a case feature is an explanation of how the features are "equivalent," in the sense that the features suggest the same classification.

Knowledge-based matching uses 38 domain-independent heuristics to evaluate the quality of a path [4, Appendix C]. The purpose of the heuristics is to find the strongest explanation and to prune weak explanations. When selecting from a set of relations to extend a path, the heuristics evaluate the potential contribution of each relation to the developing explanation. This is a function both of:

– The individual relation and its qualifiers. For example, the heuristics penalize the inclusion of weak correlational relations such as "sometimes implies" in a causal explanation.
– The overall explanation constructed thus far. For example, one heuristic prevents ascribing the function of an assembly to a particular part. This heuristic would prune an explanation that begins "*steering wheel* is part of *car* which has function *transportation* . . . ."

The depth bound for the search relating an exemplar feature and a case feature is a function of the importance of the exemplar feature to the exemplar's category. If the feature is necessary, Protos will search extensively, allowing weak explanations to be found. If the feature is moderately important, the search either will find a strong explanation or fail. If the feature is spurious, Protos will not search at all.

In calculating the overall match strength between a case and an exemplar (step 6.3) each feature of the exemplar contributes a factor between 0 and 1. The contribution of an unmatched feature with importance $i$ is $1 - i$ (for example, 0 for an essential feature). The contribution of a matched feature is the strength of the explanation relating the feature to a case feature (1 for a direct match; a fraction for an explained match). The overall match strength is the product of these factors for all of the exemplar's features (cf., the similarity function of Medin and Schaffer's context model [33]). An important property of this definition of match strength is that matching numerous unimportant features does not compensate for failing to match an important one.

Using matching knowledge, the similarity of related cases is more accurately estimated. However, the matching knowledge in a weak domain theory is not

---

GIVEN: a case (*NewCase*) to classify, and an exemplar (*Exemplar*).
To determine the similarity of *NewCase* and *Exemplar*:

6.1 Assign a high match strength to each feature of *Exemplar* that directly matches a feature of *NewCase*.
6.2 For each feature of *Exemplar* that is not directly matched, search matching knowledge for the best explanation relating it to a feature of *NewCase*. Assign a match strength corresponding to the quality of the explanation.
6.3 Compute the overall similarity of *Exemplar* and *NewCase* using the match strength of each matched exemplar feature and the importance of each unmatched exemplar features.

If the match between *NewCase* and *Exemplar* is sufficiently strong, *Exemplar's* category is used to classify *NewCase*, and the match between *Exemplar* and *NewCase* is used to explain this classification. Indexing knowledge is acquired by discussing this classification and explanation with the expert, as follows.

6.4 IF the expert rejects the classification or explanation
    THEN Request new matching knowledge from the expert.
6.5 ELSE (the expert accepts the classification and explanation)
    IF some features of *Exemplar* are unmatched
6.6 THEN Request feature-to-feature explanations from the expert.
    IF the match is very strong
6.7 THEN Discard *NewCase*.
6.8 ELSE Retain *NewCase* as an exemplar.
6.9     Construct feature-to-category explanations.
6.10    Estimate featural importances.

Fig. 6. The Protos algorithms for using and learning matching knowledge. Steps 6.1–6.3 describe how Protos uses matching knowledge to determine the similarity of a case and an exemplar. Steps 6.4–6.10 describe how Protos acquires matching knowledge.

**matching**. It uses matching knowledge and a collection of heuristics to evaluate explanations.

During knowledge-based matching of an exemplar and a case, the exemplar is a model for interpreting the case. It determines which features are important for a successful match. If an important feature is absent from the case description, Protos attempts to infer it from the case features using matching knowledge. Unlike the models used by other expectation-driven classifiers

perfect, and these imperfections can cause the similarity of unrelated cases to be overestimated. For example:

- Featural importances are generally ball park approximations of a quantity whose exact value is unknown. Small numerical differences in featural importance values, which ought to be negligible, can accumulate during match-strength calculation and distort the similarity estimate.
- Expert-supplied explanations of relations between concepts can be overly general, and inadvertently "explain away" the significant differences between unrelated cases (cf. "promiscuous theories" in [17]).

By causing the similarity of unrelated cases to be overestimated while causing the similarity of related cases to be accurately estimated, matching knowledge can result in the misclassification of cases that would be correctly classified using a simple feature-counting measure of similarity. In Protos, this problem is approached in two ways. First, matching knowledge is revised whenever it leads to a misclassification (step 6.4). Secondly, a new case is not matched against every exemplar. Protos' method for selecting the exemplars with which to match a new case is discussed next.

### 4.3. Indexing the domain theory

In Protos, a new case is matched only with those exemplars most likely to be correct. By doing this, Protos overcomes two serious problems that arise when a new case is matched with all known exemplars:

- misclassifications due to the inappropriate use of matching knowledge, as described above;
- the inefficiency of applying the computationally expensive process of knowledge-based matching to many exemplars.

To select and order the exemplars to match with a given case, Protos uses three types of **indexing knowledge**: remindings, prototypicality, and exemplar differences. This section describes this knowledge, how it is used (see the upper part of Fig. 7) and how it is learned (see the lower part of Fig. 7).

The first type of indexing knowledge, **remindings**, indexes categories and exemplars by a new case's features (cf., [27, 50] and "cue validity" in [45]). Protos uses remindings as cues to the case's classification. A reminding from a feature to a category, such as *backrest* indexing *chair* (Fig. 8), suggests that the feature to a category is the most general classification for cases described with the feature. A reminding from a feature to an exemplar, such as *pedestal* indexing *chair1* (Fig. 8), suggests that the exemplar will match cases described with the feature (cf., "idiosyncratic information" in [32]). Each reminding has an associated strength, which is used to order the list of candidate exemplars.

When searching for an exemplar that matches a new case, Protos first collects remindings to categories (step 7.1 in Fig. 7). Related categories are

GIVEN: a case (*NewCase*) to classify.

To find an exemplar matching *NewCase*:

7.1 Collect [remindings] from *NewCase*'s features to categories.
7.2 Combine remindings to related categories.
7.3 Retain the N categories with the strongest remindings.
7.4 Select, in order of [prototypicality], several exemplars of each category.
7.5 Collect [remindings] from *NewCase*'s features to exemplars, and add these to the list of exemplars. Order this list by reminding strength.
    REPEAT (consider the exemplars in decreasing order)
7.6    Let *Exemplar1* be the exemplar with the next highest reminding strength.
7.7    Determine the similarity of *NewCase* and *Exemplar1*.
    UNTIL a sufficiently strong match is found.
7.8 Use [exemplar differences] from *Exemplar1* to locate a better match (*Exemplar2*).

*Exemplar2*'s category is used to classify *NewCase* and the match between *Exemplar2* and *NewCase* is used to explain this classification. Indexing knowledge is acquired by discussing this classification and explanation with the expert, as follows.

IF the expert rejects the classification or explanation
7.9    THEN Reassess the [remindings] from *NewCase*'s features.
    ELSE (the expert accepts the classification and explanation)
7.10    Increase [prototypicality] of *Exemplar2*.
    IF *NewCase* is retained as an exemplar
7.11    THEN Learn [remindings] for *NewCase*.
    IF *NewCase* was initially classified or explained incorrectly
7.12    THEN Record [exemplar differences].

Figure 7. The Protos algorithms for using and learning indexing knowledge. Steps 7.1–7.8 describe how Protos uses indexing knowledge to find an exemplar matching a given case. Steps 7.9–7.12 describe how Protos acquires indexing knowledge. Boxes highlight the different types of indexing knowledge. The process of matching a case with an exemplar (step 7.7) is described in Fig. 6.

combined by summing the strengths of duplicate remindings and by inheriting remindings from general categories to subcategories (step 7.2). Only the N strongest combined remindings are returned (step 7.3).[2] Protos then selects

[2] In the current implementation, N = 5.

classifications. Censors are derived from *mutual exclusion* relations used in explanations.

Remindings are not foolproof. The explanation from which a reminding is derived might change. For example, a reminding from a feature *f* to a category *C* might be derived from the explanation that "*f* causes *C*." Later, the domain expert might change the explanation to "*f* sometimes causes *C*," or "*f* causes $C_2$ which has specialization *C*." Protos does not check remindings when matching knowledge is altered. Rather, a reminding is reassessed only when it suggests an incorrect classification (step 7.9). Protos uses the current matching knowledge to explain the relationship between the classification and the case feature that evokes the reminding. From this explanation Protos derives a replacement for the faulty reminding.

The second type of indexing knowledge, **prototypicality**, orders the exemplars within a category according to their record of success in previous classifications. When a new case reminds Protos of a category, the exemplars of that category are matched with the case in order of decreasing prototypicality (step 7.4). For example, given a case with remindings to *chair* but no remindings to particular exemplars, Protos attempts to match the case with *chair1* before *chair2* (Fig. 8). Prototypicality is a heuristic estimate of the psychological notion of "family resemblance" [47], which is the degree to which an exemplar is similar to other category members. Prototypicality is incrementally learned: if a match between a case and an exemplar is accepted by the expert then the exemplar's prototypicality is increased by an amount proportional to the strength of the match (step 7.10).

The third type of indexing knowledge, **exemplar differences**, indexes exemplars by the features that distinguish them from exemplars with similar descriptions (cf., "indexing of failures" in [28, 29, 54]). After finding an exemplar that matches a new case, Protos hillclimbs to the best matching exemplar (step 7.8). For example, if the case partially matches *chair2*, but has the unmatched feature *armrests*, *chair1* is suggested by the exemplar difference relating *chair1* to *chair2* (Fig. 8).

Protos learns an exemplar difference by matching a new case to a "near miss" [60] before matching the case to an exemplar preferred by the expert (step 7.12). The near miss and the preferred exemplar may be members of the same category or different categories. Protos relates them by their differences to improve classification accuracy on subsequent cases. Relating only those pairs of exemplars that were actually confused during classification avoids the problem of recording a plethora of exemplar differences.

**4.4. An example of Protos in clinical audiology**

The Protos classification and learning algorithm (Fig. 9) combines the algorithms for matching and selecting exemplars. This section applies the

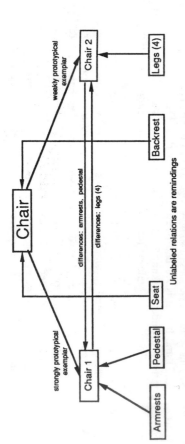

Fig. 8. The indexing knowledge for *chair*. In Protos, this knowledge overlays the network of matching knowledge (Fig. 4).

several of the most prototypical exemplars (defined below) to represent each category (step 7.4). Finally, Protos collects remindings from case features to particular exemplars (step 7.5). The result is an ordered list of exemplars to try matching with the new case.

Protos learns a reminding by compiling an expert-supplied explanation of a case feature (step 7.11). For example, Protos derives a reminding from *seat* to *chair* (Fig. 8) from the explanation:

*seat* enables *holds*(*person*) which is the function of *chair*.

Protos heuristically analyzes each explanation to determine the category or exemplar to which the reminding should refer and the strength of the reminding. As in the previous example, a reminding often refers to the last term in an explanation. However, some remindings are derived from a portion of the explanation. For example, one heuristic applies to explanations of the form:

$\langle$case feature$\rangle \ldots category_1$ has specialization $category_2 \ldots$

and derives a reminding from $\langle$case feature$\rangle$ to $category_1$, the most general category named. The strength of a reminding is a function of the relations and qualifiers used in the explanation. For example, from the explanation:

*fur* is usually required by *mammal* which has specialization *cat*.

Protos derives a moderate strength reminding from *fur* to *mammal*.

Some remindings, called **censors**, are negative associations between case features and categories or exemplars. A censor from a feature to a category suggests that cases described with the feature should not be classified in the category. Protos uses censors to remove entries from the set of candidate

GIVEN: a case (*NewCase*) to classify.

1   Collect and combine remindings from *NewCase*'s features. Retain only the *N* strongest combined remindings.

2   Create a list of exemplars ordered by reminding strength.

REPEAT

  REPEAT (consider the exemplars in decreasing order)

3     Let *Exemplar1* be the exemplar with the next highest reminding strength.

4     Determine the similarity of *NewCase* and *Exemplar1*.

  UNTIL a sufficiently strong match is found.

5   Use exemplar differences from *Exemplar1* to locate a better match (*Exemplar2*).

6   Use *Exemplar2*'s category to classify *NewCase* and use the match between *Exemplar2* and *NewCase* to explain this classification. Discuss this classification and explanation with the expert:

  IF the expert rejects the classification or explanation

  THEN Reassess the remindings from *NewCase*'s features.

7

8     Request new matching knowledge from the expert.

9   ELSE (the expert approves the classification and explanation)

10     Increase prototypicality of *Exemplar2*.

    IF some features of *Exemplar2* are unmatched

11     THEN Request feature-to-feature explanations from the expert.

    IF the match is very strong

12     THEN Discard *NewCase*.

13     ELSE Retain *NewCase* as an exemplar.

14     Construct feature-to-category explanations.

15     Estimate featural importances.

16     Learn remindings for *NewCase*.

17     IF *NewCase* was initially classified or explained incorrectly

    THEN Record exemplar differences.

UNTIL the expert approves the classification and explanation.

Fig. 9. The Protos classification and learning algorithm, combining the algorithms in Fig. 6 and Fig. 7.

| | |
|---|---|
| age_gt_60 | history(noise) |
| air(mild) | s_neural(profound,2k) |
| bone(unmeasured) | acoustic_ref_u(elevated) |
| speech(poor) | acoustic_ref_c(elevated) |
| static(normal) | o_acoustic_ref_u(normal) |
| tymp(a) | o_acoustic_ref_c(elevated) |

Fig. 10. The features of *NewCase*.

action—e.g., Figs. 10–13 are screen-dumps of actual Protos output—and Protos' internal processing.

After training Protos with 175 cases, the expert asks Protos to classify *NewCase*, which has the features (symptoms and test results) listed in Fig. 10. There are remindings from some of these features to diagnostic categories, but no remindings to individual exemplars (Fig. 11). Protos combines these remindings to produce an ordered list of possible classifications for *NewCase* (Fig. 9, step 1). Duplicate remindings (such as the four remindings to *cochlear*) are summed, and remindings to general categories are inherited by subcategories. As a result, remindings to the general categories *cochlear*, *age-induced cochlear*, and *otitis-media* are inherited by their shared subcategory *age-induced cochlear with otitis-media*.

The strongest combined reminding is to the category *age-induced cochlear with otitis-media*. Protos attempts to confirm this classification (steps 3 and 4)

NewCase Features

- age_gt_60
- air(mild)
- history(noise)
- speech(poor)
- tymp(a)
- acoustic_ref_c(elevated)
- acoustic_ref_u(elevated)
- o_acoustic_ref_c(elevated)

Category Remindings

- age-induced cochlear with otitis-media
- age and noise-induced cochlear
- noise-induced cochlear
- age-induced cochlear
- normal_ear
- acoustic_neuroma
- cochlear
- mixed
- otitis_media
- possible_menieres
- bells_palsy

Fig. 11. Remindings from *NewCase*'s features to diagnostic categories.

algorithm to a typical case that Protos processed in the clinical audiology domain. The dialogue in Fig. 1 provides an outline of this section. There, the interaction between Protos and the expert on this case is given in an abridged form. This section presents and discusses the unabridged form of the inter-

by explaining the similarity of *NewCase* and a prototypical exemplar, *Patient163* (Fig. 12). The match is strong, and there is no exemplar-difference knowledge that indexes a better match (step 5). The match is presented to the expert, who rejects it as incorrect (step 6).

In response to the expert's rejection, Protos reassesses the indexing and matching knowledge that led to the misclassification. First, Protos verifies the remindings by searching the domain theory for feature-to-category explanations (step 7). Then, Protos discusses with the expert the matching knowledge that overestimated the similarity of *NewCase* and *Patient163* (step 8). In the current match, there are no feature-to-feature explanations to be discussed, because there are only direct matches. There are some unmatched features, and Protos asks the expert to reconsider their importances. The expert tells Protos that one of these features, *acoustic_ref_u(absent)*, is actually very important for category membership. Consequently, Protos' assessment of the similarity of the two cases decreases.

Protos attempts to classify *NewCase* using its second strongest reminding, which is to the category *age and noise-induced cochlear*. Protos selects a prototypical exemplar and explains its similarity to *NewCase* (steps 3 and 4). The result is shown in Fig. 13. Most of the features match directly, and the *speech* feature is matched using the knowledge:

> IF the category is *age and noise-induced cochlear*
> THEN *speech(poor)* is usually equivalent to *speech(very_poor)*.

| NewCase | Exemplar of Age-Induced Cochlear with Otitis Media: Patient163 |
|---|---|
| air(mild) | air(mild) |
| bone(unmeasured) | bone(mild) |
| tymp(a) | tymp(c) |
| speech(poor) | speech(poor) |
| static(normal) | static(normal) |
| age_gt_60 | |
| s_neural(profound,2k) | s_neural(moderate,3k) |
| history(noise) | |
| acoustic_ref_u(elevated) | acoustic_ref_u(absent) |
| acoustic_ref_c(elevated) | acoustic_ref_c(elevated) |
| o_acoustic_ref_u(normal) | o_acoustic_ref_u(elevated) |
| o_acoustic_ref_c(elevated) | o_acoustic_ref_c(absent) |

Fig. 12. Match between *NewCase* and an exemplar of *age-induced cochlear with otitis-media*.

Of the four unmatched exemplar features, two are believed to be important: *s_neural(severe,1k)* and *bone(abnormal)*. The expert accepts the classification and the explanation.

Because important features are unmatched, Protos solicits explanations from the expert (step 11). He tells Protos that

> *bone(unmeasured)* is sometimes equivalent to *bone(abnormal)*

but is unwilling to equate the value of feature *s_neural* in the exemplar with its value in *NewCase*. Because this important exemplar feature remains unmatched, Protos retains *NewCase* as an exemplar of *age and noise-induced cochlear* (step 13).

Protos acquires more matching knowledge by constructing feature-to-category explanations for the new exemplar (step 14). It constructs most of the explanations using existing knowledge, and the expert adds:

> *acoustic_ref_c(elevated)* is spurious to *age and noise-induced cochlear*
>
> *s_neural(profound,2k)* is sometimes consistent with *cochlear*
>     which has specialization *age-induced cochlear*
>     which has specialization *age and noise-induced cochlear*.

*NewCase* introduced features into the domain theory, and Protos estimates their importance to the category *age and noise-induced cochlear* (step 15).

| NewCase | Exemplar of Age & Noise-Induced Cochlear: Patient054 |
|---|---|
| air(mild) | air(mild) |
| bone(unmeasured) | bone(abnormal) |
| tymp(a) | tymp(a) |
| speech(poor) | speech(very poor) |
| static(normal) | static(normal) |
| age_gt_60 | age_gt_60 |
| s_neural(profound,2k) | s_neural(severe,1k) |
| history(noise) | history(noise) |
| acoustic_ref_u(elevated) | acoustic_ref_u(normal) |
| acoustic_ref_c(elevated) | acoustic_ref_c(normal) |
| o_acoustic_ref_u(normal) | o_acoustic_ref_u(normal) |
| o_acoustic_ref_c(elevated) | o_acoustic_ref_c(elevated) |

Fig. 13. Match between *NewCase* and an exemplar of *age and noise-induced cochlear*.

Because acoustic_ref_c(elevated) was explained to be spurious, Protos considers it unimportant. Protos heuristically evaluates the explanation that relates s_neural(profound,2k) to the category. Because the relation is qualified by "sometimes," it infers that s_neural(profound,2k) is moderately important to age and noise-induced cochlear.

Protos adds indexing knowledge for the new exemplar (step 16). Because s_neural(profound,2k) is explained to occur with any type of cochlear hearing loss, Protos derives a reminding from s_neural(profound,2k) to cochlear. The presence of the qualifier "sometimes" causes Protos to assign only a moderate strength to the reminding.

Recall that Protos initially misclassified NewCase by matching it with Patient163, the exemplar of age-induced cochlear with otitis-media. Protos records this near-miss by adding exemplar-difference knowledge (step 17). Protos asks the expert which features reliably distinguish the exemplars and then annotates the relationship. Before concluding, Protos asks the expert to provide any additional information he wishes, and he declines.

## 5. Evaluating Protos

In this section we empirically evaluate Protos' competence at the learning and classification task defined in Section 2. First we describe the results of training Protos in the audiology domain. We then compare the classification accuracy achieved by Protos to that achieved by human audiologists and by several other programs, including simplified versions of Protos. Some of these programs have a potential advantage in this comparison because they are specifically designed to achieve high classification accuracy without regard for explanatory adequacy. On the other hand, a potential advantage for Protos is that it acquires, and uses for classification, a considerable amount of domain knowledge that the other programs are not designed to use. These comparisons are intended to determine the significance of Protos' results in audiology and to identify the aspects of Protos that are most important in achieving these results.

### 5.1. Protos' competence at the knowledge acquisition task

To evaluate Protos, we applied it to the task in clinical audiology of identifying a patient's hearing disorder. This domain was chosen for three reasons. First, it is a representative application of heuristic classification. Patients are assigned to diagnostic categories as a result of uncertain inferences involving features such as symptoms, test results, and patient history. Second, an interested expert was available to serve as Protos' teacher. Third, a graduate program in audiology at the University of Texas provided a population of expert and student diagnosticians to whom Protos could be compared.

Protos was trained and tested in clinical audiology by Dr. Craig Wier, an expert audiologist and a professor of Speech Communication at the University of Texas at Austin. Cases were chosen at random from the Speech and Hearing Laboratory of the Methodist Hospital in Houston, Texas.[3] A case was considered correctly diagnosed if Dr. Wier and the laboratory clinicians agreed. (Of an original set of 230 cases, they disagreed on 4, which were not used for Protos' training or testing.) Protos' classification accuracy is the percentage of cases which it correctly diagnosed.

Dr. Wier interacted directly with Protos without a knowledge engineer's assistance. He trained Protos with 200 cases in 24 diagnostic categories. This is approximately the number of cases seen by a student during graduate school preparation for state certification. After this training, Protos was tested with 26 different cases. Learning was "turned off," and the expert provided no explanations. Protos' competence is evident in the following figures, which describe its classification accuracy, efficiency, and autonomy gain.

Table 1 reports Protos' classification accuracy during training and testing. Accuracy improved during training, culminating in 100% agreement with the expert during testing. Moreover, Protos' misclassifications were usually plausible categories that the expert judged were more specific than the evidence permitted.

Classification efficiency was measured in two ways, by the storage required for classification, and by the effort required to find a correct match. Figure 14 illustrates the growth of Protos' storage requirements, as measured by the number of categories, indices, and exemplars. Overall, Protos retained 120 exemplars of 24 diagnostic categories. Figure 15 reports the number of exemplars retained in several common categories. Some categories, such as normal and unknown cochlear hearing loss, are highly polymorphic, whereas others, such as fixation, are not. During the first 100 training cases, exemplar retention was 86%. There are two reasons for this high rate of retention. First,

Table 1

Percentage of correct classifications. "First class correct" is the percentage of cases in which the strongest combined reminding which produced a matching exemplar resulted in the correct classification. "Preferred class correct" is the percentage of cases in which the strongest match Protos found was the correct classification. The 24 training cases that introduced new categories were excluded from these calculations.

| Cases | First class correct | Preferred class correct |
| --- | --- | --- |
| Training | 57.7 | 81.7 |
| Test | 92.3 | 100.0 |

[3] Professor James Jerger graciously provided access to the patient records.

Protos was learning two-thirds of its diagnostic categories from these cases, including many of the highly polymorphic categories. Second, the conditional explanation capability was added to Protos after the first hundred cases had been presented.[4] The expert estimates 30–40 fewer exemplars would have been retained with conditional explanations. This is consistent with Protos' lower rate of exemplar retention during the second hundred cases.

Table 2 reports the number of categories considered and the number of exemplar matches attempted by Protos, on average, before (and including) making a correct match. Both numbers increased at approximately the same rate as the number of categories and exemplars. The disproportionate increases that occurred with cases 151–200 were due to the large number of atypical cases in that group.[5]

Protos discussed every successful match with the expert, not just the strongest one. The classification could be accepted or rejected. If accepted, the expert would assess the adequacy of the explanation. The expert rarely disagreed with Protos' explanations.

The number of matches Protos discussed with the expert is a measure of Protos' autonomy. Table 3 shows that most of Protos' classification effort was

Table 2
Protos' mean effort to find a correct match ("*" indicates data unavailable)

| Cases | Classifications | Exemplars |
|---|---|---|
| 1–50 | 2.7 | * |
| 51–100 | 2.8 | * |
| 101–150 | 2.5 | 4.6 |
| 151–200 | 4.0 | 7.4 |
| test | 3.7 | 5.3 |

Table 3
Matches discussed with the expert

| Cases | Matches discussed (per case) |
|---|---|
| 1–50 | 1.7 |
| 51–100 | 1.6 |
| 101–150 | 1.5 |
| 151–200 | 1.9 |
| test | 1.1 |

[4] The experiment was not restarted because the expert's time was limited.
[5] Dr. Wier counted seven atypical cases in this group, compared with two in the previous group of 50 cases.

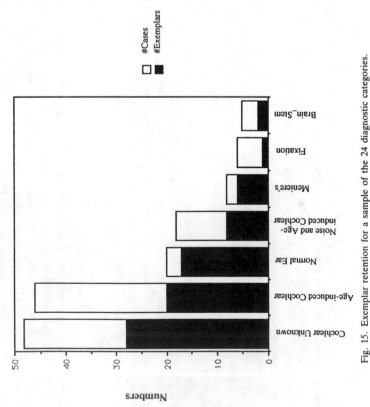

Fig. 14. Protos' acquisition of categories, exemplars and indexing knowledge.

Fig. 15. Exemplar retention for a sample of the 24 diagnostic categories.

independent of the expert. An indication that Protos gained autonomy is that the number of matches discussed with the expert remained constant as the number of exemplars and categories grew.

### 5.2. The classification accuracy achieved by audiologists

Protos' classification performance was compared with that of 19 clinicians from the Department of Speech Communication of the University of Texas. Two were supervisors of the department's clinical practicum. The other 17 were graduate students with more than one year of clinical experience. On average, the subjects did considerably less well than Protos, although one supervisor performed almost as well (Table 4).

The student clinicians commonly complained that some cases could not be diagnosed because information that they believed was essential was missing from the case descriptions. The case descriptions in the audiology data are extremely incomplete, supplying, on average, less than half the possible features. However, the clinical supervisors found the case descriptions adequate.[6]

### 5.3. The classification accuracy achieved by ID3

The incompleteness of the case descriptions was also an obstacle for ID3, a well-known concept formation program that learns decision trees from examples. In [44], Quinlan describes four ways to adapt ID3 to cope with incomplete case descriptions. Each of these variants of ID3 was implemented, applied to the 200 audiology training cases, and evaluated by classifying the 26 audiology test cases with the resulting decision trees [18]. None of the variants of ID3 achieved high classification accuracy. The highest accuracy, a mere 38%, was achieved by treating "missing" as a feature-value. The other variants, which represent various methods of estimating missing features, achieved considerably lower classification accuracies.

In [44], the methods of estimating missing features perform well on data with the following properties:

- The percentage of features that are missing, called the "ignorance level," is very small. Quinlan claims that "in practice, an ignorance level of even 10% is unlikely" [44, p. 99].
- Missing features are randomly distributed across cases.

The methods perform poorly on the audiology data because the data exhibits neither of these properties. The data has an ignorance level exceeding 50%.[7] Furthermore, missing features are not distributed randomly throughout the audiology data set. For example, yes/no features are always missing when their value is "no." More generally, features are missing when they are known to be irrelevant for classification or redundant with features already present in the case description.

Protos performs well given data in which missing features have the properties exhibited by the audiology data. Although the ignorance level is very high, important features either were given or were inferable. Unimportant features, which may be missing in some cases and present in others, have little effect on the matching process.

### 5.4. The classification accuracy achieved by simple exemplar-based programs

Kibler and Aha [25] describe three similarity-based exemplar learning programs, called Proximity, Growth, and Shrink. Like Protos, these programs learn by retaining exemplars, and they classify a test case by assigning it to the category of the exemplar that best matches the test case. Unlike Protos, they do not use knowledge during classification: a test case is matched against all exemplars, and the strength of a match is determined by the number of features that are identical in the exemplar and the test case. The programs differ from each other only in the rule used to decide whether to retain a new training case as an exemplar.

The matching algorithm in Kibler and Aha's programs is reasonably well-suited to data whose missing features exhibit the properties of the audiology data. Consequently, these algorithms have a much better chance of achieving high classification accuracy on the audiology data than did any of the variants of ID3. And indeed, when the programs were implemented and tested, Shrink and Growth achieved a classification accuracy of 65%, and Proximity achieved a classification accuracy of 77% [30]. The method of calculating match strength in Kibler and Aha's programs can be replaced with Protos' method by

[7] Very high ignorance may be quite common in practice. For example, Ruberg et al. [48] report a 50% ignorance level.

Table 4
Correct classifications by clinicians. Each clinician rank-ordered his diagnoses of each case. "Preferred class correct" is the percentage of cases in which the clinician's top-ranked diagnosis was correct. "Any class correct" is the percentage of cases in which the clinician listed the correct diagnosis.

| Subjects | Preferred class correct | Any class correct |
| --- | --- | --- |
| Supervisor 1 | 85% | 92% |
| Supervisor 2 | 69% | 81% |
| Student (mean) | 69% | 73% |

[6] From years of teaching, our domain expert believes that novice audiologists frequently rely on unnecessary data. The reliance of novice diagnosticians on unnecessary data has also been reported in formal studies. e.g., [20].

assuming that no distinct features are equivalent and that all features have the same importance. When this was done, the performance of Shrink and Growth did not change, but Proximity achieved a classification accuracy of only 62% [30]. This suggests that the low-level details of Protos' match strength calculation could be improved.

### 5.5. The effect of deleting knowledge from Protos on classification accuracy

Protos derived indexing and matching knowledge from the explanations supplied by the expert. To determine the degree to which Protos' high classification accuracy depended on these two types of knowledge, an ablation study [14] was conducted in which various combinations of Protos' knowledge were used to classify the audiology test cases. Because this type of study would be very difficult to run on Protos itself, a program, called M-Protos, was constructed specifically for these experiments. M-Protos differs from Protos in many ways, notably that it cannot acquire knowledge. However, its classification process is sufficiently similar to Protos' that the results of the experiments apply equally to M-Protos and Protos. Details of M-Protos and of the experimental results are given in [30].

In the absence of indexing knowledge, M-Protos matches all exemplars with the given test case. In the absence of matching knowledge, M-Protos reduces the match strength a fixed amount for every feature in the exemplar that does not occur in the test case. M-Protos is considered to have correctly classified the test case if the strongest of its attempted matches is an exemplar in the correct category. Given all of the audiology training cases, and no indexing or matching knowledge, M-Protos achieved a classification accuracy of 65%, similar to that achieved by Kibler and Aha's programs. The accuracy dropped to 58% when matching knowledge was added. With indexing knowledge, but no matching knowledge, M-Protos achieved 92%. With both indexing and matching knowledge, M-Protos, like Protos, achieved 100% classification accuracy.

For the most part, these results are consistent with the general philosophy of exemplar-based programs. Classification accuracy is primarily achieved by using direct match and a large, well-indexed set of exemplars; knowledge-based matching boosts classification accuracy, but is not its primary source. Lack of indexing knowledge resulted in the inappropriate use of matching knowledge and a concomitant increase in misclassifications (as discussed at the end of Section 4.2.2).

However, the dependence of classification accuracy on matching knowledge in this experiment was surprisingly small. This may be explained by peculiarities of our audiology training that will not necessarily arise in other domains, or even in the audiology domain given different training. With the case language used in our experiments, direct match worked well. In a typical correct match between an exemplar and a case, 8 of the 11 exemplar features matched features in the case, and 7 of these matched directly. Thus, there was limited opportunity to use matching knowledge, either to increase the strength of the correct match or to reduce the strength of incorrect matches. Furthermore, much of the matching knowledge that did exist was expressible only as conditional explanations of feature equivalence, a form of explanation that was not available during the first half of training. This prevented a significant body of matching knowledge from being entered by the expert.

## 6. Summary

Our research developed a successful approach to the task of concept learning for heuristic classification. This task differs from the usual concept learning task in three ways. A program for this task must explain its classifications, accommodate incomplete case descriptions, and learn domain-specific knowledge for inferring case features needed for classification.

Our approach to this task is exemplar-based. Concepts are learned by retaining exemplars, and new cases are classified by matching them to similar exemplars. This approach has strong psychological support, but it raises two problems: measuring similarity and efficiently finding an exemplar to match. We solve these problems by augmenting exemplars with matching knowledge and indexing knowledge. A new case is classified by using indexing knowledge to find an exemplar and using matching knowledge to explain similarity. By interleaving heuristic classification and knowledge acquisition, this approach permits a program to start at a level of utter incompetence and to achieve a level of expert competence.

To evaluate our approach, we built the Protos program and applied it to the task in clinical audiology of identifying a patient's hearing disorder from symptoms, test results, and history. This evaluation yielded many encouraging results:

- After a reasonable amount of training, Protos achieved very good classification accuracy without using excessive computational resources.
- Protos' classification accuracy is comparable to that of experienced human experts, and is significantly better than that of the machine learning alternatives we examined. The two main reasons for this are (1) Protos' ability to deal with incomplete case descriptions and (2) Protos' use of indexing and matching knowledge derived from explanations provided by the expert.
- Most of the explanations Protos generated for a case's classification were acceptable to the expert.
- Protos gained autonomy. The number of matches Protos discussed with the expert remained constant as the number of exemplars and categories grew.

The evaluation of Protos also revealed several shortcomings, which we are addressing with our current research. The first shortcoming is that Protos adds new knowledge without considering its relation to existing knowledge. This allows inconsistencies to go undetected until they cause a classification or explanation failure, which is sometimes undesirable. Ken Murray's research [40, 41] explores the task of integrating new information into existing knowledge. The second shortcoming of Protos is that it does not adapt its explanations to different users. The research of Liane Acker, James Lester, and Art Souther [56] explores the generation of coherent explanations that can vary in viewpoint and level of abstraction. This research and Ken Murray's both use a large-scale, multifunctional knowledge base for the domain of plant anatomy, physiology, and development [43]. The third shortcoming of Protos is its very restricted explanation language. Karl Branting's research [8] explores the representation and reuse of complex explanations for automated reasoning in weak-theory domains, using as a testbed the domain of Worker's Compensation case law.

## ACKNOWLEDGEMENT

Many of our colleagues have contributed to this research. Dr. Craig Wier trained Protos in clinical audiology and counseled us on evaluation methods and user interface design. Richard Mallory performed the ablation study. Claudia Porter, Joe Ross, and Todd Stock contributed to Protos' construction. Kenneth Murray and Adam Farquhar were instrumental in Protos' design. Liane Acker, Brad Blumenthal, Karl Branting, James Lester, Richard Mallory, and Kenneth Murray reviewed early drafts of this paper.

Support for this research was provided by grants from the Army Research Office (ARO-DAAG29-84-K0060), and the National Science Foundation (IRI-8620052), and by contributions from Apple Corporation, Texas Instruments, and the Cray Foundation. The research was conducted in the Department of Computer Sciences, University of Texas at Austin.

## REFERENCES

1. J.S. Aikins, A representation scheme using both frames and rules, in: B.G. Buchanan and E.H. Shortliffe, eds., *Rule Based Expert Systems* (Addison-Wesley, Reading, MA, 1984).
2. J. Amsterdam, Some philosophical problems with formal learning theory, in: *Proceedings AAAI-88*, St. Paul, MN (1988) 580–584.
3. E.R. Bareiss, *Exemplar-Based Knowledge Acquisition* (Academic Press, New York, 1989); also: Ph.D. Dissertation, Department of Computer Sciences, University of Texas at Austin.
4. E.R. Bareiss, B.W. Porter and K.S. Murray, Gaining autonomy during knowledge acquisition, Tech. Rept. AI89-97, University of Texas at Austin, Department of Computer Sciences, Austin, TX (1989).
5. E.R. Bareiss, B.W. Porter and K.S. Murray, Supporting start-to-finish development of knowledge bases, *Mach. Learning* **4** (1989) 259–284.
6. J.S. Bennett, ROGET: A knowledge-based system for acquiring the conceptual structure of a diagnostic expert system, *Autom. Reasoning* **1** (1) (1985) 49–74.
7. J. Boose, Personal construct theory and the transfer of expertise, in: *Proceedings AAAI-84*, Austin, TX (1984) 27–33.
8. L.K. Branting, Integrating generalizations with exemplar-based reasoning, in: *Proceedings Eleventh Annual Conference of the Cognitive Science Society* (1989).
9. L. Brooks Non-analytic concept formation and the memory for instances, in: E. Rosch and B.B. Lloyd, eds., *Cognition and Categorization* (Erlbaum, Hillsdale, NJ, 1978) 169–211.
10. W.J. Clancey, Extensions to rules for explanation and tutoring, in: B.G. Buchanan and E.H. Shortliffe, eds., *Rule Based Expert Systems* (Addison-Wesley, Reading, MA, 1984) 531–568.
11. W.J. Clancey, Heuristic classification, *Artificial Intelligence* **27** (1985) 289–350.
12. P. Clark, A comparison of rule and exemplar-based learning systems, in: P. Brazdil, ed., *Proceedings International Workshop on Machine Learning, Meta-Reasoning, and Logic*, Porto, Portugal (1988).
13. P. Clark and T. Niblett, The CN2 induction algorithm, *Mach. Learning* **3** (1989) 261–283.
14. P. Cohen and A. Howe, How evaluation guides AI research, *AI Mag.* (Winter 1988) 35–43.
15. J.H. Connell and M. Brady, Generating and generalizing models of visual objects, *Artificial Intelligence* **31** (1987) 159–183.
16. G. DeJong and R. Mooney, Explanation-based learning: An alternative view, *Mach. Learning* **1** (2) (1986).
17. T.G. Dietterich, Machine learning, in: *Annual Review of Computer Science* **4** (1990).
18. R.T. Duran, Concept learning with incomplete data sets, Master's Thesis, Tech. Rept. AI88-82, Department of Computer Sciences, University of Texas at Austin (1988).
19. D.L. Dvorak, A guide to CL-Protos: An exemplar-based learning apprentice, Tech. Rept. AI88-87, Department of Computer Sciences, University of Texas at Austin (1988).
20. P.J. Feltovich, P.E. Johnson, J.H. Moller and D.B. Swanson, LCS: The role and development of medical knowlege in diagnostic expertise, in: W.J. Clancey and E.H. Shortliffe, eds., *Readings in Medical Artificial Intelligence* (Addison-Wesley, Reading, MA, 1984) 275–319.
21. N.S. Flann and T.G. Dietterich, Selecting appropriate representations for learning from examples, *Proceedings AAAI-87*, Seattle, WA (1987).
22. A.L. Gardner, An artificial intelligence approach to legal reasoning, Ph.D. Thesis, Stanford University, Stanford, CA (1984).
23. H.L.A. Hart, Positivism and the separation of law and morals, *Harvard Law Rev.* **71** (1958) 593–629.
24. K.J. Holyoak and A.L. Glass, The role of contradictions and counterexamples in the rejection of false sentences, *J. Verbal Learning and Verbal Behav.* **14** (1975) 215–239.
25. D. Kibler and D. Aha, Learning representative exemplars of concepts: An initial case study, in: P. Langley, ed., *Proceedings Fourth International Workshop on Machine Learning*, Irvine, CA (Morgan Kaufmann, Los Altos, CA, 1987) 24–30.
26. Y. Kodratoff and J.G. Ganascia, Improving the generalization step in learning, in: R.S. Michalski, I.G. Carbonell and T.M. Mitchell, eds., *Machine Learning: An Artificial Intelligence Approach 2* (Morgan Kaufmann, Los Altos, CA, 1986) 215–244.
27. J.L. Kolodner, Maintaining organization in a dynamic long-term memory, *Cogn. Sci.* **7** (1983) 243–280.
28. J.L. Kolodner, Extending problem solver capabilities through case-based inference, in: P. Langley, ed., *Proceedings Fourth International Workshop on Machine Learning*, Irvine, CA (Morgan Kaufmann, Los Altos, CA, 1987) 167–178.
29. J.L. Kolodner and R.M. Kolodner, Using experience in clinical problem solving, Tech. Rept. GIT-ICS-85/21, School of Information and Computer Science, Georgia Institute of Technology, Atlanta, GA (1985).
30. R.S. Mallory, Sources of classification accuracy in Protos, Tech. Rept. AI89-118, Department of Computer Sciences, University of Texas at Austin (1989).
31. L.T. McCarty and N.S. Sridharan, A computational theory of legal argument, Tech. Rept. LRP-TR-13, Laboratory for Computer Science Research, Rutgers University, New Brunswick, NJ (1982).
32. D.L. Medin, G.I. Dewey and T.D. Murphy, Relationships between item and category learning: Evidence that abstraction is not automatic, *J. Experimental Psychol.: Learning, Memory and Cognition* **9** (1983) 607–625.

33. D.L. Medin and M.M. Schaffer, Context theory of classification learning, Psychol. Rev. 85 (1978) 207–238.

34. D.L. Medin and E.E. Smith, Concepts and concept formation, Annu. Rev. Psychol. 35 (1984) 113–138.

35. R.S. Michalski, A theory and methology of inductive learning, in: R.S. Michalski, J.G. Carbonell and T.M. Mitchell, eds., Machine Learning: An Artificial Intelligence Approach 1 (Tioga, Palo Alto, CA, 1983).

36. T.M. Mitchell, R.M. Keller and S.T. Kedar-Cabelli, Explanation-based generalization: A unifying view, Mach. Learning 1 (1986) 47–80.

37. T.M. Mitchell, P.E. Utgoff and R. Banerji, Learning by experimentation: Acquiring and refining problem solving heuristics, in: R.S. Michalski, J.G. Carbonell and T.M. Mitchell, eds., Machine Learning: An Artificial Intelligence Approach 1 (Tioga, Palo Alto, CA, 1983) 163–190.

38. J.D. Moore and W.R. Swartout, A reactive approach to explanation, in: Proceedings Fourth International Workshop on Natural Language Generation (1989).

39. G.L. Murphy and D.L. Medin, The role of theories in conceptual coherence, Psychol. Rev. 92 (1985) 289–316.

40. K.S. Murray, KI: An experiment in automating knowledge acquisition, Tech. Rept., AI88-90, Department of Computer Sciences, University of Texas at Austin (1988).

41. K.S. Murray and B.W. Porter, Developing a tool for acknowledge integration: Initial results, in: J.H. Boose and B.R. Gaines, eds., Proceedings Third Knowledge Acquisition for Knowledge-Based Systems Workshop, Calgary, Alta. (1988).

42. H.P. Nii, E.A. Feigenbaum, J.J. Anton and A.J. Rockmore. Signal-to-symbol transformation: HASP/SIAP case study. AI Mag. (Spring 1982) 23–35.

43. B. Porter, J. Lester, K. Murray, K. Pittman, A. Souther, L. Acker and T. Jones, AI research in the context of a multifunctional knowledge base: The Botany Knowledge Base project, Tech. Rept. AI88-88. Department of Computer Sciences, University of Texas at Austin (1988).

44. J.R. Quinlan, Induction of decision trees. Mach. Learning 1 (1986) 81–106.

45. E. Rosch, Principles of categorization, in: E. Rosch and B.B. Lloyd, eds., Cognition and Categorization (Erlbaum, Hillsdale, NJ, 1978).

46. E. Rosch, Prototype classification and logical classification: The two systems, in: E.K. Scholnick, ed., New Trends in Conceptual Representation: Challenges to Piaget's Theory? (Erlbaum, Hillsdale. NJ, 1983).

47. E. Rosch and C.B. Mervis, Family resemblance: Studies in the internal structure of categories, Cogn. Psychol. 7 (1975) 573–605.

48. K. Ruberg. S.M. Cornick and K.A. James, House calls: Building and maintaining a diagnostic rule-base, in: J.H. Boose and B.R. Gaines, eds., Proceedings Third Knowledge Acquisition for Knowledge-Based Systems Workshop, Calgary, Alta. (1988).

49. D. Rumelhart and J. McClelland and the PDP Research Group. Parallel Distributed Processing 1 (MIT Press, Cambridge, MA, 1986).

50. R.C. Schank, Dynamic Memory: A Theory of Reminding and Learning in Computers and People (Cambridge University Press, Cambridge, 1982).

51. R.C. Schank, G.C. Collins and L.E. Hunter, Transcending inductive category formation in learning, Behav. Brain Sci. 9 (1986) 639–651.

52. A.D. Shapiro, Structured Induction in Expert Systems (Addison-Wesley, Reading, MA, 1987).

53. E.H. Shortliffe, MYCIN: Computer-Based Medical Consultations (American Elsevier, New York, 1976).

54. R.L. Simpson, A comptuer model of case-based reasoning in problem solving: An investigation in the domain of dispute mediation, Ph.D. Thesis, School of Information and Comptuer Science, Georgia Institute of Technology, Atlanta, GA (1985).

55. E. Smith and D. Medin, Categories and Concepts (Harvard University Press, Cambridge. MA. 1981).

56. A. Souther, L. Acker, J. Lester and B. Porter, Using view types to generate explanations in intelligent tutoring systems, in: Proceedings Eleventh Annual Conference of the Cognitive Science Society (1989).

57. A. Tversky and D. Kahneman, Judgment under uncertainty: Heuristics and biases, Science 185 (1974) 1124–1131.

58. S.M. Weiss, A.K. Casimir and S. Amarel, A model-based method for computer-aided medical decision-making, Artificial Intelligence 11 (1978) 145–172.

59. M.R. Wick, C.L. Paris, W.R. Swartout and W.B. Thompson. eds., Proceedings AAAI'88 Workshop on Explanation (1988).

60. P.H. Winston. Learning structural descriptions from examples, in: P.H. Winston, Ed., The Psychology of Computer Vision (McGraw-Hill, New York, 1975) 157–209.

61. P.H. Winston, T.O. Binford, B. Katz and M. Lowry, Learning physical descriptions from functional definitions, examples, and precedents, in: Proceedings AAAI-83, Washington, DC (1983) 433–439.

62. L. Wittgenstein, Philosophical Investigations (MacMillan, New York, 1953).

Received February 1989; revised version received September 1989

# Improving Rule-Based Systems through Case-Based Reasoning[1]

**Andrew R. Golding**
KSL/Stanford University
701 Welch Road
Palo Alto, CA 94304

**Paul S. Rosenbloom**
ISI/University of Southern California
4676 Admiralty Way
Marina del Rey, CA 90292

## Abstract

A novel architecture is presented for combining rule-based and case-based reasoning. The central idea is to apply the rules to a target problem to get a first approximation to the answer; but if the problem is judged to be compellingly similar to a known exception of the rules in any aspect of its behavior, then that aspect is modelled after the exception rather than the rules. The architecture is implemented for the full-scale task of pronouncing surnames. Preliminary results suggest that the system performs almost as well as the best commercial systems. However, of more interest than the absolute performance of the system is the result that this performance was better than what could have been achieved with the rules alone. This illustrates the capacity of the architecture to improve on the rule-based system it starts with. The results also demonstrate a beneficial interaction in the system, in that improving the rules speeds up the case-based component.

## 1 Introduction

One strategy for improving the performance of a rule-based system is simply to extend its rule set. For many real-world domains, however, this strategy reaches a point of diminishing returns after awhile. The work reported here takes an alternative approach: it per-forms rule-based reasoning (RBR) with whatever imperfect rules are available, and supplements the rules with case-based reasoning (CBR). This enables the system to tap into a knowledge source that is often more readily available than additional rules; namely, sets of examples from the domain.

The viability of this approach depends on whether adding CBR will actually provide improved coverage of the domain, or merely redundant coverage. Section 3.2 below presents experimental evidence that in fact it provides improved coverage. The reason is that rules and cases have complementary strengths. Rules capture broad trends in the domain, while cases are good at filling in small pockets of exceptions in the rules.

The hybrid strategy is not the only way to incorporate both rules and cases into the system. An alternative is to convert all the cases into rules, or vice versa, and then work in a single representation. Either direction of the conversion has its pitfalls, however. Consider first converting a case into rules. The conversion must preserve the functionality that the case, in its CBR framework, provides. Each case effectively gives rise to a rule every time an analogy is drawn from it, as behind every analogy is an implicit rule. We could therefore represent the case by the set $R$ of all rules that it could ever give rise to. However, $R$ may be huge, as the case could produce subtly different rules for each target problem to which it is analogized. On the other hand, if we leave the case as a case, we only generate rules for target problems that we actually encounter. To economize, we might replace the plethora of rules in $R$ with fewer, more general rules. Induction programs do this by generalizing over multiple cases; this yields across-case economies as well. But no matter how we do it, we are generalizing further than CBR would have generalized from the original case, thus we run the risk of overgeneralization.

Converting in the opposite direction has analogous problems. The conversion from a rule into a set $C$ of cases must preserve the rule's coverage. That is, we must pick $C$ such that for each case covered by the rule, its nearest neighbor is one of the cases in $C$, according to the similarity metric being used. The only set $C$ that is guaranteed to do this is the full set of cases covered by the rule; but it is likely to be huge, assuming it can be generated at all. If we pare

[1] This research was sponsored by NASA under cooperative agreement number NCC 2-538, and by a Bell Laboratories PhD fellowship to the first author. Computer facilities were partially provided by NIH grant LM05208. The views and conclusions contained in this document are those of the authors and should not be interpreted as representing the official policies, either expressed or implied, of NASA, the US Government, Bell Laboratories, or the National Institute of Health. The authors would like to thank the Speech Technology Group at Bellcore, especially Murray Spiegel, for their valuable assistance in this research. We are also grateful to Pandu Nayak for helpful discussions on the ideas of this paper, and to Ross Quinlan and the AAAI reviewers for useful comments on drafts of this paper.

Finally, it should be mentioned that the system presented here was originally implemented in and shaped by the Soar architecture [Laird *et al.*, 1987]. The Soar influence will not be discussed explicitly in this paper, however.

down $C$, we run the risk that one of the cases that we delete will be misrepresented. This is because it is unpredictable what the case's nearest neighbor will be in the long run, as further cases are added to the case library. In short, converting either way between rules and cases will tend to produce an inefficient or unreliable representation. The degree to which this happens, and can be tolerated, determines whether it is better to convert or to adopt a hybrid approach. In certain domains, the conversion from cases to rules has been shown feasible by induction programs. But the conversion will leave us with two sets of rules — the original set, and the set derived from cases. The two sets must then be integrated, just as rules and cases must be integrated in a hybrid system. Thus even when it is feasible, induction solves only part of the problem. It leads to an approach of conversion followed by rule integration (see section 4).

The approach taken here has been cast as a general architecture for combining RBR and CBR. The architecture is presented in section 2. The architecture has been implemented for the full-scale task of pronouncing names. Experimental results for this implementation are given in section 3. In section 4, the architecture is compared with alternative methods for combining RBR and CBR. The final section is a conclusion.

## 2   The Architecture

The central idea of the architecture for combining RBR and CBR is to apply the rules to a target problem to produce a default solution; but if the target problem is judged to be compellingly similar to a known exception of the rules in any aspect of its behavior, then that aspect is modelled after the exception rather than the rules. Problem solving in this architecture is done by applying operators to the problem until it is solved. The central idea above is therefore realized through the following procedure:

**Until** the target problem is solved **do**:
(a)   Use the rules to select an operator to apply.
(b)   Search for analogies that would contradict this choice of operator, stopping if and when a *compelling* analogy is found.[2]
(c)   If a compelling analogy was found, apply the operator it suggests, else proceed to apply the operator suggested by the rules.

Underlying this procedure is the assumption that the rules are decent to begin with. If they are very slow, then the system will suffer when they are applied in step (a). If they are highly inaccurate, then the system

---

[2]If there are multiple compelling analogies for different operators, this procedure will only find the first one. This will not result in a wrong answer, unless there is an inconsistency in the case library or the definition of compellingness. It merely will miss the other acceptable answers corresponding to the unchosen analogies.

will get bogged down overriding them in step (b). In such cases, some alternative architecture is called for, such as one that looks for compelling analogies first, and only consults the rules if none is found.

In the next section, we describe the knowledge needed for the procedure above. We then elaborate on the major aspects of the procedure itself: indexing the cases for use in analogies, proposing the analogies, and deciding when an analogy is compelling.

### 2.1   Knowledge Sources

The architecture itself is domain-independent; its domain knowledge comes from three external sources: a set of rules, a case library, and a similarity metric. The rules specify an operator to apply in every problem-solving state. The case library is a collection of cases, where a case consists of a problem, its answer, and the chain of operators by which the answer was derived.[3] The similarity metric gauges the similarity between two problems for purposes of applying a particular operator. It will be discussed further in section 2.3.

### 2.2   Indexing

The role of CBR in the architecture is to improve the performance of the rules. It follows that the only cases from which useful analogies can be drawn are the exceptions, i.e., the cases that violate the rules. Cases that confirm the rules do not lead to any new behaviors. Moreover, the only time an exception is useful is when the rule that it violates actually fires. At that point, it becomes relevant to ask whether the exception should override the rule. These considerations lead to the indexing scheme of storing each case as a *negative exemplar* of the rules that it violates. To determine which rules these are, we basically apply RBR to the case as if it were a new problem. If, in the process, a rule $R$ says that a certain operator should apply, but the case library specifies that in fact some other operator was applied, then the case violates rule $R$. It turns out to be useful to store each case also as a *positive exemplar* of the rules that it confirms — this will help later in judging compellingness (see section 2.4). We call this scheme *prediction-based indexing* (PBI), because effectively, an exemplar is indexed by the features that the rules looked at in order to to predict which operator to apply. This is like explanation-based indexing [Barletta and Mark, 1988], except that there the rules are used to explain an observed outcome, rather than to make their own prediction of the outcome.

**Example**   For ease of exposition, we will illustrate the architecture not for name pronunciation, but for a toy version of a problem in auto insurance: to assess the risk of insuring a new client. Problem solving consists of applying just one operator, either **high** or **low**,

---

[3]Actually, the chain of operators need not be specified; the architecture can infer it from the problem/answer pair by a process of *rational reconstruction* [Golding, 1991].

```
If occ(C) = student then low      ; 'Student' rule
elseif sex(C) = M and
      age(C) < 30 then high        ; 'Young driver' rule
elseif age(C) ≥ 65 then high       ; 'Old driver' rule
else low                           ; 'Default' rule
```

Figure 1: The rules in the toy auto-insurance example. $C$ stands for a client.

| | Target | Case #1 | Case #6 |
|---|---|---|---|
| **Name** | Smith | Johnson | Davis |
| **Addr1** | Sigma Chi | Sigma Chi | Toyon Hall |
| **Addr2** | Stanford, CA | Stanford, CA | Stanford, CA |
| **Sex** | M | M | F |
| **Age** | 21 | 19 | 22 |
| **Occ** | student | student | student |
| **Make** | Chevrolet | BMW | Toyota |
| **Value** | 2,500 | 30,000 | 3,000 |

Figure 2: Selected clients in the insurance example.

which asserts the level of risk of the client. The full set of rules is shown in Figure 1. A client is represented as a feature vector; Figure 2 gives some examples. The case library contains 23 cases. Each case specifies a client and the operator applied to that client, either **high** or **low**. The cases are derived (conceptually) from the insurance history of past clients.

To illustrate PBI, we consider the first client in the case library, Johnson. Suppose that he is listed as having had the **high** operator applied. The first step of PBI is to see what the rules would have predicted. They predict **low** by the 'student' rule. Since this disagrees with the case library, Johnson is stored as a negative exemplar of the 'student' rule. As a second example, consider the client Davis, whom we will suppose is listed as **low** in the case library. Again the 'student' rule applies, but this time its prediction agrees with the case library. So Davis is listed as a positive exemplar of the 'student' rule.

### 2.3  Proposing Analogies

Proposing analogies is done by applying the similarity metric. The metric takes three arguments: the source and target problems, and the operator to be transferred from source to target. The operator establishes a context for comparing the problems. Given these three arguments, the metric returns two values: a numerical rating of the similarity (the *similarity score*), and the implicit rule behind the analogy (the *arule*). The left-hand side of the arule gives the features that were judged by the metric to be shared by the two problems, and the right-hand side gives the operator-to-be-transferred. The arule will be used for judging whether the analogy is compelling (see section 2.4).

**Example**  Continuing with the insurance example, suppose the system is asked to evaluate the risk of client Smith (see Figure 2). It starts by applying the rules to Smith. The 'student' rule matches, suggesting the **low** operator. Before accepting this conclusion, the system checks for analogies from negative exemplars of the rule. As we saw earlier (section 2.2), Johnson is one such negative exemplar. Application of the similarity metric for this domain to Johnson and Smith (with respect to the **high** operator) yields the arule:

```
If addr1(C) = Sigma Chi and
    addr2(C) = Stanford, CA and sex(C) = M
    and age(C) < 30 and occ(C) = student
then high.
```

This arule expresses the features shared by Johnson and Smith, according to the metric. The metric is very simplistic in this toy domain. It compares corresponding text fields of the two clients via literal comparison. For numeric fields, it checks whether the two numbers fall within the same interval of a predefined set of intervals. It assigns similarity scores by counting the conditions in the arule; here the score is 5.

### 2.4  Deciding Compellingness

Rather than accepting an analogy purely on the basis of its similarity score, the system subjects it to inductive verification. This entails testing out the arule of the analogy on all relevant exemplars — both negative and positive — in the case library. The test returns two results: the arule's accuracy, that is, the proportion of cases it got right; and the significance of the accuracy rating, which is 1 minus the probability of getting that high an accuracy merely by chance. The analogy is then said to be compelling iff (1) its similarity score is high enough, (2) its accuracy is high enough, and (3) either its accuracy rating has a high enough significance, or its similarity score is extremely high. The latter disjunct is an escape clause to accept analogies between overwhelmingly similar problems, even if there are not enough data for a significant accuracy reading. All "high enough" clauses above are implemented via comparison with thresholds. The thresholds are set by a learning procedure that generates training analogies for itself from the case library [Golding, 1991].

**Example**  Consider again the analogy from Johnson to Smith. Should it be judged compelling? To decide, the system first runs an inductive verification. It turns out that the arule applies to four clients in the database: Johnson and three others. Three of them are listed as **high** risk, one as **low**. This gives an accuracy of 3/4. The significance of this accuracy rating works out to be 0.648. Also, as mentioned earlier, the similarity score of the analogy is 5. The thresholds in this domain have been set to 3 for the similarity score, 0.75 for accuracy, and 0.50 for significance.[4] Thus the anal-

---

[4]These thresholds were set by hand rather than by the usual learning procedure, because the toy domain has too few cases to apply the learning procedure meaningfully.

ogy is deemed compelling, although it was marginal in the accuracy department. The upshot is that Smith is assessed as high risk, by analogy to a similar high-risk student from the same fraternity.

## 3    Experimental Results

The architecture described here was developed in the context of Anapron, a system for pronouncing surnames. In particular, the architecture was applied to two subtasks of pronunciation: transcription and stress assignment. Transcription converts a spelling into a string of phonetic segments. Stress assignment places a level of emphasis on each syllable. Although there has been little work on pronunciation within the CBR community — with a few notable exceptions [Lehnert, 1987; Stanfill, 1987] — the domain was selected for the present research for several reasons. First, both rules and cases are already available; rules have been developed in previous pronunciation efforts [Hunnicutt, 1976], and case libraries can be derived from pronouncing dictionaries of names. This makes the domain amenable to the hybrid rule/case approach. Second, pronouncing *names* in particular is an open problem [Klatt, 1987], due to the unique etymology and morphology of names. To give an idea of the size of the system, there are 619 transcription rules and 29 stress rules, covering five major languages. There are 5000 cases in the system, derived from a name dictionary of the same size. Below we give results on the overall level of performance of the system, and on the contribution of RBR and CBR to this performance.

### 3.1    Overall Performance[5]

To establish the initial credibility of the architecture for the pronunciation domain, we include here the results of a pilot study comparing Anapron with six other name-pronunciation systems: three state-of-the-art commercial systems (from Bell Labs, Bellcore, and DEC), one machine-learning system (NETtalk [Sejnowski and Rosenberg, 1987], trained on Anapron's name dictionary), and two humans. Each system was run on a test set of 400 names, and the acceptability of its pronunciations was measured. This had to be done by taking a poll of public opinion, as there is no objective standard for surname pronunciations. To hide the identities of the systems in the poll, the order of systems was randomized for each test name, and all pronunciations were read by the DECtalk speech synthesizer. The pilot study was conducted on just one

[5]The authors gratefully acknowledge the assistance on this experiment of the following people: Cecil Coker at Bell Labs, Murray Spiegel at Bellcore, and Tony Vitale at DEC, for supplying data from their systems; Tom Dietterich, for providing the non-copyrighted portion of NETtalk; John Laird, for providing a fast machine for training NETtalk; Mark Liberman, for making the test set of names available; and Connie Burton, for providing access to DECtalk.

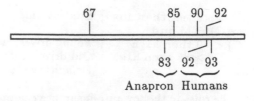

Figure 3: Results of pilot study comparing seven name-pronunciation systems. Each line marks the percentage of acceptable pronunciations for one system. The scale goes from 50% to 100%.

test subject; at this point, the exact numbers in the results should not be taken too seriously.

The test set for this experiment was drawn from the Donnelly corpus, a database of over 1.5 million surnames in the US. The names in Donnelly range from extremely common (Smith, which occurs in 676,080 households) to extremely rare (Chavriacouty, which occurs in 1 household). The test set contains 100 randomly selected names from each of four points along this spectrum: names that occurred in about 2048 households, 256 households, 32 households, and 1 household. Rare names are known to be harder to pronounce than common ones. The test set therefore represents a fairly challenging cross-section of Donnelly.

**Results**    The results of the pilot study are shown in Figure 3. The identities of most systems have been omitted due to the preliminary nature of the results. The initial indications are that Anapron performs near the level of the best commercial systems, which is barely short of human performance. One reason that the commercial systems may outperform Anapron is simply that they have better rules. Presumably, giving these same rules to Anapron would help its performance; moreover, the point of Anapron is that it can then achieve further gains by leveraging off CBR.

### 3.2    The Contribution of RBR and CBR

An experiment was run on Anapron to evaluate the effect of combining RBR and CBR in practice. The results can be taken as one example of how the architecture behaves when instantiated for a task. The experiment involved independently varying the strength of the rules and of the case library, and observing how system performance was affected on a particular test set. The rules were set to four different strengths: 0, 1/3, 2/3, and 1. Strength 1 means that all rules were retained in the system; 0 means that all rules were deleted, except *default* rules.[6] As strength decreases

[6]The rules are arranged in a partial order by specificity; more specialized rules take precedence over more general ones. A default rule is one that is maximally general. Such a rule must not be deleted, otherwise the system will no longer be guaranteed to produce an answer for every problem. Default rules constitute 137 of the 619 transcription rules and 16 of the 29 stress rules.

| Rule | Case strength | | | | | |
|------|------|------|------|------|------|------|
| strength | 0 | 1000 | 2000 | 3000 | 4000 | 5000 |
| 0 | 19 | 27 | 32 | 34 | 35 | 36 |
| 1/3 | 33 | 39 | 43 | 44 | 46 | 47 |
| 2/3 | 46 | 54 | 56 | 56 | 57 | 59 |
| 1 | 56 | 65 | 65 | 67 | 67 | 68 |

Table 1: System accuracy results. Each value is the percentage of names in the test set for which the system produced an acceptable pronunciation.

| Rule | Case strength | | | | | |
|------|------|------|------|------|------|------|
| strength | 0 | 1000 | 2000 | 3000 | 4000 | 5000 |
| 0 | 0.9 | 3.0 | 4.5 | 6.3 | 8.2 | 10.2 |
| 1/3 | 1.1 | 3.0 | 4.4 | 5.9 | 7.6 | 9.3 |
| 2/3 | 1.2 | 3.1 | 4.4 | 5.8 | 7.2 | 8.5 |
| 1 | 1.3 | 3.0 | 4.1 | 5.2 | 6.3 | 7.2 |

Table 2: System run-time results. Each value is the average time, in seconds, for the system to pronounce a name in the test set.

from 1 to 0, we delete proportionately more rules. Each weakening deletes a random subset of the non-default rules in the previous rule set. As for the case library, it was set to six different strengths: 0, 1000, 2000, 3000, 4000, and 5000. The strength is just the number of names included in the case library. Each weakening deletes an arbitrary subset of the previous case library.

System performance was measured by two parameters: accuracy and run time. Accuracy is the percentage of names in the test set for which the system produced an acceptable pronunciation. The same 400-name test set was used as in the previous experiment, except that the names were chosen to be disjoint from the case library. This time the decisions of acceptability were made by a single, harsh human judge (the first author).[7] All judgements were cached and reused if a pronunciation recurred, to help enforce consistency. The other parameter of system performance, run time, is just the average time, in seconds, for the system to pronounce a name in the test set. The data are for the system running in CommonLisp on a Texas Instruments Microexplorer with 8M physical memory, and are inclusive of garbage collection and paging.

**Accuracy Results**  System accuracy, for each combination of rule and case strength, is shown in Table 1. The important result is that accuracy improves monotonically as rule or case strength increases. The total improvement in accuracy due to adding rules is between 32% and 38% of the test set (depending on case strength). For cases it is between 12% and 17% (depending on rule strength). This shows that by combining rules and cases, the system achieves a higher accuracy than it could with either one alone — both are essential to the accuracy of the combined system. This suggests dual views of the architecture: as a means of improving rule-based systems through CBR, or improving case-based systems through RBR.

**Run-time Results**  Table 2 gives the results on run time. The interesting point here is that when the case library is large, adding rules to the system actually de-

creases run time. For example, with the case library at size 5000, increasing the rules from strength 0 to 1 lowers run time from 10.2 to 7.2 seconds per name. The basic reason is that adding rules to the system improves the overall accuracy of the rules, barring sociopathic effects. When the rules are more accurate, they will have fewer exceptions. This translates into fewer negative exemplars, and thus fewer opportunities to draw analogies. The forgone analogies result in a corresponding savings in run time. In short, adding rules to the system speeds up the CBR component. This shows that RBR and CBR do not merely coexist in the system, they interact beneficially.

## 4   Related Work

A number of other methods have been proposed in the literature for combining RBR and CBR. They fall into two basic classes, according to whether their rules and cases are independent, or whether one was derived from the other. The primary motivation for the former class of systems is to maximize accuracy by exploiting multiple knowledge sources. For the latter class of systems, it is to express their knowledge in whatever form will make problem solving most efficient.

The systems whose rules and cases were derived from each other can be further classified according to which knowledge source was derived from which. Most CBR systems that include a rule component [Koton, 1988; Hammond and Hurwitz, 1988, etc.] have cases that are derived from their rules. The cases are records of how the rules were applied to particular examples encountered previously. By reasoning from cases, the systems bypass the potentially lengthy process of solving a new problem from scratch via the rules. The systems whose rules are derived from their cases extract the rules by some generalization procedure. The systems must still keep the cases around, because their rules do not encode all of the knowledge in the cases. The rules in these systems can serve various purposes, such as enabling a more compact representation of the data [Quinlan and Rivest, 1989], or providing more efficient access to the cases [Allen and Langley, 1990].

Systems utilizing independent rules and cases are much closer in spirit to the system described here. Again the systems fall into two groups. In the first group [Rissland and Skalak, 1989; Branting, 1989], the

---

[7]The resulting scores are not directly comparable to those in section 3.1, primarily because the judge there applied native-speaker intuitions to the spoken pronunciations, whereas the first author applied more formal notions of acceptability to the written transcriptions.

focus is on deciding how and when it is appropriate to invoke RBR and CBR. For example, CABARET [Rissland and Skalak, 1989] uses heuristics for this purpose. These systems do not try to reconcile conflicts between RBR and CBR, they merely report all of the evidence.

In the second group of systems, the focus is on reconciling the conclusions of RBR and CBR. Anapron falls into this group, and so does MARS [Dutta and Bonissone, 1990]. MARS represents cases not as cases per se, but as rules derived from the cases. It acquires these rules from written documents via natural-language processing. The documents in MARS's domain of mergers and acquisitions are the rulings of the judges who decided each case. Once everything is represented as rules, MARS is able to aggregate the evidence from multiple rules using possibilistic reasoning. This requires that each rule specify a level of necessity and sufficiency with which its conclusion is implied. Thus MARS takes the approach mentioned earlier (see section 1) of converting cases to rules, and then integrating the derived and original rules.

The fundamental difference between MARS and Anapron is that MARS specifies the knowledge for drawing analogies on a per-case basis, whereas Anapron specifies it all at once in a more general form. That is, in MARS, each case is written as a rule that says which of its features must match the target problem; it also gives necessity/sufficiency values that specify its strength for purposes of aggregation. In Anapron, the similarity metric gives the equivalent knowledge for matching cases and evaluating their strength. This indicates that the two systems are appropriate in different situations. When it is practical to do the knowledge engineering of cases that MARS requires, MARS is appropriate. When it is practical to specify a similarity metric, Anapron is appropriate.

## 5   Conclusion

A general architecture was presented for improving the performance of rule-based systems through CBR. The motivation for turning to CBR was that cases are often easier to obtain than additional rules. The architecture was implemented for the full-scale problem of name pronunciation. Preliminary results indicate that the system performs near the level of the best commercial systems. However, this only reflects how the system does with its current rules and cases. The more significant finding was that the system could not have achieved this level of accuracy with its rules alone. This illustrates the capacity of the architecture to improve on the rule-based system it starts with. The results also showed that RBR and CBR interact beneficially in the system, in that improving the rules speeds up CBR. Finally, the architecture fills a new niche among rule/case hybrids — it is an accuracy-improving system; it focuses on reconciling the conclusions of RBR and CBR; and it requires weak domain knowledge in the form of a similarity metric, instead

of complex knowledge engineering of the case library.

Directions for future work include improving the system for pronunciation; applying the architecture to other domains; allowing the system to save its arules; and generating similarity metrics automatically.

## References

John A. Allen and Pat Langley. A unified framework for planning and learning. In *Proc. of Work. on Innovative Approaches to Planning, Scheduling, and Control*, San Diego, 1990. Morgan Kaufmann.

Ralph Barletta and William Mark. Explanation-based indexing of cases. In *Proceedings of the CBR Workshop*, Clearwater Beach, 1988.

L. Karl Branting. Integrating generalizations with exemplar-based reasoning. In *Proceedings of the CBR Workshop*, Pensacola Beach, 1989.

Soumitra Dutta and Piero Bonissone. Integrating case based and rule based reasoning: The possibilistic connection. In *Proceedings of the Sixth Conference on Uncertainty in Artificial Intelligence*, July 1990.

Andrew R. Golding. *Pronouncing Names by a Combination of Case-Based and Rule-Based Reasoning.* PhD thesis, Stanford University, 1991. Forthcoming.

Kristian J. Hammond and Neil Hurwitz. Extracting diagnostic features from explanations. In *Proc. of CBR Workshop*, Clearwater Beach, 1988.

Sharon Hunnicutt. Phonological rules for a text-to-speech system. *American Journal of Computational Linguistics*, 1976. Microfiche 57.

Dennis H. Klatt. Review of text-to-speech conversion for English. *J. Acoust. Soc. Am.*, 82(3), 1987.

Phyllis Koton. Reasoning about evidence in causal explanations. In *Proc. of AAAI-88*, St. Paul, 1988.

John E. Laird, Allen Newell, and Paul S. Rosenbloom. Soar: An architecture for general intelligence. *Artificial Intelligence*, 33, 1987.

Wendy G. Lehnert. Case-based problem solving with a large knowledge base of learned cases. In *Proceedings of AAAI-87*, Seattle, 1987.

J. Ross Quinlan and Ronald L. Rivest. Inferring decision trees using the minimum description length principle. *Information and Computation*, 80, 1989.

Edwina L. Rissland and David B. Skalak. Combining case-based and rule-based reasoning: A heuristic approach. In *Proc. of IJCAI-89*, Detroit, 1989.

Terrence J. Sejnowski and Charles R. Rosenberg. Parallel networks that learn to pronounce English text. *Complex Systems*, 1, 1987.

Craig W. Stanfill. Memory-based reasoning applied to English pronunciation. In *Proceedings of AAAI-87*, Seattle, 1987.

# Explaining and Repairing Plans That Fail*

## Kristian J. Hammond

*Department of Computer Science, The University of Chicago, 1100 East 58h Street, Chicago, IL 60637, USA*

ABSTRACT

*A persistent problem in machine planning is that of repairing plans that fail. One approach to this problem that has been shown to be quite powerful is based on the idea that detailed descriptions of the causes of a failure can be used to decide between the different repairs that can be applied.*

*This paper presents an approach to repair in which plan failures are described in terms of causal explanations of why they occurred. These domain-level explanations are used to access abstract repair strategies, which are then used to make specific changes to the faulty plans. The approach is demonstrated using examples from CHEF, a case-based planner that creates and debugs plans in the domain of Szechwan cooking.*

*While the approach discussed here is examined in terms of actual plan failures, this technique can also be used in the repair of plans that are discovered to be faulty prior to their actual running.*

## 1. The Problem of Plan Failure

All planners face the problem of plans that fail. As a result, most planners have some mechanism for plan repair or debugging. These range from simple replanning and backtracking [5] to analytically driven critics [16] and metaplanning techniques [27]. The most powerful approaches to repair, however, have been those that make use of the notion that a planner should first explain and then debug any failures that are detected (e.g., [21, 29]). This work builds on a tradition initially established by Sussman [24] of approaching plan repair from the point of view of developing vocabularies to construct descriptions of planning problems that can be used to select specific and thus powerful repairs.

This paper presents an approach to plan repair that uses a causal description of *why* a failure has occurred to index to a set of strategies for repairing it. This approach makes use of a set of repair rules that are indexed by the causal descriptions of the problems that they solve. The repair rules themselves are empty frames that are instantiated using the specific steps and states of a problem at hand. This combination of abstract repair knowledge and specific state information results in a repair mechanism that is both general (in that it can be applied to a wide range of problems) and powerful (in that the instantiated repairs are aimed directly at the specific details of any given problem).

The approach is embedded in the computer program CHEF, a case-based planner that creates new plans in the domain of Szechwan cooking. The difference between the approach taken in CHEF and that taken by other planners stems from CHEF's use of causal explanations of its own failures to focus on and select relevant repairs.

## 2. Repair in CHEF

CHEF's approach to plan repair is based on its ability to explain its own failures. This process of failure repair can be broken down into five basic steps:

(1) Notice the failure.
(2) Build a causal explanation of why it happened.
(3) Use the explanation to find a collection of repair strategies.
(4) Instantiate each of the repair strategies, using the specific steps and states in the problem.
(5) Choose and implement the best of the instantiated repairs.

The reasons behind most of these steps are straightforward. CHEF has to notice a failure before it can react to it at all. It has to try each of its strategies in order to choose the best one. It has to implement one of them to fix the plan. The only steps that might not seem as straightforward are the second and third steps of building an explanation and using it to find a structure in memory that corresponds to the problem and organizes solutions to it.

When CHEF encounters a failure in one of its own plans, it uses a set of causal rules to explain why the failure has occurred. This explanation includes a description of the steps and states that led to the failure as well as a description of the goals that were being planned for by those steps and states. This description is used to discriminate down to the set of abstract repair strategies appropriate to the general description of the problem. CHEF then tries to implement each of the different strategies and then choose the one best suited for the specific problem.

The problem that this technique addresses is one that crops up again and again in knowledge-intensive systems: the problem of the control of knowledge

* This paper describes work done at the Yale Artificial Intelligence Lab under the direction of Roger Schank. This work was supported by the Advanced Research Projects Agency of the Department of Defense and monitored by the Office of Naval Research under contracts N00014-82-K-0149, N00014-85-K-0108 and N00014-75-C-1111. NSF grant IST-8120451, and Air Force contract F49620-82-K-0010. It was also supported by the Defense Advanced Research Projects Agency, monitored by the Air Force Office of Scientific Research under contract F49620-88-C-0058, and the Office of Naval Research under contract N0014-85-K-010.

*Artificial Intelligence* **45** (1990) 173–228

0004-3702/90/$03.50 © 1990 — Elsevier Science Publishers B.V. (North-Holland)

This paper originally appeared in the journal, *Artificial Intelligence*, Vol. 45, Nos. 1-2, and is reprinted here with permission of the publisher, Elsevier, Amsterdam.

has encountered before. The topic of this paper, however, is its ability to repair these planning failures when it first encounters them.

CHEF consists of six modules:

(1) An *ANTICIPATOR* predicts planning problems on the basis of the failures that have been caused by the interaction of goals similar to those in the current input.

(2) A *RETRIEVER* searches CHEF's plan memory for a plan that satisfies as many of the current goals as possible while avoiding the problems that the ANTICIPATOR has predicted.

(3) A *MODIFIER* alters the plan found by the RETRIEVER to achieve any goals from the input that it does not satisfy.

(4) A *REPAIRER* is called if a plan fails. It builds up a causal explanation of the failure, repairs the plan and then hands it to the STORER for indexing.

(5) An *ASSIGNER* uses the causal explanation built by the REPAIRER to determine the features which will predict this failure in the future.

(6) A *STORER* places new plans in memory, indexed by the goals that they satisfy and the problems that they avoid.

The important module for plan repair is the REPAIRER. This module is handed a plan only after it has been run in CHEF's version of the real world, a "cook's world" simulation in which the effects of actions are computed. The rules used in this simulation are able to describe the results of the plan CHEF has created in sufficient detail for it to notice the difference between successful and unsuccessful plans.

The final states of a simulation are placed on a table of results that CHEF compares against the goals that it believes that a plan should satisfy. Plans that fail in one way or another to satisfy all of their goals are handed to the REPAIRER for repair.

CHEF's algorithm is an example of what McDermott has referred as *dependency-directed transformation* in which a preliminary plan is drawn from a library of plan schemas and then incrementally debugged, either in response to simulation or execution. Another example of this approach is Simmons' "Generate, Test and Debug" (GTD) [21], a problem solver that combines associational rules with a deep causal model. Given a problem, the association-al rules are used to generate preliminary (and potentially buggy) solutions and then the causal model is used to debug them incrementally. The main difference between the two models lies in the attitude each takes towards its domain. One of Simmons' goals in GTD is a domain-independent model of planning, while the goal in CHEF was to develop a planner that learns (through the debugging of faulty plans) how better to act and react in its domain of interest. In some sense, the attitude taken in the development of CHEF was that there is a trade-off between domain expertise and problem-solving generality, but that this expertise can be learned from weak methods.

access (McDermott [14], Stefik [23] and Wilensky [27]). In this case, the problem takes the form of choosing which plan repair, among many possible repairs, should be applied to a faulty plan. The goal is to have a planner that is able to diagnose its own failures and then use this diagnosis to choose and apply the repair strategy that will result in a corrected plan. The approach described in this paper allows a planner to do this diagnosis and repair without having to do an exhaustive or even extensive search of the possible results of applying the different plan changes that the planner has available. Further, the specific repair is selected on the basis of its ability to correct an existing problem while avoiding the introduction of any new ones.

## 3. An Overview of CHEF

Before getting into the repair method used in CHEF, it is important to understand CHEF as planner.[1] CHEF is a case-based planner that, like other case-based reasoning systems, such as those of Carbonell [3] and Kolodner et al. [10, 11], builds new plans out of its memory of old ones. Its domain is Szechwan cooking and its task is to build new recipes on the basis of a user's requests. CHEF's input is a set of goals for different tastes, textures, ingredients and types of dishes, and its output is a single recipe that satisfies all of its goals. Its basic approach is to find a past plan in memory that satisfies as many of the most important goals as possible and then modify that plan to satisfy the other goals as well.

Before searching for a plan to modify, CHEF examines the goals in its input and predicts any failures that might rise out of the interactions between the plans for satisfying them. This prediction is made on the basis of past problems that the planner has encountered rather than an exhaustive base of rules. When a failure is predicted, CHEF adds a goal to avoid the failure to its list of goals to satisfy and this new goal is also used to search for a plan. In one CHEF example, the program predicts that stir frying chicken with snow peas will lead to soggy snow peas because the chicken will sweat liquid into the pan. In response to this prediction, the program searches its memory for a stir fry plan that avoids the problem of vegetables getting soggy when cooked with meats. In doing so, it finds a past plan for beef and broccoli that solves this problem by stir frying the vegetable and meat separately. The important similarity between the current situation and the one for which the past plan was built is that the same problem rises out of the interaction between the planner's goals, although the goals themselves are different. This similarity is what allows the planner to access the plan from the past, given the description of the goal interaction in the present.

The power of CHEF lies in its ability to anticipate and thus avoid failures it

[1] For a more detailed discussion of CHEF's planning mechanisms, see [8].

## 4. Case-Based Reasoning

CHEF is part of a growing movement in Artificial Intelligence that involves the use of memory in planning (e.g., [1, 11]), problem solving (e.g., [15, 22]), language understanding [13] and diagnostic systems [12]. The main feature that links all of these systems together is that the reasoning they perform is driven by an episodic memory rather than a base of inference rules or plan operators.

Like CHEF, PLEXUS [1] and MEDIATOR [11] have tried to address issues of planning from a dynamic memory. PLEXUS' memory was designed to provide nearly right plans for an execution-time improvisional system. MEDIATOR, on the other hand, used plans pulled from memory as starting points to guide new reasoning. Together, CHEF, PLEXUS and MEDIATOR cover much of the range of planning problems that occur in the world. PLEXUS deals with those execution-time problems that can be solved by directly applying an existing plan selected from memory on the basis of environmental cues. MEDIATOR is aimed more at problems that rise out of classification errors which can be solved by building new categories in memory. CHEF, on the other hand, is aimed at problems of the interaction between planning steps that are discovered during plan execution. Like CHEF's, MEDIATOR's memory is changed as a result of its experience.

The major difference between CHEF and PLEXUS lies in the use of causal knowledge. In CHEF, all repair is based on the use of a deep domain model that provides explanations of the failures that occur. This gives CHEF the ability to repair a wide range of problems, but limits it to those problems that it has the ability to explain. PLEXUS, on the other hand, does not require a causal model in that it repairs plans by selecting alternative subplans from memory on the basis of environmental features. This frees it from the need for an explicit domain model, but also limits it in terms of both correctness and range of possible repairs. In CHEF, the analog to the improvisation in PLEXUS is the use of *object critics* to tweak an almost right plan. It is clear that both these approaches are needed in order to create a functioning case-based planner.

The major difference between CHEF and MEDIATOR is that of vocabulary. One of the major issues in CHEF is the use of abstract descriptions of planning problems in indexing. In CHEF, solutions, in the form of general strategies as well as specific plans, are indexed using a vocabulary of goal and plan interaction. In MEDIATOR, the vocabulary was more closely linked to the features of the domains in which it operated. Here the trade-off is again between the overhead involved with inference needed to apply the more abstract vocabulary and the power gained through its use. As with PLEXUS, the relationship between CHEF and MEDIATOR is a complementary one. Well-understood problems can be handled faster using the vocabulary in MEDIATOR while newer problems require the use of a domain model. The analog to the MEDIATOR vocabulary in CHEF is the network of links between surface features and memories of existing problems that is used to anticipate those problems when those features are present.

Another line of research in case-based reasoning that has shown a great deal of promise has been in the area of legal reasoning [15]. This work has centered around the use of cases, in the legal sense of the word, to support decision making and argument. Like the CHEF research, much of the thrust in this work has been aimed at the issue of representation. In particular, it has involved the use of a strategic approach to the alteration of input features so as to find relevant cases in memory. This use of strategic modification has resulted in systems that can retrieve cases from memory that are similar to but strategically different from an initial input case. By finding those cases that differ along specific dimensions, the system can reinforce its own arguments as well as anticipate problems that an adversary may throw in its way. The most exciting aspect of this work is the use of explicit strategies in the selection of features for use in indexing. This strategic approach has been all but ignored in other case-based systems yet is clearly an important aspect of human reasoning [20].

Along with the generative work in planning and problem solving, the case-based approach has been successfully used in both language understanding and diagnosis. In their work on using memory in parsing, Martin and Riesbeck [13] have advanced the idea of parsing directly into a dynamic memory by passing markers up from lexical items to concepts in memory. This activation results in predications also being passed through memory back down to particular lexical items. The overall approach involves treating understanding primarily as a recognition task in which all aspects of understanding (i.e., parsing, inference and disambiguation) are handled through the use of a single mechanism and memory. In recent work in diagnosis, Koton [12] has proposed a case-based approach to diagnosis that again treats the task as one of recognition. Using an existing expert system as a data source, Koton's CASEY was able to construct a case base that allowed it to perform the same task using less computational power and with more graceful degradation at the edges of its knowledge.

CHEF is only part of what seems to be a very fruitful approach towards reasoning. In all of these systems, the philosophy is that the search for a solution to a new problem should begin with a solution to an old one.

## 5. Indexing of Repairs

### 5.1. TOPs in understanding and repair

CHEF's approach to plan repair is based on the idea that the strategies for repairing a problem should be stored in terms of that problem. In much the same way that it makes sense to organize plans in terms of the goals that they satisfy so that they can be found when the goals arise, it makes sense to store plan repair strategies in terms of the situations to which they apply, so that they too can be found when those problems arise.

CHEF builds an explanation in response to every failure. These causal descriptions are used to discriminate between different structures in memory that describe the different interactions that can arise between steps in a plan. These structures are planning versions of the understanding TOPs suggested by Schank [17] to store information relating to complex interactions of goals. The idea behind these structures was simple: just as the concept underlying a primitive action such as ATRANS [19] could be used to store inferences relating to that action, structures relating to the interactions between these actions and the goals that they serve could also be used to store inferences that relate to the interaction. He also suggested that these structures could be used to organize episodes that they describe as well as the inferences that they relate to.

Schank argues that these structures are used for understanding in two ways: to supply expectations about a situation and to provide remindings of past situations that are similar to a current one that could be used in generalization. By having structures in memory that correspond to goal interactions rather than to individual goals or actions, an understander can have access to expectations that relate to those interactions and can learn more about them by generalizing across similar instances that they describe.

In CHEF, plan repairs are stored in terms of the problems that they solve using a set of planning TOPs that correspond to different planning problems. Each TOP organizes a set of repair strategies, which in turn suggest abstract alterations of the circumstances of the problem defined by the TOP. A TOP is defined not only by the series of steps that define the failure, it is also defined by the goals that those steps were originally designed to satisfy. Only those strategies that will fix the problem defined by a TOP, while at the same time maintaining the goals that are already satisfied by the existing steps, are found under that TOP. Any strategy that can be applied will repair the current problem without interfering with the goals that the steps involved with that problem still achieve.

A planning TOP consists of the description of a planning problem and the set of repair strategies that can be applied to solve the problem.

Like Schank's TOPs, CHEF's planning TOPs are memory structures that correspond to the interactions between the steps and states of a plan. Each planning TOP describes a planning problem in terms of a causal vocabulary of effects and preconditions. Instead of storing inferences about the situation described, however, each planning TOP stores possible repairs to the planning problem that it describes. Once a problem is recognized, the planner can use the repairs stored under the TOP that describes it to alter the faulty plan and thus fix the failure.

In CHEF, each TOP stores the repair strategies that will fix the faulty plans it

describes. These TOPs are not just descriptions of problems. They are descriptions of problems paired with the solutions that can be applied to fix the problems. The strategies under a TOP are those and only those alterations of the causal structure of the problem described by the TOP that can solve that problem. The strategies themselves are not specific repairs, they are the abstract descriptions of changes in the causality of the situation that CHEF knows about. Finding a TOP that corresponds to a problem means finding the possible repairs that can be used to fix that problem.

Each of CHEF's TOPs is stored in memory, indexed by the features of the explanation that describes the problem with which the TOP deals. To get to the strategies that will deal with a problem, CHEF has to explain why it happened and then use this explanation to find the TOP and strategies that will fix the plan. This is a simple idea: the solution to any problem depends on the underlying causality of the problem. It makes sense, then, to index solutions to problems under the causal descriptions of the problem themselves so that these descriptions can be used to access the appropriate solutions.

Planning TOPs are memory structures that correspond to the interactions between the steps and states of a plan. Each planning TOP describes a planning problem in terms of a causal vocabulary of effects and preconditions. Instead of storing inferences about the situation described, however, each planning TOP stores possible repairs for the planning problem it corresponds to. Once a problem is recognized, the planner can use the repairs stored under the TOP that describes it to alter the faulty plan and thus fix the failure.

For example, the planning TOP, SIDE-EFFECT:BLOCKED-PRECONDITION describes situations in which the side effect of one step violates the preconditions for a later one. One case of this comes from Sussman's [24] example of a planner painting a ladder before painting a ceiling and then finding that the precondition for painting the ceiling, having an available ladder, has been violated by an earlier step in the plan that has left the ladder wet. This TOP is recognized because the planner can see that a step is actually blocked and can then build the explanation that the state that blocks it is the product of an earlier step and the state itself does not satisfy any goals. Once the planner has the TOP, it is then able to apply the different general strategies for repairing the faulty plan that are stored under the structure. In this case, the strategies are:

- ALTER-PLAN:PRECONDITION: Find a way to paint the ceiling that does not require a ladder, thus avoiding the problem of the failed precondition.
- ALTER-PLAN:SIDE-EFFECT: Find a way to paint the ladder that does not leave it wet, thus negating the blocking state.
- REORDER: Paint the ceiling before painting the ladder, thus running the step with the problematic precondition before it is blocked.
- RECOVER: Do something to dry the ladder, thus reestablishing the state before it is needed for a later step.

Each of these strategies is designed to break a single link in the causal chain that leads to a failure.

The planning TOPS discussed in this paper were developed for the CHEF program and are built out of a general vocabulary of causal interactions.[2] The problems that they describe include many of those discussed by both Sussman [24] and Sacerdoti [16], but the level of detail of TOPS allows a richer description than was possible using the vocabulary of critics suggested by either of them. As a result, a planner that uses TOPS to diagnose and repair planning problems is able to describe problems in greater detail and thus suggest a wider variety of repairs for each problem encountered.

## 5.2. Controlling repair

A TOP stores those, and only those, strategies that will solve the problem corresponding to the TOP without interfering with the goals that are satisfied by the steps included in the problem. As a result, CHEF is able to control its use of repairs so as to fix existing problems without interfering with the goals satisfied by other steps highlighted in the TOP. This is an important point that deserves an example.

In a failure encountered by CHEF while creating a strawberry soufflé plan, the problem is diagnosed as a case of SIDE-EFFECT:DISABLED-CONDITION:BAL-ANCE. This TOP is distinguished by the fact that the condition that is disabled is a balance condition and the state that disables it is a side effect. That the state that undermines the plan is a side effect is important in that it allows the strategies RECOVER and ALTER-PLAN:SIDE-EFFECT to be associated with the TOP. The first of these strategies suggests finding a step that will remove the side effect state before it interferes with a later step. The second strategy suggests finding a replacement for the step that caused the side effect with a step that accomplishes the goal of the original action without producing the undesired effect. Both of these strategies depend on the fact that the state in question is a side effect, that is, a state that does not satisfy any goals that the planner is trying to achieve.

If the situation were different (e.g., if the liquid produced by pulping the strawberries satisfied one of the planner's goals), these two strategies would no longer apply. Adding a step that would remove the added liquid would violate the goal that it achieved. Replacing the step that causes the liquid with one that does not would likewise violate the goal. Changing the goals changes the strategies that can be applied to the problem because some strategies will now interfere with those goals while fixing the problem. Such differences between situations are reflected in the TOPS that are found to deal with them. If the liquid served some goal but violated a balance condition, the TOP found would

be DESIRED-EFFECT:DISABLED-CONDITION:BALANCE. Unlike the TOP, SIDE-EFFECT:DISABLED-CONDITION:BALANCE, this structure does not suggest the strategies ALTER-PLAN:SIDE-EFFECT and RECOVER, because they would fix the initial problem only at the expense of other goals.

Another important point about the relationship between planning TOPS and the strategies they store is the problem of applicability. Every strategy that is stored under a TOP will, if it can be applied, repair the problem that originally accessed the TOP. There is no guarantee, however, that a strategy can be applied in every situation. In the case of a problem CHEF encounters while stir frying beef and broccoli together,[3] one strategy, ADJUNCT-PLAN, suggests finding a step that can be run concurrent with the STIR-FRY step that will absorb the liquid produced by the beef. Unfortunately, no such step exists in CHEF's knowledge of steps. So ADJUNCT-PLAN, while it would have repaired the plan, cannot be implemented in this situation because the steps required to turn it into an actual change of plan do not exist. Each strategy describes a change that would fix a failed plan, but no strategy can be implemented if the steps that would make that change do not exist.

Each TOP describes a specific causal configuration that defines a problem. In turn, each of the strategies under a TOP describes one way to alter the configuration that will solve the problem described by the TOP. Each of the individual strategies suggests a change to one part of the overall configuration. Because the causal configurations that define these TOPS are built out of a vocabulary of interactions that is common to all of them, many share repair strategies. For example, one TOP corresponds to the situation in which the side effect of a step alters the conditions required for the running of a later step. Another corresponds to the problem of the side effect of a step itself being an undesired state. These two TOPS share the feature that a side effect of a step is interfering with the planner's goals, although in different ways. Because of this, they share the strategy ALTER-PLAN:SIDE-EFFECT which suggests finding a step to replace the original step in the plan that causes the side effect with one that achieves the same goals but does not cause the side effect. Each of these TOPS also organizes other strategies, but because some aspects of the problems that they describe are shared, they also share the strategy that suggests changes to that aspect of the problem.

The repair strategies stored under a TOP are those, and only those, that will repair the problem described by the TOP. Because each strategy alters one aspect of the problem, it may be associated with many TOPS that share that aspect.

Each of CHEF's TOPS has two components: the problem features used to index to it and the strategies that it suggests to deal with that problem. CHEF

---

[2] For a detailed discussion of this vocabulary, see Section 9.

[3] The liquid produced by stir frying the beef causes the brocolli to become soggy.

In terms of its domain, CHEF can notice that a plan has stopped when the shrimp cannot be shelled because it is too slippery, that a plan to make a soufflé fails because the batter has not risen and that a stir fried dish with fish fails because the fish has developed an iodine taste.

After CHEF has built a plan, it runs a simulation of it. This simulation is the program's equivalent of the real world rather than a part of the planning model, and a plan that makes it to simulation is considered complete. The result of this simulation is a table of descriptions that characterize the states of the ingredients used in the plan. Any compound objects created out of those ingredients are also described. The representation used by both CHEF and its simulator is a frame-like notation. In a current reimplementation of CHEF, we are doing the same work using a typed predicate calculus notation.

After running a plan to make a beef and broccoli dish, the table of results includes descriptions of the taste, texture and size of the different ingredients as well as the tastes included in the dish as a whole (Fig. 1).

Once a simulation is over, CHEF checks the states on this table against the goals that it believes should be satisfied by the plan that it has just run. These goals take the form of state descriptions of the ingredients, the overall dish and the compound items that are built along the way. No matter what its object, each compound goal defines a particular TASTE or TEXTURE for that object. Goals have the same form as the states placed on the simulator's result table, allowing CHEF to test for their presence after a simulation. CHEF tests for the satisfaction of goals by comparing expected states against those on the table of results.

Most of the failures that CHEF is able to recognize are related to the final result of the plan rather than the steps that the plan goes through on the way to that result. This is because CHEF notices failures by looking at that final product rather than monitoring the plan as it is being executed. The only failures that CHEF recognizes that are related to the running of the plan rather than its effects are those that result from the inability to perform a step because the conditions required for that performance are not satisfied.

stores its TOPs in a discrimination network, indexed by the features that describe the problem that they correspond to. In searching for a TOP, CHEF extracts these same features from its explanation of the current problem, and then the TOP suggests the strategies it stores to solve that problem.

CHEF uses sixteen TOPs to organize its repairs. The details of each are discussed in Section 7. For now, it is only important to understand that each TOP is defined and indexed by the features of a particular planning problem and organizes the two to six strategies that can be applied to the problem it corresponds to. While there are clearly more TOPs that can be used in plan repair than CHEF knows about, those it has describe the planning problems that it is forced to deal with. An expanded domain with a different set of problems, and possible reactions to them, would require an equally expanded set of TOPs and strategies.

## 6. CHEF's Repair Algorithm

As we mentioned in Section 2, CHEF's process of failure repair has five basic phases:

(1) Notice the failure.
(2) Build a causal explanation of why it happened.
(3) Use the explanation to find a collection of repair strategies.
(4) Instantiate each of the repair strategies, using the specific steps and states in problem.
(5) Choose and implement the best of the instantiated repairs.

In the sections that follow, we will discuss each of these phases as well as clarify each one with an example from the running of CHEF.

### 6.1. Noticing the failure

The first step in dealing with a failure is noticing it. CHEF is only able to recognize what we call domain failures. These are failures that can be characterized in terms of the operators and states in a domain. It is unable to recognize failures such as described by Wilensky's metagoals [27] (e.g., avoid wasting resources and avoid overly complex plans). This, however, is not because of any problem in terms of the theory of repair expressed in CHEF. It is just a byproduct of the emphasis of the program. CHEF is able to recognize three basic types of failures:

(1) failures of a plan to be completed because of a precondition failure on some step;
(2) failures of a plan to satisfy one of the goals that it was designed to achieve;
(3) failures of a plan because of objectionable results in the outcome.

```
(SIZE OBJECT (BEEF2) SIZE (CHUNK))
(SIZE OBJECT (BROCCOLI1) SIZE (CHUNK))
(TEXTURE OBJECT (BEEF2) TEXTURE (TENDER))
(TEXTURE OBJECT (BROCCOLI1) TEXTURE (SOGGY))
(TASTE OBJECT (BEEF2) TASTE (SAVORY INTENSITY (9.)))
(TASTE OBJECT (BROCCOLI1) TASTE (SAVORY INTENSITY (9.)))
(TASTE OBJECT (GARLIC1) TASTE (GARLICY INTENSITY (9.)))
(TASTE OBJECT (DISH) TASTE (AND (SALTY INTENSITY (9.))
                                (GARLICY INTENSITY (9.))
                                (SAVORY INTENSITY (9.))
                                (SAVORY INTENSITY (5.)))))
```

Fig. 1. Section of result table for BEEF-WITH-BROCCOLI.

The easiest failure for CHEF to notice is the failure of a plan to finish because of a blocked precondition on a particular step. When this occurs, the simulator stops execution of the plan and informs CHEF that the plan has failed because of a blocked precondition. This is what happens in a plan for SHRIMP-STIR-FRY that CHEF created out of its memory of a FISH-STIR-FRY plan (Fig. 2). The problem with this dish is simply that a MARINATE step has been placed before a SHELL step, making the shrimp too slippery to handle.

One type of failure CHEF recognizes is the failure of a plan to run to completion because the preconditions for a step are blocked.

More often than not, CHEF's plans run to completion. Even though a plan may run, this is no guarantee that it will run well or that it will succeed in doing all that it is supposed to do. After a plan finishes, CHEF must check its outcome to be sure that it has not failed to achieve the desired results.

CHEF evaluates its results along two dimensions. First, it has to check for any of the plan's goals that might not have been achieved. Second, it has to check for any generally objectionable states that might also have resulted from the plan.

Each of CHEF's plans has a set of goals associated with it. These goals are generated by CHEF using the general role information attached to the general plan type and the specific ingredients of the plan itself. Each role specifies the expected contribution of its fillers and each ingredient provides the particulars of that contribution.

These goals take the form of state descriptions of the ingredients, the overall dish and the compound items that are built along the way. No matter what its object, each goal defines a particular TASTE or TEXTURE for that object. These goals all have the same form as the states placed on the simulator's result table, allowing CHEF to test for their presence after a simulation.

Once a plan has been run, the goals associated with the plan are searched for on the table of results built up by the simulator. If a goal is not present, then the plan has not succeeded in achieving it. This is the second kind of failure that CHEF can recognize. It is the failure of a plan to achieve one of its goals. The failure in the beef and broccoli recipe is one of this type. CHEF finds the goal to have crisp broccoli associated with the plan, checks it against the states on the simulator's table of results and finds that the desired state is not there. Because the plan has failed to achieve one of its own goals, it is considered a failure (Fig. 3).

The second type of failure that CHEF recognizes is the failure of a plan to achieve a goal it was designed to satisfy.

The final type of failure that CHEF can recognize is a failure that results from a state that has been included rather than excluded from the results of a plan. In this case, the state is one that the planner knows to be objectionable. Its inclusion in the results of a plan is a liability rather than an asset. In this situation, the plan may actually achieve all of the goals it is designed for but also results in states that are *a priori* objectionable.

To recognize these failures, CHEF uses descriptions of the particular states that it wants to avoid. Like positive goals, these states are of the same form as the states on the simulator's table of results so they can be tested for directly. One example of this type of failure occurs as a result of CHEF's first attempt to build a stir fried fish dish. The plan CHEF creates achieves all of the goals that it was designed for but also results in a dish that has the taste of iodine. This taste is a byproduct of the fish which was treated in the same way as the chicken that was originally in the dish. CHEF recognizes this by checking the states resulting from the plan against its knowledge of states to be avoided in general (Fig. 4).

The last type of failure CHEF can recognize is the occurrence of an objectionable state in the result of a plan.

---

```
Simulating -> Marinate the shrimp in the soy sauce,
sesame oil, egg white, sugar, corn starch and rice wine.

Unable to simulate -> Shell the shrimp.
: failed precondition.

RULE: "A thing has to be handleable in order to shell it."

Some precondition of step: Shell the shrimp.
has failed.
```

Fig. 2. A SHELL step blocked by unhandleable shrimp.

---

```
Checking goals of recipe -> BEEF-AND-BROCCOLI

Checking goal ->
   It should be the case that: The broccoli is now crisp.

The goal: The broccoli is now crisp.
is not satisfied.
It is instead the case that: The broccoli is now soggy.

Recipe -> BEEF-AND-BROCCOLI has failed goals.
```

Fig. 3. Finding fault with BEEF-WITH-BROCCOLI.

By finding out the answers to these general questions, the planner can then find out how to respond to the failure while protecting the rest of the plan. This is the information that any planner would need in order to make an intelligent decision about how to react to a planning failure.

To build its explanations, CHEF uses the trace left by the forward chaining of the simulator. The links built by the simulator are a very simple set of causal connections that reflect the requirements of the domain. Steps are connected to the states that follow from them by RESULT links. States lead into new steps by filling slots and by satisfying PRECONDITIONS. The tests on preconditions are limited to tests on the texture, taste and existence of ingredients as well as their amounts and the relationship of those amounts to other ingredients. Failures are traced back from the failed states themselves through the steps that caused them, back to the conditions that caused the steps to fail, and so on back to the step that caused the unexpected condition itself.

CHEF constructs its causal explanation of failures by chaining backward through the causal links built during the simulation of the failed plans.

It is important to note that we make no claims about the details of any process model involved with constructing these explanations. We are not claiming that we have solved or even made great advances in automatic diagnosis. We do, however, stand by our claim that the form of the diagnosis must be a causal description of the states and steps that actually led to a failure. We have done some work in the use of case-based techniques in the construction of explanations in [7, 9], but it is only tentative and discussion of it is beyond the scope of this paper.

CHEF's movement through the causal network built up by the simulator is controlled by a set of explanation questions similar to those suggested by Schank [18]. These questions tell CHEF when to chain back for causes and when to chain forward for goals that might be satisfied by a particular state or step. Each answer tends to be used as the starting point for the next part of the search. For example, the answer to the question of what step caused an undesired state is the starting point in searching for the answer to the question of what condition altered the expected outcome of that step. The "questions," however, only serve to focus the basic search mechanism to the appropriate branches of the dependency structure. In the absence of a pre-existing support structure, the questions would act to guide a forward and backward chaining inference engine.

CHEF uses different sets of questions in explaining different types of failure. For failures in the results of a plan, CHEF has seven questions aimed at identifying the steps and states that have combined to cause an objectionable state or to block a desired one. For situations involving plans that cannot be completed because some precondition of a step is blocked, CHEF asks a

```
Checking goals of recipe -> FISH-STIR-FRIED

Checking for negative features ->

Unfortunately: The dish now tastes a bad taste.
In that: The dish now tastes fresh, like iodine, like sea-food,
like garlic, hot, oniony, sweet, nutty and salty.

Recipe -> FISH-STIR-FRIED has failed goals.
```

Fig. 4. Finding fault with FISH-STIR-FRIED.

## 6.2. Explaining the failure

Once a failure is noticed, it has to be explained. This is because the explanation of a plan failure is used to access the TOP and strategies that can be applied. The best way to organize plan repairs is under the descriptions of the problems that they solve so that the problem itself is a pointer to the solution. The best description in this case is a causal explanation of the problem. So the next step in dealing with a failed plan is to causally explain why the failure occurred.

This idea of explaining failure is not a new one. This approach to failure was suggested by Wilensky in his use of MAKE-ATTRIBUTION in PANDORA [28]. The goal of explanation in CHEF, however, is not simply to explain why the failure occurred. The goal is also to explain the presence of the steps and states that gave rise to the failure in terms of the planner's current goals. It is this combination of information that allows CHEF to select the set of strategies that will repair the plan while preserving the goals that it already satisfies.

CHEF's explanation of a failure is a causal description of the steps and states that led to it.

In the case of a failure due to a precondition that was not satisfied, the explanation is of the events that led up to the state that violated that condition. In the case of a failure due to an unsatisfied goal, it is an explanation of why the steps that normally lead to the goal state did not do so in this plan. In the case of a failure due to a result that includes an objectionable state, it is an case of a failure due to a result that includes an objectionable state, it is an explanation of why that state has come about. In all three cases, the actual explanation format of the explanation is a dependency tree in which the planner's actions and the initial state of the world support the existence of the problematic states.

In general, the explanation of a failure is aimed at finding out:

- *What state constitutes the failure?*
- *What caused the failure?*
- *What goals were the steps involved in the failure aimed at achieving?*

somewhat different set of questions that are designed to identify the cause of the precondition violation. Both sets of questions, however, have the overall aim of diagnosing the problem so that the appropriate repair strategies can be found and applied.

CHEF's search through the simulator's causal trace is guided by a set of explanation questions that focus on the relevant steps and states. The process used to answer these questions is simply forward and backward chaining.

When a plan fails because of a faulty result, CHEF first asks the questions that will determine the steps that caused the failure. Then it asks the questions that will determine how those steps relate to the goals of the plan. The first set takes the form of backward chaining rules while the second takes the form of forward chaining rules. The questions are:

- *What is the failure?*
This identifies the particular problem state. In situations where the failure is an unsatisfied goal, the negation of the goal state serves as the answer. In situations where an objectionable state has come about, the state itself serves.

- *What is the preferred state?*
Where a goal has not been achieved, the goal itself is the answer. Where an objectionable state has come about, the desired state of the object affected is focused on instead.

- *What was the plan to achieve the preferred state?*
This question identifies the step that has actually caused the failure. The answer is found by chaining back from the failure to the step that actually caused it to come into being. To do this CHEF traverses a RESULT link back to the step.

- *What were the conditions that led to the failure?*
With this question, CHEF is trying to identify the nonnormative conditions that caused the step to go wrong. Using the step that caused the failure as a starting point, CHEF searches back along PRECONDITION links to any states that had to be true for the original inference of the failure to be made.

- *What caused the conditions that led to the failure?*
This question identifies the actual cause of the nonnormative conditions. Continuing to chain back, CHEF identifies the causes of the state that altered the predicted conditions and thus allowed the failure to result.

- *Do the conditions that caused the failure satisfy any goals?*
This question directs CHEF's attention forward. It looks to the effects of the condition that led to the failure for any goals that it directly or indirectly satisfies.

- *What goals does the step which caused the condition enabling the failure satisfy?*
This question is similar to the last one in that it directs CHEF's attention to the goals satisfied by the step that eventually led to the failure.

In explaining inability to complete a plan because of the failed preconditions of a step, CHEF uses a slightly different set of questions.

- *What was the step that was blocked?*
CHEF begins by identifying the blocked step itself.
- *What was the condition that disabled the step?*
Checking the preconditions on the step, CHEF chains back to find the one that has failed.
- *What caused the precondition to fail?*
Next it chains back along RESULT links to the step that caused the state which in turn violated the precondition.
- *What goals does the step which caused the condition disabling the step satisfy?*
This question directs CHEF to chain forward to the goals satisfied by the step which caused the violating state.
- *Do the conditions that caused the failure satisfy any goals?*
Just as the last question looked forward to the goals satisfied by the step this question looks forward to the goals satisfied by the violating state itself.
- *What goals does the blocked step serve?*
With this question, CHEF again chains forward to find the goals served by the step that was blocked.

The answers to these questions give CHEF the same flexibility and assurance in this situation that it gets from the explanation of failures rising out of the results of a plan. It has the extended causal chain that leads back from the blocked step to the state that blocked it and then back to the step that caused that state. This gives it the knowledge of where it can change the plan. It also has the understanding of what goals the different steps satisfy. This gives it the knowledge it needs to alter a step or state while maintaining the goals that it serves.

While CHEF asks different explanation questions in different situations, the questions it asks are always aimed at building a causal chain of the states and steps that led to the failure.

One good example of the kind of explanation that is built by CHEF is found in the case of the fallen strawberry soufflé. The problem is that the added liquid from pulped strawberries disturbs the balance between the amount of liquid in the batter and the amount of whipped egg and flour used as leavening. Because there is too much liquid, the soufflé falls. One important aspect of this

ASKING THE QUESTION: 'What is the failure?'
ANSWER-> The failure is: It is not the case that: The batter is now risen.

ASKING THE QUESTION: 'What is the preferred state?'
ANSWER-> The preferred state is: The batter is now risen.

ASKING THE QUESTION:
'What was the plan to achieve the preferred state?'
ANSWER-> The plan was: Bake the batter for twenty-five minutes.

ASKING THE QUESTION:
'What were the conditions that led to the failure?'
ANSWER-> The condition was: There is an imbalance between the whipped stuff and the thin liquid.

ASKING THE QUESTION:
'What caused the conditions that led to the failure?'
ANSWER-> There is thin liquid in the bowl from the strawberry equaling 2.4 teaspoons.
was caused by:
Pulp the strawberry.

ASKING THE QUESTION:
'Do the conditions that caused the failure satisfy any goals?'
ANSWER-> The condition:
There is thin liquid in the bowl from the strawberry equaling 2.4 teaspoons is a side effect only and meets no goals.

ASKING THE QUESTION:
'What goals does the step which caused the condition enabling the failure satisfy?'
ANSWER-> The step:
Pulp the strawberry.
establishes the preconditions for:
Mix the strawberry with the vanilla, egg white, egg yolk, milk, sugar, salt, flour and butter.
This in turn leads to the satisfaction of the goals:
The dish now tastes like berries.

Fig. 5. Explanation in case of strawberry soufflé failure.

situation is that the condition that prevents the soufflé from rising is not just that there is no too much liquid. It is that there is no longer a balance between the amount of liquid and the amount of leavening. When CHEF has to chain back to find the cause of this condition it has to check the two parts of the relationship against the normative case. The part that is irregular (in this case because it is new to the plan) is then traced down as the cause of the imbalance (Fig. 5).

This explanation gives CHEF the descriptors that will index to the planning TOP and repair strategies that will propose the appropriate set of solutions.

The fact that the PULP step has the side effect of producing liquid makes it a candidate for change. The fact that it enables the addition of the strawberries to the batter, thus making the batter taste like berries, means that any change that is made to this step to avoid the side effect has to include some addition that satisfies that goal. Likewise, the fact that the liquid is itself a side effect that satisfies no goals means that the planner can add steps that remove that side effect without having to worry about any goals that the condition served. The TOP and strategies that are found using these features reflect the constraints that they place on the type of repair that can be made to the plan.

CHEF responds to failures by constructing causal explanations of why they have occurred.

This is a simple idea: the solution to a problem is based on the nature of the problem. Because of this, it makes sense to index different sets of solutions by the descriptions of different sorts of problems and then use the descriptions of the problems to find the solutions that are appropriate.

### 6.3. Getting the TOP

CHEF's repair strategies are all stored under planning TOP's, structures that correspond to different planning problems. The TOPs themselves are stored in a discrimination network, indexed by the features of the explanations they correspond to. The strategies organized under a TOP describe the alterations to the failed plans described by the TOP. These alterations are designed to repair the failure without interfering with the other goals in any plan that the TOP describes. The TOPs include structures such as SIDE-EFFECT:DISABLED-CONDITION:BALANCE and SIDE-FEATURE:ENABLES-BAD-CONDITION. The strategies include changes such as REORDER the steps, REMOVE the condition, and SPLIT-AND-REFORM the step.

To get to a TOP, CHEF uses the structure and content of the dependency tree it has built to index through a discrimination network that organizes its TOPs. The features that are important in this discrimination include the nature of the violated condition, the temporal relationship between the steps, and the nature of the failure itself, as well as the relationship between the problematic state and the planner's goals.

The explanation of a failure is used to index through a discrimination-net to a TOP that describes it in more general terms.

In the case of the strawberry soufflé failure, the condition violated in the plan was a balance requirement between two amounts, and the condition that caused the imbalance was a side effect rather than a goal state. These two facts were very important in discriminating down to the TOP that corresponds to the situation. If the condition that caused the imbalance had not been a side effect or the requirement had not been one for a balance condition, a different TOP with different strategies would have been found (Fig. 6).

The TOP that describes the problem of the fallen soufflé is indexed so that it can be found using the explanation of any situation in which a side effect of one step violates the conditions of a later step by causing an imbalance in a required relationship. Each of the strategies that is stored under SIDE-EFFECT: DISABLED-CONDITION:BALANCE is designed to deal with one aspect of this problem. If the problem had been different, a different TOP would have been found and a different set of strategies would have been suggested. The strategies under a TOP are limited by the types of changes CHEF is able to make and by the kinds of actions the domain allows. For instance, CHEF does not have the ability to have other actors perform tasks for it, so the strategy of having a step performed by a different actor is not available to it.

Each TOP organizes a set of strategies that, if implemented, will repair any problem described by the TOP.

Each of the strategies indexed under SIDE-EFFECT:DISABLED-CONDITION: BALANCE is also under other TOPs that share features with it. Each strategy suggests an alteration to the initial plan that will cause a break in a particular part of the causal chain that leads to the failure. Each change suggested by a strategy is, in principle, sufficient to repair the plan. So they are used individually and are not designed to be used in concert. Each strategy describes a single change to some link in the causal chain that leads to the failure. The strategies indexed under SIDE-EFFECT:DISABLED-CONDITION:BALANCE are:

- ALTER-PLAN:SIDE-EFFECT: Replace the step that causes the side effect with one that does not. The new step must satisfy the goals of the initial step.
- ALTER-PLAN:PRECONDITION: Replace the step that has the violated condition with a step that satisfies the same goals but does not have the same condition.
- ADJUNCT-PLAN: Add a new step that is run concurrent with the step that has the violated condition. This new step should allow the initial step to satisfy the goal even in the presence of the precondition violation.
- RECOVER: Add a new step between the step that causes the side effect and the step that it blocks. This step should remove the state that violates the precondition.
- ADJUST-BALANCE:UP: Adjust the imbalance between conditions by adding more of what the balance lacks.

Each of these five strategies suggests a change in the causal situation that will solve the current problem without affecting the other goals of the plan. They are those and only those changes that will alter the causal structure of the current faulty plan so as to remove that fault.

If the features of the problem had been different, the TOP and the strategies found would also be different. For example, if the condition violated by the side effect had not been a balance condition, CHEF would have found SIDE-EFFECT:DISABLED-CONDITION, a simpler TOP that does not include the ADJUST-BALANCE:UP strategy. Likewise, if the condition satisfied goals of its own, DIRECT-EFFECT:DISABLED-CONDITION:BALANCE would have been selected, a TOP that lacks both ALTER-PLAN:SIDE-EFFECT and RECOVER because strategies that remove the condition would alter any plan to no longer satisfy the goal achieved by the condition. So, as the situation changes, the fixes that can be applied to it change, and thus the TOP and strategies that are found to deal with it change as well.

```
Searching for top using following indices:

Failure = It is not the case that: The batter is now risen.
Initial plan = Bake the batter for twenty-five minutes.
Condition enabling failure = There is an imbalance between
   the whipped stuff and the thin liquid.
Cause of condition = Pulp the strawberry.
The goals enabled by the condition = NIL
The goals that the step causing the condition enables =
   The dish now tastes like berries.

Found TOP TOP3 -> SIDE-EFFECT:DISABLED-CONDITION:BALANCE
TOP -> SIDE-EFFECT:DISABLED-CONDITION:BALANCE has 5
   strategies associated with it:

      ALTER-PLAN:SIDE-EFFECT
      ALTER-PLAN:PRECONDITION
      ADJUNCT-PLAN
      RECOVER
      ADJUST-BALANCE:UP
```

Fig. 6. TOP for strawberry soufflé failure.

Different problem descriptions allow access to different TOPs and different TOPs organize different strategies. The causality of a situation determines the strategies that will be suggested to deal with it.

Once it has found a planning TOP, CHEF has access to a set of strategies that, if implemented, will repair its current problem. It may not be the case, however, that every abstract repair will have a real implementation in every situation. It may also be the case that the change suggested by one strategy will be better than those suggested by others. So CHEF must test each strategy and decide which to apply to the particular problem. It does this by generating the changes to the plan that the TOP's strategies suggest, choosing between those changes and then implementing the change it has chosen.

## 6.4. Applying the strategies

Once a TOP has been found, the strategies that are stored under it are applied to the problem at hand. For CHEF, applying a strategy means generating the specific change to the failed plan that is suggested when the abstract strategy is filled in with the specifics of the current situation. The idea here is to take an abstract strategy such as RECOVER and fill it in with the specific states and steps from the current problem. In this way a general strategy for repairing a plan becomes a specific change to the plan at hand.

To apply a strategy, CHEF fills the framework the strategy defines with the particulars of the current situation, turning it into a specific change rather than just an abstract alteration.

Each strategy has two parts: a test and a response. The test under each strategy determines whether or not the strategy has an actual implementation in the current situation. The response is the actual change that is suggested. In most cases, the result of the test run by the strategy is used in the response. For example, one of CHEF's strategies is RECOVER, which suggests adding a new step between two existing ones that removes a side effect of the first before it interferes with the second. The test on RECOVER checks for the existence of a step that will work for the particular problem. The response is a set of instructions that will insert that step between the two existing ones. The action that is returned when CHEF searches for the step described by RECOVER is used in building the response (Fig. 7). The general format of the strategies is to build a test and then use the response to that test in building the set of instructions that CHEF has to follow in order to implement the change directed by the strategy.

These strategies fall into four general classes of changes: some alter the sequence of events in a plan, some break single steps into multiple ones, some add new steps and others replace old steps with new ones. Each of these classes of response has a slightly different type of test associated with it. Those involving changes to the order of steps in a plan only test for conflicts that the reordering might cause. Strategies that split steps test the step to check for any problems that splitting it might cause. Strategies that add steps check a library of actions for the existence of the steps that they describe. This library has actions indexed by their effects and preconditions which makes it possible for CHEF to search for a particular action that has the effect described by a strategy. Similarly, the strategies that direct the planner to replace steps check this library for actions that meet their precondition and effect specifications.

These repair strategies make up the core of the strategies needed to deal with planning problems in general. They are not strategies that are related to the CHEF domain alone. Just as the planning TOPs are built out of a general vocabulary for describing different causal interactions, the repair strategies used by CHEF are general methods for altering plans. The vocabulary for describing TOPs is taken from a basic vocabulary of plan interactions and can describe a wide range of planning problems. Because the TOPs are products of the combination of these descriptors, however, each one is very specific. So the strategies stored under each can be equally specific. This means that the TOPs approach allows a planner to deal with a wide range of planning problems with very specific plan repairs.

This does not mean, however, that these strategies are in any way domain-specific. They are instead frames that are instantiated as specific changes to plans in response to problems that arise in all domains. With the general descriptive powers of the TOPs vocabulary, a wide range of problems can be described at this level of specificity.

Each strategy has a test that can be run to check for the conditions that have to hold for the strategy to be implemented. Each strategy also has a response, which gives CHEF the actual changes that it has to make to implement the strategy.

```
Asking question needed for evaluating strategy: RECOVER

ASKING ->
Is there a plan to recover from
There is thin liquid in the bowl from the strawberry equaling 2.4
teaspoons

There is a plan: Drain the strawberry.

Response: After doing step: Pulp the strawberry
          Do: Drain the strawberry.
```

Fig. 7. Test and response for RECOVER strategy.

In building the tests and responses during the application of a strategy to a particular problem, CHEF uses the answers to its explanation questions to fill in the specific steps and states that the strategy will test and possibly alter. The tests and responses are actually empty frames that are filled with the specifics of the current explanation. The strategy RECOVER, for example, uses the answer to the question of what condition caused the current failure to construct its test and the answer to the question of what step caused that condition to build its response. This allows it to find a step that will remove the condition and run it immediately after the condition arises. The definition of each strategy refers to the answers to the explanation questions that are important to it, making it possible to build the specific test and response at the appropriate time. Each definition begins with a binding of the existing explanation answers to variables that the strategy will then use to construct its query and response (Fig. 8). When the strategy is actually applied, the specific answers are inserted into the appropriate slots in the strategy structure.

CHEF builds the changes suggested by a strategy by filling its framework in with the appropriate answers to its earlier explanation questions.

While each of the strategies that a TOP suggests for repairing a plan will result in a successful plan if implemented, there is no guarantee that an implementation will be found for a specific correction. In the beef and broccoli case, for example, one strategy that is suggested is ADJUNCT-PLAN. This directs the planner to find a step that can be run along with the original STIR-FRY step that will continuously remove the effects of stir frying the beef as they are created. While any such addition would repair the plan, because the liquid would be removed before it could affect the broccoli, CHEF does not have knowledge of such a step so the strategy cannot be implemented in this situation.

```
(def:strat recover
  bindings (*condition* expanswer-condition
            *step* expanswer-step)
  question (enter-text ("Is there a plan to recover from "
                        *condition*)
            test (search-step-memory *condition* nil)
            exit-text ("There is a plan" *answer*)
            fail-text ("No recover plan found"))
  response (text ("Response: After doing step: " *step* t
                  "          Do: " *answer*)
            action (after *step* *answer*)))
```

Fig. 8. Definition of RECOVER strategy.

While not all strategies will be useful in all situations, most of the time many changes are suggested that the planner can make. In the example of the strawberry soufflé (Fig. 6), the five strategies associated with the TOP end up generating four possible changes that will repair the plan. CHEF generates all possible changes so that it can compare the specific changes and choose which one to actually implement on the basis of the changes themselves rather than on the basis of the abstract strategies (Fig. 9).

```
Applying "OP -> SIDE-EFFECT:DISABLED-CONDITION:BALANCE
to failure It is not the case that: The batter is now risen.
in recipe BAD-STRAWBERRY-SOUFFLE

Asking questions needed for evaluating strategy:
ALTER-PLAN:SIDE-EFFECT

ASKING ->
Is there an alternative to
Pulp the strawberry.
that will enable
The dish now tastes like berries.
which does not cause
There is thin liquid in the bowl from the strawberry equaling
2.4 teaspoons

There is a plan: Use strawberry preserves.

Response: Instead of doing step: Pulp the strawberry
          do: Use strawberry preserves.

Asking questions needed for evaluating strategy:
ALTER-PLAN:PRECONDITION

ASKING ->
Is there an alternative to
Bake the batter for twenty-five minutes.
that will satisfy
The batter is now risen.
which does not require
It is not the case that: There is thin liquid in the bowl from the
strawberry equaling 2.4 teaspoons.

No alternate plan found
```

Fig. 9. Strategies generating changes in strawberry soufflé example.

The changes suggested by the different strategies are aimed at altering different aspects of a problem. Some change the steps that caused a particular condition. some change the steps that will remove the condition itself and others change the circumstances that make the condition a problem.

Each of CHEF's strategies generates a change that is a combination of the abstract description of a repair provided by the strategy itself and the specifics of the failed plan. Because each TOP only stores those strategies that will repair the situation described by it and used to find it. any one of them will fix the plan if implemented. Because each TOP does have multiple strategies. however. not only must CHEF have a mechanism for generating these changes, it also must have one for choosing between them.

### 6.5. Choosing the repair

Once all of the possible repairs to a failed plan are generated, CHEF has to choose which one it is going to implement. To do this, CHEF has a set of rules concerning the relative merits of different changes. By comparing the changes suggested by the different strategies to one another using these heuristics, CHEF comes up with the one that it thinks is most desirable.

This set of heuristics is the compilation of general knowledge of planning combined with knowledge from the domain about what sort of changes will be least likely to have side effects. Some of these heuristics are closely tied to the domain. such as "It is easier to add a preparation step than a cooking step." and "It is better to add more of something that is already in the recipe than something new." Others are more domain-independent, such as "It is better to add a single step than to add many steps." and "It is better to replace a step than add a new step."

In the strawberry soufflé example, the final repair that is chosen is to add more egg white to the recipe. This change is generated by the strategy ADJUST-BALANCE:UP which suggests altering the down side of a relationship between ingredients that has been placed out of balance. This repair is picked because it is the least violent change to the plan that can be made and has the least likelihood of creating one problem as it solves another.

CHEF chooses between the competing changes suggested by different strategies using a set of repair heuristics designed to find the most reliable alteration.

### 6.6. Confirming the change

Once a change is selected, CHEF implements the change using its procedural knowledge of how to add new steps, split steps into pieces. remove steps and add or increase ingredients. These functions are the same as those used to

```
Asking questions needed for evaluating strategy:
ADJUNCT-PLAN

ASKING ->
Is there an adjunct plan that will disable
There is thin liquid in the bowl from the strawberry equaling
2.4 teaspoons
that can be run with
Bake the batter for twenty-five minutes.

There is a plan: Mix the flour with the egg, spices, strawberry,
salt, milk, flour and butter.

Response: Before doing step: Pour the egg yolk, egg white, vanilla,
sugar, strawberry, salt, milk, flour and butter into a baking-dish
    Do: Mix the flour with the egg, spices, strawberry, salt,
    milk, flour and butter.

Asking questions needed for evaluating strategy:
RECOVER

ASKING ->
Is there a plan to recover from
There is thin liquid in the bowl from the strawberry equaling 2.4
teaspoons

There is a plan: Drain the strawberry.

Response: After doing step: Pulp the strawberry
    do: Drain the strawberry.

Asking questions needed for evaluating strategy:
ADJUST-BALANCE

ASKING ->
Can we add more whipped stuff to BAD-STRAWBERRY-SOUFFLE

There is a plan: Increase the amount of egg white used.

Response: Increase the amount of egg white used.
```

Fig. 9 (*Continued*).

implement the plan changes made by the MODIFIER when it adds new goals to existing plans.

In the strawberry soufflé situation the final change is marginal, which is the best sort of change if it actually can repair the problem. The only difference between the original strawberry soufflé plan and the new one is that the new one has more egg white in it. Figure 10 shows the change generated by the strategy ADJUST-BALANCE:UP.

CHEF implements the changes suggested by a strategy using the same alteration functions used by the MODIFIER to add new goals to plans.

Once a change is made, the plan is simulated again to assure that the change has led to the expected result. If another failure occurs, it is once again passed through the repair process of explaining the failure, finding the TOP and applying the appropriate strategy. Although past changes will not be marked explicitly, the fact that they participate in satisfying a goal will stop the REPAIRER from removing them. For example, in order to fix a fish and peanuts recipe to avoid the problem of the iodine taste of the fish, CHEF adds the step of marinating it in rice wine. Unfortunately, this causes the fish to become soggy. In trying to fix the new failure, CHEF recognizes that it cannot just remove the marinate step, because it satisfies a goal of removing the iodine taste. Instead of removing the step CHEF replaces it with another step that satisfies the same goal, removing the iodine taste of fish, but does not add any more liquid. Rather than marinating the fish in rice wine, it marinates it in crushed ginger.

If the plan is successful, it is then indexed in memory like any other plan, except it is marked by the fact that it avoids a particular kind of failure that can be used when that failure is predicted to occur at some later date.

Because CHEF uses its plans again and again, just building them is not enough. It also has to place them in memory so that they can be accessed again. While this paper does not stress learning, it is important to note that CHEF is designed to use the explanation generated while repairing a failure to discern which features will be predictive of problems of this type. This knowledge, combined with the existence of the new plan that repairs the problem, allows CHEF to *anticipate and avoid* the problem in later planning.

If a new plan is built out of one that avoids a failure, the fact that it too avoids the same failure is associated with it. When the new plan is stored in memory, it too is stored by the token which is related to the prediction of the failure. This means that any one failure can have many plans in memory that can be used to avoid it. Each one of these is indexed by the token related to the failure and is also indexed by the goals that it satisfies and any other failures that it also avoids. Every time a once failed plan is stored in memory, the token that is associated with the prediction of a failure is used to index it in memory. This closes the repair loop, allowing the prediction of a failure to provide the information needed to find the plan that will avoid it.

## 7. CHEF's TOPs

The repair algorithm is only part of the overall approach to repair used in CHEF. An equally if not more important aspect is the theory of the content of the types of problems that tend to be encountered and the different repairs that remove them. This section will outline the different problems that rise out of the interactions between the steps and goals of a plan (represented by planning TOPs). The sections that follow will also look at the various repairs that can be applied as well as the other uses to which TOPs can be put.

CHEF's TOPs fall into five categories or families of problems. Some have to do with side effects of a step interfering with later steps, some with the features of objects enabling bad effects, and some with the problems of blocked preconditions. The TOPs within each family share features with one another. The fact that they describe similar problem situations means they must share those strategies that are designed to repair the aspects of the problem that they have in common.

```
Implementing plan -> Increase the amount of egg white used.
Suggested by strategy ADJUST-BALANCE:UP

New recipe is -> STRAWBERRY-SOUFFLE

    STRAWBERRY-SOUFFLE

    Two teaspoons of vanilla
    A half cup of flour
    A quarter cup of sugar
    A quarter teaspoon of salt
    A half cup of milk
    Two cups of milk
    One piece of vanilla bean
    A quarter cup of butter
    Five egg yolks
    Six egg whites
    One cup of strawberry
```

Fig. 10. Change generated by ADJUST-BALANCE:UP strategy.

- SIDE-EFFECT, or SE, TOPs describe problems that are generated by the side effects of STEPs.
- DESIRED-EFFECT, or DE, TOPs describe problems that are generated by the desired effects of STEPs.
- SIDE-FEATURE, or SF, TOPs describe problems generated by the features of OBJECTs that do not satisfy any goals.
- DESIRED-FEATURE, or DF, TOPs describe problems generated by the goal-satisfying features of OBJECTs.
- STEP-PARAMETER, or SP, TOPs describe problems generated by improperly set STEP parameters.

CHEF's TOPs fall into families of configurations whose members correspond to similar causal situations and organize similar repair strategies.

## 7.1. SIDE-EFFECT (SE)

The most commonly used TOPs in CHEF are from the family of TOPs that describe problems with the side effects of one step interfering with the overall plan in one way or another. There are five TOPs that belong to the general family of SIDE-EFFECT TOPs (SE):

- SE:DISABLED-CONDITION:CONCURRENT: The side effect of a step disables its own success requirements or the requirements of a concurrently run step.
- SE:DISABLED-CONDITION:SERIAL: The side effect of a step disables the success requirements of a later step.
- SE:DISABLED-CONDITION:BALANCE: The side effect of a step disables a success requirement of a later step by causing an imbalance in a required relationship.
- SE:BLOCKED-PRECONDITION: The side effects of a step violate the preconditions of a later step that are required for it to run at all.
- SE:GOAL-VIOLATION: The side effects of a step are in themselves an undesired state.

SE TOPs describe situations in which the side effects of a step interfere with the successful running of a plan.

### 7.1.1. SE:DISABLED-CONDITION:CONCURRENT (SE:DC:C)

This TOP describes situations in which a side effect of a step interferes with the satisfaction conditions of the step itself or of another step that is being run concurrent with it. Here the side effect has to occur as the step is being run, not just at the end. Likewise, the condition that is violated is not just a precondition, it is a condition that has to be true for the entire duration of the step. In CHEF these are referred to as *developing side effects* and *maintenance conditions*. One example of this situation is in the case of the BEEF-AND-BROCCOLI plan in which the liquid generated by stir frying the beef violates the maintenance condition on the step to stir fry the broccoli that the pan remain dry. As a result, the plan fails because the broccoli becomes soggy. The indices for SE:DC:C are:

- There is a failure.
- The failure is caused by a violated condition.
- The step that caused the state violating the condition is concurrent with the step which has resulted in the failure.
- The condition satisfies no goals.
- The step that causes the condition satisfies at least one goal directly or indirectly.

The strategies stored under SE:DC:C are:

SPLIT-AND-REFORM,
ALTER-PLAN:SIDE-EFFECT,
ADJUNCT-PLAN:REMOVE,
ADJUNCT-PLAN:PROTECT,
ALTER-PLAN:PRECONDITION.

Each of these strategies aims its attack at one part of the causal chain that led to the failure. For example, SPLIT-AND-REFORM suggests breaking the self-defeating single step into a series. ALTER-PLAN:SIDE-EFFECT suggests that a different step be used that does not produce the violating condition, and ADJUNCT-PLAN:REMOVE suggests that a new step be added that removes the effects altogether.

### 7.1.2. SE:DISABLED-CONDITION:SERIAL (SE:DC:S)

The complement to the TOP SE:DC:C is SE:DC:S, which differs from its sibling in that the step that causes the problem side effect occurs before the step with which the side effect interferes. The problem condition is still a side effect, but the steps involved are separate so there are more options than in the case of SE:DC:C.

The indices to this TOP differ from those of SE:DC:C only by the fact that the two steps involved are not run at the same time:

- There is a failure.
- It is caused by a violated condition.
- The step that would have achieved the desired state follows the step that caused the violating conditions.
- The condition satisfies no goals.
- The step that causes the condition satisfies at least one goal directly or indirectly.

The fact that two steps are separated in time gives the planner more options than if they had been at the same time. The strategies indexed under the TOP reflect this added flexibility:

```
REORDER.
ALTER-PLAN:SIDE-EFFECT.
ALTER-PLAN:PRECONDITION.
RECOVER.
  ADJUNCT-PLAN:REMOVE.
  ADJUNCT-PLAN:PROTECT.
```

### 7.1.3. SE:DISABLED-CONDITION:BALANCE (SE:DC:B)

A slightly different situation in which a side effect causes problems is defined by SE:DC:B. This is the situation in which the side effect of a step produces the effect of changing an existing state so as to increase an amount, in turn causing an imbalance in a relationship required for a later step. Unlike SE:DC:S, the condition caused by the earlier step is already accounted for by the plan, but not completely. The fallen soufflé in the STRAWBERRY-SOUFFLE plan is an example of this problem. The added liquid from the pulped strawberries causes an imbalance between liquid and leavening in the batter which leads to a fallen soufflé.

The difference between the features that access this TOP and those that access SE:DC:S is clear. SE:DC:B is found when the condition that is violated is a balance relationship that has to hold for a step to succeed.

– There is a failure.
– There is a violated balance condition on the step that caused it.
– The step that would have achieved the desired state follows the step that caused the violating conditions.
– The condition satisfies no goals.
– The step that causes the condition satisfies at least one goal directly or indirectly.

The strategies organized by the TOP are also the same, with the addition of two new strategies.

```
ADJUST-BALANCE:UP.
ADJUST-BALANCE:DOWN.
```

### 7.1.4. SE:BLOCKED-PRECONDITION (SE:BP)

SE:BP describes the situation in which the side effect of a step actually halts the running of the plan. This occurs in the case of the first stir fried shrimp dish CHEF creates in which the MARINADE step that is run before the SHELL step blocks the precondition on SHELL that the shrimp be handleable. The features used to access this TOP are:

– There is a blocked precondition.
– The condition that caused the block was caused by an earlier step.
– The condition satisfies no goals.
– The step that causes the condition satisfies at least one goal directly or indirectly.

The four strategies associated with this TOP are:

```
RECOVER.
REORDER.
ALTER-PLAN:PRECONDITION.
ALTER-PLAN:SIDE-EFFECT.
```

### 7.1.5. SE:GOAL-VIOLATION (SE:GV)

The TOP SE:GV describes the situation in which the side effect of a step itself is an undesired state in the present circumstances. The state generated by the step does not interfere with other steps, it is just objectionable in its own right. The features used to index to this TOP are:

– There is a failure.
– The step that caused it has no violated conditions that the planner can identify.

The strategies stored under this TOP are:

```
RECOVER.
ALTER-PLAN:SIDE-EFFECT.
ADJUNCT-PLAN:REMOVE.
```

### 7.2. DESIRED-EFFECT (DE)

A somewhat different class of TOPs are those that describe situations in which the desired effect of a step, that is a state that either directly satisfies a goal or enables the satisfaction of a goal, causes problems later in the plan. The main difference between DESIRED-EFFECT and SIDE-EFFECT TOPs is that DE TOPs do not suggest strategies designed to remove or avoid the effects that are interfering with the plan. To do so would be to undercut the goals satisfied by the interfering state.

There are four DE TOPs. They are parallel to the first four SE TOPs that were discussed in the last section. But because these correspond to situations in which the interfering state satisfies a goal, the strategies that they store are aimed at altering the aspects of the problem that are not related to the desired effect itself. The DE TOPS are:

- DESIRED-EFFECT:DISABLED-CONDITION:CONCURRENT: A desired effect of a step disables its own success requirements.
- DESIRED-EFFECT:DISABLED-CONDITION:SERIAL: A desired effect of a step disables the success requirements of a later step.
- DESIRED-EFFECT:DISABLED-CONDITION:BALANCE: A desired effect of a step disables a success requirement of a later step by causing an imbalance in a required relationship.
- DESIRED-EFFECT:BLOCKED-PRECONDITION: The desired effects of a step violate the preconditions of a later step that are required for it to run at all.

CHEF does not use the TOP DESIRED-EFFECT:GOAL-VIOLATION because it defines a situation that it never has to encounter. DE:GV describes a situation in which the goal-satisfying effect of a step is itself a state the planner wants to avoid. While this can happen in some planning situations, it is never the case that CHEF has to deal with states that both meet and violate its goals.

DE TOPs describe situations in which the desired effects of a step interfere with the successful running of a plan.

### 7.2.1. DE:DISABLED-CONDITION:CONCURRENT (DE:DC:C)

This TOP describes the ultimate self-defeating plan. The desired effects of a step infer with the conditions that it itself requires to succeed. Because the violating state is also serving the planner's goals, strategies such as ADJUNCT-PLAN:REMOVE and ALTER-PLAN:SIDE-EFFECT cannot be applied because they would negate a state that the planner wants to maintain. Only those strategies that are aimed at correcting the situation without altering the part of the causal chain leading to the failure that includes the violating state are included under this TOP.

The features that are used to find this TOP are:

- There is a failure.
- There is a violated condition on the step that caused it.
- The plan to achieve the desired state itself caused the violating conditions.
- The condition satisfies at least one goal directly or indirectly.

The strategies stored under this TOP are:

ALTER-PLAN:PRECONDITION,
SPLIT-AND-REFORM,
ADJUNCT-PLAN:PROTECT.

### 7.2.2. DE:DISABLED-CONDITION:SERIAL (DE:DC:S)

Like its brother DE:DC:C, the TOP DE:DC:S is aimed at situations in which the desired effect of a step interferes with the plan rather than a side effect that can be removed or avoided altogether. This TOP describes the situation in which the desired effect of a step violates the satisfaction conditions of a later step. The features that index to it are:

- There is a failure.
- There is a violated condition on the step that caused it.
- The step that would have achieved the desired state is different from the step that caused the violating conditions.
- The condition satisfies at least one goal directly or indirectly.

The fact that two steps are separate in time gives the planner more freedom than if they took place in parallel. The strategies under the TOP reflect this:

REORDER,
ALTER-PLAN:PRECONDITION,
RECOVER,
ADJUNCT-PLAN:PROTECT.

### 7.2.3. DE:DISABLED-CONDITION:BALANCE (DE:DC:B)

A variant of the situation in which a relationship between two states is put out of balance is DE:DC:B, which describes the situation in which the culprit is the desired effect of a step rather than a side effect. DE:DC:B is indexed by the following features:

- There is a failure.
- There is a violated balance condition on the step that caused it.
- The step that would have achieved the desired state is different from the step that caused the violating conditions.
- The condition satisfies at least one goal directly or indirectly.

The strategies organized by the TOP reflect the fact that the state causing the problems is a desired one by including only those that deal with the problem without interfering with that state. They are:

ALTER-PLAN:PRECONDITION,
ADJUNCT-PLAN:PROTECT,
ADJUST-BALANCE:UP.

### 7.2.4. DE:BLOCKED-PRECONDITION (DE:BP)

The TOP DE:BP describes the situation of one of the classic problems in machine planning: the problem of ordering the steps required to build a three-block

This is less a point about TOPs and more a point about the level of detail used to define them and describe different causal situations. Because the description of the situations leading to failures include distinctions between side effects and desired effects. CHEF is able to distinguish between cases where different strategies apply where earlier planners could not. Because it has knowledge of exactly what steps and states in the problem have to be protected, it is able to make alterations that other planners would not have the assurance to make.

The features that are used to index to DE:BP are almost identical to those used to access SE:BP, but the single difference between them has a great effect on the strategies that CHEF can apply to deal with the different situations. The features that access DE:BP are:

- There is a blocked precondition.
- The condition that caused the block was caused by an earlier step.
- The condition satisfies at least one goal directly or indirectly.

Because the planner has to protect the goals satisfied by the blocking condition it only has two strategies that it can apply to repair the situation:

> REORDER.
> ALTER-PLAN:PRECONDITION.

## 7.3. SIDE-FEATURE (SF)

In many situations, a failure will rise out of a problem having to do with a particular feature of an item in a plan rather than having to do with the effects of one step relating to the effects of another. This is the type of situation described by TOPs in the SIDE-FEATURE family of structures. These SF TOPs relate to situations in which the features of new items that have been added to plans interfere with the goals that the plans are trying to achieve. This family of TOPs is called "SIDE-FEATURE" because the TOPs in it all describe situations where a feature of an object that does not satisfy a goal interferes with the plan. This is opposed to the DESIRED-FEATURE TOPs that describe situations in which the desired feature of an object disrupts a plan.

There are three TOPs in this family that are actually used by CHEF:

- SIDE-FEATURE:ENABLES-BAD-CONDITION: An object's feature enables a step to have a faulty result.
- SIDE-FEATURE:BLOCKED-PRECONDITION: An object's feature disables a required precondition on a step.
- SIDE-FEATURE:GOAL-VIOLATION: An object's feature is itself an objectionable state.

SF TOPs describe situations in which a non-goal satisfying feature of an item interferes with the successful running of a plan.

tower [24]. In this problem, the planner has the dual goals of having block A on block B, (ON A B), and block B on block C (ON B C). Unfortunately, if it starts the tower by putting A on B, (MOVE A B), before putting B on C, (MOVE B C), it is unable to continue because of the precondition on the MOVE step that the block being moved must have a clear top (Fig. 11). Because A is on B, B cannot be moved, but having A on B is also one of the planner's goals. The effects of the first step violate the preconditions for the later one. This is the situation described by DE:BP. The desired effect of one step blocks the preconditions required to perform another step, and both steps satisfy one or more of the planner's goals. The problem is how to change the situation so that both parts of the plan can be run.

The solution that has been suggested in the past [16, 24] is to repair the plan by reordering the steps, putting B on C before putting A on B. This solution is the same as one of the two suggested by the TOP DE:BP. But DE:BP also suggests the strategy of finding some way to move the B block that does not require that it has a clear top. At the very least the approach of splitting the process of plan repair into diagnostic and prescriptive stages has allowed a gain of one new solution to this classic problem. But, quite truthfully, this is not a particularly exciting gain.

A more exciting gain lies in the vocabulary used to describe this problem at all. The vocabulary suggested by Sussman in building HACKER describes this situation as one of *Brother-goal-clobbers-brother-goal*. While this description covers cases of DE:BP, it also covers cases of SE:BP where the state blocking the goal is not a protected one. Because of this, HACKER would suggest the limited solution REORDER in cases described by SE:BP where CHEF would be able to suggest the strategies of RECOVER, ALTER-PLAN:SIDE-EFFECT, ALTER-PLAN: PRECONDITION, ADJUNCT-PLAN:REMOVE as well as REORDER. Because CHEF is able to distinguish between situations in which an interfering state serves some goals and those in which it does not, it is able to know when it can apply more powerful strategies than those planners that could not describe problems in these terms.

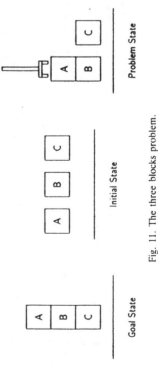

Fig. 11. The three blocks problem.

### 7.3.1. SF:ENABLES-BAD-CONDITION (SF:EBC)

The TOP SF:EBC describes situations in which some feature of an object enables a step to have a bad result. The failure CHEF encounters in building FISH-STIR-FRY is an example of this sort of situation. The taste of the fish interacts with the stir fry step to create an iodine taste. The failure is caused by a feature of the fish itself rather than by the side effect of a step leading into a later one. The features of the situation that lead to recognizing this TOP are as follows:

- There is a failure.
- There is a violated condition on the step that caused it.
- The plan to achieve the desired state has a violated satisfaction condition.
- The violating state satisfies no goals.
- The condition is an inherent feature of an object.

Because there is only one step involved in this type of situation, the strategies to deal with the failure are centered around it. But because there is an identifiable state that is related to an object feature, there is also a strategy that is aimed at removing that feature:

ALTER-PLAN:PRECONDITION,
ADJUNCT-PLAN:PROTECT,
REMOVE-FEATURE.

### 7.3.2. SF:BLOCKED-PRECONDITION (SF:BP)

Sometimes a new object is added to a plan that the steps of the plan are not designed to deal with at all. If the MODIFIER allows this to happen, it is possible that certain steps will be blocked altogether by some feature of the new object. This is the situation described by SF:BP. One example of this is the problem of adding lobster to a fish dish, replacing it for the existing fish. In this situation, the planner has to deal with the problem of the shell, either when building the plan or later when a failure points to the problem. Because the texture of the lobster does not meet the preconditions for a CHOP step, the plan cannot be run without alteration. The problem is not that one step is interfering with another. It is that one of the items in the plan does not meet the requirements for running one of its steps. The features that make it possible to recognize this situation are:

- There is a blocked precondition.
- The condition that caused the block is a feature of an object.
- The feature satisfies no goals.

The strategies that this TOP organizes are again aimed at changing the violated step itself and altering the feature of the object involved:

ALTER-FEATURE,
ALTER-PLAN:PRECONDITION.

### 7.3.3. SF:GOAL-VIOLATION (SF:GV)

Sometimes the problem with an item is not in that it leads to difficulties, but instead that it has a feature that by itself is a problem. This is the situation described by SF:GV. One example of this situation that CHEF deals with is the problem it encounters while trying to create duck dumplings. In this case, the fat from the duck itself is an objectionable feature that violates one of the planner's goals. This TOP has only those strategies that are aimed at removing the features from an item that are themselves objectionable and has no suggestions about changing the existing steps in the plan.

This situation is easy to recognize:

- There is a failure.
- The failure is an inherent feature of an object.

The strategies suggested in this situation are aimed only at changing the object itself:

ALTER-ITEM.
REMOVE-FEATURE.

### 7.4. DESIRED-FEATURE (DF)

Another family of TOPs related to the features of items rather than the interactions of steps is DESIRED-FEATURE (DF). DF TOPs all describe situations in which a feature of an object that actually satisfies a goal causes trouble. Unlike SIDE-FEATURE TOPs, DF TOPs store strategies that only alter the steps affected by the problem feature.

There are only two TOPs in this family that CHEF uses:

- DESIRED-FEATURE:DISABLED-CONDITION: A goal-satisfying feature of an object enables a faulty result from a step.
- DESIRED-FEATURE:BLOCKED-PRECONDITION: A goal-satisfying feature of an object actually blocks a required precondition of a step.

DF TOPs describe situations in which a goal-satisfying feature of an item interferes with the successful running of a plan.

### 7.4.1. DF:DISABLED-CONDITION (DF:DC)

DF:DC describes situations in which a desired feature of an object causes a step to have a bad result.

The features used to recognize this situation are:

- There is a failure.
- There is a violated condition on the step that caused it.
- The plan to achieve the desired state has a violated satisfaction condition.
- The violating state satisfies at least one goal directly or indirectly.
- The condition is an inherent feature of an object.

There are three repairs associated with this TOP:

ADJUNCT-PLAN:PROTECT.
ALTER-PLAN:PRECONDITION.
ALTER-FEATURE.

### 7.4.2. DF:BLOCKED-PRECONDITION (DF:BP)

This TOP describes a situation in which an object's feature blocks a step but the feature itself is a desired one. Because the step is actually blocked by the feature, thus removing the possibility of running an adjunct plan as in DF:DC, the strategies associated with this TOP are very limited.
The features used to recognize this situation are:

- There is a blocked precondition.
- The condition that caused the block is a feature of an object.
- The condition satisfies at least one goal directly or indirectly.

The strategies that this TOP organizes are again aimed at changing the violated step itself and altering the feature of the object involved:

ALTER-FEATURE.
ALTER-PLAN:PRECONDITION.

### 7.5. STEP-PARAMETER (SP)

The last family of TOPs relates to problems involving the amount of time a step takes and the tools it uses.
The STEP-PARAMETER family has two TOPs:

- STEP-PARAMETER:TIME: a failure is blamed on the amount of time a step has run.
- STEP-PARAMETER:TOOL: A failure is blamed on the tool used in a step.

SP TOPs describe situations in which the bad parameter of a step interferes with the successful running of a plan

### 7.5.1. SP:TIME (SP:T)

SP:T is actually two TOPs, one for steps that have run too long and one for steps that have not run long enough. These are particularly useful TOPs in the CHEF domain where cooking times have a great effect on the results of a step. While significant, however, the features used to index to the TOPs and strategies used to repair the problems described by those TOPs are trivial.
The indices for SP:T:LONG, which describes situations in which steps have been run too long, are:

- There is a failure.
- The plan to achieve the desired state has a violated satisfaction condition.
- The violated condition is a time that is greater than the time constraint on the objects of the step.

There are two strategies to deal with this problem:

SPLIT-AND-REFORM,
ALTER-TIME:DOWN.

The indices for SP:T:SHORT, which describes the reverse situation, in which a step has not been run long enough, are:

- There is a failure.
- The plan to achieve the desired state has a violated satisfaction condition.
- The violated condition is that the time on the step is less than the time required by the objects of the step.

Again there are two strategies to deal with this problem:

ALTER-TIME:UP,
SPLIT-AND-REFORM.

### 7.5.2. SP:TOOL (SP:TL)

Sometimes the instruments used in a step lead to problems of their own. Baking a soufflé in the wrong size pan, for example, will lead to the outside cooking too fast or too slowly. SP:TL describes situations in which a step fails because of an inappropriate instrument.
The indices for SP:T are:

- There is a failure.
- The instrument used causes the failure.

There is only one strategy associated with this TOP:

ALTER-TOOL.

## 7.6. Why TOPs?

In CHEF, TOPs are used to organize the repair strategies that can be applied to the problems that they describe. Strictly speaking, this is not necessary. The different strategies could each be indexed under the particular causal connection that they deal with. Instead of using a causal description of a situation to index to a TOP and then accessing the strategies that are housed under it, a planner could use the pieces of the same causal description to index directly to each of the strategies independently. Given this, what function do CHEF's TOPs really serve?

The answer to this has three parts: two within the CHEF implementation and one outside of it.

The first part of this answer is that CHEF uses its TOPs for something other than organizing repair strategies. It also uses them to guide it in learning from its failures. Along with the strategies it organizes, each TOP also indicates which features in the situation it describes should be marked as predictors of the current problem. Because each TOP corresponds to a particular causal configuration, it can store the information as to which aspects of the overall situation are important for CHEF to notice in future planning.

For example, CHEF had to repair the problem of the iodine taste of fish ruining a dish. In doing so, it diagnosed the situation as one of SIDE-FEATURE:ENABLES-BAD-CONDITION. This TOP organizes a set of strategies that can be applied to the problem. but because the TOP describes a situation in which a feature of an item interacts with a step (the taste of sea food and the STIR-FRY step), it is able to direct the planner to mark both of them as predictive of the failure. Once this is done, the co-occurrence of the two features. the goal to include sea-food and the goal to make a stir fry dish. will cause the planner to anticipate and try to avoid the failure. Neither feature alone, however, predicts this problem.

The TOP SIDE-FEATURE:GOAL-VIOLATION, which describes situations in which a feature of an item directly violates a goal, directs the learning in a slightly different direction. Like SF:EBC. SF:GV states that the feature of the object should be marked. but it does not suggest that any particular step be marked. because the feature violates one of the planner's goals independent of any step that has acted on it. CHEF diagnoses the greasy texture in the duck dumplings it builds as a case of SF:GV. because duck will have fat in any situation. As a result. CHEF marks the duck itself as predictive of a greasy texture in all circumstances.

CHEF uses its TOPs to indicate which aspect of a situation should be marked as predictive of a problem in later planning. Because the TOP corresponds to the causal circumstances of the situation, it can indicate which features are important to a current problem and which will be important to later ones. Unlike organizing repair strategies, this is a function that requires the knowl-

edge of all aspects of a planning problem. The entire description of the problem is needed to choose the features that will be marked. Even if the individual aspects of the problem could be used independently to point out individual features that were important, they would have to be combined at some point to form the proper conjunction of features that would predict a particular problem. One way or another, the configurations that correspond to the TOPs would have to be recognized.

The second answer to the question of the functionality of TOPs has to do with the prediction of failures and the indexing of plans. When CHEF anticipates a problem it has to have some way of describing that problem to its RETRIEVER so it can search for a plan that solves it. Instead of using a description that stays at the level of a specific failure (e.g., soggy broccoli). CHEF uses its TOPs to describe what it predicts and what it is looking for. CHEF also indexes the plans that deal with problems by the TOPs that described them. The prediction of a problem described by a TOP is used to find a plan that solves that problem. The TOPs allow the planner to access plans that solve problems that are analogous to current ones.

The different plans that are indexed by a single TOP are similar in that the causal configuration of the problems they solve are the same. Each TOP is used to index to the plans that deal with different instances of the single causal situation it describes. So each TOP acts as the access mechanism that links problems to the analogous plans in memory that will solve them.

One possibility that CHEF does not explore in dealing with plan failures is searching for another plan to replace its current one altogether. This would be a process similar to the initial retrieval of a plan to deal with a problem that CHEF does when it predicts one. In this case, however, it would happen after CHEF actually encounters a failure and has to recover from it. In this sort of situation, the TOPs themselves could be used to store past episodes that deal with the problems they describe. This situation demands that the plan being searched for deals with the causality of the current problem. which is described by the TOP, and so it makes sense to store these plans under the TOP itself. TOPs could carry greater weight by directly storing complete replacement plans to deal with failures as well as strategies.

Beyond this, TOPs could also be used to help deal with the problems that would rise out of a more realistic implementation of repair strategies. In a more ambitious implementation of strategies, one in which the table look-up of steps that meet certain requirements is replaced with a planner that can deal with simple state changes, the current approach to the competition between strategies would have to change. Generating all possible alterations and then choosing between them is too costly. A better approach would be to associate the successful and unsuccessful applications of a strategy to problems described by a TOP with the TOP itself. These episodes could then *focus* the planner's attention on the strategies that have been most helpful in this situation, *suggest* implementations of different strategies. and *warm* if certain strategies have had problematic results in this type of situation [6]. These functions have to be linked to the TOPs in that the competition between strategies has to be between them as they apply to the current problem. not as they apply globally to all problems.

In CHEF, TOPs organize strategies. indicate the features that will predict a failure. and link predictions of problems to the plans that solve them. They also have the potential to organize plans so that they can be suggested as replacements for failed plans and to manage better the choice between strategies that can be applied to a problem. While many of these functions could be implemented without the use of TOPs. others require TOPs because they correspond to entire causal situations and can be used to organize inferences that have to be made about those situations. The functional gains from the use of TOPs more than justifies their presence as organizing structures for planning.

## 8. The Repairs

The repair strategies used by CHEF owe a great deal to the work on plan repair that has preceded it. such as that of Sacerdoti [16]. Sussman [24] and Wilensky [28]. CHEFs repair rules. however. are somewhat more detailed than those that have gone before and make greater use of an organization that links the description of a problem to the solutions that can be applied to it.

Because many planning projects have been developed in somewhat impoverished domains many repair strategies have been overlooked because they had no application within these domains. Sussman's blocks world and Sacerdoti's pump world limited the actions of any planner working within them and thus limited the kinds of repairs that a planner could make. The failures encountered by HACKER and NOAH were usually the product of scheduling errors and were repaired by one or another variation of REORDER. They did not. in general. have to deal with questions such as the difference between a side effect and a desired effect of an action. Wilensky suggested a wider range of plan repair strategies in PANDORA. but did not provide the organization that would make them useful or give a method for actually implementing the general strategies for use when solving specific problems.

CHEF's repair strategies differ from those of past planners in that they are more specific and are organized such that a single situation can have multiple strategies applied to it.

In CHEF the repair rules are all organized under specific TOPs and each TOP is associated with a particular causal configuration. The TOP SIDE-EFFECT:DISABLED-CONDITION:CONCURRENT. for example. is accessed only when a single action has a side effect that disables states that have to be maintained during the course of that action. CHEF accesses these strategies by accessing the TOP that stores them. and the TOP is indexed by the causal explanation of the problem that corresponds to it.

For CHEF it is always the case that the repair strategies that are applied to a particular problem are those and only those that suggest changes to the causal configuration that will repair the plan. It may be that the change is not possible. because of the specifics of the problem. but if the change can be made then the plan will be repaired. In the beef and broccoli failure, one of the suggested repairs is to run an adjunct plan that will remove the liquid from the pan as the broccoli is cooking. In this case. CHEF does not know of any step to do this. but if such a step were known. such as throwing a sponge in the pan with the food. it would solve the problem. Even though it cannot find such a plan. CHEF is able to describe the kind of action it needs. in terms of the preconditions and effects of different steps.

In order to use this description to find specific plans CHEF makes use of a library of actions. indexed by their preconditions and effects and by other plans that they are similar to. When a repair strategy is applied. CHEF builds a request into this library using the general description associated with the strategy. filled in with the specifics of the problem. The general strategy is turned into a specific request for a step or set of steps in the domain that have particular preconditions and effects.

Requests to this library of steps can take two forms. They can be requests for steps that have particular results or requests for steps that are similar to given steps but have different preconditions or effects. A strategy such as ALTER-PLAN:SIDE-EFFECT. that suggests replacing an existing step with one that does not produce a particular side effect. builds a request of the second type (Fig. 12). A strategy such as RECOVER. that directs the planner to add a new step to a plan that will remove a particular state. builds a request of the first type (Fig. 13). Each one is defined as a general structure which is filled in with the current answers to CHEF's explanation questions.

For example. one problem that CHEF encounters in creating a plan for FISH-WITH-PEANUTS is that the rice wine marinade it uses to remove the iodine taste of the fish makes the fish crumble during cooking. Because it recognizes that the side effect of one plan is enabling an undesired condition, CHEF evokes the TOP SIDE-EFFECT:DISABLED-CONDITION:SERIAL, which suggests the strategy ALTER-PLAN:SIDE-EFFECT. as well as many others. ALTER-PLAN:SIDE-EFFECT is a general strategy to use a plan that achieves the initial goal but does not have the undesired side effect. Because CHEF knows the problematic state, the goal that is to be achieved. and the initial plan that has gone wrong, it is able to build a request for a step that removes the iodine taste from fish that does not have the side effect of adding liquid to the dish. This describes the plan segment in which the fish is marinated in ginger.

To apply an abstract strategy, CHEF fills in the general structure with specific information about the current situation from its explanation of the problem.

CHEF uses seventeen general repair rules in the normal course of its planning. Each one of these is associated with one or more TOPs and suggests a fix to a specific causal problem. Each one of these rules carries with it a general description of a fix to a plan, through a reordering of steps, an alteration of the objects involved or a change of actions. These general descriptions are filled in with the specific states that the planner is concerned with at the time the repair rule is suggested.

It is important to realize that these strategies, while they are designed for specific situations, are not *domain*-specific. Stated generally, they are:

- ALTER-PLAN:SIDE-EFFECT: Replace the step that causes the violating condition with one that does not have the same side effect but achieves the same goal.
- ALTER-PLAN:PRECONDITION: Replace the step with the violated precondition with one that does not have the same precondition but achieves the same goal.
- RECOVER: Add a step that will remove the side effect before the step it interferes with is run.
- REORDER: Reorder the running of two steps with respect to each other.
- ADJUST-BALANCE:UP: Increase the down side of a violated balance relationship.
- ADJUST-BALANCE:DOWN: Decrease the up side of a violated balance relationship.
- ADJUNCT-PLAN:REMOVE: Add a new step to be run along with a step that has the result of removing a problematic state as it is being created.
- ADJUNCT-PLAN:PROTECT: Add a new step to be run along with a step that is affected by an existing condition that allows the initial step to run as usual.
- ALTER-TIME:UP: Increase the duration of a step.
- ALTER-TIME:DOWN: Decrease the duration of a step.
- ALTER-ITEM: Replace an existing item with one that has the desired features but not an undesired one.
- ALTER-TOOL: Replace an existing tool with one that has the desired effect but does not cause an undesired one.
- SPLIT-AND-REFORM: Split a step into two separate steps and run them independently.
- ALTER-PLACEMENT:BEFORE: Move an existing step to run before another one.
- ALTER-PLACEMENT:AFTER: Move an existing step to run after another one.

```
(def:strat alter-plan:side-effect
  bindings (*condition* expanswer-condition
            *step* expanswer-step
            *sgoal* expanswer-step-goal)
  question (enter-text ("Is there a alternative to " t
                        *step* t
                        "that will enable " t
                        *sgoal* t
                        "that does not cause " t
                        *condition*)
            test (search-alter-memory nil *step* *condition* *sgoal*)
            exit-text ("There is a plan" *answer*)
            fail-text ("No alternate plan found"))
  response (text "Response: Instead of doing step: " *step* t
                 "    Do: " *answer*)
            action (replace *step* *answer*)))
```

Fig. 12. Definition of ALTER-PLAN:SIDE-EFFECT strategy.

```
(def:strat recover
  bindings (*condition* expanswer-condition
            *step* expanswer-step)
  question (enter-text ("Is there a plan to recover from "
                        *condition*)
            test (search-step-memory *condition* nil)
            exit-text ("There is a plan" *answer*)
            fail-text ("No recover plan found"))
  response (text "Response: After doing step: " *step* t
                 "    Do: " *answer*)
            action (after *step* *answer*)))
```

Fig. 13. Definition of RECOVER strategy.

CHEF uses its explanation of what has gone wrong to suggest the TOP, which in turn suggests a set of possible repairs. CHEF then uses the explanation again to provide the specific states and steps that convert the general repair rules into domain-specific requests for plans. Having a detailed causal description of the problems it encounters allows it to find very general repair rules and instantiate them as specific repairs.

- ALTER-FEATURE: Add a step that will change an undesired attribute to the desired one.
- REMOVE-FEATURE: Add a step that will remove an inherent feature from an item.

Each of these strategies is associated with one or more planning TOPs. Each TOP is indexed by a general description of the type of plan failure that its strategies can repair. This allows the explanation of a failure to be used to access the TOP that contains the strategies that can repair it.

## 9. A Causal Vocabulary for TOPs

Each of CHEF's TOPs corresponds to a causal configuration that describes a failure. The vocabulary that is used to build up these configurations and define the TOPs is one of causal interactions between steps and states. This vocabulary differs from those used by past planners to describe the problems they encounter primarily in that it distinguishes the effects of steps that lead to satisfied goals from those that do not. It also distinguishes problems that cause a plan to halt from those that allow the plan to run to completion but ruin the result.

CHEF's causal vocabulary is based on four classes of things that it knows about:

(1) OBJECTs, which are physical objects such as the ingredients and the utensils used in the CHEF domain.
(2) STATEs, which are features of the OBJECTs such as TASTE, TEXTURE and SIZE.
(3) STEPs, which are actions taken on OBJECTs with the aim of altering some STATEs.
(4) GOALs, which are STATEs that the planner is trying to achieve. Unlike other STATEs, GOALs are hypothetical STATEs that actual STATEs are tested against.

With the exception of a distinction between certain types of STATEs, the bulk of CHEF's vocabulary has to do with relationships between these OBJECTs, STATEs and STEPs. One important aspect of the relationships that CHEF uses to describe causal configurations is that they depend on the presence of goals. Many of the relationships change as the planner's goals change, even if the causality of the situation does not. If a STATE satisfies a goal, that fact is reflected in the description of any problems that result from it. If the goal it satisfies is no longer part of the planner's overall goal structure, the description of the situation will change to reflect this. CHEF's descriptions of causal situations depend on its goals because it has to use these description to find appropriate changes to make to its plans, and these changes cannot be such that they violate the goals already met by these plans.

The vocabulary used to describe planning TOPs is based on the different relationships that can hold between OBJECTs, STATEs, STEPs and GOALs.

One of the most powerful distinctions that CHEF's vocabulary makes use of is the distinction between different relationships between STATEs and the STEPs that cause them. CHEF understands three types of relationships:

(1) DESIRED-EFFECTs are states that result from steps that satisfy the planner's goals. This satisfaction can either be the direct result of the state matching a goal state or the indirect result of the state enabling a later step that satisfies a goal.
(2) SIDE-EFFECTs are the results of steps that do not satisfy any goals either directly or indirectly.
(3) DEVELOPING-SIDE-EFFECTs are side effects that occur during the running of a step rather than as a final result.

All of the effects of a step are linked to it by RESULT links that lead from the step to the state and RESULT-OF links that lead from the state back to the step. The effect of distinguishing between these different relationships lies in the types of strategies that each will allow. Problems having to do with SIDE-EFFECTs can be solved by making changes to a plan that remove the effects in one way or another while those having to do with DESIRED-EFFECTs cannot. Likewise, those states that are DEVELOPING-SIDE-EFFECTs can be dealt with using adjunct steps that can be added to a plan to remove the effects of the steps as they are produced.

CHEF recognizes three types of preconditions for STEPs:

(1) REQUIRED-PRECONDITIONs are those states that have to hold for a step to be run at all.
(2) SATISFACTION-CONDITIONs are those states that have to hold as a step is entered for its desired effects to result.
(3) MAINTENANCE-CONDITIONs are those states that have to hold during the entire running of a step for its desired effects to result.

STATEs that meet the preconditions of a STEP have ENABLES links going from the STATEs to the STEP. The STEP has ENABLED-BY links going from it back to the STATEs. For example, the STATE representing the texture of the crushed strawberries in a strawberry soufflé plan is linked to the MIX step by an ENABLES link and the MIX step points back to it by an ENABLED-BY link.

Along with the relationships between STATEs and STEPs there are relationships between OBJECTs and STATEs and between OBJECTs and STEPs. An OBJECT can link into a STEP in two ways:

(1) As a STEP-OBJECT, which means that the STEP acts on the OBJECT in order to change a STATE related to it.

By noticing this distinction CHEF is able to suggest strategies in cases of violated BALANCE STATES that it is not able to suggest in cases of violated ABSOLUTE STATES.

The vocabulary of TOPs is one of causal interactions. It describes the relationships between OBJECTs, STATEs, STEPs and GOALs and makes distinctions between those that serve goals and those that do not. It distinguishes between these different TOPs because the different problems described by them require different repair strategies.

## 10. Repairs Not Used by CHEF

While CHEF uses quite a few repair strategies to deal with its planning failures, there exists a whole set of these repair rules that it ignores. CHEF excludes these strategies not because they are not useful, but because they deal with problems that CHEF never encounters and suggest changes that make no sense in CHEF's domain. For example, CHEF does not have strategies to deal with planning failures having to do with interactions with other actors. The entire range of *counter-planning* strategies suggested by Carbonell [2] and Wilensky [26] that were designed to deal with problems that arise when two or more planners interact have been ignored. CHEF also ignores those strategies that require that it alter the initial goals that it is handed as its input. While the changes that CHEF makes to a plan may modify goals that it has generated on its own, it never makes any changes that require modifications of the initial goals it is given as input. This means that subgoals that CHEF is planning for may be changed, but the main goals that CHEF has remain intact.

CHEF is not able to delegate its planning tasks to others, so it does not use strategies such as ALTER-ACTOR, because the problem that this strategy solves never arises for CHEF. Likewise, although the actions controlled by the planner all have durations which can be changed, none of them have alterable rates. For example, it is not possible for CHEF to change the amount of time that it takes to chop vegetables. It can change the duration of cooking steps, but it cannot change the rates of those steps. This means that it cannot use strategies such as SPEED-UP or SLOW-DOWN. They are useful when the amount of time that an action takes to perform can be altered by the planner by changing the rate at which he performs them. These strategies allow a planner to coordinate the times when actions end, to minimize ill effects produced by the performance of an action, or maximize any positive effects produced.

In general, domains with different sorts of actions will allow a planner to use different sorts of strategies. Just as the cooking domain allows CHEF to make use of more interesting and powerful strategies than are possible in a blocks world, a more expansive domain than cooking would suggest a greater set of strategies than CHEF could make use of. The main reason for the expansion of strategies in CHEF, however, has less to do with the domain and more to do

(2) As an INSTRUMENT, which means that the STEP uses the OBJECT in order to enable a STATE change in another OBJECT.

The STATEs that CHEF knows about are actually features of OBJECTs. The different STATEs describe the TASTE, TEXTURE and SIZE of the OBJECTs as they are modified by the STEPs in the plan. Each STATE is not only the RESULT of a STEP, it is also a feature of an object. The texture of strawberries after they are pulped is the RESULT of the PULP step but it is also a feature of the strawberries.

CHEF only recognizes two types of relationships between an OBJECT and the STATEs that define its features:

(1) DESIRED-FEATURE is a feature of an OBJECT that satisfies or enables the satisfaction of a goal.
(2) SIDE-FEATURE is a feature that is incidental to the satisfaction of any current goals. It is not UNDESIRED in that it does not necessarily cause problems. It just does not satisfy any goals.

There are three relationships that a STATE can have with a GOAL:

(1) A SATISFY relationship exists when one STATE matches the preconditions of a step or the final GOAL of a plan.
(2) A VIOLATE or BLOCK relationship exists when a particular STATE of an object is supposed to SATISFY a GOAL or step precondition but does not.
(3) A DISABLE relationship exists when a state VIOLATEs the satisfaction conditions of a step.

STEPs can only relate to one another in terms of their running order in the plan. CHEF only requires two relationships to describe its failure situations:

(1) Two STEPs are SERIAL when they are run at different times.
(2) Two STEPs are CONCURRENT when they are run at the same time.

Like other features that CHEF uses to describe situations, the time sequence of two STEPs determines the strategies that can be applied to different problems involving the interactions between them.

The last set of features that CHEF uses to describe situations has to do with the nature of the STATEs it has to deal with rather than the relationship between STATEs and either STEPs or OBJECTs. The distinction here, however, still makes use of the notion of "relationship" in that it points to the fact that some states are themselves relationships between many STATEs at once. CHEF understands two sorts of STATEs:

(1) A BALANCE STATE is defined as a relationship that has to hold between two or more STATEs.
(2) An ABSOLUTE STATE is the feature of a single OBJECT.

with the addition of the vocabulary required to distinguish between goal satisfying and non-goal satisfying actions and states.

## 11. Planners and Repair

CHEF's approach to failure recovery draws a great deal from the tradition established by Sussman [24] and Sacerdoti [16] in their use of planning critics, and then extended by Wilensky [28] in PANDORA. Both Sussman and Sacerdoti suggested that planners need to know about planning errors in general to debug faulty plans intelligently. With this knowledge, a planner would not have to perform the backtracking that a STRIPS-like planner must do when it hits a dead end. Instead, it would be able to apply one of a set of planning critics, each having knowledge of a specific problem and the means to solve it, thus repairing the faulty plan by changing only the steps that participate in the failure. The primary difference between the two views of planning critics suggested by Sussman and Sacerdoti had to do with when the critics were applied. Sussman's HACKER would apply its critics while running a fully expanded plan in a careful mode while Sacerdoti's NOAH would have its critics check for plan interactions at each stage of expansion down to primitive planning steps. Sussman's approach required the assumption that the plan was linearized, while Sacerdoti's required complete knowledge of the effects of all of the actions in a domain.

There are difficulties with the critics approach presented by both Sussman and Sacerdoti, however. The first stems from the fact that they both wrote planners that functioned in somewhat impoverished domains. Sussman working in a blocks world and Sacerdoti working in a world where the problem task was the building of simple machines such as pumps. Unfortunately, in such worlds, there is usually only one plan for each goal and the effects of each plan tend to be those and only those that directly satisfy the goal being planned for. Because of this, only a limited vocabulary was needed to describe the problems the critics were confronted with and each problem required only a single transformation to solve it. As a result, the critics suggested by both Sussman and Sacerdoti only began to scratch the surface of what is needed to deal with complex domains.

In an effort to remedy these problems with critics, Wilensky suggested the idea of *metaplanning* [28]. Rather than representing abstract planning knowledge in a set of critics, Wilensky represented it in the form of metagoals and metaplans that are identical in form to the specific goals and plans of the planner's domain. When confronted with a problem stemming from plan interactions, a goal to deal with that interaction is spawned and the general planning mechanism deals with it directly. This allows the planner to notice a problem, insert a goal to deal with it into its general planning agenda, and then find plans to deal with it. Wilensky has taken the same knowledge that Sussman and Sacerdoti stored in critics, and has divided it into diagnostic knowledge which recognizes problems and prescriptive knowledge which solves them.

In building his planner, Wilensky argued that Sussman and Sacerdoti did not go far enough in taking seriously the role of goal and plan interactions, the main source of planning failures. He argued that the way to deal with problems rising out of goal and plan interactions is to elevate them to the status of goals themselves. He argued, in fact, that the basic structure of the planner should reflect the fact that it will often be encountering failures due to these interactions. This argument is continued in CHEF, and extended to include the argument that a planner needs to have a rich causal description of *why* a failure has occurred rather than just a description of *what* the failure is.

More recently, Chapman [4] has described a planner, TWEAK, that uses a simple repair strategy that grows out of a formal analysis of when a statement can be understood as provably valid in the context of a nonlinear planner. The purpose of Chapman's approach to repair, and to TWEAK in general, was not to build a practical system or to make points about repair. but was instead to make formal claims about the complexity of a provably correct and complete planner. The approach taken in CHEF, while by no means complete, is aimed at the more practical problem of finding an effective solution to a local planning failure that will be less likely than others to introduce new problems. There is a further difference in that TWEAK is concerned solely with problems in domains that can be fully described using STRIPS operators. As a result, TWEAK lacks a full notion of time or repairs that have to do with time. Many of CHEF's repair rules, however, have to do with the problems of overlapping and simultaneous actions as well as states that develop over the duration of an action.

There is little sense, however, in comparing CHEF and TWEAK in that TWEAK exists primarily to point out the complexity problems in nonlinear planning while CHEF is an attempt to avoid some of them. In particular, CHEF avoids the problem of the complexity of projection by replacing exhaustive projection with a heuristically driven process of anticipation that is based on the planner's memory of past failure rather than its full knowledge of the physics of a domain.

Another approach to repair has been suggested by Wilkins in the SIPE planner [30]. Like CHEF, SIPE is designed to repair problems detected at execution that for one reason or another were missed at planning time. Like CHEF, SIPE makes use of a taxonomy of planning problems and repairs that is used to drive what Wilkins refers to as "replanning." Unlike CHEF, however, SIPE's primary replanning strategies center around identifying problematic states and handing descriptions of the state and the desired world back to the planner. In effect, SIPE responds to failures by actually replanning rather than repairing. There is little to be gained in SIPE by building an explanation of the failure, in that no retroactive changes can be made to the plan.

For many types of problems, this strategy is a very effective one, but it is not the best when the actual goal of a system is not just to repair the plan in place, but also to save and reuse the corrected version. Rather than changing a plan so as to reinstate any missing states. CHEF attempts to change the plan in a way that allows later execution of the plan to avoid the problem altogether. In this way, the plan is required for reuse rather than continuation. More recently, we have been concerned with both aspects of this problem—continuation of a current plan as well as repair of the plan for later reuse.

## 12. Conclusions

By explaining plan failures, CHEF is able to make use of a broad range of plan repairs that a less informed system would not be able to apply reliably. The explanation gives the planner the knowledge it needs to choose those and only those repairs that will fix a plan without introducing new problems to it. As a result, strategies with greater power but less general applicability can be used with confidence. Furthermore, by dividing the task of plan repair into diagnosis and treatment, the system has the flexibility to try multiple strategies for repairing a single failure and choose the one most appropriate for the particular problem. The method as a whole gains in both range and power. Its repair strategies are applicable to a wide range of planning problems, while each strategy is itself a specific and thus powerful repair.

## REFERENCES

1. R. Alterman. Adaptive planning: Refitting old plans to new situations. in: *Proceedings Seventh Annual Conference of the Cognitive Science Society*. Irvine. CA (1985).
2. J.G. Carbonell. Subjective understanding: Computer models of belief systems. Ph.D. Thesis. Yale University. New Haven. CT (1979).
3. J.G. Carbonell. A computational model of analogical problem solving. in: *Proceedings IJCAI-81*. Vancouver. BC (1981).
4. D. Chapman. Planning for conjunctive goals. *Artificial Intelligence* **32** (1987) 333–377.
5. R. E. Fikes and N.J. Nilsson. STRIPS: A new approach to the application of theorem proving to problem solving. *Artificial Intelligence* **2** (1971) 189–208.
6. K.J. Hammond. Indexing and causality: The organization of plans and strategies in memory. Tech. Rept. 351. Yale University Department of Computer Science. New Haven. CT (1984).
7. K.J. Hammond. Learning and re-using explanations. in: *Proceedings Fourth International Conference on Machine Learning*. Irvine. CA (1987).
8. K.J. Hammond. *Case-Based Planning: Viewing Planning as a Memory Task* (Academic Press. New York. 1989).
9. K.J. Hammond and N. Hurwitz. Extracting diagnostic features from explanations. in: *Proceedings 1988 AAAI Symposium on Explanation-Based Learning* (1988).
10. J.L. Kolodner and R.L. Simpson. Experience and problem solving: A framework. in: *Proceedings Sixth Annual Conference of the Cognitive Science Society*. Boulder. CO (1984).
11. J.L. Kolodner. R.L. Simpson and K. Sycara. A process model of case-based reasoning in problem-solving. in: *Proceedings IJCAI-85*. Los Angeles. CA (1985).
12. P. Koton. Using experience in learning and problem solving. Ph.D. Thesis. MIT. Cambridge. MA (1988).
13. C. Martin and C.K. Riesbeck. Uniform parsing and inferencing for learning. in: *Proceedings AAAI-86*. Philadelphia. PA (1986).
14. D. McDermott. Planning and acting. *Cogn. Sci.* **2** (1978) 71–109.
15. E. Rissland and K. Ashley. Hypotheticals as heuristic device. in: *Proceedings AAAI-86*. Philadelphia. PA (1986).
16. E.D. Sacerdoti. A structure for plans and behavior. Tech. Rept. 109. SRI Artificial Intelligence Center. Menlo Park. CA (1975).
17. R.C. Schank. *Dynamic Memory: A Theory of Learning in Computers and People* (Cambridge University Press. Cambridge. 1982).
18. R.C. Schank. *Explanation Patterns: Understanding Mechanically and Creatively* (Erlbaum. Hillsdale. NJ. 1986).
19. R.C. Schank and R. Abelson. Scripts. plans. and knowledge. in: *Proceedings IJCAI-75*. Tbilisi. USSR (1975).
20. C. Seifert. G. McKoon. R. Abelson and R. Ratcliff. Memory connections between thematically similar episodes. *J. Experimental Psychol. Learning Memory Cogn.* (1985).
21. R.F. Simmons and R. Davis. Generate. test. and debug: Combining associational rules and causal models. in: *Proceedings IJCAI-87*. Milan. Italy (1987).
22. R.L. Simpson. A computer model of case-based reasoning in problem solving. Ph.D. Thesis. Georgia Institute of Technology. Atlanta. GA (1985).
23. M.J. Stefik. Planning and meta-planning (MOLGEN: Part 2). *Artificial Intelligence* **16** (1981) 141–169.
24. G.J. Sussman. *A Computer Model of Skill Acquisition*. Artificial Intelligence Series **1** (American Elsevier. New York. 1975).
25. A. Tate. Generating project networks. in: *Proceedings IJCAI-77*. Cambridge. MA (1977).
26. R. Wilensky. Understanding goal-based stories. Ph.D. Thesis. Research Rept. #140. Yale University. New Haven. CT (1978).
27. R. Wilensky. Meta-planning: Representing and using knowledge about planning in problem solving and natural language understanding. *Cogn. Sci.* **5** (1981).
28. R. Wilensky. *Planning and Understanding: A Computational Approach to Human Reasoning* (Addison-Wesley. Reading. MA. 1983).
29. D.E. Wilkins. Domain-independent planning: Representation and plan generation. *Artificial Intelligence* **22** (1984) 269–301.
30. D.E. Wilkins. Recovering from execution errors in sipe. *Comput. Intell.* **1** (1985) 33.

*Received November 1988; revised version received September 1989*

# Chapter 8

# Discovery and Commonsense Knowledge

Two highly desirable characteristics for knowledge-based expert systems are generality and robustness. The topics in this chapter, discovery learning and commonsense reasoning, are research directions relevant to the achievement of these goals.

One way to understand the issues of generality and robustness in relation to expert systems is to consider the distinction between weak and strong methods. The early work in artificial intelligence and learning used weak methods of problem solving. For example, Samuel's checker player used hill climbing. Strong methods were introduced in artificial intelligence with the advent of expert systems such as DENDRAL and MYCIN. The problem-solving power of these systems derived not from the use of a particular type of general problem-solving method, but rather from knowledge specific to the application domain. But when a problem requires strong knowledge to solve, lack of the correct strong knowledge leads to failure.

Expert systems use both weak and strong methods. The inference methods used in expert system shells are usually weak methods. MYCIN'S inference mechanism of backchaining is

a weak method, as are the role-limiting methods that we saw in the McDermott article in Chapter 2. However, strong method knowledge is contained in an expert system's knowledge base, such as MYCIN'S medical facts and rules. The power of an expert system is a function of its strong method knowledge, not its selection of a shell inference method.

Lack of robustness has been cited as a major limitation of expert systems. That is, they may fail precipitously upon slight modification of their knowledge bases. How brittle are expert systems? Surprisingly, there have been no studies to quantify this issue. It is well known that all software that interacts with humans is brittle. Compiler code is mainly exception coding; no one knows the extent to which the addition of exception handling mechanisms to expert systems would increase their robustness.

Discovery systems acquire knowledge via search through a space of concepts and relations that is relatively unconstrained by empirical data. They are capable of adding new knowledge to a knowledge base because they can discover new and interesting relationships and consequences of the knowledge they start with. They may use examples to check the plausibility of the discovered relationships, but they do not use examples for inductive generalization. Section 8.1 of this chapter considers two very different types of discovery systems: Lenat's AM program, which discovers new concepts in the domain of set theory, and Holland's genetic algorithms and classifier systems, which provide a weak method of optimization that is ideal when there is little or no prior knowledge about what is to be discovered. Section 8.2 describes Lenat's CYC, a knowledge-based system for commonsense reasoning that represents the largest single knowledge acquisition effort to date within the field of artificial intelligence.

# Section 8.1

# Discovery Systems

Discovery is a fundamental learning method, but the value of discovery methods for an expert system is unclear, because human experts seldom use discovery when refining and debugging their expertise.

The common usage of the term "discovery" includes a very broad range of intellectual activities, such as induction and other acts of scientific creativity. Karl Popper maintained that there could never be a logic of discovery, that is, a mechanical procedure that would produce innovations in science. This claim was addressed directly by Buchanan (1966) and has subsequently been refuted by the discoveries made by many AI learning programs.

Lenat's article on AM in Section 8.1.1 provides a classic example of a discovery system. The architecture of AM embodies many of the major elements of any discovery system. AM first defines a new concept by generalizing or specializing an existing concept, or by combining two or more existing concepts. Then it takes a multi-strategy learning approach to fill in slots of the frame that define the concept. AM then has an experimentation phase that determines the likelihood that the new concept is worth keeping.

The article in Section 8.1.2. by Booker, Goldberg, and Holland contains two essential ideas: genetic algorithms and classifier systems. Genetic algorithms are perhaps the weakest optimization method known. Therein lies their strength, for, when confronting a problem never seen before, genetic algorithms are least likely to miss the boat due to bias. The idea of classifier systems is to find the contributors to success. The article shows how genetic algorithms can be used within a classifier system framework.

# The Ubiquity of Discovery*

## Douglas B. Lenat

*Computer Science Department, Carnegie-Mellon University, Pittsburgh, PA 15213, U.S.A.*

Recommended by Bernard Meltzer

## ABSTRACT

*As scientists interested in studying the phenomenon of "intelligence", we first choose a view of Man, develop a theory of how intelligent behavior is managed, and construct some models which can test and refine that theory. The view we choose is that Man is a processor of symbolic information. The theory is that sophisticated cognitive tasks can be cast as searches or explorations, and that each human possesses (and efficiently accesses) a large body of informal rules of thumb (or heuristics) which constrain his search. The source of what we colloquially call "intelligence" is seen to be very efficient searching of an a priori immense space. Some computational models which incorporate this theory are described. Among them is AM, a computer program that develops new mathematical concepts and formulates conjectures involving them: AM is guided in this exploration by a collection of 250 more or less general heuristic rules. The operational nature of such models allows experiments to be performed upon them, experiments which help us test and develop hypotheses about intelligence. One interesting finding has been the ubiquity of this kind of heuristic guidance: intelligence permeates everyday problem solving and invention, as well as the kind of problem solving and invention that scientists and artists perform. The ultimate goals of this kind of research are (i) to de-mystify the process by which new science and art are created, and (ii) to build tools (computer programs) which enhance man's mental capabilities.*

## 1. Introduction

Much of the behavior which we regard as "intelligent" involves some sort of *discovery* process.[1] This is obvious for some of the most creative and intellectually

* This is the edited text of the "Computers and Thought" Lecture delivered at the 1977 International Joint Conference on Artificial Intelligence, held at the Massachusetts Institute of Technology, Cambridge, U.S.A., August 1977. At each two-yearly conference, such an invited lecture is given by the recipient of a prize given to a young man judged to have made the most impressive contribution to the subject since the previous conference. The lecture is intended for a lay audience. Douglas Lenat's predecessors were Chuck Rieger in 1975, Patrick Winston in 1973 and Terry Winograd in 1971. The 1975 and this one are the first of what it is hoped will be an unbroken sequence of these lectures to be published in the Journal.

This work was supported in part by the National Science Foundation (MCS77-04440) and in part by the Defence Advanced Research Projects Agency (F 44620-73C-0074).

[1] Much of the rest of "intelligence" involves algorithmic solving of well-structured problems. That topic will not be emphasized in this paper. We take the position that "algorithms known and used by experts" is just a proper subset of "knowledge experts use to reduce search".

*Artificial Intelligence* **9** (1978), 257-285

Copyright © 1978 by North-Holland Publishing Company

This paper originally appeared in the journal, *Artificial Intelligence*, Vol. 9, No. 3, and is reprinted here with permission of the publisher, Elsevier, Amsterdam.

difficult human activities (identifying an unknown chemical compound, composing a new sonnet, deriving a new cosmological model, ligating plasmids, conjecturing a new theorem, probing the internal structure of a proton, solving the *N.Y. Times* crossword puzzle, . . .). By the end of this talk we'll see that it's no less true for our everyday activities (understanding spoken English, making a joke, driving from CMU to MIT, cutting cheese, playing board games, finding our way about Boston, solving the *Pittsburgh Press* crossword puzzle, . . .).

## 1.1. Model-building in science

We in the field of Artificial Intelligence (AI) want to understand how it's possible to do such things, to understand the mechanisms of intelligence. I'll propose a theory of how humans are able to carry out such tasks, and then embody that theory in several concrete, testable models.

Scientific models are useful because they

(i) *unify* large masses of empirical data (e.g., the periodic table); and they

(ii) *predict* new effects, which subsequently can be tested for by conducting experiments (e.g., Young's two-slit interference test for the wave theory of light).

In very "hard" sciences, objective data are available about isolated and relatively simple phenomena. This enables the construction of small yet quite rigorous *predictive* models, using the language of mathematics (e.g., Maxwell's equations). But in the so-called "soft" fields, the phenomena cannot be measured precisely (the role of the family, the "life after life" reports, etc.), or are not so reproducible (the evolution of life, the origins of WWI, etc.), or (as in the case of human intelligence) cannot be easily isolated for study (e.g., the genetic component of IQ). The resulting models are usually only *descriptive*, and may often be presented in everyday prose (e.g., psychological theories of personality).[2] The physicist's model (his set of equations) is better than mere prose because it is able to draw on the power of established mathematics[3] to make *quantitative* predictions.

But planets and atoms behave in much more regular a fashion than do people. Can we build a hard, predictive sort of model for the phenomena of discovery and creativity? Or are we limited to sterile prose discussions about the mysteries of incubation and illumination [e.g., as in (Poincaré 1929) and (Polya 1954)]? Can we draw only metaphorical pictures (e.g., as in the 'hooked atoms' image that Einstein conjured up when pressed to introspect on how he attained his insights

[2] Attempts to formalize "soft" phenomena do go on continually, but the interpretation of the resultant rigorous mathematics is often a topic of heated debate [a current example is Catastrophe Theory (Kolata 1977)].

[3] The power to solve analysis problems in closed form (e.g., to solve a differential equation simply by repeatedly manipulating it according to known transformations), or the power to make approximations when necessary, or the power to somehow "run" the model (to "grind out" solutions to his equations).

(Hadamard 1945); or as in the "snake swallowing its own tail" dream that inspired Kekulé' to consider that the structure of the benzine molecule might be a *ring*)? The answer, until just twenty years ago, was unfortunately "We can't do any better." When the answer changed, a whole new science, Artificial Intelligence, was born.

## 1.2. Choosing an approach in science

Each science is differentiated from the others not merely by the set of *phenomena* it claims as its object of study, but also by the *approach* it takes [the science's *view* of those phenomena; its *paradigm* (Kuhn 1970), if you will].

So even though we've decided to study the phenomena of human intelligence (creativity, problem solving, concept formation, etc.), we must still choose a *view* of Man.

If we view Man as an actor whose internal thought processes can't be investigated, then we are called "behavioral psychologists", and we study human behavior. If we view Man as a brain, as a piece of hardware built out of neurons, then we're called "biologists" and we study neurophysiological responses (e.g., by implanting electrodes). If we view Man as a machine, as an automaton, then we're called "cyberneticists", and we investigate mathematical properties of feedback networks of simple components. If we view Man as a collection of atomic particles, then we're called foolish,[4] for this is too fine a "granularity" with which to investigate intelligence.

Another view arose about twenty years ago, from three independent sources:

(i) engineering (Donald Broadbent: Man can be viewed as an information processor with a limited memory system),

(ii) psycholinguistics (Noam Chomsky: Grammar characterizes human competence; hence, Man can be viewed as a system governed by abstract rules), and

(iii) computer science and cognitive psychology (Allen Newell and Herbert Simon: Man can be viewed as a processor of symbols).

If we adopt that view of Man, then we're working in the field of "Artificial Intelligence".

No one view of Man is "right" or "wrong"; each is adopted because from it we can build a model, which in turn has some practical consequences and uses. When I'm ill, I want to go to a doctor who practices medicine based on Man as a biological organism, not Man as an economic agent. At the present limited state of our understanding, any one view is bound to be simplistic and incomplete.[5] It is the *whole man* who lives and reacts, even though we can only *view* him, first this way, then that.

[4] Unlike the Brownian motion of atoms in a perfect gas, the fundamental information processes of intelligence are *not random*.

[5] On the other hand, we never capriciously adopt a view with impunity.

### 1.3. The foundation for artificial intelligence

Suppose we view Man as information processor (Newell, Shaw and Simon 1957), (Newell and Simon 1976). How can we construct models of intelligence that are predictive rather than just descriptive? We might build *operational* models, which can *exhibit* whatever behavior our theory called for. To do this, we need to use a general purpose symbol manipulator:

(i) a way to specify what processing gets done when,[6]

(ii) a memory in which to store symbol structures,[6] and

(iii) an "engine" that can actually cause such processing to occur.

The science of Artificial Intelligence sprang into being soon after the invention of one such computational engine: the digital computer. In fact, AI is sometimes called "Machine Intelligence".

### 1.4. The paradigm of AI research

We in AI have evolved the following paradigm:

(i) Choose some human cognitive activity (like playing chess, proving theorems, understanding spoken English).

(ii) Develop hypotheses and eventually a theory about what kinds of information processing could be taking place to produce such ability.

(iii) Incorporate that theory into a computer program, which serves as the model. Make that computer program carry out the original activity, and observe how well it does.[7]

(iv) Experiment with the program, attempting to find out where the apparent "intelligence" is really coming from.

Over the last twenty years, we've hypothesized and tested scores of models, for several different sophisticated tasks. There have been many successes (such as the Hearsay speech understanding programs), and many failures. Failure often stemmed from *underestimating* how complicated some activity is, which human beings are able to do fairly easily (for instance, driving a car, or understanding someone who's speaking into a microphone). We once thought that translation by machine could be accomplished by a program which simply looked up each word in a Russian/English dictionary. Legend has it that *"The spirit is willing but the flesh is weak"* was translated into Russian as *"The vodka is fine but the meat is rotten"*.

[6] Symbol processing is not the same as mere data processing. See (Newell and Simon 1976). It was some years after its discovery that the electronic digital computer was perceived as a general symbol manipulator.

[7] AI deviates from cognitive psychology at this stage. Psychologists would run experiments on people, to see if they really do fit the theory. We in AI are more concerned with whether the programs containing the hypothesized mechanisms are capable of *any* sort of "intelligent" behavior—even if it differs somewhat from human performance at that task.

**SOME HEURISTICS ARE ALMOST ALWAYS RELEVANT**

(a) >If X is often true, try to find out exactly where it does and doesn't hold.

(t) >If you must do some new, complicated task, try to arrange things so that the tools, subtasks, etc. are very familiar.

>Look at the extreme cases of the known relationships.

>Ignore minor details until a basic plan is formed.

**SOME HEURISTICS ARE RELEVANT WHEN DOING MATH OR SCIENCE**

>Even if a theory predicts something strongly, if a very easy test is available, do it (you may be surprised).

>The more important a step is (in a proof, an experiment, etc.), the more stringent verification to which it should be subjected.

>Design experiments so that a negative result will still be interesting.

>When preparing an article's bibliography, cite all possible referees.

**SOME HEURISTICS ARE RELEVANT WHEN DOING MATHEMATICS**

>If $f: A \times A \times \ldots \times A \to B$, and $A \subseteq B$, then see if in fact $f: A \times A \times \ldots \times A \to A$; Else try to find a subset S of A for which $f: S \times S \times \ldots \times S \to S$.

>If a set S has only a few elements, then it's no longer of interest; But it is worth trying to understand the reason why S is so small.

**SOME HEURISTICS ARE RELEVANT WHEN DOING BIOLOGY**

(a) >It's interesting to study whether a mechanism from one species also operates in another species.

(b) >When choosing which type of experimental animal to use, favor a species about which much is already known.

**SOME HEURISTICS ARE RELEVANT WHEN DOING MOLECULAR GENETICS**

(a) >It's interesting to study whether gene control signals from one species are operative in another species.

(b) >E. Coli is a favorite because much is known about its genetics; many of its plasmids have been characterized and are available.

>If you want to introduce DNA between strains of bacteria, then typical vectors to use are plasmids and lysogenic viruses.

>To check whether a gene transferred to a new host has been modified, reintroduce it into its donor.

FIG. 1. Hierarchy of heuristic rules. Note that heuristics (a) are specializations of each other, as are heuristics (b).

We've learned a lot from both the successes and the failures. Some of these experiments will be described later (Section 3); for now, I just want to present a single, very central result.

It turns out that we can model a surprising variety of cognitive activities (recognizing, problem solving, inventing) as a *search* in which the performer is guided by a large collection of informal rules of thumb, which we shall call "heuristics" or "heuristic rules". But what's really exciting is that not only can this single theory (intelligence as heuristic rule guided search) explain the behavior of the brainstorming math researcher and the wandering Boston visitor, but when we go off and build up such models in detail, we find that they can all contain many of the same—or at least similar—heuristics. If we look at many heuristics (see Fig. 1), we find that each one seems to have its own sphere of influence, its own domain of applicability, outside of which it is meaningless or useless. There exist many heuristics at all these levels; many of the specific ones are just specializations of ones at higher levels (e.g., "*study gene control signals across species boundaries*" is a special case of "*study the scope of biological mechanisms*", which in turn is a special case of "*study the scope of any phenomenon*").

## 2. Heuristic Rule Guided Search

### 2.1. The theory

There is a theory of intelligence lurking here:

1. Human cognitive tasks can be cast as *searches*, as explorations wandering toward some goal.

2. We are guided in these searches by a large collection of informal rules of thumb (which we've been calling *heuristics*).

3. We access relevant heuristics in each situation, and follow their advice.

That's it.[8] It sounds plausible; in fact, it sounds trivial. Yet the models which incorporate this theory are capable of performing many tasks which one would suppose require intelligence (organic chemistry problem solving and research, chess playing, composing musical variations, diagnosing blood infections, discovering new math concepts and conjectures, etc.) (see Fig. 2).

### 2.1.1. Intelligence and information

The theory contains two important implicit assumptions, which are worth displaying explicitly:

(i) Man is viewed as a processor of symbolic information.

(ii) Man exhibits "intelligence" by his performance at various cognitive tasks.

They say that information processing has something to do with intelligence. Let's try to justify that.

Twenty-seven years ago, Alan Turing (1950) rejected as meaningless the question "*Can machines think?*". He replaced it with a game, called the Imitation Game (now commonly referred to as the Turing Test). One version of that game would go as follows: A human interrogator is placed in an isolated room. A teletype exists in the room, and by using it he can communicate with a computer and with another human, both located in the next room. The interrogator asks them each some questions, and then must guess which is the human and which is the machine. If we can program a machine in such a way that it fools the interrogator into making the wrong identification at least 50% of the time, then we shall say that the machine (as programmed) is "intelligent". Many of you are familiar with this game. Now let me introduce you to a slightly different one:

Thirteen years ago, Keith Gunderson (1964) rejected as meaningless the question "*Can rocks think?*". He replaced it with a game, an Imitation Game. A human interrogator is placed in an isolated room. A small hole exists near the bottom of the door, through which the interrogator can shove most of his foot. On the other side of the door are located a human and a rock. Sometimes the human will stomp on the interrogator's foot, and sometimes the rock will fall on it. The interrogator then must guess which one is the human. If we can shape a rock in such a way that it fools the interrogator at least 50% of the time, then we shall say that the rock (as shaped) is "intelligent".[9]

Why does the dialogue-test sound so much less silly, so much more indicative of intelligence, than the stomping-test? Because unrestricted dialogue is open-ended;

[8] Notice the conspicuous absence of the word "representation" anywhere in the theory. To design and construct a *model* for this theory would entail grappling with representational issues, much as any running instance of an abstract algorithm must exist on some particular machine. But the validity and power of the theory are independent of representation, just as the validity and complexity of an algorithm are independent of which machine it's implemented on.

[9] During the oral presentation of this talk at IJCAI-77, the rock test was demonstrated onstage, with Allen Newell in the role of the unfortunate interrogator.

| Program | Task |
| --- | --- |
| AM | Elementary theory formation and discovery in mathematics |
| DENDRAL | Enumeration of atom-bond graphs of organic molecules |
| * EURISKO | Discovery of new mathematics and new heuristics |
| Meta-DENDRAL | Abstraction of new fragmentation rules for Dendral |
| M-METHOD | Improvisation of variations on melodies |
| * MOLGEN | Planning of molecular genetics experiments |
| MYCIN | Clinical diagnosis of blood infections |
| PECOS | Expert at coding programs in Lisp |
| * PROSPECTOR | Evaluating the mineral potential of sites |
| PUFF | Medical expert for pulmonary disorders |
| RITA | Learns how to run programs at remote Arpanet sites |
| SU/X | Combine many sources' signals into a global model |
| TEIRESIAS | Expert at extracting new Mycin rules from physicians |
| UT-ITP | Natural deduction proofs of theorems |

Fig. 2. Heuristic rule based search programs. * indicates "in progress".

it permits genuine interrogation of information and information processing capabilities. The second test doesn't. If you agree that the first test is genuine and the second one bogus, it must be because intelligence has *something* to do with sophisticated processing of massive quantities of information.

Thus it seems that the information processing view of Man is an especially good one from which to study intelligence. Before we see what happens when one tries to build models based on it, let's look at six different kinds of situations requiring intelligence, and see if our theory can handle them all.

## 2.2. Some examples supporting the theory

### 2.2.1. Everyday problem solving
Suppose we decide to plan a trip from CMU to MIT. How can we find a good route to take? We will probably obtain a detailed road map and begin *searching*. We look for some powerful rules of thumb which make our search very short, and then do some "fixing up" around the termini.

The map-makers aid us by drawing the biggest highways as very thick red lines. Needless to say, ignoring all but the red lines makes the map much simpler. (Thick red lines constrain furiously.) The very general heuristic of *planning* has reduced our search dramatically. One could imagine even a computer being able to solve it. In the next subsection, we'll show that the same kind of analysis can explain episodes of brainstorming (in particular, the inventing of some new kitchen gadget).

### 2.2.2. Everyday invention
Suppose we're confronted with the following problem: we're fond of eating cheese, but it's difficult to use to a knife to cut uniform, thin slices. Let's assume that we try to design an improved tool. We are now facing a search in an enormous space of possibilities. But we have many informal rules of thumb which may help us:

1. Sometimes, there will be a good way (perhaps a recent invention) to do something *more general* than what is strictly asked for.

2. Consider what variables affect the success/failure of the current (inadequate) technique. Look for motivation at the *extreme* cases of the various known relationships involving those variables.

3. Look carefully at what is truly wanted; maybe the problem can be completely bypassed; at least, perhaps it's over-specified.

One of them (#2) says to look for motivation at the *extreme* cases of various known relationships. We know several things about cutting thin slices (see Fig. 3.) There seems to be some relationship between the thickness of the knife and the thinness of the slices we can cut. So we might consider as an extreme the thinnest knife possible, just a knife *edge*, and perhaps we thereby invent the wire cheese cutter. Or we might look at the extreme case of the relation that says that most cheese can be cut thinner if it's softer, moreso than if it's dry and crumbly. We may ask ourselves if we can get the cheese very soft; completely molten; maybe then pour it into slice-molds, much like making a thin crepe. That's too messy. If we keep the cheese solid, and use a knife, maybe we could just get the cheese *directly under the knife-edge* completely molten; so we've invented the "hot-knife"; General Electric wil probably come out with one soon.

The thinner the knife, the thinner the slices  
The softer the cheese, the easier it is cut          [except: Brie, ...]  
The slower the slicing, the more uniform the slices  
The longer the knife, the more uniform the slices  
The rounder the whole cheese, the more irregular slices there will be  
etc.

Fig. 3. Cheese-cutting relationships.

This brainstorming seemed like fun. Incorporating heuristic rules into a computer model which could then tirelessly systematically apply them seems like a very promising direction to follow. We'll follow it in Section 3. Bear in mind, however, that inventions are rarely made with little or no search. In the cheese-cutting case, there might be hundreds of somewhat relevant heuristics, and many ways of applying each one, and only a few of these combinatorial possibilities are even remotely viable.

On the other hand, both of these other heuristics *can* be used in this situation. The first one is the "inventor's paradox": sometimes the easiest way to solve a problem is to find and solve a more general case, an apparently-harder problem. In the cheese-cutting situation, the heuristic might direct us to look at various devices which "cut": a big scissors? a paper-cutter? a light-saber? the new whirling-nylon-cord grass-cutters? It so happened that recently I came across a cheese slicer which operates remarkably like a paper-cutter (see Fig. 4).

Heuristic number three might have us build a better mousetrap: go into business selling already sliced cheese; or try to devise a "cheese press" that takes the crumbs and squeezes or melts them together into shapes that resemble cheese slices. "Kraft singles" are just such a product: processed cheese shaped into slices and then individually wrapped.

### 2.2.2.1. Judging 'Interestingness'. Let's put our theory to a most severe test, by asking whether it can account for our everyday judgments about what is and isn't "interesting". This would seem to be the realm of intuition, emotion, taste, and aesthetics—the antithesis of logical empiricism.[10] If we look, we find that texts on

[10] If in fact there is a large non-rational component to such judgments, then it is not surprising if they lie outside the power of any theory founded on a view of Man which ignores that aspect of him. So even a partial success at explaining "taste" in terms of heuristic rules would be significant.

the arts abound with "rules" of composition. They analyze artistic works in terms of symmetry, recency, unconventionality, harmony, utility, etc. A typical rule might say:

IF two apparently disparate parts of the work are suddenly recognized as being very closely related, THEN that increases the interestingness of both parts, and of the whole work as well.

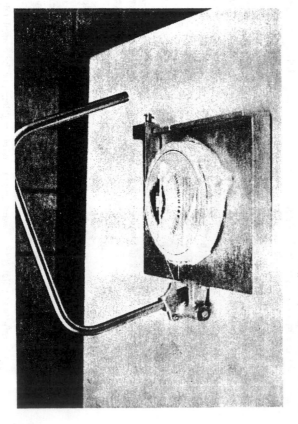

FIG. 4. Paper-cutter-like cheese slicer.

Charles Dickens' popularity is due in no small measure to his mastery of this heuristic of "coincidence": the reader is always astonished and pleased when two separate characters are discovered to be one and the same person. Escher's art is pervaded by just this sort of co-identification (consider his print where geese and fish "turn into" one another).

### 2.2.3. Scientific problem solving

Suppose we're designing a molecular genetics experiment, whose ultimate goal is to transfer a gene from one bacteria to another, by using a plasmid (a small, circular DNA molecule) (see Fig. 5). We must design a very long chain of steps (perhaps reaching into the thousands), each of the form "raise the temperature to x degrees", "add the following restriction enzyme in order to cut the DNA at a certain place", etc.

### MOLECULAR GENETICS EXPERIMENT

Transform Thy$^-$ E. Coli into Thy$^+$ E. Coli by transferring the relevant gene from the bacteriophage Phi-3-T.

#### PLAN FOR THE EXPERIMENT

1. Extract Phi-3-T DNA from bacteriophage Phi-3-T.
2. Add restriction enzymes to break the DNA into fragments.
3. Mix the fragments with E. Coli plasmids to construct hybrid plasmids.
4. Use these cloned plasmids to transform the E. Coli.
5. Verify the Thy$^+$ character of the transformed E. Coli.

#### EXPANDED PLAN

1. Extract Phi-3-T DNA from bacteriophage Phi-3-T.
   Verify the purity of the DNA by measuring UV absorption.
   Check that the molecules are intact, using electron microscope.
   Ensure adequate transforming ability in B. Subtilis.
2. Add restriction enzymes to break the DNA into fragments.
   Completely digest the DNA, by adding enzyme EcoRi.
   Use electrophoresis to estimate the molecular wts. of the fragments.
   Study, hypothesize, and test until confident of what's happening.
   Re-do the digestion, but stopping it after partially complete.
3. Mix the fragments with E. Coli plasmids to construct hybrid plasmids.
   Use EcoRi to cut out pscl01 plasmids from E. Coli.
   After mixing these with the fragments, ligate with T4 ligase.
4. Use these cloned plasmids to transform the E. Coli.
   Grow colonies, selecting for Thy$^+$
5. Verify the Thy$^+$ character of the transformed E. Coli.
   Use a curing technique to remove the hybrid plasmids from E. Coli.
   Confirm the experiment by reintroducing them into cured bacteria and testing that the observed frequencies of transform stay constant.

FIG. 5. Molecular genetics experiment.

It's a common practice to ignore certain kinds of minor steps, and to concentrate on finding a relatively small sequence of important intermediate goals. Afterwards, we can "expand" each subgoal into a detailed list of small steps (see Fig. 5, again). We solved the problem by applying a general heuristic—planning—plus several heuristics specific to molecular genetics.

The heuristic used is just the one we used previously to find a route from CMU to MIT. There, we chose to ignore all minor roads on the map. Here, we chose to ignore the minor experimental steps. This repetition is not accidental; it illustrates the commonality between everyday problem solving and scientific problem solving. Let's see if this similarity also occurs between everyday invention and scientific invention.

### 2.2.4. Scientific invention

Suppose we're confronted with the following problem: we're fond of factoring numbers, but it's difficult to use *division* to cut the numbers up in any uniform, repeatable way. E.g., one time, we may factor 12 into 2×6, another time into 3×4, and another time it crumbles into even more pieces: {1, 2, 2, 3}. We may be content with this situation, or we may try to find out more about factoring, to improve our "cutting tool"—division—or the way in which we wield it.

Such an endeavor would involve searching an enormous space (looking for a new kind of factoring; looking for new facts about factoring). But we have many rules of thumb to help us, including the three rules which were displayed earlier (at the beginning of Section 2.2.2).

One of them (#2) says to look for motivation at the *extreme* cases of various known relationships. In other words, when you've got an interesting function f from A into B, and there are some special subsets of B, extreme kinds of B's, then it's worth defining and studying the inverse images of those special parts of B, i.e., the members of A which map into those special B's (see Fig. 6). The function in this case is "Divisors-of". It maps a number into a set of numbers. (E.g., Divisors-of [12] = {1, 2, 3, 4, 6, 12}.) An extreme case would be when it mapped a number into an extreme kind of set, say an extremely *small* kind of set (e.g., into a singleton, an empty set, a doubleton, etc.).

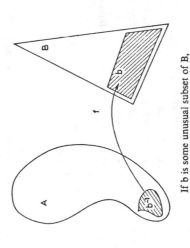

If b is some unusual subset of B,
Then isolate the subset $f^{-1}(b)$ of A.

FIG. 6. Go to extremes.

### 2.2.4.1. Judging 'interestingness'.

Even allowing that the "heuristic rule guided search", theory could account for the *discovery*—the definition—of prime numbers, could it also explain how a researcher might have noticed that they were valuable and interesting?

Let's look at how the following four heuristic rules could lead to the conclusion that "Primes" is interesting, soon after it had first been defined.

(#1) IF specializations of concept C have just been created, and the current task is to find examples of each of them, THEN one method is to look over the known examples of C; they may be examples of some of the new specialized concepts as well.

(#2) IF all examples of a concept C turn out to be examples of another concept D as well, and C was not previously known to be a specialization of D, THEN conjecture that C is a specialization of D, and raise the "interestingness" value of both concepts.

(#3) IF all examples of a concept turn out to be in the domain of a rarely-applicable function F, THEN it's worth computing all their F-values (their images under the function F), and studying that collection of F-values as a separate concept.

(#4) IF a concept has very few examples (say, less than 2), THEN it's worth trying to find out why, but the concept itself is not interesting.

The first heuristic tells us that IF we've just created some special kinds of Numbers, and we want to fill in examples of them, THEN one quick way to find such examples is to look at the known examples of Numbers, say the integers from 1 to 1000, and dump each one into whichever new specialized set(s) it belongs. If we do this, we get the following empirical results:

*Numbers with no divisors:* (none found)
*Numbers with 1 divisor:*  1
*Numbers with 2 divisors:*  2, 3, 5, 7, 11, 13, 17, 19, ...
*Numbers with 3 divisors:*  4, 9, 25, 49, 121, 169, 289, ...

Heuristic #4 says to rule out any sets which are very tiny; that immediately causes us to lose interest in the first two kinds of numbers, those with zero or one divisor. None of the heuristics have much to say about the next set of numbers (with 2 divisors); what about this final set, numbers which have precisely 3 divisors? Heuristic #2 says, IF all these numbers are also examples of some other special kind of number, THEN they'd be interesting. Well, is there anything special about all of them? Most of them seem to be odd, ..., *all of them* seem to be perfect squares. That's very unexpected and surprising. All these numbers have integer square roots; that's a very rare thing. Heuristic #3 says that in such a case it's worth actually computing what their square roots are. So let's take their square roots. Lo and behold! They're precisely the set of numbers with two divisors; i.e.

In other words, this heuristic rule says that it's worth defining and studying the set of numbers with no divisors, with just one divisor, with precisely two divisors, and maybe the set of numbers with precisely three divisors. *Voilà*, we've invented prime numbers. Notice that we used the very same heuristic (rule #2 in Section 2.2.2) that led earlier to the invention of the wire cheese cutter and the hot-knife.

primes. Heuristic #2 explains why we might have noticed this, and indicates that it would cause us to drastically increase the interestingness values of both Numbers-with-3-divisors and Primes. This heuristic was the same one we talked about before, in connection with Dickens and Escher: the rule of startling coincidence.

So we *were* able to fit this kind of judgmental evaluation of "interestingness" into the same theory.

### 3. Models

The examples I've shown you so far have been merely suggestive. The heuristics which I claimed "explained" various behaviors might really be just comments on those behaviors, ways of rationalizing in hindsight what was actually done. I claim that the heuristic rules can be an *operational* part of the theory, that predictive models can be built which use them for guidance in solving problems and making discoveries. To that end, I'm going to briefly describe a few landmark computer programs that have been written, models based on the theory of intelligence as heuristic rule guided search. These programs form but a thin sliver of the work that has gone on under the label of "Artificial Intelligence".

### 3.1. LT and GPS: General problem solving

Probably one of the earliest AI programs written was the Logic Theorist ('LT', to its friends) (Newell, Shaw and Simon 1957). It was repeatedly given symbolic logic theorems from *Principia Mathematica*, and its task was to find a formal proof of each theorem. LT had some given axioms and rules of inference. To search for a proof, in a completely exhaustive, systematic manner, could literally be an impossible undertaking! But LT had a few heuristics which constrained its search:

"... *selective principles that enable solutions to be found after examining only a relatively tiny subset of the set of possibilities. One such principle—illustrated by the methods in the Logic Theorist—is to generate only elements of the set that are already guaranteed to possess at least some of the properties that define a solution. Another principle—illustrated by the matching process in LT—is to make use of information obtained sequentially in the course of generating possible solutions in order to guide the continuing search. A third principle— illustrated by the use of similarity tests in LT—is to abstract from the detail of the problem expressions and to work in terms of the simpler abstractions.*"

(Newell and Simon 1972, p. 137)

One of LT's heuristics was *constrained generation*: if you want an entity satisfying ten specific properties P1 · · · P10, try to arrange things in such a way that you only have to consider entities already guaranteed to satisfy P1 · · · P7; then just test each one to see if it meets the final three criteria. Another principle was to *learn from your failures*: instead of just blindly backtracking, use the nature of your failure

to help guide you in the future, so you won't make exactly the same mistake again.

After they learned the power of heuristics from LT, the same group of researchers then worked on a program called GPS, for General Problem Solver. Its aim was to embed the few general heuristics above in a domain-independent form. It was hoped that *any* problem could be represented in the GPS formalism, and hence solved by GPS. It was the first program to isolate explicitly these general methods:

1. Means ends analysis: Decide what the most important difference is between the current state and the desired goal, locate an operator which is known to be relevant to reducing that kind of difference, and then try to actually apply that operator. With any luck, you'll be one step closer to the goal.

2. Setting up subgoals, equivalent to the idea of *problem reduction*, and to divide and conquer strategies.

3. Planning in an abstraction space.

Two decades of experimenting with GPS have shown that, yes, a large array of problems can be cast in terms that GPS can deal with (states, operators, difference tables), but no, GPS's few general heuristics just aren't powerful enough to solve problems as difficult as can be tackled by humans.

### 3.2. Dendral: Scientific problem solving

The next giant step along the line of development we're following was taken by Ed Feigenbaum and Joshua Lederberg at Stanford, and independently by Joel Moses here at MIT. They recognized what was lacking: expertise. After all, humans have to train in specialized fields for quite a while before they are able to solve any hard problems in them. This phenomenon might not just be a reflection of human brain frailties, it might indicate a necessary requirement for intelligent problem solving in a complex knowledge-rich domain.

In 1965 they conceived a new kind of computer program, and in the process a whole new approach for AI: they were willing to commit their programs to working on a very specific kind of problem—in Moses' case, symbolic integration; in Lederberg, Feigenbaum and Buchanan's case, the enumeration of atom-bond graphs of organic molecules (based on analysis of mass spectrograph data and nuclear mass resonance data). For instance, you type in "$C_{10}H_{22}$," and their program types back a list of all 71 structural isomers of decane. They built their program, DENDRAL, around a body of heuristics—not just a few, but a few *dozen* heuristic rules. Some of them were as general as the rules that GPS had, but most of them were specific rules of thumb which they extracted from chemists (e.g., rules for recognizing imbedded subgraphs which are impossible; knowledge of aggregates of radicals which co-occur often; heuristic estimation of the worth of pursuing a particular subproblem; rules for recognizing current subproblems which have been worked on before).

The success of this research (measured partly by the large number of articles which have been published in chemical journals) confirmed Feigenbaum's hypothesis about the tradeoff between generality and power (see Fig. 7). Heuristics are distributed along the pictured curve (and below it); the more general they are, the weaker they must be. Experiments with Dendral have demonstrated the importance of using both general heuristics and task-specific heuristics for guidance.

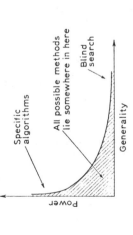

Fig. 7. Generality vs. Power.

### 3.3. AM: Scientific invention

We now jump to some quite recent research by the speaker, which involved collecting *hundreds* of heuristics, to do elementary mathematics research, open-ended discovery. This is scientific *invention*, as compared to Dendral, which performs scientific *problem solving*.[11]

*3.3.1. Math discovery as heuristic rule-guided search*

The task which this program, called *AM*, performs is the discovery of new mathematics concepts and relationships between them. The simple paradigm it follows for this task is the one specified by our theory (in Section 2.1):

1. Open-ended math research is viewed as a search, an exploration in a space of partially-developed concepts.[12]

2. AM is guided in this exploration by a collection of a few hundred heuristic rules. They are rules of varied generality which guide it to define and study the most plausible thing next.

[11] This is not the "inductive vs. deductive" issue: both Dendral and author's program (AM) perform quite inductive tasks. The difference is that Dendral is given specific problems to solve (specific mass spectra to identify), whereas AM's activities are open-ended research, with no particular goal specified.

[12] The goal of this search is ill-defined: to maximize the interestingness value of the concepts which are available for AM to develop further.

3. In each situation, AM quickly accesses relevant heuristic rules, and then follows (obeys) them.

For example, AM discovered "Multiplication" in four separate ways. This coincidence raised its interestingness value to quite a high level. One of AM's heuristic rules said '*If f is an interesting operation, Then look at its inverse*'. This rule was relevant (with f = Multiplication) and was actually followed in this context. It directed AM to define and study the relation "divisors-of". Another heuristic rule which later was obeyed (see Fig. 8) said to examine the inverse image of extrema under interesting functions. We've seen this rule before, but Fig. 8 indicates more accurately how it appeared in the AM computer program. Just as we saw before (in Section 2.2.4), AM was driven by this rule to define prime numbers.

**In English and Math notation:**

IF f: A → B is an interesting function,
and there's some interesting or extremal subset X of B,
THEN it's worth defining and naming and studying $f^{-1}(X)$.

**Roughly as it appeared in the AM program:**

```
(IF
   (CURRENT-TASK DEALT-WITH "F")
   AND (F IS-A FUNCTION)
   AND ((WORTH-OF F) IS-GREATER-THAN 600)
   AND (THERE-ARE-KNOWN-ENTRIES-FOR (BOUNDARY-OF (RANGE-OF F)))
THEN
   (FOR-EACH X IN (BOUNDARY-OF (RANGE-OF F))
      (CREATE-A-NEW-CONCEPT
         (WHOSE NAME IS "F-INVERSE-OF-X")
         (WHOSE WORTH · IS (WORTH-OF F)×(WORTH-OF X))
         (WHOSE DEFINITION IS "(LAMBDA (z) (F (z) IS-A X))"
         (WHOSE GENERALIZATION IS (DOMAIN-OF F))
         (WHOSE ORIGIN IS "Inverse image of extrema")
         (WHOSE INTEREST IS "(TIES-TO F) (TIES-TO F-INVERSE)"))))
```

Fig. 8. Go to extremes, again.

The same heuristic also directed AM to study not only various kinds of numbers having very *few* divisors, but also classes of numbers with very *many* divisors; such "maximally-divisible" numbers were also found to be interesting (by AM, by the author, and by professional mathematicians). In fact, a couple minor new results in number theory were developed regarding them. Still another time, AM was guided by the same heuristic to define and study the pairs of sets whose intersection is empty; i.e., this rule also led to the definition of the relation "Disjointness". This multiple usage of the heuristics is strong evidence that they are truly general.[13]

[13] If a supposedly general rule were only involved in one major discovery, there would always be the question of whether the rule is merely a subtle encoding of that discovery.

3.3.2. *Representation of mathematical knowledge*

What exactly does it mean for AM to "have the notion of" a concept? It means that AM *represents* that concept somehow in the computer, that there is a data structure of some kind which is meant to correspond to, and contain information about, that concept. While the entire issue of how to represent knowledge has been de-emphasized in this talk, it is helpful to glance at how some typical concepts looked (see Fig. 9).

The representation of a concept is as a collection of *facets*, or slots (e.g., Definitions, Conjectures, Worth[14]) each of which can have some associated value, or entry.

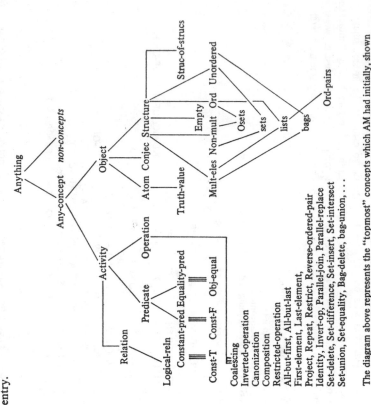

The diagram above represents the "topmost" concepts which AM had initially, shown connected via Specialization links (\\) and Examples links (⫴).

Fig. 10. Initial concepts.

[14] Unlike the other numbers appearing as part of the pictured 'Primes' concept, the number '800' is merely an estimate, an ad hoc value for the overall worth of this concept. It would be preferable to replace this by a mass of symbolic reasons, by a plausible justification for why this concept was and wasn't useful, interesting, etc. But in lieu of the ability to reason about, create, manipulate, and otherwise use such knowledge, we opt for a simple scalar, a numeric rating which in effect crudely *summarizes* these reasons.

NAME(s): Set, Non-proper Class, Collection, Finite set
DEFINITIONS:
   RECURSIVE: $\lambda$ (S) [S = {} or Set . Definition
                   (Remove(Any-member(S),S))]
   RECURSIVE QUICK: $\lambda$ (S) [S = {} or Set . Definition (CDR(S))]
   QUICK: $\lambda$ (S) [Match S with {...}]
SPECIALIZATIONS: Nonempty-set, Set-of-sets, Set-of-numbers
   BOUNDARY: Empty-set, Singleton, Doubleton, Tripleton
GENERALIZATIONS: Unordered-Structure, Collection,
   Structure-with-no-multiple-elements-allowed
IS-A: Kind-of-structure
EXAMPLES:
   TYPICAL: {{}}, {A}, {A,B}, {3}
   BARELY: {}, {A, B, {C, {{{A, C, (3,3,9), ⟨ 4, {B},A⟩}}}}}
   NOT-QUITE: {A,A}, (), {B,A}
   FOIBLE: ⟨4,1,A,1⟩
CONJEC's: All unordered-structures are sets.
INTUITIONS: Geometric: Venn diagram.
ANALOGIES: {set, set operations} ≡ {list, list operations}
WORTH: 600   [on a scale of 0–1000]
VIEW:
   PREDICATE: $\lambda$ (P) {x$\epsilon$Domain(P) | P(x)}
   STRUCTURE: $\lambda$ (S) Enclose-in-braces
               (Sort(Remove-multiple-elements(S)))
IN-DOMAIN-OF: Union, Intersection, Set-difference, Subset,
   Member, Cartesian-prod, Set-equality
IN-RANGE-OF: Union, Intersect, Set-difference, Satisfying

Fig. 9. Two typical math concepts.

NAME(s): Prime Numbers, Primes, Numbers-with-2-Divisors
DEFINITIONS:
   ORIGIN: Divisors-of(x) is-a Doubleton
   PRED.-CALCULUS: Prime(x) ≡ ($\forall$z)(z|x → z =1 XOR z = x)
   ITERATIVE: (for x > 1): For i from 2 to x−1, ¬(i|x)
EXAMPLES: 2, 3, 5, 7, 11, 13, 17
   BOUNDARY: 2, 3
   BOUNDARY-FAILURES: 0, 1
   FAILURES: 12
GENERALIZATIONS: Numbers, Numbers with an even no. of
   divisors, Numbers with a prime no. of divisors
SPECIALIZATIONS: Prime pairs, Prime uniquely-addables
CONJECS: Unique factorization, Goldbach's conjecture
ANALOGIES: Maximally-divisible numbers are converse
   extremes of Divisors-of
INTEREST: Conjec's tying Primes to Times, to Divisors-of, and
   to other closely related operations
WORTH: 800

### 3.3.3. Flow of control

AM is initially given a collection of 115 core concepts (see Fig. 10), each with only a few facets (slots) filled in. AM repeatedly chooses some facet of some concept, and tries to fill in some entries for that particular slot. Thus a "job" for AM is simply to engage in a mini-research project, to commit a simple act of discovery. Its overall task—to discover interesting concepts and conjectures—is accomplished as a composition of hundreds of these repeated attempts at little discoveries.

(Fill in Generalizations facet of "Equality concept")

    Priority = 700
    Reasons = ((No known generalizations of Equality)
        (Equality is rarely satisfied)
        (Focus of attention: recently worked on Equality))

(Check Conjecs facet of "Equality" concept)

    Priority = 500
    Reasons = ((Worth of Equality has recently risen)
        (Conjecs involving Equality have just been found)
        (Focus of attention: recently worked on Equality))

(Fill in Examples facet of "Primes concept")

    Priority = 400
    Reasons = ((No known exs of primes yet))

(Check Examples facet of "Set-union" concept)

    Priority = 350
    Reasons = ((Many examples of Set-union recently added)
        (Worth of Set-union has recently risen))

(Check Domain/range facet of "Square-root" concept)

    Priority = 300
    Reasons = ((Square-root was unable to return a value for 8)
        (Square-root was unable to return a value for 3)
        (Should check the domain/range entries for any
        operation created as an inverse))

(Fill in new Algorithms for Compose concept)

    Priority = 200
    Reasons = ((Empirical: taking too long))

Fig. 11. Agenda of jobs.

To decide which small job to work on next, AM maintains an *agenda* of jobs, a global queue ordered by priority (see Fig. 11). A typical job is '*Fill-in examples of Primes*'. The agenda may contain hundreds of such jobs. AM repeatedly selects the top-rated job from the agenda and tries to find *relevant* rules (i.e., heuristics which, when obeyed, bring AM closer to satisfying that job). Potential relevance is determined *a priori* by where the rule is stored. Each of AM's 250 heuristic rules is tacked onto the most general (or abstract) concept[15] C to which it's relevant and meaningful. The relevance of these heuristic rules is presumed to be inherited by all C's

[15] It was very important to place each heuristic on as general a concept as possible, to give it a large scope of applicability, to bring it close to the generality versus power curve.

specializations. A method which can generalize any operation can certainly generalize any composition; any heuristic that knows how to find examples of any concept can find examples of "Numbers-with-3-divisors". And so on. In other words, the aggregate of the Generalization/Specialization relationships among the *concepts* induces a similar graph structure upon the set of *heuristic rules* (see Fig. 12) (see also Fig. 1, again). This "inheritability property" permits potentially relevant rules to be located efficiently.

ANYTHING
⋮
INTEREST: The user recently mentioned C.
INTEREST: C is the result of F(x), where F and x are interesting.

ANY-CONCEPT
⋮
FILL-IN: Find the results of any operation whose range is C.
INTEREST: The Worth rating of C keeps fluctuating wildly.
CHECK: For any x, x is a C iff it satisfies the Definition of C.

ACTIVITY
⋮
FILL-IN: Run the algorithm for C on random members of its domain.
INTEREST: All the components of C's domain are identical.

OPERATION
⋮
FILL-IN: For any identity i of C, for any j, include 'C(i,j) = j'.
INTEREST: The range of C is also one of C's domain components.

| COMPOSITION | DOMAIN = RANGE-OP |
|---|---|
| INTEREST: CoC is nontrivial. | FILL-IN: Include any fixed-points of C. |
| INTEREST: F's conjecs hold for C = FoG. | INTEREST: C(x, C(y, z)) = C(C(x, y), z). |
| CHECK: Dom(F) ∩ Ran(G) is nontrivial. | CHECK: Ran(C) is not a proper subset of Dom(C). |

UNION · COMPLEMENT

Fig. 12. Induced structuring of the heuristics.

The IF-part of each potentially relevant rule is evaluated to determine whether the rule is truly relevant. If so, it's obeyed. At that time, it can direct three kinds of actions or effects:

(i) Facets of some concepts can get filled in (e.g., examples of primes may actually be found and tacked onto the "Examples" facet of the "Primes" concept).

Sets with less than 2 elements (singletons and empty sets).
Sets with no atomic elements (nests of braces).
Singleton sets.
Bags containing (multiple occurrences of) just one kind of element.
Superset (contains).
Doubleton bags and sets.
Set-membership.
Disjoint bags.
Subset.
Disjoint sets.
Singleton sets.
Same-length (same number of elements).
Same number of left parentheses, plus identical leftmost atoms.
Count (find the number of elements of a given structure).
Numbers (unary representation).
Add.
Minimum.
SUB1 ($\lambda$ (x) x$-$1).
Insert x into a given Bag-of-T's (almost ADD1, but not quite).
Subtract (except: if x $<$ y, then the result of x$-$y will be zero[71]).
Less than or equal to.
Times.
Union of a *bag* of structures.
& (the ampersand represents the creation of several real losers.)
Compose a given operation F with itself (form F.F).
Insert structure S into itself.
Try to delete structure S from itself (a loser).
Double (add 'x' to itself).
Subtract 'x' from itself (as an operation, this is a real zero[72]).
Square (TIMES(x,x)).
Union structure S with itself.
Coalesced-replace2: replace each element s of S by F(s,s).
Coalesced-join2: append together F(s,s), for each member s$\varepsilon$S.
Coa-repeat2: create a new op which takes a struc S, op F, and repeats F(s,t,S) all along
Compose three operations: $\lambda$(F,G,H) F.(G.H).
Compose three operations: $\lambda$(F,G,H) (F.G).H.
& (lots of losing compositions created, e.g. Self-insert.Set-union.)
ADD$^{-1}$(x): all ways of representing x as the sum of a bunch of nonzero numbers.

G.H, s.t. H(G(H(x))) is always defined (wherever H is), and G and H are interesting.
Insert.Delete.
Delete.Insert.
Size.ADD$^{-1}$. ($\lambda$ (n) The number of ways to partition n)
Cubing
&
Exponentiation.
Halving (in natural numbers only; thus Halving(15)$-$7).
Even numbers.
Integer square-root.
Perfect squares.
Divisors-of.
Numbers-with-0-divisors.
Numbers-with-1-divisor.
Primes (Numbers-with-2-divisors).
Squares of primes (Numbers-with-3-divisors).
Squares of squares of primes.
Square-roots of primes (a loser).
TIMES$^{-1}$(x): all ways of representing x as the product of a bunch of numbers ($>$1).
All ways of representing x as the product of just one number (a trivial notion).
All ways of representing x as the product of primes.
All ways of representing x as the sum of primes.
All ways of representing x as the sum of two primes.
Numbers uniquely representable as the sum of two primes.
Products of squares.
Multiplication by 1.
Multiplication by 0.
Multiplication by 2.
Addition of 0.
Addition of 1.
Addition of 2.
Product of even numbers.
Sum of squares.
Sum of even numbers.
& (losers: various compositions of 3 operations.)
Pairs of perfect squares whose sum is also a perfect square ($x^2+y^2-z^2$).
Prime pairs (p,p+2 are prime).

Fig. 13. Concepts discovered.

(ii) New concepts may be created (e.g., the concept "numbers which are uniquely representable as the sum of two primes" may be explicitly deemed worth studying).

(iii) New jobs may be added to the agenda (e.g., the current activity may suggest that the following job is worth considering: "Find new generalizations of the concept of prime numbers.")

### 3.3.4. *Behavior of this rule system*

AM began its investigations with scanty knowledge of one hundred elementary concepts of finite set theory. Most of the obvious set-theoretic concepts and relationships were quickly found (e.g., de Morgan's laws; singletons), but no sophisticated set theory was ever done (e.g., diagonalization). Rather, AM discovered natural numbers, rated them highly, and went off exploring elementary number theory (see Fig. 13). AM discovered scores of well-known concepts (some of them in novel ways,[16] some of them in several ways[17]), and a roughly equal number of "losers" (most of which were quickly recognized as such by AM). All this occurred in two cpu hours (see Fig. 14).

The AM project has demonstrated that that open-ended scientific theory formation (the defining and exploring of new concepts and relationships) *could* be mechanized, could be modelled as heuristic rule guided search, using a few hundred heuristics for guidance. This is a significant verification of the theory of intelligence presented in Section 2.1.

AM had some difficulties. As it ran longer and longer, the concepts it defined were further and further from the primitives it began with; while the general set-theoretic heuristics were technically valid for dealing with primes and arithmetic, they were simply too general, too weak to guide effectively. The key deficiency was AM's inability to create and modify new specific heuristics.

### 3.3.5. *The next step: EURISKO*

These findings came to light only because the AM program existed, was run, and was experimented with. Recall that the final step in the AI paradigm is to experiment with the computational model. In this case, what we've learned from AM is guiding our current efforts at writing a program which discovers new task-dependent heuristics as well as new concepts. Our new program, EURISKO, is quite ambitious, because even scientists are very poor at formulating—or even recognizing—new heuristics.

---

[16] E.g., AM restricted the operation 'Addition' to prime numbers; i.e., it asked 'For which primes p, q, r is it true that p+q = r?' In such a case, p or q must be '2', and the other two primes must be a *prime pair*.

[17] E.g., *multiplication* was discovered in four separate ways: as repeated addition, as an analogue to the Cartesian product of sets, as the cardinality of the union of the powersets of two sets, and as the total number of symbols one gets by replacing (in parallel) each element of bag X by a complete copy of bag Y.

NAME(s): Generalize-rare-predicate
STATEMENT
English: If a predicate is rarely True, create a generalization of it
IF-Current-task-deals-with: a predicate P
AND-IF: P returns "True" less than one tenth of the time
THEN-Conjecture:
C1: P is a little less interesting than expected.
C2: Generalizations of P may be more interesting than P.
Then-add-a-new-task:
"Fillin Generalizations of P" because C2
Then-modify-facet:
Reduce the Worth of P by 10%, because C1
SPECIALIZATIONS: Generalize-rare-set-predicate
BOUNDARY: Enlarge-domain-of-predicate
GENERALIZATIONS: Modify-predicate, Generalize-concept
JUSTIFYING GENERALIZATION: Hill-climbing
IS-A: Heuristic
EXAMPLES:
GOOD: Generalize "set-equality" into "same-length"
BAD: Generalize "set-equality" into "same-first-element"
CONJEC's: Special cases of this rule are MUCH more powerful than it is.
ANALOGIES: Weaken-an-overconstrained-problem
WORTH: 600 [on a scale of 0-1000]
VIEW:
ENLARGE-STRUCTURE: let the structure be $\{x \mid P(x)\}$
ORIGIN: A specialization of "Modify-predicate", via empir. induction
HISTORY
Summary of examples: 1 good, 1 bad example known; average +0.4
Summary of conjectures proposed: 3 correct, 1 unclear
Summary of tasks added to agenda: 2 added, 2 tried, 2 succeeded, +0.8
Summary of facets modified: 2 Worth lowerings, 1 verified
CPU Time used: Average 9.4 cpu seconds
Space used: Average 250 list cells

FIG. 15. Heuristic represented as a concept.

The MYCIN program (Shortliffe 1974) contains a couple hundred judgmental rules which were extracted from physicians, and it uses them to make diagnoses of various blood infections.

MOLGEN (Feitelson and Stefik 1977) (still under construction) attacks the molecular genetics experiment-planning problem discussed earlier (in Section 2.2.3).

The PROSPECTOR program (Duda et al. 1977) performs geological analysis of on-site data relayed to the computer by a human expert. It aids him in the evaluation of the mineral potential of exploration sites. Prospector's rules were gleaned from geologists, much as MYCIN's were from physicians.

These programs perform complex *problem solving*. A few programs exist which, like AM, use heuristic rules to guide them in scientific and other *invention* tasks.

---

We asked ourselves how new heuristics get discovered; we took the same kind of heuristically-guided approach to the problem that AM would have. By using general rules, we were led to ponder whether heuristics might not get discovered and reasoned about in much the same way that math concepts do (i.e., by hindsight, by manipulating existing ones, and so on). We think they might.

Machine: SUMEX, PDP-10, KI-10 uniprocessor
Language: INTERLISP, January 1975 release
Number of small support functions for AM: 200
Number of heuristics: 250
Number of Initial concepts: 115
Number of Final concepts: 300
Average Initial concept: 8 facets
Average Final concept: 11 facets
Average size of a concept: 700 list cells
Average size of a concept: 1 typed page
Total CPU Time: 1 hour
Speedup factor if user advises AM: 3
Total number of jobs executed: 200
Average time allocated per task: 30 secs.
Average time actually used by a task: 18 secs.
Number of winning concepts: 25 (estimated)
Number of acceptable concepts: 100 (est.)
Number of losing concepts: 60 (est.)

FIG. 14. Performance statistics.

So EURISKO's method for discovering and developing heuristics is therefore simply to *not distinguish* between concepts and heuristics; i.e., each heuristic is represented internally as a full-fledged concept (see Fig. 15).[18] Any heuristic which, say, can advise when it's time to generalize any concept, can also automatically tell when it's time to generalize any heuristic. Any method for creating a new concept out of old ones can be used to create new heuristics out of old ones. Evaluating the new heuristics is done just like evaluating any new concepts: by observing them in action, by gathering empirical data about them. Naturally, there are some special heuristics which are meaningful only for reasoning about other heuristics, just as there are some special heuristics that apply only to ligating plasmids.

We've taken the same AM-like approach to solving *most* of the problems that beset AM.

### 3.4. Other heuristic rule guided expert programs

There are several programs like AM in existence, knowledge based expert programs which perform under the guidance of a large collection of heuristic rules.

[18] Notice its similarity to a typical math concept.

META-DENDRAL (Buchanan and Mitchell 1977) is a theory formation program which looks over mass spectra and their correct identifications, and then abstracts that data into new fragmentation rules, which are then usable by the Dendral program, as if they had been extracted from a human expert.

The M-Method program (Zaripov 1975) for improvising variations on a given melody is based around a body of musicology rules.

Several other such programs are listed in Fig. 2.

## 4. Conclusions

### 4.1. The main points to remember

We viewed Man as a processor of symbolic information. Keeping in mind that this is but one narrow view, we found it a useful vantage point from which to study the phenomenon of intelligence.

Many cognitive tasks can be cast as explorations through more or less enormous[19] search spaces. "Intelligence" is the ability to zero in effectively on a solution, despite the apparent size of the search space.

We theorize that humans possess thousands of informal rules of thumb, of varying levels of generality and power, which they use to guide them in these searches. These rules are the prime repository for domain-specific knowledge (i.e., for expertise).

We have seen the relationships among knowledge, search, and intelligence.

Search is ubiquitous.

Knowledge reduces search.

Using knowledge is intelligent.

It is therefore meaningless to debate whether the source of intelligence lies in "search" or in "knowledge": *both* are prerequisites. They interact synergetically: each would be almost powerless without the other. Search by itself leads to small programs with impossible running times. Knowledge by itself just sits on library shelves and gets dusty.

The theory of intelligence as heuristic rule guided search contains the power of *additivity*: many small pieces of "local knowledge" combine to produce sophisticated "global effects", with a consequent ease of introducing new pieces of knowledge.

This methodology contains the power[20] afforded by *coarse granularity*: a rule can express any arbitrarily complex heuristic, can embody a meaningful chunk of domain-specific knowledge. In particular, it can have some significance to a human expert. Thus each model of the theory will be self-explaining (Feigenbaum 1977): it need only keep the user posted of each rule

[19] The less structured the domain, the larger the search space. One extreme of this "tradeoff" is an *algorithm*, which is a highly "compiled" search.

[20] Promised by general "heuristic search" (Nilsson 1971), and by some rule-based system architectures (Lenat and Harris 1977), but not by "pure" production systems (Newell 1973).

firing. Also, new heuristic rules can be added by a human expert at a level which seems "natural" to him (Davis 1977).

Several example scenarios have been presented, to show that this theory can account for everyday and scientific problem solving, invention and judging the "interestingness" of newly synthesized invention. There is a whole lattice of increasingly more specialized heuristics. Some of them, at the very top, are useful in all six types of situations.

Three kinds of models, based on this theory, were examined (LT/GPS, Dendral, and AM). The efforts are separated in time by periods of about ten years (1957, 1967, 1977) and factors of about ten in the number of heuristics they utilized (3, 30, 300). All three serve to support the theory of intelligence we've been discussing.

We saw in particular how AM is able to use its heuristics to guide attention (add and modify jobs on its agenda), to synthesize new concepts, to explore them (fill in their facets), and to evaluate their interestingness. This demonstrated that the general heuristic rules are not merely a descriptive commentary, they are an operational part of the theory. AM and its predecessors are not merely lucky accidents.

### 4.2. The goals of AI

#### 4.2.1. Toward a science of science

In the Middle Ages, only a few European artists incorporated linear perspective into their paintings. The techniques were never communicated explicitly; rather, the would-be artist had to serve as an apprentice to a master. Gradually, by example, the student learned the necessary skills. Some time between Giotto and Da Vinci, the artists wrote down, explicitly, the knowledge they were really using to create perspective. Once they did that, anyone could learn how to create such drawings. In place of mystery was understanding.

There is a similar mystique today, about how doctors can diagnose disease, how mathematicians can discover new theorems, how scientists in general are able to carry out productive research. The doing of science today is not unlike the guilds of the Middle Ages. We scientists rarely try to introspect on our own creativity, to explicate our skills.

One very significant reason for doing Artificial Intelligence research is that it starts the metamorphoses of the nature of scientific fields, from incomprehensible guilds into well-understood technical crafts. It leads to a science of science. AI programs make explicit, in a very usable form, the knowledge necessary to perform some complicated activity, thereby de-mystifying it.

#### 4.2.2. Mental enhancement

A concrete *understanding* of intelligence, as might be achieved by the above "Science of Science'', enables attempts to *synthesize* it. What good would a synthetic intellect be?

The ultimate material benefit to be derived from Science is the enhancement of (some aspect of) Man. Medicine views him as an organism, and is able to provide biological enhancement (pharmacological agents and techniques which improve his resistance to disease, his longevity, etc.) Engineering views him as a dynamic actor, and is able to provide physical enhancement (devices and techniques which enable better locomotion than legs, better communication that shouting, etc.). AI views Man as a symbol processor, and provides mental enhancement: programs and techniques which augment his ability to *reason*: automation of routine tasks (book-keeping, housekeeping[21]), aids to artists and scientists (partial automation of the "hack" side of composing, proving, diagnosing, exploring, programming), an avenue leading to the understanding (and appreciation of the sophistication) of his own intelligence, and perhaps—in the *far* distant future—even finding his way around the streets of Boston.

## ACKNOWLEDGMENT

The author wishes to acknowledge a few of the many individuals who have inspired him with their ideas which have filtered down into this talk: Jon Bentley, Woody Bledsoe, Bruce Buchanan, Edward Feigenbaum, John Gaschnig, Greg Harris, Donald Knuth, Joshua Lederberg, Merle Lenat, John McDermott, Bernard Meltzer, Donald Michie, Allen Newell, Raj Reddy, Earl Sacerdoti, Michael Shamos, Herbert Simon, and Patrick Winston.

## REFERENCES

1. Buchanan, Bruce G., Sutherland, G. and Feigenbaum, E., Heuristic Dendral: A program for generating explanatory hypotheses in organic chemistry, in: Meltzer and Michie (eds.) *Machine Intelligence 4* (American Elsevier Pub. N.Y., 1969) pp. 209–254.

2. Buchanan, Bruce G. and Mitchell, T., Model-directed learning by production rules, in: D. A. Waterman and F. Hayes-Roth (eds.) *Pattern-Directed Inference Systems* (Academic Press, New York, 1978).

3. Davis, Randall, Interactive transfer of expertise: acquisition of new inference rules, Proceedings of the Fifth IJCAI (International Joint Conference on Artificial Intelligence), Cambridge, MA (August 1977) pp. 321–328.

4. Duda, Richard O., Hart, P., Nilsson, N. and Sutherland, G., Semantic network representations in rule-based inference systems, in: D. A. Waterman and F. Hayes-Roth (eds.) *Pattern-Directed Inference Systems* (Academic Press, New York, 1978).

5. Feigenbaum, Edward A. and Feldman, J. (eds.), *Computers and Thought* (McGraw-Hill Book Company, N.Y., 1963).

6. Feigenbaum, Edward A., The art of artificial intelligence, Fifth IJCAI, Cambridge (1977) pp. 1014–1029.

7. Feitelson, Jerry and Stefik, M., A case study of the reasoning in a genetics experiment, Heuristic Programming Project Working Paper 77–18, Stanford University Computer Science Department (April 11, 1977).

8. Gunderson, Keith, The imitation game, in: A. Anderson (ed.) *Minds and Machines* (Prentice-Hall, Englewood Cliffs, N.J., 1964).

9. Hadamard, Jaques, *The Psychology of Invention in the Mathematical Field* (Dover Publications, N.Y., 1945).

10. Kolata, Gina B., Catastrophe theory: The emperor has no clothes, *Science* (April 15, 1977) p. 287. See also the spate of letters in the June 15 issue, replying to that article.

11. Kuhn, Thomas S., *The Structure of Scientific Revolutions*, 2nd ed. (University of Chicago Press, Chicago, 1970).

12. Lederberg, Joshua, Dendral-64: A system for computer construction, enumeration, and notation of organic molecules as tree structures and cyclic graphs, NASA Interim Report, 1964.

13. Lenat, Douglas B., AM: An artificial intelligence approach to discovery in mathematics as heuristic search, SAIL AIM-286, Artificial Intelligence Laboratory, Stanford University. Jointly issued as Stanford Computer Science Report No. STAN-CS-76-570, and as Stanford Heuristic Programming Project Report No. HPP-76-8 (July 1976).

14. Lenat, Douglas B., Automated theory formation in mathematics, Fifth IJCAI, Cambridge, 1977, pp. 833–842.

15. Lenat, Douglas B. and Harris, G., Designing a rule system that searches for scientific discoveries, in: D. A. Waterman and F. Hayes-Roth (eds.) *Pattern-Directed Inference Systems*, (Academic Press, New York, 1978).

16. Moses, Joel, Symbolic integration, MIT Report MAC-TR-47 (December 1967).

17. Newell, Allen, Shaw, C. and Simon, H., Empirical explorations of the logic theory machine: a case study in heuristics, RAND Corp. Report P-951 (March 1957).

18. Newell, Allen and Simon, H., *Human Problem Solving* (Prentice-Hall, Englewood Cliffs, N.J., 1972).

19. Newell, Allen, Production systems: models of control structures, Computer Science Department Report, Carnegie-Mellon University, Pittsburgh, PA (1973).

20. Newell, Allen and Simon, H., Computer science as empirical inquiry: symbols and search, 1975 ACM Turing Award Lecture, CACM 19, Number 3 (March 1976) pp. 113–126.

21. Nilsson, Nils, *Problem Solving Methods in Artificial Intelligence* (McGraw-Hill, N.Y., 1971).

22. Poincaré, Henri, *The Foundations of Science: Science and Hypothesis, The Value of Science, Science and Method* (The Science Press, N.Y., 1929).

23. Polya, George, *Mathematics and Plausible Reasoning*, Princeton University Press, Princeton, Vol. 1 (1954) Vol. 2 (1954).

24. Shortliffe, Edward H., MYCIN—A rule-based computer program for advising physicians regarding antimicrobial therapy selection, Stanford AI Memo 251 (October 1974).

25. Turing, A an M., Computing machinery and intelligence, *Mind* 59, no. 236 (1950).

26. Zaripov, R. Kh., Simulation of functions of composer and musicologist on electronic computer, Proceedings of the Fourth IJCAI, Tbilisi, USSR (1975).

*Received September 1977*

[21] Controlling the temperature, lighting, security, and other functions around the house.

# Classifier Systems and Genetic Algorithms

**L.B. Booker, D.E. Goldberg and J.H. Holland**

*Computer Science and Engineering, 3116 EECS Building,*
*The University of Michigan, Ann Arbor, MI 48109, U.S.A.*

ABSTRACT

*Classifier systems are massively parallel, message-passing, rule-based systems that learn through credit assignment (the bucket brigade algorithm) and rule discovery (the genetic algorithm). They typically operate in environments that exhibit one or more of the following characteristics: (1) perpetually novel events accompanied by large amounts of noisy or irrelevant data; (2) continual, often real-time, requirements for action; (3) implicitly or inexactly defined goals; and (4) sparse payoff or reinforcement obtainable only through long action sequences. Classifier systems are designed to absorb new information continuously from such environments, devising sets of competing hypotheses (expressed as rules) without disturbing significantly capabilities already acquired. This paper reviews the definition, theory, and extant applications of classifier systems, comparing them with other machine learning techniques, and closing with a discussion of advantages, problems, and possible extensions of classifier systems.*

## 1. Introduction

Consider the simply defined world of checkers. We can analyze many of its complexities and with some real effort we can design a system that plays a pretty decent game. However, even in this simple world novelty abounds. A good player will quickly learn to confuse the system by giving some novel twists. The real world about us is much more complex. A system confronting this environment faces perpetual novelty—the flow of visual information impinging upon a mammalian retina, for example, never twice generates the same firing pattern during the mammal's lifespan. How can a system act other than randomly in such environments?

It is small wonder, in the face of such complexity, that even the most carefully contrived systems err significantly and repeatedly. There are only two cures. An outside agency can intervene to provide a new design, or the system can revise its own design on the basis of its experience. For the systems of most interest here—cognitive systems or robotic systems in realistic environments, ecological systems, the immune system, economic systems, and so on—the first option is rarely feasible. Such systems are immersed in continually changing

*Artificial Intelligence* **40** (1989) 235–282

0004-3702/89/$3.50 © 1989, Elsevier Science Publishers B.V. (North-Holland)

This paper originally appeared in the journal, *Artificial Intelligence*, Vol. 40, Nos. 1-3, and is reprinted here with permission of the publisher, Elsevier, Amsterdam.

environments wherein timely outside intervention is difficult or impossible. The only option then is learning or, using the more inclusive word, adaptation.

In broadest terms, the object of a learning system, natural or artificial, is the expansion of its knowledge in the face of uncertainty. More directly, a learning system improves its performance by generalizing upon past experience. Clearly, in the face of perpetual novelty, experience can guide future action only if there are relevant regularities in the system's environment. Human experience indicates that the real world abounds in regularities, but this does not mean that it is easy to extract and exploit them.

In the study of artificial intelligence the problem of extracting regularities is the problem of discovering useful representations or categories. For a machine learning system, the problem is one of constructing relevant categories from the system's primitives (pixels, features, or whatever else is taken as given). Discovery of relevant categories is only half the job; the system must also discover what kinds of action are appropriate to each category. The overall process bears a close relation to the Newell–Simon [40] problem solving paradigm, though there are differences arising from problems created by perpetual novelty, imperfect information, implicit definition of the goals, and the typically long, coordinated action sequences required to attain goals.

There is another problem at least as difficult as the representation problem. In complex environments, the actual attainment of a goal conveys little information about the overall process required to attain the goal. As Samuel [42] observed in his classic paper, the information (about successive board configurations) generated during the play of a game greatly exceeds the few bits conveyed by the final win or a loss. In games, and in most realistic environments, these "intermediate" states have no associated payoff or direct information concerning their "worth." Yet they play a stage-setting role for goal attainment. It may be relatively easy to recognize a triple jump as a critical step toward a win; it is much less easy to recognize that something done many moves earlier set the stage for the triple jump. How is the learning system to recognize the implicit value of certain stage-setting actions?

Samuel points the way to a solution. Information conveyed by intermediate states can be used to construct a model of the environment, and this model can be used in turn to make predictions. The verification or falsification of a prediction by subsequent events can be used then to improve the model. The model, of course, also includes the states yielding payoff, so that predictions about the value of certain stage-setting actions can be checked, with revisions made where appropriate.

In sum, the learning systems of most interest here confront some subset of the following problems:

(1) a perpetually novel stream of data concerning the environment, often noisy or irrelevant (as in the case of mammalian vision),

(2) continual, often real-time, requirements for action (as in the case of an organism or robot, or a tournament game),

(3) implicitly or inexactly defined goals (such as acquiring food, money, or some other resource, in a complex environment),

(4) sparse payoff or reinforcement, requiring long sequences of action (as in an organism's search for food, or the play of a game such as chess or go).

In order to tackle these problems the learning system must:

(1) invent categories that uncover goal-relevant regularities in its environment,

(2) use the flow of information encountered along the way to the goal to steadily refine its model of the environment,

(3) assign appropriate actions to stage-setting categories encountered on the way to the goal.

It quickly becomes apparent that one cannot produce a learning system of this kind by grafting learning algorithms onto existing (nonlearning) AI systems. The system must continually absorb new information and devise ranges of competing hypotheses (conjectures, plausible new rules) without disturbing capabilities it already has. Requirements for consistency are replaced by competition between alternatives. Perpetual novelty and continual change provide little opportunity for optimization, so that the competition aims at satisfying rather than optimization. In addition, the high-level interpreters employed by most (nonlearning) AI systems can cause difficulties for learning. High-level interpreters, by design, impose a complex relation between primitives of the language and the sentences (rules) that specify actions. Typically this complex relation makes it difficult to find simple combinations of primitives that provide plausible generalizations of experience.

A final comment before proceeding: Adaptive processes, with rare exceptions, are far more complex than the most complex processes studied in the physical sciences. And there is as little hope of understanding them without the help of theory as there would be of understanding physics without the attendant theoretical framework. Theory provides the maps that turn an uncoordinated set of experiments or computer simulations into a cumulative exploration. It is far from clear at this time what form a unified theory of learning would take, but there are useful fragments in place. Some of these fragments have been provided by the connectionists, particularly those following the paths set by Sutton and Barto [98], Hinton [23], Hopfield [36] and others. Other fragments come from theoretical investigations of complex adaptive systems such as the investigations of the immune system pursued by Farmer, Packard and Perelson [14]. Still others come from research centering on genetic algorithms and classifier systems (see, for example, [28]). This paper focuses on contributions deriving from the latter studies, supplying some illustrations of the interaction between theory, computer modeling, and data in that context. A central theoretical concern is the process whereby structures (rule clusters and the like) emerge in response to the problem solving demands imposed by the system's environment.

### 2. Overview

The machine learning systems discussed in this paper are called *classifier systems*. It is useful to distinguish three levels of activity (see Fig. 1) when looking at learning from the point of view of classifier systems:

At the lowest level is the *performance system*. This is the part of the overall system that interacts directly with the environment. It is much like an expert system, though typically less domain-dependent. The performance systems we will be talking about are rule-based, as are most expert systems, but they are message-passing, highly standardized, and highly parallel. Rules of this kind are called classifiers. The performance system is discussed in detail in Section 3; Section 4 relates the terminology and procedures of classifier systems to their counterparts in more typical AI systems.

Because the system must determine which of its rules are effective, a second level of activity is required. Generally the rules in the performance system are of varying usefulness and some, or even most, of them may be incorrect. Somehow the system must evaluate the rules. This activity is often called *credit assignment* (or apportionment of credit); accordingly this level of the system will be called the *credit assignment system*. The particular algorithms used here for credit assignment are called *bucket brigade algorithms*; they are discussed in Section 5.

The third level of activity, the *rule discovery system*, is required because,

even after the system has effectively evaluated millions of rules, it has tested only a minuscule portion of the plausibly useful rules. Selection of the best of that minuscule portion can give little confidence that the system has exhausted its possibilities for improvement; it is even possible that none of the rules it has examined is very good. The system must be able to generate new rules to replace the least useful rules currently in place. The rules could be generated at random (say by "mutation" operators) or by running through a predetermined enumeration, but such "experience-independent" procedures produce improvements much too slowly to be useful in realistic settings. Somehow the rule discovery procedure must be biased by the system's accumulated experience. In the present context this becomes a matter of using experience to determine useful "building blocks" for rules; then new rules are generated by combining selected building blocks. Under this procedure the new rules are at least plausible in terms of system experience. (Note that a rule may be plausible without necessarily being useful of even correct.) The rule discovery system discussed here employs *genetic algorithms*. Section 6 discusses genetic algorithms. Section 7 relates the procedures implicit in genetic algorithms to some better-known machine learning procedures.

Section 8 reviews some of the major applications and tests of genetic algorithms and classifier systems, while the final section of the paper discusses some open questions, obstacles, and major directions for future research.

Historically, our first attempt at understanding adaptive processes (and learning) turned into a theoretical study of genetic algorithms. This study was summarized in a book titled *Adaptation in Natural and Artificial Systems* (Holland [28]). Chapter 8 of that book contained the germ of the next phase. This phase concerned representations that lent themselves to manipulation by genetic algorithms. It built upon the definition of the *broadcast language* presented in Chapter 8, simplifying it in several ways to obtain a standardized class of parallel, rule-based systems called *classifier systems*. The first descriptions of classifier systems appeared in Holland [29]. This led to concerns with apportioning credit in parallel systems. Early considerations, such as those of Holland and Reitman [34], gave rise to an algorithm called the *bucket brigade algorithm* (see [31]) that uses only local interactions between rules to distribute credit.

### 3. Classifier Systems

The starting point for this approach to machine learning is a set of rule-based systems suited to rule discovery algorithms. The rules must lend themselves to processes that extract and recombine "building blocks" from currently useful rules to form new rules, and the rules must interact simply and in a highly parallel fashion. Section 4 discusses the reasons for these requirements, but we define the rule-based systems first to provide a specific focus for that discussion.

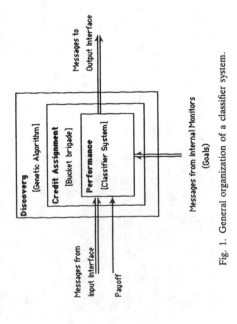

Fig. 1. General organization of a classifier system.

### 3.1. Definition of the basic elements

Classifier systems are parallel, message-passing, rule-based systems wherein all rules have the same simple form. In the simplest version all messages are required to be of a fixed length over a specified alphabet, typically $k$-bit binary strings. The rules are in the usual *condition/action* form. The condition part specifies what kinds of messages satisfy (activate) the rule and the action part specifies what message is to be sent when the rule is satisfied.

A classifier system consists of four basic parts (see Fig. 2).

– The *input interface* translates the current state of the environment into standard messages. For example, the input interface may use property detectors to set the bit values (1: the current state has the property, 0: it does not) at given positions in an incoming message.

– The *classifiers*, the rules used by the system, define the system's procedures for processing messages.

– The *message list* contains all current messages (those generated by the input interface and those generated by satisfied rules).

– The *output interface* translates some messages into effector actions, actions that modify the state of the environment.

A classifier system's basic execution cycle consists of the following steps:

*Step* 1. Add all messages from the input interface to the message list.

*Step* 2. Compare all messages on the message list to all conditions of all classifiers and record all matches (satisfied conditions).

*Step* 3. For each set of matches satisfying the condition part of some classifier, post the message specified by its action part to a list of new messages.

*Step* 4. Replace *all* messages on the message list by the list of new messages.

*Step* 5. Translate messages on the message list to requirements on the output interface, thereby producing the system's current output.

*Step* 6. Return to Step 1.

Individual classifiers must have a simple, compact definition if they are to serve as appropriate grist for the learning mill; a complex, interpreted definition makes it difficult for the learning algorithm to find and exploit building blocks from which to construct new rules (see Section 4).

The major technical hurdle in implementing this definition is that of providing a simple specification of the condition part of the rule. Each condition must specify exactly the set of messages that satisfies it. Though most large sets can be defined only by an explicit listing, there is one class of subsets in the message space that can be specified quite compactly, the hyperplanes in that space. Specifically, let $\{1, 0\}^k$ be the set of possible $k$-bit messages; if we use "#" as a "don't care" symbol, then the set of hyperplanes can be designated by the set of all ternary strings of length $k$ over the alphabet $\{1, 0, \#\}$. For example, the string $1\# \ldots \#$ designates the set of all messages that start with a 1, while the string $00 \ldots 0\#$ specifies the set $\{00 \ldots 01, 00 \ldots 00\}$ consisting of exactly two messages, and so on.

It is easy to check whether a given message satisfies a condition. The condition and the message are matched position by position, and if the entries at all non-# positions are identical, then the message satisfies the condition. The notation is extended by allowing any string $c$ over $\{1, 0, \#\}$ to be prefixed by a "–" with the intended interpretation that $-c$ is satisfied just in case *no* message satisfying $c$ is present on the message list.

### 3.2. Examples

At this point we can introduce a small classifier system that illustrates the "programming" of classifiers. The sets of rules that we'll look at can be thought of as fragments of a simple simulated organism or robot. The system has a vision field that provides it with information about its environment, and it is capable of motion through that environment. Its goal is to acquire certain kinds of objects in the environment ("targets") and avoid others ("dangers"). Thus, the environment presents the system with a variety of problems such as "What sequence of outputs will take the system from its present location to a visible target?" The system must use classifiers with conditions sensitive to messages from the input interface, as well as classifiers that integrate the messages from other classifiers, to send messages that control the output interface in appropriate ways.

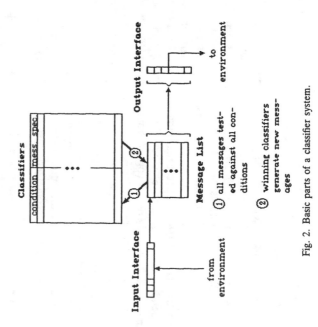

Fig. 2. Basic parts of a classifier system.

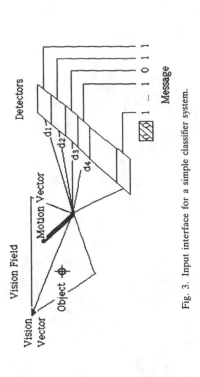

Fig. 3. Input interface for a simple classifier system.

In the examples that follow, the system's input interface produces a message for each object in the vision field. A set of *detectors* produces these messages by inserting in them the values for a variety of properties, such as whether or not the object is moving, whether it is large or small, etc. The detectors and the values they produce will be defined as needed in the examples.

The system has-three kinds of *effectors* that determine its actions in the environment. One effector controls the VISION VECTOR, a vector indicating the orientation of the center of the vision field. The VISION VECTOR can be rotated incrementally each time step (V-LEFT or V-RIGHT, say in 15-degree increments). The system also has a MOTION VECTOR that indicates its direction of motion, often independent of the direction of vision (as when the system is scanning while it moves). The second effector controls rotation of the MOTION VECTOR (M-LEFT or M-RIGHT) in much the same fashion as the first effector controls the VISION VECTOR. The second effector may also align the MOTION VECTOR with the VISION VECTOR, or set it in the opposite direction (ALIGN and OPPOSE, respectively), to facilitate behaviors such as pursuit and flight. The third effector sets the rate of motion in the indicated direction (FAST, CRUISE, SLOW, STOP). The classifiers process the information produced by the detectors to provide sequences of effector commands that enable the system to achieve goals.

For the first examples let the system be supplied with the following property detectors:

$$d_1 = \begin{cases} 1, & \text{if the object is moving,} \\ 0, & \text{otherwise;} \end{cases}$$

$$(d_2, d_3) = \begin{cases} (0,0), & \text{if the object is centered in the vision field,} \\ (1,0), & \text{if the object is left of center,} \\ (0,1), & \text{if the object is right of center;} \end{cases}$$

$$d_4 = \begin{cases} 1, & \text{if the system is adjacent to the object,} \\ 0, & \text{otherwise;} \end{cases}$$

$$d_5 = \begin{cases} 1, & \text{if the object is large,} \\ 0, & \text{otherwise;} \end{cases}$$

$$d_6 = \begin{cases} 1, & \text{if the object is striped,} \\ 0, & \text{otherwise.} \end{cases}$$

Let the detectors specify the rightmost six bits of messages from the input interface, $d_1$ setting the rightmost bit, $d_2$ the next bit to the left, etc. (see Fig. 3).

**Example 3.1.** A simple *stimulus-response* classifier.

IF there is "prey" (*small*, *moving*, *nonstriped object*), centered in the vision field (*centered*), and not adjacent (*nonadjacent*),
THEN move toward the object (ALIGN) rapidly (FAST).

Somewhat fancifully, we can think of the system as an "insect eater" that seeks out small, moving objects unless they are striped ("wasps"). To implement this rule as a classifier we need a condition that attends to the appropriate detector values. It is also important that the classifier recognize that the message is generated by the input interface (rather than internally). To accomplish this we assign messages a prefix or *tag* that identifies their origin—a two-bit tag that takes the value $(0, 0)$ for messages from the input interface will serve for present purposes (see Example 3.5 for a further discussion of tags). Following the conventions of the previous subsection the classifier has the condition

$$00\#\#\#\#\#000001 ,$$

where the leftmost two loci specify the required tag, the # specify the loci (detectors) not attended to, and the rightmost 6 loci specify the required detector values ($d_1 = 1 = moving$, being the rightmost locus, etc.). When this condition is satisfied, the classifier sends an outgoing message, say

$$0100000000000000 ,$$

where the prefix 01 indicates that the message is *not* from the input interface. (Though these examples use 16-bit messages, in realistic systems much longer messages would be advantageous.) We can think of this message as being used directly to set effector conditions in the output interface. For convenience these *effector settings*, ALIGN and FAST in the present case, will be indicated in **capital letters at the right end** of the classifier specification. The complete specification, then, is

$$00\#\#\#\#\#000001 / 0100000000000000, \text{ ALIGN, FAST} .$$

**Example 3.2.** A set of classifiers detecting a compound object defined by the *relations* between its parts.

The following pair of rules emits an identifying message when there is a moving T-shaped object in the vision field.

IF there is a centered object that is large, has a long axis, and is moving *along* the direction of that long axis,
THEN move the vision vector FORWARD (along the axis in the direction of motion) and record the presence of a moving object of type "I".

IF there was a centered object of type "I" observed on the previous time step, and IF there is currently a centered object in contact with "I" that is large, has a long axis, and is moving *crosswise* to the direction of that long axis,
THEN record the presence of a moving object of type "T" (blunt end forward) .

The first of these rules is "triggered" whenever the system "sees" an object moving in the same direction as its long axis. When this happens the system scans forward to see if the object is preceded by an attached cross-piece. The two rules acting in concert detect a compound object defined by the relation between its parts (cf. Winston's [53] "arch"). Note that the pair of rules *can be* fooled; the moving "cross-piece" might be accidentally or temporarily in contact with the moving "I". As such the rules constitute only a first approximation or default, to be improved by adding additional conditions or exception rules as experience accumulates. Note also the assumption of some sophistication in the input and output interfaces: an effector "subroutine" that moves the center of vision along the line of motion, a detector that detects the absence of a gap as the center of vision moves from one object to another, and beneath all a detector "subroutine" that picks out moving objects. Because these are intended as simple examples, we will not go into detail about the interfaces—suffice it to say that reasonable approximations to such "subroutines" exist (see, for example, [37]).

If we go back to our earlier fancy of the system as an insect eater, then moving T-shaped objects can be thought of as "hawks" (not too farfetched, because a "T" formed of two pieces of wood and moved over newly hatched chicks causes them to run for cover, see [43]).

To redo these rules as classifiers we need two new detectors:

$$d_7 = \begin{cases} 1, & \text{if the object is moving in the direction of its long axis}, \\ 0, & \text{otherwise} ; \end{cases}$$

$$d_8 = \begin{cases} 1, & \text{if the object is moving in the direction of its short axis}, \\ 0, & \text{otherwise} . \end{cases}$$

We also need a command for the effector subroutine that causes the vision vector to move up the long axis of an object in the direction of its motion, call it V-FORWARD. Finally, let the message 0100000000000001 signal the detection of the moving "I" and let the message 0100000000000010 signal the detection of the moving T-shaped object. The classifier implementing the first rule then has the form

00####01#1#001 / 0100000000000001, V-FORWARD .

The second rule must be contingent upon *both* the just previous detection of the moving "I", signalled by the message 0100000000000001 and the current presence of the cross-piece, signalled by a message from the environment starting with tag 00 and having the value 1 for detector $d_8$.

0100000000000001, 00####10#1#001 / 0100000000000010 .

**Example 3.3.** Simple memory.

The following set of three rules keeps the system on alert status if there has been a moving object in the vision field recently. The duration of the alert is determined by a timer, called the ALERT TIMER, that is set by a message, say 0100000000000011, when the object appears.

IF there is a moving object in the vision field,
THEN set the ALERT TIMER and send an alert message .

IF the ALERT TIMER is not zero,
THEN send an alert message .

IF there is *no* moving object in the vision field and the ALERT TIMER is not zero,
THEN decrement the ALERT TIMER .

To translate these rules into classifiers we need an effector subroutine that sets the alert timer, call it SET ALERT, and another that decrements the alert timer, call it DECREMENT ALERT. We also need a detector that determines whether or not the alert timer is zero.

$$d_9 = \begin{cases} 1, & \text{if the ALERT TIMER is } not \text{ zero }, \\ 0, & \text{otherwise} . \end{cases}$$

The classifiers implementing the three rules then have the form

00############1 / 0100000000000011, SET ALERT
00####1######### / 0100000000000011
00####1#######0 / DECREMENT ALERT .

Note that the first two rules send the same message, in effect providing an OR of the two conditions, because satisfying either the first condition *or* the second will cause the message to appear on the message list. Note also that these rules check on an *internal* condition via the detector $d_9$, thus providing a system that is no longer driven solely by external stimuli.

**Example 3.4.** Building blocks.

To illustrate the possibility of combining several active rules to handle complex situations we introduce the following three pairs of rules.

(A)   IF there is an alert and the moving object is near ,
      THEN move at FAST in the direction of the MOTION VECTOR .

      IF there is an alert and the moving object is far ,
      THEN move at CRUISE in the direction of the MOTION VECTOR .

(B)   IF there is an alert, and a small, nonstriped object in the vision field ,
      THEN ALIGN the motion vector with the vision vector .

      IF there is an alert, and a large T-shaped object in the vision field ,
      THEN OPPOSE the motion vector to the vision vector .

(C)   IF there is an alert, and a moving object in the vision field ,
      THEN send a message that causes the vision effectors to CENTER the object .

      IF there is an alert, and *no* moving object in the vision field ,
      THEN send a message that causes the vision effectors to SCAN .

(Each of the rules in pair (C) sends a message that invokes additional rules. For example "centering" can be accomplished by rules of the form,

      IF there is an object in the left vision field ,
      THEN execute V-LEFT .

      IF there is an object in the right vision field ,
      THEN execute V-RIGHT .

realized by the pair of classifiers

      00#########10# / V-LEFT .
      00#########01# / V-RIGHT .)

Any combination of rules obtained by activating one rule from each of the three subsets (A), (B), (C) yields a potentially useful behavior for the system. Accordingly the rules can be combined to yield distinct behavior in eight distinct situations; moreover, the systems need encounter only two situations (involving

disjoint sets of three rules) to test all six rules. The example can be extended easily to much larger numbers of subsets. The number of potentially useful combinations increases as an *exponent* of the number of subsets; that is, *n* subsets, of two alternatives apiece, yield $2^n$ distinct combinations of *n* simultaneously active rules. Once again, only two situations (appropriately chosen) need be encountered to provide testing for *all* the rules.

The six rules are implemented as classifiers in the same way as in the earlier examples, noticing that the system is put on alert status by using a condition that is satisfied by the alert message 0100000000000011. Thus the first rule becomes

$$0100000000000011, \quad 00\#\#\#\#0\#\#\#\#\#\#\#1 \,/\, FAST ,$$

where a new detector $d_{10}$, supplying values at the tenth position from the right in environmental messages, determines whether the object is far (value 1) or near (value 0).

It is clear that the building block approach provides tremendous combinatorial advantages to the system (along the lines described so well by Simon [45]).

**Example 3.5.** Networks and tagging.

Networks are built up in terms of *pointers* that couple the elements (nodes) of the network, so the basic problem is that of supplying classifier systems with the counterparts of pointers. In effect we want to be able to couple classifiers so that activation of a classifier $C$ in turn causes activation of the classifiers to which it points. The passing of activation between coupled classifiers then acts much like Fahlman's [13] marker-passing scheme, except that the classifier system is passing, and processing, messages. In general we will say a classifier $C_2$ is *coupled* to a classifier $C_1$ if some condition of $C_2$ is satisfied by the message(s) generated by the action part of $C_1$. Note that a classifier with very specific conditions (few #) will be coupled typically to only a few other classifiers, while a classifier with very general conditions (many #) will be coupled to many other classifiers. Looked at this way, classifiers with very specific conditions have few incoming "branches," while classifiers with very general conditions have many incoming "branches."

The simplest way to couple classifiers is by means of *tags*, bits incorporated in the condition part of a classifier that serve as a kind of identifier or address. For example, a condition of the form 1101## ... # will accept any message with the prefix 1101. Thus, to send a message to this classifier we need only prefix the message with the tag 1101. We have already seen an example of this use of tags in Example 3.1, where messages from the input interface are "addressed" only to classifiers that have conditions starting with the prefix 00. Because $b$ bits yield $2^b$ distinct tags, and tags can be placed anywhere in a condition (the component bits need not even be contiguous), large numbers of conditions can be "addressed" uniquely at the cost of relatively few bits.

By using appropriate tags one can define a classifier that attends to a specific set of classifiers. Consider, for example, a pair of classifiers $C_1$ and $C_2$ that send messages prefixed with 1101 and 1001, respectively. A classifier with the condition 1101## ... # will attend only to $C_1$, whereas a classifier with condition 1#01## ... # will attend to both $C_1$ and $C_2$. This approach, in conjunction with recodings (where the prefix of the outgoing message differs from that of the satisfying messages), provides great flexibility in defining the sets of classifiers to which a given classifier attends. Two examples will illustrate the possibilities:

**Example 3.5.1.** Producing a message in response to an arbitrarily chosen subset of messages.

An arbitrary logical (boolean) combination of conditions can be realized through a combination of couplings and recodings. The primitives from which more complex expressions can be constructed are AND, OR, and NOT. An AND-condition is expressed by a single multi-condition classifier such as $M_1, M_2/M$, for $M$ is only added to the message list if both $M_1$ and $M_2$ are on the list. Similarly the pair of classifiers $M_1/M$ and $M_2/M$ express an OR-condition, for $M$ is added to the message list if either $M_1$ or $M_2$ is on the list. NOT, of course, is expressed by a classifier with the condition $-M$. As an illustration, consider the boolean expression

$$(M_1 \text{ AND } M_2) \text{ OR } ((\text{NOT } M_3) \text{ AND } M_4).$$

This is expressed by the following set of classifiers with the message $M$ appearing if and only if the boolean expression is satisfied.

$$M_1, M_2/M, \quad -M_3, M_4/M.$$

The judicious use of # and recodings often substantially reduces the number of classifiers required when the boolean expressions are complex.

**Example 3.5.2.** Representing a network

The most direct way of representing a network is to use one classifier for each pointer (arrow) in the network (though it is often possible to find clean representations using one classifier for each node in the network).

As an illustration of this approach consider the following network fragment (Fig. 4). In marker-passing terms, the ALERT node acquires a marker when there is a MOVING object in the vision field. For the purposes of this example, we will assume that the conjunction of arrows at the TARGET node is a requirement that all three nodes (ALERT, SMALL, and NOT STRIPED) be marked

before TARGET is marked. Similarly, PURSUE will only be marked if both TARGET and NEAR are marked, etc.

To transform this network into a set of classifiers, begin by assigning an identifying tag to each node. (The tags used in the diagram are 5-bit prefixes). The required couplings between the classifiers are then simply achieved by coordinating the tags used in conditions with the tags on the messages ("markers") to be passed. Henceforth, we extend the notation to allow #'s in the action part of classifiers, where they designate *pass-throughs*: Wherever the message part contains a #, the bit value of the outgoing message is identical to the bit value of the message satisfying the classifier's first condition. That is, the bit value of the incoming (satisfying) message is "passed through" to the outgoing message.

On the basis, assuming that the MOVING node is marked by the detector $d_1$, the arrow between MOVING and ALERT would be implemented by the classifier

$$00\#\#\#\#\#\#\#\#\#\#\#\#1 / 01001\#\#\#\#\#\#\#\#\#\#,$$

while the arrows leading from SMALL, NOT STRIPED, and ALERT to TARGET could be implemented by the single classifier

$$00\#\#\#\#\#\#\#00\#\#\#, \quad 01001\#\#\#\#\#\#\#\#\#\# /$$
$$10001\#\#\#\#\#\#\#\#\#.$$

In turn, the arrows from NEAR and TARGET to PURSUE could be implemented by

$$00\#\#\#\#0\#\#\#\#\#\#\#, \quad 10001\#\#\#\#\#\#\#\# /$$
$$11001\#\#\#\#\#\#\#\#\#.$$

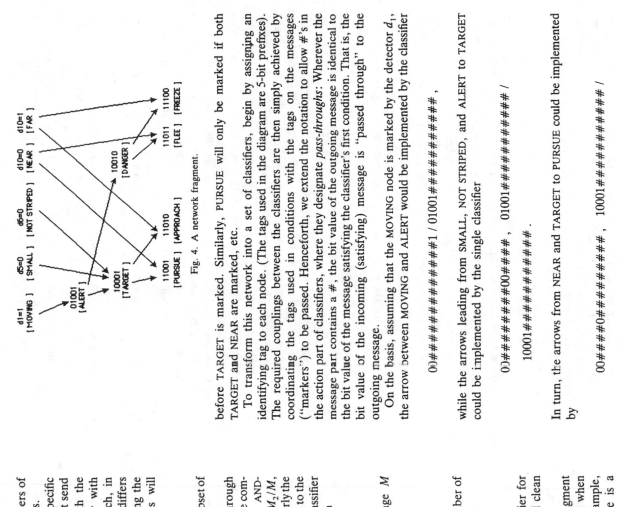

Fig. 4. A network fragment.

can be difficult to achieve in a distributed computation. Explicit machinery is needed for insuring a consistent problem solving focus, and the requisite control knowledge may be hard to come by unless the problem is inherently parallel to begin with. These two properties suggest an unconventional approach if a classifier system is to be used to build a *conventional* expert system, though the computational completeness of classifier systems assures it could be done in the usual way.

The key to understanding the advantages of classifier systems is to understand the kind of problems they were designed to solve. A perpetually novel stream of data constitutes an extremely complex and uncertain problem solving environment. A well-known strategy for resolving uncertainty is exemplified by the blackboard architecture (see [12]). By coordinating multiple sources of hierarchically organized knowledge, hypotheses and constraints, problem solving can proceed in an opportunistic way, guided by the summation of converging evidence and building on weak or partial results to arrive at confident conclusions. However, managing novelty requires more than this kind of problem solving flexibility. A system must dynamically construct and modify the representation of the problem itself! Flexibility is required at the more basic level of concepts, relations, and the way they are organized. Classifier systems were designed to make this kind of flexibility possible.

Building blocks are the technical device used in classifier systems to achieve this flexibility. The message list is a global database much like a blackboard, but the possibilities for organizing hypotheses are not predetermined in advance. Messages and tags are building blocks that provide a flexible way of constructing arbitrary hierarchical or heterarchical associations among rules and concepts. Because the language is simple, modifying these associations can be done with local syntactic manipulations that avoid the need for complex interpreters or knowledge-intensive critics. In a similar way, rules themselves are building blocks for representing complex concepts, constraints and problem solving behaviors. Because rules are activated in parallel, new combinations of existing rules and rule clusters can be used to handle novel situations. This is tantamount to building knowledge sources as needed during problem solving.

The apparently unsophisticated language of classifier systems is therefore a deliberate tradeoff of descriptive power for adaptive efficiency. A simple syntax yields building blocks that are easy to identify, evaluate, and recombine in useful ways. Moreover, the sacrifice of descriptive power is not as severe as it might seem. A complex environment will contain concepts that cannot be specified easily or precisely even with a powerful logic. For example, a concept might be an equivalence class in which the members share no common features. Or it might be a relation with a strength that is measured by the distance from some prototype. Or it might be a network of relationships so variable that there are no clearly defined concept boundaries. Rather than construct a syntactically complex representation of such a concept that would

The remainder of the network would be implemented similarly.

Some comments are in order. First, the techniques used in Example 3.5.1 to implement boolean connectives apply equally to arrows. For example, we could set conditions so that TARGET would be activated if *either* MOVING and SMALL *or* MOVING and NOT STRIPED were activated. Relations between categories can be introduced following the general lines of Example 3.2. Second, tags can be assigned in ways that provide direct information about the structure of the network. For example, in the network above the first two bits of the tag indicate the level of the corresponding category (the number of arrows intervening between the category and the input from the environment). Finally, effector-oriented categories such as PURSUE would presumably "call subroutines" (sets of classifiers) that carry out the desired actions. For instance, the message from PURSUE would involve such operations as centering the object (see the classifiers just after (C) in Example 3.4), followed by rapid movement toward the object (see the classifier in Example 3.1).

Forrest [15] has produced a general compiler for producing coupled classifiers implementing any semantic net specified by KL-ONE expressions.

A final comment on the use of classifiers: Systems of classifiers, when used with learning algorithms, are *not* adjusted for consistency. Instead individual rules are treated as partially confirmed hypotheses, and conflicts are resolved by competition. The specifics of this competition are presented in Section 5.

## 4. The Relation of Classifier Systems to Other AI Problem Solving Systems

As noted previously, many of the problem solving and learning mechanisms in classifier systems have been motivated by broad considerations of adaptive processes in both natural and artificial systems. This point of view leads to a collection of computation procedures that differ markedly from the symbolic methods familiar to the AI community. It is therefore worthwhile to step back from the details of classifier systems and examine the core ideas that make classifier systems an important part of machine learning research.

When viewed solely as rule-based systems, classifier systems have two apparently serious weaknesses. First, the rules are written in a language that lacks descriptive power in comparison to what is available in other rule-based systems. The left-hand side of each rule is a simple conjunctive expression having a limited number of terms. It clearly cannot be used to express arbitrary, general relationships among attributes. Even though sets of such expressions are adequate in principle, most statements in the classifier language can be expressed more concisely or easily as statements in LISP or logic. Second, because several rules are allowed to fire simultaneously, control issues are raised that do not come up in conventional rule-based systems. Coherency

be difficult to use or modify, a classifier system uses *groups* of rules as the representation. The structure of the concept is *modeled* by the organization, variability, and distribution of strength among the rules. Because the members of a group compete to become active (see Section 5), the appropriate aspects of the representation are selected only when they are relevant in a given problem solving context. The modularity of the concept thereby makes it easier to use as well as easier to modify.

This distributed approach to representing knowledge is similar to the way complex concepts are represented in connectionist systems (see [24]). Both frameworks use a collection of basic computing elements as epistemic building blocks. Classifier systems use condition/action rules that interact by passing messages. Connectionist systems use simple processing units that send excitatory and inhibitory signals to each other. Concepts are represented in both systems by the simultaneous activation of several computing elements. Every computing element is involved in representing several concepts, and the representations for similar concepts share elements. Retrieval of a concept is a constructive process that simultaneously activates constituent elements best fitting the current context. This technique has the important advantage that some relevant generalizations are achieved automatically. Modifications to elements of one representation automatically affect all similar representations that share those elements.

There are important differences between classifier systems and connectionist systems, however, that stem primarily from the properties of the building blocks they use. The interactions among computing elements in a connectionist system make "best-fit" searches a primitive operation. Activity in a partial pattern of elements is tantamount to an incomplete specification of a concept. Such patterns are automatically extended into a complete pattern of activity representing the concept most consistent with the given specification. Content-addressable memory can therefore be implemented effortlessly. The same capability is achieved in a classifier system using pointers and tags to link related rules. A directed spreading activation is then required to efficiently retrieve the appropriate concept.

Other differences relate to the way inductions are achieved. Modification of connection strengths is the only inductive mechanism available in most connectionist systems (see [36, 48]). Moreover, the rules for updating strength are part of the initial system design that cannot be changed except perhaps by tuning a few parameters. Classifier systems, on the other hand, permit a broad spectrum of inductive mechanisms ranging from strength adjustments to analogies. Many of these mechanisms can be controlled by, or can be easily expressed in terms of, inferential rules. These inferential rules can be evaluated, modified and used to build higher-level concepts in the same way that building blocks are used to construct lower-level concepts.

Classifier systems are like connectionist systems in emphasizing micro-structure, multiple constraints and the emergence of complex computations from simple processes. However, classifier systems use rules as a basic epistemic unit, thereby avoiding the reduction of all knowledge to a set of connection strengths. Classifier systems thus occupy an important middle ground between the symbolic and connectionist paradigms.

We conclude this section by comparing classifier systems to SOAR (see [38]), another system architecture motivated by broad considerations of cognitive processes. SOAR is a general-purpose architecture for goal-oriented problem solving and learning. All behavior in SOAR is viewed as a search through a problem space for some state that satisfies the goal (problem solution) criteria. Searching a problem space involves selecting appropriate operators to transform the initial problem state, through a sequence of operations, into an acceptable goal state. Whenever there is an impasse in this process, such as a lack of sufficient criteria for selecting an operator, SOAR generates a subgoal to resolve the impasse. Achieving this subgoal is a new problem that SOAR solves recursively by searching through the problem space characterizing the subgoal. SOAR's knowledge about problem states, operators, and solution criteria is represented by a set of condition/action rules. When an impasse is resolved, SOAR seizes the opportunity to learn a new rule (or set of rules) that summarizes important aspects of the subgoal processing. The new rule, or chunk of knowledge, can then be used to avoid similar impasses in the future. The learning mechanism that generates these rules is called *chunking*.

There are some obvious points of comparison between classifier systems and the SOAR architecture. Both emphasize the flexibility that comes from using rules as a basic unit of representation, and both emphasize the importance of tightly coupling induction mechanisms with problem solving. However, classifier systems do not enforce any one particular problem solving regime the way SOAR does. At a broader level, these systems espouse very different points of view about the mechanisms necessary for intelligent behavior. SOAR emphasizes the sufficiency of a single problem solving methodology coupled with a single learning mechanism. The only way to break a problem solving impasse is by creating subgoals, and the only way to learn is to add rules to the knowledge base by chunking. Classifier systems, on the other hand, place an emphasis on flexibly modeling the problem solving environment. A good model allows for prediction-based evaluation of the knowledge base, and the assignment of credit to the model's building blocks. This, in turn, makes it possible to modify, replace, or add to existing rules via inductive mechanisms such as the recombination of highly rated building blocks. Moreover, a model can provide the constraints necessary to generate plausible reformulations of the representation of a problem. To resolve problem solving impasses, then, classifier systems hypothesize new rules (by recombining building blocks), instead of recompiling (chunking) existing rules.

We will make comparisons to other machine learning methods (Section 7), after we have defined and discussed the learning algorithms for classifier systems.

## 5. Bucket Brigade Algorithms

The first major learning task facing any rule-based system operating in a complex environment is the *credit assignment* task. Somehow the performance system must determine both the rules responsible for its successes and the representativeness of the conditions encountered in attaining the successes. (The reader will find an excellent discussion of credit assignment algorithms in Sutton's [47] report.) The task is difficult because overt rewards are rare in complex environments; the system's behavior is mostly "stage-setting" that makes possible later successes. The problem is even more difficult for parallel systems, where only some of the rules active at a given time may be instrumental in attaining later success. An environment exhibiting perpetual novelty adds still another order of complexity. Under such conditions the performance system can *never* have an absolute assurance that any of its rules is "correct." The perpetual novelty of the environment, combined with an always limited sampling of that environment, leaves a residue to uncertainty. Each rule in effect serves as a hypothesis that has been more or less confirmed.

The *bucket brigade* algorithm is designed to solve the credit assignment problem for classifier systems. To implement the algorithm, each classifier is assigned a quantity called its *strength*. The bucket brigade algorithm adjusts the strength to reflect the classifier's overall usefulness to the system. The strength is then used as the basis of a competition. Each time step, each satisfied classifier makes a *bid* based on its strength, and only the highest bidding classifiers get their messages on the message list for the next time step.

It is worth recalling that there are no consistency requirements on posted messages; the message list can hold any set of messages, and any such set can direct further competition. The only point at which consistency enters is at the output interface. Here, different sets of messages may specify conflicting responses. Such conflicts are again resolved by competition. For example, the strengths of the classifiers advocating each response can be summed so that one of the conflicting actions is chosen with a probability proportional to the sum of its advocates.

The bidding process is specified as follows. Let $s(C, t)$ be the strength of classifier $C$ at time $t$. Two factors clearly bear on the bidding process: (1) relevance to the current situation, and (2) past "usefulness." Relevance is mostly a matter of the specificity of the rule's condition part—a more specific condition satisfied by the current situation conveys more information about that situation. The rule's strength is supposed to reflect its usefulness. In the simplest versions of the competition the bid is a product of these two factors, being 0 if the rule is irrelevant (condition not satisfied) or useless (strength 0),

and being high when the rule is highly specific to the situation (detailed conditions satisfied) and well confirmed as useful (high strength).

To implement this bidding procedure, we modify Step 3 of the basic execution cycle (see Section 3.1).

*Step* 3. For each set of matches satisfying the condition part of classifier $C$, *calculate a bid* according to the following formula,

$$B(C, t) = bR(C)s(C, t) ,$$

where $R(C)$ is the specificity, equal to the number of non-# in the condition part of $C$ divided by the length thereof, and $b$ is a constant considerably less than 1 (e.g., $\frac{1}{8}$ or $\frac{1}{16}$). The size of the bid determines the *probability* that the classifier posts its message (specified by the action part) to the new message list. (E.g., the probability that the classifier posts its message might decrease exponentially as the size of the bid decreases.)

The use of probability in the revised step assures that rules of lower strength sometimes get tested, thereby providing for the occasional testing of less-favored and newly generated (lower strength) classifiers ("hypotheses").

The operation of the bucket brigade algorithm can be explained informally via an economic analogy. The algorithm treats each rule as a kind of "middleman" in a complex economy. As a "middleman," a rule only deals with its "suppliers"—the rules sending messages satisfying its conditions—and its "consumers"—the rules with conditions satisfied by the messages the "middleman" sends. Whenever a rule wins a bidding competition, it initiates a transaction wherein it pays out part of its strength to its suppliers. (If the rule does not bid enough to win the competition, it pays nothing.) As one of the winners of the competition, the rule becomes active, serving as a supplier to its consumers, and receiving payments from them in turn. Under this arrangement, the rule's strength is a kind of capital that measures its ability to turn a "profit." If a rule receives more from its consumers than it paid out, it has made a profit; that is, its strength has increased.

More formally, when a winning classifier $C$ places its message on the message list it pays for the privilege by having its strength $s(C, t)$ reduced by the amount of the bid $B(C, t)$,

$$s(C, t + 1) = s(C, t) - B(C, t) .$$

The classifiers $\{C'\}$ sending messages matched by this winner, the "suppliers," have their strengths increased by the amount of the bid—it is shared among them in the simplest version—

$$s(C', t + 1) = s(C', t) + aB(C, t) ,$$

where $a = 1/(\text{no. of members of } \{C'\})$.

A rule is likely to be profitable only if its consumers, in their local transactions, are also (on the average) profitable. The consumers, in turn, will be profitable only if *their* consumers are profitable. The resulting chains of consumers lead to the ultimate consumers, the rules that directly attain goals and receive payoff directly from the environment. (Payoff is added to the strengths of all rules determining responses at the time the payoff occurs.) A rule that regularly attains payoff when activated is of course profitable. The profitability of other rules depends upon their being coupled into sequences leading to these profitable ultimate consumers. The bucket brigade ensures that early acting, "stage-setting" rules eventually receive credit if they are coupled into (correlated with) sequences that (on average) lead to payoff.

If a rule sequence is faulty, the final rule in the sequence loses strength, and the sequence will begin to disintegrate, over time, from the final rule backwards through its chain of precursors. As soon as a rule's strength decreases to the point that it loses in the bidding process, some competing rule will get a chance to act as a replacement. If the competing rule is more useful than the one displaced, a revised rule sequence will begin to form using the new rule. The bucket brigade algorithm thus searches out and repairs "weak links" through its pervasive local application.

Whenever rules are coupled into larger hierarchical knowledge structures, the bucket brigade algorithm is still more powerful than the description so far would suggest. Consider an abstract rule $C^*$ of the general form, "if the goal is $G$, and if the procedure $P$ is executed, then $G$ will be achieved." $C^*$ will be active throughout the time interval in which the sequence of rules comprising $P$ is executed. If the goal is indeed achieved, this rule serves to activate the response that attains the goal, as well as the stage-setting responses preceding that response. Under the bucket brigade $C^*$ will be strengthened immediately by the goal attainment. On the very next trial involving $P$, the earliest rules in $P$ will have their strengths substantially increased under the bucket brigade. This happens because the early rules act as suppliers to the strengthened $C^*$ (via the condition "if the procedure $P$ is executed"). Normally, the process would have to be executed on the order of $n$ times to backchain strength through an $n$-step process $P$. $C^*$ circumvents this necessity.

## 6. Genetic Algorithms

The rule discovery process for classifier systems uses a *genetic algorithm* (GA). Basically, a genetic algorithm selects high strength classifiers as "parents," forming "offspring" by recombining components from the parent classifiers. The offspring displace weak classifiers in the system and enter into competition, being activated and tested when their conditions are satisfied. Thus, a genetic algorithm crudely, but at high speed, mimics the genetic processes underlying evolution. It is vital to the understanding of genetic algorithms to

know that even the simplest versions act much more subtly than "random search with preservation of the best," contrary to a common misreading of genetics as a process primarily driven by mutation. (Genetic algorithms have been studied intensively by analysis, Holland [28] and Bethke [4], and simulation, DeJong [11], Smith [46], Booker [6], Goldberg [18], and others.)

Though genetic algorithms act subtly, the basic execution cycle, the "central loop," is quite simple:

*Step 1.* From the set of classifiers, select pairs according to strength—the stronger the classifier, the more likely its selection.

*Step 2.* Apply *genetic operators* to the pairs, creating "offspring" classifiers. Chief among the genetic operators is *cross-over*, which simply exchanges a randomly selected segment between the pairs (see Fig. 5).

*Step 3.* Replace the weakest classifiers with the offspring.

The key to understanding a genetic algorithm is an understanding of the way it manipulates a special class of building blocks called *schemas*. In brief, under a GA, a good building block is a building block that occurs in good rules. The GA biases future constructions toward the use of good building blocks. We will soon see that a GA rapidly explores the space of schemas, a very large space, implicitly rating and exploiting schemas according to the strengths of the rules employing them. (The term *schema* as used here is related to, but should not be confused with, the broader use of that term in psychology).

The first step in making this informal description precise is a careful definition of *schema*. To start, recall that a condition (or an action) for a classifier is defined by a string of letters $\alpha_1 \alpha_2 \ldots \alpha_j \ldots \alpha_k$ of length $k$ over the 3-letter alphabet $\{1, 0, \#\}$. It is reasonable to look upon these strings as built up from certain combinations of letters, say 11 or 0#1, as components. All such possibilities can be defined with the help of a new "don't care" symbol "*." To define a given *schema*, we specify the letters at the positions of interest, filling out the rest of the string with "don't cares." (The procedure mimics that for defining conditions, but we are operating at a different level now.) Thus, *0#1**...* focuses attention on the combination 0##1 at positions 2 through 5. Equivalently, *0#1**...* specifies a *set* of conditions, the set of *all* conditions that can be defined by using the combination 0##1 at positions 2 through 5. Any condition that has 0##1 at the given positions is an *instance* of schema *0#1**...*. The set of all *schemas* is just the set $\{1, 0, \#, *\}^k$ of all strings of length $k$ over the alphabet $\{1, 0, \#, *\}$. (Note that a *schema* defines a subset of the set of all possible conditions, while each condition defines a subset of the set of all possible messages.)

A classifier system, at any given time $t$, typically has many classifiers that contain a given component or schema $\sigma$; that is, the system has many instances of $\sigma$. We can assign a value $s(\sigma, t)$ to $\sigma$ at time $t$ by averaging the strengths of its instances. For example, let the system contain classifier $C_1$, with condition $10\#\#110\ldots0$ and strength $s(C_1, t) = 4$, and classifier $C_2$, with condition $00\#\#1011\ldots1$ and strength $s(C_2, t) = 2$. If these are the only two instances of schema $\sigma = *0\#\#1**\ldots*$ at time $t$, then we assign to the schema the value

$$s(\sigma, t) = \tfrac{1}{2}[s(C_1, t) + s(C_2, t)] = 3,$$

the average of the strengths of the two instances. The general formula is

$$s(\sigma, t) = (1/[\text{no. of instances of } \sigma]) \sum_{C \text{ an instances of } \sigma} s(C, t).$$

$s(\sigma, t)$ can be looked upon as an *estimate* of the mean value of $\sigma$, formed by taking the average value of the samples (instances) of $\sigma$ present in the classifier system at time $t$. It is a crude estimate and can mislead the system; nevertheless it serves well enough as a heuristic guide if the system has procedures that compensate for misleading estimates. This the algorithm does, as we will see, by evaluating additional samples of the schema; that is, it constructs new classifiers that are instances of the schema and submits them to the bucket brigade.

Consider now a system with $M$ classifiers that uses the observed averages $\{s(\sigma, t)\}$ to guide the construction of new classifiers from schemas. Two questions arise: (1) How many schemas are present (have instances) in the set of $M$ classifiers? (2) How is the system to calculate and use the $\{s(\sigma, t)\}$?

The answer to the first question has important implications for the use of schemas as building blocks. A single condition (or action) is an instance of $2^k$ schemas! (This is easily established by noting that a given condition is an instance of *every* schema obtained by substituting an "*" for one or more letters in the definition of the condition.) In a system of $M$ single-condition classifiers, there is enough information to calculate averages for somewhere between $2^k$ and $M2^k$ schemas. Even for very simple classifiers and a small system, $k = 32$ and $M = 1000$, this is an enormous number, $M2^k \sim 4$ trillion.

The natural way to use the averages would be to construct more instances of above-average schemas, while constructing fewer instances of below-average schemas. That is, the system would make more use of above-average building blocks, and less use of below-average building blocks. More explicitly: Let $s(t)$ be the average strength of the classifiers at time $t$. Then schema $\sigma$ is above average if $s(\sigma, t)/s(t) > 1$, and vice versa. Let $M(\sigma, t)$ be the number of instances of schema $\sigma$ in the system at time $t$, and let $M(\sigma, t + T)$ be the number of instances of $\sigma$ after $M$ new classifiers (samples) have been constructed. The simplest heuristic for using the information $s(\sigma, t)/s(t)$ would be to require that the number of instances (uses) of $\sigma$ increase (or decrease) at time $t + T$ according to that ratio,

$$M(\sigma, t + T) = c[s(\sigma, t)/s(t)]M(\sigma, t),$$

where $c$ is an arbitrary constant. It is even possible, *in principle*, to construct the new classifiers so that *every schema $\sigma$ with at least a few instances present at $t$* receives the requisite number of samples. (This is rather surprising since there are so many schemas and only $M$ new classifiers are constructed; however a little thought and some calculation, exploiting the fact that a single classifier is an instance of $2^k$ distinct schemas, shows that it is possible.)

A generating procedure following this heuristic, setting aside problems of implementation for the moment, has many advantages. It samples each schema with above-average instances with increasing intensity, thereby further confirming (or disconfirming) its usefulness and exploiting it (if it remains above average). This also drives the overall average $s(t)$ upward, providing an ever-increasing criterion that a schema must meet to be above average. Moreover, the heuristic employs a distribution of instances, rather than working only from the "most recent best" instance. This yields both robustness and insurance against being caught on "false peaks" (local optima) that misdirect development. Overall, the power of this heuristic stems from its rapid accumulation of better-than-average building blocks. Because the strengths underlying the $s(\sigma, t)$ are determined (via the bucket brigade) by the regularities and interactions in the environment, the heuristic provides a sophisticated way of exploiting such regularities and interactions.

Though these possibilities exist in principle, there is no feasible *direct* way to calculate and use the large set of averages $\{s(\sigma, t)/s(t)\}$. However, genetic algorithms do *implicitly* what is impossible explicitly. To see this, we must specify exactly the steps by which a genetic algorithm generates new classifiers.

The algorithm acts on a set $B(t)$ of $M$ strings $\{C_1, C_2, \ldots, C_M\}$ over the alphabet $\{1, 0, \#\}$ with assigned strengths $s(C_j, t)$ via the following steps:

*Step* 1. Compute the average strength $s(t)$ of the strings in $B(t)$, and assign the normalized value $s(C_j, t)/s(t)$ to each string $C_j$ in $B(t)$.

*Step* 2. Assign each string in $B(t)$ a probability proportional to its normalized value. Then, using this probability distribution, select $n$ pairs of strings, $n \ll M$, from $B(t)$, and make copies of them.

*Step* 3. Apply *cross-over* (and, possibly, other *genetic operators*) to each copied pair, forming $2n$ new strings. *Cross-over* is applied to a pair of strings as follows: Select at random a position $i$, $1 \le i \le k$, and then exchange the segments to the left of position $i$ in the two strings (see Fig. 5).

*Step* 4. Replace the $2n$ lowest strength strings in $B(t)$ with the $2n$ strings newly generated in Step 3.

*Step* 5. Set $t$ to $t + 1$ in preparation for the next use of the algorithm and return to Step 1.

Figure 6 illustrates the operation of the algorithm. In more sophisticated versions of the algorithm, the selection of pairs for recombination may be biased toward classifiers active at the time some triggering condition is satisfied. Also Step 4 may be modified to prevent one kind of string from "overcrowding" $B(t)$ (see [4, 11] for details).

Contiguity of constituents, and the building blocks constructed from them, are significant under the cross-over operator. Close constituents tend to be exchanged together. Operators for rearranging the atomic constituents defining the rules, such as the genetic operator *inversion*, can bias the rule generation process toward the use of certain *kinds* of building blocks. For example, if "color" is nearer to "shape" than to "taste" in a condition, then a particular "color"-"shape" combination will be exchanged as a unit more often than a "color"-"taste" combination. *Inversion*, by rearranging the positions of "shape" and "taste," could reverse this bias. Other genetic operators, such as *mutation*, have lesser roles in this use of the algorithm, mainly providing "insurance" (see [28, Chapter 6, Sections 2–4] for details).

To see how the genetic algorithm implicitly carries out the schema search heuristic described earlier, it is helpful to divide the algorithm's action into two phases: phase 1 consists of Steps 1–2; phase 2 consists of Steps 3–4.

First consider what would happen if phase 1 were iterated, without the execution of phase 2, but with the replacement of strings in $B(t)$. In particular, let phase 1 be iterated $M/2n$ times (assuming for convenience that $M$ is a multiple of $2n$). Under $M/2n$ repetitions of phase 1, *each instance C* of a given schema $\sigma$ can be expected to produce $s(\sigma, t)/s(t)$ "offspring" copies. The total number of instances of schema $\sigma$ after the action of phase 1 is just the *sum* of the copies of the individual instances. Dividing this total by the original number of instances, $M(\sigma, t)$, gives the average rate of increase, and is just $s(\sigma, t)/s(t)$ as required by the heuristic. This is true of every schema with instances in $B(t)$, as required by the heuristic.

Given that phase 1 provides just the emphasis for each schema required by the heuristic, why is phase 2 necessary? Phase 2 is required because phase 1 introduces no *new* strings (samples) into $B(t)$, it merely introduces copies of strings already there. Phase 1 provides emphasis but no new trials. The genetic operators, applied in phase 2, obviously modify strings. It can be proved (see [28, Theorem 6.2.3]) that the genetic operators of Step 3 leave the emphasis provided by phase 1 largely undisturbed, while providing *new* instances of the various schemas in $B(t)$ in accord with that emphasis. Thus, phase 1 combined with phase 2 provides, implicitly, just the sampling scheme suggested by the heuristic.

The fundamental theorem for genetic algorithms [28, Theorem 6.2.3] can be rewritten as a procedure for progressively biasing a probability distribution over the space $\{1, 0, \#\}^k$:

**Theorem 6.1.** *Let $P_{\text{cross}}$ be the probability that a selected pair will be crossed, and let $P_{\text{mut}}$ be the probability that a mutation will occur at any given locus. If $p(\sigma, t)$ is the fraction of the population occupied by the instances of $\sigma$ at time $t$,*

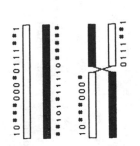

Fig. 5. Example of the cross-over operator.

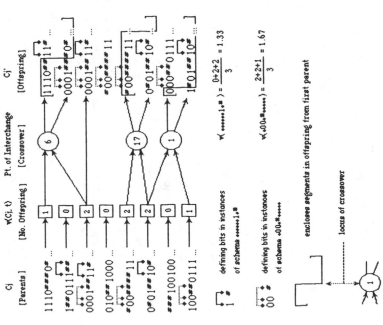

Fig. 6. Example of a genetic algorithm acting on schemas.

To gain some idea of how many schemas are so processed consider the following:

**Theorem 6.2.** *Select some bound e on the transcription error under reproduction and cross-over, and pick l such that l/k = e. Then in a population of size $M = c_1 2^{l/k}$, obtained as a uniform random sample from {1, 0}, the number of schemas propagated with an error less than e greatly exceeds $M^3$.*

**Proof.** (1) Consider a "window" of 2l contiguous loci in a string of length k such that 2l/k = e. Clearly any schema having all its defining loci within this window will be subject to a transcription error less than e under cross-over. (2) There are

$$\binom{2l}{l} \cong 2^{2l}/[\pi l]^{-1/2}$$

ways of selecting l defining positions in the window, and there are $2^l$ different schemas that can be defined using any given set of l of defining loci. Therefore, there are approximately $2^{3l}/[\pi l]^{-1/2}$ distinct schemas with l defining positions that can be defined in the window.

(3) A population of size $M = c_1 2^l$, for $c_1$ a small integer, obtained by a uniform random sampling of {1, 0}$^k$ can be expected to have $c_1$ instances of *every* schema defined on l defining positions. Therefore, for the given window, there will be approximately $M^3/(c_1)^3[\pi l]^{-1/2}$ schemas having instances in the population and defined on some set of l loci in the window.

(4) The same argument can be given for schemas of length l − 1, l − 2, . . . , and for l + 1, l + 2, . . . , with values of

$$\binom{2l}{l \pm j}$$

decreasing in accord with the binomial distribution. There are k − l − 1 distinct positionings of the window on strings of length k. It follows that many more than $M^3$ schemas, with instances in the population of size M, increase or decrease at a rate given by their observed marginal averages with a transcription error less than e. □

From the point of view of sampling theory, 20 or 30 instances of a schema σ constitute a sample large enough to give some confidence to the corresponding estimate of u(σ). Thus, for such schemas, the biases p(σ, t) produced by a genetic algorithm over a succession of generations are neither much distorted by sampling error nor smothered by "cross-talk."

It is important to recognize that the genetic algorithm only manipulates M strings while implicitly generating and testing the new instances of the very

*then*

$$p(\sigma, t+1) \geq [1 - \lambda(\sigma, t)][1 - P_{mut}]^{d(\sigma)}[u(\sigma, t)/u(t)]p(\sigma, t)$$

*gives the expected fraction of the population occupied by instances of σ at time t + 1 under the genetic algorithm.*

The right-hand side of this equation can be interpreted as follows: [u(σ, t)/u(t)], the ratio of the observed average value of the schema s compared to the overall population average, determines the rate of change of p(σ, t), subject to the "error" terms $[1 − \lambda(\sigma, t)][1 − P_{mut}]^{d(\sigma)}$. If u(σ, t) is above average, then schema σ tends to increase, and vice versa.

The "error" terms are the result of breakup of instances of σ because of cross-over and mutation, respectively. In particular, $\lambda(\sigma, t) = P_{cross}(l(\sigma)/k)p(\sigma, t)$ is an upper bound on the loss of instances of σ resulting from crosses that fall within the interval of length l(σ) determined by the outermost defining loci of the schema, and $[1 − P_{mut}]^{d(\sigma)}$ gives the proportion of instances of σ that escape a mutation at one of the d(σ) defining loci of σ.

(The underlying algorithm is stochastic so the equation only provides a bound on expectations at each time step. Using the terminology of mathematical genetics, the equation supplies a *deterministic model* of the algorithm under the assumption that the expectations are the values actually achieved on each time step.)

In any population that is not too small—from a biological view, a population not so small as to be endangered from a lack of genetic variation—distinct schemas will almost always have distinct subsets of instances. For example, in a randomly generated population of size 2500 over the space {1, 0}$^k$, any schema defined on 8 loci can be expected to have about 10 instances. (For ease of calculation, we consider populations of binary strings in the rest of this section, but the same results hold for n-letter alphabets.) There are

$$\binom{2500}{10} \cong 3 \times 10^{26}$$

ways of choosing this subset, so that it is extremely unlikely that the subsets of instances for two such schemas will be identical. (Looked at another way, the chance that two schemas have even *one* instance in common is less than $10 \times 2^{-8} \cong \frac{1}{25}$ if they are defined on disjoint subsets of loci.) Because the sets of instances are overwhelmingly likely to be distinct, the observed averages $\hat{u}(\sigma, t)$, will have little cross-correlation. As a consequence, the rate of increase (or decrease) of a schema σ under a genetic algorithm is largely uncontaminated by the rates associated other such schemas. Loosely, the rate is un-influenced by "cross-talk" from the other schemas.

large number of schemas involved ($\geq M^3$, early on). Moreover, during this procedure, samples (instances) of schemas not previously tried are generated. This implicit manipulation of a great many schemas through operations on $2n$ strings per step is called *implicit parallelism* (it is called *intrinsic parallelism* by Holland [28]).

## 7. Comparison with Other Learning Methods

The rule discovery procedures in a classifier system—genetic algorithms—are just as unconventional as the problem solving procedures. Here again, it is important to look beyond the details and examine the core ideas. In terms of the weak methods familiar to the AI community, a genetic algorithm can be thought of as a complex hierarchical generate-and-test process. The generator produces building blocks which are combined into complete objects. At various points in the procedure, tests are made that help weed out poor building blocks and promote the use of good ones. The information requirements of the process are modest: a generator for building blocks and objects, and an evaluator that allows them to be tested and compared with alternatives. It is altogether appropriate to label the procedure a weak method, if one is referring to its lack of domain-dependent requirements.

On closer examination, though, it is apparent that there are important differences between genetic algorithms and the standard assortment of weak methods. The differences are centered on the formulation of the search for useful rules. The familiar weak methods focus on managing the *complexity* of the search space, emphasizing ways to avoid computationally prohibitive exhaustive searches. Such methods use small amounts of knowledge to focus the search and prune the space of alternatives. Genetic algorithms proceed by managing the *uncertainty* of the search space. Uncertainty enters in the sense that the desirability of an element of the search space as a solution or partial solution is unknown until it has been tested. Managing complexity reduces uncertainty as more of the search space is explored; on the other hand, it is also clear that reducing uncertainty makes the search more effective, with complexity becoming more manageable in the process.

This shift of viewpoint is subtle, but has important consequences for the way the search is carried out. Typical AI search procedures use heuristic evaluation functions to prune search paths, and it often suffices that they provide bounds on test outcomes. On the other hand, uncertainty management requires the use of test outcomes (samples) to estimate regularities in the search space. Acquiring and using this knowledge as the search proceeds requires that more attention be paid to the *distribution* of test outcomes over the search space. The focus is on subspaces and the kinds of elements they contain, rather than on paths and their ultimate destinations. That is, the emphasis is on sample-based induction [33].

This point of view is captured by a weak method we will call *sample-select-and-recombine*. Assume that the elements of the search space are structured, that is, that they are constructed of components or building blocks. To find an element in this space:

*Step* 1. Draw a sample from the space.
*Step* 2. Order the elements in the sample according to some preference criterion related to the goals of the search.
*Step* 3. Use this ranking to estimate the usefulness of the building blocks present in the sample's elements.
*Step* 4. Generate a new sample by selecting building blocks on the basis of this evaluation, recombining them to construct new elements.
*Step* 5. Repeat Steps 1–4 until the desired element is found.

This method has the obvious advantage that the memory requirements are small and it can be used when a conventional generator or heuristic evaluation function is hard to find. All that is needed is a set of building blocks and a capability to order a sample in terms of a goal-relevant preference. Just as generate-and-test procedures are made more effective by incorporating as much of the test as possible into the generation process, genetic algorithms derive their power by tightly coupling the sampling and selection process. It is important that there are theoretical results that show that genetic algorithms implement the sample-select-and-recombine method in a near-optimal way.

We can make a direct comparison of this approach with more familiar AI learning procedures. This is most easily accomplished in the realm of concept learning tasks where the problem is to find a concept description consistent with a given set of (positive and negative) examples of the concept. Wilson [52] gives a detailed account of the way in which genetic algorithms acting on classifier systems learn complex multiple disjunctive concepts. Here we will refer to the description of genetic algorithms given above, and will briefly examine two well-known learning algorithms: the interference matching algorithm (Hayes-Roth and McDermott [22]), and the candidate elimination algorithm (Mitchell [39]).

### 7.1. Interference matching

Interference matching is a general technique for inferring the common attributes of several positive examples. (Interference matching is closely related to techniques, such as those examined by Valiant [49], for inferring boolean functions from true and false instances, but interference matching makes less stringent requirements on the match between problem, algorithm and representation.) A schema describing the shared characteristics is constructed using the attribute value for attributes shared, and a place holder symbol (essentially a "don't care" symbol) for attributes that differ over the examples. For example, interference matching of the two descriptors [RED, ROUND, HEAVY] and [RED, SQUARE, HEAVY] yields the schema [RED, HEAVY]. This technique can be used to compute a set of schemas accounting for all positive examples of a concept—called a *maximal decomposition*—by using the following algorithm:

Let $S$ be the list of schemas, initially empty.
Let $\{E_1, \ldots, E_N\}$ be the set of $N$ examples.
**For** $i = 1$ to $N$
  **For** $j = 1$ to $|S|$
    Form a schema $s$ by interference matching $E_i$ with the $j$th element of $S$.
    Form a new schema $s'$ by interference matching all examples that satisfy (are instances of) $s$.
    Add $s'$ to the list $S$ if it is not already there.
  Repeat until no new schemas are created (for the given value of $i$).
  Add $E_i$ to $S$ unaltered.

A simple example is given in Fig. 7.

The list of schemas comprising a maximal decomposition is the minimal complete set of nonredundant schemas that occur in the examples. For instance, in Fig. 7, the schemas ***1 and **0* are redundant because they designate the same subset of examples; they are therefore summarized by the more restrictive schema **01. The algorithm is more complicated when there is more than one concept to be learned or, equivalently, negative examples are available. A separate maximal decomposition is computed for each concept, but, in addition, a performance value rates each schema according to its ability to discriminate instances of a concept from noninstances in the set of examples.

| Examples | Maximal Decomposition |
|----------|----------------------|
| 1001     | 1001                 |
|          | ----                 |
| 1110     | 1***                 |
|          | 1110                 |
|          | ----                 |
| 0101     | **01                 |
|          | ****                 |
|          | *1**                 |
|          | 0101                 |
|          | ----                 |
| 0010     | *0**                 |
|          | **10                 |
|          | 0***                 |
|          | 0010                 |

Fig. 7. Example of a maximal decomposition.

Similar algorithms have been suggested for inferring the structure of boolean functions from presentations of true instances (see, for example, Valiant [49]).

Because a maximal decomposition is an exhaustive list of the structural characteristics of a concept, the size of the list becomes unmanageable as the number of examples grows. Hayes-Roth suggests discarding schemas with low performance values to keep the size of the list under control. This strategy can only work, though, if all the examples are available at once. If the examples occur incrementally, the performance value assigned to a schema at any given time is an estimate subject to error. The only obvious way to recover from a mistakenly discarded schema is to recompute the entire maximal decomposition.

Therein lies the major difference between interference matching and genetic algorithms. Genetic algorithms implicitly work with the building blocks for a decomposition. Iterative application of a genetic algorithm produces a population of concept descriptions in which the number of occurrences of each building block is proportional to the observed average performance of its carriers. In this sense, the population is a database that compactly and usefully summarizes the examples so far encountered. If a new example is introduced, it is assimilated by an automatic revision of the proportions of the relevant building blocks. This updating occurs without keeping explicit or exhaustive records about performance, thereby avoiding the large computational burdens associated with updating a maximal decomposition.

## 7.2. Candidate elimination

The candidate elimination algorithm is similar to genetic algorithms in that it cleverly implements a procedure that would be intractable if attempted by brute force. The basic idea is to enumerate the set of all possible concept descriptions and, for each example, remove from consideration any description that is inconsistent with that example. When there is only one description left the problem is solved. Mitchell [39] makes this idea tractable by ordering the set of possible descriptions according to *generality*. One description is more general than another if it includes as instances all the instances specified by the other description. Thus the schema **0* is more general than the schema **01. This is a partial ordering because not all descriptions are comparable—there can be several maximally general or maximally specific descriptions in the space. The key to this approach is the observation that the set of most specific descriptions and the set of most general descriptions consistent with an example *bound* the set of all descriptions consistent with the example. An algorithm therefore need only keep track of these bounds to converge to the description consistent with all examples.

In more detail, the candidate elimination algorithm maintains two sets that bound the space of consistent descriptions: the set $S$ of most specific possible descriptions, and the set $G$ of most general possible descriptions. Given a new positive example, the elements of $S$ are generalized the smallest amount that allows inclusion of the new example as an instance. Any element of $G$ that is inconsistent with this example is removed. Similarly, given a new negative example, the elements of $G$ are specialized the smallest amount that precludes the example as an instance. Any element of $S$ that includes this example as an instance is removed. This process is repeated for each new example, the set $S$ becoming more specific, and the set $G$ becoming more general, until $S$ and $G$ are identical. The concept description remaining is the one that is consistent with all the examples.

This algorithm obviously has no problems assimilating new examples and it converges to a solution quickly. The basic limitations are: (i) the $S$ and $G$ can be quite large, even for relatively simple concepts, (ii) only conjunctive concepts can be learned, and (iii) the algorithm usually fails if the data are noisy (some instances incorrect). Genetic algorithms avoid these limitations by characterizing the search space in a fundamentally different way: (i) the data set corresponding to the $S$ and $G$ sets is carried implicitly in the proportions of the building blocks, (ii) disjunctions are handled effortlessly by the parallelism of the rule set, and (iii) noise is handled effortlessly because uncertainty reduction is at the heart of the procedure. The price paid by the genetic algorithm is that it cannot use an obvious path to a solution to curtail its search unless there are strong building blocks that can be combined to construct that path.

## 8. Applications

Research on genetic algorithms has paralleled work in mainstream artificial intelligence in the sense that simpler studies of search and optimization in straightforward problem domains have preceded the more complex investigations of machine learning. This is no surprise. Search and optimization applications, with their well-defined problems, objective functions, constraints and decision variables provide a tame environment where alternatives may be compared easily. By contrast, machine learning problems, with their ill-defined goal statements, subjective evaluation criteria and multitudinous decision options, constitute an unwieldy environment not easily given to comparison or analysis. The application of GAs in search and optimization has both tested and improved GAs, and it has encouraged their successful application to search problems that have not succumbed to more traditional procedures. Accordingly this review of applications starts by examining GA applications in search and optimization.

### 8.1. Genetic algorithms in search and optimization

(Because much of the inspiration for early studies of genetic algorithms came

from genetics, much of the work described in this section was set forth using the terminology of genetics. We have not explained these terms in detail, but we have eliminated any terms that would not appear in a high-school biology text.)

The first *application* of a GA—in fact, the first published use of the words "genetic algorithm"—came in Bagley's [3] pioneering dissertation. At that time there was much interest in game playing computer programs, and in that spirit Bagley devised a controllable testbed of game tasks modeled after the game hexapawn. Bagley's GA operated successfully on "diploid chromosomes" (paired strings) which were decoded to construct parameter sets for a game board evaluation function. The GA contained the three basic operators—reproduction, cross-over, and mutation—along with dominance and inversion. At about the same time, Rosenberg [41] was completing his Ph.D. study of the simulated growth and genetic interaction of a population of single-celled organisms His organisms were characterized by a simple rigorous biochemistry, a permeable membrane, and a classical, one-gene/one-enzyme structure. He introduced an interesting adaptive cross-over scheme that associated linkage factors with each gene, thereby permitting different linkages between adjacent genes. Rosenberg's work is sometimes overlooked by GA researchers because of its emphasis on biological simulation, but its nearness to root finding and function optimization make it an important contribution to the search domain.

In 1971 Cavicchio [7] investigated the application of GAs to a subroutine selection task and a pattern recognition task. He adopted the pixel weighting scheme of Bledsoe and Browning [5] and used a GA to search for good sets of detectors (subsets of pixels). His GA found good sets of detectors more quickly than a competing "hill-climbing" algorithm. Cavicchio was one of the first to implement a scheme for maintaining population diversity.

The first dissertation to apply GAs to well-posed problems in mathematical optimization was Hollstien's [35] which used a testbed of 14 functions of two variables. The work is notable in its use of allele dominance and schemes of mating preference adopted from traditional breeding practices. Hollstien's GA located optima for his functions much more rapidly than traditional algorithms, but it was difficult to draw general conclusions because he used very small populations ($n = 16$). Frantz [17] studied positional effects on function optimatization. Specifically, he considered functions wherein the value assigned to an argument string could not be well approximated by assigning a least mean squares estimate to each component bit of the argument. (From the point of view of a geneticist, this amounts to saying there are strong epistatic interactions between the genes.) He tested the hypothesis that an inversion (string permutation) operator might improve the efficiency of a GA for such functions. Because the standard GA found near-optimal results quickly in all cases, the inversion operator had little effect. However, for substantially more difficult

[26]). Although the 1968 conference at which this paper was presented predates the first application of a classifier system by a full decade [34], schemata processors resemble modern day classifier systems in both outline and detail. The 1978 implementation of Holland and Reitman [34], called CS-1 (Cognitive System Level One), was trained to learn two maze-running tasks. It used (i) a performance system with a message list and simple classifiers, (ii) a credit assignment algorithm that retained information about all classifiers active between successive payoffs and adjusted their strengths at the time of payoff, and (iii) a GA with reproduction, cross-over, mutation and crowding that generated new classifiers. The main result demonstrated that the system could transfer its experience in a simpler maze to improve its rate of learning in a more complex maze.

Smith's [46] study of a classifier system used a purely GA approach, sidestepping the need for a credit assignment algorithm. He represented a rule *set* by a single string, obtained by stringing the rules end to end. He then devised a micro-level cross-over operator, for exchanging segments of individual rules, and a macro-level cross-over operator, for exchanging segments of rule strings (equivalent to exchanging subsets of rules). Smith successfully applied this system, LS-1 (Learning System One) to the Holland and Reitman maze-running task and to a draw poker betting task. In the draw poker task, Smith's system learned to beat Waterman's [50] adaptive poker playing program consistently, a substantial achievement given the amount of domain-specific knowledge in Waterman's program.

The next major application of classifier systems was Booker's [6] study. Booker concentrated on the formal connections between cognitive science and classifier systems. His computer simulations investigated the adaptive behavior of an artificial creature, moving about in a two-dimensional environment containing "food" and "poison," controlled by a classifier system "brain." Booker's classifier system contained a number of innovations including the use of sharing to promote "niche" exploitation, and the use of mating restrictions to reduce the production of ineffective offspring (lethals).

In 1983, Goldberg [18] applied a classifier system to the control of two engineering systems: the pole-balancing problem and a natural gas pipeline-compressor system. The simulations were in the SR (stimulus-response) format, with payoff being presented at each computational time step by a critic. In both cases Goldberg observed the formation of stable subpopulations of rules serving as *default hierarchies*. In a default hierarchy, fairly general rules cover the most frequent cases and more specific rules (that typically contradict the default rules) cover exceptions.

Wilson [51, 52], working along different lines, studied a number of applications of classifier systems. While at Polaroid, he was able to construct and test a classifier system that learned to focus and center a moveable videocamera on an object placed in its field of vision. These experiments, though successful,

problems, such as the traveling salesman problem, job shop scheduling and bin packing, Frantz's hypothesis remains a fruitful avenue of research (see Davis [8, 9], Goldberg and Lingle [19], and Grefenstette, Gopal, Rosmaita and van Gucht [21]). More recently, Bethke [4] has added rigor to the study of functions that are hard for GAs through his investigation of schema averages using Walsh transforms (following a suggestion of Andrew Barto). Goldberg [19] has also contributed to the understanding of GA-hard functions with his definition and analysis of the *minimal deceptive problem*.

De Jong's [11] dissertation was particularly important to subsequent applications of genetic algorithms. He recognized the importance of carefully controlled experimentation in an uncluttered function optimization setting. Varying population size, mutation and cross-over probabilities, and other operator parameters, he examined GA performance in a problem domain consisting of five test functions ranging from a smooth, unimodal function of two variables to functions characterized by high dimensionality (30 variables), great multimodality, discontinuity and noise. To quantify GA performance he defined online and offline performance measures, emphasizing interim performance and convergence, respectively. He also defined a measure of robustness of performance over a range of environments and demonstrated by experiment the robustness of GAs over the test set.

In Appendix A we display a representative group of GA search and optimization applications ranging from an archeological model of the transition from hunting and gathering to agriculture, through VLSI layout problems and medical image registration, to structural optimization. (A complete bibliography covering the entries in Appendices A and B is available from any one of the authors.) The broad successes in these domains have encouraged experiments with GAs in machine learning problems.

### 8.2. Machine learning using genetic algorithms

The goals for GAs in the context of machine learning have always been clear:

The study of adaptation involves the study of both the adaptive system and its environment. In general terms, it is a study of how systems can generate procedures enabling them to adjust efficiently to their environments. If adaptability is not to be arbitrarily restricted at the outset, the adapting system must be able to generate any method or procedure capable of an effective definition. (Holland [25])

The original intent, and the original outline of the attendant theory, encompassed a class of adaptive systems much broader than those concerned with search and optimization. The theoretical foundation was used as a basis for defining a series of increasingly sophisticated *schemata processors* (Holland

implicit *parallelism*, searching through and testing large numbers of building blocks while manipulating relatively few classifiers.

Competition based on rule strength, in conjunction with the parallelism of classifier systems provides several additional advantages. New rules can be added without imposing the severe computational burden of checking their consistency with all the extant rules. Indeed the system can retain large numbers of mutually contradictory, partially confirmed rules, an important advantage because these rules serve as alternative hypotheses to be invoked when currently favored rules prove inadequate. Moreover, this approach in conjunction with the genetic algorithm provides the overall system with a robust incremental means of handling noisy data. The system has no need of an archival memory of all past examples; its memory resides in the sets of competing alternatives.

## 9.2. Problems

To this point in time our problems are largely those attending a new approach wherein the experimental landmarks only sparsely cover the landscape of possibilities.

The most serious problem we have encountered concerns the stability of emergent default hierarchies. The hierarchies *do* emerge (see, for example, Goldberg [18], a first as far as we know), but in long runs there may be a catastrophic collapse in which whole subsets of good rules are lost. The rules, or rules similar in effect, are then reacquired, but this instability is highly undesirable.

Forrest [15] has demonstrated that semantic nets can be implemented simply and directly with coupled classifiers, but the question of how such structures can emerge in response to experience has been barely touched. This is, of course, more a research objective than a fault.

We also have only the faintest guidelines as to the functioning of the bucket brigade when the rule sequences are long and intertwined. Again, we have uncovered no faults, we simply have very little knowledge.

## 9.3. Techniques

There are several new techniques that should substantially increase the power and robustness of classifier systems. Chief among these is the *triggering* of genetic operators. For example, when an input message receives only weak bids from very general classifiers, it is a sign that the system has little specific information for dealing with the current environmental situation. A cross between the input message and the condition parts of some of the active general rules will yield plausible new rules with more specific conditions. This amounts to a bottom-up procedure for producing candidate rules that will automatically be tested for usefulness when similar situations recur. As another

caused him to turn to a simpler environment and a simpler version of the classifier system to better understand its behavior. In the later experiments, performed at the Rowland Institute for Science, a classifier system called ANIMAT operated in a two-dimensional environment, searching for food hidden behind obstacles. ANIMAT did not use a message list and hence could not employ a standard bucket brigade algorithm. Instead all classifiers contributing to a chosen action, the *action set*, received strength increments derived either from subsequent environmental payoff or from the bids of the next action set. This bucket brigade-like algorithm successfully propagated credit to early stage-setting rules under conditions of intermittent and noisy payoff.

A number of GA-based machine learning applications and extensions have followed the early works. A representative list, ranging from the evolution of cooperation (Axelrod [2]) and prediction of international events (Schrodt [44]) to VLSI compaction (Fourman [16]), is presented in Appendix B. There are now standard software tools for exploring these systems, including Forrest's [15] KL-ONE-to-classifier-system translator and Riolo's general-purpose, classifier system C-package.[1]

Recent work on classifier systems and genetic algorithms may be found in the books *Genetic Algorithms and Simulated Annealing* (Davis [10]) and *Genetic Algorithms and Their Applications* (Grefenstette [20]), the latter book containing papers presented at a conference held at MIT in the summer of 1987.

## 9. The Future: Advantages, Problems, Techniques, and Prospects

Up to this point we have reviewed and commented upon established aspects of classifier systems and their learning algorithms. Now we want to look to the future. Section 9.1, as a prologue, reviews some properties of classifier systems that afford future opportunities, while Section 9.2 points up some of the problems that currently impede progress. Section 9.3 outlines some untried techniques that broaden the possibilities for classifier systems, and Section 9.4 offers a look at some of the directions we think will be productive for future research.

### 9.1. Advantages

When it comes to describing advantages, pride of place goes to the genetic algorithm. The genetic algorithm operating on classifiers discovers potentially useful building blocks, tests them, and recombines them to form plausible new classifiers. It does this at the large "speedup" implied by Theorem 6.2 on

[1] Available on request from R. Riolo, Division of Computer Science and Engineering, 3116 EECS Building, The University of Michigan, Ann Arbor, MI 48109, U.S.A.

The process is reciprocal. For instance, in mathematical economics there are pieces of mathematics that deal with (1) hierarchical organization, (2) retained earnings (fitness) as a measure of past performance, (3) competition based on retained earnings, (4) distribution of earnings on the basis of local interactions of consumers and suppliers, (5) taxation as a control on efficiency, and (6) division of effort between production and research (exploitation versus exploration). Many of these fragments, mutatis mutandis, can be used to study the counterparts of these processes in classifier systems.

Similarly, in mathematical ecology there are pieces of mathematics dealing with (1) niche exploitation (models exploiting environmental regularities), (2) phylogenetic hierarchies, polymorphism and enforced diversity (competing subsystems), (3) functional convergence (similarities of subsystem organization enforced by environmental requirements on payoff attainment), (4) symbiosis, parasitism, and mimicry (couplings and interactions in a default hierarchy, such as an increased efficiency for extant generalists simply because related specialists exclude them from some regions in which they are inefficient), (5) food chains, predator-prey relations, and other energy transfers (apportionment of energy or payoff amongst component subsystems), (6) recombination of multifunctional coadapted sets of genes (recombination of building blocks), (7) assortative mating (biased recombination), (8) phenotypic markers affecting interspecies and intraspecies interactions (coupling), (9) "founder" effects (generalists giving rise to specialists), and (10) other detailed commonalities such as tracking versus averaging over environmental changes (compensation for environmental variability), allelochemicals (cross-inhibition), linkage (association and encoding of features), and still others. Once again, though mathematical ecology is a younger science than mathematical economics, there is much in the mathematics already developed that is relevant to the study of classifier systems and other nonlinear systems far from equilibrium.

In addition to attempting to adapt and extend these fragments, there are at least two broader mathematical tasks that can be undertaken. One is an attempt to produce a general characterization of systems that exhibit *implicit parallelism.* Up to now all such attempts have led to sets of algorithms which are easily recast as genetic algorithms—in effect, we still only know of one example of an algorithm that exhibits implicit parallelism. The second task involves developing a mathematical formulation of the process whereby a system can develop a useful internal model of an environment exhibiting perpetual novelty. In our (preliminary) experiments to date these models typically exhibit a (tangled) hierarchical structure with associative couplings. Such structures have been characterized mathematically as quasi-homomorphisms (see [33]). The perpetual novelty of the environment can be characterized by a Markov process in which each state has a recurrence time that is large relative to any feasible observation time. Considerable progress has been made along these lines (see [32]), but much remains to be done. In particular, we need to construct an interlocking set of theorems based on:

example, when a rule makes a large profit under the bucket brigade, this can be used as a signal to cross it with rules active on the immediately preceding time step. An appropriate cross between the message part of the precursor and the condition part of the profit making successor can produce a new pair of *coupled* rules. (The trigger is only activated if the precursor is *not* coupled to the active profit maker.) The coupled pair models the state transition mediated by the original pair of (uncoupled) rules. Such coupled rules can serve as the building blocks for models of the environment. Because the couplings serve as "bridges" for the bucket brigade, these building blocks will be assigned credit in accord with the efficacy of the models constructed from them. Interestingly enough there seems to be a rather small number of robust triggering conditions (see Holland et al. [33]), but each of them would appear to add substantially to the responsiveness of the classifier system.

*Support* is another technique that adds considerably to the system's flexibility. Basically, support is a technique that enables the classifier system to integrate many pieces of partial information (such as several views of a partially obscured object) to arrive at strong conclusions. Support is a quantity that travels *with* messages, rather than being a counterflow as in the case of bids. When a classifier is satisfied by several messages from the message list, each such message adds its support into that classifier's *support counter.* Unlike a classifier's strength, the support accrued by a classifier lasts for only the time step in which it is accumulated. That is, the support counter is reset at the end of each time step (other techniques are possible, such as a long or short half-life). Support is used to modify the bid, small support decreases it. If the classifier wins the bidding competition, the message it posts carries a support proportional to the size of its bid. The propagation of support over sets of coupled classifiers acts somewhat like spreading activation (see [1]), but it is much more directed. Like spreading activation, support can serve to bring associations (coupled rules) into play; but, as mentioned at the outset, it is meant to act primarily as a means of integrating partial information (as when several weakly bidding, general rules bearing on the same topic are activated simultaneously).

## 9.4. Prospects

The number of feasible directions for exploring the possibilities and applications of classifier systems is almost daunting. Here we will mention only some of the broader paths.

Perhaps the most important thing that can be done at this point is an expansion of the theory. Classifier systems serve as a "testbed" for concepts applicable to a wide range of complex adaptive systems. In developing a mathematics to deal with the interaction of the genetic algorithm and classifier systems we perforce develop a mathematics for dealing with a much wider range of adaptive systems.

(1) a stronger set of fixed point theorems that relates the strengths of classifiers under the bucket brigade to observed payoff statistics, (2) a set of theorems that relates building blocks exploited by the "slow" dynamics of the genetic algorithm to the sampling rates for rules at different levels of the emerging default hierarchy (more general rules are tried more often), and (3) a set of theorems (based on the previous two sets) that detail the way in which various kinds of environmental regularities are exploited by the genetic algorithm acting in terms of the strengths assigned by the bucket brigade.

In the realm of experiment, aside from interesting new applications, the design of experiments centered on the *emergence* of tags under triggered coupling offers intriguing possibilities. Tags serve as the glue of larger systems, providing both associative and temporal (model building) pointers (see Example 3.5). Under certain kinds of triggered coupling (see the previous section) the message sent by the precursor in the coupled pair can have a "hash-coded" tag (say a prefix or suffix). The purpose of this hash-coded tag is to prevent accidental eavesdropping by other classifiers—a sufficient number of randomly generated bits in the tag will prevent accidental matches with other conditions (unless the conditions have a lot of # in the tag region). If the coupled pair proves useful to the system then it will have further offspring under the genetic algorithm, and these offspring often will be coupled on to other rules in the system. Typically, the tag will be passed on to the offspring, serving as a common element in all the couplings; the tag will only persist if the resulting cluster of rules proves to be a useful "subroutine." In this case, the "subroutine" can be "called" by messages that incorporate the tag, because the conditions of the rules in the cluster are satisfied by such messages. In short, the tag that was initially determined at random now "names" the developing subroutine. It even has a *meaning* in terms of the actions it calls forth. Moreover, the tag is subject to the same kinds of recombination as other parts of the rules (it is, after all, a schema). As such it can serve as a building block for other tags. It is as if the system were inventing symbols for its internal use. Clearly, any simulation that provides for a test of these ideas will be an order of magnitude more sophisticated than anything we have tried to date. Runs involving hundreds of thousands of time steps will probably be required.

Another set of possibilities, far beyond anything we yet understand either theoretically or empirically, is fully directed rule generation. In the *broadcast language* that was the precursor of classifier systems, provision was made for the generation of rules by other rules. With minor changes to the definition of classifier systems, this possibility can be reintroduced. (Both messages and rules are strings. By enlarging the message alphabet, lengthening the message string, and introducing a special symbol that indicates whether a string is to be interpreted as a rule or a message, the task can be accomplished.) With this provision the system can invent its own candidate operators and rules of inference. Survival of these meta- (operator-like) rules should then be made to depend on the net usefulness of the rules they generate (much as a schema takes its value from the average value of its carriers). It is probably a matter of a decade or two before we can do anything useful in this area.

Another interesting possibility rests on the fact that classifier systems are general-purpose systems. They can be programmed initially to implement whatever expert knowledge is available to the designer; learning then allows the system to expand, correct errors, and transfer information from one domain to another. It is important to provide ways of instructing such systems so that they can generate rules—tentative hypotheses—on the basis of advice. Little has been done in this direction. It is also particularly important that we understand how lookahead and virtual explorations can be incorporated without disturbing other activities of the system.

Our broadest hopes turn on reincarnating in machine learning the cycle of theory and experiment so fruitful in physics. The close control of initial conditions, parameters, and environment made possible by simulation should enable the design of critical tests of the unfolding theory. And the simulations should suggest new directions for the theory. We hope to gain an understanding, not just of classifier systems, but of the consequences of competition in a changing population wherein subsystems are defined by combinations of building blocks that interact in a nonlinear fashion. In this context, classifier systems serve as a well-defined, precisely controllable testbed for a general theory.

## Appendix A. Genetic Algorithm Applications in Search and Logic

| Cat. | Year | Investigators | Description |
| --- | --- | --- | --- |
| *Biology* | | | |
| B | 1967 | Rosenberg | Simulation of the evolution of single-celled organism populations. |
| B | 1970 | Weinberg | Outline of cell population simulation including meta-level GA. |
| B | 1984 | Perry | Investigation of niche theory and specification with GAs. |
| B | 1985 | Grosso | Simulation of diploid GA with explicit subpopulations and migration. |
| *Computer science* | | | |
| CS | 1967 | Bagley | GA-directed parameter search for evaluation function in hexapawn-like game. |
| CS | 1983 | Gerardy | Probabilistic automaton identification attempt via GA. |
| CS | 1983 | Gordon | Adaptive document description using GA. |
| CS | 1984 | Rendell | GA search for game evaluation function. |

| Cat. | Year | Investigators | Description |
|---|---|---|---|
| *Engineering* | | | |
| E | 1981 | Goldberg | Mass-spring-dashpot system identification with simple GA. |
| E | 1982 | Etter, Hicks, Cho | Recursive adaptive filter design using a simple GA. |
| E | 1983 | Goldberg | Steady state and transient optimization of gas pipeline using GA. |
| E | 1985 | Davis | Outline of job shop scheduling procedure using GA. |
| E | 1985 | Davis, Smith | VLSI circuit layout via GA. |
| E | 1985 | Fourman | VLSI layout compaction via GA. |
| E | 1985 | Goldberg, Kuo | On-off, steady state optimization of oil pump-pipeline system via GA. |
| E | 1986 | Goldberg, Samtani | Structural optimization (plane truss) via GA. |
| E | 1986 | Minga | Aircraft landing strut weight optimization via GA. |
| E | 1987 | Davis, Coombs | Communications network link size optimization using GA plus advanced operators. |
| E | 1987 | Davis, Ritter | Classroom scheduling via simulated annealing with meta-level GA. |
| *Function optimization* | | | |
| FO | 1985 | Ackley | Connectionist algorithm with GA-like properties. |
| FO | 1985 | Brady | Traveling salesman problem via genetic-like operators. |
| FO | 1985 | Davis | Bin-packing and graph-coloring problems via GA. |
| FO | 1985 | Grefenstette, Gopal, Rosmaita, van Gucht | Traveling salesman problem via knowledge-augmented genetic operators. |
| FO | 1986 | Goldberg, Smith | Blind knapsack problem via simple GA. |
| *Genetic algorithm parameters* | | | |
| GA | 1971 | Hollstien | 2-D function optimization with mating and selection rules. |
| GA | 1972 | Bosworth, Foo, Zeigler | GA-like operators on simulated genes with sophisticated mutation. |
| GA | 1972 | Frantz | Investigation of positional nonlinearity and inversion. |
| GA | 1973 | Martin | Theoretical study of GA-like probabilistic algorithms. |
| GA | 1975 | DeJong | Base-line parametric study of simple GA in 5-function testbed. |
| GA | 1976 | Bethke | Brief theoretical investigation of possible parallel GA implementation. |
| GA | 1977 | Mercer | GA controlled by meta-level GA. |
| GA | 1981 | Bethke | Application of Walsh functions to schema average analysis. |
| GA | 1981 | Brindle | Investigation of selection and dominance in GAs. |
| GA | 1981 | Grefenstette | Brief theoretical investigation of possible parallel GA implementation. |
| GA | 1983 | Pettit, Swigger | Cursory investigation of GAs in nonstationary search problems. |
| GA | 1983 | Wetzel | Traveling salesman problem via GA. |
| GA | 1984 | Mauldin | Study of several heuristics to maintain diversity in simple GA. |
| GA | 1985 | Baker | Trial of ranking selection procedure on DeJong testbed. |
| GA | 1985 | Booker | Suggestion for partial match scores, sharing, and mating restrictions. |
| GA | 1985 | Goldberg, Lingle | Traveling salesman problem using partially matched cross-over and schema analysis. |
| GA | 1985 | Schaffer | Multi-objective optimization using GAs with subpopulations. |
| GA | 1986 | Goldberg | Maximization of marginal schema content by optimization of estimated population size. |
| GA | 1986 | Grefenstette | GA controlled by meta-level GA. |
| GA | 1986 | Grefenstette, Fitzpatrick | Test of simple genetic algorithm with noisy functions. |
| GA | 1987 | Goldberg | Analysis of minimal deceptive problem for simple GAs. |
| *Image processing* | | | |
| IP | 1970 | Cavicchio | Selection of detectors for pixel-based pattern recognition. |
| IP | 1984 | Fitzpatrick, Grefenstette, van Gucht | Image registration via GA to highlight selected properties. |
| IP | 1985 | Englander | Selection of detectors for known image classification. |
| IP | 1985 | Gillies | GA search for diagnostic image feature subroutines in Cytocomputer. |
| *Physical sciences* | | | |
| PS | 1985 | Shaefer | Nonlinear equation solving with GA for fitting molecular potential surfaces. |
| *Social sciences* | | | |
| SS | 1979 | Reynolds | GA-guided adaptation in hunter gatherer/agricultural transition model. |
| SS | 1981 | Smith, DeJong | Calibration of population migration model using GA search. |
| SS | 1985 | Axelrod | Iterated prisoner's dilemma problem solution using GA. |
| SS | 1985 | Axelrod | Simulation of the evolution of behavioral norms with GA. |

## Appendix B. Genetic Algorithm Applications in Machine Learning

| Cat. | Year | Investigators | Description |
|---|---|---|---|
| *Business* | | | |
| BU | 1986 | Frey | Architectural classification using CS. |
| BU | 1986 | Thompson, Thompson | GA search for rule sets to predict company profitability. |

| Cat. | Year | Investigators | Description |
|---|---|---|---|
| **Computer science** | | | |
| CS | 1980 | Smith | Draw poker bet decisions learned by pure GA (LS-1). |
| CS | 1985 | Cramer | GA learning of multiplication task using assembler-like instruction set. |
| CS | 1985 | Forrest | Interpreter to convert KL-ONE networks to CSs. |
| CS | 1986 | Riolo | General-purpose C-package for classifier system study. |
| CS | 1986 | Riolo | Letter sequence prediction task via CS. |
| CS | 1986 | Robertson | LISP version of letter sequence prediction task implemented on Connection Machine |
| CS | 1986 | Zeigler | GA searches for rule sets in symbolic rule-based system. |
| CS | 1986 | Zhou | GA builds finite automata from I/O examples. |
| **Engineering** | | | |
| E | 1983 | Goldberg | Pole-balancing task and gas pipeline control tasks learned by CS. |
| E | 1984 | Schaffer | LS-2 (see Smith) learns parity and signal problems. |
| E | 1985 | Kuchinski | GA search for battle management system rules. |
| E | 1986 | Liepins, Hilliard | Simple scheduling problem learned via CS. |
| E | 1986 | Wilson | Boolean multiplexer task learned via CS. |
| **Psychology and social sciences** | | | |
| SS | 1978 | Holland, Reitman | CS-1 learns to transfer information between maze-running tasks. |
| SS | 1982 | Booker | Animal-like automaton with CS "brain" learns in simple 2-D environment. |
| SS | 1983 | Wilson | Video eye learns to focus when driven by CS. |
| SS | 1985 | Axelrod | GA searches for rule-based strategies in iterated prisoner's dilemma. |
| SS | 1985 | Wilson | ANIMAT automaton with CS "brain" learns to acquire obstacle-hidden objects in 2-D environment. |
| SS | 1986 | Schrodt | Prediction of international events using CS. |
| SS | 1986 | Haslev (Skanland) | Past tense for Norwegian verb forms learned by CS. |

## REFERENCES

1. Anderson, J.R., *The Architecture of Cognition* (Harvard University Press, Cambridge, MA, 1983).
2. Axelrod, R., The evolution of strategies in the iterated prisoner's dilemma, in: L. Davis (Ed.), *Genetic Algorithms and Simulated Annealing* (Pitman, London, 1987).
3. Bagley, J.D., The behavior of adaptive systems which employ genetic and correlation algorithms, Ph.D. Dissertation, University Microfilms No. 68-7556, University of Michigan, Ann Arbor, MI (1967).
4. Bethke, A.D. Genetic algorithms as function optimizers, Ph.D. Dissertation, University Microfilms No. 8106101, University of Michigan, Ann Arbor, MI (1981).
5. Bledsoe, W.W. and Browning, I., Pattern recognition and reading by machine, in: *Proceedings Eastern Joint Computer Conference* (1959) 225-232.
6. Booker, L.B., Intelligent behavior as an adaptation to the task environment, Ph.D. Dissertation, University Microfilms No. 8214966, University of Michigan, Ann Arbor, MI (1982).
7. Cavicchio, D.J., Adaptive search using simulated evolution, Ph.D. Dissertation, University of Michigan, Ann Arbor, MI (1970).
8. Davis, L.D., Applying adaptive algorithms to epistatic domains, in: *Proceedings IJCAI-85*, Los Angeles, CA (1985) 162-164.
9. Davis, L.D., Job shop scheduling with genetic algorithms, in: J.J. Grefenstette (Ed.), *Proceedings of an International Conference on Genetic Algorithms and Their Applications* (Carnegie-Mellon University Press, Pittsburgh, PA, 1985) 136-140.
10. Davis, L.D., *Genetic Algorithms and Simulated Annealing* (Morgan Kaufmann, Los Altos, CA, 1987).
11. DeJong, K.A., An analysis of the behavior of a class of genetic adaptive systems, Ph.D. Dissertation, University Microfilms No. 76-9381, University of Michigan, Ann Arbor, MI (1975).
12. Erman, L.D., Hayes-Roth, F., Lesser, V.R. and Reddy, D.R., The Hearsay-II speech-understanding system: Integrating knowledge to resolve uncertainty, *Comput. Surv.* **12** (1980) 213-253.
13. Fahlman, S., *NETL: A System for Representing and Using Real World Knowledge* (MIT Press, Cambridge, MA, 1979).
14. Farmer, J.D., Packard, N.H. and Perelson, A.S., The immune system and artificial intelligence, in: J.J. Grefenstette (Ed.), *Proceedings of an International Conference on Genetic Algorithms and Their Applications* (Carnegie-Mellon University Press, Pittsburgh, PA, 1985) supplement; revised: *Phys. D* **22** (1986) 187-204.
15. Forrest, S., A study of parallelism in the classifier system and its application to classification in KL-ONE semantic networks, Ph.D. Dissertation, University of Michigan, Ann Arbor, MI (1985).
16. Fourman, M.P., Compaction of symbolic layout using genetic algorithms, in: J.J. Grefenstette (Ed.), *Proceedings of an International Conference on Genetic Algorithms and Their Applications* (Carnegie-Mellon University Press, Pittsburgh, PA, 1985) 141-153.
17. Frantz, D.R., Non-linearities in genetic adaptive search, Ph.D. Dissertation, University Microfilms No. 73-11116, University of Michigan, Ann Arbor, MI (1973).
18. Goldberg, D.E., Computer-aided gas pipeline operation using genetic algorithms and rule learning, Ph.D. Dissertation, University Microfilms No. 8402282, University of Michigan, Ann Arbor, MI (1983).
19. Goldberg, D.E. and Lingle, R., Alleles, loci, and the travelling salesman problem, in: J.J. Grefenstette (Ed.), *Proceedings of an International Conference on Genetic Algorithms and Their Applications* (Carnegie-Mellon University Press, Pittsburgh, PA, 1985) 154-159.
20. Grefenstette, J.J., *Genetic Algorithms and Their Applications* (Erlbaum, Hillsdale, NJ, 1987).
21. Grefenstette, J.J., Gopal, R., Rosmaita, B.J. and van Gucht, D., Genetic algorithms for the traveling salesman problem, in: J.J. Grefenstette (Ed.), *Proceedings of an International Conference on Genetic Algorithms and Their Applications* (Carnegie-Mellon University Press, Pittsburgh, PA, 1985) 160-168.
22. Hayes-Roth, F. and McDermott, J., An interference matching technique for inducing abstractions, *Commun. ACM* **21** (1978) 401-410.
23. Hinton, G.E. and Anderson, J.A., *Parallel Models of Associative Memory* (Erlbaum, Hillsdale, NJ, 1981).
24. Hinton, G.E., McClelland, J.L. and Rumelhart, D.E., Distributed representations, in: D.E. Rumelhart and J.L. McClelland (Eds.), *Parallel Distributed Processing, I: Foundations* (MIT Press, Cambridge, MA, 1986).
25. Holland, J.H., Outline for a logical theory of adaptive systems, *J. ACM* **3** (1962) 297-314.
26. Holland, J.H., Processing and processors for schemata, in: E.L. Jacks (Ed.), *Associative Information Processing* (American Elsevier, New York, 1971) 127-146.
27. Holland, J.H., Genetic algorithms and the optimal allocation of trials, *SIAM J. Comput.* **2** (1973) 88-105.
28. Holland, J.H., *Adaptation in Natural and Artificial Systems* (University of Michigan Press, Ann Arbor, MI, 1975).

29. Holland, J.H., Adaptation, in: R. Rosen and F.M. Snell (Eds.), *Progress in Theoretical Biology* IV (Academic Press, New York, 1976) 263–293.

30. Holland, J.H., Adaptive algorithms for discovering and using general patterns in growing knowledge-bases, *Int. J. Policy Anal. Inf. Syst.* **4** (1980) 245–268.

31. Holland, J.H., Escaping brittleness: The possibilities of general purpose learning algorithms applied to parallel rule-based systems, in: R.S. Michalski, J.G. Carbonell and T.M. Mitchell (Eds.), *Machine Learning: An Artificial Intelligence Approach 2* (Morgan Kaufmann, Los Altos, CA, 1986) 593–623.

32. Holland, J.H., A mathematical framework for studying learning in classifier systems, *Phys. D* **22** (1986) 307–317.

33. Holland, J.H., Holyoak, K.J., Nisbett, R.E. and Thagard, P.R., *Induction: Processes of Inference, Learning, and Discovery* (MIT Press, Cambridge, MA 1986).

34. Holland, J.H. and Reitman, J.S., Cognitive systems based on adaptive algorithms, in: D.A. Waterman and F. Hayes-Roth (Eds.), *Pattern-Directed Inference Systems* (Academic Press, New York, 1978) 313–329.

35. Holstien, R.B., Artificial genetic adaptation in computer control systems, Ph.D. Dissertation, University Microfilms No. 71-23773, University of Michigan, Ann Arbor, MI (1971).

36. Hopfield, J.J., Neural networks and physical systems with emergent collective computational abilities, *Proc. Nat. Acad. Sci. USA* **79** (1982) 2554–2558.

37. Jain, R., Dynamic scene analysis using pixel-based processes, *IEEE Computer* **14** (1981) 12–18.

38. Laird, J.E., Newell, A. and Rosenbloom, P.S., SOAR: An architecture for general intelligence, *Artificial Intelligence* **33** (1987) 1–64.

39. Mitchell, T.M., Version spaces: A candidate elimination approach to rule learning, in: *Proceedings IJCAI-77*, Cambridge, MA (1977).

40. Newell, A. and Simon, H.A., *Human Problem Solving* (Prentice-Hall, Englewood Cliffs, NJ, 1972).

41. Rosenberg, R.S., Simulation of genetic populations with biochemical properties. Ph.D. Dissertation, University Microfilms No. 67-17836, University of Michigan, Ann Arbor, MI (1967).

42. Samuel, A.L., Some studies in machine learning using the game of checkers, *IBM J. Res. Dev.* **3** (1959) 210–229.

43. Schleidt, W.M., Die historische Entwicklung der Begriffe "Angeborenes Auslosendes Schema" und "Angeborener Auslosmechanismus", *Z. Tierpsychol.* **21** (1962) 235–256.

44. Schrodt, P.A. Predicting international events, *Byte* **11** (12) (1986) 177–192.

45. Simon, H.A., *The Sciences of the Artificial* (MIT Press, Cambridge, MA, 1969).

46. Smith, S.F., A learning system based on genetic adaptive algorithms, Ph.D. Dissertation, University of Pittsburg, Pittsburgh, PA (1980).

47. Sutton, R.S., Learning to predict by the methods of temporal difference, Tech. Rept. TR87-509.1, GTE, Waltham, MA (1987).

48. Sutton, R.S. and Barto, A.G., Toward a modern theory of adaptive networks: Expectation and prediction, *Psychol. Rev.* **88** (1981) 135–170.

49. Valiant, L.G., A theory of the learnable, *Commun. ACM* **27** (1984) 1134–1142.

50. Waterman, D.A., Generalization learning techniques for automating the learning of heuristics, *Artificial Intelligence* **1** (1970) 121–170.

51. Wilson, S.W., On the retinal-cortical mapping, *Int. J. Man-Mach. Stud.* **18** (1983) 361–389.

52. Wilson, S.W., Knowledge growth in an artificial animal, in: J.J. Grefenstette (Ed.), *Proceedings of an International Conference on Genetic Algorithms and Their Applications* (Carnegie-Mellon University Press, Pittsburgh, PA, 1985) 16–23.

53. Winston, P.H., Learning structural descriptions from examples, in: P.H. Winston (Ed.), *The Psychology of Computer Vision* (McGraw-Hill, New York, 1975).

# Section 8.2

# Commonsense Knowledge

Commonsense knowledge and commonsense reasoning are not well-defined concepts, but are used broadly to refer to vast quantities of knowledge about the world and our interactions with it. Common sense keeps us out of trouble (some of the time) and could, therefore, keep a knowledge-based system from blundering into trouble occasionally. That is, common sense is seen as one answer to the problem of brittleness.

Commonsense and expert reasoning share a number of characteristics. They are both very knowledge-intensive modes of human reasoning. Their acquisition requires years of study, during which time a great deal of specific knowledge about the real world is acquired. They both rely on strong method knowledge, on specific facts about the real world. For both types of reasoning, inference is often mentally effortless.

There are also many differences between commonsense and expert knowledge. Commonsense reasoning can be done by everyone, whereas expert reasoning can only be done by a small fraction of the population. Commonsense knowledge is broad in scope and is not restricted to a particular domain. In contrast, human expertise is narrow and does not transfer easily between domains (e.g., the ability to memorize numbers quickly does not generalize to memorizing letters).

There are four reasons why the CYC project, described in Section 8.2.1, is important to the field of knowledge acquisition and learning. First, the CYC project is the largest knowledge-acquisition effort within artificial intelligence to date. Current machine-learning techniques are not applicable to automating early acquisition of commonsense reasoning knowledge. Therefore, CYC developed a number of manual and inter-active elicitation methods, and they have proved effective.

Second, the CYC ontology, organization, representation and inference methods have evolved from actual experience with a large knowledge base. Knowing the target structures has always been a source of power for learning systems.

Third, CYC contains the type of knowledge that may enable expert systems (and most other software programs) to escape certain types of brittleness. For some types of problem-solving failures, human performance gracefully degrades due to commonsense knowledge. CYC could provide such graceful degradation for expert systems.

Fourth, the CYC knowledge base may reach a

critical mass stage, wherein further expansion of the knowledge base can proceed automatically via natural language understanding. A critical shortcoming of natural language systems is that they are not sufficiently knowledge-intensive; they lack the knowledge needed to disambiguate input sentences into one unique parse. It is only when the number of interpretations is so reduced that a natural language system truly understands.

CYC's research methodology is exactly that which has led to most of the advances in learning for expert systems in the last twenty years. In a nutshell, CYC is taking a real-world problem that is completely beyond the state of the art, finding an empirical solution to the problem, then generalizing what is learned.

# Cyc: A Midterm Report[1]

*R. V. Guha and Douglas B. Lenat*

Computers need common sense—not only to prevent brittleness characteristic of most expert systems but also for semantic disambiguation. The Cyc knowledge base aims to resolve such ambiguities by capturing "consensus reality."

The majority of work in knowledge representation has dealt with the technicalities of relating predicate calculus to other formalisms and with the details of various schemes for default reasoning. There has almost been an aversion to addressing the problems that arise in actually representing large bodies of knowledge with content. However, deep, important issues must be addressed if we are to ever have a large intelligent knowledge-based program: What ontological categories would make up an adequate set for carving up the universe? How are they related? What are the important facts and heuristics most humans today know about solid objects? And so on. In short, we must bite the bullet.

We don't believe there is any shortcut to being intelligent, any yet-to-be-discovered Maxwell's equations of thought, any AI Risc architecture that will yield vast amounts of problem-solving power. Although issues such as architecture are important, no powerful formalism can obviate the need for a lot of knowledge.

By knowledge, we don't just mean dry, almanac-like or highly domain-specific facts. Rather, most of what we need to know to get by in the real world is prescientific (knowledge that is too commonsensical to be included in reference books; for example, animals live for a single solid interval of time, nothing can be in two places at once, animals don't like pain), dynamic (scripts and rules of thumb for solving problems) and metaknowledge (how to fill in gaps in the knowledge base, how to keep it organized, how to monitor and switch among problem-solving methods, and so on).

Perhaps the hardest truth to face, one that AI has been trying to wriggle out of for 34 years, is that there is probably no elegant, effortless way to obtain this immense knowledge base. Rather, the bulk of the effort must (at least initially) be manual entry of assertion after assertion.

Half a decade ago, we introduced (Lenat, Prakash, and Shepherd 1986) our research plans for Cyc, a decade-long, two person-century effort we had recently begun at MCC to manually construct such a knowledge base.

*After explicating the need for a large commonsense knowledge base spanning human consensus knowledge, we report on many of the lessons learned over the first five years of attempting its construction. We have come a long way in terms of methodology, representation language, techniques for efficient inferencing, the ontology of the knowledge base, and the environment and infrastructure in which the knowledge base is being built. We describe the evolution of Cyc and its current state and close with a look at our plans and expectations for the coming five years, including an argument for how and why the project might conclude at the end of this time.*

We have come a long way in this time, and this article presents some of the lessons learned and a description of where we are and briefly discusses our plans for the coming five years. We chose to focus on technical issues in representation, inference, and ontology rather than infrastructure issues such as user interfaces, the training of knowledge enterers, or existing collaborations and applications of Cyc.

## The Evolution of the Cyc Methodology

For two decades, AI research has been polarized into neats and scruffies (roughly corresponding to theoretical versus experimental approaches). After an initial strongly scruffy approach, we seem to have settled on a middle ground that combines the insights and power of each.

On the one hand, we realized that a number of mistakes made in the project's initial years would have been avoided by a more formal approach (especially in regard to the construction of the representation language). We also realized that philosophy had a lot to contribute, especially when it came to deciding on issues of ontology (Quine 1969).

On the other hand, however, there are a number of areas where we found the empirical approach more fruitful. The areas are typically still open research issues for the formalists or have not even been addressed by them, for example, codifying the most fundamental types of goals that people have.

Therefore, our approach is to largely carry out empirical research and be driven by looking at lots of examples but to keep this work supported on a strong theoretical foundation. Further, we have been driven to adopt a kind of tool-kit orientation: Assemble a collection of partial solutions to the various difficult problems Cyc has to handle, and add new tools as required. That is, for a number of problems (time, causality, inference, user interface, and so on), there aren't any known general-purpose, simple, efficient solutions, but we can make do with a set of modules that enable us to easily handle the most common cases.

*. . . an aversion to addressing the problems that arise in actually representing large bodies of knowledge with content.*

0738-4602/90/$4.00 ©1990 AAAI

The bulk of the effort is currently devoted to identifying, formalizing, and entering microtheories of various topics (such as shopping, containers, emotions). We follow a process that begins with a statement, in English, of the microtheory. On the way to our goal, an axiomatization of the microtheory, we identify and make precise those Cyc concepts necessary to state the knowledge in axiomatic form. To test that the topic has been adequately covered, stories that deal with the topic are represented in Cyc; we then pose questions that any reader ought to be able to answer after having read the story.

One of the unfortunate myths about Cyc is that its aim is to be a sort of electronic encyclopedia. We hope that this article lays this misconception to rest. If anything, Cyc is the complement of an encyclopedia. The aim is that one day Cyc ought to contain enough commonsense knowledge to support natural language understanding capabilities that enable it to read through and assimilate any encyclopedia article, that is, to be able to answer the sorts of questions that you or I could after having just read any article, questions that neither you nor I nor Cyc could be expected to answer beforehand.

Our hope and expectation is that around the mid-1990s, we can transition more and more from manual entry of assertions to (semi-) automated entry by reading online texts; the role of humans in the project would transition from the brain surgeons to tutors, answering Cyc's questions about the difficult sentences and passages. This radical change is what it means for Cyc to have a decade-long projected lifespan.

## The Evolution of the Representation Language

CycL is the language in which the Cyc knowledge base is encoded. In 1984, our representation was little more than frames. Although a significant fraction of knowledge can be conveniently handled using just frames, this approach soon proved awkward or downright inadequate for expressing various assertions we wanted to make: disjunctions, inequalities, existentially quantified statements, metalevel propositions about sentences, and so on. At least occasionally, therefore, we required a framework of greater expressive power. We were thus led to embed the frame system in a predicate calculus–like constraint language.

Moreover, there were a number of downright ad hoc aspects of the 1984 frame language, such as how inheritance worked. We kept modifying and tweaking such mechanisms, and often, this method forced us to go back and redo parts of the knowledge base so that they corresponded to the new way the inference engine worked. As the size of the knowledge base increased, this process became intolerable. We came to realize that having a clean semantics for the knowledge base was vital, declaratively expressing the meaning of inheritance, TheSetOf, default rules, automatic classification, and so on, so that we wouldn't have to change the knowledge base when we altered the implementation of one of the mechanisms.

As late as 1987, the only inferencing in Cyc was done using these few mechanisms: inheritance along instances (IS-A) links, rigid toCompute definitions of one slot in terms of others plus the running of demons (opaque lumps of Lisp code) and expert system–like production rules. The results were inefficiencies (because of the overuse of the most general mechanisms), abstraction breaking (often resorting to raw Lisp code escapes), and inadequacies (for example, given a rule "If $A$ Then $B$," and $\neg B$, Cyc couldn't conclude $\neg A$.)

For efficiency's sake, we developed dozens of specialized inference procedures, with special truth maintenance system–related (TMS-related) bookkeeping facilities for each (Doyle 1987). Then, to recoup usability, we developed a mechanical translator so that one can now input general predicate calculus–like assertions, and Cyc can convert them from this epistemological level into the form required by these efficient heuristic-level, special-purpose mechanisms (see The Current State of the Representation Language).

Originally, Cyc handled defaults in an ad hoc and frequently inadequate way. In the last two years, we have moved to a powerful and principled way of handling them. As we discuss in the section Epistemological Level and Default Reasoning, Cyc constructs and compares arguments for and against a proposition, using explicit rules to decide when an argument is invalid or when one argument is to be preferred over another.

Early on, we allowed each assertion in the knowledge base to have a numeric certainty factor (cf), but this approach led to its own set of increasingly severe difficulties. For example, one knowledge enterer might assert A and assert B and assign them cfs of 95 and 94 (on a 0–100 scale). There wasn't statistical data to support these numbers; the knowledge enterer just meant to express that both A and B were likely, and A was slightly more likely than B. The problem is that some other knowledge enterer might assert C and assert

D, and, respectively, give them cfs of 94.4 and 94.6. Certainly, neither person intended to tell Cyc that A is more certain than C or that D is more certain than B, but this is exactly what they were doing. These problems led us to go back to a simple nonnumeric scheme in which A, B, C, and D would all simply be true (nonmonotonically, that is, true by default), and in addition, there would be two explicit assertions: (moreLikelyThan A B) and (moreLikelyThan C D).

We conclude this section by listing our desiderata for the representation language in which to build our large knowledge base. The next section goes on to describe the current state of CycL, the language that strives toward these criteria. Our point here is that this list bears little resemblance to what we expected the language to be like five years ago:

First, the language should have a clear (and hopefully simple) semantics. The semantics should be declarative for two reasons: to facilitate communication with, and use by, many different problem solvers, be they human or machine and, as mentioned previously, to prevent having to discard or redo the knowledge base when the inference mechanisms change.

Second, it should provide certain inferential capabilities (including verifying conjectures, finding bindings for variables that make some statement true, planning) and provide them efficiently. Why? Only by actually building applications can the knowledge base be truly exercised and, ultimately, validated.

Third, it should provide some scheme for expressing and reasoning with default knowledge. Almost all the knowledge in Cyc is defeasible. Only about 5 percent is monotonic, and of this amount, only about 1 percent is definitional (such as the function cousins being defined as cousins(x) = children(siblings(parents(x)))).

Fourth, it should have the expressiveness of all first-order predicate calculus (FOPC) with equality (Moore 1986). It should also be able to handle (nested) propositional attitudes (McCarthy 1986a) (such as beliefs, goals, purpose, dreads). It should have facilities for operations such as reification (McCarthy 1986b) and reflection (Weyhrauch 1986). Each assertion P (fact, rule, and so on) can have various metalevel assertions about it that need to be made; for example, who asserted this and when, what arguments support P and what arguments counter it, what arguments does P participate in, what assertions are analogous to P, and in what ways and to which models (levels of granularity or other clumpings of mutually consistent asser-

> *Two of the wish list entries are at odds . . . having a clean and simple semantics and providing speedy inference.*

tions) does P belong?

Given this wish list, we could summarize the major changes in CycL over the past five years as follows: We started with a frame language whose emphasis was more on issues such as the data structures used, indexing, and interface. We have since realized the importance of a declarative semantics for the language, the need for expressive power, and the importance of making a clear distinction between what knowledge the knowledge base contains and how the knowledge base is implemented.

## The Current State of Cyc's Representation Language

The last several paragraphs considered some of the issues that heavily influenced the design of this language. This section presents the result of our striving to satisfy this wish list.[2]

### Epistemological Level and Default Reasoning

Two of the wish list entries are at odds with each other: having a clean and simple semantics and providing speedy inference. To improve inferencing abilities, we want to include special-purpose representations and inference routines, procedural attachments, and so on. However, these make it harder to provide a simple semantics. Also, although it is reasonable to expect the semantics of CycL to remain unchanged, it is likely that new constructs are going to be incrementally added to improve CycL's inferencing. The addition of such special-purpose constructs (templates for classification, inheritance, special-purpose inference mechanisms, and so on) is likely to prove bothersome to other programs that use Cyc, for example, programs that were written before the new constructs even existed and, hence, couldn't take advantage of them.

Therefore, we would like users of Cyc (both humans and application programs) to interact with the system at an epistemological level and not a heuristic level. These terms and the distinction between them are used here in the sense of McCarthy and Hayes (1987).

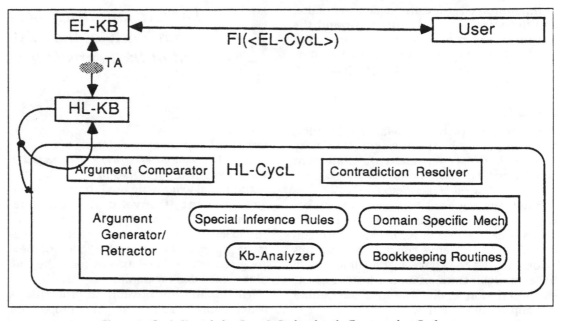

*Figure 1. Cyc's Knowledge Base Is Redundantly Expressed at Both an Epistemological Level and a Heuristic Level.*

*A user (human or application program) will usually communicate with Cyc at the epistemological level, and their utterances are translated by the tell-ask (TA) interface into heuristic-level propositions. The heuristic level consists of several modules for generating and comparing arguments for and against a given proposition.*

These observations lead to the conclusion that the knowledge base should be constructed at two levels, which is exactly what we have done. The Cyc knowledge base itself, therefore, exists redundantly at the epistemological level and at the heuristic level, and an external program (or human user) can interact with CycL at either of these levels. The epistemological level uses a language that is essentially FOPC, with a slightly different syntax and augmentations for reification and set construction.[3] It gives an account of the knowledge base in a form that has a simple semantics and, therefore, is easy to communicate in. In contrast, the heuristic level uses a variety of special-purpose representations and procedures for speedy inference. The heuristic level is the language of choice whenever any inference needs to be done.

There is a facility for automatically translating sentences from the epistemological level into the most appropriate representations in the heuristic level, and vice versa; it is called the tell-ask (TA) interface (Derthick 1990) (figure 1). Therefore, one can type epistemological-level expressions (that is, in some form like FOPC) to TA, and they are converted into the most efficient heuristic-level representation.

Both the epistemological level and the heuristic level are real parts of CycL. The epistemological level, in particular, is not just

some abstract conceptual level. For example, one could eliminate the entire heuristic level, replace it with a general-purpose problem solver, and Cyc would merely slow down (that is, the Cyc knowledge base would remain unchanged, the same conclusions would be reachable, the same problems solvable, and so on, but at [presumably] a much slower speed). One way in which some of our collaborators choose to use Cyc is at arms' length, accepting only epistemological-level expressions from the Cyc knowledge base and using their own inference engines on them.

The epistemological level is based on a language called the Cyc constraint language, which, as we remarked earlier, is essentially FOPC with equality, with augmentations for defaults and reification. It also allows some amount of reflection of the problem solver into the language and allows for predicates such as justifies that relates a sentence $Q$ to other sentences $P_1$, $P_2$, . . . that a problem solver used to deduce it. The Cyc constraint language also uses a number of modals, including beliefs, desires, and goals, whose semantics are defined by using the ability to reify propositions.

The only nonmonotonic constructs used are the closed-world assumption (CWA) and the unique names assumption. CWA, in particular, is used to provide the language with nonmonotonicity, and the default reasoning abilities were designed using CWA and the notion of arguments. The next subsection gives a brief description of this, that is, how default reasoning is done in Cyc; details can be found in Guha (1990b).

## Defaults

The syntactic structure of defaults is identical to that of defaults in circumscription (McCarthy 1987a). Thus, we represent the statement "birds usually fly" as follows:[4]

$isa(x\ Bird) \wedge \neg ab1(x) \supset flies(x)$ .

Intuitively, we want to weaken the monotonic statement "all birds fly" to get the default "birds usually fly," and we use the *ab1* predicate to do so. To derive conclusions from this axiom, we use the concept of arguments and have an argumentation axiom instead of the circumscription axiom. The intuition behind this approach is as follows:

We first axiomatize the concept of an argument as an extension of the concept of a proof. In addition to the sentences that might appear in a proof, an argument might also contain a class of sentences that have been labeled as assumptions (for example, sentences of the form $\neg ab1(Tweety)$ are assumptions). We use the ability to reify sentences to do this labeling.

If there is an argument for a sentence, we would like to believe in the truth of the sentence. However, because arguments are a weaker notion than proofs, it is possible to come up with invalid arguments; that is, those that try to make assumptions that are known to be false. It is okay for an argument to make assumptions, but if we know that an assumption made by an argument is false, then we ought to know enough to ignore this argument. We explicitly restrict our attention to arguments that are not yet known to be invalid. The details of how arguments are generated in practice, and so on, are discussed in the section The Heuristic Level: Efficient Inferencing in Cyc.

It is also possible to come up with arguments for both P and ¬P (and, indeed, to have multiple distinct arguments for each). Combining arguments is tricky and is handled as follows: Given a set of arguments for P and for ¬P, Cyc compares these arguments and decides what to add to the knowledge base—P, ¬P , or neither. We do this comparison by making arguments first-class objects in the CycL language and using axioms in the Cyc knowledge base that capture our intuitions of various aspects of default reasoning. The argumentation axiom, which captures the gist of this approach, is as follows:$(\forall a)$

> *The Cyc knowledge base itself . . . exists redundantly at the epistemological level and at the heuristic level . . .*

$(argumentFor('p, a) \wedge \neg invalidArg(a)$
$\wedge \neg(\exists a1)\ (argumentFor('\neg p, a1) \wedge \neg preferred(a,a1)$
$\wedge \neg invalidArg(a1))) \supset True('p)$ .

Additional axioms are used to specify when an argument is invalid (for example, $(True('\neg p) \wedge inArgument('p,a)) \supset invalidArg(a))$ and axioms that can conclude that one argument is preferred over another (a few of these are given later). These axioms form the core of the real default reasoning.

It is usually not possible to prove that a better counterargument to some proposition does not exist or prove that some argument is not invalid. To deal with this problem, CWA is made for the predicates *argumentFor* and *invalidArg*, and this closed-world assumption is what provides the required nonmonotonicity to the language. This axiom uses the truth predicate *True*, and to avoid the possibility of paradoxes, we (following Tarski) allow this predicate to differ from the actual truth value of the sentence for certain sentences (those that are likely to be paradoxical). In other words, the following is not an axiom schema in our knowledge base:

$True('p) \Leftrightarrow p$ .

The preference axioms and the axioms that define the predicates *argumentFor* and *invalidArg* are not part of any metatheory; they are regular axioms of the knowledge base. The salient aspect of our approach to doing default reasoning is that most of the work is done using axioms explicit in the knowledge base and not wired into the logic. This approach provides us greater flexibility and control and makes it easier to fix problems if inadequacies are detected. Adding and removing axioms from the knowledge base is strongly preferable to changing the logic, especially when a massive knowledge base already exists and assumes a certain logic.

We currently use a number of different criteria for comparing arguments: prefer inferences with shorter inferential distance (Touretzky 1987), prefer causal explanations (Lifschitz 1987), prefer constructive arguments over nonconstructive ones, and so on. We are also trying to construct a taxonomy of standard types of arguments that capture different dialectic patterns. For example, there is the concept of a narration (one kind of argument) that corresponds to giving a sequence of events that lead to some assertion (from some starting point) as an argument for why this assertion might be true.

What aspects of our default reasoning scheme need more work? Surprisingly, we would not include the logical formalism used. However, we would include issues such as what are reasonable preferences and dialectic patterns. Currently, we are actively engaged in this research (Guha 1990b).

## Microtheories and the Representation Language

One of the facilities available in CycL is the ability to say that a set of sentences constitutes a theory. For example, one set of sentences represents a naive theory of physics (NTP). Here is a typical NTP sentence, which says that if something is not supported, then it falls.[5] (Of course, this heuristic is not always true; it fails for balloons, objects in outer space, and so on. This theory should not be used when dealing with such objects.)

$$ist((\forall x \ \neg supported(x) \supset falls(x)), NTP) .$$

These theories, such as NTP, are referred to as microtheories ($\mu$Ts). They are first-class objects in the CycL language and are usually given descriptions related to their scope, when they should be used, and so on. This facility is extremely useful in forming theories and abstractions at different levels of granularity. In addition to avoiding the inconsistencies that often accompany the careless merging of different abstractions, microtheories give us a convenient formalism for using multiple representations, reasoning about when to use which one, and representing within a context (the microtheory could correspond to something like a discourse context). They also enable us to use contextual information to simplify the statement of axioms.

The description of the assumptions made by the microtheory—what is left implicit, and so on—that is associated with it form its *context* (McCarthy 1987b). A distinction is made between the *propositions* that constitute the microtheory (that is, the deductive closure of the axioms in the microtheory) and the *context* associated with it. The context is a rich (McCarthy and Hayes 1987) object and usually carries information that can be used to universalize (Quine 1969) the contextual representation of the microtheory. The addition of a fact to a microtheory always changes the theory associated with it but need not always change the context of the microtheory.

Statements about the world (as opposed to statements about a particular microtheory) have to be within some microtheory or other. One distinguished microtheory corresponds to the most expressive microtheory (MEM). In this article, as a notational convention, unless otherwise mentioned, if no microtheory is explicitly associated with a statement, the microtheory in which this statement is true is taken to be MEM. Most of the discussion of the ontology in this article is of that in MEM, although the last subsection of this section does discuss the role of microtheories in the ontology.

Here, we end our discussion of the epistemological level and proceed to a description of some of the techniques used at the heuristic level to speed up inference.

## The Heuristic Level: Efficient Inferencing in Cyc

The heuristic level is meant for doing inferencing. As opposed to the epistemological level, where we tried to avoid superfluous constructs, the heuristic level incorporates a host of logically superfluous mechanisms for improving efficiency.

**The Functional Interface to CycL.** The user can interact with Cyc at the epistemological level (figure 1) using a set of functions called the *functional interface*. The functionality of each of these is implemented at the heuristic level. The functions are Assert, Unassert, Deny, Justify, Ask, and Bundle.

**Assert:** ($\Sigma$ x KB $\rightarrow$ KB): Given a sentence $\sigma$ and a knowledge base, after Assert($\sigma$, KB), we get a new (modified) knowledge base in which $\sigma$ is an axiom.

**Unassert:** ($\Sigma$ x KB $\rightarrow$ KB): This function is the "undo" of Assert. After Unassert($\sigma$, KB), $\sigma$ is not an axiom (although it might still follow from axioms in the knowledge base).

**Deny:** ($\Sigma$ x KB $\rightarrow$ KB): This operation is similar to but stronger than Unassert. It tries to produce a knowledge base in which the sentence $\sigma$ is neither an axiom nor a theorem. Deny is stronger than Unassert in the case where $\sigma$ is currently a theorem in the knowledge base—follows from axioms Asserted into the knowledge base—but not an axiom. In such a case, Unassert would do nothing (that is, $\sigma$ would still be a theorem afterwards). It is possible that after Deny, neither $\sigma$ nor $\neg\sigma$ is a theorem or axiom, which contrasts with Assert($\neg\sigma$, KB), after which $\neg\sigma$ would be an axiom. Thus, Unasserting $\sigma$ is weaker than Denying it, which, in turn, is weaker than Asserting its negation.

**Justify: ($\Sigma$ x KB → sentences):** If sentence $\sigma$ is true in the knowledge base, then Justify($\sigma$, KB) should return a minimal subset of the knowledge base from which $\sigma$ can be derived.

**Ask: ($\Sigma$ x KB → truth-value bindings):** Ask is used to test the truth value of a statement and, if the expression contains some free variables, to find which variable bindings make it true. An optional argument (UNWANTED-BINDINGS) turns Ask into a generator; that is, each repeated call yields new sets of bindings.

**Bundle: (sequence of functional interface statements):** This facility performs a series of calls to the previous five functional interface functions as one atomic macro-operation. This operation is of great pragmatic benefit for two reasons: (1) The first few operations might violate some integrity constraints, and later ones might satisfy them again. (2) The bundling allows the heuristic level to be smart about which assertions it has to undo. For example, suppose we change an axiom from "Southerners speak with a drawl" to "Southerners over age 2 speak with a drawl." We make this change by issuing an Unassert and an Assert. Each of these two operations would cause about $n$ modifications (assuming an average lifespan of 72 years and a uniform age distribution in the population of $n$ Southerners). However, if we Bundle the two operations, then only $n/35$ modifications are done rather than $2 \cdot n$.

The concept of a functional interface, with functions such as Assert and Ask, has been around in computer science and AI for some time (Brachman, Fikes, and Levesque 1986). We tailored it somewhat for our purposes and increased its pragmatic usefulness by adding some new constructs (such as Bundle and Justify) and teasing apart old ones (such as Unassert($\sigma$, KB) versus Deny($\sigma$, KB) versus Assert($\neg\sigma$, KB)).

**Default Reasoning Modules (The Structure of the Heuristic Level).**    Most of the gain in processing speed at the heuristic level comes about because of the way we implement Ask. (Much of the complexity at the heuristic level arises from the need to do Deny and Unassert properly, but this is another issue [Pratt and Guha 1990].) The structure of the heuristic level is based on default reasoning. As we mentioned previously, defaults are implemented in CycL by way of an argumentation axiom. The argumentation axiom is just like any other axiom at the epistemological level. However, because it's used often, at the heuristic level, there are some special procedures for incorporating it so that certain special cases can be run effi-

ciently. Here, then, are the four modules that make up the structure of the heuristic level:

**Argument Generator:** Given a sentence $\sigma$, this module tries to generate an argument for it. Recall from the section on default reasoning that an argument is similar to a proof that can include assumptions.

**Argument Comparator:** Given a set $\{A_i\}$ of arguments for and against a sentence $\sigma$, this module decides on a truth value for $\sigma$ by using knowledge base axioms to check each $A_i$ for invalidity and decide which noninvalid $A_i$s are preferred over others.

**Argument Retractor:** When the truth value of a sentence $\sigma$ changes, this module ensures that truth values of other sentences that depend on $\sigma$ are also updated. Not surprisingly, the argument generator module is, in practice, tightly integrated with this module.

**Contradiction Resolver:** This module is responsible for detecting and resolving contradictions. For example, suppose we have an axiom $p \supset q$ involving no abnormality literals, and $p$ is true, yet $q$ is found to be false (because of arguments for $\neg q$). This module would notice such a contradiction and attempt to resolve it, for example, by retracting some weak (default) assertion that was used in the argument for $p$.

Given a sentence $\sigma$, Ask first tries to find arguments for it. If it can, it then tries to find arguments against it. These arguments are then compared (which can invoke preference axioms from the knowledge base and recursively involve calls on Ask), and the final truth value is decided based on this comparison. Note that the comparison process could fail (the arguments could be incomparable), which results in neither $\sigma$ nor $\neg\sigma$ being concluded.

The representation of default axioms at the heuristic level is different from that at the epistemological level. First, all the default axioms sharing the same *ab* literal are grouped into classes. For instance, the set of all rules whose antecedents (left-hand sides) contain ... $\wedge \neg ab_{37}(...)$ ... are grouped into one class. Second, each class is labeled with the *ab* literal (in this case, $ab_{37}$). Third, therefore, we can strip all the *ab* literals from all the default axioms. Fourth, although the argument generator can ignore these labels, which increases its efficiency, the argument comparator can still make use of them. However, certain precautions have to be taken against the knowledge base appearing inconsistent to the argument generator (because of some default not holding.)

Although the epistemological level has only two truth values (true and false), the heuristic level uses five truth values (true, default true, unknown, default false, and false) to label sentences in the knowledge base. True-false sentences are those that are monotonically true; that is, the addition of new facts can't cause them to be retracted (although even monotonic axioms can later be explicitly Unasserted, of course). Default true-false sentences don't have this property. Unknown is used for sentences for which there are unresolved conflicting arguments (Ginsberg 1987). The presence of five heuristic-level truth values helps in making the TMS-related bookkeeping activities more efficient.

A number of the statements at the epistemological level are of the form ($\neg ab$-$literal \supset$ $ground$-$formula$). These are called *local defaults* (and simply translate to the ground formula with a truth value of default true at the heuristic level), and the heuristic level provides special support to handle these efficiently.

### Speeding Up the Argument Generator Module.

The bulk of Cyc's time spent inferencing is done by the argument generator module. A number of techniques have been introduced to make the argument generator (and conclusion retractor) modules work more efficiently. These techniques fall into three categories: highly specialized inference rules, domain-specific inference modules, and dependency analysis of the knowledge base.

*Highly Specialized Inference Rules.* In the knowledge base, a number of axioms are instances of the following schema:

$(s1\ x\ y) \wedge (s2\ x\ z) \supset (s1\ z\ x)$ .

Here is one such axiom:

$(owner\ x\ y) \wedge (parts\ x\ z) \supset (owner\ z\ x)$ .

If the owner of JoesCar is Joe, and one of the parts of JoesCar is JoesCarsSteeringWheel, then it's reasonable to conclude that the owner of JoesCarsSteeringWheel is also Joe. Here is another example of an axiom that fits the same schema:

$(lastName\ x\ y) \wedge (sonOf\ x\ z) \supset (lastName\ z\ y)$ .

A new rule of inference, called transfers-Through, is used at the heuristic level to exploit the common syntactic structure of axioms matching this schema. Thus, the previous two axioms would be represented at the heuristic level as follows:

(transfersThrough owns parts)
(transfersThrough lastName sonOf) .

Currently, there are numerous such schemas, each of which has been made into a rule of inference, each schema corresponding to a category of axioms with isomorphic syntactic structure. Two other schemas are inheritance and automatic classification.

Associated with each such inference schema are specialized procedures for speeding up this sort of inferencing. For example, a certain amount of compilation can be done that drastically cuts down on conjunct ordering and unification at run time. Also, the stack used by Lisp itself can be used instead of using binding lists. Many of these savings are similar to those obtained by the Warren Machine–like compilation of Prolog programs (Warren 1983). In particular, each schema has specialized procedures for recognizing instances of the schema (for translating from the epistemological level to the heuristic level), applying instances of the schema to derive conclusions, and performing bookkeeping functions such as storing justifications.

We have also built a facility to help a user add new inference rule schemas. That is, one specifies a new schema, and Cyc automatically generates all the code needed to efficiently implement it—the types of specialized procedures previously itemized. Currently, this code generator can only handle schemas with no sentential variables, but even with this restriction, the code-generating facility is extremely helpful.

*Domain-Specific Inference Modules.* The previous technique—introducing specialized inference mechanisms—was based purely on the syntactic structure of the axioms and had nothing to do with the domain the axioms dealt with. However, at times, we can exploit some special properties of a set of domain-specific axioms or the domain-specific use of a set of general axioms. Some examples of such axiom clusters that Cyc currently optimizes in this way are those related to temporal reasoning and quantity arithmetic. In the case of temporal reasoning, for example, many tasks can be formulated as simple graph-search problems over the graph whose nodes are time points and whose arcs are primitive temporal relations (*before*, *after*, and *simultaneousWith*.)

In other words, a certain set of axioms about time can be compiled into a graph-search procedure. It should be noted that although at the heuristic level, nothing more than the program might be representing them, these axioms do still explicitly exist at the epistemological level.

*Dependency Analysis of the Knowledge Base.* Over the years, AI researchers have developed a number of stand-alone modules (for exam-

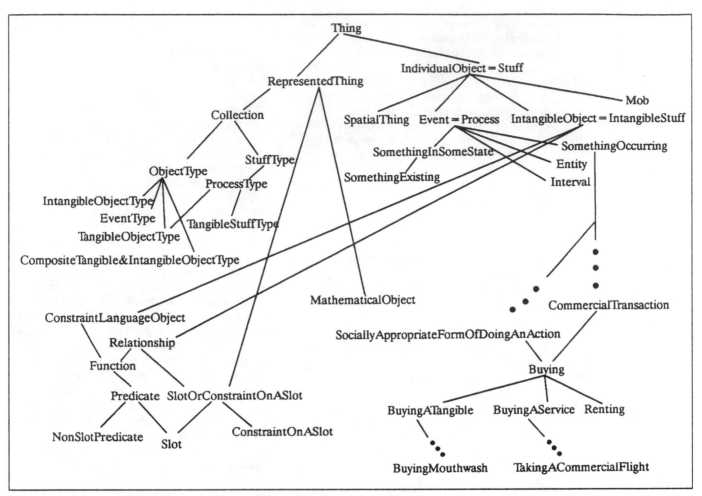

*Figure 2. Some of Cyc's Collections.*

(a) For millenia, ontologists have derived power through judicious choice of categories and predicates. Here, were see a few of Cyc's 5000 collections, related by genl and spec (superset and subset) links. Of course, because such arcs only depict one of Cyc's 4000 slots, many concepts that are closely related in the knowledge base (for example, ProcessType and Process) aren't connected in the diagram. (b) Although we make use of taxonomic classification, most of the power in the knowledge base derives from the particular axioms (facts, heuristics, and so on) such as the five depicted here (drawn from naive theories of buying, consuming, and so on). Axioms typically cut across category boundaries; for example, a single assertion about mouthwash might involve human emotions, cognitive-processing limitations, buying, liquids, hygiene, and containers. (c) Here is the way we enter the first two of these axioms into Cyc. Free variables (such as buyer, agent) are assumed to be universally quantified. We previously specified a context, a particular microtheory, in which these are full-fledged CycL epistemological-level axioms. Cyc can then lift them, adding clauses to decontextualize them as necessary. (For example, owning an object is only a necessary precondition to consuming it in the context of law-abiding, calm, responsible parties in a partially capitalistic economic setting, and so on). In each case, the tell-ask interface converts these clauses into efficient CycL heuristic-leel expressions

ple, TMSs) that could be used with any problem solver. To make them problem solver independent, their operation was usually made independent of the structure of the knowledge base on which the problem solver was operating. However, we have found that it is possible to obtain significant improvements in problem-solving efficiency by using an analysis of the structure of the knowledge base axioms.

For example, consider the problem of detecting purely self-justifying sequences of statements (for example, A justifies B, which justifies C, . . ., which justifies B, and then A

is retracted, but the rest remain). Avoiding such situations is a traditional source of space-time complexity in TMSs. However, a dependency analysis of the knowledge base axioms could reveal the circumstances in which there could possibly be circular justifications and the set of sentences that might be involved in the circular justification. Having this information can vastly reduce the time required to search for such circularities. For example, it turns out that in Cyc's current knowledge base, (1) only a small fraction of the 4000 kinds of slots could possibly participate in circular lines of reasoning and (2) such garbage-collectable chains are precisely characterizable and, hence, easily recognizable when they occur. These two knowledge base–specific properties make the problem of detecting them computationally feasible in practice, even though this detection is complex and expensive in the worst case. Although these modules are now making strong assumptions about the structure of the representation used by the problem solver, the resultant improvements in efficiency are worth it (Guha and Lenat 1989a).

In addition to the specialized inference procedures, Cyc has a general-purpose inference mechanism that is capable of a much larger (but incomplete) category of inferences. This general inference engine is similar to a unit preference resolution theorem prover, and with this inference mechanism, CycL is complete if attention is restricted to a horn subset of the knowledge base.

When dealing with mechanisms other than the domain-specific inference mechanisms, a depth-first iterative deepening procedure is used for the search. Resource-limited reasoning is implemented by using indexical functions that specify various bounds on resources (such as the time available, the cutoff depth for search).

In addition, part of these inference mechanisms is represented in Cyc, which allows Cyc to use an agenda to perform a best first search, using various heuristics to control the search strategy. However, to date, the performance of the iterative deepening strategy alone has been good enough that this metalevel (agenda) mechanism is rarely used. Here, we end the discussion of CycL and proceed to our discussion of the contents of the knowledge base.

# The Current State of Cyc's Ontology

The ontology of Cyc primarily includes categories and things in the world; it also includes reified assertions and internal machine objects such as strings, numbers, lists, and program code (figure 2).[6]

The next subsection introduces some of the basic concepts and distinctions used; the latter subsections discuss representation issues such as time, events, agents, and causality. One caveat: This discussion is only meant to give the flavor of the kind of things that are in the Cyc knowledge base; it is by no means a comprehensive overview of what is there, nor does it adequately capture the breadth of the current knowledge base. Further details on the ontology can be found in Lenat and Guha (1990).

Recall that the epistemological level is meant for communicating the contents of Cyc independent of the inferencing hacks that are used for efficiency down at the heuristic level. Hence, most of our discussion of the ontology of Cyc's knowledge base will be at the epistemological level, not the heuristic level.

We also mentioned that the knowledge base is organized in different microtheories along with information about when to use which microtheory, the information that is implicit in each microtheory, and so on. Different microtheories can use different abstractions of time, actions, space, objects that are known about, and so on. In this section, most of our discussion is in the context of the most expressive microtheory (MEM). MEM's expressiveness is a good measure of the expressiveness of the Cyc ontology as a whole. Therefore, the assertions we make have no explicitly mentioned microtheory; it should be assumed to be MEM. In the subsection Microtheories and the Ontology, we discuss the need for, and the impact of, having multiple microtheories.

## Some Basic Concepts and Distinctions

The ontology of Cyc is organized around the concept of *categories*. We also refer to them as classes or collections. The categories are organized in a generalization-specialization hierarchy (a directed graph, not a tree because each category can have several direct generalizations) (figure 2).

The Cyc predicates relating a category to its immediate supersets and subsets are, respectively, genls and specs. The instances of a category are its elements or members; the inverse of this relation is instanceOf. It should be noted that unlike many frame systems, a strong distinction is made in Cyc between the two relations instances (elements) and specs (subsets). The relation between Person and MarvinMinsky is different from the relation between Person and ComputerScientist. Another example is genls(Texan, American) and instanceOf(Lenat, Texan). Although we frequently use set-theoretic notions to talk about collections, these collections are more akin to what Quine (1969) termed natural kinds than they are to mathematical sets. This distinction becomes apparent later when we start ascribing various intentional properties to collections.

Because the generalization-specialization hierarchy is important, we start off by discussing some of its highest nodes, why they are in certain unintuitive genls-specs relations to other nodes, and so on.

The universal set is called Thing. One of its partitionings is into the two sets InternalMachineThing and RepresentedThing. Instances of InternalMachineThing include the number 5 and the string "DOG," that is, things for which the representation is provided by the Lisp substrate on which CycL is written. Instances of RepresentedThing are things such as Chair for which only a representation is provided by CycL. This distinction is useful when deciding whether to use model attachments (Weyhrauch 1986).

Another partition of Thing is into IndividualObject and Collection. IndividualObjects are elements such as Fred, TheWhiteHouse, and TheFourthOfJuly1990, that is, the non-sets. They can have parts but not instances. Instances of Collection include Thing (the set of all things), Chair (the set of all chairs), Texan (the set of all Texans), Dining (the set of all dining events), and so on.

Predicates are all strongly typed, and a single category from the Cyc hierarchy has to be specified as the type for each argument.[7] This was a conscious design decision and has tremendous heuristic power as the knowledge base is built. Namely, when knowledge enterers have an urge to define a new kind of slot, they must either select or define the domain of the slot. Usually, the slot is separately worth existing only if the domain is; so, our single category constraint frequently gives the knowledge enterers a well-needed doublecheck on what they were about to do.

It should be noted that predicates such as age and weight can't legally be applied to collections (such as Chair). To rephrase, because Chair is a set, an abstract mathematical entity, it can't have a weight or an age (it can, of course, have many other slots such as cardinality). Of course, we could discuss weight (Chair905)—the weight of an element of the set Chair—but this element is different.

In addition to collections of individuals, we also have collections of collections. For example, PersonType is a set whose elements include Person, ComputerScientist, and Texan, which themselves are collections whose elements include Lenat, Bledsoe, and so on. The hierarchy folds into itself at this level; that is, we don't have collections of collections of collections, and Collection is an instanceOf itself.[8]

The predicates themselves are first-class objects in the language and can be used as arguments to other predicates (this is a second-order–like construct that can easily be first ordered). Although some of our editing tools (and internal data structures) gather into frames the set of assertions that are binary predicates sharing a common first argument, this distinction is merely a heuristic-level (and user interface) one; there is nothing special about binary versus other arity predicates at the epistemological level.

We are now ready to discuss some of the representation issues. First, we discuss the distinction between Substances and IndividualObjects; then we proceed to how we represent events, causality, intelligent agents, and so on.

## Substances versus Individual Objects

If you take a piece of wood, and smash it into 10 pieces, each of them is still a (albeit smaller) piece of wood. However, if you do the same to a table, each piece is not a (smaller) table. Substances are usually referred to in linguistics and philosophy as *mass nouns*; some of them are obvious (sand, peanut butter, air) and some less so (time, walking). We view the concept PeanutButter as the collection of all pieces of peanut butter.

Every individual is made of some substance or other. If we don't have a single type of substance of which this individual is composed, we can define a new one (BertrandRusselStuff? ugh!); use a more general substance (AnimalMatter); or even fall back on the most general kind of substance, Substance.

Conversely, every piece of any substance—say, this particular piece of peanut butter over here—is clearly an individual. This leads to some interesting relations between substances and individuals:

Because every individual is a piece of some substance, IndividualObject $\subset$ Substance. However, any particular piece of any substance is an individual, and because the category corresponding to a type of substance is nothing but the set of its pieces, Substance $\subset$ IndividualObject.

Thus, rather surprisingly, the two properties are extensionally equivalent, which explains the IndividualObject = Substance node in figure 2. We still choose to distinguish between them because they have different intensional descriptions. The different substances (Wood, PeanutButter, Air, and so on) are all instances of the collection SubstanceType, and the collections of individuals (Table, Person, Number, and so on) are instances of ObjectType. We shortly describe how this difference in intensional description is made use of.

Certain properties are intrinsic (that is, if an individual has them, slices of this individual also have them, at least as a default), and other properties are extrinsic (that is, the parts don't inherit this property from the whole). The notion of intrinsicness is closely related to that of substances: Consider a par-

*The predicates themselves are first-class objects in the language and can be used as arguments to other predicates . . .*

*We can cut something up spatially . . . but we can also cut it up temporally.*

ticular table made entirely of wood—Table103. It inherits various default properties from Wood, which is the kind of substance it's an instance of (properties such as density, flash point), and it inherits other properties from Table, which is the kind of individual object it's an instance of (properties such as number of legs, cost, size). The former properties are intrinsic; the latter are extrinsic. This is no coincidence! We have noticed that an object (typically) inherits its intrinsic properties from whichever instances of SubstanceType it's an instance of, and it inherits extrinsic properties from whichever instances of ObjectType it's an instance of.

Thus, we now have a way of predicting for most predicates P whether it will be intrinsic. Namely, see whether P's domain is an instance of SubstanceType or ObjectType. Now we see the importance of having collections of collections; we could actually dispense with the concepts Substance and IndividualObject (because they are coextensional), but we can't do without SubstanceType and ObjectType.

For each type of substance, the granule predicate associates are the building blocks out of which the substance is built; for example, granule(Wood, PlantCell), granule(Sand, GrainOfSand), and granule(ThrongOfPeople, Person). Considering a portion of a substance smaller than a mob of its granules is risky; many of the default properties are violated as one approaches this level of granularity. Strictly speaking, we could conceptually carve a throng of people into all their heads and the rest, and neither alone would be an instance of ThrongOfPeople. Thus, we place a further restriction and say that the substancehood principle applies not only to portions much bigger than a granule but also only to portions that are just a contiguous mob of granules. As one drops below the grain size of a substance, one finds individual objects (which, in turn, are made out of substances). For example, MilitaryHardware is a kind of substance (that is, an instance of Substance-Type); its granules include guns and tanks, which are individual objects. Each instance of Gun is, in turn, made of some substance such as Iron. The granule of Iron is IronAtom, which is an ObjectType, and so on. This alternating individual-substance-individual-. . . continues at higher and lower (particle physics) levels.

## Processes, Events, and Persistent Objects

To this point, we have used the terms piece and cutting up in a loose fashion. Actually, these terms can be used in two senses—spa-tially and temporally—and we now examine them both. This leads to more general issues about events that occur over some time interval and objects that exist over some time interval.

We can cut something up spatially (as we did with the piece of peanut butter), but we can also cut it up temporally. For example, consider a process such as walking. In Cyc's ontology, we have the collection Walking, which is the set of all walking events. Consider one of its instances, a particular event in which, say, you walk to the corner mailbox and back home. Imagine a videotape of this event, and now consider some contiguous one-minute segment of the tape, say, the third minute of it. If anyone watched just this minute, they would report that this minute was itself a (albeit shorter) walking event, that is, another instance of Walking.

In the last subsection, we noted that the class Wood has an interesting property: When a member of the class (for example, Wood-enTable001) is carved into several pieces, each one is still an instance of Wood. We then said that Wood is a type of substance (that is, instanceOf(Wood, SubstanceType)), and we could use such substance-like categorization to decide on intrinsicness of properties. Here, we are seeing an analogous phenomenon: A class Walking, which is a set of events, has the property that when a member of the class is temporally carved into pieces, each one is still an instance of Walking. We say that Walk-ing is a type of temporal substance, a type of process. That is, Walking is an instance of Pro-cessType and a spec of Process. This analogy turns out to be more than superficial. Indeed, ProcessType is a spec of SubstanceType; so, Walking is an instance of SubstanceType. Sub-stanceType is partitioned into TangibleSub-stanceType and ProcessType. Wood, for example, is an instance of TangibleSubstance-Type.

Similarly, ObjectType is currently parti-tioned into TangibleObjectType and EventType. Although Walking is a type of process, WalkingToTheMailboxAndBack is not. If you imagine the third minute of the 10-minute WalkingToTheMailboxAndBack event, it is still an instance of Walking, but a stranger watching just this minute would not say that it was an instance of someone walking to a mailbox and back home—neither your home nor the mailbox might be visible anywhere on the videotape during this minute! The relationship here between Walking and Walk-ingToTheMailboxAndBack is indeed the same as the one between Wood and Table. Table is an instance of TangibleObjectType, and

WalkingToTheMailboxAndBack is an instance of EventType.

Earlier we saw that, surprisingly, Substance and IndividualObject were coextensional; with a similar argument, it turns out that Process and Event are coextensional. This is why ProcessType and EventType are actually the more useful collections to have explicitly represented rather than Process and Event.

There are now two types of intrinsicness as well: A property can be spatiallyIntrinsic or temporallyIntrinsic. If you imagine the particular event in which you walked to the mailbox and back home, it is an instance of Walking (from which it inherits default values for rate of speed, step size, amount of attention required, and so on) and an instance of WalkingToTheMailboxAndBack (from which it inherits default values for destination, duration, and so on). Sure enough, this third minute of the videotape would agree with the entire video on properties such as rate of speed but would differ radically on properties such as duration. rateOfMotion is temporallyIntrinsic, just as density is spatiallyIntrinsic.

Consider Table001, a particular table, an instance of the category Table. It persists for a lifetime, an interval of time before and after which it doesn't exist. Consider a temporal slice of Table001, such as the decade it was owned by Fred. This slice is also an instance of Table. This fact is interesting because it means that the category Table is an instance of ProcessType, and Table001 is an instance of Event! The process going on is existing.

Not surprisingly, a number of categories exist in our ontology whose instances are space-time chunks that exhibit sufficiently persistent properties that it makes sense to associate a notion of identity with these objects. The category of such things is called SomethingExisting, and this category is an instance of ProcessType. Because all physical objects (which have any persistent identity) exhibit this property, TangibleObject is an instance of ProcessType; so, anything that is spatially substance-like is also temporally substance-like, although the converse is not true.

This view of concepts such as Lenat or Table001 (that is, as Events) is interesting. We view these objects as space-time chunks, and we call the temporal pieces of these—for example, LenatDuring1990, Table001While-BeingEatenOn—subAbstractions of the larger piece. SubAbstractions can, of course, have further subAbstractions. Each maximal subAbstraction (for example, Lenat or Table001) is called an Entity; that is, entities cannot have superAbstractions. Being space-time chunks, these subAbstractions have temporal proper-

ties such as duration (the duration of Lenat is his lifespan), startingTime and endingTime.[9] This subabstraction scheme shares similarities with the histories approach of Hayes (1985).

Not all objects that have temporal extents need exhibit enough persistence to warrant a persistent identity. Consider Roger dining at a restaurant one evening. We might consider a system consisting of Roger, the waitress, the table, cutlery, food, and so on, interesting enough to create an explicit object RogerDiningEvent2317 to represent this system. However, this object has no temporally persistent properties, has poorly defined boundaries, and is of little interest after Roger walks out (except perhaps as an example in an AI article). Such objects are instances of SomethingOccurring, which is another important instance of EventType; these objects correspond to names that usually go by the names of actions, scripts, or processes, and they are rich objects (McCarthy and Hayes 1987).

The parts of an instance X of SomethingOccurring are referred to as its actors. These parts include all the persistent objects (that is, instances of SomethingExisting) that are involved in X. The actors of RogerDiningEvent2317 include the waitress, the food, the table, Roger, the bill, and so on. There are useful specializations of actors, such as performer, objectActedUpon, and instrumentInAction. The various actors in an event usually undergo some change either during or after the event occurs (that is, the subAbstractions of the actors during or just after the event are different from the subAbstractions just before).

No fixed set of slots appears in an action such as RogerDiningEvent2317. The ones that appear could depend on what happened there and how much Cyc knows about it; and in general, more details can always be added later. RogerDiningEvent2317 can later be arbitrarily elaborated along any dimension, for example, by specifying P(RogerDiningEvent2317) for predicates P that were not known at the time that RogerDiningEvent2317 was created!

It should be noted, however, that no ad hoc distinction is made about what kinds of events can cause changes in the properties of instances of SomethingExisting. In fact, because some of the properties of things change simply by their existing (for example, their age), it could well be the case that the properties of something change substantially even though it was not an actor in any instance of SomethingOccurring.

Any instance of Event can have temporal properties (duration, endsAfterTheStartOf, and

> *. . . by associating temporal extents with objects as opposed to reifications of propositions, we get a certain added expressiveness.*

so on). We use two abstractions of time to specify these temporal properties: interval based and set based.[10] Let's first discuss the *interval-based abstraction of events*. We can define a number of relations between events using the two primitives before and simultaneousWith that can hold between the starting or ending times of these intervals (which might have discontinuities in them). Thus, for example, we define the binary temporal relation startsBeforeStartOf as

$(\forall x,y)$ (startsBeforeStartOf(x, y) $\Leftrightarrow$ before (startingTime(x),startingTime(y))) .

Why do we need a second abstraction of time? The interval-based abstraction of time makes it awkward to say things such as "people don't eat and sleep at the same time" because we are not dealing with a single convex interval. In such cases, it is easier to abstract the times when *x* is eating and the times when *x* is sleeping as sets of points. Then, based on this set-based abstraction, we use set-theoretic relations such as intersects, subset, and disjoint to state axioms such as "people don't eat and sleep at the same time." In this case, the sentence would just be an assertion that for each person, the piece of time they're eating and the piece of time they're sleeping, viewed as sets of points, have an empty intersection.

It is interesting to note that by associating temporal extents with objects as opposed to reifications of propositions, we get a certain added expressiveness. For example, it is easy to express statements of the form "Fred when he was 39 liked his house as it had been 20 years earlier" in this formalism, and it is difficult to do so with formalisms that associate time with propositions (or their reifications). However, there is a high cost associated with this expressiveness. Given *n* entities and *m* intervals, we can have as many as $n \cdot m$ subAbstractions (that is, have to create $O(n \cdot m)$ objects) using the set-of-points-based abstraction; using the interval-based formalism, we would only need $O(n + m)$ objects.

A vast majority of the statements we would like to make relate coTemporal objects; that is, the temporal extents of the objects related is the same. For example, FredIn1972 could not be married to EthelIn1958. Similarly, Fred lived in House001 from 1965 through 1975 means that livesIn(FredFrom1965To1975, House001From1965To1975).[11] To exploit this regularity, we use the predicate holdsDuring. Instead of creating innumerable pairs of concepts never again needed (FredIn1958, EthelIn1958; FredFrom1965To1975 and House001From1965To1975; and so on), we just assert

holdsDuring(Fred, livesIn, House001, 1965-1975)

and

holdsDuring(Fred, marriedTo, Ethel, 1958). Similar constructs that allow temporal extents to be associated with reifications of propositions are used when dealing with predicates of arity greater than two.

It turns out to be notationally much simpler to write complex axioms (where specific instances of SomethingExisting are replaced by variables) using the subAbstraction formalism, but it is more efficient to inference using the holdsDuring predicate. The heuristic level provides special support for doing exactly this bifurcation: allowing the expressive but inefficient Subabstraction formalism for stating axioms but using the more efficient holdsDuring predicate for doing inference whenever possible.

In addition to instances of SomethingExisting, such as Fred , and instances of SomethingOccurring, such as FredBeingBorn, we also recognize changes in properties of persistent objects as first-class events. If Fred was hungry before going to the restaurant and not hungry afterwards, we can consider this change as an object. Formally, this corresponds to reifying a sentence that specifies that he was hungry at some time and not hungry at some later time into an object and making this resultant object an event (because one can associate temporal properties with it).

**Temporal Projection.** When one of the properties of an instance of SomethingExisting changes, it's not likely to affect all (or even many) of its other properties (McCarthy and Hayes 1987). For example, when Guha gets a haircut, it doesn't affect his address, languagesSpoken, birthDate, and so on. This fact is not surprising because a useful set of properties is useful in part because the properties are largely independent.

Associated with each ground formula is an

interval of persistence. Thus, if we knew that Fred was happy at time *t0*, and the persistence interval of this time was *I1*, then given any point in time between *t0* and *t0 + I1*, we can conclude that Fred was happy at this time point. Usually, we associate default periods of persistence with classes of propositions by using axioms, which are called *temporal projection axioms*. These axioms enable us to *project* (infer a good guess for) Fred's name and gender years in the future or past, his hairStyle months in the future or past, his mood seconds in the future or past, and so on, based on the values of these attributes at some given time.

These temporal projections are only defaults. If the evidence is contrary to these projections based on particular actions that have taken place, this contrary evidence usually overrides these projections. Also, if an event that is capable of changing this property is known to have taken place, even if the effects of the event can't be computed (possibly because of missing information), we don't project this property across such an event.

Associating specific finite periods of persistence with propositions has advantages over using a frame axiom (McCarthy 1987a) to allow for extended projection. It provides a simple scheme for accumulating the information at a finer granule (regarding the possibility of different events capable of changing this property that are likely to occur) into a coarser granule in terms of this interval. However, this association introduces the following problem: If our knowledge that Fred was happy (or a gun was loaded) at *t0* came from some source other than temporal projection, we are willing to say that until time *t0 + I1*, he's happy (or the gun is still loaded). However, we don't want to repeat this argument and say that at time *(t0 + I1) + I1* he's still happy, and the gun is still loaded. That is, we want to project only from a base time point where we had this other source of information (that is, some justification other than temporal projection) about the fact in which we are interested. Notice how we escape from this classic problem by making use of the ability to explicitly refer to justifications for facts (which we obtained using reflection) to state this dependence (Guha 1990a).

Temporal projection has more to it than just a frame axiom. We mentioned earlier the concept of a narrative as a kind of argument. These narratives, together with argument preference criteria based on notions of causality, are used to actually do the temporal projection. The details of this can be found in Guha (1990b).

**Causality.**    Most treatments of causality (in AI) proceed by labeling some appropriate subset of occurrences of material implication as causal. We do this labeling by using a causal relation whose argument is the reification of a sentence involving a material implication. For convenience, we refer to $((p \supset q) \wedge (causal\ '(p \supset q)))$ as (Cause *p q*). Let us take a closer look at the axioms that specify the meaning of Cause:

First, suppose we assert (Cause *p q*). Then it follows that $(p \supset q)$. In other words, Cause is a strictly stronger notion than material implication.

Second, suppose (Cause *p q*), and *p* and *q* are ground sentences and true. Then *p* and *q* must refer to events (which in Cyc is anything that can have temporal attributes). That is, *p* and *q* must have at least one object constant that is an event.

Third, suppose (Cause *p q*). Then every single event referred to in *p* must startBeforeTheEndingOf every event in *q*.

Fourth, given any atomic ground sentence *q* that refers to an event, either *q* should be basic, or there should be some sentence *p* such that (Cause *p q*) is true. Intuitively, *q* being classified as basic corresponds to the notion of it being unexplainable.

Fifth, given a statement of the form (Cause *p q*), either this statement is "basic," or a sequence of sentences exists of the form (Cause *p a*), (Cause *a b*) . . . (Cause *m q*), that is, some mechanism that implements this causal relation.

Both the fourth and the fifth axioms are extremely strong statements to make, which is why the notion of basic sentences was included. No commitment is made about which occurrences of implication are to be labeled as causal. The aim of the previous formalism is to provide a facility to state and experiment with various heuristics for doing just this labeling. As with default reasoning, we chose to have axioms in the knowledge base provide the guidance and decision making rather than wiring it in in some fashion.

**Actions and Concurrent Processes.** Each action (that is, instance of SomethingOccurring) has a set of axioms associated with it specifying its preconditions, its postconditions, and constraints on the actors during the event. A tangible object is a structured arrangement of its physicalParts (for example, Table001 breaks down into its legs, top, and so on). In much the same way, an action is a constrained arrangement of its subEvents and actors; for example, RogerDiningEvent2317 breaks down into subEvents such as ordering

*Associating specific finite periods of persistence with propositions has advantages over using a (conventional) frame axiom. . .*

food, eating, and paying the bill and actors such as Roger, the waitress, and the food, with restrictions on their arrangements and properties. Both events and tangible objects, then, can have a structure slot. An entry on a structure slot is a Structure, which, in turn, lists the parts/subEvents and the constraints on them. Several entries might be on a structure slot corresponding to orthogonal decompositions. It is significant that the constraints themselves, in both the action and tangible object cases, are often similar. For example, a set of subEvents or physical parts might be linearly sequenced or partially ordered (in time or space, respectively), nested in series, and so on.

Given a physical object and its parts, it is often possible to distinguish between different classes of parts. For example, the parts of most tables can be classified into parts meant for providing support to the top, the top itself, parts for decoration, and so on. We usually associate a predicate (which is an instance of PartSlot and a specSlot of physicalParts) with each of these classes and use these predicates to relate the parts to the overall object (rather than just using the single predicate physicalParts.)

A similar approach is taken to relating the parts of an action to the action. When dealing with actions, there are two important categories of parts—the actors and the subEvents—and there are separate categories of slots that are used to relate the actors to an action (the ActorSlots) and the subEvents to the event (the SubEventSlots). The ActorSlots define the roles played by the different actors in the event (performer, victim, instrument, and so on). Given an action and a participant actor, there are three subAbstractions of the actor related to this action, namely, the subAbstraction of the actor just before, during, and after the action. In practice, we associate the entities of the actors with the action (through the ActorSlots) and then use three ternary predicates (subAbsOfActorBefore, subAbsOfActorDuring, and subAbsOfActorAfter) to specify the exact subAbstractions of the actors.

It should be noted that there are no primitive actions into which all actions are broken down. That is, the actions are not merely macros introduced for notational convenience (for use instead of more complex sequences of primitive actions). We eschew primitive actions because we want to be able to reason at different levels of abstraction, and the a priori assigning of a set of actions as primitives goes against this ability; often, one can provide only descriptions and not definitions of the more complex actions in terms of their subEvents. In such cases, the more complex actions are not merely for notational convenience but are an epistemological necessity.

One of the problems that arises with predicting the effects of actions on the participating actors is the possibility of concurrent events. Our solution for this problem is as follows: Cyc gathers all the co-temporal events $E_i$ (cutting up events if required) that affect a particular property and collects them into a single new event $E$. Cyc then computes the net effect of $E$ on this property from the subEvents of $E$ (suppressing the direct updating of the property by the subEvents). It should be noted that the agglomeration is necessarily a nonmonotonic process because a closed-world assumption has to be made while collecting the $E_i$.

Another thorny issue is how to handle, for example, the weight of (the subAbstraction) of FredSmith on a particular day because it obviously fluctuates slightly from moment to moment. More generally, when dealing with subAbstractions of a reasonable duration, it becomes hard to specify values for most temporally intrinsic numeric attributes because of the (often slight) changes in the value of the attribute over the period of the subAbstraction. To overcome this problem, we use a class of terms corresponding to intervals in the quantity space (of the attribute). These intervals can be named (for example, around 180 pounds) and in the extreme can also be open in one direction. A calculus for performing simple mathematical operations with these intervals (provided by CycL) makes it relatively easy to use both qualitative and quantitative specifications for attributes, switch between them, and so on. Another use for these interval-based quantity terms is to specify defaults for numeric attributes (for example, height, weight) for categories that exhibit some but not too much variation in the value of these attributes (for example, the weight of newborn humans).

Interval-based quantity slots are also useful for dealing with quantities for which no acceptable measurable scale or measuring instruments have yet (or perhaps ever will) to be defined: happiness, alertness, level of frustration, attractiveness, and so on. Despite the lack of absolute units of measure, mileposts for these attribute values can be defined, and partial orders and even crude calculi can be developed.

## Composite Objects and Agents

In addition to purely physical objects (such as tables and rocks), objects such as books and people exist with which we would like to associate an intangible aspect such as a message or a mind (which also would have a temporal aspect). Given such a composite tangible-intangible object, we can separate the purely tangible parts from the purely intangible and separately represent both of them explicitly as well as represent the composite. The purely intangible parts are instances of IntangibleObject, the purely physical parts are instances of TangibleObject, and the composition is an instance of CompositeTangibleIntangibleObject.

The most important subset of CompositeTangibleIntangibleObject is Agent—the set of intelligent agents—and this subsection considers some aspects of representing agents. Agents include people (and most macroscopic animals), computer programs, corporations, and other things with intelligence, purpose, and (frequently) rationality.[12] Let us first consider why we want this distinction between the physical and nonphysical aspects of agents. Consider representing the Frankenstein monster at some point in time. We would like to be able to say that his body was *n* years old, his mind was *m* years old, and the composition was *k* years old. Rather than introduce new predicates such as ageOfMyMind, ageOfMyBody, amountOfTimeSinceMyMindAndBodyWereJoined, and so on, we would like to use the single existing predicate age; besides being simpler and cleaner, this predicate also lets us fully use the axioms involving age that are already available.

To deal with the previous example, we need to be able to explicitly talk about the physical and mental extents of a composite. Having made this distinction (and relating these using the predicates physicalExtent and mentalExtent), we associate weight not with the mental part of the Frankenstein monster nor with the composite part but only with the physical part; similarly, IQ is associated only with the mental part. Finally, age makes sense for all three aspects and has a different value for all three.

This scheme has the advantage of separating the physical aspects of composites from their mental aspects and allows us to talk about aspects that might apply to both with different values (age, interestingness, likedBy, and so on). However, in most cases, there is not a single predicate that can be used and has a different value for two or more of these units (physical extent, mental extent, composite). We would like to make use of this regularity.

In other words, we don't mind having three separate concepts for Frankenstein's monster—he was rather unusual after all—but we

shouldn't need to have three separate concepts for every composite if nothing conflicts from one to the other. We added the categories PartiallyTangible (a spec of SomethingExisting and a genl of TangibleObject) and PartiallyIntangible (a spec of SomethingExisting and a genl of IntangibleObject); so now, CompositeTangibleIntangibleObject is a spec of both of these new Partially . . . collections. IQ, for example, now makes sense for PartiallyIntangibleObjects, and weight makes sense for PartiallyTangibleObjects, and so on. Thus, we can state IQ, weight, and all the other properties right on the composite unit.

If we happen to be representing an exception, such as the monster, in which some property has a different value for the physical or mental extent, then we can create the appropriate instances of TangibleObject and IntangibleObject, just as we did previously. As a default, we also inherit the properties that talk about physical (mental) properties to the physical (mental) extents. This framework gives both the expressiveness of the separation of physical and mental parts and the efficiency of not doing this separation unless it is required.

A full description of the various issues related to agenthood that have been and are being considered in Cyc would require more space than is available here, so we just mention a few of them. One of our recent technical reports (Guha and Lenat 1989b) deals exclusively with this topic.

Agents can be collective (such as organizations and institutions) or individual (such as people). Each agent can have one or more attitudes toward any given proposition; some of the propositional attitudes currently used in Cyc include beliefs, goals, dreads, purpose, and desires. We now consider some issues related to these propositional attitudes.

A primitive notion of awareness is incorporated as follows: Each agent has a set of terms and predicates s/he is awareOf. An agent cannot have any attitude toward a sentence that involves terms s/he is not aware of. This restriction is introduced to keep us from, for example, talking about Aristotle's beliefs about the Space Shuttle.

Attributing our own beliefs to other agents (with whom we might never have directly communicated) is something frequently done. Sometimes this attributing is good (for example, when the traffic light in front of you turns green, you assume that the drivers on the cross-street share your beliefs about what this green light means), and sometimes it's bad (for example, cross-cultural mirror imaging has led to innumerable political dis-

*We eschew primitive actions because we want to be able to reason at different levels of abstraction . . .*

asters). A class of axioms called the *belief projection axioms* enables Cyc to efficiently do this sort of mirror imaging and explicitly record separate beliefs when they are known. These belief projection rules themselves are moderately interesting because they describe what it means to be a public figure, what it means to be commonsense knowledge, and so on. CycL provides special support to efficiently handle these rules at the heuristic level.

Agents can be in control of (the truth value of) propositions, which means that the controlling agent can perform the requisite actions that determine the proposition's truth value. For example, a robber holding a gun is in control of whether the gun fires and at whom. The truth value chosen by the controlling agent is assumed to be based on his/her/its desires.

This notion of agents controlling propositions is sometimes an expedient way of computing the truth value of certain propositions. If an agent is in control of a proposition P, and s/he desires P, then we can assume that P is true (modulo limited resources, conflicting goals, and so on).

The concept of control gives us an abstraction layer that allows us to skip the details of the agent planning to make P true, executing this plan, monitoring it, repairing it, and so on. For example, a teacher assigns a book report to a student and, later, needing a copy of this book, asks the student where it can be obtained. The teacher didn't have to worry about the plan the student made to get the book or read it, the details of the execution of this plan, and so on, to believe that (by the day before the book report was due) the student would have somehow obtained a copy of the book.

Just knowing that you control when you go home from work and that you want to sleep at home tonight is enough to have me call you first at home at midnight if I have to reach you at this time; that is, I don't have to worry about the plan you made to get home, the details of the execution, and so on, to believe that (by midnight, at least) you had made it home.

Agents can participate in events (actually in instances of SomethingOccurring (see the section Processes, Events, and Persistent Objects and also figure 2) in one of two modes: voluntarily or involuntarily. If an agent A participates in an event E voluntarily, s/he usually has a purpose P; P is generally one of his(her) goals, which, in turn, are the subset of his(her) desires that s/he has decided to try and achieve. Moreover, A believes that P will become true because of this event E. The con-

cept of purpose allows us to (write axioms that will) decide when an agent will participate in (or pull out of) an event.

Agents can enter into Agreements with other agents; some of the parties to an agreement might be individual agents, and some might be collective. This activity is one of the most important, frequent ones that agents carry out, and we use the remainder of this subsection to discuss it.

An *agreement* defines a set of propositions that all the participants share (although they might have different propositional attitudes toward the various clauses of the agreement!). In addition, the Agreement might also assign certain responsibilities (logically, these are also propositions) to specific participants. Agreements also usually specify certain punitive or remedial actions to be taken in case these responsibilities are not fulfilled. If the agent performing these punitive actions is a LegalSystem (such as a Government or GovernmentalAgency), then the agreement is said to be a LegalAgreement.

We distinguish between agreements in which the event that enrolled a particular agent was one in which s/he voluntarily participated and ones in which s/he didn't participate voluntarily. For agreements an agent involuntarily participates in, the constraint that s/he shares the common beliefs of the agreement is slightly relaxed.

As a default, collective agents have one or more special types of agreements associated with them, such as their charter and articles of incorporation. Often, an organization or institution will itself have (or at least act as if it has) certain desires, dreads, purposefulness, authority, and so on, that are not present in most (or perhaps even any) of the participants or members of the organization. Often, such attitudes and goals are captured in, or even caused by, the special agreements it participates in.

## Microtheories and the Ontology

The formalisms discussed in the previous few sections try to provide a general and expressive framework for representing various aspects of the world. However, as our initial statements claimed, much of the power in Cyc comes from specific partial solutions, simplified models (of time, space, a domain, and so on) that work in certain common but restricted situations and not from overarching use-neutral formalisms.

The use of single abstraction, no matter how expressive, also has bad consequences from a pragmatic standpoint. For example, one would like to be able to state something like "When x buys o from y, one of the subEvents is a paying event, in which x pays y the price of o." Given an expressive abstraction of time, we might have to write a long axiom to encode this statement—one that involves numerous uses of subAbsOfActorDuring, subAbsOfActorAfter, and so on—and most of the details being represented would be irrelevant in 99 percent of the uses of the axiom.

Thus, we would like to use much simpler abstractions if the domain we are dealing with does not require more expressive abstractions. Further, the process of formulating models for domains becomes time consuming if one is going to try and develop the *right* model for each domain.

These considerations led us to introduce the concepts of microtheories and contexts (McCarthy 1987b; Guha 1990a) that we mentioned earlier. These microtheories are first-class objects, and a number of operations are possible on them. For example, given a discourse or a problem to be solved, we can decide to create and enter a new context that leaves implicit a number of arguments to predicates, makes assumptions about the domain, and so on. We can have axioms that describe which kind of microtheory should be used for which problems, which form taxonomies or other structures of microtheories, which decide when it is necessary to change the context of a microtheory (see The Evolution of the Representation Language for a discussion on the relationship between a context and a microtheory), which have defaults that lift the contents of one microtheory into a more general one, and so on.

The ontology described in earlier sections is the most detailed one and is representative of the net-expressive power of the language. In addition to the formalism for time and actions previously mentioned, we have a lattice of simpler abstractions of these available. Some of these abstractions have only discrete time or associate time with propositions, and some even assume that the whole theory they are dealing with is about a single instant of the world and, hence, completely ignore time. A particular domain theory about, say, Buying (remember that many different theories can exist for any given domain), can use the simplest abstraction of time, actions, and so on, that are adequate for this theory.

The concept of microtheories figures prominently in the approach we are taking for developing a representation for space. After many failed attempts at developing a single general abstraction for space, we decided to

*The concept of microtheories figures prominently in the approach we are taking for developing a representation for space.*

use a number of globally inadequate but locally adequate theories of space. For example, we are working on abstractions of space that are based on (1) simple diagram-like representations, (2) computer-aided design–like representations that build solids and surfaces out of a small number of primitives, and (3) device-level representations that primarily deal with the topology of a device by using a number of primitive components and using a small number of ports for each primitive and a small number of ways in which two primitives can be connected. Although none of these abstractions is sufficient as a general approach to representing space, for any given problem, one of these (plus a few more that we are developing) if often adequate. These various abstractions of space are organized into a hierarchy because some are just refinements of others.

Contexts and microtheories are not panaceas for the problems mentioned at the beginning of this subsection. They bring their own set of problems with them. For example, we need to determine when to use which context, when a context is insufficient, when we need to enter a new context, and so on. Although it does not seem hard to come up with extremely specific heuristics that do these tasks (for example, for kinematics problems, if the velocity of the objects is less than .5c, then use Newtonian mechanics), it would be preferable to have at least a few general heuristics for these purposes (Guha 1990a). This area is one of current focus. Most of the knowledge base is currently in the theory MEM. The simpler abstractions of time mentioned earlier are available, and a few theories use these abstractions. A few general heuristics are available for solving some of the problems (such as deciding when to use which theory), and more are being developed. We expect that most of the theories of topics at a finer granule than those mentioned in this section, which we will add to Cyc, will make use of this notion of microtheories and that they will figure prominently in the overall structure and contents of the knowledge base.

## The Evolution of the Cyc Ontology

Earlier, we described the 1984–1990 evolution of the Cyc methodology and the CycL representation language. The construction of the ontology began in late 1984 with an expert system–like approach. As is apparent from Lenat, Prakash, and Shepherd (1986), issues such as the representation of time, substances, agents, and causality were largely ignored in favor of highly specific issues. However, our position has considerably changed in the interim, and these issues are now regarded as significant to the ontology.

We have worked out fairly adequate solutions to some of these ontological problems and are working on solutions for others. We differ from the rest of the AI community working on such issues in that we have refrained from agonizing over the myriad subtleties of, for example, the different formalisms for representing pieces of time; instead, we have concentrated on using the formalisms we have for actually encoding information about various domains. We have also refrained from tinkering with the logic for, for example, reasoning about pieces of time; instead we have worked within the logic described earlier (see The Evolution of the Representation Language).

In general, we did not find these solutions on the first try or even the second. Therefore, we conclude this subsection with a brief list of some of the mistakes we made and the lessons we learned along the way.[13]

We began by explicitly representing the time interval over which an event occurred. Thus, for example, we would have an event such as TrafficAccident903 and a separate object TimeIntervalOfTrafficAccident903, and only the time intervals could participate in temporal relations such as before and startsAfterTheEndOf. However, again and again, there was never anything more to say about these time interval frames, that is, beyond a pointer to the event that they represented the time interval and beyond the temporal relations in which they participated. Thus, eventually we just merged the two notions—an event and the time interval of its occurrence—and now the domain and range of temporal relations is Event (the set of all events) rather than TimeInterval. In theory, TimeInterval need no longer exist; pragmatically, a few pure time intervals do exist in the sense of there being some events whose only interesting aspects are their temporal extents, for example, TheYear1990.

By examining many cases of reasoning about the creation and destruction of objects, we were led to classify TangibleObject as a subset of Event. That is, each tangible object is running a process so to speak—the process of existing. This ontology lets us easily state temporal relations between objects, such as "Fred lived long after Aristotle." We originally viewed the Substance versus IndividualObject distinction to be crucial. We were surprised to find the two concepts *coextensional* (each portion of a substance is an individual and vice versa); similarly, TangibleSubstance is coextensional with TangibleObject; and so on. The central distinction turns out to be between, for example, TangibleSubstanceType (whose instances include, for example, Wood and Water) and TangibleObjectType (whose instances include, for example, Table and Ocean). Using this latter distinction, Cyc can, for example, predict whether a property will be extrinsic or intrinsic.

During late 1986 and early 1987, we thrashed through a series of formulations for basic property inheritance, including explicitly having frames such as TypicalPerson instead of (and at one point in addition to) TheSetOfAllPeople. We can use TypicalPerson to illustrate two troubles with prototypes:

First, one often wants to inherit along slots other than allInstances. For example, each entry on Stallone's fans slot should inherit entries such as Rocky and Cobra to its moviesSeen slot. (Of course, our use of terms such as slot and entries is just shorthand. In this case, the general nonmonotonic assertion at the epistemological level is fans(Stallone, $x$) $\land \neg ab_n(x) \supset$ moviesSeen($x$, Rocky).)

Second, we occasionally need to distinguish a predicate (such as interestingness, createdBy, likedBy) applying to the set of all people, being inherited to the typical instance of this set, or even applying (at a metalevel) to the reified Cyc concept itself. For example, the typical person is created by their parents, the frame TypicalPerson was created by Lenat, and the set of all people has no creator (all sets exist in a Platonic universe and can be neither created nor destroyed). The typical person is interesting, the concept TypicalPerson is uninteresting, the set of all people is reasonably interesting, the concept Person representing the set of all people is slightly interesting, and so on. Eventually, we dispensed with concepts such as TypicalPerson because any assertion applying to it could just as well be stated as applying to (that is, inheriting to) allInstances of Person.

Precision is generally a good thing, or (to be more precise) the ability to be precise is generally a good thing. However, in most situations, the most cost-effective behavior is to choose a level of detail and use the corresponding microtheory instead. A case in point was our partitioning of the universe (Thing) into TangibleObject (such as Rock0093), Intangible (such as the predicate mass or the set Rock of all rocks), and CompositeTangible/IntangibleObject (such as Lenat). As we discussed in detail in the sections on composite objects and agents, Cyc frequently gets the right answer without making this distinction, even though in rare cases, it is important (for example, the typical person has the same answer for how old is their mind, their body, and the joining of the two, but we can, as in Frankenstein, separate the three concepts if we need to). In these subsections, we explained our solution (that is, our current way out of this dilemma), which involves the use of PartiallyTangible and PartiallyIntangible, and we also described our current investigations into codifying and using microtheories.

## The Current State of Cyc's Environment and Infrastructure

You might have noticed several aspects of the Cyc effort that we did not even touch on in this article. Although interesting in their own right, these areas are not our main topic for research, and in each case, we have done only what we felt necessary to maximize the rate of Cyc's construction. Here is a list of a few such intentional omissions:[14]

**The Knowledge Server:** This subsystem accepts everyone's knowledge base operations; serializes them; and, in case constraint violations appear, adjudicates the resolution of the conflict. In cases of no conflict, it then broadcasts the operations to everyone else. The connections today are generally thin wire, although we expect this to change in the coming year.

**The User Interface:** We have constructed various textual and graphic tools for browsing, querying, and editing the knowledge base. Some of the graphic tools are semantic net based; one is a sort of Escheresque recursive bird's-eye view of a museum floor plan. Some of the editing tools are ideal for making point mutations and corrections; some are oriented toward sketching some brand new (and not yet well codified) area and gradually making the sketch more precise. User interface issues are tangled with knowledge acquisition (the next two items respectively describe tools for doing knowledge acquisition manually and automatically).

**The Copy and Edit Mechanism:** Most knowledge entry in Cyc involves finding similar knowledge and copying it and modifying the copy. More and more over the years, Cyc has helped in this process, and as a result, knowledge entry can be done more rapidly than we had originally estimated.

**Digitized Images:** Yes, often it's much easier to just grab a picture of an object and point to the part you mean rather than try to figure out what its name is. Cyc contains such images (from *The Visual Dictionary* [Corbell 1987]), but experienced knowledge enterers know their way around the knowledge base and rarely use them.

**Other Nonpropositional Knowledge:** Some Cyc researchers are building neural nets that we can use at the earliest (preheuristic) and latest (reduction to instinct) stages of understanding some task (for example, training a net on examples of good analogies and then letting it make hunches about potentially good new analogies, hunches that the rest of Cyc can investigate and flesh out symbolically).

**The Machine Learning Module:** This module is a symbolic learning subsystem in addition to the previous statistical, nonpropositional one. This program roams over the knowledge base, typically at night, looking for unexpected symmetries and asymmetries. These, in turn, often turn out to be bugs, usually crimes of omission of one sort or another. In rare cases today and, we expect, more frequently in future years, these turn out to be genuine little discoveries of useful but hitherto unentered knowledge.

## Present and Future Directions

This article began by explaining the need for a large, general knowledge base to overcome the brittleness (in the face of unanticipated situations) that limits software today. The need for a Cyc-like knowledge base is critical not only in expert system–like applications but also to do semantic processing for natural language understanding (disambiguation, anaphora, ellipsis) and to enable realistic machine learning and analogizing.

We then focused on criteria for an adequate representation language for this knowledge base, which drove us to the bifurcated CycL architecture, having both an expressive epistemological level and an efficient heuristic level. One of the Cyc project's most interesting accomplishments has been the construction of the TA translator, which can convert back

*Most knowledge entry in Cyc involves finding similar knowledge and copying it and modifying the copy.*

*We plan to develop an ontology of arguments and formulate and encode assorted perference criteria that are useful in default reasoning . . .*

and forth between general epistemological-level (FOPC-like) expressions and particular heuristic-level template instances. The epistemological and heuristic knowledge base levels and the TA translator are fully implemented and function as described in this article.

We discussed some of the unexpected aspects of the Cyc knowledge base's organization and contents, such as the relationships between IndividualObject, Substance, Process, and Event. We gave the flavor of some of our recent research by sketching our (still incomplete) treatment of agents and agreements. Finally, we briefly mentioned the Cyc user interface tools, knowledge server, and related issues.

Perhaps the most important theme from all these aspects of the project is that of eschewing the single general solution dream, instead assembling a set of partial solutions that work most of the time and work efficiently in the most common situations. We have seen this tenet apply to representation language design, knowledge entry methodology, control of search during inferencing, and truth maintenance as well as throughout the contents of the knowledge base. The emerging global behavior of the system should hopefully be fairly use neutral.

In the following two subsections, we discuss the directions along which we are currently working to extend both CycL and the knowledge base. In some sense, the two are extremely intertwined, in that the extensions to CycL are largely driven by the needs of the knowledge base. We then touch on other future plans and issues: new collaborations; the proliferation, standardization, and marketing of Cyc; and the expected future scenario for the demise (or at least transmutation) of the Cyc project.

### Future Plans for the Representation Language

The main focus of research on extending the reasoning abilities of the CycL language is along the following lines:

**Default Reasoning:** We plan to develop an ontology of arguments and to formulate and encode assorted preference criteria that are useful in default reasoning (to aid in choosing one argument over another).

**Microtheories:** Although the epistemological level does not require any extension to deal with these explicit contexts, it is likely that certain standard kinds of microtheories are likely to benefit from the heuristic level's providing special support for this feature.

**Metalevel:** Although there are various facil-

ities for stating and using metalevel information in Cyc, the metalevel reasoning that takes place in Cyc today is minimal because it has not yet been the bottleneck in building and running Cyc. We believe this situation might change as Cyc grows even larger, and the search for arguments grows. Metalevel reasoning in Cyc needs to be extended both by adding reasonable metalevel heuristics (for example, for identifying the small subset of the knowledge base that is even possibly relevant to answering a given query [Guha and Levy 1990]) and providing some ability for the system to improve its performance from past experience.

### Future Plans for the Ontology and the Knowledge Base

The work being done on the Cyc knowledge base is largely in the form of the development of microtheories for topics at the level of transportation, human emotions, modern buildings, and so on. Microtheories are being developed in two major areas. The first of these is a set of commonsense theories about everyday physical phenomena (in the manner of naive physics), and the second of these is a set of theories dealing with aspects of agents (such as agents having and acting on the basis of emotions, goals, limited resources).

In addition to these areas, a significant research effort is in progress on the topic of microtheories themselves, from the perspective of both formulating axioms for solving problems (such as when which theory is to be used) and cataloging the standard kinds of simplifications that can be made to theories on developing formalisms, such as for time and space, that make it easier to state axioms (that use these formalisms).

Finally, although gross size is often negatively correlated with overall knowledge base quality and power, we should mention that Cyc's knowledge base currently contains over a million assertions, and we expect almost an order of magnitude increase in the coming five years. There are currently 30,000 units, of which approximately 4,500 are types of predicates, and approximately 5,000 are collections.

### Collaborations

How are we to judge where we are going? How do we make sure that we don't go through these 10 years of labor and then find out in 1995 that we were fundamentally mistaken all along? We make sure by getting others to actually use our system.

In the past 18 months, as the Cyc representation language and ontology stabilized, we

*Microtheories are being developed in two major areas. . .
a set of common sense theories about everyday physical
phenomena . . and . . . a set of theories dealing with
aspects of agents . . .*

began to encourage collaborations with both academic researchers and industrial researchers and developers. We also held workshops and panel sessions. Finally, we once again (after a purposeful several-year hiatus to focus solely on research) began to write books and technical reports and articles, such as this one, to inform and interest our colleagues.

Cyc is still too small to have more than an anecdotal chance of improving the performance of the application programs using it, but the early results are promising. Cyc-based applications and research efforts are under way at Bellcore, Digital Equipment Corporation, NCR, US West, and Apple, and these efforts do not include the numerous Cyc-based research projects in academia. In the following paragraphs, we sketch a few of these efforts plus a few that are just beginning. Our purpose is to illustrate projects that are using the richness, scope, or size of the Cyc knowledge base.

At Digital, John McDermott, David Marques, Renata Bushko, and others have built a Cyc-based computer-sizing application. Serving as a preprocessing step for Xcon (Soloway, Bachant, and Jensen 1987), its job is to ask questions about a potential Digital customer and come up with a rough computer sizing (mainframes versus workstations, approximate number and size of file servers, and so on). The trouble with standard expert systems doing this task is that they ask too many questions, questions that can often be answered by common sense, questions that Cyc is able to guess answers for. (We don't mean that standard expert systems lack inferential abilities, just that they simply don't have the required commonsense knowledge from which to draw the inferences.)

For example, given that toy manufacturers have stringent government safety regulations and adult clothing manufacturers don't, which is more likely to be the proper match or precedent for a new potential customer who is a manufacturer of children's clothing? As another example, given that the basic business unit in a hotel is the room and at a car

rental agency is the car, use relatively deep understanding of what goes on at each place to decide that for a hospital, which is a new potential customer, the right business unit is Bed, not Room. These examples illustrate a reliance on the scope of the Cyc knowledge base. The next example illustrates a reliance on the richness and size of one particular part of the knowledge base, namely, the part dealing with predicates (and, in particular, slots.)

One speculative but fascinating line of research by Paul Cohen, Micheal Huhns, and others (Cohen and Loiselle 1988; Huhns and Stephens 1988) involves automatically guessing whether the composition of two unary functions (binary predicates, slots) s1 o s2 is equal to any known relation s3. The guess is made as follows: They assign +, -, and 0 values to 10 attributes of each predicate (such as hierarchical, composable, temporal, near, intrinsic). They then create a combination table for each of these attributes, which says, for example, "if s1 has a + value for its hierarchical attribute, and s2 has a - value, then s3 must have a + value." Given a particular s1 and s2, their values for the 10 attributes produce a set of 10 constraints on the values of these attributes for s3, which is used to constrain the search for s3's identity.

To the extent that this line of research succeeds, it teases apart the underlying deep structure of what it means to be a predicate. However, when or if the scheme fails, such failures should lead to the refining of the combination tables and assignments or, rarely, to the defining of a new primitive attribute for predicates. In any case, the point is that the research required a platform like Cyc: (1) The size of Cyc's slot space (4000+ known types of slots and other predicates) increases the chance that the resultant 10 vector matches some existing predicate. (2) The richness of slot space (categories and other interslot relationships) helps in the following way: For each particular slot $s_i$, most of the 10 primitive attributes' values for $s_i$ can be inherited or otherwise inferred rather than have to go through (in our current case)

We tell Cyc that Sam is a land animal and ask for types of body parts that Sam probably has:

    (assert '(#%allInstanceOf #%Sam #%LandAnimal))
    (ask '(#%hasPartTypes #%Sam x)) .

The question is addressed to the epistemological level. The tell-ask interface translates this question into an appropriate heuristic-level query. The heuristic level already contains an inheritance axiom that says the land animals have legs. The inheritance procedure runs and yields a simple argument that Sam has legs. Because there is no reason for invalidating this argument and because there isn't any argument for Sam not having legs, the Argument Comparison module asserts into the heuristic-level knowledge base that Sam has legs. In turn, this assertion produces a binding list for the free variable x in the formula that we Asked, above; namely,

    ((x . Legs)) .

Repeated calls to Ask can be made and will result in additional bindings for *x*. We now tell the systems that as a default, Reptiles don't have legs. The tell-ask interface translates this assertion into an inheritance axiom:

    (assert '(#%LogImplication (#%LogAnd (#%allInstanceOf x #%Reptile) (#%LogNot (#%abnormal x "reptile-with-leg")))
    (#%LogNot (#%hasPartTypes x #%Legs)))) .

We now tell Cyc that Sam is a snake, and (in case it didn't know already) that snakes are reptiles, and again ask the system if Sam has legs.

    (assert '(#%allGenls #%Snake #%Reptile))
    (assert '(#%allInstanceOf #%Sam #%Snake))
    (ask '(#%hasPartTypes #%Sam #%Legs)) .

Even though the system previously asserted that Sam had legs, the addition of the inheritance caused this conclusion to be marked as potentially stale. Thus, when we ask this query, the argument generator tries to search for an argument for the negation of the query and, sure enough, finds one. Now we have an argument for Sam having legs based on his being a land animal and an argument for Sam not having legs based on his being a reptile. The argument comparator chooses the more specific one and concludes (and asserts into the heuristic-level knowledge base) that Sam does not have legs.

*Figure 3. An Example of Interaction between the User, the Epistemological Level, the Tell-Ask Interface, and the Heuristic Level. The example is intentionally very simple and is meant to be clear rather than typical of the sophisticated inferencing that Cyc performs.*

40,000+ separate episodes of pondering and entering a +, -, or 0 entry.

One vital collaboration is that with Elaine Rich and Jim Barnett at MCC, namely, the natural language understanding project described in Barnett et al. (1990). Here, the Cyc knowledge base is stressed to its limits to disambiguate word senses, resolve anaphoric and omitted references, interpret the meaning of ellipses, and so on. Only so much can be done with syntactic analysis and discourse rules; the rest must be handed to Cyc, which creates various alternate hypothetical worlds and decides how (im)plausible each one is, for example, by seeing how metonymical the speaker would have to be in each possible world for no real-world constraints to be violated.

A number of theories in AI seem rather powerful—and might be—but have not been tested on many examples. Having a knowl-edge base with a wide scope (not just size) on which to test these theories would be useful. One example is the work of Devika Subramanian, now at Cornell University, who is testing her reformulation ideas in Cyc.

Other ongoing research collaborations include coupling with large engineering knowledge bases (with Ed Feigenbaum and Tom Gruber at Stanford University) and large databases (with Stuart Russell and Mike Stonebraker at University of California at Berkeley), standardizing knowledge interchange formats (with Mike Genesereth at Stanford), axiomatizing human emotions (with John McCarthy at Stanford), developing machine learning (with Wei-Min Shen and Mark Derthick at MCC), and using qualitative physics and analogy in children's stories (with Ken Forbus). We are also engaged in informal collaborations with Marvin Minsky, Pat Hayes, and others.

## Conclusion

What do we hope to get from our efforts? Where do we hope to be by the end of the 1990s? Here are three possible levels of success, in increasing order of optimism:

**Good:** Although not directly built on and widely used, the Cyc research might still provide some insights into issues involved in building large commonsense knowledge bases. Perhaps, it would give us an indication about whether the symbolic paradigm is flawed and, if so, how. It might also yield a rich repertoire of "how to represent it" heuristics and might at least motivate research issues in building future AI systems.

**Better:** Cyc forms the core of a knowledge base that can be used by the next generation of AI research programs to help make them more than theoretical exercises. No one doing research in symbolic AI in the early twenty-first century would want to be without a copy of Cyc, any more than today's researchers would want to be without Eval.

**Best:** Cyc's knowledge base serves as the foundation for the first true AI agent. It is something on which full-fledged natural language understanding systems, expert systems, and machine learning systems can be built. No one in 2015 would dream of buying a machine without common sense, any more than anyone today would buy a personal computer that couldn't run spreadsheets, word processing programs, communications software, and so on.

Numerous projects are under way in Japan and Great Britain and in this country at Carnegie-Mellon University, USC/Information Sciences Institute, Stanford, and elsewhere that appear similar to Cyc in some ways, but each of them has traded breadth and scope for an increased chance of success at this narrowed goal (for example, several of these projects have some form of limited machine translation as their goal).

Do we have a good chance of achieving our better goal? Because of our clipping of representation thorns and stabilizing of the representation language, inference engine suite, and high-level ontology, we believe the answer is "Yes." At the least, we now expect that the body of knowledge we accumulate in this decade will continue to exist, be used, and be extended for decades to come, with much of this accretion being done semiautomatically.

We now come to the final area we address in this article: the Cyc project's expected life expectancy and mode of demise. We expect to increasingly rely on knowledge-based natu-

> *. . . the role of humans would become much more like tutors . . .*

ral language understanding (KBNL) as the means of clarifying apparent contradictions and gaps in the knowledge base, and we expect to rely increasingly on knowledge-based machine learning (KBML) as the means of identifying these unexpected regularities and irregularities in the knowledge base. Both KBNL and KBML can gradually become more and more important ways of entering new knowledge into the knowledge base. These projects have already begun, but it's too early to look for signs of the ramp up. This particular corner is one we expect to turn in the middle part of this decade, with KBNL becoming the dominant mode of knowledge acquisition for Cyc and KBML becoming the dominant mode of policing the growing knowledge base. The role of human knowledge enterers today, manually entering assertion after assertion, is akin to teachers who must instruct by surgically manipulating brains. Turning the corner would mean that the role of humans would become much more like tutors, with a great deal of question answering going on in both directions. Much of the work in this coming decade will be driven by use as humans and application programs exercise Cyc and rely on it more and more as a substrate for intelligent behavior.

## Acknowledgments

We would like to thank Mary Shepherd for her patience and help since the inception of the Cyc project. We also want to thank Mark Derthick, Karen Pittman, Dexter Pratt, David Wallace, Nick Siegel, Wanda Pratt, John Huffman, and the other members of the Cyc group, past and present, for their help in building and testing the system. We also thank Ed Feigenbaum, Pat Hayes, John McCarthy, John McDermott, Marvin Minsky, and Stuart Russell, who have in almost orthogonal ways helped us to think more clearly about the material presented herein. We also thank John McCarthy, Charles Petrie, and Russ Greiner for reading earlier drafts of this article and giving us numerous useful comments.

# References

Allen, J. 1986. Maintaining Knowledge about Temporal Intervals. In *Readings in Knowledge Representation*, eds. H. Levesque and R. Brachman, 509–523. San Mateo, Calif.: Morgan Kaufmann.

Barnett, J.; Knight, K.; Mani, I.; and Rich, E. 1990. Knowledge and Natural Language Processing, Technical Report ACT-NL-104-90, MCC Corp., Austin, Tex.

Brachman, R. J.; Fikes, R. E.; and Levesque, H. J. 1986. Krypton: A Functional Approach to Knowledge Representation. In *Readings in Knowledge Representation*, eds. H. Levesque and R. Brachman, 411–431. San Mateo, Calif.: Morgan Kaufmann.

Cohen, P. R., and Loiselle, C. L. 1988. Beyond isa: Structures for Plausible Inference in Semantic Networks. In Proceedings of the Seventh National Conference on Artificial Intelligence. Menlo Park, Calif.: American Association for Artificial Intelligence.

Corbell, J. C. 1987. *The Visual Dictionary.* New York: Facts on File.

Derthick, M. 1990. An Epistemological Level Interface for Cyc, Technical Report ACT-CYC-084-90, MCC Corp., Austin, Tex.

Doyle, J. 1987. A Truth Maintenance System. In *Readings In Nonmonotonic Reasoning*, ed. M. Ginsberg, 259–279. San Mateo, Calif.: Morgan Kaufmann.

Ginsberg, M. 1987. Multivalued Logics. In *Readings in Nonmonotonic Reasoning*, ed. M. Ginsberg, 251–256. San Mateo, Calif.: Morgan Kaufmann.

Guha, R. V. 1990a. Contexts in Cyc, Technical Report ACT-CYC-129-90, MCC Corp., Austin, Tex.

Guha, R. V. 1990b. The Representation of Defaults in Cyc, Technical Report ACT-CYC-083-90, MCC Corp., Austin, Tex.

Guha, R. V., and Lenat, D. B. 1989a. Cycl: The Cyc Representation Language, Part 3, Technical Report ACT-CYC-454-89, MCC Corp., Austin, Tex.

Guha, R. V., and Lenat, D. B. 1989b. The World according to Cyc, Part 2: Agents and Institutions, Technical Report ACT-CYC-453-89, MCC Corp., Austin, Tex.

Guha, R. V., and Levy, A. 1990. A Relevance-Based Meta Level, Technical Report ACT-CYC-040-90, MCC Corp., Austin, Tex.

Hayes, P. J. 1985. Naive Physics 1: Ontology for Fiquids. In *Formal Theories of the Common Sense World* (chapter 3), eds. J. R. Hobbs and R. C. Moore. Norwood, N.J.: Ablex.

Huhns, M., and Stephens, L. 1988. Extended Composition of Relations, Technical Report ACA-AI-376-88, MCC Corp., Austin, Tex.

Lenat, D. B., and Guha, R. V. 1990. *Building Large Knowledge-Based Systems.* Reading, Mass.: Addison-Wesley.

Lenat, D. B.; Prakash, M.; and Shepherd, M. 1986. Cyc: Using Common Sense Knowledge to Overcome Brittleness and Knowledge-Acquisition Bottlenecks. *AI Magazine* 6:65–85.

Lenat, D. B.; Guha, R. V.; Pittman, K.; Pratt, D.; and Shepherd, M. 1990. Cyc: Toward Programs with Common Sense. *Communications of the ACM* 33(8).

Lifschitz, V. 1987. Formal Theories of Action. In *Readings in Nonmonotonic Reasoning*, ed. M. Ginsberg, 410–432. San Mateo, Calif.: Morgan Kaufmann.

McCarthy, J. 1987a. Applications of Circumscription to Formalizing Common Sense Knowledge. In *Readings in Nonmonotonic Reasoning*, ed. M. Ginsberg, 153–166. San Mateo, Calif.: Morgan Kaufmann.

McCarthy, J. 1987b. Generality in Artificial Intelligence. *Communications of the ACM* 30(12): 1030–1035.

McCarthy, J. 1986a. Epistemological Problems of Artificial Intelligence. In *Readings in Knowledge Representation*, eds. H. Levesque and R. Brachman, 23–31. San Mateo, Calif.: Morgan Kaufmann.

McCarthy, J. 1986b. First-Order Theories of Individual Concepts and Propositions. In *Readings in Knowledge Representation*, eds. H. Levesque and R. Brachman, 523–531. San Mateo, Calif.: Morgan Kaufmann.

McCarthy, J., and Hayes, P. J. 1987. Some Philosophical Problems from the Standpoint of AI. In *Readings in Nonmonotonic Reasoning*, ed. M. Ginsberg, 26–45. San Mateo, Calif.: Morgan Kaufmann.

Moore, R. C. 1986. The Role of Logic in Knowledge Representation and Commonsense Reasoning. In *Readings in Knowledge Representation*, eds. H. Levesque and R. Brachman, 335–343. San Mateo, Calif.: Morgan Kaufmann.

Pratt, D., and Guha, R. V. 1990. A Functional Interface for Cyc, Technical Report ACT-CYC-089-90, MCC Corp., Austin, Tex.

Quine, W. V. 1969. Natural Kinds. In *Ontological Relativity and Other Essays* (chapter 5). New York: Columbia University Press.

Soloway, E.; Bachant, J.; and Jensen, K. 1987. Assessing the Maintainability of Xcon-in-Rime: Coping with the Problem of a Very Large Rule Base. In Proceedings of the Sixth National Conference on Artificial Intelligence, 9824–9829. Menlo Park, Calif.: American Association for Artificial Intelligence.

Touretsky, D. S. 1987. Implicit Ordering of Defaults in Inheritance Systems. In *Readings in Nonmonotonic Reasoning*, ed. M. Ginsberg, 106–109. San Mateo, Calif.: Morgan Kaufmann.

Warren, D. H. D. 1983. An Abstract Prolog Instruction Set, Technical Report 309, SRI, Artificial Intelligence Center, Computer Science and Technology Center, Menlo Park, Calif.

Weyhrauch, R. W. 1986. Prolegmena to a Theory of Mechanized Formal Reasoning. In *Readings in Knowledge Representation*, eds. H. Levesque and R. Brachman, 309–329. San Mateo, Calif.: Morgan Kaufmann.

## Notes

1. A shortened version of portions of this paper appeared in *Communications of the ACM,* Vol. 33, No. 8, Copyright 1990, Association for Computing Machinery, Inc. By permission.

2. All the material presented on the language and the ontology has been implemented and is in use in the Cyc system unless otherwise mentioned. In a number of places in this article, we have omitted the axioms and other details. They have been worked out and in most cases are available in one of the references or can be obtained from the authors.

3. Because it includes facilities to form the set of objects $x$ satisfying a given property $P(x)$, our language is closer to Zermelo-Frankel (ZF) than to first-order predicate calculus (FOPC).

4. The isa predicate corresponds to the set-membership relation; it is sometimes called ISA, is-a, AKO, element-of, and so on. In Cyc's knowledge base, we happen to call it *instanceOf.* Also, the $ab_i$ predicates are short for *abnormal in fashion i;* so $ab_i$ corresponds to being an exception in the sense of being a bird and not being able to fly. One Cyc axiom says that birds with broken wings are abnormal in sense $ab_i$ .

5. $ist(x,y)$ means $x$ is true in theory $y$. Moreover, although supported, falls, and so on, are fluent valued functions, in this article, we often refer to them as predicates; the intended meaning should always be clear from the context.

6. Although in most cases, we use the term ontology in the sense of the objects that can be quantified over, we occasionally use it in a looser sense of the organization and structure of the knowledge base or even the predicates and objects in the epistemological-level language.

7. The same predicate can appear with different arities and argument types in different microtheories.

8. We used to, but they were never much use. Collections of collections, however, such as PersonType, SubstanceType, and EventType, have proven vital They are analogous to object-oriented systems' metaclasses.

9. The subabstraction formalism is superficially similar to the histories framework (Hayes 1985). However, there is no relation between the intersection of these histories and the frame problem (McCarthy and Hayes 1987).

10. The interval-based abstraction was developed independently of Allen (1986).

11. There are, of course, exceptions. For example, FredIn (1972) might like EthelIn (1958) more than EthelIn (1972).

12. This use of the term agent is unrelated to the linguists' usage, as in "'Kettle' is the agent in 'The kettle whistled'."

13. Rather than go through a lengthy presentation of some of the ways in which the Cyc ontology has changed over time, we refer the reader to the previous section, The Current State of Cyc's Ontology, wherein the nature and salient aspects of our fairly adequate solutions should become apparent.

14. Unless otherwise noted, each of them is fully implemented and in routine daily use.

---

**R. V. Guha** is the co-leader of the Cyc project and a Ph.D. student at Stanford University.

---

**Douglas Lenat** is principal scientist at Microelectronics and Computer Technology Corporation (MCC). He was a professor in the Computer Science Departments at Carnegie-Mellon University and Stanford University prior to his move to MCC and remains a consulting professor and industrial lecturer at Stanford today. His Ph.D. thesis (Stanford, 1976) was a demonstration that certain kinds of creative discoveries in mathematics could be produced by a computer program. This work earned him the biannual International Joint Conference on Artificial Intelligence, Inc., biannual Computers and Thought award in 1977. He was also named one of America's brightest scientists under the age of 40 by *Science Digest* in December 1984. Lenat has authored and coauthored more than 50 published papers and has written and edited several books, including *Knowledge-Based Systems in Artificial Intelligence; Building Expert Systems;* and, most recently, *Building Large Knowledge-Based Systems: Representation and Inference in the Cyc Project.* He is an editor for *IEEE Transactions on Knowledge and Data Engineering* and the *Machine Learning Journal* and was a cofounder of Teknowledge, Inc. His main research interest is in getting machines to discover new knowledge, an interest that has led him to work on a large commonsense knowledge base.

# Appendix A

# Use of the Book in a Course

## 1. Introduction

This book has been used in courses that focused on machine learning, knowledge acquisition, and knowledge-based systems. This section provides information on how the book was used in these courses.

## 2. Machine Learning

The goal of machine learning is to create computational models that allow automatic improvement of artificial intelligence programs, and to create a theoretical framework for understanding and comparing computational learning mechanisms.

There is a great advantage to introducing one of the major empirical application goals of artificial intelligence in a learning course, as it gives students a better appreciation of the nature of the difficulties faced by machine learning. The course outlined below uses knowledge-based expert systems as the empirical application area, but other major applications, such as automatic programming, natural language understanding, robotics, vision, and commonsense reasoning, are also appropriate. The advantage that knowledge-based expert systems has over these other areas is that it gives students insight into how to make learning

programs themselves more knowledge intensive.

In the course outline below, a week can be spent on each item in the outline. The number in parentheses shows the sections of the book that correspond to each item, and two or three articles can be comfortably covered in a week. When this book is used as a text at Illinois, we supplement this book with two articles on computational learning theory (Valiant, 1984; Haussler, 1988).

- Overview of Learning and KA (1.1)
- Nature of Expertise (2.1)
- Nature of Expert Systems (2.2)
- Interactive Elicitation Tools (3.1 and 3.2)
- Induction and Connectionism (4.1)
- Evaluating Inductive Methods (4.3)
- Speed-Up Learning (5.1)
- Explanation-Based Learning (5.2)
- Apprenticeship Learning (6.1 and 6.2)
- Case-Based Reasoning (7.2)
- Analogical Learning (7.1)
- Discovery Systems (8.1 and 8.2)

## 3. Knowledge Acquisition

A course on knowledge acquisition focuses on the range of tools and techniques that have been shown to be effective in creating knowledge-based systems. A course project using an expert system shell is essential in such a course. At Illinois, we use a PROLOG-based shell called MINERVA.

The outline below is for a course that focuses on Knowledge Acquisition. A week is spent on each item in the list. The sections of this book that are covered are shown in parentheses, and two or three articles can be comfortably covered in a week.

- Overview of Learning and KA (1.1)
- Nature of Expertise (2.1)
- Nature of Expert Systems (2.2)
- Classification Elicitation Tools (3.1)
- Design Elicitation Tools (3.2)
- Induction from Examples (4.1)
- Evaluating Learning Performance (4.3)
- Explanation Based Learning (5.2)
- Synthesis from Deep Models (5.3)
- Classification Apprentice Systems (6.1)
- Design Apprentice Systems (6.2)
- Case-Based Reasoning (7.2)

## 4. Term Paper Topics

This section provides examples of term paper topics. There are two primary objectives behind these paper topics. The first objective is for the student to think about how to make AI programs, including learning programs, more knowledge-intensive. The second objective is to give an appreciation of the effect of an AI program's organization, representation, and inference method on the learning problem.

### 4.1 Learning Projects and AI Subfields

**Automatic Programming.** Expert systems have shown how domain-specific knowledge can be used for problem-solving. Many believe that the limitations of current automatic programming systems are largely due to their lack of detailed knowledge of the domain (Barstow, 1985). What types of knowledge are needed? How might they be used? Can machine learning be of assistance in acquiring the needed domain knowledge? Describe the similarities and differences between learning from examples and automatic programming from examples.

**Knowledge-Based Natural Language.** We expect the size of the knowledge base needed to support natural language understanding to be several orders of magnitude larger than that needed to support an expert system. Survey the literature to locate those projects that are taking a knowledge-intensive approach to natural language. Are the learning techniques described in this book suitable to these systems, given the source constraints (nature of the input to the learning program) and the target constraints (representation and inference method of the natural language system)?

**Knowledge-Based Tutoring.** There appears to be a deep symmetry between learning and teaching in an expert domain. The learning problem, when learning from examples, is to watch a human expert and find errors in the knowledge base. The tutoring problem is to watch the student solve problems and detect when the student uses knowledge that is not in the expert system knowledge base. Discuss the similarities and differences between learning and tutoring in an expert system domain. Discuss the various ways that a knowledge-based system can serve as the basis for a tutoring program to teach the domain knowledge.

**Expert Reasoning Versus Commonsense Reasoning.** Commonsense reasoning appears to require orders of magnitude more domain-specific knowledge than expert reasoning. Probably because of this, we have little experience with creating computer programs that can demonstrate competent commonsense reasoning. What are the similarities and differences between commonsense and expert reasoning? How applicable are the techniques developed from expert systems to commonsense reasoning problems? Discuss the difference between making a learning program more capable by giving it access to commonsense knowledge and making a learning program that can learn commonsense knowledge.

**Knowledge-Based Learning.** The goal of learning for expert systems is to acquire domain knowledge to aid in problem solving. Since learning is just another type of problem-solving, perhaps domain knowledge might be of help to a learning program itself. Explore the various ways that this might be the case. How might it help in global and local credit assignment when learning from examples?

**Qualitative Reasoning.** The papers of McDermott and Chandrasekaran in Section 2.1 of this book describe a spectrum of generic problem classes. Does qualitative reasoning fit within any of these classes? Can a generic shell be created for the task of qualitative reasoning? What are the differences in representation and inference techniques needed for expert reasoning and commonsense reasoning?

## 4.2 Learning Projects and Computer Science

**Parallel Programming and Learning.** Restrictions on the programming constructs (e.g., recursion) and architecture (e.g., use of a meta-level representation for control knowledge) of a generic expert system shell have an enormous effect on the ability to accomplish global and local credit assignment in an apprenticeship learning setting. Certain restrictions on parallel programming languages (such as Shapiro's Flat PROLOG) greatly facilitate decomposition of a program into subelements that can be executed in parallel. Can the restrictions that have been made for parallel programming make the problem of debugging the knowledge structures of an expert system shell any easier?

**Software Engineering.** Three subfields of computer science appear to share very similar goals: Machine learning is concerned with automating the construction of knowledge-based programs. Automatic programming is concerned with automating the construction of computer programs. Software engineering is concerned with automating the construction of software systems. Discuss the similarities and differences between the objectives of these three fields. What similarities and differences might we expect between the solution methods that will be found someday for these three problems?

**Automatic Programming from Examples.** Do the types of problems that automatic programming research has previously attempted to automate fall into generic problem classes? If so, what are these classes? Construct the meta-level control knowledge needed for one of these classes, and demonstrate that this simplifies the automatic programming task for a particular problem that has been previously investigated in the literature. What types of domain theories underlie the domain knowledge that needs to be acquired? Does the vocabulary of the generic shell provide a way of connecting the knowledge that needs to be acquired with the underlying domain theories?

## 4.3 Learning Projects and Knowledge Representation

**Expert Systems and Uncertainty Reasoning.** Expert reasoning often requires making decisions before there is complete information. Does a knowledge representation that uses an uncertainty calculus simplify or complicate global and local credit assignment? Discuss the strengths and weaknesses of various approaches to reasoning under uncertainty such as MYCIN certainty factors and belief networks. What is the impact on learning of the different approaches?

**Blackboard Architectures for Control.** What are the advantages of a blackboard architecture over a typical rule-based system? For what problems are blackboards especially well suited? Describe how blackboard models allow the control of reasoning to be explicitly represented and reasoned about. What are the implications of a blackboard architecture for learning?

**Prolog-Metainterpreters for Expert Systems.** Logic programming languages in general, and the use of metainterpreters in particular, provide a powerful framework for knowledge-based expert systems. Describe some of the capabilities that a metainterpreter can provide.

**Meta-Level Representations.** How do meta-level representation decisions affect learnability, such as global and local credit assignment? Can the approach that appears to work successfully for heuristic classification problems be extended to other generic problem classes such as design and interpretation problems? Can the use of meta-level control knowledge for a generic problem class be applied to automatic programming and commonsense reasoning?

**Expert Systems and SOAR.** SOAR is a unified architecture for general cognition. It was originally designed with the CMU suite of "toy problems" primarily in mind. What are the strengths and weaknesses of the SOAR architecture in a knowledge-intensive domain?

## 5. Term Programming Projects

The courses that used this book had one large programming project during the term, written in PROLOG. The projects consisted of creating an expert system shell or modifying an existing expert system shell, and programming a learning method that worked in conjunction with the expert system. We used the MINERVA shell for several inductive and explanation-based learning projects (Park et al., 1989).

# Appendix B

# Guide to the Literature

This appendix provides a selected list of approximately ninety books in the area of knowledge-based systems and learning. The list is organized using the chapter and subsection structure of this book. There is also an additional special topics section.

In addition to these books, the following journals have articles on knowledge-based systems and learning: *Artificial Intelligence, Machine Learning, International Journal of Knowledge Acquisition, International Journal of Expert Systems, International Journal of Man-Machine Studies.* Journals that focus on applications of techniques include *AI Expert* and *IEEE Expert*.

## Chapter 1: Overview of Knowledge Acquisition and Learning

### General Knowledge Acquisition

Scott, A. C., Clayton, J. E. and Gibson, E., *A Practical Guide to Knowledge Acquisition*, Addison-Wesley, 1991.

Gaines, B. R. and Boose, J. H., *Knowledge Acquisition for Knowledge-Based Systems*, Academic Press, 1988.

Boose, J. H. and Gaines, B. R., *Knowledge Acquisition Tools for Expert Systems*, Academic Press, 1988.

Boose, J. H. and Gaines, B. R., *The Foundations of Knowledge Acquisition*, Academic Press, 1990.

## General Machine Learning

Shavlik, J. W. and Dietterich, T. G., (eds.), *Readings in Machine Learning*, Morgan Kaufmann, 1990.

Cohen, P. R. and Feigenbaum, E. A., (eds.), *Handbook of Artificial Intelligence*, William Kaufmann, Volume III, 1982.

Kodratoff, Y., *Introduction to Machine Learning*, Morgan Kaufmann, 1988.

Kodratoff, Y. and Michalski, R., *Machine Learning: An Artificial Intelligence Approach*, Volume III, Morgan Kaufmann, 1990.

Michalski, R. S., Carbonell, J. G. and Mitchell, T. M., (eds.), *Machine Learning: An Artificial Intelligence Approach*, Volume II, Morgan Kaufmann, 1986.

Michalski, R. S., Carbonell, J. G. and Mitchell, T. M., (eds.), *Machine Learning: An Artificial Intelligence Approach*, Volume I, Tioga Press, 1983.

# Chapter 2: Expertise and Expert Systems

## Expertise and Its Acquisition

Anderson, J., *Cognitive Psychology and its Implications*, W. H. Freeman, 1947.

Chi, M. T. H., Glaser, R. and Farr, M., (eds.), *Contributions to the Nature of Expertise*, Lawrence Erlbaum Press, 1987.

Gentner, D. and Stevens, A. L., (eds.), *Mental Models*, Hillsdale, Lawrence Erlbaum Associates, 1983.

Ericsson, K. A. and Simon, H. A., *Protocol Analysis: Verbal Reports as Data*, MIT Press, 1984.

## Expert Systems and Generic Problem Classes: General

Buchanan, B. G. and Shortliffe, E. H., *Rule-Based Expert Systems: The MYCIN Experiments of the Stanford Heuristic Programming Project*, Addison-Wesley, 1984.

Waterman, D., *A Guide to Expert Systems*, Addison-Wesley, 1988.

Engelmore, R. and Morgan, T., *Blackboard Systems*, Addison-Wesley, 1988.

Hayes-Roth, F., Waterman, D. A. and Lenat, D. B., *Building Expert Systems*, Addison-Wesley, 1983.

## Expert Systems and Generic Problem Classes: Logic Programming

Walker, A., McCord, M., Sowa, J. and Wilson, W., *Knowledge Systems and Prolog*, Addison-Wesley, 1987.

Ullman, J. D., *Database and Knowledge-Base Systems*, Computer Science Press, 1988.

Jackson, P., Reichgelt, H. and Van Harmelen, F., *Logic-Based Knowledge Representation*, MIT Press, 1989.

Sterling, L. and Shapiro, E., *The Art of Prolog*, MIT Press, 1986.

Rowe, N. C., *Artificial Intelligence Through Prolog*, Prentice Hall, 1988.

## Expert Systems and Generic Problem Classes: Uncertainty Reasoning

Shafer, G. and Pearl, J., (eds.), *Readings in Uncertainty Reasoning*, Morgan Kaufmann, 1990.

Kruse, R., Schwecke, E. and Heinsohn, J., *Uncertainty and Vagueness in Knowledge Based Systems*, Springer-Verlag, 1991.

Pearl, J., *Probabilistic Reasoning in Intelligent Systems: Networks of Plausible Inference*, Morgan Kaufmann, 1988.

Heckerman, D., *Probabilistic Similarity Networks*, MIT Press, 1991.

Kanal, L. and Lemmar, J., *Uncertainty in Artificial Intelligence*, North Holland, 1986.

Klir, G. J. and Folger, T. A., *Fuzzy Sets, Uncertainty, and Information*, Prentice Hall, 1988.

# Chapter 3: Interactive Elicitation Tools

## Eliciting Classification Knowledge

Bareiss, R., *Exemplar-Based Knowledge Acquisition*, Academic Press, 1989.

Boose, J. H., *Expertise Transfer for Expert System Design*, Elsevier, 1986.

## Eliciting Design Knowledge

Marcus, S., (ed.), *Automating Knowledge Acquisition for Expert Systems*, Kluwer Academic, 1988.

Musen, M. A., *Automated Generation of Model-Based Knowledge Acquisition*, Pitman, 1990.

Gruber, T. R., *The Acquisition of Strategic Knowledge*, Academic Press, 1989.

# Chapter 4: Inductive Generalization Methods

## Learning Classification Knowledge: Symbolic Approach

Weiss, S. M. and Kulikowski, C. A., *Computer Systems that Learn: Classification and Prediction Methods from Statistics, Neural Nets, Machine Learning and Expert Systems*, Morgan Kaufmann, 1990.

Quinlan, *C4.5: Programs for Machine Learning*, Morgan Kaufmann, 1993.

Breiman, L., Friedman, J., Olshen, R. and Stone, C. *Classification and Regression Trees.* Wadsworth Press, 1984.

Ginsberg, A., *Automatic Refinement of Expert System Knowledge Bases*, Morgan Kaufmann, 1988.

Utgoff, P. E., *Machine Learning of Inductive Bias*, Kluwer Academic Publishers, 1986.

### Learning Classification Knowledge: Neural Approach

Freeman, J. A., *Neural Networks*, Addison-Wesley, 1991.

Rumelhart, D. E. and McClelland, J. L., (eds.), *Parallel Distributed Processing: Explorations in the Microarchitecture of Cognition*, volume I, MIT Press, 1986.

Rumelhart, D. E. and McClelland, J. L., (eds.), *Parallel Distributed Processing: Psychological and Biological Models*, volume II, MIT Press, 1986.

### Learning Classes Via Clustering

Fisher, D., Pazzani, M. and Langley, P., (eds.), *Concept Formation: Knowledge and Experience in Unsupervised Learning*, Morgan Kaufmann, 1991.

### Measurement and Evaluation of Learning Systems

Weiss, S. M. and Kulikowski, C. A., *Computer Systems that Learn: Classification and Prediction Methods from Statistics, Neural Nets, Machine Learning and Expert Systems*, Morgan Kaufmann, 1990.

Anthony, M. and Biggs, N., *Computational Learning Theory*, Cambridge University Press, 1992.

Natarajan, B. K., *Machine Learning, A Theoretical Approach*, Morgan Kaufmann, 1991.

James, M., *Classification Algorithms*, William Collins and Sons, 1985.

# Chapter 5: Compilation and Deep Models

### Compilation of Knowledge for Efficiency

Minton, S., *Learning Search Control Knowledge*, Kluwer Academic, 1988.

Laird, J., Rosenbloom, P. and Newell, A., *Universal Subgoaling and Chunking: The Automatic Generation and Learning of Goal Hierarchies*, Kluwer Academic, 1986.

### Explanation-Based Learning

DeJong, G., (ed.), *Explanation Generalization in EGGS*, Kluwer Academic, 1992.

Shavlik, J., *Extending Explanation-Based Learning by Generalizing the Structure of Explanations*, Morgan Kaufmann, 1990.

### Synthesizing Problem Solvers from Deep Models

Bratko, I., Mozetic, I. and Pereira, L., *KARDIO: A Study in Deep and Qualitative Knowledge for Expert Systems*, MIT Press, 1989.

# Chapter 6: Apprenticeship Learning Systems

## Apprentice Systems for Classification Knowledge

Wilkins, D. C., *Automated Knowledge Acquisition: The Odysseus Apprenticeship Learning Program*, book manuscript.

## Apprentice Systems for Design Knowledge

Segre, A. M., *Machine Learning of Robot Assembly Plans*, Kluwer Academic, 1988.

# Chapter 7: Analogical and Case-based Reasoning

## Analogical Reasoning

Owens, S., *Analogy of Automated Reasoning*, Academic Press, 1990.

Russell, S. J., *The Use of Knowledge in Analogy and Induction*, Morgan Kaufmann, 1989.

Vosniadou, S. and Ortony, A., *Similarity and Analogical Reasoning*, Cambridge University Press, 1989.

Prieditis, A., *Analogical*, Pitman, 1988.

Helman, D. H., *Analogical Reasoning*, Kluwer Academic, 1988.

## Case-Based Reasoning

Kolodner, J. L., *Case-Based Reasoning*, Morgan Kaufmann, 1992.

Hammond, K. J., *Cased-Based Planning: Viewing Planning as a Memory Task*, Academic Press, 1989.

Ashley, K. D., *Modeling Legal Argument: Reasoning with Cases and with Hypotheticals*, MIT Press, 1990.

Bareiss, R., *Exemplar-Based Knowledge Acquisition*, Academic Press, 1989.

# Chapter 8: Discovery and Commonsense Knowledge

## Discovery Systems

Shrager, J. and Langley, P., (eds.), *Computational Models of Scientific Discovery and Theory Formation*, Morgan Kaufmann, 1990.

Piatetsky-Shapiro, G. and Frawley, W. J., (eds.), *Knowledge Discovery in Databases*, MIT Press, 1991.

Davis, R. and Lenat, D., *Knowledge-Based Systems in Artificial Intelligence*, McGraw-Hill, 1982.

Langley, P., Simon, H. A., Bradshaw, G. L. and Zytkow, J. M., *Scientific Discovery*, MIT Press, 1987.

### Genetic Algorithms

Goldberg, D. E., *Genetic Algorithms in Search, Optimization, and Machine Learning*, Addison-Wesley, 1989.

Davis, L., *Handbook of Genetic Algorithms*, Van Nostrand Reinhold, 1991.

### Commonsense Knowledge

Lenat, D. and Guha, R., *Building Large Knowledge-Based Systems*, Addison-Wesley, 1990.

Davis, E., *Representations of Commonsense Knowledge*, Morgan Kaufmann, 1990.

Hobbs, J. R. and Moore, R. C., (eds.), *Formal Theories of the Commonsense World*, Ablex Publishing, 1985.

# Other Relevant Topics

## Learning and Tutoring

Clancey, W. J., *Knowledge Based Tutoring: The GUIDON Program*, MIT Press, 1987.

Murray, W. R., *Automatic Program Debugging for Intelligent Tutoring Systems*, Morgan Kaufmann, 1988.

Wenger, E., *Artificial Intelligence and Tutoring Systems*, Morgan Kaufmann, 1987.

Johnson, W. L., *Intention-based Diagnosis of Novice Programming Errors*, Morgan Kaufmann, 1986.

Sleeman, D. H. and Brown, J. S., (eds.), *Intelligent Tutoring Systems*, Academic Press, 1981.

## Learning and Automatic Programming

Lowry, M. and McCartney, R., (eds.), *Automating Software Design*, MIT Press, 1991.

Rich, C. and Waters, R., (eds.), *Readings in Artificial Intelligence and Software Engineering*, Morgan Kaufmann, 1986.

Barstow, D. R., *Knowledge-Based Program Construction*, Elsevier, 1979.

Shapiro, E., *Algorithmic Program Debugging*, MIT Press, 1983.

## Learning and Natural Language

Berwick, R. C., *The Acquisition of Syntactic Knowledge*, MIT Press, 1985.

Pinker, S., *Language Learnability and Language Development*, Harvard, 1984.

Zernik, U., (ed.), *Lexical Acquisition: Exploiting On-Line Resources to Build a Lexicon*, Lawrence Erlbaum Associates, 1991.

Dyer, M. G., *In-Depth Understanding*, MIT Press, 1973.

## General Artificial Intelligence

Charniak, E. and McDermott, D., *Introduction to Artificial Intelligence*, Addison-Wesley, 1985.

Rich, E. and Knight, K., *Artificial Intelligence*, 2nd edition, McGraw-Hill, 1991.

Genesereth, M. and Nilsson, N., *Fundamentals of Artificial Intelligence*, Morgan Kaufmann, 1987.

Luger, G. F. and Stubblefield, W. A., *Artificial Intelligence and the Design of Expert Systems*, Benjamin-Cummings, 1989.

# Appendix C

# Addendum to Chapter 2

**References for Paper 2.1.1, Development of expertise, by J.R. Anderson:**

Anderson, J.R. (ed.) (1981). *Cognitive skills and their acquisition.* Hillsdale, NJ: Erlbaum.

Anderson, J.R. (1982). Acquisition of cognitive skill. *Psychological Review*, 89, 369-406.

Anderson, J.R. (1983). *The architecture of cognition.* Cambridge, MA: Harvard University Press.

Anderson, J.R., Boyle, C.F., Farrell, R., and Reiser, B. (1984). Cognitive principles in the design of computer tutors. *Proceedings of the Cognitive Science Program*, 2-11.

Anderson, J.R., Farrell, R., and Sauers, R. (1984). Learning to program in LISP. *Cognitive Science*, 8, 87-129.

Angell, J.R. (1908). The doctrine of formal discipline in the light of the principles of general psychology. *Educational Review*, 36, 1-14.

Bilodeau, I. McD. (1969). Information feedback. In E.A. Bilodeau (ed.), *Principles of skill acquisition.* New York: Academic Press.

Blackburn, J.M. (1936). Acquisition of skill: An analysis of learning curves. IHRB Report No. 73.

Bloom, B.S. (1984). The 2 sigma problem: The search for methods of group instruction as effective as one-to-one tutoring. *Educational Researcher*, 13, 3-16.

Boring, E.G. (1950). *A history of experimental psychology.* New York: Appleton Century.

Bray, C.W. (1948). *Psychology and military proficiency.* Princeton: Princeton University Press.

Card, S.K., Moran, T.P., and Newell, A. (1983). *The psychology of human-computer interaction.* Hillsdale, NJ: Erlbaum.

Carpenter, T.P., and Moser, J.M. (1982). The development of addition and subtraction problem-solving skills. In T.P. Carpenter, J.M. Moser, and T. Romberg (eds.), *Addition and subtraction: A cognitive perspective.* Hillsdale, NJ: Erlbaum.

Carraher, T.N., Carraher, D.W., and Schliemann, A.D. (1985). Mathematics in the streets and in the schools. *British Journal of Developmental Psychology*, 3, 21-29.

Charness, N. (1976). Memory for chess positions: Resistance to interference. *Journal of Experimental Psychology: Human Learning and Memory*, 2, 641-653.

Charness, N. (1979). Components of skill in bridge. *Canadian Journal of Psychology*, 33, 1-16.

Chase, W.G., and Ericsson, K.A. (1982). Skill and working memory. In G.H. Bower (ed.), *The psychology of learning and motivation*, Vol. 16. New York: Academic Press.

Chase, W.G., and Simon, H.A. (1973). The mind's eye in chess. In W.G. Chase (ed.), *Visual information processing*. New York: Academic Press.

Chi, M.T.H., Feltovich, P.J., and Glaser, R. (1981). Categorization and representation of physics problems by experts and novices. *Cognitive Science*, 5, 121-152.

Chi, M.T.H., Glaser, R., and Farr, M. (eds.) (1988). *The nature of expertise*. Hillsdale, NJ: Erlbaum.

Crossman, E.R.F.W. (1959). A theory of the acquisition of speed-skill. *Ergonomics*, 2, 153-166.

de Groot, A.D. (1965). *Thought and choice in chess*. The Hague: Mouton.

de Groot, A. D. (1966). Perception and memory versus thought. In B. Kleinmuntz (ed.), *Problem-solving*. New York: Wiley.

Egan, D.E., and Schwartz, B.J. (1979). Chunking in recall of symbolic drawings. *Memory and Cognition*, 7, 149-158.

Engle, R.W., and Bukstel, L. (1978). Memory processes among bridge players of differing expertise. *American Journal of Psychology*, 91, 673-689.

Fitts, O.M. and Posner, M.I. (1967). *Human performance*. Belmont, CA: Brooks Cole.

Gagne, R.M. (1973). Learning and instruction sequence. *Review of Research in Education*, 1, 3-33.

Gay, I.R. (1973). Temporal position of reviews and its effect on the retention of mathematical rules. *Journal of Educational Psychology*, 64, 171-182.

Greeno, J.G. (1974). Hobbits and orcs: Acquisition of a sequential concept. *Cognitive Psychology*, 6, 270-292.

Hayes, J.R. (1985). Three problems in teaching general skills. In J. Segal, S. Chipman, and R. Glaser (eds.), *Thinking and learning*, Vol. 2. Hillsdale, NJ: Erlbaum.

Jeffries, R.P., Turner, A.A., Polson, P.G., and Atwood, M.E. (1981). The processes involved in designing software. In J.R. Anderson (ed.), *Cognitive skills and their acquisition*. Hillsdale, NJ: Erlbaum.

Kelso, J.A.S. (ed.) (1982). *Human motor behavior: An introduction*. Hillsdale, NJ: Erlbaum.

Klatzky, R.L. (1979). *Human memory*. New York: W.H. Freeman and Company.

Koch, H.L. (1923). A neglected phase of a part/whole problem. *Journal of Experimental Psychology*, 6, 366-376.

Kolers, P.A. (1976). Reading a year later. *Journal of Experimental Psychology: Human Learning and Memory*, 2, 554-565.

Kolers, P.A. (1979). A pattern analyzing basis of recognition. In L. S. Cermak and F.I.M. Craik (eds.), *Levels of processing in human memory*. Hillsdale, NJ: Erlbaum.

Kolers, P.A., and Perkins, P.N. (1975). Spatial and ordinal components of form perception and literacy. *Cognitive Psychology*, 7, 228-267.

Larkin, J. (1981). Enriching formal knowledge: A model for learning to solve textbook physics problems. In J.R. Anderson (ed.), *Cognitive skills and their acquisition*. Hillsdale, NJ: Erlbaum.

Larkin, J.H., McDermott, J., Simon, D.P., and Simon, H.A. (1980). Expert and novice performance in solving physics problems. *Science*, 208, 1335-1342.

Lesgold, A.M. (1984). Acquiring expertise. In J.R. Anderson and S.M. Kosslyn (eds.), *Tutorials in learning and memory*. New York: W.H. Freeman and Company.

Lesgold, A., Rubinson, H., Feltovich, P., Glaser, R., Klopfer, D., and Wang, Y. (1988). Expertise in a complex skill: Diagnosing X-ray pictures. In M.T.H. Chi, R. Glaser, and M.J.

Farr (eds.), *The nature of expertise*. Hillsdale, NJ: Erlbaum.

Lewis, M.W., and Anderson, J.R. (1985). Discrimination of operator schemata in problem solving. Learning from examples. *Cognitive Psychology*, 17, 26-65.

McKeithen, K.B., Reitman, J.S., Rueter, H.H., and Hirtle, S.C. (1981). Knowledge organization and skill differences in computer programmers. *Cognitive Psychology*, 13, 307-325.

Neves, D.M., and Anderson, J.R. (1981). Knowledge compilation: Mechanisms for the automatization of cognitive skills. In J.R. Anderson (ed.), *Cognitive skills and their acquisition*. Hillsdale, NJ: Erlbaum.

Newell, A., and Simon, H. (1972). *Human problem solving*. Englewood Cliffs, NJ: Prentice-Hall.

Pillsbury, W.B. (1908). The effects of training on memory. *Educational Review*, 36, 15-27.

Polson, P., Muncher, E., and Kieras, D. (In press). Transfer of skills between inconsistent editors. *Human Computer Interaction*.

Reitman, J. (1976). Skilled perception in GO: Deducing memory structures from interresponse times. *Cognitive Psychology*, 8, 336-356.

Rosenbloom, P.S., and Newell, A. (1983). The chunking of goal hierarchies: A generalized model of practice. *Proceedings of the International Machine Learning Workshop*.

Rumelhart, D.E., and Norman, D.A. (1978). Accretion, tuning, and restructuring: Three modes of learning. In J.W. Cotton and R. Klatzky (eds.), *Semantic factors in cognition*. Hillsdale, NJ: Erlbaum.

Schmidt, R. A. (1982). *Motor control and learning*. Champaign, IL: Human Kinetics.

Schmidt, R.A., Young, D.E., Swinnen, S., and Shapiro, D.C. (1989). Summary knowledge of results for skill acquisition: Support for the guidance hypothesis. *Journal of Experimental Psychology: Learning, Memory, and Cognition*, 15, 352-359.

Schneiderman, B. (1976). Exploratory experiments in programmer behavior. *International Journal of Computer and Information Sciences*, 5, 123-143.

Schoenfeld, A.H., and Herrmann, D.J. (1982). Problem perception and knowledge structure in expert and novice mathematical problem solvers. *Journal of Experimental Psychology: Learning, Memory, and Cognition*, 8, 484-494.

Schonberg, H.C. (1970). *The lives of the great composers*. New York: W.W. Norton.

Silver, E.A. (1979). Student perceptions of relatedness among mathematical verbal problems. *Journal for Research in Mathematics Education*, 12, 54-64.

Simon, H.A., and Gilmartin, K. (1973). A simulation of memory for chess positions. *Cognitive Psychology*, 5, 29-46.

Singley, K., and Anderson, J.R. (1989). *The transfer of cognitive skill*. Cambridge, MA: Harvard University Press.

Sleeman, D., and Brown, J.S. (eds.) (1982). *Intelligent tutoring systems*. New York: Academic Press.

Soloway, E., Bonar, J., and Ehrlich, K. (1983). Cognitive strategies and looping constructs: An empirical study. *Communications of the ACM*, 26, 853-860.

Stelmach, G.E., and Requin, J. (eds.) (1980). *Tutorials in motor behavior*. Amsterdam: North-Holland.

Stratton, G.M. (1922). *Developing mental power*. New York: Houghton Mifflin.

Sweller, J.H., Mawer, R.F., and Ward, M.R. (1983). Development of expertise in mathematical problem solving. *Journal of Experimental Psychology: General*, 112, 463-474.

Thorndike, E.L. (1906). *Principles of teaching*. New York: A.G. Seiler.

Thorndike, E.L., and Woodworth, R.S. (1901). The influence of improvement in one mental function upon the efficiency of other functions. *Psychological Review*, 9, 374-382.

Weiser, M. and Shertz, J. (1983). Programming problem representation in novice and expert programmers. *International Journal of Man-Machine Studies*, 19, 391-398.

Woodrow, H. (1927). The effect of the type of training upon transference. *Journal of Educational Psychology*, 18, 159-172.

## References to Paper 2.2.1, Fundamentals of expert systems, by B.G. Buchanan and R.G. Smith:

AALPS. 1985. SRI: AI and the military. *The Artificial Intelligence Report.* 2(1):6-7.

Allen, J.F. 1984. Towards a general theory of action and time. *Artificial Intelligence* 23(2):123-154.

Allen, J.F., and Koomen, J.A. 1983. Planning using a temporal world model. *Proceedings of the Eighth International Joint Conference on Artificial Intelligence*, Karlsruhe, West Germany.

American Association for Artificial Intelligence. 1989. *Proceedings of the conference on innovative applications of artificial intelligence.* Stanford University, March 28-30, Menlo Park, Calif.

Brownston, L., Farrel, R., Kant, E., and Martin, N. 1985. *Programming expert systems in OPS5.* Reading, Mass.: Addison-Wesley.

Buchanan, B.G. 1986. Expert systems: Working systems and the research literature. *Expert Systems* 3(1):32-51.

Buchanan, B.G. 1988. Artificial intelligence as an experimental science. In J.H. Fetzer (ed.), *Aspects of artificial intelligence.* Amsterdam: D. Reidel.

Buchanan, B.G., and Shortliffe, E.H. 1984. *Rule-based expert systems: The MYCIN experiments of the Stanford heuristic programming project.* Reading, Mass.: Addison-Wesley.

Bundy, A. (ed.) 1986. *Catalogue of artificial intelligence tools.* New York: Springer-Verlag.

Chandrasekaran, B. 1986. Generic tasks in knowledge-based reasoning: High-level building blocks for expert system design. *IEEE Expert* 1(3):23-30.

Clancey, W.J. 1985. *Heuristic classification.* Technical Report KSL-85-5, Knowledge Systems Laboratory, Computer Science Department, Stanford University.

Clancey, W.J. 1985. Heuristic classification. *Artificial Intelligence* 27(3):289-350.

Clancey, W.J. 1986. From GUIDON to NEOMYIN and HERACLES in twenty short lessons: ONR final report 1979-1985. *AI Magazine* 7(3):40-60, 187.

Cline, T., Fong, W., and Rosenberg, S. 1985. *An expert advisor for photolithography.* Technical Report, Hewlett-Packard, Palo Alto, Calif.

Cohen, P.R., and Howe, A.E. 1988. How evaluation guides AI research. *AI Magazine* 9(4):35-43.

Cohen, P., and Howe, A. 1988. Toward AI research methodology: Three case studies in evaluation. *COINS Report* 88-31. (To appear in the *IEEE Transactions on Systems, Man, and Cybernetics*, 1989.)

Davis, R. 1982. Expert systems: Where are we? And where do we go from here? *AI Magazine* 3(2):1-22.

Davis, R. 1987. Robustness and transparency in intelligent systems. In *Human Factors in Automated and Robotic Space Systems.* Committee on Human Factors, National Research Council, Washington, D.C., 211-233.

Davis, R. 1989. Expert systems: How far can they go? Part 1. *AI Magazine* 10(1):61-68.

Davis, R., and Lenat, D.B. 1982. *Knowledge-based systems in artificial intelligence.* New York: McGraw-Hill.

Dreyfus, H., and Dreyfus, S. 1986. Why expert systems do not exhibit expertise. *IEEE Expert* 1(2):86-90.

Feigenbaum, E.A., Buchanan, B.G., and Lederberg, J. 1971. On generality and problem solving: A case study using the DENDRAL program. In B. Meltzer and D. Michie (eds.), *Machine intelligence* 6. New York: American Elsevier, 165-190.

Feigenbaum, E.A., McCorduck, P., and Nii, H.P. 1989. The rise of the expert company, forthcoming. New York Times Books.

Feinstein, J.L., and Siems, F. 1985. EDAAS: An expert system at the U.S. Environmental Protection Agency for avoiding disclosure of confidential business information. *Expert Systems* 2(2):72-85.

Fox, M.S., and Smith, S.F. 1984. ISIS: A knowledge-based system for factory scheduling. *Expert Systems* 1(1):25-49.

Fried, L. 1987. The dangers of dabbling in expert systems. *Computerworld* 21:6.

Gevarter, W.B. 1987. The nature and evaluation of commercial expert system building tools. *Computer* 20(5):24-41.

Goldberg, A., and Robson, D. 1983. *Smalltalk-80: The language and its implementation.* Reading, Mass.: Addison-Wesley.

Gorry, G.A. 1970. Modelling the diagnostic process. *Journal of Medical Education* 45:293-302.

Gruber, T.R. 1987. Acquiring strategic knowledge from experts. *Proceedings of the Second AAAI Knowledge Acquisition for Knowledge-based Systems Workshop*, 214-219.

Harmon, P. 1987. Currently available expert systems-building tools. *Expert Systems Strategies* 3(6):11-18.

Harmon, P., and King, D. 1985. *Expert systems: Artificial intelligence in business.* New York: Wiley.

Hayes-Roth, B. 1983. *The blackboard architecture: A general framework for problem solving.* Technical Report HPP-83-30, Knowledge Systems Laboratory, Computer Science Department, Stanford University.

Hayes-Roth, B. 1985. Blackboard architecture for control. *Journal of Artificial Intelligence* 26:251-321.

Hayes-Roth, F., Waterman, D.A., and Lenat, D.B. (eds.). 1983. *Building expert systems.* Reading, Mass.: Addison-Wesley.

Hernandez, R. 1987. Big eight firm audits with Mac. *Applied Artificial Intelligence Reporter* 4(7):9.

Hewitt, C. 1977. Viewing control structures as patterns of passing messages. *Artificial Intelligence* 8(3):323-364.

Hi-Class. 1985. AI brings smarts to PC-board assembly. *Electronics* 58:17-18.

Hickam, D.H., Shortliffe, E.H., Bischoff, M.B., and Jacobs, C.D. 1985. The treatment advice of a computer-based cancer chemotherapy protocol advisor. *Annals of Internal Medicine* 103(6):928-936.

Hollan, J.D., Hutchins, E.L., and Weitzman, L. 1984. STEAMER: An interactive inspectable simulation-based training system. *AI Magazine* 5(2):15-27.

Horn, K.A., Compton, P., Lazarus, L., and Quinlan, J.R. 1985. An expert computer system for the interpretation of thyroid assays in a clinical laboratory. *The Australian Computer Journal* 17(1):7-11.

Kahn, G., and McDermott, J. 1986. The mud system. *IEEE Expert* 1(1):23-32.

Kerschberg, L. (ed.) 1986. *Expert database systems: Proceedings of the First International Workshop.* Menlo Park, Calif.: Benjamin Cummings.

Klahr, P., et al. 1987. The authorizer's assistant: A large financial expert system application. *Proceedings of the Third Australian Conference on Applications of Expert Systems.* New South Wales Institute of Technology, Sydney, 11-32.

Kolcum, E.H. 1986. NASA demonstrates use of AI with expert monitoring system. *Aviation Week and Space Technology*, 79-85.

Kulikowski, C., and Weiss, S. 1982. Representation of expert knowledge for consultation: The CASNET and EXPERT projects. In P. Szolovits (ed.), *Artificial intelligence in medicine.* Boulder, Colo.: Westview Press, 21-55.

Laird, J.E., Newell, A., and Rosenbloom, P.S. 1987. SOAR: An architecture for general intelligence. *Artificial Intelligence* 33:1-64.

Lenat, D.B., Davis, R., Doyle, J., Genesereth, M., Goldstein, I., and Schrobe, H. 1983. Reasoning about reasoning. In F. Hayes-Roth, D.A.

Waterman, and D.B. Lenat (eds.), *Building expert systems*. Reading, Mass.: Addison-Wesley.

Lenat, D.B., Prakash, M., and Shepherd, M. 1986. CYC: Using common sense knowledge to overcome brittleness and knowledge acquisition bottlenecks. *AI Magazine* 6(4):65-85.

Lindsay, R.K., Buchanan, B.G., Feigenbaum, E.A., and Lederberg, J. 1980. *Applications of artificial intelligence for organic chemistry: The DENDRAL project*. New York: McGraw-Hill.

Marcus, S. 1987. Taking backtracking with a grain of SALT. *International Journal of Man-Machine Studies* 26(4):383-398.

McCarthy, J. 1958. Programs with common sense. *Proceedings of the Symposium on the Mechanisation of Thought Processes*. National Physical Laboratory, 77-84. (Reprinted in 1968 in M.L. Minsky (ed.), *Semantic Information Processing*. Cambridge, Mass.: MIT Press, 403-409.)

McCarthy, J. 1983. Some expert systems need common sense. *Annals of the New York Academy of Science* 426:129-137. Invited presentation for the New York Academy of Sciences Science Week Symposium on Computer Culture, April 5-8.

McCarthy, J., and Hayes, P. 1969. Some philosophical problems from the standpoint of artificial intelligence. In B. Meltzer and D. Michie (eds.), *Machine Intelligence 4*. Edinburgh: Edinburgh University Press.

McDermott, J. 1983. Extracting knowledge from expert systems. *Proceedings of the Eighth International Joint Conference on Artificial Intelligence*, Karlsruhe, West Germany, 1:100-107.

Michalski, R.S., Mozetic, I., Hong, J., and Lavrac, N. 1986. The multipurpose incremental learning system AQ15 and its testing application to three medical domains. *Proc. AAAI-86*. AAAI, Philadelphia, 1041-1045.

Michie, D., Muggleton, S., Riese, C., and Zubrick, S. 1984. RULEMASTER: A second-generation knowledge-engineering facility. In

*The first conference on artificial intelligence applications*. Silver Spring, MD.: IEEE Computer Society Press.

Miller, F.D., Copp, D.H., Vesonder, G.T., and Zielenski, J.E. 1985. The ACE Experiment: Initial evaluation of an expert system for preventive maintenance. In J.J. Richardson (ed.), *Artificial intelligence in maintenance: Proc. joint services workshop*. Air Force Systems Command, Park Ridge, N.J.: Noyes Publications, Publication #AFHRL-TR-84-25, 421-427.

Minsky, M. 1975. A framework for representing knowledge. In P.H. Winston (ed.), *The psychology of computer vision*. New York: McGraw-Hill, 211-277.

Mishkoff, H.C. 1985. *Understanding artificial intelligence*. Texas Instruments Information Publishing Center, Dallas.

Mitchell, J.M., Carbonell, J.G., and Michalski, R.S. (eds.) 1986. *Machine learning: A guide to current research*. Boston: Kluwer Academic Publications.

Mittal, S., Dym, C.L., and Morjaria, M. 1985. PRIDE: An expert system for the design of paper handling systems. In C.L. Dym (ed.), *Applications of knowledge-based systems to engineering analysis and design*. New York: ASME Press.

Moses, J. 1971. Symbolic integration: The stormy decade. *Communications of the ACM* 8:548-560.

Newell, A., and Simon, H.A. 1976. Computer science as empirical inquiry: Symbols and search. *Communications of the ACM* 19(3):113-126.

Nilsson, N.J. 1980. *Principles of artificial intelligence*. Palo Alto, Calif.: Tioga.

O'Keefe, R.M., Balci, O., and Smith, E.P. 1987. Validating expert system performance. *IEEE Expert* 2(4):81-89.

Pearl, J. 1986. Fusion, propagation, and structuring in belief networks. *Artificial Intelligence* 29:241-251.

Pearl, J. 1988. *Probabilistic reasoning in intelligent systems: Networks of plausible inference.* San Mateo, Calif.: Morgan Kaufmann.

Rauch-Hindin, W.B. 1986. *Artificial intelligence in business, science, and industry: Volume I Fundamentals, Volume II Applications.* Englewood Cliffs, N.J.: Prentice-Hall.

Richer, M.H. 1986. Evaluating the existing tools for developing knowledge-based systems. *Expert Systems* 3(3):166-183.

Richer, M.H., and Clancey, W.J. 1985. Guidon-Watch: A graphic interface for viewing a knowledge-based system. *IEEE Computer Graphics and Applications* 5(11):51-64.

Scown, S.J. 1985. *The artificial intelligence experience.* Digital Equipment Corp., Maynard, Mass.

Shafer, G., Shenoy, P.P., and Mellouli, K. 1989. Propagating belief functions in qualitative Markov trees. *International Journal of Approximate Reasoning*, forthcoming.

Sheil, B.A. 1984. Power tools for programmers. In D.R. Barstow, H.E. Shrobe, and E. Sandewall (eds.), *Interactive programming environments.* New York: McGraw-Hill, 19-30.

Smith, R.G. 1984. On the development of commercial expert systems. *AI Magazine* 5(3):61-73.

Smith, R.G., Barth, P.S., and Young, R.L. 1987. A substrate for object-oriented interface design. In B. Shriver and P. Wegner (eds.), *Research directions in object-oriented programming.* Cambridge, Mass.: MIT Press, 253-315.

Smith, R.G., Winston, H.H., Mitchell, T.M., and Buchanan, B.G. 1985. Representation and use of explicit justifications for knowledge-base refinement. *Proceedings of the Ninth International Joint Conference on Artificial Intelligence*, Los Angeles, Calif.: 673-680.

Smith, R.G., and Young, R.L. 1984. The design of the dipmeter advisor system. *Proceedings of the ACM Annual Conference*, 15-23.

Stefik, M.J., and Bobrow, D.G. 1986. Object-oriented programming: themes and variations. *AI Magazine* 6(4):40-62.

Sweet, L. 1985. Research in progress at General Electric. *AI Magazine* 6(3):220-227.

Szolovits, P., and Pauker, S.G. 1978. Categorical and probabilistic reasoning in medical diagnosis. *Artificial Intelligence* 11:115-144.

Teknowledge. 1987. *TEKSolutions: Customer success stories.* Teknowledge, Palo Alto, Calif.

Wah, B.W. (ed.) 1987. *Computer (Special issue on computers for AI applications).* IEEE.

Walker, T.C., and Miller, R.K. 1986. *Expert systems 1986.* Madison, Ga.: SEAI Technical Publications.

Waterman, D.A. 1986. *A guide to expert systems.* Reading, Mass.: Addison-Wesley.

Winograd, T. 1975. Frame representations and the procedural/declarative controversy. In D.G. Bobrow and A. Collins (eds.), *Representation and understanding: studies in cognitive science.* New York: Academic Press, 185-210.

Winograd, T., and Flores, F.F. 1986. *Understanding computers and cognition.* Norwood, N.J.: Ablex.

Zadeh, L.A. 1979. A theory of approximate reasoning. In J.E. Hayes, D. Michie, and L.I. Mikulich (eds.), *Machine Intelligence 9.* Chichester, England: Ellis Horwood Ltd., 149-195.

# Bibliography

Ashley, K. D. (1990). *Modeling Legal Argument: Reasoning with Cases and with Hypotheticals.* Cambridge: MIT Press.

Barstow, D. R. (1979). *Knowledge-Based Program Construction.* New York: Elsevier-North Holland.

Buchanan, B. G. (1966). *Logics of Scientific Discovery.* PhD thesis, Dept. of Philosophy, Michigan State University, Ann Arbor: UMI.

Buchanan, B. G. and Mitchell, T. M. (1978). Model-directed learning of production rules. In Waterman, D. A. and Hayes-Roth, F., editors, *Pattern-Directed Inference Systems*, pages 297–312. New York: Academic Press.

Buchanan, B. G. and Shortliffe, E. H. (1984). *Rule-Based Expert Systems: The MYCIN Experiments of the Stanford Heuristic Programming Project.* Reading: Addison-Wesley.

Falkenhainer, B. (1990). A unified approach to explanation and theory formation. In Shrager, J. and Langley, P., editors, *Computational Models of Scientific Discovery and Theory Formation*, pages 157–196, SanMateo, CA. Morgan Kaufmann.

Feigenbaum, E., McCorduck, P., , and Nii, H. P. (1988). *The Rise of the Expert Company.* New York: Times Books.

Feigenbaum, E. A. (1961). The simulation of verbal learning behavior. In *Proc. Western Joint Computer Conference*, pages 121–132. Reprinted in E. A. Feigenbaum and J. A. Feldman, *Computers and Thought*, McGraw-Hill, 1963.

Feigenbaum, E. A. (1977). The art of artificial intelligence: Themes and case studies in knowledge engineering. In *Proceedings of the 1977 IJCAI*, pages 1014–1029, Cambridge, Mass.

Forsythe, D., Buchanan, B. G., Osheroff, J. A., and Miller, R. A. (1992). Expanding the concept of medical information: An observational study of physicians' information needs. *Computers and Biomedical Research*, 25(2):181–200.

Gaines, B. R. and Boose, J. H. (1988a). *Knowledge Acquisition for Knowledge-Based Systems.* New York: Academic Press.

Gaines, B. R. and Boose, J. H. (1988b). Knowledge acquisition tools for expert systems. In Boose, J. H. and Gaines, B. R., editors, *Knowledge Based Systems 2*, pages xiii–xvi. New York: Academic Press.

Harandi, M. T. and Ning, J. Q. (1990). Knowledge-based program analysis. *IEEE Software*, 7(1):74–81.

Haussler, D. (1988). Quantifying inductive bias: AI learning algorithms and Valiant's learning framework. *Artificial Intelligence*, 36(2):177–221.

Hayes-Roth, F., Waterman, D. A., and Lenat, D. B. (1983). *Building Expert Systems*. Reading, Mass.: Addison-Wesley.

Hunt, E. B. (1962). *Concept Learning: An Information Processing Problem*. New York: Wiley.

Hunt, E. B. and Hovland, C. I. (1961). Programming a model of human concept formulation. In *Proc. Western Joint Computer Conference*, pages 145–155. Reprinted in E. A. Feigenbaum and J. A. Feldman, *Computers and Thought*, McGraw-Hill, 1963.

Hunt, E. B., Marin, J., and Stone, P. J. (1966). *Experiments in Induction*. New York: Academic Press.

Karp, P. D. and Wilkins, D. C. (1989). An analysis of the distinction between deep and shallow expert systems. *International Journal of Expert Systems*, 2(1):1–37.

Lenat, D. B. and Feigenbaum, E. A. (1987). On the thresholds of knowledge. In McDermott, J., editor, *Proceedings of the 1987 IJCAI*, pages 1173–1182, Milan.

McCarthy, J. (1958). Programs with common sense. In Office, H. M. S., editor, *Proceedings of the Symposium on the Mechanisation of Thought Processes*, pages 77–84, London. Reprinted in E. A. Feigenbaum and J. A. Feldman, *Computers and Thought*, McGraw-Hill, 1963.

Minsky, M. (1961a). A selected descriptor-indexed bibliography to the literature on artificial intelligence. *IRE Trans. on Human Factors in Electronics, HFE-2*, pages 39–55. Reprinted in E. A. Feigenbaum and J. A. Feldman, *Computers and Thought*, McGraw-Hill, 1963.

Minsky, M. (1961b). Steps toward artificial intelligence. *Proc. Institute of Radio Engineers*, 49(1):8–30. Reprinted in E. A. Feigenbaum and J. A. Feldman, *Computers and Thought*, McGraw-Hill, 1963.

Minsky, M. and Papert, S. (1969). *Perceptrons*. Cambridge, Mass.: MIT Press.

Nilsson, N. (1965). *Learning Machines*. New York: McGraw-Hill.

Park, Y. T., Tan, K. W., and Wilkins, D. C. (1989). MINERVA: A knowledge based system shell with declarative representation and flexible control. Technical Report UIUC-KBS-89-001, Department of Computer Science, University of Illinois, Urbana-Champaign, Illinois. Revision 3, August 1992.

Polanyi, M. (1964). *Personal Knowledge: Towards a Post-Critical Philosophy*. New York: Harper.

Rendell, L. A. and Seshu, R. (1990). Learning hard concepts through constructive induction: Framework and rationale. *Computational Intelligence*, 6:247–270.

Rich, C. and Wills, L. M. (1990). Recognizing a program's design: A graph-parsing approach. *IEEE Software*, 7(1):82–89.

Samuel, A. L. (1959). Some studies in machine learning using the game of checkers. *IBM Journal of Research and Development*, 3:211–229. Reprinted in E. A. Feigenbaum and J. A. Feldman, *Computers and Thought*, McGraw-Hill, 1963.

Scott, A. C., Clayton, J. E., and Gibson, E. (1991). *A Practical Guide to Knowledge Acquisition*. Addison-Wesley, Reading, Mass.

Smith, D. R. (1988). KIDS: A knowledge-based software development system. In *Proceedings of the AAAI88 Workshop on Automating Software Design*, page 12 pages, St. Paul, MN.

Smith, R. G., Winston, H. A., Mitchell, T. M., and Buchanan, B. G. (1985). Representation and use of explicit justifications for knowledge base refinement. In *Proceedings of the 1985 IJCAI*, pages 673–680, Los Angeles, CA.

Steier, D. M. e. a. (1987). Varieties of learning in soar: 1987. In Langley, P., editor, *Proceedings of the Fourth International Workshop on Machine Learning*, pages 300–311, California.

Valiant, L. G. (1984). A theory of the learnable. *Communications of the ACM*, 27(11):1134–1142.

Waterman, D. (1988). *A Guide to Expert Systems*. Reading, Mass.: Addison-Wesley.

Waters, R. (1985). The Programmer's Apprentice: A session with KBEmacs. *IEEE Trans. Software Engineering*, 11(11).

# Author Index

Note: Bold page numbers refer to papers appearing in this volume.

# Subject Index